TODD–SANFORD

CLINICAL DIAGNOSIS

By Laboratory Methods

THIRTEENTH EDITION

Edited by

ISRAEL DAVIDSOHN, M.D., F.A.C.P.

*Chairman, Department of Pathology, The
Chicago Medical School; Director, Department of Pathology,
Mount Sinai Hospital; and Scientific Director, Mount Sinai
Medical Research Foundation, Chicago*

BENJAMIN B. WELLS, M.D., Ph.D., F.A.C.P.

*Dean, California College of Medicine, Los Angeles; formerly
Assistant Chief Medical Director for Research and Education
in Medicine, The Veterans Administration, Washington, D.C.*

W. B. SAUNDERS COMPANY

Philadelphia 1962 London

TO OUR WIVES

Clara Davidsohn and Minnie Wells

WHO PATIENTLY ACCEPTED THE INCONVENIENCE
OF OUR LONG PREOCCUPATION WITH THIS WORK

Contributors

LLOYD G. BARTHOLOMEW, M.D.

Assistant Professor of Medicine, Mayo Foundation, Graduate School, University of Minnesota; Consultant, Section of Medicine, Mayo Clinic, Rochester, Minnesota.

JAMES C. CAIN, M.D.

Associate Professor of Medicine, Mayo Foundation, Graduate School, University of Minnesota; Consultant, Section of Medicine, Mayo Clinic, Rochester, Minnesota.

BRADLEY E. COPELAND, M.D., F.A.C.P.

Associate in Pathology, Harvard Medical School; Clinical Pathologist, New England Deaconess Hospital, New England Baptist Hospital; Coordinating Director of Laboratories, Lahey Clinic, Boston, Massachusetts.

MILTON GOLDIN, M.S.

Associate in Microbiology, The Chicago Medical School; Bacteriologist, Mount Sinai Hospital, Chicago, Illinois.

OSCAR B. HUNTER, Jr., M.D.

Professorial Lecturer in Forensic Medicine, Georgetown University; Director, Department of Pathology, Doctors Hospital, Sibley Memorial Hospital, Montgomery General Hospital, and Loudoun County Hospital, Washington, D.C.

FRANK A. IBBOTT, F.I.M.L.T.

Director of Pediatric Laboratories, University of Colorado Medical School, Denver, Colorado.

EMANUEL E. MANDEL, M.D.

Clinical Associate Professor of Medicine, State University of New York, Downstate Medical Center; Director, Department of Medicine, and Director of Medical Education, Jewish Chronic Disease Hospital, Brooklyn, New York.

RUSSELL M. McQUAY, Ph.D.

Instructor in Parasitology, The Chicago Medical School; Parasitologist, Mount Sinai Hospital, Chicago, Illinois.

FERRIN B. MORELAND, Ph.D., F.A.A.C.C.

Associate Professor of Biochemistry, Baylor University College of Medicine; Clinical Chemist, Veterans Administration Hospital; Director, Clinical Laboratory, Texas Institute for Rehabilitation and Research, Houston, Texas.

DONOUGH O'BRIEN, M.D., M.R.C.P.

Associate Professor of Pediatrics, University of Colorado Medical School; Attending Pediatrician, University of Colorado Medical Center; Consulting Pediatrician, National Jewish Hospital, Denver, Colorado.

RAYMOND A. SANFORD, M.D., F.C.A.P.

Pathologist, St. Joseph's Hospital, Mankato, Minnesota.

JAMES G. SHAFFER, Sc.D.

Formerly Professor and Chairman, Department of Microbiology and Public Health, The Chicago Medical School. Director, Microbiology and Hospital Epidemiology, The Lutheran General Hospital, Park Ridge, Illinois.

KURT STERN, M.D.

Professor of Pathology, University of Illinois College of Medicine; Pathologist, Research and Educational Hospital, University of Illinois, Chicago, Illinois.

NORBERT W. TIETZ, Ph.D.

Associate in Pathology, The Chicago Medical School; Clinical Chemist, Department of Pathology, Mount Sinai Hospital, Chicago, Illinois.

HARRY F. WEISBERG, M.D.

Clinical Associate Professor of Medicine, The Chicago Medical School; Clinical Pathologist and Associate Attending Physician, Little Company of Mary Hospital; Chief, Metabolic and Endocrine Clinic, and Associate Attending Physician, Mount Sinai Hospital; Consulting Physician, Franklin Boulevard and Central Community Hospitals, Chicago, Illinois.

HYMAN J. ZIMMERMAN, M.D., F.A.C.P.

Professor and Chairman, Department of Medicine, The Chicago Medical School; Chairman, Department of Medicine, Mount Sinai Hospital; Attending Physician, West Side Veterans Administration Hospital and Cook County Hospital, Chicago, Illinois.

Preface

FOR THE FIRST TIME in more than half a century of its publication, this edition of Todd and Sanford is a work of multiple authorship. Only in this way could we expect to offer physicians, medical students, and technologists a volume having authority, recency, and depth, and one reflecting the rapidly expanding scope of clinical pathology.

Since it is quite impossible to compress all of laboratory medicine into a single volume, we have chosen to emphasize certain topics that have compelling practical applications. Thus, the fields of hematology, microbiology, and clinical chemistry have been greatly expanded and each now appears as a series of chapters. In addition to the basic chapter on blood, there are separate chapters on blood groups and on the hemorrhagic disorders. Immunohematology, a relative newcomer in clinical pathology, received due recognition as a key to the understanding of many old pathogenetic puzzles and as a practical diagnostic tool and a guide to therapy. Microbiology is dealt with in seven chapters, including one on microbiologic methods. A chapter on clinical chemistry is devoted largely to the fundamental principles and basic techniques so essential in the modern laboratory, while various special phases of this field are handled in five new chapters: Water and Electrolytes, Microbiochemical Techniques in Pediatrics, Tests of Hepatic Function, Serum Enzyme Determinations, and Laboratory Tests Aiding in the Diagnosis of Pancreatic Disorders.

Among other topics appearing for the first time in the present edition are chapters on Statistical Tools in Clinical Pathology, Isotopology, Hospital Epidemiology, and a brief discussion of space and equipment needs in the modern clinical laboratory.

Small print is used both as a warning to those who lack time or inclination to delve into areas of less immediate practical import and as an invitation to those who may be differently minded.

Despite the pressure of many new topics in a completely rewritten text, we have carefully retained the classic and traditional subject matters where these continue to have current validity or can be used in the teaching process.

ISRAEL DAVIDSOHN, M.D.
Chicago, Illinois

BENJAMIN B. WELLS, M.D.
Los Angeles, California

Acknowledgments

A WORK OF multiple authorship requires by its very nature the willingness of the coauthors to accept the guidance of the editors. We are glad to acknowledge that our collaborators have been most gracious in this respect.

Dr. Changling Lee, Head of the Immunohematology Research Laboratory, Dr. Leigh Rosenblum, Head of the Isotope Clinic, Dr. Norbert W. Tietz, Head of the Biochemistry Laboratory, and Mrs. Gertrude Feigl, Chief Research Librarian, at the Mount Sinai Hospital in Chicago have been most helpful with suggestions, reading the manuscript and proof.

We want to express our appreciation for the cooperation of the staff of W. B. Saunders Company.

ISRAEL DAVIDSOHN, M.D.

BENJAMIN B. WELLS, M.D.

Contents

Chapter 12.   **SERUM ENZYME DETERMINATIONS AS AN AID
               TO DIAGNOSIS**

By HYMAN J. ZIMMERMAN, M.D.

Chapter 13.   **LABORATORY TESTS AIDING IN THE DIAGNOSIS
               OF PANCREATIC DISORDERS**

By NORBERT W. TIETZ, M.D.

Chapter 20.   **VACCINES AND DIAGNOSTIC SKIN TESTS** 804

By JAMES G. SHAFFER, Sc.D., *and* MILTON GOLDIN,
M.S.

Chapter 21.   **MILK AND WATER** 817

By JAMES G. SHAFFER, Sc.D., *and* MILTON GOLDIN,
M.S.

Chapter 25. **THE SPUTUM** 903

By BENJAMIN B. WELLS, M.D.

Chapter 26. **EXUDATES, TRANSUDATES, AND CEREBRO-SPINAL FLUID** 915

By BENJAMIN B. WELLS, M.D.

Appendix 1. **THE CLINICAL PATHOLOGIC LABORATORY** ... 927

Appendix 2. **CULTURE MEDIA, STAINS, REAGENTS, AND TECHNIQUES** 929

TODD and SANFORD

(1908-1962)

The History of a Book
and of a Medical Specialty

Habent sua fata libelli (books have their destinies).[1] This ancient phrase is certainly applicable to Todd and Sanford's book because of the age of the book and the influence it has exerted on clinical pathology for over half a century. What makes the history of Todd and Sanford especially interesting is that in it are mirrored the history and the development of clinical pathology in this country.

Dr. James C. Todd, a young man, age 32, Associate Professor of Pathology in the Medical Department at the University of Denver, and pathologist at Mercy, St. Anthony's, and Denver City and County Hospitals, found time in spite of his many duties to publish in 1906 and 1907, in the *Denver Medical Times* and the *Utah Medical Journal,* a series of articles entitled "Laboratory Diagnosis for the Practitioner." This led to the publication of the collected reprints of the articles in the form of a small book of 124 pages, entitled *A Syllabus of Lectures Upon Clinical Diagnosis,* dated 1906–1907. It was followed one year later by the first edition of *A Manual of Clinical Diagnosis* published by the W. B. Saunders Company in 1908.

Let us now take a look at what clinical pathology was like in those days. Bacteriology, chemistry, and physics had just begun to be applied to medical diagnosis in the living patient. At first, practicing physicians, mostly internists, practiced what we now call clinical pathology as a part of physical diagnosis. Then the busy ones among them turned over this part of the work to their younger assistants. Eventually, however, the amassed knowledge and the necessary skills became too much to be handled as a side issue; it became necessary to apply one's full time to do justice to the job. That is how the clinical pathologist came into being: He was a physician first and, when he began employing instruments and methods of precision that enabled him to go farther and to see more than was possible with his five unaided senses, he became a clinical pathologist.

The number of physicians who entered the new field was small. It required courage. The clinical pathologist of those days was looked upon as little more than a technician with a medical degree. That this attitude continued is apparent from an advertisement in the *Journal of the American Medical Association* as late as 1920, at a time when Todd's fourth edition was already two years old. Under those circumstances it required dedication to specialize in clinical pathology.

How did the clinical pathologist practice his specialty at the time when Dr. Todd began teaching? It is interesting to read about it in the Syllabus:

"A kitchen table, with a few shelves for

A

SYLLABUS OF LECTURES

UPON

CLINICAL DIAGNOSIS

By

JAMES C. TODD, M.D.

Associate Professor of Pathology, Medical Department,
University of Denver, Pathologist to Mercy,
St. Anthony's, and Denver City
and County Hospitals

*Reprinted from Denver Medical Times
and Utah Medical Journal
1906-1907*

Front page of *A Syllabus of Lectures Upon
Clinical Diagnosis.*

Front page of *A Manual of Clinical Diagnosis,*
the first edition of Todd.

A MANUAL

OF

Clinical Diagnosis

BY

JAMES CAMPBELL TODD, Ph. B., M. D.

ASSOCIATE PROFESSOR OF PATHOLOGY, DENVER AND GROSS COLLEGE OF
MEDICINE (UNIVERSITY OF DENVER); PATHOLOGIST AND CLINICAL
MICROSCOPIST TO MERCY, ST. ANTHONY'S, AND THE
DENVER CITY AND COUNTY HOSPITALS

Illustrated

PHILADELPHIA AND LONDON

W. B. SAUNDERS COMPANY

1908

Classified advertisement that appeared in the *Journal of the American Medical Association*, July 10, 1920, Advertising Section, page 25. Reproduced with permission of the American Medical Association.

bottles, screened off in a corner of the office will suffice for a laboratory." And here is the ancestor of the modern blood cell calculator: "Some workers divide a slide box into compartments by slides, one for each variety of leukocytes, and drop a coffee bean into the appropriate compartment when a cell is classified." Only two types of leukemia were recognized, myelogenous and lymphatic. No clinical importance was attached to the platelets.

The first edition of Todd, which appeared in 1908, measured 7½ x 5 inches and had 319 pages and 131 figures, including 10 color plates. The illustrations were of fine quality. The reviewers have been uniformly in accord on this item through the entire history of Todd and Sanford. As the title of the Syllabus indicated, and as was stated in the preface to the first edition, the book "had its origin some years ago in a short set of notes which the author dictated to his classes, and which has gradually grown by the addition each year of such matter as the year's teaching suggested. The eagerness and care with which the students and some practitioners took these notes and used them convinced the writer of the need of a volume of this scope." In the author's own words, "The book was meant for the student and practitioner, not for the trained laboratory worker." The emphasis was on simplicity and not on "absolute" accuracy.

The two largest chapters, occupying more than one-half of the whole book, were the second, Urine, 92 pages, and the third, Blood, 74 pages. Coagulation rated 20 lines, which included a description of the technique of coagulation time. Cytodiagnosis was emphasized by devoting to it a page of text and three illustrations, including a hint of its

possible value in the diagnosis of cancer—a harbinger of things to come.

Four years later, the second edition appeared, about one-third thicker with its title changed to *Clinical Diagnosis. A Manual of Laboratory Methods.* The inclusion in the title of the word "laboratory" was symbolic of the new emphasis.

Important additions included Benedict's test for sugar in the urine, the blood culture in typhoid fever, Wassermann tests, and a chapter of 23 pages on bacteriologic methods, in addition to discussions of special bacteriologic procedures in various places in the book, especially in the chapter on "Miscellaneous Examinations," and a separate chapter of 13 pages on "Preparation and Use of Vaccines."

Photomicrography was discussed for the first time. Photographs taken by the author were so designated, one of them as having been "taken with a Kodak."

Economic fluctuations were reflected in the price of microscopes. "A first class microscope, of either American or foreign make ...will cost in the neighborhood of a hundred dollars, exclusive of the mechanical stage." In the fourth edition, 1918, the price of the microscope dropped to $70.00, to increase to $125.00 by the time the fifth edition was published in 1925. Reference to the price was always accompanied by the statement: "It is poor economy to buy a cheap instrument." The price was quoted for the last time in the seventh edition (1931).

The binocular microscope was mentioned for the first time in the fourth edition (1918): "After one has learned to use them, the new mono-objective microscopes are extremely satisfactory, giving the impression of stereoscopic vision."

Returning to the second edition, we find a few especially interesting entries: "The hematocrit is not to be recommended for accuracy...but seems to be gaining in favor." Nowadays, of course, we recognize the hematocrit as the most accurate of the blood tests.

What we now call a monocyte was then divided into two groups: large mononuclear leukocytes and transitional leukocytes.

Band forms were not mentioned by name, although they can be seen in the illustrations (Fig. 90, p. 235).

Pernicious anemia: "It is frequently impossible to diagnose this disease from the blood examination alone." There was no mention as yet of marrow aspiration (not until the tenth edition, 1943).

"The rare and rapidly fatal anemia which has been described under the name of *aplastic anemia* is probably a variety of pernicious anemia." The morphologic findings in aplastic anemia are well expressed as "absence of any attempt at blood regeneration."

Hodgkin's disease was mentioned in parenthesis, with pseudoleukemia as the preferred term.

The third edition was published in 1914 —again substantially larger (from 469 to 585 pages). Sources of error in laboratory work were emphasized, because, as stated in the preface, "To one who sees a great deal of the work of students in the clinical laboratory it soon becomes evident that errors in microscopic diagnosis spring much less frequently from ignorance of the typical appearance of microscopic structures than from imperfect preparation of the slide, faulty manipulation of microscope, or failure to recognize extraneous matters, artefacts, and other misleading appearances."

There was a new chapter on "Serodiagnostic Methods," 52 pages long, written by Ross C. Whitman, who was Professor of Surgical Pathology and Serology at the University of Colorado. The chapter included a two-page description of a test for cancer by the German immunologist, von Dungern, and it was claimed that the test gave correct results in over 90 per cent of the cases. Another interesting item is a 15-page discussion of Abderhalden's test for fermentation reactions. The career of this test in Todd and Sanford is worth noting, for Abderhalden's ideas had many adherents in those days. Dr. Whitman must have been one of them, as evidenced by this statement: "It may be flatly asserted at the outset that, in spite of the severe criticism to which the method has been subjected, the correctness of Abder-halden's thesis has been abundantly confirmed." It is strange that the real purpose of the test and its possible clinical applications were not stated clearly. The test became a controversial issue as evidenced by the critical remarks of a British reviewer of the third edition in the Lancet,[2] as will be mentioned later. At any rate, the author was quick to recognize that the Abderhalden reaction and the von Dungern test for cancer had not been established as clinically significant. Both were dropped in the fourth edition, never to reappear.

Other changes included expansion of the space alloted to coagulation to three pages as compared with 20 lines in the first edition. Acute leukemia was treated separately for the first time, whereas, in the preceding edition, what is now acute granulocytic leukemia was dismissed with "acute cases have been described." Acute lymphocytic leukemia was not mentioned and monocytic leukemia was not recognized at all.

The firsts in the fourth edition (1918) included vital staining, the osmotic fragility test, and tests for blood grouping and cross matching. Regarding the latter, it was stated that "*if possible* it should always be done when transfusion is contemplated." In the fifth edition (1925), the recommendation was changed: "Matching of blood...*should always* be done when transfusion is contemplated." What is now called the "walking blood bank" was recommended: "In hospital work, upon the other hand, it will be found much more satisfactory to determine in advance the grouping of a number of individuals who may be willing to serve as donors upon occasion."

The war may have been responsible for a seven-year interval between the fourth and fifth editions. The size of the book increased from 7½ x 5 inches to 9 x 6 inches, and the number of pages increased from 687 to 762.

The firsts include the phenoltetrachlorophthalein test for liver function and the Kolmer complement fixation and the Kahn flocculation tests for syphilis.

Tests for urea and uric acid, formerly treated in the chapter on urine, were now in the chapter on blood together with newly added tests for creatinine, blood sugar, and carbon dioxide. It was not until 1935 that these and other tests relating to blood chemistry rated a separate chapter.

Acute infectious mononucleosis was mentioned for the first time in the fifth edition: "Within the past few years a number of cases of 'acute infectious mononucleosis' with glandular enlargement and fever have been reported by Cabot, Sprunt and Evans, Longcope, and others. The striking feature of the blood has been a marked leukocytosis with preponderance of mononuclear cells which appear to be lymphocytes or cells derived from them."

The index outline of laboratory findings in important diseases appeared for the first time and has remained a permanent fixture.

The sixth edition appeared after only two years and now was written by Todd and Sanford, for Dr. Todd's ill health had made it necessary to share the burden. The preface contained a phrase repeated from previous editions: The "size has been considerably increased." Actually this was the first edition in which the size was reduced, from 762 pages to 748.

Dr. Todd died on January 6, 1928, at the age of 54. In an obituary published in the *Journal of Laboratory and Clinical Medicine*, he was given credit for having been the first to advocate a chair of clinical pathology in medical schools.[3] At his request, a separate Department of Clinical Pathology was created in 1916 at the University of Colorado School of Medicine. Dr. Todd was sick a good part of his active life. Work on all editions of his book was done while he was bedridden or in a rocking chair.

The seventh edition was published in 1931 with Dr. Sanford as the sole author.

The Sheard-Sanford photoelectrometer (later the photocolorimeter) was mentioned for the first time as being used successfully by the inventors, but "these new methods are scarcely beyond the experimental stage and are not yet available for general use."

Blood grouping tests were recommended for determining illegitimacy of children. The technique of the Aschheim-Zondek test for pregnancy and of the more practical Friedman modification was described.

In the preface to the eighth edition (1935), Dr. Sanford stated that "Clinical pathology has become a recognized specialty in medical practice." There was, for the first time, a separate 59-page chapter on "Clinical Chemistry." Other innovations included the Addis method for counting casts and cells

Dr. James C. Todd.

in the urine and the heterophilic antibody test for infectious mononucleosis.

The ninth and tenth editions each followed after intervals of four years, each showing evidence of having kept pace with the development in this rapidly growing field. Aspiration of sternal marrow was described in the tenth edition (1943).

The eleventh edition (1948) mentioned Dr. George G. Stilwell as collaborator. For the first time, the references were listed at the end of each chapter, having been placed till then at the bottom of the pages.

Dr. Benjamin B. Wells joined Dr. Sanford as coauthor of the twelfth edition, published in 1953. Although no drastic changes were made in this edition, the book had grown to 998 pages. The chapters on blood and bacteriology were rearranged, and the chapter on clinical chemistry was brought up to date.

Dr. Sanford died on April 2, 1959 at the age of 77.[4]

At the end of this review of 12 editions and of more than 50 years of the history of Todd and Sanford, the question comes to mind: What has been the image of this book through these years?

I thought that one might find an answer in published reviews. The following journals were consulted: the *Journal of the American Medical Association*, the *American Journal of Clinical Pathology*, the *Archives of Pathology*, the *New England Journal of Medicine*, and the *Lancet*.

There is no doubt that Todd and Sanford has enjoyed a good press. The reviews were almost unanimously laudatory all through the years.

Constructive criticism has been voiced repeatedly. Its beneficial influence is apparent when one studies the changes in subsequent editions. A striking example is the previously mentioned critical remark in the review in the *Lancet* of the third edition: "With regard to the value of Abderhalden's test, criticism is not only deprecated, but somewhat fiercely resented, but we may at least express doubt as to the wisdom of including such a test in its present stage of development and with its acknowledged difficulty in a textbook avowedly intended for the practitioner and student rather than the trained laboratory workers."[2] The omission of the discussion of Abderhalden's method in the fourth edition may or may not have been the result of the criticism.

Dr. Arthur H. Sanford.

Interesting are the repeated references to the relation between the development of clinical pathology as a branch of medicine and the influence exerted by Todd and Sanford. The following quotation is from a review of the tenth edition that appeared in the *American Journal of Clinical Pathology*.[5] Referring to the 35 years that had elapsed since the publication of the first edition, it stated: "During these years clinical pathology has grown up from infancy to its present maturity and has gained recognition as a specialty of equal rank with the other branches of medicine. Todd and Sanford has played a prominent part in this development."

If it is true that "historia...magistra vitae" (history is the teacher of life),[6] what does the history of Todd and Sanford teach?

1. It was written in response to a need.
2. The first author had a clear idea of what he wanted to achieve, and he succeeded in transmitting this idea directly and indirectly to those who followed him.
3. He and those who followed him were sensitive in responding to the changing demands of the day.

These are some of the plausible explanations of the continued demand for Todd and Sanford and the resulting success.

Israel Davidsohn, M.D.

REFERENCES

1. Terentianus Maurus: De Litteris, De Syllabis, De Metris. Line 1286. Written approximately in the year A.D. 150.
2. Book review: The Lancet, *1*: 757, 1915.
3. James Campbell Todd: J. Lab. & Clin. Med., *14*: 581, 1928/1929.
4. Arthur Hawley Sanford: Am. J. Clin. Path., *32*: 273, 1959.
5. Book review: Am. J. Clin. Path., *13*: 282, 1943.
6. Cicero: De Oratore, Book II, Section 9.

Chapter 1

The Microscope

By BENJAMIN B. WELLS, M.D.

It is probable that the usefulness of no other laboratory instrument is so dependent on proper manipulation as is the usefulness of the microscope, and no other laboratory instrument is so frequently misused by beginners. Some suggestions regarding the proper use of the microscope therefore appear to be indicated. It will be assumed that the reader is already familiar with the general construction of this instrument (Fig. 1–1). A careful and frequent study should be made of the booklet that is furnished with each new microscope by the manufacturer.

ILLUMINATION

Source of Light

Good work cannot be done without proper illumination, and this is therefore the first and most important consideration

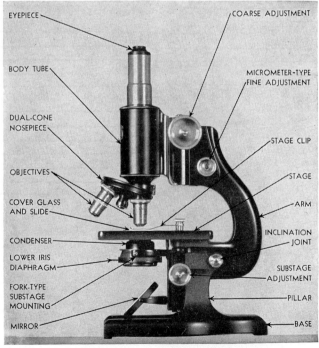

Figure 1–1. The microscope.

Figure 1–2. Small microscope lamps with daylight-glass filters.

for one who wishes to use the microscope effectively.

The light that is generally recommended as best is that coming through a white cloud, the microscope being placed by preference at a north window to avoid direct sunlight. At any other window a white window shade is desirable. Such light is satisfactory for all ordinary work. Artificial light is, however, imperative for those who must work at night and is a great convenience at all times. Properly regulated artificial light offers decided advantages over daylight for critical work. Almost any strong light that is diffused through a frosted globe will give fair results. Such a bulb may conveniently be enclosed within a metal box with small openings in the back for ventilation and a window in the front to transmit the light. All such lights have a yellow tinge, and to counteract

this a blue glass disk, usually supplied with the microscope, is placed in a supporting ring beneath the condenser.

Two types of lamps are shown in Fig. 1–2. Both can be fitted with light filters made of "daylight glass," which, when used with the nitrogen-filled tungsten lamp, transmit a light practically indistinguishable from daylight. Figure 1–3 illustrates a more expensive type of lamp but one that has a wide range of usefulness.

The microscope lamp should not stand at so great a distance from the microscope that its image fails to fill the aperture of the condenser—a condition one can readily detect by removing the ocular and looking down the tube.

Forms of Illumination

After one has arranged the microscope in proper relation to the source of light, whether this be daylight or an artificial source, the next problem is to secure an evenly illuminated field of view without mottling or any trace of shadows. This is accomplished by manipulating the mirror and the condenser. When this has been accomplished, the direction and the amount of light must be considered in relation to the character of the object under examination.

Central and Oblique Illumination. Illumination may be either central or oblique, depending on the direction in which the light enters the microscope. To obtain central illumination the mirror should be so adjusted that the light from the source is reflected directly up the tube of the microscope. This is easily done by removing the ocular and looking down the tube while adjusting the mirror. The ocular is then replaced and the light reduced as much as desired by means of the diaphragm.

In simple instruments oblique illumination is obtained by swinging the mirror to one side so that the light enters the micro-

Figure 1–3. An excellent type of microscope lamp suitable both for ordinary work and for darkfield illumination.

scope obliquely. In more complicated instruments it is obtained by means of a rack and pinion, which move the diaphragm laterally. Beginners frequently use oblique illumination without recognizing it, and they are thereby much confused. If the light is oblique, an object in the center of the field will appear to sway from side to side when the fine adjustment is turned back and forth. The amount of light admitted is also important. It is regulated by the diaphragm.

The bulk of routine microscopic work is done with central illumination; therefore, it should be used at the beginning of each microscopic examination. Each of the forms of illumination, however, central and oblique, subdued and strong, has its special uses and demands some consideration. The well-known rule, "Use the least amount of light that will show the object well," is good, but it does not go far enough.

In studying any microscopic structure one considers its color, its outline, and its surface contour. No one form of illumination shows all of these to the best advantage. It may therefore be necessary to change the illumination many times during a microscopic examination.

To see color best, use central illumination with strong light. A stained glass window, for example, shows the purest color when light is streaming through it, and therefore strong central light should be used for examining stained specimens, such as bacteria, that must be recognized chiefly by their color. In general, strong central light should be alternated with other forms of light in the examination of stained specimens.

To study the outline of an object, use very subdued central illumination. The diaphragm should be closed to the point which trial shows to be best in each case. This illumination is required for the examination of delicate colorless objects, such as hyaline casts and cholesterol crystals, which are recognized chiefly by their outline. The usual mistake of beginners is to work with the diaphragm opened too wide. Strong light will often render semitransparent structures entirely invisible.

To study surface contour, use oblique light of a strength suited to the color or opacity of the object. In routine work oblique illumination is resorted to only to study more carefully some object that has been found with central illumination, e.g., to demonstrate the cylindric shape of a hyaline cast.

Darkfield Illumination. Darkfield illumination consists of blocking out the central rays of light and directing the peripheral rays against the microscopic object from the side. Only those rays that strike the object and are reflected upward pass into the objective. The object that is being examined thus appears bright on a black background. By means of this form of illumination very minute structures can be seen, just as particles of dust in the atmosphere become visible when a beam of sunlight enters a darkened room.

When using the low power objective, darkfield illumination can be obtained by means of the ring stops with central disks, which accompany most microscopes when purchased. The stop is placed in a special ring beneath the condenser. When the regular stop is not available, one can use the glass disk, which is generally supplied with the microscope, or an extra large round coverglass in the center of which is pasted a circular disk of black paper. The size of the black disk depends on the aperture of the objective with which it is to be used and can be ascertained by trial. For best results the condenser should be oiled to the under surface of the slide and should be focused on the object that is being examined.

When the oil immersion objective is used, a special condenser is necessary. This is known as a "reflecting condenser" or "darkfield illuminator." The most desirable

Figure 1–4. Darkfield condenser with lamp attached.

Figure 1–5.   Darkfield microscope.

the darkfield condenser and illuminant in positive alignment and a rheostat control on the substage lamp (Fig. 1–5). The chief use of darkfield illumination in clinical work is for demonstration of *Treponema pallidum* in fresh material.

Use of the darkfield condenser. A small drop of the fluid to be examined is placed on a clean slide of the correct thickness and covered with a clean coverglass. The thickness of the slide is important owing to the need for accurately focusing the condenser, and the proper thickness to be used with a particular condenser is generally engraved upon its mounting. This is usually between 1 and 1.55 mm. The layer of fluid must be thin. The slide and coverglass must be free from scratches; air bubbles must be avoided as well as any excess of objects (blood corpuscles, pus cells, and so forth) other than those sought, since all of these tend to brighten the background and thus reduce contrast. Because of the short working distance of oil immersion objectives, No. 1 coverglasses are essential.

The source of light, other than a built-in lamp, may be direct sunlight or, preferably, a strong artificial light with a bull's-eye or a water-bottle condenser to deliver parallel rays to the mirror.

The regular substage condenser is removed, and the darkfield condenser is inserted in its place and accurately centered in the optical axis. To facilitate centering, a series of concentric circles is generally ruled on the top of the condenser. These circles are brought to the center of the field of a low power objective by means of centering screws provided for the purpose. A drop of immersion oil is then placed on the apex of the condenser, the slide is placed in position on the stage, and the condenser is raised until the oil is in contact with the under surface of the slide. The low power objective is now focused on the slide. If the

form of condenser for this purpose is one that is interchangeable with the regular substage condenser. One type has a lamp built in or attached beneath it (Fig. 1–4). Some manufacturers offer a condenser that allows one to change almost instantly from a bright field to a dark field and vice versa with, however, some loss of quality in both. Objectives used for darkfield illumination must be of relatively low numeric aperture (usually less than 0.9); hence, when the ordinary oil immersion objective is used, its aperture must be reduced by placing in it a "funnel stop" obtainable from the maker of the objective. Oil immersion objectives of low numeric aperture especially designed for this work, but also useful for bright-field illumination, are available. If examinations by darkfield illumination are made frequently, it is advantageous to use a specially designed darkfield microscope with

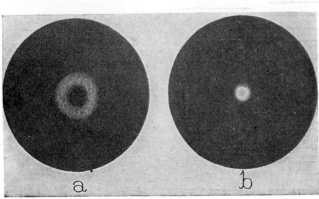

Figure 1–6.   Darkfield illumination: *a*, Circle of light seen with a low power objective when the condenser is above or below the correct focus. *b*, The bright spot of light seen with a low power objective when the condenser is correctly focused.

light is sufficiently intense and the mirror properly adjusted, a circle or a spot of light should be seen in the center of the field. A circle indicates that the condenser is decidedly above or below its correct position (Fig. 1–6). The condenser is then focused by raising or lowering it until the circle becomes a spot of light and this spot becomes as small and as bright as possible. This spot is also utilized for centering the condensers provided with the concentric centering circles just mentioned. The low power objective is finally replaced by the high power objective with which the examination is to be made, and this is brought to focus and used in the ordinary way.

For darkfield examination the various adjustments must be much more exact than for a bright field. The most frequent causes of failure to secure a satisfactory dark field with brilliantly lighted objects that appear to be self-luminous are:

1. Use of an objective with too wide an aperture. When the regular oil immersion objective is used, its aperture must be reduced by means of the stop provided by the makers.

2. Failure to focus and to center the condenser accurately. Very slight readjustments of the condenser or mirror after the examination is begun may remedy matters, provided the slide is not too thick to permit accurate focusing.

3. Inclusion of air bubbles in the preparation or in the oil above or below the slide. It is generally necessary to remove the oil and to apply it again.

4. Inclusion of too many microscopic objects in the field. This may be remedied by diluting the fluid to be examined or by reducing the thickness of the preparation by means of slight pressure on the coverglass.

The Substage Condenser

For the work in a clinical laboratory a substage condenser is a necessity. Its purpose is to condense the light on the object to be examined. For critical work the light must be focused on the object by raising or lowering the condenser by means of the screw provided for the purpose. The image of the light source will then appear in the plane of the object. This is best seen by using a low power objective and ocular. Should the image of the window frame or other nearby object appear in the field and prove annoying, the condenser may be raised or lowered slightly. It has been recommended that the condenser be re-

moved for certain kinds of work; however, this is not necessary and is seldom desirable in the clinical laboratory.

The condenser is constructed for parallel rays of light. With daylight, therefore, the plane mirror should be used, and for the divergent rays of ordinary artificial light the concave mirror, which tends to bring the rays together, is best.

It is very important that the condenser be centered accurately in the optical axis of the instrument, and most high-grade instruments have centering screws by which it can be adjusted at any time. The simplest way to recognize whether the condenser is centered is to close the diaphragm beneath it to as small an opening as possible and then to remove the ocular and look down the tube. If the diaphragm opening does not appear in the center of the field, the condenser is off center. The use of the condenser also will be considered in the following sections.

OPTICAL CONSIDERATION

Objectives and Oculars

Unfortunately different makers use different systems to designate their lenses. In this country objectives are designated by their focal lengths expressed in millimeters or by their "initial magnification," and oculars are designated by their magnifying power, indicated by an "×."

From the standpoint of color correction objectives may be divided into two classes: achromatic and apochromatic. Those in general use are of the achromatic type, and they fulfill all requirements for ordinary work. Apochromatic objectives are more highly corrected for chromatic and spheric aberration and are the finest microscope lenses produced. They give crisp images with little or no trace of color fringes, which with achromatic objectives can be seen readily about the edges of black or colorless objects lying in a bright field, and are very desirable for photomicrography and research. A compensating ocular must be used with an apochromatic objective. A third type of objective, which is made of fluorite, requires no special ocular and offers color correction midway between an apochromatic and an achromatic objective. This is sometimes designated as a "semi-apochromat."

The simple oculars that have long been used with achromatic objectives are known as "huygenian oculars." With apochromatic

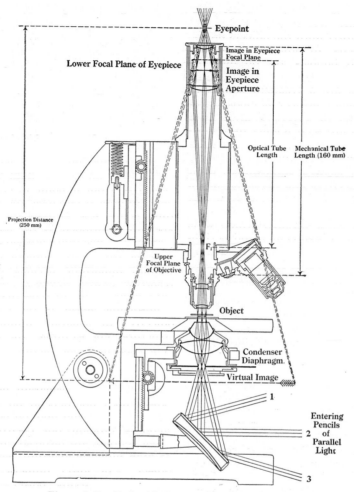

Figure 1–7. Path of light through the microscope.

objectives it is necessary to use special "compensating oculars," which are corrected to overcome certain defects in this type of objective. The same compensating oculars may be used with oil immersion and high power dry objectives of the achromatic series. Many persons who wear glasses while using a microscope find that with lower power objectives particularly there is a great advantage in using 10× "wide field" oculars, designed originally for the "Greenough type" wide field binocular microscope.

Although for critical work, especially with apochromatic objectives, the thickness of the coverglass is very important, one pays little attention to it in the clinical laboratory. A high power dry objective always requires a coverglass, but its exact thickness is unimportant in routine work. Very low power objectives and oil immersion objectives may be used without any coverglass.

The correction for the medium between objective and coverglass is very important. This medium may be air or some fluid, and the objective is hence either a "dry" or an "immersion" objective. The immersion fluid generally used is an especially prepared cedar oil, which gives great optical advantages because its index of refraction is the same as that of crown glass. It is obvious that only objectives with a very short working distance, that is, 2 mm. or less, can be used with an immersion fluid.

To use an oil immersion objective, a suitable field for study should first be found with the low power objective. A drop of immersion oil is placed on the slide, and the objective is lowered until it is in contact with the oil and almost touches the slide. This is observed with the eye on a level with the stage. Then, while the operator looks into the microscope, the objective is raised very slowly until the objects on the slide are in focus. In order to avoid the formation of air bubbles, the oil must be placed on the slide carefully without stirring it. Bubbles are a frequent source of trouble and should always be looked for when an immersion objective gives poor results. Bubbles are seen readily by removing the ocular and looking down the tube. If they are present, the oil must be removed and a new drop applied. Immediately after use both the objectives and the slide should be wiped clean with lens paper or a soft linen handkerchief.

Curvature of field, through which it is impossible to focus both center and periphery sharply at the same time, is a very noticeable defect, but it is less serious than appears at first sight, particularly for visual work. It is easily compensated for by frequent use of the fine focusing adjustment. Complete flatness of field cannot be attained without sacrifice of other, more desirable properties. Some of the finest objectives made, notably the apochromatic objectives, show decided curvature of field.

The working distance of an objective should not be confused with its focal distance. The former term refers to the distance between the front lens of the objective, when it is in focus, and the coverglass. It is always less than the focal distance, since the focal point lies somewhere within the objective, and it varies considerably with different makes. A long working distance is a very desirable feature. Some oil immersion objectives have such a short working distance that only very thin coverglasses can be used.

The formation of the microscopic image demands brief consideration (Fig. 1–7). The rays of light, which are reflected upward from the mirror and which pass through the object, are brought to a focus in a magnified, inverted real image. This can be focused to appear at different levels, but when the microscope is used in the ordinary way the image is formed at about the level of the diaphragm in the ocular. It can be seen by removing the ocular, placing a piece of ground glass on the top of the tube, and focusing on it. When viewing this image, a roll of paper or a cylindric mailing tube should be used to exclude extraneous light. This image, in turn, is magnified by the eye lens of the ocular, which produces a second real image, which is again inverted. The object, therefore, appears right side up. This can be seen on a ground glass held a few inches above the ocular, provided strong artificial light is used and the room is darkened. When the eye looks into the microscope, it does not see this real image but rather an inverted virtual image, which appears about 250 mm. in front of the eye.

Numeric Aperture

This expression, usually written N.A., indicates the amount of light that enters an objective from a point in the microscopic field. In optical language the numeric aperture is the sine of half the angle of the aperture multiplied by the index of refraction of the medium between the coverglass and the front lens. Numeric aperture is extremely important, because on it depends resolving power, which is the most important property of an objective.*

Resolving power is the capacity of an objective to separate minute details of structure. For example, the dark portions of a good half-tone picture appear gray or black to the unaided eye, but a lens easily resolves this apparently uniform surface into a series of separate dots. Resolving power does not depend on magnification. The fine lines and dots on certain diatoms may be brought out clearly and crisply (that is, they are resolved) by an objective of high numeric aperture, whereas with an objective of lower numeric aperture but greater magnifying power, the same diatom may appear to have a smooth surface with no markings at all, no matter how greatly it is magnified. Knowing the numeric aperture, it is possible to calculate how closely lines and dots may lie and still be resolved by a given objective. To state the numeric aperture, therefore, is to tell what the objective can accomplish, provided, of course, that spheric and chromatic aberrations are satisfactorily corrected. The numeric aperture of an objective usually is engraved upon the mounting.

It is an important fact, and one almost universally overlooked by practical microscopists, that the proportion of the numeric aperture of an objective that is utilized depends on the aperture of the cone of light delivered by the condenser. In practice the numeric aperture of an objective is reduced nearly to that of the condenser (which is

---

* Resolving power really depends on two factors, the numeric aperture and the wavelength of light, but the latter can be ignored in practice.

indicated by lower case letters, n.a.).* The condenser should therefore have a numeric aperture at least equal to that of the objective with which it is to be used. Lowering the condenser below its focal distance and closing the diaphragm beneath it have the effect of reducing its working aperture. A condenser, whatever its numeric aperture, cannot deliver through the air a cone of light of greater numeric aperture than 1.

From these considerations it follows that the proper adjustment of the substage condenser is a matter of great importance when using objectives of high numeric aperture. To gain the full benefit of the resolving power of such objectives, the condenser must be focused on the object under examination, it must be oiled to the under surface of the slide in the same way as the immersion objective is oiled to the cover-glass, and the substage diaphragm must be wide open. The last condition introduces a difficulty in that colorless structures will appear "fogged" in a glare of light, making a satisfactory image impossible when the diaphragm is more than three-quarters open. Wright suggested that the size of the light source should be so regulated by a diaphragm that its image, thrown on the slide by the condenser, coincides with the real field of the objective. He maintained that in this way it is possible to reduce the glare of light and to dispel the fog without closing the diaphragm.

One can easily determine how much of the aperture of an objective is in use by removing the ocular, looking down the tube, and observing what proportion of the back lens of the objective is illuminated. The relation of the illuminated central portion to the unilluminated peripheral zone indicates the proportion of the numeric aperture in use. The effect of raising and lowering the condenser and of oiling it to the slide can thus be easily seen.

Another property of an objective that depends largely on the numeric aperture is depth of focus, that is, the capacity of the objective to render details in different planes clearly at the same time. The higher the numeric aperture and the greater the magnification, the less the depth of focus. Any two objectives of the same focal length and same numeric aperture will have exactly the same depth of focus.

Depth of focus can be increased by clos-

ing down the diaphragm, thus reducing the numeric aperture. Great depth is desirable for certain work done with the lower power objective, but, when the high power objective is used, closing the diaphragm does not offer advantages to balance the loss of numeric aperture by which it is attained. In some cases, indeed, it is a real disadvantage.

Magnification

The degree of magnification should always be expressed in diameters, not times, which is a misleading term. The former term refers to increase of diameter; the latter, to increase of area. The comparatively low magnification of 100 diameters is the same as the apparently enormous magnification of 10,000 times. According to the system of rating magnification used in this country, the magnifying power of an objective is ascertained by dividing the optical tube length by the focal length of the objective. The optical tube length is usually somewhere near 165 mm., but it varies with the different objectives, and the manufacturers' catalogs must be consulted for an accurate statement of magnifying power. Some manufacturers follow the commendable plan of engraving both the focal length of the objective and the initial magnification on its barrel.

This system of rating magnification measures the enlarged image at the level of the diaphragm in the ocular, and this image is in turn magnified by the ocular; therefore, when an objective and an ocular are used together, the total magnification is the product of the two. In the case, for example, of a 1.9 mm. oil immersion objective with an initial magnification of 95 diameters, the total magnification with the 5× ocular is 475 diameters.

It is easy to find the magnifying power of any combination of objective and ocular by actual trial. Place the counting slide of a hemacytometer upon the microscope and focus the ruled lines. Adjust a sheet of paper upon the table close to the microscope in such a position that when the left eye is in its proper place at the ocular the paper will lie in front of the right eye at the normal visual distance, that is, 250 mm. The paper may be supported on a book if necessary. If both eyes are kept open, the ruled lines will appear to be projected on the paper. With a pencil, mark on the paper the apparent location of the lines that bound the small squares used in counting erythrocytes and measure the distance between the marks. Divide this distance by 0.05 mm., which is the actual distance between the lines on the slide. The quotient gives the magnification. If, for example, the lines in the image on the paper are 5 mm. apart, the magnification is 100 diameters.

---

* The numeric aperture of the objective is not reduced wholly to that of the condenser, because owing to diffraction phenomena a part of the unilluminated portion of the back lens is utilized.

The figures obtained in this way will vary somewhat, depending on whether one is near-sighted or far-sighted, unless the defect of vision is corrected with glasses.

In practice, magnification can be increased in one of two ways.

Using a High Power Objective. As a rule this is the best way, because resolving power is also increased, but it is often undesirable because of the shorter working distance and because the higher power objective often gives greater magnification than is desired or cuts down the size of the real field too much.

Using a High Power Ocular. This is the simplest method. It has, however, certain limitations. When an ocular that is too strong is used, there results a hazy image in which no structural detail is seen clearly. This is called "empty magnification" and results because the objective has not sufficient resolving power to support the high magnification. It has been aptly compared with the enlargement, by stretching in all directions, of a picture drawn upon a sheet of rubber. No new detail is added, no matter how great the enlargement.

The extent to which magnification can be satisfactorily increased by oculars depends wholly on the resolving power of the objective and consequently on the numeric aperture. The greatest total or combined magnification that will give an absolutely crisp picture is found by multiplying the numeric aperture of an objective by 400. The greatest magnification that can be used at all satisfactorily is 1000 times the numeric aperture. For example, suppose the ordinary 1.9 mm. objective has a numeric aperture of 1.30. The greatest magnification that will give an absolutely sharp picture is 520 diameters, which is obtained approximately by using a 5× ocular. Higher power oculars can be used to produce a total magnification of 1300 diameters (12.5× ocular) beyond which the image becomes wholly unsatisfactory.

SELECTING A MICROSCOPE

It is poor economy to buy a cheap microscope. For work in a clinical laboratory the microscope should preferably be of the handle-arm type and should have a large stage. It should be provided with a substage condenser, three or more objectives on a revolving nosepiece, and two or more oculars. After one has learned to use them, single objective binocular microscopes (Fig. 1–8) are extremely satisfactory; they give an impression of stereoscopic vision and also enable the worker to keep both eyes open with no feeling of strain.

The distance between the two oculars is adjustable to allow for differences in pupillary distances of different individuals. The left ocular may also be focused by turning it slightly and thus adjusting it for any slight refractive differences of the two eyes. If there is a bad refractive error, it may be necessary to have special lenses ground for the oculars in order to obtain stereoscopic

Figure 1–8. Two American binocular microscopes.

effects. Microscopists generally prefer binocular instruments when they become familiar with their use.

The most generally useful objectives are: 16 mm., 4 mm., and an oil immersion, which usually is 1.9 or 1.8 mm. The 4 mm. objective may be obtained with a numeric aperture of 0.65 or 0.85. If it is to be used for blood counting. N.A. 0.65 is preferable, since its working distance is sufficient to take the thick cover of the blood counting instrument. For coarse objects a 32 mm. objective is very desirable. The oculars most frequently used are 5× and 10×. A very low power (2×) and a very high power ocular (15×) will sometimes be found useful. The micrometer ocular is also very useful. A mechanical stage is almost indispensable for differential counting of leukocytes and certain other work in the clinical laboratory.

USE OF THE MICROSCOPE

Optically it is a matter of indifference whether the instrument is used in the vertical or inclined position. Examination of fluids requires the horizontal stage, and since much of the work in the clinical laboratory is of this nature, it is well to become accustomed to the use of the vertical microscope. While working, one should sit as nearly upright as is possible and compatible with comfort, and the height of the seat should be adjusted accordingly.

It is always best to "focus upward," which saves annoyance and probable damage to slides and objectives. This is accomplished by bringing the objective nearer the slide than the proper focus and then, with the eye at the ocular, by turning the tube up until the object is seen clearly. The fine adjustment should be used only to get an exact focus with the higher power objectives after the instrument is in approximate focus. It should not be turned more than one revolution.

There will be less fatigue to the eyes if both are kept open while using the microscope and if no effort is made to see objects that are not in distinct focus. Fine focusing should be done with the fine adjustment, not with the eye. An experienced microscopist keeps his fingers almost constantly on one of the focusing adjustments.

Although the ability to use the eyes interchangeably is sometimes very desirable, greater skill in recognizing objects will be acquired if the same eye is always used.

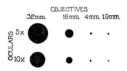

Figure 1–9. Size of the "real fields" (actual areas seen through the microscope) with various objectives and oculars and tube length of 160 mm. The size differs slightly with microscopes of different makes.

The left eye is the more convenient, because the right eye is thus left free to observe the drawing one may wish to make with the right hand. After a little practice one can cause the microscopic image to appear as if it were projected on a sheet of paper placed close to the microscope under the free eye. This gives the effect of a camera lucida and makes it very easy to trace outlines. When one is accustomed to spectacles, they should not be removed.

It is very desirable that one work with the low power objective as much as possible and reserve the high power objective for detailed study of the objects that have been found with the low power objective. This makes both for speed and accuracy. A search for tube casts, for example, with the 4 mm. objective is both time consuming and liable to failure. Even such minute structures as nucleated erythrocytes in a stained blood film are found more quickly with an 8 mm., or even a 16 mm., objective combined with a high power ocular than with an oil immersion lens. It is difficult for one who has not measured it to realize how small the "real field" is, that is, the actual area of the slide that is seen through the microscope (Fig. 1–9).

To be seen most clearly, an object should be brought to the center of the field. Acuity of vision will be greatly enhanced and fatigue lessened if all light except that which enters through the microscope is subdued. Strong light should not be allowed to fall directly on the surface of the slide, for this clouds the image, especially if a low power objective is used.

A useful pointer can be made by placing a straight piece of hair across the opening of the diaphragm of the ocular, cementing one end with a tiny drop of balsam and cutting the hair in two in the middle with small scissors. When the ocular is in place, the hair appears as a black line extending from the periphery to the center of the microscopic field. If the pointer does not appear sharply defined, it is out of focus and the diaphragm within the ocular must be raised or lowered slightly.

One often wishes to mark a particular field on a permanent preparation to refer to it again. If the mechanical stage is permanently fastened to the stage of the microscope, the vernier can be used to mark the position of an object on the slide. There are on the market several "object markers" by which a desired field can be marked with ink or by a circle scratched on the coverglass by a small diamond while the slide is in place on the microscope. The circle is easily located with a low power objective.

CARE OF THE MICROSCOPE

The microscope is a delicate instrument and should be handled accordingly. Even a slight disturbance of its adjustments may cause serious trouble. It is so heavy that one is liable to forget that parts of it are fragile. It seems unnecessary to say that, when there is unusual resistance to any manipulation, force should never be used to overcome it until the cause has first been sought. It is not uncommon to see students, and even graduates, push a high power objective against a microscopic preparation with such force as to break not only the coverglass but even a heavy slide.

To bend the instrument at the joint, the force should be applied to the pillar and never to the tube or the stage.

The microscope should be kept scrupulously clean, and dust must not be allowed to settle on it. When not in use, the instrument should be kept in its case or under a cover. A bell jar is particularly liable to strike the mechanical stage and disturb its adjustment. In the absence of a special cover a square of lintless cloth may be draped over the microscope.

Lens surfaces that have been exposed to dust should be cleaned only with a camel's hair brush. A small brush and a booklet of lens paper should always be at hand in the microscope case. Surfaces that are exposed to finger marks should be cleaned with lens paper or a soft linen handkerchief moistened with water if necessary. The rubbing should be done very gently and with a circular motion. Particles of dirt that appear in the field are on the slide, the ocular, or the condenser. Their site can be determined by moving the slide, rotating the ocular, and lowering the condenser. Dirt on the objective cannot be seen as such; it causes a diffuse cloudiness. When the image is hazy, the objective probably needs cleaning; in case of an oil immersion objective there may be bubbles in the oil.

Oil and balsam that have dried upon the lenses—an insult from which even dry objectives are not immune—may be removed with alcohol or xylol, but these solvents must be used sparingly and carefully because there is danger of softening the cement between the components of the objective. Some manufacturers now claim to use a cement that resists xylol.

When the vulcanite stage becomes brown and discolored, the black color can be restored by rubbing well with petrolatum.

MEASUREMENT OF MICROSCOPIC OBJECTS

The importance of size in identification of microscopic structures cannot be too strongly emphasized. Even very rough measurements will often prevent humiliating blunders. The principal microscopic objects that are measured clinically are animal parasites and their ova and abnormal blood corpuscles. The metric system is used almost exclusively. For very small objects 0.001 mm. has been adopted as the unit of measurement under the name *micron*. It is represented by the Greek letter μ. For larger objects, if exact measurement is not essential, the diameter of a red blood corpuscle (7 to 8 microns) is sometimes taken as a unit. Of the several methods of measurement, the most convenient and accurate is the use of a micrometer ocular. In its simplest form this is similar to an ordinary ocular, but it has within it a glass disk on which is ruled a graduated scale. When this ocular is placed in the tube of the microscope, the ruled lines appear in the microscopic field and the size of an object can be determined readily in terms of the divisions of this scale. The value of these divisions in millimeters manifestly varies with different magnifications. Their value must therefore be determined separately for each objective. This is accomplished through use of a stage micrometer—a glass slide with a carefully ruled scale divided into subdivisions, usually hundredths of a millimeter. The stage micrometer is placed upon the stage of the microscope and brought into focus. The tube of the micrscope is then pushed in or pulled out until two lines of the one scale exactly coincide with two lines of the other. From the number of divisions of the ocular scale which then correspond to each division of the stage micrometer, the value of the former in microns or in fractions of a millimeter can be easily calculated. This value, of course, holds good only for the objective and the tube length with which it was found. The counting slide of a hemacytometer may be used in place of a stage micrometer. The lines of the sides of the small squares used in counting erythrocytes are 50 microns apart. When using the counting chamber with an oil immersion objective, a coverglass must be used; otherwise the oil will fill the ruled lines and cause them to disappear. Any ocular can be converted into a micrometer ocular by placing a micrometer disk—a small circular glass plate with a ruled scale—ruled side down on its diaphragm. If the lines on this are at all hazy, the disk has probably been inserted upside down or else the diaphragm is out of its proper position. Usually it can be pushed up or down as required.

PHOTOMICROGRAPHY

Although high-grade photomicrography requires expensive apparatus and considerable skill, fairly good pictures of microscopic structures can be made by anyone with simple instruments.

Any camera that is equipped with a focusing screen or a ground glass may be used. Remove the lens but retain the shutter for making the exposures. The camera on a tripod or bench block is faced close to the ocular of the microscope. A light, tight connection between the shutter and the ocular can be made of a cylinder of paper or a cloth sleeve with drawstrings. The image will be thrown on the ground glass and is focused by means of the fine adjustment of the microscope. The degree of magnification is determined by placing the ruled slide of the blood counting instru-

ment on the microscope and measuring the image on the focusing screen. For roll film cameras without a ground glass use the lens and set it on infinity and also focus the microscope for infinity. Only trial and error can determine exposures and the area of the histologic section that will be shown.

Oil immersion objectives require more light than low power. The light should be as strong as possible in order to shorten exposures. In microscopic work the light should be carefully centered. Use colored filters between the light and the microscope. The filter should have a color complementary to that detail which it is desired to bring out strongly on the photograph. For blue structures a yellow filter is used; for red structures, a green filter. For the average stained preparation a picric acid yellow or yellowish-green filter will be found satisfactory. When it is necessary to suppress deeply stained objects or to bring out as much of the internal detail as possible, a filter of the same color should be used.

For histologic sections panchromatic plates are best. The length of exposure depends on many factors and can be determined only by trial. Either tray or tank development may be used. Use the developer recommended by the manufacturer of the film. Eastman Kodak has a low priced booklet on photomicrography.

PHASE MICROSCOPY

In 1935 Professor F. Zernike of the University of Groningen announced the application of phase contrast methods to microscopy. This technique has aroused a great deal of interest among medical and biologic workers. Several types of equipment are now available commercially as separate units or as accessories to microscopes of standard design. At present the

Figure 1–10. Phase contrast microscope accessories. (Bausch and Lomb Optical Co.) The photograph shows a rotatable, turret type condenser, a set of four objectives with phase altering patterns in the rear focal planes, a green filter, and a centering telescope.

phase microscope is essentially a research instrument, but the large number of valuable observations that have been made in cytology, bacteriology, mycology, and parasitology suggest that phase contrast methods may find an important place in the technical area of clinical microscopy. The phase microscope permits objects to be visualized by virtue of minute differences in light absorption and refractive index. Thus, it is possible to see and to photograph details that are invisible in the ordinary brightfield instrument. Phase microscopy is most valuable for the examination of specimens that are too thin or too transparent for effective study by the ordinary microscope. The full significance of this technique in medicine and clinical pathology has not been realized. The interested student should consult the excellent studies of Bennett (1951) and his associates.

ELECTRON MICROSCOPY

Many years ago it was realized that the ordinary light microscope had been developed to limits beyond which it could not be expected to further resolve the structure of objects. Fundamentally the function of a microscope is to spread out the light emitted by or reflected from an object, so that minute points or lines separated by minute distances can be distinguished from one another. There is no theoretic limit to pure magnification using ordinary light, but actual microscopic structure is revealed only to the extent that one point or line in the object of study can be distinguished from other points or lines. This important matter of resolving power depends on two factors: the wave length of the light source and the numerical aperture of the lens. The average wave length of ordinary mixed light is about 5000 Å*. It is practically impossible to construct lenses with a numerical aperture greater than 1.5. As a rough approximation the distance between two points that can just be resolved by the light microscope is given by the following equation:

$$d = 0.61 \times \frac{\lambda}{N.A.}$$

Using the limiting factors mentioned, this distance becomes:

$$d = 0.61 \times \frac{5000}{1.5}$$

* The angstrom unit, Å, is a length equal to 1×10^{-8} centimeters or 0.1 mμ.

Thus, it is seen that two points or lines must be separated by a distance of no less than about 2000 Å or 200 mμ in order to be clearly distinguished in the microscopic field.

Understanding the limits of light microscopy immediately suggests a means to surmount these limits. Ultraviolet rays range from about 100 Å to 4000Å in wave length. Using special quartz lenses and photographic equipment for recording the image, it has been possible to double the resolving power or to reduce by approximately one-half the distance between structural lines and points that can be sensed in the microscopic field. Ultraviolet microscopy has proved to have significant usefulness entirely apart from the relatively slight improvement in resolving power. Certain chemical constituents of cells, particularly the purine and pyrimidine ring components of nucleic acids, strongly absorb ultraviolet rays at characteristic wave lengths. Some of these chemical substances can be identified and certain phases of their metabolism can be followed by ultraviolet microscopy.

The electron microscope depends for its operation on the fact that a stream of electrons moving at high velocity behaves like a beam of light of very short wave length.

Figure 1–11. R. C. A. electron microscope. A human hair photographed with this instrument would appear as large as the Lincoln Tunnel.

Focusing of the electron beam is accomplished by adjustable magnetic or electrostatic fields. The image is made visible to the eye by means of a fluorescent screen or is recorded directly on photographic film. Commercially available electron microscopes are capable of resolution to as little as 20 Å or even 10 Å. Magnification can be achieved to as great as 50,000 or even 100,000 times.

Because electrons are readily stopped or deflected by any molecular particles, including gas molecules in the air, electron microscopy must be carried out in a vacuum. This imposes a severe limitation on the type of specimen that can be studied and the manner in which materials must be prepared for examination. Preparations must be completely dessicated and mounted in extremely thin films. Electron microscopic exploration of biologic material, especially the study of human and animal tissues, has only quite recently been opened up with the development of plastic embedding media and techniques for the production of extremely thin sections (Pease, 1960). (Fig. 1-11).

Electron microscopy has made important contributions to bacteriology, and the technique has become practically indispensable to the science of virology. It has made possible a detailed structural analysis of subcellular elements, such as the mitochondria, which are far below the resolving power of the ordinary light microscope. By combining biochemical and electron microscopic methods, we are beginning to approach the structural basis of normal and abnormal function at or near the molecular level. Although electron microscopic methods must now be classed among the tools of research, it seems highly probable that they will be developed along increasingly practical lines and find their way into the clinical laboratory.

REFERENCES

1. Bennett, A. H.: Phase Microscopy. New York, John Wiley & Sons, Inc., 1951.
2. Pease, D. C.: Histological Techniques for Electron Microscopy. New York, Academic Press, Inc., 1960.

Chapter 2

Statistical Tools in Clinical Pathology

By BRADLEY E. COPELAND, M.D.

Laboratory measurements are used by physicians for two purposes: to identify the diseased individual and to follow the progress of the diseased individual under medical therapy. The laboratory itself has two responsibilities to the physician: to provide the physician with an estimate of the variation in the normal human population and to guarantee the reliability of each individual measurement.

SELECTING THE ABNORMAL INDIVIDUAL

Before the abnormal can be identified, the normal population must be defined. To express the normal values of the human population clearly, one measures a series of individuals who are in normal health. The average value is calculated. The dispersion of values around the average is described by the standard deviation. The complete expression of the normal population will consist of the average, showing the center of the normal distribution, and the standard deviation, which indicates the dispersion of the population about the average.

The standard deviation is a descriptive tool, which condenses the frequency distribution of a population into a single measurement unit. Figure 2–1 shows the normal curve of the frequency distribution

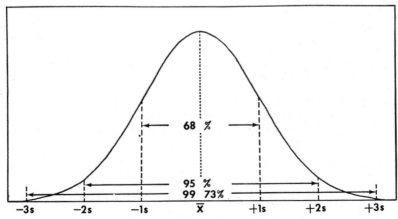

Figure 2–1. Items in normal curve included between average ($\overline{X}$) and $\pm$ 1s = 68%; $\overline{X} \pm$ 2s = 95%; and $\overline{X} \pm$ 3s = 99.7%; (s means standard deviation; $\overline{X}$ means average). (Modified from Croxton, F. E.: Elementary Statistics with Applications in Medicine. New York, Prentice Hall, Inc., 1953.)

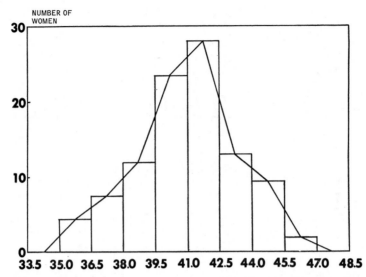

Figure 2–2. Volume of packed red cells per 100 ml. of whole blood for 100 normal young women 18 to 30 years of age. (Data from Osgood, E. E., and Haskins, H. D.: Relation between cell count, cell volume and hemoglobin content of venous blood of normal young women. Arch. Int. Med., *39*:643, 1927. Chart by Croxton, F. E.: Elementary Statistics with Application in Medicine. New York, Prentice-Hall, Inc., 1953.)

of a population. The horizontal axis (x-axis) represents the units of measurement, and the vertical axis (y-axis) represents the frequency or number of times each value occurs. The standard deviation shown in Fig. 2–1 describes the distribution of a population as follows: 68 per cent of the population is included within plus or minus (±) one standard deviation from the average; 95 per cent of the population is included within plus or minus (±) two standard deviations from the average; and 99.7 per cent of the population is included within plus or minus (±) three standard deviations from the average.

The most frequent measurements cluster around the average, whereas measurements far from the average occur less and less frequently until a point is reached where for practical purposes no normal values occur. This distribution of measurements about an average value has been shown to hold true for all types of biologic, chemical, and physical measurements. The measurements may be made upon a population of humans, a population of animals, or a series or population of inanimate objects.

DECISION CRITERION NO. 1

Does the individual differ from the normal population with respect to a particular measurement? If the value lies outside the ± three standard deviation limits (99.7 per cent), then it is clear that the individual in question does not belong to the normal population. If the value lies outside the two standard deviation limits (95 per cent) and within the three standard deviation limits (99.7 per cent), the individual possibly may not be one of the normal population. The physician would need to give extra thought and attention to this patient.

A typical normal distribution of measured values on a normal human population is shown in Fig. 2–2. The hematocrit of 100 normal young women is recorded in the frequency distribution form. The average hematocrit equals 41.0 ml. packed red cells per 100 ml. of whole blood. One standard deviation limit, including 68 per cent of the measurements, is ± 2.4 ml. packed red blood cells per 100 ml. whole blood. The two and three standard deviation limits are 4.8 and 7.2 ml. respectively. Therefore, using the average and the standard deviation value, the complete frequency distribution can be reconstructed as follows: 68 per cent of the young normal women had hematocrit values between 38.6 and 43.4, 95 per cent of the young normal women had hematocrit values between 36.2 and 45.8, and 99.7 per cent of the young normal women had hematocrit values between 33.8 and 48.2.

It is usually possible for a laboratory to measure its own normal values. Thirty or 40 normal samples collected over several months would give a reasonable approximation of the normal value for the method, the laboratory, and the geographic location. Attention should be given to the age range and to the sex distribution. Our true knowledge of normal values is still very limited. Several texts devoted to normal values are listed at the end of this chapter.

Guaranteeing Reliable Measurements. The second laboratory responsibility is to guarantee the reliability of every measurement. Two difficulties should be identified. First, no method of analysis gives exactly the same result each time it is repeated. There is an inherent variability characteristic of each measurement procedure that cannot be avoided. Second, practical considerations limit the amount of sample available for measurement. Each sample is one of a population of possible samples that could have been taken from the subject.

Quality control system for the clinical laboratory. Quality control systems have been developed to guarantee reliability and at the same time require only limited blood samples. A large number of identical samples from the same large pool are prepared and are frozen to preserve stability. Every batch of laboratory measurements is accompanied by one of the identical pool samples. The variability of repeated analyses is measured under regular operating conditions, using the identical samples, and is expressed in standard deviation units. If the quality control sample does not fall within the known limits of inherent variability, the measurements are rejected and the analyses are repeated. In this way each laboratory measurement is accompanied by a known sample, which undergoes exactly the same steps and conditions as the unknown samples.

There are several acceptable methods for setting up quality control. The system described has been found practical, but each laboratory should develop a quality control technique suitable for its own purposes.

Preparation of a quality control pool. Excess serum is salvaged daily from regular specimens and frozen in a deepfreeze until 2,000 to 3,000 ml. are collected. Hemolyzed, lipemic, and jaundiced sera are avoided. Fasting human donors may be used if the supply of serum is not available. Beef serum is available commercially and is not expensive. The pool should be thawed and mixed thoroughly. Then the pool is divided into samples (aliquots), which are convenient for storage in the deepfreeze. Pyrex screw cap tubes are convenient. Plastic vials capped to prevent evaporation are satisfactory.

It is important to remember that when frozen serum melts, pure water layers out at the top surface. Be sure to mix thoroughly before using each sample. This is the most frequent cause of out-of-control measurements. Changes of 50 to 100 per cent can be caused by incomplete mixing.

Calculation of average and standard deviation values. The average value and standard deviation for each method to be controlled should be established before the pool is put into service. Pool samples are processed with the daily measurements for 15 to 25 days. From the 15 to 25 values an average and a standard deviation are calculated.

Example: Daily Potassium Values Run for 15 Days Prior to Institution of a New Control Pool

February 5	5.7
February 6	6.0
February 7	5.9
February 8	5.7
February 9	5.7
February 11	5.9
February 12	5.7
February 13	5.7
February 14	5.8
February 15	5.7
February 16	5.9
February 18	5.7
February 19	6.0
February 20	5.8
February 21	5.6

Procedure for Calculating Average and Standard Deviation

1. Record analyses in column one.
2. Add column one.
3. Calculate average of column one (step A).
4. Calculate and record in column two the individual differences from the average.
5. Square each individual difference and record in the third column.
6. Add column three (sum of squared differences).
7. Calculate standard deviation (step B).

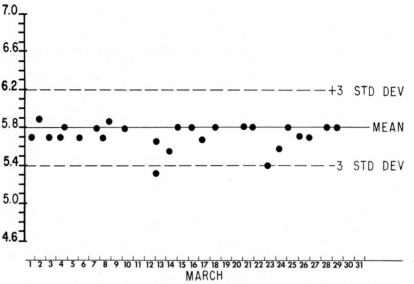

Figure 2–3. Quality control measurements of potassium (mEq./L.) for one month. (From: Copland, B. E., Newell, J., and Dolan, W.: Quality Control Manual. Chicago, Am. Soc. Clin. Pathologists, 1959.)

Daily Potassium Values

(mEq./L.)	DIFFERENCE FROM AVERAGE	SQUARED DIFFERENCE FROM AVERAGE
1. 5.7	0.1	0.01
2. 6.0	0.2	0.04
3. 5.9	0.1	0.01
4. 5.7	0.1	0.01
5. 5.7	0.1	0.01
6. 5.9	0.1	0.01
7. 5.7	0.1	0.01
8. 5.7	0.1	0.01
9. 5.8	0.0	0.00
10. 5.7	0.1	0.01
11. 5.9	0.1	0.01
12. 5.7	0.1	0.01
13. 6.0	0.2	0.04
14. 5.8	0.0	0.00
15. 5.6	0.2	0.04
86.8		0.22

In the example, the average daily potassium value is 5.8 mEq./L. The standard deviation is 0.13 mEq./L.

When beginning quality control, one should set the control limits at ± 3 SD from the average. The ± three standard deviation limits for the example are ± 0.39 mEq./L. or a range of 5.41 to 6.19 mEq./L. After the control system is well established, the limits may be narrowed to ± two standard deviations, which decreases the overall variability of reported measurements. In the example this would be ± 2 SD = 5.54 to 6.06.

Figure 2–3 shows a typical month of quality control measurements and the evaluation of these values. Note the out-of-control value on March 12. All measure-

Calculations

Step A. Average $= \dfrac{\text{total sum of analyses}}{n}$

n = number of measurements = 15

Average $= \dfrac{86.8}{15} = 5.78 = 5.8$ mEq./L.

Step B. Standard deviation $= \sqrt{\dfrac{\text{sum of squared differences from average}}{n-1}}$

Sum of squared differences from average = 0.22

$n-1 = 15-1 = 14$

Standard deviation $= \sqrt{\dfrac{0.22}{14}} = \sqrt{0.0157}$

Standard deviation = 0.13 mEq./L.

ments were repeated, and the second control on March 12 is shown.

The reliability of each laboratory measurement is in this way guaranteed to be within the predictable limits of the inherent variability of the method.

DECISION CRITERION NO. 2

When is an individual measurement considered reliable? If the quality control sample is in control, the individual sample measurements are reliable because no unusual variables are operating.

Evaluation of Change in a Single Patient: The Significant Change Limit. The physician must interpret day-to-day or month-to-month changes in his patient's measurements. He needs tools to distinguish the inherent variability change due to methodology from the real change in the patient. The information gained from quality control supplies the physician with the tool by which he can follow the progress of the patient under medical therapy from day to day or month to month. The significant change limit, three times the quality control standard deviation, is defined as that change which results from a change in the patient and not from the method.

DECISION CRITERION NO. 3

What change in successive measurements indicates a real change in the patient? A change greater than three times the quality control standard deviation is called the significant change limit.

What significant change limits indicate good laboratory performance? At present only preliminary estimates can be given. Table 1 shows the values obtained in well-run laboratories. Note that there is not complete uniformity of performance, and the final criterion should be the use to which the test is being put at the bedside. Unused precision is very expensive. The Clinical Standards Committee of the College of American Pathologists is developing a set of practical performance values for quality control.

Average Versus the Individual: A Note of Caution. In the medical literature, publications frequently indicate a real difference between the average of a normal series of individuals and the average of a series of diseased individuals. Scientifically this is important information. However, this should not lead to the conclusion that

such a comparison is useful in making the diagnosis of the disease in question. The diagnosis of disease in an individual depends upon the capacity of a test to show a complete separation of a normal population from a diseased population (Fig. 2–4, A and C). A significant difference between averages can be shown when there is considerable overlap in the two populations. For example, the difference between the

Table 1–1. **Quality Control Standard Deviation Limits**

ANALYSIS	LAB A	LAB B	LAB C	LAB D	LAB E
Blood urea nitrogen	0.60	3.3	1.2	—	0.5
Calcium	0.10	0.24	0.2	—	0.22
Carbon dioxide	0.34	2.0	—	0.33	—
Chloride	0.8	2.04	—	0.5	1.10
Cholesterol	1.8	7.3	5.0	4.51	6.0
Creatinine	0.08	0.15	—	0.04	—
Glucose	2.1	6.3	5.5	1.1	3.0
Phosphorus	0.08	0.22	0.07	0.14	0.08
Potassium	0.04	0.22	0.08	0.05	0.15
Protein-bound iodine	0.30	0.65	0.4	—	0.4
Sodium	0.70	1.8	0.2	0.87	1.4
Total protein	0.05	0.16	0.10	0.22	0.11
Transaminase	—	1.96	1.8	—	—
Uric acid	0.08	0.62	0.02	0.44	0.15

Laboratory A — Freier and Rausch; Freier and Benson
Laboratory B — New England Deaconess Hospital
Laboratory C — Lahey Clinic
Laboratory D — New England Baptist Hospital
Laboratory E — Benenson

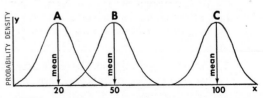

Figure 2–4. Distribution with same standard deviation or spread but different mean values. (Moroney, M. J.: Facts from Figures. London, Penguin Books, 1956.)

average male height and the average female height is significant. It cannot be inferred that, for the individual, maleness or femaleness can be identified on the basis of height.

Figure 2–4 shows examples of population overlap (A and B) and complete differentiation between populations A and C.

The usefulness of a test to identify a disease state is related to its capacity to help in a problem situation in which the diagnosis is not obvious. Many tests can clearly separate normal populations (Fig. 2–4A) from the grossly diseased population (Fig. 2–4C). The crux of the matter is this: How successful is a particular test in indicating disease in the problem case diagnostically, in the presence of other disease states, and in the early stages of the disease when symptoms and physical signs are not present, that is (Fig. 2–4), population A and population B?

Improvement of Methodology and Instrumentation. It is evident that to reduce the inherent variability of measurements, the major effort should be in the areas of methodology, instrumentation, and primary standards. A method or an instrument that is highly reproducible on a single day may show considerable day-to-day variability over the period of a year. Therefore, it is important to evaluate new methods and new instruments for their inherent variability over a year's time in order to truly evaluate their acceptability in the field. No methods currently published carry this evaluation nor do any of the new instruments. The tools are readily available for such evaluation and should be utilized. Indeed, workers in the field should demand this information.

The new instruments and new methods constantly being added only create more confusion and increase the variability of this problem, since none are accompanied by the proper credentials for reproducibility and quality control under regular operating conditions.

Technique for Comparing New Methods with Standard Methods and New Instruments with Established Instruments

1. Collect a sample pool large enough to make 20 measurements with each method or instrument.
2. Make the series of 15 to 20 measurements under actual operating conditions, including the effect of different days.
3. Compute the average and standard deviation for each series of measurements.

DECISION CRITERION NO. 4

Do the methods or instruments under investigation have the same precision, or does one show significantly better precision? If one standard deviation is one-half the other, this method or instrument can be said to be significantly more precise.

DECISION CRITERION NO. 5

Do the methods or instruments give the same average values? If the difference between the two averages is three times greater than the larger standard deviation, it can be concluded that the difference between the averages is significant. This would indicate a constant error or difference between the method or instruments.

Criteria for New Instruments

1. Precision under ideal conditions.
2. Precision under regular working conditions (quality control limits over at least a one-year period).
3. Accuracy (that is, absolute concentration level) and relation to medically accepted values.
4. A complete manual in which all parts are described.
5. Trouble-shooting guide.
6. Approximate cost estimate for yearly maintenance (20 per cent per year has been recommended).
7. Availability of parts and repair service (a four-hour repair time would be ideal).
8. Operating criteria for daily checking.

Criteria for New Methods

1. Precision under optimal conditions.
2. Precision under regular working conditions.
3. Accuracy (that is, absolute concentration level) and relation to medically accepted values.
4. Quality control limits obtainable over a year's time.
5. Number of analytical runs out of control in a one-year period.

IN SUMMARY

Laboratory measurements are useful only when interpreted with the knowledge of the normal population variation and an understanding of the inherent variability present in all instruments and methods.

The standard deviation is a descriptive tool, which is very useful to describe variation in populations. These properties make it indispensable in quality control systems and in other criteria related to the decision-making process in the laboratory and at the bedside.

REFERENCES

1. Benenson, A. S., Thompson, H. L., and Klugerman, M. R.: Application of laboratory controls in clinical chemistry. Am. J. Clin. Path., 25:87, 1955.
2. Bodansky, M., and Bodansky, O.: Biochemistry of Disease. 2nd Ed. New York, The Macmillan Company, 1952.
3. Freier, E. F., and Rausch, V. L.: Quality control in clinical chemistry. Am. J. Med. Technology, 24:195, 1958.
4. Spector, W. B. (ed.): Handbook of Biological Data. Philadelphia, W. B. Saunders Company, 1956.
5. Sunderman, F. W., and Boerner, F.: Normal Values in Clinical Medicine. Philadelphia, W. B. Saunders Company, 1949.

Chapter 3

The Urine

By RAYMOND A. SANFORD, M.D., *and*
BENJAMIN B. WELLS, M.D.

Examination of the urine is one of the most important of all medical diagnostic procedures. The fact that this body fluid is so readily available and that much of the technology applied to its study is relatively easy to accomplish has led to the reprehensible practice of routine examination *en masse*. The large number of urinalyses ordered without specific reference to the diagnostic problem at hand and often without subsequent interpretation has seriously reduced the effectiveness of this examination and has created an unwarranted disregard for it among both physicians and laboratory workers. As the end product of a complicated and delicately balanced physiologic system the urine is a valuable index to many normal and pathologic mechanisms. Not only is the urine altered by most intrinsic diseases of the kidney, but many extrarenal conditions produce changes that have important diagnostic implications. In order to assure the inherent advantages of the urinalysis certain simple technical precautions must be constantly observed. Of these there are two that eclipse all others: the urine specimen must be fresh, and the urinary sediment must be examined microscopically by someone who is thoroughly trained in this skill and genuinely interested in its results, preferably the physician himself.

The urine is an extremely complex aqueous solution of various organic and inorganic substances. Most of the substances are either waste products from the body metabolism or products derived directly from the foods eaten. Normally the total amount of solid constituents carried off in 24 hours is about 60 gm., of which the organic substances make up about 35 gm. and the inorganic substances about 25 gm.

The most important organic constituents are urea, uric acid, and creatinine. Urea constitutes about half of all the solids, or about 30 gm., in 24 hours. The chief inorganic constituents are the chlorides, phosphates, sulfates, and ammonia. The chlorides, practically all in the form of sodium chloride, make up about half of the inorganic substances, or about 13 gm., in 24 hours.

Certain substances appear in the urine only when pathologic conditions are present. The most important of these are proteins, carbohydrates, acetone, bile, and hemoglobin. Hormones appear in the urine in varying concentrations, and their detection and quantitation may have very practical clinical significance. As an illustration we may note the common pregnancy tests, which depend on the excretion of hormones. A large number of chemical end products of normal and abnormal metabolism are excreted in the urine. Determination of these substances is generally beyond the scope of the clinical laboratory, but many procedures of current research interest may ultimately find their way into standard clinical practice. In addition to the substances in solution all urine contains various microscopic structures.

Collection and Preservation of Urine Specimens. For most clinical purposes a random voided specimen is adequate. Such a specimen is suitable only for qualitative examinations, since the concentration of any solute will vary widely with the volume of water being excreted at that time. The first urine voided in the morning is usually recommended as most suitable, since this specimen is likely to have the most uniform volume and concentration and the lowest pH. The low pH insures better preservation of the formed elements. The constancy of volume and concentration will tend to make more reliable the observation of quantitative variations in the formed elements from day to day. It will be remembered that glycosuria is somewhat less likely to appear in the first morning specimen, and albuminuria, particularly the orthostatic type, is less frequently observed.

The random specimen should be freshly voided and delivered to the laboratory as quickly as possible. The urine is an excellent culture medium for many organisms, and bacterial growth with decompensation of urinary constituents begins quickly and proceeds actively. If a delay of several hours is unavoidable, the specimen should be kept in the refrigerator. When handling at ordinary temperatures is necessary, toluene is the best all-round preservative. Addition of enough toluene to form a layer on top of the urine will maintain the specimen in suitable condition for most examinations. A crystal of thymol is also satisfactory. When it is of especial importance to preserve the structure of cells and casts in the urine, 40 per cent formalin in the proportion of one drop to one ounce of specimen is the most effective agent. Calcium, most other inorganic constituents, and the nitrogen content can be well preserved over a long period of time by strong acidification with sulfuric acid.

The preservation of urobilinogen in the urine requires unusual precautions. To assure alkalinity, a half teaspoonful of sodium carbonate should be placed in the specimen bottle before the urine is voided. Unnecessary exposure to light must also be avoided. These and similar matters cannot be left to chance or in the hands of disinterested attendants. Specific directions must be issued by the physician.

A 24-hour collection is required if quantitative estimations of urinary constituents are to be made. To insure proper collection, one must issue clear and explicit directions to attendants and patients. When patients are able to cooperate, it is often found that they carry out directions more accurately than most office or hospital personnel. It is best that directions be written and that they be handed directly to the persons concerned. Many annoying misunderstandings

will be avoided if specific times are stated. The patient may be told to empty his bladder at a specific time, say 8 a.m. He should discard this urine but should save all the urine voided up to 8 a.m. of the following day. At that time he should empty his bladder whether he feels like doing so or not. The urine voided at this time should be added to the collected specimen.

Rarely, if ever, should catheterization be used for the collection of urine. It has been clearly demonstrated that even the most meticulous sterile technique will not prevent contamination of the bladder and the upper urinary tract during passage of a catheter. Fortunately the recently developed procedures of quantitative bacteriologic examination of the urine have essentially eliminated the necessity for catheterized specimens for urinalysis.

After a correct collection has been made, there follows the equally important business of labeling the specimen. In addition to identifying the patient fully, the label should note the time of collection and the special procedures that are requested.

Routine Examination. The selection of tests will vary with the circumstances. In the usual office and hospital practice it is customary to note the quantity of the specimen, the color, the transparency or appearance, the reaction, and the specific gravity. Any unusual appearance, odor, or evidence of poor preservation will, of course, be noted. Qualitative tests, generally reported in semiquantitative units, are performed for protein, sugar, and acetone bodies. The sediment is always examined carefully with the microscope.

GENERAL CHARACTERISTICS

Quantity. The average daily output of urine is between 1200 and 1500 ml. Quantities greater than 2000 ml. per day must be thought of as pathologic. A normal individual, even under conditions of severe water restriction, does not excrete less than 30 ml. of urine per hour (720 ml. a day). The limit of diuresis in the normal is about 1200 ml. an hour. An excretion of less than 30 ml. of urine per hour indicates definite oliguria. When fluid intake is restricted (no fluid for 14 hours), an excretion of more than 55 ml. an hour represents polyuria.

The quantity of urine is decreased (oliguria) in conditions of dehydration, such as severe diarrhea, prolonged vomiting, and fever without adequate fluid intake. Oliguria also occurs in diseases that interfere with circulation to the kidney, such as poorly compensated heart disease, especially during the accumulation of edema and fluid in the serous cavities. In acute renal failure and in the advanced phases of destructive intrinsic diseases of the kidney the volume of urine is usually decreased. In cases of uremia, the amount of urine is generally greatly decreased and excretion may be entirely suppressed (anuria).

The quantity of urine is increased (polyuria) as a result of excessive fluid intake, during absorption of large quantities of edema fluid (as may occur with successful treatment of cardiac decompensation), and by many nervous conditions. It is often increased in certain types of chronic renal diseases, in diabetes insipidus, and in diabetes mellitus. In diabetes mellitus, the daily quantity of urine is often as much as 2 to 5 liters.

Under normal conditions, the urine passed during the day (8:00 a.m. to 8:00 p.m.) is three to four times the volume of that excreted during the night (8:00 p.m. to 8:00 a.m.). An increasing night volume of urine is an important early sign of renal decompensation. It is usually recognized by the complaint of nocturia before laboratory confirmation is obtained. Loss of the normal day-night ratio is directly associated with a decreasing capacity to concentrate urine to a normal specific gravity. Loss of the normal day-night ratio is correlated with changes found in the concentration test, which will be described later.

Color. The color of the urine varies considerably in health and depends largely on the quantity of urine voided. Dilute urine is pale and concentrated urine is highly colored. The usual color is yellow or reddish yellow owing to the presence of several pigments, chiefly urochrome and urobilin. The presence of blood gives the urine a red or brown, smoky color. Urine containing bile is yellowish or brown, and a yellow foam forms when the urine is shaken. Many drugs and some foods give colors to the urine; these seldom have diagnostic importance.

Among clinical rarities may be mentioned the reddish urine of porphyria, the brown to black color of homogentisic acid in alkaptonuria, and the black color of melanin occasionally seen in association with extensive melanotic sarcoma.

A classic finding of diabetes mellitus is a pale greenish urine that has a high specific gravity.

Transparency or Appearance. Freshly voided normal urine is usually clear but not necessarily so. Most of the time cloudiness in the urine has no pathologic significance, but patients frequently complain of the appearance. Cloudiness may usually be ascribed to one of the following:

1. Amorphous phosphates. These form a white sediment in neutral or alkaline urine and disappear on addition of acid. This type of sediment is extremely common; it is of no clinical importance. The amount of phosphate sediment increases when the urine stands and becomes more alkaline by formation of ammonia.

2. Amorphous urates. It is less common to see a white or pink cloud of this material. It disappears on heating.

3. Pus. The white cloud and sediment due to pus cells may be grossly indistinguishable from amorphous phosphates. It does not disappear, but is increased, when acid is added.

4. Blood. A reddish brown or smoky color may be caused by the presence of blood in the urine. The gross observation must be confirmed by microscopic or chemical tests.

5. Bacteria. These produce a uniform cloud or opalescence. Bacteria sufficient to produce cloudiness are practically always those that multiply in the urine after voiding and usually have no clinical significance.

Odor. About the only practical use to be made of this observation is in detecting urines that are too decomposed to be worth examining. The fruity odor of diabetic urine may occasionally be useful, but this odor is best noted on the breath of the patient and the ketones should be determined chemically in the urine. Everyone is familiar with the mercaptan odor of urine after asparagus has been eaten. A distinctly fecal odor may be due to perforation of the intestine into the bladder. A cloudy urine with an ammoniacal odor suggests cystitis or pyelitis, usually with obstruction in the urinary tract.

Reaction. Normally the mixed 24-hour urine is acid in reaction with a pH of about 6. Individual samples may be acid, alkaline, neutral, or amphoteric. The extremes of urine pH in health are 4.7 to 8.0. Urine voided after a full meal is usually alkaline. Except under special therapeutic or dietary regimens observation of urine reaction is of little or no clinical importance. It is well to remember that formed elements often disintegrate in alkaline urine but may remain well preserved for some time if the reaction is acidic. Extreme alkalinity may be due to ammoniacal decomposition of the urine either before or after voiding. A very satisfactory method of testing the reaction of urine and roughly determining the pH is by the use of nitrazine paper.*

Specific Gravity. This is a relatively important step in the urinalysis. The specific gravity is most conveniently estimated by means of the urinometer. This is a simple instrument, but it must be used correctly and its calibrations must be checked from time to time. Unless the urine is refrigerated before examination, it is seldom necessary to make a correction for temperature in ordinary clinical work. Each type of urinometer has its temperature of calibration shown on the float. For greater accuracy add 0.001 to the reading for each 3° C. above this temperature or subtract 0.001 for each 3° C. below the temperature of calibration. Care should be taken that the urinometer does not touch the side of the tube and that air bubbles are removed from the surface of the urine. Bubbles are easily removed with a strip of filter paper. With most instruments the reading is taken from the bottom of the meniscus. A long scale on the stem is desirable because of the greater ease of accurate reading.

The normal range of specific gravity of the urine is about 1.003 to 1.030. Under pathologic conditions, an extreme variation of 1.001 to 1.060 is possible. If the specific

* Manufactured by E. R. Squibb & Sons, New York, N.Y.

gravity determined on random specimens shows a concentration in any one sample of 1.025 or more and a variation between individual samples of as much as ten points in the last two figures of the readings, it is usually not necessary to do a concentration test of renal function. A concentration test is frequently carried out when all the information it could possibly yield is already on the patient's chart in the form of random urinalyses.

The specific gravity of a random specimen has important bearing on the interpretation of other findings in the urinalysis. All proteinaceous casts (hyaline, granular, or cell-containing) tend to dissolve and disappear in dilute urine, particularly if the reaction is alkaline. Also red cells are hemolyzed in dilute urine. The apparent degree of proteinuria may also change with specific gravity; e.g., a 3 plus reaction in a concentrated urine may become a trace in a dilute sample.

Contrary to general belief it is rarely necessary to make a correction for the protein content of urine. The specific gravity is increased by only 0.003 for each 1 per cent of protein in the urine. Thus a 3 plus reading by the heat-and-acetic-acid test would raise the specific gravity by no more than about 0.001.

CHEMICAL EXAMINATION

Normal Constituents

Of the large number of organic and inorganic substances normally present in the urine only a few demand any consideration from the clinician. Table 3–1 outlines the average composition from the clinical,

Table 3–1. Composition of Normal Urine

	GRAMS IN 24 HOURS	GRAMS (APPROXIMATE AVERAGE)
Water	1000–1500	1200
Total substances in solution	55–70	60
Inorganic substances	20–30	25
Chlorides (chiefly sodium chloride)	10–15	12.5
Phosphates (estimated as phosphoric acid), total	2.5–3.5	3
Earthy (⅓ of total)		1
Alkaline (⅔ of total)		2
Sulfates (estimated a sulfuric acid), total	1.5–3	2.5
Mineral, 9/10 of total		2.25
Conjugate, 1/10 of total		0.25
Includes indican		Trace
Ammonia	0.5–1	0.7
Organic substances	30–40	35
Urea	25–35	30
Uric acid	0.4–1	0.7

rather than from the chemical, standpoint. Only the 24-hour quantities are given, since they alone furnish an accurate basis for comparison. The student cannot learn too soon that percentages mean little or nothing unless they furnish a means of calculating the elimination in 24 hours. Although the conjugate sulfates are organic compounds, they are included for the sake of convenience with the inorganic sulfates.

Among constituents that are of little clinical importance or are present only in traces are iron, carbonates, nitrates, silicates, fluorides, creatinine, hippuric acid, purine bases, oxalic acid, volatile fatty acids, pigments, and acetone.

Variations in body weight, diet, and exercise cause marked fluctuations in the total solids and in individual substances.

Chlorides. Chlorides are derived from the food and are excreted mainly as sodium chloride. The amount excreted normally is 10 to 15 gm. in 24 hours. It is much affected by the diet and is reduced to a minimum in starvation.

Excretion of chlorides is diminished in some forms of nephritis and in febrile diseases, especially in pneumonia and in inflammation, which lead to the formation of large exudates. In extensive burns there is a diminution of chlorides in the urine. Saline injections comprise an important part of the treatment. Diminution of the urinary chlorides is also sometimes observed in severe diarrhea and in other gastrointestinal disturbances. Determination of urinary chloride excretion is frequently used as an index of sodium depletion in the treatment of cardiac decompensation by low sodium diets.

Qualitative test for chlorides. The simple Fantus test will show the presence of chlorides and also indicate any great alteration in the amount. Place 10 drops of fresh centrifuged urine in a test tube and add 1 drop of 20 per cent potassium chromate solution as an indicator. Add, drop by drop, a 2.9 per cent silver nitrate solution until a permanent and distinct red-brown color appears. To assure uniform size of drops, the same dropper must be used all the time; it should be rinsed well with distilled water between uses. The number of drops of silver nitrate required to produce the red color change is equal to the approximate concentration of chloride in the urine expressed as sodium chloride in grams per liter.

Normal urine requires from 6 to 12 drops of silver nitrate. In cases of acute salt depletion the amount may be 1 to 2 drops or less.

Quantitative test for chlorides. The well-known method of Schales and Schales (1941) is simple, reliable, and sufficiently accurate for ordinary clinical work.

Reagents

1. Standard sodium chloride solution. Dry sodium chloride at 120° C. overnight. Make aqueous solution containing 1 gm. per liter, using chemical balance, volumetric flask, and distilled water.

2. 2 N nitric acid. Dilute 115.4 ml. of concentrated nitric acid to 1 liter with distilled water.

3. 0.05 N nitric acid. Dilute 25 ml. of 2N nitric acid to 1 liter with distilled water.

4. Indicator. Dissolve 100 mg. diphenylcarbazone (Eastman Kodak No. 4459) in 100 ml. of 95 percent alcohol. Store in refrigerator in dark bottle. Make fresh solution each month. Deepening color of indicator solution indicates deterioration.

5. Standard mercuric nitrate solution. Dissolve 10 to 15 gm. of mercuric nitrate in 1 liter of distilled water. Allow insoluble material to settle. Take 730 ml. of the supernatant liquid, add 100 ml. of 2N nitric acid, and dilute to 5 liters with distilled water. Titrate samples and dilute until 1 ml. of mercuric chloride is equivalent to 0.50 ml. of the standard chloride solution. This solution keeps indefinitely.

Technique

1. Dilute 0.5 ml. of urine to 5 ml. with 0.05 N nitric acid in a 50 ml. Erlenmeyer flask.

2. Add 8 drops of indicator solution.

3. Titrate with mercuric nitrate solution to the first definite and permanent pink-violet color. In urines containing high concentrations of protein, the color of the slightly turbid mixture is first salmon-red and changes after titration to deep violet. As titration proceeds slowly, the solution becomes clear or pale yellow. The end point is a sharp change to pale violet.

4. Since 1 ml. of mercuric nitrate is equivalent to 0.5 ml. of standard sodium chloride containing 1 mg. per ml., when a urine sample of 5 ml. is used, the number of ml. of mercuric nitrate used is equivalent to the mg./ml. or gm./L. of sodium chloride in the urine.

5. Multiply the number of ml. of mercuric nitrate solution used by the 24-hour volume to give the excretion rate of chloride (as sodium chloride) in gm. per 24 hours.

Phosphates. Phosphates are derived largely from the food; only a small proportion results from metabolism. The normal daily output of phosphoric acid is about 2.5 to 3.5 gm.

The urinary phosphates are of two kinds: alkaline phosphates which make up two thirds of the whole and include the phosphates of sodium and potassium, and earthy phosphates, which constitute one-third and include the phosphates of calcium and magnesium. Earthy phosphates are frequently thrown out of solution in neutral or alkaline urine and, as amorphous phosphates, form a very common sediment. This sediment seldom indicates an excessive excretion of phosphoric acid. It is usually merely an indication of diminished acidity of the urine or of an increase in the proportion of phosphoric acid eliminated as earthy phosphates. When the urine undergoes ammoniacal decomposition, some of the ammonia set free combines with magnesium phosphate to form ammoniomagnesium phosphate (triple phosphate), which is only slightly soluble in alkaline urine and is deposited in typical crystalline form.

From the clinical point of view variations in the amount of phosphates in the urine are unimportant, and no method for their determination need be given here.

Sulfates. The urinary sulfates are derived partly from the food, especially meats, and partly from body metabolism. The normal urinary output of sulfuric acid is about 1.5 to 3 gm. daily. It is increased in conditions associated with active metabolism; in general the amount that is excreted may be taken as a rough index of protein metabolism.

About nine-tenths of this sulfuric acid is eliminated in combination with various mineral substances, chiefly sodium, potassium, calcium, and magnesium (*mineral or preformed sulfates*). A tenth is eliminated in combination with certain aromatic substances, which are mostly products of protein putrefaction in the intestine but are derived in part from destructive metabolism (*conjugate* or *ethereal sulfates*). Among these aromatic substances are indole, phenol, and skatole. By far the most important of the conjugate sulfates, and

representative of the group, is potassium indoxyl sulfate.

Calcium. There may be considerable variation in the amount of calcium that is excreted in the urine. A very simple test for calcium in the urine has been devised by Sulkowitch. This is a rough quantitative test for the amount of calcium that is excreted in cases of hypoparathyroidism, hyperparathyroidism, or urinary calculi.

Sulkowitch's test (Barney and Sulkowitch, 1937). The patient should be kept on a neutral, low calcium diet before the test is begun. Save a 24-hour specimen of urine.

Reagent.

Take 2.5 gm. of oxalic acid, 2.5 gm. of ammonium oxalate, and 5 ml. of glacial acetic acid. Dissolve in distilled water and make up to 150 ml.

Technique.

1. Take equal parts of urine and Sulkowitch's reagent in a test tube.

2. Mix thoroughly and allow to stand for two or three minutes. The calcium in the urine will come down almost immediately as a fine, white precipitate of calcium oxalate.

If there is *no precipitate*, there is no calcium and the concentration of serum calcium is probably 5 to 7.5 mg. per 100 ml. If there is a *fine, white cloud*, there is a moderate amount of calcium and the value for the serum calcium is in the normal range, that is, 9 to 11 mg. per 100 ml. If the precipitate is *heavy*, like milk, or *very heavy*, the danger of hypercalcemia is present. The amount of precipitate may be graded 1, 2, 3, or 4.

Urea. From the standpoint of physiology urea is the most important constituent of the urine. It is the principal waste product of metabolism and constitutes about half of all the solids excreted. About 20 to 35 gm. of urea is excreted in the urine in 24 hours. It represents 85 to 90 per cent of the total nitrogen of the urine, and its quantitative estimation is a simple, though not very accurate, method of ascertaining the state of nitrogenous excretion. This is true, however, only in normal individuals on an average mixed diet. If the diet is low in protein, the urea may represent only 60 per cent of the total nitrogen. Under pathologic conditions the proportion of nitrogen distributed among the various nitrogen-containing substances undergoes great variation. The only accurate index of protein metabolism is, therefore, the total output of nitrogen, which can be estimated by the Kjeldahl method or by one of its modifications. When a mixed diet is being used, the nitrogen of the urine is distributed about as follows: urea nitrogen, 86.9 per cent; ammonia nitrogen, 4.4 per cent; creatinine nitrogen, 3.6 per cent; uric acid nitrogen, 0.75 per cent; and "undetermined nitrogen," chiefly in amino acids, 4.3 per cent.

Normally the amount of urea excreted in the urine is greatly influenced by exercise and diet. It is increased by copious drinking of water and by the administration of ammonium salts of organic acids.

The excretion of urea is increased pathologically in fevers and in many other conditions accompanied by increased metabolism, tissue destruction, or absorption of large exudates. A decrease in the amount of urea in the urine is due either to lessened formation within the body, such as may occur in severe liver disease, or to retention of urea, as may occur in cases of renal failure. Determination of urine urea alone is not used as a practical clinical observation. The method is used, however, as a part of the urea clearance test for the study of kidney function.

Uric Acid. Uric acid is the most important of a group of substances called "purine bodies," which are derived chiefly from the nucleins of food (exogenous uric acid), and from metabolic destruction of the nuclei of the body (endogenous uric acid). The daily output of uric acid in the urine is about 0.4 to 1 gm. The amount of the other purine bodies together is about a tenth that of uric acid. Excretion of these substances is greatly increased by a diet rich in nucleins, as sweetbreads and liver.

Uric acid exists in the urine in the form of urates, chiefly of sodium and potassium, which in concentrated urine are readily thrown out of solution and constitute the familiar sediment of "amorphous urates." This, together with the fact that uric acid is frequently deposited as crystals, constitutes its chief interest to the practitioner. It is a very common error to consider these deposits as evidence of excessive excretion of uric acid.

The greatest increase of uric acid occurs in leukemia in which there is extensive destruction of leukocytes, in diseases associated with active destruction of the liver and other organs rich in nuclei, and during absorption of a pneumonic exudate. There is generally an increase during roentgenologic treatment. The excretion of uric acid is decreased before an attack of gout but is increased for several days after the attack. An increase is also noted in cases of acute fever.

Urinary excretion of uric acid is increased by administration of 11-oxygenated adrenocortical hormones and by ACTH. Determination of the extent of rise in urinary uric acid in relation to creatinine excretion after administration of ACTH has been used as a test of the functional reserve capacity of the adrenal cortex.

Ammonia. A small amount of ammonia is always present combined with hydrochloric, phosphoric, and sulfuric acids. Estimated as NH_3, the normal average is about 0.7 gm. in 24 hours. This represents 4 to 5 per cent of the total nitrogen of the urine, ammonia standing next to urea in this respect.

Under ordinary conditions most of the ammonia that results from metabolic processes is transformed into urea. When, however, acids are present in excess, either from ingestion of mineral acids or from abnormal production of acids within the body (for example, diacetic and beta-oxybutyric acids in diabetes mellitus), ammonia combines with them and is so excreted, the urea of the urine being correspondingly decreased. This is an important part of the mechanism by which the body protects itself against acid intoxication. The ammonium salts are not, however, increased in all forms of acidosis (notably, in acidosis of nephritis).

In diabetes mellitus and in other pathologic conditions associated with excessive production of diacetic and beta-oxybutyric acids the output of ammonium salts is a very important index of the degree of acidosis. In diabetes associated with mild acidosis 1 or 1.5 gm. of ammonia may be eliminated daily; the amount may increase to 4 or 5 gm. in cases of severe diabetes and even to 8 or 10 gm. in extreme cases. The excretion of ammonia is likewise increased in pernicious vomiting of pregnancy but not in nervous vomiting; it also is increased in diseases that interfere with the power to synthesize urea, notably cirrhosis and other destructive diseases of the liver and diseases associated with deficient oxygenation. Certain drugs have a marked influence on the elimination of ammonia. Fixed alkalis and salts of organic acids decrease the elimination, while inorganic acids, such as hydrochloric acid, increase it.

The ammonia just referred to is in the form of ammonium salts and should not be confused, as it often is, with the accumulation of free ammonia, which is derived from decomposition of urea after the urine is secreted and which leads to volatile alkalinity.

Abnormal Constituents

Substances that appear in the urine only in pathologic conditions—namely, protein, sugar, acetone bodies, bile, urobilin, hemoglobin, and hematoporphyrin—are of much more interest to the clinician than are those that have just been considered. Most of these are present normally in negligible traces.

PROTEIN

Of the proteins that may appear in the urine, serum albumin and serum globulin are the most important. Mucin, proteose, and a few others are found occasionally but are of less interest.

Albuminuria. Albuminuria is a term that has been used to designate the presence of serum albumin or serum globulin in the urine. It is probably the most important pathologic change in the urine and also the most frequent. It may be either accidental or renal. The physician can make no greater mistake than to regard all instances of albuminuria as indicative of renal disease.

Accidental or *false albuminuria* is due to admixture with the urine of albuminous fluids, such as pus, blood, and vaginal discharge. The microscope will usually reveal its nature. It occurs most frequently in cases of pyelitis, cystitis, and chronic vaginitis, and the quantity of albumin is usually small.

Renal albuminuria refers to albumin that has passed from the blood into the urine through the walls of the kidney tubules or the glomeruli.

Albuminuria of sufficient degree to be recognized readily by ordinary clinical methods probably never occurs as a physiologic condition. The so-called physiologic albuminuria appears only under conditions that must be regarded as abnormal. Among these are excessive muscular exertion by persons unaccustomed to it, excessive ingestion of proteins (dietetic albuminuria), prolonged cold baths, the later stages of pregnancy and childbirth. In these conditions the albuminuria is ordinarily of slight degree and transient. Albumin is frequently present in the urine of infants, possibly because the kidney is particularly sensitive to irritants.

Certain other forms of albuminuria have still less claim to be called physiologic, but are not always regarded as pathologic. Among these is cyclic, orthostatic, or postural albuminuria. This appears at certain periods of the day, varying in different cases, and disappears after rest in bed. Most frequently the maximal output of albumin occurs late in the afternoon. This form of albuminuria occurs for the most part in neurasthenic persons during adolescence and is by no means rare. In some cases, at least, it is associated with curvature of the spinal column (lordotic albuminuria). Renal function tests usually yield results within normal limits. Tube casts may or may not be present. A considerable amount of protein that is precipitable by acetic acid in the cold has been noted in many cases. It is noteworthy that nephritis sometimes begins with cyclic albuminuria.

Pathologic Significance of Renal Albuminuria. In pathologic conditions and in many functional conditions renal albuminuria may be due to one or more of the following causes. In nearly all cases, it is accompanied by tube casts.

Circulatory changes in the kidneys. Anemia or congestion, such as occurs with excessive exercise, chronic heart disease, severe general anemia, and pressure on the renal veins (as in the later stages of pregnancy), may cause albuminuria. The quantity of albumin is usually small. Its presence is constant or temporary according to the cause.

Irritation of the kidneys. In cases of renal irritation there is slight damage to glomeruli or renal cells with cloudy swelling or even more serious degeneration, but definite nephritis is not present. The amount of albumin is generally small and the condition is transitory. Renal irritation is probably the chief cause of toxic and febrile albuminuria, and it is at least a contributing factor in the albuminuria of pregnancy. Among the agents that in toxic doses may cause albuminuria are mercury, cantharides, turpentine, mustard, arsenic, lead, and ether. In febrile diseases, particularly in acute infectious diseases, small or moderate amounts of albumin are frequently found in the urine owing chiefly to the irritant effect of bacterial toxins. This is especially true of diphtheria, scarlet fever, pneumonia, typhoid fever, and acute streptococcic infection, in any of which the renal condition may develop into true nephritis with a coincident increase in the amount of albumin.

Organic Changes in the Kidney. These changes include the inflammatory and degenerative changes commonly grouped together under the term "nephritis"; they also include the renal changes in renal tuberculosis and neoplasms. The amount of albumin eliminated in these conditions varies from minute traces to 20 gm. or even more in 24 hours, and except in acute processes, bears little relation to the severity of the disease. In acute and chronic glomerular nephritis and in syphilis of the kidney the quantity of albumin is usually very large, from 1 to 2 per cent or more. In chronic nephrosclerosis it is small; frequently no more than a slight trace. The amount is variable in renal tuberculosis and neoplasms. In amyloid disease of the kidney the quantity is usually small, and serum globulin may be present in especially large proportion.

Qualitative Tests for Albumin. Detection of albumin depends on its precipitation by chemicals or coagulation by heat. There are many tests, but none is entirely satisfactory because other substances as well as albumin are precipitated. The most common source of error is mucin. When any considerable amount of mucin is present, it can be removed by acidifying with acetic acid and filtering. Urine voided early in the evening or a few hours after a meal is most likely to contain albumin.

It is important that urine to be tested for albumin be rendered clear by filtration or centrifugation. This is too often neglected in routine work. When ordinary methods do not suffice, the urine can usually be cleared by shaking up with a little purified talc, infusorial earth, or animal charcoal and filtering. This will remove a part of the albumin by absorption, but the remainder can be detected more easily. If the urine is alkaline, sufficient acetic acid should be added to make it acid to litmus. If bacteria are abundant in an alkaline urine, some of the bacterial proteins may go into solution and respond to tests for albumin. In extremely concentrated urine, certain of the urinary salts may interfere with the test for albumin. In such cases dilution of the urine will render the result of the test more definite, even though the concentration of albumin is thereby reduced.

Albuminous urine foams markedly on shaking and the foam remains a long time. This gives a rough indication of the presence of albumin before the tests are made.

Ring or contact tests. Tests in this category are now seldom used.

ROBERTS'S TEST
Reagent
To five parts of a saturated solution of magnesium sulfate add one part of pure nitric acid.
Technique
Place the reagent in a test tube and gently layer the urine on the heavier fluid with a pipet or medicine dropper. Albumin gives a white ring, which varies in density with the amount of albumin present. When only traces of albumin are present, the white ring may not appear for two or three minutes. A similar white ring may be produced by Bence Jones protein, primary proteose, thymol, and resinous drugs. White rings or cloudiness in the urine above the zone of contact may result from excess of urates or mucus. Colored rings near the junction of the fluids may be produced by iodides, urinary pigments, bile, or indican, but these are not so frequent as they are with Heller's test.

HELLER'S TEST. This test is not quite so sensitive as Roberts's test.
Reagent
Pure nitric acid.
Technique
This test is performed in exactly the same way as Roberts's test. The reagent is more corrosive than the reagent used in Roberts's test and it must be used cautiously. If the ring appears only after two minutes, the amount of albumin is less than 0.0005 per cent.

Precipitation tests (heat tests). There are a number of tests that demonstrate the presence of albumin when the urine is heated with a reagent that contains some sort of acid. A white cloud shows the presence of protein.

HEAT AND ACETIC ACID METHOD. This procedure is widely used; it has the advantage of simplicity and suitable accuracy for clinical work.
Reagent
10 per cent acetic acid.
Technique
1. Centrifuge or filter the urine if it is not clear.
2. Fill a small Pyrex tube within one-half inch of the top. Heat the upper portion

of the urine over a small flame until boiling just begins.

3. Add 3 to 5 drops of 10 per cent acetic acid.

Clouding owing to protein appears or is intensified after the addition of acid. Some clouding owing to the presence of phosphate and carbonate salts will clear quickly on the addition of acid.

Results are reported as negative, trace, and 1 to 4 plus. In a negative test there is no clouding. A trace is described as barely visible clouding. In a 1 plus reaction, there is a definite cloud but no appearance of granularity or flocculation. A 2 plus reaction is indicated by a heavy and granular cloud without flocculation or coagulation. In the 3 plus reaction the cloud is dense and opaque; flocculation can be seen or a light coagulum is formed. In the 4 plus reaction, a thick precipitate or coagulum is formed after addition of acid.

EXTON'S SULFOSALICYLIC ACID TEST
Reagent

Dissolve 200 gm. of sodium sulfate in about 750 ml. of water with the aid of heat. Cool. Add 50 gm. of sulfosalicylic acid and dilute with water to 1000 ml.

Technique

1. Mix equal parts of urine and reagent in a test tube and warm gently in a gas flame. A white cloud shows the presence of protein, usually albumin or globulin. Bence Jones protein causes a heavy precipitate, which clears on boiling. The precipitate will again appear on cooling. Second-

ary proteoses may also cause a cloudiness when the mixture cools.

Quantitative Tests for Albumin. Accurate estimation of the amount of albumin in the urine is seldom necessary in routine clinical work. Ordinarily the information obtainable from properly conducted qualitative tests will suffice. When more definite information is required, the following simple tests are available. Of these, Kingsbury's test is by far the most accurate.

Esbach's test. The urine must be clear and of acid reaction and should not be concentrated. Always filter the urine before testing and, if necessary, add acetic acid and dilute with water, making allowance for the dilution in the final calculation.

Apparatus

Esbach's albuminometer (Fig. 3–1) is essentially a test tube with a mark U near the middle, a mark R near the top, and graduations ½, 1, 2, 3, and so forth, near the bottom.

Reagents

Dissolve 1 gm. of picric acid and 2 gm. of citric acid in distilled water to make 100 ml.

Technique

1. Fill the albuminometer tube to the mark U with urine.

2. Add the reagent to the mark R.

3. Close the tube with a rubber stopper, invert it slowly several times, and set it aside in a cool place.

4. At the end of 24 hours read the height of the precipitate. This gives the amount of the precipitate in grams per liter and must be divided by 10 to obtain the percentage.

Kingsbury's test (Kingsbury et al., 1926).

Apparatus

Artificial quantitative standards* are made from dilutions of formazin held in suspension in gelatin. These standards represent the turbidity produced by the reagent with known amounts of protein. The number of milligrams of protein per 100 ml. is indicated on each tube.

Reagent

A 3 per cent solution of sulfosalicylic acid.

Technique

1. Place 2.5 ml. of urine in a test tube measuring ½ by 4 inches.

2. Add 7.5 ml. of reagent. Mix thoroughly and allow the tube to stand for five minutes.

Figure 3–1. Esbach's albuminometer, improved form.

* Standards may be purchased from Magar Chemicals, Inc., Cornwall Landing, New York.

3. Compare by transmitted light the turbidity with that of the standard tubes, and record in milligrams per 100 ml. the amount of protein as indicated on the standard tube that most nearly matches.

MUCIN

Traces of the substances mucin, mucoid, and nucleoprotein, which are loosely designated as mucin, are present in normal urine. Increased amounts of these substances are observed in cases of irritation and inflammation of the mucous membrane of the urinary tract or the vagina. They are of interest chiefly because they may be mistaken for albumin in most of the tests. If the urine is diluted with water and acidified with acetic acid without heating, the appearance of a white cloud indicates the presence of mucin.

BENCE JONES PROTEIN

In 1847 Henry Bence Jones described a protein in the urine that had peculiar characteristics. It was precipitated by nitric acid but was soluble in boiling water and again was precipitated when the urine was cooled. The same solid precipitate, soluble by heat, was formed by adding hydrochloric acid but not to such a degree by adding strong acetic acid.

This protein is particularly pathognomonic of multiple myeloma. Proteins with somewhat similar characteristics have been observed in other conditions, such as leukemia and osteomalacia, and even in healthy young persons with high blood pressure. There is a well-founded opinion, however, that true Bence Jones protein may not be found in any condition other than multiple myeloma. Jacobson and Milner (1944) defined Bence Jones protein as a urinary protein that exhibits the characteristics originally described by Jones. They called the similar heat-coagulable substance found in other conditions "pseudo-Bence Jones protein." They also pointed out that many of the more recent tests for the Bence Jones protein are applicable to proteose, and positive results have led to the faulty conclusion that Bence Jones protein is present in the urine in several other diseases than multiple myeloma. They devised an excellent scheme for the detection of urinary proteins and for the identification of Bence Jones protein, pseudo-Bence Jones protein, nucleoprotein, heat-coagulable protein, and proteose. The reader is referred to the original article for the reasons given by these authors for the various steps in their scheme. The following abbreviated form gives the essential steps for the identification of the substances and especially for the proof that true Bence Jones protein is present.

1. Filter a fresh sample of urine and perform a ring test with cold concentrated nitric acid. If this is negative, Bence Jones protein is absent.

2. If this test is positive, perform a ring test with cold concentrated hydrochloric acid. If this is negative, Bence Jones protein is absent. If it is positive and if the ring test with nitric acid reveals a trace or more (above 0.40 per cent) of protein, dilute to a small trace with fresh, normal, protein-free urine.

3. Acidify 5 ml. of the original or diluted urine with 25 per cent acetic acid to pH 5 (as tested with nitrazine paper) and let stand for five minutes. If a precipitate forms, nucleoprotein is present. Filter through fine filter paper.

4. Warm the filtrate, or the unfiltered urine if there was no precipitate in step 3, in a water bath at 70° C. for fifteen minutes. If the urine remains clear, Bence Jones protein is absent.

5. If a coagulum forms, heat the same sample in a water bath at the boiling point for ten minutes. If the coagulum dissolves, Bence Jones protein is present.

6. If the coagulum does not dissolve, add 0.1 ml. of concentrated nitric acid to each cubic centimeter of the sample and heat at the boiling point for ten minutes. If the coagulum dissolves, Bence Jones protein is present.

7. If the coagulum does not dissolve, proceed with another sample of urine from the beginning through step 4. Centrifuge until the coagulum settles, pour off and save the supernatant fluid.

8. Suspend the precipitate in 5 ml. of protein-free normal urine, add 0.5 ml. of concentrated nitric acid, and heat at the boiling point for ten minutes. If the precipitate dissolves, Bence Jones protein is present. If the precipitate does not dissolve, pseudo-Bence Jones protein is present.

9. Filter while hot into a test tube partly immersed in a boiling water bath. Cool the filtrate. If it remains clear, Bence Jones protein is absent.

10. If a precipitate forms, add 0.5 ml. of 50 per cent sulfosalicylic acid. If the precipitate dissolves, Bence Jones protein is absent. If the precipitate persists, Bence Jones protein is present.

11. The supernatant fluid from step 7 can next be tested. Heat at the boiling point for ten minutes. If a coagulum forms, heat-coagulable protein is present. Filter while hot or, if there is no coagulum, cool the sample and add 0.5 ml. of concentrated nitric acid. If a precipitate forms, proteose is present.

CARBOHYDRATES

Various carbohydrates may be found in the urine. Dextrose is by far the most common and is the only one of much clinical importance. Levulose, lactose, and some others are encountered occasionally.

Dextrose. Dextrose and other carbohydrates are present in the urine in health in traces too small to respond to the ordinary tests. The presence of dextrose in appreciable amounts constitutes glycosuria or glycuresis and is the result of increase of dextrose in the blood (hyperglycemia), of lowered renal threshold for sugar, or both.

Transitory glycosuria is unimportant, is generally of slight degree, and may occur in many conditions, as after general anesthesia and administration of certain drugs, in some cases of hyperthyroidism, in pregnancy, and after shock and injuries of the head. Attention has been directed to glycosuria that occurs after strong emotions (anger, fear, and anxiety) owing, according to Cannon, to increased secretion of epinephrine leading to sudden mobilization of dextrose that has been stored as glycogen. The urine of a considerable percentage of a class of students will respond to tests for sugar after a long, difficult examination. The possibility must be kept in mind that a trace of sugar found in a patient's urine after a physical examination may be due to his anxiety.

Glycosuria also may occur after ingestion of an excessive amount of carbohydrates (alimentary glycosuria). The assimilation limit varies with different individuals and with different conditions of exercise. It also depends on the kind of carbohydrate. The normal limit for pure dextrose is generally stated to be about 100 to 200 gm., but more recent work has shown that in many individuals glycuresis cannot be induced by much larger amounts even up to the maximum (400 to 500 gm.) that the stomach will tolerate. Glycuresis that follows the ingestion of 100 gm. or less is definitely abnormal and indicates lowered renal threshold, diminished capacity of the liver to store dextrose as glycogen, or disturbance of carbohydrate metabolism. Excretion lasts for four or five hours.

Persistent, although not necessarily continuous, *glycosuria* has been noted in cases of injury of the floor of the fourth ventricle and in cases of renal glycosuria of which it is the essential symptom. As a rule, however, persistent glycosuria is diagnostic of diabetes mellitus and is the most important sign. The amount of dextrose eliminated in diabetes is usually considerable and is sometimes very large, reaching 500 gm. or even more in 24 hours, but it does not bear any uniform relation to the severity of the disease. Dextrose may, on the other hand, be almost or entirely controlled by careful restriction of the diet, and in cases of mild diabetes it may occur only about two or three hours after ingestion of considerable quantities of carbohydrate.

Qualitative tests for dextrose. Albumin, if present in any considerable quantity, interferes with precipitation of copper in the copper tests and should be removed by acidifying with acetic acid, boiling, and filtering.

BENEDICT'S TEST. Benedict's test will detect as little as 0.15 to 0.2 per cent of dextrose. Benedict's solution is not reduced by uric acid, creatinine, chloroform, or the aldehydes.

Reagent
Copper sulfate (pure crystallized)
        17.3 gm.
Sodium or potassium citrate
        173.0 gm.
Sodium carbonate (crystallized)
        200.0 gm.
  (or 100 gm. of anhydrous sodium carbonate)
Distilled water, to make 1000.0 ml.

Dissolve the citrate and carbonate in 700 ml. of water with the aid of heat and filter. Dissolve the copper sulfate in 100 ml. of water and pour slowly into the first solution, stirring constantly. Cool and make up to 1 liter. The reagent keeps indefinitely. It cannot be used for quantitative estimations.

Technique
1. Take about 5 ml. of the reagent in a test tube and heat to boiling to make sure that none of the copper is precipitated by heat alone.
2. Add 8 or 10 drops (not more) of the urine.

3. Heat to vigorous boiling, keep at this temperature for one or two minutes, and allow to cool slowly.

In the presence of dextrose the entire body of the solution will be filled with a precipitate, which may be red or yellow. A small amount of yellow precipitate in the blue reagent may appear to be green. When only traces of dextrose are present (less than 0.3 per cent), the precipitate may appear only on cooling. In the absence of dextrose the solution remains clear or shows only a faint bluish precipitate owing to the presence of urates. The long boiling is inconvenient, especially when there is much bumping in the tube. It will therefore generally be found more satisfactory, particularly when a large number of specimens of urine must be tested, to place the tubes in a water bath, which is kept at the boiling point for five minutes.

RECORDING RESULTS OF QUALITATIVE TESTS. Unless a quantitative estimation is made, sugar is generally reported simply as "present" or "absent." If it is desired, when recording a positive result of this test, to convey some idea of the quantity of sugar present, the following scheme is suggested.

1. S. T. (slight trace). No reduction is evident during boiling for two minutes with 8 or 10 drops of urine, but signs of reduction appear after cooling.

2. T. (trace). With 8 drops of urine the reaction occurs after boiling for about one minute.

3. M. A. (moderate amount). With 8 or 10 drops of urine the reaction occurs after boiling for 10 or 15 seconds.

4. L. A. (large amount). Reduction occurs almost immediately after adding 2 drops of urine to the boiling reagent.

Owing to the many variable factors, it is impossible to set down with any degree of accuracy the percentages of dextrose covered by the four terms.

COMMERCIALLY AVAILABLE TESTS. An important contribution to urinalysis has been realized in the development of several commercially available reagents for certain of the chemical tests. One of the earliest and most valuable of these has been the Clinitest tablets (Ames Company) for determination of urine sugar. These tablets are convenient to use, inexpensive, and as accurate as the Benedict test. In more recent times, there has been increasing interest in tests that are specific for glucose. These tests do not respond to the various nonglucose reducing substances in urine, since they are based on the enzymatic conversion of glucose to gluconic acid by the specific glucose oxidase. These tests, commercially available as Clinistix (Ames) and Testape (Eli Lilly), have proved satisfactory for glucose detection in the routine urinalysis.

Quantitative test for dextrose. On rare occasions, it may be desirable to determine the exact quantity of dextrose excreted over a period of time. Should the urine contain much dextrose, it must be diluted before making any quantitative test, allowance being made for the dilution in the subsequent calculation. Albumin, if present, must be removed by acidifying a considerable quantity of urine with acetic acid, boiling, and filtering. Any water lost during the boiling should be replaced before filtering.

The method of choice in most laboratories is Benedict's method.

BENEDICT'S TEST FOR DEXTROSE

Reagent

Copper sulfate (pure crystallized)	18.0 gm.
Sodium carbonate (crystallized)	200.0 gm.
(or 100 gm. of anhydrous sodium carbonate)	
Sodium or potassium citrate, C. P.	200.0 gm.
Potassium sulfocyanate, C. P.	125.0 gm.
Potassium ferrocyanide solution (5 per cent)	5.0 ml.
Distilled water, to make	1000.0 ml.

With the aid of heat dissolve the carbonate, citrate, and sulfocyanate in about 700 ml. of water and filter. Dissolve the copper sulfate in 100 ml. of water and pour slowly into the other fluid, stirring constantly. Add the ferrocyanide solution, cool, and dilute to 1000 ml. Only the copper sulfate need be weighed accurately. This solution is of such strength that the copper sulfate in 25 ml. is reduced by 0.05 gm. of dextrose. It keeps well.

Technique

Take 25 ml. of the reagent in a small flask and add 10 to 20 gm. of sodium carbonate crystals (or half this weight of anhydrous sodium carbonate) and a small quantity of powdered pumice stone or talc. Heat to boiling, and add the urine a little at a time, but fairly rapidly, from a buret until a chalk-white precipitate forms and the blue color of the reagent begins to fade. After this point is reached, add the urine a drop at a time until the last trace of blue just disappears. This end point is easily recognized. During the titration the mixture must be kept boiling vigorously. Loss by evaporation must be made up by adding water. Note the quantity of urine required to discharge the blue color; this contains exactly 0.05 gm. of dextrose. The percentage of dextrose can be calculated easily.

Levulose. Levulose, or fruit sugar, is seldom present in urine except in association with dextrose.

Qualitative tests for levulose. Levulose responds to all the tests that have been described for dextrose. It may be distinguished from dextrose by the following test.

BORCHARDT'S TEST. Mix about 5 ml. each of the urine and 25 per cent hydrochloric acid (concentrated HCl, 2 parts; water, 1 part) in a test tube and add a few crystals of resorcinol. Heat to boiling and boil for not more than half a minute. In the presence of levulose, a red color appears. Cool the mixture in running water, pour into a beaker, and render slightly alkaline with solid sodium or potassium hydroxide. Return to the test tube, add 2 or 3 ml. of acetic ether, and shake. If levulose is present, the ether will be colored yellow. A similar yellow color will follow administration of rhubarb and senna.

Quantitative tests for levulose. The methods used for the quantitative determination of levulose are the same as those used for dextrose; 25 ml. of Benedict's quantitative solution is reduced by 0.053 gm. of levulose.

Lactose. Lactose, or milk sugar, is sometimes present in the urine of nursing women and in that of women who have recently had a miscarriage. It is of interest chiefly because it may be mistaken for dextrose. It is not fermented by yeast but reduces copper; 0.0676 gm. of lactose will reduce 25 ml. of Benedict's quantitative solution. In strong solution it can form crystals with phenylhydrazine, but it is extremely unlikely to do so when the test is applied directly to the urine.

Rubner's test. To about 10 ml. of urine add 2 or 3 gm. of lead acetate, shake well, and filter into a test tube. Boil the filtrate, add 1 or 2 ml. of strong ammonia water, and heat again. If lactose is present, the solution turns brick red and a red precipitate will separate. The precipitate is the criterion of the test. Dextrose produces a red solution and a yellow precipitate.

Maltose. Maltose and cane sugar are of little or no clinical importance. Maltose has been found along with dextrose in cases of diabetes. It reduces copper; 0.074 gm. of maltose will reduce 25 ml. of Benedict's solution. Cane sugar (sucrose) is sometimes added to the urine by malingering patients. It does not reduce copper; hence, when it has been added, it passes unrecognized by the physician who uses the copper tests only. Both maltose and sucrose are fermentable by yeast.

Pentoses. Pentoses are so named because the molecule contains five atoms of carbon. Vegetable gums form their chief source. They reduce copper strongly but slowly; they produce crystals with phenylhydrazine but are not fermented by yeast.

Pentosuria is uncommon. It has been noted after ingestion of large quantities of pentrose-rich substances, such as cherries, plums, and fruit juices. It is said to be fairly constant among habitual users of morphine. An obscure chronic form of pentosuria, which does not cause clinical symptoms, has been observed and occurs most commonly among Jews. The pentose excreted in such cases is believed to be optically inactive arabinose, although ribose or xylose may be present in some cases.

Bial's orcinol test for pentose
Reagent
Dissolve 1.5 gm. of orcinol in 500 ml. of 30 per cent hydrochloric acid. Add 1 ml. of a 10 per cent solution of ferric chloride.
Procedure
1. Remove any dextrose that is present by fermentation.
2. Add 5 ml. of the reagent in a test tube, heat, and after removing from the flame add the urine drop by drop until not more than 2 ml. has been added. The appearance of a green color denotes the presence of pentose.

ACETONE BODIES

Acetone bodies are closely related substances—acetone, diacetic acid, and beta-oxybutyric acid—which apparently originate in the liver. Excessive production of diacetic and oxybutric acids within the body leads, by virtue of their acid nature, to the condition known as acid intoxication. Since acetone bodies are ketones, this form of acidosis is sometimes given the special name "ketosis." The existence of this condition or, rather, the tendency toward it (since there may be moderate acetonuria without definite acidosis), is shown by the presence of acetone bodies in the urine. When the condition is very mild, acetone occurs alone; as the acidosis becomes more severe, diacetic acid and beta-oxybutyric acid are also present.

The occurrence of these ketones is associated with the amount of available glycogen in the liver. When the amount of available glycogen is reduced, as in starvation or diabetes mellitus, an increase in the oxidation of fatty acids occurs, in turn causing an accelerated rate of formation of ketone bodies in the liver and consequent ketosis. If there is an adequate reserve of liver glycogen, the rate of fat metabolism, and therefore the rate of formation of ketone bodies, apparently cannot become increased sufficiently to cause ketosis. According to this physiologic concept it seems that "the flames of carbohydrate inhibit those of fat" and that fats do not "burn in the flames of carbohydrate" as was formerly thought.

Acetone. Traces of acetone that cannot be detected by the ordinary tests may be present in the urine under normal conditions. Larger amounts may be present when the intake of carbohydrate is limited and in fever or gastrointestinal disturbances.

Acetonuria finds its chief clinical importance in connection with diabetes mellitus. It occurs intermittently in some cases in which the disease is mild and fairly regularly in cases in which the disease is advanced, although much depends on the diet. It is always present in cases in which the disease is severe. Tests for acetone are fully as important as tests for sugar in diabetes. A progressive increase, as measured by the response to qualitative tests, is a grave prognostic sign, since acidosis that is due to the acetone bodies is probably the chief cause of the dreaded diabetic coma. Acetonuria can be diminished temporarily by more liberal allowance of carbohydrates in the diet.

Acetonuria due to any cause is liable to be especially severe in children, and this doubtless plays an important part in acute and chronic diseases of childhood, especially in those requiring a restricted diet. In fact, the urine of a considerable percentage of young children contains appreciable quantities of acetone under normal conditions.

Qualitative tests for acetone. The urine may be tested directly. Methods requiring distillation have been abandoned by most laboratories.

LANGE'S TEST. Lange's test is a modification of the well-known Legal's test. It is more sensitive than Legal's test and gives a sharper end reaction.

Reagents
1. Glacial acetic acid.
2. Concentrated solution of sodium nitroprusside.
3. Strong ammonia water.

Technique
1. Place 5 ml. of urine in a test tube and add 5 drops of glacial acetic acid and a few drops of the concentrated solution of sodium nitroprusside.
2. Gently run a little ammonia water on the surface of the mixture.

If acetone is present, a reddish purple ring will form immediately at the junction of the two fluids.

ROTHERA'S TEST

Reagents
1. Ammonium sulfate.
2. Concentrated solution of sodium nitroprusside.
3. Strong ammonia water.

Technique
1. Place 5 or 10 ml. of urine in a test tube and add about 1 gm. of ammonium sulfate and 2 or 3 drops of a concentrated solution of sodium nitroprusside.
2. Overlay with strong ammonia water. A reddish purple ring shows the presence of acetone.

Commercially available tests: The convenient tablet and dip-stick methods are sufficiently accurate for determination of acetone in the clinical urinalysis. They are commercially available as Acetest and Ketostix (Ames).

Diacetic Acid. Diacetic (acetoacetic) acid occurs in the same conditions as acetone. Separate tests for its presence are not carried out routinely in most laboratories.

Qualitative test for diacetic acid. The urine should be fresh. If a preservative must be used, toluene is best.

GERHARDT'S TEST

Reagent
A 10 per cent aqueous solution of ferric chloride.

Technique
1. Place a few milliliters of urine in a test tube. Add ferric chloride solution drop by drop until the phosphates are precipitated.
2. Filter and add more of the ferric chloride solution to the filtrate.

If diacetic acid is present, the urine will assume a bordeaux red color. The test is somewhat more definite if applied by the contact or ring methods. Very small amounts of diacetic acid may produce a brown color instead of the characteristic reddish brown color.

Similar colors may be produced by other substances, as phenol, salicylates, antipyrine, and sodium bicarbonate. To exclude these fallacies, it is necessary, whenever the test gives a red or violet color, to repeat it on a fresh portion of the urine as follows: To about 5 ml. of urine in a test tube add an equal volume of water and boil down to the original volume. Cool and add the ferric chloride solution. Boiling drives off diacetic acid; hence, if the color appears in this second test, it was not originally due to diacetic acid. It is not sufficient to boil the urine after the color has been brought out by the ferric chloride solution, as is sometimes advised, since the color caused by certain drugs as well as that caused by diacetic acid will then disappear.

Beta-oxybutyric Acid. Beta-oxybutyric acid has much the same significance as diacetic acid but is of more serious import. It is seldom if ever found without acetone and diacetic acid, which are detected more easily.

Hart's test
Reagents
1. Glacial acetic acid.
2. Hydrogen peroxide.
Technique
1. Dilute 20 ml. of urine with 20 ml. of water. Add a few drops of glacial acetic acid and boil mixture down to 10 ml.
2. Add 10 ml. of water, mix, and place half in each of two test tubes.
3. Add to one tube 1 ml. of hydrogen peroxide. Warm gently and cool. This transforms beta-oxybutyric acid to acetone.
4. Apply Lange's test for acetone to the mixture in each tube. A positive reaction in the tube to which hydrogen peroxide has been added shows the presence of beta-oxybutyric acid in the original sample of urine.

BILE

The pigment of bile has its origin in the never-ceasing destruction of erythrocytes within the body.

The significance of bile in the urine is practically the same as that of bile staining of the tissues, which is known as icterus or jaundice. Small amounts of bile may, however, be found in the urine when the disturbance is not severe enough to produce recognizable jaundice or, in other cases, before the jaundice supervenes. Icterus is generally caused by obstruction to the outflow of bile from the liver owing to diseases affecting the hepatic parenchyma or to conditions that obstruct the external biliary ducts. A less common but important cause is an excessive production of bilirubin associated with pathologically increased destruction of erythrocytes.

Tests for Bile Pigment. Bile pigment gives the urine a greenish yellow, yellow, or brown color, which after shaking is imparted to the foam. Cells, casts, and other structures in the sediment may be stained brown or yellow. This, however, should not be accepted as proof of the presence of bile without further tests.

Smith's test. Overlay the urine with tincture of iodine diluted with nine times its volume of alcohol. An emerald green ring at the zone of contact shows the presence of bile pigment.

Gmelin's test. This test consists in bringing slightly yellow nitric acid into contact with the urine. A play of colors, of which green and violet are most distinctive, denotes the presence of bile pigment. Blue and red may be produced by indican and urobilin, and violet by iodides. Colorless nitric acid will become yellow on standing in the sunlight. The test may be applied in the following ways: (1) by overlaying the acid with the urine; (2) by bringing a drop of each together on a porcelain plate; (3) by filtering the urine through thick filter paper and touching the paper with a drop of the acid, and (4), probably best of all, by precipitating with lime water, filtering, and touching the precipitate with a drop of the acid. In the last method bilirubin is carried down as an insoluble calcium compound, which concentrates the pigment and avoids any interfering substances.

Harrison's test (Hawkinson, Watson, and Turner's Modification, 1945). In his original test Harrison employed a 10 per cent solution of barium chloride, which forms a precipitate when mixed with an equal amount of urine. If the urine is filtered and a drop of Fouchet's reagent is added to the precipitate on the filter paper, a characteristic green color will develop if bile pigment is present. The test that will be described here is Hawkinson, Watson, and Turner's modification of Harrison's test.

Reagents

1. Fouchet's reagent. Prepare a 0.9 per cent solution of ferric chloride in a 25 per cent solution of trichloracetic acid.

2. Barium impregnated paper strips. Thoroughly soak pieces of extra thick filter paper (Schleicher and Schull no. 470) in a saturated aqueous solution of barium chloride. Dry in the air or preferably in a drying oven. Cut the impregnated paper into strips 4 inches long by ½ inch wide.

Technique

1. Place one end of the barium-impregnated paper in the sample of urine to be tested. At least half the strip should extend above the surface of the sample of urine. Allow it to stand in the urine for thirty seconds to two minutes. Withdraw the strip and place it on a piece of absorbent paper.

2. In that area corresponding to the surface of the urine there is generally more color. Place 2 or 3 drops of Fouchet's reagent directly on this area. A positive reaction is denoted by the appearance of a green color, which varies in intensity with the amount of bilirubin present.

UROBILINOGEN AND UROBILIN

When bilirubin of the bile reaches the intestinal tract, it is reduced by the action of bacteria to colorless chromogens, collectively referred to as urobilinogen. A considerable proportion, probably as much as 50 per cent, of the urobilinogen is reabsorbed from the intestine and carried to the liver in the portal blood. The remainder in the intestine, in part oxidized to the orange or brown pigments known as urobilin, passes out with the feces. Under normal conditions reabsorbed urobilinogen is almost completely metabolized in the liver or excreted with the bile. Minute amounts that escape into the systemic circulation account for the normal urinary excretion of 0.5 to 4 mg. of urobilinogen in 24 hours. When liver cells are damaged, urobilinogen may not be removed effectively from the portal blood, thus allowing an abnormally large amount to reach the general circulation and to be excreted by the kidneys. On the other hand, if the bile ducts are completely obstructed so that no bilirubin enters the intestine, the formation of urobilinogen ceases and the urine (and feces as well) may contain diminished or imperceptible amounts of the chromogens.

Whenever excessive destruction of hemoglobin causes increased formation of bilirubin and hence an increased production of urobilinogen in the intestine, there may also be abnormally large amounts of urobilinogen excreted in the urine. When not due to excessive destruction of blood, increased excretion of urobilinogen in the urine usually indicates functional incapacity of the liver. Its recognition is simple and has considerable practical usefulness as, for example, in the diagnosis of acute hepatitis, in judging the amount of damage done to the liver parenchyma by poisons, and in the chronic congestion of poorly compensated heart disease. The urinary and fecal excretion of urobilinogen is an aid in distinguishing the anemias associated with excessive destruction of blood (hemolytic anemias) from those due to other causes (iron deficiency anemia, aplastic anemia, and so on). Absence of urobilinogen from the urine is characteristic of complete biliary obstruction, although in this instance the disappearance of bile pigments from the feces is likely to have more definite diagnostic significance.

To be of value, tests for urobilinogen in the urine should be made on several successive days, since the chromogen may be absent for a day or two without demonstrable cause. It is also essential that the test be made immediately after passage of the urine or that proper conditions of preservation be observed meticulously. If there is to be any significant delay in performance of the test, as when 24-hour specimens are being examined, the urine must be collected in dark bottles or otherwise protected from light, and it must be alkalinized at all times. The latter condition is easily arranged by having a few grams of calcium carbonate in the bottle before the collection is begun. If these precautions are not observed, urobilinogen will be quickly oxidized to urobilin and a false negative test will be reported.

Quantitative Estimation of Urine Urobilinogen. Watson and his associates (1944) have develped methods for quantitative estimation of urinary and fecal urobilinogen. In principle, these tests begin by reducing all urobilin to urobilinogen with ferrous hydroxide. Urobilinogen is then combined with paradimethylaminobenzaldehyde (Ehrlich's reagent) in the presence of sodium acetate, which produces a cherryred solution. This can be compared colorimetrically with an artificial standard of phenolsulfonphthalein or a suitable mixture of dyes. By calibration against actual urobilinogen, the amount of chromogen can be calculated in milligrams. It is well to remember that the color developed with Ehrlich's aldehyde reagent is not specific for urobilinogen, and quantitative interpretation of most methods based on this reaction is more or less arbitrary. Accurate quantitative determination of urobilinogen is too demanding for ordinary clinical laboratory practice. The semiquantitative procedure described by Wallace and Diamond (1925), details of which are given in the next paragraph, is a simple and generally useful method for estimation of urine urobilinogen.

Wallace and Diamond Method for Urine Urobilinogen
Reagent

Ehrlich's aldehyde reagent. Dissolve 2 gm. of paradimethylaminobenzaldehyde in 100 ml. of a 20 per cent aqueous solution of concentrated hydrochloric acid.

Technique

1. Arrange 6 to 10 clean test tubes of the same size in a rack for serial dilution of the urine sample.

2. Place 5 ml. of water in all but the first tube.

3. Pipet 5 ml. of the urine sample into each of the first two tubes.

4. Mix the urine and water in the second tube and pipet 5 ml. into the third tube. This procedure is carried out serially to the number of tubes desired.

5. Add 0.5 ml. of Ehrlich's aldehyde reagent to each tube, mix, and allow to stand five minutes for full color development.

The color is best observed by looking vertically through the solution at a white background in bright daylight. The last dilution in which a faint pink color appears is recorded as the end point. The urine of a normal individual is expected to show color production at dilutions of 1:8 to 1:32. If the pink color can be detected only in the undiluted urine or in urine diluted 1:2, urobilinogen is considered to be decreased. A positive reaction at dilutions of 1:64 or greater represents increased urinary excretion of urobilinogen.

If the urine contains bile, it should be treated with equal parts of 10 per cent aqueous solution of barium chloride and filtered through hard paper before this test is undertaken. This procedure removes bilirubin, which otherwise may interfere with reading of the urobilinogen results. The dilution introduced by this step must be taken into account in setting up the series of tubes for the test.

Qualitative Test for Urobilin. Only traces of urobilin are present in fresh normal urine. It is now customary and much more simple to examine the urine for urobilinogen either as a freshly voided specimen or under conditions that obviate the loss of urobilinogen by oxidation. Since there are occasional instances when a qualitative test for urobilin may be useful, the technique of Schlesinger is given in detail.

Schlesinger's Test for Urobilin.
Reagents

1. Compound solution of iodine (Lugol's iodine solution).

2. A saturated alcoholic solution of zinc acetate or zinc chloride.

3. A 10 per cent solution of calcium chloride.

Technique

1. If bile pigment is present, it should be removed by adding about a fifth the volume of calcium chloride solution to the urine and filtering.

2. Place 10 ml. of filtered urine in a test tube and add a few drops of compound solution of iodine.

3. Add 10 ml. of saturated alcoholic solution of zinc acetate. A greenish fluorescence, best seen when the tube is viewed in bright sunlight against a black background and when the light is concentrated on it with a lens, shows the presence of urobilin. The fluorescence becomes more marked after an hour or two.

HEMOGLOBIN

The presence in the urine of hemoglobin or pigments directly derived from it, accompanied by few, if any, erythrocytes, constitutes hemoglobinuria. It must be distinguished from hematuria or blood in the urine, which is a commoner condition. In both conditions chemical tests will reveal hemoglobin, but in hematuria microscopic examination will reveal the presence of erythrocytes. The presence of considerable amounts of hemoglobin imparts a reddish or brown color to the urine, and there may occur a sediment of brown, granular pigment.

Benzidine Test
Reagents

1. Saturated solution of benzidine in glacial acetic acid. The benzidine labeled "For blood tests" should be employed.

2. Hydrogen peroxide.

Technique

1. Mix equal parts of the two reagents in a test tube.

2. Place a few milliliters of urine in a test tube and add an equal amount of the mixed reagents. A blue color appears in the presence of hemoglobin.

MICROSCOPIC EXAMINATION

A careful microscopic study should be a part of every routine examination of urine. It will often reveal structures of diagnostic importance in urine that seems perfectly clear, and from which only slight sediment can be obtained with the centrifuge. On the other hand microscopic examination of cloudy urine that contains an abundant sediment often does not disclose any structures of clinical significance.

Since the nature of the sediment soon changes, the urine must be examined while fresh, preferably within six hours after it is voided. If it must be kept for a much longer period, some preservative should be added, preferably 4 drops of formalin or 5 grains (0.3 gm.) of boric acid or 1 ml. of toluene for each 4 ounces (120 ml.) of urine. When possible, the specimen should be placed on ice. The sediment is best obtained by means of the centrifuge.

After the supernatant fluid is poured off, a small amount of the sediment should be transferred to a slide and covered with a coverglass. The correct amount of the sediment to be placed on the slide can be learned only by experience. It should not be so much as to float the coverglass about or so small as to leave unoccupied space beneath the coverglass. A coverglass (about 22 mm. square) provides an area sufficiently large to enable one to find any structures that are present in sufficient number to have clinical significance, provided other parts of the technique have been correct. It may be necessary, however, to examine several drops. When the sediment is abundant, drops from the upper and lower portions should be examined separately and a capillary tube used to transfer the material.

In the microscopic examination of urinary sediments, no fault is so common or so fatal to good results as improper illumination, and none is so easily corrected. The light should be central and subdued for ordinary work, but oblique illumination, obtained by swinging the mirror a little out of the optical axis, will be found helpful in identifying certain delicate structures, such as hyaline casts. The 16 mm. objective should be used as a finder; the 4 mm. is reserved for examining details. An experienced worker will rely almost wholly upon the low-power objective.

It is well to emphasize that the most common errors that result in failure to find important structures, when present, are: lack of care in transferring the sediment to the slide, too strong an illumination, and too great a magnification.

In order to distinguish similar structures, it is often necessary to watch the effect of certain reagents on them. This is especially true of the various unorganized sediments. They frequently cannot be identified by their form alone. With the structures still in focus a drop of a reagent may be placed at one edge of the coverglass and drawn underneath it by the suction of a piece of blotting paper touched to the opposite side or, better, by placing a small drop of the reagent and of the urine close together on a slide and lowering a coverglass gently over them. As the two fluids mingle, the effect on various structures may be seen.

A common error is to attempt to identify objects in urine that has dried on the slide. Satisfactory examination is impossible under such conditions. Not only are the delicate, organized structures distorted beyond recognition, but there is a confusing deposit of urinary salts. After a little experience one recognizes at a glance, from the peculiar refraction of the structures, that the urine has dried.

The record of the microscopic examination should not merely state that particular structures are present but should give an approximate idea of their number. The best plan is to record the average number of structures seen in a field of the low-power objective, although the number will vary greatly with the thoroughness of centrifugation and especially with the care with which the sediment is transferred to the slide. The approximate amount of sediment in the centrifuge tube should also be recorded.

Amorphous and Crystalline Sediments

In general these sediments have little diagnostic or prognostic significance. Most of them are substances normally present in solutions that have been precipitated either because they are present in excessive amounts or, more frequently, because of some alteration in the urine (as in reaction or concentration that may be purely physiologic, depending on changes in diet or habits. Various substances are always precipitated during decomposition, which may take place either within or without the body.

Unorganized sediments may be classified according to the reaction of the urine in which they are most likely to be found. This classification is useful, but many exceptions are to be expected, since the characteristic sediments of acid urine may remain after the urine has become alkaline and the alkaline sediments may be precipitated in a urine that is still acid.

Table 3–2. Chemical Sediments Observed in Acid and Alkaline Urine

CHARACTER OF SEDIMENT	CHEMICAL COMPOSITION OF SEDIMENT IN ACID URINE	IN ALKALINE URINE
Yellow crystals	Uric acid; soluble in solution of sodium hydroxide	Ammonium biurate; soluble in hydrochloric acid
Colorless crystals	Calcium oxalate; soluble in hydrochloric acid	Phosphate crystals; soluble in acetic acid
Amorphous material	Urates; dissolved by heat	Amorphous phosphates; soluble in acetic acid

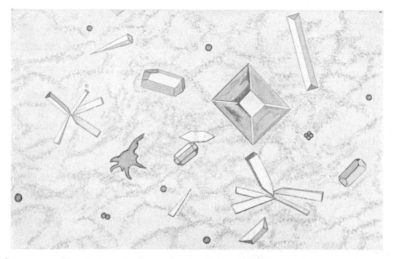

Figure 3–2. Common sediments of alkaline urine: triple phosphate crystals, calcium phosphate crystals, ammonium urate crystals, and amorphous phosphates (× 150).

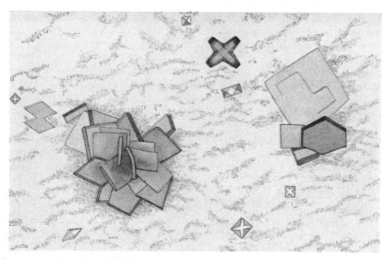

Figure 3–3. Common sediments of acid urine: uric acid crystals, calcium oxalate crystals, and amorphous urates (× 150). (Dorothy Booth, pinx.)

Uric acid, urates, and calcium oxalate comprise the deposits that are found most frequently in acid urine, but leucine, tyrosine, cystine, and globules of fat also may be found in acid urine. The reaction of the urine has less effect on the latter substances than it has on the former substances. Phosphates, calcium carbonate, and ammonium biurate may be found in alkaline urine. Other crystalline sediments, which are rarely observed and need no further comment, are calcium sulfate, cholesterol, hippuric acid, hematoidin, fatty acids, and indigo. Table 3–2 shows the chemical sediments that are observed most frequently in acid and alkaline urine.

Organized Sediments

The principal organized structures in urinary sediments are tube casts, epithelial cells, pus corpuscles, erythrocytes, spermatozoa, bacteria, and animal parasites. They are much more important than the unorganized sediments just considered. A monograph by Lippman (1957) has been one of the most valuable contributions to this particular phase of urinalysis.

Tube Casts. These interesting structures are albuminous casts of the uriniferous tubules. Their presence in the urine (cylindruria) probably always indicates some pathologic change in the kidney, although this change may be slight or transitory. Large numbers of these casts may be present in cases of temporary irritation and congestion of the kidneys. They do not in themselves, therefore, imply organic disease of the kidney. They rarely occur in urine that does not contain, or has not recently contained, albumin, and in a general way they have the same clinical significance as renal albuminuria.

Although it is not possible to draw a sharp dividing line between the different types of casts, the classification used in Table 3–3 has proved satisfactory. As will

Table 3–3.　**Types of Tube Casts Found in Urine**

1. Hyaline casts.
    a. Narrow hyaline casts.
    b. Broad hyaline casts.
2. Waxy casts.
3. Granular casts.
    a. Fine granular casts.
    b. Coarse granular casts.
4. Fatty casts.
5. Casts containing organized structures.
    a. Epithelial casts.
    b. Blood casts.
    c. Pus casts.
    d. Bacterial casts.

be seen later, practically all varieties of casts are modifications of hyaline casts. Two varieties frequently are included in the same cast.

The significance of the different varieties is more readily understood if one considers their mode of formation. Albuminous material, the source and nature of which are not definitely known but which are doubtless not the same in all cases, probably enters the lumen of a uriniferous tubule in a fluid or plastic state. The material has been variously thought to be an exudate from the blood, a pathologic secretion of the renal cells, or a product of epithelial degeneration. In the tubule the albumin hardens into a cast, which, when washed out by the urine, retains the shape of the tubule and contains within its substance whatever structures and debris were lying free within the tubule or were loosely attached to its wall. If the tubule is small and has the usual lining of epithelium, the cast will be narrow; if the tubule is large or entirely denuded of epithelium, the cast will be broad. A cast, therefore, indicates the condition of the tubule in which it is formed, but it does not necessarily indicate the condition of the kidney as a whole. In any particular case of disease of the kidney several types of casts, or even all types, may be found. Their number and the preponderance of certain types will, as is shown later, furnish a clue to the nature of the pathologic process, but further than this one cannot go with certainty. One cannot rely on the casts for accurate diagnosis of the histologic changes in the kidney.

At times during the course of nephritis the urine is suddenly flooded with great numbers of tube casts. Such "showers" of casts may be of serious import but are not necessarily so. In some cases they may result from a clearing of the plugged renal tubules coincident with improvement and increased flow of urine.

The search for casts must be made carefully. The urine must be fresh, since hyaline casts soon dissolve when the urine becomes alkaline. The urine should be thoroughly centrifuged. When the sediment is abundant, casts, being light structures, will be found near the top of the deposit. In cases of cystitis, in which casts may be entirely hidden by the pus, the bladder should be irrigated to remove as much of the pus as possible and the next specimen of urine should be examined. Heavy sediments of urates, blood, or vaginal cells may likewise obscure casts and other important structures. Vaginal cells can be avoided by catheterization. Urates can be dissolved by warming gently before centrifuging, care being taken not to use enough heat to coagulate the albumin. Blood can be destroyed by centrifuging, pouring off the supernatant urine, filling the tube with water, adding a few drops of dilute acetic acid, mixing well, and centrifuging again. This process should be repeated until the blood is completely decolorized. Too much acetic acid will dissolve hyaline casts.

In searching for casts, the low power objective should invariably be used, although a higher-power objective occasionally may be desirable in studying details as, for example, in distinguishing an epithelial cast from a pus cast. The casts are perhaps most frequently found near the edge of the coverglass. Their cylindric shape can best be seen by moving the coverglass slightly while observing them or by pressing on one edge of the coverglass with a needle, thus causing them to roll. This little manipulation should be practiced until it can be done satisfactorily. It will prove useful in many examinations.

Various methods of staining casts so as to render them more conspicuous have been proposed. These methods offer no special advantage to one who understands how to use the substage mechanism of the microscope. The "negative-staining" method is as good as any. It consists simply of adding a little India ink to a drop of urine on the slide. Casts, cells, and other substances will stand out as colorless structures on a dark background. Some workers tinge the urine faintly with eosin or compound solution of iodine, which is taken up by the casts.

Hyaline casts. Typically these are colorless, homogeneous, semitransparent, cylindric structures, which have parallel sides and usually have rounded ends. They frequently are somewhat opaque or contain a few granules, or an occasional cell or oil globule either adheres to them or is contained within their substance. Generally they are straight or curved; less commonly they are convoluted (see Fig. 3–12). Their length and breadth vary greatly; they are sometimes so long as to extend across several fields of a medium power objective but are usually much shorter; their breadth is from one to seven or eight times the diameter of an erythrocyte (Figs. 3–4 and 3–5).

Hyaline casts are the least significant of all the casts and usually occur with pale, very fine, granular casts in many transitory conditions. Small numbers are common

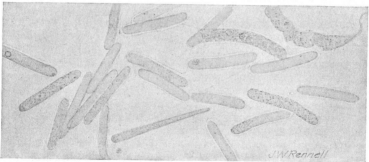

Figure 3–4. Hyaline and finely granular casts in urine; a "shower" of casts. At the upper right is a mucous shred. A portion of an actual field (× 100).

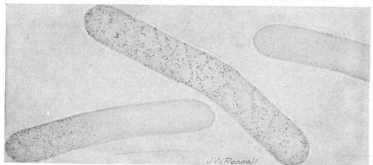

Figure 3–5. Hyaline and finely granular casts enlarged from Figure 3–4 (× 350).

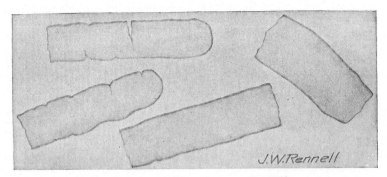

Figure 3–6.   Waxy tube casts (× 350).

after ether anesthesia, in fever, after excessive exercise, and in cases of congestion and irritation of the kidney. They are always present and are usually stained yellow when the urine contains much bile. Although they occur in all organic diseases of the kidney, they are most important in nephrosclerosis. In this disease they are seldom abundant, but their persistent presence is a significant sign of the disease. Small patches of chronic interstitial change are probably responsible for the few hyaline casts that frequently occur in the urine of elderly persons.

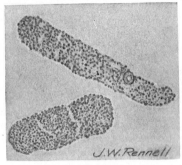

Figure 3–7.   Coarsely granular tube casts (× 350).

Very broad hyaline casts commonly indicate complete desquamation of the tubular epithelium, such as occurs in the late stages of nephritis, or they may originate in relatively normal collecting tubules.

Waxy casts. Like hyaline casts waxy casts are homogeneous when typical, but they frequently contain a few granules or an occasional cell. They are much more opaque than the hyaline variety and are usually shorter and broader. They have irregular, broken ends and sometimes appear to be segmented. They are grayish or colorless and have a dull, waxy appearance as if they had been cut from paraffin (Fig. 3–6). They are sometimes composed of material that produces an amyloid reaction. All gradations between hyaline and waxy casts may be found, and many waxy casts doubtless are merely hyaline casts that have remained in the kidney tubules for a long time.

Waxy casts occur in most cases of advanced nephritis in which they are an unfavorable sign. They are perhaps most abundant in amyloid disease of the kidney but are not distinctive of the disease, as is sometimes stated.

Granular casts. These are merely hyaline casts in which numerous granules are embedded (Figs. 3–4, 3–5, and 3–7).

Fine granular casts contain many fine granules; are usually shorter, broader, and more opaque than hyaline casts; and are more conspicuous. Their color is grayish or pale yellow.

Coarse granular casts contain granules and are darker in color than the fine granular casts. They are often dark brown owing to the presence of altered blood pigment. They are usually shorter and more irregular in outline than fine granular casts, and they more frequently have irregular, broken ends.

Fatty casts. Small droplets of fat may be seen at times in any variety of cast. Casts in which the droplets are numerous are called "fatty casts." The fat globules are not difficult to recognize. Staining with osmic acid or Sudan III will remove any doubt as to their nature.

The granules and fat droplets seen in casts are chiefly products of epithelial degeneration. Granular and fatty casts, therefore, always indicate partial or complete disintegration of the renal epithelium. The fine granular cast is the least significant and may be found with hyaline casts when the epithelium is only slightly, and perhaps not seriously, affected. Coarse granular, and especially fatty casts, if present in considerable numbers, indicate serious glomerulonephritis. Brown granular casts are most common in acute nephritis.

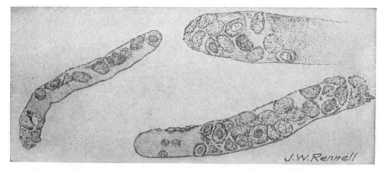

Figure 3–8. Tube casts containing renal epithelial cells (× 350).

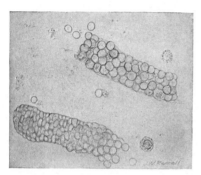

Figure 3–9. Two blood casts, one containing a leukocyte; six free erythrocytes; and two renal epithelial cells. From the urine of a child with acute nephritis (× 300).

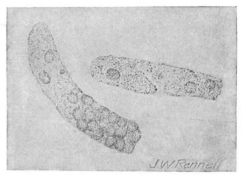

Figure 3–10. Tube casts containing pus corpuscles (× 350).

Casts containing organized structures.

Cells and other structures are frequently seen adherent to a cast or embedded within it. When these structures are numerous, their name is used to designate the cast.

EPITHELIAL CASTS. Epithelial casts contain epithelial cells from the renal tubules. The cells vary in size and are often flattened, oval, or elongated. They may be recognized as epithelial cells by irrigating with dilute acetic acid, which usually brings out the nucleus clearly. Epithelial casts always imply desquamation of epithelium, which rarely occurs except in cases of parenchymatous inflammation (Fig. 3–8). When the cells are well preserved, they indicate acute nephritis.

BLOOD CASTS. Blood casts contain erythrocytes, which usually are much degenerated (Fig. 3–9). They always indicate hemorrhage into the renal tubules, which is most common in acute nephritis, or an acute exacerbation of chronic nephritis.

PUS CASTS. Pus casts (Fig. 3–10), which are composed almost wholly of pus corpuscles, are uncommon and indicate a suppurative process in the kidney, usually pyelonephritis. Casts containing a few pus corpuscles, either alone or in combination with epithelial cells or erythrocytes, are common, especially in cases of acute nephritis. In such cases the pus corpuscles have no special significance.

BACTERIAL CASTS. True bacterial casts are rare. They indicate a septic condition in the kidney. Bacteria may permeate a cast after the urine is voided.

Structures likely to be mistaken for tube casts.

MUCOUS THREADS. Mucus frequently appears in the form of long strands, which slightly resemble hyaline casts (Fig. 3–11). Mucous threads, however, are more ribbon-like, have less well-defined edges, and usually show faint longitudinal striations. Their ends taper to a point or are split or curled and are never evenly rounded as is commonly the case with hyaline casts.

Such threads form a part of the nubecula of normal urine and are especially abundant when calcium oxalate crystals are present. When there is an excess of mucus, as in cases of irritation of the urinary tract, every microscopic field may be filled with an interlacing meshwork.

Mucous threads are microscopic and should not be confused with urethral shreds or "gonorrheal threads," which are macroscopic (0.5 to 1 cm. long) and consist of a matrix of mucus in which many epithelial and pus corpuscles are embedded.

Figure 3–11. Mucous threads in urine (× 350). These are often wrongly called cylindroids.

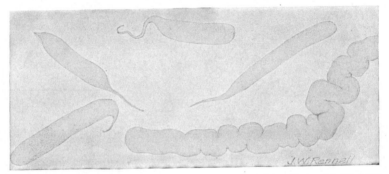

Figure 3–12. Four cylindroids and one convoluted hyaline cast (× 350)

CYLINDROIDS. This name is sometimes given to the mucous threads just described but is more properly applied to certain peculiar structures more nearly allied to casts. They resemble hyaline casts in structure but differ in that they taper to a slender tail, which is often twisted or curled on itself (Fig. 3–12). They frequently occur in the urine with hyaline casts, especially in cases of circulatory disturbance and irritation of the kidney. They have practically the same significance as hyaline casts.

MASSES OF URATES, PHOSPHATES, OR MINUTE CRYSTALS. Masses of amorphous urates, phosphates, or minute crystals (Fig. 3–13), which accidentally take a cylindric form, or shreds of mucus covered with granules may closely resemble granular casts. The gentle application of heat or appropriate chemicals will distinguish them from casts. When urine contains both mucus and granules, large numbers of these "pseudocasts," all lying in the same direction, can be produced by moving the coverglass slightly from side to side. It is possible—as in urate infarcts of infants —for urates to be molded into cylindric bodies within the renal tubules.

HAIR, WOOL, AND COTTON. Hair and fibers of wool, cotton, and similar sub-

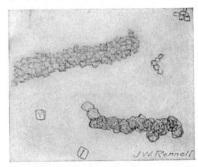

Figure 3–13. Two pseudocasts, one composed of calcium oxalate crystals and the other of uric acid (× 300).

stances could be mistaken for casts only by beginners. One can easily become familiar with the appearance of such substances by suspending them in water and examining them with the microscope.

HYPHAE OF MOLDS. Hyphae of molds frequently are mistaken for hyaline casts. Their higher degree of refraction, their jointed or branching structure, and the accompanying spores enable one to identify them.

Epithelial Cells. A few cells from the epithelium of various parts of the urinary tract occur in every specimen of urine. A marked increase in the number of these cells indicates some pathologic condition at the site of their origin. It is sometimes possible to locate their probable source from their form, notably in the case of vaginal epithelium. One should, however, be extremely cautious about making any definite statement as to the origin of any individual cell. Most cells are much altered from their original shape, and they may be so granular as a result of degenerative changes that the nucleus is obscured. Many of them contain fat globules.

Pus Corpuscles. A very few leukocytes are present in normal urine, particularly when mucus is present. They are numerous only as a result of a pathologic process. The cells are then called "pus corpuscles," and their presence constitutes pyuria. Although pus corpuscles are not so well preserved as leukocytes and show more tendency to form small clumps, when only a few are present the line of distinction between them must be drawn arbitrarily and is best based on the number present. This depends largely on the care used in preparing the slide. The majority of pus corpuscles are polymorphonuclear leukocytes.

When at all abundant, pus adds an appreciable amount of albumin to the urine and forms a white sediment resembling amorphous phosphates macroscopically. Under the microscope the pus corpuscles appear as granular spheric cells, about 10 to 12 microns in diameter, or somewhat larger than erythrocytes (Fig. 3–14). The granules are partly normal neutrophilic granules and partly granular products of degeneration. In freshly voided urine many of these corpuscles exhibit ameboid motion, assuming irregular outlines. Each pus corpuscle contains one irregular nucleus or several small, rounded nuclei. The nuclei are obscured or entirely hidden by the granules but may be brought clearly into view by running a little dilute acetic

acid under the coverglass. This enables one to distinguish pus corpuscles easily from small, round epithelial cells, which resemble them in size but have a single, rather large, round nucleus. In moderately acid urine the structure of the pus corpuscle is rather well preserved. In strongly acid urine, the corpuscles may be shrunken and irregularly shaped, suggesting ameboid forms. When the urine is alkaline, they are usually swollen, very granular, often ragged, and have a strong tendency to adhere in clumps; in decomposing urine they are soon destroyed and converted into a gelatinous substance, which gives the urine a mucilaginous consistency.

Pyuria indicates suppuration in some part of the urinary tract, such as the bladder, urethra, or renal pelvis, or may be due to contamination from the vagina, in which case many vaginal epithelial cells will also be present. Of these conditions chronic cystitis causes by far the greatest amount of pus. In general the source of the pus can be determined only by the accompanying structures (epithelium, casts) or by the clinical signs. A considerable amount of pus, appearing suddenly, originates from a ruptured abscess.

A rather accurate idea of the quantity of pus occurring from day to day may be obtained by shaking the urine thoroughly and counting the number of corpuscles per cubic millimeter with the blood-counting slide, but conditions such as ingestion of water must be kept as uniform as possible. A drop of the urine is placed directly on the slide. Dilution is not necessary unless the number of corpuscles exceeds 20,000 per cubic millimeter. The urine must not be alkaline because the corpuscles will adhere in clumps. The number of corpuscles varies from about 5000 for each cubic millimeter in cases of mild cystitis

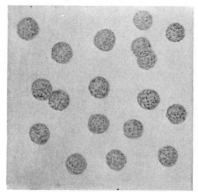 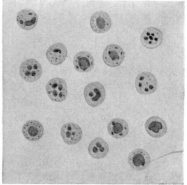

Figure 3–14. Pus corpuscles in urine: *A*, as ordinarily seen; *B*, when treated with acetic acid (× 475).

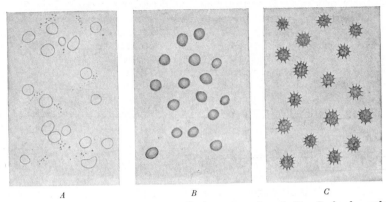

Figure 3–15.   Erythrocytes in urine: *A*, shadow cells in a case of nephritis; *B*, fresh erythrocytes; *C*, crenated corpuscles in urine of high specific gravity ($\times$ 475).

to 100,000 or 150,000 in cases of severe cystitis.

Pus adds a certain amount of albumin to the urine, and it is often desirable to know whether the albumin in a given specimen is due solely to pus. It has been estimated that 80,000 to 100,000 pus corpuscles per cubic millimeter add about 0.1 per cent of albumin. If albumin is present in much greater proportion than this, the excess is probably derived from the kidney.

Erythrocytes. Urine that contains blood is always albuminous. Very small amounts of blood do not alter its macroscopic appearance, but larger amounts alter it considerably. Blood from the kidneys is generally mixed intimately with the urine and gives it a hazy, reddish, or brown "smoky" color. When blood comes from the lower part of the urinary tract, it is not so intimately mixed with the urine and settles more quickly to the bottom; the color is brighter, and small clots are often present. A further clue to the site of the bleeding may sometimes be gained by having the patient void three separate portions. If the blood is chiefly in the first portion, the bleeding point is probably in the urethra; if the blood is chiefly in the last portion, the bleeding point is probably in the bladder. If the blood is mixed uniformly in all three portions, it probably comes from the kidney or ureter. The presence of tube casts or considerable numbers of epithelial cells of the renal type would be suggestive, and the presence of blood casts would of course point definitely to hemorrhage into the renal tubules.

Erythrocytes usually are not difficult to recognize with the microscope. Since fat, yeasts, and oxalate crystals may cause confusion, erythrocytes should be identified positively by examining them with the high power, dry objective. When very fresh, they have a normal appearance and are yellowish disks of uniform size. They are likely to be swollen in dilute urine and crenated in concentrated urine. When they have been in the urine any considerable time, their hemoglobin may be dissolved; they then appear as faint colorless circles or "shadow cells" and are more difficult to see (Fig. 3–15). The shadow cells are not always uniform in size and, although usually circular, may be oval, pear shaped, or irregular in outline. The microscopic findings may be corroborated by chemical tests for hemoglobin, although the microscope may show a few erythrocytes when the chemical tests are negative. When the erythrocytes are numerous, they are often accompanied by yellowish shreds of fibrin of various sizes.

When not the result of contamination from menstrual discharge, blood in the urine, or hematuria, is always a pathologic condition and usually is of serious import. A few erythrocytes may be found in the urine after strenuous exercise. Blood comes from the renal tubules in severe hyperemia, in acute nephritis, in exacerbations of chronic nephritis, in renal tuberculosis, and in malignant disease. Renal hematuria may also be a manifestation of the hemorrhagic disease.

Blood comes from the pelvis of the kidney in the presence of renal calculus, of which hematuria is the classic and most constant symptom. The bleeding in this condition usually is intermittent, small in amount, and accompanied by a little pus and perhaps crystals of the substance forming the stone.

Considerable bleeding from the bladder may occur in cases of vesical calculus, tuberculosis, and new growths. Small amounts of blood generally accompany acute cystitis. In Africa the presence of *Schistosoma haematobium* in the veins of the bladder is a common cause of hemorrhage (Egyptian hematuria).

Quantitative Estimation of Organized Sediments. *Addis' method of counting casts and cells.* Thomas Addis and his associates (1950) have developed a method for the quantitative estimation of formed elements in the urine. Extensive studies using this method have helped to formulate important basic principles concerning the excretion of formed elements in health and disease. Perhaps the most valuable contribution of this work has been to emphasize the importance of a properly conducted microscopic examination of the urinary sediment. The method is now seldom used in practical clinical work. It has unusual teaching value, and it can be recommended as a part of any curriculum leading to an understanding of renal disease or a technical mastery of urinalysis.

Technique

1. Save a 12-hour sample of urine, which must be measured to within ± 2 ml.

2. Transfer 10 ml. of urine to a special graduated centrifuge tube (Fig. 3–16). The narrow tip is graduated for the measuring of small amounts of sediment.

3. Centrifuge for five minutes at 1800 revolutions per minute.

4. Pour off the supernatant urine and adjust the volume of the remaining fluid with physiologic salt solution (1 to 5 ml.) so that the sediment from the 10 ml. of urine will be well distributed in the fluid by mixing thoroughly with a fine pipet.

5. Place a drop of the mixture of sediment in a hemacytometer and count the number of casts in the total ruled area, which represents the number in 0.0009 ml. Also count the erythrocytes and the leukocytes that are found in the same ruled area.

Repeat this procedure two to ten times and add the number of cells and casts that have been counted.

CALCULATION. The following formula is self-explaining: Let V = volume of urine, expressed in cubic centimeters, for 12 hours; 10 = number of milliliters of urine centrifuged; s = volume in milliliters of mixed sediment; v = volume in milliliters in which count was made; n = total number of cells or casts counted; N = number of casts or cells in 12-hour sample.

$$N = \frac{s}{v} \times n \times \frac{V}{10}$$

NORMAL VALUES AND SIGNIFICANCE. Hyaline casts normally may number as high as 5000 in the 12-hour period, although in cases of nephritis the casts of various sorts may total 50,000 to 1,000,000. Erythrocytes normally number from 0 to 500,000 (possibly even 1,000,000); in nephritis there may be an enormous increase in the number of erythrocytes in the 12-hour period (15,000,000 to 400,000,-000). Leukocytes may be present normally; usually the number of leukocytes does not exceed 1,000,000 in twelve hours. In pathologic conditions the epithelial cells and pus corpuscles may number from 2,000,000 to 50,000,000. It is evident that with such wide variations in normal subjects, a close division between normal and abnormal is impossible.

Lyttle (1933) has shown that the urine of children may normally contain slightly more albumin and casts than the urine of adults. The number of erythrocytes and leukocytes in the urine excreted in 12 hours by a normal child will be slightly less, on the average, than the number of erythrocytes and leukocytes in the urine excreted in a similar period by adults.

Spermatozoa. Spermatozoa are generally present in the urine of men after nocturnal emissions, after epileptic convulsions, and in spermatorrhea. They may be found in the urine of both sexes after coitus. They are easily recognized by their characteristic structure (Fig. 3–17). The 4 mm. objective should be used with subdued light and careful focusing.

Bacteria. Under normal conditions the urine is free from bacteria in the bladder but becomes contaminated in passing through the urethra. Various nonpathogenic bacteria are present in decomposing urine. They are easily seen with the 4 mm. objective in the routine microscopic examination, but ordinarily no attempt is made

Figure 3–16. Addis graduated centrifuge tube.

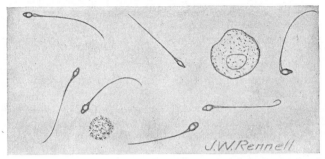

Figure 3–17. Spermatozoa in urine. A pus corpuscle and a transitional epithelial cell are also shown (× 475).

to identify them. They produce a cloudiness, which will not clear on filtration through paper.

In many infectious diseases the specific bacteria may be eliminated in the urine without producing any local lesion. *Salmonella typhosa* is present in the urine in about 30 per cent of cases of typhoid fever, and it has been known to persist for months and even years after the attack. *Mycobacterium tuberculosis* nearly always is present in the urine when tuberculosis exists in any part of the urinary tract. In cases of general miliary tuberculosis it often is present but may be difficult to find, especially when the urine contains little or no pus.

In local nontuberculous infections of the urinary tract, notably in acute and chronic pyelitis and cystitis, a variety of bacteria have been found in the urine. In more than half the cases *Escherichia coli* is present alone or in company with other bacteria. Next most frequent are the staphylococci. *Proteus vulgaris, Pseudomonas aeruginosa,* streptococci, and other organisms also have been encountered.

KIDNEY FUNCTION TESTS

It has long been recognized that changes in excretory function are associated with renal disease and that functional disturbance may be the first definite indication of anatomic damage. That certain excretory functions can be measured quantitatively has encouraged us to hope that the extent of pathologic damage may thus be estimated. More recent developments in renal physiology provide the basis for quantitative study of separate anatomic and functional segments in the nephron (Smith, 1956). Specific knowledge of renal physiology and ingenious tests of excretory function have not, however, produced a comparable body of clinically applicable procedures. There are several reasons for this disappointing issue. In the first place, changes in renal function do not necessarily indicate the existence of organic kidney disease. Renal function may be greatly depressed by pathologic conditions that are primarily extrarenal, such as heart disease that is poorly compensated or severe anemia. Moreover, the tests generally measure a gross summation of functions or an average performance of the total kidney mass, so that localized lesions, extensive focal damage, and generalized changes of less severe degree often fall well below the sensitivity of the methods. Even the most refined function tests have not shown a striking correlation with histopathologic changes in the kidney and offer at best only a crude index of clinical status.

Despite these severe limitations the excretory function tests are of definite value in the study of renal disease. Like most other laboratory procedures their results are meaningful chiefly when taken in association with other observations and a full clinical evaluation of the patient.

A very large number of renal function tests have been proposed, but only a few have received wide and continued acceptance. These few will be discussed in the following pages.

Concentration Tests. The capacity of the kidney to concentrate urine is one of the more sensitive tests for early loss of function. In view of the ease with which this observation can be made, it should take precedence over more complex methods. As the kidney loses its capacity to do osmotic work, the urinary solids must be excreted in more dilute solution, for a greater total volume is required to accomplish the same excretory function. The specific gravity of the urine, which in the normal individual fluctuates widely in response to fluid intake, becomes confined within narrower limits until it is fixed at approximately 1.010. These changes are usually expressed symptomatically as nocturia and sometimes as polyuria. The day-night ratio of urine volume, normally 3 or 4 to 1, tends toward a 1 to 1 ratio.

There are many techniques for performing the concentration test. Some are unnecessarily complex. If the patient is deprived of water during a period of 14 to 16 hours, the urine collected at the end of this time will show the maximum concentration of which the kidneys are capable. For practical purposes no other principle or test routine need be known. Thus, if a patient is allowed no water after 5 p.m. and urine specimens are collected at 7, 8, and 10 a.m. the following morning, one of the specimens will show the maximum concentration of which the individual's kidneys are capable. Under these conditions a normal adult will excrete urine of specific gravity 1.025 or greater. Failure to concentrate urine above 1.020 is indicative of renal functional impairment. In general the nearer the maximum concentration approaches 1.010, the more severe is the renal damage. It should be emphasized that a normal capacity to concentrate urine does not rule out major renal disease. Many patients show urinary sediment and other signs clearly indicative of active kidney disease while retaining the capacity to excrete a urine of 1.025 specific gravity or better.

Results of the concentration test are unreliable in the presence of any severe water or electrolyte imbalance, pregnancy, chronic liver disease, or adrenal cortical insufficiency. Obviously the test is indeterminate during the formation or excretion of edema fluid. Some test procedures require that the patient be placed on a standard diet. No doubt this precaution does eliminate certain irregularities in the results, but from the practical standpoint the test is seldom if ever worth so much effort. Patients who are taking a low protein and low salt diet may fail to concentrate urine simply because of lack of urinary solids. Not the least important factor is the patient's cooperation in the procedure.

Although the concentration test is simple and usually quite harmless, one should keep in mind some contraindications to its use. Deprivation of fluid for a minimum of 14 hours is an uncomfortable experience. In older people and particularly those with heart disease or incipient renal failure this much dehydration may prove to be a fatal stress. There is no excuse for using the test on any patient who is very ill or who has fever or is unable to cooperate.

Administration of Pituitrin or vasopressin may be used to achieve maximum urine concentration. In this test the patient need not be deprived of water or otherwise prepared; he is asked to empty his bladder and the urine is saved as the first specimen. Surgical Pituitrin is given subcutaneously in a dose of 10 units or 0.5 ml. Nothing is allowed by mouth until the test is complete. Specimens are obtained at one- and two-hour intervals after the injection. The lowest concentration consistent with normal kidney function is about 1.023. Reactions to Pituitrin are often rather uncomfortable. The test should not be used in hypertensive patients or in those who are chronically ill or debilitated. Normal individuals often fail to concentrate urine if they are physically active during the test period.

Dilution Tests. Loss of capacity to dilute urine is a later consequence of renal damage, and it is rarely so striking an observation as the loss of concentrating power. The discomfort and even the danger of administering so large a quantity of fluid as required for the test generally offset the meager value of the result.

The usual procedure is as follows: Breakfast is withheld, and the patient is given 1200 ml. of water to drink during an interval of 30 minutes. Urine is collected hourly thereafter for four hours. In the normal individual approximately 1200 ml. of urine will be excreted during this time. The largest part will be voided during the first two hours. The specific gravity of at least one of the specimens should fall to 1.003. In kidney disease with functional impairment, the quantity eliminated in the four-hour period may be much smaller, and the specific gravity of the urine may not fall below 1.010.

Phenolsulfonphthalein (P.S.P.) Test. This test, which was described by Rowntree and Geraghty in 1910, consists of the intravenous or intramuscular injection of a solution of phenolsulfonphthalein, a drug that is eliminated only by the kidneys. The amount of this drug in the urine can be estimated easily by colorimetric methods. The time of its first appearance in the urine and the quantity eliminated within a definite period are taken as a measure of the functional capacity of the kidneys. The test is harmless, extremely simple, and for general purposes the most satisfactory of the functional tests. In addition it has the advantage of being readily adapted to the observation of function in each kidney separately when urine is obtained by ureteral catheterization.

Several minor variations of the procedure have been proposed. The procedure to be outlined takes advantage of the important 15-minute excretion.

1. Give the patient 300 to 400 ml. (about two glasses) of water to promote urinary excretion.

2. Twenty to 30 minutes later inject intravenously exactly 1 ml. of solution containing 6 mg. of phenolsulfonphthalein. The dye can be administered intramuscularly, allowing approximately ten minutes' additional time for absorption. The intravenous injection is preferable, since it permits more accurate measurement, particularly at the 15-minute interval.

Note that the patient is not asked to void and discard urine at the time the dye is injected. Quantitative collection of the excreted dye is greatly improved if urine is present in the bladder at the time excretion begins.

3. Exactly 15 minutes after the intravenous administration of the dye, and again at the end of one hour and two hours, have the patient void completely. The three specimens are properly labeled and kept in separate containers.

4. Estimate the output of phenolsulfonphthalein in each of the three specimens.

A number of slightly different procedures for the estimation of phenolsulfonphthalein can be adapted to any type of colorimetry:

1. To prepare a standard, place 1 ml. of P.S.P. solution (6 mg.) in a 1000 ml. volumetric flask. Add 5 ml. of 10 per cent sodium hydroxide to bring out the maximum red color. Dilute to 1000 ml. with water and mix by inverting several times. This is the 100 per cent standard. It can be diluted with an equal amount of distilled water to make a 50 per cent standard. The latter is generally used, since no more than 50 per cent of the injected dye is likely to be excreted in any one specimen.

2. Place each specimen of urine in a volumetric flask or graduated cylinder. Note the amount of each. If a specimen is less than 40 ml., results are not dependable.

3. Add to each specimen 5 ml. of 10 per cent sodium hydroxide to bring out the

purplish red color. Dilute each with water until the color is roughly equivalent to the standard. If the urine is cloudy, it must be filtered before being compared with the standard.

Estimation can be made in any type of colorimeter. In the absence of a colorimeter one can easily make up a series of standards representing 10, 20, 30 per cent, and so on by diluting the 100 per cent standard. Standards are also available in commercial kits*; these are quite satisfactory for small laboratory work.

In the normal individual, 25 per cent or more of the dye will be excreted during the first 15 minutes after intravenous injection, and not less than 70 per cent will be excreted during the two-hour period. In the absence of cardiac decompensation or obstructive uropathy the degree of retention is a fairly accurate guide to the severity of impairment of renal function. The rate at which the dye appears in the urine depends both on the renal blood flow and the action of the tubular epithelium in removing the dye from the blood. In the absence of cardiac failure the results, especially of the 15-minute excretion test, correlate rather well with measurements of renal blood flow. Obstructive lesions of the lower urinary tract as well as delayed or incomplete emptying of the bladder make it impossible to interpret the test in terms of renal function.

The Urea Clearance Test. The concept of renal clearance can be applied to any substance that is present in the blood and is excreted in the urine. The principle was first applied by Van Slyke to urea. Urea clearance was defined as the least volume of blood (or plasma) containing an amount of urea equal to that excreted in one minute. Thus, clearance is a ratio of the urinary excretion to the average blood level determined simultaneously. Such a ratio is correlated more directly with the progress of kidney disease and shows a deviation from normal earlier in the course of renal damage than any isolated observation of a blood constituent or the urinary excretion of urea or other substance.

Procedure. Although not absolutely necessary, it is usually best to have the patient remain at rest during the test period. The test should be performed at high but falling rates of urine flow, since the onset of water diuresis alters the rate of urea reabsorption by the tubules. Prepa-

* The Dunning test for P.S.P. (Hynson, Westcott & Dunning, Inc., Baltimore 1, Maryland).

ration of the patient for urea clearance by induction of water diuresis should, therefore, begin an hour or more before the urine collections are made.

1. At least one hour before the test is to begin, give the patient 8 ml. of water per kilogram of body weight (but not more than 600 ml.).

2. At the beginning of the test the patient empties his bladder completely, discarding the specimen. The time is recorded accurately.

3. In exactly one hour the patient is asked to void again. Measure the quantity of urine exactly in ml. and divide by 60 to calculate the number of ml. per minute (V).

4. Near the midpoint of the test withdraw blood by venipuncture and determine the value for the urea nitrogen in mg. per 100 ml. (B). The exact time is unimportant, since there is very little fluctuation of blood urea over such a short interval.

5. Determine the urea nitrogen content of the urine and express as mg. per 100 ml. (U).

Calculation. The urea clearance is the number of ml. of blood cleared of urea per minute. If the quantity of urine voided is more than 2 ml. per minute, the formula used is that for "maximum clearance"

$$C_m = \frac{U \times V}{B}$$

or expressed in per cent of normal

$$C_m = \frac{100\ UV}{75\ B}$$

If the quantity of urine excreted is less than 2 ml. per minute, the formula used is that for "standard clearance"

$$C_s = \frac{U \times \sqrt{V}}{B}$$

or expressed in per cent of normal

$$C_s = \frac{100\ U\sqrt{V}}{54\ B}$$

For both technical and physiologic reasons maximum clearance is a more reliable figure than standard clearance.

Interpretation. Results falling between 75 and 125 per cent of normal have no pathologic significance. Clearance values from 40 to 60 per cent of normal indicate moderate functional impairment; values from 20 to 40 per cent are associated with marked impairment. Urea clearance less than 20 per cent of normal indicates severe renal damage. Since the proportion of urea reabsorbed by the renal tubules remains relatively constant at about 40 per cent of that filtered, the urea clearance test serves as a measure of glomerular filtration. The urea clearance expressed as a per cent of normal multiplied by 1.2 is a rough clinical estimation of glomerular filtration rate.

Other Clearance Tests. The measurement of endogenous creatinine clearance has been advocated rather widely. Creatinine clearance approaches the glomerular filtration rate, but the situation is complicated in the human, because a proportion of the creatinine is secreted in the tubules. This proportion rises somewhat unpredictably when failure of filtration occurs in renal disease. This fundamental defect is not corrected by the use of specific enzymatic methods for the measurement of creatinine.

Several more specific tests of renal function have been based on the clearance principle. For the most part these require intravenous infusion of test substances at constant rates, catheterization, and a relatively complicated laboratory facility. They are time consuming and costly. We are generally satisfied to use the results of these more refined methods as a background against which the more simple and practical methods can be interpreted.

The glomerular filtration rate can be estimated by determining the clearance of any substance that is filtered freely at the glomerulus but that is neither excreted nor reabsorbed by the tubules. A nearly ideal substance for this purpose is inulin, an inert polysaccharide. The normal glomerular filtration rate as determined by inulin clearance is about 110 to 150 ml. per minute.

Renal blood flow can be determined by using such substances as Diodrast and para-aminohippuric acid, which at low blood concentrations are removed almost completely by tubular excretion in a single circulation through the kidney. Effective renal blood flow as calculated from this type of clearance procedure is about 1000 to 1150 ml. per minute or, expressed as plasma flow, about 600 to 700 ml. per minute.

The specific determination of tubular function is somewhat more involved. Tubular secretory mechanisms can be overloaded at high blood levels of Diodrast, para-aminohippuric acid, phenol red, glucose, and other substances. Clearance rates under these circumstances, after being corrected for amounts simultaneously filtered by the glomerulus, are related to the average tubular function (expressed as tubular mass or Tm) with respect to the particular test substance.

DISEASES OF THE KIDNEY

A few of the more common forms of renal diseases will be discussed briefly. The descriptions are intended only to illustrate the manner in which clinical laboratory procedures can aid in the diagnosis and treatment of these conditions. A full presentation in this category of diseases is beyond the scope of our present purpose. The student will find adequate material in the references at the end of this chapter (refs. 2, 4, 15, and 16).

Acute Glomerulonephritis. This is a diffuse inflammatory disease of the kidneys, involving primarily the capillary endothelium and other elements of the glomerulus. The kidney tissues are not actually invaded by bacteria. The disease appears rather to be a delayed, possibly allergic, response to antecedent not concurrent infection. The infection, which precedes the nephritic episode by 10 to 20 days, is usually localized in the upper respiratory tract. Frequent examples are tonsillitis, pharyngitis, sinusitis, scarlet fever, and rheumatic fever. The infection is caused by hemolytic streptococci of the Lancefield group A. The patient may complain of swelling of the face and hands, headache, oliguria, and hematuria. In more severe cases edema becomes generalized, hypertension severe, and dyspnea marked. Anorexia, vomiting, fever, visual disturbances, delirium, nitrogen retention, and coma are manifestations in fatal cases. The disease is seldom encountered in the fully developed and classical form. We must recognize the possibility of glomerulonephritis when mild or transient signs occur. In many cases the typical urinary findings appear in patients who present no history or physical findings truly characteristic of the disease.

Urinalysis. The volume of urine may remain normal. When oliguria does occur, it is a grave prognostic sign, usually indicating severe renal damage. A period of anuria, two to four days, is not inconsistent with recovery but often marks the fatal case. Actual renal insufficiency does not occur during the acute disease, and consequently the specific gravity of the urine is normal or increased. The urine is deeply colored and often has a smoky appearance owing to the presence of red cells. Hematuria is so typical that the disease was once referred to as hemorrhagic Bright's disease. Red cells in the urine are often the first abnormality to appear and the last to disappear during healing. Gross hematuria occurs in approximately 40 per cent of cases. Failure to find red cells in the urine would place considerable doubt upon the diagnosis of glomerulonephritis.

Protein is regularly present in the urine, but the amount varies widely. A moderate number of white cells appear in the sediment, but frank pus is not seen. When they can be found, red cell casts are particularly convincing evidence of glomerulonephritis. Hyaline and granular casts may be present in the early stages of the disease, and waxy and fatty casts appear somewhat later.

Since vomiting and refusal of food are common features of acute glomerulonephritis, ketonuria is often encountered. This finding bears no essential relation to the disease itself, but it is an important danger signal, indicating that precautions must be taken against further development of acidosis, dehydration, or carbohydrate starvation.

Kidney function tests. In at least half the patients with acute glomerulonephritis renal function, as measured by the usual tests, is normal. In other patients there are varying degrees of renal failure that can be estimated by the urea clearance and the P.S.P. excretion tests. Renal insufficiency with nitrogen retention and termination in uremia is decidedly uncommon; only 2 or 3 per cent of cases follow this course. Hypertensive encephalopathy with convulsions and coma may occur in acute glomerulonephritis without significant azotemia.

Blood counts. A normochromic, normocytic anemia occurs in many patients. It may occur in the absence of nitrogen retention but is most marked when the nonprotein nitrogen is elevated. The white cell count is usually not altered significantly unless there is an associated infection.

Blood nonprotein nitrogen. Severe azotemia occurs in less than 5 per cent of cases. The discovery of marked nitrogen retention early in the course should lead one to suspect that chronic nephritis has been established previously and that the present episode is an acute exacerbation.

Other observations. During the acute attack the serum complement may be low and the antistreptolysin titer high. Serum protein levels are frequently somewhat depressed.

Chronic Glomerulonephritis. This condition is a special challenge to laboratory investigation, since the patients seldom present clinical evidence of specific diagnostic significance. Relationship to the acute episode of the disease is difficult or impossible to establish. Symptoms of hypertension and cardiac decompensation often dominate the clinical picture.

Urinalysis. Urine findings are essential to the diagnosis, but they vary widely, depending upon the activity of the disease and the stage to which it has progressed. Small amounts of protein and a few casts may for many years be the only evidence of abnormality. Red cells are found in the sediment intermittently and in important relation to the degree of activity. Hematuria, either gross or microscopic, is always a grave sign during the course of the disease. Patients in whom the nephrotic phase occurs may excrete large amounts of protein with few or no red cells.

As the disease progresses, the volume of urine becomes greater. Its specific gravity shows a diminishing fluctuation and finally becomes fixed between 1.008 and 1.012. When this point has been reached, the excretion of cells and protein may be decreased strikingly.

The most typical urine findings in chronic glomerulonephritis are: continued proteinuria of variable degree, intermittent hematuria, and progressive failure of concentration and dilution.

Kidney function tests. These procedures have their greatest usefulness in the study of chronic kidney disease. They may indicate the presence of renal insufficiency before nitrogen retention occurs; they serve to estimate the degree of functional insufficiency and the extent of renal damage. A concentration test is usually run first. After fixation of the specific gravity has taken place, this test yields no further information concerning the progress of kidney disease. Thereafter a urea clearance test is most valuable in estimating further loss of excretory efficiency until nitrogen retention becomes marked. Because of its simplicity, the P.S.P. test may be used during this period of observation, but it does not have the accuracy of the urea clearance method. With the approach of uremia blood chemical abnormalities appear and may be used to follow the further course of events.

Blood counts. Moderate to severe anemia is found regularly in chronic glomerulonephritis. The degree of anemia is often said to parallel the nitrogen retention, but there are many exceptions to this rule. In most cases the anemia is of the microcytic, hypochromic type. In some cases there is a general hematopoietic arrest, resulting in severe anemia, leukopenia, and thrombocytopenia. This situation is often characterized mistakenly as aplastic anemia or even thrombocytopenic purpura before the underlying renal disease is discovered.

The Nephrotic Syndrome. The term "nephrosis" was invented for a group of diseases supposed to be of degenerative origin and thus not properly called nephritis, or inflammatory. The concept of nephrosis has over the years become quite confused. In current usage the term "nephrotic syndrome" does not commit us to any definite concept of renal disease. The syndrome is characterized chiefly by massive proteinuria, retention of sodium, hypoproteinemia, and massive edema. The nephrotic syndrome occurs in association with kidney lesions of such widely different etiologies as chronic glomerulonephritis, intercapillary glomerular sclerosis or Kimmelstiel-Wilson syndrome, amyloidosis of the kidney, syphilitic nephrosis, thrombosis of the renal vein, and disseminated lupus erythematosus. Chronic glomerulonephritis is the pathologic basis for the nephrotic syndrome in a large proportion of cases. The so-called true or lipoid nephrosis is described as occurring principally in children. It is doubtful that this can be distinguished from the nephrotic phase of glomerular nephritis.

Urinalysis. The volume of urine is small; the specific gravity is normal or high. The excretion of chloride is low during the formation or presence of edema. The urine always contains a large quantity of protein with daily excretions of 5 to 20 gm. being noted. There is no other condition in which the loss of protein in the urine is so great. Hyaline casts may occur in large numbers. Occasionally there are a few or many white cells, but red cells do not appear. Continued absence of hematuria is an important point in the exclusion of active glomerular nephritis. Doubly refractile lipoid bodies are seen in the urinary sediment, especially in the so-called true lipoid nephrosis.

Plasma proteins. The plasma protein disturbance is characterized by a marked hypoalbuminemia. The total globulins are increased in the alpha and beta fractions, and there is a decrease in the gamma globulins. The total protein and the albumin fraction are below the critical level for edema formation; that is, the total is less than 4.5 gm. and the albumin less than 2.5 gm. per 100 ml. The protein levels are of great importance in diagnosis, in the estimation of prognosis, and in determining the response to therapy.

Blood cholesterol. There is a general increase in the blood lipids with strikingly high levels of both free and esterified cholesterol and phospholipid fractions. The plasma often appears milky. The determination of blood cholesterol is a satisfactory index to the total lipemia. Values for cholesterol concentration are usually in excess of 300 mg. per 100 ml., and levels above 1000 mg. have been reported.

Blood urea and nonprotein nitrogen. These determinations are usually within normal limits, although slight to moderate azotemia does not exclude the diagnosis.

Plasma chloride. Chloride concentration in the plasma is often normal but may be considerably increased. Sodium retention is closely related to the formation of edema in this condition, and salt restriction is a fundamental part of the therapeutic regimen.

Kidney function tests. Renal insufficiency does not occur in the typical nephrotic syndrome. The kidneys retain their normal capacity to concentrate and dilute the urine. The function tests, particularly the P.S.P. excretion test, may show slight, transient impairment, but normal results are the rule.

Basal metabolic rate. The metabolic rate is often lower than normal. The meaning of this finding is not clear. Recent studies indicate that thyroid function is normal, but significant quantities of the protein-bound hormone may be lost in the urine. Treatment with thyroid hormone usually does not improve the patient nor does it alter the metabolic rate appreciably.

Blood counts. Total white cell and differential counts are usually within normal limits. There may be a slight anemia, which becomes more severe with the onset of renal failure.

Arteriolar Nephrosclerosis. Hypertensive vascular disease results in renal failure in approximately 10 per cent of cases. Renal damage and insufficiency of less than lethal grade are much more common occurrences than this figure would suggest. The two general forms of this disease are differentiated by the rate of progress. When the progression is slow and the patient dies after many years, the term "benign hypertension" is used. When the disease progresses rapidly and the patient dies within a few months after the onset, it is described as "malignant." Benign and malignant hypertension are by no means clearly distinct, and their antemortem manifestations overlap widely.

There are no laboratory findings strictly characteristic of this disease. The chief value of laboratory methods in the study of hypertensive disease is in the determination of prognosis as indicated by the degree of renal excretory failure. Unfortunately these findings occur late in the course of the disease when they are of less practical use.

Urinalysis. During the early phases of hypertensive disease the urine remains entirely normal. A small amount of protein and a few hyaline casts are often among the first urinary findings. These may be present for years before other signs of renal damage appear. A gradually increasing urine volume, a reversal of the day-night ratio, and a diminishing capacity to concentrate the urine occur before the onset of renal decompensation. This course of events is quite like that associated with chronic glomerulonephritis. These two conditions are always difficult, and sometimes impossible, to differentiate. Red cells and other formed elements occur in the urine with very similar frequency in both diseases. Gross or microscopic hematuria is always a grave sign during the course of hypertensive disease and is particularly characteristic of the malignant form. The terminal urinary findings are those of renal failure and uremia.

Kidney function tests. As has already been indicated, the onset of renal failure occurs late in the course of hypertensive vascular disease. The practical value of the kidney function tests is, therefore, distinctly limited. Their prognostic value is often sufficient to justify their use. Selection of the procedures and interpretation of results are the same as that described in connection with chronic glomerulonephritis.

Blood counts. Anemia associated with advanced nephrosclerosis may be of the same severity and type as that associated with chronic glomerulonephritis. During the earlier course of the disease anemia is not characteristic of hypertensive vascular disease of the primary type. Anemia is more likely to indicate the presence of chronic glomerulonephritis. Leukocyte counts are not altered.

Blood chemistry. The blood chemical changes in advanced nephrosclerosis are those characteristic of renal failure and uremia.

Pyelonephritis. This disease is characterized by inflammatory, vascular, and cicatricial changes owing to the multiplication of pathogenic bacteria in the renal parenchyma and the pelvocalyceal system. Clinical interest in pyelonephritis has greatly increased since the recent introduction of quantitative studies of normal and pathogenic bacteria of the genitourinary tract (Kleeman *et al.*, 1960). These studies have indicated the prevalence and insidious character of significant infection of the urinary tract. A number of predisposing factors figure in the pathogenesis of pyelonephritis. Some of the more important of these are obstructive lesions located anywhere from the nephron to the external meatus, pregnancy in which asymptomatic bacteriuria is especially frequent, diabetes mellitus, urethral instrumentation, and disturbances of bladder innervation.

The majority of instances of pyelonephritis are caused by coliform bacteria. Less commonly infection is caused by *Proteus vulgaris, Pseudomonas aeruginosa,* and various species of staphylococcus and enterococcus.

Urinalysis. The urinary sediment in acute pyelonephritis is characterized by pus, leukocyte casts, and varying degrees of hematuria without red cell or hemoglobin casts. Quantitative proteinuria rarely exceeds 1 to 2 gm. per day. In chronic pyelonephritis the urinary findings vary widely, depending on the degree of active inflammation, the associated pathologic changes, and the presence of congestive heart failure.

The so-called "glitter cell," although not pathognomonic of pyelonephritis, is rarely seen in large numbers in other forms of renal disease. This is a large, swollen cell with cytoplasmic granules showing Brownian movement. The exact origin and identity of this cell are in some doubt.

When quantitative urine cultures show 100,000 bacteria or more per ml. of urine, they furnish important diagnostic information and a valuable guide to therapy. Since bacteriuria of this magnitude can exist in the absence of demonstrable infection of renal tissue, the correlation of bacteriologic findings with the diagnosis of pyelonephritis is not a precise one.

Acute Renal Failure. A large number of conditions characterized by sudden impairment or cessation of renal function with anuria or oliguria are included under the term acute renal failure. Among the diverse causes are surgical shock, traumatic injuries, massive hemorrhage, severe vomiting or diarrhea, transfusion reactions, and certain nephrotoxic agents. Pathologists have described the lesion as lower-nephron nephrosis and more recently as acute tubular necrosis. It may occur in the presence or absence of intrinsic renal disease.

The importance of acute renal failure as a diagnostic category is derived from the fact that the disorder can in many cases be fully reversed by proper treatment. It is therefore extremely important that the situation be recognized in its earliest phases. Without doubt the most important factors contributing to the proper diagnosis of acute renal failure are a thorough understanding of its pathogenesis and a keen awareness of the clinical setting in which it is likely to occur. A full presentation of these matters is beyond the scope of this discussion (see Franklin and Merrill, 1960).

Urinalysis. The volume of urine is small, usually less than 200 ml. per 24 hours, but actual anuria is uncommon. The occurrence of anuria should lead one to suspect obstruction of the urinary tract or acute renal failure superimposed on preexisting intrinsic disease of the kidney. The specific gravity of the urine is relatively high, 1.018 or more, and the reaction is usually strongly acid. After the first two or three days the urine specific gravity may drop to 1.010 or below. Proteinuria is often marked in the beginning but tends to clear with persistence of oliguria. Small to moderate numbers of granular casts or blood-pigment casts are commonly found.

When acute renal failure is reversed or the disease enters the diuretic phase, the urine volume increases rapidly by 50 or 100 per cent a day. A generalized description of urinary findings cannot be given for this disease category, since the wide variations that occur depend upon the etiologic factors involved and the diverse courses that the condition can take.

Blood chemistry. Blood urea nitrogen, nonprotein nitrogen, creatinine, and uric acid rise gradually or precipitately, depending on the rate of protein catabolism and the nature of the underlying cause of renal failure. Serum sodium, chloride, and calcium concentration tend to decrease.

Serum bicarbonate (carbon dioxide combining capacity) decreases as acid metabolites accumulate. Serum potassium concentration tends to increase, and its determination becomes an important guide to treatment and prognosis. At potassium concentrations of 5.5 mEq./L. toxic effects, such as electrocardiographic changes, are often observed, and levels of 7.0 mEq./L. are considered dangerous. All these findings are greatly modified by therapy, and wide variations from one case to another invalidate any generalized description. Blood electrolyte changes are especially complex during the diuretic or recovery phase.

Blood counts. The leukocyte count is often sharply increased even in the absence of obvious infection. A normocytic and normochromic anemia often appears during the course of acute renal failure even in cases not associated with hemorrhage or intravascular hemolysis.

Uremia. Uremia is the clinical condition or symptom complex that results from severe loss of renal excretory function. The highly varied clinical manifestations of uremia are poorly correlated with the many metabolic and biochemical changes that are observed during its course. The symptoms fall into two general categories: (1) complications of renal failure: dehydration; acidosis; retention of sulfate, phosphate, and all the end products of protein metabolism; and disturbances of water and electrolyte distribution; and (2) toxic manifestations: anorexia, nausea, vomiting, headache, mental disturbances, hyperirritability, convulsions, coma, stomatitis, enteritis, pericarditis, and anemia. Although nitrogen retention is a constant accompaniment of uremia and affords the most practical index to its severity, there is no evidence that urea, creatinine, or uric acid contributes significantly to the clinical symptoms. Many metabolic products, such as guanidine, phenols, indican, and so on, accumulate in the blood and tissues, but current information is insufficient to support definite conclusions concerning the role of these and other substances.

The most common causes of uremia are the acute and chronic intrinsic diseases of the kidneys. There is little to distinguish one of these from the other in their more advanced or terminal phases. There is often nothing in either the clinical or the laboratory findings to suggest the specific type of pathologic change underlying the uremic syndrome. Every patient in uremia or impending uremia must be examined carefully to exclude the possibility of obstructive lesions in the lower urinary tract. These lesions are relatively easy to discover; to fail to think about them is inexcusable. Often they are subject to treatment, and the uremic state is reversible. If obstruction is allowed to persist, and particularly if there is superimposed infection, the renal parenchyma is seriously damaged and cure becomes impossible. Some of the more common conditions in this category are:

1. Benign prostatic hypertrophy
2. Carcinoma of the prostate
3. Pelvic carcinoma, particularly carcinoma of the uterine cervix, producing bilateral ureteral obstruction
4. Tumors of the bladder
5. Urethral or ureteral strictures, stones, tumors, and so forth

Consideration must be given also to those conditions described as acute renal failure in which some or all features of uremia may appear. Acute renal failure in this concept is totally reversible, at least in its early phases, and is due primarily to the operation of extrarenal or prerenal factors. Perhaps we should call attention to the terms "postrenal azotemia," which has been used in reference to urinary tract obstruction, "renal azotemia," which is associated with intrinsic diseases of the kidney, and "prerenal" or "extrarenal azotemia," which has been used to describe a wide variety of conditions, including those now classed as acute renal failure. These terms lack current utility in that they emphasize a spectacular but physiologically unimportant finding of blood chemistry and fail to bring out important therapeutic implications, especially in reference to acute renal failure.

As stated previously, the uremic syndrome can be the end result of many different renal diseases chronic pyelonephritis, glomerulonephritis, arteriolar nephrosclerosis, diabetic nephropathy, polycystic disease, and so on. In the following generalizations it should be clear that neither clinical nor laboratory findings are uniquely related to the various antecedent causes.

Blood nonprotein nitrogen. Nitrogen retention is an invariable accompaniment of the uremic state, and failure to demonstrate it excludes the diagnosis. The opposite statement is not always true. A considerable elevation of the blood nonprotein nitrogen may be present without sign or symptom of the uremic syndrome, and the degree of azotemia is not closely correlated with the severity of the clinical manifestations. In serial observations increases or decreases in nitrogen retention reflect with considerable accuracy the progress or regression of the disease. In conditions producing chronic and slowly progressive nitrogen retention, the blood N.P.N. may be extremely high before the onset of uremia. In polycystic disease of the kidneys or in benign prostatic hypertrophy, for example, nonprotein nitrogen levels of 200 mg. per 100 ml. or more may occur before there is clinical evidence of uremia. In the more acute diseases characterized by rapidly progressive renal insufficiency, nitrogen retention may not be nearly so marked before death occurs in fully manifest uremia. In general, uremia due to intrinsic diseases of the kidney or obstructive uropathy is accompanied by blood N.P.N. values between 100 and 300 mg. per 100 ml. In acute renal failure the values tend to be somewhat lower but are too widely variable to have differential significance.

Estimations of blood urea nitrogen are almost equally suitable in the study of uremia. Since, however, there are certain extrarenal influences (such as liver damage and protein starvation), which may affect the urea level in the blood, the N.P.N. determination is more generally applicable. Elevation of blood creatinine to levels between 5 and 30 mg. per 100 ml. is an equally characteristic but somewhat later finding. A great deal of prognostic significance was once attributed to marked elevation of the blood creatinine, but this has not been borne out by later and more extensive observations. Since determination of creatinine is not very satisfactory from the technical standpoint, this determination is not recommended to replace the N.P.N. and it has no great value as a supplementary observation.

Electrolyte and fluid changes. Recent studies using more exact methods of analysis have made it quite clear that there is no one pattern of fluid and inorganic change to be expected in renal failure. Observed changes vary widely in relation to the underlying pathologic changes, the rapidity and degree of advancement, the associated metabolic and nutritional state, and the use of different therapeutic approaches. It is important to realize that the concentration of the various blood constituents represents a balance between intake, endogenous production, and renal excretion. Blood phosphate and sulfate concentrations are increased regularly. Metabolic acidosis is common and leads to greatly decreased blood bicarbonate levels. Plasma sodium and chloride concentrations are usually decreased as a result of vomiting and diminished intake and sometimes by increased renal excretion. Unless the situation is complicated by administration of large amounts of fluid, there is usually some degree of dehydration and hemoconcentration. Loss of body water tends to produce higher concentrations of the various blood solutes and to make the interpretation of blood chemistry much more difficult. Estimation of the actual fluid spaces and total body content of the various substances is not easily accomplished in the usual clinical situation.

Although total body potassium is usually reduced as a result of vomiting, diarrhea, malnutrition, and occasionally by excessive loss in the urine, plasma potassium is usually increased to some extent and potassium intoxication may occur. Hypocalcemia is a common finding and may be severe enough to lead to tetany. The latter tendency is offset by the metabolic acidosis, which increases the degree of ionization of the available serum calcium.

Urinalysis. There is nothing strictly characteristic about the urine in uremia. As a rule the volume is decreased below the minimum normal, and complete anuria may be present. Even in those instances in which renal insufficiency has produced a low fixed specific gravity, there may be a tendency for the specific gravity to rise during the terminal episode. The protein and cellular constituents are those characteristic of the renal disease and not of the uremic state itself. As a consequence of starvation and fluid loss the urine contains acetone bodies but usually not in quantities so great as those found in the urine of diabetic patients in comparable clinical condition.

Blood counts. Anemia of the normochromic or hypochromic type is found very frequently and is roughly proportional to the severity and duration of nitrogen retention. Changes in hematocrit readings reflect the degree of hemoconcentration due to loss of body water balanced against the loss of total red cell mass due to anemia. There are no other characteristic changes in the peripheral blood. Although hemorrhagic tendencies are frequent and sometimes quite severe, there are no constant changes in the known components of the hemostatic mechanism. The hemorrhagic diathesis has been attributed to increased capillary fragility and to thrombocytopenia.

REFERENCES

1. Addis, T.: Glomerular Nephritis. New York, The Macmillan Company, 1950.
2. Aller, A. C.: The Kidney: Medical and Surgical Disorders. London, J. & A. Churchill, Ltd., 1951.
3. Barney, J. D., and Sulkowitch, H. W.: Progress in the management of urinary calculi. J. Urol., 37:746–762, 1937.
4. Fishberg, A. M.: Hypertension and Nephritis. 5th ed. Philadelphia, Lea & Febiger, 1954.
5. Franklin, S. S., and Merrill, J. P.: Acute renal failure. New Eng. J. Med., 262:711–768, 1960.
6. Hawkinson, V., Watson, C. J., and Turner, R. H.: A modification of Harrison's test for bilirubin in the urine especially suited for mass and serial usage. J.A.M.A., 129:514–515, 1945.
7. Jacobson, B. M., and Milner, L. R.: Detection of urinary Bence Jones protein. Am. J. Clin. Path., 14:138–149, 1944.
8. Jones, H. B.: On a new substance occurring in the urine of a patient with "mollites assium." London, Phil. Tr. Roy. Soc., 1847, pp. 55–62.
9. Kingsbury, F. B., Clark, C. P., Williams, G., and Post, A. L.: The rapid determination of albumin in urine. J. Lab. & Clin. Med., 11:981–989, 1926.
10. Kleeman, C. R., Hewitt, W. L., and Guze, L. B.: Pyelonephritis. Medicine, 39:3–1116, 1960.
11. Lippman, R. W.: Urine and the Urinary Sediment. Springfield, Illinois, Charles C Thomas, 1957.
12. Lyttle, J. D.: The Addis sediment count in normal children. J. Clin. Investigation, 12:87–93, 1933.
13. Schales, O., and Schales, S. S.: A simple and accurate method for the determination of chloride in biological fluids. J. Biol. Chem., 140:879–886, 1941.
14. Smith, H. W.: Principles of Renal Physiology. New York, Oxford University Press, 1956.
15. Strauss, M. B., and Raisz, L. G.: Clinical Management of Renal Failure. Springfield, Illinois, Charles C Thomas, 1956.
16. Symposium on the kidney. Am. J. Med., 24:659, 1958.
17. Wallace, G. B., and Diamond, J. S.: The significance of urobilinogen in the urine as a test for liver function; with a description of a simple quantitative method for its estimation. Arch. Int. Med., 35:698, 1925.
18. Watson, C. J., Schwartz, S., Sborov, V., and Bertie, E.: Studies of urobilinogen. V. A simple method for the quantitative recording of the Ehrlich reaction as carried out with urine and feces. Am. J. Clin. Path., 14:606–615, 1944.

Chapter 4

The Blood

By ISRAEL DAVIDSOHN, M.D.

METHODS USED IN THE STUDY OF BLOOD

PRELIMINARY CONSIDERATIONS

Studies of the blood and blood-forming tissues are used in practically every phase of medical practice. Certain observations of peripheral blood are universally regarded as indispensable to the examination of all patients. These procedures and their interpretations are so numerous and important that they form a separate branch of medical science called clinical hematology, which contains a great deal of information concerning the anatomy and physiology of the blood and the laboratory methods by which this information is commonly obtained. Examinations of the blood derive their practical meaning in relation to the care of patients only as they are correlated with the entire clinical condition.

The blood consists of a fluid of complicated and variable composition, the plasma, in which are suspended erythrocytes, leukocytes, and platelets. If coagulation is prevented, the formed elements can be separated from the pale straw-colored plasma. When blood coagulates, the fluid that remains after separation of the clot is called serum. Serum differs from plasma only by loss of the protein fibrinogen, the latter being removed as insoluble fibrin threads in the process of coagulation. Serum and plasma are used for many important studies in clinical chemistry and immunology. The techniques of hematology are concerned chiefly with the cellular constituents of the blood, their number or concentration, the relative distribution of various types of cells, the presence of abnormal cells and many qualitative features.

METHODS OF OBTAINING BLOOD

There are two sources of blood for laboratory tests: capillary or peripheral blood and venous blood. Both have their advocates, advantages, and disadvantages.

Capillary or Peripheral Blood

It is claimed that what we call peripheral blood is more likely arteriolar than capillary.

For most clinical examinations, including cell counts and determination of the concentration of hemoglobin, blood is best obtained from a vein. However, for making differential blood counts and also for the enumeration of cellular elements, blood may be obtained from the lobe of an ear, the palmar surfaces of the tip of the finger, or, in the case of infants, the plantar surfaces of the great toe or the heel. In the case of the ear, the free margin of the lobe, not the side, should be punctured. Puncture can be made deliberately and slowly because there is almost no pain connected with it. The puncture should be about 3 mm. deep. It is possible to make 100 blood smears or to collect several milliliters of blood from a well-made puncture. If the patient is bedridden, the finger will be found more convenient because the approach is easier; otherwise the ear is preferable because it is less sensitive. An edematous or congested part should not be used. Free flow of blood is essential to obtain reproducible results comparable to those of venous blood. Cold and cyanotic skin is a source of errors. It is responsible for false high figures for red cell and white cell counts. It can be obviated by massage before the puncture until the skin is pink and warm. Vigorous squeezing after the puncture is another source of errors.

The site is first rubbed well with a gauze pad moistened with 70 per cent alcohol or another antiseptic to remove dirt and epithelial debris and to increase the amount of blood in the part. After allowing sufficient time for drying and for the circulation to equalize, the skin is punctured with a blood lancet (of which there are several patterns) or preferably with a short, stout, sharp, three-cornered needle, which is known as a glover's needle. The Bard-Parker No. 11 scalpel blade has been recommended as a good instrument for obtaining blood from a skin puncture. Still better is a similar blade made of stainless steel, which can be mounted in a stopper and kept immersed in alcohol. The so-called Hagedorn type and other similar needles are widely used. Glass capillary prickers have been recommended for earlobe punctures. That serum hepatitis can be transmitted by incompletely sterilized needles must be recognized. The etiologic agent is resistant to ordinary simple forms of sterilization. Many laboratory workers now insist upon individual needles or lancets for each patient and sterilize them by autoclaving after each use. Still better are disposable needles, which are likely to replace the older types.

Technique of Puncture. Whichever site is chosen, cleansing with a suitable disinfectant and drying is followed by a 2 to 3 mm. deep prick preferably with a disposable needle. The puncture is practically painless if properly made with a sharp needle. It should be made with a firm quick stab, which, however, must not be so quick or made from so great a distance that its site and depth are uncertain. A deep puncture is not more painful than a superficial and makes it unnecessary to repeat the procedure.

The first drop of blood that appears is wiped away because it contains tissue juices and the second is used for examination. If the skin at the site of the puncture is not dry, the blood will not form a rounded drop as it exudes. The blood must not be pressed out, since this dilutes it with fluid from the tissues, but moderate pressure some distance above the puncture is allowable. After the needed blood has been obtained, a pad of gauze or cotton soaked in an antiseptic is applied to the puncture and the patient instructed to apply slight pressure until bleeding has ceased. When the heel is used, it must be made warm, probably done most easily by immersion in hot water or by use of a hot water compress. Otherwise, values significantly higher than in venous blood may be obtained, especially in the newborn. On the first day of life average differences as high as 2 gm. of hemoglobin per 100 ml. may be present. The values for hematocrit, red cells, hemoglobin, platelets, and osmotic fragility are lower in peripheral blood than in venous. The leukocyte count is about the same except when the skin is cold in which case the count may be higher.

Venous Blood

Veins have become important in the modern practice of medicine in two ways: as a source of blood for the many and constantly rising number of blood tests and as an avenue for introduction of various therapeutic agents, including blood itself.

This ever-increasing need for veins as portals of entry and of exit makes it paramount to do everything in our power to preserve their patency as the condition for their usefulness, especially since the number of easily accessible good veins is limited by anatomy and since their structure is delicate and vulnerable. The chief responsibility for preservation of veins rests on medical technologists, interns, and residents, because they are the main users of veins.

Three factors are involved in a good venipuncture: the venipuncturist, the patient and his veins, and the equipment.

The Venipuncture. The venipuncture is in most instances a relatively simple procedure, but only if the obtaining of the blood specimen or the introduction of the therapeutic agent is considered the sole purpose of the operation. The operator must be aware of the old phrase in ancient medicine that the doctor's main motto should be "primum non nocere"—"the first thing is not to inflict damage." The vein that one tries to enter should be preserved for innumerable future uses. Actually the life of the patient may sometimes depend on vein patency.

The hematomas displaying all the colors of the rainbow in anticubital fossas, around wrists, and other sundry places testify eloquently to the operator's lack of skill or lack of judgment. As a rule the damage

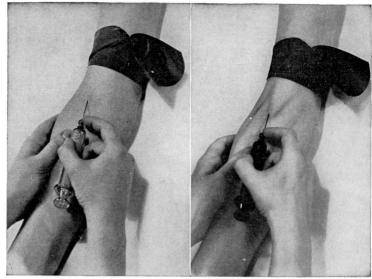

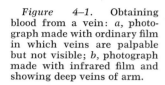

Figure 4–1. Obtaining blood from a vein: *a,* photograph made with ordinary film in which veins are palpable but not visible; *b,* photograph made with infrared film and showing deep veins of arm.

a   b

is only temporary, but it may be long lasting or even permanent. The situation is even worse when the veins by nature are difficult to find or when there has been much past use and some abuse. Enough has been said to make the point that a venipuncture is an operation that is by no means trifling and must be learned at the beginning and approached with due care and deliberation.

The Patient and His Veins. The patient should be reassured with a few words well chosen to fit the particular situation. Self-assurance and poise will do much to establish the proper rapport. The patient should be made comfortable and the approach to his arm should be convenient for the operator. There is no need to add to the difficulties by trying to do the puncture in an inconvenient position. Ambulatory patients should be seated comfortably, preferably in a chair provided with an armrest or at a table on which the arm can be placed comfortably. The operator sits at the opposite side of the table (Fig. 4–1).

The veins should be inspected and evaluated. If the patient's condition is such that he may have to receive repeated transfusions, his elbow veins should be kept intact because they are more suitable for that purpose. Veins at other sites, for example, on the dorsal surface of the hand, though delicate and less fixed, are good enough to be used for drawing of blood. When veins are deep and not felt distinctly, an attempt to enter them is bad practice because it

amounts to blind probing. One can get around this difficulty by using a tourniquet, which makes the veins more prominent and palpable for orientation. Such trial compression should be released and repeated again when one is ready for the actual puncture.

In patients with many punctures in the past and sequelae thereof, such a preliminary study of the veins is particularly important and may reveal more available veins than would seem apparent at first glance.

The Equipment. The syringe should be of the proper size for the amount of blood to be drawn. The fit of the plunger and barrel, which is borne out by the identical number of both, and the integrity of the syringe tip are things to be checked. The life and usefulness of the syringe can be prolonged if the operator rinses the syringe with cold tap water immediately after use to get rid of the blood. Disposable syringes are claimed to be gaining in popularity.

The needle also has to be chosen as to gauge and length for the job ahead. The gauge number expresses the thickness of the needle. The smaller the number, the thicker the needle. The length of the needle used depends upon the depth of the vein. The tip should be inspected most carefully. A blunt or bent tip will defeat the purpose of the puncture and will also damage the patient's vein. The needle should be tested for patency. Again disposable needles seem to be the answer to the problem of sharp needles. However, some institutions may

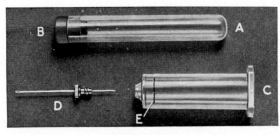

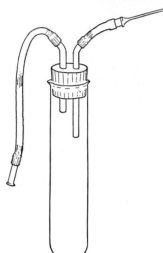

Figure 4–2 (upper). B-D Vacutainer (a blood-collecting tube). A, Vacutainer tube; B, rubber stopper; C, holder; D, double-pointed needle; E, guide line. (Becton, Dickinson and Company.)

Figure 4–2 (lower). Device for drawing blood from a vein, using a large test tube, a centrifuge tube, or a small flask. The glass delivery tube may be extended to the bottom of the container if it is desired to collect blood under a layer of liquid paraffin.

find it more convenient and economical to use regular needles and to care for them according to established standards. Rinsing the needle immediately after use, washing, sharpening, inserting a wire to maintain patency of the lumen, placing in an individual glass tube provided with cotton at the bottom or in one with a constriction on which the hub of the needle rests, plugging the test tube with cotton, and sterilization are the procedures that have stood the test of time.

There are occasional problems involving venipuncture equipment that experience has taught us to solve. The "frozen" syringe is usually the result of blood clotting before the plunger was removed. The following has been recommended to loosen the "frozen" syringe: It is first filled with water by means of another syringe and needle inserted through the tip. Then two needles of different but sufficiently close gauges are fitted together so that one is inserted into the lumen of the other. One end of this assembly is attached to the "frozen" syringe and the other to the end of a small syringe filled with water. Gentle pressure on the smaller of the two syringes may loosen the

"frozen" syringe. Other recommended procedures: gently heating the barrel under running hot water and quickly withdrawing the plunger before it also expands, or soaking in a mixture of equal parts alcohol and glycerin. To prevent such complications, experienced technologists rinse the syringe and needle with cold water immediately after use.

Method of Obtaining Blood from a Vein

It is best to have the patient lying down. If he is sitting, his arm should be firmly supported. Never have the patient standing or seated on a high stool. Although very few patients faint as a result of venipuncture, this danger must always be kept in mind. The skin is cleansed at the bend or at any other site of the elbow by rubbing well with 70 per cent alcohol or another suitable disinfectant. It is then wiped dry with sterile absorbent cotton.

A rubber tourniquet is used to increase venous pressure and to make the veins more prominent and easier to enter, but to prevent hemoconcentration the pressure should not be maintained longer than necessary.

A rubber bandage bound firmly around the upper part of the arm is a very suitable form of tourniquet. The outer end should be tucked under the last round in such a manner that a slight pull will release the bandage (Fig. 4–1). The cuff of a blood pressure apparatus answers admirably or a soft rubber tube may be used. A blood pressure cuff has the advantage that it permits adjustment of the compression to a level sufficient to reduce the flow of venous blood without stopping arterial circulation. This is usually at approximately the middle between the systolic and diastolic pressures. Also reduction or release of pressure after the needle has entered the vein is facilitated. Occasionally it will be sufficient for an assistant or even the patient to grasp the upper arm firmly. If one uses a rubber tubing as tourniquet, one can apply the proper pressure by first compressing the arm so as to suppress the radial pulse and then releasing the pressure just enough to feel the radial pulse feebly. The patient is asked to open and close his fist several times. This causes the veins to become distended. Giving the patient an active role in the procedure helps to take his mind off the puncture. Even if not seen, veins can usually be felt beneath the skin. In fat persons, veins that show as blue streaks are usually too superficial and too small.

After all preliminary steps have been taken, the skin is cleansed with a suitable disinfectant. The next step is to fix the vein in position. This is done by supporting the patient's forearm with the operator's hand and compressing and pulling the soft tissues just below the intended puncture site with the operator's thumb. The syringe is held between the thumb and the last three fingers of the other hand. The back of these fingers are rested on the patient's arm. The free index finger rests against the hub of the needle and serves as a guide. A prominent vein may be entered with a single direct puncture of skin and vein. This one-step procedure is less painful.

When veins are difficult to find, as in adults and in children, a two-step procedure is used. First the skin is punctured in the vicinity of the vein and then the vein itself is punctured. Successful entrance into the vein is followed immediately by appearance of blood in the syringe. If that does not take place, the plunger is withdrawn slightly and in most instances blood appears. Next the tourniquet may be loosened slightly if blood flows freely; otherwise it may be left as put on originally until the desired amount of blood is obtained. At this point the patient is asked to open his fist, the tourniquet is released, a small additional amount of blood is permitted to enter the syringe, the needle is withdrawn, gentle pressure is applied to the site of the puncture with a pad of dry gauze or cotton, and the patient is instructed to take over pressing the pad and to raise the outstretched arm for a few minutes. This usually stops the bleeding and prevents formation of hematoma. Occasionally a small dressing (band-aid) may be applied, mainly to prevent a stain on the rolled-down sleeve. The operator must see that the patient's condition is satisfactory before he is dismissed. If there is any sign of continued discomfort, anxiety, bleeding, or shock, the patient should be kept lying down and seen by a physician.

It is usually easy to secure 5 to 15 ml. of blood, or even more, if required. If the needle is sharp and smooth, the procedure causes the patient surprisingly little inconvenience, seldom more than does an ordinary hypodermic injection. Dull needles may be sharpened by rubbing the bevel, point forward, on a hard, fine oilstone. There is rarely any difficulty in inserting a needle into a vein except in children and in patients in whom the arm is fat and the veins are small. If desired, one of the veins about the ankle can be used. In infants, blood may be secured from the femoral or the external jugular vein and rarely, and only with approval of the attending physician, from the superior longitudinal sinus by puncturing through the posterior angle of the anterior fontanel. A short needle (about ⅜ inch) of rather large caliber is used for this latter procedure.

When the blood has been expelled, the plunger should be separated from the barrel. Otherwise the syringe may become "frozen" when the blood clots or dries. If that happens, the plunger may be loosened by one of many recommended procedures.

Instead of a syringe, many other devices for securing blood from a vein may be employed. Two of these are shown in Figure 4–2 (upper and lower) which indicates their construction in sufficient detail. They possess the advantage that the blood can be drawn directly into any desired reagent or culture medium, and they avoid the expense and difficulty of maintaining a supply of sterile syringes.

Hemolysis interferes with many examinations. It can be minimized by using clean glassware and clean and not too thin needles, by drawing the blood slowly, not faster than the vein is filling, by avoiding admixture of air with resulting frothing, and, after the blood was drawn, by removing the needle and then emptying the blood again slowly and without force into the test tube.

Complications of Venipunctures and Suggestions for Their Prevention

Immediate Local Complications. Hemoconcentration is the result of prolonged application of the tourniquet.

Failure of blood to enter the syringe is the result of several factors. Excessive pull on plunger may collapse a small vein. Remedy: using a slight back-and-forth movement and reducing the force of aspiration. Piercing the outer coat of the vein without entering the lumen may also account for the failure of blood to enter the syringe. Remedy: withdrawing slightly and reentering the vein. This complication may occasionally be followed by hematoma formation. As soon as signs of beginning hematoma are noticed, the needle should be withdrawn, local pressure applied, and venipuncture attempted on the other arm. Transfixation of the vein also accounts for failure to obtain blood. Remedy: slight withdrawal followed by gentle aspiration to see whether blood appears. If this fails, the puncture may have to be repeated. This complication is frequently followed by formation of a hematoma. The same procedure is followed as outlined in the preceding paragraph. Circulatory failure is another cause and the situation is entirely beyond the control of the operator.

In the case of these or of any other complications, failure to draw blood after two attempts should be an indication not to make further attempts but to request another operator to try.

Another not infrequent immediate complication is syncope. This is best treated by having the patient lie down, if he is not already in this position. This is to be followed immediately by calling a physician unless the operator is one.

Continued bleeding may occur in patients with a bleeding tendency, whatever the source. Local pressure as a rule solves the problem.

Late Local Complication. Thrombosis of the vein is sometimes due to trauma but occasionally to infection and resulting thrombophlebitis. These complications are extremely rare if the precautions and recommendations discussed in this chapter are observed.

Late General Complication. Homologous serum jaundice is caused by transmission of the virus by improper handling and by contamination of the needle or the syringe. Aseptic technique and use of adequately sterilized needles and syringes, and preferably disposable needles, may be expected to eliminate this source of transmitted disease.

Venipuncture in Infants

In infants and children venipuncture presents special problems because of the small size of the veins and the difficulty of control. However, even here much can be achieved by the same approach that was outlined for procedures in adults.

Restraining the infant to reduce mobility, use of sharp needles of appropriate size, careful inspection of the veins, making certain that the pressure applied with the tourniquet is not excessive (best achieved by feeling pulsation of the radial artery) will contribute to a successful venipuncture, when others may have failed or given up trying. External jugular puncture may be tried in difficult cases and is frequently successful. Occasionally the internal jugular vein may have to be used. Puncture of the superior sagittal sinus is mentioned here only to discourage its use. Any complication that would be harmless in another area, for example, a hematoma, may have serious consequences.

For hematologic examination, blood obtained by venipuncture is delivered to bottles or tubes containing a suitable anticoagulant. This transfer must be made without delay. Mixing with the anticoagulant is accomplished by thorough but gentle rotation of the container.

If no anticoagulant is used, blood smears should be prepared immediately before clotting occurs. Placing a small amount of blood on a siliconized watchglass will prevent coagulation and make the blood usable for preparation of smears and for quantitative and morphologic studies. Mixing the blood with heparin serves the same purpose, but smears of heparinized blood stained with Wright's stain have a blue background.

To obtain serum, blood is kept at room temperature or in a 37° C. incubator until a clot has formed and begins to retract and then placed in the refrigerator overnight at 4 to 8° C. To accelerate retraction the clot may be separated from the wall of the container with a platinum needle, a thin glass rod, or a wooden applicator before it is placed in the icebox. To obtain serum more rapidly, the blood may be defibrinated with glass beads or a glass rod.

ANTICOAGULANTS

The four most popular are: a mixture of ammonium and potassium oxalate, trisodium citrate, Sequestrene (EDTA), and heparin. The first three prevent coagulation by removing calcium from the blood plasma by precipitation or binding in unionized form. Heparin neutralizes thrombin.

Trisodium citrate is used to prevent coagulation of blood for transfusions. Sequestrene and heparin may be used for the same purpose but not the toxic oxalate mixture.

The mixture of ammonium (six parts) and potassium oxalate (four parts), 2 mg. per 1 ml. of blood, is probably the most widely used anticoagulant. Oxalated blood does not affect the mean corpuscular volume and may be used for hemoglobin, hematocrit, and cell counts. Its usefulness for blood films is limited to the first few minutes. The reason: Crenation of red cells, vacuolation in the cytoplasm of granulocytes, phagocytosis of oxalate crystals, artefact formation in the nuclei of lymphocytes and monocytes, and other malformations develop rapidly.

Trisodium citrate is used in a mixture of one part of a 3.8 per cent aqueous solution and nine parts of blood in blood coagulation studies and in the erythrocyte sedimentation test.

Sequestrene (EDTA) is used in a concentration of 1.0 to 2.0 mg. per 1 ml. of blood. The dipotassium or disodium salt of ethylenediamine tetra-acetic acid is becoming increasingly popular. It must be mixed thoroughly with the blood. It equals oxalate for hematocrit studies and is superior because it prevents formation of artefacts even on prolonged standing. Acceptable blood smears can be prepared after 2 to 3 hours and cell counts even after 12 hours. Also platelet counting is still possible after a few hours.

Heparin, 0.1 to 0.2 mg. per 1 ml. of blood, does not affect the corpuscular size and hematocrit. It is the best anticoagulant for prevention of hemolysis and for osmotic fragility tests. It is not satisfactory when blood smears are to be prepared, because it produces a blue background in Wright's stained slides.

Sources of Error from the Use of Anticoagulants. Even with the use of the best anticoagulant, changes take place that may lead to errors unless suitable precautions are taken. Swelling of erythrocytes raises the mean corpuscular volume (M.C.V.) and osmotic fragility and lowers the sedimentation rate. Leukocytes autolyze and prothrombin time increases. Hemoglobin is affected least. Blood smears should be prepared immediately. Quantitative studies, such as cell counts and estimation of the sedimentation rate of erythrocytes (ESR), should be completed within six hours. It is important to mix the blood thoroughly immediately after it is obtained and before it is examined if stored. This is best done by rotation for not less than two minutes. During the interval, the blood should be kept in the refrigerator at 4 to 8° C. Freezing makes the blood useless.

Preparation of Anticoagulant Tubes or Bottles. The most suitable container for collection is one of somewhat more than 5 ml. capacity with a mouth wide to permit the entry of counting pipets. The stopper must be clean and fit well so that there will be no leaking of blood even when the bottle is inverted.

The anticoagulant solution is prepared as follows:

Ammonium oxalate	1.2 gm.
Potassium oxalate	0.8 gm.
Distilled water	100.0 ml.

If this solution is to be kept in stock, add 1 ml. of 40 per cent formalin as a preservative.

Transfer 0.5 ml. of this solution to each bottle or tube and allow it to dry at room temperature or in a bacteriologic incubator. Do not dry in an oven or autoclave, since above 80° C. oxalate is converted to carbonate, which has no anticoagulant properties. *Warning:* Blood collected in this anticoagulant mixture cannot be used for chemical determinations of nitrogen or potassium.

The containers prepared in this manner are used for 5 ml. of blood. This method of collection allows repeated sampling for determination of cell counts, hemoglobin concentration, and hematocrit reading. Because the staining property of cells is not well preserved in any anticoagulant, smears for microscopic study are best prepared by taking a few drops of blood directly from the syringe or from a separate puncture of the finger or lobe of the ear.

MACROSCOPIC EXAMINATION

Important information may be obtained from the appearance of the blood. Inspection of a centrifuged blood specimen with the naked eye may furnish valuable information. The inspection should include the relative heights of the red cell, buffy coat, and plasma columns.

Estimation of the Sedimentation Rate. After the blood is transferred from the syringe into the hematocrit tube a few minutes will of necessity elapse until centrifugation is started. Inspection of the hematocrit tube at the end of 5 to 10 minutes may reveal excessive sedimentation of the red cells. If 10 per cent or more of the total blood column is cleared of red cells, the conclusion is justified that the sedimentation rate is increased. If this is the case, an accurate determination of the sedimentation rate is indicated.

In order to take advantage of this rough estimation of the sedimentation rate, the tube must be held as vertical as possible and the time of sedimentation must be noted.

The most frequent causes of an accelerated sedimentation rate detected in this crude way are severe anemia, rouleaux due to elevated serum globulin, or autoagglutinins.

The Buffy Coat. Normally a thin layer at the line of separation between the red cell column and plasma seen best in the centrifuged specimen, the buffy coat may begin to form in a relatively short time, especially in leukemia with high cell counts.

The Plasma. Green color is a sign of excessive bilirubin. The pink or reddish hue of the transparent plasma suggests hemoglobinemia. It should be kept in mind that poor technique in collecting the blood specimen is the most frequent cause of hemolysis. Cloudy plasma points to leukemia. If the specimens were not obtained within an hour or two after a fat rich meal, cloudy plasma may point to nephrosis or certain abnormal hyperglobulinemias, especially cryoglobulinemia.

THE ERYTHROCYTES

Hemoglobin

Hemoglobin, the main component of the red blood cell, serves as the vehicle for the transportation of oxygen and of CO_2. When fully saturated, each gram of hemoglobin holds approximately 1.34 ml. of oxygen. The red cell mass of the adult being about 2000 ml. contains approximately 600 gm. of hemoglobin, capable of carrying 800 ml. of oxygen.

Hemoglobin is a conjugated protein, which consists of a basic protein, the globin, and ferroheme (ferroprotoporphyrin), which serves as the prosthetic (active) group. Hemoglobin (reduced hemoglobin or Hb) consists of one molecule of globin and four molecules of hemin (each containing one molecule of iron in the ferrous state). Reduced hemoglobin (Hb) is part of the "active" hemoglobin and can combine reversibly with oxygen and carbon monoxide. When Hb is *oxygenated*, it becomes oxyhemoglobin (HbO_2), which consists of one molecule of globin and four molecules of hemin (each with one molecule of iron in the ferrous state) and is combined with oxygen. Its main function is the transport of oxygen from places of high oxygen pressure (lungs) to places of low oxygen pressure (tissues). This is possible since hemoglobin (Hb) forms with oxygen a dissociable hemoglobin-oxygen complex, oxyhemoglobin (HbO_2), which releases oxygen readily at a low oxygen pressure. The iron in the molecule remains in the ferrous or reduced form.

$$Hb + O_2 \longleftrightarrow HbO_2$$

At an oxygen tension of 100 mm. (pulmonary alveoli) approximately 95 to 96 per cent of the hemoglobin is converted to oxyhemoglobin. Another function of the hemoglobin is the transport of CO_2 from the tissues to the lung. If the ferrous iron in the molecule is oxidized to the ferric iron, as in methemoglobin, the molecule loses its capacity to combine with O_2 and CO_2.

Hemoglobinometry is one of the most frequent tests in clinical laboratories. At the same time and for good reasons it has been until recently one of the most inaccurate tests. Unavailability of stable standards, the practical need for a simple and rapid procedure for a commonly and frequently used test on one hand, and the inherent inaccuracy of most shortcut methods on the other, and the well-known defectiveness of the human eye in matching colors are only a few of the reasons that have made this one of the least reliable tests in clinical pathology, at least until relatively recently.

To all these problems, one needs to add all kinds of variations in what is called normal hemoglobin. Those associated with sex and age have been studied most thoroughly. Hemoglobin levels at various ages are shown in Figure 4-3.

Anemia is one of the most common diseases; frequently it is a complication of other diseases. Fortunately it is a condition readily amenable to successful therapy if recognized and appropriately classified, as will be seen later. The clinical diagnosis of anemia is difficult. It is based on the estimation of the color of the skin and of visible mucous membranes, both not too reliable indicators. To make matters even more complicated, anemia is frequently masked by other manifestations of many diseases. To a limited extent similar considerations apply to conditions with abnormally high hemoglobin. For all these reasons the correct estimation of hemoglobin is important and is one of the routine tests done on practically every patient.

Determining the Concentration of Hemoglobin. Quantitative estimation of hemoglobin is less tedious and, if reasonably accurate, usually is more helpful than an erythrocyte count. It offers the simplest means of detecting the existence and degree of anemia and of judging the effect of treatment of anemic conditions. Pallor observed clinically does not always denote anemia.

There are many methods for determining the concentration of hemoglobin.

The custom of recording hemoglobin in terms of percentage of an indefinite normal is grossly inaccurate and leads to much confusion. It could be compared to an attempt to set up a normal for weather and to express temperature in percentages of the arbitrary normal, disregarding geographic, seasonal, daily, and many other forms of variations in weather. No single normal standard can be applied to all ages and to both sexes. The situation is further complicated by the fact that manufacturers of different hemoglobinometers have arbitrarily selected values ranging from 13.8 to 17.2 gm. per 100 ml. of blood as the equivalent of 100 per cent. A record, therefore, means little unless one knows what instrument was used and the age and sex of the patient. Confusion is best avoided if records are made in terms of the actual amount of hemoglobin, that is, in grams per 100 ml. of blood. The reading on any type of instrument can be readily converted into the actual content of hemoglobin, expressed as grams per 100 ml. of blood, if one knows what amount of hemoglobin was adopted by the makers as 100 per cent, provided, of course, that the particular instrument is

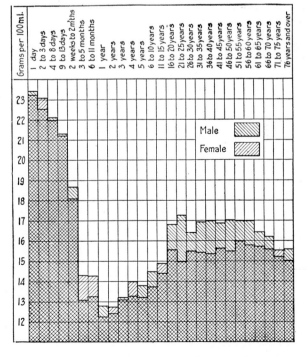

Figure 4-3. Diagram showing average hemoglobin values for both sexes at different ages (after Williamson). Some workers have obtained slightly lower values for the different ages.

accurately standardized. This calculation will be given with the description of the various instruments.

When one evaluates the relative merits of clinical laboratory tests, at least four desiderata are considered: the accuracy of a single determination as compared with a known standard; the reproducibility of a series of determinations when done by the same technician, by a group of technicians in the same laboratory, and by different laboratories; the speed from the point of view of availability in case of emergency; and the simplicity of the procedure from the point of view of economy.

It has been stated that there is probably no procedure more commonly used in clinical laboratories than hemoglobinometry, and there are few that are less satisfactory in their results (Cannon, 1955). The deficiencies may reside, in part, in inadequacies of the chosen method. In larger part, however, they result from manipulative errors in the measurement and processing of the samples of blood. The latter involves questions of technical proficiency that are entirely within the control of the analyst himself. When, however, he converts his observations, such as gasometric or photometric readings or measurements of specific gravity, to grams of hemoglobin in 100 ml. of blood, he must depend upon his own calibration or a calibration supplied by an instrument maker. If a uniform hemoglobin standard were avaliable nationally and a single method of analysis widely practiced, the individual laboratory would then have assurance not only that its results would be comparable from month to month, but that they would also be comparable with those from other laboratories employing the same standard. Inconsistencies in results that persisted under these conditions could then be clearly attributed to technical and manipulative errors.

There are at least three reasons why defining the limits of accuracy for hemoglobin determinations would be desirable. First, the prevalent opinion in circles of experienced hematologists is that there must be difference in value of at least 1 gm. of hemoglobin to be significant. On the other hand, many clinicians are disturbed when told that a change in hemoglobin of 0.2 gm. is not significant. It would be desirable to reconcile these differences so that clinicians may know when a true change in hemoglobin concentration has actually occurred as opposed to a change due to expected variation of the method.

Second, clinical pathologists need not expect from their technicians a degree of accuracy that is beyond the limits of inherent accuracy of the instruments or methods employed in their laboratories.

Finally, the standard of reproducibility will be different for one technician and for a group of technicians in a single laboratory. It will have to be different again when the results of two different laboratories are compared. The physician must recognize these facts, for otherwise he may expect from the laboratory a degree of accuracy and reproducibility of hemoglobin determination that is greater than is possible and justifiable. This is further complicated by the fact that, as a rule, the physician at the bedside is using a value obtained from the examination of a single sample and not multiple ones. Therefore, the physician must not consider as different two values that are within the range of reproducibility for the laboratory that he is using.

Hemoglobinometry. A large variety of methods is available, and no doubt too many unreliable techniques are still used. However, the increasing popularity of photometers and improved and stable standards have raised the quality of hemoglobinometry. The two most widely used procedures today are the cyanmethemoglobin method and the oxyhemoglobin method. The availability of certified and stable cyanmethemoglobin standards encourages wide use of this method.

The methods used in hemoglobinometry can be grouped into four main classes depending on the basic technique employed with variants within each class: colorimetric methods, gasometric methods, specific gravity methods, and chemical methods.

COLORIMETRIC METHODS

Principle. Hemoglobin (Hb) is measured as oxyhemoglobin or is first converted into one of several compounds, such as acid hematin, alkaline hematin, cyanmethemoglobin, and others less widely employed. The measurement is done by comparing the unknown sample with a standard. The method of comparison may be visual or photoelectric. The latter is considerably more accurate.

Direct Matching Methods. Methods that are based on the direct matching of the red color of whole fresh blood with some color standard are not satisfactory.

Tallqvist's hemoglobin scale. The Tallqvist hemoglobin scale consists of a book of small sheets of absorbent paper and a lithographed color scale representing values ranging from 10 to 100 per cent. The undiluted blood from a skin prick is collected on a piece of absorbent paper and compared with the color scale. The percentages on this scale do not have any accurate meaning. The method is not recommended, except for use at the bedside when other methods are not available and with the realization that the margin of error is between 20 and 50 per cent.

Dare's hemoglobinometer. The Dare hemoglobinometer, which employs direct matching of undiluted blood, has been used extensively. The blood is drawn by capillary attraction between two glass plates, and the color is matched with a rotating disc of tinted glass varying in thickness and depth of red color. It has been changed by the present manufacturers in an effort to make it adaptable for the estimation of the grams of hemoglobin per 100 ml. of whole blood. The instrument is expensive and not accurate. Errors of as much as 20 to 30 per cent have been reported.

Acid Hematin Methods. There are several methods that depend on converting hemoglobin into acid hematin with dilute hydrochloric acid and matching the brownish yellow color of this solution with a standard in some sort of a colorimeter or comparator.

The Sahli-Hellige hemometer. The Sahli-Hellige hemometer is equipped with permanent glass standards and a square comparison tube, which allows the value for the hemoglobin to be read as grams per 100 ml. of whole blood and also as percentages. However, 100 per cent on this instrument corresponds to 14.5 gm. per 100 ml. of hemoglobin, which is too low (Fig. 4-4 [upper]).

TECHNIQUE. Place decinormal solution of hydrochloric acid in the graduated tube to the mark 10. Obtain a drop of blood and draw it into the pipet to the 20 cu. mm. mark. Wipe off the tip of the pipet, blow its contents into the hydrochloric acid solution in the tube, and rinse well. Care must be taken not to form bubbles of air. The hemoglobin is changed to acid hematin, which is brown. Mixing should be done with a mixing rod provided with the instrument. Place the tube in the compartment of the frame, let it stand one minute, and dilute the fluid with water drop by drop, mixing after each addition, until it has exactly the same color as the comparison standards.

The intensity of color development is progressive. The maximum is reached after one hour, but after 40 minutes the changes are minimal and after 10 minutes 95 per cent of color intensity has been reached. Therefore, the reading is done after 10 or 20 minutes, but the same time interval has to be observed each time and the instrument should be standardized for that interval. The graduation corresponding to the surface of the fluid then indicates the percentage of hemoglobin. A decinormal solution of hydrochloric acid is prepared with sufficient accuracy for this purpose by adding 1 ml. of concentrated hydrochloric acid to 99 ml. of distilled water.

The Sahli-Haden hemoglobinometer. Haden (1939) has devised a Sahli type hemoglobinometer that is probably the most accurate and simple of any of these instruments. A graduated, square glass tube is used for holding the acid hematin. The Ulrich pipet is recommended for making the dilution with 0.1 N HCL. The calibrations are in grams per 100 ml. of hemoglobin and are based on allowing the blood to stand 30 minutes before making the comparison with the yellow glass standard in the instrument. This may be done either by daylight or by artificial light. If the result is read by electric light, a blue "Daylite" glass filter is used in comparison with an opal glass filter in the holder on the back of the instrument. There are three windows on the scale, and a magnifier is used in focusing on the scale. When the color of the specimen is nearest to a correct match with the central or standard color, the top window will be of lighter shade and the bottom window will be of darker shade. The reading is made by observing the point on the graduated scale to which the diluted blood has risen. Figure 4-4 (lower) illustrated the parts of this apparatus.

Sources of error in the acid hematin methods. 1. Nonhemogloin substances (protein, lipids) in plasma and cell stroma influence the color of blood diluted with acid, because the acid hematin is in colloidal suspension and not a true solution. This is also the reason why the acid hematin method is not satisfactory for photometry.

From 2 to 12 per cent of the total hemoglobin of the blood is in an inactive form, mainly as carboxyhemoglobin, methemoglobin, and sulfhemoglobin. In alkaline solutions these abnormal hemoglobins are converted to hematin, whereas acid has no such effect.

2. Adding of water to match colors is a

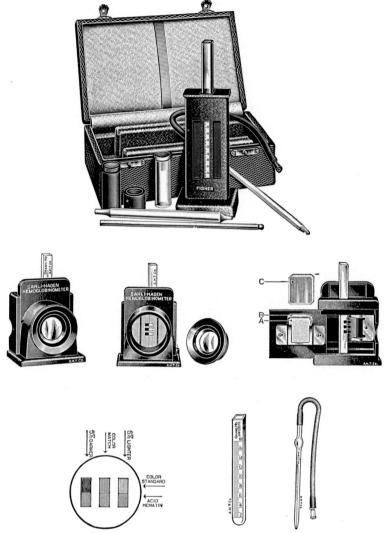

Figure 4–4 (upper).   Sahli-Hellige hemometer. (lower).   Sahli-Haden hemoglobinometer.

time-consuming and delicate procedure. If the matching point is passed, the test has to be repeated.

3. The result has to be read each time after the same interval for which the instrument was standardized. Failure to observe this rule introduces an error.

4. The difficulty of accurate matching with the brown glass standard, although it is probably the simplest glass standard available, introduces a source of error.

5. Variations due to the personal equation of the operator in matching colors are also sources of error.

In addition to these special sources of error there are other sources of error that plague all quantitative blood measuring pro-cedures: errors of the sample; errors of equipment, such as error of the pipet and calibration error; and technical errors, such as an unclean or wet pipet, improper filling of the pipet, blood adhering to the outside of the pipet, and improper mixing of blood with the acid, including air bubbles.

Alkali Hematin Method. Addition of an excess of alkali produces a true and relatively stable solution of hematin.

Method. To 0.05 ml. of blood add 5 ml. of 0.1 N NaOH. Heat in a boiling water bath for four to five minutes, cool, and read against an appropriate standard (Clegg and King, 1942).

Commercial standards are available for use with photometers.

Sources of error. The blood of the newborn and the young infant contains alkali-resistant fetal hemoglobin. This may be a significant source of error in newborns.

Oxyhemoglobin Method. A widely used method is the determination of hemoglobin as oxyhemoglobin. In this procedure 0.02 ml. of blood measured with a Sahli-type hemoglobin pipet is washed into 5.0 ml. of approximately 0.007 N ammonium hydroxide solution prepared by adding 4 ml. of reagent grade NH_4OH to 1 L. of water and mixing. Rinse pipet three times with diluting fluid. The water used in the preparation of ammonia solution must be glass distilled, because minute amounts of copper in distilled water or other diluents employed in oxyhemoglobin determinations may cause oxyhemoglobin to be converted to methemoglobin and lower the values. Shake well to ensure mixing and oxygenation of hemoglobin. The solution is read in a photometer using a green filter (540 mμ) and a 0.007 N ammonium hydroxide solution as blank. The test can be read within a few seconds or with a stoppered cuvet any time up to three days. The standard curve can be set up with one of the procedures to be listed later.

Cyanmethemoglobin Method. This method is the outcome of the long-felt need for improvement of standardization of hemoglobin determinations.

In 1941 the British Medical Research Council instituted an extensive study of the problem of standardizing hemoglobinometry and emerged with a recommended analytical procedure, a simple hemoglobinometer for general use, and a certified national hemoglobin standard for distribution to cooperating laboratories (King *et al.*, 1948).

In the United States the initiative was taken by the Army Medical Service Graduate School with a limited field trial of a cyanmethemoglobin solution proposed by Drabkin (Crosby *et al.*, 1954). The success of the Army plan so impressed the hematology study section of the National Institutes of Health that it requested the National Research Council to explore the possibility of establishing a national hemoglobin standard for general use throughout the country.

To this end the National Research Council established an *ad hoc* panel under the subcommittee on blood and related problems of the division of medical sciences. This panel has sought the cooperation of the College of American Pathologists, the American Society of Clinical Pathologists, the American Association of Blood Banks, the Department of Defense, the Veterans Administration, the National Institutes of Health, and the National Bureau of Standards. It has also maintained close liaison with the Committee on Hemoglobinometry of the Medical Research Council of the United Kingdom and with the National Research Council of Canada.

The panel gave serious consideration to the British plan but decided that, in respect to simplicity and adaptability, the cyanmethemoglobin method adopted by the U.S. Army would be more suitable for use in the United States and Canada. Among the forms of hemoglobin well adapted to photometry, cyanmethemoglobin has outstanding advantages. All forms of hemoglobin likely to be found in blood, with the exception of sulfmethemoglobin, are quantitatively converted to cyanmethemoglobin upon the addition of a single reagent.

Solutions of cyanmethemoglobin are the most stable of the various hemoglobin pigments. Drabkin (1949) has kept similar solutions for six years without deterioration. It is certainly safe to say that solutions of cyanmethemoglobin are stable for at least six months when kept in the refrigerator. Another advantage of cyanmethemoglobin solutions is that they can be standardized accurately. The absorption band of cyanmethemoglobin in the region of 540 mμ is broad rather than sharp, and consequently its solutions can be used in filter type photometers and in narrow band spectrophotometers.

The first spectrophotometric method for oxyhemoglobin was reported by Davis and Sheard (1927), and the application of the photoelectric colorimeter for the determination of the concentration of hemoglobin was first reported by Sheard and Sanford (1929). They used 0.1 per cent sodium carbonate as diluent. This method was further improved by the development of the photelometer.

Photoelectric colorimeters or photometers make it possible to determine hemoglobin with an accuracy of from ±2 to 5 per cent. However, this degree of accuracy, though possible, is not always achieved in practice. The main obstacle is the difficulty of standardizing the instrument, especially for hemoglobinometry. "Recalibration" by the manufacturer is rarely reliable and frequently creates a false sense of security. To be reliable, standardization has to be done under the conditions prevailing in the laboratory and must be checked frequently. Several photometers are available. Whichever is used, it must be used exactly according to the instructions provided by the manufacturer. Calibration of the instrument is the first step. The method differs with each make.

It is advisable to have an independent "photometric" standard in addition to the cyanmethemoglobin standards. This will help to check both the instrument and the cyanmethemoglobin standard if the photometric readings of the standard used in the test show excessive variations in duplicate readings.

Preparation of independent "photometric" standards:

Copper sulfate · 5H₂O	1.5 gm.
2 M ammonium hydroxide	500.0 ml.

Store in tightly stoppered Pyrex flasks. Keeps for a year.

Preparation of 2 M ammonium hydroxide: Dilute 136 ml. of concentrated reagent grade ammonium hydroxide to 1 L. with distilled water.

Selection and matching of cuvets

ROUND CUVETS. 1. Clean and dry several dozen cuvets inside and out.

2. Examine each cuvet and select only those free of scratches or other flaws.

3. Add 0.2 ml. of whole blood to 50 ml. of distilled water, mix well, and fill each cuvet with this solution.

4. Set the photometer at the 540 mμ band or insert the appropriate green filter.

5. Set a water blank at 100 on the transmittance scale (T) or at zero on the density scale (D). This setting should be checked frequently.

6. Insert a filled cuvet in the well. Set the galvanometer beam near the middle of the scale. Rotate the tube slowly, watching the movement of the beam. At the midpoint of the beam's swing, mark the cuvet with a diamond point pencil in relation to a stable mark on the housing of the well.

7. Repeat the same procedure with each cuvet and rotate it until the reading of the galvanometer corresponds with the reading of the first cuvet, marking each in relation to the same stable mark of the colorimeter.

8. All precautions should be taken to avoid scratching the cuvets. For that reason wooden or coated wire test tube racks are preferable.

SQUARE CUVETS. Steps 1 to 5 are identical.

6. Place each cuvet in the well. If inex-

pensive cuvets are used, only those giving identical readings should be kept. If high-grade expensive cuvets are used, a correction factor has to be determined for each and applied each time the cuvet is used.

Pipets. The 0.02 ml. pipet (Sahli) that is used to measure the blood should be accurate to ±1 per cent. Several supply houses offer 0.02 ml. pipets with a claimed accuracy of this order. However, it would appear advisable to calibrate a few such pipets in order to verify the degree of accuracy. (For technique of calibration see p. 76 ff.) The pipets should be acid cleaned and thoroughly washed with water at least once a week. They should be washed and thoroughly dried between each measurement.

The transfer pipets used to measure the diluent solution should be of a good order of accuracy and preferably within ±0.5 per cent. Some of the commercially available pipets are well within these limits. (The Bureau of Standards tolerance on 5 ml. pipets is ±0.2 per cent.) If a buret or automatic pipet is used for this purpose, it should be of the same order of accuracy.

The standard. THE PRINCIPLE. Potassium ferricyanide-cyanide solution is used. Ferricyanide converts hemoglobin iron from the ferrous to the ferric state to form methemoglobin, which combines with potassium cyanide to produce the stable cyanmethemoglobin.

The stock standard is available commercially. The exact concentration is within ±2 per cent of the value stated on the label. It is about 60 mg. of cyanmethemoglobin per 100 ml. The spectrophotometric characteristics of cyanmethemoglobin are such that D is directly proportional to the concentration. Three different concentrations of the reagent must be used for the preparation of a standard curve, the one purchased containing 60 mg. and two more with 40 and 20 mg. of cyanmethemoglobin per 100 ml. They are equivalent to 15, 10, and 5 gm. of hemoglobin per 100 ml. when blood is diluted 1:251.

DILUTION OF STANDARD. 1. Transfer 5 ml. of the stock standard to each of three large clean test tubes using a clean 5 ml. volumetric pipet. Allow the pipet to drain. Do not blow it out. Add a second 5 ml. volume of the standard to the second tube using the same pipet.

2. Rinse pipet five times with Drabkin's diluent.

3. Add 5 ml. of the diluent into tube 2 and 10 ml. into tube 3.

4. Mix contents of tube 3 and of tube 2 in the order mentioned.

5. Beginning with tube 3 and continuing with tubes 2 and 1, transfer 5 ml. of contents of each tube into each of three matched cuvets.

6. The concentration of cyanmethemoglobin in tube 1 is the same as stated on the label of the standard solution. The concentration in tube 2 is two-thirds, and in tube 3 one-third, of the standard.

7. The procedure is different if one uses the Evelyn photometer because the dilution of blood is 1:501. Therefore, 5 ml. of the stock standard is added to each of the three test tubes, followed by 5 ml. of the diluent to tube 1, 10 ml. to tube 2, and 20 ml. to tube 3. The resulting concentration of cyanmethemoglobin in tube 1 is one-half of the stock solution, one-third in tube 2, and one-fifth in tube 3.

Drabkin's Diluent Solution

Sodium bicarbonate (NaHCO₃)	1.0	gm.
Potassium cyanide (KCN)	0.05	gm.
Potassium ferricyanide		
(K₃Fe(CN)₆)	0.20	gm.
Distilled water to make	1000.0	ml.

Reagent grade quality chemicals should be used. This is a clear, pale yellow solution. It should be discarded if it turns turbid. It should be kept in a brown bottle and not more than a month's supply should be prepared.

Precautions in the use of cyanide. Salts and solutions of cyanide are poisonous, and care should be taken to avoid getting them into the mouth or inhaling their fumes. Most clinical laboratories use for the determination of uric acid a reagent containing 50 gm. of this salt per liter. In view of this, and of the fact that laboratories of clinical pathology are disciplined in the use of such dangerous materials as isotopes and virulent pathogens, it would seem that the handling of the proposed reagent constitutes a quite negligible hazard.

The concentration of cyanide in the stock standard is 50 mg. per liter. The smallest dose of potassium cyanide that has been known to kill a human is 300 mg. (Glaister, 1945). The lethal dose for a man approaches 4 liters (Sollmann, 1948). In most clinical laboratories, however, this is not a substance to be handled by irresponsible persons. Especially the salt itself must be handled with great circumspection. The following precautions have been recommended:

1. A suction bulb should be employed to fill pipets.

2. Blood should be mixed with the cyanide solution by swirling.

If the standard is prepared in the laboratory, special care must be taken in handling the chemical. If during weighing it is spilled accidentally on the bench or floor, the dry powder should be wiped up with a damp cloth. The cloth should be carefully discarded into a suitable closed container. The solution or powder should not be placed in a sink with acid. The solution may be discarded into a sink if the water is flowing freely. The solid potassium cyanide should be kept under lock and key. The standard solution is bacteriostatic and will remain free of bacterial growth if not contaminated in handling. It is recommended to place the standard in clean matched cuvets and to seal them permanently. Stoppers are not recommended. It should be stored in a refrigerator in darkness together with the blank solution at about 5° C. but not frozen. Before use, the outside of the cuvets should be wiped free of moisture, finger marks, and lint, and the standard should be permitted to reach room temperature to prevent condensation on the cuvets and formation of bubbles when the cold solution is heated suddenly by the light source. Both events may be a source of error. The standard must be discarded every six months.

Calibration of instrument with the cyanmethemoglobin standards. 1. The readings are taken at the 540 mμ band. The filter appropriate for the instrument must be in place.

2. The current is turned on and the instrument allowed to warm up according to the instructions of the manufacturer.

3. Distilled water or the diluent solution is used as blank. The absorption of light by the diluent at 540 mμ is negligible.

4. The blank is set at 100 on the per cent transmittance (T) scale or at zero on the density (D) scale.

5. The three standard tubes are placed in the cuvet well and the readings recorded beginning with the tube with the lowest concentration and proceeding with next higher concentration tubes. This standardization procedure takes about five minutes. It should be done by the beginner before each determination. Later, as experience grows and the instrument performs well and reliably, checking with the standards may be done at intervals to be determined by the operator's and supervisor's judgment.

The preparation of a standard curve and table. The following formula is used:

$$\frac{S \times D}{1000} = \text{gm. hemoglobin per 100 ml.,}$$

where S is concentration of cyanmethemoglobin standard and D is the dilution of the blood sample. For example, if the concentration of the cyanmethemoglobin standard is 60.4 and the dilution is 251, then

$$\frac{60.4 \times 251}{1000} = 15.16 \text{ gm. of hemoglobin}$$

per 100 ml.

The procedure may be facilitated by preparing a curve from which the readings of the galvanometer can be readily translated into hemoglobin values.

If the galvanometer readings are in terms of per cent of transmission (T), the readings of the standards are entered on semilogarithmic graph paper. The abscissa (bottom axis) represents grams of hemoglobin and the ordinate, the percentage of light transmittance. A line is drawn through the three points. It should pass through or very near T per cent = 100. This graph will show the value in grams of hemoglobin per 100 ml. corresponding to each reading. When many tests are done, it may be more convenient to construct a table of hemoglobin values for every possible per cent reading. Each photometer must be standardized individually against the standards and should be checked frequently.

If the meter readings are in terms of density (D), the values are plotted on linear graph paper with the density values on the ordinate and the hemoglobin in grams per cent on the abscissa. A line connecting the three points should pass through or very near zero. The readings for unknown can be translated into grams of hemoglobin.

The test. 1. Exactly 5 ml. of Drabkin's solution is transferred into each of two matched cuvets, using an accurate volumetric transfer pipet (meeting U.S. Bureau of Standards requirements of tolerance). A suction bulb, an automatic pipet, or a buret should be used, depending on the amount of work.

2. The blood sample may be taken from a freely bleeding capillary puncture or from a venous sample. The latter must be thoroughly mixed by gently tipping the tube end over end 10 to 20 times before blood is taken from it. Exactly 0.02 ml. of whole blood is transferred with an accurate standardized Sahli pipet into one of the two cuvets. Great care must be exerted to fill the pipet exactly to the mark. If the excess is minimal (not more than 2 mm.), it may be removed by touching the point of the

pipet with a cloth; otherwise the pipet has to be emptied, cleaned and dried, and the procedure repeated.

3. The blood and solution are mixed by swirling the cuvet. They are left standing for 10 minutes to permit formation of cyanmethemoglobin.

4. The second cuvet serves as a blank. (Instead of Drabkin's solution distilled water may be used.)

5. If a filter type photometer is used, the filter appropriate for the make of the instrument is put in place. If the instrument is a spectrophotometer, the wave length scale is adjusted to 540 mμ. Then proceed for the blank and unknown as described previously (see p. 75). The hemoglobin values are read from the curve or table.

The details of procedure vary with each instrument. These include calibration of the instrument with cyamethemoglobin standards, preparation of a standard curve and a standard table for hemoglobinometry, and hemoglobinometry by the cyanmethemoglobin method.

Special detailed instructions can be obtained from the manufacturer of the following photometers: Evelyn Photoelectric Colorimeter, Coleman Jr. Spectrophotometer, Fisher Clinical Electrophotometer, Klett-Summerson Photoelectric Colorimeter, Leitz Photometer, Bausch and Lomb Spectromic 20 Colorimeter, and Beckman Model B Spectrophotometer.

Sources of error—inaccuracy of the pipet. In view of the fact that 0.02 ml. Sahli pipets are accurate only to about ±5 per cent, it is desirable to reserve several carefully calibrated pipets for hemoglobin tests. Calibration of blood diluting pipets can be carried out by the following procedure recommended by Stevenson *et al.* (1951).

EQUIPMENT. Redistilled mercury; tuberculin syringe; single hole, size 0 rubber stopper; mineral oil or stopcock grease; apparatus support stand; 50 ml. beaker; weighing bottles; thermometer; analytical balance.

CALIBRATION. 1. 0.02 ml. pipets are cleaned with concentrated nitric acid, washed, and dried.

2. The equipment is kept at room temperature. The mercury and pipets are allowed to reach room temperature before calibration is started. The temperature of the mercury is recorded. Mercury is placed in the beaker. The weighing bottles are weighed and the weight recorded.

3. The plunger of the syringe is coated with mineral oil or grease and the syringe assembled. The tip of the syringe is inserted into the hole of the rubber stopper, which is then clamped vertically to a heavy apparatus support about 18 inches above the bench.

4. The proximal end of the pipet is inserted into the other end of the stopper.

5. The plunger of the syringe is slightly withdrawn. The tip of the pipet is immersed in the mercury. Slow withdrawal of the plunger fills the pipet with mercury. When the 0.02 mark is reached, the beaker is removed. If some mercury is lost in this procedure, the procedure must be repeated. The mercury is emptied into the weighing bottle. The determination should be done in duplicate. The weight of the mercury is established by subtracting the weight of the empty weighing bottle from the final weight with mercury.

6. The volume of the weight of the mercury is established by dividing the weight by a temperature correction factor:

TEMPERATURE (°C.)	CORRECTION FACTOR
20	13.547
21	13.545
22	13.543
23	13.541
24	13.539
25	13.537
26	13.534
27	13.532
28	13.530
29	13.528
30	13.526

7. The actual volume of the pipet expressed in milliliters divided by the number of milliliters supposed to be measured by the pipet (0.02) gives a correction factor for the pipet, which should be scratched on the pipet with a diamond pencil.

Example
(1) Weight of weighing
    bottle   = 39.8731 gm.
(2) Weight of weighing
    bottle plus mer-
    cury   = 40.1311 gm.
Weight of the mercury
    = (2) − (1)   0.2580 gm.
Volume of mercury delivered by pipet
$\dfrac{W}{TCF} = \dfrac{0.2580}{13.528}$ at 29° C. = 0.0191 ml.,
where W is the weight of mercury and TCF

is the correction factor for the temperature. Correction factor for the pipet = $\dfrac{VM}{SVP} = \dfrac{0.0101}{0.0200} = 0.96$, where VM is the volume of mercury delivered at prevailing temperature and SVP is the supposed volume measured by the pipet.

Other sources of error. Lipemic blood is a source of error. (This applies to all methods employing colorimetry.)

According to a recent report, false high hemoglobin values were seen in two patients with easily precipitable globulins, one with myeloma and the other with idiopathic macroglobulinemia. This was corrected by adding 0.1 gm. of K_2CO_3, which increased the alkalinity of the reagent; the globulin remained in solution. Otherwise the composition of the reagent remained identical (Green and Teal, 1959).

GASOMETRIC METHOD

Van Slyke's Oxygen Capacity Method. This is an indirect method, which estimates the amount of hemoglobin from the amount of oxygen it will absorb and utilizes the Van Slyke apparatus that is used for the estimation of carbon dioxide. It serves as an accurate method for standardizing the various hemoglobinometers but is too complicated for clinical work. The technique will be found in Van Slyke's papers (1918, 1921).

SPECIFIC GRAVITY METHOD

The specific gravity of the blood is the ratio of the weight of a volume of blood to the weight of the same volume of water at a temperature of 4° C. The normal specific gravity ranges from 1.048 to 1.066. The average for men is 1.057 and for women 1.053. There is a normal diurnal variation of about 0.003, the values in the afternoon and after meals being somewhat lower and those after exercise and at night, higher (Palowe, 1929). The specific gravity of the serum is 1.026 to 1.031 and that of the erythrocytes, 1.092 to 1.095 (Leake *et al.*, 1927).

The copper sulfate method for measuring the specific gravity of the blood is a simple and rapid procedure requiring no precision equipment. Drops of blood are permitted to fall into a series of solutions of copper sulfate of known specific gravity and one observes whether the drops sink or rise in the solutions. Upon immersion, the drops of blood become coated with a layer of copper proteinate, remain discrete for 15 to 20 seconds, and fall if their specific gravity is higher than that of the copper sulfate solution and vice versa. The accuracy of the method depends on the number of solutions used. If 16 are used with specific gravity intervals of 0.004, the gravities are accurate to 0.001. The solutions can be used repeatedly.

The Test. *Reagent.* Place 4 lb. of "fine crystals" of $CuSO_4 \cdot 5H_2O$ in a 4-liter bottle.

Add distilled water to 2500 ml. Stopper bottle and shake vigorously for five minutes. Measure the temperature of the solution. Pour off the supernatant and filter through cotton or dry filter paper into a clean 4-liter bottle. With the help of a table in the original publication (Phillips *et al.*, 1950), a volume of the saturated solution, which varies with the temperature, is diluted with a volume of distilled water to make up a stock solution with a specific gravity of 1.100. From the stock, solutions of lower specific gravities of any other desired range are prepared.

Method. Venous blood is released into the solution from a height of about 1 cm. directly from the syringe and needle or from a medicine dropper from the tube with blood collected in an anticoagulant. The drop penetrates 2 to 3 cm. below the surface. In a few seconds the drop begins to rise or continues to fall. The specific gravity of the drop does not change for another 10 to 15 seconds. If the drop is of the same specific gravity as the test solution, it will become stationary for about 10 to 15 seconds and will then resume its downward course. If it is lighter, it will rise for a few seconds and then begin to sink. If it is heavier, it will continue to fall.

The method is especially valuable for screening for hemoglobin prior to drawing of blood from donors. The same method can be used for measuring plasma protein.

CHEMICAL METHODS

The iron of the hemoglobin is separated by sulfuric acid, the protein is precipitated, and the iron is measured colorimetrically by comparison with a standard of known iron contents.

Two methods of determining the iron content of the blood have proved satisfactory: the Kennedy method and the newer Wong method. The value for the iron content may be transposed into grams of hemoglobin per 100 ml. of blood by dividing the amount of iron in milligrams per 100 ml. by 3.35, since hemoglobin contains 0.335 per cent

of iron. According to a recent recommendation of the Protein Commission of the International Union of Pure and Applied Chemistry, the iron content of hemoglobin is 0.338 per cent.

The sources of error may be those of: the sample, the method, the equipment, or the operator.

The popularity of a procedure does not mean that it is the best available as evidenced by the different degrees of popularity various procedures enjoy in different countries. Standardization studies conducted under the auspices of the British Medical Research Council and in the United States by the National Research Council have been mainly responsible for objective evaluation of the various methods. These studies have contributed much to bringing more order into the selection of methods least subject to errors of whatever source.

Errors Inherent in the Sample. The errors of the dilution methods (i.e., Sahli) are greater than when whole blood is tested. Admixtures of abnormal hemoglobins introduce errors that vary with the methods.

Errors Inherent in the Method. The alkali hematin methods have fewer errors than the acid hematin procedures.

The low cost is probably responsible for the popularity of the acid hematin method and equipment (i.e., Sahli) in this country.

The cyanmethemoglobin method has been studied exhaustively by a committee of the National Research Council and seems at present the method of choice for use with a photometer. The use of cyanmethemoglobin standard for calibration of the instrument and for the test itself eliminates one major source of error. The broad absorption band of cyanmethemoglobin in the region of 540 mμ makes it convenient to use it both in filter type photometers and in narrow band spectrophotometers. With the exception of sulfhemoglobin, all other varieties of hemoglobin are converted to cyanmethemoglobin.

Errors Inherent in the Equipment. The accuracy of equipment is not uniform, and many instruments have built-in errors of 20 per cent or more. A higher price does not guarantee higher accuracy.

The British Medical Research Council recommended in 1948 the gray-wedge photometer, a simple instrument that measures the optical density of colored liquid in daylight or with artificial light (MacFarlane *et al.*, 1948). In general, an instrument employing a fixed light source and a filter, preferably a green one, for matching oxyhemoglobin in a sample of undiluted blood reduces the sources of error.

The introduction of photometry has been a great advance, but photoelectric instruments are probably even more subject to error than are the less complicated instruments. They are potentially better, but just as other machines they must be calibrated at the beginning under conditions of actual operation in the laboratory and must be rechecked at frequent intervals. The wave length setting, the filters, and the meter readings are some of the items requiring constant checking.

The calibration of the instruments can be done with one of several reliable methods. Some of them, i.e., iron and oxygen capacity methods, are complicated and consequently not widely used. On the other hand, the cyanmethemoglobin method as a method for standardization has the advantages of simplicity and inexpensiveness. Crystalline human hemoglobin prepared according to Drabkin's method is a solution containing 1 milliatom of hemoglobin iron per liter. The three commercially available standards with certified concentrations of approximately 20, 40, and 60 mg. of hemoglobin per 100 ml. in the form of cyanmethemoglobin have been found to be stable for years. When the method is used with a properly standardized and regularly checked photometer, the error of the cyanmethemoglobin method can be reduced to ±2 per cent. This is worth noting, especially because hemoglobin pipets may have an error as high as ±5 per cent. Calibration of pipets and matching of cuvets will lessen these sources of errors inherent in equipment.

Operator's Errors. Most of the so-called human errors are the same in all technical procedures. They can be reduced by good training, meticulous understanding of the clinical significance of the test and of the necessity for a dependable method, adherence to oral and written instructions of the principles of the method, and familiarity with the equipment and with the sources of error. The technologist should be well trained in the performance of critical volumetry and be familiar with the performance of his instrument to be able to identify its misbehavior. The technologist who is patient and critical by nature and by training and who is interested not only in the *what* and *how* of his work, but also in the *why*, will be less prone to make errors than the one not so constituted.

The matching of colors is a source of errors, which can be reduced by not permitting the eye to get tired.

ABNORMAL HEMOGLOBIN PIGMENTS

The two physiologic hemoglobins, the oxyhemoglobin and the reduced hemoglobin, are readily converted into a series of compounds through the action of acids, alkalies, oxidizing and reducing substances, heat, and other agents. Lesser concentrations can be distinguished with the spectroscope. If the amounts present are still smaller (less than 10 per cent) and for quantitative measurements, spectrophotometric, colorimetric, and gasometric methods have to be used.

Methemoglobin. Methemoglobin (ferrihemoglobin) is a derivative of hemoglobin in which the ferrous iron is *oxidized* to the ferric state, methemoglobin (MHb); it consists of one molecule of globin and four molecules of hemin (with the iron in the ferric state).

Methemoglobin (MHb) is part of the "inactive" hemoglobin; it is unable to combine reversibly with oxygen and carbon monoxide. In addition, MHb causes a shift of the oxygen dissociation curve and hinders the transfer of oxygen from the blood to the tissues. Thus, abnormal amounts of MHb will result in a functional "anemia" with cyanosis (due to the decreased oxygen carrying capacity of the blood). A degree of cyanosis, comparable to the presence of 5 gm. of reduced hemoglobin (Hb) per 100 ml., will be evident with 1.5 gm. of the methemoglobin (MHb) or with less than 0.5 mg. of sulfhemoglobin (SHb) per 100 ml.

It is believed that 99.6 per cent of the iron in hemoglobin exists in the ferrous state (Hb) and 0.4 per cent in the ferric state (MHb). A small amount of MHb is always being formed, but it is reduced by the enzyme systems within the erythrocytes. Glucose is believed to be necessary as a substrate for this reduction of the MHb back to Hb. It has been reported that *normal subjects may have up to 0.24 gm. of MHb per 100 ml. of blood;* the average normal concentration of MHb, however, is about 0.06 gm. per 100 ml.

An absence of the reducing enzyme systems will result in large amounts of MHb being present. This is seen in primary (or congenital) methemoglobinemia in which an equilibrium is reached at about 40 per cent methemoglobin; polycythemia may be present as a compensatory mechanism. At concentrations of 20 per cent methemoglobin, working subjects complain of mild fatigue and have abnormally high blood lactic acid levels. However, levels of 30 to 50 per cent MHb may occur without producing severe symptoms. The lethal concentration in dogs is 85 to 90 per cent MHb; the exact level at which coma and death occur in man is not known.

Most cases of methemoglobinemia are classified as secondary methemoglobinemia. These are due mainly to poisoning with drugs and chemicals, especially those containing the nitro or amino groups. These are aniline and its derivatives, nitrates, nitrites, and some sulfonamides. Recently ferrous sulfate has been reported to produce methemoglobinemia after ingestion of very large doses.

There follows an alphabetical list of drugs, chemical (oxidizing) compounds, and some "bacteria" that change Hb to methemoglobin. This has been compiled from the work of Finch, 1948; Goodman and Gilman, 1955; Michel and Harris, 1940; and Smith *et al.*, 1950.

Acetanilid
Acetophenetidin
Alphanaphthylamine
Aniline and derivatives
   paranitraniline
Aniloethanol
Antipyrine
"Bacteria"
   Cholera vibrio
   Gärtner's bacillus
   G.I. tract nitrite-producing bacteria
   Nitrosobacilli (some)
   Pneumococcus
   Strep. viridans
Benzene and derivatives
   Dinitrobenzene
   Nitrobenzene
   Nitrosobenzene
Chlorates
Dimethylamine
Ferrocyanide
Ferrous sulfate
Formaldehyde
Hydrogen peroxide
Hydroquinone
Hydroxylacetanilide
Hydroxylamine
Iodine
Methylacetanilide
Nitrites
   Amyl nitrite
   Ethyl nitrite
   Sodium nitrite

Nitroglycerin
Ozone
Para-aminopropriophenone
Permanganate
Phenacetin
Phenylenediamine
Phenylhydroxylamine
Pyrogallol
Sulfonal (sulfon-methanol)
Sulfonamides
   Prontosil
   Sulfanilamide
   Sulfapyridine
   Sulfathiazole
Toluenediamine
Tolylhydroxylamine
Trinitrotoluene

Methemoglobin (MHb) is reduced back to Hb by the erythrocyte enzyme system. It can also be reduced (slowly) by the administration of reducing agents, such as ascorbic acid or sulfhydryl compounds (glutathione, cysteine, BAL); these are of value in the cases of primary methemoglobinemia when there is an impaired cell-reconversion mechanism. In cases of secondary methemoglobinemia, methylene blue is of great value; its rapid action is not based on its own reduction capacity but on its acceleration of the normal cell-reconversion mechanism.

Methemoglobin (MHb) can combine reversibly with various chemicals (e.g., cyanides, sulfides, peroxides, fluorides, and azides). Because of its strong affinity for cyanide, the therapy of cyanide poisoning is to administer nitrites to form MHb, which then combines with the cyanide. Thus, the free cyanide (which is extremely poisonous to the cellular respiratory enzymes) becomes less toxic when changed to cyanmethemoglobin (MHbCN).

The *normal* individual may have up to 0.24 gm. of MHb per 100 ml. of blood. The *average* normal concentration is about 0.4 per cent of the total hemoglobin or about 0.06 gm. of MHb per 100 ml. of blood.

Cyanosis may occur with concentrations of 0.5 gm. or higher of MHb per 100 ml. of blood. However, the degree of cyanosis is not necessarily correlated with the concentration of the MHb.

Sulfhemoglobin. In the presence of oxygen, hemoglobin reacts with hydrogen sulfide to form a greenish derivative of hemoglobin called sulfhemoglobin. Since oxygen is necessary for the formation, it is assumed that oxyhemoglobin reacts directly with the H_2S.

Sulfhemoglobin cannot transport oxygen,

but it can combine with CO to form carboxysulfhemoglobin. The concentration of sulfhemoglobin *in vivo* is as a rule within the range of a few per cent and seldom exceeds 10 per cent. Unlike methemoglobin, it remains in the corpuscles until they break down.

Sulfhemoglobin has been reported in patients receiving treatment with sulfonamides, aromatic amine drugs (phenacetin, acetanilid), and sulfur as well as in those with severe constipation, in cases of bacteremia due to *Clostridium welchii*, and in a condition known as enterogenous cyanosis.

Formation of sulfhemoglobin in these conditions is caused by H_2S, which is the result of bacterial action on sulfur compounds in the intestine.

Carbon Monoxide Hemoglobin (Carboxyhemoglobin, HbCO). Hemoglobin has the capacity to combine with carbon monoxide in the same proportion as with oxygen. However, the affinity of the hemoglobin molecule for carbon monoxide is 210 times greater. This means that carbon monoxide will bind with hemoglobin even if its concentration in the air is extremely low (e.g., 0.02 to 0.04 per cent). In those cases, HbCO will build up more and more until typical symptoms of poisoning appear.

HbCO cannot bind oxygen and therefore is not available as an oxygen carrier. Furthermore, the HbO_2-HbCO mixture does not release oxygen so readily as is done in normal blood, thus adding to the anoxia. If a patient poisoned with carbon monoxide receives pure oxygen, the conversion of HbCO to HbO_2 is greatly enhanced. HbCO is light sensitive and has a typical, brilliant, cherry red color.

Acute carbon monoxide poisoning has long been well known. Chronic poisoning, due to prolonged exposure to small amounts of carbon monoxide, is less well known but is assuming increasing importance. The chief sources of the gas are gasoline motors, illuminating gas, gas heaters, and defective stoves and furnaces. Exposure to carbon monoxide is thus one of the hazards of modern civilization. The gas has even been found in the air of busy streets of large cities in sufficient concentration to cause mild symptoms in persons such as traffic policemen, who are long exposed to it.

Henderson and Haggard found that healthy persons exposed to various concentrations of the gas for an hour do not experience definite symptoms (headache, dizziness, muscular weakness, and nausea) unless the concentration of the gas in the blood reaches 26 or 30 per cent of saturation, but it appears that in chronic poisoning, especially in children, serious symptoms may occur with lower concentrations. The figures reported for cases of clinical poisoning are often misleading, since the carbon monoxide largely or wholly disappears from the blood after the patient has breathed pure air for a few hours, although the symptoms may continue for a long time.

Tests for Abnormal Hemoglobin Pigments. Some information can be obtained by naked eye examination of the blood specimen. Normal appearance of the serum or plasma identifies the red cells as the site of the pigment. Shaking of normal whole blood in the air for 15 minutes imparts to it a bright red color as the reduced hemoglobin is converted to oxyhemoglobin. The blood is cherry red when the pigment is carboxyhemoglobin in carbon monoxide poisoning. The color is chocolate brown in methemoglobinemia and mauve-lavender in sulfhemoglobinemia.

The specimen must be obtained carefully to avoid hemolysis and promptly because the abnormal pigment, unlike hemoglobin, disappears rapidly on cessation of exposure and on institution of therapy. If carbon monoxide is suspected, dry sodium citrate in small well-stoppered tubes should be used. If methemoglobin is to be tested for, heparin is the anticoagulant of choice, because oxalate tends to elevate the pH and favors conversion of neutral to alkaline methemoglobin. For all other tests, dry oxalate anticoagulant is preferable. Plasma containing plasma hemoglobin is pink or red and brown in the presence of methemoglobin or methemalbumin. The red cells and the plasma or serum must be examined.

Identification of Hemoglobin Pigments. Whole blood or washed red cells are added to distilled water in a ratio of 1 to 10 or 1 to 100 depending on the concentration of the abnormal pigment. A few milliliters of the hemolyzed blood are placed in each of two test tubes. In the case of methemoglobin and methemalbumin a dark band is seen in the spectroscope between 620 and 630 millimicrons in the red portion of the spectrum between the Frauenhofer lines C and D. Sulfhemoglobin produces a similar band at 618 $m\mu$. To distinguish the pigments, two to three drops of a 5 per cent solution of potassium cyanide are added (with a dropper, not a pipet) to the second tube with blood. The band will disappear if the pigment is methemoglobin, and the color of the specimen will change from brown or black to dark red, but not if it is sulfhemoglobin or methemalbumin. Three per cent hydrogen peroxide causes the bands of sulfhemoglobin and methemoglobin to disappear. Carboxyhemoglobin and oxyhemoglobin are difficult to distinguish with the spectroscope. Both produce bands at approximately the same location (576 mμ).

Other tests. Naked eye examination of diluted blood (one drop in 5 ml. of water) shows a yellowish red color of oxyhemoglobin and pinkish or bluish red color of carboxyhemoglobin.

ALKALI TEST. Two drops each of normal blood and of the patient's blood are placed on spot plate. Two drops of 25 per cent sodium hydroxide are added to each. Carboxyhemoglobin remains unchanged. The normal control turns brown.

A simple qualitative test may be useful in an emergency and will be described.

KATAYAMA'S TEST (1888). This is one of the best of the simple tests for carbon monoxide hemoglobin. It will detect as little as 10 per cent of saturation. Place about 10 ml. of water in each of two test tubes. To one tube, add five drops of the suspected blood and to the other add five drops of normal blood to serve as a control. To each tube, add five drops of fresh orange colored ammonium sulfide. Mix gently and make faintly acid with acetic acid. The color of blood containing carbon monoxide hemoglobin becomes more or less rose red, depending on the concentration of the gas; normal blood becomes a dirty greenish brown.

CARBON MONOXIDE HEMOGLOBIN (HbCO). A very convenient method to detect HbCO is based on the reaction of this form of hemoglobin with pyrotannic acid. A convenient pocket size unit for this determination is supplied by the Mine Safety Appliance Company, Pittsburgh, Pa.

Spectrophotometric Identification of Hemoglobins. The various hemoglobins have characteristic absorption spectra, which can be determined easily, provided the laboratory is equipped with a spectrophotometer. Hemoglobin, for instance, has an absorption maximum at 565 mμ. Oxyhemoglobin has maxima at 514, 544.8, 576.9, and 640.2 mμ. Carboxyhemoglobin is characterized by an absorption peak of 535 and 570.9 mμ. Methemoglobin has maxima at 500, 540, 578, and 634 mμ, and cyanmethemoglobin has its maximum at 414 and 540 mμ.

The identification of different forms of hemoglobins by determining the absorption spectrum can be carried out in a very simple way. Approximately one-half of a drop of blood is put into a test tube and diluted with approximately 20 ml. of de-ionized or double-distilled water. The actual dilution of the hemoglobin depends on the concentration of the hemoglobin (e.g., if the hemoglobin is extremely low, one might have to add less water; if the hemoglobin content is high, one might have to dilute the specimen more). For maximal accuracy, the peak of absorption should be somewhere between 60 and 40 per cent transmittance. After the blood has been diluted with water, samples are read in a spectrophotometer using water as the blank. (The Beckman B or the Beckman DU Spectrophotometer is very satisfactory for this determination.) The absorption is read at intervals of 5 mμ between 620 and 500 mμ (see Fig. 4–5).

In the differentiation between oxyhemoglobin and carbon monoxide hemoglobin, one can take advantage not only of the different absorption spectrum but also of the following characteristic: In the case of pure oxyhemoglobin, the absorption at 576.5 mμ will be greater than that at 544.8 mμ. In the case of carboxyhemoglobin, however, the absorption at 570.5 mμ will be less than that at 535 mμ (see Fig. 4–5).

The Blood Cell Count

The study of the blood in the laboratory can be divided into two large groups of tests: tests used primarily for the diagnosis of diseases of blood, to be discussed next, and tests used primarily for the diagnosis of diseases of other organs, to be discussed in other chapters.

The diagnostic tests for diseases of blood consist of two large groups: the chemical and the morphologic. The former deal with hemoglobin and its abnormalities. The morphologic studies are divided into quantitative and qualitative tests.

The quantitative tests are concerned with the numbers of red blood cells, white blood cells, and platelets in a cubic millimeter. In the qualitative tests the appearance and structure of these cells are analyzed and classified in stained blood films.

The Complete Blood Count. The so-called complete blood count or CBC in laboratory lingo traditionally includes: red cell count, hemoglobin, white cell count, and differen-

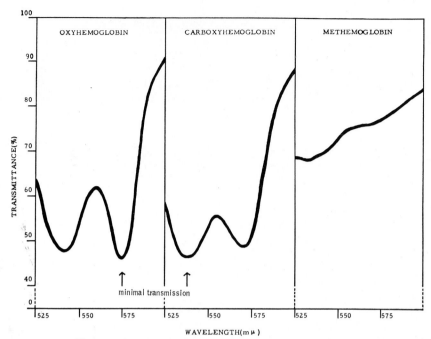

Figure 4–5. Spectrophotometric identification of hemoglobins.

tial count. For reasons to be discussed later, the red cell count has lost much of its former popularity.

The Red Cell Count

EQUIPMENT

Red Cell Counting Pipet. The basic equipment employed in the quantitative studies of all three blood elements is contained in the hemocytometer. It consists of diluting pipets and the counting chamber (Fig. 4–6).

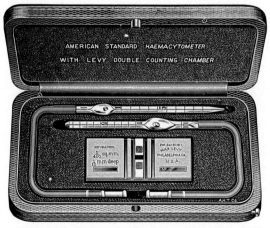

Figure 4–6. Hemacytometer, consisting of a counting chamber, a coverglass, and two pipets for diluting the blood.

The Thoma glass pipets (Fig. 4–7) consist of a graduated capillary tube, divided into ten parts and marked 0.5 at the fifth mark and 1.0 at the tenth, a mixing bulb above it containing a glass bead and, above the bulb, another short capillary tube with an engraved mark 11 on the white and 101 on the red cell pipet. The red cell pipet has a red bead in the mixing bulb and the white cell pipet a white bead. The graduations on the pipets are arbitrary. The volume of the red cell pipet is made up of one-half part at the level of the 0.5 mark, one part at the level of the 1.0 mark, and 100 parts in the bulb. When the blood is drawn to the 0.5 mark and the diluting fluid to the 101 mark, all the blood cells are washed into the bulb and the resulting dilution in the bulb is 1 to 200. The cell-free fluid in the capillary portion is not included in the total volume.

The volume of the whole red cell counting pipet is 100 times larger than the volume of the graduated portion of the stem. It contains 101 volumes from the tip to the 101 mark. After the red cell counting pipet has been filled with the blood and the diluting fluid, the graduated capillary stem of the pipet contains no blood but only diluting fluid; therefore, its contents must be expelled before the red cell suspension is introduced into the chamber.

In the white cell diluting pipet, the marks

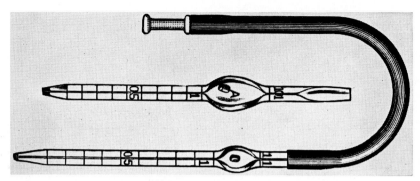

Figure 4–7. Thoma red and white cell diluting pipets.

on the capillary tube are the same as in the red pipet, but the bulb is smaller with an engraved mark 11 above it. When the blood is drawn to the 0.5 mark and diluted to the 11 mark, the dilution is 1 to 20. Again the cell-free fluid in the capillary is not included in the total volume.

According to the U.S. Bureau of Standards, the permissible error of the red cell pipet is ±5 per cent and of the white cell pipet, ±3.5 per cent. Thirty-six blood counting pipets sold by three manufacturers with a guarantee to be accurate within ±5 per cent were checked by the National Bureau of Standards. Twenty-three were found to be accurate according to the Bureau of Standards' allowable error of ±5 per cent; in 8 the error was ±10 per cent; in 2, ±15 per cent; and in 3, ±25 per cent (Cartwright, 1958). This shows that the only reliable guarantee is to purchase red cell pipets with a Bureau of Standards' certification or to send them to the Bureau of Standards for certification. This will provide a correction factor for both the 1 to 100 and 1 to 20 dilution.

The Trenner automatic pipet (Fig. 4–8) is so constructed that the capillary tube is filled by capillary attraction and the blood stops automatically at the end of the tube. This provides an accurate control of the blood column and eliminates this source of error. The pipet is more expensive and more fragile.

The rubber tubing that is attached to the pipet should be sufficiently heavy walled to resist collapse during suction and should be long enough (at least 10 inches) to permit easy reading of the graduation marks.

After use, pipets should be rinsed with tap water and then three times with distilled water, filling the bulb through the capillary end, shaking, and emptying through the large-bore end. This is followed

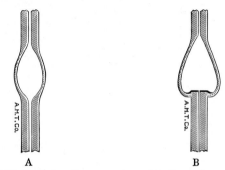

Figure 4–8. Cross section of bulb and part of stem of diluting pipets. *A,* Original Thoma pipet; *B,* Trenner automatic pipet. In the latter, blood fills the stem by capillarity and automatically stops when it reaches the bulb.

by similar treatment with acetone or 95 per cent alcohol and finally with ether using a water suction pump. The interior of the pipets should then be dried with a current of dry air. The bulb is dry if the bead rolls freely. If the lumen of the capillary pipet contains coagulated blood or other debris, it can be cleaned with a horse hair or with a special delicate, commercially available wire. If the pipet contains impurities, it should be filled with cleaning solution and allowed to stand overnight. Washing devices are available that permit cleansing and drying many pipets simultaneously. If cleansing or at least thorough rinsing cannot be done immediately after use, the pipets should be placed upright in a container with water. Utmost care must be exerted to prevent damage to the delicate point of the pipet, for even the slightest damage that affects the bore makes the pipet useless because it leads to inaccuracy in the dilution.

The Counting Chamber. Several types of counting chambers differing in design are available. The type most widely used consists of a heavy, colorless glass slide, on the middle third of which are fixed three parallel platforms extending across the slide. In the "double counting chamber," the central platform is subdivided by a transverse groove into two halves, each slightly wider than the two lateral platforms and separated from them and from each other by moats. The central platforms or "floor pieces" are exactly 0.1 mm. lower than the lateral platforms. Each of the central platforms has a so-called improved Neubauer ruling, which consists of a square measuring 3 × 3 mm.

Figure 4–9. Group of 16 small squares of improved Neubauer ruling, showing split boundary lines.

(9 sq. mm.) subdivided into nine secondary squares, each 1 × 1 mm. (1 sq. mm.). The four corner squares are used for the white cell count and are subdivided into 16 tertiary squares, each measuring 0.25 × 0.25 mm. (Fig. 4–9).

The central square millimeter is divided into 25 tertiary squares, each of which measures 0.2 × 0.2 mm. Each of these tertiary 0.2 × 0.2 mm. squares is further subdivided into 16 smaller squares, each of which measures 0.05 × 0.05 mm. The total number of the smallest 0.05 × 0.05 mm. squares in the central square is 400. As a rule, five of the tertiary squares, amounting to 80 of the smallest squares, are used for red cell counts. (It is customary to count the four corner and the central tertiary squares.)

In the so-called "Bright Line" and "Hy-Lite" hemocytometers, the ruling is made on a metallic coating on the glass, which makes the lines more distinct (Fig. 4–10).

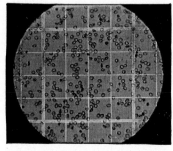

Figure 4–10. Spencer Bright Line counting chamber. The new construction makes the lines appear white against a dark background.

Hausser's counting chamber (Fig. 4–11) consists of an unbreakable Bakelite slide, which serves as a frame. In it is inserted a small removable counting glass chamber, which is made in one piece and thus avoids the troublesome loosening of parts that have

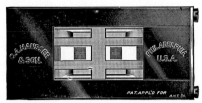

Figure 4–11. Hausser's counting chamber in Bakelite holder. The coverglass and clamps are not shown.

been cemented in place with balsam. Counting chambers with various rulings, single and double, and of different depths for counting thrombocytes, blood corpuscles, and the cells of spinal fluid, are available and are interchangeable in the Bakelite holder. All are of the "open" type. The instrument is equipped with coverglass clips.

A thick coverglass, ground perfectly plane, accompanies the counting chamber of all makes. Ordinary coverglasses have uneven surfaces and should not be used with this instrument. According to the U.S. Bureau of Standards' requirements, the coverglass must be free of visible defects and must be optically plane on both sides within ±0.002 mm. For use with objectives of short working distance, heavy coverglasses can be obtained with a flat-bottomed excavation or "well" in the center. This combines the advantage of a thin coverglass with the rigidity of a thick one.

It is evident that, when the coverglass is in place on the platform of either type of counting chamber (Fig. 4–12), there is a space exactly 0.1 mm. thick between it and the ruled platform; therefore, each square

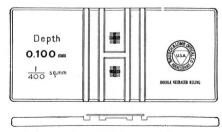

Figure 4–12. Open counting chamber. The lower figure shows the chamber in cross section with coverglass in place.

millimeter of the ruling forms the base of a space holding exactly 0.1 cu. mm.

Another style of counting chamber is illustrated in Figure 4–13. This chamber is ruled so that there are four chambers, mak-

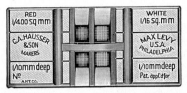

Figure 4–13. Levy counting chamber, quadruple, with two Neubauer rulings and two Fuchs-Rosenthal rulings.

ing it possible to make duplicate counts of both red and white corpuscles without the necessity for cleaning and refilling the chamber or refocusing the microscope. The two rulings for counting erythrocytes are the improved Neubauer rulings; the two additional rulings for counting leukocytes are the Fuchs-Rosenthal rulings, which originally were designed for counting cells in spinal fluid but are very convenient, because of the large area, for making leukocyte counts.

For cell counts in cerebrospinal fluid and other fluids with relatively small numbers of cells, the Levy counting chamber with the Fuchs-Rosenthal ruling is convenient. It has a depth of 0.2 mm. The ruling consists of 16 one millimeter squares with triple boundary lines. Each square is subdivided into 16 smaller squares. The cells in the entire ruled area (16 sq. mm.) are counted. The number of cells counted is divided by 16 to give the number per square millimeter. This is multiplied by the dilution factor and by 5 to give the number of cells per cubic millimeter.

Counting chambers and coverglasses should be rinsed immediately after use in lukewarm water, never in hot water. To remove dried blood and grease, soap and lukewarm water, soda bicarbonate solution, or ether may be used and then the equipment should be thoroughly washed and rinsed in running water. Strong acids or alkalies must not be used. The water may be wiped off with a clean lint-free cloth. The counting chamber and coverglass may be allowed to dry in the air. The surfaces must not be touched with gauze or linen, because they may scratch the ruled areas. A scratch across the chamber or coverglass ruins it. The chamber and coverglass should not be touched because fingerprints are difficult to

remove and may be responsible for errors. Before using, the surfaces must be absolutely clean, dry, and free from lint and water marks. After they have been cleaned they must not be touched except at the edges.

RED CELL DILUTING FLUIDS

Requirements. The diluting fluid must be isotonic to prevent lysis and crenation of the red cells. It should also contain a fixative to preserve the shape of the erythrocytes, to prevent autolysis and agglutination, and thus to make it possible to do the count even several hours after the sample was obtained, if necessary.

Of the many diluting fluids that have been used in the course of time, the following meet these requirements:

Hayem's Solution

Bichloride of mercury	0.5 gm.
Sodium sulfate	5.0 gm.
Sodium chloride	1.0 gm.
Distilled water	200.0 ml.

Gower's Solution

Sodium sulfate	12.5 gm.
Glacial acetic acid	33.3 ml.
Distilled water	200.0 ml.

Gower's solution is superior to Hayem's because it prevents rouleaux formation. In cases of hyperglobulinemia Hayem's solution may cause precipitation of protein, which interferes with counting of the red cells. Both fluids should be filtered frequently and for convenient handling should be kept in small wide-mouthed bottles.

COUNTING THE RED CELLS

This procedure consists of the following steps: drawing the blood and diluting the sample, charging the counting chamber, counting the cells and calculating the result, and cleaning the pipets and chamber in preparation for the next count.

The Sample. The skin is cleansed and sterilized, the puncture made, and the first drop of blood wiped off. The pipet is held horizontally at nearly a right angle to the line of vision so that the exact height of the column may be seen easily. The side of the tip should rest against the skin, but the end must be free and the tip immersed in the drop of blood. The red counting pipet with the 101 mark is filled from the second drop, sucking the blood to the mark 0.5 or 1 according to the dilution desired.

Complication 1. Air bubbles may enter into the pipet with the blood. This is a sure sign that one of three things is happening:

The drop is too small, or the tip is not kept immersed in it, or the tip is damaged.

If venous blood is used, the procedure has to be modified accordingly. The bottle or tube with the blood must be inverted or rotated gently but long enough to assure complete mixing and even distribution of the corpuscular elements immediately before the pipet is immersed.

Complication 2. The blood may rise beyond the mark. This can be corrected by touching the tip of the pipet to a moistened towel or a finger tip. The blood will be drawn back to the mark. If a large excess of blood has been drawn up, the pipet should be cleaned and the procedure repeated, because even though it is withdrawn, enough will remain adhering to the inside of the pipet to introduce a significant error. Painstakingly accurate technique in this part of the procedure is important, because any error is magnified 200 times by the subsequent dilution.

The blood adhering to the tip is wiped off quickly, the tip is plunged into the diluting fluid, and the fluid is sucked up to the mark 101, rotating the pipet slightly meanwhile. Again while doing so, it is best to hold the pipet nearly horizontally in order to avoid aspiration of air bubbles in the bulb, but when the bulb is almost full the pipet should be raised to the vertical position. At this stage the blood sample has been diluted 1 to 200 or 1 to 100, depending on the amount of blood taken. Except in cases of severe anemia, a dilution of 1 to 200 is preferable. At this stage, the ends of the pipet are closed with the thumb and middle finger, and the pipet is shaken for about 30 seconds to facilitate the initial mixing. The bead contained in the bulb should move freely. The shaking should be done at a 90 degree angle to the long axis of the pipet. If capillary blood is used, all these steps must be carried out rapidly to prevent coagulation before blood is mixed with the diluting fluid.

To fill the Trenner automatic pipet (Fig. 4–8), the blood is drawn by suction into the capillary portion until it is nearly full. The suction is discontinued, and if the pipet is held nearly horizontally, the blood will continue to rise to the end of the capillary portion and will automatically stop there. The diluting fluid is then immediately drawn in by suction as described for the Thoma pipet.

When it is not convenient to count the erythrocytes at once, a heavy rubber band is placed around the pipet so as to close both ends. A small piece of rubber cloth or other tough, nonabsorbent material may be inserted, if necessary, to prevent the tip from punching through the rubber. In this manner the sample may be preserved in usable condition for 24 hours or longer.

Charging the Counting Chamber. When the counting chamber and the coverglass have been cleaned, the coverglass is adjusted and clamped in place if the counting chamber is supplied with clamps. The pipet is held between the thumb and middle finger or in a special shaking machine and shaken for two to three minutes at right angles to the long axis of the pipet. A method for mixing by hand is as follows: One or two pipets are held between the thumb and fingers of one hand. The base of the hand is struck against the base of the other hand at a rate of 60 times per minute for three minutes. The first three to four drops are blown off to eliminate the cell-free fluid from the capillary tube. The pipet is held at an angle of about 35 degrees while the tip is touched to the angle between the edge of the coverglass and one of the projecting ends of the floor piece. The fluid will run under the coverglass by capillary attraction. The fluid is allowed to enter in a controlled manner. This can be done by pressure from the index finger on the open end of the pipet or from the pressure of the tongue on the mouth piece of the pipet. Care must be exercised to permit just enough fluid to fill the space beneath the coverglass. This is especially important when the chamber lacks clamps, since an excess of fluid will tend to raise the coverglass appreciably and increase the erythrocyte count. A small excess remaining at the mouth of the counting chamber can be removed by touching the drop gently with the finger but not with gauze or a towel.

The characteristics of a properly filled counting chamber are: The fluid fills the space beneath the coverglass entirely or almost entirely; none of the fluid has run over into the moat; there are no bubbles. If any of these conditions are not met, the count will not be reliable and the chamber has to be cleaned, dried, and recharged.

Counting the Cells and Calculating the Results. The cells in the chamber are permitted to settle for several minutes. Then the ruled area is surveyed with the low power objective to see whether they are evenly distributed. If they are not, the procedure has to be repeated. If the chamber is filled and the cells not counted promptly, the fluid should be protected against evaporation by placing the chamber under a Petri dish containing a moistened piece of filter paper, which is applied to the top inner surface.

A little experience is needed to learn to locate the ruled area. Modern chambers have a deeply ruled line running from the end of the platform to the ruled area. This "finding line" is quickly located with either the high power or low power objective. The best objective for counting erythrocytes is the 8 mm. or the 4 mm. objective with long working distance.

The principle of counting. The square millimeter with its 400 small squares in the center of the ruled area has a capacity of 0.1 cu. mm. One has to find the number of erythrocytes in the square millimeter, multiply by 10 to find the number in 1 cu. mm. of the diluted blood, and finally multiply by the dilution to find the number in 1 cu. mm. of undiluted blood. Instead of actually counting all the erythrocytes, it is customary to count those in only a limited number of small squares and calculate the number in the square millimeter for the dilution of 1 to 200. The volume of diluted blood contained in the chamber above the 80 small squares—five groups of 16 each—is 0.02 cu. mm. The number of erythrocytes counted in these 80 small squares is multiplied by 50 to convert the number found in 0.02 cu. mm. to the number contained in 1.0 cu. mm. The number in 1.0 cu. mm. is multiplied by 200 to correct for the dilution of 1 to 200. The combined conversion factor is $50 \times 200 = 10,000$.

In practice, a convenient procedure is as follows: With a dilution of 1 to 200, count the erythrocytes in 80 small squares and to the sum add four zeros. With the dilution of 1 to 100, count 40 small squares and add four zeros. Thus, if with 1 to 200 dilution 450 erythrocytes were counted in 80 squares, the total count would be 4,500,-000 for each cubic millimeter. This method is sufficiently accurate for most clinical purposes, provided the erythrocytes are evenly distributed. It is convenient to count five blocks of 16 small squares (Fig. 4–14), one in each corner of the square millimeter and one in the center. When using the "double counting chamber," it is convenient to count the erythrocytes in 20 small squares at the top and those in 20 small squares at the bottom in each of the ruled portions, making 80 squares in all, and to add four zeros. In order to avoid confusion

in counting erythrocytes that lie on the borderlines, the following rule is generally adopted: Erythrocytes that touch any one of the three lines or the single line on the left or the top borders of the small square should be counted as though they were within the squares, but those that touch any of the lines on the right and the bottom borders of the small squares should not be counted. In this way no cell is counted twice. The cells are counted in each small square, first from left to right, beginning with the top of four small squares, and then from right to left for the next row, and so on. The number of cells for each of the five groups of 16 squares is recorded separately and the results are added.

When the number of red cells is excessively high, e.g., in polycythemia, greater accuracy is achieved by drawing the blood in the pipet only up to the 0.3 mark. The counting is done in the usual way, but the conversion factor in $\frac{5}{3}$ of 10,000 or 16,667. Example: the number of red cells counted in 80 small squares was 500. With the usual multiplication factor of 10,000 the result would have been 5,000,000. Owing to smaller sample the conversion factor will be 16,667 and the result, 8,333,500 RBC per cu. mm.

Conversely, in anemia the number of red cells may be too small for accurate measurement. To correct for this, the blood should be drawn up to the 1.0 mark instead of the 0.5 mark. The dilution will be 1 to 100 and the conversion factor, 5000 instead of 10,000. Example: the total number of cells counted was 400. The red cell count will be $400 \times 5000 = 2,000,000$.

Another way of counting in anemias is to count cells in more squares than the standard five. The conversion factor will vary accordingly: 5000 if 10 squares are counted, 3333 if 15 squares are counted, 2500 if 20, and 2000 if 25 squares are counted, the latter being the maximum possible in one chamber. Example: Blood was diluted 1 to 200; 400 cells were counted in 25 large squares or a total of 400 small squares. The conversion factor is 2000 and the total red blood cell count, 8,000,000.

Sources of error. Counting erythrocytes is a procedure abounding with errors. It is probably the oldest micromethod in clinical pathology and consequently has the same sources of error that are common to all micromethods. In addition it is afflicted with other possible errors characteristically its own. The various sources of errors can be classified as follows: Errors due to the size of the sample or to the nature of the sample, the operator's error, errors due to equipment, and the so-called unavoidable errors (errors of the field, the counting chamber, and the pipet).

ERRORS DUE TO THE SIZE OF THE SAMPLE. One begins with a minute amount of blood. Because of the necessity for counting individual cells, the portion of the sample that will be actually examined is further decreased 200-fold. The total number of cells counted is at best 500 and as a rule smaller than that. The obtained figure has to be multiplied by 10,000. Consequently, every error built into the procedure or introduced in one way or another is also magnified 10,000 times.

ERRORS DUE TO THE NATURE OF THE SAMPLE. When capillary blood is used, there is a race with time because of imminent coagulation, which may, even if it is only partial, introduce errors by changes in the distribution of the cells or decrease of their number. Drawing a drop of blood from pale, cold, or cyanotic skin is another serious source of error, as is excessive massage to improve the flow of blood.

There are possible sources of error even when venous blood is used. Stasis due to prolonged application of the tourniquet, various degrees of coagulation of blood due

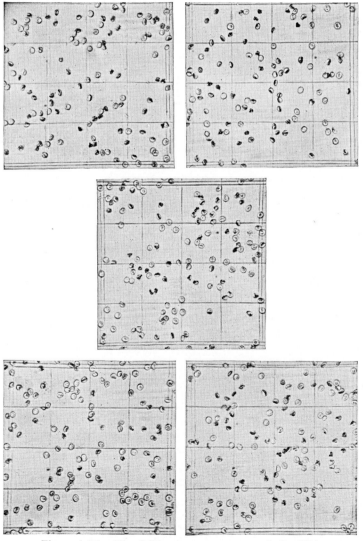

Figure 4–14. Five fields, sixteen squares each (× 430).

to delay in mixing with the anticoagulant, and hemolysis are some of the sources of possible errors. The distribution of the cells in the plasma changes rapidly due to sedimentation. Failure to mix the blood thoroughly and immediately before drawing the sample into pipet is bound to introduce an error, which is directly proportionate to the degree of sedimentation during the interval since the blood was mixed. This is accentuated in a variety of diseases in which the sedimentation is significantly accelerated. The fact that the specimen is a suspension and that the cells have to be in a uniform suspension in order to be counted correctly opens the door to other possible errors. Currents of all kinds may alter the uniformity of the suspension. Yeast cells growing in contaminated diluting fluid may be mistaken for erythrocytes.

THE OPERATOR'S ERRORS. Here belong errors due to faulty technique, such as may occur when blood and the diluting fluid are drawn into the pipet (use of an unclean or wet pipet or failure to wipe off the pipet tip), and errors introduced when the chamber is loaded and when the cells are counted. A frequent source of trouble is faulty application of the coverglass, especially when it is raised by introduction of an excess of diluted blood, or movement of the coverglass after the counting chamber has been filled. Overflowing of the suspension into the moat is another example. This may reduce the count by as much as 1,000,-000. The number of technical errors of this kind is legion. They can be reduced to a minimum in the hands of an experienced technologist.

ERRORS DUE TO EQUIPMENT. Inaccuracies in the graduations of the pipets and of the ruled areas of the counting chambers are frequent sources of error. They can be avoided by using pipets certified by the U.S. Bureau of Standards. Faulty construction may be responsible for inaccuracy in depth of the counting chamber.

Cleaning of the counting chamber with alcohol or exposure to excessive heat or intensive sunlight may soften the cement that holds the counting platform. The construction of the coverglass may also be faulty.

THE SO-CALLED "NORMAL" ERROR OF THE COUNT. This occurs even if all usual precautions have been taken to avoid errors that have been listed. When all errors inherent in the sample, technique, and equipment are controlled and two chambers are

filled from each of two pipets and the cells are counted in each chamber, the error amounts to ± 11 per cent. Accordingly, if the true red cell count is 5,000,000, chance distribution of the cells in the chamber may be responsible for variation from 4,450,000 to 5,550,000 per cu. mm. When fewer than 400 cells are counted or when only one pipet is used, the error may be as high as ± 22 per cent.

In doing a red cell count, one uses an extremely small sample. It is a common observation that different samples of the same batch differ one from the other. According to the method recommended here, erythrocytes in 80 squares are counted. It is obvious that one will not get the identical count if one particular set of 80 of the 400 available squares rather than another is used. This does not indicate necessarily maldistribution of the erythrocytes because of poor mixing. Each erythrocyte that enters the chamber takes a position among the 400 squares "at random." The distribution of erythrocytes in the counting chamber follows the law of chance, and consequently there is a variation of the number of erythrocytes which fall into each square. The chance distribution of the cells in the chamber introduces an inherent error, which cannot be controlled.

According to Poisson's law of distribution, the variation among the different squares in the chamber is given by the formula S.D. $= \sqrt{m}$ where m is the mean number of erythrocytes per unit area and S.D. is the standard deviation* of the counts in these areas. Example: The mean count per 80 squares is 500 (as for a count of 5,000,000 per cu. mm.). The S.D. of counts of different sets of 80 squares in the chamber will be $\sqrt{500}$ or 22.4. Expressed relatively as a per cent, this is $\frac{22.4}{500} \times 100 = 4.5$ per cent.

Between ± 1 S.D. are included two-thirds of the repeated counts; 67 per cent of the results based on chance distribution are included within one standard deviation on each side of the mean. Between ± 2 S.D. on each side of the mean are included 95 per cent of repeated counts. Deviations falling outside the range of twice the standard

---

* The standard deviation is a measure of variability given by the formula $\sqrt{\frac{\Sigma(x-m)^2}{N}}$ where x is the observation the variation of which is measured, m is the mean or average, N is the number of observations, and Σ stands for summation.

deviation are as a rule due to errors in technique.

Since ±2 S.D. is generally accepted as a significant limit, the error of a count of 5,000,000 per cu. mm. made in the hemocytometer chamber owing merely to the variation in the field of observation is ±2 × 4.5 = ±9 per cent. This "error of the field" measured as S.D. = $\sqrt{m}$ is the minimal error to which a single estimate of the count can be considered subject as long as the hemocytometer is used, but the error due to variation within the field of observation is not the only one to which the count as usually made is subject. Separate fillings of different standard chambers with the same blood will result in different total counts per measured unit volume in the different chambers owing to variations in calibration, variations in the filling technique, and variations in pressure of the coverglass. This may be referred to as the *"error of the chamber."*

Similarly, separate fillings of different standard pipets with the same blood will result in different total counts per measured unit volume in the different pipets. This may be referred to as the "error of the pipet." Berkson *et al.* (1940) have de-

termined the S.D. of the pipet error as 4.7 per cent of the mean count. For the total error, they gave for a count of 5,000,000 $\sqrt{4.1^2 + 4.6^2 + 4.7^2} = 7.7^*$ or about 8 per cent. Since twice the S.D. is the usually accepted limit of significance, the error of a single estimate of the erythrocyte count was given by them as ±16 per cent.

A large number of repeated counts of this kind will of course vary, and 95 per cent of them will be within the limits of ±16 per cent; 68 per cent, or about two-thirds, will be within ±8 per cent. Figure 4–15 shows the distribution of repeated estimates for a total count of 5,000,000 per cu. mm.

The conclusions of those who investigated the sources of error of erythrocyte counts can be summarized as follows: The degree of inaccuracy is greatest when only one pipet and one chamber are used. The accuracy and reproducibility increase with the increased number of cells counted but

---

* The total error is given as the square root of the sum of the squares of the constituent errors. The 4.1 per cent for the error of the field is a slight modification found by Berkson *et al.* (1940), of what is given by the Poisson distribution as 4.5 per cent. The 4.6 per cent is the error of the chamber.

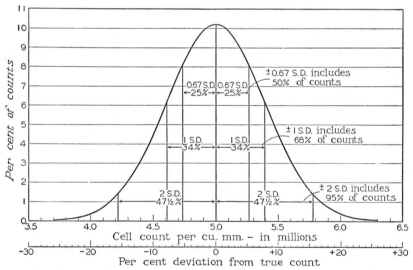

Figure 4–15. Distribution of repeated estimates of the erythrocyte count made by enumerating the erythrocytes in 80 squares of the hemacytometer chamber, for an individual with 5,000,000 erythrocytes per cubic millimeter of blood. The ordinate gives the per cent of the counts that will fall in each 100,000 interval. For instance, between 5,000,000 and 5,100,000 there will be 10.2 per cent of the counts. The standard deviation (S.D.) of the counts is 390,000, and from this may be calculated the frequency of counts falling in any interval. Between ±0.67 S.D. (the probable error) will fall 50 per cent of the counts; hence, one may expect 50 per cent to fall between 4,740,000 and 5,260,000. Between ±1 S.D. will fall 68 per cent of the counts; hence, one may expect 68 per cent to fall between 4,610,000 and 5,390,000. Between ±2 S.D. will fall 95 per cent or almost all of the counts; hence, one may expect 95 per cent to fall between 4,220,000 and 5,780,000.

only up to about 500 cells counted in each chamber. The accuracy improves with the increase of number of pipets and chambers used. It has been recommended (Ham, 1951) that the red cell counts be performed with two degrees of minimum accuracy: (1) for clinical estimation of the number of red cells and (2) if used for the calculation of M.C.V. or M.C.H. For (1) one pipet and two chambers should be used, counting in each about 500 cells and using the calculated average. For (2) two pipets and two counting chambers should be used.

The importance attached to the erythrocyte count has fluctuated in the course of history. Although it was initially considered a basic laboratory examination, its significance has faded considerably because of inherent inaccuracy, which could not be controlled with the methods available. Of the three methods available for the detection of anemia, the erythrocyte count is considered the most difficult, most time consuming, and least accurate. The volume of packed red cells (hematocrit) is recognized as the most accurate technically, easiest to perform and least consuming of the technologist's time. It may be that the present shortcomings of the erythrocyte count will be overcome with the application of electronic instruments.

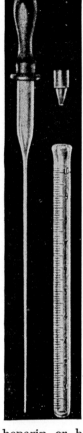

Figure 4–16. Wintrobe's hematocrit, pipet and bulb used for filling it, cap for filling it, and cap for closing. Two-thirds actual size. (Tice's Practice of Medicine; courtesy of W. F. Prior Company, Inc.) (From Wintrobe, M. M.: Clinical Hematology. 5th Edition, Lea and Febiger, Philadelphia, 1961, p. 379, Fig. 8–2.)

Hematocrit (Packed Cell Volume)

Definition. The hematocrit can be defined as the percentage of the volume of a blood sample, determined by centrifugation, needed for calculation of mean corpuscular volume and mean corpuscular hemoglobin concentration.

The Macromethod of Wintrobe (1956). *Equipment.* The Wintrobe hematocrit tube is a thick walled glass tube with a uniform internal bore and a flattened bottom. It is graduated in millimeters from 0 to 105 and has a rubber cap to prevent evaporation during the long period of centrifugation (Fig. 4–16).

Of the various forms of filling pipets available, a 2 ml. syringe with a needle long enough to reach the bottom of the hematocrit tube is probably as good as any and quite practical.

The essential requirement of a centrifuge is that it generate a centrifugal field of not less than 2500 G. at the bottom of the cup. Angle head centrifuges with an inclination of not more than 45° are widely used.

Reagent. For an anticoagulant, dried heparin or balanced oxalate is best. The latter can be used only if not less than 3 ml. and preferably 5 ml. of blood is collected. EDTA is not recommended.

Procedure. The oxalated or heparinized blood must be mixed thoroughly by not less than 30 slow and complete inversions of the container. Rolling the bottle is inadequate, and shaking is still worse because it may damage the cells.

After adequate mixing, the hematocrit tube is filled using the filling pipet or a syringe, preferably in one operation. The tip of the pipet is introduced to the bottom of the tube. As filling proceeds, the tip of the pipet is raised, but it remains under the rising blood meniscus in order to avoid foaming. The level of the blood should be noted and the tubes capped to avoid evaporation during the required centrifugation for 30 minutes at 2500 G.

Reading is done without disturbing the specimen. The result is calculated from the formula:

$$\text{Hematocrit (per cent)} = \frac{100\ L_1}{L_2} \text{ where}$$

L_1 is the height of the red cell column in mm. and L_2 is the height of the whole blood specimen (red cells and plasma).

The Micromethod. *Equipment.* A capillary hematocrit tube about 7 cm. long with a bore of about 1 mm. is recommended. The capillaries are filled with a 1 to 1000 dilution of heparin, dried at 56° C. or 37° C. and stored. Special centrifuges are available producing centrifugal fields ranging from 5000 to 10,000 G. This permits shortening of centrifugation to five minutes for the latter and ten minutes for the former.

Collection of sample. A warm but not congested skin site should be selected. The skin must be cleaned with an antiseptic and dried before the puncture. The skin puncture should be deep enough to permit free flow of blood. The first two drops of blood should be wiped away and the capillary filled by capillary attraction to within not less than 1 cm. from the end. The empty end is sealed in a small flame of a microburner or plugged with modeling clay, e.g., plasticine. The filled tubes are placed in the radial grooves of the microhematocrit centrifuge head with the sealed end away from the center.

The air at the outermost end of the capillary will be displaced in the course of centrifugation and the air gap will disappear. Leakage, especially if model clay was used for sealing, can be prevented by using a rubber gasket at the periphery of the hematocrit head to act as a cushion. Breakage of the delicate capillary can be prevented by spinning the centrifuge head first by hand, thus establishing contact between the end of the tube and the periphery of the head before turning on the motor.

The capillary tubes are not graduated. The length of the whole column, including the plasma, and of the red cell column alone must be measured in each case with a millimeter rule and a magnifying lens or with one of several commercially available automatic or semiautomatic devices. The instructions of the manufacturer must be followed.

Interpretation of results. The normal hematocrit for males is 47.0 ± 7, for females 42.0 ± 5. It is especially important for the diagnosis of anemia and polycythemia. It does not indicate the total red cell mass. The hematocrit is low in hydremia of pregnancy but the total number of circulating red cells is not reduced. The hematocrit may be normal or even high in shock accompanied by hemoconcentration but the total red cell mass may be considerably decreased due to blood loss.

Sources of error. CENTRIFUGATION. Adequate centrifugation both as to speed and duration is the sine qua non of a correct hematocrit. The red cells must be packed so that additional centrifugation does not reduce further the packed cell volume. In general, the higher the hematocrit, the more powerful the centrifugal force required. The centrifugal force means the magnitude and duration of the centrifugal field. It is expressed in units of G., the acceleration due to gravity, and is calculated from the formula:

$CG = (1.118 \times 10^{-5}) n^2 r$, where C is the numerical measure of the field, n is the speed of rotation of the centrifuge (revolutions per minute), and r is the radius of rotation measured to the tip of the centrifuge cup.

In the course of centrifugation, leukocytes, platelets, and plasma are trapped between the red cells. The error resulting from the former is as a rule quite insignificant. The increment of the hematocrit due to trapped plasma is somewhat greater than that due to leukocytes and platelets, but this too is of little practical consequence. It was calculated to be in the range of 0 to 2 per cent in the hematocrit range of 33 to 68 per cent.

THE SAMPLE. Prolonged stasis caused by constriction with a tourniquet may result in pronounced changes in hydrostatic pressure in capillaries. This source of error should be avoided.

A free flow of blood from a skin puncture for microhematocrit is essential. The hematocrit is unreliable immediately after a loss of blood, even if moderate, and immediately following transfusions.

Red Cell Corpuscular Values

Quantitative studies of corpuscular values require accurate measurement of hematocrit, red cell count, and hemoglobin, the three basic tests for the study of red cell disorders.

The red cell count is less important as a screening procedure for the detection of anemia than is the determination of the hematocrit or the hemoglobin. It may be normal in some anemias, for example, in hypochromic anemias. After the presence of anemia has been established, the red cell count is one of the three determinations needed for the calculation of the red cell corpuscular values. The other two are hemoglobin and hematocrit.

MEASUREMENT OF VOLUME AND HEMOGLOBIN CONCENTRATION OF RED CELLS

Wintrobe introduced procedures for the study of anemia which have substituted objective quantitative standards for subjective impressions: Mean corpuscular volume (M.C.V.), mean corpuscular hemoglobin (M.C.H.), and mean corpuscular hemoglobin concentration (M.C.H.C.). Three accurately determined basic values are needed: red cell count, hemoglobin, and hematocrit. Venous blood is used with heparin or balanced oxalate (ammonium and potassium oxalate) added.

M.C.V. Definition. The M.C.V. is the average volume of the individual red cells.

Calculation

$$\text{M.C.V.} = \frac{\text{hematocrit (per cent)} \times 10}{\text{red cell count (millions per cu. mm.)}}$$

Normal (N) = 87 ± 5 cubic microns per cell

Examples

Hematocrit = 20; red cell count = 1,500,000

$$\text{M.C.V.} = \frac{20 \times 10}{1.5} = 133 \text{ cubic microns (macrocytic anemia)}$$

Hematocrit = 20; red cell count = 3,000,000

$$\text{M.C.V.} = \frac{20 \times 10}{3} = 67 \text{ cubic microns (microcytic hypochromic anemia)}$$

M.C.H. Definition. The M.C.H. is the content (weight) of hemoglobin of the average individual red cell in micromicrograms ($\mu\mu$g.).

Calculation

$$\text{M.C.H.} = \frac{\text{hemoglobin (gm./100 ml.)} \times 10}{\text{red cell count (millions per cu. mm.)}}$$

N = 29 ± 2 micromicrograms ($\mu\mu$g.)

In most anemias, changes in the average size of the red cells (M.C.V.) parallel similar changes in the weight of hemoglobin in the red cells (M.C.H.). Consequently, the M.C.V. and M.C.H. show similar variations.

Examples

Hemoglobin = 6 gm.; red cell count = 1,200,000

$$\text{M.C.H.} = \frac{6 \times 10}{1.2} = 50 \ \mu\mu\text{g. (macrocytic anemia)}$$

Hemoglobin = 5 gm.; red cell count = 2,400,000

$$\text{M.C.H.} = \frac{5 \times 10}{2.4} = 21 \ \mu\mu\text{g. (microcytic hypochromic anemia)}$$

M.C.H.C. Definition. The M.C.H.C. is the average hemoglobin concentration per 100 ml. of packed red cells in per cent.

Calculation

$$\text{M.C.H.C.} = \frac{\text{hemoglobin (gm./100 ml.)} \times 100}{\text{hematocrit (per cent)}}$$

N = 34 ± 2 gm./100 ml. (increased only in spherocytosis)

Examples

Hemoglobin = 7 gm.; hematocrit = 20 per cent

$$\text{M.C.H.C.} = \frac{7 \times 100}{20} = 35 \text{ gm. per cent (macrocytic anemia)}$$

Hemoglobin = 5 gm.; hematocrit = 20 per cent

$$\text{M.C.H.C.} = \frac{5 \times 100}{20} = 25 \text{ gm. per cent (hypochromic anemia)}$$

Volume Index (V.I.). Definition. The volume index is the mean volume of red cells in proportion to the mean volume of red cells in normal blood.

Calculation

$$\text{V.I.} = \frac{\text{hematocrit} \times 2.3}{\text{red cell count (millions per cu. mm.)} \times 20}$$

$$\text{or} \quad \frac{\text{M.C.V. of patient}}{\text{M.C.V., normal}}$$

Normal = 1.0

The volume index has largely replaced the color index, because it avoids the use of normal hemoglobin in the calculation of results and is therefore more consistent.

Color Index (C.I.). Definition. The color index is the amount of hemoglobin in each erythrocyte compared with the normal amount.

Calculation. The percentage of hemoglobin is divided by the percentage of erythrocytes. The normal number of erythrocytes (100 per cent) is assumed to be 5,000,000 per cu. mm. and the normal hemoglobin, 14.5 gm. per 100 ml. of blood. The percentage of erythrocytes may be found by multiplying the erythrocyte count in millions by 20.

$$C.I. = \frac{\text{hemoglobin per cent (gm. per 100 ml.)} \times 6.9}{\text{red cell count (millions per cu. mm.)} \times 20}$$

N = 1.0

Volume of Blood and Plasma

Many methods have been devised for determining the total volume of blood. The use of these in clinical medicine is limited by inherent inaccuracies and technical difficulties. The total blood volume amounts to about 7.7 per cent or $\frac{1}{13}$ of the body weight.

There are two basic indirect methods: First, one may inject intravenously a substance that becomes diluted in plasma and enables measurement of total plasma volume. Hematocrit permits calculation of total blood volume. Second, one may inject intravenously a substance that is incorporated in the erythrocytes and permits measurement of the red cell mass and total blood volume. Plasma volume is the difference between the two, or it can be calculated from either one using the hematocrit.

For a method to be reliable the following condition should be fulfilled by a suitable substance. It should be retained only in the plasma or in the cells without passing from one to the other or into the extravascular compartment. Evans blue (Warner-Chilcott T-1824) and I^{13} tagged albumin both pass readily into the extravascular compartment. This tendency is further increased in patients with edema. In cases of impaired circulation, the time needed for mixing with the blood is changed.

DIFFICULTIES ENCOUNTERED WHEN ISOTOPES ARE USED FOR ERYTHROCYTE TAGGING

They may be eluted into plasma and measurement of total erythrocyte volume may be inaccurate. They may be adsorbed to glass surface with a loss up to 10 to 20 per cent; this results in underestimation of plasma volume. Erythrocyte measurement is based on the assumption that erythrocytes are uniformly distributed in the vascular system. This is not the case in circulatory disturbances and in splenomegaly.

Other Sources of Error. These include the need for using the hematocrit and for considering its inherent errors for calculation of total blood volume or total erythrocyte mass. The trapping of plasma in centrifugation must also be considered. Finally, the hematocrit of venous blood is not identical with the hematocrit of blood as a whole.

EVANS BLUE DYE METHOD FOR DETERMINING THE VOLUME OF BLOOD AND PLASMA

The blood volume is determined under basal conditions. The patient reports to the laboratory in the morning, having fasted since the evening meal of the previous day. He is asked to lie down quietly for at least 20 minutes before the dye is injected. All materials should be at hand so that the procedure will move smoothly and in proper time sequence. All syringes and needles must be absolutely dry; every precaution is taken to avoid hemolysis. A tourniquet is not used during the withdrawal of blood.

Apparatus. 1. A spectrophotometer or a photometer with a narrow band filter in the range of 610 to 620 millimicrons. (The procedure described here has been set up for the Coleman Model 6 Spectrophotometer using six 310 cuvets. It can be readily converted to other instruments.)

2. A means of determining the hematocrit reading.

3. Oxalated tubes to contain 10 ml. quantities of blood.

4. Three clean, dry, sterile, good quality 10 ml. syringes.

5. A stop watch for timing the injection of dye and the withdrawal of blood.

Reagents. Evans blue dye, T-1824 (Arlington), in 10 ml. vials containing 2 mg. per ml.

Technique. 1. Using a sterile, dry syringe, collect without stasis 10 ml. of blood from the antecubital vein. Detach the syringe from the needle and express the blood into a tube labeled dye-free plasma, inverting several times to insure solution of the anticoagulant.

2. Attach a syringe containing the measured amount of dye solution to the needle already in the vein, note the time, and inject the dye solution slowly. The syringe is filled and emptied at least five times with the patient's blood in order to wash out all traces of dye. The volume of dye solution to be injected is indicated in the following table:

WEIGHT OF PATIENT	DYE (NO. OF ML.)	CORRECTION FACTOR (F)
Less than 100 lb.	5.0	0.5
100 to 180 lb.	7.5	0.75
Over 180 lb.	10.0	1.0

3. Approximately nine minutes after beginning the injection of dye, a clean needle on a clean syringe is inserted into the opposite antecubital vein. Exactly ten minutes from the beginning of the injection of the dye, withdraw 10 ml. of blood; deliver this into an oxalated tube marked dyed plasma.

4. With as little delay as possible, centrifuge the two samples of blood and pipet off the plasma. The plasma should be clear, not lipemic, and contain no trace of hemolysis.

5. A cuvet containing the dye-free plasma is set in the spectrophotometer and the instrument adjusted to zero optical density at 620 millimicrons. The dyed plasma is then inserted and its optical density (D) at 620 millimicrons is noted.

6. Determine the volume of packed cells (hematocrit reading).

Calculation. *A.* The total plasma volume is determined according to the following formula:

$$\text{Plasma volume} = \frac{20\ \text{K}}{\text{D}} \times \text{F}$$

The constant "K" is the same for each lot of dye. It is determined in the following manner: Dilute 1 ml. of dye solution to 50 ml. with water in a volumetric flask. (There is enough dye remaining in each vial for this step after the 10 ml. have been withdrawn for the test.) Deliver 5 ml. of the diluted dye into a 50 ml. volumetric flask containing about 40 ml. of 0.9 per cent saline. Add 0.5 ml. of clear plasma and fill to the mark with saline. This yields a dye concentration in plasma of 0.004 mg. per ml. The optical density of this standard is determined at 620 millimicrons using a control blank of 0.5 ml. of the same clear plasma diluted to 50 ml. with 0.9 per cent saline.

$$\text{K} = \frac{\text{D}}{\text{C}} \text{(where D is optical density and C = 0.004)}$$

B. The total blood volume is calculated according to the following formula:

$$\text{Blood volume} = \frac{\text{Plasma Volume}}{100 - \text{Hematocrit}} \times 100$$

Divide the total plasma volume, and also the whole blood volume, by the patient's weight in kilograms to determine the plasma volume for each kilogram and the whole blood volume for each kilogram.

Normal values vary according to the procedure that is used. It is necessary for each laboratory group to establish its normal limits and to become acquainted with the expected variations in disease. Measurements are not likely to be valid unless the procedure is in more or less constant use and is done by technicians who have had considerable experience with the method. Using the technique outlined here, the plasma volume for men is approximately 40 to 48 ml. per kilogram of body weight and for women, 37 to 46 ml. per kg. Total blood volume in normal adult men is approximately 70 to 85 ml. per kg. and for women, 59 to 73 ml. per kg. Some workers prefer to express the blood and plasma volumes in relation to body surface rather than body weight. In our experience, no method of expression will avoid certain inconsistencies that appear when we attempt to compare results obtained in different patients under what would seem to be identical physiologic or clinical conditions.

The blood volume with T-1824 is higher than with labeled erythrocytes. Blood volume data are usually related to body weight. Differences for persons of the same weight are due to varying amounts of fat and lean tissues. Lower blood volume in women may be partly due to their greater fat content. Total blood volume at birth is about 300 ml. Differences in blood volume related to sex appear first at about 10 years of age.

Clinical Applications. Surgical patients with anemia and hemoconcentration may have a normal red cell count and hematocrit. Administration of fluid postoperatively and transfusion therapy are best guided by tests for total blood volume, plasma volume, and red cell mass. Patients may need packed red cells but not saline or plasma, or, vice versa, patients may need only plasma and not whole blood. Prior to transfusion therapy, erythrocyte counts and hematocrits may be misleading. Volume studies may help to decide if whole blood or only plasma is needed.

Fragility Tests:
Erythrocyte Osmotic Fragility Test

Destruction of erythrocytes goes on continually within the body. In certain pathologic conditions, this destruction is greatly accelerated and may lead to anemia. It is, then, of great practical interest to ascertain whether the excessive hemolysis is referable chiefly to increased fragility of the erythrocytes, as is typically the case in hereditary spherocytosis (congenital hemolytic anemia). The resistance of the erythrocytes can be measured by subjecting them to the action of various harmful agents. In clinical work, hypotonic salt solution is generally used.

Principle. Red cells suspended in hypotonic solution of sodium chloride take up water, swell, become spheroidal and more fragile, and eventually burst. The increased fragility, which leads to lysis, is determined by two main factors: It is inversely proportionate to the concentration of sodium chloride and directly proportionate to the thickness of the erythrocyte. The cell that is closest to being round or spherical (the spherocyte of hereditary spherocytosis) has the smallest volume for its contents and its capacity to expand is limited. Consequently, it bursts upon intake of small amounts of water in relatively high concentrations of the salt. Its osmotic fragility is increased and its osmotic resistance is decreased. On the other hand, the thin or flat cell in hypochromic anemia can take up considerable amounts of water and requires lower concentrations of sodium chloride to lyse. Its osmotic fragility is decreased; its resistance is increased.

The osmotic fragility test measures accurately how nearly spherical red cells are, but it does not measure the fragility of the red cells. Increased osmotic fragility or decreased resistance means spherocytosis. The degree of the latter parallels fairly accurately the degree of the former. The accuracy of the parallelism depends on the accuracy of the method employed for measuring the fragility.

Increased fragility is found in hereditary spherocytosis and in idiopathic and symptomatic acquired hemolytic anemias. Contrariwise, diminished osmotic fragility or increased resistance means excessive flatness of red cells; it is seen in the presence of jaundice, in iron deficiency anemias, in thalassemia, in sickle cell anemia, in polycythemia vera, in diseases of the liver, after splenectomy, and in a variety of anemias in which target cells are found. In thalassemia a portion of red cells may remain undissolved in 0.03 per cent saline and even in distilled water. In tests for osmotic fragility, identical amounts of blood are added to decreasing concentrations of sodium chloride solution. After a period of incubation, the highest concentration of

sodium chloride with minimum hemolysis determines beginning hemolysis; the highest concentration in which hemolysis is complete expresses the complete hemolysis.

Incipient hemolysis in higher concentrations of sodium chloride is an indicator of increased osmotic fragility of red cells. In other words, osmotic fragility of red cells is increased if hemolysis occurs in over 0.5 per cent concentration of sodium chloride. On the other hand, osmotic fragility is decreased if hemolysis is incomplete in 0.3 per cent sodium chloride.

Two tests of osmotic fragility of varying degrees of accuracy will be described.

THE SCREENING TEST

Reagents

1. Stock solution of sodium chloride. A 1 per cent solution of sodium chloride is prepared by dissolving 1.0 gm. of C.P. sodium chloride in 100 ml. of distilled water. The salt must be first dried in a desiccator

2. Dilute solutions. The 0.85 per cent solution is prepared by placing 8.5 ml. of the stock solution in a test tube and adding 1.5 ml. of distilled water. Similarly, the 0.50 per cent solution is prepared by mixing 5.0 ml. amounts of the stock solution and of distilled water.

Procedure. One milliliter of each of the two solutions is placed in one of the two tubes. One-tenth milliliter of oxalated venous blood is added. To a similar set of two tubes, blood of a normal person is added and serves as a control. The control blood must be obtained approximately at the same time as the patient's. The tubes are shaken gently, and if the tube with the 0.5 per cent sodium chloride solution shows hemolysis and the one with 0.85 per cent is not hemolyzed, the osmotic fragility of the red cells is probably increased, and a quantitative test is indicated.

QUANTITATIVE METHOD

Equipment
1. Test tube rack containing two rows of 13 matched, chemically clean and dry colorimeter tubes.
2. Ten milliliter serologic pipets.
3. Pipets calibrated to contain or deliver 0.05 ml.
   Sahli pipets delivering 20 cu. mm. have been recommended for transfer of blood.

Reagents
1. Stock solution of 10 per cent NaCl (pH 7.4)

NaCl	180.00 gm.
Na$_2$HPO$_4$	27.31 gm.
NaH$_2$PO$_4$ • 2H$_2$O	4.86 gm.

Dissolve in distilled H$_2$O and dilute to 2 L. Keeps well at room temperature in a tightly stoppered bottle.

2. Starting with a 1 per cent solution prepared from the 10 per cent solution, 50 ml. of the following solutions are made: 0.85, 0.75, 0.65, 0.60, 0.55, 0.50, 0.45, 0.40, 0.35, 0.30, 0.20, 0.10, and 0.00 per cent NaCl.

The solutions can be prepared in 50 ml. volumetric flasks as follows: To each flask the following volumes of the 1 per cent solution are added: 42.5, 37.5, 32.5, 30.0, 27.5, 25.0, 22.5, 20.0, 17.5, 15.0, 10.0, and 5.0 ml. The solutions are made up to volume (50 ml.) with distilled water. A 1.2 per cent solution of sodium chloride is prepared by diluting 6 ml. of the 10 per cent solution to 50 ml. The solutions keep well at 4° C. for weeks. They should be discarded if molds develop.

3. Freshly obtained heparinized or defibrinated blood is preferable to oxalated or citrated blood. To defibrinate, 10 to 15 ml. of aseptically drawn venous blood is placed in a sterile flask containing one glass bead (3 to 4 mm. in diameter) for each milliliter of blood. The flask should be rotated gently until the beads become coated with fibrin. The control blood should be obtained approximately at the same time.

Procedure. Five milliliters of each of the dilutions of sodium chloride are added to the 13 test tubes of each row. The second row of tubes is set up as a control. Five one-hundredths of the patient's blood is added to each tube of the first row, and the same amount of the normal control blood is added to the second row. After each transfer of blood, the pipets should be rinsed thoroughly with saline and blown out vigorously. The tubes are immediately mixed well. They are allowed to stand at room temperature for 20 minutes, remixed, and centrifuged at 2000 r.p.m. for five minutes. In a photoelectric colorimeter provided with a suitable filter, the degree of hemolysis in the supernatant (diluted 1 to 2 or 1 to 5) is measured by comparing with 100 per cent hemolysis in the tube with no saline and using the supernatant of the 0.85 per cent sodium chloride as a blank. The per cent hemolysis in each of the tubes is calculated by dividing the hemoglobin value by the value in the tube containing no

saline. A good colorimeter permits recognition of as little as 1 per cent hemolysis.

Range of osmotic fragility in normal blood:

Per Cent NaCl	Per Cent Hemolysis
0.30	97–100
0.40	50– 90
0.45	5– 45
0.50	0– 5
0.55	0

Each laboratory should determine its own normal values.

Recording of Results. Beginning hemolysis or minimum resistance is expressed by the percentage concentration of sodium chloride in the tube in which the first trace of lysis is visible. Complete hemolysis or maximum resistance is expressed accordingly. A more accurate picture is obtained by plotting on graph paper the percentage of hemolysis in each tube against the corresponding concentration of sodium chloride (Fig. 4–17).

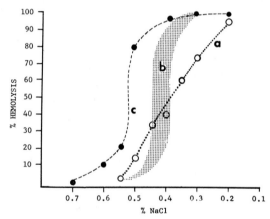

Figure 4–17. Red cell osmotic fragility. a = thalassemia; b = normal zone; c = hereditary spherocytosis.

Interpretation of Results. Although osmotic fragility is essentially a measure of spherocytosis, it provides a more objective measurement than inspection of a blood smear. A difference of more than one tube between the patient and the control is significant.

Sources of Error. 1. Chemical purity of sodium chloride is essential. Even minute impurities may act as hemolytic agents.

2. Accuracy of the sodium chloride solution.

3. The relative volumes of blood and saline. A 1 to 100 dilution is recommended, because the degree of hemolysis can be read directly in most colorimeters without fur-

ther dilution, and the minimal amount of plasma does not affect the tonicity of the solution. Because of differences between arterial and venous blood, the latter should be mixed until bright red.

4. A change of pH by 0.1 equals the change of tonicity by 0.01 per cent; specifically, a lowering of pH increases fragility.

5. A temperature rise increases fragility; a rise of 5° C. is equivalent to a change of tonicity of about 0.01 per cent. Room temperature is generally sufficiently constant.

OSMOTIC FRAGILITY AFTER INCUBATION

Incubation at 37° C. for 24 hours increases the fragility of normal erythrocytes (Fig. 4–18, 1A). The increase is even more marked for red cells of hereditary spherocytosis and of one variety of congenital nonspherocytic hemolytic anemia; hemolysis may begin between 0.70 and 0.65 per cent sodium chloride and may be complete at about 0.40 per cent (Fig. 4–18, 2A). The test permits recognition of low grade hereditary spherocytosis and together with the autohemolysis test makes it possible to distinguish various types of congenital nonspherocytic hemolytic anemia.

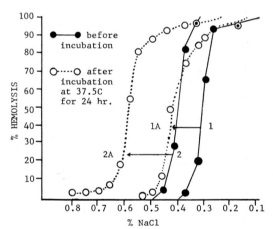

Figure 4–18. The effect of incubation on red cell osmotic fragility.

Procedure. Duplicate 2 ml. volumes of sterile, defibrinated blood in stoppered test tubes are incubated at 37° C. for 24 hours. The second test tube is included to have a spare in case of contamination. The test is set up similarly as described for the quantitative fragility test but with the addition

of a tube containing a 1.2 per cent solution of sodium chloride to serve as a blank in case of increased hemolysis.

Source of Error. Bacterial contamination.

MECHANICAL FRAGILITY

Red cells with increased osmotic fragility also show an increased mechanical fragility, but the latter may be abnormally increased when the former is normal. Sickled cells and agglutinated cells have an increased mechanical fragility. The mechanical fragility of red cells of newborn infants is about twice that of older children and adults. The procedure does not offer enough additional information to justify its inclusion here.

INDICATIONS FOR THE FRAGILITY TEST

The quantitative fragility test is time consuming and rarely rewarding. It is indicated when hereditary spherocytosis is suspected, and it may be useful in unexplained hemolytic jaundice, abnormal red cell regeneration, and splenomegaly. It is advisable to do the screening test as a preliminary procedure.

Sedimentation Rate of Erythrocytes

An increased tendency to sedimentation of erythrocytes in shed blood in certain pathologic conditions, particularly inflammation, has long been recognized as an interesting phenomenon explaining the well-known buffy coat of coagulated blood. Following the work of Fahraeus and other investigators with blood rendered noncoagulable by heparin, citrate, or oxalate, the rate of sedimentation has been actively studied and applied clinically.

The erythrocyte sedimentation rate (E.S.R.) measures the suspension stability of erythrocytes. Essentially, it is a rough measure of abnormal concentration of fibrinogen and serum globulins.

It has been found that the erythrocytes settle more rapidly in the blood of women than of men and very much more rapidly after the third or fourth month of pregnancy. In pregnancy, acceleration begins with the tenth to twelfth week, increasing moderately and progressively. Normal rates return about one month post partum. Increased speed of sedimentation is also observed in tuberculosis, in which it increases with the activity of the disease; in cancer, in which it more or less closely parallels the extent of the malignant process; in various so-called connective tissue diseases, such as rheumatic fever and rheumatoid arthritis; and in localized acute inflammation, in which the rate appears to increase with the leukocyte count.

The cause of the phenomenon is not clear. Sedimentation is the result of greater density of erythrocytes than of plasma. Many hypotheses have been suggested to explain the mechanism. According to one of them, changes in the negative electric charge of the surface of red cells and of the positive electric charge of the plasma are responsible.

Various factors have been demonstrated to play a role.

Plasma Factors. An accelerated E.S.R. (erythrocyte sedimentation rate) is favored by elevated levels of fibrinogen and to a lesser extent of globulin. These plasma components cause increased formation of rouleaux, which are sedimenting more rapidly because of their increased weight as compared with single cells. Removal of fibrinogen by defibrination lowers the E.S.R., except when plasma globulin is markedly elevated.

The effect of globulin on acceleration of the E.S.R. is less pronounced than that of fibrinogen, except in liver disease in which close correlation between the two has been noted in the presence of low fibrinogen levels. That fibrinogen and globulin are not the only responsible factors is shown by the fact that E.S.R. may be accelerated in the presence of normal levels and in patients without anemia. There is no absolute correlation between the E.S.R. and any of the plasma protein fractions. Alpha and beta globulins are more effective than gamma globulin. Albumin retards sedimentation.

Extreme increase in plasma viscosity slows down the E.S.R. by counteracting the accelerating effect of blood proteins on rouleaux formation (Eastham, 1954). Cholesterol accelerates and lecithin retards the E.S.R.

Red Cell Factors. Anemia is responsible for accelerated E.S.R. The change in the erythrocyte-plasma ratio favors rouleaux formation (Poole, 1952).

Microcytes sediment significantly more slowly and macrocytes somewhat more rapidly than normocytes. The larger the cells, the smaller the surface in relation to the volume. The sedimentation rate is directly proportionate to the weight of the cell aggregate and inversely proportionate to the surface area. Rouleaux formation is an aggregation of erythrocytes into units of larger size and proportionately decreased surface area, which is smaller in relation to the volume of the aggregate than the combined surface area of the individual cells. The result is acceleration of the E.S.R.

Anticoagulants. Sodium citrate does not affect the rate of sedimentation, but oxalates and heparin may.

Stages in the E.S.R. Three stages can be observed: (1) The initial period of aggregation. During this phase the rouleaux are formed and the sedimentation is relatively slow. It lasts about ten minutes of the one-hour observation period. (2) The period of fast settling. During this period the settling rate is constant. It lasts about 40 minutes. (3) The final period of packing continues for the balance of the hour and for a longer time afterwards.

METHODS FOR DETERMINING THE
SEDIMENTATION RATE

Since a variety of methods have been used in determining the sedimentation rate, the figures of different workers who use different methods are not comparable.

The E.S.R. may be measured in one of two ways: one measures the time it takes for the upper level of the red cell column to reach a specified point (Linzenmeyer method), and the other measures the distance covered by the upper level in a specified period of time (Westergren method). The latter is more practical and more widely accepted. The specified periods of time may be one hour (the most popular procedure) or 15 minutes (Cutler method), or the E.S.R. per minute is calculated. The latter, the Rourke-Ernstene method, gives probably the most reliable results but is the least practical method for routine work. The height of the column of blood is an important factor as is also the size of the bore of the sedimentation tube.

The more important differences in methods can be reduced to: the composition of the anticoagulant, the length of the tube and its diameter, the volume of blood used, the time of observation, and the reading and recording of results.

Wintrobe and Landsberg's Method. Equipment. Wintrobe's hematocrit tube (Fig. 4–19) is 110 mm. long, has a uniform bore of 3 mm. and a flat bottom, and is calibrated in centimeters and millimeters

Figure 4–19. Wintrobe hematocrit tube.

actly vertical position in an appropriate rack and left at room temperature.

4. The point on the millimeter scale to which the erythrocytes have fallen is the E.S.R. Readings at 15-minute intervals may give some indication of the rate of sedimentation.

5. The tube is centrifuged until packing of erythrocytes is complete, usually at 2500 G for 30 minutes. The volume of packed erythrocytes is read on the scale and recorded as the hematocrit.

Various methods have been suggested to correct for anemia, but the present consensus is not to do it, because all methods of correction are crude and frequently more misleading than helpful. Recording the hematocrit calls attention to the presence and degree of anemia or polycythemia, and this permits proper interpretation of the result of E.S.R. The normal average sedimentation in one hour as determined by this method is 4 mm. for healthy men and 10 mm. for women, with a maximal range from 0 to 9 mm. for men and 0 to 20 mm. for women. The normal figures given here are not to be correlated with those which have been obtained with other methods.

Westergren's Method. Because of its simplicity the Westergren method is widely used.

Equipment. The Westergren tube is a straight pipet 30 cm. long and 2.5 mm. in internal diameter. It is calibrated in millimeters from 0 to 200. It holds about 1 ml. The Westergren rack is also used (Fig. 4–20).

Reagent. A 3.8 per cent solution of sodium citrate.

on one side from 0 to 10 cm. and on the other from 10 to 0.

Reagent. A mixture of dried ammonium and potassium oxalate (6 mg. of the former and 4 mg. of the latter for each 5 ml. of blood) is used. The tubes in which the blood is collected can be prepared in advance by placing in them the oxalate solution and then evaporating to dryness in a hot air oven.

Technique

1. Five milliliters of venous blood are withdrawn in a dry syringe, placed in a tube or bottle containing the anticoagulant, and mixed well.

2. With a capillary hematocrit pipet, a Wintrobe tube is filled with blood to the 10 cm. mark. This is done by passing a hematocrit pipet to the bottom of the tube. As the blood is expelled gradually, the pipet is raised. This helps to avoid producing air bubbles in the tube.

3. The filled tube is placed in an ex-

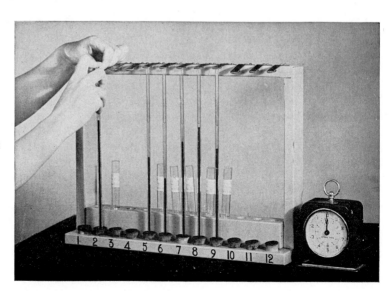

Figure 4–20. Westergren rack and tubes.

Technique

1. Exactly 0.5 ml. of the 3.8 per cent solution of sodium citrate is transferred with a graduated pipet to a tube with a mark at the 5 ml. level.

2. Five milliliters of venous blood are withdrawn in a dry syringe, and 4.5 ml. of it is placed in the tube containing the anticoagulant. The tube, now filled to the 5 ml. mark, is inverted two or three times to mix thoroughly the anticoagulant with the blood.

3. A Westergren pipet is filled exactly to the 0 mark and placed in the rack. The bottom of the tube must be pressed firmly against the rubber stopper in the base of the rack before removing the finger from the top of the tube. The tube must be held firmly by the clip at the top of the rack in an *exactly vertical* position. The rack is constructed to hold 12 or more tubes.

4. The level of the red cells is read in millimeters in exactly 60 minutes.

With this method, the normal sedimentation rate for men is 0 to 9 mm. in one hour. The rate for women is 0 to 20 mm. in one hour.

Relative Merits of the Wintrobe-Landsberg and Westergren Methods. *The Westergren method.* The higher blood column (200 mm.) gives more reliable results in blood with rapid sedimentation. The Wintrobe-Landsberg method may give normal results when the results with the Westergren method are abnormal.

The Wintrobe method. This method allows for correction for anemia. Recently doubts have been expressed regarding the value of such corrections. Occasionally paradoxical negative values may be obtained after a correction. It is recognized that the E.S.R. is of little value in patients with anemia (Fig. 4–21).

SOURCES OF ERROR

1. The anticoagulant. The exact concentration is important. If it is higher than recommended, the E.S.R. may be slowed down.

2. Hemolysis may modify the sedimentation.

3. The dimensions of the tube. The height should be not less than 100 mm. The optimum inner diameter is 2.5 to 3.75 mm.

4. The cleanliness of the tube is important, and all traces of alcohol and ether must be removed.

5. Effect of the acceleration by tilting. The red cells aggregate along the lower side while the plasma rises along the upper side. Consequently, the retarding influence of the rising plasma is less effective. An angle of even 3° from the vertical may accelerate the E.S.R. by as much as 30 per cent.

6. The filling of the tube. Bubbles affect sedimentation.

7. Temperature. Optimum 20° C. Acceptable range from 22° to 27° C. Otherwise a correction must be made for the temperature or the tube should be placed in a

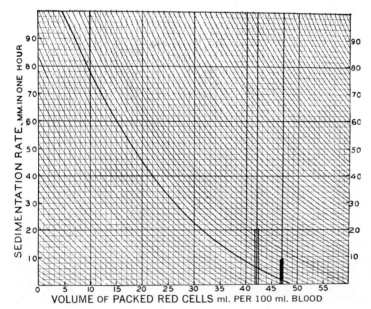

Figure 4–21. Correction chart for sedimentation time. Use of chart: First, find the horizontal line that corresponds to the mm. of sedimentation for one hour. Then follow this line until it intersects the vertical line representing the volume of packed red cells. At this point, follow the nearest curved line downward until it intersects the dark line at 42, if the patient is a woman; if a man, follow the curved line until it intersects the dark line at 47. This point of intersection represents the corrected sedimentation rate, when read on the horizonal line. (Wintrobe and Landsberg, 1935.)

constant temperature bath at 20° C. If the blood has been kept in a refrigerator, it should be permitted to reach room temperature before the test is set up.

8. Time. The test should be set up within two hours after the blood sample was obtained. Otherwise the E.S.R. may be lowered. On standing, erythrocytes tend to become spherical and less inclined to form rouleaux, hence, retarded E.S.R.

9. Anemia. A decrease in the number of erythrocytes accelerates the E.S.R.; an increase as in polycythemia retards it. This was the reason for the attempts to make a correction for the anemia, but as stated elsewhere in this chapter, the present tendency is to recognize that the value of the E.S.R. is extremely limited in the presence of anemia and that a correction for the anemia is hardly worth the effort and may be actually misleading.

10. Anisocytosis may interfere with rouleaux formation. Pronounced poikilocytosis, for example, sickling, may inhibit sedimentation.

11. Factors favoring slowing of the E.S.R.: defibrination, partial clotting with resulting defibrination, low temperature, excess of dry anticoagulant, and diameter of tube less than 2 mm.

INTERPRETATION

Many aspects of the E.S.R. have not been settled. The rate has been shown to be higher in females than in males, but it has not been settled whether this difference applies to the upper limit of normal. The same holds regarding the alleged higher rate in the aged. It may be that in both instances the lower normal red cell volume is responsible.

According to the current interpretation, the accelerated E.S.R. is a nonspecific response to tissue damage. It is only an indication of presence of the disease and somewhat vaguely of its severity. Its value is greatest when used as one evidence of subsidence of an inflammatory process.

It may help in differentiating certain conditions, e.g., myocardial infarction from angina pectoris, rheumatoid arthritis from osteoarthritis, and advanced cancer of the stomach from peptic ulcer.

It may also be elevated without apparent inflammation or necrosis, mainly in so-called dysproteinemias.

On the other hand it may be within normal limits in the presence of tissue destruction, for example, in some cases of acute myocardial infarction and acute rheumatic fever and in the presence of congestive heart failure.

The test must be used with great caution. It is most valuable in following the course of certain inflammatory processes, e.g., tuberculosis and rheumatic fever.

THE LEUKOCYTES

The White Cell Count

Equipment. The white cell pipet has a stem and a mixing chamber (Fig. 4–7). The stem is divided into ten parts, which measure the volume of the blood sample. The fifth and tenth graduations are marked as 0.5 and 1.0, respectively. The mixing chamber extends from the mark 1.0 to 11.0. It contains a white bead, which aids in the mixing. The volume of the mixing chamber is 20 times the volume of the stem at the mark 0.5 and 10 times the volume at the mark 1.0. When blood is drawn to the 0.5 mark (1 volume) and the diluting fluid to the 11.0 mark (11 volumes), the dilution of the blood sample is 1 to 20 and the dilution factor is 20. When blood is drawn to the 1.0 mark and the diluting factor to 11.0, the dilution factor is 10.

The counting chamber with the improved Neubauer ruling is used. The ruled area measures 9 sq. mm. The central square is used for counting the erythrocytes, and the four squares at the corners, each measuring 1 sq. mm., are used for counting the leukocytes.

Diluting Fluid. The diluting fluid should dissolve the erythrocytes so that they will not obscure the leukocytes. The simplest diluting fluid is a 2 per cent solution of acetic acid. More satisfactory is the following:

Glacial acetic acid	2 ml.
1 per cent aqueous solution of gentian violet	1 ml.
Distilled water	100 ml.

The fluid must be filtered frequently to remove yeasts and molds.

Technique. All recommendations made previously relating to the erythrocytes apply also to leukocytes and will not be repeated here.

1. The blood is drawn carefully to the 0.5 mark and the diluting fluid to the mark 11. This gives a dilution of 1 to 20. If the blood should accidentally go much above the 0.5 mark, it is drawn to 0.6 and the final count is multiplied by $\frac{5}{6}$.

2. The outside of the tip of the pipet is wiped off with cotton to remove any blood that may be adhering to it, making sure that the level of the blood in the lumen of the pipet was not affected.

3. The diluting fluid is drawn to fill the mixing chamber to the mark 11.

4. The pipet is held between the thumb and the middle finger, and the contents are mixed well by shaking the pipet for three minutes in all directions except in the long axis of the pipet. Pipet rotors save time and labor, and do a good mixing job.

5. The first three drops are blown out to discard the diluting fluid from the stem, which contains no blood.

6. The counting chamber is loaded exactly the same way as was described for the erythrocyte count. Loading both counting chambers and counting the leukocytes in eight instead of four squares gives more reliable results.

7. The chamber is placed on the microscope, and the light is adjusted to make the leukocytes stand out clearly when viewed with a low power objective. The four corner squares are surveyed to check the distribution of the leukocytes. Uneven distribution is caused by inadequate or improper mixing of the pipet or failure to discard enough of the diluting fluid in the pipet stem. If that happens, the counting chamber and the coverglass have to be washed and wiped dry, the mixing repeated, and the chamber reloaded.

8. The leukocytes are counted with a 16 or 8 mm. objective and a 10 × ocular. A square millimeter will be included in the field of the 16 mm. objective. The leukocytes are counted in each of the secondary squares of the four large corner squares, beginning at the extreme left of the top row, moving right, then down to the second row, then left through the four secondary squares of the second row, then down to the third row, then right along the third row, and finally down to the fourth row and from right to left along the fourth row until all the leukocytes in the 16 secondary squares have been counted. Only the cells that touch the dividing lines to the left and above are included; those touching the dividing lines to the right and below are omitted (Fig. 4–22).

The leukocytes found in all 16 small squares are added. This gives the number in 1 sq. mm. The numbers counted in all four corner squares of each chamber are added. If only one chamber is counted, the

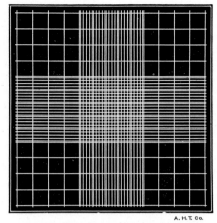

Figure 4–22. Entire area of improved Neubauer ruling.

total is divided by four to find the average per square millimeter. The average is multiplied by 10 to find the number in 1 cu. mm. of diluted blood and by the dilution to find the number in a cubic millimeter of undiluted blood. With a Neubauer or similar ruling and a dilution of 1 to 20, a convenient plan is the following: With a low power objective, the leukocytes in the square millimeters at each of the four corners of the ruled area are counted and multiplied by 50, or the count is divided by two and two zeros are added. This should be repeated on a second slide and the average taken. A general formula is:

$$\text{Number cells per cu. mm.} = \frac{cc \times d \times 10}{l.s.c.}$$

where cc is the total number of cells counted, d is the dilution factor, 10 is the factor transforming the surface of the square millimeter to the volume in cubic millimeters, and l.s.c. = the number of large squares counted.

In leukopenia, with a total count below 2500, the blood is drawn to the 1.0 mark and the dilution factor is 10.

Example: 120 cells counted in eight squares. Number of leukocytes per cu. mm.

$$= \frac{120 \times 10 \times 10}{8} = 1500.$$

In leukocytosis with high counts, red cell pipets are used, and the dilution may be 1 to 100 or even 1 to 200.

Sources of Error. The dilution factor in white cell counts is smaller than in the red cell count. This influences the inherent error. With good technique, when four large squares in each of 2 chambers are counted, the error for a count within normal limits is ±15 per cent. When only four squares are counted, the error increases to ±20 per cent.

If 100 cells are counted, the standard deviation is about $\sqrt{100} = 10$. Accordingly, if 100 cells are counted, 95 per cent of observed white cell counts of true value of 8000 cells per cu. mm. would lie within the range of 6400 to 9600. The error in the leukocyte count is less important than in the red cell counts. The difference between 8000 and 6400 is of little practical consequence.

In general the error decreases as the total leukocyte count and the number of cells included in the count increase. As many leukocytes as possible should be counted.

Impurities and debris in the diluting fluid are other possible sources of error. They can be prevented by filtering the diluting fluid frequently. Occasionally leukocytes tend to clump, especially when oxalated or heparinized blood is left standing for several hours, before samples are withdrawn for counting.

Nucleated red cells will be counted and cannot be distinguished from leukocytes with the magnification used. If their number is high as seen on the stained smear, a correction should be made according to the following formula:

$$\frac{\text{No. of NRBC*}}{100 + \text{No. of NRBC*}} \times \text{leukocyte count} = \text{absolute No. of nucleated red cells per cu. mm.}$$

Corrected count = leukocyte count per cu. mm. − nucleated red cell count per cu. mm.

Example. The blood smear shows 25 nucleated red cells per 100 leukocytes. The total white cell count is 10,000.

$$\frac{25}{125} \times 10,000 = 2500$$

10,000 − 2500 = 7500 per cu. mm.
The true leukocyte count is 7500 per cu. mm.

THE PLATELETS

The number of platelets in the platelet count depends on the method of counting. With the Rees-Ecker method, the normal range is 140,000 to 340,000 per cubic millimeter of blood. Indirect methods yield higher values. With Dameshek's method the normal range is 500,000 to 900,000.

* Number of nucleated red cells as counted in the differential count per 100 leukocytes.

Function. Small, insignificant, and fragile as the platelet is, it is known to have several functions and chances are that more will be discovered. These functions are of two kinds: First, they take part in blood coagulation by being a source of platelet factor 3 and of other factors involved in coagulation. They are essential for clot retraction. They participate in maintaining the integrity of the blood vessel wall by becoming agglutinated and sealing defects in the wall. Second, they are carriers of serotonin (5-hydroxytryptamine).

The platelets originate in the marrow from megakaryocytes. In general, whenever the number of thrombocytes is less than the critical levels of 100,000 to 50,000 per cubic millimeter of blood, a hemorrhagic tendency may become evident. Its severity is usually inversely proportionate to the number of platelets. Prolonged bleeding time, delayed and inadequate clot retraction, diminished prothrombin consumption, positive tourniquet test, and petechiae may be the other associated *in vitro* and *in vivo* findings.

APPEARANCE

Platelets are round, oval, or rod shaped, 2 to 4 μ in diameter, and are capable of ameboid movement by means of pseudopodia as evidenced by the presence of elongated platelets in stained blood smears. Considerably larger platelets can be seen when blood is regenerating rapidly and actively. In Wright stained smears, the center (the granulomere), about one-third to one-half of the platelet, is filled with fine purplish red granules, 0.03 to 0.06 μ in size. It is surrounded by the homogeneous or finely fibrillar pale blue cytoplasm (the hyalomere). The separation into a "granulomere" and "hyalomere" may be artefacts, because upon prompt fixation and staining with brilliant cresyl blue the two zones are not demonstrable. The platelet contains no nuclear material and no or almost no deoxyribonucleic acid.

Physiologic variations in number of thrombocytes are considerable. The newborn, especially during the first two days of life, have fewer platelets (150,000 to 250,000) than older infants. The number of platelets decreases progressively before menstruation, even more precipitously during the first day of menstruation. They begin to rise on the third day. Violent exercise is followed by a rise, possibly caused by a change in distribution. The number increases as one ascends to a higher altitude and is higher in winter than in summer. There are unexplained variations from day to day; hence, a single abnormal count should not be taken to indicate a pathologic condition.

The number of the platelets is the result of an equilibrium between their production in the marrow and their utilization, loss, or destruction in the peripheral blood. The normal life span of platelets has been generally estimated to be about four days, but in a recent report the use of a radioactive label showed a survival of eight to nine days. On the basis of a four-day survival period and an average 400,000 platelets per cu. mm., 100,000 platelets are formed and destroyed per cu. mm. per day. In disease, variations are often extremely great. An increase (thrombocythemia) may be due to an increase in the number, or in the activity, of the megakaryocytes. The result may be a tendency to thrombosis or, rarely and paradoxically, to hemorrhage. The latter is explained by the fact that extremely high platelet counts have an anticoagulant effect and may inhibit the generation of thromboplastin. A decrease (thrombocytopenia) is more important. There is no means of recognizing increased destruction of thrombocytes as there is in the case of erythrocytes (see reticulocytosis). Even when thrombocytes are present in normal numbers, they may be functionally defective.

CLINICAL APPLICATIONS

On the clinical side the following facts seem to be established:

1. In acute infectious diseases, the number of platelets is usually normal or subnormal; occasionally it may be increased.

2. In secondary anemia, especially in the posthemorrhagic type, the count generally is increased although it sometimes is decreased. In pernicious anemia, it nearly always is greatly diminished, and an increase should cause one to question the diagnosis of this condition.

3. It is increased in polycythemia and idiopathic thrombocythemia; after splenectomy, excitement, and tissue injury, including operations; and following injection of epinephrine (but not in the splenectomized patient).

4. The platelet count is decreased in chronic lymphocytic leukemia; it is variable but usually greatly increased in chronic granulocytic leukemia and myeloproliferative disorders. It is much decreased in acute leukemia of either form.

5. The count is somewhat increased in tuberculosis.

6. Platelet counts are of great value in distinguishing the hemorrhagic diseases. In hemophilia, the platelets are normal in number but are claimed to be defective in function. The clot, although delayed, is well formed and has normal retractile power. In thrombocytopenic purpura, on the other hand, platelets are functionally normal but greatly reduced in number. The count ranges from about 40,000 to 75,000 per cubic millimeter in cases of mild purpura to 15,000 or less in cases in which the disease is severe. The coagulation time is about normal, but the number of platelets is too small to cause normal retraction of the clot.

7. Platelets, although adequate in numbers, may be deficient qualitatively in which case the deficiency may become manifest by a prolonged bleeding time, reduced clot retraction, inadequate plasma thromboplastin generation, or increased vascular fragility. The qualitative defect may be hereditary. The platelets may be enlarged and abnormal in shape.

The Platelet Count

Platelets are difficult to count, because they disintegrate easily and rapidly and then are hard to distinguish from debris. Another source of difficulty is their tendency to adhere to glass, to any foreign body, and particularly to each other. In addition, there is evidence that they are not evenly distributed in the blood. The unavoidable error is greater than in counting erythrocytes or leukocytes but is negligible in practice because only great variations in the count have clinical significance. It is often possible to recognize a great decrease in the number of platelets by a careful inspection of stained films, provided these are made evenly and very quickly after the blood was obtained in order to avoid clumping. Therefore, a remark regarding platelets should be a part of the report on the differential count in the form of a reference to their abnormal shape and inadequacy in numbers, if noted.

Many methods have been proposed for counting platelets, but there are two groups of them. In the direct methods, the platelets are counted similarly as the red and white cells. In the indirect methods, the platelets and the red cells are counted simultaneously and then the number of platelets per cubic millimeter is calculated on the basis of the red cell count.

Each method has its merits and disadvantages. The direct methods give more accurate results in the hands of the experienced and meticulous worker. The indirect methods are somewhat easier for the less experienced who does platelet counts only occasionally. In the direct methods, the results are regularly lower than those obtained by some of the indirect methods.

Direct Methods. *Principle.* Capillary or venous blood with an anticoagulant is mixed in a red cell pipet with a diluting fluid. The platelets are counted in a hemocytometer.

Method of Rees and Ecker (1923). DILUTING FLUID. This solution preserves the erythrocytes, which may be counted in the same specimen.

Sodium citrate	3.8	gm.
Formaldehyde, 40 per cent solution	0.2	ml.
Brilliant cresyl blue	0.05	gm.
Water	100	ml.

The formula is a slight modification of the original. The reduced amount of the dye is adequate. The solution is made by adding 3.8 gm. of sodium citrate to 75 ml. of distilled water. Brilliant cresyl blue is ground in a mortar with three or four samples of distilled water of 5 ml. each. It is then filtered and mixed with the solution of sodium citrate. The formaldehyde is added and the volume brought up with distilled water to 100 ml. The mixture is allowed to stand at room temperature with occasional shaking. It is then filtered and centrifuged at 2500 G. for 30 minutes to remove any undissolved particles. The supernatant is kept in glass stoppered bottles in the refrigerator. The fluid is filtered each time before use and the unused portion is discarded.

TECHNIQUE. The pipet, counting chamber, and all other glassware must be completely free of grease and debris. Rapid work is necessary in order to prevent clumping of the platelets. The skin is cleansed with soap and water, followed by alcohol and ether or acetone. The finger is better than the ear lobe, because hyperemia and free flow of blood can be produced easily by immersion in warm water.

Venous blood gives more reproducible counts. It is best collected in a siliconed test tube. A direct, uncomplicated venipuncture and minimal contamination with tissue juice is essential.

The diluting fluid is drawn to near the 1 mark in the "red" pipet and then expelled, and blood from a freely bleeding skin puncture or from a bottle containing freshly obtained and adequately shaken venous blood is drawn exactly to the 0.5 mark. The excessive blood is rapidly wiped off the outside of the tip, and finally the diluting fluid is quickly drawn to the 101 mark. This gives a blood dilution of 1 to 200. The blood and diluting fluid are immediately mixed by shaking for three to five minutes and the first several drops are discarded. The counting chamber is filled at once, and 15 minutes are allowed for the corpuscles to settle before counting is begun. To prevent drying, the hemacytometer must be covered with a Petri dish containing moistened filter paper. The count is made with the high power, dry objective and with the 10 × ocular in the manner described for counting erythrocytes. In the counting chamber the platelets appear as highly refractile, round, oval, or elongated particles, 1 to 5 μ in size. With the Rees-Ecker diluting fluid the red cells are preserved. Proper adjustment of the light is important to distinguish the platelets from debris, yeast cells, or precipitated stain. If too many extraneous particles are present, repeating the count with a new sample of blood and with refiltered diluting fluid may be necessary, especially if loading the chamber with diluting fluid alone corroborates the suspicion.

An occasional small clump of platelets does not interfere, but if they are too many or too large, the count is valueless. The diluting fluid or the technique may be at fault, especially slow work. If the red cells have been hemolyzed, the diluting fluid is at fault.

It is best to count the platelets in two large corner squares in each of two counting chambers, or a total of four squares. The average number of platelets per 0.1 cu. mm. (large square) is multiplied by 10 to get the number present in 1.0 cu. mm. and by 200 to correct for the dilution or by a factor 2000. The result is the number of platelets per 1 cu. mm. A control count should always be made at the same time with blood from a normal person, using the same diluting fluid and exactly the same technique.

SOURCES OF ERROR IN THE DIRECT METHODS. They are the same as those inherent in the red and white cell count. Some of the special sources of error are particles that may be confused with platelets. This can be controlled by a "blank" count on the diluting fluid. If it is below 5000, a correction can be made. If it exceeds 5000 platelet-like particles, a fresh, clean diluting is needed. The error is proportionally greater as the count decreases. Doubling the amount of blood or using a white cell pipet in which the dilution factor is decreased are other ways of reducing the error. Siliconed glassware, pipets, and needles have also been recommended. Clean glassware and sterilized diluting fluid, stored in glass stoppered bottles in a refrigerator and filtered each time before use, contribute to the accuracy of the count. If hemolysis of red cells is noted, the fluid should be discarded. Oxidation of formaldehyde into formic acid may be responsible.

Counting platelets with the phase microscope. EQUIPMENT. Flat bottom counting chamber and a No. 1 or $1\frac{1}{2}$ coverslip. "Long working distance" phase condenser with $43 \times$ annulus and matching $43 \times$ phase objective and $10 \times$ eyepiece. For American Optical Company equipment, "medium dark contrast" should be specified. Siliconed Kahn test tubes.

SOLUTION. One per cent ammonium oxalate in distilled water. Stock bottle is kept in refrigerator. The amount needed for the day is removed and the unused portion discarded at end of day.

PROCEDURE. 1. About 2 ml. of venous blood, obtained with a 20-gauge needle and without a syringe, is allowed to flow directly into a clean, siliconed Kahn tube, which is kept in ice water before and after the collection. The blood is immediately diluted in red cell pipets. In another recommended procedure, a siliconed syringe is used with a minimum of suction to avoid air bubbles. The needle is removed promptly and the blood emptied gently into a siliconed test tube.

2. A red cell pipet is filled rapidly with blood to the 1 mark, then with ammonium oxalate to the 101 mark, and then rotated in a mechanical pipet rotor. The Bryant-Garrey rotors have been found satisfactory. Rotation for as long as eight hours does not affect the counts.

3. The hemacytometer is filled in the usual fashion.

4. The chamber is covered by a Petri dish for 15 minutes. A wet piece of cotton is left beneath the dish to prevent evaporation.

5. Platelets are counted in ten blocks of small squares, five blocks in each half of the chamber. The result multiplied by 2500 is the platelet count per cu. mm. The

platelets appear round or oval with a pink or purple sheen or uniformly black with more fully corrected objectives. The differentiation of platelets from other structures is easy. With this method the range of values in 95 per cent of healthy controls is from 140,000 to 440,000.

SOURCES OF ERROR. Most of the sources of error are the same as those discussed previously for the usual direct platelet count. Only freshly obtained blood can be used with this method. Preserved blood with anticoagulant added is not satisfactory. Capillary blood gives values about 2.5 per cent lower, but errors are about twice those with venous blood. Other important errors are careless venipuncture and delay in dilution.

Indirect Methods. A large drop of a 14 per cent magnesium sulfate solution is placed on the clean, dry skin. The puncture is made through the liquid. Wright's stain is used. The platelets are counted simultaneously with red cells until at least 1000 red cells have been counted. The number of platelets obtained is calculated from the ratio of the red cells to platelets and the number of red cells obtained from a count done at the same time.

Example

Number of platelets counted = 75.
Number of red cells counted = 1000.
Red cell count = 4,000,000.

Calculation: $\dfrac{1000}{75} = 13$

$\dfrac{4,000,000}{13} = 307,693$ platelets per cu. mm.

In another method, a vital stain (brilliant cresyl blue) is used. Platelets are counted and the result calculated similarly as in the Wright's stain. The range of values is higher with this method: 500,000 to 1,000,000.

Dameshek's method (1932). DILUTING FLUID. Eight grams of sucrose and 0.04 gm. of sodium citrate are dissolved in 100 ml. of distilled water and 0.15 gm. brilliant cresyl blue is added. The fluid is mixed well and filtered. Three drops of 10 per cent formaldehyde are added.

The finger tip is punctured. The first drop of blood is discarded. A large drop of diluting fluid is placed over the punctured wound. The finger is squeezed gently to obtain a small drop of blood, roughly one-fifth the size of the drop of diluting fluid. The mixture is then transferred to a coverslip, which is dropped on a slide. After 15 to 45 minutes the slide is examined with an oil immersion lens. The number of platelets is calculated as stated previously. An additional advantage is that reticulocytes can also be counted.

ACCURACY OF THE PLATELET COUNT

Differences of less than 25 per cent are not significant. Expressed another way, a difference of at least 80,000 between two successive counts on the same person may be significant. Some of the factors determining accuracy are experience, meticulous attention to detail, and the number of platelets counted. The high counts are not necessarily correct. Venous blood diluted as soon as it is obtained gives more reproducible results.

EXAMINATION OF STAINED BLOOD

Making and Staining Blood Films

The information gathered from the examination of the blood smear is extremely important. It may furnish the diagnosis as does a histologic section. It may serve as a guide to therapy and as indicator of harmful effects of chemotherapy and radiotherapy. The reliability of the information obtained depends to a considerable extent on the quality of the smears. Properly spread films are essential to accurate work. They more than compensate for the time spent in learning to make them.

There are certain requisites for success with any method: First, the slides and coverglasses must be *perfectly clean* and free of grease. They should be washed with soap and water, then with abundant, clean hot water (the water should not be permitted to cool before all the soap has been removed), followed by distilled water, and then dried and polished with a clean, lint-free cloth. From then on they must be handled by touching only their edges. Washed slides and coverglasses may be stored in 95 per cent alcohol. Dry coverglasses may also be stored in a clean, dry Petri dish.

Large numbers of slides and coverglasses may be cleaned in advance with acid cleaning solution, which is prepared as follows: Twenty-five grams of powdered potassium dichromate is dissolved in a Pyrex beaker in 25 ml. of water with the aid of heat. Let it cool and add slowly 1 L. of technical grade concentrated sulfuric acid. This step must be done cautiously because intense heat develops.

The slides and coverglasses are dropped individually into the cleaning solution and left in it for from 4 to 24 hours. The cleaning solution is poured off and the slides washed with multiple changes of tap water. The removal of the acid may be accelerated by heating. The complete removal of the acid is established when the tap water is negative with litmus paper. They should then be rinsed in distilled water. The slides and coverslips are then stored as described previously. For routine use, clean slides are available commercially.

The drop of blood must *not* be *too large*.

The work must be done *quickly*, before coagulation begins. The blood is obtained from the finger tip or the lobe of the ear, as for a blood count. Only a very small drop is required, usually about twice the size of a pinhead. The size of the drop largely determines the thickness of the film. The proper thickness depends on the purpose for which the film is made. For a study of the structure of blood corpuscles and examination for malarial parasites, it should be so thin that, throughout the greater part of the film, the erythrocytes lie in a single layer, close together but not overlapping. For routine differential counting of leukocytes, a film in which the erythrocytes are piled up somewhat is best because the leukocytes are more evenly distributed, the number of leukocytes in a given area is greatly increased, and the tedium of counting is correspondingly lessened. The film must not, on the other hand, be so thick that identification of the various leukocytes becomes difficult. In some cases of severe anemia, it is very difficult to make good films owing to the large proportion of plasma, which leads to slow drying with consequent distortion of the erythrocytes and the appearance of artefacts. To overcome this, the films should be made very thin and dried quickly.

The Two-slide Method. The coverglass method has the advantage of more even distribution of leukocytes. In every other respect the slide method is preferable. Slides are easier to handle and to label and are less fragile.

Preparation of the film. Take a small drop of blood on a chemically clean and dust-free slide about $\frac{3}{4}$ inch from the end, using care that the slide does not touch the skin. Place the slide on a table or flat surface. At the bedside it may be more convenient to hold the end of the slide away from the drop by the thumb and forefinger of the left hand and to support the other end with the small finger. With the thumb and forefinger of the right hand hold the end of a second slide against the surface of the first at an angle of 30 to 40 degrees (the free edge of the spreader slide will then be about an inch above the table) and draw it up against the drop of blood until contact is established. The drop will immediately run across the end, filling the angle between the two slides. The edge of the spreader must be absolutely smooth. If it is rough, the film has ragged tails containing many leukocytes. A "margin free" blood spreader prepared by cutting off the corners of a regular slide is preferred in some laboratories. This makes the smear narrower than the slide. Push the "spreader slide" slowly in the reverse direction along the other in the manner indicated in Figure 4–23 so that the blood flows behind the edge of the spreader slide. If the drop of blood was of appropriate size, the thin portion of the film is about 3 cm. long. The thickness of the film can be regulated by changing the angle at which the spreader slide is held, by varying the pressure and the speed of spreading, and by using a smaller or larger drop of blood. The film should not cover the entire surface of the slide. In a good film there is a thick portion and a thin portion and a gradual transition from one to the other. The film should have a smooth, even appearance and be free from ridges, waves, or holes.

The speed of spreading the film is a factor in the quality of the preparation. The faster it is spread, the more even and the thicker it is. In films of optimum thickness there is some overlap of red cells in much of the film but even distribution and separation of red cells toward the thin tail. However, in a good smear the leukocytes should not be crowded.

It is very easy by this method to make large, thin, even films, which are especially useful for studying the erythrocytes and malarial parasites. The use of the slide preparations for making differential leukocyte counts is less satisfactory because the distribution of leukocytes is not uniform.

The films should be allowed to dry in the air.

Labeling the blood films. The identification can be written with a soft lead pencil directly on the blood film.

Two-coverglass Method. This method is widely recommended, but considerable practice is required to get good results. No. 0 or No. 1 coverglasses $\frac{7}{8}$ inch square are recommended. No. 2 coverglasses are too thick for oil immersion.

Preparation of the film. Touch a coverglass (22 × 22 mm. square) to the top of a small drop of blood (about 2 to 3 mm. in size) without touching the skin and place it, blood side down, crosswise on another coverglass so that the corners appear as an eight-pointed star. If the drop is not too large and if the coverglasses are perfectly clean, the blood will spread out evenly and quickly in a thin layer between the two surfaces. Just as it stops spreading and before it begins to coagulate, pull the coverglasses quickly but firmly apart on a plane parallel to their surfaces. They should not be separated by lifting (Fig. 4–24). They should be placed smear side up on clean

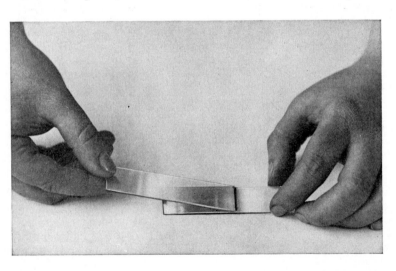

Figure 4–23. Spreading the film, two-slide method.

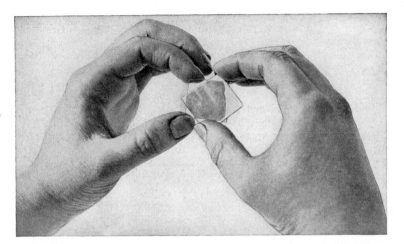

Figure 4–24. Spreading the film, two-coverglass method.

paper and allowed to dry in the air, or they may be placed back to back cornerwise in slits made in a cardboard box.

Films from venous blood may be prepared similarly by touching the tip of a hypodermic needle to a coverslip, placing on it a drop 1 to 2 mm. in size, and proceeding as described. It has also been recommended to empty the syringe quickly into the container with anticoagulant except for the last few drops, to hold it in vertical position with the tip up, and to apply gentle pressure on the plunger until a small drop of blood appears on the tip. The drop is then touched with the coverglass. Venous blood with an anticoagulant is not suitable for the study of white cells. Oxalate is probably the worst of all anticoagulants because of the presence of vacuoles and phagocytized crystals of oxalate. Blood with other anticoagulants and defibrinated blood is also less satisfactory for the study of leukocytes.

SOURCES OF ERROR IN PREPARATION OF FILMS. Separation of the slides must be done just at the right moment to get good results. If it is done too soon, the smear will not cover the entire slide and will be too thick. If it is done too late, the blood will clot and it may be difficult to pull the slides apart.

The coverglass method is especially to be recommended for accurate differential counts, since all the leukocytes in the drop will be found on the two coverglasses and thus the error due to unequal distribution can be excluded by counting all the leukocytes. The blood usually is much more evenly spread on one of the coverglasses than it is on the other.

Fixing the Film. In general, films must be "fixed" before they are stained. Stains that are dissolved in methyl alcohol, i.e., Wright's or Giemsa's stain, combine fixation with the staining process. This takes place during the first minute when the undiluted stain is applied. With aqueous stains, chemicals or heat must be used.

Chemical fixation. Soak the film one to two minutes in pure methyl alcohol or absolute ethyl alcohol, or 15 minutes or longer in equal parts of absolute alcohol and ether. One minute in a 1 per cent solution of mercuric chloride or in a 1 per cent solution of formalin in alcohol is preferred by some workers. The film must be well washed in water after fixation with mercuric chloride. Chemical fixation may precede staining with hematoxylin and eosin and with other simple stains.

Fixation with heat. This may precede any of the methods that do not combine fixation with a staining process. The best method is to place the film in an oven, raise the temperature to 150° C., and allow to cool slowly. Without an oven, the proper degree of fixation is difficult to attain.

BLOOD STAINS

The aniline dyes, which are extensively used in blood work, are of two general classes: basic dyes, such as methylene blue, and acid dyes, such as eosin. Nuclei and certain other structures in the blood are stained by the basic dyes and are hence called basophilic. Certain structures take up only acid dyes and are called acidophilic, oxyphilic, or eosinophilic. Certain other structures are stained by a combination of the two and are called neutrophilic. Recognition of these staining properties marked the beginning of modern hematology.

Polychrome Methylene Blue and Eosin

Stains. These stains, which are the outgrowth of the original time-consuming Romanowsky method, have largely displaced other blood stains for routine laboratory use. They may be recommended for all routine work. They stain differentially every normal and abnormal structure in the blood. Most of them are dissolved in methyl alcohol and combine the fixing with the staining process. Numerous methods of preparing and applying these stains have been devised, among the best known being Giemsa's and Wright's.

Wright's stain. This is a polychrome stain because it produces a variety of colors. It is a methyl alcoholic solution of an acid and a basic dye. It is one of the best and is the most widely used stain. Wright's stain certified by the Commission of Staining is commercially available. It is satisfactory and ready for use. One can also purchase the powder certified by the Commission on Staining.* The solution is prepared by dissolving 0.1 gm. of powder per 60 ml. of chemically pure absolute methyl alcohol (C.P., acetone-free). The powder (0.1 gm.) is ground in a mortar adding a few milliliters of the alcohol at a time until 60 ml. have been added and the entire stain has gone into solution. This requires 20 to 30 minutes. The stain should then be left standing for a day or two and filtered before use. The stock dye is filtered when prepared and each time when samples are taken from the stock. The dye is sensitive to contamination with water in reagents or glassware. The reagent bottle must be tightly stoppered at all times to prevent entry of water vapor. Exposure to acid or alkaline fumes must also be avoided.

Wright's directions for the preparation and use of the stain are as follows:

PREPARATION. To a 0.5 per cent aqueous solution of sodium bicarbonate add methylene blue (B.X. or "medicinally pure") in the proportion of 1 gm. of the dye to each 100 ml. of the solution. Heat the mixture in a steam sterilizer at 100° C. for one hour, counting the time after the sterilizer has become thoroughly heated. The mixture should be placed in a flask, or flasks, of such size and shape that it forms a layer not more than 6 cm. deep. After heating, allow the mixture to cool, placing the flask in cold water, if desired, and then filter it to remove the precipitate that has

formed in it. It should, when cold, have a deep purplish red color when a thin layer is viewed by transmitted yellowish artificial light. It does not show this color while it is warm.

To each 100 ml. of the filtered mixture add 500 ml. of a 0.1 per cent aqueous solution of "yellowish water-soluble" eosin and mix thoroughly. Collect the abundant precipitate, which immediately appears, on a filter. Owing to lack of uniformity in the dyes now obtainable, it may be necessary to add more or less of the eosin to obtain a satisfactory precipitate. When the precipitate appears, it may be recognized by placing a drop of the fluid on filter paper. Dry the precipitate thoroughly and dissolve it in methyl alcohol (Merck's reagent) in the proportion of 0.1 gm. to 60 ml. of the alcohol. In order to facilitate solution, the precipitate should be rubbed with the alcohol in a porcelain dish or mortar with a spatula or pestle. This alcoholic solution of the precipitate is the staining fluid. It frequently is found that freshly made solutions stain the erythrocytes blue owing to slight alkalinity; however, such solutions usually work properly after a few months.

Buffer for dilution of Wright's stain (pH 6.4): primary (monobasic) potassium phosphate (KH_2PO_4), anhydrous 6.63 gm.; secondary (dibasic) sodium phosphate (Na_2HPO_4), anhydrous 2.56 gm.; and distilled water to make 1 L. A more alkaline buffer (pH 6.7) may be prepared by using 5.13 gm. of the potassium salt and 4.12 gm. of the sodium salt.

STAINING THE FILM. 1. For best results the films should be stained as soon as they have been dried in the air but in any case not later than after a few hours. If they must be kept longer without staining, they must be fixed. In smears left unfixed for a day or more, the dried plasma stains and produces a background of pale blue. Uniform staining is difficult to achieve, because smears tend to vary in thickness except when exceptionally good technique is used in their preparation.

2. Place the slide with the air-dried film side up on a stain rack over a pan; the coverslip is placed best on a support, i.e., a cork attached to the bottom of a pan with paraffin.

3. Without previous fixation, cover the film with a noted quantity of the staining fluid with a medicine dropper. There must be plenty of stain in order to avoid too great an evaporation and consequent pre-

---

* Conn, H. J., and Darrow, M. S.: Staining procedures used by the Biological Stain Commission. Geneva, N.Y., Biotech Publications, 1943–1944.

cipitation. This step fixes the smear. When slides are used, the stain may be confined to the desired area by two heavy wax-pencil marks.

4. After two minutes, add to the staining fluid on the film an equal quantity of the buffer solution with a second medicine dropper. In some parts of the country tap water may be used with equally good results. To mix the stain with the diluent, blow gently on the diluted stain on several portions of the slide to set up gentle currents and to make an even distribution. The quantity of the fluid on the preparation must not be so large that some of it runs off. Allow the mixture to remain for three to four minutes. Look for a greenish metallic scum to appear. The margins should show a reddish tint. A longer period of staining may produce a precipitate. The time of optimum staining with the undiluted stains has to be established for each batch. Eosinophilic granules are best brought out by a short period of staining. The optimum time for the most effective combination of stain and diluent varies from batch to batch.

5. Float off the stain with a stream of water (preferably distilled), first slowly and then more vigorously, preferably from an overhead water bottle, until all traces of excessive stain have disappeared. During the entire procedure the slide must remain horizontal. The washing takes 5 to 30 seconds until the thinner portions of the film become yellowish or pink in color. The preparation should be flooded with buffered water while the stain is still on it. If the stain is poured off before rinsing, the scum tends to settle on the blood film, where it clings in spite of subsequent washing. If the color is too dark, the excessive blue can be removed by further washing. The film is dried by evaporation or by blotting gently with filter paper. The stain remaining on the back of the slide is removed with gauze moistened in alcohol.

6. The washing completed, the excessive water is drained by tilting the slide and touching a blotter with the lower edge.

7. For drying, the slide remains in the tilted position or is waved gently.

8. The coverslide, film side down, is mounted on a slide with neutral Canada balsam.

Coverglass films may be mounted temporarily by placing them, blood slide down, on a glass slide on which a drop of immersion oil has been placed. Using a drop of isobutyl methacrylate dissolved in xylol or toluol at an approximately neutral pH will give permanent mounts.

Films stained well with Wright's stain have a pink color when viewed with the naked eye and give the following picture on microscopic examination (see Plates 4–1, 4–2, 4–3, 4–5). When inspected under low power magnification of the microscope, the cells should be evenly distributed and separated from each other. The red cells are pink, not lemon yellow or red; they are lying flat without overlapping or forming rouleaux. At least eight satisfactory low power fields on a slide are present in a good preparation. They should be free from artefacts, such as vacuoles. The nuclei of leukocytes are purplish blue, the basi- and oxychromatin clearly differentiated, and the cytoplasmic neutrophilic granules lilac or violet pink. The eosinophilic granules are red and each distinctly discernible, so that one may count the individual granules. There should be only a minimum of precipitate. The areas between the cells are clear. The color of the film should be uniform without pale or dark green areas indicative of excessive staining of thick portions of film.

The blood cells appear as follows: erythrocytes, yellow or pink; nuclei, various shades of purple; neutrophilic granules, reddish lilac, sometimes pink; eosinophilic granules, bright red; basophilic granules of leukocytes and degenerated erythrocytes, very dark bluish purple; thrombocytes, dark lilac; bacteria, blue. The cytoplasm of lymphocytes is generally robin's-egg blue; that of the monocytes has a faint bluish tinge. Malarial parasites stain characteristically: the cytoplasm, sky blue; the chromatin, purplish red. These colors are not invariable; two films stained from the same bottle sometimes differ greatly. In general, a preparation is satisfactory when both the nuclei and the neutrophilic granules are distinct, regardless of their color, and when the film is free from precipitated dye. In addition, it is desirable, but not essential, that the erythrocytes be a clear pink or yellowish pink; they should not be blue. The colors are prone to fade if the preparation is mounted in a poor quality of balsam or if it is exposed to the light.

Failure to get satisfactory results with the polychrome methylene-blue-eosin stains, when they are properly used, may be due to imperfect polychroming of the powder but is most frequently due to incorrect reaction of the staining fluid. When the solution is too acid (pH too low), the erythrocytes stain bright red and the nuclei of the leukocytes are pale sky blue or even colorless. When the reaction is too alkaline (pH too high), the erythrocytes stain deep slate blue and there is little differentiation of colors. The reaction of the solution is determined partly by that of the powder when, as is the case with Wright's stain, its reaction is not accurately adjusted, but it depends to a still greater degree on the methyl alcohol, which is prone to develop formic acid as a result of oxidation on standing. A given powder may afford perfect results when dissolved in methyl alcohol from a freshly opened bottle but may produce poor results when dissolved in the same lot of alcohol after it has stood for some months exposed to the air. Deterioration of old solutions is largely due to the same cause. Pathologic blood will sometimes not stain well with solutions that are correct for normal blood.

If American Wright's stain is used, the decolorizer recommended by Schleicher (1942) is useful. Mix 0.5 ml. of acetone and 5.0 ml. of methyl alcohol with 100 ml. of freshly distilled water. After staining with diluted Wright's stain, place the slide in the decolorizer for from one to five seconds. The exact time must be determined for each individual Wright's stain preparation. Wash the decolorizer off the slide with distilled water.

SOME CAUSES OF BAD RESULTS. 1. Causes of excessively blue stain: thick films, overstaining, inadequate washing, or too high an alkalinity of stain or diluent. In such smears the erythrocytes appear blue or green, the nuclear chromatin is deep blue to black, and the granules of the neutrophilic granulocytes are deeply overstained and appear large and prominent. The granules of the eosinophils are blue or gray. Such stain can be corrected by staining for a shorter time with the stain itself and for a longer time with the diluent or by using more stain and less diluent. If these steps are ineffective, the buffer may be too alkaline and a new one should be prepared. When the water is too alkaline, the pH of the buffer may have to be raised to 6.7.

2. Causes of excessively pink stain: insufficient staining; too long a washing; mounting the coverslips before they are dry; or too high an acidity of the stain, buffer, or water. In such smears the erythrocytes are bright red or orange and not pink,

the nuclear chromatin is pale blue, and the granules of the eosinophils are sparkling brilliant red. One of the causes of the increased acidity is exposure of the stain or buffer to acid fumes. The situation may be corrected by a new batch of stain or buffer. If the local tap water is alkaline, using it in place of distilled water may improve the stain.

Causes of pale, inadequately stained red cells, nuclei, or eosinophilic granules: understaining or excessive washing. Prolonging the staining or reducing the washing may solve the problem.

3. Causes of precipitate on the film: unclean slides, drying during the period of staining, inadequate washing of the stain at the end of the staining period, especially failure to hold the slide horizontally during washing or inadequate filtration of the stain, and permitting dust to settle on the slide or smear.

Other useful blood stains. Although Wright's stain suffices for most clinical work and is to be recommended if only one blood stain is to be used, certain other stains demand brief mention.

GIEMSA'S STAIN. This widely used stain is probably the best modification of Romanowsky's stain for demonstrating blood parasites and other protozoa, and it is also highly satisfactory as a routine blood stain. Its composition is as follows:

Azur II-eosin	3.0 gm.
Azur II	0.8 gm.
Glycerin (Merck, C.P.)	250.0 ml.
Methyl alcohol (Kahlbaum I or Merck's reagent	250.0 ml.

The solution is troublesome to make and is best purchased already prepared. Blood films are fixed in methyl alcohol and are then immersed for 20 minutes or longer in a freshly prepared mixture of 1 ml. of stain and 10 ml. of distilled water. In order to prevent precipitate from forming on them, the slides or coverglass should be placed on the edge in the stain. Satisfactory results may also be obtained by placing about 30 drops of distilled water on the fixed film, adding 3 drops of Giemsa's stain, mixing, and allowing it to act for 15 or 20 minutes.

PAPPENHEIM'S PANOPTIC METHOD. In order to combine the advantages of the several stains, Pappenheim recommended the following procedure: Stain for one minute with the May-Grünwald stain; add an equal quantity of water; after one minute, pour off the fluid and stain 15 minutes with the diluted Giemsa solution. The May-Grünwald stain is the same as Jenner's stain. Wright's stain, diluted with an equal quantity of water, may be substituted for Giemsa's stain, but the time of staining should then not exceed five minutes.

JENNER'S STAIN OR THE MAY-GRÜN-WALD STAIN. Jenner's eosinate of methylene blue, dissolved in methyl alcohol, brings out leukocytic granules well and is, therefore, especially useful for differential counting. It stains nuclei poorly and is much inferior to Wright's stain for the detection of malarial parasites since it does not produce the so-called Romanowsky staining.

It may be purchased in solution, in the form of tablets, or as a powder, 0.5 gm. of which should be dissolved in 100 ml. of neutral absolute methyl alcohol. The unfixed blood film is covered with the staining solution and after three to five minutes is rinsed with water, dried in the air, and mounted.

CARBOLTHIONIN BLUE. Carbolthionin blue is especially useful for the study of basophilic granular degeneration of the erythrocytes. Nuclei, malarial parasites, and basophilic granules are brought out sharply. Polychromatophilia is also evident. The films can be fixed with an alcoholic solution of formalin or saturated solution of mercuric chloride.

PAPPENHEIM'S METHYL GREEN PY-RONINE. Pappenheim's methyl green pyronine can be used as a blood stain and is very satisfactory for study of the erythrocytes and lymphocytes and for demonstration of Döhle's inclusion bodies. All nuclei are blue to reddish purple; basophilic granules, cytoplasm of lymphocytes, and inclusion bodies are red. Polychromatophilia is well demonstrated, the affected cells taking more or less of the red color. Heat fixation is probably best.

Study of Stained Blood Films

It has been said with much truth that an intelligent study of the stained film, together with an estimation of the concentration of hemoglobin, will yield 90 per cent of all the diagnostic information obtainable by examination of the blood. The stained films furnish the best means of studying the morphology of the blood and blood parasites, and, to an experienced person, they give a fair idea of the amount of hemoglobin and of the number of erythrocytes

and leukocytes. An oil immersion objective is required.

ERYTHROCYTES

Normally the erythrocytes are acidophilic. The colors they take with different stains have been described. In a healthy person the erythrocytes, when not crowded together, appear as circular, homogeneous disks of nearly uniform size, ranging from 6 to 8 microns in diameter (Fig. 4–25).

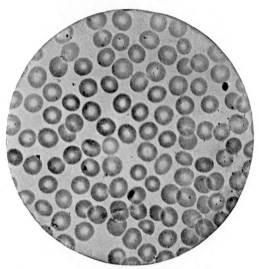

Figure 4–25. Erythrocytes of normal blood.

However, even in normal blood, there may be individual cells as small as 5.5 microns and as large as 9.5 microns. The center of each is somewhat paler than the periphery. Erythrocytes are liable to be crenated when the film has dried too slowly. In disease, erythrocytes vary in their hemoglobin content, size, shape, staining properties, and structure.

Hemoglobin Content. The depth of staining furnishes a rough guide to the amount of hemoglobin in the erythrocytes. When the amount of hemoglobin is diminished, the central pale area becomes larger and paler. This is known as hypochromia. In pernicious anemia, on the other hand, many of the erythrocytes may stain deeply and lack the pale center entirely.

Variations in Size and Shape

The erythrocytes may be abnormally small (microcytes, 5 microns or less in diameter) (Plate 4–1 [1]); abnormally large

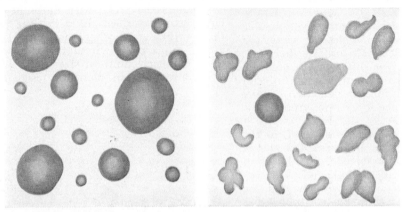

1. Anisocytosis: microcytes and macrocytes   2. Poikilocytosis

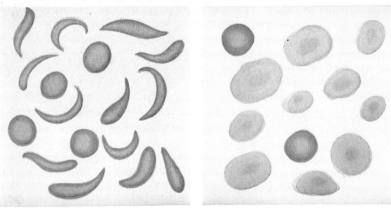

3. Sickle cells   4. Target cells (polychromatophilia)

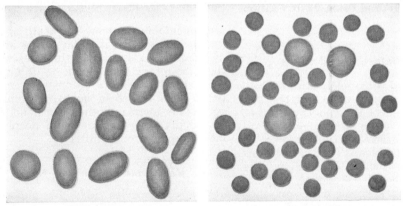

5. Ovalocytes   6. Spherocytes

Plate 4–1. Variations in size and shape of erythrocytes. (Dorothy Booth, pinx.)

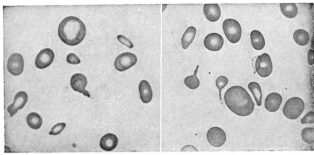

Figure 4–26. Erythrocytes showing variations in size and shape, from a case of pernicious anemia (× 750).

(macrocytes, 10 to 12 microns), or very large (megalocytes, 12 to 25 microns) (Plate 4–1 [1]). Abnormal variation in size is called anisocytosis (Plate 4–2, Fig. 4–26).

Variation in shape is often marked. Oval, pear shaped, saddle shaped, club shaped, and irregularly shaped erythrocytes are common (Fig. 4–26). These are called poikilocytes, and their presence is spoken of as poikilocytosis (Plate 4–1 [2]). Elliptic erythrocytes have been reported in healthy persons as an hereditary anomaly (ovalocytosis or elliptocytosis) (Plate 4–1 [5]), which is inherited as a mendelian dominant. Its association with anemia will be discussed later.

Spherocytes are nearly spherical erythrocytes in contradistinction to normal biconcave disks. Their diameter is smaller than normal. They lack the central pale area. They show increased fragility in hypotonic salt solutions and are found in hereditary spherocytosis and in smaller numbers in some cases of acquired hemolytic anemia (Plate 4–1 [6]). "Target cells" are erythrocytes that are thinner than normal (leptocytes) and when stained show a peripheral rim of hemoglobin with a dark, central, hemoglobin containing area. The two are separated by a pale unstained ring, which contains less hemoglobin (Plate 4–1 [4]). These cells seem to be more resistant to hypotonic salt solution than are normal erythrocytes. They are found in various chronic anemias and are particularly numerous in hereditary leptocytosis (thalassemia).

Erythrocytes that vary from the normal size and shape are present in most types of anemia, and in the severer types of anemia they are often very numerous. Irregularities are particularly conspicuous in leukemia and pernicious anemia; in some cases a normal erythrocyte is the exception. In pernicious anemia anisocytosis is especially pronounced with extremely large cells,

macrocytes, megalocytes, and oval forms, which are present side by side with microcytes. Megalocytes are rarely found in any other condition.

Variations in Staining Properties

The variations include polychromatophilia, basophilic granular degeneration, and malarial stippling.

Polychromatophilia. The affected erythrocytes do not show normal affinity for acid stains and, instead, take the basic stain (Plate 4–3 [2]). Wright's stain gives such cells a bluish tinge ranging from faint to fairly deep. The color is a mixture of the blue of residual ribonucleic acid and the red of hemoglobin. The cells are larger than normal. They lack the pale center. A supravital stain, i.e., brilliant cresyl blue, shows these to be reticulocytes. Consequently about 1 per cent of them is present in the normal person and more when regeneration is more active. They are most abundant in malaria, leukemia, pernicious anemia, and hemolytic anemia.

Basophilic Stippling (Basophilic Granular Degeneration; Basophilic Aggregation; Punctate Basophilia). This is characterized by the presence, within the erythrocyte, of irregular basophilic granules, which vary in size from scarcely visible dots to granules nearly as large as those of basophilic leukocytes (Fig. 4–27, Plate 4–3 [3]). The number

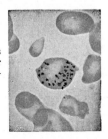

Figure 4–27. Erythrocytes showing basophilic granular degeneration with large granules (× 1000).

of these granules present in an erythrocyte commonly varies in inverse ratio to their

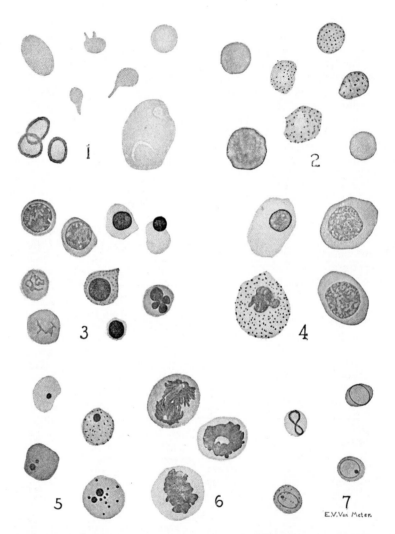

E.V.Van Meter.

Plate 4–2. Abnormal erythrocytes. All drawn from actual specimens and all stained with Wright's stain except where noted (× 1000) (1 mm. = 1 micron). 1. Variations in size, shape, and hemoglobin content; from cases of pernicious anemia and iron deficiency anemia. 2. Polychromatophilia and basophilic granular degeneration in cases of lead poisoning and pernicious anemia. 3. Normoblasts, reticulated erythrocytes, and one microblast; the top row represents stages in the development of the normoblast. The two reticulated erythrocytes are stained with brilliant cresyl blue. 4. Megaloblasts in pernicious anemia. Two show polychromatophilia and fairly typical nuclei, two have condensed nuclei, and one of these has basophilic cytoplasmic granules. 5. Nuclear particles or Howell-Jolly bodies. One cell also shows basophilic granular degeneration. 6. Mitotic figures. 7. Cabot's ring bodies. Two cells also contain nuclear particles and one shows basophilic granular degeneration (Leishman's stain). (E. V. Van Meter, pinx.)

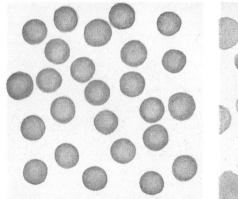

1. Normal erythrocytes   2. Polychromatophilia

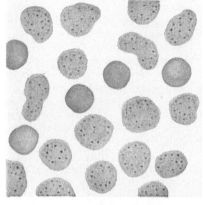

3. Basophilic stippling   4. Howell-Jolly bodies

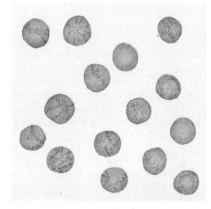

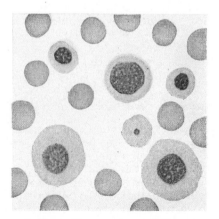

5. Reticulocytes   6. Normoblasts and megaloblasts

Plate 4–3.   Normal and abnormal erythrocytes. (Dorothy Booth, pinx.)

size. They stain deep blue with carbolthionin blue or Wright's stain. The erythrocyte containing them may stain normally in other respects or it may exhibit polychromatophilia. Polychromatophilic erythrocytes generally contain small granules, which may be so fine that the erythrocytes appear dusted with them. Basophilic stippling may also be seen in nucleated red cells. Stippling is attributed to degenerative changes in the cytoplasm involving ribonucleic acid in the young cell.

In industries employing lead, health control includes counting stippled cells in 50 fields of 50 cells each (a total of 2500 erythrocytes). The presence of 11 or more stippled cells per 2500 red cells is an indication of excessive exposure and of the need of correction. Stippling is a sign of exposure and not of lead poisoning. There is no direct relationship between the number of stippled red cells and the degree of toxicity.

Stippled cells can probably be found in every case in which there are clinical symptoms of lead poisoning, and in some cases of severe poisoning they are present in nearly every microscopic field. Except in lead exposure, the degeneration indicates a serious blood disease. It is present in severe pernicious anemia and leukemia and, much less commonly, in other forms of severe anemia.

Malarial Stippling. This term has been applied to the finely granular appearance of erythrocytes that harbor the parasites of tertian malaria. It was formerly classed with basophilic stippling but is undoubtedly different. Not all stains show it. With Wright's stain it can be brought out by staining longer and washing less than usual when ordinary blood is examined. The minute granules, "Schüffner's granules," stain purplish red. They are sometimes so numerous that they almost hide the parasites. These red cells are, as a rule, larger than normal.

Variations in Structure

The most important variation in the structure of erythrocytes in the peripheral blood is the absence of a nucleus. As a rule the nucleus in normoblasts is small, round, and sharply defined. The structure of these nuclei is different from that of the nuclei of leukocytes. As a rule, they are the most deeply stained nuclei to be seen in the blood film, being approached in this respect only by the nuclei of the smaller lymphocytes. Young normoblasts are large. Their nuclei are relatively large, and the chromatin is arranged in a more or less reticular manner with clean-cut open spaces. The openings are arranged at the periphery and, with the chromatin bars between them, suggest a wheel with broad spokes. Mitosis may be seen occasionally, especially in leukemia and untreated pernicious anemia. The cytoplasm is blue, with a mixture of red or purple as evidence of hemoglobin formation (basophilic normoblast, prorubricyte). The older normoblasts are smaller. Their nuclei also are smaller and more dense; some are entirely homogeneous and stain very deeply (pyknotic nuclei). These are likely to be situated eccentrically and sometimes appear as if they are being extruded from the normoblasts. These characteristics are shown in Figure 4–28.

With increased production of hemoglobin the blue color of the cytoplasm is progressively replaced by red (polychromatophilic normoblast: rubricyte) until it assumes the orange color of the normoblast (orthochromatic normoblast: metarubricyte). It is important to distinguish the younger normoblasts from the older ones. As a result of degenerative changes, the nuclei may be irregular in shape (Fig. 4–29) and clover-leaf forms are common. On the other hand, they may be completely broken up into fragments—the so-called Howell-Jolly bodies (Fig. 4–30) of which all but one or two may have disappeared from the normoblast. These particles are smooth, round remnants of the parachromatin of the nucleus (Plate 4–3 [4]).

The megaloblast (Plate 4–3 [6], Fig. 4–31) is a distinct cell, not merely a larger normoblast. It is present in pernicious anemia and in related macrocytic anemias. The cells of this series are not found in the normal marrow. They are all larger than the corresponding cells of the normal series. Deficiency of vitamin B_{12} or folic acid is responsible. The result is abnormal nucleic acid synthesis and defective development of the nucleus. The cells grow longer without dividing. Iron hemoglobin synthesis is as a rule essentially normal. The result of the discrepancy in the growth of the nucleus and cytoplasm is the formation of abnormally large cells with an increased amount of hemoglobin in the cytoplasm and an immature nuclear chromatin pattern.

The morphologic differences including the abnormally large size are due to the

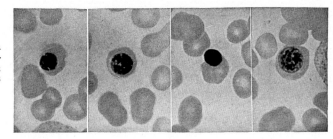

Figure 4–28. Normoblasts from cases of secondary anemia and leukemia. The next to the last is oldest; the last is the youngest of the series (× 1000).

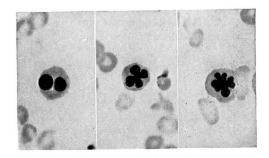

Figure 4–29. Normoblasts with irregular and fragmented nuclei (× 1000).

Figure 4–30. Nuclear particles or Howell-Jolly bodies in erythrocytes. From a case of pernicious anemia (× 1000).

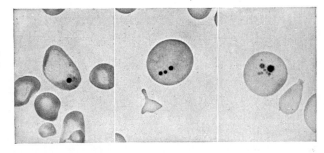

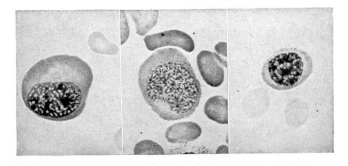

Figure 4–31. Megaloblasts showing typical nuclei; from cases of pernicious anemia (× 1000).

disproportionate maturation of the nucleus and the cytoplasm of the megaloblast, the nucleus developing much more slowly than the cytoplasm.

In the typical megaloblast (rubriblast of the pernicious anemia type) the nucleus is characteristic. The youngest cell of the series usually has nucleoli. It is large, round, or oval. The cytoplasm stains deeply blue with a light juxtanuclear zone. It has a more delicate chromatin network with larger and more numerous openings than has the nucleus of the normoblast at the corresponding stage of development (Fig. 4–31). Sometimes it appears as if it were composed of coarse granules.

As the megaloblast grows older and goes through the stages from promegaloblast (the mother cell of this series)—through basophilic megaloblast and polychromatophilic megaloblast to orthochromatic megaloblast, the nucleus becomes smaller (Fig. 4–32) and the chromatin denser, coarser, and more solidly stained. Nuclei of megaloblasts at the end stages of development may show degenerative changes (pyknosis, karyorrhexis). The end stage is a megalocyte, a larger anuclear cell without the central pale zone of the normocyte and as a rule with abundant hemoglobin. At the same time, the entire megaloblast becomes smaller and the cytoplasm shows less tendency to polychromatophilia. The recognition of megaloblasts is important, but is not always easy unless the nucleus is typical. Mitosis may occur as in the nuclei of normoblasts (Fig. 4–33).

Young nucleated erythrocytes, especially megaloblasts, are prone to exhibit polychromatophilia. In some nucleated erythrocytes, the cytoplasm is so blue and shows so little of its characteristic smooth texture that it is difficult to recognize the cell as an erythrocyte except by the character of the nucleus. Such erythrocytes are often mistaken for lymphocytes or for Türk's irritation leukocytes, an error that careful observation of the nucleus usually will prevent.

Cabot's rings are ring-shaped, figure-of-eight, or loop-shaped structures (Fig. 4–34). Occasionally they are formed by double or several concentric lines. They have been observed rarely in erythrocytes in pernicious anemia, lead poisoning, and lymphatic leukemia. They stain red or reddish purple with Wright's stain and have no internal structure (on close examination they are seen to consist of fine granules). In addition to Cabot's rings, erythrocytes may occasionally contain basophilic granules, nuclear fragments, or even complete nuclei.

The rings have been thought to be the remains of a nuclear membrane. However, Schleicher (1942) stated that Cabot's ring bodies are neither nuclear remnants nor identical with the nuclear membrane, but are laboratory creations—denatured and

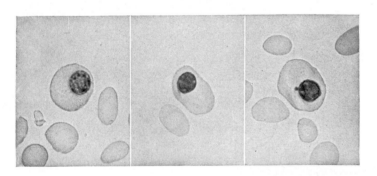

Figure 4–32. Small (aged) megaloblasts with condensed nuclei (× 1000).

Figure 4–33. Two megaloblasts in the process of mitosis. Mitotic figures are often seen in the blood especially in leukemia (× 1000).

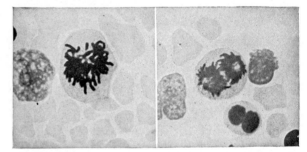

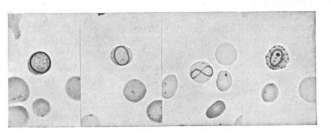

Figure 4–34. Cabot's ring bodies, Leishman's stain (× 1000).

aggregated colloid protein in cellular degeneration induced by hemolytic agents. According to others they represent endoplastic reticulum coated with ribonucleic acid. They are interpreted as evidence of defective regenerative activity.

SIGNIFICANCE OF NUCLEATED ERYTHROCYTES

Normoblasts are present normally only in the blood of the fetus and of very young infants. In the healthy adult, they are confined to the bone marrow and appear in the circulating blood only in disease, in which their presence denotes an excessive demand made on the blood-forming organs to regenerate erythrocytes. In response to this demand, immature and imperfectly formed cells are thrown into the circulation. Their number, therefore, is usually regarded as an indication of the extent to which the bone marrow reacts rather than of the severity of the disease. A contributing factor may be a "lowered bone marrow threshold," which allows immature cells to pass into the circulation more readily at some times than at others. Occasionally great numbers of nucleated erythrocytes appear rather suddenly. This is called a blood crisis, and the name is rather arbitrarily applied whenever there are more than five nucleated erythrocytes for every hundred leukocytes.

In general, normoblasts appear when regeneration of blood takes place in a normal manner although with excessive activity. They are found in severe anemia, leukemia. and pernicious anemia. They are often abundant in granulocytic leukemia. In pernicious anemia they are often difficult to find. In erythroblastosis fetalis, there are abnormally large numbers of normoblasts. This disease of the newborn is characterized by splenomegaly, an enlarged liver, jaundice, and a macrocytic anemia if the disease is caused by Rh (blood factor) incompatibility. If the disease is caused by AB blood factor incompatibility, varying numbers of spherocytes are present, but macrocytes are rare or absent. Nuclear particles, or Howell-Jolly bodies, are common in untreated pernicious anemia and have been noted in greatest numbers after splenectomy.

The presence of megaloblasts indicates a change in the type of blood formation. This is seen most characteristically in pernicious anemia, and the presence of megaloblasts in the marrow is therefore important in the diagnosis of this disease, although less significance is attached to them than formerly. They are probably present in every case of untreated disease but may be rare in patients treated adequately with vitamin B_{12} or folic acid. In patients who have not been treated adequately, they may exceed normoblasts in number—a ratio that is extremely rare in other diseases in which they have been found.

LEUKOCYTES

The total white blood cell count is determined in the counting chamber (see p. 84 ff.). The same applies to the eosinophils for which a special counting chamber is available. The percentage distribution of the different types of leukocytes and the qualitative study is done on a stained smear. Such study is called differential count. It probably yields more helpful information than any other single procedure used in examination of the blood.

Wright's stain is probably most widely used. A thin blood film is best for the study of details and identification of the cells. One should first glance over the preparation to note the general tinting of leukocytes. Two films stained side by side will often show marked differences in the color reactions of the leukocytes.

To make the differential count, the film is examined carefully with an oil immersion objective, using a mechanical stage. Each leukocyte seen is classified and the percentage of each cell type is calculated. For accuracy, 500 to 1000 leukocytes should be classified. For practical reasons, a smaller number is classified. It is imperative to count leukocytes in all parts of the film, since the different varieties may be unevenly distributed. A record of the count may be kept by placing a mark for each leukocyte in its appropriate column, ruled on paper. It is more convenient to use one of several commercially available recording tabulators (Fig. 4–35). They have a separate key for each type of blood corpuscle, and the percentages can be read directly as the instrument automatically

Figure 4–35. Blood cell calculator.

indicates when 100 corpuscles have been counted. Leukocytes that cannot be classified should be placed together in an unidentified group. In some conditions, notably leukemia, there may be many of these unidentified leukocytes.

The actual number of each variety of leukocyte in a cubic millimeter of blood is easily calculated from these percentages and the total leukocyte count. It should form part of the record if this is to be complete. An increase in actual number is an *absolute increase* and an increase in percentage only, a *relative increase*. It is evident that an absolute increase of any variety may be accompanied by a relative decrease.

One should always make it a rule, when making a differential count, to attempt to estimate the total leukocyte count from the number of leukocytes seen in a field with the low power objective. After some practice, this can be done with a considerable degree of accuracy.

One should remember that in addition to the differential count the examination of the blood smear provides an excellent opportunity to study and to note the morphology of the red cells. The number of nucleated erythrocytes seen while making the count should also be noted in the record.

It is unfortunate that differential leukocyte counts ordinarily made on films on slides are often extremely unreliable owing to irregular distribution of leukocytes, which may be very great in thin films. For this reason, many workers totally condemn the use of slides for differential counting. Undoubtedly good coverglass films allow an accurate differential count but only when every leukocyte on both coverglasses is classified, which is impracticable in routine work, since it requires classification of 8000 to 30,000 leukocytes. The distribution of leukocytes on the coverglass is not, however, more uniform than on properly prepared films on slides. A definite number of leukocytes (100 or 200) is then classified in each of three areas extending across the film—one at the beginning, one in the middle, and one at the end, and reaching to the very edges of the film. When the count is made in this way, the percentage of polymorphonuclear neutrophils (which is taken as the criterion because of the unlikelihood of errors in classification) usually agrees within two points with the true percentage as ascertained by classifying every leukocyte on two coverglass films made from the same sample.

Regarding the nomenclature and classification of some of the leukocytes, particularly those found in pathologic conditions, there is much confusion. We shall try to describe these cells with sufficient clearness to facilitate their recognition and shall, as far as possible, avoid disputed ground, particularly the tangled web of the conflicting theories of histogenesis. The student should thoroughly familiarize himself with the five types of leukocytes found in normal blood and with at least three types that are found in disease. These are myelocytes, myeloblasts, and lymphoblasts.

Table 4–1 shows the average distribution of the various types of leukocytes in the

Table 4–1. Average Distribution of Leukocytes in the Blood of Normal Persons in the United States

TYPE OF LEUKOCYTE	PER CENT
Lymphocytes	25 to 33
Monocytes	2 to 6
Polymorphonuclear neutrophils	60 to 70
Eosinophils	1 to 4
Basophils	0.25 to 0.5

blood of persons in the United States. Recent studies indicate that variations among healthy persons may be greater than has been supposed and that climatic factors or altitude may exert a decided influence. One should, therefore, hesitate to base diagnostic conclusions on slight variations in the differential count unless one has previously determined the normal for the patient.

Normal Types of Leukocytes
Lymphocyte

Lymphocytes are small mononuclear cells without specific cytoplasmic granules. They are about the size of an erythrocyte or slightly larger (6 to 10 microns), although their diameter is influenced to a great degree by the thickness of the film, being greatest in very thin films in which the leukocytes are much flattened. The typical lymphocyte has a single, sharply defined nucleus containing heavy blocks of chromatin. The chromatin stains dark blue with Wright's stain, while the parachromatin stands out as lighter stained streaks; at the periphery of the nucleus, the chromatin is condensed. The cytoplasm stains robin's-egg blue except for a clear perinuclear zone. The characteristic feature of the nucleus is that there is a gradual transition between the chromatin and the parachromatin so that it is practically impossible to tell where chromatin ends and parachromatin begins. The nucleus is generally round but is sometimes indented at one side.

Larger lymphocytes, 12 to 15 microns in diameter, with paler nuclei and more abundant cytoplasm are frequently found, especially in the blood of children, and may be difficult to distinguish from monocytes. The number of large lymphocytes is greater in thin smears, probably because their cytoplasm is easily spread out if more space is available as is the case in thin smears. The misshapen, indented cytoplasmic margins of lymphocytes are due to pressure of neighboring cells. Some believe that the larger forms are young lymphocytes, which become smaller as they grow older. Accordingly, intermediate lymphocytes are present but need not be recorded. Some workers record the large and small lymphocytes separately. In cases of lymphocytosis it is desirable to note the preponderance of one of the two forms, but there is no advantage in separating the large from the small lymphocytes in routine differential counts. In the cytoplasm of about one-third of the large lymphocytes, a variable number (usually five to ten) of rounded, discrete, reddish purple (azurophilic) granules are present. They are larger than the granules of neutrophilic leukocytes and are regarded by some authors as specific for the lymphocyte. Deviations in appearance due to degenerative influences may be seen in the nuclei and cytoplasm. The most frequent are vacuoles.

Lymphocytes are formed in lymphoid tissue, including that of the bone marrow.

They constitute about 20 to 40 per cent of all leukocytes; 1000 to 4000 are present in each cubic millimeter of blood. They are more abundant in the blood of children, averaging about 60 per cent of all leukocytes in the first year of life and decreasing to about 36 per cent in the tenth, the immature cells being especially abundant. Lymphocytes constitute about 5 to 15 per cent of the nucleated cells in the marrow.

The percentage of lymphocytes is usually moderately increased in those conditions that cause leukopenia, especially in pernicious anemia and many debilitating conditions. There is decided absolute and relative increase in the number of lymphocytes at the expense of the polymorphonuclear neutrophils at high altitudes, although the extent of this increase is somewhat uncertain. A similar increase is noted in residents of the tropics and in persons who are much exposed to the sun in temperate zones. When heliotherapy is employed, the percentage of lymphocytes seems to increase in proportion to the degree of tanning of the skin. A marked increase, accompanied by an increase in the total leukocyte count, is seen in pertussis and lymphocytic leukemia (Fig. 4–36). In the former condition, the average percentage of lymphocytes is about 60; in the latter condition, it sometimes exceeds 98. Exophthalmic goiter commonly causes a marked relative lymphocytosis, while simple goiter does not affect the lymphocyte count. In pulmonary tuberculosis, a high percentage of lymphocytes or, especially, a progressive increase is a favorable prognostic sign, while a progressive decline should be looked on with apprehension. A marked increase in the percentage of lymphocytes may be present after induction of

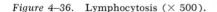

Figure 4–36. Lymphocytosis (× 500).

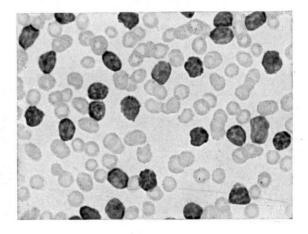

artificial pneumothorax in cases of pulmonary tuberculosis.

There is at present a tendency toward greater conservatism in ascribing diagnostic significance to lymphocytosis of moderate degree, that is, of less than 40 per cent, unless the normal for the individual has been established previously. Lymphocytic percentages as low as 15 and as high as 45 are found occasionally in apparently healthy persons.

MONOCYTE

Monocytes include leukocytes that formerly were classified as large mononuclear leukocytes, endothelial leukocytes, and transitional leukocytes (Fig. 4–37).

The monocyte is the largest corpuscle of normal blood. It generally is about two to three times the diameter of an erythrocyte (14 to 20 microns), although smaller monocytes sometimes are encountered. It contains a single nucleus, which is lobulated, deeply indented, or horseshoe-shaped. Occasionally the nucleus of a monocyte may appear round or oval. Careful inspection and adjustment of the oil immersion lens to observe the nucleus at several levels reveals that even in those cases there is an indentation of the nucleus, which is obscured by the position of the cell.

The zone of protoplasm surrounding the nucleus is relatively wide. With Wright's stain the characteristic feature of the nucleus is for the chromatin to be in strands. There is also a relatively sharp distinction between the chromatin and the parachromatin, which results in a less densely stained nucleus than that seen in the lymphocyte, while the cytoplasm is slate colored, ground glass, or "muddy" in appearance and sometimes appears dusted, uniformly or in patches, with fine reddish granules, which are very much less distinct than the granules of neutrophilic leukocytes. Occasionally bluish granules may be

seen. Digestive vacuoles may be present, occasionally containing phagocytized red cells, debris, pigment, or bacteria. The size of the cell, the width of the zone of cytoplasm, its bluish grey color, evidences of phagocytosis, and the depth of color and the folds and indentations of the nucleus, usually with the absence of peripheral condensation of nuclear chromatin and of a clear perinuclear zone, are the points to be considered in distinguishing monocytes that have a round nucleus from lymphocytes. For comparison, condensation of nuclear chromatin in clumps and at the nuclear margin, a perinuclear clear zone in the cytoplasm, and a homogeneous agranular cytoplasm are characteristic for lymphocytes. It must be borne in mind that the thickness of the film has a great influence on the apparent size of all leukocytes. They are larger and paler when flattened out in very thin films.

Comparatively little is known regarding the origin of the monocytes, and it is possible that more than one cell is included. There have been many reports by Sabin, Doan, and their associates of their studies in hematology with supravital stains (Doan and Wiseman, 1934; Sabin, 1923; Sabin et al., 1925). Monocytes constitute about 2 to 6 per cent of the total number of leukocytes in the peripheral blood—100 to 600 for each cubic millimeter of blood. Only a few pathologic conditions raise this figure to any great degree. A distinct increase, to 15 per cent or even higher, is a feature of the blood in typhoid fever and may be of some value in differential diagnosis. It is also increased in malaria in which many of the monocytes sometimes contain engulfed pigment. In chronic tetrachlorethane poisoning, a progressive increase in the percentage of monocytes (12 to 40 per cent) has been reported. Other conditions in which an increase is usual are subacute bacterial endocarditis, possibly due to proliferation of

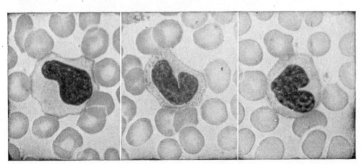

Figure 4–37. Three monocytes from normal blood (× 1000).

capillary endothelium; chronic amebic dysentery; Rocky Mountain spotted fever; trypanosomiasis; and kala-azar.

SEGMENTED NEUTROPHILIC GRANULOCYTE (POLYMORPHONUCLEAR NEUTROPHILIC LEUKOCYTE)

There is usually no difficulty in recognizing these cells. Their average diameter (about 12 microns) is decidedly less than that of the monocytes. The nucleus stains deeply; it is irregular and often assumes shapes comparable to such letters as E, Z, and S (Fig. 4–38). Frequently there appear to be several separate nuclei, hence, the widely used name "polynuclear leukocyte." On careful inspection, however, delicate filaments connecting the segments can usually be seen. Occasionally it may be difficult to recognize whether one is dealing with a segmented or nonsegmented cell, especially in thick smears. In such cases, finding that the margin of a segment can be traced from one side across the narrowed portion to the margin on the other side indicates that the lobes are overlying and that the nucleus is segmented. The cytoplasm is abundant and contains great numbers of fine neutrophilic granules. When stained with Wright's stain, the chromatin of the nucleus is purple and the cytoplasmic granules are lilac, while in the well-stained preparation the cytoplasm itself is light pink or acidophilic.

Segmented neutrophilic granulocytes are formed in the marrow from neutrophilic myelocytes. Ordinarily they constitute 50 to 70 per cent of all the leukocytes, and 3000 to 7000 are present in each cubic millimeter of normal blood. Occasionally, in normal adults, the percentage of these leukocytes may be as low as 40 or as high as 80. In children, the average varies from about 35 per cent in the first year to 50 per cent in the tenth. Any marked increase in their number practically always produces an increase in the total leukocyte count. The leukocytes of pus, pus corpuscles, belong almost wholly to this variety.

In infectious and inflammatory conditions, notably pneumonia and appendicitis, a comparison of the percentage of neutrophilic granulocytes with the total leukocyte count yields more information than a consideration of either alone. In a general way, as was first pointed out by Sondern (1906), the percentage represents the severity of the infection, or, more correctly, the degree of toxic absorption, and the response to the exogenous leukocytosis stimulating factor, while the total count indicates the patient's power of resistance. With moderate infection and good resisting powers, the leukocyte count and the percentage are increased proportionately. When the neutrophilic percentage is increased to a notably greater extent than is the total number of leukocytes, no matter how low the count, either a lost resistance or a severe infection may be inferred.

It is a matter of observation that in the absence of acute infectious disease or of inflammation directly in the blood (for example, phlebitis, sigmoid sinusitis, and septic endocarditis), a neutrophilic percentage of 85 or more points very strongly to gan-

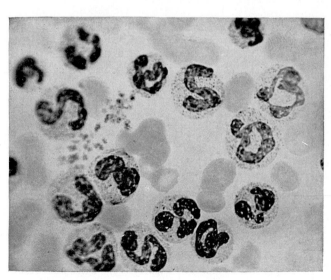

Figure 4–38. Marked polymorphonuclear neutrophilic leukocytosis (× 1000) (courtesy of Dr. W. P. Harlow).

grene or pus formation somewhere in the body. On the other hand, except in children, pus is uncommon with less than 80 per cent of neutrophils.

Exceptions to these rules occur chiefly in cases in which the patients are moribund, in children, and in typhoid and tuberculous infections.

Arneth's Classification of Neutrophilic Polymorphonuclear Granulocytes. Arneth (1904) grouped the polymorphonuclear neutrophilic granulocytes into five classes according to the number of lobes their nuclei possess. Three-fourths of the normal polymorphonuclear neutrophilic granulocytes have two or three nuclear divisions. In all five different classes Arneth numbered from left to right according to whether the leukocytes have one, two, three, four, five, or more segments. By making a count of the neutrophils according to this classification, the percentage indicates the number of youngest cells. An increase of the class with less segments at the expense of the classes with more segments is known as a "shift of the neutrophilic blood picture to the left," while the opposite condition is known as a "shift to the right."

The "Arneth index" at one time was used by adding the first and second classes and half the third class. The average normal is about 60 with variations between 51 and 65. However, the "Arneth index" is little used now, because the simplification known as the Schilling count and the even simpler filament and nonfilament counts are more practical.

The Schilling Count. The original Arneth count has been modified and criticized by many workers. One of these, Schilling (1924, 1929), has developed a much simpler classification. The technique described by this author can be applied in the course of an ordinary differential count by observation of the following forms of leukocytes: basophils, eosinophils, myelocytes, metamyelocytes having many of the characteristics of myelocytes but with indented or bean-shaped nuclei (single-lobed neutrophils), "stab" or band cells, neutrophils with more than one lobe in the nucleus, lymphocytes, and monocytes. A differential count with this classification constitutes a Schilling "hemogram" (Fig. 4–39).

The significant dividing line in the Schilling count lies in the neutrophilic group between the band cells and the cells with a segmented nucleus. In the normal blood film, there are no myelocytes or metamyelocytes, only 3 to 5 per cent of neutrophils with single-lobed nuclei, and 50 to 65 per cent of other neutrophils. A "shift to the left" is seen when the percentage increases to the left of the dividing line. A regenerative shift to the left with a high total leukocyte count occurs in acute septic infection and appendicitis. In these conditions, myelocytes and metamyelocytes appear and there is an increase in the number of band cells. The prognosis in such conditions may be made by subsequent counts; a continued or increased shift to the left is unfavorable, while a shift toward the right is an encouraging sign. There is also a *degenerative shift to the left* with a diminished total white count. There is a marked increase in the percentage of band cells with no appearance of myelocytes or metamyelocytes.

The segmented granulocytes of pernicious anemia are called "macropolycytes." They are about 50 per cent larger by measurement of their diameters than are normal segmented granulocytes. They have more nuclear segments than normal granulocytes.

	LEUKOCYTE COUNT	BASOPHILS	EOSINOPHILS	MYELOCYTES	METAMYELOCYTES OF PAPPENHEIM	BAND CELLS (NEUTROPHILS WITH A SINGLE LOBE)	SEGMENTED NEUTROPHILIC GRANULOCYTES WITH TWO OR MORE LOBED NUCLEI	LYMPHOCYTES	MONOCYTES	THICK DROP OBSERVATIONS AND REMARKS
Normal limits	5000 to 8000	0 to 1 %	2 to 4 %	0 %	0 to 1 %	3 to 5 %	51 to 67 %	21 to 35 %	4 to 8 %	

Figure 4–39. Hemogram (after Schilling).

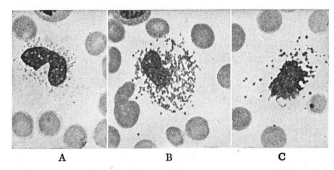

Figure 4–40. Ruptured leukocytes, showing relative size of granules; *A*, neutrophilic; *B*, eosinophilic; *C*, basophilic (× 1000).

A   B   C

They may be present before the other signs of pernicious anemia are present.

EOSINOPHILIC GRANULOCYTE (EOSINOPHIL)

The structure of these cells is similar to that of the polymorphonuclear neutrophils with the striking difference that, instead of the neutrophilic granules, their cytoplasm contains coarse, round or oval granules having a strong affinity for acid stains (Fig. 4–40). They are easily recognized by the size and color of the granules, which stain bright red with stains containing eosin. In well-stained preparations a distinct high-light can be seen on each granule. Their cytoplasm generally has a faint sky-blue tinge, and the nucleus stains somewhat less deeply than that of the polymorphonuclear neutrophils.

Eosinophils are formed in the bone marrow from eosinophilic myelocytes. Their normal number varies from 50 to 250 for each cubic millimeter of blood and they comprise 1 to 4 per cent of the leukocytes. An increase is called eosinophilia, and it is better determined by the actual number per cubic millimeter as calculated than by the percentage.

Marked eosinophilia—above 6 or 7 per cent or above 400 cells per cubic millimeter—is probably always pathologic.

BASOPHILIC GRANULOCYTE (BASOPHIL)

In general, basophilic granulocytes resemble polymorphonuclear neutrophils, except that the nucleus is less irregular (usually merely indented or slightly lobulated) and granules are larger and have a strong affinity for basic stains (Fig. 4–41). They are easily recognized. In some basophils, most of the granules may be missing owing to their ready solubility in water, leaving clean-cut openings in the cytoplasm. The granules then are a mauve color. In a well-prepared smear stained with Wright's stain, the granules are deep purple, while the nucleus is somewhat paler and is often nearly or completely hidden by the granules so that its form is difficult to distinguish. Because of their small numbers, basophils, just as eosinophils, are reported as a group without subdividing them into the various developmental stages.

Unevenly stained granules of basophils may be ring shaped and resemble *Histoplasma capsulatum* or protozoa.

There is some uncertainty as to the origin of the basophilic leukocytes. Most authors believe that they originate in the bone marrow from basophilic myelocytes. They are the least numerous of the leukocytes in normal blood and rarely comprise more than 0.5 per cent of the leukocytes. There usually are 25 to 50 basophils in each cubic millimeter.

Abnormal Types of Leukocytes

MYELOCYTES

Myelocytes are large mononuclear cells that have cytoplasm that is filled with granules (Plates 4–15, 4–16). Typically the nucleus occupies about half of the myelocyte and is round or oval or indented with its convex side in contact with the periphery of the cell. It stains rather feebly and rarely contains nucleoli. The average diameter of myelocytes (about 15 microns) is greater than that of any other leukocyte, but there is much variation in size among individual cells.

Myelocytes are named neutrophilic, eosinophilic, and basophilic myelocytes according to the character of their granules. These granules are identical with the corresponding granules in the leukocytes just described. They are, however, often less distinct and less sharply distinguished by the various stains than those of the corresponding polymorphonuclear leukocytes. In some,

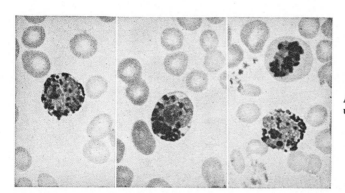

Figure 4–41. Basophilic leukocytes. At the right, in addition, a normoblast undergoing mitosis (× 1000).

the granules are few in number, the cells departing but little from the structure of the parent myeloblast. These are the "promyelocytes." In young neutrophilic myelocytes, there is a tendency to relatively large granules, which take a purple color with Wright's stain. These finally give place to true neutrophilic granules. Sometimes only a portion of the cytoplasm near the nucleus is filled with granules, the periphery, or at least one edge, retaining the smooth basophilic cytoplasm of the parent myeloblast (See Plate 4–16). Although the occurrence of two kinds of granules in the same cell is rare, a few basophilic granules are sometimes seen in young eosinophilic myelocytes. The basophilic myelocyte is usually small, and its nucleus is commonly so pale and so obscured by the granules that the cell is not easily distinguished from more mature forms.

The small neutrophilic cell with a single small, round, deeply staining nucleus, which is sometimes encountered, must not be confused with the myelocyte. Such atypical cells probably result from division of polymorphonuclear neutrophils.

Myelocytes are the bone marrow cells from which the corresponding segmented granular leukocytes are developed. They, in turn, are derived from certain nongranular cells of the bone marrow, the myeloblasts. Their presence in the blood in considerable numbers is diagnostic of granulocytic leukemia. Neutrophilic myelocytes are least significant. A few myelocytes of this type may be present in leukocytosis or in other blood diseases, e.g., pernicious anemia. In the anemia of malignant disease they suggest metastasis to bone marrow. Eosinophilic myelocytes are found, as a rule, only in granulocytic leukemia in which they are often numerous. Basophilic granulocytes are less common and are con-

fined to long standing, severe granulocytic leukemia.

MYELOBLASTS

Myeloblasts are the parent cells of the myelocytes from which they differ chiefly in the absence of specific granules. They are about the size of myelocytes. Their round or oval nuclei are poor in chromatin, have a finely reticular or so-called sieve-like structure, and contain several rather indistinct nucleoli, which are generally pale blue when stained with the usual stain and are outlined by a ring of denser chromatin (Plate 4–19). The cytoplasm, which is generally not abundant, is basophilic and stains blue with Wright's stain. In some preparations, it is characteristically smooth in texture; in others, it is finely reticular.

Myeloblasts appear in the blood in large numbers in acute granulocytic leukemia and in the terminal stages of chronic granulocytic leukemia. Their number is, therefore, important in prognosis. They may be indistinguishable morphologically from the lymphoblasts of acute lymphocytic leukemia but can usually be distinguished by the peroxidase reaction. In almost all cases of advanced granulocytic leukemia, all stages of transition between the myeloblast and myelocyte may be found.

Peroxidase Test. The technique of Goodpasture, which has been found satisfactory, is as follows:

1. Prepare dried films on slides or coverglasses in the usual way.

2. Cover the film with a measured amount of Goodpasture's stain and let stand one minute. The composition of Goodpasture's stain is as follows:

Alcohol	100.00 ml.
Sodium nitroprusside	0.05 gm.
Benzidine (C.P.)	0.05 gm.
Basic fuchsin	0.05 gm.
Hydrogen peroxide	0.5 ml.

Dissolve the nitroprusside in 1 or 2 ml. of water, mix with the alcohol, and then add the other ingredients. In order to secure satisfactory staining of the nuclei, it may be necessary to double the amount of basic fuchsin, owing probably to a difference in strength of dye.

Goodpasture's stain remains good only a few days. Without the hydrogen peroxide, the stain will give satisfactory results for about eight months. A freshly made 1 to 200 dilution of hydrogen peroxide is then used in place of water for diluting the stain on the slide. This solution is made with sufficient accuracy by adding 2 drops of hydrogen peroxide to 15 ml. of distilled water.

3. Add an equal amount of water or of the 1 to 200 dilution of hydrogen peroxide if the modification described in the preceding paragraph is used.

4. Rinse well in water, dry by blotting, and examine with an oil immersion objective. When stained by this method, the nuclei are clear red, the cytoplasm and thrombocytes are pale pink, and the erythrocytes are a buff color. Cells that give the peroxidase reaction — polymorphonuclear neutrophils, eosinophils, myelocytes, and occasionally a few granules in monocytes— contain sharply defined, deep blue granules. Such granules are lacking in lymphocytes.

Osgood and Ashworth Modification. A modification of Washburn's method by Osgood and Ashworth (1937) has been recommended as trustworthy.

Reagents

Solution 1

Alcohol	99.0 ml.
Benzidine	0.3 gm.

Dissolve

Add saturated aqueous solution of sodium nitroprusside	1.0 ml.

Solution (1) keeps well for 8 to 10 months

Solution 2

Distilled water	25.0 ml.
Fresh 3 per cent hydrogen peroxide	0.3 ml.

Test. Air dried films should be stained as soon as possible, preferably within 3 to 4 hours but definitely not later than within 12 hours after the blood has been obtained.

Procedure

1. Add ten drops of solution 1 on slide for one to one and a half minutes.

2. Add five drops of solution 2.

3. Let stand for three to four minutes.

4. Wash slide in tap water for three to four minutes.

5. Stain with Wright's stain.

Results

In neutrophilic granulocytes, there are many large blue-black granules.

In promyelocytes, the granules are fewer.

In monocytes, the granules are few, small, and blue-green.

In eosinophils, the granules are large and bronze colored.

In basophils, vacuole-like spaces remain because the granules of basophils are water soluble.

LYMPHOBLASTS

In acute lymphocytic leukemia there appears in the blood a high percentage of very young cells of the lymphocytic series that are called lymphoblasts. In many cases they are indistinguishable from the large or immature lymphocytes previously described as occasionally occurring in the blood of normal adults and more frequently in that of children. Azure granules are sometimes seen in the cytoplasm and the nucleus generally contains nucleoli (Plates 4–20, 4–21). At times the nucleus is curiously lobulated and the name "Rieder's cell" is then applied.

Lymphoblasts are sometimes morphologically indistinguishable from myeloblasts but do not give the peroxidase reaction.

TÜRK'S IRRITATION LEUKOCYTE

These are large, mononuclear, nongranular cells with a dense, opaque, strongly basophilic cytoplasm, which often contains vacuoles. With Wright's and similar stains, the cytoplasm stains almost as intensely as the nucleus although of a different color, being deep blue while the nucleus is deep purplish red. The nuclear chromatin shows no tendency to radial arrangement. Nucleoli are usually present.

The nature of the irritation leukocytes is not definitely known, and at present no diagnostic importance can be ascribed to them. Considerable numbers have been found in the blood conditions associated with irritation of the bone marrow, notably anemia, leukemia, and malaria and in the leukocytosis of pneumonia.

PLASMA CELLS

Morphologically, plasma cells are very similar to Türk's irritation leukocytes. The nucleus of the plasma cell may show a tendency toward a radial or "wheel-like" arrangement of its chromatin (see Plate 4–4).

Plasma cells are considered by some hematologists to be an altered form of the lymphocyte, the same cell that appears frequently at the site of certain types of chronic inflammation. Many hematologists believe that they develop directly from reticulum cells. They are rare in the circulating blood. Atypical plasma cells have diagnostic significance in multiple myeloma (Plate 4–22).

Degenerated Forms

Degenerated forms of leukocytes are frequently encountered but have no significance unless they are present in large numbers. They include vacuolated leukocytes and bare nuclei from ruptured cells. The former are found most frequently in cases of toxemia and leukemia. A few of the latter are present in every blood film but are especially abundant in leukemia (Fig. 4–42). They vary from fairly well-preserved nuclei without cytoplasm to mere strands of palely stained nuclear substance arranged in a coarse network—the so-called basket cells (Fig. 4–43).

Occasionally, in lymphocytic leukemia, frayed-out nuclei without cytoplasm exceed the usual lymphocytes in number. Such nuclei may represent fragile lymphocytes that have been broken in making the film.

Atypical Types

Leukocytes that do not fit in with the classification just discussed are encountered especially in high-grade leukocytosis, pernicious anemia, and leukemia. They are always more abundant in childhood. The nature of many of them is not clear, and their number is usually so small that they may be classed as "undetermined" in making a differential count.

PLATELETS

When stained with Wright's stain or similar stains, platelets or thrombocytes appear as spheric or ovoid, reddish to violet, granular bodies, 2 to 4 microns in diameter. Occasionally a thrombocyte as large as an erythrocyte is seen. When they are well stained, a delicate, pale blue, hyaline ground substance can be distinguished. In ordinary

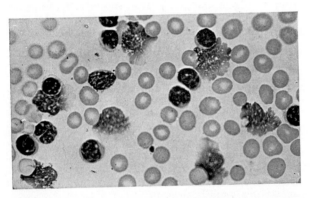

Figure 4–42. Blood in chronic lymphatic leukemia, showing many ruptured lymphocytes (× 750).

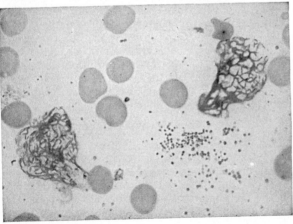

Figure 4–43. Two remnants of degenerated nuclei in a blood film. They are often called "basket cells" (× 1000).

blood films, they are usually clumped in masses. A single thrombocyte lying on an erythrocyte may be mistaken for a malarial parasite by the inexperienced, while unusually large and oval thrombocytes may similarly be mistaken for estivo-autumnal crescents (Fig. 4–44).

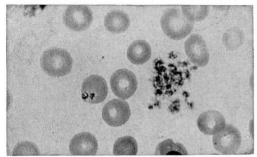

Figure 4–44. A cluster of thrombocytes and two thrombocytes lying on an erythrocyte and simulating malarial parasites (× 1000).

Thrombocytes have been much studied, but, aside from the facts mentioned under their enumeration, they have limited diagnostic value. At present the accepted explanation of their origin is that of J. H. Wright (1910), who regarded them as detached portions of the cytoplasm of certain giant cells (megakaryocytes) of the bone marrow. The megakaryocyte illustrated in Plate 4–4 is magnified about 500 diameters. If it were drawn to the scale of the other cells, it would be four times as large. The giant cells push cytoplasmic processes into the capillaries, and these break off and appear in the circulating blood as thrombocytes.

Megakaryoblasts, precursors of megakaryocytes, occasionally find their way into the blood, particularly in conditions in which the bone marrow is extremely active, as in granulocytic leukemia. The megakaryocytes are too large to pass the capillaries and are arrested in the lungs, but occasionally the smaller cells may pass the lungs and appear in the peripheral circulation.

HEMATOPOIESIS

A complete consideration of how blood corpuscles are formed in embryonic and adult life belongs in the province of histology and is of little practical importance in clinical laboratory diagnosis. In adult life the bone marrow, lymphoid structures, and connective tissues contain the precursors of the mature cells (hemocytes) found in the circulating blood in normal persons and of the immature cells found in the blood in pathologic conditions. Hematologists do not agree whether the several cells of the circulating blood have a common origin from one type of cell—the unitarian hypothesis of Downey, Ferrata, Pappenheim, and many others—or from two or more primitive blood cells, as advocated by the polyphyletists, represented by Piney, Naegeli, Schilling, Rosenthal, Osgood, Sabin, Cunningham, and Doan, to mention only a few of the well-known hematologists supporting the latter view.

The Unitarian Hypothesis

According to the unitarians, the precursor, or mother cell, of all blood cells is the undifferentiated mesenchymal cell, which is found in the adult as the reticuloendothelial cell, also called reticulum cell, a fixed tissue cell and not a blood cell. This cell has the capacity to develop into any other cell. The first step in its evolution is the stem cell, the least differentiated of the blood cells (Plate 4–4). This cell is also known as the hemohistioblast of Ferrata.

The nucleus is large in relation to the size of the cell; its chromatin is delicate and homogeneous. It contains one or more distinct nucleoli. There may be a narrow, hyaline, clear perinuclear zone. The nuclear membrane is indistinct. The cytoplasm is a deeply blue narrow band.

The Maturation of Erythrocytes. The stem cells are at first morphologically identical, but in the course of further development they give rise to all the other blood cells. The stem cell which gives rise to erythrocytes differentiates into two series of cells: the megaloblastic (the primitive or fetal type) and the normoblastic (the adult type).

The precursor of the megaloblastic series is the promegaloblast (synonyms: erythrogone, embryonic rubriblast). Its nuclear chromatin is slightly coarser, and its cytoplasm more basophilic than in the stem cell. In the next phase, the megaloblast, varying amounts of hemoglobin are present, giving rise to polychromatophilic (partial hemoglobinization) or orthochromatic (complete hemoglobinization) megaloblasts. The chromatin structure of the nucleus shows only moderate condensation. The cytoplasm may contain occasional blue granules. The megalocyte is the mature, anuclear end stage of this series.

The normoblastic series begins with the pronormoblast (synonyms: proerythroblast, prorubricyte). Its nuclear chromatin is coarsely granular; the cytoplasm is deeply basophilic. The next step is progressive condensation of nuclear chromatin, decrease of the size of the nucleus, and progressively increasing production of hemoglobin. This is the normoblast. The changes in the nucleus and cytoplasm permit recognition of early and late, polychromatophilic and orthochromatic normoblasts. In this stage a so-called Howell-Jolly body may be present—a small pyknotic mass of nuclear chromatin. The erythrocyte is a normoblast minus the nucleus; supravital stain brings out a network of dots and filaments in the polychromatophilic erythrocyte, the reticulocyte. The final phase is the normocyte, the orthochromatic normal mature erythrocyte, completely devoid of nuclear remnants, not demonstrable even with supravital stains.

The Maturation of Granulocytes. The stem cell gives rise to the myeloblast, the mother cell of this series. It is as a rule completely free of granules, although a few bright red, so-called azurophilic granules may be present. The nucleus contains one or more nucleoli. The maturation of the myeloblast proceeds along two parallel lines. One line of progression involves the nucleus; the other involves a chemical reaction that results in the formation of neutrophilic, eosinophilic, and basophilic granules.

The first stage is the transformation into a promyelocyte, the largest of the series, with beginning condensation of the nuclear chromatin, disappearance of the nucleoli, and the appearance of a small number of cytoplasmic granules, which are a mixture of azurophilic and of the specific granules.

In the second stage, the myelocyte, the nucleus is round or oval and the condensation of the nuclear chromatin is still farther advanced. The cytoplasmic granules are fully developed and abundant so that they may obscure the outline of the nucleus. In the third stage, the metamyelocyte, the nucleus becomes indented and kidney shaped, its chromatin more clumped.

In the fourth stage, the change to a band-shaped nucleus is what gave it the name of the band or staff cell, or rhabdocyte. In the fifth stage, the nucleus becomes segmented and the segments are connected with filaments of varying thickness. With progressive maturation the number of segments increases. The prognostic implications of the presence of immature granulocytes in the peripheral blood will be discussed later. The preceding description

of the maturation of the neutrophilic granulocytes applies to eosinophilic and basophilic granulocytes but with a few minor deviations.

The eosinophilic segmented granulocytes rarely have more than two segments. The granules are large, bright red, and discrete in the mature cell but may be dark gray or purplish in the immature cell.

In the basophilic series, the myelocyte has fewer granules than the corresponding neutrophilic or eosinophilic cell. The basophilic granules are coarse and irregular in all the cells of this series.

The Monocytic Series. The monoblast is the mother cell. It is a large cell, larger than the corresponding cells of the other two series. Nucleoli are prominent. The cytoplasm is finely granular and basophilic. In the next stage, the promonocyte, the nucleus tends to become indented; the cytoplasm contains a small number of slightly azurophilic granules, usually aggregated in the area of the nuclear indentation. The mature monocyte is the largest white blood cell in the peripheral blood. The indentation or lobation of the nucleus, its finely reticulated chromatin structure, and the delicate, diffuse granulation of the cytoplasm are characteristic and consistent features of this cell.

The Maturation of Platelets. The megakaryoblast, the largest of the marrow cells, is the mother cell of the platelet or thrombocyte. It has distinct and prominent nucleoli; the nuclear chromatin is dense and reticulated; and the cytoplasm is bluish gray, occasionally with a deeper bluish tinge at the periphery and a clear perinuclear zone. In the next stage, the promegakaryocyte, the nucleus becomes multilobulated; the cytoplasm increases in volume; and granules, at first azurophilic and later reddish purple, appear. In the mature megakaryocyte, platelets with eosinophilic granules appear; the cell becomes huge and irregularly shaped; platelets can be seen to separate and enter the peripheral circulation. The platelets or thrombocytes are fragments of megakaryocytic cytoplasm. They normally measure 2 to 4 microns. They consist of a refractile, granular, reddish purple chromomere or granulomere and a homogeneous hyalomere.

The Maturation of the Lymphocyte. The lymphoblast is the mother cell of the lymphocytic series. Its nuclear chromatin is somewhat coarse; its nucleoli are more distinct but are few, usually not more than two; and its basophilic cytoplasm is somewhat more abundant than the same cell components in the myeloblast or monoblast. The next stage, the prolymphocyte, occurs in two sizes, the large and small. Its chromatin is more densely clumped than is the case in the other blood cells at the same stage of development. There is, as a rule, a simple but distinctly outlined nucleolus. The cytoplasm is deeply blue and homogeneous.

The third stage, the lymphocyte, is seen in three sizes, large, intermediate, or small. The three differ not only in size, as indicated by the designation, but in addition, a disproportionately large amount of cytoplasm appears in the large lymphocyte, a small number of azurophilic granules appear in the cytoplasm of the intermediate lymphocyte (also called mesolymphocyte), and a disproportionately small amount of cytoplasm and particularly dense and clumped chromatin appear in the small lymphocyte.

The extreme unitarians believe that the lymphocyte is a multipotential cell and that it may, under certain abnormal circumstances, become dedifferentiated to the stage of a stem cell and be capable of differentiating again into any other blood cell.

The mother cell of the plasma cell is the plasmablast (synonyms: lymphoblastic plasma cell, Türk's irritation cell). The main difference between this cell and the more mature forms is the immaturity and lack of condensation of the nuclear chromatin. Nucleoli may be present although frequently indistinct. The cytoplasm is deeply blue, homogeneous, and devoid of granules.

In the second stage, the proplasmacyte is, as a rule, a tissue cell and represents an intermediate phase in the development toward the third and the most mature stage of this series, the plasma cell or plasmacyte (synonym: Marshalko cell). Its cytoplasm is abundant and deeply blue; its nucleus, as a rule, is eccentric; and its nuclear chromatin is dense and clumped and frequently presents a so-called cartwheel arrangement. The perinuclear clear zone is sharp and distinct from the basophilic cytoplasm.

The Origin of Plasma Cells. They are thought to be derived from lymphocytes. However, it is possible or even probable that other cells of the blood or tissues and even fibroblasts may develop into plasma cells.

BLOOD FORMATION

Sites of Blood Formation. Undifferentiated cells of the mesenchyme and endothelial cells of the primitive blood spaces give rise to blood cells in the embryo. Later, in due course, production of blood cells becomes organoid and the liver and spleen become the main sites. Eventually the bone marrow takes over. At birth, the marrow is active and red and contains only minimal amounts of fat. Later in childhood, only the proximal portions of the long bones and the flat bones (the skull, vertebrae, thoracic cage, shoulder, and pelvis) are the sites of blood formation. The rest of the marrow space is occupied by fat, which remains the reserve space for life. It contains stem cells capable of rapid growth and reproduction when the need arises.

Production of Blood Cells. Blood cells are formed from preexisting cells. Depending on the maturity of the cell at the time of multiplication, the division may be heteroplastic when multipotent mesenchymal embryonal cells are dividing. These cells are capable of giving rise to more than one cell form. The division is homoplastic when a more differentiated cell gives rise by mitotic division to two cells of the same kind.

CELL DIFFERENTIATION

This means acquisition of functional properties, which range from phagocytosis, an example of a relatively primitive function, to the production of complex proteins and of various structures essential for body economy.

TISSUE CELLS AND BLOOD CELLS

The former are fixed (e.g., fibrocytes and muscle cells) or are endowed with ability to move about, as a rule in response to chemical stimuli (e.g., fibroblasts and tissue leukocytes). Blood cells of the peripheral blood or hemocytes get into the circulation by being shed into circulating blood or lymph in the growing marrow and lymphoid tissues (red cells and possibly lymphocytes) or by migrating into blood with the help of ameboid motion (granulocytes).

Nomenclature

There is much confusion concerning the nomenclature and classification of cells of the blood and bone marrow. Every individual attempt to clarify this situation seems only to lead to further confusion. In 1947 a committee, sponsored by the American Society of Clinical Pathologists and the

(Text is continued on p. 142.)

Plate 4–4. Development of blood cells. This plate comprises a survey of all blood cells. The horizontal double line separates the cells that are found in the marrow and in lymphoid tissue from the mature cells below the line seen normally in the peripheral blood. The first of the two vertical double lines separates the cells produced exclusively in the marrow from the cells of the monocytic series. The second vertical double line in the upper part of the plate separates the two types of immature cells of extramedullary origin, lymphoblasts and plasmoblasts.

1. The cells near the top of the plate have a characteristically basophilic cytoplasm, are free from granules, and have large, round, or slightly oval nuclei with a delicate chromatin structure (with the exception of the nucleus of the plasma cell in the left upper corner, which will be discussed in more detail later). As presented, the primitive erythrocyte, the basophilic proerythroblast, the primitive granulocyte, the myeloblast, and the young megakaryocyte, the megakaryoblast, originate directly from the primitive reticulum cell. Blue nucleoli are seen in the nuclei of the proerythroblast, myeloblast, and lymphoblast.

Certain changes take place with progressive maturation of all blood cells. Some are common to all of them; some are different and specific for each type.

As one descends along the line of development from the top of the plate to the bottom, one sees:

The size of the whole cell and of the nucleus decreases in the erythroid, the granulocytic, and the lymphocytic series. The chromatin of the nucleus progressively loses its delicate granular structure and becomes more dense, more coarse, and clumped. The basophilia of the cytoplasm disappears completely in the cells originating in the marrow. The cells of extramedullary origin behave differently. Their cytoplasm remains basophilic but becomes less deep in the lymphocyte; it actually becomes more intense in the plasma cells.

The result of the first transformation of the reticulum cell is a so-called stem cell, a cell that has not declared its allegiance. It is neither fish nor fowl. Maybe that is why it was not included in this plate. At any rate, in the course of differentiation this cell takes on specific characteristics and becomes the proerythroblast, the myeloblast, the monoblast, the megakaryoblast, and the lymphoblast, each the mother cell of a series. From this point on, specific changes take place in each series.

2. *The erythrocyte.* Beginning with the proerythroblast, the deep blue of the cytoplasm decreases somewhat, the nucleus loses its granulation, and the nucleoli vanish; the basophilic normoblast has appeared. At first, small, indistinctly purple patches of forming hemoglobin appear in the cytoplasm. They become confluent and the whole ring of cytoplasm becomes a light purple: the polychromatic normoblast. As the amount of hemoglobin increases, so does the pink of the cytoplasm: the orthochromatic normoblast.

As all this goes on in the cytoplasm, the nucleus shrinks and its chromatin contracts into a small, round, black clump and eventually is thrown out of the cell; the erythrocyte has arrived. The cell still contains a vestige of nuclear chromatin, the reticulum, invisible in smears stained with any of the usual Romanowsky stains but recognizable by the larger size and the faint purplish gray color of the polychromatophilic erythrocyte. In a smear vitally stained with cresyl blue, for example, the nuclear remnant appears as a delicate blue network of fibrillae and dots, the reticulocyte. At this stage the cell enters peripheral blood; the reticulum disappears progressively until the fully functional mature erythrocyte has evolved.

3. *The granulocyte.* Again from the primitive reticulum cells, via the stem cell, the myeloblast has evolved.

All these transitions are rapid and distinct when measured in days. Actually they take place slowly when observed from minute to minute. As we see them during this progressive evolution, we cannot always discern the differences, no more than we can set apart a two-year-old child from one two and one-half years old, but we can as a rule distinguish between a two- and four-year-old. And so it is in the case of the five different blast cells. At first we cannot tell them apart, even as we cannot note any differences in the stem cells. In early stages of their embryonal life we have to resort to "judging a cell by the company it keeps."

Now let us go back to the changes taking place in the granulocyte. A most characteristic innovation has taken place. Granules appear in the cytoplasm, at first coarse and of indefinite color. This together with the coarsening of the nuclear chromatin and the disappearance of the nucleoli results in the promyelocyte. According to the plate, a promyelocyte should not be classified as eosinophilic, neutrophilic, or basophilic. It is just a promyelocyte and nothing else. When the differentiation into the three colors—the red, the deep blue, or the black and the in-between, the neutral—becomes clear cut, the next phase has developed: the myelocyte—the eosinophilic, the basophilic, and the neutrophilic cell. The abundance of granules is frequently so great that the structure and even the outlines of the nucleus are hazy, but its round or oval shape and the progressive coarsening of its chromatin can be made out. The brilliant dazzling red of the discrete eosinophilic granules stands out and is maintained during the remainder of this cell's functional life. Occasionally, in poorly stained smears, the granules of the neutrophilic cell appear coarse and deeper red than they should. The inexperienced may fall into this trap and report eosinophilia where it does not exist. Paying attention to the brilliancy and discreteness of true eosinophils protects against this mistake.

The basophilic myelocyte is just as distinct in its appearance as is the eosinophilic. In this case the tendency to obscure the nucleus is even greater. The granules in the basophilic cells are water soluble, and when exposed to water, the pigment disappears leaving a bunch of grape-like vacuoles.

The changes in the cytoplasm of granulocytes reach their peak in the myelocyte. Nothing of importance happens in the cytoplasm during the subsequent transformations. It is the nucleus that changes. It becomes indented and kidney shaped, and the metamyelocyte has developed. The metamyelocyte is the first cell of the series to break through the marrow-blood barrier normally and then only as an occasional cell. In the next phase, the band form, the shape of the nucleus is just what the name implies. Finally, as the cell ages, the band subdivides into segments connected with thin filaments—first two segments, then three, and so on until the usual maximum of five segments is reached. Presence of more than five segments is a sign of advanced age: polysegmentation, a shift to the right. This progressive segmentation is characteristic for the segmented neutrophilic granulocyte. The eosinophilic and basophilic segmented granulocytes have fewer segments than the neutrophil, as a rule only two segments, rarely more. Eventually, as the cell reaches the end of its useful life, it disintegrates. It swells, its outlines become vague and its cytoplasm loose, its granularity appears structureless, the segments of the nucleus fall apart, and their chromatin congeals, as shown at the bottom of the plate. Complete breakdown is the end.

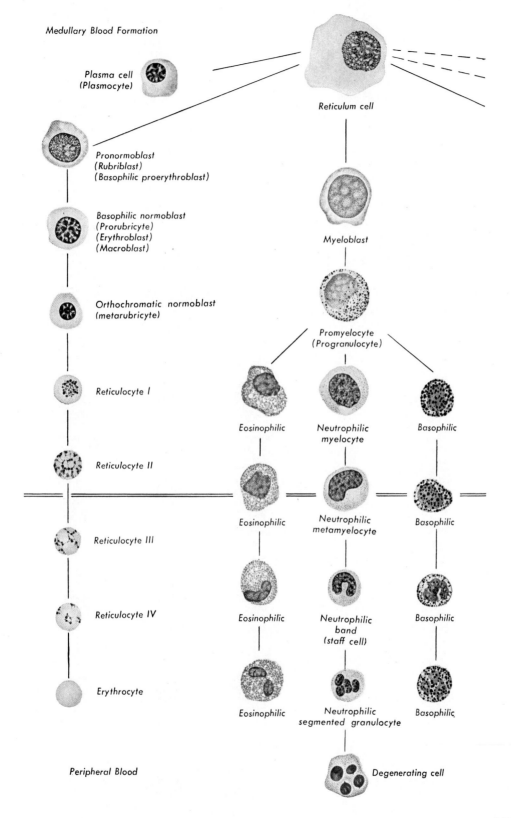

Medullary Blood Formation

Plasma cell
(Plasmocyte)

Reticulum cell

Pronormoblast
(Rubriblast)
(Basophilic proerythroblast)

Myeloblast

Basophilic normoblast
(Prorubricyte)
(Erythroblast)
(Macroblast)

Orthochromatic normoblast
(metarubricyte)

Promyelocyte
(Progranulocyte)

Reticulocyte I

Eosinophilic   Neutrophilic   Basophilic
                       myelocyte

Reticulocyte II

Eosinophilic   Neutrophilic   Basophilic
                      metamyelocyte

Reticulocyte III

Reticulocyte IV

Eosinophilic   Neutrophilic   Basophilic
                         band
                      (staff cell)

Erythrocyte

Eosinophilic   Neutrophilic   Basophilic
                  segmented granulocyte

Peripheral Blood

Degenerating cell

137

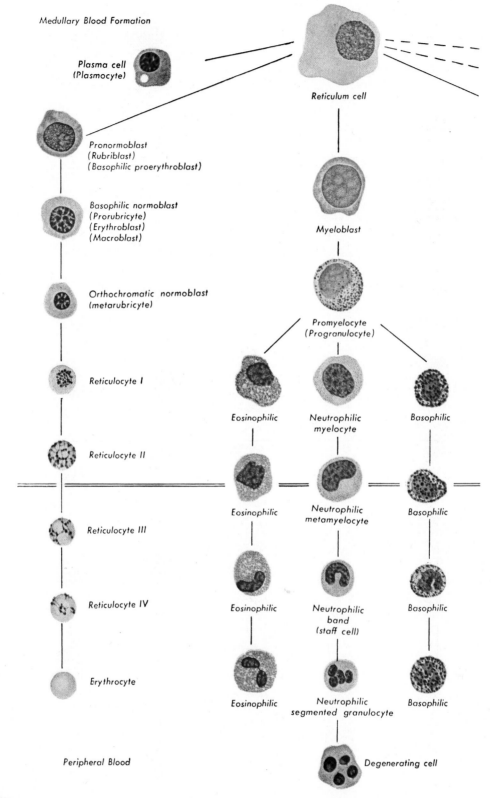

Medullary Blood Formation

Plasma cell
(Plasmocyte)

Reticulum cell

Pronormoblast
(Rubriblast)
(Basophilic proerythroblast)

Basophilic normoblast
(Prorubricyte)
(Erythroblast)
(Macroblast)

Myeloblast

Orthochromatic normoblast
(metarubricyte)

Promyelocyte
(Progranulocyte)

Reticulocyte I

Eosinophilic

Neutrophilic
myelocyte

Basophilic

Reticulocyte II

Eosinophilic

Neutrophilic
metamyelocyte

Basophilic

Reticulocyte III

Reticulocyte IV

Eosinophilic

Neutrophilic
band
(staff cell)

Basophilic

Erythrocyte

Eosinophilic

Neutrophilic
segmented granulocyte

Basophilic

Peripheral Blood

Degenerating cell

138

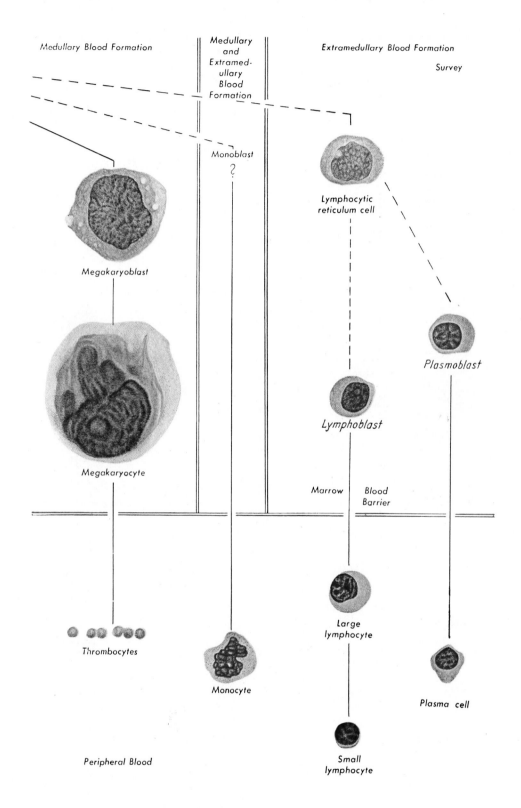

Medullary Blood Formation

Medullary
and
Extramed-
ullary
Blood
Formation

Extramedullary Blood Formation

Survey

Monoblast
?

Megakaryoblast

Lymphocytic
reticulum cell

Megakaryocyte

Plasmoblast

Lymphoblast

Marrow   Blood
Barrier

Thrombocytes

Large
lymphocyte

Monocyte

Plasma cell

Peripheral Blood

Small
lymphocyte

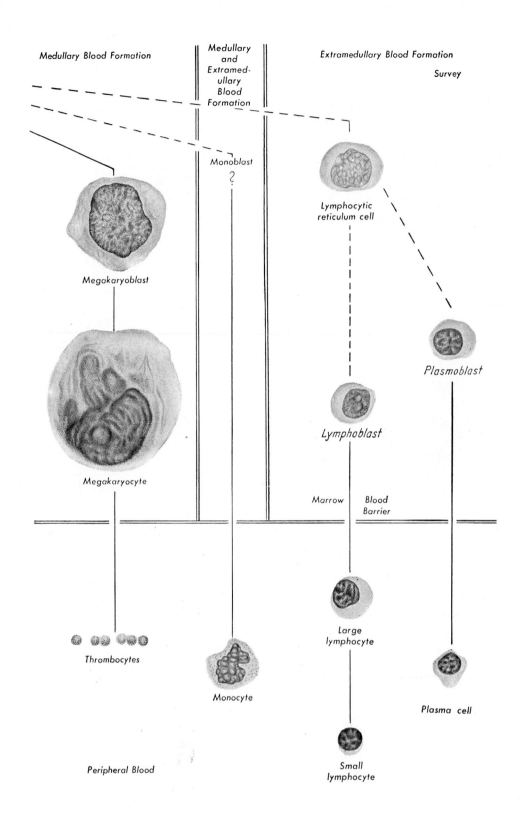

Medullary Blood Formation

Medullary and Extramedullary Blood Formation

Extramedullary Blood Formation

Survey

Monoblast
?

Lymphocytic
reticulum cell

Megakaryoblast

Plasmoblast

Megakaryocyte

Lymphoblast

Marrow   Blood
          Barrier

Thrombocytes

Large
lymphocyte

Monocyte

Plasma cell

Peripheral Blood

Small
lymphocyte

Plate 4–4. Continued. Development of blood cells.

4. The story of the *megakaryocyte* is less dramatic, possibly because much less is known about it. The megakaryoblast at the top in the third major vertical column is a giant of a cell with a restless nucleus and a homogeneous basophilic cytoplasm, which very soon begins to show a fine granularity as the cell becomes the functioning megakaryocyte. This cell is probably the largest normal cell of the body. Its octopus-like, multilobed, gigantic nucleus looks threatening. The cytoplasm spreads out like the web of a spider. Interestingly, this restless giant of a cell gives birth to the smallest formed particle of the body, the platelet or thrombocyte.

5. The next series, the *monocytic* in the fourth vertical column, is represented merely by one cell and that one only as it is seen in the peripheral blood. Where the blast form of this series should have been, a question mark fills the void because the beginning of the monocyte is shrouded in mystery. It is supposed to originate both within and outside the marrow. Nevertheless, there is no question that there is such a cell in the circulation as it is depicted at the bottom of the column. As the picture shows, it is the largest white cell in the peripheral blood. Its nucleus is irregularly lobated. It cannot be reduced to a pattern. Its chromatin structure is the most delicate and the least clearly outlined of all the white cells in the peripheral blood. Its structural haziness is made even more indefinite by the fine granulation of the abundant cytoplasm, which is described as of "ground glass" appearance.

6. The mother cell of the *lymphocyte,* as shown in the plate, stems from the embryonal reticulum cell by way of the lymphatic reticulum cell, which proceeds to the lymphoblast and then to the lymphocytes of the peripheral blood, the large and the small lymphocyte. The latter distinction is not accepted by all. It is worth repeating that in this series the basophilia of the cytoplasm of the embryonal precursors does not disappear with maturity. It assumes a lighter hue. Small numbers of deep red granules appear but only in some lymphocytes, the azurophilic granules. The mature small lymphocyte is an unassuming cell with a bare rim of cytoplasm, which is sometimes lost and leaves exposed the dense, almost structureless nucleus. In the large lymphocyte, the cytoplasm is abundant—frequently a beautiful transparent blue; the nuclear chromatin is much more loosely patterned.

7. In the *plasma cell* series, in the last right-hand vertical column, the plasmoblast is shown branching away from the lymphatic reticulum cell outside the marrow in keeping with the modern conception and not in accord with the older view that the plasma cell is a modified lymphocyte.

The top cell in the left upper corner of the plate shows a plasma cell originating directly from the primordial reticulum cell of the marrow, which is in keeping with the well-known presence of plasma cells in the marrow in health and their increase there in various conditions.

The characteristic eccentric location of the nucleus, the arrangement of the chromatin clumps, and their separation by the colorless parachromatin with the resulting resemblance to the spokes of a wheel are well shown. (Plates from Heilmeyer, L., and Begemann, H.: Atlas der Klinischen Hämatologie und Cytologie. Springer, 1955.)

American Medical Association, undertook a complete reexamination of this subject. The committee selected what its members believed to be the simplest, clearest, and most descriptive terms for the various cell forms. In addition, they tried to achieve consistency between related terms and suggested the elimination of many synonymous terms and eponyms (Committee report, 1949, 1950). At the present time, however, the suggested changes in terminology have not been generally accepted by clinical pathologists, and with few exceptions no significant change in usage is noted in current texts and medical literature. For this reason we feel that it would be unwise to burden the reader with a more detailed consideration of the matter. Since no theory of hematopoiesis has been firmly established, and since the maturation of the cells is a continuous process yielding an infinity of transitional forms, the student must be prepared to resolve a certain amount of confusion in terminology. In actual practice the situation is not nearly so difficult as it seems. For ordinary clinical purposes, reports according to any of the various systems are equally well interpreted provided the terms used are clearly defined.

EXAMINATION OF MARROW

Marrow aspiration biopsy, introduced by Arinkin in 1929, was considered at first a formidable and highly specialized procedure. It is now widely used in the diagnosis of hematologic diseases and many conditions not primarily affecting the blood system. A number of techniques have been devised by which a suitable specimen of marrow can be obtained with little discomfort to the patient. The simple aspiration type of biopsy can be carried out as an office procedure on ambulatory patients. The risks involved are minimal. They compare favorably with ordinary venipuncture and are decidedly less traumatizing than a lumbar puncture. As for any other special procedure, however, the indications for marrow examination should be clear. In each instance the physician should have in mind some reasonable prediction of its result and consequent benefit to the patient. Without exception, the peripheral blood should be examined carefully first. It is a relatively uncommon circumstance to find hematologic disease in the bone marrow either earlier or more certainly than it can be discovered in the peripheral blood. If an examiner is not able to find at least suggestive evidence of an abnormality referable to the marrow from the clinical data or the study of the peripheral blood, he is not likely to do better with the marrow.

It is estimated that the weight of the marrow in man varies from 1300 to 1500 gm. The unique feature of this organ is its extreme lability. It can undergo complete transformation in a few days and occasionally even in a few hours. This rapid transformation involves as a rule the whole organ, as evidenced by the fact that a small sample represented by a biopsy or aspiration is usually fairly representative of the whole marrow. This conclusion is in accord with results of studies of biopsy samples simultaneously removed from several sites. According to these observations, the various sites chosen for removal of marrow for studies are in most instances equally good. Consequently, the difficulty of access, the risks involved, and the discomfort of the patient are the main reasons for selection of a site in the particular patient. Occasionally the failure to obtain quantitatively or qualitatively adequate material in one site may be followed by success in another location. Also the need for repeated aspirations or biopsies may indicate the use of several different sites. The iliac bone and the vertebral spinous processes are less traumatic to the patient and seem to be more promising as sources of marrow for demonstration of cancer cells. On the other hand the iliac marrow frequently shows quantitative differences, namely, a greater admixture of peripheral blood, including lymphocytes and mature granulocytes, and a lower myeloid-erythroid (M:E) ratio. Qualitative differences are less marked.

Technique of Marrow Aspiration Biopsy

In the adult patient, the sternum, the spinous processes of the vertebrae, and the iliac crest are readily accessible areas from which bone marrow material can be obtained. In infants and young children the upper end of the tibia is frequently used to obtain marrow. The various methods of obtaining and handling material are essentially identical in principle so that comparable results are achieved by workers of equal skill and experience.

Surgical biopsy of the marrow, in which intact fragments of tissue are obtained by incision or by trephining, at one time had many advocates. These procedures have now been largely replaced by aspiration technique, which has the advantage of simplicity and less discomfort to the patient. The preparation of marrow fragments for histologic examination in sections is tedious and time-consuming. Also the stained sections are not so suitable for accurate differentiation of cell types as are the smeared preparations. Surgical biopsy may be used when it is important to see the cells in their anatomic relation to one another and to the inactive fat or connective tissue stroma (as in aplastic anemia and myelofibrosis) or in diseases that produce focal rather than diffuse changes (Hodgkin's disease, multiple myeloma, metastatic or primary malignant diseases of bone, and so on). However, aspiration should be tried first because each of the lesions listed in the preceding sentence may be demonstrated by means of an aspiration.

Aspirated marrow may be handled in several different ways. Some workers prefer to pick out visible particles from the specimen, with or without heparin, and stain these on slides. Others make films on slides using small drops of the whole material withdrawn. Satifactory results can be had either way, but particles (essentially fragments of marrow tissue) should be utilized whenever they are available. Some additional experience is required for the selection and staining of fragments, but the preparations usually have a higher technical quality and the distribution of cells is more reliable.

The technique to be outlined here is known to yield good films and to show reasonably smooth distribution of cells, and it can be carried out with a minimum of technical complexity.

Equipment. The needle must be of short, stout construction, properly molded for a firm grasp, with a short bevel and well-fitted stylet. The lumen needs to be rather large, not less than about 14-gauge. Several varieties of needles are available. A widely used needle is the University of Illinois sternal needle (V. Mueller & Co., Chicago) (Fig. 4–45). It has an adjustable guard,

Figure 4–45. University of Illinois sternal needle with adjustable guard, special locking device for the stylet, and Luer-Lok hub set into the needle. (Courtesy of V. Mueller and Co., Chicago.)

which, when properly set, would prevent perforation of the inner plate of the sternum. With each complete turn the guard moves 1 mm. The stylet can be fixed firmly. A small needle of same construction is available for infants and children.

Turkel's trephine has many advocates (Fig. 4–46). An outer 14-gauge needle, 2 cm. long, with a stylet that serves as guide for an inner trephine is passed to the periosteum. The stylet is removed and replaced by the inner 6 cm. long 17-gauge needle with a serrated tip, which cuts out a small core of bone and marrow for sections and smears.

Clean glass slides, coverslips, test tubes, and watch glasses should be available.

Five or 10 ml. syringes are better than smaller sizes because they have a stronger pull. Syringes with metal tips are preferable. An extra syringe and a *separate* small

Figure 4–46. Puncture biopsy needle of Turkel and Bethell. Two needles with stylets: an outer guiding or splitting needle, 14-gauge, 20 mm. long, and an inner trephine needle and stylet, 17-gauge.

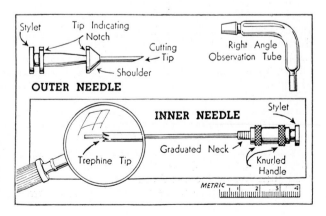

syringe for the anesthetic should be available.

Sterile equipment to be used by the operator should be ready on a marrow puncture tray. It should contain the following: towels, emesis basin, cotton sponges, hemostat, two 10 ml. syringes preferably with metal tips, 5 ml. glass syringe, two 24-gauge hypodermic needles, and two marrow needles (University of Illinois type) wrapped and sterilized. In addition: several pairs of sterile rubber gloves, procaine, alcohol, iodine, or another local antiseptic (e.g., zephiran), clean and preferably new glass slides, band-aids, and collodion.

Heparin is recognized as a good anticoagulant and probably is least objectionable for preservation of cellular detail.

TECHNIQUE OF ASPIRATION OF STERNAL MARROW

The patient should be informed and reassured concerning the nature of the procedure to put him in the proper frame of mind. The next step is to put him at ease physically by having him lie down comfortably on his back with both his arms at the sides.

Occasionally a mild, rapidly acting sedative may be indicated but not if the operation is done in the office and the patient expects to drive afterward.

The site of the puncture is selected. Find the sternomanubrial prominence (angle of Louis) and, using a skin pencil, mark this with a horizontal line. Locate the jugular notch of the manubrium and mark the midline of the sternum in its long axis. The site of puncture in the body of the sternum will lie in the midline or slightly to one side of the midline, 1 to 2 cm. below the angle of Louis, opposite the second interspace. This location is recommended, regardless of age, because it is rarely deformed and contains marrow. The outer table in that region varies from 0.2 to 5 mm. in thickness and the marrow cavity from 5 to 15 mm. in depth. The area between the costal insertions should not be used; it may be cartilaginous.

Marking lines may seem superfluous, but the operator can easily become disoriented after antiseptic solutions and sterile towels have been applied about the field, and he may introduce the needle into the connective tissue or cartilage at the sternomanubrial junction or too far from the midline.

When biopsies are to be repeated, a different site should be selected for each to avoid obtaining marrow damaged by previous punctures.

The skin is cleansed, and shaved if hairy, and a wide working area is prepared with an antiseptic solution as for any minor surgical incision. The field surrounding the puncture site is protected by sterile towels or a spinal drape. The patient's face is covered. The operator's hands should be washed thoroughly. Sterile gloves are worn. Aseptic technique should be used during the operation.

Using a solution of 1 per cent procaine, raise a skin wheal approximately 1 cm. below the point where the needle will enter the sternum. With the hypodermic needle directed upward and at an angle of about 30 to 45 degrees with the skin, the anesthetic is injected through the subcutaneous tissues and down to the periostium.

One must make sure that the patient is not sensitive to the particular anesthetic, in which case another should be chosen. Another recommended precaution is to withdraw the needle slightly at the start of the injection to make certain that the local anesthetic is not being injected intravenously.

With its stylet in place and locked in position, the marrow puncture needle is grasped firmly and introduced vertically through the anesthetized area until its point impinges upon the outer table of the bone. The guard is screwed down until it touches the skin. It is then screwed back two and a half turns. In most instances the added length, which equals the length of the bevel of the needle, permits the needle to enter the cavity on slight pressure but protects against perforations of the inner table. Some hold the needle vertically, under a 90 degree angle to the bone. Others recommend a 45 degree angle as an additional safety measure. My preference is to hold it vertically. Only a little steady pressure and a slight side-to-side rotation of the needle serve to enter the outer table of the sternum. The sudden diminution of resistance is easily felt as the needle enters the marrow cavity. It is a mistake to suppose that one must exert considerable pressure.

When the point of the needle is in the marrow, the stylet is removed and a 5 or 10 ml. syringe is attached. Using gentle aspiration, not more than 0.2 to 0.3 ml. of material is withdrawn. The small amount is more suitable for cytologic studies. When greater volumes are aspirated, only additional peripheral blood is drawn into the syringe, and the results may be completely vitiated by dilution. A slightly larger amount may be drawn if the specimen is to be concentrated by centrifugation. Many patients experience pain or distress when marrow is being aspirated. It is recommended to prepare the patients for the pain; it does not come as a surprise and is tolerated better. If material is not obtained at once, the stylet can be replaced and the needle gently manipulated. Occasionally it may be useful to inject a few drops of physiologic saline to clear the point of the needle. A "dry tap" should be a rare experience. The aspirate is transferred immediately to a paraffin coated vial or watchglass containing heparin (lot 152, Hynson, Westcott and Dunning), and the container is rotated to insure thorough mixing. The needle is withdrawn and the wound sealed with a collodion-covered pad of cotton or gauze and fastened firmly by adhesive tape.

Obtaining Marrow from Infant

A small size, special sternal 17-gauge needle is used. Otherwise the procedure is essentially the same as in adults, except that a sedative is needed as a rule.

The preferable site of puncture is also at the level of the second interspace. The sternum of the infant is essentially cartilaginous and accordingly great caution must be exercised. In infants and children the other sites to be mentioned are preferable.

Iliac Aspiration

The patient lies on one side. The site is about 1 cm. below the crest posterior to the anterior iliac spine. Actually the iliac bone can be punctured in a variety of places. The crest itself can be used in infants and children. In adults slightly greater pressure is needed to pierce the crest. Otherwise a less solid area is chosen as described.

Vertebral Spinous Process Aspiration

This site has the psychologic advantage that the patient cannot see the operation. The patient sits leaning forward or lies on his side or with his face down. The lower thoracic or lumbar vertebral spinous process is punctured. More pressure is needed than for sternal puncture. The needle should be inserted slightly to the side of the middle at right angle to the skin surface.

Tibial Aspiration

This site is frequently used in infants and young children up to about 2 years of age. It is considerably more traumatic than the iliac crest and does not furnish better marrow. The preferable site for the puncture is the superior medial surface of the tibia, inferior to the medial condyle and medial to the tibial tuberosity.

Preparation of the Aspirate for Examination

Many procedures are in use and each has its advocates. The three most frequently used are: marrow films, gross quantitative study, and histologic sections.

Preparation of Marrow Films. Delay, no matter how brief, is undesirable. To avoid delay in handling aspirated bone marrow, it is well to have an assistant on hand to prepare the smears. When small amounts of material are taken as suggested previously, films can be made in a similar manner as for ordinary blood counts. Gray particles of marrow are usually seen with the naked eye. They are the best material for the preparation of good films and serve as landmarks for the microscopic examination of stained smears.

Preparation of smears containing particles of marrow. Drops of marrow are placed on a slide a short distance away from one end. Most of the blood is sucked off with a capillary pipet leaving the particles behind. A smear 3 to 5 cm. long is made with a spreader, not wider than 2 cm., dragging the particles behind but not *squashing* them. A trail of cells is left behind. Criteria of a good preparation: particles and free marrow cells are present.

Marrow particles can also be used for preparation of imprints. One or more visible particles are picked up with a capillary pipet, the broken end of a wooden applicator, or a toothpick and transferred immediately to a slide and made to stick to it by a gentle smearing motion. The slide is air dried rapidly by waving and then is stained.

A careful cytologic study is a good index of the composition of the marrow. Qualitative changes detected by examination of well-prepared smears of adequate marrow aspirates are as a rule more significant diagnostically than any amount of quantitative data. As the marrow is being spread, the appearance of fat as irregular holes in the films gives assurance that the desired material (not peripheral blood) has been obtained. The smears are dried rapidly, whipping them through the air by exposing them to a fan.

Gross Quantitative Study. This method is usually combined with the study of smears or of histologic sections. The aspirate is transferred to a Wintrobe hematocrit tube with a capillary pipet. Some or all of the visible particles are included, depending on their use for preparation of direct smears. The tube is centrifuged at high speed (± 2500 r.p.m.) for ten minutes. Four layers can be distinguished in the centrifugate: fat, plasma, myeloid-erythroid (M:E) portion, and erythrocytes. Their height is recorded in percentages by reading on the scale of the tube. Normally the fat layer is 1 to 3 per cent of the total volume and the M:E layer, 5 to 8 per cent. The volumes of the plasma and erythrocyte layers vary considerably. The erythrocyte volume is generally more than the hematocrit because of shorter centrifugation. The admixture of sinusoidal blood, not an uncommon occurrence in marrow aspiration, may alter the proportions of the different fractions more or less significantly.

Interpretation of quantitative findings. High myeloid-erythroid and low fat values, in the absence of a significant peripheral leukocytosis, suggest marrow hyperplasia, at least local. Low myeloid-erythroid and high fat values suggest hypoplasia, at least of the aspirated sample. If the myeloid-erythroid layer is less than 2 per cent and fat is absent, the sample is mainly sinusoidal blood. Examination of histologic sections is an essential check on the quantitative data. Concentration by centrifugation is particularly valuable in group studies, but in the study of individual patients the use of particles and of histologic preparations is more advantageous. Dilution with sinusoidal blood may amount to 40 to 100 per cent in aspirates as small as 0.25 to 0.5 ml. Consequently it was suggested to use the term hemomyelogram for a differential count of marrow aspirates and to restrict the term "myelogram" to counts from which mature granulocytes have been excluded (Pontoni, 1936).

Histologic Sections. The fragments obtained by surgical biopsy or trephine, the particles visible in the aspirate, the myeloid-erythroid layer of the centrifuged specimen, or a clotted portion of the aspirate are fixed in Zenker's fluid, run through in one of several ways, and embedded in paraffin or colloidin. Adherents of this method claim that it furnishes all the information provided by the smear method, a much better picture of marrow architec-ture, and quantitative data in addition. However, the histologic section method is definitely inferior for the study of cytologic details. Another disadvantage is that particles adequate for histologic sections are not always obtained, especially in conditions in which the diagnosis depends on marrow evidence, e.g., myelofibrosis or metastatic cancer.

Berman (1953) recommended the following technique: The aspirated marrow is deposited in a paraffin-coated vial. A small amount of powdered topical thrombin is placed on a clean glass slide, dissolved in a drop of water, and allowed to dry. The marrow particles in the aspirate tend to stick to the paraffin coating. They are transferred with the broken end of a wooden applicator and placed close to each other on the thrombin-coated area on the slide. A few drops of heparinized plasma from the centrifuged aspirate are added. The plasma clots by action of thrombin. The marrow particles are included in the clot, which is transferred to a suitable fixative. The latter is changed repeatedly until it remains water clear and then run through, embedded, sectioned, and stained.

The Surgical Biopsy

The indications for surgical biopsy are: dry tap, myelofibrosis, osteosclerosis, and metastatic cancer. Smears, touch preparations and pieces of bone and marrow can be obtained in adequate amounts. Any location can be used, but the disadvantage of the sternum is that it may leave a conspicuous scar.

Staining of Marrow Preparations

Good fixation is essential. In some stain the fixation is included. Otherwise fixation has to be done separately.

1. **Wright's Stain.** The stain as it is used for blood smears is diluted with an equal quantity of absolute methyl alcohol. The slide is covered with a measured number of drops of the stain for two minutes, followed by an equal amount of buffered distilled water for four to eight minutes. The stain is rinsed as recommended for blood smears.

2. **May-Grünwald-Giemsa Stain.** The slide is covered with a measured number of drops of May-Grünwald stain for two minutes. An equal amount of buffered distilled water is added, the slide agitated for two minutes, the mixture poured off, and the

slide covered with double-strength Giemsa's stain (two drops of stock to 1 ml. buffered distilled water) for 10 to 12 minutes. The slide is rinsed in neutral distilled water until the water is clear. The slide is placed vertically and air dried.

3. **Wright-Giemsa Stain.** The technique is the same as the preceding, except that Wright's stain is substituted for May-Grünwald.

Examination of Marrow Films

The ability to interpret marrow cytology can be attained only by experience. It must be regarded more as a qualitative examination than as a quantitative test. For this reason, the examiner should be informed of the clinical nature of the patient's disease.

In general there are two ways in which a marrow film can be examined: First, by scanning several slides under low, then high dry, and finally under oil immersion magnification, and on the basis of previous experience, one can arrive at impressions concerning the number and distribution of cells in very much the same manner as the pathologist reads his sections of tissue. Second, one can actually make a differential count of large number of cells (300 to 1000) and calculate the percentage of each type of cell. Finally, a combination of both methods can be used.

The second of these methods, painstaking differential counting, is an essential part of training in this work without which accuracy in the first method may never be had. The differential count also affords an objective record from which future changes may be measured. The recognition of cell types, and particularly recognition of the maturation phase within any given series, tends to vary rather widely from one laboratory to another despite a great many efforts to standardize nomenclature with descriptions, photographs, and drawings. No average normals, or even ranges of normal, can be accepted as universal. The most valid base line is that determined in each individual laboratory, and even then, unless "group training" is used, there may be significant variations from one examiner to another. Fortunately these limitations of the method are serious only when they are not recognized. By practice and experience laboratory workers are able to obtain gratifying practical results and establish a high degree of reproducibility in their marrow

differential counts. The following procedure for the studies of marrow preparations can be recommended.

1. Naked eye inspection of the slides to select the smear containing particles.

2. Low power (16 mm.) survey of the particles to form a preliminary opinion whether the marrow is normoplastic, hypoplastic, or hyperplastic.

3. Selection of a cellular area, usually in the tail portion of the film around the particles, is followed by high power and oil immersion study of cytologic details.

The following points are particularly significant:

CELLULARITY

The degree of cellularity or whether the marrow is generally hyperplastic or hypoplastic is a difficult point to determine by examination of aspirated material. When this issue is crucial, we can be certain only by the study of histologic sections of material obtained by surgical biopsy. If aspiration is carried out in a uniform manner, and if minimal amounts of material are withdrawn, it is possible to make useful, although rather crude, estimates of cellularity.

The report should include references to the following: description of the general cellularity, type of erythropoiesis, general maturity of the erythropoietic and leukopoietic cells, and an estimate of the M:E or L:E ratio based on a count of 500 to 1000 cells.

A differential count is useful but only in special cases, for example, in leukemia to follow up the effect of therapy. Examination of more slides in the time that would otherwise be spent for differential counts is more fruitful.

MYELOID-ERYTHROID (M:E) RATIO

In the normal adult, the M:E ratio is about 3 or 4 to 1. This widely used term refers to differential counts from which mature granulocytes have not been excluded. The term "leukoerythrogenetic" (L:E) ratio refers to counts from which mature granulocytes have been excluded. The latter is a better expression of the relative proportions of leukopoiesis to erythropoiesis (Pontoni, 1936).

The M:E ratio at birth is 1.85 to 1. It rises rapidly soon afterward, and during the first two weeks of life it reaches the highest normal level of 11 to 1. It then gradually drops to the 1-to-20-year average of 3 to 1.

Interpretation. An *increased* M:E ratio, i.e., 6 to 1, may mean a reaction to an infection or may mean leukemia, a leukemoid reaction or erythroid hypoplasia. A *decreased* M:E ratio, i.e., less than 2 to 1, may mean a depression of leukopoiesis or a hyperplasia of erythropoiesis. Normoblastic erythroid hyperplasia may be the result of one of the many forms of anemia or of liver diseases or polycythemia. Megaloblastic erythroid hyperplasia may be caused by a deficiency of a red cell maturing factor as in pernicious anemia. A normal M:E ratio does not necessarily mean normal marrow.

Due to the irregular distribution of the various cell types, differential counts of nucleated marrow cells are not more than approximations. The irregularity is partly caused by the tendency of mature neutrophilic granulocytes and platelets to aggregate. A low power survey of the entire smear gives the experienced examiner a much more accurate picture of the relative proportions of the cells than a differential count. An estimate expressed as increased, normal, or reduced cellularity is all that is necessary for practical purposes.

One soon learns to note with some accuracy the expected 20 or 25 per cent of nucleated cells in the erythrocytic series without the necessity of making actual counts. A diminished proportion of nucleated red cells usually signifies bone marrow suppression or displacement by leukemic or other malignant cells. An increased number of nucleated red cells, usually seen in a generally hyperplastic marrow, characterizes the iron deficiency and hemolytic anemias in which normoblasts predominate and the macrocytic anemias in which erythroblasts, megaloblasts, or pernicious anemia-type cells predominate.

The "Normal" Marrow Differential. The data available in the literature for so-called "normal" marrow cell counts vary from investigator to investigator. One misses the generally accepted normals for the peripheral blood. The various "normal" differentials reflect the particular investigator's technique of counting and manner of interpretation. Therefore, it is best to establish one's own normals. Our own collected observations are recorded in our table of normals (Table 4–2).

Interpretation of cytologic findings. 1. Cells normally present may be increased in numbers. This includes arrest of maturation and presence of younger cells in abnormally large numbers.

2. Eosinophil counts above 5, lymphocyte counts above 20, and plasma cell counts above 5 may be significant.

3. Cells normally absent: neoplastic cells, metastatic (cancer) or primary (multiple myeloma) cells, cells seen in storage diseases (Gaucher's disease).

4. Granulomatous lesions: tuberculosis, Hodgkin's, and sarcoidosis.

5. Parasites: malaria, histoplasmosis.

MEGAKARYOCYTES

Because of their large size and unique appearance, these cells are readily recognized under low magnification. Since they tend to accumulate at the edges or thick end of the smear, it is best to look for them first at low magnification before proceeding to a more detailed study under the oil immersion lens. Attempts at actual counting of megakaryocytes are usually disappointing, and even after examining several films one is usually satisfied to state that megakaryocytes appear to be present in normal numbers or that they are absent. In direct smears made from aspirated marrow the distribution of megakaryocytes is so unpredictable that their absence should excite little concern unless associated with thrombocytopenic purpura. Smears of selected marrow fragments are more reliable for this observation. In idiopathic thrombocytopenic purpura, megakaryocytes are usually present in normal or even in increased numbers. Qualitative changes in their appearance should be noted, although they are difficult to evaluate. It has been recommended that not less than 25 megakaryocytes be examined for such a study. Morphologic evidence of immaturity, diminished or absent cytoplasmic granulation, vacuolization or hyalinization of the cytoplasm, and absence of peripheral fragmentation or "platelet production" have been noted by various observers in the study of thrombocytopenic disorders.

DISTRIBUTION OF CELL TYPES

In overt disease of the blood system, an abnormal distribution of cells is often immediately evident upon scanning the marrow smear. This may be true in the aleukemic leukemias, when the diagnosis is difficult or impossible by examination of peripheral blood, so that this group of dis-

Table 4–2. Myelogram

	FOUND	NORMAL	
		AVERAGE	RANGE
Undifferentiated cells		0.0	0 – 2.0
Myeloblasts		1.6	0.4 – 5.0
Promyelocytes		4.0	1.0 – 8.0
Myelocytes:			
Neutrophilic		12.0	5.0 –19.0
Eosinophilic		1.5	0.5 – 3.0
Basophilic		0.3	0.0 – 0.3
Metamyelocytes:			
Neutrophilic		26.4	13.0 –32.0
Eosinophilic		2.0	0.5 – 3.0
Basophilic		0.3	0 – 0.3
Segmented granulocytes:			
Neutrophilic		15.4	7.0 –30.0
Eosinophilic		2.0	0.6 – 4.0
Basophilic		0.3	0 – 0.4
Pronormoblasts		0.6	0.2 – 4.0
Basophilic normoblasts		2.4	1.5 – 5.8
Polychromatic normoblasts		10.6	5.0 –20.0
Orthochromatic normoblasts		6.6	3.0 –20.0
Promegaloblasts		0	0
Basophilic megaloblasts		0	0
Polychromatic megaloblasts		0	0
Orthochromatic megaloblasts		0	0
Megakaryocytes		0.4	0.04– 2.0
Monocytes		2.0	0.4 – 4.0
Prolymphocytes		10.0	3.0 –17.0
Lymphocytes			
Reticulum cells		1.0	0.2 – 3.0
Plasma cells		0.6	0 – 2.0
M:E ratio		3–4:1	
No. of cells classified			

eases constitutes one of the more important indications for bone marrow aspiration. In certain cases of chronic granulocytic leukemia and plasma cell myeloma, more careful study, perhaps including differential counts, may be necessary to indicate the true nature of the disease. The cell pattern in pernicious anemia and related macrocytic anemias is often helpful in diagnosis or in noting response to therapy. Other valuable uses of marrow biopsy will be discussed in relation to the various blood diseases.

PRESENCE OF MALIGNANT CELLS

In spite of the focal nature of its lesions, multiple myeloma is often diagnosed by marrow aspiration. It is less frequent, but not rare, to find other types of malignant tissue including carcinomas metastasizing to bone.

Indications for Marrow Aspiration

In the differential diagnosis of macrocytic anemia, there are some cases in which the peripheral blood picture suggests pernicious anemia, and the examination of marrow may show normoblastic and not megaloblastic regeneration of erythrocytes. In such instances the examination of the marrow may be the only means of recognizing the true nature of the condition.

In a variety of conditions, such as hemolytic, aplastic, and regenerative anemias, leukopenia, thrombocytopenic purpura, multiple myeloma, metastatic carcinoma, lipoid storage diseases, myeloproliferative disease, splenomegaly, lymph node enlargements, in various skin lesions and in other situations, marrow examination may help to the correct diagnosis or may exclude a primary disease of the blood.

In obscure fevers and suspected infections in which blood cultures were negative, culture of marrow aspirate may show growth of the infectious agent.

Examination of marrow is essential for correct diagnosis of *pancytopenia*. It may help to diagnose or rule out leukemia.

Examination of marrow smears is of little diagnostic value in the following conditions: microcytic hypochromic anemia, posthemorrhagic anemia, coagulation disorders, lymphoma, anemia of nephritis, anemia of infection, polycythemia, infectious mononucleosis, chronic granulocytic leukemia, and chronic lymphocytic leukemia (Cartwright, 1958).

Examination of histologic sections prepared from particles of marrow may be helpful in the recognition and diagnosis of neoplastic and granulomatous lesions of marrow, such as malignant lymphoma, metastatic carcinoma, multiple myeloma, sarcoidosis, tuberculosis, brucellosis, and histoplasmosis and of storage diseases, e.g., Gaucher's. This method also permits one to study the architecture of marrow that is essential for the diagnosis of aplastic anemia and myelofibrosis and may not be demonstrated with the smear method. It is in most of the conditions listed in this paragraph that "dry taps" are common. In such cases surgical biopsy may furnish suitable material. In experienced hands a "dry tap" or a film showing only peripheral blood is a significant finding and should arouse suspicion of bone marrow aplasia, replacement by malignant tissue, myelosclerosis, or similar condition.

Contraindications: Hemophilia and other major disturbances of coagulation; liver or equivalent therapy including blood transfusion during the preceding three weeks; and patients suspected of having pernicious anemia.

Hazards of Marrow Aspiration

Complications may occur during aspiration. One should be prepared to administer intravenously a short-acting barbiturate from ready-to-use sterile ampules if the patient develops convulsions.

Death has been reported from puncture of the heart and tamponade. Caution is essential. Indications for the procedure should be observed. Neophytes should be carefully trained and closely supervised. The use of sites other than the sternum should be encouraged whenever possible.

Study of Marrow Obtained at Autopsy

Samples of marrow should be obtained at every autopsy, but to secure useful material it has to be removed within two hours after death. Tissue from the following sites should be obtained: a segment of a rib and sternum, a wedge of a lumbar vertebral body, and a segment of marrow removed from the midfemur. The femoral marrow is particularly useful as an indicator of response of the marrow to hematopoietic stimuli, whereas the rib, sternum, and vertebra, which contain red marrow at all ages, are sensitive indicators of damage of various kinds.

Special Diagnostic Stain

Iron stain is useful for differentiation of anemias due to iron deficiency and blood loss from anemia of thalassemia and of pyridoxine deficiency in which iron is poorly utilized for hemoglobin synthesis.

Hemosiderin Stain

Potassium ferrocyanide	4 gm.
Distilled water	20 ml.

Add concentrated HCl until a white precipitate forms. Filter. Cover the marrow smear with filtrate for 30 minutes. Result: hemosiderin is blue; iron in ferritin and hemoglobin is not stained. Report as negative or 1+ to 4+. Marrow hemosiderin is comparable to hemosiderin in rest of body.

Interpretation. In iron deficiency the result is negative. In unstained preparations hemosiderin appears as yellow, refractile granules. Normally a small number of blue granules are seen. None or extremely rare hemosiderin granules are seen in iron deficiency states. They are numerous in infections, pernicious anemia, hemolytic anemia, hemochromatosis, hemosiderosis, hepatic cirrhosis, uremia, and cancer and after repeated transfusions.

VITAL STAINING

Vital Staining of Erythrocytes

On the assumption that ordinary staining of dried and fixed blood films shows the reactions of dead corpuscles and does not necessarily indicate the condition of the living corpuscles, attempts have been made to stain blood corpuscles in the living state. The information yielded by this so-called vital or supravital staining has to do chiefly with certain reticulated erythrocytes, which contain a coarse skein or network of granular filaments. Sometimes, apparently depending on variations in technique of staining, there are no definite filaments but only a number of discrete, coarse granules scattered irregularly through the corpuscle. The granulofilamentous substance stains sharply with many of the basic dyes when these are applied to the living corpuscles but completely fails to stain films dried in the usual manner.

As to the nature of the reticulum, little is known definitely. Some workers connect it with polychromatophilia and others with mitochondria. In any case, reticulation is apparently a characteristic of very young erythrocytes, and the number of reticulated erythrocytes in the circulating blood is prob-

ably the best available index of the activity of regeneration of blood. An increase may be interpreted as indicating both an excessive demand for new erythrocytes and a competent bone marrow; when the demand lessens or the bone marrow fails to function, the number of reticulated erythrocytes decreases.

In healthy medical students, for example, the reticulated erythrocytes comprise 0.3 to 1 per cent (usually 0.6 to 0.8 per cent) of all the erythrocytes. In young infants, the percentage is two to four times as high as it is in medical students. Some writers give higher figures, that is, 0.5 to 2 per cent for adults and 5 to 10 per cent for infants. In the various types of anemia associated with increased activity of the bone marrow, the percentage of reticulated erythrocytes ranges from 2 to 20 or even higher, the percentage running parallel with the varying activity of regeneration of blood and bearing no necessary relation to the erythrocyte count. The percentage is notably high in hemolytic jaundice.

Of the various dyes that have been used for vital staining, brilliant cresyl blue appears to be by far the most satisfactory.

The following method is very satisfactory for staining reticulocytes. Make a saturated solution of brilliant cresyl blue by placing a very small amount of dye in the bottom of a small tube (Wassermann tube) and adding distilled water to dissolve as much of the dye as possible. If the American-made dye is used, better results may be obtained if the dye is dissolved in 0.9 per cent solution of sodium chloride. Place a drop of the patient's blood on one end of a clean slide as in making an ordinary blood film. Place beside it a drop of the solution of cresyl blue, using a glass rod. Wipe off the excess stain from the glass rod, mix the blood, and the stain thoroughly. The mixture will be a light green color. Then spread the blood in the usual manner, as illustrated in Figure 4–23, and stain with Wright's stain. The reticulocytes will have the appearance shown in Figure 4–47 and Plate 4–3 [5]. A differential count then may be made.

Examine the stained film with an oil immersion objective and calculate what proportion of the erythrocytes contains reticulum or granules. As a basis for calculation, at least 1000 erythrocytes (preferably 3000) should be examined for reticulation. These should be examined on several different portions of the slide. To obviate the difficulty

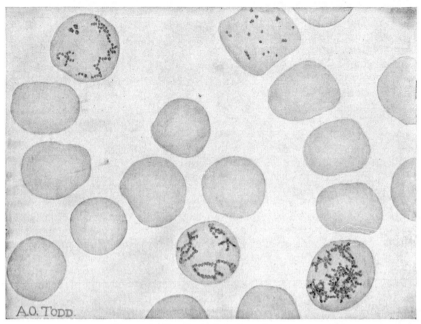

Figure 4–47. Reticulated erythrocytes.

of examining large fields that contain a confusing number of erythrocytes, the field of vision may be made smaller by placing a metal or paper diaphragm in the oculars to show about 25 cells per field.

In preparations made as just described, the leukocytes and thrombocytes are stained blue and the erythrocytes are yellowish green. The reticulated erythrocytes often are decidedly larger than the other erythrocytes. The network and granules are stained deep blue and stand out distinctly (Fig. 4–47). The only serious source of error will be particles of stain adhering to the surface of the corpuscles. The preparations retain their color well if kept away from light.

The films also may be stained with Wright's stain, which, combined with brilliant cresyl blue, produces beautiful preparations that are very satisfactory.

Vital Staining of Leukocytes

Florence Sabin has introduced a simple method for studying the leukocytes in the living conditions. This method opens a new and fertile field for research and also promises to become a useful clinical procedure. For a detailed description of this method, the reader is referred to the papers of Sabin and her coworkers (Cunningham *et al.*, 1925; Sabin, 1923; Sabin *et al.*, 1924, 1925).

A similar method has long been used for vital staining of erythrocytes, but the concentration of dye that stained the erythrocytes satisfactorily injured the leukocytes. Moreover, in the case of the erythrocytes, it was not necessary to keep the corpuscles alive during the examination.

Technique. 1. Carefully clean slides and coverglasses in the following manner: Soak them in bichromate cleaning fluid three or four days, place in running water for two or three hours, separate occasionally, rinse in three or four changes of distilled water, soak overnight, and store in 80 per cent alcohol. Before use, wipe them with a clean towel and polish the slides with jeweler's rouge applied on a piece of silk.

2. Flame the slides and flood with a very dilute solution of the selected dye in absolute alcohol; drain off excess dye and place the slides upright until dry. The film must be very thin and evenly spread. Prepared slides may be stored until needed but must be kept away from dust. Many stains will serve. Sabin preferred neutral red (specify for vital staining), because it is relatively nontoxic and is also an indicator, showing the chemical reaction of the parts of the cell that take the stain. The very dilute solution that is applied to the slides is prepared by mixing 0.4 cc. of a 1 per cent solution of neutral red in absolute alcohol

with 10 cc. of absolute alcohol. When it also is desired to bring out the mitochondria of the cells, three drops of saturated solution of Janus green in absolute alcohol may be added to each 2 cc. of the diluted solution of neutral red.

3. Receive a very small drop of blood from a puncture on a perfectly clean coverglass. Invert the coverglass on the prepared slide and immediately seal with petrolatum of high melting point or with a mixture of petrolatum and paraffin. The slide must not be cold but need not be warmed.

4. Within ten minutes place the slide on a warm stage or preferably in a microslide incubator. Examine at once with the oil immersion objective. Normally the corpuscles remain alive for at least an hour, sometimes for three or four hours.

Each lot of cleaned slides and each new bottle of diluted stain should be tested with normal blood to insure uniform conditions. Leukocytes are very sensitive to the least trace of acid that may be left on the slides and to an excess of the dye. Any coloring of the nucleus indicates injury to the cell.

Appearances of Leukocytes. Polymorphonuclear neutrophilic leukocytes are constantly moving about owing to their characteristic ameboid motion and are readily seen. Their cytoplasmic granules, which are numerous, of small size and pale red, are constantly streaming through the cytoplasm. As the leukocytes move about, the nucleus, with its several lobes, is usually in the rear part. In addition to the granules, the cytoplasm of most of these leukocytes contains one or more rounded bodies, which take the stain slowly. These are larger than the granules and are presumably digestive vacuoles, indicating phagocytic activity. They vary in color, depending on the chemical reaction of their contents. Certain leukocytes are rounded and motionless, the nucleus is structureless and nearly fills the cell, and the granules, although distinctly visible, do not take the stain. These are interpreted as dead or dying neutrophils. Their number varies at different hours; it usually is greatest near the middle of the day. The number may be greatly increased by faulty technique (excessive heat, pressure of the coverglass, and so forth).

The cytoplasmic granules of *eosinophils* and *basophils* stain with the neutral red. The basophilic granules are somewhat smaller than the eosinophilic granules and differ among themselves in size and depth of staining. Digestive vacuoles are apparently absent from both cells. Eosinophils are actively motile; basophils are slightly so.

The younger *monocytes*, with oval nuclei, are rounded and practically nonmotile. Their cytoplasm contains very fine salmon-colored granules, which are grouped around a clear spot, the centrosphere. With these fine granules are a variable number of larger red bodies, apparently digestive vacuoles. The older cells, with lobulated or saddle-shaped nuclei, are more irregular in shape, usually elongated, and are sluggishly motile. The red vacuoles are usually numerous and may displace or at least obscure the fine granules.

The cytoplasm of *lymphocytes* is clear except for a few small vacuoles that take the red stain. When Janus green is added, a clump of blue mitochondria may be seen opposite the nucleus. The nucleus is oval or indented, seldom round. The large and small lymphocytes show no locomotion. Those of intermediate size move very slowly, and the nucleus is then at the front end and its shape changes.

HEMATOLOGIC CHANGES IN DISEASE

The result of hematologic examinations, forming what we call the "blood picture," is an essential part of the clinical description of practically every disease. A normal number and distribution of cells and a normal hemoglobin concentration in the blood are so important as physiologic constants that the absence of disease can scarcely be asserted until these observations have been made. That certain diseases do not produce significant changes in the blood, is often a valuable point in differential diagnosis. Most hematologic changes are the result of pathologic processes not primarily affecting the blood or blood-forming tissues. The granulocytosis of acute suppurative diseases, the anemia of bleeding peptic ulcer, the lymphocytosis of whooping cough, and many other "blood pictures" constitute important diagnostic information, in each instance forming an essential part of the clinical description of the particular disease. It is evident, therefore, that clinical hematology is almost coextensive with the entire field of medical diagnosis.

By far less common are some of the so-called "true blood diseases" in which the first and most obvious deviations from normal are noted in the blood or blood-forming tissues. The leukemias, multiple myeloma, and some of the anemias are representative of this group. We also recognize a group of diseases, which, although not primarily involving the blood system, present such conspicuous changes in the blood picture that this feature becomes the key to diagnosis and treatment. Toxic or allergic agranulocytosis, nutritional anemia, and certain forms of aplastic anemia are suitable examples of this group. In addition, the field of clinical hematology is generally defined to include the hemorrhagic diseases or those conditions in which there is disturbance of the blood-clotting mechanism. All these divisions are arbitrary and not sharply outlined. Their consideration may serve, however, to give some general notion as to the scope and meaning of clinical hematology.

Types of Hematologic Examination

Some hazard is involved in adopting a routine or set of routines for laboratory orders, since the problem of each patient must be given individual consideration. However, certain tests are used so frequently that time and effort can be saved by putting them into groups as indicated in the following paragraphs.

Routine or Screening Examinations. It is generally considered a wise policy to include a few hematologic procedures in the examination of every patient without relation to any known or suspected diagnosis. The procedures are selected with reference to the most common diseases and abnormalities. Their chief purpose is to indicate whether or not more detailed examinations are needed. Since these tests must be done on large numbers of patients and often, it is also important that they be simple and economical and consume as little time as possible. An accurate hemoglobin determination, a total leukocyte count, and a differential leukocyte count on the stained smear are usually accepted as an adequate hematologic routine. The hemoglobin test must be the most accurate available. A total erythrocyte count should not be included in such a routine, because the procedure takes a great deal of time and, except under the most exacting technical conditions, the results are astonishingly inaccurate. In some laboratories a hematocrit reading is substituted for the hemoglobin

determination. It has the advantage of being accurate and highly reproducible even when done by the less experienced.

Special Hematologic Procedures. Almost any of the examinations on blood may be included in the routine or ordered from time to time, depending on the type of practice being conducted and the needs of the individual patient. For example, a sedimentation rate may be used in the routine of clinics in gynecology, tuberculosis, or rheumatology where the presence or absence of systemic reactions to inflammatory processes is a very common differential point. Likewise, it may be well to examine wet preparations of the blood on all Negro patients whether or not there are clinical suggestions of sickle cell disease. Single procedures, or groups of procedures, will be indicated by the nature and course of the patient's illness.

Complete Hematologic Examination or Consultation. If it is evident that hematologic changes are the primary or principal component of the patient's illness, or if the presence of such changes must be ruled out, the physician should seek a complete hematologic examination. In order to get the most immediate and effective study of the patient it may be necessary to ask for consultation with the clinical pathologist or hematologist. In any event, the purpose of this examination is to get the maximal amount of information concerning the blood system with as little discomfort to the patient and as little loss of time as possible. It is a matter of common experience that both the technical accuracy and diagnostic value of blood studies are improved when several observations are made at one time and, so far as possible, with a single sample of blood. There will, of course, be some selection of procedures, depending on the clinical findings, but the risk of making a few extra observations in this type of work is much less than the hazard involved in trying to piece together bits of information obtained at different times on separate samples of blood.

THE ANEMIAS

Definition. Anemia is a disease characterized by a reduction of the O_2-carrying substance in a certain volume of blood due to reduction below normal in the number of red blood cells per cubic millimeter, in hemoglobin per 100 ml. of blood, and in the volume of packed red cells per 100 ml. of blood. For practical purposes 12 gm. of hemoglobin may be accepted as the dividing line. Values below it indicate anemia.

The loss of hemoglobin and consequent reduction in the oxygen-carrying capacity of the blood is the most conspicuous feature of anemia and is the pathologic basis for most of the associated signs and symptoms, such as dyspnea, tachycardia, weakness, and so on. Anemia, without the addition of a qualifying or descriptive term, is not a satisfactory diagnosis and never a valid basis for treatment. In the majority of instances anemia occurs as a sign or complication of disease, often remote from the blood system itself. When anemia is encountered, a careful reevaluation of the patient's condition and a search for the underlying cause are demanded.

DEVELOPMENT OF THE ERYTHROCYTE

It takes only one to two days for the proerythroblast, the cells just one step away from the undifferentiated, multipotential stem cell, to pass through the stages of the early and late erythroblast and to mature into the normoblast, the cells with the dense homogeneous nucleus. The transformation is accomplished by enzymes utilizing metabolic substrates. The morphologic expression of the maturation is the appearance of hemoglobin molecules, which are first demonstrable in early erythroblasts, but only spectrophotometrically, and visually in late erythroblasts (Thorell, 1947). The increase of hemoglobin goes on at the expense of ribonucleic acid.

The next steps, which take another day, include expulsion of the nucleus, transformation into the reticulocyte, entrance into the circulating blood, and maturation into the fully developed red blood cell, all of which takes two to four days and is accompanied by exhaustion of the ribonucleic acid. The period of useful function of the red cell in the circulating blood is 80 to 100 days. Aging is associated with the progressive loss or deterioration of enzymes.

The most important metabolic change at the end of the red cell's life is release of iron and of the other metabolites. About 1 mg. of iron and 10 mg. of bilirubin are released into the circulation when 1 ml. of erythrocytes is destroyed (Crosby, 1957). The mature functioning erythrocyte has a lipoprotein stroma, which encloses from 200 to 300 million hemoglobin molecules. Its energy source is anaerobic glycolysis. For its physiologic function of oxygen transport

by hemoglobin, the erythrocyte needs a system of enzymes. One of them, carbonic anhydrase, is needed for the transport of carbon dioxide from the tissues to the lungs (Gabrio et al., 1956; Granick, 1949). As reduced hemoglobin is exposed in the lungs to oxygen at increasing pressures, increasing amounts of oxygen are taken up until each molecule of hemoglobin has bound four molecules of oxygen. The final product, saturated oxyhemoglobin, contains 1.34 ml. of oxygen per gram of hemoglobin.

The release of oxygen in the tissues depends on the hydrogen ion concentration. In active tissues with a high hydrogen ion concentration and a more acid pH, more oxygen is released than in resting tissues with a low hydrogen ion concentration and more alkaline pH.

The CO_2 is carried by the red cells mainly as bicarbonate; only small amounts are absorbed physically and carried as unchanged CO_2. The transformation of CO_2 to bicarbonate in the tissues and its release as CO_2 from bicarbonate in the lungs is mediated by the enzyme carbonic anhydrase.

The Hemopoietic Equilibrium. Normally the red cell count and hemoglobin levels are maintained tenaciously. They are the result of a balance between red cell destruction and production. Red cell production is controlled by and is inversely proportionate to the oxidative tissue metabolism.

The normal daily output of red cells by marrow is 20 ml. of packed cells (Crosby, 1958). The production is increased when oxygen supply to the tissues drops, as in anemia, at high altitudes, and when oxygen exchange in the lungs is impaired by pulmonary and cardiovascular diseases. The production drops with increase of oxygen transport to the tissues, as in experimental polycythemia produced by transfusions of blood or as a result of exposure to high atmospheric oxygen pressure.

ERYTHROPOIETIN

Definition. Erythropoietin is a substance in the plasma of anemic animals, plasma of animals exposed to low oxygen pressure, and plasma and urine of some anemic patients capable of stimulating red cell production in normal animals (Gurney et al., 1957; Sacks, 1958; Stohlman and Brecher, 1957).

FACTORS WHICH DETERMINE THE HEMATOLOGIC PICTURE IN ANEMIA

The formation and destruction of erythrocytes and hemoglobin are continuous processes in the body. The composition of peripheral blood reflects the existing balance between these two mechanisms. In health, a balance is maintained such that the number of erythrocytes and concentration of hemoglobin remain at a remarkably constant level. When the balance is upset by deficient formation of blood, on the one hand, or by excessive destruction or actual loss of blood, on the other, the result is anemia. In many cases it is possible to determine which phase of the balanced mechanism is at fault and in this manner to approach the true etiologic basis of the anemia. Thus, an excessive destruction of red cells is characterized by an increase in the excretion of urobilinogen (both urine and feces), elevated serum bilirubin, increase in the number of reticulocytes, leukocytosis, and other evidences of reactive hyperplasia of the bone marrow. Decrease in the formation of red cells is characterized by disappearance of reticulocytes, decrease in the excretion of urobilinogen, and often by leukopenia and other signs of inactivity of the hematopoietic tissues.

In addition to simple diminution in the concentration of hemoglobin and of the erythrocyte count in anemia, certain qualitative changes appear and may be marked in the cases in which anemia is severe. In general, these are an expression of strain put on the erythropoietic marrow, which tends to react excessively and sometimes in an abnormal manner. It may produce and release into the circulation a variable number of immature and imperfect erythrocytes (such as poikilocytes, polychromatophilic cells, and nucleated erythrocytes). In some types of anemia the regeneration of blood takes on some of the characteristics seen in fetal life, and immature red cells appear in great numbers in the marrow and even pass over into the circulating blood.

Clinical Signs of Anemia

Certain clinical signs and symptoms are directly associated with anemia per se and are more or less independent of the particular cause. For the most part these signs and symptoms are due to the diminished oxygen-carrying capacity of the blood and, therefore, are roughly proportionate to the hemoglobin concentration. It is not possible to state a critical level beyond which the vital processes are deranged, since there are always a number of factors operating at one time. Consideration must be given to the underlying disease process and its complications other than anemia, the metabolic requirements of the tissues as conditioned by the illness, the nutritional state and other factors, and the rate at which the anemia develops. When anemia develops slowly in a patient who is not otherwise severely ill, erythrocyte counts below 2,000,000 per cubic millimeter or hemoglobin concentrations as low as 6 grams per 100 milliliters may develop without producing any discomfort or physical signs as long as the patient is at rest.

In general, the anemic patient complains of easy fatigability and dyspnea on exertion. He may complain also of faintness, vertigo, and palpitation. Headache is a common symptom. Tinnitus is occasionally mentioned. Dysphagia, ulcers on the buccal mucous membrane, and glossitis have a somewhat more specific relation to the type of anemia. The more common physical findings are pallor, a rapid pulse, low blood pressure, slight fever, some dependent edema, and systolic murmurs. In addition to these general signs and symptoms there are many clinical findings characteristic of the specific type of anemia. It is not our present purpose to discuss these in full, but the point to be emphasized is that the anemias are not laboratory diseases but are conditions in which the clinical record has both specific and differential diagnostic value.

Posthemorrhagic Anemia

Anemia due to blood loss is typically a normocytic anemia, which is defined as the anemia with a normal M.C.V. and M.C.H. (Wintrobe, 1961). The morphologic characteristics are only minimal anisocytosis, poikilocytosis, and achromia regardless of the severity of the anemia. If a marked degree of these morphologic variations and normal corpuscular indexes are present together, a technical error in the latter or combined deficiencies of vitamin B_{12} or folic acid and of iron may be the explanation. Macrocytosis due to vitamin B_{12} or folic acid deficiency and microcytosis due to iron deficiency may cancel each other out and normocytic anemia is the result (see Table 4–3).

The causes of normocytic anemia are listed in Table 4–4. The normal M.C.V. of anemia following a sudden blood loss or a sudden hemolytic crisis may become transiently elevated due to outpouring of re-

Table 4–3. Morphologic Classification of Anemias

CLASS AND SEVERITY	NO. RED COR-PUSCLES	MEAN COR-PUSCULAR VOLUME VOL. / RBC	MEAN COR-PUSCULAR HEMO-GLOBIN HB / RBC	MEAN CORPUSCULAR HEMOGLOBIN CONCEN-TRATION HB / VOL.	DESCRIPTION
Macrocytic					Red cells increased in volume; mean corpuscular hemoglobin proportionally increased; increase in size and hemoglobin content of red cells roughly inversely proportional to number of cells; mean corpuscular hemoglobin concentration remains normal throughout or may be slightly reduced.
Slight	−	+	+	0	
Moderate	− −	++	++	0 −	
Severe	− − −	+++	+++	0 −	
Normocytic					Reduction in the number of red cells without any, or at most only a slight increase in mean corpuscular volume and mean corpuscular hemoglobin; mean corpuscular hemoglobin concentration normal throughout.
Slight	−	0	0	0	
Moderate	− −	+0	+0	0	
Severe	− − −	+0	+0	0	
Simple microcytic					Reduction in volume and hemoglobin content characteristically less marked than reduction in number of red cells; mean corpuscular hemoglobin concentration normal or only slightly reduced.
Slight	−	0	0	0	
Moderate	− −	−	−	0 −	
Severe	− − −	− −	− −	0 −	
Hypochromic microcytic					Reduction in volume and hemoglobin content characteristically more marked than reduction in number of red cells; *mean corpuscular hemoglobin concentration characteristically reduced.*
Slight	0	−	− −	−	
Moderate	−	− −	− − −	− −	
Severe	− −	− − −	− − − −	− − −	

Hb indicates the quantity of hemoglobin in grams per 1000 ml. of blood; Vol. = volume of packed red cells in cubic centimeters per 1000 ml. of blood; RBC, the number of red cells in millions per cubic millimeter.

+ increase; − decrease; 0 no change from the normal; 0 − no, or only slight, decrease; +0 slight or no increase. The amount of increase or decrease is indicated by the number of plus or minus signs, respectively.

Reproduced with permission from Wintrobe: Clinical Hematology. 5th Edition, 1961.

ticulocytes that are larger than mature erythrocytes. Frequently recurring blood losses or attacks of blood destruction lead to loss of iron stores and to microcytic hypochromic anemia. Sickle cell disease is an exception to the rule that in normocytic anemia anisocytosis and poikilocytosis are minimal.

In hereditary spherocytosis the large number of spherocytes reduces the M.C.V. below normal. A normochromic microcytic anemia is the result. After a hemolytic crisis, the outpouring reticulocytes and the remaining spherocytes add up to anisocytosis.

ACUTE POSTHEMORRHAGIC ANEMIA

Definition. This anemia is due to a sudden loss of blood of whatever cause.

Blood. An increased platelet count and a shortened coagulation time are the earliest manifestations and may be demonstrable in less than an hour. The next development is a moderate leukocytosis from 10,000 to

Table 4–4.   Morphologic, Etiologic, and Clinical Classification of Anemia*

TYPE OF ANEMIA	MEAN CORPUSCULAR VOLUME (cu.μ)	MEAN CORPUSCULAR HEMOGLOBIN CONCENTRATION (%)	CAUSE	CLINICAL SYNDROME
I. Macrocytic	>94**	>30	Deficiency of vitamin B_{12} or folic acid (megaloblastic macrocytic anemias)	Pernicious anemia Sprue Idiopathic steatorrhea Some cases of intestinal stricture or resection, gastrocolic fistula, celiac disease
			Faulty absorption	Other forms of chronic diarrhea "Tropical" nutritional macrocytic anemia Less frequently, dietary deficiency in temperate zones Rare cases of carcinoma of the stomach Following total gastrectomy Macrocytic anemia of pregnancy Megaloblastic anemia of infancy *Diphyllobothrium latum* infestation "Refractory megaloblastic" and "achrestic" anemia

			Overactivity of marrow (?) (nonmegaloblastic macrocytic anemias)	Conditions usually associated with normocytic anemia, especially:
				  Sickle cell anemia
				  Macrocytic hemolytic anemias of obscure etiology
				  Chronic and extensive liver disease
				  Macrocytic anemia of hypothyroidism

			Chronic radiation effect	"Internal radiation"
II. Normocytic	80 to 94	>30	Sudden loss of blood	Acute posthemorrhagic anemia, including scurvy, hemophilia, and purpura
			Excessive destruction of blood (for details see Table 4-5)	Hemolytic anemia due to: Infectious, chemical, physical, vegetable, and animal agents

Spherocytes may be present
The intrinsic structural abnormality may be morphologically apparent as:
  Spherocytosis
  Elliptocytosis
  Sickling
  Targeting
			Extracorpuscular causes	Immune reactions
				Nonimmune reactions

			Corpuscular causes (intrinsic structural abnormality)	Hereditary spherocytosis
			Abnormal hemoglobin molecule	Sickle cell anemia and other hereditary hemoglobinopathies Paroxysmal nocturnal hemoglobinuria Hereditary nonspherocytic and other hemolytic anemias
			Defective blood formation	Aplastic or hypoplastic anemia, induced by: Agents that regularly produce marrow hypoplasia (ionizing radiation, mustards, antimetabolites)

Table 4-4 (continued)

TYPE OF ANEMIA	MEAN CORPUSCULAR VOLUME (cu.μ)	MEAN CORPUSCULAR HEMOGLOBIN CONCENTRATION (%)	CAUSE	CLINICAL SYNDROME
				Agents occasionally associated with hypoplasia (antimicrobials, anticonvulsants)
				Unknown causes
				"Simple" chronic anemia associated with various inflammatory and noninflammatory diseases, especially renal disease, malignant disease, and chronic infections
				"Myelophthisic" anemia due to metastatic carcinoma in bone marrow, Hodgkin's disease, leukemia, multiple myeloma, myelosclerosis, and marble bone disease
				Pure red cell anemia
				Congenital pancytopenia (Fanconi)
				Congenital hypoplastic anemia (Diamond-Blackfan)
			Hydremia (?)	"Physiologic" anemia of pregnancy
III. Simple microcytic	<80†	>30	"Imperfect" formation of blood	Subacute and chronic inflammatory diseases and chronic noninflammatory conditions
IV. Hypochromic microcytic	<80	<30	Deficiency of iron through: Deficient diet	Diet deficient in foods containing iron, especially in infants
			Defective absorption	In association with achlorhydria
				Following gastrectomy (total or partial)
				Sprue, idiopathic steatorrhea, celiac disease, chronic diarrhea
			Continued loss of blood	Chronic alimentary or genitourinary tract bleeding
				Multiple hereditary telangiectasia
			Excessive demands for iron	Requirements for growth
				Repeated pregnancies
			Above causes in various degrees and combinations	Chlorosis
				Chronic hypochromic anemia of women
			Deficient antenatal storage or postnatal supply	Hypochromic anemia of infants
Target cells			Genetic anomaly	Thalassemia
				Hereditary sex-linked anemia

* Modified from Wintrobe: Clinical Hematology, 5th Edition, 1961, with permission of the author.
** The sign > indicates "greater than."   † The sign < indicates "less than."

35,000 and a shift to the left reaching the peak in two to five hours. Twenty-four to 48 hours later an outpouring of reticulocytes begins and becomes maximal four to seven days after the hemorrhage. There is a progressive loss of serum iron. The red cell count, hemoglobin, and hematocrit are elevated immediately following hemorrhage owing to vasoconstriction and changes in blood distribution. This is followed by a drop, which persists even though the loss of blood has stopped. Dilution by tissue fluids, which compensate for the lost blood volume, is responsible for the progressive anemia. As a rule the anemia is normocytic, but following severe hemorrhage young basophilic erythrocytes (polychromatophilia) and normoblasts appear. This may give rise to transient macrocytosis.

Regeneration following acute blood loss is progressive. The red cells return to normal levels in about four to six weeks; the hemoglobin takes about two more weeks to come back. It takes about two weeks after the blood loss for the morphologic changes to disappear and two to four days for the leukocyte count to return to normal. A persistent high reticulocyte count and leukocytosis indicate continued bleeding if an infection has been excluded.

Chronic Posthemorrhagic Anemia

When blood is lost slowly or in small quantities, the reactive mechanisms of the body are not excited; hence, both the clinical and hematologic features that characterize acute posthemorrhagic anemia are lacking. Instead of being stimulated, the hematopoietic tissues are likely to be suppressed or depleted. The leukocyte count is low, the percentage of granulocytes is decreased, reticulocytes and other evidence of red cell immaturity do not appear, the serum bilirubin is normal or diminished, and there is no increase in the urine urobilinogen. Over a period of time the anemia of chronic blood loss becomes a chronic iron deficiency anemia, the features of which will be discussed in detail in another section. Acute episodes of hemorrhage may occur during the course of chronic blood loss, in which event certain features of the hematologic picture described in the previous section may be noted. The presence of microcytic red cells containing less than the normal complement of hemoglobin is adequate evidence of chronic blood loss even in the presence of signs characteristic of acute posthemorrhagic anemia. In any instance, the source and cause of the blood loss must be found if possible, since it is toward these that definitive treatment must be directed.

Hemolytic Anemias

Definition. These anemias are caused by excessive destruction of blood.

Table 4–5. Etiologic Classification of Hemolytic Anemias*

I. Corpuscular Defects (intrinsic structural abnormality)
  A. Hereditary spherocytosis
  B. Hereditary elliptocytosis
  C. Hereditary nonspherocytic hemolytic anemia
  D. Hereditary leptocytosis (thalassemia, Mediterranean anemia)
  E. Hereditary hemoglobinopathies (S, C, D, E, G, H, I)
  F. Thalassemia and combinations of thalassemia with sickle cell disease or other hemoglobinopathies
  G. Paroxysmal nocturnal hemoglobinuria
II. Extracorpuscular Causes
  A. Chemical agents
    a. Hemolytic and toxic agents
      Acetanilid
      Allyl-propyl-disulfide
      Anilin
      Arsine
      Benzene
      Colloidal silver
      Dinitrobenzene
      Lead
      Lecithin
      Methyl chloride
      Naphthalene (moth balls)
      Nitrobenzene
      Phenacetin
      Phenylhydrazine
      Promin
      Saponin
      Toluene
      Trinitrotoluene
      Water
    b. Those depending on hypersensitivity
      Benzedrine
      Mesantoin
      Neoarsphenamine
      Pamaquine (Plasmochin)
      Paraphenylenediamine (in hair dyes)
      p-Aminosalicylic acid (PAS)
      Primaquine
      Quinine
      Sulfonamides
  B. Physical agents
    Heat and severe thermal burns
  C. Vegetable and animal poisons
    a. Vegetable poisons
      Fava bean (favism)
      Baghdad spring anemia
      Castor bean
    b. Animal poisons
      Snake venoms
      Endogenous agents
  D. Infectious agents
    1. Protozoal parasites: malaria

---

* Modified from Wintrobe, 5th Edition, 1961, with permission of the author.

Table 4–5 (Continued)

2. Nonprotozoal blood parasites: Bartonella (Oroya fever).
3. Viruses: primary atypical pneumonia, infectious mononucleosis
4. Bacteria: *Cl. welchii, V. cholerae*
E. Immune reactions
  1. Isoimmune reactions
    a. Hemolytic transfusion reactions
    b. Hemolytic disease of the newborn due to blood group incompatibility
  2. Autoimmune reactions
    a. Idiopathic hemolytic anemia
    b. Symptomatic hemolytic anemia
F. Idiopathic nonimmune hemolytic anemia
G. Symptomatic nonimmune hemolytic anemia
H. Paroxysmal cold hemoglobinuria

The classification of hemolytic anemias is based on the location of the factor responsible for the hemolysis. Those within the erythrocyte, the corpuscular defects, are as a rule hereditary. The extracorpuscular factors are as a rule acquired. The difference between the two is best demonstrated by survival studies of the red cells. When erythrocytes with a corpuscular defect are transfused into a normal recipient, their survival is about as long as it is in the original host and shorter than the survival of the recipient's red cells. Normal red cells transfused to patients with defective erythrocytes survive normally. Red cells of patients with an extracorpuscular defect survive in a normal recipient as long as his own red cells. On the other hand, normal erythrocytes transfused to patients with extracorpuscular defects survive only about as long as the recipient's own red cells.

LABORATORY FINDINGS IN HEMOLYTIC ANEMIA

They differ depending on the amount of destroyed blood and the rate of destruction. If the destruction is rapid and the quantity of destroyed blood is large, free hemoglobin and methemalbumin will be present in the plasma (hemoglobinemia and methemalbuminemia). The urine will show albumin and granular and red cell casts and may also show hemosiderin.

According to recent studies hemoglobinuria depends upon the action of haptoglobin, a hemoglobin-binding globulin. The hemoglobin-haptoglobin complex is removed from the circulation and catabolized by the reticuloendothelial system (Laurell and Nyman, 1957). This process prevents hemoglobin from appearing in the urine. However, under certain circumstances the hemoglobin-haptoglobin reaction does not operate. This happens when the plasma hemoglobin level exceeds 100 to 130 mg. per 100 ml. or when the plasma haptoglobin has been used up. Then the plasma hemoglobin passes into the urine and hemoglobinuria results. In the renal tubules a part of the hemoglobin is broken down. The iron is eliminated in the urine as hemosiderin. The remaining hemoglobin may be oxidized and eliminated as methemoglobin. The normal plasma hemoglobin level is 2 to 3 mg. per 100 ml. A rise to 5 to 10 mg. imparts to the plasma a yellow to orange color. With further increase the color becomes pink. Levels up to 25 to 30 mg. per 100 ml. are common in hemolytic anemia. Higher levels are usually indicative of intravascular hemolysis and are seen in hemolytic transfusion reactions and in paroxysmal cold and nocturnal hemoglobinurias.

Quantitative Determination of Plasma Hemoglobin. Ham modified the benzidine method of Bing and Baker for quantitative determination of plasma hemoglobin (Bing and Baker, 1931; Page and Culver, 1960). A more recent micromethod was introduced by Crosby and Furth (1956). Careful technique to avoid adding to the hemolysis is essential for correct interpretation of all tests for hemoglobin. The benzidine method does not distinguish between hemoglobin, sulfhemoglobin, and methemalbumin. The latter imparts to the plasma a brown color and can be identified with the *Schumm test*. Nine volumes of plasma or serum are overlaid with a layer of ether in a large test tube. One volume of saturated solution of ammonium sulfide is added with a pipet. After thorough mixing, the contents are poured into a hand spectroscope. An absorption band at 558 mμ indicates a positive test for methemalbumin (Page and Culver, 1960).

If the rate of destruction is not rapid, there is no hemoglobinemia or hemoglobinuria, but elevated bilirubin in the serum and increased urobilinogen in the urine and stools are found. In some cases hemosiderin may be present in the urine. The normal urobilinogen in a 24-hour specimen is 0 to 3.5 mg. in urine and 40 to 280 mg. in the stool. Following excessive hemolysis it may increase to 5 to 200 mg. in the urine and to 300 to 4000 mg. in the stool. The examination of feces is more dependable than of the urine, because it may show an increase when the urine shows none. It may show an increase even when the serum bilirubin is not raised. The latter finding is explained by the fact that the normal liver has the capacity to remove large amounts of free hemoglobin from the blood. The development of anemia as a result of hemolysis depends on the erythropoietic capacity of the marrow. Wintrobe (1961) speaks of "compensated hemolytic disease" when anemia does not follow hemolysis and of "decompensated hemolytic disease" when anemia develops.

The Blood Smear. The anemia is normocytic as a rule. It may be macrocytic. What one sees in the blood smear is nothing else but the expression of the capacity of the marrow to compensate for the lost blood. Here belong anisocytosis and poikilocytosis (usually more of the former than of the latter), reticulocytosis (much larger number of reticulocytes in massive acute hemolysis than in chronic), polychromatophilia (i.e., reticulocytes without the benefit of vital stain), and normoblasts. Macrocytosis is an expression of the presence of immature red cells, which are larger than normocytes.

When in response to excessive blood destruction the call for increased production reaches the marrow, it reacts usually as an organ and releases excessive numbers and younger forms of leukocytes and platelets together with erythrocytes. The result is leukocytosis with a "shift to the left" and thrombocytosis with abnormal and giant platelets. The other findings are spherocytes in hereditary and acquired hemolytic anemia, schistocytes (fragmented red cells), and erythrophagocytosis.

The spherocytes in acquired hemolytic anemia are larger and are called overhydrated "macrospherocytes" as distinguished from underhydrated "microspherocytes" of hereditary spherocytosis. The consequences of spherocytosis are defective rouleaux formation, which may exert a retarding influence on the sedimentation rate of erythrocytes, and a "shift to the left" of the osmotic fragility curve.

Hemolytic Anemias due to Intrinsic Structural Abnormalities

HEREDITARY SPHEROCYTOSIS

Definition. This is a hereditary corpuscular abnormality characterized by the presence of spherocytes and bouts of acute hemolysis (hemolytic crises). The cause of the crises is believed to be acute aplasia (Plate 4–5 [2]).

Increased osmotic fragility is characteristic. Occasionally the fragility of incu-

bated cells has to be tested to establish the diagnosis. It may be considerably greater than the fragility of the nonincubated cells. The antiglobulin test is usually negative. Splenectomy is as a rule curative.

HEREDITARY NONSPHEROCYTIC HEMOLYTIC ANEMIA

This anemia is clinically similar to the spherocytic disease. The osmotic fragility is normal, but it is considerably increased when done with preincubated red cells. Splenectomy does not help.

HEREDITARY OVALOCYTOSIS

Ovalocytes are abundant in the peripheral smear. The deformity is increased in sealed, moist preparations. Most patients with this cellular abnormality are not ill except about 10 to 15 per cent who develop mild anemia (Plate 4–1 [5]).

HEMOLYTIC ANEMIA OF UNDETERMINED ETIOLOGY (HEINZ BODY ANEMIA)

In hemolytic anemia produced by acetanilid (phenacetin) and following exposure to various chemicals, such as naphthalene, sodium nitrate, sodium chlorate, sulfanilamide, para-aminosalicylic acid, Isoniazid, Furadantin, certain antimalarial drugs, and certain others, so-called Heinz bodies can be demonstrated in smears stained supravitally with brilliant cresyl blue or with 0.5 per cent methyl violet in saline (Fig. 4–48).

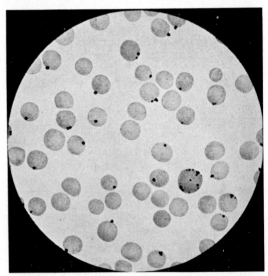

Figure 4–48. Heinz bodies, nile blue sulfate stain. The location of the granules along the cellular margin is characteristic. The larger, somewhat darker cell with many granules in the right lower quadrant just three cells away from the border of the field is a reticulocyte. (Reproduced with permission from Heilmeyer and Begemann, 1955.)

Stain for Heinz Bodies. To four drops of the methyl violet stain on a slide a drop of blood is added. The smear is covered with a coverslip, blotted with a sheet of filter paper to remove the excessive fluid, ringed with petrolatum, and examined with the oil immersion lens. Heinz bodies appear as rounded or irregularly shaped, deep purple, refractile particles (thus differing from Howell-Jolly bodies, which are always round and form siderotic granules known as Pappenheimer bodies, which are bluish black). The network in reticulocytes stains pale blue. With brilliant cresyl blue, Heinz bodies stain lighter blue than the filaments of reticulocytes. Heinz bodies can also be demonstrated in wet preparations as refractile particles ranging from being just visible up to 3 microns and tending to lie close to the periphery. Only mature erythrocytes develop Heinz bodies; reticulocytes do not. Red cells with Heinz bodies are removed from the circulation by the spleen, or, as some claim, the Heinz bodies are extracted from the red cells by splenic action.

The Pathogenesis of Heinz Body Anemia. Intracellular oxidation may lead to hemolysis and hemolytic anemia. The intensity of intracellular oxidation varies from mild, which is manifested by reduction of intracellular glutathione, through moderate oxidation, with methemoglobin appearing in the cell, to severe oxidation, with denaturation and precipitation of hemoglobin leading to formation of Heinz bodies with stainable intracellular granules.

Heinz granules may appear spontaneously in premature infants as well as in adults following splenectomy without history of drug intake, or they may be induced by chemicals. When given in therapeutic doses, drugs do not affect normal red cells but produce anemia with Heinz bodies in susceptible patients, especially Negroes (Dern et al., 1954). This happened in about 10 per cent of male Negroes who were given 30 mg. of primaquine a day. The deficiency in the susceptible red cells is believed to be in the oxidative enzyme, glucose 6-phosphate dehydrogenase (Carson et al., 1956). This form of anemia was shown to be due to a hereditary sex-linked susceptibility to drugs. Red cells exposed to the drugs showed a decrease in the concentration of reduced glutathione. Older cells were more susceptible. An unstable glutathione system is held responsible. Premature and newborn infants have an unstable glutathione system and may develop hemolytic anemia and jaundice following intake of vitamin K.

Wright's stained blood smears in drug-induced or Heinz body anemia show misshapen red cells in addition to spherocytosis and basophilic stippling. Such findings should suggest the special examination and stain for Heinz bodies. They can be seen also in wet preparations with darkfield and phase-contrast microscopy.

For controls, artificially induced Heinz bodies can be seen in normal blood to which acetylphenylhydrazine has been added. The blood turns brown and should then be examined.

The chemicals and drugs responsible for Heinz body hemolytic anemia include naphthoquinone in moth balls, which can be absorbed via the skin or inhaled by infants, and acetanilid (phenacetin) in adults.

In some cases of hemolytic anemia of indefinite etiology, also called "inclusion body" anemia, siderocytes (Pappenheimer bodies) have been described. They are rod shaped or round bodies when stained with Wright's stain and with other Romanowsky dyes. They are present in the peripheral blood only after splenectomy but can also be seen in marrow preparations in the nonsplenectomized. The marrow shows normoblastic hyperplasia.

The various forms of hemolytic anemia arranged according to etiology have been summarized in Table 4–5.

Hemolytic Anemias due to Extracorpuscular Causes

CHEMICAL AGENTS

Hemolytic and Toxic Agents. The action of chemical agents depends on the dose and on other factors many of which are known only vaguely. They range from simple substances, such as water, to some that are highly complex.

When it was used as irrigating fluid, distilled water was found responsible for acute hemolytic anemia as a result of entry into venous channels during transurethral resection (Landsteiner and Finch, 1947). In addition to anemia some of these chemicals produce methemoglobinemia, and some are responsible for cyanosis (toluene, trinitrotoluene, nitrobenzene, acetanilid, and phenacetin). Some may lead to aplastic anemia (toluene and trinitrotoluene). Promin, a sulfone derivative, makes blood turn chocolate brown. Lead administered therapeutically may produce progressive anemia with basophilic stippling, reticulocytosis, normoblastemia, Cabot's rings, Howell-Jolly bodies, and leukocytosis. In cases of chronic exposure to lead, basophilic stippling, more in the marrow than in the peripheral blood, and coproporphyrinuria are the characteristic findings. These changes produce defective erythrocytes, which are removed by the spleen.

Chemicals Causing Hypersensitivity. Such chemicals affect only few persons of the many who are exposed to them. Racial differences in the action of some of these chemicals have been demonstrated by the greater susceptibility of Negroes to pamaquin and primaquine. Survival studies have shown that erythrocytes are directly affected. Recovery from the anemia was followed by resistance to subsequent administration of the drug.

The observation that the sensitive cells formed Heinz bodies led to a test for red cell sensitivity to some drugs (primaquine, acetanilid, some sulfonamides, phenylhydrazine, sulfoxone, and phenacetin).

Test for red cell sensitivity. REAGENT. Acetylphenylhydrazine, 100 mg. per 100 ml. of buffered saline.

PROCEDURE. To 2 ml. of the reagent in a test tube, add 0.1 ml. of blood, mix well, and place in 37° C. water bath for two hours. A small drop of the blood is placed on a coverslip. The coverslip is inverted over a large drop of a 2 per cent solution of crystal violet.

RESULT. From 45 to 92 per cent of erythrocytes of a sensitive person may contain Heinz bodies. Only 0 to 28 per cent were present in nonsensitive controls (Dern et al., 1954, 1955). The same authors reported a lowering of glutathione to two-thirds of normal in sensitive red cells.

PHYSICAL AGENTS

Extensive third degree burns produce hemolytic anemia, probably because of direct damage to red cells (Ham et al., 1948).

VEGETABLE AND ANIMAL POISONS

Inhalation of pollens of the fava bean plant or ingestion of the bean itself may be followed by a fulminant hemolytic anemia. The sensitivity is racial and familial. It is claimed that a hereditary glutathione instability is responsible. It affects mainly persons of Mediterranean origin. Incomplete autoantibodies in the serum and positive direct and indirect antiglobulin tests have been reported (Marcolongo, 1953). So-called Baghdad spring anemia is similar to the anemia caused by the fava bean. Some snake venoms and ricin contained in the castor bean are strongly hemolytic.

Hemolytic anemia may also be the effect of endogenous metabolic products, but not enough is known about them.

INFECTIOUS AGENTS

Destruction of erythrocytes by plasmodia is responsible for the anemia in malaria. This is supported by the observation that the osmotic and mechanical fragility of parasitized erythrocytes is increased. Inhibition of marrow activity may be an additional factor. Fulminant hemoglobinuria (blackwater fever) is a complication of P. falciparum malaria. Its frequency after quinine therapy suggests an autoimmune mechanism mediated by the drug.

Oroya fever, a frequently fatal disease in Peru, is characterized by a hemolytic anemia and leukocytosis. *Bartonella bacilliformis* is the responsible agent.

Cold agglutinins may be responsible for hemolytic anemia complicating so-called virus pneumonia (Moeschlin et al., 1954). (For details see p. 178.)

Hemolytic anemia is one of the rare complications of infectious mononucleosis, possibly a virus disease. Hemolytic anemia of varying severity is frequent in some bacterial infections.

IMMUNE MECHANISMS. IMMUNOHEMATOLOGY

Immunohematology has been defined as the branch of medicine dealing with "diseases of blood of which the cause, the pathogenesis, or clinical manifestations have been shown to be determined by an antigen-antibody reaction" (Davidsohn, 1954).

From this definition it is obvious that immunohematologic laboratory tests comprise a wide variety of techniques with one common denominator: they are based on immunologic reactions in which blood cells participate. For reasons of convenience

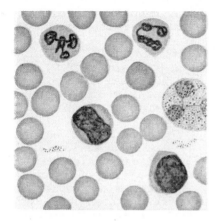

1. Normal blood

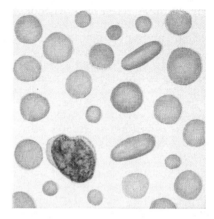

2. Hereditary spherocytosis

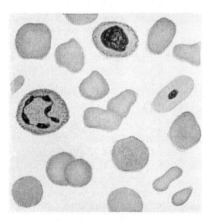

3. Untreated pernicious anemia

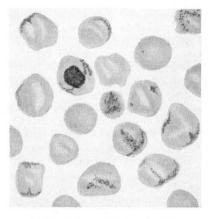

4. Treated pernicious anemia

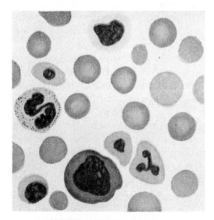

5. Fetal erythroblastosis

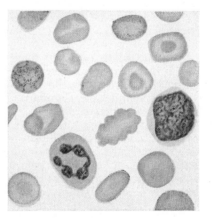

6. Hereditary leptocytosis
(thalassemia major)

Plate 4–5. Anemia. (Dorothy Booth, pinx.)

some tests belonging in this category are treated in other sections of this book as indicated by suitable references. Although all three corpuscular elements of blood may be involved in immunohematologic tests, the methodology of the tests in which white cells and platelets are involved is, as yet, not fully developed for general practical application.

IMMUNE DISEASES OF THE BLOOD AND BLOOD FORMING TISSUES

Definition. These are diseases in which an antigen-antibody reaction is involved in one or more of the following: the cause of the disease, the pathogenesis, or a diagnostic test for the disease.

Pathogenesis of Immune Diseases. *Heteroimmune diseases.* The antigen is a foreign living agent invading the host and capable of multiplying within the body of the host. The antibody is produced in the body of the host. Examples: acute acquired hemolytic anemia in virus pneumonia; the test for infectious mononucleosis.

Isoimmune diseases. The antigen comes from another person or is a part of the host (usually blood). The antibody is a part of the host or comes from another person. Examples: Hemolytic transfusion reaction, fetal erythroblastosis (hemolytic disease of the newborn), isoimmune leukopenia, and isoimmune thrombocytopenia.

Isoimmune hemolysis may be the result of transfusion of incompatible red cells or of incompatible plasma. Injection of incompatible red cells may be followed by a hemolytic transfusion reaction with its characteristic clinical picture (p. 303 ff.). Anemia is not a part of this type of hemolytic transfusion reaction, but it may trigger an autoimmune hemolytic process in the host. Injection of incompatible plasma may produce an anemia if the transfused plasma contains an excessively high titer of isoagglutinin or if it contains immune isoagglutinins in which case hemolysis may result even if the titer is low. This type of isoimmune hemolytic anemia may follow the transfusion of blood of group O to recipients of groups A, B, or AB. Isohemolysis may be the result of the action of several types of isoantibodies: (1) Isohemolysins, which are present in the serum of a relatively small number of normal persons. They may be increased considerably by various therapeutic and prophylactic immunizations. (2) Isoagglutinins, which do not hemolyze red cells *in vitro*, but *in vivo* prepare them for the hemolytic action of the reticuloendothelial system (Jandl *et al.*, 1957).

HEMOLYTIC DISEASE OF THE NEWBORN (FETAL ERYTHROBLASTOSIS). The anemia of hemolytic disease of the newborn is of the isoimmune type. The isoantibody comes from the mother via the placenta (p. 305 ff.).

The Blood Findings in Hemolytic Disease of the Newborn

Early examination of the blood usually reveals an increase of immature nucleated erythrocytes (pronormoblasts and normoblasts. On the other hand, although this finding gave the disease its name, erythroblastemia is not always present, especially if the examination is not done immediately after birth.

From 200 to 2000 nucleated erythrocytes per cubic millimeter may be present in term infants and up to 5000 in premature infants. Blood from the umbilical vein for early examination is more reliable than peripheral (capillary) blood because the erythrocyte count and the hemoglobin may be significantly altered between birth and ligation of the cord.

Generally there is a macrocytic anemia of varying severity and an increase in reticulocytes. In fetal erythroblastosis caused by ABO incompatibility, spherocytes are conspicuous. Occasionally anemia may appear suddenly on the second or third day or even later. The platelet count is frequently below the lower normal value of 150,000 to 250,-000 per cu. mm. When the nucleated erythrocyte count is high (10,000 or more per cu. mm.), the leukocyte count (which is frequently elevated) must be corrected. Frequently the differential count shows a leukemoid blood picture with many immature leukocytes including myelocytes (Plates 4–5[5], 4–7). There is pronounced normoblastic hyperplasia of the marrow.

Autoimmune Diseases. The antigen is an autoantigen (a modified part of the patient's own body). The antibody is an autoantibody (also a modified part of the patient's own body). Examples: Idiopathic and symptomatic autoimmune hemolytic anemia, autoimmune leukopenia, and paroxysmal cold hemoglobinuria.

Knowledge of autoimmune diseases goes back to the end of the 19th century but was pushed into the background by the authority of Paul Ehrlich, who coined the phrase "horror autotoxicus" with which he expressed his conviction that antibodies could not be formed in the body against its own tissues, because this would not be compatible with life. There were occasional break-throughs, such as Donath and Landsteiner's test for cold paroxysmal hemoglobinuria (1904) and studies on hemolytic anemia by the French hematologists of the beginning of the century (Chauffard and Troisier, 1908; Widal *et al.*, 1908).

The recent great advances have been made possible by the progress in our knowledge and understanding of antibodies. There are some that do not react in saline but need plasma, albumin, macromolecular substances in general, and proteolytic enzymes. These are the so-called incomplete antibodies as compared with the previously well-known so-called complete antibodies, which react well in saline. Much of this new knowledge came as a by-product of studies on the Rh factor.

All antibodies are globulins. Some antibodies react only at warm (body) temperatures and others at cold temperatures with optimums at a particular degree of temperature. Some react only at a certain pH. Some agglutinate only but do not hemolyze directly. The agglutinated red cells become subject to destructive forces in the reticuloendothelial system. Some are hemolysins, lysis taking place at only one temperature, warm or cold (monothermal). Some are hemolysins but require two temperature levels, first cold and then warm (bithermal).

Incomplete warm autohemoantibodies. DEFINITION. These are abnormal serum globulins that combine with red cells at 37° C. Demonstrable reactions, e.g., agglutination, do not occur in saline except when the red cells are treated with proteolytic enzymes, but reactions can be demonstrated in macromolecular mediums, such as serum albumin and plasma, and with the indirect antiglobulin test.

ELUTION OF AUTOANTIBODIES. Incomplete autoantibodies can be separated from the red cells by suspending the latter in small amounts of saline of suitable temperature and centrifuging at the same temperature. The supernatant contains the antibodies. Maximum elution of warm antibodies takes place at 56° C. In the body, red cells coated with these antibodies are rapidly destroyed. Warm antibodies are responsible for idiopathic and symptomatic acquired hemolytic anemia.

Warm autohemolysins occasionally are present together with warm autoagglutinins and react best at 37° C. They have not been studied sufficiently.

Cold agglutinins. Cold agglutinins are nonspecific antibodies that agglutinate the patient's own and other human erythrocytes, regardless of blood group. Reaction temperature ranges from 0° to 20° C. At 0° to 10° C. cold agglutinins are almost universal. Antibodies reacting only at such low temperatures have no pathologic significance. They are the so-called physiologic cold agglutinins.

Pathologic agglutinins also exert maximal effect at 0° but have a wider thermal amplitude. The highest temperature at which they react is as a rule 30° C.

The range of titers of physiologic cold agglutinins at 0° C. is 0 to 128. The most frequent titer: around 1 to 8. In chronic cold agglutinins disease the range is 4000 to 130,000 (maximum reported). Erythrocytes coated with cold agglutinins have increased mechanical fragility.

Hemolysins

1. Natural isohemolysins are rare. They have been reported in some of the rare blood group systems, e.g., Lewis (see p. 278).

2. Immune isohemolysins are seen following injection of incompatible blood or so-called purified specific blood group substances.

3. Bithermal autohemolysins are seen in cold paroxysmal hemoglobinuria.

Bithermal cold autohemolysins are abnormal serum globulin capable of hemolyzing the patient's own and other persons' red cells.

They combine with erythrocytes (sensitization of erythrocytes) at temperature below 20° C. They do not combine with red cells at temperature higher than 20° C. When temperature rises to 25° C., hemolysis begins. The optimum temperature for hemolysis is 40° C. The titers are low: 2 to 16; the highest recorded was 64 and even then it was transient.

4. Monothermal cold autohemolysins, having a thermal range of 15 to 30° C. (optimum: 22° C.), occur simultaneously with high titered cold agglutinins. They are the cause of excessive destruction of red cells and of hemolytic anemia. They react best at slightly acid pH (acid hemolysins), the optimum pH is 6.3 and the range, pH 6 to 7. The serum is acidified by adding 10 volumes per cent of 0.4 N HCl. The range of titers of cold monothermal autohemolysins

Plate 4–6. Hemolytic anemia.

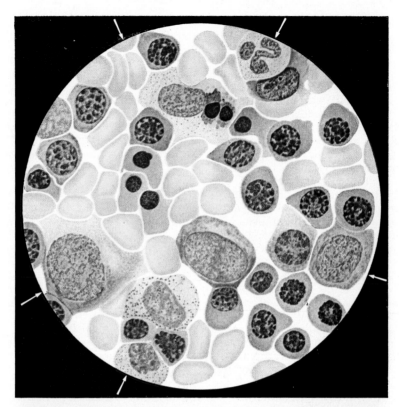

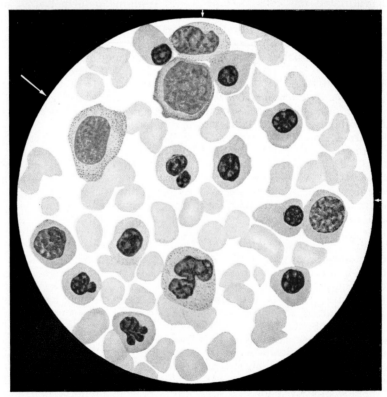

Plate 4–7. Fetal erythroblastosis.

Plate 4–6. Hemolytic anemia, marrow. The plate shows the characteristic findings of a reactive, predominantly normoblastic hyperplasia. We will start just a little to the right of the very top of the circle, at 1 o'clock, where, conveniently located for orientation, is the familiar segmented granulocyte. What seems to be a separate nucleus on the left in this cell is actually connected with a fine filament that cannot be seen here. To the right of the granulocyte, touching it and slightly deformed by it, is probably a basophilic normoblast. As we travel down the circle, we find at 2 o'clock two polychromatophilic normoblasts of which there are many in the preparation. These cells are somewhat younger than a number of almost orthochromatic normoblasts with their small dense pyknotic nuclei. One of them is impinging on or, more correctly, is being impinged upon by the second of two polychromatophilic normoblasts which we have just described. At 4 o'clock we find in a colony of eleven cells three varieties of erythroid cells. The one at which the arrow is pointing is a proerythroblast. Its chromatin is loosely knitted, and it has three distinct nucleoli and a deeply basophilic cytoplasm. Touching it toward the center of the field is a normoblast that differs from the proerythroblast just described by the coarsening of its nucleus and the almost polychromatophilic color of its cytoplasm owing to advancing hemoglobinization. This cell, which is best labeled as a polychromatophilic normoblast, is just slightly younger than the two fully ripened polychromatophilic normoblasts just above and the six just below the proerythroblast. The large cell toward the center of the field bordering on the six polychromatophilic normoblasts just described is another proerythroblast.

At 7 o'clock the arrow points at a neutrophilic myelocyte. Covering it toward the center are two polychromatophilic normoblasts, followed in the same direction by a promyelocyte. Note the difference between the fewer and coarser granules of the promyelocyte and the abundant and finer granules of the myelocyte. At 8 o'clock the arrow points at another proerythroblast distinctly younger than the one at 4 o'clock. The larger nucleus and the looser structure of the chromatin testify to its younger age. Roughly at 11 o'clock we see what looks like the cytoplasmic body of a neutrophilic myelocyte cut in half with the nucleus left outside. The amputated cell is surrounded by two basophilic normoblasts. (Plate from Heilmeyer, L., and Begemann, H.: Atlas der Klinischen Hämatologie und Cytologie. Springer, 1955.)

Plate 4–7. Hemolytic disease of the newborn (fetal erythroblastosis), peripheral blood. The erythrocytes are predominantly macrocytic and show considerable aniso- and poikilicytosis. This finding alone suggests Rh incompatibility as the cause of the erythroblastosis. In erythroblastosis caused by ABO incompatibility, spherocytes are frequent.

The predominant nucleated cells in this preparation are orthochromatic normoblasts with dense, compact, and coarse nuclei, many of them deformed and lobated. At 3 o'clock the arrow points at a polychromatophilic normoblast. Its large nucleus with its chromatin subdivided by the lighter parachromatin testifies to its younger age when compared with the more mature, almost orthochromatic, normoblast just touching it toward the center. The signs of advancing age of the latter cell are its small compact nucleus and more hemoglobin and the consequent lighter blue of its cytoplasm. A polychromatophilic normoblast with a misshaped nucleus having three finger-like projections is at 7 o'clock, another almost orthochromatic normoblast with a single knob on its nucleus is at 8 o'clock, followed clockwise by a polychromatophilic, larger, and somewhat younger normoblast. The arrow at 10 o'clock points at a neutrophilic myelocyte. Sharply at 12 o'clock is a neutrophilic metamyelocyte surrounded clockwise by an orthochromatic normoblast, a proerythroblast, the youngest cell in the preparation, and by another orthochromatic normoblast. (Plate from Heilmeyer, L., and Begemann, H.: Atlas der Klinischen Hämatologie und Cytologie. Springer, 1955.)

is 320 to 2048; the highest reported titer was 8000.

Test for Autohemolysis

Sterile clotted normal blood incubated for 24 hours shows no hemolysis or only minimal traces (0 to 0.5 per cent in a quantitative test) and only very small amounts after 48 hours (0.4 to 3.5 per cent in a quantitative test). Hemolysis is accelerated and more pronounced in hereditary spherocytosis, paroxysmal nocturnal hemoglobinuria, hemolytic anemia caused by chemicals such as acetylphenylhydrazine, acquired autoimmune hemolytic anemias with spherocytosis, and one form of congenital nonspherocytic hemolytic anemia (Selwyn and Dacie, 1954). A sample of the preincubation serum is used as a control. In a quantitative test defibrinated blood is used. The hemolysis in the serum is measured in a colorimeter.

Collection of Blood and Serum. For the study of cold autoantibodies it is best to collect the blood with a prewarmed syringe in a prewarmed test tube (both at 37° C.) and to place the tube immediately into a container with water maintained at 37° C. until it is transferred into an incubator. There it remains until it clots and the clot is retracted. Centrifugation must also be carried out at the same temperature. The serum is then removed with a capillary pipet. If cells are mixed with the serum, the specimen must be recentrifuged at 37° C. The procedure may be simplified somewhat by using a prewarmed vacutainer tube.

Red cells can be obtained from the same specimen by breaking up the warm clot, transferring them to a test tube with warm (37° C.) saline, washing with warm saline, and centrifuging at the same temperature. They can also be obtained with an anticoagulant, e.g., acid citrate-dextrose (ACD) or oxalate, but again maintaining 37° C. is essential.

For shipping by mail, the serum obtained as described and whole blood collected in ACD solution should be sent. Upon arrival at the destination the whole blood will have to be placed in an incubator before the cells are washed. Serum should be stored frozen in 1 to 2 ml. vials at −20° C. or less. Red cells will keep for two to three weeks in ACD or in another suitable solution. They can be kept for considerably longer periods at −20° C. in glycerin (Chaplin *et al.*, 1954). Once washed and suspended in saline, they must be used within a few hours.

Plate 4–8. Normal marrow. At the 12 o'clock position the arrow points to an island of six cells. Two at the top are neutrophilic myelocytes lying next to each other. The next two toward the center are a promyelocyte on the left and an eosinophilic myelocyte on its right. The visible portion of a cell partly covered by the promyelocyte is probably a normoblast. Next to it on the right is a neutrophilic segmented granulocyte.

At the bottom of the circle the arrow is directed at a metamyelocyte. Just above it is a reticulum cell, somewhat deformed and crowded by the adjacent red cells.

At 7 o'clock there is a metamyelocyte.

At 9 o'clock there is a myelocyte and next to it and below, a plasma cell.

At 10 o'clock a proerythroblast is seen, and just a short distance away clockwise are two orthochromatic normoblasts.

There is a superficial resemblance between the proerythroblast and the plasma cells. The main difference is in the size and structure of the nucleus. In the proerythroblast the nucleus is larger and the chromatin is delicately reticulated and granular. In the plasma cell it is more compact and clumped. In this reproduction of the plasma cell the separation into chromatin and parachromatin masses is not apparent. The presence of hemoglobin in the cytoplasm of the proerythroblast, even if only traces of it are present, may sometimes be another differential point. (Plate from Heilmeyer, L., and Begemann, H.: Atlas der Klinischen Hämatologie und Cytologie. Springer, 1955.)

Plate 4–9. Osteoblasts and osteoclasts.

1. The three oval-shaped cells on the left are osteoblasts. They measure about 30 microns in their longest diameter. The nucleus is somewhat eccentrically located. Its chromatin structure is coarse. It contains one or more deeply blue nucleoli. The cytoplasm is purplish blue. Within it, some distance away from the nucleus, in the part of the cell with more abundant cytoplasm, is an indefinitely outlined, light colored area, the archoplasm.

Familiarity with this marrow cell is important, because otherwise it may be mistaken for a plasma cell, and if such cells are present in sheets, they may be mistaken for cancer cells.

2. The multinucleated cell on the right is an osteoclast. It has four nuclei with a finely reticulated chromatin structure and a distinct margin. The cytoplasm is reddish purple and finely granular. It may contain coarse inclusions, which are interpreted as phagocytosed osseous debris. These cells are seen frequently in children and in osteitis fibrosa. They may have as many as 100 nuclei. Familiarity with them is essential because they also are easily mistaken for cancer cells. (Plate from Heilmeyer, L., and Begemann, H.: Atlas der Klinischen Hämatologie und Cytologie. Springer, 1955.)

Plate 4–8. Normal marrow.

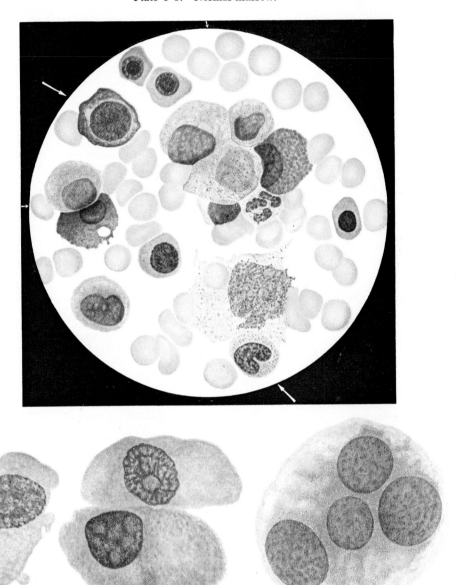

1   osteoblasts

2   osteoclast

Plate 4–9

The Red Cell Suspension. For agglutination tests a 2 per cent suspension is used, and for hemolysin tests a 4 to 5 per cent is used.

Testing for Autoantibodies. The direct antiglobulin (Coomb's) test detects antibodies attached to red cells (see p. 275). The indirect antiglobulin (Coomb's) test (ICT) detects free autoantibodies in the serum. Warm autoantibodies are detectable more readily with enzyme-treated red cells than with the ICT test (for technical details see p. 276). On the other hand, cold autoantibodies are readily detected with the indirect antiglobulin test. Successful use of the ICT depends on meticulous technique and attention to sources of error. The following outline is based on the recommendations of Dacie (1956).

The temperature. The temperature recommended for incubation must be adhered to strictly. Carrying out the test at 37° C. means carrying out the entire procedure at that temperature from the moment one obtains the blood specimen until the reading of the results. Tests at 4° C. are less informative than those at 20° C., because normal incomplete cold antibodies may interfere.

The pH. For detection of incomplete cold hemolysins, acidification of the test serum with 10 per cent by volume of 0.25 N HCl is essential before the red cells are added.

Complement. Inactivation of the test serum at 56° C. for as little as five minutes destroys its reactivity in the ICT. To use such inactivated serum one has to add one or more volumes of fresh normal serum but only after normal incomplete cold antibody has been absorbed from it. The same applies to serum that has lost its complement activity on prolonged standing.

On the other hand, the warm autoantibody of the gamma globulin type does not require complement and can be used after inactivation.

The test cells. Some warm autoantibodies are specific especially for certain types in the Rh system. Hence, cells of known Rh genotypes should be used, i.e., Rh_1, Rh_1 (CDe/CDe), Rh_2 Rh_2 (cDE/cDE), and rh (cde/cde), and not just Rh-(D)-positive and -negative cells. For screening purposes, O Rh_1 Rh_2 (CDe/cDE) cells should be used.

The antiglobulin serum. At least two dilutions have to be used—1 to 4 and 1 to 64. The former is more likely to detect cold

autoantibodies and the latter, the warm autoantibodies.

The test for autoantibodies. Fourteen test tubes are set up, seven in each of two racks.

RACK 1 (FOR INCUBATION AT 37° C.)	RACK 2 (FOR 20°C.)
Tube 1: To 0.25 ml. (five drops) of serum add 0.05 ml. (one drop) of 20 to 30 per cent suspension of ORh_1 Rh_2 (CDe/cDE) cells.	same set-up
Tube 2: As tube 1, but serum acidified with 1/10 volume of 0.25 N HCl is used.	same
Tube 3: As tube 1, but an equal volume of fresh normal serum is added to the patient's serum.	same
Tube 4: As tube 3, but both the patient's and normal serum are acidified with 1/10 volume of 0.25 N HCl.	same
Tube 5: As tube 2, but patient's serum is inactivated at 56°C. for 30 minutes.	same
Tube 6: As tube 1 but with normal serum instead of patient's serum.	same
Tube 7: As tube 2 with normal serum instead of patient's serum.	same

The racks are shaken gently at intervals. After two hours' incubation the test tubes are inspected for agglutination or hemolysis and so recorded. The cells are washed at least three times in saline and the indirect antiglobulin test carried out. This is a qualitative test. If positive, the titer of the antibody and its specificity remain to be determined.

The Gamma Globulin Neutralization Test (Dacie, 1956)

Principle. The addition of gamma globulin to antiglobulin serum permits to distinguish two types of antiglobulin reactions in autoimmune hemolytic anemia: (1) The reaction is inhibited by gamma globulin. This is the gamma globulin type which includes the majority of autoimmune hemolytic anemias due to warm autoantibodies; (2) the reaction is not inhibited by gamma globulin. This is the nongamma globulin type. This is the antibody seen in autoimmune hemolytic anemia due to cold antibodies.

The Test. *Reagents*

1. 4 per cent solution of human gamma globulin.

2. A potent antiglobulin serum diluted

1 to 4 or 1 to 8 in saline.

3. The test red cells.

Fourfold dilutions of the gamma globulin solution are set up ranging from 1 to 4 to 1 to 4096. To each dilution of the gamma globulin an equal amount of the antiglobulin serum solution is added. The mixture is incubated for a brief period (not less than five minutes). An agglutination test with the red cells is set up.

Controls

1. The test red cells with unabsorbed antiglobulin serum (the antiglobulin serum control).

2. O Rh-positive (D-positive) red cells sensitized with anti-D with the absorbed antiglobulin serum.

3. O red cells sensitized with cold agglutinins present in normal serum.

Results. None or weak agglutination reaction: The autoantibody is of the warm type. The agglutination remains essentially unchanged: The antibody is of the cold variety.

Red Cell Survival Studies

THE DIFFERENTIAL AGGLUTINATION METHOD OF ASHBY (1919)

Principle. Compatible blood possessing a blood group factor that the recipient does not possess is transferred to the recipient, e.g., O cells to recipients A or B or AB and ON cells to M or MN recipients. After the transfusion, serums with potent agglutinins for the red cells of the recipient are added to samples of the recipient's blood and the unagglutinated red cells are counted.

The Test. A sample of the recipient's blood obtained prior to the transfusion is tested first to serve as a control and for the selection of a serum reacting strongly with the cells of the recipient.

After the transfusion, 0.1 ml. of the recipient's blood is added to 4.9 ml. of 3 per cent sodium citrate. To 0.25 ml. of this suspension, 0.25 ml. of a potent agglutinating serum is added.

The optimum dilution of the agglutinating serum is determined with pretransfusion blood. The optimum dilution is one with which less than 10,000 unagglutinated red cells are found when the tested blood sample contains 5,000,000 red cells. The blood serum mixture is left at room temperature for at least two hours and then centrifuged at about 1500 r.p.m. (300 G) for one minute. The tube is shaken vigor-

ously to break up the large clumps into small ones. The specimen is permitted to settle for not more than one minute, and the upper three-fourths of the suspension is transferred with a pipet to another test tube, which is then recentrifuged for one minute. The sediment is mixed with the supernatant according to a standard procedure, i.e., 50 inversions at an angle of about 90° at the rate of one per second. A counting chamber is filled with the upper layer of the cell suspension. The cells are permitted to settle for not less than two minutes. Only the free cells are counted. The number of the unagglutinated cells is expressed in absolute numbers per cubic millimeter or as a percentage of the number present after the transfusion (Mollison, 1956).

THE RADIOCHROMIUM METHOD (Cr^{51})

Principle. Blood cells tagged with sodium chromate containing a small amount of Cr^{51} are transferred to the recipient. The survival of the tagged cells is studied in samples removed at intervals.

The Test. 20 ml. of the patient's own or donor's blood is removed, labeled and injected into the patient (for details of the technique see p. 379).

On the following pages the recognized clinical autoimmune hemolytic disease entities will be reviewed in summary fashion with special emphasis on the application of the various laboratory tests that may be useful in the diagnosis.

Classification of Autoimmune Hemolytic Anemias (AIHA)

I. Acquired hemolytic anemias caused by incomplete warm autoantibodies.

1. *Chronic idiopathic AIHA.* Slow to start, insidious, not related to another disease. The immune nature of the hemolytic process is more frequently demonstrable in this form of anemia than in the symptomatic.

2. *Symptomatic AIHA.* Accompanies chronic inflammatory, reticuloendothelial, and neoplastic diseases.

3. *Acute idiopathic AIHA.* Sudden onset; dramatic blood destruction. Usually occurs in second week after a clinically clear-cut, seemingly insignificant infection.

II. Acquired hemolytic anemias caused by cold autoantibodies, mainly agglutinins.
1. Chronic
2. Acute, transient
III. Paroxysmal cold hemoglobinuria (P.C.H.) caused by bithermal autohemolysins.
1. Chronic (syphilitic)
2. Transient (nonsyphilitic)
IV. Atypical autoimmune hemolytic anemia.

Acquired Hemolytic Anemias Caused by Incomplete Warm Autoantibodies

CHRONIC IDIOPATHIC AUTOIMMUNE HEMOLYTIC ANEMIA

Pathogenesis. Shortened survival of red cells. The etiologic role of autoantibodies in the pathogenesis of the disease is established by elution and transfer of autoantibodies to normal red cells and decrease and disappearance of antibodies as disease improves.

How do autoantibodies act? Attachment may cause various disturbances: change to spherocytes, decreased osmotic and mechanical resistance, clumped erythrocytes obstructing narrow blood passages, phagocytosis of erythrocytes, alteration in role of spleen in removing the modified red cells, disturbance of erythrocytic enzyme balance, and loss of K ions and entrance into erythrocytes of Na ions.

Clinical Findings. Pallor, slight jaundice, tachycardia, murmurs, and slight to moderate splenomegaly.

Laboratory Findings. M.C.H. normal, M.C.V. normal, normocytic normochromic anemia. Smear: anisocytosis, macrocytes (pseudomacrocytes or reticulocytes, which are basophilic), spherocytes, schistocytes.

Normoblasts may be present. Urobilinogen in the urine is increased. Signs of blood regeneration: normoblastic marrow hyperplasia. The M:E ratio is decreased.

Reticulocytes: 6 to 12 per cent and more. If reticulocytes are not increased, hypoplastic complication is probable. Direct Coombs' test (DCT)(+): addition of gamma globulin neutralizes the DCT.

Complications. Marrow hypoplasia (folic acid deficiency may be responsible), thrombocytopenia and purpura, thromboembolism, and neurologic complications with spinal cord involvement. Blood transfusion problems: difficulty of correct typing and donor selections with sensitization and its dangers resulting.

Diagnosis. Shortened survival of patient's own red cells (radioisotope technique); shortened survival of transfused red cells (Ashby or radioisotope technique); increased destruction of erythrocytes with increased urobilinogen in urine and feces; increased production of red cells (reactive); reticulocytosis; marrow hyperplasia; and demonstration of autoantibodies.

Anatomic Pathology. Spleno- and hepatomegaly, moderate. Marrow hyperplastic. Extramedullary hematopoiesis in 20 per cent of the patients. Hemosiderosis and erythrophagocytosis in spleen and liver.

SYMPTOMATIC AUTOIMMUNE HEMOLYTIC ANEMIA

Definition. Hemolytic anemia with autoantibodies and associated with another disease.

Plate 4–10. Pernicious anemia, peripheral blood. Several oval-shaped megalocytes, one of them at 11 o'clock, many macrocytes well filled with hemoglobin and without a trace of polychromatophilia, pronounced anisocytosis and extreme poikilocytosis, and the oversized polysegmented neutrophilic granulocyte add up to the characteristic picture of a macrocytic anemia of pernicious anemia type. The normoblast adds to the findings but is not essential for the diagnosis. A study of the marrow and the other laboratory tests described elsewhere in this chapter are essential. (Plate from Heilmeyer, L., and Begemann, H.: Atlas der Klinischen Hämatologie und Cytologie. Springer, 1955.)

Plate 4–11. Pernicious anemia, marrow. The youngest cell in this preparation is at 11 o'clock. It is large, its cytoplasm is deeply basophilic, and its nucleus has a fine filigreed, dispersed chromatin with several blue nucleoli barely visible through the cloud of the granular chromatin. This is a promegaloblast. Just opposite, at 5 o'clock, is a more mature polychromatic megaloblast with its more advanced condensation, which still retains its delicate structure of chromatin and has clearly visible nucleoli. Bordering on this cell toward the center of the field is a basophilic megaloblast. Then, almost in linear sequence, are another polychromatophilic megaloblast, a giant platelet, and a third polychromatophilic, smaller megaloblast. At 3 o'clock is a polychromatophilic megaloblast in mitosis.

At 12 o'clock is a neutrophilic myelocyte; touching it on its left is a ripe orthochromatic normoblast, and toward the center of the field is a promegaloblast. (Plate from Heilmeyer, L., and Begemann, H.: Atlas der Klinischen Hämatologie und Cytologie. Springer, 1955.)

Plate 4–10. Pernicious anemia, peripheral blood.

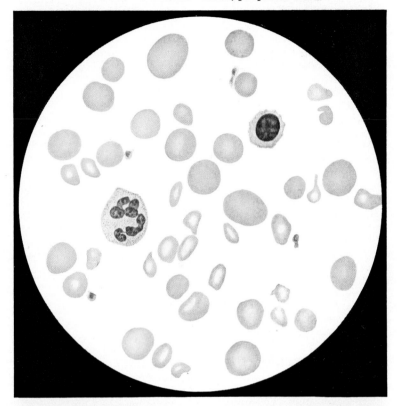

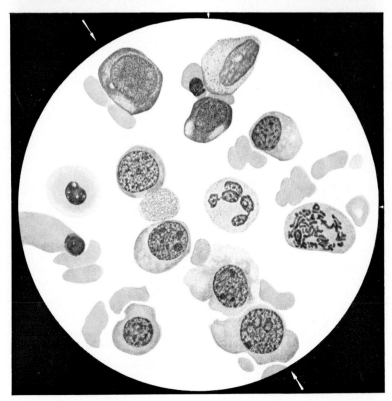

Plate 4–11. Pernicious anemia, marrow.

The clinical picture of the disease is the result of two entities: the *basic* lesion (neoplasm, lymphoma, chronic infection) and *anemia*. The anemia is frequently the minor manifestation but may be in the foreground. As a rule, the anemia disappears when the basic ailment is treated successfully. There is no fundamental difference from the idiopathic variety. Here, too, incomplete antibodies are responsible for the shortened survival of red cells.

Diseases in Which Symptomatic Autoimmune Hemolytic Anemia Occurs. Leukemia (lymphocytic, mainly; rare in chronic granulocytic leukemia and in acute leukemia), lymphoma (lymphosarcoma) (Dacie, 1954, 1960), Hodgkin's disease, myeloma, macroglobulinemias, myelofibrosis, myeloproliferative disorders, cancer (stomach, pancreas, cervix, marrow metastases), and ovarian cysts and teratomas.

Diseases in Which Hypersensitivity May Play a Part. Tuberculosis, Boeck's sarcoid, lupus erythematosus (Dubois, 1952), acute rheumatic fever, rheumatoid arthritis, periarteritis nodosa, scleroderma, and dermatomyositis.

Clinical and Serologic Findings. Essentially the same as in idiopathic.

Relation of Hemolytic Anemia to Basic Disease. Basic disease may be hidden. Anemia may be presenting first and may be mistakenly interpreted as idiopathic.

The autoimmune nature of the anemia is established by the antiglobulin test. In our series the test was positive in 97 per cent of 33 cases of idiopathic hemolytic anemia, in 50 per cent of 28 cases of symptomatic anemia, and in 28 per cent of 14 cases of hereditary spherocytosis (Davidsohn *et al.*, 1953, 1954).

The nonimmune variety of idiopathic and symptomatic hemolytic anemia differs little from the immune.

ACUTE IDIOPATHIC AUTOIMMUNE HEMOLYTIC ANEMIA

Onset is dramatic with high fever. More frequent in the young. Anemia usually noticed after early manifestations subside. Patients much more sick than in the chronic disease. Leukocytosis with shift to left.

Blood Smear. Microspherocytes, normoblasts, erythrophagocytosis.

Therapy. Transfusion may be urgent. Cortisone. Recovery usually spontaneous, more often than in chronic, with less tendency to relapses. Fatal outcome rare.

Acquired Hemolytic Anemias Caused by Cold Autoantibodies

CHRONIC COLD AGGLUTININ DISEASE

Clinical Findings. Long lasting (years and decades). No known therapy. Increased red cell destruction occasionally with hemoglobinuria. Disturbance of blood circulation in skin, especially in exposed areas, due to intravascular autohemagglutination (acrocyanosis) and hemolytic anemia. Onset usually in winter. General well being not affected. Sensation of pin pricks but no severe pain. Another diagnostic finding is that all fingers are cyanotic; after warming the hand, if one finger is dipped in cold water, only this finger becomes cyanotic.

Synonyms. Acquired hemolytic anemia of cold agglutinin type, cryoagglutinemia, cold agglutinin disease, cold agglutinin syndrome, hemopathic acrocyanosis.

Pathogenesis. Cold agglutinin is inactive at inner body temperature, but in exposed areas of skin, temperature may drop to below 30° C. with resulting agglutination. Reversible on rise of temperature. In some exposed areas skin temperature may decrease to 25° C., at which point intravascular hemolysis begins and small hemorrhagic episodes occur. Factors involved in the hemolysis: local temperature of skin, titer of antibodies, frequency and degrees of exposure, season of the year, erythrophagocytosis.

Laboratory Findings. Autoagglutination of blood samples at room temperature, difficulty in doing blood count, slight normocytic, normochromic anemia, shortened survival of erythrocytes, both patient's own and transfused, with Ashby's method and with Cr^{51}.

Serologic Tests. 1. Cold agglutinin titers from 8000 to 64,000. Optimal conditions for cold monothermal hemolysis: pH 6.5, 22° C. 2. Test for cold monothermal hemolysins:

Plate 4–12. Pernicious anemia marrow. The cells are identified by the key. The giant band cell at 6 o'clock may be pointed out as an illustration of the fact that granulocytes in pernicious anemia tend to be excessively large as do erythroid cells—and possibly for the same reason, i.e., deficiency of vitamin B_{12} and folic acid. (Plate from Heilmeyer, L., and Begemann, H.: Atlas der Klinischen Hämatologie und Cytologie. Springer, 1955.)

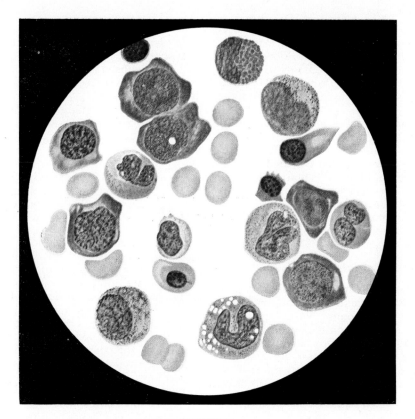

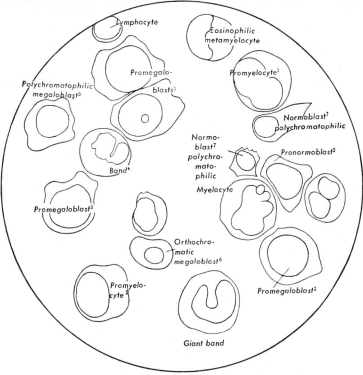

Lymphocyte

Eosinophilic metamyelocyte

Promegalo-blasts³

Promyelocyte¹

Polychromatophilic megaloblast⁵

Normoblast⁷ polychromatophilic

Band⁴

Normo-blast⁷ polychro-mato-philic

Pronormoblast²

Myelocyte

Promegaloblast³

Orthochro-matic megaloblast⁶

Promegaloblast³

Promyelo-cyte¹

Giant band

Synonyms

1. Progranulocyte

2. Rubriblast (Pernicious anemia—P.A. type)
   Basophilic proerythroblast

3. Rubriblasts (P.A. type)

4. Staff cell

5. Rubricyte (P.A. type)

6. Orthochromatic metarubricyte (P.A. type)

7. Metarubricyte

Plate 4–12

0.1 ml. of patient's serum, 0.1 ml. of normal fresh serum of same blood group (complement), 0.02 ml. 0.25 N HCl, and 0.02 ml. of 50 per cent red cells of group O or patient's own. Centrifuge. Supernatant is red.

3. Positive indirect Coomb's test (ICT) with patient's serum at 10° C.

Diagnosis. Clinically demonstrable reversibility of acrocyanosis, elevated titer of cold agglutinins, monothermal hemolysis, normoblastic hyperplasia in marrow, signs of increased blood formation (reticulocytosis, polychromatophilia, aniso- and poikilocytosis), chronic nature of changes.

Differential Diagnosis

Acute Transient Cold Agglutinin Disease. Short duration. Preceding pneumonia.

Raynaud's Syndrome. Vascular lesion (vasomotor nerves), mainly in extremities. Not all fingers uniformly involved. Cold temperature is not only factor. Reversibility by warm temperature is not so impressive. May be very painful. Serologic findings negative.

ACUTE TRANSIENT HEMOLYTIC ANEMIA CAUSED BY COLD AGGLUTININS AFTER VIRUS PNEUMONIA

Acute attack of hemolysis lasting only a few days.

Clinical Findings. The disease starts as an acute pneumonia with characteristic physical and radiologic findings. Just as recovery begins, usually in the second or third week, acute anemia sets in.

Serologic Findings. Cold agglutinins in titers of 2000 to 64,000. Monothermal cold hemolysins are demonstrable, reacting even at 30° C. Positive indirect Coombs' test (ICT) at low temperature. Direct Coombs' test (DCT) positive; it is not neutralized by gamma globulin. Other findings as in chronic cold agglutinin disease.

Diagnosis. Characteristic course. Spontaneous recovery the rule.

Paroxysmal Cold Hemoglobinuria Caused by Bithermal Hemolysins

Chronic: In congenital or late syphilis. Curable by antisyphilitic therapy.

Transient: Brief hemolytic crisis, once or a few repeats, without preceding infection.

In both forms: hemoglobinemia and hemoglobinuria, precipitated by exposure to cold, and caused by bithermal hemolysins. Cold agglutinin present but only in low nondiagnostic titers.

Pathogenesis. Cooling of body or region essential. Binding of antibody takes place below 20° C.

CHRONIC PAROXYSMAL COLD HEMOGLOBINURIA (SYPHILITIC) CAUSED BY BITHERMAL HEMOLYSINS

Clinical Findings. Attacks of acute intravascular hemolysis and hemoglobinuria brought on by exposure to cold. No symptoms during intervals. Attacks come suddenly; start about 10 minutes after exposure with general malaise, headache, nausea, occasional vomiting, chill, fever (over 40° C.), urticaria on skin exposed to chilling. The first urine passed is red-brown and then clears; normal in 24 hours.

Serology. Test for syphilis (+); Donath-Landsteiner test (+); indirect Coombs' test (+); direct Coombs' test (—).

Diagnosis. 1. Tendency to repeat brief, dramatic hemolytic crises with hemoglobinuria, chill, high fever, and other anaphylactoid general reactions.

2. Demonstration of bithermal hemolysins and absence of monothermal.

3. Positive test for syphilis.

4. Demonstration of hemolytic mechanism.

Ehrlich Finger Test. A ligature or rubber band is placed tightly around a finger. This is immersed in ice water and then in warm water (about 40° C.). The finger tip is punctured and the blood drawn into a capillary tube. The free end is sealed in the flame, and the capillary is centrifuged. Hemolysis is present. Control: blood from another finger not so treated.

5. Exclusion of chronic cold agglutinin disease.

Therapy. The only autoantibody disease with specific therapy.

THE DONATH-LANDSTEINER (D-L) TEST FOR PAROXYSMAL COLD HEMOGLOBINURIA

The Qualitative Test. One blood sample is collected in a previously warmed (37° C.) test tube and incubated at 37° C. until it clots. The other is placed in melting ice for 30 minutes and then transferred without shaking to a water bath at 37° C. Both specimens are inspected after an hour or two when the clots have retracted. In paroxysmal cold hemoglobinuria the chilled and then warmed specimen will show hemolysis of the serum. The specimen kept at 37° C. will not show hemolysis.

The Indirect Test. Serum is obtained from a specimen that has been permitted to clot at 37° C. One volume of a 50 per cent suspension of washed normal O cells is added. The suspension is placed in melting ice for 30 minutes, followed by incubation in a water bath at 37° C. for 60 minutes. Hemolysis is seen in the centrifuged specimen.

In another tube, a volume of fresh normal serum is added to the patient's serum as a source of complement to compensate for a possible complement deficiency.

A control test tube is set up as for the patient's serum but is kept at 37° C. and should show no hemolysis.

PAROXYSMAL NOCTURNAL HEMOGLOBINURIA (P.N.H.)

Principle. Recurrent hemoglobinuria, mainly during sleep or on arising, is due to increased susceptibility of the red cells to the slight decrease of pH during sleep. Hemosiderinuria is diagnostic.

TEST FOR PAROXYSMAL NOCTURNAL HEMOGLOBINURIA (P.N.H.)

Principle. Patient's red cells are hemolized by fresh (uninactivated) patient's or normal serum at 37° C. and a pH 6.5 to 7.0.

Reagents

Patient's red cells washed in saline.

Fresh normal serum.

Fresh washed normal red cells.

Procedure. One-half a milliliter of fresh normal serum is placed in each of four tubes. The serum in two tubes is acidified by adding one-tenth volume (0.05 ml.) of 0.2 N HCl. The tubes are placed in the water bath at 37° C., and 0.05 ml. of a 50 per cent suspension of the patient's washed red cells is added to one of the acidified serums and to one of the unacidified. A similar amount of the normal red cells is added to the other two tubes. After one hour's incubation, the tubes are centrifuged.

Two controls are set up: one with unacidified patient's or normal serum and another with normal cells. Hemolysis in the test with acidified serum plus the patient's red cells and no or only significantly less hemolysis in the controls with the patient's cells in the unacidified serum are positive for P. N. H. (Ham, 1939). There should be no hemolysis in the tubes with normal cells. False positive results may be obtained with blood containing a large number of spherocytes. Differentiation is possible by using serum inactivated at 56° C. for 10 to 30 minutes. P.N.H. cells will not hemolyze in inactivated serum; spherocytes will be lysed. According to Crosby (1950), addition of thrombin to the acidified serum makes the test more specific.

ALLERGIC AUTOIMMUNE HEMOLYTIC DISEASE

Principle. The *antigen* is formed in the body *from* (a) an exogenous component (allergen), which by itself is not antigenic but is a "hapten" (half antigen), and (b) a part of the host, a protein. (a) may be a simple chemical compound. (a) + (b) = antigen, which stimulates antibody production.

The basis for this process is an abnormal reactivity of the host. After antibodies have developed, there are no manifestations until new exposure occurs to the allergen. The routes of entry of the allergen may be enteral, parenteral, inhalation, or contact. Result: allergic hemolytic reaction. The autoantibody by itself cannot react with the patient's red cells until the allergen is reintroduced.

ALLERGIC AUTOIMMUNE HEMOLYTIC REACTIONS

Principle. Hemolytic crisis after oral or parenteral intake of chemical, bacterial, animal, or vegetable substances. Well-studied cases due mainly to drugs. Allergic *hemolytic mechanisms* must be differentiated from nonallergic toxic mechanisms.

VARIETIES

1. Substance acts directly as blood toxin on normal red cells. Damage due to chemical reaction with *stroma* or *hemoglobin* or *enzyme systems* of the red cells with resulting destruction. *Not immunologic.* Examples: phenylhydrazine, arsenicals, snake venoms.

2. Responsible agent is not primarily a blood toxin, but is a derivative resulting from physiologic or pathologic metabolic changes, which then directly damages the

Plate 4–13

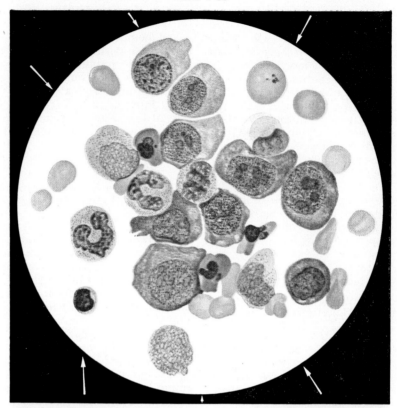

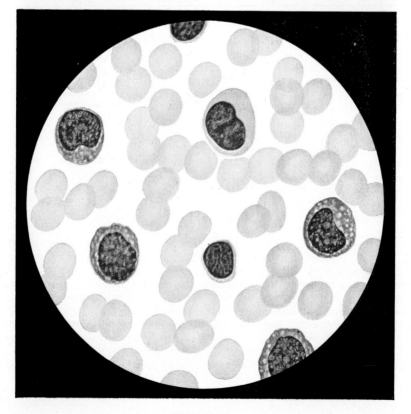

Plate 4–14

red cell. *Not immunologic.* Example: naphthalene. Predisposition may be a factor.

3. Agent and its metabolites damage only constitutionally abnormally sensitive red cells. *Not immunologic.* Examples: quinidine, sulfa compounds, phenacetin. Red cells abnormally sensitive to drugs are more common in Negroes; in Caucasoids, they occur mainly in Mediterraneans. These erythopathies are hereditary.

4. Agent reacts with red cells of sensitive persons. Acute fulminant anemia of this type follows exposure to the fava bean (see p. 164). This reaction is immunologic.

5. Responsible agent acts as hapten and combines with a body protein to a complex antigen, which stimulates production of antibodies. When the same agent is readmitted, an antibody reaction results with damage to red cells.

Mechanism. Allergic-immunologic.

Principle. Antibody reacts with patient's red cells but only in the presence of the responsible drug.

Example. The patient received a drug without a reaction. The drug is administered the second time after varying intervals, which may be years. The second administration is followed by an acute hemolytic reaction with hemoglobinuric anemia and a positive direct Coombs' test. Antibodies react directly but only after small amounts of the drug were added. No other antibodies demonstrable. The serum factor may be transferred passively to a normal person by transfusing the plasma of the allergic individual. Several hundred ml. may be needed. *Examples* of such drugs: stibophen, quinidine, phenacetin, penicillin, sulfonamides.

Summary of Immunohematologic Tests for the Diagnosis of Autoimmune Hemolytic Anemia

Available methods permit a step-by-step analysis of acquired autoimmune hemolytic anemia. The direct antiglobulin test detects cell-bound antibodies. The quantitative antiglobulin test and the gamma globulin neutralization test answer the question as to the thermal range of the autoantibodies. The specificity of the autoantibodies can be determined with the antiglobulin test, with enzyme-treated red cells, with the elution technique, and by typing and genotyping the patient's red cells. The free autoantibodies in the circulating blood can be studied with agglutination and indirect antiglobulin tests at various temperatures and with the Donath-Landsteiner test. The hemolytic autoantibody can be studied with acidified serum and with enzyme-treated red cells. The role of the complement can also be studied using appropriate set-ups.

Some Chemical Findings in the Blood and Urine in Hemolytic Anemia

The hemoglobinemia and hemoglobinuria of acute hemolysis have been discussed previously (see p. 161).

Hemoglobinuria must be differentiated from myoglobinuria, which follows destruction of muscle.

In chronic blood destruction, increase of indirectly reacting serum bilirubin and increased excretion of urobilinogen are found. The rate of blood formation and the functional capacity of the liver influence the amount of urobilinogen found in the stools. The so-called hemolytic index gives a corrected value for the hemoglobin breakdown (Miller *et al.*, 1942).

$$\text{Hemolytic index} = \frac{\begin{array}{c}\text{Daily fecal urobilinogen} \\ \text{(average of 4 days)} \\ \text{mg.} \times 100\end{array}}{\begin{array}{c}\text{Hb (gm. per 100 ml.)} \\ \times \text{ total blood volume}/100\end{array}}$$

Normal: 11 to 21.

Increased indirectly reacting serum bilirubin is not limited to hemolytic anemia but may be present in a variety of other conditions, among which those with hepatic involvement are most frequent.

Plate 4–13. Pernicious anemia, typical megaloblastic marrow. At 11 o'clock there are typical megaloblasts, arching toward the center. At 1 o'clock is a megalocyte with nuclear remnants. Beginning at 3 o'clock and running horizontally toward and beyond the center of the preparation are four promegaloblasts. At 5 o'clock an arrow points at a neutrophilic metamyelocyte and another at 6 o'clock at a reticulum cell that has lost its nucleus. One at 7 o'clock points at a lymphocyte, and finally, the arrow at 10 o'clock aims at a neutrophilic myelocyte. (Plate from Heilmeyer, L., and Begemann, H.: Atlas der Klinischen Hämatologie und Cytologie. Springer, 1955.)

Plate 4–14. Infectious mononucleosis, peripheral blood. The erythrocytes look normal. The seven white cells show some of the changes characteristically present in this disease. Five of the seven cells are larger than the average lymphocyte. The nuclei tend to be less regular in outline and indented. The nuclear chromatin is less dense. Three of the cells, at 3, 5, and 10 o'clock, have distinct nucleoli. Four of the five large cells have cytoplasmic vacuoles. Only one lymphocyte, below the center, is normal in appearance. The pleomorphism is characteristic. (Plate from Heilmeyer, L., and Begemann, H.: Atlas der Klinischen Hämatologie und Cytologie. Springer, 1955.)

BLOOD PICTURE

The morphologic findings in the peripheral blood include changes reflecting increased regeneration of blood cells, such as polychromatophilia, reticulocytosis, normoblastemia, poikilo- and anisocytosis, and in some cases spherocytosis. Leukocytosis and thrombocytosis are present frequently. The findings in the marrow correspond with those described in the peripheral blood, namely, normoblastic hyperplasia (Plate 4–6).

Summary of Tests for Hemolytic Anemia

Hemolytic anemia is caused by abnormal and excessive destruction of red cells. Eight groups of tests are available, each aimed at the detection of a different mechanism responsible for, involved in, or resulting from the destruction.

I. Intracorpuscular abnormalities. Abnormal red cell structure.

  1. Tests for osmotic fragility. These are tests for increased sensitivity of the erythrocytes to hypotonic solutions of sodium chloride (see page 96 ff.).

  2. Tests for mechanical fragility (see p. 99).

  3. Tests for autohemolysis (see p. 170).

II. Abnormal molecular structure of erythrocytes.

  4. Tests for sickling (see p. 194).

  5. Tests for abnormal types of hemoglobin (see p. 190).

III. Extracorpuscular abnormalities: abnormal antibodies.

  6. Tests for autoantibodies attached to the red cells or circulating in the plasma: antiglobulin (Coombs') tests, direct and indirect (see p. 285 ff.); the gamma globulin neutralization test.

IV. Shortened survival of red cells.

  7. Tests for shortened survival of red cells.

V. Excessive destruction of red cells.

  8. Chemical tests to demonstrate increased excretion of products of hemoglobin catabolism.

VI. Excessive regeneration.

  9. Tests for reticulocytes.

  10. Examination of bone marrow.

Hypochromic Microcytic Anemia

Definition. Anemia characterized by a decrease of hemoglobin and, to a lesser degree, of the hematocrit that are more marked than the decrease in the number of the red cells. Synonym: iron deficiency anemia.

IRON METABOLISM

Iron is an essential component of hemoglobin and of other body cells. The average diet contains 5 to 15 mg. per day. The normal adult has 4 to 5 gm. of iron in the body. Over 60 per cent of the body's iron is in the hemoglobin of circulating red cells. About 1 mg. of iron is contained in each milliliter of red cells. About 3 to 4 per cent of the body's iron is present in enzymes of the red cells and the myoglobin, and the rest is stored as ferritin, submicroscopic particles of iron in tissues, and as hemosiderin, larger particles of iron demonstrable microscopically. Very little iron is excreted from the body. Only a few milligrams of iron are absorbed daily from the food, even in the presence of an iron deficiency anemia. "Transferrin," a serum iron-binding protein, a beta globulin, transports absorbed iron. The body's iron is used again and again practically without any loss. Less than 1 mg. of iron is lost daily in the urine, bile, and other secretions. Consequently, deficient supply of iron in the diet or inadequate absorption in the diet results in iron deficiency only when either of the two or both are complicated by an increased need for iron as it exists during rapid growth in infancy and childhood or during pregnancy, or when excessive loss of blood has reduced the body's reserves of iron, as following repeated hemorrhages, excessive menstruation, and multiple pregnancies.

The numerical expressions of hypochromic and microcytic anemia are reflected in a low M.C.V., M.C.H., and M.C.H.C. The reduction of M.C.H.C. is seen only in this type of anemia.

The synonym, iron deficiency anemia, expresses the cause and points to the treatment. The only other condition with a hypochromic microcytic anemia is thalassemia, which does not respond to iron.

The causes of the iron deficiency include chronic blood loss from a variety of causes, chronic diarrhea, hookworm infestation, achlorhydria, pregnancy, and inadequate diet, especially in children and women.

Chlorosis, a form of anemia belonging in this category, used to be very common in girls up to the age of 25. It was caused by faulty nutrition. It has been infrequent since the beginning of this century. Chronic hypochromic anemia (late chlorosis) resembles chlorosis but occurs mainly in women between 20 and 50 years. It is associated frequently with achlorhydria and occasionally may be complicated by difficulty in swallowing (the Plummer-Vinson syndrome, or Waldenström's sideropenic dysphagia) (Waldenström and Kjellberg, 1939). Low plasma iron is present in all cases.

LABORATORY FINDINGS

The Blood. The stained blood smear shows microcytosis, anisocytosis, poikilocytosis (including elliptical and elongated cells), and varying degrees of hypochromia (see p. 116) (Plate 4–1). Reticulocytes are within normal limits except following hemorrhage and iron therapy. The number of red cells is rarely as low as in pernicious anemia. The hemoglobin and hematocrit may be extremely low. The fragility of red cells is normal, but occasionally there may be a slight increase in resistance.

Chemical examination may show hypoproteinemia, serum sideropenia, increase of the serum iron binding capacity, and increase of serum copper and of erythrocyte protoporphyrin. The latter may be as high as 500 micrograms per 100 ml. of red cells, whereas normally the range is 20 to 38 micrograms. Moderate increases have been reported in hemolytic and refractory anemia, leukemia, Hodgkin's disease, and multiple myeloma (from 30 to 150 micrograms). Increases comparable to those seen in iron deficiency anemia have been reported in anemia due to heavy metal intoxication and somewhat lower levels in anemia of chronic infection. The white blood cell count is normal or slightly lowered. Granulocytopenia, relative lymphocytosis, and a small number of polysegmented granulocytes may be present. The platelets are normal except in a rare case when the count may be slightly lower. Achlorhydria is common. No free hydrochloric acid, even after histamine, was reported in 50 to 60 per cent of cases (Wintrobe, 1961).

The marrow shows normoblastic hyperplasia. The normoblasts are smaller than normal and are deficient in hemoglobin. They are irregular in shape with frayed margins. Smears stained for hemosiderin show none.

LABORATORY DIAGNOSIS

Therapeutic Test. The therapeutic test is based on the reticulocyte response to oral or parenteral administration of iron. The response is directly proportionate to the severity of the anemia. The increase of reticulocytes is least pronounced following acute blood loss in patients who did not receive iron. It is pronounced following iron intake in patients with iron deficiency anemia, but the highest peaks are seen following administration of vitamin B_{12} or folic acid in patients with the corresponding deficiency anemia (Schodt, 1938).

Hemosiderin. Hemosiderin in marrow is a sensitive indicator of iron deficiency. The diagnosis is established if no hemosiderin is found in good preparations stained in the usual fashion (Wright's or Giemsa stain) or stained specially for the Prussian blue reaction.

Serum Iron. The normal range is from 80 to 180 micrograms per 100 ml. of serum. Lesser levels are present in iron deficiency but may be seen also in chronic infections and a number of other chronic diseases.

Serum Iron Binding Capacity. This determination helps to differentiate iron deficiency anemia from the other conditions with low serum iron. In iron deficiency anemia, the serum iron binding capacity is increased. It is decreased in the other conditions with low serum iron. The normal total serum iron binding capacity is 300 to 450 micrograms per 100 ml.

DIFFERENTIAL DIAGNOSIS

Pyridoxine deficiency is responsible for a hypochromic microcytic anemia resembling morphologically iron deficiency anemia. It differs by elevated serum iron, hemosiderosis, and the presence of abnormal tryptophan derivatives in the urine (Harris *et al.*, 1956).

Hypochromic anemia in *chronic plumbism* is caused by the injurious effect of lead poisoning on heme synthesis. The pronounced increase of coproporphyrin III in the urine in lead poisoning helps to establish the true nature of the anemia.

Macrocytic (Megaloblastic) Anemias
PERNICIOUS ANEMIA

Definition. A chronic anemia, characterized morphologically by macrocytosis and chemically by the absence in the gastric juice of free hydrochloric acid and of certain enzymes (achlorhydria and achylia). It is caused by deficiency of vitamin B_{12} or folic acid and, as a rule, responds promptly to their administration. Consequently, pernicious anemia is not "pernicious" any more.

Synonym. It is also called addisonian anemia, because the disease was described fully by Addison in 1855.

Pathogenesis. Deficiency in substances essential for the synthesis of deoxyribonucleic acid with resulting defects in nuclear development.

Vitamins of the B complex include B_{12} and folic acid (pteroylglutamic acid, PGA). The two are thought to be coenzymes.

Vitamin B_{12} deficiency. The essential substances are: (1) vitamin B_{12}, the extrinsic factor, which is synthesized by bacteria. It is contained in the flesh and especially in the liver of animals. (2) The intrinsic factor, which is essential for the absorption of vitamin B_{12}, is produced by the mucosa of the fundus of the stomach.

The combined vitamin B_{12} and intrinsic factors are absorbed in the small intestine. Considerable stores of vitamin B_{12} are present in the liver: 1 to 2 micrograms per gram of liver in healthy adults. Vitamin B_{12} deficiency is rare even in persons on a deficient diet except in extreme vegetarians. In most instances vitamin B_{12} deficiency is actually the result of lack of the intrinsic factors as seen in pernicious anemia, after destruction of the mucosal glands in the gastric fundus, and after total gastrectomy.

Other causes of vitamin B_{12} deficiency are disturbances of intestinal absorption as it occurs in certain diseases, for example, in sprue and regional enteritis and after resection of parts of the small intestine. Fish tapeworm infestation may have a similar effect; it is explained by absorption of vitamin B_{12} by the worm.

Folic acid deficiency. From 500 to 1500 micrograms of folic acid (90 per cent of it conjugated with glutamic acid) is present in the average daily diet. Only one-third of it is absorbed and only 4 to 5 micrograms is excreted in the urine.

Dietary deficiency of folic acid is more frequent than vitamin B_{12} deficiency, especially in chronic alcoholics, in the aged, in intestinal malabsorption, and as a complication of therapy with folic acid antagonists.

Pernicious anemia of pregnancy is suspected of being caused by a folic acid deficiency. The morphologic changes in the peripheral blood may be less pronounced, and those in the myeloid cells of the marrow are as a rule more pronounced than in true pernicious anemia.

Differential Diagnostic (Therapeutic) Test. Small daily doses of 0.5 to 2 mg. of folic acid will produce a therapeutic response. Large doses of folic acid (10 to 100 mg.) are moderately effective in vitamin B_{12} deficiency "false positive" responses. Large doses of vitamin B_{12} may be similarly effective in folic acid deficiency.

Blood Morphology. *Erythrocytes.* MACROCYTOSIS AND MEGALOCYTOSIS. The M.C.V. (mean corpuscular volume) is elevated. It may be from 95 to 110 cu.μ (cubic microns) in mild disease and considerably higher in severe. The normal M.C.V. is 82 to 92 cu.μ.

POIKILOCYTOSIS is always present and is moderate to severe. Bizarre shapes are characteristic.

ANISOCYTOSIS is also regularly present and is moderate to marked.

(Figs. 4–49, 4–50; Plates 4–3[6], 4–10, 4–11, 4–12, 4–13.)

HEMOGLOBIN as noted in blood smears is abundant. Hypochromia is rare and appears only when iron deficiency is also present. The appearance in the blood smears of excessive filling with hemoglobin is misleading and is caused by increased thickness of the cell. Consequently, the term hyperchromic anemia is inappropriate.

Abnormal cells. Polychromatophilia may be present, usually in cells of increased size. These are, as a rule, young cells (reticulocytes). Reticulocytosis is present only during therapy. Stippled cells (punctate basophilia) may be present. Howell-Jolly bodies and Cabot's rings may be seen. Basophilic, polychromatophilic, and orthochromatic megaloblastic cells are also present, especially in untreated or inadequately treated patients.

Leukocytes. Leukopenia is the rule. Large, multisegmented leukocytes with more than the upper normal of five segments (polysegmentation, macropolycytes) are present regularly and early, frequently before erythrocytic abnormalities become manifest. Their presence is referred to as "shift to the right." Shift to the left or immaturity of white cells is also present with varying numbers of myelocytes and metamyelocytes and rarely even myeloblasts. In untreated cases eosinophilia has been reported.

Platelets. Thrombocytopenia is the rule in relapse. Abnormal forms, including giant platelets, may be seen.

Abnormal cells have been described in the mucosa of the mouth, esophagus, stomach, and vagina in patients with macrocytic anemia (Graham and Rheault, 1954).

Red cell survival in pernicious anemia

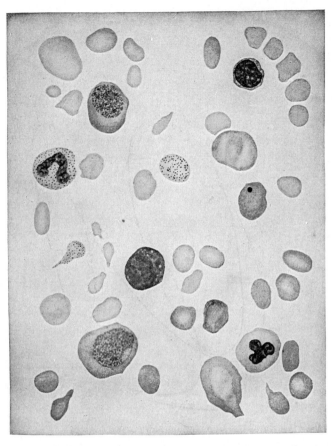

Figure 4–49. Blood cells in pernicious anemia. Note variations in size and shape of the erythrocytes; three megaloblasts, one with an irregular, deeply stained nucleus; erythrocytes showing polychromatophilia, basophilic granular degeneration, and one nuclear particle; one lymphocyte and one polymorphonuclear neutrophil. All drawn from actual cells on two slides (× 800 (0.8 mm. = 1 micron).

is shortened. Transfused normal erythrocytes survive normally in patients who have been adequately treated, but their survival is shortened in untreated patients. Red cells of patients with pernicious anemia survive normally in normal recipients.

Marrow. In untreated patients or in relapse, megaloblastic hyperplasia is the characteristic finding. Nucleated red cells constitute up to 50 per cent of the nucleated count. Megaloblasts, characterized by their large size and finely reticulated nuclear chromatin resembling a network, are present. Their cytoplasm varies from deep blue, basophilic in the younger cells (promegaloblasts), through light blue to orange and pink in the more mature cells (orthochromatic megaloblast). These colors may be diffuse or spotty (see p. 177).

Side by side with erythroid hyperplasia, myeloid metaplasia is the rule with hypertrophy especially of the metamyelocytes and band cells. Both types of cells may be of giant size with poorly staining chromatin and with a basophilic cytoplasm showing decreased granularity.

The characteristic abnormal findings revert promptly to normal as soon as specific therapy is instituted. Various complications, including severe infections, may also affect the typical marrow findings.

The Biochemical Abnormality. The absence of free hydrochloric acid in the gastric juice, even after injection of histamine, is a diagnostic finding. The total amount of gastric secretion is decreased and the enzymes pepsin and renin are reduced or absent. These changes may precede the other signs of the disease. They are not affected by therapy. A small number of cases of clinical and hematologic pernicious anemia but with free hydrochloric acid in the gastric secretion have been reported (so-called achrestic anemia.) The correct interpretation of such cases requires further studies to be mentioned later, such as assay of the patient's gastric secretion,

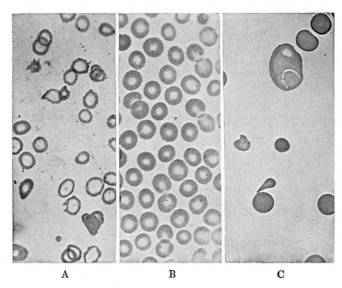

Figure 4–50. Erythrocytes in iron deficiency anemia (A) and pernicious anemia (C) contrasted with those of normal blood (B). In a case of well-marked iron deficiency anemia the erythrocytes are pale and ringlike; in pernicious anemia they are rich in hemoglobin and show marked variations in size and shape. The megalocyte in the upper part of the figure is especially characteristic of pernicious anemia (× 750).

A   B   C

the Schilling test, and the therapeutic test. Such studies have reduced cases of pernicious anemia with free hydrochloric acid to a very low incidence.

Serum iron is increased, except in cases complicated by iron deficiency.

Differential Diagnosis. *Tropical sprue.* Blood findings are as follows: Frequently macrocytic anemia is present, occasionally hypochromic microcytic, and rarely normocytic. Rarely anemia may be absent. In the macrocytic anemia, the peripheral blood and marrow findings are the same as in pernicious anemia.

Idiopathic steatorrhea (nontropical sprue) and celiac disease. In both diseases macrocytic or hypochromic microcytic or normocytic anemia may be present, as a rule less severe than in pernicious anemia. Macrocytic anemia is more common than microcytic in idiopathic steatorrhea but less frequent in celiac disease.

The *marrow* is megaloblastic in macrocytic anemia and normoblastic in microcytic. In sprue and nontropical steatorrhea, iron deficiency may be present together with vitamin B_{12} and folic acid deficiency. This combination is more frequent than in pernicious anemia. Macrocytosis and anisocytosis may result in a normal M.C.V. Iron therapy leads to macrocytic anemia and liver therapy to microcytic hypochromic anemia.

THE BIOCHEMICAL DEFECT. Free HCl may be absent, but less frequently than in pernicious anemia, and tends to respond to treatment. The large bulk, the mushy appearance, the light color, and the high fat content of the stool in sprue, idiopathic steatorrhea, and celiac disease are helpful in the differential diagnosis.

NUTRITIONAL MACROCYTIC ANEMIAS

Tropical Macrocytic Anemia. This is a rather indefinite group, seen also in subtropical and temperate zones with occasional iron deficiency anemia superimposed. In some cases, findings identical with those seen in pernicious anemia are present. In others, the findings characteristic for iron deficiency are in the foreground.

Pellagra. The anemia, which may be severe in less than 20 per cent of cases, is only rarely macrocytic. In so-called "alcoholic" pellagra, the anemia, if present, is frequently macrocytic.

Pernicious Anemia of Pregnancy. This should be differentiated from the more common, so-called physiologic anemia of pregnancy and from the iron deficiency anemia of pregnancy. The characteristic peripheral blood and marrow findings help in making the correct diagnosis. The more uniform size and shape of the red cells in the peripheral blood may help to differentiate this condition from true pernicious anemia. Megaloblastic marrow hyperplasia may be most impressive and impossible to distinguish from true pernicious anemia. Free HCl is present more frequently than in true pernicious anemia. Folic acid is more effective than liver extract, and oral administration of liver extract may help when it is not effective parenterally.

MACROCYTIC ANEMIA IN LESIONS OF THE GASTROINTESTINAL TRACT

The condition is sometimes reported as

common in cancer of the stomach. Actually the sequence is such that this neoplasm shows a significantly higher incidence in pernicious anemia.

An increased incidence of macrocytic anemia following total gastrectomy, and less frequently after partial gastrectomy and gastroenterostomy, has been reported. It has also been seen in patients with intestinal strictures and anastomoses. Macrocytic anemia resembling pernicious anemia may be seen in liver disease. Here the leukocytes look normal and the marrow is rarely megaloblastic. Achlorhydria is less frequent than in patients with hepatic disease but without macrocytic anemia.

Fish tapeworm infestation is another condition that was thought to be complicated occasionally by a pernicious anemia-like picture in the blood and marrow and by central nervous system involvement. Liver therapy is effective, as is expulsion of the worm. The present consensus is that a cause and effect association between the infestation and the blood disease is rare. According to some writers, the location of the tapeworm may be a factor. Macrocytic anemia is supposed to be more frequent when the jejunum is infested than when the tapeworm is in the ileum. According to some authors, the coexistence of the infestation and of the pernicious anemia is best explained by the simultaneous incidental presence of both conditions.

MACROCYTIC ANEMIA IN METABOLIC DISEASES

A pernicious anemia-like picture has been described in hypothyroidism. The anemia is, as a rule, only moderate. Some patients respond to combined antideficiency and thyroid therapy. In other cases in which poikilo- and anisocytosis are as a rule not pronounced, liver therapy is not effective but thyroid therapy is.

"ACHRESTIC" ANEMIA

This is a progressive, often fatal, macrocytic anemia closely resembling pernicious anemia but without certain of its features, such as absence of central nervous system involvement. Failure to respond to liver therapy and presence of free HCl are characteristics. Well-studied cases of this type are rare. The syndrome is still insufficiently delineated.

TESTS USED IN THE DIFFERENTIAL DIAGNOSIS OF MACROCYTIC ANEMIAS

Gastric Analysis. The presence of free HCl almost excludes pernicious anemia. The exceptions are extremely rare.

Therapeutic Test. Following administration of vitamin B_{12} the blood picture changes rapidly. If no response is noted within 10 to 14 days, the diagnosis of pernicious anemia is not likely.

Procedure. The patient should be on a diet low in animal products for about one week. Following this period of observation he is given daily small injections (1 to 5 micrograms) or a single large injection (30 micrograms) of vitamin B_{12}. A substantial increase of reticulocytes during the first week after the beginning of the therapy together with a general improvement in the blood picture are indicative of a vitamin B_{12} deficiency. Concomitant infection may interfere with the reticulocyte response, even in the presence of pernicious anemia, and give a "false negative" result.

The Schilling Test. *The principle.* Co^{60}-labeled vitamin B_{12}, taken orally by persons who can absorb it, is excreted in the urine if the patient is given parenterally large amounts of unlabeled vitamin B_{12}. The test may help to differentiate pernicious anemia from other macrocytic anemias. (For details see p. 380.)

Interpretation. Subnormal absorption of vitamin B_{12} that can be corrected by the simultaneous injection of vitamin B_{12} favors the diagnosis of pernicious anemia (Callender *et al.*, 1954; Glass *et al.*, 1954; Schilling, 1955).

Serum Vitamin B_{12} Level. This is determined by the growth response of certain bacteria. A positive result establishes vitamin B_{12} deficiency (Lear *et al.*, 1954; Ross, 1950).

Refractory Anemias (Aregenerative Anemias)

PRIMARY REFRACTORY (AREGENERATIVE) ANEMIA

Definition. Anemia, granulocytopenia, and thrombocytopenia, refractory to any form of therapy except transfusions and not associated with infection, chronic renal or hepatic disease, cancer, or malnutrition.

Aplastic anemia differs from refractory anemia by its acellular marrow, whereas the marrow in refractory anemia may be cellular and active in varying degrees or show findings of leukemia, myelofibrosis, or myelosclerosis.

Hypersensitive Refractory Anemias. There is a long, constantly increasing number of drugs that produce marrow damage only in some individuals after single or repeated exposures. These drugs are not capable of damaging the marrow of animals as are the chemicals in the first group. They include antimicrobial drugs (salvarsan, chloramphenicol, sulfonamides, chlortetracycline, streptomycin); anticonvulsants (Mesantoin, Tridione); antithyroid drugs (carbimazole); antihistaminics (Pyribenzamine); insecticides (DDT); and other chemicals—some known (gold compounds, atabrine, chlorpromazine, hair dyes, bismuth, mercury) and more to come.

Toxic Refractory Anemia. This is caused by a number of physical or chemical agents that produce marrow damage in all subjects exposed to a sufficient dose, including animals. Here belong ionizing radiation, mustard compounds, benzol, and antileukemic agents, such as Myleran, urethane, and antimetabolites.

Benzol Poisoning. The changes in the blood frequently include anemia alone, or in combination with leukopenia and thrombocytopenia. Occasional changes: eosinophilia, leukocytosis, and leukemoid reaction. The *marrow* may vary from aplastic or hypoplastic to hyperplastic. Occasionally extramedullary hematopoiesis may be present with splenomegaly.

Organic Arsenicals. There is no apparent relationship between the size of the dose, the frequency or duration of exposure, and the injury to the blood. The various compounds differ in their effectiveness.

In the case of some drugs, marrow damage did not appear until the second or third course of therapy (e.g., chloramphenicol).

Ionizing Radiation. The effects on blood cells depend on the radiosensitivity of the cells, the capacity of the cells to regenerate, and the survival rate of the cells in the peripheral blood.

The opinions regarding radiosensitivity of blood cells differ. A single therapeutic dose of 300 r to the sacroiliac joints and the whole length of the spine of patients with ankylosing spondylitis was followed in a few hours by a rise of the neutrophilic granulocytes.

A drop of the lymphocytes was noted first after 24 hours and continued for several days. The total white count began decreasing on the first or second day, mainly due to the effect on lymphocytes. After five days the number of the granulocytes began falling. The hematocrit had already begun to decrease at the end of the first or second day (Brown and Abbott, 1955).

The effects of massive exposure depend on the dose and sensitivity. In the acute radiation syndrome, systemic effects (prostration, fever), leukopenia, and infection may lead rapidly to death. Or thrombocytopenia and purpura may develop. This form may lead to diarrhea, dehydration, infection, aplastic anemia, hemorrhage, and death in weeks. The effect of radioactive isotopes is more gradual, more persistent, and longer lasting. Late effects of ionizing radiation include leukemia.

Blood counts at regular intervals for persons exposed occupationally to ionizing radiation have been recommended. According to Wintrobe (1961) this practice has little to recommend it. The use of film badges is more practical.

OTHER CAUSES OF REFRACTORY ANEMIA

The disease may be a terminal development in pernicious anemia, granulocytic leukemia, myelophthisic anemia, miliary tuberculosis, and occasionally in a variety of other conditions. A so-called *pure red cell anemia* with a normal leukocyte and platelet count combined with a thymoma was reported (Davidsohn, 1941; Ross *et al.*, 1954; Weinbaum and Thompson, 1955). In some patients with thymoma, pancytopenia, marrow hypoplasia, and myasthenia were present.

BLOOD FINDINGS IN REFRACTORY ANEMIA

The red cells are normal in size and shape. Polychromatophilia, stippling, normoblasts, and aniso- and poikilocytosis are conspicuously absent. There is leukopenia with a marked decrease or almost complete absence of granulocytes and a relative lymphocytosis. In severe leukopenia there is also an absolute lymphocytopenia. Thrombocytopenia, with prolonged bleeding time and poor clot retraction, is a part of the picture. The serum iron is usually decreased.

Marrow. In the typical case, the aspirate consists mainly of red cells. The lymphocytes are the predominant white blood cells. Occasionally the marrow is normocellular or even hyperplastic.

Simple Chronic Anemia

Definition. The nondescript term refers to the most common type of anemia seen in various infections and chronic systemic diseases and as a rule mild and overshadowed by the basic disease. Occasionally the basic disease may be obscured by the anemia. This is especially frequent in chronic renal disease, cancer, subacute bacterial endocarditis, hypothyroidism, and Addison's disease.

Blood. The anemia is normocytic, occasionally normochromic microcytic, the so-called "simple microcytic anemia" (Wintrobe, 1961). It is mild as a rule. There is no evidence of blood destruction or regeneration. Anisocytosis is slight and poikilocytosis insignificant.

Marrow. No hypoplasia is seen, but actually and not infrequently there is granulocytic hyperplasia with maturation arrest. Quantitative and qualitative erythroid hypoplasia has been reported in severe renal insufficiency with azotemia above 150 mg. of nonprotein nitrogen per 100 ml. of blood. Even in such a case aplasia was not seen. Failure to respond to treatment, except via the underlying disease, is the main feature of this type of anemia.

Anemia of Infection

It occurs in two main forms: the acute, occasionally severe anemia of septicemia and the chronic mild anemia of chronic infection. The serum iron is lowered and not corrected by parenterally administered iron. There are no signs of blood regeneration, indicating that the red cell formation is depressed. Studies on red cell survival showed increased destruction.

Anemia of Renal Insufficiency

Shortened survival of red cells has been reported with red cell production unable to keep pace.

Myelophthisic Anemia

Definition. Anemia due to marrow replacement by metastatic carcinoma, myelofibrosis (occasional cases of multiple myeloma), and a variety of other less well-defined conditions.

Presence of varying numbers of normoblasts and immature granulocytes is a characteristic finding and is responsible for the synonyms "leukoerythroblastic anemia" and "leukoerythroblastosis."

In the anemia of myelofibrosis or myelosclerosis, splenomegaly is frequent and the course is slow. In the so-called "agnogenic myeloid metaplasia" the marrow shows various changes but they are not leukemic. The spleen shows widespread myeloid hyperplasia.

The Blood. Normocytic anemia of varying severity is present; occasionally there is macrocytic anemia. Many normoblasts are present in the peripheral blood as well as evidence of active red cell regeneration. The leukocyte counts vary. Leukocytosis and immature granulocytes may be seen in myelofibrosis, but they are rare in the presence of cancer metastases. There is no lymphocytosis as it is seen in aplastic anemia. Thrombocytopenia may be present and atypical giant platelets are frequent.

HEREDITARY HEMOGLOBINOPATHIES

Definition. Diseases of the blood for which genetically determined physical-chemical properties of hemoglobin are responsible.

History. Chemical differences between fetal and adult hemoglobin have been known for over 100 years (Von Körber, 1866). The immunologic differences between the two hemoglobins were studied more recently (Darrow et al., 1940). A clinical entity belonging to this group, sickle cell anemia, was described by Herrick in 1910. Pauling et al. (1949) opened a new fruitful field of investigation when they reported specific and characteristic properties of sickle cell hemoglobin. Their studies initiated a new approach to the study of human hemoglobins, which led to much information of clinical importance. More than 13 different varieties of hemoglobins have already been identified. Others have been announced and await identification, and undoubtedly more will follow.

Nomenclature. By agreement, capital letters of the alphabet are used for their identification in the order of discovery, except for those which had already been associated with a particular letter at the time when the new nomenclature was agreed upon. When two or more hemoglobins are involved in a syndrome, the major is listed first; the same preference is given to thalassemia.

Biochemistry. The genetically determined hemoglobin differences are located in the globin component of hemoglobin, not in the heme. So far, significant biochemical differences have been found in Hb F (fetal hemoglobin), specifically in the total amino acid composition as compared with Hb A (normal adult hemoglobin). In the other hemoglobins, the differences seem to be in amino acid arrangement or linkage or in substitution of one or more amino acids for those usually found in Hb A.

In practically all hemoglobinopathies there is anemia of varying degrees. The anemia is hemolytic and the hemoglobin abnormality is responsible. Another finding common to most hemoglobinopathies is target cells in the peripheral blood. Their numbers vary. They are characteristic but not specific.

Identification of the Hemoglobins

Alkali Denaturation. Hb F is resistant to denaturation by highly alkaline solutions by which all other human hemoglobins are destroyed. This method is capable of detecting Hb F if present in excess of 2 per cent of the total hemoglobin.

Paper Electrophoresis. Proteins are electrically charged molecules and move at different rates of speed in an electric field. Additional differences are related to the hydrogen ion concentration of the solution employed. Most of the hemoglobins can be identified in this manner, as shown in Figs. 4–51, 4–52.

At pH 8.6, Hb C moves least and I and H move most. The other hemoglobins move as follows (from less to more): E, O, D, and S, same speed as D; L, G, and F, same speed as G; A, K, J, I, and H, same speed as I.

SUMMARY OF METHODS OF IDENTIFICATION OF ABNORMAL HEMOGLOBIN

Hb F. Alkali resistance, higher solubility, immunologic specificity, different ultraviolent spectrum, different amino acid composition.

Hb S. It is insoluble when reduced. It

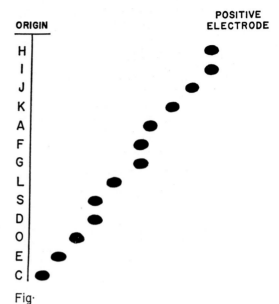

Figure 4–51. Relative migrations of the human hemoglobins after electrophoresis on filter paper in 0.05 M barbital buffer at pH 8.6. Hemoglobins H and I may be separated by filter-paper electrophoresis at pH 6.5 (phosphate buffer). Hemoglobins S and D may be differentiated by virtue of their different solubilities in phosphate buffer under standard conditions. Hemoglobins F and G may be differentiated from each other by the resistance of the former to denaturation by alkali. (Page & Culver: A Syllabus of Laboratory Examinations in Clinical Diagnosis: Critical Evaluation of Laboratory Procedures in the Study of the Patient. Revised Ed. Cambridge, Mass., Harvard Univ. Press, 1960.)

forms crystals (tactoids) and sickles in concentrated reduced solutions. This is the most convenient means of identification.

Hb D. Electrophoretic pattern is identical

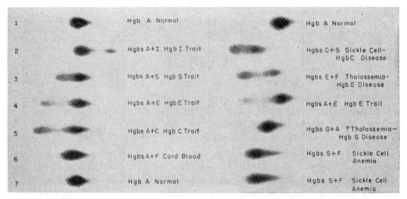

Figure 4–52. Paper electrophoresis of human hemoglobins. On the left are shown the actual runs of specimens from persons with the heterozygous Hb C, E, I, and S traits as well as that of cord blood, as compared with the electrophoretic pattern of normal hemoglobin (Hb A) alone. On the right are shown the electrophoretic patterns of sickle cell anemia, sickle cell-Hb C disease, thalassemia-Hb E disease, and thalassemia-Hb G disease. (Courtesy of Dr. Amoz Chernoff and New England J. Med.)

with S but has higher solubility when reduced; no sickling.

Hb G. Electrophoretic pattern is identical with F but not resistant to alkali denaturation.

Hb C, E, I, and J. Characteristic electrophoretic mobilities.

Hb H. Characteristic electrophoretic pattern at pH 6.5.

Some of the other recently reported hemoglobins have not been fully studied and identified. Almost 30 different ones have been named, some of them observed in newborn infants.

Recently component A_2 has been separated from Hb A in normal adults and from persons with various diseases—in one of them as much as 27 per cent. Components A_3 and A_4 have also been reported, but these latter observations have been questioned.

Distribution of the Hemoglobins

Hb F. Main hemoglobin in fetus; 60 to 90 per cent at birth. Then it rapidly decreases to 2 per cent or less after second to fourth years. In adults only traces (0.5 per cent or less) are demonstrable immunologically.

In certain hemoglobinopathies and in some blood diseases, Hb F may persist in larger amounts, especially in hereditary hemolytic anemias. It may reappear in adults when marrow is overactive, e.g., in pernicious anemia, multiple myeloma, and metastatic cancer in marrow. When Hb F is increased after the age of four years, a careful blood study is indicated to find an explanation.

Another fetal hemoglobin (P) was found during the first two or three months of intrauterine life. It is also alkali resistant. It awaits more adequate study.

Hb S. Found almost exclusively in Negroes in sickle cell trait and disease. Geographic distribution: prevalent in Africa, where it is present in up to 45 per cent of the native population, and in some regions of Central Africa, Southern Asia, and the United States (about 10 per cent in American Negroes). It has been found in isolated regions around the Mediterranean, especially in Greece. Mutations or admixtures of Negro blood are possible explanations.

Hb. C. Almost exclusively in Negroes (West Coast of Africa, up to 14 per cent of natives). In the United States, about 3 per cent.

The other hemoglobins have been located mainly in the native populations in Asia and Africa with occasional small groups in American Negroes, e.g., Hb D in 0.5 per cent.

Hb I. A rare so-called "private" hemoglobin has been found in a few families in the United States.

Genetics of Human Hemoglobins

The hemoglobin pattern of every person is determined by a pair of genes. If they are identical, the result is homozygosity; if they are different, heterozygosity. The most common pattern is homozygous hemoglobin A in the normal adult. The next in frequency is sickle cell trait with a mixture of hemoglobins A and S (from 22 to 46 per cent of the latter). In sickle cell anemia, hemoglobin S is present alone or together with F.

According to one hypothesis, four loci control human hemoglobins—three for Hb A and one for Hb F.

Suggested genetic formula for normal human hemoglobin: Hb_1A, Hb_2A, Hb_3A, Hb_4F/Hb_1A, Hb_2A, Hb_3A, Hb_4F. Each of these normal genes may be replaced by the gene for an abnormal hemoglobin. Hb_1 is supposed to control major portion of Hb A, HbS, and Hb C and probably also Hb D, E, I, and J. Hb_2 may control a fraction of Hb A and Hb G. No abnormalities have been suggested for the Hb_3A locus. Hb_4F may be the locus controlling thalassemia. Until more is known, it is advisable to limit the gene symbol to the major hemoglobin locus, Hb_1. A normal person would be homozygous for Hb A (Hb_1A/Hb_1A). A person may be homozygous or heterozygous for an abnormal hemoglobin with one or both genes for Hb A replaced by a gene for an abnormal hemoglobin: Hb_1A/Hb_1X, Hb_1X/Hb_1X. Also a different gene for each of two abnormal hemoglobins may replace those for Hb A, resulting in a mixed heterozygous formula: Hb_1X/Hb_1Y. The genetic mechanism for Hb F is apparently present at all times.

When more than one hemoglobin is present, one of them predominates. Hb A, when combined with another hemoglobin, usually is more than 50 per cent of the total. All hemoglobins suppress, in varying degrees, the expressivity of Hb F. Especially in the presence of Hb A, almost no F can be found, but Hb C, D, E, and S suppress the F less effectively. On the other hand, a thalassemia gene enhances the expressivity of Hb F and of any associated abnormal hemoglobin but suppresses Hb A. Hence, in thalassemia major large amounts of F may be present with very little A, although A is presumably homozygous. Also, in thalassemia-Hb S disease, up to 100 per cent of Hb S may be found although the patient is heterozygous for S.

Clinically Abnormal Hemoglobin Syndromes

There are four main groups:

1. Homozygous hemoglobin diseases. Both genes for Hb A are replaced by the same abnormal hemoglobin: Sickle cell anemia (S-S

disease), C-C disease, D-D disease, E-E disease.

2. Heterozygous hemoglobin trait syndromes. One gene for Hb A and one for an abnormal hemoglobin: sickle cell trait (A-S disease), Hb D trait, and Hb C trait.

3. Mixed heterozygous hemoglobin diseases. Two different abnormal hemoglobins replace Hb A: S-C disease, S-D disease.

4. Thalassemia in homozygous form or in heterozygous form in combination with any hemoglobin, again either in homozygous or heterozygous form.

HOMOZYGOUS HEMOGLOBIN DISEASES

These are the so-called pure hemoglobin diseases. Each parent transmits one gene for the same abnormal hemoglobin. So far four such diseases have been described: Hb S (sickle cell anemia), Hb C, Hb D, and Hb E disease. The details of the clinical and laboratory findings are summarized in Table 4–6.

Sickle Cell Anemia. *Clinical findings.* Chronic hemolytic anemia and episodes of painful crises. Continued and progressive severity of the disease, which is usually fatal before the age of 30, is interrupted by two kinds of crises: clinical (painful) without acute hematologic changes, and hematologic. Hematologic crises with acute drop of red cells and hemoglobin are due to acute marrow aplasia with persistent shortened survival of red cells.

Pathogenesis. Hemoglobin S is freely soluble when oxygenated, but when reduced it forms elongated molecular masses, tactoids, which are responsible for the distortion of the cells into sickles and all the consequences. The severity of the clinical manifestations is related to the amount of Hb S and to the mean corpuscular S hemoglobin concentration in the red cells.

Blood. Chronic normochromic normocytic anemia with a tendency to macrocytosis and hyperchromia, reticulocytosis, polychromatophilia, large numbers of target cells (up to 30 per cent), normoblasts, and Howell-Jolly bodies are seen regularly (Fig. 4–53). The characteristic cell deformity may be present in direct smears. Anisocytosis, poikilocytosis, hypochromia, and basophilic stippling are rare. Osmotic fragility is slightly decreased; mechanical fragility is increased. The marrow shows normoblastic hyperplasia except during aplastic crises. Occasional myelocytes and monocytes with ingested red cells may be seen. The hyperplasia leads to atrophy of the cortex and osteoporosis.

Osmotic fragility is decreased. There is moderate jaundice. There is increased serum bilirubin and urobilinogen excretion and an elevated hemolytic index.

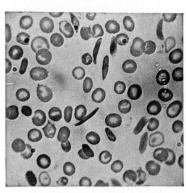

Figure 4–53. Blood in sickle cell anemia, active form, stained film. The diagnosis is best made from unstained wet preparations, in which, after a few hours, the number of crescentic and stellate forms is greatly increased (about × 500). (Courtesy of V. P. Sydenstricker.)

Red cell survival is decreased. The hemolytic anemia results from a corpuscular defect. The spleen is enlarged owing to congestion early in life. It becomes atrophic (siderofibrotic) later. Leg ulcers are frequent. The painful crises are caused by occlusive vascular phenomena. The jaundice is the result of hepatic necrosis and is often obstructive. The sudden drop of the blood level is usually caused by an acute aplasia (aplastic crisis) with absence of reticulocytes, decrease in jaundice, frequent leukopenia, and increase in plasma cells.

Electrophoresis. In S-S disease (homozygous S disease), Hb S is characteristically present between the locations of Hb A and C. There is no Hb A. From 60 to 99 per cent is Hb S; the balance is made up of Hb F. Less than 3 per cent of patients with sickle cell anemia fail to show elevated Hb F. Most of these patients are sickle cell variants (Fig. 4–52).

Homozygous Hb C Disease and Homozygous Hb E Disease. The incidence of C-C disease is about 1 to 6000 in American Negroes. Clinically, both (C-C and E-E) are similar: easy fatigability and dyspnea on effort, arthralgias, and occasional abdominal pain. True crises are not seen. Occasionally there is mild jaundice. Fertility and longevity are not affected. Moderate splenomegaly is characteristic for homozygous Hb

Table 4-6. Hemoglobin Diseases*

DISEASE	Hb TYPES	Hb F %	CLINICAL SEVERITY	CRISES	SPLENO-MEGALY	SEVERITY OF ANEMIA	RED CELL CONSTANTS	TARGET CELLS %	ANISOCY-TOSIS AND POIKILO-CYTOSIS	SICKL-ING
Homozygous										
Sickle cell anemia	S + S	2–25	+++	++++	–	+++	Normocytic normochromic	5–30	Minimal	+
Hb C disease	C + C	<7	+	–	++	±	Slightly microcytic normochromic	40–90	Minimal	–
Hb D disease	D + D	2	–	–	–	–	Microcytic normochromic	40–80	Minimal	–
Hb E disease	E + E	<7	+	–	±	±	Microcytic normochromic	25–60	Minimal	–
Mixed Heterozygous										
Sickle cell-Hb C disease	C + S (F**)	<7	– to +++	– to +++	± to +++	– to +++	Slightly microcytic, slightly hypochromic to normochromic	20–85	Minimal	+
Sickle cell-Hb D disease	D + S (F**)		++	+	– to +++	+++	?	Infre-quent	Marked	+
Thalassemia Syndrome										
Thalassemia major	A + F		++++		++++	++++	Microcytic hypochromic	10–35	+++	–
Thalassemia-Hb S disease	S + F + A		+ to ++++		+ to +++	++ to +++	Microcytic hypochromic	20–40	+++	+
Thalassemia-Hb C disease	A + C (F**)		+ to ++		?	– to ++	Microcytic hypochromic	10–30	++	–
Thalassemia-Hb E disease	E + F		+ to ++++		+ to ++++	+ to ++++	Microcytic hypochromic	10–40	+++	–

* Modified from Chernoff (1958).
** F may be present.

C disease, but it is minimal or absent in homozygous Hb E disease.

Blood. No, or only slight, predominantly normocytic normochromic anemia with an admixture of microcytes and microspherocytes occurs in Hb C and is almost always microcytic in Hb E disease. Mean corpuscular hemoglobin is normal in both. There is no significant increase in reticulocytes, but many target cells appear (40 to 90 per cent in C and 25 to 60 in E disease). Red cell survival is slightly shortened. Osmotic fragility is biphasic with a population having increased and decreased fragility. Crystals of hemoglobin in stained smears and moist preparations, especially after splenectomy, may be responsible for abdominal pains and embolism. The marrow shows moderate normoblastic hyperplasia. There is evidence of slightly increased hemolysis. Electrophoresis: almost 100 per cent of Hb C or E with less than 7 per cent Hb F. The abnormal hemoglobins are demonstrable in both parents.

Homozygous D Disease. Only two cases have been reported. Clinically, only easy fatigability.

Blood. Hemoglobin normal; erythrocytes microcytic and normochromic. Signs of only slightly increased hemolysis. Sixty to 80 per cent target cells and decreased osmotic fragility of red cells. Only Hb D present with normal levels of Hb F (less than 2 per cent).

HETEROZYGOUS HEMOGLOBIN TRAITS

The gene for the abnormal hemoglobin comes from one parent and the Hb A from the other. At least six trait combinations have been recognized: Hb S (sickle cell trait), Hb C, Hb D, Hb E, Hb I, and Hb J traits. In Hb S trait, carriers may show hematuria and splenic infarction. The other traits show no abnormal clinical symptoms or signs of disease. The quantitative blood findings are within normal limits. Sickle cells are demonstrable by special techniques in Hb S trait, and target cells are frequently present in Hb C trait.

Electrophoresis. Mixture of Hb A (the major component) and of the abnormal pigments; Hb F within normal limits.

Sickle Cell Trait. Sickle cell trait is found in about 8 per cent of American Negroes. Patients with sickle cell trait show no clinical signs of disease or hematologic abnormalities under normal circumstances. At autopsy sickling and congestion, especially in the spleen, may be present, probably as a terminal complication, because no other changes are seen, such as abnormal pigmentation or vascular or parenchymatous changes. However, patients with the trait are handicapped by being poor surgical and obstetrical risks and may react poorly under conditions of hypoxia in general and in high altitude flights. Then sickling and the various vascular complications with the parenchymatous sequelae may occur with focal necrosis of the brain, splenic infarcts, and hematuria frequently on one side, particularly on the left side, where the renal vein is longer and tortuous. Sudden death may also occur.

Tests for Sickling. *Screening test.* Examination of a Wright's stained smear may show sickled cells. Such cells do not occur in sickle cell trait.

Sealed whole blood method for demonstrating sickling. PRINCIPLE. Deoxygenated red cells sickle. Deoxygenation is achieved by creating conditions in which the available oxygen is used up by cellular metabolism in sealed preparations of whole blood while the access to oxygen is prevented. The process of deoxygenation may be enhanced by adding reducing substances to the preparation. Various methods have been recommended. Three simple and one more sophisticated method, employing a reducing agent, will be described.

1. A drop of capillary or venous blood (any anticoagulant may be used) is placed on a slide and immediately covered with a coverslip, the edges sealed with petrolatum, and the preparation incubated at room temperature. The preparation is examined for the presence of sickles at intervals for several hours and after 24 hours.

INTERPRETATION. The result is positive if not less than 10 per cent of the cells are sickled. A negative result does not exclude sicklemia because the red cells may lose their capacity to sickle before the oxygen has been exhausted.

2. A drop of blood is allowed to fall into a small tube containing 0.2 to 0.5 ml. of a mixture of equal parts of physiologic salt solution and a 3 per cent solution of sodium citrate. The blood is mixed thoroughly with the solution, and a sufficient quantity of paraffin oil is added to make a layer 1 cm. thick. No air bubbles must be trapped under the oil. The preparation is left standing for 24 hours. Then 0.2 to 0.5 ml. of a 10 per cent solution of neutral formalin in physiologic salt solution is added. This is most easily prepared by adding 0.85 gm. of

sodium chloride to 100 ml. of a 10 per cent solution of neutral formalin. Thorough mixing is assured by forcing the liquids in and out of the pipet several times. A few drops are placed on a slide and covered with a coverglass. The moist preparation is examined for sickle cells (Beck and Hertz, 1935).

3. The steps of a convenient "stasis method" are illustrated in Figure 4–54. When preparations are made by this method, the results may be read immediately; consequently, this is the method of choice for routine work (Scriver and Waugh, 1930).

4. Method employing a reducing agent.

REAGENT. Aqueous sodium metabisulfite ($Na_2S_2O_5$), 2 gm. per 100 ml., freshly prepared. The preparation, a 200 mg. capsule, is available commercially ready to use.

PROCEDURE. A drop or two of the fresh reagent is added to a drop of blood (capillary or venous) on a glass slide. A coverglass is put on the slide. The excessive blood is expressed by gently pressing the coverglass with a piece of filter paper. Sealing and waiting is not necessary.

A similar preparation but with saline instead of the reducing agent is set up as control. The preparation should be read immediately, and if negative the slide should be reexamined at intervals. The final reading must be made 30 minutes after preparation. A positive test is reliable. A negative should be repeated (Daland and Castle, 1948).

INTERPRETATION. The test does not differentiate between sickle cell anemia, sickle cell trait, or the other Hb S syndromes. It does not detect Hb S below a concentration of 7 gm. per 100 ml.

SOURCES OF ERROR. The reducing agent is unstable and may be responsible for a false negative result. The reagent deterior-

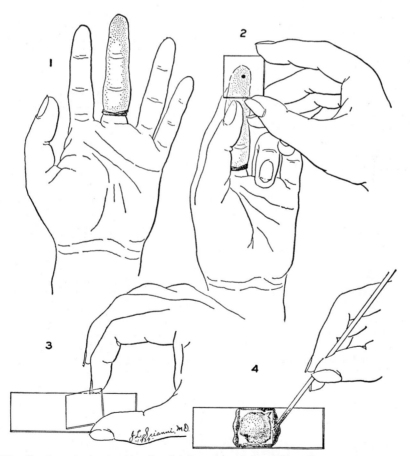

Figure 4–54. Stasis moist preparation for the detection of the sickle cell trait. 1. Rubber band constriction of finger for five minutes. 2. Collection of drop of blood from finger. 3. Coverslip preparation. 4. Sealing preparation with petrolatum. (Diggs and Pettit, J. Lab. & Clin. Med., Vol. 25.)

ates rapidly at room temperature and should be kept in the refrigerator when not in use. Repetition with a fresh reagent is indicated if the test is negative. False negative tests may also result when the amount of the Hb S is too small for detection or from admixture of alcohol (when left on the skin), from trapped air under the coverslip, or from inadequate sealing.

A positive test is diagnostic, provided distortion caused by ovalocytosis, extreme anisocytosis, and crenation as they may occur in thalassemia major have been excluded. The saline control serves this purpose.

Test for differentiation between sickle cell anemia and trait. PRINCIPLE. In sickle cell anemia, sickling takes place at a considerably higher oxygen pressure than in the trait. Equilibration of a blood sample at 37° C. with a gas mixture of oxygen (4 per cent), nitrogen (86 per cent), and carbon dioxide (10 per cent) will produce sickling of 90 per cent or more of red cells in sickle cell anemia but of less than 10 per cent in the trait.

THE TEST. Four milliliters of venous blood with an anticoagulant are placed in a large test tube or small Erlenmeyer bottle closed with a stopper containing a rubber diaphragm. The gas mixture is passed through the blood for three minutes while the containers are rotated. The bottle is shaken gently for 15 minutes at 37° C.

One-tenth to 0.5 ml. of blood is transferred without exposure to the air into 3 ml. of 10 per cent of formalin (1 part of 37 per cent formaldehyde in water and 9 parts of aqueous NaCl, 0.85 gm. per 100 ml.). This fixes the red cells and prevents reversal of the sickling on exposure to oxygen. A drop of the red cell suspension is examined under the microscope.

INTERPRETATION. Less than 10 per cent of red cells sickle in the trait, whereas 90 per cent do in the anemia. The test will differentiate the two conditions. It also permits the correct diagnosis in a patient who received a recent blood transfusion.

Electrophoretic analysis does not permit the correct diagnosis of sickle cell anemia in a patient with a recent transfusion but gives the electrophoretic pattern of sickle cell trait.

Blood of S-C and of thalassemia-S undergoes intermediate degrees of sickling (Page and Culver, 1960).

MIXED HETEROZYGOUS HEMOGLOBIN DISEASES

A different abnormal hemoglobin inherited from each parent. Only two diseases are described: sickle cell-Hb C disease and sickle cell-Hb D disease.

S-C Disease. Originally thought to be an atypical sickle cell anemia, sickling occurring in only one parent; the spleen is usually palpable, the anemia is of varying severity but not infrequently is mild, and many more target cells are present than in sickle cell anemia.

Electrophoresis. Hb S and Hb C. About one-fifth of the cases formerly diagnosed as sickle cell anemia are now recognized as S-C disease. Also, some cases of sickle cell trait are found to be S-C disease. The incidence is about one-third that of sickle cell anemia.

Clinical findings. Clinical findings are most variable, from asymptomatic to severe and more frequently are milder than in homozygous S disease. The onset is usually early in childhood, but real difficulties do not occur until the teens or later. Fatigue, dyspnea on effort, frequent upper respiratory infections, attacks of mild jaundice, and arthralgias are seen. Crises as a rule are mild and rare but may be severe and frequent. Painful crises occur more often in joints and muscles than in the abdomen. Constant hip and low back pain is often present with aseptic necrosis of the head of the femur on x-ray. Hematuria and splenic infarcts have also been described. Leg ulcers only occur occasionally. In pregnancy there is a tendency to increased frequency of crises, clinical and hematologic.

Physical findings. The body habitus is normal or stocky and in sickle cell anemia, asthenic. In remissions there are no physical abnormalities. In relapses, jaundice, muscle tenderness, and splenomegaly with marked and frequent fluctuations in size and tenderness are seen.

Blood. Mild chronic normochromic, slightly microcytic anemia is seen in some cases, but the anemia is severe in others. Only indistinct signs of hemolysis are found in remissions, but occasionally are present in severe hemolytic crises. Reticulocyte counts range from normal to high. Aniso- and poikilocytosis is mild to severe. There are many target cells, up to 85 per cent (Plate 4–1[4]).

In relapses many normoblasts appear in

the peripheral blood. The marrow, hemolytic index, and red cell survival studies parallel the clinical picture. Hb C and Hb S occur in about equal amounts. Hb F ranges from normal to 7 per cent.

Sickle cell-Hb D Disease. Little is known; too few cases have been described.

Clinical findings. These range from mild to moderate. In the latter case, they may resemble sickle cell-Hb C disease.

Electrophoresis. The pattern is indistinguishable from sickle cell anemia, because Hb S and Hb D cannot be distinguished on paper electrophoresis. Solubility studies and family investigation reveal the true nature of the condition.

The less known sickle cell-Hb G, Hb C-Hb C disease and sickle cell Hb E disease have been described but are not well studied.

THALASSEMIA

This term comprises a group of hereditary diseases resulting from multiple interrelated genetic defects in people of Mediterranean, African, and Asian ancestry.

Principle. There is a defect in corpuscular structure and in iron utilization. The defective hemoglobin is A or F.

Blood findings range from very mild, even asymptomatic, and difficult to diagnose to severe chronic microcytic hypochromic hemolytic anemia. There may be a possible genetic relationship between the thalassemia gene or genes and Hb F.

In families of patients with thalassemia, high levels of Hb F up to 80 per cent were found with only minimal clinical manifestations of thalassemia.

According to the present consensus thalassemia major is homozygous, and thalassemia minor (thalassemia trait) is heterozygous.

At least six different abnormal hemoglobins have been found in thalassemia: Hb S, C, E, D, H, and G.

Thalassemia Major (Homozygous Thalassemia, Cooley's Anemia). *Clinical findings.* Severe hemolytic anemia. Prominent facial bones, slanting eyes, and icterus add up to the "mongoloid facies." Splenomegaly.

X-ray. Thinning of the cortex of long and flat bones from marrow hyperplasia. Skull thickened and osteoporotic. "Hair on end" appearance.

Blood. Microcytic hypochromic anemia, reticulocytosis, target cells, ovalocytosis, extreme poikilocytosis with bizarre shapes, Cabot rings, Howell-Jolly bodies, nuclear fragments, siderocytes, anisocytosis, aniso-

chromia, and normoblastemia (see Plates 4–1, 4–5[6]). Indirect serum bilirubin and serum hemoglobin are elevated. Osmotic resistance is increased.

Marrow. Normoblastic hyperplasia.

Electrophoresis. Hb F is increased up to 90 per cent. Hb F can be measured with paper electrophoresis, chromatography, immunologic tests, or alkali-denaturation test (Singer *et al.*, 1951).

Hb A$_2$ ("trace" hemoglobin) is increased (Gerald and Diamond, 1958; Kunkel and Wallenius, 1955). Best demonstrated with starch-block electrophoresis.

Thalassemia Minor (Heterozygous Thalassemia; Thalassemia Minima; Cooley's Trait). *Clinical findings.* Longevity not affected. Hypochromic microcytic anemia with slight hemolytic icterus.

Blood. Red cell count normal or elevated, hematocrit and hemoglobin reduced. Reticulocytosis, normoblastemia. Many target cells and stippled cells. Serum iron high (iron therapy not effective). Splenomegaly.

Electrophoresis. Frequently elevated A$_2$, slow moving component of A (moves like E). Normally less than 3 per cent.

Marrow. Normoblastic hyperplasia.

Thalassemia and Other Hemoglobinopathies (Double Heterozygosities)

Thalassemia trait and sickle cell trait. BLOOD. Moderate anemia and morphology of thalassemia major. Characteristic blood finding: pronounced microcytosis and only slight hypochromia. In iron deficiency, both decreased proportionately. Important: family study.

Thalassemia-Hb S and thalassemia-Hb E disease. May resemble closely thalassemia major, although usually the course is milder and the onset later.

Blood findings in thalassemia-abnormal Hb disease: sickled cells when in combination with Hb S. When in combination with Hb E, spherocytes may be present.

ALKALI DENATURATION TEST FOR Hb F (SINGER *et al.*, 1951)

Principle. Blood is alkalinized and then neutralized, the nonhemoglobin is precipitated, and the remaining alkali-resistant hemoglobin is measured.

Test. *Reagents.* 0.12 N KOH or NaOH, kept in refrigerator in plastic or paraffin lined bottles (alkali solution); 50 per cent saturated $(NH_4)_2SO_4$, 1000 ml.; concentrated HCl, 2.5 ml.; (precipitating solution).

Procedure. 10 ml. of blood is washed once with saline.

To sediment add distilled H_2O, 1.5 volumes, and toluene (C.P.), 0.4 volume. Shake for five minutes. Centrifuge at 3000 r.p.m. for ten minutes (in clinical centrifuge). Discard upper two layers. Remove layer with clear red solution. Adjust concentration of hemoglobin to about 10 per cent with distilled water. Determine hemoglobin concentration (H_1). Add 0.1 ml. of H_1 hemoglobin solution to 1.6 ml. of alkaline reagent. To mix, rinse pipet five to six times while shaking the tube.

After exactly *one minute*, add 3.4 ml. of precipitating reagent. Invert tube three to four times and filter immediately. The filtrate H_2 is a 1 to 50 dilution of the original hemoglobin solution (H_1). Test for hemoglobin (H_2). Alkaline resistant hemoglobin $= \dfrac{H_2}{H_1} \times 100$.

Interpretation. In normal adult blood, the filtrate is almost colorless with less than 2 per cent of initial hemoglobin. Blood with Hb F (if more than 2 per cent) is brown to red.

BLOOD IN PREGNANCY

"Normal" Hematologic Values

1. Hemoglobin is consistently lower than normal and will be discussed in greater detail.

2. Erythrocyte sedimentation rate is increased beginning with the third month. It returns to normal beginning with the third postpartum week.

3. Leukocytes (mainly granulocytes) may show a slight increase in the third trimester. The increase is more pronounced in primiparas. The leukocyte count rises frequently to 15,000 to 20,000 immediately post partum.

4. Platelets may be slightly decreased during the third trimester. The increase becomes more pronounced during labor.

5. The marrow shows a slight normoblastic hyperplasia during the final weeks of the pregnancy.

6. Iron binding capacity may be slightly increased during the second trimester and is frequently and significantly increased during the third trimester.

7. Plasma volume begins to increase in the second trimester and becomes pronounced (up to 40 per cent above normal) during the third. It returns to normal promptly after childbirth.

8. Red cell mass shows a moderate decrease (about 200 ml.) during the first two months followed by a slight increase during the remainder of the pregnancy (about 270 ml. in the ninth month) and a drop during labor to below normal values. It returns to normal post partum but more slowly than the plasma volume.

9. Red cell fragility is slightly increased. The increase is more pronounced in anemia.

10. Plasma proteins drop progressively. They return to normal rapidly after childbirth.

Anemia in Pregnancy

IRON DEFICIENCY ANEMIA

Moderate normochromic normocytic anemia in pregnancy is the rule rather than the exception. Some writers call it physiologic. It has been reported in 88 per cent of pregnant women. A variety of factors contribute to this situation. Primiparas may enter their childbearing career with an iron deficiency brought on by periodic blood losses in menstruation, which may be aggravated by dieting and faulty food habits. In multiparous women the deficiency is increased by further loss of iron in each successive pregnancy and lactation. The iron requirements during a pregnancy amount to about 725 mg. This requires correction for the amount of iron that would have been lost with each menstruation. The fetus derives its initial iron stores from the mother.

Another factor is the plasma volume, which is normal during the first trimester, rises slightly during the second, and may reach a level 40 per cent above normal in the third trimester. All this adds to a slightly lower hemoglobin to begin with (14 gm. $\pm$ 0.5 gm.), an average of 13 gm. ($\pm$ 1 gm.) in the second trimester, and an average of 12 gm. ($\pm$ 1 gm.) in the third.

Red cell values of about 3,500,000 and hematocrit readings of about 33 per cent have been reported. Temporary increases of blood values have been recorded in the third trimester (thirty-second to thirty-fourth weeks). Following delivery the antepartum "normal" is reestablished with varying speed, which is accelerated by iron medication. Red cell counts and hematocrit values rise more rapidly than hemoglobin.

In addition to the so-called "physiologic" anemia of pregnancy, more severe hypochromic microcytic iron deficiency anemia occurs, usually when the hemoglobin drops to below 10 gm. Infection, toxemia of pregnancy, protein deficiency, decreased gastric secretion, and multiple pregnancies are the contributing factors.

MEGALOBLASTIC ANEMIA

The incidence of this form shows striking geographic differences. It is less frequent in the United States than in England. It is seen frequently in India and in the tropics, especially in advanced pregnancy and early after childbirth, more often in young multiparas under 35 years of age, and in women with poor dietary habits. Marrow examination is needed for the diagnosis, especially when clear-cut iron deficiency is absent. It may be indicated even in the presence of low hemoglobin values, because combined megaloblastic and iron deficiency anemias may exist. Albuminuria and purpura may also be present.

The peripheral blood picture is similar to but not identical with that seen in true pernicious anemia. Aniso- and poikilocytosis are less pronounced. Leukopenia is present less regularly. The marrow resembles addisonian pernicious anemia closely, except that normoblastic hyperplasia may be present simultaneously with the megaloblastic. Folic acid deficiency seems to be the immediate cause. The anemia subsides after termination of pregnancy.

POLYCYTHEMIA

Definition. An increase of erythrocytes above 6.9 million in men and 6.3 million in women.

Classification. Two main forms of the disease are recognized: Polycythemia vera synonyms: erythremia, Vaquez-Osler disease, Osler's disease and secondary polycythemia. Relative polycythemia caused by loss of plasma is best included among secondary polycythemias.

Polycythemia Vera

Clinical Findings. Affected patients exhibit a peculiar and striking cyanotic countenance. There is a tendency to thrombosis. Splenomegaly is present in the majority of patients and is accepted as diagnostic. The liver is enlarged but less frequently. The disease is somewhat more frequent in men. It begins in middle age; the prevalence is highest after 50. It is known to occur in combination with hypertension (Gaisböck's syndrome) and with hepatic cirrhosis (Mosse's syndrome).

Pathogenesis. The pathogenesis has not been established. None of the suggested explanations have prevailed. It is considered as one of the myeloproliferative disorders. This fits well with the abnormal proliferation of all three marrow elements with resulting findings in the marrow and peripheral blood.

The erythrocytes of the circulating blood number 7,000,000 to 12,000,000 per cubic millimeter. Erythrocyte counts of more than 15,000,000 have been recorded. The value for the hemoglobin ranges from 18 to 24 gm. per 100 ml. of blood. The M.C.V., M.C.H., and M.C.H.C. are normal or low. In the cases with excessively high numbers of erythrocytes, the cells are abnormally small; otherwise the cellular volume would exceed that of the whole blood. As would be expected, the total volume of the blood is usually increased. It may be two to three times greater than normal. The increase is brought on by a rise in the total erythrocyte mass and correspondingly in the hematocrit. Resistance of the erythrocytes to hypotonic saline solutions is increased. The viscosity of the blood is high, and it may be difficult to prepare good smears. The blood coagulates rapidly. The E.S.R. is reduced. The platelet count is usually above the normal average, sometimes 1 million and more. Macrocytes, microcytes, polychromatophilic erythrocytes, and normoblasts may be found but are not a prominent feature of the disease. Moderate polymorphonuclear neutrophilic leukocytosis is the rule, and a number of these patients may show a leukemoid reaction with immature granulocytes and normoblasts. Large masses of platelets may be seen. Alkaline phosphatase is greatly increased with values up to 200.

The marrow shows general hyperplasia of all cell types. In some cases, especially late in the disease, the myeloid cells including the basophils proliferate most actively. Occasionally myelofibrosis sets in.

Complications. Leukemia may develop late in the disease; an incidence of 20 to 80 per cent has been reported (Miale, 1958).

The course of polycythemia vera is chronic; mild symptoms may be present for years but the disease is ultimately fatal.

Secondary Polycythemia

Definition. A secondary increase in the number of erythrocytes results from hypoxia in decreased atmospheric pressure under various circumstances, e.g., high altitude and concentration of blood due to severe diarrhea, burns, chronic acquired or congenital heart disease, chronic pulmonary disease, or other causes. In cases of burns, there is marked hemoconcentration as the fluid portion of the blood leaks into the tissues. The concentration of hemoglobin has been found to be reduced after hemorrhage and increased during shock. In shock, there is reduction in the plasma volume, which results in hemoconcentration. In anaphylactic shock, the same hemoconcentration as is found in surgical shock has been noted by some investigators. Hemoconcentration occurs several hours before blood pressure sinks to critical levels. Studies of blood concentration made early may show a rising curve that acts as a warning signal of the more serious circulatory failure that will follow unless active treatment is immediately carried out.

HEMATOPOIESIS IN THE NEWBORN AND INFANT

In the seven-to-ten-week-old (18 to 38 mm. long) embryo, about 25 per cent of the circulating red cells are nucleated. At the intrauterine age of four or five months (length 160 to 250 mm.), the number of nucleated red cells is reduced to less than 1 per cent. It has been reported that the number of erythrocytes increases with the progression of pregnancy by about 500,000 every four weeks from 1 million per cu. mm. at eight weeks of intrauterine life (Fruhling et al., 1949). In addition to age, other factors, prenatal and postnatal, influence the blood picture.

1. One such factor is size. In single ovum twins with common placental circulation, differences in body weight are reflected in corresponding differences in the numbers of erythrocytes and levels of hemoglobin, for example, 25 gm. of hemoglobin and 7,500,000 erythrocytes in the larger twin and 3.7 gm. and 1,800,000 erythrocytes in the smaller (Klingberg et al., 1955).

2. Bleeding from the fetal into the maternal circulation is evidenced by the presence of elevated amounts of fetal hemoglobin in the maternal circulation of anemic infants (O'Connor et al., 1957).

3. At the time of clamping the cord as much as 100 to 125 ml. of placental blood may be added to the newborn if tying of the cord is postponed until the pulsation of the cord ceases. In a study of newborns whose cords had been clamped late, the average capillary red cell counts were 400,000 higher one hour after and 800,000 higher 24 hours after birth as compared with newborns whose cord had been clamped early (DeMarsh et al., 1941, 1948).

4. Capillary blood (obtained by skin prick) gives higher red cell and hemoglobin values than venous (cord, sinus). The differences may amount to about 500,000 for the former and about 3.0 gm. for the latter. The slowing of capillary circulation and the resulting loss of fluid may be the responsible factor. Examination of venous blood furnishes more consistent results than capillary.

5. Dramatic changes take place in the blood and marrow during the first few days and even during the early hours after birth. These are reflected in the values of all formed elements and in the rapid fluctuations. The number of erythrocytes tends to reach a peak during the first 24 hours, remains at this plateau for about two weeks, and then declines slowly.

The calculated average of 480 erythrocyte counts in capillary blood was reported as 5,640,000 with a range of 3,500,000 to 8,230,000. The calculated average of 249 counts in venous blood was 4,820,000 with a range of 3,100,000 to 6,850,000 (Smith, 1959). Both compilations were based on examinations done during the first postnatal day. It is apparent that the high counts are seen mainly in capillary blood, whereas values obtained in venous blood are not significantly different from what one finds in healthy older children.

Nucleated red cells are most numerous at birth with 8 per 100 white blood cells in the cord blood at term and 25 per cent in premature infants at 24 weeks (Fruhling, 1949). In full-term infants, the number of normoblasts declines rapidly to about 1 per cent during the first 24 hours. The normal reticulocyte count at birth ranges from 1 to 6 per cent during the first 24 hours. It may rise somewhat during the first few hours and decline beginning with the third day to about 1 to 3 per cent (Gairdner et al., 1952; Seip, 1955).

The calculated average of 526 hemoglobin tests in capillary blood during the first 24 hours was reported as 19.85 gm. with a range of 12.3 to 27.5 gm. Similarly, the calculated average of 289 tests on venous blood was reported as 17.0 gm. with a range of 12.5 to 24.6 gm. (Smith, 1959). There is frequently an initial increase in the hemoglobin level of venous blood at the end of 24 hours as compared with that of cord blood. The level remains constant for about three days. It is followed by a drop beginning with the fourth day, becoming more pronounced during the second week, and continuing until anemia is present, normally in the second and third months.

The hematocrit ranges from 46 to 60 per cent in cord blood at birth. It is lower in prematures: Smith quoted 42.5 per cent in six-month prematures with monthly increases of about 3 per cent and an average of 53 per cent in newborns at term. After birth, there is usually an increase during the first 48 hours, followed by a slow but continuous decline down to about 46 per cent after two weeks and about 35 per cent between the second and fourth months.

Macrocytosis is usually present at birth. The average mean corpuscular volume (M.C.V.) is about 100 cu. microns. A sharp drop takes place during the first 24 hours. The drop continues at a less rapid pace to reach about 82 cu. microns at six months. Mean corpuscular hemoglobin (M.C.H.) shows a similar course: 37 $\mu\mu$g. at birth, 34 $\mu\mu$g. at 20 days, and 26 $\mu\mu$g. at six months. Average mean corpuscular hemoglobin concentration (M.C.H.C.) in cord blood was reported as about 33 gm. per 100 ml. of erythrocytes with a slight rise to about 34 gm. between the first and tenth days, to 35 gm. at two months, and a slow but steady decline to a minimum level during the second year (Guest and Brown, 1957).

The high erythrocytic values at birth are explained by the stimulating effect on the marrow of the partial anoxia *in utero*, which becomes more progressive with the growth of the fetus. With the change in the environment and improved oxygenation after birth, the stimulus to blood production ceases abruptly with resulting lowering of all the erythrocytic values and later a more gradual development of a "physiologic" anemia. The role of hypoxia is illustrated by reports of continued high erythrocytic values in the neonatal period in infants with congenital heart disease. These infants do not develop "physiologic" anemia (Rudolph *et al.*, 1953).

Another factor that contributes to the lowered values is the shortened survival of neonatal erythrocytes (Hollingsworth, 1955).

There are conflicting reports in the literature regarding osmotic resistance of fetal blood, but the consensus is that it is not significantly different from the resistance in later life. The evidence in favor of lowered mechanical resistance of fetal blood is slightly more convincing.

The White Blood Cells

The total white cell count at birth and during the first 24 hours varies within wide limits. The numbers range from 4000 to 40,000, granulocytes being the predominant cell and a large proportion of them being nonsegmented with occasional myelocytes and without evidence of disease. According to most opinions there are increases of the total number and of the granulocytes during the first 24 hours. The count begins to drop progressively at the beginning of the second day mainly owing to 'a decrease of granulocytes. According to a careful study by Forkner (1929) during the first day the average was a total white cell count of 25,000 with 69 per cent neutrophilic granulocytes, 2 per cent eosinophils, 7 per cent monocytes, 18 per cent lymphocytes, and 4 per cent myelocytes. Ten days later the corresponding figures were 13,000, 29 per cent, 3 per cent, 17 per cent, 49 per cent, and 0.2 per cent.

In premature infants examined on the first day, the total white cell count is usually lower (average: about 7500). The number of immature white cells in the differential count is higher, and the replacement of granulocytes by lymphocytes takes place somewhat later than in term infants.

The dramatic variations in the total white cell count and in the differential count suggest caution in correlating such findings with clinical manifestations of disease. The platelet count is in the lower normal range at birth and during the first week and then rises rapidly to adult levels.

DISEASES AFFECTING LEUKOCYTES

The examination of leukocytes includes two technical phases. In the quantitative phase, one determines the number of all the white cells, the total white blood count (WBC), and the relative and absolute numbers of the various forms of white cells. In the qualitative phase, one determines the deviations from the normal in appearance and structure of the cytoplasm and nuclei. Examination also includes two anatomic phases: examination of peripheral blood (capillary or venous) and examination of marrow (obtained from sternum, tibia, iliac, or spinous process).

The purpose of the study of leukocytes is, first, to help in establishing a diagnosis. Occasionally the examination alone may furnish a positive specific diagnosis, for example, in leukemia. More frequently it may be diagnostically helpful together with other clinical or laboratory data, for example, in acute appendicitis or infectious mononucleosis. Another purpose is to help in establishing a prognosis. For example, a low white blood count in acute appendicitis or pneumonia is considered prognostically unfavorable.

Finally, study of the leukocytes is helpful in following the course of disease. For example, toxic effects of radiotherapy and chemotherapy may be recognized early by examination of leukocytes.

Examination of leukocytes may also reveal the existence of an entirely unsuspected disease. For example, leukemia may be found in a patient with the clinical picture of an acute infection, or infectious mononucleosis may be found in patients whose disease clinically resembles leukemia.

For this and other reasons the white blood count is one of the so-called routine tests, which, according to recommendations of organizations supervising hospitals, have to be done on every patient admitted to the hospital regardless of disease.

The Normal White Blood Count

For techniques employed in the study of leukocytes, see p. 103ff.

According to studies with radioactive phosphorus and C^{14}-labeled thymidine, neutrophilic and eosinophilic granulocytes remain in the marrow for four to six days before entering the peripheral blood, where their average survival is 9 to 13 days with a maximum of 21 days (Ottesen, 1954). The survival of lymphocytes is 100 to 200 days (Christensen and Ottesen, 1955).

It is generally agreed that a white blood count falling within the range of 5000 to 10,000 per cu. mm. is within normal limits. By this is meant that a study of large numbers of apparently healthy individuals showed that 80 per cent of them had white blood counts ranging between the two values mentioned. About one person in five will have a count either higher or lower than the mentioned values. If 95 per cent of those tested were included as normals, the range would be 4000 to 11,000. According to the best judgment of the examiners, the 20 per cent beyond the 80 per cent range showed no perceptible signs of abnormality or illness.

Some factors responsible for this wide range of normal are known but many more are not known. For example, it is known that the condition of the host plays an important part, as was shown by Garrey and Bryan (1935). According to their studies the upper limits of normal, under basal conditions, are 3000 to 4000 cells per cu. mm.

After the first few years of life most of the white blood cells are granulocytes, which are produced in the bone marrow. Therefore, the condition of the bone marrow and the release mechanism, both variables, have a bearing on the total number of white blood cells. It seems that the release of the granulocytes from the bone marrow occurs at regular intervals. The highest total count and the highest number of neutrophilic leukocytes are seen late in the afternoon. This is known as diurnal variation. The conception that food intake influences the total white count has been given up, at least as it concerns the normal individual. The influence of allergy will be discussed later.

Basal conditions and prolonged rest lower the white blood count. Muscular activity, especially if excessive, raises the total white count. As a rule, the increase is in granulocytes, sometimes in lymphocytes. It has been shown that during exercise the spleen tends to contract excessively. It is possible that this causes an increase of the peripheral white blood count by expelling the stored blood and leukocytes with it. Cold showers or massage may raise the white blood count up to 25,000. Mental factors, such as pain, may produce leukocytosis.

There is no evidence that sex influences the white blood count except in the last month of pregnancy, when variations from the normal seem to be exaggerated, and during labor when there is as a rule a striking increase in the total white count ranging from 15,000 to 30,000. It lasts a few days and returns to normal after four days to two weeks post partum.

Age is one of the important factors influencing the white blood count, quantitatively and qualitatively. Fluctuations of white blood cells are common at all ages, but they are greatest in infants and only slightly less so in childhood.

In the newborn baby the average count

is quoted as 15,000 with occasional values as high as 45,000 and a rapid drop on the second day continuing until about the tenth day. Nucleated red blood cells in the newborn, especially in the premature, may cause errors in leukocyte counts if proper corrections are not made. After ten days, until the age of about seven years, the range is 4500 to 15,500. This range is narrowed to 4000 to 13,000 in the age period of 8 to 18 years. From then on the values quoted for adults prevail (Table 4–7).

Table 4–7. The Normal White Blood Count

	RANGE per cu. mm.	AVERAGE per cu. mm.
Newborn		
1st day	3,600–45,000	15,000
2nd day	5,000–13,000	10,000
3rd–10th days	5,000–13,000	7,500
Infants		
10 days to 7 years	5,500–15,500 (95% value)	10,400
Adolescents	4,000–13,000 (95% value)	8,400
Adults	5,000– 8,000 (80% value)	

Variations similar to those for the total white blood count also prevail with regard to the relative proportions of the different white blood cells, the so-called differential blood count (Table 4–8). According to Wintrobe the range of neutrophilic granulocytes in adults is 54 to 62 per cent. According to Osgood, in the newborn the average is 60 per cent on the first day; it drops to 38 per cent on the fifth day and continues approximately at the same level with a range of 16 to 60 per cent. In adolescents, the average increases to 48 per cent and the range to 25 to 70 per cent.

Band cells are found in 0 to 5 per cent of white blood cells in the adult. As high as 25 per cent occur in the newborn infant during the first day of life; they increase up to 17 per cent during the first year of life and then slowly reach the values seen in the adult. Values over 10 per cent in the differential count are abnormal.

Eosinophils range from 1 to 5 per cent with an average of 3 per cent in adolescents and adults. The values are slightly higher in children.

Basophils are rare: they range from 0 to 1 per cent.

Normal values for lymphocytes in adults range from 20 to 40 per cent of the white blood cells. In the newborn the average is 30 per cent on the first day with a slow rise up to 45 per cent on the fourth day. Until the age of 14 years the average is 48 per cent and the range, 20 to 70 per cent. The average drops to 42 per cent and the range to 22 to 62 per cent in adolescents.

Prevalence of lymphocytes over neutrophilic leukocytes may sometimes continue far beyond the age mentioned and into adult life. The reason for persistence of infantile lymphocytosis is unknown.

Monocytes are quoted as averaging 4 per cent of white blood cells in adolescents and adults with a range of 1 to 6 per cent; an average of 5 per cent, with a range of 0 to 12 per cent in newborn and infants up to 4 years of age; and an average of 3 per cent and a range of 0 to 7 per cent in children 4 to 13 years of age.

The wide range of variations in the total white blood count and in the relative proportions of the different white cells makes it apparent that relative figures expressed in percentages are of limited value and frequently misleading. Therefore, it is important to calculate and to use the absolute values of these cells per cubic millimeter. Familiarity with and use of absolute values help to prevent erroneous conclusions. The finding of 10 per cent lymphocytes in a differential count would at first suggest reduction in the number of these cells but assumes an entirely different aspect when it is expressed in absolute numbers of a total white count of 25,000. The absolute values are listed in Table 4–8. The absolute values are calculated from the total white count and the percentage according to the formula:

$$\text{Absolute no.} = \frac{\text{WBC}}{100} \times \text{per cent of cell type}$$

For example, total WBC = 20,000
% of eosinophils = 12
Absolute no. of eosinophils per cu. mm.
$$= \frac{20,000}{100} \times 12 = 2400$$

The Differential Count

In addition to the study of the numbers of leukocytes of the three types (granulocytes, lymphocytes, and monocytes)—the quantitative study—evaluation of the blood picture includes consideration of the age of the cells—the qualitative study. From this point of view most attention has been

Table 4–8. The Normal Differential Count (95 per cent values)

	RELATIVE VALUES		ABSOLUTE VALUES	
	Average %	Range %	Average per cu. mm.	Range per cu. mm.
Segmented neutrophilic granulocytes				
Newborn–1st day	60		9000	
Newborn–2nd day			6000	
5 days to 14 years	38	16–60		
8 to 14 years			3250	
15 to 19 years	48	25–70		
Adolescents	48	25–70	4000	1500–7500
Adults	60	50–70	4500	2500–7000
Band cells				
Newborn–1st day	25			
1st year	17			
Adults	3	0–5		0–500
Eosinophils				
Under 14 years	2.8	0–8		0–600
Over 14 years	3.0	1–5	200	50–500
Basophils	0.5	0–1	40	0–100
Lymphocytes				
Newborn–1st day	30			
Newborn–4th day	45			
4 to 7 years	48	20–70	5000	1500–8500
8 to 14 years	48	20–70	4000	1500–6500
15 to 19 years	42	22–62	3250	1500–5000
Adults	30	20–40	3000	1000–4000
Monocytes				
All age groups			375	285–500
Birth to 4 years	5	0–12		
4 to 14 years	3	0–7		
14 years and over	4	1–6	300	50–600
Disintegrating cells	5	0–12	400	0–1200

given to cells of the granulocyte series. Several methods of classifying granulocytes according to the degree of maturation have been suggested. Arneth (1904) was the first to attempt practical prognostic evaluation of granulocytes by dividing them into five classes according to the number of segments. Band cells and cells younger than these form Class I. The other classes are determined by the presence of two, three, four, and five segments. About 35 per cent of the segmented cells have two segments; 41 per cent, three segments; 17 per cent, four segments; and not more than 2 per cent have five segments, which is the highest number of segments in normal granulocytes.

Arneth worked out an elaborate but impractical system of grading. In addition to its complexity, the weakness of the Arneth system was emphasis on classification of segmented cells, which are prognostically least important.

Schilling's differential count enjoys the greatest popularity (Schilling, 1929). The granulocytes are divided according to their age in four groups: myelocytes and younger cells, metamyelocytes, bands, and segmented cells. In normal blood myelocytes are absent and metamyelocytes may be seen occasionally. The frequency of the other cells is shown in Table 4–8. In hemograms (graphic presentations of differential counts) the cells are usually listed from left to right in order of increasing maturity; therefore, an increase of immature forms is spoken of as a "shift to the left."

A "shift to the left" or an increase of immature granulocytes in the differential count means inability of the marrow to produce or release enough mature granulocytes in response to an excessive demand. Instead immature cells are sent out as substitutes. This myeloid or marrow insufficiency is usually temporary. The shift to left may be "regenerative" if the total count is high and mature cells are present in ample numbers or "degenerative" if the count is normal or low, the mature cells are below normal numbers, and the nuclei of the immature cells are shrunken and pyknotic, i.e., show signs of degeneration.

In a "shift to the right" there are fewer band cells and an increase of polysegmented "aged" cells, a phenomenon seen especially in pernicious anemia.

Filamented cells are those in which segments or lobes are connected with a distinct thin filament of chromatin. The filament must be thin. A mere thinned-out portion of the nucleus is not sufficient to classify them as filamented.

Toxic Granulation. Damaging action of severe infections and of other toxic conditions is manifested in so-called "toxic" granules of the cytoplasm. These are basophilic granules unevenly distributed if large and diffusely distributed if small. They are peroxidase positive. Damage takes place early in the development of the cell, probably at the stage of granule formation (Fig. 4–55).

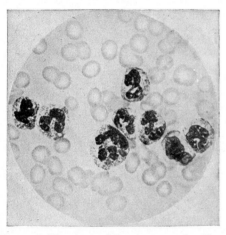

Figure 4–55. Acute lobar pneumonia (Jenner-Giemsa stain). "Toxic" granules in all segmented and nonsegmented polymorphonuclear neutrophils. Note anisocytosis of the leukocytes and also large polymorphonuclear neutrophils.

Basophilia of the cytoplasm and vacuolization are other signs of toxic damage.

A so-called degenerative index, based upon the number of segmented granulocytes showing basophilic granules, was proposed by Kugel and Rosenthal (1932). It is computed by dividing the total number of neutrophils into the total number of cells with toxic granules. For example, if the total percentage of neutrophils is 75 and 55 of them show basophilic granulation, then 73 per cent show this change and the degenerative index is 73. The higher the index, the more serious the prognosis. The quality of the stain has an important bearing on the appearance of the granulocytes.

Toxic granulation may be simulated by artifacts caused by imperfect staining. It may also be confused with basophilic granules. The latter are uniform and dark blue. Toxic granules are smaller and black.

Doehle's Inclusion Bodies. These are inclusions in the cytoplasm of polymorphonuclear neutrophils (Fig. 4–56). Their na-

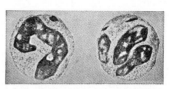

Figure 4–56. Doehle's inclusion bodies in leukocytes. From a case of scarlet fever. Methyl green pyronine stain (× 1500). (L. W. Hill.)

ture has not been definitely determined. The typical "inclusion bodies" are about the size of micrococci or a little larger; some of them are pear shaped; others appear as short rods or cocci lying in pairs. Smaller, discrete, punctiform granules are sometimes seen but do not have the same significance. It now seems well established that typical inclusion bodies have some diagnostic value. They apparently are found in many or even in the majority of the polymorphonuclear neutrophilic leukocytes in every case of scarlet fever early in the disease. A few may be found in diphtheria, pneumonia, and some other infectious diseases but never in rubella and rarely in measles. They are also present in burns.

The inclusion bodies appear blue in preparations stained with Wright's stain, but long staining with methyl green pyronine is preferable (see p. 115). When stained with the latter stain, nuclei are purplish and the bodies bright red.

The Alder Anomaly. A dense azurophilic granulation in all white blood cells was described by Alder (1939, 1950). Their significance is unknown.

Chediak-Higashi Syndrome. This is a lethal anomaly of leukocytes in infants combined with other abnormalities (albinism, photophobia, lymphoma, and leukemia) (Chediak, 1952; Higashi, 1954). Granulocytes and monocytes contain giant cytoplasmic peroxidase-positive granules, which are green in granulocytes.

THE ACCURACY OF THE DIFFERENTIAL COUNT

The accuracy of the differential count is directly proportionate to the numbers of cells counted, and the error is increased in relation to the total white blood count unless a proportionately large number of cells is counted. In other words, the higher the total white count, the larger the number of cells that must be counted to obtain an accurate differential count. The following table has been found useful:

Normal—100 cells

Leukocytosis—200 or 300 cells

Leukemias—500 cells

Marrow

The total weight of the marrow in the adult is about 2600 gm., which is more than the weight of any other organ except circulating blood, skeletal muscles, and bones. Approximately one-half of marrow is functioning red marrow; the remainder is space-occupying yellow, fatty marrow.

Fat marrow may be replaced at any time by functioning marrow. This change may occur at an astoundingly rapid rate, especially in the young. That explains the extreme changes that may be seen in the peripheral blood on slight provocations, especially in the young.

Age. In the newborn, only red marrow is present. With growth, recession of red marrow takes place from the distal ends of the extremities (centripetal). In the normal adult, red marrow is found only in bones of trunk, skull, and proximal ends of femur and humerus. In hyperplasia, the transformation of fat to red marrow progresses in centrifugal direction.

Maturation. Erythrocytes grow in intersinusoidal capillaries, which can open to the general circulation but which normally are closed until the cells reach a certain stage of maturation. When that is reached, the capillary reopens into general circulation and the cells are thrown out as reticulocytes, of which there is normally about 1 per cent. It is probable that in cases of special need—for example, loss of blood in large quantities—the release or the washing out of the intersinusoidal capillaries takes place before the cells mature. The formation of granulocytic cells is extrasinusoidal. It is assumed that they get into the circulation by ameboid motion. This is not present in myeloblasts and progranulocytes but is present in increasing degrees in myelocytes and metamyelocytes (Plate 4–8).

Marrow Changes

Hyperplasia. Hyperplasia may be defined as an increase of cellular marrow at the expense of fat marrow. In extreme degrees even bone may be replaced by proliferating marrow cells (osteoporosis).

Hyperplasia may involve all marrow components (general hyperplasia) or only one (for example, granulocytic hyperplasia), or any combination of them. Hyperplasia may also be generalized and involve most or many bones or may be local and limited to one region or bone. Hyperplastic marrow may consist of fully differentiated cells or of cells arrested at various stages of maturation. The peripheral blood may reflect the hyperplasia of marrow by showing a corresponding increase of fully differentiated or immature cells (marrow hyperplasia with normal marrow-blood threshold), or the hyperplasia of the marrow may not be manifest by a corresponding increase in the circulating blood (marrow hyperplasia with elevated marrow-blood threshold).

Hypoplasia. Hypoplasia may be defined as a decrease of cellular marrow and replacement by fat, connective tissue, bone, metastatic cancer, malignant lymphoma, Hodgkin's disease, or multiple myeloma. Hypoplasia of marrow may or may not be accompanied by pancytopenia.

All elements of marrow may be affected (general marrow hypoplasia) or only one or any combination of them. Excessive hyperplasia of one or more marrow elements may be responsible for hypoplasia of the others. For example, in granulocytic leukemia, the granulocytes may be hyperplastic to the extent of interfering with the normal growth of red blood cells and megakaryocytes with resulting anemia and thrombocytopenia.

Aplasia. Aplasia may be defined as an extreme degree of general marrow hypoplasia.

Leukocytosis

Definition. Leukocytosis is an increase of the total leukocyte count above the upper normal limit of 10,000 per cu. mm. or a relative increase in neutrophils above 80 per cent.

The white blood picture is regulated by a complex mechanism that is not yet fully understood. The central nervous system is probably one of the more important factors.

Hydrogen ion concentration may be another factor. During the early phase of neutrophilia there is a tendency toward acidosis. This can be confirmed experimentally; acidosis brings about a neutrophilic leukocytosis and alkalosis, a lymphocytosis. In diabetic acidosis there is a leukocytosis with a shift to the left just as in sepsis, but in alkalosis of tetany leukocytes show low values with a relative lymphocytosis.

THE RELATION OF THE HYPOPHYSIS AND ADRENALS TO LEUKOCYTES

In the alarm reaction of Selye (1950), of which infection is one cause, there is an activation of the suprarenals. According to Dougherty et al. (1944), corticotropic hormone of the hypophysis causes a drop of lymphocytes in the peripheral blood and disintegration of lymphocytes in lymph nodes, spleen, and thymus. This reduction of lymphocytes can be caused not only by the corticotropic hormone of the pituitary but also by the hormones of the adrenal itself, especially 11-oxycorticosteroids. The breakdown of lymphocytes liberates globulin, especially gamma globulins, the protein fraction in which most antibodies are present.

MOBILIZATION OF LEUKOCYTES

Leukocytes are produced in the marrow. They leave the marrow by ameboid movement when attracted to a focus of inflammation by chemotactic substances. The passage through the walls of blood vessels is facilitated by the tendency of leukocytes in circulating blood to flow along the margins when circulation slows down.

This so-called margination of leukocytes has been explained as follows: In suspensions flowing in tubes, on slowing up of circulation the heaviest particles get into the axis and the lightest go to the periphery. Leukocytes are lighter than red cells. They stick to the endothelium because of their natural stickiness, which is further increased with a rise of the surface tension. The latter is brought on by the acid metabolic products of the inflammatory focus.

There are about 5 billion leukocytes in a milliliter of pus. Therefore, all the leukocytes of the circulating blood are sufficient just for 10 ml. of pus. This relative scarcity of granulocytes is further accentuated by their short life span—only about 9 to 13 days in circulating blood, with slight differences upward and downward, depending on the variety of the cells (granulocyte, monocyte). These data have been arrived at with the help of recent studies employing leukocytes labeled with radioisotopes. In purulent foci, the life span is considerably shorter.

PHYSIOLOGIC LEUKOCYTOSIS

(See Table 4–9).

PATHOLOGIC LEUKOCYTOSIS

The term means an increase of leukocytes in disease (see Table 4–10). As a rule it is neutrophilia, an increase of segmented granulocytes. The neutrophilia may be relative—an increase in the differential count —or absolute—an increase of the total number of the cells—or both. The latter is the most frequent finding.

Sometimes the relation of leukocytosis to disease is not easily demonstrable. Attention must be paid to the presence of immature cells, eosinophils, and monocytes. Still more important is correlation with the clinical condition of the patient. A leukocyte and differential count by itself is of little value as an aid to diagnosis unless it is related to the clinical condition of the patient. Only then is a correct and useful interpretation possible.

INFECTIOUS LEUKOCYTOSIS

The characteristic pattern of infectious leukocytosis is made up of three component parts: progressive neutrophilic leukocytosis (neutrophilic phase), increase of young forms (shift to left), and drop of eosinophils —all three reaching their peak when the infection is at its peak. When the infection begins to subside and the fever drops, a gradual transformation in the blood picture takes place: the total number of leukocytes goes down, and the number of monocytes increases (the monocytic phase of infection). A relative lymphocytosis (lymphocytic phase) and an increase of eosinophils are signs of advancing recovery.

The neutrophilic phase represents the period of active resistance to infection. When the process of defense is finished and the peak is passed, the monocytic phase follows, and the end phase or the phase of recovery is lymphocytic. One could also say that the fight against the infection is characterized by neutrophilia, overcoming of the infection by monocytosis, and healing by lymphocytosis.

Leukocytic, monocytic, and lymphocytic reactions may occur without infection in a variety of circumstances, such as severe muscular exertion, menstruation, during anesthesia and operations, following perspiration in baths at high temperature, following exposure to high temperatures in hyperthermia, and in response to stimulation by foreign substances. Similar blood

Table 4–9. Physiologic Leukocytosis

Definition: increase of leukocytes due to factors other than disease or injury

CAUSE	CELL TYPE	MECHANISM
Acute anoxia	Neutrophilic granulocytes	
Adrenalin	Neutrophilic granulocytes and lymphocytes	Contraction of spleen. Occurs also after splenectomy
Artificial fever	Neutrophilic granulocytes (may be preceded by leukopenia)	
Cold showers, massage	Neutrophilic granulocytes	Emptying of depots. Accelerated blood flow
Dehydration	Neutrophilic, eosinophilic, and basophilic granulocytes; lymphocytes; monocytes	Concentration
Emotional disturbance, excitement, pain, nausea, vomiting	Neutrophilic granulocytes	Nervous mechanism. Accelerated blood flow
Ether anesthesia	Neutrophilic granulocytes	Struggling during excitation may be responsible.
Ether spray of skin	Neutrophilic granulocytes	
Exercise	Neutrophilic granulocytes or lymphocytes	Accelerated blood flow. Emptying of depots (spleen, liver, lungs), but occurs even after splenectomy. Increased adrenalin output
Labor	Neutrophilic granulocytes	Emptying of depots. Accelerated blood flow
Newborn state	Neutrophilic granulocytes	
Sunlight: ultraviolet irradiation	Lymphocytes	

There are as a rule no immature neutrophilic granulocytes in the circulating blood in leukocytosis of this type (no significant shift to left), and the eosinophilic leukocytes and monocytes do not disappear from the blood as they do in leukocytosis due to infections.

Table 4–10. Pathologic Leukocytosis

CAUSE	CELL TYPE
Allergy	Eosinophilic granulocyte
Brucellosis	Lymphocyte, monocyte
Convulsions	Neutrophilic granulocyte or lymphocyte*
Drugs and poisons	
ACTH	Neutrophilic granulocyte
Adrenalin	
Camphor	Neutrophilic and eosinophilic granulocyte
Copper sulfate, phosphorus, carpine	Eosinophilic granulocyte
Tetrachlorethane, adrenalin	Monocyte, neutrophilic granulocyte, and lymphocyte
Other (acetanilid, arsenicals, benzol, CO, digitalis, lead, phenacetin, turpentine, venoms)	Neutrophilic granulocyte
Erythrocytosis (polycythemia)	Neutrophilic, eosinophilic, basophilic granulocyte
Hemolysis	Neutrophilic granulocyte
Hemorrhage	Neutrophilic granulocyte
Hodgkin's disease	Neutrophilic and eosinophilic granulocyte, monocyte
Infectious lymphocytosis	Lymphocyte
Infectious mononucleosis	Lymphocyte
Leukemia	Granulocyte, lymphocyte, or monocyte
Loeffler's syndrome, periarteritis nodosa, pernicious anemia	Eosinophilic granulocyte
Toxemias:	
diabetic acidosis, eclampsia, gout, uremia	Neutrophilic granulocyte
Tuberculosis	Neutrophilic and eosinophilic granulocyte, lymphocyte, monocyte
Tumors involving	
marrow and serous cavities	Neutrophilic and eosinophilic granulocyte
ovarian tumor	Eosinophilic granulocyte
GI tract and liver	Neutrophilic granulocyte
Typhoid fever	Lymphocyte

* Pathogenesis: (1) Emptying of depots (spleen, liver, lungs) but occurs even after splenectomy. (2) Increased adrenalin output.

changes may accompany tissue breakdown when its products are not disposed of in the usual physiologic way. The same may be seen in some diseases of the central nervous system and following experimental irritation of the central nervous system.

NEUTROPHILIA

Infectious Neutrophilia. *General infections.* These are systemic infections caused by various bacteria, fungi, spirochetes, and viruses. In some of these conditions the leukocytosis may be preceded by a transient initial leukopenia, particularly if the infection is overwhelming. It is thought that the severe damage rapidly uses up the available leukocytes and that the leukopenia persists until the marrow can meet the demand. On the other hand, there are bacterial infections that depress the marrow, especially its granulocyte producing or releasing capacity, with resulting leukopenia. Here belong typhoid fever, paratyphoid fever, and tuberculosis, except when complicated by a secondary infection or in special forms as tuberculous meningitis, peritonitis, and pleuritis.

Local infections. Here belong appendicitis, salpingitis, otitis media, mastoiditis, and various other circumscribed accumulations of pus, usually caused by one of the pyogenic bacteria, such as streptococci, staphylococci, and pneumococci. The size of the abscess is less important than the pressure exerted within it. The effect on the blood picture is decreased with organization of a limiting pyogenic membrane, even though the accumulation of pus within persists.

Toxic Neutrophilia. *Endogenous intoxications.* These include uremia, eclampsia, gout, diabetic acidosis, and burns. A chemotactic substance attracting granulocytes from the marrow or a substance specifically stimulating the marrow may be responsible. In burns, it may be absorption of denatured proteins. In eclampsia, convulsions may be a contributory factor.

Drugs and poisons. Various chemicals and drugs such as lead, mercury, potassium chlorate, digitalis, adrenaline, and many others may cause toxic neutrophilia. Among them are chemicals which under certain circumstances are known to produce severe neutropenias (benzol, sulfonamides, arsphenamine).

Posthemorrhagic Neutrophilia. This may occur especially if hemorrhage has taken place into a serous cavity (peritoneum, pleura, joint, subdural space). Leukocytosis following a hemorrhage into the lumen of an intestine also belongs in this category.

Leukocytosis following intracranial hemorrhage is probably caused at least in part by increased intracranial pressure. In some cases of posthemorrhagic neutrophilic leukocytosis, rapid absorption of a chemotactically active component of the blood is incriminated.

Neutrophilia due to Tissue Destruction. Here belongs neutrophilia following injections of turpentine; in myocardial infarction; after operations; in cancer of liver, gastrointestinal tract, or bone marrow, especially with extensive necrosis; in burns; after rapid hemolysis of red cells; in hemolytic crises of hemolytic anemia; and in hemolytic transfusion reactions.

DETERMINANTS OF NEUTROPHILIC LEUKOCYTOSIS

Host Factors. 1. Age. Children respond more intensely and more rapidly to a leukocytogenic stimulus than adults.

2. Resistance. An ill-defined property frequently highly specific for a certain microorganism.

3. Marrow efficiency or reserve. Capacity of the marrow to respond rapidly and efficiently to leukocytogenic stimuli.

4. Localizing ability of body in response to invasion by infectious agents. The more localized the process, the more pronounced the neutrophilia and vice versa.

The Infectious Agent. 1. Specific leukocytogenic properties of microorganisms, especially pyogenic bacteria.

2. Virulence of microorganisms. There is within limits a direct relationship between virulence of the infecting microorganism and the degree of neutrophilia. This property is frequently conditioned by the spreading ability or invasiveness of the microorganism, as opposed to the localizing ability of the host.

A highly virulent microorganism endowed with a high degree of invasiveness may produce only a mild neutrophilic leukocytosis even with a severe infection.

It is claimed, and it is probably correct within wide limits, that the height of leukocytosis is an indicator of the resistance of the individual and that the degree of the shift to the left is an indicator of the severity of the infection. In keeping with this conception, a simultaneous fall of the former and a rise of the latter are prognostically unfavorable.

Prognostic conclusions in the study of leukocytes can be drawn from quantitative data, such as height of leukocyte count, decrease in number of eosinophils, number of lymphocytes (see Hodgkin's disease), and number of monocytes in relation to lymphocytes (see tuberculosis) and from qualitative data, such as a shift to left and toxic granulation of leukocytes.

The following are hematologic signs of recovery from infectious diseases:

1. Drop of the total leukocyte count and of the number of neutrophils.

2. Disappearance of shift to the left.

3. Increase in number of monocytes (except in tuberculosis; see p. 223).

4. Increase of eosinophils when they were decreased or absent during the height of the disease.

5. Increase in number of lymphocytes.

6. Disappearance of toxic granulation.

Therefore, the following are unfavorable hematologic signs:

1. A moderate or slight rise in the total number of leukocytes associated with a marked shift to the left during the height of the disease.

2. Failure of eosinophils to reappear in the end stages of an infectious disease when they were absent before.

3. Absolute reduction of lymphocytes.

4. Excessive number of cells with toxic granulation.

Specifically, in tuberculosis, in addition to the increase of monocytes, the disappearance of young leukocytes is a prognostically poor sign. Therefore, improvement is indicated by a drop of monocytes and reappearance of young leukocytes and increase in the number of lymphocytes.

Eosinophilia

Definition. Eosinophilia is an increase of eosinophilic granulocytes above the highest normal of 500 per cu. mm. counted just like white blood cells with a special diluent.

The close association of eosinophilic leukocytes with allergy, broadly conceived, is impressive. One could easily correlate practically all eosinophilias with one form of allergy or another. An individual host factor has to be assumed to explain variations in eosinophil response. The eosinophils in the blood come from the marrow; those in the tissues come from the blood.

CONDITIONS CHARACTERIZED BY EOSINOPHILIA

1. Allergic diseases: bronchial asthma, hay fever, angioneurotic edema, urticaria, erythema multiforme. Eosinophils are found in the peripheral blood, marrow, sputum (in bronchial asthma), nasal and conjunctival discharges (in hay fever), and urticarial skin lesions and vesicles. Blood eosinophilia is usually only mild or moderate.

The exact role of eosinophils in the allergic immunologic reaction has not been determined. Histamine, which is the substance involved in such reactions, is supposed to attract eosinophils chemotactically.

2. Skin disorders of various kinds. In some of them the allergic background is apparent, for example, allergic eczema and dermatitis venenata; in others it may be surmised. There is frequently a clear-cut direct relation between the degree of eosinophilia and extent of cutaneous involvement.

3. Parasitic infestations. Eosinophilia is more pronounced if tissues are invaded (for example, trichinosis) than when parasites are inhabiting the lumen of a viscus (for example, tapeworm). The role of free exchange of tissue fluids (metabolic continuity) is evident by disappearance of eosinophilia in some forms of infestation when encystment occurs (for example, cysticercosis).

In trichinosis eosinophils begin to rise in the blood within days after infection. The peak of the eosinophilia, from 40 to 60 per cent, is during the third or fourth weeks (Gould, 1945).

Leukocytosis and eosinophilia extending over months are seen in visceral larva migrans (dog and cat roundworm) infestation. In this condition pulmonary lesions (Loeffler's syndrome) may be present. In Loeffler's eosinophilic pneumonitis, the fleeting pulmonary infiltrates are thought to be caused by passage of the parasites from the blood into the alveoli of the lung. (Regarding local tissue eosinophilia in Loeffler's syndrome, see item 11 in this section.)

Another parasitic infestation with eosinophilia is creeping eruption caused by larvae of the dog or cat hookworm.

Eosinophilia may be absent in severe infestations with trichinae. The prognosis in such cases seems aggravated.

4. Eosinophilia of various degrees is seen in many infectious diseases. Some of them (for example, scarlet fever) have cutaneous rashes, probably of allergic nature; some

(like brucellosis) have granulomatous lesions with obvious allergic overtones. It is possible that the blood and tissue eosinophilia of Hodgkin's disease is of a similar nature.

Neutrophilia depresses eosinophilia. This is well shown in the disappearance of eosinophilia when a lesion that is responsible for eosinophilia (for example, echinococcus cyst) becomes infected, suppurates, and is followed by neutrophilia. The same phenomenon is also observed in acute infections (for example, pneumococcus pneumonia).

It is in infectious diseases that the depression of eosinophilia by neutrophilia is particularly noticeable.

Chorea may show eosinophilia, although other forms of rheumatic fever do not.

5. Alimentary eosinophilia. Relation to food allergy is suggestive. It is seen in patients with pernicious anemia. The claim that liver therapy is responsible is negated by reports of eosinophilia in patients with pernicious anemia before the era of liver therapy.

In so-called allergic diarrhea there is a large number of eosinophils in the mucous discharge.

6. Blood diseases. In chronic granulocytic leukemia, general marrow hyperplasia may be responsible for the eosinophilia as well as for the basophilia. Eosinophilia may be seen in pernicious anemia to be replaced by eosinopenia in late stages. Marrow eosinophilia may be present in thrombocytopenic purpura. Eosinophilic leukemia is discussed with other leukemias.

7. Splenectomy is frequently followed by eosinophilia and lymphocytosis. Neutrophilia, if previously present, recedes. This may last for several months. On the other hand, injection of splenic extracts in animals has been reported to produce eosinopenia. This suggests that hyposplenism may favor eosinophilia and hypersplenism, eosinopenia.

8. The constitutional element in eosinophilia is exemplified in familial eosinophilia. In some reported cases infestation with parasites and subclinical allergy have not been excluded.

9. There is no satisfactory explanation for occasional instances of moderate and even severe eosinophilia, general or local, in patients with various neoplasms and a variety of other conditions (for example, ovarian cysts. Eosinophilia is seen more frequently in neoplasms involving serous surfaces and bone and in those with excessive necrosis.

10. Various drugs have been reported to be responsible for eosinophilia: pilocarpine, physostigmine, digitalis, phosphorus, benzol, parenterally administered liver extracts, and insulin. On the other hand, atropine is supposed to depress the eosinophils.

11. Local tissue eosinophilia with or without blood eosinophilia: here belong eosinophilic granuloma, polyps of the nose, intestinal eosinophilia, chronically inflamed pleura, and Loeffler's syndrome.

12. Familial eosinophilia is linked by some with a genetically determined allergic condition and by others with the effect of a common parasitic infection.

Eosinopenia

Definition. Eosinopenia is a decrease below the lowest normal of 50 per cu. mm. It is seen most frequently in the presence of infectious neutrophilia in severe infections. In Cushing's syndrome the count ranges from 0 to 30 per cu. mm. It results from hyperactivity of the adrenal cortex. After major surgical operations there is a drop within four to six hours in the presence of adequate adrenal function. In postoperative shock not associated with massive hemorrhage, a normal or high eosinophil count indicates adrenal insufficiency.

Eosinopenia is seen after electric shock therapy, in eclampsia, and in labor.

The eosinopenia following parenteral administration of certain adrenal cortical hormones and of substances (ACTH and epinephrine) that increase the output of these hormones is the basis for a test for adrenal function.

Thorn et al. (1948) recommended a test for evaluation of adrenal cortical function based on the development of eosinopenia following the injection of ACTH (adrenocorticotropic hormone). Absence of a significant drop of eosinophils is interpreted as evidence of adrenal cortical insufficiency. At the present time, the value of the test is limited (Huntsman et al., 1959).

Technique of Absolute Eosinophil Count. Regular or special (Fuchs-Rosenthal) counting chamber and a special staining fluid are used (Randolph, 1944). The technique of counting white blood cells described on p. 103 applies to counting of eosinophils.

Basophilia

Definition. Basophilia is an increase of basophilic granulocytes in the peripheral blood beyond the normal range of 1 per cent.

Basophilia is seen most frequently in chronic granulocytic leukemia, myeloid metaplasia (extramedullary myelopoiesis), and polycythemia. Relative basophilia may be transient following irradiation. Basophilia may be present in chronic hemolytic anemia and following splenectomy. In some infections basophils disappear at the same time as eosinophils, and then both reappear when recovery sets in. Tissue basophils, mast cells, are entirely different from basophilic granulocytes.

Basopenia

In view of the rarity of these cells in normal persons, a decrease cannot be readily detected and interpreted except in acute infections, when basophils disappear at first together with the eosinophils and reappear later with the lowering of the neutrophilia.

Lymphocytosis

Definition. Lymphocytosis is an increase in the number of lymphocytes in the peripheral blood above the normal range of 1000 to 4000 per cu. mm. in the adult and 1500 to 8500 in the child.

Relative lymphocytosis is present in various conditions in which there is a neutropenia. True lymphocytosis is present in various infections but mainly late in the disease and during recovery. It is common in exanthems (for example, German measles) and also has been reported in brucellosis and secondary and congenital syphilis. It is considered a good omen in tuberculosis. In thyrotoxicosis, lymphocytosis is present frequently. In some of these patients there is also splenomegaly (Means, 1948). In pertussis, lymphocytosis may be high early in the catarrhal stage and persist all through the entire course and late in convalescence.

INFECTIOUS LYMPHOCYTOSIS

This infectious and contagious disease of unknown etiology, described by C. H. Smith (1941), involves a high lymphocyte count and occurs mainly in children. The incubation period is 12 to 21 days. The disease sometimes occurs without systemic manifestations and sometimes with vomiting, fever, abdominal discomfort, signs suggesting involvement of the nervous system, cutaneous rashes, upper respiratory infections, and diarrhea. Usually the high white count (20,000 to 40,000 and higher) precedes the clinical manifestations. From 60 to 95 per cent of the cells in the differential count are mature, adult, small lymphocytes, not like those seen in infectious mononucleosis. There is usually an increase of the eosinophils. The lymphocytosis lasts three to five weeks and longer. There are no other blood changes. The marrow is not characteristic. Increase of lymphocytes has been observed but is probably due to admixture of peripheral blood. Lymph node enlargement is rare and minimal when present. The spleen and liver are rarely if ever enlarged. Lymph node biopsy may show reactive follicular hyperplasia but no characteristic changes.

The presumptive and differential tests for infectious mononucleosis are both negative. (For details regarding tests for infectious mononucleosis see p. 217ff.) In some cases there has been an increase of white cells in the cerebrospinal fluid with about 40 per cent lymphocytes. The disease is distinctly infectious and contagious. The course is benign.

There is another form of infectious lymphocytosis, chronic in its course, with a leukocytosis of 10,000 to 25,000, with 60 to 80 per cent lymphocytes of normal appearance, and with a slight increase of eosinophils, monocytes, and plasma cells. As a rule the children have enlarged tonsils, lymph nodes, and spleen and a history of recurrent upper respiratory infections. The marrow shows no abnormalities.

Infectious Mononucleosis

Definition. Infectious mononucleosis is an acute self-limited infectious disease of the reticuloendothelial tissues, especially of the lymphatic tissues, with characteristic clinical, hematologic, pathologic, and specific serologic changes.

The main reason for clinical interest in infectious mononucleosis is that it imitates many diseases, some of them serious, some inviting surgical intervention, and some with serious prognostic implications. The brief sketch of the clinical manifestations of the disease and the three tables that follow illustrate the difficulties of differential diagnosis (Davidsohn and Lee, 1962).

Onset. The onset is vague, indefinite, and similar to the onset of other infectious diseases. This stage lasts about four to five days.

Duration. The disease proper lasts, as a rule, from 7 to 21 days.

Clinical Picture. Fever varies from mild to moderate, occasionally up to 106° F. Chills, sweats, headache, dizziness, malaise, pharyngitis, tonsillitis, retro-orbital aching, irritability, prostration, and asthenia may be seen, all of varying severity.

Lymph Nodes. Enlargement may vary from slight to marked but is usually not too excessive, averaging about the size of a plum. The enlargement may be simultaneous with the onset of fever or may follow or even precede it. It develops rapidly, sometimes in a matter of hours. There is no perilymphadenitis. As a rule, there is tenderness but it is transient. It is important to look for it because it differentiates this type of lymph node enlargement from that seen in leukemia.

As a rule, cervical lymph nodes are the first to be enlarged, first on one side and then on the other, and then other regions are affected, including mediastinal and inguinal. The enlargement is transient but occasionally has a tendency to persist for a long time.

Spleen. There is frequent splenomegaly of varying degrees. Occasionally the spleen may be enlarged without noticeable lymph node enlargement. It is frequently tender and the enlargement sometimes persists for a long time.

Liver. The liver is less frequently enlarged than the spleen and occasionally tender.

The various *complications*, the anatomic lesions underlying them, and the resemblance to various diseases are all shown in Tables 4–11, 4–12, and 4–13.

Relapses are not uncommon. Occasionally there may be several, and some may be more severe than the original attack.

Recurrences are rare, but they do occur sometimes after intervals of months or even years.

Death occurs as a rule only from complications, for example, ruptured spleen, involvement of the central nervous system, cerebral hemorrhage, and complicating septic infection.

Sequelae. Prolonged state of exhaustion. The various complications will be discussed (p. 214).

Contagiousness of the usual sporadic form

Table 4–11. **Diseases Simulated by Infectious Mononucleosis**

DIAGNOSES MADE IN OUR SERIES (106 CASES) PRIOR TO BLOOD COUNT AND SEROLOGIC TESTS	No. cases	ADDITIONAL DIAGNOSES RECORDED IN THE LITERATURE
Agranulocytosis	1	Angioneurotic edema
Appendicitis	1	Asthma
Brucellosis	2	Bacterial endocarditis,
Diphtheria	4	subacute
Duodenal ulcer	1	Chickenpox
Gastroenteritis	1	Encephalitis
Hodgkin's disease	2	Erysipelas
Infectious hepatitis	3	Erythema multiforme
Influenza	7	Erythema nodosum
Leukemia	4	Glottis edema
Measles	1	Hyperthyroidism with
Meningitis	1	lymphocytosis
Nephritis	1	Infectious lymphocytosis
Pharyngitis	7	Myocarditis (abnormal
Pharyngitis, ulcerative	2	ECG)
Pneumonia	1	Mumps
Pneumonia, virus	4	Obstructive jaundice
Purpura	2	Poliomyelitis
Scarlet fever	1	Rheumatic fever, acute
Serum disease	2	Scarlet fever
Sinusitis, frontal	1	Stomatitis, herpetic
Streptococcus sore throat	5	Syphilitic cervical
Tonsillitis, acute follicular	3	adenitis
Tonsillitis, acute ulcerative	1	Syphilis, secondary
Tuberculous lymphadenitis	1	Thrombocytopenic purpura
Vincent's angina	4	Trichinosis
	63	Tuberculosis, miliary

is probably slight. Epidemics do occur and many have been described, sometimes of very large proportions, in schools and homes for children.

Age. The disease has been observed in patients from 3 months to 70 years, but the disease occurs rarely above college age. Most epidemics have been in adolescents and children.

Sex. Males are affected more frequently than females (ratio 2 to 1).

The greater frequency of the diagnosis of the disease among nurses and college and medical students is probably explained by better medical supervision. The disease has been described in all parts of the world and in all races.

DIFFERENTIAL DIAGNOSIS

The diagnostic difficulties in infectious mononucleosis are illustrated by a report of

Table 4–12. Why Does Infectious Mononucleosis
Simulate So Many Diseases?

CLINICAL FINDINGS IN 106
CASES OF INFECTIOUS MONONUCLEOSIS

	NO. CASES	PER CENT
Lymphadenopathy	101	95.3
Fever	93	87.7
Pharyngitis	64	60.4
without membrane	50	47.2
with membrane	14	13.2
Splenomegaly	51	48.1
Headache	26	24.5
Hepatomegaly	24	22.6
Prostration	11	10.4
Emesis	10	9.4
Pain in abdomen	8	7.6
upper abdomen	6	5.7
lower abdomen	2	1.9
Stiffness or pain in neck	6	5.7
Skin rash	5	4.7
Epistaxis	3	2.8
Icterus	3	2.8
Loss of weight	2	1.9
Diarrhea	2	1.9
Arthritic pains	2	1.9
Purpura	2	1.9
Gingivitis	2	1.9
Convulsions	1	0.9
Toothache	1	0.9
Albuminuria	14	13.2
Positive test for syphilis	3	2.8
Relapses (17 days to 2 months)	7	6.5
Recurrence (1 year)	1	0.9

234 patients with infectious mononucleosis of whom only 25 (10.7 per cent) were admitted with the correct admission diagnosis. Sixty-nine (29.5 per cent) were diagnosed as diphtheria and 98 (41.9 per cent) as possible diphtheria. The other diagnoses were, in order of frequency: pharyngitis, Vincent's angina, lymphadenitis following scarlet fever, infectious hepatitis, suspected typhoid fever, and pneumonia (Leopold, 1958).

According to recent reports, the clinical picture of acquired toxoplasmosis may resemble infectious mononucleosis, especially in a form of the disease characterized by enlarged lymph nodes (Siim, 1960). The similarity may be even more pronounced, since in some of the cases reported, lymphocytes resembling those seen in infectious mononucleosis have been found (Couvreur and Desmonts, 1961).

The nature of the anatomic lesions and of the signs and symptoms that explain the differential diagnostic difficulties are correlated in Tables 4–11, 4–12, and 4–13.

COMPLICATIONS IN THE ACUTE STAGES OF INFECTIOUS MONONUCLEOSIS

Respiratory System. Extreme dyspnea may occur in the presence of severe inflammatory and ulcerative lesions of the pharynx and in laryngeal edema. Tracheostomy may have to be resorted to as a life-saving operation (Breza, 1951; Kouba et al., 1961). Fatal cases have been reported (Beck et al., 1953).

Hemolytic Anemia may occur.

Purpura is, as a rule, not severe. It may be combined with thrombocytopenia (Holzel, 1954). Cutaneous purpura in the form of a hemorrhagic eruption is most frequent. Involvement of the urogenital and gastrointestinal tracts are rare.

Heart. Leibowitz (1953) reviewed the cases of cardiac involvement occurring up to 1953. Since then, several more have been reported. The clinical and electrocardiographic manifestations of pericarditis may be manifested earlier than those of infectious mononucleosis at a time when clinical, hematologic, and serologic signs of the underlying mononucleosis are still absent. The electrocardiographic changes may be detectable long after the clinical manifestations of infectious mononucleosis have disappeared and after the laboratory findings return to normal (Roseman and Barry, 1957). Occasionally cardiac involvement may be serious or even fatal (Fish and Barton, 1958).

Central Nervous System. Many cases of Guillain-Barré syndrome have been described (Durfey and Allen, 1956).

Rupture of the Spleen may occur in the acute stage of the disease (Carlisle and Shiffman, 1957). Prompt recognition and immediate surgical intervention may be life-saving.

The Liver. Involvement of the liver demonstrable by biopsy is common in infectious mononucleosis. Some claim that it is the rule. Clinical jaundice is rare, but cases have been reported in which jaundice and acute pharyngitis were the only clinical manifestations of infectious mononucleosis with positive hematologic and serologic findings (Cattan et al., 1961).

The jaundice is, as a rule, hepatocellular with both conjugated and nonconjugated bilirubin fractions in the serum, bilirubin and elevated urobilinogen in the urine, and other manifestations of hepatocellular damage, including the histologic findings and results of various laboratory tests (Zimmerman, H. J.: Personal communication).

Table 4–13. Some Differential Diagnostic Problems in Infectious Mononucleosis

SIGNS AND SYMPTOMS	ANATOMIC LESIONS	RESEMBLANCE TO
Sore throat	Ulcerative or membranous pharyngitis	Diphtheria
Painful and stiff neck; occasionally convulsions and coma	Rapidly enlarged retrocervical lymph nodes. Acute hyperplastic lymphadenitis. Pleocytosis in cerebrospinal fluid may be present	Meningitis (serous meningitis may be present)
Generalized lymphadenopathy	Acute hyperplastic lymphadenitis	Leukemia
Abdominal pain and tenderness	Rapidly enlarged abdominal lymph nodes	
right lower quadrant		Acute appendicitis
left upper quadrant	Acute splenomegaly. Acute diffuse hyperplasia	Acute pleuritis; perinephritic abscess
acute tenderness and pain in right upper quadrant	Acute diffuse hepatitis; periportal infiltrations; enlarged lymph nodes around common bile duct	Acute hepatitis, especially if jaundice present
acute general abdominal pain, followed by shock	Ruptured spleen	Acute abdominal emergency
Cough (resembling whooping cough)	Enlarged mediastinal lymph nodes	Pertussis; Hodgkin's disease; tuberculosis
Cutaneous rashes		Exanthematous disease (measles); scarlet fever especially if angina is present; secondary syphilis, especially if enlarged inguinal lymph nodes and positive test for syphilis are present
Puffiness around eyes	Swelling of retrobulbar tissues	Trichinosis
Toothache	Acutely swollen submandibular lymph nodes	Pulpitis
Hematuria	Specific infiltration of renal parenchyma or purpuric renal hemorrhage	Acute glomerulonephritis

In one study thymol turbidity was abnormal in 69 per cent of the cases and cephalin flocculation in 83 per cent (Gelb et al., in press).

According to Wróblewski, when infectious mononucleosis is complicated by hepatitis, there is a rise in serum glutamic oxalic transaminase (SGO-T) and serum glutamic pyruvic transaminase (SGP-T) at a time when liver function tests may be normal or inconclusively affected as measured by conventional tests (Wróblewski, 1958).

Infections. Those due to pyogenic bacteria (sinusitis, otitis, bronchopneumonia) can be readily controlled, but staphylococcus infection may be serious or even fatal. Virus infection may be difficult to control. A fatality due to measles complicating infectious mononucleosis has been reported (Kouba et al., 1961).

Other Complications. These include nasopharyngeal hemorrhage, jaundice, hemolytic anemia, hematuria, myositis or myalgia, hemoptysis, and uterine bleeding. Congenital malformation of heart has been reported following infectious mononucleosis of mother during first trimester.

Late Complications. Chronic lesions of the liver have been reported (Kouba and Mašek, 1960).

BLOOD FINDINGS

There are no changes in the red blood cells and in platelets except in rare cases of complicating hemolytic anemia and thrombocytopenia. There is an increase of white blood cells ranging from 12,000 to 25,000 and sometimes higher. The highest counts in adults that have been observed were 40,000, but counts as high as 70,000 have been seen in children. The leukocytosis is usually brief. The total white count is, as a rule, within normal limits within a week or two.

The increase is due to a rise in lymphocytes. These cells show characteristic changes, which can be summed up as follows:

1. Hyperplasia or an increase in their number.

2. Hypertrophy or an increase in size of the individual cells.

3. Nuclear changes are characterized by an increased density of the chromatin and by changes in shape (Plate 4–14). They show deep indentations and many are lobated, resembling in general outlines nuclei of monocytes. The cytoplasm shows basophilia, a decrease of azurophilic granules, and frequently marked vacuolar degeneration. Some cells resemble plasma cells; some have nucleoli. Some cells resemble monocytes (monocytoid deviation). Occasionally cells show anaplasia and resemble prolymphocytes. It is in these cases that one has to consider lymphocytic leukemia in the differential diagnosis.

The polymorphism of the lymphocytes is the striking feature of the differential blood picture (see Plate 4–14).

Not infrequently there are rapid and, as a rule, transient rises in the number of monocytes. The term mononucleosis refers to an increase of lymphocytes and not of monocytes. From 60 to 90 per cent of the cells in the differential white count are lymphocytes. Usually the mononucleosis remains for weeks but may persist for months and longer.

The neutrophils are relatively decreased in proportion to the rise of the lymphocytes. Early in the disease there may be a transient shift to the left with an increase of band cells and metamyelocytes. The eosinophils are within normal limits.

The cytologic changes are by no means pathognomonic of infectious mononucleosis. Similar cells in similar numbers may be found in other diseases, especially in upper respiratory infections in children, in liver diseases, and especially in viral infections, e.g., infectious hepatitis, viral pneumonia, varicella, mumps, and exanthemas of children.

CEREBROSPINAL FLUID

Pressure is slightly increased. There is frequently pleocytosis—as a rule, only moderate—but cell counts as high as 1000 per cu. mm. have been seen. All, or almost all, the cells in the cerebrospinal fluid are mononuclear. The globulin is increased. In 125 patients studied for involvement of the central nervous system, the cerebrospinal fluid was abnormal in 35 and the electroencephalogram in 47 (Silberstein et al., 1948).

OTHER LABORATORY FINDINGS

Serologic Tests for Syphilis. Occasional positive results have been observed, usually only transient and becoming negative after a few days or weeks. Transient false positive Kahn tests in the blood serum and in the cerebrospinal fluid were reported in a 20-year-old man who had positive tests for infectious mononucleosis but no other signs of either disease (Sobel and Simons, 1959).

Urine. Traces of albumin may be found in the urine.

PATHOLOGY

In addition to the previously mentioned gross changes in lymph nodes, spleen, and liver, recent studies have shown extensive microscopic changes, not only in lymph nodes but also in the spleen, liver, and other tissues. In the lymph nodes there is a complete transformation of the architecture with crowding of the parenchyma by proliferation of large cells resembling reticulum cells. Some of them have a striking resemblance to the so-called abnormal lymphocytes seen in the peripheral circulation.

In the spleen, which is large and extremely soft, similar changes are present. The follicles are small and compressed by the proliferating cells. The capsule and trabeculae are thinned out and eaten away by the proliferation. This explains the ease with which the spleen ruptures on slight trauma or increase of intra-abdominal pressure. In many places there are subintimal infiltrations in the trabecular veins, and one can see masses of cells pouring out from the infiltration into the lumen of the blood vessels.

In the liver, massive infiltration is present in the periportal spaces, consisting of large cells resembling those seen in the spleen, lymph nodes, and the peripheral blood. Sometimes there is also infiltration within the sinusoids.

In cases with pulmonary lesions that are seen sometimes, there are massive peribronchial infiltrations, which explain some of the changes seen in the x-ray. Such findings may suggest the diagnosis of virus pneumonia (Arendt, 1950). Occasionally large masses of infiltrating mononuclear cells are seen within the alveoli in pneumonia-like fashion.

Infiltrations have also been seen in the kidneys, in various parts of the central nervous system, and in peripheral nerves. The lesions in the liver explain the abnormal liver function tests.

Recent electron microscopic studies have thrown new light on the disease. In a light and electron microscopic study of inguinal lymph nodes, removed at different stages of the disease from three young men with clinical infectious mononucleosis, ultramicroscopic particles were seen in all of them (Reinauer, 1959). The possibility that they may be viral inclusions was considered but not claimed. Reinauer interprets the characteristic changes seen in the light microscope as diagnostic.

SEROLOGIC TESTS

There are several tests for infectious mononucleosis.

The Presumptive Test. This test is based

Table 4–14. The Presumptive Test for Infectious Mononucleosis

Principle: The test is based on the agglutination of sheep red cells by the serum of patients with infectious mononucleosis.

Technique:

The physician: Obtain 5 to 10 ml. of blood under aseptic precautions. Send to the laboratory.

The laboratory:

Reagents:

Serum inactivated for 30 minutes at 56° C. 2 per cent suspension of sheep red cells.

Procedure:

Set up 13 tubes in a rack. Place 0.4 ml. of 0.85 per cent saline in the first tube and 0.25 ml. in each of the remaining tubes.

Add 0.1 ml. of the inactivated serum to the first tube, mix and transfer 0.25 ml. to the second tube, and so on until the twelfth tube is reached. Discard 0.25 ml. from the twelfth tube (Table 4-15). The serum dilutions are 1:5, 1:10, and so on.

Add 0.1 ml. of the 2 per cent suspension of sheep cells to each tube, including the thirteenth, which is the control. The final dilutions are 1:7, 1:14, and so on. Shake each tube.

Reading of results:

Let stand at room temperature. When speed is indicated, reading may be done after 15 minutes. If the result is positive (agglutination in dilutions 1:224 or higher), the test may be considered completed except that the final titer will be higher after two hours' incubation. If negative (titer less than 1:224), repeat reading at intervals as frequent as convenient. Final negative result (titer less than 1:56) should *not* be recorded until after two hours' incubation. If speed is not a factor, the results may be read only once, at the end of two hours.

Results are read after shaking the test tubes to resuspend the sediment. Check with the naked eye. If no clumping is visible, place the tube horizontally on the stage of the microscope and read with a low power objective (scanning lens, e.g., 25 mm. or 35 mm.), permitting viewing of a test tube.

The titer is the reciprocal value of the highest serum dilution still showing agglutination.

on an increase of antisheep agglutinins. Such agglutinins are present, in low titers, in the blood of most people. Their normal titer is as a rule less than 1 to 112. The titer is elevated in serum disease, sometimes to high levels, and in a variety of infections, especially those of the upper respiratory system. Another cause of the elevated titer of antisheep agglutinins is transfusion of blood to which blood group-specific substances have been added to neutralize the isoagglutinins. The test is nonspecific. If positive in a titer of 1 to 224 or more, it may be considered as confirming the diagnosis of infectious mononucleosis if the clinical and hematologic findings are characteristic for the disease (Paul and Bunnell, 1932). Details regarding the presumptive test are summarized in Tables 4–14, 4–15, and 4–16.

Table 4–15. The Presumptive Test for Infectious Mononucleosis

Interpretation of Results

The finding of a titer of 224 or higher, in a person who has not received an injection of horse serum or of horse immune serum in the recent past, and who presents a clinical picture and hematologic findings suggestive of infectious mononucleosis, indicates with a high degree of probability the presence of infectious mononucleosis.

Antisheep agglutinins in titers up to 56 may be found in normal persons and in patients with a variety of diseases. Occasionally, also, titers of 112 may be found in such persons.

When titers of 224 or higher occur in patients with serum disease, or following injection of horse immune serum;

When the presumptive test shows titers of 224 or higher, but the characteristic clinical or hematologic findings of infectious mononucleosis are absent;

When the test shows titers of 112 or less, but the characteristic clinical or hematologic findings of infectious mononucleosis are present

Then the differential test for infectious mononucleosis is indicated.

The Differential Test. The principle of the differential test is that absorption of serum with a suspension of a Forssman antigen (guinea pig or horse kidney) removes antisheep agglutinins in the serum of patients with serum disease and various other infections but not in the serum of patients with infectious mononucleosis. Here a substantial part of the antibodies remains after absorption. On the other hand, absorption with a suspension of beef cells removes the antisheep agglutinins in infec-

Table 4–16. Technique of Presumptive Test for Infectious Mononucleosis

TUBES	SALINE ml.	SERUM ml.	SERUM DILUTIONS	2 PER CENT SHEEP CELLS ml.	FINAL DILUTIONS OF SERUM
1	0.4	.1	1:5	.1	1:7
2	0.25	0.25 of 1:5	1:10	.1	1:14
3	0.25	0.25 of 1:10	1:20	.1	1:28
4	0.25	0.25 of 1:20	1:40	.1	1:56
5	0.25	0.25 of 1:40	1:80	.1	1:112
6	0.25	0.25 of 1:80	1:160	.1	1:224
7	0.25	0.25 of 1:160	1:320	.1	1:448
8	0.25	0.25 of 1:320	1:640	.1	1:896
9	0.25	0.25 of 1:640	1:1280	.1	1:1792
10	0.25	0.25 of 1:1280	1:2560	.1	1:3584
11	0.25	0.25 of 1:2560	1:5120	.1	1:7168
12	0.25	0.25 of 1:5120	1:10,240*	.1	1:14,336
Control 13	0.25	—	—	.1	

* Discard 0.25 ml. from last tube.

Table 4–17. The Differential Test

Principle

Antisheep agglutinins in *infectious mononucleosis* are NOT absorbed by Forssman antigen (guinea pig or horse kidney); they are NOT of the Forssman type.

Antisheep agglutinins in *serum disease* and in *normal persons* are readily absorbed by Forssman antigen; they are of the Forssman type.

Antisheep agglutinins in *infectious mononucleosis* are readily absorbed by beef cells.

Antisheep agglutinins in *conditions other than infectious mononucleosis* may or may not be absorbed by beef cells.

MATERIALS	PREPARATION OF ANTIGENS

1. Test tubes
  (a) for absorption: 85 x 13 mm. (inside diameter) rounded bottom and no lips.
  (b) for agglutination: 75 x 10 mm. (inside diameter)
2. Blood serum (0.5 ml. will suffice) inactivated for 30 minutes at 56° C.
3. 2 per cent suspensions of sheep erythrocytes
4. Capillary pipets
5. Physiologic salt solution
	1. Guinea pig kidney
	  Organs are stored frozen until needed and then thawed and washed with physiologic saline until washings are free of blood. They are now mashed into fine pulp and made into a 20 per cent suspension in physiologic saline. The suspension is boiled one hour on water bath, and loss by evaporation is made up with distilled water.
	2. Horse kidney
	  A 2 per cent suspension in physiologic saline is prepared. Otherwise the procedure is the same as for guinea pig kidney.
	3. Beef red cells
	  They are washed three times with physiologic saline and packed by centrifuging. One volume of packed cells is suspended in four volumes of saline, and the suspension is boiled on water bath for one hour. Loss by evaporation is made up with distilled water. To all antigens, phenol is added to make a 0.5 per cent solution. Can be kept in icebox for many months.

tious mononucleosis but leaves them in some of the other bloods. It is this combination of no, or incomplete, removal of antibodies with Forssman antigen and complete removal with beef cells that is characteristic for infectious mononucleosis (Tables 4–17, 4–18, 4–19, 4–20, and 4–21).

Specificity of the differential test. In only two cases in our experience with the test, extending over 26 years, has it been positive in patients without a history or evidence of the disease. One patient had rheumatoid arthritis; the other was a young man with Hodgkin's disease. There were no

Table 4–18. Differential Test

Procedure

1. Place in test tube (85 x 13 mm.) 1 ml. of thoroughly shaken Forssman antigen suspension.
2. Add 0.2 ml. of serum.
3. Shake and let stand at room temperature for three minutes.
4. Centrifuge at 1500 r.p.m. for ten minutes or longer till supernatant is perfectly clear.
5. Remove the supernatant fluid with a capillary pipet, making sure not to take particles along.
6. Set up as many tubes (75 x 10 mm.) as needed, according to the titer of the presumptive test. Add 0.25 ml. of physiologic saline to each tube except the first.
7. Add 0.25 ml. of the absorbed serum to the first and second tubes.
8. Mix the second tube and transfer 0.25 ml. to the third tube, and so on. Discard 0.25 ml. from the last tube. The serum dilutions are 1:5, 1:10, 1:20, and so on.
9. Add 0.1 ml. of the 2 per cent suspension of sheep cells. Shake well. Final dilutions of serum are 1:7, 1:14, and so on.
10. Absorption with boiled beef cells. Follow the same procedure as above, using 1.0 ml. of the thoroughly mixed 20 per cent suspension of beef cells.
11. Let stand at room temperature. When speed is indicated reading may be done after 15 minutes. If test is positive, which means:
    (a) in test tubes containing serum treated with Forssman antigen, agglutination in the same dilution as the presumptive test or in not more than three dilutions or tubes below that of the titer of the presumptive test, and
    (b) no agglutination in test tubes containing serum treated with beef cell antigen,
    then the test can be reported as positive for infectious mononucleosis.
    If the result is negative, which means:
        more than three tubes' difference in the agglutination as compared with the titer of the presumptive test (or agglutination remaining after absorption with beef cell antigen),
    repeat reading at intervals as frequent as convenient. Final negative results should NOT be recorded until after two hours incubation.
    If speed is not a factor, results may be read only once, at the end of two hours.

---

clinical or blood changes suggestive of infectious mononucleosis. The diagnosis of Hodgkin's disease was made on a lymph node and confirmed by autopsy (Pessin). Other cases of Hodgkin's disease and of serologically established infectious mononucleosis present simultaneously have been reported previously (Massey *et al.*, 1953).

With these two exceptions, among the many hundreds of cases studied, the differential test was positive only in infectious mononucleosis and was negative in all other diseases. The differential test is a specific and qualitative test. The height of the titer is not important.

On the basis of 600 carefully studied cases, Bender (1958) concluded that there is no satisfactory evidence that a positive differential test for infectious mononucleosis can be duplicated by any other condition.

As a rule, the test is positive when the patient presents symptoms of the disease or when he is first examined. The test may be negative early in the disease and may remain negative as long as three weeks. Therefore, if the first test is negative and if clinical and hematologic findings still suggest the disease until at least the third week from onset, it is necessary to repeat the test. The test remains positive for weeks and sometimes months after the clinical symptoms have disappeared.

In some of the other reported cases of alleged infectious mononucleosis, the presumptive test alone was used and not the complete differential test; in others the recommended technique was not followed, e.g., centrifugation was used to accelerate the incubation period, or the tests were kept in the refrigerator overnight. The latter modification brings into play cold agglutinins, which may increase the titer considerably, but not specifically, with resulting false positive readings.

Details regarding the differential test are summarized in Tables 4–17, 4–18, 4–19, 4–20, and 4–21.

The Beef Hemolysin Test for Infectious Mononucleosis. *Principle.* Elevated titers of hemolysin for beef erythrocytes are present in infectious mononucleosis (Peterson *et al.*, 1956).

Procedure

1. Inactive serum at 56° C. for 30 minutes.

2. Wash beef erythrocytes three times and make a 2 per cent suspension with saline (0.85 per cent NaCl and 0.01 per cent $MgSO_4$).

3. Make a 1 to 15 dilution of guinea pig complement and keep at 4° C.

4. Set up eleven 12×75 mm. test tubes. Add milliliters of saline and serum specified in the following table.

5. Mix and transfer 0.5 ml. from the preceding tube to the next tube, beginning with the first tube and discarding 0.5 ml. from the seventh tube.

6. Add beef cell suspension, complement, and water to the tubes specified in the following table.

TUBE	1	2	3	4	5	6	7	8	9	10	11
Saline (ml.)	0.8	0.5	0.5	0.5	0.5	0.5	0.5	0.5	0.9	1.0	
Serum (ml.)	0.2								0.1		
Beef cell 2% (ml.)	0.5	0.5	0.5	0.5	0.5	0.5	0.5	0.5	0.5	0.5	0.25
Complement, 1:15 (ml.)	0.5	0.5	0.5	0.5	0.5	0.5	0.5	0.5			
Water (ml.)											1.25
Reciprocal of dilution	15	30	60	120	240	480	960				

Controls	complement	serum	erythrocytes	50% hemolysis standard
Tube	8	9	10	11

Table 4–19. The Differential Test

Interpretation of Results

In serum of patients with infectious mononucleosis, absorption with Forssman antigen will result in a partial removal of the agglutinin for sheep red cells, but, as a rule, not less than one-fourth of the original titer will still be present in the serum after absorption. For example, an original titer of 1:112 may be reduced to 1:28 after absorption with Forssman antigen.

If all or almost all (more than 90 per cent) of the sheep agglutinins have been removed by absorption with Forssman antigen, this speaks against infectious mononucleosis.

On the other hand, so far no other condition has been found, except infectious mononucleosis, in which Forssman antigen fails to remove sheep agglutinins from the serum.

The absorption with beef red cells is a confirmatory procedure in infectious mononucleosis, since absorption with beef cells removes all or almost all (more than 90 per cent) of the sheep agglutinins from the serum. Failure of beef cells to remove sheep agglutinins speaks against infectious mononucleosis.

It may be preferable to do the absorption with Forssman antigen and with beef cell antigen in EVERY case. The absorption with beef cells is essential in patients with elevated titers of antisheep agglutinins if no clinical or hematologic findings are present suggestive of infectious mononucleosis. In most of these instances the antisheep agglutinins will be completely removed by Forssman antigen, but, in rare instances, the absorption may be incomplete. The use of the beef cell antigen will then be decisive.

EXAMPLES

PRESUMPTIVE TEST	TITER OF DIFFERENTIAL TEST AFTER ABSORPTION WITH		RESULT
	FORSSMAN ANTIGEN	BEEF RED CELLS	
(a) 1:224	1:112	0	POSITIVE for infectious mononucleosis
1:224	0	1:112	NEGATIVE for infectious mononucleosis
1:224	1:56	0	POSITIVE for infectious mononucleosis
1:224	1:56	1:56	NEGATIVE for infectious mononucleosis
1:224	1:28	0	POSITIVE for infectious mononucleosis
1:224	1:14	0	NEGATIVE for infectious mononucleosis
1:224	1:7	0	NEGATIVE for infectious mononucleosis
(b) 1:56	1:56	0	POSITIVE for infectious mononucleosis
1:56	1:56	1:28	NEGATIVE for infectious mononucleosis
1:56	1:28	0	POSITIVE for infectious mononucleosis
1:56	1:14	0	POSITIVE for infectious mononucleosis
1:56	1:7	0	POSITIVE for infectious mononucleosis
(c) 1:28	1:28	0	POSITIVE for infectious mononucleosis
1:28	1:14	0	POSITIVE for infectious mononucleosis
1:28	1:7	0	POSITIVE for infectious mononucleosis

Table 4-20. Results of the Differential Test for Infectious Mononucleosis

DIAGNOSIS	PRESUMPTIVE TEST SRBC[a] AGGLUTINATED	DIFFERENTIAL TEST A		B	
		ANTIBODY ABSORBED BY FA[b]	SRBC AG-GLUTINATED AFTER AB-SORPTION	ANTIBODY ABSORBED BY BCA[c]	SRBC AG-GLUTINATED AFTER AB-SORPTION
Forssman heterophilic antibody in normal serum	Yes (1:56 or lower in about 98%)	Yes	No	[d]	[d]
Forssman heterophilic antibody in horse serum sickness or sensitization	Yes (usually 1:112 or higher)	Yes	No	Yes	No
Various assorted conditions	Yes (may be elevated)	Yes or no	Yes or no	Yes or no	Yes or no
Heterophilic antibody of infectious mononucleosis	Yes (as a rule elevated but may be 1:56 or less)	No[e]	Yes	Yes	No

[a] Sheep red blood cells.
[b] Forssman antigen.
[c] Beef cell antigen.
[d] Absorption is incomplete in approximately one-third of normal persons; if absorption is incomplete, agglutination is present.
[e] Titer after absorption not more than three tubes lower than in presumptive test.

Table 4-21. Positive Differential Test in Cases with Low Titers in Presumptive Test (1:56 or less)

	NUMBER OF TESTS	TESTS WITH TITERS OF 1:112 OR LESS
First tests (early in disease)	267 (in 267 patients)	46 (17.2%)
Follow-up tests (3 to 18 weeks after onset of symptoms)	107 (in 69 patients)	39 (36.5%)
Total number of tests	374 (in 267 patients)	85* (22.7%)

* In these 85 tests infectious mononucleosis could *not* be diagnosed with the *presumptive* test.
Only the *differential* test made it possible to establish the *serologic* diagnosis of the disease.

7. Incubate in water bath at 37° C. for 15 minutes.

8. After centrifugation, compare the degree of hemolysis of tubes 1 to 10 with tube 11. Those tubes that show greater degrees of hemolysis than tube 11—the 50 per cent hemolysis standard—are recorded as positive. Control tubes 8, 9, and 10 should show no hemolysis.

Interpretation. A titer of 480 or higher

is considered to be presumptive evidence for the diagnosis of infectious mononucleosis. False positive tests have been encountered in patients without clinical or hematologic evidence of infectious mononucleosis. The specificity of the test is comparable with that of the presumptive test for infectious mononucleosis (Davidsohn, 1938; Davidsohn and Stern, 1951).

Wöllner's Enzyme Test for Infectious Mononucleosis No. 1*. *Principle:* Dilutions of serum are set up with normal sheep cells and with sheep cells previously treated with papain (Wöllner, 1955).

Procedure

1. Preparation of stock solution of papain: Grind 1 gm. of papain into 100 ml. of 0.85 per cent sodium chloride solution in a mortar; separate and discard the undissolved sediment. Divide the supernatant solution in aliquots of 0.5 ml. and keep frozen.

2. Preparation of the dilute papain solution: To 0.5 ml. of stock solution of papain, add 4.5 ml. of buffered saline, which is prepared by adding one volume of 0.15 M, pH 7.3, Sörenson phosphate buffer to nine volumes of 0.85 per cent sodium chloride solution.

3. Add one volume of packed sheep cells

* Slightly modified in our laboratory.

(previously washed three times) to two volumes of dilute papain solution.

4. Incubate in water bath at 37° C. for 30 minutes with frequent gentle mixing.

5. Wash the papain-treated cells three times and make a 2 per cent suspension with 0.85 per cent sodium chloride solution.

6. Make a 2 per cent suspension of washed but untreated sheep cells.

7. Inactivate serum at 56° C. for 30 minutes. Set up two rows of ten tubes. Make serial twofold dilutions with 0.85 per cent sodium chloride in a volume of 0.25 ml. and with dilutions of 1/5, 1/10, 1/20, and so on, up to 1/2560. (For details, see procedure for presumptive test for infectious mononucleosis, p. 217.)

8. Add 0.1 ml. of untreated sheep cell suspension to each tube of one row, and add papain-treated cell suspension to each tube of the other row.

9. Incubate at room temperature for two hours.

10. Record agglutinations as ++++ (large clump), +++ (large and small clumps), ++ (distinct small clumps), + (barely visible small clumps), +w (microscopic agglutination), and − (no agglutination).

Interpretation of results. In serum of patients with infectious mononucleosis the titer of agglutinins is higher with normal sheep cells, whereas in normal serum and in conditions other than infectious mononucleosis the titer is higher with papain-treated red cells. The value of this test is limited because about 30 per cent of serums of patients with infectious mononucleosis do not react as described.

Wöllner's Enzyme Test for Infectious Mononucleosis No. 2*. *Principle.* The serum is absorbed with papain-treated sheep red cells and then tested for agglutinins with normal and with papain-treated sheep cells (Wöllner, 1956).

Procedure

1. Inactive serum at 56° C. for 30 minutes.

2. Prepare papain-treated sheep cells as in Wöllner's Test 1 and make a 20 per cent suspension.

3. Add 0.3 ml. of inactivated serum to 1.5 ml. of 20 per cent papain-treated sheep cell suspension.

4. Incubate at room temperature for 15 minutes with frequent gentle mixing.

5. Separate the supernatant by centrifugation.

* Slightly modified in our laboratory.

6. Set up two rows of ten tubes; make serial twofold dilutions with 0.85 per cent sodium chloride in a volume of 0.25 ml. and with dilutions of 1/5, 1/10, 1/21, and so forth, up to 1/2560.

7. Prepare 2 per cent suspensions in 0.85 per cent sodium chloride of papain-treated and untreated sheep cells, and add 0.1 ml. of the former to each tube of one set and of the latter to each tube of the other set.

8. Incubate at room temperature for two hours.

9. Record agglutinations as ++++ (large clump), +++ (large and small clumps), ++ (distinct small clumps), + (barely visible small clumps), +w (microscopic agglutination), and − (no agglutination).

Interpretation. In infectious mononucleosis, the agglutinin titer of the absorbed serum titrated with untreated cells is always four or more tubes higher than the one titrated with papain-treated cells. In conditions other than infectious mononucleosis, papain-treated cells absorb the sheep agglutinin completely or give a higher titer than the untreated cells. This is a highly specific test. Data from our laboratory confirm Wöllner's observation.

ETIOLOGY

The etiology of the disease is not known, although it is suspected to be caused by a virus. Successful transmissions of the disease from monkey to man, from man to monkey, and from man to man have been reported but require confirmation.

Misao and Kobayashi (1955, 1960) inoculated mice with marrow and lymph node tissue of patients with infectious mononucleosis. From the mice they isolated a microorganism and called it *Rickettsia sennetsui*. Volunteers inoculated with material obtained from the mice developed infectious mononucleosis and a positive differential test. However, according to Eyquem (1961) the serologic tests were not of the kind seen in human infectious mononucleosis in Europe.

EPIDEMIOLOGY

The peaks of morbidity in a military academy occurred in February and August exactly on the forty-fifth day following vacations. Hoagland (1955) postulates transmission by passionate kissing for which the vacation period offers greater opportunities. The incubation in 71 of 73 patients was 42 to 49 days following intimate oral contact in one series. In 68 per cent of another series the incubation was 31 to 60 days. Other epidemiologic observations indicate that kissing is by no means the only means of transmission.

There is reason to believe that there are carriers of the disease who are free of clinical manifestations.

The possible role of "Mono Annies" in the epidemiology of the disease has been suggested, drawing the analogy from Typhoid Marys (Godden, 1960).

Lymphopenia

Lymphopenia is present in infants with hypogammaglobulinemia and agammaglobulinemia. Susceptibility to various infections is the consequence. It follows administration of adrenocortical hormones. It is present characteristically in Hodgkin's disease and lymphosarcoma.

Monocytosis

Monocytosis is an increase of monocytes above the normal of 500 per cu. mm. The normal range in the peripheral blood is 1 to 6 per cent.

Monocytosis is present during the recovery stage from acute infections and is usually considered a favorable sign except in tuberculosis. An increase of monocytes in tuberculosis is a poor prognostic sign. An index has been developed expressing the ratio of monocytes to lymphocytes. The absolute number of lymphocytes is divided by the absolute number of monocytes, and if the quotient is higher than 1, the prognosis is better than if it is lower.

Monocytosis may be present in subacute bacterial endocarditis. In this condition monocytes may show phagocytosis of other blood cells, red blood cells, and leukocytes. It may be present in Hodgkin's disease; in mycotic, rickettsial, protozoal, and viral infections, as well as in various lipoid storage diseases, such as Gaucher's disease and Niemann-Pick disease.

Blood and Marrow Findings in Diseases of Blood-producing Tissues

MALIGNANT LYMPHOMA

The terminology of lesions referred to in the heading of this section is still in a state of confusion. For example, some use the term lymphoma to indicate malignant lesions of lymphoid tissues. Some include all neoplastic or borderline neoplastic or hyperplastic lesions of blood producing tissues under this heading. One popular medical dictionary defines lymphoma as "a benign tumor composed of lymphatic tissue." Another dictionary defines it as "any tumor made up of lymphoid tissue." To avoid misunderstanding, the term malignant lymphoma is used here. A classification of malignant lymphoma is given in Table 4–22.

Transitions from one type of malignant lymphoma to another are known to occur. Changes from aleukemic to leukemic forms are even more common, except for Hodgkin's granuloma. The leukemic phases may be transient.

Table 4–22. Classification of Malignant Lymphomas*

GENERAL CLASSIFICATIONS	SUBCLASSIFICATION	TERMS TO BE AVOIDED	LEUKEMIA VARIANT
Lymphoma (type unclassified)		Lymphoblastoma	
Lymphocytic sarcoma		Lymphosarcoma	Lymphosarcoma cell or lymphocytic
Reticulum cell sarcoma		Reticulosarcoma	Histiocytic
		Reticuloendotheliosis	Monocytic
Follicular lymphoma		Giant follicular lymphoma	Lymphocytic
		Giant follicular lympho-blastoma	Occasionally, so-called notched cell or lymphosarcoma cell
		Brill-Symmers disease	
Hodgkin's disease	Hodgkin's paragranuloma	Hodgkin's lymphoma	
	Hodgkin's granuloma	Hodgkin's lymphoblastoma	
	Hodgkin's sarcoma	Hodgkin's lymphogranulomatosis	

* Modified from Table 1 in Fourth Report of the Committee for Clarification of the Nomenclature of Cells and Diseases of the Blood and Blood-forming Organs. Am. J. Clin. Path., *20:* 562–579, 1950.

HODGKIN'S DISEASE

Jackson and Parker (1947), who devised a classification for this disease, recognized three forms: paragranuloma, granuloma, and sarcoma. The paragranuloma is comparatively the least malignant in its course, and the microscopic picture shows least variation from the normal, but each of these forms contains the Sternberg-Reed cells.

The paragranuloma shows no necrosis, and the predominant cell is the adult lymphocyte. Sternberg-Reed cells are few. Eosinophils are rare. Plasma cells are quite common. This form may pass into granuloma at any time.

Many authors doubt that paragranuloma is an entity as distinctly discernible as claimed by Jackson and Parker, especially on histologic grounds. On the other hand the great variation in the clinical course is undeniable.

Blood Picture. Normocytic, sometimes severe, anemia is seen in about 50 per cent of cases.

The leukocyte count may be elevated, normal, or reduced (leukopenic). The differential count shows neutrophilia, lymphocytopenia, monocytosis, and eosinophilia. Either all, or any combination, of these may be present.

Neutrophilic leukocytosis is seen, especially when lymph nodes are involved, and neutropenia, when bone marrow is involved. The blood changes seem to depend on the stage of the disease and on some individual, as yet unknown, factors.

The most frequent finding is a moderate leukocytosis with white cell counts ranging from 12,000 to 25,000 per cu. mm. and a relative and even absolute lymphopenia. In the differential count the lymphocytes may decrease below 10 per cent. A slight shift to the left may be present in the neutrophils. The pathogenesis of this change is impairment of lymphocytogenic properties of reticuloendothelial tissues by the disease. As a rule lymphopenia is prognostically a poor omen.

Monocytosis is frequent with values of 10 per cent or higher. Eosinophilia has been described in about 20 per cent of cases and may be extreme. The platelet count may be increased, normal, or decreased, especially with marrow involvement.

Marrow Findings. Frequently there is a shift to the left of the granulocytes, slight monocytosis, and eosinophilia. As a rule findings are not characteristic. Amyloid degeneration of various grades is sometimes present in various organs and with it plasma cell hyperplasia in the marrow. The marrow may be diagnostic when Hodgkin's granuloma with its characteristic pattern, including Sternberg-Reed giant cells, is seen in a biopsy and occasionally in marrow puncture smears.

LYMPHOSARCOMA (LYMPHOCYTIC)

Lymphopenia may be present similar to that seen in Hodgkin's disease, but as a rule there is no leukocytosis except in the leukemic variant.

MACROGLOBULINEMIA

This variant of malignant lymphoma (Waldenström's disease, lymphocytic-plasmocytic leukemia) is characterized by hyperglobulinemia, fibrinogenopenia, anemia, and bleeding tendency from mucous membranes. Microscopic sections of lymph nodes and marrow aspirates show cells resembling plasma cells and lymphocytes with large PAS-positive cytoplasmic granules. The elevated serum gamma globulin has an extremely high molecular weight of 1 million with sedimentation constant of 18 to 20 Svedberg units. These macroglobulins make up 3 to 5 per cent of the normal serum proteins. In macroglobulinemia they amount to 20 per cent or more. The Sia test (water dilution test) is strongly positive.

THE SIA TEST

Procedure. Into a test tube containing distilled water a drop of serum is permitted to fall from a pipet. Normally the drop disappears, leaving a faint haziness. In macroglobulinemia, the precipitate is heavy, does not dissolve, and drops to the bottom. It can be further identified. The test is negative when only small or moderate, and occasionally even large, amounts of macroglobulin are present. It is not diagnostic by itself. It may be positive in rheumatoid arthritis. The diagnosis of the disease can be made definitive only by ultracentrifuge analysis of the serum.

LEUKEMIC VARIANTS OF LYMPHOMAS

Lymphomas may become leukemic, in which case the neoplastic cells are invading the peripheral circulation. This change is most common in chloroma. It is next most frequent in lymphocytic sarcoma. Frequently the blood picture is that of typical chronic or subacute lymphocytic leukemia. In some cases the characteristic neoplastic cells permit a diagnosis of lymphosarcoma cell leukemia. Leukemic transformation is less frequent in follicular lymphoma and reticulum cell sarcoma, and does not occur in Hodgkin's disease.

LEUKEMIA

Definition. Leukemia is an acute or chronic systemic disease of the white blood cell producing tissues characterized by: hyperplasia of leukocytes (granulocytes, lymphocytes, or monocytes) and their precursors, frequently but not invariably with corresponding quantitative and qualitative changes in the circulating white blood cells and infiltration of organs and tissues in a widespread and irregular manner similar to the behavior of malignant lymphomas.

There are at the present time three different conceptions regarding the nature of leukemia.

1. Leukemia is a neoplasm of the marrow or of the lymphatic or reticuloendothelial tissues as the case may be.

2. It is a hyperplastic condition of the corresponding tissues.

3. Leukemia is closely related to but not identical with neoplastic diseases arising in hemopoietic tissues. According to this opinion the malignant nature of leukemias has not been definitely established.

Some of the differences between the normal and leukemic leukocytes are shown in Table 4–23. The low agglutinability of the leukemic leukocyte and the lower alkaline phosphatase reactivity (particularly pronounced when compared with leukocytes in the leukemoid reaction) are in sharp contrast with the faster rate of amino acid synthesis and cystine and cysteine incorporation by leukemic cells.

Classification. According to the consensus of the members of the Committee for Clarification of the Nomenclature of Cells and Diseases of the Blood and Blood-forming Organs, the leukemias should be classified in the Standard Nomenclature of Disease under the etiologic category of "new growth originating in specialized mesenchymatous tissue" (Jordan, 1942) (Table 4–24). Favoring the inclusion of leukemias under malignant tumors, in the judgment of the Committee, is the fact "that the therapy currently used for these diseases (i.e., leukemias) is the same as is used for unquestioned malignant neoplasms."

The fourth report of the Nomenclature Committee defines leukemias as neoplastic diseases arising in hemopoietic tissues in which the type cells appear in the blood or are disseminated diffusely through the marrow. If the cell series cannot be identified, then the leukemia should be included in the category "type unclassified." Usually that means an acute leukemia of unidentified "blast cell" type.

According to the report of the Committee, the name of the most undifferentiated of the cells of each series of white blood cells should carry the suffix -blast and the second stage, the prefix pro-, and except in the granulocytic series all cells that are more mature than the -blast stage have names with the suffix -cyte. The name of the fourth stage in the granulocytic and erythrocytic series is to have the prefix meta-.

Table 4–23. The Leukemic Leukocyte

	LEUKOCYTE	
	Leukemic	Normal*
Agglutinability[1]	±	+
Amino acid synthesis[2]	100 +[5] 100 + +[6]	100
Cysteine and cysteine incorporation[3]	100 + +	100
Alkaline phosphatase[4]	low	100 100 +[7]

1. Tullis, 1953
2. Baker *et al.*, 1957
3. Weisberger *et al.*, 1954, 1955
4. Valentine and Beck, 1951; Valentine, 1956
5. Chronic granulocytic leukemia
6. Acute leukemia
7. Leukemoid reactions

* The figure 100 is used to express the normal. 100 + and 100 + + mean above normal.

SUMMARY

I. Classification

1. Chronologic, based on duration
   a. fulminant
   b. acute
   c. subacute
   d. chronic

(*Continued on page 227*)

Table 4–24. Classification of Leukemia*

GENERAL CLASSIFICATION	SUBCLASSIFICATION	TERMS TO BE AVOIDED	PREDOMINANT CELL	VARIANTS	LONGEVITY[g]
Leukemia blast cell (type unclassified)	Acute[a] leukemic[b] subleukemic[c] aleukemic[d]	Stem cell leukemia	Unclassified blast cell (undifferentiated)		Under 12 mo.
Lymphocytic	Acute leukemic subleukemic aleukemic	Lymphoblastic leukemia Blast cell leukemia	Lymphoblast		Under 12 mo.
	Subacute[e] leukemic subleukemic aleukemic	Lymphadenosis Lymphatic, lymphoid or lymphogenous leukemia	Partially differentiated lymphocyte	Associated with lymphocytic sarcoma	12–24 mo.
	Chronic[f] leukemic subleukemic aleukemic		Well-differentiated lymphocyte		Over 24 mo.
Granulocytic neutrophilic	Acute leukemic subleukemic aleukemic	Myeloblastic leukemia	Myeloblast	Micromyeloblastic Monocytoid (Naegeli) Chloroma	Under 12 mo.
	Subacute leukemic subleukemic aleukemic	Myeloid, myelogenous, myelocytic leukemias	Partially differentiated granulocyte		12–24 mo.
	Chronic leukemic subleukemic aleukemic	Myelosis	Well-differentiated granulocyte	Subclinical Eosinophilic Basophilic Leukoerythroblastic Polycythemic Thrombocythemic Megakaryocythemic Megakaryocytic Acute relapsing Myelofibrotic Osteosclerotic	Over 24 mo.
Monocytic	Acute leukemic subleukemic aleukemic		Monoblast		Under 6 mo.
	Subacute leukemic subleukemic aleukemic	Reticuloendotheliosis Schilling or Naegeli type leukemia	Partially differentiated monocyte	Associated with reticulum cell sarcoma	6–12 mo.
	Chronic leukemic subleukemic aleukemic		Well-differentiated monocyte		Over 12 mo.

Table 4–24 *(concluded)*

GENERAL CLASSIFICA- TION	SUBCLASSIFICA- TION	TERMS TO BE AVOIDED	PREDOMINANT CELL	VARIANTS	LONGEVITY[g]
Plasmocytic	Acute leukemic subleukemic aleukemic		Plasmoblast		
	Subacute leukemic subleukemic aleukemic		Partially differenti- ated plasmocyte	Associated with multiple myeloma of corresponding degree of cell ma- turity	Unpredict- able
	Chronic leukemic subleukemic aleukemic		Well-differentiated plasmocyte		

* Modified from Table 1 in Fourth Report of the Committee for Clarification of the Nomenclature of Cells and Diseases of the Blood and Blood-Forming Organs. Am. J. Clin. Path. 20: 562–579, 1950, and from Table 22 in R. Philip Custer: An Atlas of the Blood and Bone Marrow. Philadelphia, W. B. Saunders Company, 1949, p. 244.

[a] Acute leukemias have an expected duration of life that is counted in months from the onset of the first symptom. The onset is typically with fever, stomatitis, and bleeding into the skin from the gums and mucous membranes. The predominant cell in the marrow and in the blood in leukemic cases is the blast form, with the single exception that in some of the acute leukemic lymphocytic leukemias, it is a cell indistinguishable morphologically from the lymphocyte or prolymphocyte. Except in the lymphocytic type, cells more differentiated than the pro-stage of the involved series are rare or absent.

[b] Leukemic leukemias are defined as those leukemias in which the leukocyte count in the blood is above 15,000 per cu. mm. and the type cells are present in the blood in sufficient number to permit the diagnosis of the type of leukemia.

[c] Subleukemic leukemias are defined as those leukemias in which the leukocyte count in the blood is below 15,000 per cu. mm. It is often much below normal, in the 100 to 4000 range, yet the type cells of the particular variety of leukemia are present in the blood in sufficient numbers to suggest the diagnosis.

[d] Aleukemic leukemias are defined as those leukemias in which the leukocyte count in the blood is below 15,000 per cu. mm., often as low as 100 to 4000 per cu. mm., but the type cells either are absent or are so few, usually less than one per 1000 cells, that it is impossible to make the diagnosis from examination of the blood alone.

[e] Subacute leukemias are defined as those leukemias with an expected duration of life longer than in acute, but shorter than in chronic leukemia, from the onset of the first symptom. The onset is more insidious than in acute cases, but eventually all develop fever, stomatitis, and bleeding into the skin from the gums and mucous membranes within three months from the onset of symptoms. The predominant cell in the marrow and blood in leukemic cases is the pro-stage of the involved series, and an increased number of blast cells is always found. Except in the lymphocytic type, cells more differentiated than the pro-stage of the involved series are rare or absent.

[f] Chronic leukemias are defined as those leukemias with an expected duration of life of one to twenty years or more (average three to five years), depending on the type, from the onset of the first symptom. Fever, stomatitis, and hemorrhages into the skin or from the gums and mucous membranes rarely develop within the first year. The most differentiated stage of the involved series is always present in addition to the less differentiated cells. In the lymphocytic type only the lymphocyte is usually found and prolymphocytes are rare or absent.

[g] The life expectancy of leukemias has been prolonged considerably by modern chemotherapy.

2. Cytologic, based on predominant cell
   a. blast cell leukemia, for undifferen-tiated types
   b. granulocytic leukemia
      acute (myeloblastic)
      chronic
   c. lymphocytic leukemia
      acute (lymphoblastic)
      chronic
   d. monocytic leukemia
      acute (monoblastic)
      chronic
   e. neutrophilic leukemia
   f. eosinophilic leukemia
   g. basophilic leukemia
   h. thrombocytic leukemia
   i. plasmocytic leukemia
   j. lymphocytic sarcoma cell leukemia
3. Based on functional capacity of release mechanism (marrow-blood and tissue-blood barrier)
   a. leukemic
   b. subleukemic
   c. aleukemic

4. Based on association with a definite neoplastic lesion of the same cytologic composition as the leukemic cells
    a. chloroma
    b. myeloblastoma
    c. myeloma (plasma cell leukemia)
    d. lymphocytic cell sarcoma

II. General Data

1. Age
    a. all forms may occur at any age
    b. acute leukemia most frequent below 20
    c. chronic granulocytic most frequent between 20 and 50
    d. chronic lymphocytic most frequent over 50
2. Sex: males more commonly affected

III. Etiology

Unknown except for isolated observations of etiologic significance.
1. Eight to ten times as frequent in radiologists as in other medical specialists
2. Hereditary predisposition in man suggestive
3. Various agents, including radiation, capable of producing the disease in animals and man
4. Transmissible in some animals by cell-free filtrate
5. Transmissibility in man not demonstrated

IV. Chronic Leukemia

A. CLINICAL FINDINGS

1. Insidious onset; not infrequently symptomless for a long time, especially chronic lymphocytic leukemia, so-called subclinical leukemia.
2. Significant clinical findings:

	GRANULOCYTIC	LYMPHOCYTIC
Lymph nodes	Moderate enlargement, late	Early and pronounced
Spleen	Greatly enlarged	Moderate enlargement
Skin lesions	Rare	More common
GI tract infiltration	Rare	More common
Bone tenderness	Rare	Moderately frequent (sternum)
Retinopathy	Common	Uncommon

3. Symptoms
    a. Symptoms from enlarged spleen, liver, lymph nodes, and other organs are caused by: anatomic enlargement, interference with specific function of organ by replacement of its normal tissues with leukemic infiltration, interference with function of neighboring organs by pressure, and infarction of spleen with pain and tenderness.
    b. Symptoms from anemia are the result of cardiac dilatation, tachycardia, palpitation, dyspnea, cardiac failure, and edema; anemia aggravates prognosis.
    c. Symptoms from increased metabolic rate are explained by weight loss, nervousness, perspiration, cachexia; this leads occasionally to diagnosis of hyperthyroidism.
    d. Marrow replacement (usually late in disease) may result in hemorrhagic tendency from thrombocytopenia; the latter aggravates prognosis.
    e. Pain in bones is most frequent in chronic lymphocytic leukemia but also occurs in other forms; x-ray may show osteoporosis and periosteal infiltration.

B. LABORATORY FINDINGS

1. Blood thick due to large number of leukocytes.
2. Heavy buffy coat on centrifugation of blood to which anticoagulant has been added.
3. Variable anemia, usually late. Occasionally high red counts may be seen, espe-

Plate 4–15. Chronic granulocytic leukemia, peripheral blood. The leukocytosis, the shift to the left, the presence of the whole gamut of the granulocytic series except the segmented granulocyte, and the three basophilic granulocytes in a single field add up to the typical picture of chronic granulocytic leukemia. The key will facilitate identification of the individual cells. (Plate from Heilmeyer, L., and Begemann, H.: Atlas der Klinischen Hämatologie und Cytologie. Springer, 1955.)

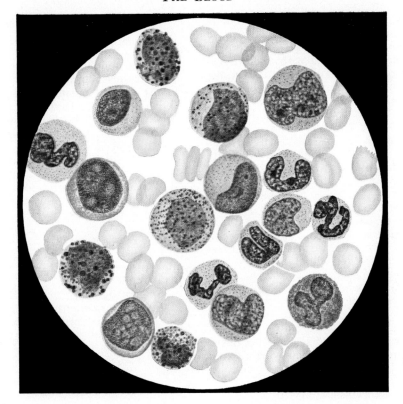

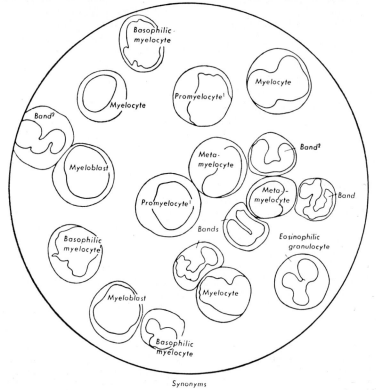

Basophilic myelocyte

Myelocyte

Promyelocyte[1]

Myelocyte

Band[2]

Myeloblast

Meta-myelocyte

Band[2]

Promyelocyte[1]

Meta-myelocyte

Band

Bands

Basophilic myelocyte[1]

Eosinophilic granulocyte

Myeloblast

Myelocyte

Basophilic myelocyte

Synonyms

1. Progranulocyte

2. Staff cell

Plate 4–15

cially early in chronic granulocytic leukemia, which may actually be preceded by a polycythemia In all forms of leukemia, there is hemolytic anemia with a shortened survival of erythrocytes. In chronic lymphocytic leukemia, autoimmune hemolytic anemia with a positive antiglobulin test is common. Not infrequently the anemia is caused or aggravated by hypersplenism. This can be demonstrated by differences in surface counts over the spleen and liver following administration of labeled patient's own red cells. If the spleen-to-liver ratio is 2 to 1, splenectomy has been recommended. Another cause of anemia in such patients was found to be accelerated plasma iron half-time clearance owing to a trapping mechanism with resulting retarded utilization of iron by the red cells.

4. Platelet count

a. Frequently increased in granulocytic form with terminal drop.

b. May be decreased late in lymphocytic form.

c. Low counts are of serious prognosis.

d. Hemorrhage may occur with normal and high platelet counts. Cause: vascular damage.

5. High leukocytosis

a. More frequent in granulocytic leukemia (100,000 to 800,000).

Segmented forms, 30 to 70 per cent
Myelocytes, 30 to 50 per cent
Blast cells, 0 to 10 per cent
Both eosinophilic and basophilic forms are increased (Plates 4–15, 4–16).

b. Lymphocytic form has monotonous picture with 90 to 99 per cent adult small lymphocytes. Total count, about 100,000 with lower and moderately higher figures common (Plates 4–17, 4–18).

c. Normal counts and leukopenic forms are not unusual.

6. Urine: albumin, casts, RBC.

7. Basal metabolic rate elevated in chronic granulocytic and late in chronic lymphocytic leukemia.

8. Blood chemistry: elevated uric acid and total nonprotein nitrogen. Sometimes negative nitrogen balance. Low plasma protein (in advanced cases). Lipids may be elevated. Cholesterol normal or low. Phosphorus and serum alkaline phosphatase may be elevated.

V. Acute Leukemia

A. CLINICAL FINDINGS

1. Onset sudden and course short.

2. Weakness, prostration, rapidly developing anemia, purpura, and gingivitis.

3. Joint and periarticular pain are not infrequent with bone involvement.

4. Disease is fulminating in nature and may resemble a sepsis.

5. Organ enlargement and infiltration are usually less conspicuous.

6. Features are found in the following types most frequently but not enough for differential diagnosis:

a. Monocytic
Ulcerative gingivitis
Cervical gland enlargement and occasional tenderness

b. Lymphoblastic
Splenomegaly
Liver enlargement (50 per cent)
Generalized lymphadenopathy

7. Marrow studies are indicated for differentiation of the forms.

B. LABORATORY FINDINGS

1. Data applicable to all acute leukemias

a. At first moderate, later rapidly developing severe anemia, normochromic and normocytic. Nucleated red cells present in peripheral blood.

b. Low platelet count (if normal, question diagnosis). Rise of platelet count may be earliest sign of remission.

c. Prolonged bleeding and clot retraction time.

d. Occasionally prolonged clotting time.

e. Hemorrhagic tendency (positive tourniquet test).

f. Hemocytology: count elevated (moderately up to 100,000, frequently much lower); may be normal or even subnormal (leukopenic). Type cell: blast cell of one of three types. Few or no intermediate cells up to level of segmented cells, lymphocytes, or monocytes (leukemic hiatus).

g. High basal metabolic rate.

h. Elevated uric acid and total nonprotein nitrogen. Nitrogen balance may be negative. These changes may be present also in chronic leukemia but less frequently.

Plate 4–16.   Chronic granulocytic leukemia, marrow. Here, as in the peripheral blood smear, all stages of development of granulocytes from the myeloblast through promyelocyte, myelocyte, metamyelocyte, band form, and segmented cell are present. The basophilic granulocytes are equally prominent. (Plate from Heilmeyer, L., and Begemann, H.: Atlas der Klinischen Hämatologie und Cytologie. Springer, 1955.)

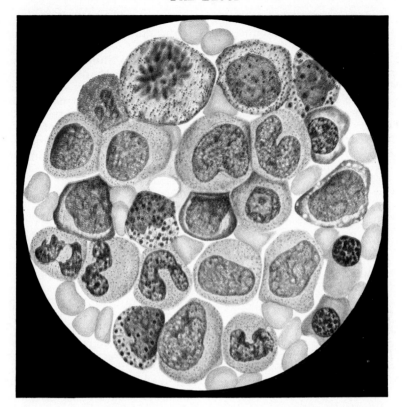

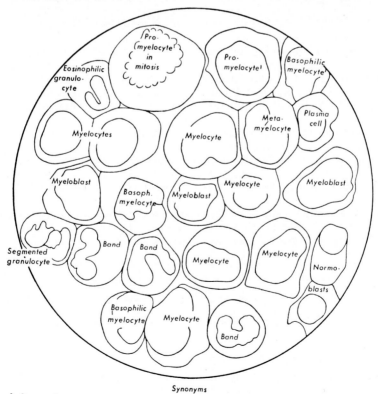

1. Progranulocyte

Synonyms

Plate 4–16

i. Marrow: replacement with blast cells. Undifferentiated in blast cell leukemia and correspondingly differentiated in the other three forms of acute leukemia (Plate 4–20).

2. Acute granulocytic

a. Type cell: myeloblast. Small numbers of progranulocytes. No further intermediate cells until level of segmented cell; leukemic hiatus. Sometimes micromyeloblasts may be difficult to differentiate from lymphocytes.

b. Auer bodies (rod-shaped cytoplasmic inclusions); if present, exclude acute lymphocytic leukemia (Plate 4–19).

3. Acute lymphocytic

a. Type cell: lymphoblasts. Occasional prolymphocytes; remainder lymphocytes (Plate 4–21).

4. Monocytic

a. Type cell: monoblast; occasional promonocytes; remainder monocytes. Auer bodies exclude acute lymphocytic leukemia.

b. Naegeli type. Acute granulocytic leukemia with transient monocytic phase.

c. Schilling type. True monocytic leukemia.

5. Blast cell leukemia if differentiation of blast cells impossible. Presence of even small numbers of progranulocytes, prolymphocytes, and promonocytes helps to identify type of acute leukemia.

DISCUSSION

The volume of writing on the cause and nature of the disease is inversely proportional to what is actually known about it. The fatal outcome is one of the few things on which there is fairly general agreement, but there are dissenting voices even on this point.

Leukemia is a collective term, which includes several entities. The nature of the disease is largely a mystery. Isolated bits of information have been accumulating that will eventually add up and explain the puzzle.

Several factors have been discovered that have some bearing on leukemia. Constitutional factor: familial inherited disposition in certain families with several members of the family affected. External factors: x-ray, benzol.

Neoplastic Nature of Leukemia. The neoplastic nature of the disease in animals has been established by experimental studies. The same transplant may produce leukemia in some animals and true tumors in others. Intravenous injection of leukemia cells, even of a single cell, produces leukemia. Carcinogens, such as benzpyrene and methylcholanthrene, and x-rays have produced experimental leukemia.

Tumor-like growth and transitions between tumors and leukemia have also been observed in animals as well as in man.

Arguments in Favor. Tendency to grow without restraint. Shift in ratio of nucleus to cytoplasm in favor of nucleus. Increased number and size of nucleoli. Atypical mitoses.

Arguments Against. So-called primary tumor in the usual form cannot be demonstrated. The disease has a pronounced systemic character and distribution.

The leukemic lesions in various tissues and organs have been interpreted as metastases by some authors who favor the neoplastic hypothesis. The argument against such interpretation runs as follows: There are cases of extramedullary myeloid metaplasia in septic infections, in anemias, and in osteosclerosis, which certainly have nothing to do with tumors and in which the extramedullary myelopoiesis can in no way be differentiated from similar lesions in a true granulocytic leukemia. The same holds true for material obtained by sternal puncture in cases of granulocytic hyperplasia, which frequently cannot be differentiated from chronic granulocytic leukemia.

Another argument against the neoplastic hypothesis is the multiformity of the cellular structure. All stages of development of granulocytic and erythroid cells, including megakaryocytes, are represented. Such degree of differentiation speaks against a neoplastic nature. It is true that in acute granu-

---

Plate 4–17. Chronic lymphocytic leukemia, marrow. A monotonous picture. The predominant cell is the lymphocyte. It has replaced the native marrow cell to a considerable degree. The arrow at 2 o'clock points to a plasma cell with its eccentrically located nucleus. At 4 o'clock is a neutrophilic myelocyte. At 9 o'clock there is a promyelocyte, above and below it are normoblasts, and to its right is an eosinophilic myelocyte. (Plate from Heilmeyer, L., and Begemann, H.: Atlas der Klinischen Hämatologie und Cytologie. Springer, 1955.)

Plate 4–18. Chronic lymphocytic leukemia, peripheral blood. The five lymphocytes have a somewhat less dense chromatin. This is the only deviation from the normal, and even that is not impressive. The two degenerating cells are commonly seen in this disease. (Plate from Heilmeyer, L., and Begemann, H.: Atlas der Klinischen Hämatologie und Cytologie. Springer, 1955.)

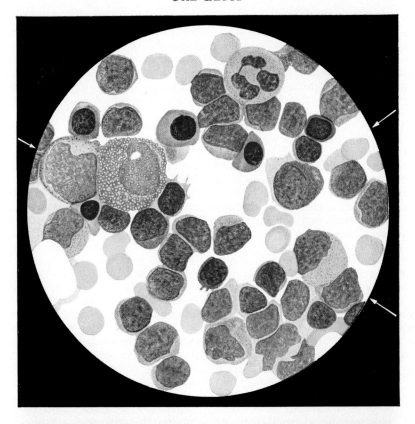

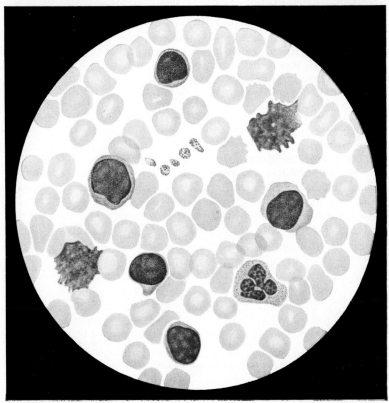

Plate 4–17
Plate 4–18

locytic leukemia the lesion is monotonously myeloblastic. Hence, the inference by some that at least this form of leukemia is a neoplasm. Even that cannot be sustained, because in some cases of agranulocytosis one finds in the marrow nothing but myeloblasts, a reversible lesion, which as a rule returns to normal.

It is on the basis of all these observations that some have concluded that leukemias are hyperplastic systemic diseases.

The fact that leukemia is irreversible and as a rule fatal is used by some in support of its neoplastic nature. The answer to this is that prior to the discovery of liver therapy pernicious anemia had had the same attributes. The advocates of the hypothesis of neoplasia argue that in some cases of leukemia there are localized tumor-like proliferations with a malignant type of growth and that there are true tumors of blood producing organs that show transitions to leukemias. However, these are isolated cases with features that set them apart from the usual case of leukemia. They are not sufficiently convincing to be used as a basis for developing a hypothesis regarding the nature of all leukemias. It is possible that leukemia may be associated with a true neoplasm. There is a difference between recognizing leukemia as a neoplasm, the possibility that a neoplasm may develop on the basis of leukemia, and the development of leukemia from a lymphoma.

According to some authors leukemia is a precancerous stage of a cancer of hematopoietic tissues. The experiments in animals could then be explained in such a way that in cases in which leukemia has already become transformed into cancer, a transplantation of cells at that stage of leukemia would produce cancer.

Nature of Acute Leukemia. According to some authors acute leukemia is a form of leukemia, equivalent to other forms. According to others it is not a true leukemia but a reactive process in response to certain stimuli (for example, septic infections). On the other hand, it is possible that the infections are the result and not the cause of acute leukemia. Also, other stimuli are considered as possible causes of acute leukemia, such as benzol, x-rays, and various drugs (for example, sulfonamides).

Much has been written about cases of cured acute leukemias. As a rule, such reports must be viewed with great suspicion. However, when cases of this kind have been observed by reliable hematologists, including Naegeli, the possibility of their occurrence cannot be denied. Some try to get around it by speaking of a so-called "myeloblastic reaction." Some go even further and see in every acute granulocytic leukemia a reactive disturbance of the bone marrow and claim that the term acute leukemia does not apply to them.

There are true cancers of blood producing organs that show hematologic findings identical with those seen in certain forms of leukemia: chloroma, myeloblastoma, lymphosarcoma.

INCIDENCE

In 1939 to 1940, 5286 deaths were attributed to leukemia in the United States —0.39 per cent of all deaths and 3.6 per cent of deaths due to cancer. The death rate from leukemia has increased steadily in the United States from 39 per million in 1940 to 65 per million in 1954 for the total population. However, when the United States total population is divided into those under 55 and those 55 and over, the rate of leukemia deaths increased from 27 per million in 1940 to 35 per million in 1954 for those under 55 years of age, while it increased from 109 to 208 per million for those 55 years or over; i.e., the increase

---

Plate 4–19. Acute granulocytic leukemia, peripheral blood. The large myeloblasts with the immature granular and reticulated chromatin and the somewhat indistinct nucleoli are characteristic. The cytoplasm shows no granules in some of the cells and varying numbers of different distinctness in the others. The peroxidase stain in the right half of the smear shows varying numbers of oxidase-positive granules in all the cells. That all cells have the peroxidase positive granules, whereas granules are seen in only a few of those stained with the regular stain, indicates that the granules demonstrated by the two stains are not identical. The Auer bodies in three of the cells on the left side are characteristic for this type of leukemia. (Plate from Heilmeyer, L., and Begemann, H.: Atlas der Klinischen Hämatologie und Cytologie. Springer, 1955.)

Plate 4–20. Acute lymphocytic leukemia, marrow. The erythrocytes show a normocytic normochromic anemia. The lymphoblasts with immature nuclei, many of them indented, with a reticulated delicate chromatin structure, multiple nucleoli, and only a narrow rim of agranular pale blue cytoplasm are characteristic. Two degenerating cells, two normoblasts, and one cell in mitosis are present.

This preparation is from an adult, in whom an acute lymphocytic leukemia is extremely rare. According to some authors, the disease can be diagnosed in an adult only if it develops in a patient with a chronic lymphocytic leukemia. (Plate from Heilmeyer, L., and Begemann, H.: Atlas der Klinischen Hämatologie und Cytologie. Springer, 1955.)

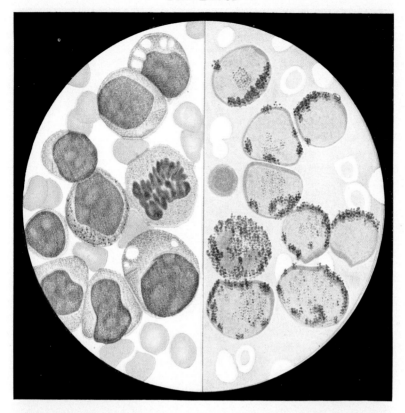

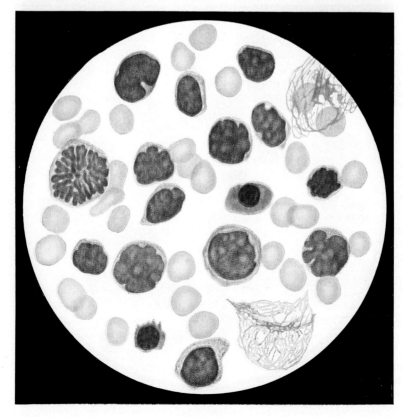

Plate 4–19
Plate 4–20

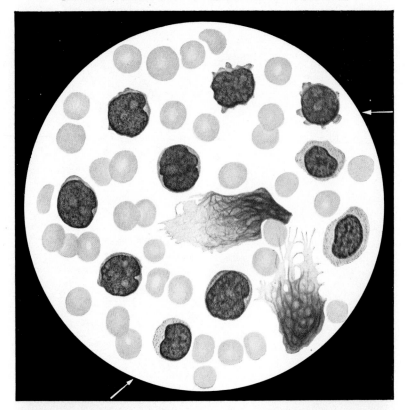

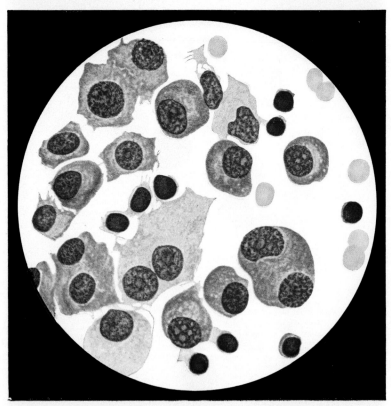

Plate 4–21
Plate 4–22

in rate for the younger group is 30 per cent, but for 55 and over, the increase is 91 per cent. Since world-wide fallout x-radiation affects the total population and affects the young more than the old, fallout cannot be responsible for the increase in leukemia deaths (Dacquisto, 1959).

The figures for 1958 are 3.4 deaths per 100,000 population for those under 20 and 27.1 per 100,000 for those 60 and over (United States National Office of Vital Statistics).

Chronic granulocytic leukemia is the most frequent form. Statistics on the relative incidence of various types of leukemia vary greatly, but Rosenthal's statement comes pretty close to actuality. He claims that the relative incidence of granulocytes, lymphocytes, and monocytes in the peripheral blood is about the same as the incidence of the corresponding three types of leukemia.

Occupation. The disease is more prevalent among physicians than among white males in the general population (1.7 times as frequent) and particularly frequent among radiologists and persons exposed to radiation. Among radiologists it is 8 to 10 times as frequent as in nonradiologists. Chronic exposure to radiation is the probable explanation of the greater frequency among radiologists (Henshaw and Hawkins, 1944). This is supported by animal experiments. It seems to be also more frequent in restaurant workers and typographers (Gram and Nielsen, 1932).

Heredity. About 35 cases of multiple occurrence have been described in members of the same family. It may be important that in some instances of multiple occurrence, different members of the families had different forms of leukemia.

Age. Up to age of 20 acute leukemia predominates; from 20 to 50, chronic granulocytic; above 50, chronic lymphocytic. Monocytic leukemia, which is most commonly acute, favors middle age and is rarely seen before the age of 30.

Sex. The disease is more prevalent in males, especially lymphocytic and monocytic.

Serologic Aspects. Patients with chronic leukemia are poor antibody producers. They have low titers of natural antibodies (anti-sheep agglutinins, isoagglutinins) (Davidsohn, 1938). Also immune antibodies may be low; for example, agglutinins for *S. typhosa* (Widal test) have been low in leukemic patients who contracted typhoid fever. This suggests that the reticuloendothelial system of patients with chronic leukemia is inadequate. In acute leukemia the titers of isoantibodies have been normal or high normal.

Experimental Production. In man, leukemia has been attributed to exposure to various chemicals (for example, benzol, pyridine, aniline dyes) and to x-rays. In animals, especially white mice, injections of benzol produce leukemia or leukemia-like conditions in about 15 per cent. Polycyclic hydrocarbons, estrogens, and irradiation also produce leukemia. Even oral administration of methylcholanthrene produced leukemia in rats (Shay *et al.*, 1950).

Leukemia occurs in several animal species and can be transmitted from animal to animal. The experimental conditions vary from species to species. Carcinogens, x-rays, and estrogens can induce leukemia in mice. The incidence of spontaneous leukemia in mice is decreased by thymectomy. Also, diet low in cystine reduces the incidence of leukemia induced by carcinogen. Spontaneous leukemia in mice is delayed by underfeeding. Immunity to transplanted leukemia can be produced by inoculation of sublethal doses of cells, injections of suspensions of normal tissue cells of certain genetic constitution, and administration of heat-killed leukemic cells, leukemic cell extracts, or normal defibrinated blood.

Plate 4–21. Acute lymphocytic leukemia, peripheral blood. This preparation is from the same adult patient as in Plate 4–7. The lymphocytes at 3 o'clock (just below the arrow) and at 4 and 7 o'clock are more mature as indicated by the presence of azurophilic granules in their cytoplasm and, in the case of the lymphocyte at 4 o'clock, also by the more compact structure of the chromatin. This mixture of lymphoblasts with occasional mature lymphocytes is indicative of acute lymphocytic leukemia developing in a patient with chronic leukemia. (Plate from Heilmeyer, L., and Begemann, H.: Atlas der Klinischen Hämatologie und Cytologie. Springer, 1955.)

Plate 4–22. Multiple myeloma, marrow. The cells resemble plasma cells, but there are pronounced differences. The perinuclear zone in some and the paranuclear *hof* in the others are prominently present in most cells. Multinucleated cells are common. The nucleus:cytoplasm ratio is strongly in favor of the nuclei. Nucleoli are present in most cells. The cells are more pleomorphic than are usual plasma cells. The name myeloma cells is appropriate. (Plate from Heilmeyer, L., and Begemann, H.: Atlas der Klinischen Hämatologie und Cytologie. Springer, 1955.)

Fowl leukemia can be transmitted by filtrate; therefore, it is thought to be caused by a virus. It has certain features of a neoplasm.

In man leukemia is not transmissible, not even by blood transfusions.

ACUTE LEUKEMIAS

General. The onset of the disease is sudden and differs strikingly from the insidious onset of chronic leukemia. The disease resembles an acute infectious or even a septic condition. Other changes include fever, rapidly developing anemia, and signs of granulocytic insufficiency with ulcerations of mucous membranes, especially of the mouth and throat, and purpura. Enlargement of lymph nodes, spleen, and liver is not very pronounced. Rheumatoid pains, sometimes resembling acute rheumatic fever, are frequent. Marked prostration and general malaise may be present. The course is rapidly progressive. Acute leukemia may imitate a variety of diseases. Some authors speak of fulminant leukemia when the course is extremely rapid and the patient dies in a few weeks.

Lymph node enlargement is conspicuous only in acute monocytic leukemia, especially cervical. Moderate generalized lymph node enlargement is more frequent in acute lymphocytic leukemia. In monocytic leukemia cervical lymph nodes are also tender.

The spleen is only slightly enlarged, except in acute lymphocytic leukemia when it may be moderately or even greatly enlarged.

Lesions in the mouth, with swelling, ulceration and hemorrhages in the gums, are especially frequent in monocytic leukemia but may also occur in other forms. Mucosal ulcerations may also be present in other parts of the gastrointestinal tract. Also, these lesions are more frequent in monocytic leukemia.

In addition to rheumatoid pains previously referred to, there may also be tenderness of bones and swelling and tenderness of joints. The responsible pathologic lesion: subperiosteal leukemic infiltrations.

Blood Findings. Anemia is present almost without exception—certainly in any case with fully developed clinical manifestations. It is usually normocytic. Frequently young nucleated red cells are present. Thrombocytopenia of moderate to marked degree is the rule with abnormally formed and excessively large platelets. Prolonged bleeding time and clot retraction time and positive tourniquet test are present. Coagulation time may be prolonged. The leukocyte count as a rule is slightly elevated but may be normal or below normal. A combination of anemia, thrombocytopenia, and leukopenia is a frequent finding in acute leukemia (see Plates 4–19, 4–21).

The frequent hemorrhagic tendency is explained by thrombocytopenia or vascular damage, sometimes caused by endothelial injury and sometimes by perivascular infiltration.

The predominant cell is an immature blast cell, most frequently a myeloblast in the adult and a lymphoblast in the child. If differentiation is not possible, the term of blast cell leukemia may be used.

Acute Granulocytic Leukemia. Cell type: myeloblast.

Cell morphology. The nucleus shows a fine reticulated structure of chromatin without condensations. There is no nuclear membrane. There are several distinct nucleoli. The cytoplasm is homogeneous without granules or with occasional azurophilic granules. More mature forms between the blast forms and mature granulocytes are absent or scarce. This gap between the immature myeloblasts and the mature segmented leukocytes is known as leukemic hiatus or gap and is characteristic of many cases of acute granulocytic leukemia.

The presence of more than an occasional myelocyte and metamyelocyte suggests an acute phase or relapse of a chronic leukemia. The same holds if a myeloblastic blood picture is present but thrombocytopenia and purpura are absent or if there is splenomegaly (Plate 4–19).

Auer bodies are characteristic: rod-shaped peroxidase-positive bodies in cytoplasm of myeloblasts. They may be present occasionally in myelocytes and monocytes.

Acute Lymphocytic Leukemia. Cell type: lymphoblast.

Cell morphology. Granular or stippled chromatin, somewhat coarser than in a myeloblast. Usually only one or two somewhat indistinct nucleoli, not so many and not so sharply outlined as in a myeloblast. The chromatin tends to be condensed at the edges suggesting a nuclear membrane. There is frequently a clear perinuclear zone. The cytoplasm is basophilic and homogeneous without granules. It is important to look carefully for granules in cytoplasm. If these are present, the possibility is that one is dealing with myeloblastic leukemia (Plate 4–21).

Some writers question the existence of

an acute lymphocytic leukemia outside of early childhood.

Acute Monocytic Leukemia. Cell type: monoblast.

Cell morphology. The nucleus has a very delicate reticular chromatin in the form of a finely meshed network and is frequently folded, indented, or coarsely and incompletely segmented. Nucleoli are less frequent and less prominent than in lymphoblasts, and still less than in myeloblasts.

The cytoplasm is basophilic with few or no granules. The outline of the cytoplasmic margin is irregular and pseudopodium-like. Phagocytes containing cellular and nuclear particles, pigment granules, and red cells are seen.

There is usually a good admixture of monocytes in various stages of maturation. In the monocytes the cytoplasm is grayish-blue, of ground glass appearance, with innumerable purplish-pink granules, which are difficult to separate from each other.

Two forms of the disease are recognized. The first is the so-called Naegeli type, which is a monocytic form of myeloblastic leukemia with numerous myeloblasts; the number of monoblasts and monocytes varies from day to day and frequently gives way to an increase of myeloblasts. The second is the so-called Schilling type, which is a true monocytic or histiomonocytic leukemia. According to Downey, in the Schilling type the monocytes are derived from the reticulo-endothelial system, and in the Naegeli type from myeloblasts.

CHRONIC LEUKEMIA

Clinical Findings. The disease may be present for a long time, even with increased white blood count and enlarged spleen and lymph nodes, before there are clinical manifestations of disease. The earliest signs of disease come from one or more of the following changes: pressure of enlarged spleen, liver, or lymph nodes; symptoms from increased metabolism; loss of weight; nervousness; perspiration; and deterioration of the nutritional state. Fever and bleeding occur late. In a patient without any signs or symptoms of disease, leukocytosis should suggest the possibility of an early leukemia.

Lymph nodes are enlarged mainly in lymphocytic and less frequently in granulocytic leukemia. In either case enlargement is only moderate, and there are no adhesions to each other or to skin. There is no tenderness and no change in the skin overlying the lymph nodes.

In the spleen, enlargement is most pronounced in chronic granulocytic leukemia. Infarcts and perisplenitis may produce clinical symptoms.

Blood in Chronic Leukemia. *Macroscopic appearance.* In advanced cases the blood is thick and sticky, and even smears are difficult to prepare. In the hematocrit tube there is a thick layer of the buffy coat. This is particularly true in chronic granulocytic leukemia in which there is also a thick layer of platelets.

Red cells. In early stages of chronic leukemia there may be no anemia but it appears sooner or later. Its intensity varies. As a rule, it is normocytic with anisocytosis; poikilocytosis is rare. Normoblasts, polychromatophilia, basophilic stippling, and reticulocytosis may be present, especially in granulocytic leukemia, even with slight or moderate anemia but not in lymphocytic leukemia.

Platelets. Early in the disease the platelet count is normal or slightly increased. Later it may be markedly increased. Increase from subnormal to normal, or a fall from excessively high to normal, is indicative of clinical improvement. A persistently low count is a poor prognostic sign.

In chronic lymphocytic leukemia, the platelet count is usually not increased and is sometimes low; if it is considerably reduced, the prognosis is poor.

White cells (Plates 4–15, 4–18). In chronic granulocytic leukemia the white cell count is greatly increased, ranging from 50,000 to 300,000 and even higher. Myeloblasts are usually few; myelocytes and metamyelocytes are numerous. Myelocytes may be increased to 50 per cent. The blood smear may be as cellular as a smear of a normal sternal marrow.

There is an increase of eosinophils and basophils, the latter 3 to 20 per cent. The number of basophils is usually higher than in any other disease.

A leukocytosis with fewer immature white cells offers a better prognosis than when the outpouring of undifferentiated cells is more pronounced. The presence of large numbers of undifferentiated white cells early in the disease is a particularly ominous prognostic indicator.

In chronic lymphocytic leukemia the white count is lower than in granulocytic and ranges from 30,000 to 100,000. The differential blood picture is monotonous. It shows mainly small lymphocytes with very little cytoplasm. The number of cells with azurophilic granules and the number of azurophilic granules in the individual cells are reduced. The nuclear chromatin is less dense than in normal lymphocytes. The cells vary only moderately in size. The nuclei, especially of the large lymphocytes, frequently show indentation.

Anemia in Leukemia. Causes: replacement of erythropoietic tissue in the marrow and excessive hemolysis of red cells. Hemosiderosis is the anatomic evidence of the hemolytic process.

Anemia is frequently more severe in lymphocytic leukemia than in granulocytic, probably due to marrow replacement. Hemolytic anemia with autoantibodies is common in chronic lymphocytic but extremely rare in chronic granulocytic leukemia. Hypoplastic anemia (myelophthisis) may develop occasionally.

Increased basal metabolic rate is frequent in chronic granulocytic and lymphocytic leukemias and in acute leukemia, usually directly proportional to the severity of the disease. Possible cause: increased protein catabolism. After irradiation it rises for a few days and then returns to normal for varying periods of time. Clinically, there is a striking difference from the changes seen in exophthalmic goiter, although there is some nervousness, tremor, and irritability. For example, there is frequently no loss of weight as in hyperthyroidism.

MICROSCOPIC TISSUE CHANGES IN CHRONIC LEUKEMIA

Granulocytic Leukemia. Infiltrations of granulocytic cells occur in various organs but are usually earliest and most pronounced in spleen, liver, and lymph nodes. They may be present in any and all tissues. The infiltrating granulocytic cells are of all grades of maturity. In the liver the infiltrations are, as a rule, more pronounced within the sinusoids in contrast to lymphocytic leukemia where they are located predominantly in periportal areas.

There are three schools of thought regarding the origin of the extramedullary myelopoietic foci in leukemia:

1. They are produced by metaplasia of multipotential mesenchyme in order to compensate for the marrow replaced or damaged by the leukemic process (compensation for marrow function) or in response to the specific leukemic stimulus (enhancement of marrow function).

2. They are implants of the leukemic blood cells (colonization).

3. They are metastases from leukemic marrow.

In some instances the extramedullary foci are not limited to granulopoiesis but contain all three elements of marrow in varying proportions and are then referred to as foci of hematopoiesis.

Extramedullary hematopoiesis is not limited to leukemia. It occurs in any condition in which marrow is encroached upon by: invasion of nonmarrow tissue (for example, metastatic carcinoma); excessive growth of tissue normally present in the marrow (for example, hyperplasia of erythroid elements in pernicious or hemolytic anemia); or hyperplasia of connective or osseous tissues, myelofibrosis or myelosclerosis. Myeloid metaplasia in the spleen may assume tremendous proportions (so-called myeloid metaplasia syndrome).

Rohr (1949) claimed that extramedullary granulopoiesis is the source of myeloblasts and myelocytes in the peripheral blood. This alone is apparently not sufficient as evidenced by aleukemic leukemias with splenomegalies. Apparently a release mechanism must be added to extramedullary myelopoiesis.

Lymphocytic Leukemia. The accumulations in various organs and tissues consist of lymphocytes. They are thought to be due to metaplasia of the mesenchyme. This explanation holds also for lymphocytic infiltrations in the marrow.

Marrow Findings (Plates 4–16, 4–17, 4–20).

Acute leukemia. Diffuse and progressive replacement of marrow and fat by undifferentiated cells takes place with thinning of trabeculae and cortex. New chemotherapeutic agents (for example, Aminopterin) have been reported to cause replacement of leukemic infiltrations by normal marrow.

Chronic granulocytic leukemia. Gross: gray or grayish red and abundant even in locations normally devoid of cellular marrow, for example, in long bones.

Microscopic: granulocytic hyperplasia. Change of E:G (erythrogranulocytic) ratio from the highest normal of 1 to 6 to about 1 to 10 and higher.

Cytology: increase of granulocytic cells of all types with an overabundance of cells at each end of the granulocytic spectrum—myeloblasts and progranulocytes at one end and band and segmented forms at the other—and depression of nucleated red cells late in the disease. Frequently there is an increase of megakaryocytes, usually with an accompanying thrombocythemia. Eosinophilic and basophilic granulocytes are frequently more numerous.

Acute granulocytic leukemia. Many myeloblasts and undifferentiated red cells.

Eosinophilic leukemia. Hyperplasia of eosinophilic granulocytes. Basophilic granulocytes may also be more numerous if the peripheral blood shows an increase.

Chronic lymphocytic leukemia. Frequently no changes. In advanced cases there is replacement by lymphocytes. An increase of lymphocytes over 50 per cent is indicative of lymphocytic leukemia.

SOURCES OF ERROR. (1) Admixture of peripheral blood may be responsible for misleading results. (2) Lymph follicles, which are present in about 10 per cent of older persons. Marrow biopsy may be more helpful.

Monocytic leukemia. Large numbers of monoblasts, promonocytes, and monocytes. Sections of marrow biopsies resemble a reticulum cell sarcoma.

SPECIAL FORMS OF LEUKEMIA

Histiocytic Leukemia (Histiocytic-monocytic Leukemia, Leukemic Reticuloendotheliosis). The predominant cell is the undifferentiated mesenchymal cell with a bluish, homogeneous, agranular cytoplasm and a round or indented nucleus. The cytoplasmic border is smooth and not indented by the adjacent red cells. Clinical findings: splenomegaly, normocytic anemia (which may be hemolytic), thrombocytopenia and purpura and frequently leukopenia. The marrow shows large numbers of reticulum cells. The lymph nodes, liver, spleen, and other viscera are similarly infiltrated. The disease is usually chronic.

Stem Cell Leukemia. This is a variety of acute leukemia in which the predominant cells are primitive undifferentiated leukocytes, which cannot be classified as one of the three blast forms. The cells are small and round, and the nuclei are round with a delicate chromatin structure, one or more nucleoli, and a narrow zone of basophilic agranular cytoplasm. There is a superficial resemblance to small lymphocytes. The course is, as a rule, that of acute or even fulminant leukemia.

Plasmocytic Leukemia. Almost always a part of multiple myeloma with corresponding marrow findings. Infiltration of various tissues with plasmocytes.

Thrombocytic (Megakaryocytic) Leukemia (Essential Thrombocythemia). Extremely rare and a doubtful entity. Most reported cases have probably been chronic granulocytic leukemia with excessive proliferation of megakaryocytes. The marrow shows hyperplasia of megakaryocytes of various grades of maturation without accompanying granulocytic hyperplasia. Some cases of the disease have been seen with extremely large numbers of platelets. At autopsy there is widespread and diffuse infiltration with megakaryocytes and immature granulocytes.

Chloroma. An acute myeloblastic leukemia with formation of tumors originating from periosteum, especially of skull, orbits, nasal sinuses, ribs, and vertebrae. These locations cause exophthalmus with disturbances of vision. Chloroma is a true cancer having destructive tendencies and forming hematogenous metastases. The sectioned surface of the tumor shows a green color owing to protoporphyrin. It fades on exposure and can be restored with hydrogen peroxide and preserved by glycerin. There are aleukemic and leukemic forms, the latter with chloroma cells in the blood. Clinically, the latter cases are identical with acute granulocytic leukemia.

Myeloblastoma. This condition differs from chloroma only by absence of pigment.

Eosinophilic Leukemia. Occurs but is extremely rare. Acute and chronic forms have been described with tissue changes similar in every way to those in other forms of leukemia, except that most of the cells in the tissues as well as in the circulating blood have been adult differentiated forms of eosinophilic granulocytes. It is difficult or impossible to differentiate this lesion from reactive hyperplastic changes, especially early in the disease. Leukocytosis and eosinophilia, no matter how high, are not sufficient to establish the diagnosis of leukemia; both can be seen in parasitic infestation. But the diagnosis can be made when there are in addition the other components that add up to the total picture of leukemia. This includes enlargement of spleen and lymph nodes, progressive anemia, thrombocytopenia, and normoblastemia.

Basophilic Leukemia. Still less frequent than eosinophilic, but both chronic and acute cases have been described. It should be kept in mind that mast cells that resemble basophilic granulocytes are present in large numbers in the skin and marrow in urticaria pigmentosa.

Neutrophilic Granulocytic Leukemia. Similar to eosinophilic and basophilic, but the cell type is the segmented granulocyte with very few immature forms.

Preclinical (Preleukemic) Leukemia. The stage of leukemia characterized by vague symptoms and occasional immature cells in the blood smears. On further observation some of these patients may show progressive development of leukemia.

Lymphocytic Sarcoma. Two main forms of this condition are recognized. One begins as a local lesion and later shows aggressive growth and metastases. This form was described by Kundrat and is known under his name. The cell type is a lymphocyte with nuclear irregularities and variations in size and shape of the whole cell and of the nucleus. It may begin in any part of the body. There are no changes in the blood until late, when anemia may be present, caused by the systemic effect of the malignant disease, by marrow replacement, or in most cases by hemolytic anemia frequently associated with autoantibodies. (For a discussion of autoantibodies, see p. 166ff.) In some cases lymphopenia develops, probably caused by widespread involvement of lymphocytogenic tissues. There are rare cases with a leukemic picture: lymphosarcoma cell leukemia (Sternberg's leukosarcoma). The sarcomatous blood cells show characteristics of cancer cells with nuclear irregularities in shape, size, and staining and with several nucleoli. The second form is systemic from the beginning but otherwise identical with the former. Lymphocytic sarcoma with leukemia is usually a phase of or the end stage in the course of lymphocytic sarcoma.

Myeloma (Plasmocytoma). Develops from plasmocellular reticulum cells, which are the cell type. Attempts to differentiate lymphocytic, myelocytic, erythroblastic, and mixed cell myelomas are not justified. There are occasional leukemic cases with varying numbers of myeloma cells in the circulating blood (see plasmocytic leukemia, p. 241).

According to Hoff (1950), at the beginning the myeloma is diffuse with generalized plasma cell proliferation in the marrow (Plate 4–22). He called this stage aleukemic or leukemic plasma cell leukemia, depending on the blood picture. In due course the neoplastic character becomes manifest in the form of what we call multiple myeloma. The latter shows characteristic metabolic changes. Bone destruction leads to calcium mobilization with increase of calcium in the serum and metastatic calcification.

Proteins in the blood are increased, especially globulin. This increase is responsible for the tendency to rouleaux formation and accelerated sedimentation rate of erythrocytes to be described. There are variants of the disease differing in the form of the globulin, which contributes mainly to the rise. They are differentiated as alpha, beta, and gamma myelomas or plasmocytomas. Electrophoresis of the serum proteins may show a characteristic finding, a so-called myeloma spot, most frequently in the gamma globulin zone and occasionally in the beta-1 or in the alpha globulin fraction. The finding of the characteristic change in electrophoretic mobility together with a pronounced elevation of serum globulin in the range of at least twice the normal is strong evidence of the presence of multiple myeloma. Another protein commonly present in multiple myeloma is macroglobulins. They precipitate from cooled serum and redissolve on warming. A simple way of detecting them is to test the erythrocyte sedimentation rate at 37° C. and at 10° C. It is extremely rapid at the higher temperature, but there is no sedimentation at the lower temperature. When cold agglutinins are present, the result is just the opposite.

The proteins are precipitated in renal tubules. Bence Jones proteinuria is present in about 50 per cent of the cases. This results in obstruction and elimination of the nephron. Progressive fibrosis, destruction of renal parenchyma, and eventually renal insufficiency are the outcome.

Plasmocytosis

Plasma cells (plasmocytes) are rare in normal peripheral blood. They are increased in a variety of chronic infections, in allergic states, in the presence of neoplasms, and whenever the serum gamma globulin is elevated. They are moderately increased in cutaneous exanthemas, infectious mononucleosis, syphilis, subacute bacterial endocarditis, sarcoidosis, and collagen diseases. Their increase is usually linked with an increase in lymphocytes, monocytes, and eosinophils. These four cells form the antigen-antibody quartet.

Marrow. Normally less than 1 per cent of plasma cells are present. An increase beyond 2 per cent is significant. Increases up to 20 per cent of plasma cells may be found in a variety of conditions other than myeloma, including metastatic carcinoma, chronic granulomatous infections, conditions linked with hypersensitivity, and following administration of cytotoxic drugs. On the other hand, they are decreased or absent in agammaglobulinemia.

Leukemoid Reactions

Definition. A blood picture that looks like leukemia but is not. Here belongs leukocytosis of 20,000 or higher with a shift to the left, or lower counts, even below normal, but with considerable numbers of immature granulocytes and similar quantitative or qualitative changes in lymphocytes. Depending on the predominant cell, leukemoid reactions may be neutrophilic, eosinophilic, lymphocytic, or monocytic.

CLASSIFICATION

Congenital. Pelger-Huet's congenital cell defect, a familial trait, involves failure of granulocytes to differentiate beyond the band stage and to form segments. It is transmitted by a non-sex-linked dominant gene. It is more common in some regions than in others (Begemann and Champagne, 1952). The differential count shows occasional myelocytes and metamyelocytes and many band forms.

Neutrophilic Leukemoid Reactions. 1. Hemoclastic crisis in hemolytic anemia. Normoblasts are commonly present in the peripheral blood.

2. Hemorrhage (WBC from 50,000 to 100,000).

3. Hodgkin's disease. Occasional counts over 100,000 with many eosinophils.

4. Various infections
   a. Tuberculosis (lymphocytic leukemoid reactions also possible).
   b. Pneumococcus, meningococcus, and streptococcus infections; gas gangrene; diphtheria; leptospirosis; malaria.
   c. Congenital syphilis (lymphocytic leukemoid reaction also possible).

5. Burns

6. Eclampsia

7. Mustard gas poisoning

8. Vascular thrombosis and infarction, e.g., mesenteric thrombosis, tissue necrosis

9. Marrow replacement by tumors including multiple myeloma and myelosclerosis (also eosinophilic, and lymphocytic leukemoid reactions possible). Normoblasts are characteristically present in the peripheral blood.

10. Myeloid metaplasia in the various myeloproliferative diseases.

Eosinophilic Leukemoid Reactions. High leukocytosis with total cell count in leukemic ranges and a high percentage of eosinophils but with few or no immature cells. Usually occurs in children and may present differential diagnostic problems. As a rule, they are not leukemias. The further course with subsidence of the eosinophilia solves the problem. A parasitic infestation is usually the cause.

Erythroblastosis. Normoblasts in peripheral blood in patients with or without anemia, frequently with a neutrophilic leukemoid blood picture. The finding of a moderate anemia with normoblasts in the peripheral blood is fairly common in metastatic carcinoma involving bone marrow.

Lymphocytic Leukemoid Reactions. These reactions occur in infectious lymphocytosis, infectious mononucleosis, pertussis, and varicella.

A leukemoid blood picture may be seen in a variety of infections for which various infectious agents are responsible. The reaction is irregular, even with the same infectious agent. The same microorganisms in the majority of cases do not produce this kind of leukemoid blood picture. Hence, the conclusion is drawn that leukemoid blood pictures are frequently determined by the host reaction.

Myeloblastic leukemia-like pictures with severe anemia, fever, and splenomegaly have been seen especially in tuberculosis with involvement of lymph nodes and spleen.

The differential diagnosis from leukemia is not always easy. Most important is the marrow examination, which is more helpful in the differentiation of lymphocytic leukemia than of granulocytic.

The increase of eosinophilic and basophilic granulocytes characteristically present in granulocytic leukemia is absent in the leukemoid blood picture. The leukemic hiatus of acute leukemia is absent.

The alkaline phosphatase cytochemical test in neutrophils is weak or negative in granulocytic leukemia and positive in nonleukemic cells (Kaplow, 1955). The reaction is particularly strong in leukemoid reactions. The values are also high in polycythemia and myeloid metaplasia.

THE TEST

1. Fixative:
   Formalin (36 to 39 per cent formaldehyde) 10 ml.
   Absolute methyl alcohol 90 ml.
   30 seconds at $0 \pm 5°$ C.
2. Substrate freshly prepared:
   Sodium alpha naphthyl acid phosphate 35 mg.
   Fast blue R.R. 35 mg.
   0.05 M propanediol buffer, pH 9.75 35 ml.

The substrate is filtered immediately before use. Incubate 10 min. Wash. Counterstain.

The result, the "score," is the value obtained from the study of 100 mature neutrophils. The cytoplasmic granules in neutrophils stain brown or black.

Unstained cells	score as 0
Cells stained diffusely	score as 1
Cells with moderate numbers of granules	score as 2
Cells with diffuse granulation	score as 3
Cells stained deeply black	score as 4

In normal controls the scores ranged from 16 to 53 with an average of 30 (Page and Culver, 1960). In leukemoid reactions, in polycythemia, and in myeloid metaplasia the scores were high and in chronic granulocytic leukemia, low or entirely absent.

Sometimes only prolonged observation may reveal the true nature of the condition, and occasionally the correct diagnosis is not made until the autopsy.

Leukopenia

Definition. A reduction of the total leukocyte count below 5000. Neutropenia is a decrease in neutrophilic granulocytes below 2000 per cu. mm.

CAUSES

Leukopenia is usually due to a drop in the number of granulocytes, because they are numerically the most frequent white blood cells (neutrophilic leukopenia). The life span of granulocytes is only a few days. Anything that interferes with the production of granulocytes rapidly brings about a leukopenia. Occasionally a lowering of the number of lymphocytes may be responsible (lymphocytic leukopenia).

Leukopenia may be transient, as seen frequently in early stages of infectious diseases and of localized severe infections. This has been explained by the depletion of the peripheral circulation of its leukocytes, which concentrate in the area of the infection. As soon as the bone marrow catches up with the production, the leukopenia is replaced by a leukocytosis (Table 4–25).

Table 4–25. Causes of Leukopenia

Toxic marrow depression
  Bacterial toxins: typhoid, paratyphoid, and brucellosis
  Viruses: influenza, measles, rubella, mumps, smallpox, dengue fever, psittacosis
  Protozoa: malaria, kala-azar
  Overwhelming infections, for example, septicemia, miliary tuberculosis
  Diseases of liver, for example, infectious hepatitis, portal cirrhosis
  Chemicals *
Metabolic marrow depression: cachexia, dietary deficiency
Cytotoxic marrow damage: nitrogen mustard, x-ray, radium, benzol
Hypersplenism (splenogenic marrow depression): splenomegaly of any type
Autoantibodies
Allergic granulocytic shift: chemicals and drugs, barbiturates
Marrow replacement: pernicious anemia, chronic hemolytic anemia, metastatic carcinoma, Gaucher's disease, aplastic anemia
Cause undetermined: for example, disseminated lupus erythematosus †; pernicious anemia, Addison's disease

---

* Neutrophilic leukopenia can be produced by amidopyrine, dinitrophenol, organic hair dyes, phenobarbital, quinacrine (Atabrine), sulfonamides, trinitrotoluene, tripelennamine hydrochloride (Pyribenzamine), neoarsphenamine, potassium arsenate, gold, aprobarbital (Alurate), thiouracil, and urethane.

Here belong drugs used in the treatment of leukemia that interfere with the growth and mitosis of leukocytes: Leukeran, Myleran, 6-mercaptopurine, triethylenemelamine, and antifolics; some of them, e.g., nitrogen mustard, produce lymphocytic leukopenia.

† In terminal stages neutrophilic leukocytosis may supplant leukopenia and is prognostically a bad omen.

Members of the Salmonella group produce a mild initial leukocytosis followed by neutropenia with relative and absolute lymphocytosis and occasionally also with monocytosis. In typhoid fever there is hyperplasia, especially of the erythropoietic and reticuloendothelial elements. Focal necrosis may also be present.

The leukopenia of measles is usually observed after the appearance of the rash. Blood counts done during the incubation period show a moderate neutrophilic leukocytosis with a shift to the left. The leukopenia persists for about a week. Plasmocytes are frequently seen in the blood smears. The thrombocytes are normal. In rubella, neutropenia and lymphopenia are present from the beginning and are followed before the end of the first week by a lymphocytosis with a relatively high number of plasmocytes (over 10 per cent).

Some bacteria, viruses, and protozoa have a direct depressing effect on the bone marrow. In overwhelming infections an effect similar to paralysis seems to be exerted on the bone marrow.

The leukopenia seen in diseases of the liver has not been explained satisfactorily. The elimination of the detoxifying function of the liver may play a part.

The same drugs that produce a depressing effect may under other circumstances, especially in smaller doses, produce a leukocytosis, and under other circumstances the effect may be directly on the circulating blood and probably of allergic nature.

The leukopenia seen in cachexia and in dietary insufficiencies probably has a metabolic basis. This is suggested by experiments in animals in which the administration of *Lactobacillus casei* factor helps to correct the leukopenia brought about by a protein-deficient diet.

The direct cytotoxic action of such agents as x-ray and radium and of chemicals, such as nitrogen mustard, benzol, and others, has been demonstrated. In acute radiation sickness an initial transient neutrophilic leukocytosis is followed during the second week by leukopenia and neutropenia.

The leukopenia of splenomegaly of various types has been attributed to hypersplenism, a hypothetical concept according to which the spleen exerts a hormonal depressing effect on the marrow leading to leukopenia, thrombocytopenia, and anemia, to any one of the three, or to any combination of the three.

Evidence has been accumulating that there are antibodies capable of clumping leukocytes of all varieties under proper experimental conditions (leukoagglutinins). The data thus far gathered permit a few general statements. The substance in the serum responsible for the agglutination of leukocytes has the characteristics of an antibody. It is present in the gamma globulin fraction. Both group-specific and non-specific leukoagglutinins have been described (Moeschlin and Schmid, 1954). In most instances leukoagglutinins were found in persons with leukopenia, which suggests that they are an autoantibody (Dausset *et al.*, 1954). Leukopenia in the newborn may be produced by leukoagglutinins coming from the mother.

The disappearance of the granulocytes during allergic reactions is thought to be due to a shift of the cells from the circulating blood to certain areas involved in the allergic reaction. Leukopenia in allergic reactions is set apart from those due to marrow depression because the leukocytes disappear very rapidly, indicating that the leukopenia is not due to a marrow depression but to a shift of the circulating granulocytes on an allergic basis.

In various conditions, such as metastatic carcinoma, the leukopenia is due to a replacement of the granulocytogenic areas of the marrow. In Gaucher's disease, in pernicious anemia, and in chronic hemolytic anemia, the proliferating cells encroach upon the granulocytic elements. In aplastic anemia the damaging agent, known or unknown, interferes with the normal granulocyte-producing capacity of the marrow.

Finally, there are leukopenias of undetermined origin. Here belong the leukopenias of lupus erythematosus disseminatus, pernicious anemia, Addison's disease, cyclic neutropenia occurring at 21-to-28-day intervals, and familial neutropenia. The diagnosis and cause of leukopenia can frequently be made by examining the marrow. One may find a hyperplastic, replaced, normal, or hypoplastic marrow. Leukemia, pernicious anemia, and various infections (for example, kala-azar and malaria) can thus be found.

Reactive Noninflammatory Monocellular Leukopathies

Here belong diseases in which one type of leukocyte is predominantly affected.

AGRANULOCYTOSIS

Synonyms. Acute granulocytopenia, malignant neutropenia, agranulocytic angina.

Clinical Findings. High fever, malaise, and ulcerative lesions, first in the pharynx and later in intestinal tract. If proper measures are not instituted, patient may succumb to a septic infection.

Laboratory Findings. Moderate to severe leukopenia as low as a few hundred cells; granulocytopenia with few or no granulocytes in the peripheral blood smear; relative lymphocytosis and monocytosis; and, as a rule, no anemia and no thrombocytopenia.

Cause. Natural or acquired hypersensitiveness to various drugs. Aminopyrine

(Pyramidon) was the first drug to have been shown to be responsible. Later a long list of drugs was shown to produce the disease, including sulfa drugs. Some patients may develop severe agranulocytosis following first administration of the drug or after a short period of administration. More frequently signs of disease appear after prolonged administration, especially after repeated courses. In such cases, there are at first mild to moderate manifestations (skin rash, fever), which warn that the drug should be discontinued. As a rule, these patients have at the same time leukopenia and granulocytopenia of varying severity. Consequently periodic leukocyte counts may be useful in recognizing approaching disease.

Pathogenesis. Drug allergy. The drug is thought to acquire antigenicity by combining with the patient's blood proteins. This results in formation of autoantibodies against leukocytes and consequently leukopenia. The role of allergic hypersensitivity is supported by observations of acute attacks following the first exposure to a drug or of a similar attack in a person who took the same drug in the past repeatedly without a reaction.

It is assumed that the drug combines with a protein in the host, which imparts to the drug antigenic properties. This autoantigen stimulates the development of autoantibodies against the leukocytes. The autoantibodies react with the autoantigen when the second dose of the chemical is given. This mechanism is similar to the one described as responsible for the allergic autoimmune hemolytic anemia (p. 179). Discontinuing the offending drug is followed by clinical and hematologic recovery.

Marrow. Several types of changes have been reported.

1. Normal cellularity is present. The granulocytes show arrest of maturation, usually at the promyelocyte level with occasional myelocytes and metamyelocytes, and no band forms or segmented granulocytes. The other marrow cells are not affected.

2. Hyperplasia of the granulocytic portion of the marrow with an arrest of maturation similar to the one described in the preceding paragraph.

3. Aplasia of the granulocytic portion of the marrow with preservation of the erythroid elements, reticulum cells, plasma cells, megakaryocytes, and lymphocytes. Islands of lymphoid tissue may be prominent.

4. Relatively insignificant changes in the normal marrow elements but an increase in reticulum and plasma cells.

5. Myeloblastic marrow similar to what is seen in acute granulocytic leukemia. Some patients of this type develop acute granulocytic leukemia. Other patients get over the myeloblastic phase and recover. This course of events is interpreted as a myeloblastic reaction complicating agranulocytosis.

Autopsy in **Rapidly Fatal Cases.** Focal necrotic lesions with microabscesses and bacterial colonies without inflammatory reactive changes around them.

Differential Diagnosis. One of the most important considerations in the differential diagnosis of agranulocytosis is the occasional case that resembles acute granulocytic leukemia. The similarity may be further accentuated by marrow changes similar to those of acute leukemia. There may also be similarity to monocytic leukemia.

The usual conception is that the lesion in agranulocytosis is limited to the granulocytogenic portion of the marrow. There are those who claim that the damage is not limited to the granulocytogenic tissue of the marrow, but because of the short life span of granulocytes it takes less time for the effect of the damage to become noticeable. It takes weeks before damage to the erythrogenic tissue becomes manifest because of the long life span of erythrocytes. Thrombocytes have a very short life span, but on the other hand megakaryocytes are highly resistant to damage. Therefore, they may produce thrombocytes for a long time before the damage advances sufficiently to interfere with their productivity.

In some cases there is a direct damaging or destructive action on granulocytes because they disappear too rapidly from the circulation; this would not be the case if the injury were only at the bone marrow level. When agranulocytosis persists, in many cases there is a drop of thrombocytes. That leads to thrombocytopenic purpura combined with agranulocytosis. Still later anemia may ensue and pancytopenia results (also known as panmyelophthisis). Then all the formed elements of the blood, red and white cells and thrombocytes, are affected. In some cases the marrow is not damaged, but on the contrary is cell-rich or even hyperplastic.

It is possible that the three conditions in which the three marrow elements are involved are not fundamentally different entities but different stages of the same disease.

There is strong evidence in favor of a constitutional factor in agranulocytosis in the form of lessened resistance of the bone marrow to damaging influences (constitutional marrow inferiority). Families have been observed in whom several members have been affected by agranulocytosis and the other conditions mentioned. The existence of dominant hereditary weakness of the granulocytogenic tissues of the marrow has been suggested.

Agranulocytosis, pancytopenia, and acute leukemias can all be caused by various agents, such as x-ray, radium, benzol, and similar substances and certain drugs as aminopyrine, arsphenamine, and sulfonamides. All these drugs have strong antitissue properties. They have antibiotic, antithyroid, antihistaminic, anticonvulsive, and various other "anti" effects. The reaction to these substances occasionally resembles allergic reactions. The three diseases cannot always be differentiated from each other by marrow changes.

THE MYELOPROLIFERATIVE SYNDROMES

Definition. The hypothesis of the myeloproliferative syndromes is based on the conception of the functional unity of the marrow, not only horizontally as it functions after birth, but vertically by including the periods which precede the participation of marrow in blood production in fetal life. The tissues involved in fetal production of blood may regain their capacity to produce blood cells in response to certain stimuli.

This concept is based on the well-known participation of megakaryocytes in the hyperplasia of chronic granulocytic leukemia and of granulocytes and megakaryocytes in polycythemia; on the frequent observation of polycythemia as a precursor of granulocytic leukemia; and on many other similar situations.

According to this concept myelofibrosis is also a part of this large group, as is extramedullary myeloid metaplasia involving the spleen, liver, and other tissues.

As our knowledge of the so-called Di Guglielmo's disease or erythroleukemia has increased, it too seems to fit well into the concept consistently and convincingly championed by Dameshek (1951, 1958) (Dameshek and Baldini, 1958).

The participation of the various cellular elements in the myeloproliferative disorders is shown in Table 4–26.

Myelofibrosis (Myelosclerosis)

Definition. Replacement of marrow by connective tissue.

Cause. Damage by radiation, chemical, or bacterial toxins. The process may also be a hyperplastic proliferation of fibroblasts with formation of connective tissue.

Clinical Course. Susceptibility to infections, especially respiratory. Chronic course.

Blood. Pancytopenia, normocytic anemia, normoblastemia.

Marrow. Aspiration results frequently in a dry tap. Biopsy shows replacement by connective tissue with foci of plasma cells, histiocytes, Ferrata cells, and mast cells.

Table 4–26. The Myeloproliferative Disorders

SYNDROMES	Myelostimulatory Factors				
	BONE MARROW				POTENTIAL BONE MARROW
	ERYTHRO-BLASTS	GRANU-LOCYTES	MEGA-KARYOCYTES	FIBROBLASTS	MYELOID METAPLASIA OF SPLEEN AND LIVER
Chronic granulocytic leukemia	±	+++	+ to +++	+	++
Polycythemia vera	+++	++	++ to +++	+ to +++	+ to +++
Idiopathic or agnogenic myeloid metaplasia of spleen	±	±	+++	+ to +++	+++
Megakaryocytic leukemia	±	±	+++	+	+ to +++
Erythroleukemia (including Di Guglielmo syndrome)	+++	+	±	±	+ to +++

Degrees of proliferation: + slight
++ moderate
+++ marked

Reproduced with the author's permission from Dameshek (1951).

In some instances progressive myelofibrosis or sclerosis is compensated by myeloid metaplasia in various organs especially spleen, liver, and lymph nodes (see next section). This may lead to a leukemoid blood picture with immature granulocytes and normoblasts. A hemolytic anemia is also frequent, sometimes of the autoimmune variety with a positive antiglobulin test. The condition may remain at this level, or it may develop into a full-fledged granulocytic leukemia.

Myeloid Metaplasia Syndrome

Definition. A syndrome of circulating immature red and white blood cells, mild anemia, hepatosplenomegaly, and extramedullary hematopoiesis.

Pathogenesis. Replacement of marrow by one of many disease processes, for example, myelosclerosis. Damage to marrow by toxic agents. Compensatory extramedullary hematopoiesis.

Symptoms and Signs. Insidious onset with weakness, vague pains, weight loss. Immature circulating red and white cells out of proportion to anemia. Marked splenomegaly, moderate hepatomegaly, and sometimes adenopathy; myeloid metaplasia in organs.

Peripheral Blood. An outpouring of immature white and red cells. The latter may show extreme aniso- and poikilocytosis and tear-shaped forms (Dameshek, 1951). Thrombocytopenia may be present and megakaryocytes may appear in the peripheral blood. The phosphatase reaction is strongly positive. The condition may develop into a granulocytic leukemia.

Marrow. Hyperplastic, hypoplastic, or normal. Functionally inadequate. Myelofibrosis or myelosclerosis.

Erythremic Myelosis (Erythroleukemia, Di Guglielmo's Disease)

This is a proliferative disorder involving the precursors of the erythrocytes. The marrow is crowded with primitive red cells, which are large and have one or more bizarre shaped nuclei with nucleoli and many mitoses. There is a hiatus between these embryonal erythroid elements at one end of the developmental scale and the mature erythrocyte at the other. This gap is similar to the one in acute leukemia. The other marrow elements are reduced. The peripheral blood shows normocytic, or in some cases macrocytic, anemia, thrombocytopenia, and a leukoerythroblastic picture with many nucleated red cells in all stages of maturation with few reticulocytes but with pronounced aniso- and poikilocytosis. Megalocytes and hypersegmented neutrophilic granulocytes are not infrequent. The autopsy findings show enlargement of spleen, liver, and lymph nodes and diffuse infiltration with the primitive erythroid cells.

Most cases of the disease show a rapid course resembling that of an acute leukemia, but occasionally the disease may take a more chronic course.

Cases have been reported in which both erythroid and granulocytic elements participated actively in the proliferation, hence, the name erythroleukemia.

Hypersplenism

Definition. A condition characterized by exaggeration of some of the normal functions of the spleen such as: phagocytosis and destruction of sequestered, overaged or abnormal blood cells; and humoral, possibly hormonal, control of certain marrow functions, specifically cytogenesis or release of marrow cells (Doan and Wright, 1946). Broadly speaking, hypersplenism may be expressed as a cytopenia involving any one or all of the formed elements of the blood.

Entities such as hereditary spherocytosis, thrombocytopenic purpura, certain instances of agranulocytosis, and others may be included in this category. Apart from the well-known entities mentioned here, the diagnosis of hypersplenism is extremely difficult and is often a matter of exclusion or clinical speculation. One expects to find in the bone marrow a compensatory hyperplasia of the element, or elements, being destroyed by splenic action. Injection of adrenalin, by producing contraction of the spleen, may increase the appearance in the peripheral blood of cells previously reduced below their normal number. This phenomenon is rejected by many observers as a valid test of hypersplenism; at best the results are irregular.

Hypersplenism is not a nosologic or gross anatomic or histiopathologic entity. Perhaps the only accepted criterion of diagnosis is the prompt and permanent restoration of normal hematocytology after removal of the spleen.

Clinical Findings. Splenomegaly of varying degrees. Occasionally the clinical syndrome may be present without demonstrable splenomegaly.

Laboratory Findings. Pancytopenia, reticulocytosis and polychromatophilia, slightly increased RBC fragility, and normal or hyperplastic marrow.

Hypersplenism may be primary (idiopathic) without demonstrable cause or the result of various diseases, all of them producing stasis in, or hyperplasia of, splenic pulp and eventually splenomegaly (secondary hypersplenism).

Here belong: portal hypertension following cirrhosis of the liver or thrombosis of the splenic vein (Banti's syndrome); congestive splenomegaly in chronic cardiac failure; rheumatoid arthritis (Felty's syndrome); chronic infectious diseases (e.g., malaria, syphilis, tuberculosis); kala-azar; Gaucher's disease and other lipid and non-lipid histiocytoses; and Hodgkin's disease. All these diseases have in common blood stasis or hyperplasia of histiocytes, monocytes, or lymphocytes.

In autoimmune acquired hemolytic anemia and idiopathic thrombocytopenic purpura, the spleen takes part in the process by producing autoantibodies, which attack the autologous antigen.

In certain chronic hypoplastic anemias the role of the spleen in the control of blood destruction is apparent from the fact that splenectomy reduces the requirement for blood transfusions.

In all these conditions anemia, leukopenia, and thrombocytopenia have been seen and have been, in some cases, relieved by splenectomy.

The L.E. (Lupus Erythematosus) Cell Test

The L.E. cell was described by Hargraves *et al.* in 1948.

Principle. A substance present in the gamma globulin fraction of the plasma or serum of patients with disseminated lupus erythematosus, the so-called L.E. factor, reacts with the nucleoprotein of white cell nuclei. It is claimed, but this has not been fully established, that the L.E. factor is an antibody. The transformed nucleoprotein acquires chemotactic properties and attracts phagocytes, usually segmented neutrophilic granulocytes and occasionally monocytes. Rarely other leukocytes may act as phagocytes. The phagocytes with the ingested nuclear material are the L.E. cells. The phenomenon for L.E. cell formation requires the presence in the serum of the L.E. factor,

damaged leukocytes, and normal active leukocytes. The L.E. factor is the agent that acts on the damaged leukocyte, the substrate, and transforms it into homogeneous round blobs. The latter acquire chemotactic properties as a consequence of the chemical transformation. The normal leukocytes ingest the transformed nuclei.

Morphology. The L.E. cell contains two nuclei. The nucleus of the phagocyte is flattened out at the periphery of the cell. Its chromatin structure is well preserved. The bulk of the cytoplasmic portion of the cell is occupied by the ingested transformed nuclear mass, the substrate or "glob." The cytoplasm forms a narrow margin at the periphery. In the fully developed L.E. cell, the normal chromatin structure of the ingested nucleus is absent and is replaced by a purplish, homogeneous, amorphous, round mass, which varies in size but is usually larger than the erythrocytes in the same preparation. A phagocyte may engulf more than one nucleus. It is possible that in some cases the multiple nuclei are segments of a granulocyte that have not yet merged. The transformation of the nucleus is a progressive process. The stages can be followed step by step. The early chemotactic action of the transforming or transformed nucleus may attract several neutrophilic granulocytes, which surround it and form a so-called "rosette." This finding is not diagnostic.

Nucleophagocytosis is a fairly common finding and is fundamentally different from the L.E. cell phenomenon. In such cases, the phagocyte is more frequently a monocyte but may be a granulocyte. The phagocytized nucleus retains the intact chromatin pattern. It may show degenerative changes, mainly pyknosis that is diffuse or appears along the margins, and nuclear vacuoles. The inclusion is frequently smaller than in a true L.E. cell. These are the so-called "tart cells" (Figs. 4–57, 4–58).

Several tests and modifications have been recommended.

TEST NO. 1 (ZIMMER AND HARGRAVES, 1952)

1. About 8 ml. of venous blood is collected in a sterile, dry, chemically clean test tube, allowed to clot, and left at room temperature for about two hours or at 37° C. for 30 minutes.

2. The clot is fragmented with several wooden applicators. What remains of the clot is removed from the bloody serum. The

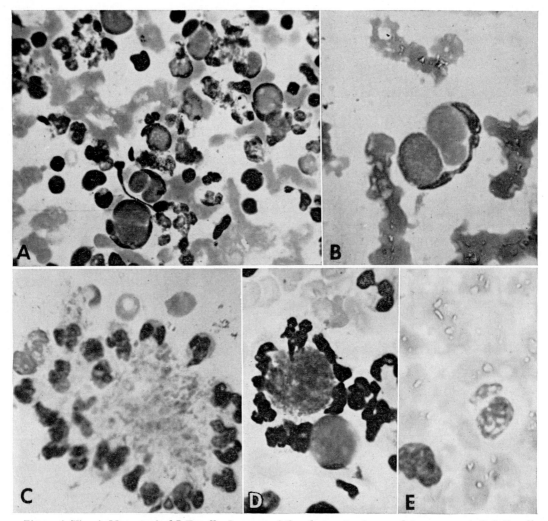

Figure 4–57.   *A.* Many typical L.E. cells. In some of the phagocytes two nuclei are present. *B.* L.E. cell. The phagocyte is embracing two nuclei. The one to the right with the more uniform structure is the more typical. A deep indentation appears along the outer periphery of the one closer to the nucleus of the segmented phagocyte. The indentation may mean that the ingested nucleus was also from a segmented granulocyte or that the phagocyte has ingested three nuclei. The nucleus to the left has still vestiges of its chromatin structure. *C.* A so-called rosette. *D.* L.E. cell and a rosette. At the bottom is a typical L.E. cell. Just above is the rosette. *E.* In the center of the field is a vague outline of a cell containing two nuclei. The one at the top is the nucleus of a segmented granulocyte. The nucleus below it is less readily identified. Both are in relatively good stages of preservation. This is an example of phagocytosis but not an L.E. cell.

serum-cell mixture remaining after the removal of the clots is centrifuged for five minutes at 2000 r.p.m.

3. Most of the supernatant serum is removed with a pipet, leaving a column of about 1 cm. This together with the visible gray buffy coat layer is transferred to several Wintrobe hematocrit tubes.

4. The tubes are centrifuged for about five minutes at 1500 to 2000 r.p.m. or until three distinct layers (plasma, buffy coat, and red cells) have formed.

5. The serum is discarded carefully with a pipet, leaving a layer of 1 or 2 mm. above the buffy coat and the buffy coat layer. The latter is transferred drop by drop to slides on which it is mixed. Smears are made and stained with Wright's stain.

6. The slide is surveyed with the low and high power of the microscope to locate areas suggestive of the presence of L.E. cells. These areas are then examined with the oil immersion objective.

In our laboratory the following modifica-

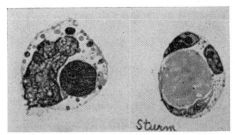

Figure 4–58. On the left is a monocyte with a phagocytized pyknotic nucleus (to be differentiated from L.E. cells). On the right is a neutrophil with a felt-like, purple staining mass in the cytoplasm. (Permission for reproduction from "The Morphology of Blood Cells," by L. W. Diggs, was obtained from Abbott Laboratories.)

tion of the method used in the preparation of smears has been found satisfactory (Mudrik).

1. From each hematocrit tube most of the serum is removed, leaving a column of serum measuring about 5 mm. above the packed cells.

2. A pipet is now inserted 2 mm. below the lower level of the serum to remove the concentrated leukocytes together with the serum (Fig. 4–59A). In this way the leukocytes are diluted mainly with serum, resulting in a mixture containing relatively few erythrocytes.

3. The serum-cell mixture from one Wintrobe tube is then placed on a slide (Fig. 4–59B). Additional preparations can be made from each of the other Wintrobe tubes.

4. A second slide is placed diagonally upon the serum-cell mixture on slide 1. (Fig. 4–59C). The mixture is allowed to spread. When fibrin is abundant, some pressure should be applied in order to separate the leukocytes from the fibrin threads. The top slide is then raised abruptly vertically from the bottom slide, but the slides should not be pulled apart horizontally. The bottom slide is held in slanting position (Fig. 4–59D). The erythrocytes and serum flow toward the edge, while the leukocytes and fibrin threads (if any) remain in the center.

5. The smaller particles are removed with the short edge of a new clean slide and are used for the preparation of the final smear as follows: The short edge of the slide to which the material adheres is placed parallel to the long edge of a second slide, pushed forward at an angle of approximately 5 degrees almost to the edge of the horizontal slide (Fig. 4–59E), and then lowered in such a manner that the

surfaces of the two slides come into complete contact (Fig. 4–59F). Finally the slides are pulled apart with the two surfaces maintaining contact until separation is completed. When preparing the smears, the smaller particles rather than the larger ones are selected in order to insure more homogeneous preparation.

With this technique we have been able to observe, in positive cases, more intact L.E. cells than with the other methods previously employed. This has been particularly true in patients with leukopenia.

The Report. The number of the characteristic cells is recorded until 1000 granulocytes have been counted. The report should make reference to this quantitative relation.

The presence of not yet fully transformed inclusions (questionable or pre- L.E. cells) and of rosettes should be noted, although they are not diagnostic. They indicate the need for examining more than 1000 leukocytes.

Phagocytosis of nuclei with preserved chromatin structure ("tart" cells) need not be reported.

This technique is one of several so-called direct methods. In indirect methods the serum comes from the patient, and the leukocytes come from another person.

TEST NO. 2 (MAGATH AND WINKLE, 1952)

1. Prepare the blood sample as for Test No. 1.

2. The clot is removed and passed through a copper wire screen of 30-mesh per inch, using the bottom of a test tube or a pestle. A special sieve and pestle are commercially available (Scientific Products Company). The effect of this procedure is twofold: the fibrin remains on the sieve, and some of the leukocytes are damaged.

3. The filtrate is transferred to several Wintrobe hematocrit tubes.

Continue with steps 4, 5, and 6 as in Test No. 1.

TEST NO. 3 (ZINKHAM AND CONLEY, 1956)

1. Ten milliliters of venous blood is placed in a tube containing three drops of a 1 per cent aqueous solution of heparin (delivered with a 21-gauge needle) and ten glass beads, 4 mm. in diameter.

2. Let stand at room temperature for 90 minutes.

3. Rotate in a Shen type rotator set at 30 r.p.m. for 30 minutes. Transfer to one or

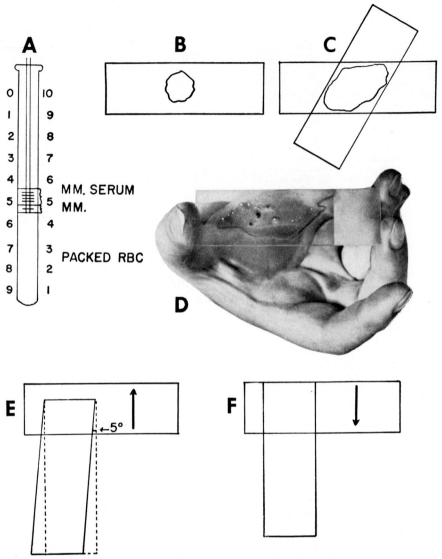

Figure 4–59. (See text for explanation.)

more Wintrobe hematocrit tubes. Continue with steps 4, 5, and 6 as in Test No. 1.

TEST NO. 4 (SLIDE TEST OF SNAPPER AND NATHAN, 1955)

This is an indirect method.

1. A substrate of leukocytes is prepared by placing a few drops of normal blood on a glass slide within a rubber ring about 0.8 cm. in diameter and 0.2 cm. high. Two such preparations are made on each slide. The slides are placed in a Petri dish, the bottom of which has been covered by moistened filter paper. After incubating at room temperature for one hour, the clot and ring are removed by pushing them off (without lifting) and the slide is washed with serum to remove the excessive free red cells. (The use of saline as a wash would distort the leukocytes.) The slides are then dried. They have been kept at room temperature as long as five weeks without losing their potency.

2. In order to test the blood of a suspected patient, a small piece of a number 2 coverslip is placed on either side of the substrate area as a pillar. Then a large drop of finger blood is put on a square, 22 mm. wide coverslip and inverted over the substrate area resting on the glass pillars.

3. The preparation is incubated at room temperature for two hours in a Petri dish, the bottom of which has been covered by a piece of moistened filter paper.

4. The coverslip is removed by pushing it off the glass slide. The substrate is washed to remove excessive red cells with either the patient's serum, if it is available, or normal serum. This step is not always necessary. Saline should not be used as a wash, because it distorts the leukocytes and causes poor staining.

5. The slides are stained with Wright's stain in the usual manner.

TEST No. 5 (CAPILLARY L.E. CELL TEST) (MUDRIK et al., 1961)

1. Collect blood from finger or ear lobe puncture in four or more 1.5 × 75 mm. heparinized capillary tubes (used in microhematocrit determination). Fill at least three-fourths of each tube.

2. Seal the red end of each tube with Critoseal, Critocaps (both used in microhematocrit determination), or children's modeling clay.

3. Centrifuge in an International Hematocrit Centrifuge (8000 × G) for one minute or in an International Clinical Centrifuge (700 × G) for five minutes. Any other horizontal centrifuge may be used, provided a rubber cushion is used to avoid the breakage of capillary tubes.

4. Insert a wire stylet into capillary tube and mix plasma and buffy coat thoroughly by rotating either the stylet or the tube 15 times. The stylet is from a 20-gauge, three-inch hypodermic needle, and its tip is slightly bent. This step is important because it brings the plasma L.E. factor and leukocytes into close contact and, at the same time, traumatizes the leukocytes, a process that has proved to be an important factor in the formation of L.E. cells.

5. Incubate tubes at room temperature for two hours or at 37° C. for 30 minutes. Prolonged incubation does not increase the yield of L.E. cells.

6. Centrifuge again as in step 3.

7. Break tubes about 2 mm. below the buffy coat level with the aid of an ampule file. The 2 mm. erythrocyte column serves to prevent the loss of buffy coat during the following operation.

8. Deliver the buffy coat layer to a glass slide with a smallpox vaccination bulb. Care should be taken that no excess plasma is delivered to the slide.

9. Make the smear by placing another slide on top of the buffy coat, compressing gently, and pulling slides away from each other at parallel planes. Our experience has shown that this procedure distributes the cells on the L.E. smears more evenly than the conventional method used in making blood smears.

10. Stain with Wright or Giemsa stain as usual.

11. If previously drawn venous blood of the patient is already available, either clotted or unclotted, the buffy coat is concentrated by means of centrifugation, transferred to capillary tubes, and treated as outlined in steps 2 to 10.

12. If only serum or plasma of the patient is available, mix one drop of either with buffy coats from two to three capillary hematocrit tubes of a normal person, incubate the mixture in a capillary tube, and proceed as outlined in steps 5 to 10. Buffy coat of bone marrow may also be used but is less satisfactory.

The two alternate methods outlined in steps 11 and 12 make it unnecessary to puncture the patient, but otherwise the regular procedure (steps 1 to 10) is preferable.

The capillary test has several advantages: (1) It does not require special equipment, such as rotating machine or sieve. (2) All reagents involved in the test come from the patient. (3) About 40 cu. mm. of patient's blood is needed. (4) It can be done in the same capillary tubes that are used for routine microhematocrit determination, and actually the hematocrit test can be done with the same specimen. (5) The plasma L.E. factor is incubated chiefly with leukocytes rather than with a mixture consisting of considerably larger numbers of erythrocytes than leukocytes, as is the case in the other tests. The erythrocytes take no part in the reaction. Therefore, reducing their number creates a more favorable medium for the leukocyte plasma reaction. (6) The incubation is performed in a minimum of space (less than 10 cu. mm.), which facilitates phagocytosis. (7) After the capillary tube is broken, practically all the formed and concentrated L.E. cells are delivered onto a small area of a glass slide.

The capillary test has been shown to be highly sensitive and specific in our laboratory.

OTHER TESTS FOR SYSTEMIC LUPUS ERYTHEMATOSUS

Complement fixation, antiglobulin consumption, passive hemagglutination, latex fixation, bentonite flocculation, tests for precipitin against DNA or p-toluene sulfonic acid, leucocyte-agglutination inhibition, and detection of nuclear antibodies by immunofluorescence technique have been reported, but none of them is suitable for clinical use as yet.

SPECIFICITY OF THE L.E. CELL TEST

The L.E. cell test is positive in most patients with disseminated lupus and in some cases of rheumatoid arthritis. It has been reported in thrombocytopenic purpura and rarely in postnecrotic cirrhosis (lupoid cirrhosis), periarteritis nodosa, scleroderma, and dermatomyositis; in sensitization to hydralazine, penicillin and tetanus antitoxin; in rheumatic fever, miliary tuberculosis, erysipelas, and chronic discoid lupus erythematosus; and in an assortment of other conditions. Recently such reports seem to be less frequent, suggesting that faulty interpretation or technique may have been responsible for some such reports in the past.

PROPERTIES OF THE L.E. FACTOR

It is stable in the frozen state and resists repeated freezing and thawing. It passes the Seitz filter. It is destroyed by heating at 65° C. for 30 minutes but resists 60° C. for 15 minutes. It is inhibited by heparin in concentrations higher than 0.75 mg. per 10 ml. and by alcohol and phenol.

It has been found also in the urine and pleural fluid and in the cord blood of children of mothers with the disease.

The L.E. factor is not limited in its activity to leukocytes. It reacts with nuclei of hepatic, splenic, and renal cells; with cancer cells; and with nuclei of cells of various animal species.

The nature of the chemical change involved in the transformation of the nucleus has been widely discussed. Various hypotheses have been suggested, such as depolymerization of DNA, alteration of the cell membrane, and others, but agreement has not been reached, except for the obvious fact that the L.E. factor reacts in some direct fashion with the nucleus.

REFERENCES

Abbe, E.: Ueber Blutkörper-Zählung. Jenaische Sitzungsber., 1879, pp. xcviii-cv.

Albritton, E. C.: Standard Values in Blood. Philadelphia, W. B. Saunders Company, 1952.

Alder, A.: Ueber konstitutionell bedingte Granula-tionsveränderungen der Leukozyten. Deutsches Arch. klin. Med., 183:372, 1939; Schweiz. med. Wchnschr., 80:1095, 1950.

Arendt, J.: The roentgenological aspect of infectious mononucleosis. Am. J. Roentgenol., 64:950–958, 1950.

Arinkin, M. J.: Intravitale Untersuchungsmethodik des Knochenmarks. Folia haemat., 38:233, 1934.

Armand-Delille, P. R., Hurst, A. R., and Sorapure, V. E.: Familial eosinophilia. Guy's Hosp. Rep., 80: 248, 1930.

Arneth, J.: Die neutrophilen weissen Blutkoerperchen bei Infektionskrankheiten. Jena, F. Fischer, 1904.

Ashby, W.: The determination of the life of the transfused blood corpuscles in man. J. Exper. Med., 29:267, 1919.

Beck, G. E., Wild, C., and Scazziga, B.: Un cas mortel de maladie de Pfeiffer. Rev. méd. Suisse Rom., 73:654, 1953.

Beck, J. S. B., and Hertz, C. S.: Standardizing Sickle Cell Method and Evidence of Sickle Cell Trait. Am. J. Clin. Path., 5:325–332, 1935.

Begemann, N. H., and Champagne, A. V. L.: Homozygous form of Pelger-Huet's nuclear anomaly in man. Acta haemat., 7:295, 1952.

Bender, C. E.: Interpretation of hematologic and serologic findings in the diagnosis of infectious mononucleosis. Ann. Int. Med., 49:852, 1958.

Berkson, J.: Some difficulties of interpretation encountered in the application of the chi-square test. J. Am. Statist. A., 33:526–536, 1938.

Berkson, J., Magath, T. B., and Hurn, M.: Laboratory standards in relation to chance fluctuations of the erythrocyte count as estimated with the hemocytometer. J. Am. Statist. A., 30:414–426, 1935.

Berkson, J., Magath, T. B., and Hurn, M.: The error of estimate of the blood cell count as made with the hemocytometer. Am. J. Physiol., 128:309–323, 1940.

Berlin, N. I., Hennessy, T. G., and Gartland, J.: Sternal marrow puncture: The dilution with peripheral blood as determined by P[32] labelled red cells. J. Lab. & Clin. Med., 36:23, 1950.

Berman, L.: A review of methods for aspiration and biopsy of bone marrow. Am. J. Clin. Path., 23:385, 1953.

Berman, L., and Axelrod, A. R.: Fat, total cell and megakaryocyte content of sections of aspirated marrow of normal persons. Am. J. Clin. Path., 20:686, 1950.

Berman, L., and Axelrod, A. R.: Aspiration of sternal bone marrow. Am. J. Clin. Path., 17:61, 551, 557, 631, 1947; 18:898, 1948; 23:385, 1953.

Berman, L., Axelrod, A. R., Goodman, H. L., and McClaughry, R. I.: So-called "lupus erythematosus inclusion phenomenon" of bone marrow and blood: Morphologic and serologic studies. Am. J. Clin. Path., 20:403–418, 1950.

Beutler, E.: The hemolytic effect of Primaquine and related compounds: A review. Blood, 14:103–139, 1959.

Bing, F. C., and Baker, R. W.: The determination of hemoglobin in minute amounts of blood by Wu's method. J. Biol. Chem., 92:589, 1931.

Block, M., Smaller, V., and Brown, J.: An adaptation of the Maximow technique for preparation of sections of hemopoietic tissues. J. Lab. & Clin. Med., 42:145, 1953.

Brecher, G., and Cronkite, E. P.: Estimation of the Number of Platelets by Phase Microscopy. In Tocantins, L. M.: The Coagulation of Blood. New York, Grune & Stratton, Inc., 1955, p. 41.

Brecher, G., Schneiderman, M., and Cronkite, E. P.: The reproducibility and constancy of the platelet count. Am. J. Clin. Path.,23:15, 1953.

Breza, J., cited by Kouba, K.: Inf. mononukleóza a jeji zriedk. komplikácie v oblasti hor. dych. ciest. Bratisl. lék. Listy, 31:313, 1951.

Brown, W. M. C., and Abbott, J. D.: The effect of a single dose of x-rays on the peripheral blood count of man. Brit. J. Haemat., 1:75, 1955.

Callender, S. T., Turnbull, A., and Wakisaki, G.: Estimation of intrinsic factor of Castle by use of radioactive vitamin B12. Brit. M. J., 1:10, 1954.

Cannan, R. K.: Proposal for the distribution of a certified standard for use in hemoglobinometry. Am. J. Clin. Path., 25:376, 1955.

Carlisle, P., and Shiffman, M. M.: Spontaneous splenic rupture in mononucleosis. California Med., 86:257, 1957.

Carson, P. E., Flanagan, C. L., Ickes, C. E., and Alving, A. S.: Enzymatic deficiency in primaquine-sensitive erythrocytes. Science, 124:484, 1956.

Cartwright, G. E.: Diagnostic Laboratory Hematology. 2nd Ed. New York, Grune & Stratton, Inc., 1958.

Cartwright, G. E., and Wintrobe, M. M.: The anemia of infection. XVII. A review. Advances Int. Med., 5:165, 1952.

Castle, W. B.: Development of knowledge concerning the gastric intrinsic factor and its relation to pernicious anemia. New England J. Med., 249:603, 1953.

Castle, W. B.: Disorders of the blood. In Sodeman, W. A. (Ed.): Pathologic Physiology: Mechanisms of Disease. 2nd Ed. Philadelphia, W. B. Saunders Company, 1956.

Cattan, R., Rey, M., and Maghsoudnia, H.: Mononucleose infectieuse icterigene. Renseignements fournis par la biologie et la ponctionbiopsie. Nouv. Rev. franç. hémat., 1:329, 1961.

Chalmers, J. N. M., and Boheimer, K.: Pure red-cell anaemia in patients with thymic tumors. Brit. M. J., 2:1514, 1954.

Chaplin, H., Crawford, H., Cutbush, M., and Mollison, P.: Post-transfusion survival of red cells stored at 20° C. Lancet, 1:852, 1954.

Chase, M. W.: The cellular transfer of cutaneous hypersensitivity to tuberculin. Proc. Soc. Exp. Biol. & Med., 59:134, 1945.

Chauffard, A., and Troisier, J.: Anémie grave avec hémolysine dans la sérum; ictère hémolysinique. Semaine méd., 28:345, 1908.

Chediak, M. D.: Nouvelle anomalie leucocytaire de caractère constitutionnel et familial. Rev. hemat., 7:362, 1952.

Chernoff, A. I., and Singer, K.: Studies on abnormal hemoglobins. IV. Persistence of fetal hemoglobin in erythrocytes of normal children. Pediatrics, 9:469, 1952.

Chernoff, A. I.: Immunologic studies of hemoglobins. I. Production of antihemoglobin sera and their immunologic characteristics. II. Quantitative precipitin test using anti-fetal hemoglobin sera. Blood, 8:399, 413, 1953.

Chernoff, A. I.: The human hemoglobins in health and disease. New England J. Med., 253:322–331, 365–374, 416–423, 1955.

Chernoff, A. I.: Human hemoglobins: Current status. Am. Pract. & Digest Treat., 9:569–581, 1958.

Chernoff, A. I., Minnich, V. M., Chongchareonsuk, S., Na-Nakorn, S., and Chernoff, R.: Clinical, hematological, and genetic studies of hemoglobin E. J. Lab. & Clin. Med., 44:780, 1954.

Chernoff, A. I., Minnich, V., and Chongchareonsuk, S.: Hemoglobin E. Hereditary abnormality of human hemoglobin. Science, 120:605, 1954.

Christensen, B., and Ottesen, J.: The age of leukocytes in the blood stream of patients with chronic lymphatic leukemia. Acta haemat., 13:289, 1955.

Clegg, J. W., and King, E. T.: Estimation of hemoglobin by alkaline hematin method. Brit. M. J., 2:329, 1942.

Comens, P.: Experimental hydralazine disease and its similarity to disseminated lupus erythematosus. J. Lab. & Clin. Med., 47:444, 1956.

Committee for Clarification of the Nomenclature of Cells and Diseases of the Blood and Blood-forming Organs: Report I. Am. J. Clin. Path., 18:443–450, 1948; Report II. Ibid., 19:56–60, 1949; Reports III, IV, and V. Ibid., 20:562–579, 1950.

Condensation of the First Two Reports of the Committee for Clarification of the Nomenclature of Cells and Diseases of the Blood and Blood-forming Organs. Blood, 4:89–96, 1949.

Cooke, W. E.: The macropolycyte. J. Lab. & Clin. Med., 19:453–462, 1934.

Couvreur, J., and Desmonts, G.: Toxoplasmose acquise et mononucléose infectieuse. Diagnostic différentiel et frequence respective. Nouv. Rev. franç. hémat., 1:345, 1961.

Crosby, W. H.: Paroxysmal nocturnal hemoglobinuria. A specific test for the disease based on the ability of thrombin to activate the hemolytic factor. Blood, 5:843, 1950.

Crosby, W. H.: The red cell and some of its problems. Ann. Rev. Med., 8:151, 1957.

Crosby, W. H.: Treatment of haemochromatosis by energetic phlebotomy. One patient's response to the letting of 55 litres of blood in 11 months. Brit. J. Haemat., 4:82, 1958.

Crosby, W. H., and Furth, F. W.: A modification of the benzidine method for measurement of hemoglobin in plasma and urine. Blood, 11:380, 1956.

Crosby, W. H., Munn, J. I., and Furth, F. W.: Standardizing a method for clinical hemoglobinometry. U.S. Armed Forces M. J., 5:693–703, 1954.

Cunningham, R. S., Sabin, F. R., Sugiyama, S., and Kindwall, J. A.: The role of the monocyte in tuberculosis. Bull. Johns Hopkins Hosp., 37:231–280, 1925.

Custer, P. R.: An Atlas of the Blood and Bone Marrow. Philadelphia, W. B. Saunders Company, 1949.

Custer, P. R., and Bernhard, W. G.: The interrelationships of Hodgkin's disease and other lymphatic tumors. Am. J. M. Sc., 216:625, 1948.

Dacie, J. V.: The presence of cold hemolysins in sera containing cold hemagglutinins. J. Path. & Bact., 62:241, 1950.

Dacie, J. V.: Hemolytic Anemias. New York, Grune & Stratton, Inc., 1954.

Dacie, J. V.: Practical Hematology. 2nd Ed. New York, Clinical Publishing Co., Inc., 1956.

Dacie, J. V.: The Haemolytic Anaemias. Congenital and Acquired. Part I. The Congenital Anemias. 2nd Ed. New York, Grune & Stratton, Inc., 1960.

Dacie, J. V., and White, J. C.: Erythropoiesis with particular reference to its study by biopsy of human bone marrow: A review. J. Clin. Path., 2:1, 1949.

Dacquisto, M. P.: Leukemia, radiation and fallout. Med. Times, 87:1407–1410, 1959.

Daland, G. A.: Color Atlas of Morphologic Hematology with a Guide to Clinical Interpretation. Cambridge, Harvard University Press, 1951.

Daland, G. A., and Castle, W. B.: A simple and rapid method for demonstrating sickling of the red blood cells; The use of reducing agents. J. Lab. & Clin. Med., 33:1082, 1948.

Dameshek, W.: A method for the simultaneous enumeration of blood platelets and reticulocytes. Arch. Int. Med., 50:579, 1932.

Dameshek, W.: Some speculations on the myeloproliferative syndromes. Blood, 6:372–375, 1951.

Dameshek, W.: Pernicious anemia, megaloblastosis and the di Guglielmo syndrome. Blood, 13:1085–1088, 1958.

Dameshek, W., and Baldini, M.: The di Guglielmo syndrome. Blood, 13:192–194, 1958.

Dameshek, W., and Henstell, H. H.: The diagnosis of polycythemia. Ann. Int. Med., 13:1360–1387, 1940.

Dameshek, W., Henstell, H. H., and Valentine, E. H.: The comparative value and limitations of the trephine and puncture methods of biopsy of the sternal bone marrow. Ann. Int. Med., 11:801, 1937.

Darrow, R. R., Nowakovsky, S., and Austin, M. H.: Specificity of fetal and of adult human hemoglobin precipitins. Arch. Path., 30:873, 1940.

Dausset, J.: Immuno-hematologie et maladies d'auto-aggression. Schweiz. med. Wchnschr., 83: 1037–1042, 1953.

Dausset, J., Nenna, A., and Brecy, H.: Leukoagglutinins. V. Leukoagglutinins in chronic idiopathic or symptomatic pancytopenia and in paroxysmal nocturnal hemoglobinuria. Blood, 9:696–720, 1954.

Davidsohn, I.: Infectious mononucleosis. Am. J. Dis. Child., 49:1222, 1935.

Davidsohn, I.: Serologic diagnosis of infectious mononucleosis. J.A.M.A., 108:289, 1937.

Davidsohn, I.: Test for infectious mononucleosis. Am. J. Clin. Path., 8:56, 1938.

Davidsohn, I.: Isoagglutinin titers in serum disease, in leukemias, in infectious mononucleosis, and after blood transfusions. Am. J. Clin. Path., 8: 179, 1938.

Davidsohn, I.: Hemochromatosis, thymoma, severe anemia and endocarditis in a woman. Ill. M. J., 80:427–432, 1941.

Davidsohn, I.: Immunohematology, a new branch of clinical pathology. Am. J. Clin. Path., 24: 1333–1349, 1954.

Davidsohn, I., and Lee, C. L.: The laboratory in the diagnosis of infectious mononucleosis. M. Clin. North America, 46:225, 1962.

Davidsohn, I., and Oyamada, A.: Specificity of auto-antibodies in hemolytic anemia. Am. J. Clin. Path., 23:101–115, 1953.

Davidsohn, I., and Spurrier, W.: Immunohematologic studies in hemolytic anemia. J.A.M.A., 154: 818–821, 1954.

Davidsohn, I., and Stern, K.: The differential test for infectious mononucleosis. Am. J. Clin. Path., 21:1101–1113, 1951.

Davis, G. E., and Sheard, C.: The spectrophotometric determination of hemoglobin. Arch. Int. Med., 40: 226, 1927.

DeMarsh, Q. B., Alt, H. L., and Windle, W. F.: Effect of depriving infant of its placental blood on blood picture during first week of life. J.A.M.A., 116:2568, 1941.

DeMarsh, Q. B., Alt, H. L., and Windle, W. F.: Factors influencing the blood picture of the newborn. Am. J. Dis. Child., 75:860, 1948.

Denst, J., and Mulligan, R. M.: The distribution of bone marrow in the human sternum. Am. J. Clin. Path., 20:610, 1950.

Dern, R. J., Weinstein, I. M., LeRoy, G. V., Talmage, D. W., and Alving, A. S.: The hemolytic effect of Primaquine. J. Lab. & Clin. Med., 43: 303, 1954; 44:171, 439, 1954; 45:30, 40, 1955.

Diggs, L. W.: The blood picture in sickle cell anemia. South. M. J., 25:615–620, 1932.

Diggs, L. W., and Pettit, V. D.: Comparison of methods used in detection of sickle-cell trait. J. Lab. & Clin. Med., 25:1106–1111, 1940.

Di Guglielmo, G.: Les maladies erythremiques. Rev. hémat., 1:355, 1946.

Diwany, M.: Sternal marrow puncture in children. Arch. Dis. Child., 15:159, 1940.

Doan, C. A.: Clinical implications of experimental hematology. Medicine, 10:323–371, 1931.

Doan, C. A., and Wiseman, B. K.: Monocyte, monocytosis and monocytic leukosis: Clinical and pathological study. Ann. Int. Med., 8:384–416, 1934.

Doan, C. A., and Wright, C. S.: Primary congenital and secondary acquired splenic panhematopenia. Blood, 1:10–26, 1946.

Donath, J., and Landsteiner, K.: Ueber paroxysmale Haemoglobinurie. München. med. Wchnschr., 51: 1590–1593, 1904.

Donohue, D. M., Motulsky, A. G., Giblett, E. R., Pirzio-Biroli, G., Viranuvatti, V., and Finch, C. A.: The use of chromium as a red-cell tag. Brit. J. Haemat., 1:249, 1955.

Donohue, W. L., and Bain, H. W.: Chediak-Higashi syndrome. A lethal familial disease with anomalous inclusions in the leukocytes and constitutional stigmata. Pediatrics, 20:416, 1957.

Dougherty, T. F., Chase, J. H., and White, M.: Demonstration of antibodies in lymphocytes. Proc. Soc. Exper. Biol. & Med., 57:295–298, 1944.

Downey, H.: Handbook of Hematology. New York, Paul B. Hoeber, Inc., 1938.

Downey, H., and McKinlay, C. A.: Acute lymphadenosis compared with acute lymphatic leukemia. Arch. Int. Med., 32:82–112, 1923.

Downey, H., and Stasney, J.: Infectious mononucleosis. Part II. Hematologic studies. J.A.M.A., 105:764–768, 1935.

Drabkin, D. L.: Standardization of hemoglobin measurement. Am. J. M. Sc., 217:710, 1949.

Dubois, E. L.: Acquired hemolytic anemia as the presenting syndrome of lupus erythematosus disseminatus. Am. J. Med., 12:197, 1952.

Dubois, E. L., and Freman, V.: A comparative evaluation of the sensitivity of the L.E. cell test performed simultaneously by different methods. Blood, 12:656–670, 1957.

Duckman, S., Merk, H., Lehmann, W., and Regan, E.: The importance of gravity in delayed ligation of the umbilical cord. Am. J. Obst. & Gynec., 66: 1214, 1953.

Duke, W. W.: The relation of blood platelets to hemorrhagic disease; Description of a method for determining the bleeding time and report of three cases of hemorrhagic disease relieved by transfusion. J.A.M.A., 14:1185–1192, 1910.

Durfey, J. Q., and Allen, J. E.: The Guillain-Barré syndrome as a manifestation of mononucleosis. New England J. Med., 254:279, 1956.

Eastham, R. D.: The erythrocyte sedimentation rate and the plasma viscosity. J. Clin. Path., 7:164, 1954.

Ebaugh, F. G., Jr., Emerson, C. P., and Ross, J. F.: The use of radioactive chromium[51] as an erythrocyte agent for the determination of red cell survival in vivo. J. Clin. Invest., 32:1260, 1953.

Edington, G. M., and Lehmann, H.: Case of sickle-cell hemoglobin C disease and survey of hemoglobin C incidence in West Africa. Tr. Roy. Soc. Trop. Med. & Hyg., 48:332, 1954.

Efrati, P., and Jonas, W.: Chediak's anomaly of leukocytes in malignant lymphoma associated with leukemic manifestations. Blood, 13:1063, 1958.

Emerson, C. P., Ham, T. H., and Castle, W. B.: The influence of resonating organic compounds on the integrity of red cells. Washington, D.C., Conference on the Preservation of the Formed Elements and of the Proteins of the Blood. American National Red Cross, 1949.

Emerson, C. P., Jr., Shen, S. C., Ham, T. H., and Castle, W. B.: The mechanism of blood destruction in congenital hemolytic jaundice. J. Clin. Invest., 26:1180, 1947.

Eyquem, A.: Les inconnues de la mononucleose infectieuse. Nouv. Rev. franç. hémat., 1:304, 1961.

Fadem, R. S., and Yalow, R.: Uniformity of cell counts in smears of bone marrow particles. Am. J. Clin. Path., 21:541, 1951.

Finch, C. A.: Methemoglobinemia and sulfhemoglobinemia. New England J. Med., 239:470–478, 1948.

Finland, M., Peterson, O. L., Allen, H. E., Samper, B. A., and Barnes, M. W.: Cold agglutinins. J. Clin. Invest., 24:451, 1945. (A series of six papers.)

Fish, M., and Barton, H. R.: Heart involvement in infectious mononucleosis. Arch. Int. Med., 101: 636, 1958.

Forkner, C. E.: Studies on living blood cells of newborn. Bull. Johns Hopkins Hosp., 45:75, 1929.

Freeman, J. A., and Samuels, M. S.: The ultrastructure of a "fibrillar formation" of leukemic human blood. Blood, 13:725, 1958.

Friberg, L., and Martensson, J.: Case of panmyelophthisis after exposure to chlorophenothane and benzene hexachloride. Arch. Indus. Hyg., 8:166, 1953.

Fruhling, L., Roger, S., and Jobard, P.: L'hematologie normale (tissues et organes hematopoietiques) de l'embryon, du foetus et du nouveau-né humains. Sang, 20:313, 1949.

Gabrio, B. W., Finch, C. A., and Huennekens, F. M.: Erythrocyte preservation: A topic in molecular biochemistry. Blood, 11:103, 1956.

Gairdner, D., Marks, J., and Roscoe, J. D.: Blood formation in infancy. II. Normal erythropoiesis. Arch. Dis. Child., 27:214, 1952.

Garrey, W. E., and Bryan, W. R.: Variations in white blood cell count. Physiol. Rev., 15:597–638, 1935.

Gelb, D., West, M., and Zimmerman, H. J.: Serum enzymes in disease. IX. Analysis of factors responsible for elevated values in infectious mononucleosis. Am. J. Med., in press.

Gerald, P. S., and Diamond, L. K.: The diagnosis of thalassemia trait by starch block electrophoresis of the hemoglobin. Blood, 13:61, 1958.

Gilmour, D., and Sykes, A. J.: Westergren and Wintrobe methods of estimating E.S.R. compared. Brit. M. J., 2:1496, 1951.

Glaister, J. J. P.: Medical Jurisprudence and Toxicology. 8th Ed. Edinburgh, E. & S. Livingstone, Ltd., 1945, p. 558.

Glass, G. B. J., Boyd, L. J., Gellin, G. A., and Stephanson, L.: Uptake of radioactive vitamin B12 by the liver in humans. Arch. Biochem., 51:251, 1954.

Godden, J. O.: "Come to the Mono. Breakfast." Nova Scotia M. Bull., 39:189, 1960.

Godman, G. C., and Deitch, A. D.: A cytochemical study of the L.E. bodies of systemic lupus erythematosus. I. Nucleic acids. II. Proteins. J. Exper. Med., 106:575, 593, 1957.

Godman, G. C., Deitch, A. D., and Klemperer, P.: The composition of the L.E. and hematoxylin bodies of systemic lupus erythematosus. Am. J. Path., 34:1, 1958.

Goldberg, S., Glynn, L. E., and Bywaters, E. G. L.: An anomaly of the sedimentation rate in rheumatic diseases. Brit. M. J., 1:202, 1952.

Goodman, L., and Gilman, A.: The Pharmacological Basis of Therapeutics. 2nd Ed. New York, The Macmillan Co., 1955.

Gould, S. E.: Trichinosis. Springfield, Illinois, Charles C Thomas, 1945.

Graham, R. M., and Rheault, M. H.: Characteristic cellular changes in cells of nonhemopoietic origin in pernicious anemia. J. Lab. & Clin. Med., 43:235, 1954.

Gram, H. C., and Nielsen, R.: Incidence of leukemia in Denmark. Ugesk. laeger, 94:437–443, 1932.

Granick, S.: The chemistry and functioning of the mammalian erythrocyte. Blood, 4:404, 1949.

Green, P., and Teal, C. F. J.: Modification of hemoglobin in order to avoid precipitation of globulins. Am. J. Clin. Path., 32:216, 1959.

Greenberg, M. S., Kass, E. H., and Castle, W. B.: Studies on the destruction of red blood cells. XII. Factors influencing the role of S hemoglobin in the pathologic physiology of sickle cell anemia and related disorders. J. Clin. Invest., 36:833, 1957.

Gregersen, M. I.: A practical method for the determination of blood volume with the dye T-1824; A survey of the present basis of the dye method and its clinical applications. J. Lab. & Clin. Med., 29:1266–1286, 1944.

Guest, G. M.: Osmometric behavior of normal human erythrocytes. Blood, 3:541, 1948.

Guest, G. M., and Brown, E. W.: Erythrocytes and hemoglobin of the blood in infancy and childhood. Am. J. Dis. Child., 93:486, 1957.

Gurney, C. W., Goldwasser, E., and Pan, C.: Studies on erythropoiesis. VI. Erythropoietin in human plasma. J. Lab. & Clin. Med., 50:534, 1957.

Haden, R. L.: A new Sahli type hemoglobinometer. J. Lab. & Clin. Med., 25:325–327, 1939.

Ham, T. H.: Studies in destruction of red blood cells. I. Chronic hemolytic anemia with paroxysmal nocturnal hemoglobinuria: An investigation of the mechanism of hemolysis, with observations on five cases. Arch. Int. Med., 64: 1271, 1939.

Ham, T. H.: A Syllabus of Laboratory Examinations in Clinical Diagnosis. Cambridge, Harvard University Press, 1951.

Ham, T. H., Gardner, F. H., and Wagley, P. F.: Studies on the metabolism of hemolytic anemia and hemoglobinuria occurring in patients with high concentrations of cold agglutinins. J. Clin. Invest., 27:538, 1948.

Ham, T. H., Shen, S. C., Fleming, E. M., and Castle, W. B.: Studies on the destruction of red blood cells. IV. Thermal injury. Blood, 3:373, 1948.

Hargraves, M. M.: Production in vitro of the L.E. cell phenomenon; Use of normal bone marrow elements and blood plasma from patients with acute disseminated lupus erythematosus. Proc. Staff Meet. Mayo Clin., 24:234, 1949.

Hargraves, M. M.: The L.E. cell phenomenon. Advances Int. Med., 6:133, 1954.

Hargraves, M. M., and Opfel, R. W.: Systemic lupus erythematosus and the blood. In Tocantins, L. M. (Ed.): Progress in Hematology. New York, Grune & Stratton, Inc., 1956, vol. 1.

Hargraves, M. M., Richmond, H., and Morton, R.: Presentation of two bone marrow elements; The "tart" cell and the "L.E." cell. Proc. Staff Meet. Mayo Clin., 23:25, 1948.

Harris, J. W.: Studies on destruction of red blood cells. VIII. Molecular orientation of sickle cell hemoglobin solutions. Proc. Soc. Exper. Biol. & Med., 75:197, 1950.

Harris, J. W., Price, J. M., Whittington, R. M., Weisman, R., Jr., and Horrigan, D. L.: Pyridoxine responsive anemia in the adult human. J. Clin. Invest., 35:709, 1956.

Haserick, J. R., and Lewis, L. A.: Blood factor in acute disseminated Lupus Erythematosus. II. Induction of specific antibodies against L.E. factor. Blood, 5:718–722, 1950.

Haserick, J. R., and Sundberg, R. D.: The bone marrow as a diagnostic aid in acute disseminated lupus erythematosus; Report on Hargraves "L.E." cell. J. Invest. Dermat., 11:209–213, 1948.

Heilmeyer, L., and Begemann, H.: Atlas der klinischen Haematologie und Cytologie. Berlin, Springer-Verlag, 1955.

Henshaw, P. S., and Hawkins, J. W.: Incidence of leukemia in physicians. J. Nat. Cancer Inst., 4: 339–346, 1944.

Herrick, J. B.: Peculiar elongated and sickle-shaped red blood corpuscles in a case of severe anemia. Arch. Int. Med., 6:517–521, 1910.

Higashi, O.: Congenital gigantism of peroxydase granules. Tohoku J. Exper. Med., 59:315, 1954.

Hoagland, R. J.: The transmission of infectious mononucleosis. Am. J. M. Sc., 229:262, 1955.

Hoff, F.: Klinische Physiologie und Pathologie. Stuttgart, Georg Thieme, 1950.

Hollingsworth, J. W.: Lifespan of fetal erythrocytes. J. Lab. & Clin. Med., 45:469–473, 1955.

Holzel, A.: Petechial enanthem of infectious mononucleosis. Lancet, 2:1054, 1954.

Huisman, T. H. J., and Prins, H. K.: Chromatographic estimation of four different kinds of human hemoglobin. J. Lab. & Clin. Med., 46:255, 1955.

Huntsman, D. B., Doggett, M. C., and Holtkamp, D. E.: Hinkleman's solution as a diluent for counting eosinophils. Am. J. Clin. Path., 31:91–92, 1959.

Israëls, M. C. G., and Wilkinson, J. F.: Achrestic Anaemia. Quart. J. Med., 5:69, 1936; 9:163, 1940.

Itano, H. A.: Third abnormal hemoglobin associated with hereditary hemolytic anemia. Proc. Nat. Acad. Sc., 37:775, 1951.

Itano, H. A.: Solubilities of naturally occurring mixtures of human hemoglobin. Arch. Biochem., 47: 148, 1953.

Itano, H. A., Bergren, W. R., and Sturgeon, P.: The abnormal human hemoglobins. Medicine, 35:121, 1956.

Itano, H. A., and Neel, J. V.: New inherited abnormality of human hemoglobin. Proc. Nat. Acad. Sc., 36:613, 1950.

Itano, H. A., and Pauling, L.: A rapid diagnostic test for sickle cell anemia. Blood, 4:66, 1949.

Ivy, A. C., Nelson, D., and Bucher, G.: The standardization of certain factors in the cutaneous "venostasis" bleeding time technique. J. Lab. & Clin. Med., 26:1812–1822, 1941.

Jackson, H., Jr., and Parker, F., Jr.: Hodgkin's Disease and Allied Disorders. New York, Oxford University Press, 1947.

Jackson, J., Jr.: The protean character of the leukemias and of the leukemoid states. New England J. Med., 220:175, 1939.

Jackson, J., Jr., Merrill, D., and Duane, M.: Agranulocytic angina associated with the menstrual cycle. New England J. Med., 210:175, 1934.

Jacobson, L. O., Marks, E. K., and Lorenz, E.: The hematological effects of ionizing radiations. Radiology, 52:371, 1949.

Jacobson, L. O., Marks, E. K., Robson, M. J., Gaston, E., and Zirkle, R. E.: The effects of spleen protection on mortality following x-irradiation. J. Lab. & Clin. Med., 34:1538, 1949; 36:40, 1950.

Jandl, J. H., Jones, A. R., and Castle, W. B.: The destruction of red cells by antibodies in man. I. Observations on the sequestration and lysis of red cells altered by immune mechanisms. J. Clin. Invest., 36:1428, 1957.

Jordan, E. P.: Standard Nomenclature of Disease. 3rd Ed. Philadelphia, The Blakiston Co., 1942, p. 1022.

Kaplan, H. S.: On the etiology and pathogenesis of the leukemias: A review. Cancer Res., 14:535–548, 1954.

Kaplow, L. S.: Histochemical procedure for localizing and evaluating leukocyte alkaline phosphatase activity in smears of blood and marrow. Blood, 10:1023, 1955.

Katayama, K.: Ueber eine neue Blutprobe bei der Kohlenoxydvergiftung. Virchows Arch. Path. Anat., 114:53–64, 1888.

Kidd, P.: Elution of an incomplete type of antibody from the erythrocytes in acquired hemolytic anemia. J. Clin. Path., 2:103, 1949.

King, E. J., Wootton, I. D. P., Donaldson, R., and Sisson, R. B.: Determination of haemoglobin. VI. Test of the M.R.C. Grey-Wedge Photometer, Lancet, 2:971–974, 1948.

Klemperer, P., Gueft, B., and Lee, S.: Nucleic acid depolymerization in systemic lupus erythematosus. J. Mt. Sinai Hosp., 16:61, 1949.

Kline, D. L., and Cliffton, E. E.: The life span of leukocytes in the human. Science, 115:9, 1952.

Klingberg, W. G., Jones, B., Allen, W. M., and Dempsey, E.: Placental parabiotic circulation of single ovum human twins. Am. J. Dis. Child., 90: 519, 1955.

Kouba, K., and Mašek, K.: Chronische Leberschaedigung bei infektiöser Mononukleose. Ztschr. ges. inn. Med. 15:244, 1960.

Kouba, K., Viklicky, J., and Sramkova, L.: Letale Fälle von infektiöser Mononukleose. Virchows Arch. Path. Anat., 334:173, 1961.

Kracke, R. R., and Parker, F. P.: The etiology of granulopenia (agranulocytosis); With particular reference to drugs containing the benzene ring. Am. J. Clin. Path., 4:453–469, 1934.

Kugel, M. A., and Rosenthal, N.: Pathologic changes occurring in polymorphonuclear leukocytes during the progress of infections. Am. J. M. Sc., 183: 657–667, 1932.

Kunkel, H. G., and Wallenius, G.: New hemoglobin in normal adult blood. Science, 122:288, 1955.

Kurnick, N. B.: The pseudo L.E. cell phenomenon, with report of a case. Blood, 12:382, 1957.

Kurnick, N. B., Pariser, S., Schwartz, L. E., Lee, S. L., and Irvine, W.: Studies on desoxyribonuclease in systemic lupus erythematosus. Nonparticipation of serum desoxyribonuclease in the "L.E. phenomenon." J. Clin. Invest., 31:1036, 1952.

Kurnick, N. B., Schwartz, L. I., Pariser, S., and Lee, S. L.: The role of DNase and a nuclease inhibitor from leukocytes in the L.E. cell phenomenon. J. Clin. Invest., 31:645, 1952.

Landsteiner, E. K., and Finch, C. A.: Hemoglobinemia accompanying transurethral resection of the prostate. New England J. Med., 237:310, 1947.

Laurell, C. B., and Nyman, M.: Studies on the serum haptoglobin level in hemoglobinemia and its influence on renal excretion of hemoglobin. Blood, 12:493, 1957.

Leake, C. D., Kohl, M., and Stebbins, G.: Diurnal variations in the blood specific gravity and erythrocyte count in healthy human adults. Am. J. Physiol., 81:493, 1927.

Lear, A. A., Harris, J. W., Castle, W. B., and Fleming, E. M.: The serum vitamin B12 concentration in pernicious anemia. J. Lab. & Clin. Med., 44:715, 1954.

Lederer, M.: A form of acute hemolytic anemia probably of infectious origin. Am. J. M. Sc., 170: 500–510, 1925.

Lederer, M.: Three additional cases of acute hemolytic (infectious) anemia. Am. J. M. Sc., 179:228–236, 1930.

Leeksma, C. H. W., and Cohen, J. A.: Determination of the life of human blood platelets using labelled di-isopropylfluorophosphate. Nature, 175: 552, 1955.

Leibowitz, S.: Infectious Mononucleosis. New York, Grune & Stratton, Inc., 1953, p. 163.

Leitner, S. J., Britton, C. J. C., and Neumark, E.: Bone Marrow Biopsy. New York, Grune & Stratton, Inc., 1949.

Leopold, P. G.: Beitrag zur Klinik der infektiösen Mononukleose. Ztschr. ges. inn. Med., 13:456, 1958.

LeRoy, G. V.: Hematology of atomic bomb casualties. Arch. Int. Med., 86:69, 1950.

Letter concerning system of nomenclature for varieties of human hemoglobin. Blood, 12:90, 1957.

Limarzi, L. R.: Evaluation of bone marrow concentration techniques. J. Lab. & Clin. Med., 32: 732, 1947.

Loge, J. P.: Spinous process puncture. A simple clinical approach for obtaining bone marrow. Blood 3:198, 1948.

MacFarlane, R. G., King, E. J., Wootton, I. D. P., and Gilchrist, M.: Determination of hemoglobin. Lancet, 1:282, 1948; 2:263, 1948.

Mackenzie, G. M.: Paroxysmal hemoglobinuria, a review. Medicine, 8:159, 1929.

Madison, F. W., and Squier, T. L.: Etiology of primary granulocytopenia (agranulocytic angina). J.A.M.A., 102:755, 1934; J. Allergy, 6:9, 1934.

Magath, T. B., Berkson, J., and Hurn, M.: Error of determination of erythrocyte count. Am. J. Clin. Path., 6:568–579, 1936.

Magath, T. B., and Winkle, V.: Technic for demonstrating "L.E." (lupus erythematosus) cells in blood. Am. J. Clin. Path., 22:586–587, 1952.

Marcolongo, F.: Anemia emolitiche acquisato. Recenti progr. med., 15:137, 1953.

Massey, F. C., Lane, L. L., and Imbriglia, J. E.: Acute infectious mononucleosis and Hodgkin's disease occurring simultaneously in the same patient. J.A.M.A., 151:994, 1953.

McKinlay, C. A.: Infectious mononucleosis. Part I. Clinical aspects. J.A.M.A., 105:761–764, 1935.

Means, J. H.: The Thyroid and Its Diseases. Philadelphia, J. B. Lippincott Company, 1948, Vol. II.

Miale, J. B.: Laboratory Medicine—Hematology. St. Louis, The C. V. Mosby Company, 1958.

Michel, H. O., and Harris, J. S.: The blood pigments. J. Lab. Clin. Med., 25:445, 1940.

Miescher, P.: The antigenic constituents of the neutrophilic leukocyte with special reference to the L.E. phenomenon. Vox Sanguinis, 2:145, 1957.

Miescher, P., and Strässle, R.: New serologic methods for the detection of the L.E. factor. Vox Sanguinis, 2:283, 1957.

Miller, E. B., Singer, K., and Dameshek, W.: Use of the daily fecal output of urobilinogen and the hemolytic index in the measurement of hemolysis. Arch. Int. Med., 70:722, 1942.

Miller, S. E.: A Textbook of Clinical Pathology. 6th Ed. Baltimore, The Williams & Wilkins Co., 1960, p. 78.

Minot, G. R., and Lee, R. I.: The blood platelets in hemophilia. Arch. Int. Med., 18:474–495, 1916.

Misao, T., and Kobayashi, Y.: Studies on infectious mononucleosis (glandular fever). I. Isolation of etiologic agent from blood, bone marrow and lymph node of patients with infectious mononucleosis by using mice. Kyushu J. M. Sc., 6:145, 1955.

Misao, T., and Kobayashi, Y.: Encyclopédie Médico-chirurgicale. 1960.

Mitus, E. J., Mednicoff, I. B., and Dameshek, W.: Alkaline phosphatase of mature neutrophils in various polycythemias. New England J. Med., 260:1131, 1959.

Moeschlin, S., and Schmid, E.: Investigation of leukocyte agglutination in serum of compatible and incompatible blood groups. Acta haemat., 11: 241–250, 1954.

Moeschlin, S., Siegenthaler, W., Gasser, C., and Hässig, A.: Immunopancytopenia associated with incomplete cold hemagglutinins in a case of primary atypical pneumonia. Blood, 9:214, 1954.

Moeschlin, S., and Wagner, K.: Agranulocytosis due to the occurrence of leukocyte-agglutinins. Acta haemat., 8:29, 1952.

Mollison, P. L.: Blood Transfusion in Clinical Medicine. 2nd Ed. Springfield, Illinois, Charles C Thomas, 1956, pp. 587.

Moloney, W. C., and Kastenbaum, M. A.: Leukemogenic effects of ionizing radiation on atomic bomb survivors in Hiroshima City. Science, 121: 308, 1955.

Moloney, W. C., and Lange, R. D.: Cytologic and biochemical studies on granulocytes in early leukemia among atomic bomb survivors. Texas Rep. Biol. & Med., 12:887, 1954.

Mudrik, P.: Personal communication.

Mudrik, P., Lee, C. L., and Davidsohn, I.: A capillary test for "L.E." cells. Am. J. Clin. Path., 35: 516–519, 1961.

Nathan, D. J., and Snapper, I.: On the interaction of dead leukocytic nuclei, L.E. factor and living leukocytes in the L.E. cell phenomenon. Blood, 13: 883–893, 1958.

Neely, F. L., Baria, W. H., Smith, C., and Stone, C. F., Jr.: Primary atypical pneumonia with high titer of cold hemagglutinins, hemolytic anemia, and false positive Donath-Landsteiner test. J. Lab. & Clin. Med., 37:382, 1951.

O'Connor, W. J., Shields, G., Kohl, S., and Sussman, M.: The occurrence of anemia of the newborn in association with the appearance of fetal hemoglobin in the maternal circulation. Am. J. Dis. Child., 93:10, 1957.

Osgood, E. E., and Ashworth, C. M.: Atlas of Hematology. San Francisco, J. W. Stacey, Inc., 1937, p. 206.

Osgood, E. E., and Seaman, A. J.: The cellular composition of normal bone marrow as obtained by sternal puncture. Physiol. Rev., 24:46, 1944.

Ottesen, J.: On the age of human white cells in peripheral blood. Acta physiol. scandinav., 32:75, 1954.

Owen, Ch. A., Jr.: The diagnostic use of radioactive isotopes. Postgrad. Med., 24:449, 669, 1958; 25: 83, 196, 1959.

Page, L. B., and Culver, P. J.: A Syllabus of Laboratory Examinations in Clinical Diagnosis: Critical Evaluation of Laboratory Procedures in the Study of the Patient. Rev. Ed. Cambridge, Mass., Harvard University Press, 1960.

Palowe, D.: The specific gravity of the blood: Its clinical significance. J. Lab. & Clin. Med., 14:811, 1929.

Paul, J. R., and Bunnell, W. W.: Presence of heterophilic antibodies in infectious mononucleosis. Am. J. M. Sc., 183:90, 1932.

Pauling, L., Itano, H. A., Singer, S. J., and Wells, I. C.: Sickle cell anemia, a molecular disease. Science, 110:543, 1949.

Pease, G. L.: Granulomatous lesions in bone marrow. Blood, 11:720, 1956.

Perry, S., Craddock, C. G., Jr., Paul, G., and Lawrence, J. S.: Lymphocyte production and turnover. Arch. Int. Med., 103:224, 1959.

Pessin, S. B.: Personal communication.

Peterson, E. T., Walford, R. L., Figueroa, W. G., and Chishom, R.: Ox cell hemolysin in infectious mononucleosis and in other diseases. Am. J. Med., 21:193, 1956.

Pfeiffer, E.: Drüsenfieber, Jahrb. Kinderh., 29:257–264, 1889.

Phillips, R. A., Van Slyke, D. D., Hamilton, P. B., Dole, V. P., Emmerson, K., and Archibald, R. M.: Measurement of specific gravities of whole blood and plasma by standard copper sulfate solutions. J. Biol. Chem., 183:305, 1950.

Pizzolato, P., and Stasney, J.: Quantitative cytologic study of multiple sternal marrow samples taken simultaneously. J. Lab. & Clin. Med., 32:741, 1947.

Pontoni, L.: Su alcuni rapporti citologici ricavati dal mielogramma. Haematologica, 17:833, 1936.

Poole, J. C. F., and Summers, G. A. C.: Correction of E.S.R. in anaemia. Experimental study based on interchange of cells and plasma between normal and anaemic subjects. Brit. M. J., 1:353, 1952.

Price-Jones, C.: The variation in the sizes of red blood cells. Brit. M. J., 2:1418–1419, 1910.

Propp, S.: An improved technic of bone marrow aspiration. Blood, 6:585, 1951.

Quick, A. J.: The diagnosis of hemophilia. Am. J. M. Sc., 201:469–474, 1941.

Raman, K.: A method of sectioning aspirated bone marrow. J. Clin. Path., 8:265, 1955.

Randolph, T. G.: Blood studies in allergy. 1. The direct counting chamber determination of eosinophils in propylene glycol aqueous stains. J. Allergy, 15:89–96, 1944.

Rath, C. E., and Finch, C. A.: Sternal marrow hemosiderin. J. Lab. & Clin. Med., 33:81, 1948.

Rebuck, J. W.: The functions of the white blood cells. Am. J. Clin. Path., 17:614, 1947.

Reddy, D. G.: A new needle for obtaining undiluted bone marrow. Am. J. Clin. Path., 22:1137, 1952.

Rees, H. M., and Ecker, E. E.: An improved method for counting blood platelets. J.A.M.A., 80:621–622, 1923.

Reimann, H. A., and de Berardinis, C. T.: Periodic (cyclic) neutropenia, an entity. Blood, 4:1109, 1949.

Reinauer, H.: Morphologische Befunde an Lymphknoten bei infektiöser Mononukleose. Virchows Arch. path. Anat., 332:56, 1959.

Rigas, D. A., Koler, R. D., and Osgood, E. E.: New hemoglobin possessing higher electrophoretic mobility than normal adult hemoglobin. Science, 121:372, 1955.

Rigas, D. A., Koler, R. D., and Osgood, E. E.: Hemoglobin H. J. Lab. & Clin. Med., 47:51, 1956.

Rohr, K.: Das menschliche Knochenmark. 2nd Ed. Stuttgart, Georg Thieme, 1949.

Roseman, D. M., and Barry, R. M.: Acute pericarditis as the first manifestation of infectious mononucleosis. Ann. Int. Med., 47:351, 1957.

Rosenthal, M. C., Pisciotta, A. V., Komminos, Z. D., Goldenberg, H., and Dameshek, W.: The Autoimmune hemolytic anemia of malignant lymphocytic disease. Blood, 10:197, 1955.

Rosenthal, N., and Sutro, C. J.: The blood picture in pneumonia; with special reference to pathological changes in the neutrophils. Am. J. Clin. Path., 3:181–197, 1933.

Ross, G. I. M.: Vitamin B_{12} assay in body fluids. Nature, 166:270, 1950.

Ross, J. F., Finch, S. C., Street, R. B., and Strieder, J. W.: The simultaneous occurrence of benign thymoma and refractory anemia. Blood, 9:935, 1954.

Rubinstein, M. A.: Aspiration of bone marrow from the iliac crest. J.A.M.A., 137:1281, 1948.

Rudolph, A. M., Nadas, A. S., and Borges, W. H.: Hematologic adjustments to cyanotic congenital heart disease. Pediatrics, 11:454, 1953.

Sabin, F. R.: Studies of living human blood cells. Bull. Johns Hopkins Hosp., 34:277–288, 1923.

Sabin, F. R., Austrian, C. R., Cunningham, R. S., and Doan, C. A.: Studies on the maturation of myeloblasts into myelocytes and on amitotic cell division in the peripheral blood in subacute myeloblastic leucemia. J. Exper. Med., 40:845–871, 1924.

Sabin, F. R., Cunningham, R. S., Doan, C. A., and Kindwall, J. A.: The normal rhythm of the white blood cells. Bull. Johns Hopkins Hosp., 37:14–67, 1925.

Sacks, M. S.: Erythropoietin. Ann. Int. Med., 48:207, 1958.

Sandoz: Atlas of Hematology. Basle, Switzerland, Sandoz Ltd. 1952. (May be purchased from Sandoz Blood Atlas, 68 Charlton St., New York 14, N.Y.)

Sanford, A. H., and Magath, T. B.: A new centrifuge tube for volume index determinations (modified Haden method). J. Lab. & Clin. Med., 15:172–173, 1929.

Sanford, A. H., and Sheard, C.: The determination of hemoglobin with the photoelectrometer. J. Lab. & Clin. Med., 15:483–489, 1930.

Schilling, R. F.: The effect of gastric juice on the urinary excretion of radio-activity after the oral administration of radioactive Vitamin B_{12}. J. Lab. & Clin. Med., 42:860, 1953; 45:926, 1955.

Schilling, V.: Das Hämogramm in der Poliklinik. I. Biologische Kurven der Leukocytenbewegung als Grundlage der praktischen Bewertung einmaliger Blutuntersuchungen. Ztschr. klin. Med., 99:232–247, 1924.

Schilling, V.: The Blood Picture and Its Clinical Significance (Including Tropical Diseases); A Guidebook on the Microscopy of Blood. (Translated by R. B. H. Gradwohl). Eds. 7 and 8. St. Louis, The C. V. Mosby Company, 1929.

Schleicher, E. M.: The origin and nature of the Cabot ring bodies of erythrocytes. J. Lab. & Clin. Med., 27:983–1000, 1942.

Schleicher, E. M.: Staining aspirated human bone marrow with domestic Wright stain. Stain Technol., 17:161–164, 1942.

Schleicher, E. M.: Isolation of particles from aspirated sternal marrow for biopsy. Am. J. Clin. Path., 17:909, 1947.

Schleicher, E. M.: A new apparatus for isolation and preparation of aspirated bone marrow particles. Am. J. Clin. Path., 20:476, 1950.

Schleicher, E. M.: An improved hematoxylin-eosin stain for sections of marrow units. Stain Technol., 28:119, 1953.

Schodt, E.: Observations on blood regeneration in man. III. The rise in reticulocytes in patients with hematemesis or melana from peptic ulcer. Am. J. M. Sc., 196:632, 1938.

Schwartz, H. C., and Spaet, T. H.: Hemoglobin G: Fifth abnormal hemoglobin. Clin. Res. Proc., 3:51, 1955.

Schwartz, H. C., Spaet, T. H., Zuelzer, W. W., Neel, J. V., Robinson, A. R., and Kaufman, S. F.: Combinations of hemoglobin G, hemoglobin S and thalassemia occurring in one family. Blood, 12: 238, 1957.

Scriver, J. B., and Waugh, T. R.: Studies on a case of sickle-cell anaemia. Canad. M. A. J., 23:375–380, 1930.

Seip, M.: The reticulocyte level and the erythrocyte production judged from reticulocyte studies in newborn infants during the first week of life. Acta paediat., 44:355, 1955.

Seligson, D. (Ed.): Standard Methods of Clinical Chemistry. Vol. II. Hemoglobin., New York, Academic Press, 1958, pp. 49–60.

Selwyn, J. G., and Dacie, J. V.: Autohemolysis and other changes resulting from the incubation in vitro of red cells from patients with congenital hemolytic anemia. Blood, 9:414, 1954.

Selye, H.: Stress. 2nd Ed. Montreal, Acta Inc., 1950.

Shackman, N. H., Swiller, A. I., and Morrison, M.: Syndrome simulating acute disseminated lupus erythematosus. Appearance after hydralazine (Apresoline) therapy. J.A.M.A., 155:1492–1494, 1954.

Shay, H., Gruenstein, M., and Glaser, L.: Uniform transfer to random bred rats of lymphatic leukemia induced by gastric instillation of methylcholanthrene. Proc. Soc. Exper. Biol. & Med., 75: 753–754, 1950.

Sheard, C., and Sanford, A. H.: A photo-electric hemoglobinometer; Clinical applications of the principles of photo-electric photometry to the measurement of hemoglobin. J. Lab. & Clin. Med., 14:558–574, 1929.

Siim, J. C.: Clinical and Diagnostic Aspects of Human Acquired Toxoplasmosis. Human Toxoplasmosis. Copenhagen, Einar Munksgaard Forlag, 1960, pp. 53–79.

Silberstein, J. K., Bernstein, T. C., and Stern, T.: Demonstration of heterophile antibodies in the cerebrospinal fluid from patients with infectious mononucleosis. J. Lab. & Clin. Med., 33:1204, 1948.

Singer, K., Chernoff, A. I., and Singer, L.: Studies on abnormal hemoglobins. I. Their demonstration in sickle cell anemia and other hematologic disorders by means of alkali denaturation. Blood, 6: 413, 1951.

Singer, K., Josephson, A. M., Singer, L., Heller, P., and Zimmerman, H. J.: Studies in abnormal hemoglobins. XIII. Hemoglobin S-thalassemia disease and hemoglobin C-thalassemia disease in siblings. Blood, 12:593, 1957.

Singer, K., Motulsky, A. G., and Wile, S. A.: Aplastic crisis in sickle cell anemia: Study of its mechanism and its relationship to other types of hemolytic crisis. J. Lab. & Clin. Med., 35:721, 1950.

Sloan, A. W.: The normal platelet count in man. J. Clin. Path., 4:37, 1951.

Smiley, R. K., Cartwright, G. E., and Wintrobe, M. M.: Fatal aplastic anemia following chloramphenicol (Chloromycetin) administration. J.A.M.A., 149:914, 1952.

Smith, C. A.: The Physiology of the Newborn Infant. 3rd Ed. Springfield, Illinois, Charles C Thomas, 1959, pp. 160–161.

Smith, C. H.: Infectious lymphocytosis. Am. J. Dis. Child., 62:231–261, 1941.

Smith, E. B., and Custer, R. P.: Rupture of the spleen in infectious mononucleosis. Blood, 1:317, 1946.

Smith, E. W., and Conley, C. L.: Filter paper electrophoresis of human hemoglobins with special reference to the incidence and clinical significance of hemoglobin C. Bull. Johns Hopkins Hosp., 93: 94, 1953.

Smith, R. P., Jones, C. W., and Cochran, W. E.: Ferrous sulfate toxicity. Report of a fatal case. New England J. Med., 243:641, 1950.

Snapper, I., and Nathan, D. J.: The mechanics of the L.E. cell phenomenon studied with a simplified test. Blood, 10:718–729, 1955.

Sobel, H. J., and Simons, R. B.: False positive spinal fluid Kahn test in infectious mononucleosis. U.S. Armed Forces M. J., 10:855, 1959.

Sollmann, T. H.: Manual of Pharmacology. 7th Ed. Philadelphia, W. B. Saunders Company, 1948, p. 713.

Sondern, F. E.: The value of the differential leukocyte count in diagnosis. Am. J. M. Sc., 132:889–891, 1906.

Stevenson, G. F., Smetters, G. W., and Cooper, J. A. D.: A gravimetric method for the calibration of hemoglobin micropipets. Am. J. Clin. Path., 21: 489–491, 1951.

Stohlman, F., Jr., and Brecher, G.: Humoral regulations of erythropoiesis. III. Effect of exposure to simulated altitude. J. Lab. & Clin. Med., 49:890, 1957.

Student: On the error of counting with a haemacytometer. Biometrika, 6:351–360, 1907.

Sundberg, R. D.: Sternal aspiration. Staff Meet. Bull. Hosp. Univ. Minnesota, 17 (26):389, 1946.

Sundberg, R. D., and Lick, N. B.: "L.E." cells in the blood in acute disseminated lupus erythematosus. J. Invest. Dermat. 12:83, 1949.

Sunderman, F. W., Copeland, B. E., MacFate, R. P., Mortens, V. E., Neumann, H. N., and Stevenson, G. F.: Hemoglobin standardizations. A commentary on procedures to insure reliable hemoglobinometry. Am. J. Clin. Path., 25:489–493, 1955.

Sunderman, F. W., MacFate, R. P., MacFadyen, D. A., Stevenson, G. F., and Copeland, B. E.: Symposium on clinical hemoglobinometry. Am. J. Clin. Path., 23:519–598, 1953.

Thompson, J. S.: An in vivo study of antileukemic serum. Blood, 10:1228, 1955.

Thomsen, O.: A method for direct count of the blood plates in the blood. Acta. med. scandinav., 53: 507–516, 1920–1921.

Thorell, B.: Studies on the formation of cellular substances during blood cell production. Acta. med. scandinav. Supp. 200, 1947.

Thorn, G. W., Forsham, P. H., Prunty, F. T. G., and Hills, A. G.: The response to pituitary adrenocorticotropic hormone as a test for adrenal cortical insufficiency. J.A.M.A., 137:1005–1009, 1948.

Timmes, J. J., Averill, H. H., and Metcalfe, J.: Splenic rupture in infectious mononucleosis. New England J. Med., 329:173, 1948.

Tocantins, L. M.: The mammalian blood platelet in health and disease. Medicine, 17:175, 1938.

Toporek, M., Bishop, R. C., Nelson, N. A., and Bethell, F. H.: Urinary excretion of Co^{60} vitamin B_{12} as a test for effectiveness of intrinsic factor preparations. J. Lab. & Clin. Med., 46:665, 1955.

Türkel, H., and Bethell, F. H.: Biopsy of bone marrow performed by a new and simple instrument. J. Lab. & Clin. Med., 28:1246, 1943.

Turnbull, E. P. N., and Walker, J.: Haemoglobin and red cells in the human foetus. II. The red cells. Arch. Dis. Childhood, 30:102, 1955.

Tuttle, A. H.: The human hemoglobins. J. Chronic Dis., 6:528–551, 1957.

Valentine, W. N.: The biochemistry and enzymatic activities of leukocytes in health and disease. In Progress in Hematology (L. M. Tocantins, Ed.): New York, Grune & Stratton, Inc., 1956, Vol. 1.

Valentine, W. N., and Beck, W. S.: Biochemical studies on leukocytes. I. Phosphatase activity in health, leukocytosis, and myelocytic leukemia. J. Lab. & Clin. Med., 38:39, 1951.

Valentine, W. N., and Beck, W. S.: Biochemical studies on leukocytes. Phosphatase activity in chronic lymphatic leukemia, acute leukemia and miscellaneous hematologic conditions. J. Lab. & Clin. Med., 38:245, 1951.

Valentine, W. N., and Neel, J. V.: Hematologic and genetic study of transmission of thalassemia (Cooley's anemia: Mediterranean anemia). Arch. Int. Med., 74:185, 1944.

Van Loghem, J. J., and Van der Hart, M.: Varieties of specific auto antibodies in acquired hemolytic anemia (II). Vox Sanguinis, 4:129, 1954.

Van Slyke, D. D.: Gasometric determination of the oxygen and hemoglobin of blood. J. Biol. Chem., 33:127–132, 1918.

Van Slyke, D. D., and Stadie, W. C.: Determination of gases of blood. J. Biol. Chem., 49:1, 1921.

Vaughan, S. L., and Brockmyre, F.: Normal bone marrow as obtained by sternal puncture. Blood, Special Issue No. 1, pp. 54, 1947.

Vejlens, G.: The distribution of leukocytes in the vascular system. Acta. path. et microbiol. scandinav., Suppl., 33:1, 1938.

Von Körber, E.: Über Differenzen des Blutfarbstoffes. Inaugural Dissertation. Dorpat., 1866. Cited by Bischoff, H.: Ztschr. ges. exper. Med., 48:472, 1926.

Waitman, W. B.: Effect of room temperature on sedimentation rate of red blood cells of man. Am. J. M. Sc., 212:207, 1946.

Waldenström, J.: Incipient myelomatosis or essential hyperglobulinemia with fibrinogenopenia—a new syndrome? Acta med. scandinav., 117:216, 1944.

Waldenström, J., and Kjellberg, S. R.: The roentgenological diagnosis of sideropenic dysphagia (Plummer-Vinson's syndrome). Acta radiol., 20:618, 1939.

Walsh, J. R., and Zimmerman, H. J.: The demonstration of the "L.E." phenomenon in patients with penicillin hypersensitivity. Blood, 8:65–71, 1953.

Warren, S., and Bowers, J. Z.: The acute radiation syndrome in man. Ann. Int. Med., 32:207, 1950.

Wasserman, L. R., Stats, D., Schwartz, L., and Fudenberg, H.: Symptomatic and hemopathic hemolytic anemia. Am. J. Med., 18:961, 1955.

Wegelin, C.: Schilddrüse, in Drüsen mit innerer Sekretion. Vol. 8, Handbuch der speziellen pathologischen Anatomie und Histologie (F. Henke and O. Lubarsch, Eds.) Berlin. Springer-Verlag, 1926.

Weinbaum, J. G., and Thompson, R. F.: Erythroblastic hypoplasia associated with thymic tumor and myasthenia gravis. Am. J. Clin. Path., 25:761, 1955.

Weiner, W.: Eluting red-cell antibodies: A method and its application. Brit. J. Haemat., 3:276, 1957.

Weiner, W., Battey, D. A., Cleghorn, T. E., Marson, F. G. W., and Meynell, M. J.: Serological findings in a case of hemolytic anemia. Brit. M. J., 2:125, 1953.

Wells, I. C., and Itano, H. A.: Ratio of sickle cell anemia hemoglobin to normal hemoglobin in sicklemics. J. Biol. Chem., 188:65, 1951.

Westergren, A.: Studies of the suspension stability of the blood in pulmonary tuberculosis. Acta. med. scandinav., 54:247–282, 1921.

Widal, F., Abrami, P., and Brulé, M.: Auto-agglutination des hématies dans l'ictère hémolytique acquise. Compt. rend. Soc. biol., 64:655–657, 1908.

Williamson, C. S.: Influence of age and sex on hemoglobin. Arch. Int. Med., 85:505, 1916.

Wintrobe, M. M.: The volume and hemoglobin content of the red blood corpuscle; Simple method for calculation, normal findings, and value of such calculations in anemias. Am. J. M. Sc., 177:513–523, 1929.

Wintrobe, M. M.: The size and hemoglobin content of the erythrocyte; Methods of determination and clinical application. J. Lab. & Clin. Med., 17:899–912, 1932.

Wintrobe, M. M.: Clinical hematology. 5th Ed. Philadelphia, Lea & Febiger, 1961.

Wintrobe, M. M., and Landsberg, J. W.: A standardized technique for the blood sedimentation test. Am. J. M. Sc., 189:102–115, 1935.

Wöllner, D.: Ueber die serologische Diagnose der infektiösen Mononukleose nach Paul-Bunnell mit nativen und fermentierten Hammelerythrozyten. Ztschr. Immunitätsforsch., 112:290, 1955.

Wöllner, D.: Differenzierungsmethoden zur serologischen Diagnose der infektiösen Mononukleose. II. Die Differentialagglutination mit nativen und papainisierten Hammelerythrozyten nach Absorption mit Meerschweinchennierenzellen und papainisiertem Hammelblut. Ztschr. Immunitätsforsch., 113:301, 1956.

Wright, J. H.: The histogenesis of the blood platelets. J. Morphol. 21:263, 1910.

Wróblewski, F.: Advances in Clinical Chemistry (H. Sobotka and C. P. Stewart, Eds.). New York, Academic Press, Inc., 1958, p. 335.

Zimmer, F. E., and Hargraves, M. M.: The effect of blood coagulation on lupus erythematosus cell phenomenon. Proc. Staff Meet. Mayo Clin., 27:424–430, 1952.

Zimmerman, H. J., Walsh, J. R., and Heller, P.: Production of nucleophagocytosis by rabbit antileukocytic serum. Blood, 8:651, 1953.

Zinkham, W. H., and Conley, C. L.: Some factors influencing the formation of L.E. cells. Bull. Johns Hopkins Hosp., 98:102–119, 1956.

Zuelzer, W. W., Neel, J. V., and Robinson, A. R.: Abnormal hemoglobins. In Tocantins: Progress in Hematology, Vol. 1, pp. 91–137. New York, Grune & Stratton, Inc., 1956.

Chapter 5

Blood Groups and Their Application

By KURT STERN, M.D.

IMMUNOHEMATOLOGY OF RED CELLS

Red cell antigens are chemical structures imparting specific properties to the surface of the red cell and are at present detectable only by the reactivity of red cells with antibodies corresponding to the antigens (homologous antibodies). Most of these antigen-antibody reactions involve clumping or *agglutination* of the red cells. Therefore, the antibodies are called *hemagglutinins* and the antigens, *hemagglutinogens*.

Isoagglutinogens and *isoagglutinins* are the antigens and antibodies, respectively, which differentiate red cells of some individuals from those of others belonging to the same species. *Heteroagglutinins* are antibodies that react with red cell antigens of different species. With few exceptions clinical immunohematology deals with isoagglutinogens and isoagglutinins. It is customary to differentiate between "natural" and "immune" agglutinins, the former term applying to agglutinins occurring without any known cause, such as transfusion or injection of blood or other antigenic substances eliciting antibody formation. On the other hand immune isoagglutinins result from deliberate or unintentional immunization (*isosensitization*), such as may occur from injection or transfusion of blood or from the entry of fetal red cells into the maternal circulation. In addition to agglutination some hemoantibodies may also hemolyze red cells: *hemolysins (isohemolysins)*. Hemolysins are most fre-quently the result of immunization and are much rarer than isoagglutinins.

From the preceding remarks it can be concluded that, in addition to morphologic variations of red cells in health and especially in disease, and in addition to chemical differences in red cell structure dependent on the presence of variants of hemoglobin, immunohematologic ("serologic") characteristics predicated on the presence or absence of surface chemical properties of red cells permit their differentiation and classification into a large number of well-defined blood groups as defined by their reactions with specific hemagglutinins. These characteristics of red cells are called blood factors. They possess three important properties: they are detectable on the basis of specific reactivity with corresponding antibodies producing agglutination or lysis; they are inherited according to Mendelian laws; and they appear at certain stages of fetal development and are fully formed either at birth or in early postnatal development and persist throughout life.

At present 11 independent and well-defined blood group systems are known. They are made up of at least 45 identifiable blood factors, in addition to which more than a dozen other factors have been described without being assigned to any system. If red cells were to be tested for the presence of all these factors, several million different phenotypes could be differentiated (Race and Sanger, 1958). This imparts to blood from different persons an individuality suggesting that some time in

263

Table 5–1. The Blood Group Systems

BLOOD GROUP SYSTEM	ORIGINAL DISCOVERY	
	YEAR	AUTHORS
ABO	1900	Landsteiner
MNS	1927	Landsteiner and Levine
P	1927	Landsteiner and Levine
Rh-Hr	1937	Landsteiner and Wiener
Kell	1946	Coombs, Mourant, and Race
Lewis	1946	Mourant
Lutheran	1946	Callender and Race
Duffy	1950	Cutbush, Mollison, and Parker
Kidd	1951	Allen, Diamond, and Niedziela
Diego	1954	Levine, Koch, McGee, and Hill
Js	1957	Giblett
Unclassified factors with very high or very low frequency	1952–1961	Several workers

the not too distant future each person's blood may be identifiable by its blood factors.

As can be seen from Table 5–1, immunologic definition of red blood cells has advanced especially rapidly during the last 15 years. This has been due to a large extent to development of new sensitive and specific techniques for demonstration of antigen-antibody reactions. Some of the factors responsible for the continuing progress in this branch of immunohematology are the increased use of blood transfusions, the relative ease in procuring material for study, and the fact that results of this work have not only proved of great clinical value but also have contributed to our knowledge in such basic sciences as immunology, genetics, and anthropology.

Theory of Blood Group Systems

1. The ABO System. It is no coincidence that the ABO system was the first to be discovered. This is the only blood group system in which plasma and serum regularly contain agglutinins reacting with blood factors present in the red cells of other persons. Such random interactions of serums and red cell suspensions actually were the method by means of which Landsteiner demonstrated the presence of ABO blood groups. In addition to the "natural" occurrence of the isoagglutinins two other factors aided the detection of isoagglutination in the ABO system: it

occurs over a wide thermal range including so-called room temperature (20 to 25 C.), and isoagglutinins responsible for agglutination in the ABO system are of the so-called complete type, which means that attachment of the antibody to the red cell possessing the homologous blood factor is followed automatically by agglutination.

In his first reports Landsteiner differentiated three types of blood: one class was not clumped by the serum of any other person, and because of this apparent absence of agglutinogens this group was designated by the numeral "0," which later was converted into the letter "O." A second group of blood specimens was agglutinated by serums of other persons and was designated as group A. The red cells of the persons whose serums agglutinated group A red cells in turn were agglutinated by the serums of persons of group A, and blood having this isoagglutinogen was called group B. A few years later a fourth, rare type of blood was discovered, the red cells of which were agglutinated both by isoagglutinins anti-A and anti-B and which therefore was called group AB. The preferable terms for designation of isoagglutinins are anti-A and anti-B, as shown by their reactivity, instead of older terms, such as those using Greek letters (α, alpha, and β, beta) or a and b. It is fortunate indeed that international agreement has provided for acceptance of a uniform (Landsteiner or international) nomenclature according to which we differentiate four groups: O, A, B, and AB. This has eliminated the use of numerical nomenclatures previously proposed that were arbitrary and much more subject to clerical errors and confusion.

Table 5–2 shows the distribution of isoagglutinogens and isoagglutinins in the ABO system. It is apparent that two "laws" can be easily formulated: the serum of a person does not contain isoagglutinins capable of agglutinating his own red cells, and the serum of a person does contain the

Table 5–2. Isoagglutinogens and Isoagglutinins in the ABO System

BLOOD GROUP	ISOAGGLUTINOGEN(S) IN RED CELLS	ISOAGGLUTININ(S) IN PLASMA OR SERUM	APPROX. FREQUENCY IN U.S. CAUCASOIDS PER CENT
O	None	anti-A, anti-B	45
A	A	anti-B	41
B	B	anti-A	10
AB	A, B	none	4

isoagglutinin(s) that react with the iso-agglutinogen(s) absent from his red cells.

There are considerable variations in the reactivity of the blood factors. For example, a serum containing anti-B, when tested against a series of specimens of group B, may produce agglutinations differing considerably in strength from one specimen to the next. Technical factors, which also affect rapidity, intensity, and titer of agglutination, will be dealt with later.

Subgroups of A. In addition to the variable agglutinability of all blood factors certain blood specimens of group A and AB are consistently less agglutinable than others.

It was shown by means of absorption tests that certain weakly agglutinable cells of group A are not able to absorb completely anti-A, whereas complete absorption is accomplished by using comparable quantities of red cells with strong agglutinability. These observations have been generally accepted as proof of a qualitative difference between the A blood factor in strongly and weakly agglutinable red cells. The majority of group A cells belong to subgroup A_1 (strongly agglutinable), whereas the weakly agglutinable specimens are designated as subgroup A_2. Similarly red cells of group AB are subdivided into subgroups A_1B and A_2B. Table 5–3 lists the relative incidence of subgroups of A including rarer subgroups designated as A_3, A_4, A_o, and A_m.

The main importance of the subgroups of A lies in the lesser agglutinability of A_2 and A_2B, for example, which may lead to mistakes unless suitable techniques are used. A further complicating factor is represented by the presence of isoagglutinins in a small percentage of blood specimens that react within the group A specifically with red cells of other subgroups: e.g., the serum of a person of subgroup A_2 or A_2B may have anti-A_1, agglutinating A_1 and A_1B cells. In contrast to anti-A and anti-B, which are present regularly according to Landsteiner's laws (see Table 5–2), these antibodies are found only infrequently and

Table 5–3. **Subgroups of A and AB**

GROUP	SUBGROUP	APPROXIMATE FREQUENCY OF SUBGROUP (PER CENT OF GROUP) IN U. S. CAUCASOIDS	ANTI-A (SERUM OF GROUP B)	ANTI-A₁ (ABSORBED SERUM OF GROUP B)	ANTI-A₁ LECTIN	ANTI-A (SERUM OF GROUP O)	ISOAGGLUTININS IN SERUM REGULAR	ISOAGGLUTININS IN SERUM IRREGULAR
A	A_1	78	+	+	+	+	anti-B	anti-A_2(O, H) (very rare)
	A_2	22	+	−	−	+	anti-B	anti-A_1 (in 1–2% of A_2 persons)
	A_3	rare	+w (see text)	−	−	+w (see text)	anti-B	anti-A_1 (in 50% of A_3 persons)
	A_o	very rare	−	−	−	+	anti-B	anti-A_1 (commonly)
	A_m	extremely rare	−	−	−	−	anti-B	anti-A_1
AB	A_1B	70	+	+	+	+***	none	anti-A_2(O, H)
	A_2B	30	+	−	−	+***	none	anti-A_1 (in 30% of A_2B persons)
	A_3B etc.**	extremely rare	+w or −	−	−	+***	none	anti-A_1 (commonly)

* + Agglutination
+w Weak agglutination
− No agglutination

** Combinations of B with other subgroups of A
*** Reflects also agglutination of factor B by anti-B

therefore are called "irregular isoagglutinins." They are usually of low titer and can be best detected when the agglutination is performed at temperatures around 4° C. At room temperature and especially at body temperature (37° C.) agglutinations by these antibodies are weak or absent. Certain special features are found in two of the rarer subgroups: when red cells of subgroup A_3 are exposed to anti-A serum, only a small number of red cells are agglutinated, as can be seen especially well on microscopic examination. A_0 red cells are clumped in most instances by anti-A in serum of group O but only rarely by anti-A present in group B. This phenomenon is not dependent on the titer of the isoagglutinins.

General properties of isoagglutinogens A and B. By suitable methods the isoagglutinogens A and B can be demonstrated as early as the second month of fetal life. However, as a rule they are not completely developed at birth. Specifically, red cells of group A or AB of newborn infants react in most instances as if they would belong to subgroup A_2 or A_2B. By the age of one year isoagglutinogens have reached full strength.

Although they were originally discovered in the red cells, the term "blood factors" A and B is to a certain extent a misnomer, since large amounts of A and B antigens are present in tissues other than blood. Within the blood itself they are probably present also in leukocytes and platelets. They are found abundantly in exocrine glands, such as the salivary glands and pancreas, as well as in the gastric mucosa and the Malpighian layer of the skin. Demonstration of the antigens in tissues is not feasible by agglutination tests but is best accomplished by specific absorption of added antibody. A and B antigens also occur in other species and even in bacteria. It is conceivable that introduction of such antigenic material into the body may be the stimulus for formation of isoagglutinins early during life.

Highly purified preparations with A and B blood group activity have been obtained from various sources, including human meconium. Witebsky, Morgan and associates, and Kabat have made outstanding contributions to the elucidation of the chemistry of A and B blood group substances. They are complex polysaccharides containing glucosamine and galactosamine, immunologic specificity apparently depending on relatively small terminal portions of these macromolecules. Commercially available, purified, protein-free preparations of group-specific substance A are derived from porcine gastric mucosa and those of group-specific substance B from equine gastric mucosa. Such material has several useful applications. First, it can be safely injected into suitable persons in order to elevate titers of isoagglutinins anti-A or anti-B for preparation of diagnostic antiserums. Second, when added to blood containing the corresponding isoagglutinins, A and B substances at least partially neutralize these antibodies, and this was expected to increase the safety of group O blood for use as "universal donor." That this purpose is not always accomplished will be discussed subsequently (p. 267). Third, group-specific substances A and B are of considerable usefulness in various laboratory techniques to be outlined later (pp. 295, 297).

Secretors of A and B. In addition to the previously mentioned wide distribution of A and B substances throughout the human body, the corresponding blood group specific substance(s) are also found in glandular secretions, such as saliva and gastric juice, of roughly 80 per cent of persons of group A or B, respectively. Such persons are called "secretors." In the remaining 20 per cent, called "nonsecretors," blood group specific substances in tissues are present only as alcohol-soluble compounds, probably in the form of lipopolysaccharides, and this prevents their appearance in the aqueous secretions. On the other hand in tissues of secretors blood group specific substances occur in alcohol-soluble as well as in water-soluble forms. The property of being a secretor is transmitted genetically and depends on the presence of at least one of a pair of allelic genes designated as Se. Persons who are nonsecretors are homozygous for the gene se (sese). Meconium of fetuses and infants who are secretors contains large amounts of blood group specific substance, reflecting concentration of material secreted during fetal life.

Isoagglutinins. As inferred from the "laws of Landsteiner," isoagglutinins anti-A or anti-B are regularly present in persons lacking the corresponding agglutinogen(s) in their red cells. It has been established that isoagglutinins develop postnatally. Isoagglutinins present in the newborn, as demonstrable in cord blood specimens, represent without exception maternal isoagglutinins transmitted transplacentally. Such passively transferred antibodies disappear gradually, and as a rule the infant begins to produce its own isoagglutinins some time between the third and sixth months of postnatal life. This strongly suggests that the isoagglutinins are the result of some subtle antigenic stimulation, possibly through microorganisms or food, which inevitably occurs postnatally. Absence of isoagglutinins corresponding to an isoagglutinogen present in the same person may be explained by the fact that such antibodies would be absorbed immediately by antigen present in red cells and tissues and thus never appear in the circulation.

Although on the basis of this concept the term "natural" isoagglutinins may appear to be a misnomer, since they also result from some form of antigenic stimulation, practical considerations make it desirable to differentiate isoagglutinins developing in the "natural" course of events from those resulting from specific antigenic stimulation. Such antigenic stimulation includes transfusion of incompatible blood, entry into maternal circulation of red cells of a fetus with incompatible ABO group (e.g., a pregnant woman of group O with fetus A or B), and administration of group-specific substances including antigens closely related to A or B, such as those present in some bacterial vaccines (tetanus) or horse serum or those that may result from infections (E. coli). In these instances it can be demonstrated that in addition to increase in quantity, anti-A and anti-B antibodies have acquired certain properties that characterize "incomplete" antibodies to be described later on (p. 274). Two specific properties of incomplete anti-A and anti-B isoagglutinins of considerable practical importance are mentioned now. First, frequently they possess not only the capacity to agglutinate but also to hemolyze red cells containing the corresponding isoagglutinogen. Since this hemolysis is dependent on presence of complement, it is apparent only with use of fresh serum or after addition of complement. Inactivation at 56° C. for 30 minutes destroys complement and prevents hemolysis while the corresponding agglutinin activity remains unaffected. Second, although the group-specific substances A and B are well capable of neutralizing "complete" anti-A and anti-B isoagglutinin, the corresponding "incomplete" antibodies are much less readily neutralized. Detailed outlines of the procedures used for demonstrating this property, its practical applications, and interpretation of the results of such tests will be discussed later.

As are most antibodies, isoagglutinins anti-A and anti-B are found in the gamma globulin fraction. This has acquired a certain clinical significance in the disturbances of plasma proteins extensively studied by Bruton (1952), Good (1956), and others, namely, acquired and congenital hypogammaglobulinemia and agammaglobulinemia. As a rule in such conditions isoagglutinins normally expected on the basis of the person's ABO group are either absent or present in unusually low titers. Hence the absence during routine blood grouping tests of an expected isoagglutinin in the adult should arouse suspicion of lack or decrease in the serum gamma globulin fraction. Rarely isoagglutinins are present only as incomplete antibodies that are not detectable unless appropriate techniques are used (pp. 274ff). The physiologic absence of isoagglutinins in the serum of the newborn up to the age of three to six months has already been referred to.

In recent years plant extracts have been prepared containing proteins that specifically agglutinate red cells of certain human blood groups. In accord with the recommendation of Boyd (1954) these plant substances are called lectins. Lectins capable of differentiating between subgroups of A are especially useful, inasmuch as they agglutinate only A_1 and A_1B cells but not red cells A_2, A_2B, A_3, and so on.

Inheritance of ABO groups. The fundamental principle of genetic transmission of the ABO characters is based on the fact that each of one autosomal chromosome pair carries one locus on which one of the three alleles—A, B, or O—must be present (Fig. 5–1). Table 5–4 lists the resulting phenotypes and genotypes and their relative frequency in the U.S. Caucasoid population. Three facts deducible from the table are worthy of mention: persons of group O are always homozygous; persons of group AB are always heterozygous; and persons of group A and B may be either homozygous or heterozygous (their phenotypes at present not susceptible to determination by laboratory tests). In other words there is no reliable reagent available by means of which the presence of the O agglutinogen can be demonstrated in red cells possessing A or B agglutinogen. However, it is best to avoid interpreting this fact as evidence for genetic "dominance" of A and B over O, since it only reflects the lack of suitable reagents. Table 5–4 also presents information concerning inheritance of phenotypes of subgroups of A and AB.

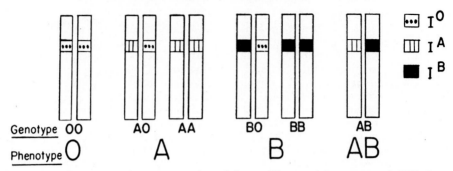

Figure 5-1. Diagrammatic representation of locus (I) containing genes of ABO factors.

Table 5-4. ABO Phenotypes and Genotypes in U. S. Caucasoid Population

BLOOD GROUP PHENOTYPE	GENOTYPE	INCIDENCE (PER CENT)
O	OO	45
A_1	A_1O	25
	A_1A_1	4
	A_1A_2	3
A_2	A_2O	8.5
	A_2A_2	0.5
B	BO	9.3
	BB	0.7
A_1B	A_1B	2.8
A_2B	A_2B	1.2

Braces: A_1A_1 and A_1A_2 → 32; A_1A_2 and A_2O/A_2A_2 → 41; A_2O and A_2A_2 → 9; BO and BB → 10; A_1B and A_2B → 4.

A_1, when present together with A_2, imparts to blood the phenotypic property A_1. Thus one cannot differentiate between the homozygote A_1A_1 and the heterozygotes A_1A_2 or A_1O. By the same token persons of group A_2 may have either genotype A_2A_2 or A_2O. In all these instances proof for zygosity of persons of group A_1, A_2, or B can reliably be established only by means of family studies; that is, heterozygosity can be proved by finding that one of the parents or children of the person in question belongs to group O. Further implications of the laws of inheritance of ABO groups will be discussed subsequently in connection with their application in medicolegal problems, specifically exclusion of parentage (p. 314).

2. The MNS System. By contrast with the circumstances relating to the discovery of A and B agglutinogens, knowledge of M and N blood factors was derived from immunologic studies of Landsteiner and Levine (1927) in which animals of another species—rabbits—were injected with human blood. In addition to the expected species-specific hemoantibodies, serums of rabbits immunized with human red cells of one person also contained antibodies that differentiated between two classes of human red cells. After such serum was suitably absorbed with red cells belonging to one class, the remaining antibody agglutinated approximately 80 per cent of all blood specimens; the blood factor present in such blood was called "M." Blood specimens not containing the M factor and some of the M blood were found to be agglutinated by another antibody present in rabbits injected with human red cells free of the M factor. This second factor was called "N." As shown in Table 5–5, there are three possible combinations of M and N; namely, either of them may occur alone or combined with the other. When only one is present, they are homozygotes— MM or NN, respectively—whereas MN obviously is a heterozygote. It is apparent that, by contrast with the findings in the ABO system, no red cell can be devoid of both M-N factors. In other words in the MN system there is nothing corresponding to group O in the ABO system. Analyses of large series of specimens typed for M and N showed that incidence of the three types—M, N, and MN—was identical in persons of the four ABO groups. Thus ABO

Table 5-5. The MN System

PHENOTYPE	GENOTYPE	APPROXIMATE FREQUENCY (U.S. CAUCASOID) PER CENT
M	MM	28
N	NN	22
MN	MN	50

and MN groups were proved to be independent of each other. Two differences between the MN and ABO systems are worthy of mention. M and N factors are present only in red cells and certain tissues but never in body fluids and secretions and isoagglutinins anti-M and anti-N are not only of extremely rare "natural" occurrence but are also hardly ever produced as a result of isosensitization. In such rare exceptions anti-M isoagglutinins are encountered somewhat more frequently than anti-N. Only a few cases have been recorded in the literature in which clinical manifestations, such as transfusion reactions or hemolytic disease of the newborn, could be traced to anti-M or anti-N. Hence no consideration need be given to M and N factors in clinical medicine and specifically in pretransfusion tests. They are used in medicolegal and anthropologic studies. M and N are fully developed in red cells at birth and are apparently formed at an earlier stage of fetal development than A and B antigens.

As has been found subsequently in other blood group systems, the original simplicity of the MN system underwent numerous modifications after new data and facts became available. Weakly reacting forms of M and N have been encountered on rare occasions and designated as "M$_2$" and "N$_2$." Similar to weakly reacting subgroups of A, they may be missed because of low agglutinability and thus give rise to erroneous interpretations. An extremely rare third allele of M and N has been described and called "M^g" (Allen, 1958), the presence of which is important in connection with exclusion of parentage.

Several agglutinogens discovered during the last decade have eventually been found to belong to the MN system. Two allelic factors, called "S" and "s" (Walsh and Montgomery, 1947), are regularly associated with M and N. In other words each M or N agglutinogen is accompanied by and inherited with either the S or s agglutinogen. A rare antibody, discovered by Wiener and Unger (1953) in a Negro patient and designated by them as anti-U, was subsequently shown to react with all red cells containing factors S or s. Thus persons capable of forming this antibody lack both S and s and presumably are homozygous for a third allele, called S^u. This rare blood type occurs almost exclusively in Negroes. Additional agglutinogens less regularly encountered include He and Hu first described in African Negroes. Also two

blood factors originally assumed to occur only in a few families and called "Mi^a" (Levine et al., 1951) and Vw (van der Hart, Bosman, and Van Loghem, 1954) have been shown to be part of the MNS system.

3. **The P System.** Simultaneously with the discovery of M and N Landsteiner and Levine (1927) established by means of anti-human red cell rabbit serums that human red cells contained a factor that they called "P". This agglutinogen was found to be present in roughly 75 per cent of U. S. Caucasoid adults. A much higher incidence of P-positive blood—over 95 per cent—was found in Negroes. Presence of P is independent of ABO, MN, and other blood group systems. There are considerable genetically transmitted differences in agglutinability of P-positive blood cells. Although P is a poor isoantigen, low-titered anti-P is found occasionally in human serum, reacting best at low temperatures. A relationship of the P antigen to Echinococcus has been demonstrated: patients with this disease were shown to produce high-titered anti-P, and injection of echinococcal antigen into rabbits resulted in specific immune serum (Levine and Celano, 1959). Normal serums of some pigs, horses, and rabbits may also contain anti-P agglutinin. The relationship of the Tj^a factor to the P system, which has been established within the last few years, will be discussed in the section on "private and universal" blood factors. Clinical implication of P in transfusion reactions or other manifestations of isosensitization is exceedingly rare.

4. **The Rh System.** The Rh factor, like the MN and P blood factors, was discovered during animal experimentation. Landsteiner and Wiener (1940) injected rabbits and guinea pigs with red cells of the Rhesus monkey (Macaca rhesus) to study immunologic relationships of higher mammals. In addition to expected hemoantibodies for Rhesus red cells the serum of rabbits so treated agglutinated approximately 85 per cent of human red cells. The significance of this discovery soon exceeded by far that of the M, N, and P factors when by fortunate coincidence and even more by ingenious reasoning Levine and Stetson (1939) and Levine, Burnham, Katzin, and Vogel (1941) demonstrated a clinical significance of the Rh factor that neither before nor since then has been possessed by any other blood groups except the ABO system. Specifically, hitherto unexplained hemolytic complications of

blood transfusions, as well as the cause of hemolytic disease of the newborn (erythroblastosis fetalis), were shown to be the result of incompatibility in the Rh system as evidenced by the finding of Rh isoantibodies in human serum indicative of isosensitization.

The Rh system differs both from the ABO system and the MN system. In the Rh system isoagglutinins are normally absent in persons lacking the corresponding blood factor by contrast with the ABO system. On the other hand, after red cells containing the Rh factor have been introduced into a person lacking it, Rh antibodies develop frequently by contrast with the MN system.

Extensive investigations were carried out soon after the discovery of the Rh factor with outstanding contributions by Wiener, Levine, Diamond, Witebsky and others in this country and Race and Sanger in England as well as numerous other workers throughout the world. Two different systems of terminology have developed from this work: one was originally proposed by Wiener, while a different set of notations elaborated by Race and Fisher in England was generally accepted in England and most parts of Europe and is also widely used in this country. It is not intended to discuss the relative merits of the two nomenclatures and to present specifically the serious objections based on principles of immunogenetics raised by Wiener against the Fisher-Race terminology, but the fact remains that both nomenclatures have today become firmly established in different parts of the world. For this reason anybody working in the field must be familiar with both of them. In this presentation the recommendations by a committee appointed by the National Institutes of Health in 1949 have been followed: i.e., to use the notations of Wiener with the Fisher-Race notations added in parentheses. Table 5–6 contains a parallel listing of the most important notations expressed in both terminologies.

The Rh-Hr factors. On the basis of

the early work the conclusion was justified that the population could be divided into two main groups: one with red cells that were agglutinated by Rh antibodies and called Rh-positive and another with red cells that were not agglutinated and called Rh-negative. However, further work soon disclosed the presence of at least two other Rh factors. This situation is similar to the one previously discussed for the association of S and s with M and N blood factors. The most important Rh factor was designated as Rh_0 by Wiener and as D by Fisher and Race. The two factors frequently associated with $Rh_0(D)$ were named $rh'(C)$ and $rh''(E)$. When suitable tests are done for these three factors, it is possible to differentiate eight different types as shown in Table 5–7: (1) If none of them is pres-

Table 5–7. The Eight Main Rh Types

| RH FACTORS* | | | RH TYPE** | | GENERAL |
Rh_0 (D)	rh' (C)	rh'' (E)	W.	F.R.	DESIGNATION
1. −	−	−	rh	cde	
2. −	+	−	rh'	Cde	
3. −	−	+	rh''	cdE	} Rh-negative
4. −	+	+	rh'rh'' or rh$_y$	CdE	
5. +	−	−	Rh_0	cDe	
6. +	+	−	Rh_1	CDe	
7. +	−	+	Rh_2	cDE	} Rh-positive
8. +	+	+	Rh_1Rh_2 or Rh_z	CDE	

* +present
−absent
** W. = Wiener notations
    F.R. = Fisher-Race notations

ent, the blood is called Rh-negative, rh (cde); (2), (3), and (4) are rather rare types in which only $rh'(C)$, $rh''(E)$, or both are present; (5) Rh_0 (cDe) may occur by itself; or (6) it may be combined with $rh'(C)$ in which event it is called Rh_1 (CDe); or (7) in combination with $rh''(E)$ in which event it is called Rh_2 (cDE); (8) finally, all three factors may be present and yield the type Rh_1Rh_2 or Rh_z (CDE). Since for practical purposes, such as blood transfusions and prenatal tests, the $Rh_0(D)$ factor is most important, the first four types lacking this factor are designated as Rh-negative and the last four possessing it, Rh-positive.

The subsequent developments in the Rh system almost invariably were connected

Table 5–6. The Five Main Rh Factors

| DESIGNATION BY | | PRESENT IN | |
WIENER	FISHER-RACE	RH-POSITIVE BLOOD	RH-NEGATIVE BLOOD
Rh_0	D	always	never
rh'	C	frequently	rarely
rh''	E	frequently	rarely
hr'	c	frequently	almost always
hr''	e	frequently	almost always

with discoveries of "new" isoantibodies in pregnant women or recipients of blood transfusions. By means of statistical analysis these antibodies could be shown to react specifically with blood factors distributed irregularly in persons of different Rh types; e.g., they were more frequently found in Rh_o-(D)-positive than in Rh_o-(D)-negative individuals. Hence they presumably belonged to the Rh system. An important advance was the recognition that absence of factors rh'(C) and rh''(E) was regularly associated with presence of a reciprocal blood factor detectable by some of these isoantibodies. In Wiener's system the blood factor determined by absence of rh' was called hr'; the reversal of the letters Rh to Hr is intended to indicate the reciprocal relationship between Rh and Hr factors. In the Fisher-Race system small letters are used, such as c for hr' in juxtaposition to C(rh'). Table 5–8 shows the reaction of

Table 5–8. The Rh-Hr Phenotypes and Genotypes

RH TYPE	REACTIONS* WITH ANTISERUMS FOR hr' (c)	hr'' (e)	PHENOTYPES** W.	F.R.	POSSIBLE GENOTYPES** W.	F.R.	APPROXIMATE FREQUENCY IN U.S. CAUCASOID POPULATION***
rh	+	+	rh	cde	rr	cde/cde	14.0
rh'	+	+	rh'rh	Ccde	r'r	Cde/cde	1.1
	−	+	rh'rh'	CCde	r'r'	Cde/Cde	Rare
rh''	+	+	rh''rh	cdEe	r''r	cdE/cde	0.4
	+	−	rh''rh''	cdEE	r''r''	cdE/cdE	Rare
rh'rh'' (rh_y)	+	+	rh_yrh	CcdEe	r'r''	Cde/cdE	Rare
					r^yr	CdE/cde	Rare
	−	+	rh_yrh'	CCdEe	r^yr'	CdE/Cde	Rare
	+	−	rh_yrh''	CcdEE	r^yr''	CdE/cdE	Rare
	−	−	rh_yrh_y	CCdEE	r^yr^y	CdE/CdE	Rare
Rh_o	+	+	Rh_o	cDe	R^or	cDe/cde	2.4
					R^oR^o	cDe/cDe	0.1
Rh_1	+	+	Rh_1rh	CcDe	R^1r	CDe/cde	30.6
					R^1R^o	CDe/cDe	2.6
					R^or'	cDe/Cde	Rare
	−	+	Rh_1Rh_1	CCDe	R^1R^1	CDe/CDe	16.9
					R^1r'	CDe/Cde	1.1
Rh_2	+	+	Rh_2rh	cDEe	R^2r	cDE/cde	12.5
					R^2R^o	cDE/cDe	0.2
					R^or''	cDe/cdE	Rare
	+	−	Rh_2Rh_2	cDEE	R^2R^2	cDE/cDE	2.7
					R^2r''	cDE/cdE	0.2
Rh_1Rh_2 (Rh_z)	+	+	Rh_zRh_o	CcDEe	R^1R^2	CDe/cDE	12.9
					R^1r''	CDe/cdE	Rare
					R^2r'	cDE/Cde	Rare
					R^zr	CDE/cde	0.2
					R^zR^o	CDE/cDe	Rare
					R^or^y	cDe/CdE	Rare
	−	+	Rh_zRh_1	CCDEe	R^zR^1	CDE/CDe	0.2
					R^zr'	CDE/Cde	Rare
					R^1r^y	CDe/CdE	Rare
	+	−	Rh_zRh_2	CcDEE	R^zR^2	CDE/cDE	Rare
					R^zr''	CDE/cdE	Rare
					R^2r^y	cDE/CdE	Rare
	−	−	Rh_zRh_z	CCDEE	R^zR^z	CDE/CDE	Rare
					R^zr^y	CDE/CdE	Rare

* + present   ** W = Wiener notations   *** Rare = frequency of 0.1% or less
  − absent   F.R. = Fisher-Race notations

the Hr antibodies with red cells of different Rh types and also indicates the relative frequencies of the corresponding phenotypes and genotypes. In addition to the significance of the Hr factors as occasional causes of incompatibility in blood transfusions or of maternal isosensitization, they make it frequently possible to establish the probability of a person's having a certain Rh genotype. This in turn is important in prognosis of future pregnancies of Rh-sensitized women. Having some information regarding the husband's genotype, one is able to state at least that there may be a 50 per cent chance for birth of an Rh-negative child (see p. 277). It must be stressed that to date no isoantibody has been detected having a reciprocal relationship to the $Rh_o(D)$ antigen. In other words anti-$hr_o(d)$ has never been convincingly demonstrated.

In addition to the five well-established and readily determined Rh-Hr factors (Table 5–6), some more rarely encountered isoantibodies that have been described permitted recognition of the following additional Rh factors: $C^w(rh^w)$ is related to, but different from, the "regular" $rh'(C)$ factor. Since most but not all anti-rh' (anti-C) serums also contain anti-C^w, one may suspect the presence of the C^w factor in a blood specimen that is agglutinated by some anti-rh'(C) serums and not by others. This suspicion may be confirmed by the reaction with "pure" anti-C^w antibody. Much rarer, and hence hardly ever of clinical significance, are other alleles of rh'(C), such as C^x and C^u, and of rh''(E), designated as E^w and E^u. Some antibodies react with Rh factors the exact nature of which has not as yet been established and which actually may reflect presence of specific combinations of other known Rh factors. For example, an Rh factor designated as "f" (hr) appears to be present in red cells of persons whose genes for hr'(c) and hr''(e) are on the same chromosome. Possibly analogous "position" effects are responsible for isoantibodies reacting with factor V.

Variants of Rh_o factor. Considerable practical importance must be assigned to $Rh_o(D)$ variants, which can be recognized by their atypical behavior in laboratory tests commonly employed for Rh typing (see p. 284). When such blood specimens were tested with a battery of serums containing Rh antibodies, it was noted that agglutination was produced by some but not by other serums. Furthermore so-called "complete" or "saline agglutinating" Rh antibodies (see p. 284) were not capable of clumping these red cells. On the other hand, when more sensitive methods were used, e.g., the antiglobulin technique (see p. 285), it was always possible to demonstrate union of Rh antibody with $Rh_o(D)$ antigen present in these specimens. These weakly reacting variants of the $Rh_o(D)$ factor, commonly designated as D^u, require special methods for their detection *in vitro*. At the same time—and this is important—*in vivo* D^u blood behaves similarly to "regular" Rh_o-positive blood as far as isosensitization by means of blood transfusions or pregnancy is concerned. Reference will be made in subsequent sections (p. 301) to procedures for selection of blood for transfusions or prenatal testing in order to avoid erroneous identification of D^u-positive blood as Rh-negative.

The strength of D^u antigens varies greatly from one specimen to the next—from strong antigens almost approaching the reactivity of the regular $Rh_o(D)$ factor to weak D^u specimens that are most difficult to detect *in vitro*.

The D^u factor does not appear to be an antigen distinctly different from the Rh_o (D) factor, since it is neither possible to produce an antibody specific for D^u nor to separate by absorptions the portion of an anti-$Rh_o(D)$ serum that reacts with the regular $Rh_o(D)$ factor from that reacting with the D^u factor.

In addition to D^u factors, which are transmitted genetically, another form of weakly reacting $Rh_o(D)$ factor has been encountered that results from a "gene interaction," namely the rh'(C) factor, which depresses the reactivity of the $Rh_o(D)$ antigen. This is important in connection with exclusion of parentage, since seemingly Rh-negative parents may give rise to an offspring found to be Rh-positive.

Variants of the D^u type are much more common among Negroid than Caucasoid persons. Furthermore, in line with the greater frequency of the Rh type $Rh_o(cDe)$ among Negroids, D^u is found frequently without simultaneous presence of the rh' (C) and rh''(E) factors, whereas this is only rarely the case in Caucasoid persons.

A behavior opposite to that of D^u, namely, unusually strong reactivity of $Rh_o(D)$, has been found in exceedingly rare blood specimens in which it is not possible to demonstrate presence of any of the other Rh or Hr factors. The Rh type thus produced has been called -D-(Rh_o); according to Race and Sanger (1958), it may reflect a gene deletion and has been found to be inherited. Red cells with this factor, even when present in heterozygous form, have the unusual property of being agglutinated even in saline suspensions by incomplete anti-Rh serums (see p. 274). The practical significance of -D- is predicated on serious difficulties encountered in transfusing persons with this Rh type, because they are capable of, and frequently do, develop antibodies for the other Rh factors: rh'(C) and hr'(c), rh''(E), and hr''(e). Therefore, blood donors used for them must have the same rare Rh type as they themselves. Implications of the -D- factor for exclusion of parentage will be discussed later (see p. 316).

Discoveries by Unger and Wiener (1957) have acquainted us with additional factors complicating the Rh system. Several observations were reported of apparently Rh_0-(D)-positive persons who formed antibodies reacting specifically with all other Rh_0-(D)-positive cells except their own, but this has now been explained by attributing a mosaic nature to the Rh_0 (D) factor. Very rarely Rh_0-positive blood specimens may occur in which one small part of this mosaic is missing. Such blood specimens have been designated as Rh^a, Rh^b, and Rh^c, and their possessors are thus capable of forming antibodies against the A, B, or C portion of Rh_0, such antibodies agglutinating "regular" Rh-positive blood specimens carrying these segments of the "mosaic."

Antigenicity of Rh factors. In medicine the significance of blood factors is based on their capacity to isosensitize in transfusions or pregnancies. The $Rh_0(D)$ factor is by far the most antigenic, and the other Rh factors are much less likely to produce isosensitization. Antibodies for rh'(C) are frequently found together with anti-$Rh_0(D)$ antibodies in the Rh-negative pregnant woman whose fetus or child was type Rh_1 and hence possessed both antigens. A similar combination of anti-$Rh_0(D)$ and anti-rh''(E) antibodies occurs less frequently in women subjected to antigenic stimulation by a fetus with type $Rh_2(cDE)$. Rarely factors other than $Rh_0(D)$ induce formation of antibodies in Rh-positive persons, their antigenicity decreasing in the following order: hr'(c), rh''(E), rh'(C), and hr'' (e). By contrast with A and B factors, Rh factors have not been unequivocally demonstrated outside of blood cells, which therefore are the only agent capable of bringing about Rh sensitization. In addition to pregnancy and blood transfusions, intramuscular injection of blood may be responsible for development of Rh antibodies.

Rh antibodies. With exceedingly rare exceptions Rh antibodies do not occur without preceding antigenic stimulation, such as sensitization by pregnancy, blood transfusion, or deliberate immunization consisting most commonly of repeated intravenous injections of blood. Heteroantibodies agglutinating Rh-positive red cells can also be produced in guinea pigs injected with Rhesus monkey or human blood, but the reliability of such antiserums was found to be inadequate for practical use.

Soon after discovery of the Rh factor it was noted that Rh antibodies were detectable only in approximately 50 to 70 per cent of patients with hemolytic transfusion reactions or women with erythroblastotic infants. Incubating the serum-red cell mixtures for prolonged periods of time at 37° C. increased the sensitivity of tests for Rh antibodies but still failed to demonstrate the presence of Rh antibodies in many instances in which they were expected on the basis of clinical findings. These contradictions between serologic and clinical findings necessitated a search for new and more sensitive hemagglutination techniques capable of detecting hemoantibodies reacting differently from those known heretofore, such as anti-A, anti-B, anti-M, and anti-N. The term "complete" antibodies is recommended for those that react readily with saline-suspended red cells and do not require special procedures except certain periods of incubation or centrifugation (see Table 5–9). The classical examples for such antibodies are isoagglutinins anti-A and anti-B. Optimal temperatures for these antibodies vary with the specific antibody, but as a rule they are "cold agglutinins," the highest titers being observed around 4° C. Higher reactivity at 37° C. is exhibited by antibodies presumably induced by specific antigenic stimulation, such as complete Rh antibodies, which may be called "warm agglutinins." Finally a third class of isoantibodies is most reactive at 18 to 20° C. ("room temperature"). In general, high-titered antibodies, though showing higher activity at certain temperatures, are also demonstrable when tested at other temperature ranges. Nevertheless, when one is concerned with practical laboratory work, it is important to realize that false negative

Table 5–9.   Categories of Rh Antibodies

CATEGORY	SYNONYMS OR SUBDIVISIONS	CHARACTERISTIC PROPERTIES	IMMUNOLOGIC SIGNIFICANCE	CLINICAL SIGNIFICANCE
A. Complete Antibodies	Saline agglutinins Bivalent agglutinins (Wiener) Thermostable agglutinins (Diamond)	Agglutinate Rh-positive, saline-suspended red cells; weakened or destroyed by heating over 60° C.	Formed in early stages of isosensitization	Rarely capable of traversing placenta and causing hemolytic disease of the newborn
B. Incomplete Antibodies	I. Blocking antibodies (Wiener)	Combine with antigenic sites of Rh-positive red cells without producing agglutination and prevent agglutination of such "blocked" red cells by subsequently added complete Rh antibodies	Formed in later stages of isosensitization, and considered to be hyperimmune isoantibodies (Diamond)	Readily capable of traversing placenta and responsible for moderate to severe forms of hemolytic disease of the newborn
	II. Serum albumin agglutinins Univalent agglutinins (Wiener) Thermostable agglutinins (Diamond) Cryptagglutinoids (Hill & Haberman)	Combine with antigenic sites of Rh-positive red cells but produce agglutination only under one or several of the following conditions: a. suspension of red cells in albumin or other macromolecular media; b. addition of antiglobulin (Coombs) serum to "coated" cells; c. enzyme treatment of red cells. Antibody activity resistant to heating over 60° C.	Formed in later stages of isosensitization, and considered to be hyperimmune isoantibodies (Diamond)	Readily capable of traversing placenta and responsible for moderate to severe forms of hemolytic disease of the newborn

results may be obtained when low-titered antibodies are tested at temperatures far from their optimal thermal range.

Hemoantibodies not readily detectable when added to saline-suspended red cells containing the corresponding agglutinogen are best called "incomplete." One of the fundamental properties of incomplete antibodies is the capacity to unite readily with homologous antigenic sites on the red cell but without manifest agglutination. One of the first methods for detecting the presence of incomplete antibodies was based on the assumption that antigenic sites occupied by incomplete antibodies could not be available for combination with complete antibodies. Hence red cells first exposed to incomplete antibodies should fail to be agglutinated when subsequently exposed to complete antibodies of the identical specificity. The correctnesss of this reasoning was proved experimentally (Wiener, 1944). Although this method has a rather low sensitivity, it is important because it furnished proof for one of the basic properties of incomplete antibodies—union with an antigen that prevented reaction with cor-

responding complete antibodies—which led to their designation as "blocking antibodies." Bacterial antibodies of this type have been known from previous studies. They have recently been investigated more intensively.

A second, more sensitive method for demonstration of incomplete antibodies, frequently used for practical work (p. 290), consists of substitution for the saline medium by macromolecular substances, such as human serum or plasma, serum proteins, especially serum albumin, as well as other colloidal solutions, such as gelatin, gum acacia, and polyvinyl pyrrolidone (PVP). In other words, when Rh-positive red cells suspended in albumin are added to a serum containing incomplete Rh antibodies, agglutination occurs after suitable periods of incubation or other procedures (centrifugation, warming on slide). This method is apparently based on the fact that molecular configurations of incomplete antibodies differ from those of complete antibodies, thus necessitating the presence of a medium in which the electrostatic forces repelling red cells from each other can be overcome more readily than is the case in saline media. Many practical applications, such as Rh typing (see p. 283), make use of this property of incomplete antibodies.

A third method with a wide range of practical applications in immunohematology and immunology is the antiglobulin test developed by Coombs.

Antiglobulin (Coombs) test. There are two basic premises for the correct understanding, performance, and application of antiglobulin tests. First, human isohemoantibodies are globulins, in most instances gamma globulin. Second, addition of antiglobulin antibody to human red cells coated with isoantibody (i.e., globulin) results in agglutination of the coated red cells. For practical purposes such antiserums (antihuman globulin serum) may be produced by injection of human globulin into animals of a variety of species; rabbits and goats are most commonly employed. Figure 5–2 represents schematically the sequence of events in the antiglobulin test: in the first step (I) incomplete antibodies unite with, or "coat," the red cells; this may occur *in vivo* or *in vitro*. The second step (II), addition of the antiglobulin reagent, is followed by the final event (III), agglutination of the globulin-coated red cells.

There are two main applications of the antiglobulin test. (1) The direct antiglobulin test is designed for demonstration of *in vivo* coating of red cells. Basically a positive test shows agglutination of the suitably prepared red cell suspension after addition of the antiglobulin serum. The main indications for this test are diagnosis of hemolytic disease of the newborn (p. 311) and of autoimmune hemolytic anemia (p. 312) and investigation of hemolytic transfusion reactions (p. 305). (2) In the indirect antiglobulin test incomplete antibodies are permitted to react *in vitro* with red cells containing the corresponding agglutinogen; after suitable periods and conditions of incubation of the red cell serum mixtures, antiglobulin serum is added to the suitably prepared red cells. The main applications of the indirect antiglobulin test are:

a. Detection of incomplete antibodies (e.g., incomplete anti-$Rh_o(D)$) by means of incubation of $Rh_o(D)$-positive red cells with the serum to be tested. Analogous procedures may be used for incomplete antibodies of other specificities, including anti-A and anti-B.

b. Detection in red cells of blood factors for which homologous antibodies are available in the incomplete form either exclusively or prevalently; e.g., Kell and Duffy (p. 287). This method is also used for demonstration of weakly reacting Rh_o variants (D^u, see p. 284).

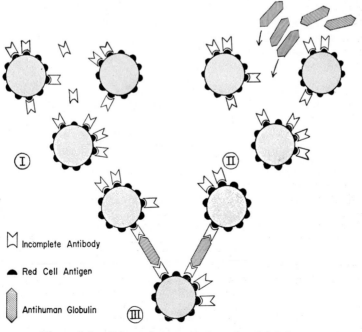

M Incomplete Antibody

▲ Red Cell Antigen

Antihuman Globulin

Figure 5–2. Schematic presentation of antiglobulin test.

c. Demonstration of autoantibodies in the serum of patients with autoimmune hemolytic anemia.

d. Antiglobulin reactions also may be used for demonstration of other antigen-antibody reactions involving white cells, platelets, and tissue cells.

e. Since addition of gamma globulin neutralizes antiglobulin antibody and thus prevents the agglutinating activity of antiglobulin for coated red cells, the test has also been adapted to demonstrate the presence of hypogammaglobulinemia and agammaglobulinemia.

Enzyme treatment of red cells. In the most recent method developed for detection of incomplete antibodies, red cells treated with proteolytic enzymes, such as trypsin, papain, ficin, and bromelin, become agglutinable by incomplete antibodies in a similar fashion as would be expected from complete antibodies. In other words incomplete antibodies are capable of agglutinating saline-suspended, enzyme-treated red cells possessing the homologous blood factors. The enzyme techniques are fairly simple; their results are easier to read than those in some of the other methods for detection of incomplete antibodies; and they exceed them also in sensitivity as far as detection of Rh antibodies is concerned. On the other hand some antigenic sites of other blood factors are destroyed or markedly weakened in reactivity after enzyme treatment, and hence this technique cannot be employed for detection of antibodies for M, N, Duffy, and some other blood factors.

Thus it is often necessary to utilize several of the techniques for detection of incomplete antibodies for Rh and other blood factors, referred to in the preceding discussion and summarized in Table 5–9. No final decision is possible at present as to whether different methods (antiglobulin tests, blocking tests, and enzyme tests, for example) are detecting the same or different varieties of incomplete antibodies. The latter possibility is considered likely by many investigators and would thus represent another instance of "heterogeneity of antibodies," which has been established for certain serologic phenomena.

Specificity of Rh antibodies. Depending on the antigenic compositions of the injected red cells and of the red cells of the recipient, antibodies with specificity for one or more Rh factors may be present in the same serum. The following general conditions must be met in isoimmunization to Rh factors or for that matter to any other antigen: the blood factor must be absent in the sensitized person; the blood factor must be present in the sensitizing blood; and the blood factor must be of sufficient antigenic strength. Other factors are the number of separate antigenic stimulations, the amount of blood involved in each stimulation, the time intervals between stimulations, and the individual variations in ability to produce antibodies. In line with the preceding statements about relative antigenicity, anti-Rh_0(D) antibodies are most commonly encountered. Rh-negative women bearing fetuses with type Rh_1 (CDe) have also an opportunity to form antibodies to rh'(C), an event occurring in a majority of such pregnancies. If, on the other hand, a woman happens to be rh' (Cde) herself, pregnancy with an Rh_1 (CDe) fetus makes possible only formation of anti-Rh_0(D). Such examples could be multiplied and apply equally to sensitization by blood transfusions. Knowledge of exact specificity of isoantibodies is important for two reasons: for selection of blood transfusions for isoimmunized recipients, including treatment of erythroblastotic babies, and for proper utilization in laboratory tests of antiserums, which may contain more than one antibody. Another important consideration concerns the possibility that antibodies with different specificity may also have different reactivity, as defined in the preceding section; e.g., a serum may contain anti-Rh_0(D) as incomplete antibody and anti-rh'(C) as complete antibody. Hence the selection of techniques used for detection of such antibodies is of critical importance. As will be discussed in connection with antibody identification, testing for specificity of Rh antibodies requires availability of red cell panels, which, on the basis of their antigenic composition, permit discrimination between antibodies of different specificity.

Inheritance of Rh factors. In general the inheritance of Rh factors follows the same principles as those discussed in connection with the ABO and MN factors. Rh factors present in any one individual must have been inherited from one or both of his parents. If, for example, a person inherits the rh'(C) factor from both parents, he is homozygous: rh'rh'(Cde/Cde). On the other hand a person heterozygous for rh'(C) has only one parent of type rh' (Cde) while the other may be Rh-negative (cde); his genotype is rh'rh(Cde/cde).

Table 5–8 lists the genotype and gene notations according to the Wiener and Fisher-Race nomenclatures.

Three facts must be stressed in connection with Rh genotypes. First, laboratory tests are limited to determination of genotypes for factors rh'(C) and rh''(E), and they cannot establish homozygosity or heterozygosity for factor Rh_o(D). Second, even when homozygosity or heterozygosity for one of the Rh factors has been established, there is frequently uncertainty as to location of the genes on the two chromosomes; e.g., a person found to be Rh_1Rh_2hr'-positive and hr''-positive (CcDEe) may belong to one of six genotypes (cf. Table 5–8). Third, the most reliable evidence for presence of a specific Rh genotype is derived from knowledge of Rh types of parents and offspring of the person under test. In most other situations one can only refer to the most probable genotype on the basis of statistical information relating phenotypes to genotypes in populations of known ethnic background. In Table 5–10 the probability for association of the most common phenotypes of Rh-positive persons with heterozy-gosity has been estimated on the basis of the distribution of Rh types in the U. S. Caucasoid population.

Information on the genotype is of prognostic value in cases of husbands of women sensitized to one of the Rh factors. Knowledge of inheritance of Rh factors is indispensable for interpretation of Rh types in connection with exclusion of parentage as discussed subsequently (p. 315).

5. The Kell, Duffy, and Kidd Blood Group Systems. Factors making up these systems have been discovered relatively recently, and instances of hemolytic disease of the newborn or hemolytic transfusion reactions have furnished the opportunity for discovery of a "new" antibody, permitting definition of the corresponding blood factor. The basic information concerning the incidence of Kell, Duffy, and Kidd blood factors in the U. S. Caucasoid population is contained in Table 5–11. For practical purposes one should be aware of the following characteristic features of these two systems:

1. Among these blood factors Kell (K) is most and Kidd (Jk^a,Jk^b) is least anti-

Table 5–10. Evaluation of Zygosity for Rh Type*

PHENOTYPE		REACTIONS** WITH ANTI-hr' (ANTI-c)	ANTI-hr'' (ANTI-e)	MOST PROBABLE GENOTYPE		CHANCES % FOR GENOTYPE BEING HETEROZYGOUS RH_o-POSITIVE
Rh_1	CDe	+	(+)	R^1r	CDe/cde	88
Rh_1	CDe	−	(+)	R^1R^1	CDe/CDe	6
Rh_2	cDE	(+)	+	R^2r	cDE/cde	98
Rh_2	cDE	(+)	−	R^2R^2	cDE/cDE	9
Rh_o	cDe	(+)	(+)	R^or	cDe/cde	96
Rh_1Rh_2	CDE	+	+	R^1R^2	CDe/cDE	10

* Applied to U. S. Caucasoid population
** Results listed in parentheses can be anticipated on the basis of phenotype; hence the tests need not be done.

Table 5–11. The Kell, Duffy, and Kidd Blood Group Systems

BLOOD GROUP SYSTEM	PHENOTYPE		GENOTYPE		COMMON DESIGNATION	APPROXIMATE FREQUENCY (%) IN U. S. CAUCASOID POPULATION
Kell	K	}	Kk		Kell-positive	6.9
			KK		Kell-positive Cellano-negative	0.1
	k		kk		Kell-negative	93
Duffy	Fy^a	}	Fy^aFy^b Fy^aFy^a	}	Duffy-positive	48 17
	Fy^b		Fy^bFy^b		Duffy-negative	35
Kidd	Jk^a	}	Jk^aJk^b Jk^aJk^a	}	Kidd-positive	50 23
	Jk^b		Jk^bJk^b		Kidd-negative	27

genic. That anti-Kell antibodies are not found more frequently as a result of iso-sensitization by transfusion or pregnancy is explained by the low incidence of Kell in the general population. Since as a rule at least two antigenic stimulations are necessary for development of antibodies, chances for a Kell-negative person to be sensitized (e.g., by two blood transfusions with Kell-positive blood) are less than one in 100.

2. Sensitization to the Cellano factor (k) occurs extremely rarely because roughly only one out of 1000 persons is susceptible to such sensitization by virtue of being homozygous for the Kell factor (KK).

3. The Duffy factor, Fy^a, is only weakly antigenic, and hence corresponding antibodies are encountered only infrequently. This holds true to an even greater extent for the allele, Fy^b, and antibodies for Jk^a and Jk^b.

4. As a rule antibodies for Kell, Duffy, and Kidd factors are best, or exclusively, detectable by the indirect antiglobulin technique. This is important in connection with crossmatching tests, which may fail to reveal incompatibility caused by such antibodies if this technique is not employed. Some examples of Kidd antibodies react best with enzyme-treated red cells subjected to the antiglobulin technique. On the other hand the Duffy agglutinogens are readily destroyed by proteolytic enzymes, such as trypsin, papain, and ficin, and hence such techniques are unsuitable for detection of Duffy factors and anti-Duffy antibodies.

5. Within the last years the Kell system has become more complex with the discovery of additional alleles designated as Kp^a and Kp^b, which are associated with K and k in a similar fashion as are rh'(C) and rh''(E) with Rh$_0$(D). Antibodies for these new factors are so rare that one need not consider them in everyday laboratory work.

6. Considerable racial variations have been established for Kell, Duffy, and Kidd factors. For example, in U. S. Negroids the incidence of Kell-positive persons is much lower—2 per cent—than among U. S. Caucasoids (Table 5–11). In the Duffy system, Negroids are found whose blood possesses neither of the Fy^a—Fy^b factors, but they may carry instead a hypothetical third allele. The frequency of the Jk^a factor is greater in the U. S. Negroid (over 90 per cent) than in the U. S. Caucasoid population.

7. Family studies have shown Kell, Duffy, and Kidd factors to be inherited according to Mendelian genetics and to be independent of the other blood group systems.

6. **The Lewis Blood Group System.** In this system two blood factors, detectable by their corresponding antibodies, are called Le^a and Le^b. Both are seen frequently as "natural" antibodies of low titer. In some instances they possess hemolytic activity and, if present in high concentration, may be responsible for complications in blood transfusions.

All Le^a-positive persons, which make up about 20 per cent of adult Caucasoids, have been found to be nonsecretors of group-specific substance, A and B.

Although in adults the incidence of Le^a-positive individuals is 20 per cent, a much higher incidence (80 per cent) is found in newborns. To explain this discrepancy, it has been suggested that in adults anti-Le^a reacts only with red cells homozygous for the Le^a factor, whereas in newborn and young infants heterozygous red cells (Le^a Le^b) also give positive reactions. This by contrast with other blood factors represents an example of recessive inheritance.

A certain percentage of blood specimens, the frequency varying in different racial groups, possesses neither Le^a nor Le^b factors. While among Caucasoids this blood type is found in about 6 per cent, it reaches much higher proportions among Negroids. Such persons are capable of forming antibodies for both Le^a and Le^b.

7. **The Lutheran Blood Group System.** The factor Lu^a occurs in approximately 8 per cent of Caucasoids. More recently its allelomorphic factor, Lu^b, also has been discovered by its corresponding antibody. Lu^b is present in all Lu^a-negative and in the majority of Lu^a-positive individuals. Since Lutheran antibodies occur rarely and are low-titered complete antibodies, their clinical significance is exceedingly limited. Only exceptionally has anti-Lu^b been implicated in transfusion reactions. Evidence for linkage of Lutheran genes to secretor genes has been presented.

8. **Other blood factors.** In addition to the nine blood group systems discussed so far and summarized in Table 5–1, a number of other blood factors discovered in recent years require more studies before their final classification. Some of these factors were originally found only in members of one family—"private" or "family" factors. The opposite behavior, namely almost universal occurrence, has been reported for

other blood factors that were absent in only one or a few individuals; familial distribution of the absence of such factors was observed and indicates a genetic mechanism.

In the course of further studies one of three developments may eventually take place with the "new" blood factors: they may turn out to belong to one of the nine known blood group systems; they may be found to represent new, independent blood group systems, the main factor showing much greater frequency in some ethnic groups than in others; or they may remain "family factors," possibly attributable to rare mutations.

Examples of the first eventuality—assignment to "old" blood group systems of blood factors originally considered to be "family factors"—are Mi^a and Vw, which have been recognized as belonging to the MNS system. A particularly interesting example in this category is the universal factor Tj^a, the absence of which was first discovered by Levine (1951) in a patient whose serum was found incompatible with all blood specimens of the same ABO group tested except her own and that of her sister. This property, called "Tj^a-negative," was subsequently encountered in approximately 20 other persons from ten families residing in different parts of the world. Sanger (1955) noted that all Tj^a-negative persons were also P-negative and was able to prove the association of Tj^a with the P system. In all Tj^a-negative persons tested so far, anti-Tj^a antibody was present in the serum, even though there was no known previous antigenic stimulation. Anti-Tj^a in most instances acts as hemolysin in the presence of complement.

Other factors of universal distribution are Ve, I, and Yt^a. In this connection it should be noted that serums of persons possessing antibodies for the blood factors U (MNS system), Cellano (k), Lu^b, and hr″ (e) will be found to agglutinate more than 98 per cent of random blood specimens tested and thus may at first glance arouse the suspicion that they are antibodies for one of the universal blood factors. Obviously such findings pose serious difficulties in connection with blood transfusions, and their solution requires cooperation of many blood banks. In such situations the "rare blood donor file," established by the American Association of Blood Banks, may prove valuable.

The second trend—development of a new blood group system—is exemplified by the Diego factor (Di^a), which was originally discovered in one single family but subsequently was shown to occur with frequencies of up to 10 to 45 per cent in certain populations, such as among certain South and North American Indians, and in Mongoloid populations (China, Japan). Similarly the recently discovered Sutter blood factor (Js^a) is present in a sizable proportion of U. S. Negroids but exceedingly rare in other races.

Additional "family blood factors" have been reported. Their clinical importance is based on their etiologic role in isolated instances of hemolytic disease of the newborn and complications of blood transfusions. Further studies are needed to fully assess their significance (cf. Stern, 1962).

Hemagglutination Techniques

I. General Principles

1. Specimen. Clotted blood is preferable, since it permits testing both for blood factors in red cell suspensions prepared from the clot and for antibodies in the serum. As soon as possible after clotting, the blood specimen should be placed into the refrigerator unless further work proceeds immediately. The only exception is in the case of cold agglutinins; in such specimens serum should be separated from the clot before refrigeration, since otherwise cold agglutinins may be absorbed by the clot. As a rule blood grouping tests can be reliably carried out on properly preserved clotted specimens for periods up to five days, although the preservation of the reactivity of blood factors varies greatly with different blood group systems as well as with individual specimens. Tests for antibodies in the serum can be performed for several weeks with refrigerated and for up to two years with frozen specimens. Testing for blood factors on red cells from oxalated or citrated blood should be done within 24 hours; plasma is poorly suited for antibody tests. Blood from skin punctures may be directly transferred into physiologic saline and used for blood group tests.

2. Preparation of red cell suspensions. Depending on the specific technique employed, 2, 5, 10, or 50 per cent red cell suspensions are required. These can be prepared by transferring freshly obtained blood from a skin puncture into saline or by suspending in saline the packed red cells obtained from citrated or oxalated blood. Preservative anticoagulant solutions are also available that permit preservation of red cells for one month or longer.* This is most useful for controls and panel cells of known antigenic composition. Most frequently suspensions are made by gently breaking up blood clots with an applicator stick and transferring the red cell aggregates into saline or other suspending media.

In order to acquire skill in preparing red cell suspensions of specific concentrations, the following technique should be followed:

a. To about 5 ml. of physiologic saline add several drops of whole blood (fresh, citrated, oxalated, or fragments of clots)

b. Centrifuge for sufficient length of time in order to pack the red cells

c. Withdraw the supernatant fluid as completely as possible

d. Add 0.1 ml. of the packed red cells to a test tube containing 4.9 ml. of physiologic saline and mix well. Remove any small clots that may be present. This represents a 2 per cent suspension of red cells in saline. After one has acquired sufficient practice, one need not measure the amounts of red cells and suspending media but can estimate the density of the suspension by its appearance. Analogous procedures are used for preparation of red cell suspensions of different concentrations and in various media (e.g., serum, bovine albumin). All red cell suspensions must be refrigerated when not in use. They are unsuitable if they show hemolysis and should be used within 12 hours after preparation.

Equipment

a. Test tubes: for collection of blood (100 mm. long, 13 mm. wide) and for hemagglutination tests (75 mm. long, 10 mm. wide)

b. Test tube racks

c. Centrifuge†

d. Waterbaths

* a. Modified Alsever's Solution: 2.05 gm. dextrose, 0.8 gm. sodium citrate, 0.05 gm. citric acid, and 0.45 gm. sodium chloride are dissolved in 100 ml. distilled water; pH is expected to be 6.1. (Bukantz, S. C., Rein, C. R., and Kent, J. F.: Studies in complement fixation. II. J. Lab. & Clin. Med., *31:* 994, 1946.)

b. Serum-lactose Solution: 10 gm. lactose, 1.53 gm. dextrose, 1.38 gm. sodium citrate, and 0.5 gm. citric acid are dissolved in 100 ml. distilled water and mixed with 100 ml. of serum from person of group AB (serum must be free of irregular and cold agglutinins). (Stern, K., Busch, S., and Malkin, L.: Preservation of red cells for *in vitro* testing. Proc. Am. Assoc. Blood Banks, 6th Annual Meeting, 1953, p. 106.)

† The Hemofuge (MacAlaster-Bicknell) and Serofuge (Clay-Adams) are especially useful for rapid centrifugation, washing of red cells, and miscellaneous procedures in hemagglutination tests.

e. Miscellaneous: wooden applicators, capillary pipets, rubber bulbs, and so forth.

Reagents

a. Physiologic saline solution

b. Blood grouping serums:
   Anti-A serum (minimum titer with A_1 cells 1:256)‡
   Anti-B serum (minimum titer 1:256)‡
   Anti-A, B serum (serum of group O (minimum titer 1:256 with A_1 and B cells)
   Anti-A_1 serum (absorbed anti-A serum; plant lectins)
   Anti-Rh_o(D) serum (minimum titer 1:32)
   Anti-rh'(C) serum (minimum titer 1:32)
   Anti-rh''(E) serum (minimum titer 1:32)
   Anti-hr'(c) serum (minimum titer 1:32)
   Anti-human globulin (Coombs) serum
   Miscellaneous antiserums for other blood factors, such as hr''(e), K (Kell), and Fy^a, as required.

c. Bovine or human albumin (22 per cent or 30 per cent)

Antiserums must be refrigerated when not in use. Reagents and blood specimens for hemagglutination tests must be handled aseptically, since bacterial contamination may cause serious sources of error, leading to both falsely negative and falsely positive results.

Positive and negative controls must be run daily with all antiserums.

The following specific techniques for the most commonly employed hemagglutination tests have been shown to give reliable results. Numerous variations of these methods are available and may be equally successful in the hands of properly trained and experienced persons. One must also keep in mind that the commercial antiserums commonly used have been standardized to give optimal results with certain techniques; hence the instructions accompanying such antiserums must be closely followed.

II. ABO Grouping

1. Six-tube technique. 1. Separate the serum from red cells or clot of unknown specimen.

‡ In order to minimize errors, blue dye is added to commercial anti-A serum and yellow dye to anti-B serum.

2. Prepare a 2 per cent suspension in saline of the red cells of the unknown specimen.

3. For each specimen 6 test tubes are labeled, showing in addition to proper identification of the unknown specimen the following information: Tube 1—anti-A; tube 2—anti-B; tube 3—anti-A,B; tube 4—A; tube 5—B; tube 6—O.

4. Place one drop of the anti-A serum into tube 1, one drop of the anti-B serum into tube 2, and one drop of the anti-A,B serum into tube 3.

5. Add two drops each of the serum of the unknown specimen to tubes 4, 5, and 6.

6. Add one drop each of the 2 per cent red cell suspension in saline of the unknown specimen to tubes 1, 2, and 3.

7. To tube 4 add one drop of a 2 per cent red cell suspension in saline of group A cells; to tube 5 add one drop of a 2 per cent red cell suspension in saline of group B cells; and to tube 6 add one drop of a 2 per cent suspension of red cells in saline of group O cells.

8. Mix the contents of all tubes by shaking the test tube rack.

9. Depending on the speed necessary for completing the test, one of two alternatives may be chosen:

a. The test tubes may be left at room temperature (20 to 25° C.) for at least two hours.

b. After two to three minutes the tubes may be centrifuged (one minute at 1500 r.p.m. in clinical centrifuge or one-half to one minute in Serofuge or Hemofuge).

10. After incubation or centrifugation the red cell suspensions are redispersed by tapping the tubes. Presence of agglutination is checked with the naked eye, with the scanning lens of a microscope, and, if results are doubtful or negative, microscopically (16 mm. objective) after placing a drop on a slide.

11. All results are immediately entered in the proper work record, using preferably "plus" signs for agglutination and "minus" signs for absence of agglutination.

INTERPRETATION. 1. The results of an ABO grouping test can be accepted as valid only if the findings obtained in the first three test tubes with known antiserums agree with those obtained in the second three test tubes with known red cell suspensions; this second part of the test is called "confirmation," "check," or "reverse" grouping. Figure 5–3 schematically compares the results in the four main ABO groups in such tests when both the un-

known red cells and the unknown serum are tested. If at all possible, it is desirable that two different persons perform ABO groupings, one testing with known antiserums and the other with known cells. After they have completed the tests and recorded their readings independently, the results should be compared for final interpretation.

2. Absent or weak agglutination with the unknown serum may be simulated by hemolysis of the known red cells; this suggests the presence of hemolytic anti-A or anti-B antibody. It is important to record such findings (using the letter "H" for hemolysin), since they affect significantly the selection of blood to be used as "universal donor" or for transfusion of "universal recipients." The assumption that hemolysis is due to anti-A or anti-B must be confirmed by repeating the test with the serum after its inactivation in a water bath at 56° C. for 30 minutes; use of the inactivated serum is expected to result in agglutination instead of hemolysis.

3. If discrepancies in the two parts of ABO grouping are observed, the test should be repeated in order to rule out some mistake in the previous test. If a second test reveals the same discrepancy, the following possibilities are to be considered:

a. Cold agglutinins. They may cause agglutination of the known cells by the unknown serum regardless of its ABO group. This must be confirmed by testing the unknown serum with its own red cells at 4° C. for 1 to 2 hours. Under these conditions cold agglutinins produce agglutination, which disappears after transfer of the specimen to a water bath at 37° C. for 5 to 10 minutes. (For further tests for cold agglutinins, see p. 890ff.)

b. Agglutination of the unknown red cells by known antiserums that conflict with the results obtained in the confirmation grouping may be due to coating of the red cells by autoantibodies. Confirmation of this phenomenon is obtained by performing on the unknown red cells the direct antiglobulin (Coombs) test and obtaining positive results. In order to obtain in such cases a reliable ABO grouping, the red cells should be washed several times with large amounts of physiologic saline solution following which they are more likely to give adequate results.

c. Unexpected agglutination ob-

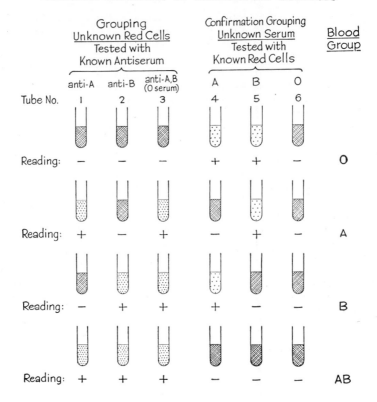

Figure 5–3.   Schematic outline of ABO grouping test.

tained with the unknown serum may reflect presence of *irregular agglutinins*, such as Rh antibodies, which react with the corresponding blood factor in the suspensions of the known red cells. This must be verified by demonstration of such irregular antibodies (see antibody identification, p. 287).

d. Discrepancies between the two parts of ABO grouping tests may be found in specimens of subgroups of A and AB. Most commonly these are specimens of group A_2 or A_2B containing anti-A_1 in their serums. Thus agglutination of the unknown red cells with anti-A serum may be associated with agglutination of known group A red cells by the unknown serum. Clarification in such cases is obtained by establishing the subgroup of A of the specimen (see p. 283) and by testing the unknown serum with suspensions of A_1 and A_2 cells. The latter test should be done at room temperature as well as at ice box temperature, since these antibodies as a rule act best at low temperatures. Group O cells must

be included as control for presence of nonspecific cold agglutinins.

e. As mentioned previously, serums of newborn and young infants may not contain the isoagglutinins expected from the reactivity of their red cells (cf. p. 266). Hence in infants use of the unknown serums is not a reliable procedure (cf. crossmatch tests, p. 302). Much less frequently isoagglutinins may be absent in older children and adults because of hypogammaglobulinemia or agammaglobulinemia or for unknown reasons.

COMMENTS. 1. It is recommended to place the serum into the test tube first and to follow with addition of the red cell suspension. In this way the error of omitting addition of the serum can be avoided.

2. The red cell suspensions of groups A, B, and O must be prepared freshly on the day of use. It is recommended to prepare each suspension from a pool of three different red cell specimens in order to reduce variations in individual reactivity and to guarantee that A_1 cells are present among the A cells. Some workers prefer

to use only red cells known to be A_1 for this purpose.

2. Slide grouping tests. 1. Prepare a 10 per cent suspension in saline of the red cells to be tested.

2. Mark the left side of a clean glass slide "anti-A" and the right side "anti-B."

3. Add to the left side a drop of anti-A grouping serum and to the right side a drop of anti-B grouping serum.

4. Next to the drops of anti-A serum and anti-B serum add one drop of the 10 per cent suspension of the unknown red cells. Be careful not to cause confluence of the drops on the left and right sides of the slide.

5. With one-half of an applicator stick mix the red cell suspension with the anti-A serum, and with the other half mix the red cell suspension with the anti-B serum.

6. Gently rock the slide back and forth and observe the mixture for one minute unless agglutination occurs earlier.

7. Enter the results as "plus" for agglutination and as "minus" for absence of agglutination.

8. It is necessary to confirm the slide grouping by testing the unknown serum with the known red cell suspensions of groups A, B, and O as indicated in the previous section.

COMMENTS. 1. Instead of a 10 per cent red cell suspension, small drops of blood obtained directly from skin punctures or whole oxalated or citrated blood not older than 24 hours may be used. In such cases one must avoid adding excessive amounts of blood to the antiserum, since this may interfere with adequate reading of the test and also may produce falsely negative results because of antigen excess.

2. Slow and weak agglutinations may occur with blood specimens of subgroups A_2, A_2B, A_3, A_3B, and so forth. This may result in falsely negative readings, since drying of the mixture may take place before the agglutination becomes clearly visible.

3. In some blood banks it is customary to do a preliminary ABO grouping for the donor record by adding to a drop of anti-A and anti-B serum one drop of blood from a skin puncture of the prospective donor. Results of such tests must be considered preliminary, since a certain percentage of weak subgroups of A and AB may be erroneously classified as O and B, respectively.

3. Determination of subgroups of A and AB. 1. To a properly identified test tube add one drop of anti-A_1 serum (absorbed anti-A serum) or of anti-A_1 lectin.

2. Add one drop of a 2 per cent red cell suspension in saline of the unknown specimen.

3. Let stand at room temperature for 15 minutes.

4. Centrifuge for one-half to one minute and check for presence of agglutination.

5. Controls with known red cells of group A_1 and group A_2 must be included with each test. Results are valid only if the expected positive and negative results are obtained with these controls.

INTERPRETATION. Anti-A_1 serum or anti-A_1 lectin agglutinates only cells of group A_1 or A_1B. Specimens that are not agglutinated are most commonly group A_2 or A_2B. The rare subgroup A_3 or A_3B can be recognized by the fact that on microscopic examination only a few small agglutinates are found surrounded by large numbers of nonagglutinated red cells even when potent anti-A serums are tested with the unknown red cells. Red cells of the rare subgroup A_o have the property of being agglutinated by most anti-A,B serums (serums of group O persons) while anti-A serums are not capable of doing so.

III. Rh Typing

1. Determination of Rh_o (D) factor with antiserums containing incomplete Rh antibodies (blocking, conglutinating, modified slide test serums). 1. Prepare a 5 per cent red cell suspension of the unknown specimen in its own serum or in group AB serum found to be free of any agglutinins.

2. Into a properly labeled test tube place one drop of the antiserum.

3. Add one drop of the 5 per cent red cell suspension and mix well.

4. Incubate in a water bath for 30 minutes at 37° C.

5. Roll the tube gently in order to redisperse the red cells.

6. Check for agglutination with the scanning lens of the microscope. If agglutination is present, record the result after checking it microscopically.

7. If agglutination was absent, centrifuge for one to two minutes at 1500 r.p.m.

8. Resuspend the red cells as before and check for agglutination with the naked eye and the scanning lens. If agglutination is absent or doubtful, check by placing a drop of the mixture on a slide and examine with the 16 mm. objective of the microscope.

9. Enter the results in the workbook.

COMMENTS. 1. Instead of incubating for one-half hour followed by centrifuga- .

tion, the test may be incubated for two hours at 37° C. and read without centrifugation.

2. A modification of this test can be used by the experienced worker: Instead of preparing a 5 per cent suspension in their own serum of the unknown red cells, one may transfer with an applicator stick ("stick method") a sufficient number of red cells into the test tube containing the anti-Rh typing serum to make an approximately 5 per cent suspension.

3. Agglutinations with anti-Rh serums are less solid and more easily dispersed than those produced by anti-A and anti-B serums. Hence the serum-red cell mixtures should never be shaken but should be gently twisted or rolled until the red cells are resuspended.

4. With each run of Rh typings, controls must be included in which the same antiserum is tested with specimens of known Rh-positive and Rh-negative red cells.

2. Rh typing with antiserums containing complete antibodies (saline test serums). The procedure is identical with the preceding one, except that a 2 per cent red cell suspension of the unknown specimen is prepared in saline. One drop of this suspension is added to 1 drop of the antiserum. Incubation of the serum-red cells mixture for two hours at 37° C., or incubation for 30 minutes followed by centrifugation, may be used.

COMMENTS. 1. In view of the limited availability of saline anti-Rh serums their use should be restricted to special cases, such as checking doubtful results obtained with antiserums containing incomplete antibodies.

2. Saline Rh antiserums should not be used for Rh typing of newborn infants with hemolytic disease of the newborn; because of coating of red cells with Rh antibodies falsely negative results may be obtained in such specimens.

3. Specimens of patients with autoimmune hemolytic disease (see p. 313) may be difficult to type using incomplete Rh antibodies, since suspension of red cells in any serum may bring about agglutination. In this situation repeated washing of the red cells and use of the saline test is recommended.

3. Slide test for Rh typing. 1. On a properly labeled glass slide place 1 drop of anti-Rh serum containing incomplete Rh antibody.

2. To the drop of antiserum add 2 drops of either whole blood (either directly obtained from skin puncture or oxalated or

Figure 5–4. Heated viewing box for Rh testing.

citrated blood not older than 24 hours, or a 50 per cent cell suspension prepared from clotted blood in its own serum).

3. Mix serum and red cells and distribute over a large area of the slide.

4. Place the slide on a heated viewing box (Fig. 5–4), bringing the temperature of the mixture to 40 to 45° C.

5. Gently rock the slide back and forth and observe for agglutination.

6. Observe the test for two minutes unless agglutination occurs earlier.

7. At the end of the two-minute period record presence of agglutination with a "plus" and absence of agglutination with a "minus" sign.

COMMENTS. 1. Only Rh antiserums with incomplete antibodies (blocking, albumin agglutinin, slide test serums) can be used.

2. Use of too dilute a red cell suspension or addition of too small an amount of red cell suspension to too much antiserum are common sources of falsely negative results.

3. Another important cause of falsely negative tests is inadequate warming of the mixture. The reaction may be speeded up by preheating glass slides on the viewing box.

4. Falsely positive results may result from autoagglutination or rouleaux formation.

5. Partial or complete drying of the mixture must be avoided, since this makes reading of the test difficult or impossible.

4. Tests for weak Rh_o variants (D^u). 1. Prepare in saline a 2 per cent suspension of the red cells to be tested.

2. Add 2 drops of Rh antiserum with incomplete antibodies to a properly labeled test tube.

3. Add to the test tube 2 drops of the 2 per cent red cell suspension.

4. Incubate the red cell-serum mixture

for 30 minutes in a water bath at 37° C.

5. Fill the test tube with the red cell-serum physiologic saline mixture and resuspend the red cells in the entire volume.

6. Centrifuge for 30 to 60 seconds.

7. Decant the supernatant as completely as possible and replace with physiologic saline.

8. Repeat such washing of red cells three times.

9. Remove the supernatant of the last washing as completely as possible.

10. Resuspend the packed red cells in 2 drops of physiologic saline.

11. Add 1 drop of antihuman globulin (Coombs) serum to the red cell suspension and mix.

12. Centrifuge for one minute.

13. Check for presence of agglutination.

CAUTION. Each test must be accompanied by a control prepared by adding 2 drops of bovine albumin (20 to 30 per cent) to 2 drops of red cell suspension used in the main test. This control is treated in the same way as the test itself.

INTERPRETATION AND COMMENTS. 1. Agglutination observed in the main test and absence of agglutination in the control indicate the presence of the weakly reacting $Rh_o(D^u)$ factor.

2. If the control also shows positive results, the test may be repeated in order to rule out a technical error. If the control continues to give positive results, this suggests coating of the red cells with auto-antibody. This can be confirmed by the direct antiglobulin (Coombs) test (cf. method V, A). Determination of the D^u factor in a patient with a positive direct antiglobulin test is not possible.

3. Since there are a great many variants of the D^u factor differing from each other in reactivity, it is not uncommon that the red cells of the same persons may be found at one time to react as D^u, whereas subsequently when different anti-Rh serums are used they may be found as "regularly" Rh_o-(D)-positive in tests using method III, 1. However, as a rule negative results are obtained with such specimens when tested with the saline test tube method (III, 2).

4. In rare instances D^u specimens possess such weak reactivity that even the test just described fails to give a positive result. In some of these instances presence of D^u can be demonstrated if the cells are first treated with papain (cf. p. 288) and then subjected to incubation with anti-Rh serum, followed by the antiglobulin test as just described.

IV. Rh Subtyping. In instances to be discussed in connection with pretransfusion (cf. p. 301) and prenatal testing (cf. p. 310), it is necessary to test for other Rh factors. Tests for rh'(C) and rh''(E) are usually done in persons negative for Rh_o (D) while Hr factors are of interest in connection with tests for Rh genotypes (cf. p. 277).

The techniques are identical with tests for $Rh_o(D)$. Test tube techniques are preferred, and depending on the availability of antiserums with complete or incomplete antibodies, tests are carried out with corresponding techniques (III, 1 or III, 2).

Antiserums are also available that contain antibodies for the three Rh factors, $Rh_o(D)$, rh'(C), and rh''(E). Such antiserums may be used parallel with anti-$Rh_o(D)$ serum. If positive results are obtained with anti-Rh_o''' (anti-CDE) serum and negative results with anti-$Rh_o(D)$ serum, this indicates the presence of rh'(C) and/or rh''(E). Suitable tests using specific anti-rh'(C) and anti-rh''(E) serums decide the question. On the other hand negative results rule out presence of both rh'(C) and rh''(E).

In subtyping for Rh and Hr factors, it is essential to include known positive and negative controls in order to assure validity of the tests.

V. The Antiglobulin (Coombs) Test

A. The direct antiglobulin (Coombs) test. 1. Place 5 to 10 drops of blood in a test tube (100 mm. long; 13 mm. wide) and fill with physiologic saline.

2. Mix contents and centrifuge for one minute at 1500 r.p.m. in order to pack the red cells.

3. Decant the supernatant as completely as possible. Repeat the washing three times, each time removing as much of the supernatant as possible.

4. Prepare a 2 per cent suspension in saline of the red cells.

5. In a test tube (75 mm. long; 10 mm. wide) place 2 drops of the antihuman globulin (Coombs) serum.

6. Add 2 drops of the red cell suspension and mix. Let stand for five minutes.

7. Centrifuge for one minute at 500 r.p.m. and check for agglutination with the naked eye and with the microscope.

8. Include controls without which the test is valueless.

a. POSITIVE CONTROL. 1. Prepare 2 per cent suspension in saline of known Rh-positive red cells of a healthy person.

2. Place into a small test tube 1 drop of an anti-Rh$_0$ (anti-D) slide test serum meeting the minimum requirements of the National Institutes of Health and diluted with saline 2 to 4 times.

3. Add 2 drops of the cell suspension.

4. Incubate for 30 minutes at 37° C.

5. Centrifuge the mixture of cells and serum and decant serum as completely as possible.

6. Wash cell sediment three times with tubefuls of saline, followed each time by centrifugation and by as complete removal of supernatant as possible.

7. After the third washing add saline to the packed cells to the original volume.

8. Add 2 drops of anti-human serum to the cell suspension and let stand at room temperature for five minutes. If agglutination is observed, this is recorded.

9. If no agglutination is visible, centrifuge at low speed for one minute (500 r.p.m.). Check again for agglutination.

B. NEGATIVE CONTROL. Proceed in the same manner as with the positive control but use known Rh-negative red cells of a healthy individual.

INTERPRETATION. 1. A positive direct antiglobulin (Coombs) test is indicated by agglutination of the test and the positive control and absence of agglutination in the negative control. Although microscopic checking of doubtful results is recommended, the presence of a few small agglutinates visible only microscopically should be regarded as a doubtful result. In such cases the test should be repeated, preferably with a different antiglobulin reagent.

2. Coating of red cells of groups A and B with the corresponding isoagglutinins anti-A and anti-B in newborn infants is often difficult to detect by means of the direct antiglobulin (Coombs) test. For best results the test should be centrifuged immediately after addition of the antiglobulin serum. Specifically standardized antiglobulin reagents may prove most suitable.

3. Positive direct antiglobulin tests are most commonly found in infants with hemolytic disease of the newborn, in patients with autoimmune hemolytic anemia, and in recipients of incompatible blood transfusions.

B. The indirect antiglobulin test. 1. Prepare a 2 per cent red cell suspension of the specimen to be used. NOTE: This may be either a specimen of known antigenic composition if the test is to be used for demonstration of an unknown antibody (e.g., anti-Duffy or anti-Kell), or it may be a specimen of unknown antigenic composition if demonstration of an unknown antigen with a known antibody, such as anti-Duffy or anti-Kell, is intended.

2. Into a properly labeled test tube place 2 drops of the serum to be used.

3. Add 2 drops of the red cell suspension.

4. Incubate the red cell-serum mixture for 30 minutes to two hours, depending on the reactivity and sensitivity of the serum.

5. If no agglutination has occurred after incubation, fill the test tube with physiologic saline and centrifuge.

6. Follow the same steps (No. 2, 3, 5 to 7) as outlined for the direct antiglobulin (Coombs) test.

7. In order to assure validity of the test, controls must be included in which either red cells of known antigenic composition or antibodies of known specificity are used in parallel with the main test.

COMMENTS. 1. The indirect antiglobulin (Coombs) technique cannot be used with red cells known to give a positive direct antiglobulin test.

2. The indirect antiglobulin technique is frequently used for determination of certain blood factors, such as Duffy, Kell, and Kidd.

3. The indirect antiglobulin test may also be used for demonstration of antibodies for these blood factors.

4. The indirect antiglobulin test is one of the most reliable methods for crossmatching tests (cf. p. 296).

5. A modification of the indirect antiglobulin test, with increased sensitivity in some instances, is based on use of enzyme-treated red cells. However, this method cannot be used for demonstration of anti-Duffy, anti-S, and some other rarely encountered antibodies reacting with blood factors that are destroyed by proteolytic enzymes. Caution also must be exerted concerning falsely positive results owing to the great sensitivity of the technique.

VI. Tests for Other Blood Factors

1. MN typing

Reagents

The anti-M and anti-N typing serums commonly used are prepared by injecting rabbits with human red cells of type OM or ON and absorbing these immune serums with reciprocal red cells (N after injection of M cells; M after injection of N cells) until agglutination specific for one of the two types is obtained. In using anti-M and anti-N typing serums, it is important to follow closely the instructions of the manu-facturer, since specificity and sensitivity of the tests have been standardized for these conditions.

Technique

1. Prepare a 2 per cent suspension in saline of the red cells of the unknown specimen. Controls of known blood groups and types must include M, N, and MN cells in combination with A, B, and O so that all groups, subgroups, and types are represented (for example: A_2M or A_2BM; A_1BMN or A_1MN; BM; ON).

2. Set up two rows of five tubes each.

3. To each tube of the first row add 1 drop of anti-M serum.

4. To each tube of the second row add 1 drop of anti-N serum.

5. To the first tubes of each row add 1 drop of a 2 per cent suspension of the unknown cells.

6. To the second tubes of each row add 1 drop of the first control suspension. To the third tubes of each row add 1 drop of the second control suspension. To the fourth tubes of each row add 1 drop of the third control suspension. To the fifth tubes of each row add 1 drop of the fourth control suspension.

7. Shake. Incubate for two hours at room temperature (about 20° C.), shaking tubes at 15-minute intervals.

8. Shake tubes gently and check for agglutination with naked eye. If no clump-ing is visible, place the tube horizontally on the stage of the microscope and read with the scanning lens. Clumping of the un-known cells with the anti-M serum indi-cates the presence of factor M. Clumping of the unknown cells with the anti-N serum indicates the presence of factor N. If the unknown cells are clumped by both

Example

TYPING SERUM	SUSPENSION OF UNKNOWN RED CELLS		
	(a)	(b)	(c)
1st row anti-M	+	−	+
2nd row anti-N	−	+	+
Results:	M	N	MN

TYPING SERUM	RED CELL SUSPENSIONS OF CONTROLS			
1st row				
anti-M	A_2M (+)	A_1BMN (+)	BM (+)	ON (−)
2nd row				
anti-N	A_2M (−)	A_1BMN (+)	BM (−)	ON (+)

serums, both factors are present. The test is invalid unless the controls show the following results: Cells of type M must be clumped with anti-M serum, cells of type N with anti-N serum, and cells of type MN with both serums.

2. Kell and Duffy typing

Reagents

Anti-Kell and anti-Duffy typing serums as a rule contain incomplete antibodies, which react best in the antiglobulin tech-nique.

Technique

1. Prepare a 2 per cent suspension in saline of the red cells of the unknown specimen.

2. Into a properly labeled test tube, place 1 drop of anti-Kell (anti-Duffy) serum.

3. Add to the serum 2 drops of the 2 per cent red cell suspension.

4. Incubate for one hour in a water bath at 37° C.

5. Wash with physiologic saline three times and proceed as outlined in the direct antiglobulin test (V, A, steps No. 5 to 7).

INTERPRETATION. 1. Agglutination ob-tained in the test indicates that specimen is Kell-positive (K) or Duffy-positive (Fy^a), depending on the type of serum used.

2. Positive and negative controls, using red cells of known antigenic composition, must be included with each test, and the results are valid only if these controls give the expected results.

3. Miscellaneous blood factors. In cer-tain conditions a variety of other blood factors may have to be determined, such as P, Lewis, and Lutheran factors. In all such instances availability of potent and reliable antiserums is critical. The reactiv-ity of such antiserums must be known, specifically whether they contain complete or incomplete antibodies, and optimal con-ditions of time and temperature of incuba-tion must be observed. Positive and nega-tive controls must always be included in order to assure validity of the results.

VII. Screening for and Identification of Isoantibodies. The following procedures are designed to detect and identify isoanti-bodies other than anti-A and anti-B in serum of persons of any of the ABO groups. Such tests as a rule are required in con-nection with either blood transfusion ther-apy or isosensitization associated with preg-nancy. Most commonly these tests concern the presence of Rh antibodies in $Rh_0(D)$-

negative persons. More rarely antibodies for blood factors other than $Rh_o(D)$ may be detected in Rh-positive persons or antibodies for some other blood factors in serum of Rh-negative and Rh-positive persons.

The following techniques deal mainly with tests for Rh antibodies. Modifications necessary for detection and identification of antibodies other than anti-Rh are discussed subsequently. One of two general approaches may be utilized for screening for Rh antibodies: (a) individual red cells of known Rh phenotypes may be used in order to detect presence and determine specificity of Rh antibodies, or (b) a pool of red cells prepared from two or three specimens possessing the commonly involved Rh factors may be employed for screening only. If positive results are obtained with pooled red cells (b), the test is repeated with individual red cells (a) in order to provide information concerning specificity of the Rh antibodies. Whenever pooled red cells are used, it is important that at least 30 per cent of the red cells forming the pool contain each blood factor for which antibodies are sought.

Several methods may be employed in order to have available red cells of known antigenic composition whenever needed. Members of the blood bank staff, laboratory, or hospital may be typed for such blood factors and blood obtained at appropriate times. All such blood specimens should be of group O in order to eliminate any confusing results resulting from isoagglutination by anti-A and anti-B. Blood donors readily available when needed may be used in a similar fashion, or blood specimens recently drawn may be tested for presence of the blood factors needed in order to select specimens with the desired antigenic composition. Finally panels of red cell suspensions of known antigenic composition are available commercially with periods of usefulness ranging from two to four weeks (cf. p. 280 for preservative solutions suitable for such purposes).

1. Papain-treated red cell technique (Kuhns and Bailey, 1950). This is one of the most sensitive techniques for demonstration of Rh-Hr antibodies.

A. PAPAIN TREATMENT OF RED CELLS

I. Reagents

   1. Stock solution of papain (1 per cent): suspend 1 gm. of papain in 100 ml. of 0.9 per cent physiologic saline and, after vigorous shaking, filter. This suspension when stored at 4° C. is stable for one month.

   2. Sörenson phosphate buffer: Mix 76.8 ml. of $\frac{1}{15}$M Na_2HPO_4 with 23.2 ml. of $\frac{1}{15}$M KH_2PO_4; expected pH: 7.3.

   3. Buffered saline: mix 9 volumes of physiologic saline with 1 volume of the buffer (2).

   4. Working solution of papain (0.1 per cent): on the day of use mix 9 volumes of buffered saline (3) with 1 volume of the stock solution of papain (1). Keep refrigerated when not in use. This solution must be prepared fresh daily.

II. Red Cell Suspensions

   1. Minimum requirement: O $Rh_1Rh_2(CDE)$; O rh(cde).

   2. If O Rh_1Rh_2 cells are not available, cells of types O $Rh_1(CDe)$ and O $Rh_2(cDE)$ may be either used individually or equal parts of their suspensions may be mixed.

   3. For identification of specificity of Rh antibodies the following additional red cells are needed: rh'(Cde), $Rh_o(cDe)$, and rh" (cdE).

III. Technique

   1. In a large test tube prepare red cell suspension in amount sufficient to yield 0.5 ml. of packed red cells.

   2. Wash red cells three times with large volumes of physiologic saline and pack red cells after last washing.

   3. Add 1.0 ml. of the buffered working solution of papain to 0.5 ml. of packed red cells and mix.

   4. Incubate the red cell-papain mixture for 30 minutes in water bath of 37° C. Agitate mixture at frequent intervals.

   5. Centrifuge mixture at moderate speed and remove supernatant.

   6. Wash the red cell sediment three times with saline.

   7. After the last washing remove the supernatant as completely as possible and add physiologic saline to make a 2 per cent suspension of the red cells.

NOTE: Papain-treated red cells react reliably only for 24 hours and hence must be prepared fresh on the day of use.

B. Screening Test. 1. Label with proper identification as many test tubes for each serum to be tested as different types of red cells are to be used. NOTE: The minimum consists of two test cells: Rh-positive red cells for the main test and Rh-negative red cells as control [cf. A. II. (1)].

2. Into each test tube place 2 drops of the unknown serum.

3. To each tube add 1 drop of the appropriate suspension of papain-treated red cells and mix.

4. Incubate all test tubes in a water bath of 37° C. for 30 minutes.

5. Check for agglutination with the naked eye and with the scanning lens. If results are doubtful, place one drop of suspension on a slide and check microscopically (16 mm. objective).

Interpretation. 1. Absence of agglutination in all tubes indicates absence of Rh antibodies.

2. Agglutination of Rh-positive cells in the absence of agglutination of Rh-negative cells indicates presence of Rh antibodies. Specificity of the antibodies can be deter-

mined by using test cells of different Rh phenotypes as shown in Table 5–12. Results of such tests also indicate whether antibodies react specifically with only one of the Rh factors or whether a combination of antibodies with different specificities is present.

3. The test is valid only if simultaneously run positive and negative controls—serums known to contain Rh antibodies or to be free of Rh antibodies, respectively—give the expected results.

4. In prenatal testing a red cell suspension from the husband should be included whenever available, provided his wife does not possess isoagglutinins reacting with AB blood factors present in the husband's red cells.

5. If agglutination occurs with Rh-positive and Rh-negative red cells, the following possibilities must be considered:

a. Autoagglutinins: this can be confirmed by finding a positive direct antiglobulin test on the red cells of the blood specimen tested. Furthermore the serum of the specimen tested with its own papain-treated red cells will produce agglutination.

b. Unsuitability of test cells. This may be due to bacterial contamination, coating with globulin, or improper preservation.

Table 5–12.   Interpretation of Screening Tests for Rh Antibodies

					PANEL CELLS*		
Serum No.	rh cde	rh' hr'-pos. Ccde	Rh₀ cDe	rh'' hr''-pos. cdEe	Rh₁ hr'-neg. CCDe	Rh₂ hr''-neg. cDEE	Antibodies Present for Factor(s)
I	−	−	−	−	−	−	none
II	−	−	+	−	+	+	Rh₀(D)
III	−	+	−	−	+	−	rh'(C)
IV	−	−	−	+	−	+	rh''(E)
V	+	+	+	+	−	+	hr'(c)
VI	+	+	+	+	+	−	hr''(e)
VII	−	+	+	−	+	+	Rh₀(D), rh'(C)
VIII	−	−	+	+	+	+	Rh₀(D), rh''(E)
IX	−	+	+	+	+	+	Rh₀(D), rh'(C), rh''(E)

* All cells group O.
+ Agglutination.
− Absence of agglutination.

c. Bacterial contamination of the serum tested (cf. bacteriogenic agglutination, p. 299).

d. Presence of antibody owing to a factor (which is present in all test cells) other than $Rh_o(D)$. One of such antibodies is anti-hr'(c). As indicated in Table 5–12 identification of anti-hr'(c) is possible if the panel includes red cells of type Rh_1hr'-negative (CCDe), which are not agglutinated by this antibody.

CAUTIONS AND COMMENTS. 1. The papain-treated red cells must not be incubated for periods exceeding 30 minutes, since falsely positive results may be obtained after prolonged incubation.

2. Other enzymes, such as trypsin, ficin, and bromelin, may be used with similar results as papain. The techniques recommended for their use must be observed closely.

2. Indirect antiglobulin (Coombs) technique (including test for complete or saline agglutinins). I. Test cells of similar composition as those mentioned for the papain technique are used.

II. *Technique*

1. Prepare 2 per cent red cell suspensions in saline of the test cells.

2. For each serum specimen to be tested, identify properly as many test tubes as test cells are to be used.

3. Into each test tube place 2 drops of the serum to be tested.

4. To each tube add 2 drops of the 2 per cent suspension of the appropriate test cell suspension.

5. Incubate the red cell-serum mixtures in a water bath at 37° C. for two hours.

6. Check for agglutination with the naked eye and with the scanning lens and microscopically if in doubt.

7. If no agglutination is observed, proceed with washing of red cell suspensions and addition of antiglobulin serum as outlined in section V (antiglobulin test, p. 285).

INTERPRETATION. 1. If agglutination is observed in step 6, this indicates presence of complete (saline) Rh antibodies.

2. If agglutination is absent in step 6 and occurs after completion of step 7, this indicates presence of incomplete Rh antibodies.

3. Presence and absence of agglutination observed with different test cells is interpreted as outlined for papain technique (Table 5–12).

3. Albumin technique (Hattersley)

I. *Reagents*

1. Bovine or human albumin (22 or 30 per cent).

2. Test cells, as outlined in papain technique.

II. *Technique*

1. Prepare a 2 per cent suspension of the test cells in bovine albumin.

2. For each serum specimen to be tested identify properly as many test tubes as test cells are used.

3. Into each test tube place 2 drops of the serum to be tested.

4. To each test tube add 1 drop of the appropriate suspension of the test cells in bovine albumin and mix.

5. Without waiting, centrifuge the red cell-serum mixture for three minutes at 1200 r.p.m.

6. Check for agglutination macroscopically and with the scanning lens.

7. If no agglutination is noted, incubate test tubes for one hour in a water bath of 37° C.

8. Centrifuge for one minute at 500 r.p.m.

9. Gently resuspend the red cells and check for agglutination with the naked eye and microscopically.

INTERPRETATION AND COMMENTS. 1. The centrifugation in step 5 is intended to eliminate falsely negative results caused by antibody excess, which may be responsible for a prozone phenomenon.

2. The following additional sets may also be included in the test: (a) red cells of the unknown specimen suspended in their own serum (2 per cent) and treated in the same way as the other tubes; (b) addition to 2 drops of the unknown serum of 1 drop of 2 per cent suspensions in saline of the test cells, run parallel with the test tubes containing albumin-suspended red cells. Positive results with red cells of set (a) indicate presence of autoagglutinins. Positive results obtained with saline-suspended red cells suggest the presence of complete (saline) Rh antibodies.

4. Slide test (Diamond-Abelson)

I. *Reagents*

50 per cent suspension of O Rh-positive and O Rh-negative test cells.

II. *Technique*

1. Place 1 drop each of the unknown serum on two glass slides, one of which is identified as "Rh+," and the other as "Rh−."

2. To the first slide add 2 drops of the

50 per cent suspension of O Rh-positive blood; to the second slide add 2 drops of the 50 per cent suspension of the O Rh-negative blood.

3. On each slide mix the serum with the cell suspension and spread over large area.

4. Place the slides on a heated viewing box (cf. Fig. 5–4, p. 284).

5. Gently rock the slides back and forth, and observe up to three minutes unless agglutination occurs earlier.

INTERPRETATION. Agglutination of the Rh-positive red cells and absence of agglutination of Rh-negative red cells indicates the presence of Rh antibodies. NOTE: The sensitivity of the techniques 1 to 4 for detection of Rh antibodies decreases in this order of enumeration: papain technique, indirect antiglobulin (Coombs) technique, Hattersley test, and Diamond-Abelson test.

5. Detection and identification of other antibodies

I. TEST CELLS. Red cell suspensions possessing known blood factor and red cell suspension free of blood factor for which antibodies may be present in the serum tested.

II. TECHNIQUES. Whenever the presence of an irregular antibody is suspected in a serum, it should be tested with appropriate red cell suspensions, using the following three techniques: saline-suspended red cells; indirect antiglobulin technique; and papain-treated red cells. Although the first part of the indirect antiglobulin test also permits evaluation of the presence of complete antibodies reacting with saline-suspended red cells at 37° C., it is also advisable to test for the presence of complete antibodies reactive at lower temperatures, specifically at 20 to 25° C. (room temperature) and at 4 to 6° C. (ice box temperature). A single set using saline-suspended red cells may be first incubated and read at room temperature and then transferred to the ice box, preferably overnight. The general procedures for antibody screening are those outlined before. In some instances it also may be advisable to use bovine albumin-suspended test cells in a procedure analogous to the Hattersley test (VII, 3).

INTERPRETATION. 1. Exclusion of antibody specificity: Presence of antibodies is conclusively ruled out for those blood factors that are represented by test cells not agglutinated by the unknown serum under the various testing conditions. For example, if test cells containing the Kell factor (K)

are not agglutinated, this is evidence for absence of anti-K antibody in the serum under study.

2. Tentative identification of antibody specificity: This is facilitated by finding a "common denominator" in test cells that were agglutinated by the serum tested; e.g., if all test cells agglutinated contain the Duffy factor (Fy^a), this is presumptive evidence for presence of anti-Fy^a in the serum tested.

3. Definitive identification of antibody specificity: After a tentative identification of the antibody specificity has been made, a definitive identification should be attempted by the following methods:

a. The serum is tested with a minimum of six separate red cell specimens, three of which contain the antigen in question and three of which do not contain it (e.g., if tentative identification of anti-Kell antibody is made, test the serum with three Kell-positive and three Kell-negative red cell specimens). If agglutination is obtained with all red cell specimens containing the incriminated antigen and no agglutination is obtained with red cell specimens free of this antigen, the tentative antibody identification has been confirmed.

b. The serum is absorbed with red cell suspension containing the incriminated antigen (red cell suspension #1) and with red cell suspension free of this antigen (red cell suspension #2).

Using the same red cell suspension as used for absorption (#1), parallel titrations are set up with

  I. the unabsorbed serum,
  II. the serum after absorption with red cell suspension #1,
  III. the serum after absorption with red cell suspension #2.

If titrations I and III yield results differing only slightly from each other and if titration II yields significantly lower values or even disclosed disappearance of the antibody, this corroborates the tentative identification of the antibody.

c. If at all possible, the complete blood formula of the red cells of the person with the antibody should be determined. With rare exceptions the antigen for which the antibody is specific should be found absent in the red cells of the sensitized person; e.g., a person with anti-rh″(E) antibody in the serum has red cells that are negative for rh″(E).

6. Controls, sources of error, and supplementary suggestions. 1. One of the most common pitfalls in attempts to identify irregular hemoantibodies is caused by the presence of nonspecific agglutinins, which clump red cell specimens indiscriminately. The best method of detecting such antibodies is to include in each test the red cells of the same person whose serum is tested. Agglutination found in this suspension suggests the presence of nonspecific agglutinins (complete or incomplete cold agglutinins or warm autoagglutinins). In some of these cases the presence of autoantibodies may be confirmed by finding a positive direct antiglobulin test with the red cells of the specimen tested.

2. Cell controls: In order to be sure that test cells have not undergone some changes making them agglutinable in a nonspecific fashion, always include controls consisting of 2 drops of saline and 2 drops of the corresponding red cell suspension. Agglutination found in any of these "cell controls" invalidates results obtained in the main test.

3. Helpful information on probable identity of the antibody may be derived from its behavior at different temperatures and in different techniques:

a. Anti-P, anti-M, and anti-N most commonly react better, or only, at low temperatures and with saline-suspended red cells.

b. Anti-Fyª antibodies as a rule react only with the indirect antiglobulin technique and give negative results with papain-treated red cells.

c. MN factors are destroyed by proteolytic enzymes and cannot be detected with this technique.

d. Rh-Hr antibodies react best with papain-treated red cells and when present in low titer may give positive results only with this technique.

e. Antibodies resulting from isosensitization by blood transfusions or pregnancy are as a rule incomplete antibodies and give best results with papain and antiglobulin techniques; "natural" antibodies for which the cause of sensitization is not known react best with saline-suspended red cells.

f. Some antibodies give much stronger reactions with red cells homozygous for the respective factor, while red cells heterozygous for the factor are agglutinated either weakly or not at all ("double dose effects"); e.g., anti-M may agglutinate MM cells much more strongly than MN cells.

4. More than one antibody may be present. This possibility is suggested when in the course of the tentative antibody identification two or more test cell specimens agglutinated by the serum tested are found not to contain a common antigen. Definitive identification of multiple antibodies requires absorption tests.

5. Red cell suspensions should not be used for longer than 12 hours after preparation even if stored at 4° C.

VIII. Titration of Antibodies. Serial dilutions of the serum to be tested are prepared. To each serial dilution add the test cells containing the blood factor(s) reacting with the antibodies tested. After completion of the test agglutinations are observed and recorded. The highest dilution of the serum showing agglutination is the reciprocal of the antibody titer; e.g., if agglutination is observed in the serum dilution of 1:32 but agglutination is absent in the serum dilution of 1:64, the titer is recorded as 32. The following techniques refer to titration of Rh antibodies. With suitable modification of the nature of test cells these techniques can be applied to titration of other isoantibodies.

1. Titration of complete (saline) Rh antibodies

Technique

1. Prepare 2 per cent suspensions in saline of O Rh-positive test cells. Test cells of type O Rh_1Rh_2(CDE) or pooled test cells of types O Rh_1(CDE) and O Rh_2(cDE) may be used. If so desired, parallel titrations may also be done with separate suspensions of test cells; e.g., in order to compare titers obtained with Rh_1(CDe) and with Rh_2 (cDE) cells.

2. For each serum to be titrated set up as many rows of ten test tubes as test cells are to be used.

3. Into the first tube of each row place 2 drops of the undiluted serum.

4. In a separate dilution tube prepare a 1:2 dilution of the serum by mixing an equal number of drops of serum and physiologic saline.

5. In separate dilution tubes an equal number of drops of the 1:2 serum dilution and physiologic saline are mixed, resulting in a dilution of 1:4. Such dilutions are continued until the dilution of 1:512 is reached.

6. Into the second tube of each row place 2 drops of serum dilution 1:2; into the third tube place 2 drops of serum dilution 1:4, and so on.

7. To each tube add 1 drop of the 2 per cent suspension of the appropriate test cells.

8. Mix the contents of the tubes and incubate in a water bath of 37° C. for two hours.

9. Check for agglutination with the naked eye, with the scanning lens of the microscope, and with low power objective (16 mm.) if result is doubtful.

Alternative procedure to steps 4 to 6: If only one test cell suspension is used, one may proceed as follows: a. Into all but the first of the ten tubes place 2 drops of saline. b. To the second tube add 2 drops of the serum tested, and after mixing the contents transfer 2 drops to the third test tube. Continue with this procedure until the tenth test tube from which, after mixing of contents, 2 drops are removed and discarded. Thus again a twofold serial dilution up to 1:512 has been prepared. If a high antibody titer is expected, one may prepare a primary serum dilution of 1:5 or 1:10 and then proceed with twofold serial dilutions; i.e., 1:5, 1:10, 1:20, and so on.

2. Indirect antiglobulin (Coombs) technique. The test is set up in the same way as outlined for complete (saline) agglutinins. Serum-test cell mixtures remaining free of agglutination after the period of incubation are converted into the antiglobulin test by following the procedures outlined in V.

3. Albumin technique. The procedure is identical with that described for complete (saline) agglutinins, except that the suspending medium for the red cells is 20 to 30 per cent bovine albumin and the serum is diluted with serum of a person of group AB instead of with physiologic saline. The diluent serum must have been shown previously to be free of irregular agglutinins. The test is read after incubation for two hours in a water bath of 37° C.

4. Papain technique. Papain-treated red cells are prepared as outlined in technique VII, 1, and added to serum dilutions prepared as outlined for the titration of saline agglutinins. The test is read for agglutination after incubation for 30 minutes in a water bath at 37° C.

5. Volumetric titration. In most laboratory procedures use of capillary pipets for titrations is satisfactory; that is, the required number of drops of serum, serum dilutions, or red cell suspensions is delivered from pipets with tips of 1 to 2 mm. diameter. For each red cell suspension and for each serum a clean pipet must be used. Transfer of serial dilutions of the same serum may be carried out with the same capillary pipet provided the contents are expressed as completely as possible between each dilution and the pipet is rinsed each time by drawing up clean physiologic saline

solution a few times and discarding the contents as completely as possible. This can be facilitated by setting up three containers with saline in which the pipets are rinsed twice, transferred to the next, and kept in the third container. By having several pipets available simultaneously, the transfer of serum is probably reduced to an insignificant minimum. Nevertheless even with this technique traces of higher serum concentrations are transferred to the next dilution. In general one must keep in mind that results of titrations are only quantitative approximations and by no means approach the accuracy of chemical quantitative tests.

Volumetric titrations provide for an increased accuracy. In this technique serums and red cell suspensions are measured in quantities of 0.1 ml., using a separate calibrated pipet each time. Otherwise the procedures are those outlined before. Volumetric techniques are mandatory for determination of the titer of antiserums used for blood grouping procedures; e.g., anti-A, anti-B, anti-$Rh_o(D)$. Their use is also desirable when one wishes to obtain information on the comparative antibody titer of two different specimens, such as may be needed in prenatal tests. Such comparison of antibody titers is valid only when the two or more serum specimens are tested simultaneously, using volumetric methods and the same test cell suspension. This is necessitated by the observation that, even in the same laboratory, titers run at different times may vary depending on test cells and diluents used.

IX. Titration of Isoagglutinins Anti-A and Anti-B. Because of special considerations given to anti-A and anti-B isoagglutinins in connection with selection of blood for transfusions and diagnosis of hemolytic disease of the newborn, the following methods of quantitative estimations are presented separately.

A. Screening procedure for elimination of "high-titered" isoagglutinins. In order to avoid use of potentially "dangerous universal donors" (cf. p. 302), a screening procedure capable of detecting "high-titered" group O blood is carried out in most blood banks. There is no unanimity as to what represents a "high titer." The following procedure is based on the assumption that any agglutinating activity of anti-A and anti-B persisting in a 1:100 dilution is to be considered as high titered. According to other workers the critical borderline may be as low as 1:50 or as high as 1:250.

The technique given next may be suitably modified if a different critical titer is chosen.

Technique

1. Into a large test tube place 9.9 ml. of physiologic saline.

2. To the test tube add 0.1 ml. of the serum to be tested with an accurately calibrated serologic pipet.

3. Mix carefully by expelling the contents of the pipet into the saline, drawing up fluid, and expelling it several times. Stopper and mix by inverting the tube. This produces a dilution of 1:100.

4. Identify one of two tubes as "A" and the other as "B".

5. Add 0.1 ml. of the diluted serum to each of the two tubes.

6. To the tube marked "A" add 0.1 ml. of a 2 per cent suspension of red cells of group A, and to the tube marked "B" add 0.1 ml. of a 2 per cent suspension of red cells of group B.

7. Let stand at room temperature for 15 minutes and centrifuge for one minute.

8. Check for presence of agglutination with the naked eye and, if in doubt or if result is negative to the naked eye, microscopically after placing a drop of the serum-cell mixture on a slide.

INTERPRETATION. If the diluted serum agglutinated A or B cells, the titer of anti-A or anti-B exceeds 100; such blood is designated as "high titered" and is eliminated from use as "universal donor." If the diluted serum did not agglutinate A or B red cells, it is designated as "low titered," and the blood may be selected for potential use as "universal donor."

NOTE: 1. Specific tests are required before low-titered blood of group O can be safely given as universal donor (cf. section X, Crossmatch Techniques, Minor Crossmatch for Universal Donor and Recipient).

2. If the presence of hemolysin for A or B cells has been noted in the ABO grouping (cf. II, 1, p. 281), such blood should be designated as "high titered" (even if the saline dilution of 1:100 failed to agglutinate A or B cells) and be excluded from use as universal donor.

3. If the titer exceeded 100 for one blood group but not for the other, such blood may be considered for use as universal donor for a recipient of the blood group for which the titer did not exceed 100.

B. Detection and titration of incomplete isoagglutinins. The following techniques represent attempts to distinguish between complete ("natural") and incomplete ("immune") anti-A and anti-B isoagglutinins; as a rule the latter result from specific antigenic stimulations, such as administration of incompatible blood, pregnancy of a woman with a fetus of an incompatible ABO group, or administration of antigens widely distributed in nature and chemically related to A and B group-specific substance. Since the properties differentiating complete and incomplete anti-A and anti-B cannot be demonstrated regularly, it is advisable to test more than one method in each instance.

The following differences are most readily established: (1) thermal range: complete isoagglutinins show higher titers at 4° C. than at 37° C., while the converse is true frequently for incomplete isoagglutinins; (2) incomplete isoagglutinins yield higher titers with papain-treated red cells than with saline-suspended untreated red cells, while this is not true for complete isoagglutinins; and (3) in the presence of group-specific substance A and B incomplete isoagglutinins may agglutinate red cells suspended in macromolecular medium. The same may be accomplished with the indirect antiglobulin (Coombs) technique. This is not the case with complete isoagglutinins.

Reagents

1. 30 per cent bovine albumin.

2. Serum of person of group AB that is free of irregular isoagglutinins.

3. Test cell suspensions:
   a. 2 per cent suspension in saline of cells of group A_1
   b. 2 per cent suspension in saline of cells of group B
   c. 2 per cent suspension in saline of cells of group O
   d. papain-treated red cells of group A_1
   e. papain-treated red cells of group B
   f. papain-treated red cells of group O
   g. 2 per cent suspension in bovine albumin of cells of group A_1
   h. 2 per cent suspension in bovine albumin of cells of group B
   i. 2 per cent suspension in bovine albumin of cells of group O.

4. Antihuman globulin (Coombs) serum.

5. Group-specific substance A and B.

1. Test for Thermal Optimum of Agglutination

1. Prepare two sets of twofold dilu-

tions of the serum to be tested if it is of group O. If the serum is from a person of group A or B, only one such set is needed. If, on the other hand, one deals with the serum of a pregnant woman and the red cells of her husband are available, a third, or second set, respectively, is prepared for testing with his red cells. In the case of possible transfusion sensitization, the red cells of the donor should also be used.

2. To each tube of one of these sets add 1 drop of the 2 per cent suspension of A cells; to each tube of the other set add 1 drop each of the 2 per cent suspension of B cells. To tubes of the third set, if present, add 1 drop each of the 2 per cent suspension of the husband's or donor's red cells.

3. Incubate in a water bath of 37° C. for two hours.

4. Read and record agglutinations.

5. Resuspend the red cell suspensions and transfer into an ice box, preferably for incubation overnight.

6. Read and record agglutinations present after ice box incubation.

INTERPRETATION. Titers significantly higher (more than one dilution tube) after incubation at 37° C. than after ice box incubation speak in favor of presence of incomplete isoagglutinins.

2. Test with Papain-treated Red Cells

1. Simultaneously with preceding test prepare additional sets of twofold serial dilutions in saline of the serum to be tested for use with papain-treated red cells of groups A_1 and B and of the husband, if available.

2. Incubate mixtures of serum dilutions and papain-treated red cells for 30 minutes in a water bath of 37° C.

3. Read and record presence of agglutination.

INTERPRETATION. Significantly higher titers obtained with papain-treated red cells as compared with those of saline-suspended red cells speak in favor of presence of incomplete isoagglutinins.

3. Neutralization Technique

1. Mix equal parts of the serum and of group-specific substances A and B.

2. For each test cell suspension (A_1, B, husband's red cells) to be used, prepare two sets of twofold serial dilutions of the mixture of the serum with group-specific substance, using physiologic saline as diluent for one set and serum of group AB for the other.

3. To each tube of the saline dilution series add one drop of the corresponding 2 per cent red cell suspension in saline (group A_1, group B, husband's red cells).

4. To each of the test tubes of the serum dilutions prepared with group AB serum, add one drop of the corresponding albumin-suspended red cells.

5. Incubate all titrations for two hours at room temperature.

6. Read and record the results.

INTERPRETATION. As a rule neutralization with group-specific substance reduces or completely inhibits the isoagglutination of saline-suspended red cells. On the other hand, in the presence of incomplete anti-A and anti-B, testing of the neutralized mixture with albumin-suspended red cells shows unchanged strength of agglutination. Thus, absence of agglutination with saline-suspended red cells and presence of agglutination with albumin-suspended red cells exposed to serum mixed with group-specific substance speaks in favor of the presence of incomplete isoagglutinin.

NOTE: (1) If, after mixing equal parts of serum and group-specific substance, neutralization is incomplete, the proportion of group-specific substance should be increased, e.g., by adding four volumes of group-specific substance to one volume of serum. The subsequent procedures are analogous to those described.

(2) The presence of incomplete isoagglutinins in "neutralized" serum may be also demonstrated by means of the indirect antiglobulin test: serial dilutions of the neutralized serum are incubated with saline-suspended red cells in a water bath of 37° C. for two hours and checked for agglutination. Dilution tubes not showing agglutination are converted into the indirect antiglobulin test. If the indirect antiglobulin test produces a significant increase of titer as compared with the first reading, this speaks in favor of presence of incomplete isoagglutinins.

C. Detection of incompatible isoagglutinin in serum of newborn infants. The direct antiglobulin (Coombs) test frequently fails to detect coating of red cells of newborn infants with anti-A or anti-B isoagglutinin. Nevertheless the serum of such infants may contain incompatible isoagglutinin, e.g., anti-A in an infant A or anti-B in an infant B. For their detection the following methods are suitable.

Reagents

Test cell suspensions; see IX, B, Reagents 3.

Procedure

1. Into each of six properly identified test tubes place 2 drops of the serum to be tested.

2. To the first tube add 2 drops of saline-suspended red cells of group A_1; to the second, 2 drops of saline-suspended red cells of group B; and to the third, 2 drops of saline-suspended red cells of group O.

3. To the fourth, fifth, and sixth test tubes add 2 drops each of papain-treated red cells of groups A_1, B, and O, respectively.

4. Incubate the mixtures of serum and saline-suspended red cells in a water bath of 37° C. for two hours and check for presence of agglutination.

5. Test tubes not showing agglutination are converted into the indirect antiglobulin test and checked again for agglutination.

6. Test tubes with the serum and papain-treated red cells are incubated for 30 minutes in a water bath of 37° C.

7. The tubes are centrifuged for one-half minute and checked for agglutination.

INTERPRETATION. 1. Presence of agglutination with saline-suspended red cells (step 4) before the indirect antiglobulin test indicates presence of complete agglutinins.

2. Absence of agglutination before, and presence of agglutination after, the antiglobulin test as well as agglutination of papain-treated red cells indicates presence of incomplete agglutinins.

3. Presence of incompatible agglutinin is associated with subclinical or clinical hemolytic disease of the newborn caused by maternal isosensitization to A or B factors.

NOTE: Use of both antiglobulin and papain techniques is recommended, since in some instances only one of them may yield positive results. If so desired, titration of the isoagglutinins may be performed. Cells of group O serve as control for presence of isoantibodies other than anti-A and anti-B.

X. Crossmatching Tests. After blood has been selected for transfusion according to the principles detailed in a subsequent section (cf. p. 300), suitable tests *in vitro*—crossmatching tests—must be performed in each instance in order to insure absence of incompatibility between the blood to be transfused and the blood of the prospective recipient. Most importantly, one must make sure in the *"major crossmatch"* that the serum of the recipient does not contain isoantibodies capable of reacting with the transfused red cells. Of secondary, though sometimes considerable, importance is absence in the *"minor crossmatch"* in the transfused plasma of isoagglutinins capable of reacting with the recipient's red cells. It is essential that the tests be capable of detecting both complete and incomplete antibodies.

I. Major crossmatch tests

1. INDIRECT ANTIGLOBULIN TECHNIQUE

1. Prepare a 2 per cent suspension in saline of the red cells of the prospective donor.

2. Separate the serum of the recipient from a specimen of clotted blood obtained within 24 hours.

3. Into a properly identified test tube place 2 drops of the recipient's serum.

4. Add to the tube 2 drops of the 2 per cent suspension of the donor's red cells.

5. Centrifuge immediately for one minute.

6. Check for presence of agglutination.

7. If no agglutination is present, place in a water bath of 37° C. and incubate for 15 minutes.

8. Wash the red cells three times with tubefuls of saline, following the procedures outlined for the antiglobulin technique (cf. p. 286).

9. After the last washing discard the supernatant and resuspend the red cells in the one drop of saline remaining in the tube.

10. Add 2 drops of the antiglobulin serum, centrifuge for one minute, and check for agglutination macroscopically and microscopically.

INTERPRETATION. 1. Agglutination observed in step 6 indicates incompatibility caused by complete antibodies.

2. Agglutination that does not occur in step 6 but is found after performance of the antiglobulin (Coombs) test indicates incompatibility caused by incomplete antibodies.

2. ACTIVATED PAPAIN TECHNIQUE

Activated Papain Reagent

One gm. of papain is ground in a mortar with 100 ml. of buffer (equal parts of 0.15M Na_2HPO_4 and 0.15M KH_2PO_4). After filtration of the solution, 0.3 gm. of l-cysteine hydrochloride is added, and the mixture is incubated for one hour in a water bath of 37° C. The pH of the solution should be 6.4 to 6.7. The reagent is frozen in 2 ml. quantities, which are thawed as needed.

Technique

1. Into a properly identified test tube place 2 drops of the recipient's serum, 2 drops of the 2 per cent suspension in saline of the donor's red cells, and 2 drops of the activated papain reagent.

2. Incubate the test for 15 minutes in a water bath of 37° C.

3. Centrifuge for 30 seconds and check for agglutination macroscopically and microscopically.

INTERPRETATION. Presence of agglutination indicates incompatibility caused by either complete or incomplete antibodies. This test is more sensitive than the indirect antiglobulin technique for detection of trace amounts of Rh-Hr antibodies. It may be converted into the indirect antiglobulin technique after the incubation period, thus detecting anti-Kell and some but not all anti-Duffy antibodies.

II. Minor crossmatch test. Proceed in the same way as outlined for the major crossmatch but use serum of the donor and red cell suspension of the recipient.

NOTE: In many laboratories the minor crossmatch is only performed through step 6 of the indirect antiglobulin (Coombs) technique. In this way only complete agglutinins may be detected, and it is therefore important to prescreen serums of donors for presence of incomplete antibodies, especially Rh antibodies in Rh-negative donors.

III. Crossmatch for selection of universal donors and transfusion of universal recipients. The blood to be selected should not have anti-A or anti-B hemolysin (cf. II, 1) and should have an anti-A or anti-B titer of less than 100 (cf. IX, A, p. 293). Nevertheless the minor crossmatch in such instances may always be expected to produce agglutination, since the serum of the donor contains an isoagglutinin reactive with the red cells of the recipient. The following technique (Grove-Rasmussen) is recommended for the minor crossmatch in order to avoid transfusion of potentially dangerous isoagglutinins.

1. To 0.1 ml. of the donor's serum add 0.3 ml. of solution of group-specific substances A and B.

2. Incubate the mixture at room temperature for five minutes.

3. To 0.1 ml. of this mixture add 0.1 ml. of a 2 per cent suspension in saline of the recipient's red cells.

4. Shake the tube and incubate for 15 minutes in a water bath of 37° C.

5. Convert into an indirect antiglobulin (Coombs) test.

INTERPRETATION. If agglutination is observed at the end of the test, it is not safe to transfuse the recipient with the blood selected.

NOTE: The modified minor crossmatch test and these considerations are not required if packed or resuspended red cells are to be transfused, that is, without the supernatant plasma. The test cannot be applied when the red cells of the recipient show a positive direct antiglobulin (Coombs) test.

XI. Miscellaneous Tests. Several laboratory tests utilize hemagglutination, though they are not related to any of the specific blood factors described in the preceding sections: they may employ human red cells or red cells of a different species (heteroagglutinins). One important category is represented by autoagglutinins, i.e., antibodies capable of agglutinating the red cells of the same person from whom the serum is derived. They may be active either as "cold" or "warm" antibodies and be detectable by methods described for either complete or incomplete antibodies. These autoagglutinins are of particular importance in connection with the diagnosis of autoimmune hemolytic anemia. "Cold" autoagglutinins, usually referred to as cold agglutinins, form the basis of ancillary tests in diagnosis of viral (atypical) pneumonia (cf. p. 174).

Heteroagglutinins for sheep red cells have been found to be increased in certain conditions, such as infectious mononucleosis, serum disease, and miscellaneous infections. Demonstration of increased titer and changes in absorption properties of sheep agglutinins is a part of the diagnostic test for infectious mononucleosis, as outlined in detail in another context (cf. p. 217ff.).

Increased titers of agglutinin for sheep red cells previously sensitized with subthreshold amounts of antisheep hemolysin have been observed in serums of patients with rheumatoid arthritis (RA factor). As shown in subsequent work, other techniques can be used to detect this serum factor (cf. p. 891ff.).

XII. Sources of Error in Hemagglutination Tests

A. False negative results

1. LACK OF SENSITIVITY OF AGGLUTINOGEN (BLOOD FACTOR) IN RED CELLS. Some agglutinogens, specifically A and B, are poorly developed in newborns and in-

fants, reaching their full development with the age of approximately one year. Recent evidence has also been presented that such diseases as leukemia and cancer may in exceedingly rare cases change the reactivity of A and B factors. Reference to weakly reacting Rh factors has been made previously. An important extraneous factor lowering the reactivity of blood factors is the age of the blood specimen, especially if kept in a saline suspension and if not preserved at ice box temperature. Blood collected with an anticoagulant as a rule does not retain its full reactivity for more than one to two days. Clotted blood specimens properly preserved are fully reactive for at least five days, and the minimum reactivity needed for crossmatch tests is preserved for three weeks. Collection of blood in ACD solution has been found to provide better preservation of agglutinability of blood factors than is the case in clotted blood.

2. FAULTY CONCENTRATION OF RED CELL SUSPENSIONS. Too high a concentration may lead to an antigen excess, preventing union of the isoantibody with blood factors. On the other hand too dilute a red cell suspension may interfere with observation of weak agglutinations.

3. FAULTY PROPORTION BETWEEN ANTIBODY AND RED CELL SUSPENSION. False negative reactions, representing prozone phenomena, may result from an excess of antibody in proportion to the amount of antigen present (i.e., quantity of red cells). Such "zoning" is especially common in undiluted serum with high titer of incomplete Rh antibodies.

4. INADEQUATE ANTIBODY TITER IN SERUM. This is especially important in connection with blood grouping serums, such as anti-A, anti-B, and anti-$Rh_o(D)$, for which minimum titers have been established by the Division of Biologics Standards of the National Institutes of Health (cf. p. 280). This assures the reliability of tests done with commercially distributed grouping serums. On the other hand, search for antibodies in unknown serums may give falsely negative results if the titer is below a certain threshold, especially if combined with a poorly reacting blood factor in the red cells used. Contrary to testing serums the titers of antibodies in unknown serums are not subject to control. This makes it mandatory to use in such tests the most reactive form of red cell antigen available.

5. PRESENCE OF HEMOLYSIN IN SERUM TESTED. Since no agglutination for the specific blood factor tested may occur as a result of hemolysis, this may be erroneously interpreted as a negative result. Suspicion, however, should be raised by the absence or paucity of detectable red cells. Inactivation of such serum (30 minutes in water bath of 56° C.) destroys hemolytic reactivity of the antibody so that agglutination can be observed in a test repeated with the inactivated specimen.

6. DEVIATION FROM OPTIMAL TEMPERATURE. Since some hemoantibodies react best at ice box and others at body temperature, it is important to observe such optimal temperatures in testing of low-titered antibodies in order not to miss weakly positive results.

7. INADEQUATE PERIODS OF INCUBATION. The lower the titer of the antibody and the poorer the reactivity of the blood factor (agglutinogen), the longer must be the periods of incubation in order to produce visible agglutination. Centrifugation and other forms of mechanical agitation may be used in order to shorten periods of incubation.

B. False positive results

1. PRESENCE IN THE SERUM OF UNSUSPECTED AGGLUTININS. This may occur with typing serums as well as with unknown specimens to be screened for presence of certain antibodies. Interfering antibodies most commonly encountered are cold agglutinins, warm autoagglutinins, and irregular agglutinins of specific nature, such as anti-P and anti-Rh. Careful prescreening of grouping serums is a critical procedure. In the case of unknown serums suitable red cell controls must be included in order to detect presence of unexpected agglutinins.

2. ROULEAUX FORMATION OR PSEUDO-AGGLUTINATION. This is a reflection of the same phenomenon that is responsible for sedimentation of red cells in which the red cells adhere to each other, presenting a "stack of coins" appearance. Rouleaux formation is favored by the presence in serum of increased amounts of asymmetric protein molecules, such as fibrinogen and globulin, and by large surfaces, such as occurs in slide tests. Extreme rouleaux is commonly associated with certain diseases producing hyperproteinemia and hyperglobulinemia, such as multiple myeloma, kala-azar, Boeck's sarcoid, and cryoglobulinemia. The gross appearance of rouleaux may sometimes be difficult to differentiate from

true agglutination, but as a rule the true nature of the phenomenon can be readily distinguished microscopically (cf. Fig. 5–5). In rouleaux formation individual red cells can be seen to separate readily from each other after mechanical agitation, such as tapping on the slide, whereas this does not occur in true agglutinates. Actually mechanical agitation favors true agglutination. Furthermore red cell agglutinates exhibit deformation and discoloration of the red cells, while red cells in rouleaux retain the normal appearance. Dilution of serum with saline inhibits rouleaux formation, whereas true agglutination is not affected unless the titer is at a critically low level.

3. BACTERIAL CONTAMINATION. Certain microorganisms, such as *Vibrio cholerae*, "activate" receptors present in all red cells, designated as "*T agglutinogen,*" which react with the *T agglutinin* present in all serums except that of newborn infants. Such agglutination is independent of the presence or absence of any other blood factors (Hübener-Thomsen phenomenon). Bacterial contamination of the serum may impart to it the capacity to clump all red cells independent of presence or absence of any blood factors (Davidsohn and Toharsky, 1940, 1942). It is obvious therefore that all precautions of asepsis must be

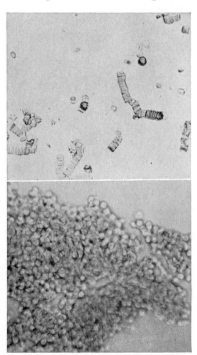

Figure 5–5. Microscopic appearance ($\times$ 415) of rouleaux (upper part) and true agglutination (lower part).

taken in handling specimens and reagents used for hemagglutination.

In addition to technical errors experience has shown that the most serious mistakes in hemagglutination work, especially those related to blood transfusions, are the results of carelessness or human fallibility. This includes failures to establish proper identity of blood specimens, donors, and patients; mix-up of specimens after collection; as well as excessive haste in performance of tests. Although emergencies arise especially frequently in connection with blood transfusions, this must never be an excuse for short cuts, which jeopardize the reliability of tests. Probably in no other area of laboratory work does a greater responsibility rest with the technologist and other members of the staff concerning adequate performance of tests. Errors resulting from such work are not subject to any review or medical judgment by the physician by contrast with the situation applying to other laboratory tests. It is well known that even fatal reactions may follow administration of incompatible blood. Hence proper organization of the work, adequate education, and constant alertness of the staff entrusted with such duties are imperative.

Practical Applications of Hemagglutination Tests

I. Blood Transfusion. The numerous clinical considerations pertaining to hemotherapy cannot be discussed within the framework of this chapter. For information on this subject the reader is referred to monographs by Mollison (1962); Wiener (1948); De Gowin, Hardin, and Alsever (1949); and the "Technical Methods and Procedures" published by the American Association of Blood Banks (1960). The main purpose of the following outline is to discuss laboratory tests needed for the proper collection, processing, and selection of blood for transfusions.

1. Prescreening of potential blood donors. The two main considerations in accepting potential blood donors are protection of the donor against any possible ill effects from the loss of blood and protection of the prospective recipient against any untoward effects from the transfusion. The first consideration necessitates that donors can be accepted only if they fulfill certain minimum requirements as to age, height, weight, and hemoglobin. In the most commonly employed screening test for hemoglobin, a drop of blood is permitted to fall into a solution of copper sulfate of known specific gravity. If the drop of blood descends to the bottom of the solution rather than floating or rising to the surface, the specific gravity of the blood is greater than that of the copper sulfate solution (see p. 77). According to general practice, male donors should have a minimal hemoglobin concentration of 13.5 gm. per 100 ml.; that is, the drop of blood should have a specific gravity greater than a copper sulfate solution with specific gravity 1.055, while for female donors a minimal hemoglobin concentration of 12.5 gm. per 100 ml. is required, corresponding to a specific gravity exceeding that of a copper sulfate solution with specific gravity 1.053. For his own protection a donor should not give blood more frequently than intervals of eight to ten weeks and not more often than five times a year. The second consideration—protection of the recipient—requires the donor to be free of any infectious or contagious disease, including tuberculosis, rheumatic fever, and syphilis, and temperature, pulse, and blood pressure should be within the normal range. Donors who have had malaria or viral (infectious) hepatitis should never be accepted.

An adequate record of prescreening tests and answers to pertinent questions obtained from the prospective donor should be prepared and retained. Proper methods of identification of the donor and his record are of utmost importance prior to the collection of blood.

2. Collection of blood. Although a variety of containers (glass, plastic) and methods (gravity, vacuum) can be employed for collection of blood and technical skill is important, the following precautions are most important: (a) elimination of any mistake in identity of donor and container assured by proper identification of the blood container and pilot tubes collected simultaneously; (b) aseptic handling of the collection and the container in order to avoid bacterial contamination; (c) use of proper anticoagulant and preservative solutions; (d) immediate refrigeration of the blood after collection; (e) storage of the blood in refrigeration equipment maintaining a temperature range of 4 to 6° C.

3. Processing of blood. The following tests are mandatory before blood can be released for transfusional use: (1) ABO grouping (p. 280); (2) $Rh_o(D)$ typing (p. 283); (3) tests for presence of D^u (p. 284), rh'(C), and rh"(E) (p. 285) when blood

has been found to be $Rh_o(D)$-negative; (4) serologic test for syphilis (p. 839ff). Additional desirable tests are: screening of isoagglutinin titer in serum of group O blood (p. 293); screening for irregular antibodies of all serums, particularly for Rh antibodies in serums of $Rh_o(D)$-negative donors (p. 287); and identification of irregular antibodies when present (p. 291).

Only in special circumstances, such as unexplained difficulties in crossmatching or investigation of transfusion reactions (p. 303), is it necessary to carry out Rh subtyping (p. 285) of $Rh_o(D)$-positive blood or tests for subgroups of A in A and AB blood.

An optional procedure employed in some blood bank laboratories is performance of the thymol turbidity test in an attempt to detect donors with abnormal liver function suggestive of a possible carrier state of viral hepatitis. Although some workers have presented evidence that use of this test lowers the incidence of homologous serum jaundice resulting from blood transfusions, others have failed to confirm this impression. In general it must be emphasized that at present no laboratory test available is capable of detecting, or ruling out with certainty, the presence of the hepatitis virus in blood.

At least once a day, and again before issuance, all units of blood should be inspected in order to detect any abnormal appearance, such as discoloration, hemolysis, and cloudiness, that may be an indication of faulty preservation or bacterial contamination. It is good practice to run bacterial cultures (see p. 835) periodically on units of blood that have not been issued before the three-week period of useful shelf-life has ended or that have to be discarded for other reasons, such as positive serologic tests for syphilis. Results of such cultures provide information on the sterility of the collecting equipment and proper asepsis in handling and storage of blood.

4. Selection of blood. Adequate selection of blood requires close and intelligent cooperation between clinicians and blood bank staff. With rare exceptions, as explained later on, adequate pretransfusion tests are required for proper selection of blood. Clotted blood (quantities of 5 to 10 ml. are desirable) should be obtained from the prospective recipient within 24 hours before anticipated administration of blood and should be subjected to ABO grouping (p. 280) and $Rh_o(D)$ typing (p. 283). In the case of infants or debilitated patients presenting difficulties for venipuncture, blood may be obtained by skin punctures in capillary tubes, which are centrifuged in order to yield red cell suspensions and serum for the crossmatch tests.

The primary consideration in selection of blood is to provide a unit of the same ABO group as that of the recipient. Furthermore $Rh_o(D)$-positive recipients should receive $Rh_o(D)$-positive blood, whereas for $Rh_o(D)$-negative recipients blood of type rh (cde) should be used, that is, blood not only lacking $Rh_o(D)$ but also $rh'(C)$ and $rh''(E)$. Such blood should also have been proved by suitable tests not to possess a weak Rh_o variant (D^u). The pilot tube of a unit satisfying these criteria is then utilized for crossmatching tests as outlined previously (p. 296). Evidence of compatibility in major and minor crossmatch tests must be established before release of blood for transfusion.

Although not mandatory, it is desirable to screen the serum of the recipient for the presence of irregular antibodies concomitantly with or prior to crossmatching, since this may disclose irregular antibodies, including autoantibodies and cold agglutinins. If unexpected incompatibility is encountered in crossmatching tests, all possible sources of error should be investigated, preferably by repeating the test with a new specimen of the recipient and using other donor pilot tubes of suitable ABO and Rh type. Cold agglutinins are a common source of unexpected incompatibility, and their presence can be confirmed as outlined on p. 890ff. Selection of blood for patients with autoimmune hemolytic anemia often poses difficult problems, since complete compatibility can rarely be obtained. Testing with numerous units, possibly by using serial dilutions of the patient's serum, may disclose some blood specimens that are less incompatible and hence presumably more suitable for transfusion. The clinician should be advised of the findings in such cases before blood is released for transfusion. All specimens of pilot tubes of the units and of recipients used for crossmatching should be preserved under refrigeration for at least five days after administration of the transfusion, since these specimens are indispensible for proper investigation of transfusion reactions if such occur (p. 303).

New specimens for crossmatching tests must be obtained from the recipient and used for selection of blood whenever more than 24 hours have elapsed since a previous transfusion. In other words it would be a serious error to use a blood specimen obtained prior to a transfusion given two or three days before and to use it to select blood for a new transfusion, because subthreshold levels of irregular antibodies may have been present in the earlier specimen and may have escaped detection. The intervening transfusion then could have stimulated a rapid rise of such antibodies that could produce gross incompatibility with subsequently given blood, thus leading to serious hemolytic reactions.

In addition to serologic factors there are other important considerations in selection of blood, such as the quantity of blood to be transfused. Basically this depends on medical judgment. Units commonly available contain 450 to 500 ml. of blood. In specific conditions it is advisable to give smaller amounts in order not to overload the circulation; on the other hand much larger amounts may be needed for replacement of blood volume. For either volume replacement or treatment of anemia a single unit of blood is rarely if ever truly indicated. In other words such a patient probably does not even need this single unit of blood and therefore should not be exposed to the various risks involved in every transfusion. Nobody who is aware of the hazards of transmission of disease, isosensitization, and similar potential untoward effects of blood transfusions can ever justify hemotherapy merely as a "tonic" or symptomatic treatment. Furthermore blood is always in short supply and must be reserved for those in need of massive blood replacement during surgery, current demands being especially high in connection with open-heart surgery.

Close cooperation between clinician and hemotherapist is also required in connection with qualitative aspects of blood for transfusion, such as the age of stored blood. When replacement of blood volume is the indication for transfusion, blood of the appropriate type with the longest shelf-life is to be used so as to avoid excessive loss from overaging. On the other hand, for patients with certain diseases, blood within specified age limits is necessary or preferred. Patients needing blood because of inadequate erythropoiesis or excessive red cell destruction should be given blood not older than five days, since this will provide red cells with maximum survival. Likewise transfusions to patients with hemorrhagic diseases should utilize blood not older than five to seven days, because some of the coagulation factors may deteriorate during more prolonged storage. Patients with advanced renal or cardiovascular disease should not receive blood older than seven days, since plasma potassium concentrations of blood increase with storage and may be injurious to such recipients. Analogous considerations hold true for patients with advanced liver disease in relation to rising ammonia levels in stored blood.

Of particular importance are indications for use of certain blood fractions instead of whole blood: packed red cells are preferable for recipients with impaired myocardial reserve when they require replacement of red cell mass. Coagulation factors for treatment of some hemorrhagic disorders are best provided by fresh plasma, especially in hemophilia; fibrinogen should be given to patients with hypofibrinogenemia; and pooled plasma is indicated when there is need for expansion of plasma volume. Platelet concentrates may, at least temporarily, combat serious hemorrhagic manifestations resulting from thrombocytopenia. In open-heart surgery citrated blood cannot be used, but instead heparinized blood must be employed. Finally certain donors should be specifically excluded from use for certain patients: namely, the husband should never be a donor for his wife or a child for his mother. It is also not advisable to transfuse a patient with the blood of the same donor more than once. All these restrictions are based on the greater liability to isosensitization that has been proved to be associated with these circumstances of transfusions.

5. Selection of blood for newborn and young infants. Because isoagglutinins are not formed until a few months after birth (cf. p. 266), reliable crossmatching tests cannot be performed with the serum of newborn or young infants. Any isoagglutinins present in such infants are derived from the maternal serum as a result of transplacental transmission. Hence it is mandatory that the major crossmatching test in selection of blood for infants be carried out with the serum of the mother. If the child is between one to three months of age, the major crossmatch test should be done with both the serum of mother and the serum of infant, since passively transferred as well as actively formed isoagglutinins may be present at this age. Additional considerations apply to transfusion of infants with hemolytic disease of the newborn as discussed in the subsequent section (p. 312).

6. "Universal" donor and "universal" recipients. In some circumstances it may be necessary to deviate from the rule of administering blood of the same ABO group as the recipient (e.g., when Rh-negative blood of type B or AB is not available). Use of O Rh-negative blood is then necessary for recipients who are A or B, or AB Rh-negative recipients may be transfused with A or B Rh-negative blood. However, whenever a transfusion involves "universal donors" or "universal recipients," precautions must be taken in order to eliminate the risk of damaging the recipient's red cells by the transfused isoagglutinins. The safety of such transfusions should be established by the following criteria: The serum of the blood to be used should not possess hemolysin for the red cells of the prospective recipient; e.g., group O blood with anti-A hemolysin should not be used for a recipient of group A or AB. The titer of the reactive isoagglutinin should be less than 1:100 (cf. p. 293). The minor crossmatch test should be performed with the neutralized serum of the donor as outlined on p. 297. Only if this test fails to show agglutination is it safe to use the "universal" donor for a recipient of another blood group or to transfuse the "universal" recipient with the blood tentatively selected.

Another situation in which "universal" donor blood may have to be used is the "emergency" transfusion when the urgency of replacement of blood volume precludes spending any time for pretransfusion tests. In this event it is best to use O Rh-negative (cde) blood with low titers of anti-A and anti-B. The decision to administer blood without pretransfusion tests must be made by the physician in charge, since it involves definite calculated risks: in rare instances the patient may already possess an antibody for one of the factors in the transfused blood. In addition there is the delayed risk of isosensitization. Obviously this procedure is therefore only justified in a true emergency but not in pseudoemergencies, such as failure to request on time or to prepare blood for surgery or similar circumstances.

7. Administration of blood transfusions. Although technical aspects cannot be dealt with in this context, it is important to be aware of the need for strict observance of the following precautions:

All safeguards must be taken to insure proper identity of the blood selected and of the patient to be transfused. Some of the most serious transfusion accidents have resulted from human errors in identification of recipient and donor blood. Strictest asepsis must be observed in administration of the blood. Excessive speed or excessively slow administration of blood must be avoided. No solution other than physiologic saline or glucose in physiologic saline should be administered through the same set as blood. Specifically, so-called isotonic glucose solution in water should be avoided, since it was found capable of hemolysing blood mixed with it. Finally, close observation of the patient during the transfusion is essential to detect as soon as possible any untoward reactions that may occur.

8. Investigation of transfusion reactions. The main purpose of such investigations is to rule out or prove that a specific reaction reflects hemolysis of transfused red cells brought about by antibodies present in the recipient or, more rarely, destruction of recipient's red cells by transfused antibodies. Table 5–13 lists the common clinical symptoms as well as the classic laboratory findings that characterize the main categories of transfusion reactions. It must be stressed that absence of clinical symptoms does not conclusively eliminate a specific cause of a reaction. On the other hand certain clinical findings, such as urticarial eruptions, may occur in more than one type of reaction and therefore by themselves do not permit definitive diagnosis. Finally some reactions including hemolytic ones may be asymptomatic and escape detection unless there is careful follow-up of the recipient immediately or soon after the transfusion, preferably including a check of his hematologic status in order to obtain valid indications for survival of the transfused red cells.

The most common potential causes of hemolytic transfusion reactions are listed in Table 5–14 with reference to the ABO, Rh, and other blood group systems that may be involved.

Whenever a patient exhibits untoward reactions during or following blood transfusion, such as chills and fever, skin eruptions, drop or rise in blood pressure, hemoglobinuria, jaundice within hours or a few days, and symptoms of renal failure such as oliguria and progressive azotemia, a complete and thorough investigation must be carried out. In order to make this possible, the pretransfusion specimen of the recipient and the pilot tube of the unit used must be preserved for at least five days as mentioned previously. It is also desirable to return the container after conclusion of the transfusion to the blood bank so that blood remaining in it will be available for testing of identity and for detecting possible bacterial contamination.

As soon as a reaction is noted, a blood specimen of the recipient must be obtained and a urine specimen collected. Urinary output should be subsequently measured as long as indicated.

Table 5–15 lists the tests to be carried out on blood and urine specimens. Of particular importance are repeat tests for the ABO group and Rh type of the recipient's pre- and posttransfusion specimens, the donor pilot tube, and the blood remaining

Table 5–13. Transfusion Reactions

TYPE OF REACTION	MOST CHARACTERISTIC CLINICAL SYMPTOMS	MOST CHARACTERISTIC LABORATORY FINDINGS
Hemolytic	Precordial pain Lumbar pain Chills Drop in blood pressure Oliguria → anuria Jaundice	Hemoglobinemia Hemoglobinuria Azotemia → uremia Elevation of indirect serum bilirubin
Pyrogenic (febrile)	Chills or fever	Isoleukoagglutinins (in approx. 30 per cent of cases)
Allergic	Urticarial eruptions	———
Bacterial contamination	Severe hypotension Shock Anuria	Gram negative rods in direct smear of unit of transfused blood
Circulatory overload	Acute heart failure Pulmonary edema	———

Table 5–14. Common Causes of Hemolytic Transfusion Reactions Based on Blood Group Incompatibility

A. ANTIBODY PRESENT IN RECIPIENT

RECIPIENT WITH		
BLOOD GROUP	ANTIBODY	TRANSFUSED WITH BLOOD OF GROUP
O	anti-A and anti-B	A, B, or AB
A	anti-B	B or AB
B	anti-A	A or AB
rh(cde) rh'(Cde) rh''(cdE)	*anti-Rh_o(D)	Rh_1(CDe), Rh_o(cDe), Rh_2(cDE), or Rh_1Rh_2(CDE)
rh(cde)	*anti-rh'(C)	Rh_1(CDe), Rh_1Rh_2(CDE), or rh'(Cde)
rh(cde)	*anti-rh''(E)	Rh_2(cDE), Rh_1Rh_2(CDE), or rh''(cdE)
Rh_1(CDe)	*+anti-rh''(E)	Rh_2(cDE), Rh_1Rh_2(CDE), or rh''(cdE)
Rh_2(cDE)	*+anti-rh'(C)	Rh_1(CDe), Rh_1Rh_2(CDE), or rh'(Cde)
Rh_1Rh_1(CCDe)	*+anti-hr'(c)	rh(cde), Rh_o(cDe), Rh_1rh(CcDe), Rh_2(cDE), or Rh_1Rh_2hr'-positive (CcDE)
X-negative[++]	anti-X[++]	X-positive[++]

* always result of isosensitization
[+] occurs only exceptionally
[++] refers to blood factors such as Kell (K), Duffy (Fy^a), and so forth

B. ANTIBODY PRESENT IN DONOR

DONOR WITH		TRANSFUSED INTO RECIPIENT
BLOOD GROUP	ANTIBODY	HAVING BLOOD OF GROUP
O	"immune" or incomplete anti-A or anti-B	A, B, or AB
A	"immune" or incomplete anti-B	B or AB
B	"immune" or incomplete anti-A	A or AB
rh(cde) rh'(Cde) rh''(cdE)	*anti-Rh_o(D)	Rh_1(CDe), Rh_2(cDE), Rh_o(cDe), or Rh_1Rh_2(CDE)
X-negative[+]	anti-X[+]	X-positive[+]

* always result of isosensitization
[+] refers to blood factors Kell (K), Duffy (Fy^a), and so forth

in the container if available. Crossmatching tests must be repeated with both pretransfusion and posttransfusion specimens, using sensitive methods for detection of incomplete antibodies.

It has recently been shown that some pyrogenic (febrile) reactions are caused by presence of leukoagglutinins in the recipient. Persons most likely to develop leukoagglutinins are recipients of multiple previous transfusions and multiparous women, the latter apparently being sensitized by fetal leukocytic antigens (Dausset, 1954; Payne, 1957; and Brittingham, 1957). The presence of leukoagglutinins may be detected by tests described on p.

317. Demonstration of this etiology of pyrogenic febrile transfusion reactions is important practically, since considerable difficulties are encountered in hemotherapy of such patients, especially if they require repeated transfusions because of conditions such as aplastic anemia or myelofibrosis. If pyrogenic reactions are found to be associated with presence of leukoagglutinins or if this mechanism is suspected even though it is not established, they can be in most instances readily eliminated by using for transfusion a red cell mass prepared in such a manner as to be practically free of leukocytes.

When it is suspected that a reaction may

Table 5–15. Laboratory Tests Capable of Determining Nature of Transfusion Reaction

A. ESSENTIAL TESTS

MATERIAL NEEDED RECIPIENT	DONOR	TEST(S)	OPTIMUM TIME OF EXAMINATION AFTER REACTION FROM	TO	CAPABLE OF DETECTING
Pretransfusion blood specimen	Pilot tube; blood remaining in container.	ABO and Rh typing	Immediate		Technical or clerical errors
Pretransfusion specimen	Pilot tube	Crossmatch	Immediate		Incompatibility
	Blood remaining in container	Bacteriologic study (smear, culture)	Immediate		Bacterial contamination
Posttransfusion blood specimen					
a. citrated or oxalated		Microscopic examination	Immediate	6–12 hours	Presence of clumps
b. red cell suspension		Direct anti-globulin test	Immediate	12–48 hours	Coating of red cells by antibody
c. plasma or serum		Hemoglobin	Immediate	48 hours	Hemoglobinemia (intravascular hemolysis)
d. serum		Indirect bilirubin	24 hours	72 hours	Hyperbilirubinemia*
e. serum		Urea N or NPN	36 hours		Azotemia
Urine		a. Hemoglobin	Immediate	48 hours	Hemoglobinuria (intravascular hemolysis)
		b. Volume	Immediate	Recovery	Oliguria (renal failure)

B. CORROBORATIVE TESTS

Red cells		Complete typing	Immediate	6–12 hours	Blood factor incompatible with serum of donor
Serum		a. Antibody screening	Immediate	6–12 hours	Antibody specific for blood factor in red cells of donor
		b. Antibody titer	Immediate	4–5 days	Low titer (e.g., anti-A in B recipient after transfusion of A blood)
		c. Antibody titer	6 days	Several months	Rising titer (e.g., anti-A in B recipient after transfusion of A blood)
Urine		Protein	Immediate	Variable	Proteinuria
Kidney biopsy or autopsy		Histopathologic study	36 hours	10 days	Hemoglobinuric nephrosis

* To compare with pretransfusion specimen if possible.

be due to bacterial contamination of the transfused blood, thorough bacteriologic examination must be carried out by means of direct smears as well as by culture of the blood. (For methods suitable for this purpose, see p. 835ff.) It must be specifically emphasized that such cultures must be incubated not only at 37° C. but also at 30 to 32° C. and preferably even at lower temperatures, since the contaminating organisms may be cryophilic (that is, they may grow best, or exclusively, at low temperatures).

II. Hemolytic Disease of the Newborn (Fetal Erythroblastosis)

1. Etiology. Levine and associates (1941) advanced the hypothesis that hemolytic disease of the newborn may be the result of formation of Rh antibodies in an Rh-negative woman carrying an Rh-positive fetus. This has since been amply confirmed by numerous clinical and laboratory studies. One of the most direct pieces of evidence has been the recent demonstration of Rh-positive red cells, obviously derived from the fetus, in the peripheral blood of Rh-negative pregnant women by means of fluorescein-labeled antiserums (Cohen, Zuelzer, and Evans, 1960).

Statistically, infants with clinical evidence of erythroblastosis are most frequently Rh-positive infants of Rh-negative mothers possessing Rh antibodies. Although in earlier work Rh antibodies were not readily detectable in all these women, this was subsequently accomplished by use of techniques capable of detecting incomplete antibodies (cf. p. 274). It is now well known that, in addition to $Rh_o(D)$, feto-maternal differences in many other blood factors may induce maternal isosensitization and hemolytic disease, although this occurs much more rarely. Of specific interest is ABO incompatibility as a cause of maternal isosensitization: expectant mothers may form "immune" or incomplete antibodies in addition to "natural" isoagglutinins already present, and transplacental transmission of the antibodies may produce clinical symptoms similar to those resulting from other incompatible antibodies. As a rule, however, severe clinical disease owing to A and B sensitization is much rarer than that caused by Rh sensitization. Subclinical forms or mild disease expressed as slight jaundice appearing before the third day of life, spherocytosis, and moderate reticulocytosis are observed more frequently.

2. Pathogenesis. Entry into the maternal circulation of fetal red cells is especially common during and right after delivery. This may explain why Rh antibodies often are first detected a few weeks after delivery. As a rule Rh antibodies do not develop during the first pregnancy of an Rh-negative woman bearing an Rh-positive fetus, unless they were stimulated by preceding transfusion of Rh-positive blood. Most commonly two or three pregnancies are needed for development of Rh antibodies. Frequently, even a much larger number of pregnancies with Rh-positive fetuses does not lead to formation of Rh antibodies in Rh-negative women. On the basis of statistical analyses of large series only approximately one out of ten Rh-negative women potentially exposed to Rh sensitization by pregnancy actually develops antibodies.

Once antibodies are present they may pass to the fetus transplacentally. According to Wiener this is much more likely with incomplete than with complete antibodies; this concept has been amply confirmed by appropriate tests on serum of cord blood specimens. Apparently this reflects the larger molecular size of complete antibodies as compared with incomplete ones.

The most severe form of hemolytic disease (hydrops fetalis) is the result of damage to fetal red cells of sufficient severity to cause intrauterine death. If, on the

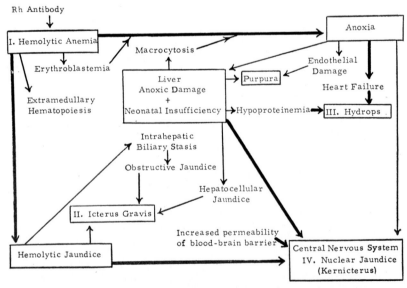

Figure 5–6. Pathogenesis of fetal erythroblastosis. (Davidsohn, 1960.)

other hand, the child is born alive, it may present one of two forms of disease. The first, more serious form is characterized by rapid development of jaundice resulting from the postnatal breakdown of red cells and entails the risk of damage of certain portions of the central nervous system by bilirubin (indirect, nonesterified) and other heme metabolites (nuclear jaundice, hyperbilirubinemic encephalopathy, generally known as kernicterus). This form is designated icterus gravis. The second, milder form of the disease is associated with a gradual destruction of the red cells coated with Rh antibody and leads to a hemolytic anemia similar to that found in patients with other causes of accelerated red cell breakdown. Figure 5–6 correlates the most important clinical, pathologic, and clinicopathologic findings in these three forms of hemolytic disease (Davidsohn, 1960). The pathogenesis of hemolytic disease caused by other forms of maternal isosensitization is in all essential points analogous to that

Table 5–16. Differential Diagnosis of Fetal Erythroblastosis in Live Born Infants

	F.E.*	C.S.	A.I.	P.I.	I.D.	I.N.	I.P.	PJK§	H.D.N.	C.M.B.D.	C.M.H.
1. Familial incidence	+++	+	−	−	−	±	+	−	−	−	−
2. Splenomegaly	+++	+++	+	±	+	+	±	−	−	−	+
3. Hepatomegaly	++	++	±	±	+	−	±	−	−	+	+
4. Enlarged placenta†	±	++	−	−	−	−	−	−	−	−	−
5. Anemia	++	++	++	±	+	−	±	−	±	−	−
6. Leukocytosis	++	++	++	++	+	−	±	−	±	−	−
7. Leukemoid blood picture	++	++	++	+	+	−	−	−	±	−	−
8. Erythroblastemia‡	++	++	+	−	+	−	−	±	±	−	+
9. Severe and early jaundice	++	++	+	+	+	−	−	− (+ 3rd day or later)	−	−	−
10. High blood bilirubin	++	++	+	+	+	+	+	+	−	+	−
11. Indirect van den Bergh reaction	++	++	+	±	+	+	+	+	−	−	−
12. Bile in urine	++	++	+	−	+	−	±	−	−	+++	−
13. Purpura	±	+	±	±	±	−	−	+ (lung, brain)	+++	+	−
14. Edema, general	±	+	−	−	−	−	−	−	−	−	−
15. Edema, local	±	+	−	−	±	−	−	−	−	−	−
16. Extramedullary hematopoiesis at term	+++	+++	±	−	+	−	−	−	−	−	+
17. Hepatic biliary stasis	+++	+++	+	−	+	−	+	−	−	+++	−
18. Liver cell damage	+++	+++	±	±	+	−	−	−	−	+++	−
19. Hemosiderosis	+++	+++	±	±	+	−	−	−	−	−	−
20. Nuclear jaundice (kernicterus)	+	−	−	−	−	−	−	+	−	−	−
21. Positive tests for syphilis	−	+++	−	−	−	−	−	−	−	−	−
22. Father Rh+, mother Rh−, infant Rh+	++ (in 95%)	−	−	−	−	−	−	−	−	−	−
23. Rh antibodies in mother's blood	++ (in over 90%)	−	−	−	−	−	−	−	−	−	−
24. Coombs test	++	−	−	−	−	−	−	−	−	−	−

+++ always present; ++ rarely absent; + frequently present; ± may be present; − absent.

* Abbreviations: F.E.—Fetal erythroblastosis; C.S.—Congenital syphilis; A.I.—Antenatal infection; P.I.—postnatal infection; I.D.—Inclusion disease; I.N.—Icterus neonatorum; I.P.—Icterus praecox; PJK syndrome or sixth day disease; H.D.N.—Hemorrhagic disease of newborn; C.M.B.D.—Congenital malformation of bile ducts; C.M.H.—Congenital malformation of heart.

† The average weight of a normal placenta is about one-seventh of the total body weight.

‡ Erythroblastemia indicates the presence of immature nucleated erythrocytes in the circulation in excess of 1000 per cu. mm.

§ Prematurity-Jaundice-Kernicterus syndrome; new entity in premature babies (Aidin, Read: M. Press, 226: 88–93, 1951).

Reprinted from: Davidsohn, I.: Blood Groups. Chicago. M. School Quart. 16: 9, Autumn, 1954.

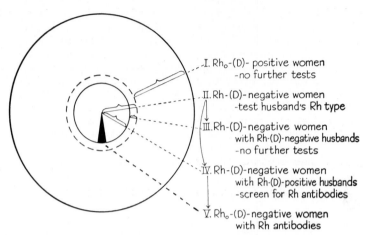

Figure 5–7. Prenatal screening tests.

described for the disease associated with Rh sensitization. At the same time it must be emphasized that none of the clinical, pathologic, and clinicopathologic findings is strictly specific for the disease, since they can also be found in a number of other conditions. Points of differential diagnostic significance are listed in Table 5–16.

3. Prenatal diagnosis. Because of the nonspecificity of clinical, pathologic, and hematologic findings in hemolytic disease of the newborn, the results of serologic tests are of paramount importance. Furthermore, if at all possible, the potential occurrence of the disease should be evaluated prenatally in order to be prepared for proper neonatal treatment without delay. For this reason certain prenatal tests should be carried out on all expectant mothers. According to the general scheme of such tests indicated in Fig. 5–7, the first and crucial test is that for the $Rh_o(D)$ factor. If the patient is found to be $Rh_o(D)$-positive, as a rule no further tests are necessary. On the other hand all $Rh_o(D)$-negative women are potential candidates for Rh sensitization provided their husbands are $Rh_o(D)$-positive. For that reason the serums of such patients should be screened for presence of Rh antibodies. The solid black segment in the innermost circle of Fig. 5–7 represents the approximate percentage of Rh sensitized women one may expect to detect upon prenatal testing. It is the infants of these women in whom hemolytic disease may become manifest provided they are Rh-positive.

Table 5–17 outlines schematically prenatal tests the results of which to a certain extent permit predicting the likelihood of disease in the infant. Table 5–18 contains

additional tests that should be carried out in Rh-sensitized pregnant women in order to obtain some prognostic information concerning the severity of disease to be expected. Repeated screening for Rh antibodies is desirable, since a negative test early in pregnancy may induce a false sense of security responsible for failure to search for and detect subsequent development of Rh antibodies. On the other hand if Rh antibody testing was done only close to term and showed a positive result, the length of exposure of the fetus to Rh antibodies cannot be established. Furthermore, repetition of antibody examinations during various stages of pregnancy may detect a rise in antibody titer. Such a rise can be accepted as significant only if the two specimens to be compared are tested simultaneously with the same technique, reagents, and test cells. Such titrations should preferably be done volumetrically (cf. p. 293). If in this manner a rise in antibodies is established, this can be taken as proving almost conclusively that the fetus carried in the respective pregnancy is Rh-positive, since presumably its red cells have provided the additional antigenic stimulus.

There is no unanimity of opinion whether or not valid prognostic information can be derived from the relative amounts—titers— of Rh antibodies in individual patients. Statistically they seem to be useful, inasmuch as "high" titers of Rh antibodies are more likely to be followed by manifest or severe disease in the newborn than "low" titers. What is to be considered as "high" or "low" titer depends on the techniques employed and therefore must be established empirically in each laboratory. Definite

Table 5-17. Prenatal Tests: Potential HDN

NO.	WHO?	LABORATORY TESTS WHAT?	WHEN? (STAGE OF GESTATION)	RESULT OF TEST	APPROXIMATE PER-CENTAGE IN TOTAL POPULATION OF PREGNANT WOMEN	FURTHER TEST(S) INDICATED
1.	*All* pregnant women	Rh type (and ABO group)	First trimester	Rh-positive	85	None*
				Rh-negative	15	Rh type of husband (2.)
2.	Husbands of Rh-negative pregnant women	Rh type (and ABO group)	First trimester	Rh-negative	2	None*
				Rh-positive	13	Screening for Rh antibodies of wife (3.)
3.	Rh-negative pregnant women with Rh-positive husbands	Screening for Rh antibodies	First trimester	negative	12–12.5	Repeat screening (4.)
				positive	0.5–1	See Table 5-18
4.	Rh-negative pregnant women with Rh-positive husbands	Repeat screening for Rh antibodies	6th month	negative	**	Repeat screening (5.)
				positive	**	See Table 5-18
5.	Rh-negative pregnant women with Rh-positive husbands	Repeat screening for Rh antibodies	8–9th month	negative	**	Repeat screening (6.)
				positive	**	See Table 5-18
6.	Rh-negative pregnant women with Rh-positive husbands	Repeat screening for Rh antibodies	2–4 weeks postpartum	negative	**	None
				positive	**	See Table 5-18

* Except when obstetrical history indicates HDN, stillbirth or unexplained neonatal death in previous pregnancy (see Table 5-19).
** Undetermined

Reprinted with permission of publisher from: Stern, K.: Hemolytic disease of the newborn: Prenatal and neonatal problems in diagnosis. Med. Times, *85*: 1255-1265, 1957.

prognostic significance can be assigned only to the finding of complete antibodies; they are less likely to produce disease, since they do not reach the fetus so readily as do incomplete antibodies. Finally the length of exposure to antibodies influences both the likelihood and degree of clinical disease: short periods of exposure are less likely to produce serious disease than longer periods. At the same time one must remember that these criteria have only general validity and that exceptions to the rule do occur. A change of opinion has taken place concerning the prognostic evaluation of the past obstetrical history. Undoubtedly a previous neonatal death attributable to maternal isosensitization is an unfavorable factor. Nevertheless, in roughly one out of three or four pregnancies with an Rh-posi-

tive fetus following a previous stillbirth caused by Rh sensitization, a live Rh-positive child may be delivered who though diseased may be treated successfully with replacement transfusion.

Once Rh sensitization of an Rh-negative woman has taken place, the prognosis for subsequent pregnancies is significantly affected by the zygosity of her husband for the Rh factor. In this situation Rh genotyping (cf. tests outlined on p. 277) is of considerable importance, because the results permit estimation of the odds for the likelihood of an Rh-negative child from a subsequent pregnancy (cf. Table 5–10). Obviously no amount of Rh antibodies can do any damage to a fetus or infant lacking the corresponding antigen.

As early as 1943 Levine noted a striking

Table 5–18. Prenatal Tests: Probable HDN

	LABORATORY TESTS		WHEN? (STAGE OF GESTATION)	RESULT OF TEST	INTERPRETATION	FURTHER TEST(S) INDICATED
NO.	WHO?	WHAT?				
1.	Rh-negative pregnant woman with positive screening test for Rh antibodies	Rh antibody titer	First trimester or as soon as discovered	High titer	Disease of infant likely if Rh-positive and high titer present before 8th month	
				Low titer	Serious disease of infant less likely	No. 2, 3, 4
				Trace	Disease of infant unlikely unless rise occurred before 8th month	
2.	Husband of pregnant woman with Rh antibodies	Zygosity for Rh factor	Whenever possible	Probably homozygous	All infants probably Rh-positive	
				Probably heterozygous	50% chance of an Rh-negative child?	No. 3, 4
3.	Previous children and parents of husband	Rh type	Whenever possible	One of children or parents Rh-negative	Husband proved heterozygous Rh-positive with 50% chance for each future child to be Rh-negative	—
				None of children or parents Rh-negative		
4.	Rh-negative pregnant woman with Rh antibodies	Repeat Rh antibody titer	Once monthly until 6th mo.; once biweekly after 6th mo.	No change	?	
				Rise	Infant almost certain to be Rh-positive; disease likely if rise to high titer occurred before 8th month	No. 5
5.	Rh-negative pregnant woman with Rh antibodies	Rh antibody titer	2–4 weeks postpartum	No change	Important as baseline for Rh antibody titer in subsequent pregnancy	—
				Rise		

Reprinted with permission of publisher from: Stern, K.: Hemolytic disease of the newborn: Prenatal and neonatal problems in diagnosis. Med. Times, *85:* 1255–1265, 1957.

difference in incidence of ABO heterospecific and homospecific pregnancies in Rh-sensitized as compared with nonsensitized Rh-negative women. Homospecific pregnancies are those in which the mother does not possess isoagglutinins (anti-A, anti-B) capable of reacting with the red cells of the fetus, whereas such isoagglutinins are present in heterospecific pregnancies. According to the distribution of ABO groups in the U. S. Caucasoid population, approximately one-third of all pregnancies is expected to be heterospecific and the remaining two-thirds, homospecific. A much higher incidence—80 to 85 per cent—of homospecific pregnancies was noted by

Table 5-19. Neonatal Tests for Diagnosis of HDN

INFANTS TO BE TESTED	TESTS ON INFANT	FINDINGS SUGGESTING HDN	SUPPLEMENTARY TESTS ON		PROBABLE ETIOLOGY OF HDN: MATERNAL ISO-SENSITIZATION TO
			MOTHER	FATHER	
All infants born to Rh-negative women	Rh type	Positive	See Tables 5–17 & 5–18	See Tables 5–17 & 5–18	Rh factor: Rh_o (D)
	Direct (Coombs) AGT*	Positive			
	Hemoglobin } RBC }	Decreased			
	Serum bilirubin	Elevated within first 6–24 hours			
All infants born to women with history of previous child with HDN, previous stillbirth or unexplained neonatal death and any infant showing otherwise unexplained jaundice and/or anemia	Hemoglobin } RBC }	Decreased or normal	ABO group and Rh type (including subtype)	ABO group and Rh type (including subtype)	(a) Rh factor other than Rh_o (D): hr′(c), rh′(C), rh″ (E);
	Serum bilirubin	Elevated within first 6-24 hours	Screening for Rh antibodies	Search for blood factor(s) differing from those of wife	(b) blood factors: Kell, Duffy, Kidd;
	Rh type and ABO group	(a) & (b) Rh-positive or Rh-negative (c) A or B (Mother O) A or AB (Mother B) B or AB (Mother A)	Screening for antibodies reacting with red cells of husband and/or infant		(c) A, B
	Direct (Coombs) AGT*	(a) & (b) positive (c) negative	Search for blood factor(s) differing from those of husband and infant		
	Witebsky test	(c) positive			
	Incompatible antibody (anti-A or anti-B)	(c) positive			

* AGT = Antiglobulin test

Reprinted with permission of publisher from: Stern, K.: Hemolytic Disease of the Newborn: Prenatal and Neonatal Problems in Diagnosis. Med. Times, *85:* 1255–1265, 1957.

Levine and many subsequent investigators in sensitized Rh-negative women. Also experimentally it was confirmed that injection of ABO-incompatible, Rh-positive red cells is much less likely to induce Rh sensitization than injection of ABO-compatible red cells (Stern, Davidsohn, and Masaitis, 1956). Thus determination of the ABO group of husband and wife may also furnish information of prognostic significance. If the red cells of the husband are incompatible in the ABO system with the serum of his wife (heterospecific mating), this entails a lesser chance for Rh sensitization than does a homospecific mating in which the serum of the wife is compatible with the red cells of her husband in the ABO system. For this reason Rh sensitization is almost never found in O Rh-negative women married to AB Rh-positive husbands, since in this mating all children must be heterospecific; that is, incompatible in the ABO group with the mother.

4. Neonatal tests. Table 5–19 lists tests helpful or essential for diagnosis of hemolytic disease of the newborn. Certain tests should be done routinely on all infants born to Rh-negative women with Rh antibodies and on infants whose Rh-negative mothers have not been adequately tested prenatally. Special consideration must be given to infants whose mothers have a history of isosensitization to blood factors other than Rh, including A and B. Finally, extensive testing is required, as outlined in Table 5–19, when infants unexpectedly develop clinical symptoms suggestive of hemolytic disease. With exceedingly rare exceptions the presence of clinical hemolytic disease of the newborn owing to Rh incompatibility can be ruled out if the direct antiglobulin (Coombs) test is negative. On the other hand a positive direct antiglobulin (Coombs) test may be associated not only with manifest disease but also with latent disease in which no other abnormal clinical or laboratory findings are obtained. Proper interpretation of laboratory tests is essential for establishing indication for treatment of hemolytic disease with replacement transfusion. (Detailed discussion of this problem may be found in the monographs of Mollison, 1962, and Allen and Diamond, 1958.) The four critical laboratory tests are the direct antiglobulin (Coombs) test; hemoglobin or hematocrit of cord blood; reticulocyte count; and indirect serum bilirubin repeated every six hours through the first two to three days of life. Abnormalities in these tests together with abnormal clinical findings or history of a previously diseased child as a rule furnish the main indications for replacement transfusion, which is the treatment of choice since it offers the greatest assurance of recovery and especially of prevention of bilirubin encephalopathy.

Controversial opinions have been expressed about the frequency with which a positive direct antiglobulin (Coombs) test is obtained in infants with AB hemolytic disease. Recent work has indicated that this variability reflects mainly the differences in selection of antiglobulin serums for the test; reagents particularly suitable for detection of coating of red cells with anti-A and anti-B can be prepared and give positive results. Another important confirmatory test for diagnosis of hemolytic disease of the newborn caused by AB sensitization is demonstration of the incompatible agglutinin in the serum of the infant; i.e., anti-A in infants of group A, anti-B in infants of group B, and so forth. These antibodies are as a rule demonstrable only by techniques suitable to detect incomplete antibodies, such as papain-treated red cells or the indirect antiglobulin technique (cf. p. 295) (Zuelzer and Kaplan, 1954; Stern, Davidsohn and Buznitsky, 1957).

5. *Transfusion therapy in hemolytic disease of the newborn.* The basic rule for selecting compatible blood for infants with hemolytic disease of the newborn is to use blood compatible with the mother. In other words the major crossmatch is done with the serum of the mother and the red cells of the donor. Blood for replacement

transfusions should preferably be not older than three days. If it differs in the ABO group from that of the infant, one must make sure that the isoagglutinin reactive with the infant's red cells is not of the "immune" type (cf. p. 302). For simple transfusions given merely to correct anemia, similar criteria for selection of blood apply. As to quantitative factors successful replacement transfusions require at least 70 ml. of blood per pound of weight; in simple transfusions not more than 10 ml. of blood per pound should be given. For the latter purpose it may be preferable to use packed red cells rather than whole blood, since in this way more red cell mass can be administered.

After replacement transfusions or in untreated cases with latent disease the following laboratory tests are essential for follow-up purposes: direct antiglobulin (Coombs) test, indirect serum bilirubin, hemoglobin or hematocrit, and reticulocyte count. It is also recommended to test a postpartum specimen from a sensitized mother about three to four weeks after delivery, since a rise in titer may occur at that time. Therefore, the antibody level ascertained at that time furnishes the most reliable baseline of comparison in future pregnancies.

III. Autoimmune Hemolytic Anemia. Immunohematologic tests applied to this condition are significant for three reasons. First, the unequivocal diagnosis of the disease requires demonstration of autoantibodies. Second, autoantibodies may represent a source of error in the proper interpretation of results of ABO and Rh typing tests. Finally, hemotherapy of patients with this disease may meet with considerable difficulties and therefore necessitate modifications of laboratory tests used for selection of blood—specifically of crossmatching tests.

Diagnosis. Diagnosis of autoimmune hemolytic anemia proceeds in three steps, as indicated in Figure 5–8: (1) establishment of accelerated destruction or shortened survival of red cells; (2) demonstration of extracorpuscular factors as the cause of this red cell destruction; and (3) identification of the extracorpuscular factors as autoantibodies. Since most autoantibodies are incomplete, the techniques most suitable for their detection are the indirect antiglobulin (Coombs) test and the use of enzyme-treated red cells. As a first step the direct antiglobulin (Coombs) test should always be done on the red cells of the patient. If this test is positive and does not reflect passive transfer of isoantibodies (e.g., hemolytic disease of the newborn) or transfusion of incompatible blood within the recent past, it is prima facie evidence for the presence of autoantibodies. On the other hand negative direct antiglobulin (Coombs) tests are occasionally found in some cases of autoimmune hemolytic anemia, probably more frequently in patients during or after intensive steroid therapy (Davidsohn, 1954). In such instances it is essential to test the serum of the patient for autoantibodies by having it act on random samples of cells of group O. Since most autoantibodies are of the "warm" type, these tests should be incubated at 37° C. In other instances "cold" autoantibodies are encountered, requiring incubation at 4° C. In either event, after incubation of saline-suspended red cells, the test is converted into the indirect antiglobulin technique (cf. p. 286); as an alternative the patient's serum may be tested with papain-treated red cells (cf. p. 288).

By merely suspending red cells that are heavily sensitized with autoantibodies in their own serum or in macromolecular medium, such as bovine albumin, agglutination may take place. Although this technique may be used for demonstrating the presence of autoantibodies, the phenomenon is more important as a source of error in ABO grouping and Rh typing. In such tests agglutinations may occur that are not the results of specific antigen-antibody reactions but merely reflect agglutination of antibody-coated cells in macromolecular medium. This is particularly prone to occur in slide techniques for ABO grouping, the nonspecific clumping leading to erroneous classification of a blood sample as AB. The error can be readily detected by suspending the red cells in their own serum or in the serum of a person of group AB. By the same token, nonspecific and frequently erroneous results may occur in Rh typing of "coated" red cells when these tests use incomplete antibodies necessitating suspension of red cells in macromolecular medium. For this reason it is preferable to use saline agglutinating antiserums for Rh typing of such samples in order to eliminate this source of error. In extreme cases it may be impossible to obtain reliable Rh types of such red cell specimens. Likewise in the presence of a positive direct antiglobulin (Coombs) test it is not possible to determine the blood factors that require as a rule the indirect antiglobulin technique, such as factors D^u, Kell, and Duffy.

Therapy. Hemotherapy of patients with autoimmune hemolytic anemia depends primarily on medical decisions as to whether to transfuse at all and, if so, what quantities and what forms of blood are to be used. Since in severe cases of autoimmune hemolytic anemia as a rule, it is not possible to find any blood that is completely compatible, one must attempt to select the least incompatible blood. For this purpose sensitive techniques, such as the indirect antiglobulin (Coombs) test or the use of enzyme-treated red cells, including the cysteine-papain technique (p. 296), are used with serial dilutions of the patient's serum. As a control one may use the red cells of the patient exposed to his own serum. In this way one is able to select among numerous units the one with the lowest titer or the weakest degree of agglutination. According to studies of several authors (Weiner (1953); van Loghem (1954); Davidsohn (1953)) some autoantibodies possess specificity for certain blood factors. If such specificity is suspected or established, it is a helpful guide in selection of blood. The minor crossmatch in such cases cannot be carried out by means of the indirect antiglobulin (Coombs) test if the direct antiglobulin (Coombs) test on the patient's red cells is positive. For discussion of hematologic findings and their significance in the diagnosis and treatment of autoimmune hemolytic anemia see chapter on hematology (p. 172ff.).

IV. Medicolegal Applications

1. Exclusion of parentage. This appli-

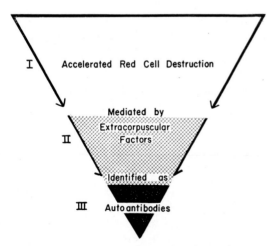

Figure 5–8. Steps in diagnosis of autoimmune hemolytic anemia.

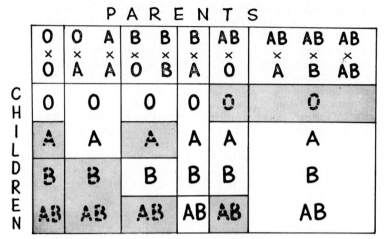

Figure 5–9. Use of the ABO system for exclusion of parentage. Children of groups in shaded area are excluded.

cation is based on the Mendelian inheritance of blood factors referred to previously (cf. p. 263). The following general principles must be understood in order to interpret properly blood grouping for possible exclusion of parentage:

1. Each person inherits one paternal and one maternal allele for each blood factor.

2. In logical consequence of this mode of inheritance a person can be either homozygous or heterozygous for each blood factor.

3. In the case of some blood factors it is possible to distinguish between homozygotes and heterozygotes, whereas for other blood factors this is not possible.

4. A person cannot possess a blood factor that is absent from the blood of both father and mother.

5. A blood factor cannot be absent in a person if one of his parents is homozygous for this factor.

6. If a parent is heterozygous for a factor of which both alleles can be demonstrated by suitable tests, his child must possess a blood factor corresponding to one of these two alleles.

By applying these principles to the ABO system, persons with certain ABO groups can be excluded from parentage as indicated in Fig. 5–9. While such tests most commonly are utilized for exclusion of paternity, the same rules apply to exclusion of maternity. Therefore, the matings shown in Fig. 5–9 are not specified as to sex of the parent. Principle 4 mentioned in the preceding section permits formulation of the *first law of inheritance:*

> *Factors A or B cannot appear in a child unless present in one or both parents.*

Principle 6 applied to the ABO system permits formulation of the *second law of inheritance:*

> *A parent of group AB cannot have a child of group O.*

Finally principle 5 adapted to the ABO system results in the *third law of inheritance:*

> *A parent of group O cannot have a child of group AB.*

In many thousands of tests done for medicolegal purposes or genetic studies no exception whatsoever was found to the first law of inheritance. On the other hand two cases are on record of children of group O born to mothers of group A_2B without any possible doubt of maternity. Hence exclusions based on the second and third laws of inheritance may have to be considered somewhat less stringent than those based on the first law of inheritance. Nevertheless it must be realized that apparent violations of the second and third laws of inheritance are exceedingly rare; they possibly result from mutations, an assumption supported by the finding that at least one of the infants of group O with an AB mother showed multiple congenital abnormalities.

Figure 5–10 summarizes possible exclusions from parentage of children of certain MN types. The laws of inheritance of MN factors may be also derived from general principles of Mendelian inheritance. Principle 4 applied to the MN system results in the *fourth law of inheritance:*

> *A child cannot possess M or N unless these factors are present in the blood of one or both parents.*

Principle 5 gives rise to the *fifth and sixth laws of inheritance:*

A parent of type M cannot have a child of type N.

A parent of type N cannot have a child of type M.

Because of the complexity of factors and phenotypes of the Rh system (cf. Table 5–8) Rh testing for exclusion of parentage requires additional considerations. If properly carried out it can contribute a great deal. As a rule factors $Rh_0(D)$, rh'(C), rh''(E), and hr'(c) are determined. Factor hr''(e) may be also determined provided reliable and potent antiserums are available. Results of such Rh tests, as interpreted by general principles of inheritance, permit the following conclusions:

1. None of the Rh factors [$Rh_0(D)$, rh'(C), rh''(E), hr'(c), hr''(e)] can be present in a person unless one or both parents possess the corresponding factor.

2. A parent lacking the rh'(C) factor cannot have a child without the hr'(c) factor; vice versa, a parent lacking the hr'(c) factor cannot have a child without the rh'(C) factor.

3. A parent lacking the rh''(E) factor cannot have a child without the hr''(e) factor; vice versa, a parent lacking the hr''(e) factor cannot have a child without the rh''(E) factor.

The chances for excluding a person from parentage of a specific child are approximately 25 per cent by use of the ABO groups alone; the chances rise to 31 per cent when ABO and MN factors are determined and to approximately 50 per cent by testing for ABO, MN, and Rh factors. These figures are derived from tests on the U. S. Caucasoid population and depend critically on the distribution of the factors in the population. There are several reasons why other blood group systems discussed in the previous sections are not utilized for exclusion of parentage: (a) sufficient quantities of potent and specific antiserums are not available; (b) in some of these systems studies of inheritance based on knowledge of alleles have not yet reached a stage warranting acceptance of results for medicolegal purposes; and (c) even without these restrictions of validity the actual gain would be rather minimal. Wiener and Wexler (1958) stated that combined use of all other known blood factors would at most add only 12 to 15 per cent to the chances of exclusions. Finally it must be emphasized that blood grouping tests as described can only be used for exclusion of parentage but never for establishing parentage. Exceptions to this rule are exceedingly rare: if the child and one parent possess one of the unusual "private" or "family factors," (cf. p. 278) this may be considered as strong presumptive evidence for parentage.

TECHNICAL CONSIDERATIONS IN TESTS FOR EXCLUSION OF PARENTAGE. Although the techniques employed for this purpose are essentially the same as those described in the previous sections, it cannot be emphasized enough that proper performance of parentage tests requires a good deal of experience and expertness. This includes use of adequate red cell controls in order to assure specific and sensitive performance of the antiserums. It is advisable to use more than one antiserum for the tests, especially for MN and Rh factors. The ABO grouping may be supplemented by use of anti-A_1 serum (cf. p. 283) in order to subgroup A and AB into A_1 and A_1B or into

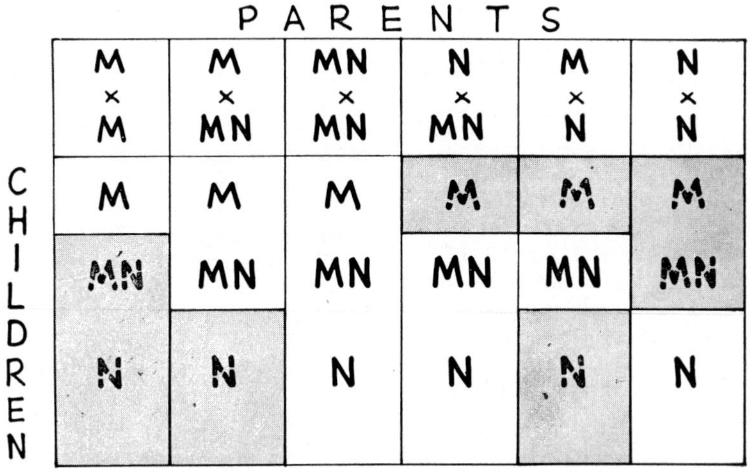

Figure 5–10. Use of the MN system for exclusion of parentage. Children of groups in shaded areas are excluded.

A_2 or A_2B. In this way it is possible to utilize consideration of inheritance of A_1 as an additional means for exclusion of parentage. As shown in Table 5–4, while persons of A_1 may be either homozygous or heterozygous for this factor, in either event their red cells react as A_1. Hence one may derive an additional law of ABO inheritance:

> A person of A_1B cannot have a child of group A_2; vice versa, a person of group A_2 cannot have a child of group A_1B.

CAUTIONS FOR INTERPRETATIONS OF EXCLUSIONS OF PARENTAGE. Apart from the exceedingly remote possibility that mutations are responsible for violations of laws of inheritance, some specific qualifications must be kept in mind when interpreting exclusion of parentage.

1. ABO system. Possible presence of weak subgroups of A must not be overlooked. Furthermore exclusion based on differences in subgroups cannot be considered valid if it concerns a child under the age of one year, since tests for subgroups of A are unreliable at this age. Finally exceedingly rare cases have been reported of "suppressor genes," which when present in one of the parents in homozygous form make it impossible to detect A or B factors in the red cells, although the factor may be present in his offspring because he is heterozygous for the suppressor gene.

2. MN system. A third allele, M^g, of exceedingly rare occurrence may lead to an apparent violation of the laws of inheritance of MN types, as described previously: e.g., a person who seemingly is type N but actually is type M^gN may have a child M from a mother M, the true type of the child being MM^g. Furthermore there are weak subgroups of $N(N_2)$ that may be missed and thus lead to erroneous typing and interpretation.

3. Rh system. The apparent absence of $Rh_o(D)$ can only be used for exclusion of parentage provided suitable tests have also shown absence of Rh_o variants (D^u factor). Otherwise, for example, a person could be erroneously excluded as the parent of an Rh-positive child because he and the other parent were found to be Rh-negative. This is especially important in connection with the Rh_o variant (D^u), when it represents a suppression of reactivity of $Rh_o(D)$ because of presence of $rh'(C)$.

The rare type $\overline{R}h_o(-D-)$ may lead to misinterpretations, inasmuch as its presence invalidates the laws of inheritance formulated for factors $rh'(C)$, $hr'(c)$, rh'' (E), and $hr''(e)$. Suitable tests and consideration of Rh types of parents and child can eliminate these pitfalls (Stern, 1959).

Properly executed and interpreted blood grouping tests are now accepted as evidence for exclusion of parentage in the courts of 14 states. Because of the medicolegal importance of these tests a special committee of the American Medical Association has issued periodic reports that incorporate the latest developments in this field and thus serve as guide for all those engaged in this work.

2. *Identification of blood stains and secretions.* Blood grouping tests can provide valuable evidence in connection with possible identity of blood stains found on clothing, utensils, and instruments presumably involved in assault with the blood of persons involved in crime or accidents (Davidsohn, 1958). However, such tests are by no means so simple as those routinely used, because only rarely is material available that is fresh enough to permit preparation of red cell suspensions capable of being reliably agglutinated by the corresponding antiserums. Most commonly it is necessary to prepare extracts of the blood stains or spots in which specific blood factors are demonstrated by mixing the extract with known antiserum (e.g., anti-A) and determining that in this mixture agglutinating activity has been inhibited or neutralized. Thus material eluted from a blood stain and found capable of significantly inhibiting anti-A serum presumably has contained blood factor A. In order to control sources of error, such as nonspecific absorption of antibody, suitable controls must be included, and adequate performance and interpretation of these tests requires considerable experience. Similar considerations apply to the demonstration of A and B substances in the saliva of secretors. Presence of A and B in such saliva permits testing traces of saliva derived from sealing of envelopes. The sensitivity and specificity of such tests must be assured by proper controls. Because of the special expertness required, they should not be done in the average blood grouping laboratory. This may also apply to identification of blood by species; that is, in cases in which a blood stain might be of human or animal origin. Specific precipitin tests must be carried out in order to prove such identity. Presence of factors other than A, B, Le^a, and Le^b in secretions or in tissues other than blood has not been conclusively established, and hence at present such tests are outside the area of practical application.

V. **Anthropologic and Genetic Applications.** Blood factors represent the most readily accessible and demonstrable genetic markers. This fact together with the significant differences in distribution of blood factors found in populations of different racial origin makes their study one of the most valuable and reliable means of anthropologic classification. Details of this fascinating discipline are outside of the scope of this text; those interested in such information are specifically referred to the classic monograph on the subject by Mourant (1954).

An application still in the early stage utilizes blood groups for following somatic mutations as they arise spontaneously or under the impact of mutagenic agents and disease (Atwood, 1958). In some instances it has been also possible to use blood groups as chromosome markers and to establish association with certain other genetically transmitted defects or peculiarities (Lawler). So far only a few specific instances of this type have been established but future applications are conceivable. That one or the other alleles of certain blood factors—e.g., A and O—may be more commonly associated than other alleles with specific diseases, such as diabetes, pernicious anemia, gastric ulcer, or gastric cancer, has been described, but the validity and significance of the phenomenon are still debatable. Evidence adduced in favor of association between specific blood factors and disease is purely statistical. Hence a great deal of additional intensive study will be required before one may accept it as valid.

IMMUNOHEMATOLOGY OF LEUKOCYTES

This area of immunohematology, as well as that concerned with platelets, is only in an early stage of development. Although immunologic phenomena involving leukocytes had been suspected for some time, it was only within the last decade that conclusive proof was furnished for isoantigenic differences between leukocytes in man. In addition to isoantibodies, autoantibodies for white cells have been demonstrated and presumably are associated with certain clinical conditions.

1. Isoleukoagglutinins

Multiple blood transfusions as well as pregnancies have been shown to be capable of producing isoagglutinins for leukocytes in a manner similar to isosensitization to red cell antigens (Dausset, 1954; Payne, 1957; Brittingham and Chaplin, Jr., 1957; and van Loghem, 1957). The main clinical significance of leukoagglutinins derives from their association with pyrogenic (febrile) transfusion reactions in approximately one-third of such cases. Since such patients tolerate leukocyte-poor blood without any untoward reaction, it is logical to assume a causal relationship between isosensitization to leukocytes and such transfusion reactions. Much less commonly, but documented by a number of recent case reports, neonatal neutropenia may result from transplacental transfer of isoleukoagglutinins formed by a pregnant woman for maternal white cells of her fetus presumably containing isoantigens of paternal origin absent in the mother. This, in analogy to red cell isosensitization, might be well designated as "leukolytic disease of the newborn." Thus there is little doubt for the existence of leukocyte groups. They have been shown to be independent of red cell factors and as yet have not been classified. This makes it necessary to utilize arbitrarily selected panels of white cell donors whenever serums suspected of containing leukoagglutinins are to be tested. It has been recommended that six to twelve different white cell donors be used in order to assure inclusion of the various leukocyte isoantigens.

Technique for Tests for Isoleukoagglutinins (Payne, 1957). Leukocytes are separated from whole blood by methods of differential sedimentation. Following incubation of the leukocyte suspension with the serum to be tested, the presence or absence of agglutination is established by microscopic examination (Fig. 5–11).

Reagents.

1. Serum to be tested; inactivated at 56° C. for 30 minutes.

2. 4 per cent solution of polyvinylpyrrolidone (PVP) in saline; adjusted by means of N/10 NaOH to pH of 6.8 to 7.2.*

3. 3 per cent acetic acid.

4. Control serum free of leukoagglutinins and irregular red cell antibodies (inactivated at 56° C. for 30 minutes).

Preparation of Leukocyte Suspension

1. Approximately 15 ml. of blood from a group O donor is rapidly transferred into an Erlenmeyer flask containing six glass beads and rotated gently for approximately

---

* 6 per cent dextran may be used instead of PVP.

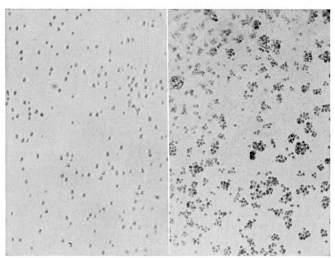

Figure 5–11.   Leukoagglutinin tests. Left: negative test; right: positive test. (Courtesy of Dr. Rose Payne.)

ten minutes in order to defibrinate the sample.

2. The defibrinated blood may be removed with a 10 ml. pipet.

3. In a test tube add to 4 parts of the defibrinated blood 1 part of the PVP solution.*

4. Mix by inverting the stoppered tube several times. Place the tube with the mixture into a beaker at an angle and incubate in a water bath at 37° C. The red cells will sediment in 30 minutes to one hour, depending on the sedimentation rate of the particular blood sample.

5. Carefully remove the supernatant mixture of serum and PVP, the bottom layer of which contains the majority of leukocytes and few erythrocytes. Platelets are absent because they have been used up in the process of defibrination.

6. Add inactivated serum of group O sufficient to yield a concentration of 3000 to 5000 leukocytes per cu. mm.

NOTE: The leukocyte suspensions must be prepared freshly on the day of the test and kept in the refrigerator until used.

Agglutination Test

1. In a Kahn test tube add 0.05 ml. of the leukocyte suspension to 0.1 ml. of the inactivated serum to be tested.

2. Incubate the mixture for 75 minutes in a water bath at 37° C.

3. Lyse the red cells by adding 0.1 ml. of 3 per cent acetic acid. Agitate gently.

4. Withdraw the sediment from the bottom of the tube, transfer to slide, and

---

* 6 per cent dextran may be used instead of PVP.

examine for agglutination with 100 × objective.

2. Autoleukoagglutinins

These are presumably associated with leukopenias, the etiology of which corresponds to that of autoimmune hemolytic anemia. However, detection of autoantibodies for white cells is difficult to accomplish. Dausset (1960) has reported that autoantibodies can be consistently demonstrated by means of the direct antiglobulin consumption test. This rather complex test has as its first step exposure of the presumably sensitized leukocytes to an antihuman globulin serum of known titer. If the leukocytes actually were coated with autoantibodies, a considerable amount of the antiglobulin antibody would be consumed for it becomes fixed to the white cells. Therefore, when tested in parallel with the original antiglobulin serum, the supernatant shows a significant drop in the antiglobulin titer.

IMMUNOHEMATOLOGY OF PLATELETS

Although similar considerations apply to the immunohematology of platelets and white cells, corresponding laboratory tests must take into account the additional problems of lability of platelets. Isothromboagglutinins may be the result of multiple transfusions as well as of maternal isosensitization. Although ABO and Rh antigens have been shown to be present in platelets, they are not responsible for platelet agglutinins, which apparently reflect other isoantigenic differences. The techniques for detection of platelet antibodies are cumbersome, difficult to reproduce, and hence not ready for routine applications. This holds true even more for autoantibodies for platelets (autothromboagglutinins). Dausset has successfully applied the direct antiglobulin consumption test for detection of platelet autoantibodies; the principle and technique are analogous to those described in the preceding section on leukocyte autoantibodies. A rather unique phenomenon concerns the thrombolytic effect of serum of patients who develop thrombocytopenia as an expression of hypersensitivity to certain drugs (sedormid, quinidine). When their serum is mixed with platelets *in vitro*, thrombolysis occurs but only if the incriminated drug has been also added (Ackroyd, 1949; Harrington *et al.*, 1951).

REFERENCES

1. Ackroyd, J. F.: The pathogenesis of thrombocytopenic purpura due to hypersensitivity to sedormid (allyl-isopropyl-acetyl-carbamide) Clin. Sc., 7:249–285, 1949.
2. Allbritton, E. C.: Standard Values in Blood. Philadelphia, W. B. Saunders Company, 1952.
3. Allen, F. H., Jr., Corcoran, P. A., Kenton, H. B., and Breare, N.: M^g, a new blood group antigen in the MNS system. Vox Sang., 3:81–91, 1958.
4. Allen, F. H., Jr., and Diamond, L. K.: Erythroblastosis Fetalis. Boston, Little, Brown & Company, 1958.
5. American Association of Blood Banks: Technical Methods and Procedures of the American Association of Blood Banks. 3rd Ed. Chicago, American Association of Blood Banks, 1960.
6. Atwood, K. C.: The presence of A$_2$ erythrocytes in A$_1$ blood. Proc. Nat. Acad. Sc., 44:1054–1057, 1958.
7. Boorman, K. E., and Dodd, B. E.: Blood Group Serology. Boston, Little, Brown & Company, 1957.
8. Boyd, W. C., and Shapleigh, E.: Specific precipitating activity of plant agglutinins (lectins). Science, 119:419, 1954.
9. Brittingham, T. E., and Chaplin, H., Jr.: Febrile transfusion reactions caused by sensitivity to donor leukocytes and platelets. J.A.M.A., 165:819–825, 1957.
10. Bruton, O. C.: Agammaglobulinemia. Pediatrics, 9:722–727, 1952.
11. Cohen, F., Zuelzer, W. W., and Evans, M. M.: Identification of blood group antigens and minor cell populations by the fluorescent antibody method. Blood, 15:884–900, 1960.
12. Coombs, R. R. A., Mourant, A. E., and Race, R. R.: A new test for the detection of weak and incomplete Rh agglutinins. Brit. J. Exper. Path., 26:255–256, 1945.
13. Dausset, J.: Leuco-agglutinins. IV. Leuco-agglutinins and blood transfusion. Vox Sang., 4:190–198, 1954.
14. Davidsohn, I. D.: Isoagglutinin titers in serum disease, in leukemias, in infectious mononucleosis, and after blood transfusions. Am. J. Clin. Path., 8:179–196, 1938.
15. Davidsohn, I.: Fetal erythroblastosis. J.A.M.A., 127:633–638, 1945.
16. Davidsohn, I.: Laboratory aids to diagnosis and therapy. Annual Review of Medicine, 3:231–264, Annual Reviews, Inc., Stanford, 1952.
17. Davidsohn, I.: Indications and contraindications for whole blood and its various fractions. Am. J. Clin. Path., 24:349–364, 1954.
18. Davidsohn, I.: Immunohematology, a new branch of clinical pathology. Am. J. Clin. Path., 24:1333–1349, 1954.
19. Davidsohn, I.: ABO incompatibility as a cause of hemolytic disease of the newborn. Obst. & Gynec., 8:318–322, 1956.
20. Davidsohn, I.: Identification of blood stains. Illinois Med. J., 114:56–63, 1958.
20a. Davidsohn, I.: Fetal erythroblastosis and the Rh and other blood factors. In J. P. Greenhill: Obstetrics, 12th ed., Philadelphia, W. B. Saunders Company, 1960, Chapter 49, pp. 620–631.
21. Davidsohn, I., and Levine, P., and Wiener, A. S.: Medicolegal application of blood grouping tests. J.A.M.A., 149:699–706, 1952.
22. Davidsohn, I., and Oyamada, A.: Specificity of auto-antibodies in hemolytic anemia. Am. J. Clin. Path., 23:101–115, 1953.
23. Davidsohn, I., and Schirmer, E.: Normal anti-M isoagglutinins. Proc. Chicago Path. Soc., October 13, 1941.
24. Davidsohn, I., and Spurrier, W.: Immunohematologic studies in hemolytic anemia. J.A.M.A., 154:818–821, 1954.
25. Davidsohn, I., and Stern, K.: Diagnosis of hemolytic transfusion reactions. Am. J. Clin. Path., 25:381–383, 1955.
26. Davidsohn, I., and Stern, K.: Blood transfusion reactions: Their causes and identification. Med. Clinics of North America, 44:281–292, 1960.
27. Davidsohn, I., Stern, K., Strauser, E. R., and Spurrier, W.: Be, a new "private" blood factor. Blood, 8:747–754, 1953.
28. Davidsohn, I., and Toharsky, B.: The production of bacteriogenic hemagglutination. J. Infect. Dis., 67:25–41, 1940.
29. Davidsohn, I., and Toharsky, B.: Bacteriogenic hemagglutination. II. J. Immunol., 43:213–225, 1942.
30. Davidsohn, I., and Toharsky, B.: The Rh blood factor: An antigenic analysis. Am. J. Clin. Path., 12:434–441, 1942.
31. Decastello, A., and Sturli, A.: Ueber die Isoagglutinine im Serum gesunder und kranker Menschen. München. med. Wchnschr., 49:1090–1095, 1902.
32. De Gowin, E., Hardin, R. C., and Alsever, J.: Blood Transfusion. Philadelphia, W. B. Saunders Company, 1949.
33. Diamond, L. K., and Abelson, N. M.: Detection of Rh sensitization; evaluation of tests for Rh antibodies. J. Lab. & Clin. Med., 30:668–674, 1945.
34. Diamond, L. K., and Abelson, N. M.: The demonstration of anti-Rh agglutinins: an accurate and rapid slide test. J. Lab. & Clin. Med., 30:204–212, 1945.
35. Good, R. A., and Zak, S. J.: Disturbances in

gamma globulin synthesis as "experiments of nature." Pediatrics, *18*:109–149, 1956.

36. Grove-Rasmussen, M., Shaw, R. S., and Marceau, E.: Hemolytic transfusion reaction in group A patient receiving group O blood. Am. J. Clin. Path., 23:828–832, 1953.

37. Harrington, W. J., Minnich, V., Hollingsworth, J. W., and Moore, C. V.: Demonstration of a thrombocytopenic factor in the blood of patients with thrombocytopenic purpura. J. Lab. & Clin. Med., 38:1–10, 1951.

38. Hattersley, P. G., and Fawcett, M. L.: Prozone phenomenon in Rh blocking serums. Am. J. Clin. Path., 17:695–703, 1947.

39. Hektoen, L.: Iso-agglutination of human corpuscles. J. Infect. Dis., 4:297–302, 1907.

40. Kabat, E. A.: The Blood Group Substances. New York, Academic Press, Inc., 1956.

41. Kuhns, W. J., and Bailey, A.: Use of red cells modified by papain for detection of Rh antibodies. Am. J. Clin Path., 20:1067–1069, 1950.

42. Landsteiner, K.: Zur Kenntnis der antifermentativen, lytischen und agglutinierenden Wirkungen des Blutserums und der Lymphe. Zentralbl. f. Bakt., 27:357–362, 1900.

43. Landsteiner, K., and Levine, P.: A new agglutinable factor differentiating individual human bloods. Proc. Soc. Exper. Biol. & Med., 24:600–602, 1927.

44. Landsteiner, K., and Levine, P.: Further observations on individual differences of human blood. Proc. Soc. Exper. Biol & Med., 24:941–942, 1927.

45. Landsteiner, K., and Wiener, A. S.: An agglutinable factor in human blood recognized by immune sera for rhesus blood. Proc. Soc. Exper. Biol. & Med., 43:223–224, 1940.

46. Landsteiner, K., and Wiener, A. S.: Studies on an agglutinogen (Rh) in human blood reacting with anti-rhesus sera and with human antibodies. J. Exper. Med., 74:309–320, 1941.

47. Landsteiner, K., and Wiener, A. S.: Tests for Rh factor with guinea pig immune sera. Proc. Soc. Exper. Biol. & Med., *51*:313, 1942.

48. Levine, P.: Serological factors as possible causes in spontaneous abortions. J. Hered., 34:71–80, 1943.

49. Levine, P., Bobbitt, O. B., Waller, R. K., and Kuhmichel, A.: Isoimmunization by a new blood factor in tumor cells. Proc. Soc. Exper. Biol. & Med., 77:403–405, 1951.

50. Levine, P., Burnham, L., Katzin, E. M., and Vogel, P.: The role of isoimmunization in the pathogenesis of erythroblastosis fetalis. Am. J. Obst. & Gynec., 42:925–937, 1941.

51. Levine, P., and Celano, M. J.: Antigenicity of P substance in echinococcus cyst fluid coated onto tanned rabbit cells. Fed. Proc., *18*:580, 1959.

52. Levine, P., Katzin, E. M., and Burnham, L.: Isoimmunization in pregnancy: its possible bearing on the etiology of erythroblastosis fetalis. J.A.M.A., *116*:825–827, 1941.

53. Levine, P., and Stetson, R. E.: An unusual case of intragroup agglutination. J.A.M.A., *113*: 126–127, 1939.

54. Levine, P., Stork, A. H., Kuhmichel, A. B., and Bronikovsky, N.: A new human blood factor of rare incidence in the general population. Proc. Soc. Exper. Biol. & Med., 77:402–403, 1951.

55. Mollison, P. L.: Blood Transfusion in Clinical Medicine. 3rd Ed. Oxford, Blackwell Scientific Publications, 1962.

56. Morgan, W. T. J., and King, H. K.: Studies in

immunochemistry; Isolation from hog gastric mucin of polysaccharide-amino acid complex possessing blood group A specificity. Biochem. J., 37:640–651, 1943.

57. Mourant, A. E.: The Distribution of Human Blood Groups. Springfield, Illinois, Charles C Thomas, 1954.

58. Owen, R. D., Stormont, C., Wexler, I. B., and Wiener, A. S.: Medicolegal applications of blood grouping tests. J.A.M.A., *164*:2036–2044, 1957.

59. Payne, R.: Leukocyte agglutinins in human sera: Correlation between blood transfusions and their development. A.M.A. Arch. Int. Med., 99:587–606, 1957.

60. Potter, E. L.: Rh. Chicago, Year Book Publishers, 1947.

61. Public Health Service Regulations: Part 73: Section 73.300 to 73.306. Bethesda, Maryland, U.S. Department of Health, Education, and Welfare, 1958.

62. Race, R. R., and Sanger, R.: Blood Groups in Man. 3rd Ed. Springfield, Illinois, Charles C Thomas, 1958.

63. Sanger, R.: An association between the P and Jay systems of blood groups. Nature, *176*: 1163–1164, 1955.

64. Scientific Committee of the Joint Blood Council, Inc., and Standards Committee of the American Association of Blood Banks: Standards for a Blood Transfusion Service. Rev. Ed. Washington, D.C., and Chicago, Joint Blood Council, Inc., or American Association of Blood Banks, 1960.

65. Stern, K.: Clinical value of serologic examinations related to blood groups in pregnant patients. Am. J. Obst. & Gynec., 75:369–375, 1958.

66. Stern, K.: Consideration of the R^{ox} (-D-) gene in the interpretation of parentage. Am. J. Clin. Path., 31:496–498, 1959.

67. Stern, K.: Hazards and safeguards in hemotherapy. Chicago Med. School Quart., 20:121–132, 1959.

68. Stern, K., Busch, S., and Buznitsky, A.: A crossmatching test using activated papain. Am. J. Clin. Path., 27:707–713, 1957.

69. Stern, K., Busch, S., and Buznitsky, A.: Experiences and experiments with cross-matching procedures. Proc. Sixth Congress Internat. Soc. of Blood Transfusions, Bibliotheca Haematologica Fasc., 7:420–423, 1958.

70. Stern, K., Davidsohn, I., and Buznitsky, A.: Neonatal serologic diagnosis of hemolytic disease of the newborn caused by ABO incompatibility. J. Lab. & Clin. Med., 50:550–557, 1957.

71. Stern, K., Davidsohn, I., Jensen, F. G., and Muratore, R.: Immunologic studies on the Be^a factor. Vox Sang., 3:425–434, 1958.

72. Stern, K., Davidsohn, I., and Masaitis, L.: Experimental studies on Rh immunization. Am. J. Clin. Path., 26:833–843, 1956.

72a. Stern, K.: Unusual blood types as a cause of disease. Med. Clinics North America, 46:277–294, 1962.

73. Unger, L. J., and Wiener, A. S.: Observations on blood factors Rh^A, Rh^B, and Rh^C. Am. J. Clin. Path., 31:95–103, 1957.

74. van der Hart, M., Bosman, H., and Loghem, J. J., van: Two rare human blood group antigens. Vox Sang., 4:108–116, 1954.

75. Walsh, R. J., and Montgomery, C.: A new human isoagglutinin subdividing the MN blood groups. Nature, *160*:504–505, 1947.

76. Weiner, W., Battey, D. A., Cleghorn, T. E., Mar-

son, F. G. W., and Meynell, M. J.: Serological findings in a case of haemolytic anaemia, with some general observations on the pathogenesis of this syndrome. Brit. Med. J., *ii:* 125–128, 1953.

77. Wiener, A. S.: Blood Groups and Blood Transfusions. 3rd Ed. Springfield, Illinois, Charles C Thomas, 1948.

78. Wiener, A. S.: A new test (blocking test) for Rh sensitization. Proc. Soc. Exper. Biol. & Med., *56:*173–176, 1944.

79. Wiener, A. S.: Conglutination test for Rh sensitization. J. Lab. & Clin. Med., *30:*662–667, 1945.

80. Wiener, A. S.: Rh-Hr Blood Types. New York, Grune & Stratton, 1954.

81. Wiener, A. S., Davidsohn, I., and Potter, E. L.: Heredity of the Rh blood types. II. Observations on the relation of factor Hr to the Rh blood types. J. Exper. Med., *81:*63–72, 1945.

82. Wiener, A. S., and Peters, H. R.: Hemolytic reactions following transfusion of blood of the homologous group. Ann. Int. Med., *13:*2306–2322, 1940.

83. Wiener, A. S., Unger, L. J., and Gordon, E. B.: Fatal hemolytic transfusion reaction caused by sensitization to a new blood factor U. J.A.M.A., *153:*1444–1446, 1953.

84. Wiener, A. S., and Wexler, I. B.: Heredity of the Blood Groups. New York, Grune & Stratton, 1958.

85. Witebsky, E., and Klendshoj, N. C.: The isolation of blood group specific B substance. J. Exper. Med., *72:*663–667, 1940.

86. Witebsky, E., and Klendshoj, N. C.: The isolation of an O specific substance from gastric juice of secretors and carbohydrate-like substances from gastric juice of non-secretors. J. Exper. Med., *73:*655–667, 1941.

87. Witebsky, E., Klendshoj, N. C., and Swanson, P.: Preparation and transfusion of safe universal blood. J.A.M.A., *116:*2654–2656, 1941.

88. Zuelzer, W. W., and Kaplan, E.: ABO heterospecific pregnancy and hemolytic disease: Study of normal and pathologic variants. IV. Pathologic variants. A.M.A. Am. J. Dis Child., *88:*319–338, 1954.

Chapter 6

Laboratory Diagnosis of Hemorrhagic Disorders

By EMANUEL E. MANDEL, M.D.

One of the outstanding characteristics of blood is its property to remain liquid while circulating through the vascular system, at the same time retaining its ability to coagulate when the vascular system is injured. That blood clots when it is shed but is usually liquid intravascularly was well known to the ancient Greeks and Romans. They distinguished between the serum, the buffy coat, and the blood clot. Some 2000 years after the discovery was made that a solid substance could be separated from the blood by whipping, Malpighi (1666) observed strands of fibers remaining after a clot of blood was washed. Nearly two centuries later, Buchanan (1845) noted that adding fresh serum to plasma resulted in prompt formation of fibrin. The agent in the serum responsible for this effect was thought by Schmidt (1893, 1895) to be an enzyme, which he termed "thrombin." Schmidt also postulated the existence in plasma of a precursor of thrombin (later named "prothrombin"), which required for its activation a substance contained in tissues. After Hammarsten (1877) had isolated fibrinogen, and Arthus and Pagès (1890) had demonstrated the anticoagulant effect of oxalate and thus the importance of calcium for coagulation, Morawitz (1904) combined the available data into the following classic theory: prothrombin plus calcium plus tissue thrombokinase (thromboplastin) yields thrombin; fibrinogen plus thrombin yields fibrin. Shortly thereafter, the concept of blood-borne, in-

trinsic thromboplastin was initiated when Bordet and Delange (1912) suggested that the platelets furnished cytozyme (synonymous with thromboplastin).

The soundness of these historic observations can be illustrated readily by correlating them with some of the tests currently used. Normal venous blood collected in a plain glass tube remains liquid for 8 to 12 minutes until, quite suddenly, it becomes viscous and gels moments later. These changes encompass what are now recognized as the three phases of coagulation, I, II, III (see Table 6–1). If an aliquot of the same freshly drawn blood sample is promptly mixed with a drop of fresh normal serum, the total clotting time is reduced to one to three seconds. Oxalated or citrated blood or plasma is clotted just as promptly by the same treatment, indicating that calcium is not essential for this reaction. Fresh serum contains a substance (thrombin) that forms in the course of clotting and is capable of rapidly converting fibrinogen to fibrin (phase III; thrombin time). When oxalated blood or plasma is incubated at 56° C. for a few minutes and centrifuged, no clot forms when fresh serum or thrombin solution is added to the supernatant because fibrinogen has been precipitated during the incubation. Adding calcium chloride to oxalated normal plasma in proper concentration and proportion is followed by the formation of a fibrin clot within two or three minutes (recalcification time). This period is shortened to 12 to 14

322

Table 6–1. Tests of Blood Coagulation and Their Interpretation

SUBSTRATE	CONVENTIONAL REAGENTS			CLOTTING TIME	CLOTTING PHASES*	INTERPRETATION
	CaCl$_2$	TISSUE EXTRACT	FRESH SERUM (THROMBIN)			
Freshly drawn venous blood	−	−	−	8–12 min.	I+II+III	Adding tissue extract (= extrinsic thromboplastin) circumvents slow generation of intrinsic thromboplastin (phase I): either agent interacts with prothrombin to form thrombin (II), which, in turn, converts fibrinogen to fibrin (III). Calcium is essential in phases I and II but not in phase III.
	−	+	−	12–20 sec.	II+III	
	−	−	+	1–3 sec.	III	
Oxalated plasma:						
Normal	+	−	−	2–3 min.	I+II+III	Platelets are required for intrinsic (I) but not for extrinsic (II) thromboplastin activity or for thrombin action (III).
Slow-spun, platelet-rich	+	+	−	12–14 sec.	II+III	
	−	+	−	No clot	II	
	−	−	+	1–3 sec.	III	
Normal†	+	−	−	4–5 min.	I+II+III	
Fast-spun, platelet-poor	+	+	−	12–14 sec.	II+III	
	−	−	+	1–3 sec.	III	
From "coumarinized" subject (a few days after treatment was started)	+	−	−	2–3 min.	I+II+III	In *hypoprothrombinemia* the defect is in the extrinsic system (II).
	+	+	−	>14 sec.	II+III	
From hemophilia patient	+	−	−	>3 min.	I+II+III	In *hemophilia* the defect is in *intrinsic* thromboplastin generation (I), which depends on platelet and plasma factors.
	+	+	−	12–14 sec.	II+III	

* Phase I: Formation of intrinsic thromboplastin
Phase II: Conversion of prothrombin to thrombin
Phase III: Conversion of fibrinogen to fibrin
† Or from thrombocytopenic patient

seconds if a tissue (brain or lung) extract is added simultaneously to the plasma (tissue thromboplastin time or "prothrombin" time, phase II), but it is lengthened indefinitely if tissue thromboplastin is added without calcium. Thus, recalcification is required for the formation of thrombin from some inactive precursor(s), whether or not tissue thromboplastin is added. Obviously, active thrombin cannot be contained in circulating blood.

Since the "tissue thromboplastin time" is much shorter than the "recalcification time," one must assume that adding calcium alone results in spontaneous but slow generation of a substance having thromboplastin-like activity (intrinsic thromboplastin, phase I), which takes much longer than the interaction of preformed tissue thromboplastin with prothrombin to form thrombin. The short "thromboplastin time," in turn, is always longer than the "thrombin time" (using each reagent in optimal concentration) and evidently includes both phases: conversion of thrombin precursor (prothrombin) to thrombin *and* of fibrinogen to fibrin. Platelet-poor plasma yields a longer recalcification time than platelet-rich plasma but practically the same thromboplastin or thrombin time, indicating that platelets contribute essentially to the formation of intrinsic thromboplastin but not to the conversion of prothrombin to thrombin or of fibrinogen to fibrin. However, platelets do have an accelerating influence upon the conversion of fibrinogen (see Fig. 6–1, Table 6–3), detectable with finer methods.

INJURY AND HEMOSTASIS (ARREST OF BLEEDING)

When injury of a blood vessel results in bleeding, reflex vasoconstriction normally occurs and is maintained for several min-

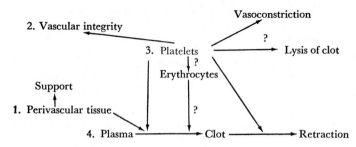

Figure 6–1. The normal hemostatic mechanism. Question marks signify pathways that have been suggested but not clearly established.

utes. Blood flow in the vessel is thereby slowed down and, if the vessel is small enough, completely stopped. Thromboplastin released from endothelium or tissues brings about production of thrombin, which, in turn, contributes to agglutination (white thrombus) and lysis of platelets and to the formation of a fibrin clot. Meanwhile "intrinsic" thromboplastin is formed and results in more thrombin.

A vasoconstrictive substance released from the platelets is presumed to add to the reflex vascular contraction and prolongs its effect. As fibrin retracts under the influence of the "retracto-enzyme" of the platelets, nascent thrombin is expressed, which tends to agglutinate more platelets (autocatalytic reaction) and thus may cause further growth of the thrombus. At the same time, thrombin is adsorbed on fibrin (which is considered by Quick to be the most important "antithrombic" substance), thus limiting the clot-promoting effect of thrombin. According to Quick, hemostasis depends on the continuous, slow production of thrombin. Fibrin is less important. In persons with complete lack of fibrinogen in the blood,

bleeding is controlled more readily than in those with a defect in thrombin formation. Inadequate hemostasis, therefore, may be due to a defect in the mechanism of reflex vasoconstriction, increased permeability of capillaries, lack of vasoconstrictor substance, hypinosis (decreased fibrinogen), or insufficiency of thrombin, which, in turn, may result from deficiency of the plasma or platelet factors required for its production (hemophilioid disorders, thrombocytopathies).

The role of perivascular tissue, blood vessels, and intravascular elements in the normal hemostatic mechanism is illustrated in Figure 6–1. Defects in hemostasis may result from abnormality of tissues, blood vessels, blood cells, especially platelets, or composition of plasma. They will be discussed in this order.

The term "hemorrhagic disorder" refers to deviations from the normal state that are potential or evident causes of bleeding. Hence, usual causes of bleeding, i.e., direct or indirect trauma, menstruation, or uterine hemorrhage incident to childbearing, are not within the scope of this chapter unless they are complicated or precipitated by a hemorrhagic diathesis.

HEMORRHAGIC DISORDERS DUE TO ABNORMALITY OF THE BLOOD VESSELS AND TISSUES (NONTHROMBOCYTOGENIC PURPURAS)

This group of hemorrhagic disorders (Table 6–2) is characterized by a local or generalized bleeding tendency, chiefly involving skin or mucous membranes or both; it is not accompanied by a quantitative platelet deficiency or a demonstrable defect of plasma clotting factors. No attempt has been made in this classification to distinguish between vascular and tissue factors, since their respective share in the pathogenesis of a bleeding diathesis cannot be clearly defined at our present state of knowledge. The routine and traditional tests

for systemic vascular integrity, namely the bleeding time and tourniquet test, are normal, with infrequent exceptions (Table 6–2). The classic separation of the nonthrombopenic from the thrombopenic purpuras is not nearly so clearcut as might appear on the surface: Some of the generalized vascular disorders listed, such as scurvy and anaphylactoid purpura, have on occasion been found associated with a numerical platelet deficiency, and the possibility of a functional platelet defect (thrombasthenia) in the presence of a nor-

Table 6-2

A. Hemorrhagic Disorders due to Generalized Vascular Abnormality, and Tests of Vascular Function

	TOURNIQUET TEST	BLEEDING TIME
Congenital		
Pseudohemophilia A	± *	P *
Purpura simplex (familial)	±	N *
Cutis laxa (Ehlers-Danlos syndrome)	−	N
Pseudoxanthoma elasticum	−	N
Acquired (secondary or symptomatic vascular purpuras)		
Purpura of infectious diseases and of intoxication	±	N
Scurvy	+	P
Purpura simplex (secondary)	±	N
Purpura senilis	±	N
Anaphylactoid purpura (Henoch-Schoenlein)	±	N
Purpura fulminans	±	N or P

B. Hemorrhagic Disorders due to Congenital Localized Vascular Abnormality

Hereditary hemorrhagic telangiectasias (Osler-Weber-Rendu)
Hemangiomas and aneurysms
Idiopathic pulmonary hemosiderosis
Idiopathic hematemesis and melena

* +, positive; −, negative; ±, may be positive or negative; P, prolonged; N, normal.

mal platelet count has, in most instances, not been considered or investigated. In fact, it is probable that the present grouping will be modified as more is learned about the integrated functions of vascular endothelium, platelets, and humoral factors. At any rate, the vasular lesions represented in this classification usually result in either increased permeability (abnormal fragility) or poor contractility of capillaries and precapillaries, or a combination of such defects. The disorder may be congenital (hereditary) or acquired and may involve certain localized areas of the vascular bed or the entire capillary system.

CONGENITAL DISORDERS

Osler's disease is listed as a localized vascular abnormality even though the lesions may be widespread throughout large areas of the body surface and organ systems; the blood vessels outside the lesions are considered normal, both structurally and functionally. The lesions consist of circumscribed collections of noncontractile and dilated capillaries which may give rise to arteriovenous aneurysms. Frequently they are not prominent in infancy or childhood; hence, bleeding of a serious nature may not occur until the adult age. The disease is hereditary, affects both sexes, and is transmitted as a Mendelian dominant. Tests of systemic capillary function are usually negative in this disorder and in the other congenital but localized vascular anomalies listed. The diagnosis rests on clinical manifestations, supported at times by x-ray findings (involvement of heart or lungs).

The term *"pseudohemophilia"* denotes a congenital disorder that is similar clinically to hemophilia but is associated with a normal clotting time and prolonged bleeding time, i.e., just the opposite of the findings in the classic disease. Apparently at least three different "hemophilic" syndromes have been designated with the prefix "pseudo" (see p. 336).

Pseudohemophilia A has been described as a hereditary disease transmitted as a non-sex-linked dominant, in marked contradistinction to classic hemophilia, which ordinarily occurs only in males. In fact, women are said to be affected more often than men. The bleeding is capillary in nature, manifesting itself chiefly in frequent epistaxis and easy bruising; at times prolonged and severe bleeding is incident to menstruation, accidental trauma, or surgical operation. Hematuria, melena, and bleeding from the gums and into muscles or joints occur but are rare. Both the bleeding tendency and the result of the bleeding time test show a great deal of fluctuation in severity so that a negative examination does not rule out the diagnosis.

Purpura simplex refers to the finding of "easy bruising" in certain families, especially their female members, and of occasional eruptions in the form of crops of petechiae (minute bleeding into the skin) with or without bleeding from mucous membranes. These symptoms occur in the absence of any demonstrable clotting defect. The tourniquet test may be positive, while the bleeding time is normal.

These tests are usually negative in *cutis laxa* and in *pseudoxanthoma elasticum*. Cutis laxa denotes a developmental anomaly of connective tissue that shows a familial incidence and is transmitted as a dominant gene. The manifestations include increased friability of blood vessels and pseudotumors over bony prominences, the result of hematomas. Relatively trivial trauma may result in subcutaneous hematoma or in gaping, slow-healing wounds. Pseudoxanthoma elasticum represents an inborn anomaly of elastic connective tissue that is probably transmitted as a recessive or irregularly dominant hereditary trait. The skin, eyes, heart, peripheral blood vessels, and gastrointestinal tract may be involved, the latter occasionally giving rise to hemorrhage.

ACQUIRED DISORDERS

Secondary or Symptomatic Vascular Purpura

Spontaneous purpura and bleeding into the skin or mucous membranes are manifestations of a large variety of systemic diseases, especially infections, intoxications, nutritional deficiencies, and other metabolic disorders. Although the noxious agent alone may cause vascular damage, its combination with a reduction in the number of platelets and with an alteration in plasma clotting factors may be more common than is currently realized. This may also be true of concomitant impairment of platelet function (thrombasthenia).

Certain infections are particularly prone to be associated with hemorrhagic skin lesions. In infectious mononucleosis petechiae often appear on the palate early in the disease. In smallpox, measles, and scarlet fever the eruption may become hemorrhagic; in typhus and other rickettsial diseases the purpuric eruption is caused by direct involvement of capillaries by the causative agent. In subacute bacterial endocarditis, meningococcemia, and other septicemias, petechiae may, at least in part, be due to septic emboli (white center of the lesion).

The purpura and bleeding tendency of uremia have for a long time been blamed on vascular damage; recently a defect in platelet function has been shown to be a common finding. Similarly, in scurvy the bleeding manifestations have been attributed to a defect in the "cement" substance of the vascular (capillary) wall and to ensuing increased permeability, although occasional thrombocytopenia has been observed. The recent discovery of platelet factor 3 deficiency in a case of scurvy, promptly responding to treatment with vitamin C, suggests this as an alternate or additional mechanism.

The use of numerous chemicals and drugs such as iodine, phenobarbital, isoniazid, and salicylates, has been associated with purpuric eruptions. To what extent a platelet or plasma factor defect may occur in these capillary bleeding states, cannot be clearly determined from the literature. Thrombocytopenia is a frequent manifestation of reactions to certain drugs, especially quinine and Sedormid.

Table 6-3.   Clotting Factors in Platelets

NO. OF FACTOR	INTRINSIC CONSTITUENT	PHYSIOLOGIC EFFECT	RESULT OF DEFECT
1	no	Accelerates conversion of prothrombin to thrombin; identical with plasma factor V	Analogous to deficiency of plasma factor V
2	yes	Accelerates conversion of fibrinogen to fibrin	May contribute to bleeding tendency in thrombopenia (?)
3	yes	Thromboplastinogenase, piastrin (Quick); essential for formation of intrinsic thromboplastin; contained in lipid extract of platelets	Congenital (Von Willebrand-Jürgens) and acquired thrombasthenic states; often associated with abnormal bleeding time and tourniquet test†
4	yes	Antiheparin activity in vitro*; contained in aqueous extract of lipid-extracted platelets	Isolated defect has not been described; usually coincides with factor 3 defect
5	no	"Clottable factor"; possibly identical with fibrinogen	?
6	yes	Retractozym (Fonio); responsible for retraction of clot; biologic effect upon hemostasis is not clear	Congenital (Glanzmann-Naegeli) and acquired thrombasthenic states†
7	no?	Antifibrinolysin	?
8	no	Serotonin; previously suspected of contributing to hemostasis by vasoconstriction; possibly serves to initiate fibrinolysis (see Fig. 6-1.)	None evident (no influence on hemostasis)

* See thrombin time (p. 350).

† Von Willebrand-Jürgens syndrome is characterized by prolonged bleeding time and abnormal prothrombin consumption and thromboplastin generation; Glanzmann-Naegeli syndrome, by deficient clot retraction but normal results of the tests listed in the table except for a variable bleeding time. It is now established that clot retraction is due to an active enzyme system in viable platelets, similar to the one existing in muscle fibers.

The tourniquet test may be found positive in *senile purpura* and in acquired simple purpura, just as in the congenital or familial disorder mentioned previously, but the bleeding time is usually normal. This laboratory pattern is also encountered in anaphylactoid purpura, while in the fulminant disease both tests may be positive.

Senile purpura, occurring almost exclusively in women, is attributed to reduced elasticity of tissue resulting from degeneration of collagen fibrils. Most lesions are confined to the dorsal and radial surfaces of the forearm and hand. In the absence of a complicating vitamin C deficiency or blood disease, this hemorrhagic diathesis illustrates the protective function of the perivascular tissue, somewhat analogous to the congenital syndrome of cutis laxa.

The acquired form of *purpura simplex* denotes a tendency to easy bruising and to developing petechial lesions in adults, chiefly women, over a period of many years, not manifestly associated with active or preceding infection or other conceivably inciting noxious agent and usually not interfering seriously with general well-being.

Anaphylactoid purpura (acute vascular purpura) is a systemic disease, appearing usually in children and characterized by a purpuric eruption or bleeding from internal organs. An acute infection, especially a sore throat, often precedes the onset by two to three weeks. At times, sensitizing drugs, insect bites, active immunization, or allergenic foods may take the place of the infectious process in initiating the pathologic chain of events. The rash usually appears suddenly and is often followed by joint symptoms, gastrointestinal disturbance, or renal involvement. The petechial and ecchymotic lesions occur chiefly about the joints, in the limbs, and on the buttocks. Joint symptoms may vary from short-lived arthralgia to marked swelling and prolonged pain, most often of the metacarpus, knee, and elbow. Although a distinction has been made between Schoenlein's syndrome (with predominant skin and joint involvement) and Henoch's disease (characterized by abdominal symptoms), the common denominator is considered to be a diffuse angiitis, the organs of greatest involvement differing from patient to patient. The pathologic findings and clinical manifestations resemble both polyarteritis nodosa and rheumatic fever. Etiologically, anaphylactoid purpura has been included by some authors in the group of diseases of hypersensitivity, together with acquired hemolytic anemia, systemic lupus, idiopathic thrombocytopenia, rheumatic fever, and glomerulonephritis (Stefanini and Dameshek, 1955).

Depending upon involvement of internal organs, such as the liver, spleen, and bone marrow, abnormalities in platelets and in plasma proteins may occur. Thus, thrombocytopenia and circulating anticoagulants have been observed as well as decreases in humoral clotting factors (prothrombin and factors V and VII) (Table 6–4).

Purpura Fulminans

This term denotes an acute syndrome, occurring mainly in children, with diffuse petechiae and ecchymoses attended by chills, fever, a septicemia-like downhill course, and a tendency to circulatory collapse. In some instances, this picture can be ascribed to acute adrenocortical insufficiency secondary to toxemia or to intra-adrenal hemorrhage occurring in the course of acute bacterial infections, especially meningococcemia (Waterhouse-Friderichsen syndrome). In other cases, when no primary infectious process can be recognized, the disease is interpreted as representing hyperacute angiitis re-

Table 6–4. Hemorrhagic Disorders Due to Deficiency of Plasma Clotting Factors

PLASMA FACTORS NO.	NAME	HEREDITARY DISORDER	PATHOGENESIS OF ACQUIRED DEFECT
I	Fibrinogen	Hypo- A- > fibrinogenemia	Hepatic (hematopoietic) disorders Defibrination syndrome Excessive fibrinolysis Circulating inhibitors (EDTA, Dextran)
II	Prothrombin	Hypoprothrombinemia	Avitaminosis K Hepatic (hematopoietic) disorders Circulating anticoagulant
(III	Tissue thromboplastin	Not known	(Not known)
IV	Calcium	Not known	Hyper- or dysglobulinemia
V	Ac-globulin (proaccelerin)	Parahemophilia, hypoproaccelerinemia	Hepatic or hematopoietic disorders Circulating anticoagulant
VI	Serum Ac-globulin	As above	As above
VII	Proconvertin	Hypoproconvertinemia	Same as II
VIII	Antihemophilic factor (AHF) (thromboplastinogen)	(Classic) hemophilia A; Vascular hemophilia (plasma and capillary defect)	Circulating anticoagulant Defibrination syndrome or increased fibrinolysis
IX	Plasma thromboplastin component (PTC)	Hemophilia B, Christmas disease	Avitaminosis K (prolonged) Hepatic disease (advanced) Circulating anticoagulant
X	Stuart (-Prower) factor	Stuart factor deficiency	Avitaminosis K (prolonged) Hepatic disease (advanced) Idiopathic (?), toxic (?)
?	Plasma thromboplastin antecedent (PTA)	Hemophilia C, Rosenthal's syndrome	Hepatic or hematopoietic disorders
?	Hageman factor (HF)	Hageman trait	None reported

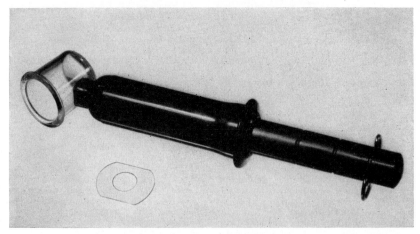

Figure 6–2.   Petechiometer.

lated to, or identical with, severe anaphylactoid purpura. Associated defects in platelets and in plasma clotting factors, as well as abnormal circulating anticoagulants (heparin-type antithrombin), have been encountered.

TESTS OF VASCULAR FUNCTION

Clinical Tests of Capillary Permeability (Determination of Increased Fragility or Decreased Resistance of Capillaries)

TOURNIQUET TEST

Principle. By partially obstructing venous blood flow of the arm, the intracapillary pressure is increased and may give rise to extravasation of blood in the form of petechiae. With standardized pressure and time of application, the number of petechiae reflects the degree of increased capillary fragility.

Equipment. Sphygmomanometer; stethoscope.

Procedure A (Quick, 1957). With the blood pressure cuff applied to the upper arm, a pressure midway between systolic and diastolic levels is maintained for five minutes. Fifteen minutes after release of the inflated cuff, petechiae are counted within a circular area 5 cm. in diameter just below the elbow pit. A count greater than five is abnormal and denotes increased capillary fragility.

Procedure B (Göthlin, 1933). The blood pressure cuff is applied to the upper arm and inflated to provide a pressure of 35 mm. Hg for 15 minutes. Upon release, the petechiae are counted with a magnifying lens within a circular area 6 cm. in diameter in or just below the elbow pit. One hour after release of the cuff the procedure is repeated with a pressure of 50 mm. Hg, and

the number of newly formed petechiae is added to the double count of the first test. *Normal range:* 8 to 12 petechiae.

SUCTION TEST

Principle. Application of negative pressure of sufficient degree to the skin and, indirectly, to extravascular tissues causes extravasation of blood, the extent of which provides a measure of capillary permeability.

A 2 cm. diameter suction cup is applied for one minute. The normal capillary resistance, as measured on the exterior surface of the upper arm at the level of the base of the heart, ranges between 200 and 250 mm. Hg, and the average normal value in the supraclavicular fossa is between 140 and 180 mm. Hg.

Equipment. "Petechiometer,"* consisting of a plastic suction cup 2 cm. in diameter connected with a barrel, which houses a piston and springs (Fig. 6–2).

Procedure. The lips of the cup are lubricated and held firmly to the midportion of the upper arm (hairless area) in close contact with the skin. Graded release of the plunger after it has first been pushed in all the way provides a negative pressure of 100, 200, or 300 mm. Hg. Suction is released after one minute, and petechiae within a circle 1 cm. in diameter (plastic disk) are counted five minutes later. *Normal range:* 0 to 2 petechiae at 200 mm. Hg (medium position of plunger).

Bleeding Time (Test for Capillary Contractility)

Principle. This test measures the time required for bleeding to stop after a stand-
* Supplied by Beutlich, Inc.

ardized stab wound. The result is influenced by the size and shape of the instrument; the force applied in setting the injury; the depth of the puncture; and the location, texture, and vascularity of the area of skin selected. The accuracy and reproducibility of results depend on standardization of all these factors.

DUKE'S METHOD (1910)

Equipment. (Sterile) Spring-Lancet (or Bard-Parker blade No. 11) or preferably a sterile, disposable, commercially available blood lancet; filter paper (small circular sheets); microscope slides.

Procedure. While a slide is held behind and in close contact with the ear lobe, the latter is pierced with the spring-lancet adjusted to 2 mm. of cutting depth (with use of the blade or disposable lancet, the ear lobe must be stabbed through with a single hard stroke for fairly comparable results). Every half minute thereafter, a fresh spot of filter paper is applied to the wound until the bleeding has stopped and no longer causes the paper to be stained. *Normal range:* two to five minutes.

IVY'S METHOD (1935)

Equipment. Same as in the Duke method, plus a sphygmomanometer.

Procedure. The same manipulation outlined for the Duke method is followed but applied to the inner aspect of the forearm (just distal to the antecubital pit) during application of a blood pressure cuff to the upper arm, inflated to 40 mm. Hg. The incision should be 2 mm. in length and depth. *Normal range:* one-half to six minutes.

ADELSON-CROSBY IMMERSION METHOD (1957)

Equipment. Same as that used in the Ivy method plus physiologic saline at 37° C. and a hemoglobinometer. A disposable lancet or Bard-Parker blade No. 11 is anchored in a cork stopper with tip of blade projecting exactly 4 mm.

Procedure. The duration of bleeding caused by puncture of the hypothenar while the blood pressure cuff compresses the upper arm at 40 mm. Hg, as well as the amount of blood lost during this period, is measured and, in addition, the skin temperature is controlled. Upon inflicting the stab wound and starting the stopwatch, the hand, previously dipped in the warm salt solution for three minutes and dried, is reintroduced into the bath, and oozing of blood is observed until it ceases (= bleeding time). The volume of blood lost is derived from measurement of hemoglobin in both the patient's blood (H) and the saline bath (h), using the formula:

$$\text{Blood loss (ml.)} = \frac{Vh}{H \times 100}, \text{ where V}$$

is the volume of saline in the beaker.

Bleeding time

    Upper limit of normal: seven minutes

    Doubtful range: seven to eight and one-half minutes

    Abnormal range: more than eight and one-half minutes

Blood loss

    Normal: less than 0.22 ml.

    Doubtful: 0.22 to 0.3 ml.

    Abnormal: above 0.3 ml.

HEMORRHAGIC DISORDERS DUE TO INTRAVASCULAR FACTORS (DEFECTS IN COAGULATION)

CELLS

Platelets

Platelets play a central role in the hemostatic mechanism, as illustrated in Figure 6-1. They were not included in Morawitz's original scheme, since their thromboplastic function was not recognized until 1912 (Bordet and Delange). Subsequently platelets were regarded as a source of thromboplastin when blood clotted in the absence of contamination with tissue juice. However, platelets will not reduce the clotting time of recalcified platelet-poor plasma to less than 60 to 80 seconds (Biggs and Macfarlane, 1957); by comparison, the clotting time is reduced to 12 seconds or less when a potent tissue extract (Table 6-1) or "intrinsic" thromboplastin is added.

The function of platelets in the coagulation process can be readily demonstrated with blood collected and centrifuged at high speed in the cold without exposing it to a glass surface. The resulting platelet-poor *native* plasma, after incubation at 37° C., clots after a long delay or not at all. Similarly, thrombocytopenic blood yields a prolonged plasma recalcification time and, with severe platelet deficiency, also a prolonged whole blood clotting time; furthermore, the prothrombin consumption of such blood is markedly reduced (see p. 357). All these clotting times can be "corrected" by adding normal platelets. In addition to their role in coagulation, platelets have at least two other biologic functions: *clot retraction* and *vascular hemostasis*.

Although the purpose of *clot retraction* is not clear, it depends upon the presence of platelets as intact *cellular elements* and apparently is distinct from their clot-promoting *chemical* action. The latter may be substantially reduced in some thrombasthenic states (without a numerical decrease), while retraction may proceed normally, and vice versa. The degree of impairment of retraction in thrombocytopenia is roughly proportional to the depression in the number of platelets, especially with counts below 100,000 per cu. mm. At least two other factors influence retraction, namely, the fibrinogen concentration and the blood cell mass (hematocrit) although in inverse proportions: The higher the number of red cells (e.g., in polycythemia) or the fibrinogen level, the less the degree of retraction.

The influence of platelets upon *vascular function* can be documented on the basis of at least four empirical facts: Thrombocytopenia is usually associated with purpura; the contraction of nail-bed capillaries, which can normally be elicited by pinprick or other direct irritation, is deficient in thrombocytopenia; platelets accumulate at sites of minute injury to small blood vessels; and skin wounds are prone to bleed longer and more profusely in patients with platelet defects.

Accordingly, tests for platelet function may be classified as follows:

Tests of coagulation:
Prothrombin consumption (p. 357)
Thromboplastin generation test (p. 358)
Plasma clotting time (without and with added heparin) (p. 347)
Whole blood clotting time (abnormal only in severe platelet deficiency) (p. 345)
Tests for clot retraction:
Qualitative test for presence or absence of retraction (see below)
Estimation of degree of retraction or of retraction time (p. 331)
Tests for vascular integrity:
Capillary fragility or permeability: tourniquet test (and its various

modifications) and suction test (p. 328)
Capillary contractility: bleeding time (p. 328)
Morphologic observations of capillaries: in nail bed, conjunctivae, and other areas.

In addition to enumeration of platelets, evaluation of their size, shape, and structure, and study of their precursors in the marrow, the megakaryocytes, these tests represent the current scope of routine laboratory studies pertaining to platelets.

The three main functions of platelets may be disturbed to varying degrees in thrombocytogenic disorders. Marked reduction of platelets (less than 50,000 per cu. mm.) may affect most or all of the tests listed. However, even under these circumstances, the degree of respective functional impairment may vary from patient to patient and in the same patient from time to time. This is particularly true with regard to vascular contractility (bleeding time). A patient with 15,000 platelets per cu. mm. may show relatively little purpura, while another with a considerably higher platelet count and without other demonstrable clotting defect may show widespread bleeding into the skin and other organs. Similarly, splenectomy in a patient with thrombopenic purpura may be promptly followed by shortening of the previously prolonged bleeding time before a noticeable rise occurs in the platelet count, and treatment with adrenocorticotropic hormone or adrenal steroids may be attended by much clinical improvement without a significant increase in the number of platelets. Although the latter phenomenon may perhaps be explained by a combined increase in production and peripheral utilization of platelets, the mechanism of such utilization and its relation to vascular integrity remain obscure.

TESTS FOR CLOT RETRACTION

Principle. This term refers to the spontaneous contraction of the blood clot and the associated separation of transparent serum. Both the timed diminution in the size of the clot (from the initial size) and the volume of serum, as well as the time required for these effects, may serve as measures of retraction.

Qualitative Test (Stefanini and Dameshek, 1955)

Equipment. Glass test tube, about 15 × 150 mm.

Procedure. Venous blood (collected

without special attention to contamination with tissue fluid) is placed in the tube and, after clotting, incubated at 37° C. for one hour. Reduction in the size of the clot or the appearance of serum between the clot and the wall of the tube signifies that retraction has occurred and may provide a rough estimate of the degree of retraction.

By pouring off the serum and measuring its volume, approxiate quantitation is possible: Clot retraction (in per cent) equals milliliters of serum × 50. This computation applies if the volume of venous blood tested is 2 ml. Otherwise clot retraction (in per

cent) $= \dfrac{\text{ml. of serum} \times 100}{\text{ml. of blood}}$. *Normal range:* 20 to 65 per cent.

When native, platelet-rich plasma is used instead of whole blood, the influence of the red cell mass on retraction is eliminated, making the result a more direct and dependable measure of platelet function. With 1 ml. of plasma, clot retraction (in per cent) equals milliliters of serum × 100. *Normal range:* 40 to 70 per cent.

Quantitative Tests

Measurement of volume of serum expressed (Adreassen, 1943) (combined with rough estimation of clotting time). EQUIP-MENT (Fig. 6–3). Paraffined or siliconized tapered test tube (15 × 160 mm.) cut off at the bottom ("home made" adaptation); twisted glass rod, not paraffined, inserted in a stopper; graduated centrifuge tube; hematocrit tube; 37° C. water bath; centrifuge.

PROCEDURE. Two milliliters of freshly drawn blood are placed in the paraffined test tube, held upside down with the stopper (armed with the glass rod) providing the base, and incubated in the water bath. The volume of packed cells (hematocrit) is measured on an aliquot of the blood. The clotting time of the blood may be determined by tilting the tube at intervals of one minute until it ceases to flow and appears gelled. One hour after clotting has occurred, the graduated centrifuge tube is attached to the open end of the paraffined test tube, and the entire apparatus is inverted, permitting the hemorrhagic serum to flow to the bottom of the graduated tube while the clot adheres to the glass rod. After another hour, the graduated tube is centrifuged for 15 minutes at a moderate speed and the volume of serum (without the volume of red cells) is recorded. Clot retraction (i.e., per cent expressed serum of total preformed serum) $= \dfrac{\text{ml. serum} \times 50}{1 - \text{hematocrit}}$. *Normal range:* 58 to

Figure 6–3. Glassware for clot retraction test.

97 per cent with a mean of 78 per cent. Note: When the clotting time is markedly prolonged (hemophilia), the clot may not adhere to the rod and may drop to the bottom of the centrifuge tube after the inverting maneuver. Increased fibrinolysis may cause the same phenomenon, or it may prevent clot formation altogether.

Clot retraction time (Hirschboeck, 1948). EQUIPMENT. Bard-Parker blade No. 11, or, preferably, a disposable blood lancet; Sahli hemoglobin pipet; test tube with castor oil (USP).

PROCEDURE. After either venous or fingertip puncture, 20 cu. mm. of blood is measured with the Sahli pipet and deposited on the castor oil surface as a large single drop (this manipulation should not take more than 20 seconds). The tube is kept at room temperature and inspected after 10, 15, and 20 minutes and then every two to three minutes. Visible dimpling of the clot surface and extrusion of a droplet of serum denote the beginning of clot retraction and the endpoint of the test. Duplicate tests should always be done; the values should be not more than three minutes apart. *Normal range:* 20 to 45 minutes; average, 33 minutes.

Longer periods are seen in thrombocytopenia, thrombasthenia, polycythemia, and hyperinosis and in hemophilioid disorders associated with prolonged clotting time. Periods shorter than 20 minutes may be indicative of a thrombotic tendency.

PLATELET FACTORS

In vitro analysis of platelets and correlation with clinical deficiency states has resulted in description of a number of platelet clotting factors, designated by Arabic numerals for differentiation from plasma factors (Table 6–3). Some of the clotting properties of platelets, as well as many other substances contained in these tiny cell fragments, were soon found to be "extrinsic baggage," i.e., adsorbed and carried along by platelets but not contributing essentially to specific platelet function. Included among these presumably extrinsic platelet constituents are not only many of the plasma clotting factors, such as fibrinogen, factors V and VIII, and others (Table 6–4) but also albumin, enzymes, and hormones. Of the latter category, serotonin shows a comparatively high concentration in platelets under normal conditions, but the only role this substance seems to play in the total clotting process concerns, perhaps, the initiation of fibrinolysis. Of the eight factors that have been described separately (listed in Table 6–3), only four are now considered to represent intrinsic cellular properties. Of these, *retractozym* is probably the most speculative substance, since no extract of platelets has thus far been found to be capable of replacing active and intact thrombocytes in eliciting clot retraction. In spite of the designation, there is no evidence that a single enzyme is responsible for this process (see footnote, Table 6–3).

Much experimental work is currently devoted to the analysis of the thromboplastic function (platelet factor 3). The factor is contained in crude, phospholipid-rich extracts of platelets. Of the various chromatographically identifiable fractions of this extract, which include ethanol-, serine-, and inositol phosphatide, lecithin, and sphingomyelin, the first three mentioned have been shown to successfully replace platelets in various tests, such as thromboplastin generation and prothrombin consumption. Extracts of brain, egg yolk, and soybean have been found to have very similar activity.

HEMORRHAGIC DISORDERS DUE TO ABNORMALITY OF PLATELETS (THROMBOCYTOGENIC PURPURAS OR THROMBOCYTOPATHIES)

Disorders due to abnormality of platelets

may be classified from various points of view. A division between quantitative deviation (significant increase or decrease) and functional abnormality (thrombasthenia) is most commonly used and is presented in Table 6–5. It is to be stressed, however, that in both thrombocytopenia and thrombocytosis platelets are frequently abnormal in function, and patients with thrombasthenia may occasionally show a numerical deficiency as well. Subdivision of the thrombocytopenias into the idiopathic and symptomatic varieties is time-honored and popular but only constitutes a temporary expedient pending further elucidation of the pathogenesis of the "idiopathic" form. The term "symptomatic" denotes association with other systemic diseases but is not a clear-cut, logical counterpart to "idiopathic" or "essential," since the etiology of many of these diseases is unknown, making the cause of the thrombocytopenia no less ob-

Table 6–5. Hemorrhagic Disorders Due to Abnormality of Platelets (Thrombocytogenic Purpuras; Thrombocytopathies)

I. Thrombocytopenia
  A. Congenital
    1. Neonatal (transient)
    2. Erythroblastosis fetalis
    3. Persistent (primary)
    4. Giant hemangioma
    5. Incidental to systemic disease (secondary)
  B. Acquired
    1. Idiopathic (primary)
      a. Chronic
      b. Acute
    2. Symptomatic (secondary)
      a. Infection
      b. Chemical agents: drugs, toxins, foods
      c. Physical agents: ionizing radiation, extensive burns, heatstroke
      d. Blood disorders: leukemia, anemias (hypoplastic, myelophthisic, pernicious), hypersplenism, massive gastrointestinal bleeding and massive transfusions, thrombotic thrombocytopenic purpura
      e. Metabolic and endocrine dysfunction: hepatic failure, uremia, "hyperestrogenosis"
II. Thrombasthenia
  A. Congenital
    1. Von Willebrand-Jürgens disease (thrombopathia)
    2. Glanzmann-Naegeli syndrome (thrombasthenia)
    3. Variations and combinations of (1) and (2)
  B. Acquired: probably occurring in each of the categories under I. B. and, perhaps, III
III. Thrombocytosis
    1. Idiopathic (primary): thrombocythemia
    2. Secondary: associated with other myeloproliferative disorders, such as polycythemia, leukemia, and myelofibrosis
    3. Reactive and hyposplenic (acute and chronic)

scure than that of the idiopathic form. Moreover, an immune mechanism accounts for the platelet deficiency not only in many cases that conform clinically to the idiopathic type but undoubtedly also in manifestly symptomatic cases (drug hypersensitivity, acute infections).

The incidence of an *immune mechanism* responsible for thrombocytopenic purpura cannot be estimated reliably because of analytical-technical difficulties, which seriously interfere with the accuracy and reproducibility of results and therefore with acceptance of such procedures. Were it not for these difficulties, division between the immune and nonimmune types of thrombocytopathies might be more logical than the present tabulation. Perhaps the most reasonable principle to follow in classifying platelet disorders would be that employed with respect to red blood cells, namely, the analysis of an existing (numerical or qualitative) abnormality of platelets in blood on the basis of *production* (bone marrow), *destruction* or utilization, and *loss* from the body: increased or decreased *thrombocytopoiesis*, increased *thrombocytolysis* or thromboagglutination (thrombosis), and *hemorrhage*. A quantitative or qualitative deficiency may conceivably be central in origin, i.e., caused by a marrow defect, or secondary to damage incurred in the peripheral vascular system (analogous, for example, to autoimmune hemolytic anemia).

Although such a breakdown into etiologic factors of a positive or negative nature may well be attempted, practical laboratory techniques are not available to apply this principle for routine diagnostic purposes. There is no procedure known that would enable one to identify or measure structural or chemical derivatives of platelet breakdown, as in the case of red blood cells. Furthermore, the very nature of the platelets—their stickiness and tendency to readily lyse or clump—interferes with *in vitro* observations of morphologic or serologic qualities and of deviations from the normal.

As another means of classifying thrombocytopenias, a distinction between *amegakaryocytic* and *megakaryocytic* forms has been advocated (Stefanini and Dameshek, 1955). Study of bone marrow is indeed desirable in every case of platelet deficiency, but it does not necessarily furnish a satisfactory etiologic clue. Thus, a reduction in the number of megakaryocytes has been observed in patients diagnosed as having idiopathic thrombocytopenic purpura (ITP), even though, in this condition, the marrow commonly shows a normal or increased number of these precursors of platelets. It may well be that a circulating antiplatelet agent not only causes accelerated removal of platelets and morpho-logic alteration (arrest of maturation) of megakaryocytes but may even shorten their life span and interfere with their reproduction.

That the spleen may play an important etiologic role in platelet disorders has been known since 1916 when Kaznelson used splenectomy successfully to treat a patient suffering from thrombocytopenia. A hyperactive spleen (hypersplenism) may not only cause direct destruction of platelets in excessive amounts but apparently may also inhibit release of platelets from the marrow, contribute to the production of platelet-agglutinating and lytic (?immune) factors, and adversely affect the integrity of the vascular endothelium. Although the exact mechanism of splenic action upon platelets and other blood cells, especially its humoral aspects, are far from clear, distinction of *hypersplenic* from *nonhypersplenic* thrombopathies would be of practical therapeutic value. However, in many instances of the disease, such distinction is a complex task requiring careful clinical judgment and can, at present, be substantiated in retrospect only by splenectomy.

Correlation of the presence of an immune mechanism (if it can be estimated reliably) and hypersplenism has been shown to be close, but many exceptions occur; i.e., some patients with proved circulating platelet agglutinins are not improved by splenectomy. The size of the spleen is no better index of splenic function. Improvement often follows removal of a normal-size or slightly enlarged spleen in ITP, but extirpation of a large spleen in lymphoma or leukemia may not help. Hence, classification of thrombocytopenias on the basis of the size of the spleen (as determined by x-ray or palpation) is useful in bedside diagnosis but does not coincide with pathogenic grouping.

Classification of platelet disorders may be attempted on the basis of structural alteration of platelets. Variations in size, pseudopod formation, granularity, proportion of chromomere to hyalomere, and other features have been associated with specific functional changes and disease entities. For adequate resolution of structural details, phase and electron microscopy is required. Results of current investigations in this field must be awaited with much interest; they do not serve practical diagnostic purposes at present.

Thrombocytopenia. Reduction in the number of platelets is characterized clinically by petechiae and ecchymoses of the skin and mucous membranes. Prolonged oozing of blood may occur from superficial injuries or from an apparently intact mucosa. The clinical picture of hemorrhagic diathesis due to platelet deficiency is generally distinguished from that of the disorders of plasma clotting factors (coagulopathies) by the type of bleeding. Coagulopathies are characterized by larger hemorrhages into skin, muscle, and joints, while thrombocytogenic bleeding usually results in petechiae of the skin and mucous membranes and a tendency to internal bleeding. Petechiae are usually more numerous over dependent parts because of increased venous pressure; they may be confluent and thus produce the picture of larger ecchymoses, but the petechial type is usually still evident at the margins of the lesion. Bleeding from the gums and nose and hematoma of the tongue are common.

Congenital thrombocytopenia. Reduction or absence of platelets in the newborn may be the result of at least five factors:

1. A *platelet antibody* transmitted from the mother through the placenta may cause transitory thrombocytopenia. Occasionally the mother may show no clinical evidence of thrombocytopenia.

2. In *erythroblastosis fetalis*, diminution of platelets is a common finding, due largely either to antibody formation against platelets, as well as against red cells, or to hypersplenism in addition, perhaps, to hepatic dysfunction and to other, not clearly recognized factors.

3. Congenital *absence* or *reduction* of *megakaryocytes* may occur with, or rarely without, deficiency of myeloid and erythroid elements in the bone marrow (*congenital hypoplastic anemia*) and may, on occasion, be associated with other abnormalities, e.g., in the Fanconi syndrome.

This hereditary disorder, which was first described in 1926, consists of pancytopenia, hypoplasia of the marrow, and other, often multiple, congenital anomalies, such as patchy brown pigmentation of skin, dwarfism, microcephaly, hypogenitalism, strabismus, digital and renal malformations, and mental retardation. The syndrome is transmitted by an autosomal recessive gene with variable penetrance and usually occurs in siblings (Hsia, 1959).

In contrast to these hypomegakaryocytic cases, a syndrome of purpura, bloody diarrhea, eczematoid dermatitis, and recurrent ear infection has been described, associated with a marrow rich in megakaryocytes but with little evidence of platelet formation. The syndrome seems to occur in males only and to be transmitted by a sex-linked recessive gene (Ratnoff, 1958).

4. Another rare cause of neonatal thrombocytopenia is *giant hemangioma*, which apparently results in sequestration of platelets in the neoplasm. Removal of the hemangioma is followed by remission of the platelet deficiency.

5. Thrombocytopenia in the newborn may be secondary to congenital *leukemia, syphilis*, and bacterial, protozoal, or viral *infections*, including cytomegalic inclusion disease.

Acquired thrombocytopenia. IDIOPATHIC (ESSENTIAL; "ITP"; MORBUS WERLHOFII). This disease shows a predilection for children and young female adults (45 per cent of the patients are less than 15 years of age) but may occur at any age. In the *chronic* form, the onset is insidious with occasional bleeding from the nose or gums or with "easy bruising." The bleeding tendency may be intermittent or continuous, but fluctuation in the degree of this tendency is the rule. In women, bleeding from the genital tract in the form of meno- and metrorrhagia is common and often misinterpreted as due to local or endocrine factors.

Gastrointestinal hemorrhage, hematuria, and hemorrhages into the lungs resulting in circumscribed consolidation in the x-ray film, central nervous system, and eye (vitreous, retina) occur in about this order of frequency. Typical of full-fledged thrombocytopenia are bruises developing in the course of a physical examination at the sites of palpation and percussion. In the majority of cases, the prognosis is good even without specific treatment, such as ACTH, "steroids," or splenectomy. Hemorrhagic diathesis, as a rule, persists until death, but its intensity usually lessens with advancing age. Periods of increased bleeding tendency alternate with an oligosymptomatic state of varying duration. Exacerbations are often precipitated by infections, pregnancy, puberty, or the menopause. In women, especially, a relationship to the menstrual cycle is often demonstrable; the bleeding tendency is greatest just before and at the time of menstruation, a phenomenon that corresponds to the physiologic reduction of platelets coinciding with menstrual flow. In some instances, blood loss at the time of delivery may not be unusually great so that this disease is not by itself an indication for interruption of pregnancy. However, a precipitous fall in the platelet count and serious external and internal bleeding may occur close to term and at times may prove fatal.

The *acute* form develops suddenly, often apparently in completely healthy patients. The hemorrhagic diathesis is generally more severe than in the chronic form, and platelet counts may drop below 20,000 per cu. mm. Blood loss may be so severe and extensive as to result in marked anemia. The duration is often not more than a few weeks. Complete recovery is frequent, but similar attacks may occur months or years later. In about one-third of the cases, a chronic course ensues.

SYMPTOMATIC OR SECONDARY THROMBOCYTOPENIA. Depression of the platelet count and associated hemorrhagic features may occur in connection with acute or chronic *infections*, exposure to *drugs* and to numerous *chemical substances* of inorganic or organic nature, with *radiation* of various types, especially ionizing radiation, and in diseases involving the *bone marrow* or the *spleen* or both. Elaborate listings of individual drugs and toxins have been published (Miale, 1958; Wintrobe, 1961).

Acute or severe infections, such as the acute viral exanthemas of childhood, may cause a decrease in platelets, presumably both by action upon circulating platelets and by depression of the marrow. The destructive action upon platelets probably involves antibody production, in addition, perhaps, to a nonspecific clumping agent, such as can be observed in peptone and anaphylactic shock (Quick, 1957). There is no correlation between the severity of the thrombocytopenia or purpura and the severity of the infection. At times, the infection (mumps, measles) may be so mild as to be completely overlooked so that the thrombocytopenia is designated as "idiopathic." Most cases of acute ITP probably should be attributed to an infectious process and others to hypersensitivity reactions to other types of noxious agents, particularly drugs.

When splenomegaly is a distinct feature of the disease, the possibility of a hypersplenic mechanism's causing or contributing to the thrombocytopenia must be considered, especially in the case of chronic infections, such as hematogenous tuberculosis or histoplasmosis. Many drugs and other chemicals produce thrombocytopenia by means of a similar immune mechanism, which, in at least some instances, involves the formation of certain antibodies. Agglutination of normal platelets by the patient's serum can be demonstrated only if a solution of the noxious substance, such as quinine or Sedormid, is added to the test tube. A direct toxic effect upon the bone marrow undoubtedly results from exposure to certain chemicals, such as benzene, DDT, and nitrogen mustards. A similar effect on circulating platelets has been ascribed to other agents, especially ristocetin (Gangarosa *et al.*, 1960).

Physical agents such as excessive heat (heat stroke), and particularly ionizing radiation, depress platelets primarily or entirely by inhibition of bone marrow function. This is also true, as a rule, of leukemia and myelophthisic processes. Inhibition cannot be attributed entirely to invasion of the marrow and replacement by foreign tissue but to a metabolic-enzymatic derangement as well. It is not unusual to find a relatively small portion of marrow (occasionally none) replaced by tumor tissue but accompanied by significant depression of platelets. Thrombasthenia is a common feature in leukemia with or without thrombocytopenia. The presence of platelet antibody complicating these diseases cannot be excluded, and in some instances a hypersplenic mechanism has been suggested by a persistent rise in platelets after splenectomy. This mechanism must be considered especially when associated with depression of red and white cells in any instance of splenomegaly, whether due to chronic infection (kala a-azar, tuberculosis), granulomatous disease (sarcoidosis), portal vein thrombosis, Gaucher's disease, rheumatoid arthritis, cirrhosis, or other splenomegalic disorders.

Hypersplenism may be a feature of systemic lupus erythematosus, but since splenectomy may cause worsening of the course of the disease, other pathogenetic mechanisms must be considered (Rabinowitz and Dameshek, 1960). Evidence of lupus has recently been found in cases previously diagnosed as ITP, and the exact relation of these two diseases remains to be elucidated, as does their fundamental nature. For the time being, one may assume that both diseases represent examples of hypersensitivity, the target in ITP being largely confined to the platelets and capillary endothelial system, whereas in disseminated lupus erythematosus it is extended to include the entire hematopoietic and vascular structures.

Massive blood loss may cause a temporary reduction in circulating platelets until the megakaryocytes succeed in compensating for the deficiency. The relatively slight thrombocytopenia may be considerably aggravated by transfusion with platelet-poor blood. Even freshly drawn blood is platelet-poor if collected in uncoated glass bottles, because a "coagulant agglutinin" forms when blood comes in contact with a foreign surface, such as glass (Quick, 1957). The nonspecific platelet-agglutinating action of glass-bottled blood may cause a significant drop in the recipient's platelets, even without preceding hemorrhage, and contribute to hemorrhagic complications. This depletion of thrombocytes may be avoided by collecting and keeping blood or plasma for transfusion in siliconized bottles or in plastic containers.

The thrombocytopenia of a hemolytic transfusion reaction is, at least in part, due to agglutination or lysis of platelets, as well as to thrombosis or hemagglutination in capillaries. This is also presumably part of the mechanism in sickle cell crisis and especially in thrombotic thrombocytopenic purpura.

The drop in platelets frequently seen in cirrhosis and at times in severe cases of acute hepatitis has usually been attributed to a hypersplenic effect. A possible direct action of the liver upon platelet production must be seriously considered, analogous to the well-known influence of hepatic disease upon erythro- and leukopoiesis (Watson *et al.*, 1947). Similarly, inhibition of the marrow in renal disease (uremia) may affect megakaryocytes with resulting depression of the number and quality of the platelets. The menstrual depression of the platelets, as contrasted to their regular rise coinciding with ovulation, and the occasional cases of thrombocytopenia precipitated or aggravated by pregnancy, especially immediately preceding parturition, suggest a direct hormonal influence upon platelet formation, presumably more complex than is inferred from the term "hyperestrogenosis" (Quick, 1957).

It should be reemphasized that the number of platelets and the degree of purpura (or length of bleeding time) generally show poor correlation. Some purpuric manifestations usually occur with counts below 100,-000 per cu. mm., but they may be pronounced with concentrations well above this level and minimal with a count of 50,000 or less. Distinct improvement in purpura and a shortening of the bleeding time often herald recovery from acute thrombocytopenic purpura before a significant increase in the platelet count can be detected. Similarly, the diffuse oozing of blood from abdominal vessels at the time of splenectomy for ITP stops as soon as the splenic vessels are ligated, while the number of circulating platelets does not increase until hours later. Finally, ACTH and cortisone frequently have a beneficial effect upon bleeding tendency and distinctly shorten the bleeding time without altering substantially the platelet count. Hence, the existence of a circulating vasotropic substance may be assumed, which is in some way connected with platelets, opposed by the spleen (and possibly estrogen) and enhanced by ACTH or adrenal steroids. In addition, the presence or absence of thrombasthenia complicating thrombocytopenia may modify the intensity of hemorrhagic manifestations.

Thrombasthenia. *Congenital.* Functional abnormality of the platelets was, until recently, considered to be restricted to congenital disorders. Two syndromes were recognized: *hereditary hemorrhagic thrombasthenia* (Glanzmann-Naegeli) and *constitutional thrombopathy* (Von Willebrand-Jürgens). The former was characterized by deficient clot retraction as the only abnormality of blood (with a normal bleeding time) and the latter, by a prolonged bleeding time but normal clot retraction. In both groups of patients, the purpuric type of bleeding was observed, with superficial hemorrhages into the skin, oozing from mucous membranes, easy bruising, and excessive bleeding from small cuts and abrasions.

Subsequent observers attempted to characterize these two groups of "nonthrombopenic purpura" more clearly. Laboratory criteria of the Glanzmann type, in addition to deficient clot retraction, were stated to include increased capillary fragility (positive tourniquet test) and decreased adhesiveness but normal size of the platelets and normal prothrombin consumption (with a normal or prolonged bleeding time). Hereditary transmission was suggested to be recessive—autosomal in character. The Willebrand-Jürgens variety, presumed to be transmitted by a dominant gene, was described as showing normal clot retraction but prolonged bleeding time, increased capillary fragility, and abnormal prothrombin consumption and thromboplastin generation, frequently in association with giant-size platelets (Table 6–3).

The large body of literature that has accumulated on this subject in recent years is somewhat confusing because of discrepancies in terminology, incomplete reporting of laboratory results, and differences in laboratory techniques. It has, however, become apparent that the classification just cited is artificial and ought to be abandoned. Von Willebrand's name has been associated with at least three types of hemostatic disorders (see p. 325), of which only one includes a platelet defect (with prolonged bleeding time and deficiency of platelet factor 3 but with normal clot retraction).

The other two types are pseudohemophilia A, considered to represent a purely vascular anomaly (proposed to be a blending of Osler's and Von Willebrand's disease, "systemic capillary telangiectasia"), and vascular hemophilia (pseudohemophilia B). The latter type denotes a combination of a capillary defect (prolonged bleeding time) with a decrease in factor VIII (or occasionally other plasma factors) (Table 6–6).

Acquired. Evidence is rapidly accumulating that a functional platelet defect is a common complication of a variety of systemic diseases. It appears that thrombasthenia may complicate thrombocytopenia of either the idiopathic or symptomatic variety and that it may occur in the presence of a normal and even a substantially increased platelet count. Much credit for this discovery should probably go to the thromboplastin generation test.

Aside from the primarily thrombocytopenic disorders, conditions that have been associated with thrombasthenia include *renal insufficiency, cirrhosis* of the liver, nutritional deficiency, such as *scurvy,* and *blood dyscrasias* of various types, especially leukemia. The qualitative defect may be demonstrated by only one of several tests, or it may involve all demonstrable platelet functions. Because of its frequent association with other types of hemostatic deficiency involving capillary permeability or plasma factors or both, recognition of thrombasthenia may be difficult and depends on careful performance of the thromboplastin generation test. To what extent thrombasthenia may be responsible for an existing bleeding tendency or be the precursor of bleeding may depend on the degree of deviation from the normal as shown by the tests employed, i.e., the degree of prolongation of the bleeding time or clotting time in the thromboplastin generation test, the platelet suspension being the only reagent derived from the patient. Thrombasthenia frequently lessens and disappears with clinical improvement; it may be marked at the time of gastrointestinal hemorrhage from the esophageal varices of a patient with hepatic cirrhosis and be absent two weeks after bleeding has stopped, when he appears to be recovering. Since massive blood loss alone may be followed by transient thrombocytopenia or thrombasthenia, the exact causal relationship in such cases is not clear and requires further study.

Thrombocytosis and Thrombocythemia. Increased activity of the bone marrow often includes accelerated *proliferation of megakaryocytes* and thrombocytosis, i.e., a rise in the number of circulating platelets above the normal range. This occurs regularly following *fractures,* especially of the neck of the femur, and in other types of *trauma,* including *surgical operations,* the maximal increase occurring between the seventh and twentieth postoperative days. *Splenectomy* is followed by a more immediate and greater increase than other operations. Acute *rheumatic fever,* suppurative *infections, asphyxiation,* and *acute hemorrhage* may result in thrombocytosis, while chronic blood loss or massive gastrointestinal bleeding may be associated with a reduction in the platelet count followed by an increase. Aside from these acute reactive forms, more *persistent thrombocytosis* is encountered in *myeloproliferative diseases,* especially in chronic granulocytic leukemia, erythremia, and myelofibrosis. It has also been observed in *Hodgkin's disease, metastatic carcinoma,* and *hyperadrenalism* and in functional or structural *hyposplenism,* such as splenic vein thrombosis, splenic atrophy, and the postsplenectomy state. Venous thrombosis in some of the conditions mentioned may, at least in part, be a result of the rise in circulating platelets. During the postoperative period after splenectomy, venous and arterial occlusions by thrombi are frequent complications.

When excessive proliferation of megakaryocytes is sustained, resulting in an elevation of the platelet count to one or several millions per cubic millimeter of blood, the term *thrombocythemia* is applied, analogous to leukemia and polycythemia. First described by di Guglielmo in 1920 under the name of *piastrinemia,* it is a rare myeloproliferative disorder limited to the megakaryocytes and their products, the platelets. The spleen, often greatly enlarged, may show distention of the cords by thrombocytic masses, in addition to extramedullary hematopoiesis confined to megakaryocytic foci. Thus, this organ fulfills the important job of removing platelets from the circulation, opposing the excessive productivity of the megakaryocytes; removal of the spleen is contraindicated and may be followed by serious vascular occlusive complications. Irrespective of splenectomy, thrombocythemia may be associated with the contrasting aspects of both *hemorrhagic diathesis* and *thrombosis.* The former may follow the pattern of thrombocytopenia but at times may also include some hemophilioid features, e.g., deep muscle hematomas and hemarthroses. These complications may perhaps be attributed to *thrombosis* and *secondary vascular injury* resulting from the high platelet count.

Consequently the hemorrhagic tendency is likely to be at least twofold: defect in platelet or plasma factors, and ischemia and vascular injury consequent to capillary thrombosis. The latter feature is, to some extent, analogous to observations in sickle cell anemia and in the platelet thrombosis syndrome (thrombotic thrombocytopenic purpura).

Red Blood Cells

Although red blood cells are known to contain a potent thromboplastic agent that is comparable in action to platelet factor 3, it is not certain to what extent, if any, this plays a role in normal hemostasis (Fig. 6–1). Posthemorrhagic anemia is frequently associated with an increase in platelets, whereas anemia due to various blood dyscrasias is associated with a decrease. A marked rise in red cells (primary or secondary polycythemia) or abnormal shape (sickle cell anemia) enhances the viscosity of the blood. This may cause occlusion of small blood vessels by slowing down of the circulation and mechanical plugging. Thrombosis of capillaries and of precapillary vessels may lead to ischemic necrosis of the vessel wall and of surrounding tissue and, secondarily, to bleeding. Associated hemostatic defects frequently encountered in erythremia include an increase in platelets and a decrease in fibrinogen.

White Blood Cells

Leukocytes per se are ordinarily not considered to play a role in hemostasis. Proteolytic ferments of leukocytes trapped in a thrombus may contribute considerably to its dissolution. A marked rise in white cells, such as occurs in leukemia, increases the viscosity of the blood and may lead to vascular obstruction and ischemic necrosis as well as to hemorrhagic manifestations, much the same as polycythemia or sickling. Both platelets and plasma clotting factors are frequently deranged in leukemia. Moderate thrombocytosis is common in the chronic granulocytic form, while pronounced thrombocytopenia is the rule in acute leukemia; in either instance, functional abnormality of the platelets may be an important causative factor in bleeding. Of the plasma clotting factors, members of the prothrombin complex (e.g., factors V, VII, and X) are most frequently deficient. Abnormal circulating anticoagulants and increased fibrinolysis may also occur.

PLASMA FACTORS (HEMOPHILIOID DISORDERS OR COAGULOPATHIES)

The Coagulation Mechanism. Primary hemostasis, i.e., cessation of bleeding from injured blood vessels, is the result of functional integrity of the vascular wall, of the platelets, and presumably of tissue thromboplastin. Secondary hemostasis or the sealing of the gap and formation of a fibrin clot depend upon interaction between platelets and plasma factors. The end product of this interaction is a proteolytic enzyme, thrombin, which converts the dissolved fibrinogen into solid fibrin. This conversion of fibrinogen, consisting essentially of splitting "fibrinopeptides" from the fibrinogen molecules, which then join to form interlacing fibrin strands, is very rapid; under optimal conditions and concentrations of the reactants, it may take as little as one second. Calcium ions are not required for this conversion process to take place, but their presence in physiologic concentrations accelerates the effect of thrombin and increases the mechanical strength of the fibrin clot. In addition, a specific accelerator substance contained in plasma has been postulated.

Except for any deficiency of fibrinogen, an interference with its conversion, or a lytic influence upon fibrin, any disturbance of the coagulation process must be reflected in the end product of the enzymatic chain reaction, thrombin. This key substance is formed from its precursor, prothrombin, by the splitting of a prosthetic group from the latter through the proteolytic (?) action of thromboplastin. In a wider sense, the term "thromboplastin" may be applied to any substance that accelerates the clotting of recalcified plasma. Although tissue thromboplastin is present in practically all body cells (except blood cells) and presumably contributes to primary hemostasis at the site of vascular injury, it ordinarily does not enter the circulation except under unusual circumstances, e.g., abruptio placentae. Tissue thromboplastin requires for its full activation the plasma "accelerator factors," namely, factors V, VII, and X. They are also called "accessory factors." Together with factor II, they form the "prothrombin complex." Formation of a blood-borne, prothrombin-converting principle or intrinsic thromboplastin (also called "prothrombinase") occurs as a result of the interaction of platelet factor 3 with all the known plasma clotting factors numbered from IV on up, except for factor VII (Tables 6–4, 6–6; Fig. 6–4).

The initiation of this chain reaction, i.e., what causes the plasma factors to "interact," is a question that touches upon the fundamental problem of the mechanism that permits blood to remain liquid in circulation while retaining the potentiality of solidifying at any time. According to Quick, maintenance of the fluidity of blood is probably due in part to the nature of the endothelial lining of blood vessels and partly to the stability and nonreactivity of the circulating clotting factors. Clotting is usually initiated by the escape of tissue thromboplastin into the blood at the site of injury to a blood vessel. This thromboplastin, with the aid of the accelerator factors, promptly liberates thrombin from prothrombin. Thrombin not only converts fibrinogen into fibrin but also activates a postulated plasma factor, prephase accelerator or PPA,* which in turn "labilizes" platelets. These agglutinate, forming a "white thrombus," and at the same time release their factor 3, piastrin. The latter interacts with the various plasma factors to form intrinsic thromboplastin. The result is further production of thrombin (autocatalytic cycle).

This hypothesis obviously leaves unanswered the question of what activates plasma factors, since platelet factor 3 apparently does not have this property. Intravenous injection of a potent platelet extract into rabbits does not cause demonstrable intravascular clotting. Moreover, extravascular (tissue) thromboplastin would seem to be a prerequisite for clot formation, even though blood carefully collected in a test tube without admixture of tissue juice (two-syringe technique) is able to clot. The suggestion that a clotting factor contained in red blood cells, which was recently discovered and shown to have platelet factor 3-like activity *in vitro*, may have the physiologic role of initiating the thrombinogenic reaction remains to be substantiated.

Discovery of the Hageman factor has provided a supplementary hypothesis attempting to fill the void just mentioned. Thus, this factor may be activated (or its inhibitor inactivated) by endothelial injury or by glass (or by some other adsorbent), giving, in turn, the signal for the chain reaction that leads to formation of intrinsic thromboplastin and of thrombin (Ratnoff, 1958).

A totally different view considers the maintenance of fluidity of the blood to be the result of a constant interplay of positive and negative forces, e.g., co-

* A hypothetical substance whose existence remains to be proved (Fisch and Duckert, 1959).

agulant and inhibitory factors. The latter may play an important role that is as yet not well understood. Under normal conditions, the only physiologically important inhibitor, according to Quick, is fibrin, which acts as a potent antithrombin by adsorbing nascent thrombin, thereby greatly limiting the autocatalytic action of thrombin. Thus, when thrombin production is slight, as with minor injuries or in many hemorrhagic disorders, and is matched by the adsorbing capacity of available fibrin, no free thrombin becomes available and the clotting process is quickly terminated, at least until fibrin retracts and releases serum containing thrombin. In freely circulating blood, thrombin is removed as quickly as it is being released and is disposed of promptly. In the presence of a slow or stagnant circulation and in shed blood, even small amounts of thrombin may eventuate in a large clot that obstructs a major blood vessel or fills a test tube.

Aside from anticoagulant factors and fibrin, a decoagulant system may play a role in the delicate balance between clot-promoting and clot-inhibiting forces. It has been suggested that fibrinolysis takes place at all times, normally dissolving fibrin at the same rate as it is being formed. Evidence for this theory has been adduced from the observations that a thin coat of fibrin may be found (with special histologic techniques) to line both the intima and the platelets and that the turnover of clotting factors is more rapid than that of most other plasma proteins. Exaggeration of fibrinolytic activity may lead to hemorrhage, while its decrease (possibly by lipemia) may enhance thrombotic tendency and perhaps inception of atheroma by subendothelial deposition of fibrin.

Defects in Coagulation due to Abnormality of Plasma Factors. The term "plasma factors" is used here in a comprehensive sense, including the following groups: the ten factors (excluding factors III and VI) listed in Tables 6–4 and 6–6, generally referred to as "clotting factors"; circulating anticoagulants and abnormal plasma proteins (globulins), which may exercise anticoagulant activity by interfering physicochemically with the normal processes of

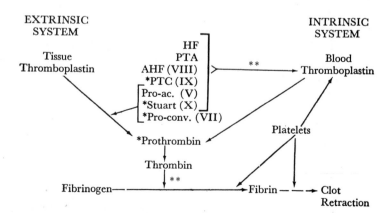

Figure 6–4. A schema of coagulation. (For abbreviations of plasma factors see Table 6–6.)

Table 6–6. The Plasma Clotting Factors and Disorders Related to their Abnormal
Concentration or Function

FACTOR I (FIBRINOGEN)

Historical Data

A soluble protein in blood was postulated to be converted to a coagulum by fermenting action in 1835 (Buchanan). Fibrinogen named and isolated in 1877 (Hammersten). First congenital deficiency described in 1920 (Rabe and Salomon); first acquired deficiency described in 1924 (Opitz and Silverberg); reported as obstetrical complication in 1935 (Dieckmann) and in 1949 (Moloney). Fibrinolysis recognized as cause of hemorrhage in 1941 (Reimann).

Physicochemical Data

It is precipitated irreversibly from plasma by heating to 56° C.; adsorbed by Al(OH)$_3$ and Mg(OH)$_2$; soluble in saline; fairly stable on cold storage; contained in Cohn plasma fraction I and in AgP and AdP; removed from decalcified plasma by bentonite (thereby separated from factor VIII!); converted into fibrin by minimal quantities of thrombin (in proportions up to 100,000 to 1). Normal level in plasma: 200 to 400 mg. per 100 ml.

Clinical Data

CONGENITAL DEFICIENCY

1. Afibrinogenemia (Ap-inosis): non-sex-linked recessive trait. Bleeding during early childhood (umbilical cord, cerebral) and subsequently (skin, mucous membranes) upon slight injury (puncture); easy bruising. Compatible with normal longevity; comparable with mild to moderate hemophilia but without hemarthroses. Increased susceptibility to infections (?). Occasional combination with thrombocytopenia.

2. Hypofibrinogenemia (hypo-inosis): heterozygous state; usually asymptomatic.

ACQUIRED ABNORMALITY

A. Decrease:
  1. Reduced production: diseases of the liver (and possibly of the reticuloendothelial system, such as hepatic failure or metastases; erythremia and leukemia.
  2. Increased utilization or removal:
    a. Defibrination: as obstetrical complication and in postoperative states, especially after lung surgery; thrombotic thrombocytopenic purpura.
    b. Fibrino-(geno-)lysis: hepatic cirrhosis; leukemias and other hematopoietic disorders; neoplasms, especially cancer of prostate.
    c. Combination of (a) and (b).
    d. Inactivation: following injection of EDTA (ethylene diamine tetra-acetic acid), and dextran.
Hemorrhagic diathesis depends on degree of deficiency and extent of associated defects, if any.
B. Increase: in pregnancy, nephrosis, acute and chronic infections, rheumatic fever and myocardial infarct, tumors (especially when associated with inflammatory reaction), and multiple myeloma.
C. Dysfibrinogenemia (abnormal fibrinogen—cryofibrinogen): in myeloma, metastatic tumors.

FACTOR II (PROTHROMBIN)

Historical Data

Precursor of thrombin postulated in 1895 (Schmidt). One-stage test described in 1935 (Quick:

prothrombin time). Relation to vitamin K discovered in 1939 (Waddell). First congenital (pure ?) deficiency reported in 1941 (Rhoads and Fitz-Hugh). Deficiency in newborn described in 1937 by Brinkhous et al. (prothrombin complex).

Physicochemical Data

It is precipitated by (NH$_4$)$_2$SO$_4$ at 50 per cent saturation; adsorbed from oxalated plasma by Mg(OH)$_2$, BaSO$_4$, Al(OH)$_3$, Ca$_3$(PO$_4$)$_2$, Seitz filtration. Relatively labile between 40 and 60° C.; inactivated at 85° C. In nearly pure state dissolved in 25 per cent sodium citrate, it converts gradually to thrombin. It is an S-containing glycoprotein present in α globulin and in AgP but not in AdP or serum (mostly consumed in normal clotting process). Normal level in plasma: about 0.2 mg. per ml.; 0.14 per cent of plasma proteins.

Clinical Data

CONGENITAL DEFICIENCY

1. *Hemorrhagic disease* of the newborn: Hypoprothrombinemia contributes to (but is often present without) frank bleeding tendency and usually responds to vitamin K or is prevented by such treatment of mother before delivery.

2. Persistent and isolated *hypoprothrombinemia* is a very rare recessive trait, similar to mild hemophilia with bleeding after tooth extractions, muscular hematomata, hemarthroses, and hematuria.

ACQUIRED DEFICIENCY

a. Lack of vitamin K: nutritional deficiency, malabsorption.
b. Hepatocellular disease.
c. Primary and secondary hematopoietic disorders, e.g., pernicious anemia, leukemia; propylthiouracil medication.
d. Antivitamin K medication (coumarin, salicylate).
e. Antiprothrombinemic activity: EDTA, sodium citrate intravenously.

FACTOR III (TISSUE THROMBOPLASTIN)

SYNONYM. Thrombokinase (used in German-speaking countries).

Historical Data

Intravascular clotting after intravenous injection of brain extract described in 1834. Action upon prothrombin to form thrombin shown in 1893 (Schmidt).

Physicochemical Data

Contained in acetone-extracted brain, dried and suspended in saline; resistant to heating up to 58° C. Loses holothromboplastic activity at 60° C. but retains platelet factor 3 activity (lipoid factor). Requires activation by accessory factors (V, VII, and X) in presence of calcium for optimal conversion of factor II.

FACTOR IV (CALCIUM)

Historical Data

Importance for clotting demonstrated by oxalate inhibition of *in vitro* clotting in 1890 (Arthus and Pagès). Requirement for clotting of bound rather than ionized calcium shown in 1940 (Quick). *In vivo* binding by excessive globulins or abnormal proteins causing clotting defect (and osteoporosis) proposed in 1959 (Wayne et al.).

Table 6–6 (*Continued*)

Physicochemical Data

It is removed from plasma (or tied up and made unavailable for coagulation process) by EDTA, oxalate, citrate, and fluoride and by ion exchange resins. Minimal concentration for optimal coagulation *in vitro* = 0.001 M for human and 0.004 M for canine plasma. This minimal concentration is increased with reduced prothrombin activity caused by vitamin K deficiency or coumarin effect. Essential in phases I and II of coagulation and required for optimal effect of thrombin in phase III. Normal level in plasma: 4.5 to 5.5 mEq. per L. Hypocalcemia per se has never been shown to interfere with clotting mechanism, but hyper- and dysglobulinemia (sarcoidosis, myeloma) may cause binding of calcium to (abnormal) globulins, resulting in a hemostatic defect even in the presence of chemical hypercalcemia.

FACTOR V (PROACCELERIN)

SYNONYMS: Labile factor, Ac-globulin.

Historical Data

A thermolabile component of prothrombin was postulated upon observing mutual correction of stored and "Dicumarol" plasma in 1943 (Quick). Congenital deficiency (parahemophilia) was described in 1947 (Owren).

Physicochemical Data

It is precipitated by $(NH_4)_2SO_4$ at 33 per cent saturation and also at pH < 4.0 and > 10.0; not adsorbed by $BaCO_3$, $BaSO_4$, $Ca_3(PO_4)_2$, $Al(OH)_3$, or Seitz filtration. Stable at pH 5.0 to 9.0; labile at pH > 10.0 and at room temperature; readily inactivated by heating to 58° C. and by trypsin or fibrinolysin; decays in oxalated plasma upon standing, even at 0° C.; much more stable in citrated plasma. Present in AdP and CP but absent from AgP and AgS; a water-soluble globulin, the concentration of which in plasma (greater in rabbit or dog than in human) is not influenced by dietary lack of vitamin K, coumarin-type medication, or biliary obstruction; required in the coagulation process for intrinsic thromboplastin generation and prothrombin conversion.

Clinical Data

CONGENITAL DEFICIENCY

Parahemophilia (hypoproaccelerinemia), due to autosomal recessive trait, non-sex-linked. A mild hemophilia-like disease with bleeding from mucous membranes, e.g., gums and nose, after tooth extraction and small cuts; tendency to ecchymoses, bruises, and menorrhagia (death reported in one instance at menarche) but compatible with normal pregnancy and parturition. Bleeding time is prolonged in some cases. Heterozygotes may have slightly prolonged "prothrombin" time.

ACQUIRED DEFICIENCY

1. Reduced production: common in hepatocellular disease, primary or secondary (including postoperative states, leukemia, systemic infections).
2. Circulating anticoagulant.
3. Increased fibrinolysis.

FACTOR VI (ACCELERIN)

SYNONYMS. Serum Ac-globulin, serum accelerator.

Historical Data

This factor was proposed in 1947 as the active principle formed from factor V during the coagulation process (Owren) but is now obsolete as a separate entity.

FACTOR VII (PROCONVERTIN)

SYNONYMS. Serum prothrombin conversion accelerator (SPCA), stable factor, cofactor V, co-thromboplastin, prothrombinogen (this latter term is used by Quick to denote a postulated inactive precursor of prothrombin, a concept which is not generally accepted).

Historical Data

Discovery of clot-promoting capacity of aged serum in 1904 (Bordet and Gengou). Identification of factor in 1949 and congenital and acquired deficiencies described in 1951 (Alexander).

Physicochemical Data

A nondialyzable protein readily adsorbed from oxalated plasma and serum by $BaSO_4$, $BaCO_3$, $Al(OH)_3$, $Ca_3(PO_4)_2$, and Seitz asbestos filters and eluted by citrate. Resistant in serum to 37° C. for at least four hours and to 45° C. for at least six minutes, but is destroyed at 56° C. within 2½ minutes, or at pH < 5.0 and > 9.0; it is not precipitated with globulins from serum or plasma at pH 5.0 to 5.2 or pH 5.7 to 5.8, respectively. Present in AgP and AgS; absent from CP and AdP. Accelerates conversion of II, maximally at tenfold concentration. Activated to convertin during coagulation (especially in glass) and gradually during aging of plasma. Half-life in normal man: 5.5 to 10.8 hours. Normal level: < 0.07 per cent of serum proteins:

Clinical Data

CONGENITAL DEFICIENCY

1. *Hemorrhagic disease of the newborn:* manifested by bruises, melena, intracranial hematoma; responds to vitamin K or prevented by such treatment of mother.
2. *Hereditary disorder:* due to autosomal recessive gene of intermediate expression and high penetrance. Homozygous state always causes hemorrhagic diathesis but with different severity from patient to patient. Bleeding from mucous membranes, especially nose and gums; hemorrhages into skin; rare hemarthroses. Heterozygous (carrier) state is probably quite common, detectable by slight increase in "prothrombin" time.

ACQUIRED ABNORMALITY

Decrease (see factor II):
   a. Lack of vitamin K
   b. Hepatocellular disease
   c. Hematopoietic disorders
   d. Antivitamin K treatment
   e. Circulating anticoagulant
Increase: pregnancy

FACTOR VIII (AHG, ANTIHEMOPHILIC GLOBULIN)

SYNONYMS. Antihemophilic factor (AHF), thromboplastinogen.

Historical Data

Correction of prolonged clotting time of a hemophiliac by *in vitro* addition of normal plasma fraction was shown in 1910 (Addis) and of normal "deprothrombinized" plasma in 1927 (Frank and Hartmann); by intravenous injection of a globulin fraction in 1937 (Patek and Taylor). Slow conversion (consumption) of prothrombin upon clotting of hemophilic blood was noted in 1939, corrected after transfusion of normal blood (Brinkhous).

Table 6–6 (*Continued*)

Physicochemical Data

A globulin or globulin-associated substance contained in Cohn fraction I and beta globulin and precipitable by alcohol or acetic acid; also present in Seitz-filtered P, CP, and AdP from which it is precipitable in the cold by CO_2 (for purpose of purification) and by 25 per cent saturation with $(NH_4)_2SO_4$. Activity is reduced 50 per cent at 56° C. in ten minutes and nearly 100 per cent after 30 minutes, but only gradually (30 to 60 per cent) after three-week storage under blood bank conditions and more slowly in fresh frozen plasma (50 per cent lost in one month, then stable for many months). It is fully consumed in clotting process; readily inactivated by thrombin or fibrinolysin. Half-life in circulation = 4 to 11 hours. Normal human plasma levels show considerable individual variations, constituting about one-fifth that of canine, porcine, or bovine plasma but exceeding equine level.

Clinical Data

CONGENITAL DEFICIENCY

A. Classic hemophilia, hemophilia A, is due to a female sex-linked, recessive trait, but familial history (mutation) is absent in up to 50 per cent of cases (mutation). Rare homozygous state causes clinical disease in female. Severity of symptoms differs in rough relation to plasma level of AHF: severe = < 1 per cent, moderate = 1 to 5 per cent, mild = 5 to 35 per cent of normal. Typical history is of bleeding in a male since early childhood and of abnormal bleeding in other members of family but restricted to males. Fatal bleeding may rarely occur after severing of umbilical cord. Often first alarming blood loss is related to dentition; subcutaneous, intramuscular, and articular hematomas are common, but bleeding from nose or gums is rare. Especially dangerous are hematoma of pharynx and larynx and in retrobulbar space; hematuria may cause urinary obstruction; retro- or intraperitoneal hematoma may lead to error in clinical diagnosis and to unwarranted surgical procedures.

B. Pseudohemophilia B (vascular or angiohemophilia) represents an association of AHF deficiency (usually mild to moderate) with a capillary defect, manifested by petechiae and prolonged bleeding time. Transmission is due to a non-sex-linked dominant trait with varying expressivity. A specially prepared plasma fraction (I–O) given intravenously corrects both defects (Nilsson *et al.*, 1959).

ACQUIRED ABNORMALITY

A. Deficiency
   a. Antithromboplastinogenemia: due to a circulating inhibitor (antibody) causing hemophilia-like disorder; especially reported in connection with pregnancy and delivery and systemic L.E.
   b. Release of tissue thromboplastin or thrombin (experimentally) into circulation is followed by clotting in multiple sites and consumption of AHF and other plasma factors (possibly associated with increased fibrinolysis).

B. Increase in AHF activity has been postulated to occur regularly with advancing age and especially in patients with coronary heart disease. (This physiologic increase, if verified, may account for the reputed improvement of classic hemophilia with advancing age.)

FACTOR IX (PLASMA THROMBOPLASTIN COMPONENT, PTC)

SYNONYMS. Christmas factor (named after a family in which the congenital defect was first discovered by Biggs *et al.*, 1952), plasma thromboplastin factor B, facteur antihemophilique B.

Historical Data

Mutual correction of clotting time of blood of two hemophiliacs was first noted in 1944 and 1950 (Koller *et al.*). Congenital hemophilia-like state other than AHF deficiency was reported in 1952 from three separate laboratories (Aggeler *et al.*, Biggs *et al.*, Schulman and Smith).

Physicochemical Data

A protein (?) contained in Cohn fractions III and IV–1, in alpha and beta fractions, and in AgS, AgP, and CP (decreased in CP after two to three weeks of patient's exposure to the drug); absent from Cohn fraction I and AdP. Removed from oxalated plasma by Seitz filtration; eluted from $BaSO_4$ precipitate of oxalated plasma by sodium citrate. Not removed from plasma by alcohol or acetic acid but by 40 to 50 per cent $(NH_4)_2SO_4$ saturation; resistant to heating to 56° C. for ten minutes. PTC is activated in the course of the clotting process or by contact of plasma with glass.

Clinical Data

CONGENITAL DEFICIENCY

1. Hemorrhagic disease of newborn: see factor VII.
2. Hemophilia B, hemophilioid state C, Christmas disease: hereditary pattern and symptomatology are identical with that of hemophilia A. Occasional combinations of AHF and PTC deficiency occur. Incidence of syndromes A:B = 9:1.

ACQUIRED ABNORMALITY

A. Decrease (see factor VII):
   1. Lack of vitamin K (prolonged)
   2. Hepatocellular disease (advanced)
   3. Antivitamin K treatment (prolonged)
B. Increase: postulated as responsible for part of thrombophilic tendency (analogous to experiments with serum-induced venous thrombosis).

FACTOR X (STUART FACTOR)

SYNONYMS. Stuart-Prower factor

Historical Data

Factor X was recognized as distinct from factor VII on the basis of studies of patients with congenital so-called "stable factor" deficiency (Hougie *et al.*, 1957).

Physicochemical Data

It is stable in serum at 37° C. for 30 minutes at pH 6 to 9 but quickly inactivated outside this range. In oxalated serum, 70 per cent activity is present after exposure to 28° C. for 168 hours; 25 per cent at 37° C. for 240 hours; 22 per cent at 56° C. for 2½ minutes; and none above 56° C. for 30 minutes. Saline eluate is more stable. Factor X is contained in AgS, AgP, and (perhaps reduced) in CP but absent from AdP; present in $BaSO_4$ eluate and in α globulin on electrophoresis; required for intrinsic thromboplastin formation and for prothrombin conversion.

Clinical Data

CONGENITAL DEFICIENCY

Stuart Factor Deficiency:

1. Hemorrhagic disease of newborn (see factor VII).

Table 6–6 (Concluded)

2. Hereditary disorder is due to a highly penetrant but incompletely recessive autosomal trait. Homozygous cases show frequent epistaxis, hematomata, and menorrhagia; bleeding upon slight trauma and at operations; and occasional hemarthroses. Heterozygotes may be mildly affected or normal clinically with reduction in factor X level to 20 to 52 per cent of normal and prolongation of "prothrombin" time by one to three seconds.

ACQUIRED DEFICIENCY
Usually part of defect in "prothrombin complex" (see factor VII):
1. Lack of vitamin K (prolonged)
2. Hepatocellular disease (severe and advanced)
3. Antivitamin K treatment (prolonged)

PTA (PLASMA THROMBOPLASTIN ANTECEDENT)

Historical Data
Mutual correction of prolonged clotting times of blood from patients with hemophilioid syndrome with blood from patients with AHF or PTC deficiency was discovered in 1953 (Rosenthal, 1955) and resulted in definition of separate clinical entity.

Physicochemical Data
It is precipitated from plasma at 20 to 33 per cent $(NH_4)_2SO_4$ saturation. Heating serum at 58 to 60° C. for ten minutes impairs its corrective effect. The deficiency in plasma tends to disappear after storage at −15° C. for 4 to 62 days. Present in AgP, AdP, AgS, AdS, and CP in which it decreases after two to three weeks of patient's exposure to coumarin.

Clinical Data
CONGENITAL DEFICIENCY
Hemophilia C (Rosenthal's syndrome, PTA deficiency) is due to an autosomal dominant trait with high degree of penetrance and variable expression; transmitted by either male or female to either male or female progeny. Relatively mild hemophilia-like disease occurs in varying degrees, clotting times ranging from normal to 30 minutes. Bleeding is rarely spontaneous but usually follows trauma or surgical procedure; occasional hemarthroses, pur-

pura, and prolonged bleeding time have been observed.

ACQUIRED DEFICIENCY
It occurs in combination with other clotting defects in hematopoietic disorders and liver disease and after prolonged coumarin treatment.

HF (HAGEMAN FACTOR)
SYNONYMS. Plasma thromboplastin factor E (PTF-E), fifth factor of plasma thromboplastin formation.

Historical Data
A familial hemorrhagic trait characterized by markedly prolonged clotting time of venous blood in glass, but absence of evidence of a bleeding tendency was discovered in 1955 (Ratnoff, 1958).

Physicochemical Data
Activity is contained in euglobulin fraction precipitated from normal human plasma by acidification and dilution; heat stable (inactivated after ten minutes at 70° C.); not consumed in clotting process and not readily adsorbed; hence, present in AgP, AgS, AdP, AdS, CP.

Clinical Data
CONGENITAL DEFICIENCY. Hageman trait is devoid of any clinical manifestations; transmitted as autosomal recessive characteristic (regularly found in ducks).

ACQUIRED DEFICIENCY. None observed.

Legend
P   Plasma
AdP   Adsorbed plasma (with $BaSO_4$, $Al_2(OH)_3$)
AgP   Aged plasma
AdS   Adsorbed serum
AgS   Aged serum
CP   Coumarin plasma (from patient treated with a coumarin derivative for two to three days).
TP   Thromboplastin
OP   Oxalated plasma

hemostasis; and circulating decoagulants (the fibrinolytic system).

The Recognized Plasma Clotting Factors and the Three Phases of Coagulation

The laboratory diagnosis of plasma factor deficiency rests primarily on localization of the defect in the overall chain reaction of the clotting process, i.e., whether it affects thromboplastin formation (phase I), prothrombin conversion (phase II), or fibrinogen conversion (phase III), or combinations of these (Table 6–1). Additional helpful criteria, especially of a differential diagnostic nature, are provided by "cross-matching" tests (not to be confused with pretransfusion tests), adsorbability, and fate of the apparent defect in the clotting process, i.e., whether it is present in plasma or serum or in both.

The four major patterns of isolated, single defects and pertinent screening tests are evident from Table 6–7: (1) impairment of thromboplastin generation due to deficiency of either AHF, PTC, or PTA (and HF), revealed by the prothrombin consumption test or the partial thromboplastin time; (2) impairment of both thromboplastin generation and prothrombin conversion as indicated by the one-stage prothrombin time (Quick), caused by deficiency of either factor V or X; (3) poor prothrombin conversion, caused by diminished activity of either factor VII or prothrombin; and (4) deficiency in fibrinogen conversion. Some of the routine differential diagnostic steps within each of the first three groups are implied in the right-hand part of Table 6–7. (Differentiation between PTA and HF deficiency, which is not afforded by the tabulated information, is indicated in the

Table 6–7. Typical Results in Isolated Deficiencies of Plasma Clotting Factors

PATTERNS OF IMPAIRED MECHANISM	DEFICIENT FACTORS	TESTS FOR				ABNORMAL RESULTS CORRECTED BY †					
		PHASE I		II	III	OP	AdP	CP		AgP	AgS
		SERUM PCT	PLASMA PTT	PLASMA PT	PLASMA TT			SHORT	LONG		
1 Thromboplastin Generation	VIII	D	I	N	N	+	+	+	+	−	−
	IX	D	I	N	N	±,+	−	±,+	−	±,+	+
	PTA (and HF)*	D	I	N	N	+	+	+	+	+	+
2 Prothrombin Conversion	V	D	I	I	N	+	+	+	+	−	−
	X	D	I	I	N	+	−	+	−	+	+
3 Prothrombin Conversion	II	N	N–I	I	N	+	−	+	−	+	−
	VII	N	N	I	N	+	−	−	−	+	+
4 Fibrinogen Conversion	I Reduced	N	N–I	I	I	+	+	+	+	+	−
	I Absent	N	∞	∞	∞	+	+	+	+	+	−
Circulating anticoagulant or abnormal plasma proteins		N–D	N–I	N–I	N–I	−	−	−	−	−	−

The whole blood clotting time and the calcium clotting time in plasma should typically be prolonged in each of the deficiencies listed except for factor VII deficiency, when they are normal, and in complete absence of fibrinogen, when no clotting occurs at all.

PT   Prothrombin time (one-stage Quick's method)
PTT   Partial thromboplastin time
PCT   Prothrombin consumption test
TT   Thrombin time
OP   Oxalated plasma (see Table 6–9)
D   Decreased
I   Increased
N   Normal
∞   Infinity (no clot)

* Distinction between PTA and HF deficiency may be made (a) on clinical grounds and (b) by means of two simple laboratory tests. Ad (a): HF deficiency is characteristically associated with normal hemostasis, i.e., absence of any bleeding disorder. Ad (b): (1) OP heated to 58° C. for ten minutes (inactivating PTA factor) will "correct" prolonged calcium clotting time of plasma in HF deficiency but not PTA deficiency. (2) Oxalated test plasma, exposed to ground glass, will shorten ("correct") the long calcium clotting time of normal plasma in a siliconized tube if the test plasma is deficient in PTA but not if deficient in HF.

† Usual proportion of test plasma to "correcting agent" (plasma or serum) is 10 to 1. If this proportion results in only slight or no correction, the defect is likely to be due to either low fibrinogen or a circulating anticoagulant. This distinction can be made by repeating the test, mixing equal parts of test plasma and reagent. Complete correction signifies low fibrinogen level in the test plasma; incomplete or no correction denotes inhibitory activity in the test plasma.

AgP (Aged Plasma). Oxalated plasma is kept at refrigerator temperature in an unstoppered and uncoated glass tube for about two weeks. A drop in prothrombin time from an initial 12 to 13 seconds to 40 seconds denotes loss of factor V activity (usually associated with loss of VIII although not demonstrable with this test). The specimen may then be stored in small aliquots at −20° C. for weeks without change in clotting activity.

AdP (Adsorbed Plasma). "Deprothrombinized" plasma: Oxalated plasma treated with dry BaSO₄ or citrated plasma treated with Al(OH)₃ (throughout this text, the term "adsorbed plasma" refers to BaSO₄-treated oxalated plasma). From 50 to 100 mg. of BaSO₄ (c.p.) are added to 1 ml. of oxalated plasma. The mixture is stirred for three minutes and permitted to stand for two minutes. After the adsorbent has been removed by rapid centrifuging for five minutes, the supernatant plasma should yield a PT of no less than five minutes, indicating practically complete elimination of prothrombin and the "serum factors": VII, X, and IX (loss of the latter not being demonstrated by the test). AdP may be stored at −20° C. for weeks, retaining most of its factor V activity and close to 50 per cent of its initial factor VIII activity. (Use of rabbit or ox plasma instead of human plasma is preferable in many instances because of their greater factor V content.) If citrated plasma is to be "deprothrombinized," BaSO₄ is unsuitable but Al(OH)₃ must be employed (Miale, 1958). This has the disadvantage of removing some fibrinogen.

AdS (Adsorbed Serum). Fresh serum treated in the same manner described for AdP.

AgS (Aged Serum). Serum from venous blood, which was collected in a glass tube and incubated at 37° C. for two hours. The tube should contain two to three glass beads and for maximal glass contact should be inverted several times before clotting occurs. The serum removed by routine centrifuging may be stored in small aliquots at −20° C. for extended periods without loss of activity (VII, IX, X, HF, PTA).

CP. Oxalated or citrated plasma from a patient treated with a coumarin-type drug; short: for two to three days (low in VII activity); long: for more than two weeks (low in VII, X, II, and IX activities).

legend.) Additional and more specific differential analysis can be made by cross-matching with samples of serum or plasma with known clotting defects; these, however, are not readily available and are therefore not considered here as a part of routine diagnosis.

With the use of these three screening tests, e.g., the thrombin time, one-stage prothrombin test, and prothrombin consumption—one for each of the three phases of the coagulation mechanism, respectively—an existing single clotting defect can, as a rule, be classified in terms of these phases. In many instances, the thrombin time may not be needed, since observation of a firm and normal-size clot with either of the other two tests, even if this endpoint is reached with some delay, provides assurance against a significant deficiency in fibrinogen. On the other hand, the presence of a circulating anticoagulant active against individual factors, total thromboplastin or thrombin, or the existence of abnormal plasma proteins that inactivate certain factors may be interpreted falsely in terms of a clotting factor deficiency.

Hence, a test for circulating anticoagulants is desirable as a part of the initial screening procedure. Whole blood clotting time, the most commonly used and age-old procedure, lends itself to this purpose. However, the wide normal range and the well-known technical shortcomings of the test greatly detract from its diagnostic utility. The calcium clotting time in oxalated or citrated blood or plasma can be standardized more conveniently and is, indeed, more suitable for the detection of circulating inhibitors, since aliquots of the test material can be applied readily to serial dilution techniques. On the other hand, the whole blood clot serves conveniently in routine screening for impairment of clot retraction and abnormal increase in fibrinolysis.

Thus, the classification of a hemostatic defect due to deficiency or inhibition of a plasma clotting factor may be achieved by testing for (a) circulating anticoagulant and fibrinolytic activity, (b) impairment of fibrinogen conversion (phase III), (c) impairment of prothrombin conversion (phase II), (d) deficient generation of intrinsic thromboplastin (phase I) (utilizing basic and relatively simple test procedures, such as (a) whole blood clotting or plasma calcium clotting time, (b) thrombin time, (c) the one-stage "prothrombin" test of Quick, (d) the prothrombin consumption test) (Table 6–8).

If the screening tests for phase I or II give abnormal results and a circulating inhibitor has been excluded, identification of the specific clotting defect can usually be made by means of the same respective test procedure, using as "corrective" or cross-matching reagents plasma and serum secured either from healthy donors (specially prepared) or from patients known to suffer from a specific hemorrhagic disorder.

TESTS OF OVER-ALL COAGULATION PROCESS

Whole Blood Clotting Time (WBCT). *Principle.* This test provides a measure of the time required for free flowing blood to

Table 6–8. **Interpretation of Results of Screening Tests**

TESTS	NORMAL RESULT	BORDERLINE OR ABNORMAL RESULT
WBCT CaT	Absence of clotting defect, except for VII deficiency Admixture of tissue fluid masking phase I defect Mild phase I or II defects	Deficiency in Phases I, II (except factor VII), or III Circulating anticoagulant Dysproteinemia
Thrombin time*	Normal phase III (normal fibrinogen, absence of excessive antithrombin (heparin) activity)	Excessive antithrombin activity (endogenous or injected heparin) Low or absent (no clot) fibrinogen Dysproteinemia
One-stage prothrombin time (Quick)	Normal phase II factors and fibrinogen Absence of circulating inhibitor against II, V, VII, X, thromboplastin or thrombin	Deficiency of II, V, VII, X, or I Circulating inhibitor in phase II or III (antithromboplastin, antithrombin)
Prothrombin consumption test	Absence of marked deficiency of prothromboplastin (phase I) Deficiency of prothrombin Deficiency of VII	Deficiency in phase I, including factors V and X Circulating anticoagulant active against one of the prothromboplastins

* Platelet-poor plasma. Platelets tend to interfere with heparin activity (antiheparin platelet factor) and may therefore shorten clotting time.

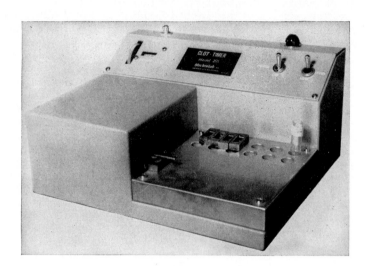

Figure 6–5. Instrument for automatic recording of clotting time. The Clot-Timer affords automatic timing of clot formation by means of a wire or a rod provided with a cross bar (rotor), which rotates through the liquid test sample (blood or plasma) and stops as soon as a fibrin strand produces contact between the rotating part and another, nonmovable rod. The temperature is kept at 37° C. by thermostatic control. To determine whole-blood clotting time, a large drop of blood (from the second syringe in the two-syringe technique) may be placed on a plastic plate provided for this technique, and a wire is made to rotate through the blood until it is arrested as a result of incipient fibrin formation. In addition, flat metal cuvets ("boats") of 0.36 ml. capacity may be used with the rotor, especially for determining the calcium clotting time and the one-stage prothrombin time.

solidify (clot) after it has been removed from the body. The results are greatly influenced by a number of physical factors, such as the nature of the surface and diameter of the test tube (and of the syringe and needle used in collecting), temperature, and agitation of the blood sample. Clotting is accelerated by contact with glass, by smaller size of the tube, by higher temperature (up to 38° C.), by turbulence (bubbling), by unduly rapid rate of flow of the blood into the syringe (enforced negative pressure), and especially by admixture of tissue fluid with the blood sample. Tissue thromboplastin results in circumventing the first phase of coagulation, thereby masking any defect in intrinsic thromboplastin formation. Only if these multiple factors are carefully controlled and the test is carried out on "a fixed volume of blood in a (glass) test tube of a fixed diameter at a constant temperature" can it be regarded as representing the "intrinsic coagulative power" of the blood (Quick, 1957). Continual practice with alert attention to details is essential, because "the determination of clotting time is the *simplest,* the most *informative,* and technically the most *difficult* of all common laboratory procedures" (Jaques, 1955).

Modified Lee-White Method

Equipment

Two syringes, 5 or 10 ml. in capacity, one coated with silicone

No. 20 needle, coated with silicone
Test tubes, 13 × 100 mm.
Glass rods
Water bath at 37.5° C.
Stopwatch

PROCEDURE. Blood is collected through a "clean" venipuncture by the two-syringe technique. After 1 or more ml. of blood (which may be used for clot retraction or for tests on serum) have entered the first, nonsiliconized syringe, this is detached from the needle and replaced with the siliconized syringe. Following gentle withdrawal of 2 or more ml. of blood (carefully avoiding collapse of vein or turbulent flow), 1 ml. is transferred without needle into each of two clean, dry test tubes prewarmed to 37° C., care being taken to avoid any agitating, foaming, bubbling, or splashing. The tubes are placed in a 37° C. water bath. One of the tubes is tilted, at first every 30 seconds and, if clotting has not occurred after 10 minutes, every 60 seconds. If clotting is delayed beyond 20 minutes, tilting may be done every five minutes. As soon as clot formation is noted (absence of flow upon tilting), tube No. 2 in the water bath is tilted as described for tube 1. The period elapsing from the moment the blood entered the second syringe until it gelled in tube 2 represents the clotting time. *Normal range:* six to ten minutes. At temperatures less than 37° C., such as in a 25° water bath or at room temperature, the normal range may extend to 15 minutes or more.

With use of silicone-coated tubes, the clotting time is prolonged to a normal range of 25 to 45 minutes. Although much more time consuming, this procedure is also more sensitive and more likely to uncover a hemophilioid defect when the plain glass technique yields a normal value.

The *incipient clotting time* (as against the period required for total clot formation) can be estimated by placing a glass rod in each test tube and withdrawing it gently every 30 seconds (instead of tilting), first in tube 1 and then in tube 2. Beginning of clotting is denoted by a fine fibrin thread. *Normal range* (in uncoated tubes): three to four minutes, followed by a solid clot two to six minutes later. This interval between incipient and total clotting is often markedly prolonged in hemophilioid disorders. Automatic timing of initial clot formation may be achieved by means of the Clot-Timer but requires modification of the procedure (Fig. 6–5).*

The tubes containing the blood clot may be kept in the water bath and inspected one to two hours later for estimation of clot retraction (see p. 330) and after 12 to 24 hours for evidence of fibrinolysis. Normally most of the solid clot is still present after overnight incubation. With accelerated fibrinolysis, part or all of the clot may be dissolved (see p. 365).

Capillary method

Equipment

Capillary glass tubes, about 1 mm. in diameter, 5 cm. long

Sterile needle or spring lancet or preferably a disposable blood lancet

70 per cent alcohol

Stopwatch

PROCEDURE. The finger tip or infant's heel is cleansed with alcohol and dried. A deep puncture is made. Two drops of free flowing blood are discarded before blood is drawn up in five to six tubes (at the same time the stopwatch is started), filling them only three-fourths full. The tubes are tilted at 30-second intervals until the flow of blood ceases. Then a short segment of tube is broken off every 30 seconds until a fibrin thread is seen to connect the fragments, denoting the endpoint. *Normal range:* three to five minutes.

Because of the almost inevitable contamination of blood with tissue juice, this procedure is acceptable only for monitor-

* The Clot-Timer is manufactured by Mechrolab, Inc., Mountain View, Calif.

ing anticoagulant treatment with heparin (which, as an antithrombin, is not influenced by tissue thromboplastin) and when venipuncture is unusually difficult, as with small children. A normal result does not exclude a defect in intrinsic thromboplastin formation (hemophilia).

Calcium Clotting Time (CaT) (Coagulation Time of Decalcified Blood or Plasma Upon Recalcifying; Recalcification Time). Principle. This test measures the time required for a fibrin clot to form in decalcified blood or plasma after addition of calcium chloride.

Decalcification, accomplished by mixing sodium oxalate or citrate with freshly drawn blood in a fixed proportion, precludes clotting until counteracted by added calcium, which reinitiates the clotting process. The recalcification test, as applied to whole blood and platelet-rich (slow-spun) plasma, normally yields clotting times considerably shorter than the whole blood clotting time for reasons not fully understood (Table 6–1). Presumably clotting is initiated before decalcifying is complete, and some clotting factors are activated when the plasma is allowed to stand (especially factors VII and IX) so that a shorter time is needed for adequate thrombin formation upon recalcifying.

The same pitfalls and precautions apply here as mentioned in the preceding description of the whole blood clotting time (p. 345). In particular, admixture of tissue juice tends to shorten the calcium clotting time and to cause it to approach the "prothrombin time," thus circumventing intrinsic thromboplastin generation and masking a hemophilia-type defect. If properly standardized and performed, the test provides information concerning the total coagulative power of the blood, similar to the whole blood clotting time. The great advantage over the latter is that the test need not be performed at or near the bedside or immediately upon blood collection, but the harvested specimen can be transported and the test carried out with delay of 30 to 60 minutes. Moreover, repeated analyses are possible without further venipunctures, and different types of tests can be performed on aliquots of a single sample (such as thrombin time, prothrombin time and partial thromboplastin time, especially when a portion is rapidly centrifuged to obtain platelet-poor plasma) (Table 6–9).

It should be emphasized that careful adherence to technical details in collecting blood and in centrifuging, transferring, and

Table 6–9. Preparation and Application of Decalcified Plasma*

TYPE OF PLASMA	COLLECTION AND PROCESSING	APPLICATION IN METHODS
Platelet-rich, oxalated	4.5 ml. of blood + 0.5 ml. of 1.34% Na oxalate, centrifuged at 50 G. for ten minutes; supernatant plasma is transferred to another tube.	Calcium time † Prothrombin time ‡ Fibrinogen ‡ Thromboplastin generation and "correction" studies after adsorption with BaSO₄‡
Platelet-rich, citrated	4.5 ml. of blood + 0.5 ml. of 3.8% Na citrate, centrifuged and transferred as stated above.	Calcium time † Prothrombin time ‡ Fibrinogen ‡ Thromboplastin generation and "correction" studies after adsorption with Al(OH)₃‡
Platelet-poor, citrated	4.5 ml. of blood + 0.5 ml. of 3.8% Na citrate; the platelet-rich supernatant is centrifuged at 1500 G. for at least 30 minutes.	Calcium time † Prothrombin time ‡ Partial thromboplastin time † Thrombin time † Fibrinolysis (quantitative) † Prolonged storage for future "correction" studies (especially in case of hemophilic donor) †

* Plasma may be kept from clotting without admixture of an anticoagulant by exposing it to ice water temperature from the moment of venipuncture and avoiding any glass contact, as noted below†. This is called native plasma. It may be prepared to be platelet-rich or platelet-poor and utilized for various purposes, such as tests for clot retraction (p. 330) and prothrombin consumption (both as substrate in step 1 of the basic procedure and as "corrective" reagent; p. 357). Cold storage at −20° C. permits preservation of clotting activities for prolonged periods of time, especially when silicone-coated tubes are used.

† Two-syringe technique (p. 346), silicone-coated glassware, including pipets, and a temperature of 0 to 4° C. are required until actual performance of test; this is usually done in uncoated tubes at 37° C.

‡ One-syringe technique, plain glassware, and room temperature are usually adequate for collection and brief storage (one to two hours).

storing plasma is necessary for reliable results. Thus, contact with a glass surface tends to shorten the clotting time during the first few hours after collection, especially with use of citrate as an anticoagulant, by activating "prothrombinogen" (Quick) and factors IX and VII. After longer standing and exposure to temperatures exceeding 4° C., the thermolabile factors, VIII and V, tend to decrease in concentration and cause a prolonged clotting time.

Modified Howell method

Equipment

Same as for whole blood clotting time, plus 1.34 per cent sodium oxalate or 3.8 per cent sodium citrate

Physiologic saline solution (0.85 per cent)

Solution of calcium chloride, 0.02 M. (All these reagents should be stored at refrigerator temperature; saline should be prepared fresh every week.)

Centrifuge tubes, 15 × 100 mm., silicone coated

Smaller test tubes, 10 × 75 mm., non-siliconized

Nongraduated (Pasteur) pipets, silicone-coated

Delivery pipets marked at 0.1 and 0.2 ml.; silicone-coated

Centrifuge (preferably refrigerated)

Beaker with ice water.

PROCEDURE. A 4.5 ml. sample of blood collected with the two-syringe technique (see p. 346) is added to 0.5 ml. of anticoagulant in a siliconized centrifuge tube previously placed in ice water. The plasma is promptly separated (see Table 6–9 for centrifuging speed) and placed in another iced, silicone-coated tube, using a coated pipet.

The test is performed on 0.1 ml. of plasma mixed with 0.1 ml. of saline in a small, plain, glass tube after three minutes of incubation in the water bath; 0.1 ml. of calcium chloride solution (kept at 37° C.) is forcibly blown into the tube and the stopwatch started. After the tube has been shaken to insure complete mixing, it is kept in the bath for another 60 seconds and then removed every 15 seconds to determine the endpoint, i.e., a fibrin clot.*

* Automatic timing can be achieved with use of the Clot-Timer (Fig. 6–4).

Normal range: 90 to 120 seconds for platelet-rich plasma; 105 to 150 seconds for platelet-poor plasma.

Heparin tolerance test; protamine tolerance test (clotting time of recalcified plasma with heparin or protamine). PRINCIPLE. The degree of lengthening of the clotting time caused by a fixed amount of heparin in the reaction tube (as compared with a control system) reflects the presence of heparin inhibiting (clot accelerating) activity. Hence, this is a test for hypercoagulability. In addition, by performing the test on both platelet-rich and platelet-poor aliquots of the same plasma, the normally present antiheparin activity of platelets can be tested. This activity is regarded as deficient if the presence of platelets fails to cause substantial shortening of the clotting time below that of the platelet-poor sample.

The same procedure, replacing heparin with protamine, may be used for recognition and assay of heparin-like activity of a plasma that shows evidence of a circulating anticoagulant (see p. 363).

13 patients who developed thromboembolic complications (Gardikas *et al.,* 1959). The value of the test remains questionable because of the wide normal range.

Test for circulating anticoagulants. PRINCIPLE. In order to determine whether a prolonged clotting time of whole blood or recalcified plasma is caused by a defect in plasma factor(s) or by a circulating anticoagulant, a small volume (one-tenth) of normal plasma is added to the patient's blood or plasma. Full "correction" to a normal clotting time denotes a defect in clotting factor(s), since these are abundantly present in normal blood; failure of the clotting time to shorten materially is indicative of inhibitory activity. This is often powerful enough to prolong the clotting time of normal plasma or blood when one-tenth the volume of the patient's plasma is added.

EQUIPMENT. Same as for previous test.

PROCEDURE. The clotting time is determined in serial dilutions of the patient's plasma with normal plasma (doubling the volumes is desirable for greater accuracy in pipetting).

REAGENTS		CLOTTING MIXTURES						
Saline (ml.)		0.2	0.2	0.2	0.2	0.2	0.2	0.2
0.02 M CaCl₂ (ml.)		0.2	0.2	0.2	0.2	0.2	0.2	0.2
Citrated plasma (ml.)	Patient	0.2	0.18	0.14	0.10	0.06	0.02	0.0
	Normal	0.0	0.02	0.06	0.10	0.14	0.18	0.2
Clotting time in seconds		300	300	300	300	240	210	120

EQUIPMENT. Same as for previous test, plus solutions of heparin in saline containing 0.1, 0.3, and 0.5 units per ml. (stable in refrigerator for several weeks). One unit equals approximately 10 μg.

PROCEDURE. The test is performed on four aliquots of citrated plasma, simultaneously or in rapid succession of one another. In three of the four tubes the plain saline moiety is replaced by the three heparin solutions, respectively. *Normal range* (in platelet-poor plasma): 3.8 minutes ($\pm$ 1.7) with 0.1 unit, 5.7 minutes ($\pm$ 3.2) with 0.3 unit, 9 minutes ($\pm$ 3.4) with 0.5 unit of heparin per milliliter of saline.

These results were obtained in 200 subjects tested before they underwent major operations. Postoperatively, values showed a distinct tendency to drop, especially in

INTERPRETATION. Suppose the patient's plasma showed a prolonged clotting time of 300 seconds. The normal range for platelet-rich plasma is 90 to 120 seconds and 105 to 150 seconds for platelet-poor plasma. The result indicates that the patient has a potent anticoagulant, because normal clotting was reached only in the test tube that did not contain the patient's plasma.

If the clotting defect were due to a plasma factor deficiency, the correction would have taken place with a small amount of normal plasma added to the patient's plasma, because normal plasma has abundant quantities of most plasma clotting factors.

Discovery of an inhibitor by this procedure ordinarily requires further analysis to determine in which phase of the clotting process it is active, i.e., whether it is an antithrombin, antiprothrombin (complex)

or antiprothromboplastin (see p. 339). For this purpose, the test for the respective phase yielding an abnormal result, i.e., TT (thrombin time), PT (one-stage prothrombin time), or prothrombin consumption test, may be applied to the serial dilution of the patient's with normal plasma in the same proportions as shown previously. In the prothrombin consumption test, native instead of citrated plasma is used (p. 348). The test may also be performed on whole blood collected simultaneously from both the patient and a control subject or on the patient's whole blood admixed to cold-stored, normal, native plasma (Tables 6–9, 6–14).

In routine practice, a mixture of equal volumes (0.1 + 0.1 ml.) is first tested; in the absence of "correction," serial dilutions may be prepared for titration of the anticoagulant concentration.

Thrombelastography. An estimate of the overall coagulability and quality of the clot can be obtained with an instrument, the thrombelastograph. This method permits automatic graphic registration of the period of time required by whole blood or recalcified plasma for initial fibrin formation, consolidation of the clot, and rate of fibrinolysis and of the firmness (elasticity) of the clot. For details of apparatus and procedure, the reader is referred to pertinent publications (De Nicola, 1957).

The whole blood clotting time (WBCT), often called simply "clotting time," and the calcium time (CaT) may be expected to uncover a deficiency in any phase of the clotting process. Indeed, abnormally long clotting times under standard conditions always denote abnormality (factor deficiency or inhibitory activity). They do not necessarily indicate a bleeding tendency, since in the Hageman trait, a prolonged clotting time (in glass) is characteristically associated with normal hemostatic function. A normal WBCT or CaT, on the other hand, is frequently encountered in the presence of bleeding disease; this is typical of a numerical or functional platelet defect—except in very severe cases of thrombocytopenia—and it is also common in mild to moderate coagulopathies (plasma factor deficiencies).

For practical purposes, a normal clotting time rules out an abnormally low level of fibrinogen or a heparin-type anticoagulant but not defects in the action or formation of thrombin or thromboplastin. For this reason, numerous technical modifications have been devised to make the test a more sensitive and a more dependable measure of "overall" disturbance in coagulation. The least sensitive procedure is the capillary tube method. Because of the inevitable admixture of tissue fluid, a normal value excludes only fibrinogen deficiency and other types of impairment in phase III. Hence, it may be used in monitoring heparin activity in the course of anticoagulant treatment. The WBCT is rendered more sensitive by performing it in siliconized glass tubes or at a standardized temperature below 37° C., e.g., 25° C., but at the same time it becomes far more

time consuming. The CaT tends to be more sensitive than the WBCT in glass tubes, i.e., it is more often abnormal, including cases of moderate platelet deficiency (when performed on slow-spun plasma). But again, a normal calcium clotting time does not exclude a defect in either phase I or II.

Tests for Phase III of Coagulation

Thrombin Time (TT). *Principle.* This test measures the time required for clot formation in decalcified plasma after admixture of a standardized thrombin solution.

Since conversion of fibrinogen to fibrin represents the end point in most tests of coagulation, scrutiny of this third phase of the clotting process should precede analysis of earlier phases. Although thrombin is capable of accomplishing this conversion by acting upon purified fibrinogen preparations, the reaction is influenced by temperature, pH, calcium concentration, and the colloidal state of the substrate. Among the recognized clot-promoting, accelerating factors active in plasma under standard conditions are platelets (factor 2), a plasma accelerator (possibly albumin) and calcium. The thrombin time does not correlate well with fibrinogen concentration; in fact, it tends to be prolonged with an increase in fibrinogen beyond the normal range, as well as with marked reduction in fibrinogen, reaching infinity in afibrinogenemia. Aside from these quantitative and possibly also qualitative alterations of fibrinogen, prolongation of the thrombin time may be due to reduction in the "plasma accelerator," deficiency in platelet factor 2 (minimized by use of platelet-poor plasma in the test), abnormal composition of plasma proteins (hyper- and paraglobulinemia), and antithrombic activity.

Equipment. Same as for the calcium clotting time, plus stock thrombin solution containing 100 units per milliliter in 50 per cent glycerol (Rapaport and Ames, 1957). This is prepared as follows: The contents of one vial of Parke-Davis Topical Bovine Thrombin is dissolved in 5 ml. of oxalated saline (one part of 0.1 M oxalate and five parts of isotonic saline) and is adsorbed with 100 mg. of $BaSO_4$ (CP) for 20 minutes at 37° C. After centrifuging, the clear supernatant (5 ml.) is transferred to a 125 ml. flask and mixed with 20 ml. of saline, followed by 25 ml. of glycerol. This solution is stable at 0 to 4° C. for many weeks. It may be stored in 0.5 ml. or 1.0 ml. quantities in stoppered small glass tubes. A 1 to 10 dilution of this stock in saline provides the working thrombin solution for the test. It is stable in a silicone-coated tube (to prevent adsorption of thrombin onto glass) for 20 minutes at 37° C.

Procedure. A 0.2 ml. sample of ice cold, platelet-poor plasma (see Table 6–9 for details of preparation) is placed in a small glass tube and incubated at 37° C. for three minutes. Thereafter, 0.1 ml. of the preincubated dilute thrombin is added and the clotting time noted.* *Normal range:* 11 to 14 seconds (a control plasma should always be tested simultaneously).

Definite prolongations of TT are encountered in a variety of clinical disorders, especially in hepatocellular diseases, acute and chronic leukemias, lymphosarcoma, systemic granulomas, multiple myeloma, malnutrition, and renal disease. At the present state of ignorance about the nature and significance of the plasma accelerator or of nonheparin antithrombin, two differential tests may be helpful when a markedly prolonged TT is encountered: heparin assay to reveal the presence of a heparin-like inhibitor ("correction" with protamine) and measurement of fibrinogen.

Heparin assay. "Correction" of an abnormally long TT by either protamine or toluidine blue—agents with heparin-neutralizing capacity—denotes the presence of heparin in the test plasma.

The following routine test system lends itself to this analysis (Quick, 1957).

are prepared as follows: A stock heparin solution containing 1 mg. (100 units) per ml. of distilled water is further diluted with water to prepare solutions of 0.01, 0.02, 0.03, 0.04, and 0.06 mg. per ml. Adding 0.1 ml. of each solution per 2 ml. aliquot of plasma (in iced, siliconized tubes) results in heparin concentrations of 0.5, 1.0, 1.5, 2.0, and 3.0 μg. per ml. of plasma.

According to Figure 6–6, the test plasma just mentioned, which is platelet-poor, appears to contain 1 μg. of heparin per ml. (corresponding to a TT of 25 seconds). The two curves in Figure 6–6 demonstrate the effect of platelets upon the TT and the necessity for distinguishing between platelet-poor and platelet-rich plasma when performing the test.

Positive results in the heparin assay test must be considered when interpreting abnormal findings, if any, obtained with other clotting tests on the same plasma. Increased heparin activity may be responsible for a prolonged prothrombin time and may invalidate the prothrombin consumption test.

Measurement of Fibrinogen by a Rapid Method (Adamis, 1960). *Principle.* This method determines the fibrinogen level of a test plasma by applying the "prothrombin" test, to standard defibrinated plasma to which the test plasma is added in fixed proportions. Defibrinated plasma requires

REACTANTS	CLOTTING MIXTURES (IN ML.)					
Normal plasma (platelet-poor)	0.2	0.2	0.2	—	—	—
Test plasma (platelet-poor)	—	—	—	0.2	0.2	0.2
Protamine sulfate (0.5% in saline)	—	0.01	—	—	0.01	—
Toluidine blue (0.1% in distilled H₂O)	—	—	0.01	—	—	0.01
Dilute thrombin (10 units per ml.)	0.1	0.1	0.1	0.1	0.1	0.1
Clotting times (seconds) (examples)	12	10	10	25	13	12

Since, in this experiment, the prolonged TT of the test plasma (25 seconds) was fully "corrected" by the antiheparin agents, the presence of heparin-like activity has been established. In order to estimate the heparin titer in a patient's blood, normal plasma containing known concentrations of heparin may be substituted for the test plasma in the clotting system. By plotting the observed clotting times against these heparin concentrations, a curve is obtained that affords estimation of the heparin level in the test plasma (Fig. 6–6).

The heparinized normal plasma samples

*For automatic recording of end point, see p. 347 and Figure 6–5.

an outside source of fibrinogen in order to clot when mixed with tissue thromboplastin and calcium; hence, the fibrinogen concentration of the added test plasma determines the clotting time, the latter being inversely proportional to the concentration.

Equipment. Same as for prothrombin and thrombin time tests, plus 0.02 M CaCl₂; imidazole buffer, pH 7.2, prepared by mixing 18.6 ml. of 0.1 N HCl (pH = 1.08) and 25 ml. of 0.2 M imidazole solution (1.36 gm. dissolved in distilled water to a total volume of 100 ml.); and defibrinated plasma (substrate reagent), which is prepared as follows:

A mixture of equal volumes of human

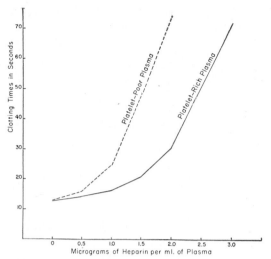

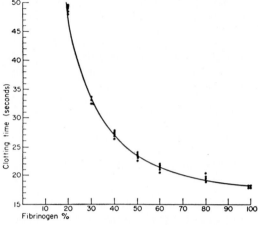

Figure 6–6. Effect of heparin level upon thrombin time of normal plasma. The two types of plasma were prepared in accordance with Table 6–9. The thrombin reagent contained 10 units per ml. of saline.

Figure 6–7. Correlation of clotting times with plasma fibrinogen levels. Since 100 per cent fibrinogen equals 300 mg. per 100 ml., a clotting time of 20 seconds corresponds to 80 per cent fibrinogen or to 240 mg. per 100 ml.; a clotting time of 25 seconds, to about 45 per cent fibrinogen or to 135 mg. per 100 ml.; and so on. (From Adamis, D. M.: Rapid method for determination of plasma fibrinogen. Proc. Soc. Exper. Biol. & Med., *103*:107, 1960.)

and bovine plasma (citrated, platelet-poor) is defibrinated with thrombin, using 5 units in 0.1 ml. of saline per milliliter of plasma. After allowing it to stand 30 minutes at room temperature, the clotted plasma is filtered through gauze and again treated with thrombin, using 1 unit in 0.3 ml. of saline. After refiltering, the procedure is repeated twice to insure complete defibrination. The plasma, which contains optimal concentrations of prothrombin and accessory factors (V, VII, and X), remains at room temperature for another two hours for inactivation of thrombin. When it is then kept at −20° C. in stoppered test tubes, this reagent is stable for at least eight months. It is stable indefinitely if lyophilized and kept at 4° C. in small aliquots, being reconstituted to the original volume of the plasma with distilled water when a test is to be done.

Procedure. Oxalated test plasma is adsorbed with BaSO$_4$ (50 mg. per ml.) for five minutes and centrifuged rapidly for another five minutes. A fivefold dilution of the supernatant with the buffer is used in the test, 0.1 ml. being mixed with equal volumes of defibrinated plasma, thromboplastin, and calcium and the clotting time recorded. Only clotting values between 50 and 20 seconds should be considered, since the accuracy of the method is best in that range (standard error = ± 1.9 seconds). With clotting times below or above this range, higher or lower dilutions, respectively, with buffer must be prepared and used in the test.

Computation of the fibrinogen concentration of a test plasma is made using a standard curve prepared by plotting clotting times against fibrinogen values secured on aliquots of the same respective plasma samples by means of a standard chemical method (Fig. 6–7). (For another rapid and even simpler method of estimating fibrinogen applicable chiefly to normal and increased concentrations, see p. 354.)

TESTS FOR PHASE II OF COAGULATION

One-stage Prothrombin Time (Quick) (Plasma Thromboplastin Time*). *Principle.* The addition of tissue (brain) thromboplastin† to recalcified (citrated or oxalated) or native plasma under standard conditions normally results in a clotting time that, for the particular thromboplastin reagent used, is well reproducible within a narrow range. The term "prothrombin time" was coined when the notion was prevalent that prothrombin was the only plasma constituent whose interaction with tissue thromboplastin and calcium resulted in thrombin. Hence, the clotting time appeared to be a direct measure of prothrombin in the absence of any fibrinogen deficiency: the less prothrombin, the longer the "prothrombin time." It was learned subsequently that aside

* This description is suggested in accord with similar terms, i.e., calcium time, thrombin time.

† A commercially available, dependable brain thromboplastin preparation may be used. The most consistent results are obtained with acetone-dehydrated rabbit (or human) brain prepared and stored in accordance with Quick's technique.

from factors II (prothrombin) and I (fibrinogen), both a "labile" and a "stable" factor were required for normal results of the test. This discovery was, in part, based on mixing experiments involving different plasmas yielding abnormally long prothrombin times. Aged (oxalated) plasma (deficient in factor V) and freshly drawn plasma from a patient treated with bishydroxycoumarin (deficient in stable factor) were found to "correct" each other's clotting defect. More recent studies of patients with congenital stable factor deficiency resulted in the realization that they had to be divided into two qualitatively different groups and that the stable factor included at least two separate clotting agents—factors VII (proconvertin) and X (Stuart factor).

Equipment. Same as for the calcium time, without the siliconized glassware.

Procedure. A 0.1 ml. sample of oxalated or citrated plasma and 0.1 ml. of thromboplastin (preincubated at 37° C.) are placed in a 13 × 100 mm. test tube and incubated in the 37° C. water bath for a few seconds; then 0.02 M CaCl₂ (also prewarmed) is forcibly blown into the tube, the stopwatch clicked, and the tube placed in the bath and shaken lightly. A few seconds before clotting is expected, the tube is removed from the bath, held against a distant light source, and tilted slightly up and down until the incipient web of fibrin is seen, denoting the endpoint.* *Normal range* (with Difco thromboplastin): 12 to 14 seconds.

* The Clot Timer provides automatic recording of the endpoint (Fig. 6–4).

The clotting time can become shorter and decrease to eight seconds in citrated (not oxalated) plasma stored in a nonsiliconized glass tube at refrigerator temperature for one or a few days. This phenomenon has been explained by Quick as the result of conversion of inactive prothrombin (prothrombinogen) to active prothrombin and has been attributed by others to activation of factor VII (proconvertin).

Results are reliable only if the test is done within 60 minutes on plasma that has been kept at room temperature. Further delay in testing requires storage close to 0° C. or freezing to avoid loss of factor V (labile factor).

A prolonged prothrombin time may be expressed in terms of concentration of "prothrombin" or "prothrombin activity" by preparing various control plasma dilutions and determining their respective prothrombin times (analogous to the heparin assay curve; see p. 352). As diluent, either saline or deprothrombinized (adsorbed) plasma may be used, but clotting times differ with plasma concentrations less than 50 per cent, being more prolonged in the saline than in the adsorbed-plasma series (Table 6–10, Fig. 6–8). Thus, a clotting time of 19 seconds in a test plasma may be interpreted as representing 30 to 35 per cent prothrombin activity from the saline dilutions but only 10 per cent on the basis of adsorbed plasma dilutions. Undoubtedly the longer clotting times observed with saline dilutions stem from the attendant reduction in concentration of factors V and I,

Figure 6–8. Human prothrombin time curve. This curve is based on use of rabbit brain thromboplastin prepared in accordance with Quick's directions. Plasma dilutions are made with saline.

Commercial preparations of thromboplastin do not yield a clotting time of 12 seconds with undiluted normal plasma so consistently as Quick's preparation. Clotting times of 13 or 14 seconds or longer require plotting of curves more or less parallel with the one shown but situated above it on the graph. The conventional (therapeutic) margin of safety is then raised accordingly, always, however, coinciding with the range of 100—20 per cent of "prothrombin" concentration. (Reproduced with the author's permission from Quick, A. J.: Hemorrhagic Diseases. Philadelphia, Lea & Febiger, 1957.)

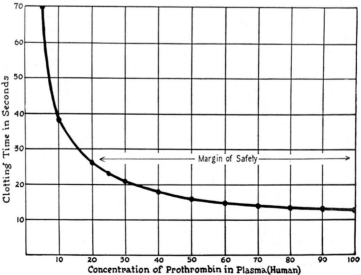

Table 6–10. Effect of Diluting Oxalated Plasma with Saline and with Adsorbed Plasma on One-stage Prothrombin Time in Humans*

CONCENTRATION OF PLASMA IN PER CENT (= PER CENT "PROTHROMBIN" ACTIVITY)		CLOTTING ("PROTHROMBIN") TIME IN SECONDS
SALINE	ADSORBED PLASMA	
100	100–50	12
—	40	12½
70	—	13
—	30	13½
60	—	14
50	—	15
—	20	16
40	—	17
35	—	18
—	10	19
30	—	19½
25	—	21–22
20	—	24–26
10	—	37–40
5	—	55–65

* Modified from Quick, A. J.: Hemorrhagic Diseases, Philadelphia, Lea & Febiger, 1957, Table 24, page 383.

which make this system less specific for the vitamin K-sensitive factors (II, VII, and X) than the adsorbed plasma technique. Hence, for purposes of monitoring oral anticoagulant therapy (which may depress factor VII alone, or VII and II, or the entire complex), the adsorbed plasma technique would seem to be preferable.

For practical purposes, reporting the prothrombin time in seconds is sufficient, provided the control result is also furnished, for instance, 25 seconds (control: 12 seconds). If per cent "prothrombin" activity is also to be stated, the dilution method used must be reported. The conventional aim of oral anticoagulant therapy is prolongation of the prothrombin time two to two and one half times the pretreatment level (or the control value). Hence, with a control of 12 seconds, a patient value of less than 24 seconds would denote inadequate anticoagulation, while a clotting time greater than 30 seconds may be regarded as indicative of an excessive bleeding tendency.

Combined Estimation of Prothrombin Time and of Fibrinogen by Photoelectric Method. *Principle.* In this modification of the method previously described, a photoelectric instrument is substituted for the naked eye to detect incipient fibrin formation. At the same time, the total amount of fibrin formed is estimated on the basis of the optical density of the clot (Volk *et al.*, 1952).

Equipment. Same as for prothrombin time, plus Coleman Spectrophotometer, Model 6A; Micro-adapter*; microcuvets, 6 × 75 mm.*; and 0.1 ml. pipets with narrow tip* or tuberculin syringe with small-gauge needle.

Procedure. A 0.1 ml. sample of *citrated*† plasma and 0.1 ml. of thromboplastin (Difco) are placed in a cuvet at 37° C. for three minutes. At the same time as 0.1 ml. of $CaCl_2$ is swiftly blown into the cuvet, a stopwatch is started and the optical density of the cuvet is recorded in the photometer at wave length 500 mμ.

As soon as movement of the light beam is noted on the density scale to the left, the stopwatch is stopped; this is the prothrombin *time*. The *distance* the beam travels on the scale until it comes to a standstill denotes completion of clotting. The difference between final and initial optical densities times 100 represents the "clot density" (d): Fibrinogen (mg. per 100 ml.) = 18d + 120 (=empirical formula).

The prothrombin time values furnished by this method tend to be somewhat shorter (0.5 second) than with the visual technique. The method lends itself to routine work in a hospital laboratory and may be superior to the visual technique because of the greater objectivity of the results. The simultaneous estimate of fibrinogen provides useful information, especially with marked increase of fibrinogen, as is commonly found in acute myocardial infarction and active rheumatic fever. The increased level of fibrinogen has been found to be a more dependable measure of clinical progress than the sedimentation rate. Estimation of a decrease in fibrinogen with this method is limited to levels exceeding 120 mg. per 100 ml., since in the formula just given a clot density of 0 would yield a fibrinogen value of 120.

The normalcy of results of the prothrombin time depends upon adequate concentrations of four plasma clotting factors, II, V, VII, and X, aside from a normal fibrinogen level and absence of a circulating anticoagulant active in the second or third stage of clotting. Next to the WBCT, this test, because of its simplicity and good reproducibility, is probably the most widely used

* Wilkens-Anderson Company, Chicago, Illinois.
† Oxalated plasma cannot be used because its greater turbidity obscures changes in optical density caused by clotting.

Table 6–11. Clinical Disorders and Deficiency of Clotting Factors Resulting in Prolonged Prothrombin Time

DISORDERS	DEFICIENCY OF PLASMA FACTORS				
	I§	V§	II	VII‖	X‖
Congenital					
Hemorrhagic disease of newborn*	−	−	+	++	+
Hereditary disorders (with single defects) persisting beyond early infancy	+	+	+	+	+
Acquired					
Vitamin K deficiency*					
Early or mild	−	−	−	++	−
Advanced	−	−	+	++	+
Hepatocellular disease	±	+	+	++	±
Hematopoietic disorders					
Leukemia	±	+	+	+	±
Pernicious or myelophthisic anemias	±	+	+	+	±
Polycythemia	+	−	+	+	−
Thrombocytopenia	−	−	+	+	−
Uremia	−	−	+	+	−

+ May occur.

++ Occurs frequently.

± Occurs rarely (advanced or severe cases only).

− Usually does not occur.

* Vitamin K deficiency:

  1. Deficient synthesis (newborn).

  2. Deficient intestinal absorption: malabsorption syndrome; absence or reduction of bile flow into intestine due to either hepatocellular or biliary tract disease; interference with vitamin synthesis in gut due to change in bacterial flora (antimicrobial treatment).

  3. Deficient utilization by liver cells: hepatocellular disease.

  4. Vitamin K antagonists.

§ Present in BaSO₄ adsorbed plasma; absent from aged serum.

‖ Present in aged serum, absent from BaSO₄ adsorbed plasma but present with factor II in the BaSO₄ eluate from this plasma ("serum factors").

clotting procedure; differential analysis of an abnormal result is attempted only in the exceptional laboratory or in specific cases. Yet determination of anticoagulant activity and recognition of the type of clotting factor deficiency present may often contribute to clinical diagnosis and be important in treatment (Table 6–11). Thus, in jaundice, factor V deficiency eliminates avitaminosis K as the sole cause of the prolonged "prothrombin time" and of bleeding, if present, and indicates hepatocellular disease; parenteral administration of the vitamin cannot be expected to correct the defect. Similarly, in hemorrhagic disease of the newborn, factor V deficiency suggests either liver disease or a congenital disorder, while confinement of the abnormality to "serum" factors strongly implicates vitamin K deficiency and points to the corrective therapy. In general, rational treatment of a bleeding disorder manifesting itself in a prolonged prothrombin time depends upon the specific defect present, since factor V is uninfluenced by vitamin K treatment and

may be insufficiently supplied (because of its instability) when transfusion of stored blood is considered. Hence, at the least, distinction between "plasma" (V) and "serum" (VII and X) deficiency should be made and, indeed, can be accomplished with simple modifications of the basic test procedure, outlined in Table 6–12.

Oral anticoagulants are known to depress factor VII readily and effectively within 24 hours, prothrombin and Stuart factor following suit within a few days and PTC only after two or more weeks of exposure. The need for differential analysis of the prolonged prothrombin time induced by coumarin derivatives is strongly suggested by experimental evidence concerning the influence of a reduced "prothrombin complex" upon intravascular clotting and a clinical correlation of hemorrhagic and thromboembolism with individual factor deficiency. Depression of factor VII alone appears to furnish little assurance, if any, against vascular thrombosis. On the other hand, hemorrhagic complications of coumarin treatment are more prone to occur when factors other than VII are decreased. Therefore, it seems to suffice no longer to monitor such treatment with a prothrombin time and to try to keep it within two and two and one-half times the normal, as is ordinarily the custom. The aim of treatment must be

Table 6–12. Sequence of Analytic Steps in Differential Diagnosis of an Abnormal One-stage "Prothrombin" Test

SEQUENCE OF STEPS	"REAGENT"	INTERPRETATION		
		FULL CORRECTION	PARTIAL CORRECTION	NO CORRECTION
1	OP	Deficiency of II, V or SF Next step: 2	Deficiency of I or weak C A Next step: CaT, TT	C A Next step: CaT, TT
2	AdP	Deficiency of V Next step: 2a (confirmation)	Deficiency of V and other factor(s). Next: 3, 2a (confirmation)	No deficiency of V Next: 3, 2a (confirmation)
3	AgS	Deficiency of SF Next: 3a, b	Deficiency of SF and II or V. Next: 3a, b; 4	No deficiency of SF Deficiency of II Next: 4 (confirmation)
4	AdP + AgS	Deficiency of V or SF No deficiency of II	Deficiency of V or SF Deficiency of II	No deficiency of V or SF Deficiency of II
2a	AgP	No deficiency of V	Deficiency of V (in part)	Deficiency of V
3a	CS	Deficiency of X	Deficiency of X (in part)	No deficiency of X
3b	VV	Deficiency of VII	Deficiency of VII (in part)	No deficiency of VII

OP, AdP, AgS, AgP, CS. See Table 6–7, legend. Roman numerals refer to plasma clotting factors (Tables 6–4 and 6–6). Bovine, or preferably rabbit, AdP should be used in this test because their factor V activity is greater than that of human plasma (2 or 50 times, respectively).

SF   Stable factor: includes both factors VII and X.
CA   Circulating anticoagulant.
TT   Thrombin time.
CaT   Calcium clotting time.

VV A solution of 5 mcg. of Russell's viper venom (Stypven) per ml. of saline (1 to 200,000), containing either cephalin or Inosithin (see p. 359): The contents of one vial of the venom, i.e., 0.5 mg., is dissolved in saline and transferred quantitatively to a 50 ml. volumetric flask, which is then filled with saline to the mark (1 to 100,000). A 0.3 per cent suspension of Inosithin in saline is prepared separately. Mixing equal parts of the two reagents furnishes VV. (Each of the three reagents may be kept in small aliquots at −20° C. for prolonged periods without loss of activity; however, once thawed, viper venom should not be refrozen but discarded.) For preparation of cephalin, see p. 358 (Rodman *et al.*, 1958).

When a prolonged prothrombin time is to be analyzed to determine the nature of the defect, the sequence of steps indicated in this table should be followed. Usual reaction mixture:

Control or test plasma	0.10 ml.
Saline or "reagent" (other than VV)	0.01 ml.
Thromboplastin (brain extract)	0.10 ml.
0.02 M CaCl₂	0.10 ml.
Total volume	0.31 ml.

In step 4, 0.01 ml. of each reagent (AdP and AgS) is added, resulting in a final volume of 0.32 ml. Each corrective procedure is to be applied to both test plasma and control plasma for optimal standardization and interpretation of results. This is necessary because some shortening (one-half to one second) of the clotting time may occur when a "reagent" is added to the control plasma, especially in the case of AgS, which normally contains activated factor VII (convertin). Control plasma is available commercially in vials or ampules or may be prepared in large batches as a pool of plasma from ten or more apparently "normal" subjects, divided into small aliquots, and either frozen or lyophilized and kept cold for prolonged storage. Citrated plasma has greater stability than oxalated plasma. Abnormal control plasma from subjects with known isolated clotting defects, i.e., with deficiency of II, V, VII, or X, is very desirable for better standardization but not readily available.

From the table, it is apparent that step 1 is required only if CA and a deficiency of I (fibrinogen) have not previously been ruled out (CaT, TT), while step 2 should be taken only after these two types of defect have been excluded. In the event of partial correction, step 1 should be repeated, using equal parts of test plasma and OP (0.05 + 0.05 ml.) to rule out *marked* deficiency of factors. Complete correction now denotes the latter, especially of I (fibrinogen), while incomplete correction signifies a weak CA.

In the course of oral anticoagulant therapy of patients who initially had a normal prothrombin time, the routine differential analysis of the iatrogenic defect involves steps 3 and 3b only. Full correction with AgS means SF deficiency without prothrombin deficiency; partial correction, with such deficiency; full correction in the VV test confines the deficiency to factor VII; partial correction denotes associated deficiency of X. Deficiency of II (prothrombin) may, in addition, be tested directly by TAMe assay (Mindrum and Glueck,

1959) or by the two-stage method (Ware and Seegers, 1949). Desirable substitute "reagents":

For AdP + AgS (step 4):	OP from a patient with congenital II deficiency
For AgP:	OP from a patient with congenital V deficiency
For CS:	AgS from a patient with congenital VII deficiency
For VV:	AgS from a patient with congenital X deficiency

In step 3b (VV test), VV takes the place of thromboplastin in the reaction mixture:

Control or test plasma	0.1 ml.
VV	0.1 ml.
CaCl₂	0.1 ml.
Total volume	0.3 ml.

Viper venom provides factor VII activity. Hence, in plasma with isolated factor VII deficiency, it yields a normal clotting time, whereas brain extract results in a prolonged clotting time. On the other hand, because of the lack of a lipoid factor, which is contained in brain extract, viper venom furnishes longer clotting times in lipid-poor than in lipemic plasma. This source of error is eliminated by saturating the VV reagent with "lipid," as described previously. The prothrombin test system with the VV reagent is thus sensitive to a deficiency of II, V, or X. If V (proaccelerin) deficiency has been ruled out in step 2, and II (prothrombin) deficiency in step 3, a prolonged VV clotting time denotes deficiency of X (Stuart factor).

The test can be modified so that it will become specific for (a) combined II and X deficiency or (b) X deficiency alone by supplying (a) factor V or (b) factors V and II in the reaction mixture. For this purpose, the test or control plasma is diluted with nine parts of adsorbed beef plasma rich in factor V:

1:10 diluted plasma	0.1 ml.
VV	0.1 ml.
CaCl₂	0.1 ml.

Ad (a) If adsorption is carried out in the usual manner with BaSO₄ or Al(OH)₃, the clotting time is influenced by changes in either factor II or X (normal: 20 to 22 seconds). Ad (b) Adsorption of the beef plasma carried out by a special procedure so as to result in removal of stable factors VII and X, but retention of much of its prothrombin content furnishes a test system that is sensitive only to X (Stuart factor) deficiency (Sise *et al.*, 1958).

The dilute system referred to under (a) is preferable to the reaction mixture with undiluted test plasma because of the factor VII potency of the VV reagent, which tends to overshadow deficiency of either II or X and to provide borderline results difficult to interpret. Thus, a patient clotting time of 12 seconds with a control time of 11 seconds may be regarded as a variant within the normal range; in the dilute system, the difference may be magnified to three or more seconds and become diagnostically valid. As a general rule, only clotting time differences of more than one second (in the relatively crude tests using undiluted test or control plasma) are to be interpreted as significant and exceeding the range of technical error. In the diluted (VV) system, a clotting time difference of three or more seconds is usually diagnostically significant. For greater precision and for quantitative assay of individual clotting factors, dilute test systems are altogether preferable. They are, however, more complex and are not needed for routine clinical purposes.

356

depression of prothrombin, and perhaps even of factor IX (PTC), sufficient to interfere with the thrombotic tendency but not severe enough to give rise to spontaneous bleeding. The optimal therapeutic levels of prothrombin and of PTC have not been established. This information will become available only if estimation of the "serum" factors and of prothrombin can be done more routinely (as indicated in Table 6–12).

It should be clearly recognized that a prothrombin time of 25 seconds, for example, found in three different patients who are treated with a coumarin derivative may, upon differential analysis, turn out to be due to factor VII depression alone in one instance (complete correction with aged serum and with Russell's viper venom; no correction with coumarin serum; Table 6–12); to VII and II deficiency in the second case (partial correction with aged serum and venom; none with coumarin serum); and to VII, II, and X in the third instance (partial correction with any of these; full correction with aged plasma). The last two cases may also have PTC or PTA depression, i.e., an acquired hemophilia, which, however, cannot be recognized with this technique. Although patient three probably is least likely to develop a thrombotic complication, he is most likely to develop bleeding. Such information is of clinical importance (Table 6–12).

TESTS FOR PHASE I OF COAGULATION

For evaluation of *phase I* of the clotting mechanism, namely, *intrinsic thromboplastin formation*, at least three practical methods are available: the prothrombin consumption test, the partial thromboplastin time, and the thromboplastin generation test (TGT). The partial thromboplastin time would, because of its simplicity in technique, be the screening method of choice were it not for the fact that the reagent is not commercially available but must be "home made." Instability in potency of the reagent has been encountered when it is stored at the recommended temperature of −20° C., as well as differences in reproducibility of results from one batch of brain extract to the next. Therefore, this test does not lend itself to routine use until a dependable reagent becomes generally available.

The test system is that of the prothrombin time, with cephalin (an ether extract of acetone-treated brain) and calcium acting upon platelet-poor plasma. The mean clotting time of normal plasmas, tested under standard conditions, is 76 seconds with a standard deviation of ± 13 (Rodman *et al.*, 1958).

Prothrombin Consumption Test (Serum Prothrombin Time). *Principle.* This test provides a measure of the amount of prothrombin remaining in the serum after the blood or plasma has clotted under standard conditions.

The test consists of two successive steps:

(1) clotting of freshly drawn blood or of native plasma, resulting in separation of serum, and (2) transfer of that serum to another clotting system for estimation of the serum prothrombin. This system is a modified prothrombin time performed on "deprothrombinized" rabbit plasma, prothrombin being supplied by the serum (from step 1). Since this is the only source of prothrombin in the system and the only variable, the clotting time in step 2 is dependent upon the serum prothrombin concentration. The latter, in turn, represents the balance between the original total plasma prothrombin and that portion of prothrombin which interacted with intrinsic thromboplastin in the process of clotting (step 1). The amount of thromboplastin generated determines the amount of prothrombin consumed during the same period. With the normal rate of intrinsic thromboplastin generation, most of the preformed prothrombin is consumed, i.e., converted into thrombin, and the small residual quantity of serum prothrombin results in a long plasma prothrombin time. A slow rate of intrinsic thromboplastin formation caused by defect in either the platelets or one of the prothromboplastins, or by the presence of inhibitory activity, is associated with an increased quantity of residual serum prothrombin and, accordingly, with a short clotting time in step 2. If this occurs, the test system may be used for differential analysis to determine the cause of the abnormality: platelet defect, plasma factor deficiency, or circulating anticoagulant (Table 6–13).

Equipment. Same as for prothrombin time, plus adsorbed rabbit plasma (stored in small aliquots—0.5 to 1.0 ml.—at −20° C.).

Procedure. Step 1: One milliliter of blood, collected by the two-syringe technique and placed in a small glass tube, is incubated at 37° C. From the moment a firm clot has formed (= clotting time), incubation is continued for exactly one hour. This incubation is interrupted after 15 minutes for rapid centrifugation of the blood for one to two minutes in order to separate the clot from the serum and to keep the nascent thrombin from being adsorbed to and inactivated by fibrin and thus to facilitate the autocatalytic reaction.

Step 2: At the end of the one-hour incubation period, the serum is transferred and 0.1 ml. is added to a mixture of rabbit plasma, tissue thromboplastin, and 0.02 M $CaCl_2$, contained and incubated in a small glass tube. The volume of each of the four

Table 6–13. Differential Analysis of Abnormal Prothrombin Consumption Test

REAGENTS	INTERPRETATION	
	FULL CORRECTION	NO CORRECTION
	No CA	CA
OP	Def. of platelets or factor(s)	
TP(60)	Def. of platelets	No def. of platelets Def. of factor(s)
AdP	Def. of V, VIII, PTA, or HF	No def. of V, VIII PTA, or HF
AgS	Def. of IX, X, PTA, or HF	No def. of IX, X, PTA, or HF

OP, AdP, AgS, CA. See Table 6–12, legend
TP(60) Tissue thromboplastin (rabbit brain extract) heated to 60° C. for 20 minutes
Def. Deficiency

Performance of Test:

Step 1
  Basic Test:
    Patient's blood or plasma* 1.0 ml.
    0.85% saline 0.1 ml.
  Correction Test:
    Patient's blood or plasma* 1.0 ml.
    Reagent 0.1 ml.

Incubate in plain glass tube for one hour; then perform prothrombin consumption test (step 2).†
  Note: When TP(60) is the correcting reagent, 0.05 ml. is used together with 0.05 ml. of saline.‡ A 5 per cent inosithin emulsion or a suspension of washed normal platelets in saline—about 20 x 10^5 per cu. mm.—may be substituted for TP(60) in 0.1 ml. volumes (see TGT procedure, p. 359). In the interest of expediency and convenience, all "corrective" tests are set up simultaneously if the initial serum prothrombin time has either been found or is expected to give an abnormal result. Five tubes are prepared for step 1, containing, respectively, 0.1 ml. of saline (control), OP, AdP, AgS, and TP(60)-saline mixture (see previous note); 1 ml. of fresh blood (or native plasma) is added to each tube, followed by incubating, rimming, centrifuging, and reincubating, as described in the text. At the end of one hour's incubation, all tubes are placed promptly in ice water to slow down the continuous process of conversion of prothrombin in each and to insure the validity of results in step 2, which is to follow without delay.

Step 2
  a. Serum (from step 1)   0.1 ml.
    Adsorbed (rabbit) plasma†   0.1 ml.
    Thromboplastin (brain extract)   0.1 ml.
    0.02 M CaCl₂   0.1 ml.
    Total volume   0.4 ml.

  b. Serum (from step 1)   0.1 ml.
    Adsorbed plasma†   0.1 ml.
    Normal aged serum   0.05 ml.
    Thromboplastin   0.1 ml.
    0.02 M CaCl₂   0.1 ml.
    Total volume   0.45 ml.

Ad (a) Incubate in 37° C. bath for one minute before adding CaCl₂; then blow the latter solution in, start stopwatch, and measure time required until first appearance of fibrin formation. A clotting time of less than 16 seconds with use of adsorbed rabbit plasma, or 20 seconds with adsorbed human plasma, is considered abnormal (= deficient prothrombin consumption).

Ad (b) If the routine prothrombin time was distinctly prolonged (due to deficiency of factor II, VII, or X), the prothrombin consumption test may be falsely negative (longer than 16 or 20 seconds, respectively) in spite of an associated prothromboplastin defect (factors VIII, IX, X, PTA). In such a case, step 2 should be repeated with the addition of normal aged serum in order to make up for deficiency of factor VII or X in the patient's serum.

The aged serum will cause considerable shortening of the clotting time in step 2 if deficiency of either factor VII or X, or both, is present and will result in an abnormally short clotting time (less than 16 or 20 seconds, depending on the type of adsorbed plasma used) if significant deficiency of a prothromboplastin or of platelets exists.

ingredients is 0.1 ml. The time required for fibrin to form is measured as described for the prothrombin time (p. 352). *Normal:* > 16 seconds (usually 17 to 45).

The test can be made more sensitive by using platelet-rich native plasma instead of whole blood (in the first step). The increased incidence of abnormal results with this modification may be attributed to the "buffer action" of the red blood cells, which, according to Quick, contain activated platelet thromboplastin factor and may thereby contribute to thromboplastin generation in the whole blood system (see Fig. 6–1).

Not infrequently the prothrombin consumption test yields a normal or borderline result with mild intrinsic thromboplastin defects, especially in the case of functional platelet deficiency and of PTA hemophilia. Therefore, if suspicion of such an abnormality is justified on clinical grounds or on the basis of other laboratory evidence, e.g., morphologic appearance of platelets, the thromboplastin generation test is applicable. This test is also preferred in the event of an abnormal prothrombin test and the likelihood of multiple hemostatic deficiencies.

Thromboplastin Generation Test (Biggs and Macfarlane, 1957; Miale, 1958). *Principle.* In this procedure, again, the basic system of the one-stage "prothrombin" test is utilized. However, the thromboplastin added to this system is not tissue (brain) extract but intrinsic (blood) thromboplastin formed by the interaction of three separate fractions of the test person's blood: platelets, adsorbed plasma, and serum (Fig. 6–10). This thromboplastic activity is tested at fixed time intervals on fresh, platelet-poor plasma (substrate). If the latter contains adequate concentrations of prothrombin and fibrinogen, a minimal clotting time of less than 12 seconds is usually observed within six (usually two to four) minutes of incubating the three fractions mentioned (in fixed dilutions) with calcium, indicating that this thromboplastin (prothrombin converting) activity is more potent than activated tissue thromboplastin. A minimal clotting time (MCT) exceeding 12 seconds or one that is shorter but delayed beyond

---

* Platelet-rich, native supernatant plasma of fresh blood collected with strict silicone (two-syringe) technique, kept in ice bath, and cold-centrifuged at low speed for ten minutes (see Table 6–9). Volumes in the test may be doubled for greater precision in pipetting when performing step 2.

† Rabbit plasma is required for a normal clotting time of 16 seconds or longer. With use of human plasma, containing far less factor V activity and being therefore less reliable, a clotting time of less than 20 seconds is usually abnormal.

‡ TP(60) must be tested before use to ascertain loss of its holothromboplastic activity (demonstration of ineffectiveness in plasma prothrombin time).

six minutes of incubation denotes a deficiency in thromboplastin generation.

By substituting one or two of the patient's three blood fractions with normal fractions and combining with either the patient's or a control person's substrate (platelet-poor plasma), the specific defect or defects can usually be determined, as shown in Table 6–14, and anticoagulants detected and identified as to site or mode of action. The test system also affords quantitation of the existing defect. Use of plasma or serum from patients with a known single clotting defect, if available, may add to the reliability of results and the expediency of the test. However, the procedure is sufficiently time-consuming to be employed only when other, simpler tests fail to furnish a satisfactory diagnosis. The preparation of the various blood fractions required for the test, especially the repeated washing and centrifuging of platelets, takes several hours. If the platelets can be absolved from any responsibility for poor thromboplastin generation, an extract of brain or soybean may be used instead with considerable saving of time and effort.*

Equipment. Same as for the calcium clotting time and the one-stage prothrombin test, but the molarity of $CaCl_2$ is 0.025; plus one additional stopwatch; microscope and ancillary facilities for platelet counting; wooden applicators; and (preferably, though not essential) adsorbed oxalated plasma from a hemophilia A patient and serum from a hemophilia B patient. The AHF-deficient plasma may be stored at −20° C. in aliquots of 0.2 to 0.5 ml. contained in small siliconized tubes for at least six months without significant loss of activity (factors V, PTA, and HF). PTC-deficient serum (providing factors X, PTA, and HF) may be stored safely under the same conditions in uncoated tubes.

Collection of blood and preparation of blood fractions. With the two-syringe technique, blood is collected into three tubes (or multiples thereof, as desired). From the first syringe, 3 or more ml. is placed in a plain glass tube containing two to three glass beads; from the second, silicone-

coated syringe, 4.5 ml. is added to each of two tubes, one (coated) containing 0.5 ml. of sodium citrate and the other, which may or may not be coated, containing 0.5 ml. of sodium oxalate (Table 6–9, Fig. 6–9).† Each of the three tubes is quickly stoppered or covered with wax paper and repeatedly inverted to insure thorough clotting in tube 1 and to avoid any clotting in tubes 2 and 3 before the blood is well mixed with anticoagulant.

The first tube is incubated at 37° C. for two hours to inactivate residual prothrombin and any traces of thrombin; the serum harvested after routine centrifuging is diluted tenfold with saline for use in the test.

By means of differential centrifugation (Table 6–9), the precooled citrate tube furnishes both substrate (platelet-poor plasma) and the platelet suspension. After initial centrifuging of the citrated blood, the supernatant platelet-rich plasma (PRP) is transferred into a silicone-coated, graduated centrifuge tube, its volume recorded, and the platelets counted. Following the subsequent rapid centrifugation, the supernatant platelet-poor plasma (PPP) is transferred to another coated tube and kept at 0 to 4° C. for use as undiluted substrate in the test. The platelets packed in the bottom of the tube ("platelet button") are washed twice with several milliliters of saline. After the saline from the second washing has been poured off, it is replaced with a volume of saline adjusted (on the basis of the plasma platelet count) to provide a suspension of 250,000 platelets per cu. mm. For example, if 2 ml. of available PRP contained 300,000 platelets per cu. mm., then the volume of saline to be added to the platelet button is $\frac{300,000}{250,000} \times 2 = 2.4$ ml. In general the volume of saline = $\frac{\text{No. platelets in PRP}}{250,000} \times$ ml. PRP.

For each of these platelet suspensions, gentle but thorough stirring is required, using wooden applicator sticks or thin, silicone-coated glass rods.

Plasma secured from the oxalated blood sample by cold centrifuging is adsorbed with $BaSO_4$ (Table 6–7, legend) for removal of factors II, IX, and X (factor VII is also removed but plays no part in thromboplastin generation or in prothrombin conversion with intrinsic thromboplastin). The prothrombin time of this adsorbed plasma

---

* Normal blood fractions (platelet reagent, adsorbed plasma, serum, and substrate) are available commercially (TGTR, Warner-Chilcott, Inc.). The platelet reagent consists of a chloroform extract of brain. Each batch should be tested for potency before use in control tests. Another commercial product, which may be used instead of normal platelets, is Inosithin, an alcohol-insoluble extract of soybean used as a 0.02 per cent saline suspension (Associated Concentrates, Long Island, New York) (Hyun *et al.*, 1960).

† Oxalated plasma may also be secured from the first syringe.

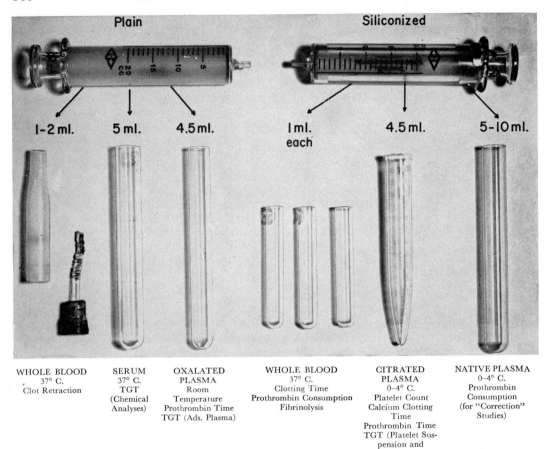

Figure 6–9. Glassware used in collecting blood for complete evaluation of clotting mechanism (coagulation profile). *TGT*—thromboplastin generation test; *Ads.*—BaSO$_4$-adsorbed plasma.

should be no less than five minutes. A five-fold dilution with saline, kept at 0 to 4° C., is used in the test.

The contents of each blood fraction in clotting factors contributing to results of the test are listed in Figure 6–10. As soon as the fractions (platelet suspension, serum, adsorbed plasma, and substrate) are ready, the test may be performed, preferably the same day. The fractions usually retain their respective activity when stored as follows: platelets, at 0–4° C., but not frozen, for one to two days; serum, at 0 to 4° C., for at least two weeks; adsorbed plasma, frozen in a siliconized tube, for one week; substrate, frozen in a siliconized tube, for several weeks.

Performance of test. As illustrated in Figure 6–10, equal volumes (usually 0.3 ml.) of serum (diluted 1 to 10), adsorbed plasma (1 to 5), and platelet suspension (250,000 per cu. mm.) are mixed in an uncoated tube (15 × 100 mm.), which is placed in a 37° C. water bath. Promptly thereafter, an equal volume of 0.025 M CaCl$_2$ is added, the tube shaken briefly, and stopwatch No. 1 started. Exactly one minute later, 0.1 ml. of this incubation mixture and 0.1 ml. of the CaCl$_2$ solution are transferred to the first of eight smaller tubes (8 × 75 mm.) previously incubated for one to two minutes with 0.1 ml. of substrate (PPP) in each. As the mixture and calcium are blown simultaneously into the substrate, stopwatch No. 2 is started to serve in determining the clotting time in this tube, in accordance with the one-stage prothrombin test technique (p. 354). The same pro-

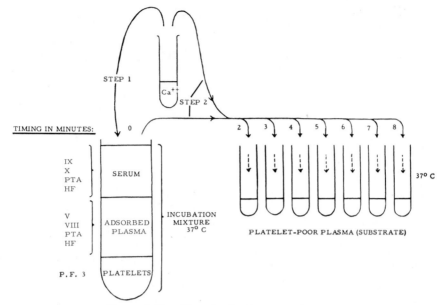

Figure 6–10. Thromboplastin generation test.

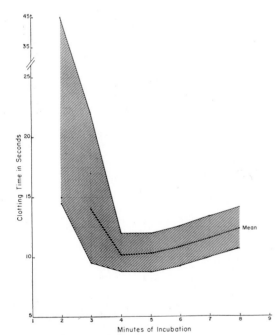

Figure 6–11. Thromboplastin generation test; normal range and mean.

cedure is carried out at 2, 3, 4, up to 8, minutes from the moment calcium was added to the incubation mixture. Clotting times are conveniently recorded as shown in Table 6–14.

A "normal run" should be done either before or promptly after the "patient run," especially if the latter gives an abnormal

result. If the control reagents yield an MCT of less than 12 seconds well before the seventh minute of incubation, they may be considered adequate (Fig. 6–11). A prolonged MCT observed with the patient's reagents, or a normal MCT reached after the sixth minute is indicative of poor thromboplastin formation. Such a result requires further analysis to determine which of the patient's blood fractions are responsible. As a matter of routine, each of the control fractions, except the substrate, is now replaced by a patient fraction in the control system and the results tabulated, followed by the opposite combination (confirmatory test); the respective patient reagent is substituted by the control reagent in the "patient run." As soon as any of these substitution "runs" appears to identify the defective patient reagent, the analysis may be terminated. Thus, if the patient's platelet suspension combined with control serum and plasma yields a prolonged MCT, and the inverse system (control platelets with patient's serum and plasma) yields a normal result, the patient has a functional platelet defect (thrombasthenia) and presumably neither a serum nor a plasma defect (Table 6–14, patient A).

If the patient's platelets in an otherwise adequate control system yield a borderline value (12 to 13 seconds), a suspension of 125,000 per cu. mm. may be prepared and tested; normal platelets will still furnish a MCT shorter than 12 seconds, while a low-

Table 6-14. Tabulation of Results of Thromboplastin Generation Test

REAGENTS		SOURCE OF REAGENTS																			
		PATIENT A			B				C				D				E				
(Incubation Mixture) Platelets (25 x 10⁴/cu. mm.)		N	P	N	N	N	N	N	N	N	N	N	N	N	N	N	N	N	N	N	N
Serum (1:10)		N	N	P	P	P	N	$\frac{P}{IX}$	N	P	N	N	P	N	P	P	P	P	N	P	$\frac{1P}{9N}$
Adsorbed plasma (1:5)		N	N	P	N	N	P	N	P	N	N	$\frac{P}{VIII}$	N	P	P	N	N	N	P	P	N
Substrate		N	N	N	N	N	N	N	N	N	N	N	N	N	N	N	N	N	N	N	N

CLOTTING TIMES IN SECONDS

MINUTES OF INCUBATION		PATIENT A			B				C				D				E				
2		19.4	45+	17.0	45+	45+	11.8	45+	45+	28.7	23.6	32.0	42.0	25.0	28.0	36.0	45+	45+	45+	45+	36.4
3		8.0	45+	35.0	45+	45+	9.8	45+	45+	29.6	11.8	30.5	30.0	14.6	17.2	28.2	45+	45+	45+	45+	25.6
4		8.0	39.8	30.0	45+	45+	10.7	45+	45+	28.8	11.6	29.0	25.0	10.4	11.6	25.4	45+	45+	45+	45+	14.2
5		7.8	27.0	27.0	45+	45+	11.0	45+	45+	28.2	11.8	27.6	22.0	11.2	10.8	20.2	45+	45+	45+	38.6	11.4
6		8.0	24.0	24.4	45+	29.0	13.2	35.5	45+	29.0	12.2	29.6	22.6	12.8	11.2	21.6	45+	40.2	45+	36.2	12.0
7					40.2	29.0	25.0	27.6	44.0	30.0	13.2	30.8	24.2	14.2	13.6	23.0	45+	38.2	42.0	35.4	12.6

		PATIENT A	B	C	D	E
Deficiency		Platelet Factor 3	Serum Factor IX	Plasma Factor VIII	Plasma-serum PTA or HF	Plasma-serum Factors?
Diagnosis		Thrombasthenia	Hemophilia B	Hemophilia A	Hemophilia C or Hageman trait	Circulating anticoagulant

N Normal (control) subject
P Patient
$\frac{P}{IX}$, $\frac{P}{VIII}$, $\frac{P}{N}$ Mixture in equal parts of (a) patient's serum with IX-deficient serum; (b) patient's plasma with VIII-deficient plasma; (c) patient's serum or plasma with control serum or plasma.
$\frac{1P}{9N}$ Mixture of patient's serum with control serum in proportion of 1 to 9.

grade deficiency in platelet factor 3 may now manifest itself in a distinctly prolonged MCT. On the other hand, if the patient's platelets yielded a normal result when normal platelets were replaced in the control system, but normal platelets did not rectify the prolonged MCT when used in the patient system, his platelets can be assumed to release normal quantities of platelet factor 3, and the search for the defect must go on. In like manner, substitution of patient's serum or adsorbed plasma in the normal system, and vice versa, will rule in or out a defect in either of these fractions.

The substitution process usually is not extended to the substrate, since this has been found to be the source of an abnormal MCT only in deficiency of either prothrombin or fibrinogen. The former should be detected with the routine one-stage prothrombin test, which would yield a prolonged clotting time not corrected by aged serum (p. 356). Similarly, fibrinogen deficiency would be readily discovered with the routine screening tests, e.g., WBCT, prothrombin time, or TT. These tests should always precede the TGT. Hence, whether the patient's or the control subject's substrate is used is usually irrelevant.

The finding of a serum defect without a plasma defect denotes deficiency of either factor IX or X. If the prothrombin time is normal, Stuart factor deficiency is excluded and factor IX is implicated (Table 6–14, patient B). If the prothrombin time is prolonged, the diagnosis is either deficiency of factor X or a combination of two or more deficiencies, such as factor IX and factor VII. Differential analysis of the prothrombin time is usually helpful in making this distinction, but serum from a factor IX- or X-deficient person, if available, provides the most direct and reliable approach to differential diagnosis. If IX-deficient serum, added to the incubation mixture so that it replaces 25 to 50 per cent of the patient's serum, fails to correct the TGT result, the patient must have a factor IX deficiency in addition to a defect in the prothrombin complex. If it corrects, he probably has an isolated factor X deficiency.

Analogous considerations apply to the finding of a defect in the patient's adsorbed plasma fraction, with his serum behaving normally. The diagnosis of factor VIII (AHF) deficiency is established in the presence of a normal prothrombin time (Table 6–14, patient C). If the latter is abnormal, differential analysis between factor V deficiency and a multiple factor deficiency is necessary, such as deficiency of factors V and VIII, e.g., a hemophiliac with acute hepatitis. Since factors V and VIII are both heat labile, normal plasma exposed to 37° C. or even to average room temperature for 12 or more hours will become deficient in these factors. Such a specimen may be used to advantage for practice. Again analysis of the one-stage prothrombin time usually clarifies the situation, but use of either V- or VIII-deficient plasma affords the most direct and conclusive evidence. If adsorbed VIII-deficient plasma is substituted for one-fourth to one-half the patient's adsorbed plasma in the incubation mixture and fails to correct, the diagnosis of AHF deficiency (hemophilia A) must be made. If it corrects, the patient's plasma presumably is deficient in factor V.

Brief mention should be made of two more diagnostic constellations that may be encountered upon differential analysis of abnormal thromboplastin generation tests: (a) The patient's serum and adsorbed plasma yield normal results when substituted individually in the control system but furnish prolonged clotting times when combined in either the control or patient "run" (Table 6–14, patient D). (b) The patient's serum and adsorbed plasma give prolonged clotting times whether used singly or in combination in the control system (patient E).

Ad (a) In the first instance, a defect must be postulated that is corrected by either control serum or control (adsorbed) plasma, since both must be excluded from the incubation mixture to result in an abnormal MCT. Since PTA and HF are the factors present in normal serum and are not eliminated from plasma by the usual adsorption technique, the diagnosis is PTA or HF deficiency. The differential analysis between these two factors is indicated in the legend to Table 6–7.

Ad (b) Abnormal activity displayed by both the patient's serum *and* plasma constitutes evidence for either multiple factor deficiency or circulating anticoagulant. If, in the control "run," substituting one half the control serum or plasma with the respective patient's reagents results in a normal MCT, a double deficiency (serum *and* plasma) must be assumed, suggesting a combination of hemophilia A and B. An abnormal result caused by this maneuver establishes evidence for the presence of inhibitory activity against one of the prothromboplastins in the patient's serum and plasma. A minute quantity of the latter agents in an otherwise normal system may cause an abnormal MCT. In other words, the proportion of patient's to control serum (or plasma) may have to be reduced to 1 to 9 or less in order to secure a normal value (patient E; cf. p. 349).

Aside from the routine diagnosis of hemorrhagic disorders, the TGT has many other applications. Thus, it may be used for assay of an isolated deficiency, utilizing the principle of determining the minimal amount of control reagent (or of a purified factor preparation) that can correct the abnormal clotting time. Furthermore, recognition of hypercoagulability may be attempted by means of the test. For this purpose, higher dilutions of either serum or plasma, or both, are used so that the normal MCT is increased and unusual shortening may be discernible (Spittel *et al.*, 1960). Details of these procedures are beyond the scope of this book.

Circulating Anticoagulants and Abnormal Globulins

The highly reactive products of the coagulation system, thromboplastin and thrombin, are probably balanced by several inhibitors. Thus, normal plasma or serum has antithrombic activity, and a fraction has been isolated from normal plasma exhibiting anticoagulant activity to factor VIII. It has been claimed that an inhibitor exists physiologically for each clotting factor, especially prothrombin and factors V and VII. The significance of these and other anticoagulant "factors" in maintaining the normal

Table 6–15. Disorders Associated with Acquired Circulating Anticoagulants

1. Hemophilia A, B, or C
2. Hemorrhagic diathesis during or following pregnancy
3. Systemic L.E. and other "collagen" diseases
4. Miscellaneous diseases: leukemia and other neoplasias, cirrhosis, pemphigus

fluidity of the blood remains to be determined. The only physiologically important and the most potent inhibitor is, according to Quick, fibrin (antithrombin I), which adsorbs nascent thrombin in the course of clotting (see pp. 324, 339).

Antithrombin(s), as well as inhibitors to other clotting factors and to platelets, may occur in excessive concentration and give rise to hemostatic defects (Table 6–15). Aside from platelet antibodies (lysins, agglutinins) causing thrombocytopenic purpura, circulating inhibitors of plasma clotting factors may be acquired by patients with hemophilia A, B, or C; women during or following pregnancy; and in connection with certain systemic diseases, chiefly those involving alteration in plasma proteins ("collagen" diseases, leukemia, other neoplastic disorders). In turn, the finding of hyperglobulinemia or of abnormal globulins (dys-, paraproteinemia) should make one suspect interference with normal hemostatic functions. Excessive or abnormal globulins have been shown to chelate with some of the normal clotting factors, such as factor V, to interfere with conversion of fibrinogen to fibrin and to tie up calcium, causing a "functional" hypocalcemia.

In most instances, the anticoagulant action may be related to an abnormal immune mechanism and can be located in the gamma globulin fraction of plasma or serum. Thus, in hemophilia, inhibitory activity against the deficient clotting factor may develop after transfusion of blood and, especially in the instance of AHF deficiency, of Cohn fraction I (containing purified factor VIII). It would appear that in congenital absence of a clotting factor, its introduction into the circulation initiates a specific antibody reaction, thereby often aggravating the bleeding tendency. The occurrence of spontaneous

anticoagulants in connection with pregnancy may be compared with other types of autosensitization in this state. In one instance, the inhibitor was detectable in an infant for several weeks after birth.

Similarly, hypersensitivity may be the common denominator for the development of clot inhibition and of many other pathologic features in systemic L.E. and other disorders associated with profound disturbance of protein metabolism. In the majority of these cases, activity of the anticoagulant is confined to the first phase of coagulation, i.e., it is an anti- (pro-) thromboplastin. The anticoagulant effect of some abnormal globulins is probably incidental to their particular physical properties. Much of the time, the effect is noticed chiefly in the third phase of coagulation (thrombin time).

Although demonstration of a circulating inhibitor of blood clotting is a fairly rare experience, this possibility must be considered in every instance of a hemorrhagic disorder or abnormal results of clotting tests. Presence of an active anticoagulant may be responsible for severe symptoms and may complicate problems of clinical diagnosis and therapy. Hence, its detection and determination of mode of action are important tasks for the laboratory (see Table 6–17). If normal plasma does not readily correct the clotting defect encountered upon routine testing of a patient's plasma, an inhibitor is indicated rather than a double defect. This conclusion also presents itself if both the patient's adsorbed plasma and serum yield abnormal thromboplastin generation when other reagents in the TGT system (platelets, substrate plasma) are normal. This test is most useful in determining the site of action of an anti-(pro-) thromboplastin, while the prothrombin and thrombin times lend themselves readily to analysis of anticoagulant activity in phases II and III, respectively.

The basic principle applied to detection of anticoagulant action arises from the usual observation that a minute quantity of normal blood or plasma added to an apparently defective blood or plasma fails to correct the abnormal result of the test being applied, whether it is the whole blood clotting time, the calcium clotting time of plasma, the prothrombin time, the prothrombin consumption test, or the thrombin time (p. 349). With deficiency of a clotting factor, full correction is usually attained, since normal plasma contains each of these factors in abundant quantities. (The only exception is fibrinogen deficiency in which equal parts of normal and test plasma may be required to correct a prolonged clotting time.) As a rule, in the presence of an inhibitor, an inverse proportion of normal to patient's plasma of 10 to 1 is required for full or nearly complete correction. In other words, a small quantity of normal plasma will correct the abnormal clotting test of a factor-deficient plasma, whereas a small volume of inhibitor-containing plasma added to nor-

Table 6–16. Site of Action of Circulating Anticoagulant

PROTHROMBIN CONSUMPTION TEST	PROTHROMBIN TIME	THROMBIN TIME	INHIBITION OF
D	N	N	Prothromboplastins: VIII, IX, PTA
D	I	N	Thromboplastin (tissues and blood): V, (X)
N	I	N	Tissue thromboplastin, II or VII
D or N	I or N	I	Thrombin

For abbreviations, see Table 6–7, legend.

mal plasma will cause the latter to react abnormally. In the TGT, this correction principle applies to normal serum or adsorbed plasma, as the case may be, for detection, localization, or titration of the inhibitory activity.

EXOGENOUS ANTICOAGULANTS

Aside from heparin, which is often used for the purpose of anticoagulation, certain types of medication have an incidental anticoagulant effect, especially plasma expanders, such as dextran and polyvinyl pyrrolidine (PVP) and ethylenediaminetetraacetic acid (EDTA), a detoxifying agent that can be used to facilitate removal of heavy metals from the body. The hemostatic defect caused by dextran manifests itself chiefly (and was uncovered) by a prolonged bleeding time, presumably resulting from physical adsorption of the large molecules on platelets and thereby interfering with their function. The delaying effect of EDTA upon clotting is due not only to its chelating action on calcium, which is minimized by use of the calcium salt, but also to its effect upon fibrinogen. The antihemostatic action of PVP seems complex, including damage to both endothelium and megakaryocytes and to agglutination of platelets with resulting thrombocytopenia (Davidsohn and Stern, 1957).

Fibrinolysis

Excessive fibrinolytic activity of the circulating blood, causing hemorrhagic manifestations, is an infrequent observation. When it occurs, it is usually serious in extent and often disastrous in outcome.

The physiologic significance of the fibrinolytic system is still poorly understood except that, quite generally, it is instrumental in dissolving intravascular thrombi and is responsible for reliquefying blood after death. The decoagulant process may not be less complex in terms of number of "factors" and their interaction than the clotting mechanism per se. There is evidence for close interaction between the two mechanisms so that they may well be regarded as parts of a single overall system concerned with maintaining fluidity of the blood and with defense of the organism against blood loss and infection. The latter task is suggested by the increase in circulating fibrinogen with systemic inflammation, deposition of fibrin in areas of active infection, and its dissolution when the host's immune forces win the upper hand (example: bacterial pneumonia). The unity of the mechanism is apparent from the fact that fibrinolysin readily inactivates various clotting factors, especially factors V and VIII, and that enhancement of fibrinolytic action can be detected at the time of clotting or even before. Experimental evidence indicates that the release of serotonin from platelets may initiate this enhancement.

The schematic representation of the fibrinolytic system in Figure 6–12 shows that the key substance, plasmin, is normally present in the form of a precursor, comparable to prothrombin, which is activated to the effective lytic enzyme by various factors contained in tissues, biologic fluids, bacteria, and other substances, e.g., plasma and urine activators (urokinase), trypsin, strepto- and staphylokinase, chloroform, other organic solvents, and peptone.

Enhanced fibrinolytic activity has been encountered in physiologic states, such as hypoxia, mental stress, and severe physical exercise. Experimentally, it can be produced by injection of epinephrine, acetylcholine, pyrogens (bacterial polysaccharides), and pharmacologic agents, especially nicotinic

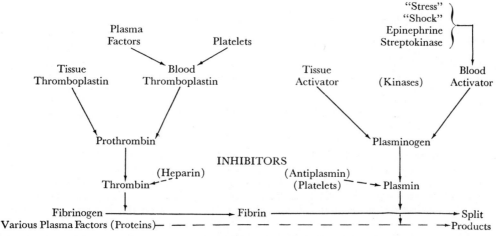

Figure 6–12. Schema of coagulation and decoagulation (fibrinolysis).

Table 6–17. Increased Fibrinolytic Activity of Blood

PHYSIOLOGIC STATE	PATHOLOGIC STATE
Causes	
Stress (physical, emotional)	Postoperative state (especially lung operations)
Fever (pyrogens)	Obstetrical complications: Abruptio placentae, amniotic fluid
Anoxia	embolism, retained dead fetus
Pharmacologic agents (epinephrine,	Neoplastic disease (especially prostate, lungs)
nicotinic acid)	Cirrhosis of liver
	Sarcoidosis
	Hematopoietic disorders: leukemia, thrombocytopenic states, erythremia
Effects	
Increase in circulating activator	Invasion of tissue activator into circulation
Thrombolysis	Hypoplasminogenemia
	Hyperplasminemia
	Fibrinogenolysis
	Hypofibrinogenemia
	Multiple hemostatic defects
	Overt hemorrhagic state

Table 6–18. Laboratory Pattern of Hemorrhagic Disorders (Screening Tests)

DISORDERS	WHOLE BLOOD CLOTTING TIME	BLEEDING TIME	TOURNIQUET TEST	CLOT RETRACTION	ONE-STAGE "PROTHROMBIN" TEST	PROTHROMBIN CONSUMPTION	THROMBIN TIME
Thrombocytogenic Disorders							
Cytopenia	−	+	+	+	−	+	±
Asthenia*							
V. Willebrand's pattern	−	+	+	−	−	+	−
Glanzmann's pattern	−	−	±	+	−	−	−
Hemophilias							
Plasma defect (VII, IX, PTA)	+	−	−	−	−	+	−
Combined plasma and vascular defect	+	+	±	−	−	+	−
Hemophilioid Disorders							
Deficiency of V	+	−	−	−	+	+	−
Deficiency of X	+	−	−	−	+	±	−
Deficiency of II	+	−	−	+	+	−	−
Deficiency of VII	−	±	−	+	+	−	−
Hypofibrinogenemia	+	±	−	−	+	−	+
Hyperplasminemia	+**	±	±	±§	+§	+§	+§
Circulating anticoagulants, abnormal globulins	+	±	±	−	±	±	±‖

+ Abnormal.

− Normal.

* Functional defect. Various combinations of the two patterns occur with normal, decreased, or increased number of platelets.

§ Clot redissolves, or no clot.

‖ Positive result denotes antithrombin (heparin or other) or abnormal globulin, to be distinguished by protamine titration and electrophoresis.

acid. The increase in fibrinolysis can be attributed to an increase in circulating activator rather than to the activated enzyme itself. Pathologic fibrinolytic activity is usually attributed to either release of abnormal amounts of plasminogen activator from tissues or entrance of thromboplastic material into the circulation (resulting in defibrination and secondary fibrinolytic response). Fibrinolytic purpura is caused not only by lysis of fibrin or of circulating fibrinogen, since the hemorrhagic diathesis in this condition may be much more severe and life-threatening than in congenital

BLOOD COAGULATION: LIST OF NORMAL VALUES

See Page

Bleeding Time   328

  Duke's method: 2 to 5 minutes
  Ivy's method: 5 to 6 minutes
  Adelson-Crosby method
    Bleeding time: 7 minutes
    Blood loss: less than 0.22 ml.

Calcium Clotting Time (CaT)   347

  Modified Howell method
    Platelet-rich plasma: 90 to 120 seconds
    Platelet-poor plasma: 105 to 150 seconds

Capillary Permeability Tests   328

  Tourniquet test
    Quick's method: Not more than 5 petechiae in a circle 5 cm. in diameter
    Göethlin's method: Not more than 8 to 12 petechiae in a circle of 6 cm. in
      diameter
  Suction test: 0 to 2 petechiae at 200 mg. Hg

Clot Retraction   330

  Stefanini-Dameshek method
    Whole blood: 20 to 65 per cent
    Platelet-rich plasma: 40 to 70 per cent
  Adreassen's method: 58 to 97 per cent; mean, 78 per cent

Clot Retraction Time   331

  Hirschboeck's method: 20 to 45 minutes; average, 33 minutes

Clotting Time   345

  Whole blood clotting time (modified Lee-White technique): 6 to 10 minutes
    At lower temperature: up to 15 minutes or longer
    With siliconized tube: 25 to 45 minutes

  Incipient clotting time: 3 to 4 minutes   347

  Capillary method: 3 to 5 minutes   347

Fibrinogen: 200 to 400 mg./100 ml.   351, 354

Fibrinolysis: No visible lysis in 24 hours   347, 365

Prothrombin Time (Quick): 12 to 14 seconds   352

Prothrombin Consumption Test: > 16 seconds; usually 17 to 45 seconds   357

Thrombin Time (TT): 11 to 14 seconds; depending on concentration of reagent   350

Thromboplastin Generation Test (TGT): clotting time less than 12 seconds   358
  within 6 minutes of incubation

afibrinogenemia. The excess of fibrinolytic enzyme inactivates other clotting factors, resulting in a multifocal hemostatic defect.

In the routine investigation of a bleeding disorder (Table 6–17, 6–18, Fig. 6–9), provision should always be made for detecting excessive fibrinolytic activity, if present. Thus, the clot resulting from one of the screening tests—usually the whole blood clotting time or prothrombin time—should regularly be incubated at 37° C. for several hours (preferably overnight). A grossly noticeable decrease in the size of the clot or its complete disappearance denotes excessive fibrinolytic activity. This finding may at times furnish the explanation for abnormal results with other clotting tests, such as the prothrombin time or the prothrombin consumption test, since plasmin is known to inactivate several of the clotting factors, especially factors V, VII, and VIII. Once excessive fibrinolysis has been recognized, its quantitative measurement is indicated, and a qualitative study may be desirable. The latter would consist of determining whether the excessive fibrinolysis encountered is due to an increase in circulating activator or in active plasmin or to a change in the plasminogen level (the latter may be decreased as a result of accelerated conversion to plasmin). Since practical methods for this differential analysis remain to be developed, a simple procedure will be described that permits detection of excess of total fibrinolytic activity. A quantitative assay of fibrinolysis was reported by Hougie and Ayers (1960). Its clinical value remains to be established. A succinct review of methods measuring fibrinolysis was published by von Kaulla and Schultz (1958).

SIMPLE SCREENING TEST FOR INCREASED FIBRINOLYSIS (STEFANINI AND DAMESHEK, 1955)

Principle. This method utilizes a normal plasma clot (or bovine fibrin) as a substrate to determine the fibrinolytic activity of test plasma.

Equipment. Same as for thrombin time; also (optional) purified bovine fibrinogen, 600 mg. per 100 ml. of saline.

Procedure. Platelet-poor plasma is prepared (Table 6–9) from citrated venous blood collected from both the patient and a control subject. Ice water temperature is maintained from the moment of venipuncture, and no delay should be allowed between the steps in the procedure. From each of the two plasmas, 0.5 ml. is transferred to a cold test tube and mixed. In addition, 1.0 ml. of each plasma is placed into separate tubes. All three tubes are now transferred from the ice bath into a 37° C. bath, and 0.1 ml. of saline containing 10 units of thrombin is added to each tube with immediate mixing. Each clot is then observed at frequent intervals (at least every 30 minutes for the first six hours) for detection of complete lysis. Normally, no noticeable lysis occurs in 24 hours.

Lysis time can be shortened, and the test made more convenient, by substituting for the normal plasma purified bovine fibrinogen, which contains little antifibrinolysin.

REFERENCES

Aballi, A. J., Banus, V. L., de Lamerens, S., and Rozengvaig, S.: Coagulation studies in the newborn period. III. Hemorrhagic disease of the newborn. A.M.A. Am. J. Dis. Child., 97:524, 1959.

Adamis, D. M.: Rapid determination of plasma fibrinogen. Proc. Soc. Exp. Biol. & Med., 103:107, 1960.

Addis, T.: The pathogenesis of hereditary haemophilia. J. Path. & Bact., 15:427, 1910.

Adelson, E., and Crosby, W. H.: A new method to measure bleeding time. The "immersion" method. Acta haemat., 18:281, 1957.

Adreassen, M.: Haemofili i Denmark. Copenhagen, Munksgaard, 1943.

Aggeler, P. M., White, S. G., Glendening, M. B., Page, E. W., Leake, T. B., and Bates, G.: Plasma thromboplastin component (PTC) deficiency: A new disease resembling hemophilia. Proc. Soc. Exper. Biol. & Med., 79:692, 1952.

Alexander, B.: Clotting factor VII (proconvertin) synonyms, properties, clinical and clinico-laboratory aspects. New England J. Med., 260:1218, 1959.

Alexander, B., Goldstein, R., Landwehr, G., and Cook, C. D.: Congenital SPCA deficiency: a hitherto unrecognized coagulation defect with hemorrhage rectified by serum and serum fractions. J. Clin. Invest., 30:596, 1951.

Arthus, M., and Pagès, C.: Nouvelle théories chimique de la coagulation du sang. Arch. physiol. norm. et path., 2:739, 1890.

Biggs, R., Douglas, A. S., Macfarlane, R. G., Dacie, J. V., Pitney, W. R., Merskey, C., and O'Brien, J. R.: Christmas disease, a condition previously mistaken for haemophilia. Brit. M. J., 2:1378, 1952.

Biggs, R., and Macfarlane, R. G.: Human blood coagulation and its disorders. Springfield, Charles C Thomas, 1957.

Bird, R. M., Hammarsten, J. F., Marshall, R. A., and Robinson, R. R.: A family reunion. A study of hereditary hemorrhagic telangiectasia. New England J. Med., 257:105, 1957.

Bordet, J., and Delange, L.: La coagulation du sang et la génèse de la thrombine. Ann. Inst. Pasteur, 26:657, 739, 1912.

Brinkhous, K. M.: A study of the clotting defect in hemophilia; the delayed formation of thrombin. Am. J. M. Sc., 198:509, 1939.

Buchanan, A.: On the coagulation of the blood and other fibriniferous liquids. Med. Gazette. 18:50,

1835–1836; London Med. Gazette, 1:617, 1845.

Cetingil, A. I., Ulutin, O. N., and Karaca, M.: A platelet defect in a case of scurvy. Brit. J. Haemat., 4:350, 1958.

Dausset, J., and Bergerot-Blondel, Y.: Acceleration of fibrinolysis of blood-clots by dilution with saline and human serum. Lancet, 2:123, 1956.

Davidsohn, I., and Stern, K.: Disturbance of hemostasis in rabbits treated with polyvinyl pyrrolidone (PVP). J. Mount Sinai Hosp., 24:777, 1957.

DeNicola, P.: Thrombelastography. Springfield, Charles C Thomas, 1957.

DeNicola, P.: Platelet count and thrombelastographic maximum amplitude in experimental thrombocythemias. Throm. Diat. Haemorrh., 3:615, 1959.

Dieckmann, W. J.: Blood chemistry and renal function in abruptio placentae. Am. J. Obst. & Gynec., 31:734, 1936.

Dische, F. E., and Benfield, V.: Congenital factor VII deficiency. Haematological and genetic aspects. Acta haemat., 21:257, 1959.

Dormer, L., Mach, O., and Brabcova, S.: Elektrophorese der Blutplättchen. Acta haemat., 20:369, 1958.

Duke, W. W.: The relation of blood platelets to hemorrhagic disease; Description of a method for determining the bleeding time and coagulation time and report of three cases of hemorrhagic disease relieved by transfusion. J.A.M.A., 55:1185, 1910.

Fisch, U., and Duckert, F.: Some aspects of kinetics of the first stages of blood thromboplastin formation. Throm. Diat. Haemorrh., 3:98, 1959.

Fountain, J. R., and Holman, R. L.: Acquired fibrinogen deficiency associated with carcinoma of the bronchus. Ann. Int. Med., 52:459, 1960.

Gangarosa, E. J., Johnson, T. R., and Ramos, H. S.: Ristocetin-induced thrombocytopenia: Site and mechanism of action. Arch. Int. Med., 105:83, 1960.

Gardikas, C., Tsakayannis, E., and Thomopoulos, D.: Post-operative changes in the results of coagulation tests. Acta haemat., 21:129, 1959.

Gardner, F. H.: Autoerythrocyte sensitization—A form of purpura producing painful bruising following autosensitization to red blood cells in certain women. Blood, 10:675, 1955.

Gollub, S.: Hemorrhagic diathesis associated with massive transfusion. Surgery, 45:204, 1959.

Göthlin, G. F.: Outline of a method for determination of the strength of the skin capillaries and the indirect estimation of the individual vitamin C standard. J. Lab. & Clin. Med., 18:484, 1933.

Gurevich, V., and Thomas, M. A.: Idiopathic pulmonary hemorrhage in pregnancy: Report of a case suggesting early pulmonary hemosiderosis with clinical recovery after steroid therapy. New England J. Med., 261:1154, 1959.

Hammarsten, O.: Zur Lehre von der Faserstoffgerinnung. Pflüger's Arch. ges. Physiol., 14:211, 1877.

Henstell, H. H., and Feinstein, M.: Interference of abnormal plasma proteins with the clotting mechanism. Am. J. Med., 22:381, 1957.

Hirschboeck, J. S.: The effect of operation and illness on clot retraction: A description of a new method. J. Lab. & Clin. Med., 33:347, 1948.

Hougie, C., and Ayers, F.: Lipaemia and fibrinolytic potentiality. Lancet, 1:186, 1960.

Hougie, C., Barrow, E. M., and Graham, J. B.: Stuart clotting defect. I. Segregation of an hereditary hemorrhagic state from the heterogeneous group heretofore called "stable factor" (SPCA, proconvertin, factor VII) deficiency. J. Clin. Invest., 36:485, 1957.

Hougie, C., and Glover, H. M.: The hemophilioid

states. A.M.A. Arch. Int. Med., 103:239, 1959.

Hsia, D. Y.: Inborn Errors of Metabolism. Chicago, The Year Book Publishers, Inc., 1959.

Hutchinson, H. E., Stark, M., and Chapman, J. A.: Platelet serotonin and normal haemostasis. J. Clin. Path., 12:265, 1959.

Hyun, B. H., Dawson, E. Z., Butcher, J., and Custer, R. P.: Studies on soybean phosphatide (Inosithin) as a platelet substitute. Am. J. Clin. Path., 33:209, 1960.

Ivy, A. C., Shapiro, P. R., and Melnick, P.: The bleeding tendency in jaundice. Surg. Gynec. & Obst., 60:781–784, 1935.

Jaques, L. B.: Determination of the clotting time of whole blood. In Tocantins, L. M.: The Coagulation of Blood. New York, Grune & Stratton, Inc., 1955. Chapter III.

Jim, R. T. S.: A Study of the plasma thrombin time. J. Lab. & Clin. Med., 50:45, 1957.

Jürgens, J., and Beller, F. K.: Klinische Methoden der Blutgerinnungsanalyse. Stuttgart, Georg Thieme Verlag, 1959.

Kaznelson, P.: Verschwinden der hämorrhagischen Diathese bei einem Falle von essentieller Thrombopenie (Frank) nach Milz Extirpation. Splenogene thrombolytische Purpura. Wien. klin. Wchnschr., 29:1451, 1916.

Koller, F., Kruse, G., and Luchsinger, P.: Über eine besondere Form der hämorrhagischen Diathese. Schweiz. med. Wchnschr., 80:1101, 1950.

Kupfer, H. G., Ebbels, B. J., Miller, J. N., Thoma, G. W., and Russi, S.: Essential thrombocythemia. Ann. Int. Med., 48:685, 1958.

Kwaan, H. C., Lo, R., and McFadzean, A. J. S.: On the lysis of thrombi experimentally produced within veins. Brit. J. Haemat., 4:51, 1958.

Langdell, R. D., Adelson, E., Furth, F. W., and Crosby, W. H.: Dextran and prolonged bleeding time. J.A.M.A., 166:346, 1958.

Lewis, J. H., and Didisheim, P.: Differential diagnosis and treatment in hemorrhagic disease. A.M.A. Arch. Int. Med., 100:157, 1957.

Lewis, J. H., Zucker, M. B., and Ferguson, J. H.: Bleeding tendency in uremia. Blood, 11:1073, 1956.

Lozner, E.: Differential diagnosis, pathogenesis and treatment of the thrombocytopenic purpuras. Am. J. Med., 14:459, 1953.

Mandel, E. E., and Lazerson, J.: Thrombasthenia in liver disease. New England J. Med., 265:56–61, 1961.

McKay, D. G., Kliman, A., and Alexander, B.: Experimental production of afibrinogenemia and hemorrhagic phenomena by combined fibrinolysis and disseminated intravascular coagulation. New England J. Med., 261:1150, 1959.

Malpighi: Opera Omnia, 1666. Quoted by Pickering.

Miale, J. B.: Laboratory Medicine—Hematology. St. Louis, The C. V. Mosby Company, 1958.

Mills, S. D.: Purpura in childhood. J. Pediatrics, 49:306, 1956.

Mindrum, G., and Glueck, H. I.: Plasma prothrombin in liver disease: Its clinical and prognostic significance. Ann. Int. Med., 50:1370, 1959.

Moloney, W. C., Egan, W. J., and Gorman, A. J.: Acquired afibrinogenemia in pregnancy. New England J. Med., 240:596, 1949.

Morawitz, P.: Beiträge zur Kenntnis der Blutgerinnung. Deutsches Arch. klin. Med., 76:215, 1903–1904.

Morlock, C. G., and Hall, B. E.: Association of cirrhosis, thrombopenia and hemorrhagic tendency. A.M.A. Arch. Int. Med., 72:69, 1943.

Naeye, R. L.: Hemophilioid factors: Acquired deficiencies in several hemorrhagic states. Proc. Soc.

Exp. Biol. & Med., *94:*623, 1957.

Nilsson, I. M., Blombäck, M., and Blombäck, B.: Von Willebrand's disease in Sweden. Acta med. scandinav., *164:*263, 1959.

Opitz, H., and Silberberg, M.: Afibrinogenämie und Thrombopenie infolge ausgedehnter hepato-lienaler Tuberkulose. Klin. Wchnschr., *3:*1443, 1924.

Owren, P. A.: Parahaemophilia: Haemorrhagic diathesis due to absence of a previously unknown clotting factor. Lancet, *1:*446, 1947.

Patek, A. J., and Taylor, F. H. L.: Hemophilia II. Some properties of a substance obtained from normal human plasma effective in accelerating the coagulation of hemophilic blood. J. Clin. Invest., *16:*113, 1937.

Perry, S., and Baker, M.: Coagulation defects in leukemia. J. Lab. & Clin. Med., *50:*229, 1957.

Pickering, J. W.: The Blood Plasma in Health and Disease. New York, The Macmillan Co., 1928.

Quick, A. J.: The prothrombin in hemophilia and in obstructive jaundice. J. Biol. Chem., *109:*lxxiii, 1935.

Quick, A. J.: Calcium in the coagulation of the blood. Am. J. Physiol., *131:*455, 1940.

Quick, A. J.: On the constitution of prothrombin. Am. J. Physiol., *146:*212, 1943.

Quick, A. J.: Hemorrhagic Diseases. Philadelphia, Lea & Febiger, 1957.

Rabe, F., and Salomon, E.: Über Faserstoffmangel im Blut bei einem Falle von Hämophilie. Deutsches Arch. klin. Med., *132:*240, 1920.

Rabinowitz, Y., and Dameshek, W.: Systemic lupus erythematosus after "idiopathic" thrombocytopenic purpura. Ann. Int. Med., *52:*1, 1960.

Rapaport, S. I., and Ames, S. B.: Clotting factor assays on plasma from patients receiving intramuscular or subcutaneous heparin. Am. J. M. Sc., *234:*678, 1957.

Ratnoff, O. D.: Hereditary defects in clotting mechanism. Adv. Int. Med., *9:*107, 1958.

Reimann, F.: Purpura thrombolytica. Acta med. scandinav., *107:*95, 1941.

Rhoads, J. E., and Fitz-Hugh, Jr., T.: Idiopathic hypoprothrombinemia—an apparently unrecorded condition. Am. J. M. Sc., *202:*662, 1941.

Rodman, N. F., Barrow, E. M., and Graham, J. B.: Diagnosis and control of the hemophiliod states with the partial thromboplastin time (PTT) test. Am. J. Clin. Path., *29:*525, 1958.

Rogers, J.: Menstruation and systemic disease. New England J. Med., *259:*675, 1958.

Rosenthal, R. L., Dreskin, O. H., and Rosenthal, N.: Plasma thromboplastin antecedent (PTA) deficiency: Clinical, coagulation, therapeutic and hereditary aspects of a new hemophilia-like disease. Blood, *10:*120, 1955.

Scharfman, W. B., Hosley, H. F., Hawkins, T., and Propp, S.: Idiopathic thrombocytopenic purpura. J.A.M.A., *172:*1875, 1960.

Schmidt, A.: Zur Blutlehre, Leipzig, 1893; Weitere Beiträge zur Blutlehre, Bergmann, Wiesbaden, 1895.

Schulman, I., and Smith, C. H.: Hemorrhagic disease in an infant due to deficiency of a previously undescribed clotting factor. Blood, *7:*794, 1952.

Setna, S. S., and Rosenthal, R. L.: Intermediate stages in platelet alterations during coagulation.

Acta haemat., *19:*209, 1958.

Sherry, S., Fletcher, A. P., and Alkjaersig, N.: Fibrinolysis and fibrinolytic activity in man. Physiol. Rev., *39:*343, 1959.

Singer, K., and Ramot, B.: Pseudohemophilia type B. A.M.A. Arch. Int. Med., *97:*715, 1956.

Sise, H. S., Lavelle, S. M., Adamis, D., and Becker, R.: Relation of hemorrhage and thrombosis to prothrombin during treatment with coumarin-type anticoagulants. New England J. Med., *259:*266, 1958.

Sjølin, K. E.: Classical hemophilia (AHF deficiency) and Christmas factor (PTC deficiency) as simultaneous defects. Acta med. scandinav., *159:*7, 1957.

Spaet, T. H., and Kropatkin, M.: Studies on "prothrombin derivatives" in vitamin K deficiency. A.M.A. Arch. Int. Med., *102:*558, 1958.

Spittel, J. A., Jr., Pascuzzi, C. A., Thompson, J. H., Jr., and Owen, C. A., Jr.: Acceleration of early stages of coagulation in certain patients with occlusive arterial or venous diseases: Use of a modified thromboplastin generation test. Proc. Staff Meet. Mayo Clin., *35:*37, 1960.

Stefanini, M., and Dameshek, W.: The Hemorrhagic Disorders. New York, Grune & Stratton, Inc., 1955.

Tocantins, L. M.: The Coagulation of Blood—Methods of Study. New York, Grune & Stratton, Inc., 1955.

Valberg, L. S., and Brown, G. M.: Haemorrhagic capillary disorder associated with antihaemophilic globulin deficiency. Medicine, *37:*181, 1958.

Van Creveld, S., Ho, L. K., and Veder, H. A.: Thrombopathia. Acta haemat., *19:*199, 1958.

Verstraete, M., and Vandenbroucke, J.: Occurrence and mode of action of endogenous circulating anticoagulants. J. Lab. & Clin. Med., *48:*673, 1956.

Volk, B. W., Losner, S., Jacobi, M., and Lazarus, S. A.: Studies on clot density. Am. J. Clin. Path., *22:*99, 1952.

Waddell, W. W., and Guerry, DuP.: Effect of vitamin K on the clotting time of the prothrombin and the blood. With special reference to unnatural bleeding of the newly-born. J.A.M.A., *112:*2259, 1939.

Ware, A. G., and Seegers, W. H.: Two-stage procedure for quantitative determination of prothrombin concentration. Am. J. Clin. Path., *19:*471, 1949.

Watson, C., Schultz, A., and Wikoff, H.: Purpura following estrogen therapy, with particular reference to hypersensitivity to (diethyl) stilbestrol and with a note on the possible relationship of purpura to endogenous estrogens. J. Lab. & Clin. Med., *32:*606, 1947.

Wayne, L., Goldsmith, R. E., Glueck, H. I., and Berry, H. K.: Abnormal calcium binding associated with hyperglobulinemia, clotting defects and osteoporosis: A study of this relationship. Proc. Central Soc. Clin. Research, *32:*102, 1959.

Wintrobe, M. M.: Clinical Hematology. 5th Ed. Philadelphia, Lea & Febiger, 1961.

Wright, I. S.: Concerning the functions and nomenclature of blood clotting factors, with a preliminary report of the profile of blood clotting factors in young males. Ann. Int. Med., *51:*841, 1959.

Chapter 7

Isotopology: Applications in the Clinical Pathology Laboratory

By OSCAR B. HUNTER, JR., M.D.

Isotopes are a comparatively new addition to the tools available to the clinical pathologist. Although they have been available for 20 years in usable form, the practical use of these elements in the clinical pathology laboratory has only recently become widespread. The basis for the practical application of isotopes is their capacity to mix with normal elements. One is able to follow the course of these elements through the chemical and biologic processes of the body and in this way determine and quantitate certain bodily functions, hence, the designation, "tracer substances" or "tracers." The only limitations placed upon the utilization of these elements are those imposed by our ability to conceive of new ways to integrate them into metabolic and chemical processes. A wide variety of elements having different physical constants can be used, depending upon the need and the purpose. However, isotopes must be used according to established rules so that they may be followed through a selected metabolic process without causing damage to the tissues by their capacity to produce ionization.

In this chapter, the use of isotopes in the study of bodily functions will be outlined. After a brief discussion of the theoretic background, each test will be described and the procedure outlined in detail.* Space limitations make it impossible to include much information on the physics of the isotopes. For this aspect of the subject, the student is referred to reliable texts listed in the bibliography (Harnwell and Stephens, 1955; Hollaender, 1954; McMillan, 1947; Quimby *et al.*, 1958).

* Miss Nellie May Bering, M.T. (A.S.C.P.), has given much assistance in detailing the procedures.

FUNDAMENTAL PRINCIPLES

The use of isotopes as tracer substances depends on three basic factors: decay factor, metabolic factor, and isotope dilution.

The decay of isotopes varies, but for each element and for each isotope of each element there is a constant rate of decay to the state of the basic stable element. The rate of decay is expressed as the half life of the isotope. Ideally the half life should be long enough to permit use of the isotope as a measure of a given function of the body but short enough so that it does not remain in the body too long and cause injury. Thus, I^{131} is a satisfactory isotope, having a half life of 8.08 days. If given in tracer amounts, it permits adequate time for study but at the same time decays rapidly enough to be within safe limits.

In selecting an isotope, one must consider its role in metabolism. I^{131} is ideal for the study of thyroid function, since it is metabolized almost exclusively by the thyroid gland. Co^{60} in vitamin B_{12} is ideal for the study of pernicious anemia, since it can be used as a tracer for the metabolic process in question.

The isotope dilution factor must be considered, because the isotope should be available in sufficient concentration to be differentiated from background radiation. If I^{131}-tagged serum albumin is not localized in the tumor in greater concentration than in the surrounding tissue, it is of little value for tumor localization.

INSTRUMENTATION

Isotope detection depends on energy released in alpha (α), beta (β), and gamma (γ) rays. For all practical studies beta and gamma rays are the only ones used. Beta rays are electrons with limited penetrability. They are able to traverse only 1 cm. of tissue and for this reason are not suitable for the study of deep organs. They may be detected readily in body fluids. Gamma rays have an infinite power of penetration. Therefore, they are used as tracers in the body and in body fluids.

Accuracy of determination depends on: the uniform assaying of standards and unknowns, the use of reliable instruments, and adherence to adequate limits of mean deviation by doing adequate counts for the sample.

UNIFORM ASSAYING

Usually the standard is an isotope source outside the body, while the unknown is within the body or body fluid. The sample to be measured should be in a limited area. Ideally, to be accurate for measurement, an isotope source should be a point source. Under such circumstances the radiation measurement can be calculated to be inversely proportional to the square of the distance between the source and the detector.

Point sources are necessarily only theoretic. Hence, it becomes necessary to minimize the variation between the standard source and the unknown. This is accomplished by having the standard source as nearly geometrically identical to the unknown as possible.

Consideration should be given to: the type of radiation from the specimen, the biologic variation, i.e., the concentration or dilution of the isotope by biologic processes, the size and shape of the specimen, and radioactive reflection and absorption.

The radiation used for tracer work is almost entirely of the beta and gamma types. Beta radiating isotopes are used almost exclusively in assays of body fluids. Gamma radiating isotopes have a wide application, including the study of body fluids, secretions, urine, and feces.

Biologic processes that concentrate elements as tagged materials make function studies feasible. In other instances the lack of concentration or actual dilution in body fluids helps to make the assay possible.

It is important to establish identical or nearly identical conditions for comparing the activity of isotopes. Most determinations depend on the comparison of the radioactivity of a standard with that of an unknown. Counting the radioactivity of the standard should be carried out under circumstances as similar as possible to those under which the unknown is counted. For example, the standard for thyroid uptake of I^{131} should be comparable to the thyroid of a living patient. For that purpose a phantom or dummy is used, containing an amount of I^{131} equal to that given the patient. Fluid specimens should be compared to standards in similar containers in approximately the same volume.

Finally, the problem of reflection and absorption of radioactivity needs to be considered. If the counter is directed at different walls in measuring the patient and the standard, different reflected radiation may be encountered.

These factors are important and must be considered in setting up conditions for assay. The principle of measuring under conditions as closely identical as possible is a good one to follow.

INSTRUMENTS

All instruments used to detect radioactive isotopes actually measure the ionization produced by alpha and beta particles and their electrical charges. Gamma rays and neutrons produce ionization by collision with atomic particles, resulting in a knocking out of electrons or of other neutrons and protons.

Gamma ray activity may be classified into three effects:

1. Photoelectric effect: ejection of an orbital electron from an atom with absorption of the photon of energy.

2. Compton effect: ejection of an orbital electron and continuation of the gamma ray at a lower peak of energy.

3. Pair production: When the gamma ray of sufficient energy passes close to a nucleus, two electrons are split off, one positively charged and the other negatively charged.

These gamma ray effects are the detected ionization that instruments enable us to quantitate.

Geiger-Müller Counter

This instrument detects radiation by identifying ionization of a gas within a tube containing a mixture of 90 per cent argon and 10 per cent ethyl alcohol; the alcohol is used to quench excessive discharging. The tube contains an insulated axial wire, which

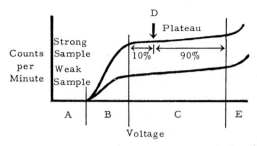

Figure 7–1. The Geiger-Müller curve. *A,* Insufficient current to produce flow of ions. *B,* Increased voltage to produce a detectable pulse. *C,* Voltage optimum for production of plateau. *D,* Geiger-Müller plateau. *E,* Excessive voltage—an avalanche of ions is produced.

is connected to the positive pole of a battery while the wall of the tube is connected to the negative pole. A meter placed in the line will show any ionization of the gas by radiation.

The voltage differential between the poles is the activity force, and the flow of charged particles to either pole depends on this differential. The flow of ionized particles follows a curve depending on the voltage, which is known as the Geiger-Müller curve. At very low voltage no detection will register. By increasing the voltage, one can detect an increasing number of ions until a plateau is reached. In this area moderate variations in voltage produce little change in the number of ions detected; above this level, however, a continuous discharge or avalanche of ions occurs. This is harmful to the detector and will burn it out. The counter is best used in the plateau area where voltage variation produces little change in the ions detected. Here the ionizing effect produces an electrical impulse, which can be counted and used to quantitate the amount of radiation (Fig. 7–1).

Scintillation Counter

Sodium iodide crystals give off a small amount of light when ionizing radiation penetrates them. These crystals are encased in an aluminum jacket open at the end. The end is sealed to a photomultiplier tube, which has a photosensitive layer next to the crystal and an electronic multiplier. The multiplier builds up each ionizing effect to an electrical pulse of sufficient strength to activate a scaler device.

The scintillation counter operates on the same general principle as the Geiger counter with a minimal voltage necessary to activate the tube and a small plateau in which small variations of voltage produce little change in counts. Increasing the voltage beyond this level produces an avalanche of counts called a dynode noise. Each counter has a separate plateau, and this should be checked from time to time for accurate results.

Scalers

The scaler is used to measure impulses produced in the counters. These are either mechanical or electronic, and the counts may be made by binary or decimal scales. Scalers are used on pre-set times or pre-set counts; the most commonly used scalers measure counts per minute.

Spectrometers

The energy of radiation produces light in sodium iodide crystals in proportion to the strength of the radiation. This in turn produces a proportionally strong pulse in the scintillation counter. The strength of these pulses can be measured and specific isotopes identified by their detected gamma radiation.

In this manner the radiation from single isotopes of a mixture can be determined. This is done by a spectrometer equipped with an electronic window, which can admit pulses of selected heights without admitting those higher or lower. Such a device permits one to count separate isotopes and to count only primary radiation and no scatter or Compton effect. It also permits a reduction in the effect of background, meaning universally existing radiation.

Operation of Spectrometer and Scintillation Counter. To operate these instruments one should first establish the normal curve for the counter. The scaler should be allowed to warm up for 30 minutes. A standard radiation source is then placed before the counter. Counts can then be plotted against voltage and the curve drawn. The proper operating voltage for each counter is the midpoint of the plateau.

The spectrometer may be plugged into the circuit and a cesium source placed before the counter. The high voltage regulator on the scaler may be turned up so as not to interfere with the spectrometer. A 10 volt window may be set with the center of the window at 0.662 mev. (million electron volts). The voltage regulator then should be varied to test the counts at the highest level. Following this the instrument may be used, resetting the window at the energy level for the particular isotope desired. The energy levels for gamma radiation of frequently used isotopes are:

I^{131}	0.364 mev.
Cr^{51}	0.320 mev.
Fe^{59}	1.3 mev.
Co^{57}	0.123 mev.
Co^{60}	1.1 mev.
Au^{198}	0.411 mev.

Collimation

Collimation utilizes the principle of shielding so as to measure radiation from a limited point of a radiation source. It also aids in reducing the effects of background radiation. Different collimators may be used and are an important adjunct to accurate radiation measurement. There are three essential types of collimators: flat field, straight bore and focusing.

The flat field collimator is designed to detect a relatively large area of radiation, while the straight bore type usually has a single small hole in a lead nose piece and measures radiation in a very limited area. The focusing collimator is designed to use a larger scintillation counter with multiple holes directed toward a focus point in front of the instrument. Theoretically this permits smaller quantities of isotopes to be used (Fig. 7–2).

The Isotope Dilution Principle

Tracer studies involving isotopes depend on the concentration by specific organs, the dilution in body fluids, and the elimination in excreta and secreta.

The application of these three factors permits quantitative evaluation of functions of some organs. These functions can be quan-

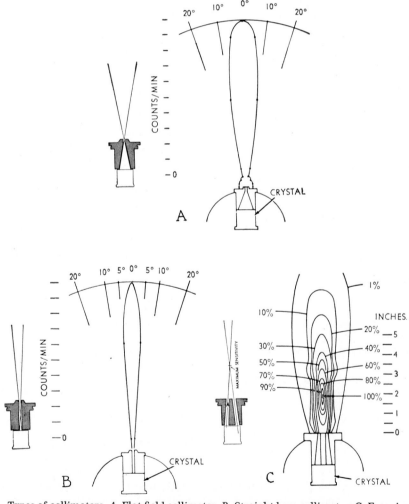

Figure 7–2. Types of collimators. *A,* Flat field collimator. *B,* Straight bore collimator. *C,* Focusing collimator.

titated, but unlike ordinary chemicals the problem of decay of isotopes must always be taken into account.

Blood volume studies are the best example of the application of the dilution principle. In this case, estimates of the total volume of the blood are made on the basis that the total value is proportional to the dilution of the introduced isotope. This can be expressed as an equation (shown at bottom of page).

This does not account for the variations in rate of isotope decay. If the half life is short, an appreciable difference may result in any long-term study. Thus, the time factor related to the half life of the isotope must be considered. For example, in a study involving Cr^{51}, which has a half life of 27.8 days, an observation made 26 days after introduction of Cr^{51} would show only half the radioactivity that was present at the start of the study, regardless of any biologic factors causing reduction in the concentration of the isotope. This problem may be eliminated in many instances if one cancels out the decay factor by placing in the standard at the beginning of the study the identical dose of the isotope that is being administered to the patient. Samples taken from the patient then can always be compared with the standard, which is decaying at the same rate.

Calibration and Counting

Assays of radioactive samples are subject to errors familiar to mathematicians but frequently overlooked by physicians. These errors result from the variability of decay of the isotope and the limitations of the instruments used for counting. Therefore, it is necessary to know the error or errors involved in the procedure and to establish conditions of testing that will reduce the errors to a minimum. This may be done by varying the quantity of counts in the sample or by varying the time of the observation. The error may also be decreased by reducing the background radiation.

Thus, in any count the standard error may be determined by the following formula:

$$SD = \sqrt{\frac{N_c}{t_c^2} + \frac{N_b}{t_b^2}}$$ in which SD = standard deviation, N_c = observed number of counts in the sample, N_b = observed number of counts in the background, t_c = time counted for sample, and t_b = time counted for background (Quimby et al., 1958). Computations of the standard error indicate that the counts of a given sample will fall within these limits in 68 per cent of the cases and outside these limits in 32 per cent of the cases; this is called 68 per cent confidence. To obtain results that have 90 per cent confidence, in which the counts will fall within the limits 90 per cent of the time, the formula is supplied with a new constant, K = 1.645; for 95 per cent confidence, K = 1.96.

I^{131} TESTS OF THYROID FUNCTION

I^{131} Uptake Curve (Astwood and Stanley, 1947; Dobyns, 1955)

Normally, iodine taken into the body is metabolized, much of it by the thyroid gland, and is used to iodinate tyrosine, which in turn forms the active thyroid hormones, triiodothyronine and thyroxine. These are bound to the protein, thyroglobulin, within the thyroid gland. The uptake of iodine by the thyroid follows a curve illustrated in Figure 7–3. Using this curve, one may determine thyroid function by comparing the uptake of I^{131} with the normal. Any time interval may be used, such as 2, 6, 12, and 24 hours. For practical purposes the 24-hour interval seems to be accurate and convenient. According to some, in hyperthyroidism a 4-hour interval is most accurate. Interfering factors in the interpretation of this test must be considered; they are detailed in Table 7–1.

I^{131} uptake should be measured with a scintillation counter equipped with a cylindrical collimator that will "see" the entire gland. The crystal should be placed approximately 15 cm. from the neck and at the same distance from the standard for measurements. If a pulse height analyzer is used, more accurate determinations may be made.

$$\frac{\text{Total blood volume}}{\text{Isotope volume}} = \frac{\text{Injected isotope concentration (expressed in counts)}}{\text{Diluted isotope concentration (expressed in counts)}}$$

or $TV = \dfrac{IC_1 \times IV}{IC_2}$

when TV = total blood volume, IC_1 = injected isotope concentration, IC_2 = diluted isotope concentration, and IV = volume isotope standard.

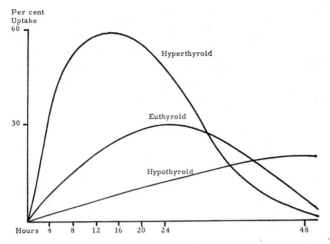

Figure 7–3. Typical thyroid uptake curves for I¹³¹.

Table 7–1. Chemicals and Drugs that Interfere with the 24-Hour I¹³¹ Thyroid Uptake

GROUP	DETAILED ITEMS	RECOMMENDED TIME BEFORE I¹³¹ TEST IS DONE	VALIDITY OF I¹³¹ TESTS PERFORMED SOONER
Dietary iodine	Foods	0	
	Iodized salt	0	All valid
Inorganic iodine, enteric	Iodide	7 days	Hyperthyroid results valid.
	Lugol's solution	7 days	Euthyroid or hypothyroid
	Hydriodic acid	7 days	results doubtful.
	Bromides (unpurified)	3 days	
Organic iodine, enteric	Entero-vioform	30 days	
	Diodoquin	30 days	
	Enterosept	30 days	As above
Iodine compounds, topical	Iodine tincture	14 days	
	Iodine ointment	14 days	
	Iodoform	2 months	As above
Iodine compounds used in radiography	Pyelography		
	Diodrast	30 days	
	Neo-Iopax	30 days	
	Urokon	30 days	As above
	Cholecystography		
	Telepaque	6 months	
	Priodax	6 months	
	Cholografin	6 months	As above
	Bronchography		
	Lipiodol	2–10 years	
	Iodochlorol	2–10 years	
	Dionosil	30 days	As above
	Myelography		
	Pantopaque	2–10 years	As above
	Salpingography		
	Skiodan acacia	30 days	
	Salpix	30 days	As above
Thyroid compounds	Thyroid, desiccated	21 days	Hyperthyroid results valid.
	Thyroxin	21 days	Euthyroid results valid.
	Diiodotyrosine	30 days	Hypothyroid results doubtful.
Antithyroid and other drugs	Thiouracil	8 days	Hyperthyroid results valid.
	Propylthiouracil	8 days	Euthyroid and hypothyroid
	Tapazole	8 days	results doubtful.
	Thiourea	8 days	
	Imidazole	8 days	
	Thiocyanate	10 days	
	Perchlorates	10 days	
	Cortisone	8 days	
	ACTH	8 days	
	Estrogen derivatives	8 days	

I^{131} *Conversion Ratio* (Clark *et al.*, 1949)

This procedure is of some help in confirming the results of the uptake, but by itself the test is not dependable. It is recommended only in hyperthyroidism.

Salivary Ratio (Thode *et al.*, 1954)

This determination is of value in hypothyroidism. It serves to confirm the clinical impression; otherwise it is of little use.

The Procedure

Radioiodine[131] Thyroid Uptake

1. A number of doses of I^{131} should be prepared before the patient reports to the laboratory. The doses are placed in the phantocube and counted at a measured distance from the end of the scintillation probe. One of these doses is chosen as the standard.

2. The patient is questioned regarding intake of substances that may interfere with this study and regarding possible contraindications to the test, such as pregnancy. The patient is given a dose of I^{131}. The test tube containing the dose is washed three times with water, and the patient drinks each of these washings.

3. The patient is instructed to avoid salt, seafood, and cabbage and to return to the laboratory in 24 hours.

4. A short time prior to the patient's return to the laboratory the standard is counted in the same manner as was done when the doses were prepared. The room background radiation is measured.

5. The patient's neck is palpated to find the thyroid gland. The scintillation probe is then adjusted at a measured distance from a point just above the isthmus of the gland and the gland counted for three minutes. We usually repeat this by repositioning the probe to see whether the positioning is good and to make sure that the probe did not move during the counting. The variation between the two counts should be less than 2 per cent.

6. A thigh background count is done before each uptake.

7. The thigh background value is subtracted from both the readings of the patient to determine the ccpm (corrected counts per minute). The room background is similarly subtracted from the reading of the standard.

8. The patient's corrected counts per minute are divided by the standard corrected counts per minute (times 100) (equal to 100 per cent of the dose) to obtain the per cent uptake by the gland.

9. Normal: 15 per cent to 45 per cent.

I^{131} Conversion Rate

1. When the patient reports to the laboratory for the second time, draw a 10 ml. sample of blood.

2. Separate the serum from the blood and place 3.0 ml. in a test tube. Mark this level with a glass marking pencil.

3. Count the serum in the well scintillation counter for three minutes. This value is equal to the whole serum activity.

4. After counting the serum, determine the radioactive protein-bound iodine (PBI^{131}) as follows: Add 6.0 ml. of 10 per cent trichloracetic acid to the sample, mix well, centrifuge, and pour off the supernatant. Wash precipitate three times with 5 per cent trichloracetic acid, mix well, centrifuge each time, and pour off supernatant.

5. Add 3 per cent NaOH to the precipitate up to the 3.0 ml. mark. Break up the precipitate and mix well until it goes into solution.

6. Read the dissolved precipitate the same way the serum was read. *Important:* check the room background radiation before each series is read. It has been found to vary.

7. Subtract the background to obtain the following values: whole serum activity (corrected) in counts per minute and radioactive protein-bound iodine (corrected) in counts per minute.

8. Calculations:

$$\text{Conversion rate} = \frac{PBI^{131} \times 100}{\text{Whole serum}} \; I^{131}$$

9. Normal conversion rate: 15 per cent to 50 per cent

Another test for evaluation of suspected hyperthyroidism is the PBI^{131} determination (Silver *et al.*, 1955; Newburger *et al.*, 1955). The thyrobinding index is used for the diagnosis of thyroid activity.

THE THYROBINDING INDEX (TBI)

This *in vitro* test determines the I^{131}-triiodothyronine (T3) binding power of the plasma and is a reflection of the number of free thyrobinding sites present. The patient's plasma is incubated with an anion exchange resin containing I^{131}-labeled triiodothyronine. If only a small amount of the patient's own thyroid hormone is present in the plasma, a large amount of I^{131}-T3 will be taken up from the resin, and this is usually the case in hypothyroidism. In hyperthyroidism, in which most of the thyrobinding sites are occupied with the patient's own hormone, only a small amount of the I^{131}-T3 will leave the resin.

Standard Plasma

Standard plasma is prepared by pooling the plasmas from 20 euthyroid persons and giving it the arbitrary value of 1.00. If this test cannot be performed on the day the blood is drawn, the plasma should be removed and frozen. All plasmas used as standards must remain frozen until time of use and once thawed out should not be refrozen for future use.

Preparation of the Labeled Resin and Resin Tubes

In a 25 ml. flask place:
1. 15 ml. of distilled water
2. 0.25 micrograms of l-triiodothyronine-I^{131} (0.05 ml. of Triomet q.s. to 5 ml. of distilled H_2O. Take 2 ml. of this dilute solution of Triomet and add to the 15 ml. of distilled H_2O in the first step).
3. 5 gm. (dry weight) of a strongly basic, anion exchange resin (IRA 400), salt form (= 9 gm. wet weight for Amberlite IRA 400).

This mixture is shaken for 30 minutes. At the end of this time the resin is filtered, washed once with distilled water, and allowed to dry at room temperature.

Approximate 0.1 gm. portions of this labeled resin are placed in individual glass tubes (100 × 16 mm.). These tubes are counted in a standard well counter. The amount of resin in each tube is adjusted to give equal (within 2 per cent) activity in each tube. The tubes are then left at room temperature until used but for no longer than two weeks.

Method. The plasma to be tested and the *standard plasma* are treated identically as follows:
1. 2 ml. of the plasma to be tested is added to each *resin tube*. (EDTA or double oxalate, but *not* heparin, may be used as anticoagulants.)
2. The stoppered tubes are shaken at 35° C. for 90 minutes, and at the end of that time the resin is allowed to settle to the bottom of the tube.
3. 1 ml. of plasma is removed and its activity measured in a suitable well counter.

4. Calculations:
$$TBI = \frac{\text{Activity of Test Plasma} \times \text{TBI of Std. Plasma}}{\text{Activity of Std. Plasma}}$$
5. Interpretation of results (Scholar, 1961)
   Hyperthyroid: less than 0.86
   Euthyroid: 0.86 to 1.20
   Hypothyroid: greater than 1.20

BLOOD VOLUME

Radioiodinated Human Serum Albumin (I^{131} HSA) (Crispell et al., 1950)

This method requires accurate timing and meticulous technique. Since radioiodinated human serum albumin is diffusable, specimens of blood must be withdrawn as soon as possible after mixing in the blood. Ten minutes is the best time. Shorter periods do not allow for mixing; longer periods allow for diffusion, which gives greater values than actually exist. The method is sufficiently accurate for clinical use.

1. I^{131} HSA is made up to a concentration of 6 to 10 microcuries per ml. in sterile normal saline solution, and this is used as a working solution.

2. A dose of I^{131} HSA (usually 3 to 5 μc.) is withdrawn from the working solution bottle and expelled into a 1000 ml. volumetric flask (being careful to keep the needle and syringe sterile). To the I^{131} HSA add water up to the mark.

3. Exactly the same amount is again drawn into the same needle and syringe from the bottle containing the working solution of I^{131} HSA.

4. Inject this into the patient's vein, being careful not to inject subcutaneously. The syringe and needle should not be rinsed with blood, since a similar rinsing was not done with the standard.

5. After ten minutes, a 10 ml. sample of blood is drawn from the opposite arm without stasis and put into a heparinized tube, and 3.0 ml. of blood is placed into a container with a dry anticoagulant suitable for hematocrit determinations.

6. Centrifuge the first specimen, remove 3.0 ml. of plasma, and place in a test tube. Place 3.0 ml. of standard in a second test tube.

7. A background count is made on the well before reading the samples.

8. The plasma and standard are each counted for three minutes. The background is subtracted to obtain the corrected counts per minute.

9. Calculations:

$$\text{Plasma volume} = \frac{\text{ccpm of standard} \times \text{volume of standard (1000 ml.)}}{\text{ccpm of patient's plasma}}$$

$$\text{Total blood volume} = \frac{\text{Plasma volume}}{1.00 - \text{corrected hematocrit*}}$$

Red cell volume = total blood volume — plasma volume

*Correction factor = 0.91
(Fields and Seed, 1961, p. 56).
10. Normals (Fields and Seed, 1961):
Total blood volume = 73 ml. per kg. (±5 ml.)
Plasma volume = 43 ml. per kg. (±5 ml.)
Red cell volume = 30 ml. per kg. (±5 ml.)

Chromium[51] (Cr[51])

This method is accurate. Its chief drawback is the necessity for tagging the red cells, a process that requires 45 minutes. Errors result from diffusion of the chromium and destruction of the red cells.

Cr[51] Blood Volume (Ascorbic Acid Method)
(Quimby et al., 1958)

1. A sterile Vacutainer is used, containing anticoagulant solution.
2. Place 10 to 15 ml. of blood in the Vacutainer containing the anticoagulant and 20 μc. Cr[51] as Na_2CrO_4.
3. Incubate at 37° C. for 45 minutes, agitating gently at 15-minute intervals.
4. At the end of the incubation period, inject 50 mg. of ascorbic acid into the bottle and mix.
5. Inject intravenously 6.0 ml. of whole blood containing tagged cells. The remaining whole blood is used for the standard.
6. After 20 minutes draw 20 ml. of blood from the opposite arm without stasis, put 17 ml. into a tube containing 0.1 ml. of heparin, and mix. The remaining 3.0 ml. is put into a container with a dry anticoagulant suitable for hematocrit determinations.
7. Label four test tubes: patient's plasma (Pt. P.), patient's whole blood (Pt. W.B.), standard plasma (Std. P.), and standard whole blood (Std. W.B.).
8. Depending on the counts in the standard, a 1 to 10 dilution is usually found necessary for the Std. W.B.
9. Transfer 3.0 ml. of Pt. W.B. into a labeled test tube; make a 1 to 10 dilution of the Std. W.B. with saline and transfer 3.0 ml. of the dilution into a test tube.
10. Centrifuge the specimens for plasma. (Caution: Be sure the sample was thor-

oughly mixed when whole blood was removed and that, after centrifuging, the cells are packed to eliminate trapping of too much plasma between the cells.)
11. Count 3.0 ml. of Pt. P. and 3.0 ml. of Std.P., and place the tubes prepared in step 9 in a well scintillation counter for three minutes.
12. Calculations (shown at bottom of page)
   Note: 6 = ml. of whole blood injected
   c/hct = corrected hematocrit
   Std. = Standard
   W.B. = Whole blood
   ccpm = corrected counts per minute
Red cell volume = TBV × c/hct (c/hct of the patient)
Plasma volume = TBV × 1.00 — c/hct (c/hct of the patient)
13. Normals (Sterling and Gray, 1950):
   Total blood volume = 53–76 ml. per kg.
   Red cell volume = 25–34 ml. per kg.
   Plasma volume = 28–42 ml. per kg.

Cr[51] Red Cell Survival (Weinstein and LeRoy, 1953)

1. Sterile Vacutainers are prepared with 0.1 ml. of heparin. Commercially available bottles containing ACD solution and NIH formula A can also be used as an anticoagulant.
2. Place 10 to 15 ml. of blood in the bottle containing the anticoagulant and 100 μc. Cr[51] as Na_2CrO_4.
3. Incubate at 37° C. for 45 minutes, agitating gently at 15-minute intervals.
4. At the end of the incubation period, inject 50 mg. of ascorbic acid into the bottle and mix.
5. Inject intravenously 6.0 ml. of whole blood containing the tagged cells.
6. Twenty-four hours later draw a 3 to 5 ml. sample of blood. Place in a test tube containing dry ammonium–potassium oxalate and use as the 100 per cent survival of the erythrocytes at time "0."
7. Samples of blood are drawn three times during the first week (including the

$$\text{Total blood volume} = \frac{6 \times \{\text{ccpm of Std. W.B.} - [\text{ccpm Std. P.} \times (1 - \text{c/hct of Std.})]\}}{\text{ccpm of Pt. W.B.} - \text{ccpm Pt. P.} \times [1 - \text{c/hct of Pt.}]}$$

24-hour specimen) and twice a week for at least three weeks.

8. It is not necessary to read the samples of blood until all have been collected; this will eliminate the need for calculating decay.

9. Read 3.0 ml. of whole blood in the well scintillation counter.

Calculations:

% red cell survival =

$$\frac{(\text{ccpm of 3.0 ml. of W.B. at "X" time}) \times 100}{\text{ccpm of 3.0 ml. of W.B. at 24 hours}}$$

10. Using linear graph paper, plot the per cent survival of whole blood as the ordinate against time as the abscissa.

11. The "half time" is the day on which 50 per cent of the labeled cells have disappeared from the circulating blood and is determined by plotting whole blood activity on a linear graph.

12. By this method the normal "half time" is 25 to 35 days.

$Co^{60}B_{12}$ *Test for Pernicious Anemia*

This procedure is useful in classifying megaloblastic anemias. The chief error arises from the failure to collect urine specimens accurately. A large amount, also known as a flushing dose, of nonradioactive B_{12} is best given after one hour, although an interval of four to six hours may be used. The flushing dose should be large enough to saturate the tissue fluids and to bind sites with B_{12} that will permit the excretion of the ingested dose. Gaffney *et al.* (1959) showed that one hour is adequate. If the vitamin $B_{12}Co^{60}$ excretion is low, the test must be repeated with the intrinsic factor to confirm the diagnosis of pernicious anemia. Defects in intestinal absorption may be detected by this method, since results of both procedures will be low in such instances. Treatment with vitamin B_{12} should be withheld for at least three days before the test.

Schilling Test $Co^{60}B_{12}$ (Schilling, 1953; Glass *et al.*, 1954)

PART A

1. Two doses of Co^{60} are prepared, 0.5 $\mu c.$ each; one dose is the standard and the other is given to the patient.

2. The $Co^{60}B_{12}$ containing 0.5 $\mu c.$ Co^{60} as radiocyanocobalamin is given orally to a fasting patient with an empty bladder.

3. One hour later a "flushing dose" of B_{12} containing 1000 micrograms of crystalline nonradioactive B_{12} is administered intramuscularly.

4. Have the patient collect *all* urine for the next 24 hours and return the specimen to the laboratory. (*Note:* Failure to collect all urine voided during the 24-hour period introduces considerable error.)

5. When the urine is received, measure and record volume; if less than 1000 ml., fill up with water to 1000 ml.

6. Prepare standard by diluting 0.5 $\mu c.$ of Co^{60} to 1000 ml.

7. Read 3.0 ml. of the urine sample and 3.0 ml. of the standard in the well scintillation counter. The ccpm may be low. If this is true, count for a longer time. If necessary, count for 10 to 15 minutes.

8. Calculations:

% $Co^{60}B_{12}$ excreted =

$$\frac{\text{ccpm of 3.0 ml. of urine} \times \text{vol. of urine} \times 100}{\text{ccpm of 3.0 ml. of the standard} \times \text{dilution factor}}$$

9. Normal range: 7 per cent or more, of dose administered is excreted in the urine in the first 24 hours. Patients with pernicious anemia excrete only from 0 to less than 3 per cent of the radioactive vitamin if it is given alone, but from 3.1 to 30 per cent if the intrinsic factor was given simultaneously.

PART B

1. If less than 7 per cent of dose administered is excreted in the urine in the first 24 hours, the examination is repeated. At the time the patient is given 0.5 $\mu c.$ of Co^{60}, he is also given a capsule containing 60 micrograms of intrinsic factor.

2. The same procedure is followed as outlined in Part A.

3. If the excreted amount of Co^{60} rises to normal levels, the diagnosis of pernicious anemia is established; if the excretion of Co^{60} does not rise following administration of the intrinsic factor, the patient has a malabsorption syndrome.

Measurement of fecal excretion has shown only about 30 per cent recovery in the normal, compared with three times as much in pernicious anemia even in remission.

Radioactive Iron (Fe^{59})

Radioactive iron may be used to study anemia. The following procedures may be performed to determine the cause of various types of anemia:

1. Oral Fe^{59} absorption studies (Moore et al., 1944).

2. Plasma Fe^{59} clearance studies (Huff et al., 1950).

3. Fe^{59} utilization studies (Burwell et al., 1953).

4. Plasma iron turnover studies (Boswell and Mallett, 1955).

Radioactive iron supplied as iron citrate (Fe^{59}) may be utilized in a study of iron activity in the body. A comparatively small dose of the iron as ferrous citrate may be given. Approximately 4 micrograms of iron with an activity of 4 to 5 microcuries is given by mouth after a period free from oral or parenteral iron therapy. According to some authors, in the absence of hydrochloric acid in the stomach, iron is absorbed poorly through the gastrointestinal tract. Collection of stools over the subsequent four days may help to evaluate the degree of absorption from the gastrointestinal tract. One interfering problem in this type of procedure is decreased mobility of the gastrointestinal tract as a result of which the iron is not eliminated through the stool. Consequently, the amount excreted may be relatively small in the first few days. If the specimens on the fourth day contain more than 2 per cent of the given dose, additional stool specimens should be collected over subsequent 24-hour periods until the amount present is found to be below 2 per cent of the administered dose. We have found that 10 to 20 per cent of the iron is absorbed in the gastrointestinal tract by normal individuals. The quantity found in the stools may be extremely low in patients with iron deficiency anemia or with polycythemia vera. Patients with adequate iron stores excrete 80 to 90 per cent. Those who have an excess of iron excrete more in the stool. It is necessary to differentiate the individual who has enough iron from one whose intestinal absorption is deficient because of inadequate hydrochloric acid in the stomach or defects of the intestinal mucosa.

Plasma Iron Disappearance Time

The study of plasma iron disappearance after injection of a known amount of radioactive iron[59] allows one to determine the approximate quantity of iron stores in the body. A dose of 20 microcuries of Fe^{59} as ferrous citrate is incubated with a sample of the patient's plasma and then injected into the patient. The incubation period allows for the tagging of the plasma with the iron and produces an iron protein fraction.

According to some authors, preliminary incubation with the patient's plasma is not necessary (Hallberg and Silvell, 1960; Lentino et al., 1960). The injected iron is cleared from the plasma at a relatively rapid rate initially, which gradually slows so that 50 per cent of the radioactive iron is removed from the plasma in 60 to 120 minutes. In individuals with an iron deficiency in whom the iron stores are relatively small, the clearance time is much more rapid. According to some authors, in individuals whose iron stores are filled, the absorption is much slower and may go on for days before the 50 per cent mark has been reached. In accord with this concept, iron disappearance is a direct measurement of the iron stores of the body and not of any red cell activity.

On the other hand, according to other authors, iron clearance is accelerated in polycythemia, the leukemias, hemolytic anemia, pernicious anemia, the anemias of infection (Bush, Ashenbrucker, Cartwright, and Wintrobe, 1956), cancer, and iron deficiency. Plasma iron clearance is decreased in aplastic conditions of the bone marrow (Wasserman, Rashkoff, Leavitt, and Port, 1956). This rate of disappearance can be used as an index of erythropoiesis provided the body stores of iron are normal (Rambach, Cooper, and Alt, 1955).

Plasma Iron Turnover

The plasma iron turnover may be calculated by comparing the plasma disappearance rate with the amount of iron present in the serum. In this way one is able to determine the amount of plasma iron that is metabolized in any one day. Normally the body metabolizes 26 to 30 milligrams per day, or according to the body weight it may be expressed as 0.4 to 0.45 milligrams per kilogram per day. In active hematopoiesis the iron turnover is much more rapid. In aplastic anemias and anemias in which the iron utilization is poor, the plasma iron turnover is below this figure.

Iron[59] Utilization Procedure

The amount of iron[59] that is actually metabolized in the red cells may be calculated by obtaining daily samples of whole blood from the patient. The iron utilization usually shows a rise at a relatively rapid rate for two to seven days. Following that period, the iron in erythrocytes remains at a relatively stable level for a long time. The measurement and graphing of the iron utilization against time and days is expressed in a curve, which can be compared with the normal. In severe anemias in which there is active regeneration, iron is used at a more rapid rate than normally, while in patients with aplastic anemias the iron incorporation into the red cells is depressed and the curve is relatively flat from the beginning. Comparison of these curves can be of diagnostic value. Iron utilization may also be calculated by *in vivo* counts. These may be determined by graphing the corrected counts per minute per given period of time over the liver, spleen, and sacrum, utilizing the thigh or knee for a background count. In hemolytic anemia, the sacrum, where hematopoiesis is active, reflects an early increase in red cell production. Ultimately the iron will be deposited from the hemolyzed red cells, usually in the liver and spleen, and in hypersplenism the spleen will have more of the iron deposited. In aplastic anemias, the liver, spleen, and bone marrow will show poor iron utilization, while in anemias with relatively active regeneration, the sacrum may show higher counts than the liver and spleen.

Oral Fe⁵⁹ Absorption Study

1. Patient reports to the laboratory in a fasting state and should not have had any iron therapy, oral or parenteral, for one week prior to the test.
2. Blood is drawn for serum iron, hemoglobin, and hematocrit. A dose of radioactive iron is given orally (approximately 3 to 4 micrograms of iron with an activity of 4 to 5 microcuries of Fe⁵⁹ as ferrous citrate).
3. At the same time a standard of Fe⁵⁹ is also prepared and counted.
4. The patient is given uniform sized containers and is instructed to collect all stool specimens passed each day for four days.
5. The specimens are returned to the laboratory and the fourth-day specimen is counted; if the specimen contains more than 2 per cent of the administered dose, the patient is requested to collect several additional specimens.
6. The specimens and standard are diluted to equal volume and mixed thoroughly.
7. The specimens and standard are counted by placing them above the well

scintillation counter. After removal of the lead shielding cap, the specimens are 4.0 cm. above the crystal.

8. Calculations:

$$\% \text{ Fe}^{59} \text{ excreted} = \frac{\text{ccpm of specimen} \times 100}{\text{ccpm of standard}}$$

The total excretion for the four days is reported.

Plasma Fe Disappearance and Plasma Fe Turnover

1. Draw 30 ml. of blood from patient. Place 15 to 20 ml. in a container with heparin and label "Plasma Fe." Send 10 ml. to laboratory for serum Fe determination.
2. Centrifuge tube labeled "Plasma Fe" and withdraw, using sterile technique, at least 8 ml. of plasma. Tag this plasma with approximately 20 μc. of Fe⁵⁹ as ferrous citrate.
3. Incubate at 37° C. for 30 minutes.
4. Inject 6.0 ml. of Fe⁵⁹-tagged plasma into patient.
5. Draw 10 ml. samples of heparinized blood at intervals of 10, 30, 45, 60, 120, 180, and 240 minutes.

Calculations

1. Plasma iron disappearance rate.
a. Draw 3.0 ml. quantities of plasma at 10, 30, 45, 60, 120, 180, and 240 minutes and count in a well scintillation counter.
b. Using semilogarithmic paper, plot ccpm in the plasma as the ordinate against time as the abscissa; this is a time exponented curve and forms a straight line. (In low counts there are exceptions to this.) Extrapolate back to time "0"; this value equals the ccpm in plasma at time "0."
c. The time at which the disappearance curve reaches one-half the value of time "0" is referred to as the "plasma disappearance ½" (PD ½) or "half time." To determine this, divide the ccpm at time "0" by 2; this gives 50 per cent of the ccpm. Where this value intersects the straight line previously plotted, the PD ½ is calculated. N = 60 to 120 minutes.
2. Plasma iron turnover (PIT) (calculation shown at bottom of page).

PV is determined with radioactive iron according to the isotope dilution principle.

$$\text{PIT} = \frac{(0.693) \ (\text{PV in ml.}) \ (\text{serum Fe mg./ml.}) \ (24 \text{ hr./day})}{\text{PD } \frac{1}{2} \text{ hr.}}$$

$0.693 = \log \text{ of } 2$

Activity at 0 time is obtained by extrapolation of the plasma Fe^{59} activity during the first hour in a semilogarithmic system (Hallberg and Silvell, 1960). If a spectrometer is available, PV may be determined with I^{131} HSA or Cr^{51}.

Serum Fe. Usually serum iron is reported in micrograms per cent; if so, multiply serum Fe by 10^{-5}.

PD ½ hr. = PD ½, which must be converted from minutes to hours.

24 hr. per day = to obtain plasma iron turnover per day.

N = 26 to 30 mg. per day or 0.4 to 0.45 mg. per kg. per day.

In Vivo *Counting of Liver, Spleen, and Sacrum*

1. The ccpm's are corrected for body activity by counting over the knee.

2. Two graphs are plotted: one graph for the first four hours and a second graph for the 25 to 30 days during which *in vivo* counts are obtained at specified intervals. Plot the ccpm at the site as the ordinate against the time (days) as the abscissa on linear graph paper.

3. All sites counted are plotted on the same graph for comparison.

Intestinal Absorption Studies (Sanders *et al.*, 1956)

I^{131} tagged fats may be used to determine the digestive and absorptive capacities of the intestinal tract. Triglyceride tagged with I^{131} may be given orally, and the capacity of pancreatic enzymes to digest this material may be determined by estimating the quantity of I^{131} absorbed into the blood from the intestinal tract.

To differentiate between the malabsorption syndrome and poor pancreatic fat digestion, one may use oleic acid tagged with I^{131}. In malabsorption syndromes both types of fats are poorly absorbed, whereas in pancreatic disorders only the triolein is poorly absorbed, while the oleic acid is absorbed normally.

The normal curve for fat absorption may be seen in the accompanying figure.

Within two hours approximately 0.5 to 1 per cent per liter of the ingested dose is found in the blood and in four hours, 2.5 to 3.5 per cent; after six hours the quantity present will be 2 to 3 per cent per liter.

Stool specimens from normal persons, measured over a period of four days, usually show less than 5 per cent of the ingested dose. This procedure is a more sensitive measure of malabsorption.

In performing this test, it is wise to give the patient Lugol's solution prior to the beginning of the test to saturate the thyroid gland. This will eliminate any absorption of I^{131} into the thyroid as a result of the procedure.

Errors may result from mechanical problems, such as eating prior to the test. In addition, mechanical defects in the stomach preventing release of the meal into the intestinal tract because of narrowing of the pylorus or any similar defect will produce abnormal results. Delayed excretion of the stool will of course produce other errors in the results. Since I^{131} is excreted in the urine, it is important that the fecal specimen not be contaminated with urine. These factors should be considered in evaluating the results of the test.

TYPICAL NORMAL TRIOLEIN AND OLEIC ACID BLOOD LEVELS*

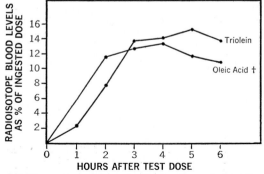

* Chart adapted from Ruffin, T. M., *et al.*: M. Clin. North America, 41:1575, 1957.

Procedure Kaplan *et al.*, 1958)

1. Prior to starting the test, the patient is given ten drops of Lugol's solution three times a day for one to two days and then reports to the laboratory while fasting.

2. The patient is weighed and the carrier meal is prepared.

3. The carrier meal is composed of 200 ml. of peanut oil, 200 ml. of water, and 15 ml. of Tween 80 (emulsifying agent).

4. Add 50 μc. of triolein I^{131} to 155 ml. of the carrier meal and homogenize for three to five minutes.

5. The patient drinks 75 ml. of the labeled mixture. Wash the container with water, which is then given to the patient.

6. To make the standard, add 1 ml. of the labeled carrier meal to 99 ml. of unlabeled carrier meal. Mix and then count 3 ml. in a well counter for five minutes.

7. Save 75 ml. of labeled carrier meal as a standard to compare with the stool specimen.

8. Draw whole blood specimens at two, four, and seven hours after the meal is ingested, and count 3 ml. of each specimen in a well counter for five minutes.

9. Save all stool specimens for 72 hours in a glass or plastic container. It is important that the patient avoid contaminating the stool specimen with urine.

Calculations

1. Blood (% per liter of whole blood)
   A. % activity per liter of blood of ingested triolein I^{131} =
   $$\frac{\text{activity per liter of blood}}{\text{activity ingested}} \times 100$$
   Activity per liter of blood = (counts of blood per 3 ml.) (333.3)
   Activity ingested = (counts of standard) (volume of ingested carrier) (33.3)
   B. Normal (Kaplan et al., 1958)
   2 hr. = 0.55–2.64% per liter; average, 1.25.
   4 hr. = 1.37–3.52% per liter; average, 2.14.
   7 hr. = 1.05–3.07% per liter; average, 1.75.
2. Stools
   A. The 72-hour stool specimen is homogenized, placed above the well scintillation counters, and counted for five minutes.
   B. Dilute the saved 75 ml. of labeled carrier to the same volume as the 72-hour stool. Homogenize and count for five minutes.
   C. % excreted = $\dfrac{\text{ccpm of specimen}}{\text{ccpm of standard}}$ $\times 100$
   N = less than 5%

REFERENCES

1. Astwood, E. B., and Stanley, M. M.: Use of radioactive iodine in the study of thyroid function in man. West. J. Surg., 55:625, 1947.
2. Boswell, T. H., and Mallett, B.: Diurnal variation in the turnover of iron through the plasma. J. Clin. Sci., 14:235, 1955.
3. Burwell, E. L., Brickley, B. A., and Finch, C. A.: Erythrocyte life span in small animals, Am. J. Physiol., 172:718, 1953.
4. Bush, J. A., Ashenbrucher, H., Cartwright, G. E., and Wintrobe, M. M.: The anemia of infection. XX. The kinetics of iron metabolism in the anemia associated with chronic infection. J. Clin. Invest., 35:89, 1956.
5. Clark, D. E., Moe, R. H., and Adams, E. E.: Rate of conversion of administered inorganic radioactive iodine into protein bound iodine and plasma, as made in evaluation of thyroid function. Surgery, 26:331, 1949.
6. Crispell, K. R., Porter, B., and Nieset, R. T.: Studies of plasma volume using human serum albumin tagged with radioactive iodine. J. Clin. Invest., 29:513, 1950.
7. Dobyns, H. M.: Iodine I^{131} in Thyroid Diagnosis. Radioisotopes in Medicine. Oak Ridge Institute of Nuclear Studies. Washington, D.C., Atomic Energy Commission, 1955.
8. Fields, T., and Seed, L.: Clinical Use of Radioisotopes, A Manuel of Technic. 2d ed. Chicago, Yearbook Publishers, Inc., 1961.
9. Gaffney, G. W., Watkins, D. M., and Chow, B. F.: Vitamin B_{12} absorption. J. Lab. & Clin. Med., 53:525, 1959.
10. Glass, G. B. J., Boyd, L. J., Gellin, G. A., and Stephanson, L.: Uptake of radioactive vitamin B_{12} by the liver in humans: Test for measurement of intestinal absorption of vitamin B_{12} and intrinsic factor activity. Arch. Biochem., 51:251, 1954.
11. Hallberg, L., and Silvell, L.: Iron absorption studies. Acta med. scandinav., Suppl. 358, 168:7, 1960.
12. Harnwell, G. P., and Stephens, W. E.: Atomic Physics. New York, McGraw-Hill Book Co., Inc., 1955.
13. Hollaender, A.: Radiation Biology. New York, McGraw-Hill Book Co., Inc., 1954.
14. Huff, R. L., Hennessy, T. G., Austin, R. E., Garcia, J. F., Roberts, B. M., and Lawrence, J. H.: Plasma and red cell iron turnover in normal subjects and patients having various hematopoietic disorders. J. Clin. Invest., 29:1041, 1950.
15. Kaplan, E., Edidin, B. O., Fruin, R. C., and Baker, L.: Intestinal absorption of iodine^{131} labeled triolein and oleic acid in normal subjects and in steatorrhea. Gastroenterology, 34:901, 1958.
16. Lentino, W., Collier, C., and Rubenfeld, S.: Radioactive iron techniques in clinical practice. J.A.M.A., 173:87, 1960.
17. McMillan, E. M.: Lecture Series in Nuclear Physics. Washington, D.C., U. S. Government Printing Office, 1947.
18. Moore, C. V., Dubach, R., Minnish, V., and Roberts, H. K.: Absorption of ferrous and ferric radioactive iron by human subjects and by dogs. J. Clin. Invest., 23:755, 1944.
19. Newburger, R. A., Silver, S., Yohalem, S. B., and Feitelberg, S.: Uptake and blood level of radioactive iodine in hyperthyroidism. New England J. Med., 253:127, 1955.
20. Owen, Charles A.: Diagnostic Radioisotopes. Springfield, Ill., Charles C Thomas, 1959.
21. Quimby, E. H., Feitelberg, S., and Silver, S.: Radioactive Isotopes in Clinical Practice. Philadelphia, Lea & Febiger, 1958.
22. Ramback, W. A., Cooper, J. A. D., and Alt, H. L.: The uptake of radioiron in the bone marrow as a measure of erythropoiesis. J. Lab. & Clin. Med., 46:941, 1955.
23. Ruffin, J. M., Keever, I. C., and Chear, W. C., Jr.: Use of radioactive labeled lipids in study of intestinal absorption, a clinical appraisal. M. Clin. North America, 41:1517, 1957.
24. Sanders, A. P., Isley, J. K., Sharpe, K., Baylin,

G. J., Shingleton, W. W., Hymans, J. C., Ruffin, J. M., and Reeves, R. J.: Radioiodine recovery in feces following an I^{131} labeled fat test meal. Am. J. Roentgenol., 75:386, 1956.

25. Schilling, R. F.: A new test for intrinsic factor activity. J. Lab. & Clin. Med., 42:946, 1953.

26. Scholar, J. F.: Original procedure distributed at the Convention of the Society of Nuclear Medicine, June, 1961.

27. Silver, S., Newburger, R. A., Yohalem, S. B., and Feitelberg, S.: Method for determination of radioiodine levels in blood plasma. J. Mt. Sinai Hosp., 21:296, 1955.

28. Sterling, K., and Gray, S. J.: Determination of circulating red cell volume in man by radioactive chromium. J. Clin. Invest., 29:1614, 1950.

29. Thode, H. G., Jainet, C. H., and Kirkwood, S.: Studies in diagnostic tests of salivary glands and thyroid gland function with radioiodine. New England J. Med., 251:129, 1954.

30. Wasserman, L. R., Rashkoff, I. A., Leavitt, D., Mayer, J., and Port, S.: The rate of removal of radioactive iron from the plasma—an index of erythropoiesis. J. Clin. Invest., 31:32–39, 1952.

31. Weinstein, I. M., and Beutler, E.: The use of chromium[51] and iron[59] in a combined procedure to study erythrocyte production and destruction in normal subjects, and in patients with hemolytic or aplastic anemia. J. Lab. & Clin. Med., 45:616, 1955.

32. Weinstein, I. M., and LeRoy, G. V.: Radioactive sodium chromate for the study of survival of red blood cells. J. Lab. & Clin. Med., 43:368, 1953.

Chapter 8

Clinical Chemistry

By FERRIN B. MORELAND, Ph.D.

BASIC LABORATORY MANEUVERS

Before describing the principles involved in the several types of analytical methods used in clinical chemistry, it may be useful to consider some basic techniques and fundamentals that are important in any chemical procedure.

Weighing

The amount of most chemicals to be used in the laboratory is measured by weight. Liquids and gases are generally measured by volume, but even these are sometimes weighed. Some chemicals are weighed directly for immediate use. Most often they are weighed and then put into solution so that the portion for actual use can be measured by volume. Sometimes the weight must be known precisely; at other times an approximate weight is all that is needed. Accurate weighing takes more time and requires the use of expensive equipment. It is therefore important in each instance to know how precisely the weighing must be done.

Several types of weighing devices should be available in a clinical laboratory. The most precise is the analytical balance. There are many kinds of analytical balances on the market. They vary in accuracy, sensitivity, and convenience, and their cost is determined by these features. For usual purposes an analytical balance should have a sensitivity of about 1/20 of a milligram (0.05 mg. or 0.00005 gm.) and a capacity of about 200 gm. An analytical balance consists essentially of a beam balanced in the center on a knife-edge with pans hung from the ends. The pans are also suspended on knife edges to minimize friction. Material to be weighed is placed on one pan (usually the left) and weights are placed on the other (usually the right). To protect the delicate knife edges and the smooth surfaces on which they rest, the balance is equipped with a mechanism for lifting the knife edges and stabilizing the beam when anything is being added to or removed from the pans or when the equipment is not in use. It is also necessary that the balance be enclosed in a case to protect it from dust and from air currents, both of which would affect the apparent weight obtained. The simplest, and therefore least expensive, type of analytical balance requires the handling of weights on the right pan down to 10 mg. Differences of less than 10 mg. (sometimes 5 mg.) are measured by moving a "rider" along graduations on the beam from 0 at the center knife edge to 10 mg. (or 5 mg.) over the knife edge of the right pan. A little more convenience is obtained by adding graduations to the left side of the beam. Weighing is made much faster by suspending from the beam a fine link chain whose effective length can be varied and whose weight can be read from a dial. Such a chain usually covers a range up to 100 mg. By eliminating the 10 mg. rider from the beam a larger rider can be used; this is set in notches to cover the range from 100 mg. to 1 gm. A "keyboard" may be used to add and remove weights in the 10 to 1000 mg. range. Other conveniences available include a magnetic damper to bring the beam rapidly to rest and a mechanism for easily adjusting the zero index to the actual zero point.

It is necessary to have an adequately accurate set of weights for use with an analytical balance. There is no point in trying to weigh to an accuracy of 0.1 mg. with weights that are accurate only to 0.1 gm. For use with the analytical balance a set of weights of at least Class S of the National Bureau of Standards classification should be available. Class C weights are useful for rough balances weighing to no better than 0.1 gm.

An analytical balance is used for weighing standards and for a few components of reagents. For weighing most of the chemicals used in the preparation of clinical laboratory reagents, less precision is needed, and a less expensive but more rapid type of balance should be available. The least expensive type of balance for this purpose is the trip balance, which may have one or two platforms or pans. This type of balance may have one or more beams with movable riders or weights on them to avoid the use of loose weights on the right pan. When working properly, this type of balance is sensitive to about 0.1 gm. One defect of this type of balance is its tendency to shift its zero point. When either end of the beam touches bottom, the zero point is likely to shift in that direction and make accurate weighing difficult.

A more stable and accurate instrument is the torsion balance; it is also much more expensive than a trip balance. A good compromise, which combines a sensitivity of about 0.01 gm. and a moderate price, is the triple-beam type of balance (Fig. 8–1).

The two most important considerations in the use of any balance are cleanliness and gentleness. With the more sensitive analytical balances the weight of fingerprints may be appreciable. Also the moisture and salt from fingers may cause corrosion. Anything that is weighed on an analytical balance should be handled with a forceps or clean gauze. Weights should be handled with special precautions, using forceps of soft metal or with ivory tips. Never place a chemical directly on the pan of a balance. On the analytical balance use a watch glass or weighing bottle to contain the chemical. For rough weighing of inert chemicals paper can be used to protect the pans from direct contact. Any spilled chemicals should be cleaned away at once.

The process of weighing is always relative. The final weight is no more accurate than the initial zeroing of the balance. This zero balancing must include the weighing paper or vessel, or these must be weighed separately and a proper allowance made for them. The weight of a sheet of paper is usually not negligible. Do not assume that a balance will read zero with nothing on it; it usually will not. Most balances have adjustable weights mounted on screws, which can be turned one way or the other to bring the empty reading to zero. Some balances are zeroed by adjusting the screws of their feet. Another way to zero is to add weights to one pan or the other until balance is attained and then to add or subtract this extra weight from the final weight.

Mixing

Directions to mix are frequently omitted from laboratory instructions, because it is

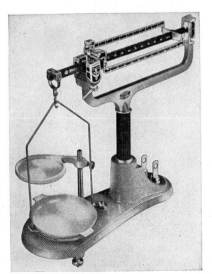

Figure 8–1. Triple-beam balance. (Courtesy Ohaus Scale Corp.)

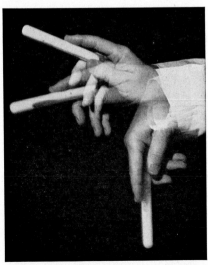

Figure 8–2. Mixing by wrist flipping.

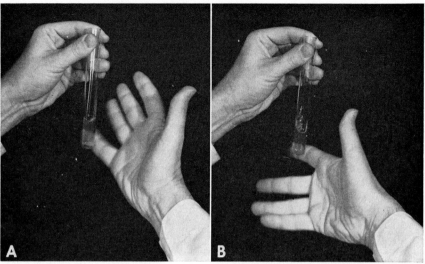

Figure 8–3. Mixing by finger flipping.

Figure 8–4. Vortex mixer.

Figure 8–5. Tube buzzer.

second nature to experienced workers and therefore taken for granted. There are certain layering tests in which careful avoidance of mixing is important, but these are rather exceptional. Unless otherwise specified, whenever two solutions are put together or when a solid or liquid reagent is added to another, *always mix*, preferably (and sometimes necessarily) after each of a series of additions.

The most obvious method of mixing is to stopper and shake. This is also one of the most effective. There are several other ways to mix, and a suitable one will be selected for the circumstances. One of the most useful is the flipping technique, which is done by holding the test tube between

the thumb and first finger and flipping up and down with a wrist action (Fig. 8–2). (Practice this technique first with a test tube of water!) Another method, particularly useful for stirring up solid material in the bottom of a tube, is to hold the tube tightly between the thumb and forefinger of one hand and to rapidly strike the bottom of the tube with the four fingers of the other hand in succession (Fig. 8–3). There are also available commercially several types of tube mixing devices or tube buzzers (Figs. 8–4, 8–5). These can be very useful. For prolonged stirring, as in dissolving a solid in a liquid, mechanical stirring is best. Many types of stirrers, electric or air driven, are on the market. Perhaps the most useful is the magnetic stirrer in which a motor driven magnet drives a second magnet placed in the beaker or flask to be stirred. Stirring magnets encased in glass or plastic are available. A combination hot plate-magnetic stirrer is a useful piece of equipment.

Dissolving

Getting solids into solution can waste a lot of time. There are a few tricks to help speed the process, but the best approach is to do something else while the dissolving is going on. Watching does not help.

Use may be made of a mechanical stirrer, such as a magnetic mixer. Heat also helps if the material involved is heat stable. Heat affects solubility in two ways: it speeds the dissolving process, and as a rule it increases solubility. If heat is used in preparing a saturated solution, it is sometimes possible to dissolve more than will remain in solution at room temperature. This may result in an undesirable excess of solid or even a broken bottle when the solution cools.

Some materials are readily soluble but may become difficult to dissolve if not properly handled. Anhydrous sodium carbonate is one of these. The powder should be placed in a dry beaker or flask and the water suddenly added from another open vessel. With immediate shaking, solution is rapid. If the powder is allowed to get wet before it is shaken thoroughly with water, it may cake and dissolve only very slowly.

Another method to speed solution involves getting the solid up off the bottom. As the material on the bottom dissolves, it forms a saturated solution, which then prevents further dissolving until it diffuses up into the more dilute solution above. A perforated cone or test tube can be set in the top of a cylinder, which is filled with solvent. Solid placed in the cone or tube is then immersed in the top of the liquid and

dissolves rapidly as the heavier solution is formed and streams downward. Another simple trick is to use a glass stopper cylinder with solvent and solid in it. The cylinder is inverted to let the solid settle to the top (Fig. 8–6). It is then carefully turned part way back, leaving the solid near the top just below the liquid level. Rapid solution results.

Filtration

Filtration and centrifugation are used to separate solids from liquids. Filtration is usually done through paper but may sometimes better be done through cloth, cotton, or glass wool, especially when rapid filtration is desired. Common sense should suggest the filter medium, depending on the size and character of the solid particles being removed and on the chemical activity of the liquid. Filter papers are available in many types and degrees of porosity (Table 8–1). Papers of low mineral or "ash" content—relatively expensive papers —are needed for only such special determinations as calcium or phosphate. Fritted glass filters, though fairly expensive, are very useful and do not add paper fibers to the filtrate. Suction, properly applied, may speed filtration; it is usually used with fritted glass filters. Sometimes the first portion of a filtrate is cloudy. It can often be cleared by refiltering through the same paper when the precipitate itself acts as an additional filtering medium.

Centrifugation

Centrifugation is frequently more satisfactory than filtration for separating a solid from a liquid. It avoids possible contamination by the paper and usually yields a larger volume than filtration. Centrifugation does not always produce clear solu-

Figure 8–6. Rapid dissolving in a graduated cylinder.

Table 8–1. Types and Characteristics of Filter Papers

WHATMAN NO.	EQUIVALENT SCHLEICHER AND SCHUELL NO.	CHARACTERISTICS
Unwashed		
1	596	Medium; medium weight, speed, and retentiveness
2	597	Dense; more retentive, less rapid
3	598	Thick; heavy, strong, quite retentive
4	604	Soft; very rapid, less retentive
5	602	Very dense; very retentive, filters slowly
Single acid washed (HCl)		
30	497	Medium; fairly rapid and retentive
31	410	Soft; more rapid, less retentive
32	402	Retentive
Double acid washed (HCl and HF)		
40	589, white ribbon	Medium; medium speed and retentiveness
41	589, black ribbon	Soft; more rapid, less retentive
41H	589-IH	Hard, rapid, strong
42	589, blue ribbon	Dense; more retentive, less rapid
44	590	Thin; very retentive
Hardened		
50	507, 576	Retentive
52	589WH	Medium speed and retentiveness
54	589BH	More rapid, less retentive

tions, but it can be supplemented by subsequent filtration, which will be more rapid because of removal of most of the solid.

There are various sizes and types of centrifuges on the market. The effectiveness of a centrifuge (i.e., the centrifugal force developed) depends on the speed of rotation and on the distance of the sample from the center of rotation. The instruction to spin at, for example, 2000 r.p.m. (revolutions per minute) is indefinite. The effect will be greater in a large centrifuge than in a small one at the same speed. At 2000 r.p.m. a tube placed with its contents 4 inches from the axis will develop a force 454 times that of gravity; at 8 inches the force will be double or $908 \times g$. In other words, to develop a centrifugal force of 400 g, a tube 4 inches from the center would have to spin at 1880 r.p.m.; a tube 8 inches from the center would require only 1330 r.p.m. The centrifugal force increases in direct proportion to the distance from the center of rotation but increases as the square of the speed. Therefore, doubling the speed of a centrifuge is far more effective than doubling its size. This is expressed in the formula $RCF = krv^2$. RCF is relative centrifugal force, r is the radius or distance from the center of rotation, v is velocity in revolutions per minute, and k is 0.0000284 when r is in inches or 0.0000112 when r is in centimeters.

Some centrifuges allow the tubes to swing out horizontally as they spin; some hold the tubes at a fixed angle. The former arrangement leads to a flat upper surface of the sedimented solid layer; the latter leaves the solid surface at an angle. Since the angle centrifuge has less air resistance than the swinging cups, it develops more speed for the same motor power.

Owing to the great force developed in the centrifuge, all rotating parts must be balanced carefully to prevent vibration, which may damage the machine and be a serious hazard to the people around it. Always place cups and tubes in the centrifuge in pairs opposite one another. Tubes are paired for equal weight. A nearly empty tube must not be opposite a nearly full one. If necessary, put in extra tubes filled with a suitable amount of water to equalize odd tubes. For high speeds the opposite cups must be even more carefully balanced by setting them with the metal tube and trunnion carrier on a two-pan trip balance and adding or removing fluid until they balance. This balancing can be with fluid within the tube or with water in the space between the glass and metal tubes. Never use mercury to balance a centrifuge. It will amalgamate with the brass and weaken the bottom of the metal cup. Always be sure there is a rubber pad in the bottom of the metal cup. With conical glass tubes these pads must be checked and changed frequently, since the pointed tips tend to dig through them.

Follow the manufacturer's instructions regarding regular lubrication of the centrifuge. Replace the carbon brushes on the motor as needed; this may be indicated by excessive sparking.

Measurement of Volume

The measurement of volume is one of the most frequent manipulations in clinical chemistry. Blood, urine, spinal fluid samples, and a very large number of liquid reagents are measured volumetrically. Some are measured in large volume, some in small; some must be measured precisely, others only approximately. For this reason a variety of volumetric ware must be available. These include pipets, burets, volumetric flasks, and graduated cylinders.

Volumetric glassware is available in several grades according to the accuracy of calibration. The most precise conforms to specifications in Federal Specification DD-V-581a and in National Bureau of Standards Circular C-434 for Class A ware. The tolerance for Class B ware is about twice that for Class A. (A table showing Class A and B tolerances is included in the front of the Kontes Technical Glassware catalog. The Pyrex and Kimble catalogs show the tolerance that the manufacturers have set for each item; some are Class A, some Class B, some of wider tolerance. The former Normax ware was Class A, and Exax was Class B. Kimax is a borosilicate glass like Pyrex and may or may not be Class A. Kimble also makes a cheaper grade with greater tolerance called Tekk.)

Pipets. Pipets may be graduated at one point or at many; they may be calibrated to contain or to deliver. They may be calibrated to deliver by drainage or by having the last drop blown out. They may be calibrated to deliver to the tip or to some other base above the tip.

The so-called measuring pipets include serologic and Mohr pipets (Fig. 8–7). These differ from one another in that the serologic pipets are calibrated to the tip, whereas the Mohr calibration stops above the constricted portion. For special applications there are modifications of these with large-bore tips or with long, thin tips.

All these pipets are graduated at intervals so they can be used for measuring odd volumes or for dispensing several samples from one filling. There may be inaccuracies in the intermediate calibrations owing to variations in the inside diameter of the pipet. Only the total volume, not the intermediate points, is checked in manufacture.

Most measuring pipets that are graduated to the tip are calibrated for blowout. The Folin-Wu pipet, however, is calibrated for drainage only. Most manufacturers mark pipets that are to be blown out with either two etched rings or a sanded band near the upper end.

Volumetric or transfer pipets are calibrated to deliver only one volume (Fig. 8–8). They have one calibration mark above a bulb in the pipet. These pipets

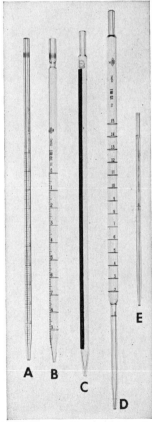

Figure 8–7. Types of measuring pipets. *A* and *B.* Serologic pipets, 1 and 10 ml. Graduated to tip; calibrated for blowout delivery as indicated by frosted band near top. *C.* Mohr pipet, 10 ml. Graduated for delivery to a base above the tip. *D.* Folin-Wu blood pipet, 15 ml. Graduated to the tip. Calibrated for drain-and-touch delivery, not blowout. *E.* Folin micro-blood pipet, 0.1 ml. Graduated to the tip. Calibrated to contain (TC) and must therefore be rinsed. All the other pipets in this and Fig. 8–8 are calibrated to deliver (TD).

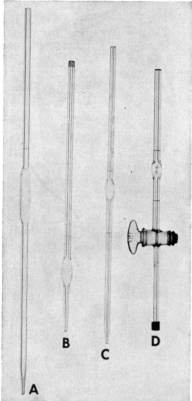

Figure 8–8. Types of volumetric pipets. *A.* Transfer pipet, 5 ml. Graduated to the tip. Calibrated for drain-and-touch delivery. *B.* Ostwald-Folin pipet, 2 ml. Graduated to the tip. Calibrated for blowout delivery. *C* and *D.* Van Slyke-Neill pipets, 1 ml. Graduated for delivery between two marks. Pipet *D* has a rubber tip to fit the bottom of the cup on the Van Slyke blood gas apparatus for anaerobic delivery.

pipet and is calibrated for blowout rather than merely for drainage. This makes it somewhat more accurate for use with more viscous liquids, such as blood.

Two modifications of these pipets are useful in handling samples for analysis in the Van Slyke blood gas apparatus. One change is the addition of a second mark below the bulb; delivery of the calibrated volume is between the two marks. The other alteration is the addition of a stopcock to control delivery of the sample.

The pipets we have discussed so far have been calibrated "to deliver," some to deliver by drainage and some by blowout. In addition to these, there are also pipets calibrated "to contain." When full, the "to deliver" pipets, which have the letters "TD" marked on them, contain a larger amount than do the "to contain" pipets marked "TC," because the former contain not only the calibrated volume that they will deliver but also the liquid that will remain, wetting the inside of the pipet when delivery is finished. In order to get the full calibrated volume out of a "TC" pipet, it must be rinsed. Usually these pipets are of small volume, and rinsing increases the accuracy of delivery, especially of viscous liquids, such as blood. The 20 microliter hemoglobin pipet and the 0.1 ml. Folin microblood sugar pipet are of this type.

Pasteur pipets are useful for transferring small volumes of liquid, for separating serum, and so on. They are made by drawing a piece of glass tubing out with a long tip and are used with a rubber medicine dropper bulb. They are available from laboratory suppliers as disposable pipets.

The use of pipets. The pipets we have been describing are normally filled by suction. This is usually done by mouth. If the fluid being pipetted is toxic or offensive, another source of suction may be used. A plain rubber bulb may be used to draw up the liquid; it is then quickly slipped off and the pipet controlled by finger as usual. There are also several special types of rubber bulbs with valves, which are designed for controlling pipets. Of these the Pumpet is easily handled, being designed for one-hand operation (either right or left). It requires, however, a sensitive touch; if you have good dexterity you should like it. Another, which is easier to control, is the Propipette.

In addition to these do-it-yourself pipets there are a number of automatic ones. Some of these are designed for gravity refilling and emptying by proper manipula-

measure their volume more accurately than the measuring pipets. They are calibrated to deliver by drainage with the tip touching the side of the receiving vessel as they empty. This procedure leaves a drop of the same size in the tip each time. For most accurate measuring, the tip should be constricted so that the liquid draining from the walls of the pipet keeps up with the bulk of the fluid as it drains out. This makes delivery slow. A good compromise is to use a pipet with a somewhat larger bore at the tip. Let it drain freely until the liquid is at the bottom of the bulb; then partially close the top of the pipet to assure slow final drainage. Kimble states, however, that their pipets are calibrated for unrestricted delivery and no wait.

A commonly used modification of this single-calibration pipet is the Ostwald-Folin pipet. This has a bulb placed low on the

tion of a stopcock. (A selection of this type can be seen in the catalog of the Scientific Glass Apparatus Co. of Bloomfield, N. J.) Others are pump operated. The Aupette and the Cornwall pipettor are hand pumped, having check valves and a glass syringe, which is spring loaded for automatic refilling following each delivery. Motor driven models are also available.

Seligson (1957) has described another device for measuring samples and diluent or reagent, eliminating the use of a pipet and volumetric flask. It consists of the pipet, A, a calibrated tube, B, and a trap, C (Fig. 8–9). Suction is applied at the trap. Suction may be provided by a fish tank aerator, which has been made to suck air, by a slow-running water pump, or by a rubber bulb. To operate the automatic pipet, the sample, often in the tube in which it was collected, is placed under the pipet tip. The sample is drawn up slowly until it reaches the elbow entering the trap. The stopcock is turned 90° clockwise to lock the desired volume of sample in the pipet. The tip is wiped, the reaction vessel or test tube cuvet is placed under the tip, and the stopcock is turned another 90° clockwise. This allows reagent or diluent in the calibrated tube to flow through the pipet and flush out the contents of the tip. The volume of reagent can be adjusted to make a desired dilution of sample. When a suitable volume of reagent has passed through the pipet, the stopcock is turned 90° clockwise to its original position, the tip wiped, and the operation repeated with

a new sample. As the new sample ascends the pipet, it moves the film of reagent ahead of it, and by the time the sample reaches the elbow entering the trap, the pipet contains the new sample uncontaminated with reagent. The operation is continued with as many samples as desired. The pipet is most convenient and accurate when used with 0.1 to 0.2 ml. volumes but has been used effectively with volumes ranging from 0.02 to 1.50 ml.

Burets. A buret is like a measuring pipet but has a stopcock for easy accurate control of delivery. As with measuring pipets, the accuracy of the intermediate marks cannot be assumed without checking unless precision bore burets are used. As with pipets calibration can be done by weighing water delivered between marks and calculating the volume from the specific gravity of water at that temperature.

Several conveniences can be built into burets. One is a two-way stopcock to allow easy refilling of the buret from a reservoir. Another is an automatic zero arrangement at the top. One of the best advances in burets is the use of Teflon instead of glass for stopcocks. These need no grease as glass cocks do and so avoid the troublesome fouling of the inside of buret barrel and tip. Also they do not freeze when allowed to stand for some time with alkaline solutions. Teflon cocks are available in the same general design as glass ones; they have, however, a steeper taper and the barrel surface is specially finished.

A buret is most conveniently handled as shown in Fig. 8–10; an Erlenmeyer flask allows effective continuous mixing by swirling as the titrant is added from the buret.

Graduated Cylinders. Graduated cylinders

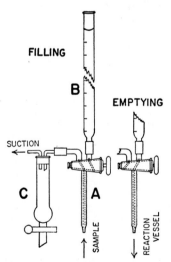

Figure 8–9. Significant features of the automatic pipet. A, pipet and 3-way stopcock; B, calibrated tube; and C, waste receiver (Seligson, D.: Am. J. Clin. Pathol., 28:200, 1957).

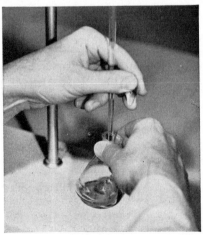

Figure 8–10. Buret titration.

are useful for volume measurements that do not have to be very precise. As with other graduated ware, the total volume is probably quite accurate but intermediate points are less reliable. Measurements in the lower portion give increasingly larger percentage errors. The size of cylinder used should be chosen so that the volume measured occupies a considerable portion of the cylinder. Do not use a 100 ml. cylinder to measure 1 or 2 ml. Mixing cylinders are glass stopper, graduated cylinders. They are particularly useful for making solutions and dilutions.

Volumetric Flasks. Volumetric flasks, like volumetric pipets, are precision measuring instruments. The most accurate dilutions are made with these two pieces of equipment. Two problems arising with volumetric flasks might be mentioned. The first is getting a weighed amount of solid into the flask in making up a solution. It is difficult to transfer material from a watch glass into the neck of a flask without spilling; even the transfer from a weighing paper is hazardous. The best procedure is to transfer the solid to a beaker and dissolve it and then to pour the solution into the flask, rinsing in the final traces. Water is added only until the solution is somewhat below the neck of the flask so that by swirling the solid can be completely dissolved and well mixed. Water is finally added until the bottom of the meniscus is on the calibration mark. The next problem is to mix the solution thoroughly so that it will be of uniform concentration throughout. This requires inversion of the flask, shaking, rerighting it so that the bubble comes back to the top, and repeating this process 15 or 20 times.

Chemicals

Just because a bottle is labeled "Sodium Chloride" does not mean that there is not even a small amount of sulfate, iodide, or potassium in it. Purity of chemicals is a matter of degree. For any chemical test we want to be sure that there is not enough of any other substance in the chemicals used to give an abnormal reaction. In a quantitative test we want to know exactly how much of the desired compound there is in the standard. For these reasons we usually use "reagent grade" chemicals. These are more expensive than less carefully purified grades of chemicals. By using judgment one can sometimes save money without loss of accuracy. However, the difference in cost is usually not enough to risk a poor result, and it is better to use the best grade when there is any doubt.

Several grades of chemicals are available. Time was when the term "C.P." or "chemically pure" designated the best available. However, some distributors started marking their chemicals "reagent grade" or "analytical grade." These terms are now widely used for the most highly purified chemicals, and "C.P." may designate a grade slightly less pure. The American Chemical Society has established standards of purity for many chemicals; any that meet these requirements may be labeled "A.C.S." Several suppliers list in their catalogs or on the label the maximum limits of impurities in their chemicals. Two companies, J. T. Baker and Fisher, put the actual analysis on the label so that one can tell exactly how much of an impurity is present in a particular bottle. This is frequently of help.

Other grades of purity are "U.S.P." and "N.F.," which mean that these chemicals meet the tests listed in the United States Pharmacopeia or the National Formulary; these grades are good enough for human consumption but may not be pure enough for some chemical purposes. "Technical" and "purified" are less pure grades.

Sometimes even reagent grade chemicals contain far less than 100 per cent of the named compound. The maximum limits of impurities may show only very small allowances, but the chemical may still contain a large amount of some other, sometimes unmentioned, impurity. If the "assay" is given this may help. Look at the label on a bottle of sodium hydroxide. Note that the sum of the allowable impurities, including a considerable amount of carbonate, does not equal the difference between the assay for sodium hydroxide and 100 per cent. In this particular case the difference is largely water. In other cases it may be something more important. For example, "molybdic acid" contains about 15 per cent ammonia; this is undesirable for certain tests in clinical chemistry, and the pure "molybdenum trioxide" must be used instead. Also "metaphosphoric acid" contains about 60 per cent sodium metaphosphate.

Another important consideration in the use of chemicals is the degree of hydration or the amount of water of crystallization they contain. Sometimes the anhydrous compound is stable; sometimes it has such an avidity for water that it cannot be weighed accurately. It then becomes necessary to use a stable hydrate of the compound. For example, copper sulfate is weighed as its pentahydrate. Sometimes a salt exists in more than one degree of hydration; thus, disodium hydrogen phosphate is available as the dodecahydrate, the heptahydrate, and the dihydrate, as well as the anhydrous form ($Na_2HPO_4 \cdot 12H_2O$, $Na_2HPO_4 \cdot 7H_2O$, $Na_2HPO_4 \cdot 2H_2O$, and Na_2HPO_4). The dihydrate is the most stable and is preferable for weighing. Naturally it will take more of the hydrate than of the anhydrous salt to give a stated amount of phosphate. If instructions call for a different hydrate than the one you wish to use, you can calculate the required amount by multiplying the stated amount by the ratio of the molecular weights of the two forms. Thus, if 12 gm. of $Na_2HPO_4 \cdot 12H_2O$ (mol. wt. 358) is called for and you wish to use $Na_2HPO_4 \cdot 2H_2O$ (mol. wt. 178), you would take

$$12 \times \frac{178}{358} = 6.0 \text{ gm.}$$

Usually the concentration of a solution is expressed in terms of the anhydrous salt. However, for some compounds that are available only as the hydrate, the percentage is of the hydrate. Thus, 10 per cent sodium tungstate solution is traditionally made by dissolving 10 gm. of $Na_2WO_4 \cdot 2H_2O$ in water and diluting to 100 ml.

In order for a chemist to know what is going on in a reaction and to be able to anticipate or evaluate abnormal reactions or interferences, he should know what compounds he is using in a determination. This would preclude the use of proprietary reagents of undisclosed composition. There are several of these on the market for protein precipitation, for urine preservation, and for the determination of cholesterol, for example. Although these may give good results under normal conditions, there is no way to predict what may happen with an abnormal specimen.

Expressing Concentration

There are several methods in use in clinical chemistry for expressing the concentration of solutions. The simplest and most common is percentage. There are, however, several ways to express percentage. One is to express per cent in grams of solute per 100 ml. of solution; this, ordinarily the most useful, is "per cent weight per volume" or "% (w/v)" and is meant if no other basis is expressed; it is the definition used in the U. S. Pharma-

copoeia. Another basis is grams of solute per 100 gm. of solution; this is "% (wt.)" and is more used than useful. It is, for example, the basis on which concentrated sulfuric acid is said to be 96 per cent; i.e., 100 gm. of solution contains 96 gm. of H_2SO_4. Since this solution has a specific gravity of 1.84, 100 gm. occupies a volume of 100/1.84 or 54.3 ml. It therefore contains 96 gm. of H_2SO_4 in 54.3 ml., or 177 gm. of H_2SO_4 per 100 ml., and is 177 per cent (w/v).

A common error in using the term "per cent" is to use it to mean per cent of concentrated without saying so. For example, a solution made by diluting 10 ml. of concentrated hydrochloric acid to 100 ml. is sometimes called 10 per cent hydrochloric acid. Actually, since concentrated hydrochloric acid is a 44 per cent (w/v) solution, the tenfold dilution is only a 4.4 per cent solution. One must read the instructions in making the solution in order to be sure what is meant and then label the solution so that other people using it will also know how it was made.

Another use of "per cent" is to designate "per cent saturated." This is usually the ratio of the volume of water added to the volumes of the water plus the saturated solution times 100. Thus, if 100 ml. of water is added to 100 ml. of saturated ammonium sulfate, the resulting solution is called 50 per cent saturated. If the solute is a liquid, we may express percentage on a volume basis as milliliters of solute per 100 ml. of solution or per cent (v/v).

Another method of expressing dilution is sometimes used and is liable to misinterpretation. This is use of the expression "dilute the solution one to three" or "a 1:3 dilution." This could mean either "dilute one volume to three volumes" or "dilute one volume with three volumes of water." The expression 1:1 can of course mean only "dilute one volume with one volume;" the expression 1:100 is usually taken to mean "dilute one volume to 100 volumes." The directions for making the solutions may clarify the meaning, but they frequently do not. It would be preferable to use the unambiguous term $1 + 3$ or $1 \rightarrow 3$.

For very dilute solutions we may express the concentration in milligrams (mg.) or micrograms (γ, μg., or mcg.; not ug.) of solute per 100 ml. of solution and thus have mg. per cent or mcg. per cent. These terms are frequently used to express concentration of certain constituents in blood. For even smaller concentrations we may occasionally need to use nanograms (ng.; 0.001 mcg.) or picograms (pg.; 0.001 ng.).

To compare solutions on the basis of amounts that will react chemically, we must have another basis than per cent. For this purpose we express concentration as molarity or equivalence. A molar (M) solution contains one gram-molecular weight in one liter. An equivalent or normal (N) solution contains one gram-equivalent per liter or one mole divided by the valence of the multivalent ion or by the number of monovalent ions in the molecule. Thus, for sodium hydroxide (m.w.40) a molar solution and a normal solution are both 40 gm./l. or 4 per cent. For sulfuric acid (m.w. 98) a molar solution contains 98 gm./l. and a normal solution, 49 gm./l. Solutions one-thousandth as strong as these are expressed as millimolar (mM.) or milliequivalent (mEq.). In some cases we are interested in the number of milliequivalents in a volume other than one liter. We therefore commonly use the symbol mEq. to mean one milliequivalent (one-thousandth of an equivalent weight) rather than a concentration of one-thousandth normal. For the latter we say mEq./liter.

To convert from mg. per cent to mEq./l., multiply by the valence, divide by the molecular or atomic weight, and multiply by 10. The 10 is necessary to convert from the basis of 100 ml. to 1 liter. To convert from vol. per cent to mEq./l., divide by the molecular volume (22.3 for CO_2) and multiply by 10. For protein and for phosphate the effective valence varies with pH because of the change in degree of ionization. At the normal pH of blood, 7.4, the effective valence of phosphate is 1.8. To convert gm. per cent of serum protein to mEq./l., multiply by 2.43.

Calculating Concentration. There are two types of calculations that are frequently made involving volume and concentration of solutions. One is in the preparation of a dilution from a stronger solution. The other is in calculating the concentration of a solution by knowing how much of it will react exactly with a known volume of another solution of known concentration. The first of these two types of calculations can be made readily if concentrations are expressed in normality or in per cent weight for volume. The second type of calculation can be made with concentration in normality. Both are based on the obvious fact that as we increase the volume of a portion of a solution, we proportionally decrease its concentration. Quantita-

tively this is expressed by the statement that the volume times the concentration of one solution equals the volume times the concentration of an equivalent solution:

$$V_1N_1 = V_2N_2 \text{ or}$$

$$V_1\%_1 = V_2\%_2 \text{ (for per cent [w/v]).}$$

We will use the first expression a little later in calculating the results of titrations. We also use it and the second equation in making dilutions. Thus, if we have a 2.5 normal solution of sodium hydroxide and want to make a liter of 0.1 N solution, we can calculate the volume to take:

$$V_1N_1 = V_2N_2$$

$$x \times 2.5 = 1000 \times 0.1$$

$$2.5x = 100$$

$$x = \frac{100}{2.5} = 40,$$

or 40 ml. of 2.5 N sodium hydroxide diluted to 1 liter with water will give us a 0.1 N solution.

Similarly, to make a liter of 70 per cent alcohol from 95 per cent alcohol, we could calculate

$$V_1\%_1 = V_2\%_2$$

$$x \times 95 = 1000 \times 70$$

$$x = 1000 \times \frac{70}{95} = 737.$$

If we dilute 737 ml. of 95 per cent alcohol to 1 liter with water, the result will be 70 per cent alcohol.

A special case of this formula is frequently helpful: interchange the volume of one solution for the concentration of the other and vice versa. Thus, 70 ml. of 95 per cent alcohol will make 95 ml. of 70 per cent (and therefore 700 ml. of 95 per cent will make 950 ml. of 70 per cent). Or 0.1 ml. of 2.5 N sodium hydroxide will make 2.5 ml. of 0.1 N (therefore, 10 ml. of 2.5 N will make 250 ml. of 0.1 N).

Calculations

There are numerous occasions when computations must be made in the practice of clinical chemistry. Almost all these are simple arithmetic manipulations. However, there are a few ways in which simplification can be introduced. Although logarithms, calculating machines, or an abacus will increase speed or accuracy of calculations, a slide rule is the most practical aid

(Fig. 8–11). A few minutes' instruction from someone who knows how or from the booklet accompanying the rule will enable you to start using it. After a little use you will be adept, rapid, and confident with it. The slide rule is used primarily for multiplying and dividing, but it can also be used for obtaining logarithms and anti-logarithms, squares and square roots. The C and D scales will be the most used; the CF and DF scales are time savers, and the CI and CIF scales are frequently helpful. The A scale is used to obtain squares and the L, logarithms. For clinical laboratory use these scales should be present; others, such as S (sine), T (tangent), and LL (log log), are superfluous.

An important concept to keep in mind, especially when calculating by hand with long multiplication and division, is that of significant figures. It is not "how many decimals should I carry?" but how many total significant figures? Illustration will best explain what is meant by significant figures. The number 2104 has four significant figures; 0.2104 has four; 210.4 has four; 210.400 has six (the last two decimals indicate that the true value is between 210.399 and 210.401, while 210.4 is between 210.3 and 210.5); and 0.0002104 has four (the first three zeros to the right of the decimal point are not significant, they merely establish the decimal point; 1.1 centimeters, 0.011 meters, and 11 millimeters each indicate the same precision and each has two significant figures).

Let us illustrate by making a calculation of the result from a colorimetric determination in which the colorimeter readings were 213 and 197, the concentration of the standard was equivalent to 35 mg. per cent, and the formula is $x = \dfrac{213}{197} \times 35$. Then $x = \dfrac{7455}{197}$. This divides out to be 37.8426⁺. How much of this should be reported? Taking at face value the three figures given, one would conclude that the report should be 38, since one of the figures involved, the 35, has only two significant figures or an accuracy of less than 1 part in 100. Actually, in making a standard solution, care would be taken that there would be at least four significant figures or an accuracy of 1 part in 1000; the concentration of the standard should therefore be expressed as 35.00 mg. per cent. Now the colorimeter readings are seen to be the limiting factor. These each have three significant figures with an apparent accuracy of about 1 in 200; the result should therefore also have three significant figures and be expressed as 37.8 mg. per cent. This is on the basis of the mathematics of the figures alone. But chemistry also rears its ugly head. If it is known that repeat determinations on the same solution will vary by, say, 20 colorimeter scale units, then the accuracy is only about 20 in 200 or 1 in 10, and only two significant figures should be used. We would then report the result only as 38 mg. per cent. One must use common sense, judgment, and experience to decide how many decimals to use. The common failing is to use too many and to indicate an accuracy that was not attained. A good rule is to report one more place than you are sure of or than is of clinical significance.

ANALYTICAL METHODS

Gravimetric Methods

Sometimes a material being analyzed can be precipitated from solution as an insoluble compound and its amount determined by weighing. For the weight to indicate the amount of the material we are interested in, the composition of the insoluble compound must be known, the precipitate must be pure, and precipitation must be complete. For accurate work, the process requires experience in careful

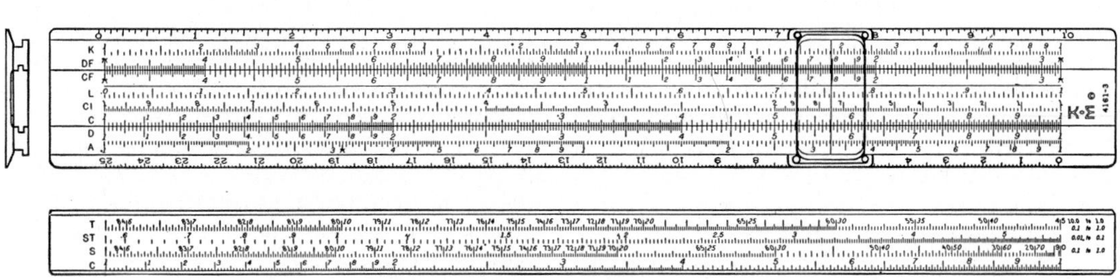

Figure 8–11.   Slide rule. (Courtesy Keuffel & Esser, Inc.)

filtering methods, washing of precipitates, drying, igniting of residues, and use of a sensitive analytical balance. Since other techniques are usually simpler and more rapid, gravimetric procedures are infrequently used in clinical chemistry. Some laboratories still measure the excretion of hippuric acid following a dose of sodium benzoate by isolating and weighing it. The mineral content of bone can be determined by ashing and weighing. Beside the removal of insoluble compounds a soluble substance may be removed by extraction with a solvent. The solvent can be removed by evaporation and the residue purified and weighed. This technique is commonly used for the determination of fecal fat.

One other application of weighing is in the determination of specific gravity, which is weight per unit volume or grams per milliliter. This determination can be done by measuring a known volume into a stoppered weighing bottle or into a beaker under a layer of oil (to retard evaporation) and weighing on an analytical balance. Or the liquid may be weighed directly in the pipet. This technique is valuable for amounts of sample too small to use with a hydrometer. Most commonly specific gravity is determined with a hydrometer, a float with a long stem that carries a calibrated scale. The hydrometer floats low or high in the liquid depending on the specific gravity. It can be used to measure the concentration of alcohol, to indicate how much charge there is in a storage battery, or to indicate the amount of dissolved solids in urine. This last application is the common one in the clinical laboratory, using a hydrometer adapted to the specific gravity range of urine. In the use of a hydrometer, several precautions must be observed. The hydrometer must be checked for accuracy at least at one point, especially if it is the type with an enclosed paper scale, which may slip. A urinometer can be checked in distilled water. The temperature of the sample must be the same as that of the calibration of the hydrometer or a correction factor must be applied. The hydrometer must float freely, not being in contact with the side of the vessel. There must be no bubbles clinging to the hydrometer. These two requirements may be met by giving the float a spin as it is put into the liquid.

Volumetric or Titrimetric Methods

The amount of a substance in solution can be determined by measuring the amount of a solution of known concentration that reacts with a measured amount of the unknown solution. These methods, which are familiar to every student who has had a didactic course in quantitative analytical chemistry, involve intelligent selection and use of well-calibrated volumetric glassware—volumetric flasks, pipets, and burets. Standard volumetric solutions are prepared by very accurate weighing of specially purified chemicals. Indicators must be chosen that will show when the equivalence point has been reached. There are several types of volumetric determinations in use in clinical chemistry. Some are based on the reaction between an acid and a base, some on oxidation-reduction reactions, and some on the formation of an insoluble or an un-ionized compound.

ACIDIMETRY

Acidimetry, involving titration of an acid and a base, is used in gastric analysis for determining the amount of HCl in gastric juice. It is also used in some laboratories for the determination of serum bicarbonate and for the fractionation of fecal lipid into free fatty acid and neutral fat. Two requisites for acidimetry are a standard solution of exactly known concentration and a suitable indicator for signaling the endpoint of the titration. The commonly used acids and alkalis (hydrochloric acid, sulfuric acid, nitric acid, sodium hydroxide, potassium hydroxide, ammonium hydroxide) are not suitable for primary standards, since they cannot be purified so that we can know exactly what we are weighing. The acids listed and ammonium hydroxide are solutions in water; sodium and potassium hydroxide are solids but have such a strong affinity for both water and carbon dioxide that they cannot be weighed accurately. There is a way in which hydrochloric acid can be used as a primary standard, since it forms a constant boiling mixture at about a 20 per cent concentration. By distillation of a solution and collection of the final constant-boiling portion, a solution of accurately known composition can be obtained. This will vary with the barometric pressure. From this, portions may be weighed to make standard solutions of desired concentration. A simpler procedure is to make a standard solution from a solid acid or acid salt. One of the most suitable compounds is potassium acid phthalate. This can be purchased in highly purified form from commercial sources. For a somewhat higher price the compound is available with a certificate from the National Bureau of Standards, showing the exact purity of the particular lot and giving instructions for its use. Oxalic acid is also a fairly satisfactory primary standard.

Directions for Preparing One-normal and One-tenth Normal Solutions of Acid and Base (Hydrochloric Acid and Sodium Hydroxide). *Preparation of primary standard.* Dry some potassium acid phthalate in an open bottle for two hours or overnight at 120° C. or use oxalic acid without drying. Weigh out 20.42 gm. of the phthalate or 6.304 gm. of oxalic acid ($H_2C_2O_4 \cdot 2H_2O$). Transfer to a beaker and dissolve in water. Pour the solution into a volumetric flask. Rinse the beaker with water, adding to the solution in the flask. Dilute to the mark and mix well. If a 100 ml. volumetric flask is used, the solution will be exactly 1 N; if 1000 ml., exactly 0.1 N.

Preparation and standardization of sodium hydroxide solution. In many applications it is necessary or preferable that the sodium hydroxide solution be carbonate free. Owing to the presence of carbon dioxide in the air and the avidity of sodium hydroxide for it, this cannot be attained without some special precautions. The first step is to prepare a concentrated sodium hydroxide solution in which carbonate is not soluble. After the carbonate has settled, the clear, carbonate-free supernatant is diluted with freshly boiled and cooled distilled water. The solution is permitted only minimum contact with air. It is stored in a bottle equipped with a soda lime tube. If the solution is to be used for titration, the bottle is conveniently attached to a buret by a siphon; the buret should also be equipped with a soda lime tube at the top.

If it is not important that the solution be carbonate free, it can be made directly from solid; in this case, weigh out about 5 per cent excess to allow for carbonate and water in the hydroxide. Even if carbonate content is unimportant, it is usually more convenient to use a stock concentrated solution to make up dilute solutions. The normality of the stock can be determined by titration; this will speed up making of solutions of approximate concentrations.

PREPARATION OF CONCENTRATED SODIUM HYDROXIDE (50 PER CENT BY WEIGHT). To 1 liter of water in a 2- or 3-liter borosilicate glass (Kimax or Pyrex) flask in a sink (there is nothing worse to spill than hot concentrated alkali), add 1100 gm. of sodium hydroxide, or to 410 ml. of water add 1 pound of sodium hydroxide. Mix while the solid is being added so that it will not cake. The solution will get very hot. Let cool. Transfer to a bottle and let stand a few days for the carbonate to settle.

When the normality of the dilute sodium hydroxide has been determined, as will be described, calculate back to find out the normality of the concentrated solution and mark this on the bottle. This value will be helpful in preparing dilutions; the exact normality of the dilution should, however, be checked. Make this back calculation, using the formula $V_1N_1 = V_2N_2$. Taking the concentrated sodium hydroxide as solution 1 and the dilution as solution 2, this might, for example, work out as

$$5.9x = 1000 \times 0.113$$

$$x = \frac{113}{5.9} = 19.2$$

or the concentrated sodium hydroxide is 19.2 N.

PREPARATION OF DILUTE SODIUM HYDROXIDE (0.1 N or 1 N). If the normality of the concentrated sodium hydroxide has not been determined, measure out 5.9 ml. of the concentrated solution (do not pipet by mouth; use a rubber bulb) and dilute it to 100 ml. with water (freshly boiled and cooled if a carbonate-free solution is desired) to make a 1 N solution; dilute 5.9 ml. of concentrated sodium hydroxide to 1 liter for 0.1 N solution. If the normality of the concentrated solution is known, calculate the volume to be used from the formula $V_1N_1 = V_2N_2$. Taking the concentrated sodium hydroxide as solution 1 and the dilution as solution 2, the formula might, for example, work out as

$$x \times 17 = 100 \times 1, \text{ or } x \times 17 = 1000 \times 0.1$$

$$x = \frac{100}{17} = 5.9$$

Therefore, 5.9 ml. of concentrated sodium hydroxide diluted to 100 ml. would give a 1 N solution and diluted to 1000 ml. would give a 0.1 N solution; or 59 ml. of concentrated sodium hydroxide would make 1000 ml. of 1 N solution. Store in a polyethylene or borosilicate glass (Pyrex or Kimax) bottle with a rubber or plastic stopper.

STANDARDIZATION OF SODIUM HYDROXIDE SOLUTION. Into a 125 ml. Erlenmeyer flask carefully pipet 10 ml. of standard acid (the phthalate or oxalic acid prepared above; use either 1N or 0.1N of all solutions) and add two drops of 1 per cent phenolphthalein in 70 per cent alcohol. From a buret, with continuous swirling of the flask, add sodium hydroxide solution. A pink color will appear where the stream enters the acid solution; as the endpoint is approached, the pink will disappear more slowly; as this occurs, decrease the rate at which the alkali is added. The endpoint is the first pink you can see that remains for 15 seconds after mixing. Read the buret before and after the titration and subtract to obtain the ml. of NaOH used. Calculate the concentration of the sodium hydroxide from the formula:

$$\text{normality of NaOH} = \text{normality of acid (0.1 or 1)} \times \frac{10}{\text{ml. NaOH}}$$

or calculate the titer or factor for the sodium hydroxide. The "factor" is the number by which the nominal or approximate normality is multiplied to obtain the exact normality. With this procedure

$$\text{f of NaOH} = \frac{10}{\text{ml. NaOH}}.$$

If it is desired to adjust the sodium hydroxide to exact normality, the amount of water to be added to each 10 ml. of alkali is the difference in the volume of NaOH used in the titration and 10 ml. Thus, for example, if 9.6 ml. of NaOH solution was required to titrate 10 ml. of acid, add $10 - 9.6$ ml. $= 0.4$ ml. for each 10 ml. If you have 980 ml. of solution, add $98 \times 0.4 = 39$ ml. of water. Then recheck by titration.

Preparation of dilute hydrochloric acid (0.1 N or 1 N). If an approximately 0.1 or 1 N solution is desired for use as such, add 105 ml. of water to 10 ml. of concentrated hydrochloric acid for 1 N or add 1 liter of water to 8.8 ml. of concentrated hydrochloric acid for 0.1 N. If you are using an analyzed brand of hydrochloric acid, such as J. T. Baker, you can calculate more closely the amount of hydrochloric acid to dilute by first calculating the normality of the concentrated hydrochloric acid from the data on the label:

$$\frac{\text{Sp. gr.} \times \text{assay (\% by wt.)} \times 10}{36.5 \text{ (equiv. wt. HCl)}} = \text{N.}$$

This might, for example, be

$$\frac{1.188 \times 37.2 \times 10}{36.5} = 12.1 \text{ N}$$

To calculate the amount to be used to make 1 N,

$$12.1x = 100 \times 1$$
$$x = 8.3.$$

Dilution of 8.3 ml. of concentrated HCl to 100 ml. with water or addition of 111 ml. of water to 10 ml. of concentrated acid would give an approximately 1 N solution. A similar calculation could be made for preparing a 0.1 N solution of HCl or for preparing solutions of H_2SO_4, HNO_3, and so forth.

If you are preparing the dilute HCl to be standardized and adjusted to exactly 1 N or 0.1 N, slightly more concentrated HCl should be used to ensure that the dilution will not be weaker than the desired normality. For this purpose add 90 or 1000 ml. of water to 10 ml. of concentrated HCl for 1 N or 0.1 N respectively, or use 2 or 3 per cent more than the amount calculated from the actual analysis of the concentrated HCl.

Standardization of hydrochloric acid solution. Proceed as in the standardization of sodium hydroxide, but in place of the standard acid use exactly 10 ml. of the approximate HCl solution just prepared and titrate with standardized NaOH. Calculate the normality of the hydrochloric acid solution,

$$\text{N of HCl} = \frac{\text{N of NaOH} \times \text{ml. of NaOH}}{10}$$

or calculate the factor for the hydrochloric acid,

$$\text{f of HCl} = \text{f of NaOH} \times \frac{\text{ml. NaOH}}{10}.$$

Calculations. The formula for calculating results of a titration is the same as for making a dilution from stock solution: the volume of one solution times its normality is equal to the volume of the other solution times its normality, or $V_1N_1 = V_2N_2$.

Thus, for the first titration, in which the normality of the sodium hydroxide was unknown and it was found, for example, that it required 9.6 ml. to titrate 10 ml. of the standard acid,

$$10 \times 0.1 = 9.6 \times x$$

$$x = \frac{10 \times 0.1}{9.6} = 0.1042 \text{ N NaOH.}$$

For exact calculation of how much the sodium hydroxide solution must be diluted to reach the desired normality, we may use this same formula. In the example we used 9.6 ml. of NaOH to titrate 10 ml. of standard acid and found that the NaOH was 0.1042 N. If we have 980 ml. of this, then

$$980 \times 0.1042 = 0.1x$$

x = 1021 ml., or add 41 ml. of water.

OXIDATION-REDUCTION TITRATIONS

Oxidation-reduction titrations are also sometimes used in clinical chemistry. Here an added indicator is sometimes needed, but sometimes the color change of one of the compounds serves to show the endpoint. Iodometric titrations are of this class. These are not used commonly in any of our procedures but may be used, for example, in the standardization of phenol for phosphatase determinations. The titration of the dissolved oxalate precipitate with permanganate in the determination of calcium is a redox titration, the permanganate oxidizing the oxalate; the color of permanganate itself shows when an excess has been added.

PRECIPITATION TITRATIONS

A precipitation titration is used in the determination of chloride with either silver nitrate or mercuric nitrate. In these a color indicator is used that will show when an excess of the titrant has been added.

CHELOMETRIC TITRATIONS

The chelometric titration, depending on the formation of an un-ionized compound, is utilized in the determination of calcium or magnesium by titration with a solution of ethylene dinitrilotetraacetate (ethylenediamine tetraacetic acid, EDTA). A number of different color indicators have been proposed for these titrations.

Gasometric Methods

If the substance whose concentration we wish to know is a gas or can be made to react to produce a gas, we can determine that substance by measuring the volume of the gas in a calibrated apparatus at known temperature and pressure or more accurately by measuring with a manometer the pressure that the gas exerts when brought to a definite volume at a known temperature. These methods are used particularly for the determination of the total carbon dioxide content of serum or the

oxygen content and capacity of blood. However, they may also be used for potassium, glucose, lipids, urea, and many other compounds; for most of these, other methods are more suitable.

The most common apparatus used for

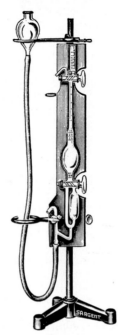

Figure 8–12. Van Slyke volumetric blood gas apparatus.

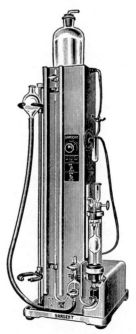

Figure 8–13. Van Slyke-Neill manometric blood gas apparatus.

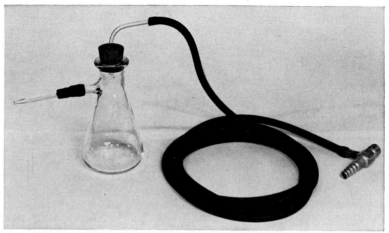

Figure 8–14. Vacuum pickup for mercury.

gasometric measurement in clinical chemistry are those devised by Van Slyke and his colleagues (Peters and Van Slyke, 1932). The volumetric form, in which the volume of gas is measured, is shown in Fig. 8–12, and the manometric form, in which the pressure is measured, is shown in Fig. 8–13. There are available a number of modifications of both. The apparatus may be shaken by hand or by motor. In one recent model a magnetic stirring bar has been enclosed within the gas evolution chamber. The volumetric apparatus may have a small trap at the bottom to catch any air that may leak in through the rubber tubing or at its connection to the glass apparatus. The manometric apparatus may be all in one piece or it may have ground glass joints, which make it easier to clean or to replace a broken portion; they also increase problems of leakage. There are also at least two microgasometers on the market made by Micro Metric Instruments Co. and by Scientific Industries, Inc. The latter can be had in a combination with a microburet.

One hazard, which should be kept in mind in using any of these instruments, is the poisonous nature of mercury, especially the vapor and droplets from finely divided mercury when it gets ground under foot. Spillage should be kept to a minimum by careful technique and any that is spilled should be cleaned up. There are a couple of commercial mercury collectors on the market. However, the simplest and most effective is a vacuum cleaner, which can be assembled easily from a filter flask, a medicine dropper, and some rubber tubing (Fig. 8–14). This, attached to a vacuum pump or aspirator, will pick up droplets of mercury or will suck up the puddle made by wiping together spilled mercury with a towel. Remember also that mercury will amalgamate with copper, silver, and gold; so keep jewelry, especially rings, out of the way.

Another apparatus for analysis of small samples of blood for carbon dioxide, oxygen, or carbon monoxide does not use mercury. This is the Scholander-Roughton apparatus (1943). It is not difficult to use and a few hours will suffice to learn how. The determination of carbon dioxide is rather tricky, but the apparatus is well adapted to oxygen determination.

Colorimetric Methods

Colorimetry is the most used of the techniques of quantitative analysis in clinical chemistry. Its value lies in its simplicity and sensitivity, two essential attributes for most clinical chemical determinations. If a material can be converted into a colored derivative, one can estimate the amount of the material by estimating the amount of color.

Visual Colorimetry. One of the simplest forms of colorimetry is dilution colorimetry. Here a standard colored solution is prepared corresponding to a concentration less than that of any sample to be analyzed. The unknown is treated to produce color, and its solution is diluted until it appears visually to have the same intensity as the standard. From the amount of dilution required the concentration in the original can be calculated. This method is sometimes used in the bedside determination of hemoglobin.

The disadvantage of this dilution technique is the relative insensitivity of the eye, so that precise measurements of concentration cannot be made. By using a "visual colorimeter" instead of looking at two tubes of colored solution, an increase of precision can be attained. This instrument places the appearance of the two solutions side by side in the same field. Such an instrument is shown in Fig. 8–15. The plungers are fixed, the cups movable. The depth of solution between the plunger and the bottom of the cup is varied until the two fields match. Then, assuming that the depth of solution is inversely proportional to the concentration of colored material and knowing the concentration in the standard, one can calculate the concentration of the unknown:

$$C_x = \frac{R_s}{R_x} C_s$$

where C_x and C_s are concentrations of unknown and standard respectively and R_s and R_x, the readings (depth in millimeters). To calculate the concentration of the constituent under investigation that was present in the blood or urine sample rather than in the final solution, this equation can be expanded:

$$C_x = \frac{R_s}{R_x} \cdot W_s \cdot \frac{V_x}{V_s} \cdot D \cdot \frac{V_c}{V_t}$$

where

W_s is the weight of the material in the volume of standard solution taken;

V_x and V_s are the final volumes of unknown and standard solutions respectively;

V_c is the volume to which the calculation is being made (usually 100 ml. or 1 liter for blood or the 24-hour volume for urine);

V_t is the volume of unknown solution taken for color development;

D is any dilution made in the sample before the volume V_t is taken for analysis.

C_x is now the amount of unknown in the volume V_c.

The visual colorimeter requires that a standard be prepared each time an unknown is run (not entirely a disadvantage). It has the advantage over a photoelectric instrument that it is not dependent on electric power and would still be useful in case of a disaster. For this reason one should be familiar with its use.

Photoelectric Colorimetry. Certain advantages (and some disadvantages) can be attained by substituting a photoelectric cell for the eye for measuring color intensity. There are many forms of photoelectric colorimeters, both filter photometers and spectrophotometers, on the market. All of them operate by measuring the amount of light that gets through the colored solution. Usually, in order to increase specificity, sen-

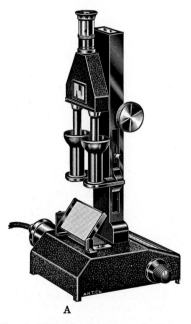

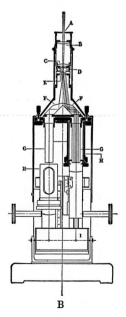

A   B

Figure 8–15. A, Klett biocolorimeter. B, Construction of Duboscq colorimeter (Bausch and Lomb). A, Eye point; B, eye lens; C, collective lens; D, coverglass; E, biprism; F, rhomboid prism; G, plungers; H, cup; I, mirror.

Figure 8–16. Single photocell photometer. $B =$ battery; $L =$ lamp; $F =$ filter; $A =$ tube containing solution; $P =$ photoelectric cell; $R_1R_2 =$ potentiometers; $G =$ meter. (Harrow, B., *et al.*: Laboratory Manual of Biochemistry. 5th Ed.)

sitivity, or range, we restrict the measurement of intensity to color of a particular wave length. If the wave length of the light used for the observation is selected by use of a colored glass, the instrument is called a filter photometer; if wave length is selected by a prism or a diffraction grating, the instrument is termed a spectrophotometer. The advantage of the latter is that the wavelength is continuously variable and that we can get light of any desired color. With a filter photometer we are restricted to the particular filters at hand.

Photoelectric colorimeters can be grouped into single photocell and double photocell types. Figure 8–16 illustrates the single photocell and Fig. 8–17, that with two photocells. The two-photocell instrument is more stable, since it compares the response of two photocells receiving light from the same source. Variations in intensity of the light, caused by fluctuations in line voltage, will affect the reading of a single-photocell instrument but not that of the double-cell type.

There are two ways of expressing the amount of light coming through the colored solution. One is as *transmission;* this is the fraction of the light striking the colored solution that comes through the solution $(T = I/I_o)$. This fraction is usually multiplied by 100 to give the per cent transmission ($\% T$). The second method of expression is as *absorbance,* the amount of light *not* passing through the colored solution. It is, however, a logarithmic value ($A = \log 1/T = -\log T = 2 - \log \% T$). It is the same as optical density, a commonly used but less suitable term. Obviously the darker a solution, the less its per cent transmission and the greater its absorbance or optical density. Different brands of instruments vary in the scales they use. The Leitz, for example, uses $\% T$; the Coleman and Spectronic 20 have both $\% T$ and A; the Lumetron has $\% T$ and $A \times 10$; the Fisher has $\% T$ and $A \times 100$; and the Klett uses $A \times 500$. Absorbance, or a function thereof, is much more convenient to use, since it is proportional (approximately or exactly) to concentration. The difference in concentrations or colors of two solutions is the difference in their absorbances; the reading for a blank can be subtracted from the reading of a determination to give a net reading. This obviously cannot be done with transmission readings.

When absorbance readings are proportional to concentration,

$$\frac{R_x}{R_s} = \frac{C_x}{C_s}$$

or

$$C_x = \frac{R_x}{R_s} \cdot C_s$$

This equation can be expanded to

$$C_x = \frac{R_x}{R_s} \cdot W_s \cdot \frac{V_x}{V_s} D \cdot \cdot \frac{V_c}{V_t}$$

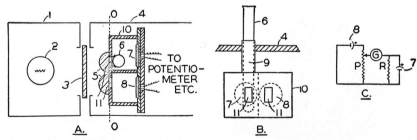

Figure 8–17. Diagrammatic details of Klett-Summerson photoelectric colorimeter. *A.* Schematic view of the rear half of the instrument, in section from above. *B.* View across the line in *A,* looking toward the front of the instrument. *C.* Wiring diagram of the photoelectric cell circuit. 1, lamp housing; 2, lamp; 3, light filter; 4, instrument housing; 5, compensating lenses; 6, test tube; 7, "working" photoelectric cell; 8, "reference" photoelectric cell; 9, metal tube (light shield); 10, photoelectric cell compartment housing; 11, light slits in compartments; P, 400-ohm potentiometer; R, 400-ohm fixed resistance; G, low-sensitivity galvanometer. (Summerson, W. H.: J. Biol. Chem., *130*:149, 1939.)

exactly as for visual colorimetry except that the ratio of readings is inverted.

When a given test is performed in the same way repeatedly, all the components of this equation are the same each time and can be collected into a single constant; thus,

$$C_x = \frac{R_x}{R_s} \cdot K$$

If it is established by using the instrument, reagents, and technique that the reading of the standard is reproducible from day to day, then R_s may also be included with K to give a factor, f, by which the reading of the unknown is multiplied to give the concentration in the specimen.

$$f = C_s/R_s$$

$$C_x = f \cdot R_x$$

Table 8-2.   Per Cent Transmittance-Absorbance

% TRANSMITTANCE	OPTICAL DENSITY	KLETT READING	% TRANSMITTANCE	OPTICAL DENSITY	KLETT READING
100	0.000	0.0	50	0.301	150.5
99	0.004	2.0	49	0.310	155.0
98	0.009	4.5	48	0.319	159.5
97	0.013	6.5	47	0.328	164.0
96	0.018	9.0	46	0.337	168.5
95	0.022	11.0	45	0.347	173.5
94	0.027	13.5	44	0.357	178.5
93	0.032	16.0	43	0.367	183.5
92	0.036	18.0	42	0.377	188.5
91	0.041	20.5	41	0.387	193.5
90	0.046	23.0	40	0.398	199.0
89	0.051	25.5	39	0.409	204.5
88	0.056	28.0	38	0.420	210.0
87	0.061	30.5	37	0.432	216.0
86	0.066	33.0	36	0.444	222.0
85	0.071	35.5	35	0.456	228.0
84	0.076	38.0	34	0.469	234.5
83	0.081	40.5	33	0.482	241.0
82	0.086	43.0	32	0.495	247.5
81	0.092	46.0	31	0.509	254.5
80	0.097	48.5	30	0.523	261.5
79	0.102	51.0	29	0.538	269.0
78	0.108	54.0	28	0.553	276.5
77	0.114	57.0	27	0.569	284.5
76	0.119	59.5	26	0.585	292.5
75	0.125	62.5	25	0.602	301.0
74	0.131	65.5	24	0.620	310.0
73	0.137	68.5	23	0.638	319.0
72	0.143	71.5	22	0.658	329.0
71	0.149	74.5	21	0.678	339.0
70	0.155	77.5	20	0.699	349.5
69	0.161	80.5	19	0.721	360.5
68	0.168	84.0	18	0.745	372.5
67	0.174	87.0	17	0.770	385.0
66	0.181	90.5	16	0.796	398.0
65	0.187	93.5	15	0.824	412.0
64	0.194	97.0	14	0.854	427.0
63	0.201	100.5	13	0.886	443.0
62	0.208	104.0	12	0.921	460.5
61	0.215	107.5	11	0.959	479.5
60	0.222	111.0	10	1.000	500.0
59	0.229	114.5	9	1.046	523.0
58	0.237	118.5	8	1.097	548.5
57	0.244	122.0	7	1.155	577.5
56	0.252	126.0	6	1.222	611.0
55	0.260	130.0	5	1.301	650.5
54	0.268	134.0	4	1.398	699.0
53	0.276	138.0	3	1.523	761.5
52	0.284	142.0	2	1.699	849.5
51	0.292	146.0	1	2.000	1000.0

In these calculations, remember, we have used colorimeter readings which are in absorbance units or some function thereof ($10 \times A$, $100 \times A$, or $500 \times A$). If the readings are in T or %T, they must first be converted to A (or one of its functions) before calculation can be made (unless a %T slide rule is used).

These calculations have all been based on the assumption that a straight-line relationship exists between concentration and colorimeter reading. It is an important part of standardizing any determination to establish the absorbance-concentration curve, using various amounts of the standard and actually plotting the curve. If a straight line results, the calculations just described may be made. If the relationship between concentration and absorbance is not a straight line, the graph must be used to convert readings to concentration, or concentration values corresponding to various readings may be taken from the graph and arranged in a table.

With the graphic (or tabular) method colorimeter readings in terms of T (or %T) may be used. In plotting the results, a straight line will be expected only if absorbance vs. concentration is plotted on rectilinear paper or if transmission vs. concentration is put on semilogarithmic paper with the colorimeter readings on the logarithmic scale.

In this discussion we have used R_s and R_x to represent the amount of color developed by the compound being analyzed. Actually in most determinations some of the final color that is measured results from the reagents or from constituents of the sample other than the compound being determined. For this reason we set up blanks, usually consisting of the reagents but substituting water for the sample, a "reagent blank." Sometimes a second blank is necessary to compensate for color present in the sample: a "sample blank," "serum blank," or "urine blank." The reagent blank would be subtracted from both standard and unknown before calculation; the sample blank would also be subtracted from the unknown.

There are two ways the blank can be subtracted from the total reading. First, the colorimeter can be set to zero absorbance with distilled water (or some other reference solution or air), both blank and standard or unknown read, and the blank subtracted from the other readings. This can be done only if readings are in absorbance or some function of it. If readings are made in %T, they must be converted to absorbance before the subtraction can be made. Second, the subtraction can be made on the colorimeter by setting to zero absorbance using the blank solution. Sometimes one procedure is easier, sometimes the other. If the same analysis is being made on a considerable number of samples, it is easier to set the instrument with the blank and let the instrument do the subtracting. If only one or two samples are being run on several different determinations, it might be easier to leave the colorimeter at the same distilled water zero setting. Also, if the blank color is not stable, the instrument should not be set at zero with it. The zero setting should be made with a stable reference so that it can be rechecked.

How often should the zero absorbance (100% T) setting (and also the zero % T setting on a few instruments, such as the Spectronic 20) be checked? As often as necessary. Start off by checking frequently; if no change is found, check less often. With some of the less stable instruments it may be necessary to check and readjust after almost every reading; others may remain steady for hours.

Cuvet Selection. "Cuvet" is just a fancy word for the test tube or other container in which the colored solution is placed in the colorimeter. Obviously, if we want to know the absorbance of the colored solution, anything else we put in the light path, including the cuvet and any dirt, scratches, or flaws that may be on it, must be the same for each solution. The best way to keep dirt (including fingerprints) constant is to avoid it. The cuvet should be wiped off routinely and checked for cleanliness each time it is placed in the instrument. Scratches are of no concern if they remain the same as when the tube is first used. Appearance of additional scratches will affect the calibration. Flaws and variations in the thickness and optical properties of the glass at various points on the cuvet mean that any one tube will not read the same in all positions. Therefore, the tube should be in the same position each time it is used. This is conventionally attained by always having the brand mark on the cuvet turned toward (or away from) the operator. This should not be a sensitive spot (slight change in position or rotation of the tube should not affect the reading). Actually it is not necessary to have more than one cuvet. Usually, however, it is more convenient to have a series of matched tubes available.

Matched cuvets can be purchased for the

colorimeter. However, the uniformity of these cuvets should not be assumed without checking them. It is much less expensive to select cuvets from ordinary test tubes. First select tubes that will fit easily into the instrument. They must be small enough to go in without binding but large enough to give steady readings. This latter consideration is unimportant in some instruments; e.g., in the Coleman junior spectrophotometer, tubes much smaller than the opening will give completely reproducible results. In other instruments the problem is almost insurmountable; e.g., in the Leitz, round tubes cannot be used satisfactorily at all because of the change in reading as they are shifted. For most Klett-Summerson colorimeters sufficient tubes can be selected from a box of 15 × 125 or 15 × 150 mm. Kimax lipless test tubes. For the Spectronic 20 use 13 × 100 mm. or 18 × 150 mm. test tubes or both; for the Coleman junior, use 10, 12, or 18 mm. test tubes or preferably both 10 and 18 mm. tubes.

In selecting tubes for optical match, be sure the tubes are clean inside and out. It is wise to form the habit of wiping each tube off and looking at it for cleanliness immediately before inserting in the instrument. Tubes should always be placed in the holder in the same relative position, preferably with the brand label directly facing you.

Place a sufficient quantity of distilled water in each tube. Insert one of the tubes in the instrument. Adjust to a Klett reading of 50, an absorbance or optical density of 0.1, or 80 per cent transmission (green filter or wave length 540 mμ). Now read each of the other tubes, marking the reading on it with a wax pencil. When you have finished, decide whether you have enough tubes that read the same (whatever the reading is) for use as a matched set without correction or whether corrections should be marked on each tube. The tubes should now be marked with an identifying mark or with the correction, using a diamond-point pencil or a vibrating tool.

To be used interchangeably, tubes should match within 2 Klett units (0.004 optical density or 0.5% T). For determinations in which the net reading, unknown minus blank, is less than 50 on the Klett (0.1 absorbance or over 80% T), tubes of perfect match should be used.

One other consideration in the choice of cuvet is the size of the sample available; conversely the final volume of solution must be sufficient for the cuvet and the instrument being used. Although the Klett-Summerson colorimeter provides for large rectangular cells, it has no provision for tubes smaller than the 14 or 15 mm. test tubes used routinely. These require a minimum volume of 4.5 ml. when round-bottom tubes are used. The microcuvets with flat bottoms require about 2.5 ml. The Spectronic 20 provides for ½, ¾, or 1 inch tubes; minimum volumes for these are about 3, 5, and 8 ml. respectively. The Coleman junior has provision for tubes from 25 mm. maximum down to capillary tubes, minimum volumes being as follows:

TUBE SIZE (MM.)	MINIMUM VOLUME (ML.)
25	10.0
19	5.5
12	1.5
10	1.0
4	0.09
0.8	0.007

Some procedures, even in the Coleman manual, are written to reflect a 5 ml. final volume with instructions to read in a 19 mm. tube. Some Coleman junior instruments require a volume of nearer 5.5 ml. for reading. One can check the volume required for an instrument by placing 4.5 ml. of a colored solution in a cuvet in the instrument, reading, adding 0.1 ml. portions, and reading after each addition. When an adequate volume is present, no further change in reading will occur. If more than 5 ml. is required, the instrument may be made to operate on this volume by cutting a slice from a cork and placing it in the cuvet adapter under the cuvet, making use of some of the waste volume, which is normally below the light beam. Be careful not to raise the tube so much that the curved portion is in the light beam. This procedure can be used to determine minimum volume for other cuvets and instruments. Note that the Klett-Summerson uses the principle of decreasing waste volume below the light beam with the flat-bottom microtubes.

Although the microtubes provided for by Coleman do make possible readings on very small volumes, they have the disadvantage of decreasing the light path in the solution and thus decreasing sensitivity and accuracy. The new microsystem cuvets provide a longer light path but still require only 0.1 ml.; the Coleman uses a 10 mm. cell with flat ends and the Spinco, 6 mm. tubes with curved ends. The Coleman microcuvet can be used in the Junior spectrophotometer; the Spinco requires a special spectrophotometer.

Operating Instructions for Colorimeters

Visual

BAUSCH AND LOMB. Place empty cups in correct position on colorimeter (they should be numbered the same as the colorimeter and as left or right). Raise the racks until the plunger touches the inside bottom of the cup. The scales should read zero; if not, adjust the scales to zero or correct each subsequent reading for the variation.

Place the same colored solution in both cups, rinsing cups and plungers if necessary; fill the cups about half full. Set the cups at 20.0 mm. See that there are no bubbles under the plungers.

Set the instrument in front of a good light source. Look through the eyepiece. Adjust the mirror (preferably using the milk glass reflector) and the position of the colorimeter itself so that the two halves of the field look the same (adjust the focus of the eyepiece if necessary). Now check for proper adjustment by running one cup up or down and coming back to visual match. The reading should, of course, be 20 again. If not, readjust the instrument.

The instrument is now ready for use. Do not disturb the position of the colorimeter, mirror, or light until readings have been completed. Place the unknown solution in the left cup and set it at 20.0. Place the standard in the right cup and read. When finished, rinse cups and plungers with distilled water and invert cups on a paper towel in front of the instrument to drain.

In using the colorimeter, be sure that there is enough solution in the cup so that the plunger is immersed when taking readings. Also be careful that there is not so much solution that it overflows when the cup is run up. Some reagents are extremely corrosive to glass or metal. Wash off any spills immediately. Be careful not to get solutions on the metal collar around the plunger or on the metal shield of the cups. This may ruin the determination and damage the instrument.

KLETT. The procedure is the same as for the Bausch and Lomb except that instead of using an outside light source, an internal light may be used. This may be adjusted by loosening the setscrew on the socket and moving the light.

Photoelectric

KLETT-SUMMERSON. Before turning the light on, see that the galvanometer needle is on the line. This is adjusted by the knob on top of the galvanometer. (Once this adjustment is made, this knob is never touched during use of the instrument.)

See that the proper colored glass filter is in place. With the shorting switch on the right side of the instrument in the OFF (down) position, turn the light on and let the instrument warm up for 15 or 20 minutes.

Insert a tube containing the blank or reference solution into the cuvet well and with the dial set at zero reading turn the shorting switch ON. Using the knob on top of the instrument near the filter holder, adjust the diaphragm so that the needle comes to the line. Turn the shorting switch OFF. Replace the blank solution with the solution to be read (in the same tube or a matching one), turn the switch ON, and bring the needle to the line with the large knob on the front of the instrument that turns the dial. Read the dial (this value is absorbance times 500).

SPECTRONIC 20. This instrument may be equipped with a type 5581 photocell for use at wave lengths below 650 mμ or with a type 1P40 photocell and a red filter for use at longer wave lengths. The type 5581 may be used at wave lengths above 650 if it is sufficiently sensitive and if the red filter is used with it.

To operate the instrument, turn it ON with the switch of the left, lower front knob (this is the amplifier control knob). After a few minutes' warmup, bring the needle to infinity on the absorbance (optical density) scale (0 on the transmittance scale). Set the wave length to the desired value with the knob beside the wave length scale window.

Insert a tube containing the blank or reference solution into the cuvet well (this opens the shutter in the light path). Adjust the needle to zero absorbance (100 per cent transmittance) with the right hand, front knob. Replace the blank solution with the solution to be read (in the same tube or a matching one) and read the scale, preferably in absorbance (optical density).

FISHER. Turn the lower left knob to ADJ GAL and see that the galvanometer needle is on the line. This is adjusted by the knob on top of the galvanometer. (Once this adjustment has been made, the knob is never touched during use of the instrument.)

See that the proper colored glass filter is in place. Turn the lower left knob to the same letter as is on the filter holder.

Insert a tube containing the blank or reference solution into the rear cuvet well and a matched tube containing the solution to be measured into the front cuvet well. Move the carrier against its stop with the rear tube in the light path. Close the cell compartment door.

With the dial set at the zero reading on scale A, depress the lamp button (in the center of the dial knob). Bring the galvanometer needle back to the line by turning the initial null knob. Keep the lamp turned on long enough to be sure that equilibrium has been reached and that the galvanometer will not drift from the index line.

Without releasing the lamp button, push the carrier back against the rear stop, putting the front tube (solution to be measured) in the light path.

Still holding down the lamp button, bring the needle back to the line by turning the large knob on the front of the instrument. Release the lamp button.

Read the dial, preferably on scale A (absorbance × 100).

Be sure that a tube of one solution reads the same in either position of the cuvet carrier; or, the blank and unknown can be read in the same well without moving the carrier.

COLEMAN JUNIOR SPECTROPHOTOMETER. Turn both fine and coarse galvanometer knobs as far as they will go counterclockwise. Turn the light on (switch on back of instrument); let warm up for ten minutes or longer. Adjust the galvanometer reading to zero transmission (left end of scale) by using the control under the hood of the galvanometer or by moving the scale itself. Set the wave length scale to the desired value, using the λ knob.

Insert a tube containing the blank or reference solution into the cuvet well. (The cuvet holder should be turned so that its key is in the slot and the light passes through the slots. The zero transmission reading may be checked by turning the cuvet holder 90° without disturbing the galvanometer knobs). Adjust the galvanometer reading to zero absorbance (right end of scale) with the coarse and then the fine galvanometer knobs.

Replace the blank solution with the solution to be read and read the galvanometer (preferably on the absorbance or optical density scale).

LUMETRON. See that the galvanometer reads zero on the lower scale, that the proper colored glass filter is in place, and that coarse and fine knobs are turned counterclockwise. Turn the light on by moving the toggle switch from BATT to AC. Let warm up a few minutes.

Insert matched tubes containing a blank or control solution and the solution to be measured into the cuvet holder. Pull carrier forward (putting blank tube in light path). Adjust galvanometer to zero absorbance (upper red scale). Push carrier back (putting solution to be measured in light path) and read meter (preferably on upper scale, which is absorbance × 10).

Be sure that one tube of one solution reads the same in either position of the cuvet carrier. This can be changed by turning the recessed screwhead, which is between the two cuvet wells and to their right. Or blank and unknown can be read in the same well without moving the carrier.

LEITZ. See that the galvanometer reads zero, that the proper colored glass filter is in place, and that the knob on the front of the instrument is turned counterclockwise. Turn the light on with the toggle switch on the front of the instrument. Let warm up a few minutes.

Insert a tube containing the blank or reference solution into the cuvet well. Using the knob on the front of the instrument, adjust the galvanometer to 100. Replace the blank solution with the solution to be read (in the same tube or a matching one) and read.

ALL MAKES. Be sure to check zero readings frequently enough to know that the instrument has not changed. Some of the instruments are steady; some are rather unstable and must be reset frequently.

Standardization. Among the greatest sources of error in clinical chemistry laboratory work are inadequately trained technicians who do not know how to or do not understand the necessity of standardizing their own determinations and instrument manufacturers who present precalibrations with the statement or the implication that they are reliable. Precalibrations are reliable only if exactly the same technique is followed by the technician with exactly equal reagents as those used by the manufacturer and if there has been no change in the response of the instrument. No precalibration should be used unless it is first checked by the technician who will use it.

Standardization is ordinarily done by preparing a solution containing an exactly known concentration of the compound being determined and running it through the analytical procedure. Sometimes some of the preliminary steps of the analysis can be (or even should be) omitted. Thus, in some methods for the determination of glucose, tungstic acid is added to blood to remove the proteins. However, with a pure aqueous glucose solution containing no protein, no precipitate would form and the tungstic acid would remain and would interfere in the reaction. Sometimes some constituent of the sample other than the compound being determined will affect the result. Thus, serum proteins will affect the reading obtained with bromsulfalein; therefore, the standard should also contain serum. In this example it is easy to get serum free of the constituent being sought. In some cases the constituent is present normally and serum cannot be added without affecting the amount of the compound present. Therefore, to get the effect of serum it is necessary to make the determination on a serum low in content of the compound being determined and on a second sample of the same serum containing a known additional amount of the compound and to consider the difference in readings as the result of the added amount of standard. Fortunately this is infrequent, and pure solutions usually suffice for accurate standardization

Sometimes it is difficult or impossible to obtain in pure form the material being determined. There are two ways in which this problem is handled. In the enzyme determinations, e.g., amylase, phosphatase, and transaminase, instead of determining the amount of these compounds, we determine the amount of some material that is used up or formed in the reaction that the enzyme catalyzes under certain well-defined conditions. Thus, we may measure amylase activity by determining the amount of maltose formed or of starch used up or measure phosphatase by the amount of phenol or phosphate split off a substrate.

In some instances, when it is difficult to obtain a pure standard, as in the case of hemoglobin or bilirubin, a different approach is used. For hemoglobin we may analyze a blood sample by a different method, for example, by determining its iron content or oxygen capacity and by calculating from this and from the known iron content or oxygen capacity of hemoglobin the hemoglobin content of the blood sample. We can now use this blood to standardize the hemoglobin method. Such analyzed hemoglobin solutions are now available commercially for laboratories that

do not have the time or facilities to do the standardization themselves.

Another approach is to use a substitute or artificial standard. Here a colored solution is prepared and its absorbance is compared with that of a carefully, sometimes tediously, prepared pure standard. Thereafter the artificial standard may be used in place of the natural one. This procedure has certain limitations. The method used in the routine determination must be one that is reproducible, always giving the same color intensity for the same amount of material. It could not, for example, be used for the determination of cholesterol or glucose, for these do not always give the same absorbance for the same concentration. The determination of hemoglobin by the alkali hematin method meets these requirements. Gibson and Harrison (1945) have described a solution of inorganic salts that is suitable as an artificial standard for hemoglobin. It may be prepared in the laboratory or purchased (from W. H. Curtin & Co., P. O. Box 118, Houston, Texas) in sealed tubes for use in the colorimeter. For the standardization of bilirubin, Moreland, O'Donnell, and Gast (1950) proposed using the color developed in the determination of sulfanilamide. They carefully purified several samples of bilirubin and determined the bilirubin equivalent of the sulfanilamide reaction.

Another problem arises in the use of these artificial standards: the question of their applicability to instruments other than the one on which they were calibrated. Different kinds of photoelectric colorimeters differ in spectral quality of the light source and in the band-width of the light passed by the filter or grating. If the wave length-absorbance curve for the artificial standard is the same as that of the color from the determination, then the standard should be usable on various instruments. This is true of the artificial alkali hematin standard and of the use of the sulfanilamide and bilirubin reactions. It is not true of the use of a copper sulfate solution as a standard for the thymol turbidity determination as proposed by Ducci (1947) for the Evelyn photoelectric colorimeter. The copper sulfate solution and the turbid solutions have quite different wave length-absorbance curves. Therefore, the turbidity equivalence of the copper sulfate will be different in different instruments or at different wave lengths.

How often should standards be run in

colorimetric determinations? As for the question on checking the zero setting of the colorimeter the answer is: as often as necessary. Some reactions are highly reproducible, being relatively insensitive to slight differences in temperature, light intensity, time of heating, or other technical variations and relatively unaffected by the age of reagents or the slight differences in different batches of reagents. If the instrument used is likewise stable, standardization need be done only occasionally. On the other hand, some reactions are sensitive to these conditions, and a standard must be run with each batch of unknowns. Other reactions must be standardized each time a new batch of reagents is made or at intervals as a reagent ages. The frequency of standardization, then, will vary with determinations, and judgment and experience are necessary for the efficient use of standards.

Technicians who do not have the time or facilities to prepare their own standards can purchase them from any reliable chemical supply dealer. The technician must, however, be acquainted with the properties of these standards; some suppliers are overoptimistic about their stability or remiss in cautioning against deterioration. Also many different versions of standards exist for different methods of determining the same compound. Not all are interchangeable. For example, cholesterol standard may be made up in chloroform or in acetic acid. The technician must be aware of what she needs in a standard and must specify carefully to be sure the suppliers will understand.

This brings us to another type of preparation, which has become available in the last few years. This is the *control serum,* which is now available from several sources, notably the Clinical Chemistry Control Serum and Abnormal Clinical Chemistry Control Serum of Hyland Laboratories. This is human serum that has been freeze dried and carefully analyzed. Each vial is accompanied by an analysis of that particular lot. These preparations should not, however, be used for standards. This would double the uncertainty of the results by adding the possible variations of the manufacturer's analysts to those of the technician. These preparations are valuable, because they enable the technician to see whether she is getting correct results. If one does not agree with the furnished value, a careful search should be made for a possible source of error. A less expensive way of providing daily evidence of control is to prepare one's own pool of serum, freeze it in individual tubes, and use one tube each day to check the reproducibility of results.

Standardization should be extended to cover as much as possible of the range of concentrations one expects to encounter. Sometimes the upper limit of a determination is set by the reagents; thus, in some methods for blood sugar there is sufficient copper present for only about 400 mg. per cent glucose. When concentrations above this are met, a smaller sample must be used. At other times the upper limit is determined by the optical density of the colored solution. There are two ways beside dilution in which this may be decreased. Remember that optical density is not an inherent property of a solution but rather is a property of a certain solution in a particular cuvet at a specified wave length. By using a smaller cuvet, the optical density will be less; therefore, if the standardization is done in two sizes of cuvets, a wider range can be covered with no change in procedure. Also by reading at two wave lengths the range can be increased. For example, in the determination of blood sugar the blue solution is usually read with blue light. By shifting to red, the optical density is greatly increased and low blood sugar concentrations can be read more accurately. Standards and blanks must, of course, be read at the same wave length as the unknowns.

Fluorimetric Methods

Fluorescence is the property of a compound of emitting light of a longer wave length than the light illuminating it. Some compounds fluoresce in visible light; many others require ultraviolet activation (or even x-irradiation). Several compounds of importance in clinical chemistry fluoresce, e.g., quinine, quinidine, porphyrins, epinephrine and norepinephrine, thiamine, and riboflavin. Fluorimetric measurements differ from colorimetric measurements in that the photocell is placed at the side of the cuvet, reacting to light that comes out at right angles to the illuminating beam. Means must be provided for regulating the wave length of both the incident and the fluorescent light. This may be done with either filters or prisms. The primary filter or monochromator setting should be chosen to give maximum fluorescence; the secondary should filter out all stray incident light and pass the maximum of the fluorescent light. Fluorescence is a very sensitive technique and can measure very small amounts of material. Most of the discussion of colorimetry applies to fluorimetry.

Flame Photometry

Colorimetry, or absorption photometry, measures the light that gets through a solution; the light absorbed by a colored material is a measure of the amount of the constituent being determined. Flame photometry measures the amount of light produced when an element is excited by the heat of a flame. It is based on the flame tests used in general chemistry that show that sodium produces a yellow flame; potassium, a violet flame; and lithium, strontium, and calcium, a red flame. If we provide a reproducible means of getting the sample into the flame and of measuring the intensity of the light produced, we will have a flame photometer. Like absorption photometers, flame photometers may be single or double photocell; the wave length of the light may be selected by colored glass or interference filters or by prisms. The flame photometer may be a self-contained instrument or it may be an attachment put on a spectrophotometer. The sample, diluted serum or urine or tissue extract, is carried into the flame as a vapor or spray. The solution may be fed through an atomizer and carried in the air supply to the burner, or it may be atomized by a straight tube directly into the flame. The flame may be city gas, hydrogen, or acetylene burning in air or oxygen. If the light from the element being determined (usually sodium or potassium, sometimes calcium) is measured directly in a single photocell instrument, the rate of atomization and the gas and air pressures must be held very close, since variation in these would cause variations in the readings. The double photocell instrument is used with the internal standard method. A carefully measured amount of another element, usually lithium, is added to the diluted sample, and the amount of light produced by it and by the element being determined are both measured. The relative intensities are used to calculate the concentration of the unknown. This technique requires less precise regulation of atomization and of flame and leads to increased stability.

Sodium and potassium levels are readily determined by flame photometry. Good technique is essential to get correct results: care in making dilutions and care to avoid contamination from the water used for dilution and from the glassware. Much distilled water is not sufficiently pure. It can be purified easily by running through a monobed deionizer, such as the Barnstead Bantam demineralizer. Water with a conductivity less than that of 0.3 parts per million of sodium chloride is satisfactory and not difficult to attain. Glassware must be washed carefully and rinsed thoroughly with good distilled water. Both the sample and the lithium solution must be measured carefully.

Calcium can be estimated at the concentration that exists in serum with the hot-flame instrument. But even here we are working at the limit of sensitivity and stability. It is essential to work carefully and to go back and forth from standard to unknown several times in order to obtain a reliable reading. It is largely a matter of personal preference whether the flame or chemical method should be used for calcium.

As with colorimeters some flame photometers are read directly from the current generated by the photocells. Others use an amplifier circuit to increase sensitivity. The latter type usually is satisfactory when working properly but, as with any electronic equipment, it may cause trouble. The simpler instruments are generally more reliable.

Chromatographic Methods

Chromatography is a very useful, relatively simple technique for separating substances that cannot be separated easily by other means. The name derives from the fact that it was first used by the Russian botanist Tswett for the separation of colored compounds from plant leaves. Most of the applications of the process involve colorless compounds, and various methods of detecting them are used.

The procedure is based on the relative degree of adsorption of the dissolved compounds being separated on a solid material over which the solution flows slowly. It also depends on the relative solubility of the compounds being separated in two liquid phases. Of these two liquid phases one is fixed and the other moving; one may be water adsorbed on the supporting solid (e.g., paper contains about 15 per cent water) and the other is the solvent moving across the solid. Owing to these differences in adsorption or solubility some of the compounds move more rapidly than others.

This may be taken advantage of in two ways: the compounds may be found at different places on the adsorbent or they may appear at different times in the stream emerging from the adsorbent. Sometimes the various compounds may all be adsorbed together at first and then be moved differentially across the adsorbent by a second, eluting solvent. Or, rather than for separating several compounds, chromatography may be used simply to purify a single substance by using an adsorbent that will stop the substance and let some or all of the impurities pass on. The desired compound is then removed by a solvent that will specifically dissolve it without taking any of the adsorbed impurities.

This general procedure may be applied in several different ways. The adsorbent may be a granular or powdered solid placed in a vertical column, and the solution of the compounds to be separated may be allowed to dry. This end of the strip is then compounds to be separated have appreciable vapor pressures at temperatures that can be used, a small sample of the solution to be resolved can be applied to one end of a column of adsorbent. From this end, then, a stream of gas may be passed through to move the compounds being separated. This is called gas chromatography.

The most commonly used technique is paper chromatography in which a drop of the solution being analyzed is placed near one end of a strip of filter paper and allowed to dry. This end of the strip is then dipped into a solvent without allowing the applied spot to dip into the liquid. The solvent moves along the strip by capillary attraction either with or against gravity. After a suitable time the strip is removed, dried, and examined. If the compounds are colored, no further treatment may be necessary; or the compounds may be visible under ultraviolet light. Usually, however, the paper has to be sprayed with a reagent, which will react with the compounds to develop a color. To improve the separations, two-dimensional paper chromatography may be used. The solution is spotted near the corner of a sheet of filter paper, and one edge is immersed in a solvent. After a time the sheet is removed, dried, and then turned 90°, and the edge along which the first movement occurred is immersed in a second solvent, which now spreads the compounds across the paper, separating mixtures that moved together in the first solvent.

Since under the same conditions a given compound always moves at the same rate with respect to the solvent front, we can characterize compounds by their R_f, or the distance they have moved divided by the distance the solvent has moved. Sometimes the R_f is so small that we allow the solvent to move off the far edge of the paper. In this case we can add a known compound for reference and express the movement of our compound in relation to this reference compound. Thus, R_g could be the distance moved by some sugar divided by the distance that glucose has moved. Amino acids from a protein hydrolysate are usually separated by two-dimensional papergramy; in this case a map can be prepared, using known amino acids in the same solvent system and noting their final positions. Comparison of the unknown with the map will show which amino acids it contains.

Paper chromatography is useful in clinical chemistry for separating porphyrins, for the identification of sugars in urine,

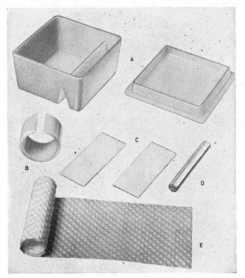

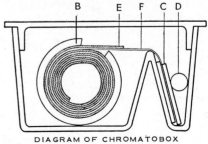

DIAGRAM OF CHROMATOBOX

Figure 8–18. Chromatobox. *A*, box and lid; *B*, holding ring for coiled paper in Teflon band; *C*, glass plates; *D*, glass rod; *E*, Teflon band; *F*, paper strip.

and for the study of urinary amino acids in such diseases as hepatolenticular degeneration (Wilson's disease), cystinosis, and the Fanconi syndrome.

A wide variety of equipment is available for chromatography. Some separations can be made on paper strips suspended in a test tube or mixing cylinder. Paper sheets can be handled in a beaker, battery jar, or cylindrical glass jar. Elaborate cabinets may be used for larger scale work. The Chromatobox provides a convenient, inexpensive means of doing one-dimensional paper chromatography in a small space. By rolling the paper strip inside a Teflon band, a 19-inch strip can be accommodated in a box 3 inches square and 2 inches high (Fig. 8–18). The band has a surface pattern of raised points to minimize contact with the paper and to prevent distortion of the chromatographic pattern. The box has a small compartment for the 10 to 15 ml. of solvent required and a larger one for the rolled paper. (Chromatobox is a trade name; Research Specialties Co. is the sole U. S. distributor for the item, which is available from E. H. Sargent and Co.)

Electrophoretic Methods

Electrophoresis is the movement of charged particles in an electric field. It has been applied to the movement of cells in suspension and of colloidal particles. It is useful in clinical chemistry for the identification of proteins. The rate of movement depends not only on the intensity of the electric field but also on the size, shape, and electric charge of the colloidal particle or molecule. Therefore, different proteins move at different rates. These rates vary with pH and the variation is not the same for all proteins. Therefore, in making identification it may be helpful to perform electrophoresis at more than one pH.

Free and zone electrophoresis differ from each other in that in the former a solution of the charged particles is placed directly in the electric field and analyzed. In the latter the solution being analyzed is "supported" on filter paper, a layer of starch granules, an agar gel, or some other solid or semisolid medium. This latter technique is simpler in decreasing the interference from diffusion and in providing stability to the separated fractions, since they are in a solid medium rather than a liquid. As with chromatography the greatest use of electrophoresis is made with filter paper as the supporting medium. The usual procedure is to dampen a strip of paper with buffer solution, place a small sample of the solution to be analyzed near the middle of the strip, and dip the ends of the strip in buffer solution into which electrodes are placed. After several hours the strip is removed, dried, stained if necessary, and examined. If the materials being separated are colored, as with hemoglobin, staining may be unnecessary. The technique may be made quantitative by measuring the intensity of the color of the several fractions. This may be done by cutting out each spot, eluting the color into solution, and measuring its intensity in a photoelectric colorimeter or by passing the intact strip through a densitometer (i.e., between a light and a photoelectric cell) and observing the relative intensities. This process may be done automatically with a densitometer that draws a curve showing relative intensities along the strip and also integrates the curve to give a quantitative measure of each component.

Potentiometric Methods

Differences in concentration of ions produces an electrical potential, which may be measured with suitable electrodes and measuring equipment. In clinical chemistry, methods based on this principle have been described for determining hydrogen and chloride ions.

For determining hydrogen ion concentration or pH, a glass electrode is used, which consists of a mercury-acid or a silver-silver chloride system behind a thin glass membrane. A calomel half-cell completes the cell. A vacuum tube potentiometer is used to measure the potential. The glass electrode is fragile and must be handled carefully. It is also affected by drying and should be kept wet or soaked for several hours before being used. Temperature affects the potential and must be considered. Most commercial pH meters have temperature compensation circuits. Many types of both potentiometers and electrodes are available. The meter may be large or small, portable or fixed, more or less sensitive, battery-operated or line-operated, and more or less expensive.

A pH meter is actually used only to compare the pH of two different solutions, since it must be standardized with a solution of known pH before it can be used; the determinations are therefore no better than the accuracy of the standardizing buffer solution. As with a colorimeter this initial setting must be checked frequently enough to avoid error from drift.

Electrodes may be chosen for many applications. For measurements within the case of the instrument shielded leads are not needed. For outside use longer shielded leads may be useful; this type is adapted to titration or to intragastric measurements. Special electrodes for small volume and for anaerobic specimens are available. There are also electrodes designed for immersion in a constant temperature bath. For determination of blood pH it might be well to caution that mineral oil on the glass electrode may give an erroneously high reading.

Potentiometric methods have also been used for other ions. A titration method for serum and urine chloride, adaptable to microsamples, has been described. Mercury and silver electrodes are used. Silver nitrate is added from a buret until the potentiometer response indicates that all the chloride ions have reacted.

CARBOHYDRATES

Carbohydrates are organic compounds containing carbon, hydrogen, and oxygen. Some of their derivatives may also contain nitrogen, though this is unusual. The carbohydrates include the sugars and compounds that yield sugars on hydrolysis. The sugars may be monosaccharides, which are simple, single sugar molecules, or disaccharides, which are composed of two monosaccharides joined through an oxygen by elimination of a molecule of water. The polysaccharides contain many molecules of monosaccharides joined together and have lost the characteristics of sugars. Chemically the monosaccharides are polyhydroxy aldehydes or ketones and are therefore easily oxidized, which is to say they are reducing compounds. If the

two sugars of a disaccharide are joined through the active aldehyde or ketone groups, the disaccharide will not be a reducing sugar; if the aldehyde or ketone of one monosaccharide is joined to a hydroxyl group of the other, there will still be one free aldehyde or ketone group and the disaccharide will be a reducing sugar although not so active as the monosaccharides. The polysaccharides consist of long chains of monosaccharides joined through the aldehyde or ketone of one to a hydroxyl of the next. They therefore have one active group on the end, but in such a large molecule this is insufficient to make it a reducing compound. A monosaccharide may have as few as two or as many as seven carbons in its chain. These are designated from the chain length as dioses, trioses, tetroses, pentoses, hexoses, and heptoses. The nature of the active group may be shown by designating them as ketoses and aldoses. Actually the monosaccharides exist mostly in a ring form with an oxygen bridge between the first and fifth carbon atoms as shown in Fig. 8–19 rather than as the free aldehydes. In this form the hydroxyl group on the first carbon can be either on the same side as or on the opposite side from the hydroxyl on the second carbon; these two forms are called α and β. They are interconvertible in solution and whichever we start with, the same equilibrium mixture results.

The stability of different types of carbohydrates with various reagents differs considerably. The di- and polysaccharides are all split by acid into monosaccharides, which are stable. The nonreducing carbohydrates (the polysaccharides and sucrose) are stable in alkaline solution, while the reducing sugars break down. There are a number of chemical reactions that are used as qualitative and quantitative tests for carbohydrates.

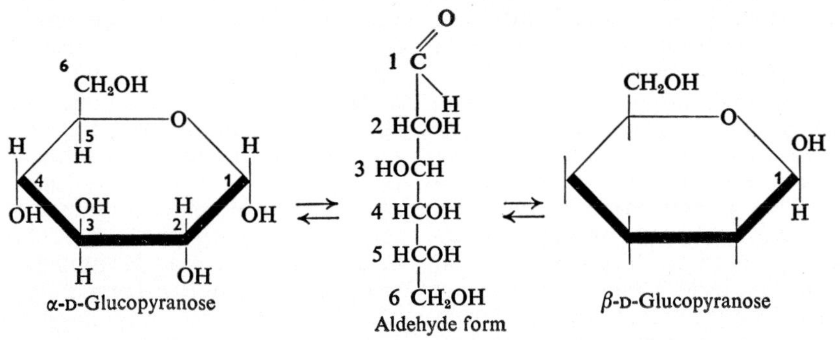

Figure 8–19. Equilibrium forms of glucose. (Harrow, B., and Mazur, A.: Textbook of Biochemistry. 7th Ed.)

Table 8–3. Carbohydrates of Interest in Clinical Chemistry

	NATURE OR HYDROLYSIS PRODUCTS	REDUCING	FERMENTABLE	DIFFUSIBLE
Monosaccharides				
Xylose	Aldopentose	+	−	+
Xyloketose	Ketopentose	+	−	+
Glucose	Aldohexose	+	+	+
Fructose	Ketohexose	+	+	+
Galactose	Aldohexose	+	−	+
Disaccharides				
Sucrose	Glucose + fructose	−	+	+
Maltose	Glucose	+	+	+
Lactose	Glucose + galactose	+	−	+
Polysaccharides				
Starch	Glucose	−	−	−
Glycogen	Glucose	−	−	−
Inulin	Fructose	−	−	−
Dextran	Glucose	−	−	−
Cellulose	Glucose	−	−	−

The reducing power of sugars is the basis of tests that use (a) copper or iron reagents, such as Benedict's test and Clinitest and the quantitative determination by the Folin-Wu, Benedict, Nelson-Somogyi, and the ferricyanide methods, or (b) picric or dinitrosalicylic acid. In the copper tests the sugar reacts in alkaline solution, being oxidized by the cupric ion, which is simultaneously reduced to cuprous and precipitates as the red cuprous oxide. The formation of cuprous oxide is the basis of Benedict's qualitative test and Clinitest. In the quantitative determinations the cuprous oxide is allowed to react with a phosphomolybdic or arsenomolybdic acid, reducing it to a blue color, which is measured in a colorimeter. In the determination by ferricyanide the glucose may be estimated by the decrease in the yellow ferricyanide color (this reaction is used in the Autoanalyzer method), or the ferrocyanide may be allowed to react with ferric ions to produce an intense blue color as in the Folin-Malmros micromethod. Unfortunately this last reaction is quite variable, and it is difficult to obtain reproducible results with it.

Glucose may be oxidized enzymatically to gluconic acid; hydrogen peroxide is formed in this reaction and may be induced to oxidize some colorless material to a colored compound. This is the basis of the tests for glucose with glucose oxidase. Qualitatively this is used in Tes-Tape and in Clinistix, Uristix, and Combistix. It may also be used quantitatively, the Glucostat method being a commercial form of this test. Since the enzyme is specific for glucose, the methods based on it should give true blood glucose values. However, there may be other compounds in the blood or urine that will also react with hydrogen peroxide and will therefore compete with the color-producing reaction and cause low results.

The carbohydrates of interest in clinical chemistry are listed in Table 8–3. Xyloketose is a pentose, which a few people excrete in the urine. This trait is familial and seems to cause no symptoms. It is important that this sugar not be confused with glucose lest the patient be treated as a diabetic. Glucose, also known as dextrose, is the common sugar of the body and of the blood. It is the one usually given when intravenous sugar is desired, although fructose is sometimes administered. It may occur in the urine when the blood sugar is elevated or, in a few people, even with a normal blood sugar. Fructose, also known as levulose, occurs free in honey along with glucose. It is utilized more readily by the diabetic than is glucose. It is rarely found in the urine. Galactose is not normally encountered free but is of importance because of its occurrence in lactose and in certain compound lipids found in the nervous system. In infants lacking the enzyme phosphogalactotransferase, galactose cannot be utilized; it accumulates in the body and is excreted in the urine. This condition of galactosemia may be harmful, and milk is usually eliminated from the infant's diet. Therefore, the recognition of galactose is occasionally of importance.

Sucrose, either cane or beet, is the common food sugar. Since it consists of a glucose molecule combined through its aldehyde group with the ketone group of a fructose molecule, it is not a reducing sugar. It is easily hydrolyzed into glucose and fructose by the enzyme sucrase or invertase or by acid. It is not formed in the animal body. Maltose is important chiefly because it is a breakdown product of the digestion of starch. The enzyme amylase splits starch down through dextrin to the disaccharide stage. Maltose remains if no maltase is present to split it to glucose. Hydrolysis of starch by acid, of course, proceeds to glucose. In the saccharogenic methods for determining amylase in serum or other fluids, it is maltose that is actually determined. Lactose is the sugar of milk and is therefore a normal food of infants; only rarely is it not properly metabolized. It sometimes appears in the urine during late pregnancy or lactation and should not be mistaken for glucose.

Starch is a polysaccharide of glucose. Actually starch is a mixture of two types of glucose polymers, amylose and amylopectin. Amylose is a linear or non-branched 1:4 polymer in which the aldehyde group of one glucose is combined to the hydroxyl group on the fourth carbon of the next glucose. Amylopectin contains 1:6 branches off the main chain with a second glucose combining through its aldehyde group to the hydroxyl on the sixth carbon of one of the glucose units in the chain. Starch is used in the laboratory as an indicator for iodine, with which it forms a dark blue compound, and as a substrate for amylase in the determination of this enzyme.

Glycogen is the polymeric storage form of glucose in the animal body. It is branched like amylopectin but gives a red color with iodine. Inulin is a polymer of fructose found in certain plants. It is sometimes used in the laboratory in the measurement of kidney function. Dextran is a 1:6 polymer of glucose that is formed by certain microorganisms. It is water soluble and not metabolized in the animal body. It is sometimes used as a blood substitute or plasma extender, since it is a large enough molecule to be only slowly lost from the blood. Cellulose is a structural material of plants; it is a 1:4 polymer of β-glucose. It is not hydrolyzed by enzymes of the human body. It is used in the laboratory chiefly in the form of filter paper and cotton.

There are several other carbohydrates that occur in the body but thus far are not likely to be encountered in the clinical laboratory. These include glyceraldehyde and dihydroxyacetone, which occur during the breakdown of glucose, and ribose and deoxyribose, which occur in nucleic acids. Certain carbohydrate derivatives also occur: glucuronic acid, in which the aldehyde group of glucose has been oxidized to a carboxyl group, is attached to a number of cyclic hydroxy compounds before excretion, including steroids, bilirubin, and a number of drugs. Glucosamine occurs with glucuronic acid in heparin and in cartilage.

Quantitative Determination of Glucose

The amount of glucose in the blood is increased following a meal. The determination of glucose on a random sample of blood is therefore of little value as a first estimate of a person's ability to metabolize glucose. The blood should be drawn sufficiently long after the last meal so that the food is completely digested and absorbed and any excess is stored. This is normally in the morning before breakfast and yields a "fasting blood sugar" or FBS. Fasting here means not only no breakfast but no cream or sugar in coffee; no tea or coke; no drugs that might affect the blood sugar, such as coffee or cigarettes; and no emotional disturbance that might cause the liberation of glucose into the blood. Fasting does not mean no water; the patient should be permitted water as usual.

Normally there is 70 to 90 mg. per cent of glucose in the blood; an increase above this is called *hyperglycemia* and a decrease is called *hypoglycemia*. Actually glycemia refers to any sugar in the blood with no specific reference to glucose. The terms hyper- and hypoglucemia would be better; the rise following a meal is called *alimentary hyperglycemia*. The most frequent cause of hyperglycemia in a fasting patient is diabetes mellitus. This consists of a relative deficiency in insulin and may be caused by pancreatic insufficiency or by adrenal or pituitary hyperfunction. Hyperglycemia may rarely be due to decreased kidney function. Hypoglycemia may be due to increased pancreatic activity (as in an islet cell tumor), to subnormal adrenal function, or to decreased reabsorption by the kidney tubules (decreased renal threshold).

A number of methods are in use for the determination of blood sugar. The Folin-Wu method is sensitive to a number of reducing compounds other than glucose and should not be used; it averages about 20 mg. per cent above the true glucose value but may be as much as 200 mg. per cent higher. Benedict improved on the Folin-Wu method by increasing the specificity of the reagent for glucose; however, this method does not produce a stable color. Somogyi decreased the effect of nonglucose reducing compounds with an improved method for precipitating the proteins from the blood, using zinc hydroxide-barium sulfate instead of tungstic acid as Folin and Wu had done. Combination of Somogyi's precipitation and copper reagent with Nelson's arsenomolybdate color reagent has produced a stable, specific, sensitive method for determining glucose in blood or cerebrospinal fluid or even urine.

SOMOGYI-NELSON METHOD (REINHOLD, 1953)

Proteins are removed by treating the sample with barium hydroxide and zinc sulfate, forming the two insoluble compounds, zinc hydroxide and barium sulfate, which combine with the proteins and carry them down. When the protein-free filtrate is heated with an alkaline copper reagent, the glucose reduces the cupric ions to cuprous. The red cuprous oxide precipitate is then allowed to react with an arsenomolybdate reagent, and the colorless hexavalent molybdenum is reduced to a lower valence with an intense blue color. Both of these oxidation-reduction reactions are incompletely defined in terms of absolute chemical equivalence. Under specific and standardized conditions, however, the reactions yield results having quantitative significance, the intensity of the blue color being proportional to the amount of glucose originally present.

Reagents

1. Protein precipitants. (a) 5 per cent zinc sulfate. Dissolve 50 gm. of $ZnSO_4 \cdot 7H_2O$ in water and dilute to 1 liter. (b) 0.3N barium hydroxide. Dissolve 45 gm. of $Ba(OH)_2 \cdot 8H_2O$ in water and dilute to 1 liter. Filter if cloudy. Store this and (a) in well-stoppered containers filled to capacity.

The concentrations of the working solutions of Zn and Ba are not so important as the requirement that they exactly neutralize one another. To titrate, measure 10 ml. of $ZnSO_4$ solution into a 250 ml. flask and add approximately 50 ml. of H_2O and 4 drops of phenolphthalein indicator.

Slowly titrate with $Ba(OH)_2$, using continual agitation. (Note: too rapid addition of the $Ba(OH)_2$ will give a false endpoint.) The titration is carried out until 1 drop of $Ba(OH)_2$ turns the solution a faint pink. The result should be such that 10 ml. of $ZnSO_4$ require 10 ml. of $Ba(OH)_2 \pm 0.05$ ml. If one or the other of the two solutions is too strong, add distilled water in appropriate quantities and repeat the titration. Store the solutions in aspirator or siphon bottles; the one containing the barium hydroxide should carry a soda-lime tube in the stopper. The solutions should be tested in advance by preparing a trial filtrate from blood. Filtration should proceed rapidly to give a clear filtrate with little tendency to foam. If faults are noted, repeat the titration and adjust solutions accordingly.

2. Copper reagent, solution A. Dissolve 50 gm. of Na_2CO_3 (anhydrous or the equivalent amount of a hydrate), 50 gm. of Rochelle salt, 40 gm. of $NaHCO_3$, and 400 gm. of Na_2SO_4 (anhydrous or the equivalent amount of a hydrate) in about 1600 ml. of water and dilute to 2 liters. Filter if necessary. This solution should be stored where the temperature will not fall below 20° C. A sediment may form after a few days; this may be filtered off without detriment to the reagent.

3. Copper reagent, solution B. Dissolve 150 gm. of $CuSO_4 \cdot 5H_2O$ 1 liter of water. Add 0.5 ml. of concentrated H_2SO_4.

4. Alkaline copper reagent. Prepared on the day it is to be used by measuring 4 ml. of copper reagent B into a 100 ml. mixing cylinder and diluting to 100 ml. with copper reagent A. Mix well.

5. Arsenomolybdate color reagent. Dissolve 100 gm. of ammonium molybdate in 1800 ml. of distilled water. Add 84 ml. of concentrated sulfuric acid and mix. Add 12 gm. of disodium orthoarsenate ($Na_2 HAsO_4 \cdot 7H_2O$) dissolved in 100 ml. of water. Mix and place in an incubator for 24 to 48 hours at 37° C. (An alternative, although less desirable, method is to heat to 55° C. for about 25 minutes while stirring actively.) Decomposition of the reagent is characterized by precipitation of a bright yellow compound. Prepared by the first method, it is stable indefinitely when stored in a glass-stopper brown bottle.

6. Stock standard glucose solution. Weigh 1.000 gm. of purest dextrose (National Bureau of Standards, obtainable from chemical suppliers). Transfer to a 100 ml.

volumetric flask and dilute to the mark with 0.2 per cent benzoic acid solution; 1 ml. contains 10 mg. of glucose.

7. 50 mg. standard (I). Dilute 0.5 ml. of stock solution to 200 ml. in a volumetric flask with 0.2 per cent benzoic acid solution; 0.5 ml. contains 0.0125 mg. of glucose.

8. 100 mg. standard (II). Dilute 1 ml. of stock solution to 200 ml.; 0.5 ml. contains 0.025 mg. of glucose.

9. 200 mg. standard (III). Dilute 2 ml. of stock solution to 200 ml.; 0.5 ml. contains 0.05 mg. of glucose. Standards diluted with benzoic acid keep indefinitely at room temperature.

10. Benzoic acid solution, 0.2 per cent. Place approximately 4 gm. of benzoic acid in a 3 liter Pyrex flask. Add 2 liters of water. Heat to boiling but do not boil.

MACROPROCEDURE. Measure 1 ml. of blood, spinal fluid, or urine into a 50 ml. Erlenmeyer flask. (If the qualitative test indicates that the urine contains over 0.3 per cent glucose, dilute the urine accurately to bring it into the 0.1 to 0.3 per cent range. Multiply by this extra dilution to obtain the final result.)

Add 15 ml. of water and mix.

Add 2 ml. of barium hydroxide while rotating flask.

Add 2 ml. of zinc sulfate solution while mixing.

Shake vigorously. Filter through Whatman No. 1 paper or equivalent.

Measure 0.5 ml. of barium-zinc filtrate, 0.5 ml. of standard, and 0.5 ml. of water (for a blank) into separate tubes (test tubes or photometer cuvets approximately 15×125 mm.).

Add 1 ml of alkaline copper reagent and mix each tube by tapping.

Place a marble on top and heat in a vigorously boiling water bath for 20 minutes, or place in a pressure cooker (see comment 3) for five minutes at 115° C.

Place tubes in water at room temperature for one minute.

Add 1 ml. of arsenomolybdate reagent and mix.

Dilute to the 10 ml. mark with water or add 7.5 ml of water. Mix by inverting.

Measure the absorbance at 540 mμ by means of a photocolorimeter, using the blank for setting the zero.

CALCULATION. R_x is the reading of the unknown, and R_s is the reading of the standard. Using standard I (0.0125 mg. of glucose):

$$\frac{R_x}{R_s} \times 50 = \text{mg. glucose per 100 ml. blood,}$$

spinal fluid, or urine.

Using standard II (0.025 mg. of glucose):

$$\frac{R_x}{R_s} \times 100 = \text{mg. \% glucose.}$$

Using standard III (0.05 mg. of glucose):

$$\frac{R_x}{R_s} \times 200 = \text{mg. \% glucose.}$$

For urine samples, multiply also by any preliminary dilution that was made. Multiply also by the number of hundreds of ml. in the total specimen, and divide by 1000 to convert mg. to gm. Report grams of glucose in the specimen (this may be gm./24 hours, gm./6 hours, or other, depending on the specimen). The general equation would be:

$$\frac{R_x}{R_s} \times \frac{50, 100, \text{ or } 200 \text{ (depending on std. used)}}{1000}$$
$$\times \text{ dilution } \times \frac{\text{vol. of specimen}}{100}$$
$$= \text{gm./specimen.}$$

If 1 ml. of urine was diluted to 10 ml. before protein precipitation, if standard II had read 105 and the unknown read 180, and if the specimen volume was 1750 ml., the calculation would be:

$$\frac{180}{105} \times \frac{100}{1000} \times 10 \times 17.5 =$$
$$30 \text{ gm. glucose/specimen.}$$

SEMIMICROTECHNIQUE. Pipet 1.5 ml. of water into a centrifuge tube.

Draw cutaneous blood into a 0.1 ml. pipet and expel it into the water. Rinse the pipet two or three times by drawing up and expelling the solution into the centrifuge tube.

Add 0.2 ml. of Ba(OH)$_2$ solution and mix.

Add 0.2 ml. of ZnSO$_4$ solution and mix the contents of the tube thoroughly by tapping.

Allow the tubes to stand for three to five minutes and centrifuge for five minutes.

Pipet 0.5 ml. samples of the supernatant fluid, of each standard, and of water (for a blank) into separate tubes and carry out the analysis and calculation as described in the procedure for larger blood samples.

COMMENTS. 1. Glucose disappears by glycolysis from whole blood at an unpredictable rate. If it is not feasible to stop this process at once by adding the protein precipitating reagents, other precautions must be taken to prevent loss of glucose. This can be done by refrigeration or by addition of fluoride. The addition of 10 mg. of sodium, potassium, or ammonium fluoride per ml. of blood or the addition of 1 drop of 20 per cent potassium fluoride (20 gm. of KF or 33 gm. of KF · 2H$_2$O dissolved in water and diluted to 100 ml.) per 5 ml. of blood will preserve the glucose at room temperature.

2. Inclusion of the sodium sulfate in the copper reagent inhibits reoxidation of cuprous oxide by air and makes unnecessary the constricted tubes used in the Folin-Wu and Benedict procedures.

3. The 20-minute heating time can be reduced to 5 minutes by using a small autoclave (household pressure cooker). This should take 2½ minutes to reach 15 p.s.i. pressure (115° C.), leaving 2½ minutes for holding at this temperature.

4. This method provides rectilinear proportionality beyond the limits of instrumental accuracy. If the Klett-Summerson reading is over 350 or if absorbance is over 0.7, the colored solution may be diluted with a mixture of 1 volume of arsenomolybdate reagent and 9 volumes of water; or the test can be repeated, using 0.1 ml. of filtrate and multiplying the result by 5. If the result is still high, as may be the case with urine from a patient with diabetes mellitus, the filtrate may be diluted with water and 0.5 ml. of the dilution used to repeat the determination. The result would be multiplied by this extra dilution. If the Klett-Summerson reading is below 50 or if the absorbance is less than 0.1, there are three methods that can be used to increase the reading. First, the test may be repeated by adding 0.5 ml. of the 50 mg. per cent standard to the 0.5 ml. of filtrate and by subtracting 50 from the final result. Second, the concentration of the filtrate may be doubled by reducing the volume of water added to the blood; instead of using 15 ml., use 5 ml. and divide the final result by 2. Third, readings can be made with red light rather than blue. Read all solutions (blank, standard, and unknowns) with a red filter or at 650 mμ.

Glucose Tolerance Tests

In patients whose blood sugar is normal or only slightly elevated, the ability of the body to metabolize glucose may be investigated by increasing the load on body mechanisms, as is done by investigating the functional capacity of the liver, kidney, and intestine, for example. If the blood sugar is markedly elevated, a glucose tolerance test is superfluous just as is a urea clearance test when the blood urea nitrogen is elevated or a bromsulfalein test when the patient has jaundice.

There are several forms of the glucose tolerance test in use. The simplest and easiest, and the one that should usually be done, is the two-hour postprandial glucose determination. In this test the patient is given a breakfast containing 100 gm. of carbohydrate, and the blood glucose is determined two hours later. The glucose concentration should be below 120 mg. per cent at two hours.

The commonest procedure for the oral glucose tolerance test is, unfortunately, to draw blood for a fasting sugar and then to give the patient 50 or 100 gm. of glucose, or 1 gm. per kilogram of ideal body weight, and determine the blood sugar one, two, and three hours afterward; sometimes blood is also drawn at one-half hour or at four, five, and six hours. If this type of test must be done, Hoffman (1959) suggests that a glucose dose of 1 gm. per kilogram be used for adults and children over 12 years; for younger children, 2 gm. per kilogram; and for infants, 3 gm. per kilogram. Moreover, blood samples should be taken at 0, 60, 90, and 150 minutes. The glucose should be given with about seven times its weight of water (e.g., for a 70 kg. man give 70 gm. of glucose and 490 ml. of water), since more concentrated solutions must dilute themselves by absorbing water into the intestinal tract before the glucose can be absorbed into the blood.

The term "tolerance" refers to the ability of the body to handle glucose. Therefore, high tolerance is indicated by a small rise in blood glucose after its oral administration; low tolerance means a high blood glucose response. In a normal person the glucose will rise to about 140 mg. per cent in 45 to 60 minutes and will return to normal in one and one-half to two and one-half hours, the most valuable diagnostic point being two hours, when the value should be under 120 mg. per cent. In most normal persons the glucose concentration falls below normal for a time, coming back to normal within about 30 minutes. In a person with diabetes mellitus the curve rises higher and returns to normal more slowly. According to Hoffman (1959), "In the mild diabetic, the peak is above 140 mg. per 100 ml. and may be as high as 200 mg. per cent. The return to normal usually requires more than two and one-half hours. Also, there is usually no dip below the base level as in the normal person. Such a curve (as shown in Fig. 8–20) is called a diabetic curve, particularly if it is accompanied by glycosuria at the time of the peak level. But it must be remembered that such curves are frequently found in the nondiabetic hospital population, especially during acute illness, after trauma, after emotional stress, and after a low carbohydrate diet. It is also not infrequently seen in elderly persons with arteriosclerosis or with cardiac impairment. Most significantly, it has been found in a large percentage of middle-age obese persons. These individuals, after successfully losing weight by going on a reducing diet, often subsequently show normal glucose tolerance curves.

"The glucose tolerance curve obtained in a more severe diabetic (if one is foolish enough to try the test in such cases) shows a high base or fasting level; a rise to a peak of 300 mg. or more per 100 ml., the peak being usually delayed for two or three hours; and then a slow fall toward normal requiring many hours to reach the base level. In fact, in some instances the administration of 100 gm. of glucose to a severe diabetic for a glucose tolerance test may result in failure of the blood sugar level to return to the original level unless insulin is given. Obviously glucose tolerance tests are contraindicated in persons with fasting hyperglycemia and glycosuria.

"The author has not been very much impressed with the value of glucose tolerance tests for the diagnosis of diabetes in hospital practice. In most instances of diabetes, the diagnosis can be made from the morning blood glucose value and from the association of glycosuria with a typical history and symptomatology. In the absence of glycosuria and fasting hyperglycemia, blood glucose determination and urinalysis an hour after a breakfast of orange juice, cereal with sugar, two pieces of toast, and a glass of milk will usually permit a diagnosis of hyperglycemia and glycosuria. However, even this test, which has the advantage of simplicity, has the same drawback as the more formal glucose tolerance test in that it is influenced by previous diet, the emotional state, acute illness, especially infection or trauma, exercise, and obesity. The glucose tolerance test is more important for ruling out diabetes than for ruling it in. In other words, a normal curve is more significant than a moderately abnormal one. Therefore the test has value for insurance purposes, for dissipating fear of diabetes in members of a family in which there is a diabetic, and for determination of the presence of renal glycosuria or of an unusual reducing reaction of a urine specimen."

The five- and six-hour glucose tolerance tests are usually requested to aid in the diagnosis of hypoglycemia. It would be much more to the point to draw a blood sample at the time the patient is showing the symptoms in order to establish or rule out hypoglycemia. The shape of the three-hour glucose tolerance curve may then be a clue to the type of hypoglycemia.

Glucose tolerance is impaired by fasting or by a low carbohydrate intake. If the patient's carbohydrate intake has been poor, a tolerance test may result in a diabetic curve; the same patient on a good diet might show a normal tolerance. If there is any doubt that the patient's carbohydrate intake has been adequate, he should be placed on a diet containing at least 250 gm. of carbohydrate per day for three days, or his diet may be supplemented with a liter of 10 per cent glucose daily for three days.

Intravenous Glucose Tolerance Test. The oral test depends not only on the ability of the body to handle glucose but also on the rate of glucose absorption from the intestine. This latter is affected in some diseases, particularly hyper- and hypothyroidism. To eliminate this effect, it is

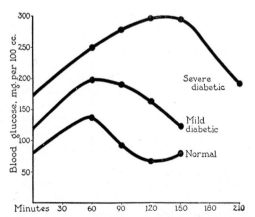

Figure 8–20. Typical oral glucose tolerance curves in normal and diabetic subjects. (Hoffman, W. S.: The Biochemistry of Clinical Medicine. 2nd Ed. Chicago, The Year Book Publishers, Inc., 1959.)

sometimes desirable to administer the glucose intravenously. A dose of 0.5 gm. per kilogram of ideal body weight is usual and is given intravenously by the physician as a 20 per cent solution. One ml. of 50 per cent glucose per kilogram is diluted to about 2½ times its volume with injectable distilled water, and this is given by intravenous drip at a constant rate such that the total volume is given in a half hour (e.g., for a 70 kg. patient, 70 ml. of 50 per cent glucose is diluted to about 175 ml. and given at the rate of 6 ml. per minute).

Rapid Intravenous Glucose Tolerance Test (Rate of Disappearance of Glucose). Amatuzio (1953) has used the disappearance rate of glucose from the blood following intravenous administration in the diagnosis of diabetes.

The patient should have been on an adequate carbohydrate intake.

Take a blood sample for determination of fasting blood sugar (FBS) (5 ml. in an oxalated bottle; protect against glucolysis).

Inject 25 gm. of glucose as a 30 per cent solution in water within four minutes (25 ml. of 50 per cent glucose and distilled water q.s. up to 40 to 45 ml. in each of two 50 ml. syringes).

Take another blood sample four minutes after the glucose administration. Call this zero time. Take further specimens 3, 6, 16, 26, 36, 46, and 56 minutes after this. Protect all bloods against glucolysis by sending them to the laboratory as drawn or by refrigerating them.

CALCULATION. From each blood sugar value subtract the FBS value, giving the "glucose excess." Plot these values on the logarithmic scale of semilogarithmic paper against time on the linear scale.

Determine from the graph the time at which the blood sugar is one-half the maximum (zero time) value.

Divide 69.3 by this time (in minutes) to obtain the glucose disappearance rate in per cent per minute.

$$\frac{69.3}{t} = \text{per cent per minute}$$

Amatuzio (1953) found a group of normals to range from 3.0 to 4.8; mild diabetics, 0.9 to 2.5; and severe diabetics, 0.2 to 1.6.

Identification of Urine Sugars

Some of the sugars that may occur in urine (glucose, fructose, galactose, lactose, sucrose, and xyloketose) can be distinguished on the basis of tests or properties described earlier. All the sugars mentioned except sucrose are reducing sugars and will therefore give positive tests with Benedict's reagent or Clinitest. The sugars other than glucose will usually not be present in amounts large enough to give more than a 2+ reducing test. If a positive test for reducing sugar is obtained, the next step would be to try Clinistix (as such or in Uristix or Combistix) or Tes-Tape; if these give a positive test, glucose is present. Other sugars may also be present. Remember that a positive test for one compound does not rule out other compounds that do not respond to that test. If the enzyme test is negative, glucose is absent and reduction was due to some other sugar.

Ketose (Lasker and Enklewitz test). Fructose or xyloketose can be shown by treating 1 ml. of the urine with 5 ml. of Benedict's qualitative reagent at 55° C. for 10 minutes or overnight at room temperature.

Pentoses. Xyloketose, ribose, and other pentoses will give a red color with Tauber's test. To 0.2 ml. of urine add 1 ml. of 2 per cent benzidine in glacial acetic acid. Heat to boiling, cool in running water, and add 2 ml. of water. If large amounts of protein are present, remove by adding to urine an equal volume of 10 per cent trichloroacetic acid, mix, and filter; use filtrate for the test.

Fermentation Test. Rub up a piece of fresh baker's yeast the size of two peas or a chinaberry with about 10 ml. of urine. Completely fill a 6 × 50 mm. lipless test tube with the mixture and pour the remainder into a 15 to 18 mm. test tube. Cover the small tube with a small piece of paper, invert, and drop into the larger tube. Let stand for an hour or two at 35 to 40° C. or for several hours at room temperature. Examine for gas accumulation within the small tube. Fermentation indicates the presence of glucose, fructose, or sucrose. The presence of nonfermentable sugars can be shown by centrifuging the mixture after fermentation is complete and applying Benedict's test, which will still be positive if galactose, lactose, or a pentose is present.

Chromatography (cf. p. 412) offers a more definitive method of demonstrating the presence of sugars in urine. Owing to the relatively low Rf's of the sugars, the chromatography should be done by a technique that permits the solvent to move a distance greater than the length of the paper sheet. This can be done by descending chromatography, allowing the solvent to drip off the lower edge of the sheet, or by ascending chromatography with the pad technique (a second sheet or two of paper is folded and clipped against the top of the chromatogram sheet). This allows more solvent to move across the sheet, moving the sugars further and improving separation. For this the chromatogram may be suspended from a glass rod held by rubber or polyethylene caps inside a circular or rectangular glass jar. Or a long paper strip may be folded into a rack made from plastic drapery pleaters to decrease the vertical length.

Whatman No. 4 paper is suitable for this chromatography when a rapid flow of solvent is desired. Flow will be more rapid along the major axis of the fibers of the paper. This can be determined by admitting water slowly onto the paper to form a spot. The longer diameter of the elliptical spot indicates the major axis of the fibers. If descending chromatography is to be used and the solvent is allowed to drip off the end of the paper, the lower end of the paper should be serrated with a point directly below each spot at which a sample is to be placed.

Prepare a standard by dissolving 50 mg. of each of the sugars that are suspected in the urine in 10 ml. of normal sugar-free urine; prepare another standard with glucose only.

On the paper sheet or strip draw a soft pencil line about an inch from one end. Mark this line at 1-inch intervals. With a fine pipet apply 5 to 50 microliters (0.005 to 0.05 ml.) of the urine being investigated and of the standards to marks on the paper sheet. The amount used will depend on the concentration of the sugars. The spots should be kept small. If necessary apply the solution repeatedly, drying the spot between applications. A hair dryer is convenient for this.

After the sample spots are dry, place the paper in position in the jar and dip the end where the samples were placed in the solvent, taking care that the spots remain well above the liquid. Apply the pad to the upper end if one is being used. A suitable solvent for separating sugars, especially when the pad technique or descending chromatography is used, is prepared by adding 20 ml. of water to 80 ml. of isopropanol; it has the advantages of being nontoxic and of having no obnoxious odor.

Cover the jar and allow the run to proceed overnight (16 to 20 hrs.). If pentose is present, a shorter run may be necessary. At the end of the run remove the paper and hang it up to dry.

To locate the sugars, prepare an aniline-diphenylamine reagent: dissolve 10 ml. of aniline and 10 ml. of diphenylamine (use caution in handling these toxic materials) in 100 ml. of acetone and add 10 ml. of 85 per cent phosphoric acid. The amine phosphates may precipitate on mixing but should return to solution after shaking or after the addition of a few drops of water.

When the paper is dry, pour the location reagent into a suitable tray and dip the paper through it. Now hang the paper or lay it on another clean paper and heat it in an oven at 95 to 100° C. for a few minutes. Note the location and color of the spots. Outline the spots with a soft pencil so that their positions will not be lost if the color fades out. Table 8–4 gives the

Table 8–4. R_g and Color of Urine Sugars by Paper Chromatography Test

SUGAR	R_g	COLOR
Xylulose	155	gray-brown
Ribose	137	gray-brown
Xylose	130	gray-brown
Arabinose	112	gray-brown
Fructose	105	brown
Mannose	105	gray-blue
Glucose	100	blue
Galactose	80	blue
Sucrose	80	brown
Maltose	47	blue
Inositol	35	
Lactose	32	blue
Glucuronic acid	20	brown

R_g and color developed for several sugars under the conditions just described.

LIPIDS

Lipids are organic compounds containing mostly carbon and hydrogen along with some oxygen; some of the compound lipids also contain nitrogen and phosphorus. In general, the lipids are insoluble in water and soluble in organic solvents, such as hydrocarbons (petroleum ether, gasoline, and benzene), halogenated hydrocarbons (chloroform, carbon tetrachloride, and dichloroethane), and ether. They are the greasy substances. Chemically they are fatty acid esters or compounds that can form such esters.

Lipids are usually classified into three

groups: simple, compound or conjugated, and derived. The simple lipids are esters of fatty acids and an alcohol; they include the true fats or neutral fats, the waxes, and the sterol esters.

The *true fats* are esters of glycerol with three molecules of fatty acid and are therefore also called triglycerides. The three molecules of fatty acid may be the same or different. The fats are named from the fatty acids that compose them. Thus, a triglyceride containing three molecules of oleic acid is called triolein; one containing one molecule of palmitic acid and two of stearic acid is palmitodistearin.

Fatty Acids. The fatty acids of natural fats are mostly straight chained and have an even number of carbon atoms. Some have one, two, or three double bonds. The human body seems to be able to introduce one double bond into a fatty acid but not more. There is some indication that the body requires a small amount of the di- and triunsaturated fatty acids; these must therefore be included in the diet and are called "essential" fatty acids. The amount required is small and the likelihood of dietary insufficiency is remote. Most of the fatty acids of body fats are 16 to 20 carbons in length with smaller amounts of the ones with shorter chains. The commonest are palmitic (16 carbon, saturated), stearic (18 carbon, saturated), and oleic (18 carbon, one double bond).

There has been considerable interest recently in the degree of unsaturation of dietary fatty acids, since there is evidence that blood cholesterol is increased by increased amounts of dietary saturated fatty acids and decreased by dietary fatty acids with two or more double bonds. Animal fats are higher in saturated fatty acids and vegetable fats higher in unsaturated. Hydrogenation, as used in converting liquid vegetable fats (corn oil, cottonseed oil, and coconut oil) into solid shortenings for cooking (e.g., Spry, Crisco, and Flair), decreases the unsaturation of the fatty acids.

There is normally a small amount of free fatty acids (FFA) in the blood that are also called unesterified fatty acids (UFA) or nonesterified fatty acids (NEFA). This fraction is apparently much more important in metabolism than its small amount would indicate; its turnover rate is high; i.e., a large amount is formed and removed per unit of time. The metabolism of FFA seems to be related to carbohydrate metabolism.

Besides the fats the class of *simple lipids* includes the waxes. These are esters of a fatty acid with a monohydric alcohol of high molecular weight. Spermaceti, for example, is largely an ester of palmitic acid with the 16-carbon alcohol, cetyl alcohol; beeswax is rich in the palmitic ester of myricyl alcohol, which has 30 carbons.

A special group of the waxes is that in which the alcohol is cholesterol—the cholesterol esters, which occur in the blood. The cholesterol esters of the blood are formed in the liver; the portion of the total cholesterol of the blood that is in the ester form is an indication of liver function.

The *conjugated lipids* contain a nonlipid material combined in the molecule. Some contain phosphoric acid, some contain a nitrogenous moiety, and some contain a sugar; not all contain glycerol.

One group of conjugated lipids is the phospholipids. These contain phosphoric acid in place of one of the fatty acids esterified on glycerol; attached to the phosphoric acid is also a nitrogenous compound. In lecithin the nitrogen portion is choline (trimethylhydroxyethylammonium hydroxide); in cephalin it is serine (α-amino-β-hydroxypropionic acid) or ethanolamine. Owing to the possible variations in the two fatty acids there are many different cephalins and lecithins. Other phospholipids, rarely of concern in the clinical laboratory perhaps because of our ignorance, are the plasmalogens, the sphingomyelins, and the phosphoinositides. The first are similar to lecithin or cephalin except that one of the fatty acids is replaced by an aldehyde; the second contain no glycerol and the third contain no nitrogen.

The cerebrosides or glycolipids contain no glycerol or phosphorus but include a sugar, usually galactose and sometimes glucose.

The *derived lipids* include the fatty acids just discussed and the sterols. The sterols, broadly defined, are high-molecular weight alcohols, including the aliphatic wax alcohols. However, the term is commonly restricted to compounds having a structure similar to that of cholesterol. There are many physiologically important compounds with a similar structure, which, lacking an alcohol group, are not sterols. These compounds are called steroids. The steroid nucleus is the cyclopentanoperhydrophenanthrene group. (Phenanthrene is a three-ring homolog of benzene. *Perhydro* means that all the double bonds are hydrogenated.

A cyclopentane group forms the fourth ring.) Other sterols of interest beside

Phenanthrene

Cyclopentanoperhydrophenanthrene

Cholesterol

cholesterol are ergosterol and 7-dehydrocholesterol. On ultraviolet irradiation the B-ring of these compounds is broken, giving products with vitamin D activity.

The steroids also include the bile acids and a number of hormones (estrogens, androgens, adrenal corticoids). The bile acids have no double bonds, have a hydroxyl group on carbon 3, and may have one or two more on carbons 7 or 12. They also have a side chain on carbon 17 containing five carbons, the terminal one of which is a carboxyl group, and a molecule of glycine or taurine coupled onto the carboxyl group in an amide linkage. In alkaline solution the bile acids are good emulsifying agents.

Glycocholic acid

Quantitative Determination of Total Serum Lipids

This can be done by extracting the lipids from the serum, purifying them, evaporating off the solvent, and weighing the lipid residue. A simpler method, which gives clinically useful results is that of Kunkel,

Ehrens, and Eisenmenger (1948); it is based on the capacity of a saline phenol solution to precipitate the lipids specifically from serum; the amount of lipid is measured by the turbidity thus produced.

Reagent

Dissolve 12 gm. of sodium chloride in water, add 1 ml. of liquid phenol, and dilute to 100 ml. Keep in the refrigerator.

PROCEDURE. Measure 0.25 ml. of fasting serum into 4.5 ml. of reagent (or 0.1 ml. serum into 1.8 ml. reagent). Mix. Let stand 30 minutes, shake, and read with the red (No. 66) filter or at the wave length used for thymol turbidity, having set zero absorbance with the reagent.

CALCULATION. Convert colorimeter reading to Maclagan units as in the determination of thymol turbidity. The result may be reported thus or converted to mg. per cent total lipid by multiplying by 16.6 and adding 267. Normal is 16 to 30 units or 530 to 765 mg. per cent.

INTERPRETATION. After a mixed meal containing fat, the serum lipid concentration gradually rises for three to five hours. Return to normal may require as long as ten hours. A disproportionate increase in neutral fat causes turbidity or lactescence of the serum. If there is a proportionate increase in phospholipids, the fat is kept in solution and the milkiness does not appear. Serum lipids are normally almost entirely combined with protein to form lipoprotein. The lactescence is due to submicroscopic globules of fat or chylomicrons. The serum lipids are elevated even in the postabsorptive state in persons with uncontrolled diabetes mellitus, in persons with ketosis from other causes such as starvation, and in persons with nephrosis or the nephrotic stage of glomerulonephritis. In obstruction of the biliary system and usually in hypothyroidism serum cholesterol is increased. There are two idiopathic diseases of lipid metabolism; in one the cholesterol is increased and in the other the triglycerides are increased.

Determination of Fat in Feces

A normal person digests and absorbs almost all the fat of his diet; the fat in the feces is excreted largely in the intestinal tract. If there is interference with digestion or absorption, the dietary fat will remain in the intestinal lumen and appear in the feces. The microscopic examination of feces is usually unsatisfactory for estimating the fat content. A semiquantitative color test, useful for screening purposes, was described by Goiffon (1949). For quantitative determination in feces or food the fat is extracted with a solvent and weighed, or the fatty acids derived from it may be titrated.

NILE BLUE TEST FOR FECAL FAT

Reagents
1. Nile blue, 0.05 per cent in water.
2. Sodium carbonate, 20 per cent.
3. Hydrochloric acid, 10 per cent. Dilute 40 ml. of concentrated HCl to 100 ml. with water. Mix.
4. Ammonium oxalate, saturated (try 7 gm. of the monohydrate per 100 ml. of water).

PROCEDURE. Dilute a representative portion of the specimen with nine volumes of water.

In a test tube place:

   1 ml. of this suspension
   1 ml. of water
   2 drops of 10 per cent HCl
   1 drop of saturated ammonium oxalate.

Heat to boiling for a few seconds. Cool. Decant the liquid into a small beaker. Wash the test tube with 2.5 ml. of 20 per cent sodium carbonate, adding to the beaker.

Add 15 ml. of water and 1 ml. of Nile blue solution.

Read at once.

Negative	— (pink turning to gray)
Doubtful	+ (blue gray, the color of overcast sky)
Positive	++ (azure blue)
Strongly positive	+++ (royal blue)

INTERPRETATION. According to Demole and Howard (1958), when the Nile blue reaction is negative, the fecal fat never exceeds 5 per cent by weight. A clearly positive reaction (++ or +++) always corresponds to a fat content above 5 per cent, indicating "chemical steatorrhea."

QUANTITATIVE DETERMINATION OF FECAL FAT

Collection of the Specimen. The result of this determination is usually expressed as grams per 100 gm. of dry specimen; if the sample represents a 24-hour period, the result could be expressed as grams per 24 hours. If it is desired to know the wet weight of the specimen or the amount of fat per 100 gm. of specimen as voided, it

will be necessary to protect the sample from drying out before the analysis is made. Some of the containers commonly used for fecal samples do not give this protection. A suitable container is a 16-oz. glass jar having a screw cap as large as the full diameter of the jar, such as that supplied by W. H. Curtin & Co. under their number 12353-10C (but not listed in their catalog) for about 30 cents each. If it is desired to know the weight of the specimen, as for 24-hour samples, the capped jar can be weighed before being given to the ward personnel or patient, and the weight can be recorded on a label on the jar; reweighing on return will then give specimen weight without transfer.

Principle of Determination (Neufeld, 1952). By heating a weighed, acidified fecal specimen under xylene in a reflux apparatus with a moisture trap, it is possible to extract simultaneously the fat and fatty acids and to determine the moisture content. After evaporation of an aliquot of the xylene and purification with petroleum ether, the residue is weighed. If desired the residue can be dissolved in warm alcohol and titrated with standard alkali to

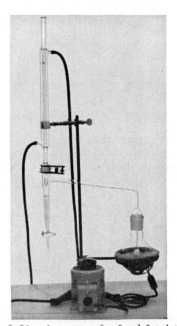

Figure 8–21. Apparatus for fecal fat determination. The 500 ml. flask with a 45/50 standard taper joint is connected at a distance of 6 to 8 inches to a moisture trap. The trap has a small funnel supported on three indentations to prevent water droplets from floating back with returning xylene. The trap is graduated 0.1 ml. to 5 ml. and 0.2 ml. to 20 ml. The trap is connected to the reflux condenser, which has a drip tip, by a ball and socket joint, since a ground joint here tends to freeze.

fractionate the lipid into neutral fat and free fatty acid.

Apparatus

1. The special apparatus used is shown in Fig. 8–21. A heating mantle and variable transformer are highly desirable for heating the boiling flask; if these are used, the flask should have a round bottom. A hot plate or even a burner (hazard: xylene is inflammable!) can be used; in such a case a flat-bottom flask may be preferable.

2. Cork ring to set the boiling flask in, if round bottom.

3. Balances (*a*) to weigh several hundred grams to 0.1 gm., (*b*) to weigh a small flask to 0.01 gm., and (*c*) to weigh a small beaker to 0.001 gm.

Reagents

1. Hydrochloric acid, concentrated, reagent grade.

2. Xylene, any pure or commercial grade boiling between 130 and 150° C. (caution: inflammable).

3. Petroleum ether, boiling range 40 to 60° C. (caution: highly inflammable).

4. Sodium or potassium hydroxide solution, about 0.1N, standardized (cf. p. 399).

5. Ethyl alcohol, 95 per cent, or ethyl alcohol denatured with isopropyl alcohol.

6. Phenolphthalein, 1 per cent in 50 per cent ethyl alcohol, or thymol blue, 0.2 per cent in 50 per cent ethyl alcohol.

(Reagents 4 to 6 are needed only if fractionation into fat and free fatty acid is to be done.)

PROCEDURE. Weigh the boiling flask and a glass stirring rod, which protrudes about 1 to 1½ inches above the neck of the flask, to the nearest 0.1 gm.

Mix the specimen until it is homogeneous. A Waring blender or similar mixer is useful.

Transfer 15 to 18 gm. of specimen into the boiling flask without getting any on the neck or sides. A wide-neck funnel may be used.

Reweigh the flask with rod and specimen to the nearest 0.1 gm.

Add 3.0 ml. of concentrated HCl and mix by means of the glass rod, which is left in the flask during the extraction.

Add about 200 ml. of xylene and connect the flask to the apparatus.

Reflux at a moderate rate (3 to 6 drops per second) until no further water collects in the trap (usually 25 to 45 minutes).

Record the volume of water collected.

Subtract 2.7 ml. to account for the HCl added.

Reweigh the boiling flask and its contents, including the rod, to the nearest 0.1 gm.

Weigh a 50 ml. Erlenmeyer flask to the nearest 0.01 gm.

Transfer 25 ml. of the xylene solution to this flask and immediately reweigh to obtain the weight of the aliquot.

Evaporate to dryness on a steam bath, using a stream of air (caution: xylene is inflammable).

Extract the residue with several small portions of petroleum ether (caution: highly inflammable), pooling the ether solutions in a graduated 12 or 15 ml. centrifuge tube, to a total volume of 12 ml. A Pasteur pipet is convenient for these transfers.

Cork the tube and centrifuge.

Weigh a 20 ml. beaker to the nearest 0.001 gm.

Pipet 10 ml. of the petroleum ether extract into the beaker.

Evaporate on the steam bath or on a warm, enclosed-element hotplate (without a thermostat and without using the switch unless these are explosion-proof) to constant weight. (The residue will be liquid when warm.) Record the final weight.

If it is desired to determine the amount of free fatty acid, add a little alcohol and warm to dissolve the residue. Titrate with 0.1N alkali to the phenolphthalein (pink) or thymol blue (blue or green) endpoint (since the fat residue is usually yellow, the yellow to green endpoint with thymol blue may be sharper than the yellow to yellowish red with phenolphthalein).

CALCULATION. *Weight of fat in fecal aliquot* $= \dfrac{P \times Xt \times Et}{Xa \times Ea}$ *gm.*

where P = weight of fat residue

= wt. of beaker with residue − wt. of beaker

Xt = weight of xylene solution after extraction

= wt. of boiling flask and contents after extraction − wt. flask and rod − wt. of dry fat-free fecal aliquot.

Weight of dry, fat-free aliquot = F − wt. of fat in fecal aliquot (see next section for F); use 10 × P for weight of fat in fecal aliquot. This should introduce no appreciable error; if desired, the result may then be recalculated by using the weight of fat in the fecal aliquot just found (calculation shown at bottom of page).

Interpretation. On an average mixed diet the daily amount of fecal fat may range from 2 to 6 gm. This corresponds to 10 to 25 per cent of the dry weight of the stool. Usually some 50 to 80 per cent of this is split fat (free fatty acids plus soaps).

This normal fecal fat equals in amount about 5 to 10 per cent of the amount of fat in the diet. Actually most of it is not directly dietary in origin; 2 gm. or more may be excreted even in starvation. Some of the endogenous fat is bacterial but most is free and originates from the bile and intestinal secretions.

The total fat excretion is increased in pancreatic deficiency (lack of digestion) or in intestinal wall deficiency (sprue, lack of absorption) when the diet contains 50 gm. or more of fat. Theoretically the proportion of split fat to neutral fat should distinguish between these two types of steatorrhea; unfortunately the time of transit gives opportunity for splitting even by decreased pancreatic secretion, and intestinal wall and bacterial enzymes may be active even in the absence of pancreatic lipase. Therefore the partition is of little value.

Quantitative Determination of Cholesterol

Many methods have been proposed for this determination. In the past it has generally been done by extracting serum with an alcohol-ether mixture, evaporating off the solvent and dissolving the cholesterol (both free and esterified) in chloroform, or by extracting with an alcohol-acetone mixture, hydrolyzing with KOH, precipitating with digitonin, and dissolving in acetic acid. To the chloroform or acetic acid solution of cholesterol were added acetic anhydride and sulfuric acid to develop a green color (Liebermann-Burchard reaction). Recently several direct methods for determining cholesterol without extraction or precipitation have been proposed by adding serum directly to the color-producing reagents. These may be either acetic acid–acetic anhydride–sulfuric acid, these plus paratoluene sulfonic acid, or ferric chloride–acetic acid–sulfuric acid.

Et = vol. of petroleum ether solution = 12 ml.
Xa = weight of xylene aliquot
= wt. of small flask and xylene aliquot − wt. of flask
Ea = vol. of petroleum ether aliquot = 10 ml.

$$\% \text{ fat in dry feces} = \frac{\text{weight of fat in fecal aliquot (just described)} \times 100}{F}$$

$$= \frac{P \times Xt \times Et \times 100}{Xa \times Ea \times F}$$

where F = dry weight of fecal aliquot = WF − FW,
where WF = wet weight of fecal aliquot
= wt. boiling flask, rod, and feces − wt. flask and rod
and FW = wt. of fecal moisture
= vol. H_2O collected in trap − 2.7 (vol. of H_2O from HCl).

$$gm. \text{ fat}/24 \text{ hrs.} = \frac{\text{weight of fat in fecal aliquot (just described)} \times \text{wt. of 24-hr. feces}}{\text{wt. of wet fecal aliquot}}$$

$$= \frac{\text{wt. fat in fecal aliquot} \times Ft}{WF}$$

$$= \frac{P \times Xt \times Et \times Ft}{Xa \times Ea \times WF}$$

where Ft = weight of 24-hour fecal specimen
= wt. of jar with sample − wt. of jar

$$\% \text{ fatty acid (\% of the total fat)} = \frac{\text{ml. std. NaOH} \times f \text{ of NaOH} \times 0.0268 \times 100}{P}$$

where f = actual normality of NaOH ÷ 0.1 = N × 10,
0.0268 = gm. fatty acid equivalent to 1 ml. 0.1N NaOH,
P = weight of fat residue.

$$\% \text{ moisture in feces} = \frac{(\text{vol. } H_2O \text{ collected} - 2.7) \times 100}{WF}$$

The direct methods, while simpler, are liable to error from bilirubin, protein, and other sources. The direct determination of cholesterol has been advocated, particularly by commercial interests selling reagents for which they will not disclose the composition and for which no careful comparison with an extraction method has been published. Even though a series of determinations by a direct and by an extraction method may average the same, an occasional individual sample may be quite different by the two methods. For this reason it is felt that a preliminary purification step is desirable, preferably extraction and possibly precipitation; neither procedure will eliminate bromide error if the ferric chloride procedure is being used.

The Bloor method, adding acetic anhydride and sulfuric acid to a chloroform extract, suffers from the disadvantage that free and esterified cholesterol do not produce the same amount of color per mol, and the result will therefore be affected by the ratio of free to ester cholesterol. The ferric chloride reaction has the advantages over the Liebermann-Burchard method of producing an increased color intensity, a more stable color, and an equal chromogenic value of free and esterified cholesterol; it has the disadvantage of being affected by bromide.

The separation of free and esterified cholesterol can be done in several ways: by precipitation of the free cholesterol by digitonin or tomatine, by selective solvent extraction, or by chromatography. The fractionation of total cholesterol is of value as a liver function test, but it is no better than some other tests that are easier to do.

FERRIC CHLORIDE METHOD
(Crawford, 1958; Chiamori, 1959; Leffler, 1959)

Principle. In the method to be detailed two alternative preliminary steps are described. In one, the free and ester cholesterol are extracted from serum, and the proteins are precipitated, with Bloor's mixture of alcohol and ether or with isopropanol. A portion of this, after or without evaporation to dryness, is treated with a ferric chloride-acetic acid reagent (which is more stable than the ferric chloride-sulfuric acid reagent sometimes used). In the other the serum is treated directly with the ferric chloride-acetic acid reagent, and the proteins are precipitated by heating the mixture. In either case sulfuric acid

is next added; heat is evolved and a color is produced—light brown at first, turning to an intense reddish-purple. In microadaptations the amount of heat produced may not be sufficient to raise the temperature to the degree required for full color development; in this case the tubes are immersed briefly in a boiling water bath.

Choice between the alternatives will depend on convenience, personal preference, and the amount of color obtained in the blanks.

Reagents

1a. Bloor's reagent. 3 volumes of 95 per cent ethanol and 1 volume of ethyl ether; ethanol denatured with methanol is satisfactory if 5 per cent water is added. (Caution: highly inflammable.) Or 1b. Isopropanol, reagent grade. (Caution: inflammable.)

2. Stock ferric chloride solution, 5 per cent. Dissolve 2.5 gm. of $FeCl_3 \cdot 6H_2O$, reagent grade, in glacial acetic acid. Transfer to a 50 ml. glass stopper volumetric flask, rinsing in and diluting to volume with acetic acid. Mix well. Store in refrigerator where the acetic acid will freeze. Thaw out just before use. Discard when precipitate appears.

3. Ferric chloride reagent, working solution, 0.1 per cent. Prepare fresh by diluting 1 ml. of stock to 50 ml. with glacial acetic acid. Mix well. A buret with a Teflon stopcock would be useful to dispense this and the next reagent.

4. H_2SO_4, concentrated, reagent grade.

5. Cholesterol standard. Use either A or B, according to whether extraction or precipitation procedure is used.

A. Stock standard (200 mg. per cent). Dissolve 200 mg. of cholesterol in Bloor's reagent or isopropanol and dilute to 100 ml. Mix well. Stopper tightly, preferably in a screw cap bottle. Store in refrigerator.

Working standard (40 mcg./ml.). Dilute 1 ml. of stock standard to 50 ml. with Bloor's reagent or isopropanol.

B. Stock standard (66.7 mg. per cent.). Dissolve 66.7 mg. of cholesterol in glacial acetic acid and dilute to 100 ml. with acetic acid. Mix well.

Working standard (40 mcg./3 ml.). Prepare freshly by measuring 1 ml. of stock standard and 1 ml. of ferric chloride stock (5 per cent) into a 50 ml. volumetric flask and diluting to the mark with glacial acetic acid. Mix well. Use 3 ml.

6. Digitonin solution. 0.5 per cent digitonin in 95 per cent ethanol.

7. Petroleum ether. Boiling range 30 to 60° C. (Caution: highly inflammable.)

Apparatus.

To avoid undesirable bubble formation, it is preferable to mix the concentrated sulfuric acid with the overlying ferric chloride–acetic acid reagent without shaking the test tube. This can be done by using a large (25 mm.) test tube and swirling or by stoppering the tube and inverting. Rubber or cork stoppers are undesirable because of the likelihood of interfering contamination. Two possible solutions are to close the test tubes with polyethylene caps (e.g., Curtin 18824 or Aloe 78305) or to use tubes with Teflon-lined screw caps (Kimble 45066-A). Another means for mixing, less satisfactory than inversion, is to use a footed stirring rod.

Evaporation.

To aid the evaporation of the solvent when the tubes are immersed in a 60 to 80° C. bath, a stream of air or nitrogen is useful. This can be obtained from a compressed air line, a laboratory air compressor (Cole-Parmer offers their small 7062 for about $40), a cylinder of compressed air or nitrogen, or an aquarium compressor (e.g., Sears Roebuck & Co. 71-8874 for about $20). A convenient manifold is made by inserting 3-inch lengths of small stainless steel tubing (or hypodermic needles with the hubs removed) into a length of heavy-walled rubber tubing; this can be laid across the top of a row of tubes in a rack in the water bath. Or suction can be used, although this requires stoppering each tube; Leffler (1959) has described such an arrangement.

Procedure for Total Cholesterol. *Extraction* (alternate to precipitation; see next section). To about 15 ml. of Bloor's reagent or isopropanol in a 25 ml. volumetric flask add exactly 0.5 ml. of serum. Maximum dispersal is obtained by blowing the serum rapidly from the pipet held just above the surface of the solvent.

Let stand 30 minutes at room temperature with occasional swirling.

Dilute to the mark with solvent. Mix by slow inversion ten times.

Filter through Whatman No. 1 paper, covering the funnel with a watchglass to retard evaporation.

Pipet a 1 ml. aliquot into a tube. This volume is suitable for most sera; it may be increased or decreased if the cholesterol content is low or high. (Pipet 2 ml. into another tube if esters are to be determined or 3 ml. for free cholesterol.)

Into a second tube place 1 ml. of Bloor's reagent or isopropanol for a blank.

Into a third tube place 1 ml. of cholesterol working standard in solvent.

To each tube add 2 ml. of ferric chloride reagent.

Proceed with Color Development (following section).

If appreciable color develops in the blank tube or if blanks are erratic, modify this procedure by omitting the solvent from the blank and evaporating it off from the unknown and standard (or use standard B); then add 3 ml. of ferric chloride reagent and proceed with Color Development.

Precipitation (alternate to extraction). Measure 14.9 ml. of working ferric chloride reagent into a test tube.

Rinse 0.1 ml. of serum into it.

Mix well and let stand 10 to 15 minutes.

Heat in a 60° C. bath for two minutes with occasional shaking.

Let cool to room temperature.

Centrifuge.

Measure 3 ml. of supernatant into a tube.

Into a second tube measure 3 ml. of ferric chloride reagent for a blank.

Into a third tube measure 3 ml. of working cholesterol standard B in ferric chloride reagent.

Proceed with Color Development.

Color development. To one tube at a time add 2 ml. of concentrated H_2SO_4, letting it flow down the side of the tube to form two layers. *Immediately* mix thoroughly and then proceed to the next tube.

Let stand ten minutes.

Read within $1\frac{1}{2}$ hours at 560 mμ or with a No. 54 Klett filter, recording absorbance or a function thereof (e.g., Klett-Summerson readings). Set to zero with blank.

CALCULATION

f = 200 ÷ Rdg. std.

f × Rdg. unk. = mg. % total cholesterol.

Microprocedure. The extraction procedure can be reduced to use 0.1 ml. of serum by starting with 3 ml. of solvent in a 5 ml. volumetric flask or graduated test tube, diluting to 5 ml. Filter and continue as just outlined. Likewise either extraction or precipitation can be done with 50 microliters of serum and 2.5 ml. of solvent or 7.45 ml. of reagent and no further change. Or for a Klett microtube or a Coleman 10 or 12 mm. tube the final amounts of extract, ferric chloride reagent, and sulfuric acid can be cut to 0.4, 0.8, and 0.8 ml. respectively or, for the precipitation procedure, 1.2 ml. of supernatant and 0.8 ml. of sulfuric acid. With these smaller amounts of reagents, if the initial brown does not promptly progress to the reddish-purple, heat the tubes in a boiling water bath for one minute.

Procedure for Cholesterol Esters. Pipet 2 ml. of Bloor's reagent or isopropanol extract into a large (19 to 25 mm.) test tube.

Add 0.5 ml. digitonin solution. Mix.

Evaporate to dryness at 60 to 80° C., using a stream of air or nitrogen if desired.

Add about 5 ml. petroleum ether.

Bring to a boil in a 60° C. bath.

Let cool, stopper, and centrifuge.

Decant supernatant fluid into another test tube.

Repeat the petroleum ether extraction, combining the extracts.

Evaporate to dryness as before.

Let cool.

If total cholesterol is being done by the extraction procedure without evaporation, add 1 ml. of Bloor's reagent or isopropanol and 2 ml. of ferric chloride reagent; mix to dissolve the residue.

If total cholesterol is being done by the precipitation procedure or if the solvent is being evaporated off, add 3 ml. of ferric chloride reagent, place in boiling water bath exactly five minutes, and let cool to room temperature.

To this, as well as to the total cholesterol tube, standard, and blank, add sulfuric acid and proceed as for total cholesterol (see Color Development just described for total cholesterol).

Calculation for esters is the same as for total except f = 100 ÷ Rdg. std.; or use same f = 200 ÷ Rdg. std. and multiply Rdg. unk. by f × 0.5 to obtain mg. per cent cholesterol esters (i.e., f for esters = ½f for total because of the use of 2 ml. of filtrate instead of 1 ml.).

$$\% \text{ ester cholesterol} =$$
$$\frac{\text{mg. } \% \text{ ester cholesterol}}{\text{mg. } \% \text{ total cholesterol}} \times 100$$

Free cholesterol =
total cholesterol − ester cholesterol

$$\% \text{ free cholesterol} =$$
$$\frac{\text{mg. } \% \text{ free cholesterol}}{\text{mg. } \% \text{ total cholesterol}} \times 100$$
$$= 100 - \% \text{ ester cholesterol}.$$

Procedure for Free Cholesterol. Pipet 3 ml. of Bloor's reagent or isopropanol extract into a test tube.

Add 0.5 ml. of digitonin solution. Mix.

Let stand 15 minutes.

Centrifuge.

Carefully pour off the supernatant and discard.

Let the inverted tubes stand on a piece of filter paper for a few minutes to drain.

Blow in 4 ml. of acetone, directing the stream into the precipitate to produce maximum dispersion.

Centrifuge, decant, and drain as before.

Dry the residue with a stream of air.

If total cholesterol is being done by the extraction procedure without evaporation, add 1 ml. of solvent and 2 ml. of ferric chloride reagent; mix to dissolve the residue.

If total cholesterol is being done by the precipitation procedure or if the solvent is being evaporated off, add 3 ml. of ferric chloride reagent, place in boiling water bath exactly five minutes, and let cool to room temperature.

To this, as well as to the total cholesterol tube, standard, and blank, add sulfuric acid and proceed as for total cholesterol (see Color Development, p. 430).

Calculation for free cholesterol is the same as for total except that f = 66.7 ÷ Rdg. std.; or use the same f = 200 ÷ Rdg. std. and multiply Rdg. unk. by f × 0.333 to obtain mg. per cent free cholesterol (i.e., f for esters = ⅓ f for total because of the use of 3 ml. of filtrate instead of 1 ml.).

$$\% \text{ free cholesterol} =$$
$$\frac{\text{mg. } \% \text{ free cholesterol}}{\text{mg. } \% \text{ total cholesterol}} \times 100$$

Ester cholesterol =
total cholesterol − free cholesterol

$$\% \text{ ester cholesterol} =$$
$$\frac{\text{mg. } \% \text{ ester cholesterol}}{\text{mg. } \% \text{ total cholesterol}} \times 100$$
$$= 100 - \% \text{ free cholesterol}.$$

COMMENT. The presence of interfering quantities of bromide is easily detectable early in an analysis as a distinct yellow color appearing in the supernatant fluid and the protein precipitate after addition of the ferric chloride reagent, in contrast to the usual straw color. The removal of bromide, when present, can be done by shaking 1 ml. of serum with 25 to 50 mg. of silver iodate and centrifuging, as Rice and Lukasiewicz (1957) did, if the extraction procedure is being used. However, in the precipitation procedure the excess silver iodate interferes with the color reaction. Removal of bromide can be done for either procedure by batchwise use of an ion exchange resin. Approximately 1 ml. of serum and 200 mg. Dowex 2 (Cl⁻ form, 200 to 400 mesh) are placed in a test tube and mixed continuously on a shaking machine for ten minutes. The sample for analysis is then removed from the supernatant fluid.

DIRECT DETERMINATION OF TOTAL CHOLESTEROL (MORELAND, 1960)

In view of the interferences that have been reported in direct methods of cholesterol determination, such a method cannot be recommended at present for reliable work. However, there may be occasions when the simplicity of these methods outweighs their errors, such as in screening tests or in a series of determinations at short intervals in which changes in concentration are of prime concern and error is likely to be constant.

The occurrence of protein error owing to the presence of glyoxylic acid in the acetic acid used can be checked by carrying a purified protein solution, such as Armour's Protein Standard Solution, through the procedure in place of serum and comparing it with the blank. Use of a control serum, such as Hyland Clinical Chemistry Control, will also give indication of error arising from the reagents. Neither of these controls will, of course, eliminate error owing to the serum, such as an increased bilirubin or hemolysis. The criticism leveled at Liebermann-Burchard methods of light sensitivity presumably is not of concern here, since this has been shown (Kabara, 1954) to have no effect when the color produced is read at a wave length above 580 mmu. The error owing to the difference in chromogenicity of free and ester cholesterol is also obviated, since this occurs only in the presence of chloroform.

Reagents

1. Acetic mixture. Mix 2 volumes of acetic acid and 3 volumes of acetic anhydride (caution: inflammable). This reagent appears to be stable.

2. Cholesterol reagent. To 5 volumes of the acetic mixture add 1 volume of concentrated sulfuric acid, reagent grade. Let cool at least 20 minutes. This reagent is unstable and should be prepared shortly before use. Do not pipet by mouth; a buret with a Teflon stopcock is desirable.

PROCEDURE. To 5 ml. of the cholesterol reagent add 0.2 ml. of serum (rinse if a TC pipet was used; caution). Mix.

Prepare a blank with 5 ml. of reagent and 0.2 ml. of water or of Armour Protein Standard.

Prepare a standard with 5 ml. of reagent and 0.2 ml. of Hyland Clinical Chemistry Control or Warner-Chilcott Versatol.

Read each tube after 5 minutes but within 15 minutes with the 66 filter or at 640 mμ (calculation shown at bottom of page).

INTERPRETATION. The normal range for total serum cholesterol is 150 to 250 mg. per cent, the free cholesterol making up 26 to 30 per cent of this and ester cholesterol, 70 to 74 per cent.

In obstructive jaundice the total serum cholesterol rises chiefly because of an increase in free cholesterol with a more moderate rise in the ester form. Thus, the ester ratio decreases below normal even though the amount of ester cholesterol increases.

In liver cell damage the proportion of esters decreases. The obstructive aspect may raise the free cholesterol so that the total is normal. With progression of the disease both total cholesterol and percentage of esters decrease.

Cholesterol also increases in hypothyroidism, the nephrotic syndrome, and untreated diabetes. It decreases in hyperthyroidism. Owing to the influence of other factors the cholesterol concentration is not a reliable diagnostic guide to thyroid function; however, changes in cholesterol are a good measure of the effectiveness of treatment. The rise of cholesterol in nephrosis and in diabetes is part of the general rise in cholesterol in any derangement of fat metabolism. There is also an idiopathic hypercholesterolemia.

There is actually no "free" cholesterol in the blood, the term as just used meaning only unesterified. All the cholesterol, whether esterified or not, is carried in the blood along with other lipids in association with protein in the form of lipoprotein. The lipoproteins can be fractionated on the basis of their specific gravity by high speed centrifugation after appropriately increasing the plasma density with salts. The triglyceride content decreases and the protein and phospholipid content increases with the density of the fraction. Cholesterol increases at first and then decreases in the heaviest fraction. The incidence of athero-

CALCULATION. $\dfrac{\text{Absorbance of serum} - \text{absorbance of blank}}{\text{Absorbance of standard} - \text{absorbance of blank}} \times$ concentration of standard (mg. %) = mg. cholesterol per 100 ml. serum.

sclerosis seems to be related both to hyper-cholesterolemia and to the increase in the lighter lipoproteins (the "Sf 12-20" class).

Cholesterol concentration and solubility seem also to be related to phospholipid concentration. An increase in phospholipid tends to increase cholesterol concentration; a decrease leads to deposition of cholesterol.

Because of the combination of cholesterol in the lipoproteins, perhaps with a protective protein layer on the outside of the particles, the cholesterol, as well as the other lipids, is not extractable from serum by petroleum ether or other nonpolar solvents but requires a polar solvent, such as alcohol, to free the lipid from the protein and extract it.

NITROGENOUS COMPOUNDS

The classification of foodstuffs into carbohydrates, fats, and proteins is sometimes carried over to the multitude of organic compounds occurring in the body. Here, however, we encounter many compounds that do not fit the definitions of these three main classes. This is particularly true of a large number of nitrogen-containing compounds, which are in general derived from proteins but which, unlike the proteins, are of relatively small molecular weight, being crystalloids rather than colloids. They therefore pass through dialyzing membranes, and most of them pass through the capillary walls, cell walls, and the glomerulus. The nitrogenous compounds of the body include the proteins and the nonprotein nitrogenous constituents. The proteins include the hemoglobins, fibrinogen, and the serum proteins; the last are somewhat arbitrarily divided into albumin and globulin and further into α_1-, α_2-, β-, and γ-globulins. The nonprotein nitrogenous compounds include a large number and variety of compounds; those most commonly determined in a clinical chemistry laboratory and to be described in this chapter are urea, creatine, creatinine, uric acid, the amino acids, ammonia, the porphyrins, and porphobilinogen; others are considered in the chapters on liver function and hormones.

Proteins

Proteins are high molecular weight organic compounds characterized by containing nitrogen. As noted previously, some carbohydrates and lipids contain nitrogen atoms, but it is only with the proteins that this element is typical. The proteins on hydrolysis yield α-amino acids, having an amino ($-NH_2$) group attached to the carbon next to the carboxyl group; that is, a carboxyl and an amino group are both attached to the carbon next to the end, the alpha carbon. One of the simplest amino acids is alanine, CH_3-CHNH_2-COOH. About 20 other different amino acids occur in natural proteins. These differ from alanine in having other configurations in place of the CH_3- group. These may be simply a hydrogen (as in glycine), an aliphatic or a sulfur-containing chain, or an aromatic or a heterocyclic ring structure. Some amino acids contain an additional carboxyl or amino group beyond those attached to the alpha carbon. These make the amino acids containing them more acid or more basic than the average. Other groups occurring in amino acids include hydroxyl, phenyl, sulfhydryl, indole, and imidazole. In the proteins, amino acids are combined together to form polypeptide chains by condensation of the α-amino group of one with the α-carboxyl of another to form the peptide linkage,

$$HO-\overset{O}{\overset{\|}{C}}-\overset{H}{\overset{|}{\underset{R}{C}}}-\overset{H}{\overset{|}{N}}-\overset{O}{\overset{\|}{C}}-\overset{H}{\overset{|}{\underset{R}{C}}}-\overset{H}{\overset{|}{N}}-H.$$

Proteins thus have a backbone of repeating

$$-\overset{H}{\overset{|}{C}}-\overset{H}{\overset{|}{N}}-\overset{O}{\overset{\|}{\underset{R}{C}}}-$$

links; variation exists because of the differing R groups, which represent the portion of the amino acids beyond the α-carbon. The patterns of the amino acids in the polypeptide chains appear to be determined by the ribonucleic acids of the cells. Not only is there variation in what amino acids make up the chain, but there is also cross linkage between active groups not involved in the peptide link, especially $-SH$ groups, which are oxidized to $-S-S-$ links.

The classification of proteins is not an easy matter because of the many unrelated characteristics that these compounds show. A grouping based on one property may be unsatisfactory when another property is considered. Thus albumins may be defined as proteins that are soluble in water and globulins as those that require a little salt to make them dissolve; or we may say that albumins require saturation of their solution with ammonium sulfate to precipitate them whereas globulins will be precipitated by half saturation with the same salt. But what, then, of proteins that are soluble in pure water but that are salted out by half saturation with ammonium sulfate?

The proteins are usually divided into

a. simple proteins containing only amino acids.

b. conjugated proteins containing also some nonamino acid prosthetic group, and

c. the derived proteins, which are really not proteins at all but partially hydrolyzed proteins.

The *simple proteins* include

1. albumins, soluble in water and salt solutions.

2. globulins, soluble in dilute salt solutions.

3. albuminoids, insoluble in water and salt solutions.

The albumins and globulins are heat coagulable; that is, they are made less soluble by heating in solution and precipitate out if the pH of the solution is near that at which there is no net ionic charge on the molecule (the isoelectric point or IEP).

The globulins will precipitate if the salt content of their solution is decreased by dialysis or by simple dilution with water. This is why serum becomes turbid if diluted with water rather than with saline.

Albumin and especially globulin are not single protein species but mixtures. Electrophoresis or precipitation by different salt concentrations shows many globulins to exist in serum. The separation of serum proteins into "albumin" and "globulin" was for many years (and still is in some laboratories) done by Howe's method of precipitation at 21.5 per cent Na_2SO_4. Careful studies, particularly by electrophoresis, have shown that this salt concentration leaves most of the α-globulin in solution, and a concentration of 26 per cent gives truer separation. Electrophoresis or the use of several salt concentrations allows us to separate the globulins into, commonly, α_1, α_2, β, and γ. These fractions are not sharply defined, and for a given serum sample different values will be obtained with the several differently graded salt concentrations that have been proposed; even electrophoresis is not definitive, different results being obtained with different buffers and supporting media (e.g., paper, starch, and agar).

The *conjugated* proteins may be divided into

1. nucleoproteins containing nucleic acid (made up of ribose or deoxyribose, purines and pyrimidines, and phosphoric acid)

2. mucoproteins containing sugar amines, sugars, and uronic acids

3. glycoproteins containing only a small amount of carbohydrate

4. lipoproteins (prosthetic group: a lipid)

5. chromoproteins (e.g., hemoglobin)

6. metalloproteins (prosthetic group: a metallic ion)

7. phosphoproteins.

DETERMINATION OF SERUM PROTEINS

The hemoglobins are discussed in Chapter 4. We will confine our attention to fibrinogen and the major serum proteins in this chapter. The difference between serum and plasma proteins is, of course, fibrinogen, since this protein separates out as fibrin in the clotting process. Fibrinogen cannot, however, be measured by determining the protein content of plasma and serum and subtracting. Since the amount of fibrinogen is small, the possible error in each total protein determination is large compared to the fibrinogen concentration. Also the anticoagulant usually causes a shift of fluid from cells to plasma that would diminish the difference between total protein of the two fluids. Plasma is the liquid portion, which, on standing or on centrifuging, separates from a sample of blood to which an anticoagulant was added; serum is the liquid portion that separates from clotted blood.

A number of methods have been used for determining the total amount of protein in serum or in other biologic samples. One of the classic methods is the Kjeldahl procedure in which the sample is digested with concentrated sulfuric acid and heat, thereby converting the nitrogen of the protein and of most of the other nitrogenous compounds into ammonium sulfate. The ammonia can be determined by making the solution alkaline, distilling it into acid, and titrating or by letting it react with Nessler's reagent to develop a color that can be measured. If there are nonprotein nitrogenous compounds in the sample, these must be corrected for; this is usually done by removing the protein by precipitation and determining the nonprotein nitrogen (NPN) and subtracting it from the protein nitrogen. Knowing the amount of nitrogen derived from the protein in the sample, we can calculate the amount of protein present if we know the proportion of nitrogen in the protein. It has been traditional to take this as 16 per cent and therefore to multiply protein nitrogen by 6.25 to obtain protein. Unfortunately not all proteins contain the same proportion of nitrogen and this factor is not applicable to all proteins. It is not actually correct for human serum proteins, and the factor varies for different protein fractions, as shown by Sunderman (1957) and others. For human serum total protein the factor is 6.54.

Other methods for determining protein have included weighing after purification and drying, a tedious procedure; measuring the turbidity produced when a precipitating agent is added to a solution of the protein, a method frequently used for urine and cerebrospinal fluid; measuring the specific gravity or refractive index of the protein solution, parameters likely to be affected by nonprotein materials; and measuring some characteristic group or linkage of the protein molecule, such as hydroxyphenyl groups or peptide linkages.

One of the difficulties in the quantitative determination of proteins lies in the qualitative changes in the proteins that occur in disease. If a new protein appears that has a different nitrogen or tyrosine content, methods based on these components will give results that are affected by this qualitative change and will not reflect only the change in amount of protein.

The so-called "biuret" reaction uses an alkaline copper sulfate reagent. It depends on the peptide links that characterize protein and appears to be very little affected by qualitative changes in the protein.

Total Serum Proteins (Kingsley, 1942)

Reagents

1. Biuret reagent. Prepare concentrated carbonate-free NaOH and determine its concentration as described on p. 399. Calculate the volume of this solution that contains 69 gm. of NaOH (this should be of the order of 100 ml.). Measure this volume into a 500 ml. graduated cylinder. Add water to the 300 ml. mark. Add 100 ml. of 1 per cent solution of copper sulfate pentahydrate. Mix well. The solution should be clear. Store in a clean polyethylene or borosilicate glass bottle with a polyethylene or rubber stopper. This reagent is stable for months at room temperature. The formation of a slight sediment does not appear to impair its usefulness. Do not pipet by mouth.

2. Sodium chloride, 0.9 or 0.85 per cent.

3. Protein standard. Prepare a standard by analyzing a batch of serum for protein content by the Kjeldahl method. (Convert protein nitrogen to protein by multiplying by 6.54, since Sunderman (1957) has shown human serum protein to contain 15.3 per cent nitrogen. This will give slightly higher results than with standards based on the traditional 6.25 × N, as presumably are Hyland and Versatol.) Or use one of the commercially available standardized protein solutions (e.g., Armour Protein Standard Solution; multiply nitrogen by 6.25 to obtain protein since this is bovine albumin) or analyzed control serums (Hyland Clinical Chemistry Control, Warner-Chilcott Versatol). Use this in place of the serum in the test; dilute standards may be made by using less serum and adding a corresponding volume of saline.

4. Ether.

PROCEDURE. To 1.9 ml. of 0.9 per cent sodium chloride in a test tube or cuvet add 0.1 ml. of serum (rinse if using a TC pipet).

Measure 2 ml. of saline into another tube for a blank.

To each tube add 4 ml. of biuret reagent (caution: strong alkali). Mix.

Add 2 or 3 ml. of ether to remove any turbidity due to lipids.

Stopper, shake vigorously, and centrifuge.

Set to zero absorbance with blank, green No. 54 filter or, for better sensitivity, a No. 56 or 59 filter or at 580 mμ.

Read unknowns in absorbance or a function of it, such as Klett units.

CALCULATION

$$f = \frac{\text{conc. of std.}}{\text{rdg. std.}}$$

f × rdg. unknown = % protein (or gm. % protein).

MICROPROCEDURE. The determination can be done on 50 mcl. of serum, using half the amounts just prescribed.

Albumin (Bracken and Klotz, 1953)

Reagents

1. Methyl orange stock, 0.1 per cent in water.

2. Buffer solution. Dissolve 21 gm. of citric acid monohydrate in 135 ml. of 1 N NaOH and enough water to make 1 liter. Adjust to pH 3.5 by adding concentrated HCl.

3. Buffered methyl orange reagent. Dilute 1 volume of methyl orange stock to 100 volumes with buffer solution. Mix. Keeps indefinitely in the dark if a few crystals of cresol are added to prevent growth of fungus.

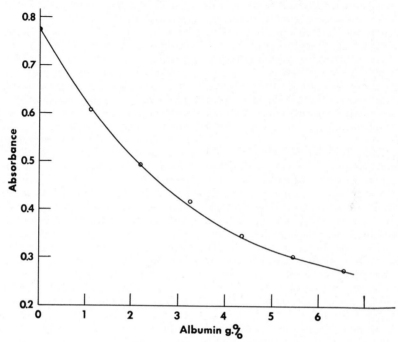

Figure 8–22. Sample calibration curve for determination of albumin with methyl orange.

4. Standard. Use Armour Protein Standard Solution (No. 3200), which is an albumin solution. Multiply the nitrogen content as shown on the vial by 6.25 to obtain albumin.

PROCEDURE. Pipet 5 ml. of buffered methyl orange into a test tube or cuvet.

Add 0.2 ml. of serum. Mix by inversion.

Read with No. 54 filter or at 550 mmu. and zero with water.

CALCULATION. Read result from standard curve or from table prepared from the curve.

STANDARDIZATION. Prepare standards equivalent to approximately 0, 1, 2, 3, 4, 5, and 6 per cent albumin. Obtain the exact values by multiplying the nitrogen content of the standard by 6.25, dividing by 6, and

multiplying by the approximate concentration. Make preliminary dilutions of standard with saline for tubes 1, 2, 4, and 5 as indicated in Table 8–5. Add 0.2 ml. of this dilution, of Armour standard or of saline, as indicated in the Final Standard portion of Table 8–5, to 5 ml. of buffered methyl orange in test tubes or cuvets as in Procedure. Read. Plot readings against actual concentrations of standards but use tube numbers for marking major lines on the graph (i.e., set up graph as indicated in Fig. 8–22 and plot readings and the actual concentrations wherever they fall). Example:

TUBE	% ALBUMIN	A
0	0	0.778
1	1.09	0.606
2	2.18	0.494
3	3.27	0.419
4	4.36	0.347
5	5.45	0.303
6	6.54	0.274

The standardization must be repeated for each new batch of reagent. The absorbance readings of the 0 and 6 per cent standards should be of the order of 280 and 110 on the Klett-Summerson colorimeter (No. 54 filter) or 0.78 and 0.27 on the Coleman junior with 19 mm. cuvets. If the Coleman is used, be sure that 5.2 ml. is adequate for the particular instrument (see p. 407).

MICROPROCEDURE. The procedure just

Table 8–5. Tube Dilutions for Standardization (Albumin by Methyl Orange)

TUBE NO.	PRELIMINARY DILUTION STANDARD (ML.)	SALINE (ML.)	FINAL STANDARD DILUTION (ML.)	STANDARD (ML.)	SALINE (ML.)
0					0.2
1	0.1	0.5	0.2		
2	0.1	0.2	0.2		
3				0.1	0.1
4	0.2	0.1	0.2		
5	0.5	0.1	0.2		
6				0.2	

described can be followed using 2.5 ml. of buffered methyl orange and 0.1 ml. of serum or 1 ml. of reagent and 40 mcl. of serum.

Globulin

Determine total protein and albumin. Subtract. The difference is globulin.

If an "A/G ratio" is requested, report the concentrations obtained for albumin and for globulin without dividing one by the other; this is usually what is wanted. If you are prevailed on to do the division, be sure to report the actual values as well as the quotient. An abnormal quotient alone will not show whether the abnormality is due to a decrease in albumin or to an increase in globulin or both.

Total Protein and Albumin (Reinhold, 1953)

The procedure just described for albumin is much simpler, but for those who prefer a salting-out technique such a method will now be described. This procedure uses the sodium sulfate-sulfite solution described by Reinhold, which, when properly used, gives results approximating those obtained by electrophoresis. Most laboratories formerly used, and some still do, the 23 per cent sodium sulfate solution of Howe; however, this gives high values for albumin and low for globulin.

Reagents

Use reagents 1 to 4 as for total serum protein.

5. Sulfate-sulfite solution. Place 208 gm. of anhydrous sodium sulfate and 70 gm. of sodium sulfite in a 2-liter beaker or flask.

To 900 ml. of water in a separate container add 2 ml. of concentrated sulfuric acid.

Add the acidified water suddenly to the salts with stirring. (This is a good place for a magnetic mixer.) When the salts are dissolved, transfer to a volumetric flask and dilute with water to 1 liter. The pH is not critical if it is above 7. (Before measuring pH, dilute 1 ml. to 25 ml. with water.) Store in glass or polyethylene stopper bottles at a temperature above 25° C.

PROCEDURE. If temperatures fall below 25° C., precipitation of sodium sulfate may occur.

To 7.5 ml. of sulfate-sulfite solution in a 15 × 125 mm. test tube add 0.5 ml. of serum with mixing.

Mix by inversion.

Immediately remove 2 ml. of the mixture to another test tube or a cuvet (for total protein determination).

To the remaining 6 ml. add 2 to 3 ml. of ether.

Invert the tube (upside down and back) ten times in 30 seconds (do not shake or albumin may be precipitated).

Centrifuge.

Tilt the tube to permit insertion of the tip of a transfer pipet past the globulin cake.

Without transferring any of the precipitate, remove 2 ml. of the clear albumin solution to another test tube or cuvet.

Measure 2 ml. of sulfite-sulfate solution into a tube for blank.

To each tube add 4 ml. of biuret reagent* and 2 to 3 ml. of ether.

Stopper, shake vigorously (*caution: strong alkali), and centrifuge.

Set up standards also, using procedure for total protein only.

Set to zero absorbance with blank, using green No. 54 filter, or (for better sensitivity) a No. 56 or 59 filter or at 580 mμ.

Read unknowns and standards.

CALCULATION

$$f = \frac{\text{conc. of std.}}{\text{rdg. of std.}}$$

f × rdg. of total protein tube = total protein, per cent.

f × rdg. of albumin tube = albumin, per cent.

Total protein − albumin = globulin.

If an "A/G ratio" is requested, report the values just obtained without dividing one by the other; this is usually what is wanted. If you are prevailed on to do the division, be sure to report the actual values as well as the quotient. An abnormal quotient alone will not show whether the abnormality is due to a decrease in albumin or to an increase in globulin or both.

INTERPRETATION. Normal values for total serum protein are 6.6 to 7.6 gm. per 100 ml. and for albumin, 3.8 to 4.6 gm. per cent, using standards based on 6.25 × nitrogen, or 6.9 to 7.9 per cent for total protein and 4.0 to 4.8 per cent for albumin, using standards based on a factor of 6.54.

Total protein may be decreased by malnutrition, prolonged liver insufficiency, or excessive protein loss as by hemorrhage or proteinuria (nephrosis); it may be increased by dehydration or hyperglobulinemia. Globulins increase in infection and liver disease and in multiple myeloma. In these cases the albumin is usually decreased so that unless the globulin increase is marked, the total protein may be unchanged.

QUANTITATIVE DETERMINATION OF PROTEIN IN CEREBROSPINAL FLUID

Precise Method. Because of the low concentration of protein normally found in cerebrospinal fluid, the biuret method used for blood serum is not sufficiently sensitive. Folin and Ciocalteu in 1927 described the use of a phosphomolybdic-phosphotungstic acid reagent for the determination of substances, which, like protein, contain tyrosine and tryptophane. In 1951 Lowry and his colleagues improved the sensitivity and usefulness of the reagent by pretreating the protein with an alkaline copper (biuret) reagent. This has been applied to the determination of protein in cerebrospinal fluid (Daughaday *et al.*, 1952).

Reagents

1. Alkaline tartrate solution. Dissolve 20 gm. of sodium carbonate and 0.5 gm. of sodium or potassium tartrate in a liter of 0.1N NaOH.

2. Copper sulfate solution. Dissolve 1 gm. of the pentahydrate in water and dilute to 1 liter.

3. Alkaline copper reagent. Add 45 ml. of the alkaline tartrate solution to 5 ml. of the copper sulfate solution. Mix. Make fresh daily.

4. Stock phenol reagent. This is one you may wish to purchase. In a 1½ or 2 liter round-bottom, ground-joint flask dissolve 100 gm. of sodium tungstate (dihydrate) and 25 gm. of sodium molybdate (dihydrate) in 700 ml. of water. Add 50 ml. of 85 per cent phosphoric acid and 100 ml. of concentrated hydrochloric acid. Insert a water-cooled reflux condenser and boil gently for ten hours. Turn off the heat and remove condenser. Add 150 gm. of lithium sulfate; wash down with 50 ml. of water. When this has dissolved, add 5 to 10 drops of 30 per cent H_2O_2 or of bromine. Boil gently for 15 minutes without a condenser to remove the excess oxidizing agent (if bromine was used, be sure to have a good fume hood). The solution should be clear golden-yellow. If it is greenish, repeat the peroxide or bromine treatment. Cool the reagent to room temperature and dilute to 1 liter. Filter if necessary through glass wool or a sintered glass filter. Store in a brown bottle (or in the dark) with a glass or polyethylene stopper.

5. Dilute phenol reagent. To 1 ml. of the stock reagent add 50 ml. of water and titrate with standard 0.1 N sodium hydroxide to a phenolphthalein endpoint. Now dilute the stock reagent with water so that 1 ml. is equivalent to 9 ml. of 0.1 N NaOH (e.g., if the titration required 22 ml. of 0.1 N NaOH, 9 volumes of the stock reagent should be diluted to 22 volumes; or dilute 90 ml. of stock reagent to ten times the volume of the sodium hydroxide used in the titration). A dilution to about double volume will usually be required. Each new batch of stock reagent should be titrated.

6. Protein standard. Use the Armour Protein Standard Solution or some normal serum on which the protein concentration has been determined. Dilute with 0.85 or 0.9 per cent sodium chloride to give a 40 mg. per cent (0.04 per cent) protein solution (this would require just over 0.5 ml. diluted to 100 ml.). This standard may be preserved with benzoic acid. Or use a 13 mg. per cent tyrosine solution in 0.1 N hydrochloric acid (this is equivalent to 50 mg. per cent protein).

PROCEDURE. To 5 ml. of the alkaline copper reagent add 0.1 ml. of spinal fluid (centrifuged if the cell count is elevated) or of standard.

Mix.

Let stand 15 minutes.

Add rapidly 0.5 ml. of the dilute phenol reagent.

Mix *immediately* and *thoroughly.*

Let stand 30 minutes.

Read within several hours with a Klett-Summerson No. 66 filter or at 700 to 750 mmu. and zero with water.

Blank. To 0.5 ml. of spinal fluid (and of standard if protein, rather than tyrosine, was used) in small test tubes, add 0.05 ml. of 60 per cent perchloric acid (if the cerebrospinal fluid sample is small, use 0.2 ml. spinal fluid and 0.02 ml. of acid).

Mix. Stopper and let stand for 15 minutes.

Centrifuge.

Carry 0.1 ml. of supernatant through the procedure described for the spinal fluid.

Multiply the reading by 1.1 because of the dilution with perchloric acid (calculation shown at bottom of page).

CALCULATION

$$f = \frac{\text{concentration of standard } (= 40 \text{ or } 50)}{\text{reading of standard} - (\text{reading of standard blank} \times 1.1)}$$

Concentration of CSF protein, mg.% = $f \times$ [reading of CSF − (reading of CSF blank × 1.1)]

= approx. (f × rdg. of CSF) − 6.

Daughaday *et al.* (1952) found the blank value to range between 3 and 9 mg. per cent and suggested using 6 mg. per cent routinely as the blank instead of determining it each time. However, Svensmark (1958) finds the blank may be as high as 45 mg. per cent and recommends determining it for each sample. If the result of a determination using 6 mg. per cent as the blank yields a protein value in the normal range, then it should be unnecessary to determine the blank; if the apparent protein concentration is elevated, then the blank should be measured.

INTERPRETATION. Normal values are in the range of 20 to 45 mg. per cent. Aside from the obvious elevation caused by hemorrhage into the cerebrospinal fluid or during puncture, the greatest increase in protein occurs in meningitis with values of 500 to 2000 mg. per cent. Concentrations of 50 to 500 mg. per cent may be seen in the nonpurulent meningitides, such as tuberculous and syphilitic meningitis, and in aseptic meningeal reaction. A moderate elevation may occur in various conditions involving the neural tissue of the brain or spinal cord (e.g., encephalitis, poliomyelitis, central nervous system syphilis, and general paresis).

Rapid bedside method. To 1 ml. of 2 per cent Na_2CO_3 in 0.1 N NaOH in a small test tube add 2 drops of spinal fluid (from a dropper not from the spinal needle).

Add 1 drop of 1 per cent copper sulfate in 2 per cent sodium acid tartrate.

After five minutes add 1 drop of stock (undiluted) phenol reagent. Mix *immediately.*

Compare after five minutes with standards made from 1, 2, and 4 drops of 7 mg. per cent tyrosine in 0.1 N HCl. If the drops of standard are of the same size as of the spinal fluid, these standards will be equivalent to 25, 50, and 100 mg. per cent protein.

A set of standards may be used for a month without serious error if to each standard tube is added 3 drops (0.1 ml.) of 1 M acetic acid and the tube is well stoppered.

Turbidimetric method for cerebrospinal fluid protein (Denis and Ayer, 1920). A less precise but somewhat simpler determination of the protein content of spinal fluid is based on the measurement of the turbidity produced by treating the cerebrospinal fluid with sulfosalicyclic acid.

Reagents

1. Sulfosalicylic acid, 3 per cent. Dis-

solve 30 gm. of sulfosalicylic acid in water and dilute to 1 liter. Mix. Stable.

2. Saline solution, 0.85 or 0.9 per cent sodium chloride. Stable.

PROCEDURE. Centrifuge spinal fluid if not clear.

To 1 ml. of clear spinal fluid in a test tube or cuvet add 4 ml. of 3 per cent sulfosalicylic acid. Mix.

Let stand ten minutes. If there is evident flocculation, repeat using 0.1 ml. of spinal fluid and 0.9 ml. of 0.85 or 0.9 per cent sodium chloride; multiply result by 10.

Read within an hour with red No. 66 filter or at 650 mmu. set to zero with water.

CALCULATION. Calculate mg. per cent protein from factor, graph, or table as established by Standardization.

STANDARDIZATION. This is done exactly as for urine protein except that the HCl tube is omitted.

QUANTITATIVE DETERMINATION OF PROTEIN IN URINE (FOLIN AND DENIS, 1914)

The degree of turbidity produced when sulfosalicylic acid is added to urine is used as a measure of the amount of protein in the urine.

Reagents

1. Sulfosalicylic acid, 3 per cent. Dissolve 30 gm. of sulfosalicylic acid in water and dilute to 1 liter. Mix.

2. Hydrochloric acid, 0.6 per cent. Dilute 15 ml. of concentrated hydrochloric acid to 1 liter with water. Mix.

PROCEDURE. Measure the volume of the 24-hour urine specimen.

If the urine is alkaline, make it just acid with concentrated HCl added dropwise with stirring.

Pipet 1 ml. of urine into each of two test tubes or cuvets.

To one tube add 4 ml. of 3 per cent sulfosalicylic acid and mix. If the precipitate flocculates instead of remaining uniform in turbidity, dilute a portion of the urine tenfold and repeat with 1 ml. of the dilution.

To the second tube of urine or dilution add 4 ml. of 0.6 per cent HCl for a blank.

Read with the red No. 66 filter or at 650 $m\mu$. set to zero with blank.

If the protein concentration is over 300 mg. per cent, dilute the urine tenfold and repeat, multiplying the final value by 10.

CALCULATION. Calculate mg. per cent protein from factor, graph, or table.

$$\text{mg.\% protein} \times \frac{\text{24-hour volume}}{100} = \text{mg.}$$

protein/24 hours. This divided by 1000 = gm. protein/24 hours.

Standardization. Determine the protein content of a portion of nonhemolyzed, nonicteric serum (p. 434). Dilute the serum to a protein concentration of 6 gm. per cent using 0.9 per cent NaCl. Make standards as follows:

> 300 mg. per cent: dilute 0.5 ml. of the 6 per cent to 10 ml. with saline; mix by inversion.
>
> 200 mg. per cent: to 2 ml. of the 300 mg. per cent add 1 ml. of saline; mix by inversion.
>
> 100 mg. per cent: to 2 ml. of the 300 mg. per cent add 4 ml. of saline; mix by inversion.
>
> 50 mg. per cent: to 2 ml. of the 100 mg. per cent add 2 ml. of saline; mix by inversion
>
> 25 mg. per cent: to 1 ml. of the 100 mg. per cent add 3 ml. of saline; mix by inversion.

Measure 1 ml. of each standard into each of two test tubes or cuvets, add sulfosalicylic acid and HCl, and read as under Procedure.

Subtract the reading of the HCl tube from that of the one with sulfosalicylic acid.

Plot the net readings against concentration of the standards. If the curve is a straight line, a factor can be calculated; otherwise use the curve or a table made from it.

Quantitative Determination of Fibrinogen in Plasma (Parfentjev et al., 1953)

Fibrinogen is the soluble protein of circulating blood and of plasma that is converted in the clotting process to the insoluble fibrin, which forms the network of the blood clot. When there is insufficient formation of fibrinogen by the liver or excessive fibrin formation and deposition, the blood will not clot and hemorrhage may result. However, it must be remembered that there are many other causes of defective clotting (Chapter 6).

The simplest and most effective way of finding whether there is sufficient fibrinogen in the blood to form a clot is to draw some blood without an anticoagulant, place it in a test tube, and let it stand five or ten minutes. Then turn the tube over. If the blood stays in the tube, the fibrinogen concentration is adequate; if it does not, clean up the mess. If the blood does not clot, there may be a deficiency of fibrinogen or of one of the other clotting factors (or an excess of a clotting inhibitor). In this case, or if you do not want to wait ten minutes in the first place, add a small amount of some kind of thrombin preparation. This will speed up clotting and will make up for any deficiency in clotting factors other than fibrinogen.

If the physician has need for a more precise estimate of fibrinogen concentration, the turbidimetric precipitation method is simple and satisfactory. It is based on the fact that fibrinogen is the most easily salted out of all the plasma proteins.

Reagents

1. Precipitating reagent. Dissolve 13.33 gm. of ammonium sulfate, 1.0 gm. of sodium chloride, and 2.5 mg. Merthiolate in water and dilute to 100 ml. Adjust to pH 7 with 10 N NaOH. The Merthiolate is a preservative and is not necessary to the functioning of this reagent.

2. Sodium chloride, 0.85 per cent.

3. Sodium chloride, 1 per cent.

Procedure. Pipet 0.5 ml. of plasma into each of two test tubes or cuvets.

To one add 0.5 ml. 0.85 per cent NaCl, mix, and add 9.0 ml. of precipitating reagent.

To the other add 9.5 ml. of 1 per cent NaCl for a blank.

Invert repeatedly to mix well.

Read with the blue No. 42 filter.

Calculation. (Reading of test − reading of blank) × f = fibrinogen, gm. per cent. For f, see Standardization.

Standardization. Prepare a 1 per cent solution of commercial fibrinogen (to contain about 0.5 per cent fibrinogen).

Determine the protein content of this solution before and after heating an aliquot to 55° C. and removing the coagulum on a glass rod. This difference is fibrinogen. (Use a micro-Kjeldahl procedure or the procedure outlined for cerebrospinal fluid protein to analyze the standard.)

Use this standardized fibrinogen solution for the Procedure just described. Calculate the factor:

$$f = \frac{\text{gm. \% fibrinogen in standard}}{\text{reading of standard} - \text{reading of blank}}$$

Optical density readings should be kept between 0.1 and 0.4 (50 to 200 Klett-Summerson).

Interpretation. Fibrinogen is normally present at 0.2 to 0.4 gm. per 100 ml. of plasma.

Semiquantitative Test for Fibrinogen. This test, although it lacks precision, is accurate and uses reagents the laboratory is likely to have for the prothrombin determination.

Reagents

1. Simplastin
2. Diagnostic plasma, Warner-Chilcott
3. 0.85 or 0.9 per cent sodium chloride.

PROCEDURE. Draw blood as for a prothrombin determination.

Centrifuge to obtain plasma.

Dilute 0.1 ml. plasma with 0.7 ml. saline. Mix.

Blow 0.1 ml. of diluted plasma into 0.2 ml. Simplastin in a 10 × 75 mm. tube.

Let stand five minutes at room temperature.

Gently tilt tube to horizontal to observe amount and type of clot.

INTERPRETATION. 1. Solid or large sliding clot: sufficient fibrinogen (over 150 mg. per cent).

2. Moderate sized clot with some liquid: borderline (75 to 125 mg. per cent).

3. Small clot to fibrin strands: low fibrinogen (under 75 mg. per cent).

4. No visible sign of fibrin formation: very low fibrinogen (less than 30 mg. per cent).

STANDARDIZATION. To familiarize yourself with the relation of fibrinogen to type of clot, carry out the following controls:

Dilute 0.1 ml. Diagnostic Plasma in each of four test tubes with the following volumes of saline to provide the fibrinogen concentrations indicated:

Saline, ml.	Fibrinogen, mg. per cent
1.5	150
2.3	100
3.1	75
4.7	50

Carry these dilutions through the Procedure just described.

QUANTITATIVE DETERMINATION OF MUCOPROTEIN (SEROMUCOID) IN SERUM (MENINI *et al.*, 1958)

Mucoprotein is a serum protein that contains about 20 per cent carbohydrate. It makes up 1 to 2 per cent of the serum proteins. Electrophoretically it travels with the α_1-globulins. It remains in solution when proteins are precipitated by perchloric, trichloroacetic, or sulfosalicylic acids but is precipitated by phosphotungstic acid. The latter precipitate can be redissolved and the mucoprotein determined by reagents for either carbohydrate or protein. The separation by use of a protein precipitant is not clearcut, about 30 per cent of the mucoprotein coprecipitating with the other proteins. The extent of this loss depends on several factors: the dilution of

the serum at the precipitation step, the method of mixing the serum with the perchloric acid, the time and temperature of contact between supernatant and precipitate, and the NaCl concentration of the diluted serum. These factors make it essential that the perchloric acid precipitation be carried out with scrupulous attention to reproduction of technique and timing. If these precautions are observed, the results, though not representing the total amount of mucoprotein, still give a constant percentage of that present in the serum. If the requirements are not adhered to, duplicate analyses may differ by as much as 20 per cent. It is also essential to remove the serum promptly from the clot (within one to two hours). The serum should be frozen if the analysis is not to be done at once. Plasma should not be used. The patient need not be fasting.

Reagents

1. Sodium chloride, 0.85 per cent
2. Perchloric acid, 1.8 M. Dilute 14 ml. of 72 per cent acid to 100 ml. with water.
3. Phosphotungstic acid, 5 per cent in 2 N HCl.
4. Perchloric acid, 0.6 M. To one volume of reagent 2 add two volumes of water.
5. Alkaline copper reagent, and 6. Phenol reagent (see reagents 1 through 4, p. 438).
7. Tyrosine standard, 13 mg. per cent in 0.1 N HCl.
8. Filter paper. Whatman No. 5 or Munktell No. 00.

PROCEDURE. To 4.5 ml. of 0.85 per cent sodium chloride add 0.5 ml. of serum. Shake gently.

Add 2.5 ml. of 1.8 M perchloric acid drop by drop while shaking.

Let stand exactly ten minutes.

Filter through Whatman No. 5 paper, covering funnel with a watchglass to retard evaporation. If necessary, the filtration is repeated several times through the same paper until the filtrate is clear.

To 5 ml. of filtrate add 1 ml. of phosphotungstic acid. Shake gently.

Let stand ten minutes.

Centrifuge at 2000 r.p.m. for ten minutes.

Discard the supernatant fluid; let tube stand on filter paper to drain.

Wash the precipitate with 10 ml. of 0.6 M perchloric acid, mixing with a glass rod, tube buzzer, or Vortex mixer.

Centrifuge, discard fluid, and drain.

Add 6.5 ml. of alkaline copper reagent. Shake until the precipitate is completely dissolved.

In two other tubes place 0.2 ml. of tyrosine for a standard and 0.2 ml. of water for a blank. To each add 6.5 ml. of alkaline copper reagent.

Add 1 ml. of phenol reagent to each tube and mix *immediately* by vigorous shaking.

Place tubes in the dark for one hour.

Read with the red No. 66 filter or at 700 to 750 mμ (calculation shown at bottom of page).

INTERPRETATION. The normal range for this procedure for mucoproteins is given as 5.7 to 12.5 mg. per cent as tyrosine. Other methods give quite different normal ranges because of the differences in analytical procedure or in basis of reporting. Thus, determination of the carbohydrate moiety yields a normal of 12 mg. per cent as hexose; measurement of protein by the biuret reagent gives 61 mg. per cent as protein; and determination with the phenol reagent leads to 3.4 mg. per cent as tyrosine or 80 mg. per cent as mucoprotein. The method just described, using the protein technique of Lowry *et al.* (1951), gives values about three times those obtained by Winzler with the phenol reagent alone, since the Lowry procedure involves peptide linkages as well as phenol groups.

The serum mucoprotein concentration may fluctuate significantly either above or below the normal range. Increase is believed to be due to release of mucoprotein by tissue cells as an acute response to inflammatory or proliferative diseases. However, there would seem to be little reason to prefer the mucoprotein determination to such an easily performed procedure as the sedimentation rate for following the course of these disorders.

Decreased values may occur in adrenocortical or hepatic insufficiency. It is usually low in "medical" jaundice and elevated in "surgical." It has been reported to be one of the best tests in making this distinction between hepatocellular and obstructive liver disease.

DETECTION OF CRYOGLOBULINS (STEFANINI AND DAMESHEK, 1955)

Cryoglobulins are proteins that separate out of solution or cause the serum or plasma to gel when cooled below body temperature and disappear again on rewarming to 37° C. Sometimes they appear at room temperature but refrigeration is usually necessary to demonstrate them.

PROCEDURE. Collect fasting blood and place tube at once in water at 37° C. If no anticoagulant was added, let clot for one hour.

Separate serum or plasma (oxalate, citrate, or heparin) at 2000 r.p.m. for ten minutes.

Transfer aliquots (about 2 ml.) to each of two serology test tubes.

Incubate one at 4° C. and the other at 37° C. for four hours.

Cryoglobulins produce no change in serum or plasma at 37° C.

In the refrigerated test tube two significant changes may be observed:

1. Plasma or serum may appear clotted *in toto*.
2. Plasma or serum may appear divided into two layers, the upper containing the normal plasma or serum, faintly stained with bilirubin, and the lower represented by cryoglobulin, whitish in color, which has precipitated to the bottom of the tube.

The appearance of the refrigerated tube containing cryoglobulin reverts to normal when rewarmed to 37° C.

MACROGLOBULINS

Macroglobulins are high molecular weight proteins, which can be demonstrated in the ultracentrifuge but not by techniques available in most clinical laboratories. They usually show an abnormal band in the electrophoretic pattern.

ELECTROPHORETIC SEPARATION OF SERUM PROTEINS WITH QUANTITATIVE DETERMINATION OF ALBUMIN AND α_1-, α_2-, β-, AND γ-GLOBULINS

The basic principles of electrophoresis were described briefly on p. 414. The equipment for paper electrophoresis consists essentially of two or three pieces: a chamber for supporting the wet paper while an electric potential difference causes the proteins to migrate; a power supply to furnish a steady potential difference; and a densitometer to quantitate the protein after staining. The densitometer may be replaced

---

CALCULATION

$$\frac{\text{Reading of unknown} - \text{reading of blank}}{\text{Reading of standard} - \text{reading of blank}} \times 0.026 \times \frac{7.5}{5} \times \frac{100}{0.5} =$$

$$\frac{\text{Reading of unknown (net)}}{\text{Reading of standard (net)}} \times 7.8 = \text{mg. tyrosine}/100 \text{ ml. serum.}$$

by an ordinary photometer to measure the amount of dye eluted from the cut paper.

There are several systems on the market that are useful for paper electrophoresis of serum proteins. Some systems are better in one respect, some in another. Because it may be advantageous to produce results that can be compared with those obtained in other laboratories rather than because these systems are necessarily better than others, mention might be made of the Spinco system, the modified Grassmann-Hannig equipment of Arthur H. Thomas Company, and the LKB apparatus distributed by Sorvall. This must not be taken to indicate that many other makes are not so convenient or so accurate.

For those who prefer to assemble their own equipment, the following procedure is given.

Equipment

1. Power supply, Heathkit; can be purchased in kit form; easily but not quickly assembled at a considerable saving in cost if one has the time; or completely assembled; obtainable from a local electronics or sound equipment dealer for about $60.

2. Glass plates, 5″ × 12″, of ¼″ plate glass with edges ground to remove the sharpness and to avoid cut fingers; two required.

3. Spring clamps. Hargrave No. 2 spring clamps available from a hardware or welding supply dealer; six required.

4. Wood blocks to support glass plates so that spring clamps will clear table.

5. Wood blocks to support electrode vessels (butter dishes) so that top is just below end of glass plates.

6. Polyethylene butter dishes for electrolyte vessels. These each have one slot cut in the cover just large enough to allow insertion of an electrode and another beside it ¹⁄₁₆″ wide for insertion of the ends of the paper strips. A baffle of ⅛″ Lucite or other hard plastic is shaped to fit lengthwise into the dish and to make separate compartments for electrode and paper. Two required.

7. Refrigerator dish and cover.

8. Electrodes, carbon, 5″ × ⅜″ × 2½″, purchased from Pennsylvania Carbon Co., 1509 Fairmount Ave., Philadelphia 30, Pa., as Grade 351. This comes in 6″ length and can be cut with a hack saw to fit. About $2. Two required.

9. Siphon. Rubber tubing 16″ long with a U-bend of glass tubing in each end and fitted with a pinch or screw clamp.

10. Whatman No. 3 MM paper, 1″ wide roll.

11. Staining and washing trays and racks. One can improvise here but the Spinco items are very convenient. Four trays and one rack required.

12. Micropipets, to measure 5 or 10 microliters.

13. Sample striper, to apply serum sample to paper strips. Spinco No. 300–805 or Lab Glass No. 3–1030. Optional.

Reagents

1. Barbital buffer, pH 8.6, ionic strength 0.083. Dissolve 3.12 gm. of diethylbarbituric acid and 17.1 gm. of sodium diethylbarbiturate in water and dilute to 1 liter. Stable two weeks at room temperature or two months in refrigerator. Remake if mold appears.

2. Dye solution. To 0.1 gm. of bromphenol blue and 50 gm. of zinc sulfate heptahydrate add 25 ml. of 95 per cent ethanol. Mix well and add 5 per cent (v/v) acetic acid to dissolve and to dilute to 1 liter.

3. Wash solution. Acetic acid, 5 per cent (v/v).

4. Fixative solution. Acetic acid, 5 per cent (v/v), and sodium acetate trihydrate, 0.3 per cent.

PROCEDURE. Coat one side of each glass plate with Desicote and let dry; or coat with silicone grease, wiping off the excess. In using the plates, place the coated sides next to the paper.

Set up the electrode vessels and one glass plate with their supports.

Insert the electrodes in their slots; they stand on edge.

Add barbital buffer to each electrode vessel until the liquid is just above the upper edge of the baffle.

Fill the siphon with buffer (e.g., by drawing it up into the siphon with a Propipette placed on the upper end). Close the clamp. Place the ends of the siphon in the two dishes. Open the clamp to let the level in the two vessels equalize.

Cut four strips of 1″ Whatman No. 3 MM paper 14″ long.

With a soft pencil, mark a light line across the center of each strip for application of samples.

Mark each strip with an identifying number or name.

Lay out clean paper towels or blotting paper to accommodate the four strips.

Holding the two ends of a strip, dip the strip through buffer in a refrigerator dish, wetting all except the very ends. Lay each strip on the blotting material. Blot to remove excess buffer.

Place the four strips on the glass plate, which has been put in position. Leave about $\frac{3}{16}''$ between strips and at each edge. Do not insert the ends of the strips in the electrode vessels yet.

Apply serum to the center lines of the strips. With a micropipet measure 5 mcl. and spot it in the center of the line; or measure 10 mcl., transfer it to the wires of the sample striper (clean with cotton moistened with acetone if the serum will not spread out), and apply it uniformly across the strip, pressing only gently.

If you wish to visualize the albumin to see how far it migrates, use a jaundiced serum or mix a little of the dye solution with a portion of one of the serums.

Even if fewer than four samples are being run, use four strips on the plates for uniformity of current density.

When samples have been applied to the strips, lay the second plate on top, treated side down.

Apply six clamps to the plates, spacing uniformly.

Seal the edges of the plates with vaseline or other grease to prevent evaporation from the sides of the outer strips, which would distort the patterns.

Insert the ends of the strips into buffer in the electrode vessels. Turn on the power supply, leaving it on Standby. Wait about ten minutes for capillarity to establish equilibrium moistening of the paper and for the power supply to warm up.

Clamp off the siphon.

Connect the electrodes to the power supply with wires having spring clips on the end.

Turn power supply to On. (Caution: do not touch wires, electrodes, or strips while power is on; danger of high voltage!) Adjust voltage to 300.

Let run until the albumin has migrated 4 to 5 inches as indicated by the bilirubin or dye or four to five hours if no marker was used; or for 16 to 18 hours at 100 volts.

Turn off the power supply.

Tear off the portions of the strips that extend beyond the plates.

Remove the clamps and carefully lift off the top plate.

Dry the strips in an oven at 100 to 110° C. for 20 to 30 minutes.

Immerse the dry strips in the dye solution for at least six hours or overnight.

Wash for six minutes each time in two changes of wash solution.

Immerse in fixative solution for six minutes.

Blot between clean papers.

Dry in the oven for about 15 minutes.

The blue color may be further intensified by exposing the strips to ammonia vapor; this is particularly desirable if a densitometer is to be used, but it is unnecessary if elution is to be done.

The strips may be evaluated by visual examination in comparison with normal serum.

Or the results may be quantitated with a densitometer, either by pulling the strip through, reading at regular intervals and plotting a curve, or by reading the center of each spot or strip and taking this density as proportional to dye and therefore approximately proportional to protein.

Or the dye may be eluted and measured. Cut the strip at the points where the staining is lightest, thus obtaining a section for each of the five protein fractions. Also cut a portion of the strip, where there is no apparent staining, for use as a blank. If the blank represents an appreciable portion of the color for any fraction, the width of the blank section and of each fraction should be measured in millimeters and a proportional blank subtracted from each fraction, since the fractions will vary in width. To elute, place each section in a test tube or cuvet containing 5 ml. of 0.01 N NaOH. Let stand 30 minutes with occasional mixing. Remove the paper, which should now be white. Centrifuge if fibers are floating in the eluate. Read each tube with a No. 54 filter or at 540 mμ against a water zero.

Even if the results are quantitated by photometry of some type, the dyed strip should be examined. Some abnormalities show up better qualitatively than quantitatively.

CALCULATION. The density of each solution (corrected for the blank) divided by the sum of the densities of all fractions times the total protein concentration (determined according to p. 435) gives the concentration of each protein fraction in serum.

The percentage of the total protein that each fraction represents can be calculated without knowing the total protein. However, these values are not so useful as the concentrations of each fraction, since these relative values are interdependent. Thus, with a markedly elevated γ-globulin, if all the other fractions were normal, they would be low as percentages of the total protein.

INTERPRETATION. Paper electrophoresis of protein is subject to variations owing to type of paper, rate of migration, nature and pH of buffer, dye used, and a number of other factors. One of the most disturbing errors is due to the "tailing" of albumin. Because the albumin, the fastest fraction, moves across the paper, some of it is adsorbed and held by the paper. Thus, when pure albumin is subjected to electrophoresis, there is some protein found in the area between the point of application and the bulk of the albumin. In electrophoresis of a mixture of proteins, such as serum, this means that results for albumin will be low and those for globulins correspondingly high. It is reported that this tailing does not occur on cellulose acetate or agar.

The γ-globulin is usually slightly behind the point of application and will include any insoluble protein that has not moved. The γ-globulin has actually moved in the electric field in the same direction as the albumin. Its net backward movement demonstrates the electroendosmotic movement of water in the opposite direction because of the interaction of water and the paper in the electric field. This movement of water carries the proteins in the opposite direction from the electric migration.

Another variable is the dye-binding power of the various protein fractions, which may not all be the same.

The rate of migration (voltage applied) and uniformity of pressure on the plates will affect the uniformity of migration and compactness of the fractions. The higher voltages produce more heat. If poor patterns are obtained, it may be desirable to try a different voltage.

Variations in either pH, ionic strength (concentration), or nature of the buffer will affect the pattern. Higher ionic strengths in general give sharper boundaries but increase the likelihood of denaturation of protein. Quite different patterns may be obtained, for example, with borate-EDTA buffer, which gives a larger number of fractions in both albumin and globulin. Variations in the temperature and time of drying may affect the dye-binding capacity of the proteins and therefore should be kept constant.

The technique of dyeing will have considerable influence on the values obtained:

concentration of dye, solvent, time of dyeing, technique of washing the dyed strips, method of elution, and solvent. The results will also depend on how the quantitation is done; if by densitometry, on how the intensity of the spots is evaluated, on the linearity of the densitometer response to changes in amount of dye, and on the decision as to where one fraction ends and another begins.

From all this it is seen that the results obtained for protein fractionation by paper electrophoresis depend on the technique and equipment used. Normal values will vary and should be established for each particular setup. For example, four sets of normal values for four different techniques are shown in the following table. The first two columns are those published by Spinco (Ehrmantraut, 1958) for their A and B procedures respectively; the third column contains Sunderman's values (1957) for his modification of the Grassmann-Hannig procedure, which uses horizontal strips suspended in air; the last column contains Bowman's figures (1954) for electrophoresis between plates but using a different dye than that just recommended. Values are in gm./100 ml. of serum.

	SPINCO A	SPINCO B	FLAT, AIR	FLAT, PLATES
Albumin	3.6	4.5	3.7	4.1
α_1-Globulin	0.4	0.3	0.4	0.4
α_2-Globulin	0.8	0.7	0.7	0.7
β-Globulin	1.0	0.7	0.9	0.8
γ-Globulin	1.2	0.8	1.5	1.0

Albumin is rarely elevated. It may be decreased by low protein intake (malnutrition), by albumin loss from severe hemorrhage or into the urine, or by liver damage when synthesis is impeded. It may also be decreased in response to an increase in globulins. In nephrosis, in addition to the decreased albumin, there is a marked increase in α_2-globulin with a decrease in the other globulins, particularly the gamma. In chronic liver disease the γ-globulin is usually increased.

In multiple myeloma the most characteristic finding is the presence of a band of abnormal protein, which has been called the M-protein. It occurs as a rather intense, fairly narrow band most often found with the γ-globulins and less often between the β and γ fractions, with the β, or rarely between α_2 and β. Sometimes it is obvious; sometimes it appears only as an increase in one of the fractions. It may sometimes be seen more clearly on the stained strip than on the densitometer record. In agammaglobulinemia there is only a faint γ-globulin band.

ELECTROPHORESIS OF PROTEINS OF URINE AND OTHER FLUIDS

The technique just described for serum can also be used for separating the proteins of urine and other fluids. It is almost always necessary to concentrate the urine before applying to the paper. The protein content should be at least 1.5 per cent.

Place an appropriate volume of urine (20 to 40 ml.) into a small cellophane bag (a piece of cellophane tubing knotted at the end after being wetted) and concentrate to 2 ml. or less, according to the original protein content, by extracting the crystalloid solution with a 15 per cent solution of carboxymethylcellulose or a 25 per cent solution of polyvinyl pyrrolidinone. Place in the refrigerator while concentrating. The technique is useful for studying the urine proteins in some cases of multiple myeloma and may occasionally reveal the presence of abnormal proteins when the study of serum does not do so.

Nonprotein Nitrogenous Compounds

In addition to the determination of individual compounds of this group the determination of the total nonprotein nitrogen (NPN) is sometimes done as a measure of kidney function. The specific determination of urea, or of creatinine if urea is markedly elevated, is now usually preferred.

For the determination of NPN, of the specific constituents, and of a number of nonprotein substances, protein must first be removed from the blood, serum, or plasma. The proteins are removed by the addition of an anion or cation, which combines with the protein to form an insoluble product, or by the addition of two solutions that will react to form a precipitate, which carries the protein down with it by coprecipitation. For a few determinations, such as calcium and phosphate, an acid precipitation is necessary and trichloroacetic acid is commonly used. For most, however, a more neutral filtrate is desirable. These are usually obtained by precipitation with tungstic acid or zinc hydroxide. Several modifications of each have been proposed. Many other precipitants have been advocated but have not been generally used; some are used for specific determinations.

DEPROTEINIZATION WITH TUNGSTIC ACID

Reagents

1. Sodium tungstate, 10 per cent. Dissolve 100 gm. of reagent grade (preferably "according to Folin") sodium tungstate dihydrate in water and dilute to 1 liter. Mix. Stable.

A satisfactory sodium tungstate gives a solution that is neutral or faintly alkaline to phenolphthalein. The sample should be discarded if it is so alkaline that more than 0.4 ml. of 0.1 N acid is required to neutralize 10 ml. of the 10 per cent solution with phenolphthalein as indicator. Acid-reacting tungstate may be used if the 10 per cent solution is brought to neutrality or to very faint alkalinity with sodium hydroxide.

2. Sulfuric acid, $\frac{2}{3}$ normal (0.667 N), or

3. Sulfuric acid, $\frac{1}{12}$ normal (0.0833 N). Dilute 2.0 or 2.5 ml. of concentrated acid to 1 liter (always pour concentrated sulfuric acid into water, never vice versa). Titrate with standardized 1 N or 0.1 N NaOH and adjust if necessary. Stable.

PROCEDURES. **A. Original Folin and Wu Method (1919).** To 1 volume of oxalated blood add 7 volumes of water. Mix.

Add 1 volume of 10 per cent sodium tungstate (equal to volume of blood). Mix.

Add slowly with mixing (preferably by swirling in an Erlenmeyer flask or wide mouth bottle) 1 volume of $\frac{2}{3}$ N H_2SO_4.

Insert a rubber stopper and give a few vigorous shakes. A dark brown coagulum should form. Should it fail to do so, coagulation is incomplete owing probably to use of too much oxalate. In such cases add a few drops of 2 N (10 per cent) solution of sulfuric acid, shake vigorously, and allow the mixture to stand for five minutes for the coagulum to change from bright red to dark brown before filtering.

Filter through paper and collect the clear filtrate. If the first that comes through is cloudy, return it to the funnel. The filtrate should show no acid when tested with Congo red paper. If the value for the uric acid is to be determined, Benedict recommended that the mixture be allowed to stand 10 to 20 minutes after the sulfuric acid is added and before filtering.

Each milliliter of the clear filtrate represents 0.1 ml. of blood. It will serve for determinations of nonprotein nitrogen, urea, uric acid, creatinine, blood sugar, and other substances and may be kept without deterioration for two days or longer if covered with a few drops of toluene or xylene, stoppered, and kept refrigerated.

For serum, plasma, or cerebrospinal fluid use less of the reagents: 1 volume of sample, 8 volumes of water, and $\frac{1}{2}$ volume each of tungstate and $\frac{2}{3}$ N H_2SO_4.

B. Haden's Modification (1923) of Folin's Method. Haden simplified the previous method of making a protein-free blood filtrate by combining the water and acid to make a twelfth-normal solution of sulfuric acid. The improved method consists of laking one volume of blood with eight volumes of twelfth-normal solution of sulfuric acid. Add one volume of 10 per cent solution of sodium tungstate, shake the mixture well and filter.

C. Van Slyke's Modification (1928) of Haden's Method. Van Slyke further modified the Haden method for making a protein-free blood filtrate. Mix one part of a 10 per cent solution of sodium tungstate with eight parts of twelfth-normal solution of sulfuric acid. One part of oxalated blood is added directly to nine parts of this mixture. This produces a clear, protein-free filtrate without any laking of the blood. In this respect the method is similar to Folin's modified method for protein precipitation.

D. Folin's Modified Method (1930). Folin published a modified method for removing proteins from blood. This method produces a water-clear solution with no laking of erythrocytes. It is claimed for this extract that more accurate determinations can be made for blood sugar and uric acid and that urea determinations are identical with those obtained with the older method. It is of no advantage for serum or plasma.

Reagents

1. Tungstate-sulfate solution. Dissolve 15 gm. of anhydrous sodium sulfate and 6 gm. of sodium tungstate dihydrate in water and dilute to 1 liter. Mix. Stable.

2. Sulfuric acid, $\frac{1}{3}$ N. Make as for $\frac{2}{3}$ N except half as strong.

TECHNIQUE. Transfer to a small flask 8 volumes of tungstate-sulfate solution.

Add 1 volume of oxalated blood. Mix by occasionally shaking very gently.

After five minutes or longer add slowly from a pipet, with constant but gentle mixing, 1 volume of a third-normal solution of sulfuric acid.

Filter or centrifuge for ten minutes at a moderate speed. The supernatant fluid should be water-clear.

DEPROTEINIZATION WITH ZINC HYDROXIDE

This method is used in the determination of blood glucose (p. 418). In this modification barium hydroxide is used in place of the alternative sodium hydroxide. This has the advantage that the barium ion precipitates the sulfate so that the precipitants are removed, leaving no added ions in the filtrate.

QUANTITATIVE DETERMINATION OF UREA IN BLOOD OR URINE (ORMSBY, 1942, AND BARKER, 1944)

Blood is deproteinized; urine is diluted. The specimen is then heated with diacetyl monoxime and immediately treated with persulfate. The colored product that results is estimated photometrically.

Reagents

1. Sodium tungstate, 10 per cent. See p. 446.

2. Sulfuric acid, $\frac{2}{3}$ N. See p. 446.

3. Urea stock standard. Dissolve 1.072 gm. of desiccator-dried, reagent grade urea in about 250 ml. of water. Rinse into a 500 ml. volumetric flask. Add 0.14 ml. of concentrated H_2SO_4 and dilute to 500 ml. Mix. Keep in refrigerator. Stable one year. One milliliter contains 1 mg. urea nitrogen (100 mg. per cent; used as filtrate, equivalent to 1000 mg. per cent).

4. Urea working standard for routine use. Dilute 2 ml. of stock standard to 100 ml. with 0.01 N H_2SO_4 and mix. One milliliter contains 0.02 mg. urea nitrogen (2 mg. per cent; used as filtrate, equivalent to BUN of 20 mg. per cent).

5. Diacetyl monoxime, 3 per cent. Dissolve 3 gm. of diacetyl monoxime (2, 3-butanedione-2-oxime) in water and dilute to 100 ml. Mix. Keep in refrigerator. Stable three months.

6. Sulfuric acid, 50 per cent. Place 500 ml. of water in a 2 liter Erlenmeyer or Florence flask. Add, slowly and with continuous mixing, 500 ml. of concentrated sulfuric acid. Work over a sink. The solution will get hot. (Never add water to concentrated sulfuric acid; always the reverse.) Let cool. Transfer to a 1-liter mixing cylinder or volumetric flask and dilute to 1 liter with water. Stable.

7. Potassium persulfate, 1 per cent. Dissolve 1 gm. of potassium persulfate in water and dilute to 100 ml. Keep in refrigerator. Stable one week.

PROCEDURE. For blood, serum, or plasma prepare a tungstic acid, protein-free filtrate (diluting the specimen 10-fold in so doing).

For urine dilute 1 ml. to 100 ml. with water (using a volumetric pipet and a volumetric flask or mixing cylinder).

Into separate test tubes pipet 2 ml. of filtrate or of urine dilution, 2 ml. of water for a blank, and 2 ml. of urea working standard. (If BUN is or may be high, set up another tube with 1 ml. of filtrate and 1 ml. of water.)

To each tube add 0.25 ml. of 3 per cent diacetyl monoxime (kept in refrigerator) and 4 ml. of 50 per cent sulfuric acid. Mix thoroughly by flipping.

Cover each tube with a glass marble (buy a sack at the dime store; you'll only confuse your purchasing agent).

Place the rack of covered tubes in a boiling water bath for ten minutes.

Remove tubes from boiling bath and *immediately* add 0.25 ml. of 1 per cent potassium persulfate (kept in refrigerator) to each; immediately mix with a footed stirring rod.

Let stand 15 minutes.

Read with the blue No. 42 filter or at 475 mμ. set to zero with blank. (If readings are too high, sensitivity can be decreased by reading at a lower wave length; standards and unknowns must of course be read at the same wave length.)

If reading is between 400 and 800 on the Klett-Summerson or absorbance of 0.8 to 1.6, dilute with an equal volume of water, reread, and multiply by 2.

If reading is greater than this, repeat the determination after diluting 1 ml. of filtrate or urine dilution to 10 ml.; multiply result by 10.

CALCULATION. For blood, serum, or plasma calculate mg. per cent urea nitrogen from factor, graph, or curve as established by Standardization.

For urine calculate as for blood and then multiply by 10 (since blood was diluted 10-fold and the urine 100-fold). Now multiply by the number of hundreds of ml. in the specimen to obtain the mg. of urea nitrogen in the specimen. If this number is large, divide by 1000 and report as grams.

STANDARDIZATION. Into four 100 ml. volumetric flasks pipet respectively 1, 2, 3, and 10 ml. of stock standard.

Dilute to the marks and mix well. These correspond to filtrates from bloods containing 10, 20, 30, and 100 mg. per cent BUN respectively when using 2 ml. When one uses 1 ml. and 1 ml. of water, the stand-

ards correspond to 5, 10, 15, and 50 mg. per cent.

Set up 2 ml. of each of these seven different standards as well as a zero BUN (blank) with 2 ml. of water.

Carry through the Procedure just described and read.

Draw the absorbance-concentration curve. This is S-shaped rather than a straight line. The variance from linearity will depend on the instrument used, and wave length chosen and on details of the technique. If the major portion of the curve is straight and in line with the origin, a factor may be used. Or a series of factors may be calculated for different portions of the curve. Or results may be read from the curve or from a table constructed from it.

The factor on the Klett-Summerson colorimeter with a No. 42 filter will be about 0.12; absorbance of the 20 mg. per cent standard on the Coleman at 475 in 12 mm. cuvets is about 0.65.

COMMENT. It is customary in many places to report urea in terms of its nitrogen content rather than in terms of urea itself. This merely makes comparison with the total NPN easier. Since the molecular weight of urea is 60, of which the nitrogen in it is 28, urea concentration is just over twice the urea nitrogen value.

After the heating period and addition of persulfate, there is competition between two reactions, which cause increase and decrease respectively in the color intensity. Maximum intensity for low concentrations of urea is reached sooner than for high ones, and it would be better to read those in the normal range at once and only the high ones after 15 minutes. For practical reasons it is easier to read all samples, standards as well as unknowns, at 15 minutes.

Diacetyl monoxime is not stable even in the solid form in unopened bottles. A freshly made solution may therefore not be good. Check each new batch with at least one standard. If the color developed is much less than usual, use a new lot of reagent.

INTERPRETATION. The normal range of blood urea nitrogen (BUN) is 5 to 20 mg. per cent. No significance is ordinarily attached to low values. High values may be "renal" or "prerenal" in origin. The chief value of the test is in detecting and following impaired excretion in kidney disease, but other causes of hyperazotemias must be kept in mind. Elevations may also occur in the impairment of kidney function, in dehydration, or in shock. Prerenal causes include increased protein catabolism of fever or cancer, roentgen therapy of leukemia or lymphoma, gastrointestinal hemorrhage, or transfusions. Urea nitrogen may rise as high as 400 mg. per cent but usually does not exceed 200 mg. per cent. Determination of blood creatinine is frequently helpful in deciding whether an increased BUN is renal in origin or not.

Urinary urea nitrogen is normally about 10 to 15 gm. per 24 hours. It reflects the dietary protein intake.

UREA CLEARANCE (MÖLLER *et al.,* 1928)

A small amount of kidney dysfunction may be present even with a normal BUN. A more sensitive measure is obtained by relating the amount of urea excreted in the urine per minute to the concentration in the blood. This is done by the formula $C = \dfrac{UV}{BT}$ where C is the "clearance" in ml. of blood per minute, U and B are the urea (or urea nitrogen) concentrations in mg. per cent in urine and blood respectively, V is the volume of urine in milliliters, and T the time in minutes of excretion that the urine represents. The clearance is thus expressed as the volume of blood that will contain the amount of urea excreted in the urine in one minute.

It is preferable to keep the urine flow above 2 ml. per minute so that this formula for "maximal" clearance will apply. Van Slyke found that at smaller flows the test could be salvaged by using a modified formula for "standard" clearance:

$$C = \frac{U}{B}\sqrt{\frac{V}{T}}$$

The urea clearance test should be done only if the blood urea nitrogen concentration is below 20 mg. per cent or if there is question as to whether a slightly increased BUN is due to renal or prerenal causes.

PROCEDURE. The patient may have breakfast.

Have the patient drink a glassful of water.

Have the patient void, emptying the bladder completely and discarding the urine. Note the time at the completion of voiding. (The physician should be prepared to catheterize if the patient cannot void or cannot empty the bladder completely.)

Save all the urine voided during the test (the next two hours).

An hour after the initial voiding the patient should drink another glass of water and empty his bladder again. Save this urine with any voided during this first hour. Note the time.

Now take a blood sample for urea determination.

At the end of the second hour have the patient again empty his bladder completely. Save this as a second specimen with any voided during the second hour. Note the exact time.

Mark each specimen with the time interval in minutes that it represents. This is important; it is unimportant that the time be exactly an hour.

Analyze the blood and each urine sample for urea. Express all the results in the same terms (e.g., mg. per cent).

Calculate the urea clearance for each urine specimen, using the maximal or standard clearance formula, depending on the rate of urine flow. If desired, calculate the clearance as "per cent of normal" by multiplying the clearance in ml. of blood per minute by 100 and dividing by the normal value; this latter is 75 for maximal and 54 for standard clearance.

The two urine samples are taken to check the accuracy of urine collection, the

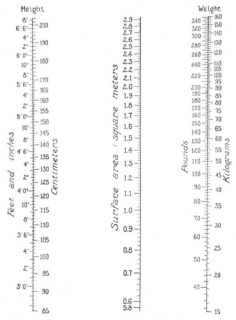

Figure 8–23. Nomogram for estimating surface area from weight and height, according to DuBois's formula. A straight line drawn from a point corresponding to the height of the individual on the left-hand scale to that of his weight on the right-hand scale crosses the middle line at a point indicating his surface area. (From Boothby.)

most likely source of error in the procedure. The results calculated from the two should agree within 10 per cent.

For greater accuracy in adults, and almost necessarily for children, the clearance should be corrected for surface area, determined from height and weight (see Fig. 8–23). The normals just quoted are for adults with an average surface area of 1.73 sq. m. The calculation then becomes:

$$\text{Maximum urea clearance} = \frac{UV}{BT} \times \frac{100}{75} \times \frac{1.73}{A} \text{ per cent of normal, and}$$

$$\text{Standard urea clearance} = \frac{U}{B} \times \frac{100}{54} \times \sqrt{\frac{V}{T} \times \frac{1.73}{A}} \text{ per cent of normal,}$$

where A is the patient's surface area (from Fig. 8–23).

QUANTITATIVE DETERMINATION OF CREATININE IN BLOOD AND URINE
(FOLIN AND WU, 1919; BONSNES AND TAUSKY, 1945)

Creatinine is usually determined by the red color produced by an alkaline picrate solution. The reaction is not specific for creatinine. The amount of other chromogens in urine is small. In normal, whole blood perhaps half the color is due to creatinine, but in serum or plasma it amounts to around 80 per cent (when the creatinine is elevated, the percentage of other chromogens decreases). It is therefore preferable to do the determination on serum or plasma rather than on whole blood.

Reagents

1. Sodium tungstate, 10 per cent, and sulfuric acid, $\frac{2}{3}$ N. (See p. 446.)

2. Picric acid, saturated. Place 14 gm. of picric acid in a bottle and add 1 liter of water. Let stand a day with occasional shaking before use. Let settle and decant or siphon off with care to avoid getting any solid particles.

Most reagent grade picric acid (which contains 10 to 20 per cent of water to reduce the hazard of explosion) is satisfactory. The solution should be checked the first time a new batch is used: the absorbance of the alkaline picrate should not be over twice that of the picric acid.

3. Sodium hydroxide, 10 per cent. Most conveniently prepared by dilution of concentrated NaOH (p. 399) (10 per cent = 2.5 N). Keep in a borosilicate glass or, prefer-

ably, a polyethylene bottle. If a glass bottle is used, it should not have a glass stopper.

4. Alkaline picrate solution. Mix 5 volumes of saturated picric acid with 1 volume of 10 per cent sodium hydroxide. Make fresh just before use.

5. Creatinine stock standard. Weigh out 0.100 gm. of pure, dry creatinine; transfer quantitatively to a 100 ml. volumetric flask. Fill about $\frac{2}{3}$ full with water and add 0.8 ml. of concentrated HCl. When all the creatinine is dissolved, dilute to 100 ml. Mix well. 1 ml. = 1 mg. (100 mg. per cent; when used in place of 1 → 4 blood filtrate, = 400 mg. per cent). Stable in refrigerator.

6. Creatinine working standard. Dilute 1 ml. of stock standard to 100 ml. with water. Mix well. 1 ml. = 0.01 mg. (1 mg. per cent; when used in place of 1 → 4 blood filtrate, = 4 mg. per cent). Keeps one month in refrigerator.

PROCEDURE. Prepare a Folin-Wu tungstic acid filtrate of serum or plasma (described on p. 446), diluting only fourfold instead of tenfold; i.e., to 1 volume of serum add 2 volumes of water, $\frac{1}{2}$ volume of 10 per cent sodium tungstate, and $\frac{1}{2}$ volume of $\frac{2}{3}$ N N_2SO_4 unless a high value is expected, when the usual tenfold dilution is made.

For urine pipet 1 ml. of specimen into a 100 ml. volumetric flask or mixing cylinder and dilute to volume with water. Mix.

Pipet 4 ml. of filtrate or dilution or 4 ml. of water for a blank into test tubes or cuvets.

Add 2 ml. of alkaline picrate solution. Mix.

Let stand 15 minutes.

Read with the green No. 54 filter or at 520 mμ.

If absorption is too great, repeat the determination with a smaller amount of filtrate or dilution made up to 4 ml. with water and multiply result accordingly.

CALCULATION. For blood serum or plasma calculate mg. per cent creatinine from factor, graph, or curve as established by Standardization.

For urine calculate as for blood; then multiply by 25 or 10 (since blood was diluted 4- or 10-fold and urine, 100-fold). Now multiply by the number of hundreds of ml. in the specimen to obtain the mg. of creatinine in the specimen. If this number is large, it may be divided by 1000 and reported as grams.

STANDARDIZATION. Into appropriately

labeled tubes or cuvets pipet 0, 0.5, 1, 2, 3, 4, and 5 ml. of creatinine working standard.

Add 5, 4.5, 4, 3, 2, 1, and 0 ml. of water respectively to make a total volume of 5 ml. in each tube.

To each tube add 2.5 ml. of alkaline picrate solution. Mix.

Let stand 15 minutes and read as above.

The tubes are equivalent to $1 \rightarrow 10$ filtrates made from serums containing 0, 1, 2, 4, 6, 8, and 10 mg. per cent respectively or to $1 \rightarrow 4$ filtrates of serum containing 0, 0.4, 0.8, 1.6, 2.4, 3.2, and 4 mg. per cent respectively.

Plot readings against equivalent concentration.

If a straight line is obtained, a factor may be calculated and used. In any case the curve or a table made up from it can be used for calculation.

INTERPRETATION. Normal values for serum or plasma creatinine are in the range of 0.5 to 1.2 mg. per cent. Significance of changes is much the same as for urea except that the prerenal factors have little effect. Ordinarily urea values are of more importance when normal or slightly increased; creatinine values are more important when increases are more marked.

CREATININE CLEARANCE TESTS

This can be done the same as for the urea clearance (p. 449) except that water need not be forced to maintain a high urine flow. Calculation is by the "maximal" clearance formula and is expressed as ml. per min. per 1.73 sq. m. rather than as per cent of normal. Normal values are 80 to 110 ml. per min. per 1.73 sq. m. Creatinine clearance is a good measure of glomerular filtration when serum creatinine concentration is in the normal range. At higher concentrations some creatinine is excreted by the tubules as well.

DETERMINATION OF CREATINE IN SERUM OR URINE
(FOLIN AND WU, 1919)

Creatine is converted to creatinine by heating in an acid solution. By determining creatinine before and after heating, creatine can be estimated.

Reagents are the same as for creatinine.

PROCEDURE. Prepare a filtrate of serum or a dilution of urine as for creatinine.

Pipet 4 ml. into a graduated test tube or a Pyrex or Kimax graduated cylinder.

Add 1.67 ml. of saturated picric acid. Mix.

Cover with aluminum foil or a marble.

Heat in an autoclave or pressure cooker at 155° C. for 10 minutes, at 130° C. for 20 minutes, at 120° C. (15 p.s.i.) for 30 minutes, or in a boiling water bath for 60 minutes.

Adjust to 5.67 ml. with water if necessary.

Add 0.33 ml. of 10 per cent NaOH. Mix.

To another 4 ml. of the original filtrate or dilution and to 4 ml. of water add 2 ml. of alkaline picrate solution.

Let all tubes stand 15 minutes.

Read as for creatinine.

CALCULATION. Convert readings into mg. per cent creatinine.

Subtract preformed creatinine (unheated) from total (heated). Multiply by 1.16 to obtain creatine.

INTERPRETATION. Normal serum creatine is 0.2 to 0.6 mg. per cent.

Children normally excrete some creatine in the urine; adults, little or none. Creatine excretion increases in starvation, muscle wasting, pregnancy, and hyperthyroidism.

QUANTITATIVE DETERMINATION OF URIC ACID (CARAWAY, 1955; HENRY *et al.*, 1957)

In alkaline solution uric acid reduces a complex phosphotungstate with the production of a blue color.

Reagents

1. Phosphotungstic acid. Dissolve 30 gm. of sodium tungstate (reagent grade) in 300 ml. of distilled water in a flask with a ground glass joint. Add 32 ml. of 85 per cent *o*-phosphoric acid and several carborundum grains (No. 12). Attach a reflux condenser and boil gently for two hours. Cool to room temperature and add water to a total volume of 1 liter. Add 16 gm. of $Li_2SO_4 \cdot H_2O$ and dissolve. The reagent is stable in a refrigerator.

This reagent is merely a 2.5-fold dilution of the reagent described by Folin and Denis (1914) with lithium sulfate added. The inclusion of lithium sulfate was suggested by the early observation of Folin that the presence of lithium salts tends to suppress the formation of turbidity in the reaction.

2. Sodium carbonate, 14 per cent. Dissolve 14 gm. of anhydrous sodium carbonate in water and dilute to 100 ml. Store in a polyethylene bottle. Stable.

3. Uric acid stock standard. Add 100 mg. of uric acid and 60 mg. of Li_2CO_3 to approximately 50 ml. of water in a 100 ml. volumetric flask. Warm to approximately

60° C. in order to dissolve the ingredients, cool to room temperature, and add water to 100 ml. The reagent is stable in a refrigerator. 1 ml. = 1 mg.

4. Uric acid working standard. Dilute 1 ml. of stock to 100 ml. with water. Mix well. Prepare fresh daily. 1 ml. = 0.01 mg.; 1 mg. per cent; used as filtrate, equivalent to 10 mg. per cent.

PROCEDURE. For serum (oxalated plasma or whole blood should not be used) prepare a protein-free filtrate (see p. 446).

For urine, if the specimen is cloudy, warm sample to 60° C. for ten minutes to ensure dissolving of any urates and then centrifuge. Dilute 1 volume accurately to 100 volumes with water.

Pipet 3 ml. of filtrate or dilution into a test tube or cuvet.

Pipet 3 ml. of water into another tube for a blank.

Pipet 3 ml. of working standard into a third tube.

To each tube add 1 ml. of 14 per cent sodium carbonate. Mix.

Add 1 ml. dilute phosphotungstic acid. Mix at once.

Let stand 15 minutes at room temperature.

Read within the next 30 minutes with red No. 66 filter or at 710 mμ set to zero with blank (which should be colorless) or set to zero with water and subtracting blank from each unknown.

CALCULATION. For serum calculate mg. per cent uric acid from factor, graph, or curve as established by Standardization.

For urine calculate as for serum and then multiply by 10 (since serum was diluted 10-fold and urine, 100-fold). Now multiply by the number of hundreds of ml. in the specimen to obtain the mg. of uric acid in the specimen. If this number is large, it may be divided by 1000 and reported as grams.

STANDARDIZATION. Make up a 2 mg. per cent working standard by diluting 1 ml. of stock standard to 50 ml. with water. Mix. Prepare standard tubes as follows:

WORKING STD., 2 MG. PER CENT, ML.	H₂O, ML.	EQUIV. MG. PER CENT, SERUM
0	6	0
1	5	3.33
2	4	6.67
3	3	10.0
4	2	13.33
5	1	16.67
6	0	20.0

Carry these tubes through the Procedure just described, beginning with the addition of the sodium carbonate but adding 2 ml. of each reagent.

Plot readings against equivalent serum concentration. If a straight line is obtained, a factor may be calculated and used. In any case the curve or a table made up from it can be used for calculation.

The standardization should be checked by running a 10 mg. per cent equivalent standard along with unknowns as decribed in Procedure.

INTERPRETATION. Normal values for serum uric acid are 3 to 5.5 mg. per cent. Increases are found in gout, in familial hyperuricemia, in kidney disease, in toxemia of pregnancy, and in leukemia and other diseases involving breakdown of nuclear material.

Normal uric acid excretion is around 0.7 gm. per day.

DETERMINATION OF AMMONIA IN BLOOD (McDERMOTT AND ADAMS, 1954; TRAEGER et al., 1954; FAULKNER AND BRITTON, 1960)

A very small amount of ammonium ions exists in blood. More is formed as the blood stands. Hence the blood must be analyzed immediately on being drawn. Carbon dioxide in the atmosphere above the blood minimizes the release of ammonia from other compounds and is used in the collection bottle. Potassium carbonate will release the ammonium ions from the blood as ammonia, which can then diffuse into boric acid. The ammonia in this weak acid can be directly titrated with dilute hydrochloric acid.

Apparatus

1. Conway diffusion dishes, porcelain, with glass covers (Arthur H. Thomas No. 4472-F.). Minimum of six required for determination.

2. Microburet. Rehberg type (Arthur H. Thomas No. 2461-A) or syringe type (MicroMetric Instrument Co.)

Reagents

1. Hydrochloric acid, approximately 0.1N, accurately standardized, factor used in calculation (p. 399).

2. Hydrochloric acid, 0.003 N. Dilute 3 ml. of 0.1 N HCl to 100 ml. on the day of use. Mix well.

3. Boric acid, 1 per cent.

4. Indicator solution. Choose one of these three according to your reaction to the endpoint. *Bromcresol green*, 0.1 per cent in 95 per cent ethyl alcohol (straight or denatured with methanol or isopropanol). Yellow in acid, blue in alkali. *Tashiro*. To 150 mg. methyl red and 75

mg. methylene blue add 100 ml. of 50 per cent ethyl alcohol. Let stand with occasional mixing until dissolved (one to two days). Endpoint is a blue-gray or a dirty blue. *Methyl purple* (Fleisher Chemical Co.). Purple in acid, green in alkali.

5. Potassium carbonate, saturated. Dissolve approximately 300 gm. of anhydrous potassium carbonate in 200 ml. of water with heat and stirring. Pour into reagent bottle while still warm. Solid carbonate should separate on cooling.

6. Ammonia stock standard. Dissolve 94 mg. of dry ammonium sulfate in ammonia-free water and dilute to 100 ml. Mix well. 20 mg. per cent N.

7. Ammonia working standard. Dilute 1 ml. of stock standard to 100 ml. with ammonia-free water. Mix well. 200 mcg. per cent NH_3 N.

8. Petrolatum, white or *Ucon lubricant*, 75-H-90,000, Carbide and Carbon Chemicals Company.

COLLECTION OF SPECIMEN. Ammonium oxalate must, of course, not be used. Prepare 50 ml. Erlenmeyer flasks by adding 2 drops of 20 per cent potassium oxalate and drying at a moderate temperature. Just before use flush the flask out with pure CO_2 (not 5 per cent) and stopper. (Histopathology or microbiology department may have a cylinder of CO_2.) Draw 5 ml. of blood, rapidly transfer to the flask, and quickly restopper. Mix to dissolve the oxalate.

PROCEDURE. The determination should start 20 minutes after collection of the blood. This usually means setting up the dishes before going for the blood.

Prepare the Conway dishes by lightly greasing the top of the inner ring and placing a ring of petrolatum on the glass plate where it will fit the outer rim. It may help also to place two lines of petrolatum across the bottom of the outer chamber (at 6 and 12 o'clock) to prevent the carbonate and blood from mixing prematurely. Prepare four dishes for blanks and standards as well as two for each blood sample being analyzed.

Pipet approximately 1 ml. of boric acid solution into the inner well. Rinse by removing with a pipet, medicine dropper, or disposable Pasteur pipet and rubber bulb. Pipet a fresh 1 ml. into the well. Add one drop of indicator solution, holding the dropper vertical so that all drops will be the same size. In all dishes the solution should now have the same color. If not,

continue rinsing that dish until no color change occurs.

Pipet 1 ml. of saturated potassium carbonate solution into one side of the outer well of each dish. Cover two dishes and set aside as blanks.

Pipet 1 ml. of blood or standard, in duplicate, into the other side of the outer well of the remaining dishes (four dishes if one blood sample is being analyzed). (Blood should be pipetted 20 minutes after collection.)

Cover immediately with the greased glass.

After the cover is securely in place, carefully rotate the dish to mix alkali and blood without mixing the inner and outer wells.

Mark the time of mixing and the type of sample on the cover.

Let stand at room temperature for 20 minutes.

Before the time is up, fill the microburet with fresh 0.003 N HCl.

At the end of the 20 minutes titrate each center well. (Practice first until you can recognize the endpoint; set up a few standards and run them before trying a blood.)

Record the amount of HCl to titrate each dish.

CALCULATION. Subtract the average blank from each standard and unknown. ml. HCl $\times$ HCl factor $\times$ 4200 = mcg. per cent NH_3 N (ammonia nitrogen). (If the HCl is exactly 0.003 N, factor = 1.) The standard should come out 200 mg. per cent.

INTERPRETATION. Normal ammonia nitrogen by this procedure is 20 to 120 mcg. of ammonia nitrogen per 100 ml. of blood. It may be elevated in severe liver disease.

EXERCISE. Figure out why the multiplier in the calculation is 4200.

QUANTITATIVE DETERMINATION OF AMINO ACIDS IN URINE (BRAY, 1957)

The basicity of the amino groups of amino acids is destroyed by formaldehyde, and the carboxyl groups can then be titrated.

Reagents

1. Phosphotungstic acid, 10 per cent in 2 per cent HCl. To 20 gm. of reagent grade phosphotungstic acid add 185 ml. of water and 10 ml. of concentrated hydrochloric acid. Mix to dissolve.

2. Phenolphthalein, 0.5 per cent in alcohol.

3. Barium hydroxide, solid.

4. Hydrochloric acid, 0.1 N (see p. 399).

5. Sodium hydroxide, 0.1 N (see p. 399).

6. Neutralized formalin. To formalin add a couple of drops of phenolphthalein solution and sufficient 0.1 N sodium hydroxide to produce a faint pink.

PROCEDURE. Dilute the 24-hour urine to 2000 ml.

Measure 200 ml. into a 500 ml. flask.

Add 200 ml. of 10 per cent phosphotungstic acid. Mix.

Let stand three hours or overnight.

Pour off 250 ml. of clear supernatant into another flask.

Add 1 ml. of 0.5 per cent phenolphthalein.

Add solid barium hydroxide until decidedly pink.

Let stand one hour and filter.

Measure duplicate 100 ml. portions into 250 ml. Erlenmeyer flasks.

Add 0.1 N hydrochloric acid until barely pink.

Add 20 ml. of neutralized formalin.

Titrate with 0.1 N sodium hydroxide until pink again.

For a blank add 20 ml. of neutralized formalin to 100 ml. of water and titrate to phenolphthalein end point with 0.1 N NaOH.

CALCULATION. Subtract blank from average of urine titrations.

ml. 0.1 N NaOH $\times$ 0.056 = gm. amino acid nitrogen per 24 hours.

INTERPRETATION. Normal excretion is 0.10 to 0.29 gm. per 24 hours. Excretion is increased in liver impairment (including Wilson's disease), gout, pneumonia, leukemia, and other diseases involving tissue destruction and in the "inborn errors" of amino acid metabolism.

QUALITATIVE DETECTION OF CYSTINE IN URINE

Cystine is reduced by cyanide to cysteine, which reacts with nitroprusside to produce a red color.

Reagents

1. Sodium cyanide, 5 per cent. Dissolve 1 gm. of NaCN in water (caution: poisonous). Should be fresh.

2. Sodium nitroprusside, 5 per cent. Dissolve 1 gm. of sodium nitroprusside (nitroferricyanide) in 20 ml. of water. Prepare fresh.

PROCEDURE. To 5 ml. of urine add 2 ml. of 5 per cent sodium cyanide (do not pipet by mouth). Mix.

Let stand ten minutes.

Add 5 drops of fresh 5 per cent sodium nitroprusside. Mix.

Normal urines show a pale brown or occasionally faint flesh color, and with cystinuric urines a rather stable magenta color is obtained.

The urine must be free of protein. If necessary, add a little acetic acid, heat to boiling, and filter.

REFERENCES

1. Amatuzio, D. S., Stutzman, F. L., Vanderbilt, M. J., and Nesbitt, S.: Interpretation of the rapid intravenous glucose tolerance test in normal individuals and in mild diabetes mellitus. J. Clin. Invest., 32:428–435, 1953.
2. Barker, S. B.: The direct colorimetric determination of urea in blood and urine. J. Biol. Chem., 152:453–463, 1944.
3. Bonsnes, R. W., and Tausky, H. H.: On the colorimetric determination of creatinine by the Jaffe reaction. J. Biol. Chem., 158:581–591, 1945.
4. Bowman, R. O., Gast, J. H., and Moreland, F. B.: Zone electrophoresis of serum or plasma. Recommended Biochemical Procedures for Hospital Laboratories, 1954, p. E-4.
5. Bracken, J. S., and Klotz, I. M.: A simple method for the rapid determination of serum albumin. Am. J. Clin. Path., 23:1055–1058, 1953.
6. Bray, W. E.: Amino acids in urine. In Clinical Laboratory Methods. 5th Ed. St. Louis, The C. V. Mosby Company, 1957, p. 77.
7. Caraway, W. T.: Determination of uric acid in serum by a carbonate method. Am. J. Clin. Path., 25:840–845, 1955.
8. Chiamori, N., and Henry, R. J.: Study of the ferric chloride method for determination of total cholesterol and cholesterol esters. Am. J. Clin. Path., 31:305–309, 1959.
9. Crawford, N.: An improved method for the determination of free and total cholesterol using the ferric chloride reaction. Clin. Chim. Acta., 3:357–367, 1958.
10. Daughaday, W. H., Lowry, O. H., Rosebrough, N. J., and Fields, W. S.: Determination of cerebrospinal fluid protein with the Folin phenol reagent. J. Lab. Clin. Med., 39:663–665, 1952.
11. Demole, M. J., and Howard, E. M.: Use of the Nile blue reaction in diagnosis of steatorrhea. Am. J. Dig. Dis., 3:549–556, 1958.
12. Denis, W., and Ayer, J. B.: A method for the quantitative determination of protein in cerebrospinal fluid. Arch. Int. Med., 26:436–442, 1920.
13. Ducci, H.: The thymol test of Maclagan. J. Lab. Clin. Med., 32:1266–1272, 1947.
14. Ehrmantraut, H. C.: The clinical significance of paper electrophoresis. Joint meeting of Pacific Northwest Society of Pathologists and the Northwest Region, College of American Pathologists, May, 1958.
15. Faulkner, W. R., and Britton, R. C.: The determination of blood ammonium by a modification of the Conway technic. Cleveland Clin. Quarterly, 27:202–214, 1960.
16. Folin, O.: Unlaked blood as a basis for blood analysis. J. Biol. Chem., 86:173–178, 1930.
17. Folin, O., and Denis, W.: The quantitative determination of albumin in urine. J. Biol. Chem., 18:273–276, 1914.
18. Folin, O., and Wu, H.: A system of blood analysis. J. Biol. Chem., 38:81–110, 1919.

19. Gibson, Q. H., and Harrison, D. C.: An artificial standard for use in estimation of hemoglobin. Biochem. J., *39:*490–497, 1945.

20. Goiffon, R.: Arch. mal. app. dig. *38:*559, 1949; described by Demole and Howard.[11]

21. Haden, R. L.: A modification of the Folin-Wu method for making protein-free blood filtrates. J. Biol. Chem., *56:*469–471, 1923.

22. Henry, R. J., Sobel, C., and Kim, J.: A modified carbonate-phosphotungstate method for the determination of uric acid and comparison with the spectrophotometric uricase method. Am. J. Clin. Path., *28:*152–160, 1957.

23. Hoffman, W. S.: Glucose tolerance tests. In the Biochemistry of Clinical Medicine. 2nd Ed. Chicago, Year Book Publishers, 1959, pp. 70–72.

24. Kabara, J. J.: The light insensitivity of the Liebermann-Burchard reaction during spectrophotometric determination of cholesterol. J. Lab. Clin. Med., *44:*246–249, 1954.

25. Kingsley, G. R.: The direct biuret method for the determination of serum proteins as applied to photoelectric and visual colorimetry. J. Lab. Clin. Med., *27:*840–845, 1942.

26. Kunkel, H. G., Ehrens, E. H., and Eisenmenger, W. J.: Application of turbidimetric methods for estimation of gamma globulin and total lipid to the study of patients with liver disease. Gastroent., *11:*499–507, 1948.

27. Leffler, H. H.: Estimation of cholesterol in serum. Am. J. Clin. Path., *31:*310–313, 1959.

28. Lowry, O. H., Rosebrough, N. J., Farr, A. L., and Randall, R. J.: Protein measurement with the Folin phenol reagent. J. Biol. Chem., *193:*265–275, 1951.

29. McDermott, W. V., and Adams, R. D.: Episodic stupor associated with an Eck fistula in the human with particular reference to the metabolism of ammonia. J. Clin. Invest., *33:*1–9, 1954.

30. Menini, E., Falholt, W., and Lous, P.: Seromucoid and protein-bound hexoses in serum. I. Methods for their routine determination in the clinical laboratory. Acta med. scandinav., *160:*315–322, 1958.

31. Möller, E., McIntosh, J. F., and Van Slyke, D. D.: Studies of urea excretion. II. Relationship between urine volume and the rate of urea excretion by normal adults. J. Clin. Invest., *6:*427–465, 1928.

32. Moreland, F. B.: Letter to the editor. Clin. Chem., *6:*176–177, 1960.

33. Moreland, F. B., O'Donnell, W. W., and Gast, J. H.: Determination of total serum bilirubin. Fed. Proc., *9:*207, 1950.

34. Neufeld, O. E.: A rapid method for determining fecal fat. J. Clin. Path., *5:*288–289, 1952.

35. Ormsby, A. A.: A direct colorimetric method for the determination of urea in blood and urine. J. Biol. Chem., *146:*595–604, 1942.

36. Parfentjev, I. A., Johnson, M. L., and Cliffton, E. E.: The determination of plasma fibrinogen by turbidity with ammonium sulfate. Arch. Biochem. Biophys., *46:*470–480, 1953.

37. Peters, J. P., and Van Slyke, D. D.: Quantitative Clinical Chemistry. Vol. II. Methods. Baltimore, The Williams & Wilkins Co., 1932, pp. 230–232.

38. Reinhold, J. G.: Glucose. Standard Methods of Clinical Chemistry, *1:*65–70, 1953.

39. Reinhold, J. G.: Total protein, albumin, and globulin. Standard Methods of Clinical Chemistry, *1:*88–97, 1953.

40. Rice, E. W., and Lukasiewicz, D. B.: Interference of bromide in the Zak ferric chloride-sulfuric acid cholesterol method and means of eliminating this interference. Clin. Chem., *3:*160–162, 1957.

41. Scholander, P. F., Roughton, F. J. W., *et al.*: Microgasometric estimation of the blood gases. J. Biol. Chem., *148:*541–580, 1943; *169:*173–181, 1947.

42. Seligson, D.: An automatic pipetting device and its application in the clinical laboratory. Am. J. Clin. Path., *28:*200–207, 1957; Tech. Bull., *27:*152–159, 1957.

43. Stefanini, M., and Dameshek, W.: Screening test for detection of cryoglobulins. In the Hemorrhagic Disorders. New York, Grune & Stratton, Inc., 1955, pp. 244–245.

44. Sunderman, F. W., Jr., and Sunderman, F. W.: Clinical application of the fractionation of serum proteins by paper electrophoresis. Am. J. Clin. Path., *27:*125–158, 1957.

45. Svensmark, O.: Determination of protein in cerebrospinal fluid. A comment on the Lowry method. Scand. J. Clin. & Lab. Invest., *10:*50–52, 1958.

46. Traeger, H. S., Gabuzda, G. J., Jr., Ballou, A. N., and Davidson, C. S.: Blood "ammonia" concentration in liver disease, and liver coma. Metab., *3:*99–109, 1954.

47. Van Slyke, D. D., and Hawkins, J. A.: A gasometric method for determination of reducing sugars, and its application to analysis of blood and urine. J. Biol. Chem., *79:*739–767, 1928.

Chapter 9

Water and Electrolytes

By HARRY F. WEISBERG, M.D.

Describing electrolyte concentrations in the blood and other body tissues in terms of milligrams per 100 ml. is not adequate for the proper understanding of the balance of the positively charged and negatively charged electrolytes present in the body. Substances do not react with each other gram for gram or milligram for milligram but do react in proportion to their equivalent weights. The chemical definition of an *equivalent weight* of a substance is that weight which will displace or otherwise react with 1.008 gm. (1 gram-atomic weight) of hydrogen or combine with 8.00 gm. (½ gram-atomic weight) of oxygen. Since the concentrations of the various electrolytes in the body are extremely small, they are expressed in terms of milliequivalents; a milliequivalent is 1/1000 of an equivalent weight. When the various electrolytes are expressed in terms of milliequivalents per liter, one can see a balance that cannot be seen when values are expressed in milligrams per 100 ml. This is seen in Table 9–1, which compares representative concentrations of serum or plasma electrolytes expressed as milligrams per 100 ml. and as milliequivalents per liter.

Electrolytes are usually determined in serum or plasma rather than in whole blood, since there is an unequal distribution of electrolytes between the serum component of the blood and the red blood cells. Any anemia or change in hematocrit reading will cause an alteration when the electrolytes in whole blood are determined, whereas the determination of the electrolyte in serum or plasma will remain constant

no matter what the actual red blood cell count.

Table 9–2 lists the various electrolytes in normal serum or plasma and the various data necessary to convert milligrams per 100 ml. to milliequivalents per liter; in addition the normal ranges are expressed in both forms in the table.

An *anion* is a negatively charged ion that migrates to the positively charged electrode (anode) when an electric current is passed through an aqueous solution containing an electrolyte, e.g., sodium chloride.

Table 9–1. Representative Concentrations of Serum or Plasma Electrolytes*

| | EXPRESSED AS: | |
ELECTROLYTE	MG./100 ML.	MEQ./L.
Cations:		
Sodium	326.0	142
Potassium	20.0	5
Calcium	10.0	5
Magnesium	2.4	2
Total cations	358.4	154
Anions:		
Bicarbonate	60.5†	27
Chloride	365.7	103
Phosphate	3.4	2
Sulfate	1.6	1
Organic acids	17.5	5
Proteinate	6500.0	16
Total anions	6948.7	154

* Slightly modified from Weisberg, H. F.: Water, Electrolyte and Acid-Base Balance. Baltimore, The Williams & Wilkins Company, 1953. Reproduced with permission of the publisher.

† Volumes (milliliters) of carbon dioxide per 100 ml.

Table 9–2. Normal Ranges of Venous Serum or Plasma Electrolytes and Data Necessary for Conversion of mg./100 ml. to mEq./L.*

ELECTROLYTE	CALCULATED AS:	CONVERSION FACTOR †	NORMAL RANGES	
			MG./100 ML.	MEQ./L.
Cations:				
Sodium	Na	0.435	310 –345	136 –150
Potassium	K	0.256	16 – 22	4.0– 5.6
Calcium	Ca	0.500	9 – 11	4.5– 5.5
Magnesium	Mg	0.833	1.6– 2.9	1.4– 2.4
Anions:				
Bicarbonate	CO_2 combining	0.450	55 – 65	25 – 29
	power		45 – 55‡	20 – 25‡
Chloride	Cl	0.282	348 –375	98 –106
	NaCl	0.171	573 –620	98 –106
Phosphate, inorganic	P	0.580	3 – 4	1.7– 2.3
			4 – 6§	2.3– 3.5§
Sulfate, inorganic	S	0.625	0.3– 2.0	0.2– 1.3
Organic acids	Lactic acid, etc.	—	14 – 28	4 – 8
Proteinate	Plasma proteins	2.43	6 – 8‖	14.6– 19.4

* Modified from Weisberg, H. F.: Water, Electrolyte and Acid-Base Balance. Baltimore, The Williams and Wilkins Company, 1953. Reproduced with permission of the publishers.

† Conversion factor × mg./100 ml. = mEq./L.

‡ For infants

§ For children

‖ Grams per 100 ml.

A *cation* is a positively charged ion that migrates to the negatively charged electrode (cathode) when the electric current is passed through a solution of sodium chloride. Sodium chloride in water will dissociate into sodium and chloride ions, and these ions—anions and cations—are intermingled in the solution.

The correct definition of an *acid*, both for the chemistry laboratory and for biology and medicine, is that substance which is able to give a proton (the proton-donor of Brønsted). A *base* is a substance capable of accepting a proton (proton-acceptor) to form an acid. The proton is the hydrogen ion, H^+, or the hydrated hydrogen ion, H_3O^+, called the hydronium ion. Thus, the cations, sodium, potassium, calcium, and magnesium, have positive charges and are neither base nor acid. However, the anions are "bases" in the sense that they can combine with a hydrogen ion (proton) to form an acid according to the concept of Brønsted. In describing the positively and negatively charged ions of blood, we can best speak of them as cations and anions. However, as will be seen later, when discussing acid-base balance, the terms acid and base can be used, provided there is an understanding of the Brønsted system of proton-donors and proton-acceptors.

CATIONS

Sodium

Dietary sodium is usually obtained as sodium chloride, the amount ingested varying according to the taste of the individual. Because of this the exact minimal daily requirement of sodium for man is not known. In the adult approximately 40 to 90 mEq. of sodium are excreted per liter of urine or an average of approximately 110 mEq. per 24 hours. In a young child the daily requirement for sodium is approximately 50 mEq. per day, and in infants of about one year the requirement is approximately 17 mEq. per day.

The daily exchange of sodium is about the same for infants and adults; the daily exchange for the adult is about 3 to 6 per cent of the total sodium contained in the body and about 4 per cent for a child. This exchange of sodium is brought about by the ingestion via the gastrointestinal tract and the loss via urinary excretion. Sodium is also lost via the sweat. In a fasting individual without any sodium intake the urinary loss of sodium will occur for the first two days and then drop to minimal values, provided no abnormal losses of water occur. When sodium is lost from the body, there is also a loss of extracellular water to maintain a normal osmotic equilibrium.

Various formulas have been devised to compute the sodium concentration in serum from the chloride and bicarbonate concentrations. Such formulas do not apply if there is any abnormal alteration of bicarbonate; they are worthless, especially with the introduction of flame spectrophotometry by which sodium determinations can be done very easily.

Contrary to the former belief that sodium is always extracellular and not found within the cells, it has been shown that sodium is present within the cells, the amount depending upon conditions existing in the extracellular compartment. Energy-producing reactions are believed to be necessary for the transfer of the sodium ion across the cell membrane. The amount of intracellular sodium is 10 to 35 mEq. per liter of cell water. Normal intracellular sodium is reported to be equal to about one-sixth to one-ninth of the total extracellular sodium or to about one-half to almost the entire amount of extracellular bicarbonate. In the adult there is about 1.09 gm. of sodium per kilogram (fat-free), and in the newborn the sodium content is 1.78 gm. per kilogram. The average man contains about 65 gm. of sodium in his body; about 38 gm. are extracellular, 21 gm. are in the bones, and about 6 gm. are found within the cells. The intracellular sodium acts as an additional buffer, protecting the pH of the extracellular fluid.

Undoubtedly the quickest method of determining sodium concentrations is with a flame photometer. The sodium of the blood is almost entirely in the plasma or serum fraction. The normal range for serum sodium is 136 to 150 mEq. per liter or approximately 310 to 345 mg. per 100 ml. The range of whole blood sodium is about 75 to 100 mEq. per liter or 170 to 225 mg. per 100 ml.

Method of Trinder (1951)

Principle. Serum is added to an alcoholic solution of magnesium uranyl acetate. Sodium is precipitated as sodium magnesium uranyl acetate, and the proteins are precipitated by ethyl alcohol. The precipitated proteins and precipitated sodium salts are removed by centrifuging, and the excess uranyl in the supernatant fluid is read against a blank that contains a known concentration of uranyl.

Reagents

a. Magnesium uranyl acetate solution.

Mix 8 gm. of uranyl acetate, $UO_2(C_2H_3O_2)_2 \cdot 2H_2O$, 30 gm. of magnesium acetate, $Mg(C_2H_3O_2)_2 \cdot 4H_2O$, and 30 ml. of glacial acetic acid with 150 ml. of water and heat to dissolve chemicals. Boil for two minutes, cool, dilute to 200 ml. with distilled water, and make up to 1 L. in a volumetric flask with absolute ethyl alcohol. Place solution in a glass-stoppered brown bottle, and add 1 ml. of 1 per cent sodium chloride solution. Mix and let stand for several days until the precipitated sodium magnesium uranyl acetate has settled out. Use the clear supernatant solution.

b. Potassium ferrocyanide, $K_4Fe(CN)_6 \cdot 3H_2O$, 20 per cent solution in water. Keep in a brown bottle.

c. Acetic acid, 1 per cent solution (v/v).

d. Standard sodium solution (200 mEq./L.). Dissolve 1.17 gm. of dry sodium chloride in distilled water and make up to 100 ml. volume in a volumetric flask.

Technique

1. Pipet 5 ml. of the magnesium uranyl acetate reagent into centrifuge tubes: one tube for the blank, one tube for a standard, and one tube for each unknown.

2. For each unknown add 0.1 ml. of serum, using a "to contain" washout pipet, and agitate the solution vigorously by blowing through the pipet.

3. To the "blank" centrifuge tube add 0.1 ml. of distilled water.

4. Stopper and let tubes stand for five minutes to allow formation of precipitate of the triple acetate salt.

5. Shake tubes vigorously for 30 seconds and centrifuge for one minute.

6. Into 100 ml. volumetric flasks add 2 ml. of the supernatant fluid, and then add about 80 ml. of 1 per cent acetic acid solution and 2 ml. of the 20 per cent potassium ferrocyanide solution, filling to the mark with 1 per cent acetic acid.

7. Mix and read in a colorimeter within the next ten minutes using a transmission of 480 millimicrons.

8. For this determination the unknown is used to set the colorimeter at 100 per cent transmission or zero optical density, and the blank is then read to determine the concentration of each tube containing sodium.

9. Preparation of standard curve. Using the 250 mEq. per liter standard sodium solution, prepare a series of dilutions so that each will contain 50, 100, 150, 200, and 250 mEq. of sodium per liter of solu-

tion. Treat 0.1 ml. of each of these in the same way as the unknown. When carrying out tests of unknowns, prepare a check standard solution using 0.1 ml. of the 150 mEq. per liter standard sodium solution.

METHOD OF TALBOTT AND KING (1952)

This bedside screening procedure is intended primarily for urine but can also be used for serum and other biologic fluids.

Principle. The test is based upon the standard procedure of chemical analysis with uranyl acetate.

Reagents
  a. In a weighed 1 L. beaker place 40 gm. of reagent grade uranyl acetate, 24 gm. of 30 per cent acetic acid, and enough water to make a total weight of 260 gm. contained in the beaker.
  b. A similar beaker is filled to the same weight of 260 gm. by adding 110 gm. of zinc acetate, 12 gm. of 30 per cent acetic acid, and distilled water to make up the rest.

Both beakers are heated separately on a steam bath and are covered with watch glasses to prevent evaporation; the contents are stirred frequently. Heating is continued for two to three hours until the solution is nearly complete. The hot liquids are then placed in a 1 L. beaker, cooled, placed in a dark bottle, and filtered before use.

Technique
  1. In a small, clean test tube place 1 drop of the sample to be tested. Rinse dropper well with distilled water before reusing.
  2. Using the same dropper, add 8 drops of the reagent and mix gently.
  3. Read in eight minutes.
  4. Classify the test as negative through 5+, depending upon the rapidity of fall of the particles; the amount, size, and density of the particles; the amount of precipitate rimming the tube above the fluid line; and the heaviness of the precipitate or white-colored solution.
  5. Standards should be made using sodium chloride to correspond to the ranges of 1+ through 5+. A 1+ is a range of 0 to 45 mEq., 2+ equals 45 to 90, 3+ equals 90 to 149, 4+ equals 149 to 267, and 5+ equals 267 to over 445 mEq.

Comments. False readings may result when urine is tested for the sodium content. Solutions may become turbid after the reaction owing to a soft, cloudy filtrate apparently composed of acid urates. The test should be repeated with a drop of urine that has been heated and the reagent added prior to cooling.

If albuminuria prevents accurate interpretation of the test, the urine should be mixed with sulfosalicylic acid and filtered before use in the test.

Complete reaction requires from six to ten minutes, and therefore the sodium concentration is read at eight minutes. For a screening test, however, it may be sufficient to read at three or four minutes, especially when comparing with standard sodium chloride solutions as controls.

Potassium

On a normal average diet there is no deficiency of potassium, since this element is found in practically all foodstuffs. The adult takes in about 60 mEq. of potassium per 24 hours; the exact minimal daily requirement of potassium for man is not known. Normally about 80 to 90 per cent of the potassium is excreted in the urine; the remainder is excreted in the feces and to a small extent in the sweat. In contrast to a fasting adult in whom sodium excretion will soon decrease, the excretion of potassium continues while the adult is fasting or on a diet adequate in calories but potassium-free. About 40 to 50 mEq. of potassium are lost per day in the urine; this daily loss is more important in children. The daily exchange of potassium in the adult is 1 to 2 per cent of the total body potassium content, whereas in a one-year-old child the exchange is 14 per cent of the total body potassium.

Potassium is the major cation found inside cells. The body content of potassium in the adult is 2.65 gm. per kilogram (fat-free) and 1.90 gm. per kilogram in the newborn.

The normal range of potassium concentration in the serum or plasma is 4.0 to 5.6 mEq. per liter or about 16 to 22 mg. per 100 ml. Most of the potassium in the blood is contained in the red blood cells, and since this can vary with hematocrit it is preferable to determine serum or plasma potassium levels. Whole blood potassium ranges from about 38 to 64 mEq. per liter or 150 to 250 mg. per 100 ml. Since the red blood cells contain so much more potassium than does the serum, it is essential to avoid hemolysis in obtaining the specimen; diffusion of potassium out of the red cells should be avoided by determining the potassium as soon as possible.

METHOD OF JACOBS AND HOFFMAN (1931)
(MODIFIED BY BARRY AND ROWLAND, 1953)

Principle. The potassium is precipitated directly from the serum as a potassium-sodium cobaltinitrite salt, $K_2NaCo(NO_2)_6 \cdot H_2O$. After suitable washing the amount of cobalt in the precipitate is determined colorimetrically, using the green color produced after the addition of choline chloride by the action of sodium ferrocyanide. A standard potassium solution may be treated similarly, or a cobalt solution already standardized against a known potassium solution may be used directly.

Reagents
a. Sodium cobaltinitrite reagent:
Solution A: Dissolve 25 gm. of cobaltous nitrate, $Co(NO_3)_2 \cdot 6H_2O$, in 280 ml. of water, and then add 12.5 ml. of glacial acetic acid and about 10 mg. of potassium chloride. *Solution B:* Dissolve 120 gm. of sodium nitrite in 180 ml. of water. Approximately 220 ml. of solution will be obtained.
Add 210 ml. of solution B to all of solution A. Draw air through the mixture until all the nitrous fumes have been removed; this may require a few hours. Store the reagent in a refrigerator at 0° C. and filter before using. The reagent will keep for approximately one month. Before using it, allow to attain room temperature and shake to insure saturation at the higher temperature before filtering.
b. Choline chloride: Stock 10 per cent (w/v) aqueous solution, which is stored in the cold. Just before use this is diluted to prepare a 1 per cent solution that is utilized in the procedure.
c. Ethyl alcohol, 35 per cent (v/v) solution.
d. Ethyl alcohol, 70 per cent (v/v) solution.
e. Sodium ferrocyanide, 2 per cent aqueous solution. Dissolve 2 gm. of $Na_4Fe(CN)_6 \cdot 10H_2O$ in distilled water and dilute to 100 ml. Store in the dark. Do not use if a precipitate forms.
f. Standard potassium solution (10 mg./ml.). Dissolve 2.228 gm. of pure dry potassium sulfate in water and make up to 100 ml. The working standard solution (20 mg./100 ml. or 0.2 mg./ml.) is made by diluting 2 ml. of the stock standard to 100 ml. with distilled water.
g. Standard cobalt solution. Dissolve 0.506 gm. of cobalt ammonium sulfate in water and make up to 1 liter. This salt is preferred to cobaltous nitrate or cobaltous sulfate, both of which are hygroscopic. The cobalt solution is equivalent to 0.1 mg. of potassium per milliliter. It should be standardized against the working standard potassium solution (0.2 mg. per milliliter) by performing the test as described. Once standardized, the cobalt solution keeps well.

Technique
1. Pipet 1 ml. of serum into a centrifuge tube graduated at 6 ml.
2. Add 3 ml. of the cobaltinitrite reagent from a pipet by blowing out rapidly to aid mixing. Immediately complete mixing by rotating the tube between the palms of the hands. (A stirring rod should not be used.)
3. The mixture is allowed to stand for two hours at a temperature of 15° C. or above.
4. Centrifuge for ten minutes at a moderate speed.
5. Remove the supernatant fluid by inverting the tube and allowing it to drain on a filter paper for a short time.
6. Wipe the mouth of the tube and add 5 ml. of 35 per cent aqueous ethyl alcohol, washing down the sides of the tube.
7. Mix the precipitate with a glass rod.
8. Recentrifuge for five minutes, and again invert the tube and drain off the supernatant.
9. Tube and precipitate are washed two more times with 5 ml. portions of 70 per cent aqueous ethyl alcohol in the same fashion.
10. Add 3 ml. of distilled water to the tube, mix with the stirring rod, and heat the tube in a boiling water bath until the precipitate has dissolved.
11. Allow to cool and add 1 ml. of 1 per cent choline chloride solution; mix thoroughly.
12. Then add 1 ml. of a freshly prepared 2 per cent solution of potassium ferrocyanide.

13. Dilute to the 6 ml. mark with distilled water and mix well.

14. A cobalt standard should be treated in the same way, diluting 2 ml. of the cobalt standard to 6 ml. as in step 13.

15. If necessary, centrifuge to remove the slight cloudiness caused by the small amount of protein present.

16. The color will fade slowly and so should be measured within 30 minutes at a wave length of 600 millimicrons, using a reagent blank set at 100 per cent transmission.

17. Standard potassium solutions containing 15, 20, 25, and 30 mg. of potassium per 100 ml. treated in the same way as serum will give a standard curve covering the values of serum potassium usually found.

Comments. The modification of Barry and Rowland (1953) has eliminated many of the inaccuracies of the original Kramer and Tisdall (1921) method. These were dilution of the serum with water, insufficient time for the precipitation, and solution of some of the precipitate during washing. In addition the possibility of incomplete precipitation owing to the solubility of potassium sodium cobaltinitrite in the precipitating reagent has been overcome by saturating the latter with this substance. Rapid addition of the cobaltinitrite reagent is used instead of dropwise addition to insure the same sodium-potassium ratio before precipitation begins. If the temperature of precipitation of serum is within 3° C. of the temperature at which the standard curve was prepared, the curve may be used repeatedly. However, it is a wise precaution to run a standard with each set of determinations.

The centrifuge tubes must be cleaned to be sure that all traces of potassium ferrocyanide are removed; they should be left in cleaning solution made of chromate in sulfuric acid, rinsed thoroughly in water, heated for one-half hour in boiling distilled water, and finally rinsed again in distilled water.

Ammonium salts interfere since ammonium cobaltinitrite is also very insoluble. Therefore, any contamination with ammonium salts should be avoided, and the estimation should be done on fresh serum and not on serum that may have stood for some time and become contaminated with bacteria.

METHOD OF KEITEL AND KEITEL (1953)

Principle. This simple rapid turbidimetric method depends upon the formation of a potassium sodium cobaltinitrite precipitate.

Reagents

a. Potassium standard (3 mEq./L.). Dissolve 0.224 gm. of potassium chloride and 8.12 gm. of sodium chloride and dilute to 1 liter.

b. Potassium standard (5 mEq./L.). Dissolve 0.373 gm. of potassium chloride and 8.12 gm. of sodium chloride and dilute to 1 liter.

c. Sodium cobaltinitrite solution (15 per cent). Dissolve 15 gm. of reagent grade $Na_3Co(NO_2)_6$ and dilute to 100 ml. with distilled water.

Technique

Special equipment needed for this procedure is Sahli hemoglobin pipets calibrated at 0.01 and 0.02 ml., microscope culture slides (depression slides), pieces of black paper or overexposed x-ray film, and rubber tip glass stirring rods.

1. Transfer 0.02 ml. of unhemolyzed blood to each of the two depressions on one of the culture slides.

2. Transfer 0.02 ml. of each of the 3 mEq. per liter and 5 mEq. per liter standard potassium solutions to the depressions of the second slide.

3. Add 0.01 ml. of the sodium cobaltinitrite reagent to each of the specimens in the following order: (1) to an unknown, (2) to the 3 mEq. per liter standard, (3) to the 5 mEq. per liter standard, and (4) to the duplicate unknown.

4. Each sample is then mixed thoroughly for five seconds with a rubber tip stirring rod, using a rapid circular motion, the rod being wiped dry between stirrings. Note: Rapid, complete mixing of the solutions is essential to insure an even distribution of the precipitate.

5. Place the test slide on a glossy black x-ray film, and compare the intensity of the precipitate formed by the standard solutions with the unknowns. The precipitate is best seen when light is directed across the slide.

Comments. The 5 mEq. per liter standard potassium solution develops a diffuse, whitish-yellow, cloudy precipitate within 10 seconds, but the 3 mEq. per liter standard solution remains clear for about 20 seconds and then slowly develops a faint white precipitate around the periphery. At low temperatures the sodium potassium cobaltinitrite precipitate forms sooner and is more pronounced than it is at higher temperatures. The temperatures of the standard and the unknowns must be the same. The readings can often be completed within 30 seconds and must be made within about five minutes. Classification of the unknowns is made as follows: (1) if the precipitate contains less than that found in the 3 mEq. per liter standard, (2) if the precipitate is about the same as the 3 mEq. per liter standard, (3) if the precipitate is an amount intermediate between the 3 mEq. per liter and 5 mEq. per liter standards, (4) if the precipitate is about the same as the 5 mEq. per liter standard, and (5) if the precipitate is greater than the 5 mEq. per liter standard.

Grossly lipemic serum cannot be used unless it is cleared by shaking 4 parts of ethyl ether with 1 part of serum for one minute and centrifuging. The supernatant ether and fatty plasma layer are removed, and the remaining plasma is then used for the potassium determination. Both standard potassium solutions should be run each time a test is done; if a distinct difference is not present, either a fresh lot of the cobaltinitrite reagent should be made or the standards checked. Do not read the unknown if either it or the standards contain a localized precipitation of the cobaltinitrite salt. The test slides should be kept scrupulously clean and free of abrasions so that the fine sodium-potassium cobaltinitrite precipitate is evenly distributed and can be clearly identified. Contamination of serum with red or white cells will give a falsely high value. When doing a determination of potassium in urine, the urine should be diluted 1:20.

Calcium

The requirement for calcium varies from individual to individual and even in the same individual at various times. Factors that regulate the absorption and retention of calcium in normal individuals are: normal gastric acidity to allow for the absorption of soluble calcium salts, adequate supply of vitamin D to aid in absorption of calcium, normal fat digestion, a proper ratio of calcium and phosphorus in the diet, and a large enough intake to allow for precipitation of insoluble calcium salts in the intestine.

The urinary excretion of calcium accounts for 20 per cent of the calcium excreted and is influenced by the calcium intake, skeletal size, kidney regulation of anions and cations, and various endocrine factors. Approximately 80 per cent of the calcium excreted is via the feces as insoluble salts. An adult will be in calcium equilibrium when the intake is 10 mg. per kilogram of body weight. An ample intake of calcium for an adult will be provided by two to three glasses of milk per day. Calcium is never absorbed completely from the gastrointestinal tract; calcium is also present in the gastrointestinal juices secreted into the gut. These juices contain 5 to 10 mg. of calcium per 100 ml. and therefore serve as an important factor in the reabsorption of calcium and in the adjustment of cell permeability. About 99 per cent of the body calcium is situated in the bones and teeth; the remainder is presumably present in the extracellular fluid and not within the cells. It is very probable, however, that small amounts of calcium are present within tissue cells outside the skeletal system. The body content of calcium in the adult is 20.1 gm. per kilogram (fat-free) and 9.2 gm. per kilogram in the newborn.

Recently several methods have been described, utilizing flame photometry to determine the calcium concentration in the blood. Some instruments require organic solvents to intensify the calcium emission line; other instruments, such as the Coleman flame photometer, have been utilized to determine calcium directly, using a rather low temperature flame. All the calcium in the blood is present in the plasma. The normal range for total serum or plasma calcium is between 9 and 11 mg. per 100 ml. or 4.5 to 5.5 mEq. per liter. In infants, especially prematures, with adequate intake of vitamin D the serum level of calcium may be as high as 12 to 13 mg. per 100 ml. The calcium present in serum is found in three major fractions: a portion bound to protein, a portion that is ionized, and an un-ionized, diffusible complex of calcium citrate. This aspect of calcium metabolism is discussed further under ionized calcium.

METHOD OF CLARK AND COLLIP (1925) (MODIFICATION OF KRAMER AND TISDALL, 1921)

Principle. The calcium of blood serum is precipitated as calcium oxalate. The precipitated calcium oxalate is washed free of excess oxalate, and the precipitate is then converted to oxalic acid, which is titrated with a standard potassium permanganate solution. One milliliter of 0.01 N potassium permanganate is equivalent to 0.2 mg. of calcium.

Reagents

a. Ammonium oxalate, 4 per cent. Dissolve 4 gm. of ammonium oxalate in distilled water and dilute to 100 ml. Filter before using.

b. Sulfuric acid, 1 N. To a 1 L. volumetric flask partly filled with distilled water add with caution 30 ml. of concentrated sulfuric acid. Dilute to mark with distilled water. Mix well.

c. Ammonium hydroxide, 0.35 N. Dilute 2 ml. of concentrated ammonium hydroxide to 100 ml. with distilled water.

d. Ammonium hydroxide, 4 N. Dilute 22 ml. of concentrated ammonium hydroxide to 100 ml. with distilled water. This reagent is used in the determination of urine calcium.

e. Sodium oxalate, 0.1 N. Accurately weigh 6.701 gm. of pure, dry, reagent grade sodium oxalate. Transfer with 1 N sulfuric acid through a funnel into a 1 L. volumetric flask, cool, and dilute to mark with 1 N sulfuric acid. Mix thoroughly. This solution is stable for several months.

f. Sodium oxalate, 0.01 N. Pipet exactly 10 ml. of the 0.1 N sodium oxalate to a 100 ml. volumetric flask and dilute to mark with 1 N sulfuric acid. This solution is used for the standardization of the 0.01 N permanganate solution. Even though it is stable, it should be prepared weekly.

g. Potassium permanganate, 0.1 N stock solution. Dissolve 4.2 gm. of reagent grade potassium permanganate crystals in water. Dilute to 1100 ml. in a graduated cylinder (use a 1 L. cylinder plus 100 ml. of water). Allow to stand in the dark for two to three days to insure complete solution and stabilization. Filter through glass wool or with gentle suction through a 3-inch Buchner funnel lined with asbestos. Keep in refrigerator.

STANDARDIZATION OF STOCK PERMANGANATE. Pipet 25 ml. of 0.1 N sodium oxalate into a white, porcelain casserole. Add 1 ml. of concentrated sulfuric acid. Warm to about 70° C. and titrate with the permanganate solution just described in the buret. The first permanent pink is the end point. Let T equal the milliliters of permanganate needed to titrate 25 ml. of 0.1 N sodium oxalate. To a 1 L. volumetric flask add 40 (25–T) ml. of water and dilute to the mark with permanganate solution. This is exactly 0.1 N permanganate.

Titrate again for accuracy. Store in a brown bottle in the dark.

h. Potassium permanganate, 0.01 N. Pipet exactly 10 ml. of the 0.1 N potassium permanganate into a 100 ml. volumetric flask. Dilute to the mark with distilled water and mix. This solution changes its strength with dilution and on standing; it should be titrated each time before a calcium determination is done.

STANDARDIZATION. A 2 ml. buret graduated to 0.01 or 0.02 ml. should be used. Pipet 2 ml. of 0.01 N sodium oxalate into a heavy duty centrifuge tube. Heat in boiling water for one minute. Titrate with a 0.01 N permanganate solution to the first pink color (against a white background; look through the end of the tube rather than the side when determining the endpoint). Place back in boiling water to make sure the solution is hot when nearing the end point. Use the following formula, when calculating the correction factor, to correct for the variation in strength of the potassium permanganate:

$$F = \frac{2}{\text{ml. of permanganate used}}$$

The titration should require 1.9 to 2.1 ml. of permanganate; if not, make up fresh 0.01 N potassium permanganate.

i. Phenol red solution, approximately 0.04 per cent in water. This solution is used in the determination of urine calcium.

j. Acetic acid, 10 per cent. Dilute 10 ml. of glacial acetic acid to 100 ml. with distilled water. This reagent is used in the determination of urinary calcium.

Technique

1. To a heavy duty centrifuge tube with a sharp conical point, which has been cleaned recently in chromate cleaning solution and dried after thorough rinsing in distilled water, add 2 ml. of distilled water, 2 ml. of serum, and 1 ml. of ammonium oxalate solution, which has been filtered just before use.

2. Mix well by tapping and allow to stand at least one hour (preferably overnight to insure complete precipitation of the calcium as the oxalate salt).

3. Centrifuge thoroughly to pack the precipitate at the bottom of the centrifuge tube.

4. Carefully decant the supernatant fluid without losing any of the precipitate. Allow the tube to drain for five or ten minutes inverted on a pad of filter paper. Then carefully dry the mouth of the tube with a soft cloth or with dry filter paper.

5. Add 1 drop of 0.35 N ammonium hydroxide solution and tap the end of the tube to break up the precipitate. Then pipet 3 ml. of this ammonium hydroxide solution, allowing to drain down the side of the tube while rotating the tube, thus washing down all the oxalate.

6. Repeat centrifugation, washing, and draining as before.

7. Repeat the centrifugation, washing, and draining.

8. Add 1 drop of 1 N sulfuric acid and tap the end of the tube to break up the precipitate. Then add 2 ml. of 1 N sulfuric acid, washing down the sides of the tube. Note: If a stirring rod has been used, be sure to wash it down as well.

9. Place the tube in a boiling water bath for exactly one minute.

10. Titrate the unknown solution with the 0.01 N permanganate to a faint pink end point that is comparable in color and time of disappearance to that obtained when the permanganate was standardized. Place back in water bath as with the standard to make sure that the end point is reached while the solution is hot.

Calculations. One milliliter of 0.01 N sodium oxalate solution (or of 0.01 N potassium permanganate solution) is equivalent to 0.2 mg. of calcium, as shown in the following formulas.

$$1 \text{ ml.} \times 0.01 \text{ N} = 0.01 \text{ mEq.}$$

$$\frac{0.01 \text{ mEq.} \times 40 \text{ (atomic weight of calcium)}}{2 \text{ (valence of calcium)}}$$
$$= 0.2 \text{ mg. of calcium}$$

$$0.2 \times \text{ml. of permanganate (0.01 N)} \times \frac{100}{2}$$
$$= \text{mg. of calcium per 100 ml. of serum}$$

or

$10 \times$ ml. of permanganate used $\times$ F = mg. of calcium per 100 ml. of serum.

In the determination of calcium in urine, pipet exactly 1 to 5 ml. of urine, depending upon the expected calcium content, into a centrifuge tube. Add 1 drop of phenol red indicator, and then add 4 N ammonium hydroxide drop by drop until the indicator is pink. Immediately add 10 per cent acetic acid drop by drop until the indicator just turns yellow. Add 1 ml. of 4 per cent ammonium oxalate solution, mix well, and allow to stand for one to two hours at room temperature. Then proceed with the centrifuging and washing as in the serum calcium but wash the precipitate an additional two times.

METHOD OF FERRO AND HAM (1957)

Principle. Calcium is precipitated as the insoluble salt of chloranilic acid. It is washed free of excess chloranilic acid, using isopropyl alcohol. The precipitate of calcium chloranilate is then dissolved in the tetrasodium salt of ethylenediamine-tetra-acetic acid. The resulting pink solution is compared photometrically against similarly prepared standards and blanks.

Reagents

a. Chloranilic acid, 1 per cent. Dissolve 1 gm. of chloranilic acid in 50 ml. of distilled water containing 7 ml. of 1 N sodium hydroxide. Mix and dilute to 100 ml. with distilled water. The pH of the solution should be between 3.5 and 11; if the pH is higher than 11, additional 0.1 gm. quantities of chloranilic acid are added to reduce the pH below 11. Filter through a Buchner funnel containing a fine pad, such as Seitz No. S1. The solution is stable at room temperature for three to four months and at refrigerator temperature for about one year. If crystals separate on refrigeration, use the clear supernatant or allow the solution to warm to room temperature and shake to dissolve the crystals; allow any excess crystals to settle for a few minutes and then use the supernatant solution.

b. Ethylenediaminetetra-acetic acid, tetrasodium salt, 5 per cent. Dissolve 5 gm. of tetrasodium ethylenediaminetetra-acetate (EDTA) in 100 ml. of distilled water, bringing to mark in a volumetric flask.

c. Isopropyl alcohol, 50 per cent. Dilute 50 ml. of reagent grade isopropyl alcohol to 100 ml. with distilled water.

d. Calcium standard (1 ml. = 0.1 mg. calcium). Weigh exactly 0.2497 gm. of reagent grade calcium carbonate (Iceland spar). Wash into a 1 L. volumetric flask; gradually add 10 ml. of 1 N hydrochloric acid, using it to rinse down the sides of the flask. When solution is complete, dilute to volume with distilled water and mix thoroughly.

Technique

1. Into 12 ml. heavy duty, conical, Pyrex test tubes, which have been thoroughly cleaned with sulfuric acid-chromic acid cleaning solution, add the following reagents: Into the tube containing the unknown pipet 2 ml. of serum. Into the tube containing the standard pipet 2 ml. of the standard calcium solution. Add 2 ml. of water to the tube serving as a blank.

2. To each of the tubes add 1 ml. of

the chloranilic acid reagent. The tubes containing protein should be constantly agitated by twirling to redissolve any precipitated protein.

3. Allow the tubes to stand at room temperature for at least 30 minutes.

4. Centrifuge at approximately 1800 r.p.m. for ten minutes.

5. Decant the supernatant and allow the tubes to drain for two to three minutes on some absorbent paper, such as filter paper. Note: An angle centrifuge does not firmly pack the precipitate that may be lost when the tube is inverted to drain; therefore, a centrifuge with free-swinging trunion cups should be used in order to obtain a tightly packed button of precipitate.

6. Wipe the lip of the tube free of the last drop.

7. Blow in 5 ml. of the 50 per cent isopropyl alcohol to break up the precipitate. The precipitate should be broken up and resuspended in this reagent. Mix the solution.

8. Centrifuge, decant, and drain as before. Note: The supernatant may be cloudy owing to the presence of a small amount of protein; this will not affect the results.

9. Add 2 drops of distilled water to each tube with the packed precipitates. After allowing to stand one minute, gently tap the tube to break up the button of precipitate. This can be done by striking the bottom of the tube sharply against the palm of the hand until the mat breaks loose and the precipitate is suspended in the water. If necessary, use a small glass rod to break up the precipitate.

10. Add 5 ml. of the sodium EDTA to each tube.

11. Stopper tubes and invert several times until the precipitate is completely dissolved. Avoid vigorous shaking; if shaking is necessary, allow the foam to settle before reading in photometer.

12. Using the reagent blank to set the photometer at 100 per cent transmission and utilizing a wave length of 520 millimicrons, read the tubes within five minutes after complete clearing.

Calculations. Compute the value of calcium by comparing the standard curve prepared by various dilutions of the standard calcium solution; or the values can be calculated by reading the density of the unknown, dividing by the density of the standard, and multiplying by 10.

Comments. A semimicro procedure, utilizing the Ferro and Ham technique, can be performed by using 0.5 ml. of serum with 0.25 ml. of the chloranilic acid and finally suspending the precipitate in 1.1 ml. of the EDTA reagent. This volume is sufficient to fill a Coleman Jr. 10 × 75 mm. cuvet.

IONIZED CALCIUM

It has been assumed that about one-half the total calcium of the serum is bound to protein and is therefore physiologically inactive. The remaining half is composed primarily of ionized calcium and an un-ionized citrate complex. Only the ionized calcium is involved in the control of muscle irritability. McLean and Hastings (1935) were able to determine the ionized calcium, utilizing a biologic assay technique. They reported the range of normal ionized calcium as 4.25 to 5.25 mg. per 100 ml. or 2.1 to 2.6 mEq. per liter. They have constructed a nomogram from which the amount of ionized calcium present can be determined if the total calcium and the total protein are known. Previously Greenwald (1931) had proposed a formula in which 0.87 mg. of calcium was considered to be bound to each gram of protein present. Thus, the ionized calcium was equal to the total calcium minus (0.87 × total protein expressed as grams per 100 ml.).

More recently Nordin and Fraser (1956) have reported that only about one-third of the calcium is bound to protein rather than one-half. Their formula for the portion bound to protein is: protein-bound calcium equals (7.6 × albumin) plus (2.9 × globulin) minus 3.1. Thus, the protein-bound calcium is expressed as per cent of total calcium, and the albumin and globulin are expressed as grams per 100 ml. of serum. For example, if a serum contains 10.8 mg. of total calcium per 100 ml., 4.6 gm. per cent of albumin, and 2.1 gm. per cent of globulin, then the protein-bound calcium is equal to (7.6 × 4.6) + (2.9 × 2.1) − 3.1, or 38 per cent. Therefore, 10.8 times 0.38 equals 4.1 mg. of calcium as protein-bound calcium per 100 ml. of serum and 6.7 mg. of diffusible calcium per 100 ml. of serum.

Because of the difficulty in using the McLean and Hastings nomogram, Zeisler (1954) devised a simple formula, which in normal ranges of total calcium and total protein expresses very well the concentration of ionized calcium. The formula is:

$$Ca^{++} = \frac{6\,Ca - \dfrac{P}{3}}{P + 6}$$ in which the total calcium is expressed as milligrams per 100 ml. and total protein as grams per 100 ml.

The ionized calcium, which is obtained from the formula, is also expressed as milligrams per 100 ml. Rose (1957) has described the determination of ionized and ultrafilterable calcium of normal human serum, utilizing a chemical method. This technique depends upon the ultrafiltration of plasma followed by the determination of ionized and total calcium in the ultrafiltrate. In order to obtain an ultrafiltrate of plasma, the carbon dioxide tension of the plasma must be kept constant and at the same tension as in the body fluid from which it came. It is necessary to assume that the act of ultrafiltration does not in itself alter the ionized calcium of the plasma. The actual values obtained by Rose for the total calcium in the ultrafiltrate are 6.05 to 6.35 mg. per 100 ml. These are higher than would be expected from the results of McLean and Hastings, who found ionized calcium of plasma to be 4.25 to 5.25 mg. per 100 ml. The nonionized ultrafilterable calcium (possibly a citrate complex) was 0.15 to 0.51 mg. per 100 ml.; this agrees very well with the value of McLean and Hastings, who reported the nonionized ultrafilterable calcium to be less than 0.6 mg. per 100 ml.

Toribara and co-workers (1957) have described a simple ultrafiltration apparatus, which can be obtained from the Will Corporation, Rochester, New York. The use of a large laboratory centrifuge is required in order to obtain the proper pressure for ultrafiltration. They report that at physiologic pH and temperature 60 to 70 per cent of the total serum calcium is found to be ultrafilterable. This correlates very well with the "biologically active" calcium described by Yendt et al. (1955). McLean and Hastings, utilizing the frog heart method, reported "ionic calcium" to be about 52 per cent of the total calcium. Toribara et al. have calculated the normal serum concentration of the complexes of calcium as citrate, phosphate, and bicarbonate to be 12 per cent of the total calcium. When this is added to the 52 per cent of the ionized calcium of McLean and Hastings, the value 64 per cent is again very close to the ultrafilterable calcium.

Magnesium

It is estimated that the magnesium requirement during the growth period is less than 10 mg. per day. Magnesium is so widespread in foods that a magnesium deficiency is rarely seen in individuals who are partaking of their normal food intake. Approximately 60 per cent of the dietary magnesium is excreted via the feces and 40 per cent via the urine. It is probable that the same factors that control calcium absorption also govern the absorption of magnesium. The intermediary metabolism of magnesium resembles that of phosphorus; both are present in bone and within tissue cells. The body content of magnesium in the adult is 0.36 gm. per kilogram (fat-free) and 0.27 gm. per kilogram in the newborn. Magnesium also governs neuromuscular irritability and is important for the coenzymes in the metabolism of carbohydrates and proteins.

Magnesium has also been analyzed by flame photometry but requires much more specialized apparatus because of the low concentration in the blood. The normal concentration is 1.4 to 2.4 mEq. per liter or approximately 1.6 to 2.9 mg. per 100 ml. Wacker and Vallee (1957) have utilized a multichannel flame photometer to obtain good results for the determination of magnesium. More recently Teloh (1958) and VanFossan and co-workers (1959) have also reported modifications of flame photometric techniques to determine magnesium.

METHOD OF NEILL AND NEELY (1956)
(MODIFICATION OF KUNKEL et al., 1947)

Principle. The blood serum or plasma proteins are precipitated by means of tungstic acid. An aqueous solution of titan yellow is added to the water-clear filtrate, and sodium hydroxide is added to develop the red magnesium hydroxide-titan yellow complex. Gum ghatti is used to stabilize the color lake. Since calcium intensifies the color of this titan yellow complex, calcium is added to the standard in order to compensate for the effect of the calcium in the serum.

Reagents

a. Gum ghatti, 0.1 per cent. Powdered gum ghatti, 0.1 gm., is suspended in a muslin bag in 100 ml. of distilled water for 24 hours. The solution does not deteriorate at room temperature. (Heagy [1948] reported that polyvinyl, 0.1 per cent, can be used in place of the gum ghatti solution.)

b. Titan yellow, 0.05 per cent. Dissolve 0.1 gm. of the powdered dye in 200 ml. of distilled water.

c. Sodium tungstate solution, 10 per cent.

d. Sodium hydroxide, 4 N solution.

e. Sulfuric acid, 0.67 N solution.

f. Stock standard magnesium chloride solution. Dissolve 8.458 gm. of magnesium chloride, $MgCl_2 \cdot 6H_2O$, in distilled water and dilute to 1 L. in a volumetric flask. This solution contains 1000 micrograms per milliliter or 1 mg. per milliliter.

g. Working standard magnesium chloride solution. Dilute 1 ml. of the stock standard solution to 200 ml. with distilled water to give a concentration of 5 micrograms of magnesium per milliliter. Volumes of 1, 2, 3, 4, and 5 ml. made up to a volume of 5 ml. in each case and representing 5, 10, 15, 20, and 25 micrograms of magnesium are utilized in setting up the standard curve.

h. Calcium chloride. Dissolve 16.13 mg. of $CaCl_2 \cdot H_2O$ in distilled water and make up to 100 ml. in a volumetric flask, giving a final concentration of 0.05 mg. of calcium per milliliter of solution.

Technique

1. Dilute 1 ml. of serum with 5 ml. of distilled water.

2. Add 2 ml. of 10 per cent sodium tungstate and 2 ml. of 0.67 N sulfuric acid.

3. Mix and then centrifuge for five minutes at 2500 r.p.m.

4. To 5 ml. of the supernatant, protein-free solution add 1 ml. of distilled water, 1 ml. of the 0.1 per cent gum ghatti solution, 1 ml. of the 0.05 per cent titan yellow solution, and 2 ml. of 4 N sodium hydroxide solution.

5. At the same time prepare a reagent blank by putting 1 ml. of the calcium chloride solution and 5 ml. of distilled water into a test tube. Treat similarly to the test just described.

6. Prepare a standard by adding 1 ml. of the calcium chloride solution, 2.5 ml. of the working standard magnesium solution, and 2.5 ml. of distilled water into a tube.

7. Set the photometer at 100 per cent transmission, using distilled water as a blank and utilizing a wave length of 540 millimicrons.

Standard curve. Readings of optical density are converted to magnesium concentrations by reference to a standard curve. The curve is prepared by carrying out the color reactions just described on 5 ml. samples of solutions containing 5, 10, 15, 20, and 25 micrograms of magnesium, replacing the 1 ml. of distilled water added to the protein-free supernatant in the test (step 4) with 1 ml. of calcium chloride solution containing 0.05 mg. of calcium. The standard blank is 5 ml. of distilled water.

Calculations. Magnesium in milligrams per 100 milliliters is calculated from the optical density of the test ($O.D._u$), optical density of the blank ($O.D._B$), and optical density of the standard ($O.D._s$) as shown in the following formula:

$$\frac{O.D._u - O.D._B}{O.D._s - O.D._B} \times C_s \times \frac{100}{0.5}$$

By using the standard just described, this will simplify out to the optical density of the unknown divided by the optical density of the standard times 2.5 to give the magnesium value in milligrams per 100 milliliters: $\dfrac{O.D._u}{O.D._s} \times 2.5$

Comments. Diffusible magnesium forms about 70 per cent of the total magnesium and can be calculated from the serum proteins and total serum magnesium by referring to the paper by Willis and Sunderman (1952).

Total Base (Total Cations)

The determination of total "base" is not done routinely, especially since the advent of the flame photometer, which allows for the direct determination of sodium and potassium and also for determining calcium and magnesium values of serum.

Sunderman (1945) has described an electrometric method for determination of total base in which the serum conductivity is determined with a conductivity apparatus and requires the chemical determination of the total serum proteins. If the total proteins are assumed to be 6.38 gm. for a normal range of 6.0 to 6.9 gm. per 100 ml., an error of 1 per cent will result. A nomogram has also been formulated to avoid calculations; thus, the conductivity value with or without the protein concentration is used to determine the total base. The normal values reported by Sunderman for total base were 142 to 149 mEq. per liter, which varied by 1.5 per cent from the chemical analyses for each of the cations, sodium, potassium, calcium, and magnesium. Since the sodium value was approximately 135 mEq. per liter and the potassium, calcium, and magnesium approximately 11, Sunderman reported a method for determining serum sodium by assuming a factor of 11 for the other cations; thus, sodium equals total base minus 11.

Boesen and Loud (1956) have described a conductrimetric screening test for the total electrolytes, both anions and cations.

A bedside determination of total cations is described by Scribner and Wiegert (1954), utilizing synthetic exchange resins. Serum is put through a column containing a cation exchange resin that almost completely removes sodium, potassium, calcium, and magnesium. A chemically equivalent amount of hydrogen is released; part of the hydrogen reacts with the bicarbonate in the serum to form carbonic acid, which escapes. The amount of hydrogen ion that has reacted with the serum bicarbonate can be determined on a separate sample, and the remainder of the hydrogen ion released from the exchange column is determined by titrating to a pH of 7.4 with standard sodium hydroxide. The amount of base or cation used in this titration and the value of the serum bicarbonate reflect the total amount of hydrogen ion released, which in turn equals the concentration of total cations in the serum.

ANIONS

Chloride

The exact requirement of chloride for the adult is not known. The urinary excretion of chloride suggests that most reported chloride requirements are too high. In the adult the daily exchange of chloride is about 2 to 7 per cent of the total body chloride, and in the child the daily turnover of chloride is about 4 per cent of the body content of chloride. Chloride losses usually follow those of sodium; however, the proportions will differ, since the loss of chloride can be compensated for by an increase of the serum bicarbonate. Such compensatory changes do not occur when sodium is lost and therefore requires the loss of body water. Chloride losses will produce the same effects in intracellular and extracellular compartments as are seen with the loss of potassium. A deficiency of either chloride or potassium will lead to a deficit of the other.

Chloride plays an integral role in the buffering action when oxygen and carbon dioxide exchange in the erythrocytes, the "chloride shift." When blood is oxygenated, chloride travels from the red blood cells to the plasma, while bicarbonate leaves the plasma and enters the red blood cells. This shift in the ratio of cell chloride to plasma chloride also occurs when the blood becomes more alkaline; thus, venous blood will have a lower plasma chloride concentration in comparison to the oxygenated arterial blood. Water travels in the same direction as chloride; the erythrocytes become dehydrated when blood is oxygenated. Normal serum or plasma chloride concentration is 98 to 106 mEq. per liter. By contrast the amount of chloride found within the cells may range up to about 25 mEq. per liter of cell water. The body content of chloride in the adult is 1.56 gm. per kilogram (fat-free) and 2.0 gm. per kilogram in the newborn.

Method of Schales and Schales (1941)

Principle. Chloride combines with mercuric ions to form unionized mercuric chloride. Even though no precipitate is formed, the nondissociated mercuric chloride is just as effective in removing the chloride from the solution. The end point is recognized by the appearance of mercuric ions in solution; this recognition of mercuric ions is made possible by various indicators, such as urea and sodium nitroprusside. In the Schales and Schales method use is made of s-diphenylcarbazone, which changes from colorless or light yellow to an intense blue when combined with mercuric ions. It is essential that the pH at the end point be between 1 and 2 (Asper et al., 1947).

Reagents

a. Mercuric nitrate solution. Dissolve 2.9 to 3.0 gm. of mercuric nitrate, $Hg(NO_3)_2 \cdot H_2O$, in a few hundred milliliters of distilled water and add exactly 20 ml. of 2 N nitric acid. Dilute to mark in a 1 L. volumetric flask with distilled water.

b. Standard sodium chloride solution. Reagent grade sodium chloride is dried at 120° C., and 584.5 mg. is dissolved in distilled water and made up to 1 L. in a volumetric flask. This solution contains 0.01 mEq. of chloride per milliliter. It is used for the standardization of the mercuric nitrate solution each day before the tests are done.

c. Diphenylcarbazone indicator. Dissolve 100 mg. of s-diphenylcarbazone (Eastman Kodak Co. No. 4459) in 100 ml. of 95 per cent ethyl alcohol. Keep in a brown, glass dropper bottle in the refrigerator. Do not allow it to come into contact with rubber. A new solution should be prepared each month. If the end point becomes sluggish, prepare a new solution, even before the end of the month.

Standardization of the Mercuric Nitrate Reagent

a. Measure 2.0 ml. of the standard sodium chloride solution into a test tube.

b. Add 4 drops of indicator.

c. Titrate with mercuric nitrate reagent from the special buret.

d. Calculate the factor,

$$F = \frac{1}{\text{titration}} \times (100).$$

This factor is the milliequivalents of chloride in serum equivalent to a titration of 1 ml.

Technique

1. To a 25 ml. Erlenmeyer flask add 2 ml. of distilled water.

2. Using a "to contain" pipet, add 0.20 ml. of serum, rinsing several times.

3. Add 0.06 ml. (4 drops) of the diphenylcarbazone indicator. The color is salmon red in a slightly turbid mixture.

4. Using a microburet calibrated in 0.01 to 0.05 ml., titrate with the mercuric nitrate solution. The color changes will be to a deep violet and then a light yellow, and the end point will be a violet color which can be seen quite readily.

Calculations. Milliequivalents of chloride per liter in serum (or spinal fluid done the same way) is equal to the titration of the unknown times factor F.

Comments. Titration of plasma or serum involves a change of colors in the end point; color at first is salmon red, changing to deep violet when the titration has begun and then becoming pale yellow or colorless. The end point is denoted by a sharp change to a pale violet color. If the test is done on a protein-free filtrate, an intense violet-blue color is seen when the first drop of excess mercuric nitrate solution is added. The protein present in the serum does affect the titration, and the results will be 1 to 3 mEq. higher than when done on a filtrate of whole blood or of plasma or serum.

A method for urine or spinal fluid uses 0.5 ml. of urine or spinal fluid. Add 5 ml. of 0.05 N nitric acid and then titrate as just described.

The pH is extremely important in the Schales and Schales method; confer article by Asper *et al.* (1947). Kirman *et al.* (1958) have modified the Schales and Schales technique to eliminate the personal error in reading the end point by using the Beckman automatic titrator.

Scribner (1950) has described a bedside determination of chloride based upon the method of Schales and Schales. Another method of calculating without using the filtration factor would be to consider T_s as the milliliters of mercuric nitrate required for the titration of 2 ml. of the standard solution (which would be equal to 0.02

mEq.) and T_u as the milliliters of mercuric nitrate reagent required to titrate 2 ml. of serum or equivalent volume of filtrate. Then the formula for milliequivalents of chloride per liter of serum is equal to $\frac{T_u}{T_s}$ times the concentration of the standard times $\frac{1000}{2} = \frac{T_u}{T_s} \times 100.$

METHOD OF VAN SLYKE AND HILLER (1947)

Principle. Phosphotungstic acid is added to serum or plasma to precipitate the proteins. The mixture is then shaken with an excess of solid silver iodate and filtered. The insoluble silver iodate reacts with the chlorides present to form insoluble silver chloride and soluble iodate, the latter passing into the filtrate. Upon addition of iodide to the filtrate the iodate reacts to produce free iodine, which is then titrated with standard thiosulfate solution with starch as an indicator.

Reagents

a. Precipitated silver iodate free from iodates and silver salts. Test the silver iodate for purity. Into a 50 ml. Erlenmeyer flask measure 25 ml. of the phosphoric-tungstic acid solution, add 0.5 gm. of silver iodate, stopper, and shake vigorously for one minute; then read the temperature immediately. Filter through S & S No. 589 Blue Ribbon filter paper. Into a 50 ml. flask measure 10 ml. of the clear filtrate, add 1 gm. of sodium iodide, and titrate immediately with 0.02303 N thiosulfate solution, shaking gently until the solution in the flask is pale yellow. Add 2 drops of 1 per cent starch solution and continue the titration until the solution suddenly turns colorless. The volumes of 0.02303 N thiosulfate solution titrated should be 0.52 ml. at 20° C., 0.74 ml. at 30° C., and 0.90 at 35° C., the intermediate variations being approximately linear.

b. Sodium iodide. Use reagent grade sodium iodide and keep it in a brown bottle in the dark. Each supply of sodium iodide should be tested for the presence of free iodine before using it and should be tested once a month thereafter. To 10 ml. of phosphoric-tungstic acid solution add 1 gm. of sodium iodide and 2 drops of 1 per cent starch solution. There should be no blue color.

c. Starch solution. Make up 100 ml. of 25 per cent sodium chloride solution. Weigh out on a rough balance 1 gm. of soluble starch. Add a few milliliters of sodium chloride solution and make a smooth suspension of the starch. Add the remaining sodium chloride solution gradually while stirring. Boil gently for ten minutes. The suspension will gradually clear while boiling. This reagent will keep indefinitely.

d. Phosphoric-tungstic acid solution. For each liter of the solution to be made weigh on a rough balance 6 gm. of reagent grade sodium tungstate, $Na_2WO_4 \cdot 2H_2O$. Dissolve the sodium tungstate in 990 ml. of distilled water and add 10 ml. of phosphoric acid (sp. gr. 1.72). Mix thoroughly.

e. Standard chloride, 0.1 M solution. Dry some sodium chloride at 175° C. for three hours. When cool, weigh out 2.9225 gm., transfer to a 500 ml. volumetric flask, and dilute to mark with distilled water.

f. Sodium thiosulfate, approximately 1 N stock solution. Weigh on a rough balance 160 gm. of reagent grade, anhydrous sodium thiosulfate or 250 gm. of $Na_2S_2O_3 \cdot 5H_2O$. Weigh on a rough balance 1 gm. of borax (sodium tetraborate, $Na_2B_4O_7 \cdot 10H_2O$); dissolve it in about 250 ml. of distilled water. Add the borax solution to the thiosulfate solution. Add distilled water to make a total volume of 1 L. and mix thoroughly. Transfer the solution to a 1 L. glass-stoppered Pyrex bottle.

g. Sodium thiosulfate solution, 0.02303 N. Measure out 2 L. of distilled water. Weigh out 4.35 gm. of sodium tetraborate on a rough balance. Put into a 250 ml. volumetric flask and put into solution. Dilute to volume. Add 125 ml. of this solution to the 2 L. of distilled water. Add 50.63 ml. of the 1 N sodium thiosulfate solution, stopper the flask, and mix the contents thoroughly. This solution should be standardized once a month and every time a new lot of sodium tungstate and silver iodate is used.

Standardization of 0.02303 N sodium thiosulfate solution. Into a 50 ml. Erlenmeyer flask transfer 1 ml. of 0.1 M sodium chloride solution in duplicate; add 25 ml. of phosphoric-tungstic acid solution. Add 0.3 gm. of silver iodate measured with a roughly calibrated, specially prepared spoon. Stopper the flask and shake vigorously for 40 seconds. Filter through S & S No. 589 Blue Ribbon filter paper. Into a 125 ml. Erlenmeyer flask pipet 20 ml. of the clear filtrate. Add 2 gm. of sodium iodide with sufficient accuracy from a specially calibrated spoon. Titrate immediately with 0.02303 N sodium thiosulfate solution, being careful to shake the flask only gently during the titration to avoid the loss of free iodine. Deliver the thio-

sulfate in rapid drops but not a stream until the color of the solution in the flask becomes a pale yellow. Add 4 drops of 1 per cent starch solution and continue the titration a drop at a time until the blue solution suddenly becomes colorless. The titration should require 20 ml. of the thiosulfate solution if it is exactly 0.02303 N. If the volume titrated deviates by more than 0.1 ml., either change the figures in the calculation or dilute the thiosulfate solution to exactly the correct normality.

Technique

1. Measure 0.5 ml. of serum into a 50 ml. Erlenmeyer flask.

2. Add 12.5 ml. of phosphoric-tungstic acid solution.

3. Add 0.3 gm. of silver iodate from a calibrated spoon, stopper, and shake flask for about 40 seconds.

4. Filter through S & S No. 589 filter paper. The filtrate must be perfectly clear.

5. Pipet 5 ml. of the clear filtrate into a 50 ml. Erlenmeyer flask.

6. Just before titrating, add 1 gm. of sodium iodide, using the roughly calibrated spoon, and immediately start to titrate with 0.02303 N sodium thiosulfate solution from a 25 ml. buret with gentle shaking of the flask. Deliver the thiosulfate in rapid drops but not a stream until the color of the solution in the flask is pale yellow.

7. Add 2 drops of 1 per cent starch solution and continue the titration until the blue color suddenly becomes colorless. Note: When a series of analyses is being done, treat each portion of filtrate with sodium iodide just before it is titrated.

Calculations. Millimoles of chloride per liter = ml. thiosulfate titrated × 10 × 2

Mg. of NaCl per 100 ml. = ml. thiosulfate titrated × 58.5 × 2

Comments. A microprocedure can be followed, utilizing 0.02 ml. of serum, 0.5 ml. of phosphoric-tungstic acid, and approximately 15 mg. of silver iodate. For the test, 0.2 ml. of clear filtrate is used and 0.05 gm. of sodium iodide is added just before titration. The titration is accomplished by using 0.02303 N thiosulfate solution, which has been diluted 1:2. When the pale yellow color is reached, add 1 drop of the starch solution and titrate until colorless. For the calculation:

$$mEq. \text{ of Cl per liter} = \frac{\text{ml. of thiosulfate}}{\text{ml. used in standard titration}} \times 100$$

Kingsley and Dowdell (1950) have modified the iodometric determination of chloride, utilizing a colorimetric procedure that is not sensitive to temperature changes and that does not require the addition of any thiosulfate as previously required by other modifications. The method is claimed to be extremely reproducible and uses a wavelength of 480 millimicrons.

Baginski *et al.* (1958) have described three indirect microprocedures, utilizing a polarographic method, a silver dithizone technique, and a mercuric chloranilate technique. The polarographic method requires an internal standard technique, and the two absorptiometric procedures involve an exchange of chloride for the anion of silver dithizonate or mercuric chloranilate with the concomitant liberation of dithizone or chloranilic acid.

Recently the electrometric titration of chloride has become popular because the instruments are produced commercially; it allows the direct titration of chloride in various biologic fluids utilizing microquantities of serum, and requires only one to two minutes for the entire titration. For procedural directions the brochures supplied with the Cotlove apparatus (1958) should be reviewed.

Bicarbonate

The classic diagram of Gamble (Fig. 9–1), showing the various cations and anions comprising the electrolytes of the blood, may be easily misinterpreted to mean that the various electrolytes are static and remain in one position on their respective positive or negative sides. This is not true, for the various cations are moving about and are in balance with the various anions, which are also moving about. Alkali reserve or alkaline reserve is a term applied to the concentration of plasma bicarbonate, total carbon dioxide content, part of the sodium, and total cations. The term alkali reserve is derived from that time in history when the bicarbonate of blood was regarded as undissociated sodium bicarbonate; sodium bicarbonate was one of the alkalies of the alchemist. Bicarbonate ions serve as a reserve in the sense that they can be displaced partially by other anions. However, at the present time alkali reserve has more than one meaning, depending upon the individual use made of it. The confusion regarding the terminology of alkali reserve is shown in Fig. 9–2.

There are at least five different meanings

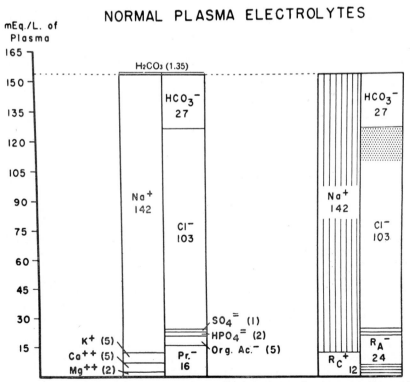

Figure 9–1. The Gamblegram. R_C+ represents residual cations; R_A- represents residual anions. (Modified from Weisberg, H. F.: Water, Electrolyte and Acid-Base Balance. Baltimore, The Williams & Wilkins Company, 1953. Reproduced with permission of the publisher.)

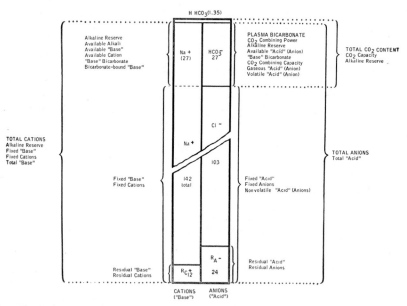

Figure 9–2. The web of terminology. The terms in capitals are preferred and should be used. (From Weisberg, H. F.: A better understanding of anion-cation ("acid-base") balance. Surg. Clinics of N. America, *39:* 93, 1959. Reproduced with permission of the publisher, W. B. Saunders Company.)

of the word "base." (1) Base has been used to mean the principal ingredient of a compound; thus, sodium is the base of sodium oxide, which is capable of forming the alkali, sodium hydroxide. Another example: phosphorus is the acidifiable base of phosphoric acid. (2) Base has also been defined in many dictionaries as a substance that reacts with an acid to form a salt. (3) According to the Arrhenius theory of ionization in aqueous solutions a base is a substance that contains a hydroxyl ion and causes the disappearance of the acid properties in the neutralization reaction. Conversely an acid is a substance that when dissolved in water dissociates to yield a hydrogen ion and some negative ion. The interaction of an acid and a base, therefore, is considered to be the combination of the hydrogen ion released from the acid and the hydroxyl ion released from the base to produce water. A base, therefore, has come to be identified with a substance having a hydroxyl ion.

(4) According to the more recent Brønsted schema a base is a substance that can gain a proton, thus forming an acid; conversely an acid is a substance that can lose a hydrogen ion (proton), thus forming a base. The Brønsted schema is important in that it also considers reactions in nonaqueous solvents in which no ions would be formed. It is unlikely that extremely small protons could remain free and un-captured by other molecules or ions in the solution. Water molecules can capture protons released from other substances to form the hydrated hydrogen ion or hydronium ion. According to the Brønsted schema, therefore, we are dealing with the exchange of protons and not with simple dissociation. Such changes exist between the proton donor (acid) and its conjugate proton acceptor (base). Thus, carbonic acid is an acid and its conjugate base is bicarbonate anion; bicarbonate is a base in the Brønsted schema and not an acid as it was called in the old schema (Fig. 9–2).

(5) Another chemical meaning of base is that considered in the Lewis theory of acid and base, which defines a base as a substance that has a lone pair of electrons, which may be used to complete the stable group of another atom. According to this theory, the proton per se is the acid.

Many a hospital laboratory lists the term CO_2 to avoid the confusion of the terms seen in various books—carbon dioxide content, carbon dioxide capacity, carbon dioxide combining power, and carbon dioxide combining capacity; these terms do not have the same meaning. For proper evaluation of carbon dioxide gas in the blood, "arterial plasma" should be used; such arterial plasma or serum is obtained from an artery, from a capillary by fingertip puncture, or from "arterialized blood" from a vein (the arm being kept in warm water for several minutes to arterialize the blood before venipuncture). True plasma is obtained by collecting blood anaerobically, and if any equilibration or alteration in the partial pressure of carbon dioxide is necessary, the changes are made before the blood cells are separated from the plasma. Such true plasma will represent the buffering action of the plasma or serum and also of the red blood cells. By contrast separated plasma is also obtained by anaerobic collection of the blood, but the blood cells are separated from the plasma before any equilibration or change in the partial pressure of CO_2 is made; such separated plasma will represent only the buffering action of the plasma or serum. A greater change in carbon dioxide content can be withstood by true plasma in comparison to separated plasma before any change in pH occurs.

The total carbon dioxide content measures the sum of bicarbonate, carbonic acid, and dissolved carbon dioxide present in the patient's plasma or serum. It is determined on the true plasma at the partial pressure of carbon dioxide present in the patient's body without any equilibration with carbon dioxide; a correction is made to 37° C.

The carbon dioxide capacity measures the sum of bicarbonate, carbonic acid, and dissolved carbon dioxide present in the plasma after equilibration to a partial pressure of carbon dioxide of 40 mm. of mercury. It may be equal to, or greater or less than, the carbon dioxide content (which is done without equilibration). The carbon dioxide capacity is determined on true plasma equilibrated with carbon dioxide from the technologist's alveoli, or by use of a gas mixture containing 5.5 per cent carbon dioxide, to a partial pressure of carbon dioxide of 40 mm. of mercury (the tension of carbon dioxide found in normal alveolar air) at room temperature. The capacity will be equal to the content if the partial pressure of carbon dioxide in both determinations (by equilibration or as found in the patient's blood) equals 40 mm. of mercury. When the partial pressure of the carbon dioxide in the patient's blood is less than 40 mm. of mercury, the capacity will be greater than the content; when the partial pressure of carbon dioxide is greater than 40 mm. of mercury, the capacity will be less than the content.

The carbon dioxide capacity is not the same as the carbon dioxide combining power. These two terms have been interchanged; the term carbon dioxide combining capacity, which is also used, could refer to either of the other two terms.

The determination of carbon dioxide combining power is a procedure done in most clinical laboratories, usually on blood plasma or serum collected "aerobically." The carbon dioxide combining power represents the concentration of bicarbonate ion in the patient's plasma equilibrated to a partial pressure of carbon dioxide of 40 mm. of mercury. The technique is the same as for the carbon dioxide capacity, but it is performed on separated plasma (which should be collected anaerobically). A correction is made for the dissolved carbon dioxide. The plasma or serum concentration of bicarbonate ion can be calculated from the total carbon dioxide content and the pH of the blood from the Henderson-Hasselbalch equation. The bicarbonate content may be determined directly by a modified titration method (Nadeau, 1953) or the value of the carbon dioxide combining power will represent the concentration. The average normal bicarbonate concentration in the adult is 27 mEq. per liter.

Table 9–3 gives the factors, f_B, necessary to calculate the bicarbonate concentration if the total carbon dioxide content and the pH are known. The factor for the determined pH value is obtained from the table; the factor multiplied by the total carbon dioxide content gives the value for the bicarbonate concentration.

Carbonic acid in the plasma represents the undissociated acid as well as the carbon dioxide dissolved in the plasma. The ratio of the dissolved carbon dioxide to the undissociated carbonic acid is about 700 to 1000:1. Because of the common-ion effect there is very little hydrogen ion or hydronium ion floating around in the blood. The preponderant bicarbonate salts are almost completely ionized or dissociated, and thus the hydrogen ion is displaced to form water and carbon dioxide, which is dissolved in the blood, or very small amounts of carbonic acid. The carbonic acid concentration can be calculated from the total carbon dioxide content and the pH, utilizing the Henderson-Hasselbalch equation; the average normal concentration in the adult is 1.35 mM. (or mEq.) per liter. The partial pressure of carbon dioxide (P_{CO_2}) is a measure of the undissociated carbonic acid, which is mainly dissolved carbon dioxide. The average P_{CO_2} in venous blood is 46 mm. of mercury and in arterial blood, 40 mm. of mercury; in the lung alveoli the tension

Table 9–3. Bicarbonate Factors, f_B, Obtained from pH to Calculate Plasma (or Serum) Bicarbonate Concentration from the Total Carbon Dioxide Content

$$[HCO_3^-] = f_B \times [CO_2 \text{ content}]$$
$$[H_2CO_3] = [CO_2 \text{ content}] - [HCO_3^-]$$

| pH | BICARBONATE FACTORS (f_B) | | | | | | | | | |
	0.00	0.01	0.02	0.03	0.04	0.05	0.06	0.07	0.08	0.09
6.8	0.833	0.836	0.840	0.843	0.846	0.849	0.852	0.855	0.858	0.860
6.9	0.863	0.866	0.868	0.871	0.874	0.876	0.878	0.881	0.883	0.886
7.0	0.888	0.890	0.892	0.895	0.897	0.898	0.901	0.903	0.905	0.907
7.1	0.909	0.911	0.912	0.914	0.916	0.918	0.920	0.922	0.923	0.925
7.2	0.927	0.928	0.930	0.931	0.932	0.934	0.935	0.936	0.938	0.939
7.3	0.940	0.942	0.943	0.944	0.945	0.947	0.948	0.949	0.950	0.951
7.4	0.952	0.953	0.954	0.955	0.956	0.957	0.958	0.959	0.960	0.961
7.5	0.962	0.962	0.963	0.964	0.965	0.965	0.966	0.967	0.968	0.969
7.6	0.969	0.970	0.971	0.971	0.972	0.972	0.973	0.974	0.974	0.975
7.7	0.975	0.976	0.976	0.977	0.977	0.978	0.978	0.979	0.979	0.980
7.8	0.980									

Table 9–4. Carbonic Acid (Including Dissolved CO_2) Factors, f_C, Obtained from pH to Calculate Plasma (or Serum) Carbonic Acid Concentration from the Total Carbon Dioxide Content

$$[H_2CO_3] = f_C \times [CO_2 \text{ content}]$$
$$[HCO_3^-] = [CO_2 \text{ content}] - [H_2CO_3]$$

| pH | CARBONIC ACID FACTORS (f_C) | | | | | | | | | |
	0.00	0.01	0.02	0.03	0.04	0.05	0.06	0.07	0.08	0.09
6.8	0.167	0.164	0.160	0.157	0.154	0.151	0.148	0.145	0.142	0.140
6.9	0.137	0.134	0.132	0.129	0.126	0.124	0.122	0.119	0.117	0.114
7.0	0.112	0.110	0.108	0.105	0.103	0.102	0.099	0.097	0.095	0.093
7.1	0.091	0.089	0.088	0.086	0.084	0.082	0.080	0.073	0.077	0.075
7.2	0.073	0.072	0.070	0.069	0.068	0.066	0.065	0.064	0.062	0.061
7.3	0.060	0.058	0.057	0.056	0.055	0.053	0.052	0.051	0.050	0.049
7.4	0.048	0.047	0.046	0.045	0.044	0.043	0.042	0.041	0.040	0.039
7.5	0.038	0.038	0.037	0.036	0.035	0.035	0.034	0.033	0.032	0.031
7.6	0.031	0.030	0.029	0.029	0.028	0.028	0.027	0.026	0.026	0.025
7.7	0.025	0.024	0.024	0.023	0.023	0.022	0.022	0.021	0.021	0.020
7.7	0.020									

Table 9–5. P_{CO_2} (Partial Pressure of Carbon Dioxide) Factors, f_P, Obtained from pH to Calculate P_{CO_2} from the Total Carbon Dioxide Content

$$P_{CO_2} = f_P \times [CO_2 \text{ content}]$$
$$[H_2CO_3] = P_{CO_2} \times 0.03$$
$$[HCO_3^-] = [CO_2 \text{ content}] - [H_2CO_3]$$

| pH | P_{CO_2} FACTORS (f_P) | | | | | | | | | |
	0.00	0.01	0.02	0.03	0.04	0.05	0.06	0.07	0.08	0.09
6.8	5.57	5.47	5.33	5.23	5.13	5.03	4.93	4.83	4.73	4.66
6.9	4.56	4.46	4.40	4.30	4.20	4.13	4.06	3.96	3.90	3.80
7.0	3.73	3.66	3.60	3.50	3.43	3.40	3.30	3.23	3.16	3.10
7.1	3.03	2.96	2.93	2.86	2.80	2.73	2.66	2.60	2.56	2.50
7.2	2.43	2.40	2.33	2.30	2.26	2.20	2.16	2.13	2.06	2.03
7.3	2.00	1.93	1.90	1.86	1.83	1.76	1.73	1.70	1.66	1.63
7.4	1.60	1.56	1.53	1.50	1.46	1.43	1.40	1.36	1.33	1.30
7.5	1.26	1.26	1.23	1.20	1.16	1.16	1.13	1.10	1.06	1.03
7.6	1.03	1.00	0.96	0.96	0.93	0.93	0.90	0.86	0.86	0.83
7.7	0.83	0.80	0.80	0.76	0.76	0.73	0.73	0.70	0.70	0.66
7.8	0.66									

of carbon dioxide is 36 mm. of mercury. Alveolar CO_2 can now be determined by infrared analysis (Collier *et al.*, 1955).

Tables 9–4 and 9–5 list the factors obtained from the pH value to calculate the carbonic acid concentration (including the dissolved carbon dioxide) and the partial pressure of carbon dioxide (P_{CO_2}). The respective factor, f_C or f_P, is multiplied by the total carbon dioxide content to obtain the proper parameter.

In most laboratories the expression volumes per cent of carbon dioxide, which means milliliters of carbon dioxide gas dissolved in 100 ml. of blood or serum, has been replaced by the term milliequivalents or millimoles per liter. Under standard conditions one mole (1 M.) or 1000 millimoles (1000 mM.) of carbon dioxide gas occupy 22.26 L. or 22,260 ml. Volumes per cent times 10 equals the milliliters of carbon dioxide per liter, and therefore the following equation can be used:

$$mM./L. = \frac{Volumes\ per\ cent \times 10}{22.26} \quad or$$

$$mM./L. = \frac{vol.\ \%}{2.226}$$

The mathematics of division can be simplified to convert to milliequivalents per liter by multiplying the milliliters of CO_2 per 100 ml. (volumes per cent) by the factor 0.450 (see Table 9–2).

Since carbon dioxide, expressed as millimoles, represents the determination of bicarbonate and 1 mM. of carbon dioxide will yield 1 mEq. of bicarbonate, the two terms can be interchanged so that CO_2 determinations can be expressed as milliequivalents per liter or as millimoles per liter.

CO₂ Content

Determination of the CO_2 content is the technique to be preferred, since this represents the concentration of carbon dioxide in the blood at the partial pressure found in the patient's body. This determination has been stated to require special care in the collection and handling of the plasma or serum to insure that the content of gas does not change until the analysis is completed; the blood should be collected without exposure to air and transferred immediately to a tube containing mineral oil. Centrifugation theoretically should be done with paraffin oil or mineral oil on top of the blood and a cork floating in the mineral oil to keep the gas pressure under standardized conditions. However, the collection of blood in a "Vacutainer" tube does not require the cork or mineral oil, since the small test tube (e.g., 5 ml. capacity) can be filled completely and the centrifugation done in the same tube without removing the stopper. When the test is to be done, the stopper is removed rapidly and the aliquot is removed. The tube is then restoppered immediately to preserve the sample if it is desired for a second determination or a pH determination.

Manometric Technique of Van Slyke and Neill (1924). The usual Van Slyke manometric apparatus consists of a manometer graduated in millimeters and usually read to 0.1 mm.; a reaction chamber or buret is used in which the blood gases are extracted and which is calibrated at 0.5 and 2.0 ml. (volumes to which the gas can be compressed when taking manometer readings) and at 50 ml. (volume used to extract gases). The reaction chamber is contained within a water jacket with a thermometer used to determine the temperature of the water. An intricate piece of glass tubing connects the manometer and the buret and this is called the "W." There are four stopcocks in the apparatus. Stopcock A is a three-way stopcock allowing the addition of material via the graduated cup or addition funnel to the buret chamber and also permitting the removal of material via the side ejection tube. Stopcock B is between the leveling bulb and the buret and allows for control of the mercury reservoir with the use of the leveling bulb. Stopcock V is at the top of the mercury manometer. Stopcock W is above stopcock B at the top of the "W" and allows for ejection of gas and water, which may accumulate at the top of the mercury in this glass manifold.

Most types of manometric Van Slyke apparatus today are controlled by a motor and rheostat to allow shaking of the buret with its water jacket. However, there are two recent models of the apparatus that should be mentioned. One has a manometer connected to the "W" by means of a ground glass joint; this joint usually requires grease to prevent air from seeping into the system. The advantage of such a joint is that it allows for easier cleaning of the glass parts. Another model of the Van Slyke apparatus is equipped with a magnetic stirring device and timer in addition to the glass ball-and-socket joints. Because magnetic stirring occurs within the buret chamber so that the entire apparatus does not have to be shaken, the two joints, one between the manometer and the "W" and the second between the "W" and the buret, hold well and do not permit much leakage.

Principle. The carbon dioxide of the blood exists chiefly in the form of bicarbonate, which is decomposed to carbon dioxide by the addition of lactic acid. The amount of gas present in a definite volume is determined by the pressure it exerts in a manometer. The released gases are adjusted to a known volume (e.g., water meniscus at 2 ml.), and the pressure (p_1) of the gas volume is read on the manometer. The carbon dioxide is absorbed with alkali, and the pressure (p_2) is read with the volume of residual gas at the same volume as before (2 ml.). The pressure fall, $p_1 - p_2$ millimeters of mercury, is the pressure that the carbon dioxide gas exerted at 2 ml. The volume that the carbon dioxide would occupy at 0° C. and 760 mm. of mercury is calculated by multiplying the pressure fall (P) by a factor that is a function of the observed temperature.

Reagents

a. Caprylic alcohol. A 10 per cent silicone antifoam agent can be used instead of the alcohol.

b. Lactic acid, approximately 1 N. Dilute 10 ml. of concentrated lactic acid (sp. gr. 1.20) to 100 ml. with distilled water.

c. Lactic acid, approximately 0.1 N. Dilute 1 N lactic acid 1 to 10 with distilled water, which has been boiled to remove the dissolved carbon dioxide.

d. Sodium hydroxide, 5 N. Dilute 27 ml. of 18 N NaOH to 100 ml. with freshly boiled and cooled distilled water. Place solution in a bottle protected from air with a soda lime tube. Note: The 18 N NaOH is prepared by dissolving a known weight of NaOH in an equal weight of water. Let stand in a paraffin-lined or polyethylene bottle to let the carbonates settle out.

e. Trimethylene glycol drying agent (Eastman Kodak).

f. Distilled water, boiled to remove carbon dioxide and protected by a soda lime tube.

Maintenance of apparatus. The most common source of error in the manometric technique is leakage around the stopcocks. Therefore, all stopcocks should be lubricated frequently so that they turn smoothly without sticking and have a complete film of lubricant between the plug and the barrel.

If moisture collects in the manometer,

it can be removed by adding 1 ml. of the trimethylene glycol through stopcock V and allowing it to flow down the manometer for about 10 cm. It is then forced out by raising the mercury in the manometer up through stopcock V. The small amount of trimethylene glycol remaining on the walls of the manometer will not affect the accuracy of the manometer reading.

When the apparatus is not in use, stopcocks A and B should be open. However, stopcocks V and W are always kept closed and sealed with mercury. The leveling bulb should be at the lower position, the buret chamber and the addition cup should be filled with distilled water, and the cup should be covered with parafilm or a beaker.

TESTING THE DRYNESS OF THE MANOMETER. With the buret empty of gases and fluid and stopcock A closed, lower the mercury level to the 2 ml. mark and then close stopcock B. The mercury surface in the manometer should be above that in the buret chamber by a height nearly equal to the vapor pressure of the water, depending on the room temperature.

If the value for the height of the mercury is not as given in Table 9–6, the dehydrating fluid should be renewed as just described. The oft-stated test for dryness of the Van Slyke buret, raising the mercury to obtain a "click," should not be done. It is not accurate and usually results in breakage of the apparatus.

Table 9–6. **Vapor Pressure of Water in Relation to Room Temperature**

ROOM TEMPERATURE (° C.)	VAPOR PRESSURE (MM. HG)
15	12.7
16	13.6
17	14.5
18	15.4
19	16.4
20	17.5
21	18.6
22	19.8
23	21.0
24	22.3
25	23.7
26	25.2
27	26.7
28	28.3
29	30.0
30	31.8
31	33.6
32	35.6
33	37.7
34	39.8

TESTING FOR LEAKS. Add 3.5 ml. of distilled water into the buret chamber and extract the dissolved air present by shaking for two minutes. Then reduce the gas volume to the 2 ml. mark and read the pressure in the manometer. Re-extract and then read the pressure again. If the temperature is the same and no leaks are present, the pressure reading should not change. If a leak exists, a slow increase in the readings of the manometer will occur.

Cleaning the Buret at Start of the Day's Work

1. Open stopcock A to the side ejection tube.

2. Close stopcock B.

3. Raise leveling bulb with mercury to the upper position.

4. Open stopcock B; close when all the water is out of the buret. (Do not allow too much mercury to escape via the ejection tube.)

5. Place leveling bulb in lower position. Close stopcock A and then open stopcock B.

6. Add 10 to 15 ml. of approximately 0.1 N lactic acid to the buret via the addition cup. Allow the 0.1 N lactic acid to enter the chamber by opening stopcock A.

7. Close stopcock A.

8. Lower the mercury in the chamber to the 50 ml. mark by opening stopcock B and lowering the leveling bulb below table level. Then close stopcock B and return leveling bulb to the lower position.

9. The buret is shaken by a motor or by the magnetic stirrer for one-half minute.

10. The acid and extracted gases are then ejected via the ejection tube as in steps 1 to 4. Note: Be sure that all air collected in the trap below stopcock W is removed.

Technique. The apparatus should be absolutely clean and free of leaks. The mercury should fill the buret chamber, and both capillaries of stopcock A should be sealed and closed with mercury. Stopcock B is open and the leveling bulb is in the lower position.

1. Add 1 drop of caprylic alcohol to the capillary in the addition funnel.

2. Add 1 ml. of carbon dioxide-free distilled water.

3. Using a Van Slyke pipet, run in 1 ml. of serum under the water in the addition cup, holding the pipet tip near the bottom of the cup.

4. With cautious manipulation of stopcock A draw the serum and water into the reaction chamber. Do not allow any air to enter.

5. Add 1.5 ml. of the 1 N lactic acid through the cup and draw into the chamber by opening stopcock A. Do not allow air to enter.

6. Seal and close stopcock A with a drop of mercury.

7. Evacuate the buret chamber by lowering the leveling bulb below table level. When the mercury reaches the 50 ml. mark, close stopcock B.

8. Shake the buret by means of its motor or magnetic control for two minutes.

9. Place leveling bulb in upper position. By careful manipulation of stockcock B mercury is readmitted slowly and without swirling until the gas volume in the buret chamber is reduced to the 2 ml. mark. (The meniscus of the water solution is at the 2 ml. mark.) Then close stopcock B. Note: The adjustment of the gas volume should not take over one-half to one minute. If the fluid meniscus passes the 2 ml. mark, more CO_2 will be reabsorbed than is accounted for in the calculations. Therefore, readjustment must be made by again lowering the mercury level to the 50 ml. mark and re-extracting for one minute.

10. Tap manometer with finger and take reading p_1.

11. Lower the leveling bulb below table level and open stopcock B so that the mercury level of the chamber is about $\frac{1}{4}$ to $\frac{1}{2}$ inch below the upper shoulders of the chamber.

12. Close stopcock B and place leveling bulb in lower ring support.

13. Place about 0.5 ml. of the 5 N NaOH into the addition cup. By manipulation of stopcock A slowly run 0.2 ml. of the NaOH into the buret chamber for absorption of the carbon dioxide.

14. After the alkali has been added, a few drops of mercury are admitted via the cup to dislodge any alkali adhering to the underside of the stopcock and to seal the stopcock.

15. After the CO_2 is absorbed (in about 30 seconds), mercury is readmitted from the leveling bulb by manipulating stopcock B until the meniscus of the solution is again at the 2 ml. mark.

16. Read the manometer for p_2.

BLANK. Repeat the carbon dioxide method just described to determine the "c" correction factor by the blank analysis, using 2.5 ml. of the 1 N lactic acid. The "c" correction factor is the sum of two components: the amount of gas yielded by the reagents and the fall in the manometer reading between p_1 and p_2 by the introduction of a given volume of the absorbent solution.

Calculations. $P = p_1 - p_2 - c$. The partial pressure P is multiplied by the appropriate factor for the temperature of the water jacket around the buret chamber. The temperature factors given in Table 9–7 are for the stated conditions, using 1 ml. of serum and a total volume in the buret of 3.5 ml. and reducing the gas volume to the 2.0 ml. mark.

Standardization of the technique can be accomplished by using pure anhydrous sodium carbonate to make a concentration of 25 mEq. per liter. To make 100 ml. of this standard 25 mEq. per liter solution requires 0.2650 gm. of sodium carbonate per 100 ml. The solution should be stored in a paraffin-lined or polyethylene bottle and should be used in the same fashion as the serum. This solution will keep for only a few weeks.

Table 9–7. Temperature Factors for Manometric Method Using 1.0 ml. of Serum

TEMPERATURE OF WATER JACKET ($^\circ$ C.)	CALCULATION OF CO_2	
	MILLIEQUIVALENTS (MEQ./L.)	VOLUMES PER CENT (ML./100 ML.)
15	0.1229	0.2733
16	0.1222	0.2719
17	0.1215	0.2704
18	0.1208	0.2690
19	0.1202	0.2675
20	0.1196	0.2662
21	0.1190	0.2648
22	0.1183	0.2634
23	0.1177	0.2620
24	0.1171	0.2607
25	0.1165	0.2594
26	0.1160	0.2581
27	0.1154	0.2569
28	0.1149	0.2557
29	0.1143	0.2545
30	0.1138	0.2533
31	0.1133	0.2522
32	0.1128	0.2511
33	0.1123	0.2500
34	0.1118	0.2489

Comments. The caprylic alcohol is used to prevent foaming, which would obscure the meniscus. Instead of caprylic alcohol a 10 per cent silicone antifoam reagent can also be utilized.

During the shaking process, when there is a vacuum in the buret chamber, the mercury meniscus in the manometer should not move more than a few millimeters. If the mercury rises appreciably, it indicates a leak at the reaction chamber stopcock; if the mercury falls, it indicates a leak at the manometer stopcock.

Acetone is used to clean the apparatus; if this is not sufficient, alcoholic potassium hydroxide (13.2 gm. of powdered KOH, 85 per cent pure) is dissolved to make up 1 L. in absolute alcohol; this is a N/5 solution and can be used to remove all the grease and dried protein). To clean a manometer, open the cock at the top, draw the mercury into the leveling bulb, and disconnect the rubber tube leading to the bulb. Replace with tubing from a suction flask. Apply strong suction and draw water and then alcoholic potassium hydroxide solution through the manometer from the top. Dry with acetone and then draw air through the tube to remove all traces of the acetone. If necessary, instead of the potassium hydroxide solution, chromic-sulfuric acid cleaning solution may be used followed by water, acetone, and air. When the manometer is filled with clean mercury, evacuate the tube several times to detach the film of air adjacent to the glass. The air bubble is then expelled through the cock at the top of the manometer.

To clean the extraction chamber between analyses, eject the solution remaining from the previous analysis through the cup and remove with suction. Lower the level of the mercury to the bottom of the chamber and admit 10 to 15 ml. of water. Shake the chamber for a few seconds. The water is ejected through the cup; then add 1 ml. of 1 N lactic acid, lower the mercury level, extract by shaking, and then eject the gases and the solution through the cup. Any solution adherent to the walls is so nearly gas-free that it will cause no error in subsequent analyses. Do not allow the air to enter the chamber, since it will form a thin film on the wall and must be removed by evacuating or by cleaning. Silicone grease should not be used for the stopcocks because alkali is used in this method.

Volumetric Technique of Van Slyke and Cullen (1917). The usual Van Slyke volumetric apparatus consists of a buret in which the blood gases are extracted and which is calibrated with many subdivisions up to 1.0 ml. and at 1.25, 1.50, 2.00, 2.50, and 50.0 ml. It has two stopcocks. The upper one is a three-way stopcock, allowing the addition of material via the graduated cup or addition funnel to the buret chamber and also permitting the removal of material via

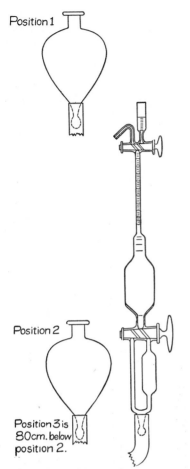

Position 1

Position 2

Position 3 is
80cm. below
position 2.

Figure 9–3. Van Slyke's apparatus for determination of the concentration of carbon dioxide in blood, showing the three positions of the mercury bulb. The bulb is connected to the apparatus by a heavy rubber tube, which is merely indicated in the drawing. The apparatus is set up on an iron ring stand.

the side ejection tube. The lower stopcock also has three-way borings connecting the buret chamber to a trap (wide tube on right side) and to the narrow side-arm tube on the left side. Some models have water jackets around the buret and motors to shake the apparatus; more recent models have a magnetic stirrer with built-in timer. The three positions of the mercury bulb reservoir shown in Fig. 9–3 should be known in order to perform the technique to be described next.

Principle. Serum or blood contains carbon dioxide primarily in the form of bicarbonate ion. In order to measure this potential carbon dioxide, it must be freed from combination, utilizing lactic acid, which is a stronger acid than carbonic, to convert the bicarbonate ion to carbonic

acid. The carbonic acid (carbon dioxide) is extracted under vacuum. Complete removal of the gas is not possible with one extraction, but if the amount of solution and the ratio of the liquid phase to the gas phase are kept constant, the residue of carbon dioxide remaining in solution can be calculated from the solubility coefficient and the temperature and pressure. At the same time correction is made for the dissolved oxygen and nitrogen that are also released by the extraction *in vacuo.* The actual volume of carbon dioxide extracted can be determined by absorbing the carbon dioxide with an alkali, such as sodium hydroxide.

Reagents

Same as described under manometric gas apparatus. Note: This procedure is for the determination of carbon dioxide content, utilizing the volumetric apparatus. The apparatus should be absolutely clean and free of leaks. The mercury should fill the buret chamber, and both capillaries of the upper and lower stopcocks should be sealed and closed with mercury.

Technique

1. Add one drop of caprylic alcohol to the bottom of the cup.

2. Open the lower stopcock to connect to the trap on the right side and, by controlling the upper stopcock, allow the caprylic alcohol to run down into the capillary tube above the upper stopcock. Mercury bulb should be at position 2.

3. Add a few drops of mercury over the caprylic alcohol in the capillary tube and seal the stopcock with mercury, allowing the caprylic alcohol to enter the apparatus.

4. Place 2 ml. of 0.1 N lactic acid in the cup. (This can be an approximate measurement using the markings on the cup.)

5. Pipet 1 ml. of plasma or serum into the cup and run it into the chamber underneath the acid layer. This is accomplished by keeping the leveling bulb in position 2, opening the lower stopcock, and controlling the delivery of the serum and the lactic acid by means of the upper stopcock. The lactic acid is run in until the mercury reaches the 2.5 ml. mark on the pipet.

6. Close both stopcocks and remove the excess lactic acid from the cup. Place a drop of mercury in the cup and open the upper stopcock to fill the capillary tube and the bore of the cock to act as a seal. Close the cock.

7. Lower the mercury bulb to posi-

tion 3, which is 80 cm. below position 2, open the lower stopcock, and draw the level of the mercury (not the aqueous mixture) to the 50 ml. mark, which is just above the lower stopcock. Close the lower stopcock.

8. Return the mercury bulb to position 2 and remove the apparatus from the stand. Extract the carbon dioxide from the solution by removing the chamber from the holder, and without inverting, shake for two minutes to liberate the gas. Place the apparatus back in the stand carefully and allow the solutions to drain for one minute. Note: Some volumetric CO_2 apparatus designs have a motor or magnetic stirrer attached for shaking.

9. Lower the leveling bulb to position 3, and open the lower stopcock to connect the chamber with the trap on the right underneath the lower cock. Drain the fluid (except for one or two drops) from the chamber down into the lower trap, being careful that no gas enters. It is best to control the flow of the fluid by means of the lower stopcock rather than by using the leveling bulb. Close the lower stopcock.

10. Turn the lower stopcock to connect to the sidearm, which is the narrow tube below the lower stopcock, and allow the mercury to rise slowly in the apparatus by raising the mercury leveling bulb.

11. Raise the leveling bulb, and place at such a height that the surface of the mercury is at exactly the same level as the mercury in the apparatus. The small amount of aqueous fluid can usually be neglected. Note: If more than 2 or 3 cm. of solution is above the mercury, the height of the mercury in the leveling bulb should be raised one-thirteenth of the height of the aqueous column above the inside mercury column.

12. Close lower stopcock and place the leveling bulb back in position 2. Read the volume of gas (at the aqueous meniscus, not at the mercury level). Read this volume and record the temperature of the environment and the barometric pressure at the time of the determination.

Note: When doing the determination using plasma or serum, the reading of the total gas volume may be taken as the finish of the determination. Since no alkali is used, it is not necessary to wash the apparatus between such analyses. However, if whole blood is analyzed, so much oxygen is mixed with the carbon dioxide that it is necessary to absorb the carbon dioxide with alkali and also to wash the apparatus between readings.

Calculation of carbon dioxide content by volumetric apparatus. When the carbon dioxide is determined on plasma or serum, the total gas volume contains a certain amount of air carried into the apparatus in the form of gas dissolved in the plasma and in the 0.1 N lactic acid mixed with carbon dioxide. The correction necessary for this may be calculated from the solubility of air in water at room temperature and in plasma at 38° C. with sufficient accuracy for most purposes. The air correction factor is given for each degree of temperature in Table 9–8 and should be subtracted from the sum of the total observed CO_2 and the air volume to obtain the volume of CO_2 extracted from 1 ml. of plasma or serum. Table 9–8 includes the

Table 9–8. Factors for Calculation of CO_2 Content by Volumetric Method Using 1.0 ml. of Serum

ROOM TEMPERATURE (° C.)	AIR CORRECTION FACTOR *	MULTIPLICATION FACTOR †	
		mEq./L.	ML./100ML.
15	0.048	44.9	100.2
16	0.048	44.7	99.5
17	0.048	44.4	98.9
18	0.047	44.2	98.3
19	0.047	43.9	97.8
20	0.046	43.7	97.2
21	0.046	43.4	96.6
22	0.045	43.1	96.0
23	0.045	42.9	95.4
24	0.045	42.6	94.8
25	0.044	42.3	94.2
26	0.044	42.1	93.6
27	0.044	41.8	93.1
28	0.043	41.5	92.4
29	0.043	41.3	91.8
30	0.043	41.0	91.2
31	0.043	40.7	90.6
32	0.042	40.4	90.0
33	0.042	40.2	89.4
34	0.042	39.9	88.4

* To be subtracted from sum of observed volume of carbon dioxide plus air.

† These factors must be multiplied by $\frac{actual\ barometric\ pressure}{760}$ or $\frac{B}{760}$ (see Table 9–9).

factors by which the milliliters of carbon dioxide extracted from 1 ml. of plasma or serum are multiplied to give the final result in terms of milliequivalents per liter or as volumes per cent of CO_2. These multiplication factors have to be multiplied by the correction for barometric pressure or $\frac{B}{760}$.

Table 9–9 lists the factors to convert the

Table 9–9. Factors to Convert Actual Barometric Pressure Readings to $\dfrac{B}{760}$

ACTUAL BAROMETRIC READING (B)	$\dfrac{B}{760}$
732	0.963
734	0.966
736	0.968
738	0.971
740	0.974
742	0.976
744	0.979
746	0.982
748	0.984
750	0.987
752	0.989
754	0.992
756	0.995
758	0.997
760	1.000
762	1.003
764	1.006
766	1.008
768	1.011
770	1.013
772	1.016
774	1.018
776	1.021
778	1.024

actual barometric pressure reading to the standard $\dfrac{B}{760}$.

Comments. The apparatus should be kept clean with well-greased stopcocks and should always be kept filled with fresh distilled water to prevent dirt from getting in and to avoid expansion of the mercury, which might crack the apparatus. Before each run of determinations the test for leaks should be done; this should never be omitted. It is performed by sealing both capillaries at the top stopcock with mercury, closing it, and drawing the mercury to the 50 ml. mark. The stopcock grease is not strong enough to prevent leakage unless the capillaries and their bores in the plug are filled with mercury. If no alkali is used in the technique, silicone grease may be used for the stopcocks. After being drawn to the 50 ml. mark, the mercury is then allowed to rise to the top stopcock and to strike it gently. This is done slowly. A sharp click should be produced; a muffled or soft click is an indication of the presence of air. Any air present should be expelled and the test for leaks repeated until no air is obtained.

Kopp-Natelson Microgasometer (1951, 1957). This apparatus utilizes only 0.03 ml. of serum or plasma to determine the amount of carbon dioxide present in the blood plasma or serum. Primarily it will determine the CO_2 content in blood collected anaerobically. O'Mara and Faulkner (1959) have mechanized the Kopp-Natelson microgasometer so that it is under precise fingertip control and eliminates all the handling of the apparatus.

CARBON DIOXIDE CAPACITY

The carbon dioxide capacity is performed in the same fashion, utilizing the manometric or the volumetric apparatus of Van Slyke or the Kopp-Natelson microgasometer. It is done on blood drawn anaerobically that is equilibrated to a partial pressure of 40 mm. of mercury before the red blood cells are separated. The partial pressure of 40 mm. of mercury represents the pressure of carbon dioxide found normally in the alveoli of the lung. Equilibration may be done by proper exhalation of alveolar air by the technician (or utilization of an apparatus delivering 5.5 per cent carbon dioxide).

Whole blood is placed in a separatory funnel, and the technician blows alveolar air into the funnel and then rotates the funnel in order to equilibrate the blood sample with the alveolar atmosphere within the separatory funnel (see Fig. 9–4).

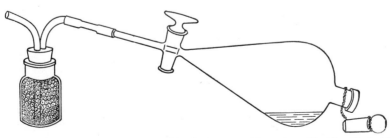

Figure 9–4. Apparatus used for saturating blood plasma with carbon dioxide. Air is blown from the lungs into the tube at the left, the stopper is inserted, and the separatory funnel rotated. The air passes among the glass beads in the bottle, which remove its moisture. (After Van Slyke.)

Alveolar air is that air expired at the end of a normal expiration after a normal inspiration. Unfortunately, however, many technicians take a deep breath and then exhale; this is not a true sample of alveolar air. Other factors contributing to abnormal alveolar air samples are smoking and colds, which cause variations in the concentration of carbon dioxide in different individuals.

Carbon Dioxide Combining Power

The method of determining the carbon dioxide combining power also utilizes the volumetric or manometric Van Slyke apparatus, but the blood is equilibrated to a partial pressure of 40 mm. of mercury by using serum or plasma obtained presumably under anaerobic conditions after the red blood cells have been separated. Caraway and Fanger (1955) have modified the Kopp-Natelson microgasometer technique to be able to obtain the carbon dioxide combining power rather than the carbon dioxide content.

Rosenthal and Buscaglia (1958) have described a simple apparatus for equilibration of the specimen with carbon dioxide, utilizing a small tank of gas containing 5.5 per cent carbon dioxide and 94.5 per cent nitrogen and a needle valve assembly for regulating the flow of the gas to saturate the sample in a test tube. Use of such an apparatus will result in a saving of time for the technician and will give a greater degree of precision in the analyses of the carbon dioxide combining power and of the carbon dioxide capacity.

Utilizing the volumetric apparatus of Van Slyke, which is present in most general laboratories, the following calculations can be used to determine the carbon dioxide combining power, which will reflect the concentration of bicarbonate in the blood. The observed volume of gas (step 12 in the technique listed on p. 479) times 100

Table 9–10. Correction Factors for Volumetric Determination of CO_2 Combining Power

OBSERVED VOLUME OF GAS (ML.)	CORRECTION FACTOR
0.20–0.30	10
0.31–0.51	11
0.52–0.73	12
0.74–0.96	13
0.97 and up	14

minus the correction listed in Table 9–10 will equal the number of milliliters of carbon dioxide found as bicarbonate in 100 ml. of serum or plasma.

Protein

Protein is also one of the electrolytes of the blood, and at the normal blood pH of 7.4 the protein, which is a zwitterion, exists as an anion having a negative charge. The amount of protein present in the blood will determine the amount of protein anions present; thus, the factor for conversion of protein to the electrolyte equivalent is grams of protein per 100 ml. times 2.43, which equals milliequivalents of proteinate per liter (see Table 9–2).

The factor 2.43 is a good approximation of the equivalents of protein under normal conditions and normal pH. The isoelectric point of proteins varies and will affect the combining capacity of the carboxyl groups in the protein. The formulas that give a more accurate description of the milliequivalents of the various proteins are shown at the bottom of the page.

Phosphorus

Phosphorus is present in practically all foods and is absorbed from the gastrointestinal tract more efficiently than calcium or magnesium. If the dietary intake of calcium from milk is sufficient to meet the minimum daily requirements, phosphorus requirements will also be satisfied. On an adult diet with less milk consumption the intake of phosphorus usually exceeds that of calcium. The metabolism of phosphorus follows that of calcium in many respects. About 10 to 20 per cent of the phosphorus, however, is found in body tissues other than bone; it is the major anion found within the cells. Phosphorus of soft tissues seems to have priority over bone for necessary metabolic processes. Of the phosphorus that is excreted from the body, about 40 per cent is excreted via the feces and 60 per cent via the urine. An average total of about 30 mEq. of phosphate calculated as phosphorus or 0.93 gm. are excreted per day via the urine. Vitamin D has little effect on phosphorus absorption via the gastrointestinal tract; however, it does increase the rate of reabsorption via the renal tubules. Other factors affecting the urinary

mEq. albumin/L. = 0.125 (gm. alb./L.) (pH − 5.16)
mEq. globulin/L. = 0.077 (gm. glob./L.) (pH − 4.89)
mEq. total protein/L. at pH 7.35 = (0.273 × gm. alb./L.) + (0.189 × gm. glob./L.)

output of phosphorus (as for calcium) are intake, acid-base regulation, and endocrines.

The normal plasma phosphorus level is 1.7 to 2.3 mEq. per liter or 3 to 4 mg. per 100 ml. In children the level is higher, being 2.3 to 3.5 mEq. per liter or 4 to 6 mg. per 100 ml. The serum or plasma phosphorus is mainly in the form of inorganic phosphate. The serum phosphorus is high in hypoparathyroidism and low in hyperparathyroidism. In patients on prolonged milk and alkali intake the serum phosphorus may be normal or elevated, whereas the serum calcium is high. During periods of active growth serum phosphorus is elevated, presumably owing to the effect of growth hormone; this is reflected in the higher levels seen in children. The phosphorus present within the cells is essentially present as organic combinations. It is the largest anion component found within the cells, about 80 mEq. per liter of cell water. The phosphorus content in the adult is about 11.6 gm. per kilogram (fat-free) and 5.4 gm. per kilogram in the newborn.

Dryer and his co-workers (1957) have described a method for determining inorganic phosphorus, using microquantities of plasma or serum. Reduction of the molybdenum is accomplished by the use of p-semidine hydrochloride solution containing sodium bisulfite. This reagent gives reproducible colors and a low color blank.

METHOD OF FISKE AND SUBBAROW (1925)

Principle. The inorganic phosphorus present in a trichloroacetic acid, protein-free filtrate of serum in the form of the orthophosphate reacts with molybdate in acid solution. The blue color is formed from the resultant phosphomolybdate after the addition of a reducing agent to form a colloidal solution of molybdenum blue. Various methods have different reducing agents used. In the method of Fiske and Subbarow aminonaphthosulfonic acid reagent is used.

Reagents

a. Trichloroacetic acid stock. Dissolve 100 gm. of trichloroacetic acid in distilled water. Dilute to 100 ml. in a volumetric flask.

b. Trichloroacetic acid, 5 per cent. Dilute 5 ml. of the stock trichloroacetic acid solution to 100 ml.

c. Sulfuric acid, 10 N. Add 300 ml. of concentrated sulfuric acid to 75 ml. of distilled water. Mix well and cool. To check, dilute 10 ml. of this solution to 100 ml.

in a volumetric flask, mix, and titrate a 10 ml. portion with standard 1 N NaOH. From the titration results adjust the original solution to make it exactly 10 N, if necessary.

d. Molybdate reagent. Dissolve 25 gm. of reagent grade ammonium molybdate in about 200 ml. of water. In a 1 L. volumetric flask place 300 ml. of 10 N sulfuric acid and add the molybdate solution. Dilute with washings to 1 L. with distilled water. Mix; the solution is stable indefinitely.

e. Sodium bisulfite, 15 per cent. To 30 gm. of reagent grade sodium bisulfite in a beaker add 200 ml. of distilled water from a graduated cylinder. Stir to dissolve and if turbid allow to stand, well stoppered, for several days and filter. Keep well stoppered.

f. Sodium sulfite, 20 per cent. Dissolve 20 gm. of reagent grade, anhydrous sodium sulfite in water. Dilute to 100 ml. and filter if necessary. Keep well stoppered.

g. Aminonaphtholsulfonic acid reagent. Place 195 ml. of 15 per cent sodium bisulfite solution in a glass stopper cylinder. Add 0.5 gm. of 1,2,4-aminonaphtholsulfonic acid. Add 5 ml. of 20 per cent sodium sulfite solution. Stopper and shake until the powder is dissolved. If solution is not complete, add more sodium sulfite, 1 ml. at a time with shaking, but avoid an excess. Transfer to brown, glass-stoppered bottle and store in the refrigerator. This solution keeps for about one month.

h. Standard phosphate solution, stock. Dissolve exactly 0.351 gm. of pure, dry potassium dihydrogen phosphate in water and transfer quantitatively to a 1 L. volumetric flask. Add 10 ml. of 10 N sulfuric acid and dilute to the mark with distilled water and mix. This solution contains 0.4 mg. of phosphorus in 5 ml. of reagent.

i. Standard phosphate solution, working. Dilute 5 ml. of the stock phosphate standard solution with 5 per cent trichloroacetic acid in a 100 ml. volumetric flask. This solution contains 0.004 mg. of phosphorus per milliliter.

Technique

1. Measure 9.5 ml. of 5 per cent trichloroacetic acid into a test tube.
2. Add with shaking 0.5 ml. of fresh serum or plasma and mix.
3. Allow to stand for five to ten minutes and centrifuge until clear. (If necessary, filter through Whatman No. 40 or No. 42 filter paper.)
4. Measure 5 ml. of the filtrate into a 10 ml. volumetric flask.

5. Add 1 ml. of the ammonium molybdate reagent and mix.
6. Add 0.4 ml. of aminonaphthol-sulfonic acid reagent and mix.
7. Prepare a blank by using 5 ml. of 5 per cent trichloroacetic acid, 1 ml. of molybdate reagent, and 0.4 ml. of the aminonaphthol-sulfonic acid reagent.
8. Prepare a standard by using 5 ml. of the working standard solution, 1 ml. of the molybdate reagent, and 0.4 ml. of the aminonaphthol-sulfonic acid reagent.
9. Dilute unknowns, blank, and standard to 10 ml. with distilled water and mix.
10. After ten minutes read in spectrophotometer, setting blank at 100 per cent transmission and using a wave length of 690 millimicrons.

Calculations. Milligrams of inorganic phosphorus =

$$\frac{\text{Density of unknown}}{\text{Density of standard}} \times 0.02 \times \frac{100}{0.5} \times \frac{10}{5} =$$
$$\frac{\text{Density of unknown}}{\text{Density of standard}} \times 8$$

A standard curve may also be prepared by diluting various quantities of the dilute working standard and working through the method.

Sulfate

Sulfate of the blood has been determined by various methods, e.g., by precipitation as barium sulfate and estimation gravimetrically, colorimetrically, or turbidimetrically or by exchange with iodate giving a gasometric technique. The precipitation of sulfate as benzidine sulfate will allow titration of the benzidine sulfate as an acid using an alkali, or the benzidine may be estimated colorimetrically. Various reagents giving color with the benzidine have been used. The method of choice to be described is that of Letonoff and Reinhold (1936), using sodium beta-naphthoquinone-4-sulfonate as the color reagent.

If the sulfate is expressed as sulfur, the normal blood serum contains 0.3 to 2.0 mg. per 100 ml. or 0.2 to 1.3 mEq. per liter. If the sulfate is expressed as inorganic sulfate ($SO_4^=$), the concentration in the serum will be 0.9 to 6 mg. per 100 ml. or 0.2 to 1.3 mEq. per liter. Since red cells contain sulfur-containing amino acids and proteins, the blood used should be separated

as soon as possible to avoid hemolysis. The amount of sulfate in the whole blood is about twice that found in serum; it is best to do the determination on serum. The inorganic sulfate of the serum is increased early in renal insufficiency, even before other tests reveal any change in renal function. Increases have been noted in nephritis up to 6 to 8 mg. of sulfur (S) or 18 to 24 mg. of sulfate ($SO_4^=$) per 100 ml. of serum. Any case of nitrogen retention in the blood is accompanied by an increase in the serum inorganic sulfate.

Nalefski and Takano (1950) have modified the turbidimetric method of Dennis, using uranyl acetate to remove the phosphates and protein and preparing a stable standard barium sulfate sol. This method requires the use of a photonephelometer.

METHOD OF LETONOFF AND REINHOLD (1936)
(MODIFIED BY KLEEMAN et al., 1956)

Principle. Benzidine, a weak organic base, forms a stable salt with strong mineral acids. The sulfate salt is insoluble in the presence of excess benzidine in acid solution and especially in the presence of organic solvents, e.g., acetone and alcohol. Powdered glass is used to avoid loss of the precipitate during the wash. The wash solution used is a mixture of ethyl ether and ethyl alcohol in which the benzidine sulfate is considerably more insoluble than in either acetone or alcohol. Addition of the colorimetric reagent, sodium beta-naphthoquinone-4-sulfonate, to the benzidine in alkaline solution develops a red-brown color, which changes to red on the addition of acetone.

Reagents

a. Trichloroacetic acid, 10 per cent. Dissolve 10 gm. of trichloroacetic acid and dilute to 100 ml. with distilled water.

b. Benzidine, 1 per cent. Dissolve 1 gm. of the colorless compound and dilute to 100 ml. in a volumetric flask with 95 per cent ethyl alcohol. Keep in refrigerator. Discard when solution becomes colored.

c. Alcohol-ether wash solution (2:1). Add 50 ml. of ethyl ether to 100 ml. of 95 per cent ethyl alcohol.

d. Alkaline sodium borate. Dissolve 10 gm. of sodium borate (borax) and dilute to 1 L., using 0.1 N NaOH as the solvent. Keep in a polyethylene bottle.

e. Powdered glass (Fisher Scientific Co. No. S248). Wash with 0.1 N HCl and water. Dry in air and store in a glass bottle.

f. Acetone, analytical reagent grade.

g. Sodium 1,2-naphthoquinone-4-sulfonate. Dissolve 200 mg. in distilled water and dilute to 100 ml. in a volumetric flask. Keep in refrigerator; stable for cne week. If the solution is colored, shake with activated charcoal and filter; the solution should be pale yellow. It is best to wash the activated charcoal first in a Buchner funnel with approximately 0.1 N HCl and water and to air dry before use.

h. Sulfate standard (1 mg. sulfur per 100 ml.). Prepare anhydrous sodium sulfate by drying at 100° C. and then cooling in desiccator. Weigh 44.5 mg. and dissolve in water and dilute up to 1 L. Cover solution with a small amount of mineral oil.

Technique

1. Place 1.0 ml. of clear, unhemolyzed serum in a test tube and add 5 ml. of 10 per cent trichloroacetic acid.

2. Mix and allow to stand for ten minutes.

3. Centrifuge for 15 minutes at 2000 r.p.m.

4. Transfer a 2 ml. aliquot to a conical centrifuge tube.

5. Add 5 ml. of 1 per cent benzidine solution.

6. Mix and place in the refrigerator for at least three hours (or overnight if convenient).

7. Add a knife tip (3 to 5 mg.) of powdered glass.

8. Mix and centrifuge at 2000 r.p.m. for 15 minutes.

9. Decant and drain for one minute on a gauze pad in an inverted position.

10. Wipe the mouth of the tube.

11. Add 10 ml. of alcohol-ether wash solution, mix, and recentrifuge.

12. Allow to drain as before.

13. Repeat washing once more and then allow to drain again.

14. Add 1 ml. of alkaline borate solution and mix gently to resuspend the precipitate.

15. Place tubes in a water bath at 60° C. and mix occasionally until the precipitate dissolves.

16. Add 10 ml. of water and mix.

17. Add 1 ml. of sodium 1,2-naphthoquinone-4-sulfonate solution.

18. Allow tubes to stand for five minutes.

19. Add 2 ml. of acetone and mix. Note: An identical number of minutes should elapse between the addition of the color reagent and of the acetone to each tube. Centrifuge and then decant the supernatant into the colorimeter tube for reading.

20. A blank using 1 ml. of water should be run through the procedure just outlined.

21. A standard solution using 1 ml. of the standard sulfur solution should be used instead of the serum and taken through the steps as for the unknown.

22. Set the blank at 100 per cent transmission, using a wave length of 490 millimicrons.

Calculations. A standard curve may be determined, using various dilutions of the standard solution just listed; or

$$\frac{\text{Density of unknown}}{\text{Density of standard}} \times 1 = \text{mg. of sulfur per 100 ml.}$$

In order to obtain milliequivalents of sulfur per liter, divide milligrams per 100 ml. by 1.6.

Ketone Bodies

The ketone bodies—acetone, acetoacetic acid, and betahydroxybutyric acid—are found in the blood in very low concentrations, namely 2 to 4 mg. per 100 ml. Once the blood level exceeds 6 to 8 mg. per 100 ml. expressed as acetone, the ketone bodies will be found in the urine. Under normal conditions the ketone bodies present in the blood exert very little effect as part of the total 5 mEq. of organic acid anions. However, in diabetic acidosis, starvation acidosis, and other conditions the greatly increased amounts of ketone bodies will depress the concentration of bicarbonate in the blood.

In diabetes elevations up to 300 to 400 mg. per 100 ml. may be seen. In normal urines up to 50 mg. per day are seen, while in diabetes 1 to 5 gm. per 100 ml. may be found; most of this is in the form of betahydroxybutyric acid, which does not react in the test to be described. The test is valuable in distinguishing between true diabetic acidosis in which the serum ketone bodies will exceed 50 mg. per 100 ml. and surgical conditions in the diabetic in which the blood level rarely exceeds 20 mg. per 100 ml.

METHOD OF DUMM AND SHIPLEY (1946)

Principle. Sodium nitroprusside in the presence of a weak alkali will give a purple color with acetoacetic acid and with acetone. Betahydroxybutyric acid does not give a positive test. The test applied to acetoacetic acid is five to ten times more sensitive than when applied to acetone.

Reagents

Acetone test powder. Grind separately, to make a fine powder, each of the following ingredients:

Sodium nitroferricyanide	1 gm.
Ammonium sulfate, dry	20 gm.
Sodium carbonate, anhydrous	20 gm.

Mix the three powdered ingredients without grinding in a screw top bottle. The mixture must be kept dry at all times and under such conditions is stable for three months or longer. Note: Instead of preparing powder as described, commercially available tablets or powder for the determination of acetone may be used.

Technique

1. Place a pinch of the mixed powder, approximately 5 mm. in diameter, on a circle of white filter paper.

2. Add one drop of serum or plasma without stirring.

3. A positive test is indicated by a red to purple color.

4. If a positive test is obtained with undiluted serum, make successive dilutions by adding water to the sample, testing each dilution as just described; e.g., start with 1 ml. of serum, add 1 ml. of distilled water, mix, and use one drop to test. If still positive, add another milliliter of water to the tube, mix, and test with one drop of diluted serum or plasma.

Calculations. This test is sensitive enough to determine 10 mg. of acetone per 100 ml. of serum. Thus, the dilution factor multiplied by 10 gives the approximate concentration of ketone bodies, expressed as acetone, present in the original serum. For example, assume that the dilution of 1 ml. of serum plus 9 ml. of water gave a positive test and that 1 ml. of serum and 10 ml. of water gave a negative test. Therefore, the dilution factor would be 10 times 10 or 100 mg. of acetone per 100 ml. of serum plus or minus 10 mg.

Comments. In order to check the reliability of the test, a known acetone solution of about 50 mg. per 100 ml. may be prepared and used as serum. To 100 ml. of distilled water add 2 drops of pure acetone and mix well. This should be approximately 50 mg. per 100 ml.

Lactic Acid

The lactic acid of blood is usually determined by conversion to acetaldehyde, which is then measured by titrimetric or colorimetric methods. A gasometric method that has also been described is based upon oxidation with permanganate to produce carbon dioxide. When obtaining a blood specimen for determination of lactic acid, it is extremely important that precautions be used to avoid conversion of the blood glucose to lactic acid owing to glycolysis on standing; the use of fluoride as an anticoagulant will help prevent such glycolysis. With serum or with the use of anticoagulants, such as oxalate or heparin, the protein-free filtrate should be prepared as soon as possible after drawing the blood. The blood should be drawn without stasis from a resting subject in the postabsorptive condition.

METHOD OF BARKER AND SUMMERSON (1941)

Principle. The protein-free filtrate is treated with copper sulfate and calcium hydroxide to remove glucose and other interfering substances. An aliquot of the resulting solution is heated with concentrated sulfuric acid to convert the lactic acid to acetaldehyde, which is then treated with p-hydroxydiphenyl to produce a condensation product that has a purple color; the intensity of the color reaction is enhanced in the presence of copper ions.

Reagents

a. Trichloroacetic acid, 10 per cent. Dilute 10 ml. of concentrated trichloroacetic acid to 100 ml. with distilled water. Prepare fresh each week.

b. Trichloroacetic acid, concentrated. Dissolve 100 gm. of crystalline trichloroacetic acid in distilled water and dilute to 100 ml. Preserve in a Pyrex, glass stopper bottle. This reagent is stable indefinitely.

c. Copper sulfate, 20 per cent. Dissolve 20 gm. of crystalline copper sulfate, $CuSO_4 \cdot 5H_2O$, in distilled water and dilute to 100 ml. Do not filter.

d. Calcium hydroxide powder, reagent grade.

e. Copper sulfate, 4 per cent. Dilute 20 ml. of the 20 per cent copper sulfate solution to 100 ml. with distilled water and mix.

f. Sulfuric acid, concentrated. This should be reagent grade and iron-free. It is dispensed from a buret suitably protected from the absorption of atmospheric moisture. The buret stopcock should not contain any grease; lubricate with a little of the concentrated acid.

g. p-Hydroxydiphenyl reagent. In a 250 ml. beaker place 1.5 gm. p-hydroxydiphenyl, $C_6H_5C_6H_4OH$. Add 5 ml. of 2.5 N NaOH and 10 ml. of distilled water. Heat until solution is complete, stirring constantly. Dilute to 100 ml. with distilled water. Preserve in a brown glass bottle; stability is approximately six months at room temperature. This reagent should be discarded when the reagent blank shows an appreciable increase in transmission.

h. Sodium hydroxide, 2.5 N.

i. Lactic acid, stock standard (1 ml. contains 1 mg. of lactic acid). In a 100 ml. volumetric flask place 106.6 mg. of recrystallized lithium lactate, $LiC_3H_5O_3$. Add approximately 80 ml. of distilled water and shake until dissolved. Add 2 drops of concentrated sulfuric acid and dilute to volume with distilled water. Preserve in refrigerator; stability indefinite.

j. Lactic acid, working standard (1 ml. contains 0.03 mg. of lactic acid). In a 100 ml. volumetric flask place 3 ml. of the stock lactic acid solution and dilute to volume with distilled water. Prepare just before use.

Technique

When mixing or shaking, glass stopper tubes must be used; never use a finger or the palm of the hand, for this introduces a considerable positive error. At no point is filtration allowed.

1. In a 15 ml. glass stopper centrifuge tube place 9 ml. of 10 per cent trichloroacetic acid and 1 ml. of the sample, which is added drop by drop while constantly agitating the tube. Stopper and shake vigorously for 30 seconds.

2. In another 15 ml. glass stopper centrifuge tube prepare the reagent blank by adding 9 ml. of 10 per cent trichloroacetic acid and 1 ml. of distilled water. Stopper and mix.

3. Allow to stand for five minutes and centrifuge at 1500 r.p.m. for three minutes. Do not filter.

4. Transfer 2 ml. of each centrifugate to a correspondingly marked, accurately graduated, glass stopper 15 ml. centrifuge tube.

5. To each tube add 1 ml. of 20 per cent copper sulfate solution and mix.

6. Dilute to 10 ml. with distilled water. Stopper and mix.

7. Add approximately 1 gm. of calcium hydroxide, using a spoon spatula known to hold approximately 1 gm. (since the exact measurement is unimportant). Stopper and shake vigorously for 30 seconds. If the mixture is not bright blue in color, add more calcium hydroxide.

8. Allow to stand for 30 minutes, repeating the shaking at ten-minute intervals.

9. Centrifuge at 1500 r.p.m. for five minutes. Do not filter.

10. Transfer 1 ml. of each clear centrifugate to a correspondingly marked 18 × 150 mm. Pyrex test tube. This should be done by inserting the tip of the pipet beneath the surface of the fluid, holding the index finger over the tip of the pipet to prevent the ingress of any of the surface film. After withdrawal of the pipet wipe off any adherent particles with clean tissue.

11. To each tube add 0.05 ml. of 4 per cent copper sulfate and mix. (One drop from a capillary tip dropper will be sufficient.)

12. Add 8 ml. of concentrated sulfuric acid drop by drop from a buret, constantly agitating the tubes by lateral shaking until the components are thoroughly mixed.

13. Place the tubes in boiling water for five minutes.

14. Cool under running tap water to at least 20° C.

15. Add 0.1 ml. of p-hydroxydiphenyl reagent, allowing the reagent to fall directly into the acid while constantly shaking to disperse the precipitate, which forms uniformly throughout the solution. Note: Adequate mixing is essential.

16. Place the tubes in a water bath at 30° C. for at least 30 minutes, redispersing the precipitated reagent by lateral shaking at ten-minute intervals. The solution should now have a violet-blue color; a reddish-purple color at this stage indicates too high a temperature and the analysis must be repeated.

17. Place in vigorously boiling water for exactly 90 seconds. The solution should be perfectly clear and reddish purple in color.

18. Cool to room temperature under running tap water.

19. Measure the transmittance of the sample against the reagent blank set at 100 per cent transmission, using a wave length of 565 millimicrons.

Preparation of Calibration Table. In a series of six accurately calibrated, 10 ml. volumetric flasks place 0, 2, 4, 6, 8, and 10 ml. of the dilute lactic acid standard and dilute to volume with distilled water. These standards represent concentrations of lactic acid equivalent to 0, 15, 30, 45, 60, and 75 mg. per 100 ml. Prepare just before use and proceed according to the technique just described.

Comments. The venous blood of normal individuals in a resting state usually contains 5 to 20 mg. of lactic acid per 100 ml. of venous blood. During severe exercise this value may rise to over 100 mg. per 100 ml., and this will decrease rapidly during recovery. Whenever there is a deficient supply of oxygen to the tissues, as in pneumonia or congestive heart failure, the blood lactate content will be increased. The presence of excessive amounts of lactic acid in the blood will cause a decrease of the blood bicarbonate and result in metabolic acidosis. As soon as the lactate is utilized by the tissues, the acidosis will disappear. This method is very sensitive and can be applied to 0.1 ml. or less of blood.

ACID-BASE BALANCE

The concentration of the hydrogen ion in the blood is extremely small, namely 0.00000004 mole (M) per liter or 4×10^{-8} moles per liter. Since the molecular weight of hydrogen is about 1, the concentration can also be expressed as 4×10^{-8} gm. per liter. Because of difficulty in handling such numbers, Sørensen introduced the concept of pH, which is defined as the negative logarithm of the concentration of hydrogen ion.

$$pH = - \log [H^+]$$

The square brackets [ ] represent the molar concentration of the substance. Thus, the cumbersome number 0.00000004 M per liter becomes 7.4 in the pH scale. The blood pH (concentration of hydrogen ion) is protected and controlled by the buffers—bicarbonate : carbonic acid system, hemoglobin, protein, and phosphate—present in the blood. The normal range of pH of the blood is 7.35 to 7.45; the pH range compatible with life is 6.8 to 7.8. Acid-base balance can be described by the Henderson-Hasselbalch equation:

$$pH = pK + \log \frac{base}{acid}$$

The major buffer system of the blood is the bicarbonate : carbonic acid system. Referral to the Brønsted schema of acids and bases will show that carbonic acid is the proton donor of this system and that bicarbonate anion is the conjugate proton acceptor or conjugate base. Thus, none of the cations, sodium, potassium, magnesium, and calcium, are base nor are they acid. They are cations. The anions of the blood are all potential proton acceptors, meaning that they can react with a hydrogen ion. The anions, therefore, are "bases" in the

Brønsted schema. This is completely different from the old terminology in which the cations were called bases and the anions were called acids.

Thus, the Henderson-Hasselbalch equation can be rewritten to be expressed as:

$$pH = pK + \log \frac{HCO_3^-}{H \cdot HCO_3}$$

The bicarbonate : carbonic acid system is the true acid-base relationship, which reflects the pH or the concentration of free hydrogen ions in the blood. The concentration of carbonic acid in the blood is determined by the functional capacity of the respiratory system, and the concentration of the bicarbonate ion is determined by functional capacity of the kidneys. The other blood buffers (hemoglobin, protein, and phosphate) play their role and via the kidneys determine the ultimate concentration of bicarbonate ions of the blood. The negative logarithm of the dissociation constant of carbonic acid is represented by pK and at body temperature is equal to 6.1.

$$
\begin{aligned}
pH &= 6.1 + \log \frac{27}{1.35} \\
&= 6.1 + \log 20 \\
&= 6.1 + 1.3 \\
&= 7.4
\end{aligned}
$$

Much confusion has resulted concerning the terms acidosis and alkalosis. Previously these terms had been reserved for the decrease or increase, respectively, of the alkaline reserve. They have also been used to represent a fall in pH (increased acidity) or a rise in pH (decreased acidity) of the blood. Other investigators prefer to use the terms acidemia and alkalemia to represent the changes in blood pH. However, the term acidosis should mean a fall in pH below the level of 7.35 and alkalosis should mean a rise in pH above the level of 7.45 without the use of the term alkaline reserve, which should be discarded.

Bicarbonate Deficit

Other names for this condition are metabolic acidosis, primary alkali deficit, and uncompensated alkali deficit. This condition may be caused by an excessive production of organic acid anions, excessive loss of cations, retention of anions, therapy with mineral acids or salts, and other miscellaneous conditions. Thus, a falling concentration of bicarbonate ions to 13.5 mEq. per liter will change the bicarbonate :

carbonic acid ratio to 10:1 instead of the normal 20:1; with the decrease of the ratio there is a decrease of the pH, which is equal to 7.1.

Bicarbonate Excess

Synonyms for this condition are metabolic alkalosis, primary alkali excess, and uncompensated alkali excess. This condition may be caused by excessive loss of anions; body deficit of potassium; therapy with alkaline salts; and x-ray, ultraviolet, or radium therapy. An increase in the bicarbonate ion concentration, for instance, to 40 mEq. per liter, would increase the ratio to 30:1 instead of the normal 20:1; the increased ratio would result in an increased pH, which would be equal to 7.58.

Carbonic Acid Excess

This condition has also been called respiratory acidosis, primary carbon dioxide excess, uncompensated carbon dioxide excess, gaseous acidosis, and hypoventilation. Some major causes are depression of the respiratory center, excessive inhalation of carbon dioxide, cardiac disease, mechanical asphyxia, respiratory muscle paralysis, and pulmonary disease. The primary pathologic alteration is impaired respiratory function so that there is an increase in the concentration of carbonic acid, for example, to 2 mEq. per liter, resulting in a decrease of the normal ratio to 13:1 instead of 20:1. This decreased ratio results in a decreased pH, which is equal to 7.21.

Carbonic Acid Deficit

Synonyms for this condition are respiratory alkalosis, primary carbon dioxide deficit, uncompensated carbon dioxide deficit, gaseous alkalosis, and hyperventilation. Conditions that may result in such imbalance are stimulation of the respiratory center, fever or external high temperature, anoxic anoxemia owing to high altitudes, hyperventilation syndrome, and hysteria and anxiety. The primary pathologic change is the result of a blowing-off of carbonic acid, which causes an increase of the ratio; for example, if the carbonic acid is 0.67 then the ratio would be 40:1 instead of 20:1. The increased ratio means an increased pH, which is equal to 7.7 in this case.

pH

Most pH determinations today are done by electrometric means, using pH meters rather than photometric methods. Hastings and Sendroy (1924) described the various indicators, temperature control, and other conditions necessary for diluting the plasma in the colorimetric determination of plasma pH by means of test tube comparisons. Van Slyke *et al.* (1949) have reinvestigated the procedure, utilizing a spectrophotometer, and have described a photometric method for the determination of the pH of plasma and of urine. Singer *et al.* (1955) have described their determination of the plasma pH, utilizing a modification of the Shock and Hastings pipet.

Electrometric Techniques. Various descriptions have been published, utilizing the glass electrode pH meter. The individual commercial setups are accompanied by brochures, which should be consulted. It should be pointed out that the pH of the blood and plasma will be affected by temperature. Rosenthal (1948) has given a formula that states that for every degree below 37.5° C. at which the pH is determined, 0.015 unit should be subtracted from the observed pH. Others, such as Wilson (1951) and Holaday (1954), have used incubators to maintain the electrodes at body temperature. Astrup and Schrøder (1956) have described an apparatus in which the electrodes are maintained at 37.5° C. by water circulating from a water bath; Straumfjord (1958) also described a water-jacketed electrode. Sanz (1957) has described a capillary electrode that uses blood drawn from the fingertip directly into the electrode. A thorough discussion of the practical aspects of routine pH determinations is given in a series of articles by Gambino (1959).

WATER BALANCE

The normal adult who indulges in routine activities will have an intake and an output of water balanced in the range of 1500 to 3000 ml. per day. The mythical 70 kg. adult male may be in water balance with an intake of 2500 ml. This amounts to about 24 per cent of his extracellular fluid, which is contained in the interstitial and intravascular compartments. A normal intake will be maintained for the adult if he is supplied with 30 ml. of water per kilogram of body weight. This will supply approximately 1 L. for loss owing to insensible perspiration and 1 L. for urine excretion. A minimum total water output for the average adult is about 1500 ml. per day; about 900 ml. are required for insensible perspiration and 600 ml. for minimum urine excretion.

The total body water consists of about 70 per cent of the total body weight. This is divided into the intracellular fluid, about 50 per cent of the total body weight, and the extracellular fluid, making up the other 20 per cent. The extracellular fluid is divided into the interstitial fluid, comprising about 15 per cent of the total body weight, and the intravascular fluid or plasma volume, which makes up about 5 per cent of the total body weight. The concentrations of the electrolytes within the plasma are summarized in Table 9–2.

In order to compare the concentrations of electrolytes within the plasma to those of the interstitial and intracellular fluid, the usual method of describing concentration of electrolytes in blood expressed as milliequivalents per liter of plasma or milliequivalents per liter of serum has to be changed to milliequivalents per liter of plasma or serum water. In this way similar units are used to express the electrolyte concentrations per liter of water in the intracellular compartment and the interstitial compartment. Since plasma contains approximately 92 per cent water, the various electrolytes will be about 8 per cent higher in concentration when expressed on the basis of per liter of plasma water. Thus, instead of 154 mEq. being the total cation concentration, it will now be approximately 167 mEq. per liter of plasma water, and the anions similarly will be increased to 167 mEq. per liter of plasma water. In contrast the total electrolyte concentration in the interstitial fluid is approximately 155 mEq. per liter of water because of the Donnan-Gibbs equilibrium. The protein concentration within the interstitial fluid is much less, amounting to approximately 1 mEq. per liter of interstitial compartment water; on the other hand the chloride concentration is elevated to make up for this difference, being about 115 mEq. per liter of water.

Though the relative concentrations, except for the conditions of proteins and chloride just described, are similar in the intravascular or plasma volume compartment and the interstitial compartment, there is a decided difference in the presumed concentration of electrolytes within the intracellular compartment. The sodium is much less evident, and potassium is the major cation present within the cells. In addition magnesium plays a major role as one of the intracellular cations. In describing the anions, the major anion is phosphate, which is found in organic form within the cells; proteins make up the second largest anion component within the cells. Bicarbonate is reduced to approximately 10 mEq. per liter of water, and practically no organic acids are present for analysis within the cells.

Under ordinary circumstances approximately 1500 ml. of urine are excreted daily via the urinary tract. This is a very small percentage of the total volume of water passing through the kidneys. The total glomerular filtrate, 120 ml. per minute, will amount to approximately 180 L. per day. Of this, approximately 85 per cent is reabsorbed in the proximal convoluted tubules owing to the "obligatory" reabsorption of water and solutes. The remaining 15 per cent of the water presented to the kidney tubules is reabsorbed passively; continued active reabsorption of sodium creates an osmotic force that causes the reabsorption of water. The amount of water reabsorbed in the distal tubules (and collecting ducts) is under the influence of the antidiuretic hormone of the posterior pituitary; antidiuretic hormone supposedly opens the hypothetical pores in the epithelial lining, an action analogous to the action of the antidiuretic hormone on the skin of amphibians. In the presence of normal amounts of antidiuretic hormone practically all the water presented to the distal convoluted tubules will be reabsorbed so that only approximately 1000 ml. of water are excreted as the daily urine. In the complete absence of the antidiuretic hormone diabetes insipidus will result, and volumes up to 20 or 25 L. of urine output per day have been reported. In such conditions the specific gravity of the urine will be very low, since there is no abnormal amount of electrolytes being excreted.

The total solute output per day has a very definite relationship to the urine solute concentration and to the total urine volume. The usual adult intake of food results in an output of 1200 milliosmoles (mosM.) of solutes. At normal concentrations of approximately 0.8 osM. per liter as exemplified by urine with a specific gravity of 1.020, these solutes can be excreted in a daily urinary output of approximately 1500 ml. of fluid. Under fasting conditions the total output of solutes per day is 800 mosM.; at a concentration seen in a specific gravity of 1.020 the amount of urine per day needed for such excretion will be 1000 ml. of fluid. The administration of 100 gm. of carbohydrate in the form of glucose to such fasting individuals will cut the solute load to 400 mosM. per day and, under similar concentrations, will be excreted in a total volume of 500 ml. per day. The protein-free glomerular filtrate issuing from the proximal renal tubules has a solute concentration of approximately 0.3 osM. per liter. This urine will have a specific gravity of about 1.008 to 1.010. The average maximal solute concentration in urine is 1.4 osM. per liter with a specific gravity of 1.035. Under these conditions a person with normal kidneys excreting 1200 mosM. per day can, under average maximum urine concentration, excrete these solutes in approximately 750 ml. of fluid. The fasting patient with an excretion of 800 mosM. per liter who can concentrate maximally will accomplish this in a volume of 500 ml. of fluid. The fasting patient who is given 100 gm. of carbohydrate can excrete his 400 mosM. load in a total volume of 250 ml. of fluid.

The daily urinary excretion of various electrolytes will vary with the intake. If a reduction occurs in the dietary intake of sodium, there will be a concomitant decrease of the sodium in the urinary output. However, even on a potassium-free diet, some potassium will always be lost in the urine as a result of negative nitrogen balance owing to tissue protein breakdown. In the adult the average excretion per liter of urine is 40 to 90 mEq. of sodium, 20 to 60 mEq. of potassium, and 40 to 100 mEq. of chloride provided renal function is normal.

One of the major sources of fluid loss to the body is via the gastrointestinal tract. Under normal circumstances only 50 to 200 ml. of water are lost in the semisolid feces. However, during the course of a day approximately 8 L. of fluid are secreted into the gastrointestinal tract via the juices from the salivary glands, bile, pancreatic juice, and intestinal juice. Thus, approximately 8 L. must be reabsorbed, a volume approximately two to three times that of the normal plasma volume. The concentration of electrolytes will vary in the various secretions of the gastrointestinal tract. The gastric secretions are high in chloride and low in sodium content; the potassium concentration is about three times that found in plasma. Fluid obtained from the pancreatic or ileal regions of the intestinal tract has a high sodium and a relatively low chloride content, but the potassium concentration is again higher than that found in plasma. The bile secretion has a composition approximating that of the extracellular fluid, whereas juices from the jejunal region of the gastrointestinal tract have almost equal concentrations of sodium and chloride.

Plasma Volume

The plasma is the only compartment of the body water that is easily accessible for various determinations. For routine purposes the volume of the intracellular fluid is not determined; the extracellular fluid, which consists of the interstitial fluid, and the intravascular fluid (plasma volume) are the other compartments. The plasma volume bears a direct relationship to the weight of the individual. For the adult male the average plasma volume is 4.5 per cent of the body weight; this can be expressed as 45 ml. of plasma per kilogram of body weight with a range of plus or minus 5 ml. per kilogram. In the adult female the average plasma volume is 4 per cent of the body weight or 40 ml. per kilogram with a range of 35 to 45 ml. per kilogram. In the newborn infant the plasma volume is higher, having an average of 5.5 per cent of the body weight, or 55 ml. per kilogram, with a range of 50 to 60 ml. per kilogram.

Plasma volume may be determined indirectly by use of the following formula:

$$PV_2 = PV_1 \times \frac{Hb_1 (1 - Hct_2)}{Hb_2 (1 - Hct_1)}$$

in which PV_1 is the initial (assumed) plasma volume, PV_2 is the new (calculated) plasma volume, Hct_1 and Hct_2 are the initial (previous) and new hematocrit determinations, respectively (expressed as fractions of unity), and Hb_1 and Hb_2 are the initial (previous) and new hemoglobin determinations, respectively. In the use of this formula it is assumed that the hematocrit and hemoglobin determinations are accurate and represent all parts of the vascular bed. The initial plasma is also assumed; the assumed plasma volume can be calculated from the percentage of the body weight as just discussed. Thus, $PV_2 - PV_1$ will be equal to the positive or negative change in the plasma volume in the patient.

Another formula involving only the determination of the total serum proteins has also been used for the serial observations of a patient:

$$PV_2 = \frac{PV_1 \times SPr_1}{SPr_2}$$

where PV_1 and PV_2 are the initial (assumed) and new (calculated) plasma volumes, respectively, and SPr_1 and SPr_2 are the initial and the new total serum protein values, respectively. In the use of this formula certain precautions must be remembered: no large amounts of protein should be entering the blood circulation, as in the case of transfusions of whole blood, plasma, or concentrated serum albumin, and none should be leaving, as occurs in hemorrhage, burns, trauma, or the rapid accumulation of ascites, transudates, and exudates. Again using the formula, $PV_2 - PV_1$ equals the loss or gain of plasma volume.

METHOD OF GREGERSON (1938, 1944)

Principle. Evans Blue or Tolidene-1824 is a blue dye that binds totally to serum albumin and is therefore retained within the plasma space. Since the dye escapes from the blood very slowly, a knowledge of the exact quantity of dye injected into the blood and the determination of the concentration in the plasma will allow the calculation of the entire space in which the dye has been diluted.

It is extremely important that the syringe used for the injection of the dye be accurately calibrated so that the exact volume injected is known; all the injected solution must enter the blood. Lipemia and hemolysis should be absent. Evans Blue has an absorption maximum at 610 millimicrons; however, in the presence of plasma protein the absorption maximum shifts to 620 millimicrons.

Reagents
a. Evans Blue dye, which is available commercially in ampules containing 5 ml. of a 0.5 per cent aqueous solution.
b. Vials of sterile saline suitable for intravenous injection, 50 ml. size.
c. An accurately calibrated 10 ml. syringe, calibrated so that the exact quantity is known, e.g., 9.995 ml., for the injection.

Technique. The patient should be fasting to avoid lipemia and should be at rest before the test is performed. Glassware and instruments should be thoroughly cleaned and dry. The syringes and needles should be coated with silicone to reduce hemolysis; samples should be discarded if there is much visible hemolysis. The test tubes to receive the samples should contain a small amount of dry heparin or sodium-potassium ammonium oxalate anticoagulant. The blood specimens should be drawn after the tourniquet is released to avoid stasis, which will distort the hematocrit reading; a difference of hematocrit readings between the blank plasma sample and the dye plasma sample indicates stasis in drawing of the blood. A macrohematocrit should be done, spinning the tubes at 3000 r.p.m. for at least 30 minutes.

1. Empty a 50 ml. vial of sterile saline except for 7 or 8 ml., which will remain inside. Transfer the contents of one vial (5 ml. of a 0.5 per cent aqueous solution) of T-1824 Evans Blue dye to the saline bottle and mix thoroughly.

2. Fill the accurately calibrated 10 ml. syringe with the diluted dye. The calibration factor must be known for this syringe.

3. Withdraw a 10 ml. sample from the patient, who is in the postabsorptive state and resting and whose tourniquet has been released before the blood sample is taken. Place the blood in a test tube containing a minute amount of dry heparin. Mix gently.

4. Leave the needle in place and inject the dye from the calibrated syringe, making certain that all the dye enters the vein. This can be done by rinsing the syringe three times with blood and reinjecting. Note the time.

5. Without stasis (tourniquet released) withdraw 10 ml. of blood from the opposite arm of the patient 15 minutes after the original injection of the dye. Place the blood in a dry test tube containing dry heparin.

6. Aliquots of the control blood and of the dye-containing blood should be taken to do the macrohematocrit.

7. Centrifuge the blood specimens to obtain clear plasma.

8. Standard solution. Remove exactly 1 ml. of the diluted dye remaining in the saline bottle and dilute to 500 ml. with distilled water in a volumetric flask.

9. Using distilled water as a blank, set at 100 per cent transmission, set the spectrophotometer at 620 millimicrons, and read the optical densities of the control plasma, the dye-tinged plasma specimen,

and the diluted standard (calculations shown at bottom of page).

Comments. Various dyes, such as Evans Blue, Congo Red or Brilliant Vital Red, may be used to measure the plasma and blood volumes. However, Evans Blue is the dye of choice, since its blue color allows the use of red filters or wavelengths in the red part of the spectrum to minimize the effects of hemolysis. Shapiro (1951) has described a simplification, which requires only one determination without a control plasma in cases of emergency. He feels that the plasma blank, although theoretically correct, is of questionable value in view of problems arising from differences in turbidity and hemolysis between the blank and the dyed specimen. Caster *et al.* (1953) have described a direct method using Zephiran as the solvent rather than saline to avoid the errors caused by the absorption of the dye on the glass surface and on the plasma proteins themselves. Salt concentrations and pH effects will also cause variations in the amount of absorption of the dye. These authors have adapted the method for use with only 0.02 ml. of plasma in the experimental animal.

METHOD WITH I^{131}

Storaasli and his associates (1950) employed human albumin tagged with I^{131} to determine the plasma volume of humans. Erickson *et al.* (1953) have described an improved method for the determination of the blood volume, using a scintillation counter. Levey *et al.* (1953) have described the various laboratory factors influencing the use of radioactive iodine to determine plasma volume. The values obtained by such techniques are: total blood volume, 60 to 85 ml. per kilogram; plasma volume, 35 to 60 ml. per kilogram; and red cell volume, 25 to 40 ml. per kilogram. These results are quite reproducible by various techniques. Blood cell mass and blood volume and plasma volume are also being investigated with the use of radioactive isotopes of phosphorus, potassium, iron, and chromium.

Water Content of Tissues

The water content of tissues has always been determined in the past by oven drying, usually for 72 hours, and then obtaining the difference in weights before and after drying. MacDonald and associates (1959) have described a rapid method for the determination of water in serum, utilizing a desiccation technique with an infrared lamp for a period of three hours. The most rapid method for determining water content, especially of blood or serum and plasma, is by the use of the Karl Fisher reagent, which can determine blood and tissue water *in vivo* and *in vitro*. Davis and his co-workers (1953) have described a method using an electrometric endpoint for this titration. Mitchell and Smith (1948) have written a book on the subject of aquametry.

Total Body Water

The total body water is approximately 70 per cent of the body weight when computed on a fat-free or lean muscle mass basis.

Calculations

O.D. (due to dye) = (O.D. of dye + plasma) − O.D. of plasma control

$$\text{Plasma volume} = \frac{\text{Volume of dye injected} \times \text{O.D. standard} \times \text{dilution of standard}}{\text{O.D. of plasma due to dye}}$$

$$\text{Total blood volume} = \frac{\text{plasma volume}}{1 - (0.96 \times \text{Hct.})}$$

Red cell volume = total blood volume − plasma volume

Sample calculations:

Amount of dye delivered by calibrated syringe = 9.995 ml.

O.D. of 1:500 dilution of standard = 0.195

O.D. of control sample = 0.215

O.D. of 15-minute unknown = 0.540

Hematocrit = 52 per cent

$$\text{Plasma volume} = 9.995 \times \frac{0.195}{0.325} \times 500 = 2998 \text{ ml.}$$

$$\text{Total blood volume} = \frac{2,998}{1 - (0.96 \times 0.52)} = 5181 \text{ ml.}$$

Red cell volume = 5181 − 2998 = 2183 ml.

Because the fat content of the body varies from patient to patient and depends especially on the sex, the total body water ranges between 50 and 73 per cent of the total body weight in the adult male with an average of about 60 per cent; in the adult female the range is 44 to 65 per cent of body weight with an average of 54 per cent. In the newborn the total body water is much greater, ranging from 70 to 83 per cent with an average of 77 per cent. Friis-Hansen and associates (1951) have derived a formula that correlates the total body water in liters to the body weight in kilograms for children weighing up to 20 kg.; the formula, however, will fit quite well with the data available for adults. The standard deviation for the formula was plus or minus 7.4 per cent. The formula is:

Total body water =
(0.55 × body weight in kg.) + 0.51.

The body water can be estimated clinically using antipyrine, which is injected intravenously and is then rapidly and evenly distributed throughout the body of man. Blood samples taken at intervals before and after the injection are deproteinized and treated with sodium nitrite. The concentration of 4-nitrosoantipyrine formed is then measured in a Beckman spectrophotometer, using a wavelength of 350 millimicrons (ultraviolet). By extrapolation to zero time the initial plasma concentration is determined. From this information and the amount of antipyrine injected, the body water is calculated. This method has been described by Brodie and co-workers (1949).

Total Osmolarity

In contradistinction to the determination of total base or total cations described previously, the total osmolarity determines the osmotic effects of both the anions and cations present in the blood. The total osmolarity varies from 290 to 310 mosM. per liter. The basis of the determination is that of freezing point determination, which requires a special apparatus and is rather expensive. The results, however, show that there may be some changes in total osmolarity that are not correlated to changes in total electrolyte concentration as determined chemically.

CLINICAL CORRELATIONS

"A fact in itself is nothing. It is valuable only for the idea attached to it, or for proof which it furnishes." —Claude Bernard

Up to now the words in this chapter have described how to accumulate "facts" or figures. The data so gathered will be of no use to the physician unless they help answer a question. Are the data consistent with the suspected clinical condition? What progress is being made in therapy? It must be emphasized that if certain laboratory data do not fit into the suspected clinical diagnosis, the diagnosis based upon a competent history and physical examination usually takes precedence to the laboratory facts.

Replacement of required water for a patient varies with the daily maintenance needs and according to what prior losses have occurred and what losses are continuing. The total body water content of a person will vary inversely with the total fat content ("obesity"). Thus, an obese individual has less body water, denoting a larger per cent daily turnover and, more important, a smaller reserve to combat dehydration without the development of untoward symptoms. In the usual routine laboratory the total body water is not determined. In research laboratories the total body water is determined by measuring the volume of distribution of a substance that can penetrate all the cells of the body; e.g., heavy water (D_2O), tritiated water (HTO), or derivatives of antipyrine. The extracellular compartment can be determined by measuring the volume of distribution of a substance that does not penetrate the cell membrane (e.g., inulin, mannitol, sucrose, thiocyanate, sulfate, bromide, thiosulfate, sodium, and chloride). Low values for extracellular fluid result from the use of inulin, since it does not fully penetrate the interstices of connective tissue, and higher values probably result with chloride since it does enter some cells (e.g., gastric mucosa) and is more concentrated in the connective tissue than in free extracellular fluid. Since the intracellular fluid compartment is calculated by the difference, it is obvious that such values are subject to criticism.

As mentioned previously, total body water varies inversely with content of body fat; the greater water content in males is correlated to the smaller fat content in this sex. In addition the water content changes with age, so that the average water content in a geriatric male is 51 per cent, and in the geriatric female 45 per cent, of the total body weight.

The only body compartment easily accessible for evaluation of the concentration of electrolytes is the intravascular compartment—the blood. The plasma volume is only about 5 per cent of the body weight, so that the mythical normal 70 kg. adult male has a plasma volume of about 3500 ml. Even if the plasma volume is determined (by injection of Evans Blue T-1824 or by using radioactive-labeled substances) in addition to determining the concentration of electrolytes in the plasma, the resulting product will yield the total amount of the particular substance in the vascular tree, and no information is garnered concerning the total amount present in the body. For instance, a patient with congestive heart failure and edema will have an excess of total body water and total body sodium. The blood concentration of sodium may be normal or even, more likely, decreased. On the other hand a patient with a total body potassium deficit owing to severe malnutrition may have an elevated, normal, or decreased potassium concentration in his serum.

Although plasma volumes can be determined under routine conditions, many laboratories do not perform this procedure or only carry it out on patients prior to or after major surgery. The combination of plasma volume and serum concentration of the substance can be of great use in medical problems, e.g., early congestive heart failure, to differentiate dilution hyponatremia from hyponatremia owing to severe salt restriction. The same low value for serum sodium may be seen in both conditions, but the plasma volume will probably be increased (or "normal") in the former and normal (or "decreased") in the latter condition.

The average total body water of the young adult male has been given as 60 per cent of the body weight; the usual average for the intracellular and extracellular compartments are 45 and 15 per cent, respectively, of the body weight. The intracellular water is computed as the difference between the total body water and the water held in the extracellular spaces. Recent advances in radioactive tracer work have shown that the value for the intracellular compartment is too large, because the extracellular compartment now includes more than the intravascular fluid and interstitial fluid included previously in this category. The plasma volume water is 4.5 per cent of the body weight. The interstitial fluid compartment (12 per cent of the body weight) also includes the lymph and a rapidly equilibrating phase of the connective tissue. The major portion of the connective tissue and cartilaginous tissue contains water equal to 4.5 per cent of the body weight. Extracellular water found in bone also equals 4.5 per cent of the body weight. The smallest amount of water (1.5 per cent of the body weight) is found in the transcellular compartment, which is formed by the transport activity of certain cells: certain cells of the gastrointestinal tract (e.g., salivary glands, pancreas, liver and biliary tract, mucous membranes, and the intraluminal fluid), "epidermal" cells (e.g., skin and mucous membranes of the respiratory tract), kidneys, cerebrospinal fluid, humors of the eye, and endocrine secretions (e.g., thyroid and gonads). Thus, the body water comprises 60 per cent of the body weight (adult male), but the new values for the intracellular and extracellular compartments are 33 and 27 per cent, respectively, of the body weight.

The osmotic pressures of the serum and urine are usually expressed in terms of milliosmoles per liter. There is a semantic difference, depending upon the technique of measurement, between osmolarity and osmolality; for our purposes the two terms may be considered synonymous. Most work has been reported in terms of milliosmoles per liter; e.g., the milliosmolar concentration of normal plasma is about 290 mosM. per liter of plasma, and on the basis of per liter of plasma water the concentration is about 310 mosM. Talbot *et al.* (1959) use the reciprocal or milliliters per milliosmole; their normal range is 270 to 285 mosM. per liter, which is equivalent to 3.7 to 3.5 ml. per milliosmole.

A decreased blood volume will be marked by circulatory dysfunction as evident by hypotension, weak thready pulse, cold clammy extremities, and cyanotic mottling of the skin; such circulatory insufficiency is best treated by proper replacement of the blood volume constituents. If the circulatory embarrassment is the result of cardiac or vascular failure rather than hypovolemia, the better treatment would be vasopressor agents rather than volume replacement. Table 9–11 shows various examples of reduced blood volume and some determinations that allow for a proper differential diagnosis. A "pure" body water deficit (e.g., owing to diabetes insipidus) of 120 ml. per kilogram would produce a 20 per cent reduction of the blood volume; the concentrations of sodium, total protein, and hemoglobin, the hematocrit, and the solute/water ratio would be increased, and the water/solute ratio would be decreased. If electrolytes are lost in addition to the

Table 9–11. Theoretical Types of Hypovolemia*

CONDITION	REQUIRED DEFICIT† (ml./kg.)	SODIUM (mEq./L.)	SERUM PROTEIN (gm./100 ml.)	HEMATO-CRIT (ml./100 ml.)	HEMO-GLOBIN (gm./100 ml.)	RATIOS SOLUTE WATER (mosM./L.)	RATIOS WATER SOLUTE (ml./mosM.)
Normal	—	N	N	N	N	N	N
Body water deficit	120	I	I	I	I	I	D
Extracellular water and solute deficit	75	N–D	I	I	I	N	N
Plasma deficit	15	N	N–D	I	I	N	N
Whole blood deficit	16	N	N–D	N–D	N–D	N	N
Deficit of electrolytes and cells	—	D	D	D	D	D	I

* Based on Talbot *et al.* (1959)
† To produce a 20 per cent reduction of blood volume.
N Normal
I Increased
D Decreased

water, resulting in a deficit of extracellular fluid, only a deficit of 75 ml. per kilogram is needed to produce a 20 per cent reduction in blood volume; such losses may be seen in vomiting, diarrhea, profuse sweating, or adrenal insufficiency. The accompanying changes in concentration are shown in Table 9–11. However, a loss directly from the vascular tree causes a more immediate reduction of blood volume. A deficit of only 15 ml. of plasma per kilogram of body weight (such as that found in patients with burns or severe proteinuria) or a deficit of whole blood (hemorrhage) of 16 ml. per kilogram will result in such hypovolemia (Table 9–11).

The ratio of water to solutes (or solutes to water) is reversed in the presence of hypervolemia, such as that seen in body water excess with edema or in left heart failure. There is an increased value for milliliters per milliosmole and a decreased value for milliosmoles per liter. Such solute ratios may also be seen in hypovolemia resulting from the loss of erythrocytes or serum proteins or extracellular electrolytes. In these cases (with a decreased value of milliosmoles per liter) the values for sodium, protein, hemoglobin, and hematocrit will be decreased (Table 9–11). It is evident, therefore, that elevation of a sodium value does not designate the cause to the physician. A history and physical examination will help point the way, and laboratory examinations may be required to prove that hyponatremia is due to retention of water resulting from congestive heart failure or to severe restriction of sodium intake in a cardiac patient.

A physician may be confronted with a patient exhibiting tetanic convulsions. Is it due to hypocalcemia or hypomagnesemia, to water intoxication or alkalosis, or to organic brain disease? Any one of these conditions may be the cause. A positive Chvostek or Trousseau sign would speak against water intoxication or an organic lesion, but it will not distinguish among hypocalcemia, hypomagnesemia or alkalosis as the cause of the increased neuromuscular irritability. Alkalosis may be determined by using a pH meter to test the blood pH. Magnesium levels are not done routinely. There may be an actual decrease of the total calcium (e.g., hypoparathyroidism), or the total calcium may be normal or even elevated and the physiologically active ionized calcium decreased because of increased binding to an increased amount of protein present in the blood (e.g., myeloma).

The McLean and Hastings nomogram or the Zeisler formula for calculating the ionized calcium from the total calcium and total protein is accurate only over the normal ranges of concentration and only if the serum proteins are "normal." Although such calculations are fraught with a potential error, they are better than none. A quick method of determining the serum level of calcium as a cause of tetany is the Sulkowitch test for urine calcium. This qualitative test is not too good for determining the amount of calcium excreted in the urine, since normal individuals have a 1 to 2 + excretion value (which depends upon the dietary intake of calcium). However, the Sulkowitch test is of excellent value in following a patient after a parathyroidectomy to be sure that the dietary intake of calcium is sufficient or to determine whether hypocalcemia is the cause of the convulsions in the patient mentioned previously. A negative Sulkowitch reaction denotes that the renal threshold for calcium excretion has not been exceeded; this implies that the serum total calcium level must be below 7.5 mg. per 100 ml.

If intravenous calcium therapy is to be given to such a patient, a blood specimen should be taken prior to therapy for subsequent determination of the levels of calcium, phosphorus, alkaline phosphatase, and total proteins for proper evaluation of the status of the parathyroids and bone metabolism. At leisure the urinary excretion of calcium and phosphorus should be determined on a known low calcium intake (Aub diet), or the determination of tubular reabsorption of phosphate (TRP) should be done for a more complete evaluation of the status of the parathyroid glands. It must be remembered that chronic renal insufficiency may result in secondary involvement of the parathyroid glands.

Phosphorus is involved with calcium metabolism, but it is also related to the pituitary growth hormone. The serum level of phosphorus is elevated in children (Table 9–2). This is presumably due to growth hormone activity. The serum phosphorus (in the absence of parathyroid or renal disease) is elevated in periods of active growth as in children or in patients with excessive growth hormone activity (e.g., the active phases of gigantism or acromegaly). Conversely the phosphorus level is decreased during active transfer of sugars from the blood to the cells. Glucose enters the cells as glucose-6-phosphoric acid, presumably in the form of the potassium salt of this strong acid.

This transfer of phosphorus with glucose has been shown to occur in the course of a glucose tolerance test. The phosphorus and potassium levels in the blood are virtual mirror images of the changing levels of glucose during the course of the tolerance test in a normal individual. In severe diabetes there is no drop of the phosphorus (and potassium) level correlating to the impaired passage of glucose into the cells. Minor impairment of the phosphorus change is seen in patients with relatively mild diabetes. This finding is of great advantage in the temporary therapy of acute hyperkalemia if no vivodialysis apparatus is available. Thus in a 2-month-old child (5 kg.) with a serum potassium level of 7 mEq. per liter the potassium level was brought down to 5 mEq. per liter by the intravenous administration over a 24-hour period of 300 ml. of 10 per cent glucose in water to which 10 units of regular insulin had been added.

So far mention has been made primarily of the cations. Phosphorus was discussed in relation to calcium metabolism and to carbohydrate metabolism. It should be emphasized that phosphorus will be elevated in the presence of renal insufficiency with retention of nitrogenous products (azotemia). In addition sulfate is elevated early in the course of renal insufficiency—even prior to the elevation of the nitrogenous components. Unfortunately sulfate is not determined in most laboratories, but when it can be done it is of great help in evaluating early cases of renal insufficiency. Another group of anions not usually determined in the course of electrolyte studies is the organic acids. Normally lactic acid and pyruvic acid, for example, are found in small quantities, the total concentration being equal to 5 mEq. per liter. In the course of congestive heart failure, liver dysfunction, or severe exertion the lactate level can and does rise very quickly to high levels. In the presence of diabetic acidosis, starvation acidosis, or relative lack of carbohydrate in the diet there is a great increase in the concentration of ketone bodies in the blood. Usually an accumulation of phosphate, sulfate, lactate, or ketones will result in a decreased bicarbonate (carbon dioxide content, for example).

Plasma proteins are usually considered as part of liver function, but it should not be forgotten that this large amount (by weight) of material in the blood does act as anions, since at the pH of the blood the protein molecules (zwitterions) have a negative charge. The variations in plasma proteins do not have so great an effect on the concentration of bicarbonate as do the other anions (which are excreted by the kidneys).

Chloride ion usually follows the same pattern of metabolism as sodium, but when the bicarbonate level is altered the chloride is usually changed in a reciprocal fashion. Noteworthy to remember, however, is the correlation of chloride with potassium in cases of metabolic alkalosis as seen in primary hyperaldosteronism; there is a hypokalemic, hypochloremic, metabolic alkalosis. Somewhat forgotten today is the major retention of chloride ion in cases of lobar pneumonia; the lack of knowledge is correlated to the lack of exposure to full-blown cases of lobar pneumonia. In this respiratory disorder there is a great retention of chloride in the tissues (and blood) until the "crisis" at which time the practically nonexistent urinary chloride excretion increases tremendously with the consequent loss of the retained chloride from the tissues and blood.

The average physician does not take advantage of the use of a battery of electrolyte determinations for the best evaluation of his patient. A routine electrolyte study should be performed on all patients who are to undergo gastrointestinal surgery or a laparotomy and on all patients, no matter how minor their ailments, who are past 50 years of age. The basic electrolyte battery consists of sodium, potassium, chloride, bicarbonate (e.g., carbon dioxide content), and pH determinations—all done at the same time. One can quickly check on the electroneutrality by adding the cations sodium and potassium and the anions chloride and bicarbonate; the respective values (Table 9–1) are 142 + 5 = 147 and 27 + 103 = 130. The average patient who does not exhibit any tetany can be assumed to have a normal level of calcium and magnesium, so that the total cations would be 147 + 7 = 154 mEq. per liter. The difference between the 154 cation value and the 130 anion value is 24, showing that the sulfate, phosphate, organic acids, and proteinate are normal (Table 9–1 and Fig. 9–1).

An example of pathologic changes is seen in a young adult diabetic male whose four major electrolytes are found to be: sodium 122, potassium 4, chloride 79, and carbon dioxide content 5. Adding 122 + 4 + 7 (for calcium and magnesium) equals 133 mEq. per liter. Adding 79 + 5 + 24 (for "normal" residual anions) equals 108 mEq. per liter, leaving a deficit of 25 mEq. of anions, which consist of ketone bodies, and perhaps a small rise of the sulfate and phosphate, depending upon the status of the kidneys.

The total electrolyte osmolarity of this diabetic patient is 222 mosM. per liter instead of the normal 289 mosM. per liter. However, the osmolar deficit is not 67 mosM. per liter, because the increased sugar present in the blood of this diabetic patient is exerting an osmotic effect greater than that owing to a normal blood sugar level. A sugar concentration of 100 mg. per 100 ml. exerts an osmotic pressure of 5.5 mosM. per liter. If the patient has a blood sugar of 650 mg. per 100 ml., the "excess" 550 mg. of sugar per 100 ml. will exert an "extra" osmotic effect of 30 mosM. per liter. Thus, the milliosmolar deficit is not 67 but 37 mosM. per liter. If any azotemia is present, the elevated urea will exert an "extra" osmotic effect. A normal urea nitrogen of 20 mg. per 100 ml. exerts an osmotic pressure of about 7 mosM. per liter. If the patient's urea nitrogen were 75 mg. per 100 ml., the "excess" 55 mg. of urea nitrogen per 100 ml. would exert an "extra" osmotic effect of 19 mosM. per liter. Thus, the final net milliosmolar deficit would be only 18 mosM. per liter. Our diabetic patient exhibits hyponatremia, hypochloremia, and a decreased bicarbonate, but the "tonicity" of his plasma is closer to his normal because of the elevated blood sugar and elevated urea nitrogen. Thus, the ratios of solutes to water (milliosmoles per liter) and of water to solutes (milliliters per milliosmole) are fairly close to normal and the blood volume is close to normal.

The last value of the "electrolyte battery," the pH, denotes the ratio of bicarbonate to carbonic acid. In this case the pH was 7.06. The various factors for pH 7.06 can be obtained from Tables 9–3, 9–4, and 9–5 to calculate the actual bicarbonate as 4.5 mEq. per liter, the carbonic acid as 0.5 mM. per liter, and the P_{CO_2} as 15.5 mm. Hg. That there has been some compensation of the metabolic acidosis owing to diabetes is shown by the reduced carbonic acid (and reduced P_{CO_2}); partial compensation is achieved by processes leading to respiratory alkalosis. Such changes are portrayed in Fig. 9–5, which pinpoints the status of the patient (carbon dioxide content 5 and pH 7.06) at a point at which the ratio of bicarbonate to carbonic acid is about 9 to 1; this is actually so with the calculated values (4.5 and 0.5).

A patient with duodenal obstruction has the following electrolyte data: sodium 138, potassium 5, chloride 49, carbon dioxide content 42, and pH 7.55. The total cations 138 + 5 + "7" equal 150, and the total anions 49 + 42 + "24" equal 115. The anion deficit of 35 mEq. is actually made up by the presence of 5 mEq. of residual anions (phosphate and sulfate) and 30 mEq. of ketone bodies. Despite the greatly increased concentration of keto-acids, the blood pH is alkaline because of the increased ratio of bicarbonate to carbonic acid. The factors for pH 7.55 from Tables 9–3, 9–4, and 9–5 will yield an actual bicarbonate of 40.5 mEq. per liter, a carbonic acid of 1.5 mM. per liter, and a P_{CO_2} of 48.7 mm. Hg. This is an uncompensated metabolic alkalosis ("normal" carbonic acid and P_{CO_2}), even though a high concentration of keto-acids is present. Figure 9–5 shows the ratio of bicarbonate to carbonic acid at pH 7.55 to be about 28 to 1; the calculated value for the respective concentrations 40.5 and 1.5 is 27 to 1.

An elderly patient with emphysema is admitted to the hospital with findings of sodium 142, potassium 5, chloride 86, carbon dioxide content 44, and pH 7.30. Using the factors in Tables 9–3, 9–4, and 9–5, the actual bicarbonate is found to be 41.3 mEq. per liter; the carbonic acid, 2.7 mM. per liter; and the P_{CO_2}, 88 mm. Hg. A condition of respiratory acidosis is present and has been partially compensated by renal mechanisms leading to metabolic alkalosis. The total cations 142 + 5 + "7" equal 154, and the total anions 86 + 41 + "24" equal 151, representing "complete" balance and no alterations of the osmolarity of the plasma. Fig. 9–5 shows the ratio of bicarbonate to carbonic acid at pH 7.30 to be 16 to 1; the calculated value for the respective concentrations 41.3 and 2.7 is 15 to 1.

A two-year-old child is admitted to the hospital because of severe hyperpnea. An electrolyte study reveals sodium 136, potassium 4, chloride 105, and carbon dioxide content 13. The total cations 136 + 4 + "7" equal 147, and the total anions 105 + 13 + "24" equal 142. There is no imbalance or, perhaps, a negative imbalance of 5 mEq. of anions. In addition the urine is found to contain some ketone bodies and a trace of reducing substances. The findings of hyperventilation, low carbon dioxide, glycosuria, and ketonuria can easily lead the physician down the path to a diagnosis of diabetic acidosis. In this case therapy with insulin is contraindicated until a more definitive diagnosis can be made. In all youngsters presenting such findings, the possibility of salicylate intoxication must be considered.

A blood pH will confirm the accurate history; at this stage (during the early period) the pH is found to be 7.65. The true diagnosis is respiratory alkalosis owing to salicylate intoxication, which causes the hyperpnea by stimulation of the central nervous system; the glycosuria and ketonuria are the result of depletion of liver glycogen by the salicylates. Reference to Tables 9–3, 9–4, and 9–5 yields an actual

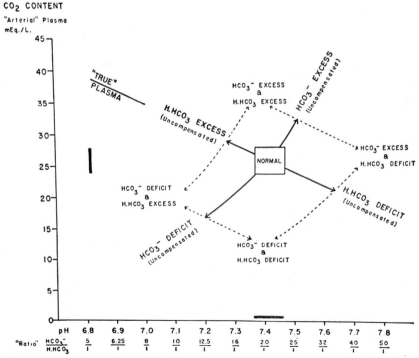

Figure 9–5. Dynamics of acid-base balance. (From Weisberg [1959]; modified from Weisberg [1953] after Davenport.)

bicarbonate of 12.64 mEq. per liter, a carbonic acid of 0.36 mM. per liter, and a P_{CO_2} of 12 mm. Hg. Thus, there has been some attempt at compensation of the respiratory alkalosis (low P_{CO_2}) by renal changes leading to metabolic acidosis (further lowering of the bicarbonate). Figure 9–5 shows the ratio of bicarbonate to carbonic acid at pH 7.65 to be about 37 to 1; the calculated value for the respective concentrations 12.64 and 0.36 is 35 to 1.

At a later stage of salicylate intoxication there may be a shift of the blood pH to the acid side, which would complicate the differential diagnosis between diabetes and salicylism. Even in the face of a low pH the physician must consider and rule out salicylate intoxication before instituting insulin therapy. If facilities are available for determining the blood salicylate level, the problem can be easily solved. However, even in the absence of such laboratory facilities, the diagnosis can be made in the emergency room by the utilization of Gerhardt's test for diacetic acid. Gerhardt's ferric chloride test for diacetic acid is a poor test in comparison to the nitroprusside tests to determine acetoacetic acid. It will be recalled that salicylates interfere with Gerhardt's test. Therefore, Gerhardt's test should be performed on two portions of urine, one of which has been acidified with concentrated nitric acid and boiled for at least one minute and then cooled prior to performing the test. The various reactions and their connotations are shown in Table 9–12. It should be emphasized that both diacetic acid and salicylate may be present in the same urine specimen; this is especially so in the case of an adult diabetic who has been taking aspirin.

Another simple test to help the thinking physician is the determination of ketone bodies in the blood or urine, preferably the former, utilizing the Dumm and Shipley test. In diabetic acidosis the plasma ketones are usually greater than 50 mg. per 100 ml., whereas the level is usually under 20 mg. in cases of salicylate intoxication. Again it must be remembered that both conditions may coexist in the same patient and that it behooves the physician to utilize all his capabilities to arrive at a clinical diagnosis; then proper laboratory tests should be performed to gather "facts" for "proof" of the diagnosis.

REFERENCES

1. Asper, S. P., Jr., Schales, O., and Schales, S. S.: Importance of controlling pH in the Schales and Schales method of chloride determination. J. Biol. Chem., 168:779, 1947.
2. Astrup, P., and Schrøder, S.: Apparatus for anaerobic determination of the pH of blood at 38 degrees C. Scand. J. Clin. & Lab. Invest., 8:30, 1956.
3. Baginski, E. S., Williams, L. A., Jarkowski, T. L., and Zak, B.: Polarographic and spectrophotometric micro serum determination of chloride. Am. J. Clin. Path., 30:559, 1958.
4. Barker, S. B., and Summerson, W. H.: Colorimetric determination of lactic acid in biological material. J. Biol. Chem., 138:535, 1941.
5. Barry, J. M., and Rowland, S. J.: Determination of blood serum potassium by an improved sodium cobaltinitrite method. Biochem. J., 53:213, 1953.
6. Boesun, E., and Loud, P. A.: A preliminary communication on a conductimetric screening test for electrolytes. J. Clin. Path., 9:137, 1956.
7. Brodie, B. B., Axelrod, J., Soberman, R., and Levy, B. B.: The estimation of antipyrine in biological materials. J. Biol. Chem., 179:25, 1949.
8. Caraway, W. T., and Fanger, H.: Ultramicro procedures in clinical chemistry. Am. J. Clin. Path., 25:317, 1955.
9. Caster, W. O., Simon, A. B., and Armstrong, W. W.: A direct method for the determination of Evans blue using Zephiran as a solvent. J. Lab. & Clin. Med., 42:493, 1953.
10. Clark, E. P., and Collip, J. B.: Tisdall method for determination of blood calcium with a suggested modification. J. Biol. Chem., 63:461, 1925.
11. Collier, C. R., Affeldt, J. E., and Farr, A. F.: Continuous rapid infrared CO_2 analysis. J. Lab. & Clin. Med., 45:526, 1955.
12. Cotlove, E., Trantham, H. V., and Bowman, R. L.: An instrument and method for automatic, rapid, accurate and sensitive titration of chloride in biologic samples. J. Lab. & Clin. Med., 51:461, 1958.
13. Davenport, H. W.: The ABC of Acid-Base Chemistry. 4th ed. Chicago, The University of Chicago Press, 1958.
14. Davis, F. E., Kenyon, K., and Kirk, J.: A rapid titrimetric method for determining the water content of human blood. Science, 118:276, 1953.
15. Dryer, R. L., Tammes, A. R., and Routh, J. I.:

Table 9–12. Differential Diagnosis Utilizing Gerhardt's Test

REACTIONS OF URINE SPECIMENS*		DENOTES†	
NON-BOILED	BOILED	DIACETIC ACID	"SALICYLATE"
−	−	0	0
(−	+ Reactions do not occur.)		
+	−	+	0
+	+ Same color	0	+
+	+ Less intense color	+	+

* + Positive ("red") color   † 0 Absence
− Negative (no color)   + Presence

A new reagent for the determination of phosphorus. J. Biol. Chem., 225:177, 1957.

16. Dumm, R. M., and Shipley, R. A.: The simple estimation of blood ketones in diabetic acidosis. J. Lab. & Clin. Med., 31:1162, 1946.

17. Edelman, I. S., and Leibman, J.: Anatomy of body water and electrolytes. Am. J. Med. 27: 256, 1959.

18. Erickson, J. R., McCormick, J. B., and Seed, L.: An improved method for the determination of blood volume using radioactive iodinated human serum albumen. Science, 118:595, 1953.

19. Ferro, P. V., and Ham, A. B.: A simple spectrophotometric method for the determination of calcium. Am. J. Clin. Path., 28:208, 1957.

20. Ferro, P. V., and Ham, A. B.: A simple spectrophotometric method for the determination of calcium. II. A semimicro method with reduced precipitation time. Am. J. Clin. Path., 28:689, 1957.

21. Fiske, C. H., and Subbarow, Y.: The colorimetric determination of phosphorus. J. Biol. Chem., 66:375, 1925.

22. Friis-Hansen, B. J., Holiday, M., Stapleton, T., and Wallace, W. M.: Total body water in children. Pediatrics, 7:321, 1951.

23. Gambino, S. R.: Variation of plasma pH with temperature of separation. Am. J. Clin. Path., 32:270–301, 1959.

24. Greenwald, I.: The relation of concentration of calcium to that of protein and inorganic phosphate in serum. J. Biol. Chem., 93:551, 1931.

25. Gregerson, M. I.: An analysis of colorimetric methods in relation to plasma volume determinations. J. Lab. & Clin. Med., 23:423, 1938.

26. Gregerson, M. I.: A practical method for the determination of blood volume with dye T-1824; a survey of the present basis of the dye-method and its clinical applications. J. Lab. & Clin. Med., 29:1266, 1944.

27. Hastings, A. B., and Sendroy, J., Jr.: Studies of acidosis; colorimetric determination of blood pH at body temperature without buffer standards. J. Biol. Chem., 61:695, 1924.

28. Heagy, F. C.: The use of polyvinyl alcohol in the colorimetric determination of magnesium in plasma or serum by means of Titan Yellow. Canad. J. Res., 26E:295, 1948.

29. Holaday, D. A.: An improved method for multiple rapid determinations of arterial blood pH. J. Lab. & Clin. Med., 44:149, 1954.

30. Jacobs, H. R. D., and Hoffman, W. S.: A new colorimetric method for the estimation of potassium. J. Biol. Chem., 93:685, 1931.

31. Keitel, H. G., and Keitel, N. B.: Rapid simple method for the determination of serum potassium. J.A.M.A., 153:799, 1953.

32. Kingsley, G. R., and Dowdell, L. A.: Direct iodometric colorimetric determination of blood chloride. J. Lab. & Clin. Med., 35:637, 1950.

33. Kirman, D., Morgenstein, S. W., and Feldman, D.: A modified microtechnic for determining chloride. Am. J. Clin. Path., 30:564, 1958.

34. Kleeman, C. R., Taborsky, E., and Epstein, F. H.: Improved method for determination of inorganic sulfate in biologic fluids. Proc. Soc. Exper. Biol. & Med., 91:480, 1956.

35. Kramer, B., and Tisdall, F. F.: Clinical method for quantitative determination of potassium in small amounts of serum. J. Biol. Chem., 46:339, 1921.

36. Kramer, B., and Tisdall, F. F.: Simple technique for determination of calcium and magnesium in small amounts of serum. J. Biol. Chem., 47:475, 1921.

37. Kunkel, H. O., Pearson, P. B., and Schweigert, B. S.: The photoelectric determination of magnesium in body fluids. J. Lab. & Clin. Med., 32:1027, 1947.

38. Letonoff, T. V., and Reinhold, J. G.: A colorimetric method for the determination of inorganic sulfate in serum and urine. J. Biol. Chem., 114:147, 1936.

39. Levey, S., Hower, J., and Loughridge, R. H.: Laboratory factors influencing the determination of plasma volume using human albumin tagged with I131. J. Lab. & Clin. Med.,41:316, 1953.

40. McLean, F. C., and Hastings, A. B.: The state of calcium in fluids of the body. J. Biol. Chem., 108:285, 1935.

41. McLean, F. C., and Hastings, A. B.: Clinical estimation and significance of calcium ion concentrations in the blood. Am. J. M. Sc., 189:601, 1935.

42. MacDonald, A., Pomeroy, J. S., and Gardner, M. H.: A rapid method for the determination of water in serum. Am. J. Clin. Path., 31:563, 1959.

43. Mitchell, J., Jr., and Smith, D. R.: Aquametry. New York, Interscience Publishers, Inc., 1948.

44. Nadeau, G.: Simple method for combined determination of plasma bicarbonate, pH and chloride. Am. J. Clin. Path., 23:710, 1953.

45. Nalefski, L. A., and Takano, F.: A photonephelometric method for the determination of sulfate in biologic fluids. J. Lab. & Clin. Med., 36:468, 1950.

46. Natelson, S.: Routine use of ultramicro methods in the clinical laboratory; Estimation of sodium, potassium, chloride, protein, hematocrit volume, sugar, urea and nonprotein nitrogen in fingertip blood; Construction of ultramicro pipets; A practical microgasometer for estimation of carbon dioxide. Am. J. Clin. Path., 21:1153, 1951.

47. Natelson, S.: Microtechniques of Clinical Chemistry for the Routine Laboratory. Springfield, Illinois, Charles C Thomas, 1957.

48. Neill, D. W., and Neely, R. A.: The estimation of magnesium in serum using Titan Yellow. J. Clin. Path., 9:162, 1956.

49. Nordin, B. E. C., and Fraser, R.: The effect of intravenous calcium on phosphate excretion. Clin. Sc., 13:477, 1954.

50. Nordin, B. E. C., and Fraser, R.: A calcium-infusion test. I. Urinary excretion data for recognition of osteomalacia. Lancet, 1:823, 1956.

51. O'Mara, T. F., and Faulkner, W. R.: A mechanized Natelson microgasometer. Am. J. Clin. Path., 31:34, 1959.

52. Rose, G. A.: Determination of the ionized and ultrafilterable calcium of normal human plasma. Clin. Chim. Acta, 2:227, 1957.

53. Rosenthal, H. L., and Buscaglia, S.: Determination of carbon dioxide combining power. A simple gas apparatus for equilibration of carbon dioxide. Am. J. Clin. Path., 28:391, 1958.

54. Rosenthal, T. B.: The effect of temperature on the pH of blood and plasma in vitro. J. Biol. Chem., 173:25, 1948.

55. Sanz, M. C.: Ultramicro methods and standardization of equipment. Clin. Chem., 3:406, 1957.

56. Schales, O., and Schales, S. S.: Simple and accurate method for determination of chloride in biological fluids. J. Biol. Chem., 140:879, 1941.

57. Scribner, H. B.: Bedside determination of chloride: a method for plasma, urine and

other fluids and its application to fluid balance problems. Proc. Staff Meet. Mayo Clin., 25:209, 1950.

58. Scribner, B. H., and Weigert, H. T.: Bedside determination of total base in serum. J.A.M.A., 155:639, 1954.

59. Shapiro, S. L.: A suggested simplification of blood volume analysis using the dye T-1824. Science, 114:73, 1951.

60. Singer, R. B., Shohl, J., and Bluemele, D. B.: Simultaneous determination of pH, CO_2 content, and cell volume in 0.1 ml. aliquots of cutaneous blood; a modification of the Shock and Hastings technic. Clin. Chem., 1:287, 1955.

61. Storaasli, J. P., Krieger, H., Friedell, H. L., and Holden, W. D.: The use of radioactive iodinated plasma protein in the study of blood volume. Surg. Gynec. & Obstet., 91:458, 1950.

62. Straumfjord, J. V.: Determination of blood pH. Standard Methods of Clinical Chemistry, 2:107, 1958.

63. Sunderman, F. W.: Measurement of serum total base. Am. J. Clin. Path., 15:219, 1945.

64. Talbot, N. B., Richie, R. H., and Crawford, J. D.: Metabolic Homeostasis. Cambridge, Mass., Harvard University Press, 1959.

65. Talbott, G. D., and King, W.: A bedside method for semiquantitative sodium analysis. Stanford M. Bull., 10:82, 1952.

66. Teloh, H. A.: Estimation of magnesium in serum by means of flame spectrophotometry. Am. J. Clin. Path., 30:129, 1958.

67. Toribara, T. Y., Teripka, A. R., and Dewey, P. A.: The ultrafilterable calcium of human serum; ultrafiltration methods and normal values. J. Clin. Invest., 36:738, 1957.

68. Trinder, P.: A rapid method for the determination of sodium in serum. Analyst, 76:596, 1951.

69. Van Fossan, D. D., Baird, E. E., and Tekell, G. S.: A simplified flame spectrophotometric method for estimation of magnesium in serum. Am. J. Clin. Path., 31:368, 1959.

70. Van Slyke, D. D.: Portable form of manometric gas apparatus and certain points in technique of its use. J. Biol. Chem., 73:121, 1927.

71. Van Slyke, D. D., and Hiller, A.: Nomogram for correction of low urine chloride values determined by the silver iodate reaction. J. Biol. Chem., 171:467, 1947.

72. Van Slyke, D. D., and Cullen, G. E.: Studies of acidosis. I. The bicarbonate concentration of the blood plasma; its significance, and its determination as a measure of acidosis. J. Biol. Chem., 30:289, 1917.

73. Van Slyke, D. D., and Hiller, A.: Application of Sendroy's iodometric chloride titration to protein-containing fluids. J. Biol. Chem., 167:107, 1947.

74. Van Slyke, D. D., and Neill, J. M.: The determination of gases in blood and other solutions by vacuum extraction and manometric measurements. J. Biol. Chem., 61:523, 1924.

75. Van Slyke, D. D., and Sendroy, J., Jr.: Carbon dioxide factors for manometric blood gas apparatus. J. Biol. Chem., 73:127, 1927.

76. Van Slyke, D. D., and Stadie, W. C.: Determination of gases of blood. J. Biol. Chem., 49:1, 1921.

76. Van Slyke, D. D., and Stadie, W. C.: Carbon dioxide factors for manometric blood gas apparatus. J. Biol. Chem., 49:1, 1921.

77. Van Slyke, D. D., Weisiger, J. R., and Van Slyke, K. K.: Photometric measurement of plasma pH. J. Biol. Chem., 179:743, 1949.

78. Van Slyke, D. D., Weisiger, J. R., and Van Slyke, K. K.: Photometric measurement of urine pH. J. Biol. Chem., 179:757, 1949.

79. Wacker, W. E. C., and Vallee, B. L.: A study of magnesium metabolism in acute renal failure employing a multichannel flame spectrometer. New Eng. J. Med., 257:1254, 1957.

80. Weisberg, H. F.: Water, Electrolyte and Acid-Base Balance. Baltimore, The Williams & Wilkins Company, 1953.

81. Weisberg, H. F.: A better understanding of anion-cation ("acid-base") balance. Surg. Clin. N. Amer., 39:93, 1959.

82. Willis, M. J., and Sunderman, F. W.: Studies in serum electrolytes. XIX. Nomogram for calculating magnesium ion in serum and ultrafiltrates. J. Biol. Chem., 197:343, 1952.

83. Wilson, R. H.: pH of whole arterial blood. J. Lab. & Clin. Med., 37:129, 1951.

84. Yendt, E. R., Connor, T. B., and Howard, J. E.: In vitro calcification of rachitic rat cartilage in normal and pathological human sera with some observations on the pathogenesis of renal rickets. Bull. Johns Hopkins Hosp., 96:1, 1955.

85. Ziesler, E. B.: Determination of diffusible serum calcium. Am. J. Clin. Path., 24:588, 1954.

Chapter 10

Microbiochemical Techniques
in Pediatrics

By DONOUGH O'BRIEN, M.D., M.R.C.P., and
FRANK A. IBBOTT, F.I.M.L.T.

In recent years pediatricians have come to make steadily increasing demands on the clinical biochemical laboratory. Such a development was, in particular, the logical consequence of realizing the importance of correcting distortions in volume and in quality of the body fluids in the metabolic diseases. It became desirable to develop methods that required only small quantities of blood and serum—in the first place because observations were likely to be required repeatedly, especially in small infants, and in the second place because the practice of taking larger blood samples from the femoral, jugular, or even scalp veins is notoriously disturbing to the very sick infant. In children's hospitals and to a lesser extent in general hospitals with large pediatric departments this progress has been expanded to include the whole range of clinical chemistry, and some particularly elegant techniques have recently been developed for the detection of congenital enzymatic defects in the homozygous and heterozygous states, as for example, that of the red cell phosphogalactotransferase in galactosemia.

The practice of micromethods in the large general clinical laboratory tends frequently to be avoided owing to the widely held belief that it is not possible to obtain sufficiently reliable results unless there is available a chemist who has been especially instructed in these methods and who has

had long experience with them. As with any skill, of course, frequent practice is essential to achieve perfection, but an appreciation of the fundamentals of microtechniques will eliminate much unsatisfactory work. In practice it has been found unnecessary to resort to ultra-microprocedures, which do not always fit into the routine of busy clinical laboratories or of changing staffs, although the automatic polyethylene delivery pipets of Sanz, which are being marketed with an appropriate spectrophotometer by Beckman, Inc., as an ultra-microanalysis system, may well restore confidence in these techniques (Fig. 10–1). In the methods described later, 0.1 ml. is the most general measurement of serum or plasma, and it requires no more than 0.23 ml. of plasma to give consistently trustworthy results for sodium, potassium, chloride, and CO_2 estimations. The purpose then of this chapter is not to promote micromethods exclusively but, first, to emphasize that the competent mastery of a relatively small number of techniques can satisfy the principal demands of a pediatric department and, second, to point out that a significant number of these techniques can be incorporated with profit into the routine of any chemical laboratory on account of their economy in time and materials, reproducibility, and robustness. The following paragraphs briefly review certain technical aspects that are of special im-

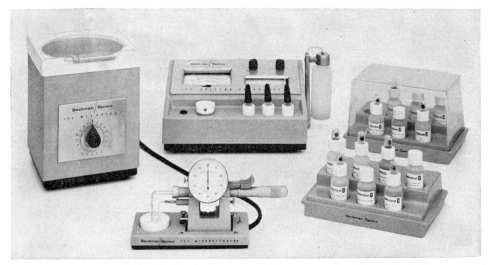

Figure 10–1.   The Beckman/Spinco ultra-microanalytical system.

portance when using small amounts of biologic materials.

COLLECTION OF BLOOD

An adroitly performed heel prick is less traumatic for a small infant than any one of the conventional venipunctures, and it has the additional advantage that it is more simple to repeat frequently. In general it has been found that ether is the most satisfactory agent with which to clean the skin, for the blood will then remain in discrete drops, whereas alcohol will cause the blood to spread; moreover, should any alcohol come in contact with the blood, hemolysis will occur. It is inadvisable to use ether on patients in incubators, and in these cases Wescodyne has proved satisfactory, the skin having been wiped dry with sterile cotton before the puncture is made. The apparatus taken to the bedside is illustrated in Fig. 10–2 and contains the following equipment: ether; Wescodyne; 2½ inch Hagedorn needles, a fresh one sterilized in a cotton plugged test tube for each patient (Hemolets have not been found satisfactory); and rimless, 1½ inch × ⅜ inch Pyrex blood collecting tubes, each containing 0.01 ml. (10 units) of aqueous heparin solution and a layer of mineral oil, capped with a B and D No. 411CU rubber cap, and labeled with an H. If serum is required, the heparin is omitted and the tube labeled accordingly. The tray also contains PCV tubes, screw cap vials containing 3 mg. of potassium oxalate, made by evaporation of 0.1 ml. of 3 per cent potassium oxalate solution, and junior size

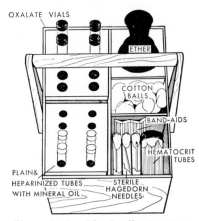

Figure 10–2.   Blood collecting tray.

Band-Aids. In order to avoid hemolysis and contamination with tissue fluid after a needle puncture, it is essential to obtain a free flow of blood, and this may require a little gentle "milking"; squeezing must not be resorted to at any time. The small vein running posteriorly to the internal malleolus and onto the sole of the foot is likely to yield very freely, and this should be pierced at the point where it passes onto the sole whenever possible. A careful and deliberate puncture should be made in contrast to the rapid "stab," which may be used on the fingertip. The blood should drip freely into the collecting tube and should fall at once through the mineral oil. It is permissible to touch the top of the tube onto the drop, but the skin surface should at no time come in contact with the tube, for hemolysis is then almost certain to occur. In the rare instances in which an adequate blood sample proves difficult to get, it is often useful to warm an infant's or a child's foot in a bowl of water at about 37° C. for some two minutes. After the extremity has been dried, it is usually possible to obtain a free flow of blood.

Directly after the collection a cotton ball is placed on the puncture site and pressure applied for a short time. When the blood flow has ceased, a Band-Aid is placed over the puncture site. The tube of blood is covered with the rubber cap and the specimen labeled with the patient's name and the date. When the sample is returned to the laboratory, a Hagedorn needle is passed very gently between the blood and the wall of the tube to release any clot in the unheparinized tubes; the cap is then replaced and the sample spun down for about five minutes at 3000 r.p.m. in a clinical centrifuge.

PIPETS FOR MICROMETHODS AND THEIR USE

The pipets used are those normally found in a biochemical laboratory with certain additions. A pipet calibrated "to contain" is capable of greater accuracy than one calibrated "to deliver," and the former should be used for the measurement of samples and standard solutions whenever possible. Examples of the first type are 0.1 ml. and 0.2 ml. Folin pipets "to contain" and Kirk transfer pipets (Microchemical Specialties), available in a wide range of capacities. One of the cheapest and most satisfactory means of pipetting off serum or plasma with these pipets is a tuberculin syringe with about ¾ inch of flexible rubber or plastic tubing attached to the nozzle. The plunger of the syringe is lubricated with a thin film of rubber grease or silicone grease and mineral oil. A special syringe control is available for Kirk pipets. These pipets must be used as illustrated in Fig. 10–3. The pipet should be held vertically, allowing the tip to enter the sample. If there is a layer of mineral oil, a few moments must be allowed until the oil has retreated from the tip, and then the plunger of the syringe is gently withdrawn until the sample has been drawn up exactly to the mark. The walls above the mark should not be wetted, because this will introduce an error. The outside of the pipet is then wiped with a tissue and all adhering liquid removed, the sample now being slowly expelled into a diluent. Usually the sample will sink in a steady stream to the

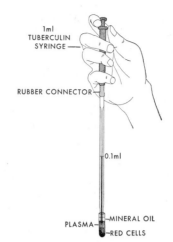

Figure 10–3. Technique for pipetting off plasma.

bottom, in which case diluent from near the top is taken up to the mark and very slowly expelled, care being taken that the pipet tip remains quite still so that the descent of the dilute sample will not be disturbed. This washing process is repeated once. It is possible in this manner to make accurate transfers of plasma and of aqueous and organic solutions. When the diluent is a protein precipitant, it is much more satisfactory to wash the serum or plasma into distilled water and, subsequently, to add the protein precipitant in double strength rather than to wash the serum directly into the more dilute precipitant.

An example of a pipet calibrated "to deliver" is the Lang-Levy pipet, which derives its precision from the fact that the zero point is self-setting. The sample is drawn a short distance above the constriction, and then the meniscus is allowed to adjust itself within the constriction. In emptying, the tip is placed in contact with the side of the receiving vessel, and a slight positive pressure is applied via a mouthpiece and tubing to start the delivery. The pipet is allowed to empty by gravity, and when the meniscus stops moving, the remainder of the fluid is carefully blown out. This type of pipet should be used only when it is not possible to use a "washout" pipet.

CLEANING OF GLASSWARE

When estimations are carried out on small quantities, it is of the utmost importance to set high standards in the cleaning of glassware. An overnight soak in Haemosol solution (1 oz. to 1 gallon of water) and a rinse in tap water followed by a thorough brushing in dilute (1:100) aqueous 7X or Sterox SE solution gives satisfactory cleaning. The process is completed by six rinses in tap water followed by two with deionized water.

Glassware for serum iron is soaked in EDTA solution or in dilute hydrochloric acid for one to two hours in addition to the cleaning just described. Similarly glassware for calcium estimation by the calcein method is also previously treated with EDTA, being subsequently rinsed with distilled water and deionized water.

DEIONIZED WATER

Deionized water should be of very high standard and is satisfactorily prepared by passing once-distilled water through a column of Amberlite MB-3 and then storing it in plastic aspirators. It should be used for the preparation of all aqueous solutions and as a diluent in all methods.

A SELECTION OF THE BIOCHEMICAL MICROTECHNIQUES MOST FREQUENTLY NEEDED IN PEDIATRICS

The most commonly used procedures are set out in the ensuing pages. Except for flame photometry, which is described in Chapter 8, this assembly comprises the greater part of the spectrum usually demanded by pediatricians and includes the following determinations for blood, plasma, or serum: CO_2 content, chloride, calcium, phosphorus, bilirubin, alkaline phosphatase, blood urea nitrogen, proteins, glucose, xylose, mucoprotein tyrosine, and total cholesterol. In each case the principle of the technique is briefly discussed with some additional notes on the interpretation. All the chemicals listed for these techniques should be of reagent grade.

Plasma CO_2 Content

The Kopp-Natelson microgasometer is a robust piece of apparatus capable of measuring plasma CO_2 content on 0.03 ml. of plasma. In practice the only difficulties with this apparatus are small leaks around the joints and stopcocks. These can be prevented by careful greasing with a high vacuum, nonsilicone preparation, but it is also desirable to have available a spare manometer and gas chamber, which can be quickly substituted while the other set is being cleaned. Teflon stopcocks are advisable.

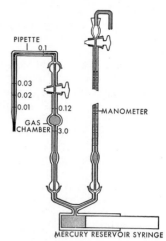

Figure 10–4. Schematic representation of Natelson microgasometer.

When using micromethods, it is impractical to measure CO_2 combining power, and for this reason there arises the rather minor disadvantage of having to take samples for CO_2 content under mineral oil.

The apparatus is illustrated in Fig. 10–4, and the method (Natelson, 1951) is as follows.

Reagents

1. Lactic acid, approx. 1 N. Make 10 ml. of lactic acid up to 100 ml. with distilled water.

2. Sodium hydroxide, approx. 3 N. Dissolve 12 gm. NaOH in and make up to 100 ml. with distilled water.

3. CO_2 standard (22.4 m. mols/L.). Dry anhydrous Na_2CO_3 at 260° C. for one-half hour. Cool in a desiccator; then weigh out 2.382 gm. Dissolve this amount in and make up to 1000 ml. with freshly demineralized water. Store a few milliliters under mineral oil in a screw cap vial containing about 3 ml. of mercury.

Preparation of reagent vials. Into labeled, screw cap vials place the following (all volumes are approximate):

1. 2 ml. mercury, 4 ml. 1 N lactic acid, 2 ml. caprylic alcohol.
2. 5 ml. mercury, 4 ml. 3 N NaOH.
3. 5 ml. mercury, 4 ml. freshly deionized water.
4. 1 N lactic acid to be used for rinsing between tests.

A 50 ml. beaker containing distilled water for rinsing is also needed.

Technique

1. Draw up 0.03 ml. specimen and 0.01 ml. Hg into pipet.
2. Add 0.03 ml. lactic acid, 0.01 ml.

Hg, 0.01 ml. caprylic alcohol, and 0.01 ml. Hg.

3. Add 0.1 ml. freshly deionized water, and Hg to 0.12 ml. mark.

4. Close stopcock and draw back mercury meniscus to 3 ml. mark.

5. Shake for one minute.

6. Advance to 0.12 ml. and read manometer (P_{S_1}).

7. Advance Hg to top of manometer and open chamber stopcock.

8. Add 0.1 ml. NaOH, and Hg to 0.12 ml. mark.

9. Close stopcock and draw back to 3 ml. mark.

10. Advance to 0.12 ml. and read manometer (P_{S_2}).

11. Rinse with water, lactic acid, and water again.

With each batch carry out a blank estimation omitting sample. ($P_{B_1} - P_{B_2}$) = blank.

Calculation. ($P_{S_1} - P_{S_2}$ − blank) × Factor = millimols/L. CO_2.

FACTORS FOR ESTIMATION OF CO_2 CONTENT

Temperature °C.	Factor
17	0.242
18	0.240
19	0.238
20	0.237
21	0.236
22	0.235
23	0.234
24	0.233
25	0.232
26	0.231
27	0.230
28	0.229
29	0.228
30	0.227
31	0.225
32	0.224

Plasma and Sweat Chloride

The measurement of plasma chloride, particularly in association with CO_2 content, offers in children a good index of acidosis and alkalosis and of the overall osmolality of the extracellular water, provided there is no excessive lipemia. Normal values lie between 97 and 104 milliequivalents per liter, much lower values being found in such conditions as pyloric stenosis, in other instances of persistent vomiting, in overhydration, and in rarer states in which intracellular tonicity has changed with a resultant migration of sodium and chloride into the cell. Somewhat high values normally occur in the thirsted small infant at around the fourth day of life. High

chloride values will also be found in hyperchloremic acidosis and in hypertonic dehydration.

Sweat chloride is probably the single most significant test in the diagnosis of fibrocystic disease of the pancreas. The range of values from the literature for normals of 24.8 mEq. per L. (2.0 to 111.8), and 121 mEq. per L. (49.6 to 220) for fibrocystic patients, suggests a rather greater degree of overlap, in spite of the wide difference in the means, than is generally experienced in any one laboratory. This is probably because the figures are compiled from a number of sources using different methods (Barbero, 1959). As a general rule it is rare for a normal person to have more than 50 mEq. per L. of chloride in his sweat and for a fibrocystic patient to have less. Some patients with chronic bronchitis or asthma as well as presumed heterozygotes for fibrocystic disease may have intermediate values.

Cerebrospinal fluid chloride can also be estimated, using a procedure identical to that for serum. Normal values range from 110 to 128 mEq. per L., being slightly low (103 to 116 mEq./L.) in acute purulent bacterial meningitis and lower still (94 to 100 mEq./L.) in the later stages of tuberculous meningitis.

Undoubtedly the simplest and best method for the estimation of chloride in serum, sweat, or cerebrospinal fluid is the amperometric one of Cotlove et al. (1958). However, for laboratories not equipped with a chloridometer the following adaptation, from Van Slyke and Hiller (1947), of Sendroy's iodometric procedure is given. The nature of the reaction involved is set out in the equations:

$$Cl^- + AgIO_3 \rightleftharpoons IO_3^- + AgCl$$
$$IO_3^- + 5I^- + 6H+ \rightleftharpoons 3I_2 + 3H_2O$$
$$I_2 + 2S_2O_3^- \rightleftharpoons 2I^- + S_4O_6^-$$

Provided the silver iodate is absolutely free of soluble iodate, the procedure should give rise to no difficulties.

Iodometric Procedure

Reagents

1. Silver iodate, A.R. Must be free of soluble iodate.

2. Potassium iodide, A.R. Finely crystalline.

3. Starch glycollate indicator. Add 0.1 gm. sodium starch glycollate to 5 ml. ethanol and 100 ml. water and boil for a few minutes. Regular starch indicator is also suitable.

4. Sodium chloride standard (100 mEq./L.). Dissolve 5.8450 gm. of dry sodium chloride in and make up to 1000 ml. with ion-free distilled water.

5. Phosphotungstic acid. Dissolve 6 gm. of $Na_2WO_4 \cdot 2H_2O$ in 500 ml. of de-ionized distilled water containing 10 ml. of syrupy phosphoric acid. The whole is shaken and further diluted to 1000 ml. with distilled water.

6. Sodium thiosulfate stock, 0.4606 N. Dissolve 57.15 gm. $Na_2S_2O_3 \cdot 5H_2O$ or 36.43 gm. anhydrous $Na_2S_2O_3$ in and dilute to 500 ml. with water. Add 1 ml. $CHCl_3$. This solution is standardized against potassium iodate.

7. Sodium thiosulfate, dilute, 0.01151 N. Dilute 25 ml. of stock to 1000 ml. Add 1 ml. $CHCl_3$.

Technique. Into 1 ml. of phospho-tungstic acid in a 5 ml. glass stopper tube wash 40 μl. of serum, plasma, or standard. Add approximately 15 mg. of silver iodate from a calibrated glass measure. Stopper and shake the tube for 40 seconds; then centrifuge at 2500 r.p.m. for one minute and pipet 0.5 ml. of supernatant off into a small test tube. One small crystal (40 to 50 mg.) of potassium iodide is added, and the contents are titrated with the dilute thiosulfate solution from a 2 ml. buret. When the yellow color is barely visible, a drop of 0.1 per cent starch indicator is added and the titration continued until the blue color disappears.

Calculation. 100 × titration of 0.01151 N $Na_2S_2O_3$ in ml. = mEq./L. of chloride.

Sweat Chloride. In infants and older children an area of clean skin on the back, abdomen, or flexor surface of the arm is washed with distilled water and dried with tissues. A preweighed, 5.5 cm. diameter, No. 42 Whatman filter paper contained in a wide-mouth plastic bottle is then applied with forceps and covered with polyethylene film. The latter is secured at the skin margins by plastic adhesive tape. The child is then wrapped in blankets and artificial heat applied as well, if necessary, so as to induce profuse perspiration. After 40 to 60 minutes the filter paper is carefully uncovered and immediately transferred back to the plastic bottle with the forceps. Both filter paper and bottle are reweighed, the difference representing the weight of sweat collected.

Reagents

1. Standard chloride solution, 4 mEq. per L. Dilute standard for plasma chloride estimation 1:25 with water.

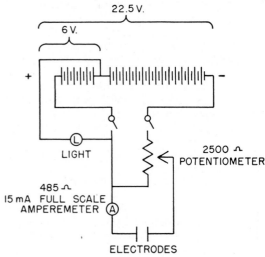

Figure 10–5. Circuit for iontophoresis apparatus. (Gibson and Cooke: Pediatrics, 23:545, 1959.)

2. 0.3 M (approx.) H_3PO_4 solution. Dilute 20 ml. concentrated H_3PO_4 to 1000 ml. with deionized water.

3. Other reagents are as for plasma estimation.

Technique. Ascertain the amount of sweat on the filter paper or gauze by determining the difference in weight. Add sufficient water to bring the volume up to 5 ml., assuming that 1 ml. of sweat weighs 1 gm. Shake vigorously. Transfer the liquid to a glass stopper tube, expressing as much liquid from the paper as possible. Centrifuge.

Into glass stopper tubes pipet 1 ml. of sweat dilution or 4 mEq. per L. standard.

Add 0.5 ml. of the 0.3 M H_3PO_4 solution, followed by 15 mg. of silver iodate.

Shake for 40 seconds and centrifuge.

Into a clean tube pipet 0.5 ml. of supernatant fluid, add 40 to 50 mg. KI, and titrate with sodium thiosulfate solution exactly as for plasma.

Calculation

$$4 \times \frac{\text{titration of test}}{\text{titration of standard}} \times \frac{5}{\text{original weight of sweat}}$$

= mEq. per L. sweat

Babies younger than six weeks do not sweat profusely, and thus it is advisable to delay the sweat electrolyte test until they are about three months old. Even at this age, however, a small number of deaths have been reported when sweating has been produced over the whole body. Thus, the collection of sweat by means of an iontophoresis technique (Gibson and Cooke,

1959) has many advantages to offer at all ages. The apparatus circuit is illustrated in Fig. 10–5, the electrodes being 3 cm. diameter metal discs curved to fit snugly on the arm or leg.

In this procedure the positive electrode is placed over a 5.5 cm. diameter filter paper moistened with four drops of 0.2 per cent pilocarpine nitrate on the anterior surface of the forearm. The negative electrode is similarly placed on the back of the arm but with gauze soaked in normal saline making the contact. A current of 2 milliamperes is passed for ten minutes; the electrodes are removed and the skin washed with ion-free water and dried. A weighed, 5.5 cm. diameter filter paper is applied over the site of the positive electrode, and sweat is collected in the usual manner after covering the site and sealing it with polyethylene film.

Serum Calcium

The range of normal values for total serum calcium depends to some extent on the method employed. In the following method, which is that of Diehl and Ellingboe (1956), the range lies between 9.4 and 11.2 mg. per 100 ml. These values are slightly lower than those for the oxalate precipitation method and on average 0.8 mg. per 100 ml. below those obtained by flame photometry. Much higher values, between 12 and 18.0 mg. per 100 ml., are found in idiopathic hypercalcemia, vitamin D intoxication, and hyperparathyroidism. By contrast low serum calcium levels are encountered in hypoparathyroidism, in pseudohypoparathyroidism, in chronic renal failure secondary to hyperphosphatemia, in all forms of rickets, in postacidotic hypocalcemia, in hypoalbuminemia, and in infantile tetany.

In this method calcium in highly alkaline solution forms a bright yellow-green fluorescent complex with calcein, a condensate of iminoacetic acid and fluorescein. In the presence of disodium dihydrogen ethylenediamine tetra-acetate the calcium is chelated, and the calcein reverts to an orange-red nonfluorescent form. This technique is quite reproducible and accurate and is unaffected by magnesium. The endpoint is not entirely satisfactory in daylight or in yellow artificial light and should never be read in direct sunlight. It can be improved by using white fluorescent lighting and by observing from above against a black background. By far the best result, however, is obtained by using polaroid sun glasses and viewing the reaction under a long-wave ultraviolet lamp. The endpoint is indicated by an abrupt disappearance of the bright yellow-green fluorescence.

This method has an additional advantage in that it can be simply adapted for the assay of calcium in urine with the use of morpholine. Mix thoroughly 2 ml. of urine, 1 ml. of 66 per cent sodium tungstate, and 2 ml. of morpholine; allow to stand for one hour. Centrifuge and titrate a 20 μl. aliquot of supernatant as for serum (Horner, 1955).

The technical details here relate to the use of the Beckman Spinco microtitrator (Fig. 10–6), but the procedure can be simply adapted to other microburets by the use of a magnetic stirrer. If necessary the quantities can be scaled up.

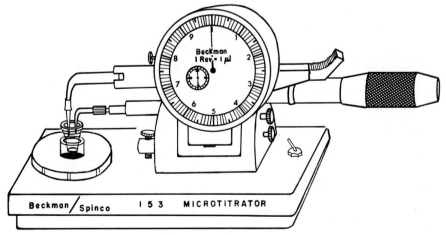

Figure 10–6. Microtitrator for serum calcium estimation.

Reagents (Store in Polyethylene Containers)

1. Calcium standard (10 mg./100 ml.). Dissolve 250 mg. of dry calcium carbonate (A.R.) in 6.0 ml. of 1 N HCl. Heat to boiling in a beaker until the excess HCl has been driven off. Cool to 25° C. Wash the contents of the beaker into a 1000 ml. volumetric flask and make up to the mark with ion-free water.

2. Potassium hydroxide (1.25 N). Dissolve 7.0 gm. of potassium hydroxide (A.R.) in about 70 ml. of ion-free water to which 0.05 gm. of KCN is added. The volume is finally made up to 100 ml. with ion-free water.

3. Calcein (25 mg./100 ml.). Dissolve 25.0 mg. of calcein in 0.25 N aqueous NaOH and make up to 100 ml. The indicator is stored in 30 ml. aliquots in brown polyethylene bottles.

4. Disodium dihydrogen ethylenediamine tetra-acetate (EDTA) (0.02 N). Reagent grade EDTA is dried at 110° C. for four hours and cooled in a desiccator for twelve hours. Dissolve 0.372 gm. in ion-free water and make up to 100 ml. It is stored in 30 ml. aliquots in polyethylene bottles.

Apparatus. Beckman Spinco Microtitrator with disposable titration cups and polyethylene semiautomatic pipets.

Technique. Into an appropriate series of titration cups pipet reagents as follows:

Blank.	20 μl.	ion-free water
	100 μl.	1.25 N KOH.
	10 μl.	calcein solution
Standard.	20 μl.	5 mEq. per l. calcium standard
	100 μl.	1.25 N KOH.
	10 μl.	calcein solution
Tests.	20 μl.	of serum
	100 μl.	1.25 N KOH.
	10 μl.	calcein solution

Mix the contents of all cups, and with 0.02 N EDTA in the microtitrator titrate under a small ultraviolet lamp (G.E.C. 100 W. H4AG) until fluorescence disappears. If there is no ultraviolet source available, the endpoint should be viewed against a black background, using overhead white fluorescent lighting. The calculation is shown at the bottom of the page.

Serum Phosphorus

In normal children the serum phosphorus varies between 4 to 6.5 mg. per 100 ml. Higher levels between 4.2 to 9.5 mg. per 100 ml., however, are found in the newborn period. Elevated serum phosphorus levels are found in chronic renal disease, in hypoparathyroidism and pseudohypoparathyroidism, as well as in tetany of the newborn when this is caused by excessive phosphorus retention. Elevated levels are not always found in the tetany occurring in infants of diabetic mothers who are often normophosphatemic. Low serum phosphorus on the other hand is encountered in rickets associated with malabsorption syndromes, in renal tubular dystrophies, in postacidotic hypocalcemia, and in primary hyperparathyroidism.

The present method depends on the formation of phosphomolybdate when serum is added to ammonium molybdate and the subsequent extraction of the phosphomolybdate into an organic solvent. An intense blue color is formed when the extracted phosphomolybdate is reduced by stannous chloride. The most important sources of error come with any delays, either in removing the serum from the red cells, when phosphorus may be split from esters in the cells, or in precipitating the serum proteins, which may lead to the release of inorganic phosphorus from phospholipid and hence an incorrectly high result. The supernatant after protein precipitation will keep for at least 48 hours. The method to be given in detail is that of McDonald and Hall (1957).

Reagents

1. 60 per cent perchloric acid.

2. 4 per cent perchloric acid. Dilute 60 per cent perchloric acid 1:15 with water.

3. Extraction solution: 15 parts petroleum ether (B.P. 100–120° C.) added to 85 parts isobutyl alcohol.

4. 5 per cent ammonium molybdate in 4 N H_2SO_4.

5. 43 per cent $SnCl_2 \cdot 2H_2O$ in concentrated HCl. Each day dilute 1:400 with 18 N H_2SO_4 (e.g., 0.1 ml. to 40 ml.).

6. Standard:
   Stock (1 mg. P/ml.). Dissolve 4.394 gm. KH_2PO_4 in water and dilute to 1 liter. Add a few drops of $CHCl_3$.
   Intermediate (100 μgm./ml.). Dilute 10 ml. stock standard plus 3.3 ml. 60 per cent $HClO_4$ to 100 ml. with water.

$$\frac{\text{Titration reading of test} - \text{titration reading of blank}}{\text{Titration reading of std.} - \text{titration reading of blank}} \times 10 = \text{mg. calcium per 100 ml.}$$

Working (1 μgm./ml.). Dilute 5 ml. intermediate standard to 500 ml. with 2 per cent $HClO_4$.

Technique

1. Into a glass stopper test tube pipet 2.4 ml. water.
2. Wash in 0.1 ml. serum or plasma.
3. Add 2.5 ml. 4 per cent $HClO_4$. Mix and let stand for at least 15 minutes (will keep satisfactorily overnight in the refrigerator at this stage).
4. Centrifuge for five minutes at 3000 r.p.m.
5. Into clean, glass stopper tubes pipet:
   2 ml. supernatant fluid or 1 ml. water + 1 ml. 4 per cent $HClO_4$ for blank or 2 ml. working standard.
   0.5 ml. ammonium molybdate solution.
   2.5 ml. extracting solution.
6. Shake vigorously for 90 seconds.
7. Centrifuge for about ten seconds at 3000 r.p.m.
8. Into a clean, glass stopper tube pipet:
   2 ml. supernatant fluid.
   0.3 ml. absolute ethanol. Mix.
   0.2 ml. dilute $SnCl_2$ solution. Mix.
9. Read after 15 minutes at 625 mμ.

Calculation

$$\frac{(\text{O.D. sample} - \text{O.D. blank})}{(\text{O.D. standard} - \text{O.D. blank})} \times 5 =$$
mg. P per 100 ml.

The standard curve is linear up to the equivalent of 10 mg. per 100 ml.

Serum Bilirubin

For the pediatrician the estimation of bilirubin has its greatest importance in the newborn period when the level is the prime index for exchange transfusion in the prevention of kernicterus. The upper limits of physiologic values for total bilirubin are:

Age	Premature	Full Term
24 hours	up to 8 mg./100 ml.	5 mg./100 ml.
48 hours	up to 12 mg./100 ml.	9 mg./100 ml.
3rd-5th day	up to 24 mg./100 ml.	12 mg./100 ml.

After one month: 0–0.3 conjugated, 0.1–0.7 unconjugated as mg./100 ml.

Neonatal jaundice may be caused by Rh, ABO, or other blood group incompatibilities; by sepsis; and in the small premature infant simply by hepatic immaturity in the conjugation of bilirubin. Although a level of 20 mg. per 100 ml. is generally accepted as an indication for exchange transfusion, this procedure is not without risk in the smaller babies, and for that reason rather higher levels may be tolerated when they occur on or after the third day of life.

The following method adapted from Lathe and Ruthven (1958) is a quick and reliable diazotization procedure. It is important, however, when a single tube or cuvet is used for all readings, to make sure that there is no contamination of the blanks by diazo reagent.

Reagents

1. 1.0 per cent sulfanilic acid in 0.2 N HCl.
2. 20 per cent $NaNO_2$ (aqueous). Store in refrigerator.
3. 0.5 per cent $NaNO_2$. Dilute stock 0.5 ml. to 20 ml. with water. Store in refrigerator.
4. Mixed diazo reagent. Prepare fresh each day. Mix 5 ml. sulfanilic acid solution and 0.15 ml. 0.5 per cent $NaNO_2$.
5. Absolute methanol.
6. Standard. The problem of producing an entirely satisfactory standard solution has not yet been completely solved because of a number of difficulties. For example, commercially available bilirubin is often impure, making it necessary for each batch to be assayed carefully. A solution of bilirubin dissolved in chloroform gives a diazo pigment of higher intensity than a solution of bilirubin dissolved in a protein medium. Even when a pure sample has been successfully dissolved in a protein solution, the resulting standard starts to deteriorate significantly after three hours. A suitable criterion of bilirubin purity is that it should have a molar extinction coefficient in chloroform of 60,000, assuming a molecular weight of 584. Dissolve 10 mg. bilirubin in 1 ml. 0.05 N NaOH. Dilute to 50 ml. with 5 per cent human serum albumin solution. This standard should be used as soon as possible and is treated exactly as a serum sample. Dilutions may be made in 5 per cent human serum albumin to calibrate the photometer, which should give a linear relation with optical density.

Technique

1. Into a 75 × 12 mm. test tube pipet 2.7 ml. water.
2. Wash in 0.1 ml. serum.
3. Mix.
4. Into a second test tube pipet 1.4 ml. of the diluted serum. Use this for the test.
5. Use the remainder for the blank.

6. To TEST add 0.35 ml. diazo solution. Mix.

7. To BLANK add 0.35 ml. sulfanilic acid solution. Mix.

8. Read O.D. of each tube exactly as the standards after ten minutes from the time of adding the diazo or blank solutions. This is measure of the conjugated bilirubin.

9. Return solutions to their tubes.

10. To each tube add 1.75 ml. methanol and mix thoroughly.

11. Read after ten minutes as just described. (Total bilirubin.)

12. Results are calculated using the optical density value of the 20 mg. per 100 ml. standard. Although it is possible to repeat this only at intervals, better control can be effected by the use of a commercially available lyophilized standard serum. Be careful to use this serum within three hours after it is dissolved.

N.B.: Take care to avoid contamination of the BLANKS with diazo reagent from the TESTS via the cuvet or transfer pipet.

Calculations.

Conjugated.

$$\frac{\text{O.D. test} - \text{O.D. blank}}{\text{O.D. Standard}} \times 10 =$$

mg. conjugated bilirubin
   per 100 ml. serum
Total.

$$\frac{\text{O.D. test} - \text{O.D. blank}}{\text{O.D. Standard}} \times 20 =$$

mg. total bilirubin per 100 ml. serum

Serum Alkaline Phosphatase

Alkaline phosphatase activity is increased in two groups of diseases: those affecting liver function and those affecting osteoblastic activity in the bones. In hepatic disease an increased alkaline phosphatase is generally accepted as an indication of biliary obstruction. In the second group the serum phosphatase activity is increased in primary hyperparathyroidism, in secondary hyperparathyroidism due to chronic renal disease, and also in the various forms of rickets whether these are due to vitamin D deficiency, malabsorption, or renal tubular dystrophies. Levels may also be increased in von Recklinghausen's disease with bone involvement and a variety of malignant infiltrations of bone. Low values for the alkaline phosphatase are found in hyperthyroidism and in the rare condition of idiopathic hypophosphatasia in which low values are associated with rickets and the excretion of phosphoethanolamine in the urine. Normal values in childhood vary considerably (Child Research Council, 1960). Between one and three months they range from 4.4 to 13.6 Bessey Lowry units (B.L.U.); thereafter there is a steady fall to between 3.4 and 9.1 B.L.U. for the 3-year to 10-year age group. At puberty, values rise again, averaging 7 B.L.U. for the range between 3.4 and 15.5 This rise occurs at a slightly younger age in girls than in boys. After the pubertal rise there is a steady fall until the adult range of 0.8 to 2.3 B.L.U. is reached at about 16 years. Boys have slightly higher levels than girls during this period.

The most suitable method for the estimation of alkaline phosphatase in serum in children is probably that of Bessey, Lowry, and Brock (1946). In this procedure serum is added to a solution of p-nitrophenyl phosphate in an alkaline buffer. The amount of phosphatase is reflected in the production of p-nitrophenol, which has a pronounced yellow color. The addition of base inactivates the phosphatase and dilutes the color to a convenient concentration for measurement. The blank is measured after making the solution acid, when the yellow color of the p-nitrophenol disappears.

Reagents

1. Alkaline buffer. Dissolve 7.50 gm. amino acetic acid and 0.095 gm. anhydrous $MgCl_2$ (or 0.203 gm. $MgCl_2 \cdot 6H_2O$) in about 750 ml. water. Add 85 ml. 1 N NaOH and dilute to 1000 ml. A few drops of chloroform are also added and the pH checked with a meter to be 10.5.

2. Buffer substrate. Dissolve 0.1 gm. p-nitrophenyl phosphate (Sigma 104) in about 20 ml. water in a 50 ml. volumetric flask. Add 25 ml. of the buffer and dilute to 50 ml. with water. The pH should be 10.4. After mixing, distribute in 1 ml. amounts in 100 × 13 mm. test tubes. These are stoppered and stored in the deep freeze.

3. Stock standard, p-nitrophenol, 10 millimols per liter. Dissolve 1.3911 gm. p-nitrophenol and make up to 1000 ml. with water. This solution is stable for one year at 4° C.

Calibration Curve

Working Standard (stable for 24 hours only; discard excess dilution).

  a. Pipet into a 1 liter volumetric flask 5.0 ml. p-nitrophenol standard solution.

  b. Add distilled water to 1 liter.

c. Mix thoroughly.

Pipet the solutions indicated according to the following chart into six test tubes:

WORKING STD. (ML.)	WATER (ML.)	0.02 N NaOH (ML.)	EQUIV. TO FOLLOWING B.L. UNITS SERUM ALKALINE PHOSPHATE
1	9	1.1	1
2	8	1.1	2
4	6	1.1	4
6	4	1.1	6
8	2	1.1	8
10	0	1.1	10

Read and record the optical density of each of these mixtures at 410 mμ (400 to 420 mμ), using 0.02 N NaOH in the reference tube.

Plot the calibration curve, which will not necessarily be a straight line. This curve should be set up initially to establish the calibration. Thereafter it need be checked only when some change occurs in the conditions for color measurement.

Technique

1. Take two tubes from the freezer and place in the 37° C. water bath for not less than five minutes.
2. Without taking the tubes from the bath, wash 0.1 ml. serum or plasma into one tube and 0.1 ml. water into the other.
3. Start stop watch as serum is added.
4. Exactly 30 minutes later add 10 ml. 0.02 N NaOH. Remove from the bath and mix.
5. Read O.D. at 410 mμ in Beckman.
6. Add 0.1 ml. concentrated HCl to each, mix, and read again.

Calculation (shown at bottom of page).

When a value greater than 10 B.L.U. is obtained, the test should be repeated with a smaller volume of serum.

Blood Urea Nitrogen

The estimation of various nitrogenous metabolites in serum is at best a rather crude gauge of renal decompensation. Nonetheless these estimations are of substantial clinical value, and in our opinion the blood urea nitrogen is the most useful criterion and one of the easiest to adapt to small amounts of blood.

In the present method blood is exposed to urease after which the proteins are precipitated. The ammonia formed is estimated colorimetrically by use of Nessler's solution. The normal values at all ages range up to 20 mg. per 100 ml., although it should be remembered that in small infants on a very high nitrogen intake the value may rise over 30 mg. per 100 ml. without evidence of renal disease.

Reagents

1. Stock standard. Dissolve 471.4 mg. $(NH_4)_2SO_4$ in water and dilute to 1 liter.
2. Working standard. Dilute 5 ml. stock standard to 100 ml. with water.
3. Control solution (20 mg. urea nitrogen per 100 ml.). Dissolve 428.6 mg. urea in water and dilute to 1 liter.
4. Nessler's reagent:

Solution A. Place 150 gm. potassium iodide, 100 gm. iodine crystals, 100 ml. deionized water, and 140 to 150 gm. Hg in a 500 ml. flask. This is shaken continuously for 7 to 15 minutes or until the iodine has nearly disappeared. After cooling in running water, the solution becomes pale red and with continued shaking it becomes a greenish color (about 15 minutes in all). After decanting this supernatant solution, the remaining mercury is washed with water, and the solution and washings are diluted to 2 liters with water.

Solution B. Standardize 2.5 N NaOH by titration against standard acid. For use, mix 150 ml. H_2O, 150 ml. solution A, and 700 ml. solution B.

5. Urease suspension. One tablet urease (25 mg.) is ground up in 6 ml. deionized water. This should be made up fresh each day.
6. Sodium tungstate, 1.25 per cent $Na_2WO_4 \cdot 2H_2O$ in water.
7. Sulfuric acid, 0.66 N.
8. Gum ghatti solution. To a beaker containing about 700 ml. water add 0.5 gm. finely powdered gum. This is stirred with an electric stirrer, filtered, and made up to 1000 ml. with water. Then 0.5 ml. saturated alcoholic $HgCl_2$ is added. The solution is stored at room temperature.

Technique. Into a test tube marked at 4 ml. place approximately 1 ml. water. Wash in 0.1 ml. blood or CONTROL solution. For the REAGENT BLANK use a similar tube containing approximately 1 ml. water. Add 0.15 ml. freshly shaken

$$\frac{(\text{O.D. test alk.} - \text{O.D. test acid}) - (\text{O.D. blank alk.} - \text{O.D. blank acid})}{\text{O.D. of standard equivalent to 1 B.L. unit.}} = \text{B.L. units}$$

urease suspension and incubate at 37° C. in a water bath for 20 minutes. Remove from the bath, add 1.2 ml. 1.25 per cent sodium tungstate solution and 0.15 ml. 0.66 N H_2SO_4, and make up to 4 ml. with water. Mix by inversion and centrifuge for two minutes at 3000 r.p.m.

1. Unknown, control, and reagent blank. Pipet 2 ml. supernatant into a test tube.

2. Standard. Pipet 2 ml. working standard into a test tube.

3. Color blank. Pipet 2 ml. water into a test tube.

4. To each add 2 ml. gum ghatti followed by 0.8 ml. Nessler's solution. Mix by tapping. After five minutes read each solution against water at 470 mμ. (N.B.: If O.D. of test is 1.5 or more times that of the standard, take a smaller aliquot of supernatant fluid, add water to 2 ml., followed by gum ghatti and Nessler's solution as just described. Adjust calculation appropriately.)

Calculation.

$$\frac{U - B}{S - B} \times 20 \text{ mg. urea N per 100 ml.}$$

Normal Values. 10 to 20 mg. per 100 ml.

Estimation of Serum Proteins by the Kjeldahl Method

In the estimation of serum proteins there are some attractive shortcuts. Total proteins, for example, can be measured by refraction methods and total proteins and the albumin fraction separately by the biuret method. In our experience, however, the present Kjeldahl method is not only quick but exceedingly reliable and reproducible. However, for clinical purposes the estimation of the albumin-globulin ratio gives information that is of significantly less value than that offered by the separation of the albumin and the various globulin fractions by electrophoresis. The optimum way of

estimating serum proteins in a clinical laboratory is therefore to estimate total protein by the Kjeldahl method and the several fractions by electrophoresis whenever this is possible. Although this entails some delay in obtaining a final answer, the actual technician time consumed in applying, developing, and calculating an electrophoretic strip is rather less than that involved in separating out albumin as a fraction and estimating its nitrogen content separately. Details of electrophoretic procedures and of scanning and elution methods are described in Chapter 8, but for the benefit of those laboratories not equipped for electrophoresis the method for the separate estimation of albumin is given here. The normal values for serum protein fractions in the plasma are given in the following table. It is important to emphasize that during the first four months of life there is a substantial fall in the levels of gamma globulin, which rise only slowly thereafter to a normal adult level at around four years of age. Smaller rises, but without the dip at three months, occur in alpha-2 and beta globulins.

The technique of the Kjeldahl procedure is simple and involves, first, the conversion of protein nitrogen to ammonium sulfate by digestion with concentrated sulfuric acid and a selenium catalyst. After the digest is alkalinized, the ammonia is steam distilled into a boric acid indicator solution (Conway, 1958), which is then back titrated with acid. The method to be set out has been derived from a number of sources (Hiller *et al.*, 1948; Fawcett, 1954), and special attention is called to the apparatus, which is illustrated in Fig. 10–7; it is not only simple but avoids a transfer of the digest.

Reagents

1. Concentrated sulfuric acid.

2. Standard ammonium sulfate solution. Dissolve 2.3581 gm. $(NH_4)_2SO_4$ in

PROTEINS IN PLASMA	FIRST WEEK		4 MONTHS	12 MONTHS		4 YEARS+
	PREMATURE	FULL TERM	PREMATURE	PREMATURE	FULL TERM	
Total	5.29	5.97	5.76	6.47	6.41	6.79
	SD 0.72	SD 0.80	SD 0.10	SD 0.47	SD 0.40	SD 0.43
Albumin	3.38	4.17	3.90	3.76	4.48	4.58
	SD 0.35	SD 0.65	SD 0.53	SD 0.37	SD 0.28	SD 0.40
Alpha-1	0.21	0.17	0.23	0.35	0.22	0.22
	SD 0.08	SD 0.04	SD 0.08	SD 0.09	SD 0.06	SD 0.06
Alpha-2	0.39	0.38	0.57	0.77	0.54	0.57
	SD 0.12	SD 0.04	SD 0.13	SD 0.18	SD 0.13	SD 0.11
Beta	0.46	0.38	0.63	0.86	0.62	0.62
	SD 0.07	SD 0.11	SD 0.14	SD 0.10	SD 0.12	SD 0.06
Gamma	0.85	0.87	0.43	0.72	0.55	0.81
	SD 0.28	SD 0.26	SD 0.16	SD 0.22	SD 0.03	SD 0.24

water and make up to 1000 ml. (1 ml. contains 0.5 mg. nitrogen).

3. 0.01436 N HCl. Standardize by distilling (see following section on distillation and titration) the ammonia from 2 ml. of the standard into boric acid reagent and titrating. Adjust strength of HCl so that titration is exactly 5 ml.; i.e., 1 ml. HCl = 0.2 mg. N.

4. 0.9 per cent NaCl.

5. Hengar selenium catalyst granules.

6. Sodium sulfate. Dissolve 27.73 gm. of anhydrous Na_2SO_4 in water and make up to 100 ml. Store at 37° C.

7. *Stock indicator solutions* (for boric acid reagent):

I. 100 mg. phenolphthalein dissolved in 95 per cent ethanol and made up to 100 ml.

II. 33 mg. bromcresol green and 66 mg. methyl red dissolved in 95 per cent ethanol and made up to 100 ml.

8. Boric acid reagent. Dissolve 10 gm. boric acid in about 1400 ml. water. Add 400 ml. 95 per cent ethanol, 70 ml. solution I, and 20 ml. solution II. Make up to 2000 ml. and mix. Adjust the color if necessary to a cherry red with 1 N HCl. Do not take the color to the extreme acid limit of the indicator. Ten milliliter amounts of this reagent may be measured out conveniently and with sufficient accuracy with a dispenser.

9. 0.1 per cent phenolphthalein in 95 per cent ethanol.

10. 60 per cent NaOH. Into a 2000 ml. Pyrex beaker measure approximately 400 ml. water. While stirring it with an electric stirrer, add gradually 600 gm. NaOH pellets. Continue to stir until cool. Make up to 1000 ml. and store in a plastic bottle.

Technique

a. *Digestion.* Into a small test tube pipet 2.4 ml. 0.9 per cent NaCl solution. Wash in 0.1 ml. serum. Mix. Into each of two Kjeldahl digestion flasks pipet 1.0 ml. of dilute serum followed by 0.5 ml. concentrated H_2SO_4 and a Hengar granule.

Heat the flasks on a digestion rack, gently at first to boil off the water, and then more strongly until the contents become colorless. Continue for another ten minutes; the whole digestion should take about 30 minutes. Allow to cool. Add about 1.0 ml. distilled water to each tube. Run a reagent blank frequently, especially when any new batch of reagent is used.

b. *Distillation and titration.* The steam-distillation apparatus (Fig. 10–7) should be set so that it delivers 10 to 12 ml. of cold

distillate every two minutes. An apparatus blank should be run to ensure that it is ammonia-free. This is done by attaching a clean, empty digestion flask and distilling into 10 ml. boric acid reagent for two minutes. The titration should be not greater than 0.1 ml. of 0.01436 N HCl.

Provided the apparatus is clean, continue with the reagent blank and the serum estimations. Place a 50 ml. conical flask containing 10 ml. boric acid reagent under the condenser of the distillation apparatus. Add 4 drops 0.1 per cent phenolphthalein solution to each digestion flask. Then, holding a digestion flask so that its lowest third is submerged in cold water, add 60 per cent NaOH solution, shaking constantly during the addition. As soon as the contents turn magenta, quickly steam the ground-glass joint and attach the flask to the steam-distillation apparatus. When the distillate appears in the condenser, start a timer. After two minutes detach the digestion flask and titrate the boric acid reagent with 0.01436 N HCl back to the cherry-red color.

The correction for NPN can be calculated with sufficient accuracy from the blood urea nitrogen according to the following table derived from that given by Harrison (1949):

BLOOD UREA NITROGEN	FACTOR FOR CONVERTING BUN INTO SERUM NPN
up to 23 mg./100 ml.	0.9
24 to 47 mg./100 ml.	0.8
48 to 70 mg./100 ml.	0.7
71 to 93 mg./100 ml.	0.6
94 and over mg./100 ml.	0.55

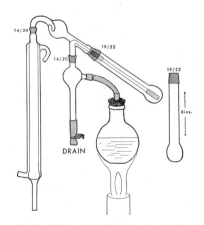

Figure 10–7. Micro-Kjeldahl steam-distillation apparatus.

Calculation. 0.5 (test − blank) = gm. nitrogen per 100 ml.

Total protein in gm. per 100 ml. = gm. nitrogen per 100 ml. − NPN × 6.25.

Serum Albumin

A simple albumin:globulin ratio is not of great value and whenever possible quantitated electrophoretic fractions should be reported. However, the following method (Majoor, 1947; Kingsley, 1942; Jackson, 1959) for serum albumin is proved and reliable. The most important practical point is to ensure that all glassware and solutions are kept as near to 37° C. as possible during the procedure.

Technique. Wash 0.2 ml. of serum into 3.0 ml. of 27.73 per cent sodium sulfate in a glass stopper tube, mix, and incubate at 37° C. for three hours. Add 1.5 ml. of ether and mix the contents by inversion 20 times, allowing the ether vapor to escape at intervals. The mixture is then centrifuged at 2000 r.p.m. for ten minutes with warm water in the centrifuge bucket. The tube is then gently slanted to dislodge the button of precipitated globulin, and a Pasteur pipet is gently inserted to remove the subnatant fluid into another tube.

Calculation. Albumin in gm. per 100 ml. = 6.25 [0.32 (test-blank) − NPN in gm. per 100 ml.]

Serum and Cerebrospinal Fluid Glucose

Differences in the glucose content of red cells and plasma, as well as the effect of cell enzymes *in vitro*, make the assay of glucose more reliable in serum (separated within 30 minutes from the cells) than in whole blood. The estimation is important in diabetes and in detecting the low values in premature infants in the first few days of life. The measurement of serum glucose is also necessary in various tolerance tests, including those after doses of leucine, glucagon, insulin, and glucose itself; and in the investigation of idiopathic hypoglycemia of infancy and of various pituitary and adrenal disorders. In the normal newborn, fasting levels range between 20 and 80 mg. per 100 ml., but occasionally values of 10 mg. per 100 ml. or even less are encountered in infants who appear to be in perfect health. Thereafter the normal fasting level ranges between 60 and about 105 mg. per 100 ml.

Cerebrospinal fluid glucose is normally between 40 and 80 mg. per 100 ml. It is low or absent in acute purulent bacterial meningitis and between 10 and 20 mg. per 100 ml. in the early stages of tuberculous meningitis.

Of the various methods available for measuring serum glucose, those involving glucose oxidase have the advantage of being specific, but some of the procedures do involve a delay of nearly an hour before a result can be obtained. The following method adapted from that of Marks (1959) is both specific and quick and, provided a rather strict timing schedule is adhered to, the results are reproducible and the standards linear.

Reagents

1. Distilled water.
2. 5 per cent $ZnSO_4 \cdot 7H_2O$ in water.
3. 0.3 N NaOH. These precipitants should be equivalent. Titrate one against the other, using phenolphthalein as indicator. Dilute the stronger to match the weaker.
4. 1 per cent o-tolidine in absolute ethanol. Store in the refrigerator.
5. Fermcozyme 653A, supplied by Fermco Labs., Inc., Chicago, Illinois. Keep refrigerated.
6. Acetate buffer, 0.15 M, pH 5.0. Dissolve 14.29 gm. sodium acetate·3H_2O in about 900 ml. water. Using a pH meter, bring to pH 5.0 by the addition of glacial acetic acid (about 2.6 ml.). Make up to 1000 ml. with water.
7. Peroxidase solution. Dissolve 20 mg. peroxidase in acetate buffer and make up to 100 ml. (Keeps several months in refrigerator.)
8. Mixed enzyme reagent. To about 80 ml. acetate buffer add 0.5 ml. Fermcozyme. Mix. Then add 5 ml. peroxidase solution. Mix. Add 1.0 ml. o-tolidine solution. Mix and make up to 100 ml. with buffer. Store in dark bottle in refrigerator; it lasts at least a week.
9. *Glucose Standards.*

Stock. Dissolve 375 mg. glucose in saturated aqueous benzoic acid solution and make up to 100 ml.

Working (equivalent to 150 mg. per 100 ml.). Dilute the stock solution 1:100 in saturated benzoic acid solution.

Technique. Into a tube containing 3.1 ml. water, wash 0.1 ml. serum or spinal fluid. Add 0.4 ml. 0.3 N NaOH, mix, and follow with 0.4 ml. 5 per cent $ZnSO_4 \cdot 7H_2O$. Mix again; let stand for five minutes. Then centrifuge.

Subsequently 1.0 ml. of supernatant fluid from each test is pipeted into a separate tube. If the spinal fluid has a normal protein content, wash 25μl. into 1.0 ml. water and continue with next step.

Standards are set up with each batch as follows:

EQUIVALENT VALUE	WATER	WORKING STANDARD
0 mg./100 ml.	1.0 ml.	0 ml.
75 mg./100 ml.	0.5 ml.	0.5 ml.
150 mg./100 ml.	0 ml.	1.0 ml.

All the tubes are placed in a rack in a 20° C. water bath together with the bottle of mixed enzyme reagent. When all are at 20° C. (that is, after about five minutes), 3.0 ml. of reagent is added to each tube at half-minute intervals, mixing after each addition. The color is read at exactly nine minutes in the absorptiometer at 625 mμ, using water as the reference.

The calibration is linear up to at least 300 mg. per 100 ml. blood. If the color is too high, however, less supernatant fluid should be used and the volume made up with water. The color is maximal at nine minutes, but the calibration is linear for at least 20 minutes, provided the time of reading remains constant for both tests and standards.

d-Xylose Absorption Test

Malabsorption states may occur in small children as a sequel to any severe illness and in particular to gastroenteritis. Nevertheless the most common diagnostic problems for which absorption tests are required are in the diagnosis and differentiation of the celiac syndrome and fibrocystic disease of the pancreas. In the latter condition the diagnosis is now most effectively made by measuring the sweat chloride, and absorption tests only play a supportive part in the diagnosis, although it may clearly be important to know whether malabsorption is occurring as a gauge of the need for, or efficiency of, pancreatin therapy. In the malabsorption of fibrocystic disease a vitamin A-alcohol tolerance test is probably the quickest and most convenient for a reasonable degree of reliability. Xylose absorption, however, may be normal in states of pancreatic insufficiency so that this test is the test of choice both in diagnosing and assessing treatment in the celiac syndrome.

The procedure is carried out as follows (Benson et al., 1957; Roe and Rice, 1948):

The fasting child is given 10 ml. per kg. of a 5 per cent solution of d-xylose and is subsequently fasted and thirsted for five hours. The urine is collected over this period, and after recording the total volume, an aliquot is preserved in the deep freeze. Blood samples are taken before the test starts and at 60 and 120 minutes after the xylose is given. In a normal person the serum xylose should reach a level between 25 and 40 mg. per 100 ml. at one hour, a level that should be maintained for another 60 minutes. In malabsorption states, the highest level obtained is around 10 mg. per 100 ml. In the urine of a normal person an average of 26 per cent of ingested xylose is excreted with a range from 16 to 33 per cent. In malabsorption states, the mean is 5.2 per cent and the range, 3.2 to 10.4 per cent.

Reagents

1. p-Bromoaniline reagent. Thiourea is added to glacial acetic acid in excess of the amount that will dissolve. Approximately 4 gm. of thiourea per 100 ml. of acetic acid is used. Decant 100 ml. of acetic acid saturated with thiourea and dissolve 2 gm. of pure p-bromoaniline (Eastman Kodak Company) in it. Keep the p-bromoaniline reagent in a dark glass bottle and prepare once weekly.

2. 0.3 N NaOH.

3. 5 per cent $ZnSO_4 \cdot 7H_2O$. Reagents 2 and 3 should be equivalent (see blood glucose).

4. Stock standard. 1 per cent d(+) xylose in saturated benzoic acid. Working standard (5 mg./100 ml.). Dilute stock solution 1:200 with saturated benzoic acid.

Technique

1. Into a tube containing 1.0 ml. of distilled water wash 0.2 ml. of whole blood followed by 0.4 ml. of 0.3 N NaOH. After mixing, 0.4 ml. 5 per cent $ZnSO_4$ is added and the mixing repeated. The tube is then centrifuged at 3000 r.p.m.

2. To separate 10 ml. test tubes, add in duplicate as follows:

TEST (BLOOD)	TEST (URINE)	STANDARD
0.5 ml. of supernatant from step 1	0.5 ml. of a 1:200 dilution of urine	0.5 ml. of working standard

3. To all tubes add 2.5 ml. of p-bromoaniline reagent.

4. Incubate one of each pair of tubes in a water bath at 70° C. for ten minutes. Then cool to room temperature under running water. The unheated tubes serve as blanks. Keep blanks at 20° C.

5. Set tubes in dark for 70 minutes and then read in absorptiometer in 1 cm. or preferably 2 cm. cells or in Beckman D.U. at 520 mμ.

Calculation

$$\text{mg. per 100 ml. xylose (blood)} = \frac{\text{O.D. test} - \text{O.D. blank}}{\text{O.D. std.} - \text{O.D. blank}} \times 50$$

$$\text{gm. per 100 ml. xylose (urine)} = \frac{\text{O.D. test} - \text{O.D. blank}}{\text{O.D. std.} - \text{O.D. blank}}$$

Serum Mucoprotein Tyrosine

The present practice of ambulatory treatment of rheumatic fever with relatively large doses of steroids has entailed some re-evaluation of the laboratory tests for diagnosis and assessment of this disease. At the present time the most valuable procedure both in the initial stages of the disease and in determining progress with or without steroids is the serum mucoprotein tyrosine. The normal mean by the method to be given (Weimer and Moshin, 1953; Winzler, *et al.*, 1948; O'Brien and Ibbott, 1959) is 3.3 mg. per 100 ml. with a standard deviation of 1 mg. per 100 ml. The assay depends, first, on the separation of the mucoproteins from other serum proteins, using perchloric acid, in which the former are by definition soluble. The mucoproteins are themselves then precipitated by phosphotungstic acid, redissolved in sodium carbonate, and quantitatively assayed on the basis of the color produced by the reaction between their exposed tyrosine residues and Folin and Ciocalteu's reagent. It is particularly important to follow the directions for this method meticulously in order to ensure reproducibility. Great care must be taken not to lose any of the very small precipitate of mucoprotein, especially when aspirating the supernatant liquid. Phenol should be excluded from the room while the tests are being conducted.

Reagents

1. 1.2 M $HClO_4$ (200 ml. 60 per cent $HClO_4$ and 1300 ml. water). Mix and standardize.

2. 5 per cent phosphotungstic acid in 2 N HCl.

3. 15 per cent aqueous Na_2CO_3.

4. Folin and Ciocalteu reagent. Dissolve 100 gm. $Na_2WO_4 \cdot 2H_2O$ and 25 gm. $Na_2MoO_4 \cdot 2H_2O$ in about 700 ml. water in a 2 liter round-bottom flask. Add 50 ml. of syrupy 85 per cent phosphoric acid and 100 ml. concentrated HCl. Reflux for ten hours in an all-glass apparatus. Add 150 gm. lithium sulfate, 50 ml. water, and a few drops of bromine. Boil without a condenser for about a quarter of an hour to remove excess bromine. Cool, make up to one liter with water, and filter through glass wool. The solution should have no greenish tint. Dilute 1:3 with water for use.

5. Tyrosine standard.

Stock. Dissolve 100 mg. tyrosine in and make up to 100 ml. with 0.1 N HCl.

Working. Dilute stock 1:25 with 0.1 N HCl (4 mg./100 ml.).

Technique

Serum samples can be stored for several weeks in the refrigerator or freezer without changes in the mucoprotein level. The procedure consists of precipitation and color development steps.

A. *Mucoprotein Precipitation.* Into 1.8 ml. of water wash 0.2 ml. serum and mix thoroughly. Then add 2.0 ml. 1.2 M perchloric acid drop by drop while shaking, again mixing well.

When the mixture has been allowed to stand for exactly ten minutes, it is filtered through Whatman No. 42, 5.5 cm. filter paper.

2.0 ml. filtrate, which must be completely clear, is then pipetted into a glass stopper tube marked at 2 ml., and 0.4 ml. of 5 per cent phosphotungstic acid is added. The solution is mixed and set aside for 15 minutes. At the end of this time it is centrifuged for 20 minutes at 2500 r.p.m., when the supernatant is removed with a bulb pipet and discarded. The precipitate is then washed with 1.5 ml. of 5 per cent phosphotungstic acid, the tube centrifuged again, and the clear liquid aspirated and discarded as before. Then 0.6 ml. of 15 per cent aqueous sodium carbonate is added to the washed mucoprotein to bring it into solution.

B. *Color Development.* To the mucoprotein solution is added 0.8 ml. water, followed by 0.3 ml. of dilute Folin and Ciocalteu reagent. Finally, after mixing immediately, make up to 2 ml. with water. Set up standard and blank tubes as indicated in the following table:

STANDARD	BLANK

0.6 ml. water
0.2 ml. working
    standard solution
0.6 ml. 15 per cent
    Na₂CO₃. Mix.
0.3 ml. dilute phenol
    reagent. Mix.
Make up to 2 ml. with
    water.
	0.8 ml. water
	
	0.6 ml. 15 per cent
	    Na₂CO₃. Mix.
	0.3 ml. dilute phenol
	    reagent. Mix.
	Make up to 2 ml. with
	    water.

Incubate all tubes in a water bath at 37° C. for 20 minutes. Read in absorptiometer, 1 cm. cells, at 680 mμ.

Calculation

$$8 \ \mu g. \times \frac{R-B}{S-B} \times \frac{100}{0.1 \times 1000} = \frac{R-B}{S-B} \times$$

8.0 = mg. mucoprotein tyrosine/100 ml.

Serum Cholesterol

Serum cholesterol in the normal child varies within such wide limits that its estimation has only a very limited application indeed. On the first day of life the normal mean is 74 mg. per 100 ml. (48 to 98 mg. per 100 ml.), and this value rises to 132 mg. per 100 ml. (69 to 173 mg. per 100 ml.) between the third day and the end of the first year. Thereafter normal levels are only a little lower than in the adult, ranging from 138 to 242 mg. per 100 ml. with a mean of 188 mg. per 100 ml.

Cholesterol levels are characteristically elevated in diabetes, nephrosis, hypothyroidism, and biliary obstruction and in those rare cases of idiopathic hypercholesterolemia and hyperlipemia; they are depressed in hyperthyroidism and hepatitis, and sometimes in cases of severe anemia or infection. In none of these instances does the measurement of serum cholesterol rank as more than a subsidiary test; in nephrosis, for example, serum protein electrophoresis provides a substantially more sensitive index of diagnosis and progress.

The differential measurement of free and esterified cholesterol has been advocated as a test of diffuse liver disease. Here there is a decrease in the ester fraction as there is also in infants during the first month of life. The estimation of these fractions is a time consuming operation and certainly in pediatric practice is not warranted.

The cholesterol method to be given was adapted from that of Carr and Drekter (1956) and was developed at the Hospital for Sick Children in London (see O'Brien

and Ibbott, 1959, p. 49). It is certainly the method of choice on the basis of reproducibility, accuracy, and ease of performance. In this instance cholesterol is measured by the Liebermann-Burchard color reaction after the serum proteins have been removed by precipitation—but without the necessity for any preliminary extraction, saponification, or precipitation of the cholesterol itself. The only drawback to this technique is that with raised bilirubin levels an interfering red color is produced. In these instances, one must resort to a more elaborate digitonin precipitation method (Colman and McPhee, 1956).

Reagents

1. Glacial acetic acid, reagent grade.
2. Acetic anhydride, reagent grade. Keep tightly stoppered.
3. 80 per cent acetic acid, reagent grade.
4. Concentrated sulfuric acid, reagent grade. Keep tightly stoppered.
5. Cholesterol (stock standard solution), 400 mg. per 100 ml. Dissolve 400 mg. of recrystallized cholesterol (m.p. 148° C.) in about 50 ml. of glacial acetic acid. Dilute to 100 ml. with glacial acetic acid. (Dilute standard solution.) Dilute stock standard 1:10 in glacial acetic acid.
6. Sulfuric acid–acetic acid reagent 1:1 (v/v). Pour 100 ml. of concentrated sulfuric acid very slowly onto 100 ml. of glacial acetic acid in a 500 ml. Pyrex flask, mixing all the time by gentle rotation. Cool to room temperature before use. This solution is stable for six months in a stoppered bottle.
7. Dehydrating reagent. Mix 10 ml. of sulfuric acid–acetic acid reagent 1:1 with an equal volume of glacial acetic acid. Solution is stable six months.

Technique. Into a series of 15 ml. Pyrex stopper tubes containing 0.9 ml. of glacial acetic acid, wash 0.1 ml. aliquots of each test serum and allow to stand for two to three minutes. For the standard add 0.5 ml. of dilute standard to 0.5 ml. of 80 per cent acetic acid and for the blank add 0.5 ml. of glacial acetic acid to 0.5 ml. of 80 per cent acetic acid in similar tubes.

Add 4 ml. of acetic anhydride to all tubes, allowing the reagent to flow freely into each sample without touching the wall of the tube. The tubes are stoppered and mixed by rotation; those with precipitate are centrifuged for five minutes at 2000 r.p.m. Into a second series of test tubes pipet out two 2 ml. aliquots for test and serum blank from each serum tube and one

2 ml. amount from the standard and blank tubes. To the serum blank tubes add immediately 0.5 ml. of glacial acetic acid and read subsequently whenever convenient. To all the remaining tubes add one drop of dehydrating reagent, allowing it to fall directly into the solution. In a few seconds the tube should become hot, and if it does not one further drop may be added in the same manner. The tubes are now left for about ten minutes in a water bath at 25° C., preferably but not essentially in the dark and never in direct sunlight. Care must be taken to assure that the mouths of the tubes do not become contaminated with water.

At exactly one-minute intervals add 0.4 ml. of sulfuric acid–acetic acid reagent to all the tubes in the water bath, again so as not to touch the walls of the tubes. Mix by tapping. Read each tube exactly 20 minutes after the last reagent is added, preferably in 2 cm. cells or in the Beckman D.U. using 50 × 10 × 4.3 mm. cells at 620 mμ.

Calculation

$$\frac{O.D.\ test - O.D.\ serum\ blank}{O.D.\ std. - O.D.\ reagent\ blank} \times 200$$
= mg. cholesterol per 100 ml.

REFERENCES

1. Barbero, G. J.: Diagnosis of cystic fibrosis of the pancreas. Pediatrics, 24:658–665, 1959.
2. Benson, J. A., Culver, P. J., Ragland, S., Jones, C. M., Drummey, G. D., and Bougas, E.: The d-xylose absorption test in malabsorption syndromes. New Eng. J. Med., 256:335–339, 1957.
3. Bessey, O. A., Lowry, O. H., and Brock, M. J.: A method for the rapid determination of alkaline phosphatase with five cubic millimeters of serum. J. Biol. Chem., 164:321–329, 1946.
4. Carr, J. J., and Drekter, I. J.: Simplified rapid technic for the extraction and determination of serum cholesterol without saponification. Clin. Chem., 2:353–368, 1956.
5. Child Research Council: Unpublished data, 1960.
6. Colman, D. M., and McPhee, A. F.: An improved method for determination of total serum cholesterol. Am. J. Clin. Path., 26:181–186, 1956.
7. Conway, E. J.: Microdiffusion Analysis and Volumetric Error. New York, The Macmillan Company, 1958, Ch. X, p. 99.
8. Cotlove, E., Trantham, H. V., and Bowman, R. L.: An instrument and method for automatic, rapid, accurate, and sensitive titration of chloride in biologic samples. J. Lab. & Clin. Med., 51:461–468, 1958.
9. Diehl, H., and Ellingboe, J. L.: Indicator for

10. Fawcett, J. K.: The semi-micro Kjeldahl method for the determination of nitrogen. J. Med. Lab. Tech., 12:1–22, 1954.
11. Gibson, L. E., and Cooke, R. E.: A test for concentration of electrolytes in sweat in cystic fibrosis of the pancreas utilizing pilocarpine by iontophoresis. Pediatrics, 23:545–549, 1959.
12. Harrison, G. A.: Chemical Methods in Clinical Medicine. London, J. & A. Churchill, Ltd., 1949, Ch. XIX, p. 380.
13. Hiller, A., Plazin, J., and Van Slyke, D. D.: A study of conditions for Kjeldahl determination of nitrogen in proteins. J. Biol. Chem., 176:1401–1420, 1948.
14. Horner, W. H.: The determination of calcium in biologic material. J. Lab. & Clin. Med., 45:951–957, 1955.
15. Jackson, S. H.: Methods of Clinical Chemistry in Pediatrics. Toronto, The Hospital for Sick Children, 1959, p. 46.
16. Kingsley, G. R.: The direct biuret method for the determination of serum proteins as applied to photoelectric and visual colorimetry. J. Lab. Clin. Med., 27:840–845, 1942.
17. Lathe, G. H., and Ruthven, C. R. J.: Factors affecting the rate of coupling of bilirubin in the van den Bergh reaction. J. Clin. Path., 11:155–161, 1958.
18. Majoor, C. L. H.: The possibility of detecting individual proteins in blood serum by differentiation of solubility curves in concentrated sodium sulfate solutions. J. Biol. Chem., 169:583–594, 1947.
19. Marks, V.: An improved glucose-oxidase method for determining blood, c.s.f. and urine glucose levels. Clin. Chim. Acta, 4:395–400, 1959.
20. McDonald, I. W., and Hall, R. J.: The conversion of casein into microbial proteins in the rumen. Biochem. J., 67:400–405, 1957.
21. Natelson, S.: Routine use of ultramicro methods in the clinical laboratory. Am. J. Clin. Path., 21:1153–1172, 1951.
22. O'Brien, D., and Ibbott, F.: Laboratory Manual of Pediatric Microbiochemical Techniques. Denver, University of Colorado Medical Center Press, 1959, p. 97.
23. Ibid., p. 49.
24. Roe, J. H., and Rice, E. W.: A photometric method for the determination of free pentoses in animal tissues. J. Biol. Chem., 173:507–512, 1948.
25. Van Slyke, D. D., and Hiller, A.: Application of Sendroy's iodometric chloride titration to protein-containing fluids. J. Biol. Chem., 167:107–124, 1947.
26. Weimer, H. E., and Moshin, J. R.: Serum glycoprotein concentrations in experimental tuberculosis of guinea pigs. Am. Rev. Tuberculosis, 68:594–602, 1953.
27. Winzler, R. J., Devor, A. W., Mehl, J. W., and Smyth, I. M.: Studies on the mucoproteins of human plasma. J. Clin. Investigation, 27:609–616, 1948.

Chapter 11

Tests of Hepatic Function

By HYMAN J. ZIMMERMAN, M.D.

THE LIVER is a complex organ, which performs many metabolic functions. More than 100 tests of hepatic functions have been based on the hundreds of reactions that have been shown to occur in the liver. Many of these have been abandoned after early study. A few have been found to be clinically useful. In Table 11–1 is shown a classification of the types of functions performed by the liver and of the types of tests that have been based on these functions.

Classic experiments in hepatic physiology have shown that removal of large portions of the liver of normal animals may leave some types of hepatic function unimpaired. This has led many authors to emphasize the great reserve power of the liver and to suggest that mild hepatic disease will not be exposed by tests of he-

Table 11–1. Classification of Types of Hepatic Function and Related Tests

FUNCTION	TEST	COMMENT
Bilirubin	Serum bilirubin level and partition (direct and indirect fraction)	Very useful.
	Urine bilirubin	Very useful.
	Urine urobilinogen	Very useful.
	Fecal urobilinogen	Very useful.
Carbohydrate Metabolism	Glucose ⎫ Fructose ⎬ tolerance tests Lactate ⎭	Not usually applied to the study of liver disease.
	Galactose tolerance	Some value in differential diagnosis of jaundice. Used in some clinics.
	Epinephrine ⎫ Glucagon ⎬ tolerances	Helpful in the diagnosis of glycogen storage disease but not generally in other hepatic disease.
Protein Metabolism	Serum protein level Albumin, globulin, gamma globulin level; electrophoretic analysis	Very useful in detecting hepatic and nonhepatic diseases.
	Flocculation and turbidometric test	Very useful in detecting hepatic and nonhepatic diseases.
	Plasma mucoprotein levels	Not widely used. May be of value.
	Amino acid levels in blood and urine	Of research rather than ordinary clinical value.
	Blood ammonia levels	Useful in understanding, diagnosis, and treatment of hepatic coma.
	Blood urea levels	Of clinical interest; late and insensitive reflection of liver damage.

Table 11–1.   Classification of Types of Hepatic Function and Related Tests *(continued)*

FUNCTION	TEST	COMMENT
Lipid Metabolism	Plasma cholesterol and cholesterol ester level	Definite but limited usefulness.
	Cinnamic acid tolerance test	An interesting test with clinical applicability yet to be demonstrated.
	Bile acid levels and fractionation	Recently introduced; quantitative measures await adequate clinical trial.
Foreign Substance Excretion	Dye excretion tests Rose bengal	Old test, rarely used. Recently revived as radioactive rose bengal test. Requires further study.
	Sulfobromphthalein (BSP)	Most sensitive measure of liver function. Very useful.
Detoxification and Synthesis	Hippuric acid excretion	Formerly widely used, recently replaced by other procedures.
	Prothrombin time response to vitamin K administration	Limited clinical applicability.
	Plasma levels of other coagulation factors	Of interest, but clinical applicability to liver disease study remains to be demonstrated.
Serum Enzyme Levels	Alkaline phosphatase } Transaminases }	Very useful and widely used in study of liver disease.
	Cholinesterase	Not widely used.
	(See Chapter 12 for other serum enzymes.)	
Levels of Serum "Metals" and Electrolytes	Serum iron and iron-binding capacity	Helpful in the diagnosis of hemochromatosis; limited usefulness in differential diagnosis of jaundice
	Serum ceruloplasmin and copper levels	Helpful in the diagnosis of hepatolenticular degeneration.
	Serum zinc levels	Abnormal in "alcoholic" cirrhosis; clinical applicability not adequately studied.
	Serum magnesium levels	Relationship of abnormality to liver disease or to associated factors remains to be evaluated.
	Serum sodium and potassium levels	Abnormality reflects complication of liver disease, not liver function.
Vitamin Metabolism	Serum vitamin A levels Serum vitamin B_{12} levels and tolerance tests	Proposed for differential diagnosis of jaundice; questionable value. May prove to be useful.
Histology of Liver	Needle biopsy	See text.

patic function. The relevance of such experiments to clinical problems, however, may be questioned. Diffuse though mild disease, such as viral hepatitis or early cirrhosis of the liver, produces impairment of many tests of hepatic function with the severity of disease reflected in the degree of hepatic dysfunction. Disturbed hepatic function does not necessarily mean hepatic disease, since some nonhepatic diseases also may produce impairment of liver function. Nevertheless the occurrence of abnormal hepatic function can usually be found to have a rational basis when considered in the light of the clinical problem.

No one test of liver function is sufficient for clinical analysis of most problems. From the many tests that have been devised, a group of procedures that are most applicable to the particular clinical problem should be selected. In the following pages the physiologic basis for hepatic function testing is discussed, a number of individual tests of liver function are analyzed, the batteries of tests that are considered useful are presented, and the results in various diseases are illustrated.

BILIRUBIN METABOLISM

Knowledge of bilirubin metabolism is essential for the proper understanding of hepatic disease. Bilirubin is a product of hemoglobin from which it is formed in the cells of the reticuloendothelial system. Here the protoporphyrin is separated from the iron and globin portions of the molecule and the ring is opened to form bilirubin (Fig. 11–1). The bilirubin is transported through the blood (loosely attached to albumin) to the liver. In the liver bilirubin is conjugated with glucuronic acid* to form the diglucuronide (Fig. 11–2), which is excreted by the liver into the duodenum. In the intestines bacterial enzyme action converts bilirubin, through a group of intermediate compounds, to several related compounds collectively referred to as "urobilinogen" (Fig. 11–1). A portion (estimated to be as high as 50 per cent) of the "urobilinogen" is reabsorbed into the blood and re-excreted by the liver. Normally small amounts (1 to 4 mg. per 24 hr.) are excreted in the urine. When the Watson "two-hour method" (see appendix to this chapter) is used, normal individuals have less than 1 Ehrlich unit per two-hour specimen. Fecal urobilinogen levels in normals range from 50 to 250 mg. per day or 300 Ehrlich units per 100 gm. The metabolism of bilirubin is summarized in Fig. 11–1.

* Approximately 10 per cent of the bilirubin excreted by the liver is conjugated with the sulfate radical.

Determination of the level of serum bilirubin was first performed by van den Bergh and Muller, who found that bilirubin in normal serum reacted with the Ehrlich diazo reagent (diazotized sulfanilic acid) only when alcohol was added. Their observation that bile pigment in human bile reacted with the diazo reagent without the addition of alcohol led to the recognition that some change in bilirubin had been effected by the liver. Van den Bergh called the form of bilirubin that reacted with the diazo reagent without the addition of alcohol "direct" and the variety that reacted only in the presence of alcohol "indirect." Serum from patients with jaundice owing to excessive hemolysis gave the indirect reaction, while in the serum of patients with jaundice owing to obstruction of the biliary tree the increased serum bilirubin levels gave the "direct" reaction. The response of the serum to the van den Bergh test has been the basis for several classifications of jaundice. The physiochemical reasons for the different types of response have been clarified only during the past several years.

The properties of indirect and of direct bilirubin and several of the theories to explain these differences are summarized in Table 11–2. It is clear that indirect bilirubin is "free" or unconjugated bilirubin en route to the liver from the reticuloendothelial system where it has been formed. The unconjugated bilirubin is nonpolar and

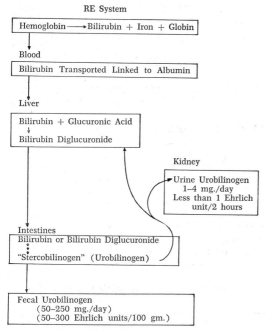

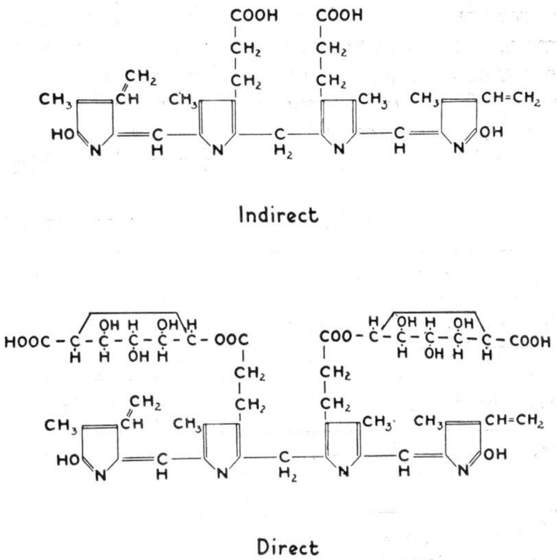

RE System

Hemoglobin ⟶ Bilirubin + Iron + Globin

Blood

Bilirubin Transported Linked to Albumin

Liver

Bilirubin + Glucuronic Acid
Bilirubin Diglucuronide

Kidney

Urine Urobilinogen
1–4 mg./day
Less than 1 Ehrlich
unit/2 hours

Intestines
Bilirubin or Bilirubin Diglucuronide
"Stercobilinogen" (Urobilinogen)

Fecal Urobilinogen
(50–250 mg./day)
(50–300 Ehrlich units/100 gm.)

Figure 11–1. Schematic representation of bilirubin metabolism.

Indirect

Direct

Figure 11–2. The structure of indirect and direct bilirubin. Note that direct bilirubin is bilirubin diglucuronide and that indirect is unconjugated bilirubin. The monoglucuronide, not shown here, may have the glucuronate group attached to either propionate side chain.

Table 11–2. Comparison of Properties of Direct and
Indirect Bilirubin

	DIRECT (CONJUGATED)	INDIRECT (UNCONJUGATED)
Structure	Bilirubin diglucuronide	Bilirubin
Old concept of structure	Bilirubinate ion	Bilirubinglobin
Type of compound	Polar	Nonpolar
Solubility		
Water	+	–
Alcohol	+	+
Van den Bergh reaction	Direct	Indirect
Diffusibility into tissues	Good	Poor
Presence in urine	+	–

therefore not soluble in water. Consequently it will react with the diazo reagent only in the presence of an agent (alcohol) in which it and the diazo reagent are soluble. The lack of solubility in water also is the presumed basis for the failure of indirect bilirubin to appear in the urine in more than trace amounts. Direct (conjugated) bilirubin is the diglucuronide, a polar compound. It is therefore soluble in water solution, reacting "directly" with the diazo reagent, and able to appear in the urine.

Recent studies have shown that bilirubin may also exist as the monoglucuronide (Fig. 11–2). Although the diglucuronide is formed in the liver, the monoglucuronide can be formed in the hepatectomized animal. The extrahepatic sites of monoglucuronide formation are as yet undemonstrated.

Qualitative analysis of serum bilirubin

according to the type of van den Bergh reaction as "indirect" or "direct" has been replaced by quantitative determination of the amount of "direct" and of total bilirubin, the difference being presumed to represent "indirect" bilirubin. A commonly used method, that of Malloy and Evelyn (1937), has been replaced in many laboratories by the modification of Ducci and Watson (1945). In this method the amount of bilirubin that has reacted with the diazo reagent at the end of one minute is determined. This "one-minute" bilirubin presumably represents the "prompt, direct-reacting" bilirubin of van den Bergh. The total bilirubin is measured 15 minutes after the addition of methyl alcohol. The difference between the total and one-minute bilirubin values is the "indirect" bilirubin.

The level of bilirubin in the serum of normals in our laboratory is less than 1 mg. per 100 ml. This is almost entirely unconjugated bilirubin. In some laboratories the normal upper limit is reported to be as high as 1.5 mg. The upper limit of normal for conjugated bilirubin varies from 0.2 to 0.4 mg. in different laboratories. Levels of total serum bilirubin above 2.5 mg. per 100 ml. usually produce jaundice.

Jaundice has been classified by various authors according to pathophysiology, etiology, or both. The three most widely applied classifications are shown in Table 11–3. The classification of McNee (1923) is based on etiology, and that of Rich (1930) is based on mechanisms. The classification of Ducci (1947), modified after Lichtman (1953), is based on both.

McNee proposed that jaundice be categorized as hemolytic, toxic and infectious, and obstructive. Others have substituted the

Table 11–3. Comparison of Three Well-known Classifications of Jaundice

PRINCIPAL CAUSE	MC NEE	RICH	DUCCI
Inability to convert bilirubin to glucuronide	—	—	Prehepatic
Excessive hemolysis	Hemolytic	Retention	Prehepatic
Hepatocellular damage	Toxic and infectious	Regurgitation and retention	Hepatic-hepatocellular
Hepatic disease with "obstructive" type of jaundice; normal parenchymal function	—	Regurgitation	Hepatic-hepatocanalicular
Mechanical obstruction of bile passages	Obstructive jaundice	Regurgitation	Posthepatic

term "hepatocellular" or "hepatogenous" for the "toxic and infectious" category. This classification has no place for constitutional hepatic dysfunction and for the jaundice that, although due to hepatic disease, may simulate obstructive jaundice (intrahepatic cholestasis, cholangiolitic hepatitis, hepatocanalicular jaundice). These defects are remedied by the rational classification of Ducci, which includes the categories of McNee.

Rich, on the basis of presumed pathophysiologic mechanisms, has divided jaundice into "retention" and "regurgitation" types. *Retention jaundice* refers to hyperbilirubinemia in which there is retention of indirect bilirubin because it has not been converted to direct bilirubin and excreted by the liver. This category includes hemolytic jaundice and the jaundice resulting from the inability to conjugate bilirubin with glucuronide or to excrete bilirubin into the biliary tree (constitutional hepatic dysfunction).

In *regurgitation jaundice* there is elevation of the "direct" and "indirect" bilirubins. The "direct" bilirubin elevation reflects bilirubin that has been conjugated and excreted by the liver but regurgitated into the blood, because of lack of patency of the biliary tree. Regurgitation jaundice characterizes anatomic obstruction of the biliary tree. The term has also been used to refer to hepatocellular jaundice, because the presence of increased levels of direct bilirubin in the blood and of bilirubin in the urine led to the inference that "indirect" had been converted to "direct" bilirubin during passage through the hepatic parenchymal cell but had been "regurgitated" into the blood. Hepatocellular jaundice has been considered to have an important element of retention as well as of regurgitation.

The classification of Ducci retains the categories of McNee and the principles of the Rich classification. It is based on the presumed site of the physiologic or anatomic abnormality. The categories are prehepatic, hepatic, and posthepatic jaundice.

Prehepatic jaundice is that variety of jaundice in which the increased serum bilirubin is mainly indirect and, therefore, has not been conjugated by the liver. This category includes hemolytic jaundice and constitutional hyperbilirubinemia (constitutional hepatic dysfunction, Gilbert's disease), a condition in which the elevated serum bilirubin level consists almost entirely of unconjugated bilirubin. It has been suggested that the defect in constitutional hyperbilirubinemia is a genetic inability to properly conjugate or excrete bilirubin. A similar but more severe condition described by Crigler and Najaar has been demonstrated to involve a defect in the conjugating mechanisms for bilirubin. (See articles by Billing and Lathe, 1958, and by Schmid, 1957.)

Hepatic jaundice has been divided by Ducci into two subcategories, hepatocellular jaundice and hepatocanalicular (cholangiolitic) jaundice. Hepatocellular jaundice is similar to the "toxic and infectious" category of the McNee classification. Hepatocanalicular jaundice is the variety of hepatic disease that in the laboratory, and at times in its clinical features, closely simulates obstructive jaundice.

Posthepatic jaundice refers to obstructive jaundice. This may result from carcinoma of the head of pancreas or bile ducts, from pancreatitis, or from gallstones in the common duct. Rarely, diseased lymph nodes at the porta hepatis or invasion of the liver by carcinoma may produce obstructive jaundice.

Hemolytic jaundice occurs because excessively rapid destruction of erythrocytes results in the production of bilirubin at a rate exceeding the ability of the liver to conjugate and excrete it. As stated previously, the hyperbilirubinemia, accordingly, consists of indirect bilirubin. Increased production of bilirubin results in an increase in the amount of urobilinogen formed (Fig. 11-3 C). Increased fecal urobilinogen is, therefore, characteristic of hemolytic icterus. Often there is an increase in the urine content of urobilinogen. Presumably this results from the reabsorption of greater amounts of urobilinogen than can be re-excreted by the liver. Bilirubin does not appear in the urine in "pure" hemolytic jaundice, since the elevated level of serum bilirubin represents largely the "indirect" type. In constitutional hepatic dysfunction and in the Crigler-Najaar syndrome the bilirubin elevation resembles that of hemolytic jaundice, being almost entirely indirect, but the fecal and urine urobilinogen content is normal or depressed, since the rate of bilirubin entry into the duodenum is depressed (Fig. 11-3 B).

Obstruction of the biliary tree (common bile or hepatic duct) produces jaundice by preventing the entry into the duodenum of bilirubin that has been conjugated. The bilirubin is regurgitated into the blood, raising the serum level of direct-reacting bilirubin, which appears in the urine. The

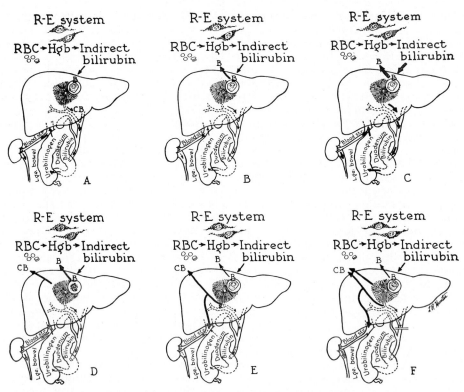

Figure 11–3. Diagrammatic representation of (*A*) normal bilirubin metabolism and the site of defect in (*B*) constitutional hepatic dysfunction, (*C*) hemolytic jaundice, (*D*) hepatocellular jaundice, (*E*) hepato-canalicular (cholangiolitic) jaundice, and (*F*) posthepatic jaundice. In the diagrams, *B* represents un-conjugated and *CB* conjugated bilirubin.

exclusion of bilirubin from the duodenum results in "clay-colored" stools and very low levels of urobilinogen in the stool and urine (Fig. 11–3 F).

The hepatocellular type of hepatic jaundice results from injury to the parenchyma (viral hepatitis, toxic hepatitis, cirrhosis). Hepatic damage theoretically might be expected to produce a retention type of jaundice with impaired conjugating ability. Indeed late in convalescence the jaundice may be of the retention type. During the more deeply jaundiced phase of hepatitis, however, there are features similar to those of obstructive jaundice. Thus, in hepatitis there is a distinct increase in the direct-reacting bilirubin fraction with bilirubin in the urine. The degree of exclusion of bilirubin from the duodenum, however, is much less marked than in obstructive jaundice. Stools usually are only somewhat lighter than normal but may be clay colored. The urobilinogen content of the stool is usually decreased but rarely to the levels character-istic of obstructive jaundice. Even though amounts of bilirubin entering the duodenum are less than normal, liver damage prevents adequate hepatic clearing from the blood of the urobilinogen reabsorbed from the duodenum. Urine urobilinogen, therefore, is often increased in some stages of hepa-tocellular jaundice (Fig. 11–3 D).

It has been presumed, therefore, that in hepatitis, as in obstructive jaundice, much of the bilirubin presented to the liver cell is conjugated and excreted into the canal-iculi but regurgitates back into the blood, perhaps because of necrotic cells or in-creased permeability of the canaliculi. Recent evidence suggests that a significant fraction of the elevated bilirubin level in patients with hepatocellular jaundice is the monoglucuronide, apparently formed in extrahepatic sites.

The hepatocanalicular type of hepatic jaundice simulates obstructive jaundice very closely (Fig. 11–3 E). It has also been called "cholangiolitic," a term based on the theory that jaundice occurs because bilirubin regurgitates into the blood through defects in the cholangioles. It has also been called intrahepatic cholestasis, a term that describes the fact that bile flow into the duodenum is inhibited by intrahepatic disease. This type of jaundice is seen most commonly with certain drug reactions (chlorpromazine, organic arsenicals, methyltestosterone); it is thought to occur occasionally as a result of viral hepatitis or it may be "idiopathic."

Tests

Determination of the total serum bilirubin level is useful in measuring the depth and progress of jaundice. Determination of the direct and indirect fraction has been of some value in the differential diagnosis of jaundice. When the direct fraction is less than 15 per cent of the total bilirubin value, the jaundice is very likely to be retention (prehepatic jaundice) in type—either owing to hemolysis or to constitutional hepatic dysfunction (Table 11-4). Little specific aid in the distinction of hepatic from posthepatic jaundice can be obtained from the relative levels of direct and indirect bilirubin. The direct fraction may constitute more than 50 per cent of the total bilirubin in either hepatic or posthepatic jaundice. Levels of the direct fraction that constitute between 15 and 50

per cent of the total bilirubin are infrequent in posthepatic jaundice and are more characteristic of hepatic jaundice. Attempts to define the level of monoglucuronide and of diglucuronide, while of interest, have not proved of specific differential diagnostic value.

Testing for urine bilirubin (urine "bile") is useful in the differential diagnosis of jaundice. The presence of bilirubin in the urine shows that the jaundice is of the regurgitation type, i.e., hepatic or posthepatic. Bilirubin may also be present in the urine of patients without jaundice, as in early or anicteric hepatitis, in metastatic carcinoma, or in early obstruction of the biliary tree.

Decreased *fecal urobilinogen* is characteristic of obstructive (posthepatic) jaundice but may also be found in patients with hepatocellular jaundice. An extremely low level (below 5 mg. or 5 Ehrlich units per day) of stool urobilinogen is strong evidence that the jaundice is posthepatic. An increased level of fecal urobilinogen (above 250 mg. or 300 Ehrlich units per day) is evidence of hemolysis. When fecal urobilinogen levels are being determined as

Table 11-4. **Differential Features of Various Types of Jaundice (According to Modified Ducci Classification)**

CATEGORY OF JAUNDICE	CAUSES	URINE BILIRUBIN	URINE UROBILINOGEN	FECAL UROBILINOGEN	SERUM BILIRUBIN (DIRECT/TOTAL RATIO)
Prehepatic					
Retention type	Constitutional hepatic dysfunction* of Gilbert and of Crigler-Najaar type	0	N or ↓	N or ↓	<0.15
	Late convalescent hepatitis	0	↑ or N	N	<0.15
Production type	Hemolytic states	0	↑ or N	↑	<0.15
Hepatic					
Hepatocellular	Cirrhosis, hepatitis (viral or toxic) Other causes of hepatic necrosis	+	N or ↑†	N or ↓	0.15-0.70
Hepatocanalicular	"Cholangiolitic" form of viral hepatitis "Cholangiolitic" type of jaundice from drugs, e.g., methyl testosterone, chlorpromazine, organic arsenicals. Primary biliary cirrhosis	+	N ↓ or ↑	↓	>0.50
Posthepatic	Obstruction of biliary tree Carcinoma of pancreas or bile ducts Choledocholithiasis Other obstructive lesions	+	↓ or N	↓	>0.50

* A variety of constitutional hepatic dysfunction recently described by Dubin and Johnson and by Sprinz (Dubin-Sprinz syndrome) should be classified as hepatic jaundice.

† In hepatitis depends on the stage of the disease (Fig. 11-4).

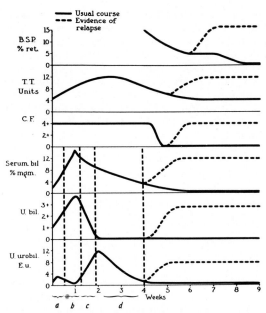

Figure 11–4. Diagrammatic representation of laboratory abnormalities during the course of viral hepatitis. Note that early in the course (phase *a*) there is presence of bilirubin and increased amounts of urobilinogen in the urine with elevated serum bilirubin levels. This is followed by the phase (*b*) of deepening jaundice with decreasing urine urobilinogen and increased urine bilirubin, after which there is an increase in urine urobilinogen (phase *c*) as the serum and urine bilirubin begin to decrease. In phase *d* bilirubin often disappears from the urine, but serum bilirubin levels are still distinctly elevated. Most patients show or are observed only in phases *c* and *d*, but some show this complete pattern. Modified from Watson and Hoffbauer (1947).

measures of hemolysis, they should be correlated with the degree of anemia (see chapter on hematology).

Urine urobilinogen levels are decreased in posthepatic jaundice and in some phases of hepatic jaundice. Increased levels are observed usually in hemolytic jaundice and with subsiding hepatitis. Increased levels also may be a sensitive measure of hepatic damage even in the absence of jaundice, as in some patients with cirrhosis of the liver, metastatic carcinoma, or congestive heart failure.

Studies of urine and stool pigments are extremely useful to the clinician, but there are several pitfalls in the application of bile pigment study to the analysis of jaundice. Very low levels of urobilinogen in the stool are characteristic of obstructive jaundice but may also occur in patients who have received "broad-spectrum" antibiotics. These agents suppress the intestinal bacteria, which convert bilirubin to urobilinogen. On the other hand normal levels of

stool urobilinogen and even increased levels of urine urobilinogen may be found in patients with incomplete obstructive jaundice. During the course of viral hepatitis (Fig. 11–4) urobilinogen and bilirubin content of the urine may be characteristic of hepatocellular jaundice (phases a and c) and of obstructive jaundice (phase b) and may even simulate hemolytic icterus (phase d). Hemolytic icterus may be complicated by hepatic necrosis (as in sickle cell anemia) and thus by hepatocellular jaundice or by pigment stones obstructing the common duct and producing posthepatic jaundice.

Other tests based on bilirubin metabolism have been devised. The *bilirubin tolerance test* consists of administering a known amount of bilirubin and observing the rate of disappearance from the blood. This test is a sensitive measure of hepatic function but has not been adopted widely because it is laborious and expensive. The *urobilinogen tolerance test* consists of the measurement of urine urobilinogen excretion after the intravenous administration of stercobilin. This test is also too complicated for general use.

METABOLIC TESTS

A number of hepatic function tests have been based on the role of the liver in carbohydrate, protein, and fat metabolism. Those tests related to carbohydrate metabolism have been least useful and those related to protein metabolism most useful. Only one commonly used test of hepatic function relates to lipid metabolism.

Carbohydrate Metabolism

Patients with hepatic disease may have hypoglycemia; diminished tolerance for administered glucose, galactose, fructose, or lactate; and decreased hepatic glycogen stores, the last being measured by the blood sugar response to administered epinephrine or glucagon.

Hypoglycemia occurs regularly in hepatectomized animals, occasionally in patients with acute hepatic necrosis, but rarely in patients with chronic liver disease. It has been described in biliary cirrhosis, in primary or metastatic carcinoma of the liver, and in the hepatic congestion of heart failure. The incidence of hypoglycemia in hepatic disease, however, is low.

Glucose tolerance is characteristically abnormal in patients with cirrhosis of the liver. There is a rapid rise of the blood sugar value to abnormal levels and a slow return to normal. This pattern in patients with liver disease can be distinguished from that of diabetes mellitus by the normal or low fasting blood sugar in liver disease and the occurrence of subnormal values by the fifth hour after the glucose has been given. Although the oral or intravenous glucose tolerance test is of interest in the study of patients with hepatic disease, it is of little specific value in diagnosis in these patients.

The *galactose tolerance* test has been applied to the study of liver disease for many years. The normal liver is able to convert galactose to glucose, which is stored as glycogen. In patients with hepatic disease this ability is defective. Administration of galactose results in persistence of abnormal blood levels for several hours and in urinary excretion of abnormal amounts of galactose. This test yields abnormal results in patients with hepatocellular jaundice but normal results in patients with obstructive jaundice of brief duration (less than three weeks). Accordingly it has been advocated by some workers for the differential diagnosis of jaundice, but it is not widely used.

The *fructose tolerance* test, based on a principle similar to that of galactose tolerance, has found no clinical application. Elevated blood levels of lactic acid have been described in patients with severe liver disease. This observation and a *lactic acid tolerance test* have been described as tests of hepatic function but also have not been applied extensively to clinical problems.

The *epinephrine tolerance test* is used to estimate hepatic glycogen stores by observing the blood sugar response to a standard dose of epinephrine. Normal individuals show a blood sugar rise of 40 to 60 mg. per 100 ml. within one hour after the epinephrine has been given. Patients with hepatic disease (cirrhosis, hepatitis) and patients with genetic deficiency in glycogenolytic enzymes (glycogen storage disease) show a subnormal response. The test has not been applied widely to the diagnosis of liver disease but has been useful in clinical research and for the diagnosis of glycogen storage disease. The *glucagon tolerance test,* a recent modification of this test, has involved the use of glucagon, instead of or combined with epinephrine, to produce glycogenolysis. In either epinephrine or glucagon tolerance tests the sub-

ject should receive a high-carbohydrate diet for three days before the test.

Lipid Metabolism

The liver is importantly involved in many phases of lipid metabolism, including the synthesis, esterification, and excretion of cholesterol. Only the determination of the free and esterified *cholesterol* levels of the serum has been applied intensively to the study of hepatic disease. In normal individuals (in the United States) the serum cholesterol level ranges between 150 and 250 mg. per 100 ml. with approximately 70 per cent (100 to 170 mg. per 100 ml.) esterified. In general the cholesterol level is normal or depressed in hepatocellular jaundice and elevated in obstructive jaundice. In patients with hepatitis the total cholesterol level may be mildly depressed or normal, but the level of esterified cholesterol is usually moderately decreased. In severe hepatitis or cirrhosis the serum cholesterol (total and esterified) levels may be markedly depressed. In patients with obstructive jaundice the blood cholesterol level is usually elevated to levels of 250 to 500 mg. per 100 ml. Greater elevations occur occasionally but are more characteristic of so-called "intrahepatic obstruction" ("cholangiolitic hepatitis" and "primary biliary cirrhosis"). In "primary biliary cirrhosis" levels up to 1800 mg. per 100 ml. may be observed. It is generally stated that patients with obstructive jaundice usually have a normal ($2/3$) cholesterol-ester/total cholesterol ratio. Strictly speaking, this is not true. Although the degree of depression of the ratio is characteristically less than that seen in hepatic disease, moderate degrees are regularly seen. Determination of the cholesterol level is widely used in the diagnosis of hepatic disease. Technically the procedure is somewhat difficult and involves meticulous care and technique. Hypocholesterolemia occurs not only in hepatic disease but also in hyperthyroidism, in the malabsorption syndrome, and in other states of hyponutrition.

Bile acids are formed from cholesterol in the liver. Normally they include dihydroxy and trihydroxy "cholic acids" and are excreted as conjugates of glycine (glycocholic acid) and taurine (taurocholic acid). The simple and qualitative methods used in the past (Hays's and Pettenkofer's tests) have shown increased blood and urine levels of bile acids in patients with obstructive jaundice. The lack of satisfactory quantitation and the demonstration that bile acids may also be found in the urine of patients with hepatocellular jaundice prevented the clinical application of these procedures. Quantitative methods have been applied recently to the study of patients with hepatobiliary disease, and characteristic patterns have been found. They may prove to have clinical application.

The *cinnamic acid* tolerance test is an interesting test of hepatic function that couples two reactions known to occur in the liver. These are fatty acid oxidation and conjugation. The normal liver oxidizes (beta oxidation) cinnamic acid to benzoic acid, which in turn is conjugated with glycine to form hippuric acid. Abnormal hepatic function is reflected in the decreased excretion of hippuric acid. This test has found little clinical application.

Protein Metabolism

Amino acid metabolism, urea synthesis, and protein metabolism occur in the liver. Evidence of defects in each of these areas may be observed in patients with hepatic disease. These include abnormal plasma levels of amino acids, proteins, urea, and ammonia and abnormal urine levels of amino acids. Several measures of hepatic function have been based on these phenomena.

Serum Protein Levels. A number of plasma proteins are formed in the liver. These include albumin, fibrinogen, and some of the alpha and beta globulins. Accordingly changes in the plasma (or serum) proteins form the basis for important laboratory aids to the diagnosis of hepatic disease. Depression of serum albumin is characteristic of chronic hepatic disease. For reasons that are not clear, the *serum globulin* level is often elevated in patients with chronic hepatic disease (cirrhosis).

The procedures used to evaluate serum protein changes in patients with liver disease include determination of serum albumin and globulin levels, serum electrophoresis, and several turbidometric ("flocculation") tests. The turbidometric tests reflect largely changes of the gamma globulin and albumin levels.

The *serum albumin* level is considered a reliable index of severity and prognosis in patients with chronic hepatic disease. In patients with cirrhosis there is a positive correlation between the degree of hypoalbuminemia and the severity of the ascites. Patients who show a rise of the albumin level have a more favorable prognosis than those whose levels remain low. In patients with acute hepatic disease (viral or toxic hepatitis) serum albumin levels are usually normal or only mildly depressed. Those who develop subacute hepatic necrosis ("subacute yellow atrophy") frequently have moderate to marked hypoalbuminemia.

The total serum globulin level is often elevated in patients with cirrhosis. The degree of elevation is usually moderate in Laennec's and in biliary cirrhosis with levels of 3 to 5 gm. per 100 ml. In postnecrotic cirrhosis elevations also may be moderate but at times are marked with values in the range of 6 to 9 gm. per 100 ml. occasionally observed. Levels in patients with acute hepatitis are usually normal or only mildly elevated but in occasional patients may exceed levels of 4 gm. per 100 ml. In patients with obstructive jaundice the globulin level is usually normal.

Serum electrophoresis (see section on clinical chemistry) is useful to demonstrate the globulin fraction elevated. In Laennec's and postnecrotic cirrhosis it reveals that the hyperglobulinemia represents largely gamma globulin elevation. In biliary cirrhosis the alpha-2, beta, and gamma fractions show an increase, while in obstructive jaundice the gamma globulin level is usually normal but the alpha-2 and beta fractions are increased. The serum protein abnormalities in patients with hepatic disease are listed in Table 11–5.

The *total serum protein* level in patients with cirrhosis is occasionally low, often normal, and at times even elevated. Reversal of the "A/G ratio" has been emphasized in this and in other hyperglobulinemic diseases. Reference to the A/G ratio, however, is needlessly awkward and imprecise. A low A/G ratio may occur because there is either hyperglobulinemia or hypoalbuminemia or both. The term should be abandoned and the depression or elevation of the respective protein values described.

Flocculation Tests. A large number of tests have been developed, which reflect abnormality of plasma proteins. These reactions, which have been called the "flocculation tests," "globulin reactions," or tests of the "serum colloidal stability," have been very useful to the clinician. In Table 11–6 are listed a few of these procedures with an indication of the presumed related protein abnormalities.

Table 11–5. Abnormalities of Serum Proteins in Liver Disease (Magnitude of Change Indicated by Number of Arrows)

	ACUTE HEPATITIS	CIRRHOSIS (LAENNEC'S)	CIRRHOSIS (POSTNECROTIC)	CIRRHOSIS (BILIARY)	OBSTRUCTIVE JAUNDICE	METASTATIC CARCINOMA
Albumin	N or ↓	↓↓	↓↓	↓	N or ↓	↓
Globulin	N or ↑	↑	↑	↑	N	N
Alpha-1	*	*	*	*	*	*
Alpha-2		N	N	↑	↑	↑↑
Beta	↑	↑	↑	↑↑↑	↑↑	N
Gamma	↑	↑↑	↑↑↑	↑	N	N

* Values not sufficiently consistent to be useful in study of hepatic disease.

Table 11–6. List of Some Flocculation Tests Including Serum Protein Abnormalities That They Reflect (after Maclagan, *et al.*, 1952)

	PRECIPITATING REAGENT	PROTEIN FRACTIONS PRODUCING ABNORMALITY	ALBUMIN INHIBITION
Cephalin flocculation	Cephalin-cholesterol emulsion	γ	+
Thymol turbidity	Supersaturated solution thymol	$\gamma\,(\beta)$	(+)
Colloidal gold	Colloidal gold	γ	+
Zinc sulfate turbidity	ZnSO₄	γ	(+)
Takata-Ara	HgCl₂	$\gamma\,(\beta)$	+
Cadmium sulfate	CdSO₄	$\gamma\,(\alpha\beta)$	+

These tests have in common the tendency to be abnormal in patients with intrinsic hepatic disease (hepatitis, cirrhosis) and to be normal in patients with obstructive jaundice. Indeed serum from patients with obstructive jaundice has the property of inhibiting the flocculation or turbidity tests when mixed with serum that gives a positive reaction. The responsible factor for this inhibition may be a phospholipid. In patients with various systemic diseases characterized by hyperglobulinemia (Table 11–7), the flocculation tests also may yield abnormal results. The various tests differ in the relative incidence of abnormality in various diseases. Of greatest application and interest (in the United States) are the cephalin-cholesterol flocculation and thymol turbidity tests. In the European literature there are more references to the use of other flocculation tests.

The *cephalin-cholesterol flocculation test* is based on the observation that diluted hyperglobulinemic sera added to an emulsion of cephalin-cholesterol leads to the flocculation and precipitation of the cephalin-cholesterol with globulin. The test is positive in approximately 90 per cent of patients with hepatitis and in approximately 60 per cent of patients with cirrhosis (Fig.

Table 11–7. Classification of Diseases Associated with Hyperglobulinemia

I. Infections (especially chronic)
   A. Bacterial (subacute bacterial endocarditis, chronic suppurative infections, granulomatous infections)
   B. Spirochetal (syphilis)
   C. Viral (lymphogranuloma venereum, psittacosis)
   D. Fungal (histoplasmosis, coccidiodomycosis)
   E. Protozoal (leishmaniasis, malaria)
   F. Helminthic
II. Liver disease (cirrhosis)
III. Collagen disease (rheumatoid arthritis, lupus erythematosis, polyarteritis nodosa, scleroderma)
IV. Neoplastic (multiple myeloma, lymphomas, and leukemia but rarely in carcinoma except for bronchogenic carcinoma)
V. Miscellaneous (sarcoidosis)

11–5). The test depends on hypergammaglobulinemia and the degree of inhibition produced by the serum albumin. Albumin decrease contributes to a "positive" cephalin-cholesterol flocculation. It has been stated that a qualitative change in the albumin molecule also contributes to a "positive" cephalin flocculation result.

"False-positive" results may be obtained

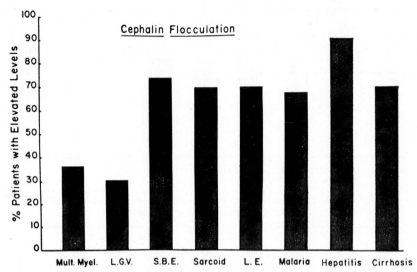

Figure 11–5. Incidence of abnormal cephalin flocculation results in various hyperglobulinemic diseases and in hepatitis and cirrhosis.

with sera that have been frozen and allowed to stand at ice box temperature for periods of one to seven days or that have been heated to 56° C. for 30 minutes. If the reaction mixture is exposed to light, "false-positive" reactions also occur. It is of interest that the sera of a number of normal laboratory animals yield positive cephalin flocculation tests (dogs, rabbits).

The *thymol turbidity test* was developed by Maclagan, who discovered that a buffered solution to which thymol had been added as a preservative became turbid when serum from patients with liver disease was added. This test has been standardized and widely applied to the study of patients with hepatic disease. The addition of one volume of serum (usually 0.1 ml.) to 60 volumes (usually 6.0 ml.) of a barbital-sodium barbital buffer supersaturated with thymol results in variable degrees of turbidity, depending on the degree of elevation of gamma globulin. The beta globulin fraction also has been considered to play a role, since the precipitate is a thymol-globulin-lipid complex. The degree of turbidity has been expressed in arbitrary units (Maclagan units), which may be determined by visual comparison with a turbidity standard or by use of a spectrophotometer. Normal individuals have values below 4 units in our laboratory. In some laboratories values as high as 5 or even 6 units have been considered normal.

Elevated levels are observed in approximately 80 to 90 per cent of patients with acute viral hepatitis and in 20 to 70 per cent of patients with cirrhosis, depending on the stage and type (Fig. 11–6). During the course of viral hepatitis the thymol turbidity becomes abnormal a few days after the cephalin flocculation test but may remain abnormal after the latter has already become normal (Fig. 11–4).

Abnormal values for the thymol turbidity and cephalin flocculation tests occur in other hyperglobulinemic diseases (Figs. 11–5, 11–6). These include subacute bacterial endocarditis, rheumatoid arthritis, chronic suppurative disease, disseminated lupus erythematosus, sarcoidosis, hematogenous tuberculosis and histoplasmosis, malaria, and lymphogranuloma venereum. In multiple myeloma abnormal thymol turbidity values are less common, presumably because the hyperglobulinemia usually results from elevation of fractions other than the normal gamma globulin.

Technical "false-positive" results may be obtained with sera that have a high lipid content. In fact the thymol turbidity test has been applied to the estimation of fat absorption by observing changes after ingestion of a fat-containing meal.

The *thymol flocculation* test is an extension of the thymol turbidity test. It consists of estimating the flocculum that is formed after the thymol turbidity test tube has been allowed to stand for 18 hours. This test has been recommended by some workers as more specific and sensitive than the turbidity test.

Turbidometric Estimation of Gamma Globulin Levels. There are several turbidometric procedures in which the turbidity produced correlates quantitatively with the gamma globulin concentration of the serum. Some of these tests depend on the tendency for gamma globulin to be precipitated by low concentrations of metallic ions in solutions of low total ionic strength.

Kunkel (1947) has applied this principle to the development of the *zinc sulfate turbidity test*. The addition of one volume of serum (usually 0.1 ml.) to 60 volumes (usually 6.0 ml.) of a 0.024 per cent zinc sulfate solution in barbital buffer of low ionic strength results in a turbidity proportional in degree to the gamma globulin concentration of the serum. The turbidity is expressed in Kunkel units, normal individuals having less than 12 units (in our laboratory). This test is of value in distinguishing hepatocellular from obstructive jaundice and in following the levels of gamma globulin in cirrhosis and other hyperglobulinemic diseases. Another method of estimating gamma globulin level turbidometrically is that described by de la Huerga and his associates in which the turbidity measured after serum is diluted 1 to 50 with 18.9 per cent ammonium sulfate in 2.93 per cent sodium chloride solution.

Mucoprotein Determinations. Determination of the serum mucoprotein level has been introduced recently into the study of patients with hepatic disease. It has been observed that patients with intrinsic hepatic disease (hepatitis or cirrhosis) have low levels of this group of proteins, presumably because their synthesis by the liver is depressed. Since the patients with obstructive jaundice have been found to have normal or elevated serum mucoprotein levels, this determination has been offered to assist in the differential diagnosis of jaundice but has not been adopted widely.

Amino aciduria. It has been known for a long time that patients with acute hepatic necrosis ("acute yellow atrophy") have leucine and tyrosine crystals in the urine. These amino acids represent, at least in part, products of autolyzed hepatic tissue. Other amino acids are found in the urine of patients with severe cirrhosis or hepatitis (toxic or viral). This amino aciduria reflects the elevated levels of blood amino acids that result from impaired amino acid metabolism by the liver as well as from the release from necrotic tissue already described.

These observations may be applied to the study of hepatic disease. Demonstration of amino aciduria by paper chromatography is preferable to and more reliable than the laborious search for characteristic tyrosine and leucine crystals. Amino acid content of the blood and urine, however, has found less routine than research application. Tests of hepatic function that have been based on the impaired ability of the damaged liver to metabolize amino acids include the *tyrosine tolerance*, the *methionine tolerance*, the *glycine tolerance*, and the *protein hydrolysate tolerance* tests. Each of these procedures may reveal a defect in the disappearance of administered amino acids from the blood of patients with hepatic disease, but they have not been applied extensively to the study of clinical problems.

Blood Ammonia Determination. A relationship between elevated levels of blood

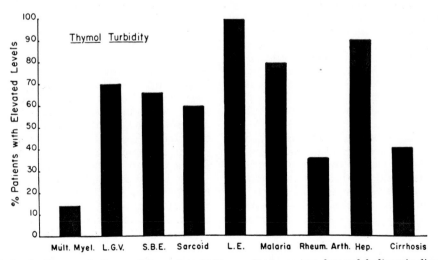

Figure 11–6. Incidence of abnormal thymol turbidity results in various hyperglobulinemic diseases and in hepatitis ("Hep.") and cirrhosis.

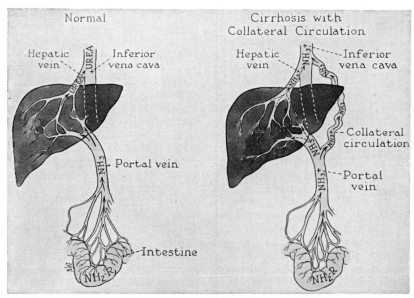

Figure 11–7. Pictorial representation of intestinal formation of ammonia in normal and cirrhotic individuals and of the role of the normal liver in removing ammonia brought to it by the portal blood. Figure also shows the production of elevated plasma ammonia levels by "shunting" of blood through the collateral circulation or by impaired hepatic parenchymal function.

ammonia and liver disease has been recognized for the past 30 years and suspected for the past 60 years. It is uncertain whether ammonia, as measured in the blood, represents this substance as such or ammonia released from some bound state by chemical manipulation. At any rate the amount of ammonia released from blood or plasma by treatment with alkali has been shown to be relatable to the severity of the liver disease.

The two chief methods that are available for ammonia determination are the microdiffusion method of Conway (1950), in which plasma or blood is used, and the simpler method of Seligson (1951), using whole blood. By the method of Conway normal individuals have plasma ammonia levels under 100 micrograms per 100 ml. (in our laboratory). By the method of Seligson, as modified by Bessman (1959), the levels are under 100 micrograms per 100 ml. of whole blood.

Studies have shown conclusively that the major source of blood ammonia is the gastrointestinal tract, although a minor contribution is made by the kidney. Bacteria, particularly those in the area of the cecum, release ammonia from nitrogen-containing foods. This ammonia, as well as ammonia ingested as ammonium salts or released from urea by urea-splitting organisms, is absorbed into the portal vein. The liver normally removes most of the ammonia from the portal vein blood, converting it to urea. Little ammonia escapes from the liver into the hepatic vein to be carried to the systemic circulation.

Elevated blood ammonia levels in patients with hepatic disease appear to depend on two mechanisms, "shunting" of portal blood past the liver and impaired parenchymal function (Fig. 11–7). In patients with cirrhosis and extensive collateral portal circulation elevation of the ammonia levels has been ascribed largely to the shunting of portal blood past the liver. Hepatic vein catheterization studies have shown that patients with severe hepatitis or cirrhosis remove less than normal amounts of ammonia from the portal blood, perhaps as a manifestation of defective urea synthesis.

Elevated ammonia levels are seen in impending or fully developed hepatic coma owing to cirrhosis or severe hepatitis and occasionally in severe heart failure, azotemia, cor pulmonale, and erythroblastosis fetalis. Also they have been described in animals and in one human with an Eck fistula and in animals in shock.

The use of the blood ammonia determination has been of assistance in the recognition of impending or established hepatic coma. As much or more, however, can be learned by proper clinical appraisal of the patient or by use of electroencephalography. Blood ammonia determination may be useful for monitoring the efficacy of treatment of hepatic coma. An additional application has been suggested recently. In patients with cirrhosis and hemorrhage from esophageal varices blood ammonia levels are elevated, whereas in noncirrhotic patients with gastrointestinal bleeding owing to duodenal ulcer the ammonia levels are usually normal. Combining the ammonia level with the determination of bromsulphthalein excretion is of assistance in recognizing gastrointestinal bleeding in cirrhotic patients. Measuring the plasma ammonia level after a standard dose of an ammonium salt has been recommended as an aid in estimating the patency of a portocaval "shunt."

FOREIGN SUBSTANCE EXCRETION

It has been known for many years that certain dyes are removed from the circulation and excreted almost entirely by the liver. The dyes that have been studied include azorubin S, rose bengal, phenoltetrachlorphthalein, phenoltetraiodophthalein, and sodium phenoltetrabromphthalein sulfonate (bromsulfalein, sulfobromphthalein). Several tests of liver function have been based on this principle. Of these the two most popular have been the rose bengal and sulfobromphthalein (BSP) excretion tests.

Rose Bengal Excretion

Rose bengal excretion is the first test of liver function, based on the elimination of dyes by the liver, that received significant clinical application. In this test the dye is administered parenterally, and either excretion of the dye into the duodenum or retention in the blood is measured. For technical reasons this procedure has been considered inferior to the bromsulfalein test and abandoned. Rose bengal excretion has been recently revived with the introduction of rose bengal "tagged" with I^{131}. When this substance is given, the rate of preferential accumulation of the radioactivity over the liver and its rate of disappearance from the liver have been used to help detect hepatic disease. This test has been introduced too recently to adequately appraise its clinical usefulness, although it has been suggested as a means of distinguishing posthepatic from hepatic jaundice.

Sulfobromphthalein (BSP) Excretion

The BSP excretion test is one of the most widely used measures of hepatic function. It is also the most sensitive test of liver function. Normal results with this procedure can, for practical purposes, be considered to exclude active parenchymal hepatic disease.

Dye is administered intravenously and the completeness of disappearance from the blood is determined. The BSP is almost completely cleared from the blood by the normal liver. (In hepatectomized animals less than 20 per cent of the dye may be removed by extrahepatic tissue.) It appears to be transferred from the blood to the parenchymal cell, temporarily stored, and excreted as a metabolite or conjugate into the bile. The two factors involved in BSP excretion by the liver are normal parenchymal cell function and an adequate hepatic circulation.

Several standardized tests have been based on the ability of the liver to remove BSP from the blood. In the most widely used procedure a dose of 5 mg. per kg. of body weight is administered intravenously, and a blood specimen is obtained 45 minutes later. (In the original method, the dose of BSP was 2 mg. per kg., and the specimen was drawn at 30 minutes.) The dye level at 45 minutes is expressed as the per cent of dye "retained," i.e., not excreted. A level of 10 mg. per 100 ml. is considered to represent 100 per cent retention (see appendix to this chapter for details).

Normal individuals have less than 5 per cent retention at 45 minutes. Abnormal degrees of retention occur in patients with obstructive or hepatocellular jaundice. It is therefore of little diagnostic value to perform the BSP excretion test in patients with jaundice that may be either hepatocellular or obstructive. It is our practice to perform BSP excretion in such patients only when the bilirubin level is below 4 mg. per 100 ml. Although there is evidence that in hepatocellular jaundice the BSP retention at any particular degree of hyperbilirubinemia is greater than in obstructive jaundice, this is of no value in the differential diagnosis of jaundice. The estimation of the amount of BSP retained in the blood may be interfered with by the presence of bilirubin in excessive amounts if the estimation is done by visual colorimetry or with a photoelectric colorimeter in which specific filters are used. On the other hand, if a spectrophotometer that can establish a precise wavelength is used, BSP levels can be estimated quite satisfactorily in the presence of hyperbilirubinemia. As indicated previously, this is of little diagnostic value. In hemolytic jaundice, BSP excretion is normal.

Abnormal results also are observed in patients who are not jaundiced if there is parenchymal hepatic disease, biliary tract disease, or extrahepatic disease (Table 11–8).

Table 11–8. Diseases Characterized by Abnormal BSP Excretion

I. Parenchymal hepatic disease
  A. Cirrhosis
  B. Fatty metamorphosis
  C. Viral hepatitis
  D. Toxic hepatitis
  E. Infectious mononucleosis
II. Biliary tract disease
  A. Common bile duct obstruction (with or without jaundice)
  B. Cholelithiasis and cholecystitis
III. Extrahepatic disease
  A. Circulatory
    1. Congestive heart failure
    2. Hepatic vein occlusion (Chiari's syndrome)
    3. ? Shock
    4. Spinal cord injuries
  B. Systemic disease producing infiltrative lesions of liver
    1. Metastatic carcinoma
    2. Lymphomas and leukemias
    3. Granulomatous disease (tuberculosis, histoplasmosis, sarcoidosis)
    4. Amyloidosis
  C. Nonspecific (fever, chronic and debilitating diseases)

Excretion of BSP is regularly impaired in patients with disease of the hepatic parenchyma. In Laennec's cirrhosis normal excretion is rarely found. Retention may be slight (5 to 15 per cent) when the degree of cirrhosis is slight or marked (15 to 50 per cent) when there is severe and "active" disease. When there is ascites or portal hypertension owing to Laennec's cirrhosis, there is a high degree of BSP retention. In postnecrotic cirrhosis impaired BSP excretion is also frequent, although patients with "healed" postnecrotic cirrhosis, even with severe portal hypertension, may occasionally have normal parenchymal function as measured by BSP excretion.

In fatty metamorphosis of the liver BSP "retention" is frequent and, in general, parallels in degree the intensity of the fatty metamorphosis. Indeed impaired BSP excretion may be the only abnormal hepatic function in such patients.

In patients with viral hepatitis BSP excretion is, of course, abnormal during the icteric phase. It remains abnormal, however, after jaundice has subsided and may be abnormal before jaundice has appeared. Similarly, in patients with toxic hepatitis, BSP retention is regularly present. Most patients with infectious mononucleosis (with or without jaundice) have impaired BSP excretion.

In patients with biliary tract obstruction, even when incomplete and producing no jaundice, BSP excretion is usually impaired. Dye excretion is also abnormal in patients with cholecystitis and cholelithiasis.

Patients with nonhepatic disease also may have impaired BSP excretion. In heart failure the BSP retention, which is regularly found, is proportional in degree to the severity of the heart failure, especially as reflected in the degree of venous pressure elevation. In hepatic vein occlusion (Chiari's syndrome) the mechanisms are similar to those of heart failure. Impaired hepatic blood flow and hepatic cell anoxia appear to contribute to the dysfunction. Shock may result in a minimal to moderate degree of BSP excretion. The impairment of BSP excretion observed in paraplegic patients has been ascribed to alterations in hepatic blood flow.

Certain nonhepatic diseases impair liver function by producing infiltrative lesions in the liver. These include metastatic carcinoma, the lymphomas and leukemia, the systemic granulomatous diseases (disseminated tuberculosis, histoplasmosis, coccidioidomycosis, sarcoidosis), and amyloidosis. In metastatic carcinoma, with enough involvement to produce hepatomegaly, there is a 90 per cent incidence of impaired BSP excretion, ranging in degree from 5 to 50 per cent retention. In the other diseases cited, the degree of retention is less.

Other nonhepatic diseases lead to impaired BSP excretion by different mechanisms. Febrile illnesses with fever of more than 103° F. usually produce some abnormality of this function. Certain chronic and "debilitating" diseases, such as rheumatoid arthritis, also may lead to moderate impairment of this function.

It is apparent that the BSP excretion test is of greatest value in the patient with little or no jaundice. A normal result is extremely helpful in excluding hepatic parenchymal disease. Patients with gastrointestinal hemorrhage owing to a peptic ulcer usually have normal or minimally abnormal BSP excretion results (less than 15 per cent retention). Patients with esophageal varices owing to cirrhosis almost always have moderate to marked degrees of BSP retention (15 to 50 per cent) with the occasional exception in postnecrotic cirrhosis referred to previously. This test is also useful in measuring the severity of liver disease and in assessing the completeness of recovery (e.g., in hepatitis). It is of aid in detecting hepatic damage in patients who have been exposed to hepatotoxins. It is of help in the recognition of metastatic carcinoma. The extrahepatic causes of impaired BSP excretion do not pose a diagnostic problem if clinical appraisal of the patient is properly done. The dye excretion test also has been used to determine hepatic blood flow by hepatic vein catheter, measuring the extraction of BSP by the liver and applying the Fick principle.

DETOXIFICATION AND SYNTHESIS

A number of conjugating reactions occur in the liver. The conjugation of bilirubin with glucuronide to convert the "indirect" to the "direct" bilirubin has been discussed. Steroid hormones are metabolized by the liver, and metabolites are excreted as conjugates of glucuronide and other substances. Similarly certain foreign substances are conjugated in the liver and, if toxic, converted to nontoxic products.

Hippuric Acid Excretion

One conjugating mechanism that has been applied as a measure of liver function is the synthesis of hippuric acid in the liver by the conjugation of benzoic acid with glycine. The test consists of administering a standard amount of benzoic acid orally or sodium benzoate intravenously and determining the amount of hippuric acid excreted in a specific period of time. The ability to synthesize hippuric acid depends not only on the conjugating enzyme systems of the liver but also on the availability of glycine stores in the liver. Furthermore the hippuric acid formed is measured by its concentration in the urine. This depends, therefore, on renal function, which must be intact to use hippuric acid excretion as a reflection of hepatic function. The hippuric acid excretion test devised by Quick (1940), which involved an oral dose of benzoic acid, has been applied widely and in some centers has been considered a good measure of hepatic function. Excretion of hippuric acid after a standard dose of benzoic acid has been found to be decreased in patients with intrinsic hepatic disease, such as cirrhosis or severe hepatitis. It has been advocated for use in the differential diagnosis of jaundice, since in early obstructive jaundice excretion of hippuric acid is generally normal. Although popular a decade ago, this test has fallen into disuse.

Prothrombin Level and Vitamin K Response

It has been known for a long time that patients with severe hepatic disease as well as those with obstructive jaundice may have coagulation defects. It was observed in 1940 that vitamin K deficiency results in hypoprothrombinemia and that vitamin K, which is fat soluble, requires bile salts for absorption. This led to the recognition that bleeding tendencies in obstructive jaundice could be improved by the parenteral administration of vitamin K. The hypoprothrombinemia of obstructive jaundice then was considered to be due to vitamin K deficiency resulting from lack of absorption. The hypoprothrombinemia of the patient with parenchymatous hepatic disease was not restored to normal by parenteral administration of vitamin K.

On this basis a test of hepatic function was devised. Administration of a standard dose of vitamin K to a patient with obstructive jaundice usually restores prolonged prothrombin time to normal, whereas it fails to do so in patients with the hypoprothrombinemia of intrinsic hepatic diseases. This test has been considered to be of some value for the differential diagnosis of jaundice. In a patient with deep jaundice the restoration of an abnormal prothrombin time to normal by vitamin K administration may be considered good evidence that jaundice is obstructive. Lack of improvement of the marked prolongation of the prothrombin time may be considered good evidence that the jaundice is hepatocellular. There are several pitfalls to the application of this procedure. Patients with obstructive jaundice may have only a mildly prolonged prothrombin time; the difference after administration of vitamin K, therefore, may be insufficient to provide a conclusive answer. Furthermore, in intrinsic hepatic disease (even with deep jaundice), parenchymal dysfunction at times may be relatively slight, and the response of the hypoprothrombinemia may be similar to that of obstructive jaundice. This is particularly characteristic of "cholangiolitic hepatitis."

It has been recognized recently that coagulation defects in patients with hepatic

**Table 11–9.   Clotting Abnormalities in Patients
with Liver Disease***

Deficiency	PTC
	(PTA)†
	(Stuart factor)†
	Factor X
	Prothrombin
	Factor V (labile factor, AC globulin)
	Factor VII (stable factor, proconverter)
	(Fibrinogen)†
Excess	Fibrinolysin

* Thrombocytopenia, sufficiently marked to produce coagulation, also may occur.

† Factors in parentheses are rarely deficient, or the reported observations have been debated.

disease or even with obstructive jaundice may include factors other than prothrombin deficiency (Table 11–9). Thus, in intrinsic hepatic disease the blood may show not only prothrombin deficiency, but there may also be decreased levels of P.T.C., Factor V, Factor X, and even of Factor VII. Furthermore increased fibrinolysins may occur in hepatic disease. In obstructive jaundice, in addition to the prothrombin abnormality, there may also be a deficiency of proconvertin (Factor VII) (see Chapter 6).

In spite of these difficulties response of the prothrombin time to parenteral vitamin K may be a useful ancillary measure in the differential diagnosis of jaundice.

ENZYME LEVELS OF BLOOD*

More than 40 enzymes have been demonstrated in the sera of humans and animals (see Chapter 12). Alkaline phosphatase, the first of these to be studied in hepatic disease, has been extensively applied to the differential diagnosis of jaundice. Another enzyme that has been studied in the serum of patients with liver disease is cholinesterase. Since 1953, when glutamic oxaloacetic transaminase (GOT) was demonstrated in the serum of humans, this and the related enzyme, glutamic pyruvic transaminase (GPT), have been studied extensively in various disease states. In Chapter 12 the applicability of serum enzymes to the study of disease in general is considered. In the present discussion we will consider the value of serum alkaline phosphatase, cholinesterase, and transaminase determinations in the diagnosis of hepatic disease.

* References relevant to this section will be found at the end of Chapter 12.

Alkaline Phosphatase (Table 11–10)

Early interest in the serum alkaline phosphatase was related to the elevated levels seen in patients with bone disease, presumably a reflection of increased osteoblastic activity since the osteoblast is rich in this enzyme. This was soon followed, however, by the observation that values of alkaline phosphatase were also increased in patients with obstructive (posthepatic) jaundice. When the obstruction is complete and prolonged, the serum enzyme activity is almost always increased with levels often above 25 Bodansky units (normal, 1 to 4 B.U.). Levels below 25 units, however, may be observed in patients with obstructive jaundice, especially when of brief duration or when the obstruction is incomplete. Biliary obstruction resulting from carcinoma produces higher values than those observed in patients with benign lesions producing obstruction. One variety of obstructive jaundice with normal alkaline phosphatase levels in the serum is that seen in infants with congenital atresia of the extrahepatic biliary tree. In these patients the serum alkaline phosphatase level is not elevated unless bony lesions of hepatic rickets develop. In contrast, infants with intrahepatic biliary atresia show striking elevations of serum alkaline phosphatase values.

Elevated levels of serum alkaline phosphatase also occur in hepatocellular jaundice. Approximately 90 per cent of patients with viral hepatitis or with toxic hepatocellular jaundice have elevated serum alkaline phosphatase values. Almost all of these have values below 15 Bodansky units (B.U.). Approximately 5 per cent of patients with hepatocellular jaundice may have levels of 15 to 25 units. In otherwise characteristic viral hepatitis it is rare to have alkaline phosphatase levels above 25 units. In jaundiced patients with higher levels posthepatic jaundice should be considered.

Occasional patients with hepatic disease may present a laboratory and clinical picture simulating obstructive jaundice. This has been called "cholangiolitic hepatitis" or "intrahepatic cholestasis" and in some instances has been considered to be a variant of hepatitis. A similar entity has been noted to follow adverse reactions to certain agents, such as chlorpromazine, methyltestosterone, and organic arsenicals. Patients with cholangiolitic hepatitis have values of alkaline phosphatase at least as high as

Table 11–10. Alkaline Phosphatase Values in Hepatobiliary Disease

DISEASE	INCIDENCE ALK. PHOSPH. ELEVATION	USUAL RANGE OF VALUES	INCIDENCE OF VALUE > 20 B.U.
1. Jaundiced states			
Hepatic jaundice			
Hepatocellular	80–100%	5–15 B.U.	5%
Hepatocanalicular	100%	15–70 B.U.	30%
Posthepatic			
Obstruction due to neoplasm	95–100%	20–40 B.U.	80%
Obstruction due to gallstone	95–100%	10–25 B.U.	40%
Congenital atresia of bile ducts	100%		
Intrahepatic	20–30%	N–15 B.U.	0
Extrahepatic		50–70 B.U.	100%
2. Jaundice absent or present			
Infectious mononucleosis	60–70%	5–40 B.U.	20%
Cirrhosis, Laennec's	40%	5–15 B.U.	5%
Cirrhosis, postnecrotic	50%	5–35 B.U.	15%
Cirrhosis, biliary, primary	100%	15–100 B.U.	50%
3. No jaundice			
Space-occupying carcinoma			
Carcinoma	80%	5–70 B.U.	20%
Tuberculosis	50%	5–50 B.U.	10%
Sarcoidosis	40%	5–18 B.U.	15%
Amyloidosis	Frequent	5–100 B.U.	—
Stone in common duct or in one hepatic duct	Frequent	5–90 B.U.	—

those observed in patients with posthepatic jaundice.

The serum alkaline phosphatase level is of value in the differentiation of hepatocellular from obstructive jaundice with several qualifications. As stated previously, levels in the "obstructive" jaundice range may occur in intrinsic hepatic disease, and levels in the "hepatocellular" range may be seen in patients with incomplete biliary obstruction. When taken with other measures of liver disease and clinical features, it is a useful diagnostic aid.

Serum alkaline phosphatase elevation may also occur in nonjaundiced patients with hepatobiliary disease. In patients with "space-occupying" lesions of the liver, such as granulomatous disease, metastatic or primary carcinoma of the liver, liver abscess, and amyloidosis, the degree of alkaline phosphatase elevation may at times be striking (50 to 100 B.U.) with little or no rise in the serum bilirubin values. This pattern of hepatic dysfunction is useful in the recognition of these "space-occupying" lesions, particularly in the recognition of metastasis to the liver in patients with carcinomatosis.

There is another type of disease associated with normal or only slightly elevated serum bilirubin levels but with distinctly increased alkaline phosphatase levels. This is occlusion of one hepatic duct or incomplete occlusion of the common bile or hepatic duct. This condition should be kept in mind, particularly in dealing with patients with cholelithiasis who develop this "dissociated" pattern of hepatic dysfunction.

Levels of alkaline phosphatase in Laennec's cirrhosis are usually normal or only mildly elevated. In postnecrotic cirrhosis the levels are generally somewhat higher. In biliary cirrhosis elevated levels of alkaline phosphatase are regularly seen. In obstructive biliary cirrhosis the elevations are modest, usually under 15 B.U., except during bouts of ascending cholangitis. In patients with primary biliary cirrhosis, considered by many to be a sequel to cholangiolitic hepatitis, alkaline phosphatase levels in the range already described for cholangiolitic hepatitis may be seen.

The basis for elevated serum levels of alkaline phosphatase in patients with hepatobiliary disease is obscure. Impaired hepatic excretion of enzyme formed in bone or liver or both has been suggested. Increased formation of alkaline phosphatase by, or release from, hepatic cells also has been suggested as a possible mechanism.

Transaminase

Enzymes that catalyze the reversible transfer of an alpha amino group from an amino acid to an alpha keto acid (Fig. 11–8)

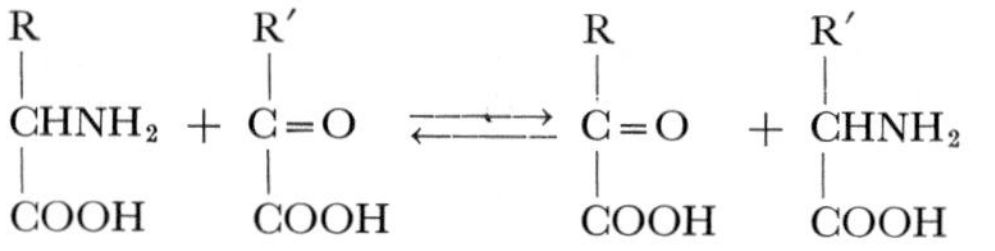

$$\underset{\substack{|\\ \text{COOH}}}{\overset{\substack{R\\|}}{\text{CHNH}_2}} + \underset{\substack{|\\ \text{COOH}}}{\overset{\substack{R'\\|}}{\text{C}=\text{O}}} \rightleftarrows \underset{\substack{|\\ \text{COOH}}}{\overset{\substack{R\\|}}{\text{C}=\text{O}}} + \underset{\substack{|\\ \text{COOH}}}{\overset{\substack{R'\\|}}{\text{CHNH}_2}}$$

Figure 11–8. Prototype of transamination reactions.

were first demonstrated in animal tissue by Braunshtein and Kritzmann in 1937. These authors called the enzymes *aminopherases*. Although a large number of substrate-specific transaminases have been demonstrated in various animal tissues, only two have been described in the serum, *glutamic oxaloacetic transaminase* (GOT) and *glutamic pyruvic transaminase* (GPT). Abnormal levels of GOT are seen in patients with hepatic disease, myocardial and skeletal muscle necrosis, and other diseases to be described. Glutamic pyruvic transaminase (GPT) elevations are absent or slight in disease that does not involve the liver primarily or secondarily.

Glutamic Oxaloacetic Transaminase. Glutamic oxaloacetic transaminase (GOT) is an enzyme that catalyzes the reversible transfer of the amino group from glutamic to oxaloacetic acid (Fig. 11–9). It has been demonstrated in the serum and tissues of all animals studied. In man it is found in cardiac, hepatic, skeletal muscle, renal, and cerebral tissue in decreasing concentrations. The recognition of the high myocardial content of this enzyme led to the observation, in 1953, that patients with acute myocardial infarction had elevated levels in the serum for a few days after the infarction. Shortly thereafter studies in several laboratories showed high serum levels of this enzyme in patients and animals with acute hepatic necrosis.

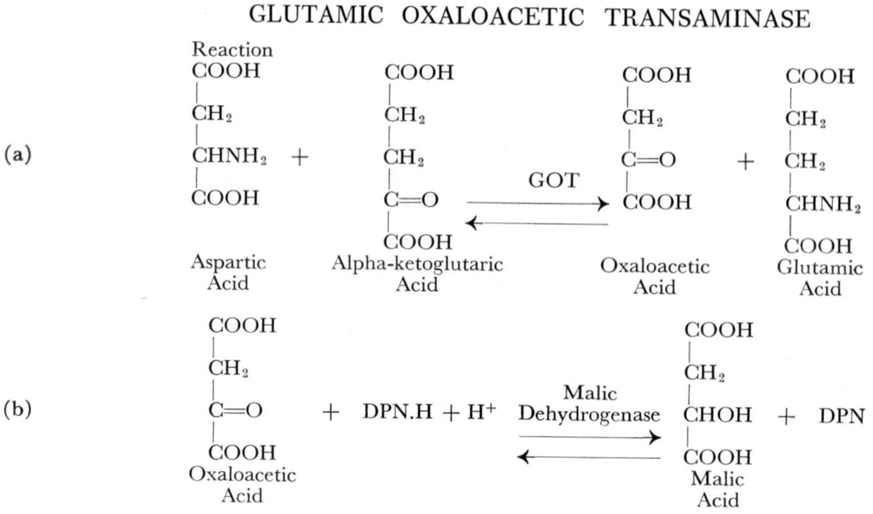

GLUTAMIC OXALOACETIC TRANSAMINASE

Figure 11–9. Reaction catalyzed by GOT, principles of assay methods, and conditions in which increased serum levels are observed.

Method of assay is based on measurement of rate of formation of product (oxaloacetic acid) of the reaction. This may be done (1) indirectly, by the coupled reaction (b), in which the rate of DPNH oxidation, in the presence of added malic dehydrogenase is a measure of oxaloacetic acid formed (method of Karmen), or (2) directly, by one of several colorimetric methods that depend on the formation of the dinitrophenylhydrazone of oxaloacetate or its decarboxylation product (pyruvate).

Conditions in which abnormal serum levels of enzymes are observed are rated (in each major category) in the order of decreasing levels.

A. Hepatic Disease
    Hepatic necrosis
        Hepatitis (infectious, toxic), infectious mononucleosis
        Cirrhosis
        Hematogenous tuberculosis
        Hepatic congestion
    Metastatic carcinoma
    Obstructive jaundice
B. Other Disease
    Myocardial infarction
    Skeletal muscle necrosis
    Hemolysis (slight)
    Pancreatitis (acute)
    Renal necrosis
    Cerebral necrosis

The activity of this serum enzyme was first demonstrated by a chromatographic technique, which was too laborious for routine use. The methods that have been used for routine determination have included the spectrophotometric procedure of Karmen (1955) and several simplified color-imetric procedures (Fig. 11–9 and Chapter 12). Most laboratories express the value in "Karmen units." The normal range is 6 to 40 units per ml. of serum.

The range of values of GOT in patients with various types of hepatic disease and in myocardial infarction is shown in Fig. 11–10. Striking elevations (400 to 4000 units/ml.) are observed in the serum of almost all patients with acute hepatic necrosis (viral hepatitis, carbon tetrachloride poisoning). Patients with posthepatic jaundice and cholangiolitic hepatitis have more modest elevations (usually less than 300 units/ml.). In patients with cirrhosis of the liver there is a 60 to 70 per cent incidence of elevated GOT levels (also below 300 units/ml.).

Approximately half the patients with metastatic carcinoma have elevated serum GOT levels in the same range as patients with cirrhosis and posthepatic jaundice. Less frequently such moderately elevated GOT levels are observed in patients with lymphoma and leukemia. In 80 per cent of patients with infectious mononucleosis moderate (100 to 600 units) GOT elevations are observed. Patients with myocardial infarction usually show GOT levels of less than 400 units. The incidence and significance of GOT elevations in patients with this and other nonhepatic conditions are discussed in Chapter 12.

Glutamic Pyruvic Transaminase. This enzyme catalyzes the reversible transfer of an amino group from glutamic to pyruvic acid (Fig. 11–11). It also has been found to be widely distributed in humans. The high hepatic content compared to the relatively low concentration in myocardial and other tissues has led to the application of GPT determination to the study of hepatic disease.

The methods used for determination of this enzyme in the serum are similar to those used for GOT assay. Both spectrophotometric and colorimetric methods have been employed. The normal range for this enzyme in Karmen units is almost the same as that for the GOT (6 to 36 units/ml.).

Patients with viral hepatitis and other forms of hepatic necrosis show striking elevations of the serum GPT level (1000 to 4000 units). The incidence of GPT abnormality in patients with posthepatic jaundice, cholangiolitic hepatitis, and metastatic carcinoma is approximately the same as that of the GOT in these conditions. In patients with Laennec's cirrhosis of the liver the incidence and degree of GPT elevation is less than that of GOT increase. It has been our experience that GPT elevation is greater than GOT increase in 75 per cent of patients with viral hepatitis, a lower figure than that reported by De Ritis and his associates (1956). The relative elevations of GOT and GPT in other diseases are shown in Table 11–11. Levels of GPT are normal or only minimally elevated in patients with myocardial infarction.

Clinical Value of Transaminase Determination. The determination of the serum transaminase is of distinct clinical aid. Dif-

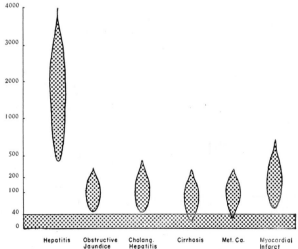

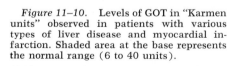

Figure 11–10. Levels of GOT in "Karmen units" observed in patients with various types of liver disease and myocardial infarction. Shaded area at the base represents the normal range (6 to 40 units).

GLUTAMIC PYRUVIC TRANSAMINASE

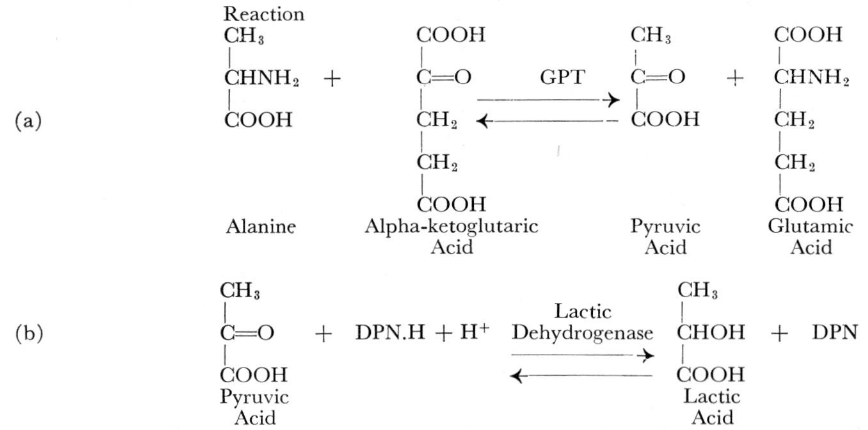

Reaction

(a)

$$\underset{\text{Alanine}}{\overset{\text{CH}_3}{\underset{\text{COOH}}{|}}\text{CHNH}_2} + \underset{\substack{\text{Alpha-ketoglutaric}\\\text{Acid}}}{\overset{\text{COOH}}{\underset{\text{COOH}}{|}}\overset{|}{\underset{|}{\overset{|}{\text{C}=\text{O}}}\overset{|}{\text{CH}_2}\overset{|}{\text{CH}_2}}} \quad\underset{\text{GPT}}{\overset{\longrightarrow}{\longleftarrow}}\quad \underset{\substack{\text{Pyruvic}\\\text{Acid}}}{\overset{\text{CH}_3}{\underset{\text{COOH}}{|}}\overset{|}{\text{C}=\text{O}}} + \underset{\substack{\text{Glutamic}\\\text{Acid}}}{\overset{\text{COOH}}{\underset{\text{COOH}}{|}}\overset{|}{\text{CHNH}_2}\overset{|}{\text{CH}_2}\overset{|}{\text{CH}_2}}$$

(b)

$$\underset{\substack{\text{Pyruvic}\\\text{Acid}}}{\overset{\text{CH}_3}{\underset{\text{COOH}}{|}}\overset{|}{\text{C}=\text{O}}} + \text{DPN.H} + \text{H}^+ \quad\underset{\text{Dehydrogenase}}{\overset{\text{Lactic}}{\underset{\longleftarrow}{\longrightarrow}}}\quad \underset{\substack{\text{Lactic}\\\text{Acid}}}{\overset{\text{CH}_3}{\underset{\text{COOH}}{|}}\overset{|}{\text{CHOH}}} + \text{DPN}$$

Figure 11–11. Reaction catalyzed by GPT, principles of assay methods, and conditions in which increased serum levels are observed.

Method of assay is based on measurement of rate of formation of product (pyruvic acid) of the reaction. This may be done (1) indirectly by the coupled reaction (b) in which the rate of DPNH oxidation, in the presence of added lactic dehydrogenase is a measure of pyruvic acid formed (method of Karmen), or (2) directly, by one of several colorimetric methods, which depend on the formation of the dinitrophenylhydrazone of pyruvate.

Conditions in which abnormal serum levels of enzyme are observed, arranged in the order of decreasing levels:

A. Hepatic Disease Abnormalities
   Hepatic necrosis; e.g., hepatitis (infectious, toxic), infectious mononucleosis, cirrhosis
   Obstructive jaundice
   Metastatic carcinoma
   Hepatic congestion (centrilobular liver cell necrosis) secondary to heart failure or hepatic vein thrombosis
B. Other Abnormalities (Slight)
   Myocardial infarction
   Acute pancreatitis

ferentiation of hepatic (hepatocellular) from posthepatic jaundice is facilitated by determining the GOT or GPT values, since levels above 300 units/ml. are rare in patients with posthepatic jaundice. In the hepatocanalicular (cholangiolitic) type of hepatic jaundice the GOT (or GPT) levels are like those of posthepatic jaundice. Likewise in cirrhosis of the liver, even with deep jaundice, the moderate GOT level and the lower GPT level are in contrast with the high levels of both transaminases observed in acute viral hepatitis. Determina-

tion of GOT, GPT, or both is useful in the early recognition of viral or toxic hepatitis and is, therefore, helpful in studying patients exposed to hepatotoxic drugs. Elevations of the GPT level appear to reflect acute hepatic disease somewhat more specifically than is true of the GOT values. The level of either enzyme, particularly the GOT, may be elevated in patients with extrahepatic disease (see Chapter 12).

Cholinesterase

The cholinesterase of the serum has been referred to as pseudocholinesterase to distinguish it from the true cholinesterase of certain tissues (Fig. 11–12). The tissue enzyme acts only on acetylcholine, while the serum enzyme hydrolyzes both acetylcholine and other choline esters. Serum cholinesterase has been applied to the study of patients with hepatic disease for more than 20 years. Methods used for its determination include electrometric, manometric, and colorimetric procedures.

In patients with hepatic disease low levels of serum cholinesterase are characteristic. Depressed serum cholinesterase values are observed in patients with viral hepatitis,

Table 11–11. Comparison of Serum GOT and GPT in Various Conditions

Acute hepatic necrosis	GOT < GPT
Obstructive jaundice	GOT ≦ GPT (human)
Obstructive jaundice	GOT > GPT (experimental)
Cirrhosis	GOT > GPT
Congestive hepatomegaly	GOT ≦ GPT
Metastatic carcinoma	GOT ≧ GPT
Chlorpromazine jaundice	GOT < GPT
Infectious mononucleosis	GOT < GPT
Myocardial infarction	GOT > GPT
Skeletal muscle necrosis	GOT > GPT

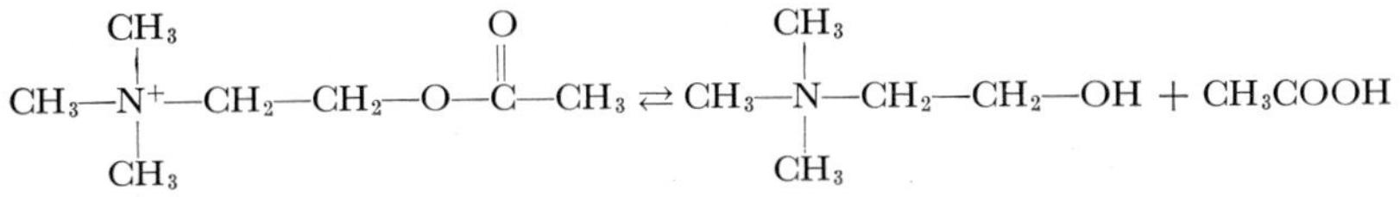

$$CH_3—\overset{\underset{|}{CH_3}}{\overset{|}{N^+}}—CH_2—CH_2—O—\overset{\overset{O}{\|}}{C}—CH_3 \rightleftarrows CH_3—\overset{\underset{|}{CH_3}}{\overset{|}{N}}—CH_2—CH_2—OH + CH_3COOH$$
$$\underset{CH_3}{|} \qquad\qquad\qquad\qquad\qquad\qquad \underset{CH_3}{|}$$

Figure 11–12. Reaction catalyzed by cholinesterase, principles of one assay method, and conditions in which increased serum levels are observed.

Method of assay is based on measurement of pH change resulting from acetic acid liberated.

Conditions in Which Serum Cholinesterase Level is Abnormal
A. Hepatic Disease Abnormalities
   1. Hepatitis
   2. Cirrhosis
   3. Metastatic carcinoma (may be depressed or normal)

   4. Obstructive jaundice (may be depressed or normal)

B. Other Abnormalities
   1. Malnutrition (hypoalbuminemia)
   2. Anemias
   3. Acute infections
   4. Myocardial infarction
   5. Dermatomyositis
   6. Nephrotic syndrome

cirrhosis, metastatic carcinoma, and the hepatic congestion of heart failure and in those with amebic hepatitis or abscess. In patients with acute hepatitis levels of the enzyme are lowest at the peak of the disease and return to normal with recovery. Accordingly the level of this serum enzyme has been considered to be of some value as an index of recovery and prognosis. In cirrhosis with jaundice or ascites cholinesterase values are usually depressed, while an uncomplicated cirrhosis the levels are often normal. It has been reported that persistent depression of the cholinesterase level in cirrhotic patients is a poor prognostic sign.

In patients with obstructive jaundice serum cholinesterase levels are often normal, but when the obstruction is prolonged and complete and when complicated by ascending cholangitis, the serum cholinesterase level may be low.

The level of this enzyme also may be depressed in patients with malnutrition, acute infections, anemias, myocardial infarction, and dermatomyositis. Since in these patients with nonhepatic and with hepatic disease depressed serum cholinesterase levels are observed when the serum albumin level is below normal, it has been suggested that the cholinesterase depression reflects impaired hepatic protein synthesis. This is consistent with the observation that patients with the nephrotic syndrome (characterized by an increased rate of albumin synthesis but low serum albumin levels) may have increased serum cholinesterase levels.

SERUM "METALS"

Abnormal levels of certain metallic substances are found in patients with some hepatic diseases. Elevated serum *iron* levels and reduced iron-binding capacity are observed in patients with hemochromatosis and transfusion hemosiderosis and may be of aid in diagnosis. Acute elevations of serum iron levels are observed in viral hepatitis and in other patients with acute hepatic necrosis. It has been observed that patients with obstructive jaundice usually have normal serum iron levels. This has led to the application by European and South American workers of the serum iron level determination to the differential diagnosis of jaundice. This application, however, has not been adopted widely in this country.

Elevated blood levels of "free" *copper* and abnormal amounts of tissue copper have been observed in patients with Wilson's disease (hepatolenticular degeneration). This elevation of "free" copper is associated, in most patients with this disease, with decreased levels of ceruloplasmin, a copper-carrying protein that is also an enzyme (copper oxidase). Diagnosis of Wilson's disease is aided by the demonstration of increased levels of free copper in the plasma and urine and of depressed levels of ceruloplasmin in the plasma.

Abnormal levels of other metallic ions of the blood have been described in patients with chronic hepatic disease. Depressed serum levels of *zinc* have been reported in patients with "alcoholic cirrhosis." The significance of this observation remains to be determined. Lower than normal serum *magnesium* levels have been reported in alcoholic patients with delirium tremens and with cirrhosis. Among the factors considered responsible is malnutrition. In cirrhotics with ascites the *hyponatremia* commonly observed is considered to be a "redistribution" phenomenon. *Hypokalemia* is frequent in patients with hepatic coma, perhaps resulting in part from the alkalosis secondary to hyperventilation.

LIVER FUNCTION TESTS BASED ON ROLE OF LIVER IN VITAMIN ECONOMY

Deficiency in a number of vitamins is prone to occur in the malnourished alcoholic patient. Accordingly in alcoholic cirrhosis evidence of beriberi, pellagra, and scurvy may be observed. In addition abnormal levels of vitamins A and B_{12} have been described in patients with hepatic disease.

Depressed plasma levels of vitamin A are characteristic of patients with parenchymal hepatic disease. The observation that patients with early obstructive jaundice usually have normal levels has led to the application of vitamin A level determination to the differential diagnosis of jaundice. The dependence of the absorption of this fat-soluble vitamin on an adequate concentration of bile salts in the duodenum, however, also leads to depressed levels in obstructive jaundice. Accordingly this determination is of little value in the differential diagnosis of jaundice.

Vitamin B_{12} is stored in the liver. In patients with acute viral hepatitis very high plasma levels of this vitamin are observed, presumably resulting from release by necrotic hepatic cells. Somewhat elevated levels are observed in cirrhosis also. A test of hepatic function based on the estimation of the hepatic "uptake" of an oral dose of vitamin B_{12} labeled with radioactive cobalt has been described. The clinical value of these determinations remains to be confirmed by adequate trial.

LIVER BIOPSY

In considering the laboratory approach to the diagnosis of hepatic disease, reference should be made to needle biopsy of the liver. This procedure, which has been widely used during the last decade, is of assistance in the diagnosis of hepatic and nonhepatic disease.

It is particularly useful in the differential diagnosis of hepatomegaly. It may be helpful in defining the specific cause of hepatocellular jaundice (e.g., hepatitis or cirrhosis). The application of needle biopsy to the differentiation of hepatic from posthepatic jaundice, however, is limited. The procedure is hazardous in patients with complete obstruction of the common bile duct. Furthermore, in those instances in which the differential diagnosis is difficult on clinical and biochemical grounds, the

Table 11–12. Indications and Contraindications for Liver Biopsy

INDICATIONS [*]	CONTRAINDICATIONS [†]
Hepatomegaly	Clotting defects
Jaundice	(abnormal bleeding time, co-
Ascites	agulation time, or capillary
Gastrointestinal	fragility or history of recent
bleeding	hemorrhagic tendency)
Systemic disease	Presumptive diagnosis of post-
e.g.,	hepatic jaundice
Hematogenous	Severe anemia
tuberculosis	Uncooperative or unduly appre-
Sarcoidosis	hensive patient
Amyloidosis	Infection in area to be traversed
	by biopsy needle, e.g., right
	lower lobe pneumonia or infec-
	tion of right pleural space
	(empyema)

[*] The need to perform biopsy for these indications depends on the ability to establish the diagnosis by other criteria.

[†] The contraindications are relative and each must be individually weighed to assess its significance.

histologic distinction is also difficult. Liver biopsy may be of assistance in the diagnosis of the cause of ascites and in the differential diagnosis of gastrointestinal hemorrhage. Of interest has been the usefulness of this procedure in the diagnosis of systemic diseases that produce recognizable lesions in the liver (Table 11–12). The indications and contraindications also are shown in Table 11–12.

LABORATORY APPROACH TO THE DIFFERENTIAL DIAGNOSIS OF HEPATIC DISEASE

A large number of tests of hepatic func-

Table 11–13. Procedures Useful in the Diagnosis of Hepatic Disease

Serum bilirubin (total, direct and indirect)
Urine bilirubin (qualitative)
Urine urobilinogen (2-hour or 24-hour urine)
Stool urobilinogen (24- or 72-hour specimen)
BSP excretion (in the nonjaundiced patient)
Serum protein determination (albumin, globulin)
  Electrophoresis and gamma globulin estimation elective
Flocculation tests
  Cephalin cholesterol
  Thymol turbidity
Serum cholesterol (Total)
  Ester fraction elective
Serum alkaline phosphatase
GOT, GPT
Liver biopsy

Table 11–14. Laboratory Aids to the Differential Diagnosis of Jaundice

	DIRECT	INDIRECT	URINE UROBIL.	URINE BIL.	STOOL UROBIL.	T.T.	C.F.	CHOL.	ALK. PHOS.	GOT
Prehepatic										
Consitutional hepatic dys-function	N	↑	N	0	N or ↓	N	N	N	N	N
Hemolytic	N or (↑)*	↑	↑	0	↑	N	N	N	N	N
Hepatic										
Hepatocellular	↑	↑	↑	+	N or ↓	↑	+	N or ↓	<15 B.U.	500–4000
Hepatocanalicular (cholangiolitic)	↑	↑	N or ↑	+	↓	N or ↑	N or +	↑↑	>15 B.U.	<400
Posthepatic	↑	↑	N	+	↓↓	N	N	↑	>15 B.U.	<400

* Increases are slight; see Table 11–4.

Table 11–15. Laboratory Aids to the Differential Diagnosis of Hepatomegaly*

	BSP	T.T.	C.F.	BIL.	ALB.	GLOB.	ALK. PHOSPH.	GOT	GPT
Hepatitis	↑	↑	↑	↑	N, ↓	↑, N	↑	↑	↑
Cirrhosis	↑	↑	↑	↑	↓	↑	↑	↑	↑
Metastatic carcinoma	↑	N	N	N	N, ↓	N	↑	↑	↑
Infectious mononucleosis	↑	↑	↑	↑	N	P, ↑	↑	↑	↑
Extrahepatic disease				See Table 11–18.					

* No grading of the degree or incidence of abnormality has been included.

Table 11–16. Laboratory Aids in the Differential Diagnosis of Ascites*

	BSP	T.T.	C.F.	BIL.	ALB.	GLOB.	ALK. PHOSPH.
Cirrhosis	↑↑↑	↑	+	↑	↓	↑	↑
Carcinomatosis	↑, N†	N	0	N	N, ↓	N	↑↑↑
Tuberculosis	↑, N†	↑	+	N	N, ↓	↑	↑↑
Heart failure	↑↑	N	0	↑	N, ↓	N	↑

* Transaminases (GOT, GPT) add little to this differential diagnosis.
† Degree of abnormality depends on presence of lesions in liver; results will be normal if only peritoneum is involved.

Table 11–17. Laboratory Aids to the Differential Diagnosis of Gastrointestinal Hemorrhage

	BSP	T.T.	C.F.	BIL.	ALB.	GLOB.	NH₃
Peptic ulcer	N	N	N	N	N	N	N
Alcoholic gastritis*	N, ↑	N, ↑	N, +	N, ↑	N, ↓	N, ↑	N, ↑
Esophageal varices							
Intrahepatic portal block (cirrhosis)	↑	↑, N	+	↑	↓	↑	↑
Extrahepatic portal block	N	N	N	N	N	N	↑

* Results of liver functions depend on degree of liver disease present.

tion have been described or mentioned in the preceding material. Only some of these are readily applicable to clinical problems. A "battery" of tests, which we use regularly in the diagnosis of hepatic disease, is shown in Table 11–13. In patients with jaundice whose serum bilirubin level is greater than 4 mg. per 100 ml., the BSP excretion test is not performed. In Tables 11–14, 11–15, 11–16, and 11–17 are shown patterns of hepatic dysfunction characteristic of the causes of jaundice, hepatomegaly, ascites, and portal hypertension, respectively. The patterns shown represent those most frequently observed in each instance. Exceptions occur and the patterns should be regarded only as guides.

HEPATIC FUNCTION IN NONHEPATIC DISEASE

Abnormal results with one or more tests of hepatic function may be obtained in patients with a variety of extrahepatic diseases. These have been considered at times to reflect on the value and specificity of liver function testing. Even in nonhepatic disease, however, fairly consistent patterns of hepatic function may be observed. In Table 11–18 is shown a classification of nonhepatic diseases in terms of the type of hepatic dysfunction observed and the presumed basis for it. Understanding of these patterns should make it possible to avoid confusing hepatic with nonhepatic disease and to assist in the diagnosis of disease in each category.

CONCLUSIONS

A selected group of laboratory procedures, based on a few of the many reactions known to occur in the liver, has been applied to the study of patients with hepatic disease. The ways in which these tests may be applied are summarized in

Table 11–19. Application of Liver Function Tests (and Biopsy)

I. Diagnostic aids to:
  A. Recognition of presence or absence of hepatic disease
  B. Differential diagnosis
    1. Hepatomegaly
    2. Jaundice
    3. Ascites
    4. Gastrointestinal hemorrhage
  C. Recognition of nonhepatic disease
    (hematogenous tuberculosis, sarcoidosis, amyloidosis, and infectious mononucleosis, for example)
II. Estimating severity in known hepatic disease
  A. Monitoring convalescence (hepatitis, cirrhosis)
  B. Preoperative evaluation
    1. In patient with recent hepatic disease
    2. In patient with extrahepatic disease that may affect liver status and function, e.g., hyperthyroidism and cholelithiasis.
III. Teaching and research

Table 11–18. Liver Function in Nonhepatic Disease

I. Abnormality of a number of different types of function similar to intrinsic hepatic disease (BSP, T.T., C.F., bilirubin, proteins), e.g., pneumococcal pneumonia and infectious mononucleosis.
II. Dissociated patterns
  A. BSP only or predominantly,
    e.g., heart failure, shock, spinal cord injury
  B. BSP and alkaline phosphatase
    Observed in patients with "space-occupying lesions" of liver, e.g., metastatic carcinoma, granulomata of liver (tuberculosis, sarcoidosis), amyloidosis, abscess
  C. Flocculation test abnormality and globulin level increase
    Diseases with hyperglobulinemia, e.g., rheumatoid arthritis, systemic lupus erythematosus, subacute bacterial endocarditis, tuberculosis, sarcoidosis, lymphogranuloma venereum
III. Combinations of dissociated patterns (II B + II C)
  A. Hyperglobulinemic diseases with space-occupying lesions, e.g., tuberculosis or sarcoidosis with granulomas in the liver
  B. Subacute bacterial endocarditis + heart failure
IV. Diseases with normal hepatic function,
    e.g., peptic ulcer, chronic nephritis

Table 11–20. Pitfalls in Application of Liver Function Test

I. Owing to atypical patterns of hepatic dysfunction
  A. Jaundice present
    1. Hepatic disease with normal parenchymal function or high alkaline phosphatase
    2. Obstructive jaundice with secondary hepatocellular damage or low alkaline phosphatase levels.
    3. Combination of two types of jaundice, e.g., hemolytic with obstructive jaundice ("pigment" stones) or hemolytic with hepatocellular damage (sickle cell anemia).
  B. Jaundice absent
    1. Space occupying lesions (metastatic carcinoma, granuloma, abscess) producing elevated alkaline phosphatase levels and BSP retention but no jaundice.
    2. Hyperglobulinemic disease with abnormal flocculation test results.
    (e.g., rheumatoid arthritis, disseminated lupus erythematosus)
II. Owing to dependence on only one or two tests of liver function

Table 11–19. It should be recalled that there are a number of pitfalls in the application of the tests to the diagnosis and management of hepatic disease (Table 11–20). Correlation of laboratory results with clinical features should obviate most of these potential difficulties.

METHODS

1. The following methods, performed regularly in our laboratory, are described in detail: serum bilirubin, urine bilirubin and urobilinogen, fecal urobilinogen, BSP excretion, cephalin-cholesterol flocculation, thymol turbidity, and zinc sulfate turbidity.

2. The following methods are described in general terms: epinephrine tolerance test, blood ammonia level, galactose tolerance test, hippuric acid excretion test, and "prothrombin time" response to vitamin K administration.

3. Serum alkaline phosphatase and the transaminase determinations are described in Chapter 12.

Bilirubin in Serum

Method. Malloy and Evelyn (1937), modified by Annino (1958) and by Ducci and Watson (1945).

Principle. Total bilirubin is measured by adding methanol, which permits reaction of indirect (and direct) bilirubin with Ehrlich's diazo reagent. Direct bilirubin is measured separately by adding Ehrlich's diazo reagent and water. Indirect bilirubin is estimated by subtracting the direct bilirubin value from the total level.

Material. Serum.

Reagents
1. Methyl alcohol, absolute, reagent grade.
2. Diazo blank solution (dilute hydrochloric acid). Dilute 15 ml. concentrated hydrochloric acid to 1 liter with water.
3. Diazo reagent:
   a. Solution A. To 985 ml. of distilled water 15 ml. of hydrochloric acid are added; then 1 gm. of sulfanilic acid is added, stirring until dissolved.
   b. Solution B. Sodium nitrate, 0.5 gm. in 100 ml. solution (distilled water). (Should be refrigerated.)
   c. To prepare the diazo reagent, 0.3 ml. of solution B is added to 10 ml. of solution A. This should be prepared daily.

Procedure
1. Dilute 1.0 ml. of serum to 10 ml. with distilled water.
2. Four tubes are prepared as follows:
   a. 3.0 ml. of water and 0.5 ml. of diazo blank.
   b. 3.0 ml. of water and 0.5 ml. of diazo reagent.
   c. 3.0 ml. of methyl alcohol and 0.5 ml. of diazo blank.
   d. 3.0 ml. of methyl alcohol and 0.5 ml. of diazo reagent.
3. Determination of the "total" bilirubin level. Add 2.0 ml. of serum (diluted 1 to 10) to tubes c and d. Mix and read after 30 minutes.
4. Determination of the direct (conjugated) bilirubin level. Add 2.0 ml. of serum (diluted 1 to 10) to tubes a and b. Mix and read in exactly one minute.
5. Optical density is determined at 540 mμ in any standard spectrophotometer.
6. Calculations:
   a. Bilirubin concentration may be calculated by use of the following formula:

$$D_u - D_B \times \frac{Cstd}{Dstd} = \text{Mg. per cent bilirubin}$$

   D_u = density of unknown
   D_B = density blank
   Cstd = concentration of standard solution
   Dstd = density of standard solution

   b. A standard "curve" may be prepared and the results read directly from the curve. The optical density used for this reading is that of the unknown minus the blank (see standardization).
7. High values. Sera with bilirubin levels higher than 50 mg. per 100 ml. must be diluted for accurate results to be obtained.

Standardization
1. Bilirubin stock solution (10 mg. per 100 ml.). Dissolve 10 mg. pure bilirubin in approximately 50 ml. of chloroform with slow heating on a hot plate. After cooling to room temperature, the solution is diluted with chloroform to exactly 100 ml. and stored in a brown bottle in a refrigerator.
2. Standards:
   a. To give a standard equivalent to a serum with a concentration of 2

mg. per 100 ml. (diluted 1 to 10), stock solution is diluted 1 to 50 with chloroform. To make one equivalent to 4 mg. per 100 ml. the stock solution is diluted 1 to 25, and to give one equivalent to 10 mg. per 100 ml. the stock solution is diluted 1 to 10, and so forth.

b. An artificial standard, dilute potassium permanganate solution, has been described but is less satisfactory than a true bilirubin standard.

3. Preparation of curve. The standards are measured by the "total bilirubin" method (see Procedure) with determination of optical density at 540 mμ and construction of the curve.

4. Results are expressed in mg. of total bilirubin (Procedure 3) and of direct bilirubin (Procedure 4). Indirect bilirubin may be calculated as the "total" minus the "direct."

Precautions and Comments. Reagents should be added exactly in the proportions and order listed. Deviations from the procedure may result in protein precipitation, which may invalidate the results. The upper limit of normal is 1.0 mg. for the total bilirubin value and 0.2 mg. for the direct fraction.

Icterus Index

This test, devised by Meulengracht (1932), consists of measuring the intensity of the golden yellow color imparted to the serum by bilirubin. This is done by comparing the serum color with the color of standard solutions of dichromate. One unit of icterus index has been defined as the color of a 1 to 10,000 solution of potassium dichromate. This test has been supplanted by the serum bilirubin determination in many laboratories. For the details of the procedure the texts by Ham (1950) or by Hawk, Oser, and Summerson (1954) may be consulted.

Urine Bilirubin Tests

General Comments. A number of methods have been devised for the demonstration of bilirubin in the urine. The "foam" test is of little value and should not be used. The methylene blue test is only useful as a rapid screening procedure for a large number of urines. The most sensitive tests depend on concentration of bilirubin by absorption on precipitated calcium or barium chloride or on talc, followed by its oxidation

or diazotization to produce a characteristic color reaction. Controlled oxidation of bilirubin to the green biliverdin has been accomplished by ferric chloride in trichloracetic acid (Fouchet's reagent) or ferric chloride in a hydrochloric acid (Obermeyer's reagent). These are superior to the methods involving progressive oxidation by nitric acid or iodine. Several sensitive tests involving the diazotization of bilirubin with several modifications of Ehrlich's diazo reagent have been devised but have been too laborious for practical application. Related to these is a procedure introduced by Free and Free (1953) and widely adopted. This simple method involves the concentration of bilirubin on a special cellulose-asbestos mat with an unusual affinity for the pigment and the development of a color reaction with a diazonium salt (p-nitrobenzene, diazonium p-toluene sulfonate). This procedure may be performed with a commercially available "kit." Several of the other methods also are the basis of commercially produced "kits" for urine bilirubin determination.

Only one method will be described in detail (Harrison spot test).

Method. Harrison (1937).

Principle. Precipitation of bilirubin with barium chloride. The bilirubin is oxidized to biliverdin by ferric chloride.

Reagents

1. 10 per cent barium chloride solution. Dissolve 10 gm. of barium chloride in distilled water and dilute to 100 ml.

2. Fouchet's reagent. Dissolve 25 gm. of trichloracetic acid in 100 ml. of water. Dissolve 1 gm. of ferric chloride in 10 ml. of water and add to the trichloracetic acid solution. Mix and store in a brown bottle.

Procedure. To 5 ml. of urine add 5 ml. of barium chloride solution. Mix and filter. Spread the filter paper bearing the precipitate on a piece of dry filter paper. Add 3 drops of Fouchet's reagent to the precipitate. The appearance of a green color indicates the presence of bilirubin.

Comments. This test is known as the "Harrison spot test." Modifications of this procedure have been devised by Watson and Hawkinson (1946) and by Franklin (1949). When the procedure is performed as just described, the filtrate may be used for the urine urobilinogen determination to be outlined.

Urine Urobilinogen Determination

Method. Watson and associates (1944).

General Comments. The several urine

and fecal pigments, which are collectively referred to as urobilinogen, give the same quantitative reaction with Ehrlich's aldehyde reagent (p-dimethylaminobenzaldehyde). This reaction, which results in a characteristic cherry-red color, serves as the basis for the quantitative determination of "urobilinogen" in the stool and urine to be described. In the stool or urine (after being passed) the colorless urobilinogen may be oxidized to orange-yellow pigments known as urobilin.

In performing quantitative tests for 24-hour urine urobilinogen excretion or for fecal urobilinogen content, the urobilin formed must first be reduced to urobilinogen with the ferrous sulfate and then the colorimetric reaction with Ehrlich's aldehyde reagent produced. This method is laborious. Many laboratories perform the semiquantitative tests for urine urobilinogen devised by Watson and his associates and which are to be presented. A two-hour urine is collected and the reaction with Ehrlich's aldehyde reagent performed directly. Since substances other than urobilinogen account for some of the final color development with the Ehrlich's aldehyde reagent, the results are reported in "Ehrlich units" rather than in milligrams of urobilinogen. The intensity of the color reaction may be measured by use of a comparator block with permanent standards prepared from pontocyl dyes (see following section). The same dyes may be used to prepare a standard curve for a photoelectric colorimeter or spectrophotometer. The Wallace and Diamond (1925) method for urobilinogen (not to be described) also depends on the reaction between urobilinogen and the Ehrlich reagent. In this procedure Ehrlich's aldehyde reagent is added to various dilutions of urine. The highest dilution of urine showing the characteristic cherry-red color is the endpoint. Normals have a value of 1 to 20 or less.

The Watson method is preferred to the Wallace and Diamond method for several reasons. The Watson method is more quantitative, expressing the urobilinogen excretion per unit of time, namely, a two-hour period. The use of saturated sodium acetate stops the reaction in 15 seconds. This minimizes the reaction of other chromogens with the Ehrlich reagent. It may be necessary to remove the bilirubin when it is present in the urine in large enough amounts to interfere with the urobilinogen reaction. This may be done by precipitating the bilirubin with barium chloride and filtering.

Reagents

1. Ehrlich's aldehyde reagent (Watson modification). Dissolve p-dimethylaminobenzaldehyde in a mixture of 150 ml. of concentrated hydrochloric acid and 100 ml. of distilled water. This solution should be stored in a dark bottle.

2. Saturated solution sodium acetate. Dissolve approximately 1000 gm. of sodium acetate ($NaC_2H_3O_2 \cdot 3H_2O$) in enough distilled water to give 1 liter of solution. This mixture should be heated to approximately 60° C. On cooling, there should be a large excess of crystals.

3. Color standard. Stock solution of pontocyl dyes for standardization includes 95 mg. pontocyl violet (6R, 150 per cent) and 5 mg. pontocyl carmine 2B. (Both dyes can be obtained under these designations from E. I. duPont de Nemours and Company, Incorporated, Wilmington, Delaware.) These two dyes are dissolved in 1000 ml. of 0.5 per cent glacial acetic acid.

Procedure

1. The patient empties the bladder at 1 or 2 p.m. and discards the urine. He then drinks a glass of water. Exactly two hours later the patient voids again. The entire specimen is collected, the volume is measured, and an aliquot of the fresh urine is promptly tested. If there is a high concentration of bilirubin, it should be removed by precipitation with an equal volume of a 10 per cent solution of barium chloride.

2. Performance of reaction

   a. Unknown tube

   In this tube 2.5 ml. of fresh urine and 2.5 ml. of Ehrlich's aldehyde reagent are mixed. Then, without delay, 5 ml. of saturated sodium acetate are added with thorough mixing.

   b. Blank tube

   This tube is prepared as is the unknown, except that the saturated solution of sodium acetate is added before the Ehrlich's aldehyde reagent.

   c. Colorimetric measurement

   1. This may be performed in a block colorimeter using permanent standards. The latter may be obtained commercially or prepared. We prefer to perform the determination in a photoelectric

colorimeter or spectrophotometer, using the dilutions of the stock color standard shown in the next paragraph to prepare a standard curve.

2. Preparation of standard curve. The following concentrations of standard dye mixture are prepared by the dilutions of the stock solution as shown with the urobilinogen value indicated in "Ehrlich units":

VOLUME OF STOCK SOLUTION (DILUTED TO 100 ML. WITH 0.5% GLACIAL ACETIC ACID)	TOTAL CONCENTRATION OF DYE IN FINAL STANDARD (MG./100 ML.)	UROBILINOGEN VALUE (EHRLICH UNITS/100 ML.)
20.40 ml.	2.040	0.6
17.00 ml.	1.700	0.5
13.60 ml.	1.360	0.4
10.20 ml.	1.020	0.3
8.50 ml.	0.850	0.25
6.80 ml.	0.680	0.20
5.10 ml.	0.510	0.15
3.40 ml.	0.340	0.10
1.70 ml.	0.170	0.05

By using these standard solutions, a standard curve is prepared with the colorimeter or spectrophotometer at 565 mμ.

3. Reading and calculation. The optical density at 565 mμ of the "unknown tube" minus the "blank tube" is determined. From the standard curve the urobilinogen concentration (in Ehrlich units per 1000 ml. of final solution) is determined. In the calculation this is multiplied by 4 (for the dilution) and by the factors shown at bottom of page.

If the urine has been treated with the barium chloride solution to remove the bilirubin, this dilution factor must also be considered (i.e., multiply the result by 2).

Precautions and Comments. A similar colorimetric reaction with the Ehrlich aldehyde reagent is produced by porphobilinogen. This may be distinguished from urobilinogen by the differential solubility of the "aldehyde product" of these two compounds in chloroform and water.

(See section on urine examination.) Very high values for urobilinogen may be falsely produced by BSP (if this test has been done), which may be excreted in the urine in amounts large enough to produce a color similar to the urobilinogen product on alkalinization. This can be recognized by the fact that the deep color develops only after the sodium acetate has been added and that the color of the blank is as intense as that of the unknown.

Normals have 1.0 Ehrlich unit or less in a two-hour urine. The diseases that produce elevated or depressed levels have been discussed. Falsely low values may be produced by permitting the urine to stand exposed to the light for more than a few minutes before testing.

Fecal Urobilinogen Determination

Method and Principle. The semiquantitative rapid method developed in Watson's laboratory involves the same reaction and technique that have been described for the measurement of urine urobilinogen. It may be applied to a random stool specimen and the results are expressed per 100 gm. of feces.

Reagents

1. Ehrlich's aldehyde reagent (Watson modification): as described previously.

2. Saturated solution of sodium acetate: as described previously.

3. 20 per cent ferrous sulfate solution.

4. 10 per cent sodium hydroxide solution.

Procedure. Ten grams of feces from a well-mixed specimen are ground to a thin paste with a small amount of water and then suspended in a total volume of 300 ml. of water. After the solids have settled, the supernatant is decanted and to it is added 100 ml. of 20 per cent ferrous sulfate solution followed by 100 ml. of 10 per cent sodium hydroxide solution. This suspension is filtered and the filtrate treated as was the urine in the procedure outlined previously. The urobilinogen value obtained from the standard curve is multiplied by 50 for the stool dilution and by 4 for the dilution introduced by adding the aldehyde reagent and the sodium acetate.

Comments. The method here described is very satisfactory for the study of he-

$$\frac{\text{Urobilinogen}}{100 \text{ ml. final solution}} \times 4 \times \frac{\text{Vol. urine in 2 hrs.}}{100} = \text{Ehrlich units urobilinogen excreted in two hours}$$

patobiliary disease. For the study of anemia and hemoglobin metabolism a four-day stool collection is more reliable. Nevertheless elevated values (above 300 Ehrlich units/100 gm. of feces) constitute presumptive evidence for hemolysis. The normal range by this method is 50 to 300 Ehrlich units per 100 gm. of feces. Levels below 10 units are observed in obstructive jaundice or in patients receiving "broad-spectrum" antibiotics.

Cephalin-Cholesterol Flocculation

Method. Hanger (1939), modified by Neefe (1946).

Principle. An aqueous, emulsified mixture of cholesterol and cephalin obtained from sheep brain is added to diluted serum. Normal serum permits the suspension to remain. The serum of patients with liver disease and at times with other diseases associated with abnormal levels of plasma proteins shows various degrees of separation of the emulsion, leaving a deposited flocculum and a clarified supernatant. Such "positive" reactions are graded as described under "Procedure."

Material. Serum.

Reagents
1. Cephalin-cholesterol mixture obtained commercially. It contains 100 mg. partially oxidized cephalin and 300 mg. cholesterol.
2. Ether, U.S.P.
3. Cephalin-cholesterol emulsion.
   a. A "stock" solution is prepared by adding 8 ml. of ether to the vial containing the cephalin-cholesterol mixture. This stock solution is stable if kept in the refrigerator.
   b. The emulsion is prepared by adding 1.0 ml. stock solution to 35 ml. freshly distilled water at 65° C. This should be stirred well while slowly bringing the mixture to a boil. The volume then should be concentrated to 30 ml. at low heat, after which the emulsion is cooled and used. It must be freshly prepared on the day of use.

Procedure
1. Add 1.0 ml. of emulsion, 0.2 ml. of serum, and 4.0 ml. of normal saline solution to a centrifuge tube. Shake thoroughly, stopper, and allow tube to stand in a dark room for 48 hours. The result is read by inspection at 24 and 48 hours as 0, 1+, 2+, 3+, or 4+. A "4+" re-

action denotes complete flocculation, leaving a water-clear supernatant fluid. A "0" result indicates the same degree of turbidity as is seen in the control tube.
2. A control tube containing 4.2 ml. of saline solution and 1.0 ml. of emulsion should always be prepared at the beginning of the test. The degree of turbidity in the serum being tested is compared with that of the control. Whenever possible, it is helpful to perform the procedure on a known "negative" and "4+" serum for comparison.

Comments and Precautions. Positive results may be obtained in patients with acute and chronic hepatic disease and also in patients with extrahepatic diseases with hyperglobulinemia. In most laboratories a value of 3+ or 4+ at the 48-hour reading is considered "positive," while a value of 0, 1+, or 2+ is considered normal. These results should be standardized for the individual laboratory by studying a series of normal sera.

Thymol Turbidity Test

Method. Maclagan (1944), as modified by Shank and Hoagland (1946).

Principle. Thymol, in barbital buffer at low ionic strength, added to serum produces distinct turbidity in patients with liver disease and with a number of other diseases causing abnormality of plasma proteins. The results are expressed in units related to an arbitrary standard.

Material. Serum.

Reagents. Thymol buffer. Add 1.03 gm. sodium barbital, 1.38 gm. barbital, and 3 gm. crystalline thymol (U.S.P., recrystallized) to 500 ml. distilled water. Heat to boiling, shake, and cool. Dust the surface with powdered thymol and allow the solution to stand overnight at room temperature (20 to 25° C.). Shake and filter to remove the thymol crystals that have formed. Annino (1958) recommends filtering for a second time after two days of refrigerator storage. The solution is stored in the refrigerator and used as needed until it becomes cloudy.

Procedure
1. Into a cuvet are measured 4 ml. thymol buffer and 0.1 ml. serum; the tube is agitated and then allowed to stand for 30 minutes. The degree of turbidity is determined by measuring the optical density at 650 mμ in a standard spectrophotom-

eter or by using the equivalent filter in a photoelectric colorimeter. A cuvet containing the thymol buffer is used as the blank. The result is expressed in arbitrary units, using a standard barium sulfate solution (or colloidal glass suspension) to prepare a standard curve. The test also may be performed by visual comparison of the turbidity with gelatin standards as described by Maclagan (1952).

2. Preparation of barium sulfate standard. A suspension of barium sulfate is made by diluting 3.0 ml. of 0.092 M barium chloride to 100 ml. with 0.2 N sulfuric acid at 10° C. The particle size of the precipitated barium sulfate at this temperature yields a relatively stable suspension. A standard curve may be established by preparing 5-unit, 10-unit, and 20-unit turbidity standards. The 5-unit standard is prepared by adding 0.68 ml. of the barium sulfate suspension to 2.32 ml. of 0.2 N sulfuric acid; the 10-unit standard is prepared by adding 1.35 ml. of the barium sulfate suspension to 1.65 ml. of 0.2 N sulfuric acid and the 20-unit standard by adding 2.70 ml. of 2 N sulfuric acid to 0.30 ml. of the barium sulfate suspension. Since the suspensions become less stable at room temperature, the cuvets should be well shaken before readings are made. Using a blank of distilled water, one can obtain a straight-line relationship between the optical density of various dilutions of the barium sulfate standard at 650 mμ.

Precautions and Comments. The hyperglobulinemic and hepatic diseases in which abnormal results are obtained with this procedure have been discussed. Serums with increased lipid levels may yield "false-positive" turbidity. Accordingly postprandial specimens may yield higher values than those obtained in the fasting state. Normal values in our laboratory are less than 4 units.

Zinc Sulfate Turbidity Test

Method. Kunkel (1947).

Principle. Gamma globulin is precipitated by low concentrations of heavy metals. The method of Kunkel depends on the capacity of very small amounts of zinc sulfate in a barbital buffer at low ionic strength to produce turbidity when mixed with serum. The results are expressed in units related to an arbitrary standard.

Material. Serum.

Reagents. Buffered zinc sulfate solution. Dissolve 24 mg. of zinc sulfate (ZnSO$_4$·

7H$_2$O), 280 mg. of barbital, and 210 mg. of sodium barbital in distilled water and dilute to make 1.0 liter of solution.

Procedure. Mix 0.1 ml. of serum with 6.0 ml. of the buffered zinc sulfate solution. Allow this to stand for 30 minutes and then read in a spectrophotometer or photoelectric colorimeter at 650 mμ using the buffered zinc sulfate solution as the blank. The result may be determined from the standard barium sulfate described for the thymol turbidity determination. The normal value is 12 units or less.

Comments and Precautions. The procedure is simple to perform and yields an estimate of the gamma globulin level of fair reliability. Turbidity of the serum due to high lipid levels may give falsely elevated values. The upper limit of normal is 12 units.

Sulfobromphthalein (Bromsulfalein, BSP) Excretion Test

Method. Rosenthal and White (1925), modified by Mateer (1943), and by Seligson and his associates (1957).

Principle. A measured amount of BSP is injected intravenously. The liver rapidly removes the dye and excretes it into the bile. If liver function is impaired, excretion is delayed and a larger proportion of the dye remains in the serum. The dye concentration in the serum is measured after addition of alkali to convert any dye present to the colored sodium salt. Corrections for turbidity and serum color interference are made by using a serum blank.

Material. Serum.

Reagents

1. BSP in solution (50 mg./ml.) is used for injection into the patient and as a "stock" solution from which to prepare standard. This is commercially available in sterile ampules.

2. Alkaline buffer pH 10.6 to 10.7. This is made by dissolving 12.2 gm. of sodium basic phosphate Na$_2$HPO$_4$·7H$_2$O), 1.77 gm. of sodium phosphate (Na$_3$PO$_4$·12H$_2$O), and 3.20 gm. of sodium-p-toluene sulfonate in distilled water and diluting to 500 ml. The solution should be adjusted to a pH of 10.6 or 10.7 with 1 N NaOH or 1 N HCl.

3. Acid reagent. This is prepared by dissolving 69 gm. of sodium acid phosphate (NaH$_2$PO$_4$·1H$_2$O) in 250 ml. distilled water.

Procedure

1. Administration of dye. The test is best done with the patient in the fasting state. The patient is weighed and the quantity of BSP required is calculated. (A dosage of 5 mg. per kg. is generally accepted. The test is described accordingly. For the method based on 2 mg. per kg. dosage other sources may be consulted.) Using the commercially available BSP solution, which contains 50 mg. per ml., the number of ml. of solution required is equal to the patient's weight (in pounds) divided by 22. This amount of BSP solution is drawn into a sterile syringe and injected into an antecubital vein with extreme care to prevent extravasation of dye into the surrounding tissue.

2. Obtaining blood specimen. Exactly 45 minutes after the dye is administered a 10 ml. sample of blood is taken from a vein, preferably from the opposite arm. The syringe used to withdraw the blood should be dry and should not be the same one used to administer the dye. After the blood has clotted, the serum should be removed with care to avoid hemolysis.

3. Determination of the amount of dye remaining in the blood. Place 0.5 ml. of serum in a cuvet and add 3.5 ml. of alkaline buffer. Mix gently and read in a photoelectric colorimeter or spectrophotometer at or near 580 mμ using water as a reference. Add 0.1 ml. of acid reagent. Mix gently and read again. The optical density reading representing the amount of dye "retained" is the O.D. obtained with the alkaline buffer minus the O.D. with the acid buffer. The per cent of dye "retained" may be read from the standard curve to be described or may be calculated from the following formula:

$$\text{Per cent retention} = \frac{\text{O.D. serum}}{\text{O.D. standard} \times \text{per cent retention standard}}$$

4. Preparation of standard curve.
   a. Preparation of the BSP standards is based on the assumption that there are 50 ml. of plasma per kg. of body weight. Injection of 5 mg. per

kg. would yield, therefore, a 10 mg. per cent solution of BSP in plasma. Accordingly, 100 per cent dye retention would correspond to a 10 mg. per cent BSP solution. In preparing the standard curve, use the optical density of the BSP solution of each of the concentrations shown in the following table after treatment as described for the serum sample in section 3.

   b. Stock solution (50 mg. per ml.) is diluted 1 to 500 with distilled water to give a 10 mg. per cent solution of BSP. The standard solutions are made by mixing this solution with distilled water as follows:

ML. 10 MG.% BSP SOLUTION	ML. WATER	DYE RETENTION IN SERUM REPRESENTED BY THIS SOLUTION
1	9	10%
2	8	20%
3	7	30%
4	6	40%
5	5	50%
6	4	60%
7	3	70%
8	2	80%
9	1	90%
10	0	100%

Comments and Precautions. Care should be taken to avoid injecting the dye into the subcutaneous tissue. A clean, dry syringe should be used to withdraw the blood. It should not be the same syringe used to give the dye. Blood should be withdrawn from a vein other than the one used to administer the dye. Normal adults retain 4 per cent or less of the administered dye by the method described.

Epinephrine Tolerance Test

The test is designed to measure the adequacy of glycogen stores or of glycogenolytic enzymes. It is well, as in doing the glucose tolerance test, to prepare the patient for this procedure by administering a high-carbohydrate diet for three days. On the day of the test the fasting blood sugar level is determined, and the patient is given an intramuscular dose of 0.01 mg. of epinephrine per kg. of body weight. The blood sugar level is determined 30 and 60 minutes after the epinephrine is administered. Normal individuals show a rise of at least 50 mg. per 100 ml. by 60 minutes.

Patients with glycogen storage disease, parenchymatous liver disease, and wasting diseases show a subnormal rise.

Blood Ammonia Determination

The addition of alkali to plasma or blood releases free ammonia. This diffuses out of the blood or plasma and is trapped by acid. The ammonia is determined by titration with alkali to determine the unbound acid (method of Conway) or by nesslerization (method of Seligson and Seligson). Both methods are sensitive and quite reliable. The method of Seligson as modified by Bessman is easier to perform and lends itself better to study of multiple samples. The details of these methods may be obtained by consulting the review by Bessman (1959).

Galactose Tolerance Test

The ability to utilize galactose as a measure of liver function has been tested by one of two related techniques. The oral galactose tolerance consists of administering a large single dose of galactose (40 gm.) and determining the excretion of galactose in the urine during the succeeding five hours. Normals excrete small amounts (less than 2 gm.). Patients with liver disease excrete more than 3 gm. with this procedure. Abnormally large quantities of galactose also may appear in the urine of patients with increased intestinal absorption (e.g., in hyperthyroidism). Accordingly an intravenous test has been devised. In this procedure the blood galactose level is determined 75 minutes after intravenous dose of galactose has been given. Normal individuals have less than 5 mg. per 100 ml. of the sugar at this time. Patients with hepatic disease have higher levels. A modification of the intravenous galactose tolerance test measuring the galactose clearance per minute has been described.

Hippuric Acid Excretion Tests

The test measures the ability of the liver to conjugate benzoic acid with glycine to form hippuric acid. A standard dose of sodium benzoate is given and the urinary excretion of hippuric acid is measured. In the oral hippuric acid tolerance test 6 gm. of sodium benzoate in 30 ml. of water is given orally followed by 100 ml. of water. The urine passed during the succeeding four hours is collected and its hippuric acid content determined. Normal individuals excrete more than 2.5 gm. during the four-hour period. In the intravenous hippuric acid tolerance test 1.77 gm. of sodium benzoate in 20 ml. of water is injected slowly into a vein and 200 ml. of water is given orally. Normal individuals excrete more than 1 gm. of hippuric acid in the urine during the succeeding hour. Less than 2.5 gm. excreted in four hours in the oral test or less than 1 gm. in one hour in the intravenous test is seen in patients with hepatic disease. The hippuric acid content of the urine may be determined gravimetrically or by titration after concentration, acidification, separation, and washing. Other methods of separation of the hippuric acid before titration and a chromatographic method have been described.

Response of Prothrombin Time to Vitamin K Administration

This test has been applied to the differential diagnosis of jaundice. Prothrombin deficiency may occur as a result of inadequate absorption of the fat-soluble vitamin K in obstructive jaundice or because of inability of the damaged liver of hepatocellular jaundice to synthesize prothrombin. The prothrombin time is determined before and 24 hours after the administration of 10 mg. of synthetic vitamin K. Patients with obstructive jaundice usually show a return of prothrombin time to, or almost to, normal (85 to 100 per cent). Patients with hepatocellular jaundice and a prolonged prothrombin time usually show less or no improvement.

REFERENCES

Liver Function (General)

1. Annino, J. S.: Clinical Chemistry: Principles and Procedures. Boston, Little, Brown & Co., 1958, pp. 182–207.
2. Culver, P. J., McDermott, W. V., and Jones, C. M.: Diagnostic value of selective interference with certain excretory processes of the liver. Gastroenterology, 33:163, 1957.
3. Ham, T. H.: A Syllabus of Laboratory Examinations in Clinical Diagnosis. Cambridge, Massachusetts, Harvard University Press, 1950.
4. Hanger, F. M.: Meaning of liver function tests. Am. J. Med., 16:565, 1954.
5. Hawk, P. B., Oser, B. L., and Summerson, W. H.: Practical Physiological Chemistry, 13th Ed. New York, Blakiston Division, McGraw-Hill Book Co., Inc., 1954.
6. King, W. E.: Liver Function. In, Jones, F. A.: Modern Advances in Gastroenterology. Second Series. New York, Paul B. Hoeber, Inc., 1958.

7. Lichtman, S. S.: Diseases of the Liver, Gall Bladder and Bile Ducts. 3rd Ed. Philadelphia, Lea & Febiger, 1953, vol. 1.
8. Mateer, J. G., Baltz, J. I., Priest, R. J., and Fischbein, J. W.: Diagnosis of biliary tract disease, present status of liver function tests, liver biopsy and duodeno-biliary drainage. Med. Clin. N. Am., 40:437, 1956.
9. Popper, H.: Liver disease—morphologic considerations. Am. J. Med., 16:98, 1954.
10. Popper, H., and Schaffner, F.: Liver: Structure and Function. New York, McGraw-Hill Book Co., Inc., 1957.
11. Reinhold, J. G.: Chemical evaluation of the functions of the liver. Clinical Chem., 1:351, 1955.
12. Schiff, L. (Ed.): Diseases of the Liver. Philadelphia, J. B. Lippincott Company, 1956.
13. Sherlock, S.: Diseases of the Liver and Biliary System. 2nd Ed. Oxford, Blackwell Scientific Publications, 1958.
14. Snell, A. M.: Liver function tests and their interpretation. Gastroenterology, 34:675, 1958.
15. Spellberg, M. A.: Diseases of the Liver. New York, Grune & Stratton, Inc., 1954.

Bilirubin Metabolism and Jaundice

16. Billing, B. H., and Lathe, G. H.: Bilirubin metabolism in jaundice. Am. J. Med., 24:111, 1958.
17. Cayer, D., and Henry, O., Jr.: The diagnosis of jaundice: an evaluation of the procedures commonly utilized in differential diagnosis. Geriatrics, 11:191, 1956.
18. Ducci, H.: Contribution of the laboratory to the differential diagnosis of jaundice. J.A.M.A., 135:694, 1947.
19. Ducci, H., and Watson, C. J.: The quantitative determination of the serum bilirubin with special reference to the prompt-reacting and the chloroform-soluble types. J. Lab. Clin. Med., 30:293, 1945.
20. Franklin, M.: New tablet test for urine bilirubin. J. Lab. Clin. Med., 34:1145, 1949.
21. Free, A. H., and Free, H. M.: Simple test for urine bilirubin. Gastroenterology, 24:414, 1953.
22. Hanger, F. M.: Diagnostic problems in jaundice. Arch. Int. Med., 86:169, 1950.
23. Harrison, G. A.: Chemical Methods in Clinical Medicine. 2nd Ed. London, J. & A. Churchill, Ltd., 1937.
24. Hoffman, H. N., II, Whitcomb, F. F., Jr., Butt, H. R., and Bollman, J. L.: Bile pigments of jaundice. J. Clin. Invest., 39:132, 1960.
25. Klatskin, G., and Bungards, L.: An improved test for bilirubin in the urine. New Eng. J. Med., 248:712, 1953.
26. Malloy, H. T., and Evelyn, K. A.: The determination of bilirubin with the photoelectric colorimeter. J. Biol. Chem., 119:481, 1937.
27. McNee, J. W.: Jaundice. A review of recent works. Quart. J. Med., 16:390, 1923.
28. Mellinkoff, S., Tumulty, P. A., and Harvey, A. M.: Differentiation of parenchymal liver diseases and mechanical biliary obstruction. New Eng. J. Med., 246:729, 1952.
29. Meulengracht, E.: Blood sugar curve in various forms of icterus. Acta Med. Scandinav., 79:32, 1932.
30. Rich, H. R.: Pathogenesis of forms of jaundice. Bull. Johns Hopkins Hosp., 47:338, 1930.
31. Sborov, V. M.: Physiology of symptoms (VI). Jaundice. Am. J. Dig. Dis., 4:65, 1959.
32. Schmid, R.: Some aspects of bile pigment metabolism. Clin. Chem., 3:394, 1957.
33. Van den Bergh, A. A. H., and Muller, P.: Ueber eine direkte un eine in direkte Diazoreaction auf Bilirubin. Biochem. Ztschr., 77:90, 1916.
34. Wallace, B. B., and Diamond, J. S.: The significance of urobilinogen in the urine as a test for liver function, with a small quantitative method for its estimation. Arch. Int. Med., 35:698, 1925.
35. Watson, C. J.: Regurgitation jaundice. J.A.M.A., 114:2427, 1940.
36. Watson, C. J.: The importance of the fractional serum bilirubin determination in clinical medicine. Ann. Int. Med., 45:351, 1956.
37. Watson, C. J., and Hawkinson, V.: Semiquantitative estimation of bilirubin in urine by means of barium-strip modification of Harrison's test. J. Lab. Clin. Med., 31:914, 1946.
38. Watson, C. J., Schwartz, S., Sborov, V., and Bertie, E.: Studies of urobilinogen V. A simple method for the quantitative recording of the Ehrlich reaction as carried out with urine and feces. Am. J. Clin. Path., 14:605, 1944.
39. Weiss, D. L., Athanasiadou, P., Long, E., and Reiner, M.: Laboratory tests for the general practitioner. I. Urinary bilirubin. South. M. J., 49:757, 1956.

Tests Based on Carbohydrate Metabolism

40. Althausen, T. L.: Liver function tests in the differential diagnosis of jaundice. Am. J. Med., 4:208, 1948.
41. Campbell, J. A., and Tagnon, H. J.: The intravenous glucose tolerance test in liver disease. New Eng. J. Med., 234:216, 1946.
42. Colcher, H., Patek, A. J., Jr., and Kendall, F. E.: Galactose disappearance from the blood stream. Calculation of a galactose removal constant and its application as a test for liver function. J. Clin. Invest., 25:768, 1946.
43. Conn, J. W.: Diagnosis and management of spontaneous hypoglycemia. J.A.M.A., 134:130, 1947.
44. Kinsell, L. W., Michaels, G. D., Weiss, H. A., and Barton, H. C., Jr.: Studies in hepatic glycogen storage. I. Adrenalin-induced hyperglycemia as an index of liver function. Am. J. Med. Sci., 217:554, 1949.
45. Moyer, J. H., and Womach, C.: Glucose tolerance. II. Evaluation of glucose tolerance in liver disease and comparison of the relative value of three types of tolerance tests. Am. J. Med. Sci., 216:446, 1948.
46. Van Itallie, T. B., and Bentley, W. B. A.: Glucagon-induced hyperglycemia as an index of liver function. J. Clin. Invest., 34:1730, 1955.

Tests Based on Lipid Metabolism

47. Billing, B. H., Harlam, R. M., Hein, D. E., Conlon, H. J., Hamilton, D. L., Mindrum, G. M., and Schiff, L.: Serum and liver lipids in patients with and without liver disease. J. Lab. Clin. Med., 45:363, 1955.
48. Carey, J. B., Jr.: The serum dihydroxy-trihydroxy bile acid ratio in liver and biliary tract disease. J. Clin. Invest., 35:695, 1956.
49. Man, E. B., Kartin, B. L., Durlacher, S. H., and Peters, J. P.: The lipids of serum and liver

in patients with hepatic diseases. J. Clin. Invest., 24:623, 1945.

50. Rudman, D., and Kendall, F. E.: Bile acid content of human serum. I. Serum bile acids in patients with hepatic disease. J. Clin. Invest., 36:530, 1957.

51. Saltzman, A., and Caraway, W. T.: Cinnamic acid as a test substrate in the evaluation of liver function. J. Clin. Invest., 32:711, 1953.

Serum Proteins and Flocculation Tests

52. Bigwood, E. J., Crokaert, R., Schram, E., Soupart, P., and Vis, H.: Amino aciduria. In Advances in Clinical Chemistry. New York, Academic Press, Inc., 1959, vol. 2, p. 201.

53. Bruger, M., and Oppenheimer, E.: The present status of liver function tests including the observations on the newer flocculation procedures. Bull. New York Acad. Med., 25:16, 1949.

54. Ducci, H.: The flocculation tests in the differential diagnosis of jaundice. Gastroenterology, 15:628, 1950.

55. Greenspan, E. M., and Dreiling, D. A.: Serum mucoprotein level in differentiation of hepatogenic from obstructive jaundice. A.M.A. Arch. Int. Med., 91:474, 1953.

56. Hanger, F. M.: Serological differentiation of obstructive from hepatogenous jaundice by flocculation of cephalin cholesterol emulsions. J. Clin. Invest., 18:261, 1939.

57. de la Huerga, J., and Popper, H.: Estimation of serum gamma globulin concentration by turbidimetry. J. Lab. & Clin. Med., 35:459, 1950.

58. Kunkel, H. G.: Estimation of alterations of serum gamma globulin by a turbidimetric technique. Proc. Soc. Exp. Biol. Med., 66: 217, 1947.

59. Kunkel, H. G., and Hoagland, L.: Mechanism and significance of the thymol turbidity test for liver disease. J. Clin. Invest., 31:1060, 1947.

60. Maclagan, N. F., Martin, N. H., and Lunnon, J. B.: The mechanism and interrelationships of the flocculation tests. J. Clin. Path., 5:1, 1952.

61. Martin, N. H., and Neuberger, A.: Protein metabolism and the liver. Brit. Med. Bull., 13:113, 1957.

62. Neefe, J. R.: Results of hepatic tests in chronic hepatitis without jaundice; Correlation with clinical course and liver biopsy findings. Gastroenterology, 7:1, 1946.

63. Oberman, H. A., and Kulesh, M. H.: Turbidimetric determination of the concentration of gamma globulin in serum. Am. J. Clin. Path., 30:519, 1958.

64. Schmid, R.: The zinc turbidity test and its clinical application. J. Lab. Clin. Med., 36: 52, 1950.

65. Shank, R. E., and Hoagland, C. L.: A modified method for the quantitative determination of the thymol turbidity reaction of serum. J. Biol. Chem., 162:133, 1946.

66. Shay, H., Berk, E. J., and Siplet, H.: The thymol turbidity test as a measure of liver disease with special reference to comparison of the turbidity at 18 hours with that at 30 minutes ("18 hour turbidity ratio"). Gastroenterology, 9:641, 1947.

67. Stillerman, H. B.: Thymol turbidity test in various diseases. J. Lab. Clin. Med., 33:565, 1948.

68. Viollier, G.: Tentative classification of some current types of liver damage on the basis

of electrophoretic serum analysis. In Hepatitis Frontiers. Boston, Little, Brown and Co., 1957, p. 423.

69. Walshe, J. M.: Observations on symptomatology and pathogenesis of hepatic coma. Quart. J. Med., 20:421, 1951.

70. Wilson, T. E., Brown, C. H., and Hainline, A., Jr.: The zinc sulfate turbidity test. Gastroenterology, 32:483, 1957.

71. Zimmerman, H. J., West, M., and Gelb, M.: Clinical significance of hyperglobulinemia. G.P., 20:137, 1959.

Blood Ammonia Levels

72. Bessman, S. P.: The role of ammonia in clinical syndromes. Ann. Int. Med., 44:1037, 1956.

73. Bessman, S. P.: Blood ammonia. In Advances in Clinical Chemistry. New York, Academic Press, Inc., 1959, vol. 2., p. 201.

74. Conway, E. J.: Microdiffusion Analysis and Volumetric Error. 3rd Ed. New York, D. Van Nostrand Company, Inc., 1950.

75. McDermott, W. V., Jr.: The role of ammonia intoxication in hepatic coma. Bull. N. Y. Acad. Med., 34:357, 1958.

76. Seligson, O., and Seligson, H.: A microdiffusion method for the determination of nitrogen liberated as ammonia. J. Lab. & Clin. Med., 38:324, 1951.

77. Traeger, H. S., Gabuzda, G. J., Jr., Ballou, A. N., and Davidson, C. S.: Blood "ammonia" concentration in liver disease and liver coma. Metabolism, 3:99, 1954.

Dye Excretion Tests

Sulfobromphthalein

78. Mateer, J. G., Baltz, J. I., Marion, D. F., and MacMillan, J. M.: Liver function tests. A general evaluation of liver function and an appraisal of the comparative sensitivity and reliability of the newer tests. J.A.M.A., 121: 723, 1943.

79. Rosenthal, S. M., and White, E. C.: Clinical application of bromsulfalein test for hepatic function. J.A.M.A., 84:112, 1925.

80. Seligson, D., Marino, J., and Dodson, E.: Determination of sulfobromphthalein in serum. Clin. Chem., 3:638, 1957.

Rose Bengal

81. Taplin, G. V., Meredith, O. M., Jr., and Kade, H.: The radioactive I[131]-tagged) rose bengal uptake-excretion test for liver function using external gamma-ray scintillation counting techniques. J. Lab. Clin. Med., 45: 665, 1955.

82. Westover, J. L., Greenfield, M. A., and Norman, H.: A clinically useful liver function test using radioactive rose bengal. J. Lab. Clin. Med., 54:174, 1959.

Hippuric Acid Synthesis

83. Quick, A. J.: Clinical application of hippuric acid and prothrombin tests. Am. J. Clin. Path., 10:222, 1940.

84. Zieve, L., Hill, E., and Nesbitt, S.: Studies of liver function tests combined intravenous bromsulfalein-hippuric acid-galactose tolerance test. J. Lab. Clin. Med., 36:705, 1950.

Blood Prothrombin and Other Clotting Factors

85. Alexander, B.: Coagulation, hemorrhage and thrombosis. New Eng. J. Med., 252:526, 1955.

86. Unger, P. N., and Shapiro, S.: Prothrombin response to the parenteral administration of large doses of vitamin K in subjects with normal liver function and in cases of liver disease: A standardized test for the estimation of hepatic function. J. Clin. Invest., 27: 39, 1948.

Serum Iron Levels

87. Editorial: Some aspects of iron metabolism. Ann. Int. Med., 42:458, 1955.
88. Finch, S. C., and Finch, C. A.: Idiopathic hemochromatosis, an iron storage disease. Medicine, 34:381, 1955.
89. Mandel, E. E.: Serum iron and iron-binding capacity in clinical diagnosis. Clin. Chem., 5:1, 1959.
90. Ramsay, W. N. M.: Plasma iron. In Advances in Clinical Chemistry (Editor: H. Sabotka). Academic Press, Inc., 1958, vol. 1, pp. 2–39.
91. Stone, C. M., Jr., Rumball, J. M., and Hassett, C. P.: An evaluation of serum iron in liver disease. Ann. Int. Med., 43:229, 1955.
92. Wallerstein, R. O., and Mettier, S. R.: Iron in Clinical Medicine. Berkeley, University of California Press, 1958, pp. 5–57, 105–113.

Serum Copper and Ceruloplasmin Levels

93. Bearn, A. G.: Genetic and biochemical aspects of Wilson's disease. Am. J. Med., 157:442, 1953.
94. Butt, E. M., Nusbaum, R. E., Gilmour, J. C., and DiDio, B. A.: Trace metal patterns in disease states. II. Copper storage diseases, with consideration of juvenile cirrhosis, Wilson's disease and hepatic copper of the newborn. Am. J. Clin. Path., 30:479, 1958.
95. Walshe, J. M.: Current views on the pathogenesis and treatment of Wilson's disease. A.M.A. Arch. Int. Med., 103:155, 1959.

Serum Zinc Levels

96. Vallee, B. L., Wacker, W. E. C., Bartholomay, A. F., and Hoch, F. L.: Zinc metabolism in hepatic dysfunction. II. Correlation of metabolic patterns with biochemical findings. New Eng. J. Med., 257:1055, 1957.

Vitamin B12 Levels in Liver Disease

97. Kristensen, H. P. Ø.: The blood vitamin B12 level in liver disease. Its significance for prognosis and differential diagnosis. Acta Med. Scandinavica, 163:515, 1959.
98. Rachmielwitz, M., Stein, Y., Aronovich, J., and Grossowicz, N.: The clinical significance of serum cyanocobalamin (vitamin B12) in liver disease. A.M.A. Arch. Int. Med., 101: 1118, 1958.

Vitamin A Levels in Liver Disease

99. White, D. P., Bone, F. C., Ruffin, J. M., and Taylor, H.: Further observations on the value of plasma vitamin A determinations in the differential diagnosis of jaundice. Gastroenterology, 14:541, 1950.

Liver Biopsy

100. Volwiler, W., and Jones, C. M.: The diagnostic and therapeutic value of liver biopsies, with particular reference to trocar biopsy. New Eng. J. Med., 237:651, 1947.
101. Ward, J., Schiff, L., Young, P., and Gall, E. A.: Needle biopsy of liver; further experiences with malignant neoplasm. Gastroenterology, 27:300, 1954.
102. Zamchek, N., and Klausenstock, O.: Medical progress: Liver biopsy; risk of needle biopsy. New Eng. J. Med., 249:1062, 1953.
103. Zamchek, N., and Sidman, R. L.: Needle biopsy of the liver; its use in clinical and investigative medicine. New Eng. J. Med., 249:1020, 1953.

Liver Function in Hepatic Disease

104. Ahrens, E. H., Payne, M. A., Kunkel, H. G., Eisenmenger, W. J., and Blondheim, S. H.: Primary biliary cirrhosis. Medicine, 29:299, 1950.
105. Baggenstoss, A. H., and Stauffer, M. H.: Post-hepatic and alcoholic cirrhosis. Gastroenterology, 22:157, 1952.
106. Bearn, A. G., Kunkel, H. G., and Slater, R. J.: The problem of chronic liver disease in young women. Am. J. Med., 21:3, 1956.
107. Cameron, G. R., and Muzaffar Hasan, S.: Disturbance of structure and function in liver as result of biliary obstruction. J. Path. & Bact., 75:333, 1958.
108. Hoffbauer, F. W.: Clinical aspects of jaundice resulting from intrahepatic obstruction. J.A.M.A., 169:1453, 1959.
109. MacDonald, R. A., and Mallory, G. K.: Natural history of post-necrotic cirrhosis. A study of 221 autopsy cases. Am. J. Med., 24:334, 1958.
110. Post, J., and Rose, J. V.: Clinical, functional and histologic studies in Laennec's cirrhosis of the liver. Am. J. Med., 8:300, 1950.
111. Ratnoff, O. D., and Patek, A. J.: Postnecrotic cirrhosis of the liver; study of 45 cases. J. Chronic Dis., 1:266, 1955.
112. Sborov, V. M., and Keller, T. B.: The diagnosis of hepatitis. Gastroenterology, 19:424, 1951.
113. Snell, A. M.: Biliary cirrhosis. Med. Clin. N. Am., 40:432, 1956.
114. Watson, C. J., and Hoffbauer, F. W.: The problem of prolonged hepatitis with particular reference to the cholangiolitic type, and to development of cholangiolitic cirrhosis of liver. Ann. Int. Med., 25:195, 1946.
115. Watson, C. J., and Hoffbauer, F. W.: Liver function in hepatitis. Ann. Int. Med., 26: 813, 1947.
116. Werther, J. L., and Korelitz, B. I.: Chlorpromazine jaundice. Am. J. Med., 22:351, 1957.
117. Zimmerman, H. J.: The evolution of alcoholic cirrhosis. Med. Clin. N. Am., 39:241, 1955.

Chapter 12

Serum Enzyme Determinations
as an Aid to Diagnosis

By HYMAN J. ZIMMERMAN, M.D.

Enzymes, organic catalysts that are responsible for most of the chemical reactions of the body, are found in all tissues. Analysis of the enzyme activity of digestive juices, of various tissues, and of formed elements of the blood has been of value in the understanding of normal and abnormal physiology. Determination of several serum enzymes has been applied for several decades to the diagnosis of pancreatic disease (amylase, lipase), hepatic disease (alkaline phosphatase), and prostatic carcinoma (acid phosphatase). Interest in the study of serum enzymes in disease was intensified by the demonstration in 1953 that there was in the serum a transaminase (glutamic-oxaloacetic transaminase), the assay of which was helpful in the diagnosis of cardiac and hepatic disease. During the past few years a large number of enzymes have been demonstrated in the serum (Table 12–1).

Some serum enzyme determinations have been so widely applied to clinical problems as to be considered routine laboratory procedures (Table 12–2, column A): Others, though clearly shown to reflect various disease states, are being applied only to investigative problems or are being determined as "routine" procedures in relatively few hospital laboratories (Table 12–2, column B). Others need further study to establish their clinical applicability (Table 12–2, column C).

In the chapter on liver function tests the serum levels of alkaline phosphatase, the transaminases, and cholinesterase are discussed with reference to the diagnosis of hepatic disease. In this chapter the enzymes that have been demonstrated in the serum will be considered in a more general fashion. The principles of the methods applied to enzyme assay will be discussed, followed by an analysis of the significance of the enzymes shown in Table 12–2, column A. The analysis of the enzymes in Table 12–2, column B will be brief; a few of the other serum enzymes will receive comment. The diagnostic application of serum enzymes will be considered both in the light of present application and of potential usefulness. Brief reference will be made to enzymes of the formed elements of the blood and to enzymes of other body fluids.

METHODS OF MEASURING SERUM ENZYME ACTIVITY

The amount of enzyme present in any tissue or body fluid is not measured directly. It is inferred from the activity, i.e., the work that the enzyme performs in catalyzing a chemical reaction. Thus, when the concentration of an enzyme in the serum is discussed, the term "concentration" is a semantic convenience and should be understood to mean activity. The rate of a reaction catalyzed by an enzyme is directly proportional to the enzyme concentration. Measuring reaction rates under standard

Table 12–1. Classification and Tabulation of Enzymes Demonstrated in the Serum with Indication of Type and Degree* of Abnormality in Disease

TYPE OF ENZYME	INFECTIOUS HEPATITIS	MONO.†	CIRRHOSIS	MET. CA†	OBST. JAUNDICE†	HEART FAILURE	MYO-CARDIAL INFARCTION	PROGRES-SIVE MUSC. DYST.†	OTHER ABNORMALITIES
A. Carbohydrate Metabolism									
1. Glycolytic									
a. Phosphoglucomutase	++	−	N	+	+	−	−	−	
b. Phosphohexose isomerase	+++	++	+	+	+	+	++	+	Granulocytic leukemia. See Fig. 12–3.
c. Fructose 1,6-diphos-phate aldolase	+++	+	+	+	N or +	+	++	+++	Leukemia, pancreatitis, delirum tremens, megaloblastic anemia See Fig. 12–4.
d. Fructose aldolase	+++	−	−	N	N	−	N	N	
e. Lactic dehydrogenase	+ or N	++	+ or N	++	+ or N	+	++	++	See Fig. 12–5.
2. Hexose Monophosphate Shunt									
a. 6-Phosphogluconic dehydrogenase	++	−	N	N or +	−	−	−	−	
b. 5-Phosphoriboisomerase	N	−	++	++	+	−	−	−	
3. Citric Acid Cycle									
a. Malic dehydrogenase	+++	−	+	−	+	+	++	−	Megaloblastic anemia, hemolytic anemia See Fig. 12–6.
b. Fumarase	+++	−	+	−	+	−	−	−	
c. Isocitric dehydrogenase	+++	+++	N or +	++	N	+	N	N	See Fig. 12–7.
4. Amylase	N	N	N or D	N	N	N	N	N	See Table 12–2.
5. β-Glucuronidase	++	−	−	−	−	−	N or +	−	Carcinoma, pregnancy
B. Lipid Esterases									
1. Lipase	N	N	N	N	N	N	N	N	Chronic pancreatitis, acute pancreatitis
2. Cholesterol Esterase	D	−	D	N or D	N	−	−	−	
C. Nonlipid Esterases									
1. Cholinesterase	D	−	D	D	N or D	N or D	D	N	See Table 12–5.
2. Phosphatases									
a. Alkaline	+	+	+	++	+++	+	N	N	See Table 12–4.
b. Acid	N	N	N	N	N	N	N	N	Carcinoma of prostate Gaucher's disease
c. 5-Nucleotidase	+	−	+	++	+++	−	−	−	Normal in bone disease
d. Adenosine triphos-phatase	+	−	+	+	++	−	−	−	Elevated in bone disease
3. Deoxyribonuclease	+	−	−	−	N	−	−	N	Acute hemorrhagic pancreatitis
4. Ribonuclease	N	−	N	N	N	+	+	−	Uremia, leukemia
D. Protein and Amino Acid Enzymes									
1. Proteolytic Enzymes (Trypsin)	−	−	−	−	−	−	−	−	Acute pancreatitis
2. Peptidases									
a. Leucine, aminopeptidase	+++	+++	+	++	+	−	−	N	Pregnancy, carcinoma of pancreas, pancreatitis
b. Aminotripeptidase	++	++	+	++	++	−	−	−	

Table 12–1. Classification and Tabulation of Enzymes Demonstrated in the Serum with Indication of Type and Degree* of Abnormality in Disease (*Contd.*)

TYPE OF ENZYME	HEPATITIS	INFECTIOUS MONO.†	CIRRHOSIS	MET. CA†	OBST. JAUNDICE†	HEART FAILURE	MYO-CARDIAL INFARCTION	PROGRES-SIVE MUSC. DYST.†	OTHER ABNORMALITIES
3. Amino Acid Substrates									
a. Transaminases									
1. Glutamic oxaloacetic transaminase	+++	++	+	+	+	+	++	++	See Table 12–5.
2. Glutamic pyruvic transaminase	+++	++	+	+	+	+	N or +	++	See Table 12–6.
b. Urea cycle									
1. Ornithine carbamyl transferase	+++	–	+	++	–	–	–	–	Acute cholecystitis
2. Arginase	++	–	+	–	–	–	–	–	
E. Other Enzymes									
1. Glutathione Reductase	++	–	+	+++	–	–	–	–	

*   +—slight increase
  ++—moderate increase
+++—marked increase
  N—no change
  D—depressed
  ——insufficient information
† Infectious Mono.—infectious mononucleosis
  Met. Ca—metastatic carcinoma
  Obst. Jaundice—obstructive jaundice
  Progressive Musc. Dyst.—progressive muscular dystrophy

Table 12–2.   Classification of Serum Enzyme Determinations According to Clinical Applicability

A	B	C
Well established for routine use:	Well studied and of some clinical value but not widely or routinely applied:	Promising but require further study:
Amylase	Cholinesterase	Fructose aldolase
Lipase	Aldolase	6-Phosphogluconic dehydrogenase
Alkaline phosphatase	Isomerase	5-Phosphoriboisomerase
Acid phosphatase	Lactic dehydrogenase	Malic dehydrogenase
GOT	Pepsinogen	Isocitric dehydrogenase
GPT	Ceruloplasmin	β-Glucuronidase
	Leucine-aminopeptidase	Cholesterol esterase
	Ornithine carbamyl	5-Nucleotidase
	Transferase	Adenosine triphosphatase
		Trypsin
		Peptidases
		Arginase
		Glutathione reductase

conditions of substrate and cofactor concentration, pH, and temperature serves as a measure of enzyme activity or concentration. The reaction rate may be measured by observing the disappearance of substrate, the appearance of a product, or the reduction or oxidation of coenzymes, such as DPN or TPN (Table 12–3). Bodansky (1959) has classified the techniques that may be applied to the measurement of these changes as follows: actually measuring the rate of change by repeated observation during the course of a reaction, measuring the amount of time required to effect a predetermined change, and determining the amount of change at the end of a given period of time.

The principle of the method used appears with each enzyme discussed, and details of the method for assay of a few of the enzymes are presented at the end of this chapter.

Table 12–3. Methods of Measuring Serum Enzyme Activity

PRINCIPLE	EXAMPLES
A. Disappearance of substrate	Amylase assay by following disappearance of starch
B. Appearance of products	Transaminase assay by measuring oxaloacetate formed (GOT) or pyruvate formed (GPT)
	a. Directly
	b. Indirectly by coupled reaction (see GOT assay in Chapter 11)
C. Following coenyzme change	
1. Reduction of coenzyme	Isocitrate dehydrogenase assay by following reduction of TPN
2. Oxidation of reduced coenzyme	Malic dehydrogenase assay by following oxidation of DPNH$_2$

Table 12–4. Conditions in Which the Level of Serum Amylase Is Abnormal

ELEVATED	DEPRESSED
Acute pancreatitis*	Chronic pancreatitis*
Pancreatic pseudocyst	Chronic hepatic insufficiency
Epidemic parotitis	Newborns
Mumps meningoencephalitis	
Intestinal obstruction	
Acute cholecystitis	
Perforated and penetrating peptic ulcer	
Uremia	
Cystic fibrosis of pancreas (early)	
Carcinoma of pancreas	
(After morphine)	
(After cholangiography)	

* Degree of serum amylase elevation in acute exacerbation of chronic pancreatitis is variable.

Serum Amylase (Diastase)

Amylases are enzymes that hydrolyze starch into smaller molecules. There are two main varieties found in nature, alpha and beta amylases. Only alpha amylase is found in mammals. This enzyme has been found in a number of tissues, but its high content in the pancreas and salivary glands is of particular clinical interest.

Methods. A number of methods have been used to determine the serum amylase activity. These fall into the two following categories:

1. The disappearance of starch as measured by the starch-iodine reaction or by the decrease in viscosity of the starch solution.

2. The appearance of reducing sugar. Many of the methods are satisfactory for clinical use. The measurement by the method of Somogyi (1938) of the amount of reducing sugar formed is widely used.

Levels in Disease. Increased levels of this serum enzyme are observed in acute pancreatitis (see Chapter 13). Almost all patients with this disease have transiently (one to three days) elevated levels of serum amylase. The degree of elevation may vary from levels just above the normal (pancreatic edema) to striking elevations (acute hemorrhagic pancreatitis). A brief period of elevation is so characteristic of acute pancreatitis that persistence of increased levels beyond three or four days is suggestive evidence that a pancreatic pseudocyst has developed.

Mild to moderate elevations in the level of serum amylase also have been observed in patients with acute cholecystitis, intestinal obstruction, perforated and penetrating peptic ulcer, and renal insufficiency (Table 12–4). Epidemic parotitis is characterized by a moderate degree of elevation of the serum amylase level. This may reflect release of enzyme from the diseased parotid glands or the pancreas (mumps pancreatitis). Patients with mumps meningoencephalitis frequently have elevated serum amylase levels, even when there is no clinical evidence of salivary or pancreatic involvement.

Lower than normal serum amylase values may be seen in patients with exocrine pancreatic insufficiency and have also been reported in patients with chronic hepatic disease.

The serum amylase determination is the most important laboratory aid in the diagnosis of acute pancreatitis. The occurrence of elevated levels in patients with acute cholecystitis, intestinal obstruction, and perforated peptic ulcer—conditions that must be distinguished from pancreatitis—imposes some limitations on the clinical application of the procedure. Correlation with other features of the clinical problem, however, usually permits distinction.

Serum Lipase

Lipases are enzymes that catalyze the hydrolysis of ester linkages between the fatty acids and glycerol of the triglycerides and phospholipids. The lipase of the serum appears to be largely of pancreatic origin. Its application to the study of pancreatic disease is discussed in Chapter 13.

Methods. The various methods for assay of this enzyme depend on the release of fatty acid from ester linkages. The use of triglycerides of long-chain fatty acids (e.g., olive oil) as substrates has the advantage of more specifically measuring true lipase activity than does the use of esters of short-chain fatty acids, such as tributyrin, alpha-naphthyl laurate, and beta-naphthyl laurate. Olive oil as a substrate has had the disadvantage of poor solubility and slow hydrolysis. The method (a modification of the Cherry and Crandall method [1932]) described by Tietz, Borden, and Stapleton (1959), which uses as substrate an emulsification of olive oil, appears to preserve the specificity of an appropriate triglyceride and to be technically feasible.

Clinical Application. The use of serum lipase determination has not achieved the popularity of the serum amylase determination in the diagnosis of pancreatic disease. This is in part the result of the greater difficulty in determining and evaluating serum lipase levels and in part because the degree of lipase elevation is less dramatic than that of serum amylase in acute pancreatitis. Nevertheless elevations of serum lipase are approximately as frequent as those of serum amylase in patients with acute pancreatitis and tend to subside more slowly during the period of recovery. In patients with chronic pancreatic disease (chronic pancreatitis, carcinoma of the pancreas) serum lipase elevations may occur while serum amylase levels are usually normal.

Phosphatases

The phosphatases of the blood, more properly called phosphomonoesterases, include two main types. The "alkaline phosphatase" has a pH optimum of approximately 9, while the "acid phosphatase" has its optimal activity at a pH of approximately 5. Although there is evidence that alkaline and acid phosphatases both include several different enzymes, it has been convenient for clinical purposes to consider each a single enzyme.

Alkaline Phosphatase. The application of alkaline phosphatase determination to the study of hepatic disease is discussed in Chapter 11. Some of the methods available for the measurement of alkaline phosphatase activity are shown in Table 12–5. The method used in our laboratory is that of Bodansky (1933).

The demonstration that bone is rich in alkaline phosphatase and that normal plasma (or serum) contains the same or a similar enzyme led to the study of serum alkaline phosphatase levels in patients with diseases of bone. Elevated levels of the enzyme occur in patients with bone diseases characterized by increased osteoblastic activity (Table 12–6). These include osteitis deformans, rickets, osteomalacia, hyperparathyroidism, healing fractures, and osteoblastic bone tumors, both primary and secondary. Growing children and pregnant women in the third trimester have "physiologically" elevated serum alkaline phosphatase levels.

Lower than normal levels are observed in patients with hypophosphatasia, an inborn error of metabolism, and in malnourished patients.

The alkaline phosphatase determination is useful in the recognition of diseases of bone, especially osteitis deformans, hyperparathyroidism, and bone neoplasms. Hepatic disease as a cause of serum alkaline phosphatase elevation usually can be distinguished by other laboratory procedures and clinical features. The increased levels of this enzyme in normal, growing children should be kept in mind when attempting to apply the serum alkaline phosphatase levels to the diagnosis of rickets.

Acid Phosphatase. This enzyme, first

Table 12–5. Methods Most Widely Used to Measure Serum Alkaline Phosphatase Activity*

METHOD	SUBSTRATE	BASIS OF ASSAY	UNIT	NORMAL RANGE
Bodansky	β-glycerophosphate	mg. phosphorus liberated	1 mg. P/ml./60′	1–4 units
Shinawora-Jones-Reinhart	β-glycerophosphate	mg. phosphorus liberated	1 mg. P/100 ml./60′	2.8–8.6 units
King-Armstrong	phenylphosphate	mg. phenol liberated	1 mg. phenol/100 ml./30′	3–13 units
Bessey-Lowry-Brock	p-nitrophenyl-phosphate	mM p-nitrophenol liberated	1 mM p-nitrophenol/100 ml./30′	1.8X Bodansky units

* Modified from Gutman (1959).

Table 12–6. Conditions in Which the Serum Alkaline Phosphatase Level Is Increased*

HEPATOBILIARY DISEASE		BONE DISEASE		OTHER CONDITIONS	
Obstructive jaundice	↑↑↑	Osteitis deformans	↑↑↑	Healing fractures	↑
Biliary cirrhosis	↑↑↑	Rickets	↑↑	Normal growth	↑
Cholangiolitic hepatitis	↑↑↑	Osteomalacia	↑↑	Pregnancy (last trimester)	↑
Occlusion of one hepatic duct	↑↑↑	Hyperparathyroidism	↑↑		
Space-occyping lesions	↑↑	Metastatic bone disease			
(granuloma, abscess, metastatic carcinoma)					
Viral hepatitis	↑				
Infectious mononucleosis	↑				
Cirrhosis	↑				

Depressed Values
Hypophosphatasia
Malnutrition
* Degree of increase indicated by number of arrows.

demonstrated in the urine in 1925, was found to be much more prevalent in male than in female urine. It was soon shown that prostatic tissue contains this enzyme in high concentration. Another acid phosphatase, distinguishable from that found in the prostate, is present in erythrocytes and platelets. The methods used for determination of acid phosphatase are similar to and include the same substrates as those used for alkaline phosphatase assay.

Elevated serum levels of acid phosphatase are seen in patients with prostatic carcinoma that has metastasized. One-half to three-fourths of patients with carcinoma of the prostate that has extended beyond the capsule have elevated acid phosphatase levels. Patients with prostatic carcinoma still confined within the capsule usually have normal serum levels of this enzyme. However, patients with benign prostatic hypertrophy may have slight elevations of the serum acid phosphatase level after vigorous prostatic "massage." Since other tissues, such as erythrocytes, may also release acid phosphatase into the serum, minor elevations of enzyme levels may reflect such an origin rather than the prostate. Accordingly efforts have been made to distinguish "prostatic" acid phosphatase from enzymes of erythrocyte and other origin. The efforts to distinguish "prostatic" acid phosphatase from erythrocyte acid phosphatase have been based on the differential effect of various inhibitors on enzymes from these two sources (Table 12–7). Such efforts do not appear to be necessary when the apparently specific method of Bodansky (beta-glycerophosphate as substrate) is used (Woodard, 1959). When the King-Armstrong method (phenylphosphate as substrate) is used, and

Table 12–7. Effect of Inhibitors on Acid Phosphatase of Prostate and Other Tissues*

INHIBITOR	INHIBITION OF PROSTATIC PHOSPHATASE	INHIBITION OF ERYTHROCYTE PHOSPHATASE
Ethyl alcohol 40%	+	−
L(+)−Tartaric acid acid 0.02 M	+	−
Formaldehyde 2%	−	+
Cupric sulfate 0.001 M	−	+

* + represents marked inhibition
− represents minimal inhibition

particularly when the acid phosphatase levels are only slightly elevated, the use of inhibitors may be of assistance. The inhibition of prostatic acid phosphatase by tartrate and the lack of inhibition by cupric ion, compared to the lack of inhibition of erythrocyte acid phosphatase by tartrate and the inhibition by cupric ion, are the properties most commonly utilized (Table 12–7).

Elevations of the serum acid phosphatase using the method of Bodansky usually reflect carcinoma of the prostate (as discussed previously), especially if the levels exceed 5 Bodansky units. When the method of Gutman (1959) (phenylphosphate as substrate) or the King-Armstrong method is used, other diseases may yield abnormal levels occasionally. Such elevations are frequent in Gaucher's disease and occasional in osteitis deformans.

Acid phosphatase determination has been useful in detecting metastases from carcinoma of the prostate. As a diagnostic clue to the presence of resectable carcinoma of the prostate, however, it is of no value.

Transaminases

The application of the serum transaminases to the study of hepatic disease and the principles of assay for these enzymes are discussed in Chapter 11. Glutamic oxaloacetic transaminase (GOT) levels of the serum are elevated in patients with hepatobiliary disease, cardiovascular disease, muscle disease, and some miscellaneous conditions. Glutamic pyruvic transaminase (GPT) levels are elevated in the serum of patients with hepatic disease. In other conditions elevations are negligible unless there is hepatic involvement.

Glutamic Oxaloacetic Transaminase. This enzyme is elevated in diseases involving the tissues that are rich in it. In Table 12–8 are also shown the tissues with the highest GOT concentration and the categories of disease that may show abnormal levels. The GOT levels in patients with disease of the liver are discussed in Chapter 11 and in Table 11–14 and Fig. 11–10 of that chapter.

Extensive studies have shown that 92 to 98 per cent of patients with acute myocardial infarction have elevated serum GOT levels, which are usually four to ten times the upper limit of normal. These develop 6 to 12 hours after the time of infarction, usually returning to normal by the third or fourth day (Fig. 12–1). Secondary rises can be correlated with other features, suggesting extension or recurrence of myocardial infarction. Experimental work with animals suggests that the degree of rise of serum GOT is related to the extent of myocardial necrosis. This has been difficult to prove in patients.

In patients with electrocardiographic and clinical criteria of "coronary insufficiency," rather than myocardial infarction, elevated serum GOT levels may occur. It is not clear whether this represents myocardial necrosis, which has not been recognizable by other means, or "leakage" of the enzyme into the serum even without frank myocardial necrosis. Nevertheless for treatment purposes we have considered such patients to have sustained a myocardial infarction.

Mild elevations of the serum GOT levels have been reported in patients with pulmonary infarction. The incidence has varied from 0 to 30 per cent and the elevations are slight to moderate. Animal studies also have yielded inconclusive results on the occurrence of elevated serum GOT levels in experimental pulmonary infarction.

In patients with congestive heart failure and in those with marked tachycardia mild to moderate degrees of GOT elevation may occur. These have been attributed to the hepatic necrosis secondary to hepatic congestion. Patients with pericarditis also have been reported to have a 50 per cent incidence of moderately elevated GOT levels. The incidence and mechanism of occurrence of elevated enzyme levels in patients with rheumatic fever are not clear. Slight serum

Table 12–8. Tissues Rich in GOT and Conditions in Which the Serum Enzyme Is Abnormal*

A. Tissue content of GOT (descending order of concentration)

   1. cardiac
   2. hepatic
   3. skeletal muscle
   4. kidney
   5. brain
   6. pancreas
   7. spleen
   8. lung
   9. serum

B. Conditions in which serum GOT is elevated

   1. *Cardiac disease*
     myocardial infarction
     pericarditis
     cardiac arrhythmias
     acute rheumatic fever (?)
     postcardiac surgery and catheterization
     heart failure

   2. *Hepatic disease*
     acute hepatitis (viral, toxic, infectious mononucleosis)
     cirrhosis
     hepatic congestion
     space-occupying lesions (granuloma, metastatic carcinoma)
     obstructive jaundice

   3. *Other diseases*
     pulmonary infarction
     acute pancreatitis
     renal infarction (experimental animals)
     cerebral necrosis
     dermatomyositis
     progressive muscular dystrophy
     delirium tremens
     hemolysis (slight)
     gangrene (slight)

C. Conditions in which serum GOT is depressed

   1. Pregnancy (abnormal pyridoxal metabolism)

* In acute hepatitis, values above 300 units are usual. In all the other conditions shown the levels are usually below this value. Almost all patients with acute myocardial infarction have elevated values during the first few days. In the other cardiac diseases listed, elevations are less frequent and usually are slight.

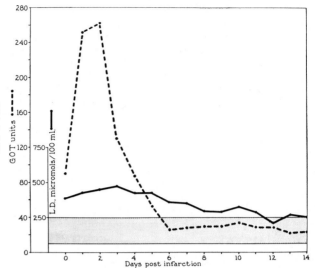

Figure 12–1. GOT and L.D. levels after myocardial infarction (mean of values for 35 patients). Note that the GOT rise is greater but more transient than that of L.D. Day "0" is the day of infarction.

GOT elevations have been reported after cardiac catheterization and mitral commissurotomy.

Glutamic oxaloacetic transaminase determination is not necessary for the diagnosis of myocardial infarction in most patients with classical clinical and electrocardiographic evidence of this condition. This determination is of value in patients whose electrocardiographic changes are insufficiently helpful, e.g., those with left bundle branch block or Wolfe-Parkinson-White syndrome or in those with electrocardiographic abnormalities remaining from previous infarction, which may obscure acute changes. Determination of this serum enzyme is also of value in recognizing the recurrence or extension of an infarction during convalescence. Normal values obtained at the proper time are of value in excluding a diagnosis of myocardial infarction.

Patients with disease or injury producing inflammation or destruction of skeletal muscle also may have elevated serum GOT levels. Patients with progressive muscular dystrophy, dermatomyositis, and trichinosis may have elevated levels, while those with amyotrophic lateral sclerosis, myasthenia gravis, and nerve section do not manifest elevated serum GOT levels. Gangrene of the extremities and surgical or other trauma may produce slight GOT elevations. In patients with cerebrovascular accidents serum GOT elevations have been inconstantly reported.

Elevated serum GOT levels in patients with hepatic disease are discussed in Chapter 11. In acute pancreatitis both normal and elevated levels have been reported. It has been suggested that obstruction of the biliary tree by the edematous pancreas and the presence of associated hepatic disease or of delirium tremens may contribute to the elevated GOT levels in these patients.

Glutamic Pyruvic Transaminase (GPT). This enzyme is also discussed in Chapter 11. In patients with myocardial infarction elevations of the serum levels of GPT are slight or absent. Heart failure or shock with the attendant hepatic necrosis may lead to elevated GPT levels. The chief application of determination of this serum enzyme is in the diagnosis of hepatobiliary disease.

Glycolytic Enzymes

A number of enzymes involved in glycolysis have been demonstrated in the serum (Figs. 12–2 to 12–8). Several of these enzymes were first shown to be in the serum by Warburg and Christian. These authors suggested that the excessive glycolysis, which Warburg had found to be characteristic of neoplastic tissue, would be reflected in increased serum levels of the glycolytic enzymes in animals and humans bearing tumors. A number of subsequent reports have confirmed their observation. In patients with extensive carcinoma elevated levels of several of these enzymes (phosphohexose isomerase, aldolase, and lactic dehydrogenase) have been observed. These elevations have served as a guide to chemotherapy, particularly in carcinoma of the breast and prostate.

Elevated levels of these enzymes also have been observed in patients with megaloblastic and hemolytic anemias and in granulocytic and acute leukemias but not in patients with chronic lymphocytic leukemia, aplastic anemia, or iron deficiency anemias. Aldolase and "isomerase" levels are high in patients with acute viral or toxic hepatitis, but lactic dehydrogenase levels are only slightly to moderately elevated in these patients. Other glycolytic enzymes (phosphoglucomutase, fructose-6-aldolase), which have been demonstrated in the serum, require further study for clear delineation of their value as reflections of particular disease entities.

Phosphohexose Isomerase (PHI). This glycolytic enzyme catalyzes the conversion of glucose-6-phosphate to fructose-6-phosphate (Figs. 12–2, 12–4). First studied in the serum of tumorous rats by Warburg and Christian, PHI levels of the serum have been investigated in patients with carcinoma and other diseases during the past few years.

The activity of PHI is assayed by using glucose-6-phosphate as substrate. The rate of formation of fructose-6-phosphate using the Seliwanoff reaction (resorcinol) is a measure of PHI activity. No standard unit of activity has been agreed upon, although several have been suggested.

Phosphohexose isomerase levels have been used as an index of metastases in patients with carcinoma of the breast and prostate and to monitor the response to therapy. Other diseases in which elevations are observed are listed in Table 12–1 and Fig. 12–2. Determination of this serum enzyme, however, has not been applied extensively to clinical medicine. Reference to Table 12–1 and Fig. 12–4 may be of assistance in contemplated clinical applications of this procedure.

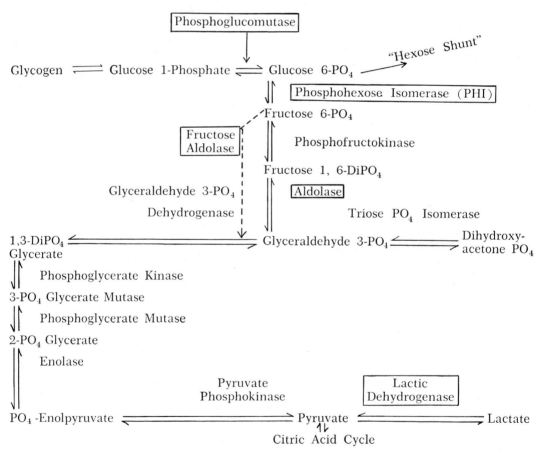

Figure 12–2.   Scheme of glycolytic pathway of carbohydrate metabolism. Enzymes demonstrated in human serum are shown in boxes.

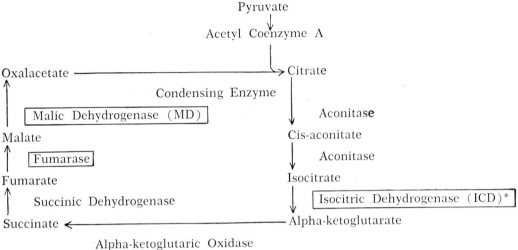

THE TRICARBOXYLIC ACID CYCLE

Pyruvate

Acetyl Coenzyme A

Oxalacetate ——————————————→ Citrate

Condensing Enzyme

Malic Dehydrogenase (MD)   Aconitase

Malate   Cis-aconitate

Fumarase   Aconitase

Fumarate   Isocitrate

Succinic Dehydrogenase   Isocitric Dehydrogenase (ICD)*

Succinate ←——————————————— Alpha-ketoglutarate

Alpha-ketoglutaric Oxidase

* Strictly speaking, the ICD of the serum differs from that of the citric acid cycle. The ICD demonstrated in the serum is TPN-linked, while that of the citric acid cycle is DPN-linked.

Figure 12-3. Scheme of citric acid cycle pathway of carbohydrate metabolism. Enzymes demonstrated in human serum are shown in boxes.

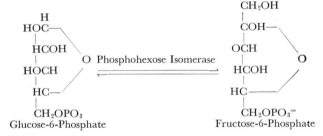

Glucose-6-Phosphate   Fructose-6-Phosphate

Figure 12-4. Reaction catalyzed by phosphohexose isomerase, principle of method used for assay, and list of some of the diseases showing abnormal levels.

Method is based on measurement of product. Fructose-6-phosphate plus resorcinol yields a colored compound; the intensity of the color is measured.
Conditions characterized by abnormal levels (the listing in each category is in the order of decreasing incidence or degree of abnormality):

A. HEPATIC DISEASE ABNORMALITIES

Hepatic necrosis
Viral hepatitis
CCl$_4$ poisoning

Infectious mononucleosis
Cirrhosis
Metastatic carcinoma
Obstructive jaundice

B. OTHER ABNORMALITIES

Myocardial infarction
Chronic granulocytic leukemia
Muscular dystrophy (progressive)
Hemolysis
Carcinoma metastatic to sites other than liver

Aldolase (Fig. 12–5). This glycolytic enzyme catalyzes the cleavage of fructose-l-6-diphosphate into two triose molecules (glyceraldehyde phosphate and dihydroxyacetone phosphate).

Methods. Several methods have been devised for this assay, based on the rate at which the trioses are formed. This is determined by forming the colored dinitrophenylhydrazone.

Elevated values of serum aldolase are observed in the diseases shown in Table 12–1 and Fig. 12–5.

Serum aldolase determination has been applied to the study of neoplastic disease, as indicated previously. Marked elevations are frequent in patients with hepatic necrosis, granulocytic leukemia, myocardial infarction, skeletal muscle necrosis, and other conditions listed in Fig. 12–5. Determination of the level of this serum enzyme has been primarily for purposes of clinical investigation rather than for routine application to clinical problems.

Lactic Dehydrogenase (L.D.). This enzyme catalyzes the reversible oxidation of lactic to pyruvic acid (Figs. 12–2, 12–6). It is widely distributed in mammalian tissues,

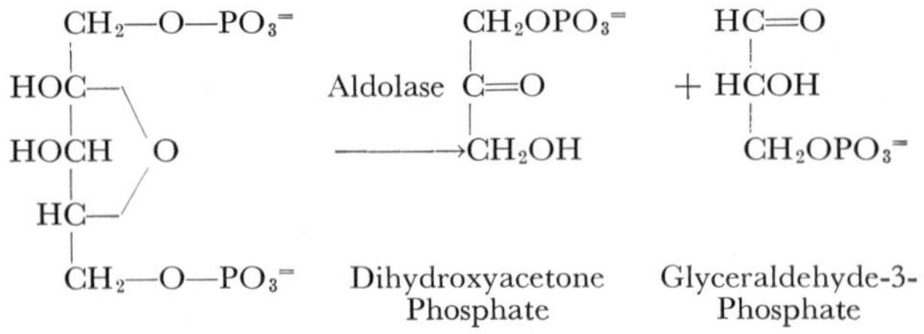

$$CH_2\!-\!O\!-\!PO_3^= \qquad CH_2OPO_3^= \qquad HC\!=\!O$$
$$HOC\!-\!\qquad Aldolase\ \ C\!=\!O \qquad +\ HCOH$$
$$HOCH\ \ O \qquad \longrightarrow CH_2OH \qquad CH_2OPO_3^=$$
$$HC\!-\!$$
$$CH_2\!-\!O\!-\!PO_3^= \qquad \substack{\text{Dihydroxyacetone}\\ \text{Phosphate}} \qquad \substack{\text{Glyceraldehyde-3-}\\ \text{Phosphate}}$$

Figure 12–5. Reaction catalyzed by "aldolase," principle of method used for assay, and list of some of the diseases showing abnormal levels.

Method is based on measurement of product. Products of reaction plus dinitrophenylhydrazine yield a dinitrophenylhydrazone with a characteristic color, the intensity of which can be measured.

Conditions characterized by abnormal levels (the listing in each category is in the order of decreasing incidence or degree of abnormality):

A. HEPATIC DISEASE ABNORMALITIES

    Hepatic necrosis
      Hepatitis
      CCl₄ poisoning
      Infectious mononucleosis

    Obstructive jaundice
    Cirrhosis
    Metastatic carcinoma

B. OTHER ABNORMALITIES

    Leukemia
    Pneumonia
    Acute pancreatitis
    Delirium tremens
    Myocardial infarction
    Skeletal muscle necrosis
    Myxedema
    Megaloblastic anemia

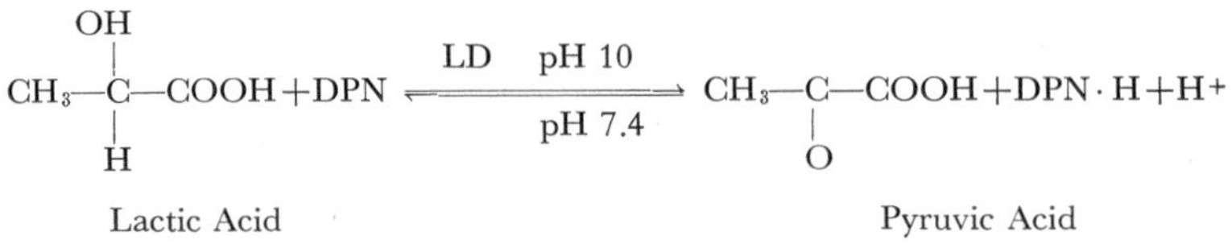

$$\begin{array}{c} OH \\ | \\ CH_3\!-\!C\!-\!COOH + DPN \end{array} \underset{pH\ 7.4}{\overset{LD\quad pH\ 10}{\rightleftharpoons}} \begin{array}{c} \\ \\ CH_3\!-\!C\!-\!COOH + DPN\cdot H + H^+ \\ | \\ O \end{array}$$

$$\substack{H}$$

Lactic Acid   Pyruvic Acid

Figure 12–6. Reaction catalyzed by lactic dehydrogenase, principle of two chief methods of assay, and list of some of the diseases showing abnormal levels.

Method is based on changes in state of coenzyme. At a pH of 10 enzyme activity is assayed by measuring the appearance of DPN•H. At a pH of 7.4 enzyme activity is measured by measuring the disappearance of DPN•H.

Conditions characterized by abnormal levels (the listing is in the order of decreasing incidence or degree of abnormality):

  1. *Hematologic Diseases*
      Megaloblastic anemia
      Sickle-cell anemia
      Severe hemolytic crisis
      Acute leukemia, chronic granulocytic leukemia

  2. *Cardiac Diseases*
      Myocardial infarction
      Congestive heart failure

  3. *Hepatic Diseases*
      Metastatic carcinoma
      Hepatitis
      Cirrhosis
      Obstructive jaundice

  4. *Other Conditions*
      Delirium tremens
      Progressive muscular dystrophy
      Renal disease
      Carcinoma
      Growth
      Infectious mononucleosis
      Myxedema

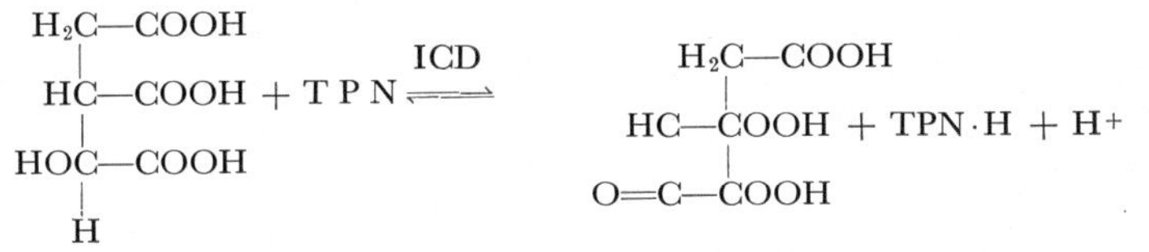

$$\begin{array}{c} H_2C\!-\!COOH \\ | \\ HC\!-\!COOH \\ | \\ HOC\!-\!COOH \\ | \\ H \end{array} + T\,P\,N \xrightarrow{\;\;ICD\;\;} \begin{array}{c} H_2C\!-\!COOH \\ | \\ HC\!-\!COOH \\ | \\ O\!=\!C\!-\!COOH \end{array} + TPN\!\cdot\!H + H^+$$

Figure 12–7. Reaction catalyzed by isocitric dehydrogenase and principle of method of assay.

Method is based on change in state of coenzyme. Rate of appearance of TPN•H is measured spectrophotometrically.

Abnormal levels are most characteristic of acute hepatitis. Lower and less frequent are the abnormal levels in patients with metastatic carcinoma.

being rich in myocardium, kidney, liver, and muscle.

Methods. Spectrophotometric and colorimetric methods have been applied to the assay of this enzyme. In the spectrophotometric method the rate of change in concentration of DPNH is determined. The reaction may be measured by following the disappearance of DPNH (pyruvate + DPNH $\xrightarrow{\text{L.D.}}$ lactate + DPN) at a pH of 7.4 or by following the appearance of DPNH (lactate + DPN $\xrightarrow{\text{L.D.}}$ pyruvate + DPNH) at a pH of 10. The results have been expressed as units or as micromols of DPN altered.

Serum L.D. elevations are observed in patients with myocardial infarction, extensive carcinomatosis, megaloblastic anemia, granulocytic and acute leukemia, and sickle cell anemia. Only slight to moderate elevations are seen in patients with hepatic disease. Growing children have been reported to have higher levels than adults. Early reports of elevated levels in pregnancy have not been supported by more recent studies.

The pattern of serum L.D. elevation in myocardial infarction is quite characteristic. Elevated levels are observed in almost all patients within a few hours of the occurrence of infarction. Although the degree of elevation is not so striking as in the case of GOT, the elevated levels persist for a longer period (10 to 14 days) (Fig. 12–1). Several authors have emphasized the value of L.D. determination in the diagnosis of myocardial infarction. Although the occurrence of elevated levels in the other diseases just listed and shown in Table 12–1 and Fig. 12–6 are of interest, there has been no widespread clinical application of serum L.D. assay.

"Citric Acid Cycle" Enzymes

Several of the enzymes identified in the serum have been considered to be citric acid cycle enzymes (Figs. 12–3, 12–7, 12–8) released into the blood. Although they are

shown as such in this discussion, this concept is currently being revised. Enzymes of the citric acid cycle are "particulate," being located in the mitochondria, and are less likely to enter the blood than the "soluble" cytoplasmic enzymes. Furthermore the isocitric dehydrogenase (ICD) (Fig. 12–7) found in the serum requires TPN as the coenzyme, while the citric acid cycle ICD is a DPN-linked enzyme. Malic dehydrogenase activity has been demonstrated in the cytoplasm and mitochondria. Fumarase appears to be a mitochondrial enzyme.

Isocitric dehydrogenase (ICD) (Fig. 12–7) has been reported to be a sensitive measure of hepatic disease, being increased up to 40-fold in the serum of patients with hepatic necrosis but much less elevated or normal in patients with obstructive jaundice and cirrhosis. We have observed distinct elevations of the level of this serum enzyme in metastatic carcinoma (to liver and perhaps bone).

Malic dehydrogenase (Fig. 12–8) levels

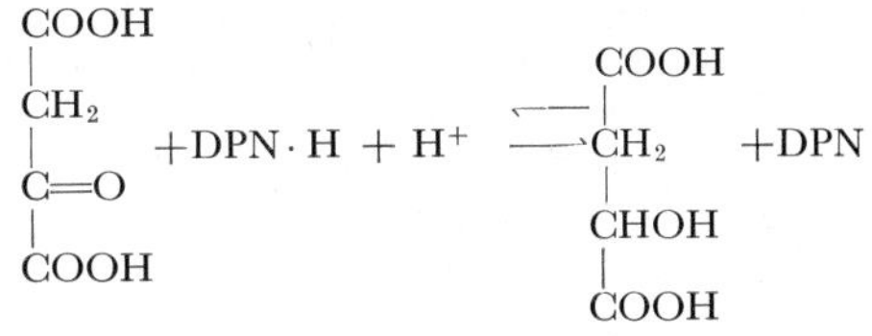

$$\begin{array}{c} COOH \\ | \\ CH_2 \\ | \\ C\!=\!O \\ | \\ COOH \end{array} + DPN\!\cdot\!H + H^+ \xrightleftharpoons \begin{array}{c} COOH \\ | \\ CH_2 \\ | \\ CHOH \\ | \\ COOH \end{array} + DPN$$

Oxaloacetic Acid   Malic Acid

Figure 12–8. Reaction catalyzed by malic dehydrogenase, principle of method of assay, and some of the diseases showing abnormal levels.

Method is based on change in state of coenzyme. Rate of disappearance of DPN•H is measured spectrophotometrically.

Conditions characterized by abnormal levels; the listing is in the tentative order of decreasing degree or incidence of abnormality.

Acute hepatitis
Megaloblastic anemia
Myocardial infarction
Metastatic carcinoma
Hemolytic anemia
Cirrhosis
Myocardial infarction

of the serum are elevated in patients with metastatic carcinoma, myocardial infarction, hepatic necrosis, hemolytic anemia, and megaloblastic anemia. *Fumarase* levels have been reported to be elevated in patients with hepatic necrosis. The clinical usefulness of the enzymes in this group remains to be established.

Hexose "Shunt" Enzymes

Several of the enzymes of the hexose monophosphate shunt have been demonstrated in the serum. Reports have appeared on the occurrence of elevated serum levels of glucose-6-phosphate dehydrogenase and of 6-phosphogluconic dehydrogenase in patients with hepatic disease. The clinical significance and applicability of assay of these serum enzymes remain to be established.

Other Serum Enzymes

Many other enzymes have been demonstrated in the serum (Table 12–1). These are too numerous for individual description in this discussion, but there are a few that warrant special mention. These include ornithine carbamyl transferase, an enzyme that has been reported to reflect, sensitively and specifically, hepatic disease; plasma pepsinogen, an enzyme precursor that reflects function and disease of the stomach (high levels in patients with peptic ulcer, low levels in patients with pernicious anemia); ceruloplasmin, a copper-carrying protein that is also an enzyme and the serum levels of which are depressed in patients with hepatolenticular degeneration (Wilson's disease); and the other enzymes listed in Table 12–1. The possible clinical significance of these enzyme determinations is shown in that table.

POSSIBLE CAUSES FOR ABNORMAL LEVELS OF SERUM ENZYMES

There are several theoretical mechanisms by which serum enzyme levels might be increased (Table 12–9).

Tissues that have normal enzyme content may release several of the enzymes upon undergoing necrosis or an alteration of cell permeability. Thus, elevations of serum levels of amylase, lipase, trypsin, leucine aminopeptidase, and deoxyribonuclease have been reported in patients with acute pancreatitis. Similarly in hepatitis and in myocardial infarction a number of enzymes found in the liver and myocardium appear to be released into the blood in abnormal amounts.

Tissues with increased enzyme concentration also may contribute to increased levels of the respective serum enzyme; e.g., rapidly growing tissues (carcinoma and embryonic tissue) have an abnormal carbohydrate metabolism characterized by an increased rate of glycolysis. Glycolytic enzymes have been found in increased concentration in some neoplasms. It has been postulated that the high glycolytic activity of neoplastic tissue is the basis for the elevated levels of some of the glycolytic enzymes (phosphohexose isomerase, aldolase, lactic dehydrogenase).

Impaired excretion may explain elevations of serum amylase in patients with renal failure and of the transaminases in patients with obstructive jaundice.

Lower than normal levels of some serum enzymes may also be observed, presumably because of impaired synthesis. Examples of this state include the depressed serum cholinesterase levels that are characteristic of chronic liver disease and the depressed serum alkaline phosphatase level observed in the inborn error of metabolism entitled hypophosphatasia.

The clinical value of serum enzyme determination is summarized in Table 12–10. (The section in the chapter on liver function tests relating to the application of serum enzymes in liver disease should be read in conjunction with this material.) There is widespread and routine clinical application of determination of serum amylase levels in the diagnosis of acute pancreatitis, of alkaline phosphatase levels in the recognition of bone and hepatobiliary disease, of acid phosphatase levels in the diagnosis of disseminated prostatic carcinoma, and of GOT levels in the diagnosis of cardiac and hepatic disease. Of value but less widely applied is the determination of GPT activity in the recognition of hepatobiliary disease and of levels of the glycolytic enzymes, which have a limited application to the diagnosis and management of neoplastic disease. The results obtained with a number of other serum enzymes in various disease states are summarized in Table 12–1. In Table 12–11 the combinations of enzyme abnormalities that may be expected in various diseases are shown. The application of serum enzyme activity to clinical problems is being studied

Table 12–9.   Hypothetical Mechanisms for Enzyme Abnormalities

HYPOTHETICAL MECHANISM	EXAMPLE	ENZYMES	REMARKS
1. Elevated Serum Enzyme Levels			
A. Cellular necrosis or increased cell membrane permeability	Myocardial infarction	Phosphohexose isomerase Aldolase Lactic dehydrogenase Malic dehydrogenase Ribonuclease Glutamic oxaloacetic transaminase	
	Hepatitis	Phosphoglucomutase Phosphohexose isomerase Aldolase Lactic dehydrogenase 6-Phosphogluconic dehydrogenase Malic dehydrogenase Fumarase Isocitric dehydrogenase β-Glucuronidase Alkaline phosphatase 5-Nucleotidase Adenosine triphosphatase Deoxyribonuclease Leucine aminopeptidase Amino tripeptidase Glutamic oxaloacetic transaminase Glutamic pyruvic transaminase Glutathione reductase Arginase Ornithine carbamyl transferase	The elevated alkaline phosphatase levels may also represent increased enzyme production by the liver as well as impaired biliary excretion.
	Progressive muscular dystrophy	Glutamic oxaloacetic transferase Glutamic pyruvic transaminase Phosphohexose isomerase Aldolase Lactic dehydrogenase	
B. Increased enzyme content of cells or tissues	Neoplastic tissue	Members of glycolytic cycle (aldolase, isomerase, lactic dehydrogenase)	
	Osteoblastic bone disease, i.e., Paget's disease	Alkaline phosphatase Adenosine triphosphatase	
C. Impaired excretion of enzyme	Uremia Obstructive jaundice	Amylase Phosphoglucomutase Phosphohexose isomerase 5-Phosphoriboisomerase Malic dehydrogenase Fumarase Alkaline phosphatase 5-Nucleotidase Adenosine triphosphatase Peptidases Glutamic oxaloacetic transaminase Glutamic pyruvic transaminase	
D. Unknown factors	Megaloblastic anemia	Lactic dehydrogenase Malic dehydrogenase 6-Phosphogluconic dehydrogenase Aldolase Isomerase	May be the result of increased enzyme content of precursor cells or of increased destruction and production of precursor cells
	Leukemia	Lactic dehydrogenase Aldolase Isomerase Ribonuclease	

Table 9 *(continued)*

HYPOTHETICAL MECHANISM	EXAMPLE	ENZYMES	REMARKS
2. Depressed Serum Enzyme Levels			
A. Decreased formation of enzyme	Hepatitis	Cholinesterase Cholesterol esterase	
B. Lack of cofactors (?)	Pregnancy	Transaminases	Possible defect in pyroxidine metabolism

Table 12–10. Serum Enzyme Determinations in Common Use

ENZYME	HELPFUL IN THE DIAGNOSIS OF:
Amylase	Pancreatic disease
Lipase	Pancreatic disease
GOT	Hepatic disease, myocardial infarction, muscle disease
GPT	Hepatic disease
Alkaline phosphatase	Hepatobiliary and bone disease
Acid phosphatase	Prostatic carcinoma

in many laboratories. It may be expected that this field will undergo considerable change during the next few years.

ENZYMES OF THE FORMED ELEMENTS OF THE BLOOD

During the past few years considerable attention has been devoted to the metabolic activity and enzyme content of erythrocytes, leukocytes, and platelets. In this brief summary the broad outlines of the work will

Table 12–11. Patterns of Enzyme Abnormality in Disease*

	AMYLASE	ALK. PHOSPH.	ACID PHOSPH.	CHOLIN-ESTERASE	GOT	GPT	L.D.	ALD.	PHI	ICD
Acute Pancreatitis	↑↑↑	N, ↑	N	N	N, ↑	N, ↑	N, ↑	N, ↑	N, ↑	N
Myocardial Infarction	N	N	N	↓	↑↑	N	↑	↑	↑	N
Hepatitis	N, ↓	↑	N	↓	↑↑↑↑	↑↑↑↑	↑, N	↑↑↑	↑↑↑	↑↑↑
Obstructive Jaundice	N	↑↑↑	N	N, ↓	↑↑	↑↑	↑, N	↑	↑	↑
Metastatic Carcinoma										
Liver	N	↑↑↑	N	N, ↓	↑↑	↑↑	↑↑	↑↑	↑↑	↑
Bone	N	↑↑†	N†	N, ↓	N	N	↑↑	↑↑	↑↑	↑
Elsewhere	N	N	N	N	N	N	↑	↑	↑	—
Megaloblastic Anemia	N	N	N	↓	N	N	↑↑↑	↑↑↑	↑↑↑	↑
Granulocytic Leukemia	N	N	N	N, ↓	N, ↑	N, ↑	↑↑	↑↑	↑↑	—
Lymphocytic Leukemia	N	N	N	N, ↓	N, ↑	N, ↑	N	N	N	—
Progressive Muscular Dystrophy	N	N	N	N	↑	N	↑, N	↑↑↑	↑	—

* Direction of arrows indicates direction of change; number of arrows indicates magnitude of change.

N = no change

† Alkaline phosphatase levels are elevated in osteoblastic metastases. Acid phosphatase levels are elevated in metastases from prostatic carcinoma.

be described and the few areas of clinical application mentioned.

Erythrocyte Enzymes

A large number of enzymes have been demonstrated in the mammalian erythrocyte. Most of the studies related to the metabolism and enzymatic machinery of the human red blood cell have been of investigative interest rather than being suited to immediate clinical application. Assay of enzymes related to galactose metabolism has been found to be of value in the diagnosis of galactosemia, and the study of one of the "hexose shunt" enzymes has been shown to be of value in the recognition of the genetically-determined, drug-induced hemolytic anemias.

Galactosemia is an inborn error of metabolism characterized by a specific defect in the utilization of galactose, which results in widespread tissue damage. The defect has been found to be deficiency of the enzyme phosphogalactose-uridyl-transferase. The resulting accumulation of galactose-1-phosphate is considered responsible for the development of cataracts, liver disease, renal disease, and other abnormalities. Although the most important site of the biochemical lesion is, of course, the liver, the hereditary enzyme deficiency can be demonstrated by studying the erythrocyte. Accordingly a clinically feasible test for the diagnosis of galactosemia has been introduced.

A genetic defect in erythrocyte metabolism has been found to be responsible for an unusual susceptibility to drug-induced hemolytic anemia in some individuals. Recognition of this inborn error is facilitated by demonstrating the reduced concentration of glucose-6-phosphate dehydrogenase in the erythrocyte. For other means of studying this phenomenon, the publications of Altman (1959), Beutler (1959), Marks and Gross (1959), and Szeinberg, Sheba, and Adams (1958) should be consulted.

Leukocyte Enzymes

The study of leukocyte enzymes has been hampered somewhat by the difficulty of freeing leukocytes from contaminating platelets. Nevertheless histochemical and biochemical studies have revealed data of interest on the alkaline phosphatase content as well as the activity of other enzymes of the leukocyte. The leukocyte alkaline phosphatase determination has proved of some limited clinical application. The leukocytes of patients with chronic myelocytic leukemia and chronic lymphocytic leukemia contain considerably lower than normal concentrations of alkaline phosphatase, while the leukocytes of patients with nonleukemic leukocytosis and myeloproliferative disease have higher than normal concentrations of the enzyme.

Platelet Enzymes

The enzymatic machinery of the platelet has been studied in only a preliminary fashion. No clinically practical applications are as yet available.

ENZYME CONCENTRATION IN OTHER BODY FLUIDS

Measurement of enzyme activity in the urine, serous effusions, cerebrospinal fluid, and gastrointestinal juices has been applied to the diagnosis of various diseases.

The application of urine amylase determination to the diagnosis of pancreatic disease has been supplanted in most laboratories by serum amylase measurement (see Chapter 13). Likewise determination of urinary pepsinogen levels as a diagnostic aid to the recognition of pernicious anemia or of peptic ulcer has been considered unreliable by many workers. It has been replaced in some laboratories by measurement of the plasma pepsinogen level.

Determination of the levels of lactic dehydrogenase in serous cavity effusions has recently been proposed as a method of demonstrating neoplastic involvement of the serosal surface. In such circumstances the serous fluid usually shows higher levels of L.D. than does the serum. Rarely, nonneoplastic effusions (e.g., tuberculosis) may show this phenomenon. The basis for the elevated L.D. is presumably the abnormally high glycolytic activity of the neoplastic cells. The clinical value of this promising diagnostic adjunct remains to be established by further studies.

Cerebrospinal fluid enzyme levels are relatively independent of the serum levels. Increased spinal fluid levels of glutamic oxaloacetic transaminase, lactic dehydrogenase, ribonuclease, and glutathione reductase have been described in patients with various diseases of the central nervous system. The levels of one or more of these enzymes are increased in patients with cerebrovascular hemorrhage, thrombus or embolism, meningitis, and neoplasms of the central nervous system. The clinical application and value of spinal fluid enzyme determination remain to be established.

METHODS

The principles of enzyme assay in general and of a number of serum enzymes in particular have been discussed in the body of this chapter. Details of the methods for the assay of the transaminases and phosphatases will be described in this section. Details of the amylase and lipase determination are discussed in Chapter 13.

Alkaline and Acid Phosphatase Determination

Method. Bodansky (1933).

Principle. The various methods available for phosphatase determination depend on the measurement of one of the products of hydrolysis of phosphate-monoesters. The method of Bodansky depends on the liberation of inorganic phosphate from beta-glycerophosphate. Alkaline phosphatase activity is determined by incubating serum with the substrate, β-glycerophosphate, at a pH of 9.0. After incubation the amount of inorganic phosphorus liberated is determined by the Fiske-Subarrow method. The degree of activity is expressed in Bodansky units. One Bodansky unit corresponds to the liberation of 1 mg. of inorganic phosphorus per 100 ml. serum per hour at 37° C. Acid phosphatase is determined by the same method but at a pH of 5.0 The normal limits are 1 to 4 units for alkaline phosphatase and 1 to 2 units for acid phosphatase.

Material. Serum.

Reagents

1. Substrate.

    a. For alkaline phosphatase determination: Into a 1000 ml. volumetric flask place successively 20 ml. of petroleum ether, 800 ml. of water, 5.0 gm. of sodium β-glycerophosphate, and 4.24 gm. of sodium diethyl barbiturate. After the material has dissolved, dilute with water to 1000 ml., reading at the ether-water interphase. Check the pH, which should be 9.0. Transfer (under the hood) to bottles containing about 1 inch of petroleum ether and use a glass stopper. It is advisable to store this reagent in several small bottles rather than in one large one.

    b. For acid phosphatase determination: This is similar to the alkaline phosphatase substrate. After adding the petroleum ether, 800 ml. of water, 5.0 gm. of sodium β-glycerophosphate, and 4.24 gm. of sodium diethylbarbiturate, 50 ml. of acetic acid should be introduced. After these components have dissolved, dilute the solution to 1000 ml., reading at the water-ether interphase.

2. 10 per cent trichloracetic acid solution.

3. Reagents for inorganic phosphorus determination.

    a. Trichloracetic acid, 5 per cent aqueous solution.

    b. Sulfuric acid, 10 N.

    c. Molybdate solution. Add 200 ml. of 12.5 per cent ammonium molybdate solution to 300 ml. 10 N sulfuric acid. Dilute to 1 liter with distilled water.

    d. Aminonaphtholsulfonic acid reagent. Add 0.5 gm. of 1,2,4-aminoaphtholsulfonic acid to 195 ml. of 15 per cent sodium bisulfite solution followed by 5 ml. of 20 per cent sodium sulfite. Shake until the powder is dissolved. Store in brown glass bottle in the cold. This solution may be used for one month.

    e. Standard phosphate solution for preparation of standard "curve" or to compare with "unknowns."

Procedure

1. Add 4.5 ml. of the substrate to each of two test tubes and place in 37° C. water bath for ten minutes.

2. To one of these tubes add 0.5 ml. of serum and to the other, 0.5 ml. of water to serve as a blank. After mixing, place in 37° C. water bath for exactly one hour. Place the tubes in an ice bath for five minutes and add 5.0 ml. of 10 per cent trichloracetic acid. Mix, let stand for ten minutes, and centrifuge or filter through low-ash filter paper.

3. Preparation of serum for inorganic phosphorus determination: Add 0.5 ml. of serum to 9.5 ml. of 5 per cent trichloracetic acid. Mix, let stand for ten minutes, and centrifuge or filter through low-ash filter paper.

4. Treat filtrates from (2) and (3) as follows: Place 5.0 ml. of each into 10 ml. graduated cylinders. Add 1.0 ml. of molybdate solution and 0.4 ml. of the aminonaphtholsulfonic acid reagent. Dilute to 10 ml. with distilled water, mix, and allow to stand for five minutes. Determine the optical density in a spectrophotometer at 690 mμ. Convert the readings to mg. of inorganic phosphorus from a standard curve.

5. The phosphatase activity in mg. of inorganic phosphous liberated is the difference between the inorganic phosphorus in the serum-substrate tube (2) and in the serum (3) expressed as mg. per 100 ml. If the liberated phosphate is 60 ml. per 100 ml. or higher, the rate of hydrolysis is inhibited. Accordingly, when this occurs, the incubation should be repeated with the time shortened to 30 or 15 minutes as needed. In calculating the results, they should be multiplied by a factor of 1.8 (30 minutes) or 3.3 (15 minutes).

Glutamic-Oxaloacetic Transaminase

Method. Karmen (1955), modified by Steinberg, Baldwin, and Ostrow (1956).

Principle. The reactions involved in this assay are shown in Fig. 11–9 of Chapter 11. The spectrophotometric assay is based on the transamination of aspartic acid with α-ketoglutaric acid to form oxaloacetic and glutamic acids; the rate of formation of oxaloacetic acid is measured by reducing it to malic acid by adding exogenous malic dehydrogenase and DPNH. The rate of this reaction is measured by serial determination of the progressive decrease in concentration of DPNH in an ultraviolet spectrophotometer (340 mμ). The method of Karmen originally described for the Beckman DU spectrophotometer has been adapted to the use of a modified Bausch and Lomb spectrophotometer (Spectronic 20"). Colorimetric methods have been described by Reitman and Frankel (1957) and by Umbreit and his associates (1957).

Material. Serum.

Reagents

1. Phosphate buffer, 0.1 M, pH 7.5. Make up 13.97 gm. buffer quality anhydrous K_2HPO_4 and 2.69 gm. buffer quality anhydrous KH_2PO_4 to 1 liter with distilled water. This should be stored in the cold.

2. L-aspartic acid, sodium salt, 0.2 M. Dissolve 2.662 gm. L-aspartic acid in 70 ml. of the phosphate buffer solution (1) and adjust to a pH of 7.5 with 1 M NaOH (approximately 20 ml. required). Then dilute to 100 ml. with the phosphate buffer solution.

3. Reduced diphosphopyridine nucleotide (DPNH). Dissolve 10 mg. of $DPNH_2$ (70 per cent pure) or 7.5 mg. of $DPNH_2$ (90 per cent pure) in 10 ml. of the phosphate buffer solution (diluted 1 to 10 with buffer as in the assay procedure; the optical density [O.D.] of this solution is approximately 0.5 at 340 mμ). This should be kept frozen until used.

4. Malic dehydrogenase (M.D.). Commercial preparations of stated potency are available. A solution of the enzyme in the phosphate buffer containing 800 M.D. units per ml. should be prepared. Since diluted enzyme is less stable than undiluted enzyme, small amounts should be prepared as needed and refrigerated.

5. Alpha-ketoglutaric acid, sodium salt, 0.1 M. Dissolve 1.47 gm. of α-ketoglutaric acid in 70 ml. of the phosphate buffer and adjust the pH to 7.5 with 1 N NaOH (this requires approximately 20 ml.). The volume is then brought to 100 ml. with the phosphate buffer solution. This should be kept frozen.

Procedure

1. For each serum to be assayed, two Beckman 1 cm. cuvets are prepared as follows:

	Tube #1 (control)	Tube #2 (assay)
Aspartate 0.2 M	0.5 ml.	0.5 ml.
M.D. (800 U/ml.)	0.1 ml.	0.1 ml.
DPNH (0.75 or 1.0 mg./ml., see description)	0	0.3 ml.
Serum	0.2 ml.	0.2 ml.
Phosphate buffer, 0.1 M (pH 7.5)	2.0 ml.	1.7 ml.

2. The tube contents are mixed thoroughly and the tubes allowed to stand for 30 minutes at room temperature. This preincubation permits the oxidation of variable amounts of DPNH by intrinsic dehydrogenase activity of the serum. If the optical density of the solution falls below 0.200 at the end of this period, an additional 0.1 ml. of the DPNH solution should be added before step 3.

3. The tubes are then brought to the temperature chosen for the assay (25 or 37° C.), 0.2 ml. of α-ketoglutarate solution is added to each tube, and the contents are once more thoroughly mixed.

4. Two minutes after the addition of the α-ketoglutarate solution readings are begun with the spectrophotometer set at 340 mμ. Using the control tube as a blank, read the optical density of the assay tube at exactly 2, 4, 6, 8, 10, and 12 minutes. When the GOT activity is low, the readings may be carried on for a longer period. When the GOT activity is so high that the DPNH is oxidized too rapidly for accurate determination, the serum should be diluted 1 to 2 or 1 to 4 and so on, as needed.

5. The GOT concentration actively is expressed in units that reflect the rate of decrease of optical density. One unit equals a decrease of optical density of 0.001 (in the Beckman DU spectrophotometer) at 25° C. The formula is as follows:

$$\text{GOT (U/ml. serum)} = \frac{\text{O.D.}_2 - \text{O.D.}_1}{t_2 - t_1} \times \frac{1}{\text{ml. serum}} \times 1000$$

O.D.$_1$ = Optical density at t_1 (first reading)
O.D.$_2$ = Optical density at t_2 (last reading)

Correction to the value at 25° C., if the procedure is carried out at another temperature, may be accomplished by reference to a chart published in the report of Steinberg et al. (1956). Likewise correction for the different light path of the Bausch and Lomb spectrophotometer (if used instead of the Beckman DU) is described by these authors.

Comments. This method is relatively simple. Falsely high values are produced by marked hemolysis. Falsely low values may result from depletion of the DPNH by excess dehydrogenase activity as indicated by a starting optical density of less than 0.200. Only when the Beckman DU spectrophotometer is used can the optical density change be equated with units. Other spectrophotometers have different light paths and a correction must, accordingly, be introduced. Before the value can be calculated by the formula just shown, the linearity of the results should be confirmed by inspection of the values or by "plotting" the results on a graph. If there is a "lag" in the early part of the determination or if the curve "flattens" during the last several readings, the most linear portion of the curve should be selected for analysis. (This should be at least eight minutes in duration.) Normal individuals have less than 40 units per ml. Serum may be maintained in the frozen state without an appreciable decline in GOT activity. Even at 5° C. the serum value of GOT is maintained for at least four to five days.

Glutamic-Pyruvic Transaminase

Method. Wroblewski and LaDue (1956) as modified in the Technical Bulletin No. 410 of the Sigma Chemical Company (1958).

Principle. The reactions involved in this assay are shown in Fig. 11–10 of Chapter 11. The spectrophotometric and colorimetric assays are analogous to those used for the GOT determination. The spectrophotometric assay is based on the transamination of alanine with α-ketoglutaric acid to form pyruvic acid and glutamic acid. The rate of formation of pyruvic acid is measured by reducing it to lactic acid by adding exogenous lactic dehydrogenase and DPNH. The rate of this reaction is measured by serial determination of the progressive decrease in concentration of DPNH in an ultraviolet spectrophotometer (340 mμ). The method of Wroblewski and LaDue, originally described for the Beckman DU spectrophotometer, may be adapted to the use of a modified Bausch and Lomb spectrophotometer ("Spectromer 20") in a manner similar to that described for the GOT determination. A simple colorimetric method has been described by Reitman and Frankel (1957).

Material. Serum.

Reagents (all may be obtained commercially)

1. Phosphate buffer, 0.1 M, pH 7.5 (see GOT method).

2. L-alanine, 0.2 M. Dissolve 1.782 gm. of l-alanine in 70 ml. of the phosphate buffer (1), adjust to a pH of 7.5 (with a few drops of 1 N NaOH or HCl), and dilute to 100 ml. with phosphate buffer. Refrigerate when not in use.

3. Reduced DPN (see GOT method).

4. Lactic dehydrogenase (L.D.). Commercial preparations of stated potency are available. A solution of the enzyme in the phosphate buffer, containing 8000 units per ml., should be prepared.

5. Alpha-ketoglutaric acid sodium salt, 0.1 M. (see GOT method).

Procedure

1. For each serum to be assayed, two Beckman 1 cm. cuvets are prepared as follows:

	Tube #1 (control)	Tube #2 (assay)
Alanine 0.2 M	0.5 ml.	0.5 ml.
L.D. (8000 U/ml.)	0.1 ml.	0.1 ml.
DPNH (1.0 mg./ml.)	0	0.3 ml.
Serum	0.2 ml.	0.2 ml.
Phosphate buffer 0.1 M (pH 7.5)	2.0 ml.	1.7 ml.

2. Procedure described in steps 2, 3, 4, and 5 of the GOT method should be followed.

REFERENCES

General

1. Bodansky, O.: Diagnostic applications of enzymes in medicine; General enzymological aspects. Am. J. Med., 27:861, 1959.
2. King, E. J.: Enzymes in clinical biochemistry. Clin. Chem., 3:507, 1957.
3. King, E. J.: Editorial. Am. J. Med., 27:849, 1959.

4. Van Rymenant, M., and Tagnon, H. J.: Enzymes in clinical medicine. New Eng. J. M., *261*:1325 and 1373, 1959.

5. Warburg, O., and Christian, W.: Gärunopfermente im blutserum von tumorratten. Biochem. Ztschr., *314*:399, 1943.

6. West, M., and Zimmerman, H. J.: Serum enzymes in hepatic disease. M. Clin. N. Amer., *43*:371, 1959.

7. White, L. (ed.): Enzymes in blood. Ann. N. Y. Acad. Med., *75*:1–384, 1958.

8. Wroblewski, F.: Increasing clinical significance of alterations in enzymes of body fluids. Ann. Int. Med., *50*:62, 1959.

Amylase

9. Janowitz, H. D., and Dreiling, D. A.: The plasma amylase. Source, regulation and diagnostic significance. Am. J. Med., *27*:924, 1959.

10. Somogyi, M.: Micromethods for estimation of diastase. J. Biol. Chem., *125*:399, 1938.

Lipase

11. Cherry, I. S., and Crandall, L. A., Jr.: The specificity of pancreatic lipase: Its appearance in the blood after pancreatic injury. Am. J. Physiol., *100*:266, 1932.

12. Tietz, N. W., Borden, T., and Stapleton, J. D.: An improved method for the determination of lipase in serum. Am. J. Clin. Path., *31*:148, 1959.

Alkaline Phosphatase

13. Bodansky, A.: Phosphatase studies. II. Determination of serum phosphatase. Factors influencing the accuracy of the determination. J. Biol. Chem., *101*:93, 1933.

14. Brem, T. H.: Use of hepatic function tests in diagnosis of amebic abscess of liver. Am. J. Med. Sci., *229*:135, 1955.

15. Gutman, A. B.: Serum alkaline phosphatase activity in diseases of the skeletal and hepatobiliary systems. Am. J. Med., *27*:875, 1959.

16. Mendelsohn, M. L., and Bodansky, O.: Value of liver function tests in diagnosis of intrahepatic metastases in nonicteric cancer patient. Cancer, *5*:1, 1952.

17. Roberts, W. M.: Variations in phosphatase activity of blood in disease. Brit. J. Exp. Path., *11*:90, 1930.

18. Ross, R. S., Iber, F. L., and Harvey, A. M.: Serum alkaline phosphatase in chronic infiltrative disease of liver. Am. J. Med., *21*:850, 1956.

Acid Phosphatase

19. Woodard, H. Q.: The clinical significance of serum acid phosphatase. Am. J. Med., *27*:902, 1959.

Cholinesterase

20. Molander, D. W., Friedman, M. M., and LaDue, J. S.: Serum cholinesterase in hepatic and neoplastic diseases. Preliminary report. Ann. Int. Med., *41*:1139, 1954.

21. Moore, C. B., Birchall, R., Horack, H. M., and Batson, H. M.: Changes in serum pseudocholinesterase levels in patients with diseases of the heart, liver or musculoskeletal system. Am. J. Med. Sci., *234*:538, 1957.

22. Vorhaus, L. J., and Kark, R. M.: Serum cholinesterase in health and disease. Am. J. Med., *14*:707, 1953.

23. Wilson, A., Calvert, R. J., and Geoghegan, H.: Plasma cholinesterase activity in liver disease: Its value as a diagnostic test of liver function compared with flocculation tests and plasma protein determinations. J. Clin. Invest., *31*:815, 1952.

Transaminases

24. DeRitis, F., Coltori, M., and Giusti, C.: Diagnostic value and pathogenic significance of transaminase activity changes in viral hepatitis. Minerva Med., *47*:161, 1956.

25. Karmen, A.: A note on the spectrophotometric assay of glutamic-oxaloacetic transaminase activity in human blood serum. J. Clin. Invest., *34*:131, 1955.

26. Mason, J. H., and Wroblewski, F.: Serum glutamic oxaloacetic transaminase activity in experimental and disease states. A.M.A. Arch. Int. Med., *99*:245, 1957.

27. Reitman, S., and Frankel, S.: A colorimetric method for determination of serum glutamic oxaloacetic and glutamic pyruvic transaminase. Am. J. Clin. Path., *28*:56, 1957.

28. Steinberg, D., Baldwin, D., and Ostrow, B. H.: A clinical method for the assay of serum glutamic-oxaloacetic transaminase. J. Lab. & Clin. Med., *48*:144, 1956.

29. Technical Bulletin No. 410. St. Louis, Sigma Chemical Co., 1958.

30. Umbreit, W. W., Kingsley, G. R., Schaffert, R. R., and Siplet, H.: A colorimetric method for transaminase in serum or plasma. J. Lab. & Clin. Med., *49*:454, 1957.

31. Wroblewski, F.: Clinical significance of alterations in transaminase activities of serum and other body fluids. Advances Clin. Chem., *1*: 313, 1958.

32. Wroblewski, F.: The clinical significance of transaminase activities of serum. Am. J. Med., *27*:911, 1959.

33. Wroblewski, F., and LaDue, J. S.: Serum glutamic pyruvic transaminase in cardiac and hepatic disease. Proc. Soc. Exp. Biol. Med., *91*:569, 1956.

Enzymes of Erythrocytes and Leukocytes

34. Altman, K. I.: Some enzymologic aspects of the human erythrocyte. Am. J. Med., *27*:936, 1959.

35. Beutler, E.: The hemolytic effect of primaquine and related compounds: A review. Blood, *14*: 103, 1959.

36. Marks, P. A., and Gross, R. T.: Drug-induced hemolytic anemias and congenital galactosemia. Bull. New York Acad. Med., *35*:433, 1959.

37. Szeinberg, A., Sheba, C., and Adam, A.: Selective occurrence of glutathione instability in red blood corpuscles of the various Jewish tribes. Blood, *13*:1043, 1958.

38. Valentine, W. N.: The biochemistry and enzymatic activities of leukocytes in health and disease. Prog. Hematol., *1*:293, 1956.

Chapter 13

Laboratory Tests Aiding in the Diagnosis of Pancreatic Disorders

By NORBERT W. TIETZ, PH.D.

The pancreas is hidden deeply in the retroperitoneal space in the abdomen. It is almost inaccessible for direct examination. The value of radiologic examination is also limited. Hence, pancreatic function tests and other laboratory tests for diagnosis of disorders of this organ are of great importance. However, none of the available laboratory tests have proved to be diagnostic and great care is necessary when interpreting results. The value of the tests is limited chiefly because the pancreas has a large functional reserve (normal secretory function may be present, even if only a part of the organ is functioning, provided the connection with the pancreatic duct is maintained). The value of laboratory tests is also limited because some of the enzymes secreted by the pancreas can also originate from other sources, because incomplete obstruction caused by tumors or other causes may permit normal flow of digestive juices into the duodenum without changes in the blood enzymes, and because increase in blood enzymes can result from extrapancreatic disorders or the administration of drugs. In spite of the limitations laboratory tests can be of considerable aid to the clinician. The tests that have been selected are thought to be the most useful of those available for the diagnosis of pancreatic disorders at the present time. Reviews published by Popper and Necheles (1959), Necheles and Kir-

shen (1957), and Janowitz and Dreiling (1959) can be consulted by those interested in pursuing the subject further.

ENZYMES

The normal pancreas secretes a number of enzymes. In some disorders these appear in the blood in increased amounts or are impeded in their flow into the duodenum. The clinically most important enzymes are amylase, lipase, and trypsin.

Serum Amylase

Amylase hydrolyzes starch, glycogen, and dextrines. The route by which amylase (and lipase) enters into the general circulation is not known. It is believed that it originates in the acinar cells of the pancreas and that a part enters the blood directly or via the ductules. In acute pancreatitis or in pancreatic injury pancreatic juice diffuses out of the duct system into interstitial spaces of the gland, the mesocolon, the mesentery, and the peritoneal cavity. This is thought to be due to changes in pressure, changes in the permeability of acinar cells, or disruption of the acinar limiting membrane (Janowitz and Dreiling, 1959; Necheles and Kirshen, 1957; Popper and Necheles, 1959). The pancreatic fluid then enters the blood circulation by means of the lymphatic channels and especially by way of the portal vein (Janowitz and Dreiling, 1959).

The increase in amylase levels in blood depends not only on the release of the enzyme by the acinar cells but also on the continued secretion in the presence of obstruction (Lemon and Byrnes, 1949). There is evidence that amylase is not absorbed normally from the intestinal tract (Janowitz and Dreiling, 1959). After the enzyme reaches the blood, it is excreted by the kidneys. It is unlikely that the liver aids in its excretion, since no amylolytic activity has been found in the bile. It follows that the amylase level in blood represents the difference between the amount of enzyme entering the circulation and that being cleared by the kidneys. Since the release of enzyme by the pancreas decreases with progressing pancreatic disease while the kidneys continue their excretion, enzyme levels do not stay elevated.

For example, in acute pancreatitis the amylolytic activity usually returns to normal within one to three days after the onset of the disease. For that reason amylase determination should be done as soon as possible if it is to be of diagnostic significance. Increases in serum amylase in acute pancreatitis, though significant, may be absent. Bockus and co-workers (1955) studied 94 cases and found 11 cases with normal amylase levels (even in patients dying from the disease), 42 with elevations up to 500 units, and 41 with values above 500 units (normal: 30 to 180 units). Similar high values have been observed in obstruction of the pancreatic duct. As in acute pancreatitis these values decrease after several days. In tumors of the pancreas increase in serum amylase is rare. Although high serum amylase levels are usually associated with acute pancreatitis, other conditions can also cause similar elevations.

Amylase in Intra-abdominal Diseases. Perforated peptic, gastric or duodenal ulcers, even if not in direct contact with the pancreas, may cause elevations of serum amylase. Values over 1000 units have been reported. These elevations seem to be due to absorption of amylase from the peritoneal cavity. In one series 19 of 35 patients with intestinal obstruction had amylase values above normal with two cases of 1600 and 2000 units. Absorption of enzymes from capillaries or lymphatics of the damaged bowel or from the peritoneum after seepage through the intestinal wall is thought to be responsible. Increased serum amylase is sometimes seen after abdominal operations. This might be caused by minor trauma to the blood supply of the pancreas or by partial duodenal obstruction with a resulting rise in intraductal pressure. Enzyme elevations have even been reported after operations far remote from the pancreas.

Miscellaneous Conditions Causing Increase in Serum Amylase. Another cause for increased serum amylase is retention of the enzyme owing to renal insufficiency. In one series of 111 cases 29 had amylase levels between 200 and 1000 units. Ruptured ectopic pregnancy, peritonitis, typhoid enteritis, and acute diseases of the salivary glands, such as mumps, are among the other causes for increased serum amylase. Morphine, codeine, and meperidine (Demerol) may cause a transient spasm of the duodenal musculature and of the sphincter of Oddi, resulting in slight serum amylase increases. Morphine sulfate in a dose of 16 mg. was found to produce slight elevations, which do not occur before five hours but which may persist as long as 24 hours. The serum amylase values after administration of provocative drugs will be discussed in a separate paragraph.

Low serum amylase values have been found in abscesses of the liver, acute hepatocellular damage, cirrhosis, cancer of the liver and bile duct, and cholecystitis. Jaundice alone and chronic diseases of the gallbladder do not influence amylase levels. Amylase is usually absent in newborns. It appears approximately at the age of two months and reaches normal levels at the end of the first year (Somogyi, 1941).

Urinary Amylase

Renal clearance of amylase is in the range of 1 to 3 ml. per minute and is only slightly altered by water-induced diuresis. It appears, therefore, that amylase is filtered but not reabsorbed and that it has no renal threshold (McGeachin and Hargan, 1956). Little else is known about the mechanism of amylase excretion.

For some unknown reasons urinary amylase in acute pancreatitis or obstruction of the pancreatic duct is sometimes more elevated than is serum amylase, and the increased levels may persist over a longer period. In cases of pancreatic carcinoma with obstruction of the pancreatic duct urinary amylase levels may also be elevated occasionally.

The method of Wohlgemuth (1908), which is usually employed in such studies, is not so reliable as the Somogyi serum amylase test because of the greatly varying concentration and composition of the urine.

Most increases in serum amylase, whatever the cause, will affect urine amylase in the same way. Hence, the need for cautious interpretation of results.

Serum Lipase

Serum lipase catalyzes the hydrolysis of fatty acid esters. Its main known source is the pancreas, but it is also produced in the mucosa of the stomach, in the small intestine, and possibly in other tissues. The pancreatic portion of the enzyme is produced in the acinar cells and reaches the blood in the same way as amylase. The best substrate for lipase determination is neutral fat (trigylceride esters with long-chain fatty acids). However, specificity of this enzyme is only relative, since it splits esters ranging from short-chain fatty acids with monohydroxy alcohols up to long-chain fatty acid esters with glycerin.

In general, changes in serum lipase levels have the same significance as those of amylase. However, there are differences that favor the lipase determination. In acute pancreatitis elevated levels of this enzyme decrease more gradually and can be found for as long as 14 days, while amylase usually returns to normal within one to three days. Our group studied serum lipase levels in 35 cases of proved pancreatitis, using a modified technique (see p. 587). According to our results lipase remains elevated longer than amylase and the increase is more pronounced. In two cases serum amylase was within the normal range but lipase was significantly elevated (Tietz et al., 1959). Serum lipase, in contrast to amylase, is increased in approximately 40 to 50 per cent of cases of carcinoma of the pancreas, in about 60 per cent of cases of carcinoma of the ampulla of Vater, and occasionally in chronic pancreatitis. Serum lipase levels may be normal in advanced disease of the pancreas if no functioning pancreatic tissue remains. Lipase is normal in acute diseases of the salivary glands.

Urinary Lipase

Lipase is excreted by the kidneys and can be demonstrated in the urine. It has been found elevated in hemorrhagic pancreatitis and in some cases of renal impairment.

The determination of lipase in the urine presents difficulties because of the presence of an inhibitor. Presently available lipase methods are either too tedious or not fully reliable.

Leucine Amino Peptidase

Leucine amino peptidase (LAP) is found in amost all human tissues and also in serum, urine, and bile. Goldbarg (1958) and Rutenburg (1958) developed a method for its assay in serum and urine and found significant elevations of this enzyme in carcinoma of the pancreas. Although such elevations were found in all 18 investigated cases and were confirmed by Perry and Gibson (1960), the test seems to have only limited diagnostic value, because elevations have also been reported in obstructive jaundice, infectious hepatitis, metastatic cancer, acute pancreatitis, and pregnancy. In addition urinary LAP is elevated in lymphomas and leukemia and following operation. Further use of this test will have to show whether it might be of value in excluding carcinoma of the pancreas.

Trypsin in Stool

Trypsin, a protein-splitting enzyme in the pancreatic juice, was formerly thought to be a single enzyme but is now known to consist of trypsin, chymotrypsin, and carboxypolypeptidase. Trypsin is secreted first as an inactive precursor, trypsinogen, and then activated in the intestines by enterokinase (or by calcium or bile). The enzyme is excreted in feces and can be demonstrated there. Patients with pancreatic insufficiency usually have little or no tryptic activity in the stool (Shwachman and Galim, 1949). Stool trypsin determinations are of value only in infants and children, since in adults negative results have been seen frequently even in the absence of pancreatic disorders.

However, these tests are of limited value, especially because of the possible presence of proteolytic bacteria. Therefore, the test can be considered only as a screening procedure, and a culture for proteolytic bacteria should always be done if the result is positive unless a control with antitrypsin is run at the same time (see p. 589).

The Effect of Provocative Drugs on Serum Enzyme Levels

Disappointment in the use of the various pancreatic function tests stimulated a number of investigators to measure serum enzyme levels before and after administration of provocative drugs. Administration of the hormone secretin* causes no elevations of blood enzymes in normal individuals. In the presence of pancreatic duct obstruction, whatever the cause, serum amylase and lipase levels increase significantly after secretin, provided there is a sufficient amount of parenchymal tissue still functioning. Simultaneous administration of secretin and of drugs producing an obstructive action (morphine sulfate, methacholine chloride, or Urecholine) will result in an increase in blood enzymes in most individuals with sufficient acinar cell function. Snape and coworkers (1949) studied a number of controls and patients with various pancreatic diseases by determining serum amylase in a fasting blood specimen and then giving 10 to 15 mg. of morphine sulfate, followed after 30 minutes by 1 unit of secretin per kg. of body weight. Further amylase studies were done on specimens withdrawn 15, 30, 60, and 90 minutes after secretin. In control patients the average base level was 133.5 units with an average peak level of 389.3 units at 30 to 60 minutes. Values in patients with pancreatitis were significantly higher, and those in patients with carcinoma of the pancreas significantly lower, than the control levels Snape *et al.,* 1949; Wirts and Snape, 1951).

Although some authors have obtained good results with these tests, there is much variation and overlap in results in normals and in patients with various pancreatic disorders (Janowitz and Dreiling, 1959, Necheles and Kirshen, 1957).

* Secretin is a hormone produced by the upper intestinal mucosa and released on contact with hydrochloric acid or gastric chyle. It reaches the pancreas via the blood and stimulates the acinar cells to produce an increased volume of fluid with high bicarbonate content. The concentration of enzymes in the pancreatic juice after stimulation is unaltered, but the total amount excreted is increased.

Examination of Pancreatic Juice (Secretin Test)

The most direct way of determining pancreatic function is measurement of volume and analysis of pancreatic juice for bicarbonate and enzyme content after stimulation of the pancreas with secretin.

Dreiling (1950, 1954), Andersen (1942), and Gibbs (1950, 1953) studied the composition of pancreatic juice in normal individuals and in various pancreatic disorders (see Table 13–1). The normal for lipase secretion is 7000 to 14,000 units per hour (135 to 225 units per kg.), and 20 to 40 units per hour (0.35 to 0.7 units per kg.) is considered normal for trypsin secretion (Cantarow and Trumper, 1955). There is a wide variation of values, even in normal persons. The test has little or no value in the diagnosis of mild cases of chronic pancreatitis and in carcinoma of the tail of the pancreas (Lagerlöf, 1942; Wirts and Snape, 1951). Normal secretion in these conditions can probably be ascribed to the functional reserve of the pancreas. In cases of decreased acinar function earliest abnormalities are usually found in amylase and lipase secretion. Decreases in trypsin, total volume, and bicarbonate follow with progression of the disease (Cantarow and Trumper, 1955; Dreiling, 1953).

In general it is sufficient to analyze the duodenal drainage for one of the enzymes only. Amylase is the enzyme of choice in adults. If the test is to be done in infants, trypsin should be determined, since the amylase production of infants is extremely low and there is interference from salivary amylase (Andersen, 1942). The duodenal fluid of infants must be collected over ice, since trypsin is readily inactivated at room temperature.

Abnormalities in the concentration of pancreatic juice have been reported in cases of chronic pancreatitis, pancreatic cysts, hemochromatosis, cystic fibrosis, cal-

Table 13–1. Normal Values of Secretin Response and Critical Values for Volume, Bicarbonate, and Amylase in the 60-minute Specimen (According to Dreiling, 1950, Modified)

	TOTAL VOLUME (ML.)	TOTAL VOLUME (ML./KG.)	HCO_3^- MAX. CONCENTRATION (MEQ./L.)	TOTAL HCO_3^- (MEQ.)	TOTAL AMYLASE (UNITS)	TOTAL AMYLASE (UNITS/KG.)
Observed Range	91–270	1.6–4.8	88–137	13.2–23.7	204–1621	3.7–22.8
Mean	164.7	2.72	107.7	17.81	722.4	10.3
Critical Value	102	1.7	91	14.1	173	2.9

cification, and carcinoma of the pancreas, and edema of the pancreas. Findings in these conditions are very similar and are of relatively little value in the differential diagnosis. Some authors feel that the relative proportion of the different fractions may give additional information.

Pancreatic neoplasms alter the response to secretin, depending on the location of the lesion and degree of duct obstruction (Dreiling, 1953; Dreiling and Hollander, 1948). The secretion tends to be reduced in volume but normal in composition. If a tumor does not obstruct the major duct, response to secretin is usually normal. Acute inflammation causes destruction of secreting cells, which in turn results in a decrease in both volume and concentration of the fluid (Dreiling, 1953). Chronic pancreatitis results mainly in a decrease in bicarbonate but causes less of a decrease in the amylase content of the secretion (Comfort et al., 1949; Dreiling and Hollander, 1948). In sprue pancreatic function is usually unaltered (Comfort et al., 1949). The interested reader can find additional information in the literature (Diamond and Siegal, 1940; Dreiling, 1954; Wirts and Snape, 1951).

The greatest value of the secretin test is probably the possibility of excluding pancreatic dysfunction, as in fibrocystic disease, and in the differential diagnosis of steatorrhea of pancreatic origin from that owing to sprue or celiac disease.

The secretin test has additional advantages. A portion of the duodenal contents can be used for cytologic studies (Bothereau et al., 1951; Lemon and Byrnes, 1949). The first collection following administration of secretin should be examined for that purpose. Simultaneous determination of the icterus index or bilirubin in duodenal contents may furnish information about gallbladder function. Normally the fluid is faintly yellow at first; then the color turns lighter and remains so throughout the test period. This is explained by the closure of the sphincter of Boyden, which prevents the release of bile accumulated in the gallbladder. If the gallbladder is nonfunctioning or absent, the pancreatic juice is deeply bile stained.

Technique of the Secretin Test. Patients should be in the fasting state. Infants or children can be sedated with Seconal. A double-lumen gastroduodenal tube should be introduced under fluoroscopic guidance in such a way that the shorter end of the tube lies in the stomach and the longer end is distal to the ampulla of Vater. Constant suction is then applied and aspiration is continued until the duodenal fluid becomes clear and not contaminated by gastric juice (after approximately 20 minutes). At this time 1 unit of secretin per kg. of body weight is given intravenously, and specimens of duodenal and gastric content are collected at ten-minute intervals. Each specimen obtained from the stomach is examined for pH (Hydrion paper). A sudden drop in acidity indicates contamination by duodenal fluid. The various ten-minute specimens from the duodenum are analyzed for pH, volume, and occult blood. Sudden changes in pH or volume indicate contamination by gastric juice. The presence of occult or overt blood may be helpful in pinpointing gastrointestinal bleedings. After 60 minutes all duodenal specimens are pooled and analyzed for volume and bicarbonate content and for amylase, lipase, or trypsin activity. The pH can be determined with Hydrion paper or the pH meter; bicarbonate concentration may be determined with a Van-Slyke gasometer, amylase according to Somogyi (see p. 585), lipase according to Tietz et al., (see p. 587), and trypsin according to Varley's modification of the procedure by Lagerlöf (see p. 588).

ABSORPTION TESTS

The absorption tests to be listed are based on the theory that proper pancreatic function is essential for normal absorption of certain substances. Although lack of proper absorption might have several causes, normal absorption would more or less exclude pancreatic deficiency. However, the pancreas does have a large functional reserve, and absorption may be normal in the presence of pancreatic disorders. Absorption tests are most valuable in the diagnosis of fibrocystic disease of the pancreas.

The Vitamin A Tolerance Test

Serum vitamin A levels in children with cystic fibrosis of the pancreas and in adults with pancreatic insufficiency are usually below the normal range of 15 to 60 μg. per 100 ml. or at its lower limit. Oral administration of large amounts of vitamin A in oil causes only slight increases in the serum vitamin A in these patients. Persons with normal absorption show rises from 200 to 600 μg. of vitamin A per 100 ml. of serum.

Technique. A fasting blood specimen is collected and 5000 units of vitamin A (in oil) per kg. of body weight are given by mouth. Further blood specimens are drawn 3, 6, and 24 hours later. The patient may drink water or consume light meals during the first 6 hours, have full meals during the second 6 hours, and then should fast until withdrawal of the 24-hour specimen. All specimens are analyzed for vitamin A content (see p. 590).

Fat Absorption Tests

These tests are based on the theory that normal absorption of fat can take place only in the presence of normal pancreatic function (in this case, secretion of lipase). Several approaches have been used to measure the rate of fat absorption from the intestinal tract.

The most commonly used test is the determination of the total fat in a fasting serum specimen and in specimens withdrawn three and six hours after administration of a high fat meal (Hirsch et al., 1953).

The optical density of the serum before and after administration of a fat meal has also been used as a measure of fat absorption. This test is much simpler to do but is less accurate, since turbidity of serum does not always represent its actual fat content. A method, such as the one suggested by Schwartz and co-workers (1952), may be used for such serum turbidity measurements.

In both of these procedures absorption curves tend to be flat in patients with impaired fat absorption.

More recent procedures are based on the administration of I^{131}-labeled triolein and oleic acid on separate days and the determination of the per cent of I^{131} found in the blood. Normal absorption of I^{131}-labeled triolein indicates that pancreatic function is probably normal or not greatly impaired, since absorption of this compound to any significant extent must be preceded by lipolytic hydrolysis. Absorption of only oleic acid suggests impaired pancreatic function. Failure of absorption of oleic acid indicates a malabsorption syndrome of non-pancreatic origin. The analysis of I^{131} in stool, in addition to that of blood, increases the accuracy of the test and is, therefore, preferred by some.

Results obtained with these procedures are more accurate than those obtained with chemical tests, but availability of an isotope laboratory is essential (Berkowitz et al., 1959; Duffy and Turner, 1958; Kaplan et al., 1958).

The Lipiodol Test

The Lipiodol test (Delory et al., 1956; Groen, 1948; Silverman and Shirkey, 1955) is based on the ability of normal children to absorb iodized oil and subsequently to excrete the iodine in the urine in a high concentration. Children with impaired pancreatic function, as in fibrocystic disease of the pancreas, absorb little Lipiodol, and therefore urine iodine concentrations are low. This test, which is only a screening procedure, is easy to perform but carries the risk of an iodine reaction in some patients. It is advisable to administer 0.5 gm. of potassium iodide to all patients the evening before the test and to proceed with the test only if no rashes, rhinitis, headache, conjunctivitis, or other side effects are observed (Groen, 1948).

Technique. A urine specimen is collected. The patient is then given 0.5 ml. of Lipiodol (40 per cent) per kg. of body weight by mouth or stomach tube (not less than 5 and not more than 10 ml.). The second urine specimen is collected 12 to 18 hours after Lipiodol administration. Both specimens are checked for iodine (see p. 591). A positive test in a 1:4 dilution or higher is said to exclude fibrocystic disease of the pancreas. In one suggested procedure the Lipiodol is given with breakfast and its absorption followed with x-rays. Iodine excretion is determined in both urine and stool. Such an elaborate approach seems hardly justifiable for clinical use.

ELECTROLYTE COMPOSITION OF SWEAT AND SALIVA

It has been found that the sodium and chloride contents of sweat in patients affected by fibrocystic disease of the pancreas are significantly elevated, even in the absence of gastrointestinal or respiratory symptoms or when no pancreatic insufficiency can be demonstrated by other tests. The chloride concentration of sweat in normal individuals is between 4 and 60 mEq. per L. with a mean of 32 mEq. per L. Patients with cystic fibrosis of the pancreas have values of 60 to 160 mEq. per L. with a mean of 133 mEq. per L. Concentrations above 70 mEq. per L. are considered diagnostic. The sodium content of normal sweat (10 to 90 mEq. per L.)

overlaps the values obtained in patients with cystic fibrosis (80 to 190 mEq. per L.) (see Kaiser *et al.*, 1956).

False normal results can be obtained in pure salt depletion, which is common in the affected group of patients during hot weather. Additional electrolyte studies on serum help to avoid misinterpretation of results in such instances. Elevated sweat electrolyte composition has also been reported in meconium ileus, in adrenal insufficiency, and in some cases of renal disease.

The sweat test is the most valuable single test in the diagnosis of fibrocystic disease of the pancreas. In most affected infants it becomes positive between three and five weeks of age.

The amount of sweat necessary to perform the sweat test is sometimes hard to obtain, and modified procedures have been devised. These tests are based on the appearance of a white precipitate of silver chloride on an agar plate (Shwachman and Galim, 1956) or on a commercially available paper prepared with silver salts that have been in contact with the skin of the patient. Such tests should be used only for screening purposes, since results are not so reliable as those obtained from direct measurement of sweat electrolyte contents.

Similar elevations of sodium and chloride have been found in the saliva of patients with fibrocystic diseases of the pancreas (Kaiser *et al.*, 1956), but the results of these determinations are inconsistent and by no means so reliable as those obtained from sweat. (Procedures for obtaining sweat are described on p. 591.)

STOOL EXAMINATIONS

The analysis of feces for various constituents was once used widely to measure pancreatic function. The simplest approach is the microscopic identification and demonstration of excess of undigested cell nuclei and meat fibers (creatorrhea), of increased fat (steatorrhea), and of increased starch (amylorrhea) (Hoffman, 1954). Demonstration of these conditions is suggestive of impaired absorption (see next section). In severe cases the feces are usually pale, bulky, and foul smelling. In steatorrhea of pancreatic origin fat droplets usually appear in the feces on standing.

Unfortunately these tests have no diagnostic value in mild cases of pancreatic disease and in those cases in which the acute phase has subsided. In addition some patients with severe pancreatic insufficiency may have almost normal digestion owing to the compensatory mechanism of the body and the activity of microorganisms. On the other hand patients with celiac disease or sprue may have stools similar to those of patients with pancreatic insufficiency (because of increased intestinal motility). The quantitative assay of fat and nitrogen in the stool is more helpful, but it also has its limitations.

Fat in Stool. Ingested fat is normally split by pancreatic lipase into fatty acids and glycerol or monoesters of glycerol, and the products of hydrolysis are absorbed by the intestinal tract. Therefore, the stool content of neutral fat, free fatty acids, and soaps is relatively low. If the amount of total fat exceeds 25 per cent of the dry matter, one may consider the stool abnormal. Increase of the neutral fat portion to 11 per cent of the dry matter or 55 per cent of the total fecal fat represents a deficiency in fat-splitting activity. If the amount of hydrolyzed fat (soaps and free fatty acids) exceeds 16 per cent of the dry matter or 75 per cent of the total fat, the condition is usually due to deficient fat absorption. There are conditions (for example, gastrocolic fistula) in which the neutral fat portion is elevated to the same extent as in pancreatic disorders. Obstructive jaundice is sometimes accompanied by a total stool fat content of up to 75 per cent of dry matter. It has been suggested that the large amount of fecal fat in this disorder is largely due to the excretion of fat by the intestinal mucosa rather than to diminished absorption (Cantarow and Trumper, 1955).

Fractional analysis of fecal fat can thus be of some help in diagnosing or excluding pancreatic insufficiency but is of no value in differentiating specific pancreatic conditions.

Nitrogen (Protein) in Stool. The feces of normal individuals usually do not contain more than 5 to 10 per cent of the nitrogen of the food ingested. Increase in the nitrogen content, especially to 25 per cent or above, can be interpreted as evidence of pancreatic insufficiency, provided intestinal motility and absorption are normal. The nitrogen content is increased also in sprue, but it seldom exceeds 17 per cent of the ingested nitrogen.

Microscopic Examination of Stool. The microscopic examination for meat fibers is a means of differentiating between pancreatic disorders and increased intestinal motility owing to other causes. Meat fibers with sharp, angular ends and transverse striations are only found if pancreatic enzymes are greatly diminished or absent. Feces of patients with increased intestinal motility owing to nonpancreatic causes may also contain meat fibers, but these have rounded ends and no transverse striations (Cantarow and Trumper, 1955).

MISCELLANEOUS FINDINGS IN PANCREATIC DISEASES

A significant number of patients with acute and chronic pancreatitis, as well as with carcinoma of the body and tail of the pancreas, show a decreased glucose tolerance. Fasting hyperglycemia is observed in acute pancreatitis but only in 15 to 30 per cent of cases of chronic pancreatitis. Glycosuria has been reported in 5 to 25 per cent of cases of acute pancreatitis.

Serum calcium levels are decreased to the range of 8.0 to 8.5 mg. per 100 ml. in the majority of cases of acute pancreatitis and occasionally are as low as 7.0 mg. per 100 ml. These changes have been observed 24 to 72 hours after the attack and are attributed to sudden withdrawal of calcium from extracellular fluids by its fixation as calcium soaps (Cantarow and Trumper, 1955; Lipp and Hubbard, 1950; Popper and Necheles, 1959).

METHODS

Determination of Amylase in Serum and Duodenal Contents

Principle. Amylase hydrolyzes starch into reducing sugars (mainly maltose and glucose). The reducing sugars in the sample, in a serum control, and in a starch blank are determined with the Folin-Wu method. The reducing power of the sample −(serum blank + starch blank) calculated as mg. glucose per 100 ml. is considered as being the amylolytic activity in units.

Reagents

1. Copper sulfate (5 per cent). Dissolve 50 gm. of $CuSO_4 \cdot 5H_2O$ in water, transfer to a 1000 ml. volumetric flask, and dilute to mark. Store in glass stopper bottle.

2. Sodium tungstate (6 per cent). Dissolve 60 gm. of $Na_2WO_4 \cdot 2H_2O$ in a 1000 ml. volumetric flask, dilute to mark with water, and mix.

3. Alkaline copper solution. Add 40 gm. of anhydrous sodium carbonate and 7.5 gm. of tartaric acid to a 1 liter volumetric flask that contains approximately 400 ml. of distilled water. After these reagents are completely dissolved, 4.5 gm. of copper sulfate ($CuSO_4 \cdot 5H_2O$) are added and dissolved. The contents of the flask are then brought to 1 liter with distilled water and mixed by inversion. If a red sediment forms on standing, the supernatant fluid or liquid is decanted or filtered into another container.

4. Phosphomolybdic acid solution. To a 2 liter Erlenmeyer flask or beaker add 400 ml. of 10 per cent sodium hydroxide, 70 gm. of molybdic acid (H_2MoO_4), 10 gm. of sodium tungstate (Na_2WO_4), and 400 ml. of distilled water. Add a few glass beads and boil the solution for 30 minutes (to remove all ammonia) and cool. The contents are transferred to a 1 liter volumetric flask with the aid of enough water to bring the volume to approximately 700 ml. Place flask in a cold water bath and add cautiously 250 ml. of 85 per cent phosphoric acid, dilute to 1 liter with water, and mix. The solution should not be blue.

5. Starch paste. Place 100 gm. cornstarch U.S.P. into a 2000 ml. Erlenmeyer flask, add 1000 ml. of 0.01 N HCl, and stir for one hour. Allow the starch to settle down, decant supernatant, and add 1000 ml. of 0.05 per cent NaCl solution. Repeat the washing with NaCl, decant, and spread the washed starch on a filter paper until dry. This purified starch is very stable and can be kept for future use if stored in a dry place.

Grind 3 gm. of purified starch in a mortar, add 10 ml. of H_2O, and transfer this suspension into 180 ml. of boiling water. Rinse the mortar with an additional 10 ml. of water and add this to the solution. Boil for one minute with agitation and then keep the solution for 15 minutes in a 100° C. water bath. During the heating process place an inverted beaker over the mouth of the flask to minimize evaporation. If kept in the refrigerator, this solution is stable for at least one week.

6. Acid-sodium chloride (1 per cent). Dissolve 10 gm. of NaCl in some distilled water, transfer to a 1 liter volumetric flask, and add 3 ml. of 0.1 N HCl. Dilute to mark and mix.

7. Glucose standard.

Stock (10 mg. per ml.). Desiccate some reagent grade glucose for at least three days before use. Place

5.0 gm. of glucose into a 500 ml. volumetric flask and dissolve in saturated (0.3 per cent) benzoic acid. Dilute to mark with benzoic acid. Keep in refrigerator.

Working standard (0.2 mg. per ml.). Dilute 2 ml. of the stock standard to 100 ml. with distilled water in a volumetric flask. This solution must be made up daily.

Method

1. Into each of two test tubes add 5 ml. of starch paste and 2 ml. of acid NaCl solution. Mark one tube "test" and the other "blank" and place both tubes into a water bath at 40° C. for five minutes.

2. Add 1 ml. of serum to the "test" and 1 ml. of water to the "blank" and mix well.

3. Incubate both tubes for exactly 30 minutes at 40° C.

4. Prepare a serum control by adding 1 ml. serum, 2 ml. acid NaCl, and 5 ml. water to a third test tube marked "control."

5. Add to the "control," and immediately after 30 minutes' incubation also to the "test" and "blank," 1 ml. of 5 per cent copper sulfate solution. Mix well and subsequently add 1 ml. 6 per cent sodium tungstate.

6. Mix all tubes well, allow to stand about five minutes, and filter content through Whatman No. 40 filter paper or centrifuge. The filtrate obtained represents a 1:10 dilution. The reducing power of these filtrates can be determined with the following Folin-Wu method or with any one of its revisions:

Folin-Wu method. 1. Transfer 2.0 ml. of protein-free filtrate to a 25 ml. graduated Folin-Wu tube.

2. Prepare a blank by pipetting 2.0 ml. of water into a Folin-Wu sugar tube.

3. For standards use two Folin-Wu tubes marked "S-1" and "S-2." To S-1 add 1.0 ml. of the working standard plus 1.0 ml. of water. To S-2 add 2.0 ml. of the working standard.

4. Add to all tubes 2.0 ml. of alkaline copper reagent. Mix.

5. Place the tubes in a vigorously boiling bath for eight minutes.

6. Transfer the tubes without shaking to a cold water bath for four minutes.

7. Add 2.0 ml. of phosphomolybdic acid to each tube and mix. After one minute (when effervescence has ceased) dilute to 25 ml. with distilled water.

8. Stopper all tubes and mix by inversion. Allow to stand for 8 minutes.

9. Read all samples in a spectrophotometer at 420 mμ, using the blank to set instrument at 100 per cent transmission. Calculate amount of reducing substance from a chart or standard curve.

Calculations. The reducing power of the "test" depends on the reducing substances in the specimen and starch as well as on the reducing sugars formed during the incubation period (owing to the amylolytic activity). The "control" measures only the reducing substances in the original serum. The "blank" measures any reducing substance that may be present in the starch solution. Therefore, reducing power of "test"—"control"—"blank" is equal to the amylase level in units.

Remarks and Sources of Error

1. Prepare a standard curve for values up to 400 mg. glucose per 100 ml. If the "test" has a reducing power equivalent to more than 400 mg. of glucose, the test should be repeated, using less filtrate (e.g., 1.0 ml. instead of 2.0 ml.) and making up the difference by adding distilled water or saline. Multiply the final result by the dilution factor employed.

2. The use of an improperly prepared or old starch paste, inaccurate timing of incubation, and incorrect temperature of the water bath are the most common sources of error.

3. If the reducing power of the "blank" reaches any appreciable level, the test must be repeated with a new starch paste.

4. If duodenal fluid is to be analyzed, a 1:100 dilution with saline should be used, and results should be multiplied by 100 and corrected for the total volume.

5. Somogyi (1960) has recommended a modified starch paste and stated that the reducing power of the filtrate can be determined with the Folin-Wu method or with any of the methods measuring true glucose.

Normal Values. Normal values are expressed in Somogyi units. One unit equals 1 mg. of reducing substances per 100 ml. of serum, calculated as glucose. Although Somogyi in his original paper (1941) gave 30 to 180 units as the normal range, probably all values above 150 units should be considered abnormal.

Determination of Amylase in Urine

Principle. Different dilutions of urine, buffered to pH 6.1, are mixed with a 0.2 per cent starch solution. After incubation at 38° C. for 30 minutes iodine is added to all tubes. The last tube in which no blue color appears is considered the dilution of urine that is just capable of digesting the starch.

Reagents

1. Phosphate buffer, pH 6.1.

Solution A. Dissolve 11.876 gm. of disodium phosphate ($Na_2HPO_4 \cdot 2H_2O$) in freshly boiled water and dilute to a volume of 1000 ml.

Solution B. Dissolve 9.078 gm. of monobasic potassium phosphate (KH_2PO_4) in freshly boiled water and dilute to a volume of 1000 ml.

Prepare the phosphate buffer of pH 6.1 by mixing 15 ml. of solution A with 85 ml. of solution B. Check the pH with a pH meter.

2. Starch solution 0.2 per cent. In a test tube shake 0.2 gm. of starch with a few ml. of cold water. The paste is washed into approximately 80 ml. of boiling water. When cool, the solution is washed into a volumetric flask and brought up to a volume of 100 ml. with water. This solution should be made up every few days and kept in the refrigerator.

3. Iodine solution (approximately 0.1 N). Dissolve 12.7 gm. of iodine crystals in a solution containing 20 gm. of potassium iodide in water. Dilute with water to 1000 ml. Use triple beam balance and not analytical balance for weighing the iodine.

4. Iodine solution (approximately N/50). Prior to use, dilute the 0.1 N stock solution 1:5 with distilled water.

Method

1. Prepare a 1:5 dilution of urine by adding 1 ml. of urine to 4 ml. of phosphate buffer solution of pH 6.1.

2. Place seven test tubes in a rack and add 2 ml. of buffer pH 6.1 to tubes 2 to 7. Then add 2 ml. of buffered urine to tubes 1 and 2. Mix.

3. Remove 2 ml. from tube 2 and add to tube 3. Mix well. Continue this procedure through tube 7, discarding the last 2 ml. The dilution is 1:5 in tube 1, 1:10 in tube 2, and so on. The dilution in tube 7 is 1:320.

4. Add 1 ml. of a 0.2 per cent starch solution to each tube, mix, and incubate all tubes for 30 minutes in a 38° C. water bath.

5. Cool all tubes for one minute in a cold water bath and add 3 drops of approximately N/50 iodine solution to each tube. Note the last tube in which no blue color is produced.

Calculations. One Wohlgemuth unit of amylolytic activity is defined as the number of ml. of 0.1 per cent starch solution digested by 1 ml. of urine in 30 minutes at 38° C.

Example. Let the dilution of the urine in the last tube that shows no blue color be 1 in 20.

This tube contains 2 ml. of a 1:20 dilution of urine. That means that $\frac{2}{20}$ ml. of urine contain just sufficient amylase to digest 1 ml. of a 0.2 per cent starch solution (or 2 ml. of a 0.1 per cent starch solution) in 30 minutes.

One ml. of urine, therefore, digests $\frac{20 \times 2}{2} = 20$ ml. of 0.1 per cent starch solution, which is equivalent to 20 Wohlgemuth units.

The number of units per ml. in the last tube with no blue color will be as follows:

Tube 1 =   5 units per ml.
Tube 2 = 10 units per ml.
Tube 3 = 20 units per ml.
Tube 4 = 40 units per ml.
Tube 5 = 80 units per ml.
Tube 6 = 160 units per ml.
Tube 7 = 320 units per ml.

Normal Values

Random specimen: 2 to 50 units per ml.

24-hour specimen: 6 to 30 units per ml.

Remarks and Sources of Error. Values obtained with a 24-hour urine specimen are more valuable than those obtained with a random specimen. The urine may be preserved with a little toluene. The total urine volume should always be reported. This procedure will give falsely low results if the starch solution is old or if the N/50 iodine solution has not been prepared on the same day it is used.

Determination of Lipase in Serum and Duodenal Contents

Principle. Lipase hydrolyzes triglycerides (for example, olive oil) to fatty acids and glycerine or its mono- and diesters. The liberated fatty acids are titrated with N/20 NaOH, using thymolphthalein as indicator.

Reagents*

1. Olive oil emulsion. Add 0.2 gm. of sodium benzoate and 7.0 gm. of gum arabic (acacia) U.S.P. to 93 ml. of distilled water and mix in blender until dissolved. Slowly add 93 ml. of olive oil U.S.P. and continue mixing for five minutes. This emulsion is

* All reagents are available commercially.

stable for six months if stored at 10 to 14° C. Exposure to heat or freezing will destroy it. Shake the emulsion vigorously before use.

2. N/20 NaOH.

3. Thymolphthalein. Dissolve 1 gm. of thymolphthalein in 95 per cent ethanol and dilute to 100 ml.

4. Buffer pH 8.0. Dissolve 0.8583 gm. of sodium diethyl barbiturate and 0.4183 gm. of diethyl barbituric acid in approximately 90 ml. of hot water. After cooling, transfer the solution to a 100 ml. volumetric flask and dilute to the mark with water. Check and adjust the pH to 8.0 at 27° C. Add 3 drops of toluene or chloroform as preservative and keep the reagent refrigerated. Discard the reagent if bacterial contamination has occurred.

Method

1. Into each of two test tubes marked "blank" and "test" pipet 2.5 ml. distilled water, 3.0 ml. olive oil emulsion, and 1.0 ml. buffer of pH 8.0.

2. Into the "test" test tubes pipet 1.0 ml. serum and mix well. If duodenal fluid is to be analyzed, two determinations should be carried out: one test with a 1:10 and another with a 1:100 dilution of duodenal fluid instead of serum.

3. Pipet 1.0 ml. serum or diluted duodenal fluid into a 50 ml. Erlenmeyer flask labeled "blank" and store this flask in the refrigerator.

4. Incubate "test" and "blank" tubes in a water bath at 37° C. for six hours. In case of an emergency, run tests in duplicate and incubate one set for three hours only.

5. Pour contents of "blank" tube into the Erlenmeyer flask stored in the refrigerator. Pour contents of "test" tube into a clean 50 ml. Erlenmeyer flask.

6. Pipet 3.0 ml. 95 per cent ethanol into "blank" and "test" test tubes, shake, and add to respective Erlenmeyer flasks.

7. Add 4 drops thymolphthalein to "blank" and "test" and titrate to a light blue color with N/20 NaOH.

8. Subtract "blank" reading from "test" reading. The difference between these readings represents the units of lipase per ml. of serum. If a three-hour incubation time was used, results should be doubled. In case of duodenal fluid results should be multiplied by dilution and total volume.

Remarks and Sources of Error. The buffer and the serum should be pipetted with volumetric and Oswald-Folin pipets, respectively. The olive oil emulsion can best be pipeted with a 10 ml. serologic pipet or with an automatic syringe-type pipet.

The pH of the buffer is critical. Incorrect adjustment causes low results. Serum lipase, when frozen or stored in a refrigerator, is stable for several days. Slight hemolysis does not interfere with the test, but strongly hemolyzed specimens should not be used.

The dilution for duodenal fluid determinations is necessary, since the buffer used in the procedure is not effective enough to compensate for the alkaline pH of the duodenal content. In addition the extremely high lipolytic activity of some duodenal fluids would cause an excessive production of free fatty acids, which in turn would inhibit the reaction.

Normal Values. Values up to 1.0 unit lipase per ml. of serum should be considered normal and those up to 1.2 units per ml. as borderline (Tietz *et al.*, 1959).

Determination of Trypsin in Duodenal Contents

Principle. Casein, when incubated at 30° C. with duodenal contents at a pH of 9.0, is hydrolyzed, and the increase in carboxyl groups is determined by titration with N/10 alcoholic KOH. Since alcohol suppresses the basic properties of the amino acids, the titration can be carried out directly.

Reagents

1. Casein solution. Place 30 gm. of casein in a 500 ml. flask, add 300 ml. of distilled water, and shake vigorously for five minutes. Then add 20 ml. of 1 N ammonium hydroxide and shake for an additional 20 minutes. Bring the volume to 500 ml. with distilled water. The reagent is stable for four days if kept in the refrigerator.

2. Buffer solution. Mix 120 ml. each of 1 N ammonium hydroxide and 1 N ammonium chloride and add 160 ml. of distilled water. Keep reagent refrigerated.

3. N/10 alcoholic KOH. Mix 1 part of 1 N KOH with 9 parts of absolute alcohol.

4. Thymolphthalein (0.5 per cent) in 95 per cent ethanol.

Method. Prepare a 1:1 dilution of duodenal fluid with glycerol immediately after collection of the specimen. Keep this solution refrigerated.

1. Pipet 2 ml. of the 1:1 dilution of duodenal contents into a test tube. Allow the pipet to drain well.

2. Place the tube in a water bath at 30° C. for 5½ minutes and add 2 ml. of buffer solution. After exactly 30 seconds add 3 ml. of the casein solution. Shake well and incubate the tube for 20 minutes.

3. Measure into each of two 250 ml. flasks 38 ml. of 95 per cent alcohol, 3 ml. of water, and 1 ml. of indicator. Mark one flask "blank" and one flask "test."

4. Exactly 20 minutes after addition of the casein pour the contents of the test tube into the flask marked "test" and rinse the test tube well with the contents of the flask.

5. Into the flask marked "blank" add 2 ml. of duodenal contents (1:1), 2 ml. of buffer, and 3 ml. of casein solution.

6. Titrate both flasks with alcoholic N/10 KOH to the first appearance of a blue color.

7. Add 72 ml. of boiling 95 per cent alcohol to each flask (the blue color will disappear) and continue titration until the same blue color appears in both flasks. It is essential that this titration be carried out rapidly.

Calculation. Subtract "blank" reading from "test" reading, determine the units from the following chart, and multiply this figure by total volume of duodenal contents per hour (shown at bottom of page).

Normal Values. Trypsin is excreted at the rate of 20 to 40 (Lagerlöf) units per hour or 0.35 to 0.7 units per kg. body weight per hour (Lagerlöf, 1942, and Varley, 1958).

Determination of Trypsin in Stool

Principle. A stool emulsion is placed on an x-ray film. Presence of trypsin is indicated by the digestion of the gelatin layer after a one-hour incubation at 37° C.

Method

1. Place 4 ml. saline into a glass stopper cylinder and add stool until the meniscus reaches the 5 ml. mark (1:5 dilution). Mix well.

2. Place one large drop of this emulsion on the gelatin side of an unexposed x-ray film. The film is clipped to a cardboard to prevent curling and placed in a Petri dish containing a wet filter paper to prevent drying of the stool.

3. Add 5 ml. of saline to the 1:5 stool emulsion, mix, and place one drop of this 1:10 dilution on the same or a separate x-ray film.

4. Incubate the film for one hour at 37° C. (or for two hours at room temperature).

5. After incubation wash film under a gentle stream of cold water. A clearing at the site of the drops indicates enzyme activity. The degree of activity is estimated as follows:

A beginning (slight) digestion with the 1:5 dilution is read as 1+.
A moderate digestion with the 1:5 dilution is read as 2+.
A moderate digestion with the 1:10 dilution is read as 3+.
A complete digestion with the 1:10 dilution is read as 4+.
No change on the surface of the x-ray film or just some roughness is considered negative.

Remarks and Sources of Error. Any x-ray film cut in squares of approximately 1″ × 1.5″ can be used, but dental films are most convenient. The film should not be stored longer than the expiration date and it should be unexposed and undeveloped. When a film is being used for the first time, an adequate control should be run.

Sufficient moisture in the Petri dish is necessary for the enzymatic reaction and to prevent caking of the stool.

Some microorganisms have proteolytic activity. However, Shwachman (1949) demonstrated that the activity is relatively slight compared to that of pancreatic juice.

To detect interference by bacterial proteases, one drop of a 0.2 per cent solution of a commercially available specific antitrypsin in saline may be added to a separate stool emulsion. The antitrypsin inhibits the pancreatic trypsin but not bacterial proteases. A test is considered positive only

ML. N/10 POTASSIUM HYDROXIDE	UNITS TRYPSIN	ML. N/10 POTASSIUM HYDROXIDE	UNITS TRYPSIN	ML. N/10 POTASSIUM HYDROXIDE	UNITS TRYPSIN
0.10	0.037	0.80	0.335	1.50	0.78
0.20	0.075	0.90	0.385	1.60	0.87
0.30	0.115	1.00	0.44	1.70	0.97
0.40	0.157	1.10	0.50	1.80	1.07
0.50	0.200	1.20	0.56	1.90	1.18
0.60	0.245	1.30	0.63	2.00	1.28
0.70	0.290	1.40	0.70		

if the control with antitrypsin shows no digestion of the x-ray film (Meites, 1960).

Urine has a strong proteolytic activity, and contamination of stool with urine, therefore, must be avoided.

Enzyme therapy must be discontinued for three days prior to the test.

Stool specimens should be examined within 24 hours after collection.

The Vitamin A Tolerance Test and the Determination of Vitamin A and Carotenoids in Serum

Principle. Serum proteins are precipitated by alcohol, and vitamin A and carotenoids are extracted by petroleum ether. The carotenoids are determined by colorimetric reading of the petroleum ether layer at a wave length of 440 mμ.

Vitamin A content is determined by evaporating the petroleum ether and adding antimony trichloride to the residue. The blue color produced (Carr-Price reaction) is read in a colorimeter at a wave length of 620 mμ. Since carotenoids also give a slight color in this reaction, a correction factor is applied.

Administration of Vitamin A. Directions for administration of the vitamin A for a tolerance test and instructions for collection of blood specimens are given on p. 582.

Reagents

1. Antimony trichloride, 22 per cent. Place 11.0 gm. of antimony trichloride, analytical grade, in a 50 ml. volumetric flask, dissolve in anhydrous chloroform, and fill to mark. If necessary, the chloroform should be redistilled from anhydrous sodium carbonate. Keep the reagent in a tightly stoppered brown bottle.

2. Ethanol, 95 per cent.

3. Petroleum ether, low boiling.

4. Beta-carotene standard. Purify beta-carotene by dissolving 100 mg. beta-carotene (Eastman No. 3702) in 2 ml. chloroform and reprecipitating with 20 ml. methanol. The filtered precipitate should be washed with a few drops of methanol and dried in a vacuum desiccator. Transfer 30.0 mg. purified beta-carotene to a 100 ml. volumetric flask, dissolve, and dilute to volume with petroleum ether. Prior to use dilute 1.0 ml. of the stock standard to 100 ml. with petroleum ether. This diluted standard contains 3 gamma beta-carotene per ml.

5. Vitamin A stock standard (10

gamma per ml.). Transfer 10 mg. of vitamin A alcohol (or 11.47 mg. vitamin A acetate) to a 1000 ml. volumetric flask and dilute to volume with petroleum ether. A standardized concentrate of vitamin A is also suitable for preparing this standard solution. Before using, dilute the stock standard 1:10 with petroleum ether.

Method for Carotenoid and Vitamin A Determination

1. Into each of two 5 ml. glass stopper centrifuge tubes pipet exactly 1.0 ml. serum, 2.0 ml. 95 per cent ethanol, and 2.0 ml. petroleum ether. Stopper tubes tightly and shake vigorously for ten minutes.

2. Centrifuge the stoppered tubes and transfer 1.0 ml. of the petroleum ether layer (top) into a microcuvet (for example, a 10 × 75 mm. Coleman cuvet).

3. Read immediately in a spectrophotometer (or colorimeter) at a wave length of 440 mμ against a petroleum ether blank. Calculate carotenoid values from calibration curve or chart.

4. Evaporate the petroleum ether to dryness by placing the cuvets into a water bath of 40 to 45° C. and by gently blowing dry air (or nitrogen) into the cuvet. A stream of dry air can be obtained by passing the air first through a bottle containing silica gel. The tubes must be absolutely dry to avoid cloudiness in the Carr-Price reaction.

5. Set the spectrophotometer to a wave length of 620 mμ and adjust to 100 per cent transmittance, using the antimony trichloride solution as blank.

6. Add exactly 1.0 ml. of the 22 per cent antimony trichloride solution and read immediately, since the blue color produced is extremely evanescent. Any cloudiness that might develop at this point is usually due to moisture in the cuvet or in the antimony trichloride solution. In such a case the test must be repeated, taking precautions to avoid moisture.

Calculations

Carotenoids. Determine the amount of carotenoids per cuvet from the standard curve and carry out the following calculations:

$$\frac{\text{gamma carotenoids/cuvet} \times \text{dilution} \times 100}{\text{ml. serum used}}$$

= gamma carotenoids/100 ml. serum

If this procedure is followed with respect to quantities, the equation reduces to:

gamma carotenoids/cuvet × 200 = gamma carotenoids/100 ml. serum.

Vitamin A. Determine the amount of

vitamin A per cuvet from the standard curve and carry out the following calculations:

gamma vitamin A/cuvet × dilution × 100

ml. serum used

− (0.075 × gamma carotenoids)
= gamma vitamin A/100 ml. serum.

If the quantities used are those given in the procedure, the equation reduces to:

gamma vitamin A/cuvet × 200

− (0.075 × gamma carotenoids)
= gamma vitamin A/100 ml. serum.

Subtraction of gamma carotenoids × 0.075 is necessary to correct for the amount of color produced by the carotenoids.

Calibration

Carotenoids. Prepare a calibration curve by using solutions of beta-carotene in petroleum ether (see reagents) in concentrations of 0.5, 1.0, 1.5, 2.0, 2.5, and 3.0 gamma per ml.

Vitamin A. The calibration curve for vitamin A is prepared by using aliquots of a solution of vitamin A alcohol in petroleum ether (see reagents), resulting in concentrations of 0.5, 1.0, 1.5, 2.0, 2.5, and 3.0 gamma vitamin A per cuvet. Proceed as outlined in steps 4 to 6 of procedure.

Normal Values. The normal carotenoid level (mainly beta-carotene and xanthophyll) is 100 to 300 gamma per 100 ml. serum, calculated as beta-carotene. Vitamin A is normally found in serum in concentrations of 15 to 60 gamma per 100 ml. (approximately 50 to 200 U.S.P. units).

Remarks and Sources of Error. The Carr-Price reaction gives a color with carotenoids as well as with vitamin A. The carotenoids, therefore, have to be determined before the vitamin A content can be calculated.

All reagents used must be water free, since moisture results in cloudiness and erroneous results.

One International and USP unit of vitamin A is defined as 0.30 gamma of vitamin A alcohol or 0.344 gamma of vitamin A acetate, and 0.6 gamma of pure beta-carotene is considered to have the activity of one unit of vitamin A (Carr and Price, 1926, and Koch and Hanke, 1953).

The Lipiodol Test

Principle. The principle of the test and the procedure for the administration of Lipiodol are explained on p. 583.

Method

1. Place five test tubes in a test tube rack and add 0.5 ml. distilled water to tubes 2 through 5.

2. Add 0.5 ml. of urine to tubes 1 and 2.

3. Mix tube 2 and transfer 0.5 ml. to tube 3. Continue with this procedure and discard 0.5 ml. from tube 5. The tubes now contain 0.5 ml. of urine or urine and distilled water in dilutions 1:1, 1:4, 1:16, and 1:32, respectively.

4. Add to each tube 5 drops of freshly prepared 8 N nitric acid, mix, and add 3 drops of a fresh 1 per cent starch solution.

The presence of a blue color is read as positive. A faint color, which disappears after five minutes, or a colorless solution is considered negative.

Normal Values. Patients with normal pancreatic function show a positive test in a urine dilution of 1:4 or above.

Remarks and Sources of Error. The starch used in the procedure should be reasonably fresh, and the nitric acid must be prepared directly before use. The test is only valid if the urine specimen prior to administration of the drug was found to be negative for iodine.

Interruption of meals during the test is not necessary, but enzyme therapy must be discontinued at least 48 hours before the test (Silverman and Shirkey, 1955).

The Sweat Test

Collection of Sweat. The back of the child is carefully washed with distilled water, and two gauze sponges on top of each other are placed on either side of the spine. The sponges should be approximately 2″ × 2″ in size and should be cleaned with distilled or deionized water, dried, and weighed exactly in a labeled Petri dish before use. A plastic sheet approximately 4″ × 4″ is put on top of the gauze and tightly sealed with surgical tape. A plastic bag is then placed around the child and tied around the neck. Sweating can be accelerated by wrapping the patient in an additional blanket or by using a heating lamp. After a sufficient amount of sweat is collected (usually after 15 to 60 minutes), the gauze is removed and sent to the laboratory in the same Petri dish. (Use a forceps to prevent contamination and cover Petri dish to prevent evaporation.) Note: Avoid overheating the child. Do not prolong the sweating period beyond 60 minutes.

Recovery of Sweat. Weigh sponges and Petri dish exactly to determine the amount of sweat collected, and recover the sweat by placing the sponges in a funnel and washing them with deionized water. Also rinse the Petri dish. The washings are collected in a volumetric flask. This procedure is simple but has the disadvantage that the sweat is not in the original concentration and that the dilution factor has to be calculated. It has been recommended recently that a golf-tee be placed point down in a 15 ml. conical centrifuge tube and that the sponges be put on top of the tee. The tube, tightly sealed with a rubber cap, is then centrifuged at moderate speed. The sweat will accumulate in the tip of the tube in its original concentration. If this procedure is used, weighing of the sponges is not necessary. (See also p. 508.)

Analysis of Sweat. The concentration of sodium or chloride in sweat can be determined with any of the common laboratory procedures. A proper dilution for the sodium determination can easily be calculated if the chloride analysis is done first, since Na and Cl results parallel each other fairly closely.

Normal Values

Na: 10 to 90 mEq. per L.

Cl: 4 to 60 mEq. per L.

Remarks and Sources of Error. Falsely high results can be obtained if the skin of the child is not cleaned properly or if contaminated sponges are used. Some laboratories have abandoned the use of sponges and collect the sweat with a capillary tube directly from the bag and the skin of the patient. The amount of sweat collected with such a procedure is greater, but results are less reliable since evaporation can cause an increase in electrolyte concentration.

REFERENCES

1. Andersen, D. H.: Pancreatic enzymes in the duodenal juice in the celiac syndrome. Am. J. Dis. Child., 63:643, 1942.
2. Berkowitz, D., Sklaroff, D., Woldow, A., Jacobs, A. G., and Likoff, W.: Blood absorptive patterns of isotopically-labeled fat and fatty acid. Ann. Int. Med., 50:247, 1959.
3. Bockus, H. L., Kalsen, M. H., Roth, J. L. A., Bogoch, A. L., and Stein, G.: Clinical features of acute inflammation of pancreas. Arch. Int. Med., 96:308, 1955.
4. Bothereau, N. R., Draper, F. H., and Gibbs, G. E.: Demonstration of a tumor involving the pancreas through the use of duodenal drainage and the intravenous injection of secretin. Am. J. Digest. Dis., 18:70, 1951.
5. Cantarow, A., and Trumper, M.: Clinical Biochemistry. Philadelphia, W. B. Saunders Company, 1955.
6. Carr, F. H., and Price, E. A.: LXIV. Colour re-

actions attributed to vitamin A. Biochem. J., 20:498, 1926.
7. Comfort, M. W., et al.: External pancreatic secretion as measured by the secretin test in patients with idiopathic steatorrhea (nontropical sprue). Gastroenterol., 13:135, 1949.
8. Delory, G. E., Israels, S., and Jonasson, H.: The iodized oil (Lipiodol) test for fat absorption. A.M.A. Arch. Dis. Child., 92:24, 1956.
9. Diamond, J. S., and Siegal, S. A.: The secretin test in the diagnosis of pancreatic disease with a report of 130 tests. Am. J. Digest. Dis., 7:435, 1940.
10. Dreiling, D. A.: Studies in pancreatic function. V. The use of the secretin test in the diagnosis of pancreatitis. Gastroenterol., 24:540, 1953.
11. Dreiling, D. A.: The technic of the secretin test: normal ranges. J. Mt. Sinai Hosp., 21:363, 1954–55.
12. Dreiling, D. A., and Hollander, F.: Studies in pancreatic function. Gastroenterol., 11:714, 1948.
13. Dreiling, D. A., and Hollander, F.: Studies in pancreatic function. II. A statistical study of pancreatic secretion following secretin in patients without pancreatic disease. Gastroenterol., 15:620, 1950.
14. Duffy, B. J., Jr., and Turner, D. A.: The differential diagnosis of intestinal malabsorption with I131-fat and fatty acid. Ann. Int. Med., 48:1, 1958.
15. Gibbs, G. E.: Secretin test with bilumen gastroduodenal drainage in infants and children. Pediatrics, 5:941, 1950.
16. Gibbs, G. E.: Cystic fibrosis of the pancreas. Maryland Med. J., 2:644, 1953.
17. Goldbarg, J. A., and Rutenburg, A. M.: The colorimetric determination of leucine amino peptidase in urine and serum of normal subjects and patients with cancer and other diseases. Cancer, 11:283, 1958.
18. Groen, J.: Absorption and metabolism of Lipiodol after oral administration. Method for the study of fat absorption and fat metabolism in man. Am. J. Med., 4:814, 1948.
19. Hirsch, E. F., Carbonaro, L., Biggs, A. D., and Phillips, F. L.: Postprandial hypolipemia of pancreatic fibrocystic disease. A.M.A. Arch. Dis. Child., 86:721, 1953.
20. Hoffman, W. S.: The Biochemistry of Clinical Medicine. Chicago, Yearbook Publishers, Inc., 1954.
21. Janowitz, H. D., and Dreiling, D. A.: The plasma amylase. Am. J. Med., 27:924, 1959.
22. Kaiser, E., Kunstadter, R. H., and Mendelsohn, R. S.: Electrolyte concentrations in sweat and saliva. A.M.A. J. Dis. Child., 92:369, 1956.
23. Kaplan, E., Edidin, B. D., Fruin, R. C., and Baker, L. A.: Intestinal absorption of iodine 131-labeled triolein and oleic acid in normal subjects and in steatorrhea. Gastroenterol., 34:901, 1958.
24. King, E. J.: Micro-analysis in Medical Biochemistry. New York, Grune & Stratton, Inc., 1951, p. 136.
25. Koch, F. C., and Hanke, M. E.: Practical Methods in Biochemistry. Baltimore, The Williams & Wilkins Company, 1953.
26. Lagerlöf, H. O.: Pancreatic Function and Pancreatic Disease Studied by Means of Secretin. New York, The Macmillan Co., 1942.
27. Lagerlöf, H. O.: Pancreatic function and pancreatic disease studied by means of secretin. Acta Med. Scand. (Suppl.), 128:1, 1942.
28. Lemon, H. M., and Byrnes, W. W.: Cancer of

the biliary tract and pancreas. J.A.M.A., *141:* 254, 1949.

29. Lipp, W. F., and Hubbard, R. S.: The serum calcium in acute pancreatitis. Gastroenterol., *16:* 726, 1950.

30. McGeachin, R. L., and Hargan, L. A.: Renal clearance of amylase. Proc. Soc. Exper. Biol. & Med., *89:*129, 1956.

31. Meites, S.: Manual of Clinical Chemistry. Columbus, The Children's Hospital, 1960.

32. Necheles, H., and Kirshen, M. M.: The Physiologic Basis of Gastrointestinal Therapy. New York, Grune & Stratton, Inc. 1957, pp. 294–321.

33. Perry, W. F., and Gibson, C.: Assessment of clinical usefulness of serum leucine aminopeptidase determinations. Report given at the meeting of the American Association of Clinical Chemists, Montreal, Canada, 1960.

34. Popper, H. L., and Necheles, H.: Pancreas function tests. Med. Clin. North Am., *43:*401, 1959.

35. Rutenberg, A. M., Goldbarg, J. A., and Pineda, E. P.: Leucine aminopeptidase activity. Observations in patients with cancer of the pancreas and other diseases. New England J. Med., *259:*469, 1958.

36. Schwarz, L., Woldow, A., and Dunsmore, R.: Determination of fat tolerance in patients with myocardial infarction. Method utilizing serum turbidity changes following a fat meal. J.A.M.A., *149:*364, 1952.

37. Shwachman, H., and Galim, N.: A simple test for the determination of excess chloride in the skin in cystic fibrosis of the pancreas. New England J. Med., *255:*999, 1956.

38. Shwachman, H., Patterson, P. R., and Laguna, J.: Studies in pancreatic fibrosis: A simple diagnostic gelatin film test for stool trypsin. Pediatrics, *4:*222, 1949.

39. Silverman, F. N., and Shirkey, H. C.: A fat absorption test using iodized oil, with particular application as a screening test in the diagnosis of fibrocystic disease of the pancreas. Pediatrics, *15:*143, 1955.

40. Snape, W. J., Wirts, C. W., and Friedman, M. H. F.: Evaluation of pancreatic function by means of induced hyper-amylasemia following morphine and secretin (Proc. Am. Fed. Clin. Research). In Am. J. Med., *6:*23, 1949.

41. Somogyi, M.: Diastatic activity of human blood. Arch. Int. Med., *67:*665, 1941.

42. Somogyi, M.: Modifications of two methods for the assay of amylase. Clin. Chem., *6:*23, 1960.

43. Tietz, N. W., Borden, T., and Stepleton, J. D.: An improved method for the determination of lipase in serum. Am. J. Clin. Path., *31:*148, 1959.

44. Varley, H.: Practical Clinical Biochemistry. New York, Interscience Publishers, Inc., 1958, p. 306.

45. Wirts, C. W., and Snape, W. J.: Evaluation of pancreatic function tests. J.A.M.A., *145:*876, 1951.

46. Wohlgemuth, J.: Über eine neue Methode zur quantitativen Bestimmung des diastatischen Ferments. Biochem. Ztschr., *9:*1, 1908.

Chapter 14

Gastric and Duodenal Contents

By JAMES C. CAIN, M.D., *and* LLOYD G. BARTHOLOMEW, M.D.

Many ingenious methods have been devised to obtain the secretions of the stomach, and it appears reasonable to hope that examination of the gastric contents in health and disease may shed light on the state of the patient's health.

EXAMINATION OF GASTRIC CONTENTS

The gastric contents consist essentially of water, free hydrochloric acid, combined hydrochloric acid, pepsin, rennin, mineral salts (chiefly acid phosphates), particles of undigested and partly digested food, and various products of digestion in solution. The amount and character of the gastric contents vary with the state of digestion. In pathologic conditions there may be added new substances, such as various microscopic structures and certain organic acids, especially lactic acid.

Gastric digestion consists mainly of the action of pepsin on proteins in the presence of hydrochloric acid and of curdling of milk by rennin. The fat-splitting ferment, lipase, of the gastric juice has extremely little activity except on previously emulsified fats, such as those of milk and egg yolk.

Pepsin and rennin are secreted by the gastric glands as zymogens, namely pepsinogen and renninogen, which are converted into pepsin and rennin by hydrochloric acid. Hydrochloric acid is secreted chiefly by the fundus of the stomach. It at once combines loosely with the proteins of the food and forms acid metaprotein, the first step in the digestion of protein. Hydrochloric acid that thus is combined loosely with protein is called "combined hydrochloric acid." The acid that is secreted after all the proteins present have been converted into acid metaproteins remains as "free hydrochloric acid"; together with pepsin it continues the process of digestion.

In normal persons the character and amount of gastric secretion obtained by gastric intubation vary greatly. Such factors as age, sex, temperature, emotions, state of digestion, type of test meal, degree of dilution or neutralization by swallowed saliva or by regurgitated duodenal contents, amount of gastric dilatation, and position of the tip of the tube all cause variations in gastric secretion in normal persons. Thus, only vague limits of normal can be suggested, as follows: The volume under fasting conditions averages 25 to 50 ml., more than 150 ml. being definitely abnormal; the height of the response after a test meal is 20 to 40 units or degrees of free hydrochloric acid and 30 to 60 units or degrees of total acidity. The normal gross characteristics are as follows: fairly fluid, no food particles, pearly gray, usually little mucus, usually no bile, sharp sour odor, and no blood.

It is the clinician's responsibility to ask himself what he expects to learn from a gastric analysis. This is not a dangerous test but it is not entirely innocuous. Although it is a time-honored procedure, its usefulness actually is limited. The presence or absence of free hydrochloric acid is often pertinent, and it is occasionally helpful to know whether the amount of free hydrochloric acid is high, low, or normal. The amount and character of the fluid seldom are diagnostic, yet in specific instances they may give a clue to the diagnosis. Some of the more elaborate and refined tests using the collection of gastric juice as part of their technique may prove of real diagnostic value. These tests require careful standardization, and thus frequently are utilized only in research. More elaborate studies include the augmented histamine test, the 12-hour collection of nocturnal secretion, the insulin test, paper electrophoresis of gastric juice, electrogastrography, and cytologic study of the gastric sediment. Because of the disagreeable aspects of passing a gastric tube the so-called tubeless gastric analysis is used frequently in some laboratories. Its value is even more uncertain than that of the time-honored routine gastric analysis.

Obtaining the Gastric Contents

Technique for Passing the Gastric Tube. Gastric juice is secreted continuously in varying amounts. In clinical work it is desirable to obtain the juice with as little mechanical or psychologic trauma as possible. Various types of tubes have been devised for removal of the gastric contents. It is preferable to use a small tube with an opening at the tip and several holes in the side near the tip.* If retained food particles are present, it occasionally may be necessary to revert to one of the larger tubes; such tubes should be used with great care, preferably being passed only by one trained in such a procedure.

It is important to assure the patient that introduction of the tube cannot possibly harm him and that, if he can control the spasm of his throat, he will experience only a minimal choking sensation. Explanation of the procedure, as well as a demonstration of the tube to the patient prior to its passage, is frequently reassuring. The tube should be chilled in ice water in order to reduce nausea. The use of glycerin or other lubricants is usually unnecessary.

With the patient seated on a chair, his clothing protected by towels or a large apron, and his head tipped forward, the tip of the tube, held as one would hold a pen, is introduced far back into the pharynx. The technician stands to the right of the patient with the tip of the tube in the right hand and the remainder coiled in the left hand. Instruct the patient to open his mouth and then pass the tube over

* A number of tubes have been designed by such workers as Sawyer, Jutte, Levin, Rehfuss, and Lyon.

the top and middle of the tongue. When the tip of the tube reaches the posterior wall of the pharynx, tell the patient to close his mouth lightly on the tube and to swallow. Push gently and firmly on the tube. Wait until the patient resumes deep breathing through his mouth; then have the patient swallow again, while the tube again is pushed downward.

Repeat these procedures until the tube enters the esophagus. Pass the tube gently and not too rapidly into the stomach. Saliva should be expectorated. It is not necessary to hurry, and it is most important that the patient be kept at ease to enable him to relax. Breathing through the mouth must be encouraged at all times. Pass the tube to the second mark (55 cm.). During the remainder of the procedure the tube may be placed between the teeth and cheek on either side, the patient holding a towel over his mouth against the protruding tube.

With a large glass syringe gently aspirate the gastric contents. If material is not recovered when the tube is inserted to the second mark, remove the syringe and withdraw the tube about 3 cm. and aspirate again. This procedure may be repeated until the tube is withdrawn to the first mark if necessary. Do not use strong suction in aspirating the gastric contents. At times it may be convenient and less traumatic to pass the small gastric tube through an unobstructed nostril.

Technique for Study of Gastric Contents

ROUTINE QUALITATIVE EXAMINATION

A routine qualitative examination is conveniently carried out in the following order:

1. Give the patient a test meal after an overnight fast.

2. At the height of digestion, usually in one hour, remove 10 to 25 ml. of the gastric contents with a gastric tube.

3. Measure the contents and examine them macroscopically.

4. Filter the contents. A suction filter is desirable, and its use may be necessary when much mucus is present. (Some clinical pathologists prefer to titrate the gastric contents without filtering.)

5. During filtration examine the material microscopically and make qualitative tests for free hydrochloric acid and lactic acid.

6. When sufficient filtrate is obtained, make quantitative estimations of total

acidity, free hydrochloric acid, and combined hydrochloric acid (if necessary).

7. Make other tests that appear to be pertinent, such as tests for blood, pepsin, or rennin.

8. If free hydrochloric acid is present in the specimen removed at the end of the first hour, wait 15 minutes, empty the stomach completely, and examine the contents as in step 6. This concludes the test.

Fractional Gastric Analysis

A fractional gastric analysis is done if the test just described fails to show the presence of free hydrochloric acid. Small samples (10 to 25 ml.) are taken at 15-minute intervals during the second hour. Each sample is examined grossly, measured, and titrated. These results and the time each specimen was taken are recorded. If free hydrochloric acid appears in any of the 15-minute samples, titrate and record the amount. At this point the stomach can be emptied completely and the test concluded. A benzidine test may be done on a portion of the first specimen if gross blood is present in subsequent fractions.

Test Meals and Stimulants

As already noted, gastric juice is secreted continuously, but quantities sufficiently large for examination are often not obtainable under fasting conditions. In clinical work, therefore, it is desirable to stimulate secretion by means of food, which is the natural and most efficient stimulus, before attempting to collect the gastric contents. Different foods and chemicals stimulate secretion to different degrees; hence, for the sake of uniform results certain standard test stimulants have been adopted. It is customary to give the test meal in the morning, since the stomach is most likely to be empty at that time.

Ewald's Test Breakfast. This test breakfast consists of a roll or two slices of bread without butter and two small cups (300 to 400 ml.) of water or a similar amount of tea without cream or sugar. The bread should be well masticated. The gastric contents are removed one hour after ingestion of the meal. This period should be calculated from the beginning of ingestion of the meal, not from its completion. The one disadvantage of this meal is that the bread contains a variable amount of lactic acid and numerous yeast cells.

A modified Ewald test breakfast consists of eight arrowroot cookies and two glasses (400 ml.) of water. This meal is extremely satisfactory and is used in most gastric laboratories.

Clinical evaluation. This is a simple physiologic meal given routinely in most laboratories.

Riegel's Test Meal. This test meal consists of 400 ml. of bouillon, 150 to 200 gm. of broiled beefsteak, and 150 gm. of mashed potatoes. The meal should be thoroughly masticated, for it has a tendency to clog the gastric tube.

Clinical evaluation. This meal is physiologic but difficult to standardize completely. It is seldom used as a routine test.

Alcohol. Alcohol may be used to stimulate gastric secretion. A total of 50 ml. of a 7 per cent solution of ethyl alcohol is instilled into the stomach by means of a small stomach tube. Aspirate the stomach in a fasting state at 5-minute intervals for 15 minutes before feeding the alcohol and afterward at 10- or 15-minute intervals for one hour, saving a 10 ml. portion for testing and then returning the remainder to the stomach. Each sample is examined grossly, measured, and titrated. A curve is usually plotted, showing the volume and titratable acidity for each period.

Clinical evaluation. This test is simple to perform but is not physiologic. The stimulus probably is that of irritation of the gastric mucosa with liberation of histamine.

Histamine. Histamine hydrochloride, or preferably histamine phosphate, is administered hypodermically after the patient has fasted for at least 12 hours. The dose originally advised, namely 0.1 mg. for each 10 kg. of body weight, may cause a disagreeable reaction. Gompertz and Cohen (1929) have shown that a total dose of 0.25 mg. of histamine may be used satisfactorily. The dose given is for histamine itself; the actual dose of histamine phosphate that is administered is 0.19 mg. per 10 kg. of body weight, which is equivalent to 0.1 mg. of histamine. The reaction comes on rapidly. Flushing of the face, quickening of the pulse, and, at times, physical discomfort result. Caution must be exercised in the choice of patients who are given histamine, and the tests should not be used routinely. The aspirated secretion is measured and titrated in the usual manner, and the results are best recorded graphically by plotting curves.

Clinical evaluation. This procedure is not physiologic; it has disagreeable side effects and must be used with caution. This is the test used to determine the stomach's capability for secreting hydrochloric acid, for histamine is probably the most potent stimulant of gastric secretory function that is available.

Augmented Histamine Test (Card, 1956; Kay, 1953). In an attempt to minimize the impediments inherent in the usual gastric analysis and to bring some degree of quantitation into the procedure, a technique has been evolved for the assay of the activity of parietal cells based on the use of a maximal stimulus from a large dose of histamine. Protection against the systemic effect of histamine is afforded by the preliminary administration of an antihistaminic preparation.

In this procedure the secretion of hydrochloric acid in normal and pathologic states is not augmented by proportionately larger doses of histamine. Thus, it is inferred that all the parietal cells are maximally stimulated. Preliminary studies indicate that the results of these tests are reproducible in the same persons within a 5 per cent error.

Technique

1. Place the patient in the left lateral decubitus position and localize the tip of the tube roentgenographically in the so-called residual pool just to the left of the vertebral column.

2. With a continuous suction at a negative pressure of less than 40 mm. of mercury obtain a 45-minute basal collection.

3. Inject intramuscularly 100 mg. of pyrilamine maleate (Neoantergan) to produce an antihistamine effect. The gastric juice collected for the next 30 minutes is discarded.

4. Thirty minutes after injection of the antihistaminic, inject histamine acid phosphate subcutaneously in a dose of 0.4 mg. per 10 kg. of body weight.

5. Discard the gastric contents collected during the next 15 minutes. Titrate the collections for the subsequent 30 minutes and express the values as milligrams of hydrochloric acid (maximal secretion).

Results. The average basal secretion in normal persons is 72 mg. of hydrochloric acid; in patients with gastric ulcer the average is 113 mg., and in patients with duodenal ulcer it is 265 mg. The average maximal secretion is 422, 478, and 837 mg. in these three groups, respectively. Wide variation on either side of the mean values may be noted. After gastric resec-

tion a reduction of the maximal secretion of acid to 25 per cent of the preoperative levels is considered to indicate good surgical results. Difficulties in complete collection from the stomach after operation make this phase of the test more difficult and probably less reliable than the preoperative phase.

Clinical evaluation. At the present time the main field of usefulness for the augmented histamine test appears to be in the experimental physiologic laboratory.

Water. Water alone will stimulate the gastric mucosa and can be used as a test meal.

Clinical evaluation. It is a poor stimulus and is not recommended.

Caffeine. Caffeine, in a dose of 0.2 gm. in 200 ml. of water, may be introduced through the gastric tube as a test meal. The test is accomplished in essentially the same manner as is the procedure using alcohol.

Clinical evaluation. It is not physiologic. It produces few side effects and is not so potent a secretory stimulus as is histamine. It is a satisfactory test but is not widely used.

Egg Albumin. Heckmann (1933) used as a test meal 80 ml. of freshly prepared egg albumin with 130 ml. of distilled water to which 4 gm. of Witte's peptone was added. The mixture was stained with 2 drops of a 2 per cent solution of methylene blue, heated to body temperature, and filtered through gauze. This fluid meal may be administered through a gastric tube, and 10 ml. portions of the gastric contents may be removed at regular intervals for titration by the fractional method.

Clinical evaluation. This is a semiphysiologic but abnormal meal. The liquid meal is easy to administer, but its preparation is inconvenient for a busy laboratory and it is rarely used.

Motor Test Meal. A meal containing a slice of roast beef, a green vegetable (spinach), a large serving (1 tablespoonful) of raisins, a piece of toast, and regular or decaffeinated black coffee is served at midnight. The patient is instructed to eat the food slowly and to chew it well. The patient is not to eat or drink anything after the meal until the stomach is aspirated the following morning. Aspirate the gastric contents, determine the volume, examine for particles of food (remnants of the test meal), and record the results. Under normal conditions there usually will be a volume of less than 100 ml., and none of the remnants of the test meal can be identified.

Clinical evaluation. This is a physiologic test that frequently gives information relative to gastric emptying.

Insulin Test (Hollander, 1946). The main purpose of the insulin test is to determine the completeness and effectiveness with which the vagal innervation of the stomach has been destroyed by vagotomy. The physiologic basis of the insulin test stems from the capacity of insulin to stimulate both motor and secretory mechanisms in the stomach by way of the vagus nerve. Transection of all vagal fibers to the stomach will prevent the usual gastric responses to such stimulation. The stimulus to the vagal center in the brain is caused by the hypoglycemia induced by the insulin. Unless the blood sugar is reduced to 50 mg. or less per 100 ml., a response will not be induced regardless of the dose of insulin. If the level of blood sugar is maintained by giving glucose or by the administration of epinephrine, the insulin effect does not occur.

The insulin test is performed in the following manner (Hollander, 1946). The fasting patient is brought to the laboratory and weighed accurately. The dose of insulin (0.3 unit per kilogram of body weight) is calculated, and the material is placed in a sterile syringe preparatory to giving it intravenously. In some laboratories a standard dose of 20 units of insulin is used. The gastric tube is passed, and the stomach is emptied completely. A sample of blood is obtained so that the baseline value for blood sugar can be measured; a macromethod or, preferably, a micromethod may be used for the blood sugar. The insulin is injected intravenously; thereafter, every 15 minutes for the next 90 minutes, a sample of the gastric contents is aspirated and a sample of blood is drawn. It is essential that the patient be instructed to expectorate all saliva, for, soon after the insulin is given, the patient will begin to salivate and perspire. It is important that a physician give the insulin and carefully watch the patient for any sign of a reaction.

At the conclusion of the test the physician may give 50 ml. of a 50 per cent solution of dextrose intravenously or, if this is not deemed necessary, the patient may be given a glass of orange juice or several lumps of sugar. The amount of sugar in each sample of blood is determined, the volume of each sample of the gastric contents is measured, and each sample of gastric juice is titrated for free hydrochloric acid and total acids. A time chart is prepared, showing these various values. If the level of sugar in any sample of blood is 50 mg. or less per 100 ml., the stimulus of the insulin is considered to have been adequate.

The test is considered to give positive results if the values for free hydrochloric acid and total acidity are greater than those obtained in the baseline sample. This indicates some intact vagal fibers. Negative results occur when the values for free hydrochloric acid and total acidity do not exceed those observed in the baseline sample.

Some precautions are necessary with this procedure. It is important that the stomach be emptied completely at the time of the baseline aspiration and that the patient meticulously expectorate all saliva. Atropine or similar parasympathetic agents should not be used for 24 hours prior to the test. The gastric aspiration must be done in such a way that neutralization of the gastric juice from the intestinal contents does not occur.

Clinical evaluation. This is a practical and useful test for determining the completeness and effectiveness of vagotomy. The performance of this test should be carefully supervised by a physician.

Nocturnal 12-Hour Gastric Aspiration. It is generally accepted that the human stomach, even in the absence of food, secretes its juices continually. The volume and concentration of the acid vary greatly in different disease states and even from hour to hour in the same person. Generally this test is begun about 5:30 p.m., starting with the usual Ewald type of test meal and aspirating the stomach at the end of one hour. This specimen is measured for volume and for concentration and output of free hydrochloric acid.

The gastric tube is left in place for the next 12 hours. Gentle, continuous suction is applied to the tube. At the end of the 12-hour period the total volume of gastric acid is measured as well as the concentration and output of free hydrochloric acid. A criticism of this test is that the stomach presumably is kept empty at all times. Experimental evidence shows that the presence of acid in the antrum of the stomach has a tendency to reduce the gastric secretion of acid. On the other hand, if suction were to be applied only at intervals, some of the gastric juice would escape into the duodenum and thus a true 12-hour total secretion would not be obtained. The technique using continuous suction appears to be preferable.

Levin (1951) studied patients by means of this 12-hour, nocturnal, continuous-suction method and found significant differences between normal persons and patients who had duodenal ulcer, gastric ulcer, or gastric carcinoma. The volume, concentration, and output of acid were greatest in patients with duodenal ulcer. No significant difference was noted between the volume of gastric secretion of normal persons and that of patients with gastric ulcer, but the output of acid tended to be less in the latter. The lowest secretory rate occurred in gastric carcinoma.

Clinical evaluation. This test is disagreeable, for the tube must be left in all night. It probably does not represent normal physiologic conditions but often gives valuable information concerning the total long-term secretion of the stomach.

Tubeless Gastric Analysis. An indirect method of detecting the presence of free hydrochloric acid has been accomplished by the so-called tubeless gastric analysis. The first practical method for estimating the gastric acidity without use of the gastric tube was introduced in 1950 by Segal and associates. Initially a quinine resin compound was employed as an indicator, but more recent investigations have dealt with dye resin compounds. One such compound consists of a carboxylic acid cation-exchange resin in which hydrogen cations have been replaced by dye cations (azure A). In the presence of dilute hydrochloric acid, the dye cations are displaced by the hydrogen cations of free hydrochloric acid. Significant replacement of the dye cations occurs in the lower range of pH (less than 3) with maximal displacement at pH 1.5. The released dye cations are absorbed from the small intestine and excreted in the urine where the discoloration from the dye is readily recognized.

Technique

1. Breakfast is withheld and the initial morning specimen of urine is discarded.

2. A gastric stimulant (usually 500 mg. of caffeine sodium benzoate) is taken orally with approximately 500 ml. of water. In some instances histamine phosphate has been given parenterally.

3. A specimen of urine is collected in one hour to serve as the control sample.

4. The dye resin compound is taken orally, again with a sufficient amount of water.

5. Two hours later the bladder is emptied, and the entire specimen of urine is saved for analysis.

6. The two-hour specimen is then compared with a known standard. The results of this comparison may denote either the absence of detectable amounts of dye, indicating that free hydrochloric acid was not secreted, or the presence of dye, signifying the presence of free hydrochloric acid. Some gross quantitation of the amount of free hydrochloric acid may be ascertained from the concentration of the dye in the urine. An overall correlation of 95 per cent is claimed with the gastric-tube method.

Clinical evaluation. This procedure avoids the discomfort associated with passage of a gastric tube and appears to have a high degree of correlation with methods employing direct aspiration of gastric contents. Both falsely positive and falsely negative results have been reported. The simplicity of the test makes it well suited for mass screening studies for achlorhydria. Its disadvantages include the time factor involved and, unless the procedure is done under close supervision, the complete dependence on the accuracy of the patient in carrying out instructions. Other information that may be obtained by use of the gastric tube, such as the presence of blood, particles of food, or a large residual volume of gastric juice, is of course unavailable by this method. The accuracy of the test may be diminished in the presence of pyloric obstruction, impairment of absorption in the small intestine, hepatic disease, and decreased renal function.

Physical Examination of the Gastric Contents

Under normal conditions 50 to 200 ml. of fluid can be obtained one hour after an Ewald test breakfast has been administered. Larger amounts point to motor insufficiency or hypersecretion; amounts less than 20 ml. may indicate too rapid an emptying of the stomach or incomplete removal. On standing, the gastric contents separate into two layers; the lower consists of particles of food, whereas the upper layer is an almost clear, faintly yellow fluid. The extent to which digestion has taken place can be estimated roughly from the appearance of the food particles.

The *reaction* is frankly acid in health

and in nearly all pathologic conditions. It may be neutral or slightly alkaline in some cases of gastric carcinoma or severe chronic gastritis or when the contents are contaminated by a considerable amount of saliva.

A small amount of *mucus* is present normally. Mucus from the stomach is recognized by its characteristic slimy appearance when the fluid is poured from one vessel to another. It is seen more frequently in fluid that has been used to wash the stomach than in the fluid removed after a test meal. If the mucus is full of air bubbles and if it floats, it is probably from the nasopharyngeal region.

A trace of *bile* is common as a result of excessive straining while the tube is in the stomach. Large amounts are rarely found and generally point to obstruction distal to the ampulla of Vater. Bile produces a yellowish or, more frequently, a greenish discoloration of the fluid. When a gastrocolic fistula is present, the gastric contents may have a strong fecal odor.

Blood often is recognized by simple inspection, but more frequently a chemical test is required for confirmation. It is bright red when fresh, whereas it is dark, resembling coffee grounds, when older. Vomiting of blood, or hematemesis, may be mistaken for pulmonary hemorrhage or hemoptysis. In the former condition the fluid is acid in reaction, usually dark red or brown and clotted, whereas in hemoptysis it is brighter red, frothy, and alkaline, usually being mixed with a variable amount of mucus. When the blood is small in amount and bright red, the possibility that it originates from injury by the tube must not be overlooked.

Particles of food eaten hours or even days previously may be found. They indicate deficient motor power or pyloric obstruction.

Search always should be made for bits of tissue from the gastric mucous membrane or tumors. These, when examined by a pathologist, sometimes may lead to the correct diagnosis.

Chemical Examination of the Gastric Contents

A routine chemical examination of the gastric contents involves qualitative tests for free hydrochloric acid and organic acids and the quantitative estimation of total acidity, free hydrochloric acid, and sometimes combined hydrochloric acid. Other tests are applied when indicated. In the routine examination qualitative tests are performed before quantitative tests.

QUALITATIVE TESTS

Free Acids. The presence or absence of free acids without reference to the kind is determined easily by the use of Congo red, although this test is not much used in practice. A thick piece of filter paper that has been soaked in a solution of Congo red, dried, and cut into strips may be used.

Free Hydrochloric Acid
DIMETHYLAMINO-AZOBENZENE TEST
  Reagent
  A 0.5 per cent alcoholic solution of dimethylamino-azobenzene.
  Technique
  To a small amount of the filtered gastric juice in a test tube, or to a few drops in a porcelain dish, add a drop of the reagent. If free hydrochloric acid is present, a cherry-red color appears at once. The intensity of color varies with the amount of acid present (Fig. 14–1, *a*). Although this test is extremely delicate, organic acids will produce a similar reaction when they are present in large amounts (more than 0.5 per cent). The color produced by organic acids, however, tends to be orange-red instead of cherry-red.

GUENZBURG'S TEST. This test is less delicate than the dimethylamino-azobenzene test, but it is more reliable because the reagent reacts only with free hydrochloric acid.
  Reagent
  Dissolve 2 gm. of phloroglucin and 1 gm. of vanillin in 30 ml. of absolute alcohol. This reagent should be freshly prepared.
  Technique
  Mix a few drops of the reagent with an equal amount of gastric juice. Slowly evaporate to dryness over a flame, taking care not to scorch the mixture. The appearance of a rose-red color indicates the presence of free hydrochloric acid. If only a yellow stain is produced, the reaction is negative (Fig. 14–1, *d* and *e*).

Organic Acids
  Lactic Acid. Lactic acid is the commonest organic acid and is considered to be typical of the organic acids that appear in the gastric contents. It is a product of bacterial activity. Acetic and butyric acids are sometimes present. Their formation is closely connected with that of lactic acid. Tests for

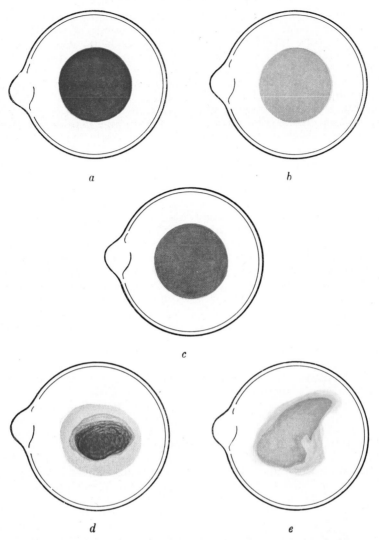

Figure 14–1. Dimethylamino-azobenzene test: *a*, free hydrochloric acid present; *b*, neutral reaction after titration with N/10 sodium hydroxide. Test for total acidity; phenolphthalein indicator; *c*, after titration with N/10 sodium hydroxide. Guenzburg's test; *d*, positive reaction; *e*, negative reaction. (Dorothy Booth, pinx.)

acetic or butyric acid rarely are performed. When these acids are abundant, they may be recognized by their odor on heating. Butyric acid gives the odor of rancid butter. From a clinical standpoint it is rarely necessary to test for organic acids.

Lactic acid is never present at the height of digestion in health. Although often present early in digestion, it disappears when free hydrochloric acid begins to appear. Small amounts may be introduced with the food. Pathologically, small amounts may be present whenever stagnation of the gastric contents and a deficiency of hydrochloric acid occur. The presence of notable amounts of lactic acid (more than 0.1 per cent by Strauss's test) is suggestive of gastric carcinoma. It is not usually necessary to test for lactic acid if free hydrochloric acid is present.

MODIFIED UFFELMANN'S TEST

Reagents

a. Phenol solution. Add 16 ml. of melted phenol crystals to 1000 ml. of distilled water.

b. A 10 per cent solution of ferric chloride in distilled water.

c. A 1 per cent solution of lactic acid in water.

Technique

1. In a test tube place 5 ml. of the phenol solution. Add a few drops of the

ferric chloride solution until a solution with an amethyst-blue color is formed.

2. To a second tube transfer 2.5 ml. of the resulting solution, which is to be used as a control. Add a few drops of the lactic acid drop by drop until the amethyst-blue solution becomes canary yellow.

3. To the other tube add filtered gastric juice drop by drop. If the color changes to match exactly the color of the control tube, lactic acid is present.

SIMON'S MODIFICATION OF KELLING'S TEST. To a test tube of distilled water add a sufficient amount of a 10 per cent solution of ferric chloride to give a faint yellowish tinge. Pour half of this into a second test tube to serve as a control. To the other tube add a small amount of gastric juice. Lactic acid gives a distinct yellow color that is readily recognized by comparison with the control. The color is seen best when the tubes are viewed from above over a sheet of paper.

STRAUSS'S TEST. This is a good test for clinical work, since it gives a rough idea of the quantity of lactic acid present and is not sufficiently sensitive to respond to the traces of lactic acid introduced by some test meals. Strauss's instrument (Fig. 14–2) is essentially a separatory funnel with a mark at 5 ml. (ccm.) and one at 25 ml. Fill to the 5 ml. mark with filtered gastric juice and to the 25 ml. mark with ether. Shake thoroughly for 10 or 15 minutes, let stand until the ether separates, and then, by opening the stopcock, allow the gastric juice to run out. Fill to the 25 ml. mark

Figure 14–2. Separatory funnel for Strauss's lactic acid test. (Sahli.)

with water and add 2 drops of a 10 per cent solution of ferric chloride. Shake gently. If lactic acid is present in a concentration of 0.1 per cent or more, the water will assume a strong greenish-yellow color. A slight tinge will appear when lactic acid is present in a concentration of 0.05 per cent.

Pepsin and Pepsinogen. Pepsinogen itself has no digestive power. It is secreted by the gastric glands and is transformed into pepsin by the action of a free acid. Although pepsin digests proteins best in the presence of free hydrochloric acid, it has a slight digestive activity in the presence of organic acids or combined hydrochloric acid. Pepsin is rarely or never absent in the presence of free hydrochloric acid. Tests for pepsin are rarely necessary.

Rennin. Rennin is the milk-curdling ferment of the gastric juice. It is derived from renninogen through the action of hydrochloric acid. Deficiency of rennin has the same significance as does deficiency of pepsin, and it is recognized more easily. A test for rennin is not necessary unless free hydrochloric acid is absent. Absence of both free hydrochloric acid and rennin may indicate achylia.

Test for rennin. Add 5 drops of filtered gastric juice to a test tube containing 5 ml. of fresh milk and place it in an incubator or in a vessel of water at about 40° C. Coagulation of the milk in 10 or 15 minutes indicates that a normal amount of rennin is present in the gastric juice.

Blood. Blood is present in the vomitus in many pathologic conditions. When it is noted in the gastric contents removed after administration of a test meal, it should cause one to suspect the presence of gastric ulcer or carcinoma. Blood can be found in the gastric contents in nearly half of all cases of carcinoma of the stomach. When blood is present, it is necessary to exclude the possibility that it might have been swallowed or that it might have resulted from injury to the stomach by the stomach tube.

Test for blood in gastric contents. Extract with ether in order to remove any fat that may be present. Fat usually is not present in gastric contents that have been removed after administration of a test meal. Artificial gastric juice that has been prepared for use in the classroom may be strongly acid. As a result the blood pigment may go into solution in the ether and be discarded unwittingly.

To 10 ml. of the fat-free gastric juice add 3 or 4 ml. of glacial acetic acid and shake the mixture thoroughly with about 5 ml. of ether. Let it stand for a short time, remove the ether, which forms a layer above the gastric juice, and use half of the ether extract for the guaiac or benzidine test. Separation of the ether may be facilitated by adding a small amount of alcohol. If a positive reaction is obtained, the remainder of the ether extract may be examined spectroscopically after treating it so as to develop the bands of hemochromogen.

When brown particles are present in the fluid, the hemin test may be applied directly to them.

QUANTITATIVE TESTS

Total Acidity. The substances that contribute to the total acidity are free hydrochloric acid, acid salts (mostly phosphates), and, in some pathologic conditions, the organic acids.

Töpfer's method for determining the total acidity
    Reagents
      a. Indicator. This consists of a 1 per cent alcoholic solution of phenolphthalein.
      b. Decinormal solution of sodium hydroxide. The physician will find it advisable to have this solution prepared by a chemist or to purchase it from a chemical supply house.
    Technique
    1. In an evaporating dish or small beaker place 10 ml. of the filtered gastric contents and add 3 or 4 drops of the indicator. When only a small quantity of gastric juice is available, 5 ml. may be used for this test, but the result will not be so accurate as that obtained with 10 ml.
    2. Add the decinormal solution of sodium hydroxide drop by drop from a buret until the gastric juice assumes a rose-red color that does not become deeper on the addition of another drop of the solution (Fig. 14–3, B and B'). Most workers accept the first appearance of a permanent pink as the endpoint, just as they do in titrating other fluids with phenolphthalein as an indicator. Owing to the interaction of phosphates it is advisable to carry the titration of gastric juice a little further, as here indicated. When this point is reached, all the acid has been neutralized. The end reaction will be sharper if the fluid is saturated with sodium chloride. A sheet of white paper beneath the beaker facilitates recognition of the change in color.

CALCULATION. In clinical work the acidity is expressed by the number of milliliters of the decinormal solution of sodium hydroxide that would be required to neutralize 100 ml. of the gastric juice, each milliliter representing 1 degree or unit of acidity. Hence, multiply the number of milliliters of the sodium hydroxide solution required to neutralize 10 ml. of gastric fluid by 10, which gives the degrees or units of acidity. The acidity may be expressed in terms of hydrochloric acid, if one remembers that each degree or unit is equivalent to 0.00365 gm. of hydrochloric acid. Someone has suggested that 365 is the number of days in the year and that the last figure, namely 5, indicates the number of decimal places, making a convenient way to remember this figure.

Example. Suppose that 7 ml. of decinormal solution is required to bring about the end reaction in 10 ml. of gastric juice; then $7 \times 10 = 70$ degrees or units of acidity; expressed in terms of hydrochloric acid, $70 \times 0.00365 = 0.255$ per cent.

Free Hydrochloric Acid. In gastric juice that has been obtained after administration of an Ewald test breakfast, the normal value for the free hydrochloric acid as determined by the method of Töpfer is 20 to 40 degrees, which is equivalent to a 0.1 to 0.2 per cent concentration of hydrochloric acid. In the presence of disease the value may be considerably higher or free hydrochloric acid may be absent entirely.

Töpfer's method for determining the concentration of free hydrochloric acid
    Reagents
      a. Indicator. This consists of a 0.5 per cent alcoholic solution of dimethyl-amino-azobenzene.
      b. Decinormal solution of sodium hydroxide.
    Technique
    1. Place 10 ml. of filtered gastric contents in a beaker and add 4 drops of the indicator. If free hydrochloric acid is present, a red color appears immediately.
    2. Add the decinormal solution of sodium hydroxide drop by drop from a buret until the last trace of the red color just disappears and a canary-yellow color appears (Fig. 14–3, A and A'). Some workers have thought that it is not necessary to continue the titration until a canary-yellow color appears; however, when the titration

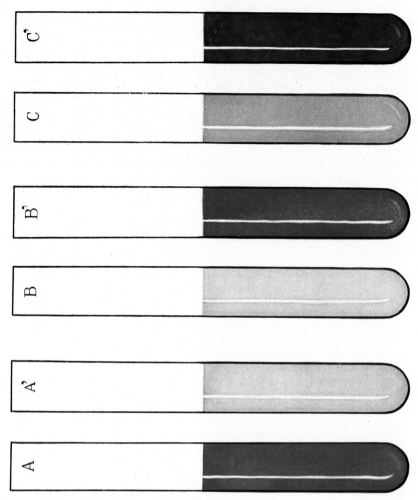

Figure 14–3. A, Gastric fluid to which a few drops of a 0.5 per cent solution of dimethylamino-azobenzene has been added. A' is A after titration with a decinormal solution of sodium hydroxide. B, gastric fluid to which a 1 per cent solution of phenolphthalein has been added. B' is B after titration with a decinormal solution of sodium hydroxide. C, Gastric fluid to which a 1 per cent solution of alizarin has been added. C' is C after titration with a decinormal solution of sodium hydroxide. (Dorothy Booth, pinx.)

is not continued until this color is present, it is more difficult to determine the endpoint.

3. Note the number of milliliters of sodium hydroxide solution used in the titration and calculate the value for free hydrochloric acid in 100 ml. of gastric juice according to the method employed in determining the total acidity.

Combined method for determining the total acidity and the concentration of free hydrochloric acid. When it is impossible to obtain sufficient gastric juice for all tests, a single portion of 10 ml. may be used to determine the total acidity and the concentration of free hydrochloric acid. This method frequently is used routinely, re-

gardless of the amount of gastric juice available.

First, determine the concentration of free hydrochloric acid by the method just described. Then add 4 drops of a 1 per cent alcoholic solution of phenolphthalein and determine the total acidity according to the method of Töpfer described on p. 605. The total number of milliliters of decinormal solution of sodium hydroxide used in both titrations is used to calculate the total acidity (Fig. 14–1, *a, b,* and *c*).

Combined Hydrochloric Acid. If free hydrochloric acid is present, it may be assumed that the amount of combined hydrochloric acid is normal; therefore, the concentration of combined hydrochloric acid need not be determined in cases in which free hydrochloric acid is present. When free hydrochloric acid is absent, it is important to know whether any acid is being secreted. In such cases determination of the concentration of combined hydrochloric acid becomes of great value. After administration of an Ewald test breakfast the normal value for the combined hydrochloric acid is about 10 to 15 degrees, depending on the amount of protein in the meal. In cases in which Riegel's test meal is employed, the values are somewhat higher. From a clinical standpoint this test is rarely indicated.

Töpfer's method for determining the concentration of combined hydrochloric acid
Reagents
a. Indicator. This consists of a 1 per cent aqueous solution of sodium alizarin sulfonate.
b. Decinormal solution of sodium hydroxide.
Technique
1. Place 10 ml. of filtered gastric juice in a beaker and add 4 drops of the indicator.
2. Titrate with the decinormal solution of sodium hydroxide until the appearance of a violet color that has a slightly bluish tinge. The titration should be continued until the color does not become deeper on the addition of another drop of sodium hydroxide. It is difficult without practice to determine when the right color has been reached. The color that determines the endpoint is not always the same; therefore, it is better to watch for a change of color than it is to try to obtain the correct shade. The shade that denotes the endpoint can be duplicated approximately by adding 2 or 3 drops of the indicator to 5 ml. of a 1 per cent solution of sodium carbonate (Fig. 14–3, *C* and *C'*).
CALCULATION. Calculate the number of milliliters of decinormal solution of sodium hydroxide that would be required to neutralize 100 ml. of gastric juice. This gives in degrees the value for all the acidity except that owing to combined hydrochloric acid. The value for the combined hydrochloric acid can be obtained by deducting this amount from the total acidity, which has been determined previously.
Example. Suppose that 5 ml. of decinormal solution of sodium hydroxide was required to produce the purple color in 10 ml. of gastric juice; then $5 \times 10 = 50$,

which represents all the acidity except that owing to combined hydrochloric acid. Suppose now that the total acidity already has been found to be 70 degrees or units; then $70 - 50 = 20$ degrees or units of combined hydrochloric acid, and $20 \times 0.00365 = 0.073$ per cent.

Acid Deficit. When free hydrochloric acid is absent, it is probably more helpful to estimate the deficit of acid than to determine the value for the combined hydrochloric acid. The deficit of acid shows how far the acid secreted by the stomach falls short of saturating the protein (and bases) of the meal. It represents the amount of hydrochloric acid that must be added to the fluid before the presence of free hydrochloric acid becomes apparent. It is determined by titrating with decinormal solution of hydrochloric acid, using dimethylaminoazobenzene as an indicator, until the fluid assumes a red color. The deficit is expressed by the number of milliliters of the solution of hydrochloric acid required for 100 ml. of the stomach fluid. This test is of little practical significance.

Organic Acids. There is no simple, direct method for determining the amount of organic acids. After the total acidity has been measured, the organic acids may be removed from another portion of the gastric filtrate by shaking thoroughly with an equal volume of neutral ether, allowing the fluids to separate, and repeating this process until the gastric juice has been extracted with eight or ten times its volume of ether. The total acidity then is determined, and the difference between the two measurements indicates the amount of organic acids.

Hydrogen Ion Concentration. The hydrogen ion concentration may be determined by using standard buffer solutions or by comparison with the color chart that is now generally employed. The range will be from 1.05 to 7; true "anacidity" with a pH of 7 is a rare condition. The indicators to be used and the range of pH of each are as follows: thymol blue, 1.2 to 2.8; bromophenol blue, 3 to 4.6; methyl red, 4.4 to 6; bromcresol purple, 5.2 to 6.8; bromothymol blue, 6 to 7.6; and phenol red, 6.8 to 8.4.

Pepsin. No direct method for the quantitative determination of pepsin is simple enough for routine use. The following methods are sufficiently accurate for clinical purposes.

Hammerschlag's method
Reagent
A 0.4 per cent solution of hydrochloric

acid. Add 4 ml. of dilute hydrochloric acid, U.S.P., to 96 ml. of water.

Technique

1. To the white of an egg add 12 times its volume of 0.4 per cent solution of hydrochloric acid, mix well, and filter. The resulting solution will contain 1 per cent egg albumin.

2. Place 10 ml. of this solution of egg albumin in each of three test tubes or beakers and number them.

3. Place 5 ml. of gastric juice in tube 1, 5 ml. of water and 0.5 gm. of pepsin in tube 2, and 5 ml. of water in tube 3.

4. Place the tubes in an incubator for one hour.

5. Calculate the amount of albumin in each tube by using the method of Esbach.

INTERPRETATION OF RESULTS. The amount of albumin in tube 3 is the amount of albumin in the test solution. The difference between the amounts of albumin in tubes 3 and 2 represents the amount of albumin that would be digested by normal gastric juice. The difference between the amounts of albumin in tubes 3 and 1 represents the amount of albumin digested by the gastric juice that is being tested.

SOURCES OF ERROR. Certain sources of error can be eliminated by diluting the gastric juice several times before the test is performed.

Mett's Method. This method generally is used in preference to Hammerschlag's technique.

Reagents

a. Mett's tubes of egg albumin. Beat the whites of one or two eggs lightly and filter. Pour the filtrate into a wide test tube. Stand a number of capillary glass tubes, 1 or 2 mm. in diameter, in the test tube. When the capillary tubes are filled, plug the ends with bread crumbs and coagulate the albumin by heating in water at a temperature just below the boiling point. Dip the ends of the tubes in melted paraffin and preserve the tubes until needed. If bubbles are present, they will disappear in a few days. For use, the tubes should be cut into lengths of about 2 cm. Discard any tube in which the albumin has separated from the wall.

b. A N/20 solution of hydrochloric acid.

Technique

1. Place 1 ml. of filtered gastric juice and 15 ml. of the hydrochloric acid in a small beaker.

2. Put two or three Mett's tubes of albumin in the beaker and place it in an incubator for 24 hours.

3. Measure as accurately as possible in millimeters the height of the column of albumin that has been digested. A millimeter scale and a hand lens or, preferably, a low-power microscopic objective and an ocular micrometer may be used for this purpose. Square the average length of the digested column and multiply by the degree of dilution, namely 16. The maximal figure thus obtained is 256, representing a digested column of 4 mm.

Microscopic Examination of the Gastric Contents

A drop of unfiltered gastric contents is placed on a slide, covered with a coverglass, and examined with 16 mm. and 4 mm. objectives with the opening of the diaphragm much reduced. A drop of greatly diluted compound solution of iodine allowed to run under the coverglass aids in distinguishing the various structures. As a rule the microscopic examination is of limited value.

Under normal conditions little is to be seen except great numbers of starch granules and an occasional epithelial cell, yeast cell, or bacterium. Starch granules are recognized by their concentric striations and by the fact that they stain blue with solutions of iodine when undigested; they stain reddish, owing to erythrodextrin, when partially digested. These colors, however, do not show clearly unless the solution of iodine is extremely dilute.

Pathologically, remnants of food from previous meals, erythrocytes, pus corpuscles, sarcinae, and excessive numbers of yeast cells and bacteria may be encountered.

Remnants of Food. The presence of remnants of food from previous meals indicates deficient gastric motility or obstruction.

Erythrocytes. Blood is best recognized by the chemical tests that have been described previously. Although the appearance of erythrocytes occasionally is normal, they generally are so degenerated that only granular pigment is left. When microscopic examination discloses only a few fresh erythrocytes, they probably are the result of irritation of the gastric mucosa by the tube.

Pus Corpuscles. Pus rarely is encountered in the gastric contents removed after a test meal. Since the corpuscles usually

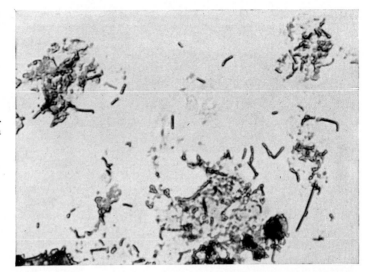

Figure 14–4. Boas-Oppler bacilli in case of gastric carcinoma (× 970).

are partially digested, only the nuclei are seen. The nuclei appear as small, highly refractile bodies lying in clusters of two, three, or four. Swallowed sputum always must be considered as a source of these corpuscles.

Sarcinae. These are small spheres arranged in cuboid groups, which often are compared with bales of cotton. They frequently form large clumps and are easily recognized. They stain brown with a solution of iodine. They signify fermentation, but their presence is of little or no diagnostic importance.

Yeast Cells. As already noted, a few yeast cells may be found under normal conditions. The presence of considerable numbers is evidence of retention and fermentation. They stain yellow to brown with a solution of iodine.

Bacteria. Numerous bacteria may be found in the gastric juice, especially in the absence of free hydrochloric acid.

Lactobacillus of Boas-Oppler. The lactobacillus of Boas-Oppler, which probably is identical with *Lactobacillus acidophilus* or *L. bulgaricus*, is of special significance when found in the gastric contents. It is said to occur in cases of extensive carcinoma of the stomach. Carcinoma probably furnishes a favorable medium for its growth.

The bacilli (Fig. 14–4) are large (5 to 10 microns long) and nonmotile, usually being arranged in clumps or end to end in zigzag chains. They stain yellow or brown with a solution of iodine. The lactobacillus of Boas-Oppler is gram positive. Although it is easily seen with the 4 mm. objective in unstained specimens, it is best recog-

nized in fixed smears that have been stained with a simple bacterial stain or by Gram's method. The stained smears should be examined with the oil-immersion objective.

Bacteriologic examination frequently discloses a few large, nonmotile bacilli that are mistaken for the lactobacillus of Boas-Oppler. The presence of Boas-Oppler organisms should not be reported unless the bacilli are arranged in clumps or end to end in chains.

Mycobacterium tuberculosis. In cases of suspected pulmonary tuberculosis in which acid-fast bacilli are not found in the sputum, it is often helpful to culture the gastric contents for the presence of *Mycobacterium tuberculosis*.

METHOD OF FOLEY AND ANDOSCA. Foley and Andosca (1943) described a satisfactory method that utilizes the concentration technique of Hanks and associates (1938).

Apparatus

1. An all-glass Luer type of syringe.

2. A Levin or Sawyer tube. The tube must be prepared carefully. Wash it with hot water and soap and then run tap water through it for 30 minutes. Boil the tube in a weak solution of sodium carbonate for 30 minutes and then place it in the refrigerator overnight.

Reagents

a. Digestor. Make a solution containing 1 per cent of sodium hydroxide, 0.2 per cent of potassium alum, and 0.002 per cent of bromothymol blue.

b. An approximately 2.5 N solution of hydrochloric acid (25 per cent of concentrated hydrochloric acid by volume)

c. A 1 per cent solution of ferric chloride in distilled water.

Technique

1. The gastric contents should be removed early in the morning before the patient has had breakfast. Pass the tube nasally into the stomach. Aspirate 30 to 50 ml. of gastric contents with the Luer syringe. Great caution must be exercised in handling the aspirated gastric contents and the containers, tube, and syringe.

2. Mix 5 ml. of the aspirated gastric contents with an equal volume of the digestor. Place the mixture in a water bath at 37° C. for 30 minutes and shake occasionally.

3. Add the 2.5 N solution of hydrochloric acid drop by drop while shaking until the color of the indicator denotes approximate neutrality.

4. Shake for 30 seconds. If flocculation does not occur in less than five minutes, add 0.2 ml. of the ferric chloride solution and shake again.

5. Centrifuge the flocculated sample for five minutes at high speed to pack the sediment.

6. Discard the supernatant fluid and transfer the sediment to mediums suitable for the cultivation of tubercle bacilli. Preparation of stained smears of gastric contents for acid-fast bacilli is not recommended because of the common occurrence of saprophytic acid-fast bacteria.

7. The sediment also may be used to inoculate guinea pigs.

The Gastric Contents in Disease

In the diagnosis of gastric disorders the physician must be cautioned against relying too much on the results of examination of the gastric contents. Even when repeated studies are made, the laboratory findings never should be considered apart from the clinical findings.

Gastric Obstruction. Evidence of retention and fermentation is the chief characteristic of this condition. The concentration of hydrochloric acid is commonly diminished. The value for pepsin may be normal or slightly diminished. Lactic acid may be detected in small amounts, but it is usually absent when the stomach has been washed before the test meal is given. Both motility and the absorptive power are deficient. Microscopic examination commonly discloses sarcinae, bacteria, and great numbers of yeast cells. Remnants of food from previous meals can be detected with the naked eye or microscopically.

Chronic Gastritis. There is no characteristic pattern of gastric secretory activity in this ill-defined clinical syndrome. It is frequently stated that the amount of free hydrochloric acid may be normal or increased in the early stages of chronic gastritis, whereas it may be decreased or absent in the late stages. The values for pepsin and rennin often are diminished in cases in which the disease is well developed. Mucus frequently is present. Gastric motility and absorption generally are deficient.

Achylia Gastrica (Atrophic Gastritis). This condition may be a terminal stage of chronic gastritis. Sometimes it is associated with a blood picture similar to that of pernicious anemia. The hydrochloric acid and the gastric ferments are decreased in amount and sometimes are absent. The value for the total acidity may be as low as 1 or 2 degrees when determined by the method of Töpfer. Small amounts of lactic acid may be present. Gastric absorption and motility are not greatly affected. Achylia is not considered so significant as it formerly was thought to be. It may be present in apparently healthy persons.

Carcinoma of the Stomach. In many instances of gastric carcinoma the gastric contents are not significantly altered. There is, however, ample evidence of an increased incidence of gastric carcinoma associated with low gastric acidity or anacidity. The frequent relationship of hypoacidity and carcinoma of the stomach has led to the hope that some simple screening test, such as tubeless gastric analysis, may be useful in the mass detection of early carcinoma. Recent techniques have made it possible to obtain freshly desquamated gastric cells for cytologic study, and thus it is hoped that the early diagnosis of small, malignant gastric lesions will be possible. Unfortunately many carcinomas of the stomach are far advanced when the first symptoms become evident. The results of the gastric analysis should be considered only in conjunction with the clinical and roentgenologic findings.

Chemical examination discloses blood in the gastric contents in nearly half of all cases of gastric carcinoma. Occult blood is present in the stools in nearly every instance.

Gastric Ulcer. In some cases of gastric ulcer the concentration of free hydrochloric acid is increased; in most cases, however, it is normal or decreased. Blood often is present in the gastric contents. Occult blood usually is present in the feces;

in some cases, however, it occurs only intermittently. The diagnosis must be made chiefly on the basis of the clinical and roentgenologic findings.

Duodenal Ulcer. Classically, duodenal ulcer is associated with hyperacidity and an increased volume of gastric secretion. In some cases, however, the gastric acidity is normal or even low. It is doubtful that an active duodenal ulcer is ever present in the absence of free hydrochloric acid. As in gastric ulcer the results of gastric analysis should be considered only as an adjunct to the clinical and roentgenologic findings.

Pernicious Anemia. For practical purposes pernicious anemia always is associated with achlorhydria, even after use of histamine as a stimulant. As is true of other causes of achlorhydria, there appears to be an increased incidence of carcinoma of the stomach associated with pernicious anemia.

EXAMINATION OF DUODENAL CONTENTS

Withdrawal of the Duodenal Contents

The duodenal contents may be withdrawn by means of one of the gastric tubes previously described or by some modification of these tubes (Fig. 14–5). The tubes usually are marked with a series of rings to indicate the distances from the incisor teeth to the cardia, pylorus, and duodenum. It is advantageous to attach a small glass tube to the proximal end of the rubber tube and to attach a short piece of rubber tubing to the proximal end of the glass tube. The glass tube serves as a window and the small piece of rubber tubing serves for the attachment of the syringe. A tube

was first demonstrated by Einhorn in 1909. Many modifications, notably those of Jutte and of Rehfuss, have appeared; these differ chiefly in the shape and weight of the metal tip and in the arrangement of the perforations. The Jutte tube has a wire stylet that facilitates introduction of the tube as far as the stomach.

When chief interest centers in the pancreatic ferments, it may be well to give the patient a cup of bouillon 30 minutes before the tube is to be introduced; ordinarily, however, a test meal is not given. The patient should abstain from food for about 12 hours prior to the test and should take only occasional sips of water. The tube is introduced into the stomach in the manner already described for the gastric tube. The patient then is placed on his right side with the hips elevated 15 or 20 cm. (6 or 8 inches). The movements of the stomach, aided by gravity, carry the tip of the tube through the pylorus into the duodenum, usually within 30 to 45 minutes.

Fluid should begin to drip from the free end of the tube soon after the tip has reached the stomach. If it does not do so, siphonage should be started by injecting a few milliliters of warm water. It is well to wash the stomach out with warm water injected and withdrawn by means of an all-glass syringe. Leave the tube in position and start siphonage. Advance the tube slowly 2.5 cm. (1 inch) at a time at ten-minute intervals until the tube reaches a position such that the incisor teeth are about midway between the second and third marks on the tube. When the tube enters the duodenum, the first fluid that appears may be turbid, yellow, and acid in reaction owing to the mixture of gastric

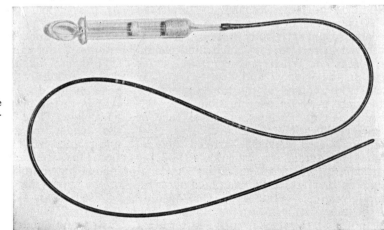

Figure 14–5. Sawyer tube attached to aspirating syringe.

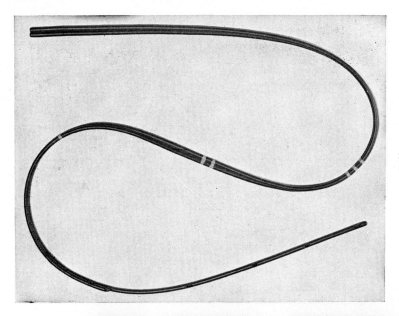

Figure 14–6. Double-barrel tube for aspirating duodenal and stomach contents.

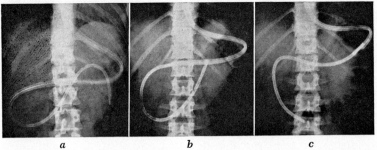

a   *b*   *c*

Figure 14–7. Roentgenologic demonstration of position of the tube: *a*, tube has passed too far into duodenum; *b*, tube in proper position; *c*, tube has not entered duodenum properly.

and duodenal contents. After 10 or 15 minutes, the fluid siphoning from the tube becomes light golden yellow, clear, alkaline, and somewhat viscid.

Should the flow be interrupted, injection of a few milliliters of warm water usually will re-establish it. Occasionally, after the tube is in the duodenum, the fluid may become somewhat cloudy and opalescent as observed in the window. Such fluid should be discarded. When it becomes clear as seen in the window and drips as a clear fluid from the end of the tube, collect the fluid once more for examination.

Although an Einhorn duodenal tube or some modification of this tube is most commonly used, a double-barreled tube designed by Ågren and Lagerlöf (1936) is particularly useful in obtaining duodenal contents that are to be examined for pancreatic enzymes (Fig. 14–6). One opening of the tube should lie in the stomach and the other in the duodenum. The terminal parts of both passages are perforated with small holes except for 10 cm. of the duodenal portion, which is meant for the pyloric region. The tube is so constructed that it passes easily through the pylorus and does not readily coil up in the stomach. Its passage should not be forced at any time if any type of obstruction is met, because resistance will disappear in a few minutes if the patient is placed on his right side. It may take from one to five hours for the insertion of this tube to the proper position for duodenal drainage. When the tube is in the proper place, clear, alkaline, bile-colored fluid should be obtained from the duodenum, and gastric juice that is not stained with bile should be obtained from the stomach. Roentgenologic examination may be used to confirm the position of the tube (Fig. 14–7). Fluoroscopy may be used as an aid during manipulation of the tube. When the tube is in place, the gastric and duodenal contents are aspirated continuously by means of a suction pump, keeping a negative pressure at a level of 20 to 30 mm. of mercury.

Physical Examination of Duodenal Contents

Normally duodenal fluid is clear, colorless, or light yellow, distinctly viscid, and slightly alkaline to litmus. Admixture of acid gastric juice causes the duodenal fluid to become somewhat cloudy and opalescent. Cloudiness caused by bacteria and pus corpuscles may be present in inflammation of the duodenum or biliary passages.

Chemical Examination of Duodenal Contents

Ferments. Absence of or great diminution in one or all of the pancreatic ferments, namely amylase, lipase, and trypsin, indicates deficient pancreatic secretion or occlusion of the pancreatic duct. Their quantitative estimation in duodenal fluid yields much the same information as does their quantitative measurement in the feces, but it is more reliable. Pancreatic fluid from a fistulous tract may show little or no proteolytic activity. The methods now considered to be most satisfactory are described in Chapter 8.

Bilirubin. There is generally a sufficient amount of unaltered bile pigment to give the duodenal contents at least a tinge of yellow, and the depth of color is a rough but useful guide to the amount of bile present, despite the presence of a variable amount of urobilin. The amount may be recorded as 1+, 2+, or 3+, indicating small, moderate, and excessive amounts, respectively. Sometimes the fluid is dark yellow, brown, or even chocolate-brown. The presence of bile rules out complete obstruction of the common bile duct. Its absence means only that bile is not entering the duodenum at that time. In jaundiced patients the repeated absence of bile in the material obtained during duodenal drainage suggests either complete obstruction of the common bile duct or, more rarely, a temporary cessation of the secretion of bile by the liver.

Urobilin. Urobilin is a reduction product of bilirubin. Its nature and significance are considered in Chapter 11. A small amount of urobilin is present in the duodenal contents normally; however, the chromogen, urobilinogen, is found only when an excessive amount of urobilin is present.

The presence of urobilinogen and an increase in the quantity of urobilin have the same significance as does an increase in the amount of these substances in the feces. In each case certain theoretic and practical objections can be raised, yet the quantitative estimations of urobilin in feces and in duodenal contents appear to have about equal clinical value, and the results constitute an index of the activity of destruction of blood. These measurements are at times valuable in the diagnosis of the hemolytic anemias, and they may be helpful in a study of anemia of doubtful origin.

A satisfactory clinical method for determining the amount of urobilin is that of Wilbur and Addis (1914), which Schneider (1916) applied to the duodenal contents as follows:

1. To 10 ml. of duodenal contents add 10 ml. of a saturated alcoholic solution of zinc acetate. Shake well and filter.

2. To 10 ml. of the filtrate add 1 ml. of Ehrlich's reagent (p. 549). Mix and let stand in a dark place for 15 minutes.

3. Examine with a spectroscope and dilute with 60 per cent alcohol until the bands of both urobilin and urobilinogen have disappeared. Calculate the dilution value for 1000 ml. of duodenal contents, remembering that the filtrate used represents 5 ml. of duodenal fluid. If, for example, the urobilin and the urobilinogen bands disappear when the 10 ml. of filtrate is diluted to 80 and 40 ml., respectively, the dilution value of 5 ml. of duodenal fluid is 16 for urobilin and 8 for urobilinogen; for 1000 ml. it would be 200 times as much or 3200 and 1600, respectively, with a total dilution value of 4800.

Schneider found the maximum for healthy medical students to be about 1000 dilutions with urobilinogen never present. In pernicious anemia and hemolytic icterus urobilinogen is generally present, and the total dilution value usually reaches 3000 to 5000. More accurate methods for the determination of urobilinogen will be found in Chapter 11.

Microscopic Examination of Duodenal Contents

The duodenal fluid must be examined within a few minutes after it is secured; otherwise the cellular elements may be damaged or destroyed by the ferments. The method is the same as that for fresh urine. Normally only an occasional leukocyte or epithelial cell can be found. In pathologic conditions such cells may be present in increased numbers but definite diagnostic inferences cannot be drawn. A great excess of pus corpuscles would suggest inflammation of the duodenum or biliary tract. *Strongyloides stercoralis* and *Giardia lamblia* have been found, sometimes in great numbers. In cases in which cystic and vegetative forms of *Entamoeba histolytica* are found, infestation of the liver or biliary passages with these parasites may be inferred.

Bacteriologic Examination of Duodenal Contents

At the present time extremely little of clinical value can be learned from a bacteriologic study of the duodenal contents. Normally the duodenal fluid is sterile or contains only a few gram positive cocci.

EXAMINATION OF FRESH BILE

Magnesium sulfate applied locally to the mucosa of the duodenum, makes it possible to collect and segregate bile from the different parts of the biliary tract. Cytologic and bacteriologic study of bile obtained in this manner may yield information of value in the differential diagnosis of cholecystitis, cholelithiasis, and choledochitis.

The procedure may be outlined as follows: Introduce about 50 ml. of a sterile 25 per cent saturated solution of magnesium sulfate very slowly into the duodenum through a duodenal tube, which is left in place for three to five minutes. Siphon off the stimulant with the first sample of duodenal contents, which is discarded. Magnesium sulfate introduced directly into the duodenum appears to relax the sphincter of the common bile duct, thereby inducing drainage of the entire biliary tract. Equal parts of Phospho-Soda (Fleet) and water also make a satisfactory stimulant for the flow of bile. The duodenal contents are siphoned into a series of sterile bottles or large tubes. Golden-yellow bile from the common bile duct appears soon and is designated "A." This bile may appear without the use of a stimulant. After a few minutes it rather suddenly gives place to a darker, more viscid bile, which is supposed to come from the gallbladder and which is designated "B." If this type of bile does not appear reasonably soon, repeat the stimulation or introduce warm water. This portion usually amounts to 30 to 75 ml., and it is succeeded by a clear, light-yellow bile of low specific grav-

ity, which is assumed to be freshly secreted bile from the liver and which is designated "C." The various portions are collected separately, and their color, viscosity, turbidity, and general appearance, as well as the presence or absence of mucus, are noted. They are also examined microscopically, chiefly for abnormal sediments, and culturally for bacteria.

Jones (1924) has shown that in cholelithiasis the sediment, after centrifugation at high speed, contains characteristic bile-stained epithelium or leukocytes, cholesterol crystals, amorphous yellow bilirubin, or darker yellowish-brown crystals of calcium bilirubinate.

REFERENCES

1. Ågren, G., and Lagerlöf, H.: The pancreatic secretion in man after intravenous administration of secretin. Acta med. Scandinav., 90: 1–29, 1936.
2. Card, W. I.: Studies of gastric secretion in duodenal ulcer. Proc. Roy. Soc. Med., 49:509–510, 1956.
3. Foley, J. A., and Andosca, J. B.: Value of examination of gastric contents for tubercle bacilli. Ann. Int. Med., 19:629–633, 1943.
4. Gompertz, L. M., and Cohen, W.: The effect of smaller doses of histamin in stimulating human gastric secretion. Am. J. M. Sc., 177: 59–64, 1929.
5. Hanks, J. H., Clark, H. F., and Feldman, H.: Concentration of tubercle bacilli from sputum by chemical flocculation methods. J. Lab. & Clin. Med., 23:736–746, 1938.
6. Heckmann: Zur Frage der Belastungsproben des Magens; Magensaftuntersuchungen mittels einer Eiweiss-Peptonlösung, Ztsch. ges. exper. Med., 87:506–528, 1933.
7. Hollander, F.: The insulin test for the presence of intact nerve fibers after vagal operations for peptic ulcer. Gastroenterology, 7:607–614, 1946.
8. Jones, C. M.: The rational use of duodenal drainage; An attempt to establish a conservative estimate of the value of this procedure in the diagnosis of biliary tract pathology. Arch. Int. Med., 34:60–78, 1924.
9. Kay, A. W.: Effect of large doses of histamine on gastric secretion of HCl; Augmented histamine test. Brit. M. J., 2:77–80, 1953.
10. Levin, E.: Nocturnal gastric secretion. In Sandweiss, D. J.: Peptic Ulcer: Clinical Aspects, Diagnosis, Management. Philadelphia, W. B. Saunders Company, 1951, pp. 83–90.
11. Schneider, J. P.: The splenic pathology of pernicious anemia and allied conditions: A duodenal method of estimating hemolysis. Arch. Int. Med., 17:32–41, 1916.
12. Segal, H. L., Miller, L. L., and Morton, J. J.: Determination of gastric acidity without intubation by use of cation exchange indicator compounds. Proc. Soc. Exper. Biol. & Med., 74:218–220, 1950.
13. Wilbur, R. L., and Addis, T.: Urobilin: Its clinical significance. Arch. Int. Med., 13:235–286, 1914.

Chapter 15

The Feces

By BENJAMIN B. WELLS, M.D.

As commonly practiced, an examination of the feces is limited to a search for intestinal parasites or ova. Much of value can, however, be learned from other simple examinations, particularly from careful inspection. Anything approaching complete analysis is, on the other hand, a waste of time for the clinician.

The normal stool is a mixture of water; undigested and indigestible remnants of food, such as starch granules, particles of meat, and vegetable cells and fibers; digested foods excreted before absorption can take place; products of the digestive tract, such as altered bile pigments, enzymes, and mucus; products of decomposition, such as indole, skatole, fatty acids, and various gases; epithelial cells shed from the wall of the intestinal canal; and bacteria, which are always present in enormous numbers. In the presence of pathologic conditions abnormal amounts of normal constituents, blood, pathogenic bacteria, animal parasites and their ova, and biliary and intestinal concretions may be present.

The stool to be examined should be passed into a clean vessel without admixture of urine. The examination should not be delayed more than a few hours to avoid the changes caused by decomposition. No disinfectant should be used when search for amebae is to be made; the vessel must be warm, and the stool must be kept warm until examined. In examining for protozoa, a saline cathartic should be given to insure the passage of a watery stool. A jar or bottle that is sent to the laboratory nearly full of feces should be opened with great care; otherwise the gases that may have formed may force the fecal material out with a spurt and soil the hands. More detailed directions for the collection and preservation of feces will be found in Chapter 17.

MACROSCOPIC EXAMINATION

Quantity. The amount of feces varies greatly with the diet and other factors. The average amount is about 200 gm. in 24 hours, but it may be much larger when a vegetable diet is being used.

Frequency. One or two stools in 24 hours may be considered normal, yet one in three or four days is common among healthy persons. The individual habit should be considered in every case.

Form and Consistency. Soft, mushy, liquid stools follow the administration of cathartics and accompany diarrhea. Copious, purely serous discharges without fecal matter are significant of Asiatic cholera, although they are sometimes observed in other conditions. Hard stools accompany constipation. Rounded, scybalous masses are common in habitual constipation and indicate atony of the muscular coat of the colon. Flattened, ribbon-like stools result from obstruction in the rectum, generally a tumor or a stricture.

Color. The normal light or dark brown color is due chiefly to urobilin, which is formed from bilirubin by reduction processes in the intestine, largely the result of bacterial activity. The stools of infants are yellow owing partly to their milk diet and partly to the presence of unchanged bilirubin.

Diet and drugs cause marked changes in the color of the stools. Milk produces a light yellow color; cocoa and chocolate, a dark gray; various fruits, a reddish or black color; spinach, a dark green; and iron and bismuth, a dark brown or black.

Pathologically the color is important. A golden yellow color is generally due to unchanged bilirubin. Green stools are not uncommon, especially in the diarrhea of childhood. They are sometimes passed by apparently healthy infants; they alternate with normal yellow stools and have little significance unless accompanied by symptoms. The color is due to biliverdin or sometimes to chromogenic bacteria. Putty-colored or "acholic" stools occur when bile is deficient owing to obstruction of outflow or to deficient secretion. The color results less from the absence of bile pigments than from the presence of fat. Similar stools, which have a greasy appearance and manifestly consist largely of fat or its derivatives, are common in conditions like tuberculous peritonitis, which interfere with absorption of fats, and in pancreatic disease.

Large amounts of blood produce tarry, black, usually viscid stools when the source of the hemorrhage is in the stomach or upper part of the intestine and dark brown to bright red stools if the source is nearer the rectum. When diarrhea exists, the color may be red, even if the source of the blood is high in the gastrointestinal tract. Red streaks of blood on the outside of the stool are due to lesions of the rectum or anus. Amounts of blood too small for recognition by simple inspection are designated occult blood and require chemical tests.

Odor. Products of decomposition, chiefly indole and skatole, are responsible for the normal offensive odor. The strength of this odor depends largely on the amount of meat in the diet and on the activity of putrefactive bacteria in the intestine. If a vegetable or milk diet is being used, the odor is much less. A sour odor owing to fatty acids is normal for nursing infants and is noted in mild diarrhea of older children. In the severe diarrhea of childhood a putrid odor is common.

Mucus. Excessive quantities of mucus are easily detected with the naked eye and signify irritation or inflammation. When the mucus is small in amount and intimately mixed with the stool, the lesion is probably in the small intestine. Larger amounts that are not well mixed with fecal matter indicate inflammation of the large intestine. Stools composed almost wholly of mucus and streaked with blood are the rule

in dysentery, ileocolitis, and intussusception.

In so-called mucous colic or membranous enteritis shreds and ribbons of altered mucus, sometimes representing complete casts of portions of the bowel, are passed, especially after an enema. In the ordinary, formed stool they usually pass unrecognized unless the feces is well mixed with water. These may appear as firm, irregularly segmented strands and may simulate tapeworms. The mucus sometimes takes the form of brown or black, jelly-like masses.

Animal Parasites. See Chapter 16.

CHEMICAL EXAMINATION

Most chemical examinations of the feces are in the category of research technique and are neither available nor necessary for ordinary clinical work. Only a few simple observations are usually made in the clinical laboratory.

Reaction

This observation has little practical value. Normally the reaction is either slightly acid or slightly alkaline. Much depends on the diet. Excess of carbohydrate produces acidity and excess of protein, alkalinity. Pathologic variations occur in gastrointestinal disorders, but clinical correlations are of no great value. Indicator papers or other standard methods can be used to determine the hydrogen ion concentration.

Fermentation

Excessive carbohydrate fermentation, resulting from intestinal indigestion of carbohydrates, is manifested by the formation of gas and by an acid reaction. The stool is usually soft and mushy, and bubbles of gas may be present. The bubbles become much more evident after the stool has stood in a warm place for 12 hours. Then the stool, when stirred with a stick, gives a crackling sound. As the gas forms, the reaction becomes increasingly acid. A similar bulky, frothy stool, which has these characteristics when freshly passed, is typical of sprue. A normal stool contains few or no gas bubbles even after it has stood 24 hours. Special diets and special procedures for the determination of gas formation, such as Schmidt's well-known test, may be employed but usually are not necessary.

Intestinal indigestion of protein, on the other hand, is manifested by evidences of putrefaction, that is, foul-smelling stools, a strongly alkaline reaction, and little formation of gas.

Blood

When present in large amounts, blood produces such marked changes in the appearance of the stool that it is not likely to be overlooked. Traces of blood (*occult blood*) can be detected only by special tests. Recognition of occult blood is most valuable in diagnosis of gastric carcinoma and ulcer. It is constantly present in practically every case of carcinoma of the stomach and is always present, although usually intermittently, in cases of active peptic ulcer. Traces of blood also accompany malignant disease of the bowel, the presence of certain intestinal parasites, and other pathologic conditions.

Detection of Occult Blood. Tests for occult blood are generally based on the capacity of hemoglobin and its derivatives to catalyze the oxidation of various chromogenic substances. The most widely used test substances are benzidine, guaiac, and orthotolidin. The large number of suggested procedures represent minor variations on this basic reaction, attempting to make the test sufficiently sensitive to detect the presence of blood while at the same time giving a minimum number of falsely positive reactions. None of the tests is entirely specific. When the issue is important, the test should always be repeated on several occasions. To properly evaluate a positive result, the patient must have been on a meat-free diet for three to six days. A positive result can be due to swallowed blood from the mouth or respiratory tract; these sources can usually be ruled out. A large amount of fat in the feces can interfere with the test reaction, but it is rarely, if ever, worthwhile to carry out an ether extraction of the feces.

A test using gum guaiac as the indicator has been widely accepted and appears to give few false reactions.

Reagents

a. Hydrogen peroxide 3 per cent.

b. Acetic acid, glacial reagent.

c. Saturated solution of gum guaiac in 95 per cent ethyl alcohol.

Technique

1. A small bit of feces, usually obtained during digital examination of the rectum, is smeared on a piece of filter paper or ordinary blotting paper.

2. To this add 1 drop of the guaiac solution, 1 drop of glacial acetic acid, and 1 drop of hydrogen peroxide.

A positive reaction is indicated by the appearance of a blue or dark green color within 30 seconds. Other colors or delayed reactions should be regarded as negative. This same procedure using a saturated solution of benzidine in glacial acetic acid in place of the guaiac preparation has also been widely recommended. Benzidine has the disadvantage of giving more false positive reactions.

Several commercial test preparations are now available for this test. The Hematest Reagent Tablets,* which use orthotolidin as the indicator, offer a convenient method for office or small laboratory units.

Bile

Normally unaltered bile pigment is never present in the feces of adults. In inflammatory conditions producing diarrhea, it may be carried through unchanged. The determination of bilirubin derivatives, urobilinogen and others, in the feces and the clinical significance of tests for these substances are discussed in relation to hematology and liver function in other sections of this book.

MICROSCOPIC EXAMINATION

Care must be exercised in the selection of portions of the feces for microscopic examination. A random search will often reveal nothing of interest. Samples from several different portions of the specimen should be examined even when the stool is apparently homogeneous. A small bit of the stool or any suspicious looking particle is placed on a slide, thinned with water if necessary, and covered with a coverglass. The layer should be just thin enough so that newsprint can be read through it when the slide is placed on the paper. A large slide—about 2 by 3 inches—with a correspondingly large coverglass will be found convenient. Most of the structures that one desires to see can be found with a 16 mm. objective. Details of structures must be studied with a high power objective. Since size is always an important consideration in the identification of microscopic structures, particularly in the case of parasites and their ova, frequent use of the ocular micrometer is essential. Detailed studies of

* Available from the Ames Company, Elkhart. Indiana.

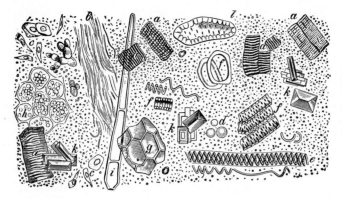

Figure 15–1. Microscopic elements of normal feces: *a*, Muscle fibers; *b*, connective tissue; *c*, epithelial cells; *d*, leukocytes; *e*, spiral vessels of plants; *f–h*, vegetable cells; *i*, plant hairs; *k*, triple phosphate crystals; *l*, stone cells. Scattered among these elements are microorganisms and debris (v. Jaksch).

food residues using standard diets are now rarely used.

The bulk of the stool consists of granular debris. Among the recognizable structures (Fig. 15–1) encountered in normal and pathologic conditions are: remnants of food, epithelial cells, pus corpuscles, erythrocytes, crystals, bacteria protozoa, and ova of animal parasites.

Remnants of Food. Remnants of food include a great variety of structures, which are very confusing to the student. Considerable study of normal feces is necessary for their recognition.

Vegetable fibers are generally recognized by their spiral structure or their pits, dots, or reticulate markings; vegetable cells, by their double contour and the chlorophyll bodies that many of them contain. These cells are likely to be mistaken for the ova of parasites. Vegetable hairs frequently look much like the larvae of some of the worms. A careful examination will, however, easily distinguish them because of the homogeneous and highly refractile wall, the distinct central canal that extends the whole length of the hair, and, especially, the absence of motion.

Starch granules sometimes retain their original form but are ordinarily not recognized except by their staining reaction. Potato starch appears in colorless, translucent masses somewhat like sago grains or flakes of mucus. When undigested, starch is stained blue by compound solution of iodine; when slightly digested, it stains red.

Muscle fibers are yellow and, when poorly digested, appear as short, transversely striated cylinders with rather squarely broken ends (Fig. 15–2). The ends generally are rounded and the striations are faint, or only irregularly round or oval, yellow masses, which bear little resemblance to normal muscle tissue, are found. If a

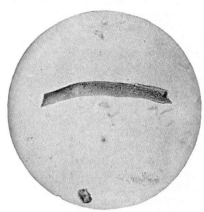

Figure 15–2. Poorly digested muscle fiber in feces showing striations and ragged ends (× 200).

little eosin solution is run under the coverglass, muscle fibers will take up the red color and stand out distinctly.

Fats occur in three modifications: neutral fats, fatty acids, and soaps. Neutral fats are present in very small amounts or not at all when an ordinary diet is used. They appear as droplets or yellowish flakes, depending on their melting point. They stain strongly with Sudan III. Fatty acids take the form of flakes like those of neutral fat or of needle-like crystals, which are generally aggregated into thick balls or irregular masses in which the individual crystals are difficult to make out. When treated with Sudan III, the amorphous flakes are stained a lighter orange than are the neutral fats, while the crystals are not stained. Soaps—chiefly calcium soap—appear partly as well-defined, yellow, amorphous flakes or rounded masses, suggesting eggs of parasites, and as coarse crystals. They do not stain with Sudan III and do not melt into globules when warmed as do the fatty acids. Mineral oil or castor oil taken as a cathartic may appear in the stool in such an amount as to interfere with an examination for parasites.

Connective tissue consists of colorless or yellowish threads with poorly defined edges and indefinite longitudinal striations. When treated with a 30 per cent solution of acetic acid, the fibers swell up and become clear and homogeneous. Elastic fibers, which are often present along with connective tissue, are more definite in outline and branch and anastomose. They are rendered more distinct by acetic acid.

An excess of any of these structures may result from excessive ingestion or deficient digestion.

Body Cells. A few epithelial cells, derived from the wall of the alimentary canal, are always present. They show all stages of disintegration and are often unrecognizable. A marked excess in the number of these cells is due to inflammation of some part of the bowel, usually the colon, if the cells are well preserved. Squamous cells come from the anal orifice; otherwise the type of the cell gives no clue to the site of the lesion.

Pus corpuscles are present in inflammatory and ulcerative conditions of the intestine. The number of the pus corpuscles roughly corresponds to the extent and severity of the lesion except in cases of amebic dysentery in which any considerable number of pus corpuscles indicates superimposed infection. If the pus is well mixed with the stool, the source of infection is high in the gastrointestinal tract, but in this case the pus is likely to be more or less completely digested and hence unrecognizable.

Unaltered erythrocytes are rarely seen unless their source is the colon, rectum, or anus. When the bleeding is in the small intestine, erythrocytes can seldom be recognized as such and chemical tests must be used.

Crystals. Various crystals may be found, but few have any significance. Slender, needle-like crystals of fatty acids and soaps and triple phosphate crystals are common. Characteristic octahedral crystals of calcium oxalate appear after ingestion of certain vegetables.

Bacteria. In health, bacteria—mostly dead—constitute about a third of the weight of the dried stool. In general it appears that they are beneficial although not necessary to existence. Ordinarily it is both difficult and unprofitable to identify them.

More than 50 different species have been isolated from the feces. Some of these are found only occasionally; some are present so constantly as to be recognized as normal inhabitants of the human intestine. Bacteriologic studies of the gastrointestinal tract are described in Chapter 16.

Animal Parasites and Ova. Methods and interpretations dealing with intestinal parasites and ova are contained in Chapter 16.

Bacteria, Protozoa, Helminths, and Arthropods of Medical Importance

By JAMES G. SHAFFER, Sc.D., MILTON GOLDIN, M.S., *and*
RUSSELL M. McQUAY, JR., Ph.D.

This chapter discusses either singly or by groups, various microorganisms (bacteria, protozoa, and helminths) of medical importance as well as some of the important arthropod vectors of disease. The fungi, rickettsia, and viruses are covered in separate chapters. It is not the plan here to present an extensive key to the identification of the organisms, which can be found in Bergey's *Manual of Determinative Bacteriology* (7th Edition) or Skerman's *Guide to the Identification of the Genera of Bacteria*. Rather, the critical identifying characteristics of the organisms, the diseases with which they are commonly associated, and the sites from which they are commonly isolated will be presented. Tables and flow sheets for the identification and differentiation of various species and groups will be given where they can be of use.

FLUORESCENCE MICROSCOPY

The development within recent years of techniques for conjugating antibodies with fluorescein and the application of these techniques to identification of specific microorganisms introduce the prospect that within a few years fluorescent antibody (FA) techniques will add a valuable tool in the clinical microbiology laboratory. Thus, it is desirable at this point to describe a broad outline of FA techniques. This is included here, rather than in the chapter on Microbiologic Methods, because these methods have not yet been developed to a point at which they can be included in the routine of microbial identification, nor is it yet clear just where they will best fit into the scheme of procedure. It may be that, in some cases, FA will completely replace time-consuming cultural methods; in other cases preliminary identification of microorganisms may be followed by cultural confirmation. It is probable that FA will replace some of the older serologic methods of making final identification of bacteria, and there is already evidence that indicates that the technique can be applied to the identification of viruses in tissue smears, sections, and other material. A great deal of investigative work is now in progress in various laboratories, which will no doubt elucidate the role that FA may play in clinical microbiologic work. Clinical microbiologists should be prepared to adapt these methods to their routine procedures at the earliest possible moment, since it is probable that FA will offer the opportunity to speed up microbiologic diagnosis.

The basic principle on which fluorescent antibody techniques depend is the nature of the combination of specific antibody with antigen. In the direct method the antibody coats the antigen (bacteria and protozoa, for example) and cannot easily be removed. If such an antibody has been rendered fluorescent by conjugation with fluorescein and all the nonantibody globulin is removed by washing, all that is left is that which is attached to the antigen. Thus, if the antigen is a bacterial cell and is viewed with an appropriate optical system, the fluorescent outline of the bacterial cell can be seen easily. The specificity of the test, as in any serologic procedure, depends on the purity of the antibody in the conjugated serum. To produce such a specific serum, one can immunize an appropriate animal with an organism (antigen) and absorb the serum to remove all but the specific, identifying antibody. For example, an animal may be given a series of inoculations with a suspension of Group A hemolytic *Streptococcus pyogenes* and by appropriate absorption the cross-reacting antibodies can be removed. The absorbed serum then contains specific Group A antibodies and when conjugated with fluorescein can be used to identify these organisms in smears.

An indirect FA technique may also be used. The basic principle of this method is as follows: The specific antiserum is not labeled with fluorescein. It is allowed to react with the antigen and the nonantibody globulin is washed off. If one is using a rabbit antiserum, the antigen is now coated with rabbit serum globulin. Treatment of this preparation with fluorescein-labeled antirabbit globulin results in a specific combination of this labeled antibody with the rabbit globulin already specifically attached to the antigen. When the nonantibody globulin is washed off, the antigen now can be seen as in the case of the direct technique. This indirect method has the advantage of reducing the number of labeled antiserums needed, since, if all diagnostic antiserums were produced in the rabbit, one would need only a fluorescein-labeled antirabbit globulin. Such a serum can be produced by inoculation of rabbit globulin into a sheep or other suitable animal. The indirect technique can be used for the detection of antibody in the serum of patients by combining such serum with specific organisms, such as *Toxoplasma,* and then using a fluorescein-labeled antihuman globulin serum.

An inhibition method has been used also for the purpose of checking the specificity of the reactions with a given antigen-antibody system. This will be outlined later. There is also a complement staining method, which is at present rather complex but may be quite useful in certain types of work.

Use of Fluorescence Microscopy as a Diagnostic Technique in Bacteriology. The following is a brief history of the development of fluorescent antibody techniques and a general outline of the materials and methods now in use. More detailed discussions will be found in the references and in the current literature.

Prior to the introduction of fluorescein isothiocyanate the conversion of amino fluorescein to fluorescein isocyanate for labeling serum globulin was a task that presented a major obstacle to many laboratories. This conversion required the use of phosgene gas, an extremely toxic reagent, and therefore the number of laboratories with facilities necessary for preparing labeled antiserums was limited. In addition to the toxicity of phosgene gas, the fluorescein isocyanate was unstable and had to be prepared immediately before mixing with the serum globulin to be conjugated. However, with the introduction of fluorescein isothiocyanate a stable reagent became available that greatly simplified the entire procedure for conjugating this derivative of fluorescein to serum globulin.

Essentially the procedure being used at present by most workers involves using half-saturated ammonium sulfate for repeated precipitation of serum globulin, which contains the antibodies. The precipitate is then dialyzed to remove the ammonium sulfate. The concentration of the precipitated globulin is usually adjusted to a concentration of about 1.0 per cent, and a calculated amount (0.05 mg. per mg. of protein) of fluorescein isothiocyanate is added. This step is carried out at 5° C., and the globulin-fluorescein isothiocyanate mixture is gently shaken for about 18 hours at 5° C.

After this the preparation is usually absorbed with an anionic resin to remove materials that are responsible for certain nonspecific staining. Originally pig liver powder or a like material prepared from other animal organs was used to absorb the conjugated globulin. However, these powder absorptions require a procedure that sometimes results in excessive dilution of the conjugated globulin. Unless specified otherwise, most methods used at the

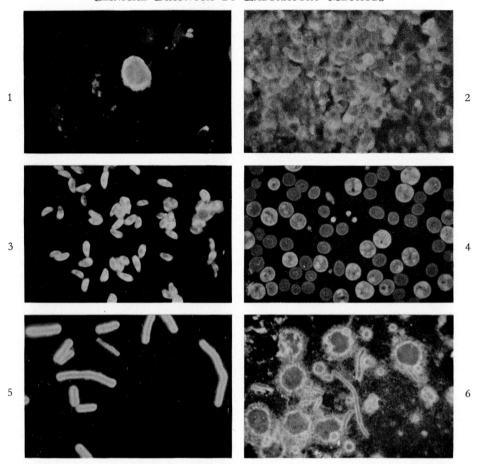

Figure 16–1 A.   Fluorescent antibody staining* of microorganisms. 1. *Entamoeba histolytica* in dried smear from culture (× 1050). 2. *Toxoplasma gondii* in spleen of infected mouse. Tissue fixed in alcohol-acetic acid and embedded in paraffin (× 1050). 3. *Toxoplasma gondii* in peritoneal exudate of infected mouse (× 1050). 4. *Plasmodium berghei,* a parasite of rodents, as seen in rat blood during preliminary studies of human malaria. 5. *Bacillus anthracis* in an impression smear from the liver of a mouse. Homologous antibody was prepared by injecting whole encapsulated antigen. Note both encapsulated and stripped forms (× 600). 6. *Pasteurella pestis* in smear of fluid aspirated from bubo of a fatal case of plague. Homologous antibody prepared by injecting whole-cell antigen. Note bizarre forms of plague bacilli and specifically stained soluble antigen surrounding tissue cells (× 1050). (From Cherry, W. B., Goldman, M., and Carski, T. R.: Fluorescent Antibody Techniques. U.S. Department of Health, Education, and Welfare, 1960.)

* By the direct method.

present time utilize an anionic resin for absorption or the absorption is omitted. If the preparation is absorbed, a period of one to two hours at 5° C. usually suffices, after which the material is placed in a cheesecloth bag and centrifuged to collect the absorbed conjugate.

The next step in the labeling procedure is another period of dialysis to remove the unconjugated fluorescein isothiocyanate. Dialysis is conducted at 5° C. in buffered saline until the dialysate no longer fluoresces when exposed to the beam of a Wood's light. After dialysis the conjugated globulin is centrifuged, if cloudy, to re-

move any precipitate. Merthiolate can be added as a preservative to give a final concentration of 1:10,000. The conjugated globulin is now ready for use. Small aliquots may be kept at 5° C. for immediate use, but the bulk of the conjugate should be kept frozen. Slow dissociation of the conjugate may occur when it is stored for long periods of time. Before the conjugate is used, these derivatives of fluorescein should be removed by dialysis.

A second important consideration in this technique is the light source, microscope, and various heat-absorbing, exciter, and barrier filter combinations. Although fluor-

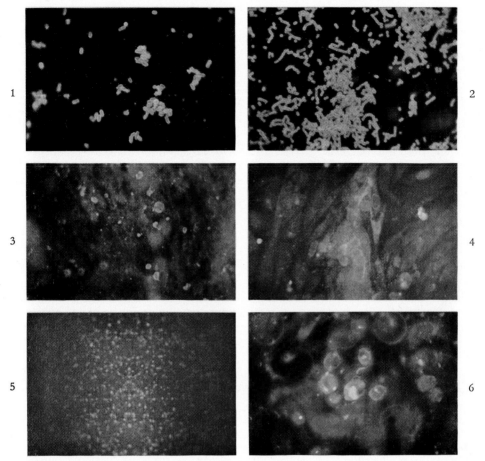

Figure 16–1 B. Fluorescent antibody staining* of microorganisms. 1. *Escherichia coli* in feces from a case of infantile diarrhea. Stained with pooled antibodies for enteropathogenic types of *E. coli* (× 600). 2. Group B streptococci in pure culture (× 600). 3. Rabies virus in impression smear of the brain of a mouse infected with street virus. Note the large aggregates of stained antigen (Negri bodies) and the numerous smaller particles that stain (× 210). 4. Simian foamy agent in a culture of monkey-kidney tissue on a coverslip. Two days after inoculation. Note stained antigen in nuclei of the multinucleate cells whose formation was induced by the infection (× 210). 5. *Rickettsia prowaseki* (epidemic typhus) in a smear of egg yolk sac. Stained with homologous antibody (× 210). 6. Polio virus type I in monkey-kidney tissue cultures, 12 hours postinoculation. Stained by complement method, using antipolio monkey serum and guinea pig complement followed by labeled anti-guinea pig complement (× 210). (From Cherry, W. B., Goldman, M., and Carski, T. R.: Fluorescent Antibody Techniques. U.S. Department of Health, Education, and Welfare, 1960.)

* By the direct method except for polio virus in 6.

escence microscopy with a bright-field microscope can be used for certain preparations, it is advisable to use a darkfield condenser for routine work. One of two major types of condensers, cardioid or paraboloid, may be used for this purpose. The immersion oil used for these darkfield condensers should be of a very low fluorescence type.

Most light systems in use at present employ a mercury lamp or carbon arc varying in power from 100 to 1000 watts. A number of light units are available commercially, and a great deal of care should be exercised in the selection of a particular unit. The more expensive units feature a closed system and can be set up more permanently than the less expensive types, which use a separate light housing from which an open beam of light must be focused onto a mirror beneath the microscope condenser. This type frequently requires realignment of the light beam and produces a considerable amount of "stray" light, which can be disconcerting to the observer.

A heat-absorbing filter is incorporated into the system to remove light near and beyond 600μ. This is necessary to prevent such light from cracking or breaking the primary filter. The primary or exciting light filter usually passes light from 300 to 425μ, depending upon the particular filter employed, and the barrier or ocular filter is usually one that will pass light of wavelengths above 400μ. The combinations of exciter and barrier filters used for virus and tissue section work are usually different from those for bacteria; hence, the various systems should be studied to find the one most suitable for the specimens to be studied routinely.

The three major techniques now in use are essentially as follows: In the direct method smears of the material to be examined may be fixed with heat or methanol or, in some cases, fixation is not necessary. Then the smear is flooded with the conjugated globulin reagent containing a specific antibody. This complex is usually incubated for 30 to 60 minutes at 37° C. in a moist chamber. Following this the smear is washed twice, the first time in buffered saline for five to ten minutes and then in tap water for another five to ten minutes. This washing is for the purpose of removing all uncombined conjugated globulin. A small drop of buffered glycerol is placed on the smear and a coverslip is added. The smear is then ready for examination.

In the indirect method the smear is treated with unlabeled antiserum exactly as in the direct test. This is the primary combining reaction. After this smear has been incubated and washed, fluorescein-labeled antiglobulin homologous to the globulin of the animal species whose serum is used in the primary reaction (e.g., if rabbit serum was the primary reagent, use labeled sheep antirabbit globulin) is added and the smear incubated and washed again as in the primary reaction. The smear is then mounted in buffered glycerol and examined.

The inhibition test is used as a control for the specificity of a reaction. In this test duplicate smears are used. One smear is treated with a mixture of unlabeled homologous antiserum and labeled homologous antiserum. The second smear is stained with a mixture of unlabeled normal serum and labeled homologous antiserum. Staining is carried out as in the direct test. When the stained smears are examined, the first preparation (unlabeled homologous antiserum plus labeled homologous anti-serum of the same species) should not fluoresce, but the second smear (stained with normal serum and labeled homologous antiserum of the same species) should fluoresce. This technique may also be used to detect antibody in unknown (patient's) serum. It requires a great deal of standardization, and before one attempts to use this method it should be thoroughly understood. The overall technique is too lengthy for this presentation. It is to be suspected that the direct and indirect methods will be much more useful in the clinical laboratory.

As FA work progresses, the new applications of this technique that will no doubt evolve will make possible changes and refinements of present techniques. Detection of antigen in tissues has been reported as well as the successful demonstration of antibody. Streptococci have been detected in smears made from throat swabs from patients with acute streptococcal pharyngitis, and a rapid method for detecting human influenza virus infection utilizing nasal smears has been described. FA studies have been extended to include members of the following genera of bacteria: *Leptospira*, *Hemophilus*, *Malleomyces*, *Streptococcus*, *Salmonella*, *Treponema*, *Pasteurella*, *Shigella*, *Escherichia*, and rumen bacteria. The technique has also been used in the detection of numerous viruses and some protozoa. An FA procedure for testing serums of patients suspected of being infected with *Toxoplasma gondii* has been developed; it appears to be as reliable as the methylene-blue dye test and yet far simpler. These cited cases represent but a few adaptations of fluorescence microscopy as a tool for studying and identifying microorganisms.

Various labeled antiserums can be obtained from commercial sources at rather nominal cost, since, if properly used, a little serum goes a long way (Fig. 16–1).

THE GRAM POSITIVE COCCI

The first group of bacteria to be considered is that comprising the gram positive cocci. The most important type species, their most important characteristics, and their occurrence are shown in Table 16–1. Certain additional information, not shown in the table, may be of help. The medium of choice for isolation of the members of this group is blood agar, since some of the organisms are fastidious in their growth requirements and one of the important identifying and differentiating character-

Table 16-1. Characteristics of the Gram Positive Cocci

SPECIES	DISEASES AND OCCURRENCE IN BODY	MORPHOLOGY AND GRAM STAIN	APPEARANCE ON BLOOD AGAR	PRIMARY DIFFERENTIATING CHARACTERISTIC
Diplococcus pneumoniae (pneumococcus)	Lobar pneumonia, eye infections, meningitis, otitis media, septicemia	Gram +, lance-shaped, encapsulated diplococcus	Small, shiny, transparent colonies, elevated in center. Alpha hemolytic	Optochin sensitive. Bile soluble. Quellung reaction
Streptococcus pyogenes (beta streptococcus)	Bronchopneumonia, follicular tonsillitis, nephritis, septicemia, scarlet fever, rheumatic fever, osteomyelitis, erysipelas	Gram +, spherical cocci, occurring in chains and pairs	Small colonies. Beta hemolysis	May be grouped and typed by Lancefield's technique
Streptococcus viridans group (green streptococcus)	Subacute bacterial endocarditis. Normal inhabitant of nasopharynx	Gram +, spherical cocci, occurring in chains and pairs	Small, raised, convex, opaque colonies. Alpha hemolytic	Optochin negative. Not bile soluble
Streptococcus faecalis (enterococcus)	Urinary infections, septicemia (may be found in blood). Normal inhabitant of intestinal tract	Gram +, round cocci, occurring in chains and pairs	Small colonies. May be beta, alpha, or gamma hemolytic	Grows in media containing 6.5% NaCl; heat resistant; may be antibiotic resistant. Lancefield's Group D
Streptococcus anhemolyticus (gamma streptococcus group)	Nasopharynx, intestinal tract, sputum, wounds	Gram +, round cocci, occurring in chains and pairs	Small colonies. No hemolysis	Primarily nonpathogenic
Staphylococcus aureus (*pyogenes*)	Skin, nasopharynx. Boils, carbuncles, food poisoning, osteomyelitis, impetigo, septicemia, pneumonia	Gram + round cocci, occurring in characteristic grapelike clusters	Large gold-pigmented colonies; usually beta hemolytic	Most pathogenic strains are coagulase, DNA, phosphatase, mannitol positive
Staphylococcus epidermidis (*albus*)	Skin and mucous membranes. Not generally pathogenic	Gram +, round cocci, occurring in characteristic grapelike clusters	Large, white, opaque colonies; usually nonhemolytic	Coagulase negative, DNA negative, phosphatase negative

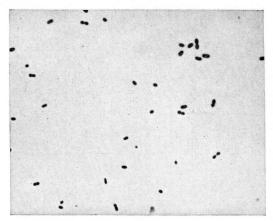

Figure 16–2. Pneumococcus, pure culture. Note the typical lanceolate shape and diplococcus arrangement. Fuchsin; × 1050. (Burrows: Textbook of Microbiology, 17th Ed.)

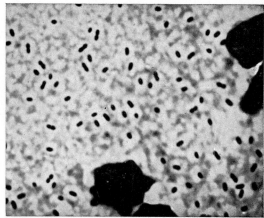

Figure 16–4. Pneumococcus in the peritoneal fluid of a mouse. Note the capsules. Fuchsin; × 2200. (Burrows)

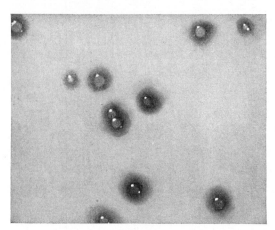

Figure 16–3. Colonies of the pneumococcus on blood agar. The areas of green hemolysis have been accentuated in the photograph. × 3. (Burrows)

istics is their effect on blood. One may incorporate sodium azide, phenylethyl alcohol, or other material to inhibit growth of gram negative bacilli when this is needed. Specialized media for this group are also widely used; these will be described where appropriate.

Diplococcus pneumoniae (pneumococcus) contains many antigenic types, which are determined by differences in their polysaccharide capsule. At one time it was very important to type these organisms (the quellung reaction), but since the advent of antibiotics, this has become less important in practice. Colonies of *D. pneumoniae* are small, moist, and 0.5 to 1.0 mm. in diameter and have a characteristic area of alpha (green) hemolysis surrounding them; they are indistinguishable from

colonies of *Streptococcus viridans* (Figs. 16–2 and 16–3). It is also not possible to differentiate these organisms by gram stain.

The simplest way to differentiate between these organisms is to pick a colony, streak it heavily on one-fourth of a blood agar plate, and apply an optochin disk.* *D. pneumoniae* is inhibited by optochin (ethylhydrocupreine hydrochloride), and a zone of inhibition will be seen around the disk after incubation. No zone appears with *S. viridans* or other alpha hemolytic streptococci. *D. pneumoniae* is also bile soluble and inulin positive, and these tests may be done if desired. White mice are highly susceptible to infection with *D. pneumoniae*. Virulent, smooth strains are encapsulated but change readily to the rough, nonencapsulated variants *in vitro* (Fig. 16–4).

Alpha hemolytic *Streptococcus faecalis* (enterococcus) is also difficult to differentiate from *D. pneumoniae* and *S. viridans* on blood agar (Fig. 16–5). *S. faecalis* will grow in medium containing 6.5 per cent NaCl and the others will not.

A medium termed "SF broth" is useful for the differentiation of Group D streptococci from other streptococci. *S. faecalis*, which belongs to Group D, grows in this medium and ferments dextrose, changing the color of the indicator from purple to yellow. *S. faecalis* will also resist heating at 60° C. for 30 minutes and grows on media containing bile salts (e.g., MacConkey's). It is also frequently resistant to antibiotics. Gamma-type streptococci colonies vary considerably in size, and are

* Available commercially.

gray and translucent. No hemolysis occurs. Anaerobic and micro-aerophilic streptococci are occasionally encountered in wound infections and septic conditions. They correspond in their general biologic characteristics to the aerobic forms.

Streptococcus pyogenes can be divided into numerous groups and types by the methods of Lancefield (1933) and others. Most of the human pathogens fall into Lancefield's Group A, although a few are found in Groups C and G. The presence of small, hard, white colonies 0.5 to 1 mm. in diameter, surrounded by a clear zone of hemolysis that reveals gram positive cocci tending to form chains, is diagnostic of *S. pyogenes* and can be so reported (Fig. 16–6). Microscopic examination of the hemolyzed zone reveals no intact erythro-

cytes. Gram stains from a blood culture may reveal such organisms, and this finding is strongly suggestive (Fig. 16–7).

If cultures are inoculated by the pour plate method, the hemolytic zones of beta streptococci are clearer. One method is to add the inoculum to a tube containing 10 ml. of infusion broth. One or two loopfuls are transferred to a similar second tube, which is shaken vigorously. One milliliter is then pipetted into a tube containing 20 ml. of melted blood agar base, which has been cooled to 45° C. One milliliter of sheep blood* is then added and the mixture rotated and poured into a Petri dish. After solidification the dish is incubated for 24 to 48 hours and examined for beta hemolytic colonies.

It is important to determine the serologic group to which beta hemolytic streptococci belong, since the presence of Group A streptococci may necessitate therapy, other groups usually being insignificant. A simple procedure that is fairly accurate is to plate the streptococci on blood agar and to apply a bacitracin disc† to the inoculated surface. A definite zone of inhibition of growth around the disc indicates presumptively that the organism belongs to Lancefield Group A.

Serologic grouping of streptococci is not difficult using Maxted's (1953) enzyme preparation, Rantz's (1955) autoclave procedure, or the classical Lancefield tech-

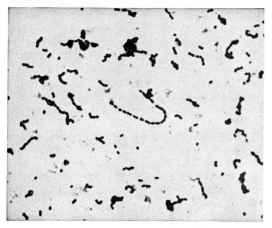

Figure 16–5. Streptococcus faecalis. P strain isolated from focal infection. Smear from pure culture. Fuchsin; × 1050. (Burrows)

---

* Sheep blood has one advantage over other types of animal blood for the isolation of beta hemolytic streptococci, because it inhibits the growth of *Hemophilus hemolyticus*. This organism, usually a saprophyte, forms a colony on blood agar that may be mistaken for *Streptococcus pyogenes*.

† Available commercially.

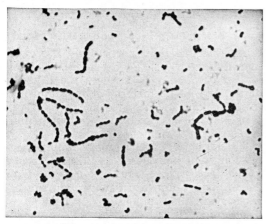

Figure 16–6. Streptococcus pyogenes. Recently isolated scarlet fever strain. Note the tendency to diplococcus arrangement in the chains. Fuchsin; × 1050. (Burrows)

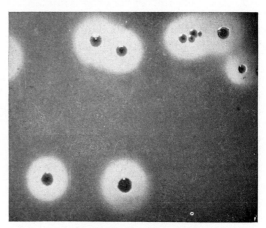

Figure 16–7. Streptococcus pyogenes. Pure culture on blood agar showing β hemolysis. × 5. (Burrows)

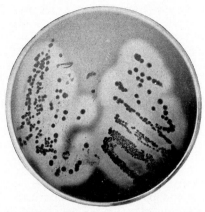

Figure 16–8. Blood agar culture of hemolytic *Staphylococcus aureus* in case of conjunctivitis (× 900). (Thygeson in Transactions of the American Ophthalmological Society.)

nique (see p. 899). These precipitation reactions depend on the presence of group specific polysaccharides, the C-substances.

Staphylococcus aureus is easily identified when it is typical, producing its gold pigment and usually having a zone of beta hemolysis surrounding the colonies (Fig. 16–8). Some strains do not hemolyze all types of blood and this must be kept in mind. The most reliable indicator of pathogenicity in *S. aureus* is considered to be the coagulase test, but unfortunately unless carefully standardized the test is subject to many sources of error. This test may be done as follows:

1. Place 2 or 3 drops of an 18-hour broth culture of the *S. aureus* in a sterile test tube (10 x 100 mm.). One may use colonies from a plate by emulsifying a large loopful in 2 or 3 drops of broth.

2. Add 0.5 ml. of plasma (human or rabbit) diluted 1:5 with physiologic saline and mix thoroughly by shaking. Desiccated or lyophilized plasma can be purchased for this purpose.

3. Place the tube in a 37° C. water bath or incubator for three hours. Most positive strains will clot the plasma within one hour. Those not clotting at three hours are re-examined after incubation for an additional 18 hours. Any degree of clotting is considered positive.

Coagulase tests can also be done in plates containing fibrinogen (Bovine Fraction I) or plasma. Coagulase positive colonies produce distinct zones of opacity after overnight incubation.

Yet another method is the slide test for coagulase (Cadness-Graves, 1943), but this is useful primarily as a rough screen-

ing procedure. Place a small drop of water on a slide and emulsify organisms from a single colony in it. Then add a small drop of plasma and mix thoroughly. If clumping of the organisms occurs in 5 to 15 seconds, the test is positive. If no clumping occurs, the organism should be tested by one of the other procedures. This test measures "bound" rather than "free" coagulase.

It has been found recently that estimation of deoxyribonuclease activity of staphylococci is considerably easier, more economical, and probably a better indication of potential pathogenicity than is the coagulase test. Details of this test may be found in the article by Weckman and Catlin (1957).

Another useful test is the estimation of phosphatase activity. This is accomplished by adding 0.01 per cent phenolphthalein phosphate to melted blood agar base. Swabs are plated in the usual way. After overnight incubation the plate is exposed to the fumes from a bottle of concentrated ammonia. Phosphatase positive colonies turn bright pink, while others remain unchanged. This test correlates very well with the coagulase and deoxyribonuclease activity.

Many other tests for determination of the potential virulence or pathogenicity of staphylococci are available. Most of these reactions are impractical for the clinical laboratory. Details of these reactions may be found in the references.

1. Egg yolk opacity test
2. Hyaluronidase production
3. Toxin production (plate or embryonated eggs)
4. Alpha hemolysin
5. Leukocidin production
6. Necrotoxin production
7. Virulence in rabbits or mice
8. Ammonium molybdate chemical test (A.M.C.)

Another reaction, particularly useful in identifying enterotoxigenic food poisoning strains of *S. aureus*, involves the capacity of the organisms to ferment mannitol and to propagate in the presence of 7.5 per cent NaCl. These tests can be run simultaneously in mannitol-salt agar.

All staphylococci that are coagulase negative may be considered as *Staphylococcus epidermidis*. These are not typable with bacteriophage and are usually, but not always, nonpathogenic.

The emergence of considerable numbers of antibiotic resistant strains of *S. aureus*, especially in the hospital environment, has created a serious problem. It is important that antibiotic sensitivity tests be done on all cultures of *S. aureus* isolated from patients in order to guide therapy. Precautions must be taken to avoid transmission of the organism within the hospital environment. (See Chapter 22.)

S. aureus is antigenically rather heterogenous, although certain definite antigen types have been described. A more workable classification is obtained by means of bacteriophage typing. This procedure has considerable usefulness in epidemiologic studies but should probably not be attempted in small laboratories and, at least at present, does not contribute greatly to diagnosis.

THE GRAM NEGATIVE COCCI

The gram negative cocci of medical importance all belong to the genera *Neisseria* and *Veillonella*. Two of the species, *N. gonorrhoeae* (gonococcus) and *N. meningitidis* (meningococcus), are well-recognized human pathogens. There are several nonpathogenic species, most important of which are *N. catarrhalis* and *N. sicca*. They are nonpathogenic inhabitants of the normal throat and mucous surfaces of man, and it is necessary to be able to differentiate them from the pathogens. Table 16–2 summarizes the most important characteristics of these species. It will be seen in the table that *N. meningitidis* and *N. gonorrhoeae* require enriched media and CO_2 for growth. The CO_2 is not so critical with *N. meningitidis* but should always be used. *N. catarrhalis* and other nonpathogenic *Neisseria* grow well on ordinary agar. Anaerobic *Neisseria* are placed among the *Veillonella*.

The oxidase test is very useful in picking colonies of *Neisseria* in mixed cultures from vaginal and urethral smears. The test is performed as follows:

Oxidase Reagent

Di- or tetra-methyl paraphenyl-
ene diamine hydrochloride   1.0 gm.
Distilled water (fresh)   100.0 ml.

The test is performed by dropping the oxidase reagent on the colonies. Oxidase positive colonies become black rather rapidly. The reagent is quite unstable and must be made fresh every few days. Some prefer to use discs impregnated with the reagent.[*]

All *Neisseria* are oxidase positive, but there are certain other microorganisms that are also positive (certain of the gram negative bacilli, yeasts, and fungi). Thus, it is necessary to do a gram stain of the colony to make sure it is a gram negative diplococcus. Subculture can be made from the oxidase positive colonies, provided sterile oxidase reagent has been used. It must be done immediately, since too long an exposure to the reagent will destroy the bacteria (Fig. 16–9).

N. meningitidis may be isolated from the spinal fluid, blood, throat, and nasopharynx or from the petechiae that may occur in the skin. This organism is divided into four antigenic types. Final identifica-

[*] Available commercially.

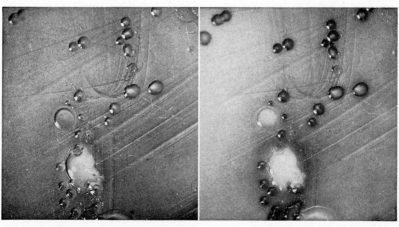

Figure 16–9. The oxidase test for the identification of meningococcus colonies. Mixed culture on blood agar. *Left,* colonies of meningococci and contaminants before the application of tetramethyl-*p*-phenylene-diamine solution. *Right,* the same colonies after the application of the reagent. Note that the meningococcus colonies show the development of color first about the edges, and there is slight discoloration of the medium. × 5. (Burrows)

Table 16-2.   Characteristics of the Gram Negative Cocci

SPECIES	DISEASES AND OCCURRENCE IN BODY	MORPHOLOGY AND GRAM STAIN	MEDIUM OF CHOICE AND CONDITIONS FOR GROWTH	PRIMARY DIFFERENTIATING AND IDENTIFYING CHARACTERISTICS
Neisseria meningitidis (meningococcus)	Meningitis (epidemic meningitis), meningococcemia, mild sore throat (may precede meningococcemia and meningitis)	Gram negative, bean shaped diplococci with adjacent sides flattened. May be seen in polymorphonuclear leukocytes in spinal fluid and in petechiae	Chocolate or blood agar. Growth greatly improved by 10% CO_2	Colonies 1 to 4 mm. in diameter, bluish white, opaque. Oxidase positive. Ferment dextrose and maltose, not sucrose. Agglutinated by polyvalent antiserum
Neisseria gonorrhoeae (gonococcus)	Acute urethritis in male and female, chronic infection of urogenital tract, gonococcal arthritis, ophthalmia neonatorum	Gram negative, bean shaped diplococci. Occur in polymorphonuclear leukocytes in urethral smears	Chocolate agar, GC medium. Requires 10% CO_2	Colonies 1 to 4 mm. in diameter, oxidase positive. Ferment dextrose, not maltose or sucrose
Neisseria catarrhalis	Normal inhabitant of throat. May be found in catarrhal conditions in upper repiratory tract	Gram negative, spherical diplococci with adjacent sides flattened	Grows well on most ordinary media	Colonies 1.5 to 5 mm. in diameter, oxidase positive. Do not ferment dextrose, maltose, or sucrose. Grow at room temperature.
Neisseria sicca	Normal inhabitant of respiratory tract of man	Gram negative diplococci with adjacent sides flattened	Grows well on most ordinary media	Colonies dry, crumbling. Sometimes hemolytic, oxidase positive
Veillonella sp.	Digestive and vaginal tract of humans. Occasionally pathogenic	Gram negative, minute, spherical diplococci	Weakly hemolytic on blood agar. Obligate anaerobe	Acid and gas from glucose. Nitrate positive, anaerobic

tion as *N. meningitidis* can be made by noting agglutination with a polyvalent antiserum (agglutinates all types) or capsular swelling (quellung reaction). For epidemiologic purposes it is often desirable to determine the actual type, but species identification is usually enough for diagnosis (Fig. 16–10).

N. gonorrhoeae is antigenically quite heterogeneous, but it is not likely to be confused with any other organism. Its morphology and culturally fastidious nature as well as clinical evidence usually leave little doubt about its identity (Figs. 16–11, 16–12, 16–13). Carbohydrate fermentations may be helpful but are not easy to perform. Morphologically similar organisms, which can be confused with gonococci, are occasionally encountered in the vagina or conjunctiva. These are either nonpathogenic *Neisseria* or members of the tribe Mima (see p. 638). Nongonococcal urethritis, particularly in males, is apparently increasing in incidence.

THE GRAM NEGATIVE ENTERIC BACILLI

This is a complex and often confusing group of bacteria. The validity of classification into a number of genera has been generally accepted. There are, however, many intermediates, and the boundaries between species often become indistinct, leaving one with the impression that this is really a spectrum of organisms in which the specific boundaries are not very sharp. Some of the genera have been studied extensively, especially the *Salmonella*, with the result that many species have been described. In many cases these species dif-

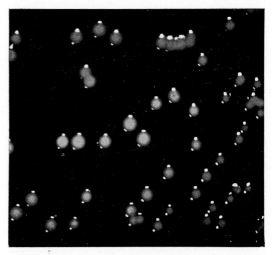

Figure 16–12. Colonies of the gonococcus on blood agar. × 6. (Burrows)

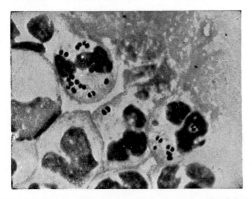

Figure 16–10. Meningococci in cerebrospinal fluid in a case of epidemic spinal meningitis (× 1500).

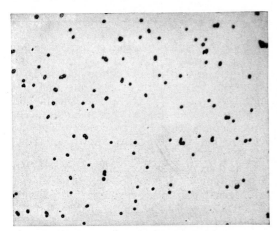

Figure 16–11. The gonococcus from pure culture. Fuchsin; × 1050. (Burrows)

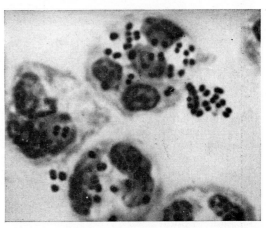

Figure 16–13. Urethral smear from gonorrhea. Gram stain. Note the intracellular and extracellular position of the gonococci and their typical coffee-bean shape and arrangement in pairs. × 2400. (Burrows)

Table 16–3. The Gram Negative Enteric Bacteria

SPECIES	DISEASE IN MAN	SOURCE OF INFECTION (OCCURRENCE IN NATURE)	SOURCES OF CULTURE IN MAN
Salmonella typhi	Typhoid (enteric) fever	Human (man to man) cases and carriers	Blood culture (first 10–14 days) Stool culture (after 10–14 days) Urine culture (late in disease) Carrier (stool culture)
Salmonella paratyphi A *Salmonella paratyphi B* *Salmonella paratyphi C*	Enteric fever (typhoid-like)	Same as *S. typhi*	Same as *S. typhi*
Salmonella enteritidis *Salmonella typhimurium* *Salmonella choleraesuis* Other salmonellas, many species	May cause enteric fever, food poisoning	Primarily animal pathogens but may establish carrier state in man	Same as *S. typhi* in enteric fever; otherwise just stools. Other organs, joints. Stool culture: seldom invade blood sufficiently for positive cultures.
Shigella dysenteriae *Shigella sonnei* *Shigella flexneri* *Shigella boydii*	Bacillary dysentery (shigellosis)	Human (man to man) cases and carriers	Stool culture: rarely invade blood
Proteus morganii	Possible cause of diarrhea in infants and children	Probably human	Stool culture
Proteus vulgaris *Proteus mirabilis* *Proteus rettgeri*	Urinary tract infections, wound infections	Normal inhabitant of GI tract; widely dispersed in nature	Urine culture, wound cultures
Escherichia coli	Urinary tract infections, terminal septicemia, infant diarrhea (enteropathogenic strains)	Normal inhabitant of lower GI tract. Pathogenic strains probably of human origin	Urine cultures Blood cultures in septicemia Stool cultures
Aerobacter aerogenes *Klebsiella pneumoniae* (Friedländer's bacillus)	Probably nonpathogenic. Friedländer's pneumonia, meningitis, urinary tract infections	Normal inhabitant in man and animals. Found in soil	Stool culture Sputum and throat Spinal fluid Urine cultures
Paracolobactrum coliforme *Paracolobactrum aerogenoides* *Paracolobactrum intermedium* *Paracolobactrum arizonae*	Possible cause of diarrhea in some cases	Probably human. *P. arizonae* in animals	Stool culture
Pseudomonas aeruginosa	Urinary tract infections, wound infections	Human. Occurs also in nature	Urine cultures Cultures from wounds
Alcaligenes faecalis	Low-grade pathogen	Human	Stool culture Urine culture Blood culture (rare)
Vibrio comma	Asiatic cholera	Human (cases and carriers)	Stool culture

fer only in minor ways and the number of species is rather cumbersome.

Table 16–3 shows the occurrence and pathogenic importance of the better known species of gram negative enteric bacteria. It is beyond the scope of this book to discuss the more exact identification of species within the complex groups of enteric bacteria. For more detailed discussions one may refer to the various textbooks and laboratory guides, some of which are listed in the bibliography.

The schemes for identification of the gram negative enteric bacteria to be given here emphasize generic identification and only proceed to species in certain special cases. Separation of the groups is determined primarily by fermentation of lactose, the formation of acid or acid and gas from dextrose, motility, effect on urea, and production of H_2S. By use of media containing proper ingredients, the isolation and identification can be accomplished according to the diagram shown in Table 16–4.

The use of selective, inhibitory, and enhancement media for primary inoculation of a fecal culture is discussed in Chapter 17. The purpose of these media is to inhibit gram positive organisms and to separate the lactose fermenting enteric bacilli from the nonlactose fermenters. The non-

Table 16–4. Isolation and Preliminary Identification of *Salmonella* and *Shigella* Cultures*

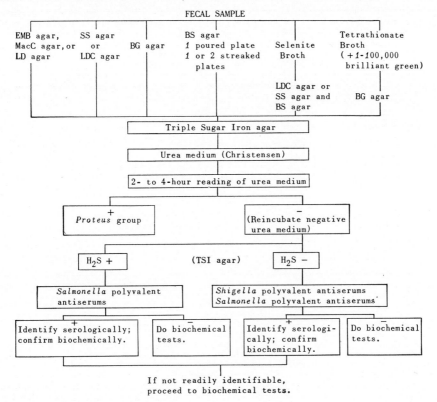

EMB agar - Eosin methylene blue agar
MacC agar - MacConkey's agar
LD agar - Leifson's desoxycholate agar
LDC agar - Leifson's desoxycholate citrate agar
SS agar - *Salmonella-Shigella* agar
BS - Bismuth sulfite agar
BG agar - Brilliant green agar

* From Edwards, P. R., and Ewing, W. H.: Identification of Enterobacteriaceae. Minneapolis, Burgess Publishing Company, 1955.

lactose fermenters include all the recognized enteric pathogens as well as the *Proteus* group, *Pseudomonas, Alcaligenes,* and the paracolons. Their colony characteristics may be seen in Table 16–5 and Figs. 16–14 to 16–22.

Further identification of the nonlactose fermenting bacilli is accomplished, as shown in Table 16–6, by transfer from the isolated colorless colonies to triple sugar iron (T.S.I.) or Kligler's iron agar and urea medium. It is well to make separate transfers from several colonies of different types, if available. Urea medium is used for the identification of *Proteus*, which breaks down the urea, rendering the medium alkaline (red). This occurs rapidly (two to four hours). Some other organisms, such as *Aerobacter*, may break down urea slowly so that a positive result after 18 to 24

hours has little significance. Some workers add tryptophan to the urea medium and use it to test for indol production after 24 to 48 hours' incubation.

T.S.I. agar is a multipurpose medium designed to provide a tentative differentiation of the enteric bacilli. It contains lactose (1.0 per cent), sucrose (1.0 per cent), dextrose (0.1 per cent), and an iron salt. It is tubed as slants with a deep butt and a relatively short slant. The center of the colony from the original culture is touched with a straight wire and stabbed into the butt, care being taken not to go completely to the bottom of the tube. The wire is then streaked over the slant. Acid production is indicated by a change in the color of the medium from red to yellow. Gas production is shown by the appearance of the bubbles in the medium along and around

Table 16–5. Appearance of Colonies of Enteric Organisms on Differential Plating Media

GROUP	E.M.B. AGAR	S.S. AGAR	BRILLIANT GREEN AGAR	BISMUTH SULFITE AGAR
E. coli	Flat; deep purple with metallic sheen	Inhibited; may develop as large, opaque pink or red colonies	Large opaque, yellowish-green colonies inhibited to some extent	Inhibited, large, mucoid, glistening, brown
Klebsiella - A. aerogenes	Light blue, metallic sheen; occasionally in depressed center	Inhibited; large, white or cream colored; opaque	Inhibited; large greenish-yellow colonies	Raised, mucoid, lenticular in shape, greatly inhibited
S. typhi	Colorless, translucent	Colonies colorless but may have light tan, light pinkish, or yellow appearance or a yellow or tan center; 1–5 mm.	Transparent pink colonies. Grow rather sparsely	Fully developed colonies are convex, 1–3 mm., black with lustrous surface surrounded by brownish-black zone
Salmonella	Colorless, translucent	Colonies sometimes larger than above; otherwise similar	Transparent pink to deep fuchsia colonies. Occ. brownish	Colonies similar to above but larger and tending toward a dark brown rather than black; usually very lustrous
Paracolon	Same as *Salmonella*	Clear, transparent colonies similar to *Salmonella*. Occ. black centered	Same as *Salmonella*	Some appear as light green, flat colonies with dark green centers. Some are greenish-brown colonies with dark centers
Proteus	Colorless, may spread. Fuzzy edges	Usually small, transparent, water-clear colonies; may have fuzzy or veil-like edge. Sometimes show black centers	Greatly inhibited	Similar to coliform group. Usually bright to brownish-green with darker centers. No spreading
Shigella	Small, round, translucent colorless	Colonies similar to above; *S. sonnei* may grow especially large with yellow centers and irregular edges.	No significant growth. Some strains of *S. alkalescens* appear same as *Salmonella*.	Inhibited, light or dark green, smooth, glistening colony. Some ameboid in shape
Pseudomonas	Oval or lenticular, colorless, irregular edges, may be mucoid	Transparent grayish colonies usually rough with irregular edges	Deep pink to purplish colonies, usually fuzzy edges	Greenish-brown colonies, sometimes with darker centers. Similar to paracolons
Alcaligenes faecalis	Colorless, small	Colorless, clear, transparent, small	Inhibited	Inhibited; dark green to black, dry

the stab line. Fermentation of lactose is indicated by the development of acid and gas in the slant and butt. Fermentation of sucrose alone is indicated by an acid slant and butt. Fermentation of dextrose only (*Salmonella, Shigella,* paracolon) is indicated by an acid butt, either with or without gas, and a slant that remains alkaline (red). The production of hydrogen sulfide is indicated by the presence of blackening of the medium as a result of the formation of iron sulfide. T.S.I. slants should be

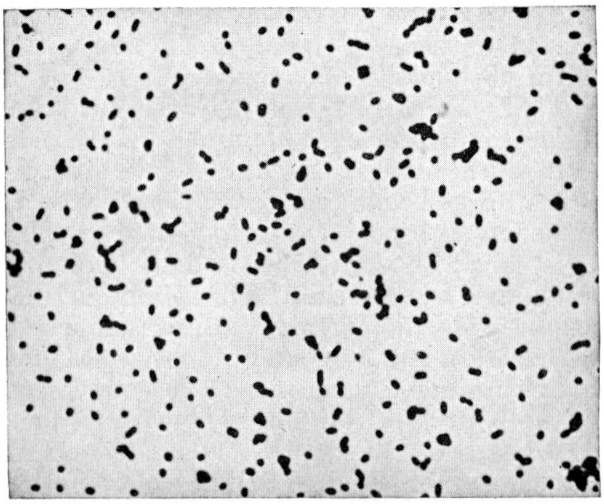

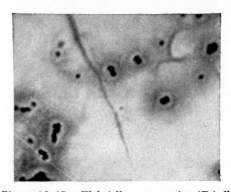

Figure 16–14. Coliform bacilli. Smear from a pure culture. Note the coccobacillary form. Fuchsin; × 1050. (Burrows)

Figure 16–15. Klebsiella pneumoniae (Friedländer's bacillus) in pure culture on blood agar, showing capules. Crystal violet; × 1200. (Burrows)

read at 24 hours, since on longer incubation the reaction may revert to alkaline and the results may be quite confusing. In Table 16–7 are shown the characteristic reactions of the main groups on T.S.I. medium.

Following the reading of the urea and T.S.I. results one should do spot agglutinations with polyvalent antisera as indicated in Table 16–4 and report the findings. Further identification of the organism depends on biochemical studies and on spe-

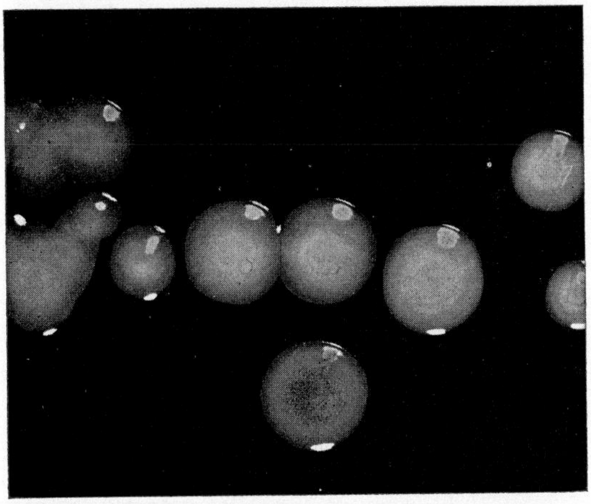

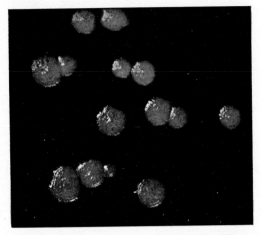

Figure 16–19. Colonies of typhoid bacillus on nutrient agar. Note the characteristic "maple-leaf" irregular margin and slightly roughened glistening surface. × 6. (Burrows)

Figure 16–16. Colonies of Friedländer's bacillus on blood agar. Note the large size and mucoid appearance. × 3. (Burrows)

Figure 16–17. *Proteus vulgaris* colony on blood agar. Note the swarming exhibited as successive waves of growth. (Dack.)

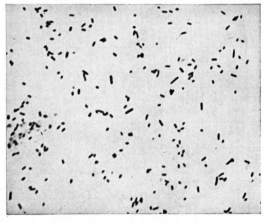

Figure 16–20. *Shigella flexneri.* Smear from a pure culture. Fuchsin; × 1050. (Burrows)

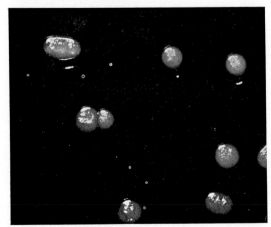

Figure 16–18. Colonies of *Salmonella typhimurium* (*aertrycke*) on nutrient agar. Twenty-four-hour culture. × 3. (Burrows)

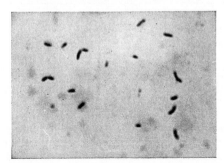

Figure 16–21. *Vibrio cholerae;* pure culture in peptone water. Gram stain; × 1200. (Burrows)

Table 16–6.　Biochemical Reactions of Enterobacteriaceae

	DEXTROSE	LACTOSE	SUCROSE	MANNITOL	INDOL	METHYL RED	VOGES-PROSKAUER	SIMMON'S CITRATE	UREA	H$_2$S (TSI)	MOTILITY	KCN	LYSINE DECARBOXYLASE	PHENYLALANINE DEAMINASE
E. coli	AG	AG	V	AG	+	+	–	–	–	–	V	–	+	–
E. freundii	AG	AG	V	AG	V	+	–	+	sl	+	+	+	–	–
Klebsiella-Aerobacter	AG	AG	AG	AG	–	–	+	+	sl	–	V	+	V	–
Paracolobactrum coliforme	AG	sl	V	AG	+	+	–	–	–	–	V	–	+	–
Paracolobactrum intermedium	AG	sl	V	AG	V	+	–	+	sl	+	+	+	–	–
Paracolobactrum aeroginoides	AG	sl	AG	AG	–	–	+	+	sl	+	V	+	V	–
Paracolobactrum arizonae	AG	sl	–	AG	–	+	–	+	–	+	+	–	+	–
Salmonella paratyphi A	AG	–	–	AG	–	+	–	–	–	+	+	–	+	–
Salmonella other sp.	AG	–	–	AG	–	+	–	+	–	+	+	–	+	–
Salmonella typhi	A	–	–	A	–	+	–	–	–	+	+	–	+	–
Shigella dysenteriae	A	–	–	–	–	+	–	–	–	–	–	–	–	–
Shigella flexneri	A	–	–	A	+	+	–	–	–	–	–	–	–	–
Shigella boydii	A	–	–	A	–	+	–	–	–	–	–	–	–	–
Shigella sonnei	A	sl	sl	A	–	+	–	–	–	–	–	–	–	–
Shigella alkalescens-dispar	A	–	V	A	+	+	–	–	–	–	–	–	–	–
Proetus vulgaris	AG	–	AG	–	+	+	–	+	+	+	+	+	–	+
Proteus mirabilis	AG	–	sl	–	–	+	–	+	+	+	+	+	–	+
Proteus morganii	AG	–	–	–	+	+	–	–	+	–	+	+	–	+
Proteus rettgeri	A	–	sl	A	+	+	–	+	+	–	+	+	–	+
Proteus inconstans (Providence)	AG	–	sl	–	+	+	–	+	–	–	+	+	–	+

A　= Acid
G　= Gas
V　= Variable
sl　= slow or delayed

cific agglutination. Antisera for the agglutination test are available commercially and the technique is simple. It can be done as follows: A loop of the growth from the T.S.I. is emulsified in a drop of saline on a clean slide. A drop of the antiserum is added and mixed by gentle rotation. In a positive test clumped bacteria can usually be seen macroscopically, but it may be necessary to check with the microscope under low power. A control with saline substituted for the antiserum is essential. For agglutination of possible *Shigella* cultures the organisms should be boiled for 30 minutes to destroy heat-labile K antigens. The use of six "H" sera (a, b, c, d,

Table 16–7. Interpretation of Reactions on Triple Sugar Iron Agar

BUTT	REACTION SLANT	H₂S	POSSIBLE ORGANISMS
Acid, gas	Acid	None	*Escherichia** *Klebsiella-Aerobacter* *Proteus* Paracolons
Acid, gas	Alk.	+	*Salmonella* *Proteus* Paracolons
Acid, no gas	Alk.	None	*Salmonella*† *Shigella* Paracolons *Proteus*
Alk.	Alk.	None	*Alcaligenes* *Pseudomonas* Mima-Herellea

* *E. freundii* produces H₂S.
† *S. typhi* produces a small amount of H₂S in the butt.

i and 1, 2, 3, 5) in conjunction with the O and Vi sera will allow satisfactory identification of most of the strains of *Salmonella* found in human disease.

Specific agglutination of suspected *S. typhi* requires special comment. Freshly isolated strains often have Vi antigen, and such organisms may not agglutinate with the *S. typhi* antiserum. One can obtain specific anti-Vi sera and, if available, this should be used. If such sera are not available, the Vi antigen can be destroyed by placing the suspension of the bacteria in a boiling water bath for 10 to 15 minutes. Following this the organism should ag-

glutinate with the routine anti-*S. typhi* serum.

To establish an exact identification of the species of organism, it is necessary to do further studies, since there are sometimes confusing cross reactions in the agglutination tests; i.e., some of the paracolons (*Paracolobactrum*) share antigens with some of the *Salmonella*. This can be accomplished by doing biochemical studies and agglutinations with species-specific antisera. Bacteriophage suspensions specific for *Salmonella* are available and may also be useful in identification. Smaller laboratories may have to send cultures to laboratories specialized in these techniques. Some of the characteristic biochemical reactions of the members of this group of bacteria are shown in Table 16–6. It must be realized that variations from the reactions listed will occasionally be encountered.

Some of the newer biochemical tests for the differentiation of the enteric bacteria are very useful and simple to perform and deserve to be widely applied. The techniques are not described here but can be found in the references (Edwards and Ewing, 1955; Kaufmann, 1954; and Moeller, 1955).

1. KCN inhibition: *Salmonella*, *Shigella*, and *Escherichia* do not grow in KCN, whereas *Klebsiella-Aerobacter*, Paracolon, and *Proteus inconstans* (Providence) do.
2. Lysine decarboxylase: *Arizona*, *Salmonella*, and *Escherichia* are positive; *Shigella*, *Proteus*, and Providence are negative.
3. Phenylalanine deaminase: *Proteus* and

Figure 16–22. The colonial morphology of *Vibrio cholerae* on bile-salt agar in mixed culture with coliform bacilli. The minute, translucent, raised colonies of the cholera vibrio contrast with the roughened appearance of coliform bacillus colonies in the presence of taurocholate. × 10. (Burrows)

Providence are positive; the other groups are negative.
4. Leucine decarboxylase: All members of the *Proteus* and Providence groups are positive.
5. Ornithine decarboxylase: *Aerobacter* and nonpigmented *Serratia* can decarboxylate ornithine; *Klebsiella* cannot.

Identification of Enteropathogenic Types of Escherichia coli

Since the pioneer work of Kaufmann starting in 1943 on the antigenic analysis of *Escherichia coli,* it has been found that certain serologic varieties are associated with diarrhea in infants and children. Severe cases, both sporadic and epidemic, in which the etiology was formerly unknown have been proved to be caused by these serotypes. Consequently it is essential to isolate and identify these organisms from clinical cases and from carriers.

Biochemical differences between the enteropathogenic strains and the normal types of *E. coli* are insufficient to differentiate them adequately from each other. Type differentiation thus depends entirely on their serologic behavior.

E. coli possesses three types of antigens —O, K, and H. The O or somatic antigens are not inactivated by heat. The K antigens, also somatic antigens, occur as sheaths or envelopes, which block the O agglutination. They are destroyed by heat at 100° C. The K antigens consist of three varieties known as L, A, and B. H antigens are the flagellar antigens found only in the motile strains.

In typing the enteropathogenic strains of *E. coli,* it is necessary to determine both the O antigen and the B variety of K antigen. The serologic types that most commonly are associated with diarrheal diseases are listed in Table 16–8.

Technique. Material for culture should

Table 16–8. Enteropathogenic Strains of *E. coli* Antigens

O (SOMATIC)	K (SHEATH ENVELOPE OR CAPSULAR)
26	B6
55	B5
86	B7
111	B4 (*E. coli neapolitanum*)
112	B11 (*S. guanabara*)
119	B14
124	B17
125	B15
126	B16
127	B8
128	B12

be collected before specific therapy is instituted. Specimens may be taken from freshly soiled diapers or collected by means of rectal swabs. If stools must be held for several hours before inoculation of media, they should be emulsified in buffered glycerol-saline.

Specimens should be streaked on EMB or MacConkey's agar and, using a light inoculum, on a blood agar plate. The blood agar is used because certain strains are inhibited on EMB or MacConkey's and also because it is easier to avoid contaminants when picking colonies from this medium. Sorbitol agar may also be useful, since enteropathogenic strains of *E. coli* tend to be sorbitol negative. It is necessary, however, to use the other media, since sorbitol positive strains of enteropathogenic *E. coli* are occasionally encountered. Sorbitol negative strains should be checked with the acriflavine dye test. The test is done by suspending a colony in a drop of normal saline solution and adding one drop of neutral acriflavine (1:500 aqueous). If no agglutination occurs within one minute, the colony is then typed with antiserum. Those that agglutinate may be discarded as nonpathogens. In addition to these media the procedure for the isolation of *Salmonella* and *Shigella* and parasitologic examination must be followed and a specimen collected for possible virus isolation. (See Table 16–9.)

After overnight incubation at 37° C. typical strains of *E. coli* are picked to nutrient agar slants for serologic study. There are no distinct differences in colonial morphology between the pathogenic and nonpathogenic serotypes; hence colonies must be picked at random. However, enteropathogenic strains may give off a definite spermatic odor on first isolation, and when they are present, they tend to predominate. The nutrient agar slants are incubated overnight and then tested with OB and O antisera.

Serologic Typing. In typing the enteropathogenic *E. coli,* the O antigen and the B variety of K antigen must be determined. Since the B antigen masks the O agglutinability of living cultures, the culture must be boiled before the O antigens can be determined. The OB antiserums* contain the agglutinins for both the O and B antigens; the O antiserums* are used only after the B antigen has been destroyed by heating.

* Available commercially.

A drop of polyvalent OB antiserum is placed on a slide, and a small loopful of the culture from the agar slant is emulsified in the serum to give a homogenous suspension. The slide is then rotated for one to two minutes and agglutination observed macroscopically. The clumping must be rapid and strong; otherwise it should be ignored. If positive, individual (specific) OB antiserums are used. Alternatively it is also possible to test individual colonies directly from the plates in OB antisera. If strong agglutination occurs either in the polyvalent antiserums or in any of the individual serotypes, a preliminary report that an enteropathogenic *E. coli* is present can be given and further serologic and biochemical tests done to confirm this and to determine the specific serotype.

If positive agglutination occurs in the OB antiserum, the O antigen must be determined. This can be done by first heating a saline suspension of the culture for 30 minutes at 100° C. and adding 0.5 per cent formalin. Serial dilutions of the specific antiserums are then made in small test tubes so that a series of dilutions ranging from 1:20 to 1:2560 in 0.5 ml. of saline are prepared. These dilutions depend on the original titer of the antiserum. To each of these dilutions 0.5 ml. of the cooled formalinized broth cultures is added. The tubes are then incubated at 50° C. for 16 to 18 hours. Cultures showing agglutination in dilutions of at least 1:160 or more are considered to have the same O antigen as the corresponding antiserum. If agglutination is not distinct except in low dilutions, this should be considered as negative for that particular O antigen. If strong agglutination occurs in more than one antiserum, this probably indicates a mixed culture, and the original agar slant should be streaked for purity and individual colonies retested.

It is also possible to test the O antigens by the slide test, but this should always be confirmed by the test tube procedure. The unboiled culture is tested on a slide with OB antiserums and a boiled culture with O antiserums. Agglutination in both antiserums is strong evidence for the identification of that serotype.

The final step in the identification is to check the strain biochemically to show that it belongs to the *E. coli* group (see Table 16–9).

The classification of the genus *Paracolobactrum* (paracolon) is rather complex. The species may be designated according to their position in relation to the other *Enterobacteriaceae*. Thus, the species are *P. coliforme* (related to *E. coli*), *P. aerogenoides* (related to *A. aerogenes* and including the Hafnia group), *P. intermedium* (intermediate), and *P. arizonae* (Arizona group). On the basis of serologic and biochemical characteristics the paracolons may be grouped into three categories now designated as the Arizona, Ballerup-Bethesda, and Providence groups. Many of the paracolons are slow lactose fermenters and indol positive, and these reactions may be used as a differential test. A number of strains have antigens in common with certain other enteric bacilli. Some are associ-

Table 16–9.   Outline of Procedure for Examination of Stool Specimens in Cases of Diarrhea in
Infants and Children

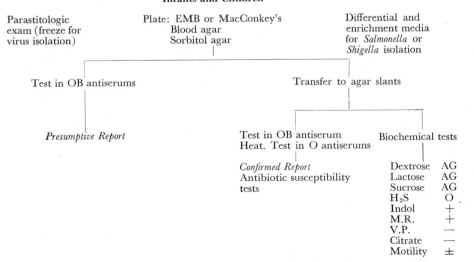

| Parasitologic exam (freeze for virus isolation) | Plate: EMB or MacConkey's Blood agar Sorbitol agar | Differential and enrichment media for *Salmonella* or *Shigella* isolation |

Test in OB antiserums   Transfer to agar slants

Presumptive Report   Test in OB antiserum   Biochemical tests
                              Heat. Test in O antiserums

                              Confirmed Report   Dextrose   AG
                              Antibiotic susceptibility Lactose   AG
                              tests   Sucrose   AG
                                                         H₂S   O
                                                         Indol   +
                                                         M.R.   +
                                                         V.P.   −
                                                         Citrate   −
                                                         Motility   ±

ated with diarrhea and appear to have pathogenic potential. Thus, this group seems to represent intermediate organisms. They pose definite problems in the clinical microbiologic laboratory that require careful study and experience to solve.

The genus *Serratia* includes gelatin-liquefying strains of gram negative bacilli, many of which produce red pigment. Occasionally they have been encountered as causative agents in chronic infections.

Pseudomonas aeruginosa is characterized by an almost complete lack of fermentative activity. It produces a pleasant, fruity odor and soluble pigments, which diffuse into the medium giving a yellow-green color. Sabouraud's maltose agar is useful to enhance pigment production.

Some strains do not show any pigments and may be confused with other organisms.

Figure 16–23. Colonies of *Pseudomonas fluorescens* on nutrient agar; 24-hour culture; × 3. (Burrows)

Two methods can be used to identify such *Pseudomonas* strains: (1) the gluconate test (Haynes, 1951), which is based on the capacity of *Pseudomonas* to oxidize gluconate to ketogluconate. A gluconate substrate tablet* is placed in a test tube with 1 ml. of sterile water. A heavy suspension of the organism is made in the tube and incubated overnight at 37° C. A test for reducing sugar is then done, using Benedict's solution or a Clinitest tablet. A positive test is indicative of *Pseudomonas*. (2) The cytochrome oxidase test of Gaby (1958) consists of adding 0.3 ml. of 1.0 per cent oxidase reagent (p-aminodimethylanaline oxalate) and 0.2 ml. of a 1.0 per cent ethanol solution of alpha-naphthol to an overnight broth culture of the organism. The rapid appearance of a blue color after shaking the tube thoroughly indicates the presence of cytochrome oxidase, characteristic of *Pseudomonas*.

Alcaligenes faecalis does not produce acid or gas on carbohydrates. It characteristically turns litmus milk alkaline. It is morphologically similar to all the other gram negative enteric bacteria.

THE MIMA-HERELLEA GROUP

These poorly defined organisms are frequently isolated from a wide variety of clinical material. In some cases they are undoubtedly primary pathogens. Morphologically they are short, plump, encapsulated, gram negative bacilli on primary isolation. They do not ferment carbohydrates and on T.S.I. slants produce alkaline slants and butts, thereby resembling *Pseudomonas* and *Alcaligenes* with which they are frequently

* Available commercially.

Table 16–10. Differentiation of Mima-Herellea Group from Other Gram Negative Bacilli

	DEXTROSE	LACTOSE	SUCROSE	LITMUS MILK	NITRATE	CITRATE	SS AGAR	MOTILITY
Mima polymorpha*	−	−	−	NC	−	−	−	−
Herellea (*B. anitratum*)	Ox	Ox	−	A, coag.	−	+	−	−
Pseudomonas aeruginosa	Ox	−	−	Alk, pep	+	+	+	+
Alcaligenes faecalis	−	−	−	Alk	±	+	±	+
Enteric bacteria	Ferm	Ferm	Ferm	Var.	+	±	±	±

NC — No change
Ox — Oxidize
Coag — Coagulation
A   — Acid
Alk — Alkaline
Pep — Peptonization
Ferm — Fermentation

* *M. polymorpha* var. *oxidana* is oxidase positive.

confused. They can be differentiated from other groups by means of the reactions listed in Table 16–10. (See Hugh and Leifson, 1953, and Aiken, et al., 1956).

HEMOPHILUS, BORDETELLA, MORAXELLA, AND CALYMMATO-BACTERIUM (DONOVANIA)

The species of gram negative bacilli belonging to the genera *Hemophilus* and *Bordetella* are fastidious organisms requiring enriched media, usually factors contained in blood or potato (Figs. 16–24, 16–25). Table 16–11 shows the medically important species of these genera.

The need for "X" and "V" factors by the hemophilic bacteria is of considerable importance in diagnostic bacteriology. The "X factor" is heat stable and is associated with hemoglobin, and the "V factor" is heat labile and associated with yeast and whole blood. Chocolate agar seems to make these factors more readily available; hence it is a better medium than blood agar.

Colonies of *H. influenzae* tend to be very small, and it may be necessary to examine the plates from spinal fluid and other cultures with a magnifying lens. Of consid-

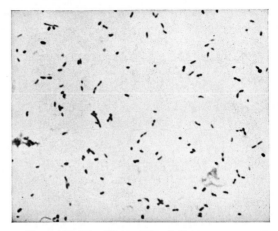

Figure 16–26. *Hemophilus influenzae*, pure culture. Note the variability from coccoid to bacillary form and the presence of longer filaments. Fuchsin; × 1050. (Burrows)

erable help in the successful isolation of *H. influenzae* is the "satellite phenomenon." This occurs when *H. influenzae* and *Staphylococcus aureus* grow together on blood or chocolate agar. The colonies of *H. influenzae* close to the staphylococcus colonies become much larger, apparently owing to production of growth factors, which diffuse from the staphylococcus colonies. In practice, exudate from the throat or nasopharynx or the spinal fluid is first streaked over the plate, and then a streak of *Staphylococcus aureus* is made across the plate. Sometimes this will produce positive cultures in which, without the staphylococcus, no colonies of *H. influenzae* appear.

There are at least six antigenic types of *H. influenzae* (a to f), determined by a specific capsular polysaccharide. Most of the pathogenic strains are Type b. Typing can be accomplished by the Neufeld capsular swelling technique using specific antiserums. *H. influenzae* causes severe meningitis in children and sometimes in adults. It also causes bronchopneumonia and tracheobronchitis (Figs. 16–26, 16–27).

The genus *Bordetella* includes two species that formerly were classified as *Hemophilus* (*pertussis* and *parapertussis*) and one as *Brucella* (*bronchiseptica*).

B. pertussis, the causative agent of whooping cough, can be readily isolated, provided proper technique is employed (Fig. 16–28). Material collected from the trachea, bronchi, or nasopharynx by means of flexible wire swabs is much superior to the classical "cough plate" procedure. Specimens cultured on Bordet-Gengou agar containing penicillin (0.3 unit per ml.)

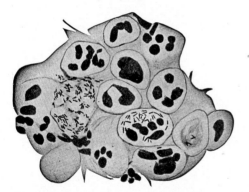

Figure 16–24. Koch-Weeks bacillus in conjunctivitis: × 900. (Axenfeld, Kolle, and Wassermann.)

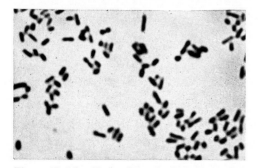

Figure 16–25. *Hemophilus duplex* (Morax-Axenfeld bacillus); pure culture. Gram stain; × 2400. (Burrows)

Table 16–11. Characteristics of *Hemophilus* and *Bordetella* (Gram Negative Bacilli)

SPECIES	DISEASES IN MAN AND SITE	GROWTH REQUIREMENTS X FACTOR	V FACTOR	MEDIUM OF CHOICE	HEMOLYSIS	REMARKS
Hemophilus influenzae (Pfeiffer's bacillus)	Bronchopneumonia, meningitis, conjunctivitis, throat infection	+	+	Chocolate or blood agar + 10% CO_2	Neg.	Exhibits satellite phenomenon with *Staphylococcus aureus*. Encapsulated, irridescent colonies
Hemophilus hemolyticus	Normal in nose and throat	+	+	Same as *H. influenzae*	Pos.	May be found in normal throat. Questionably pathogenic. Inhibited by sheep blood
Hemophilus ducreyi (Ducrey's bacillus)	Soft chancre (chancroid)	+	−	Clotted heated rabbit blood	Slight	Difficult to culture. Occurs as short chains
Hemophilus aegyptius (Koch-Weeks bacillus)	Acute conjunctivitis	+	+	Rabbit blood agar	Neg.	Agglutinates human red blood cells. Nonencapsulated. Satellitism
Bordetella pertussis	Whooping cough	−	−	Bordet-Gengou medium, charcoal agar	Pos.	Colonies are raised and white (half-pearl) and have a hazy zone of hemolysis.
Bordetella parapertussis	Whooping cough (few cases)	−	−	Bordet-Gengou medium	Pos.	Grows readily on nutrient agar. Citrate positive
Bordetella bronchiseptica	Rarely causes pneumonia. Whooping cough-like disease	−	−	Blood agar	Pos.	Antigenically related to *B. pertussis* and *Brucella*. Motile
Moraxella lacunata (Morax-Axenfeld diplobacillus)	Angular conjunctivitis	−	−	Loeffler's medium	Variable	Diplobacilli. Liquefies coagulated serum. Related organism, *M. liquefaciens*, grows on blood agar.
Calymmatobacterium granulomatis (Donovania)	Granuloma inguinale	−	−	Enriched heart infusion. Yolk sac of chick embryo	Neg.	Difficult to culture; stained smears (Wright's) from lesion show bacilli with large capsules (Donovan bodies).

and diamidinodiphenylamine dihydrochloride (2 mcg. per ml.) reveal characteristic colonies in almost pure culture in 48 to 72 hours. Adsorbed agglutinating antiserum (Phase 1) for this organism is available and is useful in differentiating it from the closely related *B. parapertussis* and *B. bronchiseptica*.

Actinobacillus mallei is the cause of glanders in horses and occasionally in man. The organism is a nonmotile, pleomorphic, gram negative rod, which grows poorly ex-

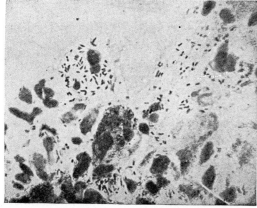

Figure 16–27. Influenza bacilli in spinal fluid in a case of meningitis (× 1000).

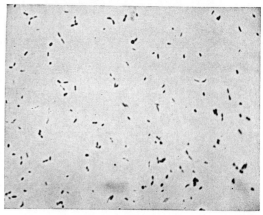

Figure 16–28. *Hemophilus pertussis*, pure culture. Fuchsin; × 1050. (Burrows)

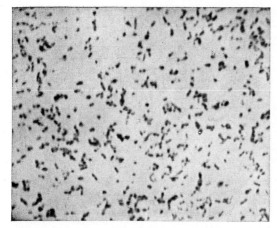

Figure 16–29. Actinobacillus mallei in pure culture. The generally poor staining is apparent, and bipolar staining may be observed in some of the cells. Methylene blue; × 1250. (Burrows)

cept on 4 per cent glycerol agar (Fig. 16–29). *Pseudomonas pseudomallei* produces a similar disease known as melioidosis. It is a motile, gram negative rod, which grows slowly on MacConkey's agar and ferments various carbohydrates. The so-called "Strauss reaction" is useful for identifying these organisms, although it is not specific. Intraperitoneal injection of male guinea pigs will reveal a white caseous exudate in the scrotal sac in positive cases.

BRUCELLA AND PASTEURELLA

The *Brucella* and *Pasteurella* are gram negative bacilli that are primarily pathogens of animals but are transmissible to man either by direct contact or by means of arthropod vectors. *Brucella* produces undulant fever (brucellosis) in man, a disease that usually is chronic and presents serious diagnostic problems. The organisms tend to be disseminated in the tissues and can be cultured in the laboratory only by blood or bone marrow culture. The organisms usually multiply slowly in blood culture, and it may be necessary to hold the cultures for four to six weeks before detectable growth occurs. There are three species of the genus: *Brucella abortus*, *Brucella melitensis*, and *Brucella suis*. All species grow well on tryptose or trypticase soy agar and on Albimi agar (Fig. 16–30). An excellent medium for isolating these organisms from contaminated material is that of Kuzdas and Morse (1953). All strains grow better under 10 per cent CO_2, and *Br. abortus* will not grow without it on primary isolation. The differentiation of

A

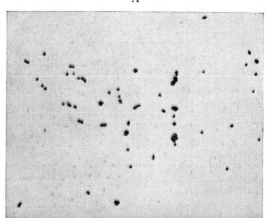

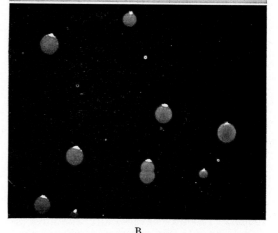

B

Figure 16–30. Brucella melitensis, pure culture: *A*, note the coccobacillary appearance. Fuchsin; × 1050; *B*, on liver infusion agar. × 4. (Burrows)

Table 16–12.   Differentiation of *Brucella*

	CO_2 REQUIRE- MENT	H_2S PRODUC- TION	INHIBITED BY*	
			1:6000 THIONIN	1:25,000 BASIC FUCHSIN
Brucella abortus	+	+ (3 to 4 days)	−	+
Brucella melitensis	−	+ (1 day)	+	+
Brucella suis	−	+ (3 to 4 days)	+	−

* There is considerable variation in the dye concentration recommended by the various authors.

the *Brucella* can be accomplished by means of the reactions shown in Tables 16–12 and 16–13. Various serologic tests have

Table 16–13. Characteristics of *Brucella* and *Pasteurella*

SPECIES	ANIMAL RESERVOIR	DISEASE IN MAN	MEDIUM OF CHOICE FOR ISOLATION	IDENTIFYING CHARACTERISTICS	REMARKS
Brucella abortus	Cattle, sometimes pig or goat	Undulant fever (brucellosis)	Blood culture – 10% CO_2 Tryptose agar – 10% CO_2	Inhibited by thionine but not fuchsin. Requires CO_2; slow hydrolysis of urea. Colonies blue-gray, smooth, glistening	Causes abortion in cattle
Brucella melitensis	Goats, sometimes cattle or pigs	Same	Blood culture Tryptose agar	Not inhibited by thionine or fuchsin. Does not require CO_2	Causes abortion in goats
Brucella suis	Bovine, sometimes cattle or goats	Same	Blood culture Tryptose agar	Inhibited by fuchsin but not thionine. Rapidly hydrolyzes urea. Does not require CO_2	Causes abortion in pigs
Pasteurella tularensis	Rodents	Tularemia	Blood culture, glucose-cystine agar	Small, droplike colonies. Cells tend to show budding and filament formation	Absolute requirement for cystine
Pasteurella pestis	Rodents (rats, ground squirrels)	Bubonic plague, "black plague" (pneumonia)	Infusion or blood agar	Organisms pleomorphic; bipolar staining. Colonies small dew-drop-like, nonhemolytic	Pathogens for mice and guinea pigs.
Pasteurella multocida	Widely distributed in animals	Pneumonia, septicemia, meningitis	Rabbit blood agar	Bipolar staining. Encapsulated. Varies from mucoid to virulent irridescent phase. Grows on ordinary media and T.S.I. agar	Common in laboratory animals. Susceptible to penicillin

been employed as aids in the diagnosis of brucellosis, but each has its disadvantages (see p. 888). This can also be said of skin testing with Brucellergen.

Pasteurella tularensis is one of the most dangerous microorganisms to handle in the laboratory. It is highly infectious and laboratory infections occur frequently. Patients with a history of exposure to wild rodents (rabbits, beavers) and who have an initial skin lesion followed by fever may be suspected of having tularemia. The organism forms minute, mucoid, transparent colonies on Francis's glucose cystine-blood agar under 10 per cent CO_2 after four to seven days at 37° C. A minute, pleomorphic, gram negative coccobacillus with an absolute requirement for cystine that agglutinates with *P. tularensis* antiserum can be considered as a positive identification (Fig. 16–31).

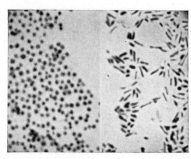

Figure 16–31. Pasteurella tularensis. Note change from coccoidal to bacillary form in 24 hours on fresh culture medium. (Francis.)

Pasteurella pestis is the causative agent of plague (bubonic or pneumonic). Fortunately few cases of plague have occurred in man in recent years. The organism exists in the rodent population over a wide area of the western United States and causes widespread epidemics, especially in ground squirrels (sylvatic plague).

Bacteriologic diagnosis of plague is not difficult. Direct smear and gram stain from aspirates of buboes or sputum (pneumonic plague) may reveal gram negative bacilli with bipolar granules in large numbers, which can be grown on trypticase soy agar plates (Fig. 16–32). The organism must be handled with extreme care in the laboratory. The use of the new fluorescent antibody techniques are of great aid in rapid identification of this organism (see p. 618).

Pasteurella multocida (septica) is an organism commonly found in a wide variety of animal species and has occasionally been isolated from man. It grows well on blood agar, forming small, translucent colonies. Smears show it to be an ellipsoidal, gram negative rod with a characteristic bipolar staining. It is H_2S, indol, and nitrate positive and forms gas in dextrose, sucrose, sorbitol, and galactose. An important differential point is that most strains are sensitive to penicillin. Almost all strains are pathogenic for rabbits and mice (Fig. 16–33).

Streptobacillus moniliformis is a gram negative, highly pleomorphic bacillus. It

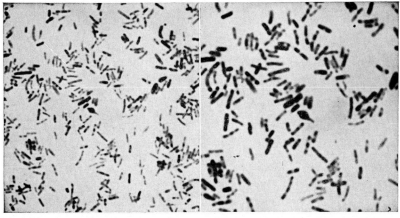

Figure 16–32. The plague bacillus. Smear from pure culture; fixed in methyl alcohol and stained with methylene blue to show bipolar staining. Note the involution forms present even at 24 hours' incubation. *Left,* × 1050; *right,* × 1800. (Burrows)

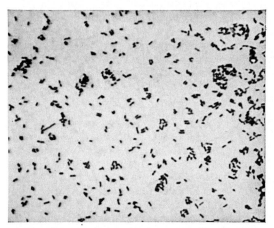

Figure 16–33. Pasteurella multocida. Smear from a pure culture. Fuchsin; × 1050. (Burrows)

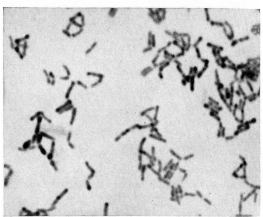

Figure 16–34. Metrachromatic granules and bipolar staining in the diphtheria bacillus. Note the differences between these organisms and the plague bacilli. Methylene blue; × 1975. (Burrows)

tends to occur in chains, requires media enriched with blood or serum, and may be cultured from lesions. The causative agent of one form of rat bite fever in man, it is primarily a pathogen of mice and rats and is transmitted to man accidentally.

THE GRAM POSITIVE BACILLI

Corynebacterium diphtheriae *and the Diphtheroids*

Corynebacterium diphtheriae is the cause of diphtheria and is strictly a pathogen of man. It is a gram positive bacillus that has characteristic cellular morphology. From the lesion or from observation of growth from Loeffler's or Pai's slants stained by Albert's technique or alkaline methylene blue, one sees considerable pleomorphism.

Most cells are slender, slightly curved rods, which may have beads or bands of deep staining material (metachromatic granules). These cells tend to lie side by side in rafts or to form peculiar "Chinese letter" arrangements (Fig. 16–34). Also there occur the so-called "snow shoe" forms. *C. diphtheriae* occurs as four types—gravis, mitis, intermedius, and minimus—and the cellular morphology differs somewhat for each type.

As indicated in a previous section, the identification of *C. diphtheriae* depends to a considerable extent on the colony morphology on tellurite agar and the cellular morphology on Loeffler's or Pai's medium. Colonies of *C. diphtheriae* gravis tend to be large (3 to 5 mm.), with a wrinkled appearance and an irregular edge. They are dark gray in color and may have a clear periphery. Mitis colonies tend to be smaller, dark gray, shiny, and buttery in consistency with a regular edge and a slightly raised center. Intermedius colonies are small, 0.5 to 1 mm. in diameter, with a dark gray or black center and a clear periphery. Minimus colonies are very small and are easily missed (Figs. 16–35 to 16–38).

The cell of C. diphtheriae gravis is less granular and banded than the others. There are usually some metachromatic granules, "snow shoe" forms, rafts, and "Chinese letters." In this regard gravis is most nearly like the diphtheroids. Mitis, intermedius, and minimus tend to be longer and more granular or banded.

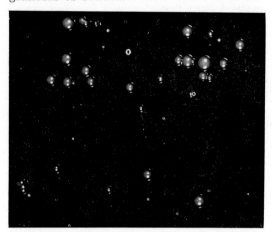

Figure 16–35. Colonies of *Corynebacterium diphtheriae* on blood agar. Note the smooth, raised, translucent appearance and relatively small size. × 2. (Burrows)

C. diphtheriae does not invade the blood sufficiently to produce positive blood cultures. However, it can usually be isolated with ease from lesions in the throat or from the skin in cutaneous diphtheria. The organisms may disappear from the throat of a patient within one or two weeks after recovery, only to reappear at about the fifth or sixth week. It is therefore imperative that all convalescent patients be observed for six to eight weeks to be certain that they are not acting as carriers of the disease. Some individuals remain carriers for extended periods and present serious problems, because the carrier state is difficult to clear.

The diphtheroids (C. pseudodiphtheriticum and others) are normal inhabitants of the throat and skin and have little if any pathologic significance. Their importance is in their morphologic resemblance to C. diphtheriae, especially gravis (Fig. 16–39). Most diphtheroids do not produce dark gray or black colonies on tellurite but some do. They are usually smooth and glistening, not wrinkled like gravis. Occasionally one must do toxicity studies to differentiate the organisms. The toxicity test is always the final test for virulence of a suspected C. diphtheriae (see p. 729). Some differences in biochemical activity exist between the gravis, mitis, intermedius, and minimus strains and the diphtheroids. Mitis strains tend to be hemolytic on blood agar and gravis ferments starch, while the diphtheroids are quite inactive. Gravis also tends to grow as a pellicle on the surface of fluid media.

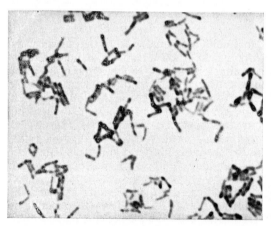

Figure 16–36. The diphtheria bacillus, gravis strain, pure culture on blood agar. Methylene blue stain. Note the bipolar staining and the club-shaped forms. The lightly stained cells with deeply stained areas are characteristic of gravis morphology. × 1200. (Burrows)

Figure 16–37. The diphtheria bacillus, intermedius strain, pure culture on blood agar. Methylene blue stain. Note the irregular staining and barred appearance characteristic of the intermedius variety. × 1200. (Burrows)

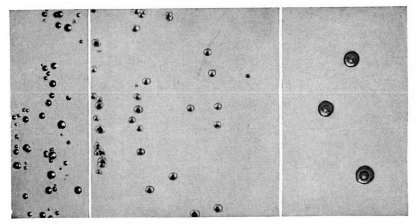

Figure 16–38. The varieties of the diphtheria bacillus on chocolate tellurite agar. *Left,* mitis type; note the characteristic raised, small black colony. *Center,* intermedius type; the lighter color, beginning radial striation, and small size are apparent. *Right,* gravis type; the gray color, larger size, raised center, and radial striation are evident. (Burrows)

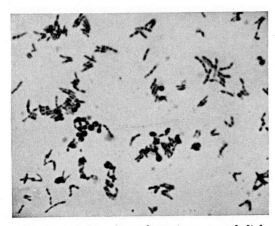

Figure 16–39. Corynebacterium pseudodiphtheriticum. Smear from pure culture stained with alkaline methylene blue. Note the irregular staining, club-shaped forms, and general close resemblance to *C. diphtheriae.* × 1050. (Burrows)

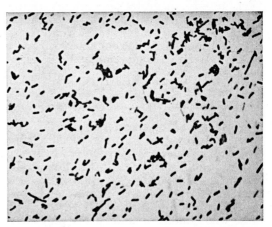

Figure 16–40. Listeria monocytogenes. Smear from a pure culture. Fuchsin; × 1050. (Burrows)

Some diphtheroids are anaerobic and are occasionally encountered in certain infections. They resemble *Actinomyces israelii* culturally and morphologically. However, the diphtheroids grow more quickly than *Actinomyces,* are invariably catalase positive, produce acid, clot litmus milk, and do not ferment xylose, salicin, or raffinose. Their significance is not understood.

Listeria *and* Erysipelothrix

Listeria monocytogenes is found occasionally as the cause of meningitis in humans. In the domestic rabbit it causes a severe inflammatory reaction when inoculated into the lower eyelid (Anton's test). When the rabbit is inoculated in-travenously or intraperitoneally, a severe monocytosis results. Morphologically *L. monocytogenes* is a gram positive, motile bacillus that may resemble diphtheroids, or, when the rods are short, it may resemble *Streptococcus pyogenes* (Fig. 16–40). The medium of choice is probably rabbit blood agar, and on this medium it produces a zone of beta hemolysis. Indeed its colonies may be mistaken for *S. pyogenes,* except that they tend to be larger and the hemolytic zone not so clearcut.

Erysipelothrix insidiosa (rhusiopathiae) is widely distributed in nature, causing erysipelas in swine and septicemia in mice. It may be isolated from infections in birds, turkeys, and ducks and causes erysipeloid in man, especially in fish handlers. It is a gram positive bacillus that varies from a slender rod to short forms resembling cocci

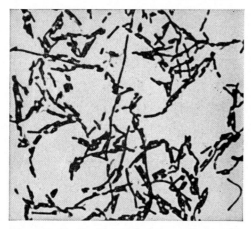

Figure 16–41. Erysipelothrix rhusiopathiae. Pure culture. Note the similarity of this microorganism to the actinomycetes; × 1000. (Kral.)

Figure 16–42. Bacillus anthracis, 48-hour culture on nutrient agar. Crystal violet stain. The spores appear as unstained areas. Note the typical arrangement of the bacilli in coiled chains; × 1200. (Burrows)

(Fig. 16–41). It grows on ordinary media and produces hemolysis on blood agar, which tends to be green at first, later changing to a slight but definite clear zone. Unlike *Listeria,* it is nonmotile and catalase negative.

Bacillus *and* Lactobacillus

All members of the genus *Bacillus* are gram positive, spore-forming bacilli. There are two species of particular interest: *Bacillus subtilis* and *Bacillus anthracis. B. anthracis* is the cause of anthrax in animals. It is transmissible to man and constitutes an occupational disease among those who handle animals, hides, and wool. In man the infection may appear as a skin lesion (malignant pustule), which usually remains localized but may progress to a rapidly fatal septicemia. Infection may occur by the respiratory route (wool sorter's disease), and when this occurs it often results in fatal septicemia.

The organism can frequently be demonstrated in gram stained smears from the lesions and may be cultured on ordinary nutrient media. The colonies are rough, flat with irregular edges approximately 3 mm. in diameter, and nonhemolytic. Gram stain reveals tangled coils of long chains of large, square-ended rods. In culture the organisms are not capsulated, but capsules may be seen in smears from infected animals. No spore formation occurs in the infected animal but occurs readily on exposure to air (Figs. 16–42 to 16–45).

A reliable and simple test for the recognition of *B. anthracis* is the "perlschnurtest" or string-of-pearls test originally de-

Figure 16–43. Colonies of *Bacillus anthracis* on nutrient agar. Twenty-four-hour culture. Note the large size and coarse texture suggestive of R variants; × 3. (Burrows)

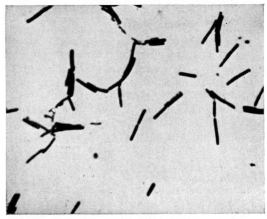

Figure 16–44. Bacillus subtilis, 24-hour culture on nutrient agar. Crystal violet stain. No spores have formed as yet. Note the typical arrangement of the bacilli; × 1200. (Burrows)

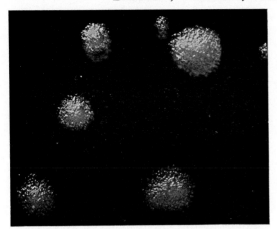

Figure 16–45. Colonies of *Bacillus subtilis* on nutrient agar. Twenty-four-hour culture. Note the resemblance to colonies of the anthrax bacillus; × 3. (Burrows)

Figure 16–46. *Lactobacillus* sp. isolated from the mouth. Morphologically identical with *L. acidophilus.* Note the diplobacillary form and palisade arrangement of the cells; × 2500. (Harrison.)

scribed by Jensen and Kleemeyer in 1953. The test is done as follows:

1. Prepare tryptose agar plates containing 0.5 unit of penicillin per ml. of medium.

2. Streak these plates with the suspected culture and incubate them for three to six hours at 37° C.

3. Place a coverslip on the inoculated portion of the plate and examine it under oil immersion.

4. Within three to six hours *B. anthracis* cells swell up into round forms, giving the distinct appearance of a string of pearls. After 15 to 18 hours of incubation growth ceases. Other species of the genus *Bacillus* do not give this reaction.

B. subtilis (the hay bacillus) is a nonpathogenic organism that is widely distributed in nature. Most of its importance lies in its close resemblance to *B. anthracis.* It can be differentiated by inoculation of a broth suspension of the organism subcutaneously into a guinea pig. *B. subtilis* does not produce disease, but *B. anthracis* will kill the guinea pig in from 36 to 48 hours. *B. subtilis* is a motile organism and *B. anthracis* is not motile.

The lactobacilli contain a number of species. Some are of considerable interest to the diagnostic bacteriologist. *Lactobacillus acidophilus* is probably identical with Döderlein's bacillus, which is a normal inhabitant of the vaginal tract and is usually present in large numbers. *L. acidophilus* also occurs in large numbers in the intestinal tract of man and animals as a normal inhabitant. It is a rather large, gram positive bacillus, occurring singly or

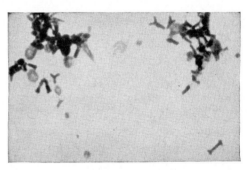

Figure 16–47. *Lactobacillus bifidus.* Note the Y-shaped forms. (Dack.)

in pairs. Colonies are small on ordinary media (Fig. 16–46).

Lactobacillus bifidus is closely related to *L. acidophilus.* It tends to appear early in the digestive tract of breast-fed infants and may comprise 90 per cent of the total flora. Cells of this organism exhibit an interesting type of bifurcation (Fig. 16–47).

Lactobacillus bulgaricus is of interest, since it appears to be identical with or closely related to the Boas-Oppler bacillus, which was first seen in 1895 in the gastric juice of patients with gastric carcinoma.

Some strains of the lactobacilli are aerobic and facultatively anaerobic, some are microaerophilic, and some are anaerobic.

Anaerobic Gram Positive Bacilli
(Clostridium)

A number of species belonging to the genus *Clostridium* are pathogenic for man. These pathogenic clostridia all produce potent toxins, some of which are among the most toxic substances known to man (the exotoxins). *Cl. tetani* causes tetanus, *Cl. botulinum* causes botulism, and some species cause gas gangrene (*Cl. perfringens* [welchii], *Cl. septicum*, *Cl. novyi* [oedematiens], *Cl. histolyticum*).

None of these organisms is an active invader of tissue. *Cl. tetani* and the gas gangrene organisms are usually introduced into wounds and multiply in necrotic tissue where anaerobic conditions exist. Usually culture from such wounds reveals that other anaerobic bacteria or aerobic bacteria are also present, and it is necessary to separately identify the various organisms. Thus, in diagnostic work it is best to streak the material on plates and to incubate anaerobically. The material sub-

mitted for culture is usually tissue that can be macerated for culture and gram stain.

Cl. botulinum probably never multiplies *in vivo*. It multiplies in food (home canned vegetables), producing its potent enterotoxin, which is then ingested by man or animals. One may be able to demonstrate or to culture organisms from the suspected food or the toxin by injection into mice with suitable controls of animals protected with antitoxin. Toxins A, B, and E are the most commonly found in human disease.

The clostridia are widely distributed in nature, especially in soil where there are animals. These organisms (*Cl. tetani*, *Cl. perfringens*) are normal inhabitants of the intestinal tract of numerous animal species.

The identification of the clostridia de-

Table 16–14. Colony Form, Morphology, and Reactions on Blood Agar of Some Representative Species of Clostridia*

SPECIES	COLONY FORM ON BLOOD AGAR*	HEMOLYSIS	VEGETATIVE MORPHOLOGY†	SPORES‡	PATHOGENICITY FOR GUINEA PIGS
C. perfringens	A	+	T, C	OE, R	+
C. butyricum	A	−	T	OE	−
C. botulinum (types B-E)	B, E	+	T	OE	+
C. histolyticum	C	+	S	OE	+
C. septicum	DG, F	+	S to T	OE, V	+
C. tertium	C	+	S	OT	−
C. sporogenes	D	+	S to T	OE	−
C. fallax	B	+	S to T, C	OE, R	+
C. tetanomorphum	E	V	S to T	ST	−
C. tetani	F, G	+	S	ST	+

K E Y
* Colony forms on blood agar:
  A. Large, raised colonies; smooth to slightly ridged with entire to undulate margins, 2–4 mm.
  B. Smaller colonies; smooth to irregular with entire undulate or serrate margins, 1–3 mm.
  C. Minute colonies, raised, smooth to irregular; entire to irregular margins with short rhizoids, 0.2–1 mm.
  D. Large colonies, raised; very irregular with wide-spreading, coarse rhizoids, 3–6 mm.
  E. As D but smaller, finer rhizoids, 1–2 mm.
  F. Irregular granular colonies with delicate spreading rhizoids to irregular rhizoid-like structures without a definite central colony.
  G. Tendency to swarm.
† Vegetative morphology:
  S—slender rods; T—thick rods; C—capsulated.
‡ Spore morphology:
  O—Oval; S—spherical; E—eccentric; T—terminal; R—rare; V—variable in size, shape, and position.

___

* Modified from Sterne, M., in Dubos, R. J.: Bacterial and Mycotic Infections of Man. 3rd Ed. Philadelphia, J. B. Lippincott Company, 1958.

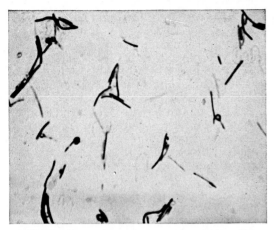

Figure 16–48. Clostridium tetani in pure culture. Young, actively growing culture showing beginning spore formation. Note the refractile, unstained spores; the drumstick appearance when these are attached to the cells; and the tendency of the vegetative cells to remain attached end to end. Fuchsin; × 1150. (Burrows)

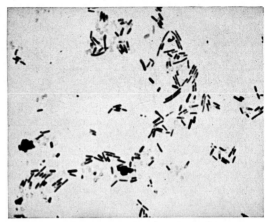

Figure 16–49. Clostridium septicum from pure culture. The tendency to form elongated vegetative cells is apparent. Fuchsin; × 1050. (Burrows)

pends on cellular morphology, spore formation, and cultural characteristics (see Tables 16–14 and 16–15). Since some of these organisms have a tendency to spread (swarming) in a thin film over a plate, it is well to use a cultural technique designed to prevent spreading. Sorbic acid, polymyxin B, chloral hydrate, sodium azide, and other substances are very useful for isolating clostridia from mixed cultures

(see references). The plates should be incubated for 48 hours or more, since colonies develop slowly. Gram stain will show gram positive rods that are likely to be quite variable but frequently are short and plump. *Cl. tetani* is long and slightly curved with a large, round, terminal spore that is characteristic (Fig. 16–48). Most other species have oval, subterminal spores (Figs. 16–49 to 16–51).

An excellent and simple technique for the rapid presumptive identification of clostridia is that of Kaufman and Weaver (1960). A layer of liver veal agar contain-

Table 16–15. Biochemical Reactions of Some Representative Species of Clostridia

SPECIES	MILK	H₂S	INDOL	GELATIN LIQUEFACTION	NITRATE REDUCTION	MOTILITY	DEXTROSE	MALTOSE	LACTOSE	SALICIN
C. perfringens	St.*	V	−	+	+	−	+	+	+	V
C. butyricum	St.	−	−	−	−	+	+	+	+	+
C. botulinum (types B-E)	AD	−	−	+	−	+	+	+	−	+
C. histolyticum	CD	+	−	+	−	+	−	−	−	−
C. septicum	ACG	−	−	+	+	+	+	+	+	+
C. tertium	ACG	−	−	−	+	+	+	+	+	+
C. sporogenes	D	+	−	+	+	+	+	+	−	−
C. fallax	ACG	+	−	−	+	+	+	+	V	V
C. tetanomorphum	−	−	−	V	−	+	+	+	−	−
C. tetani	C	+	+	+	+	−	−	−	−	−

* A—acid; C—clot; D—digestion; G—gas; St.—stormy fermentation; V—variable.

ing 0.004 per cent neutral red is poured into a Petri dish and allowed to solidify. A layer of the same medium to which the specimen has been inoculated is then poured on this and finally another layer of sterile medium. The plates are incubated for 18 to 48 hours in a Brewer jar or similar device in an atmosphere of hydrogen. The plates are then examined under an ultraviolet light. Colonies of clostridia can be recognized by a distinct zone of golden yellow fluorescence. This shows as a zone of yellow fluorescence under ordinary illumination. No facultative anaerobes and only rare obligate anaerobic organisms display this fluorescence. Other tests for confirmation and identification

may then be performed from the isolated colonies.

The gas gangrene group are highly saccharolytic and if inoculated into litmus milk medium produce large amounts of gas, which results in a foamy appearance called "stormy" fermentation.

These organisms tend to become gram negative in older cultures and this may be confusing. Space does not permit a more detailed discussion of these organisms; this can be found in the references.

ANAEROBIC STREPTOCOCCI

The anaerobic streptococci are poorly defined, but such organisms (anaerobic or microaerophilic) are found associated with various types of conditions in which they may be significant. They may be present in chronic abscesses of various types, in pilonidal cysts, and in umbilical lesions. They are also present in some cases of puerperal sepsis. Sometimes microaerophilic streptococci are isolated from the blood of patients with chronic diseases. These organisms grow rather slowly, and cultures should be incubated anaerobically at 37° C. for 48 to 72 hours before examination.

BACTEROIDES

The genus *Bacteroides* includes a number of species but is rather poorly classified. These are gram negative, anaerobic bacilli, which are normal inhabitants of the gastrointestinal tract and can be found on the mucous surfaces of the nose and throat. Occasionally they are isolated in

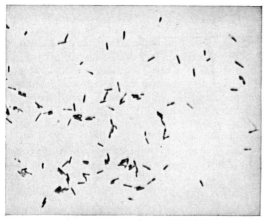

Figure 16–50. Clostridium welchii from pure culture. Note the relatively smaller size of these bacteria and the central spores. Fuchsin; × 1050. (Burrows)

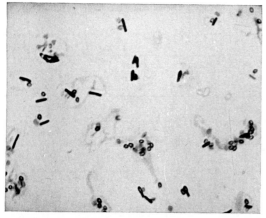

Figure 16–51. Clostridium botulinum type A from pure culture. Note the subterminal swollen spores and free unstained spores admixed with the vegetative cells. Fuchsin; × 1050. (Burrows.)

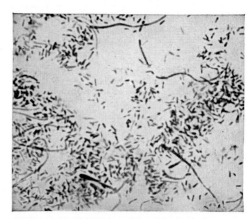

Figure 16–52. Bacteroides funduliformis. The swollen and filamentous forms and poorly staining "ghost cells" are typical of the usual stained smear preparations; × 1000. (Dack.)

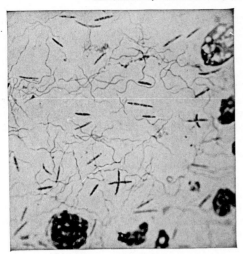

Figure 16–53. Borrelia vincentii in case of ulcerative stomatitis (× 1200).

blood culture or from wounds and joint fluids.

They are difficult to culture, requiring special media and prolonged incubation. They are oxygen sensitive and most strains require 5 per cent CO_2. Most strains appear to grow very well in fluid thioglycollate medium but may require as much as five days to grow. Some do not grow well on the surface of agar plates (Fig. 16–52).

Fusobacterium fusiforme is probably a normal inhabitant of the throat of man. It is a large, gram negative bacillus, occurring in pairs with blunt ends together and outer ends pointed. It grows on ordinary agar media under anaerobic conditions. This organism is almost invariably present in considerable numbers along with a spirochete (*B. vincentii*) in Vincent's angina. It is not known whether the organism contributes in the causation of this condition. It is occasionally found in anaerobic wound infections (Fig. 16–53).

SPIROCHETES

There are four genera of spiral and curved bacteria among which there are a number of human pathogens. The genera are *Borrelia, Treponema, Leptospira,* and *Spirillum.* The important species are listed in Table 16–16 with certain of their important characteristics. *Borrelia* and *Trepo-*

Table 16–16. Characteristics of the Spirochetes and Spirilli

SPECIES	DISEASE IN MAN	MODE OF TRANSMISSION	CULTIVATION	MORPHOLOGY	LABORATORY DIAGNOSIS	DISTRIBUTION
Borrelia recurrentis	European relapsing fever	Human body louse	Yes, special medium	Rather delicate, loose coils	Demonstration of spirochete in blood smear stained by Giemsa. Mouse inoculation. Blood taken at onset of relapse	Europe
Borrelia novyi	American relapsing fever	Ticks	Same	Same	Same	America
Borrelia vincentii	Vincent's angina (trench mouth)	Probably contact	No	Same	Demonstrate spirochetes in smears from lesions together with fusiform bacilli.	Worldwide
Treponema pallidum	Syphilis, bejel	Direct contact (venereal)	No	Delicate, tight coils	Darkfield examination of fluid from chancre or secondary rash. Serologic test. Fontana's stain	Worldwide
Treponema pertenue	Yaws	Contact (nonvenereal). Bite of flies	No	Same	Darkfield or Giesma stain from lesion. Serologic test for syphilis	Mediterranean area, tropical Far East, Haiti, northern South America
Treponema carateum	Pinta (carate)	? insect vector	No	Same	Darkfield on early lesion. Serologic test for syphilis	Central and South America
Leptospira icterohaemorrhagiae	Weil's disease (infectious jaundice)	Rats to man	Yes, Fletcher's or Cox's medium	Tight coils, hooked ends	Blood culture, inoculation of blood into guinea pig or weanling hamsters. Serologic tests on paired serums	Worldwide
Leptospira canicola	Canicola fever	Dogs to man	Same	Same	Same	Worldwide
Spirillum minus	Ratbite fever	Rat bite	No	Short, thick cells	Inoculation of blood into guinea pig or mouse. Demonstration in blood smear. Cultivation in peptone water (pH 8.5)	Japan, U.S.

nema are similar, being delicate, spiral organisms in which the 6 to 12 coils are rather loose; they tend to bend in the center. (See Fig. 16–55.)

Borrelia appear in the blood at the onset of relapses and may be demonstrated in Giemsa stained blood smears, where they appear as wavy, hair-like organisms. Blood can be inoculated into mice or rats. Large numbers appear in the blood after a few days. Mice often carry these organisms naturally, and great care must be exercised to make sure the mouse colony is free of the *Borrelia*. Culture of these organisms is difficult.

T. pallidum is best demonstrated by darkfield microscopy (see p. 3). In the absence of darkfield equipment one may stain smears from the aspirate of the chancre by Fontana stain. The india ink method to be described may also be used. No cultural methods are available (Figs. 16–54, 16–55).

Leptospira icterohaemorrhagiae, the causative agent of Weil's disease, is widely distributed in the infected individual and appears in the blood early in the disease. After 10 to 14 days the organisms are present in considerable numbers in the urine. These organisms are rather easily cultured in fairly simple medium containing rabbit

serum, peptone, and Ringer's solution, and Cox and Larson (1957) have shown that they can be cultured on simple solid media. Blood or urine may be inoculated intraperitoneally into a guinea pig, or into mice. The organisms can be demonstrated in the blood after a few days or in the tissues at necropsy. The *Leptospira* have tight coils and one or both ends are hooked. In darkfield preparations they are seen to rotate very rapidly.

Patients with Weil's disease show striking antibody responses, and agglutination or complement fixation tests on acute and convalescent sera are useful in diagnosis. Antigens are available for testing antibody rises against the various other species of *Leptospira*.

In addition to Weil's disease members of the *Leptospira* are responsible for certain other diseases in various parts of the world, e.g., swamp fever in Europe (*L. grippotyphosa*) and swineherd's disease (*L. pomona*). There are a large number of serotypes of these organisms based on differences in agglutination—lysis and cross-absorption tests. The differentiation of these strains is of considerable epidemiologic importance.

India Ink Method for Spirochetes. A relatively simple means of demonstrating spirochetes in blood or urine involves the use of India ink. It requires a good grade of ink.* A small drop of the India ink is mixed with 1 or 2 drops of the specimen. This mixture is then spread over the slide and allowed to dry. On examination with the oil immersion lens the spirochetes appear white on a brown or black background. Some India inks contain wavy vegetable fibrils and bacteria that may be misleading, and exudates sometimes agglutinate the ink particles, making this type of preparation unsatisfactory.

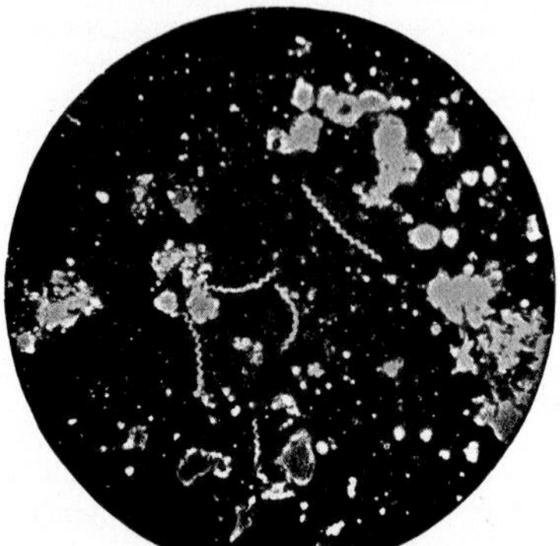

* Not all India inks are suitable. It is advisable to select a bottle with a minimum amount of bacteria and to add phenol or tricresol as a preservative.

Figure 16–54. Treponema pallidum (× 1000); darkfield preparation.

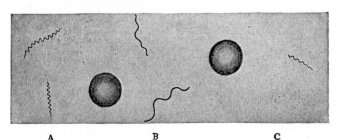

Figure 16–55. A, Treponema pallidum; B, Borrelia refringens; C, Treponema microdentium. Two erythrocytes (× 1200).

A   B   C

THE ACID-FAST BACTERIA
(*MYCOBACTERIUM*)

A number of acid-fast bacteria are pathogenic for man. *M. tuberculosis* (human) and *M. bovis* (bovine) have long been recognized for their role in human tuberculosis and have been studied extensively. In recent years two new groups of acid-fast organisms, apparently capable of causing tuberculosis, have been recognized—the so-called "yellow bacilli" and *M. fortuitum.* These are large, acid-fast bacteria that are not pathogenic for rabbits and guinea pigs but usually are pathogenic for mice. Their pathogenicity is not yet completely understood. *M. avium* has been reported in cases of chronic involvement of localized lymph nodes, but the extent of its pathogenicity in humans is not clear. The relation of Hansen's bacillus (*M. leprae*) to leprosy seems fairly well established, although final, undisputed proof of its primary role in the disease has not yet been accomplished.

In Table 16–17 are shown some of the important characteristics of the most important mycobacteria. Numerous similar organisms exist in nature and infect a number of warm- and cold-blooded animal species.

The diagnosis of tuberculosis depends on clinical, x-ray, and bacteriologic findings. Every effort must be made to demonstrate the organism in sputum, urine, or other material by acid-fast stain, cultures, and animal inoculations. In pulmonary tubercu-

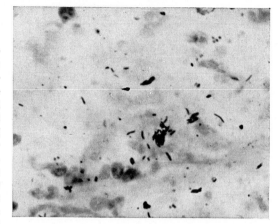

Figure 16–56. Myobacterium tuberculosis. Acid-fast stained smear of tuberculous sputum. × 1050. (Burrows)

losis the sputum, laryngeal and bronchial secretions, or gastric contents are examined. The presence of acid-fast bacilli is highly suggestive, and when this is followed by a positive culture or positive findings in the inoculated animal, it may be definitive. Acid-fast stains can be done on tissue smears and sections and may be very helpful.

The human and bovine tubercle bacilli are slender, straight, or slightly curved rods, which occur singly or in clumps. They frequently have metachromatic granules, which may give them a beaded appearance, or they may be bipolar, giving the organism a dumbbell appearance. The nonpathogenic acid-fast bacilli tend to be less gran-

Table 16–17. Characteristics of the Mycobacteria

SPECIES	DISEASE IN MAN	TRANSMISSION	PATHOGENICITY FOR ANIMALS GUINEA PIG	RABBIT	FOWL	CULTURAL CHARACTERISTICS
Mycobacterium tuberculosis (hominis)	Primarily pulmonary tuberculosis	Man to man	++++	+	0	Slow growth—2–6 wks.; granular, wrinkled colonies; strict aerobe, grows on surface of liquid media
Mycobacterium bovis (bovine)	Tuberculosis of viscera or bone, sometimes pulmonary	Unpasteurized milk or milk products	++++	++++	0	Slow growth—2–6 wks.; small, flat, smooth colonies; strict aerobe. Inhibited by glycerin above 0.25%
Mycobacterium avium	Mild chronic infection of submaxillary lymph nodes	?	0+	++	++++	Growth not so slow as human and bovine; smooth colonies. Optimal temp. 40° C. No pellicle in fluid medium
"Yellow bacilli"	Primarily pulmonary tuberculosis	?	0	0	?	May be highly pathogenic for mice. Produce bright yellow pigment on exposure to visible light
Mycobacterium fortuitum	Glandular tuberculosis	?	0	0	0	Causes renal lesions in mice. Not photochromogenic; grows rapidly
Mycobacterium smegmatis	Nonpathogenic	—	0	0	0	Grows rapidly. Normal inhabitant of human genitourinary tract
Mycobacterium phlei	Nonpathogenic	—	0	0	0	Widely distributed in nature. May be present in sputum or gastric washings. Grows rapidly with pigmented colonies
Mycobacterium leprae (Hansen's bacillus)	Leprosy (Hansen's disease)	Probably man to man	0	0	0	Not cultivable; may be demonstrated by acid-fast stain of smears from lesions

Table 16–18. Differentiation of Atypical Acid-fast Bacteria

FEATURES	RAPID GROWERS	PHOTOCHROMOGENS	SCOTOCHROMOGENS	NONPHOTO-CHROMOGENS OR BATTEY GROUP
Associated with human disease	Probably not except for *M. fortuitum*	Yes	Abscesses or scrofula. Probably not otherwise important	Probably yes.
Pigment	Usually not	Ivory in dark; yellow to orange in light	Yellow to orange in dark or light	Mostly nonchromogens. Few pigmented
Colony characteristics	Smooth or rough	Generally smooth. Some rough	Smooth	Smooth. Remain smooth on subculture
Microscopy		Larger than true tbc. Vacuolated and beaded	Larger than true tbc. Vacuolated and beaded	Pleomorphic
Cord formation	+ and −	+ (loose cords)	−	−
Neutral red reaction	−	−	−	−
Catalase reaction	+++	+++	+++	+++
Drug resistance	Resistant to antituberculous drugs	Usually resistant to PAS. Variably to SM and INH.	Resistant to antituberculous drugs	Resistant to antituberculous drugs
Guinea pig virulence (depends on size of inoculum)	−	Subcutaneous usually without effect. Intracardial may be fatal in three weeks	−	−
Mouse virulence (depends on size of inoculum)	(*M. fortuitum* said to be pathogenic)	Moderately pathogenic by IV or IP routes. Lesions in lung after 10 weeks	Generally not	+ and −

ular and are not so strongly acid-fast as the pathogens (Figs. 16–56, 16–57). In culture the pathogens tend to be shorter and thicker than when seen in sputum with less granulation. Culturally the human and bovine bacilli grow best at 37° C., the avian strain grows well at 42° C., and the nonpathogens grow at much lower temperatures. At 37° C. the nonpathogens grow much more rapidly (sometimes in two to three days) and usually produce considerable pigment. Human tubercle bacilli are not inhibited by glycerin, while bovine strains are to a considerable extent. There are numerous special media on which these organisms can be cultured (Fig. 16–58).

Recently both clinicians and bacteriologists have become aware of the common

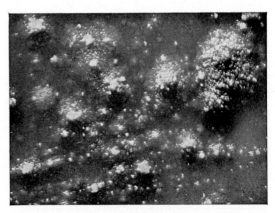

Figure 16–57. Colonies of the human variety of the tubercle bacillus, H-37 strain, on Löwenstein's medium, 5 weeks' incubation. × 3. (Burrows)

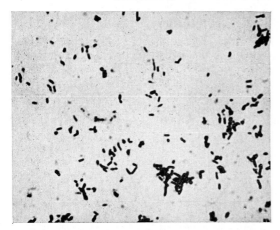

Figure 16–58. Avian tubercle bacillus. Acid-fast stain of a smear from a pure culture. × 1050. (Burrows)

occurrence of acid-fast bacilli that differ from the true tubercle bacilli in several important cultural respects. There seems little doubt that these organisms, the so-called "atypical" or "anonymous" mycobacteria, cause tuberculosis-like disease in humans. In general these organisms produce smooth, pigmented colonies; have a low degree of virulence for guinea pigs; and are usually resistant to isoniazid and para-aminosalicylic acid. A clearcut classification of these organisms is not yet possible until more is learned about them. The method of classification currently used, based on the recommendations of Runyon is summarized in Table 16–18.

A simple procedure that is helpful in differentiating nonpathogenic acid-fast organisms from virulent strains of *M. tuberculosis* is as follows: three tubes of Löwenstein-Jensen medium are inoculated uniformly with the unknown organism (see Table 16–19). Tube 3 contains 10 μg. per ml. of INH (isonicotinic hydrazide). Tubes 1 and 3 are incubated for three weeks at 37° C. and tube 2 is kept at room temperature.

Virulence Tests for M. Tuberculosis

Neutral Red Test (Dubos and Middlebrook, 1948; Morse, Dail, and Olitsky, 1953). A loopful of culture from the surface of solid medium or approximately 1 ml. from the growth in liquid medium is transferred to a corked 15 ml. conical centrifuge tube containing 5 ml. of 50 per cent methanol. The tube is allowed to stand 30 to 60 minutes at 37° C. and is then centrifuged thoroughly. The sediment is resuspended in another 5 ml. portion of methanol and re-incubated for another hour. The sediment is then suspended in 5 ml. of buffer (NaCl, 5 gm.; sodium barbital, 1 gm.; distilled water, 100 ml.; 0.05 per cent neutral red, 0.2 ml.). The tube is allowed to stand at room temperature for one hour, shaken at 15-minute intervals, and examined with a bright light and a hand lens. Colonies of virulent strains stain light pink to deep red. Avirulent organisms do not change the color of the dye, the buffer remaining clear amber in color. Adequate controls should accompany each test, consisting of known virulent and avirulent strains. The test must be done in a hood or safety cabinet because of the danger of spread of virulent tubercle bacilli.

Niacin Test (Konno and Sbarra, 1959). Add 0.1 ml. of the heavy growth from a ten-day-old culture of organisms in Dubos's liquid Tween-albumin medium to 3 ml. of the same medium in a screw cap tube. Add 1 ml. of 4 per cent aniline in 95 per

Table 16–19. Interpretation of Results of Tests for Pathogenic Acid-Fast Bacteria

TUBE	INCUBATION TEMPERATURE	GROWTH				
1	37° C.	+	+	+	+	+
2	24° C.	−	−	−	+	+
3 (I.N.H.)	37° C.	−	+	+	+	−
Catalase*			−	+	+	
Interpretation		Pathogen	Pathogen	Saprophyte	Saprophyte	Saprophyte

* The catalase test is done by adding equal parts of 30 per cent hydrogen peroxide and 10 per cent Tween-80 to the growth in tube 3. Visible bubbles of gas rising from the submerged colonies within two minutes is considered a positive test.

cent ethanol and 1 ml. of 10 per cent aqueous cyanogen bromide to the tube. A distinct yellow color indicates the presence of niacin, which is characteristic of the human strains of *M. tuberculosis*. Bovine strains are doubtful or negative; the other strains are negative. Original cultures must be saved in case reactions are doubtful for animal inoculations and for sensitivity tests if necessary.

Tuberculin testing as an aid in the diagnosis of tuberculosis is discussed elsewhere (p. 811). Antibiotic susceptibility testing of the human tubercle bacillus is of considerable importance in following the course of therapy with chemotherapeutic agents. This technique is described in Chapter 17.

THE PARASITIC PROTOZOA

As indicated in a previous section, a number of protozoa are capable of living in the intestinal tract of man. None of these is a normal inhabitant, although most of them are considered nonpathogenic. However, the presence of large numbers of any one of these organisms in the stool of a patient may be viewed with some suspicion that the organism may be contributing to whatever clinical condition may exist. Most of the enteric protozoa have a worldwide distribution, and the percentage of any population harboring these organisms is determined by their living conditions, diet, and sanitary habits.

There are, in addition, several protozoa that live in the blood and tissues of man. All are pathogenic, producing such diseases as malaria, trypanosomiasis, and leishmaniasis. Their distribution is usually limited to areas where the proper arthropod vectors are present. In areas where they exist, they present serious problems in diagnosis, treatment, and prevention. In this section the fundamental characteristics of the parasitic protozoa will be related to diagnosis.

The Intestinal Amebae (Rhizopoda)

There are five well-recognized species of amebae, belonging to four genera, that are found in the human digestive tract: *Entamoeba histolytica, Entamoeba coli, Endolimax nana, Iodamoeba bütschlii* (williamsi), and *Dientamoeba fragilis*. These amebae, with one exception, exist in three forms in the digestive tract of man. The *trophozoite* or vegetative stage multiplies

by binary fission and moves about by means of pseudopods, which are quite characteristic in some of the species. The trophozoites ingest particles and contain these particles in vacuoles in their cytoplasm. In the *precyst* stage the trophozoite rounds up, the inclusions are extruded, and the cell wall thickens. The nucleus may divide during this period. The *cyst* is an extension of the precyst. The cell wall becomes fairly thick and resistant, and the nucleus may divide once or several times so that the cyst, depending on the species, may contain one to eight nuclei. These nuclei are much smaller than those in the trophozoite.

The differentiation of the species of protozoa depends on the size, type of pseudopod, and nuclear and cytoplasmic structure of the trophozoite and on the size and nuclear and cytoplasmic structure of the cysts and precysts. One must become thoroughly familiar with these features to do reliable parasitologic examinations (Fig. 16–59).

Entamoeba histolytica. *Entamoeba histolytica* is the most pathogenic of the enteric amebae. It produces acute amebic dysentery in tropical areas and occasionally in temperate zones, and there is little question of its direct etiologic significance in this condition. A varying percentage of various population groups in the temperate zones is infected with *E. histolytica*. Certain of these infections are asymptomatic and may remain so for extended periods. Others have an irregular course with short bouts of diarrhea intermingled with periods of constipation. There may be selective dyspepsia to certain foods, such as milk and greasy foods, with considerable gas and abdominal discomfort. It is not easy to evaluate the role of *E. histolytica* in patients with these symptoms. It is highly desirable that, in patients with chronic gastrointestinal disease in whom *E. histolytica* is found, a complete workup be done to rule out such conditions as carcinoma and ulcerative colitis before attempting to determine the role of the amebae.

The trophozoite of *E. histolytica* has certain diagnostic characteristics. The nucleus is round with a delicate ring of chromatin around the periphery, which tends to be beaded. The chromatin ring may on occasion be heavier in some areas than in others. The nucleus has a small, delicate, centrally located karyosome. The nucleus is usually about one-third the diameter of the trophozoite. The cytoplasm is delicate and may appear foamy in stained preparations with a thin cell wall. This organism characteristically ingests red blood cells, and the finding of red blood cells in the trophozoite is diagnostic. In fresh, warm specimens the trophozoites send out clear, hyaline pseudopods, which tend to continue coming out in the same direction, giving what has been termed unidirectional motion. The size of *E. histolytica* trophozoites varies from 8 to 9 microns to as much as 20 to 25 microns.

The precyst is usually round, and the cell wall is thicker than in the trophozoite. There may be one or two typical nuclei.

Characteristically there appear rather large structures called chromatoidal bars, which are cigar shaped and stain black with hematoxylin stain but remain unstained with iodine. When found, these are diagnostic but they do not always occur.

The cyst of *E. histolytica* has a heavy cyst wall with a delicate, nongranular cytoplasm. The chromatoid bars tend to disappear. There are characteristically four nuclei, although occasionally there may be eight. The nuclei are much smaller than those in the trophozoite but have the same structure. The size of the cysts varies from 5 to 15 microns.

The variation in the size of the cysts and

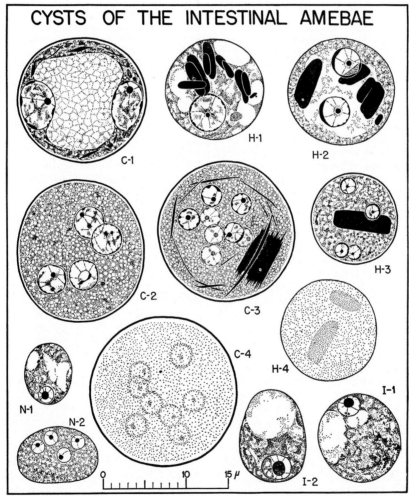

CYSTS OF THE INTESTINAL AMEBAE

Figure 16–59. C-1, Iron-hematoxylin stained binucleate cyst of *Entamoeba coli.* C-2, Iron-hematoxylin stained quadrinucleate cyst of *E. coli.* C-3, Iron-hematoxylin stained mature cyst of *E. coli.* H-1, Iron-hematoxylin stained uninucleate cyst of *E. histolytica.* H-2, Iron-hematoxylin stained binucleate cyst of *E. histolytica.* H-3, Iron-hematoxylin stained mature cyst of *E. histolytica.* N-1, Iron-hematoxylin stained uninucleate cyst of *Endolimax nana.* N-2, Iron-hematoxylin stained mature cysts of *E. nana.* I-1, I-2, Iron-hematoxylin stained mature cysts of *Iodamoeba bütschlii.* C-4, Unstained mature cyst of *E. coli.* H-4, Unstained cyst of *E. histolytica.* (Hunter, Frye, and Swartzwelder: A Manual of Tropical Medicine, 3rd Edition.)

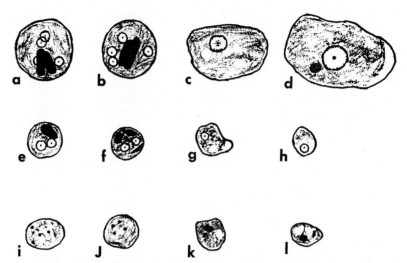

Figure 16–60. Camera lucida drawings of cysts, precysts, and trophozoites of large and small race *Entamoeba histolytica* and *Endolimax nana*. (*a, b*) Large race cysts with four nuclei and chromatoid bars; (*c, d*) large race trophozoites. (*e, f*) Small race cysts with two nuclei and chromatoid bars; (*g, h*) small race trophozoites. (*i, j*) *Endolimax nana* cysts with four nuclei; (*k, l*) *Endolimax nana* trophozoites. × 2500.

trophozoites of *E. histolytica* has led to an arbitrary classification into two races. The large race comprises those with average cyst sizes of 10 microns and over, and the small race, those with average cyst sizes under 10 microns. Evidence indicates that the two races are different in certain fundamental respects. The large race is associated with the most severe pathologic lesions, i.e., acute amebic dysentery; liver, lung, and brain abscess; and cutaneous amebiasis. The small race tends to be found in persons with chronic gastrointestinal disease in which their role is difficult to evaluate; they have not been found in liver abscess or in other extraintestinal complications. They do not ingest red blood cells and are much more difficult to culture.

Some workers have described additional small amebae, which resemble the small race very closely and are termed *Entamoeba hartmanni;* they are said to be nonpathogenic. Further study is needed to clarify the relationship between the large and small race *E. histolytica* and *E. hartmanni* (Figs. 16–60, 16–61).

The laboratory diagnosis of acute amebic dysentery is usually not difficult. Examination of warm, freshly passed stool reveals characteristic trophozoites. In the chronic or asymptomatic case of amebiasis in which the stool may be formed, it is usual to find only the cysts in the stools. The cysts may be present in very small numbers and considerable search is necessary. This is particularly true in small race infections

in which the cysts may be sparse and small. It is also important to emphasize that small race cysts are very difficult if not impossible to differentiate from *Endolimax nana* cysts in wet preparations (unstained or iodine stained). Thus, hematoxylin stained fecal smears are very important.

The number of positive findings depends on the care, diligence, and experience of the person doing the examinations. An experienced worker may be able to make a systematic search of a slide in ten minutes, but the less experienced will need more time. The number of daily stool examinations for a given patient will be determined by the degree of suspicion that exists. One should never do less than three complete stool examinations, and six are recommended. Certain structures in the stool may be confusing, and it is important to be thoroughly familiar with stool cytology. Macrophages are likely to be troublesome, since they are motile and ingest red blood cells. Their nuclear structure, however, is quite different and can be used for differentiation, especially when stained with hematoxylin. The presence of certain structures in the stool, such as Charcot-Leyden crystals, has been considered suggestive of *E. histolytica* infection. However, these structures occur also in the absence of these amebae (Fig. 16–62).

Stool culture for *E. histolytica* is a time-consuming and difficult procedure. However, when properly used, it can be helpful. Several media are available, three of the most common being the Boeck-Drbohlav coagulated egg slant, the Cleveland-Collier liver slant, and the Balamuth fluid medium. The large race can be cultured in these media relatively well, but the small race is difficult to grow. McQuay described a medium in which he cultured the small race fairly easily.

Culture methods for* Entamoeba histolytica *and certain other protozoa

BOECK-DRBOHLAV LOCKE EGG-SERUM MEDIUM. This medium may be employed for the cultivation of *Entamoeba histolytica,*

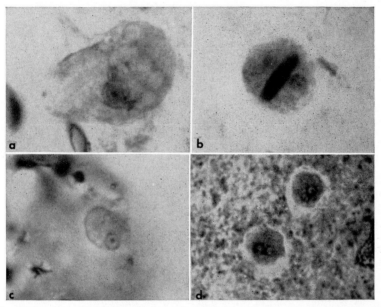

Figure 16–61. *Entamoeba histolytica,* large and small race trophozoites and cysts in fecal smears. (*a*) Large race trophozoite, showing the characteristic foamy cytoplasm and a typical nucleus with central karyosome. (*b*) Large race precyst with a single nucleus and typical large chromatoid bar. (*c*) small race trophozoite. (*d*) Two small race cysts, each with two nuclei. Modified Mallory's phosphotungstic acid stain. × 2500.

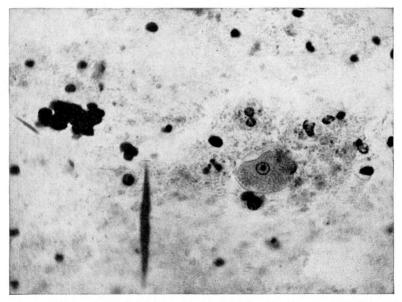

Figure 16–62. Early exudate in stool (iron-hematoxylin stain) showing trophozoite, clumped erythrocytes, pyknotic bodies, and Charcot-Leyden crystals. (Hunter, Frye, and Swartzwelder: A Manual of Tropical Medicine, 3rd Edition.)

E. coli, Endolimax nana, Dientamoeba fragilis, Chilomastix mesnili, and *Trichomonas hominis.* Transfers are made every 48 hours except in the case of *E. coli,* which requires transfers every 72 hours. About 0.5 ml. of the fluid medium at the bottom of the tube is used for each transplant.

Materials Required

1. Eggs
2. Sterile Ringer's solution

This is prepared according to the following formula:

NaCl	8.0 gm.
KCl	0.2 gm.
CaCl₂	0.2 gm.
MgCl₂	0.1 gm.
NaH₂PO₄	0.1 gm.
NaHCO₃	0.4 gm.
Distilled water	1000.0 ml.

It is then autoclaved at 15 pounds pressure for 20 minutes and allowed to cool.

3. Modified sterile Ringer's solution (serum-Ringer). Prepare by adding 0.25 gm. of Loeffler's dehydrated blood serum to 1000 ml. of Ringer's solution, which should be made up in addition to the Ringer's solution of (2). Boil serum and Ringer's solution for one hour to facilitate solution of serum. Filter and autoclave for 20 minutes at 15 pounds pressure. (Instead of the Loeffler's dehydrated blood serum, sterile human serum or sterile horse serum—inactivated and tricresol free—may be used, in which case the modified Ringer's solution should consist of 1 part serum to 8 parts of Ringer's solution. This solution is sterilized by passing through a Berkefeld filter and incubating at 37° C. to determine sterility before pouring onto egg slants.)

4. Sterile Chinese rice flour. The rice flour is sterilized by placing about 5 gm. in a test tube and plugging it with cotton. It is distributed evenly and loosely over the inner surface of tube by shaking. Then it is sterilized in a horizontal position in dry heat at about 90° C. for 12 hours, using intermittent sterilization and allowing 4 hours for each period; flour remains white if not overheated.

Technique

1. Wash four eggs thoroughly, rinse, and brush well with 70 per cent ethyl alcohol. Break into sterile Erlenmeyer flask containing glass beads and about 50 ml. of Ringer's solution. Emulsify completely by shaking. Place about 4 ml. of this material in each test tube and sterilize as follows (using autoclave as inspissator):

2. Place tubes in a preheated autoclave in such a position as to produce a slant of about 1 to 1½ inches. Close the door and vacuum exhaust valve, turn on the steam, and open the outside exhaust valve. When steam appears from this valve, close it and allow the pressure to rise to 15 pounds; then shut off steam and allow pressure to decline to zero; remove media from autoclave. Repeat on three successive days, storing media at room temperature between sterilizations.

3. To these sterile solid slants add enough modified Ringer's solution (about 5 or 6 ml.) to cover egg slant completely. Incubate at 37° C. for 24 hours to determine sterility before adding the sterile Chinese rice flour. Flour is added by taking up 0.25 ml. into a clean, sterile, dry, wide bore, 1 ml. pipet and discharging it into the liquid medium by tapping the pipet against the inside wall of the tube. The tubes are again incubated at 37° C. for 24 hours to test for sterility.

Charcoal Medium for amebae (McQuay). Charcoal medium can be used for the growth of large and small races of *Entamoeba histolytica, E. coli, Endolimax nana, Dientamoeba fragilis, Chilomastix mesnili, Trichomonas hominis,* and *Iodamoeba bütschlii.*

Diphasic medium for stool culturing and maintenance of stock strains. One liter of the charcoal agar for the slants is prepared as follows:

Na₂HPO₄•12 H₂O	3.0 gm.
KH₂PO₄	4.0 gm.
Na₃C₆H₅O₇•2 H₂O	1.0 gm.
MgSO₄•7 H₂O	0.1 gm.
Ferric ammonium citrate, brown pearls (U.S.P.)	0.1 gm.
Asparagine	2.0 gm.
Tryptone	5.0 gm.
Glycerin (reagent grade)	10.0 ml.
Distilled water	1000.0 ml.

Stir these ingredients, using gentle heat to dissolve. Remove the flask some distance from the flame and add:

Norite A (Pfanstiehl)	1.0 gm.
Bacto-agar	10.0 gm.
1 per cent solution of cholesterol in acetone (cholesterol, C.P., ashfree, for Kline test, Pfanstiehl)	25.0 ml.

Return the flask to the flame and stir frequently to prevent scorching of the agar as the mixture is brought to a slow boil. Remove from the flame and dispense while hot from a Kelly bottle in 2.0 to 3.0 ml. amounts into screw cap culture tubes. Autoclave at 15 pounds pressure for 15 minutes. Make slants without butts immediately upon removal of the tubes from the autoclave. Shake the tubes to resuspend the charcoal. Allow slants to cool until hardened.

Completely overlay the slant with sterile 0.5 per cent saline buffered at pH 7.4. One liter of this saline is prepared in the following manner:

Add 5.0 gm. of NaCl to 190 ml. of M/15 KH$_2$PO$_4$* and 810 ml. of M/15 Na$_2$HPO$_4$.†

Tap a small amount of sterile rice powder (which has been autoclaved in screw cap tubes at 15 pounds pressure for 15 minutes and dried in an oven without scorching) into overlayed media and store the media at room temperature or in the refrigerator.

Liquid medium for maintenance of stock strains of large and small race *E. histolytica* and *T. hominis:* This medium consists of the same ingredients that are used in the diphasic medium except for omission of the agar. After one liter of the base preparation is brought to a boil over a flame, one liter of the buffered saline is added and the medium is dispensed in 5.0 or 6.0 ml. amounts into screw cap tubes and autoclaved as just described. Sterile rice powder is added and the medium is ready for use.

Some workers have used proctoscopic aspirates with considerable success. These aspirates may be examined immediately or fixed with PVA and stained with one of the hematoxylin stains (see p. 933).

The diagnosis of amebic liver or brain abscess is largely clinical. In such abscesses the amebae are present in the tissues at the edge of the abscess and are only infrequently found in the pus in the center of the lesion. Thus, smears or sections made from tissue at the edge of the lesion should be examined. Lung abscess results sometimes from extension of a liver abscess through the diaphragm. In such cases the amebae can be demonstrated in aspirated material. Amebic peritonitis and involvement of other organs have been described.

Cutaneous amebiasis occurs most frequently in the perianal region and on the buttocks. Occasional cases have occurred on the abdomen as a result of the formation of a fistula from a liver abscess. Tropho-

zoites can be demonstrated from the periphery of such lesions under the layer of overhanging skin. An inoculating loop can be used to remove material to a slide.

Other Intestinal Amebae. *Entamoeba coli* is a nonpathogenic ameba that occurs usually in a higher per cent of individuals than does *E. histolytica*. It is important from two standpoints: First, it is necessary that *E. coli* be differentiated from *E. histolytica*, for it bears a considerable resemblance to the large race. Second, since this and other intestinal amebae are transmitted in the same manner as *E. histolytica*, its presence in the stool increases the suspicion that *E. histolytica* might also be present.

The trophozoite of *Entamoeba coli* is generally larger than that of *E. histolytica*, varying from 15 to 35 microns in diameter. Its nucleus has a denser ring of chromatin around the edge, and its karyosome is larger and eccentric. The karyosome may appear to be centrally located, depending on how it is oriented. The cytoplasm of *E. coli* is coarse and it does not ingest red blood cells. It may ingest bacteria. The cell wall tends to be thicker and its pseudopods are not so clear as those of *E. histolytica*. The pseudopods tend to come out in several directions and its motility is not unidirectional.

The precyst may have one or more nuclei and chromatoid bars, but the bars are likely to be shorter and thicker and to have splintered ends. The cytoplasm is rather coarse.

The ripe cyst of *E. coli* is usually larger (15 to 25 microns) than that of *E. histolytica* and usually has eight nuclei with eccentric karyosomes. The cytoplasm again is coarse, and the cell wall is heavier than that of *E. histolytica*. With experience the differentiation of *E. coli* from *E. histolytica* is not too difficult, especially with the cysts and precysts.

Endolimax nana is a nonpathogen that occurs in a varying percentage of the population. It is a small ameba and may be confused easily with the small race of *E. histolytica*. As mentioned previously, it is not easy to distinguish between these organisms in wet preparations.

Trophozoites are motile by means of clear, hyaline pseudopods and tend to be unidirectional. In unstained preparations they have a greenish coloration. Their cytoplasm is smooth and the cell wall is thin. The nucleus has a thin membrane and a large karyosome, which may fill a considerable part of the nucleus. There is a

---

* M/15 KH$_2$PO$_4$ = 9.07 gm. KH$_2$PO$_4$ (anhydrous); add distilled water to one liter.

† M/15 Na$_2$HPO$_4$ = 9.46 gm. Na$_2$HPO$_4$ (anhydrous) or 23.88 gm. Na$_2$HPO$_4$·12 H$_2$O; add distilled water to one liter.

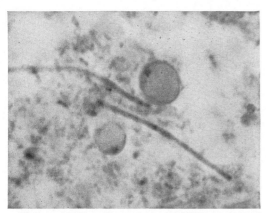

Figure 16–63. Blastocystis hominis in fecal smear showing the large, amorphous central area with nuclear staining material on the periphery of the cell. Modified Mallory's phosphotungstic acid stain. × 2500.

clear area between the karyosome and the nuclear wall, giving the appearance of a halo. The size of the trophozoite is 8 to 12 microns.

The cyst tends to vary in shape from round to oval and has a smooth cytoplasm with a moderately thick cell wall. It varies from 5 to 10 microns in diameter. There are two to four small nuclei with the same structure as in the trophozoite. In hematoxylin stained smears the cysts of *E. nana* are not too difficult to distinguish from those of the small race *E. histolytica*. The cysts do not have chromatoid bars but may contain bacilliform bodies that stain in the same manner.

Iodamoeba bütschlii is a nonpathogenic ameba characterized by a tendency to contain a large glycogen inclusion, which stains brown with iodine. The glycogen inclusion may be so large as to push the nucleus to one side of the cell. The nucleus has a large karyosome, which may be central or eccentric, and one may see bands connecting the karyosome with the thin nuclear wall. The trophozoite varies in size from 8 to 12 microns. The fully formed cyst has a heavy cyst wall; the glycogen inclusion may or may not be present and it has one or two nuclei. The cysts are 5 to 10 microns in diameter.

Dientamoeba fragilis is considered to be a pathogen with the capacity to invade the mucosa of the intestine and possibly the appendix. No cyst formation has been observed. The trophozoite of *D. fragilis* is small (5 to 10 microns). It is a delicate organism with a smooth cytoplasm and thin cell wall and may have one or two nuclei. When two nuclei are present, they

are frequently arranged at opposite ends of an oval trophozoite. The shape of the trophozoite varies, however, from oval to round. The nucleus has a beaded karyosome with the beads arranged in a rosette. Owing to its small size, this ameba is difficult to find.

Blastocystis hominis is a yeast-like organism that occurs frequently in the digestive tract of man. It is nonpathogenic but bears a close enough resemblance to protozoan cysts to cause some difficulty. It may be ovoid or spherical and 10 to 15 microns in diameter. The cytoplasm is hyaline and refractile and is enclosed in a membrane resembling a cyst wall. The outer wall of the cytoplasm is often differentiated, making the cell resemble a double-walled cyst. This outer layer contains granules and may have one or more structures resembling nuclei. The center portion of the cell is amorphous and resembles a large vacuole. One may also see dividing forms, which exhibit considerable variation in size and shape. In iodine stained preparations the nuclei are stained and the central area may be brown. In hematoxylin stained preparations the central area is gray and the periphery unstained except for the granules and nuclei (Fig. 16–63).

The Intestinal Ciliates (Ciliata)

The most important ciliate that is found in the human digestive tract is *Balantidium coli*. The infection may be harmless, or it may produce severe diarrhea and dysentery indistinguishable clinically from acute amebic dysentery. The organism is essentially a parasite of hogs, the per cent of humans in which the infections occur being quite small (less than 0.5 per cent). Infection occurs through ingestion of materials containing cysts. Butchers sometimes are infected.

Balantidium coli is a large organism, varying from 50 to 100 microns in length and from 40 to 60 microns in width. The trophozoite is motile by means of cilia, which cover the entire organism, exhibiting a directional, tumbling motion. The organism is more pointed at one end. This end contains a cleft called a peristome, which leads into a mouth called a cytostome connected to a gullet or esophagus. Food particles are taken in through this series of structures and are held in vacuoles in the cytoplasm. The cytoplasm is granular and contains, in addition to the food vacuoles, two contractile vacuoles, which can be seen to pulsate. At the blunt end of the organism there is an anal opening or cytopyge. *B. coli* has two nuclei, a kidney-shaped macronucleus, and a small, spherical micronucleus.

B. coli forms a cyst, which is round with a thick cell wall having a double outline. Young cysts contain macro- and micronuclei and a single contractile vacuole, and one can often see movement inside the cyst wall. Older cysts have only the macronucleus in a granular cytoplasm and there is no movement inside the cyst. The cysts are 45 to 65 microns in diameter.

The identification of *B. coli* in fecal preparation is not difficult, but it may require the examination of several samples to find the organism. It stains well with hematoxylin stains (Fig. 16–64).

The Intestinal Flagellates (*Mastigophora*)

Three species of flagellates are most commonly found in the human digestive tract. At least two others may be found occasionally. The flagellates are motile protozoa, their motility resulting from the possession of hair-like flagellae. The various species differ in the number and location of their flagellae, in morphology, and in size (Fig. 16–64). The three most common species are *Giardia lamblia*, *Chilomastix mesnili*, and *Trichomonas hominis*. Occasionally one may find *Embadomonas in-*

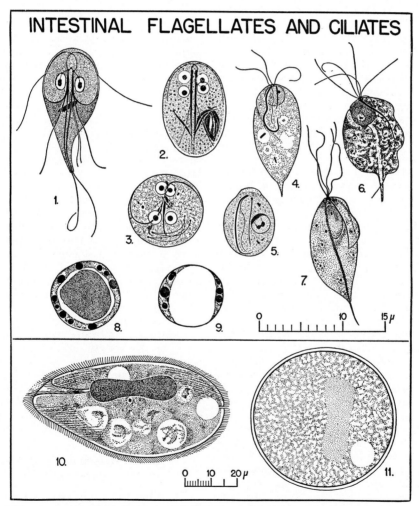

Figure 16–64. 1. Iron-hematoxylin stained trophozoite of *Giardia lamblia*. 2. Iron-hematoxylin stained cyst of *G. lamblia*. 3. Iron-hematoxylin stained cyst of *G. lamblia*, end-view. 4. Iron-hematoxylin stained trophozoite of *Chilomastix mesnili*. 5. Iron-hematoxylin stained cyst of *C. mesnili*. 6. Iron-hematoxylin stained trophozoite of *Trichomonas hominis*. 7. Iron-hematoxylin stained trophozoite of *T. vaginalis*. 8. Iron-hematoxylin stained *Blastocystis hominis*. 9. Unstained *B. hominis*. 10. Trophozoite of *Balantidium coli*. 11. Unstained cyst of *B. coli*. (Hunter, Frye, and Swartzwelder: A Manual of Tropical Medicine, 3rd Edition.)

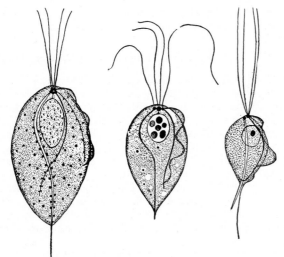

Figure 16–65. Trichomonas vaginalis, Trichomonas tenax, Trichomonas hominis (× 2000) (Powell).

testinalis and Enteromonas hominis. With the exception of Giardia lamblia these protozoa are all considered as nonpathogens. G. lamblia lives high up in the intestinal tract, and considerable evidence (mostly clinical) suggests that it may be capable of producing inflammatory changes in the intestinal wall and diarrhea. Final proof of its primary role in gastrointestinal disease is not yet available.

Giardia lamblia is a bilaterally symmetrical, pear shaped organism with a broad, rounded anterior and a tapering posterior extremity. It is usually from 12 to 15 microns in length. Space does not allow for a detailed description of the rather complex morphology of this organism (see Fig. 16–64). Trophozoites are not usually found in the stools, except in liquid stools of patients with diarrhea. When present the trophozoites exhibit motility that resembles that of a leaf in a stream of water.

G. lamblia forms a cyst, which is the most common structure present in stools. These are usually oval in shape although they may be round. The cyst wall is smooth and well defined and the cytoplasm tends to shrink away from the wall. The cytoplasm is granular and contains two to four nuclei, which have a dense and comparatively large nucleolus. Some of the structures of the trophozoite can be seen in the cyst, i.e., the axostyles, fibril, and the anterior and lateral flagella. The cyst is 9 to 12 microns in length. Sometimes the round cysts resemble those of small race E. histolytica and must be differentiated from them. This is one of the more easily recognized cysts. G. lamblia has never been cultured in vitro.

Chilomastix mesnili is a small, nonpathogenic flagellate, which may be found as either the trophozoite or the cyst in the human intestinal tract. The trophozoite is a small, pear shaped organism 13 to 24 microns long. It exhibits a spiral, jerking motion. It forms a cyst, which is also somewhat pear shaped with a characteristic thickening at the narrow end. Internally there is an axoneme and a single, rather large nucleus. The cyst is 6.5 to 10 microns long (see Fig. 16–64).

Trichomonas hominis is generally considered a nonpathogen, although it is occasionally found in considerable numbers in diarrheic stools. This organism does not form a cyst and accordingly is identified by finding the motile trophozoite in stool specimens. It is motile by means of a variable number of anterior flagella (three to five) and a single terminal flagellum. The terminal flagellum is an extension of an undulating membrane, which extends over most of the length of the organism. This undulating membrane can be seen under the microscope with reduced light and is diagnostic. The morphology of the organism is shown in Fig. 16–65. T. hominis has been cultured in several different media and its culture from feces is not difficult.

Other Trichomonads of Medical Importance

Trichomonas vaginalis is frequently associated with persistent vaginitis and has been considered to have a causative role, especially by clinicians. The patient with T. vaginalis vaginitis presents signs of vaginal inflammation and complains of itching,

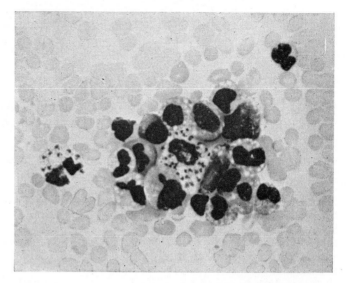

Figure 16–66. Smear from splenic pulp showing in the center a large mononuclear cell the cytoplasm of which is filled with Leishman-Donovan bodies. (A.F.I.P. No. 218689–1.)

burning, and discharge. The discharge exudes from the introitus and is frothy, creamy, yellowish, and acid and contains many vaginal epithelial cells, leukocytes, bacteria, and trichomonads. This is accompanied by inflammation over a considerable area. Infection in the urethra in the male also occurs and may be asymptomatic or symptomatic, resulting in some inflammation and discharge. Some workers believe that the infection is transmitted by sexual contact.

In the female the diagnosis can usually be made by collecting some of the frothy discharge with a speculum and emulsifying it in a drop of saline on a slide. A coverglass is applied and the preparation examined microscopically. Motile trichomonads are easily seen when present. *T. vaginalis* resembles *T. hominis* quite closely but is larger (see Fig. 16–65). The organism can be cultured although this is usually not necessary. The incidence of infection with *T. vaginalis* appears to be fairly high, surveys revealing a 13 to 31 per cent incidence in females. The incidence in males is not known with certainty.

Trichomonas tenax is sometimes found in the mouth of individuals with oral disease or with poor dental hygiene (see Fig. 16–65). It is not considered pathogenic.

THE SYSTEMIC FLAGELLATES

Genus Leishmania

The several species that compose this genus are apparently closely related to the trypanosomes. They have been grown out-

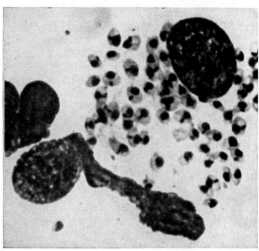

Figure 16–67. *Leishmania donovani* in stained smear from spleen puncture. (Hunter, Frye, and Swartzwelder: A Manual of Tropical Medicine, 3rd Edition.)

side the body, and their transformation in cultures into flagellated, trypanosome-like structures has been demonstrated.

They grow rather easily at room temperature in citrated blood or in N.N.N. (Nicolle, Novy, McNeal) medium. Incubation for two to three weeks is necessary before the cultures can be considered negative.

Leishmania donovani is the cause of kala-azar, an important and common disease in India and certain other areas. When stained with Wright's stain, the Leishman-Donovan bodies are round or oval, light blue structures, 2 or 3 microns in diameter, with two distinct reddish purple, chromatin masses, one large and pale (trophonucleus), the other small and deeply stained (blepharoplast) (Fig. 16–66). The parasites, which lie chiefly within endothelial cells, are especially abundant in the spleen. Splenic puncture has been used for diagnosis but is not without danger (Fig. 16–67). They may also be found, although with less certainty, in material obtained by puncture of superficial lymph nodes. Although they have been seen within endothelial leukocytes in the peripheral blood, particularly late in the disease, they are extremely difficult to find in ordinary blood films. The search may be greatly facilitated by concentrating the leukocytes. The leukocytes will form a whitish layer on top of the solidly packed erythrocytes. They should be skimmed off with a capillary pipet, spread on a slide, and stained with Wright's stain.

Napier's Serum Test for Kala-azar. This test, which has proved useful in the field where laboratory facilities are not available, is performed as follows: Place 1 cc. of clear serum in a small test tube. Add 1 drop of formalin. Shake the tube thoroughly and place it in a rack. In 3 to 20 minutes the serum will coagulate and become white and opalescent if it has been obtained from a patient who has untreated kala-azar. Normal serum remains clear and fluid. Serum of patients who have leprosy, tuberculosis, or malaria gives a somewhat similar but less pronounced reaction.

Leishmania has been found in a form of splenomegaly associated with a severe anemia occurring in young children in the region around the Mediterranean, especially Italy; this form is known as infantile kala-azar. Morphologically the parasite is indistinguishable from *Leishmania donovani*. The sandfly, *Phlebotomus argentipes*, has been shown to be the transmitting agent.

Other Species of Leishmania

Leishmania tropica resembles the parasite just described. It is found lying intracellularly in granulation tissue in cases of Delhi boil or oriental sore. A variety, sometimes described as a separate species, *Leishmania braziliensis* or *Leishmania tropica americana*, is similarly found in the ulcers of espundia, a very chronic form of mucocutaneous leishmaniasis that occurs in South Central America.

The fungus disease, histoplasmosis, may be confused with kala-azar; however, the latter disease probably does not occur in the United States, while the former occurs over a considerable area of the United States.

Genus Trypanosoma

Trypanosomes have been found in the blood plasma of a great variety of vertebrates. Many of them appear to produce no symptoms, but a few are of great pathogenic importance. Many species have been described. The forms found in the blood are easily recognized as trypanosomes, but accurate determination of species is difficult and may be impossible on the basis of their shape alone. They are elongated, spindle-shaped bodies, the average length of different species varying from 10 to 70 microns. Along one side runs a delicate undulating membrane, the free edge of which appears to be somewhat longer than the attached edge, thus throwing it into folds. Somewhere in the body, usually near the middle, is a comparatively pale-staining nucleus, and near the posterior end is a smaller, more deeply staining chromatin mass, the micronucleus or blepharoplast. A number of coarse, deeply staining granules—chromatophores—may be scattered through the cytoplasm. A flagellum arises in the blepharoplast, passes along the free edge of the undulating membrane, and continues posteriorly as a free flagellum. These details of structure are shown in Fig. 16–68.

The life history of the tryanosomes is complicated. There is an alternation of hosts, various insects playing the part of intermediate host. At least three species of *Trypanosoma* are pathogenic for man. These are pathogenic to a variable degree for some of the lower mammals, which in the wild state serve as reservoirs from which man may become infected through the agency of the insect host.

The best known trypanosome of human blood, *Trypanosoma gambiense* (Fig. 16–68), is an actively motile, spindle-shaped organism that is two to four times the diameter of an erythrocyte in length and has an undulating membrane, which terminates at the anterior end in a long flagellum. It can be seen in stained films with a medium power objective, but it is best studied with an oil immersion objective. It may be necessary to examine many slides. The parasites are more abundant in the fluid obtained by aspirating a lymph node with a large hypodermic needle. In the late stages of African sleeping sickness they can be found also in the cerebrospinal fluid. The length of the parasite varies from 15 to 33 microns. There are short, stumpy forms; long, slender forms; and intermediate forms. The parasite is transmitted by a biting fly, *Glossina palpalis*. A second species that causes sleeping sickness in Africa is *Trypanosoma rhodesiense*. The chief difference between it and *Trypanosoma gambiense* is the situation of the nucleus close to, or even posterior to, the blepharoplast. It is transmitted by the fly, *Glossina morsitans*. The antelope and other large game animals are probably the reservoir for these African trypanosomes.

Trypanosoma cruzi is the cause of Brazilian trypanosomiasis or Chagas' disease. In the febrile stage of the disease the organism is found in the peripheral blood without much difficulty. Its average length is about 20 microns. The life cycle is very complicated. In the vertebrate host multiplication takes place in the muscles and certain internal organs in which the parasites assume forms resembling *Leishmania donovani*. The early phase of the flagellated stage is passed within erythrocytes, the later phase in the blood plasma. The armadillo is probably the natural reservoir. The insect host by which the trypanosome is transmitted to man is a large bug belonging to the genus *Panstrongylus*, which is abundant in the dwellings of the poorer classes in Brazil. There are several species of which *Panstrongylus megistus* is most important and best known. De Coursey reported a case of fatal Chagas' disease observed in Panama. Besides *Panstrongylus megistus* other species of the superfamily Reduviidae have been found to be vectors. Reduviid bugs are found also in the United States. Opossums, armadillos, bats, dogs, and squirrels have all been found to be natural hosts. Packchanian demonstrated that a Texan strain of *Trypanosoma cruzi* found in a blood-sucking insect, *Triatoma*

heidemanni, was capable of infecting man with a disease clinically identical with Chagas' disease.

Trypanosoma lewisi, a very common and apparently harmless parasite of gray rats, especially sewer rats, is interesting because it closely resembles the pathogenic forms and is easily obtained for study. Its posterior end is more pointed than that of *Trypanosoma gambiense*.

Trypanosoma evansi, *Trypanosoma brucei*, and *Trypanosoma equiperdum* produce respectively surra, nagana, and dourine, which are common and important diseases of horses, mules, and cattle in the Philippines, East India, and Africa.

The Sporozoa

A number of protozoa of the group belonging to the Sporozoa (subclass Telosporida) are parasitic, and there are three genera that contain species parasitic in man. These are *Isospora hominis*, *Eimeria gubleri* and *stiedae*, and *Plasmodium vivax*, *malariae*, *falciparum*, and *ovale*. The latter species are the causative agents of malaria in man. Each of the sporozoa has a life cycle involving propagation by means of sporulation. In some the life cycle is quite complex, involving sexual and asexual reproductive cycles (*Plasmodium*).

ISOSPORA HOMINIS

Isospora hominis has been found in human feces. Apparently it causes no particular disturbance. Diagnosis depends on the recognition of oocysts in the feces. These are colorless, ovoid bodies, measuring about 14 by 28 microns. They have a clearcut, definite wall, which usually consists of two or more layers. When they first pass out of the body, the protoplasm is unsegmented and appears as a rounded, granular mass that does not fill the cyst, as in Fig. 16–69. They might easily be mistaken for the eggs of some unknown

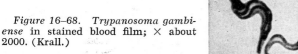

Figure 16–68. Trypanosoma gambiense in stained blood film; × about 2000. (Krall.)

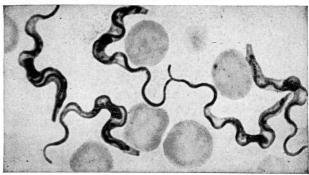

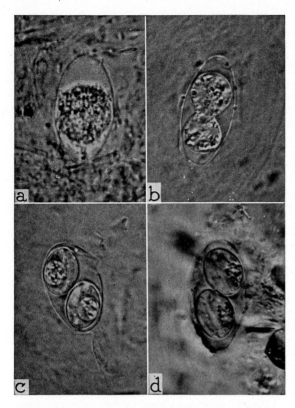

Figure 16–69. Isospora hominis (× 1000). *a*, Oocyst in stool at time of passage. *b*, Beginning formation of two sporocysts. *c*, Sporocysts formed (36 hours); large residual mass; sporozoites not completely formed; oocyst wall ruptured by pressure. *d*, Mature oocyst (56 hours). (Magath, in Am. J. Trop. Med., March, 1935.)

worm. To gain an idea of their general appearance, one may study the contents of the whitish nodules in the liver of an infected rabbit.

Genus Eimeria

The literature contains reports of a few cases in which human beings have been infected with *Eimeria gubleri*. This species has not been studied thoroughly; therefore, it is not known whether it is the same as *Eimeria stiedae,* which is commonly found in rabbits and has been studied extensively.

Eimeria stiedae, when fully developed, is ovoid in shape; it is about 30 to 50 microns long and has a shell-like integument. The parasite develops within the epithelial cells of the bile passages. Its presence in rabbits causes the formation of whitish nodules, which usually have caseous contents. On reaching the adult size, the parasite divides into a number of spores or merozoites, which enter other epithelial cells and repeat the cycle. A sexual cycle, which suggests that of the malarial parasite but does not require an insect host, also occurs. By conjugation of microgamete with macrogamete a zygote is formed. This acquires a definite membranous wall and thus becomes an oocyst, which passes out with feces. Its contents then divide into a

number of sporozoites. The cyst remains quiescent until it reaches the stomach of a new host, usually through contaminated food. Here the wall of the cyst is digested, and the sporozoites are set free to travel to the liver and enter epithelial cells where they initiate a new cycle.

A number of related species of *Eimeria* have in very rare instances been found in man. In most of these cases the oocyst was large and spherical.

Genus Plasmodium

In the class Sporozoa and in the suborder of blood parasites usually called Haemosporidia is found the genus *Plasmodium,* which includes all the parasites causing malaria in man and other animals. Although malaria is now rare in the United States, it is still a very important disease in much of the world and is responsible directly or indirectly for much debilitation and death.

Four species of the protozoan *Plasmodium,* the generic name of the etiologic agent, are known, viz., *vivax, falciparum, malariae,* and *ovale.* Transmission from man to man is through the bite of certain species of infected female *Anopheles* mosquitoes. The disease, although generally referred to as malaria, may be specifically

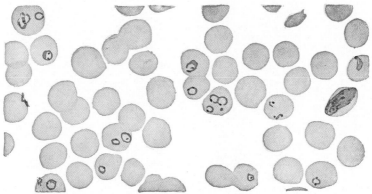

Estivo-autumnal malaria; exact reproduction of a portion of a field showing an exceptionally large number of parasites.

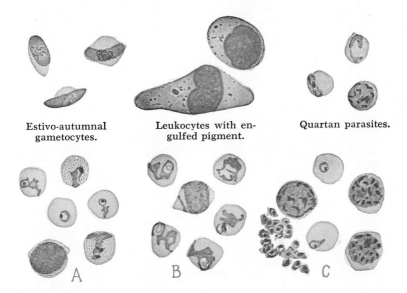

Estivo-autumnal gametocytes.   Leukocytes with engulfed pigment.   Quartan parasites.

Figure 16–70. Tertian parasites. *A,* Eight hours after chill showing malarial stippling, five young parasites, and one gametocyte from two slides. *B,* Twenty-four hours after chill; five half-grown parasites and one gametocyte. *C,* During chill; one presegmenter, two segmenters, a cluster of freshly liberated merozoites, and two very young parasites, from one slide. (J. W. Rennell, pinx.)

designated by the name of the etiologic agent as shown at the bottom of the page.

The life cycle of the malaria parasite in man is shown in Fig. 16–71. Man is the intermediate host in whom the asexual cycle, schizogony, occurs, and the mosquito is the definitive host in which gametogony and sporogony take place.

Man becomes infected as sporozoites from infected mosquitoes are injected into the peripheral circulation during the bite. Pre-erythrocytic development takes place in

PLASMODIUM	CLASSIC NOMENCLATURE	MODERN NOMENCLATURE
vivax	benign tertian malaria	vivax malaria
ovale	ovale malaria	ovale malaria
malariae	quartan malaria	malariae malaria or quartan malaria
falciparum	estivo-autumnal (EA); subtertian malaria; malignant tertian	falciparum malaria

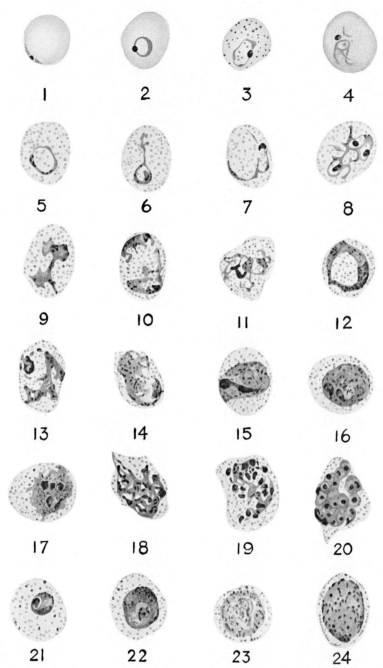

Figure 16–71. Plasmodium vivax. 1. Normal-size erythrocyte with marginal ring form trophozoite. *2.* Young signet-ring form of trophozoite in macrocyte. *3.* Slightly older ring form trophozoite in erythrocyte showing basophilic stippling. *4.* Polychromatophilic erythrocyte containing young tertian parasite with pseudopodia. *5.* Ring form of trophozoite showing pigment in cytoplasm of an enlarged cell containing Schüffner's stippling. This stippling does not appear in all cells containing the growing and older forms of *Plasmodium vivax,* but it can be found with any stage from the fairly young ring form onward. *6* and *7.* Very tenuous medium trophozoite forms. *8.* Three ameboid trophozoites with fused cytoplasm. *9, 11, 12,* and *13.* Older ameboid trophozoites in process of development. *10.* Two ameboid trophozoites in one cell. *14.* Mature trophozoite. *15.* Mature trophozoite with chromatin apparently in process of division. *16, 17, 18,* and *19.* Schizonts showing progressive steps in division (presegmenting schizonts). *20.* Mature schizont. *21* and *22.* Developing gametocytes. *23.* Mature microgametocyte. *24.* Mature macrogametocyte. (From *Manual for the Microscopical Diagnosis of Malaria in Man* by Aimee Wilcox, Bulletin No. 180, National Institute of Health, 1942.)

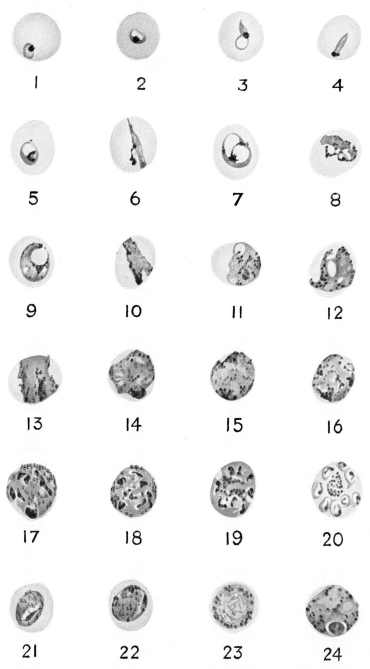

Figure 16–72.   Plasmodium malariae. 1. Young ring form trophozoite of quartan malaria. *2, 3,* and *4.* Young trophozoite forms of the parasite showing gradual increase of chromatin and cytoplasm. *5.* Developing ring form of trophozoite showing pigment granule. *6.* Early band form of trophozoite—elongated chromatin, some pigment apparent. *7, 8, 9, 10, 11,* and *12.* Some forms which the developing trophozoite of quartan may take. *13* and *14.* Mature trophozoites—one a band form. *15, 16, 17, 18,* and *19.* Phases in the development of the schizont (presegmenting schizonts). *20.* Mature schizont. *21.* Immature microgametocyte. *22.* Immature macrogametocyte. *23.* Mature microgametocyte. *24.* Mature macrogametocyte. (From *Manual for the Microscopical Diagnosis of Malaria in Man* by Aimee Wilcox, Bulletin, No. 180, National Institute of Health, 1942.)

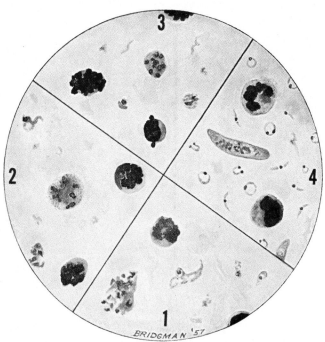

Figure 16–73. The human plasmodia as seen in thick film: *1, Plasmodium vivax:* young and older trophozoites and schizont; *2, P. ovale:* developing trophozoite and schizonts, one within a "ghost cell"; *3, P. malariae:* trophozoites and schizont; *4, P. falciparum:* young trophozoites and gametocyte. (Markell and Voge: Diagnostic Techniques in Medical Parasitology.)

the parenchymal cells of the liver at which time there is a progressive development through several stages that eventually results in the development of merozoites. These merozoites either initiate the erythrocytic cycle by rupturing from the cell and penetrating red cells or penetrate other liver parenchymal cells to continue the exoerythrocytic phase.

Once the asexual phase of the cycle is begun in the red cells, the parasite develops, beginning with ring forms and progressing through the trophozoite to the early and mature schizonts. This process, known as schizogony, is a 48-to-72-hour process, depending upon the species, and begins with a primary splitting of the chromatin, continuing until merozoites are formed. These merozoites rupture from the mature schizonts and penetrate new red cells. This rupture of the red blood cells is associated with the chill and fever that characterize clinical malaria. After several asexual cycles some tend to become sexually differentiated forms, the male or microgametocyte and the female or macrogametocyte, while the majority continue the erythrocytic cycle. The gametocytes do not contribute to the production of symptoms and remain alive as long as the red cell lives, about 120 days. The paroxysm, chill and fever, is somewhat characteristic and occurs every 72 hours with *P. malariae* infections but at 48-hour intervals with the

other three species. Different broods of organisms may give irregular paroxysms, which may be quotidian rather than strictly tertian or quartan.

Only the gametocytes are infective for the mosquito. In the stomach of the female mosquito they mature as microgametes and macrogametes. The microgametes exflagellate and fertilize the macrogamete to become a zygote. The zygote elongates and becomes actively motile and is called an ookinete. This form penetrates the stomach wall and rounds up on the outside of the wall to become an oocyst. As it matures to a sporocyst, slender sporozoites develop, and these break out and migrate to the salivary glands where they are retained until the next blood meal, at which time they enter the blood of the human.

Differentiation of Species. Walker (1952) has given a concept of the basic facts of malaria that have an important bearing on the recognition of the species under the microscope as shown at the top of p. 673.

Species diagnosis is important according to Walker to insure the immediate treatment of *falciparum* malaria in which completely unpredictable symptoms may develop. Furthermore in *vivax* malaria it is useful to be able to estimate from the observation of the developmental stage of the majority of the parasites when the next paroxysm may be expected.

Differential diagnosis of malaria may be

Malaria

Falciparum	*Vivax* or Quartan
Only cells containing young parasites (or gametocytes) seen in peripheral blood. Older stages in red cells adherent to endothelial lining, interfering with function (anoxia) of organism involved; hence protean symptoms.	All infected cells circulate freely and continually.
Paroxysmal symptoms with schizogony; anemia from blood destruction	
Adequate treatment controls attack	

Cured because
  pre-erythrocytic stage is exhausted with primary attack.
	May relapse because
	  pre-erythrocytic stage reseeds liver cells. Relapse of parasitism occurs when immunity decreases.

Gametocytes appear late; persist some days.	Gametocytes only with asexual forms.

made by examining either thin or thick films, but one must be cautious with scanty infections. Figures 16–70 to 16–72 show the parasites as they are seen within red cells in thin film preparations.

Thick film diagnosis is a little more challenging, because the red cells are destroyed and the parasites are not spread out; however, more positive findings will be reported using thick films. Parasites that show purplish-red chromatin and blue cytoplasm are stained properly. White cells can be used as a guide to staining (Fig. 16–73).

Blood from a suspected individual should be taken at six-to-eight-hour intervals, and one need not necessarily wait until the rise in temperature before taking the blood. (For the technique of making and staining blood films, see Chapter 4.) Multiple infections are possible but do not occur regularly.

Toxoplasma Gondii

Toxoplasma gondii is the causative agent of toxoplasmosis in man and animals and was originally described from a North African rodent, the gondi. In human adults the infection is usually asymptomatic and unrecognized, although occasional symptomatic and fatal cases occur. In children the disease may produce a syndrome involving the central nervous system and the viscera. Congenitally acquired infection occurs and is manifest in the infant or young child as an encephalitis accompanied by such features as chorioretinitis, hydrocephalus or microcephaly, micro-ophthalmos, intracerebral calcification, and mental retardation. Convulsions may occur. In such cases parenchymal and reticuloendothelial cells are generally affected, and lesions occur in the brain, spleen, kidneys, adrenals, and lymph nodes.

Serologic studies indicate that infection with *T. gondii* is fairly widespread in the population, although active cases in adults are, as mentioned previously, rare. Such active cases usually have prolonged remittant fever with such accompanying features as pneumonitis, encephalitis, and myocarditis. There may be a rash, generalized lymphadenitis, and myositis accompanied by generalized aching and pain. In some areas 50 per cent or more of the population at age 20 years show a positive serologic test.

T. gondii, when it occurs in the free stage, is curved or crescent shaped, measuring 4 to 6 microns in length and 2 to 3 microns in width with one extremity more rounded than the other. When stained by Wright's or Giemsa's method, the cytoplasm is blue and the nucleus is a red or purple, irregular structure occupying one-fifth to one-fourth of the cell. The nucleus lies near the rounded end of the organism. The cells tend to occur singly or in pairs (Fig. 16–74).

When *T. gondii* is found in the parenchymal or reticuloendothelial cells, the organisms lose their crescent shape and may be confused with the leishmanias. They occur singly or in clusters in these tissue cells. In certain instances, especially in the brain of mice, *T. gondii* occurs as clusters of organisms called pseudocysts.

The diagnosis of toxoplasmosis depends on demonstration of the organisms in blood, bone marrow, cerebrospinal fluid, or exudates from serous cavities by staining or by intracerebral or intraperitoneal inoculation of these materials into mice. After three to six weeks the inoculated mice are sacrificed, and lymph nodes, spleen, liver, brain, and peritoneal fluid are examined grossly and with stained smears. If no positive findings are noted, another group of

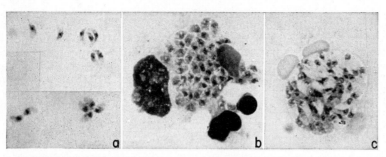

Figure 16–74. Toxoplasmata as seen (a) free in stained films of peritoneal exudate or tissue, (b) intracellularly, and (c) as pseudocyst in film of brain. Wright's stain (× 800) reduced from a photomicrograph with a magnification of 1000 diameters. (Courtesy of Dr. A. B. Sabin in J.A.M.A., vol. 116.)

mice should be inoculated with suspensions of tissue from the first group and examined similarly. This should be repeated at least one further transfer before giving a negative report.

Serologic tests are of value as presumptive evidence of toxoplasmosis. Complement fixation, the Sabin-Feldman dye test, or fluorescent antibody techniques may be used. Since few laboratories are equipped to do these tests, 10 ml. of blood should be collected aseptically and sent to an appropriate laboratory (usually the state health department laboratory). It is not usually possible to demonstrate the organism in congenital cases; thus, it is usually necessary to do serial serologic tests on the blood of both the mother and the infant. Skin tests (toxoplasmin) are of some value and are discussed on p. 814.

THE HELMINTHS

Two phyla of worms (helminths) are of medical importance: Nemathelminthes (roundworms) and Platyhelminthes (flatworms, viz., flukes and tapeworms).

Diagnosis of these helminthic infections in the clinical laboratory is based upon the demonstration of the ova, larvae, or other stages of the parasite in body fluids, stools, and tissues or in the environment. The life cycles of the helminths may be quite complex, and one should know something of these life cycles to be better able to decide what examinations are needed. The most important human helminths are presented in Table 16–20.

The Nematodes

Distinguishing features of the nematodes are as follows: cylindrical shape, nonsegmented body, tapered ends, and a cuticular covering. The intricate digestive system is complete with both mouth and anus. The nematodes are diecious, and generally the

males are much smaller and more slender than the female worms.

Several females of the nematodes are viviparous, but generally ova are produced in quantities each day, a fact that makes diagnosis easier. Some of the common nematode ova are seen in Fig. 16–75. The reproductive organs are bilaterally symmetrical, tubular, and coiled within the body. An excretory system and a nervous system exist, but vascular and respiratory systems do not.

Enterobius Vermicularis. The seatworm or pinworm causing human enterobiasis or oxyuriasis is *Enterobius vermicularis* (*Oxyuris vermicularis*). This common helminth is widely distributed in families and in institutions. Broadly speaking, sanitation is not a primary factor in its dissemination; rather it is neglected individual hygiene that permits rapid spread of the infection. This infection occurs at all economic levels.

The female worm is distinctive in possessing a long, narrow, sharply pointed tail, the characteristic from which it gets the name pinworm. Females measure 8 to 13 mm. in length and 0.5 mm. in diameter; the male is 2 to 5 mm. in length and 0.5 mm. in diameter with a ventrally curved posterior end. The adults possess cephalic alae or wings at their anterior end (Fig. 16–76).

The site of predilection of the adult worms is the neighborhood of the cecum. The gravid female migrates to the anus where she crawls about on the perianal folds and deposits large numbers of eggs. These eggs are fully embryonated, are immediately infective, and only need to be swallowed for reinfection or to establish an infection in a new host.

Since ova and adults are seldom seen in feces, specific diagnosis rests upon the recovery of the eggs or adult females from the perianal region. Although there are numerous methods available, the best known is the Graham scotch tape technique (Fig. 16–77). It is advisable for tape samples to be taken from each member of the family upon awakening on three successive days, because the female worms may not migrate each night. These tapes should be submitted to the laboratory. The egg has a thick hyaline shell with one flattened side and a larva within. There is a violet tint to the space surrounding the larva within the shell. Frequently the larva is slightly motile. The ovum measures 50 to 60 microns in length and 20 to 30 microns in width (Fig. 16–78). The laboratory technologist should be cautioned about the infectiousness of the ova on the scotch tape preparations.

Scotch tape technique for pinworms after Graham. Ova are not readily found

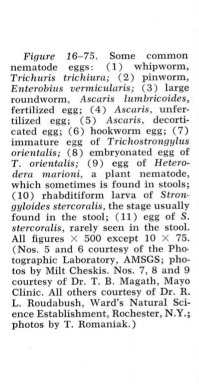
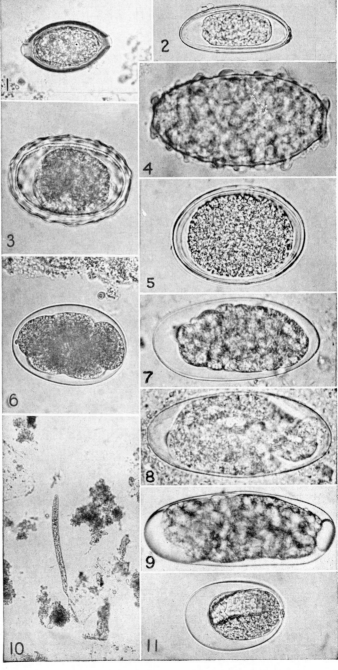

Figure 16–75. Some common nematode eggs: (1) whipworm, *Trichuris trichiura;* (2) pinworm, *Enterobius vermicularis;* (3) large roundworm, *Ascaris lumbricoides,* fertilized egg; (4) *Ascaris,* unfertilized egg; (5) *Ascaris,* decorticated egg; (6) hookworm egg; (7) immature egg of *Trichostrongylus orientalis;* (8) embryonated egg of *T. orientalis;* (9) egg of *Heterodera marioni,* a plant nematode, which sometimes is found in stools; (10) rhabditiform larva of *Strongyloides stercoralis,* the stage usually found in the stool; (11) egg of *S. stercoralis,* rarely seen in the stool. All figures × 500 except 10 × 75. (Nos. 5 and 6 courtesy of the Photographic Laboratory, AMSGS; photos by Milt Cheskis. Nos. 7, 8 and 9 courtesy of Dr. T. B. Magath, Mayo Clinic. All others courtesy of Dr. R. L. Roudabush, Ward's Natural Science Establishment, Rochester, N.Y.; photos by T. Romaniak.)

Table 16-20. Diseases Caused by Helminths

DISEASE	PARASITE	COMMON NAME	GEOGRAPHICAL DISTRIBUTION	VECTOR	CLINICAL DIAGNOSIS	LABORATORY DIAGNOSIS
Enterobiasis; oxyuriasis; pinworm infection	Enterobius vermicularis	Pinworm	Cosmopolitan	Anus to mouth; eggs spread on fomites	Pruritus ani; abdominal cramps and pain; diarrhea; or no symptoms	Eggs on perianum picked up on scotch tape; adult females on surface of stool or on scotch tape
Ascariasis	Ascaris lumbricoides	Roundworms	Cosmopolitan	Embryonated ova from soil; eggs in contaminated water or food	Pneumonitis (in early stages); allergic symptoms; abdominal pain or discomfort; intestinal blockage	Eggs in feces; adult worms
Trichuriasis; trichocephaliasis; whipworm infection	Trichuris trichiura (Trichocephalus)	Whipworm	Cosmopolitan	Embryonated ova from soil; eggs in contaminated water or food	Allergic symptoms or no symptoms; secondary bacterial invasion; bloody diarrhea	Eggs in feces
Ancylostomiasis; uncinariasis; hookworm disease; hookworm infection	Ancylostoma duodenale Necator americanus	Old World hookworm New World hookworm	Tropical and subtropical 45° N. to 30° S. latitude	Filariform larvae in soil	May be no symptoms; pulmonary, intestinal pain	Eggs or rarely larvae in feces; larvae in cultures
Strongyloidiasis; Cochin China diarrhea	Strongyloides stercoralis	Threadworm	Cosmopolitan	Filariform larvae in soil	Watery diarrhea; pneumonitis; hepatitis; abdominal pain	Larvae in feces, sputum, duodenal contents; larvae and free-living adults in cultures
Trichinosis; trichiniasis; trichinelliasis	Trichinella spiralis	Trichina worm	Cosmopolitan	Consumption of infected pork, raw or insufficiently cooked	Gastrointestinal symptoms may be mild; painful respiration; myocardial damage; muscle pain; edema of face	Adults in feces (early in infection); muscle biopsy; skin and serologic tests
Bancroft's filariasis; wuchereriasis	Wuchereria bancrofti	Bancroft's filaria	Asia; Africa; South America; Near East; India	Mosquitoes (Culex, Aedes, Anopheles)	Blocked lymph nodes may produce elephantiasis; toxic reactions	Microfilariae in peripheral blood with nocturnal periodicity
Malayan filariasis	Wuchereria malayi	Malayan filaria	Malay peninsula; Asia	Mosquitoes (Culex, Aedes, Anopheles)	Blocked lymph nodes may produce elephantiasis; toxic reactions	Microfilariae in peripheral blood
Loiasis; eye worm infection	Loa loa	African eye worm	Central and West Africa	Bite of tabanid fly (Chrysops)	Calabar swellings; allergic manifestations; eosinophilia	Microfilariae in peripheral blood in daytime
	Acanthocheilonema perstans	The persistent filaria	Tropical Africa; Venezuela; Brazil; Argentina	Culicoides	Allergic state with eosinophilia	Microfilariae in peripheral blood nonperiodic
	Mansonella ozzardi	Ozzard's filaria	Tropical America	Culicoides	Nonpathogenic or allergic state	Microfilariae in peripheral blood
Guinea worm infection; dracunculiasis	Dracunculus medinensis	Guinea worm	Egypt; Africa; Near East; Russia; India, East Indies, Carribean area; Brazil; Guianas	Consumption of water contaminated with infected Cyclops	Cutaneous blisters and ulcers; anaphylactic symptoms	Adult worms in skin; skin tests; larvae in blister or ulcer
Onchocerciasis	Onchocerca volvulus	The convoluted filaria	Mexico; Guatemala; Africa	Simulium (black fly)	Fibrous nodules on trunk; arms or legs; blindness may develop	Microfilariae from nodular fluid or adults and microfilariae from biopsy

Disease	Organism	Common name	Geographic distribution	Mode of infection	Symptoms	Diagnosis
Broad fish tapeworm infection	*Diphyllobothrium latum*	Broad fish tapeworm	North Central U.S.; Canada; Europe; Russia; Japan; Israel	Consuming infected raw or insufficiently cooked fresh-water fish	Anemia; no symptoms; digestive disturbances; weakness; loss of weight	Eggs in feces; chains of segments passed; entire worm following therapy
Beef tapeworm infection	*Taenia saginata*	Beef tapeworm	Cosmopolitan	Consuming raw or insufficiently cooked infected beef	Diarrhea; increase in appetite; slight irritation of mucosa; obstruction	Eggs or proglottids (single or chains) in feces; entire worm after therapy
Pork tapeworm infection	*Taenia solium*	Pork tapeworm	Cosmopolitan	Consuming raw or insufficiently cooked infected pork or pork products	Vague abdominal discomfort; persistent diarrhea; serious complications with the bladder worm; eosinophilia	Eggs or proglottids in the feces; entire worm after therapy; surgical removal of bladder worm
Dwarf tapeworm infection	*Hymenolepis nana*	Dwarf tapeworm	Cosmopolitan	Anus to mouth infection; contamination of food or drink from human excreta	Toxemia; diarrhea; abdominal pains; may have no symptoms	Eggs or adults in feces; adults after therapy
Hymenolepiasis diminuta infection	*Hymenolepis diminuta*	Rat tapeworm	Cosmopolitan	Infective state in insects or certain arthropod species that are accidentally swallowed	Emaciation	Ova in feces; adult after therapy
Echinococcosis; hydatid disease	*Echinococcus granulosus*	Hydatid worm	Argentina; New Zealand; Australia; U.S.A.; Europe	Fingers, food, or drink contaminated with eggs from dog feces	Symptoms depend upon the location of cysts; allergic reaction	Precipitin, skin tests; aspiration of cysts is dangerous
Manson's schistosomiasis	*Schistosoma mansoni*	Blood fluke	Brazil; Venezuela; Puerto Rico; Africa	Fresh water harboring infected snails producing infective cercariae	Spleen and liver enlargement; intestinal fibrosis; bloody mucus; urticaria; toxemia	Ova in feces (occasionally in urine); serologic and skin tests; rectal or hepatic biopsy
Schistosomiasis japonica	*Schistosoma japonicum*	Blood fluke	Phillipines; Japan; Formosa; China; Celebes	Fresh water harboring infected snails producing infective cercariae	Spleen and over enlargement; intestinal fibrosis; bloody mucus; uricaria; toxemia	Ova in feces; serologic and skin tests; rectal or hepatic biopsy
Bilharziasis; vesical schistosomiasis	*Schistosoma haematobium*	Blood fluke	Africa; Israel; Greece; Spain; Portugal	Fresh water harboring infected snails producing infective cercariae	Chronic cystitis with secondary infection; genital organs damaged; hematuria; painful micturition	Ova in urine (occasionally in feces); skin and serologic bladder scrapings
Fasciolopsiasis	*Fasciolopsis buski*	Giant intestinal fluke	Far East; India; China; East Indies	Consumption of encysted metacercariae on aquatic plants	Intestinal inflammation; diarrhea; edema; ascites; toxemia	Ova in feces; adults occasionally after therapy
Fascioliasis	*Fasciola hepatica*	Liver fluke	U.S.A.; South America; Europe; Africa	Metacercariae on aquatic vegetation	Enlarged liver; mechanical and toxic irritation of the liver	Eggs in feces
Clonorchiasis	*Clonorchis sinensis*	Chinese liver fluke	Orient	Consuming infected fish flesh raw or insufficiently cooked	Blocking of bile ducts; jaundice; cirrhosis; toxemia	Eggs in feces
Paragonimiasis	*Paragonimus westermani*	Lung fluke	Orient; Africa; South America	Consuming infected raw crabs or crayfish	Cough, hemoptysis; pneumonitis; chest pain	Eggs in sputum or feces

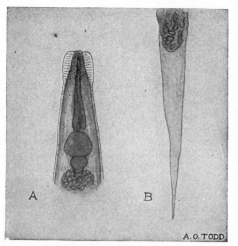

Figure 16–76. Head and tail of female pinworm, *Enterobius vermicularis. A,* Head showing the two cuticular appendages and the beginning of the esophagus with its bulbous expansions; *B,* tail showing sharply pointed tip (× 35).

in stools, because the gravid female does not lay her eggs to be mixed with feces. Rather the female migrates, usually at night while the individual is resting, and deposits her eggs on the perianum. These eggs can be picked up best by using a scotch tape method early in the morning before getting out of bed or at least before defecation. Since the worms may not migrate each night, scotch tape preparations should be made on three successive mornings.

1. Apply a strip of scotch tape 2½ to 3 inches in length on the upper side, beginning at one end, of a tongue blade. A small portion of the end on the opposite portion of the tongue blade should be folded on itself. This provides a nonsticky surface for handling the tape.

2. To obtain a sample, pull the folded tab so that the sticky side of the tape is freed, still leaving enough of it stuck to the tongue blade.

3. Carry the freed tape over the end of the blade so that the sticky side is out.

4. Hold the tongue depressor with the thumb and second finger and hold the tape to the tongue blade with the forefinger.

5. Press the sticky surface onto the right and left perianal folds but do not insert the blade into the rectum.

6. Replace the tape onto the tongue blade. (These blades can be sent by mail to the laboratory.)

7. Transfer the tapes to microscope slides.

8. Pull tape back from the slide, leaving a small portion attached.

9. Add a drop of toluene and replace the tape on the slide. (The toluene clears everything except the ova and adults.)

10. Smooth out the tape with a piece of gauze, which should be disinfected. Examine the ova and adults under the low power objective.

Ascaris lumbricoides. *Ascaris lumbricoides* is the intestinal roundworm (Fig. 16–79) that resides in the small intestine and causes ascariasis. The adult female worm measures 20 to 40 cm. in length and is about 5 mm. thick or about the size of a lead pencil with most of the worm given to reproductive organs; the males, 10 to 30 cm. long, are more slender and have a ventrally curved tail. The cuticle is pinkish-white in color. *Ascaris* worms, in spite of their size, have trilobate lips at their anterior end, an outstanding characteristic that aids in the identification of small immature worms as well as the adults of this genus.

The fertilized ovum (Figs. 16–75, 16–80) is broadly oval, measuring 45 to 75 microns in length by 35 to 50 microns in breadth. The thick shell has an outer albuminous covering, which is coarsely mammilated and is stained with bile to a golden brown or yellow color. Those fertilized ova that have lost their albuminoid coat are denoted as decorticated, and they must be differentiated from hookworm ova. In all fertilized eggs there is a conspicuous, crescentic, clear space at each pole between the contents and the shell.

When only female worms are present or in early infections, only unfertilized ova may be found (Fig. 16–81). There is much variation in structure from one unfertilized egg to another, but they are longer and narrower than the fertile ova and have a thinner shell. Internally there is a mass of coarse granules, which fill the shell. The inexperienced technician may overlook these ova, since some are extremely irregular in outline and may show little likeness to *Ascaris* ova.

Adult female ascarids deposit about 200,-000 ova per day during the year or two of lifespan. These ova become infective for man only after a two-week or longer period of embryonation in the soil. *Ascaris* larvae may be seen in the sputum of infected individuals.

Strongyloides stercoralis. *Strongyloides stercoralis* is the threadworm of man pro-

a. Cellulose-tape slide preparation

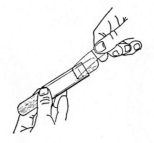

b. Hold slide against tongue depressor one inch from end and lift long portion of tape from slide

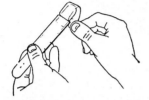

c. Loop tape over end of depressor to expose gummed surface

d. Hold tape and slide against tongue depressor

e. Press gummed surfaces against several areas of perianal region

f. Replace tape on slide

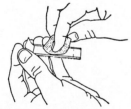

g. Smooth tape with cotton or gauze

Note: Specimens are best obtained a few hours after the person has retired, perhaps at 10 or 11 P.M., or the first thing in the morning before a bowel movement or bath.

Figure 16–77.   Use of cellulose tape slide preparation for diagnosis of pinworm infections. (Adapted from Brook, Donaldson, and Mitchell, 1949.)

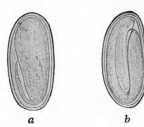

a   *b*

Figure 16–78.

Figure 16–78.   Eggs of *Enterobius vermicularis*: *a*, Freshly deposited, with tadpole-like embryo; *b*, 12 hours after deposition, with nematode-like embryo ($\times$ 500). (After Fantham, Stephens, and Theobald.)

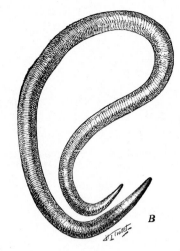

Figure 16–79. The common roundworm, *Ascaris lumbricoides*, natural size; A, male, B, female. (After Brumpt.)

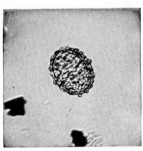

Figure 16–80. Egg of *Ascaris lumbricoides,* surface view (× 250).

ducing Cochin-China diarrhea or strongyloidiasis, a condition that is very refractory to therapy. The 2 mm. long parasitic female (Fig. 16–82), which may be pathogenic, is buried in the mucosa of the duodenum. Since the ova are deposited in the mucosa, they rarely are seen in the stool (Fig. 16–83); rather the first larval stage, the rhabditiform larva, is observed. These must be differentiated from those of the hookworms, *Rhabditis hominis* and *Trichostrongylus*. The rhabditiform larva measures 225 by 16 microns and possesses

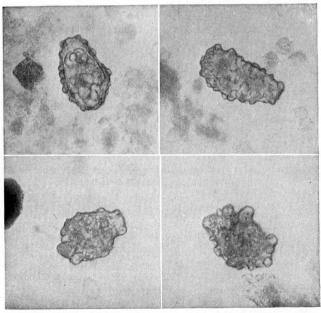

Figure 16–81. Unfertilized ova of *Ascaris lumbricoides*, showing the great irregularity in shape. Some of these eggs are extremely difficult to identify (× 250).

a conspicuous, ovoidal, genital anlage (primordium) nearly midway and ventral in the body. In addition the buccal capsule is short as evidenced by the close proximity of the esophagus to the anterior tip. The larvae are actively motile and have a snake-like, whipping motion. Under favorable conditions these rhabditiform larvae, which pass out with the feces onto moist, warm soil, develop into free-living males or females or into the infective filariform stage.

Filariform larvae may develop also within the intestine from rhabditiform larvae, and autoinfection (hyperinfection) may take place as the larvae penetrate the mucosa. If these filariform larvae are in the stool or in cultures, they must be differentiated from the rhabditiform larvae and from the filariform larvae of the hookworm. They are characterized by a notched tail and a body that is nearly evenly divided into esophagus and gut, the latter being more granular and set off by a distinct line of demarcation. When in moist warm soil, the filariform larvae come to the surface from which they penetrate the skin of the host. Subsequent to penetration they migrate to the lungs whence they are coughed up and swallowed to become parasitic females in the duodenum.

Diagnosis is based upon finding the distinctive rhabditiform or filariform larvae in the feces or the former in duodenal contents. It is possible for an individual to have a mixed infection of hookworm and *Strongyloides*. Frequently the larvae are seen in the stool in a molting stage between the rhabditiform and filariform and cannot be specifically identified, but cultivation for 24 to 48 hours (see Appendix, p. 936) will produce free-living adults (Fig. 16–84) and filariform larvae of *Strongyloides* but only rhabitiform larvae of hookworm. About eight days are required for the filariform larvae of hookworm to develop. The laboratory worker should be cautioned against self-contamination with stools or cultures containing filariform larvae of *Strongyloides*.

Trichuris trichiura. *Trichuris trichiura* (*Trichocephalus trichiura*) is commonly called the whipworm and causes trichuriasis (trichocephaliasis). The adults (Fig. 16–85) are 3.5 to 5.0 cm. long with an attenuated, whip-like anterior end and a thicker posterior portion, which is bluntly rounded in the female and coiled like a watch spring in the male. The worms are pinkish-white in color. The characteristic ova (Fig. 16–86) are football-shaped with mucus plugs at either pole. They are golden brown with a thick shell and measure 50 to 54 microns long and about 23 microns wide.

Embryonated ova in the soil are infective when ingested by man, and larvae hatching

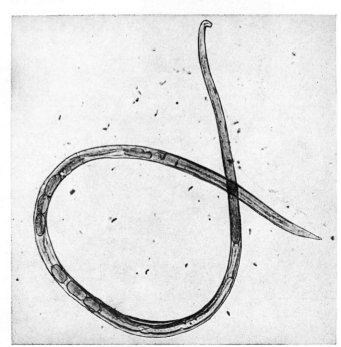

Figure 16–82. Strongyloides stercoralis, parasitic female. (Photomicrograph by Zane Price.)

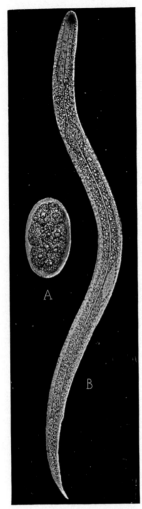

from the ova in the region of the duodenum merely descend to the large intestine where they develop into adults. They may live several years during which time each female produces approximately 5000 ova per day.

Trichostrongylus orientalis. A number of species of *Trichostrongylus* have been found in man, although they are primarily parasites of herbivorous animals. The larvae from the soil are ingested with contaminated food. The adults are small and live in the jejunum and upper ileum of man. Diagnosis is based upon finding the ova (Fig. 16–75) in the feces. They measure 75 to 91 microns in length and 39 to 47 microns in diameter. They resemble hookworm ova in that they have a thin shell, but they are more nearly pointed at one end and are larger. The rhabditiform larva possesses a characteristic small knob at the tip of the tail (see Table 16–21). They may be found in feces or in cultures (see Appendix, p. 936). These worms are refractory to therapy, but they are essentially nonpathogenic.

Heterodera marioni. *Heterodera marioni* is a true parasite of plants, but man has been shown to harbor ova of this organism, which are swallowed with parasitized vegetable tissues, such as onion roots. These ova (Fig. 16–75) are passed in human feces and must be differentiated from hookworm and *Trichostrongylus* ova. They are 82 to 120 microns in length and 24 to 43 microns in breadth. They are elongated and

Figure 16–83.   A, Egg of *Strongyloides stercoralis* (parasitic mother worm) found in stools in a case of chronic diarrhea; *B,* rhabditiform larva of *Strongyloides stercoralis* from the stools. (William Sydney Thayer in J. Exper. Med.)

Figure 16–85.   Whipworms (*Trichuris trichiura*). *A,* Females; *B,* males. The posterior portion of the male is usually coiled as is shown at the right. Photographs of mounted specimens. Natural size.

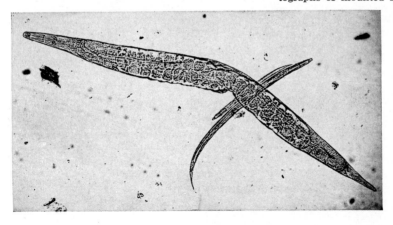

Figure 16–84. Strongyloides stercoralis, free-living female and larvae. (Photomicrograph by Zane Price.)

Table 16–21. Differentiation of Larvae of Hookworm, *Strongyloides*, *Rhabditis*, and *Trichostrongylus*

CATEGORY	*Strongyloides*	HOOKWORM	*Rhabditis hominis*	*Trichostrongylus*
		Rhabditiform Larvae		
Shape	Short, stout	Short, stout	Short, stout	Short, stout
Size (average)	225 x 16 microns	275 x 17 microns	240–300 x 12 microns	480 microns
Anterior	Short, narrow buccal cavity; esophagus near anterior tip	Long, narrow buccal cavity; esophagus distal from anterior tip	Long buccal cavity with thick cuticle	Long buccal cavity
Posterior	More blunt	Sharply pointed	Pointed	Bead-like swelling at tip
Genital anlage (primordium)	Conspicuous on ventral side halfway down midgut	Inconspicuous	Inconspicuous	Inconspicuous
Internal structures	Well developed for feeding	Well developed for feeding	Well developed for feeding	Well developed for feeding
		Filariform Larvae		
Shape	Long, slender	Long, slender	None	Long, slender
Size	700 microns	700 microns	None	690 microns
Anterior	Rounded	Rounded	None	Rounded
Posterior	Notched tail	Pointed tail	None	Bluntly rounded with a minute, sharp terminal process
Internal structures	One-half esophagus, one-half gut with line of demarcation; nonfeeding stage	Remnants of esophagus and gut; nonfeeding feeding stage	None	Pseudofilariform type; nonfeeding stage

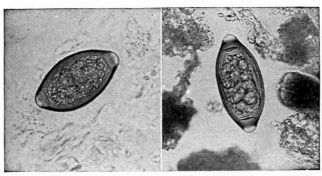

Figure 16–86. Ova of *Trichuris trichiura* in feces (× 500).

ovoid with rounded ends and contain several globular masses in addition to the large granular mass.

The Hookworms

The hookworms, *Ancylostoma duodenale* and *Necator americanus*, account for the diseases ancylostomiasis or uncinariasis and necatoriasis, respectively. *A. duodenale* is called the Old World hookworm, while the latter is called the New World hookworm.

The adult hookworms are small, cylindrical, pinkish-white with a dorsal flexion. The

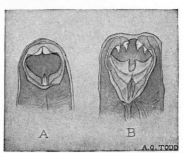

Figure 16–87. Heads of hookworms showing mouth parts. *A, Necator americanus; B, Ancylostoma duodenale.* Since the head of the hookworm is sharply curved backward, the upper part of the figure represents the ventral surface. (After E. R. Stitt.)

683

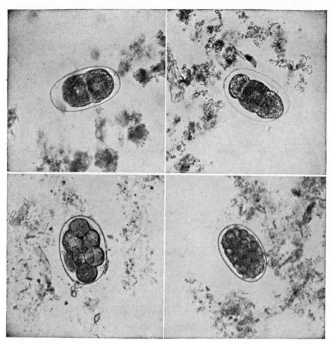

Figure 16–88. Ova of *Necator americanus* in feces. The egg showing three cells is a lateral view of a four-cell stage (× 250).

male worm measures 1 cm. in length and 0.5 mm. in width, while the female is slightly larger. *Ancylostoma* is larger than *Necator*. Males possess a fan-shaped bursa at their posterior end. Spicules are separate in *Ancylostoma* but fused in *Necator*. The shape of the adults is of diagnostic importance, for although there is a curvature of the head in *Ancylostoma*, *Necator* shows a pronounced dorsal flexion, which is hook-like. The buccal capsule reveals diagnostic features. In *Necator* cutting plates are seen in contrast to teeth in *Ancylostoma* (Fig. 16–87).

The ova (Fig. 16–88) of the two genera are identical except for a slight variation in size. *Ancylostoma* ova are 56 to 60 microns in length and 36 to 40 microns in breadth, whereas *Necator* ova are 64 to 76 microns and 36 to 40 microns. These ova, which possess a hyaline shell, are unsegmented or in the four-cell stage when passed in the fresh stool. These must be differentiated from *Trichostrongylus* and *Heterodera* ova. Occasionally larvae may be seen within the ova, especially in stools that have been standing without refrigeration for a few days.

The rhabditiform larvae have a long buccal cavity as evidenced by the position of the esophagus (see Table 16–21). These larvae must be differentiated from those of *Strongyloides, Rhabditis hominis,* and *Trichostrongylus*. Rhabditiform larvae may appear in cultures in a few days, but eight days are required for the filariforms (see Appendix, p. 936). The laboratory worker should be cautious when handling cultures containing the filariform larvae.

The Cestodes

The cestodes or tapeworms are common parasites of man. The adult tapeworms dwell in the small intestine and consist of a family of segments or proglottids, which are attached to the wall by means of suckers or in some instances by hooklets situated on the rostellum of the scolex or head. This chain of segments is called a strobila. Behind the scolex is the neck region from which the worm grows longer. Posterior to the neck one sees immature, mature, and gravid segments, the latter being the oldest and displaying distinctive uterine designs. Segments may be hermaphroditic. Ova in the uterus generally are released by disintegration of the segment but in one genus are expelled through a birth pore.

Tapeworms utilize one or more intermediate hosts in which the larval stage is found. Consumption of the viable larval stage results in infection in man.

Differentiating the tapeworms (Fig. 16–89, 16–90) may be achieved by a study of their ova, segments, and scolices, as the case may be. To study the uterine design of the gravid segment, press the segment between two wide glass slides and hold the segment against a good light source. Segments, which may be passed singly or in chains, are frequently brought to the physician. These should be placed in saline and sent to the laboratory for identification. The scolex, however, remains attached to the intestinal wall and the worm continues to grow. Since the neck region behind the scolex is the source from which the worm grows, it is imperative to search for the head following therapy. The entire post-therapy specimen should be submitted to the laboratory where a search should be made by straining the specimen through a coarse sieve.

Taenia solium is the pork tapeworm, occurring wherever man consumes raw or insufficiently cooked pork, but it is extremely rare in the United States. Infective cysticerci, *Cysticercus cellulosae*, which are small bladders containing a scolex, are found in the pork. Man also may harbor the cysticerci. Extraordinary caution should be taken by the laboratory technologist in handling the adult worm or stools containing *Taenia* ova, since the ova are immediately infective.

The adult worm is 2 to 4 meters in length, and although numerous cysticerci may be swallowed, usually only one worm develops to maturity. The scolex (Fig. 16–90) has four suckers and a rostellum with a double row of 25 to 30 hooklets; therefore, it is an "armed" scolex. The gravid segments (Fig. 16–90) are longer than they are wide and contain a branched uterus. From the main uterine stem 7 to 14 main branches arise on one side only. This number is of diagnostic importance, because it differentiates these segments from those of *T. saginata*. Species diagnosis cannot be made on the basis of ova alone, because the eggs of the taenias are morphologically identical (Fig. 16–89). These

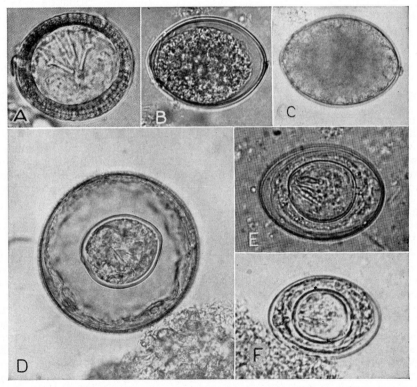

Figure 16–89. Some cestode eggs: A, Human tapeworm, *Taenia sp.* × 750. B, Broad tapeworm of man, *Diphyllobothrium latum.* × 500. C, Broad tapeworm of man, *Diphyllobothrium latum.* × 500. D, Rat tapeworm, *Hymenolepis diminuta.* × 650. E, Dwarf tapeworm, *Hymenolepis nana.* × 750. F, Dwarf tapeworm, *Hymenolepis nana* (note polar filaments). × 750. (Figs. B and F courtesy of Lt. L. W. Shatterly, School of Aviation Medicine, Gunter AFB, Alabama; all others courtesy of Dr. R. L. Roudabush, Ward's Natural Science Establishment, Rochester, New York; photos by T. Romaniak.)

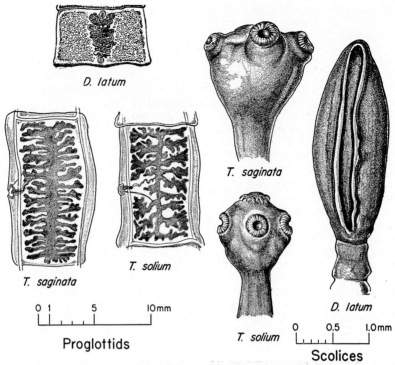

D. latum

T. saginata

T. solium

T. saginata

0 1   5   10mm

Proglottids

T. saginata

T. solium

D. latum

0   0.5   1.0mm

Scolices

Figure 16–90.   Scolices and gravid proglottids of some tapeworms of man. (Mackie, Hunter, and Worth: Manual of Tropical Medicine, 2nd Edition.)

eggs, which are 30 to 40 microns in diameter, are spherical with a thick, radially-striated brown shell that contains a hexacanth onchosphere.

Taenia saginata, the beef tapeworm of man, is commonly found in the United States. This worm may be 4 to 10 meters in length with as many as 2000 segments; thus, it is larger than *T. solium*. Usually only one worm develops to maturity even though many cysticerci may be consumed in raw or insufficiently cooked beef. The scolex (Fig. 16–90) has four suckers but is "unarmed" and about the size of a large pinhead. The gravid segments (Fig. 16–90) are longer than they are wide and are characterized by the presence of 15 to 30 main lateral branches on one side of the uterine stem. The ova (Fig. 16–89) cannot be differentiated from those of *T. solium*. They are, however, infective for cattle but not for man. In the musculature of cattle the larval stage (*Cysticercus bovis*) develops and serves as the source of infection for man (Fig. 16–91).

The dwarf tapeworm, *Hymenolepis nana*, differs from the larger tapeworms in that there may be hundreds of adult worms in a host, whereas only one of the other tapeworms of man develops to maturity.

The adult (Fig. 16–92) is 1 to 4.5 cm. long and 0.4 to 0.7 mm. wide. The "armed" rostellum may be invaginated or evaginated and embraces 24 to 30 hooklets. Segments, which may number 200, are broader than long. Eggs escape only when the segments disintegrate. Characteristic ova (Fig. 16–89) are found by routine stool examination, but in light infections sedimentation is helpful. They are hyaline and nearly spherical and possess a thin outer shell and a hexacanth embryo. From each pole arise four to eight slender filaments or hair-like structures, which spread toward the center over the embryo. Considerable focusing may be necessary to locate these filaments. These eggs are immediately infective; thus, hyperinfection may occur. When swallowed, they hatch in the small intestine, and the onchospheres burrow into the villi where they become cysticercoid larvae. These leave the villi and descend farther down the small intestine where they attach themselves and grow to maturity.

Hymenolepis diminuta, the rat tapeworm, measures 20 to 60 cm. in length and about 4 mm. in width. The scolex is "unarmed" but there are four suckers. The distinctive ova, which measure 56 to 80 microns by 24 to 40 microns (Fig. 16–89) and which may be observed in the stool, are of diagnostic importance. They are broadly oval and brown in color with a thick shell, possessing an outer thickening that is frequently striated. There are no polar filaments but there is an onchosphere.

Dipylidium caninum or the dog tapeworm causes dipylidiasis in man, more particularly in children who may acquire the infection by accidentally ingesting infected fleas from infested pets, such as cats and dogs.

Adult *D. caninum* range from 15 to 70 cm. in length. The scolex is "armed." The mature and gravid proglottids have a bilateral set of reproductive organs and are longer than they are wide. The ova, 36 to 60 microns in diameter, are found in clusters or packets in the stool. Each cluster may have 8 to 25 ova, each ovum containing six hooklets.

Diphyllobothrium latum, the broad fish tapeworm, is the animal parasite causing diphyllobothriasis in man. Man becomes infected upon consuming infected freshwater fish, which are eaten raw or improperly cooked. The adult worms may reach a length of 10 meters with as many as 3000 segments, and generally only one worm develops, although multiple infections are known, in which case the worms are smaller. The "unarmed" scolex (Fig. 16–90) is characteristically spoon-shaped and possesses two slit-like grooves, or bothria, which are placed laterally. The mature and gravid proglottids are broader

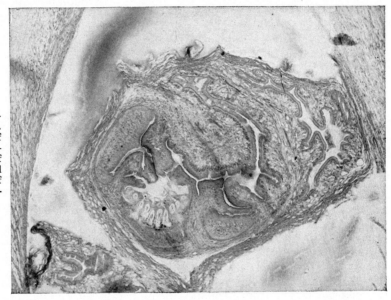

Figure 16–91. Cysticercus of *T. solium* in brain. Note slight tissue reaction of host, rostellar hooks, and laterally placed suckers of parasite. (Hunter, Frye, and Swartzwelder: A Manual of Tropical Medicine, 3rd Edition.)

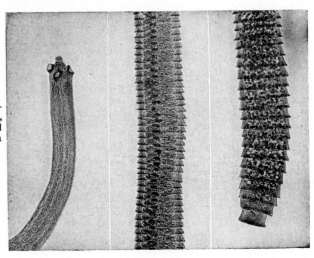

Figure 16–92. Dwarf tapeworm (*Hymenolepis nana*), head, middle segments, and terminal segments. Note the protruded rostellum and the three suckers. From stained and mounted specimens (× 30).

than they are long with a rosette-shaped uterus (Fig. 16–90), which is centrally located. Single segments are seldom seen but chains may be passed. Ova are liberated through a birth pore into the lumen of the intestine to be passed with the feces where they are easily found, although they may be few in number or absent for a time after a large chain of segments has broken off. These ova (Fig. 16–89) with a mass of granules inside measure about 45 to 56 microns and are yellowish-brown in color. An operculum or lid is present and may be observed if sufficient pressure is placed on the coverslip to open it.

The Trematodes

The trematodes or flukes are dorsoventrally flattened, unsegmented worms, which are leaf-like. The majority are hermaphroditic, but the schistosomes or blood flukes are diecious; i.e., there are males and females.

Most adult species have two radially striated suckers, one oral and one ventral (the acetabulum). The digestive tract is incomplete, and most of the body is occupied by organs associated with the reproductive system. Thousands of eggs are found in the uterus.

Diagnosis of most fluke infections depends upon finding their ova (Fig. 16–93) in the feces. The life cycles are complex with one or two intermediate hosts required.

Fasciolopsis buski. *Fasciolopsis buski* is the giant intestinal fluke of man and is found primarily in the duodenal region. Infection in man results from the ingestion of metacercariae from aquatic plants. Bloody diarrhea, severe toxic or obstructive symptoms, or even death may occur in heavy infections. The adults (Fig. 16–94) are 2 to 7.5 cm. in length and 0.8 to 2.0 cm. in width. They may be seen following therapy. The yellowish-brown ova (Fig. 16–93) have a thin shell, a small operculum, and granular contents. They measure 135 by 80 to 85 microns.

Echinostoma ilocanum. The adult flukes of the family to which the *Echinostoma* belong are distinguished by possessing a horseshoe-shaped collar of spines on the dorsal and lateral sides of the oral sucker. The adults (Fig. 16–95) live in the small intestines, and they measure under 1 cm. in length and 0.2 cm. in width. Man becomes infected by consuming raw freshwater snails harboring metacercariae. Diag-

nosis is difficult, because the ova resemble those of other flukes; however, adults can be diagnosed after therapy.

Heterophyes heterophyes and *Metagonimus yokogawai.* The small, oval heterophyid worms are attached to the intestinal wall. *Metagonimus yokogawai* and *Heterophyes heterophyes* measure about 1.4 to 0.6 mm., and the latter possesses a genital sucker in addition to the oral and ventral suckers. Infections in man are acquired through consumption of raw and pickled fish. The yellowish-brown ova (Fig. 16–93) contain a miracidium and an operculum, which is set on opercular shoulders that are thickened. The ova measure 26.5 to 30 by 15 to 17 microns and must be differentiated from *Clonorchis sinensis.*

Clonorchis sinensis. *Clonorchis sinensis* (*Opisthorchis sinensis*) is the Chinese liver fluke of man inhabiting the bile ducts, gallbladder, and pancreatic duct. The adult is 10 to 25 mm. in length and 3 to 5 mm. in width. The light yellowish-brown ova (Fig. 16–93), which measure 29 by 16 microns, are readily found in the feces. They have an operculum and an abopercular, commashaped thickening on the shell and a miracidium inside. These ova must be differentiated from those of *Heterophyes* and *Metagonimus.* Man becomes infected by consuming the metacercariae from raw or insufficiently cooked fresh-water fish. The adult worms may live for many years. Other opisthorchids, such as *O. felineus* and *O. viverrini,* have also been found in man.

Fasciola hepatica. *Fasciola hepatica* (Fig. 16–96), the sheep liver fluke, is 3 cm. by 1.2 cm. and establishes itself in the bile ducts. The characteristic anterior end projects like a cone and is 3 to 4 mm. long. The ova, which appear in the feces, are yellowish-brown, oval, and operculated and measure about 130 to 140 by 76 to 90 microns but cannot be differentiated easily from those of *Fasciolopsis buski* and the echinostomes. Adult worms are seen only at autopsy. Infection in man follows the consumption of metacercariae on aquatic vegetation.

Schistosoma mansoni. Manson's schistosomiasis is caused by the blood fluke, *Schistosoma mansoni,* which has a preference for the smaller branches of the inferior mesenteric vein in the region of the lower colon, but they may be found in other foci also. The males are 1 cm. in length, and the females are 1.6 cm. long (Fig. 16–97). The body of the male is flattened

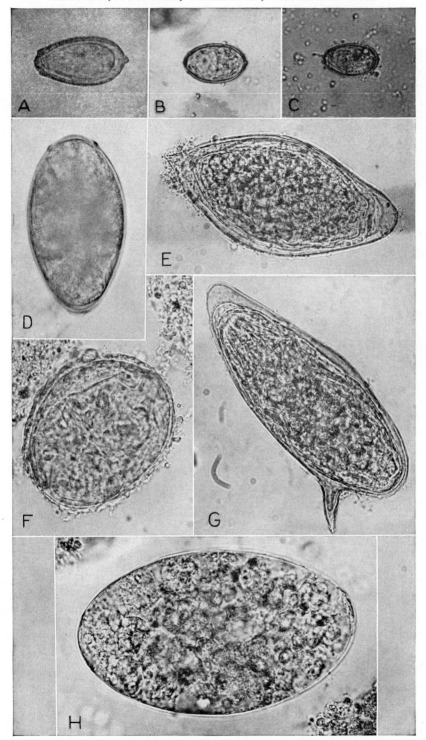

Figure 16–93. Some trematode eggs: A, Chinese liver fluke, *Clonorchis sinensis.* B, *Heterophyes heterophyes.* C, *Metagonimus yokogawai.* D, Lung fluke, *Paragonimus westermani.* E, Vesical blood fluke, *Schistosoma haematobium.* F, Oriental blood fluke, *Schistosoma japonicum.* G, Manson blood fluke, *Schistosoma mansoni.* H, Large intestinal fluke, *Fasciolopsis buski.* All figures × 500 except A, which is × 830. (Fig. A courtesy of Dr. E. C. Faust, in Brenemann: Practice of Pediatrics, W. F. Prior Co. Figs. B and C courtesy of Lt. L. W. Shatterly, MSC, School of Aviation Medicine, Gunter AFB, Alabama. All others courtesy of Dr. R. L. Roudabush, Ward's Natural Science Establishment, Rochester, New York; photos by T. Romaniak.)

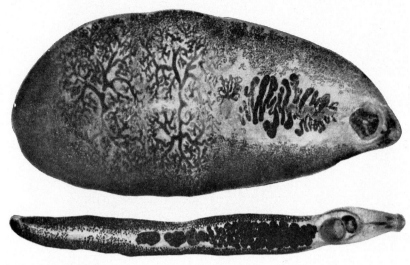

Figure 16–94. Fasciolopsis buski. (Photomicrograph by Zane Price.)

B

Figure 16–95. A, *Echinostoma* sp.; B, anterior end of *Echinostoma* showing circumoral spines. (Photomicrographs by Zane Price.)

with its lateral edges curled ventrally, forming a gynecophoral canal in which the slender female resides. The characteristic ova (Fig. 16–93) appear in the feces and occasionally in urine or may be recovered by rectal biopsy or hepatic puncture. Special concentration or sedimentation techniques (see Appendix, p. 937) on feces may be necessary for diagnosis, because relatively few ova may pass the barrier from the lumen of the venule to the lumen of the intestine in a given time. Each ovum has a conspicuous lateral spine, is yellow in color, contains a ciliated miracidium, and measures 112 to 162 by 60 to 70 microns. Degenerate ova may have the shape of normal ova but contain granules and globules in lieu of the miracidium. Viable ova can be detected by searching for the four beating flame cells (solanocytes) within the miracidium held captive in the egg shell. Diagnosis of the infection or viability of the ova can be determined by egg hatching techniques (see Appendix, p. 937) that allow for the release of the ciliated mira-

cidium, which swims about and can be seen by the naked eye or with a hand lens. Skin tests and serologic tests are also available.

The ova are laid in the lumen of the venules, pass the barrier across the tissues into the lumen of the intestine, and pass out with the feces. The egg is mature when passed and hatches in fresh water, releasing a ciliated miracidium. This miracidium seeks out an appropriate snail host and becomes a mother sporocyst in which daughter sporocysts develop. These forms migrate to the liver of the snail and there give rise to fork-tailed cercariae, which emerge from the snail and swim about ready to penetrate the skin of man. Once through the skin the anterior portions of the cercariae enter the circulatory system and are transported to the specific sites in the body as follows: *S. japonicum*, superior mesenteric venules; *S. mansoni*, inferior mesenteric venules; *S. haematobium*, vesical plexus.

Schistosoma japonicum. Schistosoma

japonicum is the oriental blood fluke, which inhabits the superior mesenteric venules around the small intestine. The males are 2.2 cm. and the females, 2.6 cm. in length. The ova (Fig. 16–93), which contain a miracidium, are more spherical than the other two schistosomes and possess a minute lateral spine, which is very difficult to detect, especially since the surface of the ovum attracts debris that masks the shell. They are 74 to 106 by 55 to 80 microns in size. Egg hatching techniques may reveal motile miracidia. Special concentration or sedimentation techniques may be needed to recover the ova from the feces (see Appendix, p. 937).

Schistosoma haematobium. See genitourinary tract parasites, next section.

Paragonimus westermani. Lung fluke infection in man is caused by *Paragonimus westermani*. The adult worms, which are seldom seen except at autopsy, are reddish-brown in color and thick-bodied, measuring 0.8 to 1.6 cm. in length, 0.4 to 0.8 cm. in width, and 0.3 to 0.5 cm. in thickness. Their yellowish-brown ova (Fig. 16–93) are thick-shelled, operculated with a thick-

ened opercular rim, and measure 80 to 120 by 48 to 60 microns. They may be seen in the sputum or in feces if the sputum is swallowed. Man becomes infected after ingesting raw or insufficiently cooked crabs or crayfish.

Helminths Inhabiting the Genitourinary Tract

Two helminths are known to primarily inhabit the genitourinary tract. They are *Schistosoma haematobium* and the giant kidney worm, *Dioctophyma renale*, which is very rare in man.

Schistosoma haematobium. Bilharziasis or urinary schistosomiasis is caused by *Schistosoma haematobium*, the blood fluke that inhabits the vesical plexus. The male is 10 to 15 mm. long and 1 mm. broad; the female is 2 cm. long. Their yellowish ova (Fig. 16–93) are oval, elongated, and possess a characteristic terminal spine. They measure 120 to 190 by 50 to 73 microns. They may be recovered from urine and less commonly in feces. Sedimentation or centrifugation of a large morning sample of urine may be necessary for the demonstration of the ova. Egg hatching techniques (see Appendix, p. 937) may

Figure 16–96. Fasciola hepatica. (Photomicrograph by Zane Price.)

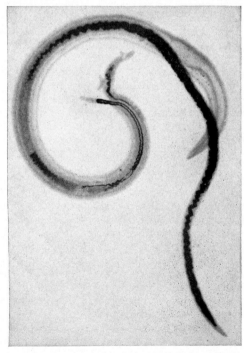

Figure 16–97. Schistosoma mansoni, male and female *in copulo.* (Photomicrograph by Zane Price.)

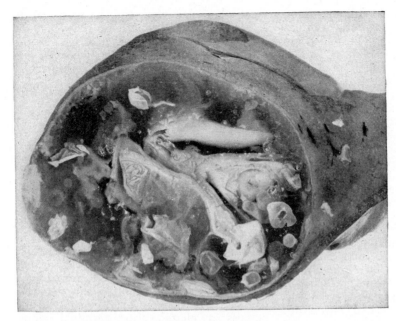

Figure 16–98. Echinococcus granulosus, section through unilocular hydatid cyst containing daughter cysts. (Courtesy of Ash and Spitz, Pathology of Tropical Diseases, Armed Forces Institute of Pathology, No. 31,977.)

reveal motile miracidia. Diagnosis may be made by observing the characteristic ova in urine, by finding ova in the bladder wall biopsy material, or by carrying out intradermal or certain serologic tests.

Dioctophyma renale. *Dioctophyma renale* is the giant kidney worm. Diagnosis is based upon the recovery of the characteristic ova in centrifuged or sedimented urine. These ova are brownish-yellow and barrel shaped with thick shells, which have depressions. They measure 66 by 42 microns. The female, 200 to 1000 by 5 to 12 mm., is a large, reddish worm with a hexagonal mouth encircled by two rings of papillae. The male is smaller and has a terminal bursa with a single spicule. The worm can be recovered at autopsy.

Tissue-inhabiting Helminths

Taenia solium (Cysticercosis). Cysticercosis is the disease in man caused by the larval stage, *Cysticercus cellulosae,* of the tapeworm *Taenia solium.* Thus, man may serve as the intermediate as well as the definitive host of the pork tapeworm. The eggs are infective for man; therefore, there is danger of infection from handling the adult worms or becoming contaminated with feces containing ova.

Ova that are swallowed hatch in the vicinity of the duodenum where the onchospheres penetrate the intestinal wall and enter the blood. From the blood they may be carried to all parts of the body, especially the brain and the eye. The elongate,

ovoid, fluid-filled bladder, 0.6 to 1.8 cm., develops in several months. Inside, a denser spot, the scolex, can be demonstrated. Specific diagnosis may be made following surgical removal of the cysticercus, which in serial section shows hooklets and suckers.

Echinococcus granulosus (Hydatid Disease). Man is not the definitive host of *Echinococcus granulosus.* Dogs harbor the adult worm, usually in great numbers. Man, cattle, and sheep serve as intermediate hosts for the larval stage of hydatid cysts (Fig. 16–98), which cause echinococcosis or hydatid disease.

The adult worm, the smallest of the tapeworms, is 2.5 to 5.0 mm. long and is composed of a scolex and neck and immature, mature and gravid proglottids. The gravid segment contains many ova, which resemble those of *Taenia.* Ova from dog feces reach the digestive system of man where the hexacanth embryos are set free and find their way to the liver, lungs, or other organs in which they slowly develop into hydatid cysts, which vary considerably in size. From the inner layer of the cyst wall brood capsules and daughter cysts bud. Within the former, scolices or "hydatid sand" (Fig. 16–99) bud. Brood capsules with "hydatid sand" inside develop within the daughter cysts. This sand is composed of ovoid organisms, which are 0.2 to 0.3 mm. long and have four lateral suckers and an "armed" rostellum, which may be invaginated or evaginated. This type of hydatid is known as the unilocular cyst. Two other types may occur: the alveolar or multilocular, and the osseous, which involves the bones. Some cysts may be sterile, i.e., without the "hydatid sand."

Laboratory diagnosis may be made by finding the scolices, brood capsules, or daughter cysts in the cysts after surgical removal. Skin testing and x-ray are also aids in diagnosis.

Multiceps multiceps (**Coenurus Disease**). *Multiceps multiceps* adult worms are found in dogs and the larval stage (coenurus), in cattle, sheep, and man. The disease is known as coenurosis.

Ingested ova hatch in the small intestine where the onchosphere penetrates the intestinal wall, enters the circulation, and migrates to various sites in the body, particularly the central nervous system. The embryo transforms into a bladder-type worm, the coenurus, which differs from a cysticercus by possessing multiple heads invaginated from the wall into the bladder cavity. Diagnosis is made at autopsy.

Sparganosis. Man may acquire the sparganum, the larval stage of a species of *Diphyllobothrium*, by ingestion of the infected fresh-water copepod *Diaptomus*; by ingesting raw infected flesh of certain frogs, snakes, and birds; or by applying a poultice of infected flesh of frogs on open wounds or the eye.

The sparganum, which can be removed by surgery, is distinguished by its elongated ribbon shape with no transverse segmentation but with a pseudosucker and no scolex. The living sparganum elongate and contract like typical tapeworms.

Onchocerciasis. Onchocerciasis is a dis-

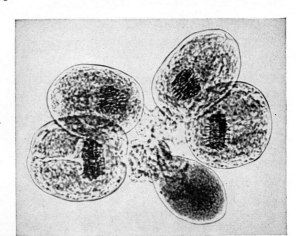

Figure 16–99. *Echinococcus granulosus*, hydatid sand. (Photomicrograph by Zane Price.)

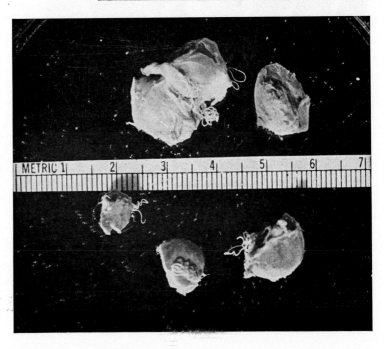

Figure 16–100. *Onchocerca volvulus* nodules. Portions of contained adult worms protruding. (Photograph by Zane Price.)

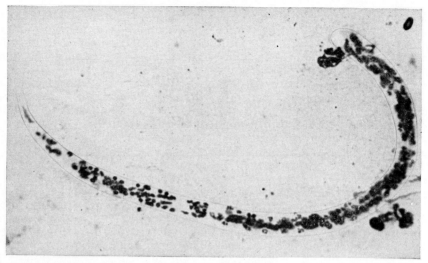

Figure 16–101. Onchocerca volvulus, microfilaria from scarification preparation. (Photomicrograph by Zane Price.)

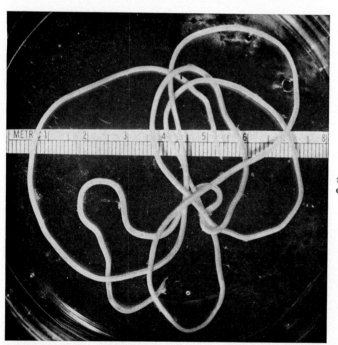

Figure 16–102. Dracunculus medinensis, female worm removed surgically. (Photograph by Zane Price.)

ease in which the adult filarial parasite, *Onchocerca volvulus,* is found in the skin and other tissue where it may produce fibrous nodules. Within the nodule (Fig. 16–100) are the cream-white colored adults. The female may be 35 to 50 cm. long and 0.5 mm. or less in diameter, while the males are smaller. The microfilariae leave the nodule and migrate in the skin. They do not appear in peripheral circulation. Specific diagnosis rests upon finding the characteristic unsheathed microfilariae (Fig. 16–101) by means of scarification smears or skin biopsy.

Dracunculus medinensis. *Dracunculus medinensis* is the guinea worm of man. The worm (Fig. 16–102) is elongated and cylindrical with males 2 cm. or less in length and females 70 to 120 cm. in length and 0.9 to 117 mm. in diameter. The mature females develop in body cavities and migrate when gravid into subcutaneous tissues. The larvae (Fig. 16–103) are released from a blister formed on the skin and are

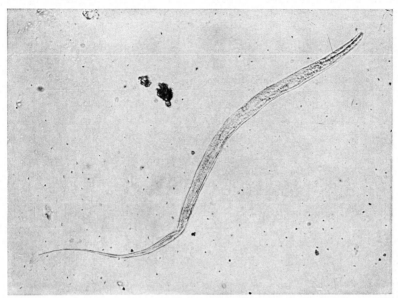

Figure 16–103. Larva of *D. medinensis* as discharged from cutaneous lesions; note long tapering tail. (Mackie, Hunter, and Worth: Manual of Tropical Medicine, 2nd Edition.)

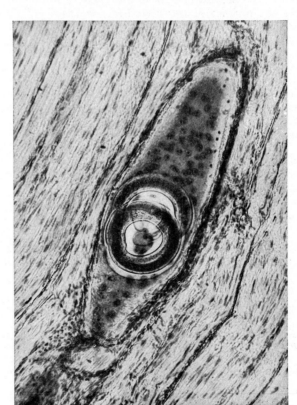

Figure 16–104. *Trichinella spiralis,* larva in muscle. (Photomicrograph by Zane Price.)

discharged from the lesion into water in which copepods live. Man gets the infection by ingesting infected copepods. Larvae may be recovered from the ulcer, but adult worms are recovered by surgical intervention or by slowly winding them on sticks each day until they have been completely removed.

Trichinella spiralis. *Trichinella spiralis* is the trichina worm responsible for producing the disease known as trichinosis, trichiniasis, or trichinelliasis. The adult worms inhabit the small intestine where the females give birth to living larvae, which migrate to the skeletal muscles of the body after entering the circulatory system. The larvae coil themselves in the muscle fibers and become encapsulated (Fig. 16–104) and eventually the capsule becomes calcified.

Man becomes infected after the consumption of insufficiently cooked or raw pork or pork products containing encapsulated larvae. Pigs are infected from uncooked garbage. When the infected meat is ingested by humans, the ingested encapsulated larvae are released and penetrate into the mucosa of the intestine and there develop into adults in several days. The adult males measure 2 mm. or less with a breadth of 0.04 mm., while the females are 2 to 4 mm. long and 0.06 mm. wide. These adults may be observed microscopically in the stools of patients with diarrhea during the first few weeks of the infection. They live in the intestine about eight weeks before they die.

The diagnosis in humans usually rests upon the history of having eaten improperly prepared pork and also upon clinical symptoms. Specific diagnosis may be made by muscle biopsy of skeletal muscles, such as the deltoid, biceps, or gastrocnemius. Skin tests and serologic tests are of distinct aid in diagnosis (see p. 814).

Visceral Larva Migrans

The disease known as visceral larva migrans may develop in children following the consumption of ova of the dog and cat ascarids, *Toxocara canis* and *T. cati*. The ova hatch in the intestine, and the larvae migrate into such organs as the liver, lungs, brain, and eye. Specific diagnosis is made by finding the larvae in biopsy material from the liver. One may suspect this condition in a dirt-eating child with a history of contact with infected dogs or cats and manifesting hepatomegaly, chronic nonspecific pulmonary disease, and high eosinophilia. Serologic tests using a purified worm antigen are available.

Cutaneous Larva Migrans

Creeping eruption results from the migration of the larvae of dog and cat hookworms, *Ancylostoma braziliense* and *A. caninum*, in the epidermis of man. The larvae are in moist, sandy soil, such as beach areas, along the Florida and Gulf Coast areas. Diagnosis is based upon the observation of the characteristic tunnel-like lesions following exposure.

Blood Helminths

The filariae are long thread-like nema-

Table 16–22. **Differential Characteristics of Filarial Worms in Man**

FILARIA	GEOGRAPHICAL DISTRIBUTION	VECTOR	ADULT SITE IN BODY	PERIODICITY	MICROFILARIAE LOCATION	SHEATH	NUCLEUS
Wuchereria bancrofti	Tropical and subtropical areas	Mosquito	Lymphatic system, lower extremities	Nocturnal with most strains	Peripheral blood	Yes	No nuclei to the tip of tail
Wuchereria malayi	Southern Asia; East Indies	Mosquito	Lymphatic system, upper extremities	Nocturnal	Peripheral blood	Yes	Two nuclei to tip of tail
Loa loa	Africa	*Chrysops* fly	Wandering in subcutaneous tissues and across the eyeball	Diurnal (daytime)	Peripheral blood	Yes	Nuclei to the tip of the tail
Acanthocheilonema perstans	Africa; South America	*Culicoides*	Body cavities; mesentery; perirenal and retroperitoneal tissies	None	Peripheral blood	No	Nuclei to the tip of tail
Mansonella ozzardi	Africa; South America	*Culicoides*	Body cavities; mesentery	None	Peripheral blood	No	No nuclei to tip of tail
Onchocerca volvulus	Africa; Central and South America	*Simulium*	Subcutaneous tissues	None	Lymph spaces of skin; subcutaneous nodules; rarely in peripheral blood	No	No nuclei to tip of tail

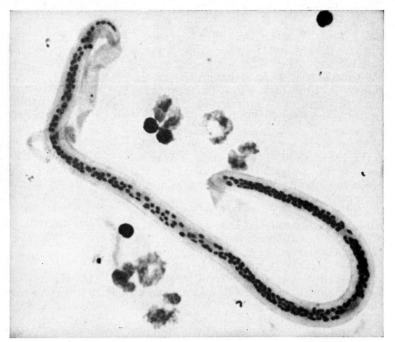

Figure 16–105. Microfilaria of *Wuchereria bancrofti* in thick blood film. (Photomicrograph by Zane Price.)

todes that usually are diagnosed by the isolation of the microfilariae from peripheral blood. The adult worms are in various sites in the body (Table 16–22). Figure 16–106 shows the differential features of the main species of microfilariae seen in man.

Wuchereria bancrofti causes Bancroftian filariasis or wuchereriasis. The adults are located in the lymphatics where they are tightly coiled. The males measure 2.5 to 4.0 cm. and the females 5 to 10 cm. in length. The females produce microfilariae 200 to 245 microns long that are sheathed (Fig. 16–105); the sheath is actually the egg membrane. These microfilariae do not have nuclei to the tip of the tail.

The microfilariae of this species tend to exhibit nocturnal periodicity. That is to say, the greatest number of organisms may be recovered from the peripheral circulation at night, usually between 10:00 p.m. and 2:00 a.m. There is a nonperiodic type, however.

Specific diagnosis may be made by finding the adult worm or microfilariae in material from biopsy or the microfilariae in peripheral blood, either in thick films or by concentration methods. Serologic and skin tests are available also.

Wuchereria malayi is incriminated in the disease called Malayan filariasis. The adult worms are similar to *W. bancrofti*, but the sheathed microfilariae, 175 to 230 microns,

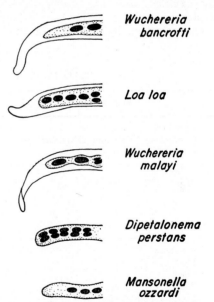

Wuchereria bancrofti

Loa loa

Wuchereria malayi

Dipetalonema perstans

Mansonella ozzardi

Figure 16–106. Differentiation of the species of microfilariae found in the human blood on the basis of posterior ends of the larvae. Note the distribution of nuclei, their presence or absence in the extreme caudal portion, and the presence or absence of a sheath. (Markell and Voge: Diagnostic Techniques in Medical Parasitology.)

that appear in peripheral blood do have body nuclei to the tip of the tail with the two distal nuclei distinctly separated from the others (Fig. 16–106).

Loiasis is caused by *Loa loa*, which is

commonly called the African eye worm. Males measure 30 mm. long, and the females are 70 mm. They live in subcutaneous tissues but migrate and produce raised areas called Calabar swellings. As the worms pass across the bridge of the nose or in front of the eyeball, they cause much discomfort. The microfilariae (Fig. 16–106) may be found in the peripheral blood in the daytime as sheathed forms, which possess a continuous row of nuclei to the tip of the tail. Frequently it may be years after the Calabar swellings or the adults are observed before microfilariae are recovered.

Adults of the persistent filaria, *Acanthocheilonema perstans* or *Dipetalonema perstans*, are found in various body cavities. The microfilariae (Fig. 16–106), which show no periodicity and which are found unsheathed in peripheral blood, are about 200 microns long and 4.5 microns wide. They are characterized by having nuclei that extend to the tip of the tail.

Mansonella ozzardi adults also inhabit body cavities, and the unsheathed, nonperiodic microfilariae (Fig. 16–106), which are characterized by the lack of nuclei to the tip of the tail, are found in peripheral blood.

ARTHROPODS OF MEDICAL IMPORTANCE

Arthropods are multicellular, segmented invertebrates that have a chitinous exoskeleton and paired articulated appendages. This is the largest phylum in the animal kingdom. Many species are of medical importance, for they may cause human disease, transmit pathogenic microorganisms to man as mechanical vectors, or act as biologic vectors when they serve as an essential host for a part of the life cycle of certain animal parasites (see Table 16–23).

Class Arachnida

This class is characterized by the following: forms with body divided into cephalothorax and abdomen; adults with four pairs of legs; absence of antennae and wings; and respiration by gills, booklungs, or tracheae or through cuticle. The most important members of this class are scorpions, spiders, ticks, and mites.

Table 16–23. Diseases Transmitted by Arthropods

VECTOR	DISEASE TRANSMITTED
CRUSTACEA	
Copepod—*Cyclops* and *Diaptomus*	*D. latum* infection; guinea worm
Crayfish and crabs	*P. westermani* infection
ARACHNIDA	
Mites	Tsutsugamushi fever (scrub typhus); rickettsial pox
Ticks	Tularemia; Russian spring-summer encephalitis; Q fever; Colorado tick fever; Rocky Mountain spotted fever
INSECTA	
Lice	Epidemic typhus; relapsing fever; trench fever
Fleas	Plague; murine typhus; *Dipylidium caninum* infection
Bugs	Chagas's disease (American trypanosomiasis)
Beetles (some species)	*Hymenolepis diminuta* infection
Blood sucking flies	
Phlebotomus (sand fly)	Leishmaniasis; pappataci fever; bartonellosis
Glossina (tsetse fly)	African trypanosomiasis
Simulium (black fly)	Onchocerciasis
Culicoides (midge, gnat)	*Acanthocheilonema perstans* and *Mansonella ozzardi* infections
Chrysops (deer fly)	Loiasis; tularemia
Culex mosquito	Filariasis; viral encephalitides
Anopheles mosquito	Malaria; Bancroftian filariasis; Malayan filariasis
Aedes mosquito	Yellow fever; dengue; viral encephalitides; Bancroftian filariasis
Mansonia mosquito	Malayan filariasis

Scorpions. Scorpions (Fig. 16–107) sting their prey and introduce neurotoxic venom by means of their caudal stinger. An ascending paralysis may be accompanied by respiratory failure, especially in children. The adult scorpions occur in and around houses in warm moist or dry areas and are nocturnal or hide themselves in dark places.

Spiders. The black widow spider, *Latrodectus mactans* (Fig. 16–108), is the best known of the poisonous spiders and is widely distributed throughout the western hemisphere.

The adult female *L. mactans* is a lustrous black on its dorsal surface, and a diagnostic red spot, which usually resembles an hourglass, appears on the midventural surface.

The spherical abdomen gives the spider the appearance of a shoebutton, a name by which it is sometimes called.

The spider inhabits trash piles, outhouses, hollow stumps, lumber piles, cellars, and garages. The females are about 13 mm. in length, and the males are about half this size.

Arachnidism (spider poisoning). As the spider bites the human victim, the toxin is injected into the skin. Within one hour severe pain develops with redness and swelling at the site of the bite. Abdominal cramps develop followed by pains in the muscles of the legs, chest, and back. In time, marked board-like rigidity develops. These acute symptoms may persist for 12 to 48 hours. Accompanying the muscu-

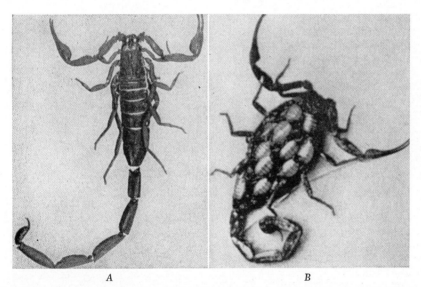

A   B

Figure 16–107. *A*, Male specimen of scorpion (*Centruroides*). × 1. (After C. C. Hoffmann, Anat. del Inst. de Biol., Mexico, from Faust, in Brennemann's Practice of Pediatrics; courtesy of W. F. Prior Company.) *B*, *Centruroides sculpturatus*, female with newly born young. × 1. (After Stahnke, Turtox News; courtesy of General Biological Supply House.)

Figure 16–108. Black widow spiders, *Latrodectus mactans.*

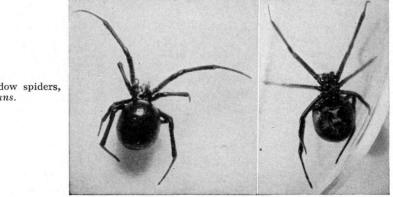

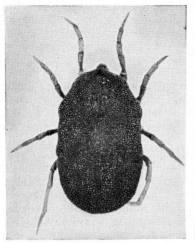 

Figure 16–109. Ornithodoros parkeri. Ticks of this genus are vectors of relapsing fever caused by *Borrelia.* (Courtesy of R. A. Cooley.)

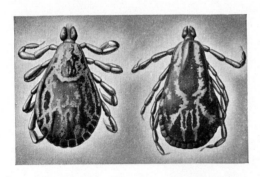

Figure 16–110. Dermacentor andersoni and *Dermacentor variabilis;* vectors of Rocky Mountain spotted fever rickettsias. (Courtesy Sharp & Dohme, Inc.)

lar rigidity one may observe excessive perspiration, nausea, vomiting, headache, elevated temperature and blood pressure, and leukocytosis. Some cases are fatal. Specific antivenin is available.

Ticks. Ticks differ from mites in the following ways: they are larger; have no hairs; have a leathery integument; and have an exposed, armed hypostome and a pair of legs. There are soft-bodied ticks (*Argasidae*) (Fig. 16–109) and hard-bodied ticks (*Ixodidae*) (Fig. 16–110).

The soft-bodied ticks have no hard plate on the dorsum, the mouthparts are ventral to the anterior end, and the spiracles are behind the third pair of coxal segments. The hard-bodied ticks possess a dorsal plate, which is anterior only in the female but covers the entire dorsum in the male. The mouthparts extend beyond the anterior portion; and the spiracles are located behind the fourth pair of coxal segments.

Certain *Ornithodoros* species, soft-bodied ticks, are important vectors of endemic relapsing fever, and hard-bodied ticks may

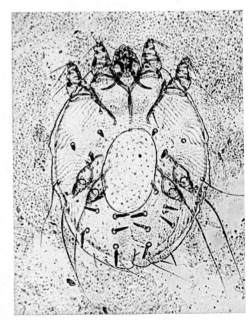

Figure 16–111. Sarcoptes scabiei, adult female. (Photomicrograph by Zane Price.)

transmit rickettsiae, viruses, and bacteria. The rickettsial diseases transmitted are Rocky Mountain spotted fever, Q fever, fièvre boutonneuse, and tick typhus. Viral diseases transmitted are Russian spring-summer encephalitis and Colorado tick fever. Tularemia, a bacterial disease, is also transmitted. *Dermacentor andersoni*, a hard-bodied tick, is the chief vector of Rocky Mountain spotted fever.

Ticks may harm man by mechanical in-

jury of their bites, by transmission of micro-organisms, and by tick paralysis.

Tick paralysis. This disease occurs mostly in young children and is characterized by an ascending flaccid paralysis. The tick is attached to the body, usually near the base of the brain or along the spinal column. The disease has a rapid onset and death may occur. Removal of the tick usually results in gradual recession of paralysis and abatement of symptoms.

Mites. Mites are smaller and longer than ticks and do not have a leathery integument. The hypostome, if present, may be without teeth. On the cephalothorax of some mites spiracles are present. Mites serve as vectors of certain human diseases. They may penetrate the skin directly, causing injury, as in scabies.

Sarcoptes scabiei, the itch mite (Figs. 16–111, 16–112), is cosmopolitan in its distribution and causes a disease known as scabies or sarcoptic mange in man. The female is about 0.5 mm. in length, and the male is smaller. The adults tunnel in the superficial layers of the skin (Fig. 16–113),

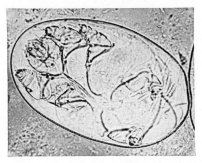

Figure 16–112.   *Sarcoptes scabiei* egg containing fully developed larva. (Photomicrograph by Zane Price.)

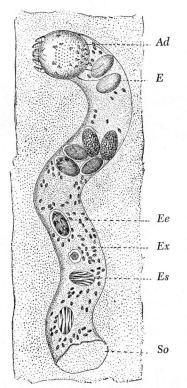

Figure 16–113.   *Sarcoptes scabiei.* Diagram of a subcutaneous burrow; *Ad,* adult female; *E,* eggs; *Ee,* embryo egg; *Ex,* excrement; *Es,* egg shell; *So,* skin orifice. (After Railliet in Brumpt.)

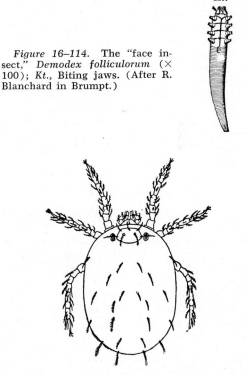

Figure 16–114.   The "face insect," *Demodex folliculorum* (× 100); *Kt.,* Biting jaws. (After R. Blanchard in Brumpt.)

Figure 16–115.   The North American chigger, *Trombicula irritans* (larva, × 100). (Ewing, A Manual of External Parasites, Charles C Thomas.)

producing lesions. These lesions are located in the soft folds of the body in areas such as the interdigital spaces, flexor surfaces of the wrists and forearms, popliteal folds, inguinal region, and the back, although other areas except the head may be involved. An intense itching develops from the minute vesicles. Scratching introduces secondary bacterial invasion with scab formation. The parasite and its eggs may be removed from the tunnel by needle or skin scrapings, which are placed in 20 per cent potassium hydroxide for clearing and are examined under the low power field. Suspected areas may be examined by the use of hand lens before scrapings are made.

Demodex folliculorum, the follicular mite (Fig. 16–114), parasitizes the hair follicles or sebaceous glands. In man it produces mild dermatitis, which may be evidenced by acne, blackheads, and keratosis. Material from the glands may be examined under the low power objective. The female is larger than the male, which measures 40 to 300 microns.

Trombiculid mites. (Fig. 16–115). Eight-legged adults of the trombiculid mites do not parasitize man; however, the six-legged larvae attack man, producing a severe dermatitis.

Eutrombicula alfreddugèsi is called the red bug, chigger, or harvest mite. These mites infest grasses and bushes, particularly berry bushes, and attack man as he brushes against these infested objects. They burrow into the skin, causing intense itching. The larvae are just visible to the unaided eye.

Trombicula akamushi and other related species produce larvae that transmit tsutsugamushi fever or scrub typhus, a rickettsial disease.

Class Insecta

Insects, also called hexapoda, are characterized by having a body divided into head, thorax, and abdomen. There are three pairs of legs. Usually two pairs of wings are present, but there are some species without them.

Lice. Human lice are distinctively flattened dorsoventrally and are wingless with piercing sucking mouthparts. The three species of lice that parasitize man are: *Pediculus humanus* var. *capitis* (Fig. 16–116), *Pediculus humanus* var. *corporis*, and *Phthirus pubis* (Fig. 16–117).

The head louse, *P. humanus* var. *capitis*, lays its eggs or nits on the hairs. Their

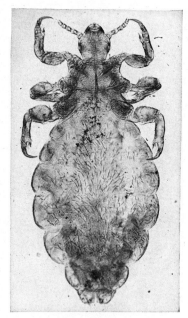

Figure 16–116. *Pediculus humanus.* (Photomicrograph by Zane Price.)

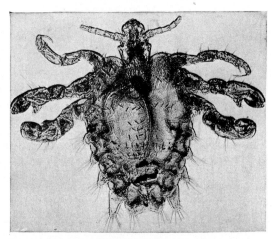

Figure 16–117. *Phthirus pubis.* (Courtesy of Army Medical Museum.)

claws are designed for clasping fine hairs of the head. The adults are 2 to 3mm. long. *P. humanus* var. *corporis* lays its eggs in seams of woolen clothing and visits the host for a blood meal. *Phthirus pubis*, the crab louse, on the other hand, has claws designed for clasping the coarse hairs of the pubic region and axilla, the eyebrows, and the chest hairs. The adult is shorter and broader than *Pediculus*, because the abdomen is more compressed.

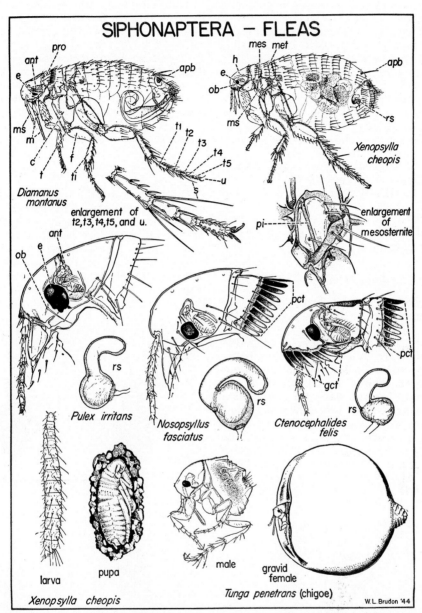

Figure 16–118. Siphonaptera. Certain characters used in identification: *ant*, antenna; *apb*, antepygidial bristle; *c*, coxa; *e*, eye; *f*, femur; *gct*, genal ctenidium; *h*, head; *m*, mouth parts; *ms*, maxillary palpus; *mes*, mesothorax; *met*, metathorax; *ms*, mesosternite; *ob*, ocular bristle; *pct*, pronotal ctenidium; *pi*, perpendicular incrassation of mesosternite; *pro*, pronotum; *rs*, receptaculum seminis; *s*, spine at tip of second tarsus; *t*, trochanter; *ti*, tibia; *t1* to *t5*, tarsus 1, 2, 3, 4, 5; *u*, ungues. (Hunter, Frye, and Swartzwelder: A Manual of Tropical Medicine, 3rd Edition.)

When man is infested with lice, the condition is referred to as pediculosis, which in sensitized individuals may be severe. Body lice are vectors of such diseases as epidemic typhus, trench fever, and relapsing fever.

Fleas. Fleas are bloodsucking, wingless, brown, laterally compressed ectoparasites with hind legs developed for jumping. The adults vary from 1.5 to 4 mm. in length (Fig. 16–118).

Salivary secretions of the flea may produce a lesion at the site of the bite. Fleas also serve as vectors of plague and endemic typhus and may mechanically spread bacterial and viral disease.

A flea of tropical America and Africa, *Tunga penetrans* or the chigoe flea is exceptional in that it burrows into the skin of the feet.

Xenopsylla cheopis, the tropical rat flea, is incriminated as one of the important vectors of plague.

The Bugs (Hemiptera)

Only two families of bugs are of any medical importance, the bedbugs and Reduviidae.

The bedbugs, *Cimex lectularius* (Fig. 16–119), frequently bite man, causing irritation. They infest houses, hotels, and tenement houses, hiding in furniture, floors, and walls during the day and coming out to feed at night. They are brown, flattened, oval insects without wings. The area of the bite may produce swelling, itching, and scratching and may produce secondary bacterial invasion. The bedbug may act as a mechanical transmitter of disease. However, there is no evidence of biologic transmission, although they have been observed experimentally as carriers of pathogenic organisms.

The Reduviidae are the kissing bugs. The reduviid bugs or "cone-nose bugs" (Fig. 16–120) feed on blood, and certain species are responsible for the transmission of Chagas's disease, which is caused by the hemoflagellate, *Trypanosoma cruzi*. One outstanding species is *Panstrongylus megistus* (*Triatoma magista*). The bite of the bug is not always painful. The infective stage of *T. cruzi* is deposited with the feces, and the puncture wound becomes contaminated.

Mosquitoes and Flies

The Diptera are the true flies and include mosquitoes and flies. They usually have two wings with the halteres as the second pair. The mouthparts are adapted for sucking and in some instances for piercing.

Mosquitoes are flies that are slender and delicate. Those that suck blood play an important role in the transmission of human diseases, such as malaria, filariasis,

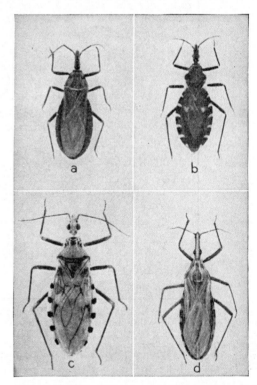

Figure 16–120. Four species of Reduviidae. (*a*) *Triatoma protracta.* (*b*) *Triatoma sanguisuga.* (*c*) *Panstrongylus geniculatus.* (*d*) *Mestor pallescens.* (Herms: Medical Entomology, by permission of The Macmillan Company.)

Figure 16–119. The common bedbug, *Cimex lectularius*, male (× 5). In the female the posterior end of the abdomen is more rounded. (Cleared with sodium hydroxide to bring out the structure more clearly.)

dengue, yellow fever, and some of the encephalitides. The mosquitoes can be differentiated from other flies by the presence of scales on the wings and a proboscis, which is adapted for piercing and sucking. The antennae are long with 15 joints.

Many species of the several genera of mosquitoes serve as vectors of human diseases. The genera incriminated are *Anopheles, Culex, Aedes,* and *Mansonia.* Differential diagnosis is based upon many varied morphologic structures, details of which can be found in textbooks on entomology. The principal differences between culicine and anopheline mosquitoes are shown in Figs. 16–121 and 16–122.

The Nonbloodsucking Flies. The nonbloodsucking flies are the filth flies, which have fleshy mouthparts adapted for sucking liquids. The adult flies may be mechanical transmitters of disease, but the larvae may invade the broken or unbroken skin or develop from ingested fly eggs to produce a condition known as myiasis (see Fig. 16–123).

Specific myiasis. Eggs or larvae from certain filth flies are deposited on the tissues of the specific host, and the larva becomes parasitic as it invades the area. Examples of flies that produce this type of myiasis are the screwworm, *Calliphora (Cochliomyia) americana* and *C. macellaria;* the botfly, *Dermatobia hominis;* the sheep botfly, *Oestrus ovis;* the cattle botfly, *Hypoderma;* and *Gasterophilus.*

Semispecific myiasis. Eggs or larvae of the semispecific flies are deposited in rotting vegetable matter or in open wounds and sores.

Accidental myiasis. Eggs of the accidental myiasis-producing flies are laid in feces or decaying organic matter or on food. Man becomes infected by ingestion of the eggs or larvae or by contamination of wounds. Examples are *Musca domestica* and *Fannia.*

Figure 16–121. Heads of *Culex* (*Culex pipiens*) showing the straight proboscis, the jointed palpi, and external to these the hairy antennae. The male is distinguished from the female by the longer hairs on the antennae. Note that the palpi of the male are about as long as the proboscis, while those of the female are very much shorter (compare with Fig. 16–122).

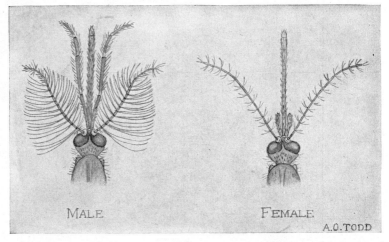

Figure 16–122. Heads of *Anopheles* (*Anopheles maculipennis*). The sexes are distinguished by the antennae as noted under Fig. 16–121. The palpi of *Anopheles* are nearly the same length as the proboscis in both sexes.

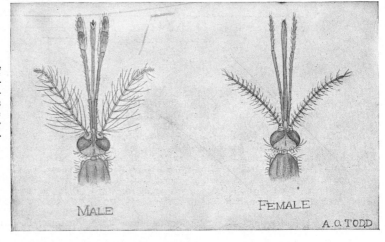

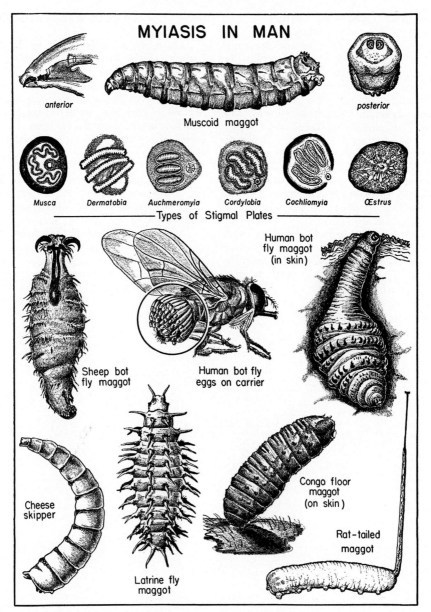

Figure 16–123. Dipterous larvae causing myiasis in man. (Hunter, Frye, and Swartzwelder: A Manual of Tropical Medicine, 3rd Edition.)

REFERENCES

1. Aiken, M. A., Work, M. K., and King, E. O.: A study of a group of gram negative bacteria resembling the tribe Mimeae (De Bord). Pub. Health Lab., *14:*126–136, 1956.
2. Alston, J. M., and Broom, J. C.: Leptospirosis in Man and Animals. Baltimore, The Williams & Wilkins Company, 1958.
3. Bang, F. B., Hairston, N. G., Graham, O. H., and Ferguson, M. S.: Studies on *schistosomiasis japonica.* II. Methods of surveying for *schistosomiasis japonica.* Am. J. Hyg., *44:* 315–323, 1946.
4. Barber, M., and Kuper, S. W. A.: Identification of *Staphylococcus pyogenes* by the phosphatase reaction. J. Path. & Bact., 63:65–68, 1951.
5. Bearn, A. G., Jacobs, K., and McCarty, M.: *Pasteurella multocida* septicemia in man. Am. J. Med., *18:*167–168, 1955.
6. Beaver, P. C.: The detection and identification of some common nematode parasites of man. Am. J. Clin. Path., 22:481–494, 1952.
7. Beaver, P. C.: Larva migrans. Exper. Parasitol., 5:587–621, 1956.
8. Belding, D. L.: Textbook of Clinical Parasitology. 2nd Ed. New York, Appleton-Century-Crofts, Inc., 1952.
9. Belding, D. L.: Basic Clinical Parasitology.

New York, Appleton-Century-Crofts, Inc., 1958.

10. Bickerstaff, E. R.: Cerebral cysticercosis. Common but unfamiliar manifestations. Brit. Med. J., 1:1055–1058, 1955.

11. Bowers, E. F., and Jeffries, L. J.: Optochin in the identification of Strep. pneumoniae. J. Clin. Path., 8:58–60, 1955.

12. Breed, R. S., Murray, E. G. D., and Smith, N. R.: Bergey's Manual of Determinative Bacteriology. 7th Ed. Baltimore, The Williams & Wilkins Company, 1957.

13. Brug, S. L.: Endamoeba williamsi; the amoeboid form of the iodine cysts. Indian J. Med. Res., 6:386–395, 1919.

14. Buhler, V. B., and Pollak, A.: Human infection with atypical acid fast organisms. Am. J. Clin. Path., 23:363–374, 1953.

15. Burrows, R. B., Swerdlow, M. A., Frost, J. R., and Leeper, C. K.: Pathology of Dientamoeba fragilis infections of the appendix. Am. J. Trop. Med. & Hyg., 3:1033–1039, 1954.

16. Burrows, R. B.: Endamoeba hartmanni. Am. J. Hyg., 65:172–188, 1957.

17. Burrows, W.: Textbook of Microbiology. 17th Ed. Philadelphia, W. B. Saunders Company, 1959.

18. Cadness-Graves, B., Williams, R., Harper, G. J., and Miles, A. A.: Slide test for coagulase-positive Staphylococci. Lancet, 1:736–738, 1943.

19. Carter, B., Jones, C. P., Alter, R. L., Creadrek, R. N., and Thomas, W. L.: Bacteriodes infections in obstetrics and gynecology. Am. J. Obst. & Gynec., 1:491–510, 1953.

20. Carter, C. H., and Liese, J. H.: Specific staining of various bacteria with a single fluorescent antiglobulin. J. Bact., 76:152–154, 1958.

21. Cary, S. G., Lindberg, R. B., and Faber, S. E.: Slide agglutination technique for the rapid differentiation of Mima polymorpha and Herellea from the Neisseria. J. Bact., 75:43–45, 1958.

22. Clark, W. M., and Cowan, S. T.: Biochemical methods for bacteriology. J. Gen. Microbiol., 6:187–197, 1952.

23. Coons, A. H., Creech, H. J., and Jones, R. N.: Immunological properties of an antibody containing a fluorescent group. Proc. Soc. Exper. Biol. & Med., 47:200–202, 1941.

24. Coons, A. H., and Kaplan, M. H.: Localization of antigen in tissue cells. II. Improvements in a method for the detection of antigen by means of fluorescent antibody. J. Exper. Med., 91:1–13, 1950.

25. Cooper, G. N.: The prolonged survival of upper respiratory tract and intestinal pathogens on swabs. J. Clin. Path., 10:226–230, 1957.

26. Cox, C. D., and Larsen, A. D.: Colonial growth of Leptospirae. J. Bact., 73:587–589, 1957.

27. Dack, G. M.: Food Poisoning. 3rd Ed. Chicago, University of Chicago Press, 1956.

28. Dobell, C.: The Amoebae Living in Man—A Zoological Monograph. London, Bale Sons and Danielson, Ltd., 1919.

29. Dobell, C., and Jepps, M. W.: A study of the diverse races of Entamoeba histolytica distinguishable from one another by the dimensions of their cysts. Parasitology, 10:320–330, 1918.

30. Dubos, R. J.: Bacterial and Mycotic Infections of Man. 3rd Ed. Philadelphia, J. B. Lippincott Company, 1958.

31. Dubos, R. J., and Middlebrook, G.: Cytochemi-

cal reaction of virulent tubercle bacilli. Am. Rev. Tuberc., 56:698–699, 1948.

32. Dwork, K. G., Rossien, A. X., and Friedman, D.: The diminutive Endamoeba histolytica; A review of the literature of small race amebas with additional notes based on a recent survey. Mississippi Valley Med. J., 77:113–117, 1955.

33. Edelman, M. H., and Spingam, C. L.: Clonorchiasis in the United States. J.A.M.A., 140:1147–1150, 1949.

34. Edwards, P. R., and Ewing, W. A.: Identification of Enterobacteriaceae. Minneapolis, Burgess Publishing Company, 1955.

35. Edwards, P. R., Fife, M. A., and Ewing, W. H.: Newer biochemical methods in the recognition of Shigellae and Salmonellae. Am. J. Med. Tech., 22:28–35, 1956.

36. Edwards, P. R., McWhorter, A. C., and Fife, M. A.: The Arizona group of Enterobacteriaceae. Occurrence and distribution. Bull. World Health Org., 14:511–528, 1956.

37. Elek, S. D.: Staphylococcus pyogenes and its relation to disease. Edinburgh, E. & S. Livingston, Ltd., 1959.

38. Ewing, W. H.: Enteropathogenic Escherichia coli serotypes. Ann. N.Y. Acad. Sc., 66:61–70, 1956.

39. Faust, E. C.: Human Helminthology. 3rd Ed. Philadelphia, Lea & Febiger, 1949.

40. Faust, E. C., Ingalls, J. W., and See, J. K.: The diagnosis of Schistosomiasis. III. Technics for the recovery of the eggs of Schistosoma japonicum. Am. J. Trop. Med., 26:559–584, 1946.

41. Faust, E. C., and Russell, P. F.: Clinical Parasitology. 6th Ed. Philadelphia, Lea & Febiger, 1957.

42. Feldman, H. A.: The clinical manifestations and laboratory diagnosis of toxoplasmosis. Am. J. Trop. Med. & Hyg., 2:420–428, 1953.

43. Felsenfeld, O. F.: Significance of the small varieties of Endamoeba histolytica. Proc. Am. Fed. Clin. Res., 2:58–62, 1945.

44. Fildes, P.: Growth requirements of hemolytic influenza bacilli and the bearing of these upon classification of related organisms. Brit. J. Exper. Path., 5:69–74, 1924.

45. Frenkel, J. K.: Host, strain and treatment variations as factors in the pathogenesis of toxoplasmosis. Am. J. Trop. Med. & Hyg., 2:390–416, 1953.

46. Gaby, W. L., and Free, E.: Differential diagnosis of Pseudomonas-like organisms in the clinical laboratory. J. Bact., 76:442–444, 1958.

47. Girges, R.: Pathogenic factors in ascariasis. J. Trop. Med. & Hyg., 37:209–214, 1934.

48. Goldman, M.: Cytochemical differentiation of Endamoeba histolytica and Endamoeba coli by means of fluorescent antibody. Am. J. Hyg., 58:319–328, 1953.

49. Goldman, M.: Staining Toxoplasma gondii with fluorescein labelled antibody. I. The reaction in smears of peritoneal exudate. J. Exper. Med., 105:549–556, 1957.

50. Goldman, M.: Staining Toxoplasma gondii with fluorescein labelled antibody. II. A new serologic test for antibodies to Toxoplasma based upon inhibition of specific staining. J. Exper. Med., 105:557–573, 1957.

51. Goldwasser, R. A., and Shepard, C. E.: Staining of complement and modifications of fluorescent antibody procedures. J. Immunol., 80:122–131, 1958.

52. Haynes, W. C.: *Pseudomonas aeruginosa*—its characterization and identification. J. Gen. Microbiol., 5:939–950, 1951.

53. Hoare, C. A.: Handbook of Medical Protozoology. Baltimore, The Williams & Wilkins Company, 1949.

54. Hugh, R., and Leifson, E.: The taxonomic significance of fermentative versus oxidative metabolism of carbohydrates by various gram negative bacteria. J. Bact., 66:24–26, 1953.

55. Jacobs, L.: The biology of toxoplasma. Am. J. Trop. Med. & Hyg., 2:365–389, 1953.

56. Jensen, J., and Kleemeyer, H.: Die bakterielle Differential diagnose des Antrax mittels eines neuen spezifischen Tests "Perlschnurtest." Zschr. für Bakt. Parasitenk., 159:494–500, 1953.

57. Jepps, M. W., and Dobell, C.: *Dientamoeba fragilis*, n.g., n.sp., a new intestinal amoeba from man. Parasitology, 10:352–360, 1918.

58. Kalz, G.: The human leptospiroses. Am. J. Med. Sc., 233:320–333, 1957.

59. Kaufman, L., and Weaver, R. H.: Use of neutral red fluorescence for the identification of colonies of Clostridia. J. Bact., 79:292–294, 1960.

60. Kaufmann, F.: Enterobacteriaceae. 2nd Ed. Copenhagen, Einar Munksgaard Forlag, 1954.

61. Konno, K., and Sbarra, A. J.: Differentiation of human tubercle bacilli from atypical and fast bacilli. III. Modification of the niacin test using Tween-albumin liquid medium. Am. Rev. Tuberc., 79:810–812, 1959.

62. Kudo, R. R.: Protozoology. 4th Ed. Springfield, Charles C Thomas, 1954.

63. Kuntz, R. E.: Biology of the Schistosome complexes. Am. J. Trop. Med. & Hyg., 4:383–413, 1952.

64. Kurtin, J. J.: Studies in autopsy bacteriology. Am. J. Clin. Path., 30:239–243, 1958.

65. Kuzdas, C. C., and Morse, E. V.: A selective medium for the isolation of brucellae from contaminated materials. J. Bact., 66:502–504, 1953.

66. Lancefield, R. C.: A serological differentiation of human and other groups of hemolytic streptococci. J. Exper. Med., 57:571–595, 1933.

67. Leise, J. M., Carter, C. H., Friedlander, H., and Freed, S. W.: Criteria for the identification of *Bacillus anthracis*. J. Bact., 77:655–660, 1959.

68. Levinson, M. L., and Frank, P. F.: Differentiation of group A from other beta-hemolytic streptococci with bacitracin. J. Bact., 69:284–287, 1955.

69. Lindenberg, R. B., Mason, R. P., and Cutchins, E.: Selective inhibitions in the rapid isolation of Clostridia from wounds. Bact. Proc., 53–54, 1954.

70. Mackie, T. J., and McCartney, J. E.: Handbook of Practical Bacteriology. 10th Ed. Edinburgh, E. & S. Livingstone, Ltd., 1960.

71. Mackie, T. T., Hunter, G. W., and Worth, C. B.: A Manual of Tropical Medicine. 2nd Ed. Philadelphia, W. B. Saunders Company, 1954. (3rd Ed., Hunter, G. W., Frye, W. W., and Swartzwelder, C., 1961.)

72. Magath, T. B.: The epidemiology of hydatid (*Echinococcus*) disease in Canada and the United States. Arch. Intern. Hidatidosis, 5:55–80, 1941.

73. Manson-Bahr, P. H.: Manson's Dysenteric Disorders. 2nd Ed. Baltimore, The Williams & Wilkins Company, 1945.

74. Markell, E. K., and Voge, M.: Diagnostic Medical Parasitology. Philadelphia, W. B. Saunders Company, 1958.

75. Maxted, W. R.: Preparation of streptococcal extracts for Lancefield grouping. Lancet, 2:255–256, 1948.

76. Maxted, W. R.: The use of bacitracin for identifying group A hemolytic streptococci. J. Clin. Path., 6:224–226, 1953.

77. McClung, L. S.: The anaerobic bacteria with special reference to the genus *Clostridium*. Ann. Rev. Microbiol., 10:173–192, 1956.

78. McLeod, J. W.: The types mitis, intermedius and gravis of *Corynebacterium diphtheriae*. Bact. Rev., 7:1–41, 1943.

79. Middlebrook, G., Dubos, R. J., and Pierce, C.: Virulence and morphological characteristics of mammalian tubercle bacilli. J. Exp. Med., 86:175–184, 1947.

80. Moeller, V.: Simplified tests for some amino acid decarboxylases and for the arginine dehydrolase system. Acta Path. & Microb. Scand., 36:158–172, 1955.

81. Moody, M. D., Ellis, E. C., and Updyke, E. L.: Staining bacterial smears with fluorescent antibody. IV. Grouping streptococci with fluorescent antibody. J. Bact., 75:553–560, 1958.

82. Moore, M. S., and Parsons, E. I.: A study of a modified Tinsdale medium for the primary isolation of *Corynebacterium diphtheriae*. J. Infect. Dis., 102:88–93, 1958.

83. Morse, W. C., Dail, M. C., and Olitsky, I.: A study of the neutral red reaction for determining the virulence of *M. tuberculosis*. Am. J. Pub. Health, 43:36–39, 1953.

84. Pai, S.: A simple egg medium for the cultivation of *B. diphtheriae*. Chinese Med. J., 46:1203–1204, 1932.

85. Parsons, E. I., Frobisher, M., Moore, M. S., and Aiken, M. A.: Rapid virulence test in the diagnosis of diphtheria. Proc. Soc. Exper. Biol. & Med., 88:368–370, 1955.

86. Prevot, A. R.: Biologie des maladies du aux anaerobies. Paris, Editions Flammarion, 1955.

87. Rantz, L. A., and Randall, E.: Use of autoclaved extracts of hemolytic streptococci for serological grouping. Stanford Med. Bull., 13:290–291, 1955.

88. Reed, R. W., Gwin, W. F., Crosby, J., and Dobson, P.: Listerioses in man. Canad. M. A. J., 73:400–402, 1955.

89. Rogers, K. B., Dowse, J. E., and Hall, J. T.: Techniques used in the routine examination of specimens for the specific serological types of *Escherichia coli*. J. Clin. Path., 12:191–192, 1958.

90. Rowatt, E.: The growth of *Bordetella*: A review. J. Gen. Microbiol., 17:297–326, 1957.

91. Sabin, A. B.: Toxoplasmosis: Current status and unsolved problems. Introductory remarks. Am. J. Trop. Med. & Hyg., 2:360–364, 1953.

92. Sapero, J. J., Hakansson, E. G., and Louttit, C. M.: Occurrence of two significantly distinct races of *Endamoeba histolytica*. Am. J. Trop. Med., 22:191–208, 1942.

93. Schaub, I. G., Foley, M. K., Scott, E. G., and Bailey, W. R.: Diagnostic Bacteriology. 4th Ed. St. Louis, The C. V. Mosby Company, 1958.

94. Schaudinn, F.: Untersuchungen über die Fort-

pflanzung einiger Rhizopoden. Vorläufige Mitteilung. Arb. K. Gesundheitsamtes (Berlin), *19*:547–576, 1903.

95. Scherp, H. W.: *Neisseria* and neisserial infections. Ann. Rev. Microbiol., *9*:319–334, 1955.

96. Shaffer, J. G., Shlaes, W. H., Steigmann, F., Conner, P., Stahl, A., and Schneider, H.: Small race *Entamoeba histolytica*. Gastroenterology, *34*:981–995, 1958.

97. Skerman, V. B. D.: A Guide to the Identification of the Genera of Bacteria. Baltimore, The Williams & Wilkins Company, 1959.

98. Smith, D. T.: Zinnser's Textbook of Bacteriology. 11th Ed. New York, Appleton-Century-Crofts, Inc., 1956.

99. Smith, L.: Introduction to the Pathogenic Anaerobes. Chicago, University of Chicago Press, 1955.

100. Society of American Bacteriologists: Manual of Microbiological Methods. New York, McGraw-Hill Book Co., Inc., 1957.

101. Spink, W.: The Nature of Brucellosis. Minneapolis, University of Minnesota Press, 1956.

102. Stirewalt, M. A., and Evans, A. S.: Serologic reactions in *Schistosoma mansoni* infections. I. Cercaricidal, precipitation, agglutination, and CHR phenomena. Exper. Parasitol., *4*: 123–142, 1955.

103. Stokes, E. J.: Clinical Bacteriology. Baltimore, The Williams & Wilkins Company, 1955.

104. Stuart, R. D.: Transport media for specimens in public health bacteriology. Public Health Reports, 74:431–437, 1959.

105. Swartz, M. N., and Kunz, L. J.: *Pasteurella multocida* infections in man. New England J. Med., *261*:889–895, 1959.

106. Tobie, J. E.: Certain technical aspects of fluorescence microscopy and the Coons fluorescent antibody technique. J. Histochem. and Cytochem., 6:271–277, 1958.

107. Todd, J. C., Sanford, A. H., and Wells, B. B.: Clinical Diagnosis by Laboratory Methods. 12th Ed. Philadelphia, W. B. Saunders Company, 1953.

108. U.S. Dept. of Health, Education, and Welfare: Recommended procedures for laboratory investigation of hospital acquired *Staphylococcus* disease. Atlanta, Georgia, U.S. Public Health Service, Communicable Disease Center, 1958.

109. Von Prowazek, S.: *Entamoeba*. Arch. protistenk., *25*:273–285, 1912.

110. Walker, A. J.: Laboratory diagnosis of malaria. Am. J. Clin. Path., *22*:495–500, 1952.

111. Weckman, B. G., and Catlin, B. W.: Desoxyribonuclease activity of micrococci from clinical sources. J. Bact., *73*:747–753, 1957.

112. Weed, L. A., and Dahlin, D. C.: Bacteriologic examination of tissue removed for biopsy. Am. J. Clin. Path., *20*:116–132, 1950.

113. Weiler, T. H.: The diagnosis of *Schistosoma mansoni* infections. Am. J. Trop. Med., *27*: 41–44, 1947.

114. Wenyon, C. M., and O'Connor, F. W.: Human intestinal protozoa in the Near East; An inquiry into some problems affecting spread and incidence of intestinal protozoal infections. Wellcome Bureau of Scientific Research (London), *4*:218, 1917.

115. Willis, A. T., and Hobbs, G.: Some new media for the isolation and identification of clostridia. J. Path. & Bact., *77*:511–521, 1959.

Chapter 17

Microbiologic Methods

By JAMES G. SHAFFER, Sc.D., *and* MILTON GOLDIN, M.S.

Speed and accuracy have always been of great importance in the clinical bacteriology laboratory, and the advent of numerous specific chemotherapeutic and antibiotic drugs has served to re-emphasize this need. Improved methods for the isolation and identification of microorganisms are constantly being developed, and it is imperative that medical bacteriologists constantly re-evaluate their techniques with the view of adapting new equipment and media to their own routines. Fortunately, improved media both for routine and special purposes are now available in dehydrated form or already prepared in tubes or plates and can be obtained from several commercial sources. It is no longer necessary, and in most cases is not desirable, to go through the time-consuming procedure of preparing media from basic ingredients. Certain general principles may be used to guide the laboratory in its operation.

In some cases the direct gram stained smear may permit tentative identification of an organism, but most often culture on appropriate media is essential for both the tentative and final identifications. To that end, appropriate inoculations on certain basic media have to be made. In order to choose the proper procedure, the nature and source of the material to be cultured must be known, and some information about the condition of the patient should be available. The latter will help to select the suitable type of examination and the most direct approach for the isolation and identification of the offending microorganism.

With the battery of antibiotic drugs now available it is in many cases desirable to know the antibiotic susceptibility of an or-

ganism at the earliest possible moment. At times this is of more immediate importance than an exact identification. For that purpose pure cultures of the organism have to be available for testing. Consequently antibiotic testing techniques are a part of bacteriologic methods and will be dealt with in that way here and not as a separate subject.

There are points in the operation of a diagnostic microbiologic laboratory that cannot be overemphasized. Proper collection of material for examination and its transport to the laboratory are of utmost importance. No matter how good the methods used in the laboratory, it is not possible to get satisfactory results with specimens that are collected improperly or delayed unduly in arriving at the laboratory. Under no circumstances should a specimen arriving at the laboratory with any of the infectious material on the outside of the container be accepted, because there may be potentially serious consequences to those handling the specimen. Thus, there should be complete understanding and free exchange of information between the physician and those examining the material in the laboratory both before and during the course of the procedure.

In the laboratory the proper operation depends upon the availability of properly cleaned and sterilized glassware and the preparation, appropriate handling, and choice of media and reagents. These are basic in the operation of the laboratory. In the actual operation it is of course essential to adequately organize, standardize, and develop the techniques of preparation, staining, and culturing specimens. Accuracy, speed, and efficiency are to be emphasized. The prompt recording and reporting of results are important. When possible, interim reports can be of great assistance.

In smaller laboratories, physicians' offices, and clinics where space, time, and personnel are limited, it is possible to accomplish a great deal with simple methods and a minimum of material. In larger laboratories more extensive procedures can be made available and more extensive service offered. The size of the laboratory does not necessarily determine the amount or quality of the services rendered, for experience, organization, and ingenuity can accomplish a great deal.

GENERAL TECHNIQUES OF MICRO-BIOLOGIC EXAMINATIONS

Washing Glassware

The efficiency of a laboratory can be greatly influenced by the availability of an adequate supply of glassware and containers. Ideally there should be on hand two or three times the amount required for day-to-day operation in order to provide a turn-over and to allow for efficient cleaning and sterilizing. The glassware itself should be of good quality, and the test tubes, flasks, and Petri dishes should not be of soft glass if this can be avoided. There are now available certain disposable items, such as plastic Petri dishes (either plain or divided into two, three, or four sections), plastic syringes, pipets, and coverslips. Other similar items are being developed continuously and will no doubt offer considerable advantages in certain situations.

Adequate cleaning of glassware is essential to insure the best results in microbiologic work. It is no longer necessary or desirable to use dichromate cleaning solution, although there are times when it is useful. For almost all purposes a good detergent cleaner is adequate. Test tube washers and mechanical glassware washers of various sizes and complexity are available for use in any size laboratory. In the absence of such a machine, washing can be accomplished in a sink, using stiff-bristle brushes to assist in the removal of solids, grease, and dirt from the glassware. After being washed, the glassware should be rinsed several times in running tap water to remove all detergent and then passed through at least three or four rinses in distilled water. After being rinsed, the glassware should be dried in an inverted position in an oven or allowed to dry at room temperature on a clean, dust-free table. This will suffice for test tubes, flasks, and Petri dishes, but pipets and slides require special comment.

In general the same washing procedure can be used with pipets as with other glassware, but rinsing requires special care. For this purpose an automatic pipet washer serves best, although rinsing can be accomplished by holding the pipets under the water tap and then rinsing in distilled water. New slides should be washed with detergent, rinsed, and immersed in 95 per cent alcohol. They should then be wiped dry with a soft lint-free cloth and stored in a covered container or slide dispenser. Used slides should be cleaned with an abrasive soap, such as Bon Ami, before washing in detergent. This is important because it is necessary to remove all adherent bacteria and debris. If bacteria are left on the slide, there may be difficulty in interpreting subsequent gram stains. Etched slides should be discarded, since bacteria or other material may be caught in crevices and may not be removed on cleaning. One can obtain prewashed slides commercially if desired.

Plugging, Capping, and Assembly of Glassware

Before sterilization of test tubes, flasks, and pipets, it is necessary that they be plugged with cotton or that a cap be applied. If cotton plugs are to be used, it is desirable to use a good grade of long-fiber, nonabsorbent cotton. Synthetic plastic materials for plugging are now available. Many workers prefer a rolled plug, made by taking an appropriate size portion of the cotton and rolling it to a diameter that fits snugly into the orifice of the tube or flask. If kept dry, such plugs may be used repeatedly. The plugs should be of sufficient length to extend about one inch into the tube, leaving enough outside for easy removal. Other workers merely stuff the cotton into the opening with a pencil or similar tool. Such plugs cannot be reused. For large tubes or flasks it is desirable to wrap the cotton in a double layer of gauze. Such plugs should fit snugly into the orifice and may be tied with string to form a little bag. There are several alternatives to the use of cotton plugs for tubes and flasks. Screw cap tubes and flasks of many sizes are available. They have the great advantage of delaying evaporation of stored media and reagents and have found wide use in the laboratory. One can also use caps of aluminum, stainless steel, or certain other materials.

Plugging of pipets must be done with care. If the plug is too tight, it will offer too much resistance and make it difficult to draw up materials, and if it is too loose the plug may slip down into the barrel of the pipet and contaminate what it touches. Pipets can be obtained with constrictions, which prevent the dropping of the plug. After being plugged, the pipets can be wrapped individually in paper or packed in specially designed stainless steel cans for sterilization and storage.

Petri dishes should be assembled after drying and may be wrapped in paper, either singly or in packages of two to four, before sterilization. Metal cans with removable racks provide an efficient means of packing and storing Petri dishes (Fig. 17–1).

Syringes may be wrapped in paper, either assembled or unassembled, or may be placed in appropriate size glass tubes provided with a pad of cotton in the bottom. Syringe needles can be put up in various ways, a very good one being to place them individually in constricted tubes specially designed for the purpose. It is important that they be handled so as to avoid damage to the point.

Sterilization of Glassware and Reagents

There are four general methods of sterilizing glassware and reagents, each of which has its special advantages, depending on the material and its projected use. These are moist heat (autoclaving or inspissating), dry heat (oven), filtration, and use of chemical agents.

Moist heat sterilizing is most frequently accomplished by using steam under pressure in an autoclave or pressure cooker. Many types and sizes of autoclaves are used: horizontal or vertical, single or double wall, gas or electrically heated, or operation on a steam line (Figs. 17–2, 17–3). There are single or double wall, automatic or manually operated machines suitable for any laboratory. Small, table model, electrically operated autoclaves have been developed recently and can be used in small laboratories or physicians' offices. These have many advantages over the pressure cooker. The standard autoclaving procedure requires a pressure of 15 lb. per square inch and a temperature of 121° C. (250° F.) for 15 minutes for most materials. In manually operated autoclaves it is imperative that all the air be allowed to escape before closing the escape valve, since air-

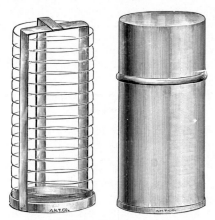

Figure 17–1.   Petri dish holder.

Figure 17–2.   Portable automatic autoclave. (Courtesy of the Wilmot Castle Co., Rochester, New York.)

steam mixtures will not produce the required temperature even though the pressure is the required 15 lb. When large quantities of material are being autoclaved, it may be necessary to sterilize for more than 15 minutes to insure proper sterility. One can use heat indicators of various types that are designed to record the temperature reached inside packages.

Most of the routine media and salt solutions used in the laboratory may be sterilized by autoclaving. However, certain media containing carbohydrates, serum, or egg and solutions of vitamins or other growth factors may be damaged by the autoclave temperature. Such materials may be sterilized by filtration or inspissation.

Glassware may be sterilized in the autoclave, but it is then necessary to provide some means of drying. Most double wall autoclaves can be run under vacuum and evacuated after the sterilization is complete in order to remove moisture.

Dry heat sterilization is accomplished in an oven, either operated by gas or electricity. Such sterilization requires a higher temperature and a longer time than autoclaving. A good standard to use is 160° C. for two hours. This temperature will not char paper, cotton, or gauze. In packing material in an oven for sterilization, it is important to leave adequate space on the shelves to allow for free circulation of air. If this is not done, the material on the lower shelves closest to the source of heat will get too hot, while the upper shelves may not reach the required temperature (Fig. 17–4).

Test tubes, pipets, Petri dishes, flasks, syringes, and needles should be sterilized in dry heat, since it is desirable that these materials be dry for use and for storage. Rubber goods and certain other materials are adversely affected and must not be sterilized in an oven. When sterilizing screw cap glassware, it is desirable to leave the caps slightly loose during sterilization and to tighten them after removal from the oven.

Handling Contaminated Materials

The problem of disposal of contaminated glassware, media, swabs, and specimen cartons in a laboratory is of considerable importance in order to avoid spread of infectious material throughout the laboratory area and its surroundings and to avoid cross-contamination of media, which may result in serious errors. All bench tops should be of good construction with a hard, smooth surface and should be kept uncluttered. They should be washed frequently with a good disinfectant.

Porcelain or stainless steel containers with snug fitting tops are needed for the discard of contaminated glassware. Butcher pans, which can be obtained from restaurant supply houses, are quite good. For

Figure 17–3. Modern laboratory autoclave with automatic controls. (Courtesy of the Wilmot Castle Co., Rochester, New York.)

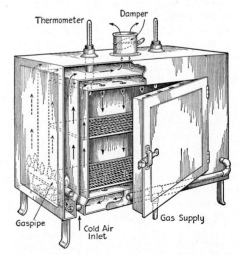

Figure 17–4. Hot air sterilizer. (From Belding, D. L., and Marston, A. T.: A Textbook of Medical Bacteriology. D. Appleton-Century Company, Inc., 1938.)

pipets one can use cylindrical jars or rectangular pans containing disinfectant. These items should be placed conveniently to provide ready access. Once an item is discarded, it should never be removed from the discard pan until the pan and its contents have been autoclaved. After autoclaving, the glassware can be removed and washed. Pipets do not ordinarily need to be autoclaved, provided they are sufficiently immersed in disinfectant.

Specimen cartons, applicators, tongue depressors, cotton, and other combustible materials should be discarded into a garbage pail with a tight cover. Lining the pail with a waterproof paper bag is recommended so that the bag can be removed and placed directly into an incinerator. All infectious materials, such as sputum from tuberculous patients, must be autoclaved before they are discarded.

Preparation, Dispensing, and Sterilization of Media

Most of the media used in diagnostic work can now be obtained from several sources in dehydrated form. Each of the firms producing such media has descriptive catalogues or pamphlets, which give ingredients, recommended use, and method of preparation for each medium. The principles of preparing, dispensing, and sterilizing media are essentially the same, whether one uses the dehydrated form or starts from the beginning and adds the various ingredients separately. All the basic media contain a peptone and certain salts to which may be added growth promoting substances or agar, depending on the need. Since numerous peptones of superior quality are now available commercially, it is no longer necessary to prepare infusions and extracts, although this may be desirable for large laboratories for reasons of economy.

There should be available a good balance for weighing the ingredients of the medium. If dehydrated media are used, one does not need an analytic balance but may use a good trip balance or its equivalent. But if one is to make media, adding all the ingredients individually, an analytic balance should be used.

Instructions for reconstituting dehydrated media are given on the label of each bottle, and it is only necessary to weigh out the required amount of the powder and to add distilled water. It is important to use an Erlenmeyer flask of sufficient size to allow adequate stirring or shaking to dissolve the medium. For example, if one is making one liter of medium, it is desirable to use a two-liter flask. If the medium does not contain agar, it may dissolve without heating, but all media containing agar require the application of heat to raise the temperature to 100° C. or thereabouts. This heating should never be done over an open flame, because there is danger of scorching the medium or breaking the flask. The flask should be placed in a boiling water bath and stirred or shaken thoroughly at frequent intervals until the agar is melted. One can determine when the agar is melted by inspecting the sides of the flask during shaking. If flecks of agar can be seen, the agar is obviously not melted and heating should be continued. These media should be dispensed into appropriate containers while still hot (above 45° C.), else they will solidify and need to be remelted. If prolonged heating is necessary, volume may be decreased owing to evaporation and it may be necessary to add distilled water to replace the loss. Certain types of dehydrated media can be dissolved without heating. Directions to this effect are supplied with the media.

Except under special circumstances, no pH adjustment is necessary with dehydrated media. When this is necessary or when one starts with basic ingredients, relatively simple methods of adjustment are available (see p. 715). A pH of about 7.0 is used for most bacteriologic work, although some bacteria require higher or lower pH values.

The methods of dispensing the dissolved media into tubes or flasks depends on the type of medium and the purpose for which it is to be used. Fluid media (e.g., infusion broth) may be pipetted into tubes using a serologic pipet or an automatic pipet calibrated to deliver the desired amount. It is not necessary to use sterile tubes for this purpose, although at times this has considerable advantage, especially in handling material that needs to be inspissated. For larger instillations one may use specially constructed flasks with delivery tubes at the bottom to which may be attached a standard glass filling device.

Media containing agar must be dispensed while hot (50° C. or above). Media containing sufficient agar to be solid on cooling (1.5 per cent or more) are used ordinarily for agar slants or Petri dishes. For slants the medium is dispensed into test tubes, autoclaved in the vertical position, and then cooled in a slanted position on the table top. The amount of medium per tube is determined by the length of slant and butt desired. To pour Petri plates, the agar medium must first be sterilized in flasks or tubes and then poured to a depth of $\frac{1}{8}$ to $\frac{1}{4}$ inch into sterile plates. Since the medium tends to dry out when stored in Petri dishes owing to the large surface, the medium should be stored in flasks or test tubes, melted in a boiling water bath, and poured into the Petri dish just before use. The melted agar is cooled to 50 to 55° C. before pouring the plates to prevent condensation of moisture on the walls of the container. Semisolid media (0.1 to 0.75 per cent agar) are tubed and sterilized in the same manner as fluid media.

It is often necessary to add carbohydrates or other substances to media for special studies. In some instances these materials can be weighed and dissolved in the medium before sterilization, but in other cases heat may adversely affect the substance and it must be added aseptically to the sterilized base. For carbohydrate fermentation tests it is necessary to use a base medium free of carbohydrate to which the desired carbohydrate, such as dextrose or maltose, is then added to produce a 0.5 to 1.0 per cent concentration. It is convenient to add the desired carbohydrate aseptically, using a filtered 10 to 20 per cent solution, to a previously sterilized base medium. Such base media containing an indicator (bromthymol blue, bromcresol purple, or phenol red) are readily available. The indicator changes color when acid is produced by bacteria.

To detect gas production, one can place an inverted vial or Durham tube (3 × 20 mm.) in the medium (Fig. 17–5). When autoclaved, this vial fills with medium. Gas production is indicated when a bubble of gas appears in the vial after bacterial propagation. If one uses semisolid agar (0.5 per cent agar), the vial is unnecessary, because gas production will be revealed by bubbles in the medium.

There are now available sterile discs of dehydrated fermentation media, which, when added aseptically to tubes with sterile distilled water, provide a medium for fermentation tests. There are also discs containing various carbohydrates that may be added to a suitable base in the same manner or may be placed on agar plates. These materials seem ideally suited for use in small laboratories.

For sterilization of media, in most cases autoclaving at 15 lb. pressure for 15 minutes is satisfactory. If the medium is in screw cap tubes, the caps should be left loose before autoclaving and tightened after removal from the autoclave. Some carbohydrates and other materials are changed or destroyed by the high temperatures. Media containing carbohydrates, Loeffler's medium, and certain of the media for TB cultures (Petragnani and Löwenstein's media, for example) can be inspissated by exposing the media to free-flowing steam in an inspissator for one hour on each of three successive days. There are various types of inspissators and Arnold sterilizers available (Fig. 17–6).

Adjusting the Hydrogen Ion (pH) Concentration of Culture Media. The colorimetric method for the adjustment of the pH of culture media is widely used and has the advantages of speed and simplicity. There are limitations to this procedure, however, and for more accurate work a potentiometer ("pH meter") is necessary.

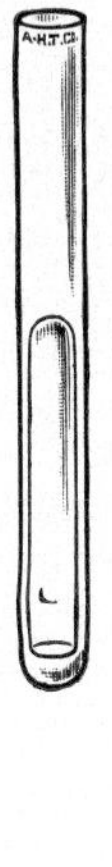

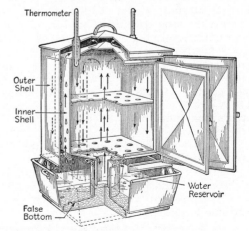

Figure 17–5. Durham's fermentation tube, consisting of a small tube inverted in a standard culture tube. When a liquid culture medium is present, the air in the inner tube is driven off during sterilization.

Figure 17–6. Arnold steam sterilizer. (From Belding, D. L., and Marston, A. T.: A Textbook of Medical Bacteriology. D. Appleton-Century Company, Inc., 1938.)

Table 17–1. Characteristics of Indicators Used in Bacteriology

COMMON NAME	INDICATORS CHEMICAL NAME	N/10 NaOH PER 0.1 GM. TO MAKE SODIUM SALT (ML.) *	CONCENTRATION RECOMMENDED (% DYE IN 50% ETHYL ALCOHOL)	SENSITIVE RANGE (pH)	COLOR CHANGE (ACID TO ALKALINE)
Thymol blue (acid range)	Thymol sulfonphthalein	2.15	0.04	1.2– 2.8	Red to yellow
Bromphenol blue	Tetrabromophenol sulfonphthalein	1.49	0.04	3.0– 4.6	Yellow to blue
Bromcresol green	Tetrabromo-m-cresol sulfonphthalein	1.43	0.04	3.8– 5.4	Yellow to blue
Chlorcresol green	Tetrachloro-m-cresol sulfonphthalein	1.92	0.04	4.0– 5.6	Yellow to blue
Methyl red	Dimethylaminoazobenzene-o-carboxylic acid	—	0.02	4.4– 6.4	Red to yellow
Chlorphenol red	Dichlorophenol sulfonphthalein	2.36	0.04	4.8– 6.4	Yellow to red
Bromcresol purple	Dibromo-o-cresol sulfonphthalein	1.85	0.04	5.2– 6.8	Yellow to purple
Bromthymol blue	Dibromothymol sulfonphthalein	1.60	0.04	6.0– 7.6	Yellow to blue
Phenol red	Phenol sulfonphthalein	2.82	0.02	6.8– 8.4	Yellow to red
Cresol red	o-Cresol sulfonphthalein	2.62	0.02	7.2– 8.8	Yellow to red
Metacresol purple (alk. range)	m-Cresol sulfonphthalein	2.62	0.04	7.4– 9.0	Yellow to purple
Thymol blue (alk. range)	Thymol sulfonphthalein	2.15	0.04	8.0– 9.6	Yellow to blue
Phenolphthalein	Dihydroxyphthalophenone	—	0.05	8.3–10.0	Colorless to red

NOTE: To produce aqueous solutions of indicators, add the indicated quantity of N/10 NaOH to 0.1 gm of the indicator; triturate in a mortar; then add distilled water to 250 ml. Indicator conc. = 0.04%.

* Most of these indicators are now available in water-soluble forms, making the addition of alkali unnecessary.

Table 17–2. Amounts of M/15 Solutions of Primary Potassium Phosphate and Secondary Sodium Phosphate That Must Be Mixed to Make a Series of Standard Solutions of Different Hydrogen Ion Concentrations

pH	6.4	6.6	6.8	7.0	7.1	7.2	7.3	7.4	7.5	7.6	7.7	7.8	8.0	8.2	8.4
M/15 solution of primary potassium phosphate (cc.)	73	63	51	37	32	27	23	19	15.8	13.2	11	8.8	5.6	3.2	2.0
M/15 solution of secondary sodium phosphate (cc.)	27	37	49	63	68	73	77	81	84.2	86.8	89	91.2	94.4	96.8	98.0

Methods using paper strips or "universal indicators" are satisfactory only for crude estimations.

Colorimetric method. The colorimetric method depends on the definite color certain substances assume when they are added to a solution at a particular pH. These substances are called indicators. Commonly used indicators in bacteriology are bromthymol blue, which is yellow at pH 6.0, yellowish green at pH 6.2 to 7.0, bluish green at 7.0, and bright blue at 7.6, and phenol red, which is yellow below pH 6.8, pale pink at 7.0, and deep red at 8.4. Table 17–1 lists the characteristics of the indicators commonly used in bacteriology.

Reagents

1. 0.04 per cent alcoholic solution of bromthymol blue.

2. N/1 and N/10 solutions of sodium hydroxide should be kept in containers that are lightly coated with paraffin or in polyethylene bottles.

3. A series of standard phosphate solutions of varying pH concentrations, made as follows (according to Sorensen):

a. Prepare a M/15 acid or primary phosphate solution by dissolving 9.078 gm. of crystalline KH_2PO_4 in freshly distilled ammonia-free water and make up to 1000 ml.

b. Prepare a M/15 alkaline or secondary sodium phosphate solution by dissolving 11.876 gm. of $Na_2HPO_4 \cdot 2H_2O$ and make up to 1000 ml.

c. To make standard solutions of different hydrogen ion concentrations, mix the two phosphate solutions in the proportions indicated in Table 17–2.

d. Place 10 ml. quantities of these standard buffer solutions in a series of hard glass test tubes of uniform diameter. Add 0.5 ml. of the 0.04 per cent solution of bromthymol blue indicator to each tube and seal with a paraffined cork. Sets of standard color tubes covering a wide range of hydrogen ion concentrations can be purchased and are generally satisfactory.

Procedure

a. Place the standard color tube representing the pH value desired in one of the end holes of the front row of the comparator block shown in Fig. 17–7. If the desired value falls between two of the standards, place these in the end holes of the front row. Place a tube of the untreated medium in back of each.

b. In a test tube of the same diameter place 10 ml. of the medium to be adjusted. Media containing agar must first be liquefied by heat. Add 0.5 ml. of the 0.04 per cent solution of bromthymol blue and mix thoroughly.

c. Add N/10 solution of NaOH from an accurate buret a little at a time, mixing after each addition until the color matches that of the standard chosen or falls between the standard next above or below. For comparison the tube is placed in the middle hole of the front row of the comparator with a tube of distilled water in back of it. Note the amount of decinormal solution required to bring the 10 ml. of medium to the desired reaction. This amount is then the amount of normal solution that must be added per 100 ml. of medium to secure this reaction.

For example, assume that there are 2000 ml. of medium to be adjusted to a pH of 7.8 and it requires 0.6 ml. of N/10 NaOH to bring the tube containing 10 ml. of medium to the same color as the standard tube marked pH 7.8. It would therefore require 120 ml. of N/10 NaOH to adjust 2000 ml. of medium. Since the addition of this amount would increase the volume too much, it is necessary to add 12.0 ml. of N/1 NaOH.

d. After the alkali has been added, the pH should again be determined as a check. Most media, particularly those containing carbohydrates, become slightly more acid during sterilization. It is therefore advisable to make a check determination on a 10 ml. portion of the sterilized product that has been withheld for this purpose.

The same procedure can be followed using HCl if the medium is too alkaline, although this is seldom necessary. Other indicators besides bromthymol blue can also be used (Table 17–1).

Determination of the pH after growth of a culture can be done by taking aliquots of

Figure 17–7. A color comparator (Clark's model) for use in adjusting reaction of culture mediums by the colorimetric method.

the culture and testing them in the potentiometer. Proper precautions must be taken when testing cultures of pathogenic bacteria. A simpler method is the spot plate procedure. One loopful of culture is placed in the concave depression of a white porcelain plate. One drop of indicator solution is mixed and the pH estimated by noting the resulting color and comparing it to the color chart for the indicator used. Another procedure is to add one or more drops of indicator solution to 1.0 ml. aliquots of the culture that have been transferred to small test tubes. The same amount of indicator solution is added to 1.0 ml. volumes of standard buffer solutions in similar tubes. The standard tube most closely matching the unknown is determined by visual examination.

In the case of the Clostridia it is best to read the pH after growth by the spot plate procedure just described, because many strains will destroy the indicator in the media rapidly and thus give erroneus results.

Preparation of Blood and Chocolate Agar. Media containing whole blood are the most commonly employed media in the diagnostic laboratory, and the type of blood, the agar base, and the technique of preparation are very important for the proper isolation of microorganisms.

The type of blood used in making blood or chocolate agar depends in most cases on what is available. Some laboratories can get human blood from blood banks; others have access to defibrinated rabbit, sheep, or horse blood. Although certain of these may have advantages over others in special situations, any one is satisfactory for most purposes. The blood should not be more than a few days old unless collected in a special preserving solution, such as Alsever's. If the blood is too old, the red cells are likely to be fragile and may hemolyze, making the blood agar unsuitable for use.

There are several good blood agar bases that can be obtained commercially. One should not use just any peptone agar, because some contain agents detrimental to the blood and the results will be undesirable.

To make blood agar, the sterile blood agar base contained in a flask is melted in a boiling water bath and cooled to 50 to 55° C. (This cooling is essential, because higher temperatures will adversely affect the blood when it is added to the agar.) Blood is then added to the melted agar (5 ml. of blood per 100 ml. of medium) and thoroughly mixed by rotating the flask. After it is mixed, the agar is carefully poured into sterile Petri dishes to a depth of $\frac{1}{8}$ to $\frac{1}{4}$ inch. The depth to which the plate is poured is of considerable importance, since one is often interested in the presence or absence of hemolysis. If the agar is too thick, the hemolysis may be missed. Too vigorous shaking should be avoided, since air bubbles may make the agar rough. Air bubbles that do appear in the plates may be removed by passing a Bunsen flame quickly over the surface before the agar has set. Some workers prefer to place a layer of plain agar over the bottom of the plate and superimpose a thin layer of 10 per cent blood agar over this.

To make chocolate agar, the flask containing the medium with blood added is placed in a water bath at 70° C. and shaken gently until it has attained a definite chocolate color. This takes usually about five minutes. Excessive heating should be avoided. The agar should then be cooled to 50 to 55° C. and poured into sterile Petri dishes.

Blood and chocolate agar can be stored in the refrigerator at 4° C. for several days but should not be used if there is evidence of excessive drying or, in the case of blood agar plates, if the blood has darkened or otherwise changed its appearance. All blood and chocolate agar plates should be incubated overnight and checked for sterility before use. Addition of Bacto-Supplement B or Fildes's peptic blood digest stimulates growth of the more fastidious organisms.

Preparation of Coagulated Serum or Egg Media. The preparation of Loeffler's serum medium and coagulated egg media requires special technique. If these are autoclaved in the usual manner, the resulting medium is unsatisfactory for use. The ingredients are mixed thoroughly, avoiding bubbles, and tubed in the same manner as for other media. Because these media coagulate on heating, they must be slanted during heating. They may be sterilized by inspissation. They are coagulated on the first day and are then merely heated in the inspissator on the two succeeding days for one hour each day.

An autoclave can be used with this type of medium, but special procedures must be used. Layers of tubes should be placed in an enamel pan in a slanted position with several thicknesses of newspaper or similar material beneath the bottom layer of tubes, between the layers of tubes, and above the top layer to prevent too rapid heating or cooling. Not more than two layers of tubes should be used, for otherwise the insulating effect may prevent sufficient heating of the middle layers. Some workers use other materials but paper serves well. The autoclave is first brought up to 15 lb. pressure without releasing the air from the inner chamber. After about 15 minutes the air is slowly released, maintaining the pressure at 15 lb. until the air has all been replaced with steam and the temperature has reached 121° C. This temperature is then maintained for 15 minutes and the pressure allowed to fall slowly. If these media are made in screw cap tubes, the tubes may be stored at 4° C. for indefinite periods of time.

Methods of Examination of Specimens

The examination of specimens received in the microbiology laboratory involves two general types of procedures. First, they may be examined by direct smear, stained or unstained, and, second, they may be cultured on appropriate media.

When certain specimens are being submitted for bacteriologic or mycologic examination, properly prepared and stained preparations may give excellent leads as to what media to inoculate or what further examination can be done. A preliminary report on such observations may, as in the case of spinal fluid, urethral smears, and sputum, be of definite value to the physician in the management of the patient.

Clean slides must be used to make smears, and the slide must be marked adequately for identification and for delineation of the area in which the smear is to be placed. A slide may be divided into several sections with a marking pencil and several smears placed on the same slide, provided they are all to be stained identically.

One or two inoculating loopfuls of the material to be smeared are spread evenly over the designated area of the slide and allowed to dry. The dried smear is then passed rapidly through a flame to heat-fix the material to the slide. This is an essential step for most staining procedures.

There are several staining procedures used in bacteriologic work, the most common and useful being that of Gram or one of its many modifications. Loeffler's methylene blue, the acid-fast stain, spore stains, capsule stains, and flagella stains may be useful for special purposes.

Gram's staining is most likely to yield

valuable information and should be done in all cases when staining is indicated. It is also used routinely for the examination of cultures to determine purity and for purposes of identification. Two of the best modifications of the gram stain follow:

Hucker's Modification of Gram's Stain

Solutions

1. Ammonium oxalate crystal violet

SOLUTION A

Crystal violet (90 per cent dye content)	2 gm.
Ethyl alcohol (95 per cent)	20 ml.

SOLUTION B

Ammonium oxalate	0.8 gm.
Distilled water	80 ml.

Mix solutions A and B

2. Iodine solution (mordant)

Iodine	1 gm.
Potassium iodide	2 gm.
Distilled water	300 ml.

3. Counterstain

Safranin O (2.5 per cent solution in 95 per cent ethyl alcohol)	10 ml.
Distilled water	100 ml.

Procedure. After the smear has been dried and heat-fixed, proceed as follows:

1. Stain smears one minute with the ammonium oxalate crystal violet. If stains are too heavy and difficult to decolorize, use less crystal violet.
2. Wash in tap water not more than two seconds.
3. Immerse in iodine solution (mordant) for one minute.
4. Wash in tap water and blot dry (do not rub).
5. Decolorize 30 seconds with gentle agitation in 95 per cent ethyl alcohol. Blot dry.
6. Counterstain ten seconds with safranin.
7. Wash in tap water.
8. Dry and examine.

Results: Gram positive organisms stain blue; gram negative, red.

Burke's Modification. This modification of the gram stain has the advantage that all solutions are aqueous and the decolorization is more vigorous, resulting in easier differentiation of the organisms in thick preparations.

Solutions

1. Alkaline Gentian Violet

SOLUTION A

Gentian or crystal violet	1 gm.
Distilled water	100 ml.

SOLUTION B

NaHCO₃	1 gm.
Distilled water	20 ml.
Add Merthiolate (1:20,000)	

2. Iodine Solution

Iodine	1 gm.
KI	2 gm.
Distilled water	200 ml.

3. Decolorizing Solution

Ether	1 volume
Acetone	3 volumes

4. Counterstain

Safranin O (85 per cent dye content)	0.5 gm.
Distilled water	100 ml.

Procedure

1. Flood slide with solution A. Then add 3 to 5 drops of solution B, depending on the size of the flooded area, and allow to stand one minute. Wash well with water.
2. Cover with iodine solution and let stand one minute or longer.
3. Rinse with water.
4. Decolorize at once with the ether-acetone mixture, adding it to the slide drop by drop until no more color comes off in the drippings. Care must be taken to avoid excessive decolorization.
5. Wash with water.
6. Counterstain 10 to 15 seconds with the safranin O.
7. Wash in tap water.
8. Dry and examine.

Results: Gram positive organisms stain blue; gram negative, red.

The techniques for the various other stains will be found in the sections describing the particular specimen with which these stains are most frequently used. Some of the less commonly used stains, e.g., spore and flagella stains, will be found in the appendix (p. 931). In general these are the techniques recommended in the *Manual of Microbiological Methods* (Ref. 61).

Aerobic Culture Methods

The most frequently used item of equipment in the bacteriology laboratory is the inoculating loop. This can be made of platinum wire, nichrome wire, or other similar material and inserted in a holder. One should also have a straight wire for stab inoculations and for picking isolated colonies from streaked plates. Numerous types, most of which are satisfactory, are available at low cost from commercial sources.

CO_2

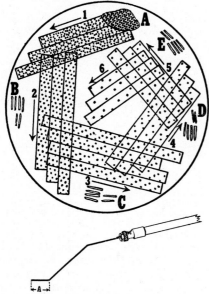

Figure 17–8. Method of streaking a plate so as to secure well-isolated colonies. The original material is deposited at *A*. The wire is afterward sterilized in the Bunsen flame. The material is then streaked with the flat part of the wire at 1, 2, 3, 4, 5, and 6, the wire being thrust into the agar to remove excess organisms, as at *B*, *C*, *D*, and *E*, after each series of parallel strokings. Isolated colonies are almost invariably found at the areas numbered 4, 5, and 6. The wire used in streaking is shown below the plate. The flat portion at *A* is brought into contact with the agar from tip to "heel." (From Frobisher, M., Jr.: Fundamentals of Bacteriology, 4th Ed.)

Culture methods in the laboratory are designed for essentially three purposes: isolation, identification, and maintenance or preservation. The first two are most important in diagnostic work.

The isolation of bacteria from specimens submitted to the laboratory is almost invariably accomplished by streaking on the surface of an agar plate. The purpose of streaking is to spread an inoculum so as to insure the appearance of isolated colonies on incubation. Most such isolated colonies will be pure cultures of an organism and may be picked for the next step—identification. The characteristics and the cellular morphology will also assist in final identification. It is therefore imperative that a suitable streaking technique be used.

A recommended technique is as follows: With a sterile inoculating loop place two loopfuls of the material near the edge of the plate. The loop should then be sterilized in the flame and allowed to cool. It should then be applied to the material on the plate and streaked using a gentle pressure in the manner illustrated in Fig. 17–8.

Each of the streaking techniques is designed to insure that at some place dilution will be sufficient to provide isolated colonies for study and transfer.

The streaked plates are incubated in an inverted position, media side up, at 37° C. and examined at 24- and 48-hour intervals. The various colonies should be observed carefully and individual ones fished for gram stain and for transfer to appropriate media for further study. Fishing of colonies may be done with a loop if the colony is well separated from other colonies, but it may be better to use a straight wire for this, especially if the colonies are close together. It is essential that gram stains be done on all colonies to study staining characteristics, morphology, and purity.

Pour plates are sometimes used on certain types of specimens, i.e., urine or blood. The pour plate is made by placing a measured amount of the material in a sterile Petri plate and pouring in melted agar (cooled to 50° C.). The plate is then rotated to mix the material thoroughly throughout the medium. After solidifying at room temperature, the plate is inverted, incubated at 37° C., and examined for colonies. This technique has the advantage of giving quantitative bacterial counts. For heavily contaminated specimens dilution must be made.

Agar slants are used frequently for maintenance of cultures or for certain biochemical studies. The slant is inoculated from a colony picked from a plate or from a broth culture. A loop is used to transfer the inoculum to the slant and is streaked over the entire slant. Slants are used only with pure cultures and are not for isolation. It is sometimes necessary to stab into the butt of a slant, as with Kligler's iron agar for enteric organisms. This is done with a straight wire, stabbing carefully in a straight line into the center of the tube. The stab should never be made completely to the bottom of the tube. Slants are examined after 24 and 48 hours of incubation, and gram stains are made to check purity of the culture.

Semisolid media are used for motility or biochemical studies and are stabbed with a straight wire. The stab is not extended to the bottom of the tube. Motility is read by examining for migration of growth away from the stab line; thus it is important that the stab be made with care.

Broth media (e.g., infusion and extract media) are used for maintenance of cultures and other studies (such as carbohydrate fermentation). They are inoculated by transfer from colonies or other growth with a loop or wire. Propagation of bacteria in such media is indicated by the development of cloudiness. It is important to ascertain growth in fermentation media, since failure of growth results in no change of the indicator and may lead to false negative interpretation. Gram stains should be done on all broth cultures to determine the purity of the culture and to make sure no contamination has occurred.

For short-term storage of cultures one should use broth or agar slant cultures, since Petri dishes tend to dry out unless sealed with a rubber or plastic band.

Incubation in an Atmosphere of 10 Per Cent CO₂. To obtain an atmosphere of 10 per cent carbon dioxide for assistance in the culture of numerous organisms, the simplest and probably most useful method is to use the candle jar. This is simply a jar or can with a tightly fitting top into which Petri dishes can be placed along with a smokeless candle. The candle is lighted and the lid sealed tightly with plasticine or tape. When the candle burns out, the atmosphere contains approximately 10 per cent carbon dioxide. Other methods have been described, but most are complex and not necessarily any more dependable than the candle jar.

Anaerobic Culture Methods

Most of the recognized pathogenic bacteria are aerobic or facultatively anaerobic and propagate well in an atmosphere free of oxygen; others are microaerophilic, preferring reduced oxygen concentrations.

Several pathogenic and nonpathogenic bacteria are incapable of propagation in the presence of oxygen and require a low oxidation-reduction potential. These are classified as obligate anaerobic bacteria.

Special methods are necessary for the isolation and study of anaerobic bacteria. The techniques are essentially of three types: the use of media containing reducing substances that eliminate oxygen from the medium; the use of media and methods by which oxygen can be excluded from the medium; and the use of anaerobic jars, plates, and incubators from which oxygen (air) can be removed and replaced with hydrogen or nitrogen.

One of the most useful media for anaerobic culture is Brewer's fluid thioglycollate medium. This medium contains sodium thioglycollate, which absorbs oxygen from the medium. It also contains a low concentration of agar, which limits convection, thus reducing the absorption of oxygen from air. Cysteine or reduced iron filings may also be used with or in place of the sodium thioglycollate. Other useful media are cooked meat and litmus milk, both of which can be obtained in dehydrated form. Before use these media should be heated in a boiling water bath for 10 to 15 minutes to drive off dissolved oxygen.

Fluid media serve well for study and identification of anaerobic bacteria but are not generally satisfactory for isolation of cultures from lesions or feces unless handled in a special manner as with spore bearers (see p. 722). For isolation it is desirable to streak plates of blood agar, infusion agar, or thioglycollate agar. Such plates are then placed in an anaerobic jar or other special container and the oxygen removed. The Brewer anaerobic jar is satisfactory for this purpose (Fig. 17–9). This jar is equipped with a special top, which contains an electrically heated platinum coil. The air is exhausted from the jar and replaced with hydrogen, exhausted again, and refilled with hydrogen. Then the jar is connected with electric current, which heats the platinum coil. This catalyzes the reaction between hydrogen and oxygen to form water, thus removing all remaining oxygen. Several other types of jars or containers are available, i.e., the Brewer anaerobic plate (Fig. 17–10) or Spray dish (Fig. 17–11), and function adequately if properly used.

One of the problems most frequently en-

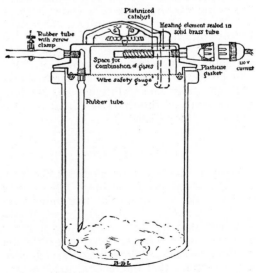

Figure 17–9. Brewer anaerobic culture jar.

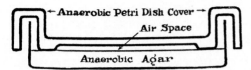

Figure 17-10.   Cross-section showing use of Brewer anaerobic Petri dish cover.

Figure 17-11.   Dish for Spray method.

countered with the anaerobes is that of spreading overgrowth. Various methods of avoiding this are available, such as use of chloral hydrate, increased agar (4 per cent), and certain antibiotics (polymyxin B, neomycin, and similar substances).

Most of the pathogenic anaerobes, such as, *Cl. tetani*, *Cl. perfringens*, and *Cl. botulinum*, produce spores that are resistant to heat of a degree capable of destroying all vegetative bacteria. It is often possible in attempting to culture these anaerobes from feces, suspected food, or wound swabs to inoculate fluid thioglycollate, cooked meat or infusion broth, or deep agar shake tubes. The culture is then put in a water bath at 75° C. for 10 to 15 minutes. This will destroy all vegetative forms (aerobic or anaerobic), and the spores will generate at incubator temperature and grow out. This may be more successful than attempts at plating. (Anaerobic techniques are detailed in the texts of Smith [1955] and Mackie and McCartney [1960].)

Choice of Media

Many media are now available for use, and one of the problems in all laboratories is the choice of media for particular purposes. Practically, particularly in small laboratories, it is desirable to limit the number of media and to choose those that offer the greatest usefulness. Once media are chosen, it is important that the technologist become thoroughly familiar with each. This is best accomplished by constant use and careful observation. Changes in media should be made when improved formulae become available but should be done with care. Cultures on new medium should be run alongside the old for a time in order to decide whether or not the new medium offers advantages in the particular laboratory.

Media may be divided into categories as follows: isolation media, enrichment media, media for maintenance, identifying or differentiating media (such as carbohydrate fermentation, hemolysis, or indol), and media for storage.

Isolation media are used to streak out specimens, such as urine or spinal fluid. They may be used for general isolation or for the selective isolation of a particular organism or group of organisms.

To be used for general isolation, a medium has to be capable of supporting a large variety of pathogenic and nonpathogenic bacteria. Blood and cholocate agar are such media and find wide usage in routine isolation work. Special media are designed for isolation of certain bacteria when their presence is suspected and may be used by larger laboratories, but for most laboratories blood and cholocate agar, used either under atmospheric conditions or in the CO_2 jar, should serve very well. These general isolation media are satisfactory with such specimens as spinal fluid, urine, and throat swabs in which the number of types of bacteria is not excessive, but when one deals with fecal culture it becomes necessary to use selective media.

Selective media incorporate substances inhibitory to propagation of a group of bacteria but allow other groups to grow. Thus, for enteric culture, media such as eosin methylene blue (EMB) and salmonella-shigella (SS) contain certain dyes and other ingredients, which inhibit gram positive organisms and allow the gram negative enteric bacilli to propagate. If, on the other hand, one wishes to isolate enterococci or staphylococci in enteric work, one can incorporate such a substance as sodium azide in blood agar, which inhibits the gram negative bacilli.

Enrichment media may be used to good advantage, particularly in enteric cultures. Such media are designed to enhance the propagation of certain organisms without favoring others. Such a medium is Selenite F, which may be used to good advantage in the isolation of *S. typhi* from stools (see p. 740).

Identification media are of various types

and range from the fluid base with specific carbohydrates added, through semisolid motility media and urea media for aid in identifying members of the genus *Proteus*, to the more complex media, such as Kligler's or triple sugar iron medium for aid in differentiation among *Salmonella*, *Shigella*, and *Escherichia*. Certain media, such as blood agar, may serve a dual purpose. In addition to its usefulness for primary isolation blood agar is very useful in establishing the tentative identity of a number of bacteria. Observations of colony morphology, effect on blood (hemolysis), and growth characteristics, as well as the gram staining characteristics and cellular morphology, are very useful, especially with gram positive cocci (Fig. 17–12).

Maintenance media may be of various types. Infusion broth is satisfactory for many of the less fastidious organisms as are infusion agar slants. For some organisms one needs an enriched medium, and blood or chocolate agar slants can be used. Certain organisms, i.e., *Diplococcus pneumoniae*, produce considerable amounts of acid from dextrose and tend to autolyze. In these cases a medium with only a little fermentable carbohydrate is advisable, else the culture may be lost. In general, cultures are best maintained by lyophilization.

Aside from these general statements, the experienced bacteriologist must be guided in the choice of media for use in any instance by the type of specimen, the nature of the suspected clinical condition, and the results of a preliminary examination of the specimen, such as gram stain.

In the section to follow there will be presented a set of procedures and certain alternatives for differentiating specimens of different types. First, there will be a list of the normal and abnormal microorganisms commonly found in the particular material or area involved, and then the routine of isolation, identification, and reporting of findings will be described. In a later section the primary identifying characteristics of the various organisms will be given. The procedures to be described represent an attempt to strike some balance between the purely academic or scientific and the practical approach that so often is necessary in small institutions.

The methods included here are obviously not the only ones that are appropriate. They have been used by the authors or are recommended by responsible workers. Each individual laboratory may make improvements and modifications of recommended techniques to fit its own special situation. Detailed procedures not described below can be found in many of the excellent textbooks listed in the references.

SPECIFIC METHODS FOR MICROBIOLOGIC EXAMINATION OF SPECIMENS

Mouth, Sputum, and Bronchial Secretions

MOUTH

Many organisms can be isolated from cultures taken from the normal mouth, and almost all organisms might conceivably be found there at one time or another. Some are found more frequently than others. There are spirochetes demonstrable in

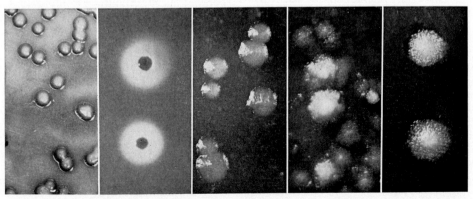

Figure 17–12. Morphologic types of bacterial colonies. *From left to right,* the raised, smooth, viscous colonies of the gonococcus on chocolate agar; β-hemolytic streptococcus colonies on blood agar showing the cleared zones of hemolysis and the slightly matt, slightly irregular edge of the typical colony; colonies of the typhoid bacillus on nutrient agar showing the typical irregular edge (maple leaf appearance) and irregular but smooth surface; colonies of the tubercle bacillus on Löwenstein's medium showing the characteristic roughened appearance; and colonies of the anthrax bacillus on nutrient agar in the typically rough, virulent form. (Burrows.)

scrapings from the base of the teeth, and lactobacilli, staphylococci, and a few other organisms may be found almost routinely in the mouth. The protozoa, *Entamoeba gingivalis* and *Trichomonas tenax*, sometime occur in the mouth and can be demonstrated in scrapings from the teeth. *E. gingivalis* may be associated with gingivitis, but its etiologic significance is not fully established.

In the mouth region organisms that may be of definite pathogenic significance include: anaerobic streptococci, *Staphylococcus, M. tuberculosis;* Vincent's organisms, *Treponema pallidum,* various viruses, and fungi. For methods of isolation and identification see sections on the various specific organisms and on the viruses.

Sputum

Organisms Normal to the Sputum. Sputum is frequently a more or less purulent exudate containing material from the lungs. "Normal" organisms are those picked up during passage through the nasopharynx. The possibility of an admixture of nonpathogenic, acid-fast bacteria is important and must be kept in mind.

The following organisms may be found in the sputum and are of possible pathogenic significance: *Diplococcus pneumoniae, Staphylococcus aureus, Streptococcus pyogenes, Klebsiella pneumoniae, Hemophilus influenzae,* and *Mycobacterium tuberculosis.* Infrequently found organisms include such fungi as *Actinomyces, Histoplasma capsulatum,* and *Coccidioides immitis* and such parasites as *Strongyloides stercoralis, Ascaris lumbricoides,* and *Trichomonas hominis.*

Collection of Sputum. The technique of collection of sputum is important not only to assist in the proper examination but also to avoid contamination of the outside of containers and of the surroundings and to prevent undue risk to those handling the material. Wide-mouth bottles with screw caps are best, but waxed paper cartons with tightly fitting tops may be used. Ideally the containers should be sterile, but this is not absolutely essential provided they have not been used previously or, in the case of glass bottles, have been thoroughly cleaned and dried. The patient should be carefully instructed about the proper procedure before collection.

It is important to distinguish sputum from saliva and postnasal discharges, and care should be taken to insure that only sputum is collected. It is desirable to rinse the mouth well before collection and then to raise the sputum by coughing. If difficulty is encountered in raising sputum, it sometimes helps to have the patient lie a few minutes with head and shoulders below the chest. Since infants and small children tend to swallow sputum and cannot be induced to cough so readily as adults, it is frequently necessary to perform gastric, bronchial, or laryngeal washings and to examine the aspirate. This is particularly useful in cases of suspected tuberculosis.

Early morning collection of sputum and immediate transport to the laboratory is to be recommended. Collection over a 24-to-72-hour period is sometimes desirable for tuberculosis, but this is not suitable for routine bacterial examination.

The procedure for examination of sputum in the laboratory depends on the suspected condition. It is always desirable to make direct smears and stains. In acute bacterial pneumonias such smears often reveal large numbers of organisms, such as *Diplococcus pneumoniae* and *Staphylococcus.* In certain other types of pneumonia (e.g., viral) bacteria may be very sparse. Prompt reporting of such findings may be of great value to the physician in guiding therapy.

To make smears, one should pick material from the more purulent portion of the sputum, flecks of mucus, and especially any blood tinged material. Care must be used in examining gram stains of such preparations, since the morphologic appearance of an organism may be misleading. For example, staphylococci quite frequently are seen in pairs and may be mistakenly reported as resembling *D. pneumoniae.* It is also important to report on cytologic components of the material, especially pus cells, and to note the presence of ingested bacteria.

Some of the material similar to that used for staining should be used for culture. Since most of the bacteria found in acute pneumonia grow well on blood agar, this is the medium of choice. The various gram positive cocci, *Staphylococcus, Streptococcus,* and *Diplococcus,* found in such conditions produce characteristic colonies on this medium, and tentative identification can be made after from 18 to 24 hours' incubation. If the gram stain has shown small gram negative bacilli, one may wish, especially in children, to inoculate a chocolate agar plate (*H. influenzae*) or, if the bacilli are larger, an EMB plate (*K. pneumoniae*). The inoculated plates should be incubated 18 to 24 hours and examined, taking care to study the colonies, the effect on the medium, and predominance of organisms. Typical colonies should be picked and stained with the gram stain. Tentative identification can often be made at this point, and a report on findings should be made. It should be made clear that such reports are tentative with final identification to follow. Further study of the isolated organisms depends on the tentative identification. It may be desirable to do antibiotic susceptibility tests, especially if such organisms as *Staphylococcus aureus* or *K. pneumoniae* are isolated. For methods of final identification of specific organisms see the section listing the basic characteristics of the species (Chap. 16).

Examination of Sputum for Acid-fast Organisms. In suspected cases of tuberculosis special staining and cultural procedures are necessary. Ideally inoculation into guinea pigs should also be done, although with improved media available this is not emphasized so much as formerly.

Since *M. tuberculosis* and other acid-fast organisms cannot be stained by gram stain, it is necessary to use one of several acid-fast staining procedures. Smears are prepared in the same manner as for the gram stain. One must, however, use only new slides. The stain must be made up in distilled water and dropped on the slide from bottles. Immersion of the slide in Coplin jars is not recommended.

The following acid-fast staining techniques may be used:

Ziehl-Neelsen method

Solutions

1. Carbolfuchsin Stain

SOLUTION A

Basic fuchsin (90 per cent dye content)	0.3 gm.
Ethyl alcohol (95 per cent)	10.0 ml.

SOLUTION B

Phenol	5.0 gm.
Distilled water	95.0 ml.

Mix solutions A and B.
2. Loeffler's Alkaline Methylene Blue

SOLUTION A

Methylene blue (90 per cent dye content)	0.3 gm.
Ethyl alcohol (95 per cent)	30.0 ml.

SOLUTION B

Dilute KOH (0.01 per cent by weight)	100 ml.

Mix solutions A and B.
Procedure
1. Stain dried smears three to five minutes with the carbolfuchsin, applying enough heat for gentle steaming. Do not allow to evaporate; add more stain as needed.
2. Rinse in water.
3. Decolorize in 95 per cent ethyl alcohol that contains 3 per cent by volume of HCl until only a suggestion of pink remains.
4. Wash in tap water.
5. Counterstain with the methylene blue stain for 30 seconds.
6. Wash in water.
7. Dry and examine.
Results: Acid-fast organisms stain red; others, blue.

Gross "cold" method

Solutions
1. Basic Fuchsin Solution. Add 25 ml. of 4 per cent alcoholic basic fuchsin solution to 75 ml. of 6 per cent aqueous phenol. To this add 3 to 4 drops of Tergitol #7 (Carbon and Chemical Corp.) and stir thoroughly.
2. Methylene Blue Solution. Add 30 ml. of 1.5 per cent alcoholic methylene blue solution to 100 ml. of 0.01 per cent aqueous KOH.
Procedure
1. Stain dried smear in the basic fuchsin solution five to ten minutes without heating.
2. Rinse in warm water.
3. Flood with acid alcohol for 30 to 60 seconds (3 ml. of concentrated HCl in 97 ml. of ethyl alcohol).
4. Rinse in cold water.
5. Counterstain three to five minutes with the methylene blue solution.
6. Rinse in water.
7. Dry and examine.
Results: Acid-fast organisms stain red; others, blue.

The finding of acid-fast organisms in sputum and gastric washings does not establish the diagnosis, although it is highly suggestive. Nonpathogenic acid-fast organisms do occur in these areas (*M. smegmatis* and *M. phlei*, for example) and can only be differentiated by culture or animal inoculation. Thus, the reports on the stained smear of necessity read "acid-fast organisms seen" or "no acid-fast organisms seen."

Concentration techniques may be used

routinely to prepare samples for culture and animal inoculation. In addition, acid-fast stains on smears from concentrates may reveal organisms when stains on the direct smear are negative.

Concentration of the sputum is accomplished by liquefaction, using one of several reagents (sodium hydroxide, sodium hypochlorite, trisodium phosphate). This not only liquefies but also destroys bacteria other than the acid-fast organisms so that they do not overgrow the culture or adversely affect the inoculated animal.

Technique of concentration

1. Place 2 to 4 ml. of sputum in a suitable test tube, preferably a pointed centrifuge tube, and add an equal volume of 4 per cent NaOH.

2. Shake for five to ten minutes or until liquefaction has occurred. The shortest time is most desirable, since on longer exposure the alkali may adversely affect acid-fast bacteria.

3. After liquefaction, centrifuge at 3000 r.p.m. for 15 to 30 minutes.

4. Aseptically remove the supernatant fluid to a disinfectant solution.

5. Add one drop of phenol red indicator to the sediment.

6. Neutralize by adding 2 N HCl drop by drop to a faint pink endpoint. This is an important step and must be done carefully.

The concentrate is then used to make smears for acid-fast staining, to inoculate special media (Löwenstein-Jensen or Petragnani's, for example), or to inoculate guinea pigs. Penicillin (50 to 100 units) may be added to the concentrate to help inhibit the growth of contaminating organisms.

To inoculate media, three or four drops are spread over each of several slants, and the slants are sealed to prevent evaporation and incubated at 37° C. The media should be incubated with the slant face horizontal for the first 24 hours to avoid settling of the entire inoculum into the point of the slant. Since nonpathogenic acid-fast bacteria grow faster than the pathogens, the appearance of colonies of acid-fast bacteria in the first three to eight days of incubation probably indicates this type of organism. The pathogenic acid-fast organisms may produce visible colonies in 10 to 14 days, but often this takes four to six weeks. For descriptions of the type of growth and cell morphology, see section on basic characteristics of species (p. 653).

Animal Inoculation. The guinea pig is the animal of choice for inoculation, because it is highly susceptible to both the human and bovine strains of *M. tuberculosis*. At least two guinea pigs should be inoculated with each specimen. The inoculum should be as large as possible, up to 0.5 ml., and may be given intraperitoneally, subcutaneously in the groin, or intramuscularly in the thigh muscle. The subcutaneous route is probably preferable, although some workers prefer the intramuscular or intraperitoneal route to avoid local abscess formation. The animal should be checked weekly after the third week, noting evidence of disease and enlarged lymph nodes. At the end of six weeks autopsy should be performed on one animal to examine for enlarged, caseous lymph nodes and disseminated tubercles throughout the various organs. Acid-fast stained smears from the lesions should reveal acid-fast bacteria. The second animal should be held for several more weeks before autopsy. If after from four to six weeks an animal shows no visible evidence of infection, a tuberculin test may be done (0.1 ml. of 1:100 old tuberculin administered subcutaneously in the flank). A positive test is strong evidence of infection. Intraperitoneal injection of such an animal with tuberculin may produce rapid death.

Cough Plates. The cough plate is used in the culture of *Bordetella pertussis* from cases of whooping cough. The plate is made with Bordet-Gengou medium (glycerin-potato agar containing 20 per cent blood and 0.3 to 1 unit of penicillin per ml.). The plate is held a few inches in front of the mouth of a child suspected of having whooping cough, and the child is encouraged to cough on the plate. The plate is incubated at 37° C. for two to four days and checked for the appearance of typical hemolytic, half-pearl colonies of *B. pertussis*. Some workers prefer to use a nasopharyngeal swab (described in the next section), which is streaked on Bordet-Gengou agar plates. This is considered to be superior to the cough method for isolating *B. pertussis*.

THROAT, NASOPHARYNX, AND SINUS DRAINAGE CULTURES

Organisms normal to the throat and nasopharynx include: *Streptococcus viridans, Staphylococcus epidermidis, Neisseria catarrhalis,* diphtheroids, *Escherichia coli,* *Aerobacter aerogenes,* nonhemolytic streptococci, and *Proteus* sp.

Organisms that may be of pathogenic importance include: *Diplococcus pneumoniae,* *Streptococcus pyogenes, Staphylococcus aureus* (coagulase positive), *Neisseria meningitidis, Hemophilus influenzae, Bordetella pertussis, Corynebacterium diphtheriae, Candida albicans, Actinomyces israelii,* and *Borrelia vincentii.*

In evaluating cultures from the throat or nasopharynx, it is important to remember that an unusual predominance of a particular organism, even though it may be considered a normal inhabitant, may have some significance and such a finding should be reported. The list of organisms just given is not a complete one, and a given situation might cause a so-called normal inhabitant to exert a deleterious effect. One cannot tell whether the predominance of one organism represents a cause or a result of some process.

Collection and Examination of Specimens. Throat and nasopharyngeal cultures are collected with cotton swabs. These may be prepared by twisting a pledget of a good grade of absorbent cotton on the end of a wooden applicator stick. One or several of the swabs may be placed in a test tube and sterilized by dry heat. Cotton swabs can also be purchased at low cost. Alginate swabs, if available, are highly recommended for taking cultures.

To collect the culture, insert the swab through the mouth, being careful not to touch the tongue, cheek, or other oral surface. The tongue may be depressed with a tongue depressor. Any obvious lesions (abscesses, follicles, or plaques) in the throat or tonsillar surfaces or any visible crypts should be explored vigorously with the swab, rotating it and getting beneath the surface. It is not sufficient simply to pass the rotating swab gently over the surface. If no obvious lesions are present, the swab should be vigorously rotated over tonsillar and other surfaces, especially any inflamed areas. In these cases it is well to obtain material from the nasopharyngeal area, which is behind and above the uvula. For this purpose a swab made with a bent wire, which may be inserted well up into the nasopharyngeal region, has definite advantages.

The nasopharyngeal swab has the advantage of avoiding much contamination with the normal flora and is particularly useful in cases of suspected whooping cough. Cultures taken from the upper nasopharynx have been found particularly successful in our experience with children. For this purpose a very thin swab on a flexible aluminum or copper wire (19-gauge) is inserted through the previously cleared nasal passage, being careful to avoid touching the sides. It is inserted until it meets definite resistance and there gently rotated. Such swabs may yield nearly pure cultures of organisms in cases of bronchial pneumonia and meningococcal infection and may be very useful in whooping cough. It cannot be too strongly emphasized that care in the collection and handling of swabs will be most rewarding in terms of results.

It is imperative that swabs not be allowed to dry out before transfer to culture media. This can be avoided by transporting the specimen to the laboratory immediately and inoculating the media, by inoculating the media at the bedside, or by placing the swab in a tube containing sterile infusion broth or Stuart's transport medium immediately after collection. If too much broth

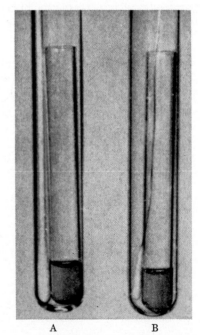

A   B

Figure 17–13. Throat and nasopharyngeal swab outfit. *A,* wooden swab for collection of material from the throat and tonsils and for general use; *B,* wire swab for the collection of nasopharyngeal specimens. Both are contained in sterile test tubes plugged with cotton. When used, the swabs are immersed in the broth in the inner tube. (From Kolmer, J. A., Spaulding, E. H., and Robinson, H. W.: Approved Laboratory Technic. 5th Ed., Appleton-Century-Crofts, Inc., 1951.)

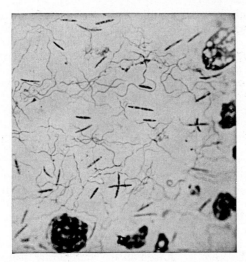

Figure 17–14. *Borrelia vincentii* and fusiform bacilli from the throat of a patient with Vincent's angina ($\times$ 1200).

is used, the resulting dilution may result in too sparse a growth on the inoculated plates (Fig. 17–13).

Blood agar is the medium of choice in most cases for inoculation of throat and nasopharyngeal swabs. Other, special media may and should be used in certain cases. *Hemophilus influenzae* and *Neisseria meningitidis* propagate better on chocolate agar under CO_2. When diphtheria is suspected, special methods should be used (see p. 729).

When a direct smear is to be examined, it is advisable to collect two swabs, one of which is smeared over a marked area on a clean, dry slide. In most cases, the smear should be gram stained, but special stains may be desired, especially in cases of suspected diphtheria or Vincent's infection. The results of examining direct smears should never be considered definitive but may be used to guide cultural procedures. Any reports made from such an examination must be descriptive and tentative.

The streaking of plates with swabs may be done in several ways, the primary goals being to obtain representative growth of the organism and to provide isolated colonies for study. One may rub the swab back and forth over one-fourth to one-third of the agar plate with continuous rotation. This may be followed by streaking with the inoculating loop at a 90° angle to the swab streaks, crossing over the swabbed area each time and covering all the rest of the plate. Some workers prefer to moisten the swab with broth before streaking on the plate. Another method is to emulsify the swab with broth before streaking on the plate. The swab can also be emulsified in 0.25 to 0.5 ml. of infusion broth by vigor-

ous agitation before streaking out three or four loopfuls of the broth emulsion. When bedside inoculation of media can be done, the first method may be used, but when some time elapses between collection and inoculation, emulsification is probably best to avoid drying.

The inoculated plates are incubated at 37° C. and examined after 24 hours at which time the colonies are studied carefully. Incubation in an atmosphere of 10 per cent CO_2 enhances growth of *N. meningitidis* and certain other organisms. Colony size, color, shape, effect on blood, and gram stain are guides to tentative identification of the organisms present and will suggest means of final identification. The use of a hand lens or other magnifier is recommended, since colonies of some organisms (e.g., *Hemophilus influenzae*) may be very small. A tentative report of the findings should be made, and the plates may be reincubated for another 24 hours.

When diphtheria is suspected, special methods are indicated. It is necessary to rule out Vincent's disease and moniliasis and to differentiate between diphtheria and follicular tonsillitis (*Streptococcus pyogenes*). The membranous lesion or follicles must be explored with the swabs vigorously enough to break the surface. At least two and preferably three swabs should be taken.

The first swab should be smeared on two clean slides and one stained with gram stain. In Vincent's infection one will see numerous spirillae (*B. vincentii*) and fusiform bacilli (large, curved, gram negative bacilli) with tapering ends. Such a finding is highly suggestive (Fig. 17–14). The second slide should be stained with either

Albert's or Loeffler's alkaline methylene blue (see acid-fast counterstain, p. 725). Albert's stain is preferable.

Albert's stain

Solution

Toluidine blue	0.15 gm.
Methyl green	0.20 gm.
Acetic acid (glacial)	1.0 ml.
Ethyl alcohol (95 per cent)	2.0 ml.
Distilled water	100 ml.

Procedure

1. Make smears as usual and fix with heat.
2. Stain five minutes in the staining solution.
3. Drain without washing.
4. Treat one minute in a modified Lugol's solution (iodine, 2 gm.; KI, 3 gm.; distilled water, 300 ml.).
5. Wash briefly in tap water.
6. Dry and examine.

Results: Metachromatic granules stain black; bars of diphtheria cells stain dark green or black; bodies of cells stain light green.

To stain with Loeffler's alkaline methylene blue, cover the fixed slide with the stain for a few seconds, wash in tap water, dry, and examine. The metachromatic granules stain dark blue to violet.

For morphologic descriptions of *C. diphtheriae* refer to the section describing the various species of microorganisms (p. 643). One must examine these direct smears carefully and interpret the findings with caution. Failure to see typical *C. diphtheriae* does not rule out their presence in the throat. Positive findings must be correlated with clinical findings, since there are nontoxic *C. diphtheriae* that are morphologically and culturally typical. This does not negate the value of the direct smear but does imply caution.

Three media should be inoculated in cases of suspected diphtheria: Loeffler's serum of Pai's slant, a tellurite agar plate, and a blood agar plate. There are several suitable tellurite media, among them Mueller's tellurite medium, Tinsdale's medium, and chocolate blood tellurite medium. If two swabs are available, one should be streaked over the entire Loeffler's slant and on the surface of the tellurite agar. The other swab should be streaked on the blood agar plate. All media should be incubated at 37° C.

Growth on the Loeffler's slant should be checked after 12 to 18 hours of incubation. More than 24 hours of incubation is not recommended, since overgrowth of other organisms may obscure the *C. diphtheriae*. Smears are made from the growth on the slant and stained with Albert's or Loeffler's alkaline methylene blue stain. These stained smears are examined for the presence of morphologically typical *C. diphtheriae*.

The blood agar plate is examined after 24 hours for typical small beta-hemolytic colonies of *Streptococcus pyogenes*. The presence of numerous such colonies is suggestive of follicular tonsillitis, but one must still rule out *C. diphtheriae* because the two organisms may occur together in cases of diphtheria.

The tellurite plate is incubated for 48 hours and examined for the typical black or gray colonies of *C. diphtheriae*. Since certain other organisms, e.g., staphylococci, yeasts, and diphtheroids, may produce black colonies on this medium, it is necessary to do gram stains to determine the type of organism present. It is well to be familiar with the differences between the microscopic appearance of *C. diphtheriae* on tellurite medium and a specimen yielding morphologically typical bacilli after growth on the Loeffler's slant. Another tellurite plate should be streaked from the growth on the Loeffler's medium. Likewise, failure to see typical organisms from Loeffler's, when suggestive colonies are found on the tellurite plate, should be followed by inoculation of a Loeffler's slant from the colony on the tellurite medium.

As indicated before, there are morphologically and culturally typical *C. diphtheriae* that are not toxigenic, that is, do not produce toxin, and are consequently nonpathogenic. Perhaps the simplest way to determine this is to grow a pure culture of the isolated organism on a Loeffler's slant for 24 to 48 hours and wash off the growth in 3 to 4 ml. of infusion broth. Add the broth to the slant and rotate vigorously between the hands. Inoculate 0.5 ml. of the suspended culture intraperitoneally into each of two guinea pigs, one of which has been protected by giving intraperitoneally 500 to 1000 units of diphtheria antitoxin a few hours previously. The unprotected guinea pig should die within four or five days, and the protected one should show no ill effects. The protected guinea pig should always be included to show that no toxic organisms other than *C. diphtheriae* are present. The toxicity test is not so important in clinically typical cases but is very important in following convalescents and in detecting carriers or doubtful cases.

There are other techniques of toxicity testing, utilizing the skin of rabbits, day-old chicks, or filter paper diffusion methods (see Parsons et al., 1955). For methods of examination of the throat and of the sputum for fungi and viruses see Chapter 18 and Chapter 19.

Cerebrospinal Fluid Cultures

Normally the cerebrospinal fluid is sterile. In meningitis, the following organisms may be found: Neisseria meningitidis, Diplococcus pneumoniae, Hemophilus influenzae, Streptococcus pyogenes, Staphylococcus aureus, Mycobacterium tuberculosis, Listeria monocytogenes, Escherichia coli, Klebsiella pneumoniae, and Pseudomonas aeruginosa. Under some conditions almost any other microorganism may be found in the spinal fluid. (For fungi and viruses see Chapters 18 and 19.)

Some of these organisms occur much more frequently in meningitis than others, and some have a definite age distribution. Hemophilus influenzae occurs most frequently in young children and seldom in adults. N. meningiditis occurs frequently in children but also affects older age groups and may occur in epidemic form. Other organisms are sometimes found in spinal fluid. Occasionally, as a result of injuries, bacteria of the normal flora may gain entry. Thus, any finding must be checked thoroughly before a final decision is made about its etiologic significance.

When cerebrospinal fluid is collected for bacteriologic examination, it must be transported to the laboratory immediately and examined at once. This is particularly important in meningococcal infection, since this organism tends to autolyze rapidly and thus may be missed. Speed is only slightly less important in other forms of meningitis, since the early initiation of appropriate treatment is of the greatest urgency.

In the bacteriologic examination of cerebrospinal fluid the gram stained smear is extremely important. The specimen should be centrifuged at 2000 r.p.m. for ten minutes and the supernatant discarded. The sediment is used for smear and culture. A loopful of the sediment is spread on a clean slide, gram stained, and examined immediately. The presence of gram negative, bean shaped, intra- or extracellular diplococci is indicative of Neisseria meningitidis. Small gram negative bacilli may indicate Hemophilus influenzae, especially in children. These are most difficult organisms to find,

since one quite frequently finds strands of proteinaceous material in such preparations that are hard to distinguish from bacteria. These examinations require care and experience. The presence of gram positive cocci indicates Diplococcus, Streptococcus, or Staphylococcus, and it is difficult to differentiate among them. Large gram negative bacilli may be suggestive of Escherichia or Klebsiella. When present, these organisms are often filamentous and may be plentiful.

It is also important to note the relative number and types of cells present on the smear. In general, polymorphonuclear leukocytes are indicative of bacterial infection, but a predominance of lymphocytes points to viral involvement. The findings of this direct examination should be reported immediately.

For culture the media of choice are blood and chocolate agar, and it is well to inoculate each specimen on plates of both media if possible. N. meningitidis and H. influenzae grow best on the chocolate agar. These plates should be incubated under 10 per cent CO_2. It is also desirable to inoculate a tube of fluid thioglycollate medium for possible anaerobic organisms.

Some workers recommend that enriched semisolid agar (ascitic fluid plus dextrose) be poured into the original tube containing the spinal fluid sediment after the other cultures have been made. Such a culture may be positive in cases in which no colonies appear on the agar plates.

The cultures are examined after 24 to 48 hours, and colonies are studied, picked, and gram stained. Further cultures for identification depend on these findings. Reports should be issued at this point with any tentative or final identifications that can be made.

The examination of spinal fluid in cases of suspected tuberculous meningitis requires special comment. Since M. tuberculosis is usually not present in large numbers, it may be difficult to demonstrate. As much spinal fluid as possible should be obtained (10 ml. if possible). Several different specimens may be pooled if available. The fluid should be centrifuged and the sediment used to make smears for acid-fast stains or for cultures, or guinea pig inoculation. The finding of acid-fast organisms on the stained smear is diagnostic. Several tubes of TB media should be inoculated and examined periodically for at least eight weeks.

Not infrequently a pellicle will form in

spinal fluid from patients with tuberculous meningitis if the specimen is allowed to stand in the collection tube in the refrigerator. This pellicle should be sedimented and examined carefully by smear and culture.

In the absence of positive findings on gram stained smears in cases of suspected meningococcal or *H. influenzae* meningitis, one may do a ring precipitin test using specific antimeningococcal or anti-influenzal antiserum. Some of the spinal fluid is drawn up in a capillary tube, and then some of the antiserum is carefully drawn up so that the two are in contact. The capillary tube is then set in plasticine on the desk. If after 20 to 30 minutes a white ring forms at the juncture of spinal fluid and serum, the test is positive. This is the result of the presence of soluble bacterial antigens in the cerebrospinal fluid, and the test is fairly specific. For mycologic and viral studies see Chapters 18 and 19.

Urine Cultures

Organisms that may be found in urine include *Escherichia coli, Paracolobactrum* (paracolon), *Proteus, Pseudomonas aeruginosa, Streptococcus pyogenes, Staphylococcus aureus,* enterococci, *Mycobacterium tuberculosis, Salmonella sp., Leptospira, Alcaligenes faecalis, Herellea,* and *Klebsiella.* (For fungi see Chapter 18.)

As it passes out through the urethra, the urine may become contaminated with certain bacteria, especially *E. coli* and staphylococci. This is more likely to happen in the female. Consequently the method of collection of urine for culture is important. Those who interpret the results of urine cultures must know how the specimen was collected. It is best to collect the urine with a sterile catheter in a sterile container. However, no matter how much care is used, there is the very real danger of introducing bacteria into the urinary tract with the catheter, and this may have serious implications in an already-ill patient. Attempts have therefore been made to use techniques that avoid the use of a catheter. In the male one may collect the middle portion of the urine, collecting from midstream, allowing the first portion to wash out most contaminating organisms. In the female one may cleanse the area around the urethra prior to urination and then collect in the middle portion, again from midstream, as in the male.

Recent investigations indicate that concentration of the urine by centrifugation is not desirable and may be misleading in cultural investigations, except possibly when tuberculosis is suspected.

Urine should be cultured within one hour after collection, or, if this is impossible, it should be stored in a refrigerator at 4° C. until cultured.

Quantitation is desirable but not absolutely essential and can be accomplished by using a standard, commercially available inoculating loop (0.01 ml.). One loopful of the urine is placed on an appropriate plate and streaked out completely over the surface of the plate. This is best accomplished with a bent wire with the bend about one-half inch from the end of the wire. The number of colonies appearing on the plate is then multiplied by 100 to estimate the number of bacteria in 1 ml. of the urine. If desired, one may do plate counts, using standard plate counting technique.

Since gram positive bacteria (streptococci and staphylococci) and gram negative enteric bacilli (*E. coli*, paracolon, and *Proteus*) may be found in urinary tract infections, it is desirable to streak the urine on a blood agar plate and on one of the selective media for gram negative bacteria, such as EMB or MacConkey's. Both plates should be streaked as described previously, incubated at 37° C., and examined after 24 and 48 hours. Further procedures for identification of the organisms depend on the type of colonies seen. Antibiotic susceptibility tests on these isolates may be of great importance and should be done at the earliest possible time.

In suspected tuberculous infection of the urinary tract, examination of the sediment of centrifuged urine should be made. The morning collection of urine is advisable. Smears of the sediment should be stained with the Ziehl-Neelsen acid-fast stain. Since nonpathogenic acid-fast bacteria, such as *M. smegmatis,* may occur normally in the urinary tract, the demonstration of acid-fast organisms in stained smears should be interpreted with caution and must be confirmed by culture or animal inoculation.

Since the urine is usually contaminated with other bacteria, the urinary sediment should be digested as described for sputum in preparation for culture and animal inoculation. It is advisable to add penicillin to the sediment. Some prefer to add 2 ml. of tannic acid (5 per cent) per liter plus 2 to 3 drops of nitric acid (30 per cent). The specimen is allowed to stand in the

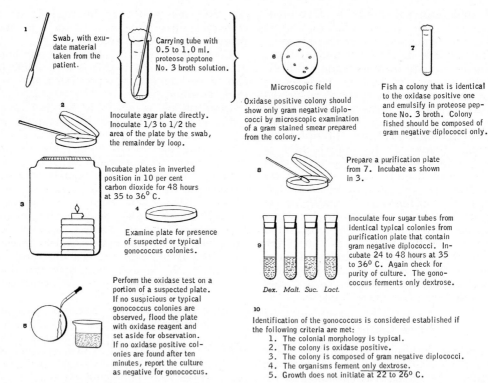

1   Swab, with exudate material taken from the patient.

Carrying tube with 0.5 to 1.0 ml. proteose peptone No. 3 broth solution.

2   Inoculate agar plate directly. Inoculate 1/3 to 1/2 the area of the plate by the swab, the remainder by loop.

3   Incubate plates in inverted position in 10 per cent carbon dioxide for 48 hours at 35 to 36° C.

4   Examine plate for presence of suspected or typical gonococcus colonies.

5   Perform the oxidase test on a portion of a suspected plate. If no suspicious or typical gonococcus colonies are observed, flood the plate with oxidase reagent and set aside for observation. If no oxidase positive colonies are found after ten minutes, report the culture as negative for gonococcus.

6   Microscopic field

Oxidase positive colony should show only gram negative diplococci by microscopic examination of a gram stained smear prepared from the colony.

7   Fish a colony that is identical to the oxidase positive one and emulsify in proteose peptone No. 3 broth. Colony fished should be composed of gram negative diplococci only.

8   Prepare a purification plate from 7. Incubate as shown in 3.

9   Dex.   Malt.   Suc.   Lact.

Inoculate four sugar tubes from identical typical colonies from purification plate that contain gram negative diplococci. Incubate 24 to 48 hours at 35 to 36° C. Again check for purity of culture. The gonococcus ferments only dextrose.

10   Identification of the gonococcus is considered established if the following criteria are met:
1. The colonial morphology is typical.
2. The colony is oxidase positive.
3. The colony is composed of gram negative diplococci.
4. The organisms ferment only dextrose.
5. Growth does not initiate at 22 to 26° C.

Figure 17–15.   Suggested steps for the isolation and identification of the gonococcus by culture. (U.S. Dept. of Health, Education, and Welfare. Public Health Service Publication No. 499.)

refrigerator overnight. The sediment is then collected and treated with sodium hydroxide.

Urethral, Prostatic, and Vaginal Exudates

The normal flora of the urethral orifice of the male includes *E. coli*, diphtheroids, and *Staphylococcus epidermidis*. The prostate and its secretions are normally sterile. In the female the urethral and vaginal areas normally have a considerable microbial flora, which is largely dependent on the glycogen content of the vaginal epithelium. This may include Döderlein's bacillus (*Lactobacillus sp.*) in large numbers, the coli-aerogenes group, staphylococci, streptococci (aerobic and anaerobic), yeasts, *Bacteroides, Veillonella,* and *Mycobacterium smegmatis.*

Pathogenic microorganisms of the region of the genital tract include: *Neisseria gonorrhoeae, Treponema pallidum, Hemophilus ducreyi* and *H. vaginalis, Calymmatobacterium* (Donovania) *granulomatis, Streptococcus pyogenes* (Groups B and D), anaerobic streptococci, *Staphylococcus aureus,* organisms of the pleuropneumonia group (PPL) or *Mycoplasma, Candida albicans, Trichomonas vaginalis,* and viruses of lymphogranuloma venereum and herpes.

The demonstration and identification of *N. gonorrhoeae* and *T. pallidum* as aids in the diagnosis of gonorrhea and syphilis are perhaps the most important procedures to carry out on urethral and vaginal exudates.

GONORRHEA AND NONSPECIFIC URETHRITIS

The microbiologic diagnosis of gonorrhea depends on the demonstration of *N. gonorrhoeae* in gram stained smears or culture of the exudate from the urethra of the male or from the vaginal secretions of the female. In the male acute gonorrhea manifests itself by a burning sensation accompanied by a purulent and rather continuous, brownish tinged exudate. This exudate should be collected on an inoculating loop, gently smeared on a clean slide, and stained with the gram stain. In gonorrhea the smear will reveal large numbers of pus cells with varying numbers of intra- and extracellular gram negative, bean shaped diplococci. Such a finding can be considered diagnostic. It is important to point out that only a very few of the thousands of pus cells on the slide may contain bacteria, and sometimes it requires considerable search to find one. In chronic gonorrhea or in treated cases the number of bacteria may be small, and they may be mostly extracellular. In such cases culture may be necessary, whereas it is not usually necessary in the acute stages.

The medium of choice for cultivation of *N. gonorrhoeae* is chocolate agar or GC medium, although other special media may be used (Griffin and Raeker, 1956; Griffin and Reider, 1957). The organism has an absolute requirement for an atmosphere of 10 per cent CO_2, unless a special medium is used that obviates this necessity. Exudate taken with an inoculating loop or a swab should be promptly streaked over the entire warmed agar plate and the plate incubated in the CO_2 jar (Fig. 17–15). For methods of identification see section on specific organisms (p. 627).

Since the infection tends to migrate up the urinary tract and may localize in the prostate, it may be necessary in chronic gonorrhea to examine the discharge result-ing from prostatic massage. The discharge should be collected in a sterile container and examined immediately by a gram stained smear and culture.

Not infrequently one encounters in the male a urethral discharge that is nongonorrheal. These discharges usually occur in the morning and tend to be cloudy but not purulent or mucoid as in gonorrhea. Gram stains from such discharges reveal large numbers of pus cells. Sometimes no bacteria are seen, or there may be sparse, gram positive cocci, usually *Staphylococcus*. Other specimens may have large numbers of small, gram negative, pleomorphic bacilli, which vary in morphology from bacilli to cocci that occur in pairs. These organisms may be intra- and extracellular and, but for their size, might be confused with *N. gonorrhoeae*. The culture of such organisms is difficult and their identity uncertain. Such conditions have been termed nonspecific urethritis and pose definite diagnostic and therapeutic problems.

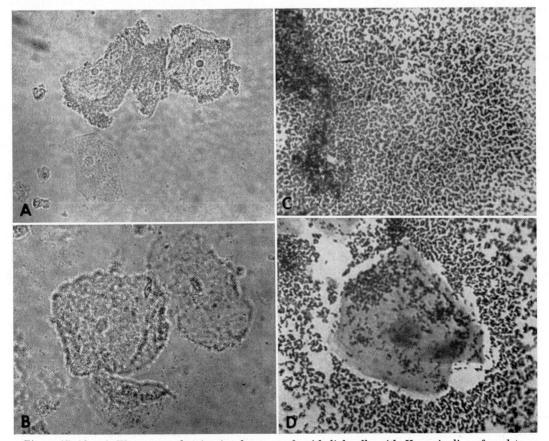

Figure 17–16. A, Wet mount showing involvement of epithelial cells with *H. vaginalis*, referred to as "clue cells." Uninvolved epithelial cell is seen in lower part of field. *B*, Higher magnification of epithelial "clue cells." *C, D*, Direct smears of vaginal discharge. Note large number of *H. vaginalis*. (Gardner, H. L., and Dukes, C. D.: Am. J. Obst. & Gyn., 69:962, 1955.)

The diagnosis of gonorrhea in the female presents certain problems. The disease may be asymptomatic, or it may manifest itself only by an increased vaginal discharge. Swab specimens for smear and culture may be taken from the cervix, vagina, or urethra as determined by the examining physician. Owing to the complex bacterial flora and the presence of epithelial cells the examination of gram stained smears from such material is difficult, and failure to find typical intra- and extracellular gram negative diplococci cannot be considered final. This is especially true of chronic, longstanding infections. Thus, in the female, culture is a necessary adjunct in attempting to make a diagnosis. Swabs should be streaked over the surface of a chocolate or GC agar plate and the plate incubated in the CO_2 jar. The addition of a few drops of a 250 units per ml. solution of polymyxin B to half the agar plate before inoculating it with the swab is of considerable help in suppressing overgrowth by coliform organisms (Crookes and Stuart, 1959).

It is possible to culture urine sediments from either the male or the female. The urine should be the first morning specimen and should be sedimented and the sediment cultured immediately.

If conditions other than gonorrhea are suspected, the cultural methods will depend on the clinical impression. Puerperal fever in the female is caused usually by aerobic or anaerobic streptococci or staphylococci. Inoculation of swabs on blood agar or fluid thioglycollate and the use of anaerobic methods should reveal these organisms. An organism recently shown by Gardner and Dukes (1955), Brewer, Halpern, and Thomas (1957), and others to be a cause of leukorrhea, vaginitis, and cervicitis is known as *Hemophilus vaginitis*. This is a a small, pleomorphic, gram negative bacillus. On wet mounts of the discharge epithelial cells may be seen covered with such large masses of this organism as to obliterate the cell membrane—the so-called "clue cell." Characteristically there is an almost complete absence of leukocytes in the preparation. Cultures on rabbit blood agar under 10 per cent CO_2 show small, pinpoint, "dewdrop" colonies (Fig. 17–16). For methods of mycologic and viral study see Chapters 18 and 19.

SYPHILIS

Syphilis in the female frequently produces lesions in the cervix, vagina, and surrounding areas, and in the male the chancre may occur in the urethra or on the penis. The bacteriologic diagnosis of syphilis depends on demonstration of the spirochete, *Treponema pallidum*, by darkfield microscopy or by silver impregnation staining. In exposed chancres material for examination is collected by first cleansing the surface and then grasping the lesion between thumb and forefinger and expressing the clear amber fluid by pressure. The operator should always wear rubber gloves and dispose of contaminated material in disinfectant solution. The expressed fluid may then be touched with a clean coverslip and the slip applied to a clean new microscope slide. Alternatively the fluid may be collected with a capillary pipet. The coverslip is sealed around the edge with petrolatum and the preparation promptly examined by darkfield microscopy. Considerable care and experience are required in making this examination. Sometimes nonpathogenic spirochetes are present. These are usually much less delicate than *T. pallidum*. (See section on specific organisms, p. 651.)

For cervical, vaginal, or other unexposed lesions it is necessary to visualize the lesion with a speculum or other instrument and to collect exudate with a Pasteur pipet or inoculating loop. This is placed on a slide and covered with a coverslip as just described. No methods are available for culturing *T. pallidum*.

Another condition occurring in the same region is soft chancre (chancroid), which is caused by *Hemophilus ducreyi*. Gram stained smears from the lesion may reveal small gram negative bacilli arranged in rows. Culture from the lesion may be made on enriched media or clotted rabbit blood but is frequently unsuccessful.

A rare condition, granuloma inguinale, is a granulomatous lesion, usually involving an inguinal lymph node. Stained aspirates from these lesions reveal gram negative bacilli with large capsules (Donovan bodies). The causative agent (*Calymmatobacterium granulomatis*) is very difficult to culture.

For methods of diagnosing vaginal moniliasis and Trichomonas vaginitis see sections on mycology and parasitology.

Skin Lesions: Wounds, Boils, Furuncles, and Exudates

Normally the skin may be contaminated with various saprophytic and potentially pathogenic bacteria. It is probable that the microorganisms present on the skin and mucous surfaces at any time depend on the environment, the area of skin and its nature, and certain other unknown factors. Bacteria on the skin may be either "transient" or "resident"; the latter seem to be constantly present and consist primarily of gram positive cocci (Evans et al., 1950).

When lesions occur in or upon the skin and microbiologic examination is desired, certain basic principles should be observed. Material for smears and culture should be taken from an area as close to normal tissue as possible, that is, the edge or base of an ulcer or boil after removal of pus or debris. In certain instances it is not profitable to culture pus or necrotic material. Pus may be completely sterile, even though the lesion from which it is derived may be caused by a specific bacterium. On the other hand it may be heavily contaminated with saprophytic bacteria, and the culture may yield nothing but confusion. One should culture for anaerobic bacteria (Cl. tetani, Cl. perfringens, and anaerobic streptococci), especially in deep or penetrating wounds.

In certain conditions in which skin rashes occur, the causative organism may sometimes be demonstrated in the lesions of the rash. In meningococcemia, incision of the bright red petechiae, followed by a gram stained smear and culture on chocolate agar, may reveal the typical gram negative diplococci. Certain of the viral diseases (smallpox and herpes) that produce skin lesions can be examined by stained smear and inoculation into embryonated eggs or animals (See Chapter 19).

The most common cause of boils, furuncles, and carbuncles is Staphylococcus aureus, although other organisms, such as Streptococcus pyogenes and certain anaerobic organisms, may rarely be involved. Cultures from such lesions should be taken with care to avoid contamination with organisms from the skin surface. The area around and over the lesion should be thoroughly cleansed with 70 per cent alcohol and allowed to dry. Pus or other material in the lesion should be removed and a sterile swab used to explore the base of the lesion. More than one swab may be used, depending on the number of procedures to be done. The swab should be emulsified in a small amount of infusion broth. The broth suspension should be streaked on a blood agar plate and inoculated into a tube of fluid thioglycollate medium for detection of anaerobes. Also, when possible, one should streak a second blood agar plate and incubate in the anaerobic jar. A swab should be smeared on a slide and stained with gram stain. Such a stained smear may suggest the type of organism involved.

If the organism cultured proves to be Staphylococcus aureus, it is important to do tests for antibiotic susceptibility and to test for coagulase and deoxyribonuclease activity.

In superficial infections, such as impetigo or acne, the surface area should be cleansed thoroughly before cultures are taken. The surface of lesions should then be broken and material collected on swabs, as in boils and furuncles. Staphylococci, streptococci (aerobic and anaerobic), Corynebacterium acnes, and certain anaerobic bacteria may be present in such conditions. It is not always easy or possible to assess the role of the isolated organisms in these conditions, especially in acne. In impetigo the causative agent is usually either Streptococcus pyogenes or Staphylococcus aureus.

Blood agar is the medium of choice as well as fluid thioglycollate medium for isolation of anaerobes. It may be desirable to inoculate two blood agar plates and to incubate one in the anaerobic jar.

Wound culture technique is determined in large measure by the existing situation. The site and method of taking material for culture are determined by the nature of the wound and whether evidence of obvious infection exists. Numerous organisms may be involved, depending on the amount of dirt and debris that may have been introduced. Wounds involving considerable trauma or penetrating wounds may contain anaerobes, such as Cl. tetani or Cl. perfringens. Thus, it is essential to do both aerobic and anaerobic cultures.

Recently infection of surgical incisions with antibiotic-resistant Staphylococcus aureus has become a serious problem. In certain areas, wound infection with C. diphtheriae is not uncommon. In such situations there may be membrane formation similar to that in the throat in classic diphtheria. Cultural techniques in this situation are similar to those described previously for diphtheria.

Cultures for Infections of the Eye

Eye secretions may have certain of the normal skin inhabitants in small numbers, such as Staphylococcus epidermidis and diphtheroids, but cultures from the normal eye, including the conjunctiva, should be relatively free of microorganisms (Cason and Winkler, 1954).

The following organisms are of pathologic importance: *Diplococcus pneumoniae, Hemophilus aegyptius* (Koch-Weeks), *Klebsiella pneumoniae, Staphylococcus aureus, Moraxella lacunata* (Morax-Axenfeld), *Pseudomonas aeruginosa,* and *Neisseria gonorrhoeae.*

Eye infections are accompanied by inflammation (pink eye) and increased secretion of tears, which may become purulent. The most common bacteria involved are listed in the preceding paragraph, although the presence of any other bacteria in considerable numbers in infected eyes should be cause for suspicion.

Cultures from infected eyes should be taken by swabbing the inflamed area and streaking on blood or chocolate agar. Inoculation should also be made into infusion broth. At the same time smears should be made for staining by gram or Giemsa stain. Viral infections, such as trachoma, inclusion blennorrhea, and herpes, are common in some areas and must be considered. (See Chapter 19.)

Cultures of the Ear, Mastoid, Sinuses, and Antrum

A variety of organisms may be associated with lesions and abscesses in ear and in sinus infections, including *Pseudomonas aeruginosa,* members of the coli-aerogenes group, *Staphylococcus aureus,* diphtheroids, staphylococci, *Streptococcus pyogenes,* anaerobic streptococci, and alpha streptococci. Fungi may also be found in ear infections and must be considered. (See Chapter 18.)

The evaluation of cultural results from abscesses and lesions in the ear is not always easy and requires the same consideration as does the interpretation of cultures from other exposed areas, where surface contamination and secondary growth of essentially nonpathogenic bacteria may occur. The presence of certain organisms may be the result rather than the cause of an infection. Nevertheless it must be recognized that eradication of such organisms may be highly desirable.

In collecting material from sinus infections, one must take care to insure that the material actually comes from the sinus and has not become contaminated from an outside source. The same general approach to culture should be followed in these situations as that described for the other areas.

Blood Culture Technique

A variety of organisms may be found in the circulating blood and, when found, have significance, since normally the blood is sterile. Numerous febrile conditions are accompanied by bacterial invasion of the blood, and the isolation of the organism has great diagnostic significance.

Organisms that may occur in the blood are as follows: *Neisseria meningitidis, Hemophilus influenzae, Diplococcus pneumoniae, Streptococcus pyogenes, Streptococcus viridans, Staphylococcus aureus, Brucella, Salmonella typhosa,* other *Salmonella, Escherichia coli,* and *Histoplasma capsulatum.* There are occasions when such organisms as *Staphylococcus epidermidis,* certain anaerobic or microaerophilic bacteria, and others may be isolated in blood culture. These should not be written off as contaminants, even though the organism is considered a nonpathogen or a low grade pathogen, without proper evaluation of technique and repeat cultures where possible.

Blood culture is one of the most important and critical procedures in clinical microbiology. When done properly, it can be of greatest assistance in diagnosis, but when poorly done, it can introduce confusion and misunderstanding. One of the best indications for blood culture is the presence of fever, especially if it is persistent.

The time at which the blood culture is taken is important. It should always be taken before initiation of antibiotic therapy and, if possible, should be taken when the fever is rising. Once antibiotic therapy is started, the chances of obtaining a positive culture are greatly reduced if not completely nullified. The stage of the disease may be important. For example, in typhoid fever the blood culture is most likely to be positive during the first two weeks of the disease. In some conditions, such as subacute bacterial endocarditis, repeated blood cultures should be done. This is also indicated in brucellosis in which, at best, the organism is difficult to culture.

The actual procedure for blood culture can be divided into steps, each of which is of critical importance: preparation of the site for collection of blood, collection of blood, inoculation into media, incubation and examination of the blood culture, and identification of cultured organism and reporting of results.

To prepare for taking a blood culture,

the patient should be placed in a comfortable position with the vein accessible. As a rule one of the veins in the antecubital fossa is used for puncture in adults. In small children and babies blood may be collected from the jugular vein. This must be done by one experienced in such techniques. The skin over and surrounding the area of puncture should be cleansed thoroughly with alcohol or soap to remove all oily deposits and then painted with disinfectant. Tincture of iodine (3 per cent iodine in 70 per cent ethyl alcohol) is recommended. The iodine should be left on for a few minutes and the area allowed to dry before the puncture is made. The area should be wiped off with alcohol after the blood has been collected. A tourniquet is applied to the arm and tightened to suppress venous, but not arterial, flow of blood.

The materials for collection must be dry, e.g., sterilized with dry heat. There are a number of techniques for collection of blood that can be used, depending on the situation. The technique involving the least number of steps in collection and inoculation of appropriate media is the most desirable, since each step increases the possibility of contamination. One can obtain blood culture sets commercially at moderate cost. Each set consists of a rubber cap vacuum bottle containing suitable medium and a sterile rubber tube with a needle at both ends. One needle is inserted into the vein and the other through the rubber cap into the bottle. The vacuum draws the blood into the bottle. When the proper amount of blood has entered, the rubber tube is pinched off, the tourniquet is removed, and the needle is removed from the vein. If the bottle contains 50 ml. of medium, one should collect no more than 5 ml. of blood. If one wishes to do an aerobic culture, a piece of sterile cotton is placed over the needle, and air is allowed to flow into the bottle. If anaerobic culture is to be done, the needle is removed from the bottle while the rubber tube remains pinched shut. Most such bottles contain increased CO_2.

If the blood is collected with a needle and syringe, one should collect 5 to 10 ml., release the tourniquet, and remove the needle. A pledget of cotton should be applied to the site of the puncture and pressure applied for several minutes with the arm elevated. Immediately after collection the blood should be transferred directly into media or into a sterile flask or test tube containing 4 ml. of 2 per cent sodium citrate to prevent clotting. It is recommended that one use a bottle containing 50 ml. of blood culture medium and fitted with a screw cap and rubber diaphragm. The needle is inserted through the cap, and not more than 5 ml. of blood is introduced into the medium with gentle shaking. Once the medium is inoculated, it should be incubated as soon as possible.

If the blood is citrated, the tube or flask should be shaken gently and transported immediately to the laboratory for inoculation of media. Delays should be avoided, since antibody may adversely affect the organisms and citrate itself may be detrimental.

By using the blood culture sets already mentioned, one can do aerobic or anaerobic culture or both as desired. If the bottles and flasks are made in the laboratory, it is well to use a good aerobic broth as well as fluid thioglycollate medium for anaerobic culture. Both media can be obtained readily in dehydrated form. In most chronic or subacute conditions it is well to inoculate both types of media, since anaerobic or microaerophilic streptococci, *Bacteroides*, and certain similar organisms will not grow out aerobically.

In a number of conditions, such as subacute bacterial endocarditis and brucellosis, in which the number of organisms may be low, it may be desirable to culture more than 5 ml. of blood. In such instances it is better to inoculate several 50 ml. portions of media than to increase the amount of blood in each bottle. If one uses excessive blood, the natural inhibitory substances or antibodies present may prevent growth of bacteria that may be in the blood.

Some workers prefer to use a Castaneda bottle for blood culture. This is made by placing a layer of an agar medium (blood agar or infusion agar) on one side of a square or rectangular bottle, then adding aseptically 50 ml. of blood culture broth. After the blood is added, the bottle is tilted to bathe the agar, and colonies may then appear on this surface.

It is desirable to add 0.05 per cent para-aminobenzoic acid (PABA) to the blood culture medium to counteract sulfonamide drugs that may be in the blood of patients. Appropriate amounts of penicillinase may be added routinely or only in cases in which the patient has been treated with penicillin.

The conditions of incubation are important. *Brucella abortus* grows only in an atmosphere containing 10 per cent CO_2, and *N. meningitidis* and *H. influenzae* grow better in 10 per cent CO_2. Such an atmosphere will not inhibit growth of any of the other organisms.

After inoculation the cultures should be shaken to distribute the blood throughout the medium before incubation at 37° C. Daily examinations should be made. Evidence of bacterial growth may appear as cloudiness in the broth above the settled red blood cells or as obvious changes in these cells, such as hemolysis. Some bacteria do not produce cloudiness, multiplying adjacent to the red blood cell layer (*Streptococcus pyogenes*). When visible evidence of growth appears, samples should be removed for gram stain and subculture. With no visible evidence of growth, samples for gram stain and subculture should be taken at 24 to 48-hour intervals for seven to ten days and weekly thereafter.

To take a sample from the blood culture bottle, one should use a dry, sterile needle and syringe. The culture is shaken, and great care used to sterilize the top before insertion of the needle. Routinely a drop should be smeared on a slide for gram stain and one or two drops streaked on a blood agar plate. On the basis of the gram stain other media may be inoculated. For example, in a patient with clinical signs of enteric fever, the presence of gram negative bacilli suggests a *Salmonella* infection, and one should streak an EMB plate or other enteric medium. The results of the preliminary finding should be reported as soon as possible.

The results of the gram stain, the type of growth in the blood culture, and the clinical appearance of the patient will do much to determine the procedures for identification of the organism. Once growth has been detected and successful subcultures obtained, it is no longer necessary to hold the blood culture. How long negative cultures should be held is difficult to define. Growth is sometimes considerably delayed, and even in typhoid fever, cultures have become positive only after 14 to 21 days. In brucellosis it is desirable to hold cultures for four to six weeks before discarding. Most other blood cultures should be held at least 10 to 14 days. If space permits, nothing is lost by holding them longer. Progress reports on blood culture findings should be made as early as possible. Positive findings must be reported promptly and susceptibility studies initiated when indicated.

Microbiologic Examination of the Feces

The microbiologic examination of feces involves several procedures: bacteriologic examination involving culture of specific recognized pathogens; examination for cysts and trophozoites of intestinal protozoa and ova, larvae, or other significant structures of intestinal helminths; examination for viruses; and cytologic descriptions of the feces in terms of cellular elements, undigested food particles, fatty acid crystals, and yeasts. The presence of yeasts is not necessarily diagnostic in the ordinary sense but may be viewed as a reflection of conditions in the intestinal tract. Such examination often gives valuable leads about what cultural or other procedures might prove of value. For example, the presence of large numbers of pus cells might indicate a bacterial infectious process, and the presence of much undigested protein or fatty acid crystals may indicate faulty absorption.

In this section the methods for bacteriologic and parasitologic examination of feces will be described. For viral isolation see Chapter 19 and for morphologic descriptions see Chapter 16.

The decision to describe bacteriologic and parasitologic methods in the same section stems from the recognition that quite frequently both types of examination are indicated in a given patient and that ideally a laboratory should be capable of doing both simultaneously. Actually the cytologic examination may be done by the person examining for parasites, since one may better recognize cysts and ova if he is familiar with the other structures that may be present in feces. Viral studies require quite different management.

The lower portion of the intestinal tract represents a complex biologic system in which numerous species of microorganisms may normally be found. The flora may consist of vast numbers of the following organisms: *Escherichia coli, Aerobacter aerogenes, Proteus, Bacteroides, Staphylococcus, Streptococcus* (aerobic and anaerobic), *Clostridium perfringens, Clostridium tetani, Lactobacilli*, and yeasts.

It is possible that organisms are normally present in the digestive tract that have not yet been isolated and identified. Studies have indicated that the relative number of these various organisms of the normal flora fluctuates considerably from day to day. This probably depends on such things as diet and other factors affecting the physiology and biochemistry of the intestine. Of the organisms most commonly cultured from the feces, *Escherichia coli* normally predominates. *Bacteroides* occur also in large numbers but are not routinely cultured since they are obligate anaerobes. A marked shift in the relative number of these bacteria in the normal flora may indicate an abnormal situation.

A large portion of the feces is made up of bacterial cells, most of which are dead. These may be seen in smears but have little specific significance.

Certain microorganisms may be present in the intestine and seen in or cultured from feces and, although not normal inhabitants, appear to have little or no pathogenic potential. Most of the intestinal protozoa fall in this category. Some of the organisms normally present in the intestinal flora may produce disease under appropriate circumstances. It appears likely that enterotoxin producing strains of *Staphylococcus aureus* are present frequently if not always. Under special circumstances these organisms may produce severe disease. *Proteus morganii* has been suspected of contributing to diarrhea in children. Certain gram positive organisms, such as staphylococci and possibly streptococci, have been suspected of playing a role in ulcerative colitis. These relationships are difficult to evaluate and the whole subject of enteric disease needs much further study.

Occasionally patients who are given prophylactic antibiotics prior to surgery develop large numbers of staphylococci in the intestinal tract, apparently replacing to a large extent the normal intestinal flora. Such patients may go into shock unless promptly treated. This condition is known as pseudomembranous enterocolitis. Gram stain of the stools reveals large numbers of gram positive cocci, and cultures on azide blood agar or Staphylococcus Medium 110 reveal almost pure cultures of *Staphylococcus*. Other organisms may also cause this condition (clostridia and fecal streptococci, for example).

Certain serotypes of *Escherichia coli* can cause serious and sometimes fatal diarrhea in infants and children. Numerous outbreaks of diarrhea in nurseries have been caused by these *E. coli*. Interestingly enough, recent work has shown that household pets may serve as reservoirs of infection with these organisms (Mian, 1959). (See Chapter 16.)

Certain members of the normal flora of the intestine are capable of producing disease outside the digestive tract. *E. coli*, *Klebsiella*, *Proteus*, and *Pseudomonas aeruginosa* are common causes of urinary tract infection. These organisms are not infrequently found in the blood as the terminal cause of death in carcinoma and other serious debilitating diseases.

The most common enteric bacterial pathogens are as follows: *Salmonella typhi* and other salmonellas, *Shigella* (several species), *Paracolobactrum* (paracolon; pathogenicity varies), enteropathogenic *E. coli*, *Vibrio comma*, and *Staphylococcus aureus*.

The pathogenic protozoa are: *Entamoeba histolytica*, *Dientamoeba fragilis*, and *Giardia lamblia*.

The pathogenic helminths of which the ova or other structures may be found in feces are as follows: *Necator americanus*, *Ancylostoma duodenale*, *Strongyloides stercoralis*, *Trichuris trichiura*, *Ascaris lumbricoides*, *Enterobius vermicularis*, *Diphyllobothrium latum*, *Taenia saginata*, *Taenia solium*, *Hymenolepis nana* and *diminuta*, *Schistosoma mansoni*, *haematobium*, and *japonicum*, *Fasciola hepatica*, *Fasciolopsis buski*, and *Clonorchis sinensis*.

COLLECTION OF SPECIMENS FROM THE INTESTINAL TRACT

A specimen of feces for examination should ideally be the first of the morning. When they can be examined immediately, the specimens can be collected in waxed paper cartons with tight fitting tops. Collection may be made in bed pans and transferred to cartons, but if this is done care should be exercised to avoid mixing with urine. With infants, one may collect the feces from a diaper. In any case the specimen should be in the laboratory and ready for examination within 30 to 60 minutes after collection. The use of barium or mineral oil should be avoided in patients whose stools are to be collected for microbiologic examination. The presence of these substances renders stool examination very difficult. Some workers prefer saline purged stools for parasitologic examination and this can be quite useful. However, if it is possible to examine a sufficient number of normally passed stools, purgation may be unnecessary.

Fresh, unpreserved specimens are preferable, but it is not always possible to obtain them. If it is not possible to obtain fresh specimens, one can use certain preservatives. For bacterial culture one may emulsify a portion of the stool in buffered glycerol-saline. For parasitologic examination two preservative solutions should be used. The first, polyvinyl alcohol (PVA), is used for preservation of the trophozoites of intestinal protozoa, and the second, 10 per cent formalin, preserves protozoan cysts and helminth ova well. The three preservative materials are put up in screw cap vials in 10 ml. quantities and may be assembled into sets.

PRESERVATIVE SOLUTIONS

The preservative solutions are made as follows:

Buffered Glycerol-Saline

Sodium chloride	4.2 gm.
Dipotassium phosphate, anhydrous	3.1 gm.
Monopotassium phosphate, anhydrous	1.0 gm.
Glycerol	300 ml.
Distilled water	700 ml.

Dispense in bottles and autoclave. It is desirable to add sufficient phenol red to the solution to give a pink color. If the phenol red changes to yellow, discard the bottles.

Polyvinyl Alcohol Preservative (PVA)

Schaudinn's fluid (2 parts saturated aqueous solutions of $HgCl_2$ to 1 part 95 per cent ethyl alcohol)	93.5 ml.
Glycerol	1.5 ml.
Glacial acetic acid	5.0 ml.
Polyvinyl alcohol, powdered (Elvanol)	5.0 gm.

The powdered polyvinyl alcohol should be added with continuous stirring to the solution at 75° C. It can be used for several months.

10 Per Cent Formalin

Formaldehyde (U.S.P.)	10 ml.
Distilled water	90 ml.

Feces are collected in waxed cartons, and a portion the size of the end of the little finger (approximately one part feces to three parts fixative) is transferred to the vial with an applicator stick and thoroughly emulsified. The best portion of feces to choose is that containing mucus or blood.

The polyvinyl alcohol and formalin preserved material can be held indefinitely for parasitologic examination, but the glycerin broth does not preserve bacteria indefinitely and should be cultured as soon as possible.

One may use rectal swabs for bacterial culture. This is quite useful in young children. An ordinary cotton swab is moistened in broth or peptone water and inserted through the anal orifice. The swab may then be sent to the laboratory or streaked on plates of appropriate media at the bedside. Rather than use the plain swab, some prefer to place it in a lubricated rubber or plastic tube, which is cut so as to have a tapered end. The rubber tube is inserted into the anus and the swab pushed through this. Some workers prefer to take the swab culture through the proctoscope.

The number of stool examinations necessary to diagnose or to rule out a given infection has been the subject of much study. It is difficult to establish a number in any given situation, and one should perhaps never set a maximum. The number of examinations depends on several circumstances. In general, though, for both bacterial and parasitologic examinations one should examine at least three specimens collected on successive or alternate days.

For the viruses that may occur in feces see Chapter 19.

BACTERIOLOGIC EXAMINATION OF FECES

Since the feces normally contain a considerable number of different bacterial species, the isolation of any single species or group requires special techniques. The principles of fecal culture depend on the use of media designed either for enhancement or selection of particular organisms. Most of the well-recognized bacterial diseases of man (typhoid and enteric fever, bacillary dysentery, *Salmonella* food poisoning, and Asiatic cholera) are caused by gram negative enteric bacteria of the genera *Salmonella, Shigella,* and *Vibrio.* Sometimes other gram negative enteric bacilli, such as *Proteus morganii,* enteropathogenic *Escherichia coli, Alcaligenes fecalis,* and certain paracolons, may be involved. The isolation of this group of organisms depends on the use of media containing certain substances that inhibit the growth of gram positive organisms. They also contain lactose to assist in separating the coli-aerogenes bacteria from the organisms that do not produce acid from this carbohydrate. On such media the lactose fermenting bacteria produce colored colonies, although the colonies of nonlactose fermenters are colorless.

The numbers of any given pathogenic bacterium in the feces vary considerably, depending on the severity and type of infection and the stage of the disease. For example, in typhoid fever the number of *S. typhi* may be very small in the early stages but tends to increase greatly after the second week of the disease. In severe cases one may find a nearly pure culture of this organism in the stools. This may also occur with *V. comma* in cholera. In the carrier state the number of the organisms usually is quite small.

The enhancement media, selenite F and tetrathionate broth, are designed to assist in the isolation of *Salmonella* in cases in which few organisms are present. In these media *Salmonella* multiplies more rapidly than the other organisms during the first 12 to 18 hours of incubation at 37° C. Thus, if one inoculates from the fecal specimen into one of these media, incubates for from 12 to 18 hours, and then streaks from this onto the selective media, the chances of isolating these pathogens are increased.

Selective media for enteric bacterial pathogens can be divided into two groups: those that are highly selective and those that are moderately selective. The latter might better be termed differential. The most commonly used highly selective media are salmonella-shigella (SS) agar, brilliant green agar, Wilson Blair bismuth sulfite agar, and desoxycholate-citrate agar. The most commonly used less selective or differential media are eosin methylene blue (EMB) agar, Endo agar, and MacConkey's agar. It is not recommended that one use all these media, but it is well to choose one from each group. A good combination is SS and EMB, although others may serve equally well, depending on experience and need.

The routine procedure for fecal culture in the laboratory is as follows: Pick portions of the stool containing mucus or blood for inoculation of media. If the stool is liquid, it can be streaked directly on EMB and SS agar plates. Appropriate portions, particularly any blood or mucus, of formed or semiformed stools should be used to make a heavy suspension in infusion broth. The SS agar should be streaked heavily, using several loopfuls of the material, but the EMB plate should be streaked with two to three loopfuls. At the same time a portion the size of a pea should be inoculated into a tube of selenite F or tetrathionate enrichment broth and thoroughly emulsified. The enrichment culture should be incubated 12 to 18 hours at 37° C. and then streaked on a SS agar plate. The EMB and SS agar plates should be examined after 24 and 48 hours and suspicious colonies picked for further study. If suspicious nonlactose fermenting colonies are seen, this should be reported to the physician,

being careful to indicate that this is only a preliminary report. For the procedure for further identification of the enteric pathogens see Chapter 16.

It should be emphasized that, in enteric infection in which fever exists, blood culture may be of great help. The simultaneous isolation of an organism from blood culture and fecal culture is significant. Urine culture is also desirable, especially in typhoid fever.

It is frequently desirable to culture feces for *Staphylococcus* or *Streptococcus*. Here again one must use selective media. The media of choice for these organisms is blood agar containing phenylethyl alcohol, sodium azide, or other substances inhibitory to gram negative bacilli or Staphylococcus Medium 110.

For culture methods for anaerobes in feces refer to the section on anaerobic culture methods (p. 721).

EXAMINATION OF FECES FOR PROTOZOA AND HELMINTHS

A number of protozoa occur in the intestines and may persist for long periods without producing disease; some of the helminths are only mildly pathogenic. Recognition of the nonpathogenic protozoa is important for two reasons. First, they must be differentiated from the pathogenic species (*Entamoeba histolytica*, *Dientamoeba fragilis*, *Giardia lamblia*) and, second, the finding of nonpathogenic protozoa should encourage further search for pathogens, since the mode of infection is essentially the same for pathogens and nonpathogens.

The parasitic protozoa exist with some exceptions in three stages in the intestinal tract: the trophozoite or vegetative stage, the rounded precyst, and the cyst. Some of the protozoa exist only as trophozoites. For descriptions of the morphology of the various protozoan forms, see Chapter 16.

The life cycle of the helminths is much more complex than that of the protozoa, and usually only one stage is found in the stool. Most commonly this is the ovum, although other structures (larvae and proglottids, for example) are found in some cases and when found are diagnostic. These structures are described in Chapter 16.

The aims of parasitologic examination of stools are: to find and identify any protozoa or helminths present in the stool; to carry out a sufficient number of procedures with sufficient care to be reasonably sure that none of these organisms has been

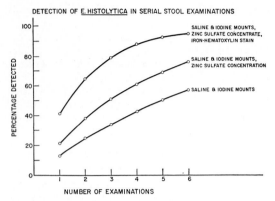

DETECTION OF E. HISTOLYTICA IN SERIAL STOOL EXAMINATIONS

SALINE & IODINE MOUNTS,
ZINC SULFATE CONCENTRATE,
IRON-HEMATOXYLIN STAIN

SALINE & IODINE MOUNTS,
ZINC SULFATE CONCENTRATION

SALINE & IODINE MOUNTS

Figure 17–17. Probability of detecting *Entamoeba histolytica* by successive stool examinations using various methods. (Adapted from Sawitz and Faust, 1942.)

missed; and to recognize and describe the cytologic and other elements in the stool in order to assist in establishing the processes that may be going on in the digestive tract. It is important that the examiner be able to recognize pus cells, macrophages, yeasts, undigested food particles, fatty acid crystals, and Charcot-Leyden crystals in order to differentiate between these and the protozoan cysts.

It has been shown repeatedly that there is a direct relationship between the number of procedures done on a stool specimen and the percentage of positive findings of protozoa and helminths. This is particularly true in the case of the important pathogen, *Entamoeba histolytica* (Fig. 17–17) (Sawitz and Faust, 1942). Routinely it is desirable to do at least four procedures on each fecal specimen: Direct smear in saline, direct smear with iodine stain, direct smear stained with iron hematoxylin or other permanent stain, and concentration of feces by Ritchie's formalin-ether method or by zinc sulfate flotation stained with iodine. The same holds for the study of preserved feces.

The direct smear in saline is done to demonstrate trophozoites of protozoa, and since one of the diagnostic characteristics of these forms is motility, this should be done immediately and provision should be made to use a warmed (37° C.) slide and saline. This is important since the motility is lost on cooling. If the stool cannot be examined immediately, it should be held in the refrigerator and warmed in the 37° C. incubator before examination. To make the preparation, two or three drops of the saline are placed on a slide, and a small portion of the fecal sample is emulsified in it. Portions containing mucus or blood are most desirable. Care should be exercised to avoid making this preparation too thick. Experience will determine the appropriate amount

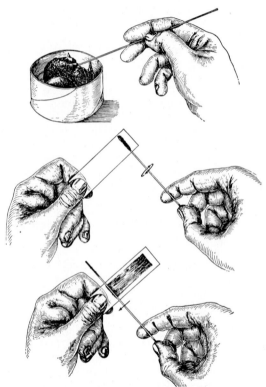

Figure 17–18. Preparation of fecal film for permanent staining. (Markell and Voge: Diagnostic Techniques in Medical Parasitology.)

of feces to use. For examination a coverslip is applied and the slide searched with the low and high dry lenses of the microscope. It is important that this be done with reduced light. In addition to the protozoan trophozoites, helminth ova and larvae may be seen in these preparations.

The iodine stained direct smear is used for the cysts and precysts of protozoa, which are stained in a characteristic manner by the iodine. The heavy cyst wall, nuclei, and other structures are revealed by this method. To make the preparation, place two or three drops of D'Antoni's iodine stain (see Appendix, p. 933) or other suitable iodine preparation on a slide and emulsify the fecal matter as in the saline preparation. Both preparations may be made on the same slide. The examination is identical in each case.

Certain of the protozoa cannot be distinguished readily from one another by direct smear examination. This is particularly true with the small races of *Entamoeba histolytica* and *Endolimax nana*. Therefore, adequately prepared and permanently stained smears are made and examined (Fig. 17–18). For this it has been a common practice to use Delafield's iron hematoxylin stain or one of its modifications (Felsenfeld and Young, 1945). Another useful stain that is somewhat easier to do is a modification of Mallory's phosphotungstic acid technique (see Appendix, p. 933). It is important that the laboratory staff be familiar with one or the other of these stains and use it routinely.

Quite frequently the number of cysts or ova in the stool is small and they may not be seen on direct smear. It is therefore necessary to use a suitable concentration method. There are several such techniques, two of which (Ritchie's formalin-ether technique and the zinc sulfate flotation) are widely used. One or the other of these is an essential part of the fecal examination.

Ritchie Formalin-Ether Concentration Method

1. Emulsify a portion of stool about the size of a walnut in 10 ml. of saline.
2. Strain the emulsion through dampened gauze into a test tube.
3. Centrifuge at 1500 to 2000 r.p.m. for two minutes. Decant the supernatant.
4. Resuspend the sediment in fresh saline, centrifuge, and decant as before.
5. Add approximately 10 ml. of 10 per cent formalin to the sediment, mix thoroughly, and allow to stand for five minutes.
6. Add 3 ml. of ether, stopper the tube, and shake vigorously.
7. Centrifuge at 1500 r.p.m. for about two minutes. This should result in four layers: a small amount of sediment containing most of the parasites and ova, a layer of formalin, a plug of fecal debris on top of the formalin, and a layer of ether.
8. Free the plug of debris from the sides of the tube by ringing with an applicator stick and carefully decant the top three layers.
9. Examine the sediment after mixing with two or three drops of iodine solution and applying a coverslip. One may also wish to use a saline preparation.

Zinc Sulfate Flotation. This method depends on the differences in specific gravity between cysts and ova and fecal debris. If a zinc sulfate solution with a specific gravity of 1.16 or 1.18 is used, the cysts and ova float, while most of the fecal debris sinks to the bottom. Trophozoites of the protozoa are destroyed and some of the more fragile cysts may be damaged, although this is not usually serious. The method is not satisfactory for operculated helminth ova.

Zinc sulfate solution. Dissolve 400 gm. of $ZnSO_4$ (U.S.P. Crystalline) in 1000 ml. of water. Check the specific gravity with a hydrometer, and add water until the specific gravity of 1.18 is obtained.

Procedure

1. Emulsify a pea-size piece of feces in distilled water in a 13×100 mm. test tube.
2. Filter the suspension through one layer of wet cheesecloth to remove large particles.
3. Centrifuge for approximately two minutes at 1800 r.p.m. and pour off the supernatant by inverting the test tube quickly.
4. Add approximately 2 ml. of tap water. Break up the sediment and fill the tube with water. Centrifuge and repeat these washings until the supernatant fluid is fairly clear.
5. Add a small amount of the zinc sulfate solution and break up the sediment. Fill the tube with the zinc sulfate solution and centrifuge. At this point the cysts and ova should be floating on the meniscus.
6. With a wire loop (5 to 6 mm. in diameter) carefully remove a few loopfuls from the meniscus and place on a slide.
7. Add one or two drops of D'Antoni's iodine stain and mix by gently rotating the slide.
8. Add a coverslip and examine for cysts and ova.

The diligence with which these examinations are done and the training and experience of the examiner determine in large measure the number of positive findings reported. Reports on stool examinations should incorporate all findings, including a description of the stool; its color; whether formed, semiformed, or liquid; its microscopic cytology; and of course any protozoan or helminthic forms seen. There are times when structures that are unidentifiable resemble protozoa. These should be reported so that the physician can decide whether or not to submit more specimens. One cannot put an upper limit to the number of specimens to be examined when a high degree of suspicion exists.

Some workers have reported success in the diagnosis of infection with *Entamoeba histolytica* by examination of proctoscopic aspirates. These aspirates are collected through the proctoscope with a serologic pipet or an appropriately prepared glass tube and rubber bulb. The mouth of the pipet is placed over a lesion (pinpoint ulcer) and mucus is sucked into the pipet. This material is then placed on a slide and examined for trophozoites. Later it may be stained with iodine for cysts. Permanent stains may be made by smearing the aspirate on a slide previously moistened with PVA fixative.

ANTIBIOTIC SUSCEPTIBILITY TESTS

Chemotherapy, i.e., the destruction of microorganisms by drugs, was initiated by the pioneer studies of Ehrlich, which culminated in the development of salvarsan for the treatment of syphilis. The sulfonamides were introduced in 1935 with Domagk's work on the use of Prontosil, the active principle of which is sulfanilamide, in the treatment of streptococcus infections in mice. Since that time dozens of new sulfonamides have been synthesized with ever increasing antibacterial activity and decreased toxicity.

The term "antibiotics" refers to substances elaborated by living microorganisms that have the capacity to inhibit the growth of other microorganisms. The story of the discovery of penicillin by Fleming in 1929, its application to the treatment of human disease, and the subsequent development of a host of new antibiotics is well known. Actually there is no clearcut differentiation between the terms "antibiotic" and "chemotherapeutic agent," because some of the antibiotics originally isolated from natural sources have also been prepared synthetically. (A notable example of this is chloramphenicol.) Consequently the terms are used interchangeably.

The sulfonamides are primarily bacteriostatic substances. They are supposed to inhibit growth by competing with the microorganism for a special enzyme system associated with the essential metabolite, para-aminobenzoic acid (Wood-Fildes). The mode of action of penicillin and other antibiotics in cellular metabolism is essentially unknown but probably depends basically upon interference with specific steps of enzymatic processes in susceptible organisms. In contrast to the sulfonamides the action of some of the antibiotics, such as penicillin, is primarily bactericidal.

The tendency of many bacteria to become resistant to antibiotics has become a problem of ever increasing importance, particularly with staphylococci and tubercle bacilli. For example, it has been found that as high as 90 per cent of strains of coagulase positive staphylococci in hospital populations are now resistant to penicillin. These resistant strains have caused an alarming number of serious infections in and outside hospitals. This emphasizes that improper use of antibiotics can lead to serious consequences and, hence, the importance of selecting the correct antibiotic with the aid of susceptibility tests.

The exact mechanism of the development of increased bacterial resistance is not clear. It is known that all bacterial populations are heterogeneous in their susceptibility to a given antibiotic. The resistant bacteria in a population may arise spontaneously as a result of mutation (Demerec, 1948) or perhaps by adaptation. In some instances resistance to an antibiotic is a function of the production of a specific enzyme that destroys the drug, e.g., penicillinase production by staphylococci. It is also possible that an organism actually can become dependent upon an antibiotic.

Many infections respond promptly to the empiric administration of one or another of the commonly used antibiotics, and bacteriologic cultures are unnecessary. However, when the diagnosis is uncertain, in cases that relapse, when the patients do not respond quickly to therapy, and when the disease is severe and fulminating, laboratory assistance is essential and may be lifesaving. The decisive factor involved in the choice of the proper antibiotic is the relative susceptibility of the invading bacterium. As used here, the terms "sensitivity" and "susceptibility" are synonymous. The term "antibiotic susceptibility" is preferable to "sensitivity," since the latter term may be confused with the allergic or hyper-sensitivity reaction to antibiotics occasion-ally encountered in patients.

Choice of Method for Antibiotic Susceptibility Testing

The most widely used methods at the present time are:

Test Tube Dilution Methods. Tubes of a nutrient vehicle containing serial dilutions of the antibiotic are inoculated with sus-pensions of the test organism. A measure of the susceptibility to the drug is manifest by failure of the organism to grow in a given dilution.

Diffusion Methods. Paper discs or strips impregnated with known amounts of anti-biotics are placed on the surface of Petri dishes seeded with the test organisms. Sus-ceptibility is indicated by a zone of in-hibited growth around the paper containing the drug.

Streak Plate Methods. Agar plates con-taining known amounts of antibiotics are streaked with the test organism, and in-hibition of growth is noted.

Other Procedures. Susceptibility can also be shown by physical or chemical changes that accompany growth, such as shift in pH, reduction of hemoglobin, and inhibi-tion of hemolysis.

The choice of the method used depends to a large extent on the facilities and ex-perience of the laboratory personnel. It does not necessarily follow that a laborious tech-nique, such as the tube-dilution method, is more accurate than a simpler technique, such as a diffusion method. By the tube method gross errors can be obtained if the following factors are not taken into consid-eration and adequately controlled: the size of the inoculum, the solubility and stability of the antibiotic being tested, the composi-tion of the culture medium used, and the growth requirements of the organisms be-ing tested. On the other hand the disc method gives results that are strictly quali-tative. The size of the zone of inhibition depends on both the solubility and diffusi-bility of the antibiotic and does not neces-sarily coincide with antibacterial activity.

The important factors in all antibiotic susceptibility testing, regardless of the pro-cedure used, are to make certain that the method is accurate and reproducible, that all steps are carried out precisely with ade-quate controls, and that the results are re-ported properly (Goldin and Davidsohn, 1954).

There are many "short cuts" practiced in antibiotic susceptibility testing that should be avoided if possible. In cases of life-threatening infections it might be advisable to attempt to determine the relative sus-ceptibility of the invading organisms di-rectly from the specimen. In general, how-ever, there is no adequate substitute for culturing the specimen, determining the possible etiologic agent, and performing accurate susceptibility tests on those or-ganisms for which tests may be useful. Susceptibility tests to the following organ-isms are ordinarily unnecessary, since they have thus far shown no tendency to change in resistance: *Streptococcus pyogenes*, *Dip-lococcus pneumoniae*, and *Neisseria menin-gitidis*. For organisms such as the following, susceptibility tests may be imperative: coli-aerogenes group, *Proteus*, *Pseudomonas aeruginosa*, *Staphylococcus aureus*, and *Streptococcus faecalis*.

Antibiotic susceptibility tests done on mixed cultures directly from the specimen are almost worthless and may even be mis-leading. Such tests should not be done.

Procedures

Test Tube Dilution Procedure. Prepare twofold serial dilutions of the antibiotics as follows: Place ten sterile 13 x 100 mm. test tubes in a rack. To each of the last nine tubes add 0.5 ml. of Penassay or trypticase soy broth. To the first and second tubes add 0.5 ml. of a solution of the anti-biotic containing 100 or 1000 units per ml. Mix and transfer 0.5 ml. from the second tube to the third tube. Continue this process until the last tube is reached and discard the last 0.5 ml.

In the same broth used for the test, prepare a 1:100 or 1:1000 dilution of the organism to be tested. Add 1.5 ml. of this suspension to each tube of the series as well as to a control tube containing no antibiotic. Incubate the tubes at 37° C. overnight and note inhibition of growth of the organisms in each tube. The least amount of antibiotic resulting in complete inhibition of growth is the endpoint and is recorded as the M.I.C. (minimal inhibitory concentration). The first tube of the series would contain 25 units per ml. if the 100-unit solution of antibiotic was used; the second, 12.5; the third, 6.25; and so on.

The concentration of antibiotic used to prepare the stock solution (which is then further diluted) depends in part on the nature and site of the infection. It is ob-vious that an organism not inhibited by

25 units per ml. of an antibiotic would be considered resistant if present in the blood, where such concentrations can seldom be obtained. On the other hand the same organism causing a superficial abscess could be considered sensitive, because high concentrations of antibiotics can be obtained readily in compresses or ointments applied to the local area.

An alternate method of performing the tube dilution test is to prepare dilutions of the antibiotics in broth, which is kept in the deep freeze at −20° C. until used. When needed, the tubes containing the antibiotics in broth are removed from the freezer, thawed, shaken thoroughly to mix, and inoculated with the broth dilution of the organism to be tested.

Synergistic or antagonistic combinations can be determined by mixing the stock solutions of the antibiotics before diluting. There is some question, however, whether this procedure correlates well with the *in vivo* activity of combinations of antibiotics. It is also possible to determine whether the antibiotic being tested has a bactericidal or a bacteriostatic effect by subculturing those tubes showing inhibition of growth in thioglycollate broth.

The results may be reported as the minimal inhibitory concentration of the antibiotic in units per ml. or simply as "susceptible," "moderately susceptible," and "resistant." These categories can be related to the results in the tube dilution test only in a rough way, and it is necessary for each laboratory to decide about the relative susceptibility or resistance of a given strain to a given antibiotic. Table 17–3 gives briefly the generally accepted method of classifying broth dilution test results for a few of the commonly used antibiotics.

The tube method of Schneierson and Amsterdam (1959) simplifies the broth dilution procedure by using only two concentrations for each antibiotic. Prepare concentrated solutions of antibiotics from standard antibiotic preparations or from commercial therapeutic parenteral packages by adding distilled water to yield a final concentration of 10,000 units per ml. of each with the exception of sulfadiazine, which is used in its original concentration, 250,000 mcg. per ml. These concentrated solutions are distributed in 1 ml. amounts in 16 x 125 mm. tubes and kept frozen at −20° C. or below until needed.

The test consists of adding 2 ml. of a 1:1000 dilution of the test organism in broth to 0.1 ml. of the desired concentration of antibiotic. After overnight incubation at 37° C., those organisms that show growth in both concentrations of the antibiotic are reported as "resistant," those in the low concentration only as "moderately resistant," and those inhibited by both concentrations as "susceptible." This implies that if the etiologic agent is susceptible to an antibiotic, treatment with average doses is suggested. If the organism is moderately resistant, massive doses would be indicated, and, if resistant, treatment with that antibiotic would be unsuccessful.

Plate Dilution Method. Penassay or trypticase soy agar is satisfactory. Organisms that grow poorly on solid media or that have a spreading tendency (*Proteus, Pseudomonas*) are best tested by a different method.

Agar medium is melted and cooled to 48° C. Serial dilutions of the antibiotic are prepared in distilled water, starting at 1000 units per ml. To the bottom of a Petri dish 1 ml. of each antibiotic dilution is added and then 9 ml. of the melted and cooled agar. The dishes are mixed by rotation and allowed to harden. Then, using a sterile cotton swab, a segment of each of several plates containing a different antibiotic concentration is streaked with a broth culture of the test organism. A control plate without any antibiotic is inoculated with each culture tested. As many as ten organisms can be used on each plate. After overnight incubation at 37° C. the plates are examined for growth. If 12 plates

Table 17–3. **Broth Dilution Test Results with Common Antibiotics**

	SUSCEPTIBLE	MODERATELY SUSCEPTIBLE	RESISTANT
Penicillin	< 0.1–0.5 units	0.5– 10 units	> 10 units
Tetracycline	< 1– 5 mcg.	5– 20 mcg.	> 20 mcg.
Chloramphenicol	< 5–15 mcg.	15– 50 mcg.	> 50 mcg.
Streptomycin or Dihydrostreptomycin	< 1– 5 mcg.	5– 20 mcg.	> 20 mcg.
Polymyxin B	< 10–25 units	25–100 units	> 100 units
Erythromycin	< 1– 2 mcg.	2– 5 mcg.	> 5 mcg.

are used, the concentration of antibiotic will decrease by halves from 100 to 50 down to 0.04 unit per ml. The concentration of antibiotic producing complete inhibition of growth is taken as the endpoint. Partial inhibition is observed by noting a decrease in the amount of growth until complete inhibition is obtained.

Agar Diffusion (Disc) Method. This method is the simplest and most rapid for the determination of susceptibility of microorganisms to antibiotics, but it is subject to the shortcomings mentioned previously.

1. The medium used can be either infusion or blood agar. For testing susceptibility to sulfonamide drugs, Mueller-Hinton agar should be used.

2. The growth from a young broth culture of the organism is streaked over the surface of the plate with a sterile cotton swab in such a manner as to allow a uniform, confluent growth. Alternatively the specimen or exudate may be suspended in broth and then streaked on the plate. This should not be a routine procedure for reasons discussed previously.

3. The inoculated plate is placed in the incubator and allowed to dry thoroughly, because extra moisture will tend to leach out the antibiotics in the filter paper and give erroneous results.

4. Discs are then placed on the plates at equidistant intervals, taking care that the medium makes contact with the entire surface of the disc. The discs may be of three types: the "wet disc" prepared by dipping sterile filter paper discs into solutions of the antibiotic just before adding them onto the plate, dried discs prepared commercially or in the laboratory, or multiple discs containing several different antibiotics in one unit. The important factor in the choice of discs is that they be of the proper potency and be carefully standardized (Fig. 17–19).

The final concentration of antibiotic in the disc for each antibiotic is computed by comparing the zones of inhibition obtained with different concentrations of antibiotics in the discs with the minimal inhibitory concentrations determined by the tube dilution method (Table 17–4).

5. The plates are incubated at 37° C. overnight or until growth develops. In some cases, particularly if heavy inoculations have been made in the morning, readings can be taken after five to six hours.

Readings are based upon the presence or absence of a distinct zone of inhibition around the discs. The diameter of the zone of inhibition varies with the antibiotic and with the test organism, and actual measurements of zone sizes should not be made. The results by this method are strictly qualitative, and the diameter of the zone of inhibition does not indicate the relative effectiveness of the antibiotic. If two strengths of antibiotics are used, results should be reported as follows:

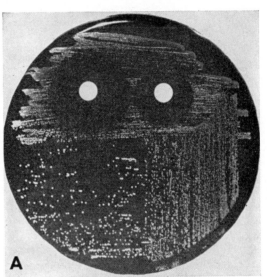

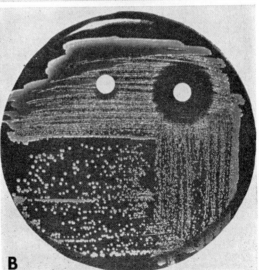

Figure 17–19. Filter paper disc method for determining sensitivity to penicillin and streptomycin. *A,* a strain of *Staphylococcus aureus* very susceptible to both penicillin (left disc) and to streptomycin (right disc). (From Milzer, A. In A Textbook of Clinical Pathology, edited by Miller, S. E. 5th Ed. Baltimore, The Williams & Wilkins Company, 1955.) *B,* another strain of *Staph. aureus* resistant to penicillin (left disc) but very sensitive to streptomycin (right disc). (From Bondi *et al.,* 1947. Reproduced through the courtesy of the authors.)

Table 17–4.   Concentrations of Antibiotics in Discs
Used in Susceptibility Testing*

	LOW STRENGTH	HIGH STRENGTH
Aerosporin	50 units	300 units
Bacitracin	2 units	10 units
Chloramphenicol	5 mcg.	30 mcg.
Chlortetracycline	5 mcg.	30 mcg.
Dihydrostreptomycin		
and streptomycin	2 mcg.	10 mcg.
Erythromycin	2 mcg.	15 mcg.
Kanamycin	5 mcg.	30 mcg.
Neomycin	5 mcg.	30 mcg.
Nitrofurantoin	25 mcg.	100 mcg.
Novobiocin	5 mcg.	30 mcg.
Oleandomycin base	2 mcg.	15 mcg.
Oxytetracycline	5 mcg.	30 mcg.
Penicillin	2 units	10 units
Ristocetin	5 mcg.	30 mcg.
Sulfonamides	50 mcg.	300 mcg.
Tetracycline	5 mcg.	30 mcg.
Vancomycin	5 mcg.	30 mcg.

* As recommended by the U.S. Food and Drug Administration, Antibiotics Division (4/1/59).

> *Susceptible:* Distinct zone of inhibition around the discs of both strengths.
> *Moderately susceptible:* Distinct zone around the highest concentration only.
> *Resistant:* No zones around any disc.

Occasionally isolated colonies can be seen growing within the zone of inhibition. These represent resistant variants of the strain of organism being tested, or perhaps contaminants, and should be gram stained or subcultured.

Susceptibility of M. Tuberculosis to Chemotherapeutic Agents

It is important from a therapeutic standpoint to know the degree of susceptibility of tubercle bacilli to the various chemotherapeutic agents used. The rapid acquisition of resistance to these drugs *in vivo* by *M. tuberculosis* creates a serious problem. It is good practice to test all positive cultures for their susceptibility during the course of treatment to see if there is any change in their response to the chemotherapeutic drug being used. Susceptibility testing of these organisms is also of some help in differentiating virulent human strains from the so-called "yellow bacillus" and the chromogens.

TECHNIQUES

Disc Procedure. This technique is essentially similar to that used for other bacteria. The base medium is prepared from Peizer's TB medium base and enrichment, which is available commercially. A heavy suspension of the organism or the clinical specimen is smeared heavily on the agar surface, and dried discs containing different concentrations of dihydrostreptomycin, isonicotinic acid hydrazide (I.N.H.), viomycin, para-aminosalicylic acid (P.A.S.), or other drugs desired are placed on the surface. The plates are then sealed and incubated for sufficient time to allow good growth; this may require two to eight weeks. The presence of zones of inhibition surrounding the discs indicates susceptibility to that agent as discussed previously.

Liquid Media. Liquid media, such as Proskauer's and Beck's or Dubos', are made up in measured volumes and sterilized. To these tubes sufficient concentrations of antibiotics are added aseptically. These usually consist of 1, 10, and 100 mcg. of streptomycin; 1, 5, and 25 mcg. of I.N.H.; and 1, 10, and 100 mcg. of P.A.S. Various combinations of these or other drugs may be used as required, and the concentrations may be varied if necessary.

Each tube is inoculated with 0.1 ml. of a 10-day-old growing culture, or a drop of a suspension of a culture is ground in a mortar with the medium. A control tube containing no drug is inoculated at the same time. All tubes are incubated at 37° C. and readings at seven-day intervals are taken. The least amount of chemotherapeutic agent that prevents growth is recorded as the susceptibility level of the strain tested.

Solid Media. This procedure has the advantage of allowing the same medium to be used for isolation and for susceptibility tests and is more satisfactory for performing this test directly from the pathologic material than is either of the two methods described previously. However, the material must contain a moderately large amount of tubercle bacilli and must be carefully digested and concentrated before it can be used successfully. Performing the test using a pure culture of the strain being tested is obviously more satisfactory, provided the delay in time is not objectionable.

Löwenstein-Jensen, Herrold's egg yolk agar, American Trudeau Society (A.T.S.), or similar media may be used. The medium is prepared as usual. Just before inspissation the required drugs are added aseptically to give the desired concentrations. The slants are then inoculated with a smooth, uniform suspension of a culture or directly from the pathologic material. Tubes containing the antibiotics may be obtained commercially. Control tubes containing no antibiotic are also included. The slants are incubated and examined weekly for six weeks. A record is kept of the number of colonies that appear in each tube. The susceptibility is expressed as the lowest concentration that completely prevents growth during the incubation period.

Antibiotic Levels in Body Fluids

The estimation of the amounts of a given antibiotic in a body fluid is not so frequently required as in the past, since very large doses are usually given. The methods briefly described can be readily adapted to the determination of other antibiotics.

PENICILLIN (METHOD OF RANDALL, PRICE, AND WEBB)

1. The test organism is *Bacillus subtilis*, N.R.R.L. strain 558.
2. Place 0.5 ml. of Penassay broth in nine small test tubes. Prepare serial dilutions of the fluid being tested (which must be sterile) by adding 0.5 ml. to tubes 1 and 2; mix and transfer 0.5 ml. from tube 2 to tube 3, and so on to tube 9. Discard 0.5 ml. from tube 9.
3. Prepare a standard for comparison by diluting penicillin of known potency (reference standard) to one unit per ml. in broth. Dilute this one unit standard exactly as for the body fluid in a second series of tubes, each containing 0.5 ml. of broth.
4. Add 1.5 ml. of a 1:100 dilution of an 18-hour culture of the test organism to all tubes. Incubate at 37° C. overnight.
5. The endpoint is last tube in which no growth occurred. Determine the concentration of the unknown by comparing the endpoint with that of the standard. For example:

Tube No.	1	2	3	4	5	6	7	8	9
Standard	0	0	0	0	0	0	0	+	+
Serum A	0	0	0	0	+	+	+	+	+
Serum B	0	0	0	0	0	0	0	0	+

In this example the standard caused complete inhibition in the seventh tube. Since this represents one unit per ml., serum A contains 0.125 unit per ml. because it required a solution eight times as strong to cause complete inhibition. Serum B thus contains 2 units per ml.

To determine potencies lower than these, it is only necessary to vary the dilution series of both the standard and the unknown.

STREPTOMYCIN (METHOD OF PRICE, NIELSEN, AND WELCH)

1. The test organism is *Bacillus circulans*, A.T.C.C. No. 9966.
2. Place 0.5 ml. of streptomycin assay broth in sterile 12 x 100 mm. tubes and make serial dilutions by halves as for penicillin.
3. Prepare a standard for comparison by diluting a streptomycin salt of known potency in broth to contain 10 mcg. of the base per ml. Serially dilute this standard in the same manner as the body fluid.
4. To all tubes add 1.5 ml. of a 1:100 dilution of an overnight culture of the test organism in broth.
5. Incubate overnight at 37° C. and consider the last tube in which no growth occurred as the endpoint.
6. The interpretation is similar to that described for penicillin.

REFERENCES

1. Aiken, M. A., Ward, M. K., and King, E. O.: A study of a group of gram negative bacteria resembling the Mimeae (De Bord). Publ. Health Lab., *14*:126–136, 1956.
2. Anderson, H. H., Bostick, W. L., and Johnstone, H. G.: Amebiasis—Pathology, Diagnosis, and Chemotherapy. Springfield, Illinois, Charles C Thomas, 1953.
3. Belding, D. L.: Textbook of Clinical Parasitology. 2nd Ed. New York, Appleton-Century-Crofts, Inc., 1952.
4. Boeck, W. C., and Drbohlav, J.: The cultivation of *Endamoeba histolytica*. Am. J. Hyg., *5*:371–407, 1925.
5. Boshell, B. R., and Sanford, J. P.: A screening method for the evaluation of urinary tract infections in female patients without catheterization. Ann. Int. Med., *48*:1040–1045, 1958.
6. Breed, R. S., Murray, E. G. D., and Smith, N. R.: Bergey's Manual of Determinative Bacteriology. 7th Ed. Baltimore, The Williams & Wilkins Company, 1957.
7. Brewer, J. H.: A modification of the Brown anaerobe jar. J. Lab. & Clin. Med., *24*:1190–1192, 1939.
8. Brewer, J. I., Halpern, B., and Thomas, B. S.: *Hemophilus vaginalis* vaginitis. Am. J. Obst. & Gynec., *74*:834–843, 1957.
9. Brooke, M. M., and Goldman, M.: Polyvinyl alcohol-fixative as a preservative and adhesive for protozoa in dysenteric stools and other liquid material. J. Lab. & Clin. Med., *34*:1554–1560, 1949.
10. Bryson, V., and Demerec, M.: Bacterial resistance. Am. J. Med., *18*:723–737, 1955.
11. Burkholder, P.: Antibiotics. Science, *129*:1457–1465, 1959.
12. Burrows, W.: Textbook of Microbiology. 17th Ed. Philadelphia, W. B. Saunders Company, 1959.
13. Cason, L., and Winkler, C. H., Jr.: Bacteriology of the eye. I. Normal flora. A.M.A. Arch. of Ophth., *51*:196–199, 1954.
14. Castenada, M. R.: Practical method for routine

blood cultures in brucellosis. Proc. Soc. Exp. Biol. & Med., 64:114–115, 1947.

15. Clark, W. M.: The Determination of Hydrogen Ions. 3rd Ed. Baltimore, The Williams & Wilkins Company, 1928.

16. Cleveland, L. R., and Collier, J.: Various improvements in cultivation of *Endamoeba histolytica*. Am. J. Hyg., 12:606–613, 1930.

17. Conn, H.: Biological Stains. 6th Ed. Geneva, New York, Biotech Publications, 1953.

18. Conner, A. B., and Mallery, O. T.: Blood culture. A clinical laboratory study of two methods. Am. J. Clin. Path., 21:785–788, 1951.

19. Cooper, G. N.: The prolonged survival of upper respiratory tract and intestinal pathogens on swabs. J. Clin. Path., 10:226–230, 1957.

20. Craig, C. F.: The Etiology, Diagnosis, and Treatment of Amebiasis. Baltimore, The Williams & Wilkins Company, 1944.

21. Crookes, E. M. L., and Stuart, C. D.: The value of aerosporin in the isolation of *Neisseria* from swabs forwarded to the laboratory in transport medium. J. Path. & Bact., 78:283–297, 1959.

22. D'Antoni, J. S.: Standardization of the iodine stain for wet preparations of intestinal protozoa. Am. J. Trop. Med., 17:79–84, 1937.

23. Dearing, W. H.: Micrococcic enteritis and pseudomembranous enterocolitis as complications of antibiotic therapy. Ann. N. Y. Acad. Sc., 65:235–242, 1956.

24. Dearing, W. H., Heilman, F. R., and Sauer, W. G.: Micrococcic (staphylococcic) enteritis following the use of Aureomycin or Terramycin. Gastroenterology, 26:38–40, 1954.

25. Demerec, M.: Origin of bacterial resistance to antibiotics. J. Bact., 56:63–74, 1948.

26. Evans, C. A., Smith, W. M., Johnston, E. A., and Giblett, E. R.: Bacterial flora of the normal human skin. J. Invest. Dermat., 15:305–324, 1950.

27. Faust, E. C., and Russell, P.F.: Clinical Parasitology. 6th Ed. Philadelphia, Lea & Febiger, 1957.

28. Faust, E. C., Sawitz, W., Tobie, J., Odom, U., Peres, C., and Lincicome, D. R.: Comparative efficiency of various technics for the diagnosis of protozoa and helminths in feces. J. Parasitol., 25:244–262, 1939.

29. Felsenfeld, O. F., and Young, V. M.: An improved method for the examination of intestinal protozoa. Am. J. Clin. Path. (Tech. Sect.), 9:47–50, 1945.

30. Flippen, H. W., and Eisenberg, G. M.: Antibiotic Therapy in Medical Practice. Philadelphia, F. A. Davis Company, 1955.

31. Frame, H. F., and Short, D. W.: Drug-induced enteritis. Lancet, 1:434–435, 1955.

32. Gardner, H., and Dukes, C. D.: *Hemophilus vaginalis* vaginitis. Am. J. Obst. & Gynec., 69:962–976, 1955.

33. Goldin, M., and Davidsohn, I.: Laboratory control of antibiotic therapy. A practical method for the general hospital. Mod. Hosp., 82:92–97, 1954.

34. Griffin, P. J., and Raeker, E.: The carbon dioxide requirement of *Neisseria gonorrhoeae*. J. Bact., 71:717–721, 1956.

35. Griffin, P. J., and Reider, S. V.: A study of the growth requirements of *Neisseria gonorrhoeae* and its clinical applications. Yale J. Biol. & Med., 29:613–621, 1957.

36. Gross, M.: Rapid staining of acid fast bacteria. Am. J. Clin. Path., 22:1034–1935, 1952.

37. Grove, D. C., and Randall, W. A.: Assay Methods

of Antibiotics. A Laboratory Manual. New York, Medical Encyclopedia, Inc., 1955.

38. Guze, L. B., and Beeson, P. B.: Observations on the reliability and safety of bladder catheterization for bacteriologic study of the urine. New England J. Med., 255:474–475, 1956.

39. Hite, K. E., Hesseltine, H. C., and Goldstein, L.: A study of the bacterial flora of the normal and pathologic vagina and uterus. Am. J. Obst. & Gynec., 53:233–240, 1947.

40. Ino, J., Neinegebauer, D. L., and Lucan, R. N.: Isolation of *Mima polymorpha* var. *oxydans* from two patients with a clinical syndrome resembling gonorrhea. Am. J. Clin. Path., 32:364–366, 1959.

41. Kolthoff, I. M., and Rosenblum, C.: Acid-base Indicators. New York, The Macmillan Co., 1937.

42. Mackie, T. J., and McCartney, J. B.: Handbook of Practical Bacteriology. 10th Ed. Edinburgh, Scotland, E. & S. Livingstone, Ltd., 1960.

43. McQuay, R. M., Jr.: Charcoal medium for growth and maintenance of large and small race of *Entamoeba histolytica*. Am. J. Clin. Path., 26:1137–1141, 1956.

44. Mian, K. A.: Isolation of enteropathogenic *E. coli* from household pets. J.A.M.A., 171:1957–1960, 1959.

45. Moore, M. S., and Parsons, E. I.: A study of a modified Tinsdale's medium for the primary isolation of *Corynebacterium diphtheriae*. J. Infect. Dis., 102:88–93, 1958.

46. Otto, J. F., Hewitt, R., and Strahan, D. E.: A simplified zinc sulfate levitation method of fecal examination for protozoan cysts and hookworm eggs. Am. J. Hyg., 33:32–37, 1941.

47. Pai, S.: A simple egg medium for the cultivation of *B. diphtheriae*. Chinese Med. J., 46:1203–1204, 1932.

48. Parsons, E. I., Frobisher, M., Moore, M. S., and Aiken, M. A.: Rapid virulence test in diagnosis of diphtheria. Proc. Soc. Exper. Biol. and Med., 88:368–370, 1955.

49. Philpot, V. B.: The bacterial flora of urine specimens from normal adults. J. Urol., 75:562–568, 1956.

50. Procedures for isolation and identification of the gonococcus. U.S. Dept. of Health, Education and Welfare. U.S. Public Health Service Publication No. 499, 1956.

51. Rammelkamp, C. H., and Lebovitz, J. L.: The role of coagulase in staphylococcal infections. Ann. New York Acad. Sc., 65:144–151, 1956.

52. Recommended procedures for laboratory investigation of hospital acquired staphylococcus disease. U.S. Dept. of Health, Education, and Welfare. Atlanta, Georgia, U.S. Public Health Service Communicable Disease Center, September, 1958.

53. Ritchie, L. S.: Ether sedimentation technique for routine stool examinations. Bull. U.S. Army Med. Dept., 8:326, 1948.

54. Sawitz, W. G., and Faust, E. C.: The probability of detecting intestinal protozoa by successive stool examinations. Am J. Trop. Med., 22:131–136, 1942.

55. Schaub, I. G., Foley, M. K., Scott, E. G., and Bailey, W. R.: Diagnostic Bacteriology. 4th Ed. St. Louis, The C. V. Mosby Company, 1958.

56. Schneierson, S. S., and Amsterdam, D.: A simplified tube procedure for the routine determination of bacterial sensitivity to antibiotics. Am. J. Clin. Path., 31:81–86, 1959.

57. Shaffer, J. G., Ryden, F. W., and Frye, W. W.:

Studies on the growth requirements of *Endamoeba histolytica*. IV. Further observations on the cultivation of *E. histolytica* and other intestinal protozoa in a clear medium without demonstrable bacterial multiplication. Am. J. Hyg., *49*:127–157, 1949.

58. Shaffer, J. G., Sienkiewicz, H. S., and Washington, J. E.: The propagation of *Endamoeba histolytica* in tissue-bearing culture without accompanying bacteria or other microorganisms. Am. J. Hyg., *57*:366–379, 1953.

59. Smith, D. T.: Zinnser's Textbook of Bacteriology. 11th Ed. New York, Appleton-Century-Crofts, Inc., 1956.

60. Smith, L.: Introduction to the Pathogenic Anaerobes. Chicago, University of Chicago Press, 1955.

61. Society of American Bacteriologists: Manual of Microbiological Methods. New York, McGraw-Hill Book Co., 1957.

62. Stokes, E. J.: Clinical Bacteriology. Baltimore, The Williams & Wilkins Company, 1955.

63. Stuart, R. D.: Transport media for specimens in public health bacteriology. Public Health Reports, *74*:431–437, 1959.

64. Sykes, G. (Ed.): Constituents of Bacteriological Culture Media. Cambridge, Cambridge University Press, 1956.

65. Tobie, J. E., Reardon, L. V., Bozicevich, J., Schick, B. C., Mantel, N., and Thomas, E. H.: The efficiency of the zinc-sulfate technic in the detection of intestinal protozoa by successive stool examinations. Am. J. Trop. Med., *31*:552–560, 1951.

66. Weckman, B. G., and Catlin, B. W.: Desoxyribonuclease activity of micrococci from clinical sources. J. Bact., *73*:747–753, 1957.

67. Wilkinson, A. E.: A note on the use of Stuart's transport medium for isolation of gonococcus. Brit. J. Ven. Dis., *27*:200–202, 1951.

68. Willis, A. S., and Cummings, M. M.: Diagnostic and Experimental Methods in Tuberculosis. 2nd Ed. Springfield, Illinois, Charles C Thomas, 1952.

69. Youmans, G. P., Ibrahim, A., Sweaney, J., and Sweaney, H. C.: A direct method for the determination of the sensitivity of tubercle bacilli to streptomycin. Am. Rev. Tuberc., *61*:569–577, 1950.

Chapter 18

Medical Mycology

By JAMES G. SHAFFER, Sc.D., *and* MILTON GOLDIN, M.S.

Many clinical pathologists and medical technologists become discouraged in their attempts to study fungi because of the unfamiliar nomenclature, the confusing synonymy and multiplicity of microscopic structures, and the widely held idea that mycologic techniques are difficult and complex. In actuality, once a few names and basic concepts are mastered, the identification of pathogenic fungi can become simpler and more rapid than that of bacteria.

In this chapter descriptions of the most important fungi are necessarily brief because of the limitations of space. More detailed descriptions may be found in the excellent texts listed in the bibliography.

Fungi are essentially plant-like organisms belonging to the phylum Thallophyta. Unlike the algae they lack chlorophyll and hence are either saprophytic or parasitic. They reproduce by spores, which germinate into long filaments called *hyphae*. As the hyphae continue to grow and branch, they develop into a mat of growth called the *mycelium* (pl. *mycelia*). From the mycelium, spores are produced in characteristic arrangements. These spores, when dispersed to new substrates, germinate and form new growths.

Reproduction of the pathogenic fungi is essentially asexual. The simplest type of reproduction is that characteristic of the *yeasts*, i.e., budding. A true yeast is a fungus that is unicellular and reproduces by budding.

Spores formed by budding are called *blastospores*. In certain fungi, e.g., *Candida*, the budding spores may elongate, remain attached to the parent cell, and form short abortive mycelia, the *pseudomycelia*.

In other fungi different types of spores are found. They may be thick-walled, resting spores, the *chlamydospores*, or may be formed by rectangular segmentation of the mycelium, the *arthrospores*. Those formed at the end of a specialized branch of the

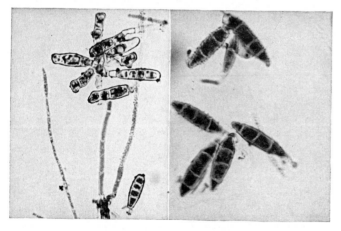

Figure 18–1. *Left,* blunt end fuseaux, *Epidermophyton floccosum.* Note the attachment to the mycelium. Mounted in Amann's lactophenol cotton blue solution; × 420. *Right,* pointed fuseaux, *Microsporum gypseum.* Mounted in Amann's lactophenol cotton blue solution; × 420. (Burrows.)

Table 18-1. Source of Specimens and Media Required for Demonstration of Fungi from Specific Types of Fungus Infections

DISEASE	TYPE OF SPECIMEN	ISOLATION MEDIUM
Superficial mycoses		
Erythrasma	Skin scrapings	None
Tinea versicolor	Skin scrapings	None
Candidiasis (moniliasis)	Skin, vaginal discharge, mucocutaneous scrapings	Sabouraud's agar; E.M.B. (CO_2)
Onychomycosis (tinea unguium)	Nail scrapings	Sabouraud's agar
Tinea capitis	Plucked hair (preferably Wood's light positive)	Sabouraud's agar
Tinea corporis	Skin scrapings	Sabouraud's agar
Tinea pedis	Skin scrapings	Sabouraud's agar
Tinea cruris	Skin scrapings	Sabouraud's agar
Systemic mycoses		
Actinomycosis	Pus from draining sinus, sputum	Thioglycollate broth; infusion agar (anaerobic)
Nocardiosis	Sputum, pus from abscesses	Sabouraud's agar; infusion broth
Blastomycosis	Scrapings from edge of skin lesions, pus from abscesses, sputum	Blood agar and antibiotics; cycloheximide agar
Candidiasis	Sputum, stools, urine, blood	Sabouraud's agar; E.M.B. (CO_2)
Coccidioidomycosis	Sputum, pus from draining sinuses, scrapings from skin lesions	Sabouraud's agar; cycloheximide agar
Cryptococcosis	Spinal fluid, sputum, urine, pus from abscesses	Sabouraud's agar; blood agar
Geotrichosis	Sputum, bronchial washings, stools	Sabouraud's agar; Littman's agar
Histoplasmosis	Blood, sternal marrow, sputum, skin scrapings, exudate from ulcers	Brain-heart infusion blood agar and antibiotics; cycloheximide agar
Sporotrichosis	Pus from ulcers, aspirated fluid from abscesses	Sabouraud's agar; Littman's agar
Aspergillosis Penicilliosis Mucormycosis	Sputum, bronchial washings, ears, biopsy material	Sabouraud's agar

hypha, the *conidiophore*, are known as *conidia*. The conidia vary greatly in size and shape, and these differences help to identify many species. Small conidia are known as *microconidia* and large, multicellular ones as *macroconidia*. Spindle-shaped macroconidia, such as those found in the genus *Microsporum*, are called *fuseaux* (Fig. 18-1).

Fungi associated with human disease can be divided into those affecting only the superficial keratinized layers of the skin— the *dermatophytes;* those capable of infecting the deeper tissues or organs within the body—the *deep* or *systemic* fungi; and those that are intermediate, i.e., capable of producing either superficial or deep infections (or both). Techniques of isolating and identifying these organisms depend on demonstrating them in tissue by direct examination and culturing them on media devised for that purpose. Success in identifying these organisms depends to a large extent on understanding the biology of the organisms and the nature of the disease in which they are involved. As in many other cases there must be a close association between the clinician and the laboratory as far as fungus diseases are concerned. The clinical impression should always be substantiated by appropriate laboratory tests, a number of which are to be described (Table 18-1).

ACTINOMYCOSIS

The *Actinomyces* and *Nocardia* groups, strictly speaking, are not true fungi, since they belong to the class Schizomycetes, which includes the bacteria. However, they do differ in many respects from bacteria and may be thought of as primitive fungi transitional to the bacteria.

Actinomycosis is caused by an obligate anaerobic organism known as *Actinomyces israeli* (*A. bovis, A. hominis*). It can mani-

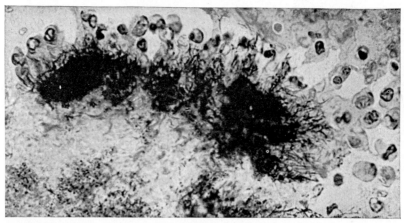

Figure 18–2. Pulmonary infection in man with *Actinomyces israeli*. Margin of a granule in lung tissue showing the ray-like structure. Note the bacteria designated *Actinobacillus actinomycetemcomitans* in the center of the granule. Gram stain; × 1000. (Humphreys.)

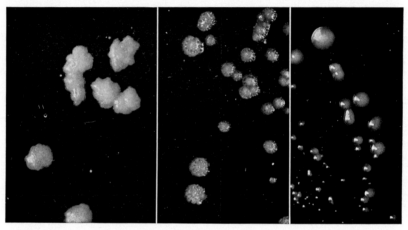

Figure 18–3.   *Actinomyces israeli,* six-day growth on brain heart infusion agar: *left* and *center*, rough type (× 3); right, smooth type (× 6). (Rosebury, Epps, and Clark.)

fest itself in a variety of clinical conditions. Most commonly the cervicofacial area is involved with swelling of the soft tissue of the face, neck, jaws, tongue, or other structures of this region; abscess formation; and multiple draining sinuses. The thoracic form is found mostly in the lungs with small abscess cavitation resembling pulmonary tuberculosis. The fungus may invade directly through the chest wall, forming numerous draining sinuses. Abdominal actinomycosis is a serious form, usually occurring by way of the cecum or appendix. A wide variety of symptoms may be produced, depending on the organ involved. Sinuses may appear in the abdominal wall, and the infection may spread to the vertebral bodies.

The disease is worldwide in distribution. The organism is normally present in the mucous membranes of the mouth, around carious teeth, and in tonsillar crypts. Trauma, teeth extractions, fractures, and other conditions that may set up anaerobic conditions predispose to invasion and infection. The infection is not ordinarily transmitted from man to man or from cattle to man.

Laboratory Diagnosis. Pus, material from draining sinuses, and sputum should be examined in the fresh state for the presence of "sulfur granules." These granules are lobulated masses composed of delicate, intertwined filaments about 1 micron in diameter, the ends of which are frequently surrounded by an eosinophilic sheath, giving a club-shaped appearance to the ends of the filaments. The apparent radiation of these club-shaped structures from the center of the granule accounts

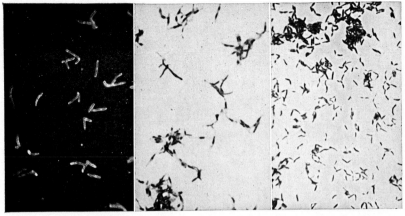

Figure 18–4. *Actinomyces israeli* from cultures. *Left,* darkfield. × 900. *Middle* and *right,* Gram stains of rough and smooth cultures respectively. × 1200. (Rosebury, Epps, and Clark.)

for the name "ray" (actino-) fungus. Not all granules show these clubs, and similar granules may be seen in other conditions. The granules are gram positive (Fig. 18–2). In some cases the granules may not be present, but only short, branching, gram positive filaments can be seen.

Culture. It is important to culture all material promptly, both aerobically and anaerobically, on suitable media, since the aerobic *Nocardia* cannot be distinguished morphologically from the anaerobic *A. israeli.* Material should be inoculated into Brewer's thioglycollate broth and deep tubes of brain-heart infusion broth and streaked in duplicate on blood agar and brain-heart infusion agar plates. All these cultures should then be incubated aerobically and anaerobically.

In broth the organism grows as small, fuzzy, white colonies in four to six days at 37° C. On streaked plates the organisms appear as small (2 to 3 mm. in diameter) colonies that are white, rough or nodular, and adherent to the agar surface (Fig. 18–3). Smears show the colonies to consist of tangled masses of delicate branching hyphae and small, fragmented, diphtheroid-like, gram positive rods (Fig. 18–4). No reliable immunologic test has been developed for this disease.

NOCARDIOSIS

This disease, which is caused by several species of aerobic actinomycetes, may manifest itself as an acute or chronic, suppurative, granulomatous infection characterized by swelling, abscess formation, and multiple draining sinuses. A primary pulmonary form that also occurs may occasionally metastasize to other organs of the body. The pulmonary form may simulate tuberculosis clinically. The organisms are gram positive, bacilliform filaments, and some stains are partially acid fast; they may be confused with *Mycobacterium tuberculosis* when seen on smears. The abdominal form may also be confused with tuberculosis. Since the treatment and control of these two diseases are entirely different, every effort must be made to differentiate the specific causative etiologic agent.

Infection of the subcutaneous tissue with bone involvement (nocardial mycetoma) is more prevalent in tropical areas. The systemic form is worldwide in distribution. In contradistinction to *Actinomyces israeli, Nocardia* occurs in nature and the infection is exogenous in origin. The organism occurs in soil and may cause infection when introduced into tissues by injury or inhalation of infectious materials. The differentiation between this organism and *Actinomyces* is summarized in Table 18–2:

Table 18–2. Differentiation Between *Actinomyces* and *Nocardia*

ACTINOMYCES	NOCARDIA
Obligate anaerobe	Aerobic
Not acid fast	Partially acid fast
Found only in human body	Found in many sources in nature (grasses, soil)
Infection primarily endogenous	Infection primarily exogenous
Sulfur granules commonly formed; clubs present	Sulfur granules not commonly produced; clubs absent
No growth on Sabouraud's agar	Grow well on Sabouraud's agar
Colonies not pigmented	Colonies frequently pigmented

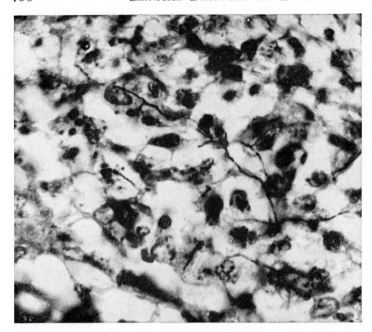

Figure 18–5. Nocardiosis. Delicate branching filaments in section of brain abscess stained by Gram's method. × 1300. (Conant *et al.:* Manual of Clinical Mycology, 2nd Ed.)

Laboratory Diagnosis. Pus from a draining sinus or abscess should be examined as a wet preparation for the presence of granules, the ends of which are usually not club shaped. Smears of this material show gram positive, intertwining, branching filaments measuring approximately 1 micron in diameter or short, diphtheroid-like elements. When stained by the Ziehl-Neelsen method, some filaments appear to be acid fast. Since this acid-fast property is only partial, the decolorization with acid alcohol must not be prolonged. One per cent sulfuric acid gives better results than hydrochloric acid as a decolorizer for this organism (Fig. 18–5).

Pus and sputum, when stained, show gram positive or acid-fast filaments. The acid-fast varieties may be mistaken for tubercle bacilli in stained sputum smears. Since the pulmonary form of nocardiosis may clinically resemble tuberculosis, it is important to differentiate this organism culturally from *M. tuberculosis.* Some strains of *Nocardia* cannot survive the acid or alkali concentration methods used for *M. tuberculosis.* It is essential to attempt to isolate these organisms before concentration is attempted.

The organisms grow well on Sabouraud's or blood agar at 37° C. or at room temperature. Media containing antibiotics or cycloheximide should not be used. In contrast to *Actinomyces israeli, Nocardia* is aerobic. Colonies appear in four to eight days. They are raised, irregular, and usually wrinkled or granular and pigmented, ranging from light tan to orange to bright red in color. The pigment is best demonstrable on Czapek-Dox agar at room temperature. On liquid media, such as thioglycollate broth, the organisms grow in the form of a wrinkled surface pellicle, the media remaining clear. This is an important differential point between this organism and "atypical" tubercle bacilli (see p. 653).

Microscopically the colonies are composed of delicate, branching, intertwining filaments, which break up into bacillary forms of variable length. The organism is gram positive and may or may not be partially acid fast, depending on the species and the media in which it is grown. *N. asteroides* is the most common species in the United States; others occasionally encountered are *N. braziliensis, N. pelletieri, N. madurae,* and *N. paraguayensis.* No reliable diagnostic skin or serologic test is available for this disease.

MADUROMYCOSIS

Maduromycosis (madura foot, mycetoma) is a chronic, progressive infection affecting the feet, hands, and rarely other parts of the body. It is characterized by severe tumefactions, abscess and sinus formation, and progressive enlargement and deformity of the infected area (Fig. 18–6). It occurs most commonly in the tropics and is probably exogenous in origin. Injury to bare feet is the most common source of

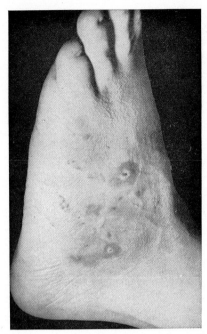

Figure 18–6. Maduromycosis of the foot, caused by *Monosporium apiospermum*. Note the swelling of the foot and the multiple discharging sinuses. (Conant *et al.*: Manual of Clinical Mycology, 2nd Ed.)

infection. Many different fungi may be involved, such as various species of *Nocardia, Allescheria boydii (Monosporium apiospermum), Madurella, Indiella,* and *Glenospora.*

THE DERMATOPHYTES

Superficial infections of the skin caused by fungi (dermatophytosis, dermatomycosis) are exceedingly common; "athlete's foot" and ringworm of the scalp are well known. Hypersensitivity to the fungi undoubtedly plays an important role in the pathogenesis of these diseases.

The fungi attack only the keratinized, dead layers of the skin, nails, and hair. A common lesion caused by these organisms is known as "ringworm" or tinea in which the lesion spreads in a circle about a healing, scaly, central portion. Clinically the dermatomycoses can be classified according to the area of the body involved. Tinea pedis, "athlete's foot," is a common infection producing a pruritic or vesicular maceration between the toes or on the plantar surfaces of the feet. Burning, itching, and pain may develop and pyogenic infections may be superimposed. Infections of the

nails, tinea unguium, may be caused by the same group of fungi as on the feet but may also be due to *Candida albicans*. These infections are difficult to diagnose clinically, since many other conditions can cause a similar picture. Ringworm of the scalp, tinea capitis, is frequently found in children and occasionally in adults. In this condition the hair becomes brittle and breaks off a short distance from the surface of the scalp. Infection by *Microsporum canis* or *M. gypseum* can result in a boggy, tumor-like mass known as a kerion. *Trichophyton schoenleini* causes a severe infection known as favus, characterized by cuplike structures (scutula) formed by the infected hair follicles (Fig. 18–7). Hairs infected by fungi may fluoresce when placed under a filtered ultraviolet light—"Woods" light.

Infection of the bearded regions, tinea barbae, may resemble those due to pyogenic bacteria. Ringworm of the groin, tinea cruris, is common in warm climates and in obese individuals. Ringworm of the body, tinea corporis, causes lesions that involve the glabrous skin anywhere on the body. The lesions advance slowly at the periphery and tend to heal in the center.

Tinea versicolor (pityriasis versicolor) is characterized by diffuse, brownish-red, scaly lesions on the trunk. The causative agent, which has never been cultured, is known as *Malassezia furfur*. It can be identified readily in skin preparations by the characteristic round, budding cells and mycelial fragments (Fig. 18–8).

Erythrasma is an eruption with brownish epidermal scales occurring in the groin or axilla. The causative agent, which has also never been successfully cultured, is called *Nocardia (Actinomyces) minutis-*

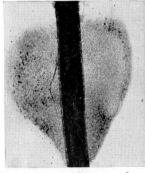

Figure 18–7. *Trichophyton schoenleini;* hair from scutulum (× 35). (Lewis and Hopper, An Introduction to Medical Mycology, The Year Book Publishers, Inc.)

Figure 18–8. Malassezia furfur: Clusters of round budding cells and mycelial elements in skin. × 700. (Conant *et al.*: Manual of Clinical Mycology, 2nd Ed.)

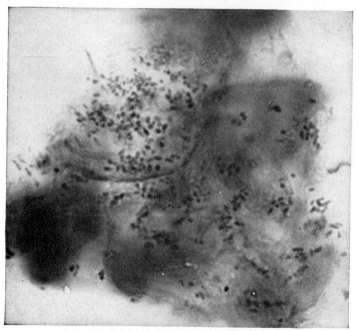

Figure 18–9. Erythrasma. Small bacillary forms seen in skin scrapings. × 1630. (Conant *et al.*)

sima and appears in skin scrapings stained with methylene blue as short, small (about 1 μ), branching filaments that are readily broken up into smaller bacillary forms (Fig. 18–9).

Otomycosis refers to fungus infections of the external ear that may be superimposed upon a bacterial infection. Organisms involved include members of the genera *Penicillium, Aspergillus, Mucor,* and *Rhizopus.* Since these organisms are common saprophytes, their relationship to this disease must be established by repeated examinations.

Mycology of the Dermatophytes

Demonstration of the fungi in infected tissue can be accomplished readily. Hair, skin, or nail scrapings from infected areas are placed on a slide and a drop of 10 to 20 per cent potassium hydroxide added. The addition of 15 ml. of Parker Superchrome blue-black ink into 15 ml. of a 20 per cent potassium hydroxide solution may enable the hyphal fragments to appear more distinctly. A coverslip is placed on top of the preparation, which is heated gently to clear and allowed to stand for 20 to 30 minutes. If the preparation is not to be examined until some time later, a drop of glycerol may be added under the coverslip. The preparation should not be allowed to dry out. When examined in a subdued light, fungi in skin or nails appear as refractile, branching fragments of hyphae (Fig. 18–10). In infected hair in potassium hy-

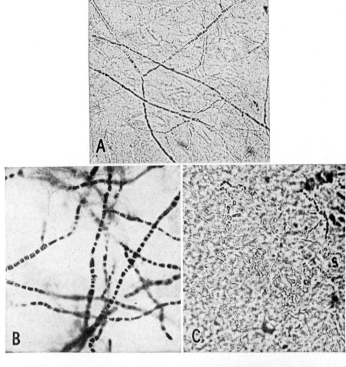

Figure 18–10. Infected skin: A. Branching hyphae that might yield in culture species of *Microsporum, Trichophyton,* or *Epidermophyton floccosum.* × 200. B. Typical close septate hyphae of *Trichophyton concentricum* in skin. × 450. C. Mosaic fungus; an artifact often seen in potassium hydroxide preparations of skin. × 200. (Conant *et al.*)

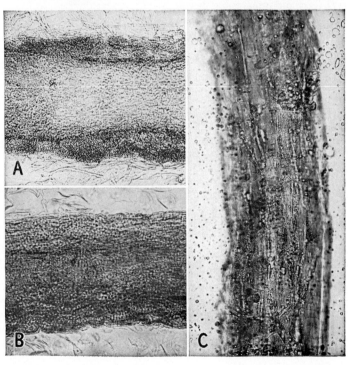

Figure 18–11. Infected hair: A. *Microsporum.* Small spores forming sheath around hair. × 110. B. *Trichophyton.* Parallel chains of arthrospores inside hair (endothrix). × 170. C. *Trichophyton.* Favus hair showing mycelial elements and numerous bubbles which are characteristic. × 220. (Conant *et al.*)

droxide preparations the spores may be seen as dense clouds around the hair stub ("ectothrix") or as linear rows inside the hair shaft ("endothrix") (Fig. 18–11). Care must be taken to avoid confusing the so-called mosaic fungi or various artifacts with true fungi. The genus and species of the infecting fungi can be established only by culture.

Cultures are made by inoculating various media; Sabouraud's, Littman's, or cyclohex-imide (Mycosel) agar are commonly used. With the exception of *Actinomyces israeli* all pathogenic fungi are aerobic. Since they are slow growing, it is best to use screw cap tubes for original isolation rather than tubes plugged with cotton. All the derma-tophytes grow well at room temperature. If the specimen is heavily contaminated with bacteria, the addition of penicillin and streptomycin (20 and 40 units, respectively, per ml. of medium) is advised. Scales, skin scrapings, and hairs, may be simply dipped into 70 per cent alcohol and placed on the surface of the agar slants. Exudates, pus, and sputum should be streaked on the surface of agar plates. If *Actinomyces* is suspected, anaerobic procedures are re-quired.

Identification of the organisms is based on the gross appearance of the colonies, the rate of growth, the pigment, and the microscopic appearance. Three distinct types of colonies may develop—the yeast, the yeast-like, and the filamentous. Yeast colonies are smooth, moist, and soft. Under the microscope they contain only oval or round, budding cells. Yeast-like colonies are also soft and smooth but may be slightly granular. Under the microscope pseudomy-celia and budding cells are seen. Filament-ous colonies show cottony-like growth pro-jecting from the agar surface. The colonies show mycelia and various types of spore formation under the microscope (Fig. 18–12).

For examination of the colonies a straight or hooked wire is used to pick a fragment of the colony to a drop of Amann's lacto-phenol cotton blue* on a slide. The fragment is separated apart gently with teasing needles and a cover glass added. Slight heating may help the stain to penetrate. The preparation is then examined for its characteristic microscopic appearance. Lacto-phenol cotton blue is

* Phenol crystals 20 gm. Glycerol 40 ml. Lactic acid 20 ml. Distilled water 20 ml. Dissolve by heat-ing gently. Add 0.05 gm. cotton blue.

also useful in examining scrapings from cases of erythrasma or tinea versicolor. If the skin scrapings are greasy, they should be washed with ether before adding the stain. Yeast-like colonies may be examined microscopically by suspending a loopful in a drop of water and covering with a cover-slip.

Fungi are best seen in fixed tissue by means of Bauer's, P.A.S. (Hotchkiss-Mc-Manus), or methenamine-silver stains rather than by the routinely used hema-toxylin-eosin technique. Mayer's mucicar-mine stain is specific for Cryptococci in tissue.

Trichophyton species are the most com-mon of the dermatophytes, causing infec-tions of the feet, nails, and hair. The fungus grows as cottony colonies that are usually pigmented light tan to red. The species are distinguished from each other by means of their colony appearance, struc-ture of the micro- and macroconidia, and various shapes of the hyphae (Fig. 18–13). Common species are T. *mentagrophytes* (*gypseum*), T. *rubrum* (*purpureum*), T. *tonsurans* (*crateriforme*), T. *schoenleini*, and T. *violaceum*. (See Table 18–3.)

Microsporum is primarily, but not ex-clusively, associated with ectothrix infec-tions of the hair. The colonies are slow growing, cottony to powdery, and light tan to brown in color. Under the microscope the spindle-shaped macroconidia are nu-merous and characteristic for the three species, M. *canis*, M. *gypseum*, and M. *audouini*.

Epidermophyton, which is primarily as-sociated with tinea cruris, forms velvety to powdery, greenish yellow, round, rapidly growing colonies. Microscopically, oval or club-shaped, multiseptate macroconidia are characteristic. There is only one species in this genus — *Epidermophyton floccosum* (*inguinale*) (Fig. 18–14, Table 18–3).

THE DEEP OR SYSTEMIC FUNGI

Fungus diseases other than those infect-ing the skin and its appendages were at one time thought to be rare. It is now recognized, either because of improved di-agnostic facilities or possibly increasing incidence of infection, that many of these conditions are more widespread than here-tofore realized. Also there is evidence that the more widespread use of antibiotics, steroids, cytotoxic drugs, and radiation pre-disposes to infection with these organisms.

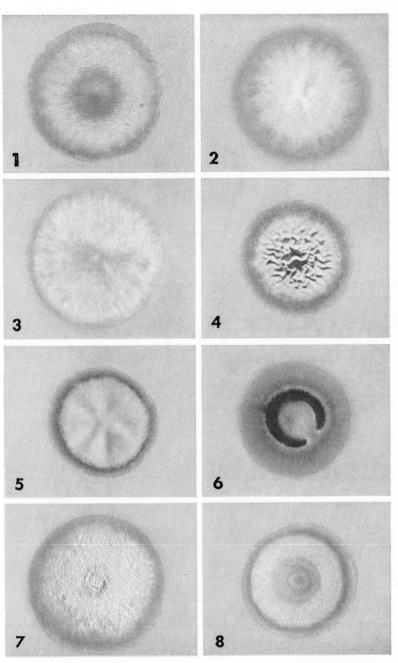

Figure 18–12. Colonies of some of the more common dermatophytes on Sabouraud's agar (× ¾). 1. *Microsporum audouini.* 2. *Microsporum canis.* 3. *Microsporum fulvum.* 4. *Trichophyton schoenleini.* 5. *Trichophyton purpureum.* 6. *Trichophyton violaceum.* 7. *Trichophyton mentagrophytes.* 8. *Epidermophyton floccosum.* (Jordan and Burrows.)

It is important to realize that all the fungi to be described, with the exception of *Cryptococcus neoformans,* exist in two phases. In the body they are invariably in the form of yeast-like organisms; when cultured at room temperature, the organisms form mycelia and the colonies are cottony masses of entangled mycelia like the dermatophytes. When cultured on appropriate media at body temperature, the colonies are nonfilamentous and yeast-like. This is the so-called yeast-to-mycelia (Y→M) transformation. An understanding of this phenomenon is essential to those working with these organisms.

Blastomycosis

Blastomycosis (Gilchrist's disease, North American blastomycosis), caused by *Blastomyces dermatitidis,* may occur as a chronic granulomatous infection of the skin and internal organs. The lungs, bones,

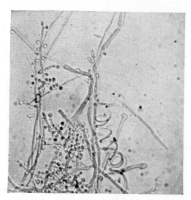

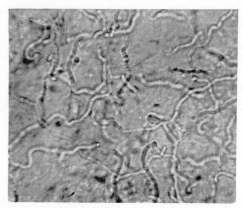

Figure 18–13. Culture of *Trichophyton gypseum* (× 348). (Lewis and Hopper, An Introduction to Medical Mycology, The Year Book Publishers, Inc.)

Figure 18–14. Epidermophyton floccosum, direct mount from scales (× 200). (Lewis and Hopper, An Introduction to Medical Mycology, The Year Book Publishers, Inc.)

Table 18–3. Cultural and Clinical Features of the Common Dermatophytes

FUNGUS	COLONY APPEARANCE	MORPHOLOGY	CLINICAL FEATURES
Trichophyton mentagrophytes (*gypseum*)	White to tan, powdery or cottony	Coils, nodular bodies, chlamydospores; microconidia in grapelike clusters	Ringworm of nails, skin. Ectothrix infections of hair
T. rubrum (*purpureum*)	Cottony to velvety. Reddish to purple pigmentation on reverse of colony	Numerous microconidia in clusters and singly along hyphae	Resistant infections of skin and nails
T. tonsurans (*crateriforme*)	Cream or yellow; folded with central crater	Elongated microconidia along sides of hyphae	Endothrix infections of hair, skin, and nails
T. schoenleini	Smooth, waxy to powdery, irregularly folded; brownish pigment	Hyphal swelling, "favic chandeliers"	Endothrix infection of hair—favus
T. rosaceum (*megnini*)	Cottony. Pale rose pigment on reverse of colony	Microconidia in clusters and singly	Ringworm of skin and nails; sycosis
Microsporum audouini	Velvety, radiating furrows; light orange pigment	Rare macroconidia; club-shaped microconidia	Human (anthropophilic) cause of epidemic tinea capitis in children
M. canis (*lanosum*)	Cottony, white mycelia with bright orange on reverse of colony	Numerous, large, multicellular macroconidia — "fuseaux"	Animal (zoophilic) species causes sporadic tinea capitis in children
M. gypseum	Powdery, rapidly growing. Buff to brown	Many thin-walled, 4-6 septate, ellipsoidal macroconidia	As above. Has been isolated from soil
Epidermophyton floccosum	Velvety to powdery. Radial furrows. Greenish-yellow	Broad, oval macroconidia in clusters	Tinea cruris

and kidneys may be involved by spread from a cutaneous lesion or from a primary pulmonary focus (Fig. 18–15). The portal of entry of the systemic form is the respiratory tract. Bone and central nervous system involvement is not rare in the disseminated form.

The disease is primarily confined to North America, and its mode of transmission is unknown. Individuals engaged in agricultural or outdoor occupations are likely to become infected.

Laboratory Diagnosis. Scrapings from lesions, sputum, and pus should be examined in 10 per cent potassium hydroxide. Characteristic thick-walled, double-contoured, single-budding yeast-like fungi 8 to 20 micra in diameter can be seen (Fig. 18–16). Hyphae are never seen in exudates or tissues. Material should be cultured on Sabouraud's (with antibiotics), cycloheximide, and brain-heart infusion agar with antibiotics at room temperature and at 37° C. At room temperature after three or four days the colonies at first are smooth and pasty but gradually become white and filamentous. Under the microscope the culture shows spherical or oval microconidia

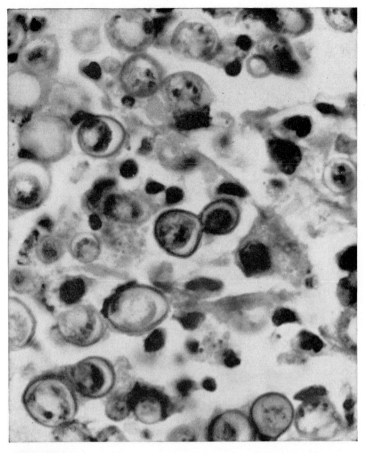

Figure 18–15. Blastomycosis of lung. Section of tissue showing budding forms. Periodic acid-Schiff stain. × 1500. (Conant *et al.*)

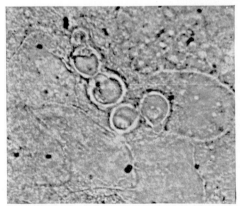

Figure 18–16. Blastomyces dermatitidis; direct mount of pus showing double-contoured budding cells (× 716). (Lewis and Hopper, An Introduction to Medical Mycology, The Year Book Publishers, Inc.)

attached directly to the hyphae or at the end of short pedicles. At 37° C. the culture is slow growing, tan, heaped, and yeast-like. Microscopically the culture is composed of double-contoured, single-budding cells resembling those found in pus or exudates.

Complement-fixing antibodies may be demonstrable in individuals with extensive or progressive disease. Since the sera may react with *Histoplasma capsulatum* antigens, the test should be done simultaneously with both. Patients with the local cutaneous form may have a negative reaction. Hypersensitivity to the skin test antigen, blastomycin, may also be demonstrable. (See p. 813.)

Coccidioidomycosis

Coccidioidomycosis (coccidioidal granuloma, valley fever), caused by *Coccidioides immitis*, is a highly infectious disease, which results in a benign, self-limited respiratory infection, or, in a small percentage of cases (about 0.25 per cent), the primary disease may develop into a progressive disseminated infection involving the skin, viscera, bones, and central nervous system. The primary pulmonary disease

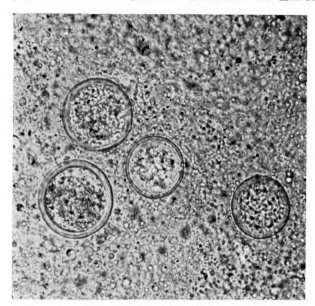

Figure 18–17. Coccidioides immitis; from purulent contents of lymph node (× 600). (Stiles and Davis: J.A.M.A., July 4, 1942.)

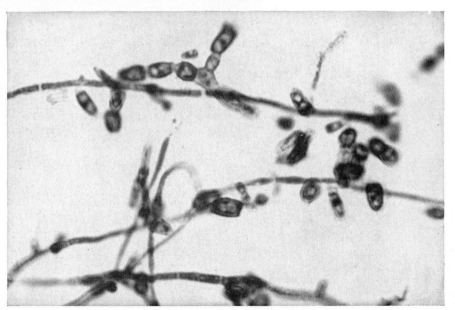

Figure 18–18. Arthrospores of *Coccidioides immitis.* Lactophenol-cotton blue preparation from culture on Sabouraud's medium; × 1135. (Havens.)

may have minimal manifestations and is often overlooked. More severe cases show symptoms of chronic pulmonary disease. There may be many years between the primary infection and the disseminated form. This disease is limited almost exclusively to the arid areas of the southwestern United States and parts of Central and South America. Humans apparently acquire the infection by inhaling dust contaminated with the infectious arthrospores or by introducing them into the skin following an injury. Laboratory workers may also become infected.

Laboratory Diagnosis. Pus, sputum, and pleural fluid should be examined as fresh preparations. The thick-walled spherule, 10 to 80 micra in diameter, filled with numerous, small (2 to 5 micra) endospores, is characteristic (Fig. 18–17). Endospores are freed by rupture of the cell wall, and "ghost" spherules may be present. Material should be cultured on Sabouraud's (plus antibiotics), Littman's, and cycloheximide agar and incubated at room temperature. Colonies appear in three to four days, at first appearing moist and membranous and later developing cottony, aerial, buff-colored mycelia. Only the mycelial phase grows in culture. Microscopically the cultures show thick, branching hyphae and numerous chains of rectangular or ellipsoidal, thick-walled arthrospores (Fig. 18–18). Typical spherules can be demonstrated by injecting a saline suspension of these spores intraperitoneally into mice. *Note: The arthrospores are highly infectious and great care must be exercised in handling them and disposing of old cultures.*

In disseminated infections persistent precipitins and complement-fixing antibodies can be demonstrated. A progressive rise in titer is a grave prognostic sign. Sensitivity to the skin test antigen, coccidioidin, indicates past or present infection. (See p. 813.)

Cryptococcosis

Cryptococcosis (torulosis, European blastomyocosis) is caused by a yeast known as *Cryptococcus neoformans* or *Torula histolytica*. The disease may involve the lungs, skin, or other parts of the body and has a predilection for the central nervous system. The primary infection may resemble a neoplasm or tuberculosis, and infection of the central nervous system may result in symptoms resembling those of bacterial meningitis. This type of infection generally terminates fatally (Fig. 18–19).

Cases of the disease occur sporadically throughout the world. It is thought that contaminated soil may be the source of infection from animals to man, but no evidence of direct transmission from man to man and animal to man has been reported. Recent work has shown that pigeon excreta may be important in the spread of the disease. In patients with Hodgkin's disease or other lymphomas the organism may disseminate rapidly from a primary focus to other organs.

Laboratory Diagnosis. *C. neoformans,* unlike all the other systemic fungi, exists only in the form of oval or spherical, single or budding organisms, 5 to 20 micra in diameter, surrounded by a gelatinous, wide, refractive capsule. The presence of this capsule is pathognomonic for this organism (Fig. 18–20).

Pus from sputum or centrifuged spinal fluid should be examined unstained by placing a small amount on a slide and gently pressing to a thin film under a coverslip. The infection is often missed in spinal fluid examinations because the organisms are confused with lymphocytes. A turbid spinal fluid with an increase in lymphocytes and globulin and a decrease in glucose should be examined for fungi as well as bacteria. The material should also be mixed with a drop of India ink* or nigrosin; then a coverslip should be added and pressed down gently. The preparation should be examined with subdued light under the high dry objective. The characteristic encapsulated budding yeast is diagnostic (Fig. 18–21).

All material should be cultured on blood and Sabouraud's agar at room temperature and at 37° C. Cycloheximide media is not satisfactory for this organism. The colonies,

* An excellent India ink preparation is made by mixing 15 ml. India ink, 30 ml. Merthiolate (1:1000 aq.), and 0.1 ml. Tween-80 (1:1000 aq.). Filter before use.

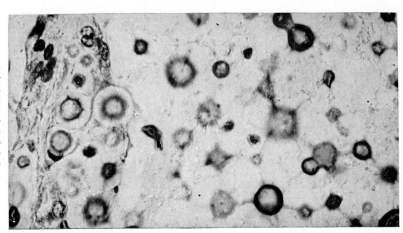

Figure 18–19. Torula meningitis in man. Growth of *Cryptococcus neoformans* in the cerebrospinal fluid. Note the budding cells, the stained capsules which give a double-contoured appearance, and the characteristic threads connecting the cells. Mucicarmine stain (staining the threads and capsules pink); × 950. (Humphreys.)

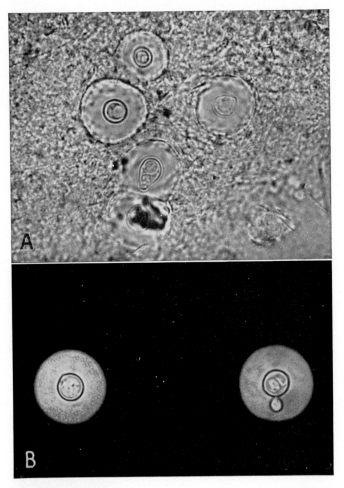

Figure 18–20. Cryptococcus neoformans: A. Pus containing the round, thick-walled budding fungus surrounded by capsule. × 850. *B.* India ink preparation of spinal fluid showing the budding fungus surrounded by capsule. × 821. (Conant *et al.*)

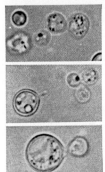

Figure 18–21. Cryptococcus hominis (Torula histolytica; Debaryomyces neoformans); budding form of fungus found in spinal fluid. (Johns and Attaway: Am. J. Clin. Path., Vol. 3.)

both at room and incubator temperatures, are yeast-like and slimy, rapidly growing, cream to brown in color, somewhat resembling colonies of *Klebsiella pneumoniae.*

Microscopically the typical encapsulated yeasts are seen. The size of the capsule varies with the strain and may be lost on primary culture. Intracerebral or intraperitoneal inoculation into mice results in the formation of gelatinous masses in the brain, lung, and abdomen from which the

budding encapsulated yeast can be demonstrated. No useful serologic or skin tests are available for this disease.

Histoplasmosis

Histoplasmosis, caused by *Histoplasma capsulatum,* causes a wide variety of clinical manifestations. Respiratory infection may be mild or severe and is usually unapparent and self-limited. The progressive disseminated infection spreads to infect the reticuloendothelial system, causing fever, malaise, hepatomegaly, splenomegaly, anemia, and leukopenia. The symptoms that occur are related to the organs involved. Mucocutaneous lesions may also occur as manifestations of the systemic disease.

The disease occurs throughout the world. There are areas of high endemicity in the United States, especially in the central Mississippi and Ohio River valleys. In some local areas as many as 80 per cent of the adult population react positively to

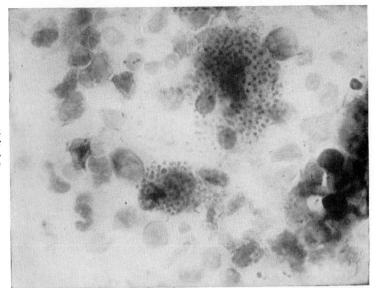

Figure 18–22. *Histoplasma capsulatum;* impression smear from rectal ulcer (× 850). (Brown, Havens, and Magath.)

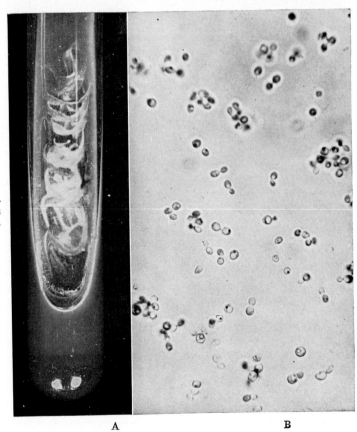

Figure 18–23. *Histoplasma capsulatum.* A. On blood agar six days at 37° C. B. From blood agar culture. × 700. (Conant *et al.*)

A   B

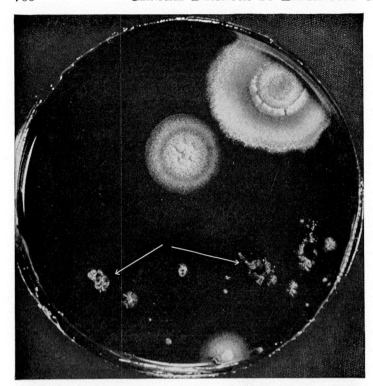

Figure 18–24. Histoplasma capsulatum. On brain-heart infusion glucose blood agar at room temperature. (After Howell, Pub. Health Rep., vol. 63 in Conant *et al.*)

histoplasmin. Infection occurs from the inhalation of the infectious spores, which exist as saprophytes in certain types of soils. There may be other, as yet unidentified, modes of infection.

Laboratory Diagnosis. Smears made from bone marrow, lymph node biopsy specimens, and mucocutaneous lesions should be stained with Wright's or Giemsa's method. The fungus appears as small (1 to 5 micra), round or oval, yeast-like cells in the cytoplasm of mononuclear cells or lying free. They appear to have a clear halo surrounding a darker stained central area (Fig. 18–22). Direct mounts or potassium hydroxide preparations are generally useless because of the intracellular localization of the organism and its small size.

Specimens of sputum, gastric or bronchial washings, and pus should be cultured on Sabouraud's, cycloheximide, and brain-heart infusion blood agar plus antibiotics at room and incubator temperatures. In addition bone marrow or blood should be inoculated in flasks of brain-heart infusion broth. All cultures should be held at least 30 days before discarding. Freshly expectorated sputum should be cultured, since the organism dies rapidly in sputum.

At 37° C. growth is slow (8 to 14 days), and the colonies are small, waxy, and membranous. Microscopically small budding organisms resembling those seen in tissues and abortive hyphae are seen (Fig. 18–23). At room temperature white mycelial growth is produced after 14 to 18 days (Fig. 18–24), and microscopic examination shows the round, thick-walled, tuberculate chlamydospores (7 to 15 micra) that are diagnostic for *H. capsulatum* (Fig. 18–25). Repeated search for these chlamydospores may be necessary, since they are occasionally sparse. They rarely grow on blood agar but can be demonstrated by transplanting the colonies to Sabouraud's agar. Intraperitoneal injection into mice sometimes gives a positive isolation when cultural procedures fail.

Complement-fixing antibodies, which react either with histoplasmin or yeast phase antigens of *H. capsulatum*, appear a few weeks after infection. Serial tests must be made throughout the course of the disease in order to demonstrate a rise in titer. Other serologic tests that may be useful are the collodion particle test of Saslaw and Campbell, the latex procedure of Carlisle and Saslaw (1958), and a precipitin reaction in agar-gel (Heiner, 1958). Positive skin tests to a standardized preparation of histoplasmin indicate past or present infection, although the skin tests of acutely ill

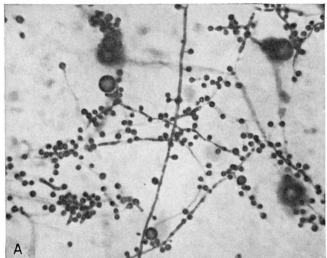

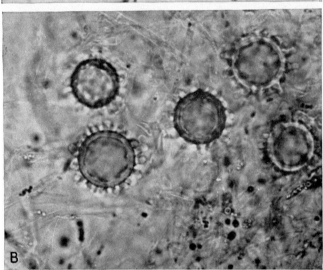

Figure 18–25. Histoplasma capsulatum from Sabouraud's glucose agar. *A.* Small, smooth, round to pyriform conidia. × 600. *B.* Large thick-walled, round, tuberculate chlamydospores. × 1150. (Conant *et al.*)

patients may become anergic during the terminal stage. (See p. 813).

Sporotrichosis

Sporotrichosis, caused by *Sporotrichum schenckii,* is a subacute infection, which follows introduction of the fungus by trauma. From the initial lesion, which begins as a small, subcutaneous pustule, the regional lymphatics are invaded. The lymph nodes show cord-like thickening, and multiple abscesses appear along the course of the infected lymphatics. Occasionally generalized infection may occur by way of the blood with or without primary cutaneous lesions, and any organ or tissue of the body may be involved.

The disease occurs throughout the world, and the fungus is widely distributed in nature. Infections occur following injury to the skin with contaminated material. Farmers, horticulturists, and miners are most frequently infected.

Laboratory Diagnosis. The organisms are difficult to demonstrate in stained smears or sections, cultures being the most reliable procedure (Fig. 18–26). Pus from lesions or swabs from infected areas should be streaked on Sabouraud's or cycloheximide agar at room temperature and at 37° C. At room temperature the colonies appear with moderate rapidity and are small, white to black, yeast-like, and without aerial mycelia. Microscopically the colony is composed of delicate, branching, septate hyphae upon which spherical or pear-shaped conidia are borne at the end of lateral branches in a characteristic tree-like cluster (Fig. 18–27).

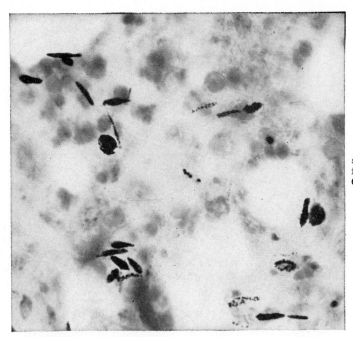

Figure 18–26. Sporotrichum schenckii. Tissue forms in smear of pus from inoculated mouse. Stained by Gram's method. × 1100. (Conant *et al.*)

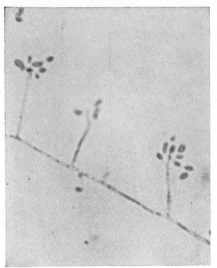

Figure 18–27. Sporotrichum schenckii, culture showing clusters of spores on hyphae (× 1000). (Lewis and Hopper, An Introduction to Medical Mycology, The Year Book Publishers, Inc.)

At 37° C. the colonies are grayish-yellow, soft, and bacterial-like. Microscopically such colonies are composed of cigar-shape, round or oval (1 to 5 micra), gram positive cells and small hyphal fragments. There are no practical serologic tests for this disease.

Other Deep Mycoses

Rhinosporidiosis is an infection of the skin or mucus membranes, usually of the nares or the face, characterized by proliferative tumor masses. It is caused by *Rhinosporidium seeberi.* It occurs primarily in tropical areas.

Chromoblastomycosis (chromomycosis) is a chronic, granulomatous infection primarily of the lower extremities characterized by formation of warty, cutaneous nodules. The causative agents are a variety of fungi of the genera *Hormodendrum* and *Phialophora.* This is also primarily a tropical disease.

South American blastomycosis (paracoccidioidal granuloma) is a disease similar to North American blastomycosis and is caused by a closely related fungus known as *Blastomyces brasiliensis.* These infections occur almost exclusively in parts of South America.

Infections Caused by Fungi That Are Primarily Saprophytic. In some cases, particularly in extremely debilitated individuals or those who have received long-term therapy with antibiotics, steroids, or antileukemic agents, severe or fatal infections may result from a variety of fungi of the genera *Penicillium, Aspergillus, Rhizopus, Mucor,* and others (Figs. 18–28 to 18–30). Rarely primary infections with these fungi occur in certain occupational groups that are exposed to heavy concentrations of spores of these organisms. Since spores of these fungi are ubiquitous, their association with disease must be confirmed by careful and repeated examinations. De-

Figure 18–28.   *Aspergillus* sp. mounted in Amann's medium. Note the fully developed sterigmata and the chains of conidia abstricted from the tips. The large dark masses are made up of free conidia. × 370. (Burrows.)

Figure 18–29.   *Penicillium* sp. mounted in Amann's medium. Note the characteristic finger-like verticillate branches and the terminal chains of conidia. × 440. (Burrows.)

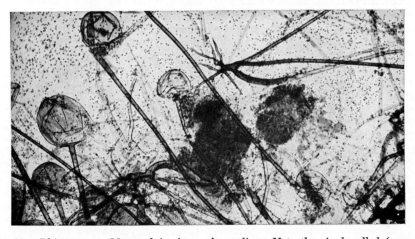

Figure 18–30.   *Rhizopus* sp. Mounted in Amann's medium. Note the single-celled (nonseptate) mycelium and ruptured, empty sporangia. The small oval bodies are free spores. The root-like structure at the base of the hyphae is the "hold-fast" by which the mold is attached to nutrient medium. × 80. (Burrows.)

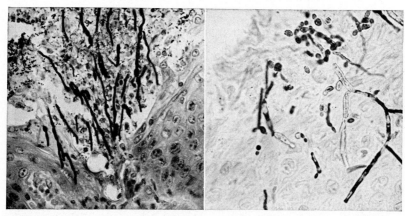

Figure 18–31. Moniliasis: invasion of the epithelial layer of the esophagus by *Canida albicans. Left,* beginning invasion of the superficial layer showing mycelium and yeast-like cells; note the gram positive micrococci accompanying the fungus. × 600. *Right,* invasion of the deeper tissue showing both mycelium and yeast-like cells penetrating the epithelium. × 950. Gram stains. (Humphreys.)

scriptions of these fungi will be found in the references.

THE INTERMEDIATE FUNGI

Certain fungi, notably the *Candida* group, may cause either superficial infections or widespread systemic disease and hence are classified as "intermediate."

Candidiasis (Moniliasis)

Candida (Monilia) albicans can cause infection of the mouth, skin, nails, or vagina or a variety of systemic diseases. Oral infection, sometimes found in newborn infants, results in thick, creamy white patches known as "thrush." Infection of the corners of the mouth is called "perlèche." A common condition found most frequently in pregnant and diabetic women is a vulvovaginal infection known as vaginal moniliasis or monilial vaginitis. Infections of the nails are known as onychia and of the cuticle as paronychia. Infection of the intertriginous areas of the body, i.e., the axilla, gluteal folds, and groin, are known as "intertrigo."

More serious infections are those involving the lungs—bronchopulmonary candidiasis—and those involving other organs of the body. Brain abscesses, endocarditis, and septicemia may be caused by this organism (Figs. 18–31, 18–32).

Candida albicans is frequently present in the skin, mucous membranes, and intestinal tract of normal individuals. Consequently infections are probably primarily endogenous in origin. Predisposing factors include diabetes, pregnancy, obesity, and avitaminosis. Occupational conditions that cause maceration of the skin predispose to cutaneous infections. Severe or fatal cases have occurred in patients treated with antibiotics; in these cases the organism proliferates abundantly to replace the normal bacterial flora. Hypersensitivity undoubtedly plays an important role in the pathogenesis of the disease. The disease is worldwide in distribution.

Laboratory Diagnosis. *C. albicans* is the only consistently pathogenic species of the several yeast-like fungi of the genus; hence, it is important to differentiate it from the other species. Skin and nail scrapings should be mounted on a slide with 10 per cent potassium hydroxide. Sputum, mucus, and pus should be crushed to a thin film and examined fresh. The material can also be stained by Gram's method or with methylene blue or lactophenol cotton blue. Candida appears in such preparations as small, oval, budding, yeast-like cells 3 to 6 micra in diameter; occasional fragments of mycelia can be seen. The organism stains intensely positive by Gram's method (Fig. 18–33).

Cultures should be inoculated on Sabouraud's, cycloheximide, or other media, a wide variety of which have been developed for this purpose. The organism grows rapidly and readily at either room or incubator temperature, appearing in two to four days as creamy, moist, flat colonies with a distinct yeasty odor (Fig. 18–34). On Levine's EMB agar containing 0.1 mg. chlortetracycline per ml. incubated at 37° C. in a 10 per cent carbon dioxide atmosphere, colonies develop as a characteristic spidery or feathery growth. A related

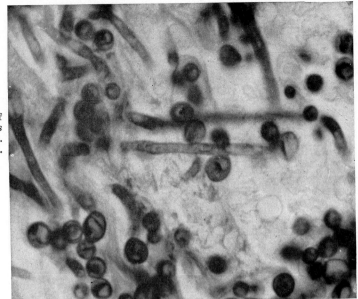

Figure 18–32. Candidiasis of brain. Growth of *Candida albicans* in ventricle in fatal meningitis. Periodic acid-Schiff stain. × 1200. (Conant *et al.*)

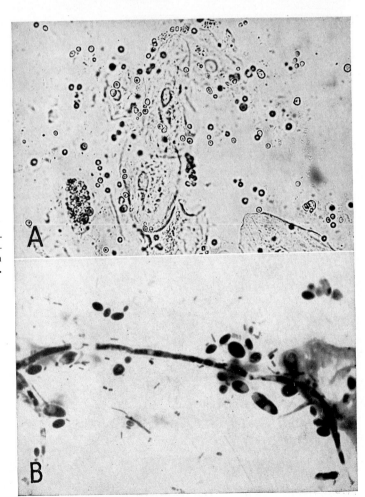

Figure 18–33. A. *Candida albicans* in sputum. Fresh preparation. × 300. B. *Candida albicans* in sputum. Gram stained preparation. × 1350. (Conant *et al.*)

species, *C. stellatoidea*, which is occasionally found in vaginitis, produces star-like colonies on blood agar. It is thought by some that this organism represents only a morphologic variant of *C. albicans* rather than a distinct species. Microscopically clusters of oval, budding blastospores are seen with occasional small fragments of mycelia.

To differentiate *C. albicans* from other species a simple procedure is as follows: A colony is picked with a straight wire, and deep cuts are made with a hooked wire into a plate of corn meal, zein, or chlamydospore agar.* A sterile coverslip is placed over the streak. After 24 to 48 hours' incubation at room temperature the preparation is examined with the low power

* An excellent medium for the demonstration of chlamydospores is Cream of Rice–Tween-80 agar, which is prepared as follows: 1 part of Cream of Rice is added to boiling tap water to which 1 per cent agar and 1 volume per cent Tween-80 are added. The medium is autoclaved and poured in plates.

Figure 18–34. Giant colony of *Candida albicans* on Sabouraud's agar. Note the smooth creamy growth characteristic of yeasts. × 3. (Burrows.)

objective through the coverslip. Along the streak *C. albicans* produces pseudomycelia-bearing clusters of blastospores and characteristic thick-walled, round chlamydospores (Fig. 18–35). Other procedures have been developed to differentiate the species of *Candida;* in most cases they are unnecessary for clinical purposes.

Although there have been many studies on the immunology of *C. albicans* and a skin test preparation known as Oidiomycin is available, none have been shown to be of value in diagnosis.

Geotrichosis

Geotrichosis is an infection caused by a yeast-like organism known as *Geotrichum candidum.* This fungus resembles *C. albicans* in many respects and may cause oral, bronchopulmonary, or systemic infections. It can be found frequently in the mouth or intestinal tract of normal individuals. Consequently the diagnosis of geotrichosis, like that of candidiasis, is justified only by repeated demonstrations of the organism and exclusion of other possible etiologic agents.

Fresh preparations or those mounted in 10 per cent potassium hydroxide or lactophenol cotton blue show oblong or rectangular arthrospores (4 to 8 micra) or larger spherical cells.

The organism grows rapidly on Sabouraud's agar at either room or incubator temperature. The colony is large and mealy and grows mostly below the surface of the agar. There are deep, radial furrows, and older colonies may have a coarse aerial

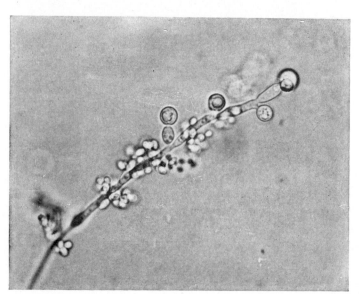

Figure 18–35. *Candida albicans;* terminal chlamydospores on corn meal agar (× 700). (De-Lamater.)

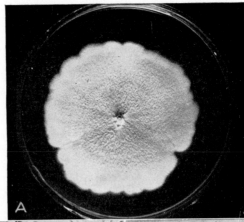

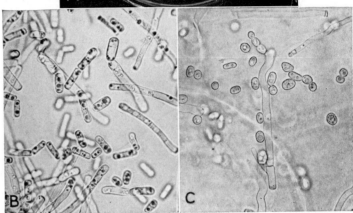

Figure 18–36. Geotrichum candidum. A. Colony on Sabouraud's glucose agar, 10 days, at room temperature. *B.* Elongate arthrospores from Sabouraud's glucose agar. × 790. (After Conant, Am. Rev. Tuberc., vol. 61.) *C.* Rounded arthrospores from Sabouraud's glucose agar. × 650. (After Smith, Am. J. Med., vol. 2.)

mycelium. Microscopically hyphae segmenting into typical rectangular arthrospores and larger spherical cells are seen (Fig. 18–36). No serologic tests are available for the diagnosis of this disease.

REFERENCES

1. Ajello, L.: Collection of specimens for the laboratory demonstration and isolation of fungi. J.A.M.A., *146:*1581–1585, 1951.
2. Baker, R. D.: Pulmonary mucormycosis. Am. J. Path., *32:*287–313, 1956.
3. Baum, G. L., and Schwartz, J.: Coccidioidomycosis: A review. Am. J. Med. Sc., *230:*82–97, 1955.
4. Beamer, P. R.: Immunology of mycotic infections. Am. J. Clin. Path., *25:*66–75, 1955.
5. Benham, R. W.: The genus *Cryptococcus.* Bact. Rev., *20:*189–210, 1956.
6. Benham, R. W.: Species of *Candida* most frequently isolated from man: Methods and criteria for their identification. J. Chron. Dis., *5:* 460–472, 1957.
7. Blank, F.: Dermatophytes of animal origin transmissible to man. Am. J. Med. Sc., *229:* 302–316, 1955.
8. Campbell, C. C., and Binkley, G. E.: Serologic diagnosis with respect to histoplasmosis, coccidioidomycosis and blastomycosis and the problem of cross reactions. J. Lab. & Clin. Med., *42:*896–906, 1953.
9. Carlisle, H. N., and Saslaw, S.: A histoplasmin-latex agglutination test. J. Lab. & Clin. Med., *51:*793–801, 1958.
10. Christie, A.: The disease spectrum of human histoplasmosis. Ann. Int. Med., *49:*544–555, 1958.
11. Conant, N. F., Smith, D. T., Baker, R. D., Callaway, J. L., and Martin, D. S.: Manual of Clinical Mycology. 2nd Ed. Philadelphia, W. B. Saunders Company, 1954.
12. Conrad, F. G., Saslaw, S., and Atwell, R. J.: The protean manifestations of histoplasmosis as illustrated in 23 cases. A.M.A. Arch. Int. Med., *104:*692–709, 1959.
13. Furcolow, M. L.: Recent studies on the epidemiology of histoplasmosis. Ann. N.Y. Acad. Sc., 72:127–164, 1958.
14. Georg, L. K.: Dermatophytes. New Methods in Classification. U.S. Public Health Service, Comm. Dis. Center, Atlanta, Ga., 1958.
15. Georg, L. K., Ajello, L., and Papageorge, C.: Use of cycloheximide in the selective isolation of fungi pathogenic to man. J. Lab. & Clin. Med., *44:*422–428, 1954.
16. Goldin, M., Libretti, A., Hoffman, A., and Kaplan, M. A.: Studies on antibodies to yeasts in bronchial asthma. Ann. Allergy, *15:*119–127, 1957.
17. Hazen, E. L., and Reed, F. C.: Laboratory Identification of Pathogenic Fungi Simplified. Springfield, Illinois, Charles C Thomas, 1955.
18. Heiner, D. C.: Diagnosis of histoplasmosis using precipitin reactions in agar gel. Pediatrics, *22:* 616–627, 1958.

19. Herrell, E. R., and Curtis, A. C.: North American blastomycosis. Am. J. Med., 27:750–766, 1957.

20. Kade, H., and Kaplan, L.: Evaluation of staining techniques in the histologic diagnosis of fungi. A.M.A. Arch. Path., 59:571–577, 1955.

21. Kao, C. J., and Schwartz, J.: The isolation of Cryptococcus neoformans from pigeon nests. Am. J. Clin. Path., 27:652–663, 1957.

22. Kurung, J. M.: The isolation of Histoplasma capsulatum from sputum. Am. Rev. Tuberculosis, 66:578–587, 1952.

23. Lewis, G. M., Hopper, N. E., Wilson, J. W., and Plunkett, O. A.: An Introduction to Medical Mycology. 4th Ed. Chicago, Year Book Publishers, Inc., 1958.

24. Littman, M. L.: Liver—spleen glucose blood agar for Histoplasma capsulatum and other fungi. Am. J. Clin. Path., 25:1148–1159, 1955.

25. Littman, M. L.: Capsule synthesis by Cryptococcus neoformans. Ann. N.Y. Acad. Sc., 20:623–648, 1958.

26. Littman, M. L., and Zimmerman, K. E.: Cryptococcosis; Torulosis, European Blastomycosis. New York, Grune & Stratton, Inc., 1956.

27. Liu, P., and Newton, A.: Rapid chlamydospore formation by Candida albicans in a buffered alkaline medium. Am. J. Clin. Path., 25:93–97, 1955.

28. McQuown, A. L.: Actinomycosis and nocardiosis. Am. J. Clin. Path., 25:2–13, 1955.

29. Moss, E. S., and McQuown, A. L.: Atlas of Medical Mycology. Baltimore, The Williams & Wilkins Company, 1953.

30. Nickerson, W. J., and Mankowski, Z.: A polysaccharide medium of known composition favoring chlamydospore formation in Candida albicans. J. Inf. Dis., 92:20–25, 1953.

31. Smith, C. E., Beard, R. R., and Saito, M. T.: Pathogenesis of coccidioidomycosis with special reference to pulmonary cavitation. Ann. Int. Med., 29:623–655, 1948.

32. Smith, C. E., Saito, M. T., Beard, R., Kepp, R., Clark, R. W., and Eddie, B. U.: Serological tests in the diagnosis and prognosis of coccidioidomycosis. Am. J. Hyg., 52:1–21, 1950.

33. Taschdjian, C.: Routine identification of Candida albicans: Current methods. Mycologia, 49:332–338, 1959.

34. Toone, E. C., and Kelly, J.: Joint and bone disease due to mycotic infection. Am. J. Med. Sc., 231:263–273, 1956.

35. Torack, R. M.: Fungus infections associated with antibiotic and steroid therapy. Am. J. Med., 22:872–882, 1957.

36. Weed, L. A.: Technic for isolation of fungi from tissue obtained at operation and necropsy. Am. J. Clin. Path., 28:70–88, 1955.

37. Weed, L. A., Anderson, H. A., Good, C. A., and Baggenstoss, A. H.: Nocardiosis: Clinical, bacteriologic and pathologic aspects. New Engl. J. Med., 253:1137–1143, 1955.

38. Weld, J.: Candida albicans. Rapid identification in cultures made directly from human material. A.M.A. Arch. Dermat., 67:473–478, 1953.

39. Zimmerman, L. E.: Fatal fungus infections complicating other diseases. Am. J. Clin. Path., 25:46–65, 1955.

Chapter 19

Viral and Rickettsial Diseases

By JAMES G. SHAFFER, Sc.D., *and* MILTON GOLDIN, M.S.

Laboratory procedures used in the diagnosis of viral and rickettsial diseases follow the same general principles as those used in the bacterial and mycotic diseases, but there are some important critical differences. Close cooperation between the physician and the laboratory is essential, since the choice of procedure is likely to be determined by clinical considerations.

Depending on the type of condition, one or more of three general approaches may be followed. First, it may be possible to demonstrate characteristic pathologic changes in stained sections of tissue biopsy specimens or to show in stained smears cell structures or inclusions typical of a certain disease (smallpox, vaccinia, herpes, trachoma, and warts). Second, an attempt may be made to isolate and identify the virus, utilizing chick embryo, tissue culture, or a susceptible animal (Arbor viruses, poliomyelitis, ECHO, Coxsackie). Third, serologic methods may be applied, utilizing acute and convalescent sera tested simultaneously by complement fixation, neutralization, hemagglutination, or hemagglutination inhibition.

An approach to the rapid, specific diagnosis of some of the viral diseases that may prove to be of great value in the near future is that of the use of fluorescent antibody methods (see p. 618). Liu (1956), for example, has shown that it is possible to diagnose influenza infection from nasal smears on the same day as the collection of the specimen. The technique, either direct or indirect, seems at this time to be most promising in the diagnosis of rabies, the pox viruses, herpes, and the L.G.V.

group. It may be that, when these techniques are perfected enough to be practical for the routine laboratory, they may replace in good part diagnostic procedures now in use, which are of value primarily only retrospectively.

In addition there are many laboratory procedures, other than those to be mentioned (cell counts, biochemical tests), that are useful in the diagnosis of viral and rickettsial diseases. They are described elsewhere in this book.

Knowledge of what specimens to collect and of how they should be handled and prepared for examination is important. Preparations for microscopic examination can be made easily and require no special equipment or material other than stains. Isolation and identification of viruses and serologic testing require special equipment, reagents, animal quarters, and incubators and have up to now been to a great extent research procedures. However, many of the reagents needed for serologic testing and tissue culture that are difficult to prepare in routine laboratories are now available commercially, and the techniques have been simplified sufficiently for routine use in smaller laboratories. Space does not permit a detailed description of all the methods that may be used in the diagnosis of viral and rickettsial diseases. Emphasis will be placed on the collection and handling of specimens, and a few simple techniques of examination will be described.

MICROSCOPIC EXAMINATION

Films, smears, or sections made from

lesions of certain viral and rickettsial diseases may be useful when properly prepared and stained. Cutaneous lesions (variola, vaccinia, herpes simplex) should be scraped with a scalpel or similar instrument and the scrapings spread thinly over a clean slide and allowed to dry. The slide should be thoroughly cleaned before use and the spreading done with care so as not to destroy the cell structure. From ocular lesions smears should be made from material expressed from the conjunctival follicles. The use of cotton pledgets is not recommended. The best stains for these preparations are Giemsa, Macchiavello, or Castaneda (see Appendix, p. 932).

It may be desirable to obtain biopsy or postmortem material for examination. Such material should be placed in a fixative immediately. Special fixatives may be used, but for general purposes Zenker's fluid with 10 per cent formalin is satisfactory. Sections stained with hematoxylin and eosin can then be examined for characteristic cells and cell structures.

MATERIAL AND METHODS FOR ISOLATION AND IDENTIFICATION OF VIRUSES AND RICKETTSIAE

The source of materials for the isolation of viruses or rickettsiae depends on the condition with which one is dealing. For most of the upper respiratory diseases throat washings are to be recommended. This includes influenza and some of the Coxsackie viruses. In poliomyelitis and the ECHO-Coxsackie infections throat washings may be used, but stools are the material of choice in most cases. In some viral diseases of the central nervous system spinal fluid may be used. In most of the viral encephalitides the virus can be isolated from the spinal fluid only in the very early stages of the disease. In fatal conditions viral isolation can be accomplished most readily with tissues obtained at autopsy. Blood may be used in some viral infections. Tissue biopsy may be done in certain diseases, especially the exanthematous conditions, such as smallpox, vaccinia, and herpes. Positive findings are significant, but failure to isolate a virus from a given specimen cannot be considered definitive.

Most laboratories, regardless of size, can collect suitable material for virus isolation, but only in the larger laboratories can actual isolation and identification be accomplished. The smaller laboratories can usually send material to larger laboratories for this purpose.

Collection of Feces

When feces are collected for virus isolation, several grams should be collected in a wide-mouth bottle or stiff paper carton. The specimen should be frozen immediately and kept in a dry ice box or electrically operated deep freezer at $-20°$ C. to $-70°$ C. Some specimens require the lower temperature if kept long. For shipment the specimen must be packed in dry ice in a suitable container. To prepare the feces for inoculation into a tissue culture or an animal the specimen is emulsified to about a 10 per cent concentration in sterile distilled water and centrifuged to remove gross particles. Then the supernatant is treated with ether or antibiotics to destroy bacteria. Penicillin (500 units per ml.) and streptomycin (2.5 mg. per ml.) are the antibiotics most frequently used. Bacterial cultures are always done prior to use of the specimen.

When it is difficult to collect feces, one may use an anal swab. The swab may be placed in 0.5 ml. of broth or other diluent and frozen, or it may be placed in a tube containing 2 or 3 ml. of 50 per cent glycerin-saline. Glycerin used for this purpose must be the purest available. Glycerin has long been used as a preservative for viruses and has the advantage of destroying bacteria in a relatively short time. It also inactivates viruses but much more slowly.

Throat Washings

Throat washings are useful in respiratory viral diseases as well as in poliomyelitis. They are collected as follows: The patient should gargle with 10 to 15 ml. of fluid, which can be broth, skim milk, or distilled water. The gargling should be done two or three times with the same fluid and the fluid collected in a sealable container. It is helpful to have the patient cough up material from the trachea. The washings are then transferred to a closed tube and frozen quickly to $-70°$ C. in dry ice or a low temperature freezer. If the washings are to be examined within two or three days, they may be treated with penicillin (500 units per ml.) and streptomycin (125 units per ml.) and stored at $4°$ C. When the frozen washings are thawed, they are also treated with penicillin and streptomycin before use in the experimental animal or tissue culture.

Collection of Material from Lesions on the Skin or Mucous Membranes

Fluid or exudate from vesicles or other superficial lesions (herpes simplex, smallpox, vaccinia, herpangina) can be collected on cotton swabs. Such swabs may be placed in 0.5 ml. of broth or other suitable diluent and frozen until use, or they may be placed in 50 per cent glycerin-saline. In either case they are handled in the same way as the anal swab. Some workers prefer to solidify the glycerin-saline by adding 1.0 per cent agar.

Collection of Tissue Specimens

The chance for virus isolation from tissues, as with most other specimens, is best in those collected in the first few days of illness or in those collected when death has occurred in the first five days or so of illness. In some diseases biopsy specimens may be taken from lesions; in others, such as the viral encephalitides, tissue can be obtained at autopsy. When possible, the tissues should be collected aseptically, but in many instances this cannot be done. In either case the tissue should be placed in sterile containers and handled aseptically thereafter. The tissue may be stored at refrigerator temperature (4° C.) for one or two days, but ideally, particularly if longer storage or shipment is necessary, the tissue should be frozen, placed in an adequately sealed container, and held at −70° C. The seal must be tight to prevent entry of carbon dioxide during storage or shipment. Shipment requires that the tissues be packed in a thermos or other suitable container with enough dry ice to last during transit.

To prepare tissue suspensions for inoculation into embryonated eggs or animals, the tissue must be ground in a mortar or suitable grinder, using sterile sand, alundum, or other suitable abrasive. It is not advisable to use an ordinary electrically driven blender because of the production of aerosols. If a blender is to be used, special precautions are essential.

When grinding tissue in a mortar, the tissue should first be ground with the abrasive and then enough distilled water added to make a paste. After further grinding, enough diluent is added to make a 10 per cent tissue suspension. The diluent to be used depends on the virus and the tissue being examined, and it is well to check on this in any specific case. Penicillin (500 units per ml.) and streptomycin (500 units per ml.) are added and the material sedimented in a centrifuge to clarify the supernatant for inoculation. Bacterial subcultures should always be done before use.

Collection of Blood and Spinal Fluid

In the early stages of some diseases the virus may be present in the blood or spinal fluid. These materials should be collected and handled aseptically throughout. It is also important to heparinize blood, since the virus may attach to the cellular elements and be absent from the serum. If the blood is not heparinized, the clot should be used. The collected spinal fluid and blood should be frozen at −70° C.

Spinal fluid may be used for animal inoculation without further treatment. Blood should be used undiluted and in several serial, tenfold dilutions, since occasionally the virus is isolated only after dilution.

Animal Inoculation

A variety of laboratory animals have been used for isolation of viruses (mice, rats, guinea pigs, hamsters, rabbits, ferrets, monkeys, chimpanzees), but the mouse is used most frequently. Some of the viruses have a rather wide host range (e.g., rabies), while others have a limited range (e.g., poliomyelitis), making it very important to choose the correct animal for inoculation. Even with viruses that have a wide range, there is often one particular laboratory animal that is more suitable than the others. It is important that the virus produce visible disease or death, since unapparent infections can be detected only by serologic means. In some instances certain strains of a given species of animal may be more susceptible than other strains of the same species. For example, some strains of mice are highly susceptible to influenza virus, while other strains are resistant. The age and condition of the animal used may be important. Old or poorly nourished animals should never be used. In many instances well-fed young adult animals are most desirable. In recent years suckling mice (one to four days old) have been used extensively with some of the viruses, especially the Coxsackie group. Another important point is to make sure that the colony from which the animals are obtained is free of infection that may confuse the issue.

The route of inoculation of the susceptible animal is important. Animals may be inoculated intracerebrally, intravenously, intraperitoneally, intranasally, subcutaneously, intracutaneously, or by mouth. It is not unusual to find that a susceptible animal may be infected regularly by one route of inoculation and only rarely by another. With influenza virus intranasal inoculation may consistently produce highly fatal disease, but the subcutaneous route will produce overt disease only infrequently.

Thus, it is important to choose the proper animal and route of inoculation to insure the best chance of virus isolation. In actual practice it may be beneficial to use more than one species of animal and to inoculate by more than one route. This is especially desirable in diagnostic work. Space does not allow for descriptions of all the inoculation techniques. These may be found in various texts and manuals, some of which are cited in the bibliography.

Inoculation into the Embryonated Egg

The embryonated hen's egg has been used extensively for virus isolation and propagation (Fig. 19–1). It has several advantages over animals: First, it has a wide range of susceptibility. Second, it is small and requires a minimum of space; consequently large numbers can be made available. Third, it is much less expensive in initial cost and maintenance. Finally, in most locations fertile hen's eggs are readily available. In some situations one must obtain the fertile eggs and incubate them to the desired age; in others one can obtain the embryonated eggs from a hatchery.

The susceptibility of the embryo to a given virus may vary somewhat with its age and also with the route by which inoculation is made. Thus, one must ascertain what age embryo and what route of inoculation to use in a given situation. The most common routes by which inoculation is accomplished are: directly into the yolk sac (psittacosis, rickettsiae), on the chorioallantoic membrane (pox viruses), into the allantoic sac, into the amniotic sac (influenza), or into the brain. Space does not allow for a description of all the various techniques. These can be found in various excellent texts and manuals, some of which are cited in the bibliography.

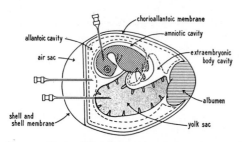

Figure 19–1. Diagrammatic representation in sagittal section of the embryonated hen's egg 10 to 12 days old. The hypodermic needles show the routes of inoculation of the yolk sac, allantoic cavity, and embryo (head). The chorioallantoic membrane is inoculated after it has been dropped by removing the air from the air sac. (Burrows.)

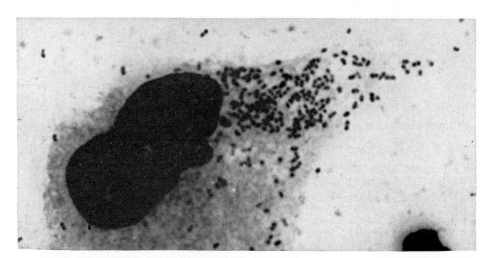

Figure 19–2. The rickettsia of tsutsugamushi disease in scrapings from a mesothelial surface of an infected guinea pig. Note the coccobacillary forms, often paired, and their intracellular location. × 2000. (Burrows.)

The recognition of the presence of a virus in the inoculated embryo depends on the production of some visible response or on the demonstration of virus by special techniques, such as a stained smear from certain tissues or the hemagglutination technique. Some viruses produce pock-like lesions on the chorioallantoic membrane, or there may be visible lesions on the embryo itself. Stained smears from such lesions may reveal typical intracellular inclusions. Some viruses and rickettsiae propagate in the yolk sac membrane but may produce only little macroscopically apparent change. However, when smears from this membrane are stained with an appropriate stain (Macchiavello or Castaneda), one may see large numbers of viral or rickettsial bodies (Fig. 19–2). Other viruses produce death of the embryo without specific visible lesions. Influenza virus, when inoculated into the amniotic or allantoic sac, may produce no visible lesions, but its presence can be detected by its capacity to cause the clumping of the red blood cells of certain species of animals (hemagglutination).

The final identification of an isolated virus depends on serologic testing with known antisera. For this the neutralization test has been used extensively. There are several techniques for doing such tests. They are not easy to perform and should only be done by laboratories with adequate equipment and trained personnel.

Complement fixation and other classic serologic tests with known antisera may also be used as aids in the identification of viruses and rickettsiae.

Tissue Culture

Tissue culture has been used in the study of viruses for some time, but only recently have techniques been developed that allow for the possibility of the extensive use of tissue culture as an aid in diagnostic work. This has resulted from the introduction of simplified procedures, the use of antibiotics to obviate some of the pitfalls of incidental bacterial contamination, and the establishment of standard lines of cultured cells e.g., HeLa). Excellent tissue culture reagents can be obtained commercially, and detailed descriptions of the techniques are available. One can also obtain tissue cultures ready for use from commercial sources.

Tissue culture methods have already contributed much valuable information in the epidemiologic investigation of certain virus diseases, among them, poliomyelitis and Coxsackie. These methods have also resulted in the isolation of numerous, previously unknown agents, such as the adenoviruses and ECHO viruses, some of which have not yet been associated with definite clinical diseases. Tissue culture methods will probably gradually replace much of the more time-consuming and expensive animal inoculation in diagnostic work. The rapid advances made in tissue culture methods should, before long, make it possible for relatively small laboratories to utilize these techniques to great advantage.

Not only can a large number of viruses be isolated and identified in tissue culture, but it is also possible to test patients' sera rapidly and economically for neutralizing antibody. Such procedures are useful in both diagnostic and epidemiologic investigations.

Serologic Tests

The diagnostic aid most widely used in viral and rickettsial diseases is serologic testing. The demonstration of a rise in titer of an antibody against a specific agent in sera collected at proper intervals may be diagnostic. Complement fixation, neutralization, hemagglutination inhibition, and agglutination may all be used. Complement fixation is used most frequently, neutralization and hemagglutination inhibition less extensively, and agglutination least frequently.

Small laboratories and private physicians obviously cannot perform all these serologic tests, but all can collect the necessary serum and send it to the appropriate laboratory for testing. Certain principles must be observed in order to insure the most satisfactory results: First, a brief clinical summary must be provided with the serum (some laboratories will not accept specimens without such a summary). Second, the blood (10 to 15 ml.) must be collected with a dry syringe and handled with aseptic technique. Third, two or more additional samples must be collected at appropriate intervals. The first sample (acute) should be taken as soon as possible after onset of symptoms, the second (convalescent) 10 to 14 days later, and, when possible, a third after one month. Since the rise in antibody titer in some cases occurs fairly late, the third specimen may be important and a fourth may be useful. Blood should be collected three to four hours after a meal, since chylous serum may be anticomplementary.

Blood collected with a syringe should be

transferred to a sterile tube and allowed to clot. The clot should be loosened from the tube by means of a sterile applicator stick or inoculating loop. The tube may then be centrifuged at 1000 to 1200 r.p.m. for 10 to 15 minutes, or it may be placed in the refrigerator overnight to allow the clot to retract. Then the serum is collected in a sterile, tightly capped vial or tube. It may be stored in the refrigerator at 4° C., or, if it is not to be tested within a few days, it should be placed in the deep freeze. The "acute" sample should always be held until the subsequent samples are collected and all tested simultaneously.

For shipment the serum may be sent unfrozen, but it is better to ship it frozen. Physicians may not have facilities for collection of serum in their offices. In such cases they may send the clotted blood sample directly to the appropriate laboratory. If this is to be done, the blood may be collected in the vacuum-type blood collection tubes without anticoagulant that are readily available commercially. In this case the blood should be sent immediately and not held until subsequent samples are taken. Whole blood should not be frozen, since this will result in complete hemolysis. The advantage of sending whole blood is that it reduces the chance of bacterial contamination, but it has the disadvantage that, if the blood is in transit too long, there may be considerable hemolysis.

Most laboratories that do serologic tests, especially the state and federal public health laboratories, will supply self-addressed mailing cartons containing sterile vials, thus simplifying the problem of shipment. It is well to find out from the laboratory what information is required with each specimen. This will save time and insure the best possible results.

SEROLOGIC TECHNIQUES

Complement Fixation. Complement fixation (CF) has, as indicated before, been used most frequently. The CF technique has varied with different laboratories, but most are modifications of the Kolmer technique, which is presented in another section (Chapter 23). Since the reagents (complement, hemolysin, and sheep red blood cells) are readily available and a number of standardized viral and rickettsial antigens are also available commercially, it is possible for moderate-size laboratories to do these tests, provided the personnel have the special training necessary to do CF tests.

One of the problems in the complement-fixation test is that serums may prove to be anticomplementary. Some serums are anticomplementary without any obvious reason, but there are some well-recognized causes of anticomplementary activity. These are bacterial contamination, use of anticoagulants, and chylous serum. All can be avoided by proper technique.

The interpretation of the results of complement-fixation tests is not difficult with experience. If simultaneous testing of multiple serums reveals a fourfold or greater rise in titer against a specific viral antigen, this may be considered significant. A twofold rise is equivocal and may be the result of technical variation. If only a single serum is available and a high titer (in most cases 1:16 to 1:32) is found, this in some cases may represent evidence of fairly recent infection with the specific agent. It is, of course, essential that the CF result be carefully correlated with the clinical picture.

NEUTRALIZATION TESTS

The neutralization test is based on the capacity of antibody to neutralize the infectious properties of viruses in a manner similar to the neutralization of toxin by antitoxin. When antibody alone is involved, such neutralization is specific, but various investigators have shown that normal serum may contain a certain amount of nonspecific neutralizing substance. This nonspecific substance is gradually lost when serum is stored at refrigerator temperature (4° C.) but is not lost when the serum is stored in the deep freeze. The full activity may be restored by adding a small amount of fresh guinea pig serum. It is important to remember this in testing paired sera, since the "acute" serum may have been stored long enough to lose the nonspecific neutralizing substance and the "convalescent" serum may be fresh when tested. This might give results indicating an antibody rise and be misleading.

The neutralization test can be used in two ways: to detect specific antibody rises as an aid in the diagnosis of disease and to identify an unknown agent after its isolation. When experimental animals are used to detect neutralization, the test is time consuming and may be fairly expensive. Not many laboratories are equipped to do it routinely. If the embryonated egg can be used, the test is better from this standpoint. Tissue culture methods make it possible for smaller laboratories to use this test to good advantage. Space does not allow detailed descriptions of the neutralization techniques. These can be found in various textbooks, manuals, and other publications (see bibliography).

Hemagglutinin Inhibition

A number of viruses have the capacity to cause the red blood cells of one or another animal species to agglutinate. Specific antibody inhibits agglutination, and this constitutes the basis for the hemagglutinin-inhibition test. This test can be done easily in routine laboratories. Serial dilutions of the serum are added to a standard amount of virus-containing fluid. The mixture is incubated at room temperature to allow reaction between virus and antibody to occur. A standard suspension of appropriate red blood cells is then added and the tubes shaken thoroughly. They are incubated at room temperature until the erythrocytes have settled out. In the absence of agglutination the cells settle as a button at the bottom of the tube, whereas agglutination is manifested by irregular dispersion of granular clumps of cells over the bottom of the tube. The hemagglutinin-inhibition titer of a serum is the reciprocal of the dilution in the last tube showing no agglutination. A fourfold or greater rise in titer between the collection of "acute" and "convalescent" serums is considered significant.

Certain serums contain nonspecific inhibitory substances, and unless these are removed the results of hemagglutinin-inhibition tests may be misleading. They can be removed in a number of ways, but treatment with trypsin appears to be best. The methods for standardization of the test can be found in various publications (see bibliography).

The hemagglutination phenomenon can be used in some instances to detect the presence of virus. For instance, one may test amniotic fluid from embryonated eggs that have been inoculated with throat washings from patients with suspected influenza. Serial dilutions of the fluid combined with suspensions of 1 per cent washed chicken or guinea pig erythrocytes will cause agglutination of the cells if virus is present. One may then identify this virus by combining it with known antiserums and testing for specific inhibition of agglutination.

Agglutination

Some viruses and rickettsiae can be prepared in a sufficiently pure form so that, when combined with serum containing antibodies, specific agglutination occurs. Since these antigens are not easy to prepare, the technique has not been used extensively.

Certain nonspecific agglutination tests have been used widely as aids in the diagnosis of viral and rickettsial diseases. The Weil-Felix test, which is described in Chapter 24, has been used in rickettsial diseases.

Certain other nonspecific agglutination tests have been used as aids in the diagnosis of viral diseases. In infectious mononucleosis agglutination of sheep red blood cells (the so-called Paul-Bunnell or presumptive test) has been used for many years. This test is not specific and must be confirmed with the specific differential test (see p. 217). Two tests have been used in primary atypical pneumonia. The first is the test for cold agglutinins, which are present in high titers in most severe and some mild cases. The second is based on the development of agglutinins against *Streptococcus* MG. The latter test is a straight agglutination using paired sera against the streptococcal antigen. Neither of these tests is specific and can only be used as aids in the diagnosis (see Chapter 24).

LABORATORY DIAGNOSIS OF VIRUS DISEASES

In the following section an attempt will be made to summarize critical information on virus diseases relating to certain diagnostic principles. In certain cases these diseases will be dealt with as groups, and others will be discussed on an individual basis. Available space does not allow extensive discussion of the diseases or of all the diagnostic techniques beyond what has been presented in the previous section.

Arthropod-borne (Arbor) Viruses

The arthropod-borne (Arbor) viruses constitute a rather large group, which produce diseases in mammals and birds (vertebrates) and which multiply in the bodies of arthropods. Their transmission from vertebrate to vertebrate depends on the arthropod host in which the virus, although it multiplies, does not produce disease. About 50 such viruses are known and new ones are still being described. In a number of instances the available information re-

Table 19-1.   Characteristics of the Arbor Viruses

VIRUS GROUP	HUMAN DISEASE	TRANSMISSION (ARTHROPOD)	OCCURRENCE IN NATURE	DISTRIBUTION (GEOGRAPHIC)	LABORATORY DIAGNOSIS — MATERIAL FOR ISOLATION	LABORATORY DIAGNOSIS — SUSCEPTIBLE ANIMAL OF CHOICE	SERO-DIAGNOSIS *	REMARKS
Group A								
Eastern equine encephalomyelitis (EEE)	Encephalitis	Mosquito	Horses, mules, pheasants, birds	Eastern U.S. and Canada, Central and So. Am., Philippines	CNS tissue	Mice (intracerebral)	CF, NT	Virus rarely isolated from spinal fluid or blood of patients
Western equine encephalomyelitis (WEE)	Encephalitis	Mosquito	Domestic and wild birds, horses, mules, deer, squirrels, pigs	Western U.S. and Canada, sometimes in eastern and southern U.S., So. Am. (Brazil)	CNS tissue	Mice (intracerebral)	CF (choice), NT, HI	
Venezuelan equine encephalitis (VEE)	Encephalitis (influenza-like)	Mosquito; direct by droplets?	Horses; birds?	Northern So. Am., Trinidad, Panama	CNS tissue, blood, nasopharyngeal washings	Mice (intracerebral)	CF, NT, HI	
Group B								
St. Louis encephalitis (SLE)	Encephalitis (many clinically inapparent infections)	Mosquito	Domestic fowl, wild birds (reservoir unknown)	U.S. from Ky. to West Coast, Trinidad	CNS tissue	Mice (intracerebral)	CF, NT, HI	Virus never yet found in spinal fluid; rarely in blood
Japanese B encephalitis (JBE)	Encephalitis	Mosquito	Domestic and wild fowl, horses, swine	Eastern Asia, Japan, Okinawa, Formosa, Guam, Philippines, Borneo	CNS tissue	Mice (intracerebral)	CF, NT, HI	Occasionally virus may be isolated from blood
Murray Valley encephalitis (Australian X disease) (MVE)	Encephalitis	Mosquito	Horses, domestic and wild fowl	Australia	CNS tissue	Chick embryo (yolk or amniotic sac), mice	CF, NT, HI	
Dengue types 1 and 2	Fever, rash, lymphadenopathy, muscle and joint pains	Mosquito		Hawaii, India, Japan, Malaya, New Guinea, Trinidad, Uganda	Whole blood or serum	Suckling mice (2–4 days)	CF, NT, HI	NT probably most reliable
Yellow fever (YF)	Hepatitis	Mosquito		Equatorial Africa and America	Serum (early in disease); liver in fatal cases	Mice (intracerebral)	CF, NT, HI	CF most specific
Louping ill, Russian spring-summer encephalitis, Central European tick-borne summer encephalitis, Kyasanur forest disease	Encephalitis	Tick	Sheep	Great Britain, Czechoslovakia, Russia, India	Blood, spinal fluid, CNS tissue	Mice (intracerebral)	CF, NT	
Group C								
Apeu, Marituba, Oriboca	Systemic	Mosquito		Brazil	—	—	CF, NT	—
Ungrouped								
California encephalitis	Encephalitis	Mosquito		Western U.S.	Blood	Mice (intracerebral)	CF, NT	Influenza-like fever
Rift Valley fever	Systemic	Mosquito	Sheep	Kenya, So. Afr., Uganda	Blood	Mice	CF, NT	History of exposure to ticks
Colorado tick fever	Systemic	Tick		Western U.S.	Blood or serum	Mice (intracerebral)	CF, NT	
Sandfly fever (pappataci, phlebotomus fever)	Systemic	Phlebotomus fly		Southern Italy, Egypt, Sicily	Blood	Mice (suckling)	CF, NT	Clinical and epidemiologic evidence and diagnosis

* CF = complement fixation   NT = neutralization test   HI = hemagglutinin-inhibition

garding these agents is fragmentary, especially regarding their geographic distribution.

Some of the Arbor viruses are related clinically and antigenically, and they have been divided into groups mostly on serologic grounds. The best known viruses are found in Groups A and B, Group C containing only a few agents. Several others are as yet ungrouped. In Table 19–1 are shown some of the important characteristics of what are at the moment the most important Arbor viruses.

Rabies

Rabies is one of the most important diseases of animals that is transmissible to man. All mammals are susceptible to the infection, which is universally fatal once symptoms have appeared. It is primarily a disease of canines, being maintained in dogs, foxes, and wolves, but also occurs frequently in skunks and less frequently in squirrels and other rodents. In Central America it is present in vampire bats, which transmit it to domestic animals and man. In the vampire bat the disease may be chronic and unapparent for a considerable time. Recently it has been found that rabies exists in insectivorous bats in widely scattered regions in the United States.

The virus is present in the saliva of infected animals and in the canine appears at this site two or three days before symptoms appear. Infection occurs by introduction of the virus into tissue, usually as the result of biting. It may also be introduced if saliva comes in contact with a fresh cut or abrasion that has broken the continuity of the skin. Any animal bite, especially of a dog, fox, skunk, squirrel, or bat, must be viewed with suspicion and every attempt made to ascertain whether the biting animal had rabies. The incubation period of rabies in humans varies from approximately two weeks to several months, there being some reports of incubation periods as long as two years. The incubation period depends on the severity of the bite and the location. Severe bites about the head and neck tend to have the shortest incubation period, while those on the extremities have the longest. It is imperative that all exposed individuals have proper treatment (Pasteur vaccine or hyperimmune serum) started at the earliest possible time, but since the treatment itself is somewhat hazardous it is of the utmost importance to determine whether the biting animal had rabies.

The diagnosis of rabies depends on a history of exposure; the clinical symptoms, which are the least dependable criteria; isolation of virus by intracerebral inoculation of mice; and demonstration of the characteristic Negri bodies in the brain, which, if properly done, is accurate and rapid. A positive finding is diagnostic, but failure to find Negri bodies does not rule out infection, especially when the brain is decomposing owing to poor handling or when the animal has been sacrificed early in the disease. Thus, it is well to do mouse brain inoculation with suspensions of salivary tissue or brain.

In all cases of animal bite all possible means of locating the animal should be tried. It should be captured alive if at all possible and observed for clinical evidence of disease. In most places the law requires that dogs showing no symptoms be impounded for 10 to 14 days. Care must be used when killing animals to avoid damage to the brain. The head should be removed with a knife and chilled but not frozen. It should be taken to the laboratory and examined immediately. If shipment is required, it must be packed in ice (not dry ice), since the brain tissue degenerates very rapidly if not cold, making microscopic examination difficult if not impossible.

Removal of the Brain. The brain is removed intact by opening the cranial cavity with a saw, bone chisel, or other suitable implement. The operator should use heavy rubber gloves and be very careful to avoid exposure to the virus. After removal the brain is placed upright on a piece of filter paper in a dish.

Preparation of Slides. Negri bodies are most frequently found in the stellate cells of the Ammon's horn (hippocampus) but may also occur in the cerebellum and cerebrum. Thus, stained smears should be made and examined from all three sites. Ammon's horn is exposed by cutting through the cerebral cortex into the lateral ventricle of the brain, making a longitudinal incision into the dorsal surface of each cerebral hemisphere. When the sides of the incision are spread apart, Ammon's horn can be seen as a semicylindrical, white, glistening body bulging laterally from the floor of the ventricle.

With a small scissors remove small transverse sections of both Ammon's horns and place them, cut surface up, on an applicator stick. Do the same with the cerebellum and cerebrum. Impression slides are then made by touching a clean slide to the cut surfaces. Touch the slide to the tissue with just enough pressure to spread a slight amount of it on the slide. Impression slides are better than smears, because they contain a maximum amount of nerve tissue in a minimum area.

Staining Procedure. While the smear is still moist, flood the slide with Seller's stain or dip it quickly into a Coplin jar filled with this stain. This stain fixes and stains simultaneously and is very dependable. Rinse the slide immediately in tap water or in M/150 phosphate buffer, pH 7.0. In some areas tap water is not suitable.

Seller's Stain

Stock solution methylene blue	
Methylene blue (85 per cent dye content)	1.0 gm.
Methyl alcohol (absolute, acetone free) to make	100.0 ml.
Stock solution basic fuchsin	
Basic fuchsin (92 per cent dye content)	1.0 gm.
Methyl alcohol (absolute, acetone free) to make	100.0 ml.

Store stock staining solutions in screw-cap bottles in a refrigerator.

Working stain	
Stock solution methylene blue	2 parts
Stock solution basic fuchsin	1 part

Mix thoroughly but do not filter. The stain improves on standing for 24 hours and may be used indefinitely if no evaporation occurs.

In the stained smear the Negri body is an acidophilic structure of varying size and shape that stains magenta to heliotrope in color (Fig. 19–3). It varies from 2 to 10 μ in size and contains one to four basophilic granules, which stain dark blue or black. The Negri body forms within the cell and is characteristically seen in the cytoplasm, but it may appear outside the cell if the cell is ruptured. Thus, the finding of typical Negri bodies is diagnostic whether they are inside or outside the cell.

Other types of inclusions that may be seen need to be differentiated from Negri bodies. In the brains of dogs and foxes the acidophilic inclusions of canine distemper or hepatitis may be seen. There are similar structures in the brains of mice, cats, skunks, woodchucks, raccoons, and squirrels. These structures stain pink to bright red, tend to be round, and are more refractile than Negri bodies. They do not have internal granules and may be differentiated on these grounds.

Inoculation of Animals. The mouse is the animal of choice for inoculation in cases of rabies. Intracerebral inoculation of 0.01 to 0.03 ml. of a 10 per cent suspension of central nervous system tissue or salivary gland into five or six mice is to be recommended in all cases of suspected rabies. The diluent for these tissue suspensions should be buffered saline, pH 7.6 to 7.8, although 0.85 per cent saline may be used. Penicillin (1000 units per ml.) and streptomycin (2 mg. per ml.) should be added to the tissue suspension, which is allowed to stand 30 minutes before use. Tissue should be taken from several parts of the brain and pooled, since virus distribution varies. If tissues are to be collected for shipment to another laboratory or for storage, they should be placed in 50 per cent glycerin, saline or frozen in a dry ice box. The suspension of tissue should be centrifuged at 1000 r.p.m. for five minutes or allowed to settle in a refrigerator for several hours before use.

Inoculated mice should be checked daily for at least three weeks, and the mice should be held for at least 30 days. Any deaths occurring within the first 48 hours are to be attributed to some other cause. Seldom do symptoms of rabies occur in less than five days. After five days, mice showing evidence of illness, such as roughing of the fur, humping of the back, sluggishness, tremors, weakness, convulsions, paralysis, or prostration, should be sacrificed; the brain should be removed and examined for Negri bodies. Touch preparations made from the cross-section of the brain and stained by Seller's stain should be examined. Presence of Negri bodies is diagnostic. Any positive or questionably positive findings should be reported immediately.

Poliomyelitis, Coxsackie, ECHO, and Lymphocytic Choriomeningitis
(Table 19–2)

The diagnosis of poliomyelitis was for many years largely a clinical one, although certain laboratory procedures (spinal fluid examination) were of some help. It was especially difficult to diagnose the nonparalytic case. In fact during nonepidemic periods these were largely missed and during epidemic periods were probably over-diagnosed. The usual diagnostic procedures for virus diseases could not be applied to poliomyelitis (Fig. 19–4). Virus isolation in most cases required the use of monkeys, which are difficult and expensive to obtain

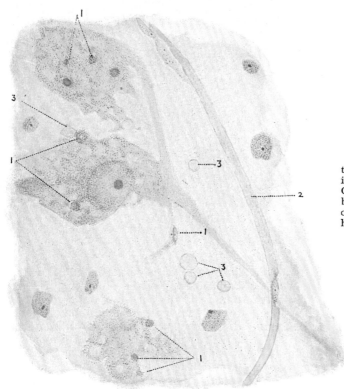

Figure 19–3. Nerve cells containing Negri bodies. Hippocampus impression (dog) stained with van Gieson's stain (× 1000). *1*, Negri bodies; *2*, capillary; *3*, free erythrocytes. (Courtesy Langdon Frothingham.)

Table 19–2. Differentiation of Enterovirus Infections

	POLIO (TYPES 1–3)	COXSACKIE TYPE A	COXSACKIE TYPE B	ECHO
Clinical Picture:				
Seasonal incidence	Summer	Summer	Summer	Summer
Age at onset	Children and young adults	Children and young adults	Children and young adults	All ages
Clinical findings:				
Fever	Frequent	Frequent	Frequent	Frequent
Headache	Frequent	Frequent	Frequent	Frequent
Paralysis	Common	Rare	Rare	Rare
Rash	Absent	Absent	Absent	Common
Diarrhea	Rare	Rare	Rare	Common (some types)
Meningitis	Common	Common	Common	Common
Herpangina	Absent	Rare	Absent	Absent
Epidemic pleurodynia	Absent	Absent	Rare	Absent
Myocarditis	Rare	Absent	Rare (infants)	Absent
Virus Laboratory Studies:				
Virus isolable from				
Nasopharynx	Occasionally	Occasionally	Occasionally	Occasionally
Spinal fluid	Occasionally	Occasionally	Occasionally	Commonly
Feces	Frequently	Frequently	Frequently	Frequently
CF tests available	Yes	No	No	No
Neutralization tests available	Yes	Yes	Yes	Yes
Serologically typable	Yes	Yes	Yes	Yes
Isolation in				
Suckling mice	No	Yes	Yes	No
Tissue culture	Yes	Variable by type	Yes	Yes

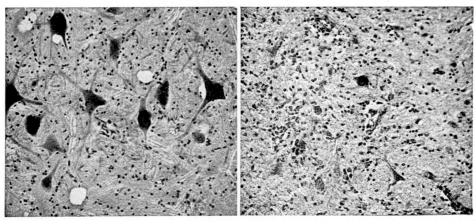

Figure 19–4. Sections through the anterior horn of monkey spinal cords. *Left,* normal monkey; *right,* monkey paralyzed with poliomyelitis showing the destruction of the large anterior horn cells and neuronophagia. Hematoxylin and eosin; × 125. (Burrows.)

and maintain. Neutralization tests had to be done using groups of monkeys and quite obviously could not be done routinely. Proper antigens were difficult, if not impossible, to prepare for the complement-fixation test.

Some years ago the Type II (Lansing) polio virus was adapted to mice, and later Type I (Mahoney) and Type III (Leon) were also adapted to mice by special methods. Using these mouse-adapted strains, it is possible to do neutralization tests on paired serums.

The demonstration that poliovirus can be propagated in tissue culture with non-neural tissues (monkey kidney and testicle and human foreskin) led within a short time to the development of methods that have made possible extensive epidemiologic and diagnostic studies. These have resulted in much better understanding of the disease, improvement in diagnosis, and the development of a vaccine. It is now possible to do virus isolations from nasopharyngeal washings or feces directly into tissue culture. Neutralization tests on paired serums can also be done using tissue culture instead of animals, and antigens for complement fixation can be made from tissue culture. Thus, any laboratory that is equipped to do tissue culture can do diagnostic poliovirus isolation and neutralization. Other laboratories may obtain antigens for complement-fixation tests on paired serums.

There are three antigenically distinct types of poliovirus, of which the accepted prototypes are Mahoney (Type I), Lansing (Type II), and Leon (Type III). Recovery from infection with one type confers long-term immunity to reinfection with that type but not to the other two. Neutralization tests do not show cross-reactions between the types, but the complement-fixation tests on human convalescent serums have revealed certain group antigens.

The immediate diagnosis of poliomyelitis is still largely based on clinical signs and spinal fluid findings, and in the paralytic form this is not too difficult. However, in nonparalytic disease it is difficult, since several other agents that cause aseptic meningitis are clinically similar and indistinguishable from poliomyelitis. The most common viruses involved are: mumps, lymphocytic choriomeningitis, ECHO, herpes simplex, herpes zoster, epidemic encephalitis, and Coxsackie Group B (some types). Some cases of "aseptic meningitis" in which *Leptospira* are involved have been described. Tuberculous and other bacterial meningitides may be difficult to differentiate clinically from those caused by virus. Laboratory assistance is, thus, necessary in these conditions.

The Coxsackie Viruses

The first strains of Coxsackie viruses were isolated from the stools of patients with paralytic poliomyelitis. It was later found that these viruses do not produce paralytic disease, but certain strains do produce aseptic meningitis. This was the first of a large group of enteroviruses, which are now divided into the Coxsackie (Groups A and B) and the ECHO viruses. New members of the group are still being found, and the classification is not yet complete. Some types in all groups have not yet been associated with definite disease entities.

Certain types (1–5) of Group B Coxsackie viruses have been shown to be associated with cases of aseptic meningitis. These tend to occur seasonally in the summer and fall. There is also evidence that some strains of Group A are associated with this disease.

Two other disease entities are associated with the Coxsackie viruses. Members of Group A, types 2, 4, 5, 6, 8, and 10, have been found to cause herpangina, which affects mainly children. Group B Coxsackie viruses are associated with epidemic myalgia or pleurodynia (Bornholm disease).

The diagnosis of Coxsackie infection can be established by virus isolation or by serologic means. The virus is present in the digestive tract and can be isolated from feces, nasopharyngeal washings, or swabs by inoculation into suckling mice (one day old) or into tissue culture, although tissue culture is much less efficient with Group A viruses (Figs. 19–5, 19–6). Adult mice and other animals are resistant to the virus. Neutralization tests utilizing suckling mice or tissue culture can be done on paired

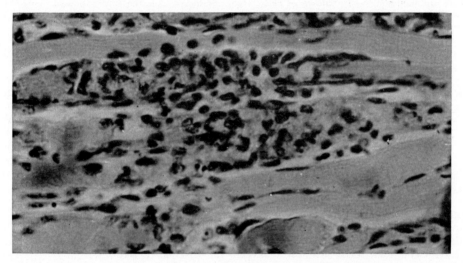

Figure 19–5. Lesion in striated muscle of a mouse infected with Coxsackie virus. Two sarcolemmic tubes with numerous mononuclear phagocytes and remnants of hyaline material within the sarcolemmic sheaths. Demarcated segmental involvement is apparent. × 500. (Godman, Bunting, and Melnick, Amer. J. Path., 1952.)

Figure 19–6. Electron photomicrograph of Coxsackie virus, Dalldorf type 2. Prepared from amniotic fluid. (Magnification × 48,000.) (Briefs, Breese, Warren, and Huebner. J. Bact., 64(2):242, 1952.)

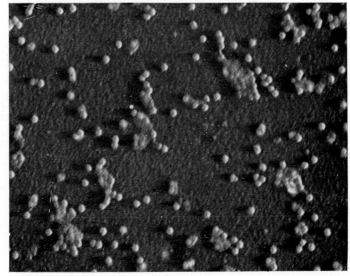

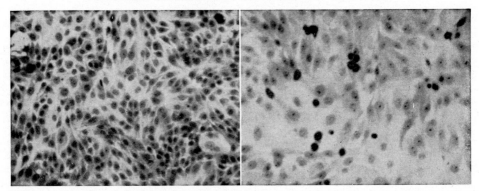

Figure 19–7. The cytopathogenic effect of ECHO virus type 1 in culture of monkey kidney epithelial cells. *Left,* uninoculated 6-day culture of cells; *right,* 24 hours after the inoculation of virus showing a few rounded cells scattered throughout the field. Carnoy fixation, hematoxylin and eosin. (Melnick, Adv. Virol.)

serums from patients. The testing of a single serum from a case is not to be recommended, since in certain areas antibody may be present in a considerable portion of the population owing to previous exposure to the virus. Complement fixation is at present of limited value.

The ECHO Virus Group

The ECHO (enteric cytopathogenic human orphan) viruses are a newly recognized group of agents that infect the human intestinal tract. They can be isolated in certain tissue cultures. Numerous antigenic types have been identified, and some have been shown to be associated with aseptic meningitis, febrile illnesses, and diarrheal diseases in infants and children during the summer months. Since this is a new group, it is to be expected that further types will be described. Much further study of these agents will be necessary to elucidate their full potential.

Melnick (1955) and Sabin (1959) have pointed out that there are no clearcut clinical indications of ECHO virus infection, but certain epidemic situations during the summer and autumn may be suggestive:

1. A high incidence of the aseptic meningitis syndrome with few or no paralytic cases.

2. Outbreaks of febrile illness associated with a high incidence of rash, especially in younger children, with or without a concomitant increase in the number of cases of aseptic meningitis.

3. Outbreaks of diarrheal disease, especially in very young infants, from which few if any of the established enteropathogenic bacteria can be recovered.

The diagnosis of ECHO virus infection depends on isolation of the virus. Such isolation can be made from feces, throat swabs, and spinal fluid by inoculation into tissue culture (Fig. 19–7). Rectal swabs may also be used. The tissue culture of choice is the one containing the kidney of rhesus or cynomolgus monkeys. Other types of tissue culture have been used. No universally useful animal has yet been found, although some of the virus stains produce disease in suckling mice.

Serologic tests so far have been useful in identification of isolated ECHO viruses but are not applicable to the diagnosis of the disease in patients.

Lymphocytic Choriomeningitis

Lymphocytic choriomeningitis is primarily a disease of animals that occasionally infects man, producing aseptic meningitis. The spinal fluid tends to have a high lymphocyte count, but the disease cannot be differentiated from other forms of aseptic meningitis. The virus can be isolated from spinal fluid, blood, and central nervous system tissue, and the mouse and guinea pig are the animals of choice. One must be certain that the stock animals are free of the virus. Neutralization and complement-fixation tests on acute and convalescent serums can be used.

Infectious Hepatitis and Serum Hepatitis

Infectious and serum hepatitis are caused by viruses, which are possibly related. Infectious hepatitis virus has been called hepatitis virus A and the serum hepatitis virus, virus B. Infectious hepatitis is

Table 19-3. Comparison of Infectious and Serum Hepatitis

	INFECTIOUS HEPATITIS	SERUM HEPATITIS
Virus	Virus A	Virus B
Incubation period, days	15–40	60–160
Type of onset	Acute	Insidious
Seasonal prevalence	Winter, autumn	Year-round
Age preference	Children, young adults	All ages
Susceptible host	Man	Man
Virus demonstrable in feces and duodenal contents	Acute phase	Not demonstrated
Virus in blood	3 days before onset and in acute phase	Incubation period and acute phase
Route of infection	Oral and parenteral	Parenteral
Duration of carrier state in:		
blood	Unknown	Many years
feces	1–2 years	Not demonstrated
Immunity:		
homologous	Present	Equivocal
heterologous	None apparent	None apparent
Prophylactic value of gamma globulin	Good	Equivocal

also called "infective hepatitis" or "epidemic jaundice," and serum hepatitis has been called "homologous serum jaundice," "syringe jaundice," "postvaccinal hepatitis," and "transfusion jaundice."

In these conditions one cannot employ the usual diagnostic techniques for diagnosis of virus diseases, since the virus has not been isolated. It is necessary to rule out other forms of hepatitis and to make the diagnosis on clinical and epidemiologic grounds (see Table 19-3).

Common Cold, Influenza, Primary Atypical Pneumonia, and Adenoviruses

The Common Cold. The pathogenesis of the common cold is still poorly understood. It is a mild disease, which appears to have several different etiologies, e.g., bacterial, viral, and allergic. Many conditions may cause symptoms that are very similar if not identical to those of the common cold, such as influenza, acute respiratory disease (ARD), primary atypical pneumonia, and

Table 19-4. Characteristics of Common Respiratory Viruses

DISEASE	NATURE OF DISEASE	EPIDEMIOLOGY	VIRUS (TYPES)	MATERIAL	LABORATORY DIAGNOSIS ISOLATION OF VIRUS	SERODIAGNOSIS *
Common cold	Mild upper respiratory disease	Worldwide, some seasonal variation	Virus, bacteria, allergy	—	—	—
Influenza	Respiratory infection. Sudden onset, fever, myalgia, pharyngitis, cough, leukopenia, 3–4 days' duration	Periodic localized epidemics, occasional pandemics	Types A, B, C, D	Throat washings in acute stage	10–14-day chick embryo (amniotic sac), intranasal into ferrets	CF, NT, HI
Primary atypical pneumonia	Onset gradual; respiratory symptoms variable	Worldwide, usually endemic. Epidemics occur frequently.	?	—	—	*Streptococcus* MG agglutinins, cold agglutinins
Adenoviruses ARD	Relatively mild, grippe-like illness	Occurs in military recruits	Adenovirus types 3, 4, 7	Pharyngeal washings, feces	Tissue culture (HeLa, KB, or human amnion cells)	CF
Pharyngitis and pharyngoconjunctival fever	Fever, sore throat, headache; may have conjunctivitis also	Probably worldwide	Adenovirus types 2, 3, 5, 7	Pharyngeal or eye secretions, feces	Same as above	CF
Conjunctivitis and keratoconjunctivitis	Sudden onset, redness of conjunctiva, edema, serous exudate	Probably worldwide	Adenovirus types 3, 7, 8	Pharyngeal or eye secretions, feces	Same as above	CF

* CF = Complement fixation
NT = Neutralization test
HI = Hemagglutinin-inhibition

abortive measles. The diagnosis tends to be largely clinical, unless one suspects influenza, ARD, or atypical pneumonia, in which case there are specific laboratory procedures that may be used (see Table 19–4).

Influenza. Influenza is caused by a virus of which four distinct antigenic types, A, B, C, and D, have been demonstrated. The antigenic composition varies from time to time. Variants of types A and B have been found in epidemics periodically over the past few years. Influenza is characteristically a mild disease, most deaths resulting from complicating pneumonias.

Laboratory confirmation of a clinical diagnosis of influenza may be made by isolation of a virus from throat washings of the acutely ill patient and inoculation into the amniotic sac of a 10- to 14-day embryonated chick embryo. Serologic tests may be done on paired serums, hemagglutinin inhibition being most commonly employed. This test is not strictly strain specific. Complement fixation using soluble antigens is considered strain specific.

Primary Atypical Pneumonia. The etiology of primary atypical pneumonia has not yet been clearly defined. The diagnosis depends on a thorough study of the patient to rule out the presence of other acute respiratory disease.

There are two nonspecific serologic tests that may be of assistance. First, it has been shown that some patients develop agglutinating antibodies against *Streptococcus* MG. Second, there may be increases in cold agglutinins for human erythrocytes, including those of group O. A fourfold or greater increase in agglutinins for *Streptococcus* MG or in cold agglutinins can be considered suggestive, but negative findings do not exclude the disease.

The Adenovirus Group. The adenoviruses were first isolated from tissue culture of human adenoid tissue. Prolonged incubation of the culture resulted in the appearance of changes in the epithelial-like cells. A number of antigenic types of adenoviruses have been found to be associated with clinical disease. They are acute respiratory disease (ARD), pharyngitis, pharyngoconjunctival fever, conjunctivitis, and keratoconjunctivitis. Laboratory confirmation of adenovirus infection depends on isolation of the virus in appropriate tissue culture (HeLa, KB, or human amnion cells) from secretions of pharynx or eye collected on swabs, or in broth washings,

or from feces. Complement fixation may be done on paired serums with the convalescent serum collected 14 to 21 days after collection of the "acute" serum.

Psittacosis, Lymphogranuloma Venereum, and Cat Scratch Fever

PSITTACOSIS

The psittacosis virus is one of a large group of viruses that are primarily pathogens of birds and mammals. Psittacosis itself, a pathogen of psittacine birds, is transmissible to man through contact with the infected bird. It is closely related, if not identical, to the virus of ornithosis found in nonpsittacine birds, such as pigeons, ducks, turkeys, and canaries. These viruses, in turn, are related to the pneumonitis viruses of several mammalian species (Figs. 19–8 to 19–10). A number of these latter agents appear capable of producing disease in man, although few proved instances have been reported.

Psittacosis in man usually results from contact with a parakeet, although other psittacines may be involved. Outbreaks of human ornithosis have occurred in workers on duck or turkey farms, and in this regard it is an occupational disease.

The psittacosis-ornithosis-lymphogranuloma group of viruses are the largest of the viruses and in size are intermediate between the viruses and rickettsiae. Their classification as viruses hinges on their intracellular multiplication. They are closely related antigenically through group antigens.

Psittacosis was originally viewed as an acute, severe, often fatal pneumonitis, but more recently it has been recognized that it is more often a subclinical disease resembling an atypical common cold. Thus, the disease has a variable course. The incubation period is 7 to 25 days. The onset is vague. It is followed by the acute stage with general malaise, coughing, fever, chills, vomiting, and headache, which may be severe. Restlessness, insomnia, delirium, and a typhoidal state with nonproductive cough and constipation may develop.

The diagnosis of psittacosis depends on clinical, x-ray, epidemiologic, and laboratory studies. A history of exposure to psittacine or other fowl is highly suggestive. In the laboratory, diagnostic procedures of critical importance are viral isolation and serologic tests. This virus is highly infec-

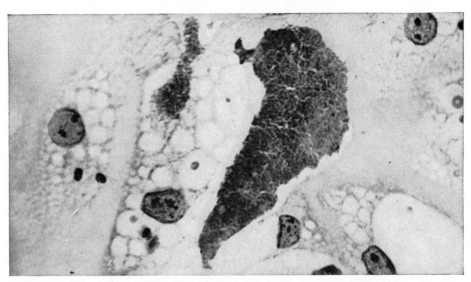

Figure 19–8. A mature intracellular vesicle of psittacosis virus in chick endodermal cell culture. May-Gruenwald-Giemsa stain; × 432. (Weiss.)

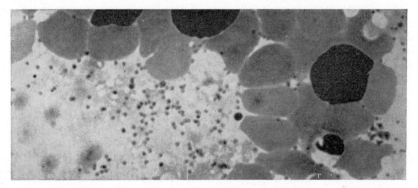

Figure 19–9. Elementary bodies of psittacosis. Impression preparation from infected mouse spleen; reduced from × 2575. (Bedson.)

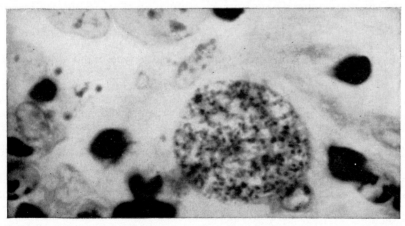

Figure 19–10. A vesicle containing elementary bodies from the lung of a mouse infected with mouse pneumonitis. Noble's stain; × 2100.

tious and consequently very dangerous to handle; numerous laboratory infections have occurred.

Serologic Tests. The serologic test of choice in psittacosis is complement fixation. Antigens for such tests are available commercially. They are usually prepared from the yolk sac of infected chick embryos and contain the heat stable, common group antigens for members of the psittacosis-ornithosis-lymphogranuloma viruses. The yolk sac antigen is now accepted as standard. The strain-specific antigens are destroyed by heating or by the addition of phenol in the preparation of the antigen. It is necessary to test simultaneously paired acute and convalescent serums from the patient, since results on single serum samples cannot be considered definitive. A rise in titer between collection of the acute and convalescent serums is indicative of infection with a member of the group. To establish the specific strain involved in the infection one can absorb the serum with the group antigen and then run the complement-fixation test using specific antigens.

Virus Isolation. For virus isolation several materials are needed: Blood should be collected during the first week of illness, before treatment, or during a relapse. The whole, defibrinated or clotted blood, but not the serum, should be frozen as soon as possible after collection. Sputum should be collected if possible; it should also be frozen as soon as possible. Pleural fluid may be collected and frozen. Vomitus may also be taken and frozen. Throat washings may be collected as in influenza. At autopsy, tissue may be taken from the part of the lung affected by pneumonia or from a piece of spleen, or liver and pleural or other effusions may be collected. The pieces of tissue should be frozen if not used within five hours. It should be re-emphasized that these materials must be handled with extreme caution.

Mice may be inoculated intranasally under light anesthesia or intraperitoneally. The material (tissue suspensions and similar material) properly treated with antibiotics may be inoculated into the yolk sac or dropped onto the chorioallantoic membrane of six- to seven-day-old chick embryos.

In the infected animal or chick embryo the virus may be demonstrated in tissue smears or sections stained by Castaneda, Macchiavello, or Giemsa stain. The virus particles are large (0.280 to 0.380 μ and bacteria-like. They are found primarily in the reticuloendothelial cells and may appear as packets staining purple with Giemsa, red with Macchiavello, or deep blue with Castaneda stain. The Frei test, extensively used as an aid in the diagnosis of lymphogranuloma venereum, may occasionally be positive.

LYMPHOGRANULOMA VENEREUM

Lymphogranuloma venereum is a venereal disease caused by a virus closely related antigenically and biologically to the psittacosis-ornithosis viruses. The characteristic lesion is the enlarged inguinal lymph node, which progresses to abscess formation. Tissue sections of the nodes reveal areas of inflammation, small foci of epithelioid cells, and some giant cells. Within the epithelioid monocytes there tend to be characteristic inclusions containing elementary bodies that stain in the same manner as the similar bodies found in psittacosis.

The virus may be isolated from bubo pus, tissue biopsy specimens, or spinal fluid. For shipment the collected material must be carefully packed in tightly sealed tubes and should not be frozen unless it is certain to be maintained in the frozen state until used. For isolation one may use young Swiss albino mice, which are most susceptible, although most laboratory mice may be used. The material should be inoculated intracerebrally, and it may be necessary to make several "blind" transfers at ten-day intervals before the mice show symptoms. The material may also be inoculated into the yolk sac of six-day embryonated eggs. Demonstration of virus in the infected animal or chick embryo is similar to that for the psittacosis virus.

There are two immunologic aids in the diagnosis of lymphogranuloma venereum. The first is the Frei test, a skin test using an antigen prepared from heavily infected yolk sac suspensions. A positive skin test with this antigen is highly suggestive, although there are cross-reactions with the psittacosis-ornithosis viruses (see Chapter 20). The second immunologic test is complement fixation, which should be run on paired serums. The antibody response in patients who receive early antibiotic therapy may be minimal or delayed, and this must be kept in mind in interpreting the results of complement-fixation tests.

CAT-SCRATCH DISEASE

Cat-scratch disease (cat-scratch fever, benign inoculation lymphoreticulosis) is an infection most frequently occurring in individuals who have been scratched by a cat. It is characterized by fever, malaise, and lymphadenitis, which may be preceded by a cutaneous lesion. Rarely the disease progresses to encephalitis. Although the causative agent has not been definitely isolated and characterized, it has been suggested that it is related to the virus of lymphogranuloma venereum. Actually one may find positive complement-fixation tests in patients with cat-scratch disease when their serums are tested with lymphogranuloma antigen. The results of such tests must be interpreted with caution, since such positive findings may have resulted from previous infection with the lymphogranuloma virus.

A skin test has been used as an aid in the diagnosis of cat-scratch fever. The antigen is prepared from human material and is not available commercially.

TRACHOMA AND INCLUSION BLENNORRHEA

Trachoma and inclusion blennorrhea are caused by viruses of the psittacosis-lympho-granuloma group. Both are characterized by the presence of typical inclusion bodies in cells in the epithelium. Trachoma is the more serious disease, having a worldwide distribution and tending to produce serious lesions in the eyes of infected individuals. This infection appears to be limited to the eye. Inclusion blennorrhea is a much milder condition than trachoma and is not worldwide in distribution. It is responsible for a benign form of conjunctivitis in the newborn that usually begins 5 to 11 days after birth. There may be a great deal of inflammation and exudate. In the adult the disease is an acute follicular conjunctivitis usually without the abundant exudate. This virus may also produce a mild urethritis in adults.

Trachoma also differs from inclusion blennorrhea in that in trachoma there may be considerable secondary bacterial infection, and bacteriologic study of the abundant exudate may be important.

Neither the virus of trachoma nor that of inclusion blennorrhea has as yet been

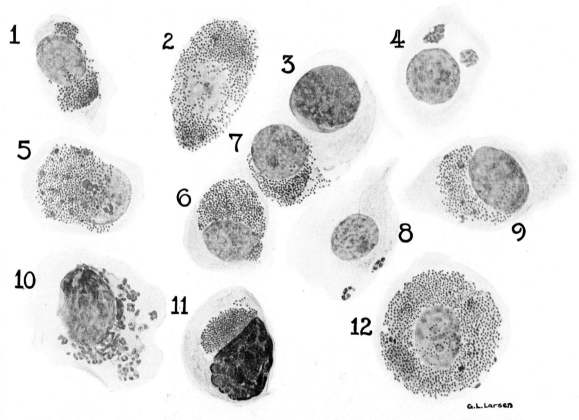

Figure 19–11. Drawing of inclusion bodies from a case of severe inclusion blennorrhea in the acute stage. Cell 3 is normal. Cells 4, 8, and 10 contain young inclusions made up of initial bodies. In cell 5 the change from initial bodies to elementary bodies is almost complete. In cells 2, 6, 7, 11, and 12 the inclusions are mature, being made up almost entirely of elementary bodies. (Phillips Thygeson in Transactions of the American Ophthalmological Society.)

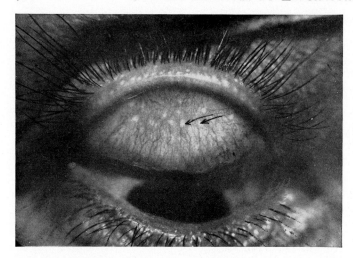

Figure 19–12. Trachoma: characteristic follicles, early infection. (Courtesy of Dr. Phillips Thygeson.)

successfully cultured in experimental animals other than monkeys and apes. Successful propagation in tissue culture has been reported. Thus, the diagnosis depends on clinical evidence and on the demonstration of the characteristic inclusions in scrapings from follicles and the affected epithelium. These scrapings should be smeared gently on a slide and stained with Giemsa stain. There are no serologic procedures or skin tests (Figs. 19–11, 19–12).

Smallpox (Variola), Vaccinia, Varicella, and Herpes Zoster

SMALLPOX

Smallpox (variola) has become a rare disease in areas where vaccination is done to a sufficient extent, but it still exists in its most virulent form in certain parts of the world, especially in the Far East. As long as the disease exists anywhere, there is the danger that during the incubation period a person with the disease will be transported to an area, such as the United States, where the disease has not been seen for a number of years.

When it occurs, smallpox must be differentiated from varicella (chickenpox). In both diseases the first skin lesions are papules, which progress to vesicles and then to pustules. In smallpox the lesions develop simultaneously, while in varicella they tend to appear in various stages.

The laboratory diagnosis of smallpox depends upon demonstration of typical inclusions in the cytoplasm of cells in stained smears from the pustules (Fig. 19–13) and on isolation of virus from blood or pustular fluid by inoculation onto the chorioallantoic membrane of embryonated eggs (10 to 13 days). Laboratory diagnosis also depends on complement-fixation or hemagglutinin-inhibition tests on paired serums from the patient and on use of the Paul test in which pustular material is inoculated on the scarified cornea of the rabbit.

VACCINIA

Generalized vaccinia sometimes occurs following vaccination for smallpox. The laboratory diagnosis can be made in a manner similar to that for smallpox.

VARICELLA AND HERPES ZOSTER

Varicella (chickenpox) and herpes zoster are caused by viruses that are apparently identical. Varicella is usually a mild disease, occurring primarily in chil-

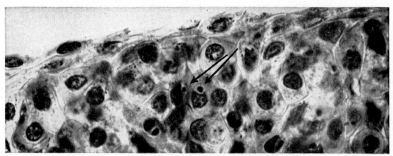

Figure 19–13. Guarnieri bodies, the intracytoplasmic inclusion bodies of vaccinia. The arrows point to two inclusions among many in the infected corneal epithelium of a rabbit's eye. Giemsa stain; × 650. (Burrows.)

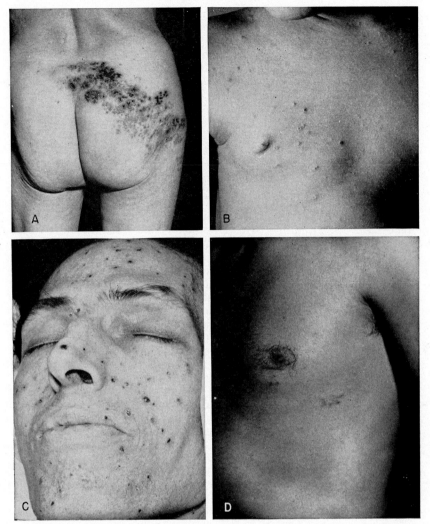

Figure 19–14.   A. Lumbosacral zoster. B. Chickenpox (varicella). C. Diffuse varicelliform lesions following zoster. The patient had Hodgkin's disease. D. Minimal lesions of zoster. The skin lesions may be slight or possibly entirely absent. (Pillsbury, Shelley and Kligman, Dermatology.)

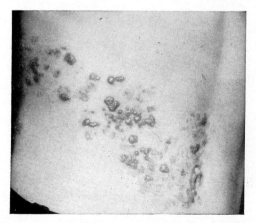

Figure 19–15.   Herpes zoster. (Courtesy of Dr. Carroll S. Wright.)

dren, for which there are no specific diagnostic laboratory test. It must be differentiated in its more severe forms from smallpox, vaccinia, and herpes simplex. This can be accomplished by means discussed in the section on these diseases (Fig. 19–14).

There are also no specific laboratory aids in the diagnosis of herpes zoster. Vesicles like those of varicella occur in areas supplied by sensory nerves of the dorsal root or extramedullary ganglia (Fig. 19–15). The lesions are very painful.

Herpes Simplex

The virus of herpes simplex produces a number of conditions in man. In the skin the virus may produce recurrent herpes simplex, which may affect any skin area but most frequently occurs at mucocutaneous junctions (cold sores); eczema herpeticum, which, as the name implies, tends to occur in individuals with eczema; or traumatic herpes, which may occur at the site of burns or other trauma. On the mucous membranes the virus may produce acute infectious gingivostomatitis, which is probably the most common primary form of herpes infection; it is the most common form of stomatitis between the ages of one and three years but may occur in all age groups (Fig. 19–16). The virus may also cause keratoconjunctivitis, which may be primary or recurrent; vulvovaginitis, which also may be primary or recurrent; and herpes progenitalis, which is usually recurrent on the glans or shaft of the penis. In the central nervous system the virus may cause

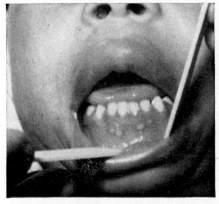

Figure 19–16. Herpetic stomatitis. (T. F. McNair Scott in Nelson, Textbook of Pediatrics, 7th ed.)

meningoencephalitis, and occasionally the primary infection may be a generalized systemic disease. In newborn infants there may be a fulminant visceral condition. Certain forms of herpes simplex infection must be differentiated from smallpox, varicella, herpes zoster, and Coxsackie (Group A) infection (herpangina).

The laboratory diagnosis depends on demonstration of typical intranuclear inclusion bodies (Cowdry, Type A) in stained smears from the lesions or in tissue sections (Fig. 19–17), on isolation of virus from tissue or vesicle fluid by inoculation into chick embryos or certain laboratory animals (mice, rabbits, guinea pigs), and on serologic tests on paired serums (neutralization or complement fixation).

The inclusion body of herpes simplex occurs in all types of infected tissues. When fully developed, it is an acidophilic mass drawn away from the edge of the nucleus with the appearance of having a halo around it. In the early stages of development the inclusion fills the nucleus and stains faintly basophilic. In epithelial lesions "ballooning cells" are present in the smears and sections.

Virus isolation may be made from vesicle fluid in the superficial lesions of the skin or mucous membranes; from saliva, spinal fluid, or clotted blood (from the clot); or from central nervous system tissue in fatal cases.

Chick embryos (12 to 13 days) are inoculated on the chorioallantoic membrane where the virus produces pock-like lesions. Adult mice may be inoculated intracerebrally, or suckling mice, which are

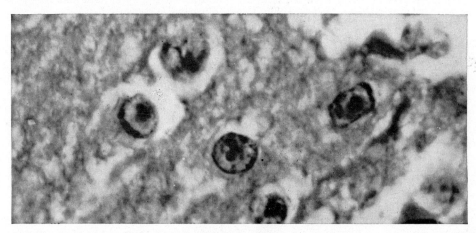

Figure 19–17. Intranuclear herpetic inclusion bodies in the human brain. (Armed Forces Institute of Pathology, No. 102644.)

highly susceptible, can be inoculated intra-peritoneally. Guinea pigs may be inoculated on the scarified skin or foot pad, and rabbits may be inoculated on the scarified cornea. In the latter two animals one may use bacterially contaminated material without antibiotic treatment. In the rabbit a keratoconjunctivitis develops in 12 hours to 7 days.

It is necessary for serologic testing that paired serums be used, since it is not uncommon to find antibodies in the serum as the result of previous experience with the virus. This is particularly true in adults. In such cases rises in antibody titer may be quite significant.

Mumps, Measles, and Rubella

MUMPS

Mumps is a well-known virus disease of childhood producing the classic parotitis, which is useful in clinical diagnosis. Complications may develop in the form of orchitis, oophoritis, encephalitis, and certain less frequent lesions, such as pancreatitis and neuritis. Encephalitis and orchitis may occur without parotitis.

Laboratory aids in the diagnosis of mumps are isolation of the virus in chick embryos and serologic tests (complement fixation and agglutinin inhibition).

Virus may be isolated from saliva on the first and second days of parotitis and from spinal fluid in cases of mumps encephalitis. Chick embryos (seven to eight days) may be inoculated into the amniotic, allantoic, or yolk sac and the embryos incubated for five to seven days. Presence of virus is then detected by hemagglutination or by complement fixation with a known antiserum.

Complement-fixing antigens that are available commercially can be used with paired serums from a patient. The results from a single serum are not usually definitive. Hemagglutinin-inhibition tests can also be done on paired serums.

MEASLES AND RUBELLA
(GERMAN MEASLES)

No routine laboratory procedures are available as aids in the diagnosis of measles or rubella. Both viruses have been cultivated in chick embryos and in tissue culture, and it has been shown that patients develop antibodies to these agents (Fig. 19–18).

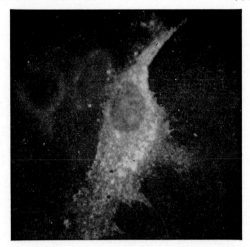

Figure 19–18. Intracellular measles virus in human epithelial cell tissue culture treated with convalescent serum and with fluorescein-labeled antiglobulin serum. × 480. (Rapp and Gordon.)

Cytomegalic Inclusion Disease (Salivary Gland Virus Infection)

A generalized disease characterized by the presence of intranuclear and intracytoplasmic inclusion bodies in the cells of several organs is occasionally encountered. In infants it is generally fatal. In older children and adults the clinical picture varies, depending on the organs involved. Diagnosis can be made by the complement-fixation and neutralization tests and by the demonstration of the typical inclusion bodies in scrapings from the mouth and in urine (Birdsong et al., 1956; Rowe et al., 1958).

RICKETTSIAE

There are a number of rickettsial diseases of man of which the best known are typhus and the spotted fevers. All these diseases, with one exception, are carried by arthropod vectors, and most are transmitted to man by the bite or the feces of the infected arthropod. In Table 19–5 the various rickettsial diseases are shown with their distribution and mode of transmission.

The diagnosis of the rickettsial diseases depends on clinical, epidemiologic, and laboratory findings. Laboratory procedures of assistance are isolation of the rickettsiae in guinea pigs or mice and observation of the animals, especially guinea pigs, for certain typical reactions, which vary with the different agents; and serologic tests on

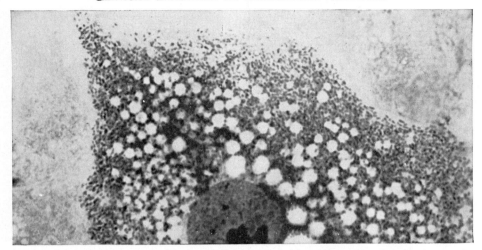

Figure 19–19. *Rickettsia prowazeki* in an infected cell from chick endoderm cultured *in vitro*. Most of the cytoplasm of the cell is occupied by rickettsias. × 1500. (Weiss.)

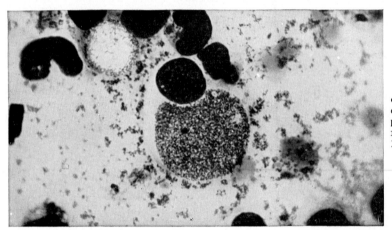

Figure 19–20. Rickettsias of Q fever in a smear of skin exudate. Note the macrophage packed with enormous numbers of the rickettsias. × 1125. (Burrows.)

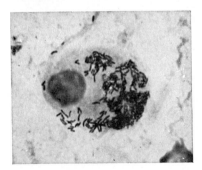

Figure 19–21. Murine typhus. Mooser cell. Intracytoplasmic rickettsiae in large serosal cell of tunica vaginalis. (Courtesy U.S.A. Typhus Commission.)

paired serums (complement fixation, rickettsial agglutination, and the Weil-Felix reaction).

During the first week of the disease rickettsiae may be isolated by inoculation of fresh or frozen whole blood intraperitone-

ally into mice or guinea pigs. Later in the disease the cellular elements should be separated from the serum or plasma by centrifugation or clotting. The cells or the ground-up clot should then be used for animal inoculation. Mice that show evidence of illness may be sacrificed and impression smears made from the spleen or scraping from the parietal peritoneum and stained with Giemsa or Macchiavello stains. The coccobacillary rickettsial bodies stain bluish purple with Giemsa stain and bright red with Macchiavello stain (Figs. 19–19 to 19–23). In the infected male pig typical scrotal lesions may occur. Impression smears from the spleen and tunica vaginalis should be stained by Giemsa or Macchiavello stain. The typical reactions of guinea pigs to the various rickettsiae are indicated in Table 19–5.

Complement-fixing antigens are available

commercially for a number of rickettsial agents and may be used with paired serums from patients. It is best, actually, to collect three serums, one during the first few days of illness, one during the second week, and one during the fourth week.

Agglutination has been used in certain rickettsial diseases (epidemic and murine typhus and Q fever). It requires the preparation of purified suspensions of the rickettsial bodies from infected yolk sac or mouse lung and may be done either in tubes or on slides.

The oldest serologic test used as an aid in

Table 19–5. Rickettsial Diseases of Man

DISEASE	AGENT	DISTRIBUTION	ANIMAL HOST	VECTOR	LABORATORY ANIMAL OF CHOICE	REACTION IN ANIMAL	SEROLOGIC DIAGNOSIS WEIL-FELIX	OTHER
Typhus Group: Endemic	R. mooseri	Worldwide	Small rodents	Flea (feces)	Guinea pig	Fever, scrotal swelling (3–10 days)	Positive OX19	Complement* fixation
Epidemic	R. prowazeki	Worldwide	Man	Body louse (feces)	Guinea pig	Fever (5–12 days)	Positive OX19	Complement fixation
Brill's disease	R. prowazeki	U.S.A., Europe	Recurrence years after original attack of epidemic typhus					Usually negative	Complement fixation
Scrub (tsutsuga-mushi fever)	R. tsutsugam-ushi	Australia, Asia, Pacific Is.	Small rodents	Mites (bite)	Mouse	Rough fur, as-cites (6–14 days)	Positive OXK	Complement fixation (50% pos.)
Spotted Fever Group: Rocky Mt. spotted fever	R. rickettsi	Western hemisphere	Small wild rodents; dogs	Ticks (bite)	Guinea pig	Fever, scrotal necrosis (3–10 days)	Positive OX19 OX2	Complement fixation
African tick fever	R. conorii	Africa, Mediterranean	Small wild rodents; dogs	Ticks (bite)	Guinea pig	Fever, scrotal swelling (3–6 days)	Positive OX19 OX2	Complement fixation
Rickettsial pox	R. akari	North Atlantic states, Russia	House mouse	Mite (bite)	Mouse	Rough fur (6–9 days)	Negative	Complement fixation
Q fever	Coxiella burnetii	Worldwide	Cattle, sheep, goats, small mammals	Ticks†	Guinea pig	Fever (5–12 days)	Negative	Complement fixation
Trench fever	R. quintana	Mexico, Europe, Ethiopia	Man	Body louse (feces)	—	—	Negative	—

* Antigens may be group (typhus or spotted fever group) or type specific.
† Man infected by inhalation of dried infected material.

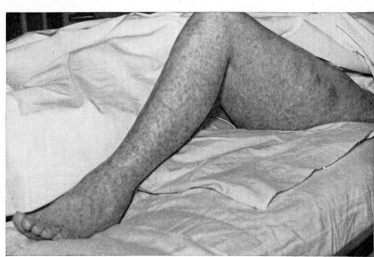

Figure 19–22. Generalized rash of Rocky Mountain spotted fever. (Courtesy U.S.P.H.S., Rocky Mountain Laboratory.)

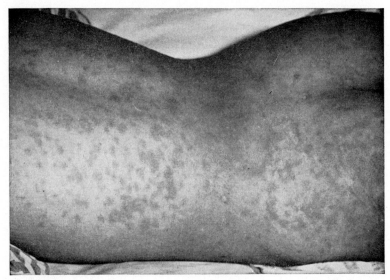

Figure 19–23. Rash of scrub typhus. (Courtesy U.S.A. Typhus Commission.)

the diagnosis of rickettsial diseases is the Weil-Felix reaction. This is based on the observation that patients with certain of these infections (typhus and spotted fever) develop antibodies that react with certain nonmotile strains of bacteria belonging to the genus *Proteus* (*Proteus* OX_{19}, OX_2, and OX_K). Although this is a nonspecific test, it is useful, since it is a simple agglutination test done on paired serums and the antibody rise occurs fairly early (late in the second week). (See section on serologic methods, p. 889.)

Patients treated with antibiotics early in the disease may have delayed antibody responses, sometimes as late as four to six weeks after the onset of symptoms. This should be remembered in evaluating the results of serologic tests, especially the complement-fixation and agglutination reactions.

REFERENCES

1. Aikawa, J. K., and Meiklejohn, G.: The serologic diagnosis of mumps: A comparative study of three methods. J. Immunol., 62:261–269, 1959.
2. Bell, J. F.: Transmission of rabies to laboratory animals by bite of a naturally infected bat. Science, 129:1490–1491, 1959.
3. Birdsong, M., Smith, D. E., Mitchell, F. N., and Corey, J. M.: Generalized cytomegalic inclusion disease in newborn infants. J.A.M.A., 162:1305–1308, 1956.
4. Buckley, S. M.: Cytopathology of poliomyelitis virus in tissue culture. Fluorescent antibody and tinctorial studies. Am. J. Path., 33:691–708, 1957.
5. Buddingh, G. J.: The nomenclature and classification of the pox group of viruses. Ann. New York Acad. Sc., 56:561–566, 1953.
6. Buddingh, G. J., Schrum, D. I., Lauier, J. C., and
    Guidry, D. J.: Studies of the natural history of herpes simplex infections. Pediatrics, 11:595–610, 1953.
7. Burnet, F. M., and Stanley, W. M.: The Viruses. 3 vols. New York, Academic Press, Inc., 1960.
8. Cheever, F. S.: Changing status of virological diagnostic service. J.A.M.A., 165:2059–2063, 1957.
9. Clarke, D. H., and Casals, J.: Techniques for hemagglutination and hemagglutination-inhibition with arthropod-borne viruses. Am. J. Trop. Med., 7:561–573, 1958.
10. Committee on Enteroviruses: The enteroviruses. Am. J. Pub. Health, 47:1556–1566, 1957.
11. Daniels, W. B., and MacMurray, F. G.: Cat scratch disease; nonbacterial regional lymphadenitis: A report of 60 cases. Ann. Int. Med., 37:679–713, 1952.
12. Diagnostic Procedures for Virus and Rickettsial Diseases. 2nd Ed. New York, Am. Public Health Assn., 1956.
13. Eichenwald, H. F., and Mosley, J. W.: Viral Hepatitis: Clinical and Public Health Aspects. Public Health Service Pub. No. 435. Washington, D.C., U.S. Govt. Printing Office, 1959.
14. Enders, J. F., Weller, T. H., and Robbins, F. C.: Cultivation of the Lansing strain of poliomyelitis virus in cultures of human embryonic tissues. Science, 109:85–87, 1949.
15. Fisher, T. N.: Diagnostic virology serving the community. Am. J. Publ. Health, 48:1184–1188, 1958.
16. Girardi, A. S., Hummeler, K., and Olshin, I.: Studies on the routine laboratory diagnosis of Coxsackie group B virus infections. J. Lab. & Clin. Med., 50:526–533, 1957.
17. Goldfield, M.: Virus meningitis. Am. J. Med. Sc., 234:91–105, 1957.
18. Gordon, R. B., Lennette, E. H., and Sandrock, R. S.: The varied clinical manifestations of Coxsackie virus infections: Observations and comments on an outbreak in California. Arch. Int. Med., 103:63–75, 1959.
19. Havens, W. P., Jr.: Hemagglutination in viral hepatitis. New Engl. J. Med., 259:1202–1206, 1958.
20. Horton, G. E.: Mumps myocarditis. Case report with review of the literature. Ann. Int. Med., 49:1228–1239, 1958.

21. Huebner, R. J.: 70 newly recognized viruses in man. Pub. Health Rep., 74:6–12, 1959.
22. Jordan, W. S., Jr., and Feller, H. E.: The relationship of complement-fixing and antihemagglutinating factors against the viruses of mumps and Newcastle disease. J. Lab. & Clin. Med., 36:369–377, 1950.
23. Kravis, L. P., Sigel, M. M., and Henle, G.: Mumps meningoencephalitis with special reference to the use of the complement-fixation test in diagnosis. Pediatrics, 8:204–215, 1951.
24. Lebrun, J.: Cellular localization of herpes simplex virus by means of fluorescent antibody. Virology, 2:496–510, 1956.
25. Liu, C.: Rapid diagnosis of human influenza infection from nasal smears by means of fluorescein-labelled antibody. Proc. Soc. Exp. Biol. & Med., 92:883–887, 1956.
26. McLean, D. L.: Patterns of infection with enteroviruses. J. Ped., 54:823–828, 1959.
27. Melnick, J. L.: Tissue culture techniques and their application to original isolation, growth and assay of poliomyelitis and orphan viruses. Ann. N.Y. Acad. Sc., 61:754–773, 1955.
28. Meyer, K. F.: Psittacosis group. Ann. N.Y. Acad. Sc., 56:545–556, 1953.
29. Olitsky, P. K., Casals, J., Walter, D. L., Ginsberg, H. S., and Horsfall, F. L., Jr.: Preservation of viruses in a mechanical refrigerator at −25°C. J. Lab. & Clin. Med., 34:1023–1026, 1949.
30. Rake, G.: The lymphogranuloma-psittacosis group. Ann. N.Y. Acad. Sc., 56:557–560, 1953.
31. Rake, G., Shaffer, M. F., and Thygeson, P.: Relationship of agents of trachoma and inclusion conjunctivitis to those of lymphogranuloma-psittacosis group. Proc. Soc. Exper. Biol. & Med., 49:545–547, 1942.
32. Rhodes, A. J.: Recent advances in the laboratory diagnosis of virus infections. Ann. Int. Med., 45:106–117, 1956.
33. Rivers, T. M., and Horsfall, F. L., Jr.: Viral and Rickettsial Infections of Man. 3rd Ed. Philadelphia, J. B. Lippincott Company, 1959.
34. Rowe, W. P., Hartley, J. W., Cramblett, H. G., and Mastrota, F. M.: Detection of human salivary gland virus in the mouth and urine of children. Am. J. Hyg., 67:57–65, 1958.
35. Sabin, A. B.: The dengue group of viruses and its family relationships. Bact. Rev., 14:225–232, 1950.
36. Sabin, A. B.: Reoviruses. A new group of respiratory and enteric viruses formerly classified as ECHO type 10. Science, 130:1387–1389, 1959.
37. Salk, J. E.: A simplified procedure for titrating hemagglutinating capacity of influenza virus and the corresponding antibody. J. Immunol., 49:87–98, 1944.
38. Sellers, T. F.: A new method of staining Negri bodies of rabies. Am. J. Publ. Health, 17:1080–1081, 1927.
39. Silber, E. N.: Respiratory viruses and heart disease. Ann. Int. Med., 48:228–240, 1958.
40. Smadel, J. E.: Status of the rickettsioses in the United States. Ann. Int. Med., 51:421–435, 1959.
41. Thygeson, P.: Etiology of inclusion blennorrhea. Am. J. Ophthl., 17:1019–1035, 1934.
42. Tierkel, E. S., and Negg, H. O.: Rabies: Methods in Laboratory Diagnosis. Atlanta, Ga., U.S. Public Health Service, Communicable Disease Center, 1957.
43. Utz, J. P., Parrot, R. H., and Kassel, J. A.: Diagnostic virus laboratory for clinical service. J.A.M.A., 163:350–352, 1957.
44. Van Rooyen, C. E., and Rhodes, J. J.: Virus Diseases of Man. 2nd Ed. New York, Thomas Nelson & Sons, 1958.
45. Wallgren, A.: Une nouvelle maladie infectieuse du systeme nerveaux central (mèningite aseptique aigüe). Acta Pediat., 4:158–182, 1924.

Chapter 20

Vaccines and Diagnostic

Skin Tests

By JAMES G. SHAFFER, Sc.D., *and* MILTON GOLDIN, M.S.

The use of vaccines of various types in the control of infectious diseases is well known (smallpox, typhoid fever, and diphtheria, for example). In this chapter only one type of vaccine will be discussed. This is the autogenous vaccine, which has from time to time been used widely in individuals with boils, carbuncles, and impetigo.

There are several varieties of this vaccine:

1. Autogenous vaccine—suspension of the organism isolated from the lesion, prepared as described in this chapter.

2. Mixed autogenous vaccine—a suspension prepared from a variety of organisms isolated from an area, such as the nasopharynx, or from sputum.

3. Stock vaccine—a vaccine ("bacterin") prepared commercially from a presumably representative strain or group of strains of bacteria.

4. Filtrates—soluble products of organisms that have grown in broth. This is sometimes mixed with the vaccine as a "vaccine filtrate."

5. Toxoid—toxins converted to nontoxic, but antigenic, substances by heat or chemicals (formalin).

The special value of autogenous vaccines would appear to be in the treatment of subacute or chronic localized infections. In these conditions circulation of blood and lymph is poor, and chemotherapeutic agents may be relatively ineffective, since they cannot readily reach the infected area. On the other hand chemotherapy may be effective in the treatment of boils and carbuncles, only to have the lesions recur on cessation of treatment. Vaccines and toxoids are frequently given for prophylaxis in such conditions. They are of little or no value in acute infections and may be contraindicated.

Best results are obtained in situations in which staphylococci are involved. Successful results have, however, been claimed in such diverse conditions as nonspecific urethritis, chronic bronchitis, bronchial asthma, sinus infections, chronic upper respiratory infections, and pustular acne. In such conditions one may wonder whether or not desensitization may be the primary factor.

The value of vaccines for the treatment of chronic or recurrent infections has long been a controversial question. Evaluation of results is difficult, and one can never be certain that beneficial results are due to the vaccine. At any rate the preparation of an autogenous vaccine on request is an important part of the work of the bacteriology laboratory, and in spite of the ever-increasing use of potent chemotherapeutic substances their use seems to be increasing.

PREPARATION OF AUTOGENOUS VACCINES

Selection of the Organism

It is essential to insure the selection of organisms responsible for the infection and to avoid contamination with other organisms, especially spore-forming bacilli, some of which produce powerful soluble toxins.

Examine a gram stain from the infected area to determine the type of organism present. Culture on plates of blood agar, in infusion broth, and in or upon other suitable media. Examine the plates for predominating colonies and make gram stains of each type and from the broth culture. If organisms different from those isolated on the primary plates are seen in the broth culture, subculture to plates of suitable media.

Select isolated colonies of the type desired and examine carefully. Re-streak to a fresh agar plate to isolate the organisms in pure culture. Select a smooth colony and transfer to the desired media for preparation of the vaccine.

Preparation of the Suspension

There are many methods of preparing the suspension. All are satisfactory, provided a representative bacterial suspension is obtained that can be administered safely to the patient. Regardless of the technique used, the following precautions must be observed:

1. Avoid the use of any media containing blood, serum, body fluids, or similar potentially antigenic materials.

2. All manipulations involved in the preparation of the suspension must be carried out with strict precautions to avoid contamination.

3. Filter the suspension to remove particles of culture media and clumps of bacteria that may clog the hypodermic needle or produce an untoward reaction in the patient.

4. The final product must be standardized to the proper density (Fig. 20–1).

5. The vaccine must be treated by heat or chemicals in such a way as to effectively kill the bacteria without denaturation of the antigenic material.

6. The sterility (freedom from viable bacteria) of the vaccine must be assured

by suitable tests before it is released for use.

Procedure I. Grow the organisms on agar slants. Add 2 or 3 ml. of sterile saline to 24- or 48-hour cultures and bring the growth into suspension by emulsifying with a wire loop and shaking. Filter the suspension through sterile cotton or glass wool into a vaccine bottle containing glass beads (Fig. 20–2). Shake the vaccine bottle vigorously. The suspension is then ready to be standardized.

This procedure is satisfactory for rapidly growing organisms, such as staphylococci, but is not suitable for mixed vaccines or those made from fastidious organisms. In these cases broth cultures are preferable.

Procedure II (Kolmer's [1951] Method). Grow the organism in pure culture in a large flask of broth overnight at 37° C. The concentration of bacteria is calculated by the counting chamber or Wright's method (see next section). Calculate the volume of suspension required to make 20 ml. of a vaccine containing 1000 million organisms per ml.

$$\frac{\text{Millions of organism desired per ml.}}{\text{Millions of organism present per ml.}} \times 20 =$$

ml. of suspension to be diluted to 20 ml.

For example, suppose the suspension count totals 4600 million per ml. Then $\frac{1000 \times 20}{4600} = 4.3$ ml. of suspension to use. In a sterile vial containing glass beads place 4.3 ml. of the suspension, 1.6 ml. of 5 per cent phenol, and 14.1 ml. of sterile saline. Tricresol (0.25 per cent) or Merthiolate (1:1000) may be used instead of phenol. Shake the suspension well. Incubate at 37° C. overnight and check for sterility.

This procedure can be modified by centrifuging the growth in the broth, decanting

Figure 20–1. Hopkins centrifuge tube. Useful for approximate count of bacteria in vaccines. The narrow portion at the bottom is graduated in hundredths of a cubic centimeter.

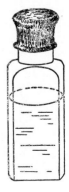

Figure 20–2. Vaccine bottle with rubber cap.

the supernatant, and resuspending the sediment with sterile saline. The suspension is then standardized as just described or by one of the methods to be outlined. This modification reduces the amount of the broth in the vaccine.

Standardization of the Suspension

WRIGHT'S METHOD

Prepare a Wright's capillary pipet with a capillary 5 to 6 inches long (Fig. 20–3). Make a mark on the stem of the capillary about 1 inch from the tip. Cleanse and prick the finger. Do an erythrocyte count. Compress the bulb of the Wright's pipet and draw 3 per cent sodium citrate solution up to the mark. Allow a little air to enter the capillary. Draw blood from the finger exactly to the mark. Then allow a little more air to enter and finally draw the well-mixed vaccine to the mark. Expel the contents of the pipet onto a watch glass and mix thoroughly by aspirating and expelling from the pipet about ten times. Prepare three or four thin films on clean glass slides.

Dry the films and fix in a saturated solution of mercuric chloride. Wash with water and stain for three to five minutes with a 1:10 dilution of carbol fuchsin or carbol thionin blue. Wash with water and allow to dry. Examine the films. There should be an even distribution of erythrocytes and bacteria with no clumps of the latter. Under the oil immersion lens count the number of erythrocytes and the number of bacteria in a number of fields until 500 or more erythrocytes have been counted. Record the number of erythrocytes and the number of bacteria counted.

Calculate as shown at bottom of page.

COUNTING CHAMBER METHOD

1. In a small sterile test tube place 0.1 ml. of the suspension and 4.9 ml. saline (1:50 dilution). Mix well. Draw to the 0.5 mark in a white blood cell counting pipet. Draw freshly filtered staining solution* to the 11 mark.

2. Shake for two to three minutes, discard the first few drops, and place a drop of the suspension on the counting chamber. Allow it to settle for about 15 minutes.

* 10 ml. of a saturated alcoholic solution of crystal violet mixed with 100 ml. of distilled water.

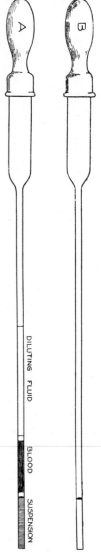

Figure 20–3. Capillary pipets: *A*, filled for counting bacteria in a vaccine by Wright's method; *B*, empty, showing wax pencil mark. The slender portion should be narrower than here represented.

3. Count the number of bacteria in at least 20 squares, focusing at different levels to count any bacteria that have not settled out. If the number of bacteria is too large for an accurate count, repeat using a 1:100 or 1:200 dilution of the suspension.

4. Divide the total number of bacteria in 20 squares by 20 to give the average per square. Multiply this figure by 400,000,000 to obtain the number of bacteria per ml. of the dilution. Then multiply by 50 (if the original dilution was 1:50) to obtain the

$$\frac{\text{No. of erythrocytes per ml.} \times \text{no. of bacteria counted} \times 1000}{\text{No. of erythrocytes counted in the film}} = \text{the number of organisms per ml.}$$

total number of organisms per ml. of undiluted suspension.

A red cell pipet may be used in a similar fashion. Draw the undiluted suspension to the 0.5 mark and the stain to the 101 mark. This is a dilution of 1:200. Mix, add to counting chamber, and count as just described. See calculation at bottom of page.*

After counting, the pipets, the coverslips and counting chamber should be placed in a disinfectant solution.

Nephelometric Method (McFarland)

This method consists of comparing the opacity of the vaccine with a series of ten standard nephelometer tubes. It is satisfactory for suspensions that are not colored.

Standards. Set up ten uniform clean test tubes of hard glass (screw caps are recommended). Add to each tube as follows:

TUBE	1% H₂SO₄, C.P.	1% BACL₂, C.P.	DENSITY APPROXIMATELY CORRESPONDING TO BACTERIAL SUSPENSION
1	9.9 ml.	0.1 ml.	300 million
2	9.8	0.2	600
3	9.7	0.3	900
4	9.6	0.4	1200
5	9.5	0.5	1500
6	9.4	0.6	1800
7	9.3	0.7	2100
8	9.2	0.8	2400
9	9.1	0.9	2700
10	9.0	1.0	3000

The tubes are hermetically sealed and labeled 1 to 10.

Procedure. One milliliter of the well-mixed bacterial suspension is placed in a tube of the same diameter as the nephelometer standard. A measured amount of saline is then added slowly with constant shaking until the density of the diluted vaccine matches that of the desired standard tube.

Calculation. The number of bacteria in 1 ml. of vaccine = the number of the corresponding nephelometer tube × the dilution. For example, 1 ml. is diluted to 5 ml. to match tube No. 3. It therefore contains approximately 900 million × 5 or 4500 million bacteria per ml.

If 30 ml. of vaccine containing 1000 million organisms per ml. is desired, the calculation is then as follows:

$$\frac{30 \times 1000 \text{ million}}{4500 \text{ million}} =$$

6.66 ml. + 23.33 saline to make 30 ml. of desired strength of vaccine

Sterilization of the Vaccine

The vaccine is sterilized by either heat or chemicals. Heating is done in the water bath, making sure that the entire suspension is immersed in the water for one hour at 60° C. Tricresol (0.25 per cent) or phenol (0.5 per cent) should be added as preservative. Merthiolate at a concentration of 1:1000 may also be used. Check for sterility.

For chemical sterilization place the desired quantity of the standardized vaccine suspension in a sterile vaccine bottle and add tricresol to a final concentration of 0.5 per cent. One milliliter of a 5 per cent solution is used for each 10 ml. of vaccine. Seal the vial with a vaccine stopper, mix thoroughly, and incubate at 37° C. for 48 hours, shaking at intervals. Check for sterility as described in the next section.

Testing for Sterility. Check the final vaccine by culturing at least 0.25 ml. from each vial in thioglycollate broth or other suitable media, depending on the type of organism from which the vaccine was originally prepared. Incubate at 37° C. for at least six to eight days. If sterile, the vaccine can then be released.

If growth occurs of the same type of organism from which the vaccine was prepared, it is permissible to reheat the suspension for one hour at 60° C. If a different organism is grown, the vaccine should be discarded and a new one prepared. For this reason it is necessary to save all the original isolations in the refrigerator until the vaccine is ready to be released. The label of the vaccine should show the type of organism it contains, the concentration, the name of the patient, and the date.

PREPARATION OF MIXED VACCINES

The process is essentially the same as for autogenous vaccines made from a single organism. Use of the so-called "shotgun" vaccines prepared by simply drawing a loop across the culture plate or the harvest of mixed flora growing on an agar slant is not recommended. By these crude pro-

---

*

$$\frac{\text{Total bacteria counted} \times 200 \times 20,000,000}{\text{No. of small squares counted}} = \text{No. of bacteria per ml.}$$

cedures the representative flora from the involved area may not be obtained. It is more likely that large numbers of rapidly growing organisms that may be saprophytes would be present. The vaccine consequently would probably be worthless.

Each organism that is to be included in a mixed vaccine must be picked from a single colony into individual tubes of infusion broth. Normal inhabitants of the mucous membranes or skin, such as coagulase negative staphylococci, diphtheroids, or *Neisseria catarrhalis*, should not be included. The growth from each tube is standardized and pooled as for an autogenous vaccine.

PREPARATION OF FILTRATES

Some authors believe that a vaccine containing the soluble toxins and metabolites of the growing bacteria is superior to the usual type.

To prepare a filtrate:

1. Grow the organism in the usual manner in a flask of infusion broth for four to five days.

2. Filter the broth through a sterile Berkefeld N, Mandler, or Seitz filter.

3. Add 0.3 per cent tricresol to the filtrate as a preservative. Take all possible precautions to prevent contamination in all stages of the process. Do not heat since this may destroy some heat-labile toxins.

4. Check for sterility in the usual manner.

5. Some authors prefer to pool the filtrate with the vaccines; others alternate injections. This is a matter of personal preference by the physician.

ADMINISTRATION OF VACCINES

Owing to the wide variations in antigenicity of organisms and susceptibilty of patients, no definite dose of a vaccine can be stated. Usually the course consists of beginning with a small dose and cautiously increasing it until the patient shows either improvement or some signs of a reaction, such as fever, exacerbation of local disease, or an inflammatory reaction at the site of injection.

For staphylococcus vaccines the usual beginning dose is about 50 million organisms (0.05 ml. of a dilution containing 1000 million organisms per ml.). The maximal dose is usually 1000 million organisms. In children the amount given is usually about half of the adult dose. For vaccines prepared with most other bacteria the beginning dose is usually 5 to 10 million and the maximum, about 100 million.

Injections are given subcutaneously once or twice per week. In some cases the vaccines are given every other day or even daily. Wide individual variation exists and depends on the situation and the physician's preference.

With regard to the usefulness of the autogenous vaccine in staphylococcal conditions, we have recently observed situations in which its use seems to be contraindicated. Several patients have been seen who gave histories of recurrent boils. There have been two groups: those with a history covering several years of recurrent lesions and those with a history of having been given an autogenous vaccine a few years previously with recent recurrences of the condition. The lesions in these individuals were characteristic, with a small necrotic center covered by a thin membrane and surrounded by a deep red area that tended to be swollen and painful. Such lesions are reminiscent of an Arthus-type reaction. Lifting the membrane from the central area revealed a shallow crater containing serous fluid, which sometimes was blood tinged but was not pus. Culture of this fluid revealed coagulase positive *Staphylococcus aureus*, which in some cases was antibiotic resistant but in others was susceptible to most common antibiotics. In most cases there was a more or less prompt response to parenteral or oral treatment with an antibiotic to which the particular organism was susceptible, but lesions have reappeared on cessation of therapy.

In several of these cases autogenous vaccines have been prepared, but their use has resulted in failure. In fact, when sufficient dosage of the vaccine was given to produce a skin reaction at the site of injection, there tended to be a flare-up of old lesions. It was therefore suspected that the lesions were, indeed, Arthus-type in nature. Serum was collected from a number of these patients before and during treatment with the vaccine, and it was found that their serum contained agglutinating antibodies to titers of 1:512 to 1:1024 against their homologous staphylococcus cultures. Thus, it would appear that some of the recurrent staphylococcal boils may progress to the point of showing Arthus-type phenomena and that in these cases the autogenous vaccine should not be used.

BIOLOGIC AND DIAGNOSTIC SKIN TESTS

Skin tests can be divided into at least three types, depending on their nature and purpose: (1) tests designed to determine possible susceptibility or resistance to an infection, such as the Schick test in diphtheria and the Dick test in scarlet fever; (2) tests for "infection allergy," which produce a delayed skin reaction and in which a positive test indicates either present or past experience with the infectious agent, such as the tuberculin test; and (3) tests for sensitivity to various types of materials to which individuals react in an exaggerated manner, as, for example, in hay fever, asthma, food idiosyncrasies, and hypersensitivity to horse serum. The skin tests to be presented in this section are mainly those in the first two categories. An extensive discussion of the third category is beyond the scope of this book.

Essentially, then, skin tests are used to reveal the presence or absence of the two conditions—hypersensitiveness or immunity. The hypersensitivity of infection, such as that revealed by tuberculin, is in general an indication of possible immunity. In the test for immunity use is made of a toxic product derived from the disease-producing agent. In normal, nonimmune individuals this substance will cause damage to the tissue when injected. The immune individual does not react in this way, since he possesses free antibody in his skin or circulation. In the concentration used, the toxin is neutralized and no lesion is produced. Tests of this sort are the Schick and Dick reactions.

In tests for hypersensitiveness antigenic material to which the normal individual does not react is injected. A positive reaction is obtained only in the hypersensitive individual. Since the individual presumably will not be hypersensitive to the agent unless actually infected, the demonstration of hypersensitiveness implies infection. There are many pitfalls in making a diagnosis solely on the basis of a positive skin test reaction. In some cases the skin test antigens are relatively nonspecific and must be considered along with other diagnostic criteria.

Diphtheria

THE SCHICK TEST FOR DIPHTHERIA

The Schick test is a widely used reaction, which is helpful in selecting individuals who may be susceptible to diphtheria. A positive reaction indicates absence of antitoxin. This may be an indication for giving prophylactic antitoxin.

The toxin can be obtained commercially and is standardized, ready for use. An intradermal injection of 0.1 ml. is given in the forearm. The positive reaction appears in three days and is characterized by a circumscribed area of hyperemia varying from 25 to 50 mm. in diameter and surrounded by distinct edema. The redness and induration gradually disappear, leaving a brownish pigmented area, which may persist three to four months (Fig. 20–4). A negative reaction may show a mild redness at the site of the injection for 24 hours but bears no resemblance to a positive test. A pseudopositive reaction occasionally occurs, apparently

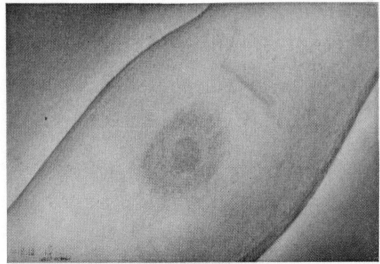

Figure 20–4. Appearance of positive Schick test five days after intracutaneous injection of 0.1 cc. of diphtheria toxin. (Courtesy Sharpe & Dohme, Inc.)

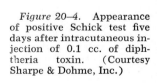

owing to an allergic reaction to the protein of the autolyzed diphtheria bacilli. This false positive reaction appears earlier than the positive reaction and is characterized by a central area of redness surrounded by a secondary pale red areola. This type of reaction can be detected with the aid of a suitable negative control established by injecting the same amount of heated toxin in the opposite forearm. The Schick test is considered highly reliable, provided the proper toxin and controls are used.

THE MALONEY TEST FOR DETECTING HYPERSENSITIVITY TO DIPHTHERIA TOXOID

Owing to a generalized allergic state or to bacterial hypersensitivity, certain individuals may show a severe local and generalized reaction following the use of toxoid, either plain or alum-precipitated. To detect this sensitivity, 0.1 ml. of plain toxoid is injected intracutaneously on the flexor surface of the forearm. A positive reaction is one in which a red area of 12 mm. or more appears within 12 to 24 hours. In cases of positive reactions the total dosage of toxoid may be given carefully in small divided doses.

Scarlet Fever

THE DICK TEST

This test is used to determine susceptibility to scarlet fever. In recent years, because of the decreasing occurrence of scarlet fever, the test is used less frequently than previously. A solution of diluted scarlet fever (Dick) toxin is injected intradermally in the same manner as the Schick test. A positive reaction is seen within 18 to 24 hours. The area around the site of the injection is intensely red, 3 to 5 cm. in diameter, and markedly swollen with sharply raised edges (Fig. 20–5). The reaction is negative when it shows no more than a faint pink streak along the course of the needle and slightly positive when there is a faint red area measuring less than 1 cm. with no swelling.

A positive reaction signifies that the individual has insufficient circulating antitoxin to the Dick toxin and is presumably susceptible to scarlet fever. Negative reactions indicate that the individual is relatively immune to the disease.

THE SCHULTZ-CHARLTON REACTION

This test may be used as an aid in the diagnosis of scarlet fever, especially in differentiating this disease from other conditions, such as measles, rubella, or drug allergies, which are characterized by a rash.

One tenth milliliter of scarlet fever (horse serum) antitoxin is injected intradermally into the area of the skin showing a bright red rash. A positive reaction appears 18 to 24 hours later and consists of a blanched area 2 to 8 mm. in diameter surrounding the needle puncture. A negative reaction shows no blanching in the red area following the injection of the antitoxin. A positive reaction indicates scarlet fever.

Convalescent scarlet fever serum will also blanch a scarlatinal rash. A positive reaction

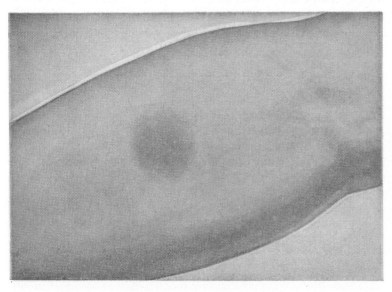

Figure 20–5. A positive Dick test showing reddish discoloration and tissue reaction at the site of injection. (Courtesy Sharpe & Dohme, Inc.)

may be more pronounced if the patient is hypersensitive to horse serum.

Tuberculin Tests

The tissues of a tuberculous person are sensitized to tuberculin (infection allergy), and a reaction occurs when a very minute quantity of tuberculin is introduced into the body. Nontuberculous persons do not exhibit such a reaction. A positive tuberculin reaction means that the individual displaying it has at some time been infected with tubercle bacilli. It does not necessarily indicate that active clinical tuberculosis is present or has ever existed. Negative reactions may be obtained in acute miliary tuberculosis because of an anergic reaction owing to massive hyposensitization. In cases of pulmonary tuberculosis the reaction with an ordinary test dose of tuberculin may be negative, but this seldom occurs in tuberculosis affecting the skin, bones, or lymph nodes.

Tuberculin tests are considered valuable in children but may be misleading in adults, since positive reactions occur in a considerable number of apparently healthy adults. In recent years it has been found that many adults with calcified lesions in the lungs and negative tuberculin tests react with histoplasmin, an antigen from the fungus *Histoplasma capsulatum*. Negative tuberculin reactions are helpful in deciding against the existence of tuberculosis except early in the initial stage of the infection or during the advanced or terminal stages of the disease. Hypersensitivity to tuberculin may also be inhibited temporarily by such factors as B.C.G. vaccination, steroid therapy, or extreme debility. When the tuberculous lesion is completely healed, the skin test occasionally converts to negative.

Old tuberculin—"O.T."—is prepared from

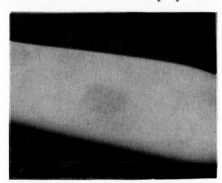

Figure 20–6. Positive tuberculin reaction at 48 hours, intracutaneous method. (Mitchell-Nelson, Pediatrics.)

tubercle bacilli grown in glycerine broth or a synthetic medium for several weeks. The cultures are steamed at 100° C. for a few hours, evaporated to $\frac{1}{10}$ volume, and passed through a filter to remove the bacteria. Fractions of culture filtrate precipitated with trichloroacetic acid or half-saturated ammonium sulfate precipitation are known as "P.P.D."—purified protein derivative. Both the O.T. and P.P.D. are standardized for biologic activity in animals and man.

The most widely used tuberculin test is the Mantoux or intradermal skin test. The forearm is cleaned with alcohol, and 0.1 ml. of the desired dilution of tuberculin is injected intradermally. When active tuberculous disease is suspected, it is customary to use a high dilution (1:10,000 or 1:100,000). If there is no reaction, a higher concentration (1:100 or 1:1000) can be used. P.P.D. is used in amounts that produce reactions corresponding in intensity to 0.01 mg. ("first strength"), 0.05 or 0.1 mg. ("intermediate strength"), and 1 mg. O.T. ("second strength"). The intermediate strength is commonly used in mass surveys. The reaction is read in 24 and 48 hours. The reaction is considered as definitely positive if there is induration of more than 10 mm. in diameter (Fig. 20–6).

Positive reactions are recorded according to the following criteria of the National Tuberculosis Association:

Doubtful (+/−)	Slight erythema and a trace of edema, which measures 5 mm. or less in diameter.
One plus (+)	Erythema and edema, which measures 5 to 10 mm. in diameter.
Two plus (++)	Erythema and edema, which measures 10 to 20 mm. in diameter.
Three plus (+++)	Marked erythema and edema, which exceeds 20 mm. in diameter.
Four plus (++++)	Erythema, edema, and central necrosis.

VOLLMER'S PATCH TEST

This consists of the application to the skin of two pieces of filter paper that have been impregnated with old tuberculin and attached to adhesive tape. The area of skin to be tested is cleansed with acetone or ether and allowed to dry. The adhesive tape is gently warmed and firmly applied to either the forearm or the interscapular region. The patch is removed after 48 hours and the reaction noted after another 48 hours. A positive reaction consists of a reddened, indurated region or of several distinct papules (Fig. 20–7).

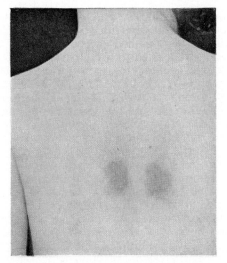

Figure 20–7. Positive tuberculin reaction with the Vollmer patch test 48 hours after removal of patch or 96 hours after patch had been applied. (Mitchell-Nelson, Pediatrics.)

This test is probably not so sensitive as the intracutaneous test, but it has the advantage of avoiding the use of a needle. The patch may become separated from the skin sufficiently to prevent the maintenance of effective contact, or the patch may be removed by the patient before completion of the test period.

VON PIRQUET'S CUTIREACTION

Two small drops of old tuberculin are placed on the skin of the front of the forearm about 2 inches apart, and the skin is slightly scarified, first at a point midway between them and then through each of the drops. A convenient scarifier is a piece of heavy platinum wire, the end of which is hammered to a chisel edge. A wooden toothpick with a chisel-shape end is also convenient. This is held at right angles to the skin and rotated 6 to 12 times with just sufficient pressure to remove the epidermis without drawing blood. In about ten minutes the excess of tuberculin is gently wiped away with cotton. No bandage is necessary. A positive reaction is shown by the appearance within 24 to 48 hours of a papule with red areola, which contrasts markedly with the small red spot left by the control scarification.

Skin Tests in Bacterial Infections

BRUCELLOSIS

Two types of antigens are used—one, a killed suspension of *Brucella* organisms, and the other, a solution of protein nucleate (Brucellergen) derived from the organism. One-tenth milliliter of the antigen is given intradermally and the reaction is read after 48 hours. A positive reaction is evinced by erythema, edema, and induration. In infected individuals the local reaction may be accompanied by an exacerbation of symptoms. The hypersensitive individual may show a systemic as well as a marked local reaction.

The use of Brucellergen may produce agglutinins against *Brucella;* hence blood for agglutination tests should be drawn before the antigen is injected. Since veterinarians may develop extreme sensitization to *Brucella,* it is best to avoid this type of skin test in these individuals.

CHANCROID

The antigen (Ducrey's or Ito-Reenstierna vaccine) is prepared from cultures of *Hemophilus ducreyi.* A positive reaction is read after 72 hours and is one in which an area of erythema of 14 mm. or more and an area of induration of 8 mm. or more appear. A positive reaction may persist for weeks. Such a reaction indicates that the patient either has an active infection or has been infected in the past. The skin hypersensitivity may last for many years.

GLANDERS

The antigen (mallein) is derived from a culture of *Actinobacillus mallei* and is used both in horses and humans. Its value in the diagnosis of human infections has not been established.

TULAREMIA

The antigen (Foshay) is prepared by treating a culture of *Pasteurella tularensis* with strong acid. A positive reaction is noticeable in 48 hours and consists of an area of erythema and induration. Skin sensitization becomes manifest during the first week of the disease and the agglutinins during the second week. Because the skin test antigen may elicit false positive agglutinins, it is necessary to draw blood for agglutination tests before the antigen is injected.

LEPROSY

The antigen used for this disease is known as "lepromin" and has both diagnostic and prognostic value in the tuberculoid type of leprosy.

Skin Tests in Mycotic Infections

BLASTOMYCIN

Many patients with North American blastomycosis (Gilchrist's disease) develop skin hypersensitivity to the filtrate of the mycelial phase of *Blastomyces dermatitidis*. This extract, known as blastomycin, is reasonably specific, although there is some cross-reaction with histoplasmosis. The reaction to the heterologous antigen is always less intense than with the homologous one. In practice this skin test antigen is usually injected simultaneously with histoplasmin, coccidioidin, and tuberculin.

A positive reaction appears within 24 to 48 hours and consists of an area of induration 5 × 5 mm. or more. A doubtful reaction consists of induration less than 5 mm. in diameter or erythema only. A negative reaction shows no induration or erythema less than 5 mm.

A positive blastomycin reaction may indicate either a past infection or a mild, chronic, or subacute infection. It may also denote improvement in cases of serious symptomatic blastomycosis, which previously have been blastomycin negative.

COCCIDIOIDIN

The skin test material for coccidioidomycosis is prepared by growing *Coccidioides immitis* in Long's synthetic broth for three to six months, filtering, and adding Merthiolate to the filtrate. Sensitivity is determined by the intracutaneous injection of 0.1 ml. of a 1:100 dilution of the standardized reagent. The immediate reaction, if it occurs, is nonspecific. A positive reaction is one in which an area of erythema and induration of 5 mm. or more appears within 24 to 72 hours.

The skin test becomes positive in 87 per cent of patients during the first week of clinical symptoms and in almost 100 per cent of patients after the second week. The antigen, thus, is probably the most sensitive available. Patients with a disseminated form of the disease may react weakly or negatively (anergy). Patients with erythema nodosum may be extremely sensitive to the antigen, which must be given in diluted form very cautiously. Patients hypersensitive to coccidioidin may react with blastomycin or histoplasmin but less strongly. It is therefore the usual practice to perform all three tests simultaneously.

Because a positive reaction persists for many years, it does not necessarily imply that active infection is present. However, a positive reaction occurring during an infection in which an earlier test was negative probably has diagnostic value. The results of the complement-fixation tests must always be compared with the results of the skin tests. Repeated skin testing with coccidioidin does not seem to interfere with subsequent serologic tests.

HISTOPLASMIN

The skin test material for histoplasmosis is prepared from *Histoplasma capsulatum* in a manner similar to coccidioidin. Sensitivity is determined by injecting 0.1 ml. of a 1:100 dilution of the standardized reagent. The immediate reaction is considered nonspecific and is ignored. A positive reaction appearing in 24 to 48 hours consists of an area of induration of 5 mm. or more. A doubtful reaction shows an area of induration of less than 5 mm. or erythema greater than 5 mm. A negative reaction shows no induration and an area of erythema less than 5 mm. A positive skin test indicates past or present infection. Acutely ill patients, however, may not develop sensitivity, or they may develop sensitivity early in the disease only to become anergic in the terminal state.

Patients sensitive to histoplasmin may cross-react with coccidioidin or blastomycin, particularly the latter. Consequently, the three antigens are best injected simultaneously.

Mass testing programs with histoplasmin have shown that the percentage of reactors in presumably normal individuals varies from 0 to over 80 per cent, depending on the geographic area. These studies have shed much light on the epidemiology of this puzzling disease.

A single injection of histoplasmin does not alter humoral antibody formation, but multiple injections may cause a rise in agglutinins and complement-fixing antibodies.

SKIN TESTS IN OTHER MYCOTIC DISEASES

Trichophytin is an extract of various species of *Trichophyton*. Its value in diagnosis is negligible, and it is used chiefly for desensitization. Oidiomycin, prepared from *Candida albicans*, similarly has no value in diagnosis. Antigens prepared for other fungus diseases, such as sporotrichosis and cryptococcosis, have not as yet been shown to possess any practical diagnostic value.

Skin Tests in Viral Diseases

THE FREI TEST

This antigen is used in the diagnosis of lymphogranuloma venereum (lymphopathia venereum, Nicolas-Favre disease) (see p. 794). The test, first developed by Frei in 1925, is widely used and practical for the diagnosis of this disease. It consists of the injection of 0.1 ml. of antigen and 0.1 ml. of control material intradermally. The test is read within 48 to 96 hours. A raised papule 6 × 6 mm. in diameter or more is considered a positive reaction, provided the reaction to the control material is 5 mm. or less. The antigen was originally prepared from pus from a bubo or from infected monkey or mouse brain. The antigen now in common use, known as "Lygranum," is made from the yolk sac of infected chick embryos. The control consists of normal yolk sac.

The test becomes positive one to six weeks after infection begins and remains positive for the life of the patient. The specificity is considered to be of high order and closely parallels the results of the complement-fixation test. Cross-reactions with psittacosis may occur occasionally.

CAT-SCRATCH DISEASE (BENIGN LYMPHORETICULOSIS)

The diagnosis of this disease is facilitated by the use of an intradermal reaction resembling the Frei test, using as an antigen heat-inactivated suspensions of infected lymph nodes or pus. (See p. 794.)

MUMPS

The antigen is prepared from infected monkey parotid gland or chick embryo allantoic fluid. It consists of the injection of 0.1 ml. of the antigen intracutaneously and 0.1 ml. of the control material (non-infected material corresponding with the antigen used). The reaction is read in 48 hours. A positive reaction, consisting of erythema and a lesion exceeding 10 mm. in diameter, indicates resistance to the mumps virus. A lesion less than 10 mm. or no area of erythema indicates susceptibility to mumps. The reaction has no diagnostic value, and the antigen may give rise to complement-fixing antibodies.

Skin Tests in Parasitic Diseases

ECHINOCOCCOSIS

The antigen employed (Casoni) consists of sterile hydatid fluid obtained by puncture of unilocular cysts from cases of echinococcosis (hydatid disease). The fluid is filtered and concentrated. An antigen obtained from the dog tapeworm, *Dipylidium caninum*, may also be used. A positive reaction is immediate in type, usually appearing within 15 to 20 minutes after the injection of the antigen. Positive reactions are not absolutely indicative of infection, since false positive reactions may occur from other cestode infections or hypersensitivity to foreign protein in the antigen. Complement-fixation, hemagglutination, and precipitation tests give more reliable results (see p. 900).

TOXOPLASMIN

The antigen is prepared from mouse peritoneal fluids rich with *Toxoplasma gondii*. The organisms are inactivated, their cell bodies are broken up, and the antigen is standardized and tested for sterility. A control antigen is treated similarly. Both materials are injected intradermally in 0.1 ml. amounts. Positive reactions, which appear after 24 or 48 hours, consist of an area of erythema and induration of over 10 mm. A positive reaction gives results similar to the Sabin-Feldman dye test, i.e., indicates the presence of antibodies to *Toxoplasma*. The considerable number of positive tests obtained in epidemiologic surveys has caused some investigators to question the specificity of the test.

TRICHINOSIS

The antigen used consists of larval extracts prepared by peptic digestion of muscles of animals infected with *Trichinella spiralis*. The test is performed by injecting intracutaneously 0.1 ml. of the antigen as well as a control from uninfected tissue. An immediate reaction, consisting of a blanched wheal with pseudopodia surrounded by a zone of erythema, appears within 10 minutes and is considered to be a valuable aid in the diagnosis of this disease, particularly in cases that present only mild symptoms (Fig. 20–8). However, as many as 10 per cent of the positive reactions may be false. It is desirable to draw blood for a precipitin, agglutination, or

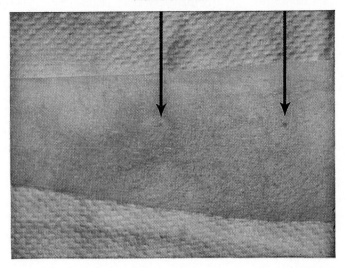

Trichinella Extract   Control

Figure 20–8. Positive intracutaneous test for trichinosis. (Courtesy of Eli Lilly and Co.)

complement-fixation test before the skin test antigen is injected.

SCHISTOSOMIASIS

Intradermal tests are conducted with cercarial or hepatopancreatic glands of infected snails (*Austrolorbis glabratus*), which are infected with *Schistosoma mansoni*. The cercariae or tissue is concentrated, washed, dried, and extracted. Reactions appear to be of a group character and are used primarily for field work in infected areas.

LEISHMANIASIS

Intradermal tests with phenolized saline suspensions of killed *Leishmania tropica* give a positive reaction in oriental sore (cutaneous leishmaniasis), but a high percentage of noninfected individuals cross-react with this antigen.

FILARIASIS

Intradermal tests are conducted with antigens prepared from the dog heart worm, *Dirofilaria immitis*. Positive reactions have been obtained in a high percentage of cases of infection with *Wuchereria bancrofti*. Since similar results have been obtained in loa loa and onchocerciasis, the reaction appears to be group specific rather than species specific.

OTHER PARASITIC SKIN TESTS

Skin tests for ascariasis, strongyloidiasis, cysticercosis, sparganosis, and various other parasitic diseases have been developed and used to some extent. None of them is cur-

rently generally available or considered to be specific enough for diagnostic purposes.

The Kveim Test

The Kveim or Nickerson-Kveim reaction for the diagnosis of sarcoidosis is occasionally used, but the value of the test is questioned by some. The antigen is prepared by grinding human sarcoid tissue, usually lymph nodes or spleen. The material is diluted 1:10 with saline and heated to 60° C. for one hour on two successive days. A preservative is added, and after suitable sterility tests the antigen is ready for use. Controls consist of suspensions of normal tissues.

The test is done by injecting 0.1 to 0.2 ml. intradermally. In a positive test a red-purple papule appears in about a week and grows gradually in size until it reaches a diameter of 3 to 8 mm. in four to six weeks. A biopsy of the papule is examined for tuberculoid granulomas resembling those of sarcoidosis. Such a reaction combined with a negative reaction in the controls is considered positive for sarcoidosis and is reported to occur in approximately 80 to 85 per cent of cases, remaining positive for the life of the patient. The specificity is considered to be of high order and closely parallels the results of the complement-fixation test. Cross-reactions with psittacosis may occur occasionally.

Tests for Hypersusceptibility

In some persons, probably as a result of

genetic factors, hypersensitivity may occur to a considerable variety of substances. When such a person is exposed to contact with the substance to which he is sensitive, toxic effects result—urticaria, hay fever, asthma, gastrointestinal disturbances, and coryza. This form of hypersensitiveness is called "atopy" and is responsible for such conditions as asthma and hay fever. Substances to which such sensitiveness can be attributed (allergens, atopens) are foods, pollens, certain drugs, animal serums and danders, and fungus spores. Tests for hypersensitiveness to these substances are carried out by means of simple skin tests, such as introducing the possible allergen through the epidermis by scratching or by intradermal injection. These procedures and their interpretations are described in detail in textbooks on allergy and clinical medicine.

REFERENCES

1. Baer, R. L., and Yanowitz, M.: Skin tests in various infectious and parasitic diseases. Arch. Derm., 62:491–501, 1950.
2. Boyd, W. C.: Fundamentals of Immunology. 3rd Ed. New York, Interscience Publishers, Inc., 1956.
3. Daniels, W. B., and MacMurray, F.: Cat-scratch disease: Nonbacterial regional lymphadenitis. Ann. Int. Med., 37:697–719, 1952.
4. Edwards, P. Q., and Edwards, L. B.: Story of the tuberculin test from an epidemiologic viewpoint. Am. Rev. Resp. Dis., 81:1–47, 1960.
5. Edwards, P. Q., and Palmer, C. E.: Prevalence of sensitivity to coccidioidin, with special reference to specific and non-specific reactions to coccidioidin and histoplasmin. Dis. Chest, 31: 3–28, 1957.
6. Enders, J. F.: Observations on immunity in mumps. Ann. Int. Med., 18:1015–1019, 1943.
7. Frenkel, J.: Dermal hypersensitivity to toxo-plasma antigens (toxoplasmin). Proc. Soc. Exp. Biol. & Med., 68:634–639, 1948.
8. Johnston, D. E.: Study of the value of bacterial vaccines in the treatment of bronchial asthma associated with respiratory infections. Pediatrics, 24:427–433, 1959.
9. Johnston, W. W., Saltzman, H. A., Bufkin, J. H., and Smith, D. T.: The tuberculin test and the diagnosis of clinical tuberculosis. Am. Rev. Resp. Dis., 81:189–196, 1960.
10. King, A J., Barwell, C. F., and Catterall, R. D.: Intradermal tests in the diagnosis of lymphogranuloma venereum. Brit. J. Ven. Dis., 32: 209–216, 1956.
11. Kolmer, J. A., Spaulding, E. H., and Robinson, H. W.: Approved Laboratory Technic. 5th Ed. New York, Appleton-Century-Crofts, Inc., 1951.
12. Loosli, C. G., Beadenkopf, W. G., Rice, F. A., and Savage, L. J.: Epidemiological aspects of histoplasmin, tuberculin and coccidioidin sensitivity. Am. J. Hyg., 53:33–57, 1951.
13. Magath, T. B.: The antigen of Echinococcus. Am. J. Clin. Path., 31:1–9, 1959.
14. Moore, M. W., and Reed, C. E.: Clinical evaluation of stock respiratory vaccine in the treatment of bronchial asthma. Ann. Allergy, 17: 722–728, 1959.
15. Palmer, C. E.: Non-tuberculous pulmonary calcification and sensitivity to histoplasmin. Pub. Health Rep., 60:513–520, 1945.
16. Raffel, S.: Immunity, Hypersensitivity, Serology. New York, Appleton-Century-Crofts, Inc., 1953.
17. Rappaport, F. T.: The immunologic properties of coccidioidin as a skin test reagent in man. J. Immunol., 84:368–373, 1960.
18. Salvin, S. B.: Current concepts of diagnostic serology and skin hypersensitivity in the mycoses. Am. J. Med., 27:97–114, 1959.
19. Saslaw, S., and Campbell, C. C.: Effect of histoplasmin skin testing on serologic results. Proc. Soc. Exp. Biol. & Med., 82:689–692, 1953.
20. Siltzbach, L. E., and Ehrlich, J. C.: The Nickerson-Kveim reaction in sarcoidosis. Am. J. Med., 16:790–804, 1954.
21. Smith, C. E., Whiting, E. G., Baker, E. E., Rosenberger, H. G., Beard, R. R., and Saito, M. T.: The use of coccidioidin. Am. Rev. Tuberc., 62: 330–360, 1948.

Chapter 21

Milk and Water

By JAMES G. SHAFFER, Sc.D., *and* MILTON GOLDIN, M.S.

MILK

The average composition of human milk and cow's milk is shown in Table 21–1.

Table 21–1. Average Composition of Human Milk and Cow's Milk Expressed in Per Cent

COMPOSITION	HUMAN MILK	COW'S MILK *
Fat	3.00–5.00	3.50–4.00
Sugar	6.00–7.00	4.30–7.00
Protein	1.00–2.25	1.50–4.00
Salts	0.18–0.25	0.20–0.70
Water	85.50–89.82	87.30–87.50

* The specimens of cow's milk used in the analysis did not include Jersey milk.

These figures are based on a large series of analyses reported by Holt.

The reaction of human milk is slightly alkaline; that of cow's milk is neutral or slightly acid. The specific gravity of each is about 1.028 to 1.032. Human milk is sterile when secreted but may contain a few bacteria from the lacteal ducts. Cow's milk, as usually sold, contains a large number of bacteria; the best milk rarely contains fewer than 1000 in each cubic centimeter. Microscopically, human milk is a fairly homogeneous emulsion of fat and is practically destitute of cellular elements. Any notable number of leukocytes indicates infection of the mammary gland.

Chemical Examinations

Chemical examination of breast milk is of great value in solving the problems of infant feeding. The sample should be the middle milk or the entire quantity from one breast, or 1 ounce should be obtained before and after nursing and the two portions should be mixed.

FAT

Leffmann-Beam Quantitative Test for Fat. This is essentially the widely used Babcock test, which has been modified for the small quantities of milk obtainable from the human mammary gland.

Apparatus
1. A special tube that fits the cup of a centrifuge (Fig. 21–1). Owing to its narrow stem the tube is difficult to fill and clean.
2. A 5 ml. pipet.

Reagents
1. Concentrated hydrochloric acid.
2. Amyl alcohol.
3. Concentrated sulfuric acid.

Technique. Exactly 5 ml. of the milk is introduced into the tube by means of the pipet, and 1 ml. of a mixture of equal parts

Figure 21–1. Centrifuge tube for milk analysis.

of concentrated hydrochloric acid and amyl alcohol is added and well mixed. The tube is filled to the 0 mark with concentrated sulfuric acid, adding a few drops at a time and agitating constantly. This is revolved in the centrifuge at 1000 r.p.m. for three minutes or until the fat has separated. The percentage of fat is then read off on the stem, each small division representing 0.2 per cent of fat.

PROTEIN

Bogg's Modification of Esbach's Test. To prepare Bogg's reagent, dissolve 25 gm. of phosphotungstic acid in 125 ml. of distilled water. Add 25 ml. of concentrated hydrochloric acid to 100 ml. of distilled water. Mix the two solutions. This reagent is fairly stable if kept in a dark glass bottle.

Technique. The technique of this test is similar to that of Esbach's test for albumin in urine. Before examination the milk should be diluted according to the probable amount of protein, and allowance for the dilution should be made in the subsequent reading. The optimal dilution is 1:10 for human milk and 1:20 for cow's milk. The dilution must be made accurately.

COMBINED METHOD FOR QUANTITATIVE DETERMINATION OF PROTEIN AND FAT

The amount of fat and protein in human milk can be estimated roughly, but accurately enough for many clinical purposes, by means of Holt's apparatus, which consists of a 10 ml. cream gauge and a small hydrometer. The cream gauge is filled to the 0 mark and allowed to stand for 24 hours. The percentage of cream then can be read on the gauge. The percentage of fat is three-fifths that of cream.

The amount of protein can be determined approximately from the specific gravity and from the percentage of fat. Since the amounts of salts and sugar seldom vary sufficiently to affect the specific gravity, a high specific gravity must be due either to an increase of protein or to a decrease of fat or both and vice versa. If the specific gravity is normal, the amount of protein is high when the amount of fat is high and vice versa. This method is not accurate with cow's milk.

LACTOSE

The protein should first be removed by acidifying with acetic acid, boiling, and filtering. The copper method may then be used as for dextrose in the urine. It must be borne in mind that lactose reduces copper more slowly than does dextrose, that longer heating is therefore required, and that 25 ml. of Benedict's solution is equivalent to 0.0676 gm. of lactose (as compared with 0.05 gm. of dextrose).

PRESERVATIVES

Formalin is the most common preservative added to cow's milk but boric acid also is used.

Test for Formalin
Reagents
1. Dilute solution of ferric chloride (approximately 10 per cent).
2. Chemically pure sulfuric acid.
Technique
1. Add a few drops of the dilute solution of ferric chloride to a few ml. of the milk.
2. Run the mixture gently on the surface of some chemically pure sulfuric acid in a test tube. If formaldehyde is present, a bright red ring will appear at the line of contact of the two fluids. This test is not specific for formaldehyde, but no other substance that is likely to be added to the milk will respond to the test. Jorissen's test for formaldehyde may also be used.

Goske's Test for Boric Acid
Reagent. Concentrated hydrochloric acid.
Technique
1. Mix 2 ml. of hydrochloric acid with 20 ml. of milk and place the mixture in a 50 ml. beaker.
2. In the mixture suspend a long strip of turmeric paper (2 cm. wide) so that its end reaches the bottom of the beaker. Allow to remain about a half hour. The liquid will rise by capillarity, and a reddish-brown color will appear at the junction of the moist and dry portions of the paper if boric acid is present. When this colored zone of the paper is touched with ammonia water, a bluish-green slate color will develop. A rough idea of the amount of boric acid that is present may be gained by comparing the depth of the color produced with that produced by solutions of boric acid of known concentration.

Bacteriologic Examination

At times it is necessary to know the types of pathogenic microorganisms that are present in a given sample of milk, especially if it is suspected that the use of such milk has been the cause of disease. Epidemics of undulant fever, bovine tuberculosis, typhoid fever, or a very virulent form of streptococcic sore throat often have been traced to a milk supply. Milk differs from water in that it is an excellent medium for the growth of many pathogenic bacteria. Usually, however, bacteriologic examination of milk consists of plating the milk in such a manner that an estimate can be made of the number of bacteria in each cubic millimeter. Standards of milk quality vary from one locality to another. Excellent milk may have only a few hundred bacteria in each ml. Milk that contains less than 10,000 bacteria on delivery would be considered very good; milk that contains less than 50,000 would be considered good. Poor milk, yet commercially usable, may contain 500,000 bacteria per ml., while milk that should not be used may contain so many bacteria that they cannot be counted.

BACTERIAL COUNT

"Standard Methods for the Examination of Dairy Products," which has been published by the American Public Health Association, should be followed in detail in making a bacterial count of milk. Briefly the technique is as follows:

1. Prepare "water blanks," sterile bottles preferably with glass stoppers. Some of these should contain exactly 99 ml. of water and others only 9 ml. Sterilize in the autoclave at 15 pounds pressure for one hour (Fig. 21–2).

2. Melt tryptone-glucose-yeast or milk-protein hydrolysate agar.

3. Shake the sample of milk thoroughly and dilute as follows: Place 1 ml. of milk in a bottle containing 99 ml. of sterile water; discard this pipet. With a sterile pipet transfer 1 ml. of the 1:100 dilution to a bottle containing 9 ml. of sterile water. With the same pipet transfer 1 ml. of 1:100 dilution to a sterile Petri dish. With a fresh sterile pipet make still another dilution by transferring 1 ml. of 1:1000 dilution to a bottle containing 9 ml. of sterile water. With this same pipet transfer 1 ml. of 1:1000 dilution to a sterile Petri dish. Finally, use a fresh sterile pipet to transfer 1 ml. of 1:10,000 dilution to a sterile Petri dish. All dilutions must be shaken 25 times before making any transfers.

4. Pour 10 ml. of melted and cooled agar into each Petri dish. The milk dilution and the agar are mixed thoroughly by gentle shaking.

5. Incubate the cultures for 48 hours at 32° C. and at 35° C.

6. Count the colonies. Only those plates are chosen in which there are not more than 300 but not less than 30 colonies in the entire Petri dish (Fig. 21–3).

7. Calculate the number of organisms for each ml. for the count and the dilution; for example, if there are 256 colonies in the plate and the dilution is 1:1000, the number of bacteria in each ml. will be 256,000.

Besides the colony count obtained by the standard plate count method, the Breed microscopic method is useful, particularly in judging the quality of milk delivered to milk-receiving stations. Special techniques

A B C

Figure 21–2. Dilution bottles with nonabsorbent stoppers. A. Screw cap Pyrex bottle, 6 oz. B. Square or rectangular bottle for special rubber stopper, 6 oz. C. Pyrex bottle, 6 oz., to be fitted with standard rubber stopper into which has been inserted a glass rod. (From Standard Methods for the Examination of Dairy Products. 10th Ed. New York, American Public Health Association, Inc., 1953.)

Figure 21–3. Quebec bacteria colony counter.

are available for determining the hygienic quality of milk and the efficiency of pasteurization. These include the methylene blue and resazurin reduction and the phosphatase and sediment tests. Detection of pathogenic bacteria in milk is a procedure best performed in specialized laboratories equipped for such purposes. These tests are described in detail in "Standard Methods for the Examination of Dairy Products" (1953).

Brucella in Milk. The organisms causing undulant fever or brucellosis are occasionally present in milk from infected animals and can present a serious public health problem. They can be isolated from milk by culture or guinea pig inoculation. The *Brucella abortus* ring test is widely used to detect the presence of agglutinins for *Brucella* in the milk of infected animals. *B. abortus* cells stained with hematoxylin or tetrazolium blue constitutes the antigen. The antigen is mixed with the milk. In milk from infected animals the agglutinated antigen rises with the cream to the top, producing a deep blue ring. In negative milk the cream ring remains white.

The technique for the bacteriologic examination of nursery formulas is described on p. 834.

WATER

The approval of water supplies for domestic purposes and the examination of water in swimming pools and at beaches is a public health problem and is usually conducted in the state board of health or municipal laboratories. However, the clinical laboratory is sometimes called on to pass judgment on the potability of drinking water and also to make a routine examination of water that is known to be usable.

The color, turbidity, and odor should be noted. Chemical examination may be made for total solid nitrogen as free ammonia and also nitrogen as albuminoid ammonia, nitrogen as nitrites or nitrates, and organic nitrogen. The amount of oxygen and chlorides, the total hardness, and the alkalinity may also be determined. All these procedures are carried out according to the standard methods as laid down by the American Public Health Association (1955).

The bacteriologic examination of water is also carried out according to standard methods. Briefly the examination is made for the number of bacteria per cubic millimeter. The sample of water in a sterile container should be shaken 25 times before plating. If it is known to have a low bacterial count, 1 ml. is plated in tryptone-glucose extract agar. If chlorine is present in the water, it is best to neutralize 100 ml. with about 0.2 gm. of sodium thiosulfate. The plates should be incubated for 48 hours at 20° C. or for 24 hours at 35° C. Use a 2½ inch lens in order to count all the colonies present. Only those plates in which there are 30 to 300 colonies should be

Figure 21–4. Membrane filter assembly. (From Standard Methods for the Examination of Water, Sewage, and Industrial Wastes. 11th Ed. New York, A.P.H.A.)

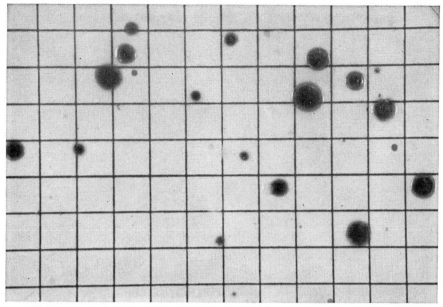

Figure 21–5.   Coliform colonies on modified Endo medium. × 10. (From Standard Methods for the Examination of Water, Sewage, and Industrial Wastes. 10th Ed. New York, A.P.H.A.)

counted. Some form of plate counter is most satisfactory for this examination.

Tests should also be made for the presence of members of the coliform group. According to the standard methods presumptive tests may be made with 10 ml., 1 ml., and 0.1 ml. of the sample of the water placed in a lactose broth fermentation tube.

If these tests are positive, confirmatory tests may be carried out by plating positive lactose tubes on Endo's or EMB agar to determine the presence of typical coli colonies. The complete test consists of picking typical coliform colonies from the plates into lactose fermentation tubes and gram staining the tubes showing gas.

A simple and customary method of testing for the presence of the coliform group of organisms is the following: Place 10 ml. of water in each of five fermentation tubes containing 10 ml. of double-strength lactose broth. If there is no gas formed in any of the tubes, *Escherichia coli* is not present in a 50 ml. sample of the water, and it is probable that it is not present in 100 ml. If one tube shows 10 per cent of gas, then there is at least one colon bacillus present in 50 ml., and the report may be made that at least two colon bacilli are present per 100 ml. of the sample of water. This amount is considered permissible in drinking water. If more than one tube contains gas, it may be well to carry out the con-

firmatory or complete tests, because the water is likely to be contaminated. If all five tubes show gas, it would be evident that there are at least ten colon bacilli per 100 ml. of the sample, and such water would be badly contaminated.

In recent years a new method of testing water supplies for the presence of coliform bacteria has been under study; it is called the membrane filter technique (Fig. 21–4). This technique involves the passage of a measured amount of the water to be tested through a standard cellulose filter, which will retain the bacteria (Millipore HA or its equivalent). Bacteria from the water sample become implanted on the filter, which is then carefully transferred to a Petri dish containing an absorbent pad saturated with an appropriate nutrient medium. The plate is inverted and incubated at 35° C. ± 0.5° for two hours. Then the filter pad is transferred to new Petri dishes containing absorbent pads saturated with differential media, such as E.H.C. Endo medium or B.G.F. medium, and reincubated for 20 ± 2 hours. Typical coliform colonies appear with a characteristic metallic sheen (Fig. 21–5).

REFERENCES

1. Maxcy, K. F.: Rosenau's Preventive Medicine and Hygiene. 8th Ed. New York, Appleton-Century-Crofts, Inc., 1958.
2. Ministry of Health, Report No. 71: The Bacterio-

logical Examination of Water Supplies. London, Her Majesty's Stationery Office, 1956.

3. Standard Methods for the Examination of Dairy Products. 9th Ed. New York, American Public Health Association, 1953.

4. Standard Methods for the Examination of Water.

Sewage, and Industrial Wastes. 10th Ed. New York, American Public Health Association, 1955.

5. World Health Organization: International Standards for Drinking Water. New York, Columbia University Press, 1958.

Chapter 22

Hospital Epidemiology

By JAMES G. SHAFFER, Sc.D., and MILTON GOLDIN, M.S.

It has been recognized for many years that the hospital environment presents special problems in the prevention of the spread of infections from patient to patient, from patient to the hospital personnel, and from hospital personnel to patients. Studies have indicated that there are increased numbers of pathogenic organisms in the hospital environment as compared to the normal environment, a finding that is not surprising in view of the fact that considerable numbers of the patients admitted are suffering from infections of various kinds. As hospital practices have evolved over the years, the recognition of these dangers has led to the development of isolation techniques applied to patients with well-recognized infectious diseases, such as the pneumonias, diphtheria, typhoid fever, and dysentery. Such specific isolation techniques have been documented thoroughly and applied effectively with good results.

Numerous developments and observations of relatively recent years have changed the situation somewhat and have renewed interest in the problems presented by the transmission of infectious agents within the hospital. Some of the problems have always been present but were no doubt overshadowed in the past by the pressing need for dealing with the large numbers of acute infectious diseases that placed enormous demands on the time of the often-inadequate hospital staff. Some new facets have resulted in part from the widespread use of the sulfonamides and the antibiotics, which has brought about important changes in the microbial flora of the hospital environment; the discovery of certain previously unknown disease-producing agents, such as the en-

teropathogenic *Escherichia coli* and certain enteroviruses; and the increased use of blood, blood derivatives, and therapeutic agents given by injection, which may result in the development of hepatitis.

THE ROLE OF CHEMOTHERAPEUTIC AGENTS

The antibiotics have had most interesting and far-reaching effects. Their use, both for therapeutic and prophylactic management of infection, resulted in the development of considerable complacency about the need for measures to prevent transmission of microorganisms within the hospital environment. Consequently carelessness resulted. It is now obvious that the widespread use of these agents within the hospital environment may be dangerous, and it has also become increasingly apparent that the prophylactic use of antibiotics is not always successful in preventing the development of infection in burns and surgical incisions. Many of the microorganisms involved in these infections are now of a type considerably different from those that caused the greatest concern in preantibiotic times. They are likely to be relatively antibiotic-resistant bacteria, normally a part of the body flora, which in the healthy, intact human host with normal resistance would not cause difficulty. However, when implanted at a suitable site in or upon a patient whose resistance is already lowered by illness, such organisms may often produce active infection, sometimes with serious consequences. This type of disease presents problems of prevention that are not easy to solve, because the organisms in-

823

volved are so widely distributed throughout the population. However, it is likely that a return to strict asepsis, which was widely practiced in the preantibiotic period, would accomplish much. This will be discussed in a general way in a later section.

Drug-resistant Organisms

Perhaps the most serious danger of the widespread use of antibiotics is illustrated by the emergence of drug-resistant strains of pathogenic *Staphylococcus aureus*. Fortunately this is the only pathogenic microorganism that has as yet exhibited this tendency to the extent of causing serious consequences. The mechanism by which resistant strains develop is not completely understood, but the result is that within the hospital environment there have appeared increasing numbers of these strains. With any given antibiotic the relative proportion of resistant to susceptible strains depends on the extent to which that antibiotic is used in the hospital. So far, the problems presented by drug-resistant *S. aureus* have been restricted almost exclusively to the hospital environment, since there has been no great increase in the relative per cent of resistant organisms in nonhospital areas. One might expect, however, that as time goes on more resistant strains will become disseminated in the general population.

In order to understand better the problems presented by the drug-resistant *Staphylococcus aureus*, it is necessary to know something of the nature of the organism. It is widely distributed in nature and is capable of survival for long periods of time in the environment attached to dust particles, droplets or droplet nuclei, various surfaces, bedclothing, and so forth. Not only does it survive for long periods, but the pathogenic strains also maintain their pathogenicity.

Numerous studies have revealed that this organism establishes itself readily in or upon the human host. It has been isolated from the throat and the nasal passages of up to 50 per cent of the personnel in certain areas of hospitals, and it is probable that all persons carry the organism periodically. Exposed areas of the skin, particularly the hands, are also commonly contaminated. Most individuals are only temporary carriers of *S. aureus*, but a few become permanent carriers of the organisms, which are constantly present in the nose and the throat or over wide areas of the skin. This poses a serious problem if the individual happens to work in a critical area of the hospital, such as the operating room or nursery.

S. aureus comprises an antigenically heterogeneous group of organisms, some pathogenic and some nonpathogenic, the classification of which is difficult. The development of successful techniques for typing the organisms with specific bacteriophages has been helpful, and in recent years this problem has been studied intensively. Such studies have revealed that certain phage types are more prone to produce epidemics within the hospital environment and that when such outbreaks occur usually only one type is involved. Sporadic cases are more likely to be caused by a variety of types. Hospital-acquired staphylococcal infections are of several types. Surgical wound infections, infection of burns and other lesions, pneumonia, skin infections in infants, and breast abscesses in newly delivered mothers are the most common, although boils and carbuncles may also occur.

Studies of hospital-acquired staphylococcal infections have revealed that the true picture of their occurrence cannot be obtained merely by tabulating the number of cases that are seen during the hospital stay of the patients. In fact the number of cases that develop after discharge from the hospital is considerably greater than the number developing during hospitalization. This is particularly characteristic of infections in infants and mothers. The situation has been compared to an iceberg in which the portion that is readily visible represents only a small portion of what actually exists. Such a finding is not surprising, since the incubation period of many of these infections lasts several days during which time no symptoms are present. This no doubt applies also to other types of hospital-acquired infection. Thus, an institution cannot truly evaluate its own situation in this regard without making every effort to follow its patients for a considerable period (14 to 21 days) after discharge.

A more complete description of *S. aureus* and its fundamental cultural characteristics will be found in Chapter 16 and in the textbooks and references listed in the bibliography. There is still much to be learned about this important bacterium, and it is hoped that an antibiotic to which resistance does not develop will be discovered.

Thus, the widespread use of antibiotic and chemotherapeutic agents has brought into sharp focus some of the general problems of hospital epidemiology. The total epidemiologic consideration facing the modern hospital still involves most of the microorganisms long recognized as serious pathogens. These are constantly being introduced into the hospital environment and must be dealt with effectively to prevent their spread within the population of the institution. These include such bacteria as *Streptococcus pyogenes* (Group A), *Diplococcus pneumoniae,* and *Neisseria meningitidis;* the various viruses that affect the respiratory system; and certain fungi, such as *Candida albicans.* In general, measures designed to control the spread of S. *aureus* will be effective in controlling the spread of most of the other organisms.

THE ROLE OF ENTEROPATHOGENS

Enteropathogenic microorganisms are another potential source of difficulty. These present somewhat different problems than the organisms just discussed, since they are usually ingested by the individual who becomes infected and are discharged from the body in the feces. A variety of organisms have been involved in outbreaks of diarrhea and dysentery in hospitals, including *Salmonella, Shigella,* enteropathogenic *E. coli* (in nurseries), and ECHO viruses. These outbreaks have been traced to carriers among the hospital personnel or patients and to breaks in technique.

In one instance we observed that cases of diarrhea were occurring in a respiratory disease ward of a children's hospital. Symptoms appeared three or four days after the patient had been admitted, and cultural examination yielded no consistent findings; that is, there appeared to be no organism common to all cases. Investigation revealed that the staff on daily rounds went from the diarrhea ward directly to the respiratory ward. When the course of the rounds was changed and precautions were taken to avoid transfer of organisms on hands and instruments, no further cases occurred.

It is important to check the personnel in critical areas periodically with adequate stool examinations. Although the protozoan parasite, *Entamoeba histolytica,* has rarely been reported as the causative agent in an outbreak in a modern hospital, its transmission may be accomplished in the same manner as the other enteric pathogens, and it is highly desirable that all infected hospital personnel be treated adequately. One report described several cases of amebiasis in a premature nursery.

Prevention of Enteric Disease

The prevention of hospital-acquired enteric disease depends on at least four precautions: (1) Adequate control of food-handling and dispensing operations, including the detection and elimination of carriers among the food-handling personnel, careful control of food preparation, dishwashing and garbage disposal, and adequate refrigeration of stored food; (2) careful attention to personal hygiene by all food handlers, physicians, nurses, and hospital employees with special attention to hand washing and the use of disinfectant soaps; (3) care in the disposal and sterilization of materials contaminated with fecal matter, such as diapers and rectal thermometers; and (4) complete isolation of patients with diarrhea and dysentery. These general measures are of the utmost importance, since it is not always possible to detect carriers when cultures are done, and even when they are done they can only be done periodically. One can never be sure what the situation is in the meantime.

THE CONTROL PROGRAM

The overall prevention of hospital-acquired infection depends almost entirely on cooperative efforts on the part of all groups involved in the operation of the institution. A control program of the type needed may be compared aptly to a chain that is only as strong as its weakest link. Ideally it is desirable to form a committee on infection made up of the most responsible person of each department concerned. The committee should formulate a definite program based on the soundest principles known. The program should be defined clearly with rules and regulations and made known to all hospital personnel. Some individual, perhaps designated as the hospital epidemiologist, should be charged with the responsibility for administering the program.

In the following discussion further attention will be given to general measures designed to prevent the spread of microorganisms within the hospital environment but will not include discussions of the isolation techniques used for the patients with specific infectious diseases who may be admitted to the hospital. The types of disease requiring isolation may be defined by health department regulations or may be determined by the committee on infections or by hospital administrative policy. It is assumed that isolation techniques are well known;

they are, at any rate, beyond the scope of this book.

In carrying out the program designed to prevent the spread of microorganisms within the hospital, the clinical microbiology laboratory plays a major role. It must be prepared, in addition to doing the regular studies on patients, to do periodic cultural studies on the members of the hospital personnel, to maintain a surveillance of sterilization procedures and the efficacy of dishwashing procedures and laundry operations, and to assist in epidemiologic follow-up on any outbreaks of infectious disease within the institution. Ideally the laboratory should be prepared to do certain environmental studies to help evaluate the efficacy of terminal disinfection of rooms occupied by patients with infectious disease and to evaluate the relative contamination of the air in various areas and under various conditions. For this it is necessary to use a standardized method for taking air samples; several methods are available. It is also desirable to work out a technique for taking cultures from surfaces of various types.

Transmission of Microorganisms

Transmission of microorganisms occurs in a variety of ways, the primary mode with any particular organism depending on the site of its localization in the infected individual and the route by which it characteristically enters its new host. At least five common means of transmission are important in hospital practice: direct, fomites (indirect), food, water, and air.

Direct Transmission. The first of these, the direct route, may be defined to include both actual physical contact and close proximity such that microorganisms can be transmitted by droplet directly through the air from the infected to the noninfected individual.

Fomite Transmission. Fomites provide an indirect means of transmission and include all inanimate objects that may be handled by or in contact with an infected individual. These include thermometers, linen, blankets, any piece of apparatus used in giving anesthesia or in doing a basal metabolism test into which a patient may breathe, pencils, stethoscopes, and surgical instruments.

Transmission in Food and Water. Food may act as a vehicle for several pathogenic microorganisms, the best known being the enteric pathogens and the organisms most commonly associated with food poisoning,

Salmonella and *Staphylococcus*. Food-borne outbreaks of streptococcal disease have also occurred, and it is entirely possible for epidemic strains of S. *aureus* to be transmitted in this way.

With modern methods of water treatment it is unlikely, under normal circumstances, that water-borne disease would occur in present-day hospitals, but it is nevertheless well to maintain constant checks on the water supply. Water may play a role in another way; it has been shown that if water carafes are allowed to stand for extended periods at the patient's bedside, considerable growth of bacteria may occur. Thorough sterilization of these containers between use and redistribution is absolutely necessary.

Transmission by Air. The role played by air in the transmission of infection has been the subject of extensive investigation for many years, and the attitude of epidemiologists toward the importance of air-borne infection has varied from time to time. The widespread dissemination of drug-resistant staphylococci and the occurrence of in-hospital infections with this and other organisms has renewed interest in the air as a possible vehicle of microbial transmission.

It is necessary for purposes of discussion to define what is generally accepted as air-borne transmission as opposed to direct contact, which has already been defined to include physical contact as well as droplet infection. This necessarily implies close proximity, since droplets settle very rapidly and present little hazard beyond a distance of 3 to 6 feet. Air-borne transmission thus implies that the organisms be suspended in the air and that they settle on an exposed surface or be inhaled in the process of breathing. Bacteria seldom, if ever, exist in the air of a room unless they are attached to another particle. Such particles are of two types, dust or droplet nuclei. The droplet nucleus has been defined as the minute remnants that remain after the evaporation of all or most of the moisture from what was originally a droplet. These two types of particles behave in different manners. Dust particles settle fairly rapidly under normal circumstances but are rather easily resuspended by any activity or by convection currents within a room. Apparently owing to their very small size, droplet nuclei remain suspended in the air for long periods of time and tend to settle out much more slowly than dust particles (Fig. 22–1).

The extent of bacterial contamination of

the air in a room or other enclosed space depends on a number of factors. Studies have shown a direct correlation between the number of air-borne bacteria and the number of persons present and the amount of their activity. The type of activity is important. Anything that stirs up dust, such as bed making, dusting, dry mopping, the common practice of puffing out a pillow, or just rapid movement about the room, has a marked effect in increasing bacterial content of the air. Sources of such bacterial contamination are not only the dust from floors and other surfaces but also bed clothing (linen, blankets, and pillows) and the clothing and hair of the persons in the room. Although many of the bacteria suspended in the air by these means are non-pathogens, such organisms as *Staphylococcus aureus*, *Streptococcus pyogenes*, alpha *Streptococcus*, and *Diplococcus pneumoniae* frequently can be isolated.

A dangerous source of air-borne bacteria is the individual with superficial infection, such as otitis media or skin lesions. Studies have shown that such lesions may release large numbers of bacteria into the atmosphere. It has also been shown that large numbers of bacteria may be released into the air during the changing of dressings on infected wounds or burns.

The laundry chute may be another source

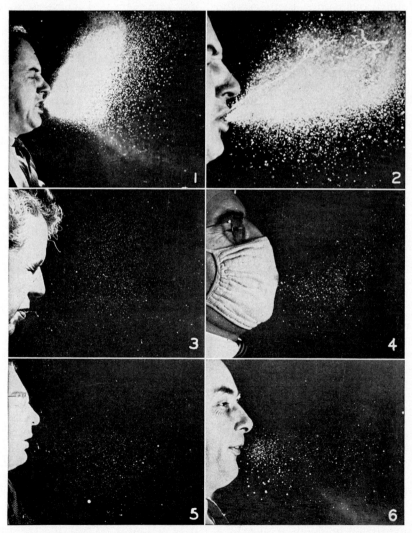

Figure 22–1. The atomization of mouth and nose secretions demonstrated by high speed photography. *1,* a violent sneeze in a normal subject; note the close approximation of the teeth, resulting in effective atomization. *2,* head cold sneeze; note the strings of mucus and the less effective atomization of the viscous secretions. *3,* a stifled sneeze. *4,* sneeze through a dense face mask. *5,* cough; note the lesser discharge than in the uninhibited sneeze. *6,* enunciation of the letter f. (Jennison.)

of air-borne contamination. When linens or other material is dropped down the chute, the air is compressed, and this causes puffs of air to come out the door on each floor as the object passes down the chute. This may result in considerable release of bacteria into the air surrounding the door. Any other situation in which a sudden puff of air is expelled from an area of contamination may release bacteria into the surrounding air.

Although epidemiologists have doubted the importance of air-borne transmission of infectious disease in the general population, this does not necessarily apply to the hospital environment for at least two reasons. First, as pointed out before, there is likely to be a considerably greater concentration of potentially pathogenic microorganisms in the hospital environment, and, second, among hospital patients there are individuals with lowered resistance who are more prone to develop disease after minimal exposure. Thus, it would seem to be imperative that great consideration be given to reducing the risk of air-borne infection.

Tuberculosis. Tuberculosis deserves special comment. Although it has characteristically been referred to as a contact disease, there is increasing evidence that it may be primarily air-borne. Such evidence has been derived in part from studies in animals and from the repeated demonstration of acid-fast organisms in the air in the hospital rooms of tuberculous patients, in laboratories, and in autopsy rooms.

Examination of Personnel

The general measures necessary for prevention of in-hospital infection must be designed to reduce the risk of both direct and indirect transmission of microorganisms from person to person. This requires control of personnel and their practices and control of the environment so as to reduce the microbial population in every way possible. In the succeeding section the measures that should be applied will be discussed.

The pre-employment examination of all personnel should include a chest x-ray or tuberculin test, nose and throat cultures, and a complete stool examination, including bacterial culture and examination for ova and parasites. Ideally at least three stool examinations should be done on successive days. For persons to be employed in nurseries and in pediatric wards the stool culture should include an examination for enteropathogenic *Escherichia coli.* When

shortages of laboratory personnel make it impossible to do three or more stool examinations on all employees, this may be limited to food handlers and to pediatric and nursery personnel. It is important that no person found carrying pathogenic microorganisms in the stool be put on duty in a critical area until the organism is eradicated. It must also be remembered that carriers often either have very few organisms in the stool or shed them only periodically; hence the need for more than a single examination. Especially if *Staphylococcus aureus* or *Streptococcus pyogenes* (Group A) is found, positive findings in nose or throat cultures should be followed up with repeated cultures to determine whether the individual is a carrier.

Following employment, periodic cultural studies on the hospital personnel are desirable. Those assigned to critical areas, such as nurseries, pediatrics and obstetric services, operating rooms, and food-handling areas, should be checked more frequently than those in administrative sections, where contact with patients may not be frequent. Since the situation within a given institution is different from that in any other institution, the frequency and extent of these studies will need to be worked out to satisfy particular needs. The purposes, possible benefits, and limitations of the cultural examination of the hospital personnel must be thoroughly understood before the program is designed.

CARRIERS AND ACTIVE INFECTIONS

The purpose of cultural examination is to discover carriers. It may be desirable to remove carriers from certain critical areas, but this may have only limited value and will depend on circumstances. A somewhat different benefit is the possibility that through these studies the personnel may be kept aware of the dangers involved and of the need for observing caution in their daily activities.

In most cases the carrier state is only transitory, especially in the nose and throat and to some extent in the intestinal tract, and a positive finding on culture signifies only that the organism was present at the time the specimen was taken. In fact at the time the culture is examined, 24 to 48 hours after the specimen is taken, the individual may no longer be carrying the organism. In order to establish the carrier state, it is necessary to do repeated cultures on all those who are positive on the first examination. Therefore, it is useless and impractical to remove individuals from duty merely on the basis of a single positive finding. This is well illustrated if one considers the situation presented by *Staphylococcus aureus* in which on any given day it may be found that over 50 per cent of the personnel in a nursery or other area have positive cultures. If such a group had cultures taken on the succeeding day, undoubtedly several of those previously positive would be negative and several of those originally negative would be positive. Fortunately none of the other well-recognized pathogens induce this carrier rate, with the possible exception of *D. pneumoniae* under most unusual circumstances.

The situation is somewhat different with the enteric pathogens, such as *Entamoeba histolytica, Giardia lamblia, Dientamoeba fragilis,* and the helminths, in which the carrier state tends to persist regularly for a long time. The same situation exists to a varying degree with the enteric bacterial pathogens. Fortunately a much lower percentage of individuals normally have positive findings of enteric pathogens, and their removal from a critical area, such as a nursery, may not result in a serious depletion of personnel. All infected persons should be removed from nurseries and food-handling activities, however, especially those who have *Salmonella, Shigella,* or *Entamoeba histolytica.*

The situation with enteropathogenic *E. coli* requires special comment. Individuals who work in nurseries are evidently exposed to special risks, and a considerable number are likely to be found carrying this organism. The carrier state is not easy to eliminate, and it may be impractical to remove all carriers from duty. Thus, all measures to prevent transmission are necessary.

Epidemiologic investigation of outbreaks of infection have indicated that the person suffering from an active infection is, as a rule, more dangerous than the carrier, undoubtedly because of the likelihood that the number of organisms present in the actively infected individual is much greater than in the carrier. It is thus imperative that individuals with evidence of active infection, i.e., upper respiratory infections, sore throat, ear infections, diarrhea, or infected lesions of the skin or nail bed, be discovered and removed from critical areas at the earliest possible moment. Employees should be removed from duty, and patients should be isolated if at all possible. This is particularly critical in the nursery, since the new-born infant tends to be highly susceptible to certain types of infection, such as staphylococcal disease, moniliasis, and dysentery. Daily inspection of all persons as they come on duty in operating rooms, nurseries, surgical wards, obstetric service, pediatric wards, central supply, and food-handling areas should be made by a competent and responsible individual. Bacteriologic examination is of little or no immediate help in most of these instances, except for diagnosis, since cultural results are not available for 24 to 48 hours and direct smears from lesions may be inconclusive.

It must be remembered that all infections have an incubation period and that this incubation period can be variable. For example, in newborn infants the incubation period for staphylococcal disease may be one to thirty days. During the incubation period of any infection, and especially in the period just prior to the appearance of symptoms, the individual may become highly infectious. Thus, the removal of an individual with clinically evident infection merely takes away a danger that has already been present for an unknown period.

Obviously, then, the discovery of carriers and active cases and their removal from the environment does not eliminate the danger of nosocomial infection. There is no question, however, that these measures will reduce the risk. To further reduce the risk, and since no individual can ever with certainty be adjudged free of potentially pathogenic microorganisms, it is necessary to design and observe procedures to prevent the transmission of organisms from hospital personnel to patient and from patient to personnel. Here it must be re-emphasized that when one speaks of "potentially pathogenic" microorganisms, one refers not only to the well-recognized pathogens but also to those organisms of the normal body flora, which, when implanted in or upon the patient whose resistance has been lowered by operation or disease, may cause serious consequences.

GENERAL MEASURES FOR PREVENTING TRANSMISSION OF MICROORGANISMS IN THE HOSPITAL ENVIRONMENT

Personnel

Since it is impossible to determine with certainty which individual is carrying a potentially pathogenic organism at any given time, and it is only possible to remove permanent carriers of certain organisms and those with active, clinically recognized infections, it is necessary to design techniques that will apply to all personnel within a given service. Services that deal with patients who are likely to be most susceptible to infection need the most stringent regulation.

No person should be allowed in a nursery who has not put on a surgical-type gown supplied from a fresh stock by the nursery. It is also necessary at all times for all nursery personnel to wear surgical caps that cover the hair effectively. This is an important consideration, since the hair is constantly exposed to dust that may be in the atmosphere and may act as a reservoir. Masks must also be worn at all times, and it is important that the type of mask be chosen carefully. The most common type in use is the standard gauze mask consisting of four or more layers of a suitable gauze of such size as to cover the nose and mouth. Its effectiveness is limited to the time it takes for the mask to become saturated with bacteria-containing moisture. When this occurs, the mask becomes a hazard rather than a protection for patient and wearer alike. The time for saturation to occur has been variously estimated from 30 minutes to one or two hours. To be effective the mask must be worn at all times and should be changed at frequent intervals, the length of such intervals depending on the situation. The mask must never be allowed to hang loosely about the neck, since this allows drying to occur and when the mask is replaced over the nose and mouth large numbers of organisms may be sprayed into the atmosphere. Unless used properly, the mask may be an actual danger and may produce a false sense of security. Another important point is that the edges of the mask may rub the skin and loosen flakes that contain bacteria. It may be desirable to use a face cream to prevent this from happening.

Care of the hands is particularly important and special attention should be given to handwashing. Hands must be scrubbed with disinfectant solutions on entry into the nursery, and the washing should be repeated between the handling of patients. Since the area under the fingernails is a good repository for microorganisms and is not easily sterilized by even the most vigorous scrubbing, it is desirable to keep the nails well trimmed at all times.

The following is an example of the need for all persons to observe precautions in order to avoid transmission of microorganisms. Numerous cases of moniliasis were occurring in the nursery of a large private hospital. Investigation by a consultant revealed that the most stringent housekeeping measures were being observed and that the nurses were required to wear caps, masks, and gowns and to wash their hands with disinfectant soap between the handling of each infant. There were no detectable breaks within the nursery. Further investigation, however, revealed that the physicians were allowed free access to the nursery to examine an infant without even washing their hands, if they so chose. As soon as the physicians were supplied with gowns, masks, and adequate handwashing facilities, no further cases of moniliasis occurred.

Recent studies have shown that shoes may become heavily contaminated with microorganisms, and it is important to supply for use by personnel in critical areas special shoes that can be sterilized after use or to provide disposable covers of some type.

The handling of babies within the nursery requires special care. All instruments used for examination should be kept in the nursery and sterilized between the examination of the infants. All blankets and linen must be laundered between uses, and all bassinets must be satisfactorily treated between occupancy. Diapers and other articles of clothing must be discarded into closed containers.

It is also of the utmost importance that formula preparation be completely supervised and in the hands of qualified individuals and that the laboratory be asked to do frequent sterility checks on randomly selected samples. All equipment (autoclaves and refrigerators, for example) used in the preparation of formulas should be checked constantly to make sure they are functioning and being maintained properly.

In other critical areas, such as operating and delivery rooms, much the same principles apply as those for the nursery. The same considerations apply to the wearing of gowns, caps, and masks and the same problems exist with shoes. There are of course certain additional precautions that have to be taken routinely. It is desirable for all personnel to change shoes as well as other articles of clothing between operations. The type of mask worn by operating room personnel has been the subject of much discussion and study. Some recommend the use of a face mask rather than the usual mask, which effectively covers only the nose and mouth. Such a mask has the advantage of preventing skin organisms, especially *S. aureus*, from being released into the atmosphere. There seems to be no general agreement about the best type of mask. All have certain advantages and disadvantages. Some use such substances as glass wool or diatomaceous earth for filtration of the air. Those most effective from the standpoint of filtration may cause difficulties in breathing. It is not within the scope of this book to describe these in detail. Regardless of the type of mask used, its limitations must be recognized.

Although the surgeon and his assistants scrub thoroughly before an operation, this does not necessarily remove all microorganisms from the hands. Organisms may be imbedded in such a way that they cannot be removed and may be brought to the surface with perspiration. Rubber gloves may be nicked during an operation, and bacteria may escape through the resulting break, although the break may be so small as to be invisible. Such an occurrence presents another hazard.

Certain general principles should be followed in all other areas of the hospital. Caps, gowns, and masks should invariably be worn when examining or otherwise dealing with a patient who has a recognized infectious disease. These articles should be discarded before approaching another patient. Hands should be washed with disinfectant solution between visits to all patients, and it must be remembered that the stethoscope represents a fomite capable of transmitting organisms from one patient to the other.

The changing of dressings on surgical incisions, lesions of the skin, and burns requires special comment. Studies have shown that the removal of dressings from infected lesions results in the escape of large numbers of bacteria into the surrounding atmosphere. Such release can be greatly reduced by removing the dressings carefully and placing them immediately in a waxed paper or plastic bag. The bag should be tied shut and discarded at the earliest possible moment in the incinerator. It also will help if the dressing is moistened before removal. All instruments used in such a procedure should also be placed in tightly closed bags and autoclaved before being removed. If a special dressing room is available, it should be used for such procedures and thoroughly cleaned after each use by removing all dressing table covers and washing all surfaces with disinfectant. At least 30 minutes

should elapse between the cleaning of the room and its use for the next patient. All personnel engaged in changing dressings should wear gowns, caps, and masks, and these should be discarded at the end of the operation.

Since the dangers of infection of surgical incisions and burns come not only from the well-recognized pathogens but also from organisms of the normal body flora, it is of the utmost importance that a number of the same general precautions used in the operating room be taken in changing dressings on noninfected wounds. The room in which the change is to be made shall be cleaned thoroughly, and no one shall be allowed in the room for 30 minutes before the procedure is to be done. This is to allow all dust-borne organisms to settle below the critical level. Masks, gowns, caps, and rubber gloves should be worn, and the surgeon and nurse or other assistant should avoid unnecessary motion during the period of removal and replacement of the dressing.

When entering patients' rooms or nurseries to take specimens, laboratory technicians must be required to observe the same precautions as the regular personnel. This is important, since technicians doing clinical microbiologic work are constantly exposed to infectious material, and their hands and clothing may be contaminated as a result.

Laboratory technicians are constantly exposed to infectious agents within their own environment and must observe all possible precautions to avoid infection. All specimens should be treated cautiously, but certain materials are particularly dangerous. Specimens from patients with tuberculosis and cultures of acid-fast organisms must be handled with extreme care. The use of bacteriologic hoods, when available, is absolutely essential. Other organisms, such as those causing psittacosis, tularemia, brucellosis, and typhus, are dangerous. Laboratory-acquired infection probably occurs much more frequently than reports in the literature indicate. Recent extensive studies have revealed the likelihood of producing bacterial aerosols during the course of performing ordinary laboratory procedures. Informative and revealing movies on this subject are available from the Communicable Disease Center of the United States Public Health Service.

Control of the Environment

In a previous section the possible role of air-borne bacteria in hospital-acquired infection was discussed. Studies conducted under a variety of circumstances have indicated that measures designed to reduce the bacterial content of the air have a definite effect on the occurrence of certain types of infectious disease. It seems obvious that dust presents the greatest problem, and it is therefore essential that all measures be taken to reduce dust to a minimum and to avoid stirring up the dust that already exists. Thus, proper housekeeping procedures are of the utmost importance. No dry mopping or dusting should ever be allowed. All floor mopping should be done with a suitable disinfectant in the water, and mop heads should be sterilized and not allowed to dry out in a mop closet. It has been shown that oiling of floors and blankets markedly reduces the hazard, presumably by trapping dust particles and preventing their resuspension in the air.

There are many sources of dust. Clothing, hair, linens, blankets, and drapes are some of the most obvious. Release of dust into the air is caused by many things, including air currents and movement. When equipment, such as lights and x-ray machines, is suspended over a patient during various procedures, there is always the danger that dust will be shaken off onto open lesions. Thus, it is well to keep such lesions protected by a suitable shield if at all possible, since it is not always possible to clean complicated apparatus completely.

Reduction of the number of bacteria in the air can be accomplished in a number of ways that may be considered adjuncts to the routine general housekeeping. Forced air ventilation, which brings in outside air and maintains a positive pressure in an enclosed space, may be used. The effectiveness of such replacement depends upon the amount of air being brought into an area and the length of time required for complete replacement. If forced air ventilation is used, the amount of outside air can be regulated; that is, 25 per cent of new air may be brought in and 75 per cent may be recirculated. In critical areas, such as operating rooms, it is highly desirable that no air be recirculated and that all the air be brought in from the outside. This air can be rendered highly pure by inserting adequate devices, such as air filters and electronic precipitators. Various studies have shown that ultraviolet lighting placed strategically in entryways and in operating rooms is effective in reducing bacterial counts. Ultraviolet rays, however, do not easily penetrate dust particles and droplets nor do they effectively penetrate blankets or linens. Bactericidal aerosols of various types have been used under certain circumstances and are fairly effective in reducing bacterial counts in the air. Such aerosols are limited in their effects on bacteria by the type of material to which the bacteria are attached.

Air replacement and filtration are the most effective means of reducing the bacterial content of the air. Ultraviolet light and aerosols are less effective, and ultraviolet has the possible disadvantage of creating a false sense of security. None of these methods can be substituted for good housekeeping. This cannot be too strongly emphasized.

Recently portable high-intensity ultraviolet light sources have been developed and can be used to assist in the sterilization of rooms occupied by patients with infectious disease who have been discharged. The efficacy of such lights in destroying microorganisms on relatively smooth and otherwise clean surfaces seems to be excellent. They are not effective for mattresses, blankets, and drapes. Such equipment may be used in lieu of scrubbing walls with disinfectant. The routine use of such a light is highly desirable in autopsy rooms after normal cleaning following a postmortem examination of an infected patient.

The sterilization of articles that cannot be autoclaved presents a problem. Such articles as shoes, rubber goods of certain types, and plastics can be sterilized effectively by using either ethylene oxide or beta-propiolactone. There is now available specially constructed equipment for use with ethylene oxide, or one can convert a standard autoclave for the use of this gas. This substance must be handled with care, however, since it is highly toxic. Being a vapor, beta-propiolactone is more effective in certain circumstances than ethylene oxide, since its penetrating capacity is greater. It may be used in the sterilization of certain remotely located areas and rooms, provided these can be sealed tightly to prevent leakage of the vapor. This vapor is highly irritating to the eyes in low concentration; thus, its presence in the atmosphere is detected easily when leakage occurs. Before using either of these agents, personnel should become thoroughly familiar with their properties and dangers.

When an outbreak of disease occurs within any area of the hospital, extensive investigation is indicated. The microbiologist and epidemiologist are bound to play a major role in this investigation and should be consulted at the earliest possible moment, since as time passes it becomes more and more difficult to determine sources of infection. The course the investigation takes and the measures taken to prevent further spread will depend on the type of infection and the situation that exists within the area or institution involved.

One must attempt to determine whether carriers provide a continuous reservoir, whether there is a single source, such as food at a given meal, and whether there are breaks in technique in the day-to-day operation of the area involved. Such information may be derived in a number of ways, such as a careful study of the nature and occurrence of the infections and the isolation of a particular microorganism from a significant number of cases. The complete identification of the microorganism in such a situation is important and can be definitive.

To take a specific example, this is perhaps the only situation in which phage typing of *Staphylococcus aureus* can be justified at the present time. If in outbreaks of staphylococcal disease all or most cases are caused by a single phage type, the search for a source of the outbreak can be narrowed. Once the type of infection is known and its source is located, the procedure for preventing recurrences should become obvious.

The occurrence of such diseases as diphtheria and meningitis in patients occupying beds in an open ward or in other areas where other patients or hospital personnel may have been exposed also presents a problem. Here again the measures taken to prevent exposed or possibly exposed individuals from developing disease will depend on circumstances. The amount of help one can get from cultural studies on contacts is limited, and in most cases perhaps such studies should not be considered. Failure to culture *C. diphtheriae*, *N. meningitidis*, *Streptococcus pyogenes*, or *H. influenzae* from the throat or nasopharynx of an individual exposed to patients with the diseases caused by these organisms does not prove the absence of the organism. One may not have swabbed the correct area, or the organisms may have been so sparse that no colonies appeared on the culture plate. Thus, the measures adopted must be determined on the basis of intimacy of contact and danger of transmission directly or indirectly to others.

The prevention of serum hepatitis is important not only in the hospital but also in doctor's offices and other places where parenteral inoculations are done. Transmission of this disease occurs when the serum of a person carrying the virus is introduced into another person. Because the minutest quantity of serum is capable of transmitting the infection, it is necessary to use extreme caution. Stylets and inoculating needles pick up enough serum to transmit the infection, and cleaning these items with alcohol between use is not sufficient to remove or destroy the virus. Thus, when a technician is doing finger punctures, a new, sterilized stylet must be used for each patient. When doing mass inoculations, such as vaccination or tuberculin testing, separate syringes and needles must be used for each individual. It is not sufficient simply to change the needle and to use the syringe for more than one inoculation. Syringes and needles must be thoroughly cleaned and sterilized between use. Disposable syringes and needles are available and should be used if at all possible. Transfusion is another potent source of transmission, and all possible precautions must be taken in the blood bank. No person with a history of jaundice should ever be used as a donor.

Since serum hepatitis usually has a very long incubation period, the consequences of carelessness may never come to the attention of the offending individual or institution.

TECHNIQUES FOR STERILITY CONTROL AND ENVIRONMENTAL STUDIES

The following section presents the most commonly requested bacteriologic checks on sterility control and environmental studies. In general these are methods that have been found reasonably satisfactory. In some instances other methods may be used if preferred. Whatever the technique chosen for a given determination, the advantages and disadvantages should be known. In some instances standards of acceptance must be set up by experience; in other cases they are prescribed by Public Health Service recommendations. In any case care, accuracy, and promptness must be used in doing and reporting on the studies. New methods for doing some of the tests are being developed constantly and should be adopted after proper evaluation and comparison with the older techniques.

Control of Heat Sterilization Procedures

The control of sterilization is very important since the use of improperly sterilized equipment can lead to disastrous consequences. Detection of faulty sterilization performance can be accomplished by the use of various mechanical devices, indicators, or culture tests. Among the mechanical devices designed to eliminate the inaccuracies of human error in sterilizer operations are recording thermometers, indicating potentiometers, and automatic time-temperature controls. Properly installed, these devices undoubtedly constitute a great safety factor and a substantial saving in personnel time. Such instruments are essential for use of the newer ethylene oxide or beta-propiolactone sterilizers.

The chemical or so-called "telltale" indicators are widely used but seem to suffer from a general lack of uniformity and standardization (Ecker, 1937). Some indicators react to a time-temperature ratio inadequate for sterilization, or the endpoints are not sufficiently clear to permit accurate interpretation of the results (Reddish, 1954, and Walter, 1937). If used, they should be placed in the center of the largest and most closely wrapped package in the load. Papers printed with chemicals that change color when adequate sterilization has presumably been accomplished are useful for some purposes but should never be used as the sole measure of control.

Culture tests are probably the methods of choice in evaluating the effectiveness of a sterilizing process. The only serious disadvantage is the delay in determining the results of culture tests. One procedure is that of Ecker (1937), who used air dried and powdered garden soil made up in paper packages. These packages are inserted in the center of the largest pack and cultured after sterilization has been completed.

Another procedure is to grow large quantities of spores of B. subtilis in a poor nutrient medium. Squares of old linen (about 1 sq. cm.) are spread out in Petri dishes, and a drop of the suspension of the spores is placed on each. They are dried in the incubator and placed in small envelopes. The envelopes are placed in areas where the steam is least likely to penetrate in the autoclave. After sterilization, the envelope is returned to the laboratory, and the piece of linen is removed under careful aseptic precautions and cultured in broth for 24 hours. If the broth is clear at the end of this time, the test is satisfactory.

Various types of bacterial spore suspensions are now available commercially. These obviate the necessity for preparing the suspensions in the individual laboratories and also have the advantage of using strains of bacteria with known thermal resistance. These are generally very satisfactory. One type found to be convenient is a suspension of spores of Bacillus stearothermophilus, which is supplied in sealed ampules containing thioglycollate broth. The ampules are placed in the autoclave in the same way as other controls and simply incubated unopened at 55 to 65° C. Ampules showing no growth after 24 to 48 hours' incubation indicate that sterilization has been properly accomplished, provided the control ampule shows growth.

Sterilization failures are the result of several factors, principally:

1. Lack of basic knowledge concerning the principles of operation and care of sterilizers.

2. Faulty equipment.

3. Failure to understand and observe the regulation of the autoclave so as to maintain a pressure of 15 to 17 lb. equivalent to 121 to 123° C.

4. Incorrect methods of packaging and wrapping material.

5. Carelessness in loading the sterilizer without due consideration of the necessity for providing for free circulation of steam throughout the load or for complete air removal.

6. Failure to time correctly the required period of exposure.

7. Failure to carry out the correct sequence of operations in the sterilizing cycle.

8. Attempts to sterilize materials that are impervious to steam, such as oils and talcum powder.

Bacteriologic Examination of Infant Formulas

A formula unit (filled bottle, nipple, and cap), which has been prepared by terminal sterilization, should be examined daily by the microbiology laboratory as a check for possible bacterial growth during the usual period of handling. This is an important safety precaution that should not be neglected. Examination should be made after the specimen has been refrigerated at +4° C. for 24 hours.

I. RINSE TEST ON ASSEMBLED NIPPLES

Preparation of Media

1. Place 50 ml. of phosphate buffer

solution (pH 7.2) into 6 oz., wide mouth, screw cap bottles. Autoclave for 20 minutes at 121° C.

2. Prepare tubes of violet-red bile agar according to the directions on the bottle of the dehydrated medium. Each tube should contain 12 to 15 ml. of agar. No autoclaving of this medium is necessary and may be detrimental.

3. Prepare tubes of plate count agar (tryptone-glucose extract or milk-protein hydrolysate) according to the directions on the bottle of the dehydrated medium. Each tube should contain 12 to 15 ml. of agar. Sterilize in the autoclave at 121° C. for 20 minutes.

Procedure

1. Remove the nipple from the nursing bottle, using sterile forceps, and place in a bottle of phosphate buffer. Shake bottle and nipple vigorously about 25 times in 7 seconds.

2. Transfer 1.0 ml. of the inoculated dilution water to each of two sterile Petri dishes, using a sterile 1.0 ml. milk dilution pipet.

3. To one dish add a tube of melted violet-red bile agar cooled to 45° C., mix, and allow to solidify. The solidified agar is then covered with 4 to 5 ml. of additional melted medium. Into the other inoculated Petri dish pour the contents of a tube of melted and cooled plate count agar and mix.

4. Invert the Petri dishes after the agar has solidified and incubate at 37° C. The violet-red bile agar plates are incubated for 24 hours and the plate count agar for 48 hours.

5. After the completion of the incubation period examine plates carefully for the presence of colonies, using a Quebec colony counter or similar device. Brick-red colonies at least 0.5 mm. in diameter appearing on the violet-red bile agar plates are considered as coliforms. Count each of these colonies, multiply by 50, and report this number as "coliform count per nipple." The accepted standard is 0 colonies. Count the total number of colonies appearing on the plate count agar dish, multiply by 50, and report as "total colony count per nipple." The maximum bacterial count allowed is less than 25 colonies per nipple.

II. Examination of the Formula

1. Invert the contents of the bottle thoroughly until the contents are homogenous before removing a sample.

2. Using a sterile milk transfer pipet, transfer 1.0 ml. of the formula to the bottom of each of two sterile Petri dishes.

3. Into one Petri dish pour violet-red bile agar and into the other pour plate count agar as described in the rinse test (step 3). Incubate and examine Petri dishes as explained previously (step 4) and report as "coliform count per ml." and "total colony count per ml." of formula. The accepted bacterial standard for formula is 0 coliform organisms and less than 25 colonies per ml.

Testing for Sterility of Blood and Plasma from the Blood Bank

Plasma must be checked carefully to assure freedom from bacterial contamination. Bank blood is occasionally contaminated, even under the best of conditions, and has been shown to have caused serious or even fatal transfusion reactions.

Plasma

1. Inoculate three tubes of fluid thioglycollate medium (conforming to N.I.H. specifications) with a sample of plasma, using sterile equipment and careful technique. The volume of broth used should be at least 15 times the volume of the inoculum. Incubate the broth as follows: one tube at 37° C., one at room temperature (22 to 25° C.), and one at refrigerator temperature (5 to 10° C.).

2. Examine cultures daily for evidence of growth for at least ten days. If the test material renders the medium so turbid that bacterial growth cannot be recognized easily, transfers should be made to fresh tubes of medium at the end of three days of incubation. Gram stains and subcultures should be made if any suspicion of growth appears at the end of the incubation period. Any organism isolated should be identified as completely as possible.

Bank Blood

The organisms most likely to be found in blood that has been contaminated and their optimal temperature requirements for growth are:

Pseudomonas sp. (2 to 30° C.)

Achromobacter sp. (20 to 37° C.)

Coliform and paracolon bacilli (2 to 37° C.)

Aerobic and anaerobic diphtheroids (20 to 37° C.)

Staphylococci (30 to 37° C.)

Consequently cultures should be made at three different temperatures as for plasma.

If only one temperature is used, 32° C. is preferable.

1. Inoculate 1 ml. in each of three tubes of thioglycollate medium and add 1 ml. to the bottom of three Petri dishes. Add tubes of melted and cooled infusion or thioglycollate agar and mix with the blood. At the same time make a gram stain of the blood.

2. The tubes and plates are incubated for at least ten days before discarding as negative. Incubate the media and examine as described previously for plasma. Identify as fully as possible any organism isolated.

Bacteriologic Examination of Food Utensils

Bacteriologic examination of swabs taken from washed utensils is an important check on the adequacy of dishwashing techniques and apparatus. The technique consists of swabbing the essential surface of the utensils to be examined, immersing the swab in diluting fluid, and culturing by standard procedures to determine total numbers of bacteria and coliforms.

Technique. A sterile, absorbent cotton swab is dipped in sterile buffered distilled water; the excess fluid is squeezed out against the side of the container and then rubbed briskly over the whole of the appropriate areas:

The inner surface of plates and bowls that would come in contact with food over an area of approximately 4 square inches.

The inner and outer surfaces of cups, mugs, and glasses to a depth of 0.5 cm. below the rim.

The inner and outer surfaces of spoons and knives.

The back and front surfaces and between the tines of forks.

Each swab is used for five similar articles. Care should be taken to prevent contamination by handling during sampling.

A greater recovery of organisms can be obtained if calcium alginate swabs are used rather than cotton (Higgins, 1950). The advantages are that cotton frequently contains substances that are toxic for the more fastidious strains of bacteria and also that the alginate swabs can be dissolved completely in buffered water containing sodium hexametaphosphate $(NaPO_3)_6$. In this way all the bacteria contained in the swab are liberated into the solution.

If cotton swabs have been used, the swab is broken off the wooden stick with a sterile forceps and allowed to drop into a screw cap jar containing 10 ml. of swabbing solution.* The containers must be kept cold and cultured within four hours. The bottle is shaken vigorously about 50 times, and 1 ml. of buffered water is added to the bottom of each Petri dish, and a tube of 10 ml. melted and cooled plate count agar is added (see p. 819). The plates are incubated for 48 hours at 37° C. The results are reported as the average plate counts of organisms removed per utensil examined.

If the alginate swabs are used, two swabs should be employed for each test, one being moistened in buffered water before use and the other kept dry. The surfaces of five articles are rubbed, first with the moistened swab and then with the dry one. Both swabs are then broken off into buffered water solution. One milliliter of sterile 10 per cent sodium metaphosphate is then added, and the bottle is shaken until both swabs have dissolved. Plate counts are then done on the solutions as described previously. If desired, pour plates can be made with violet-red bile agar for coliforms or with blood agar for pyogenic cocci.

The U.S. Public Health Service standard, based on the swabbing and standard plate count technique, allows a maximum of 100 colonies per utensil cultured. Higher counts are presumptive evidence of inadequate cleansing or antibacterial treatment or of recontamination by handling or during storage. Judgment should be made on the basis of repeated sampling.

Cultures of the Environment for Staphylococci

For smooth, impervious surfaces (dressing tables, toilet seats, and oxygen tents): Take a sterile swab, moisten with sterile saline or broth, and swab an area as wide as possible, e.g., about 2 square feet of a table top or an entire toilet seat. Streak swabs on blood agar plates, and streak heavily on mannitol salt agar or other suitable medium.

For fabrics (bedding, curtains, gowns): Uncover Petri dish of mannitol salt, phenolphthalein phosphate, fibrinogen, or similar selective medium or blood agar. Place the agar surface towards the fabric and sweep the Petri dish rapidly back and forth. Cover dish and incubate.

* To 34 gm. KH_2PO_4 in 500 ml. H_2O add 175 ml. of N/1 NaOH and dilute to 1 liter with distilled water. Adjust pH to 7.2. Add 1 ml. of this stock solution to 800 ml. of distilled water. If the material to be swabbed is likely to contain residual chlorine, add 4 ml. of N/1 sodium thiosulfate to the 1 ml. of stock solution before diluting it to 800 ml.

For dressings and gauze: Collect sample in suitable container. Drop sample in broth, shake well, and streak the broth heavily on mannitol salt agar and blood agar.

For equipment and instruments: Rub sterile swab over appropriate surfaces. Tubular instruments, such as bronchoscopes, catheters, or tracheotomy tubes, are best cultured by rinsing sterile broth through the lumen of the instrument and into a sterile container. Incubate broth overnight and then streak on mannitol salt or similar medium.

For liquids, medicaments, ointments, or water used for oxygen washing in resuscitators: Drop sample into two tubes of broth, shake well, and allow to settle. Streak broth heavily on a mannitol salt agar plate. The other broth is incubated at 37° C. overnight and then streaked on mannitol salt agar. If disinfectants, preservatives, or other inhibitory substances are suspected to be present in any of these materials, large volumes of broth or fluid thioglycollate medium should be used.

For dust: Expose numerous Petri dishes containing suitable agar - phenolphthalein phosphate, fibrinogen, mannitol salt, or Staphylococcus Medium 110 in various locations in the area under investigation. The optimal time of exposure will vary with the air currents, activity in the area, and humidity and can best be determined by experience. Floor dust and vacuum sweepings are collected in sterile containers and cultured as for liquids. More elaborate air and dust sampling devices are available, but these are intended for more quantitative

studies than are generally required in a hospital environment (Fig. 22–2).

Blood agar, phenolphthalein phosphate, and fibrinogen agar are generally incubated for 24 hours, and mannitol salt and Staphylococcus Medium 110 for 48 hours in order for staphylococci to appear on these media and for further *in vitro* studies for virulence to be performed (see p. 626).

REFERENCES

1. Anderson, R. E., Steun, L., Moss, M. L., and Gross, N. A.: Potential infectious hazards of common bacteriological techniques. J. Bact., 64:473–481, 1952.
2. Barnes, J., Pace, W. G., Trump, D. S., and Ellison, E. H.: Prophylactic postoperative antibiotics. A.M.A. Arch. of Surg., 79:190–196, 1959.
3. Bourdillon, R. B., and Colebrook, L.: Air hygiene in dressing rooms for burns or major wounds. Lancet, 1:601–605, 1946.
4. Braude, A. I., Carey, F. J., and Simienski, J.: Studies of bacterial transfusion reactions from refrigerated blood: The properties of cold-growing bacteria. J. Clin. Invest., 34:311–325, 1955.
5. Brown, J. W.: Hygiene and education within hospitals to prevent staphylococci infections. J.A.M.A., 166:1185–1191, 1958.
6. Dawson, F. W., Jansen, R. J., and Hoffman, R. K.: Virucidal activity of β-propiolactone vapor. II. Effect on the etiological agents of smallpox, yellow fever, psittacosis and Q fever. Appl. Microb., 8:39–41, 1960.
7. Ecker, E. E.: Sterilization based on temperature attained and time rates. Mod. Hosp., 48:92–98, 1937.
8. Finland, M., and Jones, W. F.: Staphylococcal infections currently encountered in a large municipal hospital; Some problems in evaluating antimicrobial therapy in such infections. Ann. N.Y. Acad. Sc., 65:191–205, 1956.
9. Fleck, A. C., Jr., and Klein, J. O.: The epidemiology and investigation of hospital-acquired staphylococcal disease in newborn infants. Pediatrics, 24:1102–1107, 1959.
10. Higgins, M.: A comparison of the recovery rate of organisms from cotton wool and calcium alginate swabs. Month. Bull. Min. Health, 9:50–51, 1950.
11. Hoffman, R. K., and Warshowsky, B.: Beta-propiolactone vapor as a disinfectant. Appl. Microb., 6:358–362, 1958.
12. Jellard, J.: Umbilical cord as reservoir of infection in a maternity hospital. Brit. M. J., 1:925–928, 1957.
13. Kilpatrick, C. F.: To organize control of cross-infections: Strengthen the role of the hospital housekeeper. Modern Sanit. & Bldg. Mainten., 10:12–14, 45–47, 1958.
14. Krugman, S., and Ward, R.: Air sterilization in an infant's ward. Effect of triethylene glycol vapor and dust-suppression measures on the respiratory cross-infection rate. J.A.M.A., 145:775–780, 1951.
15. Langmuir, A. D.: Airborne infection. In Rosenau's Preventive Medicine and Public Health. 8th Ed. New York, Appleton-Century-Crofts, 1956, ch. 2, pp. 152–167.

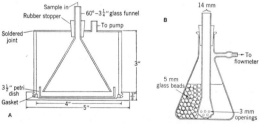

Figure 22–2. Two devices employed for the microbiologic sampling of air. *A.,* The funnel device. The air sample is drawn in through the stem of the funnel, and microorganisms become impinged on the agar surface of the medium contained in the Petri dish. (From H. de Buy *et al.:* Public Health Reports, Supplement 184, 1945.) *B.,* The bead-bubbler device. The air sample is drawn through small openings of a tube extended beneath the surface of beads covered with a liquid. Organisms become "trapped" in this liquid, which is subsequently plated or cultured. (From Wheeler *et al.:* Science, 94:445, 1941.)

16. Letourneau, C. V.: Nosocomial infections. II, III. Hospital Manag., 83:52–57, 1958.

17. Loosli, C. G., and Robertson, O. H.: Recent studies on the control of dust-borne bacteria by treatment of floors and bedclothes with oil. Am. J. Med. Sc., 209:166–172, 1958.

18. MacDonald, K.: A quantitative bacterial analysis of the air of operating and delivery rooms and related areas of a general hospital. Am. J. Hyg., 31:74–84, 1940.

19. Moulton, F. R.: Aerobiology. Washington, D.C., Am. Assn. Adv. Sci. Pub. #17, 1942.

20. Murray, W. A.: Evaluation of a phone survey in an outbreak of staphylococcal infection in a hospital nursery for the newborn. Am. J. Publ. Hlth., 48:310–318, 1958.

21. Pittman, M.: A study of bacteria implicated in transfusion reactions of bacteria isolated from blood products. J. Lab. & Clin. Med., 42:273–288, 1953.

22. Puck, T. T., Robertson, O. H., Wise, H., Loosli, C. G., and Lemon, H. M.: The oil treatment of bedclothes for the control of dust-borne infection. I. Principles underlying the development and use of a satisfactory oil-in-water emulsion. Am. J. Hyg., 43:91–104, 1946.

23. Ravenholt, O. H., Baker, E. F., Jr., Wysham, D. N., and Giedt, W. K.: Eliminating blankets as an infection source. Hospitals, 32:75–80, 1958.

24. Ravenholt, R. T., and Ravenholt, O. H.: Staph-

ylococcal infections in the hospital and community. Am. J. Publ. Hlth., 48:277–287, 1958.

25. Recommended procedures for laboratory investigation of hospital acquired staphylococcus disease. U.S. Dept. of Health, Educ. & Welfare, U.S. Publ. Health Service, Comm. Dis. Center, Atlanta, Ga., Sept., 1958.

26. Reddish, G. F.: Antiseptics, Disinfectants, Fungicides, and Sterilization. Philadelphia, Lea & Febiger, 2nd ed., 1957.

27. Skeehan, R. A., Jr., King, J. A., Jr., and Kaye, S.: Ethylene oxide sterilization in ophthalmology. Am. J. Ophthalm., 42:424–430, 1956.

28. Stedman, R. L., and Kravitz, E.: Recent studies in surface disinfection. Pub. Hlth. Rep., 71:1057–1064, 1956.

29. Sterility requirements for biological products. Federal Register, 24(190):7835, Sept. 29, 1959.

30. Stokes, E. J. Clinical Bacteriology. London, Edward Arnold, Ltd., 1955, pp. 218–249.

31. Tiedeman, W. D.: A proposed method for control of food utensil sanitation. Am. J. Publ. Hlth., 34:255–258, 1944.

32. Walter, C. W.: Bacteriology of the bedside carafe. New Engl. J. Med., 259:1198–1202, 1958.

33. Walter, C. W.: Evaluation of sterilizer indicators. Surgery, 2:585–589, 1937.

34. Wells, W. F.: Airborne Contagion and Air Hygiene. Cambridge, Mass., Harvard University Press, 1955.

Chapter 23

Serodiagnostic Tests for Syphilis

By JAMES G. SHAFFER, Sc.D., *and* MILTON GOLDIN, M.S.

The purpose of all serologic tests for syphilis is to detect in the serum of patients with this disease antibodies against *Treponema pallidum* or antibody-like substances known as "reagins." The first serologic test for syphilis was developed in 1906 by Wassermann and his colleagues, who applied the recently discovered principles of complement fixation. Tests used at the present time are of three main types—those based on the complement-fixation reaction, those based on the principle of flocculation, and those intended to detect what appear to be specific antitreponemal antibodies, utilizing living or dead *T. pallidum* suspensions.

GENERAL PRINCIPLES

The first principle to keep in mind in relation to serodiagnostic tests for syphilis is that the accepted procedures carefully worked out by the authors of the respective tests must be adhered to rigidly and that no arbitrary changes in technique are to be introduced. The techniques described in this chapter follow in detail the latest presentations by the originators of each test as described in the manual, "Serologic Tests for Syphilis" (1959).

Although serologic tests for syphilis are not absolutely specific and some serums and spinal fluids may react positively in one test and negatively in another, interpretation of conflicting serologic results in terms of diagnosis or prognosis should not be made by the laboratory technician. These decisions are within the province of the physician. Valid serologic test findings are obtained when standardized reagents and adequate controls are used, when techniques recommended for each method are adhered to strictly, and when results are reported as specified for each procedure.

The technician should test every new lot of a reagent in parallel with one that has been tried and is being used and that has been shown to possess acceptable reactivity before the new lot of the reagent is placed in routine use. This procedure is recommended regardless of the source from which the new reagent is obtained. Other factors to be considered in the control of serologic tests are discussed in the following sections.

Equipment

Water-bath temperatures should be checked each time the baths are used. The refrigerator temperature should be checked daily with a thermometer placed in the part of the refrigerator occupied by the test racks. Temperature should also be noted when the refrigerator is first opened in the morning if complement-fixation tests (16-to-18 hour fixation) are stored within.

The speeds of shaking and rotating machines should be checked by the technician each time they are used, and marked variations from prescribed speeds should not be tolerated.

Centrifuges should be equipped with tachometers so that speeds may be checked and controlled. The inside of centrifuges should be cleaned frequently to prevent dust particles from being blown into specimens.

Automatic pipetting machines should be checked daily for correct volume delivery. Should readjustment be found necessary, a volume of 25 or 50 deliveries may be collected and measured in a certified graduated cylinder.

Glassware

Only chemically clean glassware should be used. Tubes and pipets that have a film of organic material should be submerged in dichromate cleaning solution.* Rinsing of the acid or any other cleaning solution must be thorough and sufficient to remove all traces of the solution. Glassware that is etched, scratched, or damaged to a degree that interferes with its use should be discarded.

New 2×3 inch flat glass slides should be cleaned with Bon Ami, which is removed with a soft cloth after drying. Previously used paraffin-ringed slides should first be freed of paraffin, washed with soap or detergent, rinsed free of cleaning compound, and then treated as new slides. Slides should be handled by the edges while cleaning to prevent greasy fingerprints on the testing surfaces. Serums will spread within the circles on clean slides. Failure of the serums to spread is an indication that the slide is unclean and therefore should not be used.

Reagents

Antigens. All the nontreponemal tests for syphilis described herein utilize cardiolipin-lecithin antigens with the exception of the Kahn procedures. Cardiolipin is a non-nitrogenous phospholipid, which is thought to be the active principle of the beef heart extracts used originally in the preparation of antigen. As a rule it is more practical and economical to purchase these antigens rather than to attempt to prepare them individually. Each new lot of antigen should be tested in parallel with one that is being used and should produce reactions in qualitative and quantitative tests with serum and spinal fluid that are comparable with those obtained with a standard antigen. Parallel testing should be carried out on more than one day, and the differences in reactivity between the two antigens being tested should not be greater than those obtained with duplicate emulsions of the standard antigen.

It is of paramount importance that anti-

gen be stored at its recommended temperature and that the diluted antigen be used only as long as is recommended.

The standardization and preparation of the antigens for the respective tests are not described here; full descriptions of this procedure will be found in the references.

Distilled Water. Distilled water of poor quality may result from failure to clean the still or the bottle trap as frequently as needed. The kind of tap water used and the number of hours per day that the still is in operation will determine the frequency of cleaning. When a bottle or tank trap is attached to the water still, attention should also be given to keeping this section clean.

Distilled water will absorb ions of alkaline or acid gases present in the laboratory and may in this way become unsatisfactory for use in serologic tests. For this reason the use of freshly distilled water is recommended.

Saline solutions and distilled water, if stored, should be placed in hard-glass containers that are tightly stoppered to avoid changes owing to ion transfer from the glass or from absorption from the air.

Saline Solutions. Sodium chloride for use in saline solutions should be dried in the hot-air oven for 30 minutes at 160° to 180° C. to remove absorbed moisture. Heating at higher temperatures should be avoided, since it may result in decomposition of the salt. The sodium chloride may then be weighed and stored in corked test tubes to avoid daily weighing. Dissolve salts in distilled water. Shake the solution thoroughly to assure complete mixing.

Chemicals. Chemicals, such as sodium chloride and cholesterol, should be of reagent quality and should meet the specifications of the technique of the procedure. Invalid results may be obtained when substandard chemicals are employed. The reagent containers should be tightly covered and properly stored.

Reporting Results of Serologic Tests

The use of new terminology for reporting results of serologic tests for syphilis was recommended in the 1953 report of the National Advisory Serology Council to the Surgeon General of the U.S. Public Health Service. The new system provides uniformity of reporting and avoids diagnostic connotations. In accordance with these recommendations the terms *reactive,* *weakly reactive,* and *nonreactive* are being

---

* Concentrated sulfuric acid, 252 ml. Water, 300 ml. Sodium dichromate, 60 gm. Mix water and dichromate until dissolved. Add sulfuric acid cautiously, stirring constantly.

substituted for the terms *positive, weakly positive* or *doubtful,* and *negative* in reporting test results.

In reporting results of quantitative reactions, it is recommended that the endpoint titer be reported in terms of the greatest dilution in which the tested specimen produces a reactive (positive) result and that the term *dils,* a contraction of the word dilution, be used to identify these dilution reactivity endpoints. By this means reactions of identical intensity will receive the same report in terms of dils when different testing methods are employed.

Control of Test Performance

Some of the factors that influence test performance have already been described. In addition inter- and intralaboratory checks are strongly recommended.

These include the daily use of controls of graded reactivity, periodic check readings to maintain uniform reading levels among the laboratory personnel, and comparison of results obtained on control serums with those of a reference laboratory.

Serum controls should be included in each run of all serum testing procedures. With slide flocculation tests each preparation of antigen emulsion should first be examined with these control serums. In other instances these controls should be included in the test run. The results obtained with the controls should reproduce an established pattern of reactivity. In the event that these results are not acceptable, further testing should be delayed until the optimal reactivity has been reestablished.

Serum controls of graded reactivity may be prepared in the following manner:

1. Collect serums giving reactive (not weakly reactive) reactions in daily test runs in containers suitable for storage by freezing. Collect nonreactive serums in a similar manner. Do not include anticomplementary serums if control serum is to be used in complement-fixation tests.

2. Store the pooled serums in a deep-freeze unit or in the freezing compartment of a refrigerator.

3. When control serums are to be prepared, allow the frozen serums to thaw at room temperature or in the 37° C. water bath.

4. Filter the pools of serums through a Seitz filter to remove particles.

5. Measure the serum in each pool and add 1 mg. of Merthiolate powder* for each milliliter of serum.

6. Prepare preliminary dilutions of re-

* Eli Lilly and Co., Indianapolis, Indiana.

Table 23–1. **Results Obtained with Serum Dilutions Prepared for Use as Daily Controls**

DILUTIONS	REACTIVE SERUM (ML.)	NONREACTIVE SERUM (ML.)	KAHN TEST	VDRL SLIDE TEST	KLINE TEST	MAZZINI TEST	HINTON TEST	KOLMER TEST
1	1.0	1.0	R4+	R	R4+	R4+	R	R4+
2	0.8	1.2	R4+	R	R4+	R4+	R	R4+
3	0.7	1.3	R4+	R	R4+	R4+	R	R4+
4	0.6	1.4	R3+	R	R4+	R4+	R	R4+
5	0.5	1.5	R2+	R	R3+	R4+	R	R4+
6	0.4	1.6	WR1+	R	R2+	R4+	R	R3+
7	0.3	1.7	WR ±	WR	WR1+	R3+	R	R2+
8	0.2	1.8	N	WR	WR1+	WR1+	WR	WR ±
9	0.1	1.9	N	N	N	N	N	N
10	0.0	2.0	N	N	N	N	N	N

R = Reactive   WR = Weakly Reactive   N = Nonreactive

Using the results indicated in Table 23–1, a set of dilutions suitable for Kahn, VDRL slide, and Kolmer tests might be selected as follows:

Control 1 — Dilution 2
Control 2 — Dilution 5
Control 3 — Dilution 7
Control 4 — Nonreactive pool
OR

If the tests to be performed included the VDRL slide, Mazzini, and Hinton tests, a set of dilutions might be selected as follows:

Control 1 — Dilution 2
Control 2 — Dilution 6
Control 3 — Dilution 8
Control 4 — Nonreactive pool

active serum in nonreactive serum. Serial twofold dilutions may be used, or a scheme similar to the one outlined in Table 23–1 may be selected.

7. Perform all the tests regularly employed in the laboratory on these serum dilutions and record the results.

8. Select for control serums a dilution that is reactive or 4+ in all tests and one or more dilutions that show intermediate reactivity. If several tests are employed, two or more dilutions may be required to obtain critical readings in all tests.

9. Calculate the amount of each serum dilution to be prepared. This will be determined by the quantity needed for each day's testing, the period of time during which the controls will be used, and the type of storage facilities available. Control serums, properly stoppered, may be stored for approximately 60 days in a deep-freeze unit, 30 days in the freezing compartment of a refrigerator, and 7 to 10 days in a liquid state in a refrigerator.

10. Prepare the calculated volumes of each serum dilution and mix thoroughly.

11. Retest each serum mixture in all the tests in which it is to be used as a control.

12. Dispense aliquots of each dilution sufficient for one testing period into properly labeled tubes and stopper tightly with paraffin-coated corks. Arrange in sets and refrigerate. After 24 hours reset the corks and seal with plastic seals or adhesive tape as further protection against evaporation and place in freezer.

13. For daily use remove one set of controls from storage, thaw at room temperature, mix thoroughly, centrifuge, decant serum, and heat for 30 minutes at 56° C.

14. New lots of control serums should be tested in parallel with the one currently in use. The pattern of reactivity should be established before they are placed into routine use.

Collection and Handling of Specimens

Blood should be drawn before meals and placed in a clean, dry test tube. Since alcohol in the blood diminishes the intensity of reaction, 24 hours should be allowed to elapse after a period of alcoholic inebriation before taking the specimen. If the specimen is to be mailed, the equipment used should be sterile; the blood is allowed to clot at room temperature and placed in the refrigerator until ready to be tested. The clot is separated from the wall of the tube with a wooden applicator stick and the

tubes centrifuged for 10 to 15 minutes at 1800 r.p.m. The serum is separated from the clots with capillary pipets into properly labeled test tubes. Careful labeling and handling of specimens are essential to prevent errors.

For children or when venipunctures cannot be performed, sufficient blood may be obtained by fingertip puncture. A capillary tube, such as that used in microchemical procedures, can be used. The free end is sealed in a flame, the clot broken with a fine wire, and the tube centrifuged for a few minutes. Sufficient serum can then be decanted with a micropipet for a Kline or VDRL (Venereal Disease Research Laboratory) or similar test.

The serum must be clear and free of suspended particles or red cells. Excessive hemolysis can cause anticomplementary reactions in the complement-fixation tests. Excessive chyle or bile may interfere with reading the reactions.

Serum is inactivated before testing to remove the native complement, to destroy certain heat-labile anticomplementary substances that may be present, and to stabilize the serologic properties of the serum. This is done by heating the serum in the water bath at 56° C. for 30 minutes. Previously heated serum must be reheated at 56° C. for 5 minutes. Alternatively the serum may be heated for 4 minutes at 61 to 62° C., but this procedure is not ordinarily recommended because of the danger of coagulating the serum.

Spinal fluid does not usually require inactivation, but if it contains gross blood or is older than three days, it is necessary to heat for 15 minutes at 56° C.

FALSE POSITIVE SEROLOGIC TESTS FOR SYPHILIS

Although the serologic tests now in use have a high degree of specificity, a positive reaction does not necessarily prove that the patient has syphilis but merely indicates that, by the procedure used, a reagin or substance reacting with the antigen is present.

Even with the so-called "specific" treponemal tests reactions are occasionally obtained in individuals who have no evidence whatever of syphilitic infection, either past or present. The problem of differentiating a true positive from a false positive reaction can be exceedingly complex, and while the treponemal tests have been of great value, much clarification is still needed.

Table 23–2. Approximate Percentage of False Positive and Doubtful Reactions in Nonsyphilitic Conditions*

CONDITION	PER CENT
Malaria	90–100
Leprosy	60
D.P.T. immunization in children	20
Infectious mononucleosis	20
Disseminated lupus erythematosus	16–20
Lymphogranuloma venereum	20
Vaccinia	20
Infectious hepatitis	10
Periarteritis nodosa	10
Rheumatoid arthritis	5–7
Rheumatic fever	5–6
Pnumococcal pneumonia	2–5
Common cold, pregnancy, blood loss	> 1

* After Moore and Mohr (1952).

False positives can be grouped into three main categories: those owing to technical errors, which can be controlled easily by close adherence to the accepted procedure, those owing to intercurrent diseases or infections, and those found in certain individuals who by every measurable standard have no disease entity that could account for the reactions obtained. These are the so-called "biologic reactors" and are the most perplexing group.

It has been known for a long time that a wide variety of conditions unrelated to syphilis can give false positive reactions. Table 23–2 lists the approximate percentage of false positive serologic tests for syphilis obtained in certain conditions.

Infants showing positive serologic reactions owing to passive transfer of reagin from syphilitic mothers usually show negative reactions within four months after birth.

If serologic reactions are encountered that are believed to be false positives, it is necessary to check all reagents carefully, to repeat the tests using other techniques, and to repeat the tests at three-to-six-month intervals, since positive reactions owing to acute diseases usually disappear spontaneously within this period. If the positive reactions persist and no underlying disease, such as collagen disease or malaria, can be found, a treponemal test may be of great value in differentiating between a true and a false positive (p. 877).

The problems of the biologic false positive reactions emphasized a fact that is often forgotten, namely, that the most the serologic technician can be expected to do is to conduct the tests precisely as described by the author-serologists. The final decision whether a positive reaction is due to syphilis is the responsibility of the physician.

FLOCCULATION TESTS FOR SYPHILIS

The visible reaction in the flocculation tests is the result of the combination of the reagin in the serum of the patient with components of the antigen, namely, particles of lipid-coated cholesterol with or without cardiolipin. The sensitized particles are precipitated by the electrolyte present. The function of the cholesterol is to serve as centers of adsorption for the tissue lipid

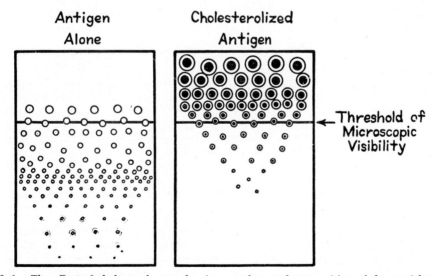

Figure 23–1. The effect of cholesterol upon the size, number, and composition of the particles in diluted antigen. (From Eagle: The Laboratory Diagnosis of Syphilis. Courtesy of C. V. Mosby Co.)

extracts resulting in the formation of larger particles, which, when coated with reagin, give macroscopically visible results (Fig. 23–1).

All the tests to be described in this section are fundamentally similar, differing mainly in the preparation of cholesterol, lecithin, and cardiolipin in the antigen and the technical details. Each of the following tests has certain advantages and disadvantages, and all give reliable results, provided the recommended techniques are adhered to strictly and standardized reagents and controls are used.

Hinton Tests

Only the standard Hinton qualitative test with serum is described here. Other Hinton tests are described in the manual, "Serologic Tests for Syphilis" (1959), pp. 16 to 19.

Equipment

Kahn shaking machine (275 to 285 oscillations per minute, with $1\frac{1}{2}$ inch stroke).

Glassware

1. Test tubes, $11\frac{1}{4} \times 100$ mm. outside dimensions, hereafter called Hinton tubes.
2. Flasks, Erlenmeyer, 125 ml. or 250 ml. capacity, with inverted V-shaped ridge in bottom that produces two semicircular compartments (Hinton flasks).

REAGENTS

1. Hinton indicator. Stock indicator for this test is an alcoholic solution containing 0.0884 per cent cardiolipin, 0.6188 per cent purified lecithin, and 0.24 per cent cholesterol. Each lot of antigen must be serologically standardized by proper comparison with an antigen of known reactivity.
2. 5 per cent sodium chloride solution.
   a. Weigh 5 gm. of previously dried sodium chloride (A.C.S.).
   b. Add the sodium chloride to 100 ml. of distilled water and heat solution in an autoclave at 15 pounds pressure for 15 minutes.
   c. Store saline solution in glass-stopper bottles at room temperature.
3. 0.85 per cent sodium chloride solution. Add the required amount (8.5 gm. to each liter) of dried sodium chloride to distilled water. This solution need not be heated and should be prepared on the day used.
4. 50 per cent solution of glycerin. Mix equal volumes of Baker and Adamson's glycerin* (reagent grade) and distilled water. This solution keeps indefinitely.

PREPARATION OF SERUMS

1. Remove serums from clots by centrifuging and pipetting or decanting.
2. Heat the serums in the 56° C. water bath for 30 minutes. Serums should not be heated before the day of testing. If it is necessary to retest a specimen, use serum freshly separated from the clot, if available. Otherwise reheat serum at 56° C. for ten minutes.

PREPARATION OF GLYCERINATED HINTON INDICATOR

1. Pipet 0.8 part of 5 per cent sodium chloride solution into one compartment of a Hinton flask.
2. Pipet one part of Hinton stock indicator into the other compartment of the flask. Care should be taken in pipetting the stock indicator solution into the flask to avoid premature mixing of the solutions. *Note:* Not less than 1 ml. nor more than 5 ml. of Hinton indicator should be mixed at one time.
3. Mix contents by shaking the flask rapidly from side to side for exactly one minute.
4. Let the mixture stand for exactly five minutes.
5. Add 13.2 parts of 5 per cent sodium solution and shake flask vigorously.
6. Add 15 parts of 50 per cent glycerin solution and shake flask until the suspension is homogeneous.
7. Store in a glass-stopper bottle or flask in the refrigerator. This suspension, referred to as glycerinated indicator solution, remains usable for at least three weeks.

HINTON STANDARD QUALITATIVE TEST WITH SERUM

1. Arrange Hinton tubes in suitable racks so that there is one tube for each serum to be tested (and also for control serums of graded reactivity). Number tubes to correspond to the identifying numbers of serums.
2. Pipet 0.5 ml. of each heated serum into its corresponding tube. *Note:* Occasionally very strongly reactive serums will elicit a nonreactive reaction when 0.5 ml. of serum is employed as the testing quantity. When this type of reaction is suspected, 0.1 ml. of serum should also be tested in addition to the 0.5 ml. quantity of serum.

* General Chemical Division, Allied Chemical and Dye Corp., New York, N.Y.

3. Pipet 0.5 ml. of the glycerinated Hinton indicator into each serum tube. *Note:* The flask containing glycerinated Hinton indicator should be shaken when taken from refrigerator. Remove the quantity of glycerinated indicator needed and return the flask to cold storage immediately.

4. Shake rack of tubes by hand until visual inspection indicates that serums and glycerinated indicator are well mixed.

5. Shake rack of tubes on Kahn shaking machine for five minutes.

6. Remove the rack from the shaking machine and place in 37° C. water bath for 16 hours. *Note:* The water bath must be uncovered during this period, and temperature should be maintained at 37° C. ± 1°.

READING AND REPORTING TEST RESULTS

1. Place a shaded cylindrical fluorescent (daylight) lamp 18 or more inches long in front of a darkened background. The lamp tube should be slightly above the level of the eyes.

2. Remove each tube from the rack carefully without disturbing the contents.

3. Hold the tube at a 45° angle at eye level close to lamp shade.

4. Look for clarification of the fluid and for presence of a ring of white flakes or white coarse granules at the meniscus.

5. Lift the tilted tube slightly above eye level and look through it toward the darkened background to determine the presence of flocculation.

6. Report findings as follows:

Reactive.	White flakes or white coarse granules at the meniscus and definite flocculation when tube is shaken.
Nonreactive.	Absence of ring or band of floccules and no flocculation or granularity when tube is gently shaken. Hemolyzed or bacterially contaminated serums frequently produce a whitish ring, which is strongly adherent to the tube.

7. Centrifuge at 2000 r.p.m. for five minutes all tubes in which clearcut nonreactive or reactive readings cannot be made.

8. Remove tubes from centrifuge and read reactions as described previously.

9. Report findings as follows:

Weakly Reactive.	Those reactions demonstrating coarse granulation at the meniscus and definite flocculation when tube is gently shaken.
Nonreactive.	All specimens failing to react

	as described under "Weakly Reactive" above.
Unsatisfactory.	Those specimens hemolyzed or bacterially contaminated unless the result is strongly Reactive.

Kahn Tests

Equipment
1. Kahn test tube racks.
2. Racks for vials.
3. Kahn shaking machine (275 to 285 oscillations per minute with a stroke of 1½ inch).
4. Microscope mirror.
5. Gooseneck-type lamp with blue inside-frosted bulb or fluorescent lamp with two tubes.

Glassware
1. Test tubes, Kahn, 12 × 75 mm., outside dimensions.
2. Pipets, Kahn, for antigen suspension, to deliver 0.25 ml., graduated in 0.0125 ml.
3. Vials, Kahn antigen suspension, with flat bottom, 15 × 55 mm. inside diameter.
4. Syringe, tuberculin, 1.0 ml. capacity, fitted with a 23-gauge, long bevel needle.

REAGENTS

1. Kahn standard antigen. This antigen is an alcoholic extract of powdered beef heart containing 0.6 per cent cholesterol. It should be serologically standardized by comparison with an antigen of standard reactivity. Standardization of each new lot of antigen includes:

Determination of titer. This represents the optimal amounts of antigen and saline required to prepare an antigen suspension that will show complete dispersion in saline and will reproduce the opalescence of the standard antigen. The label should give the titer of the antigen.

Adjustment of reactivity level. An antigen more reactive than the standard may be adjusted by the addition of cholesterolized alcohol, concentrated lecithin solution, or under-reactive antigen. An antigen less reactive than the standard may be corrected by the addition of cholesterolized alcohol, sensitizing reagent, or over-reactive antigen.

Comparative testing. Each new lot of antigen should be tested in parallel with a standard antigen on reactive, weakly reactive, and nonreactive serums.

The antigen should be stored at room temperature in the dark.

Changes in antigen owing to aging are usually reflected in the appearance of the nonreactive tests. If these reactions become too clear or if they become cloudy, the antigen should be retitrated and restandardized. The need for retitration or restandardization of this reagent occurs but rarely. Such procedures should be carried out only by a laboratory qualified to make such adjustments.

2. Saline solution. Weigh 9.0 gm. of dried, chemically pure sodium chloride reagent quality for each liter of distilled water. Dissolve salt in freshly distilled water. Shake solution thoroughly to assure complete mixing. The pH of the 0.9 per cent saline solution should not be less than 5.5 nor more than 7.0.

Kahn Tests with Serum

Preparation of Serums

1. Separate serums from clotted blood by centrifugation and by pipetting or decanting.

2. Examine each serum for absolute clarity (freedom from cells or foreign particles) by holding tube in same position and light as for reading Kahn tests. Do not report results with serums not satisfactorily cleared.

3. Heat serums at 56° C. for 30 minutes.

4. When retesting of the serum is required, the serum is reheated at 56° C. for ten minutes if an interval of more than two hours has elapsed from first heating period.

5. Re-examine each serum for freedom from particles, and recentrifuge any serums not satisfactorily cleared.

Kahn Standard Qualitative Test with Serum

1. Arrange test tubes in standard Kahn racks so that there are three tubes for each serum to be tested, including reactive serum, nonreactive serum, and saline controls. Number the first row of tubes to correspond to the serums being tested.

2. Prepare standard antigen suspension as follows:

    a. Measure into an antigen suspension vial the amount of saline solution, according to titer, required for the given amount of antigen.

    b. Measure into a second antigen suspension vial the necessary quantity of antigen. Use a 1.0 ml. pipet.

Note: The titer on the bottle of the antigen will state the amount of saline solution that must be mixed with 1.0 ml. of antigen in order to produce a suspension of standard reactivity. Usually 1.0 ml. of antigen makes sufficient suspension for 20 tests. An amount of 2.0 ml. of antigen may be used with the proportionate quantity of saline solution. Less than 1.0 ml. should not be used.

    c. Pour the saline solution into the antigen, and without stopping pour the mixture back and forth 12 times without allowing vials to drain during the mixing period.

    d. Allow the antigen suspension to stand ("ripen") for 10 minutes before using it. The suspension should not be used after 30 minutes from the time of its preparation.

3. Place thumb over mouth of mixing vial and shake suspension briskly to suspend the lipid aggregates.

4. Pipet 0.05 ml. of antigen suspension directly to the bottom of each tube of the front row of the Kahn rack, employing a Kahn antigen suspension pipet.

5. Pipet 0.025 ml. of antigen suspension directly to the bottom of each tube of the middle row of the Kahn rack.

6. Pipet 0.0125 ml. of antigen suspension directly to the bottom of each tube of the back row of the Kahn rack.

7. Add 0.15 ml. of each serum to the designated set of three tubes containing 0.05 ml., 0.025 ml., and 0.0125 ml. of antigen suspension, respectively. *Note:* Complete the addition of antigen suspension and serums to one rack before adding antigen suspension and serums to another rack.

8. Shake rack by hand for ten seconds after antigen suspension and serum have been added to all tubes in that rack.

9. Permit serum-antigen-suspension mixture to stand for three to seven minutes at room temperature.

10. Shake rack of tubes for three minutes on Kahn shaking machine.

11. Remove rack from shaking machine, and add 1.0 ml. of 0.9 per cent saline solution to each tube of the front row and 0.5 ml. of the saline solution to each tube of the middle and back rows. *Note:* Add saline solution to one rack and complete readings before adding saline solution to another rack.

12. Shake rack by hand gently for a few seconds to mix contents of tubes.

13. Read and record each tube of the rack one to two minutes after the addition of the saline solution.

14. Reread each tube 15 minutes after the addition of the saline solution in all instances in which a nonreactive result was not obtained on the first reading.

15. Place all serums giving reactive or weakly reactive results in the refrigerator overnight. The next day reheat serums for ten minutes at 56° C. and re-examine them with the standard Kahn test. If the two examinations show a difference, report the weaker result.

Table 23–3. Outline of Kahn Standard Qualitative Test with Serum

	TUBE 1 (FRONT)	TUBE 2 (MIDDLE)	TUBE 3 (BACK)
Ratios of serum:antigen suspension	3:1	6:1	12:1
Antigen suspension, ml.	0.05	0.025	0.0125
Serum, ml.	0.15	0.15	0.15

Shake rack by hand ten seconds. Allow to stand three to seven minutes. Shake rack for exactly three minutes on Kahn shaking machine.

| 0.9 per cent NaCl solution, ml. | 1.0 | 0.5 | 0.5 |

Shake rack sufficiently to mix ingredients and examine tubes for presence and absence of floccules.

Control System for the Kahn Standard

1. Reactive serum, nonreactive serum, and saline solution controls should be employed for testing each antigen suspension before it is used in the regular tests with unknown serums.

2. The antigen suspension for the control tests is pipetted immediately after it has aged for ten minutes. After pipetting the serums and saline solution, the tests are at once shaken for three minutes, and the usual amounts of saline solution added to the tubes before reading the results.

3. The antigen suspension should not be employed in the regular tests with serum or spinal fluid if typically reactive and nonreactive results are not obtained with the control serums and if the antigen-saline solution control tubes are not of the correct degree of opalescence and free from nondispersible aggregates. Failure to obtain correct results in the control system may be due to factors such as:

 a. Incorrectly prepared antigen suspension.

 b. Use of antigen suspension that has aged more than 30 minutes after time of preparation.

 c. Use of antigen suspension that has not been allowed to age ("ripen") for ten minutes after it has been prepared.

 d. Use of refrigerated or chilled antigen and saline solution.

 e. Use of antigen that has undergone some change (such as prolonged exposure to light), use of wet pipets, loose capping of bottle, and so forth.

Reading of Results

1. Place a microscope mirror on the work table with the concave side upward.

2. Adjust a reading lamp (daylight bulb or fluorescent tube) above the mirror so that the bulb image is not visible but so that the tube is held within the cone of light.

3. Place each tube to be read in a nearly horizontal position, holding it about 1 to 2 inches above the mirror.

4. View the image of the tube contents in the mirror and note degree of flocculation.

Recording Results

Record degrees of flocculation in accordance with the following outline:

 4+ Relatively large floccules.
 3+ Medium-size floccules.
 2+ Fine floccules easily distinguishable.
 1+ Very fine floccules.
 ± Extremely fine floccules just distinguishable.
 − An opalescent medium free from visible floccules.

Reporting Results

1. Report test results as reactive, weakly reactive, or nonreactive according to Table 23–4 or Table 23–5 when indicated. In all reactions in which the greatest degree of flocculation is produced by the lesser amounts of antigen suspension (tubes 2 and 3), the following scheme of reporting should be used.

2. Report other types of reactions according to Table 23–5.

Table 23–4. Reporting of Typical Reactions

SUM OF PLUSES IN THE 6-TUBE READINGS	FINAL RESULT
22 to 24	Reactive 4+
16 to 21	Reactive 3+
10 to 15	Reactive 2+
5 to 9	Weakly reactive 1+
4 *	Weakly reactive ±
3 or less †	Nonreactive

± readings are disregarded.

* A nonreactive report of a sum of 4 pluses applies to −11 and −11 on first and second readings.

† A weakly reactive (±) report of a sum of 3 pluses applies to − − 3 and to − − ± on first and second readings as well as to − − 2 and − − 1 on first and second readings, respectively.

Supplementary Steps When Reactions Obtained Appear as in Table 23-5

Step 1

1. Measure 0.05 ml. antigen suspension into the bottom of each of two Kahn tubes numbered 1 and 2.

2. Add 0.05 ml. serum (previously heated) to tube 1 and 0.1 ml. serum to tube 2.

3. Shake rack by hand ten seconds to mix contents of tubes, and allow it to stand three to seven minutes at room temperature.

4. Shake rack on Kahn shaking machine for three minutes.

5. Remove rack from shaker, add 1.0 ml. saline solution to each tube, and shake rack by hand gently to mix contents of tubes.

6. Read immediately and again 15 minutes later.

7. Consider as reactive a 3+ or 4+ reading in either tube.

Step 2

1. Prepare serum dilutions of 1:4, 1:8, and 1:16 in the following manner:

    a. Measure into each of three Kahn tubes 0.3, 0.2, and 0.2 ml. of saline solution, respectively.

    b. Add 0.1 ml. serum to tube 1 and mix. (Use a 0.2 ml. pipet.)

    c. Transfer 0.2 ml. from tube 1 to tube 2 and mix.

    d. Transfer 0.2 ml. from tube 2 to tube 3 and mix.

2. Measure 0.0125 ml. of antigen suspension to the bottom of three Kahn tubes.

3. Transfer 0.15 ml. of the 1:4, 1:8, and 1:16 dilutions of serum to tubes containing the antigen suspension, starting with the highest dilution.

4. Shake rack by hand ten seconds to mix contents of tubes and allow it to stand three to seven minutes at room temperature.

5. Shake rack on Kahn shaking machine for three minutes.

6. Remove rack from shaker, add 0.5 ml. saline solution to each tube, and shake rack by hand gently to mix contents of tubes.

Table 23-5. Types of Reactions of Standard Kahn Test Requiring Performance of Supplementary Steps 1 and 2 Before Reporting Standard Test Result

Type 1 = Greatest degree of flocculation is given with the greater amounts of antigen suspension.

Type 2 = The degree of flocculation is the same in each of the three tubes but is less than 4+.

SERUM NO.	STANDARD TEST READINGS 1ST TUBES 1	2	3	2D TUBES 1	2	3	SUM OF PLUSES OF 1ST AND 2D READINGS	REPORT STANDARD TEST
	Supplementary Steps 1 and 2 not necessary							
1	4	4	3	4	4	3	22	Reactive 4+
2	4	4	—	4	4	—	16	Reactive 4+

When supplementary steps 1 and 2 are necessary (examples below), report as follows:

A. Report Kahn standard test as REACTIVE 4+ when both steps give reactive results.

B. Report Kahn standard test as outlined in next section when one or both steps give nonreactive results.

Table 23-5 (continued)

SERUM NO.	STANDARD TEST READINGS 1ST TUBES 1	2	3	2D TUBES 1	2	3	SUM OF PLUSES OF 1ST AND 2D READINGS	REPORT STANDARD TEST
1	4	3	3	3	3	3	19	Reactive 3+
2	3	3	3	3	3	3	18	Reactive 3+
3	4	2	2	3	2	2	15	Reactive 2+
4	3	3	2	3	3	—	14	Reactive 2+
5	4	1	±	3	1	±	9	Weakly reactive 1+
6	3	±	—	3	±	—	6	Weakly reactive 1+
7	2	2	2	2	2	2	*12	Weakly reactive 1+
8	2	2	1	2	2	±	*9	Weakly reactive ±
9	2	1	—	2	±	—	*5	Weakly reactive ±
10	2	±	±	2	±	±	*4	Nonreactive
11	2	—	—	1	—	—	*3	Nonreactive
12	1	1	1	1	1	1	*6	Nonreactive
13	±	±	±	±	±	±	0	Nonreactive
14	±	—	—	±	—	—	0	Nonreactive

* When flocculation is less than 3+ in each tube of the standard test, the report of the test is not based on the sum of pluses in the 6-tube readings.

7. Read results immediately.

8. Consider as reactive a 3+ or 4+ reading in any of the three tubes.

Kahn Standard Quantitative Test with Serum

Quantitative tests are performed on all serums that are 4+ or 3+ reactive results in the Kahn standard qualitative test.

1. Prepare serum dilutions of 1:2, 1:4, 1:8, 1:16, 1:32, 1:64, and higher if necessary in the following manner:

    a. Pipet into each of five (or more) tubes 0.5 ml. of 0.9 per cent saline solution.

    b. Add 0.5 ml. of heated serum to the first tube and mix well.

    c. Transfer 0.5 ml. from the first tube to the second tube and mix well.

    d. Continue transferring and mixing from one tube to the next until all dilutions have been made. Allow the mixing pipet to remain in the last tube. *Note:* Serum dilutions should be prepared and tested within two hours of the heating or reheating of the undiluted serum.

2. Prepare antigen suspension as previously described under "Kahn Standard Qualitative Test with Serum" (p. 846) by mixing Kahn standard antigen with 0.9 per cent saline solution.

3. After the antigen suspension has stood 10 minutes (but not more than 30 minutes), place the thumb over the mouth of the mixing vial containing the suspension and shake vial briskly to obtain a uniform suspension.

4. Pipet 0.0125 ml. of antigen suspension into the bottom of five (or more) numbered Kahn tubes.

5. Add 0.15 ml. of the 1:32 dilution of serum to the antigen suspension contained in tube 5.

6. Add 0.15 ml. of the 1:16 dilution of serum to the antigen suspension contained in tube 4.

7. Continue addition of 0.15 ml. of decreasing dilutions of the serum to tubes 3, 2, and 1, respectively.

8. Shake rack by hand for ten seconds and then allow it to stand five minutes.

9. Shake rack on a Kahn shaking machine for three minutes.

10. Remove rack from shaking machine and add 0.5 ml. of 0.9 per cent saline solution to each tube. *Note:* Add saline solution to one rack and complete reading before adding saline solution to another rack.

11. Shake rack by hand a few seconds to mix contents of tubes.

12. Read each tube of the rack one to two minutes after the addition of the 0.9 per cent saline solution.

13. Note the titration endpoint, i.e., the highest dilution of serum in which a 4+, 3+, or 2+ reaction is observed.

14. Compute the quantitative titer by applying the formula S = 4D, where S is the potency of the serum in terms of Kahn units and D is the highest dilution in which a 4+, 3+, or 2+ reaction is observed.

    Examples

    a. If the highest dilution in which a 4+, 3+, or 2+ reaction is observed is 1:32, then S= 4 × 32 or 128 Kahn units.

    b. If the highest dilution in which a 4+, 3+, or 2+ reaction is observed is 1:16, then S= 4 × 16 or 64 Kahn units.

    c. If a 4+, 3+, or 2+ reaction was not observed in the 1:2 or higher dilutions, then S= 4 × 1 (1 representing tube 3 of the standard test with undiluted serum that had given a reactive 4+ or 3+ result) or 4 Kahn units.

15. Report results both in terms of Kahn units and the highest serum dilution in which a 4+, 3+, or 2+ reaction is observed.

    Examples

    a. 128 Kahn Units (1:32 dilution)

    b. 64 Kahn Units (1:16 dilution)

    c. 4 Kahn Units (1:1 dilution)

KAHN TESTS WITH SPINAL FLUID
Preparation of Saturated Solution of Ammonium Sulfate

1. To 500 gm. of reagent quality ammonium sulfate add 500 ml. of doubly distilled water in a clean, 3 to 5 liter Pyrex flask.

2. Boil until solution becomes clear.

3. Allow solution to cool to room temperature. (Preferably, let it stand overnight.)

4. Filter solution through No. 1 Whatman filter paper and store it in a glass-stopper bottle at room temperature.

Preparation of Globulin Concentrate of Each Spinal Fluid

1. Centrifuge and decant all spinal fluids to remove cellular debris and particles.

2. Measure 1.5 ml. of the spinal fluid into a Kahn test tube.

3. Add 1.5 ml. of saturated solution of ammonium sulfate to the 1.5 ml. of spinal fluid.

4. Place thumb (protected by rubber) over mouth of tube and shake tube vigorously to mix contents.

5. Place mixture in a 56° C. waterbath for 15 minutes to hasten precipitation of the globulin.

6. Remove tube from waterbath and centrifuge it at 2000 r.p.m. for 15 minutes. (The globulin precipitate will be found packed at the bottom of the tube.)

7. Decant and discard supernatant fluid by inverting and rotating tube at the same time. Cover the entire wall of the tube with the supernatant fluid to permit its even drainage, thereby preventing ammonium sulfate from crystallizing on tube wall. *Note:* In rare instances the amount of globulin is excessive. In such cases do not decant the supernatant fluid, but instead remove it with a capillary pipet.

8. Drain inverted tube for ten minutes on filter paper, tap tube gently, and use a strip of filter paper to remove any remaining drops of supernatant fluid.

9. Add 0.15 ml. of saline solution to globulin precipitate, holding point of pipet close to bottom of tube to avoid washing down any ammonium sulfate that may be adhering near mouth of tube.

10. Tap base of tube gently to redissolve the globulin and examine the resulting concentrated globulin solution for freedom from particles. *Note:* When the globulin does not completely dissolve in 0.15 ml. of saline solution, add 0.05 ml. more saline solution and shake tube gently. If the globulin is still insoluble, repeat with an additional 0.05 ml. saline solution. In rare instances the globulin will still be incompletely soluble, in which case the clear globulin solution is separated from the insoluble protein by centrifugation. If centrifugation does not clear the fluid, a trace of talc or kaolin is then added to the mixture and the tube is recentrifugated. The clear supernatant fluid (which is the globulin solution) is removed with a capillary pipet and transferred to a clean tube; it is then ready for testing with the antigen suspension.

Kahn Standard Qualitative Test with Spinal Fluid Globulin Concentrate

1. Arrange Kahn test tubes in a rack so that there is one tube for each spinal fluid globulin concentrate to be tested, including control concentrates from reactive and nonreactive spinal fluids and antigen-saline solution. Number tubes to correspond to the spinal fluids being tested.

2. Prepare standard antigen suspension as described under "Kahn Standard Qualitative Test with Serum" (p. 846).

Table 23–6. Outline of Kahn Standard Qualitative Test with Spinal Fluid

Antigen suspension, ml.	0.01
Spinal fluid globulin concentrate, ml.	0.15
Shake rack by hand ten seconds.	
Shake rack for four minutes on Kahn shaker.	
Salt solution, ml.	0.5
Read one to two minutes after the addition of saline solution and again 15 minutes later.	

3. Place thumb over mouth of mixing vial and shake vial briskly to suspend the lipid aggregates.

4. Measure 0.01 ml. of standard antigen suspension directly to the bottom of each tube, using a 0.2 ml. pipet.

5. Add 0.15 ml. of spinal fluid globulin concentrate to each corresponding tube. *Note:* Complete the addition of antigen suspension and globulin concentrate to one rack before adding antigen suspension and globulin concentrate to another.

6. Shake rack by hand for ten seconds after antigen suspension and spinal fluid concentrates have been added to all tubes in that rack.

7. Shake rack for four minutes on a Kahn shaking machine.

8. Remove rack from shaking machine and add 0.5 ml. of 0.9 per cent saline solution to each tube. *Note:* Add saline solution to one rack and complete reading before adding saline solution to another.

9. Shake rack by hand a few seconds to mix contents of tubes.

10. Read each tube of the rack as described under "Reading of Results" (p. 847), within one to two minutes after the addition of saline solution.

11. Report results in accordance with Table 23–7, averaging the two readings.

Table 23–7. Reporting Kahn Standard Qualitative Tests with Spinal Fluid

TUBE READING	REPORT
4+	Reactive 4+
3+	Reactive 3+
2+	Reactive 2+
1+	Weakly Reactive 1+
±	Nonreactive
−	Nonreactive

Kahn Standard Quantitative Test with Spinal Fluid. Quantitative spinal fluid tests are performed on spinal fluids producing reactive results in the Kahn qualitative test.

1. Prepare dilutions of spinal fluid as indicated in Table 23–8.

Table 23–8. Dilution of Spinal Fluid for Kahn Standard Quantitative Test

TUBE	SPINAL FLUID* (ML.)	SALINE SOLUTION DESIGNATED (ML.)	DILUTION
1	Quantity available	None	1:10
2	0.2	0.1	1:15
3	0.2	0.2	1:20
4	0.1	0.2	1:30
5	0.1	0.3	1:40

* Whole spinal fluid is considered a 1:10 dilution, since the qualitative test is performed with spinal fluid globulin concentrated ten times.

2. Prepare standard antigen suspension as described under "Kahn Standard Qualitative Test with Serum" (p. 846).

3. Place thumb over mouth of mixing vial and shake briskly to suspend the lipid aggregates.

4. Measure 0.01 ml. of the antigen suspension directly into the bottom of a Kahn test tube. One tube is required for each dilution of spinal fluid being tested.

5. Add 0.15 ml. of diluted spinal fluid to each tube, starting with the highest dilution.

6. Shake rack by hand for ten seconds.

7. Shake rack on Kahn shaking machine for four minutes.

8. Remove rack from shaker, add 0.5 ml. of saline solution to each tube, shake rack gently to mix contents of tubes, and read immediately.

9. Note the highest dilution of spinal fluid producing a reactive result (4+, 3+, or 2+).

10. Calculate the Kahn units according to the formula $S = 4D$, where S is the potency of the spinal fluid in terms of Kahn units and D is the highest dilution in which a 4+, 3+, or 2+ reaction is observed.

Example

a. Spinal fluid reactive at 1:10 dilution (designated) $4 \times 10 = 40$ Kahn units.

b. Spinal fluid reactive at 1:40 dilution (designated) $4 \times 40 = 160$ Kahn units.

11. Retest spinal fluids that produce only nonreactive results in the designated dilutions in the following manner:

a. Prepare a spinal fluid globulin concentrate as described under "Kahn Standard Qualitative Test with Spinal Fluid" (p. 849)

b. Add 0.6 ml. of saline solution to the 0.15 ml. of globulin solution to produce a globulin solution concentrated five times (instead of ten times). (The resulting solution is a 1:5 dilution of the globulin solution.)

c. Perform a one-tube test as prescribed for testing spinal fluid dilutions.

d. If this 1:5 dilution gives a reactive result, the quantitative titer is 20 Kahn units; if it gives a nonreactive result, the titer is based on the reading obtained with the undiluted globulin concentrate, namely 4×1 or 4 Kahn units (1:1).

Kline Tests

Equipment

1. Rotating machine adjustable to 180 r.p.m. circumscribing a circle $\frac{3}{4}$ inch in diameter on horizontal plane.

2. Ringmaker to make paraffin rings approximately 14 mm. in diameter.

3. Mold set* for spinal fluid tests, consisting of a steel mold ($3\frac{1}{8} \times 2\frac{3}{16} \times \frac{1}{8}$ inch with two wells $1\frac{9}{16}$ inches in diameter) and two metal discs ($1\frac{5}{16}$ inches in diameter $\times \frac{3}{16}$ inch thick) with central screws.

4. Slide holders for 2×3 inch slides.

5. Hypodermic needles, 22- and 25-gauge, without bevels.

Glassware

1. Pipets, 0.2 ml., graduated in 1/100 ml. to the tip.

2. Centrifuge tubes, round-bottom, 3×1 inch.

3. Bottles, round, glass-stopper, 30 ml. capacity.

4. Glass slides, 2×3 inch, plain, for paraffin rings.

5. Syringe, glass, hypodermic, 1.0 or 2.0 ml. capacity.

KLINE TESTS WITH CARDIOLIPIN NATURAL LECITHIN (CNL) ANTIGEN

Reagents

1. Antigen.* Cardiolipin natural lecithin (CNL) antigent for the Kline tests is composed of cardiolipin (0.2 per cent) and purified natural lecithin (1.8 to 2 per cent) in absolute alcohol. This reagent should be assembled from chemically standardized components and should be serologically standardized by comparison with an antigen of standard reactivity. Store at refrigerator temperature (6° to 10° C.).

2. Cholesterol solution. Dissolve 1.0 gm. of cholesterol (Pfanstiehl, ash-free, precipi-

* LaMotte Chemical Products Co., Chestertown, Maryland.

tated from alcohol) in 100 ml. of absolute alcohol and store in glass-stopper bottle at room temperature.

3. Distilled water. Distilled water suitable for the Kline tests should have a pH of 6.0–6.8 and have a minimum of positive ions or other electrolytes.

4. Sodium chloride solution (0.85 per cent). Add the required amount of dry, reagent quality sodium chloride (850 mg.) to 100 ml. of distilled water. This solution should preferably be prepared on the day of use. It may be satisfactory for as long as one week if kept in a clean glass-stopper bottle.

Preparation of Serums

1. Remove serums from clots by centrifuging and pipetting or decanting.

2. Heat serums in 56° C. water bath for 30 minutes. When re-examination of the serum on another day is required, serum should be reheated at 56° C. for five minutes.

3. Recentrifuge any serum in which visible particles have formed during heating.

Preparation of Paraffin-Ring Slides

1. Clean 2 × 3 inch glass slides.

2. Place 12 paraffin rings (14 mm. in diameter) on each slide, using a hand-operated or an electrically heated ringmaking machine. Paraffin or a mixture of two parts of paraffin and one part of petroleum, heated to about 120° C., may be used. Care should be exercised to produce rings of the prescribed diameter.

Preparation of CNL Antigen Emulsion

1. Pipet 0.85 ml. of distilled water to the bottom of a 30 ml. glass-stopper bottle.

2. Add 1.0 ml. of 1 per cent cholesterol solution. This is accomplished by allowing the cholesterol solution to drop slowly (20 seconds) from the pipet while the bottle, held at an angle, is vigorously and continuously rotated on a flat surface.

3. Continue rotation of the bottle for an additional 20 seconds.

4. Add 0.1 ml. of antigen against the side of the neck of the bottle from a 0.2 ml. pipet, avoiding the ground-glass area.

5. Place stopper in bottle and shake vigorously for one minute, throwing fluid from bottom to stopper and back.

6. Add 2.45 ml. of 0.85 per cent sodium chloride solution rapidly to the bottle and shake less vigorously for 30 seconds.

The emulsion is now ready for use and, if refrigerated, may be used for 48 hours.

Double quantities of antigen emulsion may be prepared in 30 ml. bottles.

Preliminary Test with Serum

1. Check the delivery of the hypodermic needle (25-gauge attached to a glass syringe). Adjustments should be made so that approximately 140 drops are obtained (0.007 ml. per drop) from each milliliter of antigen emulsion.

2. Complete tests with control serums of graded reactivity as described under "Kline Standard Qualitative Test with Serum."

3. Reactions with control serums should reproduce the reactivity pattern. The nonreactive serum should show complete dispersion of antigen particles and the optimum number of particles per microscopic field.

Kline Standard Qualitative Test with Serum

1. Pipet 0.05 ml. of heated serum into a paraffin ring on a glass slide.

2. Add one drop (0.007 ml.) of antigen emulsion to each serum.

3. Rotate slides on a rotating machine at 180 r.p.m. for four minutes. *Note:* When tests are performed in a hot, dry climate, slides may be covered during rotation with a box lid containing a moistened blotter to prevent excess evaporation.

4. Examine the reactions microscopically, employing a 100 × magnification.

5. Report observed results in accordance with the following outline:

   a. Typical reactions.

Nonreactive	Antigen particles dispersed, no clumping.
Weakly reactive (± or 1+)	Antigen particles in small but definite clumps.
Reactive (2+, 3+, or 4+)	Antigen particles in medium-sized or large clumps.

b. Atypical reactions. Atypical reactions are characterized by irregular feathery clumping in which smaller clumps predominate. Atypical reacting serums should be retested, in dilutions from 1:2 to 1:64, as described under "Kline Standard Quantitative Test with Serum." A reactive report is rendered if a reactive result is obtained with one or more serum dilutions.

Kline Quantitative Test with Serum

1. Add 0.5 ml. of 0.85 per cent sodium chloride solution to each of six or more tubes.

2. Add 0.5 ml. of heated serum to the first tube and mix.

3. Transfer 0.5 ml. from first to second tube and mix.

4. Continue transferring 0.5 ml. from each tube to the next and mixing until the last tube contains 1.0 ml.

5. Pipet 0.05 ml. of undiluted serum and of each serum dilution into separate paraffin rings on a glass slide.

6. Add one drop of antigen emulsion (0.007 ml.) to each serum dilution.

7. Rotate slide at 180 r.p.m. for four minutes.

8. Read and record reactions as described under "Kline Standard Qualitative Test with Serum" (p. 852).

9. Report results in terms of the highest dilution producing a reactive (2+, 3+, or 4+) result.

Examples (see bottom of page).

KLINE TESTS WITH SPINAL FLUID

Preparation of Spinal Fluid

1. Centrifuge spinal fluid at 2000 r.p.m. for five minutes and remove supernatant fluid by decanting. The pH should be 8.0 or more. Spinal fluids that are contaminated or that contain blood are unsatisfactory for testing.

2. Test each spinal fluid for the presence of sugar.

    a. Pipet 0.5 ml. of distilled water into a Pyrex tube.

    b. Add 0.25 ml. of the spinal fluid.

    c. Add one Clinitest tablet.

    d. Allow to stand until the fluid ceases boiling.

    e. Examine for green-to-orange color indicating the presence of sugar. Spinal fluids giving a negative reaction for sugar are unsatisfactory for testing.

3. Place spinal fluids in a 56° C. water bath for five minutes immediately before testing.

Preparation of Double-Ring Slides

1. Clean 3 × 2 inch glass slides with Bon Ami.

2. Place steel mold and two center disks on slide.

3. Fill spaces between discs and outer mold with hot paraffin mixture (one part of paraffin plus two parts of petrolatum).

4. Remove mold and disks from slide after paraffin has cooled. Disks may be loosened by turning the central screw to the right. The mold is removed by inserting a knife blade between the slide and mold.

Preparation of Antigen Emulsion

1. Pipet 0.6 ml. of 1 per cent cholesterol solution to the bottom of a 3 × 1 inch, round-bottom test tube.

2. Add 0.4 ml. of distilled water rapidly by removing finger from pipet and blowing in the last drop while vigorously rotating the tube on a flat surface.

3. Continue rotation of tube for an additional ten seconds.

4. Add 0.1 ml. of antigen and rotate tube vigorously for one minute.

5. Add 1.4 ml. of 0.85 per cent sodium chloride solution and rotate the tube on a flat surface for 30 seconds.

6. Centrifuge tube of antigen emulsion at 1100 r.p.m. for five minutes.

7. Decant and discard the turbid supernatant fluid. Keeping the tube inverted, wipe the excess fluid from the wall of the tube with a piece of gauze or cotton.

8. Add 0.6 ml. of 0.85 per cent sodium chloride solution to the sediment and rotate tube vigorously for 30 seconds to uniformly resuspend the antigen particles.

9. Transfer the antigen emulsion to a stoppered 13 × 100 mm. tube. This emulsion, if stored in the refrigerator, may be used for 48 hours after preparation.

Preliminary Tests with Spinal Fluid

1. Check the delivery of the hypodermic needle (25 gauge, attached to a glass syringe). Adjustments should be made so that approximately 125 drops are obtained (0.008 ml. per drop) from each milliliter of antigen emulsion.

2. Complete tests with reactive spinal fluid and nonreactive spinal fluid controls as described under "Kline Standard Qualitative Test with Spinal Fluid."

3. Clumping of antigen particles will be observed in the reactive spinal fluid. The

UNDILUTED SERUM	SERUM DILUTIONS						REPORT
1:1	1:2	1:4	1:8	1:16	1:32	1:64	
4	4	3	1	—	—	—	Reactive, 1:4 dilution or 4 dils.
4	4	4	4	2	—	—	Reactive, 1:16 dilution or 16 dils.
4	4	4	4	4	2	—	Reactive, 1:32 dilution or 32 dils.

nonreactive spinal fluid should show complete dispersion of antigen particles and the optimum number of particles per microscopic field.

Kline Qualitative Test with Spinal Fluid

1. Place the required number of doubling-ring slides in a holder while spinal fluids are being heated.

2. Pipet 0.3 ml. of the warm spinal fluid into a ringed chamber. Reactive and nonreactive spinal fluid controls should be included.

3. Add one drop (0.008 ml.) of antigen emulsion to the spinal fluid in each chamber.

4. Rotate the slides on a flat surface with moderate vigor for 30 seconds to distribute the antigen emulsion.

5. Move the slide holder back and forth rapidly (about three complete movements a second), a linear distance of $\frac{1}{4}$ to $\frac{1}{2}$ inch, for eight minutes.

6. Examine reactions microscopically at 100 × magnification and report observed results in accordance with the following outline. For ease in reading, the slide may be tilted.

Nonreactive	Antigen particles dispersed, no clumping.
Weakly reactive (± or 1+)	Antigen particles in small but definite clumps.
Reactive (2+, 3+, or 4+)	Antigen particles in medium-sized or large clumps.

Kline Quantitative Test with Spinal Fluid

1. Prepare spinal fluid dilutions of 1:2, 1:4, 1:8, 1:16, using nonreactive spinal fluid or 0.9 per cent saline solution as the diluent.

2. Test undiluted spinal fluid and each spinal fluid dilution as described under "Kline Qualitative Test With Spinal Fluid."

3. Report results in terms of the highest dilution producing a reactive (2+, 3+, or 4+) result as described under "Kline Quantitative Test with Serum" (p. 852).

Kline tests with cardiolipin synthetic lecithin (CSL) antigen are performed in the same manner as those with cardiolipin natural lecithin (CNL) antigens. The preparation of the antigen emulsion, however, is somewhat different. Details can be found in the manual "Serologic Tests for Syphilis," pp. 44–45, and in an article by Kline and Suessenguth (1958).

Mazzini Tests

The Mazzini quantitative test and tests on spinal fluid are described in the manual "Serologic Tests for Syphilis," pp. 79–83.

Equipment

1. Rotating machine, adjustable to 100 to 180 r.p.m., circumscribing a circle $\frac{3}{4}$ inch in diameter on a horizontal plane.

2. Slide holder. Made of any convenient material to accommodate 2 × 3 inch slides.

3. Hypodermic needles, 13 and 21 gauge with bevels removed.

Glassware

1. Glass slides, 2 × 3 inch, having 10 concavities, 6 mm. in diameter by 1.75 mm. in depth, for serum tests.

2. Bottles, glass-stopper or screw-cap, round, 30 ml. capacity.

3. Syringe, Luer-type, 1 or 2 ml. capacity, or an "observation tube" No. 420 LST.*

REAGENTS

1. Antigen.* Antigen for this test is an alcoholic solution containing 0.025 per cent cardiolipin, approximately 0.2 per cent lecithin, and 0.75 to 0.9 per cent cholesterol that has been serologically standardized against an antigen of known reactivity.

2. Buffered 1 per cent saline solution, pH 6.3 to 6.4.

    a. Prepare solution according to the following formula:

	gm.
Sodium chloride (C.P.)	8.1
Primary potassium phosphate (KH_2PO_4)	0.2
Secondary sodium phosphate ($Na_2HPO_4 + 12\ H_2O$)	1.7

	ml.
Distilled water	1000.0
Normal hydrochloric acid	3.2
Formaldehyde (Merck Reagent) neutral	1.0

    b. Filter and check pH of solution.

PREPARATION OF SERUMS

1. Remove serums from clots by centrifuging and pipetting or decanting.

2. Heat serums in the 56° C. water bath for 30 minutes. Serums should be reheated for ten minutes if re-examined more than four hours after the original heating period.

3. Recentrifuge any specimen in which visible particles have formed during heating.

* Serological Reagents Co., Indianapolis, Ind., and Sylvania Chemical Co., Orange, N.J.

PREPARATION OF ANTIGEN EMULSION

1. Pipet 0.4 ml. of buffered saline solution into the bottom of a 30 ml. bottle.

2. Measure 0.4 ml. of cholesterolized antigen (reading from the bottom of the pipet) with a 1 ml. pipet graduated to the tip.

3. Hold the bottle in the left hand and impart a rapid rotating motion to it as the antigen is being blown directly and at once into the saline solution from the pipet held in the right hand.

4. Mix by drawing the suspension into the pipet and blowing out exactly six times, returning all the emulsion left in the pipet into the last mixture.

5. Add 2.6 ml. of the buffered saline solution, cap the bottle, and shake from bottom to top and back 50 times in 15 seconds.

6. The emulsion then is ready for immediate use and continues usable for the entire day. Shake antigen emulsion gently each time it is used.

PRELIMINARY TESTING OF ANTIGEN EMULSION

1. Check delivery of the syringe or observation tube fitted with a 21-gauge needle. When in a vertical position, 0.01 ml. of antigen suspension per drop should be delivered.

2. Test control serums of graded reactivity and buffered saline solution as described under "Mazzini Qualitative Test with Serum." The results obtained should reproduce the reactivity pattern previously established for these serums and should show complete dispersion of the antigen particles in both nonreactive serum and buffered saline solution.

MAZZINI QUALITATIVE TEST WITH SERUM

1. Pipet 0.03 ml. of each serum into a separate concavity.

2. Add one drop of antigen emulsion (0.01 ml.) to each serum.

3. Rotate slides on rotating machine for four minutes.

Note: When employing a mechanical rotator, the speed should be 160 to 180 rotations per minute. If rotation is by hand, circumscribe a 2 inch circle 120 times per minute.

4. Read each reaction microscopically, using the low power objective (16 mm.) and a 6X ocular. Record and report all serums that are nonreactive (no clumping) and all serums that are reactive (4+).

5. Add one drop (about 0.05 ml.) of 0.9 per cent saline solution from a syringe, using a 13-gauge needle with cut-off bevel, to each test that gives a 1+, 2+, 3+, or atypical reaction.

6. Rotate the slide for a second four-minute period on a rotating machine set at 100 to 120 r.p.m. or by hand.

7. Examine microscopically, record, and report the results as follows:

a. Typical reactions

DESCRIPTION	READING	REPORT
No clumping or coarse reactions	—	Nonreactive
Very small clumps	1+	Weakly reactive
Small clumps	2+	Weakly reactive
Medium-size clumps	3+	Reactive
Large clumps	4+	Reactive

b. Atypical reactions. Atypical reactions are characterized by irregular particle aggregates of various sizes in which the small clumps and free antigen particles predominate. Atypically reacting serums should be retested according to the "Mazzini Quantitative Test with Serum."

VDRL Tests

VDRL SLIDE FLOCCULATION TESTS WITH SERUM

Equipment

1. Rotating machine, adjustable to 180 r.p.m., circumscribing a circle ¾ inch in diameter on a horizontal plane.

2. Ringmaker, to make paraffin rings approximately 14 mm. in diameter.

3. Slide holder, for 2 × 3 inch microscope slides.

4. Hypodermic needles of appropriate sizes with or without points.

Glassware

1. Slides* 2 × 3 inch with paraffin rings approximately 14 mm. in diameter.

2. Bottles, 1 ounce, round, screw-cap (Vinylite or tinfoil liners) or glass-stopper, narrow mouth.

3. Syringe, Luer-type, 1 or 2 ml.

* Glass slides with ceramic rings may also be used for the VDRL slide test with the following precautions. The rings must be high enough to prevent spillage when slides are rotated at prescribed speeds. Slides must be cleaned after each use so that serum will spread to the inner surface of the ceramic rings. This type of slide should be discarded if or when the ceramic ring begins to flake off, since these particles in the test serums may be mistaken for antigen particle clumps, thereby causing a false reactive report.

Figure 23–2.   Slides and slide holder for qualitative tests. (From Venereal Disease Research Laboratory. In Serologic Tests for Syphilis. U.S. Department of Health, Education, and Welfare, Public Health Service, 1959.)

Note: Some of the 1 ounce, glass-stopper bottles now available are unsatisfactory for preparing a single volume of antigen emulsion for these tests owing to an inward bulging of the bottom that causes the 0.4 ml. of saline solution to be distributed only at the periphery. A satisfactory emulsion may be obtained if the 0.8 ml. of saline solution covers the bottom surface of this type of bottle when double quantities of antigen emulsion are prepared. Round bottles of approximately 35 mm. diameter with flat or concave inner bottom surfaces are satisfactory for preparing single volumes of antigen emulsion.

The low cost of plastic caps is a recommendation against attempts to clean these for re-use. The use of an unclean stopper or cap can be the cause of unsatisfactory emulsions.

Reagents

1. Antigen

a. Antigen for this test is an alcoholic solution containing 0.03 per cent cardiolipin, 0.9 per cent cholesterol, and sufficient purified lecithin to produce standard reactivity. During recent years this amount of lecithin has been 0.21 per cent ±0.01 per cent.

b. Each lot of antigen must be serologically standardized by proper comparison with an antigen of known reactivity.

c. Antigen is dispensed in screw-cap (tinfoil or Vinylite liners) brown bottles or hermetically sealed glass ampules and stored at room temperature (73° to 85° F.).

d. Since the components of this antigen remain in solution at normal temperature, any precipitate noted will indicate changes owing to factors such as evaporation or to additive materials contributed by pipets. Antigen containing precipitate should be discarded.

2. Saline solutions.

a. Buffered saline solution containing 1 per cent sodium chloride

Formaldehyde, neutral, reagent grade, ml.	0.5
Secondary sodium phosphate (Na_2HPO_4 + 12 H_2O), gm.	0.093
Primary potassium phosphate (KH_2PO_4), gm.	0.170
Sodium chloride (A.C.S.), gm.	10.0
Distilled water, ml.	1000.0

This solution yields potentiometer readings of pH 6.0 ±0.1 and is stored in screw-cap or glass-stopper bottles.

b. 0.9 per cent saline solution. Add 900 mg. of dry sodium chloride to each 100 ml. of distilled water.

Preparation of Serums

1. Clear serum obtained from centrifuged, clotted blood is heated in a 56° C. water bath for 30 minutes before being tested.

2. All serums are examined when removed from the water bath, and those found to contain particulate debris are recentrifuged.

3. Serums to be tested more than four hours after the original heating period should be reheated at 56° C. for ten minutes.

Preparation of Slides

1. Clean 2 × 3 inch glass slides.

2. Paraffin rings are made by transferring heated paraffin to the slides by means of a hand-operated or an electrically heated ring-making machine. Care should be exercised to produce rings of the prescribed diameter (Fig. 23–2). *Note:* Glass slides with concavities or glass rings are not recommended for this test.

Preparation of Antigen Emulsion

1. Pipet 0.4 ml. of buffered saline solution to the bottom of a 30 ml. round, glass-stoppered or screw-cap bottle.

2. Add 0.5 ml. of antigen (from the lower half of a 1.0 ml. pipet graduated to the tip) directly onto the saline solution while continuously but gently rotating the bottle on a flat surface.

Temperature of buffered saline solution and antigen should be in the range of 23° to 29° C. at the time antigen emulsion is prepared.

Note: Antigen is added drop by drop, but rapidly, so that approximately six seconds are allowed for each 0.5 ml. of antigen. Pipet tip should remain in upper third of bottle and rotation should not be vigorous enough to splash saline solution onto pipet. Proper speed of rotation is obtained when the outer edge of the bottle circumscribes a 2 inch diameter circle approximately three times per second.

3. Blow last drop of antigen from pipet without touching pipet to saline solution.

4. Continue rotation of bottle for ten seconds more.

5. Add 4.1 ml. of buffered saline solution from 5 ml. pipet.

6. Place top on bottle and shake from bottom to top and back approximately 30 times in ten seconds.

7. Antigen emulsion then is ready for use and may be used during one day. Double this amount of antigen emulsion may be prepared at one time by using doubled quantities of antigen and saline solution. A 10 ml. pipet should then be used for delivering the 8.2 ml. volume of saline solution. If larger quantities of antigen emulsion are required, more than one mixture should be prepared. These aliquots may then be tested and pooled.

Stabilized Antigen Emulsion. If desired, VDRL antigen emulsion for use in all the VDRL tests may be stabilized by the addition of benzoic acid. The use of this stabilized emulsion makes it unnecessary to prepare fresh emulsions each day tests are performed.

Reagents

1. Benzoic acid, 1.0 per cent alcohol solution. Dissolve 1.0 gm. of reagent grade benzoic acid in 100 ml. of absolute ethyl alcohol. Store in a tightly sealed all-glass container in the refrigerator at 6° to 10° C. May be used as long as the solution remains clear.

2. VDRL antigen emulsion—prepared in either single (5.0 ml.) or double (10.0 ml.) volumes as described on p. 856.

Preparation of stabilized antigen emulsion

1. Immediately after preparation of the emulsion add 0.05 ml. of 1.0 per cent benzoic acid to each single volume (5.0 ml.) or 0.1 ml. to each double volume (10.0 ml.). Shake gently from bottom to stopper for ten seconds. Pipet benzoic acid solution with

a 0.1 ml. or 0.2 ml. capacity pipet graduated in hundredths.

2. Test each stabilized aliquot with control serums and pool all those of standard reactivity. Mix by swirling bottle gently.

Storage of stabilized antigen emulsion

1. Store stock bottle of stabilized emulsion in a tightly stoppered bottle at 6° to 10° C.

2. For use remove the stock bottle from the refrigerator, swirl gently to mix, and with a pipet remove an aliquot sufficient for one day's testing. Return the stock bottle to the refrigerator immediately to avoid warming.

3. Allow the aliquot for each day's testing to stand at room temperature at least 30 minutes before use. Check with control serums for standard reactivity each day before testing individual serums.

4. Use a new aliquot from the refrigerator each day.

5. The stock stabilized emulsion stored in the refrigerator may be used as long as it retains a standard level of reactivity as determined by testing control serum(s).

Testing antigen-emulsion delivery needles

1. It is of primary importance that the proper amount of antigen emulsion be used, and for this reason the needle used each day should be checked. Practice will allow rapid delivery of antigen emulsion, but care should be exercised to obtain drops of constant size.

2. For use in the Slide Qualitative Test and Slide Quantitative Test A, antigen emulsion is dispensed from a syringe fitted with an 18-gauge needle without point, which will deliver 60 drops of antigen emulsion per milliliter when the syringe and needle are held vertically.

3. For use in the Slide Quantitative Test B, antigen emulsion is dispensed from a syringe fitted with a 19-gauge needle without point, which will deliver 75 drops of antigen emulsion per milliliter when syringe and needle are held vertically (Fig. 23–3).

4. When allowed to stand, antigen emulsion should be mixed gently before use by rotating the bottle.

Preliminary testing of antigen emulsion

1. Each preparation of antigen emulsion should first be examined by testing serums of known reactivity in the reactive, weakly reactive, and nonreactive zones. This is accomplished by the method described under "VDRL Slide Qualitative Test with Serum."

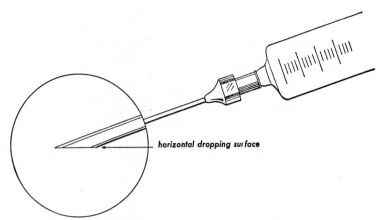

Figure 23–3. Method of testing antigen emulsion delivery needle.

These tests should present typical results, and the size and number of antigen particles in the nonreactive serum should be optimum.

2. Only those antigen emulsions that have produced the designated reactions in tests performed with control serums (reactive, weakly reactive, and nonreactive) should be used. If antigen particles in the nonreactive serum tests are too large, the fault may be in the manner of preparing antigen emulsion, although other factors may be responsible.

3. An unsatisfactory antigen emulsion should not be used.

VDRL Slide Qualitative Test with Serum

1. Pipet 0.05 ml. of heated serum into one ring of a paraffin-ringed glass slide.

2. Add one drop (1/60 ml.) of antigen emulsion onto each serum.

3. Rotate slides for four minutes. (Mechanical rotators that circumscribe a ¾ inch diameter circle should be set at 180 r.p.m. Rotation by hand should circumscribe a 2 inch diameter circle 120 times per minute.)

4. Read tests immediately after rotation. *Note:* Serum controls of graded reactivity (reactive, weakly reactive, and nonreactive) are always included during a testing period to insure proper reactivity of antigen emulsion at time tests are run.

Reading and reporting slide qualitative test results

1. Read tests microscopically with low power objective, at 100 × magnification. The antigen particles appear as short rod forms at this magnification. Aggregation of these particles into large or small clumps is interpreted as degrees of reactivity.

Reading	*Report*
No clumping or very slight roughness	Nonreactive (N)
Small clumps	Weakly reactive (WR)
Medium and large clumps	Reactive (R)

2. Zonal reactions owing to an excess of reactive serum component are recognized by irregular clumping and the loosely bound characteristics of the clumps. The usual reactive finding is characterized by large or small clumps of fairly uniform size. Experience will allow differentiation to be made between this type of reaction and the zonal picture wherein large or small clumps may be intermingled with free antigen particles. A zonal reaction is reported as reactive. In some instances this zoning effect may be so pronounced that a weakly reactive result is produced by a very strongly reactive serum. *It is therefore recommended that all serums producing weakly reactive results in the qualitative test be retested using the quantitative procedure before a report of the VDRL slide test is submitted.* When a reactive result is obtained on some dilution of a serum that produced only a weakly reactive result as undiluted serum, the report is reactive (see "Reading and Reporting Slide Quantitative Test Results," p. 861, under "VDRL Slide Quantitative Test with Serum").

VDRL Slide Quantitative Tests with Serum

All serums that produce reactive or weakly reactive results in the qualitative VDRL slide test should be quantitatively retested by one of the two methods referred to as quantitative tests A or B. Since both of these procedures, in most instances, provide for direct measurements of serum and saline solution, either method is efficient in its requirement of technician-time and amount of glassware employed. Since quantitative test A uses serum dilutions of 1:2.5, 1:5, 1:10, and so on, the alternate quantitative test B has been added for those laboratories desiring the doubling, serum-dilution scheme of 1:2, 1:4, 1:8, 1:16, and the like.

VDRL slide quantitative test A

1. Place four 2 × 3 inch glass slides containing twelve 14 mm. paraffin rings in a five-place slide holder (see Fig. 23–4).

2. Place a glass slide with two parallel strips of masking or adhesive tape in the center space of the slide holder. Numbers identifying the serums to be tested (four on the two slides above the numbered slide and four on the two lower slides) are written on the adhesive strips.

3. Prepare a 1:10 dilution of each serum to be tested quantitatively by adding 0.1 ml. of the heated serum to 0.9 ml. of 0.9 per cent saline solution, using a 0.2 ml. pipet graduated in 0.01 ml.

4. Mix the serum and saline solution thoroughly and then allow the pipet to stand in the test tube.

5. Using this 0.2 ml. pipet, transfer 0.05 ml., 0.02 ml., and 0.01 ml. quantities of the 1:10 dilution of the first serum into the fourth, fifth, and sixth rings, respectively.

6. With the same pipet transfer 0.05 ml., 0.02 ml., and 0.01 ml. of the first serum, undiluted, into the first, second, and third ringed areas, as illustrated in Fig. 23–4.

7. Repeat this procedure with each serum and the accompanying 1:10 serum dilution until each of the eight serums are pipetted onto the slides.

8. Add one drop (0.03 ml.) of 0.9 per cent saline solution to the second and fifth rings of each serum by vertical delivery from a 15-gauge* hypodermic needle fitted to a glass syringe.

9. Add one drop (0.04 ml.) of 0.9 per cent saline solution to the third and sixth rings of all eight serums by vertical delivery from the syringe fitted with the 13-gauge* needle. The six mixtures of each serum are then equivalent to dilutions of 1:1 (undiluted), 1:2.5, 1:5, 1:10, 1:25, and 1:50.

10. Rotate slides gently by hand for about 15 seconds to mix the serum and saline solution.

11. Add one drop (1/60 ml.) of antigen emulsion to each ring using a syringe and needle as described in the technique for the slide qualitative serum test (p. 858).

12. Complete tests by rotation of the slides in the manner prescribed for the

* Needles should be checked for proper drop size.

"VDRL Slide Qualitative Test with Serum" (p. 858).

13. Read results microscopically. The highest serum dilution giving a reactive result (not weakly reactive) is reported as the reactivity endpoint of the serum, e.g., reactive—1:25 dilution, or reactive—25 dils.

14. If all serum dilutions tested give reactive results, prepare a 1:100 dilution of that serum by diluting 0.1 ml. of the 1:10 serum dilution with 0.9 ml. of 0.9 per cent saline solution.

15. Pipet 0.05 ml., 0.02 ml., and 0.01 ml. amounts of this 1:100 serum dilution onto each ring and add enough saline solution to bring the volumes to 0.05 ml. Serum dilutions of 1:100, 1:250, and 1:500 are thus prepared. Test these dilutions of serum exactly as the lower dilutions are tested.

VDRL slide quantitative test B

1. Place four 2 × 3 inch glass slides with 12 paraffin rings in a five-place slide holder (see Fig. 23–4) with a numbered slide in the center space, exactly as described for "Slide Quantitative Test A."

2. Prepare a 1:8 dilution of each serum by adding 0.1 ml. of the heated serum to 0.7 of the 0.9 per cent saline solution, using a 0.2 ml. pipet graduated in 0.01 ml.

3. Mix the serum and saline solution thoroughly and then allow the pipet to stand in the test tube.

4. Using this pipet, transfer 0.04 ml., 0.02 ml., and 0.01 ml. quantities of the 1:8 serum dilution into the fourth, fifth, and sixth paraffin rings, respectively.

5. With the same pipet transfer 0.04 ml., 0.02 ml., and 0.01 ml. of the undiluted serum into the first, second, and third paraffin rings, respectively.

6. Repeat this procedure with each serum and the accompanying 1:8 serum dilution until each of the eight serums are pipetted into their respectively numbered places on the slides.

7. Add two drops (0.01 ml. in each drop) of 0.9 per cent saline solution to the second and fifth rings of each serum by vertical delivery from a 23-gauge* hypodermic needle fitted to a glass syringe.

8. Add three drops of 0.9 per cent saline solution (delivered in the same manner) of the same size to the third and sixth rings of each serum.

9. Rotate slides gently by hand for about 15 seconds to mix the serum and saline solution.

* Needles should be checked for proper drop size. Saline solutions may be delivered from a 19-gauge needle (0.02 ml. per drop) and a 15-gauge needle (0.03 ml. per drop).

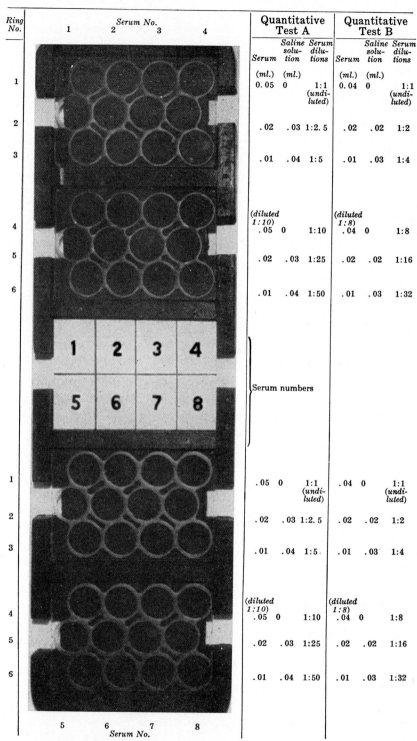

Ring No.	Serum No. 1 2 3 4	Quantitative Test A			Quantitative Test B		
		Serum (ml.)	Saline solution (ml.)	Serum dilutions	Serum (ml.)	Saline solution (ml.)	Serum dilutions
1		0.05	0	1:1 (undiluted)	0.04	0	1:1 (undiluted)
2		.02	.03	1:2.5	.02	.02	1:2
3		.01	.04	1:5	.01	.03	1:4
4		(diluted 1:10) .05	0	1:10	(diluted 1:8) .04	0	1:8
5		.02	.03	1:25	.02	.02	1:16
6		.01	.04	1:50	.01	.03	1:32
	1 2 3 4 / 5 6 7 8	Serum numbers					
1		.05	0	1:1 (undiluted)	.04	0	1:1 (undiluted)
2		.02	.03	1:2.5	.02	.02	1:2
3		.01	.04	1:5	.01	.03	1:4
4		(diluted 1:10) .05	0	1:10	(diluted 1:8) .04	0	1:8
5		.02	.03	1:25	.02	.02	1:16
6		.01	.04	1:50	.01	.03	1:32
	Serum No. 5 6 7 8						

Figure 23–4. Slides and slide holder for quantitative tests. (From Venereal Disease Research Laboratory. In Serologic Tests for Syphilis. U.S. Department of Health, Education, and Welfare, Public Health Service, 1959.)

10. Add one drop (1/75 ml.) of antigen emulsion to each ring, using a syringe and needle of appropriate size.

11. Complete tests in the manner described for the "VDRL Slide Qualitative Test with Serum" (p. 858) and read results microscopically immediately after rotation. By this method the dilutions of each serum are 1:1 (undiluted), 1:2, 1:4, 1:8, 1:16, and 1:32.

12. If all serum dilutions tested produce reactive results, prepare a 1:64 dilution of that serum in saline solution. Add seven parts of saline solution to one part of the 1:8 serum dilution, and test in three amounts as was done with the 1:8 serum dilutions. Dilutions prepared from the 1:64 dilution will be equivalent to 1:64, 1:128, and 1:256.

Reading and reporting slide quantitative test results

1. Read tests microscopically at 100× magnification as described for the qualitative procedure.

2. Report results in terms of the greatest serum dilution that produces a reactive (not weakly reactive) result in accordance with the following examples:

Method A

UNDI-LUTED SERUM 1:1	SERUM DILUTIONS 1:2.5	1:5	1:10	1:25	REPORT
R*	WR	N	N	N	Reactive, undiluted only, or 1 dil.
R	R	WR	N	N	Reactive, 1:2.5 dilution, or 2.5 dils.
R	R	R	WR	N	Reactive, 1:5 dilution, or 5 dils.
WR	N	N	N	N	Weakly reactive, undiluted only, or 0 dils.
WR	R	R	WR	N	Reactive, 1:5 dilution, or 5 dils.

Method B

UNDI-LUTED SERUM 1:1	SERUM DILUTIONS 1:2	1:4	1:8	1:16	REPORT
R*	WR	N	N	N	Reactive, undiluted only, or 1 dil.
R	R	WR	N	N	Reactive, 1:2 dilution, or 2 dils.
R	R	R	WR	N	Reactive, 1:4 dilution, or 4 dils.

*R = Reactive. WR = Weakly reactive. N = Non-reactive.

Note: Under conditions of high temperature and low humidity, which are sometimes present during the summer months in certain areas, antigen emulsion may be stored in the refrigerator but should be restored to room temperature before use. To avoid surface drying under these conditions, tests should be completed and read as rapidly as possible. Slide covers containing a moistened blotter may be employed.

VDRL TUBE FLOCCULATION TESTS WITH SERUM

Equipment
1. Kahn shaking machine (must be operated at 275 to 285 oscillations per minute).
2. Reading lamp, fluorescent or gooseneck-type.

Reagents
1. Antigen. (VDRL slide flocculation test antigen; see p. 856.)
2. Saline solutions.
   a. 1 per cent buffered saline solution. (Prepare as for the VDRL slide flocculation tests.)
   b. Unbuffered 1 per cent sodium chloride solution. Add 1 gm. of dry sodium chloride (A.C.S.) to each 100 ml. of distilled water.

Preparation of Serums
1. Clear serum, removed from centrifuged, whole, clotted blood, is heated in a 56° C. water bath for 30 minutes before being tested.
2. All serums are examined when removed from the water bath, and those found to contain particulate debris are recentrifuged.
3. Serums to be tested more than four hours after being heated should be reheated at 56° C. for ten minutes.

Preparation of Antigen Emulsion
1. Prepare antigen emulsion as described for the VDRL slide flocculation tests (see p. 856).
2. Add four parts of 1 per cent sodium chloride solution to one part of VDRL slide test emulsion. Mix well and allow to stand five or more minutes (not longer than two hours) before use. This solution will be referred to as "diluted antigen emulsion." Resuspend diluted antigen emulsion before use.

VDRL Tube Qualitative Test with Serum
1. Pipet 0.5 ml. of heated serum into a 12 × 75 mm. (outside dimension) test tube.

2. Add 0.5 ml. of diluted antigen emulsion to each serum.

3. Shake tubes on Kahn shaker for five minutes.

4. Centrifuge all tubes for ten minutes at a force equivalent to 2000 r.p.m. in No. 1, or to 1700 r.p.m. in No. 2, I.E.C. centrifuge* with horizontal heads.

5. Return tubes to the Kahn shaking machine and shake for exactly one minute. *Note:* Include reactive and nonreactive control serums in each test run.

Reading and reporting tube qualitative test results

1. Read test results *as soon as secondary shaking period is completed* by holding tubes close to the shade of a reading lamp with a black background at approximately eye level. A shaded fluorescent desk lamp or a gooseneck-type lamp with a blue bulb is a satisfactory reading light source.

2. Record results as follows:

Reactive.   Visible aggregates in a clear or slightly turbid medium. All borderline reactions— when the observer has doubt regarding visible clumping— should be reported as nonreactive.

Nonreactive.   No visible clumping or aggregation of antigen particles. Appearance slightly turbid or granular. Definite silken swirl on gentle shaking.

Note: Turbid or hemolyzed serums may cause completed tests to be too turbid for macroscopic reading and are therefore unsatisfactory specimens for this test. Zonal reactions owing to excess of reactive serum component may appear to be very weak or, in rare instances, non-reactive. Whenever a zonal reaction is suspected, another test should be performed, using 0.1 ml. of heated serum and 0.4 ml. of saline solutions in place of the original 0.5 ml. of serum. If a reactive finding is obtained with the smaller amount of serum, a reactive report should be issued.

VDRL Quantitative Tube Test with Serum

1. Pipet 0.5 ml. of freshly prepared 0.9 per cent saline solution into each of five or more test tubes (12 × 75 mm.), omitting the first tube.

2. Add 0.5 ml. of heated serum to the first and second tubes. (The first tube may be omitted if the VDRL tube qualitative test has been performed and if sufficient serum is not available.)

* International Equipment Co., Boston, Mass.

3. Mix and transfer 0.5 ml. from second to third tube.

4. Continue mixing and transferring 0.5 ml. from each tube to the next until the last tube is reached.

5. Mix and discard 0.5 ml. from last tube.

6. Add 0.5 ml. of diluted antigen emulsion to each tube and proceed as described under "VDRL Tube Qualitative Test with Serum" (p. 861).

Reading and reporting tube quantitative test results.

The greatest serum dilution producing a definitely reactive result is reported as the reactivity endpoint as shown in the following examples:

UN-DILUTED SERUM 1:1	SERUM DILUTIONS 1:2	1:4	1:8	1:16	REPORT
R*	N	N	N	N	Reactive, undiluted only, or 1 dil.
R	R	R	N	N	Reactive, 1:4 dilution, or 4 dils.
R	R	R	R	N	Reactive, 1:8 dilution, or 8 dils.

*R = Reactive. N = Nonreactive.

VDRL TESTS WITH SPINAL FLUID

Equipment

1. Kahn shaking machine (must be operated at 275 or 285 oscillations per minute).

Reagents

1. Antigen (VDRL slide flocculation test antigen, see p. 856).

2. Saline solutions.

   a. 1 per cent buffered saline solution. (Prepare as for the VDRL slide flocculation tests).

   b. 10 per cent sodium chloride solution. Dissolve 10 gm. of dry sodium chloride (A.C.S.) in 100 ml. of distilled water.

Preparation of Spinal Fluid

1. Centrifuge and decant each spinal fluid. Spinal fluids that are visibly contaminated or contain gross blood are unsatisfactory for testing.

2. Heat spinal fluid at 56° C. for 15 minutes. Cool to room temperature before testing.

Preparation of the Sensitized Antigen Emulsion

1. Prepare antigen emulsion as described

for the VDRL slide flocculation tests (see "Preparation of Antigen Emulsion," p. 856).

2. Add one part of 10 per cent sodium chloride solution to one part of VDRL slide test emulsion.

3. Mix well and allow to stand at least five minutes but not more than two hours before use.

VDRL Qualitative Test with Spinal Fluid

1. Pipet 1.0 ml. of heated spinal fluid into a 13 × 100 mm. test tube. Include reactive and nonreactive spinal fluid controls in each test run.

2. Add 0.2 ml. of sensitized antigen emulsion to each spinal fluid. Resuspend the sensitized antigen emulsion immediately before use by inverting container several times.

3. Shake racks of tubes on Kahn shaking machine for 15 minutes.

4. Centrifuge all tubes for five minutes at force equivalent to 1800 r.p.m. in No. 1, or to 1600 r.p.m. in No. 2, I.E.C. centrifuge.

5. Return tubes to Kahn shaking machine and shake exactly two minutes.

Reading and reporting qualitative test results

1. Read test results as soon as possible after the secondary shaking period by holding tubes close to the shade of a desk lamp having a black background. *Note:* Each tube may be held motionless or shaken gently during the reading. Excessive agitation should be avoided.

2. Report results as follows:

| Reactive. | Definitely visible aggregates suspended in a water clear or turbid medium. All borderline reaction in which the observer has doubt regarding visible clumping should be reported as nonreactive. |
| Nonreactive. | No aggregation, complete dispersion of particles, appearance turbid or slightly granular. Definite silken swirl on gentle shaking. |

VDRL Quantitative Test with Spinal Fluid

Quantitative tests are performed on all spinal fluids found to be reactive in the qualitative test.

1. Prepare spinal fluid dilutions as follows:
   a. Pipet 1.0 ml. of 0.9 per cent sodium chloride solution into each of five or more tubes.
   b. Add 1.0 ml. of heated spinal fluid to tube 1, mix well, and transfer 1.0 ml. to tube 2.
   c. Continue mixing and transferring

from one tube to the next until the last tube contains 2 ml. Discard 1.0 ml. from the last tube. The respective dilution ratios are 1:2, 1:4, 1:8, 1:16, 1:32, and so on.

2. Test each spinal fluid dilution as described under "VDRL Qualitative Test With Spinal Fluid."

Reading and reporting quantitative test results

1. Read each tube as described under "VDRL Qualitative Test with Spinal Fluid."

2. Report test results in terms of the highest dilution of spinal fluid producing a reactive result.

Example

SPINAL FLUID DILUTIONS					
1:2	1:4	1:8	1:16	1:32	REPORT
N	N	N	N	N	Reactive,* undiluted only, or 1 dil.
R	R	R	N	N	Reactive, 1:8 dilution, or 8 dils.
R	R	R	R	N	Reactive, 1:16 dilution, or 16 dils.

R = Reactive. N = Nonreactive.
* Reactive finding with undiluted spinal fluid in the qualitative test.

Plasmacrit (P.C.T.) Test

The plasmacrit test was originated in 1959 by Andujar and Mazurek to utilize the plasma from microhematocrit capillary tubes. The test is primarily intended as a rapid screening test and appears to be reasonably sensitive and specific. A similar reaction that has been well tested is the R.P.R. (Rapid Plasma Reagin) test of Portnoy, Garson, and Smith (1957).

Apparatus and Materials

1. Microhematocrit centrifuge.
2. A Kline or VDRL type rotator producing 180 r.p.m. in circle extensions of ¾ inch.
3. Special heparinized capillary plasmacrit tubes,* 75 mm. with an internal diameter of 1.2 mm. Ordinary microhematocrit tubes are not satisfactory for this test.
4. Sealing material. Same as for microhematocrit tubes or heat can be used but with caution to avoid hemolysis.
5. VDRL antigen and buffered saline.
6. Choline chloride.

* Available commercially.

7. Paraffin or ceramic ring plates as for the VDRL and slide test.

8. Antigen emulsion syringe. Tuberculin syringe with 25-gauge needle with bevel removed. It should be adjusted to deliver 100 drops per ml. of the antigen emulsion.

METHOD

1. From the free end of the plasma column of the microhematocrit tube measure back 22 mm. toward the packed red cells, and nick the glass here. Snap off this column (contains 0.025 ml.) of plasma, and with a small vaccine bulb blow it onto a ceramic ring.

2. One 0.01 ml. drop of antigen emulsion is added, and the mixture is agitated on the rotator for four minutes.

3. The mixture is promptly observed for clumping. The results are reported as: no clumping—*nonreactive* or *negative;* very slight clumping—*weakly reactive* or *doubtful* (the test should be repeated with another sample); moderate to marked clumping—*reactive* or *positive.* In the third category a sample of serum should be submitted for study by means of various serologic tests for syphilis.

PREPARATION OF ANTIGEN EMULSION

1. A solution of 10 ml. of 10 per cent choline chloride in 0.85 per cent saline should be made when the emulsion is prepared. It should be kept refrigerated.

2. VDRL slide antigen is prepared as specified in the technique for that test, but after the 5 ml. of antigen is ready, it is centrifuged in a conical stainless tube in an angle centrifuge at approximately 2000 g. for 15 to 30 minutes. The supernatant fluid is discarded and the emulsion of antigen is resuspended by blowing 5 ml. of 10 per cent choline chloride in saline directly onto the sediment and then vigorously shaking and tapping the centrifuge tube in the hand.

3. The emulsion will keep several days in the refrigerator but should be warmed to room temperature before use.

4. Adequate plasma controls must accompany each run. These are readily available from rejected reactive blood from the blood bank.

COMPLEMENT-FIXATION TESTS FOR SYPHILIS

In 1894 Pfeiffer showed that, when guinea pigs that had recovered from cholera were infected with *Vibrio comma,* their serum possessed strongly bacteriolytic activity against this organism. When the guinea pig serum was heated, this activity was lost. Further studies showed that the bacteriolytic activity was due to two substances, one a heat-resistant substance found only in the blood of an immune animal and the other a heat sensitive (thermolabile) substance present in the serum of nearly all warm-blooded animals, whether immune or not. Ehrlich named these substances "amboceptor" and "complement" (or alexin), respectively. The bacterium that induced the immunity and against which the bacteriolytic activity was directed was called the "antigen." According to Ehrlich the bacteriolytic power really resides in the complement, the specific amboceptor merely serving as an intermediate body or connecting link, which binds the complement to a particular kind of bacterium and thus enables the complement to act. Whenever this union of the three bodies takes place—whether within the body of an animal or in a test tube—bacteriolysis results. If the appropriate amboceptor or bacteriolysin is absent, complement, even if abundantly present, cannot be bound to the bacteria and hence does not attack them. If, on the other hand, the complement is absent, union of the amboceptor and bacteria does take place, but bacteriolysis does not occur. In such cases the bacteria are said to be sensitized and subsequent addition of complement will quickly bring about bacteriolysis.

Substances other than bacteria can act as antigens, notably red blood cells, the destruction of which is known as hemolysis. The mechanism is analogous to that described for bacteriolysis. Injection of washed erythrocytes from another species of animal induces the formation of hemolytic amboceptor, or hemolysin, which is capable of binding complement to erythrocytes of that species, thus bringing about their destruction.

When hemolysis is carried out *in vitro,* the process is easily followed by the unaided eye because of the liberation of hemoglobin from the damaged erythrocytes. When the reagents are first mixed, the erythrocytes form an opaque reddish suspension. As hemolysis proceeds, their hemoglobin diffuses out through the fluid, which eventually assumes a clear, transparent red color with no visible sediment. If hemolysis does not occur, the intact erythrocytes slowly settle to the bottom, forming a red sediment with a clear, colorless supernatant.

The part that the three substances play in hemolysis can be illustrated in the following simplified diagram (Fig. 23–5).

In the application of the complement-fixation reaction the determination of the amboceptor present in the patient's serum establishes the diagnosis of the corresponding disease. When the unknown serum is mixed with a specific antigen and complement in a test tube, one of two things will occur:

1. If the patient has the disease in question and if his blood serum therefore contains the corresponding amboceptor, "reagin," the complement will be bound or "fixed" to the antigen by the specific amboceptor and no complement will be left in the free state.

2. If the patient's serum does not contain the specific antibody, the complement will remain unbound or free in the fluid.

In either case there will be no visible change to show what has taken place, and it is therefore necessary to add an indicator that will show whether the complement still

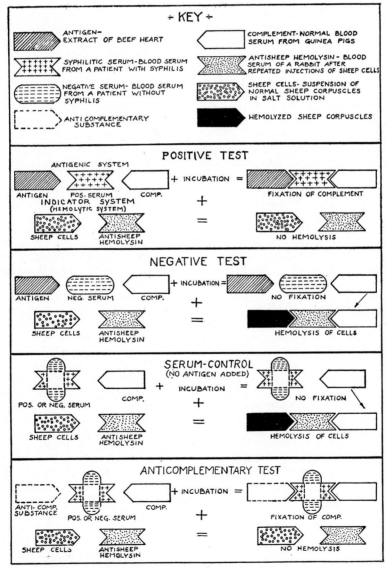

Figure 23–5.   Diagram illustrating the action of the various reagents used in the complement-fixation test. (Miller, S. E.: A Textbook of Clinical Pathology. 6th Ed. Baltimore, The Williams & Wilkins Company, 1955.)

remains free. This is done by adding sheep red blood cells and hemolytic amboceptor to these cells—"sensitized sheep cells." If free complement is present, the hemolytic system is completed and the erythrocytes will be hemolyzed. If, on the other hand, the complement has been bound to the antigen by the antibody, hemolysis cannot occur.

The phenomenon of complement fixation was applied to the serodiagnosis of syphilis by Wassermann, Neisser, and Bruch in 1906. At first, aqueous extracts of human syphilitic tissues were used as the antigen, but shortly after it was found that alcoholic extracts of normal animal tissues could be used equally well. Since the isolation of cardiolipin by Pangborn in 1941, the antigens used in the complement-fixation test for syphilis with the exception of the treponemal tests usually contain cardiolipin, lecithin, and cholesterol in proper proportions.

Since these antigens are not specific for syphilis, the reaction is due to the presence in the serum, spinal fluid, or body fluid of a substance designated as "reagin," which is not a true antibody for *T. pallidum*. Consequently, while the reactions are biologically nonspecific, they possess a remarkable degree of specificity from the practical point of view with the exceptions that have been discussed previously (p. 842).

The reaction has been applied to the diagnosis of a wide variety of diseases besides syphilis—parasitic, mycotic, viral, rickettsial, and bacterial. In many cases simpler procedures are available or the reaction has not proved sufficiently reliable to be of value. In other cases the complement-fixation reaction has considerable use; these are discussed in the appropriate section.

Kolmer Complement Fixation Test

There are many modifications of the original Wassermann technique; that of Kolmer to be described is the most widely used in this country. All complement-fixation tests are somewhat complex. Close adherence to the recommended procedures and careful standardization of all reagents is essential for accurate results.

Equipment

Racks, test tube, galvanized wire for 72 tubes.

Glassware

1. Test tubes, Pyrex, 15 × 85 mm. outside dimensions.

2. Tubes, centrifuge, graduated, 15 ml. capacity, Pyrex.

3. Tubes, centrifuge, round-bottom, 50 ml. capacity.

REAGENTS

1. Antigen. Antigen for the Kolmer tests is an alcoholic solution containing 0.03 per cent cardiolipin, 0.05 per cent lecithin, and 0.3 per cent cholesterol. Each new lot of antigen should be tested in parallel with a standard antigen in both qualitative and quantitative tests on reactive, weakly reactive, and nonreactive serums before being placed into routine use.

2. Saline solution

a. Weigh 8.5 gm. of dried sodium chloride (A.C.S.) and 0.1 gm. of magnesium sulfate or chloride crystals for each liter of saline solution.

b. Dissolve salts in distilled water. Freshly prepared saline solution should be used for each test run.

c. Place portion of saline solution sufficient for diluting complement (to be used for completing the tests) into refrigerator, allowing remainder to stand at room temperature (73° to 85° F.).

3. Sheep red cells.

Collection and Preservation of Sheep Blood. Sheep cells may be too resistant or too susceptible to the hemolytic action of complement and hemolysin. Because the reactivity level of a complement-fixation test is influenced by the quality of sheep cells employed, particular attention should be given to this test component. The effects of bacterial contamination on sheep cell reactivity are unpredictable, and only aseptically collected sheep blood in sterile containers is recommended for use in complement-fixation testing.

Red corpuscles from an occasional sheep will be found to be exceptionally resistant to the hemolytic action of complement and hemolysin. Whenever blood from an untested sheep is drawn, comparative complement and amboceptor titrations should be made, employing other sheep cells of acceptable quality.

Sheep cells are too fragile for use when a saline suspension of washed cells, prescribed by a test technique, shows any degree of hemolysis when stored overnight at 6° to 10° C.

The only recommended solution in either of these instances is to discard unsatisfactory cells and to obtain another supply of sheep blood. Freshly collected sheep blood should be refrigerated for 48 hours before being used.

4. Hemolysin. Stock glycerinated (50 per cent) sheep red cell hemolysin can be stored at refrigerator temperature for long periods of time with little loss of reactivity. A more rapid lowering of titer will be noted in the diluted hemolysin solutions. When a marked drop in titer is found or if precipitate is seen in the diluted hemolysin, the reagent should be discarded and reprepared from stock hemolysin.

A sudden drop in hemolysin titer may also be caused by the complement, sheep cells, or saline solutions used. Comparative tests should be made to determine which reagent is at fault.

5. Complement serum.

Preparation and Preservation of Complement. Guinea pig blood may possess less complement activity than the prescribed minimum or greater than the prescribed maximum. Low complement titers may be caused by improper feeding or housing of guinea pigs or, most commonly, through loss of reactivity during storage of guinea pig serum. Complement serum stored as liquid (with preservative added) at refrigerator temperature or in the frozen state should be adequately protected from partial drying as a result of evaporation. Aliquots sufficient for one day's use should be placed in containers to avoid complement destruction owing to repeated thawing and refreezing.

Some technicians are deceived by restoring dehydrated complement serum to only one-half or two-thirds of the original serum volume and then omitting the serum concentration factor when calculating complement dilution. Substandard serum may be made to appear adequately reactive in this way. This practice, used to circumvent technique restrictions, is to be discouraged.

Individual guinea pig serums may possess complement in higher titer than is optimum for some techniques. The pooling of serum from several guinea pigs will usually avoid this condition.

Cardiolipin-lecithin antigens are free of the fraction responsible for the nonspecific fixation of complement at low temperature. Pretesting of guinea pig serums and the use of egg white is therefore omitted when this type of antigen is employed.

a. Cell-free guinea pig serum can be obtained by centrifuging the tubes of blood and decanting serum from the clots when the laboratory practice is to bleed guinea pigs the day before the complement-fixation tests are performed. The serums from three or more guinea pigs should be pooled and returned to the refrigerator.

b. Dehydrated complement serum should be restored to original serum volume by dissolving in the proper amount of buffered diluent or distilled water and storing in the refrigerator.

c. Complement serum stored in the frozen state should be returned to liquid state by remaining at room temperature or at 37° C. only long enough to melt. Because the protein content of these serums will tend to collect at the bottom of the tube during thawing, these tubes of serum should be adequately mixed by inversion and returned to the refrigerator (6° to 10° C.).

Preparation

1. Select three or more large, healthy, male guinea pigs.

2. With a needle and syringe remove 5 ml. of blood from the heart and place in individual tubes identified by number.

3. After the blood has clotted at room temperature, ring with applicator stick and refrigerate for at least one hour.

4. Centrifuge and remove clear serum from the clot.

5. Pool serums from all tubes, recentrifuge, and preserve.

OR

6. If animals are to be exsanguinated, stun to anesthetize, cut the external jugular veins, and collect blood in Petri dishes or in 50 ml. centrifuge tubes.

7. Allow clotting to take place for one hour at room temperature.

8. Loosen clot from wall of container, and refrigerate for one to two hours.

9. Decant and filter serum through gauze, centrifuge, pool clear serum, and preserve.

Preservation

METHOD 1. Dehydrate complement serum from the frozen state *in vacuo* by the lyophile or cryochem methods.

METHOD 2. Add an equal part of the following solution to the complement serum:

Sodium acetate	12 gm.
Boric acid	4 gm.
Sterile distilled water	100 ml.

For use dilute 1 ml. of the preserved complement serum with 14 ml. of saline solution to prepare a 1:30 dilution. Store in refrigerator.

METHOD 3. Add 1.0 gm. of sodium chloride for every 10 ml. of guinea pig serum. Store in refrigerator.

Method 4. Freeze complement serum and retain in the frozen state until used.*

Preparation of Serums

1. Centrifuge blood specimens and separate serum from the clot by pipetting or decanting.

2. Heat serum at 56° C. for 30 minutes. Previously heated serums should be reheated for five minutes at 56° C. on day of testing.

3. Recentrifuge any serum in which visible particles have formed during heating.

Note: If complement-fixation reactions of maximum sensitivity are desired in the Kolmer quantitative test, it is necessary to remove the natural antisheep hemolysins from serums. This may be accomplished in the following manner:

a. Pipet 1 ml. of each serum into a small (12 × 75 mm.) tube and place in the refrigerator for 15 or more minutes.

b. Add one drop of washed, packed sheep red cells to each serum and mix well.

c. Return all tubes to the refrigerator for 15 minutes.

d. All tubes then are centrifuged and the serums separated by decanting. Avoid carrying over cell residue from side walls or bottom of tubes.

e. These serums then are heated at 56° C. for 30 minutes. Previously heated, absorbed serums should be reheated for ten minutes.

Preparation of Spinal Fluid

1. Centrifuge and decant all spinal fluids to remove cellular and particulate debris. Spinal fluids that are visibly contaminated or contain gross blood should not be tested.

2. Heat all spinal fluids at 56° C. for 15 minutes to remove thermolabile anticomplementary substances.

Preparation of Sheep Red Cell Suspension

1. Filter an adequate quantity of preserved sheep blood through gauze into a 50 ml. round-bottom centrifuge tube.

2. Add two or three volumes of saline solution to each tube.

3. Centrifuge tubes at a force sufficient to throw down corpuscles in five minutes

* 2 gm. per cent sodium acetate (A.C.S.) is added to complement serum before dehydration or storage in frozen state at the Venereal Disease Research Laboratory.

(I.E.C. centrifuge No. 1 at 2000 r.p.m. or I.E.C. centrifuge No. 2 at 1700 r.p.m.).

4. Remove supernatant fluid by suction through a capillary pipet, taking off upper white cell layer.

5. Fill tube with saline solution and resuspend cells by inverting and gently shaking tube.

6. Recentrifuge tube and repeat the process for a total of three washings. If supernatant fluid is not colorless on third washing, cells are too fragile and should not be used.

7. After supernatant fluid is removed from third washing, cells are poured or washed into a 15 ml. graduated centrifuge tube and centrifuged at previously used speed for ten minutes in order to pack cells firmly and evenly.

8. Read the volume of packed cells in the centrifuge tube and carefully remove supernatant fluid.

9. Prepare a 2 per cent suspension of sheep cells by washing the corpuscles into a flask with 49 volumes of saline solution. Shake flask to insure even suspension of cells.

Example

2.1 ml. (packed cells) × 49 = 102.9 ml. (saline solution required).

10. Pipet 15 ml. of the 2 per cent cell suspension into a graduated centrifuge tube and centrifuge at previously used speed for ten minutes. A 15 ml. aliquot of a properly prepared cell suspension will produce 0.3 ml. ± 0.01 ml. of packed cells.

Note: When the packed cell volume is beyond the tolerable limits just stated, the cell suspension concentration should be adjusted. The quantity of saline solution that must be removed or added to the cell suspension to accomplish adjustment is determined according to the formula shown at bottom of page.*

Example 1

Volume of cell suspension   100 ml.
Centrifuge tube (15 ml.) reading   0.27 ml.

$$\frac{0.27 \text{ ml.}}{0.3 \text{ ml.}} \times 100 \text{ ml.} = 90 \text{ ml.}$$

Therefore, 10 ml. of saline solution should be removed from each 100 ml. of cell suspension. Saline solution may be removed by centrifuging an aliquot of the cell suspension and pipetting off the desired volume of saline solution for discard.

---

* $\dfrac{\text{Actual reading of centrifuge tube}}{\text{Correct reading of centrifuge tube}} \times$ Volume of cell suspension =

Corrected volume of cell suspension

Example 2

Volume of cell suspension   100   ml.
Centrifuge tube (15 ml.) reading   0.33 ml.

$$\frac{0.33 \text{ ml.}}{0.3 \text{ ml.}} \times 100 \text{ ml.} = 110 \text{ ml.}$$

Therefore, 10 ml. of saline solution should be added to each 100 ml. of cell suspension. An adjusted cell suspension should be rechecked by centrifuging a 15 ml. portion.

11. Place flask of cell suspension in refrigerator when not in use. Always shake before using to secure an even suspension, because the corpuscles settle to the bottom of the flask when allowed to stand.

Preparation of Antigen Dilution

1. Place the required amount of saline solution in a flask and add antigen drop by drop while continuously shaking the flask. Rinse the pipet. The amount needed may be calculated from the number of tubes containing antigen in the test and titrations. The test dose constitutes 0.5 ml. of the antigen dilution indicated on the label of the bottle—usually 1:150.

2. Antigen dilution is kept at room temperature in a stoppered flask.

3. The diluted antigen should stand at room temperature for at least one hour before it is used.

Preparation of Stock Hemolysin Dilution

1. Prepare 1:100 stock hemolysin dilution as follows:

	ml.
Saline solution	94.0
Phenol solution (5 per cent in saline solution)	4.0
Glycerinized hemolysin (50 per cent)	2.0

Phenol solution should be mixed well with the saline solution before glycerinized hemolysin is added. This solution keeps well at refrigerator temperature but should be discarded when found to contain precipitate.

2. Each new lot of stock hemolysin dilution (1:100) should be checked by parallel titration with the previous stock hemolysin dilution before it is placed into routine use.

3. Dilutions of hemolysin of 1:1000 or greater are prepared by further diluting aliquots of the 1:100 dilution.

After these reagents are prepared, the complement and hemolysin titrations may be assembled.

Complement and Hemolysin Titrations

1. Perform these two titrations simultaneously in the same rack.

2. Place ten tubes (numbered 1 to 10) in one side of the rack for the hemolysin titration and eight tubes (numbered 1 to 8) in the other side for the complement titration. Add two other tubes to the rack, one for 1:1000 hemolysin solution and one for 1:30 complement dilution.

3. Prepare a 1:1000 dilution of hemolysin by placing 4.5 ml. of saline solution in a test tube and adding 0.5 ml. of 1:100 stock hemolysin solution by measuring from point to point in a 1.0 ml. pipet. Allow the solution to run into the tube a little above the level of the saline. Discard pipet. Mix thoroughly with a clean pipet, being sure to wash down all hemolysin solution adhering to the wall of the tube.

4. Pipet 0.5 ml. of 1:1000 hemolysin solution into the first five tubes of the hemolysin titration.

5. Add the following amounts of saline solution to the hemolysin titration tubes:

	TUBE NO.									
	1	2	3	4	5	6	7	8	9	10
Saline solution	None	0.5 ml.	1.0 ml.	1.5 ml.	2.0 ml.	0.5 ml.	0.5 ml.	0.5 ml.	0.5 ml.	0.5 ml.

6. Proceed as follows:

TUBE NO.	PROCESS	FINAL HEMOLYSIN DILUTION
1	None	1:1,000
2	Mix. Discard 0.5 ml.	1:2,000
3	Mix. Transfer 0.5 ml. to tube 6. Discard 0.5 ml.	1:3,000
4	Mix. Transfer 0.5 ml. to tube 7. Discard 1.0 ml.	1:4,000
5	Mix. Transfer 0.5 ml. to tube 8. Discard 1.5 ml.	1:5,000
6	Mix. Transfer 0.5 ml. to tube 9.	1:6,000
7	Mix. Transfer 0.5 ml. to tube 10.	1:8,000
8	Mix. Discard 0.5 ml.	1:10,000
9	Mix. Discard 0.5 ml.	1:12,000
10	Mix. Discard 0.5 ml.	1:16,000

7. Prepare 1:30 dilution of complement by adding 0.2 ml. of guinea pig serum to 5.8 ml. of saline solution, measuring from point to point in a 1 ml. pipet. Discard pipet. Mix thoroughly with a clean pipet, being sure to wash down all the serum adhering to the wall of the tube.

8. Pipet 0.3 ml. of 1:30 complement into each of ten tubes of the hemolysin titration.

9. Add the following amounts of 1:30 complement to the complement titration tubes:

	TUBE NO.							
	1	2	3	4	5	6	7	8
Complement 1:30	0.2 ml.	0.25 ml.	0.3 ml.	0.35 ml.	0.4 ml.	0.45 ml.	0.5 ml.	0.0 ml.

10. Add 0.5 ml. of antigen dilution to each of the first seven tubes of the complement titration.

11. Add 1.7 ml. of saline solution to each of the ten tubes of the hemolysin titration.

12. Add the following amounts of saline solution to the complement titration tubes:

	TUBE NO.							
	1	2	3	4	5	6	7	8
Saline solution	1.3 ml.	1.3 ml.	1.2 ml.	1.2 ml.	1.1 ml.	1.1 ml.	1.0 ml.	2.5 ml.

13. Add 0.5 ml. of 2 per cent sheep red cell suspension to each tube of the hemolysin titration.

14. Shake each tube of the hemolysin titration to insure even distribution of cells and place rack containing the two titrations in the 37° C. water bath for one hour. At this point the complement titration and the completed hemolysin titration stand as shown in Tables 23–9 and 23–10.

15. Remove rack from water bath and read hemolysin titration.

The unit of hemolysin is the highest dilution that gives complete sparkling hemolysis. The use of dilutions lower than 1:4000 is not recommended.

Hemolysin for the complement titration and test proper is diluted so that 2 units are contained in 0.5 ml.

16. Prepare a quantity of diluted hemolysin, containing 2 units per 0.5 ml., sufficient for the complement titration in accordance with Table 23–11.

Table 23–9. Complement Titration (First Stage)

TUBE NO.	COMPLEMENT 1:30 (ML.)	ANTIGEN DILUTION (ML.)	SALINE SOLUTION (ML.)
1	0.2	0.5	1.3
2	0.25	0.5	1.3
3	0.3	0.5	1.2
4	0.35	0.5	1.2
5	0.4	0.5	1.1
6	0.45	0.5	1.1
7	0.5	0.5	1.0
8	0	0	2.5

Table 23–10. Hemolysin Titration (Complete)

TUBE NO.	HEMOLYSIN DILUTION (0.5 ML.)	COMPLEMENT 1:30 (ML.)	SALINE SOLUTION (ML.)	SHEEP CELL SUSPENSION (2 PER CENT) (ML.)
1	1:1,000	0.3	1.7	0.5
2	1:2,000	0.3	1.7	0.5
3	1:3,000	0.3	1.7	0.5
4	1:4,000	0.3	1.7	0.5
5	1:5,000	0.3	1.7	0.5
6	1:6,000	0.3	1.7	0.5
7	1:8,000	0.3	1.7	0.5
8	1:10,000	0.3	1.7	0.5
9	1:12,000	0.3	1.7	0.5
10	1:16,000	0.3	1.7	0.5

Table 23–11.

DILUTION CONTAINING 1 UNIT PER 0.5 ML.	DILUTION CONTAINING 2 UNITS PER 0.5 ML.	TO PREPARE 2 UNIT HEMOLYSIN DILUTION, MIX: 1:100 HEMOLYSIN SOLUTION (ML.)	SALINE SOLUTION (ML.)
1:4,000	1:2,000	0.3	5.7
1:5,000	1:2,500	0.2	4.8
1:6,000	1:3,000	0.2	5.8
1:8,000	1:4,000	0.15	5.85
1:10,000	1:5,000	0.1	4.9
1:12,000	1:6,000	0.1	5.9
1:16,000	1:8,000	0.1	7.9

Table 23–12. Complement Titration (Complete)

TUBE NO.	COMPLE-MENT 1:30 (ML.)	ANTIGEN DILUTION (ML.)	SALINE SOLUTION (ML.)		HEMOLYSIN (ML.)	SHEEP CELL SUSPENSION (2 PER CENT) (ML.)	
1	0.20	0.5	1.3		0.5	0.5	
2	0.25	0.5	1.3	37° C. water bath. for 1 hour.	0.5	0.5	37° C. water bath. for 1/2 hour.
3	0.30	0.5	1.2		0.5	0.5	
4	0.35	0.5	1.2		0.5	0.5	
5	0.40	0.5	1.1		0.5	0.5	
6	0.45	0.5	1.1		0.5	0.5	
7	0.50	0.5	1.0		0.5	0.5	
8	None	None	2.5		None	0.5	

Table 23–13.

EXACT UNIT (ML.)	FULL UNIT (ML.)	TWO FULL UNITS (ML.)	DILUTION TO USE	PREPARATION COMPLEMENT SERUM (ML.)		SALINE SOLUTION (ML.)
0.3	0.35	0.7	1:43	1	+	42
0.35	0.4	0.8	1:37	1	+	36
0.4	0.45	0.9	1:33	1	+	32
0.45	0.50	1.0	1:30	1	+	29

17. Add 0.5 ml. of diluted hemolysin (containing 2 units of hemolysin) to each of the first seven tubes of the complement titration.

18. Add 0.5 ml. of 2 per cent sheep red cell suspension to all eight tubes of the complement titration. The addition of hemolysin and cells to the complement titration should be completed without delay, preferably within five minutes after rack is removed from the water bath.

19. Shake each tube of the complement titration to insure even distribution of cells and return to the 37° C. water bath for 30 minutes. The completed complement titration is shown in Table 23–12.

20. Remove rack from water bath and read complement titration. *The smallest amount of complement giving complete sparkling hemolysis is the exact unit. The full unit is 0.05 ml. more than the exact unit.*

For the complement-fixation tests complement is diluted so that 2 full units are contained in 1.0 ml.

Example

	ml.
Exact unit	0.3
Full unit	0.35
Dose (2 full units)	0.7

Dilution of complement to be employed in the test proper may be calculated by dividing 30 by the dose, i.e., $\frac{30}{0.7} = 43$ or 1:43 dilution of guinea pig serum.

Table 23–13 gives additional examples.

Occasionally hyperactive complement serums are encountered that yield titrations indicating 2 full units per milliliter in dilutions greater than 1:43. These complements should be used at 1:43 dilution to accomplish satisfactory testing. *Note:* Tubes of the complement or hemolysin titrations showing complete hemolysis may be removed and placed in the refrigerator for later use as hemoglobin solutions for the reading standards (see p. 881).

KOLMER QUALITATIVE TESTS WITH SERUM AND SPINAL FLUID

1. Arrange test tubes in wire racks so that there are two tubes for each serum and spinal fluid to be tested. Control serums of graded reactivity should be included. Number the first row of tubes to correspond to the serum and spinal fluid being tested. Three additional test tubes are included for reagent controls.

2. Pipet 0.5 ml. of saline solution into each tube of the second row.

3. Add the following amounts of saline solution to the three control tubes:

	Saline Solution ml.
Antigen control	0.5
Hemolytic system control	1.0
Corpuscle control	2.5

4. Pipet 0.2 ml. of each serum to be tested into tubes 1 and 2.

5. Pipet 0.5 ml. of each spinal fluid to be tested into tubes 1 and 2.

6. Pipet 0.2 ml. of each control serum to be tested into tubes 1 and 2.

7. Add 0.5 ml. of the antigen dilution to the first tube of each test—either serum, control serum, or spinal fluid—and to the antigen control tube.

8. Allow test racks to stand for 10 to 30 minutes at room temperature.

9. Prepare diluted complement during this interval. The amount needed is equivalent to 1.0 ml. for each tube of the test plus a slight excess.

Note: The volume of complement serum to be diluted is determined by the amount of diluted complement necessary for the test proper. Dividing the number of milliliters of diluted complement needed by the titration dilution factor (2 full units) will give the number of milliliters of complement serum needed. Calculations may be made in accordance with Table 23–14.

10. Add 1 ml. of diluted complement (containing 2 full units) to all tubes of the

Table 23–14.

COMPLEMENT TITRATION, 2 FULL UNITS	DILUTED COMPLEMENT NEEDED (ML.)	COMPLEMENT SERUM REQUIRED (ML.)	COLD SALINE SOLUTION REQUIRED (ML.)
1:43	43	1	42
1:43	215	5	210
1:37	37	1	36
1:30	210	7	203

serum, control serum, and spinal fluid tests, including the antigen control tube and the hemolytic system control tube.

11. Mix the contents of the tubes by shaking the racks well and place in the refrigerator at 6° to 8° C. for 15 to 18 hours.

12. Prepare the volume of diluted hemolysin needed for the test proper, allowing 0.5 ml. (containing 2 units)* for each tube. Prepare a slight excess. The following formula (shown at bottom of page) may be used for calculating the amounts of 1:100 hemolysin solution and diluent required to prepare the needed volume of diluted hemolysin.

Table 23–15 gives additional examples:

Table 23–15.

HEMOLYSIN TITER, 2 UNITS IN 0.5 ML.	DILUTED HEMOLYSIN NEEDED (ML.)	1:100 HEMOLYSIN REQUIRED (ML.)	SALINE SOLUTION REQUIRED (ML.)
1:3,000	30	1	29
1:4,000	120	3	117
1:2,500	25	1	24
1:2,500	250	10	240

13. Remove racks of tubes from the refrigerator at regular intervals and place immediately in the 37° C. water bath for ten minutes. The interval will be determined by the length of time necessary to add hemolysin and sheep cell suspension to each rack.

14. Remove each rack from the water bath and add 0.5 ml. of the diluted hemolysin to all tubes of the test except the corpuscle control tube.

15. Add 0.5 ml. of the 2 per cent sheep

---

* $\dfrac{100}{\text{Hemolysin titration dilution factor (2 units)}} \times \text{Volume of diluted hemolysin needed (ml.)} = \text{ml. of 1:100 hemolysin required}$

Table 23–16. Outline of Kolmer Qualitative Tests with Serum and Spinal Fluid

TUBE NO.		SALINE SOLUTION	ANTIGEN		COMPLEMENT 2 FULL UNITS		HEMOLYSIN 2 UNITS	SHEEP CELL SUSPENSION (2 PER CENT)	
	Serum (ml.)	(ml.)	(ml.)	Shake rack well. Allow to stand at room temperature for 10 to 30 minutes.	(ml.)	Shake rack well. Primary incubation 15 to 18 hours at 6° to 10° C. followed by 10 minutes in 37° C. water bath.	(ml.)	(ml.)	Shake rack well. Secondary incubation in 37° C. water bath.
1	0.2	None	0.5		1.0		0.5	0.5	
2	0.2	0.5	None		1.0		0.5	0.5	
	Spinal fluid (ml.)								
1	0.5	None	0.5		1.0		0.5	0.5	
2	0.5	0.5	None		1.0		0.5	0.5	
Controls									
Antigen		0.5	0.5		1.0		0.5	0.5	
Hemolytic system		1.0	None		1.0		0.5	0.5	
Corpuscle		2.5	None		None		None	0.5	

red cell suspension (prepared the previous day) to all tubes. The 2 per cent cell suspension should be agitated occasionally to insure even suspension of cells during the period when this reagent is being added to the complement-fixation tests.

16. Mix the contents of the tubes thoroughly by shaking each rack before returning it to the 37° C. water bath for the secondary incubation. Examine the controls at five-minute intervals. The period of secondary incubation will be determined by the length of time necessary to reproduce the predetermined reactivity pattern of the control serums. In all instances, however, the reading time should be at least ten minutes more than is required to hemolyze the antigen and hemolytic system controls but should not exceed a total of 60 minutes' incubation. When control serums are not available, the secondary incubation period will be terminated ten minutes after the hemolytic system control and the antigen control hemolyze. In no instance should this period extend beyond one hour.

17. Remove each rack of tubes from the water bath at the end of the secondary incubation period. Record observed hemolysis as described under "Preparation of Reading Standards" (p. 874) and "Reading and Reporting Test Results" (p. 874) except in those instances in which inhibition of hemolysis is noted in the control tube.

All serums and spinal fluids showing inhibition of hemolysis in the control tube should be returned to the 37° C. water bath for a period sufficient to complete one hour of secondary incubation. At the end of this period these tests are removed from the water bath, and tube readings (including control tubes) are recorded (Table 23–16).

KOLMER QUANTITATIVE TESTS WITH SERUM AND SPINAL FLUID

1. Place test tubes in wire racks, allowing eight tubes for each serum and six tubes for each spinal fluid to be tested. Include reagent controls and control serums of graded reactivity.

2. For each serum pipet 0.9 ml. of saline solution into tube 1 and 0.5 ml. of saline solution into tubes 2, 3, 4, 5, 6, 7, and 8.

3. For each spinal fluid pipet 0.5 ml. of saline solution into tubes 2, 3, 4, 5, and 6.

4. Pipet the indicated amount of saline solution into each of the following reagent control tubes:

	Saline Solution
Antigen control	0.5 ml.
Hemolytic control	1.0 ml.
Corpuscle control	2.5 ml.

5. For each serum proceed as follows:

TUBE NO.	PROCESS	SERUM DILUTION
1	Add 0.6 ml. of inactivated serum. Mix and transfer 0.5 ml. to tube 8 (control) and to tube 2.	Undiluted
2	Mix. Transfer 0.5 ml. to tube 3.	1:2
3	Mix. Transfer 0.5 ml. to tube 4.	1:4
4	Mix. Transfer 0.5 ml. to tube 5.	1:8
5	Mix. Transfer 0.5 ml. to tube 6.	1:16
6	Mix. Transfer 0.5 ml. to tube 7.	1:32
7	Mix. Discard 0.5 ml.	1:64
8		Undiluted (control)

6. For each spinal fluid proceed as follows:

TUBE NO.	PROCESS	SPINAL FLUID DILUTION
1	Add 0.5 ml. of spinal fluid.	Undiluted
2	Add 0.5 ml. of spinal fluid. Mix. Transfer 0.5 ml. to tube 3.	1:2
3	Mix. Transfer 0.5 ml. to tube 4.	1:4
4	Mix. Transfer 0.5 ml. to tube 5.	1:8
5	Mix. Discard 0.5 ml.	1:16
6	Add 0.5 ml. of spinal fluid	Undiluted (control)

7. Add 0.5 ml. of diluted antigen to the first seven tubes of each serum test, to the first five tubes of each spinal fluid test, and to the antigen control tube. Shake the racks to mix thoroughly.

8. Allow racks to stand at room temperature for 10 to 30 minutes.

9. Complete the tests as indicated in paragraphs 9 through 17 of the technique for the performance of the "Kolmer Qualitative Tests with Serum and Spinal Fluid" (p. 872).

Both qualitative and quantitative tests may be conducted in one-half volume. The amounts of complement, antigen, and other reagents needed are in this way reduced

by half. Some accuracy of operation may be sacrificed by using these reduced quantities, however, since the relative effects of measuring errors are increased. Hemolysin and complement are titrated at full volume as described for the regular test. The performance of the one-half volume tests is identical with the regular methods except that halved volumes of serum, spinal fluid, and reagents are used (Table 23–17).

Preparation of Reading Standards

1. Heat tubes of hemoglobin solution (saved from the titration or obtained from control tubes of current day's tests) in the 56° C. water bath for five minutes.

2. Prepare a 1:6 dilution of 2 per cent corpuscle suspension by adding 5 ml. of saline solution to 1 ml. of 2 per cent suspension.

3. Prepare reading standards by mixing hemoglobin solution and cell suspension in the proportions given in Table 23–18.

4. Reading standards are prepared with one-half volumes of cell suspension and hemoglobin solution when performing the one-half volume tests.

Reading and Reporting Test Results

1. All serum and spinal fluid controls should show complete hemolysis.

2. Estimate the individual tube readings

Table 23–17. Outline of Kolmer Quantitative Tests with Serum and Spinal Fluid

TUBE NO.		ANTIGEN		COMPLEMENT 2 FULL UNITS		HEMOLYSIN 2 UNITS	SHEEP CELL SUSPENSION (2 PER CENT)	
	Serum (in 0.5 ml.)	(ml.)		(ml.)		(ml.)	(ml.)	
1	0.2 (undiluted)	0.5		1.0		0.5	0.5	
2	0.1 (1:2)	0.5		1.0		0.5	0.5	
3	0.05 (1:4)	0.5		1.0		0.5	0.5	
4	0.025 (1:8)	0.5	Shake rack well. Allow to stand at room temperature for 10 to 30 minutes.	1.0	Shake rack well. Primary incubation 15 to 18 hours at 6° to 10° C. followed by 10 minutes in 37° C. water bath.	0.5	0.5	Shake rack well. Secondary incubation in 37° C. water bath.
5	0.012 (1:16)	0.5		1.0		0.5	0.5	
6	0.006 (1:32)	0.5		1.0		0.5	0.5	
7	0.003 (1:64)	0.5		1.0		0.5	0.5	
8	0.2 (undiluted, control)	None		1.0		0.5	0.5	
	Spinal fluid (in 0.5 ml.)							
1	0.5 (undiluted)	0.5		1.0		0.5	0.5	
2	0.25 (1:2)	0.5		1.0		0.5	0.5	
3	0.125 (1:4)	0.5		1.0		0.5	0.5	
4	0.062 (1:8)	0.5		1.0		0.5	0.5	
5	0.031 (1:16)	0.5		1.0		0.5	0.5	
6	0.5 (undiluted, control)	None		1.0		0.5	0.5	
	Reagent controls							
	Antigen, 0.5 ml. saline solution	0.5		1.0		0.5	0.5	
	Hemolytic, 1.0 ml. saline solution	None		1.0		0.5	0.5	
	Corpuscle, 2.5 ml. saline solution	None		None		None	0.5	

Table 23–18.

1:6 CORPUSCLE SUSPENSION (ML.)	HEMOGLOBIN SOLUTION (ML.)	EQUIVALENT COMPLEMENT FIXATION PER CENT	RECORD
3.0	0.0	100	4+
1.5	1.5	50	3+
0.75	2.25	25	2+
0.3	2.7	10	1+
0.15	2.85	5	±
....	3.0	0	−

Table 23–19. Kolmer Qualitative Test Reporting

TEST TUBE READING	CONTROL TUBE READING	REPORT	TEST TUBE READING	CONTROL TUBE READING	REPORT
4+	−	Reactive	3+	3+	Anticomplementary
3+	−	Reactive	3+	2+	Anticomplementary
2+	−	Reactive	3+	1+	Weakly reactive
1+	−	Reactive	3+	±	Reactive
±	−	Weakly reactive	2+	2+	Nonreactive
−	−	Nonreactive	2+	1+	Nonreactive
4+	4+	Anticomplementary	2+	±	Weakly reactive
4+	3+	Anticomplementary	1+	1+	Nonreactive
4+	2+	Weakly reactive	±	±	Nonreactive
4+	1+	Reactive			

Table 23–20.

UNDILUTED	SERUMS OR SPINAL FLUID DILUTIONS 1:2	1:4	1:8	1:16	1:32	1:64	REPORT
4	3	1	−	−	−	−	Reactive, 1:4 dilution or 4 dils.
4	−	−	−	−	−	−	Reactive (4+), undiluted, or 1 dil.
4	4	3	2	−	−	−	Reactive, 1:8 dilution, or 8 dils.
4	4	4	4	4	1	−	Reactive, 1:32 dilution or 32 dils.
3	1	−	−	−	−	−	Reactive, 1:2 dilution or 2 dils.
1	−	−	−	−	−	−	Reactive, (1+), undiluted, or 1 dil.
2	1	±	−	−	−	−	Reactive, (1:2 dilution, or 2 dils.
±	−	−	−	−	−	−	Weakly reactive
−	−	−	−	−	−	−	Nonreactive
4	4	4	4	4	4	4	See note following.

by comparison with the reading standards at the end of the secondary incubation period, and record degree of complement fixation noted, except for those specimens showing inhibition of hemolysis in the control tube.

3. Read the tubes that have been returned to the 37° C. water bath for a full hour's secondary incubation, estimating and recording the degree of complement fixation of each tube and control tube by comparison with the reading standards.

4. Report the results of the qualitative tests in accordance with Table 23–19.

5. Quantitative tests are reported in terms of the highest dilution giving a reactive result (1+, 2+, 3+, or 4+) as illustrated in Table 23–20.

Note: If a reactive result is obtained with the highest dilution of the regular quantitative test (1:64), higher dilutions may be prepared and tested.

6. Report the results of the quantitative tests in accordance with Table 23–21 when

Table 23–21.   Quantitative Test Reporting

(After 1-Hour Secondary Incubation at 37° C.)

TEST TUBE READING							CONTROL TUBE READING	REPORT*
4	4	4	4	4	2	—	4+	Anticomplementary
4	4	3	—	—	—	—	2+	Reactive
4	4	1	—	—	—	—	1+	Reactive
4	4	1	—	—	—	—	±	Reactive
3	2	—	—	—	—	—	±	Reactive
4	4	1	—	—	—	—	3+	Weakly reactive
3	2	—	—	—	—	—	1+	Weakly reactive
2	1	—	—	—	—	—	±	Weakly reactive
3	—	—	—	—	—	—	±	Reactive
1	—	—	—	—	—	—	±	Nonreactive
1	—	—	—	—	—	—	1+	Nonreactive
2	—	—	—	—	—	—	1+	Nonreactive
2	—	—	—	—	—	—	2+	Nonreactive

* Quantitative designations of dilution endpoints or dils are omitted.

the full-hour incubation at 37° C. is required.

Retesting Anticomplementary Serums* (Modified Sachs Method)

1. Heat 0.5 ml. of serum in the 56° C. water bath for 15 minutes. If the serum has been previously inactivated, reheat for five minutes.

2. Add 4.1 ml. of accurately titrated N/300 hydrochloric acid to the serum and invert several times. Allow to stand for 30 minutes at room temperature.

3. Centrifuge for ten minutes, save supernatant fluid, and discard sediment.

4. Add 0.4 ml. of 10 per cent sodium chloride solution to the supernatant fluid. Neutralization is not necessary.

5. Arrange two rows of five test tubes each and number 1 to 5. The second row contains the serum controls.

6. Pipet 0.5 ml. of saline solution into tubes 3, 4, and 5 of both rows.

7. To both rows:

Add 1.0 ml. of treated serum to tube 1.

Add 0.5 ml. of treated serum to tubes 2 and 3.

Mix tube 3 and transfer 0.5 ml. to tube 4.

Mix tube 4 and transfer 0.5 ml. to tube 5.

Mix tube 5 and discard 0.5 ml.

The five tubes of each row contain 0.1,

* Anticomplementary serums may also be retested by preparing serial twofold dilutions in saline, beginning with 1:2 and ending with 1:64. Each dilution of serum in 0.5 ml. amounts is tested in two tubes as test and control. Interpret test results in the same manner as described for "Retesting Anticomplementary Spinal Fluids."

0.05, 0.025, 0.012, and 0.006 ml. of serum, respectively.

8. Add 0.5 ml. of antigen dilution to each tube of the first row.

9. Add 0.5 ml. of saline solution to each tube of the second row.

10. Shake rack of tubes to mix and allow to stand at room temperature for 10 to 30 minutes.

11. Add 1.0 ml. of diluted complement to all tubes of both rows.

12. Shake rack to mix and place in refrigerator for 15 to 18 hours at 6° to 10° C.

13. Complete the test as described under "Kolmer Qualitative Tests with Serum and Spinal Fluid" (p. 872).

14. Record degree of hemolysis in both the test and control tubes.

15. All tubes of the rear row may show complete hemolysis. However, the first and second tubes of the rear row may show slight inhibition of hemolysis.

With nonreactive serums the corresponding front tubes show the same degree of inhibition of hemolysis, and if the degree is slight, a nonreactive report may be rendered. With reactive serums inhibition of hemolysis is much more marked in tubes of the front row. Report the results as reactive, weakly reactive, or nonreactive.

Retesting Anticomplementary Spinal Fluids

1. Heat the spinal fluid for 15 minutes at 56° C.

2. Arrange two rows of five test tubes each and number 1 to 5.

3. Pipet 0.5 ml. of saline solution into tubes 2, 3, 4, and 5 of both rows.

4. To both rows:

Add 0.5 ml. of spinal fluid to tubes 1 and 2.

Mix tube 2 and transfer 0.5 ml. to tube 3.

Mix tube 3 and transfer 0.5 ml. to tube 4.

Mix tube 4 and transfer 0.5 ml. to tube 5.

Mix tube 5 and discard 0.5 ml.

5. Add 0.5 ml. of antigen dilution to each tube of the first row.

6. Add 0.5 ml. of saline solution to each tube of the second row.

7. Shake rack of tubes to mix and allow to stand at room temperature for 10 to 30 minutes.

8. Add 1.0 ml. of diluted complement to all tubes of both rows, shake rack to mix, place in the refrigerator for 15 to 18 hours at 6° to 10° C., and complete test as described under "Kolmer Qualitative Tests with Serum and Spinal Fluid."

9. Interpret the results according to the following examples:

First row:	4	4	4	1	—	Reactive
Second row:	4	1	—	—	—	
First row:	4	3	2	—	—	Reactive
Second row:	4	1	—	—	—	
First row:	4	1	—	—	—	Reactive
Second row:	1	—	—	—	—	
First row:	4	4	2	—	—	Nonreactive
Second row:	4	2	1	—	—	
First row:	3	2	—	—	—	Nonreactive
Second row:	3	1	—	—	—	

TREPONEMAL TESTS FOR SYPHILIS

The immunochemical nature of the antibody "reagin" detected in syphilitic serums by the conventional serologic procedures is essentially unknown, and the antigens employed are nonspecific. Also the frequency of biologic false positive reactions, as has previously been discussed, has stimulated a great deal of investigation leading to the definitive diagnosis of syphilis by the detection of antibody that is related directly to *Treponema pallidum.*

The major step in this direction was finally achieved by Nelson in 1947 and culminated in the development of the Treponema Immobilization Test (T.P.I.) by Nelson and Mayer in 1949. Since that time it has been widely and critically tested and found to be highly specific in the diagnosis of human syphilis. Unfortunately the propagation of virulent *T. pallidum* and its preparation for the tests are too complex for the average clinical laboratory, and only laboratories especially equipped for this purpose can perform it. For this reason many modi-

fications attempting to use killed treponemas have been developed in order to make the test more practical.

Some of these are:

T.P.I.	—	*Treponema pallidum* immobilization
T.P.I.A.	—	*Treponema pallidum* immune-adherence
T.P.A.	—	*Treponema pallidum* agglutination
T.P.M.B.	—	*Treponema pallidum* methylene blue
T.P.C.F.	—	*Treponema pallidum* complement fixation
F.T.A.	—	Fluorescent treponemal antibody
R.P.C.F.	—	Reiter protein complement fixation

Reiter Protein Complement-Fixation Test

A significant advance in the field of treponemal antigens was achieved when a simple and inexpensive antigen was prepared from the avirulent Reiter strain of *T. pallidum* by D'Allesandro (1953) and by Cannefax and Garson (1957). Comparative studies have revealed that the tests using this protein antigen in a complement-fixation test (R.P.C.F.) have given results comparable with the T.P.I. or T.P.C.F. tests. The antigen is prepared by growing the Reiter strain of *T. pallidum* in a modified Brewer's fluid thioglycollate medium containing horse serum. After incubation the treponemas are washed, frozen, and thawed repeatedly and dialyzed against saline. The test is carried out on sera or spinal fluids using a one-fifth volume Kolmer technique.

One-fifth Volume Kolmer Test

Equipment

Racks, test tube, galvanized wire for 72 tubes.

Glassware

1. Test tubes, Pyrex, 12 × 75 mm. outside dimensions.
2. Tubes, centrifuge, graduated, 15 ml. capacity, Pyrex.
3. Tubes, centrifuge, round-bottom, 50 ml. capacity.
4. Pipets, 0.25 ml., or 0.5 ml. capacity.

REAGENTS

1. Antigens. The Reiter protein antigen is a relatively stable antigen. It may be stored for long periods of time in a liquid state at 6° to 10° C., in a frozen state at −20° C. or −40° C., or in the lyophilized state.

2. Saline solution, sheep red cells, hemolysin, guinea pig complement. Same as for the Kolmer Qualitative Test.

PREPARATION OF SERUMS

Heat serum at 56° C. for 30 minutes before or after preparation of the 1:5 dilution that is used in the test. Previously heated, undiluted serums should be reheated for ten minutes at 56° C. on day of testing. Diluted serum should not be reheated or retested. Recentrifugate any specimen in which visible particles have formed during heating.

PREPARATION OF SPINAL FLUIDS

Same as for the Kolmer Qualitative Test. (See p. 872.)

PREPARATION OF SHEEP RED CELL SUSPENSION

Same as for the Kolmer Qualitative Test.

PREPARATION OF ANTIGEN DILUTION

1. Place the required amount of saline in a flask or tube.
2. Draw up 0.05 ml. or more of Reiter protein antigen in the bottom half of a 0.1 ml. pipet graduated to the tip, and add to the saline. (The test dose is 0.1 ml. of antigen dilution, indicated on the bottle label, as determined by titration. The amount needed may be calculated from the number of tubes containing antigen in the test.)
3. Mix well by filling and emptying the pipet a few times in the diluted antigen solution.

PREPARATION OF STOCK HEMOLYSIN DILUTION

Same as for the Kolmer Qualitative Test.

HEMOLYSIN AND COMPLEMENT TITRATIONS

1. Place ten tubes (numbered 1 to 10) in a rack.
2. Prepare a 1:1000 dilution of hemolysin in tube number 1 by adding 0.5 ml. of the 1:100 stock hemolysin to 4.5 ml. of saline, measuring from point to point in a 1 ml. pipet. Discard pipet and with a clean one, mix thoroughly, being sure to wash down all hemolysin solution adhering to the wall of the tube.
3. Pipet 0.5 ml. of 1:100 hemolysin solution into tubes 2 through 5.
4. Add the amounts of saline solution to tubes 2 through 10 shown below.*
5. Proceed as shown at bottom of page.
6. Perform the hemolysin and complement titrations simultaneously in the same rack.
7. Use 12 × 75 mm. tubes. Place ten tubes (numbered 1 to 10) in one side of the rack for the hemolysin titration and six tubes (numbered 1 to 6) in the other side for the complement titration.
8. Pipet 0.1 ml. of each of the hemolysin dilutions (1:1000 to 1:16,000) into each of the corresponding ten tubes of the hemolysin titration.
9. Prepare a 1:50 dilution of complement by adding 0.1 ml. of guinea pig serum to 4.9 ml. of saline, measuring from point to point in a 0.2 ml. pipet. Discard pipet. With a clean 1 ml. pipet mix thoroughly,

*					TUBE NO.					
	2	3	4	5	6	7	8	9	10	
Saline Solution	0.5 ml.	1.0 ml.	1.5 ml.	2.0 ml.	0.5 ml.	0.5 ml.	0.5 ml.	0.5 ml.	0.5 ml.	

TUBE NO.	PROCESS	FINAL HEMOLYSIN DILUTION
1	None.	1:1,000
2	Mix.	1:2,000
3	Mix. Transfer 0.5 ml. to tube 6.	1:3,000
4	Mix. Transfer 0.5 ml. to tube 7.	1:4,000
5	Mix. Transfer 0.5 ml. to tube 8.	1:5,000
6	Mix. Transfer 0.5 ml. to tube 9.	1:6,000
7	Mix. Transfer 0.5 ml. to tube 10.	1:8,000
8	Mix.	1:10,000
9	Mix.	1:12,000
10	Mix.	1:16,000

			TUBE NO.			
	1	2	3	4	5	6
Complement 1:50 (ml.)*	0.25	0.20	0.15	0.12	0.10	0.0
Saline solution (ml.)	0.25	0.30	0.35	0.38	0.40	0.60

* The complement dilution should be delivered to the bottom of the tubes. The quantity of 1:50 complement in the first two tubes may be measured with a 0.5 ml. or a 0.25 ml. pipet and in the last three tubes with a 0.2 ml. pipet.

being sure to wash down all serum adhering to the wall of the tube.

10. Pipet 0.1 ml. of 1:50 complement into each of the ten tubes of the hemolysin titration.

11. Add the amounts of 1:50 complement and saline solution to the complement-titration tubes shown at top of page.

12. Complete the hemolysin titration by the addition of 2 per cent sheep cell suspension and saline solution in the amounts and in the order indicated in Table 23–22.

13. Shake each tube of the hemolysin titration to insure even distribution of cells and place rack containing the two titrations in the 37° C. water bath for one hour.

14. Remove rack from the water bath and read hemolysin titration. The unit of hemolysin is the highest dilution that gives complete hemolysis.

15. Prepare a quantity of diluted hemolysin containing 2 units per 0.1 ml., sufficient for the complement titration as shown in Table 23–23.

16. Add 0.1 ml. of diluted hemolysin (containing 2 units of hemolysin) to each of the first five tubes of the complement titration.

17. Add 0.1 ml. of 2 per cent sheep red cell suspension to each tube of the complement titration.

18. Shake each tube of the complement titration to insure even distribution of the cells and return the rack to the 37° C. water bath for one-half hour. The complete titration is shown in Table 23–24

The smallest amount of 1:50 complement giving complete hemolysis is the exact unit. For use in the test, complement is diluted so that 2 exact units are contained in 0.2 ml.

Table 23–22. Hemolysin Titration

TUBE NO.	HEMOLYSIN 0.1 (ML.)	COMPLEMENT 1:50 (ML.)	2 PER CENT SHEEP RED CELL SUSPENSION (ML.)	SALINE SOLUTION (ML.)
1	1:1,000	0.1	0.1	0.4
2	1:2,000	0.1	0.1	0.4
3	1:3,000	0.1	0.1	0.4
4	1:4,000	0.1	0.1	0.4
5	1:5,000	0.1	0.1	0.4
6	1:6,000	0.1	0.1	0.4
7	1:8,000	0.1	0.1	0.4
8	1:10,000	0.1	0.1	0.4
9	1:12,000	0.1	0.1	0.4
10	1:16,000	0.1	0.1	0.4

Table 23–23.

DILUTION CONTAINING 1 UNIT PER 0.1 ML.	DILUTION CONTAINING 2 UNITS PER 0.1 ML.	TO PREPARE 2 UNIT HEMOLYSIN DILUTION, MIX	
		1:100 HEMOLYSIN SOLUTION (ML.)	SALINE SOLUTION (ML.)
1:4,000	1:2,000	0.1	1.9
1:5,000	1:2,500	0.1	2.4
1:6,000	1:3,000	0.1	2.9
1:8,000	1:4,000	0.1	3.9
1:10,000	1:5,000	0.1	4.9
1:12,000	1:6,000	0.1	5.9
1:16,000	1:8,000	0.1	7.9

Table 23–24. Complement Titration

TUBE NO.	COMPLEMENT 1:50 (ML.)	SALINE SOLUTION (ML.)		HEMOLYSIN 2 UNITS (ML.)	2 PER CENT SHEEP RED CELL SUSPENSION (ML.)	
1	0.25*	0.25		0.1	0.1	
2	0.20*	0.30		0.1	0.1	
3	0.15*	0.35	1 hour in 37° C. water bath	0.1	0.1	½ hour secondary incubation in 37° C. water bath.
4	0.12*	0.38		0.1	0.1	
5	0.10*	0.40		0.1	0.1	
6	0.0	0.60		None	0.1	

* All measurements should be made to the bottom of the tube. The quantity of diluted complement in the first two tubes may be measured with a 0.5 ml. or 0.25 ml. pipet and in the last three tubes with a 0.2 ml. pipet.

Example

	ml.
Exact unit	0.15
Two exact units (dose)	0.30
Complement dilution used in titration 1:50	

Dilution of complement to be employed in the test proper may be calculated by dividing 50 by the dose and multiplying by the volume in which the dilution is to be contained, i.e., $\frac{50}{0.3} \times 0.2 = 33$ or a 1:33 dilution of guinea pig serum.

Table 23–25 gives other examples:

Table 23–25.

EXACT UNIT (ML.)	TWO EXACT UNITS (ML.)	TEST DOSE
0.25	0.5	0.2 ml. of 1:20 dilution
0.2	0.4	0.2 ml. of 1:25 dilution
0.15	0.3	0.2 ml. of 1:33 dilution
0.12	0.24	0.2 ml. of 1:42 dilution
0.10	0.2	0.2 ml. of 1:50 dilution

QUALITATIVE TESTS WITH SERUM AND SPINAL FLUID

1. Arrange 12 × 75 mm. test tubes in wire racks so that there are two tubes for each serum or spinal fluid to be tested. Control serums of predetermined reactivity must be included. Number the first row of tubes to correspond to the serum or spinal fluid being tested. Three additional test tubes are included for reagent controls (antigen, hemolytic system, and corpuscle).

2. Prepare a 1:5 dilution of each serum by adding 0.2 ml. of serum to 0.8 ml. of Kolmer saline. Mix well. Spinal fluid is tested undiluted.

3. Complete the tests as outlined in Table 23–26.

4. Mix contents of tubes thoroughly and return to 37° C. water bath. The period of secondary incubation will be determined by the length of time necessary to reproduce the predetermined reactivity pattern of the control serum. In all instances the reading time should be at least ten minutes more

Table 23–26. Performance of the One-fifth Volume Kolmer Test

TUBE NO.		SALINE SOLUTION	ANTIGEN		COMPLEMENT 2 EXACT UNITS		HEMOLYSIN (2 UNITS)	SHEEP CELL SUSPENSION (2 PER CENT)
	Serum (1:5 dil.) ml.	(ml.)	(ml.)		(ml.)		(ml.)	(ml.)
1	0.2	None	0.1		0.2		0.1	0.1
2	0.2	0.1	None		0.2		0.1	0.1
	Spinal fluid (ml.)			Shake rack well. Allow to stand at room temperature for 10 to 15 minutes.		Incubate 15–18 hours at 6° to 10° C. followed by 10 minutes in 37° C. water bath.		
1	0.1	0.1	0.1		0.2		0.1	0.1
2	0.1	0.1	None		0.2		0.1	0.1
Controls								
Antigen	0.2	0.1		0.2		0.1	0.1
Hemolytic system	0.3	None		0.2		0.1	0.1
Corpuscle	0.6	None		None		None	0.1

than the time necessary to hemolyze the antigen and hemolytic system controls and should not exceed a total of 60 minutes' incubation.

5. Remove each rack of tubes from the water bath at the end of the secondary incubation period and immediately place in an ice bath. Using reading standards, read and record observed hemolysis as described under "Reading and Reporting Test Results" (p. 874) except in those instances in which inhibition of hemolysis is noted in the control tube.

All serums and spinal fluids showing inhibition of hemolysis in the control tube should be returned to the 37° C. water bath. Read control tubes at five-minute intervals and record test results when complete hemolysis is observed in the control tube (not longer than one hour secondary incubation). Record test results in accordance with Table 23–21.

The sensitivity and reproducibility of the R.P.C.F. test are controlled by use of a positive control serum of known reactivity, and in this respect the test differs from the conventional Kolmer technique. The secondary incubation period is dependent upon the time necessary for the positive control serum to produce a predetermined pattern of reactivity. The R.P.C.F. test should not be performed unless one includes a positive control serum of established reactivity for determining the duration of secondary incubation. A pattern of 4+, 2+, and negative can be established with proper dilutions of the standard serum.

Quantitative Tests with Serum and Spinal Fluid

1. Place 12 × 75 mm. test tubes in racks, allowing eight tubes for each serum and six tubes for each spinal fluid to be tested. Reagent control tubes are the same as for the qualitative tests.

2. For each serum, pipet 0.2 ml. of saline into tubes 2 through 7 and 0.1 ml. into tube 8.

3. Pipet 0.2 ml. of serum (diluted 1:5) into tubes 1, 2, and 8.

4. Mix the contents of tube 2, transfer 0.2 ml. to tube 3, and so on, to tube 7. Mix contents of tube 7 and discard 0.2 ml.

5. For each spinal fluid, pipet 0.3 ml. of saline into tube 1, 0.2 ml. into tubes 2 through 5, and 0.1 ml. into tube 6.

6. Pipet 0.3 ml. of spinal fluid into tube 1, mix well, and transfer 0.2 ml. to tubes 2 and 6. Mix tube 2, transfer 0.2 ml. to tube 3, and so on to tube 5. Mix tube 5 and discard 0.2 ml.

7. Add 0.1 ml. of diluted antigen to the first seven tubes of each serum test and to the first five tubes of each spinal fluid test.

8. Add 0.2 ml. of diluted complement to all tubes.

9. Shake the racks to mix thoroughly and place in the refrigerator at 6° to 10° C. for 15 to 18 hours.

10. Complete the tests the following morning as indicated for the qualitative tests.

11. The endpoint titer is the highest dilution giving a "reactive" result. With both serums and spinal fluids the first tube is considered to be undiluted or 1 dil. Additional dilutions may be prepared and tested if no endpoint is obtained.

Retesting Anticomplementary Serums

Anticomplementary serums may be retested by preparing serial twofold dilutions in saline as described for the quantitative test, beginning with the 1:5 dilution and ending with 1:80. Each dilution of serum in 0.2 ml. amounts is tested in two tubes as test and control, as described for the qualitative test. Results of these tests may be interpreted as "reactive," without reference to titer, if the first serum dilution showing complete hemolysis in the control tube has a 3+ or 4+ reaction in the tube containing antigen. All other reactions would be reported as "Anticomplementary."

Reading Standards

1. Heat tubes of hemoglobin solution (saved from the titration) in the 56° C. water bath for five minutes.

2. Prepare a 1:7 dilution of 2 per cent sheep cell suspension by adding 0.5 ml. of 2 per cent suspension to 3.0 ml. of saline.

3. Prepare reading standards by mixing hemoglobin solution and cell suspension in proportions as follows:

1:7 CORPUSCLE SUSPENSION (ML.)	HEMOGLOBIN SOLUTION (ML.)	EQUIVALENT COMPLEMENT FIXATION	
		PER CENT	RECORD
0.7	None	100	4+
0.35	0.35	50	3+
0.175	0.525	25	2+
0.07	0.63	10	1+
0.035	0.665	5	±
None	0.7	0	−

Reading and Reporting Test Results

Reading and reporting are done in the same matter as in the Kolmer Wassermann (see p. 874).

It is likely that before long, as the R.P.C.F. antigen becomes more readily available, it will replace the conventional Kolmer complement-fixation antigen. It has been suggested that an ideal approach to the serologic diagnosis of syphilis, which would limit the need for the laborious and expensive T.P.I. test, is as follows:

1. A standard serologic test for syphilis (Kahn, V.D.R.L.). If the test is negative and there is no clinical evidence or history of syphilis, the patient is considered non-infected.

2. The R.P.C.F. done on individuals who are positive with a standard test. If the R.P.C.F. is positive, treatment for syphilis is indicated.

3. Patients with a positive standard test and negative R.P.C.F. tested by the T.P.I. If the T.P.I. is negative, the standard test is considered nonspecific. If the T.P.I. is positive, this indicates past or present infection.

According to an extensive survey conducted by the U.S. Public Health Service Serology Evaluation Research Assembly (1956–1957), the continued wide use of a cardiolipin or lipoidal antigen of good sensitivity and specificity plus the supplementary use of a Reiter protein antigen test either routinely on all specimens is recommended as a check on all reactive specimens or in questionable "false-positive" cases.

Of course, with the rapid advances being made in the serodiagnosis of syphilis, this recommendation may be altered in the near future.

REFERENCES

1. Andujar, J. J., and Mazurek, E. E.: The plasmacrit (PCT) test on capillary blood. Unheated plasma screen test for syphilis. Am. J. Clin. Path., 31:197–204, 1959.
2. Bossak, H. N., and Duncan, W. P.: Stabilized antigen emulsions for use in flocculation tests for syphilis. 1. The VDRL tests. Pub. Health Rep., 71:836–838, 1958.
3. Bossak, H. N., Falcone, V. H., Duncan, W. P., and Harris, A.: Kolmer test with Reiter protein antigen (Venereal Disease Research Laboratory Modification). Pub. Health Lab., 16:39–48, 1958.
4. Cannefax, G. R., and Garson, W.: Reiter protein complement fixation test for syphilis. Pub. Health Rep., 72:335–340, 1957.
5. D'Alessandro, G., and Dardanoni, L.: Isolation and purification of the protein antigen of the Reiter treponeme. Am. J. Syph., Gonor. & Ven. Dis., 37:137–150, 1953.
6. Deacon, W. E., Falcone, V. H., and Harris, A.: A fluorescent test for treponemal antibodies. Proc. Soc. Exper. Biol. & Med., 96:477–480, 1957.
7. Garson, W.: Recent developments in the labora-

tory diagnosis of syphilis. Ann. Int. Med., 51: 748–758, 1959.
8. Harris, A., Rosenberg, A. A., and Riedel, L. M.: A microflocculation test for syphilis using cardiolipin antigen. Preliminary report. J. Ven. Dis. Inform., 27:169–174, 1946.
9. Harris, A., Harding, V. L., and Bossak, H. N.: Serum standards for serologic tests for syphilis. J. Ven. Dis. Inform., 32:310–318, 1951.
10. Harris, A., Sunkes, E. J., Bunch, W. L., and Bossak, H. N.: An evaluation of the plasmacrit screening test for syphilis. Pub. Health Lab. 17:83–85, 1959.
11. Hinton, W. A., Stuart, G. O., and Grant, J. F.: The use of cardiolipin-lecithin in the preparation of antigen for the Hinton test. Am. J. Syph., Gonor. & Ven. Dis., 33:587–592, 1949.
12. Kahn, R. L.: Serology with Lipid Antigen. Baltimore, The Williams & Wilkins Company, 1950.
13. Kline, B. S.: Cardiolipin antigen in the microscopic slide precipitation test for syphilis. Am. J. Clin. Path., 16:68–80, 1946.
14. Kline, B. S., and Suessenguth, H.: Improved emulsion of cardiolipin, synthetic lecithin antigen for the Kline test. Am. J. Clin. Path., 30:473–476, 1958.
15. Kolmer, J. A., and Lynch, E. R.: The technic of the Kolmer complement fixation tests for syphilis employing one-fifth amounts of reagents. Am. J. Clin. Path., 12:109–115, 1942.
16. Kolmer, J. A., and Lynch, E. R.: Cardiolipin antigens in the Kolmer complement-fixation test for syphilis. J. Ven. Dis. Inform., 29:166–172, 1948.
17. Mazzini, L. Y.: Mazzini cardiolipin microflocculation test for syphilis. J. Immunol., 66: 261–275, 1951.
18. Miller, J. L., and Hill, J. H.: Studies on significance of biological false-positive reactions. J.A.M.A., 164:1461–1465, 1957.
19. Moore, J. E., and Mohr, C. F.: Biologically false positive serologic tests for syphilis. Type, incidence and cause. J.A.M.A., 150:467–473, 1952.
20. Nelson, R. A., Jr., and Mayer, M. M.: Immobilization of Treponema pallidum in vitro by antibody produced in syphilitic infection. J. Exper. Med., 89:369–393, 1949.
21. Nelson, R. A., Jr., and Diesendruck, J. A.: Studies on treponemal antibodies in syphilis. J. Immunol., 66:667–685, 1951.
22. Osler, A. G., Strauss, J. H., and Mayer, M. M.: Diagnostic complement fixation. Am. J. Syph., Gonor. & Ven. Dis., 36:140–153, 1952.
23. Pangborn, M. C.: A simplified preparation of cardiolipin, with a note on purification of lecithin for serologic use. J. Biol. Chem., 161: 71–82, 1945.
24. Portnoy, J., and Magnuson, H. J.: Treponema pallidum complement-fixation (TPCF) test for syphilis. Am. J. Clin. Path., 26:313–322, 1956.
25. Portnoy, J., Garson, W., and Smith, C. A.: Rapid plasma reagin test for syphilis. Pub. Health Rep., 72:761–766, 1957.
26. U.S. Public Health Service: Serology Evaluation Research Assembly, 1956–1957. No. 50. Washington, U.S. Govt. Printing Office, 1959.
27. U.S. Public Health Service: Serologic Tests for Syphilis. Manual No. 411. Washington, U.S. Govt. Printing Office, 1959.
28. Wallace, A. L., and Harris, A.: Preparation of Reiter protein antigen. Pub. Health Lab., 16: 27–38, 1958.

Chapter 24

Serodiagnostic Tests in Diseases Other Than Syphilis

By JAMES G. SHAFFER, Sc.D., *and* MILTON GOLDIN, M.S.

Serologic reactions are employed in the diagnosis of many bacterial, parasitic, rickettsial, and viral diseases. Some of the techniques are relatively simple and may be performed even in the smallest laboratory; others require special facilities. A variety of antigens are used. They include living or heat-killed bacterial suspensions, such as those employed in the Widal test in typhoid fever; red blood cells of animals or man, as in the anti-streptolysin O or cold agglutinin titrations; and inert particles, such as collodion or polystyrene latex, to which antigens are adsorbed in one way or another.

The process of agglutination has been considered a two-step reaction. When antigen is added to antiserum, a physicochemical combination occurs in which the antibody is adsorbed on the surface of the antigen. This first step is followed by agglutination in the presence of an electrolyte (usually in physiologic saline solution). In the absence of the electrolyte only the first step occurs, and there is no aggregation of the antibody-coated antigen. The degree of agglutination is dependent on the quantity of antibody, the concentration of the antigen, the composition of the salt solution, and the temperature of the reaction (Fig. 24–1).

Bacterial antigens exhibit one of two types of agglutination, which depend on the presence or absence of flagellar ("H") antigens. When H antigen is present, the combination with the anti-H antibody produces a floccular type of agglutination, evidently the result of entanglement of the flagellae. This type of agglutination is easily broken up by vigorous shaking (Figs. 24–2 and 24–3).

When no flagellae are present, as with non-

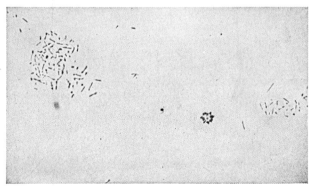

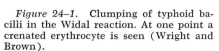

Figure 24–1. Clumping of typhoid bacilli in the Widal reaction. At one point a crenated erythrocyte is seen (Wright and Brown).

883

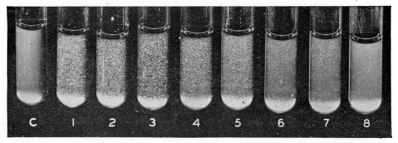

Figure 24–2. The macroscopic agglutination test—flagellar agglutination of *Salmonella*. The control tube, *C*, contains bacterial suspension but no antiserum. Successive dilutions in the numbered tubes are 1:100, 1:200, 1:500, 1:1000, 1:2000, 1:5000, 1:10,000, and 1:20,000. Note agglutination in 1:10,000 but not in 1:20,000. (From Burrows.)

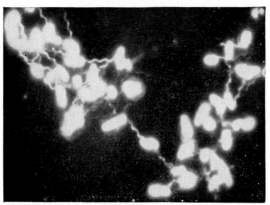

Figure 24–3. Flagellar agglutination of *Salmonella typhosa* by H antiserum: clumps of cells formed by intertwining of thickened flagellar structures, the bacterial bodies not touching one another. (From a photograph kindly supplied by Dr. Adrianus Pijper.)

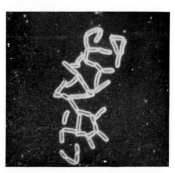

Figure 24–4. Somatic agglutination of *Salmonella typhosa* by O antiserum between slide and coverslip; polar attachment of cells gives a regular crystal-like structure in two dimensions. (From a photograph kindly supplied by Dr. Adrianus Pijper.)

motile bacteria or with motile bacteria from which the flagellae have been removed in some way, granular ("O") agglutination occurs in the presence of antibodies for the somatic antigens. These fine, granular clumps seen in O-type agglutination are much more difficult to break up by shaking (Fig. 24–4).

THE WIDAL REACTION

The Widal reaction for the diagnosis of typhoid and paratyphoid infections is widely used and, while it is relatively simple to perform, is subject to many pitfalls of performance and interpretation.

A very high per cent (approximately 98 per cent) of the pathogenic *Salmonella* occurring in the United States belong to five main serologic groups differentiated on the basis of their O or somatic antigens, which are stable. These groups are designated A, B, C (C_1 and C_2), D, and E. The H antigens of the *Salmonella* exhibit certain variations as a result of which cultures may contain combinations of species- and group-specific antigens. Those containing only species-specific antigens are said to be monophasic (Phase 1) and those with both are diphasic (Phase 2). (See Table 24–1 and p. 634.)

Vi antigens are surface antigens peculiar to *S. typhi* and a few other strains of *Salmonella*. Antibodies to the Vi antigen appear during typhoid fever but tend to disappear from the blood soon after recovery from the disease. Their presence is highly suggestive of current or recent infection. These antibodies tend to persist in carriers, disappearing only after the carrier state no longer exists (Fig. 24–5).

Classically the Widal test was done using only *Salmonella paratyphi* A, *S. paratyphi* B, and *S. typhi* H and O suspensions as antigens. Since group A infections are rare in the United States and the other groups are comparatively common, it is best to use antigens of the other serologic groups as well. Such antigens have recently become available or can readily be prepared as will be described.

The test can be done by several methods,

Table 24–1. Antigenic Structure of Representative Salmonella Types

ORGANISM	O GROUP	O ANTIGENS	GROUP ANTIGEN	H. ANTIGENS PHASE 1	PHASE 2
S. paratyphi A	A	I, II, XII	II	a	—
S. paratyphi B	B	I, IV, V, XII	IV	b	1, 2
S. choleraesuis	C₁	VI, VII	VII	c	1, 5
S. newport	C₂	VI, VIII	VIII	e,h	1, 2
S. typhi	D	IX, XII(Vi)	IX	d	—
S. enteriditis	D	I, IX, XII	IX	g,m	—
S. anatum	E	III, X	III	e,h	1, 6

Figure 24–5. Vi agglutination of *Salmonella typhosa* by Vi antiserum: side-to-side attachment eventually yields a dense mass of agglutinated cells. This is a small clump. (From a photograph kindly supplied by Dr. Adrianus Pijper.)

which include the macroscopic tube test using live or killed cultures and the rapid microscopic slide test. A sensitive test for O agglutinins is that described by Neter *et al.* (1956) by which O antigens are adsorbed to the surface of human type O erythrocytes. When these red cells are added to serum containing anti-O antibodies, they are agglutinated to high titer.

Preparation of Antigens

H Antigen. Inoculate a flask of broth with actively motile smooth strains of *Salmonella.* Incubate 24 hours at 37° C. Transfer by streaking over the entire surface of large slants or in Blake bottles of infusion agar and incubate overnight at 37° C. Wash off the growth with saline containing 0.5 per cent formalin. Wash the bacteria three times with the formalinized saline, harvest sediment, and dilute to a density approximating tube No. 3 of the McFarland scale.

O Antigen. This procedure is similar to that used for preparing the H antigen except that the organism is washed with saline containing an equal volume of absolute

ethyl alcohol. After washing, the sediment is suspended in a solution of saline containing 33 per cent ethyl alcohol and is adjusted as just described. The final concentration of alcohol should be approximately 3 per cent.

Concentrated antigens for the rapid slide tests are prepared as described previously, but the suspensions are more concentrated and gentian violet and brilliant green are added to facilitate the reading of the reactions.

Macroscopic Tube Agglutination Test
(See Table 24–2)

1. For each antigen used, arrange ten small (100 × 13 mm.) test tubes in a rack. Place 0.9 ml. saline in the first tube and 0.5 ml. in each of the remaining tubes.

2. Add 0.1 ml. of serum to the first tube. Mix, transfer 0.5 ml. to the tube No. 2, mix, transfer 0.5 ml. to tube No. 3, and so on to tube No. 9 from which 0.5 ml. is discarded.

3. Mix antigens well and add 0.5 ml. to each tube. The final dilutions are 1:20, 1:40, 1:80, 1:160, 1:320, 1:640, 1:1280, 1:2560 and 1:5120. Tube No. 10 serves as the antigen control.

4. Incubate at 37° C. for two hours and in the icebox overnight. Alternatively the tubes may be incubated at 52° C. for 15 to 18 hours. Read the reactions by holding the tube rigidly at the top and gently tap the bottom just sufficiently to stir up the sediment, which appears as clumps or masses in positive reactions. Avoid excessive agitation. The tubes may be centrifuged at approximately 1800 r.p.m. for five minutes. This may reveal agglutination that is not otherwise apparent. The antigen control should be uniformly turbid and should show no agglutination. The positive serum control should show marked agglutination, indicating satisfactory sensitivity of the antigen. If the controls are satisfactory, the reactions should be read and recorded for each tube as follows:

Table 24–2. Protocol for the Agglutination Test by the Serial Dilution Method

Tube No.	1	2	3	4	5	6	7	8	9	10
Saline (ml.)	0.9	0.5	0.5	0.5	0.5	0.5	0.5	0.5	0.5	0.5
Serum (ml.)	0.1	0.5 of tube #1*	0.5 of tube #2	0.5 of tube #3	0.5 of tube #4	0.5 of tube #5	0.5 of tube #6	0.5 of tube #7	0.5 of tube #8 discard 0.5 ml.	0
Antigen (ml.)	0.5	0.5	0.5	0.5	0.5	0.5	0.5	0.5	0.5	0.5
Final serum dilution	1:20	1:40	1:80	1:160	1:320	1:640	1:1280	1:2560	1:5120	—

* The use of separate pipets for making each of these dilutions will give more accurate and more reproducible results.

4+ = complete agglutination with solid disk of bacteria and clear supernatant fluid.
3+ = large clumps of bacteria and a clear supernatant fluid without complete settling of the bacteria to the bottom of the tube.
2+ = agglutination with incomplete clearing of the supernatant fluid.
1+ = agglutination with turbid fluid with clumps visible to the naked eye.

With the flagellar (H) antigens the agglutinated bacteria appear as soft, coarse, floccular sediments; with the alcoholic (O) antigens, as previously indicated, the agglutination is more discrete and granular and less voluminous.

Rapid Macroscopic Slide Test

1. Using a 0.2 ml. pipet graduated in 0.01 ml., place the amount of serum listed in Table 24–3 on each of five squares on a glass plate.
2. Shake the antigen bottle thoroughly and add a drop to each amount of serum, starting with the smallest amount and proceeding to the largest. The dropper used should deliver 0.03 ml. of antigen per drop.
3. Mix, using a clean toothpick for each square, starting at the smallest amount and working to the largest. After mixing, lift the plate and slowly tilt back and forth for two to three minutes. Read in a viewing box or against a flat black background. Do not allow mixtures to dry out.
4. Complete agglutination is read as 4+, 75 per cent clumping as 3+, 50 per cent as 2+, and faint agglutination as 1+. The titer is the last dilution showing definite clumping.
If all dilutions are strongly agglutinated, the serum may be diluted 1:10 or 1:20 with 30 per cent bovine albumin diluent and the test repeated. All dilutions should be run

Table 24–3. Rapid Slide Test for Typhoid and Paratyphoid

SQUARE NO.	SERUM VOLUME	PIPET READINGS	ANTIGEN	FINAL DILUTION
1	0.08 ml.	0.08 ml.	0.03 ml.	1:20
2	0.04 ml.	0.12 ml.	0.03 ml.	1:40
3	0.02 ml.	0.14 ml.	0.03 ml.	1:80
4	0.01 ml.	0.15 ml.	0.03 ml.	1:160
5	0.005 ml.	0.155 ml.	0.03 ml.	1:320

on each serum tested because of the frequent occurrence of prozones.

Interpretation

The interpretation of the Widal reaction requires caution and must be done in the light of the clinical findings. Many factors must be kept in mind, such as:
1. In regions where typhoid fever and *Salmonella* infections are endemic, a high level of natural agglutinins may be present. Also it must be kept in mind that cross-reactions are common among all enteric bacteria.
2. Anamnestic responses are encountered occasionally. By this is meant the phenomenon in which a rise in agglutinins to *S. typhi* may occur in a person who has had a previous infection or vaccination but whose present illness may be unrelated to typhoid. Such anamnestic responses may also be encountered with other agglutination tests.
3. No appreciable immunologic response can be demonstrated in some individuals, such as those with agammaglobulinemia, leukemia, and advanced carcinoma and including persons without any disease that can serve as an explanation.
4. The stage of the disease is important in determining the significance of elevated

titers of agglutinins. Typhoid bacilli can be isolated from the blood, stools, and urine before the Widal test shows a positive reaction. As the agglutinin titer increases, the number of positive cultures decreases. Only 50 per cent of patients with typhoid fever give positive reactions within one week after infection, and the percentage of positive reactions increases until about 90 to 95 per cent are positive after four weeks. If the reaction remains positive for a year or more, the patient may have become a chronic carrier. In this case the Vi agglutinins are usually elevated.

5. Antibiotic therapy, particularly if given early in the disease, may depress the titer of agglutinins. It is best to draw a sample of blood for testing before specific therapy is instituted.

6. It would be virtually impossible to determine the exact species of *Salmonella* responsible for an infection by means of this reaction, since there are so many serotypes already recognized. However, by the use of the antigens now available, the O group can be usually ascertained. For specific identification, isolation of the organisms is essential.

7. No one titer can be considered diagnostic for the reasons already mentioned. In unvaccinated individuals an H or O titer of 1:160 or higher is suggestive. In vaccinated persons the H and O titers are usually elevated. The O titer disappears in time, but the H agglutinins may persist for several years. In either case the demonstration of a rise in titer during convalescense is considerably more important than any single determination.

AGGLUTINATION TESTS FOR BRUCELLOSIS (UNDULANT FEVER)

Human brucellosis simulates many other diseases, and clinical diagnosis based on symptoms alone is difficult and often impossible. For that reason laboratory confirmation is required. Isolation of the organisms from the patient is the only absolute method, but this is sometimes difficult, especially if the number of organisms is low or if optimal cultural techniques are not employed (see p. 641). Also if antibiotics have been administered, the chances of isolating *Brucella* become even smaller.

If serologic diagnosis is done properly, the test can be of considerable diagnostic aid. The skin test with brucellergen has some value as does the opsonic index (p. 812), but the agglutination test is the most widely used and the most accurate

provided the test procedures and antigens are standardized.

Macroscopic Slide Test (Huddleston and Abel, 1928)

This test is a rapid and simple test primarily of value for screening, but the tube test (see following section) has been found to be more reliable and more accurate. The technique is identical with that used for *Salmonella* (p. 886) and will not be repeated here. The antigen used is a concentrated suspension of *Brucella abortus*, which is available commercially. This antigen serves to detect agglutinins produced by all three species of *Brucella*. In the slide test the full series of serum dilutions must be used, since a high-titered serum may show a marked prozone reaction (Fig. 24–6).

Test Tube Procedure

It has been shown recently by the Brucellosis Committee of the National Research Council (Spink *et al.*, 1954) that the procedures and antigens previously used for agglutination tests for brucellosis were frequently inconsistent and inaccurate. They have recommended a new antigen that is prepared from a smooth strain of any of the three species of *Brucella* (*B. abortus*, *B. melitensis*, *B. suis*).* The organism is grown on infusion agar, washed off with saline, inactivated by adding phenol or formalin, and finally standardized turbidimetrically.

PROCEDURE

1. Set up a series of ten small agglutina-

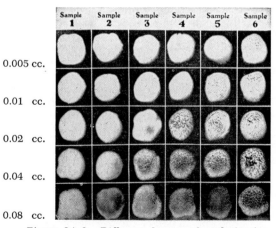

Figure 24–6. Different degrees of agglutination reactions for undulant fever and abortion disease. (Huddleson.)

* Available commercially.

tion tubes and dilute serum in saline as shown in Table 24–2.

2. Shake the antigen vial thoroughly and remove enough antigen aseptically to make a 1:100 dilution sufficient for the number of tests to be run. Dilute in 0.85 per cent saline with 0.5 per cent phenol added. Add 0.5 ml. of this dilution to each tube. The final titers are thus 1:20 in the first tube, 1:40 in the second, to 1:5120 in the ninth tube; the tenth tube serves as the antigen control.

3. An antiserum of known titer of agglutinins against *Brucella* and one without agglutinins should be run in parallel with every lot of antigen.

4. Shake all tubes and incubate for 48 hours in a 37° C. water bath. After this period allow the tubes to cool and read the reaction as in the Widal macroscopic tube test. Record the titer as the highest dilution that gives a distinct agglutination of the antigen.

Interpretation

In active cases of brucellosis owing either to *B. abortus, melitensis,* or *suis,* agglutinins appear during the second week of illness and reach the maximum in the fourth to eighth weeks.

No single titer can be considered as diagnostic, although the higher the titer, the more likely it is that the patient is infected. Titers less than 1:100 are questionable, since healthy adults living in endemic areas may have a low titer of agglutinins. A rising titer during the course of the infection is diagnostic.

Cross-agglutination may occur with tularemia and with individuals vaccinated against cholera. Prozone reactions may be seen, usually in a dilution not exceeding 1:320.

High titers may persist for years in this disease but usually drop gradually. Therapy with antibiotics apparently does not interfere with the diagnostic value of the agglutination test, but treatment with *Brucella* vaccines or the injection of antigen intradermally may result in the appearance of a high titer of agglutinins in noninfected individuals.

THE OPSONOCYTOPHAGIC (OPSONIC) INDEX

This test depends on the demonstration of increased activity of opsonins, which are supposed to sensitize bacteria for engulf-

ment by the leukocytes. The test is complex, and unless it is precisely controlled the results may be confusing.

AGGLUTINATION TEST FOR TULAREMIA

The agglutination test is the most widely used and the most reliable procedure in the diagnosis of tularemia, since *Pasteurella tularensis* is difficult to isolate and the skin test antigen (Foshay) is not generally available. The antigen used is a killed saline suspension of *P. tularensis* (Francis No. 38) preserved with Merthiolate. No attempt should be made to prepare this antigen in a laboratory not specially designed for this purpose, since the organism is highly infectious.

Procedure

1. Serial dilutions of serum in saline are prepared in 0.5 ml. amounts (see Table 24–2). An equal quantity of antigen is then added. The dilutions used range from 1:20 to 1:1280 plus an antigen control tube. If at all possible, an anti-*P. tularensis* serum of known titer should also be run as a control.

2. The tubes are shaken, placed in a 37° C. water bath overnight, and read for agglutination as in other tube agglutination tests. Owing to the prolonged incubation period sedimentation of the unagglutinated antigen may occur, but the sediment can be resuspended readily upon shaking. Agglutinated clumps of bacteria are broken up only with difficulty, and the supernatant fluid remains clear. The highest dilution of serum that gives definite clumping is recorded as the titer.

Interpretation

Titers of 1:40 or less may be observed in uninfected individuals. A rise in titer obtained in serum samples tested at weekly intervals after infection is considerably more significant than any single titer. Titers of 1:80 or higher usually appear during the second week of illness and reach higher levels during the fourth to eighth weeks. Elevated titers may persist for many years after infection. A negative test does not rule out tularemia, and the clinical findings must be considered in establishing the diagnosis.

Cross-agglutination reactions occasionally occur with *Brucella* and *Proteus* OX19; hence it is necessary to conduct parallel tests with all three antigens. The serum will generally react with the homologous antigen in the highest titer. Prozone reactions may occasionally be seen.

An excellent flocculating antigen for this test has been reported by Hunter, Burdorff, and Colbert (1958). It consists of an extract of *P. tularensis* adsorbed on cholesterol in the presence of lecithin. Tests using this antigen appear to be sensitive and specific, and no cross-reaction occurs with serum from cases of brucellosis.

THE WEIL-FELIX REACTION IN RICKETTSIAL DISEASES

Weil and Felix in 1916 isolated a strain of *Proteus* from the urine of a patient with typhus fever, which was agglutinated by the patient's serum and serum from other typhus fever patients but not by the serum of normal subjects. The original strain of Weil and Felix was a nonmotile or O strain designated as X19 thus "*Proteus* OX19." Later two additional strains OX2 and OXK (Kingsbury) were found, which proved useful in serologic tests as aids in the diagnosis of various other rickettsial diseases.

The chemical nature of the antigens that participate in this reaction have not been completely determined, but it has been shown that *Proteus* OX19 and *Rickettsia prowazeki,* the cause of typhus fever, share a common glucolipid antigen.

Although the reaction is nonspecific, its simplicity and the positive results that may be obtained as early as the second week of the disease warrant its use. Specific complement-fixation methods for the rickettsial diseases are considerably more satisfactory but also more laborious and expensive (p. 800). It is common procedure in some laboratories to check any serum that reacts in the Weil-Felix test with the complement-fixation reaction. Rickettsial agglutinations and hemagglutination procedures are also available but are not practical as yet for the clinical laboratory.

Procedure

Antigens are prepared as follows: Only a smooth, nonmotile or O variant of *Proteus* is used. The tube antigen is prepared by washing the growth of 18-to-24-hour agar slant cultures with 0.85 per cent NaCl containing 0.5 per cent formalin and by adjusting the turbidity to that of tube No. 3 of the McFarland nephelometer scale. The rapid slide test antigens are prepared in a manner similar to that used for the O antigens of *Salmonella* (see p. 885).

Macroscopic Tube Test

This is done as in the Widal reaction (see p. 886). The tests and controls are incubated in the water bath at 37° C. for two hours followed by refrigeration for 20 to 22 hours.

Rapid Slide Test

This is done in the same way as in the Widal reaction (see p. 886). Only the OX19 antigen is commonly used in the United States, since most of the rickettsial diseases encountered in this country react with it. The OX2 and OXK antigens can, of course, be included in any test if deemed necessary. Proper controls consisting of known positive and negative sera should always be included.

Interpretation

1. The typical response obtained with suspensions of *Proteus* OX19, OX2, and OXK are given in Table 24–4. It is notable that serums from patients with rickettsial pox and Q fever give negative Weil-Felix reactions.

Table 24–4. **Weil-Felix Reactions in Rickettsial Diseases**

DISEASE	*PROTEUS* OX19	OX2	OXK
Epidemic typhus	++++	+	0
Murine (endemic) typhus	++++	+	0
Scrub typhus (tsutsugamushi)	0	0	+++
Rocky Mountain spotted fever	++++	+	0
Rickettsial pox	0	0	0
Q fever	0	0	0

Serums from patients with Brill's disease (recrudescent typhus fever) frequently fail to agglutinate any of these three antigens. If this disease is suspected, complement fixation tests must be done.

2. The Weil-Felix agglutinins appear as early as the fifth or sixth day but more commonly by the twelfth day after onset. The antibodies reach their peak levels in early convalescence and disappear usually within three to five months after clinical recovery.

3. Occasionally patients with typhus or

spotted fever do not develop agglutinins. Also patients who are treated with antibiotics prior to the time the blood specimen was drawn may not demonstrate a high titer of agglutinins.

4. As in the Widal test anamnestic reactions, cross-reactions with other infections, and prozones may be encountered. In patients with recent or concurrent *Proteus* infections the results of the agglutination test may be misleading.

5. As in other agglutination tests of similar nature no one titer can be considered as diagnostic. Except in those individuals who have been vaccinated or have lived in an area where the diseases are endemic a titer of 1:160 or more is highly suggestive. However, a rise in antibody titer demonstrated in two or more serums collected at different stages of the disease is essential for the presumptive diagnosis of rickettsial diseases when the Weil-Felix reaction is employed.

COLD AGGLUTININS

The serum of most normal individuals has an antibody-like substance that will cause the agglutination of group O human erythrocytes at temperatures between 0 and 5° C. This type of substance has been termed "cold agglutinin." The agglutination is reversible, since erythrocytes clumped by cold agglutinins disperse when warmed to 37° C. This is a good method for detecting true cold agglutination.

Cold Agglutinin Titration (Method of Ellenhorn and Weiner, 1953)

1. Serum: The serum should be separated from the clot after the blood has stood at room temperature for at least one hour. Inactivation is unnecessary. Plasma may also be used for this determination.

2. Erythrocytes: Defibrinated, oxalated, or citrated human group O blood cells are used, preferably the same donor in all tests. A fresh red cell suspension should be used daily. The cells are washed three times in saline for ten minutes at 1500 r.p.m. A 1.0 per cent suspension of packed cells by volume in saline is then used for the test.

3. Place 0.8 ml. saline in the first tube and 0.5 ml. in seven other small (12 × 100) test tubes. To the first tube add 0.2 ml. serum, mix throughly, and transfer 0.5 ml. of the mixture to the second tube. With a fresh pipet mix the second tube and transfer 0.5 ml. to the third tube. In this man-

ner continue through the seventh tube from which 0.5 ml. is discarded. The eighth tube serves as the cell control. Add 0.5 ml. of the washed 1.0 per cent red cell suspension to each tube, shake thoroughly, and place in refrigerator at 2 to 5° C. overnight. The dilutions of the serum range thus from 1:8 in the first tube to 1:512 in the seventh tube.

4. Reading: This must be done as soon as the racks are removed from the refrigerator. A bright source of visible light and a stationary magnifying lens are used. A Kahn viewer is an excellent device for this purpose. The tubes are read by gentle shaking sufficient to disperse red cells into solution. Vigorous shaking will result in lower titers and an increase of negative agglutinations. Alternatively the racks can be placed in a shaking machine and shaken for four seconds at 350 one-inch excursions per minute. They are immediately removed and the tubes read without further shaking. Readings are graded as follows:

4+ = Massive agglutination of all or nearly all cells.
3+ = Large clumps with clear surrounding fluid.
2+ = Many smaller clumps with pinkness of surrounding fluid.
1+ = Minimal but definite agglutination visible.

The titer is reported as the highest dilution in which any definite agglutination is visible.

5. The tubes are then incubated for 30 minutes at 37° C. and read for the disappearance of agglutination to eliminate heteroagglutinins or antibodies other than cold agglutinins that might cause agglutination.

INTERPRETATION

Titers of 1:32 or higher are considered elevated by this technique. Elevated titers are rarely seen except in primary atypical pneumonia or in certain hemolytic anemias (see p. 173). More important than any single titer is a demonstration of a rise in titer during the course of illness.

Low titers of cold agglutinins have been demonstrated in malaria, peripheral vascular disease, and common respiratory diseases. However, primary atypical "virus" pneumonia is the only respiratory disease in which high titers or an increase in titer can be consistently demonstrated. Cold agglutinins are not related to the *Streptococcus* MG agglutinins, and either one or both may be absent in primary atypical pneumonia. Consequently it is best to perform both tests simultaneously on each serum sample when this disease is suspected (see p. 891).

Rapid Cold Agglutinin Test (Garrow, 1958)

This reaction is a simple and rapid screening test for the presence of increased cold agglutinins. It is particularly valuable in children, since it can be done from fingertip blood.

PROCEDURE

Approximately 0.2 ml. of blood obtained by fingertip or ear-lobe puncture is allowed to run into 0.2 ml. of 3.8 per cent trisodium citrate in a small (60 × 7 mm.) test tube. The tube is corked and then rubbed over the surface of the ice-cube tray of a refrigerator and left on its side in the tray for about 15 seconds. The tube is then removed and, holding it at the corked end to avoid warming, is slowly rotated so that the blood citrate mixture runs gently over the chilled glass surface. The presence of coarse floccular agglutination is recorded as "positive." No agglutination or the presence of a fine granularity is recorded as "negative." The tube is then warmed in the hand for a few seconds and re-examined to confirm that all agglutination has disappeared. A positive rapid test indicates a test tube titer of 1:64 or higher.

STREPTOCOCCUS MG AGGLUTINATION TEST

Streptococcus MG is a nonhemolytic streptococcus, which was first isolated from the lungs in fatal cases of primary atypical pneumonia. It was later isolated from the upper respiratory tract of normal individuals, and there is considerable doubt that it is directly related to the disease. However, it has been found that many patients convalescent from primary atypical pneumonia have increased agglutinins against this organism. Although these agglutinins do not appear in all cases of this disease, their detection in convalescent sera is of value as an aid in its diagnosis. The agglutinins against Streptococcus MG are not related to the cold hemagglutinins just discussed. Both cold agglutinins and anti-Streptococcus MG titrations should be performed simultaneously on sera collected at intervals whenever the disease is suspected.

Preparation of Antigen

The antigen is prepared from smooth Streptococcus MG cultures. Cultures are grown in infusion broth for 16 to 18 hours, washed three times with physiologic saline, and adjusted to a turbidity approximately equivalent to No. 5 on the McFarland scale. The suspensions are heated at 65° C. for one hour, and Merthiolate in a final concentration of 1:10,000 is added as a preservative. Such suspensions are satisfactory for use for approximately two weeks.*

Procedure

1. Dilute unheated serum with saline as shown in Table 24–2.
2. Add 0.5 ml. of the antigen suspension to each tube.
3. For each titration a similar series should be set up, using Streptococcus MG control antiserum.
4. Shake tubes thoroughly and incubate in the water bath for two hours at 37° C. followed by 18 hours in the refrigerator at 4° C. The tubes are then placed in the water bath at 37° C. for two hours after which the tubes are read.
5. Complete agglutination with a clear supernatant is read as a 4+ reaction, large clumps and clear supernatant as 3+, large clumps but incomplete clearing of the supernatant as 2+, and small clumps with incomplete clearing of the supernatant as 1+. The agglutination titer is taken as the highest dilution of serum in which reactions of 1+ or more are observed.

Interpretation

Titers of 1:20 or more are found in 50 to 80 per cent of cases of primary atypical pneumonia. Elevated titers in normal individuals or those suffering from other conditions are rare.

The demonstration of a fourfold or more increase during convalescence is more significant than the titer of a single specimen; hence, serum samples should be tested periodically during the course of the disease until late in convalescence. The absence of Streptococcus MG agglutinins does not necessarily exclude primary atypical pneumonia. Antibiotic therapy may also result in the failure of these agglutinins to be demonstrable.

SEROLOGIC TESTS FOR RHEUMATOID ARTHRITIS

In the serum of patients with rheumatoid arthritis there exists a so-called "rheumatoid factor." This or related factors occur

* Stable Streptococcus MG suspension and control antiserum are available commercially.

also in a wide variety of other diseases but are not so frequent. The factors behave like antibodies in that they produce agglutination of certain types of substances. They may actually be autoantibodies.

This agglutinating capacity was first noted by Waaler in 1940 and again by Rose in 1948, and from their studies has been developed the so-called "Waaler-Rose" test. The test has subsequently been considerably modified and improved and new tests developed. Among these new tests are the sensitized sheep cell agglutination test (Ziff [1956] modification), the FII test of Heller *et al.* (1954), the Rh sensitized human cell test (Waller and Vaughan, 1956), and many others. The sources of these procedures will be found in the references. Tests that have been shown to be rapid and simple to perform have been developed using biologically inert particles coated with human gamma globulin.

The mechanisms of these reactions are basically similar. Antibody or gamma globulin coats red cells or inert particles, which are then agglutinated by serum containing the rheumatoid factors. The rheumatoid factors have a specific affinity for gamma globulin or for a surface coated with gamma globulin. The inhibition procedure depends on the presence in normal serum of an inhibitor, which is lacking in rheumatoid arthritis serum since it is neutralized by small amounts of inherent rheumatoid factor. The inhibitor is tested by using a standard reactive rheumatoid arthritis serum and noting the drop in titer that occurs after the addition of the serum containing the inhibitor.

The inhibitors may cause inconsistent results in the various serologic tests and have led some workers to employ euglobulin or gamma globulin fractions rather than the whole serum for measuring the rheumatoid factors. Among the many modifications the ones to be described have been used widely and successfully.

Latex Fixation Tests (Singer and Plotz, 1956)

USING PATIENT'S OWN GAMMA GLOBULIN

1. A suspension of polystyrene latex particles of uniform size (0.81 micra) is diluted with distilled water until a 0.1 ml. aliquot mixed with 10 ml. of glycine buffer (pH 8.2*) matches a light transmission of 5

* 975 ml. of 0.1 M glycine and 2.5 ml. of 1 N NaOH made up to 1000 ml. with water and the pH adjusted to 8.2. 10 gm. of NaCl is added to each 1000 ml. of buffer.

per cent at 650 mμ with a red filter. This suspension is stable in the refrigerator for several months.

2. To 5 ml. of 1.64 M ammonium sulfate, 0.1 ml. of inactivated serum is added. The mixture is refrigerated for one hour and centrifuged for ten minutes at 3000 r.p.m. The supernatant is discarded and 0.5 ml. of the glycine buffer is added to the precipitate.

3. To 9.5 ml. of glycine buffer 0.05 ml. of latex particles and 0.5 ml. of the redissolved ammonium sulfate precipitate are added. Two milliliters of this mixture are transferred to a 13 × 100 mm. tube.

4. The tube is incubated in a water bath at 56° C. for 90 minutes and refrigerated overnight.

5. The tube is then centrifuged at 2300 r.p.m. for three minutes and the reaction read.

FRACTION II LATEX PARTICLE TEST

1. Serial twofold dilutions of inactivated serum are made in glycine-saline buffer, starting with a dilution of 1:20 (0.1 ml. serum and 1.9 ml. buffer). The dilutions are made by transferring 1.0 ml. serially through tubes containing 1.0 ml. of the buffer. Each tube then contains 1 ml., and the dilutions range from 1:20 to 1:5120. Serums of known titers should be included as controls.

2. To each serum dilution tube 1.0 ml. of a buffer-latex-gamma globulin solution is added. This is prepared by adding to 10 ml. of glycine buffer 0.1 ml. of stock latex and 0.5 ml. of a 1 per cent gamma globulin (lyophilized human Fraction II solution)*.

The tubes are shaken well and incubated in a water bath at 56° C. for 1½ hours. The tubes are then centrifuged at 2300 r.p.m. for three minutes and refrigerated overnight. They are then recentrifuged as described previously and read.

Agglutination is read macroscopically. The interpretation of the degree of agglutination is the same as for other similar reactions. Agglutination in a dilution of 1:160 or greater is considered positive. Seventy to 90 per cent of all serums from patients with rheumatoid arthritis react positively with this test, depending primarily on the stage of the disease. The incidence of false positive reactions in non-

* To 1 gm. of lyophilized Fraction II add glycine-saline buffer, pH 8.2, in small increments, mixing well until the globulin is completely dissolved. Refrigerate new solutions of gamma globulin for 24 hours before use. The solution should be tested with serums of known titers before use.

arthritic persons is reported to be about 2 per cent.

SLIDE LATEX FIXATION TEST (SINGER AND PLOTZ, 1958)

In this procedure 0.05 ml. of serum or 0.2 ml. of fingertip blood is placed on each of two glass slides. One drop (0.05 ml.) of 1 per cent eosin is added to one slide and one drop of 2 per cent eosin to the other. The serum and eosin are mixed thoroughly with a toothpick. Two drops of a latex suspension* are added to each slide. The suspensions are mixed thoroughly again, and the slide is tilted from side to side for three minutes. A fine granular agglutination, which appears in one to three minutes on either slide, is considered a positive reaction. Negative tests show a homogeneous reddish suspension. By this procedure the incidence of positive reactions in rheumatoid arthritis is about 85 per cent.

Bentonite Flocculation Test (Bloch and Bunim, 1959)

PREPARATION OF STOCK BENTONITE SUSPENSION†

Suspend 0.5 gm. of Wyoming bentonite (BC micron or No. 200 standard Volclay) in 100 ml. of distilled water. Homogenize in Waring blender for one minute; repeat after five minutes for one minute.

Transfer bentonite suspension to a 500 ml. glass-stopper graduate and add distilled water to make 500 ml. Shake thoroughly and allow to settle for one hour. Pour off the supernatant into six 100 ml. centrifuge tubes (heavy duty) and centrifuge at 1300 r.p.m. for 15 minutes. Use International centrifuge, size 2, with a No. 240 head. Pour off and save supernatant; discard sediment.

Centrifuge supernatant in 100 ml. tubes at 1600 r.p.m. for 15 minutes. Pour off supernatant and discard it.

Resuspend accumulated sediment from the six tubes in 100 ml. of distilled water and homogenize in Waring blender for one minute. This is the stock bentonite suspension, which remains stable for as long as six months without losing its adsorptive properties.

*Stock polystyrene latex particles, 0.81µ in diameter, diluted with distilled water until 0.1 ml. when mixed with 10 ml. of water matches a light transmission of 5 per cent at 650 mµ with a red filter.

† Detergents (often used in cleaning glassware) adherent to the surface of glassware will interfere with this test. It is important, therefore, to cleanse all glassware of this material by washing with distilled water before using.

PREPARATION OF FRACTION II SOLUTION

Lyophilized Fraction II (gamma globulin), 0.5 gm., derived from pooled normal human serum, is suspended in installments while stirring in 50 ml. of 0.06 M barbital (Veronal) buffer, pH 8.6 (made by dissolving 0.184 gm. of barbituric acid and 1.03 gm. of sodium barbiturate in 100 ml. of distilled water). This buffered Fraction II suspension may be stored in a refrigerator for one to two months. Before use it should be cleared by centrifugation at 3000 r.p.m. for ten minutes in order to remove all particulate matter, which otherwise might simulate flocculation.

PREPARATION OF SENSITIZED BENTONITE PARTICLES

Thoroughly shake the stock bentonite suspension to distribute the bentonite particles evenly. Remove 10 ml. of the uniformly dispersed particles, place in a 15 × 200 mm. culture tube, and centrifuge at 3000 r.p.m. for five minutes.

Decant the supernatant and add 1 ml. of distilled water to the sediment. Agitate the tube to resuspend the bentonite particles in the 1 ml. of distilled water.

Add 2 ml. of stock Fraction II solution and mix gently by tilting and rotating. Allow the suspension to stand 15 to 30 minutes at room temperature to permit adsorption. Add 15 ml. of distilled water again and mix gently.

Centrifuge for five minutes at 3000 r.p.m. Decant the supernatant. Resuspend the sediment with 5 ml. of distilled water, shaking thoroughly. Add another 10 ml. of distilled water and shake.

Centrifuge as described previously. Decant the supernatant and resuspend the sediment in 5 ml. of distilled water. Shake vigorously. To this suspension add 1 ml. of 0.1 per cent methylene blue dye; shake, and after five minutes add 10 ml. of distilled water and centrifuge.

Decant the supernatant, resuspend the sediment in 10 ml. of distilled water, and centrifuge. Again decant the final washing, and to the sediment add 4 ml. of 0.05 M phosphate buffer, pH 7.3 (made by dissolving 0.975 gm. of sodium phosphate and 0.185 gm. of potassium dihydrophosphate in 100 ml. of distilled water). This constitutes the sensitized bentonite particles. Add 0.1 ml. of 1 per cent polysorbate 80 (Tween 80).

PROCEDURE

The serum to be tested should be inactivated for 30 minutes at 56° C. prior to use. Microscopic slides (3 × 2 in.) with 12 rings, designed for serologic flocculation tests, are used. In each ring on the slide is placed 0.1 ml. of serial twofold dilutions of serum in phosphate-buffered saline solution at pH 7.4. One drop of sensitized bentonite suspension is added to each ring. (Prior to use the suspension should be shaken thoroughly.) The drop is of such size that a capillary pipet should dispense about 40 drops per milliliter. The slide is then rotated on a Boerner type of rotating machine at 100 to 120 r.p.m. for 20 minutes and read immediately under a microscope at low power magnification (60 ×). Drying is to be avoided.

READING OF RESULTS

A reaction is regarded as 4+ when all the sensitized particles are clumped in separate masses. There may be a few large or a number of small clumps, depending on the titer of the serum. Nevertheless the fields between the flocculi are almost clear. A reaction is regarded as 3+ when approximately three-fourths of the sensitized particles have clumped. In a 2+ reaction half of the particles are clumped and half still remain in colloidal suspension. In a 1+ reaction only one-fourth of the bentonite particles are clumped. In a negative reaction the sensitized bentonite particles remain in colloidal suspension. The result of the flocculation test is considered positive when 2+ or stronger clumping occurs in a serum dilution of 1:32 or higher. Although a negatively reacting serum does not cause any clumping in dilutions up to about 1:1000, occasionally weak flocculation may occur in dilutions of 1:1000 or higher.

With each test performed serial dilutions of a known positive and a known negative reacting serum should be included in order to detect any change in the sensitized bentonite particles. If debris has gotten into the sensitized bentonite mixture or the control negative reacting serum, false clumping may result. With experience the spurious aggregates can be distinguished readily from true flocculation. When the result of the test is positive, the flocculi are of uniform density, evenly distributed in the microscopic field, and free from "hyaline-like" material or other debris.

By this procedure about 85 per cent of verified cases of rheumatoid arthritis give positive results. The incidence of false positives is about 3 per cent.

TESTS FOR TRICHINOSIS

Trichinosis (infection with *Trichinella spiralis*) is a disease of some importance in public health work because of its mode of transmission. Human infections are not uncommon, but the clinical diagnosis may be difficult. Serologic tests have been shown to be useful, particularly in mild or clinically unrecognizable infections. Techniques that have been used are the precipitation, circumlarval precipitation, slide flocculation, complement fixation, bentonite flocculation, and others. The technique to be described is simple enough to be performed in routine laboratories.

Trichinosis Slide Test (Suessenguth and Kline, 1957)

1. Serum is inactivated at 56° C. for 30 minutes.
2. Pipet 0.05 ml. of serum onto a paraffin ringed slide as for the VDRL test for syphilis.
3. One drop of antigen emulsion* is added into the serum from a 26-gauge needle.
4. The slide is rotated on a flat surface for four minutes. The rotation should describe a circle ¾ inch in diameter and should be at the rate of 120 per minute.
5. The results are examined under the microscope with low power with the light cut down. Clumping is reported as in the VDRL test. In a negative reaction the coated crystals are completely dispersed and no clumping occurs.

Interpretation. The test becomes positive in 14 to 17 days and reaches its maximum at three to five weeks. A reaction that shows a rising titer is more significant than the results of a test on a single serum sample. For absolute proof of infection biopsy of the tendinous portions of the deltoid, gastrocnemius, or biceps muscles is to be used.

ANTISTREPTOLYSIN O TITERS

Streptolysin O is a hemolytic substance produced by almost all strains of Lancefeld Group A streptococci and a few strains of streptococci of groups C and G. Unlike streptolysin S, it is inactive in the oxidized form but is readily activated by the addition of sulfhydryl compounds. A high proportion of patients with group A streptococcal infection show an antibody response to streptolysin. Hence, the measurement of anti-

* Available commercially.

streptolysin O (ASO) levels in serum has become widely used for detecting evidence of a recent streptococcus infection. It has been particularly useful as an aid in the diagnosis of rheumatic fever and acute glomerulonephritis.

The antigen in this test is recovered from a liquid medium in which group A streptococci have grown for 18 hours. In its reduced form it is capable of lysing human or rabbit erythrocytes. Antistreptolysin O antibody is capable of neutralizing the lytic action of streptolysin O, and this fact provides the basis for the titration of serum for the presence of this substance.

Procedure

1. Inactivate the serum, which must be clear and nonhemolyzed, for 30 minutes at 56° C. Serum collected by fingertip puncture may also be used. (See C.R.P., p. 896; in this case the 1:10 dilutions of serum are omitted.)

2. Fresh human group O or rabbit red cells (preferred) are collected in a flask and defibrinated with glass beads (about five minutes at 30 to 40 shakes per minute). The cells are filtered through a double layer of gauze and washed as follows:

    a. Centrifuge at 1700 r.p.m. for ten minutes and discard supernatant.

    b. Suspend sediment in saline and repeat step (a).

    c. Centrifuge at 2000 r.p.m. for ten minutes with buffer solution and discard supernatant.

The last centrifugation must yield a colorless supernatant; otherwise the cells should be discarded. Make a 5 per cent suspension of cells for the test (2.5 ml. packed cells to 47.5 ml. buffer).

3. Dilute the serum as follows, using a fresh pipet for each dilution:

    1:10 — 0.5 ml. serum plus 4.5 ml. buffer solution.*
    1:100 — 0.5 ml. 1:10 dilution plus 4.5 ml. buffer solution.
    1:500 — 2.0 ml. 1:100 dilution plus 8.0 ml. buffer solution.

4. Remove the stopper from the antigen (Streptolysin O Reagent†) and rehydrate by adding freshly distilled water in the amount stated on the vial, inverting the vial several times until the reagent is completely dissolved. It is important that the serum be diluted and that the tubes be ready for the addition of the antigen, since the antigen must be added to the diluted serum within ten minutes after it is rehydrated.

5. Dilute the patient's serum according to Table 24–5. Add antigen and cells and incubate as indicated. The first seven tubes are usually sufficient for the preliminary titration. For each run a standardized antiserum of known titer (ASTO standard†), and two

---

* NaCl, 7.4 gm.; KH$_2$PO$_4$, 3.17 gm.; Na$_2$HPO$_4$, 1.81 gm. per liter of distilled water. Final pH adjusted to 6.5 to 6.7. Keep solution in refrigerator.

† Available commercially.

Table 24–5. Antistreptolysin O Titration

Tube No.	1	2	3	4	5	6	7	8	9	10	11	12	CELL CONTROL	LYSIN CONTROL
1:10 serum dilution	0.8	0.2	—	—	—	—	—	—	—	—	—	—	—	—
1:100 serum dilution	—	—	1.0	0.8	0.6	0.4	0.3	—					—	—
1:500 serum dilution	—	—	—	—	—	—	—	1.0	0.8	0.6	0.4	0.2	—	—
Buffer	0.2	0.8	0	0.2	0.4	0.6	0.7	0	0.2	0.4	0.6	0.8	1.5	1.0
Antigen (Streptolysin O)	0.5	0.5	0.5	0.5	0.5	0.5	0.5	0.5	0.5	0.5	0.5	0.5	0	0.5
	Shake gently. Incubate 15 minutes at 37° C.													
5% cell suspension	0.5	0.5	0.5	0.5	0.5	0.5	0.5	0.5	0.5	0.5	0.5	0.5	0.5	0.5
Value of tube in Todd units	12	50	100	125	166	250	333	500	625	833	1250	2500	—	—

Shake gently. Incubate 45 minutes at 37° C. Refrigerate overnight or centrifuge tubes one minute at 1500 r.p.m. and read.

tubes of reagent controls must be included.

6. The lysin control should be completely hemolyzed; the cell control should show no hemolysis and the titer of the ASTO standard should correspond to the labeled titer. If these controls are not correct, the test is unreliable and the discrepancies must be analyzed and corrected. The titer expressed in Todd units is the reciprocal of the highest dilution of serum showing no hemolysis when viewed by clear, strong light. For example, a serum showing no hemolysis in tubes 1 through 6, a trace of hemolysis in tube 7, and complete hemolysis in the other tubes would have an ASO titer of 250 Todd units.

Interpretation

A single determination is of little significance, but a rise in titer or a persistently elevated titer in serum over a period of several weeks may be of considerable diagnostic value. The titer that is considered elevated varies somewhat with the locality and other factors, but in general a titer of 166 Todd units or higher is definitely elevated. A repeated low titer is good evidence that the patient does not have active rheumatic fever. On the other hand a high titer does not necessarily mean that the patient is suffering from rheumatic fever or acute glomerulonephritis, but it does indicate that a focus of streptococcus infection is present. The deciding factors in diagnosis are the clinical symptoms and other relevant laboratory findings.

C-REACTIVE PROTEIN

C-reactive protein (C.R.P.) was first reported in the blood of patients during the acute phase of pneumococcal pneumonia by Tillett and Francis in 1930. It is a protein that forms a precipitate with the somatic C-polysaccharide of the pneumococcus—hence, the name C-reactive protein. Later it was found in a variety of other conditions, and, while it is nonspecific for any particular disease entity, the demonstration of C.R.P. in the blood is a sensitive indicator of inflammation of infectious or noninfectious origin. Changes in the amount of C.R.P. are useful for prognostic purposes and for indicating the efficacy of a therapeutic regimen. The list shown in Table 24–6 is only a general tabulation of the occurrence of C.R.P. in disease states, which may vary with the stage of the disease, treatment, and physical state of the patient.

Table 24–6. Presence of C.R.P. in Various Diseases

USUALLY PRESENT	IRREGULARLY PRESENT	USUALLY ABSENT
Acute rheumatic fever	Pericarditis	Skin diseases
Myocardial infarction	Rheumatoid arthritis	Upper respiratory infections (mild)
Carcinoma	Pyelitis	Renal disease
Streptococcus infections	Nephritis	Skin disease
Postcommissurotomy syndrome		Localized infections
Pneumonia		

Procedure

1. A capillary tube (0.8 mm. in diameter x 100 mm. in length) is dipped into a vial of C-reactive protein antiserum.* The antiserum is allowed to rise about one-third the length of the capillary tube. A finger is placed over the top of the tube before the tube is removed from the antiserum, and the excess is carefully wiped off.

2. With the finger still in place the capillary is then dipped into a tube of the patient's serum, which must be fresh and clear, and an equal volume drawn up. Care must be taken to avoid the interposition of air bubbles, since this will prevent mixing. Plasma is not satisfactory for this test.

3. The capillary tube is carefully inverted several times to mix the serums. A finger is placed at the end, leaving an air space at the opposite end. Excess serum and finger marks are wiped from the tube with cleaning tissue, and the tube is placed upright in plasticine, leaving an air space between the bottom of the serum column and the clay. It is convenient to employ a wooden block with a plasticine-filled groove as a pipet stand so that a series of tubes can be set up on a single stand.

4. The tube is then placed in the incubator at 37° C. for two hours and in the refrigerator overnight. Alternatively the tubes may be incubated overnight at room temperature.

5. A control serum known to contain C.R.P. should be included in every series of tests as well as a tube with normal rabbit serum in place of antiserum as a control for the possible occurrence of nonspecific precipitation.

6. The test can also be done as a micromethod by the procedure of Goldin and Kaplan (1955). Blood is drawn from the

* Available commercially.

fingertip, ear lobe, or heel in capillary tubes with an outside diameter of about 1.4 mm. The blood is allowed to clot. The clot is separated from the wall of the tube with a fine wire, and the capillary tube is centrifuged.

After centrifugation the tube is scratched with a small file just above the clot; the portion containing the clot is broken off and discarded. C.R.P. antiserum is drawn up into one-third of a finer capillary tube (outside diameter up to 1.1 mm.) A fingertip is placed over the air space of this tube, the external surfaces of the tube is wiped clean, and the antiserum is carefully placed in contact with the patient's serum in the wider capillary tube. The patient's serum is allowed to flow up the remainder of the finer tube, leaving a space of 5 to 10 mm. The fingertip is placed over the top of this capillary tube, which is then inverted and placed air space down into the modeling-clay rack. The test is completed in the usual manner.

7. A precipitate will form if the patient's serum contains C.R.P. This precipitate may appear in as little as 15 minutes, but a final reading should not be made until overnight incubation. Readings are best made against a black background with light falling obliquely from above and behind the tubes. The amount of precipitate is recorded as 4+ for maximal precipitation to 0 for no precipitation. Alternatively the number of millimeters of precipitate column can be measured, but it is necessary to take into account the variability of packing of the flocculent precipitate if this method of reading is used.

8. A recent modification of this technique uses polystyrene latex particles coated with anti-C.R.P. serum. The test is done as a slide test. Other techniques that may be used for demonstrating C.R.P. are complement fixation and gel diffusion.

Interpretation

Normal individuals do not have demonstrable C.R.P. in their serum. The presence of this protein indicates an active inflammatory process. It is almost invariably found during the active phases of rheumatic fever and rheumatoid arthritis. The protein is also demonstrable in joint fluids and exudates in these conditions. It is present during certain neoplastic diseases, myocardial infarction with necrosis, disseminated lupus erythematosus, and acute bacterial and viral infections (Table 24–6).

The amount of C.R.P. in the serum is to some degree a reflection of the extent and severity of the disease process. It can appear rapidly after the onset of a pathologic process (approximately 12 hours) and is usually completely eliminated after the stimulus is removed, as in the case of effective therapy of bacterial infections, within one or two days. Although not related to this phenomenon, the presence of C.R.P. is similar in its implications to that of an elevated sedimentation rate.

The most extensive clinical application of the C.R.P. test is in the evaluation of disease activity and therapeutic measures in acute rheumatic fever. Since the protein is present during rheumatic activity, successful suppressive therapy causes disappearance of C.R.P. from the blood. Consequently the test can be used to determine whether an adequate therapeutic response has been obtained.

The C.R.P. test is very sensitive and has no equivocal "normal range," since it is absent from the blood of normal individuals. It is important, however, to realize that the test is completely nonspecific and hence must be used in association with clinical judgment.

ANTITHYROID ANTIBODIES

The demonstration of autoantibodies in various diseases of the thyroid gland stems primarily from the work of Witebsky and Rose (1956) and Roitt and Doniach (1960) and their groups. Recent work has clearly shown that in a high percentage of patients with chronic (Hashimoto's) thyroiditis and primary myxedema, circulating antibodies against normal thyroglobulin (stored in colloid) or intracellular (microsomal) antigens can be demonstrated. A variety of techniques have been used for this purpose—precipitation in agar-gel, tanned red cell agglutination, complement fixation, and Coons' fluorescent antibody technique on fixed or unfixed tissue sections. In addition, certain of these sera have been shown to give rise to cytotoxic effects when added to human thyroid cells in tissue culture.

There seems to be little doubt that these investigations will ultimately find applications, both theoretical and practical, in diseases other than those associated with the thyroid gland.

The techniques just listed for the demonstration of circulating thyroglobulin antibodies are somewhat complex for use as routine procedures. A slide test using latex particles sensitized with thyroglobulin is available commercially but is suitable only for rough qualitative screening. The technique to be described is a practical one based on the bentonite technique for rheumatoid arthritis (see p. 893).

Bentonite Particle Test for Detection of Thyroid Antibodies (Ager, Hutt, and Smith, 1959)

Normal thyroid glands removed at autopsy are stripped of connective tissue and blended with twice their weight of physiologic NaCl solution in a blender. The resultant homogenate is centrifuged at 4000 r.p.m. to remove heavy cellular debris and fibrous tissue. This supernatant is then recentrifuged at 27,000 r.p.m. for 45 minutes at 4° C. The supernatant is used to sensitize the bentonite particles.

A 2.5 gm. portion of bentonite is added to 300 ml. of distilled water in a flask and thoroughly shaken. A 25 ml. portion of this mixture is added to a heavy wall centrifuge tube, which is centrifuged at 3000 r.p.m. for ten minutes. The supernatant is discarded and replaced with 25 ml. of distilled water; the material is mixed vigorously and then recentrifuged. This process is repeated twice. At the end of the final washing the supernatant is removed and thoroughly mixed with 2 ml. of thyroid antigen. After standing for one hour at room temperature, the sensitized bentonite particles are washed twice in physiologic NaCl solution and finally resuspended in 25 ml. of saline.

Serial dilutions of the serum to be tested are made in small glass tubes or clear plastic agglutination trays. Dilutions range from 1:5 to 1:2,500,000, using 0.25 ml. volumes and 2 per cent serum-saline as diluent. To each dilution 0.1 ml. of sensitized bentonite particles is added, and the rack or tray is placed in the refrigerator overnight. Adequate controls must, of course, be included. The pattern of deposited bentonite particles is read macroscopically. Positive agglutination is shown by a small, central, round button of agglutinated particles and negatives by a thin carpet of particles over a wide area of the bottom of the tube or cup. Weak positives show a central button with a small carpeting around.

Cases of Hashimoto's disease give titers as high as 1:25,000,000. Lower titers (1:5 to 1:250) may be found in other types of thyroid disease. Normal serums rarely react at titers above 1:5.

PRECIPITIN TESTS

These tests are utilized for many purposes, such as diagnosis of parasitic diseases, typing of various bacteria, and biologic identification of unknown proteins. Properly performed, they are extremely sensitive and highly specific. Antisera are prepared, usually in rabbits, by immunization with the known protein. The antiserum then contains precipitins, which when added to a solution of the antigen used for immunization (precipitinogen) form a visible precipitate. Excellent precipitating antigens against a wide variety of substances are available commercially.

Identification of Unknown Antigens

PROCEDURE (see Table 24–7)

The unknown substance should be diluted about 1:100. If a dried clot or blood stain is to be tested, it is eluted with sterile saline and the dilution approximated. To approximate a given dilution of serum one can make a standard 1:100 dilution of a known serum and adjust the unknown in such a way that when the known and unknown are shaken vigorously side by side, the amount of foam is similar. The solution must be clear and should meet the following conditions:

    a. It should be almost completely colorless by transmitted light.
    b. It should give only a slight cloudiness when heated with dilute nitric acid.
    c. It should foam freely on shaking.
    d. The pH should be as close to neutrality as possible. If either strongly acid or alkaline, it should be neutralized with dilute HCl or NaOH.

Arrange a series of eight small precipitin tubes and fill them by means of a capillary

Table 24–7. Protocol for Standard Precipitin Test

TUBE NO.	UNKNOWN ANTIGEN DILUTION	SERUM
1	0.5 ml. of 1:100	0.1 ml. immune serum
2	0.5 ml. of 1:100	0.1 ml. normal serum
3	0.5 ml. of 1:1000	0.1 ml. immune serum
4	0.5 ml. of 1:1000	0.1 ml. normal serum
5	0.5 ml. of 1:10,000	0.1 ml. immune serum
6	0.5 ml. of 1:10,000	0.1 ml. normal serum
Controls		
7	Saline	0.1 ml. immune serum
8	Saline	0.1 ml. normal serum

pipet. The unknown solution is carefully overlaid on the immune serum so as to form a sharp line of contact between the two fluids.

The dilutions and the various controls can be varied, depending on the system being studied. To conserve reagents the test may be conducted in capillary tubes.

A distinct white cloud should appear at the line of contact within a few minutes, deepening rapidly to a flocculant precipitate; the reaction is complete after 20 minutes.

INTERPRETATION

Provided adequate controls have been used, the reaction can be considered specific for the antiserum used. If blood stains are tested, the reaction does not prove the presence of blood but only of a protein of the species indicated. Doubt can arise in differentiating among the proteins of very closely related species, as, for example, man and monkey or sheep and goats, but this doubt can practically always be removed by the use of adequate controls. Even old stains have given good results with this technique, although stains on leather and in earth present difficulties. Various modifications of this procedure in agar gel (Oudin, Ouchterlony) are being investigated and may well prove more practical and specific than the method just described.

Grouping of Beta Hemolytic Streptococci by the Precipitin Technique

The grouping and typing of a beta hemolytic streptococcus can readily be done by the same procedure. It is necessary to prepare an extract for testing with grouping sera. Such sera are readily available commercially. Typing of streptococci within the groups can only be done in special laboratories. The determination of the type of a group A streptococcus is used primarily for epidemiologic and investigative studies and is rarely required in a clinical laboratory (see p. 625). However, the determination of the *group* to which a streptococcus belongs is an important procedure, particularly those of Lancefield group A to which the vast majority of human pathogens belong. Recent work, such as that of Moody *et al.* (1958), has shown that it is possible to group streptococci in smears by the fluorescent antibody technique. This procedure appears to show much promise. The use of bacitracin discs is recommended for presumptive identification of group A streptococci (see p. 625); for final identification the precipitin method is necessary.

Preparation of Extract. It is necessary to bring about partial disintegration of the cell wall with the release of soluble carbohydrate ("C substance") in a form that retains its serologic reactivity. Several different methods are employed for this purpose of which those of Lancefield, the autoclave method of Rantz and Randall (1945), and the enzyme procedure of Maxted (1948) will be described briefly. The latter is simpler and more rapid than the other procedures. More complete descriptions will be found in the references.

Lancefield Procedure. The organisms are grown for 18 to 24 hours in Todd-Hewitt broth. The culture is centrifuged and the supernatant discarded after which the sediment is suspended in 5 to 7 drops of N/5 HCl. This is placed in a boiling water bath for ten minutes and cooled for another ten minutes. It is then centrifuged again. The sediment is discarded and one drop of 0.01 per cent phenol red is added to the clear supernatant fluid. Buffer (1 gm. sodium acid phosphate in 100 ml. N/5 NaOH) is added drop by drop until a pale pink color develops. Following another centrifugation the clear supernatant fluid is used as the antigen for the precipitin test (Swift *et al.,* 1943).

Autoclave Procedure (Rantz and Randall). The streptococci to be grouped are grown overnight in 50 ml. of trypticase soy or tryptose phosphate broth. The cultures are centrifuged and the sediment suspended in a small amount of sterile saline. The tube is then autoclaved at 15 lb. pressure for 15 minutes and the tube again centrifuged. The clear supernatant is used for the antigen.

Enzyme Procedure (Maxted, 1948). A loopful of growth of the streptococci to be grouped is placed in 0.25 ml. of the enzyme. The enzyme consists of a powerful proteolytic substance isolated from *Streptomyces albus.* (Details for the preparation of this material can be found in the references.) The tubes are placed in a water bath at 50° C. for 90 minutes. The clear solution contains the soluble antigen that is used in the test.

RING PRECIPITIN TECHNIQUE FOR STREPTOCOCCUS GROUPING

1. A capillary tube (1.0 to 1.5 mm. in diameter) is dipped into the streptococcus

grouping antiserum and a column of 25 to 30 mm. is allowed to rise into the tube.

2. The excess serum is wiped from outside of the capillary tube, which is then dipped into the previously prepared streptococcal extract. A column equal to the antiserum is allowed to enter into the capillary tube. Care must be used to insure contact between the serum and antigen.

3. The tube containing the antiserumextract mixture is wiped, placed into a plasticine block, and incubated at room temperature. Macroscopic precipitate appears within a few minutes and is complete in 30 minutes.

A control consisting of an extract of streptococci of a known group should be included. The procedure can be repeated with different dilutions of the antigen. If no reaction occurs, one may be dealing with streptococci of a different group or a prozone reaction may be occurring. To determine this, the extract should be diluted and retested with the antiserum.

OTHER SERODIAGNOSTIC PROCEDURES

The following tests are done only in a few clinical laboratories at present, although they may assume more importance in the future. They are described only briefly here; more complete details will be found in the references.

Leptospirosis

The serologic detection of antibodies to *Leptospira* is an important adjunct in the diagnosis of this disease. Procedures used are the complement fixation, agglutination lysis, latex fixation, and macroscopic agglutination techniques. The latter reaction is simple and may be done in the same manner as that described for the Widal test. Stable antigens are now available commercially for most of the common serotypes. Antibody is frequently detectable during the second week of the disease and may be demonstrable in the serum for several years.

Toxoplasmosis

Most commonly the Sabin-Feldman dye test is used for diagnosis in this disease. This requires the use of living organisms and is slow and tedious. The complementfixation reaction and the hemagglutination procedure are probably more practical. Fluorescent antibody methods appear to show great promise in the diagnosis of this disease.

Echinococcosis (Hydatid Disease)

Complement fixation, hemagglutination, precipitation, bentonite flocculation, and intracutaneous tests are useful in the serologic diagnosis of this disease (see p. 814).

REFERENCES

1. Ager, J. A. M., Hutt, M. S. R., and Smith, G.: Detection of thyroid antibodies using bentonite particles. Nature, *184:*478, 1959.
2. Bloch, K. J., and Bunim, J. J.: Simple rapid test for rheumatoid arthritis—bentonite flocculation test. J.A.M.A., *169:*307–314, 1959.
3. Bozicevich, J., Bunim, J. J., Freund, J., and Ward, S. B.: Bentonite flocculation test for rheumatoid arthritis. Proc. Soc. Exper. Biol. & Med., *97:*180–183, 1958.
4. Carpenter, P. L.: Immunology and Serology. Philadelphia, W. B. Saunders Company, 1956.
5. Chang, R. S., and McComb, D. E.: Erythrocyte sensitizing substances from five strains of leptospirae. Am. J. Trop. Med., *3:*481–489, 1954.
6. Ellenhorn, M. J., and Weiner, D.: Variables in the determination of cold hemagglutinins. Am. J. Clin. Path., *23:*1031–1039, 1953.
7. Epstein, W. A., Johnson, A. M., and Ragan, C.: Observations of a precipitation reaction between serum of patients with rheumatoid arthritis and a preparation (Cohn fraction II) of human gamma globulin. Proc. Soc. Exper. Biol. & Med., *91:*235–237, 1956.
8. Felix, A.: Technique and interpretation of the Weil-Felix test. Tr. Roy. Soc. Trop. Med. & Hgy., *37:*343, 1944.
9. Florman, A. L., and Weiss, A. B.: Serological reactions in primary atypical pneumonia. J. Lab. & Clin. Med., *30:*902–910, 1945.
10. Garrow, D. H.: A rapid test for the presence of increased cold agglutinins. Brit. Med. J., *11:* 206–208, 1958.
11. Gilbert, R., and Coleman, M. B.: Agglutination in the diagnosis of enteric disease. Am. J. Pub. Health, 23:693–696, 1933.
12. Goldin, M., and Kaplan, M. A.: A method for obtaining blood for micro-tests; application to determination of C-reactive protein and antistreptolysin O titers. Am. J. Clin. Path., *25:* 1432–1434, 1955.
13. Goldman, M.: Staining *Toxoplasma gondii* with fluorescein labelled antibody. II. A new serologic test for antibodies to *Toxoplasma* based on inhibition of specific staining. J. Exper. Med., *105:*557–572, 1957.
14. Han, E. S.: Hemagglutination test for epidemic and murine typhus fever using sheep erythrocytes sensitized with *Proteus* OX19 extracts. Am. J. Trop. Med., *31:*243–251, 1951.
15. Harding, H. B., and Synder, R. A.: The epidemiology of primary atypical pneumonia. A.M.A. Arch. Int. Med., *105:*217–232, 1960.
16. Heller, G., Jacobson, A. S., Kolodny, M. H., and Kammerer, W. H.: The hemagglutination test for rheumatoid arthritis. II. The influence of human plasma fraction II (gamma globulin) on the reaction. J. Immunol., 72:66–78, 1954.
17. Huddleston, F. I., and Abel, E.: Rapid micro-

scopic agglutination for the serum diagnosis of Bang's abortion disease. J. Infect. Dis., 42: 242–247, 1928.

18. Hunter, C. A., Burdorff, R., and Colbert, B.: Flocculation tests for tularemia. J. Lab. & Clin. Med., 51:134–140, 1958.

19. Hunter, C. A., and Colbert, B.: Flocculation tests for brucellosis. J. Immunol., 77:232–241, 1956.

20. Jablon, J. M., Saul, M., and Saslaw, M. S.: Microtechnic for determination of titers of antistreptolysin O. Am. J. Clin. Path., 30:83–86, 1958.

21. Johnson, G. D.: The determination of antistreptolysin. J. Clin. Path., 8:296–299, 1955.

22. Kabat, E. A., and Mayer, M. M.: Experimental Immunochemistry. 2nd ed. Springfield, Illinois, Charles C Thomas, 1961.

23. Kagan, I. G., Allain, D. S., and Norman, L.: An evaluation of the hemagglutination and flocculation tests in the diagnosis of Echinococcus disease. Am. J. Trop. Med. & Hyg., 8:51–55, 1959.

24. Kolmer, J. A., Spaulding, E. H., and Robinson, H. W.: Approved Laboratory Technic. 5th Ed. New York, Appleton-Century-Crofts, Inc., 1951.

25. Koomen, J., Jr., and Morgan, H. R.: An evaluation of the anamnestic serum reaction in certain febrile illnesses. Am. J. Med. Sc., 228: 520–524, 1954.

26. Kunkel, H. G.: The rheumatoid factors. Arch. Int. Med., 170:832–836, 1960.

27. Lunde, M. N., and Jacobs, L.: Characteristics of the toxoplasma hemagglutination test antigen. J. Immunol., 82:146–150, 1959.

28. Maxted, W. R.: Preparation of streptococcal extracts for Lancefield grouping. Lancet, 2: 255–256, 1948.

29. Moody, M. D., Ellis, E. C., and Updyke, E. L.: Staining bacterial smears with fluorescent antibody. IV. Grouping streptococci with fluorescent antibody. J. Bact., 75:553–560, 1958.

30. Muraschi, T. F.: A simple screening test for the detection of leptospirosis in human beings and animals. Am. J. Pub. Health, 49:74–78, 1959.

31. Muschel, L. H., and Weatherwax, R. J.: Complement fixation in the C-reactive protein system. Proc. Soc. Exper. Biol. & Med., 87:191–194, 1954.

32. Neter, E., Gorzynski, E. A., Gino, R. M., Westphal, O., and Luderitz, O.: The enterobacterial hemagglutination test and its diagnostic potentialities. Canad. J. Microbiol., 2:232–244, 1956.

33. Norman, L., Sadun, E. H., and Allain, D. S.: A bentonite flocculation test for the diagnosis of hydatid disease in man and animals. Am. J. Trop. Med. & Hyg., 8:45–50, 1959.

34. Price, S. G., and Weiner, L. M.: Use of hemagglutination in the diagnosis of trichinosis. Am. J. Clin. Path., 26:1261–1269, 1956.

35. Raffel, S.: Immunity, Hypersensitivity, Serology. New York, Appleton-Century-Crofts, Inc., 1953.

36. Ransmeier, J. C., and Ewing, C. L.: The agglutination reaction in tularemia. J. Infect. Dis., 69:193–205, 1941.

37. Rantz, A. L., and Randall, E. A.: Modification of the technic for the determination of the antistreptolysin titer. Proc. Soc. Exper. Biol. & Med., 59:22–25, 1945.

38. Rantz, L. A., and Randall, E.: Use of autoclaved extracts of hemolytic streptococci for serological grouping. Stanford Med. Bull., 13: 290–291, 1955.

39. Roitt, I. M., and Doniach, D.: Thyroid autoimmunity. Brit. Med. Bull., 16:152–158, 1960.

40. Sabin, A. B., Eichenwald, H., Feldman, H. A., and Jacobs, L.: Present status of clinical manifestations of toxoplasmosis in man. Indications and provisions for routine serologic diagnosis. J.A.M.A., 150:1063–1069, 1952.

41. Sabin, A. B., and Feldman, H. A.: Dyes as microchemical indicators of a new immunity phenomenon affecting a protozoan parasite (Toxoplasma). Science, 108:660–663, 1948.

42. Sadun, E. H., and Norman, L.: A practical flocculation test for the seriodiagnosis of trichinosis by the state health laboratory. Pub. Health Lab., 13:147–152, 1955.

43. Schubert, J. H.: A study of the rapid slide agglutination test for brucellosis as compared with the tube agglutination test. J. Lab. & Clin. Med., 41:776–781, 1953.

44. Schubert, J. H., Holdeman, L., and Martin, D. S.: Evaluation of certain factors which affect the titers obtained with the Weil-Felix test. J. Lab. & Clin. Med., 44:194–201, 1954.

45. Shackman, N. H., Heffer, E. T., and Kroop, I. G.: The C-reactive protein determination as a measure of rheumatic activity. Am. Heart J., 48:599–605, 1954.

46. Sharp, C. G.: Laboratory diagnosis of leptospirosis with the sensitized erythrocyte lysis test. J. Path. & Bact., 76:349–356, 1958.

47. Singer, J. M., and Plotz, C. M.: Latex fixation test. I. Application to serological diagnosis of rheumatoid arthritis. Am. J. Med., 21: 888–892, 1956.

48. Singer, J. M., and Plotz, C. M.: Slide latex fixation test. A simple screening method for diagnosis of rheumatoid arthritis. J.A.M.A., 168: 180–181, 1958.

49. Spink, W. W., McCullogh, N. B., Hutching, L. M., and Mingle, C. K.: A standardized antigen and agglutination technic for human brucellosis. Am. J. Clin. Path., 24:496–498, 1954.

50. Stats, D., and Wasserman, L. R.: Cold hemagglutinins: An interpretative review. Medicine, 22:363–424, 1943.

51. Stollerman, G. H., Glick, S., Patel, D. J., Hirschfeld, I., and Rusoff, J. H.: Determination of C-reactive protein in serum as a guide to the diagnosis and management of rheumatic fever. Am. J. Med., 15:645–655, 1953.

52. Suessenguth, H., Bauer, A. H., and Greenlee, A. M.: Evaluation of the Suessenguth-Kline test for trichinosis. Pub. Health Rep., 72:939–942, 1957.

53. Swift, H. F., Wilson, A. T., and Lancefield, R. C.: Typing group A streptococci by M precipitin reactions in capillary pipettes. J. Exper. Med., 78:127–133, 1943.

54. Thomas, L., Minick, G. S., Curnen, B. C., Ziegler, J. E., Jr., and Horsfall, F. J., Jr.: Studies on primary atypical pneumonia. II. Observations concerning the relationship of a non-hemolytic streptococcus to the disease. J. Clin. Investigation, 24:227–240, 1945.

55. Tillet, W. B., and Francis, T.: Serological reactions in pneumonia with a non-protein somatic fraction of pneumococcus. J. Exper. Med., 52:561–571, 1930.

56. Todd, E. W.: Antihemolysin titers in haemolytic streptococcus infections and their significance in rheumatic fever. Brit. J. Exper. Path., 12: 248–259, 1932.

57. Turner, J. C., Nisnevitz, S., Jackson, E. B., and Birney, R.: Relationship of cold agglutinins

to atypical pneumonia. Lancet, 1:765–769, 1943.

58. Valyasevi, H., Sloan, J. M., and Barnes, L. A.: C-reactive protein in the serum in nephrosis and acute glomerulonephritis. Pediatrics, 25: 106–111, 1960.

59. Waller, M. V., and Vaughan, J. H.: The use of anti-Rh sera for demonstrating agglutination activating factor in rheumatoid arthritis. Proc. Soc. Exper. Biol. & Med., 92:198–200, 1956.

60. Wannamaker, L. W., Denny, F. W., Rammel-kamp, C. H., and Brink, W. R.: Use of Max-ted's method for group classification of hemolytic streptococci. Proc. Soc. Exper. Biol. & Med., 73:467–469, 1950.

61. Weil, E., and Felix, A.: Des Serologischen Diag-nose des Fleckfiebers. Wien. klin. Wchnschr., 29:33, 1916.

62. Witebsky, E., and Rose, N. R.: Studies on organ specificity. IV. Production of rabbit thyroid antibodies in the rabbit. J. Immun., 76:408–416, 1956.

63. Yocum, R. S., and Doener, A. A.: A clinical evaluation of the C-reactive protein test. Arch. Int. Med., 99:74–81, 1957.

64. Ziff, M., Braun, P., Lospalluto, J., Badin, J., and McEwen, C.: Agglutination and inhibition by serum globulin in the sensitized sheep cell ag-glutination in rheumatoid arthritis. Am. J. Med., 20:500–509, 1956.

Chapter 25

The Sputum

By BENJAMIN B. WELLS, M.D.

Several circumstances in recent years have greatly diminished the attention paid to detailed examination of the sputum. Chief among these are the development of more accurate roentgen diagnosis and the use of antibiotic agents. In acute bacterial infection of the lungs antibiotic therapy often so alters the character of the sputum that classic findings cannot be made even when the disease process is not entirely checked. Therefore, some of the observations contained in this chapter are seldom used in present-day practice. However, in addition to occasional practical requirements these observations have sufficient instructional value to warrant their inclusion in a work of this nature. Many of the macroscopic and microscopic studies of sputum have been displaced by more sophisticated methods of microbiology and pulmonary physiology. It is to be hoped that students and teachers will appreciate the retention of certain descriptions that have more historic interest than current utility.

Before beginning the study of the sputum the student will do well to familiarize himself with the structures that normally may be present in the mouth and that frequently appear in the sputum. Nasal mucus and material obtained by scraping the tongue and about the teeth should be studied by the method used for the examination of unstained sputum. A drop of compound solution of iodine (Lugol's solution) should be placed at the edge of the coverglass, and as it runs under its effect on different structures should be noted. A portion of the sputum should be spread on slides or coverglasses and stained by some simple stain and by Gram's method. The structures likely

to be encountered are epithelial cells of columnar and squamous types; leukocytes, chiefly mononuclear leukocytes, the so-called salivary corpuscles; food particles; *Leptotrichia buccalis;* great numbers of saprophytic bacteria; and frequently spirochetes and *Entamoeba.* These structures will be described later.

When collecting the sample for examination, the morning sputum or all the sputum that is expectorated in 24 hours should be saved. In cases of incipient tuberculosis *Mycobacterium tuberculosis* often can be found in the material that is coughed up in the morning but cannot be detected in material that is coughed up at any other time of the day. Sometimes in cases of early tuberculosis there are only a few mucopurulent flakes that contain the *Mycobacterium tuberculosis,* or the organism may be found only in a small purulent mass that is coughed up every few days. These masses may easily be overlooked by the patient.

Patients should be instructed to rinse their mouths well in order to avoid contamination with food particles, which may prove confusing in the examination, and to make sure that the sputum contains material from the lungs or bronchi. Many persons find it difficult to distinguish between material that comes from the lungs or bronchi and material that comes from the nose or nasopharynx. It is desirable that the material be raised with a distinct expulsive cough, but this is not always possible. Material from the upper air passages can usually be identified by the large proportion of mucus and the character of the epithelial cells. In some cases of chronic tuberculosis there may be no cough at all; the small masses may be raised by the action of the bronchial and tracheal cilia, and the patient may become conscious of the masses only when they reach the larynx. Patients often swallow the masses without realizing their significance. Aspiration of the stomach contents in such cases may yield material in which acid-fast organisms may be found.

The collection of sputum from asymptomatic patients or from those with unproductive cough can be aided by the inhalation of nebulized fluids, which are subsequently expelled as sputum. A heated saline-aerosol has proved quite satisfactory for the artificial production of sputum used for cytologic study in the detection of lung cancer (Bickerman *et al.*, 1958; Umiker *et al.*, 1960) and for bacteriologic diagnosis of tuberculosis.

The sputum of infants and young children is usually swallowed and cannot be collected. In such cases examination of the feces for *Mycobacterium tuberculosis* will sometimes establish a diagnosis of tuberculosis.

As a receptacle for the sputum a clean, wide-mouth bottle with a tightly fitting cork or screw cap may be used. The patient must be particularly cautioned against smearing any of the sputum on the outside of the bottle. This is probably the chief source of danger to persons who examine sputum. Disinfectants should not be added. Although some of them (phenol, for example) do not interfere with detection of the *Mycobacterium tuberculosis,* they generally alter the character of the sputum and render it unfit for further examination.

The following plan is suggested for the routine examination of sputum:

1. Spread the material in a thin layer in a large Petri dish.

2. Examine all parts carefully with the naked eye or with a hand lens. This is best done over a dark background. The portions most suitable for further examination may thus be easily selected.

3. Transfer various portions, including all suspicious particles, to clean slides; cover and examine unstained with the microscope. A wooden applicator may be used to transfer selected portions of sputum to the glass slide. The applicator is then used as a spreader and can be burned in the Bunsen flame.

4. Slip the coverglasses from some or all the unstained preparations, leaving a thin smear on both slide and coverglass.

5. Dry and fix the smears and stain one or more by a staining method for *Myco-*

bacterium tuberculosis or by Gram's method.

6. When indicated, make special examinations for capsules of bacteria and for eosinophilic cells.

After the examination has been completed, the sputum must be destroyed by heat or chemicals, and everything that has come in contact with it must be sterilized. The utmost care must be taken not to allow any of it to dry and become disseminated through the air. The sputum must be kept covered. It is a good plan to conduct the examination on a large newspaper, which can then be burned. Contamination of the work table is thus avoided. If this is not feasible, the table should be washed off with a 1:10 dilution of compound solution of cresol or with some other disinfectant and allowed to dry slowly as soon as the examination of the sputum has been completed.

MACROSCOPIC EXAMINATION

Quantity. The quantity of sputum expectorated in 24 hours varies greatly. It may be so slight as to be overlooked entirely in cases of incipient tuberculosis. It is usually small in cases of acute bronchitis or lobar pneumonia. It may be very large—sometimes as much as 1000 ml.—in advanced tuberculosis with large cavities, in edema of the lung and bronchiectasis, after rupture of an abscess, or in empyema. It is desirable to obtain a general idea of the quantity, but accurate measurement is unnecessary.

Color. Since the sputum ordinarily consists of varying proportions of mucus and pus, it may be colorless and translucent or opaque, whitish or yellow, and purulent. Yellowish green sputum is frequently seen in cases of advanced tuberculosis and chronic bronchitis. In jaundice, in caseous pneumonia, and in slowly resolving lobar pneumonia it may assume a bright green color owing to bile or altered blood pigment.

A red or reddish brown color usually indicates the presence of blood or blood pigment. Bright red blood, which most commonly occurs in streaks, is strongly suggestive of tuberculosis. It may be noted early in the disease and generally denotes an extension of the tuberculous process. One must, however, be certain that the blood-streaked mucus or mucopus is not due to nasopharyngeal infection or irritation. Blood-stained sputum is also sometimes seen in bronchiectasis. A rusty red sputum is the rule in lobar pneumonia and was at one time considered pathognomonic of the disease. Exactly similar material may be raised in cases of pulmonary infarction. Brown sputum owing to altered blood pigment follows hemorrhage from the lungs and is present in chronic passive congestion of the lungs, which is most frequently due to cardiac decompensation.

Consistency. Sputum usually is classified as serous, mucoid, purulent, seropurulent, or mucopurulent. These terms are self-explanatory. As a rule the more mucus and the less pus and serum a sputum contains, the more tenacious it is.

The rusty sputum of lobar pneumonia is extremely tenacious, so that the vessel in which it is contained may be inverted without spilling the sputum. The same is true of the almost purely mucoid sputum (sputum crudum) of beginning acute bronchitis and of that which follows an attack of asthma. A purely serous sputum, usually slightly blood tinged, is fairly characteristic of edema of the lungs.

Formerly much attention was paid to the so-called nummular sputum. This consists of definite mucopurulent masses, which flatten into coinlike disks and sink in water. It is fairly characteristic of tuberculous and bronchiectatic cavities.

Layer Formation. Some specimens of sputum show a striking tendency to separate into three sharply defined layers when a large volume is allowed to stand in a tall vessel. This is notably true in bronchiectasis, gangrene, and abscess of the lung.

Dittrich's Plugs. Although these bodies sometimes appear in the sputum, they are more frequently expectorated alone. They are yellowish or gray caseous masses; they usually are about the size of the head of a pin but sometimes may become as large as a navy bean. When crushed, they emit a foul odor. Microscopically they consist of granular debris, fat globules, fatty acid crystals, and bacteria. They are formed in the bronchi. They are sometimes expectorated by healthy persons but are observed more frequently in cases of putrid bronchitis and bronchiectasis. Patients commonly regard them as evidence of tuberculosis. The similar caseous masses that are formed in the crypts of the tonsils are sometimes also included under this name.

Lung Stones. At times during the course of chronic tuberculosis small calcified nodules of tuberculous tissue may be expectorated. These constitute the majority of the so-called pneumoliths. Small foreign bodies, bits of clothing, and similar material, which are carried into the lung by gunshot and other injuries, may sometimes remain for years and finally ulcerate into a bronchus and be expectorated, usually with hemorrhage.

Bronchial Casts. These are branching, treelike casts of the bronchi. They frequently, but not always, are composed of fibrin (Figs. 25–1 and 25–2). They are usually white or grayish in color but may be reddish or brown owing to the presence of blood pigment. Their size varies with that of the bronchi in which they are formed. Casts 15 cm. or more in length have been observed, but most bronchial casts are very much smaller. Ordinarily they are rolled into a ball or tangled mass and can be recognized only by floating them out in water. They are best seen over a black background. When examined in this manner, their treelike structure becomes evident. Gross examination usually will suffice, but

Figure 25–1. Bronchial casts (natural size) as seen when carefully spread out and viewed over a black background; usually only broken pieces are found.

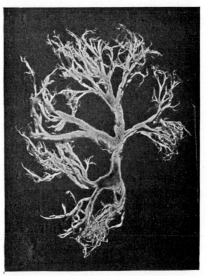

Figure 25–2. Unusually large and perfect bronchial cast. Half natural size (Spencer).

a hand lens occasionally may be required.

Bronchial casts appear in the sputum in lobar pneumonia, in fibrinous bronchitis, and in cases of diphtheria in which the lesion extends into the bronchi. In diphtheria they are usually large. In fibrinous or chronic plastic bronchitis they are of medium size and usually of characteristic structure. Their demonstration is essential for the diagnosis of this disease. In some cases they may be found every day for considerable periods; in others, only occasionally. In almost every case of lobar pneumonia the casts are present in the sputum in variable numbers during the stages of resolution. In this disease they are usually small (0.5 to 1 cm. long) and often are not branched.

MICROSCOPIC EXAMINATION

The portions of the sputum most likely to contain structures of interest should be very carefully selected as already described. The few minutes spent in this preliminary examination will sometimes save hours of work later. Opaque, white or yellow particles are most frequently bits of food but may be cheesy masses from the tonsils. Such particles, sometimes caseous, may be derived from tuberculous cavities and contain many tubercle bacilli and elastic fibers. Curschmann's spirals, small fibrinous casts coiled into little balls, or shreds of mucus with great numbers of entangled pus corpuscles may also be seen. The food particles most likely to cause confusion are bits of bread, which can be recognized by the blue color they assume when touched with a solution of iodine. Some structures are best identified without staining; others require that the sputum be stained.

Unstained Sputum

A careful study of the unstained sputum should be included in every routine examination. Unfortunately it is almost universally neglected. This examination best reveals certain structures that are seen imperfectly or not at all in stained preparations. It gives a general idea of the other structures that are present, such as pus cells, eosinophils, epithelial cells, and blood, and thus suggests appropriate stains to be used later. It enables one to select more intelligently the portions to be examined for *Mycobacterium tuberculosis*.

The particle selected for examination should be transferred to a clean slide, covered with a clean coverglass, and examined first with the 16 mm. objective and then with the 4 mm. objective. The oil immersion objective should not be used for this purpose. It is convenient to handle the bits of sputum with a wooden toothpick or with a wooden applicator that has been wrapped with cotton, which may be burned when the examination has been completed. The platinum wire used in bacteriologic work is unsatisfactory because it usually is not stiff enough. A little practice is necessary before one can handle particles of sputum readily. The bit desired should be separated from the bulk of the sputum by cutting it free with a toothpick and drawing it out on the dry portion of the glass dish. It can then be picked up by rotating the end of a fresh toothpick against it. The slide should never be dipped into the sputum and none of the sputum should be allowed to run over the edges of the slide.

The more important structures to be seen in unstained sputum are elastic fibers, Curschmann's spirals, Charcot-Leyden crystals, pigmented cells, myelin globules, the ray fungus of actinomycosis, and molds. Forming the background for these are usually pus corpuscles, granular detritus, and mucus in the form of translucent, finely fibrillar or jelly-like masses. Pus cells appear as finely granular, grayish or yellowish balls, about 10 to 12 microns in diameter, and generally are without visible nuclei. They are best studied in stained preparations.

Elastic Fibers. These are the elastic fibers of the pulmonary substance. In the lung they are distributed in the walls of the alveoli, the bronchioles, and the blood vessels. When found in the sputum, they always indicate destructive disease of the lung provided they do not come from food, which is a frequent source. They are found in abscess and gangrene of the lung, but in the majority of cases their presence indicates tuberculosis. In cases of advanced tuberculosis great numbers of elastic fibers often are present in the sputum. They rarely are found in cases of early tuberculosis when the *Mycobacterium tuberculosis* cannot be detected. After the diagnosis of tuberculosis is established, they furnish a valuable clue to the existence and rate of destruction of the lung. In gangrene of the lung, contrary to the older teaching, elastic tissue is probably always to be found in the sputum, usually being present in large fragments.

The portion of the sputum to be searched

for elastic tissue should be selected by careful inspection. Small bits of necrotic tissue or yellowish, greenish, or rusty particles, which are often minute, are most likely to contain elastic fibers. When bits of necrotic tissue or rusty particles are absent, the most purulent portion of the sputum should be taken. The selected bit is taken on a slide, and a coverglass is applied and pressed down so as to give a moderately thin preparation, which should be examined before it dries. Careful selection of the portion examined is more efficient than is the concentration method—boiling with a 10 per cent solution of caustic soda and centrifuging—which is widely recommended.

The search should be conducted with the 16 mm. objective, although a higher power objective is often needed to identify the fibers with certainty. They are slender, highly refractive, wavy fibrils with double contour and curled, often split, ends. Very characteristic are their graceful curves without sharp bends, their uniform diameter, and their smoothness, although in old sputum they may be much roughened. The fibers may lie singly or in bundles. Frequently they are found in alveolar arangement, and the original outline of the alveoli of the lungs is preserved (Figs. 25–3 and 25–4). This arangement is positive proof of their origin in the lung.

Leptotrichia buccalis, which is a normal inhabitant of the mouth, may easily be mistaken for elastic tissue with the lower power objective. It usually can be distin-

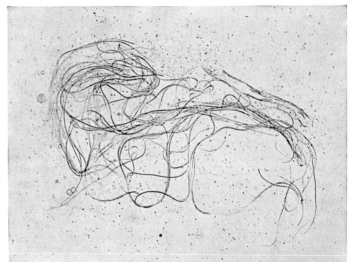

Figure 25–3. Unstained elastic fibers in sputum as seen with a low power objective (× 100).

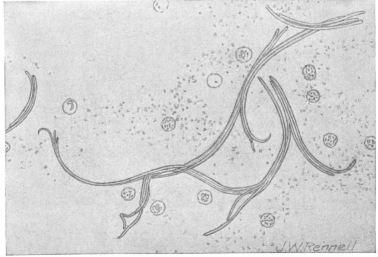

Figure 25–4. Unstained elastic fibers in tuberculous sputum, unstained, as seen with a high power objective (× 400).

guished easily when studied with the 4 mm. objective.

Fatty acid crystals, which are often present in Dittrich's plugs and in sputum that has remained in the body for some time, also simulate elastic tissue when very long, but they are more like stiff, straight, or curved needles than wavy threads. They show varicosities when the coverglass is pressed down on them, and they melt into droplets when the slide is heated.

The structures that most frequently confuse the student are cotton fibrils, which are often present as a contamination from the air. These are usually coarser than elastic fibers and are flat with one or two twists and often have longitudinal striations and frayed ends. Their color too is somewhat different. Cotton fibers lack the faint yellowish tinge of elastic tissue. Very important also is the relative degree of refractility: If the diaphragm is opened slowly, elastic fibers can be seen long after the slightly refractile strands of mucus have disappeared, but finally they also are practically lost in the glare, while cotton fibers still remain visible. In examining stained preparations, students frequently report the fibrils of precipitated mucus as elastic tissue. Elastic fibers of food are coarser, generally shorter, less frequently wavy, and not arranged in an alveolar order.

Curschmann's Spirals. These peculiar structures are found most frequently in bronchial asthma and are fairly characteristic of this disease. Although they are not present in every attack, they probably occur at some time in every case. Sometimes they can be found only near the end of the attack. They occasionally may be present in cases of chronic bronchitis and other diseases, but in these cases there is nearly always an underlying asthmatic tendency. Their nature has not been definitely determined.

Macroscopically they are whitish or yellow wavy threads frequently coiled into little balls (Fig. 25–5). Their length is rarely more than 1.5 cm., though it sometimes exceeds 5 cm. They can sometimes be definitely recognized with the naked eye. Under a 16 mm. objective they appear as mucous threads with a bright, colorless, central line—the so-called central fiber—about which are wound many fine fibrils (Figs. 25–6 and 25–7). The bright central line is best seen when the objective is raised a little above the true focus. This line has been interpreted as an optical phenomenon owing to tight coiling of the spiral. In some

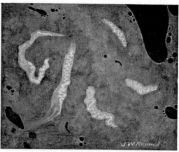

Figure 25–5. Curschmann's spirals (natural size) in asthmatic sputum as seen when pressed out between two plates of glass and viewed over a black background. Each is embedded in a mass of grayish mucus.

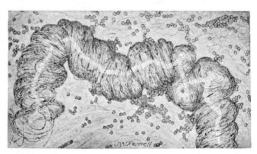

Figure 25–6. End of a large, tightly wound Curschmann's spiral (unstained) in sputum from a case of bronchial asthma (× 70).

cases one or more definite dark colored, threadlike fibers can be seen at the true focus. The spiral fibrils are loosely or tightly wound. Eosinophils are usually present within them, and sometimes Charcot-Leyden crystals also are present. Not infrequently the spirals are imperfectly formed and consist merely of twisted strands of mucus enclosing leukocytes. The central fiber is absent in these spirals.

Charcot-Leyden Crystals. Of the crystals that may be found in the sputum, the most interesting are the Charcot-Leyden crystals. They may be absent when the sputum is expectorated but appear in large numbers after it has stood for some time. They are rarely found except in cases of bronchial asthma. At one time they were thought to be the cause of this disease. They frequently adhere to Curschmann's spirals. Their exact nature is unknown. Their formation seems to be connected in some way with the presence of eosinophilic cells. They also are found in the feces in association with parasites.

The crystals are colorless, pointed, often needle-like (Fig. 25–8). Formerly they were described as octahedral, but they are now known to be hexagonal on cross-section.

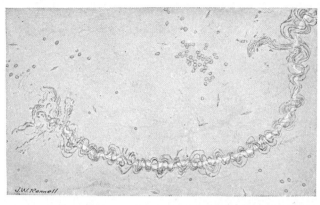

Figure 25–7.   Slender, loosely wound Curshmann's spiral (unstained) in sputum. A few Charcot-Leyden crystals also are visible (× 70).

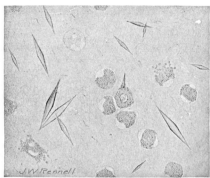

Figure 25–8.   Unstained Charcot-Leyden crystals and eosinophilic leukocytes in sputum from a case of bronchial asthma (× 475). The magnification is greater than is usually used in studying these structures.

Their size varies greatly; their average length is about three or four times the diameter of an erythrocyte.

Other crystals—hematoidin, cholesterol, and, most frequently, fatty acid needles— are common in sputum that has remained in the body for a considerable time, as in cases of abscess of the lung and bronchiectasis. Fatty acid crystals are regularly found in Dittrich's plugs. They might be mistaken for elastic fibers. Sometimes they form rounded masses with the individual crystals radially arranged, and they then bear considerable resemblance to the clumps of *Actinomyces israeli.*

Pigmented Cells. Granules of pigment are sometimes seen in ordinary pus cells, but the more common and more important pigment-containing cells are large mononuclear cells. The origin of these cells is doubtful. They were formerly thought to be the flattened epithelial cells that line the pulmonary alveoli. The present tendency is to identify them with the endothelial leukocytes, which are known to take up pigment granules readily. In view of recent studies the question of their origin must be left open. Two kinds of pigmented cells deserve mention: those which contain blood pigment, chiefly hemosiderin, and those which contain carbon. As a rule these cells also have a coarsely granular appearance owing to the presence of many small colorless myelin globules.

To the cells containing blood pigment the name "heart-failure cells" has been given, because they are most frequently found when long-continued passive congestion of the lungs has resulted from poorly compensated heart disease. The presence of these cells in considerable numbers, by directing one's attention to the heart, will sometimes clear up the cause of chronic bronchitis. They are sometimes so numerous as to give the sputum a brownish tinge. Such cells are also found in the sputum in cases of pulmonary infarction and for some time after a pulmonary hemorrhage. In fresh unstained sputum heart-failure cells appear as round, grayish, or colorless bodies filled with various size rounded granules of yellow to brown pigment (Fig. 25–9 [upper]). Sometimes the pigment appears as a diffuse staining. The nucleus is usually obscured by the pigment. The cells are large; they average about 35 microns in diameter.

To demonstrate the nature of the brown pigment, apply a 10 per cent solution of potassium ferrocyanide for a few minutes and then apply weak hydrochloric acid. Iron-containing pigment assumes a blue color. Many of the granules will, however, fail to respond. The test may be applied either to wet preparations or to dried smears.

Carbon-laden cells (Fig. 25–9 [upper]) are less important. They are especially abundant in the sputum in cases of anthracosis in which angular black granules, both intracellular and extracellular, may be so

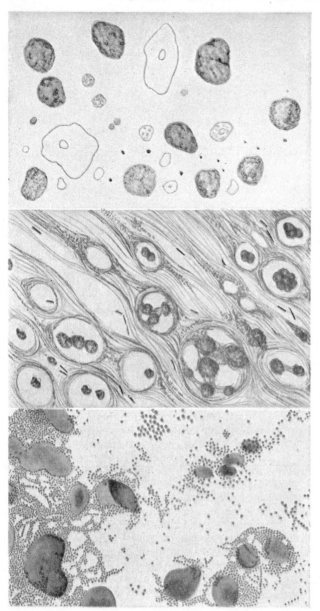

Figure 25–9. Upper, Heart-failure cells and carbon-laden cells in unstained sputum (× 200). *Center,* Tubercle bacilli and pus cells in sputum; specimen stained by Ziehl-Neelsen method (× 1000). *Lower,* Eosinophilic leukocytes in asthmatic sputum (× 1000). (Dorothy Booth, pinx.)

numerous as to color the sputum. Similar cells with smaller carbon particles are often abundant in the morning sputum of persons who inhale tobacco smoke to excess or of persons who live in a smoky atmosphere.

Myelin Globules. These have little or no clinical significance but require mention because of the danger of confusing them with more important structures, notably *Blastomyces.* They are colorless, round, oval, or pear-shaped globules of various sizes. They often resemble fat droplets, but the larger ones more frequently show peculiar concentric or irregularly spiral markings (Fig. 25–10). Such globules are abundant in the

scanty morning sputum of apparently healthy persons, and they may be found in any mucoid sputum. They may be free in the sputum, or they may be contained within the large cells that have long been known as alveolar cells but that are possibly endothelial leukocytes. The intracellular globules are generally small and when closely packed give the cells a yellowish tinge, which may mislead the unwary into calling them heart-failure cells.

Actinomyces israeli. In the sputum of pulmonary actinomycosis and in the pus obtained from actinomycotic lesions elsewhere in the body, small, gray or yellowish "sulfur" granules can be detected with the unaided eye. Without a careful macroscopic examination they are almost certain to be overlooked. The fungus can be seen by crushing one of these granules between the slide and the coverglass and examining with a low power objective (Figs. 25–11 and 25–12). The fungus can be demonstrated more clearly by running a small amount of solution of eosin in alcohol and glycerin under the coverglass. It must be remembered that clumps of organisms resembling

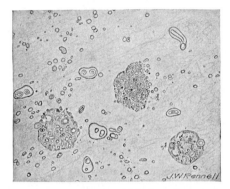

Figure 25–10. Myelin globules, free and contained within cells, in "normal morning sputum" (× 350).

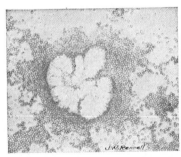

Figure 25–11. Sulfur granule (unstained, crushed beneath a coverglass) obtained from pus in a case of actinomycosis of submaxillary lymph nodes (× 60).

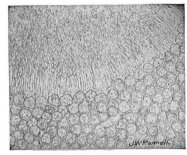

Figure 25–12. A portion of Figure 25–11 more highly magnified (× 300).

sulfur granules may be found in the tonsillar crypts. These may be present in sputum and be confused with granules arising from true actinomycotic pulmonary infection. The nature of the pathogenic actinomyces is described in more detail elsewhere.

Molds and Yeasts. The hyphae and spores of various molds are occasionally observed in sputum. The hyphae are rods, usually jointed or branched and often arranged in a meshwork (mycelium). The spores are highly refractive spheres and ovoids. Both stain well with the ordinary stains. Molds in the sputum are usually the result of contamination and have little significance. Occasionally they grow in the pus of pulmonary cavities owing to tuberculosis or other disease.

In pulmonary blastomycosis specific yeasts have been found in the sputum in large numbers. In the tissues they multiply by budding, and the presence of budding forms in the sputum is sufficient to identify them as *Blastomyces.* In cultures they form hyphae. A similar organism, *Coccidioides immitis,* which is the cause of coccidioidal granuloma of the Pacific Coast regions, does not form buds but multiplies by endosporulation. For the demonstration of both these organisms it is advisable to add a small amount of a 10 per cent solution of caustic soda and to examine an unstained smear. Both may also be studied in stained smears, but cultural methods are essential for their identification.

Animal Parasites. These are extremely rare in the sputum in this country. A trichomonad, perhaps identical with *Trichomonas hominis,* has been seen in the sputum in cases of putrid bronchitis and gangrene of the lung but its etiologic relationship is doubtful. In Japan infection with the lung flukeworm, *Paragonimus westermani,* is common and the ova are found in the sputum. The lung is not an uncommon seat for echinococcus cysts, and hooklets and scolices may appear in the sputum. Larvae of *Strongyloides stercoralis* and of the hookworm have been observed in the sputum. *Endamoeba histolytica* has been found after rupture of hepatic abscess into the lung. Ciliated body cells with cilia in active motion are frequently seen and may easily be mistaken for Infusoria.

Stained Sputum

The principal structures that are best seen in stained sputum are bacteria and cells.

BACTERIA

Examination of the sputum for the presence of bacteria is described in Chapter 17.

CELLS

These include various types of leukocytes, epithelial cells, and erythrocytes. In general a stain of the nature of Wright's blood stain is most satisfactory.

Leukocytes. Polymorphonuclear neutrophils are present as pus cells in every specimen of sputum. At times the sputum may consist of little else. They appear as granular, rounded cells, 10 to 12 microns in diameter, with several nuclei or one very irregular nucleus, which when unstained is obscured by the granules. In preparations stained by any of the usual methods the nuclei stand out clearly and their polymorphous character makes identification of these cells easy (Fig. 25–9 [center]). In old sputum the polymorphonuclear neutrophils may be much disintegrated and hence difficult to recognize even when stained. When these cells predominate in the sputum, the presence of a pyogenic infection may be assumed.

Lymphocytes are generally present in small numbers with the ordinary pus cells from which they are distinguished by the presence of a single round nucleus. In cases of early or mild pure tuberculous infection they are usually the predominating type of cell, and they may be of much help in distinguishing this disease from pyogenic infection. If in a case of known tuberculosis the "cell formula" changes from lymphocytic to polymorphonuclear, the occurrence of secondary infection is strongly suggested.

Eosinophilic leukocytes are rather constantly found in large numbers in the sputum of bronchial asthma near the time of the paroxysm. They constitute one of the most distinctive features of the sputum of this disease. However, while of much diagnostic importance, they are by no means pathognomonic of asthma. They resemble ordinary pus cells, except that their cytoplasm is filled with coarse granules having a marked affinity for eosin. Many of them sometimes are mononuclear; these are involuted forms and not myelocytes. The eosinophils are very fragile, and large numbers of free granules derived from disintegrated cells are also found (Fig. 25–9 [lower]). Eosinophils can often be recognized in unstained sputum by the coarseness of their granules (Fig. 25–8), but for

positive identification some method that includes staining with eosin must be used. A simple method is to stain the dried and fixed film two or three minutes with a saturated solution of eosin and then with Loeffler's methylene blue solution for half a minute or until the thinner portions of the film become blue. Nuclei and bacteria will be blue, and the eosinophilic granules will be bright red. Wright's or Jenner's stain will also be found satisfactory.

Endothelial leukocytes are best studied in unstained sputum. They have been described in the sections on Pigmented Cells and Myelin Globules.

Epithelial Cells. Epithelial Cells may come from any part of the respiratory tract. A few are always present, since desquamation of cells goes on constantly. Their recognition is important chiefly as an aid in deciding on the source of the portion of the sputum in which they are found. For this reason they are sometimes spoken of as "guide cells." In cases of suspected disease of the lung it is manifestly useless to study material from the nose only, yet this is frequently done. These cells have little diagnostic value, although a considerable excess would indicate a pathologic condition at the site of their origin. Any of the stains mentioned will disclose them, and they can usually be identified without difficulty in unstained sputum. In general three forms are found:

Squamous cells are large, flat, polygonal cells that have a comparatively small nucleus. When they are present in the sputum, they have come from the upper air passages. They are especially numerous in laryngitis and pharyngitis and are frequently studded with bacteria—most commonly diplococci.

Cylindric cells from the nose, trachea and bronchi are not usually abundant, and as a rule they are not identified because they are much altered from their original form, usually being round and swollen. Cylindric cells with cilia intact are rare but are sometimes seen in bronchial asthma and very acute bronchitis. When fresh, the cilia may still be in active motion and be suggestive of Infusoria.

Alveolar cells—rather large, round, or oval cells, three to six times the diameter of a red cell, with one or two round nuclei—are presumably from the pulmonary alveoli. It is probable that many of the cells that have been included in this group are really endothelial leukocytes.

Erythrocytes. Erythrocytes may be present in small numbers in almost any sputum.

When fairly constantly present in considerable numbers, they are suggestive of tuberculosis. When they are fresh, they can easily be recognized in unstained sputum or may be demonstrated by any of the staining methods that include eosin. They are, however, commonly so degenerated as to be unrecognizable and in many cases only altered blood pigment is left. Ordinarily blood in the sputum may be recognized with the naked eye.

THE SPUTUM IN DISEASE

Strictly speaking, any appreciable amount of sputum is abnormal. A great many healthy persons, however, raise a small quantity each morning owing chiefly to irritation by inhaled dust and smoke. Although not normal this can hardly be spoken of as pathologic. Ordinarily the material reaches the larynx without coughing. This condition is particularly frequent among city dwellers and among those who smoke cigarettes to excess. In the latter the amount of sputum is sometimes so great as to arouse suspicion of tuberculosis. Such "normal morning sputum" or "sputum of irritation" generally consists of small, rather dense, mucoid masses, which are translucent, white, or when due to inhaled smoke, gray in color. Microscopically there are a few pus cells but usually many endothelial leukocytes. The pus cells and the endothelial leukocytes may contain carbon particles. The endothelial leukocytes commonly show myelin degeneration, and free myelin globules may be present in large numbers. Saprophytic bacteria may be present but are not abundant.

Acute Bronchitis. In the early stage of acute bronchitis there is a small amount of tenacious, almost purely mucoid sputum, which frequently is blood streaked. This gradually becomes more abundant, mucopurulent in character, and yellowish or gray in color. At first the leukocytes commonly show myelin degeneration, and free myelin globules may be present in large numbers. Saprophytic bacteria may be abundant.

Chronic Bronchitis. In this disease the sputum is usually abundant, mucopurulent, and yellowish or yellowish green in color. Nummular masses like those that occur in tuberculosis are sometimes seen. Microscopically there are great numbers of pus cells, often much disintegrated. Epithelium is not abundant. Bacteria of various kinds, especially staphylococci, are usually numerous.

In fibrinous bronchitis there are found, in addition, fibrinous casts, usually of medium size.

In chronic bronchitis that accompanies long-continued passive congestion of the lungs, as in poorly compensated heart disease, the sputum may assume a rusty brown color owing to the presence of large numbers of the heart-failure cells mentioned previously.

Bronchiectasis. In bronchiectasis the characteristic sputum is greenish or grayish, purulent, and very abundant—sometimes as much as a liter in 24 hours—and has an offensive odor. It is thinner than that of chronic bronchitis and on standing separates into three layers of pus, serum, and frothy mucus. It contains great numbers of miscellaneous bacteria. Small hemorrhages are common. A feature of cases with a single large cavity is the periodic emptying of the cavity, usually when the patient arises in the morning; in other cases this periodic emptying is not evident.

Gangrene of the Lung. The sputum in this disease is abundant, fluid, very offensive, and brownish in color. It separates sharply into three layers on standing—a thick brownish deposit of pus, debris, and blood pigment; a clear fluid; and a frothy layer. Microscopically few cells of any kind are found. Bacteria are extremely numerous. As stated previously, elastic fibers are usually present in large fragments.

Edema of the Lung. In this disease the sputum is abundant, watery, and frothy and varies from faintly yellow or pink to dark brown. A few leukocytes and epithelial cells and varying numbers of erythrocytes are found with the microscope.

Bronchial Asthma. During and following an attack of asthma the sputum is scanty, mucoid, and very tenacious. Most characteristic is the presence of Curschmann's spirals, Charcot-Leyden crystals, and eosinophilic leukocytes.

Lobar Pneumonia. Characteristic of this disease is a scanty, rusty red, very tenacious sputum containing erythrocytes or altered blood pigment, leukocytes, epithelial cells, usually many pneumococci, and often very small fibrinous casts. This type of sputum is seen during the stage of red hepatization. During resolution the sputum assumes the appearance of that of chronic bronchitis. When pneumonia occurs during the course of chronic bronchitis, the characteristic rusty red sputum may not appear.

Pulmonary Tuberculosis. In cases of pulmonary tuberculosis the sputum is variable. In the earliest stages it may appear only in the morning and is then scanty and almost purely mucoid with an occasional yellow flake, or there may be only one small mucopurulent mass no larger than a match head. When the quantity is small, there may be no cough and the sputum may reach the larynx by action of the bronchial cilia. This is not well enough recognized by practitioners. A careful inspection of all the sputum brought up by the patient on several successive days, and microscopic examination of all yellow portions, will frequently establish a diagnosis of tuberculosis when physical signs are negative. Intelligent cooperation of the patient is essential in such cases. *Mycobacterium tuberculosis* sometimes will be found in large numbers at this stage. Blood-streaked sputum is strongly suggestive of tuberculosis and is more common in the early stages than later. It usually indicates an advancing process.

In cases in which the disease is advanced, the sputum resembles that of chronic bronchitis with the addition of *Mycobacterium tuberculosis* and elastic fibers. Nummular masses—circular, coinlike disks, which sink in water—may be seen. Caseous particles containing immense numbers of the bacilli are common. In cases in which the disease is far advanced and cavities have been present for a long time, there may be firm, spheric, or ovoid grayish masses in thin fluid—the so-called globular sputum. These globular masses usually contain many tubercle bacilli. Severe hemorrhages are frequent, and for some time after the hemorrhages occur the sputum may contain clots of blood or may be colored brown. The bacteriology of tuberculosis is discussed in more detail in Chapters 16 and 17.

REFERENCES

1. Bickerman, H. A., Sproul, E. E., and Barach, A. L.: Aerosol method of producing bronchial secretions in human subjects: Clinical technic for detection of lung cancer. Dis. of Chest, 33: 347–362, 1958.
2. Diagnostic Standards and Classification of Tuberculosis. New York, National Tuberculosis Association, 1955.
3. Umiker, W. O., Korst, D. R., Cole, R. P., and Manikas, S. G.: Collection of sputum for cytologic examination. New Eng. J. Med., 262:565–566, 1960.

Exudates, Transudates, and Cerebrospinal Fluid

By BENJAMIN B. WELLS, M.D.

PERITONEAL, PLEURAL, AND PERICARDIAL FLUIDS

The serous cavities normally contain very little fluid, but considerable quantities are frequently present as a result of pathologic conditions. The pathologic fluids are classed as transudates and exudates.

Transudates are noninflammatory in origin. Their color is light yellow or greenish yellow, and they may be clear, slightly cloudy, or opalescent. They contain only a few cells and less than 2.5 per cent of albumin, and do not coagulate spontaneously. The specific gravity is below 1.018. Microorganisms are seldom present.

Exudates are of inflammatory origin. They are richer in cells and albumin and tend to coagulate on standing. The specific gravity is above 1.018. The amount of albumin may be estimated by Kingsbury's or Esbach's method, after diluting the fluid if much albumin is present. A mucin-like substance, called serosamucin, is likewise found in exudates. It is detected by acidifying with a few drops of 5 per cent acetic acid, which produces a white cloudy precipitate. This reaction is helpful in distinguishing transudates from exudates, although some transudates become slightly turbid when acetic acid is added. Bacteria are generally present and often are numerous. When none are found in stained smears or cultures, tuberculosis should be suspected and animal inoculation should be used.

Exudates are usually classed as serous, serofibrinous, seropurulent, purulent, and hemorrhagic. In addition, chylous and chyloid exudates occasionally occur. In the chylous form the milkiness is due mainly to the presence of minute fat droplets and may be the result of rupture of a lymph vessel, usually from obstruction of the thoracic duct. Chyloid exudates are milky owing chiefly to proteins in suspension or to fine debris from broken-down cells. These exudates are most frequently seen in carcinoma and tuberculosis of the peritoneum. It may be that all milky effusions are in reality chylous, although in some (chyloids, pseudochylous) the fat is so finely divided as to take on some of the properties of colloids.

Brescia (1941) gave the following characteristics for chylous fluid obtained from the pleural cavity in cases of chylothorax: (1) The fluid has a milky appearance. (2) It does not change in appearance on standing but frequently forms a creamy top layer. (3) It has no odor; any odor that may be present is due to volatile fatty acids. (4) It is sterile. (5) It resists putrefaction. (6) It is finely emulsified. (7) It is alkaline in reaction. (8) Its specific gravity is greater than 1.012. (9) The fat content is 0.4 to 4.0 per cent. (10) The amount of protein is variable. (11) The percentage of solids is about 7. (12) Smear shows varying numbers of leukocytes with lymphocytes predominating. (13) Shaking with ether after the addition of alkaline solution causes the fluid to become clear. Tinney and Olsen

(1945) stated that if chylothorax caused by trauma to the thoracic duct is excluded, the commonest cause of an accumulation of chylous fluid is some neoplastic disease.

Cytodiagnosis

Cytodiagnosis is based on a differential count of the cells in a transudate or exudate, particularly one of pleural or peritoneal origin.

A tube of the fresh fluid, obtained by aspiration and preferably mixed at once with a little citrated salt solution to prevent clotting, is centrifuged for at least five minutes. The supernatant liquid is poured off, and smears are made from the sediment and dried in the air. The fluid must be very fresh, and the smears must be thin and quickly dried; otherwise the cells will be small, shrunken, and difficult to identify. The smears are then stained with Wright's blood stain, which has preferably been diluted previously with a third its volume of pure methyl alcohol. The smears are examined with an oil immersion objective.

Predominance of polymorphonuclear leukocytes (pus cells) points to an acute infectious process (Fig. 26–1). These cells are the neutrophils of the blood. Eosinophils and mast cells are rare. In thin smears they are easily recognized, the cytoplasmic granules often staining characteristically with polychrome methylene blue and eosin. In thick smears, on the other hand, they are often small and shrunken; they are difficult to identify and are easily mistaken for lymphocytes.

A large number, or even a preponderance, of eosinophils is seen in about 1 to 5 per cent of cases of pleural effusion. The significance is uncertain. Some of these effusions have followed artificial pneumothorax; others have been of tuberculous origin.

Predominance of lymphocytes (Fig. 26–2) generally signifies tuberculosis. They are the same as found in the blood. The cytoplasm is usually scanty, is often ragged, and sometimes is apparently absent entirely.

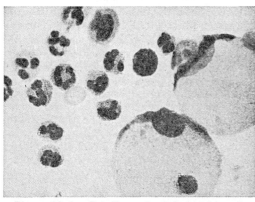

Figure 26–1. Cytodiagnosis. Polymorphonuclear leukocytes and swollen endothelial cells in acute infectious nontuberculous pleuritis. (Percy Musgrave; photo by L. S. Brown.)

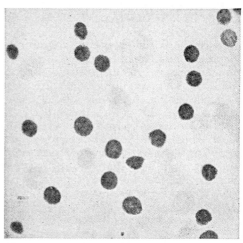

Figure 26–2. Cytodiagnosis. Lymphoid cells from pleural fluid; case of tuberculous pleuritis. (Percy Musgrave; photo by L. S. Brown.)

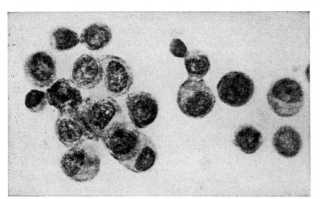

Figure 26–3. Cytodiagnosis. Mesothelial cells from transudate or mechanical effusion. (Percy Musgrave; photo by L. S. Brown.)

Tuberculous pleurisy resulting from direct extension from the lung may cause an excess of neutrophils owing to mixed infection.

Predominance of mesothelial cells, few cells of any other kind being present, indicates a transudate (Fig. 26–3). These cells are large with relatively abundant cytoplasm and contain one, sometimes two, round or oval, palely staining nuclei. Mesothelial cells generally predominate in carcinoma but are accompanied by a considerable number of lymphocytes and erythrocytes. The presence of mitotic figures suggests malignant disease.

CYTODIAGNOSTIC METHOD FOR EFFUSIONS AND EXUDATES (PAPANICOLAOU, 1954)

Cell Block. An exudate is generally clotted by the time it reaches the laboratory. To obtain a specimen for a block, it is necessary to stick a large wooden applicator into the mass and to twist and stir while pressing against the sides of the container. The excess fluid will be pressed out and a fibrin mass will collect on the applicator. The mass is wrapped in tissue paper and placed in a tissue capsule, fixed in 10 per cent formalin, and processed as a tissue.

It is important when embedding the block to spread the material well over the bottom of the embedding mold, for this gives good distribution of cells. Cut the block at 5 microns, being sure to get a representative section of the block on the slide.

Stain with hematoxylin and eosin. Staining according to the Papanicolaou method gives a good contrast. If a block of a transudate is desired and no fibrin masses are noted, mix 100 ml. of the fluid with 100 ml. of 95 per cent ethyl alcohol and centrifuge at moderate speed for 15 minutes. Place the soft mass that is formed by precipitation into some tissue paper and place in a tissue capsule. Process as just described.

Direct Smear. *Immediately* after withdrawal, centrifuge three times for five minutes at moderate speed, each time removing the supernatant fluid and adding more fluid to the sediment already in the tube. After the third centrifuging decant the supernatant fluid and make smears in the following manner.

Place a small drop of Mayer's albumin in the center of a slide and add a large drop of the sediment to it. Place another slide on top of this and allow the fluids to spread out over the slide. Pull the slides apart. Allow *only* the edges to dry before placing the slides into a fixative of equal parts of 95 per cent ethyl alcohol and petroleum ether. The slides are allowed to fix for 30 to 60 minutes. (The latter is preferred, because it assures adherence of the material to the slides during staining and washing.) The smears are stained according to the Papanicolaou technique. The hematoxylin and eosin method can also be used. Malignant cells are identified according to the accepted criteria.

The Staining Procedure: A Modification of the Papanicolaou Method by Anne Vance (1961)

1. 95 per cent alcohol (propyl alcohol can be substituted for ethyl alcohol), ten dips (15 to 20 seconds).
2. 80 per cent alcohol, ten dips (15 to 20 seconds).
3. 70 per cent alcohol, five dips (8 to 10 seconds).
4. Tap water, rinse clear.
5. Harris hematoxylin, three minutes (time changes with age of stain).
6. Tap water, rinse clear.
7. Acid alcohol, three to five dips (timing depends on strength of hematoxylin).
8. Tap water, rinse clear.
9. Lithium carbonate (10 ml. saturated solution to 200 ml. tap water), ten dips.
10. Tap water, rinse clear.
11. 70 per cent alcohol, ten dips (15 to 20 seconds).
12. 80 per cent alcohol, ten dips (15 to 20 seconds).
13. 95 per cent alcohol, ten dips (15 to 20 seconds).
14. OG₆*, two minutes.
15. 95 per cent alcohol, ten dips (15 to 20 seconds).
16. 95 per cent alcohol, ten dips (15 to 20 seconds).
17. 95 per cent alcohol (always fresh), ten dips 15 to 20 seconds).
18. EA† 36, 2½ minutes.

*OG₆: Orange G, 0.5% solution in 95% alcohol	100	ml.
Phosphotungstic acid	0.015 gm. (2)	

†EA 36: Light green SF yellowish 0.1% solution in 95% alcohol	45	ml.
Bismark brown 0.5% solution in 95% alcohol	10	ml.
Eosin yellow (water and alcohol soluble), 0.5% solution in 95% alcohol	45	ml.
Phosphotungstic acid	0.2	gm.
Lithium carbonate, saturated aqueous solution	1	drop (2)

Note: EA 36 and OG₆ can be obtained commercially.

19. 95 per cent alcohol, ten dips (15 to 20 seconds).

20. 95 per cent alcohol, ten dips.

21. Absolute alcohol, ten dips.

22. Absolute alcohol, ten dips.

23. Absolute alcohol, ten dips.

24. Two xylol rinses to clear.

25. Mount with Permount.

Note: Slides should be checked under the microscope after the ninth step to be sure that the nuclei are stained well.

COLLECTION OF SMEARS FOR EXFOLIATIVE CYTOLOGY

The patient should not have had any intravaginal examinations, douches, or therapy of any kind 24 hours prior to the cytological examination. The patient is placed upon an examining table in the lithotomy position. A speculum is introduced into the vagina and the portio vaginalis is visualized. Lubricant should not be introduced into the vagina nor should a wet speculum be used. All powder should be wiped off gloves before spatulas are handled, since the presence of starch granules will make the interpretation of the slides difficult.

Vaginal Smear. Scrap very slightly with a tongue depressor the upper lateral wall of the vagina and make a thin smear without pressure. From this smear the hormonal reading and microbiologic reading will be made.

Cervical Smear. Scrape slightly with a spatula (or a tongue depressor) the entire portio vaginalis uteri, especially the borders of an erosion, and smear on the slide.

Endocervical Smear. Introduce a cotton swab applicator into the cervical canal, rotate slightly, and make the smear.

Special Cases (Suspicion of Endometrial Cancer). A fourth smear (endometrial aspiration) should be performed, since the three smears just mentioned usually do not contain adequate material from the uterine cavity.

Hormonal Reading

For exact hormonal reading the smear must be taken gently from the lateral vaginal wall, since here the cells are fresh and are representative of those being exfoliated that day. An exact evaluation of the menstrual cyclic changes can be made only from smears prepared every day throughout one cycle. For an informative reading in sterility cases smears should be made 14 and 3 days prior to the next expected menstruation.

Fixation

As soon as each smear is spread, it should be fixed immediately while wet without any time lapse for air drying. In the office this can be accomplished by adding 5 drops of Cyto-Dri-Fix (a commercially available fixative) to the wet smear. In the hospital and clinics or whenever preferable, smears may be immersed immediately while wet into a liquid fixative consisting of equal parts of ether and 95 per cent ethyl alcohol.

COLLECTION OF MATERIALS FOR CYTOLOGIC EXAMINATION

Sputum. The sputum should be collected on three consecutive days. A 24-hour collection is of no value. The sputum must be an early morning specimen obtained by a deep cough. It should be collected in 95 per cent alcohol, or the alcohol should be added immediately after the specimen is obtained. The specimen must be brought to the laboratory within one hour.

Information to be Supplied with Request for Gynecologic Cytologic Examination

AGE:	LMP:	CLINICAL DIAGNOSIS:	
BLEEDING:	DISCHARGE:	EROSION:	VAGINAL: ☐ ENDOCERVICAL: ☐ CERVICAL: ☐
THERAPY (HORMONE? RADIATION?):	PREVIOUS SMEARS OR SPECIMENS:		YES ☐ DATE(S): NO ☐
COMMENT:			

Bronchial Washings. Washings should be collected in saline and brought to the laboratory immediately.

Urine. Urine collected for detection of cancer cells must be brought to the laboratory immediately. Equal amounts of 95 per cent alcohol may be added to the urine and the specimen transported to the laboratory within the hour.

Body Fluids. All the body fluid collected not needed for other tests should be sent to the laboratory immediately after collection. If the fluid is collected outside the hospital, at least 100 ml. of the sample should be mixed with 95 per cent alcohol and transported to the laboratory as soon as possible. In the meantime the specimen should be refrigerated.

Breast Secretions. Smear should be made and fixed immediately in a mixture of equal volumes of 95 per cent alcohol and ether.

GASTRIC LAVAGE FOR CYTOLOGIC EXAMINATION

Preparation of the Patient

For a successful cytologic examination of stomach contents it is important that the patient's stomach be prepared properly. The patient is instructed to eat a light supper the night before and no breakfast on the day of the test. The patient is encouraged to drink plenty of water to clean the stomach of any debris or retained food. If retention is encountered unexpectedly, the stomach should be cleansed with large volumes of saline solution and the cytologic examination performed the following day. The reason for the delay is that the exfoliated cells are washed away and time must be allowed for the shedding of more cells. Avoid doing cytologic examinations under any but the very best conditions.

Intubation

The patient sits upright. If dentures are present, they are removed. An iced rubber Levin tube (No. 18) or a warmed plastic tube is inserted through the mouth. With careful attention to midline placement of the tube and an assisting swallow by the patient the Levin tube is passed rapidly 55 cm. into the body of the stomach. The stomach is aspirated with a 100 ml. syringe. It is important to obtain at least a few milliliters of residue, for this indicates that the tip of the tube has reached the most dependent portion of the stomach. If no fluid is obtained, the tube should be withdrawn to the cardioesophageal junction (40 cm.) and reinserted slowly.

Lavage

Since the amount of exfoliated material obtained is directly proportional to the degree of energy expended, the lavage must be an aggressive irrigation.

First Part. One hundred milliliters of saline is rapidly injected into the stomach, quickly aspirated, and reinjected. Sometimes one-half of the syringe is allowed to fill with air to project the fluid at a faster rate. The tube is withdrawn a few centimeters, another 100 ml. of fresh saline is injected, and vigorous washing (barbotage) is continued for two minutes. The aspirate is placed immediately into 50 ml. tubes, which are immersed in an ice bath. (This procedure is important, because the cells are to be preserved.) About 300 to 400 ml. of fluid is used during the first portion of the irrigation.

Second Part. Five hundred milliliters of saline is introduced into the stomach. The patient then lies in each of the following positions for two minutes: on the right side, the back, the abdomen, and finally the left side. The fluid is withdrawn after the patient has been lying on his left side (usually about 400 ml. can be recovered). The fluid is placed in tubes immersed in an ice bath.

When the test is completed, the specimen should be delivered to the laboratory immediately. *Note:* Gastric specimens taken for chemical analysis will not be at all satisfactory for a cytologic examination.

CEREBROSPINAL FLUID

Cerebrospinal fluid is obtained by lumbar puncture between the third and fourth lumbar vertebrae with a flexible needle having a length of about 10 cm. and a bore of 1 to 1.5 mm., and provided with a stylet. For children a shorter needle is used. The needle and the stylet are sterilized by boiling, and the site of the puncture is prepared as for a venipuncture. A local anesthetic is usually used, the skin and subcutaneous tissue being infiltrated with a sterile 1 per cent solution of procaine hydrochloride. The patient should lie on one side, his head so placed on a pillow that there is no pressure on his neck and the head is in line with the vertebral column. The neck should be moderately flexed forward and the knees drawn up as far as can be com-

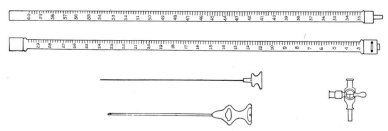

Figure 26–4. Ayer manometer with stylet, needle, and three-way stop-cock.

fortably maintained throughout the procedure.

The patient should not be draped, since this may cause disorientation with respect to the vertebral architecture. Also, when drapes slip about, they are more likely to be a source of contamination than of protection. Sterile gloves should be used. When handling the needle, it is important to avoid touching its shaft and point. Once the stylet has been returned to the surgical tray, it should not again be inserted in the needle, since this increases the danger of contamination. The site for the puncture is found by running the fingers along the spinous processes of the vertebrae until the "soft spot" between the spinous processes of the third and fourth lumbar vertebrae is found. This lies on or just above a line joining the crests of the ilia. The needle is inserted in the midline and pushed directly forward with a quick thrust until it reaches the tough spinous ligaments, when it may be pushed more slowly. A sudden cessation of resistance indicates that it has entered the spinal canal. The stylet is then removed and the fluid should flow at once. If it fails to do so, the flow usually may be started by inserting the needle a little farther or pulling it out a trifle, by inserting the stylet to dislodge anything that may have clogged the needle, or by having the patient take a deep breath.

The pressure under which the fluid appears should be noted. Normally the fluid drips rather slowly from the needle. When under high pressure, it spurts out. In the presence of obviously elevated pressure only a small amount of spinal fluid should be withdrawn as slowly as possible, and jugular compression must not be carried out. The pressure is measured by attaching the manometer with a three-way stopcock (Fig. 26–4) to the end of the needle. Spinal fluid pressure will ordinarily rise to 100 and 200 mm. Initial pressures are often somewhat higher than this owing to elevated abdominal pressure resulting from an over-

flexed position or from anxiety. When the patient is in a comfortable position and he is instructed to breathe through his mouth, the pressure will normally drop below 200 mm.

Patency of the spinal subarachnoid space can be tested by the Queckenstedt maneuver. Moderate bilateral compression on the jugular vessels is maintained until the spinal fluid pressure rises to approximately 400 mm. Compression is released and the fluid returns toward the resting level. Both the rise and fall should occur rapidly. With complete jugular compression the pressure should reach 400 mm. within about five seconds. After release the base line should be reached within ten seconds. The rate of fall is a more reliable observation than the rate of rise, since it is difficult to standardize the degree of jugular compression.

When the manometer has been removed, the first few drops of fluid are discarded, since they almost invariably contain some blood owing to passage of the puncture needle. Then approximately 3 ml. of fluid is collected in each of three sterile test tubes.

Without replacing the stylet, the needle is quickly withdrawn. No dressing is used, since it is not necessary and only serves to fix the patient's attention on the procedure. Ordinarily it is best to avoid sedation or unnecessary restriction of activities for the same reason. From beginning to end it is important to avoid any word or action that may reinforce the popular myths concerning the danger of lumbar puncture.

Laboratory examination of the cerebrospinal fluid includes: appearance, total and differential cell counts, protein concentration, glucose, chloride, bacteriologic studies by direct smear and culture, and serologic tests for syphilis. The colloidal stability tests, which reflect changes in the albumin-globulin ratio of cerebrospinal fluid, will be discussed in connection with the determination of protein concentration. These tests have lost much of the significance attributed to them in former years, and they are generally being discarded as a routine examination.

Appearance

Normally cerebrospinal fluid is water-clear and limpid. The reaction is slightly alkaline and the specific gravity is 1.003 to 1.008. The fluid may be tinged with blood owing to accidental puncture of a small vessel. The appearance of fresh blood is not to be confused with the dull red or brown color that is characteristic of true hemorrhage. When the bleeding is extensive and recent, it may have the appearance of practically pure blood. When the fluid is collected in three tubes and the third tube does not look obviously clearer than the first, subarachnoid hemorrhage must be considered. When blood is present, a tube should be centrifuged in order to note the color of the supernatant fluid. If the fluid is clear, it is unlikely that the blood has been present in the subarachnoid space for more than a few hours. If the fluid is yellow (xanthochromic), the blood has been present for more than a few hours and cannot be ascribed to the trauma of the puncture.

In spinal cord tumors and other lesions producing obstruction in the subarachnoid space, there may be an association of spinal fluid findings known as Froin's syndrome. These are great increase in protein, spontaneous coagulation, moderate pleocytosis, and xanthochromia.

In infectious meningitis the fluid may exhibit varying degrees of cloudiness from a slight turbidity to almost pure pus. Turbidity resulting from the presence of cells becomes evident when there are 500 or more cells per cubic millimeter. In less acute forms of meningitis and in tuberculous meningitis the fluid is often clear or only faintly opalescent. Turbidity owing largely to the bacterial content is especially characteristic of pneumococcic meningitis.

After standing for 12 to 24 hours, the fluid may coagulate. This occurs especially in the various forms of meningitis but rarely occurs in noninflammatory conditions. In tuberculosis the coagulum is usually very delicate and cobweb-like and is not easily seen.

Chemical Examination

Only a few of the chemical constituents of the cerebrospinal fluid are of clinical importance.

Protein

The cerebrospinal fluid of normal individuals contains 15 to 45 mg. of protein per 100 ml. Electrophoretic studies have shown that the protein components of cerebrospinal fluid are analogous to those of serum in that albumin and alpha-1, alpha-2, beta, and gamma globulin can be identified. Fibrinogen does not normally occur in the cerebrospinal fluid. A protein fraction called prealbumin (because it migrates faster than albumin in the electric field) is found in cerebrospinal fluid but not generally in serum.

Protein is increased in cerebrospinal fluid in a large number of pathologic conditions associated with an increase in permeability of the blood-brain barrier. This includes all types of inflammatory reactions of the central nervous system. The most notable increases are associated with bacterial meningitis. Less significant increases accompany viral infections (such as poliomyelitis and the various forms of viral encephalitis) and central nervous system syphilis. Even milder elevations are associated with tumors and chronic degenerative diseases. With severe inflammatory reactions fibrinogen may be sufficiently increased to allow spontaneous clotting of the fluid. Obviously all tests for protein in cerebrospinal fluid are invalidated by the presence of blood.

Qualitative Tests for Protein. The protein components that appear in the cerebrospinal fluid under most pathologic conditions have the chemical characteristics of serum globulin. Hence, the classic qualitative tests for abnormal protein were designed to demonstrate "globulin." This concept, although not a technically accurate one, is so well established in the medical literature that the following qualitative tests are retained from older editions of this work. Modern laboratory practice requires a quantitative estimation of cerebrospinal fluid protein as an element of the routine examination. Determination of the several protein fractions by chemical or chromatographic separation can be done readily, but these refinements have failed to yield very significant clinical data.

Nonne-Apelt reaction

REAGENT. Saturated solution of ammonium sulfate. Place 85 gm. of Merck's purified neutral ammonium sulfate in 100 ml. of distilled water and boil. Filter the solution when it has cooled.

TECHNIQUE. Place equal quantities of spinal fluid and saturated solution of ammonium sulfate in a test tube and mix by inverting the tube. Allow the tube to stand for three minutes.

Fluid that contains a normal amount of globulin remains clear or becomes slightly opalescent. If an excess of globulin is present, a cloudy precipitate forms.

Ross-Jones test. The technique of this test is similar to that of the ring test for albumin in urine. Place 2 ml. of a saturated solution of ammonium sulfate in a test tube and overlay with 1 ml. of spinal fluid. (The saturated solution of ammonium sulfate is the same as that employed in the Nonne-Apelt reaction.) In the presence of an excess of globulin a clearcut, thin, grayish white ring appears at the zone of contact of the two fluids within a few seconds. Under normal conditions a ring may appear after five minutes.

Pandy's test

REAGENT. Saturated solution of phenol. Add 10 gm. of phenol crystals to 100 ml. of distilled water and place in an incubator for several days.

TECHNIQUE. Place 1 ml. of the saturated solution of phenol in a test tube and add 1 drop of cerebrospinal fluid. The formation of a bluish white cloud indicates the presence of an abnormal amount of globulin.

Quantitative Test for Protein. The method described by Summerson, in the directions accompanying the Klett-Summerson Photoelectric Colorimeter (New York, 1941), is easily adaptable to most laboratory facilities and entirely adequate for clinical purposes. The proteins are precipitated by sulfosalicylic acid in the form of a suspension. The concentration of the suspension is estimated from the light transmittance in a colorimeter or a photometer.

Reagents.

1. Sulfosalicylic acid, 3 per cent aqueous solution.

2. Stock standard protein solution. This is prepared by diluting 5 ml. of normal human serum (6 to 8 gm. protein per 100 ml.) to 50 ml. with 0.9 per cent NaCl solution. The total protein content of this standard should be determined by the most accurate method available to the laboratory. This standard keeps well if stored in a refrigerator.

3. Working standard protein solution. This is prepared by diluting the stock standard with 0.9 per cent NaCl solution. A generally useful standard is about a twentyfold dilution of the stock, so that the protein content is about 35 mg. per 100 ml.

Technique

1. Place 1 or 2 ml. of cerebrospinal fluid in a colorimeter cup or a photometer cuvet and add 4 volumes (4 or 8 ml.) of the 3 per cent sulfosalicylic acid solution.

2. Treat 1 or 2 ml. of the working standard exactly as the cerebrospinal fluid and as nearly as possible at the same time.

3. Mix gently by inversion both the test and standard suspensions. Readings can be made at any time between 10 and 30 minutes after addition of the sulfosalicylic acid. Always mix again directly before reading.

4. If the cerebrospinal fluid flocculates after addition of the sulfosalicylic acid, dilute another portion of the original fluid with 0.9 per cent NaCl solution to 2 or 4 volumes (giving d = 2 or 4 in the calculation to be described) and proceed as before.

Calculation. If an ordinary light colorimeter is used, the unknown and standard are compared, preferably with a blue filter.

Mg. protein per 100 ml. spinal fluid

$$= C_s \times d \times \frac{S}{U}$$

in which C_s is the mg. protein per 100 ml. in the working standard used, d is the number of volumes to which the cerebrospinal fluid was diluted, S is the reading of the standard, and U is the reading of the unknown.

When measurement is made in a photometer, light of about 450 millimicrons wave length is used. The zero is set with a water blank.

Mg. protein per 100 ml. spinal fluid

$$= C_s \times d \times \frac{D_u}{D_s}$$

C_s and d have the same significance as before. D_u is the optical density of the cerebrospinal fluid preparation, and D, is the density of the standard.

Tests for the Albumin-Globulin Ratio

Lange's colloidal gold test. Lange's colloidal gold test was introduced in 1912 and became one of the most widely used procedures in this category. It and the mastic test are retained here largely for historic reasons. Although these tests are still used to a very limited extent, they have generally been replaced by more accurate serologic methods, when syphilis is in question, or by chemical and chromatographic methods, when subtle changes in protein fraction distribution are being studied.

Lange's test is performed by mixing cerebrospinal fluid in certain proportions with a colloidal solution of gold. Normal cerebrospinal fluid causes no change in color. In cases of syphilis and certain pathologic conditions of the nervous system the fluid induces changes in the color of the gold solution from red to purple, deep blue, or pale blue, or the solution becomes colorless. Moreover the dilution at which the maximal color change occurs is more or less characteristic of the different pathologic conditions. The typical "curves" are shown in Fig. 26–5. The most consistent and valuable results occur in cases of general paresis. In lethargic encephalitis and poliomyelitis atypical curves in the tabetic zone have been observed.

Albumin "protects" colloidal gold, while globulin causes it to precipitate. Various degrees of disturbance of the normal albumin-globulin ratio in spinal fluid may account for the various types of curves that are produced.

The test itself is relatively simple, and any difficulty may be attributed to imperfectly cleaned utensils or to a faulty reagent, the preparation of which by the usual methods is time consuming and uncertain. The reagent can be purchased ready prepared, or it can be prepared easily by the Borowskaja (1934) method.

The reagent must be absolutely transparent and of a brilliant salmon or orange-red color with no trace of blue; it must be neutral to alizarin red on the day it is used; a 5 ml. sample must be completely decolorized in one hour when added to 1.7 ml. of 1 per cent solution of sodium chloride; it must produce a typical paretic curve with a known paretic spinal fluid; and it must not produce a reaction beyond "red-blue" with a normal spinal fluid.

Borowskaja's modification of Lange's test (1934). This very simple method for making a stable colloidal gold solution has been found satisfactory. Add 1 ml. of a 1 per cent solution of gold chloride (Merck's Blue Label) to 95 ml. of distilled water.

Heat to 90° C. on an electric hot plate (not over an open gas flame) and add 5 ml. of 1 per cent solution of sodium citrate (Merck's Blue Label). Boil the solution for one to three minutes.

TECHNIQUE OF THE TEST. Arrange 12 clean test tubes in a rack. Place 1.8 ml. of fresh sterile 0.4 per cent solution of sodium chloride in the first test tube and 1 cc. in each of the others except the twelfth. In the twelfth tube place 1.7 ml. of a sterile 1 per cent solution of sodium chloride. To the first tube add 0.2 ml. of the spinal fluid, which must be free from any trace of blood. Mix well by sucking the fluid up into the pipet and expelling it, and then transfer 1 ml. to the second tube. Mix and transfer 1 ml. to the third tube, repeating this down the row to the tenth tube and discarding the last 1 ml. portion. This leaves the eleventh and twelfth tubes with salt solution only to serve as controls. To each of the 12 tubes add 5 ml. of the colloidal gold solution. Let stand at room temperature for an hour or longer, at the end of which time, in the case of a positive reaction, the solution in some of the tubes will have changed from red to purple, deep blue, or pale blue or will have become colorless. In the case of normal fluids, no change will occur. The fluid in the eleventh and twelfth tubes, which serve as controls, should be orange-red and colorless, respectively.

The results are usually charted as in Fig. 26–5 in which each column represents a tube. For the purpose of brevity the colors may be indicated by the corresponding numbers, which are placed in the same order as the tubes. Thus the "paretic reaction" in Fig. 26–5 may be expressed as 5555542100. Felton's suggestion that the type of reaction is best indicated by using the terms "Zone I" "Zone II," and "Zone III" is used in many laboratories for reporting the "paretic," "tabetic," or "meningitic" curves.

Boerner and Lukens (1934) have de-

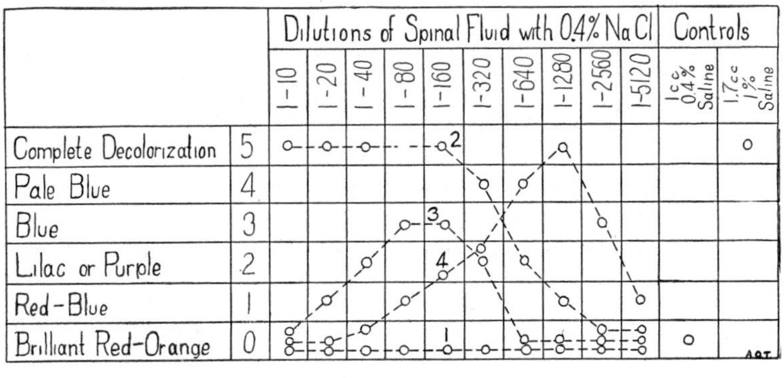

Figure 26–5. Types of reactions in colloidal gold test: 1, Normal cerebrospinal fluid, no reaction; 2, paretic type; 3, syphilitic or tabetic type; 4, meningitic type.

		Dilutions of Spinal Fluid with 0.4% NaCl										Controls	
		1–10	1–20	1–40	1–80	1–160	1–320	1–640	1–1280	1–2560	1–5120	1 cc 0.4% Saline	1.7 cc 1% Saline
Complete Decolorization	5						2						o
Pale Blue	4												
Blue	3					3							
Lilac or Purple	2			4									
Red-Blue	1												
Brilliant Red-Orange	0					1						o	

Figure 26–6. The mastic reaction in cerebrospinal fluid: *A,* in a case of dementia praecox, negative; *B,* in a case of paresis, positive. (Courtesy of J. A. Cutting.)

scribed a modification of the original technique that is more economical in the use of the gold sol. Place 1.8 ml. of a 0.4 per cent sodium chloride solution in the first tube and only 0.5 ml. of this solution in the other tubes. Add 0.2 ml. of the spinal fluid to the first tube. Mix, discard 1 ml., and transfer 0.5 ml. to the second tube. Mix and transfer 0.5 ml. of the mixture to the next tube and so on to the last tube, discarding 0.5 ml. from this tube after mixing the fluids. Then add only 2.5 ml. of colloidal gold solution to all the tubes.

Mastic test. Because of the many difficulties in the older methods of preparing satisfactory and uniform colloidal gold solutions, the mastic test was proposed as a substitute for the gold test. The reagent is inexpensive and easily made, and the test is easily carried out. Results appear to parallel those obtained with colloidal gold. They are almost uniformly positive in paresis, cerebrospinal syphilis, and tabes, but there is much less definite differentiation of the various types of reaction. Complete precipitation of the mastic corresponds to complete decolorization of the colloidal gold solution, while partial precipitation of the mastic corresponds roughly to the purple or blue of the colloidal gold test. The method following is that used by Cutting.

Reagents

1. Mastic solution. Make a stock solution by completely dissolving 10 gm. of gum mastic, U. S. P., in 100 ml. of absolute alcohol and filter. To 2 ml. of this stock solution add 18 ml. of absolute alcohol, mix well, and pour rapidly into 80 ml. of distilled water.

2. Alkaline-saline solution. Make 1.25 per cent solution of sodium chloride (C. P.) in distilled water, and to each 99 ml. of this solution add 1 ml. of a 0.5 per cent solution of potassium carbonate in distilled water.

TECHNIQUE. Take six small test tubes. In the first tube place 1.5 ml. of the alkaline-saline solution and in each of the others place 1 ml. To the first tube add 0.5 ml. of the spinal fluid, which must be completely free from blood. Mix by sucking the fluid up into the pipet and expelling it, and transfer 1 ml. to the second tube. Again mix and transfer 1 ml. to the third tube and continue down the line to the fifth tube, discarding the 1 ml. portion removed from this and leaving the sixth tube with alkaline-saline solution alone to serve as a control. Finally add 1 ml. of the mastic solution to each tube. Mix well and set aside at room temperature for 12 to 24 hours or in the incubator for 6 to 12 hours. Tubes in which the reaction is complete will show a heavy precipitate with clear supernatant fluid (Fig. 26–6).

CHLORIDES

Normal spinal fluid contains more chlorides, expressed as sodium chloride, than does blood plasma. The normal value for adults varies from 720 to 750 mg. for each 100 ml. of spinal fluid. In children the value varies from 625 mg. to 760 mg. per 100 ml.

The determination is made according to the method for plasma chloride. Use 1 ml. of spinal fluid. In acute meningitis the amount of chloride may be reduced in adults to 625 mg. per 100 ml. and to 575 mg. per 100 ml. in children. In tuberculous meningitis still smaller amounts are found. High values may be found in conditions in which the value for the plasma chloride is increased.

DEXTROSE

Cerebrospinal fluid normally contains about 0.04 to 0.07 per cent of dextrose or roughly half as much as is present in the blood. Quantitative estimation may be carried out by the methods used for blood sugar. It is advisable to determine the concentration of dextrose in a sample of the patient's blood obtained by venipuncture at the same time the spinal puncture is made. For accurate comparison these determinations should be carried out as promptly as possible after withdrawal.

Microscopic Examination

This includes a study of the bacteria and of the number and kinds of cells. Bacteriologic examination of the cerebrospinal fluid is discussed in Chapter 17.

CYTOLOGIC EXAMINATION

For cytologic examination the fluid should be as fresh as possible, since the cells tend to degenerate. To avoid formation of a coagulum, which might entangle the cells and interfere with the count, it is well to secure the fluid in two tubes. One tube that is to be used for the cytologic examination should contain a trace of powdered potassium oxalate. Early coagulation is, however, not common in the diseases in which the cell count is most important.

The routine examination should include both a total and a differential count. The total cell count is best made with a Fuchs-Rosenthal counting chamber in a manner similar to the counting of leukocytes in blood. The ruled area (Fig. 26–7) in this chamber covers 16 sq. mm. and the depth below the coverglass is 0.2 mm. The capacity is thus a trifle more than 3 cu. mm. (sixteen fifths). Unna's polychrome methylene blue or a staining fluid consisting of 0.1 gm. of crystal violet, 1 ml. of glacial acetic acid, 50 ml. of water, and a few drops of 5 per cent solution of phenol is drawn into the leukocyte pipet to the mark 1, and the fresh spinal fluid, which has been well shaken, is drawn up to the mark 11. After mixing, a drop is placed in the counting chamber and covered. The number of cells in the entire ruled area is counted, and this number is divided by 3 to obtain the number of cells in each cubic millimeter of spinal fluid. The error incident to this calculation is practically balanced by the opposite error owing to dilution.

When a Fuchs-Rosenthal chamber is not at hand, an ordinary hemacytometer counting chamber may be used. The number of cells in the ruled area is counted, the number for each cubic millimeter is calculated, and this is multiplied by 10/9 to compensate for the dilution with staining fluid.

The differential count is made as described on p. 123. A weak aqueous solution of methylene blue is probably preferable to Wright's stain for this purpose. Ordinarily only two kinds of cells are seen: lymphocytes and polymorphonuclear neutrophils.

The cells normally present are nearly all lymphocytes. They vary in number from one to five or seven in each cubic millimeter; ten is usually accepted as the maximum in health.

An increase in the cell count and a predominance of lymphocytes (more than 70 per cent) strongly suggest tuberculous meningitis or syphilitic disease of the nervous system, since these findings occur in about 90 to 95 per cent of the cases. The number of cells present in these conditions varies greatly in different cases but ordinarily is between 25 and 100 in each cubic millimeter. Similar counts are frequent in viral encephalitis and anterior poliomyelitis and may also sometimes be noted in cases of cerebral hemorrhage, tumor, and the more chronic type of epidemic cerebrospinal meningitis.

In all forms of acute meningitis the total count is high, 100 to several thousand, and polymorphonuclear leukocytes prevail. A notable number of endothelial cells may also be present, especially in cases of acute epidemic meningitis.

In lymphocytic choriomeningitis, an acute virus disease, there is a marked lymphocytic reaction of the meninges and in the choroid plexus, and the cell count is 30 to 1500 or more. The disease is characterized by marked malaise, headache, vomiting, fever, stiffness of the neck, and slow pulse. There are no bacteria in the spinal fluid.

In some cases of polyneuritis the Guillain-Barré syndrome may occur. There is no febrile reaction but motor weakness is present and the tendon reflexes are absent. There is a normal number of cells in the spinal fluid but a great increase in the amount of protein. A positive serologic test for infectious mononucleosis has been re-

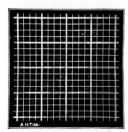

Figure 26–7. Fuchs-Rosenthal ruling of counting chamber for cells in spinal fluid.

ported in some cases of Guillan-Barré syndrome (Durfey and Allen, 1956).

REFERENCES

1. Boerner, F., and Lukens, M.: A modification of the Lange colloidal gold test. J. Lab. & Clin. Med., *19*:1007–1008, 1934.
2. Borowskaja, D. P.: Zur Methodik der Goldsolbereitung. Ztschr. f. Immunitätsforsch. u. exper. Therap., 82:178–182, 1934.
3. Brescua, M. A.: Chylothorax; Report of case in an infant. Arch. Pediat., 58:345–356, 1941.
4. Durfey, J. G., and Allen, J. E.: Guillain-Barré syndrome. New Eng. J. Med., *254*:279–283, 1956.
5. Papanicolaou, G. N.: Atlas of Exfoliative Cytology. Cambridge, Mass., Harvard University Press, 1954.
6. Tinney, W. S., and Olsen, A. M.: Significance of fluid in pleural space; Study of 274 cases. J. Thoracic Surg., *14*:248–252, 1945.
7. Vance, A.: A modification of the Papanicolaou method (personal communication), 1961.

The Clinical Pathologic Laboratory

SPACE, EQUIPMENT, AND MODERNIZATION

The changes in the modern clinical pathologic laboratory mainly involve increasing emphasis on accuracy, on quantitative versus qualitative methods, and on specific versus nonspecific results. The rising utilization of the laboratory and the resulting increase in costs and shortage of manpower are being met by simplification of methods without loss of specificity and reliability, by saving of unnecessary steps, by better organization of space, and finally by ever-increasing automation. Some of these developments are not unlike what one sees in a modern kitchen: less unnecessary motion and handling, better illumination, less odors, and less noise.

In small hospitals one central laboratory is most convenient. In larger hospitals, in addition to a central laboratory, small laboratory units are needed to permit interns and residents to carry out personally some of the simpler tests. This experience should be a part of the medical education.

The relation of the physician to the laboratory should not be limited to writing requests for tests. If that is the only link, the physician cannot possibly appreciate the various sources of error and reliability of methods and consequently will not be able to interpret the results. It should not be overlooked that it is during this stage of education of the medical student and young physician that interest in scientific aspects of medicine may be planted to lead eventually to scientific careers and significant contributions.

Should there be fewer large rooms or many smaller ones? Smaller rooms have certain advantages: more wall space for shelves, an important and most useful item in a laboratory; less noise; and the possibility of placing highly sensitive equipment in separate rooms. Chemical work requires a room large enough to permit a centrally located working area accessible from all sides. The height and width of the benches should make them easily accessible, convenient to reach, and adjustable to either standing or sitting as needed. The bench tops should be acid resistant; some of the modern plastics meet these requirements. Shelves for reagents, easily within reach of the sitting or standing technologists, are essential. Properly constructed drawers under the tables are useful. They can be used to keep various materials, such as pipets, but are not practical for reagents. The latter are kept best in wall cabinets located within easy reach. The shelves should not be too wide. It is best to have only one row of reagents on the shelves for ease of handling.

Small bench sinks with hot and cold water and vacuum pumps are a great convenience. Conveniently located outlets for gas and electricity are absolutely essential; outlets for vacuum, pressure, hot steam, and distilled water are a great convenience when needed. There should be a shelf over the sink to hold a large bottle with distilled water. Small, easily transported carts serve the double purpose of adding to the available surface area and permitting convenient transport to the glass washing area. The wall space not taken up by doors, cabinets, and other equipment should be used for benches. Much information regarding laboratory equipment, glassware, and supplies can be gathered from the study of catalogs issued by the manufacturers and dealers. For example, different procedures may require different varieties of glass, which differ in thermal and mechanical resistance, thickness, and even shape.

Daylight is desirable mainly for psychologic reasons. Southern exposure should be avoided. Adequate artificial light should be provided for each working area in addition to ceiling light.

The most convenient floor covering that is also easiest for the feet is one of the many varieties of linoleum or similar rubber substitutes. Damage by acids and stains can be easily corrected. Cement is cold, hard, and unpleasant; stone and cement are best in washing areas.

Hoods are needed especially in the chemical laboratory. They should be provided with light, electricity, gas, water, exhaust, and drain. Refrigerators are needed in each laboratory. Cold rooms are useful in larger institutions. Two smaller refrigerators are better than a large one of double capacity, for mechanical troubles will be less troublesome. The cold room serves not only for storage but is also useful for certain laboratory procedures, such as electrophoresis or chromatography. Minimum cold room requirements are outlets for electrical current, water, and drain. Illumination should be adequate but not more than what is really required to avoid overheating. In cold rooms that are used for actual work, it is advisable to reduce the air flow to the essential minimum. Too rapid a turnover of air makes the stay in the cold room too uncomfortable. An outside red light is recommended to indicate that a person is in the cold room. Another useful installation is an alarm to warn when the thermostat is out of commission.

The glass cleaning area must be provided with not less than four sinks: one for preliminary cleansing, the second for thorough washing, the third for rinsing with tap water, and the fourth with distilled water. To facilitate operation of the latter, a sizeable bottle or another source of distilled water is convenient. Proper equipment for cleaning of pipets, drain areas, drying ovens, and ample, large sized drains are also needed.

It is best to have a special room for centrifuges. If they must be in a working area, provision should be made to reduce noise.

It is convenient to have an instrumentation room for light- and vibration-sensitive equipment and for bulky instruments requiring easy access from all sides.

Suitable safety provisions are needed to protect against accidents from electric and gas installations: fireproof hose connections for Bunsen burners, instead of rubber tubing, and safe grounding of electrical connections. Gas cylinders and other bulky containers must be safely fastened against possible turning over. Access to fire exits must be kept open. Advice from safety experts is a good investment.

Rest rooms for male and female personnel are desirable. They can also be used as sleeping areas for the night technicians and for conferences at daytime.

INCREASED UTILIZATION OF THE CLINICAL LABORATORY

At the Mount Sinai Hospital in Chicago the total number of laboratory tests rose from 39,000 in 1931 to 450,713 in 1960. During the same period the bed capacity rose from slightly over 200 to 384.

There are several reasons for this increase. Not the least important is that almost each important discovery calls for new laboratory tests. The many new function tests, sensitivity tests, histochemical procedures, and immunologic methods are only a few of the many innovations.

Culture Media, Stains, Reagents, and Techniques

CULTURE MEDIA

The following bacterial culture media are most commonly used in dehydrated form (see p. 714). Details of their formulation can be found in the references listed after Chapters 16 and 17 and in the manuals obtainable from the manufacturers. It is important to follow explicitly the directions for the preparation of the various media that are supplied with the dehydrated product.

Albimi agar
Anaerobic agar (Brewer)
Azide blood agar base
Bismuth sulfite agar (Blair-Wilson)
Blood agar base
Bordet-Gengou agar
Brain-heart infusion agar
Brilliant green agar
Chapman-Stone medium
Cooked meat medium
Corn meal agar
Cystine glucose heart agar
Desoxycholate agar
Desoxycholate citrate agar
Endo's agar
Eosin methylene blue (EMB) agar
Eugonagar
Fluid thioglycollate medium (Brewer)
GC medium base
Heart infusion agar
KCN medium
Kligler's iron agar
Litmus milk
Littman's oxgall agar
Loeffler's blood serum
MacConkey's agar
Mannitol salt agar
Milk protein hydrolysate (MPH) agar
Motility test medium
MR-VP medium
Mueller-Hinton medium
Mycosel (cyclohexi-mide) agar
Nitrate agar and broth
Nutrient agar and broth
Nutrient gelatin
Peizer TB medium base
Penassay broth
Phenylethyl alcohol medium
Sabouraud's dextrose agar
Salmonella-Shigella (SS) agar
Selenite F broth
Sensitivity test medium
SF medium
Simmon's citrate agar
Sorbitol and sorbitol iron agar
Staphylococcus medium No. 110
Stuart's transport medium
TB broth base (Dubos)
Tetrathionate broth base
Tinsdale's medium
Tellurite agar base
Tellurite glycine agar
Triple sugar iron agar
Todd-Hewitt broth
Trypticase soy agar
Tryptone glucose extract agar
Tryptose agar
Urea agar and broth base
Veal infusion medium
Violet-red bile agar

A.T.S. (American Trudeau Society) Medium for M. tuberculosis

Egg yolk	500 ml.
Potato-flour water (containing 2 per cent glycerol)	500 ml.

1. The potato-flour water is made by adding 20 gm. potato flour to 500 ml. of 2 volumes per cent glycerol-water in a flask. The mixture is heated to boiling and with constant stirring cooled to 50° C.

2. Egg yolk is obtained by carefully cleansing fresh hens eggs with wet gauze, rinsing them in alcohol, and separating the egg white and yolk. A proportion of one whole egg to eleven egg yolks is used, and 500 ml. of this combination is prepared.

3. Add 500 ml. of the egg yolk to 500 ml. of potato-flour water and to this add 20 ml. of 1 per cent malachite green in 50 per cent alcohol. All ingredients are thoroughly mixed and tubed. The tubes are slanted and coagulated in the inspissator for 60 minutes at 90° C.

Tarshis Blood Medium for M. tuberculosis

Plain agar	1.5 gm.
Glycerol	1.0 ml.
Human bank blood (with A.C.D. solution)	30.0 ml.
Distilled water	69.0 ml.
Penicillin	50–100 units/ml.
The final pH is 6.8.	

Dissolve the agar in the glycerol-water by heating. Autoclave at 15 lbs. for 15 minutes. Cool to 45° C., add penicillin and blood, mix well, and dispense in suitable sterile containers.

Herrold's Egg Yolk Agar for M. Tuberculosis

Nutrient agar	23 gm.
Glycerol	10 ml.
Distilled water	750 ml.
Malachite green (2 per cent aqueous)	10 ml.

Boil to dissolve. Dispense in 150 ml. amounts in flasks. Autoclave for 15 minutes at 15 lb. Cool to 47° C. Scrub fresh eggs, rinse in water, and soak in 70 per cent alcohol for 15 minutes. Add 50 ml. of egg yolk aseptically to each flask, mix well, and tube. Check for sterility. Streptomycin, I.N.H, or other chemotherapeutic agents may be added in the desired concentrations after the egg yolk is added.

Modified Kirschner Medium for the Growth of the Tubercle Bacillus

$Na_2HPO_4 \cdot 12H_2O$	19	gm.
KH_2PO_4	2.5	gm.
Magnesium sulfate	0.6	gm.
Sodium citrate	2.5	gm.
Asparagine	5	gm.
Glycerol	20	ml.
Phenol red (0.4 per cent)	3	ml.
Distilled water	1000	ml.

Dissolve the salts before adding glycerol. The pH is approximately 7.4 to 7.6. No adjustment of pH is necessary. Bottle 9 ml. amounts in 1 oz. bottles or tubes and autoclave at 10 lb. pressure for ten minutes. Before use, add 1 ml. of sterile horse serum containing 100 units penicillin per milliliter to each 9 ml. of medium.

Lowenstein-Jensen's Medium (Holm and Lester)

Salt Solution

Monopotassium phosphate, anhydrous	2.4	gm.
$MgSO_4 \cdot 7H_2O$	0.24	gm.
Magnesium citrate	0.6	gm.
Asparagine	3.6	gm.
Glycerol	12.0	ml.
Distilled water	600	ml.

1. Dissolve the dry ingredients and glycerol in water and heat gently.
2. Sterilize in flowing steam in the autoclave for two hours and store overnight.

Final Medium

Salt solution	612 ml.
Potato flour	30 gm.
Eggs, whole	1000 ml.
Malachite green, 2 per cent aqueous	20 ml.

1. Suspend the potato flour in salt solution, being careful to break up all clumps.

2. Heat in boiling water bath (double boiler) with frequent stirring until mixture clears. Continue heating for 15 minutes in the bath. Cool to 56° C. and maintain at this temperature for one hour.
3. Wash fresh eggs (must be less than 48 hours old) in 5 per cent soap solution or in 1:1000 benzalkonium chloride for 30 minutes. Then place the eggs in running cold water to remove the antiseptic or soap solution. The eggs are then immersed in 70 per cent alcohol for 15 minutes.
4. Break eggs into a sterile flask, shake well to homogenize, and filter through four layers of sterile gauze.
5. Combine the egg fluid and the flour-salt mixture, add the malachite green solution, and mix thoroughly until the dye is evenly distributed throughout the medium.
6. Dispense in sterile tubes and sterilize as described for Petragnani's medium.

Petragnani's Medium (Frobisher Modification)

Mixture A

Milk	225.0 ml.
Potato starch	9.0 gm.
Peptone	1.5 gm.
Diced potato	150.0 gm.

Heat in a double boiler, stirring constantly, for one hour.

Mixture B

Eggs (whole)	8
Glycerol	18.0 ml.
Malachite green, 2 per cent aqueous	15.0 ml.

Mix well.

Mixture C

Dextrose	1.5 gm.
Asparagine	1.5 gm.
Distilled water	50.0 ml.

Warm until dissolved.

Mix A, B, and C in a sterile flask and strain through one layer of gauze. Tube, slant, and inspissate at 80° C. for one hour.

Coagulase Agar Medium for Staphylococci

Rabbit or human plasma (previously tested for suitability for coagulase tests) is mixed with sterile nutrient agar in a concentration of 12 to 15 per cent (V/V) at a temperature of 47° C. The mixture is poured into Petri dishes and allowed to solidify. Following spot inoculation coagulase production is indicated by the development of opacity around the colonies after overnight incubation.

Tellurite Serum Agar (Perry and Petran)

Meat infusion agar	1000 ml.
Serum, horse	50 ml.
Dextrose, 10 per cent solution	20 ml.
Potassium tellurite, 1 per cent solution	10 ml.
(pH 9.5; filter)	

Prepare the stock solutions and sterilize. Melt agar and cool to 50° C. Add each of the other ingredients aseptically. Mix well and pour into Petri dishes.

Paï's Egg Medium

Infusion broth (1 per cent dextrose)	30 ml.
Whole, mixed eggs	70 ml.
Glycerol, C.P.	8 ml.

Mix, tube, slant, and inspissate as for Loeffler's medium (see p. 718).

Fletcher's Semisolid Medium for Leptospira

1. Sterilize 1.76 liters of distilled water by autoclaving at 121° C. for 30 minutes.
2. Cool to room temperature and add 240 ml. of pooled sterile normal rabbit serum.
3. Inactivate at 56° C. for 40 minutes.
4. Add 120 ml. of melted and cooled (at not higher than 56° C.) 2.5 per cent meat extract agar at pH 7.4.
5. Dispense 5 ml. amounts into sterile 16 × 130 mm. screw-cap test tubes and 15 ml. amounts into sterile 25 ml. diaphragm-type, rubber-stopper vaccine bottles.
6. Incubate at 56° C. for 60 minutes on two successive days.

Solid Medium for Leptospira (Cox and Larson)

Tryptose phosphate broth	0.2 gm.
Agar	1.0 gm.

Dissolve in 90 ml. of distilled water, adjust the pH to 7.5, and sterilize the medium in the autoclave. Cool to 50° C. and add aseptically 10 ml. of sterile rabbit serum and 1 ml. of hemoglobin preparation. Heat at 56° C. for 30 minutes and then pour plates.

Prepare the hemoglobin by lysing washed and packed sheep erythrocytes in 20 volumes of cold distilled water. Remove the stroma by centrifugation. Sterilize by Seitz filtration.

Zein Medium for Chlamydospore Production by Candida Albicans (Reid)

Soak 40 gm. of zein in 1 liter of distilled water. Heat to 60° C. for one hour. Filter through gauze and coarse filter paper and make up to original volume. Add 15 gm. of agar, boil to dissolve, and autoclave at 121° C. for 15 minutes. Dispense as needed.

STAINS

Capsule Stain (Hiss)

Basic fuchsin (90 per cent dye content) or	0.15–0.3 gm.
Crystal violet (85 per cent dye content)	0.05–0.1 gm.
Distilled water	100 ml.

1. Grow organisms in ascitic fluid or serum medium, or mix with drop of serum and prepare smears from this mixture.
2. Dry smears in air and fix with heat.
3. Stain with one of the above solutions a few seconds by gently heating until stain rises.
4. Wash off with 20 per cent aqueous $CuSO_4 \cdot 5H_2O$.
5. Blot dry and examine. Capsules stain faint blue; cells, dark purple.

Capsule Stain (Muir's Method)

Mordant

Tannic acid	2 parts
Saturated aqueous mercuric chloride	2 parts
Saturated aqueous potassium alum	5 parts

1. Prepare an even, thin film of the bacteria. Allow to dry with heating. Cover the film or smear with a strip of filter paper cut to the shape and size of the slide and flood with Ziehl-Neelsen carbolfuchsin. Warm with a flame until it just steams for 30 seconds.
2. Rinse gently with alcohol and then with water.
3. Add the mordant for 15 to 30 seconds and wash well with water.
4. Decolorize with alcohol until faintly pink.
5. Wash with water.
6. Counterstain with methylene blue for 30 seconds.
7. Allow to dry in air and examine. Cells are stained red and capsules, blue.

Spore Stain (Bartholomew and Mittwer's Method)

1. Fix the smear by passing through flame.
2. Stain ten minutes with saturated

aqueous malachite green (7.6 per cent) without heat.

3. Rinse about ten seconds with tap water.

4. Counterstain 15 seconds in 0.25 per cent aqueous safranin.

5. Rinse and dry. Spores stain green; rest of cell, red.

Spore Stain (Schaeffer and Fulton's Method)

Malachite green (5 per cent) in distilled water. When freshly prepared, allow to stand one-half hour and filter.

Safranin (0.5 per cent) in distilled water. Flood the fixed smear with malachite green and steam gently over the flame for one-half minute. Wash thoroughly with water. Stain with safranin for one-half minute. Wash, blot, dry, and examine. Spores stain green; bacilli, red.

Flagella Stain (Leifson)*

KAl $(SO_4)_2$. $12H_2O$ or NH_4Al
  $(SO_4)_2$ · $12H_2O$ (sat. aqueous
  solution)   20 ml.
Tannic acid (20 per aqueous)   10 ml.
Distilled water   40 ml.
Ethyl alcohol, 95 per cent   15 ml.
Basic fuchsin (saturated solution in 95 per cent ethyl alcohol)   3 ml.

Mix ingredients in order named. Keep in tightly stoppered bottle.

1. Prepare slides by cleaning in dichromate cleaning solution, wash in water, rinse in alcohol, and wipe with clean piece of cheesecloth. Pass slides through a flame several times.

2. Flood slides with solution and allow to stand ten minutes at room temperature in warm weather or in an incubator in cold weather.

3. Wash with tap water.

4. Dry and examine. Flagella are well stained (red) in bacteria that do not have extremely delicate flagella.

Stain for Spirochaetes (Fontana)

Preparation of ammoniacal silver nitrate: Dissolve 5 gm. of $AgNO_3$ in 100 ml. of distilled water. Remove a few milliliters, and to the rest of the solution add drop by drop a concentrated ammonia solution until the sepia precipitate redissolves. Then add drop by drop enough of the silver nitrate solution to produce a slight cloud that persists after

* This stain is available commercially in powder form.

shaking. The stain should remain in good condition for several months.

Stain for Rickettsiae (Castaneda's Method)

Prepare a buffer-formaldehyde solution as follows: Dissolve 1 gm. of KH_2PO_4 in 100 ml. of distilled water. Dissolve 25 gm. Na_2HPO_4· $12H_2O$ in 900 ml. distilled water. Mix the two solutions so that the pH is 7.5. Add 1 ml. of formalin as a preservative.

The stain consists of a 1 per cent solution of methylene blue in methyl alcohol.

Mix 20 ml. of buffer solution with 1 ml. formalin and 0.15 ml. of the methylene blue solution. Apply the mixture to the film for three minutes and then decant without washing. Counterstain for one or two seconds with:

    Safranin, 0.2 per cent aqueous   1 part
    Acetic acid, 0.1 per cent aqueous 3 parts

Wash in running water, blot, and dry. The rickettsiae remain blue, while the protoplasm and nuclei of the cells are red.

This stain can also be used for elementary bodies, e.g., those of psittacosis. It may be modified by using Azur II in place of methylene blue.

Stain for Rickettsiae (Macchiavello's Method)

Staining solution: 0.25 gm. of basic fuchsin (90 per cent dye content) dissolved in 100 ml. of distilled water and buffered to pH 7.2 to 7.4 with the proper phosphate buffer mixture.

1. Smear a bit of tissue on a slide.

2. Dry in the air and fix with gentle heat.

3. Pour the staining solution onto the slide through coarse filter paper. Allow to stand four minutes.

4. Rinse rapidly with 0.5 per cent aqueous citric acid.

5. Wash quickly and thoroughly with tap water.

6. Counterstain about ten seconds with 1 per cent aqueous methylene blue.

7. Rinse in tap water, dry, and examine. Rickettsia stain red; cell nuclei, deep blue; cytoplasm, light blue.

Nigrosin Stain

Nigrosin   5.0 gm.
Distilled water   100   ml.
Boil 30 minutes and add:
  Formalin   0.5 ml.

Filter twice through double filter paper.

Iron Hematoxylin Stain (Heidenhain's) for Parasites

Stain

Hematoxylin crystals (Grubler)	1.0 gm.
Alcohol, 90 per cent	10.0 ml.
Distilled water	90.0 ml.

Dissolve the hematoxylin crystals in the alcohol using gentle heat and add the distilled water. Put the solution in a tightly stoppered flask and allow to ripen, preferably in the sun, for ten days. Add 100 ml. of distilled water and the stain is ready for use.

Mordant

Iron alum (violet crystals)	2.0 gm.
Distilled water	50.0 ml.

Procedure

1. Prepare smears of fecal sample and fix in Schaudinn's fixing solution (see modified Mallory's stains, below).
2. Pass smears through 70 per cent alcohol, through 70 per cent alcohol containing enough iodine to produce a port wine color, and then through 70, 50, and 30 per cent alcohol, leaving in each for five minutes.
3. Place in distilled water for ten minutes.
4. Place in mordant for six hours.
5. Rinse quickly with distilled water.
6. Place in staining solution for at least six hours or overnight.
7. Wash thoroughly with distilled water.
8. Place smears in a 1 per cent iron alum solution. This decolorizes the smear and should be continued until the nuclear detail of the amebas can be seen. This must be checked periodically by washing the slide with distilled water and checking under the microscope.
9. Wash smears in gently running water.
10. Dehydrate by placing smear in 70, 80, 95 per cent, and absolute alcohol, leaving in each for five minutes.
11. Clear in xylol and mount in balsam.

This technique is time consuming and requires experience and skill but produces excellent permanent stains.

Modified Mallory's Phosphotungstic Acid Stain for Fecal Parasites
Schaudinn's Solution

Saturated aqueous solution of HgCl$_2$	200.0 ml.
Ethyl alcohol (95 per cent)	100.0 ml.

Before use, add 5.0 ml. of glacial acetic acid to every 100.0 ml. of solution.

Mallory's Phosphotungstic Acid Hematoxylin

1. Dissolve 0.1 gm. of hematoxylin (histologic) in 50 ml. of boiling distilled water.
2. Dissolve 2.0 gm. of phosphotungstic acid in 20 ml. of distilled water.
3. After cooling, mix the hematoxylin and phosphotungstic acid and dilute to 100.0 ml. with distilled water.
4. Add 10.0 ml. of aqueous 0.25 per cent potassium permanganate.

Procedure

1. Make two slides on each fecal sample by smearing. The smear should not be too thick or it will flake off the slide.
2. Place the wet smear in Schaudinn's fluid for at least one hour or up to 24 hours.
3. Transfer slide to 95 per cent ethyl alcohol containing enough iodine to give the color of port wine for 15 minutes.
4. Transfer slide to 95 per cent ethyl alcohol for 15 minutes.
5. Transfer slide to 70 per cent ethyl alcohol for five minutes.
6. Transfer slide to distilled water for five minutes.
7. Stain with Mallory's stain for 24 to 48 hours.
8. Transfer to tap water for five minutes.
9. Transfer slide to 70 per cent ethyl alcohol for five minutes.
10. Transfer slide to 95 per cent ethyl alcohol for five minutes.
11. Tranfer slide to absolute ethyl alcohol for five minutes.
12. Transfer slide to xylol.
13. Mount in Canada balsam or clarite.

This is a relatively rapid method of staining and gives excellent results when done properly. The slides tend to fade after a period of time and are not so permanent as Heidenhain's.

D'Antoni's Iodine Solution for Staining Protozoan Cysts

Adjust a potassium iodide solution to exactly 10 per cent by the specific gravity method. To 100 ml. of a 1:10 dilution of the stock KI solution (1 per cent KI) add 1.5 gm. of iodine crystals. This stain is ready to use after standing for four days. For immediate use a small portion is filtered into a dropping bottle. This filtered solution should be discarded after ten days. Standard basic reagents to make 1000 ml. of the solution can be purchased.

REAGENTS

Modified Alsever's Solution for Preservation of Sheep Red Cells

Glucose	2.05	gm.
Sodium chloride	0.42	gm.

Trisodium citrate	0.8	gm.
Citric acid	0.055	gm.
Distilled water	100	ml.

Add to an equal volume of sheep cells. Keep at 4° C.

Solution for Spray or Bray Anaerobic Dish

40 per cent pyrogallic acid
20 per cent sodium hydroxide

Add 4 ml. of the pyrogallic acid on one side of the dish and 10 ml. of the sodium hydroxide on the other. Inoculate agar, seal, and mix the two solutions by carefully tilting the dish.

Andrade's Indicator

Distilled water	100	ml.
Acid fuchsin	0.5	gm.
Sodium hydroxide (1 N)	16	ml.

The fuchsin is dissolved in the distilled water and the sodium hydroxide is added. If after several hours the fuchsin is not sufficiently decolorized, add an additional 1 or 2 ml. of alkali. The dye content of different samples of acid fuchsin varies quite widely, and the amount of alkali that should be used with any particular sample usually is specified on the label. The reagent improves somewhat on aging and should be prepared in a sufficiently large quantity to last for several years. The indicator is used in amounts of 10 ml. per liter of medium.

Preservative Solutions for Stools

BANXGANG AND ELIOT SOLUTION

Sodium citrate	10.0	gm.
Sodium desoxycholate	5.0	gm.
Sodium chloride	9.0	gm.
Disodium phosphate (M/15 sol.)	3.0	ml.
Distilled water	1000	ml.

Titrate to neutrality to litmus with 1 N sodium hydroxide. Add 2 ml. of 1 N sodium hydroxide, dispense in bottles, and autoclave. It is advisable to add sufficient phenol red to the medium to impart a distinct color.

HANK'S DIGESTION SOLUTION

Sodium hydroxide	40	gm.
Potassium alum	2	gm.
Distilled water	1000	ml.

Add bromthymol blue, 0.04 per cent, q.s. to give deep blue color.

RINGER'S SOLUTION

| NaCl | 7.0 | gm. |
| CaCl₂ | 0.3 | gm. |

| KCl | 0.25 gm. |
| Distilled water to 1000 ml. | |

INDICATOR OF ANAEROBIASIS

Solution A

| N/10 NaOH | 6 ml. |
| Distilled water to 100 ml. | |

Solution B

| Methylene blue, 0.5 per cent | 3 ml. |
| Distilled water to 100 ml. | |

Solution C

| Glucose | 6 gm. |
| Distilled water to 100 ml. | |

Place equal volumes of each solution in test tube. Add one small thymol crystal. Boil until colorless. Place in anaerobic jar. Remains colorless if anaerobic conditions are maintained.

TECHNIQUES

Bile Solubility Test for Pneumococci

Centrifuge the growth from a 5 ml. culture of the organism in dextrose broth and resuspend the growth in 0.5 M phosphate buffer, pH 7.6, containing 2 per cent sodium chloride and 0.05 per cent sodium desoxycholate. Incubate at 37° C. for 60 minutes and examine. Colonies of pneumococci lyse under these conditions.

Test for Catalase Production

Pour 1 ml. of H_2O_2 (10 volumes per cent) over the surface of a 24-hour agar slope culture. If catalase is present, bubbles of oxygen will be released from the surface of the growth.

Preparation of Permanent Lacto-Phenol Cotton Blue Mounts for Fungi

Tease a small portion of culture apart gently on a slide, add a drop of 95 per cent alcohol, and let dry. Add a small drop of lacto-phenol cotton blue and let it set for three minutes. Place clean coverslip on top and press gently to drive out air bubbles. Let dry for three weeks. Seal coverslip with a suitable agent (collodion, asphaltum). Such preparations usually remain satisfactory for many months.

Methyl Red Test

Methyl Red Solution

Methyl red	0.1	gm.
Ethyl alcohol (95 per cent solution)	300	ml.
Distilled water, to make 500 ml.		

Add 5 drops of the indicator solution to 5 ml. of a four-to-five-day culture in MR-VP medium. A distinct red color is positive; yellow is negative.

Voges-Proskauer Reaction (O'Meara Modification)

To 5 ml. of a four-to-five-day culture in MR-VP medium add a knife point (25 mg.) of creatine and 5 ml. of 40 per cent KOH. Shake the tube thoroughly. A pink color appearing in about two minutes is positive.

Nitroso-Indol Reaction (Cholera Red Test)

Grow organism in 1 per cent tryptone broth containing 0.001 per cent potassium nitrate. After 24 hours' incubation add 2 to 3 drops of concentrated H_2SO_4. A deep rose-pink color develops if the test is positive.

Test for Nitrate Reduction

Solution A
Sulfanilic acid   8 gm.
5 N acetic acid   1000 ml.
Solution B
Alpha-naphthylamine   5 gm.
5 N acetic acid   1000 ml.

Filter through washed absorbent cotton.
Procedure
1. To 5 to 10 ml. of a culture grown in peptone broth containing 0.02 per cent potassium nitrate add 1 ml. of solution A, followed by 1 ml. of solution B added drop by drop. If nitrite is present, a pink, red, or maroon color is produced.
2. If no color develops, this indicates the absence of nitrite and may mean that the nitrate is not reduced or that both the nitrate and the nitrite have been reduced.
3. In order to determine definitely that the nitrate has not been reduced, the following procedure can be used:
   a. Add a small amount of zinc dust to the culture and the nitrate reagents.
   b. If a red color develops, the zinc has reduced nitrate to nitrite. This indicates that nitrate was present and was not reduced by bacterial action.
   c. If no red color develops, this indicates that the bacteria have reduced both nitrates and nitrites.

Tests for Hydrogen Sulfide Production-Lead Acetate Paper Method

Cut filter paper into 50 × 10 mm. strips and immerse them in a 5 per cent solution of lead acetate. Dry in air. Sterilize in a suitable container at 121° C. for 15 minutes.

Following inoculation of the liquid medium (which must contain available sulfur compounds) insert a strip of the sterilized paper between the plug and the glass with the lower end above the liquid level. Incubate.

If H_2S is liberated during the growth of the organism, the lower portion of the paper will turn black. If after incubation there has been no color change, remove the plug and add 0.5 ml. of 2 N HCl. Replace the paper and plug without delay. The addition of the acid will liberate any dissolved sulfide, which will react with the lead to yield the black lead sulfide.

Indol Production (Kovacs)

Para-dimethylaminobenzaldehyde   5 gm.
Amyl or butyl alcohol   75 ml.
Hydrochloric acid, conc.   25 ml.

Add approximately 1 ml. of reagent to a 24-to-48-hour peptone-water culture. Shake gently. The reagent rises to the surface. A cherry-red color is a positive test for indol.

Test for Indol Production-Oxalic Acid Paper

Prepare a saturated aqueous solution of oxalic acid (15 to 20 gms. per 100 ml.). Dip filter paper into this solution while warm and dry thoroughly. Cut paper into strips 10 × 90 mm. With the paper strip, form a loop under the cotton plug. Production of indol is shown by the development of a pink color on the paper during the growth of the culture.

Gelatin Liquefaction (Smith)

Streak cultures on a plate of nutrient agar containing 0.4 per cent gelatin. Incubate at 28° C. for 2 to 14 days according to rate of growth. Cover plate with 8 to 10 ml. of a solution of 15 gm. of $HgCl_2$, 20 ml. of conc. HCl, and 100 ml. of distilled water. A white opaque precipitate is formed with the unchanged gelatin, but a liquefier is surrounded by a clear zone.

Charcoal Gelatin Disc Method (Kohn)

Discs composed of formalinized gelatin and powdered charcoal (available commercially) are added to the medium and incubated at desired temperature. Gelatinase activity is indicated by a release of charcoal particles.

Differentiation of Oxidative and Fermentative Production of Acid from Carbohydrates (Hugh and Leifson)

Peptone (casein hydrolysate)	2.0 gm.
NaCl	5.0 gm.
K₂HPO₄	0.3 gm.
Agar	3.0 gm.
Bromthymol blue (1 per cent aqueous)	3.0 ml.
Distilled water	1000 ml.

Dissolve the ingredients and adjust the pH, if necessary, to 7.1. Sterilize at 121° C. for 20 minutes.

Prepare 10 per cent aqueous solutions of the carbohydrates and sterilize by Seitz filtration. Add 10 ml. of the carbohydrates aseptically to every 100 ml. of the sterile, melted medium and dispense in 5 ml. amounts into sterile 150 × 13 mm. tubes.

Inoculate two tubes of each carbohydrate with each organism by stabbing with inoculum from a fresh slope culture. Cover the surface of one tube with sterile paraffin (petrolatum).

Fermentative organisms produce acid throughout both tubes. Oxidative organisms produce acid in the open tube only. In the latter, acid appears first at the surface and then progressively toward the base. Slow oxidative reactions are sometimes preceded by a slight alkaline reaction.

Blood for Microfilarial Studies

THICK FILM PREPARATIONS

1. Thick film preparations are made about the size of a dime—not thick enough to slough off when dry—and stained with Giemsa's stain in the same manner as thick films for malaria.

2. Examine the stained smears under the low objective with increased light so that the leukocytes come into view. Examine for organisms.

3. Use oil immersion for identification of larvae.

CITRATED BLOOD

1. Mix 5 ml. of freshly drawn blood and 1 ml. of 2.0 per cent sodium citrate made up in 0.85 per cent sodium chloride solution.

2. Centrifuge at 1000 r.p.m. for ten minutes.

3. Pass a fine pipet through the red cell sediment to remove the material on the bottom of the tube.

4. Spread this sediment on a glass slide and examine for active microfilariae with the low power of the microscope. Also examine the buffy coat for microfilariae (this coat may need to be diluted with saline to see the organisms).

5. The microfilariae may live several days at room temperature in the citrated blood.

KNOTT CONCENTRATION FOR MICROFILARIAE (MODIFIED)

This technique hemolyzes the red cells and concentrates the leukocytes and microfilariae (which are killed).

1. Obtain 2 ml. of blood by venipuncture and deliver it directly into a centrifuge tube containing 10 ml. of 1 per cent acetic acid. Mix thoroughly.

2. Centrifuge at 1500 r.p.m. for one minute.

3. Decant supernatant and spread sediment out to approximate thick films on slides. Dry thoroughly.

4. Stain with Wright's or Giemsa's stain.

5. The sediment may be examined by wet mount for the dead organisms.

Culture for Larvae of Hookworm and Strongyloides

PETRI DISH SMEARS

1. Cut a piece of filter paper so that a ½ inch space remains around it in the bottom of a Petri dish.

2. Smear feces on the filter paper with a tongue depressor in a thin layer and allow to dry slightly.

3. Layer a thin film of tap water over the surface of the feces and cover.

4. Culture at room temperature for 24 to 48 hours.

5. Examine area around the filter paper under the scanning lens of a microscope.

6. Transfer organisms to microslide, using a medicine dropper.

7. Filariform larvae of Strongyloides have notched tails and appear in 24 to 48 hours. Free-living adults may be seen in 48 hours or more.

8. Filariform larvae of hookworm do not appear for eight days. However, the rhabditiform larvae may appear in 24 hours.

CHARCOAL CULTURE

1. Moisten 6 gm. of charcoal with water and add about 1 gm. of feces and mix with a tongue depressor.

2. Place the charcoal in a Petri dish to form a cone of charcoal that will cover the bottom of the dish but will only remain in contact with an area about 2 inches in diameter on the inside of the lid.

3. Incubate at room temperature for one to eight days.

4. Examine the droplets of the moisture of condensation under the scanning lens of a microscope or examine the washings of the inside of the cover.

5. The filariform larvae of *S. stercoralis* have notched tails and appear in 24 to 48 hours, while the filariform of hookworm appear in about eight days. Rhabditiform larvae, however, may appear in 24 hours at the bottom of the dish.

Examination of Sputum for Helminth Ova and Larvae

1. Comminute sputum sample with an equal amount of hydrogen peroxide (3 per cent).

2. Centrifuge at 3000 r.p.m.

3. Decant supernatant.

4. Examine sediment for ova and larvae.

Examination of the Urine for Schistosoma haematobium *and* D. renale

1. Collect a morning specimen of urine.

2. Place it in a sedimentation glass or a graduated cylinder.

3. Allow the urine to settle one-half hour.

4. Decant.

5. Centrifuge the sediment.

6. Examine sediment for ova.

Egg Hatching Methods for Schistosome Ova

URINE

1. Follow the procedure given for examination of urine through step 5, above.

2. Suspend sediment in 10 to 15 ml. of tap water.

3. Place tube in direct path of a bright light or in sunlight passing through a window.

4. Examine for motile miracidia during the next few hours using a hand lens or the unaided eye.

FECES

1. Emulsify a large quantity of stool specimen (10 to 20 gm.) in physiologic saline to prevent hatching of the ova.

2. Strain through four layers of dampened gauze into a graduated cylinder or sedimentation glass.

3. Allow to settle one-half hour.

4. Decant supernatant.

5. Suspend sediment in saline.

6. Repeat steps 4 and 5 until supernatant is clear.

7. Transfer saline-washed sediment into a small flask.

8. Add tap water to the sediment until the flask is full.

9. Darken the flask with foil or paper except for a small area at the top of the water.

10. Expose the water to a bright light source from the side.

11. Examine for motile miracidia during the next few hours with a hand lens or with the unaided eye.

Other Staining Solutions

In this section are given the formulas for a few widely used staining fluids that have not been included in the text. Other stains that are used only for special purposes are discussed in the body of the book and may be found by consulting the index.

Acid-fast Stain. Kinyoun carbolfuchsin acid-fast stain (Am. J. Pub. Health, 5:867, 1915). Formula: basic fuchsin, 4 gm.; phenol crystals, 8 gm.; 95 per cent alcohol, 20 ml.; and distilled water, 100 ml. Stain fixed smear for three minutes (no heat necessary) and continue as with Ziehl-Neelsen stain.

Basic Fuchsin. This dye should not be confused with acid fuchsin. Solutions of this dye are generally made with phenol as a mordant, and they are then very powerful bacterial stains with a strong tendency to cause overstaining. They are used chiefly to stain the tubercle bacillus.

Carbol Thionine. Saturated solution of thionine in 50 per cent alcohol, 20 ml.; 2 per cent aqueous solution of phenol, 100 ml. This stain is used as a general stain. In blood work, it is sometimes used to demonstrate the malarial parasite and to demonstrate basophilic degeneration of the red cells. The fluid is applied for one-half to three minutes, after fixation by heat, or for about a minute in a 1 per cent aqueous solution of mercuric chloride or in a 1 per cent solution of formalin in alcohol.

Crystal Violet. Crystal violet, a powerful bacterial stain, may be substituted for gentian violet in all formulas and is more satisfactory. A solution of 2 gm. crystal violet in 100 ml. methyl alcohol of the highest purity is probably the best stain for Gram's method.

Gentian Violet. This dye has long been widely used as a bacterial stain, especially for Gram's method, but is now being rapidly displaced by crystal violet and methyl violet. Methyl violet, or crystal violet, may be substituted for gentian violet.

Giemsa's Stain for Blood. Immerse the slide in stain diluted 1 to 50 for 30 to 45 minutes. Rinse gently in distilled water for three to five minutes. Dry in air and examine. Do not blot.

Hematoxylin. Hematoxylin is one of the best nuclear stains available. There are many combinations, most of which require weeks or months for "ripening." The following is a good solution, which is ready for use as soon as made:

Harris' hematoxylin. Dissolve 1 gm. hematoxylin crystals in 10 ml. alcohol. Dissolve 20 gm. ammonia alum in 200 ml. distilled water with the aid of heat, and add the alcoholic hematoxylin solution. Bring the mixture to a boil, and add 0.5 gm. of mercuric oxide. As soon as the solution assumes a dark purple color, remove the vessel from the flame and cool quickly in a basin of cold water.

Hematoxylin and Eosin (particularly for cytologic examinations). Place smear into: Water for one minute. Harris' hematoxylin for one minute. Water for one minute. Dip into acid alcohol. Water for 30 seconds. 0.5 per cent aqueous eosin for two minutes. Dip in water. Dip into increasing concentrations of alcohol to absolute alcohol. Beechwood creosote for five minutes. Xylol for five minutes. Apply coverslip with Clarite, Canada balsam, or similar substances.

Lugol's Solution (liquor iodi fortis, U.S.P.). Lugol's solution consists of iodine, 5 gm.; potassium iodide, 10 gm.; and water, 100 ml. Gram's iodine solution may be made from this by adding 14 times its volume of water.

Methylene Blue. This widely used basic dye does not readily overstain. The following solutions are useful:

Loeffler's methylene blue solution. This is one of the most useful bacterial stains for general purposes. The solution is applied at room temperature for 30 seconds to three minutes and is followed by rinsing in water. Fixation may be by heat or chemicals. The stain is composed of 30 parts of a saturated alcoholic solution of methylene blue and 1000 parts of a 1 to 10,000 aqueous solution of potassium hydroxide. It keeps indefinitely.

Pappenheim's methylene blue solution. This solution is used as a decolorizer and as a contrast stain in Pappenheim's method for staining the tubercle bacillus. Dissolve 1 gm. corallin (rosolic acid) in 100 ml. absolute alcohol; saturate with methylene blue and add 20 ml. glycerol.

Peroxidase Stain (Goodpasture). 1. Dissolve 0.05 gm. sodium nitroprusside in 1 or 2 ml. of water, mix with 100 ml. alcohol, and add 0.05 gm. benzidine (C.P.), and 0.05 to 0.1 gm. basic fuchsin. This stain will keep 8 months.

2. Prepare 1 to 200 dilution of hydrogen peroxide just before use (2 drops to 15 ml. of water).

3. The blood film is prepared in the usual manner, dried in air, within 3 to 4 hours of the time of collection.

4. Cover with Goodpasture's stain for one minute; add equal amount of hydrogen peroxide for three to four minutes. Rinse well in water and dry by blotting.

5. Neutrophilic granules of granulocytes are stained deep blue and are clearly defined. No granules are seen in the lymphocytes. Fewer and ill defined granules are seen in most monocytes.

Pyronine. Used in strong aqueous solution, this is useful as a contrast stain in Gram's method, but results are more satisfactory when the dye is combined with methyl green.

Pappenheim's Methyl Green Pyronine. This solution colors bacteria red and the nuclei of cells blue. It is, therefore, especially useful for staining intracellular bacteria like the gonococcus and the influenza bacillus. It is a good stain for routine purposes, is an excellent contrast stain for Gram's method, and is also used to demonstrate Döhle's inclusion bodies in the blood. It colors the cytoplasm of lymphocytes bright red and has been used as a differential stain for these cells. The solution is applied cold for one-half to five minutes. It consists of a saturated aqueous solution of methyl green, 3 to 4 parts, and a saturated aqueous solution of pyronine, 1 to 1½ parts. It is a good plan to keep these solutions in stock and to mix a new lot of the staining fluid about once a month. If staining with either dye is too deep, the proper balance is attained by adding a little of the other.

Because pyronine is now highly concentrated, the following formula, which has been proposed by the Commission on Biological Stains of the Society of American Bacteriologists, may prove more useful: methyl green (50 per cent dye content), 1 gm.; pyronine (Commission certified product), 0.25 gm.; ethyl alcohol (95 per cent), 5 ml.; glycerol, 20 ml.; and 2 per cent aqueous solution of phenol, 100 ml.

Reticulocyte Stain (Osgood-Wilhelm method). Place 5 drops of oxalated capillary or venous blood in a small test tube. Add 5 drops of 1 per cent brilliant cresyl blue in 0.85 per cent NaCl solution. Mix and let stand for two to five minutes. Mix and make blood smear. Counterstain with Wright's, if desired.

Safranin. A 1 per cent aqueous solution of safranin is widely used as a contrast stain in Gram's method of staining.

Sudan III. This is a valuable stain for fat, to which it gives an orange color. Scharlach R is a similar but stronger dye and may be substituted to advantage.

Physiologic Solutions, Buffers, Acid-Base Indicators, and Weights and Measures with Equivalents

Physiologic Solutions

Physiologic solutions are so made that they contain the same percentages of various salts as are found in the fluids of the animal body.

Physiologic saline solution is made of sodium chloride (C.P.), 0.85 gm. and distilled water, 100 ml.

Locke's solution consists of sodium chloride, 0.9 gm.; calcium chloride, 0.024 gm.; potassium chloride, 0.042 gm.; sodium carbonate, 0.02 gm.; dextrose, 0.25 gm.; and distilled water, 100 ml.

Ringer's solution (modified by Porter) consists of sodium chloride, 0.7 gm.; calcium chloride, 0.0026 gm.; potassium chloride, 0.035 gm.; and distilled water, 100 ml.

Buffers

A buffer is a substance or a combination of substances that, when dissolved in water, will minimize (resist) changes in pH when acid or alkali is added.

A buffer consists of a weak acid and its salt with a strong alkali or of a strong acid and its salt with a weak alkali.

SØRENSON'S PHOSPHATE BUFFER

These buffer solutions are generally useful, since the range of the mixtures is from pH 5 to 8.

Fifteenth Molar Monobasic Potassium Phosphate Solution (KH_2PO_4). Weigh exactly 9.078 gm. of monobasic potassium phosphate, and dissolve it in exactly 1 liter of distilled water. The solution must be absolutely clear and should yield no test for chlorine or sulfates.

The phosphate salt solutions should be kept in the refrigerator in Pyrex bottles.

Fifteenth Molar Dibasic Sodium Phosphate Solution (Na_2HPO_4). Expose dibasic sodium phosphate containing 12 mols of water of crystallization to ordinary atmosphere for two weeks. It should then contain 2 mols of crystallization. Dissolve exactly 11.876 gm. of this sodium phosphate in exactly 1 liter of distilled water. The solution should be absolutely clear and should yield no test for chlorine or sulfates.

Sørensen's Table of Buffer Mixtures

Na_2HPO_4 SOLUTION, ML.	KH_2PO_4 SOLUTION, ML.	pH
0.25	9.75	5.288
0.5	9.5	5.589
1.0	9.0	5.906
2.0	8.0	6.239
3.0	7.0	6.468
4.0	6.0	6.643
5.0	5.0	6.813
6.0	4.0	6.979
7.0	3.0	7.168
8.0	2.0	7.381
9.0	1.0	7.731
9.5	0.5	8.043

TRIS (HYDROXY-METHYL) AMINOMETHANE BUFFER*

Tris (hydroxy-methyl) aminomethane buffer can be used for a pH range between

* If buffers of a higher molarity are desired, the 0.1 N HCl may have to be replaced by a 1.0 N HCl.

7.0 and 9.0, but its best buffer capacity is between 7.5 and 8.5. It is practically ineffective below pH 7.0 and above pH 9.0. One advantage of the buffer is its excellent stability. The buffer can be prepared by weighing the desired amount of tris (hydroxy-methyl) aminomethane, dissolving it in water, and adjusting the pH to the desired value with HCl. For example, if 100 ml. of 0.05 M buffer is desired, place 0.5057 gm. of tris (hydroxy-methyl) aminomethane into a 100 ml. volumetric flask, dissolve in approximately 50 ml. of distilled water, add 0.1 N HCl, as indicated in the following table, and fill up to the mark with distilled water. The table shows the pH values obtained when 0.5057 gm. of tris (hydroxy-methyl) aminomethane dissolved in water is mixed with the indicated amounts of 0.1 N HCl and diluted to 100 ml.

Barbiturate Buffer (pH 8.6)
(see p. 443)

Acid-Base Indicators*

An acid-base indicator is a weak acid or a weak base, the undissociated form of which has another color and constitution than the iogenic form. An indicator does not change its color from the purely acid to the purely alkaline side at a definite hydrogen concentration, but the color change takes place over a certain range of hydrogen ion concentrations. This range is called the color change interval and is expressed in terms of pH (the negative logarithm of the hydrogen ion concentration). A great number of substances show indicator properties, although relatively few of them are practically applied for neutralization reactions and pH determinations. In general, weak acids should be titrated in the presence of indicators that change in slightly alkaline solutions. Weak bases should be titrated in the presence of indicators that change in slightly acid solutions.

ML. 0.1 N HCl ADDED	RESULTING pH AT 23°C.	RESULTING pH AT 37°C.
5.0	9.10	8.95
7.5	8.92	8.78
10.0	8.74	8.60
12.5	8.62	8.48
15.0	8.50	8.37
17.5	8.40	8.27
20.0	8.32	8.18
22.5	8.23	8.10
25.0	8.14	8.00
27.5	8.05	7.90
30.0	7.96	7.82
32.5	7.87	7.73
35.0	7.77	7.63
37.5	7.66	7.52
40.0	7.54	7.40
42.5	7.36	7.22
45.0	7.20	7.05

INDICATOR	pH RANGE	QUANTITY OF INDICATOR PER 10 ML.	COLOR ACID	ALKALINE
Thymol blue (A)*†	1.2–2.8	1–2 drops 0.1% soln. in aq.	red	yellow
Methyl orange (B)	3.1–4.4	1 drop 0.1% soln. in aq.	red	orange
Bromphenol blue (A)†	3.0–4.6	1 drop 0.1% soln. in aq.	yellow	blue-violet
Bromcresol green (A)†	4.0–5.6	1 drop 0.1% soln. in aq.	yellow	blue
Methyl red (A)†	4.4–6.2	1 drop 0.1% soln. in aq.	red	yellow
Bromcresol purple (A)†	5.2–6.8	1 drop 0.1% soln. in aq.	yellow	purple
Bromthymol blue (A)†	6.2–7.6	1 drop 0.1% soln. in aq.	yellow	blue
Phenol red (A)†	6.4–8.0	1 drop 0.1% soln. in aq.	yellow	red
Neutral red (B)	6.8–8.0	1 drop 0.1% soln. in 70% alc.	red	yellow
Thymol blue (A)#†	8.0–9.6	1–5 drops 0.1% soln. in aq.	yellow	blue
Phenolphthalein (A)	8.0–10.0	1–5 drops 0.1% soln. in 70% alc.	colorless	red
Thymolphthalein (A)	9.4–10.6	1 drop 0.1% soln. in 90% alc.	colorless	blue

The letters A or B following the name of the indicator signify, respectively, that the compound is an indicator *acid* or *base*.

† Sodium salt.   * For the acid range.   # For the alkaline range.

** Extracted from Lange, N. A.: Handbook of Chemistry. 8th Ed. Sandusky, Ohio, Handbook Publishers, Inc., 1952, pp. 942–943.

Commonly Used Acids and Alkalies*

SOLUTION	MOL. WEIGHT	SPEC. GRAVITY†	GM. PER LITER†	MOLARITY†	NORMALITY†	APPROX. NUMBER OF ML. REQUIRED TO MAKE 1000 OF 1 N SOLUTION
Conc. HCl	36.46	1.19	440	12	12	83
Conc. H_2SO_4	98.08	1.84	1730	18	36	28
Conc. HNO_3	63.02	1.42	990	16	16	64
Conc. lactic acid	90.08	1.21	1030	11	11	87
Glacial acetic acid	60.08	1.06	1060	17.5	17.5	57
Conc. NH_4OH	35.05	0.90	250	15	15	67

* Commercially available.

† Figures may vary slightly according to the lot or manufacturer.

Weights and Measures, with Equivalents

METRIC

Meter (unit of length):
Millimeter (mm.) = 1/1000 meter
Centimeter (cm.) = 1/100 meter
Kilometer = 1000 meters
Micron (μ) = 1/1000 millimeter

Gram (unit of weight):
Milligram (mg.) = 1/1000 gram
Kilogram (kilo.) = 1000 grams

Liter (unit of capacity):
Cubic centimeter = 1/1000 liter = Same measure as milliliter (ml.)

1 Millimeter = { 0.03937 (1/25 approx.) in.
1000 microns }

1 Centimeter = { 0.3937 (2/5 approx.) in.
0.0328 feet }

1 Meter = { 39.37 in.
3.28 feet }

1 Micron (μ) = { 1/25000 in.
0.001 millimeter }

1 Gram = { 15.43 grains
0.563 dram
0.035 ounce } Avoir.
0.0022 pound }
0.257 dram
0.032 ounce } Apoth.
0.0027 pound }

1 Kilogram = { 35.27 ounces (Avoir.)
2.2 pounds (Avoir.) }

1 Liter = { 1.056 (1 approx.) quarts
61.02 cubic inches
1000 cu. centimeters }

1 Sq. Millimeter = 0.00155 }
1 Sq. Centimeter = 0.1550 } sq. in.
1 Sq. Meter = 1550 }
1 Sq. Meter = 10.76 sq. feet

1 Cu. Millimeter = 0.00006 }
1 Cu. Centimeter = 0.0610 } cu. in.
1 Cu. Centimeter = 0.001 liter
1 Cu. Meter = { 35.32 cu. feet
61025.4 cu. in. }

1 Inch = 25.399 millimeters
1 Sq. Inch = 6.451 sq. centimeters
1 Cu. Inch = 16.387 cu. centimeters

1 Foot = 30.48 centimeters
1 Sq. Foot = 0.093 sq. meter
1 Cu. Foot = 0.028 cu. meter

AVOIRDUPOIS WEIGHT

1 Ounce { 437.5 grains
16 drams }
1 Pound = 16 ounces

1 Grain = 0.065 (3/50 approx.) }
1 Dram = 1.77 (3/4 approx.) }
1 Ounce = 28.35 (30 approx.) } grams
1 Pound = 453.59 (500 approx.) }
1 Pound = 27.7 cu. inches
1 Pound = 1.215 lb. Troy

APOTHECARIES' MEASURE

1 Dram = 60 minims
1 Ounce = 8 drams
1 Pint = 16 ounces
1 Gallon = 8 pints

1 Dram = 3.70 }
1 Ounce = 29.57 }
1 Pint = 473.1 } cu. centimeters
1 Gallon = 3785.4 }
1 Gallon = 231 cu. inches

APOTHECARIES' WEIGHT

1 Scruple = 20 grains
1 Dram = 3 scruples = 60 grains
1 Ounce = 8 drams = 480 grains
1 Pound = 12 ounces

1 Grain = 0.065 }
1 Dram = 3.887 }
1 Ounce = 31.10 } grams
1 Pound = 373.2 }

To convert *minims* into *cubic centimeters* multiply by 0.061
To convert *fluidounces* into *cubic centimeters* multiply by 29.57
To convert *grains* into *grams* multiply by 0.0648
To convert *drams* into *grams* multiply by 3.887

To convert *cubic centimeters* into *minims* multiply by 16.23
To convert *cubic centimeters* into *fluidounces* multiply by 0.0338
To convert *grams* into *grains* multiply by 15.432
To convert *grams* into *drams* multiply by 0.257

Temperature

CENTIGRADE	FAHRENHEIT	CENTIGRADE	FAHRENHEIT
110°	230°	37°	98.6°
100	212	36.5	97.7
95	203	36	96.8
90	194	35.5	95.9
85	185	35	95
80	176	34	93.2
75	167	33	91.4
70	158	32	89.6
65	149	31	87.8
60	140	30	86
55	131	25	77
50	122	20	68
45	113	15	59
44	111.2	10	50
43	109.4	+5	41
42	107.6	0	32
41	105.8	−5	23
40.5	104.9	−10	14
40	104	−15	+5
39.5	103.1	−20	−4
39	102.2	0.54° = ·1°	
38.5	101.3	1 = 1.8	
38	100.4	2 = 3.6	
37.5	99.5	2.5 = 4.5	

To convert Fahrenheit into Centigrade, subtract 32 and multiply by 0.555.
To convert Centigrade into Fahrenheit, multiply by 1.8 and add 32.

International Atomic Weights of the Most Commonly Used Elements*

	SYMBOL	ATOMIC NUMBER	ATOMIC WEIGHT		SYMBOL	ATOMIC NUMBER	ATOMIC WEIGHT
Aluminum	Al	13	26.98	Lead	Pb	82	207.21
Antimony	Sb	51	121.76	Lithium	Li	3	6.940
Arsenic	As	33	74.91	Magnesium	Mg	12	24.32
Barium	Ba	56	137.36	Manganese	Mn	25	54.93
Beryllium	Be	4	9.013	Mercury	Hg	80	200.61
Bismuth	Bi	83	209.00	Molybdenum	Mo	42	95.95
Boron	B	5	10.82	Nickel	Ni	28	58.69
Bromine	Br	35	79.916	Oxygen	O	8	16
Cadmium	Cd	48	112.41	Phosphorus	P	15	30.975
Calcium	Ca	20	40.08	Potassium	K	19	39.100
Carbon	C	6	12.010	Selenium	Se	34	78.96
Chlorine	Cl	17	35.457	Silicon	Si	14	28.09
Chromium	Cr	24	52.01	Silver	Ag	47	107.880
Cobalt	Co	27	58.94	Sodium	Na	11	22.997
Copper	Cu	29	63.54	Strontium	Sr	38	87.63
Fluorine	F	9	19.00	Sulfur	S	16	32.066
Gold	Au	79	197.2	Thallium	Tl	81	204.39
Hydrogen	H	1	1.0080	Tin	Sn	50	118.70
Iodine	I	53	126.91	Tungsten	W	74	183.92
Iron	Fe	26	55.85	Zinc	Zn	30	65.38

* Copied and table-extracted from Lange, N. A.: Handbook of Chemistry. 8th Ed. Sandusky, Ohio, Handbook Publishers, Inc., 1952.

Tables of Normal Values

The following lists of normal values are based on the experience in the Department of Pathology, Mount Sinai Hospital, Chicago, Illinois. Actual values may vary with different techniques or in different laboratories. All blood and serum values are given for the fasting state.

Whole Blood, Serum, and Plasma (Chemistry)

TEST	MATERIAL	NORMAL VALUE	SPECIAL INSTRUCTIONS
Acetone, qualitative	Serum	Negative	
quantitative	Serum	0.3–2.0 mg./100 ml.	
A/G ratio	Serum	1.1–1.9	
Total protein	Serum	6.0–7.8 gm./100 ml.	
Albumin	Serum	3.2–4.5 gm./100 ml.	
Globulin	Serum	2.3–3.5 gm./100 ml.	
Amino acid nitrogen	Serum	4–5 mg./100 ml.	
Alcohol (ethyl), semi-quantitative	Serum	Negative or trace	Stopper tube tightly.
Aldolase	Serum	3.8 units	
Ammonia	Plasma	20–150 μg./100 ml.	Collect with sodium-heparinate. Specimen must be analyzed immediately.
Amylase	Serum	30–150 Somogyi units/100 ml.	
Ascorbic acid (vitamin C)	Plasma	0.6–1.5 mg./100 ml.	Collect with oxalate and analyze within 20 minutes.
Barbiturates	Serum or urine	Negative	
Base, total	Serum	145–160 mEq./L.	
Bilirubin, direct	Serum	0–0.2 mg./100 ml.	
indirect		0.2–0.8 mg./100 ml.	
total		0.2–1.0 mg./100 ml.	
Bromide	Serum	0.8–1.5 mg./100 ml.	
B.S.P. (5 mg./kg.)	Serum	0–5% (45 min.)	
Calcium, total	Serum	4.5–5.5 mEq./L. 9.0–11.0 mg./100 ml. Infants: 11–13 mg./100 ml.	
Calcium, ionized	Serum	2.1–2.6 mEq./L. 4.2–5.2 mg./100 ml.	
Carbon dioxide (CO_2) content	Serum	Adults: 20–30 mEq./L. Infants: 20–28 mEq./L.	Collect under oil without stasis.
Carbon dioxide pressure (pCO_2)	Whole blood	35–45 mm. Hg	Collect in sealed heparinized syringe.
Carboxyhemoglobin	Whole blood	< 5%	
Carotene, beta	Serum	40–200 μg./100 ml.	
Cephalin cholesterol flocculation	Serum	Negative or 1+ after 24 hours	

Whole Blood, Serum, and Plasma (Chemistry)—Continued

TEST	MATERIAL	NORMAL VALUE	SPECIAL INSTRUCTIONS
Ceruloplasmin	Serum	6–15 units	
Chloride	Serum	98–108 mEq./L.	
Cholesterol, total	Serum	140–250 mg./100 ml.	
Cholesterol, esters	Serum	65%–75% of total	
Congo red test	Serum	> 60% at 1 hour	Severe reactions may occur if dye is injected twice. Check patient's record.
Copper	Serum	70–140 µg./100 ml.	
Creatine	Serum	Males: 0.2–0.6 mg./100 ml. Females: 0.6–1.0 mg./100 ml.	
Creatinine	Serum	0.7–1.5 mg./100 ml.	
Creatinine clearance (endogenous)	Serum and urine	117 ± 20 ml./min. 150–180 L./24 hours	
Cryoglobulin	Serum	Negative	Keep specimen at 37° C.
Electrophoresis, protein	Serum	Albumin 51–65% Alpha-1 globulin 3–6% Alpha-2 globulin 3.5–9.5% Beta globulin 8.6–12.6% Gamma globulin 13.6–19.6%	
Fatty acids, total	Serum	9–15 millimoles/L.	
Fibrinogen	Plasma	0.2–0.4 gm./100 ml.	Collect with K oxalate.
Gamma globulin	Serum	0.7–1.3 gm./100 ml.	
Globulin, total	Serum	2.3–3.5 gm./100 ml.	
Glucose	Serum or plasma	70–110 mg./100 ml.	Collect with oxalate-fluoride mixture.
Glucose	Whole blood	65–100 mg./100 ml.	Collect with oxalate-fluoride mixture.
Glucose tolerance, oral	Serum	Fasting 70–110 mg./100 ml. ½ hr.: 30–60 mg. above fasting 1 hr.: 20–50 mg. above fasting 2 hr.: 5–15 mg. above fasting 3 hr.: fasting level or below	Collect with oxalate-fluoride mixture.
Glucose tolerance, I.V.	Serum	Fasting: 70–110 mg./100 ml. 5 min.: Max. of 250 mg./100 ml. 60 min.: significant decrease 120 min.: below 120 mg./100 ml. 180 min.: fasting level	Collect with oxalate-fluoride mixture.
Hemoglobin, free	Serum or plasma	Negative	
17-Hydroxy Corticosteroids	Plasma	Male: 7–19 µg./100 ml. Female: 9–21 µg./100 ml. After 25 U.S.P. units ACTH, I.M.: 35–55 µg./100 ml.	Perform test immediately or freeze plasma.
Icterus index	Serum	4–6 units	
Insulin tolerance	Serum	Fasting: 70–110 mg./100 ml. 30 min.: falls to 50% of fasting 90 min.: fasting level	Collect with oxalate-fluoride mixture.
Iodine, butanol extractable	Serum	3.5–6.5 µg./100 ml.	Test not reliable if iodine-containing drugs or x-ray contrast media were given prior to test.
Protein bound	Serum	4.0–8.0 µg./100 ml.	
Iron	Serum	50–150 µg./100 ml.	Hemolysis must be avoided.
Iron binding capacity	Serum	290–380 µg./100 ml.	Hemolysis must be avoided.
17-Ketosteroids	Plasma	25–125 µg./100 ml.	Perform test immediately or freeze plasma.
Lactic acid	Whole blood (venous)	5–20 mg./100 ml.	Draw without stasis.
Lactic dehydrogenase (LDH)	Serum	<270 units	
Lead	Whole blood	0–50 µg./100 ml.	

Whole Blood, Serum, and Plasma (Chemistry)—Continued

TEST	MATERIAL	NORMAL VALUE	SPECIAL INSTRUCTIONS
Lipase	Serum	0–1.0 Tietz units	
Lipids, total	Serum	360–765 mg./100 ml.	
		9.0–15.0 mMol./L. (fatty acids)	
Neutral fat		0–200 mg./100 ml.	
Phospholipid-P		8.0–11.0 mg./100 ml.	
Magnesium	Serum	1.4–2.4 mEq./L.	
		1.6–2.9 mg./100 ml.	
Methemoglobin, quantitative	Whole blood	0–0.24 gm./100 ml. (average 0.06 gm./100 ml.)	
Non protein nitrogen (NPN)	Serum	20–35 mg./100 ml.	
Osmolality	Serum	285–295 mOsm/L.	
Oxygen, pressure (pO_2)	Whole blood (arterial)	95–100 mm. Hg	
Oxygen saturation	Whole blood (arterial)	94–100% saturation	
pH	Serum	7.35–7.45	Collect under oil without stasis. Centrifuge and perform test without delay.
Phenylalanine	Serum	3.0–5.0 mg./100 ml.	
Phosphatase, acid	Serum	0–1.1 Bodansky units	Hemolysis must be avoided. Perform test without delay or freeze specimen.
		1–3 King-Armstrong units	
		0.13–0.63 Bessey-Lowry units	
Phosphatase, alkaline	Serum	Adults:	
		1.5–4.5 Bodansky units	
		0.8–2.3 Bessey-Lowry units	
		4.0–13.0 King-Armstrong units	
		Children:	
		5.0–14.0 Bodansky units	
		2.8–6.7 Bessey-Lowry units	
		15.0–30.0 King-Armstrong units	
Phosphorus	Serum	Adults:	Separate cells from serum promptly.
		1.8–2.6 mEq./L.	
		3.0–4.5 mg./100 ml.	
		Children:	
		2.3–4.1 mEq./L.	
		4.0–7.0 mg./100 ml.	
Phospholipids	See lipids.		
Protein, total	Serum	6.0–7.8 gm./100 ml.	
albumin		3.2–4.5 gm./100 ml.	
globulin		2.3–3.5 gm./100 ml.	
Protein, fractionation	Serum	See electrophoresis.	
Salicylates	Serum	Negative	
		Therap. level 20–25 mg./100 ml.	
		Toxic level >30 mg./100 ml.	
Sodium	Serum	133–148 mEq./L.	
Sulfate	Serum	0.2–1.3 mEq./L.	Hemolysis must be avoided.
		0.9–6 mg./100 ml. (as $SO_4^=$)	
Sulfonamides	Serum or whole blood	Negative	
Thiocyanide	Serum	Negative	
Thymol flocculation	Serum	Negative or 1+ (24 hrs.)	
Thymol turbidity	Serum	0–5 units	
Transaminase: GOT	Serum	Up to 40 units	
GPT	Serum	Up to 35 units	
Urea clearance	Serum and urine	Max. clearance 64–99 ml./min.	
		Std. clearance 41–65 ml./min. or: more than 75% of normal clearance.	
Urea nitrogen	Serum	7–17 mg./100 ml.	

Whole Blood, Serum, and Plasma (Chemistry)—Continued

TEST	MATERIAL	NORMAL VALUE	SPECIAL INSTRUCTIONS
Uric acid	Serum	Male: 3.8–7.1 mg./100 ml. Female: 2.6–5.4 mg./100 ml. (Archibald method)	
Vitamin A	Serum	15–60 μg./100 ml.	
Vitamin A tolerance	Serum	Fasting: 15–60 μg./100 ml. 3 hr. or 6 hr.: Increase to 200–600 μg./100 ml. 24 hr.: Fasting values or slightly above	Administer 5000 units vit. A in oil per kg. body weight.
Vitamin C	Plasma	0.6–1.5 mg./100 ml.	Collect with oxalate and analyze within 20 minutes.
Xylose absorption	Serum	25–40 mg./100 ml. between 1 and 2 hrs. In malabsorption, maximum approx. 10 mg./100 ml.	For children, administer 10 ml. of a 5% solution of D-xylose/kg. of body weight.
Zinc sulfate turbidity	Serum	< 12 units	

Miscellaneous (Chemistry)

TEST	MATERIAL	NORMAL VALUE	SPECIAL INSTRUCTIONS
Bile, qualitative	Random stool specimen	Negative	
Chloride	Sweat	4–60 mEq./L.	
Diagnex test (tubeless gastric)	Urine	Free HCl present	
Duodenal drainage	See Chapter 13.		
Fat	Stool	Total fat 10–25% of dry matter and <5.0 gm./24 hrs. Neutral fat: 1–5% of dry matter. Free fatty acids: 5–13% of dry matter. Combined fatty acids: 5–15% of dry matter.	Keep refrigerated.
Gastric analysis			
Volume, fasting	Gastric contents	25–100 ml.	
Free HCl	Gastric contents	10–30 degrees or mEq./L.	
Combined acidity	Gastric contents	10–15 degrees.	
Total acidity	Gastric contents	20–40 degrees	
pH	Gastric contents	1.0–2.0 After stimulation with histamine: free acid 30–125 degrees or mEq./L. After stimulation with alcohol or Ewald meal: free acid 25–50 degrees or mEq./L.	
Tubeless (Diagnex blue)	Urine	Free HCl present	
Nitrogen, total	24-hr. stool specimen	10% of intake or 1–2 gm./24 hrs.	
Sodium	Sweat	10–80 mEq./L.	
Thyroid I^{131} uptake		15–45%	See Iodine in serum.
Trypsin, semiquantitative	Random stool specimen	Positive (2+ to 4+)	Freshly voided specimen needed.
Urobilinogen, qualitative	Random stool specimen	Positive	
quantitative	24-hr. specimen	40–200 mg./24 hrs.	

Hematology

TEST	MATERIAL	NORMAL VALUE	SPECIAL INSTRUCTIONS
Basophilic stippling	Whole blood	Negative	
Complete blood count:	Whole blood		
Hematocrit		Male: 40–54 volumes %	
		Female: 37–47 volumes %	
Hemoglobin		Male: 14–18 gm./100 ml.	
		Female: 12–16 gm./100 ml.	
Red blood cell		Male: 4.6–6.2 million cu. mm.	
White blood cell		5,000–10,000/cu.mm.	
Platelet count		200,000–400,000/cu. mm.	
Blood indices:	Whole blood	0.85–1.05	
Color index			
M.C.H.		27–31 micromicrograms	
M.C.V.		82–92 cu. microns	
M.C.H.C.		32–36%	
Volume index		0.85–1.05	
Coagulation tests	Whole blood		See p. 367.
Electrophoresis (hemoglobin)	Whole blood	Hemoglobin "A"	
Eosinophil count	Whole blood	100–300/cu. mm.	
Fetal hemoglobin	Whole blood	Negative	
Fragility test	Whole blood	Begins 0.45–0.39%	
		Complete 0.33–0.30%	
L.E. preparation	Whole blood	Negative	
Reticulocyte count	Whole blood	0.5–1.5%	
Sedimentation rate	Whole blood	Men: 0–10 mm./hr.	
		Women: 0–20 mm./hr.	
		Children: 0–20 mm./hr.	
Sickle cell preparation	Whole blood	Negative	
Thorn eosinophil test	Whole blood	50–90% below original level	Test is done in morning after 12-hr. fast. No food allowed during test (4 hours).

Urine

TEST	MATERIAL	NORMAL VALUE	SPECIAL INSTRUCTIONS
Addis count	12-hr. specimen	WBC 1,800,000 RBC 500,000 Casts (hyaline) 0–5,000 In children, the values for albumin and casts can be slightly higher, and the RBC and WBC slightly lower, than in adults.	Rinse bottle with some neutral formalin. Discard excess.
Aldosterone	24-hr. specimen	2–23 µg./24 hrs.	Keep refrigerated.
Albumin, qualitative	Random specimen	Negative	
quantitative	24-hr. specimen	10–100 mg./24 hrs.	
Alkapton bodies	Random specimen	Negative	
Amino acid nitrogen	24-hr. specimen	0.1–0.29 gm./24 hrs.	Preserve with thymol. Keep refrigerated.
Amylase	Random specimen	2–50 Wohlgemuth units/ml.	
	24-hr. specimen	6–30 Wohlgemuth units/ml. or up to 5000 Somogyi units/25 hrs.	
Bence-Jones protein	First morning specimen	Negative	
Bilirubin (bile), qualitative	Random specimen	Negative	

Urine—Continued

TEST	MATERIAL	NORMAL VALUE	SPECIAL INSTRUCTIONS
Blood, occult, qualitative	Random specimen	Negative	
Calcium (Sulkowitch)	Random specimen	1 +	
Calcium, quantitative	24-hr. specimen	Average diet: 30–150 mg./24 hrs. High calcium diet: 100–250 mg./24 hrs.	
Catecholamines	Random specimen 24-hr. specimen	0–14 μg./100 ml. <230 μg./24 hrs. (varies with muscular activity)	Preservative: 1.0 ml. concentrated H_2SO_4.
Chloride	24-hr. specimen	110–250 mEq./24 hrs.	
Concentration	See Dilution and Concentration.		
Coproporphyrin	Random specimen 24-hr. specimen	Adults: <20 μg./100 ml. 50–200 μg./24 hrs. Children: 0–80 μg./24 hrs.	Send fresh specimen and do not expose to direct light. Preserve 24-hr. urine with 5.0 gm. Na_2CO_3.
Creatine	24-hr. specimen	Male: 0–40 mg./24 hrs. Female: 0–100 mg./24 hrs. Higher in children and during pregnancy.	
Creatinine	24-hr. specimen	Male: 1000–1900 mg./24 hrs. Female: 800–1700 mg./24 hrs. or: 5–15 mg./kg. body wt./24 hrs.	
Creatinine clearance	See Serum.		
Cystine (qualitative)	Random specimen	Negative or trace	
Diacetic acid, qualitative	Random specimen	Negative	
Dilution and concentration	See procedure pp. 50–51.	Concentrated specimen 1.025 or higher. First diluted specimen 1.001–1.003.	
Double refractive bodies	Random specimen	Negative	
Estrogens	24-hr. specimen	Male: 4–25 μg./24 hrs. Female: 4–60 μg./24 hrs. Pregnancy: up to 45,000 μg./24 hrs.	Keep refrigerated.
Fat, qualitative	Random specimen	Negative	
Follicle stimulating hormone (F.S.H.)	See gonadotropins.		
Glucose, qualitative	Random specimen	Negative	
quantitative	24-hr. specimen	<100 mg./100 ml.	Collect with toluene.
Gonadotropic hormone, pituitary (F.S.H.)	24-hr. specimen	10–50 mouse uterine units/24 hrs.	
Hemoglobin	Random specimen	Negative	
17-Hydroxycorticosteroids	24-hr. specimen	Males: 3–10 mg./24 hrs. Females: 2–8 mg./24 hrs. Lower in children. After 25 U.S.P. units ACTH, I.M.: 200–400% increase.	Keep refrigerated. Tranquilizers interfere with test.
5-Hydroxy-indole-acetic acid, qualitative	Random specimen	Negative	Some muscle relaxants and tranquilizers interfere with test.
quantitative	24-hr. specimen	<16 mg./24 hrs.	
17-Ketosteroids	24-hr. specimen	Males: 8–20 mg./24 hrs. Females: 5–15 mg./24 hrs. Children: 12–15 yrs.: 5–12 mg./24 hrs. < 12 yrs.: less than 5 mg./24 hrs. After 25 U.S.P. units ACTH, I.M.: 50–100% increase.	Keep refrigerated. Tranquilizers interfere with test.
Alpha 17-ketosteroids/beta 17-ketosteroid ratio	24-hr. specimen	$\dfrac{9}{1}$	See 17-Ketosteroids.

Urine—Continued

TEST	MATERIAL	NORMAL VALUE	SPECIAL INSTRUCTIONS
Lead	24-hr. specimen	<100 µg./24 hrs.	Collect in specially cleaned bottles. Avoid contact with metallic bed pans.
Melanin, qualitative	Random specimen	Negative	
Microscopic examination	Random specimen	Small amounts of uric acid, calcium oxalate, or urate crystals may be present in acid urine, and small quantities of ammonium biurate, phosphate crystals, or amorphous phosphate may be present in alkaline urine.	
pH	Random specimen	4.8–7.8	
Phenylpyruvic acid, qualitative	Random specimen	Negative	
Phosphorus	24-hr. specimen	0.9–1.3 gm./24 hrs. (varies with intake.)	
Porphobilinogen, qualitative	Random specimen	Negative	Submit fresh specimen and protect from direct light.
Potassium	24-hr. specimen	25–100 mEq./24 hrs.	
Pregnancy tests:			
Frog test	Concentrated morning specimen or serum.	Positive in a normal pregnancy or tumors producing chorionic gonadotropin.	Sparine administration may cause false positive results. Barbiturates, quinine, and salicylates may cause death of animals.
Latex pregnancy test	Concentrated morning specimen.	Ditto	
Rabbit (Friedman) test	Concentrated morning specimen.	Ditto	
Mice (A-Z) test	Concentrated morning specimen.	In pregnancy, positive in dilutions up to 1 to 10 (10,000 mouse units).	
Pregnanediol		Children: Negative Male: 0–1 mg./24 hrs. Female: 1–8 mg./24 hrs. Peak: 1 week after ovulation. Peak during pregnancy: 60–100 mg./24 hrs.	Keep refrigerated.
Pregnanetriol	24-hr. specimen.	Children: <0.5 mg./24 hrs. Female: 0.5–2.0 mg./24 hrs. Male: 1.0–2.0 mg./24 hrs.	Keep refrigerated.
Protein, qualitative	Random specimen	Negative	
Protein, quantitative	24-hr. specimen	10–100 mg./24 hrs.	
P.S.P. excretion (6 mg. dye)		Dye administered I.V.:	
	15-min. specimen	20–50% dye excreted	
	30-min. specimen	16–24% dye excreted	
	60-min. specimen	9–17% dye excreted	
	120-min. specimen	3–10% dye excreted	
		Dye administered I.M.:	
	1-hr. specimen	40–60% dye excreted	
	2-hr. 10 min. specimen	20–25% dye excreted	
Serotonin	See 5-hydroxy-indole-acetic acid.		
Sodium	24-hr. specimen	130–260 mEq./24 hrs.	
Solids, total	24-hr. specimen	55–70 gm./24 hrs. Decrease with age to 30 gm./24 hrs.	
Specific gravity	Random specimen	1.002–1.030	
	24-hr. specimen	1.015–1.025	

Urine—Continued

TEST	MATERIAL	NORMAL VALUE	SPECIAL INSTRUCTIONS
Sugars (excluding glucose)	Random specimen	Negative	
Urea nitrogen	24-hr. specimen	10–15 gm./24 hrs.	
Urea clearance	See Serum.		
Uric acid	24-hr. specimen	700–850 mg./24 hrs.	
Urobilinogen, semi-quantitative	2-hr. specimen	0.3–1.0 Ehrlich units/2 hrs.	
Quantitative	24-hr. specimen	0.5–4.0 mg./24 hrs.	Collect in dark bottle with 5 gm. Na_2CO_3.
Vanil mandelic acid (3-methoxy-4-hydroxy-mandelic acid	24-hr. specimen or first morning specimen	Infants: 83 μg./kg./24 hrs. Adults: 1.8–8.4 mg./24 hrs.	No coffee or fruit 2 days prior to test.
Volume, total	24-hr. specimen	800–1800 ml./24 hrs.	

Cerebrospinal Fluid

TEST	MATERIAL	NORMAL VALUE	SPECIAL INSTRUCTIONS
Chloride		118–132 mEq./L.	These values are invalidated by admixture of blood.
Colloidal gold curve		0001111000	
Globulin (Pandy)		Negative	
Glucose		45–75 mg./100 ml.	
Pandy's test		Negative	
Protein, total		15–45 mg./100 ml.	
Xanthochromia		Negative	
Cell count		0–10	

Seminal Fluid

TEST	MATERIAL	NORMAL VALUE	SPECIAL INSTRUCTIONS
Quantity	Semen	>1.5 ml.	
pH	Semen	7.2–8.9	
Sperm motility	Semen	90%	
Sperm count	Semen	80–120 million/ml.	

Serology

TEST	MATERIAL	NORMAL VALUE	SPECIAL INSTRUCTIONS
Agglutination tests	Serum		
Widal		4-fold rise in titer between acute and convalescent sera	
Weil-Felix			
Trichinosis		0	
Brucella		< 1:80	
Tularemia		< 1:80	
Antistreptolysin O (ASO)	Serum	125 Todd units or less	
C-Reactive protein	Serum	0	
Latex-rheumatoid arthritis test	Serum	< 1:160	
Strep. MG agglutination test	Serum	< 1:40	

Index

Page numbers in *italic* indicate either an illustration or a table.